WITHDRAWN
From the
Dean B. Ellis Library
Arkansas State University

ENCYCLOPEDIA OF ARTIFICIAL INTELLIGENCE SECOND EDITION

VOLUME 2

Stuart C. Shapiro, *Editor-in-chief*

Wiley-Interscience Publication

John Wiley & Sons, Inc.

New York / Chichester / Brisbane / Toronto / Singapore

Dean B. Ellis Library
Arkansas State University

In recognition of the importance of preserving what has been written, it is a
policy of John Wiley & Sons, to have books of enduring value
published in the United States printed on acid-free paper, and we exert our
best efforts to that end.

Copyright © 1992 by John Wiley & Sons, Inc.

All rights reserved. Published simultaneously in Canada.

Reproduction or translation of any part of this work beyond that permitted
by Section 107 or 108 of the 1976 United States Copyright Act without the
permission of the copyright owner is unlawful. Requests for permission or
further information should be addressed to the Permissions Department,
John Wiley & Sons, Inc.

This publication is designed to provide accurate and authoritative
information in regard to the subject matter covered. It is sold with the
understanding that the publisher is not engaged in rendering legal,
accounting, or other professional services. If legal advice or other expert
assistance is required, the services of a competent professional person should
be sought. *From a Declaration of Principles jointly adopted by a Committee of
the American Bar Association and a Committee of Publishers.*

Library of Congress Cataloging in Publication Data:

Encyclopedia of artificial intelligence / Stuart C. Shapiro, editor-in
   -chief. — 2nd ed.
       p.   cm.
   "A Wiley-Interscience publication."
   Includes bibliographical references and index.
   ISBN 0-471-50307-X (set). — ISBN 0-471-50305-3 (v. 1). — ISBN
0-471-50306-1 (v. 2)
   1. Artificial intelligence—Encyclopedias.   I. Shapiro, Stuart
Charles.
Q335.E53   1992
006.3′03—dc20   91-37272

Printed in the United States of America
10 9 8 7 6 5 4 3 2 1
Printed and bound by Courier Companies, Inc.

ENCYCLOPEDIA OF ARTIFICIAL INTELLIGENCE
SECOND EDITION

VOLUME 2

MACHACK 6

Also known as The Greenblatt Chess Program, MACHACK 6 was written by Richard Greenblatt, Donald Eastlake, and Stephen Crocker at MIT. It was the first computer chess program to play well against humans in a chess tournament. It uses a method of forward pruning to variable depths along with the alpha-beta algorithm to determine its next move (see R. D. Greenblatt, D. E. Eastlake, and S. D. Crocker, The Greenblatt Chess Program, *Proceedings of the Fall Joint Computer Conference, 1967*, AFIPS Press, Montvale, N.J., 1967, pp. 801–810; M. Newborn, *Computer Chess*, Academic Press, New York, 1975).

J. ROSENBERG
Kilchberg, Switzerland

MACHINE TRANSLATION

Machine translation is typically composed of the following three steps: analysis of a source language sentence, transfer (word selection and structural mapping) from one language to another, and generation of a target language sentence. It incorporates the methods of natural language understanding (qv) and sentence generation. Natural language understanding is composed of parsing technology (see PARSING; PARSING, WORD EXPERT) and knowledge representation (qv). The question then arises as to whether machine translation has a particular content of its own, besides these mentioned above, which are all basic natural language technologies. The answer follows. First, there is a problem of drawing a correspondence between source language words and phrases to those of the target language. Further problems include determining what factors should decide such word selection and what cultural backgrounds of the countries where these languages are used have decisive influence on the selection of translation words and sentential styles. These problems are interesting to attack because all are central to artificial intelligence. Human translators are supposed to be doing the same in their translations works; however, research in the behavior of human translators is not advanced enough for the results to be utilized in practical machine translation systems.

There has been tremendous advancement in linguistic theories since the 1970s, and there are a few theories which are interesting from the standpoint of machine translation. However, they do not cover varieties of exceptional expressions which practical machine translation systems have to handle. A machine translation system, which is still imperfect and will never be completed, is exposed to very crude tests when the system construction reaches a certain stage. At that stage of development, the system is given a comparatively simple sentence for translation, with structures that can be analyzed by a grammar given to the system. After completion, people other than those who developed the system are asked to translate a variety of texts such as newspaper articles, science magazines, patent documents, contract documents, and commercial letters. Because the documents have not been adequately tested at the development stage, users are disappointed by the poor translation results produced by the system. Many of the failures of the system come from the fact that the dictionary and the grammar are not sufficient to accept such unexpected input sentences. There are almost infinite varieties of sentential expressions, and a few years of effort in the improvement of grammar and dictionary is not enough.

Natural language has a property of infinity in sentential structures and meanings. Some ten thousand words are normally used in everyday life. Each word has a variety of meanings and word combinations create even more meanings. Many of these cannot be explained by a standard grammar and typical meaning interpretation. Natural language can be regarded as a huge set of exceptional expressions, and as many such expressions as possible must be collected in the dictionary. It is an endless job.

There is enthusiasm for such grammar theories as lexical functional grammar and head-driven phrase structure grammar, and many experimental laboratory systems are constructed by using one of these grammar formalisms. However, such systems will not be successful as practical machine translation systems. Natural language is very complex. It is not a phenomena of natural science, and cannot be explained by a single theory. Natural language must be analyzed by the proper combination of several different principles each of which must be applied to a specific kind of linguistic phenomena. The vague total world of natural language cannot be clarified by a sharp, elegant tool. The combination of several, not sharp, but substantially powerful tools must be used. A combination of the phrase structure grammar formalism and case grammar formalism, with large and precise dictionaries that have case frame information, modality information, and many exceptional linguistic expressions, is a good model in this respect.

DIFFICULTIES OF MACHINE TRANSLATION

One of the difficulties of translation, whether it is done by a human or a machine, is that the translation of an input sentence is not unique. Various translations are possible for an input sentence, and it is very hard to decide which one is the best. The task requires constructing a box (transducer) whose input is a source language sentence and whose output is a target language sentence which conveys the same meaning. If there is a definite one-to-one correspondence between input and output, the design and construction of the box will not be so difficult. In machine translation, the input-to-output mapping is ambiguous, and the design and construction of the box cannot be achieved by a normal engineering methodology, namely a bottom-up approach from translation pairs. A top-down model-theoretic approach to machine translation must be considered. Natural language understanding systems and natural language dialogue systems consider how the human brain makes inferences and decisions, represents inside information out, and uses available information in such inference and decision making. An ideal machine translation system will be a kind of human brain system. It is only realizable by integrating research results from neurophysics, linguistics, cognitive science (qv), knowledge representation (qv), problem solving (qv), and supporting computer software.

The present-day machine translation system, unfortunately, is not advanced enough to simulate human translation activities. It performs a series of rather simple transformations on an input sentence and obtains an output sentence. The process includes some undeterministic and feedback stages, but generally speaking, is purely mechanical. The system has no world knowledge, but only a certain amount of linguistic knowledge. Almost no part of it can be properly called artificial intelligence, so they cannot produce expressions and phrases which are not explicitly given in an input sentence. The process is based on the compositionality principle, that is, a translation sentence is composed of an appropriate combination of the words or phrases whose source language words or phrases exist in the source language sentence. Many improper translations and, sometimes, failures result, particularly with complex and long input sentences. However, the systems are useful and cost-beneficial when used wisely and when weak points of the system are avoided. There are more than ten commercial systems marketed in Japan, all of which translate between English and Japanese. There are several commercial systems in the United States and Europe (Dostert and co-workers, 1978; Hutchins, 1988; King, 1987; Japan Electronic Industry Development Association, 1989).

The real difficulty in machine translation is not only in the problem of word sense; ambiguity is very often cited with regard to the inability of machine translation systems; eg, when the word "bank" is used in the sentence "I went to the bank," it is unclear which meaning is meant: a river bank, or a bank to deposit money. This problem is not solved completely in the present-day machine translation system, but will be solved by utilizing contextual information and domain knowledge (qv) about the text to be translated. In practical machine translation systems, when the ambiguity is not solvable by such information, a post-editor selects a proper solution from all the possible alternative translations. Post-editing is an obligatory step in the present-day machine translation. It is necessary not only in machine translation, but also in human translation, which goes through two steps: rough translation and post-editing. This supports the post-editing step in machine translation, which is generally considered inferior to human translation (although this is not always true).

Another difficulty in machine translation exists in the complex combination of the above ambiguity phenomena with the additional ambiguity in syntactic structure. Almost all the words in a sentence have several meanings, and the phrases in a sentence can modify several other phrases from a syntactic point of view. Therefore, the number of possible syntactic structures for a sentence of, say, twenty words, exceeds several hundred. There is no reliable method or information available to select only one right sentential structure from the many alternatives. Semantic information, contextual information, and world knowledge will play important roles in the selection of a proper solution, but there are no reliable theories which are applicable for the selection.

Current machine translation systems can analyze and translate sentences composed of less than ten words, but almost always fail to analyze and translate the sentences of more than thirty words. A reason for such failure is the ambiguity mentioned above. This is inevitable because sometimes even a human cannot understand the meaning of a long sentence at the first reading. We may feel we understand the structure and the meaning of a long sentence at the first reading, but when accurately checked we often cannot decide which phrases modify which.

To examine the real cause of the translation failure is important, although it is difficult in a large system which has over a thousand grammatical rules and tens of thousands of lexical entries. Often the cause stems from incompleteness of grammatical rules and dictionary information. A particular phrase containing unexpected adverbial phrases may sometimes put a translation system out of order. The condition for the application of a syntactic rule is not always well specified, and many unnecessary analysis trees disturb the analysis process to obtain the best result. Similar erroneous results appear when the necessary information is lacking in the dictionary and a good selection is not made for a translation word.

When causes of errors are located, the necessary improvement is taken for grammatical rules and dictionary contents, then the translation will be done correctly for the particular sentences for which the system improvements are achieved. However the improvement of a system for some sentences is sometimes harmful for other sentences which were translated correctly before the improvement. The improvement of grammar and dictionary must be done very carefully, considering varieties of possible side-effects, otherwise there will be unexpected effects for many other sentences. Improvement is difficult in a big system because the detailed behavior of a system cannot be seen and the effect of a change at a local portion to other portions cannot be estimated.

THEORIES AND METHODOLOGIES

As the above discussion demonstrates, a machine translation system is a kind of expert system. It is probably the hardest expert system to construct because a language is a monstrous system, and machine translation has to build a bridge between two such complex systems. Grammatical rules in machine translation can be regarded as production rules that find out a specific linguistic structure and transform it to another linguistic structure. However, the conditional parts of grammatical rules (the left side of a rewriting rule), that is, the conditions for the application of a particular rule, are rather simple in an ordinary grammar formalism, particularly in a context-free phrase structure grammar. Surrounding situations such as adjacent words and phrasal structures must be checked for the application of a grammatical rule. This means that a tree-to-tree transformation formalism is required for the analysis, transfer, and generation of a sentence. Even contextual information and knowledge must be used as such a condition. A difference between an ordinary expert system and a machine translation system is that the former has no good theoretical background in general but is just the accumulation of intuitive experiences, while the latter has theories such as syntactic theories and semantic theories (Grishman, 1986), although these are still very simple and imprecise. There is active research in such areas as discourse theory, situation semantics (qv), mental space theory, etc, besides the traditional linguistic theories (Brady and Berwick, 1983; Fauconnier, 1985). These theories will help the construction of machine translation systems greatly and are making rapid progress. They are, however, quite young. Therefore, it is difficult to incorporate these recent linguistic research results into existing machine translation systems at present. It will probably take another ten years to integrate all of the recent linguistics theories to achieve the next-generation machine translation systems.

Again, these theories cannot cover the whole activity of natural language because a language is a large set of exceptional expressions, and general theories are hopeless for such exceptional phenomena. Only the dictionary, which collects all these exceptions, is effective for the system, and is therefore drawing the attention of many researchers in this area (see DICTIONARY/LEXICON), as is knowledge representation in artificial intelligence. There are several researches going on in this domain. Examples are the CYC project at MCC (Lenat and Guha, 1990), and the Electronic Dictionary Project at EDR. The former aims at encoding encyclopedic knowledge in the computer in a specific representation framework. The latter involves encoding linguistic knowledge of words in a bilingual dictionary as well as monolingual dictionaries of Japanese and English. The efforts must be carefully evaluated before it is known whether the current frameworks of the encyclopedic knowledge base and the dictionaries are sufficient for various applications.

One of the research fields which has only recently gained serious attention is the comparative study of languages from the standpoint of translation. There are so many complex problems in this field that there is no methodology established yet to compare two languages. There are word level comparisons, phrase level comparisons, comparisons of grammatical structures, and comparisons of semantic, pragmatic, and culture-dependent phenomena, to mention a few, which are closely related to translation. It is well known that the French and Italian languages are very similar, as are the Japanese and Korean languages; they are close in the language family as well as in the cultural traditions. Between these closely related languages, translation is comparatively easy because word-to-word and phrase-to-phrase correspondences are simple. Also, the sentential constructions used to express a certain idea about a phenomenon or an object are almost the same, so that a deep language analysis process for machine translation is unnecessary. Shallow analysis and simple word replacement will give better translation results than the deep analysis, complex transformation, and understanding process for such language pairs.

Translation must convey the explicit and implicit information in a source language to a target language. In the case of language pairs such as the above, the simple replacement of words from one language to another and some additional simple processing will better retain delicate information from a source language sentence than does heavy analysis, which inevitably loses delicate information contained in the original sentence. Machine translation has been successful in such language pairs and has been used in everyday operations. English–French, French–Italian, English–German, and French–Spanish are successful language pairs used by the European Community, Siemens, and others. The Pan American Health Organization (PAHO) has developed their own translation systems between English and Spanish, and is using them very successfully (Vasconcellos and Leon, 1985). Speed, cost, and translation quality are said to be fairly good. Evaluation of machine translation quality must always be done by comparison with average human translation done by translators not specialized in the particular field of documents. Evaluation will become an important topic as machine translation becomes more common.

TOWARDS HUMANISTIC MACHINE TRANSLATION

Machine translation is difficult between dissimilar language families, with different cultural backgrounds, eg, English and Japanese. English is an SVO language. Many noun phrases and verb phrases have structures such as N · PP and V · PP or V · O · PP. Japanese is an SOV language and has no such structures as PP attachment from the right. Modifiers always come to the left of modifiees. Word order is rather free in Japanese, and subject and object words are often omitted. Therefore, translation necessarily entails big structural transformations and the recovery of omitted words or the deletion of redundant words, which is difficult to estimate. Because of the cultural differences, the same content is often presented in totally different expressions in these two languages, such as "I will come soon" in English, vs "I will go soon" in Japanese, and "You don't . . . No, I don't" in English, vs "You don't . . . Yes, I don't" in Japanese. Contrastive studies are essential as a basis of machine translation between two such languages.

In a sentence two components can be recognized: the core fact that a speaker wants to convey, and the speaker's attitude to the fact and to the hearer (see MENTAL MODELS). For example, the sentence "I would like to send it to you" is composed of "I send it to you" and "I would like to," with the latter expressing the attitude of the speaker toward the hearer. This part of the speaker's attitude is strongly influenced by the cultural background and by the mentality of the speaker at the time of the utterance.

Japanese people usually recognize or estimate extralinguistic information from various factors such as the speaker's sex and age, the hearer's relative position and attitude to the speaker, and official or casual situations. If the essential part of a sentence is not the factual content but rather the speaker's mentality, and if this is expressed in the way of indirect speech acts, the translation is quite difficult (McKeown, 1985). This is because the direct translation of the expression does not necessarily convey the same indirect speech act in another language and cultural world. For example, "I will consider it seriously" in Japanese sometimes means polite denial (eg, "I don't think I can" or "I don't think it is possible").

Compared to the translation of the sophisticated mentality of a sentence, it may seem that the translation of the essential fact in a sentence is not as difficult. This is not so. As mentioned, grammatical structures are completely different between different language families. Western languages such as English and French often have complex embedded structures in a sentence. The Japanese language seldom uses such structures but connects several simpler sentences (embedded phrases) in a sequence with some connectives to express the relation between these sentences. Metaphorically, the Western languages have a three-dimensional or cubic structure, and the Japanese language has linear or flat structure. Heavy structural transformations are required to bridge this structural gap. For this, a context-free phrase structure model is inadequate. A framework which transforms a tree structure to another tree structure must be introduced (Nagao and co-workers, 1985; Nagao, 1987). The Japanese language has no gender or plural and has many ellipses (eg, subject and object omissions). Good algorithms must be developed to estimate and recover this information. Contextual and situational information is important for these problems. Some studies have been done on these subjects. Particularly the usage of pronouns such as *this, that,* and *it,* in real conversational situations in Japanese have been fairly clearly distinguished by a recent study which utilizes the mental space theory (Kinsui and Takubo, 1990).

The selection of the most suitable translation word or phrase in a target language for a word or a phrase in a source language is a difficult problem. The problem lies not in choosing a word for "bank" in the sense of river bank or money bank, but in selecting a word appropriate to a context (such as the selecting among *think, consider, imagine, study, meditate,* etc). It is mapping from a source language word with vague meaning to a target language word with vague meaning whose coverage is somewhat different from the meaning of the original word. The selection is influenced not only by the word meaning, but also by the sentential structure in which the word is used. It is also affected by the sophisticated mental state of the speaker and his or her relation to the hearer. This problem, particularly in the context of contrastive study between, eg, English and Japanese, has not been studied adequately in the linguistics world.

Some trials have begun on part of the above problem, namely, the selection of a translation word according to the phrasal–sentential structure in which the word is used. One of the most promising involves storing many pairs of example phrases and their translations to compare an input partial phrase with these examples, and to extract the most similar example phrase. Then, the translation of the input phrase is done in reference to the translation of the example phrase. This principle is called *translation by analogy.* (Nagao, 1984). Humans perform this operation by consulting the dictionary for example phrases and their translations. Translation by analogy has been used in some recent research (Sumita and co-workers, 1990; Sadler, 1989). For example, it is applied to the translation of "of" in the phrase type, "A of B," in which the interpretation is quite difficult. There are many meanings in "of," and the distinction depends on the combination of the lexical meanings of A and B. The combinations are enormous, and the semantic distinction of lexical meanings of A and B and the determination of the function of "of" is difficult by the semantic primitive approach. Instead, different examples of "A of B" and their translations are stored in computer memory for comparison with the input phrase "a of b." The thesaurus is useful for determining the similarity of a and A and of b and B. When the most similar example is determined using a similarity measure based on the thesaurus nearness, the translation is produced according to the example translation.

Metaphorical interpretation of an expression is essential to the understanding and translation of a sentence. To properly perform such an interpretation, huge amounts of human knowledge ranging from academic theories to everyday customs must be accumulated, and strong associative inference processes must be performed. For example, in the sentence "I read Shakespeare," "Shakespeare" must be interpreted not as a writer but as the literary works of Shakespeare. This interpretation is performed by the inference sequence from Shakespeare to the writer to the literary works (which can be an object of "read"). However, there is still no clear definition of the conditions of the proper interpretation. It may depend on circumstances which are difficult to specify for every possible situation. This will be an interesting topic of future research.

In the future of machine translation, there will be many more problems in which artificial intelligence factors are involved. Sentence generation and dialogue interpretation and translation are typical problems that require information about the speaker's and hearer's mental states. This is called a *user model* (Kobsa, 1989), and it depends heavily on the discourse, the speaker's and hearer's intentions, speaker–hearer relations, and cultural background. Intensive future research is expected.

FROM TOY PROGRAMS TO ROBUST PRACTICAL SYSTEMS

Present-day machine translation systems are almost wholly dependent on phrase structure grammar (qv), which merges several linguistic components into one, and on case grammar (see GRAMMAR, CASE) for the recognition of core sentential structures. Case grammar includes some semantic information. One of the most widely used grammars in the academic circle today is a unification grammar which merges two elements into one. This, however, is not sufficient, because many words in a sentence influence each other at the same time. For practical systems which must process a variety of expressions, three or more elements must be checked and merged at the same time by a grammatical rule, or, tree-to-tree transformation must be introduced to cope with varieties of sentential structures. It is important for linguists to be able to write the grammatical relations of three or more elements at the same level, even though the actual checking and merging operations are done two elements at a time by the computer. Simple standard sentences will be handled by a unification grammar, but thirty years of effort in machine translation proves that such a simple-minded grammar cannot conquer the real language.

Case grammar is commonly adopted as a model to interpret natural language sentences; it is also adopted as a model of internal representation of a sentence. That is, there is an assumption that any language sentences which represent the same content can be analyzed by case grammer into the same internal representation. Case structure representation is widely considered a kind of neutral or pivot representation of the same content expressed in different languages. It is regarded as the core of a multilingual machine translation system, and hence is called the *pivot language* (Nirenburg, 1987). Ongoing debates continue as to whether the pivot method is better than the transfer method, which includes a stage that connects the internal representations of two language sentences. However, the discussion is no longer fruitful, because it has been made clear that if a multi-lingual system should handle such information as tense, modality, and other culture-dependent components of translation, there is little intersection among many different languages. Such sophisticated information can be treated only in the domain of two specific languages. Therefore, if high-quality machine translation is to be achieved, the transfer method must be adopted.

Present-day theoretical linguistics is making advances in a variety of directions, and many of these will be very useful for machine translation in the future. However, at present few of the results are in use in practical machine translation systems. At least another ten years will be necessary to construct a completely new machine translation system which will integrate all the reliable linguistic theories of morphology, syntax, semantics, and discourse, and which has the capabilities of problem solving, inferencing, and culture-dependent translation.

BIBLIOGRAPHY

J. Barwise and J. Perry, *Situations and Attitudes*, MIT Press, Cambridge, Mass., 1983.

M. Brady and R. Berwick, eds., *Computational Models of Discourse*, MIT Press, Cambridge, Mass., 1983.

B. H. Dostert, R. R. McDonald, and M. Zarechnak, *Machine Translation*, Mouton Publishers, 1978.

G. Fauconnier, *Espaces Mentaux, Edition de Minuit, 1984*, English translation: Mental Spaces, MIT Press, Cambridge, Mass., 1985.

R. Grishman, *Computational Linguistics, An Introduction*, Cambridge University Press, UK, 1986.

W. J. Hutchins, "Recent Developments in Machine Translation—A Review of the Last Five Years," *Proceedings of New Directions in Machine Translation*, Budapest, Aug. 1988.

Japan Electronic Industry Development Association, *A Japanese View of Machine Translation in Light of the Considerations and Recommendations Reported by ALPAC, U.S.A.*, July 1989.

M. King, ed., *Machine Translation Today; The State of the Art*, Edinburgh University Press, Edinburgh, UK, 1987.

S. Kinsui and Y. Takubo, "A Discourse Management Analysis of the Japanese Demonstrative Expressions," in *Advances in Japanese Cognitive Science*, Vol. 3, Kodan-sha Publishers, 1990.

A. Kobsa and W. Wahlster, eds., *User Models in Dialog Systems*, Springer-Verlag, New York, 1989.

D. B. Lenat and R. V. Guha, *Building Large Knowledge Based Systems*, Addison-Wesley, Reading, Mass., 1990.

K. R. McKeown, *Text Generation: Using Discourse Strategies and Focus Constraints to Generate Natural Language Text*, Cambridge University Press, UK, 1985.

M. Nagao, "A Framework of a Mechanical Translation Between Japanese and English by Analogy Principle," in A. Elithorn and R. Banerji, eds., *Artificial and Human Intelligence*, North-Holland, Amsterdam, 1984.

M. Nagao, "Role of Structural Transformation in a Machine Translation System," in S. Nirenburg, ed., *Machine Translation, Theoretical and Methodological Issues*, Cambridge University Press, UK, 1987.

M. Nagao, J. Tsujii, and J. Nakamura, "The Japanese Government Project for Machine Translation," in J. Slocum, ed., *Machine Translation Systems*, Cambridge University Press, UK, 1985.

S. Nirenburg, V. Raskin, and A. Tucker, "The Structure of Interlingua in TRANSLATOR," in S. Nirenburg, ed., *Machine Translation*, Cambridge University Press, UK, 1987.

V. Sadler, *Working with Analogical Semantics—Disambiguation Techniques in DLT*, Foris Publishers, 1989.

E. Sumita, H. Iida, and H. Kohyama, "Translating with Examples; A New Approach to Machine Translation," *Proceedings of the Third International Conference on Theoretical and Methodological Issues in Machine Translation of Natural Languages*, June 11–13, 1990, Austin, Tex.

M. Vasconcellos and M. Leon, "SPANAM and ENGSPAN; Machine Translation at the Pan American Health Organization," in J. Slocum, ed., *Machine Translation Systems*, Cambridge University Press, UK, 1985.

Makoto Nagao
Kyoto University

MACHINES, SELF-ORGANIZING. See Robotics.

MACLISP. See LISP.

MACSYMA

A system for solving problems in symbolic mathematics, such as integration and algebraic manipulation, MACSYMA was designed in 1968 by J. Moses and co-workers and written in 1971 by Martin and Fateman at MIT (see LAMBDA CALCULUS; W. A. Martin and R. J. Fateman, "The MACSYMA System," *Proceedings of the Second Symposium on Symbolic and Algebraic Manipulation*, ACM SIGSAM, New York, 1971, pp. 59–75; see also J. Moses, "A MACSYMA Primer," Mathlab Memo No. 2, Computer Science Laboratory, MIT, Cambridge, Mass., 1975).

M. TAIE
AT&T Bell Laboratories

MANIPULATORS. See ROBOT HANDS AND END-EFFECTORS.

MANUFACTURING, AI IN

Computer-integrated manufacturing (CIM) is, basically, the technology that embraces the full range of the unique ability possessed by the digital computer and related computer technology to enhance the capabilities of the manufacturing process. That ability has three main elements. The first is the ability of the computer to provide online, variable-program (flexible) automation of manufacturing activities and equipment. The second is the ability to provide online, moment-by-moment optimization of manufacturing activities and operations. With respect to both of these elements, it should be noted that the computer can accomplish them not only with the "hard" components of manufacturing (the manufacturing machinery and equipment, etc) but also with the "soft" components (the information flow, the handling of databases, etc). However, as is becoming more and more widely recognized, the third element of the computer's unique ability is by far the most important and powerful. This is its ability to integrate all of the constituents of the entire manufacturing process into a system which can, because of the first two elements mentioned, be flexibly automated and optimized as a whole moment by moment. This powerful ability of the computer to function as a systems tool therefore results, in the case of its application to manufacturing, in what is called the computer-integrated-manufacturing system (Merchant, 1973).

That generic CIM system is defined as a closed-loop feedback system in which the prime inputs are product requirements (needs) and product concepts (creativity) and the prime outputs are finished products (fully assembled inspected and ready for use). It is comprised of a combination of software and hardware, the elements of which include product design (for production), production planning (programming), production control (feedback, supervisory and adaptive optimizing), production equipment (including machine tools), and production processes (removal, forming, and consolidative). It is amenable to being realized by application of systems engineering and has the potential of being fully automated by means of versatile automation and of being made fully self-optimizing (adaptively optimizing); the present major resources for accomplishing this are the computer-related technologies.

The general concept of this system can be more fully appreciated by reference to Figure 1. In this particular characterization of the system, five main elements are represented by the five boxes. There is nothing hard and fast about this particular characterization of the elements of the manufacturing system. The important concept to recognize is that all of the types of activities, equipment, and processes represented by the terms in the boxes are, and must be, integral parts of any manufacturing system that is to be automated, optimized, and integrated by applying the computer to these tasks if the full benefits of CIM are to be realized.

The second point to note from Figure 1 is that the CIM system is a closed-loop system. In other words, data and information relative to what is happening downstream in the system must be fed back upstream constantly, and in real time, to continuously condition the operations and activities going on there. Without such feedback, online real-time optimization and integrated, coordinated, flexible automation become impossible. Two of the more critical feedback loops, labeled "cost and capabilities" and "performance" in Figure 1, illustrate the general nature of the two types of data and information that must be fed back to provide overall flexible automation and real-time

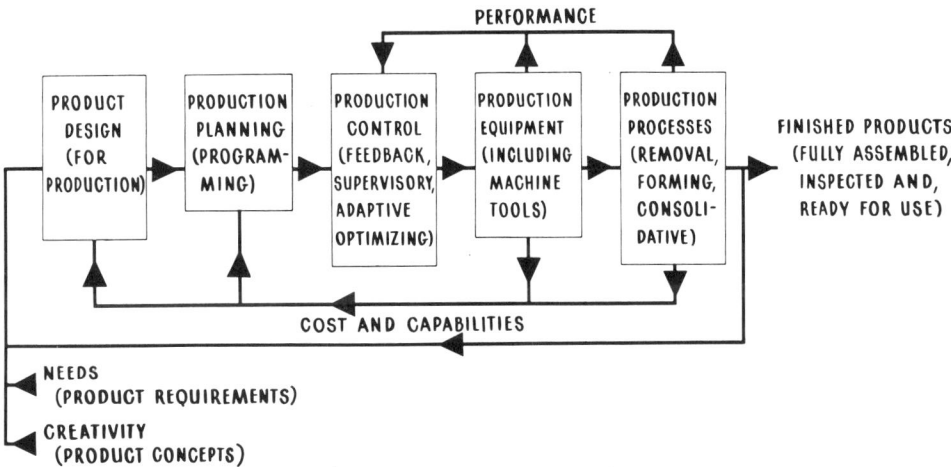

Figure 1. The CIM system.

optimization. Obviously, all data and information originating within any of the elements of the system must be able to be fed either forward or back to any of the other elements of the system where it is required.

The foregoing concept of computer-integrated manufacturing evolved during the 1960s and gradually increasing effort was devoted to its realization in practice during the 1970s, although progress was painfully slow. Nevertheless, such attention and progress led gradually toward a broadening of the concept of the CIM system that had evolved in the 1960s. By the early 1980s, it was recognized that the concept represented by Figure 1 involved primarily the technological operations of a company's system of manufacturing and that, to take full advantage of the enormous potential of computer technology to improve manufacturing capability and cost effectiveness, the concept and its application should be broadened to encompass both the technological and the business operations of a company, eg, a manufacturing enterprise. This concept was quickly espoused by the Computer and Automated Systems Association (CASA) of the Society of Manufacturing Engineers (SME) and by 1985 had evolved into the concept of the computer-integrated-manufacturing enterprise illustrated in Figure 2. As illustrated here, the current concept of CIM aims at integration of the corporate enterprise's technological manufacturing system and its business operations system, both within themselves and with each other, to accomplish overall computer integration of the corporate manufacturing enterprise. This concept of the computer-integrated manufacturing enterprise provides guidance for the major ongoing technological and managerial efforts being focused on development and implementation of full computer-automated, computer-optimized, and computer-integrated manufacturing, collectively called computer-integrated manufacturing. Despite such efforts, however, *full* computer-integrated manufacturing has not yet been realized in practice anywhere in the world. Although at this stage it is possible to integrate many parts of the system with each other, the technology is not yet sufficiently advanced to accomplish overall, closed-loop integration of the total corporate enterprise from conceptual design of the product to its delivery to the customer in finished, ready-to-use form. In particular, the greatest difficulty is being experienced in closed-loop integration of the engineering design of the product with the remainder of the technological system, and of integration of the technological system with the business operations system.

THE ROLE OF AI IN CIM

Background

The fact that CIM has not yet been fully realized anywhere is due in large part to the fact that the CIM system is not yet an intelligent system. At this stage, artificial

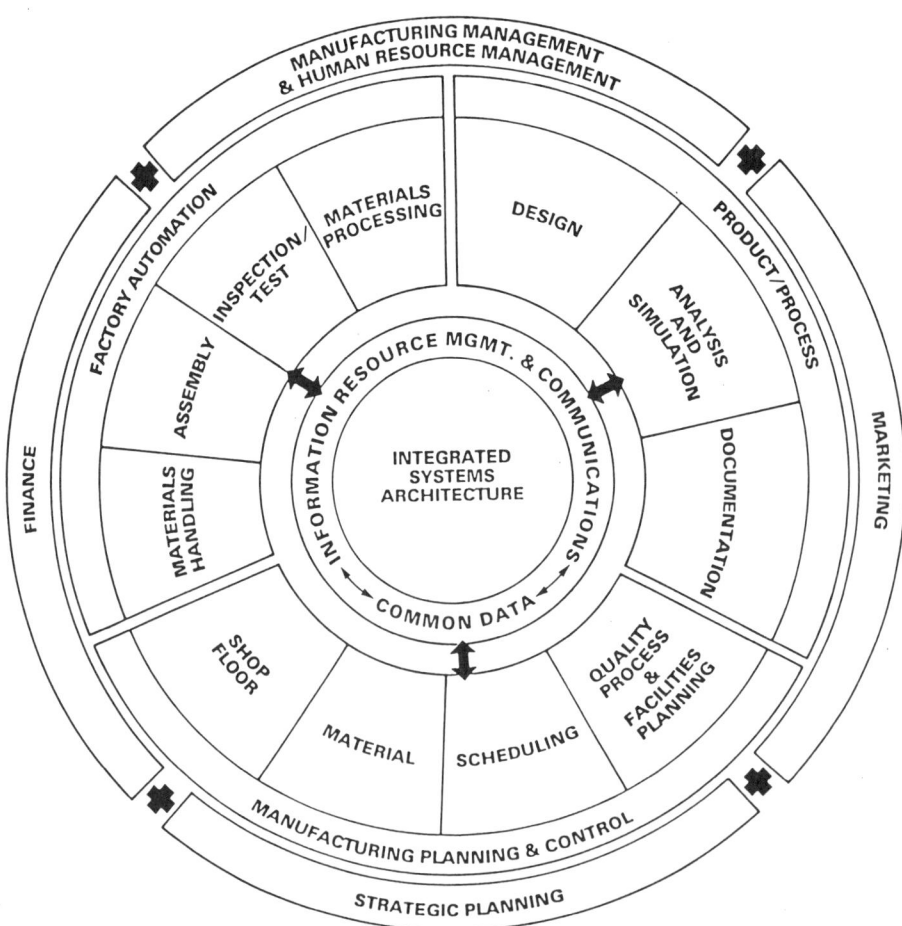

Figure 2. The CIM enterprise. CIM "wheel" developed by the Technical Council of the Society of Manufacturing Engineers' Computer and Automated Systems Association (CASA/SME, 1985). Courtesy of the Society of Manufacturing Engineers.

intelligence (AI) in the form of expert systems technology is being developed and experimentally applied to certain elements of the system, but many of these developments and applications have not yet been put into practice. Nevertheless, they exhibit considerable promise. Some examples from both the technological system and the business operations system will provide a glimpse of the developing possibilities and applications.

Computer-Aided Design

The technological system and the field of computer-aided design for production will be considered first. Gero (1985) developed methodology for modeling both single objects and assemblies of objects by using knowledge engineering techniques of first-order predicate logic implemented via PROLOG. Even though a restricted domain was used in his initial work, it demonstrated the uniformity and power of the approach. Such approaches as this have led more recently to efforts focused on applying AI to the critical problem of enabling the output of the computer-aided design (CAD) process to convey to the rest of the CIM system not only the detailed product model, but also the designer's intent. For example, Ando and Yoshikawa (1989) have succeeded in representing the designer's intent in a unified manner by utilizing a network of AI frames to represent the functions of the object being designed. This unified approach is then implemented by describing the design information about each face element of the object in a single frame and then referring all of the geometrical and functional data associated with the face element to that frame. Another approach to utilizing AI to represent and manipulate the designer's intent in production has been taken by Kimura and Suzuki (1989). This focuses on supporting efficient concurrent product and process design in CAD systems. For this purpose, they originated a new architecture for flexibly integrating all engineering activities, within which these activities can be carried out concurrently. This architecture makes it possible to represent all of the necessary product information in a product model in which the designer's intent is one of the most important items. The basic tool used for representing and manipulating that intent is based on logical constraint and its solution methods utilizing an AI-based geometric reasoner.

Production Planning

The field of production planning has seen the greatest activity so far, with most of that directed to process and operations planning. Derbyshire and Davies (1985) have developed a hybrid expert/algorithmic process-planning system for turned parts, called EXCAP. It combines a PROLOG-like expert system with a recursive planning algorithm. This has shown considerable promise for the realization of truly generative process planning. Milacic and Kalajdzic (1985) have developed the underlying theory of the utilization of expert systems technology in process planning, considering it to be the functional basis for long-term logical structuring of overall manufacturing process design. Triouleyre (1985) has developed an expert-systems-type approach to process and operations planning for forming and welding operations. It takes into account the structure of the data concerning process, product, and processing, thus enabling decisions to be arrived at readily concerning both the choice of process and the detailed operations required. Furthermore, the rules contained in the knowledge base are found to be an efficient aid in product design and in determining its ease of production. Zdeblick and Barkocy (1985) evolved an intelligent module for detailed operations planning for machining operations that, as it matures, will find its way into the production equipment itself, through the medium of intelligent control systems. There it can perform such functions as making tool selections, cut selections, and speed and feed decisions in real time just prior to actual machining of a workpiece. Preiss and Kaplansky (1985), by encoding knowledge of the milling process into a computer program using principles of artificial intelligence, have produced a system that automatically writes part programs to mill $2\frac{1}{2}$-dimension parts successfully on a three-axis numerically controlled milling machine. Iwata and Sugimura (1985) have developed, in prototype form, a knowledge-based computer-aided process-planning (CAPP) system that determines, from the CAD model of a part, the sequence of machine tools required to produce it. The knowledge base of the system includes a set of rules describing preference relations among the machining processes. Peklenik and Sluga (1989) have developed a system for process and operations planning of machining based on manufacturing process topology and an expert systems approach as a basic decision-making tool. The resulting generative process and operations-planning system is formulated in such a way that its integration into an overall CAD/CAPP/CAM system is possible. The structure of the CAPP system is based on a modular approach, with the system thereby comprising a set of independent modules. This technique significantly lowers the complexity of the process- and operations-planning procedure. The manufacturing elements of the system comprise a comprehensive body of manufacturing process topology information. The expert system developed for operations planning exhibits high flexibility and is well integrated into the overall CAPP system.

Production Control

The field of production control has had considerable activity in the application of AI, with much of it devoted to either scheduling or process control. For example, Bourne and Fox (1984) have created an AI system, called ISIS, which has been used successfully to schedule jobs at the shop-floor level in a factory. Ouchi and co-workers (1985) have developed and implemented an integrated AI system for controlling the sequencing and processing in the robotic assembly of color television sets by eleven robots. CAD data from a higher level computer is automatically transformed to control the robots. Sauve and Collinot (1987) have presented an expert system for daily estimated scheduling and real-time control of production disturbances thereto in a flexible manufacturing system (FMS). The system utilizes object-oriented language to represent the relevant information of a scheduling problem, particularly knowledge about constraints and flexibility factors in a factory. It integrates automatic generation and automatic modification of schedule plans, employing a coordination level that generates an admissible solution and a local cooperation level that deals with local modifications of the plan. Bertok and Vancza (1989) have explored and appraised the contemporary state of the art of AI applied to manufacturing control in four important areas of the subject, namely, material handling subsystems, scheduling, monitoring, and recovery. They find that, in the case of material handling subsystems, the application of expert systems combined with simulation methods helps considerably in getting optimum system design. In scheduling, two approaches are useful. For realtime scheduling, rule-based techniques can be used efficiently, whereas for attacking the combinatorial complexity of the problem, iterative reformulation can produce good results. For monitoring the operation, the combination of data-driven and function-oriented methods may give the best results. When a failure has been detected, comprehensive model-based methods should be combined with fast empirical diagnosis. To recover from an error state, a well-structured set of goals is needed for action planning. Newman (1988) has carried out and presented a quite comprehensive review of the contemporary state of the art and activity in the development and application of AI in scheduling in CIM systems, with emphasis on a flexible environment and the production of small to medium lot sizes that are subject to variation.

Production Equipment and Processes

The field of production equipment and production processes has seen somewhat less activity in the application of AI, with much of it being devoted to monitoring of machine performance and diagnosis of machine malfunctions. For example, Bel and co-workers (1985) have investigated the possibilities for applying AI to satisfy the need for efficient and flexible monitoring systems in fully automated manufacturing systems. They find that AI methodology is very well suited, not only to creating effective monitoring systems capable of dealing with the imprecise terms in which triggering situations are expressed, but also to detecting unpredicted events, specifying error-recovery strategies, and planning job input sequences. Bourne and Fox (1984) have presented a rule-based architecture, called PDS and written in the Schema Representation Language, for the online, real-time diagnosis of malfunctions in machine operations. Diagnosis is based on information acquired from tens to hundreds of sensors, which is analyzed to account gracefully for sensor degradation over time as well as spurious readings. Weck (1986) has presented a modular, flexible monitoring and diagnosis system that can be adapted to a variety of manufacturing equipment and tasks. Its simplicity of programming and ease of use make it an effective aid to process and machine diagnosis. He illustrated its application with results obtained during the monitoring of drilling tools using pattern recognition techniques. Weck and Kiratli (1987) have investigated the applicability and potential impact of knowledge-based systems in flexible manufacturing using an integrated parts-making and assembly FMS as a potential application case. Applicability was investigated using three-level expert systems both to control the FMS and to carry out diagnosis of failures in the system. They found expert systems to be useful tools, not only for assisting the users of FMSs in carrying out tasks that they formerly had to carry out manually, but also in performing tasks that were virtually impossible to perform using conventional software. They see, however, a need for considerable further development of AI software and hardware and of sensor techniques if the full potential of expert systems technology to greatly improve the capabilities of flexible manufacturing is to be realized.

Business Operations System

Efforts toward application of AI in the manufacturing enterprise's business operations system and its integration with the technological CIM system are in an appreciably earlier stage than efforts toward application in the technological CIM system just described. In fact, almost all of these efforts have so far been directed principally toward utilization of expert systems technology in supporting managerial decision making. A good overview of the contemporary state of such efforts has been presented by Paradice (1988). He reports that some degree of success has already been obtained in applying AI to such decision making in the areas of financial analysis, portfolio management, general linear program formulation, managerial problem diagnosis, and database design. Theoretical development is underway in such areas as problem formulation, management's problem domain, and the representation strategy. He illustrates the nature of such work by use of an example in the form of a laboratory prototype managerial expert system called SmartSLIM, an enhanced version of the System Laboratory for Information Management's (SLIM) decision support system.

Overall CIM System

Turning finally to consideration of the overall CIM system, considerable effort and thought have been, and are being, devoted to illustrating the extent of AI's current application in CIM and to analyzing its future role. Concerning current application, Engelke (1987) has highlighted the typical areas in CIM systems (which he calls integrated CAD/CAM systems). In the area of design, he highlights design synthesis, parametric programming, and the checking of design rules against specifications as typical. In the area of production planning, he highlights design analysis for process planning and in production control he highlights intelligent vision systems, image processing, and pattern recognition. In the areas of production equipment and processes, he highlights manipulation of randomly placed objects by robots. Looking at applications relevant to enhancing the operation of the overall system, he highlights user interfacing and engineering and manufacturing problem solving.

As for application of expert systems *per se* in the CIM system Meyer (1987) has compiled a very helpful tabulation (see Table 1) of typical expert systems already in use

Table 1. Expert Systems Manufacturing Applications[a]

System	Developer	Application
Engineering Design		
XCON	DEC	Configures all DEC VAX computer systems
HICLASS	Hughes	Knowledge base implementation for producibility aspects of small fabricated mechanical part design
VULCAN	United Technologies Corp.	Automated design of intermediate manufacturing shapes for a class of axisymmetric forged parts
Cell Design Aid	Arthur Andersen and Co.	Use for group technology flexible manufacturing cells/system design
CADHELP	DEC	CAD subsystem for assisting in the design of digital logic circuits
Knowledge System	Boeing	Integrated computation programs for vehicle designers that integrates heterogeneous software for aerospace vehicle design
EXCABL	Rockwell International	Configures control cabling for space shuttle payloads and experiments
Intelligent Optical Design Program	Los Alamos National Laboratory	Designs image-forming optical systems
Manufacturing Planning		
HICLASS	Hughes	Generates process plans and manufacturing work instructions
METCAPP	Metcut	Generates process plans for machining operations
Automated CNC Milling	Ben Gurion University (Israel)	Generates CNC part programs for CNC milling
XPSE-E	CAM-I	Generates process plans for part fabrication
Manufacturing Control		
IMACS	DEC	Generates detailed build plans from customer orders for computer hardware fabrication and assembly
ISIS	Westinghouse	Develops factory job shop schedules for detailed parts fabrication
PTRANS	DEC	Controls manufacture and distribution of DEC computer systems
ISA	DEC	Assists production control analysts in scheduling factory orders
IFES	Hughes	Models the dynamic flow of factory information
Factory Automation		
MOVE	Industrial Technology Institute	Planning assistant for material handling
Dispatcher	Carnegie Group, Inc.	Controls and monitors automated material handling systems
GMR Experimental Flexible Assembly Cell	General Motors Research Laboratory	Flexible automation assembly system programmed via graphical language
VIREC	University of Florida	Knowledge-based system for automated visual recognition of industrial parts
FMS/CML	Westinghouse, North Carolina State University	Computer simulation tool for FMS design, planning, and control
HICLASS	Hughes	Interprets design engineering notes via natural language processing and communicates producibility information to both assembly workers and design engineers
FMS Simulator	Arizona State University	Constructs FMS design models for system verification via simulation

[a] Reprinted with permission of the Society of Manufacturing Engineers.

(in 1987) in industry, in engineering design, manufacturing planning, manufacturing control, and factory automation. Kusiak (1988) has edited a comprehensive work that reviews current developments and applications of AI across the entire spectrum of CIM systems, including managerial developments and applications. Many of the papers in this volume also briefly consider the future role of AI in CIM. The work is a very helpful resource for those who wish to explore the subject of artificial intelligence in computer-integrated manufacturing in greater depth than is possible here.

FUTURE ROLE OF AI IN CIM

Concerning the future role of AI in CIM systems, Merchant (1985) has analyzed existing Delphi-type technological forecasts on the future of manufacturing to determine their implications for utilization of AI in manufacturing systems. He identified three main thrusts for the future: (1) toward the application of AI to accomplish full utilization of the product definition database, generated by CAD, as the primary source for automatic generation of all the information required throughout the rest of the system of manufacturing; (2) toward the application of AI, in conjunction with pattern-recognition techniques, to accomplish full automation of all production activities carried on throughout the system of manufacturing; and (3) toward the application of AI to accomplish overall online adaptive optimization of advanced manufacturing systems and their components.

Hatvany (1985) conducted research on appropriate approaches to the architecture of overall manufacturing systems that would be conducive to maximum effectiveness. As a result he concluded that during the past 30 years our thinking about complex computer-controlled systems has been conditioned by the concepts of hierarchic structures. However, recent advances in distributed computing power and open system architectures (particularly local-area networks) have opened the way for utilization of heterarchic structures in the future. Further, he finds that, based on the incomplete and nonalgorithmic architecture specification that ensues from this approach, these future systems will need to be able to exercise a high degree of local intelligence to cope with unforeseen situations.

However, the greatest future promise and potential impact of AI for the overall CIM system relates to the fact that the system of manufacturing, despite the best strivings of the engineering profession to arrive at fully deterministic methodologies, can never be a totally deterministic system. Among the reasons for this is the fact that the system must always have interfaces with nondeterministic elements of the real world. These include human beings, who are often far from logical or free of error in their performance, and the economic, social, and political systems of the world, with all their vagaries. Further, as pointed by Hatvany (1983), the system of manufacturing, even within a given manufacturing company, involves such an overwhelming welter of variables, parameters, interactions, activities, flows of material and information, etc, that neither a detailed, explicit algorithm for each solution procedure, nor all the facts, mathematical relations, and models available in perfect arrangement and complete form for a deterministic (and unique) answer can ever be found. What is required then, as Hatvany indicates, for realization of the full potential of CIM, is intelligent manufacturing systems capable of solving, within certain limits, unprecedented, unforeseen problems on the basis of even incomplete and imprecise information. The technology of artificial intelligence must advance considerably in capability to carry out the kinds of inference and even intuition that persons now use to overcome the problems arising from the nondeterministic nature of the overall manufacturing system before that potential can be significantly realized. As AI technology advances, however, integration of that capability into the computer-integrated-manufacturing system can assure realization of the dramatic improvement of manufacturing productivity and quality that CIM technology can provide.

BIBLIOGRAPHY

K. Ando and H. Yoshikawa, "Generation of Manufacturing Information in Intelligent CAD," *Ann. CIRP* **38**, 133–136 (1989).

G. Bel, D. Dubois, H. Farreny, and H. Prade, "Towards the Use of Fuzzy Rule-based Systems in the Monitoring of Manufacturing Processes," *Proceedings of the PROLAMAT Sixth International Conference,* AFCET, Paris, 1985, pp. 109–119.

P. Bertok and J. Vancza, "The Role of Artificial Intelligence Methods in Manufacturing Control," *Software for Factory Automation,* Elsevier, Amsterdam, 1989, pp. 337–352.

D. A. Bourne and M. S. Fox, "Autonomous Manufacturing: Automating the Job Shop," *Comput. Mag.* **17**(9), 76–88 (1984).

CASA/SME, *CIM Wheel,* 2nd ed., SME, Nov. 5, 1985 (revised).

I. Darbyshire and B. J. Davies, "EXCAP, an Expert Systems Approach to Recursive Process Planning," *Proc. CIRP Sem. Manufact. Sys.* **14**, 127–138 (1985).

W. D. Engelke, *How to Integrate CAD/CAM Systems,* Marcel Decker, New York, 1987, pp. 297–301.

J. S. Gero, "Object Modelling Through Knowledge Engineering," *Proc. CIRP Sem. Manufact. Sys.* **14**, 54–62 (1985).

J. Hatvany, "The Efficient Use of Deficient Information," *Ann. CIRP* **32**, 423–425 (1983).

J. Hatvany, "Intelligence and Cooperation in Heterarchic Manufacturing Systems," *Proc. CIRP Sem. Manufact. Sys.* **14**, 5–10 (1985).

K. Iwata and N. Sugimura, "A Knowledge Based Computer Aided Process Planning System for Machine Parts," *Proc. CIRP Sem. Manufact. Sys.* **14**, 139–152 (1985).

F. Kimura and H. Suzuki, "A CAD System for Efficient Product Design Based on Design Intent," *Ann. CIRP* **38**, 149–152 (1989).

A. Kusiak, ed., *Artificial Intelligence: Implications for CIM,* IFS Publications, Bedford, U.K., 1988.

M. E. Merchant, "The Future of Batch Manufacture," *Phil. Trans. R. Soc. London* **A275**, 357–372 (1973).

M. E. Merchant, "Analysis of Existing Technological Forecasts Pertinent to the Utilization of Artificial Intelligence and Pattern Recognition Techniques in Manufacturing Engineering," *Proc. CIRP Sem. Manufact. Sys.* **14**, 11–16 (1985).

R. J. Meyer, "AI and Expert Systems: In Pursuit of CIM," *Manuf. Eng.* **98**(2), CT15–18 (1987).

V. R. Milačić and M. Kalajdžić, "Logical Structure of Manufacturing Process Design—Fundamentals of an Expert System for Manufacturing Process Planning," *Proc. CIRP Sem. Manufact. Sys.* **14**, 153–167 (1985).

P. A. Newman, "Scheduling in CIM Systems," *Artificial Intelligence: Implications for CIM,* IFS Publications, Bedford, U.K., 1988, pp. 361–402.

T. Ouchi, M. Mibuka, K. Kouzouki, and K. Taguchi, "The Intelligent Production Control System for Color TV Assembly Process," *Proc. CIRP Sem. Manufact. Sys.* **14**, 245–255 (1985).

D. B. Paradice, "Databases and Knowledge Bases in Managerial Expert Systems," *Artificial Intelligence: Implications for CIM,* IFS Publications, Bedford, U.K., 1988, pp. 405–432.

J. Peklenik and A. Sluga, "Contribution to Development of a Generative CAPP-System Based on Manufacturing Process Topology," *Ann. CIRP* **38**, 407–412 (1989).

K. Preiss and E. Kaplansky, "Automated Part Programming for CNC Milling by Artificial Intelligence Techniques," *J. Manufact. Sys.* **4**, 51–63 (1985).

B. Sauve and A. Collinot, "An Expert System for Scheduling in a Flexible Manufacturing System," *Robot. Comput. Integr. Manufact.* **3**, 229–233 (1987).

J. Triouleyre, "Elaboration of Expert System Knowledge Based Structure," *Proc. CIRP Sem. Manufact. Sys.* **14**, 236–244 (1985).

M. Weck, "Development and Application of a Flexible, Modular Monitoring and Diagnosis System," *Comput. Ind.* **7**, 45–51 (1986).

M. Weck and G. Kiratli, "Applicability of Expert Systems to Flexible Manufacturing," in *Robot. Comput. Integr. Manufact.* **3**, 97–103 (1987).

W. J. Zdeblick and B. E. Barkocy, "Manufacturing Planning Evolution with Artificial Intelligence and Applications Toward Machining Operations," *Proceedings of the PROLAMAT Sixth International Conference,* AFCET, Paris, 1985, pp. 99–108.

M. Eugene Merchant
Institute of Advanced
Manufacturing Sciences,
Inc.

MATHEMATICAL INDUCTION. See Induction, mathematical.

MATHEMATICAL KNOWLEDGE REPRESENTATION

One of the intended applications of the MKRP (qv) system is to prove all the lemmas and theorems of a standard textbook of a particular mathematical field. With the present system, this is possible in principle (one third of a text book on semigroups and automata has, in fact, been encoded and proved) but there are problems: it is cumbersome to express typical mathematical notions in plain first-order predicate calculus, which is more like a "machine language" of the MKRP system. Encoding a text book requires a user-friendly input language that offers some higher order constructs which can be automatically translated into the "machine language" of the logical engine.

The factual knowledge of a mathematical field is highly structured, and this structure influences the search for a proof; eg, a human mathematician knows when and down to which level to expand a definition. An adequate representation for such knowledge was developed and a substantial part of the mathematical knowledge of a text book was encoded into this representation.

J. H. Siekmann
Universität Kaiserslautern

MEANS-ENDS ANALYSIS

Means-ends analysis is a term that is quite descriptive. In the context of problem-solving (qv), it refers to the process of comparing what is given or known to what is desired and, on the basis of this comparison, selecting a "reasonable" thing to do next. This definition is deliberately informal and general because it is intended to capture the essential nature of a number of different, but similar, problem-solving methods.

The use of means-ends analysis in computer programs that solve problems dates back to 1957 when it was first used in GPS (qv) (Newell, Shaw, and Simon, 1960). Since then, mean-ends analysis has been the topic of considerable research, only some of which was part of the GPS effort. This article describes most of this research; it starts with a description of GPS, partly for historical reasons, but also because it is quite easy to describe other programs given a technical description of GPS. Amazingly enough, the variant of means-ends analysis used in GPS is still one of the more elaborate and subtle problem-solving methods reported in the literature (ie, methods that have applicability in several different domains, unlike a method that can only be used, for example, in chess).

Over the years, research on GPS had at least three distinct goals: One was empirical explorations into problem solving and generality. This was important in the earlier years because little was known about how to get a computer to behave intelligently. The final version of GPS, which is the culmination of this research, is described in Ernst and Newell (1969). A second goal was the simulation of cognitive processes for the purpose of understanding the extent to which GPS can be used as a model of human problem solving. A good reference to this research is Newell and Simon (1972), which also contains several other models of human problem solving. The remaining contribution of research on GPS is its problem-solving method; it is the only one described in this entry.

Another variant of means-ends analysis is used in FDS (Quinlan and Hunt, 1968), which is described after GPS. This problem solver was designed for a certain class of theorem-proving problems. In the early seventies there was a significant research effort at Stanford Research Institute on the use of problem solving in robotics. This work was based on STRIPS (Fikes and Nilsson, 1971), a computer program that used means-ends analysis. It and one of its successors, ABSTRIPS (Sacerdoti, 1974) is described after FDS.

The last variant of means-ends analysis in this entry is MPS (Korf, 1985). This research differs from the others in that it focuses on learning good strategies for solving problems. The strategies that are learned use mean-ends analysis and are sufficiently powerful for MPS to solve difficult puzzles, such as Rubik's cube. The entry closes with a discussion of how to choose good differences for GPS. The differences are problem-dependent parameters whose purpose is to guide the search for a solution.

GPS

GPS is an acronym for general problem-solver. This name stems from the fact that it was the first problem-solving program that separated the problem-dependent and the problem-independent parts of the system in a reasonably clean way. GPS was designed to solve state space problems (Nilsson, 1971) in which there is an initial state, a set of goal states, and a set of operators. Each operator f is a partial function on states; $dom(f)$ denotes its domain. A solution to a problem is a sequence of operators that transforms the initial state into a goal state. Each intermediate state produced by one of these operators must be in the domain of the next operator in the sequence.

To solve a problem, GPS creates a hierarchy of goals;

the first goal is to transform the initial state into a goal state. Assuming that the initial state is not a goal state. GPS detects differences between them and then attempts to reduce one of these differences. For this kind of goal, GPS selects an operator that is relevant to reducing the difference and creates the goal of applying the operator. A separate goal is used for this because the initial state may not be in the domain of the operator that gives rise to a difference and the goal of reducing it.

This very brief description of how GPS works contains the three different kinds of goals that GPS uses:

- Transform a state into a set of states,
- Reduce a difference possessed by a state, and
- Apply an operator to a state.

The method for achieving a transform goal tests if the state is in the set of states. If not, the goal of reducing the largest difference between them is created, followed by the goal of transforming its result into the set of states. GPS requires the differences to be totally ordered. The method for achieving a reduce goal selects a relevant operator and creates the goal of applying it. GPS requires a table that indicates which operators are relevant to which differences. The method for achieving an apply goal tests if the state is in the domain of the operator. If not, the goal of reducing the largest difference between them is created, followed by the goal of applying the operator to the result of the reduce goal. To summarize, GPS uses three different kinds of goals, and for each there is a single method for achieving it. This is a slightly simplified picture of GPS. There was a select type of goal and other methods also. These were required for operators that mapped two states into a third state. GPS could handle such operators even though they are excluded by the state space paradigm; the details are in Ernst and Newell (1969). This entry only describes how GPS solved state space problems.

Information about differences is a problem-dependent parameter to GPS; its purpose is to make the search more efficient. More problem-solving methods designed for more than a single problem have such parameters; for example, h is such a parameter to the A* problem-solving method (Nilsson, 1971) (see A* ALGORITHM). GPS requires the following information about differences:

- The differences to be used;
- An ordering on these differences; and
- For each difference, the operators relevant to reducing it.

Intuitively, the differences are just properties of states that are appropriate for the given problem. Some of these are more difficult to remove than others, and thus they are ordered according to their difficulty. GPS employs the strategy of removing differences in order of their difficulty, the most difficult first. Any operator will be relevant to removing some differences but not others. These intuitive concepts can be used inside of GPS because it is parameterized by the information about differences, which varies from problem to problem.

A trace of GPS solving a simple problem will make the above description more concrete. The problem is the three-disk Tower of Hanoi whose initial state has three disks of different diameters stacked on the first peg in ascending order; the other two pegs are empty. There is only one goal state in which all the disks are on the third peg. The operators move the top disk from one peg to another, provided that the disk being moved is not placed on a smaller disk.

Figure 1 shows how GPS solves this problem. As always, the first goal is to transform the initial state s0 to the goal states G. Comparing the two, GPS detects that all of the disks are in the wrong positions. The second goal is to reduce the largest of these differences; d3 indicates that the position of disk 3 is incorrect, and GPS notes in goal 2 that it should be on peg 3. Goal 3 is to apply the operator that moves disk 3 to peg 3. Of course, this operator cannot be directly applied because s0 is not in its domain since the other two disks are not on peg 2. Therefore, goal 4 is created to reduce d2, the larger of these two differences. Since disk 2 cannot be moved in s0 (goal 5), disk 1 is moved to peg 3 (goals 6 and 7), which results in the new state s1. Disk 2 is then moved in s1 (goal 8) resulting in s2. Goal 9 is another attempt to move disk 3, but this cannot be done in s2, and GPS continues in a similar manner.

The indentation in Figure 1 is important because it shows the hierarchical relationship among the goals. Although this relationship is obvious for the first seven goals, note that goal 9 is a subgoal of goal 3. This is impor-

1. Transform s0 into G.
  2. Reduce d3 of s0 to peg-3.
    3. Apply disk-3 → peg-3 to s0.
      4. Reduce d2 of s0 to peg-2.
        5. Apply disk-2 → peg-2 to s0.
          6. Reduce d1 of s0 to peg-3.
            7. Apply disk-1 → peg-3 to s0.
              s1 = ((2 3) () (1))
        8. Apply disk-2 → peg-2 to s1.
          s2 = ((3) (2) (1))
    9. Apply disk-3 → peg-3 to s2.
      10. Reduce d1 of s2 to peg-2.
        11. Apply disk-1 → peg-2 to s2.
          s3 = ((3) (1 2) ())
      12. Apply disk-3 → peg-3 to s3.
        s4 = (() (1 2) (3))
  13. Transform s4 into G.
    14. Reduce d2 of s4 to peg-3.
      15. Apply disk-2 → peg-3 to s4.
        16. Reduce d1 of s4 to peg-2.
          17. Apply disk-1 → peg-1 to s4.
            s5 = ((1) (2) (3))
        18. Apply disk-2 → peg-3 to s5.
          s6 = ((1) () (2 3))
  19. Transform s6 into G.
    20. Reduce d1 of s6 to peg-3.
      21. Apply disk-1 → peg-3 to s6.
        s7 = (() () (1 2 3))
    22. Transform s7 into G.
    Success.

Figure 1. A trace of GPS solving the three-disk Tower of Hanoi problem.

tant because the operator of goal 3 is used for the operator of goal 9. Moving disk 3 in goal 12 causes goal 9 to be solved, which finally causes goal 3 to be solved, and goal 13 becomes the second transform goal, which is a subgoal of goal 1. The whole process stops with goal 22, which is trivially solved because s7 is an element of G. This causes goals 19, 13, and 1 to be solved because they are supergoals of goal 22.

The behavior depicted in Figure 1 is strongly dependent on the difference information that was used. The difference ordering is d3 > d2 > d1, and each difference indicates an incorrect position of a particular disk. An operator that moves a disk is relevant to reducing the difference that pertains to that disk. The difference information only contains difference types; in solving a problem, multiple instances or tokens of each difference may be encountered. For example, the difference (token) of goal 2 is not just that the position of disk 3 is wrong but also that its goal position is peg 3. In addition to the type of the difference, GPS uses its goal value to select a relevant operator. The version of GPS in Ernst and Newell (1969) analyzed the specification of operators to find one that produced the goal value of a difference. This version exhibits the behavior shown in Figure 1. Note that Figure 1 shows GPS at its best since it always selects the right operator for the right reason. Normally, GPS makes mistakes because its difference information is "weaker," and this gives rise to search.

Although Figure 1 gives an intuitively appealing picture of GPS, it does not show how GPS relates to other mechanical problem-solving concepts. Nilsson (1971) noted that GPS is conceptually based on a form of AND/OR trees. A technical description of GPS based on this idea follows. This description is necessarily somewhat more complex than the one in Nilsson (1971). The original problem is divided into a number of subproblems of the form (s, D); s is the initial state of the subproblem and D is the set of desired states. Such a subproblem is trivial if $s \in D$. GPS attempts to solve each nontrivial subproblem in the same way: for each operator that is relevant to reducing the largest difference between s and D, two new subproblems are created: $(s, \text{dom}(f))$ and $(f(r), D)$. A solution to the first of these results in a state r in the domain of f. The second subproblem is to transform the result of applying f to r into D. A complication is that each subproblem may have multiple solutions, and thus there may be many subproblems of the form $(f(r), D)$, one for each different r produced by a solution of $(s, \text{dom}(f))$.

This decomposition of a subproblem can be represented by the AND/OR tree in Figure 2. The root is the subproblem of transforming s into D. The operators that are relevant to reducing the largest difference between s and D are f and g and perhaps others. Each r_i is in dom(f) because it is a result of solving $(s, \text{dom}(f))$; hence, the original subproblem can be reduced to any subproblem $(f(r_i), D)$. Since some of these may not have a solution, GPS must be prepared to consider all of them. Similarly, applying f may not lead to a solution, and it may be necessary to consider other relevant operators like g. As usual, the little arc on the branches of a node indicates that all of its subnodes need to be

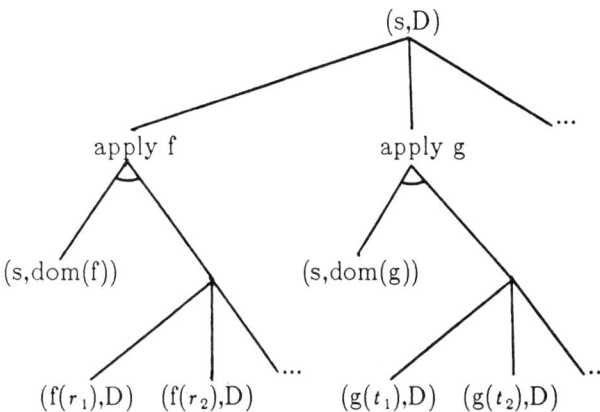

Figure 2. The AND/OR tree for the subproblem (s, D). Each r_i is a result of solving $(s, \text{dom}(f))$ and each t_i is a result of solving $(s \text{ dom}(g))$.

solved if the arc is missing. Since all of the terminal nodes are labeled with subproblems, this decomposition method can be applied recursively until trivial subproblems are encountered.

The example in Figure 3 clarifies this view of GPS. It does not have a physical interpretation, like the Tower of Hanoi, because such problems are either complicated or do not illustrate important features of GPS. The initial state is s, and G is the goal states, as indicated by the root of the tree in Figure 3. GPS attempts to apply the relevant operator f to s, which is not in its domain. To solve this sub-

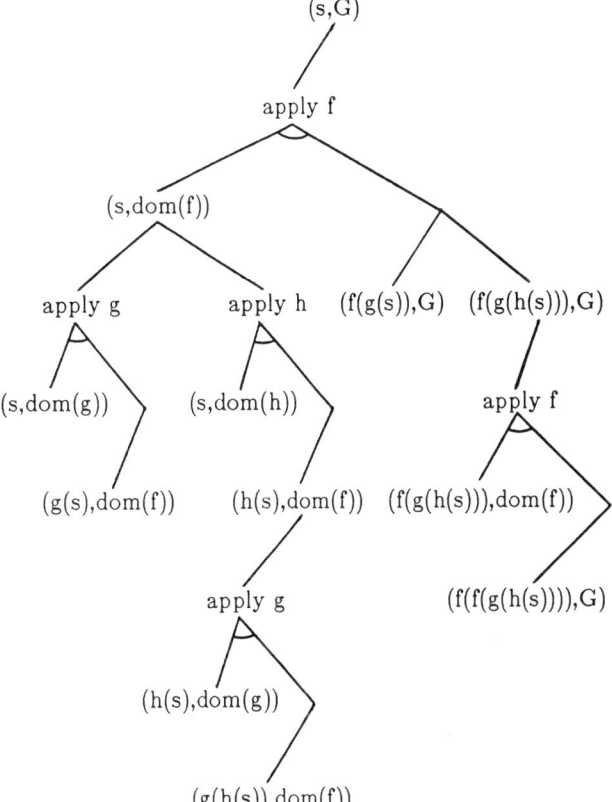

Figure 3. An example of GPS search viewed as an AND/OR tree.

problem $(s, \text{dom}(f))$, GPS attempts to apply g and h to s since they are relevant to the largest difference between s and $\text{dom}(f)$. This example assumes that all of the subproblems at the terminal nodes in Figure 3 are trivial except $(f(g(s)), G)$. Thus, g can be applied to s, and its result is in $\text{dom}(f)$. This makes $g(s)$ a result of solving $(s, \text{dom}(f))$, and the subproblem $(f(g(s)), G)$ is created. However, $(s, \text{dom}(f))$ can also be solved by applying h to s. Since $h(s)$ is not in $\text{dom}(f)$, g is applied to it. This produces another result of solving $(s, \text{dom}(f))$ because $g(h(s)) \in \text{dom}(f)$, solve the latter, f is applied again, which produces a solution; that is, $f(f(g(h(s)))) \in G$.

This example illustrates how OR nodes give rise to multiple subproblem results. Using the notation in Figure 2, the results of subproblem (s, D) are recursively defined as follows:

s is a result of (s, D) if $s \in D$; and
the results of subproblems $(f(r_i), D)$ and $(g(t_i), D)$ are also results of (s, D).

This description of GPS depicts one use of the difference ordering—to select the largest difference of a subproblem. Usually a subproblem (s, D) will have several differences between s and D. GPS only considers the largest of these differences and is prepared to apply all operators relevant to this difference. This use of the difference ordering and operator relevance restricts the number of operators used on a subproblem to some fraction of the total number of operators. Although this makes the search more efficient, the difference ordering has another use that gives a more dramatic improvement to search. GPS rejects any subproblem that is more difficult than the subproblem for which it was created. The difficulty of a subproblem (s, D) is the largest difference between s and D; thus, the difference ordering essentially defines the difficulty of subproblems. Rejecting subproblems because they are too difficult is a very powerful heuristic because it prevents large portions of the search space from ever being explored.

A precise definition of this heuristic can be given in terms of the notation in Figure 2. Subproblem $(s, \text{dom}(f))$ must be strictly less difficult than (s, D); otherwise, the former will not be attempted. The same is true of $(s, \text{dom}(g))$. The subproblem $(f(r_i), D)$ must be less difficult or as difficult as (s, D); otherwise, search will be terminated at the former. The same is true for $(g(t_i), D)$. The first of these rules controls GPS's use of recursion; that is, applying an operator so that another operator can be applied. In particular, it prohibits the use of f to transform s into $\text{dom}(f)$. The second rule controls GPS's use of iteration; that is, once an operator is applied, the result must still be transformed into D. This rule allows multiple applications of an operator because its first application may not remove the difference, but a second application of the same operator may remove the difference. Note that an operator that is relevant to a difference is not guaranteed to remove the difference. This would be too strong since most operators in the various problems that GPS has solved do not possess such guarantees.

The above is a detailed description of the GPS problem-solving method and does not attempt to describe how to use GPS effectively. The difference information is very important to GPS's performance, which may vary from an exhaustive search to no search at all. It may also cause GPS to miss all of the solutions to a problem. What constitutes good difference information is discussed in the penultimate section of this entry.

FDS

FDS (Quinlan and Hunt, 1968) is a program that was designed to solve a class of theorem-proving problems, such as proving algebraic identities. The version of means-ends analysis in FDS is in many respects similar to GPS. Differences are used to select operators, and the same kind of subproblems are created. Unlike GPS, FDS does not use a difference ordering. Instead, it orders the operators that are relevant to reducing the differences of a subproblem according to how well they remove differences and how difficult they are to apply. This is determined, not by applying the operators, but by analyzing their behavior in terms of the differences they introduce and remove. Another major deviation from GPS is that FDS uses the same set of differences for all problems. This essentially moves the difference information inside of FDS which, consequently, has no problem-dependent parameters. The relevance of operators to differences is determined by FDS through an analysis of the operator specification. This has the good effect of making FDS self-contained since no external heuristic information is required. The performance is not appreciably degraded by this; FDS has the ability to solve reasonably difficult problems. However, for some problems other differences and a difference ordering have proven to be very useful. FDS does not appear to be suitable for such problems.

STRIPS

STRIPS (qv) (Fikes and Nilsson, 1971) is a program that was designed for solving problems that a robot might encounter. An applied predicate calculus is used to represent problems in STRIPS. The representation used by other problem-solving programs is not discussed in this entry since the emphasis is on their problem-solving methods. However, in the case of STRIPS the representation seems to have had an impact on the way it solves problems. A state in STRIPS is represented by the conjunction of a set of literals, such as Inroom(Robot, Room-1), which indicates that the robot is in room 1.

The goal states are represented in STRIPS by a formula in predicate calculus; any state that satisfies it is a goal state. Operators are robot actions and can best be described by an example: Push(x, y) is

Precondition: Pushable(x), Object(y), Nextto(Robot, x), $\exists r$(Inroom(Robot,r) & Inroom (y,r) & Inroom(x,r));

Deletions: At(Robot,$1,$2), Nextto(Robot,$1), At(x,$1,$2), Nextto(x,$1), Nextto($1,x); and

Additions: Nextto(x,y), Nextto(y,x), Nextto(Robot,x).

In this operator the robot pushes object x to object y, provided that x and y are in the same room with the robot. A state is in the domain of the operator if all of the formulas in the precondition are true. The output state of the operator is formed by modifying its input state; all of the literals in the deletion list are deleted, and the literals in the addition list are added. Variables $1 and $2 match anything.

Like GPS, STRIPS starts by comparing the initial state to the goal states to detect differences between the two. A difference is a formula in the goal state (or in the precondition of an operator) that is not satisfied by the given state. It then attempts to apply an operator that is relevant to a difference. If an operator has a literal in its addition list that is part of the difference, the operator is considered relevant to the difference. In attempting to apply an operator, its precondition may not be satisfied. In this case STRIPS creates the subproblem of transforming the given state into the domain of the operator and attempts to solve it in the same way that it attempts the main problem.

The main deviations of STRIPS from GPS is that it uses no difference ordering and is committed to the particular kind of differences described above. Thus, STRIPS needs no problem-dependent parameters, like GPS's difference information, since it can determine operator relevance by a simple analysis of the operators. Although no external heuristic information is given to STRIPS, the formulation of operators is very important because the differences are embedded in their preconditions. Reformulating the operators may thus change the differences, which may have a large effect on STRIPS's performance Problems like Fool's Disks (see below) require differences that are more or less independent of the problem formulation. STRIPS has no provision for such differences and consequently would have difficulty with such problems. However, a modification of it uses a difference ordering in a very effective way, which is described next.

ABSTRIPS

ABSTRIPS (Sacerdoti, 1974) was designed for the same class of problems as STRIPS and uses a very similar representation for problems. Each literal in the precondition of an operator is assigned a criticality value whose purpose is to indicate how difficult it is to remove a difference that contains this literal. As in STRIPS, differences are formulas that are not satisfied by the given state. The criticality values are assigned in a semiautomatic way; a partial ordering on the predicates, reflecting their intuitive importance, must be given to ABSTRIPS, which then assigns the criticality values by analyzing the operator specifications.

ABSTRIPS starts by solving the problem at the highest criticality level; ie, it ignores all those literals in the preconditions of operators that have a lower criticality value. This yields a solution that is correct in the most critical literals but not in other literals. Next, it solves the problem at the second highest criticality level. This involves finding a literal at this level that was not true in the top-level solution, creating the subproblem of making it true and inserting its solution into the top-level solution. For example, suppose the problem is to move Box-1 to Box-2.

At the top level the single operator (Push(Box-1, Box-2) is a solution to the problem. But at the next level STRIPS notes that the two boxes are not in the same room. Moving Box-1 to Box-2's room is set up as a subproblem and its solution together with Push(Box-1, Box-2) constitutes a solution to the main problem. ABSTRIPS solves all of the subproblems at a particular criticality level and then moves to the next lower criticality level. Backtracking occurs when no solution to a subproblem can be found. This causes ABSTRIPS to find an alternative solution at the higher levels.

This use of criticality values is essentially the same as GPS's use of the difference ordering. ABSTRIPS only considers the most difficult differences of a subproblem, those of the current criticality level; smaller criticality values are ignored, and larger ones have already been removed. An operator can be applied to a state that is not in its domain, but at lower criticality levels the subproblem of transforming the state into its domain must be solved. This corresponds to GPS's rule that the difficulty of transforming a state into the domain of an operator must be less than the difference the operator is supposed to reduce. The reason is that the subproblem must be solved at lower criticality levels. Thus, ABSTRIPS generates the same subproblems as GPS and uses the same rules for terminating search.

The new thing in ABSTRIPS is that the order of its search is different from that of GPS. Using the notation in Figure 2, ABSTRIPS delays $(s, \text{dom}(f))$ until after $(f(r_i), D)$ has been solved. This is non-trivial because r_i, a result of the former, is unknown; ie, r_i is whatever state a solution to $(s, \text{dom}(f))$ produces, and this subproblem has not yet been solved. ABSTRIPS is very clever about this because it does not care about the lower criticality literals in r_i; it only cares about the higher ones, which it already knows. Delaying $(s, \text{dom}(f))$ can be very prudent because $(f(r_i, D)$ may not be solvable in which case $(s, \text{dom}(f))$ will never be attempted. Of course, in some cases $(s, \text{dom}(f))$ will not be solvable, and the effort in solving $(f(r_i), D)$ has been wasted.

Sacerdoti (1974) views ABSTRIPS as solving a problem in a hierarchy of abstraction spaces, each criticality level being a different abstraction space. The solution at each level forms a plan for the solution at the next lower level. Newell and Simon (1972) have proposed a similar method in which the planning space is defined in terms of the difference ordering (Newell and Simon, 1972, pp. 428–435). Basically, the difference ordering is cut in half; the more difficult half is used in the planning space; and the easier half is used in the problem space. As with ABSTRIPS, the same set of subgoals is encountered, but in a different order. This research shows that there is a definite connection between the difference ordering and planning and that such methods dramatically improve search. Empirical tests show that ABSTRIPS's search is much more efficient than that of STRIPS.

MPS

MPS (Korf, 1985) is a problem-solving method that is capable of efficiently solving some very difficult puzzles, such as Rubik's cube. MPS requires its problems to have a single goal state rather than a set of goal states. The central component of MPS is the macro table in which each column is labeled by a state component and each row is labeled by a possible value for a state component. Each entry in a macro table is a macro operator, which is a sequence of operators. At each step in the problem-solving process, a macro operator is applied to the current state s by applying the first operator in the sequence to s, the next operator to the result of the first, etc. The resulting state is the input to MPS's next step. The macro operator m_{ij} that is applied to s is selected as follows: s and the goal state have the same values for the first $j - 1$ state components (which label the first $j - 1$ columns). In addition, i is the value of the jth component of s. This is a very simple procedure; the trick is to use a macro table that leads to a solution.

Macro tables are required to have the following property: If m_{ij} is applied to any state in which the first $j - 1$ components have their goal values and component j has i as its value, the resulting state will have goal values for its first j components. In addition, the precondition of each operator in m_{ij} will be satisfied if m_{ij} is applied to a state with these values for its first j components. Needless to say, these are very strong conditions, but they can be satisfied for many problems. The first step of MPS produces a state whose first component has its goal value; after the second step the second component has its goal value; etc. Unlike the methods described above, MPS does not use any search.

The column labels correspond to the differences of GPS, and their order gives the difference ordering, the label on column 1 being the most difficult difference. Thus, the first step of MPS removes the most difficult difference, and none of the remaining steps reintroduce it. This is equivalent to GPS's rules for terminating search at more difficult subproblems. MPS contains two extensions to GPS: Macro operators are used instead of operators to reduce differences, and each macro is guaranteed to reduce the difference to which it is relevant. Banerji (1984) also argued that these extensions to GPS were needed, but he did not have a particular proposal for the implementation of the latter.

The first extension is necessary because the differences are not invariant over operators; ie, in applying a macro operator, the operators that compose it temporarily reintroduce differences that have already been removed, but they are also removed before the end of the macro application. The second extension guarantees progress unlike the relevant operators in GPS, which are only required to affect and not necessarily to fix the property to which a difference pertains.

A mechanical procedure for learning macro operators with the desired properties has been developed; space permits only a brief outline of it. A search is conducted from the goal state using the inverse of the operators; ie, they are applied, first, to the goal state, then to the states produced by these applications, etc. For each state s in this space, there is a j such that the first $j - 1$ components of s have goal values and the jth component has some nongoal value i. Then the sequence of operators on the path from the goal state to s is the inverse of a macro operator for row i and column j of a macro table. Thus, each s identifies an entry for a macro table because the inverse of a macro is just the inverse of each of its elements in the reverse order. Examining enough of the search space should identify macros for an entire macro table. However, the ordering of state components (the column ordering) is an input parameter to this procedure; it is not learned.

MPS does not create subproblems of the form "transform a state into the domain of an operator." For problems like the Tower of Hanoi they would be useful. There are two major limitations of MPS: Multiple goal states are not allowed, and the differences must be state components. Fool's Disks, described below, is an example of a problem that violates both of these conditions and hence lies outside MPS's domain of applicability.

GOOD DIFFERENCE INFORMATION

The previous sections have pointed out the importance of difference information. This section addresses the question of what properties difference information should possess to efficiently guide search. For motivation, this discussion starts with an example. Fool's Disks is a puzzle in which each state has four disks that can be rotated independently of each other; Figure 4 gives the initial state. There are eight numbers on each disk, and the goal is to align the disks so that each of the eight columns radiating from the center sums to 12. Good differences for this problem are

D3: The 16 numbers on the horizontal and vertical diameters do not sum to 48;
D2: the 8 numbers on a diameter do not sum to 24; and
D1: a radius does not sum to 12.

The difference ordering is D3>D2>D1. Using this difference information, GPS searches for a state that does not

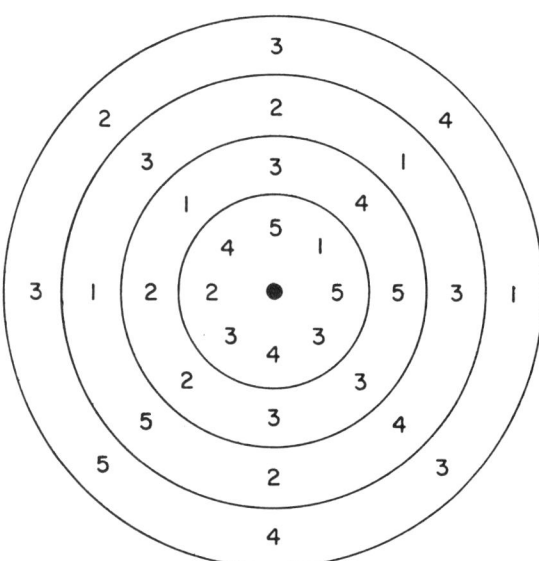

Figure 4. Initial state in Fool's Disks puzzle.

possess D3. Then, without reintroducing D3, it searches for a state that does not possess D2. And finally, it looks for a goal state without reintroducing either D3 or D2. Of course, GPS backtracks if necessary.

The invariances of the differences are important. A difference d is invariant over an operator f if, for any state s, both s and $f(s)$ either possess d or both do not. In other words, f neither introduces nor removes d. For example, D2 and D3 are invariant over 180° moves that are relevant to D1. The invariances can be tabulated as follows:

	F3	F2	F1
D3	1	0	0
D2	1	1	0
D1	1	1	1

F1 are the 180° moves; F2 are the 90° and 270° moves; F3 are the remaining moves. A 0 indicates that the difference is invariant over the operators. Note that this table is triangular: 0's above the diagonal. In general, it is this triangular property of the differences that is desirable. It is also important that the difference orderig is the row ordering in the triangular table.

Fool's Disks has two interesting features besides the triangular property. Its differences are much more complex than a single-state component, such as the first number on the third disk. Most of the problem solvers in this entry (including the version of GPS in Ernst and Newell, 1969) cannot handle such differences. The second item has to do with operator relevance. Note that a 45° move is only used to reduce D3 even though it could also reduce D1. In general, only the 1's on the diagonal indicate operator relevance. Triangularity gives a global view of invariants, ie, how different invariants relate to one another. Local invariants are not enough because, for example, using a 45° move to reduce D1 will only have the undesirable effect of reintroducing D3, which is not present when attempting to reduce D1. Triangularity also leads to a form of completeness (Banerji and Ernst, 1977): GPS will find any solution in which the differences never increase. This shows that the off-diagonal 1's should not be used in the definition of relevance.

Triangularity has been used as the basis of a method (Goldstein and Ernst, 1982) for learning difference information. The basic idea is to find a set of differences that gives rise to a triangular table. The row ordering gives the difference ordering, and the diagonal entries give operator relevance. The method starts by looking for properties that are invariant over at least one operator. Then, the properties are combined to form properties all goal states possess. These properties are potential differences, and the method attempts to form a triangular table out of them. The details are given in Goldstein and Ernst (1982).

SUMMARY

A number of different problem-solving methods have employed some form of means-ends analysis. Empirical results show that it has been rather effective in controlling search. Most of these methods use a specialization of the mechanisms found in GPS in order to remove the requirement for external information about differences. In addition to GPS's mechanisms, MPS has two important mechanisms it uses very effectively in solving difficult puzzles like Rubik's cube. Some guidelines are given for selecting differences that lead to efficient search.

BIBLIOGRAPHY

R. B. Banerji, "GPS and the Psychology of the Rubik Cubist: A Study in Reasoning about Actions," in A. Elithorn and R. B. Banerji, eds., *Artificial and Human Intelligence*, Elsevier Science, New York, 1984.

R. B. Banerji and G. W. Ernst, "A Theory for the Complete Mechanization of a GPS-type Problem Solver," *Proceedings of the Fifth International Joint Conference on Artificial Intelligence*, Cambridge, Mass., pp. 450–456, 1977.

G. W. Ernst and A. Newell, *GPS: A Case Study in Generality and Problem Solving*, Academic Press, New York, 1969.

R. E. Fikes and N. J. Nilsson, "STRIPS: A New Approach to the Application of Theorem Proving to Problem Solving," *Artif. Intell.* **2,** 251–288 (1971).

M. M. Goldstein and G. W. Ernst, "Mechanical Discovery of Classes of Problem Solving Strategies," *JACM* **29,** 1–23 (Jan. 1982).

R. E. Korf, "Macro-Operators: A Weak Method of Learning," *Artif. Intell.* **26**(1), 35–78 (April 1985).

A. Newell, J. C. Shaw, and H. A. Simon, "Report on a General Problem-Solving Program," *Proceedings at the International Conference on Information Process.*, UNESCO House, Paris, 1960, pp. 256–264.

A. Newell and H. A. Simon, *Human Problem Solving*, Prentice Hall, Englewood Cliffs, N.J., 1972.

N. J. Nilsson, *Problem-Solving Methods in Artificial Intelligence*, McGraw-Hill, New York, 1971.

J. R. Quinlan and E. B. Hunt, "A Formal Deductive Problem-solving System," *JACM* **15,** 625–646 (Oct. 1968).

E. D. Sacerdoti, "Planning in a Hierarchy of Abstraction Spaces," *Artif. Intell.* **5,** 115–135 (1974).

G. Ernst
Case Western Reserve
University

MEDIATOR

Mediator was the earliest case-based problem solver. It resolved disputes over resources in a common-sense way. Mediator used case-based reasoning for 10 different inference tasks including problem classification and elaboration, plan selection and refinement, and recovery from failure. Mediator was important in showing the usefulness of case-based reasoning, showing how subgoals can control case-based inference, showing how several different cases can be integrated to solve a single problem, and providing the basis for integrating a case-based reasoner with a goal-directed problem solver. It showed that case-based reasoning can shortcut the long inference chains required when reasoning from scratch, that a case-based reasoner can avoid mistakes made previously, and that case-based reasoning is applicable to a wide variety of reasoning tasks. [See J. L. Kolodner and R. L. Simpson, "The Mediator: Analysis of an Early Case-Based Problem Solver," *Cognitive Science,* **13**(4), 507–549 (1989).]

JANET L. KOLODNER
Georgia Institute of Technology

MEDIC

MEDIC is an experimental medical diagnostic consultant (in the domain of pulmonology) written by Turner in 1989 at Georgia Institute of Technology. It is an adaptive, "schema-based" reasoner, which uses procedural, contextual, and strategic schemas to ensure that it behaves appropriately for the problem-solving situation it is in, even as changes occur in that situation. It incorporates ideas from a generalized form of case-based reasoning (qv) and from reactive planning (qv): generalized cases and generalized plans (ie, compiled experience) are represented as schemas, which are retrieved from a memory and applied to control behavior; changes in the situation can interrupt the reasoner, which then uses contextual and strategic knowledge to decide if and how to respond. The diagnostic technique used is a simplified version of INTERNIST-1's, represented as procedural schemas. The schema-based reasoning approach used in MEDIC is currently being applied to other, more reactive domains (for example, controlling autonomous underwater vehicles). [See R. Turner, *A Schema-Based Model of Adaptive Problem Solving,* Ph.D. dissertation, Georgia Institute of Technology, Atlanta, Ga., 1989; R. Turner, "Using Schemas for Diagnosis," *Computer Methods and Programs in Biomedicine,* **30**(2/3), 199–208 (1989).]

ROY M. TURNER
University of New Hampshire

MEDICINE, AI IN

For more than 30 years, collaborating computer scientists and physicians have studied the nature of medical reasoning, with the aim of building computer programs to assist in medical decision-making. In 1959, a seminal paper introduced logic, Bayesian probability theory, and value theory to the medical community as a basis for diagnostic reasoning (Ledley and Lusted, 1959); a decade of research followed in which probabilistic reasoning programs were constructed in limited domains (Gorry and Barnett, 1968; de Dombal and co-workers, 1972). In the early 1970s, as a result of concerns about the intractability of the probabilistic approach, the focus of research shifted from purely numerical approaches to more symbolic methods, in particular, to knowledge-based techniques pioneered in early artificial intelligence systems such as DENDRAL (qv). The implementation of a number of consultation systems during those years helped to define the field of AI in medicine (AIM), and spawned the development of expert systems in other domains as well.

Four large, experimental systems (MYCIN, CASNET, INTERNIST, and PIP) are widely regarded as having set the stage for most subsequent research in the field. MYCIN (qv), a program developed at Stanford University to assist in the selection of antibiotic therapy for patients who have infectious diseases of the blood and nervous system, demonstrated that a complex heuristic approach to diagnosis and treatment could be expressed with relatively few concise rules and could explain its conclusions using a simple, recursive inference algorithm. CASNET, developed at Rutgers University, was the first system to explore the representational issues of causality in medical diagnosis and therapy, particularly in the domain of glaucoma and related diseases of the eye. INTERNIST (qv) was designed by researchers at the University of Pittsburgh to diagnose diseases and combinations of diseases within the vast domain of internal medicine. PIP (present illness program), developed at MIT and the Tufts–New England Medical Center, generated hypotheses about disease processes in patients with renal disease. These systems contributed significantly to the commercial growth of AI and are described extensively in several books that summarize the first decade of AIM research (Szolovits, 1982; Clancey and Shortliffe, 1984). In recent years, some AIM researchers have returned to the methods first introduced by Ledley and Lusted, armed with an arsenal of lessons learned from the 1970s AIM systems.

The medical diagnosis and patient-management problems addressed by these systems demonstrated the validity of an emerging AI principle: domain-specific assertions and extensive knowledge about a problem area are generally more crucial to problem-solving performance than are domain-independent principles of reasoning. Simple reasoning techniques were shown to suffice for expert-level performance, so long as the program had comprehensive and accurate knowledge of the domain.

Medical knowledge has attracted AI researchers for several reasons. Medicine is a complex discipline, rich in facts, relationships, and methods. In addition, detailed knowledge of underlying disease processes or the results of intervention is typically uncertain and thus provides a fertile testbed for methods of reasoning under uncertainty. Finally, the dissemination of medical expertise through medical advice systems could have a profound effect on health care. AIM research is important to medicine not only because computer systems will someday become routine tools in clinical practice but also because the education of doctors, which has traditionally emphasized memorization of knowledge, may increasingly emphasize the learning of effective problem-solving techniques, enhanced with the knowledge and advice provided by computer systems.

Although in the broadest sense AIM research includes applications of AI to medical image processing, medical instrumentation, and biotechnology, this article will limit discussion to medical advice systems, which attempt to represent and reason with the knowledge used by medical decision makers.

THEORETICAL BASIS

This section describes the major theoretical considerations in AIM research, including the representation of medical knowledge and the nature of medical problem solving.

Protocol Analysis

The theoretical foundation of AIM owes a great deal to psychological research from the mid-1970s. In several experiments, physicians were asked to verbalize their thoughts while solving diagnostic problems. Researchers then analyzed transcripts of those sessions. Investigations of this type (Kassirer and Gorry, 1978; Elstein, 1978) identified a general problem-solving procedure common to both expert and novice physicians: the hypothetico-deductive approach. The physcian begins to formulate hypotheses soon after beginning to gather data, and these are tested as new data are collected. The physician may generate questions solely to test an active hypothesis or to distinguish between hypotheses. Building on these results, researchers at the University of Minnesota (Feltovich and co-workers, 1984) examined the performance of both experts and novices, and found differences not in the reasoning of these people (regardless of experience, they shared the hypothetico-deductive approach) but in the richness and organization of the subjects' medical knowledge. Novices had spotty knowledge of diseases, not yet full enough or sufficiently organized to optimize the hypothetico-deductive approach. These results confirmed that performance seems to be critically dependent on domain-specific knowledge.

Medical Knowledge

Medical decision making has often been compared to decision making in more structured domains, eg, automotive diagnosis. In manufactured domains, however, the components are specifically designed and the causal relationships are fully characterized. In the natural domain of medicine, the mechanisms of disease are often poorly understood and causal relationships are difficult to describe, due to incomplete and inaccurate information.

The first-generation AIM programs captured only a small portion of the knowledge that physicians actually use in problem solving. The medical knowledge represented in these programs typically consisted of weighted associations between findings (ie, observable descriptors of a patient) and disease hypotheses or between two hypotheses. Ledley and Lusted used the technique of assigning probabilities to represent associations between findings and hypotheses. As symbolic-reasoning methods gained in popularity in the early 1970s, researchers invented new ways to represent and use associational knowledge. For example, INTERNIST associated clinical manifestations with diseases using two variables: evoking strength, to capture the strength of association, and frequency, to estimate how often patients with the disease have the finding. MYCIN expressed its knowledge in rules, with related certainty factors to gauge the degree of association. The underlying semantics of such associations were not always made clear, and there was generally no distinction made between associational and causal relationships. For example, a diagnostic system might represent a link between the hypothesis of breast cancer and the finding that the patient's mother had breast cancer. In this case, the finding is a risk factor, not a clear causal relationship, as a skiing accident might be to a fractured leg. In response to problems caused by the *ad hoc* nature of these associational representations and their inference techniques, some AIM researchers have reembraced axiomatic frameworks such as probability theory, for reasoning with uncertain, associational knowledge.

A good deal of knowledge-representation research in AIM has concentrated on causal modeling, which can incorporate temporal, anatomical, and physiological knowledge. Although pure causal modeling is rarely applicable in medicine, a presumed causal model may offer both a deeper understanding of its domain and the ability to explain its reasoning in terms acceptable to a physician. CASNET modeled the domain of glaucoma diagnosis and treatment using three levels of detail (observations, pathophysiological states, and disease categories), linked together in a causal-associational network. Following effect-to-cause links (ie, statements of what entities may cause an observed effect) from findings back toward primary disorders can indicate a common cause of multiple complaints. ABEL, a computer program developed at MIT to deal with acid–base imbalance and electrolyte disorders, further explored the advantages of partitioning causal knowledge into multiple levels of abstraction (Patil, 1981). ABEL used causal knowledge to determine how interactions among multiple diseases can alter the observed symptoms. In general, causal models can be used to interpret the temporal ordering of findings, to provide symptomatic relief by treating intermediate states along a causal pathway when the patient's primary disease is untreatable, and to avoid considering two related findings as though they provided independent support for an hypothesis.

Causal models incorporate a wide variety of knowledge; they also take a number of different forms. In qualitative causal models, variables are given qualitative values, and the model reasons symbolically about the causal relations involved. Quantitative causal models rely on mathematical relations to determine the effect of interacting forces on the model's variables. A semiquantitative causal model can combine the symbolic-reasoning potential of a qualitative model with the clarity of a mathematical model in resolving interacting forces (Widman and co-workers, 1988). In medicine, most causal relations are uncertain rather than categorical; thus causal models often must cooperate with mechanisms for managing uncertainty (see below for a more detailed description of causal-reasoning research).

Taxonomies of Biomedical Concepts

The representation of taxonomies, such as ones in which the diagnostic hypothesis space is organized as a hierarchy of diseases, has been an active area of study. For example, viral hepatitis and alcoholic hepatitis are inflammatory diseases of the liver. A representation scheme that captures this type of hierarchical relationship might allow the system to begin reasoning at an appropriate level of abstraction; for example, a program may identify a patient as having hepatitis before beginning to determine which subtype is present. The MDX system, a liver-disease diagnostic program developed at Ohio State University, contains a taxonomy of diseases that allows the system to direct its search as a progressive refinement of hypotheses, popping back to higher nodes in the hierarchy only when strong contradictions arise (Gomez and Chandrasekaran, 1981). Another control scheme that uses taxonomic knowledge extensively can be found in the design for CADUCEUS, an enhancement to INTERNIST (Pople, 1982). In CADUCEUS, multiple hierarchies classify diseases on the basis of anatomical locus, etiological agent, or other discriminating characteristic.

After years of using a taxonomy of standardized medical terms, known as the medical subject headings (MeSH) taxonomy, the National Library of Medicine (NLM) has realized that simple taxonomies do not capture the richness of relations among biomedical concepts. To address the problems caused by the diversity of knowledge structures and biomedical vocabularies, the NLM has undertaken a large project to build a Unified Medical Language System (UMLS), which will facilitate the retrieval and integration of information from many machine-readable sources, including descriptions of the biomedical literature, clinical records, factual databanks, and medical knowledge bases (Humphreys and Lindberg, 1989). A metathesaurus, a large semantic network, and an information-sources map will provide an organized approach to the systematization of medical terminology so that both humans and machines will be able to access medical information for use in such diverse applications as literature retrieval and clinical diagnosis.

Knowledge Structures

AIM systems use an assortment of abstract data types to represent medical knowledge; the diversity of data structures mirrors that of AI in general. MYCIN experimented with production rules; PIP and INTERNIST used disease frames. The AI-RHEUM system, a program for diagnosis in the domain of rheumatology, used criteria tables with which clinical experts could interact easily (Kingsland and Lindberg, 1986). The causal-associational networks of CASNET laid the groundwork for the use of network structures. Augmented decision networks (similar to augmented transition networks used in natural language research) are used in the ATTENDING systems to generate critiques of patient management plans (Miller, 1984). Neural networks, inspired by the fine structure of the brain, have been used to diagnose dementia (Mulsant, 1990). Bayesian belief networks have recently gained significant popularity as a structure for probabilistic reasoning (discussed below). Discussions of rules, frames, and causal-associational networks in the context of AIM systems have been published (Clancey and Shortliffe, 1984) as well as a discussion of Bayesian belief networks in expert-systems research (Cooper, 1989).

Inference and Control Methods

Medical decision making exists along a spectrum, from categorical (or deterministic) reasoning to probabilistic (or evidential) reasoning (Szolovits and Pauker, 1978). Categorical reasoning is exemplified by the flowchart, in which decisions are made without reservations, if conditions permit. Probabilistic reasoning is used when evidence must be weighted and combined before a decision is made. AIM systems must use a judicious combination of both types of reasoning to simulate expert behavior. Inference methods to perform evidential reasoning, both probabilistic and nonprobabilistic, have been the focus of most AIM research in inference.

There are as many control schemes as there are systems. MYCIN searches its rule set using a depth-first control strategy. The system uses backward chaining to invoke and link its rules so that a reasoning network is created dynamically. INTERNIST's control is initiated with a data-directed scheme (Miller and co-workers, 1982). Patient data first allow the program to contribute evoking strengths and frequency weights to form diagnostic hypotheses. Then a high-level algorithm chooses one of four hypothesis-directed control schemes (conclude, pursue, rule out, and discriminate), depending on how many active hypotheses there are and on how closely they are clustered by weights of evidence. This higher-level control scheme models the hypothetico-deductive approach mentioned earlier. The system can handle multiple coexisting diseases through a partitioning algorithm that allows it to focus on the differential diagnosis of subsets of findings, while holding in abeyance the additional patient data for later investigation. The MDX system employs breadth-first search of a static tree; as MDX searches deeper into its taxonomy tree, it refines hypotheses to be more specific. The ATTENDING system searches a hierarchical planning network to identify alternatives to the user's proposed plan. Systems based on Bayesian belief networks differ from earlier AIM systems in that the network structures serve as both control architectures and knowledge-representation forms, while still effecting a functional separation of knowledge and control.

Uncertainty Management

The representation and management of medical uncertainty has been a recurring issue in AIM. Ledley and Lusted acknowledge the inherent uncertainty in medical reasoning and present a method for managing it, based on Bayes's rule. Bayes's rule (see BAYESIAN INFERENCE METHODS) offers an exact method for computing the posterior probability of a disease hypothesis given the findings. Most of the first-generation diagnostic systems (Warner and co-workers, 1961; Gorry and Barnett, 1968; de Dombal et al., 1972) were based on Bayesian probability and decision theory, and made two simplifying assumptions to escape computational intractability: findings were conditionally independent given diseases and diseases were mutually exclusive and collectively exhaustive. These assumptions were found to be restrictive (Gorry, 1973), and AI techniques were suggested in part as a potential solution. The early AIM systems all used weighting mechanisms that avoided the computational and knowledge-acquisition limitations of formal statistical or probabilistic approaches. MYCIN used confirmation theory and certainty factors for its model of inexact reasoning (Shortliffe and Buchanan, 1975); the INTERNIST scoring mechanism used an empirically derived calculus of evoking strengths and frequencies. Wechsler describes a diagnostic program based on Zadeh's fuzzy set theory (Wechsler, 1976) (see FUZZY SETS AND FUZZY LOGIC).

A considerable amount of research is now focused on axiomatic frameworks, both probabilistic and nonprobabilistic (Dempster-Shafer theory (qv), fuzzy set theory), for inexact reasoning in AI. The tractability of such approaches has been enhanced by increases in the computational power of hardware, the introduction of graphical techniques for the direct creation and manipulation of complex data structures, and the development of more efficient inference algorithms. While the debate between probabilists and nonprobabilists has been raging in AI, there has been a particularly strong resurgence of interest in probabilistic approaches for AIM systems. Bayesian belief networks offer robust and expressive structures for uncertainty representation, and numerous probabilistic inference algorithms offer means for managing the ubiquitous uncertainty in medical knowledge bases.

Evaluation Functions

Just as AI chess playing programs use an evaluation function to assign scalar values to possible moves, AIM systems for patient management must compare potential treatment alternatives. The values of medical outcomes, however, are difficult to assess. What are the relative values of chronic pain versus a lifetime of paralysis versus loss of life? In cases where there is no generally accepted correct therapy, the physician will demand a reasoned argument that addresses the issues of costs and benefits in a convincing way. Medical advice systems have often considered information-gathering costs, but most systems continue to ignore the utility of actions. For example, assume that a medical advice system concludes that an infection is most probably caused by organism 1 and is much less probably caused by organism 2. Is it correct management to treat for organism 1 and not for organism 2? Perhaps not, if organism 1 causes only discomfort, whereas organism 2 can cause death, and if the treatment for organism 1 may cause kidney damage. The cost of diagnostic misclassification drives the real-life diagnostic process. Medical cost-containment pressures may force more explicit inclusion of cost–benefit considerations in future systems.

In early AIM management systems, such as MYCIN, the preferences and trade-offs used in selecting a course of action were rarely represented explicitly, but were instead compiled in the rules (Langlotz and co-workers, 1986; Rennels and co-workers, 1987). Decision theory offers normative evaluation mechanisms, employing constructs such as multiattribute value functions to model preferences and trade-offs explicitly (Farr and Fagan, 1989; Klein, 1989). Physicians have recognized the importance of incorporating patient utilities for making decisions, and methods have been explored for eliciting preferences from patients (Barry and co-workers, 1988; McNeil and co-workers, 1981) and for building patient-specific decision models (Jimison, 1988).

RESEARCH THEMES

Current topics of active AIM research are of similar importance to expert-systems research in general. This section presents seven research themes, but is by no means comprehensive. The yearly proceedings of the Symposium on Computer Applications in Medical Care is a good source of articles on active areas of AIM research (IEEE Computer Society Press, Washington, DC).

Knowledge Acquisition

A notorious bottleneck in building expert systems is the acquisition of knowledge from the expert. TEIRESIAS, a program built to interface with MYCIN, demonstrated that a program might assist in the on-line transfer of knowledge from a human expert to the consultation program's knowledge base (Davis, 1979). The expert could disagree with a conclusion, and the system would then trace through the reasoning process step-by-step, until the erroneous rule (or missing rule) was identified. The SEEK program, which operated in concert with the EXPERT tool, derived from work on CASNET, also provided assistance in recognizing how a system's knowledge base should be altered (Politakis and Weiss, 1982; Weiss and co-workers, 1986). OPAL, the knowledge-acquisition program for ONCOCIN (qv), an expert system that assists in the management of patients who have cancer and are enrolled in clinical trials, permits the entry of visual representations of cancer treatment plans; this graphical knowledge is then converted automatically into a form usable by ONCOCIN (Musen and co-workers, 1986). OPAL presents a model of oncology knowledge intuitive to expert oncologists; in general, knowledge acquisition is facilitated by a formal model of the domain that approximates the mental model used by experts. PROTEGE (qv), is a tool to help system developers build models for tasks that are soluble by skeletal-plan refinement (Musen, 1989).

Decision–Theoretic Expert Systems

As mentioned, some AIM researchers, disenchanted with the *ad hoc* nature of early AI techniques for managing uncertainty, have returned to decision–theoretic techniques first explored in the 1960s. The development of more expressive decision–theoretic representations, in particular, of Bayesian belief networks, has motivated a flurry of research in probabilistic expert systems. Excellent introductions to decision theory (qv) and belief networks in AI and in AIM have been published (Pearl, 1988; Horvitz and co-workers, 1988; Cooper, 1989; Neapolitan, 1990). A belief network is a specialization of an influence diagram, which is a graphical representation of decision alternatives and preferences (utilities). In graph–theoretic terms, a belief network is a directed acyclic graph; nodes represent domain variables and arcs represent conditional dependences between variables. Current belief-network research addresses several issues that have been cited in arguments against the use of probability theory in expert systems, including the assumption of conditional independence and problems of knowledge acquisition (qv), computational efficiency, and explanation (qv).

Figure 1 depicts a simple belief network, taken from the domain of medicine (Cooper, 1989). The key feature of belief networks is their explicit representation of conditional independence, evidenced by the lack of arcs between nodes. In Figure 1, for example, *increased total serum calcium* and *brain tumor* are conditionally independent given *metastatic cancer;* metastatic cancer may cause both an increased serum calcium level and a brain tumor, but there is no direct relationship between the calcium level and the occurrence of a brain tumor, given metastatic cancer. On the other hand, *coma* is dependent on both *increased serum calcium* and *brain tumor*. Explicit conditional independence can dramatically reduce the number of probabilities required to represent the complete joint probability space. For example, with five binary variables, there are $2^5 = 32$ probabilities in the joint space; with the belief network in Figure 1, however, only 11 probabilities are needed to represent the problem space. It has been shown that with explicit representation of conditional independence a belief network can compute the joint probability of any instantiation of all n variables as the product of only n probabilities (Shachter, 1986). Probabilistic inference using belief networks typically involves computation of the probability $P(C|E)$ of a conclusion C, given evidence E. Numerous algorithms exist for computing $P(C|E)$, when C and E are conjunctions of instantiated variables (Pearl, 1988; Lauritzen and Spiegelhalter, 1988; Neapolitan, 1990). Traditional rule-based systems that use alternative uncertainty formalisms have difficulty with this type of computation. They also require different control structures for forward and backward chaining, whereas belief networks make no directional distinctions in the propagation of information. With simple, restricted types of belief networks, inference can be performed efficiently; with more complex, multiply connected network structures, inference is more difficult. In fact, probabilistic inference using general belief networks is known to be NP-hard (Cooper, 1990). Thus, for networks that are highly connected (ie, many arcs among the nodes), the calculation of $P(C|E)$ is likely to be exponential in the number of nodes in the network. Techniques have been developed to deal with this potential intractability for complex networks, including approximation and special case algorithms.

Causal Reasoning

Early causal reasoning programs, such as CASNET (Weiss and co-workers, 1978) and ABEL (Patil and co-workers, 1981), first explored the nature of causality in medical reasoning, using multiple levels of detail and qualitative descriptions of relationships between concepts. Building on the work of Patil at MIT, the Heart Failure Program uses a mostly qualitative causal model of the cardiovascular system to assist in diagnosis and management of cardiovascular disease (Long and co-workers, 1987). The model reasons with quantitative parameters, such as cardiac output, mean arterial pressure, and systemic vascular resistance, as well as with qualitative state information. The model also serves as an organizing structure for its reasoning modules, which use a variety of techniques, including a belief network for evidence interpretation, a truth-maintenance (qv) system for state-information propagation, and signal-flow analysis for prediction of therapeutic effects. A different approach to the problem of dealing with interacting forces represented by quantitative and qualitative data is demonstrated in Widman's model of the cardiovascular system (Widman and co-workers, 1988). This model has a qualitative component and an underlying mathematical component, derived from the field of dynamic systems. The system reasons symbolically with the qualitative model and uses the dynamic systems model to simulate the qualitative model in hypothetical situations. The dynamic systems model is defined by levels (quantities), rates (flows), and delays, using first-order differential equations. To simulate the qualitative model, the system first maps qualitative variables into semiquantitative terms. For example, values such as low, normal, and high might be mapped onto the values $-1, 0$, and 1. After the simulation, the output is translated back into qualitative terms to allow further symbolic reasoning. Both the Heart Failure Program and the semiquantitative simulation approach address several problems encountered earlier in dealing with temporality and conflicting forces; they apply cooperative, mathematical models where qualitative models fail. Inspired by ad-

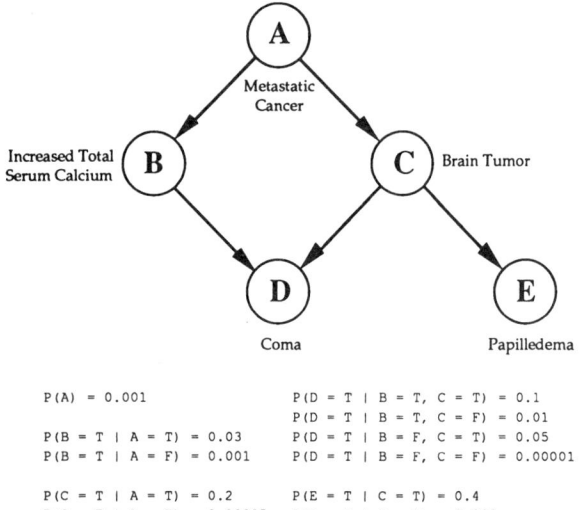

Figure 1. An example of a belief network from the domain of medicine. For each node with no direct predecessors (no incoming arcs), there exists a prior probability function, for example, the prior probability of metastatic cancer is 0.001. For each node x_i with one or more direct predecessors π_i, there exists a conditional probability function $P(x_i|\pi_i)$, for example, the probability of coma given evidence of a brain tumor, but evidence of no increased total serum calcium, is 0.01. The conditional probability is analogous to the rule "If π_i, then x_i with probability $P(x_i|\pi_i)$." This network was developed for the purpose of illustration only and is not intended to be a complete or accurate model of any area of clinical medicine. Reproduced with permission from Cooper (1989).

vances in qualitative physics (qv), an attempt to model the physiology of water balance in humans using purely qualitative abstractions of differential equations has been made (Kuipers, 1986).

It has been pointed out that there are many medical domains in which causal models are misleading or unavailable. In these domains, advice programs can base their recommendations on empirical data from the clinical literature rather than on formal causal models. To illustrate this point, ROUNDSMAN, a program to assist in the management of patients who have primary breast cancer was developed (Rennels, 1987). ROUNDSMAN reasons directly from published, experimental data, because causal models of breast cancer are too simplistic and nonpredictive for use in decisions about specific patients. Thus ROUNDSMAN selects relevant studies from the clinical literature, determines the patient stratum and treatment intervention from the articles that best match the patient and proposed plan, and analyzes the strengths and weaknesses of the studies in relation to the case at hand. ROUNDSMAN's output is a prose critique of the proposed plan in relation to the selected articles.

Temporal Reasoning and Planning

Medical advice systems are usually designed with the assumption that data are gathered and inferences are made at one point in time. Because medical diagnosis and management actually take place over time, AIM systems should allow the user to reevaluate the patient, assessing the rate of disease progression or the therapeutic response to prior treatment. The Digitalis Therapy Advisor, VM, and ONCOCIN are unusual in that they give advice on the management of patients over time. The Digitalis Therapy Advisor used the results of previous treatment to alter its model of the patient (Gorry and co-workers, 1978). For example, if predicted levels of digitalis were much higher than the measured stores, the system adjusted the "oral absorption" parameter downward. VM, a program designed to assist with the management of patients on ventilators, assumed that particular data are valid for only a certain period (Fagan and co-workers, 1984). VM could also represent temporal trends; for example, a rise in mean arterial blood pressure of 15 torr over 10 min. ONCOCIN (Tu and co-workers, 1990) extends the skeletal planning technique to the domain of chemotherapy for patients who have cancer, where the history of past events and the duration of actions are important. ONCOCIN uses stored skeletal plans of chemotherapy protocols, compiled heuristics, and a temporal database of observed patient reactions to determine the appropriate modifications to the skeletal plan for the current planning period (Kahn and co-workers, 1989).

Planning in medicine also requires techniques developed for planning under uncertainty; state-space planning techniques are not usually applicable, because the initial state and the effects of plan operators rarely can be stated with certainty. Some of the preliminary theoretical work in the area of planning under uncertainty is relevant. The trade-off–formulation task, which separates the real decisions from choices that are qualitatively inadmissible or are trivial, has been investigated (Wellman, 1988). The SUDO-PLANNER system constructs qualitative, probabilistic networks, similar to Bayesian belief networks, and uses a dominance prover to plan for partially satisfiable goals. A decision–theoretic approach to the construction of planning systems has been presented (Langlotz, 1989); the QXQ system explains and interprets the differences in expected utility among branches of a plan that is represented by a decision tree.

Strategies for the Diagnosis of Multiple Diseases

The difficult problem of diagnosing multiple coexisting diseases, initially addressed in the INTERNIST partitioning algorithm, has generated notable theoretical work on alternative diagnostic strategies. A parsimonious set cover model for diagnosis has been adopted in which the set of minimal explanations for the observed manifestations is maintained throughout the sequential hypothetico-deductive process (Reggia and co-workers, 1983). This parallel, or breadth-first, approach contrasts with INTERNIST's inference mechanism, which is essentially serial, or depth-first. The set cover model also incorporates a heuristic strategy for proposing new measurements, just as INTERNIST provided three questioning strategies for converging on a diagnosis. A general diagnostic engine (GDE) for diagnosing multiple faults in a general model has been presented in which every possible set cover, not just the minimal sets, is considered an explanation for the symptoms observed (de Kleer and Williams, 1986). Using a probabilistic representation for its hypotheses, GDE can compute the entropy of each potential measurement, and can choose the test that minimizes the expected entropy of candidate hypotheses resulting from the test. Both the set cover model and GDE assume that symptoms are set additive in that the set of symptoms of a patient with multiple diseases is the same as the set union of the symptoms of a patient with each disease separately.

Explanation and Critiquing

MYCIN was one of the first systems to demonstrate that explanation capabilities might be key to physician acceptance of computer-based decision support (Scott and co-workers, 1984). MYCIN allowed users to ask why, when they wanted to know the purpose of the system's questioning and how, when they wanted to know how the system could reach certain conclusions. Researchers at MIT enhanced the Digitalis Therapy Advisor with causal models of heart rhythm disturbances and principles of antiarrhythmia therapy to create a program called XPLAIN (Swartout, 1981), which could give the rationale behind a therapy plan. This work demonstrated that optimal explanation is facilitated by access to more abstract principles, which do not always appear in the program code. The developers of the ATTENDING system for planning of anesthesia management first proposed the critiquing approach to explanation (Miller, 1983, 1984). Rather than simulating a physician's reasoning and generating a recommended action, critiquing systems focus their analysis on the user's proposed management plan. In medical management, there is often more than one defensible therapy; thus an approach that highlights the pros and cons of each treatment alternative is more likely to be accepted by the physician. In addition, critiquing systems remain silent about the uncontroversial aspects of the plan.

Validation and Evaluation

Validation of expert-system knowledge bases is difficult and often requires automated validation tools; both static and dynamic validation methods have been used on AIM knowledge bases (Davis, 1979; Suwa and co-workers, 1982; Shwe and co-workers, 1989). Diagnosis systems usually are judged by the accuracy of their diagnosis when compared to some accepted gold standard. The program gains credibility through evaluation studies: informal ones at first and then formal ones. Several groups have carried out formal evaluations of performance (Yu and co-workers, 1979; Miller and co-workers, 1982; Aikins and co-workers, 1983; Hickam and co-workers, 1985). Evaluation in a clinical setting different from that in which the system was built can demonstrate the generalizability of the system. Fewer groups have evaluated a system's acceptability to users, and success in this area is notoriously difficult to achieve. Systems that require hands-on use by doctors encounter additional challenging design issues compared with those systems that analyze instrument data and produce a report. An informal, market research study highlights several obstacles to physician acceptance of decision-support technologies (Shortliffe, 1989). Objectives and guidelines for system validation and evaluation have been discussed in several reviews (Buchanan and Shortliffe, 1984; Wyatt and Spiegelhalter, 1989).

Recent evaluation studies of the Quick Medical Reference (QMR) diagnostic program, which uses an extended version of the INTERNIST knowledge base, have confirmed that medical advice systems can provide accurate, educationally helpful suggestions, which users value sufficiently to alter their original differential diagnoses (Bankowitz and co-workers, 1989). As programs such as QMR are distributed throughout the medical community, AIM researchers must acknowledge that the use (or misuse) of their programs may result in litigation when patients experience adverse medical outcomes (Miller, 1989).

EXAMPLE SYSTEMS

Medical advice systems were first envisioned more than 30 years ago. Since then, hundreds of systems have been built to provide diagnostic and patient-management advice in a plethora of medical domains. Some systems even provide disposition advice, or advice on where to send the patient; the DISPO Advisor is an expert system in daily use at Johns Hopkins Hospital to assist in the disposition of psychiatric patients who come to the emergency room (Barta and Barta, 1988). Many systems are now implemented on inexpensive microcomputers, a departure from the situation a mere 10 years ago, when AIM programs required mainframe or professional workstation computing power. Indeed, most developers now strive for systems that can be delivered on low cost hardware. The theoretical issues and research themes that have been mentioned are illustrated in the context of several programs that have achieved limited clinical use.

Quick Medical Reference

Of all medical advice systems developed to date, none is as large in scope or ambition as Quick Medical Reference (QMR) (Miller and co-workers, 1986). QMR contains a superset of the INTERNIST knowledge base, in which almost 600 diseases and more than 4000 possible patient findings are represented. In addition, more than 40000 links describe the possible causal, temporal, and associational interrelationships among the findings and diseases represented. QMR serves as a powerful diagnostic consultation system for internal medicine and addresses the more basic information needs of physicians. QMR's diagnostic strategy used in inferring disease hypotheses is related to INTERNIST's; numerous other information-processing functions, including electronic textbook features and case analysis features, are provided as well. With user-friendly interfaces on inexpensive microcomputers, QMR provides its users with rapid access to a vast knowledge base. Figure 2 shows an example of the kinds of

---

Associations List for Pulmonary Disease and DIARRHEA Chronic
Pairs of Diseases consistent with Entered Finding and Topic:

Atelectasis
caused-by Carcinoid Syndrome Secondary to Bronchial Neoplasm

Eosinophilic Pneumonia Acute (LOEFFLER)
caused-by Hookworm Disease

Pulmonary Legionellosis
predisposed-to-by Immune Deficiency Syndrome Acquired (AIDS)

Pleural Effusion Exudative
caused-by Pancreatic Pseudocyst

Pneumococcal Pneumonia
predisposed-to-by Carcinoid Syndrome Secondary to Bronchial Neoplasm

Pneumocystis Pneumonia
predisposed-to-by Immune Deficiency Syndrome Acquired (AIDS)

Pulmonary Hypertension Secondary
caused-by Progressive Systemic Sclerosis
or co-occurring-with Schistosomiasis Chronic Hepatic

Pulmonary Infarction
predisposed-to-by Carcinoma of Body or Tail of Pancreas
or predisposed-to-by Carcinoma of Head of Pancreas
or caused-by Hepatic Vein Obstruction

Pulmonary Lymphoma
coinciding-with Lymphoma of Colon
or coinciding-with Small Intestinal Lymphoma

Pulmonary Interstitial Fibrosis Secondary Diffuse
caused-by Progressive Systemic Sclerosis

Figure 2. A sample consultation with QMR. QMR is asked to list diseases that might account for the presence of two apparently disparate problems: pulmonary disease and chronic diarrhea. QMR generates a list of possible diagnoses, of which a subset is shown, from its knowledge base of more than 600 diseases, more than 4000 observations, and their interrelations.

questions with which QMR can assist. Note that the program uses its knowledge base to create dynamic responses to a user's query. In this case, QMR is being used to browse medical knowledge rather than to give a diagnostic interpretation for a specific patient. QMR has been widely distributed among AIM researchers for testing; in the near future, the American College of Physicians will assume responsibility for the distribution and maintenance of QMR's knowledge base. DXplain, a program developed by researchers at Massachusetts General Hospital, has goals similar to those of QMR (Barnett and co-workers, 1987).

Pathfinder and Intellipath

Pathfinder, an expert system for the diagnosis of lymph node disease, is the result of one of the earliest decision–theoretic projects, in which efficient techniques for acquiring, representing, and reasoning with probabilistic knowledge were developed (Heckerman and co-workers, 1989). Pathfinder reasons about 60 diseases that can manifest in lymph node pathology, using more than 100 morphologic, clinical, immunologic, cell kinetic, and microbiologic features. Knowledge is acquired in Pathfinder through the use of probabilistic similarity networks; these networks

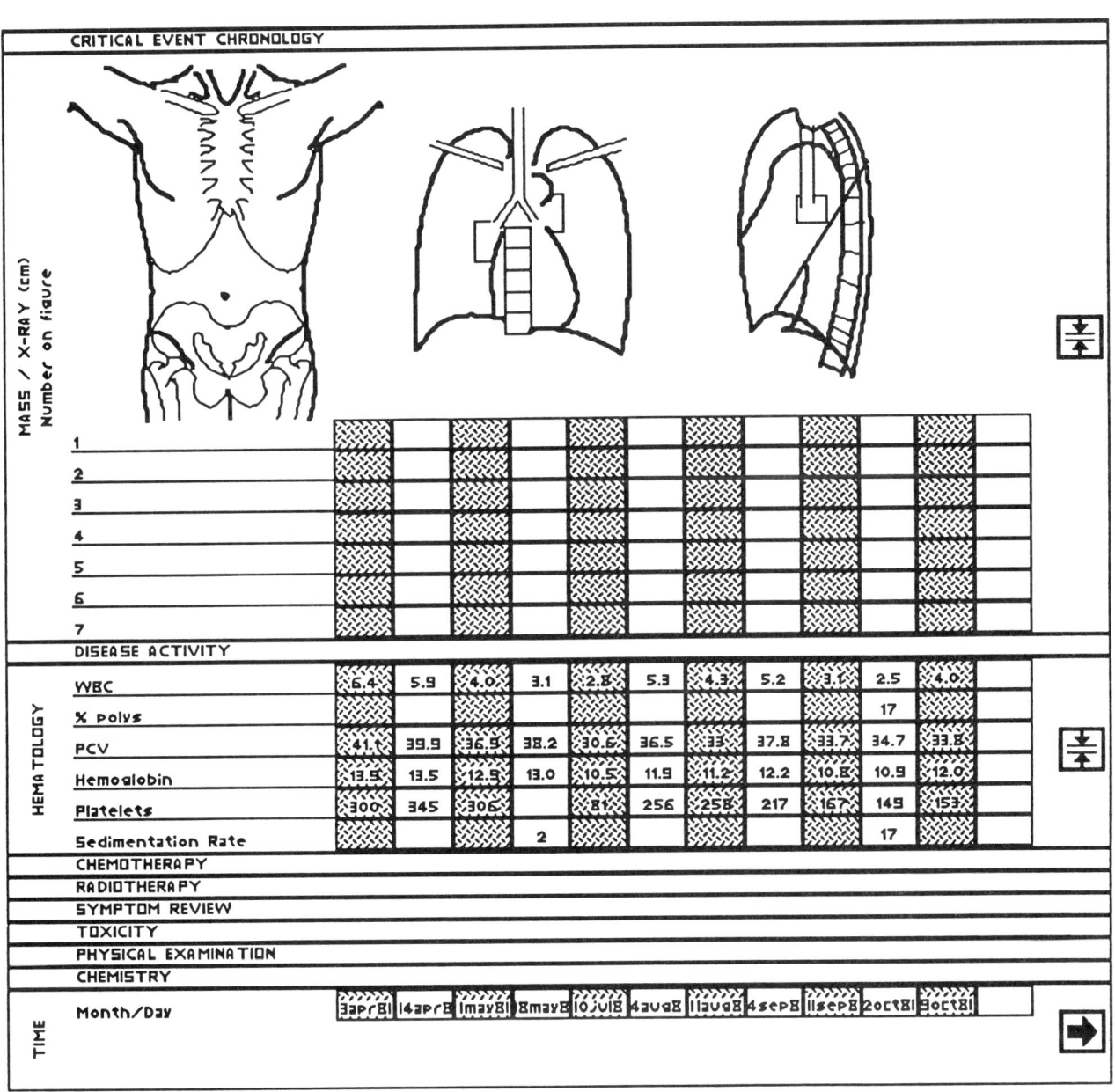

Figure 3. A portion of the flowsheet used for data entry in ONCOCIN. ONCOCIN's interface is modeled after the paper flowsheet used in oncology clinics. The physician can indicate the locations of tumors on an anatomical diagram. ONCOCIN uses the time-oriented patient data entered on this form to refine the skeletal plan of the patient's chemotherapy protocol.

allow an expert to decompose the task of building large belief networks into modular and manageable subtasks (Heckerman, 1990). Pathfinder attempts to satisfy the information needs of a nonexpert pathologist. The system provides graphical explanations of decision-theoretic inference and a set of heuristic abstractions that helps the user to access and learn from the probabilistic knowledge in the system. Intellipath is a commercial system that uses the principles developed in the Pathfinder research project to assist surgical pathologists. This system integrates probabilistic reasoning with a set of supportive informational tools, including an analogue videodisk-library of representative images, text information on diseases and microscopic features, references to the literature, and an automated report generator. The developers plan to create a belief-network knowledge base for each of 40 different pathology tissue types. There are currently about 200 Intellipath systems in use in North America.

ONCOCIN

ONCOCIN is a therapy advice system designed to assist in the treatment of patients who have cancer (Tu and co-workers, 1990). The system helps oncologists to manage patients over time, interpreting the current session in light of past information whenever necessary. ONCOCIN models 36 standard treatment protocols of clinical chemotherapy trials as skeletal plans; a large heuristic knowledge base converts a skeletal plan to a patient-specific plan. ONCOCIN tracks the therapy process over time using a temporal database and refines the plans as necessary. A central goal of this research is that the system be used regularly in a busy clinical environment, thus response times must be short. Another constraint imposed by clinical use is that the electronic format of data recording and display must not encumber the physician. ONCOCIN reasons from data gathered in graphical displays (Fig. 3), including anatomic diagrams, of the flowsheets used in chemotherapy treatments (Lane and co-workers, 1986). ONCOCIN has been field tested in Stanford Hospital's Oncology Clinic since 1986.

DISCUSSION

As computers have become more prevalent in the practice of medicine, AIM researchers have realized that the stand-alone consultation model is inadequate for medical advice systems. The evolving lesson is that decision support must be integrated into routine data-management environments; ideally, AIM systems should be easy to use, accessible through networks, and capable of exchanging data and knowledge with other programs.

Medical decision makers must be comfortable using medical advice systems in a clinical context. Several AIM systems are, or have been, in clinical use. Many of these systems, such as the Serum Protein Diagnostic Program and PUFF (Aikins and co-workers, 1983), acquire the needed information automatically from instruments, so data collection, analysis, and recommendation proceed without direct interaction with the physician. However, the need for the physician's direct interaction with the computer is a major design consideration in other AIM systems. QMR, Intellipath, and ONCOCIN all face these additional design challenges: response time must be short, data collection and analysis must be simple and intuitive to the physician, recommendations must be backed up with good explanations, and system hardware and software must be inexpensive and reliable.

Medical advice systems designed for clinical use have influenced the evolution of AI. This article has emphasized the role of AIM systems as laboratories for experiments in the representation of associational, causal, and taxonomic knowledge; in uncertainty management; and in decision-theoretic reasoning. The field of artificial intelligence in medicine will continue to serve as a proving ground for systems that reason in complex, real-world domains.

BIBLIOGRAPHY

J. Aikins, J. Kunz, E. Shortliffe, and R. Fallat, "PUFF: An Expert System for Interpretation of Pulmonary Function Data," *Comput. Biomed. Res.* **16**, 199–208 (1983).

R. Bankowitz and co-workers, "A Computer-Assisted Medical Diagnostic Consultation Service: Implementation and Prospective Evaluation of a Prototype," *Ann. Int. Med.* **110**, 824–832 (1989).

G. Barnett, J. Cimino, J. Hupp, and E. Hoffer, "DXplain: An Evolving Diagnostic Decision-Support System," *JAMA* **258**, 67–74 (1987).

M. Barry, A. Mulley, F. Fowler, and J. Wennberg, "Watchful Waiting Versus Immediate Transurethral Resection for Symptomatic Prostatism," *JAMA* **55**, 473–484 (1988).

P. Barta and W. Barta, "DISPO Advisor: Expert System for Psychiatric Disposition," *Proceedings of the Twelfth Symposium on Computer Applications in Medical Care*, 1988, pp. 12–22.

B. Buchanan and E. Shortliffe, eds., *Rule-Based Expert Systems*, Addison-Wesley Publishing Co., Inc., Reading, Mass., 1984.

W. Clancey and E. Shortliffe, eds., *Readings in Medical Artificial Intelligence: The First Decade*, Addison-Wesley Publishing Co., Inc., Reading, Mass., 1984.

G. Cooper, "Current Research Directions in the Development of Expert Systems Based on Belief Networks," *Appl. Stochastic Models Data Anal.* **5**, 39–52 (1989).

G. Cooper, "The Computational Complexity of Probabilistic Inference Using Bayesian Belief Networks," *Artif. Intell.* **42**, 393–405 (1990).

R. Davis, "Interactive Transfer of Expertise: Acquisition of New Inference Rules," *Artif. Intell.* **12**, 121–158 (1979).

F. de Dombal and co-workers, "Computer-Aided Diagnosis of Acute Abdominal Pain," *Br. Med. J.* **2**, 9–13 (1972).

J. de Kleer and M. Williams, "Diagnosing Multiple Faults," *Artif. Intell.* **32**, 97–130 (1986).

A. Elstein, L. Shulman, and S. Sprafka, *Medical Problem Solving: An Analysis of Clinical Reasoning*, Harvard University Press, Cambridge, Mass., 1978.

L. Fagan, J. Kunz, E. Feigenbaum, and J. Osborn, "Extensions to the Rule-Based Formalism for a Monitoring Task," in B. Buchanan and E. Shortliffe, eds., *Rule-Based Expert Systems*, Addison-Wesley, Reading, Mass., 1984.

B. Farr and L. Fagan, "Decision-Theoretic Evaluation of Therapy Plans," *Proceedings of the Thirteenth Symposium on Computer Applications in Medical Care*, 1989, pp. 188–192.

P. Feltovich, P. Johnson, J. Moller, and D. Swanson, "LCS: The role and development of medical knowledge in diagnostic expertise," in W. Clancey and E. Shortliffe, eds., *Readings in Medical Artificial Intelligence*, Addison-Wesley, Reading, Mass., 1984.

F. Gomez and B. Chandrasekaran, "Knowledge Organization and Distribution for Medical Diagnosis," *IEEE Trans. Sys. Man Cybernet.* **11**, 34–42 (1981).

G. Gorry, "Computer-Assisted Clinical Decision Making," *Meth. Inform. Med.* **12**, 45–51 (1973).

G. Gorry, H. Silverman, and S. Pauker, "Capturing Clinical Expertise: A Computer Program that Considers Clinical Responses to Digitalis," *Am. J. Med.* **64**, 452–460 (1978).

G. Gorry and G. Barnett, "Experience with a Model of Sequential Diagnosis," *Comput. Biomed. Res.* **1**, 490–507 (1968).

D. Heckerman, "Probabilistic Similarity Networks," *Networks* **20**, 607–636 (1990).

D. Heckerman, E. Horvitz, and B. Nathwani, "Update on the Pathfinder Project," *Proc. Symp. Comput. Applic. Med. Care* **13**, 203–207 (1989).

D. Hickam and co-workers, "A Study of the Treatment Advice of a Computer-Based Chemotherapy Protocol Advisor," *Ann. Intern. Med.* **103**, 928–936 (1985).

E. Horvitz, J. Breese, and M. Henrion, "Decision Theory in Expert Systems and Artificial Intelligence," *J. Approx. Reas.* **2**, 247–302 (1988).

B. Humphreys and D. Lindberg, "Building the Unified Medical Language System," *Proc. Symp. Comput. Applic. Med. Care* **13**, 475–480 (1989).

H. Jimison, "A Representation for Gaining Insight into Clinical Decision Models," *Proc. Symp. Comput. Applic. Med. Care* **12**, 110–113 (1988).

M. Kahn, L. Fagan, and S. Tu, "Extensions to the Time-Oriented Database Model to Support Temporal Reasoning in Medical Expert Systems," *Meth. Inform. Med.* **30**, 4–14 (1991).

J. Kassirer and G. Gorry, "Clinical Problem Solving: A Behavioral Analysis," *Ann. Intern. Med.* **89**, 245–255 (1978).

L. Kingsland and D. Lindberg, "The Criteria Table Form of Knowledge Representation in Medical Artificial Intelligence," *Proceedings of the Fifth Conference on Medical Informatics* (*MEDINFO 86*), North-Holland, Amsterdam, 1986, pp. 12–16.

D. Klein, *Interpretive Value Analysis*, Ph.D. dissertation, University of Pennsylvania, Philadelphia, 1989; also Report RC 15278 (#68173), IBM Research Division, Yorktown Heights, NY, 1989.

B. Kuipers, "Qualitative Simulation," *Artif. Intell.* **29**, 289–338 (1986).

C. Lane, J. Walton, and E. Shortliffe, "Graphical Access to Medical Expert Systems: II. Design of an Interface for Physicians," *Meth. Inform. Med.* **25**, 143–150 (1986).

C. Langlotz, *A Decision-Theoretic Approach to Heuristic Planning*, Ph.D. dissertation, Stanford University, Stanford, Calif., 1989.

C. Langlotz, E. Shortliffe, and L. Fagan, "Using Decision Theory to Justify Heuristics," in *Proceedings of the Fifth National Conference on Artificial Intelligence*, Philadelphia, AAAI, Menlo Park, Calif., 1986, pp. 215–219.

S. Lauritzen and D. Spiegelhalter, "Local Computations with Probabilities on Graphical Structures and Their Applications to Expert Systems," *J. R. Stat. Soc.* **50**, 157–224 (1988).

R. Ledley and L. Lusted, "Reasoning Foundations of Medical Diagnosis," *Science* **130**, 9–21 (1959).

W. Long, S. Naimi, M. Cristicello, and R. Jayes, "Development and Use of a Causal Model for Reasoning about Heart Failure," *Proceedings of the Eleventh Symposium on Computer Applications in Medical Care*, 1987, pp. 30–36.

B. McNeil, R. Weichelbaum, and S. Pauker, "Speech and Survival: Tradeoffs between Quality and Quantity of Life in Laryngeal Cancer," *N. Engl. J. Med.* **305**, 982–987 (1981).

P. Miller, "ATTENDING: Critiquing a Physician's Management Plan," *IEEE Trans. Pattern Anal. Machine Intell.* **5**, 449–461 (1983).

P. Miller, *A Critiquing Approach to Expert Computer Advice: ATTENDING*, Pittman, London, 1984.

R. Miller, "Legal Issues Related to Medical Decision Support Systems," *Int. J. Clin. Monit. Comput.* **6**, 75–80 (1989).

R. Miller, H. Pople, and J. Myers, "INTERNIST-1, An Experimental Computer-Based Diagnostic Consultant for General Internal Medicine," *N. Engl. J. Med.* **307**, 468–476 (1982).

R. Miller and co-workers, "The INTERNIST/Quick Medical Reference Project: Status Report," *West. J. Med.* **145**, 816–822 (1986).

B. Mulsant, "A Neural Network as an Approach to Clinical Diagnosis," *M.D. Comput.* **7**(1), 25–36 (1990).

M. Musen, *Automated Generation of Model-Based Knowledge Acquisition Tools*, Pitman, London, 1989.

M. Musen and co-workers, "OPAL: Toward the Computer-Aided Design of Oncology Advice Systems," *Proc. Symp. Comput. Applic. Med. Care* **10**, 43–52 (1986).

R. Neapolitan, *Probabilistic Reasoning in Expert Systems*, John Wiley & Sons, Inc., New York, 1990.

R. Patil, P. Szolovits, and W. Schwartz, "Causal Understanding of Patient Illness in Medical Diagnosis," in *Proceedings of the Seventh IJCAI*, Vancouver, B.C., Morgan-Kaufmann, San Mateo, Calif., 1981, pp. 893–899.

J. Pearl, *Probabilistic Reasoning in Intelligent Systems: Networks of Plausible Inference*, Morgan-Kaufmann, San Mateo, Calif., 1988.

P. Politakis and S. Weiss, "A System for Empirical Experimentation with Expert Knowledge," *Proceedings of the Fifteenth Hawaii International Conference on Systems Science*, Vol. 2, 1982, pp. 649–657.

H. Pople, "Heuristic Methods for Imposing Structure on Ill-Structured Problems: The Structuring of Medical Diagnosis," in P. Szolovits, ed., *Artificial Intelligence in Medicine*, Westview Press, Boulder, Colo., 1982.

J. Reggia, D. Nau, and P. Wang, "Diagnostic Expert Systems Based on a Set Covering Model," *Int. J. Man-Machine Stud.* **19**, 437–460 (1983).

G. Rennels, *A Computational Model of Reasoning from the Clinical Literature*, Springer-Verlag, New York, 1987.

G. Rennels, E. Shortliffe, and P. Miller, "Choice and Explanation in Medical Management: A Multiattribute Model of Artificial Intelligence Approaches," *Med. Decis. Making* **7**(1), 22–31 (1987).

A. Scott, W. Clancey, R. Davis, and E. Shortliffe, "Methods for Generating Explanations," in B. Buchanan and E. Shortliffe, eds., *Rule-Based Expert Systems*, Addison-Wesley, Reading, Mass., 1984.

R. Shachter, "Intelligent Probabilistic Inference," in L. Kanal and J. Lemmer, eds., *Uncertainty in Artificial Intelligence*, North-Holland, Amsterdam, The Netherlands, 1986.

E. Shortliffe, "Testing Reality: The Introduction of Decision-Support Technologies for Physicians," *Meth. Inform. Med.* **28**, 1–5 (1989).

E. Shortliffe and B. Buchanan, "A Model of Inexact Reasoning in Medicine," *Math. Biosci.* **23**, 351–379 (1975).

M. Shwe and co-workers, "Validating the Knowledge Base of a Therapy Planning System," *Meth. Info. Med.* **28**, 36–50 (1989).

M. Suwa, A. Scott, and E. Shortliffe, "An Approach to Verifying Completeness and Consistency in a Rule-Based Expert System," *AI Magazine* **2**, 16–21 (1982).

W. Swartout, "Explaining and Justifying Expert Consulting Programs," in *Proceedings of the Seventh IJCAI*, Morgan-Kaufmann, San Mateo, Calif., 1981, pp. 815–822.

P. Szolovits, ed., *Artificial Intelligence in Medicine, AAAS Selected Symposium*, Westview Press, Boulder, Colo., 1982.

P. Szolovits and S. Pauker, "Categorical and Probabilistic Reasoning in Medical Diagnosis," *Artif. Intell.* **11**, 115–144 (1978).

S. Tu and co-workers, "Episodic Skeletal-Plan Refinement Based on Temporal Data," *Communications of the ACM* **32**, 1439–1455 (1990).

H. Warner and co-workers, "A Mathematical Approach to Medical Diagnosis: Application to Congenital Heart Diseases," *JAMA* **177**, 177–183 (1961).

H. Wechsler, "A Fuzzy Approach to Medical Diagnosis," *Int. J. Biomed. Comput.* **7**, 191–203 (1976).

S. Weiss, P. Politakis, and A. Ginsberg, "Empirical Analysis and Refinement of Expert System Knowledge Bases," *Proc. Symp. Comput. Applic. Med. Care* **10**, 53–60 (1986).

M. Wellman, *Formulation of Tradeoffs in Planning under Uncertainty*, Report MIT/LCS/TR-427, Laboratory of Computer Science, MIT, Cambridge, Mass., 1988.

L. Widman, Y. Lee, and Y. Pao, "Toward the Diagnosis of Medical Causal Models by Semiquantitative Reasoning," in P. Miller, ed., *Selected Topics in Medical Artificial Intelligence*, Springer-Verlag, New York, 1988.

J. Wyatt and D. Spiegelhalter, "Evaluating Medical Expert Systems: What to Test and How," in J. Talman and J. Fox, eds., *System Engineering in Medicine*, Springer-Verlag, New York, 1989.

V. Yu and co-workers, "An Evaluation of MYCIN's Advice," *J. Am. Med. Assoc.* **242**, 1279–1282 (1979).

ADAM R. GALPER
EDWARD H. SHORTLIFFE
Stanford University

GLENN D. RENNELS
RAMESH S. PATIL
MIT

MEMORY-BASED REASONING. See REASONING, MEMORY-BASED.

MEMORY ORGANIZATION PACKETS

A memory organization packet (MOP) is a unit of representation and memory organization proposed in a theory by Schank (1980) to explain the way episodic information is stored in human memory. The term is also used to refer to the entire theory of memory organization built around this unit. The theory has been most fully explicated in Schank (1982). A number of computer programs that make use of MOPs have been developed to test the theory, primarily by Schank and his associates. The basic ideas behind MOPs have been used extensively in case-based reasoning.

The basic idea behind the MOP theory is that representations of information are dynamic knowledge structures that are constantly being created and changed through learning and generalization. Episodes are indexed in memory in terms of knowledge structures that have been generalized from earlier examples. Episodes are always analyzed at a number of levels simultaneously. This allows information to be stored and generalizations to be made at a variety of concrete an abstract levels during the processing of a single example. When a new episode is to be understood, information is collected from all relevant knowledge structures and applied to the new example.

Historically, MOPs developed out of the understanding theory proposed in Schank (1977)—specifically from the knowledge structure known as a script. Scripts (qv) were designed to be used to explain events comprised of stereotypical sequences of actions such as visits to restaurants and trips to the doctor. While scripts were successfully used in several language understanding programs, they did have certain problems, particularly when used for memory and learning.

The main problem is using scripts for memory and learning is that they are too large and monolithic. Several psychological experiments (eg, Bower and co-workers, 1979) showed that people would confuse events that occurred in similar local settings, even if in different scripts. So, for example, a subject who read about an action that took place in a waiting room during a dentist visit might recall it as having taken place in a story about a visit to a doctor. In addition, learning in situations involving different scripts but similar situations (such as waiting rooms) would be difficult.

The solution to these problems was to develop a system made up of a number of much smaller structures. Each structure describes a small chunk of information about events. These chunks can be used by a variety of higher level structures, providing flexibility in memory organization and learning.

The basic unit of memory in the MOP theory is the *scene*. A scene consists of actions that occur over a short period of time in service of a specific goal. MOPs then organize scenes. Schank (1982) divides scenes into three basic classes—physical, societal, and personal. Physical scenes describe events that take place at a single location. Societal scenes are tied together by a social relationship among people. Personal scenes are unified by idiosyncratic goals. MOPs can be broken down into the same three categories. In understanding, these classes lead to the questions "What happened physically?", "What happened socially?", and "What happened to the participants?". All types of memory structures are idiosyncratic, not just personal scenes and MOPs. Physical and societal MOPs and scenes describe an idiosyncratic view that a person assumes to be shared by other people.

Most events that take place are not simply isolated scenes. Scenes occur together in common patterns. This information is captured by MOP memory structures. Each MOP is a stereotypical sequence of scenes (or other MOPs) tied together physically, societally, or by a personal goal. An event is usually understood in terms of three or more MOPs, at least one at each of the physical, societal, and personal levels. In understanding, for each MOP found to be relevant, the various scenes are collected and used much as a script would be in the Schank (1977) theory. The use of the same scenes in a number of MOPs increases generality and the ability to learn.

Figure 1 lists a typical MOP from each class, along with some of their component scenes. The physical MOP contains concrete, if stereotypical, information about a trip to a grocery store. The societal MOP involves social conventions about making a purchase, and the personal MOP is a very idiosyncratic one involving the preparation of a typical dinner for a specific person.

To illustrate how MOPs are applied, the method that a person (or program) might make use of some of the structures in Figure 1 to understand a story about a person going to a grocery store and coming home to make a TV dinner will be briefly considered. Understanding such a story would involve all three MOPs in Figure 1. The physical MOP would be used to understand, for example, why the patron took a shopping cart on the way into the store. The societal MOP might be used to understand why a patron who did not have enough cash was able to write a check. Such processing could occur even if the understander only knew about checks in other situations. The personal MOP might be required to understand why the patron turned on the oven before leaving for the store.

The overall flow of understanding is to collect the various relevant physical, societal and personal scenes and match incoming events against them. This provides the explanatory part of understanding. In our example, an action in the story involving the patron at the checkout with a TV dinner, will be understood three ways: in physical terms (the check-out scene is being carried out); societally (a payment is taking place); and in terms of the patron's personal goal of having a TV dinner by which to watch television.

Crucial to the idea of MOPs is that understanding must include learning. The understander examines the cases where input was not adequately explained and determines how the relevant scenes or MOPs should be modified to enchance later understanding. Depending on whether earlier expectation violations were similar, either the generalizations underlying one or more scenes or MOPs will be changed, or this violation will be indexed so that it can be found if there are similar violations in the future. Developing an algorithm for determining exactly which structures should be modified is one of the most difficult aspects of implementing a MOP-based computer system. In people, accurately determining which structures should be modified seems to be an important component of intelligence.

The first two computer experiments that made use of MOPs were CYRUS, developed by Kolodner (1984) and IPP, developed by Lebowitz (1983). CYRUS used MOPs to store detailed descriptions of episodes about a single individual. Due to the rich nature of the descriptions and the generalizations made from them, CYRUS was able to answer a variety of questions about its memory. CYRUS was also used to study the reconstructive nature of memory retrieval and question answering. IPP used a MOP-type memory structure to organize information taken from news stories about international terrorism. The generalization-based memory created from the articles was useful both in studying the cognitive process of organizing information and as a prototype intelligent information system. The use of dynamic memory structures in text understanding was a major part of the development of IPP. MOPs were also used in BORIS (qv) (Dyer, 1983), which used them to do detailed text understanding.

MOPs have subsequently been used in a number of other computer experiments. MOPs have been used to assist language understanding, in Lebowitz's intelligent information system, RESEARCHER (1988) and Lytinen's translation system, MOPTRANS (1984). They have also been used in a number of case-based reasoning systems such as Kolodner's MEDIATOR (qv) (conflict mediation) (1989), Bain's JUDGE (criminal sentences) (1985), and Hammond's CHEF (qv) (cooking) (1989). Much related work is described in Kolodner and Riesbeck (1986) and Kolodner (1988).

BIBLIOGRAPHY

W. M. Bain, "Assignment of Responsibility in Ethical Judgments," in J. L. Kolodner and C. K. Riesbeck, eds., *Memory, Experience and Reasoning*, Lawrence Erlbaum, Hillsdale, N.J., 1985, pp. 127–138.

G. H. Bower, J. B. Black, and T. J. Turner, "Scripts in Text Comprehension and Memory," *Cog. Psychol.* **11**, 177–220 (1979).

M. Dyer, *In-Depth Understanding*, MIT Press, Cambridge, Mass., 1983.

K. J. Hammond, *Case-Based Planning*, Academic Press, Cambridge, Mass., 1989.

J. L. Kolodner, *Retrieval and Organizational Strategies in Conceptual Memory: A Computer Model*, Lawrence Erlbaum, Hillsdale, N.J., 1984.

J. L. Kolodner, ed., *Proceedings of the Case-Based Reasoning Workshop*, Morgan-Kaufmann, San Mateo, Calif., 1988.

J. L. Kolodner and C. K. Riesbeck, eds., *Memory, Experience and Reasoning*, Lawrence Erlbaum Associates, Hillsdale, N.J., 1986.

J. L. Kolodner and R. L. Simpson, "The Mediator: Analysis of an Early Case-Based Problem," *Mach. Learn.* **13**(4), 507–550 (1989).

M. Lebowitz, "Generalization from Natural Language Text," *Cog. Sci.* **7**(1), 1–40 (1983).

M. Lebowitz, "The Use of Memory in Text Processing," *Commun. ACM*, **31**(12), 1483–1502 (1988).

S. L. Lytinen, "Frame Selection in Parsing," in *Proceedings of the*

Physical	Societal	Personal
M-GROCERY-SHOP	M-PURCHASE	M-MAKE-(MY)-DINNER
get-cart	make-selection	preheat-oven
examine-fruit	determine-availability	get-tv-dinner
check-out	provide-payment	eat-and-watch-tv

Figure 1. Examples of different MOP types with some component scenes.

Fourth National Conference on Artificial Intelligence, Austin, Tex., AAAI, Menlo Park, Calif., 1984, pp. 222-225.

R. C. Schank, "Language and Memory," *Cog. Sci.* 4(3), 243-284 (1980).

R. C. Schank, *Dynamic Memory: A Theory of Reminding and Learning in Computers and People*, Cambridge University Press, New York, 1982.

R. C. Schank, *Scripts, Plans, Goals and Understanding*, Lawrence Erlbaum, Hillsdale, N.J., 1977.

MICHAEL LEBOWITZ
Morgan Stanley and Company

MENTAL IMAGERY REPRESENTATION

Issues about the nature of internal representation lie at the heart of much of AI. Mental imagery is one way in which information can be stored and used in the human brain, and the reasons it is useful for humans have direct implications for the construction of intelligent machines. A mental image is a transient perceptual representation that is formed on the basis of stored information, rather than evoked by immediate sensory input. When these data structures are present the experiences are of "seeing with the mind's eye," "hearing with the mind's ear," and so forth. In scientific psychology, the term *image* refers to the data structure, not the experience that accompanies it. Although imagery can occur in many sensory modalities, the bulk of imagery research has been in visual imagery. Thus, this article will focus on investigations of visual imagery.

HISTORICAL CONTEXT

Plato conceived of memory as images carved on a wax tablet, and imagery was inextricably interwoven with theories of thinking through most of the succeeding centuries. The British associationists, for example, conceived of thinking as sequences of images. Imagery was at the heart of theories of mental events when psychology and philosophy diverged, with both Wundt and James giving it considerable attention. However, the scientific method rests on being able to disprove hypotheses, and imagery—and mental events in general—are not publicly accessible. Furthermore, in the early 1900s it was not clear how to think of imagery. Thus, lacking sophisticated methodologies for studying mental events and theoretical constructs for conceptualizing them, it was easy for behaviorism to eschew such topics altogether. Mental events in general, and imagery in particular, were excluded from scientific psychology from roughly 1913, when Watson's famous treatise attacking imagery was published (Watson, 1913), to the early 1960s.

It is no accident that parts of psychology are now directly relevant to AI. Historically, the study of mental events became acceptable in psychology only after computers became readily available and theorists had a concrete metaphor for conceptualizing mental events. Computers rely on the representation and manipulation of information, and it is clear that the brain can be regarded as a similar kind of machine. But even so, the modern reintroduction of imagery into scientific psychology was not smooth. Indeed, only after new methodologies produced striking results did researchers in psychology and AI take imagery seriously.

A series of experiments was conducted in the early 1970s that forced researchers in both psychology and AI to consider the nature of imagery. Perhaps the best example of such work is the research investigating mental rotation of imaged objects (Shepard and Cooper, 1982; Shepard and Metzler, 1971). In a typical mental rotation experiment, subjects were asked to compare two objects (eg, three-dimensional block figures) with different orientations, and determine whether they had the same shape. When the figures were different, they differed only subtly (either by a mirror reversal or slight modification of the shape). Subjects in these experiments typically claimed to mentally rotate one of the objects to fit the orientation of the other, and the time required to make a decision increased with the number of degrees of rotation required to make one object fit the orientation of the other. Thus, despite the fact that images are not rigid, space-occupying objects that must obey the laws of physics, imaged figures have characteristics that resemble those of actual objects.

The systematic results obtained in mental rotation experiments had at least two important consequences. First, they convinced many that mental imagery should be brought back into serious scientific study, if only because such reliable, systematic effects could be found. An intense period of fruitful investigations into the properties of visual imagery took place in the 1970s and early 1980s (Kosslyn, 1980). Second, researchers considered how a computer could be programmed to mimic such results. This fueled disagreements over alternative formats for imagery representation, which resulted in the debate about the nature of imagery.

POSSIBLE IMAGERY REPRESENTATIONS

Different representations make different information explicit. Consider the difference between the pattern "A" and the description "two symmetrical diagonal lines that meet at the top and are joined roughly halfway down by a horizontal line." Both representations apply to the same thing, but one would be easier to use to determine whether the pattern has an enclosed region and, if so, what shape it is. The difference between these two kinds of representations corresponds to the difference between a depictive and a propositional representation.

A propositional representation contains a property or relation, which modifies or ties together one or more entities, called arguments. For example, a scene in which a ball is sitting on a box can be coded propositionally with the notation *on (ball, box)*. Here, *on* is a relation tying together the arguments *ball* and *box*. Notice the notation used is abstract and is not a natural language (although propositional representations are assumed to be used in language processing). The basic elements of a propositional representation are symbols that fall into classes.

On, ball, and *box* are symbols; *on* is a symbol for a certain relation and the other two are symbols for certain entities.

In contrast, a depictive representation is picturelike, using patterns of points in a functional space to store information. The space need not be physical, such as this page, but can be like an array in a computer, which specifies spatial relations purely functionally. In a depictive representation, each part of an object is represented by a pattern of points, and the spatial relations between these patterns in the functional space correspond to the spatial relations among the parts themselves in the object. An example of a depictive representation is a drawing of a ball on a box. Depictive representations do not explicitly represent a relation (eg, a symbol *on*); instead the relation between arguments emerges from the spatial positions between and among the depicted objects. In this form of representation, the basic element is a point placed in a certain location, as opposed to an abstract symbol.

THE IMAGERY DEBATE

A large amount of research has been aimed at determining which type of representation is used in imagery. The debate about the nature of imagery representation began with an article by Pylyshyn (1973), attacking the very idea of imagery on logical grounds. Pylyshyn argued that images could not be pictorial because there is no little man to look at them, no light to see by, and so forth. Kosslyn and Pomerantz (1977) summarized each of Pylyshyn's arguments, and showed that they did not rule out the idea of picturelike mental representations. This reply initiated a series of exchanges, which presented a mixture of argumentation and empirical results.

The so-called imagery debate has had two phases and has just entered a third. In the first, the focus was on the characteristics of the internal representations that underlie the experience of having visual images. In the second, the debate centered on whether the empirical support for specific characteristics was contaminated by methodological problems. And most recently, problems with relying solely on behavioral evidence to investigate imagery have led theorists to turn to facts about brain function to resolve the issue.

Phase 1: Two Forms of Representation or One?

The first phase of the imagery debate concerned how information is represented when one has the experience of a visual image. The debate focused on two alternatives. One view was that images are represented symbolically, using a sentencelike predicate calculus format; this code is a propositional representation. The propositionalists claimed that humans store all information using propositional representations (Anderson and Bower, 1973; Pylyshyn, 1973) and that the subjective visual properties of imagery are *epiphenomenal*; this means that the subjective, experiential qualities of images do not causally interact with the representations used to process information.

The other view was that images are represented spatially, using an arraylike format; this code is a depictive representation. According to this position, although propositional representations exist and are used for language and other tasks, visual imagery utilizes another form of representation. Depictivists claim that the properties of the experience of imagery reflect functional properties of the underlying representation. Hence, according to this view the depictive properties of imagery are actually used in processing information.

The propositionalists staunchly argued for the single-format position for several reasons. First, computer scientists and members of the AI community often think about mental events by analogy to LISP programs. LISP is grounded in recursive search of property lists, and these property lists correspond to propositional representations. Indeed, Pylyshyn (1984) claimed that formal understanding itself cannot be achieved if more than one type of representation are postulated. Second, many researchers found the propositionalist view attractive because it is parsimonious; if both approaches are capable of explaining the experimental results, it is simpler to theorize about only one form of representation rather than two.

However, many investigators found that the propositionalist approach faltered when confronted with the results of experiments. For example, explaining the mental rotation findings in terms of networks of propositions and lists of symbols did not appear as convincing as explaining the results in terms of depictive representations that were sequentially reoriented to solve a problem. Investigators began to explore other characteristics of visual images that strain propositional accounts.

An important difference between propositional and depictive representations is that depictive codes intrinsically represent distance between and among objects and parts. This distinction was utilized in experiments on scanning of imaged objects. For example, it was hypothesized that if distance is intrinsically represented in images, then the time required to shift attention from one location to another on an imaged object should reflect the distance between them (Kosslyn, 1973). In this study subjects were asked to close their eyes and visualize previously memorized objects. For example, a subject might visualize a boat with a motor on the left end, a porthole in the middle, and an anchor on the right end. Then, the subject would focus attention on one end of the object (eg, the one with the motor). Next, the subjects would decide whether a named part was on the object; they were to "look" for the named part and press one button if they could "see" it and another if they could not. As expected by the depictive theory, the farther the subject had to scan to find a named part, the more time was required. With regard to the example, more time would be required to verify the anchor than the porthole, presumably because it is farther away from the motor.

Results from mental scanning experiments were initially taken to support the claim that visual mental images are depictive representations. However, these results were not conclusive. Explanations for them could be provided in terms of propositional representations: subjects might memorize objects by encoding a series of linked propositions. If the object was simple, a list might be sufficient. In such a list, parts that are farther apart on the object would be farther apart on the list, and hence, would require more time to search between. More sophisticated propositional structures can also be formed, using networks of linked propositions to capture the spatial structure of objects. In this scheme, focusing attention on a part corresponds to selecting that entry, and scanning is the same thing as iterating through the structure.

A series of experiments was conducted to rule out such possible accounts. For example, the amount of distance and the number of objects scanned over independently were varied, and it was shown that more time was required to scan greater distances per se (Kosslyn and coworkers, 1978). But even these results could be countered, if it is accepted that dummy entries were added to a list to mark off distance. Many additional experiments were conducted, and arguments exchanged, in this phase of the debate. With each additional experiment, the propositional accounts became more varied and complicated, whereas the depictive accounts remained relatively simple. Thus, although no one experiment was conclusive, the weight of the evidence began to lean marginally toward the depictive position. It is fair to say, however, that most researchers who believed at the outset that images are depictive representations stayed convinced, and most who believed that images are propositional representations also remained convinced.

Phase 2: Methodological Problems?

In the second phase of the imagery debate, attention was shifted to potential methodological problems with the way imagery experiments were conducted. On the one hand, it was argued that the experimenters unconsciously led the subjects to produce the expected data (Intons-Peterson, 1983); experimenter expectancy effects have been found in other areas of psychology. On the other hand, it was suggested that asking subjects to scan imaged objects may lead them (unconsciously) to try to mimic the behavior of actually scanning real objects (Pylyshyn, 1981). If this is the case, propositionally encoded information could guide such mimicry and be responsible for image scanning results. These demand characteristics were said to be an inherent aspect of the way the task was defined.

A study was conducted in which half the experimenters were told to expect one pattern of results and the other half were told to expect a different pattern (Intons-Peterson, 1983). In this study, subjects scanned imaged displays in one part of the experiment and scanned actual displays in another part. If the experimenter expected perceptual scanning to be faster than imagery scanning, the subjects obliged. Thus it appeared that subject performance was indeed influenced by expectations held by the experimenters.

In response to these results, another study showed that experimenter expectancies do not influence the important distance effects found in previous image scanning studies (Jolicoeur and Kosslyn, 1985). Different experimenters were told to expect different effects of scanning distance. Nevertheless, scan times increased with distance in the same way in all conditions. This pattern of results was different from that expected by the experimenters, thereby showing that experimenter expectancies cannot explain the increase in scanning time with increasing distance.

The demand characteristics explanation for visual imagery effects was also examined. For instance, image scanning experiments were conducted in which the subjects were not asked to use imagery to perform the task (or even told that imagery could be helpful to do the task) (Finke and Pinker, 1982, 1983). A set of randomly located dots was presented briefly to subjects, after which the dots were replaced by an arrow. The subjects responded as to whether the arrow, if placed in the same display as the dots, would point directly to one of the dots. The subjects reported afterward that they used imagery to perform the task, although they were not asked or required to do so. The main finding was that response times increased linearly with increasing distance between the arrow and dot. It is quite unlikely that the increase in time with increasing distances was due to demand characteristics. Because no imagery instructions were given, it is unlikely that the results were influenced by propositionally encoded information about how long scanning would take in a similar perceptual situation.

In addition, it has even been found that when the subjects themselves (not the experimenters, the actual participants) are told to expect to take more time to scan shorter distances, the normal finding of increased scanning time with increasing distance is evident (Goldston and coworkers, 1985). In this situation, any unconscious influence on scanning times brought about by how subjects think scanning is conducted should have led to quite different results. Overall, the conclusion of the second phase of the imagery debate is clear. Earlier experimental results cannot be explained as simply artifacts of the methodologies used.

Phase 3: Beyond Behavioral Results

Although behavioral experiments have consistently supported the notion that visual images utilize depictive representations, there has always been an abundance of propositional counterexplanations. This problem appears to be inescapable if behavioral evidence alone is relied on (Anderson, 1978). Therefore, the next step was to look beyond behavioral evidence toward another approach to discover whether depictive representations underlie visual imagery. The goal of this approach is to understand visual images in terms of the brain systems instantiating them.

This line of research builds on behavioral evidence that imagery utilizes the same mechanisms as those used in visual perception (Finke and Shepard, 1986; Segal and Fusella, 1970). For example, there is ample neuropsychological evidence that parts of the brain important for visual perception are also used in visual imagery (Farah, 1988). The brain of a monkey with humanlike visual abilities has at least 32 distinct regions concerned with vision. About 10 of these areas represent incoming perceptual information topographically. These representations preserve two-dimensional spatial information, reflecting how the information is encoded on the retina. Thus, if visual imagery utilizes activation over these same areas in the same topographical manner, convincing evidence will be found for depictive representations. Strong evidence that some of these topographically organized areas are indeed selectively activated during visual imagery has just been discovered (Kosslyn and co-workers, unpublished).

Therefore, it seems clear that the imagery debate can in principle be resolved by a three-step procedure: (1) imagery must be conclusively shown to evoke a depictive pattern of activation in topographically organized areas of the brain, (2) the pattern of activation must vary depending on the shape of the object being imaged, and (3) imagery must be impaired when these areas are damaged. If all three conditions are met, conclusive evidence that images are depictive will be obtained.

IMAGERY AND COMPUTATIONAL SYSTEMS

Part of the original critique of imagery (Pylyshyn, 1973) hinged on the claim that depictive representations could not be used in computational systems. However, a computer simulation model was built that in fact relied on such representations (Kosslyn and Shwartz, 1977), and it was independently shown that depictive representations are computationally efficient for computing dynamic interactions among tumbling objects (Funt, 1976). To simulate depictive codes, the computer simulation model (Kosslyn and Shwartz, 1977) used a visual buffer, in which images were represented as points in an array, that functionally captured depictive features of imaged objects. In this model, the depictive representations in the visual buffer causally interacted with propositionally encoded information stored elsewhere.

Models such as this did more than demonstrate the computational sufficiency of depictive representations. They also made clear that depictive imagery processes could be implemented within computational systems. Depictive representations could be generated in the visual buffer on the basis of more abstract information, interpreted as representing parts and objects, and transformed in various ways. [Discussions of these processes have been published (Kosslyn, 1980).] In fact, this model provided accounts for nearly all documented imagery findings, such as the increased time to rotate imaged objects greater amounts.

CONCLUSION

Research in experimental psychology is beginning to provide the broad outlines of the nature of visual image representations and the neurophysiological systems in which they are produced and used. Not only do such findings illustrate that imagery is empirically and conceptually tractable but they also indicate that images are more than epiphenomena. They instead appear to be genuine depictive representations utilized by the human brain.

BIBLIOGRAPHY

J. R. Anderson, "Arguments Concerning Representations for Mental Imagery," *Psychol. Rev.* **85**, 249–277 (July 1978).

J. R. Anderson and G. H. Bower, *Human Associative Memory*, V. H. Winston, New York, 1973.

M. J. Farah, "Is Visual Imagery Really Visual? Overlooked Evidence from Neuropsychology," *Psychol. Rev.* **95**, 307–317 (July 1988).

R. A. Finke and S. Pinker, "Spontaneous Imagery Scanning in Mental Extrapolation," *J. Exp. Psychol. [Learn. Mem. Cogn.]* **8**, 142–147 (Mar. 1982).

R. A. Finke and S. Pinker, "Directional Scanning of Remembered Visual Patterns," *J. Exp. Psychol. [Learn. Mem. Cogn.]* **9**, 398–410 (July 1983).

R. A. Finke and R. N. Shepard, "Visual Functions of Mental Imagery," in K. R. Boff, L. Kaufman, and J. P. Thomas, eds., *Handbook of Perception and Human Performance*, John Wiley & Sons, Inc., New York, 1986.

B. V. Funt, *WHISPER: A Computer Implementation Using Analogues in Reasoning*, Ph.D. dissertation, University of British Columbia, Vancouver, Canada, 1976.

D. B. Goldston, J. V. Hinrichs, and C. L. Richman, "Subjects' Expectations, Individual Variability, and the Scanning of Mental Images," *Mem. Cogn.* **13**, 365–370 (July 1985).

M. J. Intons-Peterson, "Imagery Paradigms: How Vulnerable Are They to Experimenters' Expectations?" *J. Exp. Psychol. [Hum. Percept.]* **9**, 394–412 (June 1983).

P. Jolicoeur and S. M. Kosslyn, "Is Time to Scan Visual Images Due to Demand Characteristics?" *Mem. Cogn.* **13**, 320–332 (July 1985).

S. M. Kosslyn, "Scanning Visual Images: Some Structural Implications," *Percept. Psychophys.* **14**, 90–94 (July 1973).

S. M. Kosslyn, *Image and Mind*, Harvard University Press, Cambridge, Mass., 1980.

S. M. Kosslyn, T. M. Ball, and B. J. Reiser, "Visual Images Preserve Metric Spatial Information: Evidence from Studies of Image Scanning," *J. Exp. Psychol. [Hum. Percept.]* **4**, 47–60 (Feb. 1978).

S. M. Kosslyn and J. R. Pomerantz, "Imagery, Propositions, and the Form of Internal Representations," *Cogn. Psychol.* **9**, 52–76 (Jan. 1977).

S. M. Kosslyn and S. P. Shwartz, "A Simulation of Visual Imagery," *Cogn. Sci.* **1**, 265–295 (July 1977).

Z. W. Pylyshyn, "What the Mind's Eye Tells the Mind's Brain: A Critique of Mental Imagery," *Psychol. Bull.* **80**, 1–24 (July 1973).

Z. W. Pylyshyn, "The Imagery Debate: Analogue Media versus Tacit Knowledge," *Psychol. Rev.* **87**, 16–45 (Jan. 1981).

Z. W. Pylyshyn, *Computation and Cognition: Toward a Foundation for Cognitive Science*, MIT Press, Cambridge, Mass., 1984.

S. J. Segal and V. Fusella, "Influence of Imaged Pictures and Sounds on Detection of Visual and Auditory Signals," *J. Exp. Psychol.* **83**, 458–464 (Mar. 1970).

R. N. Shepard and L. A. Cooper, *Mental Images and Their Transformations*, MIT Press, Cambridge, Mass., 1982.

R. N. Shepard and J. Metzler, "Mental Rotation of Three-Dimensional Objects," *Science* **171**, 701–703 (Feb. 1971).

J. B. Watson, "Psychology as the Behaviorist Views It," *Psychol. Rev.* **20**, 158–177 (Mar. 1913).

CHAD J. MARSOLEK
STEPHEN M. KOSSLYN
Harvard University

MENTAL MODELS

A mental model is an internal representation of a state of affairs in the external world. It is thus a form of knowledge representation that is advocated by many cognitive scientists as the natural way in which the human mind constructs reality, conceives alternatives to it, and searches out the consequences of assumptions in a process of mental simulation. The origins of this theory are to be found in the work of three remarkable individuals: the philosopher Wittgenstein, the psychologist Craik, and the physiologist Marr. In his early work, Wittgenstein (1922) defended a picture theory of meaning, which he captured in a handful of propositions:

> 2.1 We make to ourselves pictures of facts.
> 2.12 The picture is a model of reality.
> 2.13 To the objects [in the world] correspond in the picture the elements of the picture.
> 2.15 That the elements of the picture are combined with one another in a definite way, represents that the things [in the world] are so combined with one another.
> 2.17 What the picture must have in common with reality in order to be able to represent it after its manner—rightly or falsely—is its form of representation.

Craik (1943) postulated a similar sort of representation, and offered one of the earliest defenses of functionalism: the doctrine that the organization of the mind is what is critical, not the fact that it is constructed out of flesh, blood, and neurons. What is striking about his conception of a strong form of artificial intelligence is that he wrote before the invention of the programmable digital computer:

> My hypothesis then is that thought models, or parallels reality—that its essential feature is not 'the mind', 'the self', 'sense data', nor propositions but symbolism, and that this symbolism is largely of the same kind as that which is familiar to us in mechanical devices which aid thought and calculation. . . .
>
> If the organism carries a 'small-scale model' of external reality and of its own possible actions within its head, it is able to try out various alternatives, conclude which is the best of them, react to future situations before they arise, utilize the knowledge of past events in dealing with the present and the future, and in every way to react in a much fuller, safer, and more competent manner to the emergencies which face it (Craik, 1943).

Wittgenstein and Craik made only programmatic proposals. Propositions are models of reality that represent its structure in an analogous way to which a picture represents reality. Human beings and other intelligent organisms construct such models on the basis of perception, transform them internally as a result of inference, and base their actions on the results. The program was plausible, but it was not until the mid-1970s that workers in the cognitive sciences were able to advance the argument any further. The rest of this article is devoted to the more important of these investigations. It considers Marr's analysis of vision in terms of mental models, the best articulated account of how perception might lead to the construction of representations of the world. It then turns to language and to the theory of comprehension that postulates that discourse is also represented in the form of models. This account leads naturally to the view that knowledge is represented in the form of models. But, if so, then inference is likely to consist in the manipulation of models. This conception of inference differs from its normal treatment in artificial intelligence as process based on formal rules of inference, and so the final section of the article outlines deductive algorithms based on models.

PERCEPTION AS THE CONSTRUCTION OF MENTAL MODELS

Marr (1982) was a major contributor to the theory of mental models, and his work on vision provided a major impetus both to psychology and artificial intelligence. He argued for the need to distinguish three levels of theorizing: the computational level gives an account of the function that must be computed and of the constraints that may have evolved to aid the process; the algorithmic level describes the procedures carrying out the computation; and the hardware level identifies, in the case of the brain, the specific neuronal mechanisms that perform the computations. In his own work, Marr succeeded in developing theories at all three levels for certain aspects of vision.

Marr's general thesis was that visual perception is a process of unconscious inference from the structure of an image to a model that makes explicit the structure of the world. The process of pure vision leads through a series of mental representations. It starts with the physical interaction between light focused on the retinas and the visual pigment in retinal cells, and it ends with the two-and-a-half–dimensional ($2\frac{1}{2}$-D) sketch, which makes explicit the relative distance and orientation (with respect to the observer) of each visible surface in the scene. For Marr, this representation is the last in the chain that is driven purely by the data. To move about safely, however, a person needs a representation that makes explicit what entities are where in the world. The $2\frac{1}{2}$-D sketch does not represent the shape of objects or the spatial relations among them. It changes as soon as the point of view changes, because the orientations of the surfaces change in relation to the viewer. Hence, Marr argued for the need for a representation that is independent of point of view. This representation is a three-dimensional (3-D) model of the world. Its construction is based not merely on the $2\frac{1}{2}$-D sketch, but also on a high level knowledge of the shapes of familiar objects. When a person walks into a room and recognizes that it contains tables, chairs, and other items of furniture, that individual can readily navigate through the room to a particular goal, say, an armchair, even if he or she has never been in the room before. This can be done because the human visual system solves three fundamental problems: it perceives the three-dimensional shapes of objects, it uses these shapes to identify objects (the *what* in the scene), and it perceives their relative locations (the *where* in the scene). A scene is a complex object made up of many component objects, and most objects in turn are made up of component parts, and so on. Hence, the perception of an object and the perception of a scene are the same tasks on two different scales.

The 3-D model is analogous to an architect's model of a scene, which makes explicit the shape of everything in the scene. Such a data-structure does not call for a 3-D layout in the hardware of the brain or computer. Its physical embodiment has merely to support a representation that functions as three dimensional. Following on from earlier work in AI, Marr and his colleagues argued that the recognition of objects from their shape depended on three components. First, the shape of an object must be described in terms of its own canonical axes, eg, a furled umbrella is a long, thin cylinder. Second, the mind contains a catalog of the shapes of objects. Each entry in the catalog is itself a model, which decomposes into the shapes of the component parts. Hence, at the top level, the overall gross shape of the object is made explicit, whereas at lower levels, the details of the object are fleshed out. Third, there are procedures for comparing the shape of an entity in the 3-D model with the entries in the catalog of shapes. The process of fitting a cataloged model to a percept is complex and by no means well understood: a specific cue about the shape of an object may provide bottom-up access to a model in the catalog. The model can then be used top-down to try to match the rest of the percept, and information about the orientation of the axes of parts of the object to its principal axis may also be used in the matching process.

Marr's scheme illustrates two distinct sorts of mental model. One sort, the 3-D model, is constructed by perception and directly represents the world. The other sort, the catalog of objects, resides in long-term memory and has been acquired as a result of individual experience. These remembered models, however, must be more complex than Marr envisaged. Many common objects, particularly artifacts such as tables, chairs, and vehicles, do not have a canonical shape. A human observer can recognize an object as a table even if it has a shape unlike any other previously perceived table. It is recognized, not because of any intrinsic feature of its 3-D shape, but because its form, dimensions, and other visible properties, are perceived as appropriate for a particular purpose (Miller and Johnson-Laird, 1976). The observer perceives the possibilities inherent in the artifact. It is a table because it has a surface that is appropriately supported to function as a work top. Inferences from form to function are deeply mysterious. They are easy for the human visual system to make, but they present a challenge that artificial intelligence has yet to meet.

COMPREHENSION AND THE CONSTRUCTION OF DISCOURSE MODELS

Human beings not only construct models of the world, as do many other species, they also communicate the content of such models. Discourse enables individuals to experience the world by proxy. A speaker describes a situation and a listener in virtue of understanding the description can imagine how the world is, at least according to the speaker. When people understand discourse, they accordingly construct a schematic model of the situation described in the discourse (Johnson-Laird, 1983). Such a representation is, of course, remote from the syntactic structure of sentences in either a natural or a mental language. A model contains, for example, one token for each individual or entity to which reference is made rather than a series of representations corresponding to each noun phrase in the discourse. These tokens are interrelated in a way that corresponds to the relations that are described as holding among the relevant individuals. Thus an indefinite noun phrase introducing an individual, "a retired admiral," leads to the insertion of a token into a discourse model, and subsequent references to the same individual, either direct ("the retired admiral") or indirect ("the old man"), are used to address the same token in order to attach to it a representation of the new information that is asserted. This general principle that co-referential noun phrases are represented by a single entity in the discourse model was independently proposed by workers in formal semantics (Kamp, 1981), linguistics, psycholinguistics (Stenning, 1977; Van Dijk and Kintsch, 1983), and artificial intelligence (Webber, 1978; Wilks and Bien, 1979).

Of course, an indefinite description does not necessarily lead to the introduction of a token. The assertion

Ann is a teacher

contains an indefinite that is used predicatively of a named individual. It would be odd to continue the discourse:

The teacher was marking the scripts

because its initial noun phrase does not seem to refer to anything in the discourse model. Similarly, discourse often uses definite descriptions without any prior mention of the relevant individuals:

Ann was in a shop. She was talking to the assistant.

The correct referential interpretation of noun phrases and other linguistic elements, such as ellipses, is accordingly no easy matter. It hinges critically on general knowledge, and it often depends on aspects of the discourse model rather than reality. Thus philosophers have often argued that a singular definite description, such as "the assistant" in the previous discourse, asserts or presupposes the existence of one and only one individual who meets the description. In fact, the speaker is referring to the only assistant who is relevant in the immediate context. Uniqueness in the discourse model rather than in reality is what controls the use and interpretation of definite descriptions. Despite many advances in the computational representation of discourse since the first programs exemplifying the role of knowledge in comprehension, a complete theory of the referential machinery of natural language is still lacking. Pronouns and other anaphoric aspects of language, including ellipses, for example,

Usually a man who has a wife wants to please her, but Arthur doesn't

present intricate problems that have so far defied explanation. Nevertheless, psycholinguists have made progress in delineating the on-line construction of models (Garnham, 1987; Oakhill and co-workers, 1989a).

A discourse model is not merely a set of interrelated tokens representing all the entities to which reference is made. It must also represent the various attributes, relations, events, and states that the discourse describes. The essential assumption here was anticipated by Wittgenstein's picture theory: the structure of a mental model is isomorphic to the structure of the state of affairs, whether perceived or conceived, that the model represents (Johnson-Laird, 1983). The construction of such models must depend on a considerable amount of background knowledge: the same knowledge enters into the interpretation of models based on perception. In the case of discourse, interpretation also depends on a general knowledge of human planning and communicative intentions (Allen and Perrault, 1981; Cohen and co-workers, 1990).

KNOWLEDGE AND MODELS

The term mental model is often used to refer to a body of human knowledge, especially knowledge of how a machine works or knowledge of a branch of science. A classic analysis of such knowledge was Hayes's (1979) account of the naive physics of liquids. His goal was to make explicit the content of everyday knowledge, but he was not concerned with how inferential processes use this knowledge. Other workers, however, have attempted to model everyday qualitative reasoning in a variety of domains. Forbus (1985) has studied the possible mechanisms underlying everyday reasoning about space and motion, and implemented several programs, including one that constructs two-dimensional spatial models in order to draw inferences about the behavior of bouncing balls. Such models are simpler than the formal theory of mechanics, but their structure appears to reflect qualitative experience of the world. The use of formal rules to reason about space is combinatorially far too complex to capture the ease with which humans reason about such matters. As students of visual imagery have argued, an internal model allows one to determine the relations among objects just as one might inspect a real diagram (Larkin and Simon, 1987). In fact, Forbus introduced the use of a hybrid representation that combines both symbolic, propositional-like, elements with the analogical use of a diagram, eg, the empty space in the diagram is divided into labeled nonoverlapping regions. Some cognitive scientists have argued that the mind represents spatial relations only by analogue representations: models contain no labels. Yet it is necessary to introduce some propositional elements in even the simplest models if they are to account for the use of, say, negation (Newell, 1990; Johnson-Laird and Byrne, 1991).

Other investigators have studied the development of successively more expert models of various domains, such as mechanics (McCloskey and co-workers, 1980), hand-held calculators (Young, 1981), and electrical circuits (Gentner and Gentner, 1983). Once again, at the heart of these studies is the idea that people learn how to make mental simulations of phenomena, either in a series of dynamic images in the mind's eye or in more abstract mental models. In the modeling of such qualitative reasoning, de Kleer (1977) drew an important distinction between envisioning a model and running it to simulate behavior. To envision a model of a device, it is necessary to consider how each component works in isolation, and to use this knowledge and a knowledge of the structure of the device to infer how it works. Envisioning could, in principle, rely on the relaxation techniques that solve constraint-satisfaction problems. More likely, human envisioning depends on tracing the propagation of causal chains through the structural model of the device.

The inferences underlying the construction and use of models are extremely subtle. On the one hand, a variety of methods have been explored in AI (Shrager and Langley, 1990; Well and de Kleer, 1990), often based on the theorists' own reasoning methods or on their conceptions of an idealized thinker. On the other hand, cognitive scientists have examined both the models that individuals develop as they progress from novice to expert and the pedagogical advantage of providing them with models of difficult domains (Gentner and Gentner, 1983). Yet there remains a hiatus between the AI models and the psychological evidence: it has so far proved almost impossible to marry the computational models with psychological evidence, particularly with respect to the structure of mental models as opposed to the content that they represent. For example, cognitive psychologists have examined how people diagnose faults (Rouse and Hunt, 1984), and AI workers have implemented model-based algorithms for diagnosis using an assumption-based truth maintenance system of the sort originally devised for nonmonotonic reasoning (de Kleer and Williams, 1987; Davis and Hamscher, 1988). These groups of researchers, however, have had little contact with each other. In one domain, deductive reasoning, there has been some success in relating psychological evidence to a specific computational account of the structure and processing of models. These results have led in turn to the development of a new sort of AI algorithm for deduction. The final sections of this article describe these developments.

HUMAN DEDUCTION AS A MODEL-BASED PROCEDURE

If perception and linguistic comprehension yield models, then, as Craik (1943) supposed, processes of inference may operate not on linguistic structures, such as the logical form of verbal premises, but on models themselves. This hypothesis was first made explicit in a theory of human deductive reasoning (Johnson-Laird, 1983). The theory readily accounts for the spontaneous deductions that individuals draw for themselves and in particular for the fact that they do not throw semantic information away. A deduction of the form:

p
$\therefore p$ or q, or both

is logically valid, ie, the conclusion must be true given that the premise is true. Yet, logically untrained individuals find it bizarre, and never spontaneously volunteer such conclusions. Their conclusions instead tend to be based on the content of the models of the premises, but they search for parsimonious conclusions that make explicit information that was not overtly stated in the premises.

The theory makes three principal predictions. First, the difficulty of a deduction depends on the number of alternative models of the premises that a reasoner must construct: the greater the number of models, the more difficult the deduction will be. Second, the characteristic errors that are made will consist either in asserting that nothing follows (because the reasoner was unable to construct a model or to discern what holds in a set of models) or in conclusions true of only some of the possible models of the premises. Third, knowledge will influence the interpretation of premises and the process of reasoning itself. The first two predictions have been corroborated experimentally for all the major domains of deduction. Difficulty depends on number of models, and errors correspond to a subset of possible models in the case of propositional reasoning, relational reasoning, quantificational reasoning, and meta-reasoning (Johnson-Laird and Byrne, 1991). Indeed, as soon as an individual must imagine more than one distinct model there is a striking decline in performance. Thus deductions based on disjunctive premises are difficult, for example,

> The fuse box is in the cupboard or the mains switch is beneath the stairs, but not both.
> The mains switch is beneath the stairs or the power circuit enters by the back door, but not both.

Each premise supports two models, but when the information from both premises is combined the result is only two distinct models:

$$C \quad D$$
$$S$$

where C denotes "the fuse box in the cupboard," S denotes "the mains switch beneath the stairs," K denotes "the mains switch in the kitchen," and D denotes "the power circuit entering by the back door." Only some adult subjects are able to draw the appropriate conclusion:

> The fuse-box is in the cupboard and the power circuit enters by the back door, or else the mains switch is beneath the stairs.

When the disfunctions are inclusive, the number of models rises to five:

$$C \quad S \quad D$$
$$ \quad S \quad D$$
$$C \quad \quad D$$
$$C \quad S$$
$$ \quad S$$

and hardly anyone is able to draw a correct conclusion. The most frequent error is to base a conclusion on only one model. It is difficult to see how a theory based on formal rules of inference could account for these phenomena. The derivation of a conclusion using formal rules is straightforward and at no point yields conclusions corresponding to single models.

When intelligent but logically untutored individuals are given the following premises:
> All of the Frenchmen in the room are wine drinkers.
> Some of the wine drinkers in the room are gourmets.

the majority draw the conclusion:
> Some of the Frenchmen are gourmets.

But, when the premises have the following content:
> All of the Frenchmen in the room are wine drinkers.
> Some of the wine drinkers in the room are Italians.

hardly anyone draws the conclusion:
> Some of the Frenchmen in the room are Italians

and most people respond correctly that there is no valid conclusion (interrelating the end terms). This phenomenon confirms the third prediction: that knowledge influences the process of deduction. Reasoners evidently are guided by their knowledge in constructing models and in deciding whether or not to search for alternative models that refute putative conclusions (Oakhill and co-workers, 1989b). In daily life, knowledge is likely to facilitate inference just as it facilitates perception, but it may render the system open to illusions in both domains.

ALGORITHMS FOR MODEL-BASED DEDUCTION

Propositional Reasoning

Human reasoners demonstrate forms of inferential intelligence that are so far lacking in computer programs. First, they are able to draw conclusions for themselves, whereas almost all deductive computer programs merely evaluate given conclusions. Second, they take into account general knowledge, whereas deductive programs tend to rely on purely formal methods. Third, they use computationally weak methods that minimize the role of search, whereas even programs proving theorems in the propositional calculus must search for the appropriate derivation. Humans often err (presumably because of the processing limitations of working memory), but it is possible to implement a deductive algorithm that combines the strengths of the human inferential system with the power of the digital computer.

The algorithm simulates the construction and evaluation of semantic representations, ie, models of the states of affairs described in premises (Johnson-Laird, in press). Hence, an assertion such as:

> There is a circle or there is a triangle, or both

yields the following set of models, in which each line represents a model of an alternative possibility:

$$\bigcirc \quad \triangle$$
$$\bigcirc \quad \neg\triangle$$
$$\neg\bigcirc \quad \triangle$$

This representation is isomorphic to a translation of the

premise into disjunctive normal form (DNF) or, equivalently, a Boolean sum of products. Given the categorical premise:

There is not a triangle

the first and third models are eliminated because they are inconsistent with the premise, but the second model survives. The following conclusion:

There is a circle

is valid because (the relevant part of) the premise model is a subset of the conclusion model:

○

In other words, there is no alternative model of the premises that refutes the conclusion. This method of reasoning does not depend on a search for a derivation: the algorithm does not have to simulate the operation of a nondeterministic automaton, because a simple deterministic procedure suffices to establish whether or not a conclusion follows from any premises.

The models are constructed recursively by a parser equipped with rules of syntax and rules of an associated compositional semantics. A central role is played by the product of two sets of models, which corresponds to the conjunction of two propositions. The product of two sets of models is a new set combining each model in one set with each model in the other set, but eliminating redundancies and those combinations that would contradict with one another.

Definition 1. The product of two sets of models, A and B, consists of the set $(A \times B)$ which is defined as follows:

$$(\forall \alpha)(\forall \beta)((\alpha \in A) \wedge (\beta \in B)) \rightarrow (\alpha \times \beta) \in (A \times B)$$

where α and β are single models, and $(\alpha \times \beta)$ has the following values:

1. *Contradictions.*

$$(\exists x)(((x \in \alpha) \wedge (\neg x \in \beta)) \\ \vee ((\neg x \in \alpha) \wedge (x \in \beta))) \rightarrow (\alpha \times \beta) = \{\ \}$$

2. *Redundancies.*

$$(\forall y)((y \in \alpha) \wedge (y \in \beta)) \rightarrow (\alpha \times \beta) = \{\alpha\ \beta\} - \{y\}$$

3. *Remaining Cases.*

$$(\alpha \times \beta) = \{\alpha\ \beta\}$$

Given the following two sets of models, for example,

$$\begin{array}{ccc} a & b & \neg c \\ \neg a & b & c \end{array}$$

$$\begin{array}{ccc} b & c & d \\ b & \neg c & d \end{array}$$

the product combines each model in the first set with each model in the second set, dropping those models that would contain an atom and its negation, and eliminating redundant occurrences of atoms:

$$\begin{array}{cccc} a & b & \neg c & d \\ \neg a & b & c & d \end{array}$$

Negation calls for the complement of a set of models.

Definition 2. The complement of a set of models A is the set $(A' - A)$, where A' is the set of all possible combinations of values of the literals in A. The complement of the following set of models, for example,

$$\begin{array}{cc} a & \neg b \\ \neg a & b \end{array}$$

is the set:

$$\begin{array}{cc} a & b \\ \neg a & \neg b \end{array}$$

The meanings of all truth-functional connectives can be defined in terms of the product and complement functions. The high level function controlling the building of models loops through the list of premises forming the product of the set of models for the current premise and the set of models for the previous premises. Because the syntactic and semantic rules are recursive, the premises can be of any arbitrary degree of complexity.

Validity is a simple relation between sets of models. Where the models of the premises and conclusion contain the same literals, the conclusion follows validly if the models of the premises are a subset of the models of the conclusion: the truth of the premises guarantee the truth of the conclusion. Where the conclusion models lack at least one literal in the premise models, for example,

$$\begin{array}{l} a \rightarrow b \\ a \\ \therefore\ b \end{array}$$

the conclusion follows validly if the premise models are a subset of the product of the premise and conclusion models: the conclusion adds no new semantic information to what is contained in the premises. This principle subsumes, of course, the cases where the premise and conclusion models have the same literals. Where the premise models lack at least one literal that occurs in the conclusion models, for example,

$$\begin{array}{l} a \\ \therefore a \vee b \end{array}$$

the missing literals must be added tautologically to the premise models: $(a \wedge (b \vee \neg b))$. The conclusion follows validly because the resulting premise models

$$\begin{array}{cc} a & b \\ a & \neg b \end{array}$$

are once again a subset of their product with the conclusion models. Validity can, therefore, be defined as follows.

Definition 3. A deduction from a set of premises to a conclusion is valid if and only if $P' \subseteq (P' \times C)$, where P' is constructed from the premise models P by adding x and $\neg x$ independently to each member of P (to form two members of P') for any literal x that is in the conclusion models C and not in the premise models P. Validly can accordingly be checked by a simple deterministic procedure that establishes whether one set of models is included in another.

An infinite number of valid conclusions follow from any set of premises, and so deductive programs generally do not draw conclusions, but rather evaluate given conclusions (Bledsoe, 1977; Robinson, 1979; Wos, 1988). Human reasoners, however, exercise a greater degree of intelligence because they can draw conclusions for themselves. They abide by two principal constraints. First, as was seen earlier, they do not normally throw semantic information away. Second, they aim for conclusions that reexpress the semantic information in the premises more parsimoniously. They never, for example, draw a conclusion that merely conjoins all the premises, even though such a deduction is valid. Of course, human performance rapidly degrades with increasingly complex problems, but the goal of parsimony provides a rational solution to the problem of nondeterminism that arises with deductive programs. An intelligent program should draw a conclusion that succinctly expresses all the information in the premises. The present algorithm behaves in this way. It is able both to evaluate given conclusions and to draw conclusions that reexpress with maximum parsimony all the information in the premises.

An Extension to the Predicate Calculus

The model theory can in principle be extended to deal with quantified deductions. The first step is to replace the use of formal rules for sentential connectives (or the resolution rule) by the algorithm based on models. This step can be taken even when the semantics of the domain is not sufficiently understood for models of relations to be constructed: it exploits the standard apparatus of the instantiation of quantifiers and their subsequent generalization. Consider, for example, the following premises, which for simplicity use the apparatus of restricted quantifiers

1. $(\forall A)(\forall B) \neg(ARB)$
2. $(\forall B)(\forall C)(BRC)$

and the following postulates that capture the symmetry and transitivity of the relation R:

3. $(\forall X)(\forall Y)(XRY \rightarrow YRX)$
4. $(\forall X)(\forall Y)(\forall Z)(XRY \wedge YRZ \rightarrow XRZ)$

What follows validly? Existing algorithms are at a loss to deal with this question because it has an infinity of possible answers. Human reasoners, however, typically respond with conclusions of the form:

$(\forall A)(\forall C) \neg(ARC)$

which is the semantically strongest valid conclusion interrelating A and C. This conclusion can be drawn by first instantiating the premises

5. $\neg(aRb)$ (universal instantiations of 1)
6. (bRc) (universal instantiations of 2)
7. $(bRc) \rightarrow (cRb)$ (universal instantiations of 3)
8. $(aRc \wedge cRb) \rightarrow (aRb)$ (universal instantiations of 4)

The next stage now proceeds, not by a search for a derivation using formal rules for the connectives, but by the construction of the corresponding models in which the relation R is left unanalyzed. The interpretation of premises 5 and 6 yields the model

$\neg(aRb)$ (bRc)

The interpretation of premise 7 yields three alternative models

(bRc) (cRb)
$\neg(bRc)$ (cRb)
$\neg(bRc)\neg(cRb)$

that combine with the previous model to yield

$\neg(aRb)$ (bRc) (cRb)

Finally, the combination of this model with the models for premise 8 yields the model

$\neg(aRb)$ (bRc) (cRb) $\neg(aRc)$

The fourth item in this model expresses a relation that is not among the premises, and the restoration of universal quantifiers within it produces the conclusion

$(\forall A)(\forall C) \neg(ARC)$.

Although this method of deduction still requires a search for the appropriate instantiations of quantified variables, it has two advantages over the use of formal rules for the connectives. First, it does not call for a search for a derivation: the construction of models depends on a simple deterministic procedure. Second, it automatically ensures that the semantically strongest conclusion will be forthcoming for each set of instantiations. An inappropriate instantiation merely fails to yield a set of models supporting a novel relation. By contrast, it is unclear how a formal derivation could be guided toward an unknown but semantically strong conclusion. In certain domains, a definition of the meaning of a relation can be used in place of premises (meaning postulates) that capture its logical properties. For example, granted the following definition of the meaning of *in the same place as*:

x is in the same place as y = x is in a place that has the same spatial coordinates as those for y

it is a straightforward matter to devise a program for spatial inference, which will put x and y into the same cell of a spatial array. Transitivity and symmetry are then emergent properties of this meaning. Everyday deductions do not call for more than a finite number of alternative (and finite) models. Hence, instead of instantiating quantifiers, a program for everyday deduction can build models in which an arbitrary number of tokens are used to represent each set. Given the premises

1. $(\forall A)(\forall B) \neg (A$ in the same place as $B)$
2. $(\forall B)(\forall C)(B$ in the same place as $C)$

the program constructs a model of the state of affairs:

$|aaa|bbbccc|$

where the vertical barriers demarcate separate places, and there are arbitrary numbers of individuals of each sort. This model supports the conclusion

$(\forall A)(\forall C) \neg (A$ in the same place as $C)$

It is impossible to construct an alternative model of the premises that refutes the conclusion, and so it is valid. In other cases, the algorithm constructs a finite set of alternative models.

CONCLUSION

The theory of mental models has its roots in philosophy and psychology, but during the last decade it has blossomed in various ways to play a part in accounts of perception, comprehension, and deduction. The theory is currently under application to inductive reasoning. If computers are ever fully to understand the world, then they will need to construct rich internal representations of it both from sensory information and from forms of linguistic communication. The evidence from cognitive science suggests that human beings construct such mental models and that much of their thinking consists, not in formal derivations from linguistic structures, but in manipulating such models in the search for plausible conclusions.

BIBLIOGRAPHY

J. F. Allen and C. R. Perrault, "Analyzing Intention in Dialogues," *AI* **15**, 143–178 (1981).

W. W. Bledsoe, "Non-Resolution Theorem Proving," *AI* **9**, 1–35 (1977).

P. R. Cohen, J. Morgan, and M. E. Pollack, eds., *Intentions in Communication*, MIT Press, Cambridge, Mass., 1990.

K. Craik, *The Nature of Explanation*, Cambridge University Press, Cambridge, UK, 1943.

R. Davis and W. Hamscher, "Model-Based Reasoning: Troubleshooting," in H. E. Shrobe and AAAI, eds., *Exploring Artificial Intelligence: Survey Talks from the National Conferences on Artificial Intelligence*, Morgan-Kaufmann, San Mateo, Calif., 1988.

J. de Kleer, "Multiple Representations of Knowledge in a Mechanics Problem-Solver," in *Proceedings of the Fifth IJCAI*, Cambridge, Mass., Morgan-Kaufmann, San Mateo, Calif., 1977, pp. 299–304.

J. de Kleer and B. C. Williams, "Diagnosing Multiple Faults," *AI* **32**, 97–130 (1987).

K. Forbus, "Qualitative Process Theory," in D. G. Bobrow, ed., *Qualitative Reasoning about Physical Systems*, MIT Press, Cambridge, Mass., 1985.

A. Garnham, *Mental Models as Representations of Discourse and Text*, Ellis Horwood, Chichester, UK, 1987.

D. Gentner and D. R. Gentner, "Flowing Waters or Teeming Crowds: Mental Models of Electricity," in D. Gentner and A. L. Stevens, eds., *Mental Models*, Lawrence Erlbaum, Hillsdale, N.J., 1983.

P. J. Hayes, "Naive Physics I—Ontology for Liquids," Mimeo, Centre pour les Études Semantiques et Cognitives, Geneva, 1979.

P. N. Johnson-Laird, *Mental Models: Towards a Cognitive Science of Language, Inference, and Consciousness*, Cambridge University Press, and Harvard University Press, Cambridge, Mass., 1983.

P. N. Johnson-Laird, *Human and Machine Thinking*, Lawrence Erlbaum, Hillsdale, N.J., in press.

P. N. Johnson-Laird and R. M. J. Byrne, *Deduction*, Lawrence Erlbaum, Hillsdale, N.J., 1991.

J. A. W. Kamp, "A Theory of Truth and Semantic Representation," in J. A. G. Groenendijk, T. Janssen, and M. Stokhof, eds., *Formal Methods in the Study of Language*, Mathematical Center Tracts, Amsterdam, The Netherlands, 1981.

J. H. Larkin and H. A. Simon, "Why a Diagram Is (Sometimes) Worth Ten Thousand Words," *Cogn. Sci.* **11**, 65–99 (1987).

D. Marr, *Vision*, W. H. Freeman, San Francisco, Calif., 1982.

M. McCloskey, A. Carramazza, and B. Green, "Curvilinear Motion in the Absence of External Forces: Naive Beliefs about the Motion of Objects," *Science* **210**, 1139–1141 (1980).

G. A. Miller and P. N. Johnson-Laird, *Language and Perception*, Harvard University Press, Cambridge, Mass., 1976.

A. Newell, *Unified Theories of Cognition*, Harvard University Press, Cambridge, Mass., 1990.

J. Oakhill, A. Garnham, and W. Vonk, "The On-Line Construction of Discourse Models," *Lang. Cogn. Proc.* **4**, 263–286 (1989a).

J. Oakhill, P. N. Johnson-Laird, and A. Garnham, "Believability and Syllogistic Reasoning," *Cognition* **31**, 117–140 (1989b).

J. A. Robinson, *Logic: Form and Function*, Edinburgh University Press, Edinburgh, UK, 1979.

W. B. Rouse and R. M. Hunt, "Human Problem Solving in Fault Diagnosis Tasks," in W. B. Rouse, ed., *Advances in Man-Machine Systems Research*, JAI Press, Greenwich, Conn., 1984.

J. Shrager and P. Langley, eds., *Computational Models of Scientific Discovery and Theory Formation*, Morgan-Kaufmann, San Mateo, Calif., 1990.

K. Stenning, "Articles, Quantifiers, and Their Encoding in Textual Comprehension," in M. Halle, J. Bresnan, and G. A. Miller, eds., *Linguistic Theory and Psychological Reality*, MIT Press, Cambridge, Mass., 1977.

T. A. van Dijk and W. Kintsch, *Strategies of Discourse Comprehension*, Academic Press, Inc., New York, 1983.

B. L. Webber, "Description Formation and Discourse Model Synthesis," in D. L. Waltz, ed., *Theoretical Issues in Natural Language Processing*, Vol. 2, Association for Computing Machinery, New York, 1978.

D. J. Well and J. de Kleer, eds., *Qualitative Reasoning about Physical Systems,* Morgan-Kaufmann, San Mateo, Calif., 1990.

Y. Wilks and J. S. Bien, "Speech Acts and Multiple Environments," in *Proceedings of the Sixth IJCAI,* Tokyo, Morgan-Kaufmann, San Mateo, Calif., 1979, pp. 451–455.

L. Wittgenstein, *Tractatus Logico-Philosophicus,* Routledge & Kegan Paul, London, 1922.

L. Wos, *Automated Reasoning: 33 Basic Research Problems,* Prentice-Hall, Inc., Englewood Cliffs, N.J., 1988.

R. Young, "The Machine Inside the Machine: Users' Models of Pocket Calculators," *Int. J. Man Machine Stud.* **15**, 51–85 (1981).

PHILIP N. JOHNSON-LAIRD
Princeton University

MERLIN

A system that implemented Newell's data-flow graphs for heuristic search (see SEARCH) encoded as schemas, MERLIN was developed around 1971 by Moore at Carnegie Mellon University. It represented Newell's Logic Theorist program, with the generators and tests derived by hand. MERLIN could prove theorems (see THEOREM PROVING) by executing the schema (see J. Moore and A. Newell, "How can MERLIN Understand?," in L. Gregg, ed., *Knowledge and Cognition,* Erlbaum Associates, Hillsdale, N.J., 1974 pp. 253–285).

K. S. ARORA
SUNY at Buffalo

META-INTERPRETATION

A meta-interpreter for a language is an interpreter for the language written in the language. It is also called a meta-circular interpreter. Some languages, ie, pure LISP (qv) and especially pure PROLOG have simple meta-interpreters. The simplicity of its meta-interpreters is considered one of the criteria for judging the power and elegance of a programming language.

Meta-interpreters by themselves are not very useful but rather a curiosity. In some cases they can clarify the semantics of the language. More interesting is that simple meta-interpreters lend themselves very well to enhancements. An enhanced meta-interpreter implements a (slightly) different language. A classic example in the context of logic programming (qv) is an interpreter that constructs, during its evaluation of an object program, a proof tree to be used as a basis for explanations in an expert system (Hammond, 1984; Sterling and Beer, 1989). An enhanced meta-interpreter is a case of language embedding, the development of an implementation for one language in another language. The naturalness and effectiveness of the embedding is an interesting base for comparing the two languages (Shapiro, 1989).

Meta-interpreters are examples of meta-programs, which are programs using another program (the object program) as data. Meta-programming in its generality raises some interesting issues concerning the representation of the object program (Lloyd, 1988) (see META-KNOWLEDGE). It is still a very active area of research in the logic programming community.

REALIZATION

In his seminal paper on LISP (qv) McCarthy (1960) illustrates the power of the language by defining a function eval, which completely specifies the evaluation for any program. In retrospect, his one-page definition of eval can be considered a meta-interpreter. Russel was the first to encode it as such. It can be enhanced to explore variants of LISP, defining new forms of variable bindings and alternative evaluation orders (Abelson and Sussman, 1987).

The topic of meta-interpreters has been studied in much greater depth in the logic programming community. Here a typical meta-interpreter does not implement the complete language but relies on the underlying implementation to perform certain functions. The degree of computational detail made explicit in the meta-interpreter determines its granularity: the more details made explicit, the finer; the less details, the coarser the granularity. It can be said that an aspect of the evaluation that is made explicit in the interpreter is reified and that all other aspects are absorbed. Most practical meta-interpreters in logic programming reify goal reduction and absorb unification.

Using solve/1 to represent the main predicate of a meta-interpreter, the object is to make the relation solve (Goal) true when Goal is true with respect to the program being interpreted. The simplest meta-interpreter absorbs everything:

solve (Goal) :- Goal

A slightly more elaborate one reifies the processing of the literals in the query. Assuming the goal conjunction terminates with true, the following can be defined.

solve (true)

solve ((A,B)) :- A, solve (B)

It is interesting to note that the meta-interpreter was part of the user interface of the first PROLOG system developed in Marseille by Colmerauer and Roussel.

The standard three-line meta-interpreter of pure PROLOG reifies the whole goal reduction process, ie, selection of a literal to be resolved on and selection of a clause, but absorbs the unification and the backtracking. It assumes existence of a predicate clause/2, which selects program clauses. The first argument contains the head literal and the second argument, the body, represented as a conjunct terminated with true.

solve (true)

solve ((A,B)) :- solve (A), solve (B)

solve (A) :- clause (A,B), solve (B)

This meta-interpreter, known as the plain or vanilla meta-interpreter, extended with features to cope with the impurities of real PROLOG is the basis of a whole class of enhanced meta-interpreters. A detailed discussion has been published (Sterling and Shapiro, 1986).

The meta-interpreters of this class have been intensively used in various applications to observe and comment on the object level computation. Examples of such applications are debugging (Sterling and Shapiro, 1986); development of expert system shells, providing explanation (Hammond, 1984; Sterling and Beer, 1989); and extension of the functionality of concurrent logic programming (qv), a.o. deadlock detection, interrupt handling, etc (Shapiro, 1989). Further reification and enhancement leads to meta-interpreters that modify the computation of the object program. Here, an important application is to provide new control strategies for the object program (Gallaire and Lasserre, 1982). Another is to support derivations based on certainty factors (Sterling and Shapiro, 1986).

PERFORMANCE OF META-INTERPRETERS

While enhanced meta-interpreters provide a simple way to increase or modify the functionality of the base language, they have one important drawback. They introduce a substantial overhead; this overhead increases with the amount of detail being reified. It is widely believed that a simple derivative of the vanilla meta-interpreter slows down the execution by an order of magnitude. There are several ways to overcome this.

1. The enhanced meta-interpreter is only considered as a first prototype of the new language. Once stabilized, the new language is implemented from scratch. This is often the case with debuggers, also sometimes in the area of expert systems.
2. The program P is transformed into a program P' exhibiting the same behavior under the original language as P does under meta-interpretation, ie, a transformation is developed that is dedicated to the particular meta-interpreter.
3. Partial evaluation of a meta-interpreter and object program. The theory developed by Futamura (1971) is an indication that the same level of optimization is achievable as in case 2; however, in practice this is often difficult.

Gallagher (1986) was the first to consider specialization of interpreters with respect to particular object programs. Interesting discussions on the topic have been published (Takeuchi and Furukawa, 1986; Sterling and Beer, 1989; Shapiro, 1989).

BIBLIOGRAPHY

H. Abelson and G. J. Sussman, *The Structure and Interpretation of Computer Programs*, MIT Press, Cambridge, Mass., 1987.

Y. Futamura, "Partial Evaluation of Computational Process—An Approach to a Compiler-Compiler," *Syst. Comput. Controls* **2**(5), 721–728 (1971).

J. Gallagher, "Transforming Logic Programs by Specializing Interpreters," in *Proceedings of the Seventh European Conference on Artificial Intelligence*, 1986, pp. 109–122.

H. Gallaire and C. Lasserre, "Metalevel Control for Logic Programs," in K. L. Clark and S.-A. Tärnlund, eds., *Logic Programming*, Academic Press, Inc., Orlando, Fla., 1982, pp. 173–185.

P. Hammond, "Micro-PROLOG for Expert Systems," in K. L. Clark and F. G. McCabe, *Micro-PROLOG: Programming in Logic*, Prentice-Hall, Inc., Englewood Cliffs, N.J., 1984, pp. 294–319.

J. W. Lloyd, "Directions for Meta-Programming," in *Proceedings of the International Conference on Fifth Generation Computer Systems*, ICOT, Tokyo, 1988, pp. 609–617.

J. McCarthy, "Recursive Functions of Symbolic Expressions and Their Computation by Machine, Part 1," *CACM*, **3**, 231–240 (Apr. 1960).

E. Shapiro, "The Family of Concurrent Logic Programming Languages," *ACM Comput. Surv.* **21**(3), 412–510 (Sept. 1989).

L. Sterling and R. D. Beer, "Metainterpreters for Expert System Construction," *J. Log. Prog.* **6**(1–2), 163–178 (Jan.–Mar. 1989).

L. Sterling and E. Shapiro, *The Art of Prolog*, MIT Press, Cambridge, Mass., 1986.

A. Takeuchi and K. Furukawa, "Partial Evaluation of Prolog Programs and Its Application to Metaprogramming," in H.-J. Kugler, ed., *Information Processing 1986*, Elsevier Applied Science Publishers, Ltd., Barking, UK, 1986, pp. 415–420.

Maurice Bruynooghe
Danny De Schreye
Katholieke Universiteit Leuven

META-KNOWLEDGE, META-RULES, AND META-REASONING

AI research involves building computer systems capable of reasoning and acting in a variety of environments. For example, these computer systems, or cognitive agents as they are sometimes called, should be capable of talking with other cognitive agents, advising people in complex tasks, and interacting with the world by perceiving situations and carrying out actions. The nature of knowledge is crucial for this research. When building these systems, one must think in terms of what they have to know to perform these tasks. Similarly, one must analyze the performance of cognitive agents in terms of their knowledge. Thus a system knows about the objects in its domain of application, about how to perform a certain activity, or about the events that take place during that activity.

Research on knowledge representation (qv) in AI concerns the search for models of knowledge that will enable systems to behave intelligently. A particular representation for knowledge is a combination of data structures and procedures that, if represented and used adequately in a program, will lead to intelligent behavior. The knowledge contained in an intelligent system is, for the most part, embodied in these data structures, generally called the knowledge base, and represents the propositions that the system knows or believes. Some of the propositions are represented explicitly, whereas others can be derived from those by applying inference rules. The process of deriving new propositions is done by the inference system, either when new information is added to the knowledge base (forward inference) or when a query is posed to the knowledge base (backward inference). Forward inference enables the cognitive agent to make new deductions with information perceived from the world, and backward inference enables the cognitive agent to find out answers to its problems (see PROCESSING, BOTTOM-UP AND TOP-DOWN).

Although the inference system allows the cognitive agent to perform reasoning, it does not allow it to act in the world. To do this, the cognitive agent needs an acting system that executes actions. Because most actions are not trivial, they must be planned first; thus the cognitive agent needs, in addition, a planning system that derives appropriate plans to be given to the acting system. The issues involved here are the subject of research in planning (qv), another field of AI. The problem in trying to formulate a plan of action to achieve some goal comes from the multiple interactions that can exist between the subactions that constitute the plan and from the fact that the agent may not have enough information to formulate the plan. It is often necessary to reason about what knowledge is needed to carry out a plan and how that knowledge can be obtained.

A typical action that these cognitive agents may need to perform is to conduct a dialogue with other cognitive agents. This action, besides the problems common to other actions, has problems of its own. They are the subject of research in natural language understanding (qv), another field of AI. One of these problems is that a cognitive agent engaging in a dialogue has to take into account the knowledge possessed by the other cognitive agent. This usually requires having a model of that agent's knowledge and reasoning about what that agent knows.

Thus the main question to be answered by these fields of AI is What kinds of data structures and procedures must the agent know about and how should they be used by the agent in order to make it behave intelligently? Research in these fields has led very soon to the conclusion that, among other things, a cognitive agent must know about objects, states, and actions. In addition, it is now strongly believed that knowledge about the extent and organization of its own and others' beliefs, about how to use its own reasoning rules, about how to perform an action, and about its own and others' performance are important aspects of intelligent behavior.

Several researchers have suggested the use of meta-knowledge, meta-rules, and meta-reasoning to accomplish the integration of all these features in a single cognitive agent. In a general sense, meta-knowledge is knowledge about knowledge as opposed to knowledge about "things in the world" (Bahr, 1979). It enables a reasoning system to "know what it knows" and to make multiple use of its knowledge (Davis, 1978). In addition to using its knowledge directly, the system may have other abilities: knowing what it knows and what it does not know (consciousness) (Bahr, 1979; Davis, 1978, 1977a; Collins, 1978; Davis and Buchanan, 1977; Davis and Lenat, 1982; Kollers and Palef, 1976; Shapiro, 1980; Morgado, 1980; Morgado and Shapiro, 1985); knowing where and how to use knowledge to infer other knowledge (planning reasoning or meta-reasoning) (Davis and Buchanan, 1977; Davis and Lenat, 1982; Morgado, 1980; Morgado and Shapiro, 1985; Davis, 1977b; Gallaire and Lassere, 1979; Genesereth, 1983; Stefik, 1980); knowing where and how to use knowledge to perform actions (planning acting) (Morgado, 1980; Morgado and Shapiro, 1985; Appelt, 1980; Moore, 1977, 1980; Smith, 1977; Morgenstern, 1986); explaining how and why it used its knowledge (explanation (Davis and Buchanan, 1977; Davis and Lenat, 1982; Morgado, 1980; Morgado and Smith, 1977; Davis, 1977b); and examining its own knowledge, modifying it, abstracting and generalizing it, and acquiring new knowledge (learning) (Davis, 1978, 1977a; Davis and Buchanan, 1977; Davis and Lenat, 1982).

FOUNDATIONS IN HUMAN COGNITION

The idea of incorporating meta-knowledge in knowledge-based systems has its foundations in human cognition. Although simulation of human cognition by a machine is not needed or even desired, AI researchers continue to search for answers in human cognition. This is reasonable on two accounts. If the goal of AI is to better understand human cognition, the theories developed in psychology must be tested through the use of computer models. If, on the other end, the goal of AI is to develop machines to help humans in activities requiring intelligence, those machines must reason and act like humans so that they can interact smoothly.

Some studies of human behavior have been described (Bahr, 1979) that demonstrate people's ability to reason about what they know and about how they reason, suggesting that meta-level knowledge and reasoning are an integral part of common cognitive activity in human experience:

> . . . the concept of meta-level knowledge captures intrinsic, common-place properties of human cognition that are central to an understanding of knowledge and intelligence.

Several cognitive phenomena illustrate the importance of meta-knowledge and meta-reasoning in human experience. For example, the tip-of-the-tongue phenomenon suggests that people have knowledge about their knowledge. This phenomenon happens when it is known that some fact is known even though it cannot be recalled. Another phenomenon that is common in human cognition is the knowing-not phenomenon (Kollers and Palef, 1976). It is illustrated when a person knows rapidly and reliably that he or she does not know something. Data were collected that suggest people know what they do not know without having to search their positive knowledge and that negative knowledge is accessed as directly as positive knowledge and sometimes even more rapidly. This phenomenon is not easily captured by common searching models of memory, where negative judgments are made only as a result of a search of positive instances that end in failure. The fact that some negative knowledge can be accessed more rapidly than some positive knowledge suggests that not even parallel processing can accommodate this fact. Another interesting phenomenon is what can be concluded from the fact that something is not known. This phenomenon has been viewed as directly related to meta-knowledge and the knowing-not phenomenon, because such reasoning presumes some awareness of not knowing some fact (Bahr, 1979). In the lack-of-knowledge inference the fact that a person would know some fact if it were true, but does not remember it, leads to the belief that it is not true. For example, if asked if the president had died one month ago, in normal circumstances it would not be a reasonable answer to say "I don't know." Although neither a positive nor a negative answer could be found, the fact that the death of the president is such an important fact, if it had occurred, it should be known about. Therefore, because a person does not know about it, he or she can conclude that the president did not die. This phenomenon was studied (Collins, 1978) and some conditions that increase certainty in these beliefs were pointed out: the relative importance of the fact and the person's expertise in the topic area. That is, the more important the fact is and the more the person's expertise in the topic area, the more certain the person is of something not being true if not remembered.

These phenomena constitute strong evidence that people have an intuitive knowledge of the extent and importance of their own knowledge. The concept of meta-knowledge captures this property of human cognition, and it seems that meta-knowledge could improve the behavior of AI reasoning systems.

MOTIVATIONS

There were also several problems faced by AI knowledge-based systems, namely expert systems (qv), that motivated the use of meta-knowledge and meta-reasoning in those systems. One problem was how to do acquisition and maintenance of knowledge. Other problems concerned the reasoning process. One problem was how to control or plan the reasoning process in those systems. Another problem was how could they explain their reasoning behavior in an intelligible manner. These problems with the reasoning process apply to any kind of activity, not just to reasoning. Finally, a more general motivation was to give these systems the capability of reasoning about knowledge that was not available previously. Each of these motivations is discussed below in greater detail.

Acquisition and Maintenance of Knowledge

The development of expert systems, ie, programs that are skillful in a specific domain of application, emphasized the importance of large stores of domain-specific knowledge as a basis for high performance (Feigenbaum, 1977). Assembling and modifying the required knowledge base is a complex process that involves great expertise and careful maintenance. This is usually an ongoing task that often extends over several years and, due to the high dependency of related facts and rules, is often error prone.

A key element of this process is the transfer of expertise from a human expert to the program. Due to the expert's lack of knowledge about programming, this usually requires the mediation of a human programmer, called the knowledge engineer. However, this transfer of knowledge through the knowledge engineer has some problems. First, the knowledge engineer is not an expert in the specific domain of application. Second, because most of the expert knowledge is heuristic and experimental, the expert is not capable of conveying it directly to the knowledge engineer. The process usually extends over many sessions in which the knowledge engineer struggles to extract the knowledge from the expert. This suggests that the expert should be able to interact directly with the program. Of course, the program has then to supply the same kind of assistance the knowledge engineer would provide and if possible in a more efficient and flexible way.

It has been suggested that meta-knowledge be used to enable the system to provide this kind of assistance (Davis, 1978, 1977a; Davis and Buchanan, 1977). Management of knowledge presents a real problem since the internal organization of the data structures and their interrelationships with other data structures are very complex. It is difficult for the expert to keep all these in memory, especially when they are constantly changing, as occurs during the initial phases of development where the refinement of successive prototypes takes place. A second problem is that documentation is usually not well organized and updated, and consequently, changing the system is not a trivial task. Another problem is that because the expert does not know about all the knowledge stored in the knowledge base, it is not easy to discover what knowledge should be added to the system to increase its performance. As the size of the domain of specific knowledge increases, maintenance becomes a more and more complex task. Systems that allow the explicit declaration of meta-level data structures in their representation schemes, ie, formalisms that allow the encoding of data structures that describe other data structures, will possibly be a solution for this problem (Davis, 1978, 1977a; Davis and Buchanan, 1977; Davis and Lenat, 1982). The system can then assist and advise the user in modifying its knowledge and can even provide expectations concerning what knowledge should be acquired next.

Planning the Reasoning Process

A second motivation for using meta-knowledge in knowledge-based systems is to control or plan the process of reasoning (Davis and Buchanan, 1977; Davis and Lenat, 1982; Davis, 1977b; Gallaire and Lassere, 1979; Genesereth, 1983; Stefik, 1980). At each cycle of the reasoning process, the system must reason about how to reason, ie, must do meta-reasoning. At a certain point, adding more object-level knowledge to the system will no longer improve performance. What is needed is some knowledge about how to use the object-level knowledge selectively. In fact, part of the definition of intelligence includes appropriate usage of information, not just brute force; so even if the amount of object-level knowledge is small, it is important to use it wisely (Davis and Buchanan, 1977).

Also, a main weakness of reasoning systems comes

from the fact that they use a severely limited and predetermined subset of reasoning strategies. It has been suggested that a significant number of strategies should be integrated into a single system (Sacerdoti, 1979). Generally, current AI paradigms have only one strategy, and even that one is embedded in the inference processor. This implicit inclusion makes the systems inflexible and hard to modify and expand. Therefore, it would be convenient to represent explicitly these strategies by meta-rules, ie, by rules that indicate how to use other rules. The strategy of the system could now be changed very easily just by changing the rules in its knowledge base. Rules could also be written describing different strategies and meta-rules of even higher order could be obtained to decide which strategy to choose in each particular situation (Davis and Lenat, 1982; Davis, 1977b; Gallaire and Lassere, 1979; Genesereth, 1983).

Explaining the Reasoning Process

An essential aspect of the interaction between cognitive agents is the explanation of their reasoning. Explanation (qv) and meta-knowledge are generally associated because both constitute a trend toward declaratively representing knowledge that previously was encoded procedurally. Moreover, if meta-rules encode strategies to plan the act of reasoning, an explanation facility gives an account of the planning decisions during reasoning. However, much more research must be done to allow the user to model a personal explanation facility in the same sense that personal strategies can be modeled, ie, to use meta-knowledge to explain reasoning.

The fundamental goal of an explanation facility is to enable a program to display a comprehensible account of the motivation for all of its actions (Davis and Lenat, 1982). It is not easy, even for an experienced programmer, to find out how a complex process of reasoning got to where it is. Trying to account for past behavior is even more difficult when dealing with an audience assumed to know nothing about programming. Comprehensibility, then, must be defined in terms of the application domain rather than in the language of computation.

Current explanation facilities are one of the main reasons for the success of expert systems. They use a goal tree built during reasoning as a basis for explanation. Because the goal tree models the control structure of reasoning, it provides a single and easy model for the system's reasoning behavior. Explanation is then viewed in terms of traversal of the goal tree and is generally activated by two commands, "why" and "how," that allow ascent or descent traversal of the tree, respectively. These commands can in general be issued consecutively to allow the entire traversal of the tree. In some systems, like TEIRESIAS (Davis and Lenat, 1982), the command "why" has an integer argument that allows the explanation of several levels of the tree to take place in a single step, and the command "how" has an argument that can refer to the number of the rule clause to be explained. TEIRESIAS also has the capability of directly examining the rules in the knowledge base to determine which clauses have already been established and which have not yet been tested. In this case the explanation facility interprets the same piece of knowledge that the inference facility is about to use. The explanations are thus expressed in terms of the contents of the rule.

It has been suggested that the goal tree, or an equivalent data structure representing the ongoing reasoning process, should be represented in the knowledge base itself, so that this knowledge could be reasoned about as any other kind of knowledge (Morgado, 1980). A system must be able to explain the course of action taken during reasoning in terms of the knowledge that was used during that reasoning and taking into account the previous interaction with the user. In order to give explanations, a system must understand what it knows and what it is doing. So, knowledge about the specific domain of application and knowledge about the ongoing reasoning activity should be encoded uniformly to allow the system to reason about them equally (Morgado, 1980). This allows the system to use rules to reason about its own reasoning behavior and, therefore, to explain it. Reasoning about a previous or ongoing activity is also a precondition to dealing with dialogues in natural language understanding. It is important to make use of what has gone on to help interpret what is coming.

Planning and Explaining Activities

What was said about reasoning can be applied to any activity in general. The interaction between knowledge, planning, and action has been the subject of much research (Morgado, 1980; Morgado and Shapiro, 1985; Appelt, 1980; Moore, 1977, 1980; Smith, 1977; Amarel, 1968). A cognitive agent must integrate a belief model with an acting model to form a single model (Morgado, 1980; Morgado and Shapiro, 1985). It must have a uniform representation for beliefs and actions to reason effectively about the interaction between knowledge and action. In particular, the system should be able to reason about what knowledge it must have to perform an action, what knowledge it may acquire by performing an action, and what knowledge it needs to plan an action (Appelt, 1980; Moore, 1977, 1980; Smith, 1977; Amarel, 1968). These are all aspects of meta-knowledge. In other words, the system must have knowledge about its own knowledge and about acting.

Pushing the Declarative Approach to Represent Knowledge

Finally, the contribution of meta-knowledge to reasoning and acting can be looked at as the ultimate move toward representing most knowledge declaratively (Morgado, 1980). This gives the system the capability of reasoning about knowledge that it could not reason about previously.

WHAT ARE META-KNOWLEDGE, META-RULES, AND META-REASONING?

Now that the background and the motivations have been presented, the main concepts talked about are defined, as well as how they relate to each other (Morgado, 1980; Morgado and Shapiro, 1985).

Knowledge and Meta-Knowledge

Meta-knowledge, like object knowledge, is composed of assertions (meta-assertions) and rules (meta-rules). Meta-assertions are beliefs about beliefs, and because a rule that is believed to hold is a belief, meta-assertions include beliefs about rules. For example, the belief that John loves Jane is an assertion, whereas the belief that Henry believes that John loves Jane is a meta-assertion representing a belief about a belief. Similarly, the belief that Henry believes that all men are mortal is a meta-assertion representing a belief about the rule that all men are mortal. Other meta-assertions that can be represented in a system are the beliefs that John loves Jane is a belief about John; all men are mortal is a rule about men; Bill doesn't know whether John loves Jane; I (the system) don't know about the fishing industry in Venezuela.

Rules tell how to derive beliefs from other beliefs. Because a rule that is believed to hold is a belief there may be rules about rules as well. These rules are called meta-rules. There are two types of meta-rules: deduction meta-rules and planning meta-rules.

Deduction meta-rules are rules that use rules to derive beliefs or that derive rules from beliefs. For example, the rule $A \rightarrow (B \rightarrow C)$ is a meta-rule that enables the system to derive the rule $B \rightarrow C$ if the belief A holds. Similarly, the rule $(A \rightarrow B) \rightarrow C$ is a meta-rule that enables the system to derive the belief C in case the rule $A \rightarrow B$ holds. Both meta-rules are represented by a proposition that has the proposition representing the rule $B \rightarrow C$ appearing on the consequent and antecedent position of the meta-rule, respectively. The second type of meta-rules, planning meta-rules, are rules that encode reasoning strategies. The distinction between deduction rules and planning rules, ie, between reasoning and meta-reasoning, is discussed below.

Reasoning and Meta-Reasoning

Believing is a state of knowledge representing the propositions that the system assumes to be true. Reasoning is the process of inference to form beliefs from other beliefs using deduction rules. The use of meta-rules has been proposed as a means of encoding strategies for reasoning (Davis and Buchanan, 1977; Davis and Lenat, 1982; Davis, 1977b). Meta-rules specify which rules should be considered and in which order they should be invoked. For example, the two rules (Davis, 1977b) appearing in Figure 1 are of this type.

Planning meta-rules must be used differently from all the other rules (deduction object rules and deduction meta-rules) because they do not express how to derive beliefs but how to plan the reasoning process. They are inference rules that specify how the deduction rules should be used.

A layered control structure was proposed to handle reasoning in the TEIRESIAS system (Davis and Buchanan, 1977; Davis and Lenat, 1982; Davis, 1977b). The basic execution cycle in TEIRESIAS consists of selecting the inference strategy to use (backward inference, forward inference, etc) and applying it to invoke all rules that are relevant to the goal. But before invoking the rules at one

Meta-rule 1:
If
1. you are attempting to determine the best stock to invest in,
2. the client's tax status is nonprofit,
3. there are rules that mention in their premise the income-tax bracket of the client, then it is very likely (0.9) that each of these rules is not going to be useful.

Meta-rule 2:
If
1. the age of the client is greater than 60,
2. there are rules that mention in their premise blue-chip risk,
3. there are rules that mention in their premise speculative risk, then it is very likely (0.8) that the former should be used before the latter.

Figure 1. Selecting and ordering planning meta-rules.

level, the system checks for rules at the next higher level that specify which rules should be selected and in what order they should be used.

This process has been seen (Morgado, 1980; Morgado and Shapiro, 1985) as a particular case of a more general acting–planning process such as another one that was proposed (Sacerdoti, 1977). Acting is the process of executing a plan. Any complex action must be planned before being performed. Planning is the process of composing a sequence of actions to be executed to achieve a predetermined goal from a given situation; it is reasoning about how to act to achieve that goal. The basic planning cycle in NOAH (qv) consists of looking for a plan to achieve the goal and of an iterative process in which new refinements of the plan are continuously expanded and criticized until a final plan is derived. The expansion phase produces a new, more detailed plan. The criticism of the new plan consists of any necessary reordering or elimination of redundant operations to ensure that the local expansions make global sense. After being constructed, a plan of actions may be executed.

Reasoning can be looked at as the sequence of actions performed in applying rules (plans for reasoning) to derive beliefs from other beliefs. Because reasoning is itself an action, and an action must be planned before being performed, then before reasoning, the system must first plan the reasoning. Because planning is reasoning about acting, and in this case, the acting is the act of reasoning, then this planning of the act of reasoning is reasoning about how to reason, or meta-reasoning, and Davis's meta-reasoning cycle can be seen as a special case of the general planning cycle.

Morgado and Shapiro conclude, then, that if an acting–planning–reasoning system uses its acting component to carry out its reasoning, its planning component will automatically perform meta-reasoning.

Connecting Theories

In philosophy there is a substantial literature on the logic of knowledge and belief (Hintikka, 1963, 1971; Linski, 1971) and on the theory of reasoning and acting (Aune, 1977; Braud and Walton, 1976; Castaneda, 1975). These topics (Appelt, 1980; Amarel, 1968; Maida and Shapiro, 1982), as well as the topics of meta-knowledge and meta-reasoning (Bahr, 1979; Davis and Lenat, 1982; Morgado, 1980; Morgado and Shapiro, 1985; Gallaire and Lassere, 1979; Genesereth, 1983; Bowen and Kowalski, 1981; Filman), and the interaction between knowledge and acting (Appelt, 1980; Moore, 1977, 1980; Smith, 1977) have also received considerable attention in AI recently. A thesis has been presented that provides an insight into the relations among these issues in AI knowledge-based systems:

> In a knowledge-representation (KR) system in which assertions and rules are represented in the same way as any other concepts, no special mechanism is needed to represent meta-knowledge, where this is understood to include beliefs about beliefs, rules about beliefs, beliefs about rules, and rules about rules. In a knowledge representation system which has an acting–planning component and which can represent actions and plans, no other mechanism is needed to handle meta-reasoning, where this is understood to include rules about the order of using rules, and reasoning about the process of reasoning. The difference between meta-knowledge and meta-reasoning as formulated above is that the former deals primarily with beliefs while the latter deals with acting. We therefore conclude that, besides the conceptual distinction between the object level and the meta-level, a valuable distinction to focus on when building KR systems which can have meta-knowledge and can do meta-reasoning is that between believing and acting (Morgado and Shapiro, 1985).

SYSTEMS WITH META-KNOWLEDGE

Two systems that have meta-level components, TEIRESIAS and MOLGEN, are briefly described.

Teiresias

In Teiresias, the concept of meta-level knowledge has been explored (Davis, 1978, 1977a, 1977b; Davis and Buchanan, 1977; Davis and Lenat, 1982) in several different forms, each of them supporting one or more of the tasks of acquisition, accumulation, and maintenance of knowledge. Schemata and rule models were built to support acquisition and accumulation of knowledge via interactive transfer of expertise from the human expert to the knowledge base. Function templates and schemata support maintenance of knowledge by giving the system a picture of its own knowledge and the way that knowledge is organized. Schemata encode knowledge about the representation of objects and about their relationship. Knowledge about inference rules is encoded in the rule models. A rule model is an abstract description of a subset of rules, built from empirical generalizations about those rules and it is used to characterize a typical member of the subset. Finally, function templates are list structures indicating the order and the type of the arguments in a typical call of a function. They are used for code dissection and generation.

Meta-rules embody strategies, knowledge that indicates how to use other knowledge (Davis and Buchanan, 1977; Davis and Lenat, 1982; Davis 1977b). It has been shown how meta-rules can be used to encode strategies and to define control regimes. Strategies are seen from the perspective of deciding which knowledge (rule) to invoke next when more than one rule may be applicable. Meta-rules in TEIRESIAS draw conclusions about object-level rules in two ways: they can make deductions about the likely utility of certain object rules or they can indicate a partial ordering between two subsets of object-level rules. It has been stressed that meta-rules should make conclusions about the utility of object-level rules, not their validity. It is claimed that it is because of this fact that it makes sense to distribute knowledge in object-level and meta-level rules. Otherwise, it would be only needed to add another premise clause to each of the relevant object-level rules.

Adding meta-rules to the TEIRESIAS system requires only a minor addition to the control structure. The system retrieves the entire list of rules relevant to the current goal. But before trying to invoke those rules, the system first looks for any meta-rules relevant to that goal. If it finds any, these are invoked first. This may draw conclusions about the likely utility and relative order of those rules. The list of object rules may be shortened and reordered by those meta-rules and only then are they used. Viewed in tree search terms, the implementation of meta-rules in TEIRESIAS can either prune the search space or reorder the branches of the tree. This process is generalized in TEIRESIAS, ie, there can be an arbitrary number of levels of knowledge, each one guiding the use of the knowledge at the next lower level. Finally, meta-rules are defended, because they enable the use of content-directed invocation. This technique allows the user to define invocation criteria, offering a richly expressive language. Meta-rules also have strong validity, because descriptions are done via direct reference to the knowledge source content itself. In meta-rules, then, the two ideas of generalized invocation criteria and content-directed retrieval are combined. The former gives a high expressiveness to meta-rules because it allows invocation of any knowledge source that fits a given description. The later gives meta-rules a strong degree of validity because there is a formal link between the knowledge source and its description. Besides this, content-directed invocation offers a strong degree of flexibility in a program, because acquisition and maintenance of knowledge becomes easier. Editing or adding an object-level rule does not require meta-rules to be edited to make sure they still apply, because meta-rules will adjust to the changes found in the edited rule. On the other hand, editing or adding a meta-rule does not cause problems either, because all the object rules to which these meta-rules apply do not need to be looked for in order to mention them in the code. Indeed, as invocation is made by a description of the code of the object rule itself, this entire operation becomes transparent to the user because again this burden for system upkeep was transferred to the program. This idea of replacing reference by name with reference by description has its problems as has been pointed out. First, it is not always clear how to generalize from a specific procedure to a general description of the capabilities desired. Second, the overhead in computer time must be considered.

MOLGEN

The fact has been recognized (Stefik, 1980) that most of the decisions a planner makes are about the reasoning process as opposed to decisions about the problem and that is raises a variety of decisions that are usually made implicitly in planning programs with rigid control structures. It is this fact that leads to the proposal of a layered approach for meta-planning, that is, for planning about planning. This meta-planning model uses operations for hierarchical planning with constraints and integrates two strategies generally used independently in planning programs: the least-commitment (conservative reasoning) and the heuristic (plausible reasoning (qv)) strategies [namely in NOAH (Sacerdoti, 1977) and HACKER (Sussman, 1975) (qv), respectively]. By integrating these techniques, MOLGEN makes sense of the use for guessing, but only as a last resort, and so, bugs are considered inevitable (as in HACKER), but only when guesses are made. Guessing is used to compensate for the lack of knowledge to solve a problem.

The control structure in MOLGEN is composed of an interpreter and three layers, called planning spaces. Each space has operators, objects, and steps and controls the creation and scheduling of steps in the next lower layer in the hierarchy. The lowest layer in the hierarchy, the domain space, is called the laboratory space. This is the space that has knowledge about the objects and operations of the specific domain, a genetic laboratory in MOLGEN. This is not a control level at all; it plays merely an execute role. The next layer in the hierarchy is called the design space. It is the space charged with designing the plans; ie, it is this layer that creates and schedules steps in the laboratory space. This is the first control layer in MOLGEN. This space defines a set of operators for designing plans abstractly and for propagating constraints among the refined subproblems in the laboratory plan. The top layer of the hierarchy is called the strategy space. The organizational idea behind the strategy space is the distinction between least-commitment and heuristic modes of reasoning. It relies on cooperation between subproblems via constraint propagation to stay in the least-commitment cycle as long as it can (conservative reasoning) resorting to guessing (plausible reasoning) only as a last choice. This is the space that has knowledge about strategy. Although the design operators plan by creating and scheduling laboratory steps, the strategy operators meta-plan by creating and scheduling design steps. Communication between spaces is done by using control messages that invoke procedures at the next lower level without knowing their names. This guarantees the communication to be uniform, but these procedures redundantly represent the knowledge about operators. Another problem is that scheduling is based on numeric priorities rather than on content-directed invocation.

In summary, MOLGEN uses layers as a way of creating abstraction. Although meta-knowledge is used to combine the least-commitment and the heuristic strategies, meta-knowledge is embedded in the interpreter in a form of two cycles that invoke the strategy operators. Therefore, MOLGEN has in the strategy space the tools to create several different control regimes, but the way they are combined to specify a particular strategy is controlled by the interpreter. In order to have other different strategies, the interpreter would have to be modified.

CONCLUSIONS

Meta-knowledge is knowledge about other knowledge as opposed to knowledge about things in the world. Meta-reasoning is planning the act of reasoning. Meta-rules are rules that talk about other rules. They can be deduction meta-rules or planning meta-rules. The planning meta-rules are rules to do meta-reasoning.

Recent work suggests that besides the conceptual distinction between the object level and the meta-level, a valuable distinction to focus on, when building knowledge-based systems that can have meta-knowledge and can do meta-reasoning, is that between believing and acting. The theories of knowledge and belief and of knowledge and action may shed some light on the issues of meta-knowledge, meta-rules, and meta-reasoning.

BIBLIOGRAPHY

S. Amarel, "On Representations of Problems of Reasoning About Actions," in D. Mitchie, ed., *Machine Learning and Heuristic Programming Machine Intelligence* **3**, Elsevier, New York, 1968, pp. 131–171.

D. A. Appelt, "A Planner for Reasoning About Knowledge and Action," in *Proceedings of the First National Conference on Artificial Intelligence,* Stanford, Calif., AAAI, Menlo Park, Calif., 1980, pp. 131–133.

B. Aune, *Reason and Action,* Reidel, Dordrecht, The Netherlands, 1977.

A. Bahr, "Meta-Knowledge and Cognition," in *Proceedings of the Sixth IJCAI,* Tokyo, Japan, Morgan-Kaufmann, San Mateo, Calif., 1979, pp. 31–33.

K. Bowen and R. Kowalski, *Amalgamating Language and Meta-Language in Logic Programming,* Technical Report, School of Computer and Information Science, Syracuse University, Syracuse, N.Y., 1981.

M. Braud and D. Walton, *Action Theory,* Reidel, Dordrecht, The Netherlands, 1976.

H. N. Castaneda, *Thinking and Doing,* Reidel, Dordrecht, The Netherlands, 1975.

A. Collins, "Fragments of a Theory of Human Plausible Reasoning," *TINLAP* **2,** 194–201, 1978.

R. Davis. "Interactive Transfer of Expertise," in *Proceedings of the Fifth IJCAI,* Cambridge, Mass., Morgan-Kaufmann, San Mateo, Calif., 1977a.

R. Davis, "Generalized Procedure Calling and Content-Directed Invocation," in *Proceedings of the AI/PL Conference,* Aug. 1977b.

R. Davis, "Knowledge Acquisition in Rule-Based Systems—Knowledge about Representations as a Basis for System Construction and Maintenance," in *Pattern Directed Inference Systems,* Academic Press, Inc., New York, 1978.

R. Davis and B. G. Buchanan, "Meta-Level Knowledge: Overview and Applications," in *Proceedings of the Fifth IJCAI,* Cambridge, Mass., Morgan-Kaufmann, San Mateo, Calif., 1977.

R. Davis and D. Lenat, *Knowledge-Based Systems in Artificial Intelligence,* McGraw-Hill Book Co., Inc., New York, 1982, pp. 227–490.

E. Feigenbaum, "The Art of Artificial Intelligence: I. Themes and Case Studies of Knowledge Engineering," in *Proceedings of the Fifth IJCAI,* Morgan-Kaufmann, San Mateo, Calif., 1977, pp. 1014–1029.

R. Filman, *Meta-Language and Meta-Reasoning,* Computer Research Center, Hewlett-Packard Laboratories, Palo Alto, Calif.

H. Gallaire and C. Lassere, "Controlling Knowledge Deduction in a Declarative Approach," in *Proceedings of the Sixth IJCAI,* Morgan-Kaufmann, San Mateo, Calif., 1979.

M. Genesereth, "An Overview of Meta-Level Architecture," in *Proceedings of the Third National Conference of Artificial Intelligence,* Washington, D.C., AAAI, Menlo Park, Calif., 1983, pp. 119–123.

J. Hintikka, *Knowledge and Belief,* Cornell University Press, Ithaca, N.Y., 1963.

J. Hintikka, "Semantics for Propositional Attitudes," in Linski, 1971, pp. 145–167.

P. A. Kollers and S. R. Palef, "Knowing Not," *Mem. Cogn.* **4-5,** 553–558 (1976).

L. Linski, ed., *Reference and Modality,* Oxford University Press, London, 1971.

A. Maida and S. Shapiro, "Intensional Concepts in Propositional Semantic Networks," *Cogn. Sci.* **6,** 291–330 (1982).

R. Moore, "Reasoning About Knowledge and Action," in *Proceedings of the Fifth IJCAI,* Morgan-Kaufmann, San Mateo, Calif., 1977, pp. 473–477.

R. Moore, *Reasoning About Knowledge and Action,* Technical Note 191, AI Center, Computer Science and Technical Division, SRI International, Menlo Park, Calif., 1980.

E. Morgado, *Believing and Acting: An Approach to Meta-Knowledge and Meta-Reasoning,* Ph.D. proposal, Department of Computer Science, SUNY at Buffalo, 1980.

E. J. Morgado and S. C. Shapiro, "Believing and Acting—A Study of Meta-Knowledge and Meta-Reasoning," in *Proceedings of the EPIA-85 (Encontro Portugues de Inteligencia Artificial),* Oporto, Portugal, 1985, pp. 138–154.

L. Morgenstern, "A First Order Theory of Planning, Knowledge, and Action," in *Proceedings of the Theoretical Aspects of Reasoning About Knowledge,* Monterey, Calif., 1986, pp. 99–114.

E. D. Sacerdoti, *A Structure for Plans and Behavior,* Elsevier Science Publishing Co., Inc., New York, 1977.

E. D. Sacerdoti, "Problem Solving Tactics," in *Proceedings of the Sixth IJCAI,* Morgan-Kaufmann, San Mateo, Calif., 1979, pp. 1077–1085.

S. C. Shapiro, *On Representing About,* extended abstract, Computer Science Department, SUNY at Buffalo, 1980.

B. Smith, "Knowledge Representation Semantics," in *Proceedings of the Fifth IJCAI,* Morgan-Kaufmann, San Mateo, Calif., 1977, pp. 987–990.

M. Stefik, *Planning and Meta-Planning, MOLGEN: Part 2,* Computer Science Department, Stanford University, Stanford, Calif., 1980.

G. J. Sussman, *A Computer Model of Skill Acquisition,* Elsevier Science Publishing Co., Inc., New York, 1975.

E. Morgado
SUNY at Buffalo

MICRO-PLANNER

MICRO-PLANNER is a subset of the programming language PLANNER (see C. Hewitt, "PLANNER: A Language for Proving Theorems in Robots," *Proceedings of the First International Joint Conference on Artificial Intelligence,* Washington, D.C., 1969, pp. 295–301). PLANNER itself has never been implemented completely, but MICRO-PLANNER was implemented by Sussman, Winograd, and Charniak (see G. J. Sussman, T. Winograd, and E. Charniak, *MICRO-PLANNER Reference Manual,* Artificial Intelligence Memo No. 203A, MIT, Cambridge, Mass., Dec. 1971). MICRO-PLANNER was intended to combine elements of a theorem prover with a normal LISP-like programming language. The mechanism used can best be described as pattern-directed procedure invocation. A theorem prover is a program that blindly searches through a database of assertions and theorems (see THEOREM-PROVING). On the other hand, a normal programming language has a fixed prespecified and inflexible flow of control. MICRO-PLANNER behaves like a theorem prover that makes use of additional procedural information. In this way it becomes possible to specify a goal to be reached instead of a detailed algorithm of how to reach it. Winograd's SHRDLU (qv) program is based on MICRO-PLANNER (see T. Winograd, *Understanding Natural Language,* Academic Press, New York, 1972). Deficiencies of MICRO-PLANNER resulted in the development of several other languages, most prominently CONNIVER (qv).

J. Geller
New Jersey Institute of Technology

MILITARY APPLICATIONS OF AI

During recent years, AI technology related activity within the military has increased dramatically. This heightened interest and expanding investment in AI by the Department of Defense (DOD) and the individual services (Army, Navy, Air Force, and Marine Corps) may be attributed to a number of factors, in particular:

1. The very real progress AI technologies have been making and demonstrating at academic centers and in commercial applications.
2. The increasing complexity of modern-day military operations, brought about in great degree by significant advances in the speed and accuracy of sensors and weapons, coupled with the rapid growth in the amount of critical information to be processed, analyzed, and assimilated under severe time constraints with limited manpower.
3. A growing awareness and acceptance by the military of the potential of AI technologies to help solve military problems.

The possible contributions of AI to defense span the breadth of military activities. Table 1 relates 14 basic AI

Table 1. Military Applications of AI Technologies[a]

Defense Applications	Signal understanding	Image understanding	Speech understanding	Non-signal understanding	Natural language understanding/generation	Information integration (fusion)	Learning	Planning/control	Resource allocation	Robotics	Distributed systems	User interfaces	Software development/maintenance	Information Management/retrieval
R&D	×	×	×	O	×	×	O	O	×	×	×	×	O	×
Manufacturing	×	O	×	×	×	×	×	O	O	O	×	×		×
Operations	O	O	O	O	O	O	O	O	O	O	O	O	×	O
Maintenance	×	×	×	×	×	×	×	×	×	×	×	×	×	O
Logistics	×	×	×	×	×	×	×	O	O		×	×		O
Personnel		×	×	×	×			×	×			×		O
Training	×	×	O	×	O	×	O	×			×	O	×	×
Intelligence collection and surveillance	×			×	×			×			×			×
Intelligence processing	O	O	×	×	×	×	×		×		O	×		×
Intelligence analysis and situation assessment			×	O	O	O	O	×	×		O	×		O
Sensor resource allocation			×			×	×	O			×	×		×
Force allocation			×	×	×	×	×	×	O		×	O		×
Force command and control	×	×	×	O	×	O	×	O	×		×	O	×	×
Route planning and navigation	×	×	×	×	×	×	O	O			×	×		×
Battle tactics			×	×	×	×	O	O			×	O	×	×
Targeting	O	O	×		×	×	×	×	O		×	×		×
Autonomous and semi-autonomous vehicles	O	O	×	×		O	O	O	×	O	×	×	×	×
Avionics	×	×	×	×		O	×	O	×	×	×	O		
Electronic warfare	O		×	×	×	O	×	×	×		×	×		×
C³ Countermeasures	O	×	×	O	×	×	×	×	×		×	×		×
Communications	×		O	×	×	×	×	×			×			×
Network control				×			×	×	O		O	×		×
Information routing			×	×	O		O	×			×	×		×
Information management and retrieval	×	×	×	×	O		O		×		×	O		O
Combat engineering and support		×	×		×	×		×	×	×	×	×		×

[a] Symbols: O, major applicability; ×, minor applicability. (McCune and Drazovich, 1983; courtesy of EW Communications, Inc.)

technologies to a number of military problem areas. Applicability to seven generic military problem areas as well as a number of more specific task domains is indicated as either major or minor. That the matrix is quite dense is not surprising; each AI technology is applicable to a wide variety of military task areas, and each problem area could profit from a number of AI techniques. Note also that the generic problem entry "operations" is rated as a potential major application area of almost all of the AI technologies considered. The more specific military task areas enumerated in the table are not only primarily operations oriented, but many are vital components in the critical operations area of command, control, communications, and intelligence (C³I). Indeed, military commanders are identifying C³I and its increasingly complex and difficult problems as perhaps the most significant areas for both near- and far-term AI technology applications (Baciocco, 1981).

Underneath the current surge of attention to military applications of AI lies a history of over 20 years of DOD support, through agencies such as the Office of Naval Research (ONR) and the Defense Advanced Research Projects Agency (DARPA), to basic AI research at a number of universities. As the discipline has progressed and promising technologies such as expert systems (qv) and natural language processing have emerged, interest has grown in applying these techniques to challenging real-world military problems. In the early 1980s, the navy took the lead among the services and established the Navy Center for Applied Research in AI at the Naval Research Laboratory to address the transition of basic AI research to naval applications. More recently, the air force has accelerated

AI research and exploratory development at the Avionics and Flight Dynamics Laboratories at Wright-Patterson Air Force Base, and has designated Rome Air Development Center at Griffiss Air Force Base as part of a long-range AI effort that includes a consortium of seven New York universities and the University of Massachusetts. The army, also, is investing in long-term AI research, exploratory development, and training of personnel, in part through liaisons with the University of Texas and the University of Pennsylvania.

A new, far-reaching program involving a number of universities, defense research and development laboratories, and private industry is the Strategic Computing Initiative (SCI). Administered by DARPA and estimated to cost about $600 million for the first five years, SCI is aimed toward developing and applying a new generation of machine intelligence technology to critical defense problems (Klass, 1985; DARPA, 1983). Three specific military areas targeted for initial technology applications are an autonomous land vehicle, an intelligent pilot's associate, and naval battle management.

Autonomous Land Vehicle. The development of the autonomous land vehicle (see ALV) with active participation by the army, emphasizes computer vision and image understanding technologies. The addition of advanced AI reasoning techniques may allow the vehicle not only to sense and react, also to but interpret its environment and then adapt its mission strategy accordingly. Initial work is concentrated on designing a vehicle that can automatically determine the path of a road and follow it. Eventually, the vehicle must also be able not only to detect an obstacle in its path but also to determine its nature (eg, a shadow, a traversable log, or a large boulder requiring a detour) and react accordingly.

Pilot's Associate. In concert with the air force, the Pilot's Associate project was conceived to provide the pilot of a single-place fighter aircraft with the support and expertise of a "phantom flight crew." Rather than addressing the automation of conventional functions in an aircraft, the project aims toward providing logical expertise in specified task areas through the concept of an integrated cockpit. Initially, the system was conceived as a construct of four major interactive expert subsystems: a situation assessment manager, a tactical-planning manager, a mission-planning manager, and a systems-status manager. Special emphasis was placed on the pilot—vehicle interface, which included advanced control, display, and automation techniques that utilized speech recognition (qv), natural language understanding (qv), and speech synthesis (qv).

Naval Battle Management. A goal of the battle management program, a joint effort with the Navy, is to demonstrate how AI technology, particularly expert systems and natural language understanding, can contribute to the development of automated decision aids for the complex combat environment. Five battle-management functions have been identified as initial application areas within fleet-command center operations. They include free requirements, capabilities assessment, campaign simulation, operations planning, and strategy assessment. These functions are well defined, yet complex, demanding, and labor intensive, requiring skill and expertise to perform and are thus promising candidates for expert system decision aids. As with the personnel they will support, expert systems developed for these applications will need to interact and cooperate with each other. Emphasis was also placed on natural language understanding, both as an interface between the expert systems and their users and as a means of automating the processing of the ever-increasing command-center message traffic, which can expand 10-fold during a crisis.

Military operations, and in particular C^3I, possess significant characteristics that have not always been prominent in other AI application domains. One such characteristic is the time-critical nature of tactical decision making: the need for appropriate, real-time response to dynamic situations. The deployment of increasingly complicated surveillance and weapons systems, both friendly and hostile, has compressed the time available for tactical decision making. Automated decision aiding (and ultimately automated decision making) under these conditions must emphasize efficient solution-space search and pruning techniques and consider finding the first solution that satisfies a given set of conditions or exceeds a specified threshold. In addition, vast amounts of diverse, often incomplete and uncertain data must be interpreted and integrated to form the tactical picture on which situation assessments and consequent tactical actions are based. Therefore, effective techniques for reasoning under uncertainty will be crucial to automated decision support (see REASONING, PLAUSIBLE).

The problem of information processing in the military is an enormous one, due both to the vast quantities of data to be handled and to the distributed nature of the generation and usage of the information. Huge databases must not only be maintained and updated but must also be quickly and efficiently accessible by a distributed hierarchy of military personnel with differing needs. The flood of incoming data must be analyzed, disseminated, integrated, stored, and presented appropriately and in a timely manner. Thus methodologies for efficient distributed database management and information interpretation and integration as well as man—machine interfaces that accommodate the specialized needs and personal preferences of the system user will be required.

The geographic and functional distribution of both C_3I assets and C^3I decision-making authority and responsibility have led C^3I to be described as an excellent example of distributed problem solving (qv). A new field of research within AI, called distributed AI, is addressing many of the difficult issues in this area (Smith, 1985). For example, how may control be most effectively distributed across a network of semiautonomous problem-solving or decision-making nodes and still ensure their cooperation in arriving at consistent and coherent problem solutions or strategies? How may tasks be assigned dynamically among often competing nodes, and in what ways should nodes communicate with each other and what kinds of information should be exchanged? In addition, how will distributed problem-solving systems recover from the failure of one or more nodes? These questions are but an indication of the challenges in developing intelligent systems for distributed problem solving in such domains as C³I.

To date, military AI application systems are still in the prototype development stage. The following sections describe a small sampling of experimental systems that are demonstrating the feasibility of applying AI techniques to a variety of military needs. Application areas include sensor-information integration for situation description and assessment, combat-resource allocation, mission planning, maintenance and troubleshooting of military equipment, training, and automated natural language understanding (qv) of military messages. A crucial issue that separates current prototype systems from operational systems is that of robustness: the ability of a system to "keep its head" and not fall apart when faced with input that is unfamiliar, violates internal system constraints, or contains unresolvable ambiguities. Many AI researchers also believe that operational systems, particularly those that are expert-system based, will need a capability to learn to survive in the complex, dynamic military environment. Although current computer systems cannot adapt and improve themselves significantly on the basis of past mistakes or acquire new abilities through observation (eg, by example or analogy), machine-learning research, which is receiving increased attention following its evolution from early network approaches to present-day knowledge-intensive techniques, is making progress toward these goals (Michalski, 1983).

SENSOR INFORMATION INTEGRATION FOR SITUATION DESCRIPTION AND ASSESSMENT

A central problem in military intelligence is the construction of coherent situation descriptions using sensor information. Situation descriptions provide crucial support to military decision makers over a wide range of activities, from local tactical operations to strategic planning. Sensor information comes from diverse sources in a variety of forms, such as intercepted communications, radar returns, intercepted radar emissions, aerial surveillance, sonar, etc. Such data are often incomplete and uncertain and may be time delayed, ambiguous, and in error. As the technology of warfare escalates, the information-integration problem grows along two dimensions: the quantity of sensor data is increasing at the same time that the variety of such information is proliferating. This combination creates a potentially overwhelming situation for the human analysts who must generate current, coherent situation descriptions and assessments under increasingly restrictive time constraints.

Perhaps the simplest form of sensor information integration occurs when returns from successive sweeps of a single radar are correlated to produce a track of some distant object. Conventional computer algorithms have long been developed for this and other routine correlation tasks. More recently, however, the techniques of AI have been applied to sensor information integration problems that normally require the attention of human analysts because their solutions often involve reasoning with incomplete, uncertain evidence. This section describes two such applications of AI technology to sensor information integration.

The ANALYST program illustrates the use of AI techniques to help generate tactical situation descriptions and assessments on the battlefield (Bonasso, 1984). Developed in the early 1980s by the MITRE Corp. as a prototype expert system for the Army, ANALYST uses reports from multiple-sensor sources to generate a real-time battlefield situation display for use by force commanders and their staffs. The premise on which the ANALYST program is based is that the existence of enemy units can be inferred from their basic war-making activities. Thus the input to ANALYST is in the form of reports involving five types of intelligence: intercepted communications, indications from shooting sensors, photo interpretation, radar interceptions, and moving-target indications. The output of ANALYST is a situation map showing suspected locations of enemy units. The process of fusing the incoming stream of intelligence reports into a coherent situation map is performed in a deductive fashion using production, or if—then, rules. An important constraint of the project was the implementation of the software on computers small enough to be deployed at a battlefield command post.

Three basic types of entities are manipulated by ANALYST. Each of the three entity types is represented using a frame hierarchy (Minsky, 1974) (see FRAMES). Thus intelligence reports, groups of seemingly related intelligence reports (activity clusters), and hypothesized battlefield entities (tanks, command posts, etc) are all stored as frames. The selection of frames as the basic data structure provides a convenient framework for storing information having taxonomic structure. For example, each photo interpretation report is a specific instance of a generic intelligence report; therefore, it inherits certain properties from intelligence reports in general. In addition, frames provide for the attachment of demon functions, which supply values for slot values that may be missing as a result of an incomplete report.

Although a good deal of information is inherent in the frame structures, the major portion of the domain knowledge available to ANALYST is stored in six distinct knowledge bases. Each knowledge base consists of a collection of if—then rules that operate on the frame entities.

The first knowledge base serves to associate each incoming intelligence report with clusters of previously processed intelligence reports from the same general geographical area. Patterns among these activity clusters are recognized by the second knowledge base, which creates a frame representing a hypothesized battlefield entity whenever one of its pattern rules fires. A corresponding symbol is placed on the system's graphical situation map to represent the entity. One of the slots in the newly created battlefield entity frame contains a likelihood that is used to indicate the strength of the evidence used to infer the entity's existence. The inference process of the first two knowledge bases is pursued in a parallel fashion for each of the five types of intelligence reports. Thus it is possible for the pattern rules of the second knowledge base to create multiple frames representing the same battlefield entity when that entity's existence is supported by more than one form of intelligence. Such duplicate entities are merged into single composite entities by the merge rules of the third knowledge base. This merging process is a crucial step not only because it removes redundancies in the situation map but also because it allows information from diverse sources to be integrated into a coherent situation description.

Tactical and terrain data are used by the fourth knowledge base to refine the descriptions of the hypothesized battlefield entities. The rules of the fifth knowledge base reinforce the existence of hypothesized battlefield entities by examining those activity clusters that were not used by any pattern rules. If a stray activity cluster is sufficiently close to some hypothesized battlefield entity, a reinforcing rule may use that unclaimed cluster to reinforce the entity's existence. One way that the refinement and reinforcement of the fourth and fifth knowledge bases is accomplished is by adjusting the values of the likelihood slots contained in the various battlefield entity frames. The sixth knowledge base serves to delete hypothetical battlefield entities that have persisted for a sufficient length of time without reinforcement.

ANALYST's rules are segregated into separate knowledge bases for control purposes. Each of the knowledge bases is applied to the incoming data in the order that they have been described. Thus all possible clusters are formed before the pattern rules are applied, all pattern rules are applied before any merging rules are applied, etc. The partitioning of ANALYST's rules into specialized knowledge bases facilitates controlling this sequential application process. ANALYST works from lower level data to higher level conclusions using a forward-chaining inference mechanism. Thus conclusions made in the then portion of an if—then rule may be used later to satisfy the if portion of some other rule. Conflict resolution, the process of deciding which rule to select when more than one rule is applicable, is handled by applying the rules in their order of appearance in the knowledge base.

ANALYST was tested using data from a computer simulation of a battlefield environment. The simulation contained models of enemy units performing some specific mission, and it simulated the intelligence observables the enemy units would produce as a result of their war-making activity. In addition, the simulation employed models of friendly sensors used to capture the intelligence observables. Two capture ratios were used in testing ANALYST: 35 and 20%. (A 35% capture ratio means that the intelligence-gathering apparatus captures only 35% out of all the possible events.) In both cases ANALYST produced a quite comprehensive situation map, even given sparse intelligence. For example, even at the 20% capture level, approximately half of the simulated battlefield entities were correctly hypothesized. In some cases hypothesized locations were accurate enough to be used as targeting data for area weapons. In addition, it may be difficult to trick the ANALYST program using decoys because it employs information from diverse intelligence sources.

Just as battlefield entities produce observable information during their activities, ships and submarines produce observable features as they transit the ocean. The observable of interest here is an acoustical signature (energy in certain narrow bands of the sound spectrum and particular harmonics of these fundamental frequencies) that is produced by the propulsion system and other equipment in the vessel. To detect and classify the ships and submarines operating in a certain sector of the ocean, the navy uses acoustical data collected by submerged hydrophone arrays located at the ocean's periphery. Each hydrophone of the array is directional, so that its sensitivity is concentrated in a cone that projects out into the ocean. The signals collected from the hydrophones are displayed in the form of a sonogram, a time series display of the acoustical energy spectrum detected at the hydrophone. Highly trained sonar analysts interpret the sonograms, and by using their knowledge of ship and submarine signature traits, sea lane characteristics, underwater sound propagation, and intelligence information, they develop a situation board that describes the current state of activity in the ocean sector in question.

The most straightforward situation for the analyst occurs when only one source presents itself on a given hydrophone channel. In that case the process of matching the incoming signature with a collection of stored references is complicated primarily by noise, changing acoustical propagation conditions, measurement errors, and the possible incompleteness of the signal data. A more difficult situation is one where radiations from several vessels are captured on the same channel and where several channels are active simultaneously. The process of disentangling these multiple signatures is challenging to even the most experienced analysts. In order to investigate the feasibility of using automated knowledge-based reasoning to aid in this complicated signal-understanding task, DARPA initiated a research project in the early 1970s involving computer scientists at the Stanford Heuristic Programming Project and also at Systems Control Technology. The resulting programs, Heuristic Adaptive Surveillance Project (HASP) and Surveillance Integration Automation Project (SIAP) (Nii and co-workers, 1982; Nii and Feigenbaum, 1978) were evaluated in the late 1970s with quite promising results.

There are several superficial similarities between ANALYST and HASP/SIAP. For example, frames are used to store static knowledge about the characteristics of vessels, and entities hypothesized by HASP/SIAP have associated weights as a measure of the confidence in the hypothesis. These weights are used in a fashion similar to ANALYST's likelihoods. HASP/SIAP represents much of its domain knowledge (qv) as production rules. In addition, the information refinement process in HASP/SIAP is similar to that of ANALYST. ANALYST successively refines intelligence reports into activity clusters and then refines activity clusters into entities. The refinement process of HASP/SIAP begins by detecting harmonic relationships between sonogram lines and associating them into harmonic sets. Harmonic sets are further related to potential shipboard noise sources, and groups of sources may suggest a specific vessel, etc.

The underlying framework for problem solving used by HASP/SIAP, however, is quite different from that of AN-

ALYST. The control strategy employed by ANALYST is to apply knowledge bases sequentially, each of which uses forward chaining and a straightforward conflict-resolution scheme. The control strategy of HASP/SIAP is a much richer one and is known as a blackboard architecture (Erman and co-workers, 1981; Case and Thibault, 1977) (see BLACKBOARD SYSTEMS). In this implementation the production rules are divided into a hierarchy of knowledge sources. The lowest level in this hierarchy consists of specialist knowledge sources that contain domain knowledge about ocean surveillance. The higher levels of the knowledge source hierarchy contain strategic knowledge about how to solve ocean surveillance problems. These problem-solving strategy rules monitor a central data structure called the blackboard, where the current best hypothesis (eg, at the highest level of analysis, the situation board postulating the most likely vessel(s) based on data available up to that time) is posted. The strategy rules determine opportunistically which of the lower level knowledge sources should be applied to the current best hypothesis to provide the most refinement. Thus all of the knowledge sources operate on the same blackboard under control of the strategy knowledge source, whose job it is to provide focus of attention for the system. The lower level knowledge sources may be invoked in either an event-driven (forward-chaining) or an expectation-driven (backward-chaining) mode. As in ANALYST, event-driven inference combines incoming data to create hypotheses at higher levels of abstraction. For example, a newly found sonogram line might be combined with other lines to form a harmonic set. Expectation-driven inference takes a higher level hypothesis and searches for lower level information to support it. For example, suppose that the current best hypothesis contains a certain type of ship known to possess several noise sources. If not all of the expected sources are present, expectation-driven inference would direct the system to look for lower level information, such as the presence of certain previously unexplained sonogram lines, to reinforce further the higher level hypothesis. Thus even though ANALYST and HASP/SIAP both address the military problem of integrating and interpreting sensor information to develop a situation description, they use dissimilar architectures to accomplish their goals.

The performance of HASP/SIAP was evaluated in a series of three experiments performed by MITRE Corp. in the late 1970s. These tests compared the expert system's performance to that of two expert sonar analysts. In all cases HASP/SIAP developed situation descriptions of similar quality to that of the experts, and in one case it outperformed a human analyst.

COMBAT RESOURCE ALLOCATION

A critical element of battle management is the allocation of combat resources, both in anticipation of and response to tactical situations. In particular, battlefield commanders have always been confronted with the problem of determining how to allocate their weapons resources so as to destroy desired targets most efficiently. A wide range of factors, pertaining both to the enemy and to friendly forces, can influence the success of a weapons-assignment strategy. For example, it may be important to consider the enemy's counterfire ability, vulnerability, etc and, at the same time, the state of readiness of friendly forces and the ease with which they can be resupplied. Furthermore, the allocation problem is compounded for modern commanders because of the ever-widening variety of weapons from which to choose.

The Marine Corps is addressing this problem with the introduction of the Marine Integrated Fire and Air Support System (MIFASS). Under MIFASS, fire and air support centers would be established to help solve weapon-to-target allocation problems. These centers would perform weapon allocation planning using information relayed from forward observers equipped with hand-held digital communications terminals. Originally, MIFASS used a heuristic algorithm for weapon-to-target assignment that approached the allocation problem in a sequential fashion by optimizing on successive weapons (Case and Thibault, 1977). However, this simple sequential scheme has several limitations: it does not consider the assignment problem as a whole, it does not allow for more than one weapon to be allocated to a target, and it ignores a significant number of battlefield factors. More recently, BATTLE, a prototype interactive decision support system that employs AI techniques to solve the weapon-to-target allocation problem, was developed at the Naval Research Laboratory to remove these limitations (Slagle and co-workers, 1983; Slagle and Hamburger, 1985).

In its first phase of operation, BATTLE examines each possible weapon-to-target pairing and calculates a measure of its effectiveness. This effectiveness calculation is performed by a computation network that is a generalization of the inference networks of PROSPECTOR (Duda and co-workers, 1979). The network, which is prepared by a military domain expert, involves an extensive set of over 50 weapon, target, and battlefield situation factors. Data for a particular battlefield situation are entered interactively by the system user under BATTLE's guidance.

In its second phase BATTLE generates a weapon allocation tree using the effectiveness measures computed in the first phase together with a user-supplied set of tactical values of the targets. Instead of searching for the optimal solution only, BATTLE allows its user to specify a value k such that the best k plans will be found. Because the size of the weapon allocation tree becomes astronomical in complex battlefield situations, it is not computationally feasible for BATTLE to explore it exhaustively. Rather, a pruning algorithm is used so that only a selected portion of the tree is explored. The pruning algorithm works by applying a heuristic each time a new node is generated. The heuristic calculation finds an upper bound for the overall destructiveness of the current partial assignment. If the upper bound indicated by the heuristic is less destructive than the kth best complete assignment found so far, the current partial path is abandoned.

As in most command and control situations, there is a certain time criticality associated with solving the weapon-to-target assignment problem. As mentioned earlier, BATTLE's first phase considers a multitude of factors in calculating the potential effectiveness of each weapon against each target. It would be time-consuming and tedious if BATTLE always insisted on asking its user all possible questions about the situation at hand, especially if some of the answers affected the outcome only marginally. To prevent this problem and thereby accelerate the interrogation process, a new questioning strategy called merit was developed (Slage and co-workers, 1984). The merit strategy ensures that BATTLE focuses its question asking so that the questions asked first are those questions whose answers will have the greatest effect on the final outcome. A cutoff value may be set so that questions having a merit value below the cutoff will not be asked. Experiments have shown that a significant reduction in the number of questions asked occurs when the merit strategy is used to guide questioning.

MISSION PLANNING

Another complex problem facing military commanders is the task of mission planning. As in other military problems, mission planning is performed at many scales, ranging from tactical to strategic. In all cases the planning process is a labor-intensive one, relying on both the common sense and the specialized training and experience of the commanders. The potential for applying AI to mission planning has long been recognized, and several existing efforts illustrate the range of applications.

Tactical air planning for the Air Force provides an example of an intermediate-level planning task facing the military. In this case the missions being planned are air strikes against designated targets. The problem is to design a plan in which aircraft and ordnance are assigned in such a way as to ensure the destruction of these targets within some predetermined probability. This planning process begins on receipt of an apportionment order issued by the Joint Task Force Commander. The resulting air tasking order, which may take 24 h to complete manually, specifies a detailed plan that satisfies the original apportionment order. To accelerate both the planning process and the replanning process, the Air Force has funded the development of a planning aid called the knowledge-based system (KNOBS) (Engelman and co-workers, 1983).

KNOBS was developed at MITRE Corp. between 1978 and 1982. Its specific domain of expertise is planning ground-strike counterair missions in the European theater. Its knowledge base contains plausible (but, for security reasons, not necessarily accurate) information about a number of potential targets and friendly air bases, generic information about aircraft and ordnance capabilities, information about antiaircraft defenses, and Air Force tactical doctrine. In a typical KNOBS interactive-planning session, the user would enter the desired target and the desired probability of destruction for that target. The user can then specify other particulars for the mission, such as the type and number of aircraft to be used, which air base should supply the aircraft, etc, or the user can have KNOBS make suggestions for each particular. An advantage of allowing KNOBS to make suggestions is that KNOBS will only make suggestions that result in a valid plan, and KNOBS will present its suggestions in an order of preference. At any point in the session the user can have KNOBS check for inconsistencies in the partially created plan. For example, the system can alert the user if the selected aircraft and airfield are too far from the designated target or if the ordnance selected cannot achieve the desired probability of destruction. The process of refining the details of the plan continues, with the user always having the option of letting KNOBS attempt to complete the plan on its own. When the plan is completely specified, KNOBS warns the user about possible antiaircraft defenses in the vicinity of the target, and the interaction is complete.

KNOBS approaches the planning process by treating each plan as an instance of a prototypical plan. Plans, as well as nearly all other objects in KNOBS, are represented using frames. Thus the construction of a valid plan consists of building an instance of a plan frame in which all slots have been filled in and the values contained in the slots define a valid plan. The validity of the plan is defined in terms of constraints that exist between the various particulars of the plan. For example, the fact that a given aircraft has only a fixed operating range defines a constraint on the distance between that aircraft's airfield and any potential target areas. In KNOBS the planning process is simplified greatly because all of the constraints are known *a priori*.

Although the approach of generating a specific plan by elaborating on a template plan is a limited one, it has been found to be useful in a variety of domains that require somewhat stereotypical planning. By modification of KNOBS's domain-dependent code, the Navy has used KNOBS to plan certain specific categories of naval missions, and NASA is investigating several applications of KNOBS relating to planning for the space shuttle. A further refined planning system is being developed for the Air Force (Courand and co-workers, 1985).

The planning cycle in the Navy is not unlike that of the air force; operational mission planning is initiated by the arrival of an operational order document, which states a mission goal in general terms. The resulting operational plan, which may take a team of commanders days or weeks to complete, specifies in detail a military plan the planners believe best satisfies the original order. To provide navy commanders with a planning tool, a knowledge-based problem-solving system called OPPLAN-CONSULTANT is being developed at the Naval Research Laboratory (Srinivasan, 1985).

OPPLAN-CONSULTANT solves planning problems in the domain of naval operational planning. Unlike KNOBS, OPPLAN-CONSULTANT is designed to be a general naval planning tool incorporating knowledge across the full spectrum of naval operational planning. The software system used to represent and operate on the domain knowledge is called calculus for knowledge processing in logic (CK-LOG). CK-LOG is a knowledge-processing system that uses a three-valued logic (true, unknown, and false) in building partial models of world states and a two-valued logic (true and false) for theorem proving. An important feature of CK-LOG is its ability to represent and reason about actions and the temporal dependencies between them. A pilot implementation of the system is currently under construction; however, it is expected that it will take several years before a sufficiently extensive knowledge base has been developed to demonstrate OPPLAN-CONSULTANT in a realistic planning environment.

MAINTENANCE AND TROUBLESHOOTING OF MILITARY EQUIPMENT

Since the early 1960s military equipment has increased steadily in complexity and variety, whereas at the same time the pool of trained technicians has been decreasing. A major cost of operations is in fault diagnosis and repair, the procurement of maintenance equipment, and the training of technicians and operators. Each of the services has problems that are unique to its mission, but all share problems of space, difficulty in providing logistics support, and limited technical manpower. These factors, coupled with the demands of operations, place heavy emphasis on speedy and accurate diagnosis and repair in the field. The various difficulties have created prime opportunities for the application of AI, and a number of efforts are underway. This discussion considers AI applications in three key military maintenance areas: automatic test equipment (ATE), built-in test (BIT), and interactive troubleshooting aids.

Automatic Test Equipment (ATE)

In any maintenance application where only a limited pool of human experts is available, the application of an expert-system-based maintenance aid is an attractive option. In electronics equipment maintenance the possibilities for immediate benefit are even more apparent. This is particularly true for aircraft electronics (avionics) because of the large number of different systems involved, the heavy reliance of modern aircraft on avionics for mission accomplishment, and the premium placed on rapid turnaround. In avionics maintenance the Navy and Air Force rely heavily on automatic test equipment (ATE) for diagnosis of faults. This reliance is especially evident in the Navy, where scarcity of space limits test equipment and manpower and spares storage. Even though many items of avionics have an intricate built-in test (BIT) with automated testing, high false removal rates, excessive levels of fault ambiguity, and the continued need for human intervention are still problems. (False removal rates as high as 85% are found, and ambiguities involving three to five circuit cards are fairly common.)

ATE makes use of test programs sets (TPS) that consist of an interface between the avionics and the ATE and software for fault diagnosis. For each different item of avionics a separate TPS must be provided. Test program generation is highly manpower intensive, and results are variable, with high costs and long delivery times common. A test sequence may take between 20 min and 12 h to diagnose system faults. Moreover, a typical Navy carrier, for example, requires more than 600 different TPS to support the avionics on its various aircraft. In many cases TPS are inadequate, either failing to identify faults in a reasonable time or producing a large ambiguity group of suspected faulty components. These factors, coupled with limited expert manpower, make ATE an especially attractive application for AI. Efforts underway in this area are applying expert systems technology toward the performance of efficient, accurate fault isolation either automatically or interactively with maintenance personnel (King, 1982; Simpson and Balaban, 1982; Cantone and co-workers, 1983; DeJong, 1984). A more near-term application of this knowledge-based approach is directed toward the automatic generation of TPS for execution on existing ATE configurations.

For electronics fault diagnosis an expert-system database typically consists of two kinds of information: detailed specifications for the equipment to be diagnosed and results of measurements. For electronics equipment, the specifications consist of such information as a functional description, interconnections, nominal values for normal operating parameters, and component values and tolerances. This kind of information must be available for each piece of equipment and is equivalent to the manuals and performance specifications that a technician would use. The additional data information in the database consists of symptoms and results of measurements. The rule base of the system consists of general diagnostic methods, rules associated with particular classes of equipment, and finally, rules unique to the specific equipment being tested. The key to the efficient utilization of expert systems in ATE is the automation of the rule and data acquisition process. This particular bottleneck to expert systems development in general is a prime candidate for automation in this application because the design data for military electronic equipment is already available in a computer-usable form from CAD—CAM databases. In addition, it is expected that at least some of the rules can be automatically captured from analysis of system functional descriptions and circuit topology. The possibility for automatic "knowledge compilation" is an important driver in applying expert systems to electronic diagnosis in ATE and should be useful in more conventional maintenance aids as well.

In fault isolation systems being developed by the Navy [such as (Fault Isolation System) (FIS) at the Naval Research Laboratory] and the air force, the concept of "functionality" is utilized to add a dimension of deep reasoning without resorting to detailed circuit analysis (DeJong, 1984; Pipitone, 1984, 1986). Most existing expert systems are limited to knowledge bases that provide shallow reasoning capability within their area of expertise. Deep reasoning is not even a reasonable objective for many application areas because the level of theoretical understanding is inadequate to permit reasoning from basic principles, and even if it were, the process would be incredibly inefficient. Electronic systems offer a potential for effective deep reasoning because their functions are fully understood and documented, and convenient partitioning of functions can permit a mix of shallow and deep reasoning to be utilized as appropriate. Under the concept of functionality, electronic equipment subsystems are considered to be more than simple nodes in a circuit. In addition to producing a value of output under a given stimulus, a subsystem is considered to provide a specified transformation of information. By reasoning about the relationship of functional elements in addition to tests made concerning nominal measured values, ambiguity about the ultimate cause of faults is expected to be greatly reduced.

A prime, long-range objective in using expert systems for diagnosis is to minimize the total testing time to unambiguously isolate the fault. An additional shorter-range goal, with substantial benefit in cost and timeliness, is the automation of TPS generation for existing ATE. The Navy project Intelligent Automatic Test Generation (IATG) incorporated the features of FIS along with a performance improvement capability based on actual test fault detection success to generate conventional TPS and will eventually perform as an on-line controller ATE. The economic benefits are potentially high for a successful diagnostic expert system because it is estimated that TPS and ATE procurement costs could be reduced by 25–50%. This is no small matter because these costs are several billion dollars a year for all the services. One key point for the application of expert systems in ATE is the already high level of commitment to automation and the fact that most of the equipment needed for immediate application exists and is designed for computer control. Significant benefits can be achieved in nonavonics applications as well, but in most cases stimulus and measurements require human intervention. The issue is addressed further in the discussion about interactive maintenance aids.

Built-in Test (BIT)

For large weapons systems off-line testing using ATE and manual methods may be impractical and inadequate. Typical characteristics of such systems are high value, long operating times, and isolation from sources of spares and test equipment during normal operations. Some typical examples are submarine and surface ships, where replacement of black boxes is not practical owing to the nature of the equipment and the difficulty in providing sufficient spares to last for a full deployment. In such circumstances the equipment is typically diagnosed and repaired in place at either the module or component level. Similarly, diagnosis and repair or the activation of redundant systems on large, long-endurance aircraft must be done in flight to ensure adequate capability levels. The Air Force has undertaken a project to develop "smart" BIT for digital systems, with the intent of minimizing false alarms, improving fault coverage, and identifying intermittent faults (Haller and co-workers, 1985; Lahore, 1984). The intent is to provide design concepts that individual designers would use to incorporate smart BIT. Although smart BIT improves performance of individual systems, two Air Force projects are looking at the overall operation of a vehicle and its systems. The integrated maintenance information system (IMIS) project is designed to provide flightline personnel with access to all onboard diagnostic data available as well as access to the supply system, scheduling data, training, and maintenance records. The B-1B aircraft would be a likely candidate for a demonstration because this aircraft incorporates extensive BIT already. In addition, the Generic Integrated Maintenance Diagnostics (GIMADS) project proposed to use AI coupled with more conventional equipment and software to address the overall diagnostics problem in an integrated system. Also, the Navy is developing an expert-system—based radar maintenance aid for the AEGIS ship combat system, a modern missile-defense system for Navy cruisers and destroyers. The complexity of the systems involved makes conventional software approaches uneconomical; however, these systems are considered excellent applications for expert system technology.

Interactive Maintenance Aids

Many military systems are not adaptable to the approach taken in avionics and large electronics systems either because they are largely mechanical and must be diagnosed in place, lack sufficient built-in sensors to diagnose, or must be repaired in the field under austere conditions. To address these cases, there is strong interest in maintenance aids that can interact with operators and technicians to guide the diagnosis, provide advice, or make technical information available in a readily usable form. Commercial work in this area has been successful (eg, the DELTA system at GE), and the military is interested in exactly the same sort of easily transportable interactive system for field use. For direct aids to a person, much more attention must be given to interfacing with the technician than is needed for ATE or BIT. Besides the more austere operating environment, the technician is likely to be less highly trained and less tolerant of system demands. Such aids must provide the required information in a readily usable form, in natural language, and with advanced graphics capabilities to be of significant utility. For maintenance aids the problem is not so much freeform communication as it is providing access to large bodies of information in a convenient way. Video disks under computer control are being explored as one solution, but the options are still open at this time. The IMIS, GIMADS, and Integrated Diagnostics projects all expect to develop some form of easily transportable aid of this sort. The army in particular has need of this type of maintenance aid because of its austere operating environment and the emphasis placed on rapid and accurate repair in the field.

The work done in diagnostic expert systems in ATE should be directly applicable to interface with a person, but voice response, natural language capability, advanced graphics, and perhaps vision and image understanding (qv) will be critical elements. The psychology of implementation is very important here, with several key issues to be considered beyond the performance of the AI system itself. To be effective, these human aids must be more than simply intelligent; they must become a partner of the maintainer to a degree well beyond existing systems. To be specifically avoided is the "smart machine—dumb human" philosophy. This approach, perhaps justified in certain instances, can only lead to failure in service due to poor job satisfaction, wasted human capability, failure to capitalize on learning as a by-product of aid, and outright sabotage. The various aspects of natural language, voice recognition, and reasoning needed to produce interactive maintenance aids are very similar to those needed in any interactive environment and need not be expanded further here. The potential for use of AI-based systems to improve human performance is especially evident in the field of diagnosis and repair. For all branches of the military-complex equipment, high costs, the need for rapid and accurate diagnosis, and the relatively high turnover rate of manpower create prime opportunities for AI applications.

TRAINING

An additional, and potentially important, use of AI technology is in training. As military operations and combat systems increase in technical complexity and personnel resources both shrink in number and increase in turnover, the efficient, yet thorough, training of military personnel is crucial to all the services. Many of the same techniques used to aid decision making can be applied to provide guidance and instruction in the training process. An important example of an intelligent, computer-based military training system is STEAMER, developed at the Navy Personnel Research and Development Center (Hollan and co-workers, 1984). STEAMER's domain is propulsion engineering. Steam propulsion systems are an integral part of most navy ships, and it is imperative that the engineers who operate them have a thorough understanding of their behavior. Although these engineers must operate the systems routinely on a day-to-day basis, their understanding must be complete enough to enable them to anticipate the behavior of the system during mechanical failures. The cost of specialized-training simulators is high for such systems, and the use of traditional simulators does not necessarily engender a deep understanding of the system being simulated. Because mathematical models exist for such systems, they may be simulated readily on a digital computer. In addition, the system in question is a physical one, making it a good target for experiments involving aiding humans in the construction of mental models.

STEAMER combines these problem features to produce a graphics-oriented trainer whose underpinnings derive from computer simulation. Users of the system are presented with a detailed digital simulation of a steam plant. Elaborate interactive-computer graphics permit users to inspect the simulated plant's operation at many different hierarchical levels. The trainees may use a mouse interface to vary settings of valves and other plant controls and watch how the changes affect the overall system. In addition, for example, trainees can manipulate fluid levels, which could not ordinarily be manipulated externally in such a plant. The latitude to introduce such changes and observe their effects may be important in developing an intuition about the system. The emphasis in the graphical depictions is to provide trainees with a display that enables them to develop a mental model of the plant's operation similar to the mental models used by experts.

The initial implementation of STEAMER relied heavily on mating a traditional digital simulation with newer AI programming techniques, such as object-oriented programming and active display icons. An important component of the overall system is an object-based graphics editor, which includes a wide range of predefined icons for displaying various levels or their rates of change. This editor has enabled nonprogrammers to build complicated steam-plant diagrams by combining primitive icons. In addition, the editor allows system builders to define their own unique display icons, if necessary. Future research will be in the area of the knowledge representations necessary to represent steam-plant-operating procedures in terms of their primitive components.

STEAMER has been used as a training aid in the Great Lakes Training Center and on Coronado Island. Preliminary results are quite encouraging; they indicate that personnel respond very positively to the interactive system and can learn the same material in a shorter period of time than with traditional instruction methods.

AUTOMATED NATURAL LANGUAGE UNDERSTANDING OF MILITARY MESSAGES

Enormous numbers of operational reports are generated and transmitted as part of daily military message traffic. These reports range from messages about employment schedules, equipment failures, and weather to messages concerning force deployment and readiness, tactics, and intelligence and are used at various levels throughout military command hierarchies. Typically operational reports obey strict formatting conventions but also contain important English narrative descriptions. Although current message-handling systems process the formatted sections by entering the data into appropriate fields in the system's database, message narrative is usually treated as adjunct information and stored in the form of remarks or comments. However, many tasks, such as message dissemination and the recognition of message trends, require information in message narrative and consequently must rely on personnel performing keyword searches and visually scanning individual message narratives, a laborious and time-consuming process.

Automation of these and other tasks in future military message systems will require computer interpretation of message content. One effort toward this end is an experimental system being developed at the Naval Research Laboratory that employs techniques of computational linguistics and AI to automatically extract information from Navy messages (Marsh and co-workers, 1983; Marsh, 1983). Initially the system is addressing a class of operational reports about shipboard equipment failure called casualty reports (CASREPs). CASREPs are an important message type, providing current information about ship readiness and equipment performance. They inform operational and support personnel about equipment casualties that could affect a unit's ability to perform its mission, as well as reporting the unit's need for technical assistance and for parts to correct the failure. The experimental system uses CASREP message content to assign a distribution list to each message and to generate a summary of the equipment failure (Froscher and co-workers, 1983).

To process such messages, the system must provide a

representation of message content that can be readily accessed and used for applications such as dissemination and summarization. This is accomplished by a message interpreter that initially decomposes the message to determine its overall structure and then performs narrative analysis to generate the structures that enable automated interpretation of English narrative. Message decomposition of reports like CASREPs is straightforward because the overall structure is known and report formatting conventions can be used to extract *pro forma* (strictly formatted) information. However, narrative analysis (the extraction and representation of the particular types of information contained in the narrative portions of a message) is more difficult, principally because the structure of the information, and often much of the information itself, is implicit in the narrative. The experimental system uses an approach to narrative analysis called information formatting, originally developed at New York University (Sager, 1981). This technique employs an explicit grammar of English and a classification of the semantic relationships within a suitably restricted domain to derive a tabular representation of the information in a message narrative. Thus in simplest terms, an information format is a large table, with one column for each type of information that can occur in a class of texts and one row for each sentence or clause in the text (see NATURAL LANGUAGE UNDERSTANDING).

The implementation of this approach first requires the development of the information format structure through the identification of the classes of objects and the relationships among them discussed in message texts within the domain. For CASREPs about electronic equipment, the objects include the equipment items and their component parts. The signals and data operated on by the equipment, the people and organizations who operate and maintain the equipment, and the documents involved in the maintenance process. These various classes of objects and their semantic relationships then have their own "slots" in the data structure, so that information can be much more readily retrieved than from the original narrative.

The transformation of the narrative portion of each message into a series of tabular format entries involves three stages of automated processing: parsing (qv), syntactic regularization, and mapping into the information format. Parsing essentially determines sentence structure and resolves lexical ambiguity, such as usage of the word *if* both as a noun abbreviation for *intermediate frequency* (a frequent occurrence in CASREPs) and as the more familiar subordinating conjunction. In the second stage the parse trees are syntactically regularized by a series of transformations to simplify the subsequent mapping into the information format. For example, passive assertions are transformed into simple active assertions, some elements missing from sentence fragments are filled in, and a subject—verb—object word order is created for sentences not having one. The third stage of processing moves the phrases in the syntactically regularized parse trees into the information format. The mapping process is controlled in large part by the sublanguage (semantic) word classes associated with each word. These classes, along with syntactic information about the word, are recorded in each word's dictionary entry, which is tailored to the domain.

CASREP information formatting is applied to two task areas: dissemination and summary generation. In each area the experimental system contains a knowledge base organized as a production system; productions operate on an initial database of working memory elements that includes data from both the *pro forma* set and the information formats. Some production rules reflect an understanding of the subject matter of the equipment failure reports, and others are based on general principles of dissemination and summarization. Taken together, the productions address such matters as malfunction, causality, investigative action, uncertainty, and level of generality. Although production rules for the dissemination system act on data extracted from both the formatted portion (eg, identity of malfunctioning equipment) and the narrative portion (eg, in requests for assistance, the type of assistance and from whom) of the message, rules for summarization deal only with message narrative (Granger, 1984). Typically, a summary consists of a single clause extracted from a section of text, thereby reducing significantly the material that must be read for such critical uses as detecting patterns of failures for particular types of equipment. Currently each summary is generated manually by reading the entire message and then selecting an appropriate clause from the "remarks" narrative as the summary. Using manual summarization expertise as the basis for its production rules, the experimental summarization system involves three steps: inference, scoring the information format entries for their importance, and finally the selection of the appropriate (highest rated) format entry as the summary. For example, words like *inhibit, impair,* and *prevent* trigger inference rules such that if part 1 impairs part 2, it can be inferred that part 1 causes part 2 to be bad, and it can also be inferred that part 1 is bad. In scoring the various format entries, the fact that *bad* is a member of the class of words signifying malfunction will cause entries associated with part 1 and with part 2 to be promoted in importance. In addition, the entry associated with part 1 will score even higher because it is a cause rather than an effect.

In an early comparison of computer-generated summaries with those generated manually on a modest set of CASREPs, the summaries agreed on approximately 83% of the messages tested. Sometimes the summarization system generated two summary lines (as a result of a tie between two format entries), although the manual summary consisted of only one sentence. Nonetheless, one of the two computer-generated summary lines was also the manual summary. On the other hand, the most significant discrepancies (except where the crucial status word in the narrative was not in the production rule system) involved the system actually selecting more specific causal information than was indicated in the manual summary.

Issues yet to be addressed in experimental system development include refinement of the format, intersentential processing, and robustness. A future option for such message systems is to perform message analysis at the point of transmission so that the message sender can be aided by the system in resolving ambiguities and avoiding crucial omissions (Marsh and co-workers, 1984). This could also result in an improvement of message system capabilities by eliminating messages of little or no information content and upgrading overall message quality.

BIBLIOGRAPHY

A. J. Baciocco, "Artificial Intelligence and C³I," *Signal* 36(1), 24–28 (Sept. 1981).

R. P. Bonasso, Jr., *ANALYST: An Expert System for Processing Sensor Returns*, MTP-83W 00002, MITRE Corp., McLean, Va., 1984.

R. R. Cantone, F. J. Pipitone, W. B. Lander, and M. P. Marrone, "Model-Based Probabilistic Reasoning for Electronics Troubleshooting," in *Proceedings of the Eighth IJCAI*, Karlsruhe, FRG, Morgan-Kaufmann, San Mateo, Calif., 1983, pp. 207–211.

K. E. Case and H. C. Thibault, *A Heuristic Allocation Algorithm with Extensions for Conventional Weapons for the Marine Integrated Fire and Air Support System*, School of Industrial Engineering and Management, Oklahoma State University, Stillwater, Sept. 1977.

G. Courand, C. O'Reilly, and J. Payne, *OCA (Offensive Counter Air) Mission Planning*, AI/DS-TR-3050-1. Advanced Information and Decision Systems, Mountain View, Calif., 1983.

DARPA, *New Generation Computing Technology: A Strategic Plan for Its Development and Application to Critical Problems in Defense*, DARPA, Arlington, Va., Oct. 28, 1983.

K. DeJong, "Applying AI to the Diagnosis of Complex System Failures," in *Proceedings of the Conference on AI*, Oakland University, Rochester, Mich., Apr. 1984.

C. Engelman, J. K. Millen, and E. A. Scarl, "KNOBS: An Integrated AI Interactive Planning Architecture," in *Computers in Aerospace IV Conference*, American Institute of Aeronautics and Astronautics, Hartford, Conn., Oct. 1983.

L. D. Erman, F. Hayes-Roth, V. D. Lesser, and R. D. Reddy, "The HEARSAY-II Speech Understanding System: Integrating Knowledge to Resolve Uncertainty," *ACM Comput. Surv.* 12(2), 213–253 (1980).

L. D. Erman, P. E. London, and S. F. Ficas, "The Design and Example Use of HEARSAY-III," in *Proceedings of the Seventh IJCAI*, Vancouver, B.C., Morgan-Kaufmann, San Mateo, Calif., 1981, pp. 409–415.

J. Froscher, R. Grishman, J. Bachenko, and E. Marsh," A Linguistically Motivated Approach to Automated Analysis of Military Messages," in *Proceeding of the 1983 Conference on AI*, Oakland University, Rochester, Mich., 1983.

R. Granger, "The NOMAD System: Expectation-Based Detection and Correction of Errors During Understanding of Syntactically and Semantically Ill-Formed Text," *Am. J. Comput. Ling.* 9(3–4), 188–196 (1984).

K. A. Haller, J. D. Zbytniewski, K. Anderson, and L. Bagnall, *Smart BIT*, Rome Air Development Center Report RADC-TR-85, June 1985.

J. D. Hollan, E. L. Hutchins, and L. Weitzman, "STEAMER: An Interactive Inspectable Simulation-Based Training System" *AI Mag.* 5(2), 15–27 (Summer 1984).

J. J. King, *Artificial Intelligence Techniques for Device Troubleshooting*, Computer Science Laboratory Technical Note Series CSL-82-9 (CRC-TR-82-004), Hewlett Packard, Palo Alto, Calif., 1982.

P. J. Klass, "DARPA Envisions New Generation of Machine Intelligence Technology," *Aviat. Wk. Space Technol.* 122(16), 46–84 (Apr. 22, 1985).

H. Lahore, *Artificial Intelligence Applications to Testability*, Rome Air Development Center Report RADC-TR-84-203, Oct. 1984.

E. Marsh, "Utilizing Domain-Specific Information for Processing Compact Text," in *Proceedings of the Conference on Applied Natural Language Processing*, 1983, pp. 99–1030.

E. Marsh, J. Froscher, R. Brishman, H. Hamburger, and J. Bachenko, *Automatic Processing of Navy Message Narrative*, NRL Report, Naval Research Laboratory, Washington, D.C., 1985.

E. Marsh, H. Hamburger, and R. Grishman, "A Production Rule System for Message Summarization," in *Proceedings of the Fourth National Conference on Artificial Intelligence*, Austin, Tex., AAAI, Menlo Park, Calif., 1984, pp. 243–246.

B. P. McCune and R. J. Drazovich, "Radar with Sight and Knowledge," *Def. Electron.* (Aug. 1983).

R. S. Michalski, J. G. Carbonell, and T. M. Mitchell, eds., *Machine Learning: An Artificial Intelligence Approach*, Tioga, Palo Alto, Calif., 1983.

M. Minsky, *A Framework for Representing Knowledge*, AI Memo 306, MIT AI Laboratory, Cambridge, Mass., 1974.

H. P. Nii and E. A. Feigenbaum, "Rule-Based Understanding of Signals," in D. A. Waterman and F. Hayes-Roth, eds., *Pattern-Directed Inference Systems*, Academic Press, Inc., New York, 1978, pp. 483–501.

H. P. Nii, E. A. Feigenbaum, J. J. Anton, and A. J. Rockmore, "Signal-to-Signal Transformation: HASP/SIAP Case Study," *AI Mag.* 3(1), 23–35 (Spring 1982).

F. Pipitone, "An Expert System for Electronics Troubleshooting Based on Function and Connectivity," in *IEEE First Conference on AI Applications*, Denver, Colo., Dec. 1984, pp. 133–138.

F. Pipitone, "The FIS Electronics Troubleshooting System," *Computer* 19(7), 68–76 (July 1986).

N. Sager, "Natural Language Information Formatting: The Automatic Conversion of Texts to a Structured Data Base," in M. C. Yovits, ed., *Advances in Computers*, Vol. 17, Academic Press, Inc., New York, pp. 89–162.

N. Sager, *Natural Language Information Processing*, Addison-Wesley Publishing Co., Inc., Reading, Mass., 1981.

W. R. Simpson and H. S. Balaban, "The ARINC Research System Testability and Maintenance Program (STAMP)," in *Proceedings of the 1982 IEEE Autoestcon Conference*, Dayton, Ohio, Oct. 1982.

J. R. Slagle, M. W. Gaynor and E. J. Halpern, "An Intelligent Control Strategy for Computer Consultation," *IEEE Trans. Patt. Anal. Mach. Intell.* 6, 129–136 (Mar. 1984).

J. R. Slagle, E. J. Halpern, H. Hamburger, and R. R. Cantone, "A Decision Support System for Fire Support Command and Control," in *IEEE Trends and Applications Conference Proceedings*, Gaithersburg, Md., May 1983, pp. 68–75.

R. G. Smith, "Report on the 1984 Distributed AI Workshop," *AI Mag.* 6(3), 234–243 (Fall 1985).

C. V. Srinivasan, *The Use of CK-LOG Formalism for Knowledge Representation and Problem Solving in OPPLAN-CONSULTANT: An Expert System for Naval Operational Planning*, NRL Report, Naval Research Laboratory, Washington, D.C., 1985.

General References

Discussion and documentation of military applications of AI are appearing in an increasing variety of sources. Defense-oriented popular publications such as *Signal, Defense Electronics,* and *Aviation Week and Space Technology* provide general articles on current and proposed military AI applications. Papers and reports from defense research laboratories, industrial defense contractors, and defense-funded university research groups remain the primary source for the more technical descriptions of these applications. However, as service-sponsored conferences and symposia on AI become more numerous, their published proceedings, along with those from the well-known national and international AI conferences, are providing additional valuable references for military applications. Examples follow.

Proceedings of the Army Conference on Application of Artificial Intelligence to Battlefield Information Management, Battelle Columbus Laboratories, Washington, D.C., Apr. 20–22, 1983.

R. Shumaker and J. E. Franklin, "Artificial Intelligence in Military Applications," *Signal Mag.* **40**(10), 29 (June 1986).

AI Magazine, American Association for Artificial Intelligence (AAAI), Menlo Park, Calif. [published quarterly].

Proceedings of the International Joint Conferences on Artificial Intelligence (IJCAI) [held biennially (odd-numbered years) since 1969, every $4 \times k + 1$ year in the United States].

Proceedings of the National Conferences on Artificial Intelligence, AAAI, Menlo Park, Calif. [since 1980, every $4 \times k$, $4 \times k + 2$, and $4 \times k + 3$ years].

J. Franklin
Planning Research Corp.

Laura Davis
Randall Shumaker
Paul Morawski
Naval Research Laboratory

MINIMAX PROCEDURE

At least two other entries in this volume (see Game-playing and Alpha-beta Pruning) discuss the idea of minimax search as it is commonly used and understood in AI. This article places the idea of minimax in context (as a very convenient simplification useful in special cases) with the rest of the field of game theory (including the way it is used in economics) (von Neumann and Morgenstern, 1947). To do this, it is necessary to go a little deeper into the discussion of the idea of a game.

GENERAL MODEL OF GAMES

Although the use of game trees (qv) to model games is almost universal in AI, the game tree cannot reflect all the aspects of games in general. Consider the game of bridge. Each team consists of two players (since their interests are the same), but since the two players in the team do not have the same information (each player knows what cards he or she holds but does not know what cards the partner holds), the game tree does not quite tell the whole story of the game. There is still a game tree, of course. The deal (a chance move) starts the game. The player on the move knows that the deal is one of the $39!/13!13!13!)$ possible ones that give the hand that is held.

What the bridge player decides to do is not based on the game state, as in chess, but on imperfect knowledge of the game state. Imperfect knowledge does not come only from chance moves, as in bridge. In Kriegspiel, chess is played on two boards, one before each player. Neither player can see the positions of the other player's pieces, but in the event that either player makes a move that is illegal in the context of the opponent's position, the umpire informs him or her. So each player's knowledge of the opponent's pieces is imperfect.

Another phenomenon that makes Kriegspiel different from the kind of games normally encountered in AI is that the players do not play alternately. If players make illegal moves and are so informed, they can try again. The illegal moves, then, yield information and allow them to play again; thus, a player can make more than one move in sequence using the illegal moves as "probes."

Returning to bridge, a player's knowledge of the other players' hands increases during the bidding, after the dummy is laid down, and as the cards fall during the plays. The point is that in a general game, one decides on moves not on the basis of the state, but on the knowledge of being in one among a possible given set of states. The result of a player's move places him or her in one of a set of states. This set may be smaller than the set reachable from the original set. Extra information may be gained on the basis of what was learned during the move. An umpire may decide, on the basis of the rules of the game, what the player is supposed to know.

STRATEGIES AND PAYOFFS

In the games usually considered in AI, a strategy is a player's initial decision as to what moves would be made at which state. If the reader feels that the idea of a strategy is unrealistic (ie, that the player makes a decision about how to move only when he is on move), then consider a strategy as a game-playing program itself. It is important to note that, given the strategy of all players in the game, the outcome of the game is determined.

The concept of strategy can be used in the general case also, but with some modification. The strategy now determines a move on the basis not of the state, but of the knowledge of the player on move about the state. One may object that the move chosen by a player may not even be a valid move, given the player's imperfect knowledge, but this can be countered by saying that the very invalidity of the move is a piece of information a player can use to enhance his or her knowledge. With Kriegspiel, this point has already been made; however, for the mathematical ramification of the idea, see the rather complex set-theoretic discussion on which von Neumann and Morgenstern (1947) based these concepts.

One of the stipulations made by von Neumann and Morgenstern was that at the beginning of the game, the player on move knows that it is the beginning of the game. So his or her choice is made with complete information, and the result of his or her move is known to the umpire. If the first move is a chance move, at least there is a probability distribution known.

One can proceed by induction from here to show that once each player's strategy is known, including a probability distribution over all the chance moves, a probability distribution over all the leaves of the game tree is known. With the payoff to each player specified by the rules at each leaf, there is an expected payoff of each player known as a function of the n-tuple of strategies, one chosen by each player.

Given the rules of a game, one can encapsulate its essential structure into what is called a game in normal form. This is a game where players, instead of choosing a move when their turns arise, are asked at the beginning of the game what their strategy is, ie, what procedure they will use to choose a move, given any state of information that may arise in the game. Each player makes this choice without any knowledge of the strategies chosen by all the other players. On the basis of these choices, the payoff to each player is determined. That is, the game is now encapsulated into n tables, one for each player, of the payoff as a function of n variables (the strategies), of which each player can control only one.

The sizes of these tables are enormous (see GAME PLAYING). But for the present, ignore the practicality of this table and consider only what one would do with it if it were accessible.

SPECIALIZATIONS: ZERO-SUM TWO-PERSON GAMES

Game theory has been studied in economics mostly in terms of the normal-form games. The problem that is posed is the following. Given n different n-dimensional matrices, each of size $k_1 \times k_2 \times \cdots \times k_n$, the first player chooses an integer between 1 and k_1, the second player between 1 and k_2, etc. The payoff to each player is given in the corresponding cell of his or her matrix. How would a player, given this matrix, decide what choice to make?

The last word has certainly not been said with regard to this problem; it is not even clear what is meant by anybody's "best" choice. The reader can be given a whiff of what is involved from the well-known game Prisoner's Dilemma: Two men have robbed a bank and have been arrested on suspicion. Each has been given the option of confessing and bearing witness against his partner in return for a full pardon. If neither confesses, the evidence would not be sufficient to convict them of the entire crime, but it would be enough to send them to jail on lesser charges. If both confess, they are both convicted. If one of the men does not confess, he gets convicted if the other confesses. So, if the two courses of action to be chosen between are "confess" and "don't confess," the 2×2 payoff matrix for each man is shown below.

	Confess	Don't
Confess	30	0
Don't	30	10

In this matrix, the two rows refer to the action of one of the prisoners, whose payoff is seen here. Not confessing is a good way for both to get lesser charges. But if the other prisoner, using that strategy, does not confess, there is great advantage to confessing and getting the full pardon due a state witness to a major crime. However, that is not a good idea if the other person confesses on the same argument; then total conviction is certain.

Leaving aside the unsolved questions of game theory, return to the case where a few things are known or at least agreed upon. This is the case when there are two players and one's gain is always the other's loss, ie, in a zero-sum game. To discuss zero-sum games, the matrix above will be used again, but its interpretation changed. The payoff shown is once again that of the player whose choices are shown as the rows. The payoff of the player whose choices are shown as columns, however, has the negative of the numbers shown on the matrix.

Looking at the above matrix from that point of view, one notes that the opponent now has a vested interest in giving up as little as possible. So if the first row is chosen, the opponent's best move is Don't, yielding zero to the player. If the player's choice is Don't, the minimum he can have is 10. So his safest move is Don't since this choice gives him the greatest value of minimum to which he can be pushed by the opponent. Similarly, the opponent can lose 30 if he chooses Confess, but only 10 if he chooses Don't. So, he minimizes his maximum loss, playing Don't and losing 10.

Thus, if both sides move conservatively, they would both play Don't. This is a rather stable situation, different from the previous one, because, unlike the previous case, no cooperation is possible between the two players; one gains exactly what the other loses. This also is a special case: the maximum over the row minima is exactly the minimum over the column maxima, ie, the matrix has a *saddle point*.

In matrices without saddle points, the players (if they are to play more than one game) can play different strategies in different games. In this case, one gets a mixed strategy, given by the chosen probability distribution over the different strategies. It can be shown in this case that there is a saddle point over the mixed strategies, ie, that there are mixed strategies p and q of the two players such that the expected payoff over the two strategies satisfies:

payoff(p, q) = max over all p' of min over all q'
  of payoff(p', q') = min over all q'
    of max over all p' of payoff(p', q')

However, this is not needed for the kinds of games usually considered in AI, most of the time, wherein the strategy maps state to move rather than knowledge to move. It can be shown that in these cases the minimax value as calculated over the entire game graph is the same as the minimax value over all strategies, and this value is indeed the saddle point of the normal-form matrix. The strategy for which this saddle point is obtained over the matrix maps each state into exactly the same move dictated by the minimax search of the game tree.

It may be worthwhile to illustrate the point by considering the three-step game shown in Figure 1. Here a, the first move, is the maximizing player's move (ie, the move of the player whose payoff is given at the leaves of the game tree); A and B are the opponent's moves (the normal "alternating move"); and $b, c, d,$ and e are the maximizer's moves again, leading to the leaves whose payoffs are as shown. The minimizer's strategies are specified by whether the left or the right branch is taken at the points A and B. A strategy where the player would go left at A

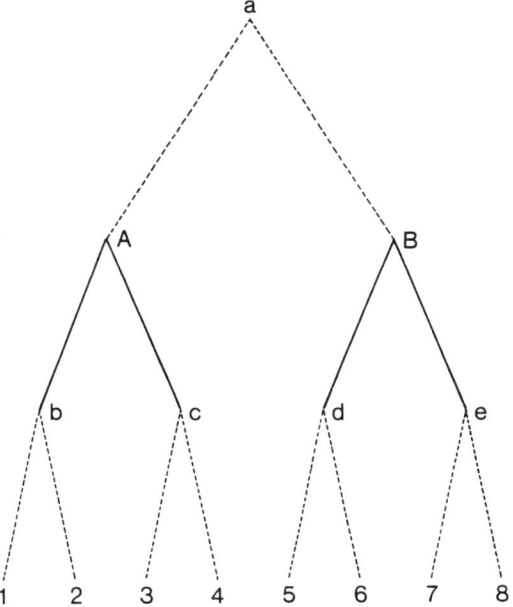

Figure 1. A three-step game.

Table 1. Strategies

i	Minimizer			
	LL	LR	RL	RR
Maximizer				
LLLLL	1	1	3	3
LLLLR	1	1	3	3
LLLRL	1	1	3	3
LLLRR	1	1	3	3
LLRLL	1	1	4	4
LLRLR	1	1	4	4
LLRRL	1	1	4	4
LLRRR	1	1	4	4
LRLLL	2	2	3	3
LRLLR	2	2	3	3
LRLRL	2	2	3	3
LRLRR	2	2	3	3
LRRLL	2	2	4	4
LRRLR	2	2	4	4
LRRRL	2	2	4	4
LRRRR	2	2	4	4
RLLLL	5	7	5	7
RLLLR	5	8	5	8
RLLRL	6	7	6	7
RLLRR	6	8	6	8
RLRLL	5	7	5	7
RLRLR	5	8	5	8
RLRRL	6	7	6	7
RLRRR	6	8	6	8
RRLLL	5	7	5	7
RRLLR	5	8	5	8
RRLRL	6	7	6	7
RRLRR	6	8	6	8
RRRLL	5	7	5	7
RRRLR	5	8	5	8
RRRRL	6	7	6	7
RRRRR	6	8	6	8

and right at B is to be denoted by LR. There are thus four possible strategies of the minimizing player. Similarly, the maximizer's strategies are given by the left and right choices made at the points a–e. There are 32 possible strategies, denoted by LLLLL to RRRRR.

It can be seen that if the maximizer chooses the strategy LLLLL and the minimizer chooses LL, the game will be at A after the first move, at b after the second move, and so end up at the leaf with value 1 after the third move following the strategy of choosing L at b. Similarly, the strategies LLLLL and RR would yield the value 3. Table 1 shows the 32 × 4 payoff matrix corresponding to the various strategy pairs. Notice that this matrix has various saddle points with value 6; they are at the intersections of the rows R--R-, with all choices at the nodes b, c, and e and of the columns LL and RL. These are exactly the values and the strategies that the extended-form minimax would yield also: The maximizer chooses the right branch at the first move. It is to the minimizer's advantage to take the left branch, forcing the game to the lower values, after which the maximizer obtains the larger of the two payoffs by taking the right branch again. This latter analysis, well known in AI and discussed in GAME PLAYING, can be clarified as follows: the maximizer's value of the nodes b–e are 2, 4, 6, and 8, respectively. The minimizer's value at A, being the minimum of 2 and 4, is 2. Similarly, the minimizer's value at B is 6. So the maximizer's value at a, the larger of 2 and 6, is 6. So the maximizer in turn plays R to B, the minimizer answers with L to node d, and the maximizer gains 6 by playing R again.

An illustration of what the situation may be when the information is incomplete clarifies some of the ramifications of the von Neumann-Morgenstern formalism, a two-step game started by the minimizer, who has three choices called 1, 2, and 3. In answer, the maximizer can make one of two moves, called L and R. So there are six possible plays, 1L, 2L, 3L, 1R, 2R, and 3R. After the minimizer's choice, the game is restricted to the plays 1L and 1R if the minimizer plays 1 and to two other corresponding sets if she plays 2 or 3. However, the maximizer, in turn, may not be informed as to what the minimizer played. If 1 was played, the maximizer is told that. In the two other cases, the maximizer is not informed what the move was, and so can surmise from the fact that no information was given that either 2 or 3 was played. So, while the umpire would know that the game had been restricted to (say) 2L and 2R, the maximizer would only know that the game had been reduced to 2L, 2R, 3L, and 3R. After the maximizer's move, the game reduces to a leaf, which may be either 2L or 3L if the maximizer plays L, or 2R or 3R if he or she plays R. So if the minimizer does not play 1, the maximizer chooses his or her own move on incomplete knowledge, and after the move, the actual play is determined.

In this case, there are three strategies determining the minimizer's first move. The maximizer has four strategies, choosing L or R depending on his or her state of knowledge. If the values of the six plays above are 4, 5, −2, 10, 10, and −2, respectively. The payoff matrix for the maximizer is as given in Table 2. The columns indicate the minimizer's choice. The rows correspond to the maximizer's four choices. For example, the strategy LR corresponds to when the maximizer decides to play L in reply to

Table 2. Payoff Matrix for Maximizer

	1	2	3
LL	4	−2	10
LR	4	10	−2
RL	5	−2	10
RR	5	10	−2

1 and to play R otherwise. Notice that the matrix has no saddle point. The maximum of the row minima occur at each row as −2. The minimum of column maxima are in column 1, at the values 5. In a game with complete information, the minimax value would be 5.

As said earlier, most of the ideas described here are not of direct applicability to AI. They appear here merely to place the AI work in context with the rest of game theory. Certain ideas of game theory applicable to AI use minimax only indirectly (see, eg, Banerji, 1980). Certain limitations to minimax and suggest alternatives and improvements (see Nau, 1983; Baudet, 1978; and Stockman, 1979).

BIBLIOGRAPHY

R. B. Banerji, *Artificial Intelligence: A Theoretical Approach*, North-Holland, Amsterdam, 1980.

G. M. Baudet, "On the Branching Factor of the Alpha-Beta Pruning Algorithm," *Artif. Intell.* **10**, 173 (1978).

D. S. Nau, "Pathology on Game Trees Revisited, and an Alternative to Mini-Maxing," *Artif. Intell.* **21**, 222 (1983).

G. A. Stockman, "A Minmax Algorithm Better Than Alpha-Beta?" *Artif. Intell.* **12**, 179 (1979).

J. von Neumann and O. Morgenstern, *Theory of Games and Economic Behavior*, Princeton University Press, Princeton, N.J., 1947.

R. B. BANERJI
St. Joseph's College

The preparation of this paper was supported by the National Science Foundation under grant MCS-8217964 and forms a part of an ongoing research on Knowledge-Based Learning and Problem-Solving Heuristics.

MKRP

The Markgraf Karl Refutation Procedure (MKRP) is a general-purpose theorem-prover for order-sorted first-order logic that was developed over a time span of more than fifteen years. It accepts type specifications and arbitrary first-order formulas, simplifies them, and translates them into clauses. If possible, the problem is split into several independent subproblems. The clause part of the system uses an extension of Kowalski's connection graph procedure [see R. Kowalski, "A Proof Procedure Using Connection Graphs," *JACM* **22**(4), 424–436 (1975); N. Eisinger, *Completeness, Confluence, and Related Properties of Clause Graph Resolution*, dissertation, University of Kaiserslautern, 1988]. The clause set is represented as a graph, where various types of edges (links) stand for various relations between literals, such as resolvability or unifiability. These links provide the basis for resolution, factoring, subsumption, tautology detection, and similar operations. Equality reasoning is based on so called P-links (see K. H. Bläsius and J. H. Siekmann, *Equality Reasoning Based on Equality Graphs*, SEKi-90, FB Informatik, Univ. Kaiserslautern). The basic algorithm is a loop:

WHILE Empty Clause Not Found and Graph Not Collapsed:

1. Select a chain of resolution, factoring, or paramodulation links.
2. Derive the final (and some intermediate) clauses generated by the corresponding sequence of operations.
3. Insert these clauses into the graph and generate the links connecting the new clauses with the old graph using link inheritance.
4. Remove the links operated upon.
5. Perform any possible reduction on the graph.

From an artificial intelligence point of view, the first step is the crucial step, and there are various heuristics and domain-specific techniques for the selection of an appropriate chain of links, ranging from the valuation of the expected length and term depth of the derived clauses, over the detection of complex resolution, factoring, and subsumption sequences with the total effect to reduce the clause graph, up to the extraction of subgraphs corresponding to complicated unit resolution chains (see G. Antoniou and H. J. Ohlbach, "Terminator," *Proceedings of the 8th IJCAI*, Karlsruhe, 1983, pp. 916–919). These domain specific techniques constitute the main body of development of the system that distinguishes it from other current theorem-proving systems. It corroborates the claim that it is possible to build a deduction system augmented by appropriate heuristics and domain-specific knowledge such that it will display an active and goal directed behavior in its striving for a proof, rather than the passive combinatorial search through very large search spaces, which was the characteristic behavior of the deduction systems of the past. Consequently, it will not generate a search space of many thousands of irrelevant clauses, but will find a proof with comparatively few redundant derivation steps.

To some extent, the data-driven mechanisms used in steps one and five have the same effect: they override the traditional theorem-proving strategies and, in combination, account for most of the system's strength. A number of mostly Boolean options is available to influence the algorithms; however, the system works largely automatically rather than interactively. The system was used to encode and prove a significant part of a textbook on automata theory. In addition, Smullian's logic puzzle book *What is the Name of This Book* was coded and proven by a group of students.

The MKRP theorem-prover consists of more than 3

MBytes of compiled code and is one of the largest software developments in the history of the field. It is currently running on the Siemens 7500 series, IBM computers, and Symbolics LISP Machines. The system has been used as the basis to develop the inference machine of the induction theorem prover at Karlsruhe (see S. Biundo and coworkers, "The Karlsruhe Induction Theorem Proving System," *Proceedings of CADE-8,* Springer-Verlag, Oxford, 1986) and, *vice-versa,* the induction prover can be called by the MKRP-System. A general description of the system is given in H. J. Ohlbach and J. H. Siekmann, *The Markgraf Karl Refutation Procedure,* Alan Robinson Festschrift, 1990. Recent extensions of the system are Unification Theory; Proof Transformation (qv); Mathematical Knowledge Representation (qv); and HADES (qv).

J. H. SIEKMANN
Universität Kaiserslautern

MOBILE ROBOTS. See ROBOTS, MOBILE.

MODAL LOGIC. See LOGIC, MODAL.

MOPS. See MEMORY ORGANIZATION PACKETS.

MORPHOLOGY

Any application using natural language needs to have mechanisms to process and interpret words. On the surface, words can be defined as a string of letters or symbols separated by blanks which combine to make phrases or sentences. However, both the definition of the word as well as the representation of underlying structure is a more complex matter. Morphology is the study of the structure and formation of words. It is one of the major subfields of linguistics along with syntax (sentential and phrasal structure), semantics (meaning), phonology (sound system), and pragmatics (usage). The basic unit of analysis for words is the *morpheme,* traditionally defined as the minimal unit of meaning. For example, the word *know* has one morpheme, and the word *knows* has two morphemes: *know* meaning "perceive, understand" and *-s* meaning "third person singular." Morphemes can be divided into two types: a free morpheme can be a word by itself, such as *know*; a bound morpheme, such as *-s*, needs to be attached to a free morpheme).

A further distinction can be made between the stem and the affix. For example, in the French verb *parler* (to speak), *parl-* is considered the stem of the word and *-er* the affix, indicating the infinitive verb form. The stem is the form to which an affix is added to build other words. In the case of *parler, parl-* is the stem for the verb conjugation paradigm, such as, *parl-ons* (we speak) or *parl-aient* (they were speaking). Affixes can be defined in terms of their position in the word. The affix *-er* which follows the stem is called a suffix, and *re-* which precedes the stem as in *re-parl-er* (to speak again) is a prefix. *Re-parl-er* is an example of a morphologically complex word, ie, a word formed of many morphemes, as opposed to *know,* which is a simple word. A morpheme added in the middle of another morpheme is an infix. For example, the language Bontoc from the Philippines has an infix *-um-* that transforms adjectives or nouns into verbs: *fikas* (strong) / *f-um-ikas* (be strong). The combination of two or more independent words into a single wordlike unit is called a compound (eg, greenhouse, blackball). Among other processes are *reduplication*, which consists of doubling a morpheme or part of a morpheme, such as in Indonesian, for example, where *rumahrumah* (houses) is the plural of *rumah* (house); paradigmatic *suppletion*, where one or more members of the inflectional or derivational paradigm of a stem appear to be an unrelated form, as in the irregular past tense "went" of the verb "go;" *shortening*, which is the clipping of an item, as in "exam" for "examination" or "dorm" for "dormitory;" *borrowing*, which consists of importing a foreign word, eg, *macho* from Spanish; *blending*, which is the combination of two morpheme parts, as in "brunch" from "breakfast" and "lunch;" the formation of an *acronym*, whereby a word is composed from a sequence of initial letters, some of which are written in uppercase ("BASIC" from beginner's all-purpose symbolic instruction code or "FORTRAN" from formula translating system), and some of which are not ("wysiwyg," meaning "what you see is what you get"); *coinage,* or *neologism,* which is the formation of new words in the language; and the adoption of words from proper nouns, eg, "lynch" coming from Judge Lynch.

Morphology varies across languages, and languages are often classified according to their morphological structure. In the traditional division of Bloomfield (1933), languages can be divided into four morphological types:

Isolating languages, which are generally made of sequences of primarily free morphemes. In Mandarin Chinese, there is no marked morpheme for specifying categories such as tense and plurality. Therefore, the free morphemes can form an ambiguous sentence. For example (Sproat, 1991), *gǒu bú ài chī qīngcài* literally means "dog not like eat vegetable" and can have at least four different translations:

"the dog didn't like to eat vegetables"
"the dogs don't like to eat vegetables"
"the dogs didn't like to eat vegetables"
"dogs don't like to eat vegetables"

Agglutinative languages, in which bound forms follow one another. In Swahili each bound inflectional morpheme carries a specified and isolatable meaning. Swahili verb stems take prefixes to indicate the person (first, second, or third) of the subject of the verb and to indicate also the tense of the verb:

ni-na-soma	I-present-read: I am reading
u-na-soma	you-present-read: you are reading
ni-li-soma	I past-read: I was reading
u-li-soma	you-past-read: you were reading
ni-ta-soma	I-future-read: I will read
u-ta-soma	you-future-read: you will read

Polysynthetic languages, in which bound morphemes are attached to each other as well. However, while in agglutinating languages the bound forms are merely concatenated, the bound forms in polysynthetic languages are merged to form words (Sadock, 1985). Highly complex words can be formed by combining several stems and affixes into a single word. Sora, a tribal language spoken in India, allows the incorporation of objects (subjects, instruments, etc) into verbs:

anim ɲamyɔten

anim ɲam -yɔ -te -n

he catch fish non-past do

"he is fish-catching or he is catching fish"

Inflecting languages or fusional languages which show a merging of semantically distinct features either in a single bound form or in closely united bound forms. For example, Latin inflectional suffixes indicate information about the mood (indicative, imperative, subjunctive), the tense (present, past), the voice (active or passive), and the person of a verb. In the verb *amo,* "I love," the inflection *-o* carries the information that the verb is first person singular present active indicative.

Given the amount of information that is contained within the morphological structure of words, a system which is capable of retrieving or generating this information serves a valuable function in natural language processing.

MORPHOLOGICAL PROCESSES

Morphological processes described here are derivation, inflection, combination (combining forms), cliticization, and compounding. Evidence for the distinctions is found in phonological, syntactic, and semantic properties. In general, affixes are ordered in their attachment to bases, with derivational affixes attaching closest, followed by combining forms, inflectional affixes, and then clitics. Morphologically complex or simple words then themselves combine into compound words.

Derivation

Derivational affixation typically consists of a base, and an affix which might change the category of the word, add semantic information, and/or change the phonology of the base. In English there are two types of derivational affixes, non-neutral (Class One) and neutral (Class Two) (Selkirk, 1982; Kiparsky, 1982; Siegel, 1974). The distinction is based on distributional and phonological properties described below (Chomsky and Halle, 1968); typical examples of noun-forming suffixes are given in Table 1. Similar tables could be constructed for suffixes forming verbs and adjectives, and for prefixes for nouns, verbs, and adjectives.

The criteria for distinguishing types of derivational affixes in English are primarily phonological. The most salient property of Class I affixes is that they usually alter the

Table 1. Suffixes That Form Nouns.

	Base	Affix	Example
Class I:			
	From nouns	-cy	(democrat, democracy)
	From verbs	-ation	(deprive, deprivation)
	From adjectives	-ity	(active, activity)
Class II:			
	From nouns	-hood	(adult, adulthood)
	From verbs	-al	(approve, approval)
	From adjectives	-ness	(happy, happiness)

stress pattern and phonology of the base; hence they are stress sensitive, or non-neutral. For example, in Table 1, the base word *active* has the main stress on the first syllable (*ác-tive*), whereas the form affixed with *-ity* has the main stress on the second syllable (*ac-tív-ity*). The pronunciation of the vowel /i/ in the second syllable changes with this emphasis. Changes in vowel quality associated with stress changes can be seen also in *deprive, deprivation* where the base *deprive* has stress on the second syllable *-príve,* but when the stress moves to the suffix *-átion,* the final vowel of the base in *deprivation* is reduced. In contrast, Class II or neutral affixes typically leave the stress (and usually the vowels) in the base word unaffected. Compare *ác-tive, ac-tív-ity* (Class I), and *ác-tiveness* (Class II). Some affixes belong to both classes. The suffix *-ment* (forming nouns from verbs) is sometimes a neutral and sometimes a non-neutral suffix; the suffix *-able* (forming verbs from adjectives) is also in the two classes. Derivational affixes typically require the base to be of a specific grammatical category. For example, the suffix *-hood* shown in Table 1 attaching to nouns to make an abstract noun can also attach to adjectives to form nouns as in *false, falsehood;* the suffix *-cy,* which in Table 1 requires a noun as a base can also attach to adjective bases to form nouns as in *normal, normalcy.*

Semantic aspects of derivational affixation are similarly complex. Many affixes are as ambiguous as their base words. For example, the suffix *-er,* used to nominalize a verb, has a multitude of uses (Rappaport, 1983) as shown in Table 2. Other suffixes found in nominalized forms are *-tion/-sion, -ation, -ment, -al,* and *-cy,* as in, for example, *calibrate/calibration, extend/extension, develop/development, arrive/arrival,* and *conspire/conspiracy.* In language analysis, the interpretation of derived nominals can be difficult since the underlying meaning of a nominal is not always transparent. For example, the phrase *Paul's examination* can mean that Paul did the examining as in "Paul's examination of the patient," or it could mean that someone examined Paul, as in "Paul's examination by the doctor." A morphological analyzer and generator might well be able to give the internal syntax of the derived word (eg, *examination* comes from *examine,* plus *-ation,* or in reverse *examine* plus *-ation* gives *examination*), but semantic characterization is far more complex. Sometimes

Table 2. Nominalizations With -er

Noun	Definition
Singer	One who sings (usually a profession)
Diner	One who is dining (not usually a profession)
Diner	A place to dine
Receiver	Thing used to receive (as in telephone receiver)
Receiver	A position in football
Cooker	Food for cooking (as in these apples are cookers)
Cooker	The device used for cooking (American 'stove')
Geographer	A person who knows about geography
3-Wheeler	A car with the property of having three wheels
Racer	Animals trained for racing
Racer	Vehicle used for racing

also the structural analysis of a word can lead to ambiguities in processing; for example, a word like *undoable* can be analyzed either as ([un-do]-able) or (un-[do-able]); the word *really* can be analyzed as ([real]-ly), the most frequent occurrence, or ([re-]ally).

Semantic ambiguities such as these add to the already difficult problem of ambiguity resolution in the automatic analysis of texts. For this reason, some system-builders chose to perform only inflectional but no derivational morphological analysis at all. However, this is a short-sighted approach since language is highly productive, so affixes such as these are used in creating new words or coinages. For example, words like *artificialization, acceptation, appleness, cherry-redness, thereness* (all attested forms occurring in a corpus) are not likely to be found in a dictionary but they are easy to understand, and they sound natural. Further, since some suffixes can attach freely to proper names (for example, *Reaganize*) it would be impossible to list all possible words.

Semi-Affixes and Combining Forms

Semi-affixes are often overlooked in the linguistics literature, but they are of particular importance in natural language analysis (Wolff, 1984). Semi-affixes are bound forms which retain word-like character. Some of them are only used as suffixes though their word character is still recognizable. Examples of suffixes are *-like* (*birdlike*) and *-worthy* (*noteworthy*). Some prefixes are *counter-* (*counterintuitive*), and *anti-* (*anti-nationalist*). What is important about words with semi-affixes is that they tend to be highly productive and usually semantically compositional (as are Class II affixes) but they also often occur optionally with hyphenation. To illustrate, observe that a word such as *perform-ance* is incorrect if hyphenated whereas *counter-intuitive* is not. Rules of hyphenation are one area of text processing that is tricky in languages like English and German. An understanding of semi-affixes helps in identifying optional and likely hyphenation spots when preprocessing text for analysis.

Combining forms are even more word-like than semi-affixes. They are especially common in technical and medical literature, for example, *oto-* as in *oto-laryngology*, or *gastro-* as in *gastro-enteritis* (Wolff, 1985). Like combining forms, they are often optionally hyphenated, and are highly productive although word formation is constrained by strict ordering of combined forms. What is peculiar about combining forms is that it is possible to find a word consisting of two bound combining forms (such as *francophile*). This is unlike other word formation processes which require at least one free form.

Inflection

The most regular and productive morphological process across languages is inflection (Matthews, 1972). Unlike derivation, which is characterized by numerous subregularities and idiosyncrasies, inflection is more predictable, notwithstanding, of course, irregular paradigms. Even if a machine-readable dictionary is used to support an application, inflectional variants are rarely listed, whereas derivational forms might be. Therefore, the necessity of implementing an inflectional analyzer or generator is essential even in the most basic of applications. Inflectional processes, as opposed to most derivational processes, does not change the grammatical category of the lexical item. Inflection alters the form of the word in number, gender, mood, tense, aspect, person, and case. In most languages, words in a sentence have to agree with one another (eg, a feminine noun in French requires a feminine adjective; a singular noun in English requires a singular verb); therefore, inflection is dependent on syntactic context whereas derivation is not. To take a simple example of noun inflection, the affix *-s* marks the regular plural subclass of English nouns, such as *table–table-s* or *car–car-s*. Other plural forms are applied to smaller categories of nouns, as in *child–child-ren, wolf–wol-ves, wife–wi-ves, watch–watch-es, person–people, foot–feet*. In the above examples, the affix *-ren* marks the plural of *child;* the affix *-es* marks the plural of *wolf* through the transformation of the voiced fricative /f/ into the voiceless fricative /v/. For these cases, a rule to generate the plural from nouns ending in *-f* would look like: -f (n. sg.) → -v/_es (n. pl.); that is, a word-final *f* in a singular noun becomes a *v* in the context of the plural inflection *es*. For another category of words such as the plural noun *people*, the singular is not obvious; one could argue for *person* to be the corresponding singular form, or one could argue that there is no singular at all. The noun *foot* has an irregular suppletive plural *feet* (irregular by synchronic standards).

In many languages, nouns and adjectives vary according to number, gender, and case. In French, the feminine form of nouns results from adding the affix *-e*, as in *chien, chienne* "dog (masculine, singular)", "dog (feminine, singular)"; *petit, petite* "small (masculine, singular)", "small (feminine, singular)". The gender and number changes are often accompanied by morpho-phonological changes, such as seen in the vowel of the final syllable in *boulanger, boulangère* "baker (masculine, singular)", "baker (feminine, singular)". The same words in a case language such as Russian or Latin have three different genders for the adjectives (feminine, masculine, and neutral) and six different cases, as in Russian: nominative, accusative, genitive, dative, instrumental, and locative.

The English verb system is relatively simple. There are only three forms: *-s* for the third person present singular,

Table 3. Russian Word Inflection

"Natasha saw the red car in the street."

Words:	Nataša	vide-l-a	krasn-uju	mašin-u	na	ulič-e
Translation:	Natasha	saw	red	car	in	street
Inflection:	subject	-l-a	-uju	-u		-e
Translation:	3rd pers sg	3rd pers sg	acc fem sg	acc fem sg		loc fem sg

-ed for the regular past and past participle, and *-ing* for the present continuous, eg, *tap, taps, tapping, tapped*. Regular spelling and sound changes accompany inflectional affixation. Other verbs such as *run* and *speak* have irregular past tenses and belong to a closed class. Thus, it is tempting to consider listing English inflectional variants rather than deriving them by rules. However, in Romance languages where the number of moods and tenses is higher (five moods and over eight simple tenses), the inflectional paradigm of a verb has many more forms, the total averaging around forty-eight. Finnish boasts over 12,000 verb inflections. The most common cases of inflectional, verb morphology are subject-verb agreement, as in the examples above, in which gender and number inflection depends on the nature of the subject, ie, whether it is singular or plural, masculine or feminine. An example of verb-object agreement would be in French: *la lettre que j'ai écrite* "the letter that I wrote," where the past participle *écrite* "wrote," agrees with the relative pronoun *que* "that," which inherits the number-gender of *lettre* "letter," ie, feminine singular.

For example, in the Russian sentence shown in Table 3, the ending of each word varies and agrees one with another. In this example, the first verbal inflection *-l-* indicates past tense, the *-a* being the marker for 3rd person singular feminine to agree with the subject *Nataša*. The suffix *-uju* on the adjective *krasn-* "red" is an accusative feminine singular marker for agreement with the feminine singular noun *mašin-u* "car", also inflected for the accusative since it is the verb object. Finally, the noun base *ulič-* (street) is inflected with a locative marker which is required by the locative preposition *na* "on" or "in". This example shows typical complexities of an inflected language in which several different agreement markers are required, such as number, case, gender.

Cliticization

Clitics, like semi-affixes, can be defined as elements that behave both like affixes and words (Klavans, 1985). However, they differ in that semi-affixes are truly part of word formation. The occurrence and attachment of semi-affixes are a result of lexical operations. In contrast, clitics occur in a syntactic structure, and strictly speaking their attachment to words is not a result of word formation rules. Clitics are, for the most part, unstressable and phonologically bound, producing a complex word from a free word and clitic combination. Semi-affixes are lexically bound morphemes like regular affixes.

The three positional types of clitic are *proclitic* (attaches to the left of the word, like a prefix), *enclitic* (attaches to the right of the word, like a suffix), and *endoclitic* (occurs inside the word, like an infix). Structurally, clitics fall into three major types: (1) second position, (2) lexical category associated (usually a verb), and (3) constituent associated. The genitive marker *'s* in English is an example of the third type of clitic that attaches to a specific constituent, regardless of where that constituent occurs in the sentence. In *my sister's pen* or *the woman I talked to's daughter* the syntactic and semantic scope of *'s* is over the entire noun phrase; however, the phonological attachment occurs between whatever word is last in the noun phrase and the possessive marker. Across languages, the most common clitic type is second position clitic. Enclitic particles in a number of Indo-European languages occur in word or phrase second position, but this tendency has been observed in languages as unrelated as Classical Greek, Finnish, many Australian Languages, Pashto, Paiute, and Czech. For example, from Finnish:

Example	:	*Minä=kö syön jäätelöä*
Word Translation:	:	I = ? eat ice cream
Meaning	:	It is *me* who is eating ice cream.
Translation	:	Am *I* eating ice cream?

Example	:	*Jäätelöä=kö minä syön*
Word Translation:	:	ice cream = ? eat
Meaning	:	Is it *ice cream* that I am eating?
Translation	:	Am I eating *ice cream*?

In these examples, the enclitic =*kö* follows the first word, indicating a question (the symbol "=" used to indicate the clitic). The question clitic only occurs in the second position allowing any major constituent in the sentence to be fronted as the focus of the question. In a neutral yes–no question, the clitic is preceded by the inflected verb. Many languages permit clitics to attach after the first word or phrase (even at the end of a sentence) in which case the scope of the clitic is over the chosen constituent. Some require the clitic to occur after the first word only. In all cases, the lexical category of the host word (ie, the word that the clitic attaches to phonologically) does not matter. In this way, cliticization differs from affixation, since affixes usually require that the base be of a specified category (eg, a noun, verb, adjective).

The next type of clitic occurs with a member of a given word class, more like affixes. Typical cases are verbal clitics in Romance languages. For example, in Spanish:

- *Ella me lo dijo ayer.*
  She me(DAT) it(ACC) told yesterday
  She told me it yesterday.

- *Dímelo mañana.*
  Tell(imperative) me(DAT) it(ACC) tomorrow
  Tell me it tomorrow.

In these two examples, the pronouns *me* (to me) and *lo* (it) occur in a specified order next to the verb. Even though in the first example the pronouns are separated orthographically from the verb, they are actually phonologically attached as proclitics to the tensed verb, as evidenced by stress assignment and some word-internal phonological rules. In the second example, the same clitics follow the verb as enclitics since the verb is in the imperative mood. Notice that the location of clitics in Spanish depends on verb tense; they are not inherently proclitics or enclitics. These clitics are more affix-like than the second position or constituent clitics since they place a categorial requirement on the word to which they attach. Thus, it is unclear whether they should be formally analyzed as affixes or clitics.

Finally, there are many languages that have optionally reduced clitic variants of words. For example, in the English sentences "Mozart is my favorite composer," and "Mozart's my favorite composer," the word *is* is part of the syntactic structure of the sentence, from the point of view of the syntax. However, it can be reduced phonologically and, like other clitics, will attach either as a proclitic or as an enclitic to whatever word is adjacent, regardless of the category of that word. The reduction of auxiliaries is not automatic with adjacency; the process is sensitive to deep syntactic structure in ways that are complex (eg, "*She is taller than I'm" is ungrammatical.).

The examples of auxiliary cliticization in English demonstrate a final characteristic of clitics that present particular problems for modularized natural language processing systems. Clitics are clearly words at the syntactic level, but they are more like affixes at the morphological and phonological level. Even more difficult, as seen in cases like English, the clitic might attach across a major constituent boundary. To give a concrete example, a morphological analyzer would have to know the basic syntactic structure of sentences like the following before knowing the correct analysis of the token *Clara's:*

Clara's decided on stopping. (Clara has . . . .)
Clara's in the kitchen. (Clara is . . . .)
Clara's mother operates efficiently. (The mother of Clara . . . .)

Since cliticization is at the syntax-phonology-morphology interface, it creates particular problems for parsers, especially since most parsing (qv) systems make a distinction between syntactic, morphological, and phonological modules.

Compounding

A compound can be defined as two or more forms which combine to build a new form (Levi, 1978). In English, compounds can be written as one word, hyphenated, or as two words, eg, *waste paper basket, waste-paper basket,* or *wastepaper basket*. Other languages have stricter rules. For example, French generally requires a hyphen but combination into one word is not permitted, as in, *un porte-clés* (key holder) but not **un porteclés* or **un porte clés*. Similarly, *un appuie-tête* (head-rest), but not **un appuie tête* or **un appuietête*. In some languages, compounds tend to be written as one word, eg, *schoenmaker* (shoemaker in Dutch), whereas in others, compound members are separated.

Compounds can be described in syntactic, intonational, and semantic terms. Structurally, compounding is a recursive binary operation. For example, the three-word noun compound *silver door knobs* consists of [*silver* [*door knobs*]]. In English, the right-hand noun *knobs* takes the plural inflectional ending; thus, compounds are said to be right-headed in English. Compounding can precede derivational affixation and vice versa, for example, in *activation vectors* the derived form *activation* is the left branch of the compound indicating that derivation preceded compounding, whereas in *boy scoutism* the derivational suffix *-ism* is attached to the entire compound, revealing that compounding preceded derivation. It is usually possible to recognize compounds by their stress pattern. In a non-compound, the right branch of a binary node is more prominent, whereas in a compound, the left branch is more pronounced. Compare *bláck sheep* (meaning an outcast) which is pronounced with stress on *black,* and *black shéep* (meaning a sheep which is black) pronounced with stress on the right branch *sheep*.

From the vantage point of category membership, most compounds in English consist of a series of nouns. Since many nouns are also verbs by zero-affixation, (ie cases where the same word converts to another part of speech as *bat, table*) the room for ambiguity in language analysis is enormous. Added to that is the problem of parsing. Given that the semantics of noun compounds is difficult to determine, and given that both left and right branching compounds occur, complexity increases exponentially as the number of nouns in a sequence increases. Few natural language processing systems have the ability to analyze noun compounds successfully, and it is not surprising that this is so because of the number of possible structures in addition to the number of possible semantic interpretations (Sproat, 1990; McDonald, 1981; Sparck Jones, 1983).

Compound verbs are rare in English, but they are widely attested in other languages. Most verb compounds in English are formed by back-formation, ie deriving a verb from a compound noun. For example, the noun–noun compound *air-conditioner* gave rise to the verb *to air condition* by removal of the *-er* suffix from the noun. The process of creating a new word by removal rather than by addition of a suffix is called back-formation. Since noun-noun compounding is far more common in English than noun–verb compounds, it should not be surprising that the majority of noun–verb compounding are a result of back-formation. Other verb compounds can be formed from verb–verb, adjective–verb, particle–verb combinations. Another common mechanism seen in verb compounds is a result of zero-affixation from an adjective–noun compound (eg *brown-bag*). Compound adjectives are less straightforward to define since they are less frequently right-headed. In fact, there are many cases where a compound functions as an adjective, but the two components are nouns (a *back-street abortionist*) or an entire phrase (*happy-go-lucky*).

The example of adjective compounds formed from nouns brings out another way to categorize compounds. In the traditional literature, compounds were analyzed with respect to their semantic compositionality. A compound is said to be *exocentric* (or *bahuvrihi* in Sanskrit), if the compound noun is semantically non-compositional. Conversely, a compound is endocentric if the compound form is a semantic hyponym of the head. Most compounds in English are endocentric. For example, a *pocket handkerchief* is a type of handkerchief, a *milktooth* is a kind of tooth, and a place which is *rat-infested* is infested. In both these cases, the meaning of the compound is related to the meaning of the right-branch (or head) noun. However, the exocentric compound *sabertooth,* is not a tooth (it is an animal) as evidenced by its plural which is *sabertooths* and not *saberteeth*. In addition are *appositional* (or *dvandva*) compounds in which the compound consists semantically of each component. For example, a *student-teacher* is both a student and a teacher.

The terms exocentric and endocentric are used ambiguously to refer to the semantic relation, in which case the test is to check if the compound is a hyponym of the head, or categorial, in which case the test for exo- and endocentricity is whether the compound is of the same part of speech. For example, *sit-in* is categorially an exocentric compound, since it is a compound noun composed of a verb and a preposition; the compound *arm chair* is endocentric categorially since it functions as a noun, and its head (chair) is a noun. As the previous discussion shows, a determination of the syntactic category of a compound cannot always be found by analyzing its parts. Furthermore, semantics of compounds are not necessarily componential. These features make compound analysis complicated in natural language processing.

THEORETICAL ISSUES

In early linguistic theory, there was no doubt that morphology was a field in its own right. In fact, early descriptive linguistics emphasized morphological structure, while ignoring syntax to a large part. Morphology was the window into the description and understanding of the language (and of language as a whole). In contrast, in early generative theory, the claim was made that morphological operations were the same as syntactic ones, namely transformational rules (Lees, 1960). Lexical items formed by transformations were then inserted into phrase markers by means of a set of context-free rewriting rules that did not differ in any formal way from the set of phrase structure rules needed for syntactic description. However, it soon became obvious that this was inadequate, and that at least some word formation might indeed require a separate set of descriptive and generative devices (Aronoff, 1983). The reinstatement of morphology led to certain theoretical consequences that are still problematic in the field today. The Strong Lexicalist Hypothesis proposes that morphology is modular, independent of other components such as syntax, phonology, semantics, or pragmatics, and with its own principles. The syntax neither manipulates nor has access to the internal form of words. However, it appears that parts of words can and do play independent roles in the syntax and that, in turn, the syntax can affect word formation processes (Everaert and co-workers, 1988). It appears that word formation might occur in several places in the grammar rather than in one isolated component.

A related problem in morphology concerns the relation between the internal morphological, semantic, and syntactic structure of words. For example, the morphological structure of a word like *unhappier* must be [un [[happy] er]] since the comparative *-er* suffix can only attach to monosyllabic or bisyllabic words. However, the meaning directly corresponding to this bracketing is *not more happy;* this is incorrect since *unhappier* in fact means *more not happy*. This implies that the semantic scope of the negative operator is narrower than the scope of the comparative, even though from a structural point of view, the comparative must be attached to the base first. Bracketing paradoxes like these raise problems concerning the relationship between types of structure imposed on words in the process of analysis. Most importantly, if a morphological analyzer can determine the internal morphological structure of a word, this structure is not always isomorphic with the semantic structure.

MORPHOLOGY IN NATURAL LANGUAGE PROCESSING SYSTEMS

Computational morphology deals with the recognition, analysis, and generation of words. The morphological processes described above can be implemented in a computational system. Inflectional morphology, because it is closely dependent on syntax and more paradigmatic, is more widely implemented in natural language systems than derivation. Theoretical issues of modularity, the nature of lexical rules, the nature of the dictionary (or lexicon), and the interaction between components, all play an important role in the design and implementation of many morphological systems. In addition, morphological theories disagree on whether the base of an inflected form is the word or the stem (Aronoff, 1976; Corbin, 1987). This actually may depend on inherent properties of the language that is being processed. System building provides deciding evidence for what is considered a base, since a system must reflect the regularities of the language. Although morphological processes have been described for many types of languages, computational morphology has mostly tackled Indo-European, Finno-Ugric, and Semitic languages.

From the most basic word frequency programs to more complex syntactic and semantic analyzers, the starting point is the word. However, words do not occur independently of one another. Morphologically related words cluster, and their distribution is affected by this property. Consider for example, a simple word frequency program. Does the user want only the tokens counted? Would it be more useful for an application to lemmatize the words, ie, to count *walk* and *walks* as two tokens of one morpheme WALK (the small capital letters indicating an underlying form), or as one token of two morphemes? Some applications, such as text understanding where the important issue is the underlying semantics of the words, might find it more useful to lemmatize, whereas others, eg a word frequency program, would not, since the goal would be to count the tokens exactly as they appear. Furthermore, some forms are unambiguously verbs or nouns, as can be detected from the morphology. Even in English, with its ambiguous verbal morphology, polysyllabic unhyphenated words that end in *-ize* are most likely verbs (93%) or compounds (7%) as in *barnsize, pintsize*. Words ending in *-tion* have a 98% likelihood of being nouns counted by type and over 99% by token. If a system is designed to lemmatize and assign a part of speech, morphology can give essential clues. The richer the morphology of a language, and the less ambiguity associated with morphological types, the easier it is for a computational system to assign a part of speech to the word, and to analyze the word to its base form.

A morphological analyzer or generator supplies information concerning the morphosyntactic properties of the words it analyzes or constructs. In principle, there are two ways to deal with morphologically related forms. One is to store all the word forms with associated relevant properties: for example, *walk* (verb present plural), *walks* (verb present singular), *walking* (verb present progressive), and *walked* (verb past); the other is to store one base form WALK (verb) with rules to relate variants. Although for languages like English, with limited verbal inflection (four per word), storage of forms is an option; for languages like Finnish, which have over 12,000 forms per verb, storage becomes costly (Koskenniemi, 1983). Furthermore, language is creative, so new words enter the language more frequently than most people realize (Aronoff, 1983). In addition, as pointed out in the section on derivation, much derivational morphology is highly productive, so storing all variants becomes an intractable problem. In fact, given the recursive nature of morphological operations, variants are theoretically infinite (Langendoen, 1981; Carden, 1983).

In most morphological analyzers and generators, there are two parts: a dictionary (qv) and a set of rules (Jäppinen, 1986; Lovins, 1968; Resnikoff, 1965; Vergne and Pagès, 1982; Winograd, 1971). The nature of the dictionary can vary. Some systems are word-based so the lexicon contains only well-formed words which serve as the base for other words (Byrd, 1983; Anshen and co-workers, 1986; Byrd and Tzoukermann, 1988). For example, a word-based system might list *distract, retract, contract*, all of which can appear as variants, such as *distraction, retracting*, and *contractable*. In contrast, a stem-based system might simply contain the stem *-tract-* with rules to account for all forms. Finally, there are mixed systems which list forms with the criterion that complex words reflect the component semantics. For example, the meaning of the word *establishment* is different from *establish* and *-ment*; it is semantically noncompositional. Thus, the mixed system would not list a word like *inducement*, the meaning of which is predictable from *induce* and *-ment*, but it would list *establishment*, meaning "a place of business." It would also allow *establish* and *-ment* as a word, meaning the act of *establishing*.

There are currently two models of analysis that are the most widely used (Klavans, 1989). One is the finite-state model and the other is the stripping approach. Furthermore, within the finite-state approach, two models can be distinguished (Alam, 1983; Bear, 1988; Karttunen, 1983; Kay, 1987; Koskienniemi, 1983; Karttunen, 1991). In one model, constraints on stems and affixes can be encoded as a finite-state network. In the other model, morphological alternations are regular and their phonological or orthographical realizations constitute a regular relation; morpho-phonological changes can be encoded by rewrite-rules. The most straightforward example of a finite-state lexicon of the first type is a simple list of all word forms. The example below shows how transitions for a Spanish morphological system (Tzoukermann and Liberman, 1990) are stored in a dictionary. The starting label of the transition is "1" and the ending label is "2" for (a). Concatenation will occur if, and only if, the ending label of a transition matches the starting label of another transition. In Table 4, (a) will link *am* in the first transition (1,2) to *amos* in (f), the fifth transition (2,100), giving *amamos*, "we love." This example shows simple concatenation but does not reflect cases where morpho-phonological rules are processed within the finite-state machine. In the case of *jugar*, the morpho-phonological changes are computed in a grammar compiler outside the finite-state system. In this system configuration, there is a rule system that takes the lexical representation of morphemes and outputs their surface representation listed under the form of the lexicon in Table 4. More sophisticated finite-state lexicons store words in letter trees and use sublexicons and continuation classes.

In the second model, the main theoretical insight is due to Johnson (1972), who demonstrated that any phonological rewrite-rule could be implemented by a finite-state transducer. Since finite-state transducers are closed under composition, any ordered set of rewrite-rules can be encoded as a single transducer (mapping directly the lexical forms to their surface forms). In Koskenniemi's work on finite-state morphology, rewrite-rules are replaced by unordered constraints (two-level rules). The two-level rules describe the correspondences between lexical and surface forms. In that respect the model is similar to the structural phonological model, but differs in its rules that do not interact with each other. In the system of Kartunnen,

Table 4. Finite-State Transitions for Spanish

	Start	End	Input	Output	Meaning
(a)	1	2	am	amar	to love
(b)	1	3	jug	jugar	to play
(c)	1	4	jueg	jugar	
(d)	1	5	juegu	jugar	
(e)	1	6	jugu	jugar	
(f)	2	100	amos		1st pers plur pres ind
(g)	3	100	amos		1st pers plur pres ind
(h)	4	100	o		1st pers sing pres ind

Koskenniemi, and Kaplan (1987), two-level phonological or orthographical rules are compiled into finite-state transducers. The goal is to allow the user to develop a set of rules for morphological generation and recognition.

Usually, stripping systems are used more for analysis than for generation. The word is stripped by pattern matching to a proposed base form (either word or stem); this proposed base might have to be altered by some spelling rules. The system proceeds until all matches are made, and then structures are suggested (Byrd and coworkers, 1986). To illustrate, one of several rules for handling the suffix -*able* is given below; the rule applies to forms like *delegable* derived from *delegate*, *litigable* from *litigate*, and *navigable* from *navigate*:

gable3te∗   (verb +transitive infinitive)
         (adjective −transitive)

Rules like these are handled by an interpreter which requires the last five letters of the spelled form to be -*gable*; it then asks whether, if three letters are removed and the letters *te* are attached, a corresponding spelling which is a transitive infinitive verb is found in the dictionary. If so, the form is said to be a nontransitive adjective, ie [*navigable* → [[*navigate*]$_{verb,+trans}$-*able*]$_{adj,-trans}$]. The rule given here is simplified, but it demonstrates how a feature-based lexicon or dictionary is used to match forms, and how affixes can carry part-of-speech changes and semantic changes. For example, the rule could have introduced a feature [possible] into the analysis, showing that a form like *navigable* has the semantic property of *possible to be navigated* rather than *has been navigated*. Alternatively, the rule could have required the base to be human, if the human feature were one of the features in the lexicon. The type of structures and analyses that result differs from system to system. Some provide a flat structure, consisting of a base and a linear sequence of affixes. Others give a richer structure so that morphological analysis is more like a grammar capable of providing detailed structures reminiscent of syntactic analyses.

One of the differences between a finite-state and a stripping model is the construction of the dictionary; a significant amount of preprocessing needs to be performed to build the transitions of a finite-state model dictionary whereas in a stripping model some of the features assigned to the words can be derived directly with little preprocessing from a machine-readable dictionary. In the finite state model shown above, processing verb entries from a machine-readable dictionary produced a list of all the possible stems for a verb. However, if no machine-readable dictionary is available, then a word list must be built, stems must be listed, and verb paradigms must be identified. At the same time, the finite-state model offers control that the stripping model does not have. Each character string in a finite-state system is handled by a pair of labels, and any operation can be achieved if, and only if, the labels match. In contrast, a stripping model defines a set of opposing features to be assigned to words; operations proceed upon the condition that there are matching features. In the stripping model, it is difficult to define a set of features distinctive enough to separate the rule operations and powerful enough to avoid rule overlapping. Although the rules in a stripping system can be written in a more flexible way, there is more predictability imposed by the finite-state formalism. Finally, an additional advantage of finite-state models is that, since they are reversible, they handle both generation and analysis with the same set of rules. Both systems have in common the fact that they produce all possible analyses, usually recursively. The application then has the often difficult task of choosing the correct analysis within the syntactic context, and of using the detailed syntactic, semantic, and phonological information that the morphological system provides.

BIBLIOGRAPHY

Y. S. Alam, "Two-Level Morphological Analysis of Japanese" *Tex. Ling. For.* **22**, 229–252 (1983).

S. Anderson, "Morphology as a Parsing Problem," *Linguistics* **26**(4), 521–544 (1988).

F. Anshen, M. Aronoff, R. J. Byrd, and J. L. Klavans, "The Role of Etymology and Word Length in English Word Formation," *Proceedings of the Conference on Advances in Lexicology*, Center for the New OED, University of Waterloo, Canada, 1986.

M. Aronoff, *Word Formation in Generative Grammar*, MIT Press, Cambridge, Mass., 1976.

M. Aronoff, "A Decade of Morphology and Word Formation" *Annu. Rev. Anthropol.*, **12**, 355–375 (1983).

M. Aronoff, "Actual Words, Potential Words, Frequency and Productivity," in S. Hattori and K. Inoue, eds., *Proceedings of the Thirteenth International Congress of Linguists*, CIPL, Tokyo, Japan, 1983, pp. 163–171.

L. Bauer, *English Word Formation*, Cambridge University Press, Cambridge, England, 1983.

J. Bear, "Morphology and Two-level Rules and Negative Rule Features," *Proceedings of the Twelfth International Conference on Computational Linguistics* (COLING), Budapest, 1988, pp. 28–31.

R. Beard, *The Indo-European Lexicon,* North-Holland, Amsterdam, 1981.

J. Bybee, *Morphology: a Study of the Relation Between Meaning and Form,* John Benjamins, Amsterdam, The Netherlands, 1985.

R. J. Byrd and E. Tzoukermann, "Adapting an English Morphological Analyzer for French," *Proceedings of the Twenty-Sixth Annual Meeting of the Association for Computational Linguistics,* Buffalo, N.Y., 1988, pp. 1–6.

R. J. Byrd, "Word Formation in Natural Language Processing Systems," *Proceedings of the Eighth IJCAI*, Karlsruhe, FRG, Morgan-Kaufmann, San Mateo, Calif., 1983, pp. 704–706.

R. J. Byrd, J. L. Klavans, M. Aronoff, and F. Anshen, "Computer Methods for Morphological Analysis," *Proceedings of the Twenty-Fourth Annual Meeting of the Association for Computational Linguistics,* New York, 1986, pp. 120–127.

L. Bloomfield, *Language,* Holt and Company, New York, 1933.

G. Carden, "The Non-Finiteness of the Word Formation Component," *Ling. Inq.* **14**, 537–547 (1983).

N. Chomsky, "Remarks on Nominalization," in R. Jacobs and P. Rosenbaum eds., *Readings in English Transformational Grammar,* Ginn, Waltham, Mass., 1970.

N. Chomsky, and M. Halle, *The Sound Pattern of English,* Harper and Row, New York, 1968.

K. W. Church, "Morphological Decomposition and Stress Assignment for Speech Synthesis," *Proceedings of the Twenty-Fourth Annual Meeting of the ACL,* New York, 1986, pp. 156–164.

D. Corbin, *Morphologie Dérivationnelle et Structuration du Lexique,* Vol. I and II, Niemeyer Verlag, Tübingen, 1987.

C. Culy, "The Complexity of the Vocabulary of Bambara," *Ling. and Phil.,* 8, 345–351 (1985).

A. M. DiSciullio and E. Williams, *On the Definition of Word,* MIT Press, Cambridge, Mass., 1987.

M. Everaert, A. Evers, R. Huybregts, and M. Trommelen, eds., *Morphology and Modularity,* Dordrecht, The Netherlands, 1988.

N. Fabb, "English Suffixation is Constrained by Selectional Restrictions, *Natural Language and Linguistic Theory,* 6, 527–540 (1988).

G. Gazdar, "Review Article: Finite State Morphology," *Linguistics,* 23(4), 597–607 (1985).

L. Henderson, M. Coltheart, A. Cutler, and N. Vincent, eds., *Linguistic and Psychological Approaches to Morphology,* 26(4), (1988).

H. Jäppinen, and M. Ylilammi, "Associative Model of Morphological Analysis: An Empirical Enquiry," *Comput. Ling.,* 12(4), 257–272 (1986).

D. C. Johnson, *Formal Aspects of Phonological Description,* Mouton, The Hague, 1972.

F. Karlsson, "A Paradigm-Based Morphological Analyzer," in F. Karlsson, ed., *Papers from the Fifth Sandinavian Conference of Computational Linguistics,* University of Helsinki, Helsinki, Finland, 1986.

L. Karttunen, "KIMMO: A General Morphological Processor," *Tex. Ling. For.,* 22, 165–186 (1983).

L. Karttunen, "Finite-State Constraints," Paper presented at the *International Conference on Current Issues in Computational Linguistics,* Universiti Sains Malyasia, Penang, Malaysia, 1991.

L. Karttunen, K. Koskenniemi, and R. Kaplan, "A Compiler for Two-Level Phonological Rules," *CSLI-Report,* Center for the Study of Language and Information, 1987.

M. Kay, "When Meta-Rules Are Not Meta-Rules," in K. Sparck Jones and Y. Wilks, eds., *Automatic Natural Language Parsing,* Ellis Horwood, Wiley, Chichester, UK, 1983, pp. 94–116.

M. Kay, "Non-Concatenative Finite-state Morphology," *Proceedings of the Third European Conference of the ACL,* 1987, pp. 2–10.

P. Kiparsky, "Lexical Morphology and Phonology," in Hanshin and I. S. Yang, eds., *Linguistics in the Morning Calm,* Seoul, Korea, 1982, pp. 3–92.

J. Klavans, "The Independence of Syntax and Phonology in Cliticization," *Language* 61, 95–120 (1985).

J. Klavans, "Computational Linguistics," in M. O'Grady, M. Dobrovolsky, and M. Aronoff, eds., *Contemporary Linguistics,* St. Martin's Press, New York, 1989.

K. Koskenniemi, *Two-level Morphology: A General Computational Model for Word-Form Recognition and Production,* University of Helsinki, Helsinki, Finland, 1983.

K. Koskenniemi and K. Church, "Complexity, Two-Level Morphology and Finnish," *Proceedings of the Twelfth International Conference on Computational Linguistics* (COLING), 1988, pp. 335–340.

D. T. Langendoen, "The Generative Capacity of Word-Formation Components," *Ling. Inq.* 12(2), 320–322 (1981).

R. B. Lees, *The Grammar of English Nominalizations,* Mouton, The Hague, 1960.

J. Levi, *The Syntax and Semantics of Complex Nominals,* Academic Press, Inc., New York, 1978.

J. B. Lovins, "Development of a Stemming Algorithm," *Mech. Transl. Comput. Ling.,* 11, 22–31 (1968).

H. Marchand, *The Categories and Types of Present-Day English Word-Formation: A Synchronic-Diachronic Approach,* 2nd ed., C. H. Beck, München, Germany, 1969.

P. H. Matthews, *Inflectional Morphology,* Cambridge University Press, Cambridge, UK, 1972.

P. H. Matthews, *Morphology,* Cambridge University Press, Cambridge, UK, 1974.

D. B. McDonald, "Compound: a Program that Understands Noun Compounds," *Proceedings of the Seventh IJCAI,* Vol. 2, Vancouver, B.C., Morgan-Kaufmann, San Mateo, Calif., 1981, p. 1061.

E. Nida, *Morphology: the Descriptive Analysis of Words,* University of Michigan Press, Ann Arbor, Mich. 1949.

M. Rappaport, "On the Nature of Derived Nominals," L. Levin and co-workers, eds., *Papers in Lexical-Functional Grammar,* Indiana University Linguistics Club, Bloomington, Ind. 1983.

H. L. Resnikoff, and J. L. Dolby, "The Nature of Affixing in Written English," Part I, *Mech. Trans. Comput. Ling.,* 8(3) (1965).

H. L. Resnikoff, and J. L. Dolby, "The Nature of Affixing in Written English," Part II, *Mech. Trans. Comput. Ling.,* 9(2) (1966).

J. Sadock, "Autolexical Syntax: A Proposal for the Treatment of Noun Incorporation and Similar Phenomena," *Natural Language and Linguistic Theory,* 3, 379–439 (1985).

S. Scalise, *Generative Morphology,* Foris, Dordrecht, The Netherlands, 1985.

E. O. Selkirk, *The Syntax of Words,* MIT Press, Cambridge, Mass., 1982.

D. Siegel, *Topics in English Morphology,* Ph.D. dissertation, MIT, Cambridge, Mass., 1974.

K. Sparck Jones, "So What About Parsing Compound Nouns?" in K. Sparck Jones and Y. A. Wilks, eds., *Automatic Natural Language Parsing,* Ellis Horwood-Wiley, Chichester, UK, 1983, pp. 104–168.

R. Sproat, *Morphology and Computation,* MIT Press, Cambridge, Mass., 1991.

R. Sproat, "Stress Assignment in Complex Nominals for English Text-to-Speech," in G. Bailly and C. Benoit, eds., *Proceedings of the Workshop on Speech Synthesis,* (ESCA), 1990, pp. 129–132.

G. Thurmair, "Linguistic Problems in Multilingual Morphological Decomposition," *Proceedings of the 10th International Conference on Computational Linguistics* (COLING), 1984, pp. 174–177.

E. Tzoukermann and M. Liberman, "A Finite-State Morphological Transducer for Spanish," *Proceedings of the Thirteenth International Conference on Computational Linguistics* (COLING), 1990.

J. Vergne, and P. Pagès, "Synergy of Syntax and Morphology in Automatic Parsing of French Language with a Minimum of Data," *Proceedings of the Ninth International Conference on Computational Linguistics* (COLING), 1982, pp. 397–405.

T. Winograd, "An A.I. Approach to English Morphemic Analysis," *A.I. Memo No. 241,* A.I. Laboratory, MIT, Cambridge, Mass., 1971.

S. Wolff, "The Use of Morphosemantic Regularities in the Medical Vocabulary for Automatic Lexical Coding," *Methods of Information in Medicine,* 23, 195–203 (1985).

S. Wolff, *Lexical Entries and Word Formation,* Indiana University Linguistics Club, Bloomington, Ind., 1983.

K. Wothke, "Machine Learning of Morphological Rules by Generalization and Analogy," *Proceedings of the Eleventh International Conference on Computational Linguistics (COLING),* 1986, pp. 289-293.

J. L. KLAVANS
IBM T. J. Watson Research Center
E. TZOUKERMANN
A.T. & T. Bell Laboratories

MOTION ANALYSIS. See VISUAL MOTION ANALYSIS.

MS. MALAPROP

This is a natural language understanding (qv) system in which the inference process is directed by frame-structured knowledge. Knowledge about mundane situations is structured in a modular hierarchy of frames (qv), thereby allowing sharing of information between frames. The system was developed around 1977 by Charniak at the University of Geneva (see E. Charniak, "Ms. Malaprop, a Language Comprehension Program," *Proceedings of the Fifth IJCAI,* Cambridge, Mass., 1977, pp. 1-7).

K. S. ARORA
SUNY at Buffalo

MULTISENSOR INTEGRATION. See SENSORS AND SENSOR FUSION.

MUSIC, AI IN

I merely report—I cannot verify—that composers already claim to have discovered musical applications of decision theory, mathematical group theory, and the idea of "shape" in algebraic topology. Mathematicians will undoubtedly think this all very naive, and rightly so, but I consider that any inquiry, naive or not, is of value if only because it must lead to larger questions—in fact, to the eventual mathematical formulation of musical theory and to, at long last, an empirical study of musical facts—and I mean the facts of the art of combination which is composition (Stravinsky and Craft, 1959).

OVERVIEW

Elaborate mathematical formulations of compositional procedure had in fact appeared well before Stravinsky's statement (Schillinger, 1941). Indeed, codifications of correct and incorrect practices have been integral to musical theory since the late Renaissance (Zarlino, 1968). It has been the advent of digital computers and AI, however, that have transformed Stravinsky's dream of empirical study into a practical reality, because it is now possible not only to formulate truly quantitative models of how composers work but also to subject these models to rigorous evaluation. AI techniques are by no means limited to modeling the process of composition; such techniques show equal promise for investigating the two other modes of human intellectual involvement with music: the cognitive processes associated with the experience of listening and the decisions undertaken by performers as they interpret musical scores.

Of the three areas (composition, listening, and performance) musical composition was initially the area of most intense activity. The most impressive results in composition have been achieved search methodologies, but music processing methodologies have also been pursued. Search methodologies originated in a crude way with Hiller and Issacson's 1957 *Illiac Suite* for string quartet (Hiller and Issacson, 1959). They follow the age-old practice of expressing musical styles as constraints, detailing what is and is not appropriate; instances of the given style may the be generated using AI search techniques. During the last 10 yrs, this approach has been greatly enhanced through the incorporation of heuristics guiding the order in which options are considered and (in rare instances) the order in which decisions are taken. Searches can be used compositionally to evaluate and catalog compositional material. They can also be used to generate compositions outright, either on a piece-by-piece basis, or following Kurzweil's vision of a record that plays a different song each time it is started. For musical theorists, composing programs provide an unprecedented empirical laboratory for investigating how aesthetic and stylistic criteria guide composers as they go about their trade. Notable empirical efforts include Ebcioglu's (1988) CHORAL, a program that harmonizes melodies in the style of J. S. Bach (Thomas, 1985; Conklin and Cleary, 1988), and CYBERNETIC COMPOSER, a program that generates compositions in jazz, rock, and ragtime genres (Ames and Domino, 1988). CHORAL has duplicated Bach's own harmonizations, occasionally, while the CYBERNETIC COMPOSER has managed to fool many unsuspecting listeners; it generated a stream of compositions for *Robots and Beyond: The Age of Intelligent Machines,* and exhibition which opened at the Boston Museum of Science in 1986. Music-processing methodologies attempt to break compositional processes down into simple, self-contained operations; their antecedents include two early examples of instantiation in computer programs: the MUSICV signal-processing program (Mathews and co-workers, 1969) and the PROJECT2 score-generating program (Koenig, 1969).

The programs that come closest to emulating human aural cognition (listening) are analytic programs that reduce note-by-note descriptions of musical scores into stylistic or structural descriptions. Areas of research include harmonic analysis, tempo-meter-rhythm analysis, and phrase parsing. Programs for harmonic analysis include the 1968 EXPLAIN program (Winograd, 1968) and another more elaborate program (Maxwell, 1988). The latter program works in three stages. Stage 1 uses rote procedures to parse the harmonic rhythm out of a polyphonic texture; a by-product of this stage is a classification of nonharmonic tones as passing tones, appoggiaturas, etc.

Stage 2 proceeds again by rote to locate and evaluate cadence points, assigning to each cadence point a heuristic strength. Stage 3 searches for a key scheme that yields strong chordal functions. This is one of a few recent analysis programs that takes the trouble (in stage 3) to consider alternative solutions. Connectionist strategies (see below) have been applied to a variety of pitch-analysis problems, with mixed results. A variety of methods has been used to distill insights into tempo, meter, and rhythm from either performances or scores. Techniques for estimating tempi from performances by analyzing rhythmic patterns have been developed (Mont-Reynaud, 1985). Connection nets have been applied to a more general problem: extracting notated rhythmic proportions from rubato performances (Desain and Honing, 1989). PDP nets have been used to infer meter from durational sequences (Jones and co-workers, in press a). Pattern-matching techniques have been applied to isolate rhythmic motives, with mixed results (Mont Reynaud and Goldstein, 1985). Phrase parsers attempt to reproduce the cognitive process of grouping notes into motives, motives into phrases, phrases into sections, and so forth; examples have been published (Tenney and Polansky, 1980; Jones and co-workers, in press b). Phrase-parsing efforts have to date been limited to unaccompanied melodies.

The area of musical performance has recently seen several promising developments, including programs that combine analytic capabilities with performance practice knowledge to interpret musical scores for totally automated performance (Sundberg and co-workers, 1983; Katayose and co-workers, 1989); programs that analyze acoustic data or keyboard input to adjust an automated accompaniment to a live soloist (Dannenberg, 1984; Vercoe and Puckette, 1985) or improvisor (Dannenberg and Mont-Reynaud, 1987); and programs that acquire and analyze psychophysical data to correlate subjective musical attributes with objective synthesis parameters, for example, loudness with amplitude or timbre with frequency modulation index (Martens, 1985).

Distinctions between composition, listening, and performance are blurred by programs that listen to (analyze) music and apply the insights gained thereby to compose and perform music. M (Zicarelli, 1987) captures motives from live performers and manipulates these motives in a variety of ways; although M is not intelligent in any sense of the word, musicians have responded to M as the most successful realization to date of the notion of an interactive compositional editor. Phrase-parsing capabilities are fundamental to the idea of an intelligent composer's assistant (Roads, 1985). Efforts to distill the essence of a musical sample to generate tables (Ames, 1989 a), stylistically similar music have resulted in two programs: Zicarelli's JAM FACTORY compiles Markov-style transition then uses these tables as compositional drivers. (A criticism of straight Markov-style analysis is that it is unable to deal with situations in which one and the same musical object serves more than one function.) EMI (Cope, 1987) distills the high level rhetoric of compositions into an augmented transition network; it also compares source melodies for intervallic and rhythmic signatures. Analysis is also an important component of programs that transcribes performance data into score output (Chafe and co-workers, 1982). One recent score-editing packaging, FINALE, actively parses out the voice leading in real-time keyboard performances.

There remain further applications of AI that are peripheral to direct musical experience but nonetheless significant. Some researchers have employed natural language processors to assist man–computer interactions (Schmidt, 1986; Garton, 1989). Automated decision making in score printing can greatly assist layout of musical symbols according to conventions of musical typography (Byrd, 1977; Maxwell and Ornstein, 1981). Other applications include the use of pattern recognition and parsing algorithms for score reading. A dramatic example of this was the performing robot exhibited at Expo '85 (Roads, 1986; Andronico and Ciampa, 1982). This robot could decipher notated scores and subsequently play them on an organ. The robot's performance capability was significant more as a robotics achievement than a musical one: as far as could be discerned after witnessing one performance, the robot gave no attention at all to performance–practice nuances.

The present survey is complicated by a lack of consensus among the computer music community as to what legitimately constitutes "intelligence" in a computer music program. Few accept the opinion that a program merits the designation "intelligent" only if it can weigh alternative solutions to a problem (CHORAL, the CYBERNETIC COMPOSER, and Maxwell's harmonic-analysis program all meet this standard). Many accept the more tolerant viewpoint that an intelligent program is one that actively makes use of at least one acknowledged AI technique: searching, heuristics, parsing, pattern matching, AI knowledge-representation schemes, neural nets, etc. Even according to this standard, few if any of the programs described in two early special "AI in Music" issues of the *Computer Music Journal* (1980) would qualify as AI programs. A series of proselytizations on the issue of AI programming languages (published in the same journal's "Machine Tongues" column) has further damaged the credibility of musical AI by relying heavily on fabricated examples instead of working applications. One survey (Roads, 1985) equates musical AI with attempts to deepen composer–computer interaction, a viewpoint that totally excludes some efforts to develop self-reliant composing programs (Hiller and co-workers, 1985). Finally, a sizable number of computer-music researchers are musicians by training who have been less concerned with doing legitimate AI than they have been with solving specific musical problems. Such people tend to have the most liberal standard of intelligence, requiring simply that a program make decisions on its own (perhaps by conditional probability) or that it in some way be aware of its environment. This is the basis of the unfortunate but now well-entrenched term *intelligent instrument* as used by people such as Spiegel (concerning her interactive composition MUSIC MOUSE) and Chadabe (concerning the performance-processing programs M and JAM FACTORY). In fairness, these programs address significant compositional issues even though they employ techniques that computer scientists will likely judge "very naive, and rightly so." Such was also the case with composing programs during the 1950s and 1960s.

CONSTRAINED SELECTION

Where computer scientists often use the word *rule* in a heuristic sense, musicians use *rule* to signify a constraint, that is, a minimal standard of acceptability. Constraints are the crudest way of imposing generalized aesthetic values on a selection process. Even so, constraints are the basis for two paradigms that have been favored for centuries by teachers of musical theory: species counterpoint (an idealization of practices by Renaissance composers such as Josquin des Pres) and the chorale harmonizations of Bach. Both paradigms teach students to reconcile their personal creative instincts with style-determined constraints such as downward resolution of dissonant tones and avoidance of parallel perfect consonances. The discipline of establishing constraints and sticking to them has been confirmed by such celebrated composers as Mozart (who supplemented his livelihood by teaching species counterpoint), Schoenberg, and Stravinksy.

The kernel of a constrained selection process appeared in composing programs as early as the *Illiac Suite*. In this work, Hiller and Isaacson enforced 16 simple melodic and harmonic constraints. These constraints were influenced by the conventions of eighteenth-century counterpoint, but were extremely crude even by elementary pedagogical standards. Pitches were selected using the following mechanism: a pitch was chosen at random from the major scale. If this pitch satisfied all the constraints, then the program went on to the next note; otherwise, the program looped. No provision was made to exclude pitches that had already been rejected. If after a set number of tries the program still didn't find an acceptable pitch, the program started the entire piece over from scratch. Examples of Hiller and Isaacson's seven melodic constraints are a constraint against any pitch repeating three or more times consecutively, and a constraint requiring any "skip" to be followed by a "step;" among their nine harmonic constraints are restrictions excluding dissonant intervals such as seconds and sevenths (restrictions that eighteenth-century pedagogues never imposed), constraints forbidding motion in parallel perfect consonances, and requirements for contrary motion. The element of randomness in their decision mechanism promoted unbiased choices within the universe of correct music defined by the constraints.

For almost two decades, Hiller and Isaacson's mechanism remained the primary way composing programs dealt with constraints. It was applied not only to pitches but also to other musical attributes such as rhythm and timbre. By the late 1970s, two serious defects had become apparent. The first of these defects was that the mechanism was incapable of dealing with situations in which none of the available options passed all the constraints. The second defect was that to avoid potential conflicts between constraints, formulations were sometimes forced to incorporate elaborate qualifications and special cases.

The first defect was resolved by adding the capability to backtrack, revise one or more earlier sources of conflict, and try again. Backtracking strongly enhances a composing program's ability to cope with very stringent constraints. It clearly models the behavior of a human composer in the act of applying a pencil eraser, and as such, pinpoints the difference between composition, which by definition happens in nonreal time, and improvisation, composition's real-time cousin. Polansky implemented casual backtracking in the program for his 1976 *Four Voice Canons*. Ebcioglu's (1983) investigations of species counterpoint used rigorous backtracking without heuristics; Ames's (1983) composition *Gradient* applied a similar approach to six-voice counterpoint in pan-chromatic style. An alternative way of ensuring quality control is forward chaining. This approach seems to have been used in an early composing program (Gill, 1963). Forward chaining is also the inference strategy for Maxwell's harmonic-analysis program.

HEURISTICS

Heuristics (that is, selection processes that are rule-based in the computer science sense of rule) eliminate many qualifications and special cases by replacing absolute judgments of acceptability with relative judgments of preference. Heuristics are attractive because they direct a program toward good choices and, therefore, permit it to spend much less time recovering from bad ones. They are particularly important to programs operating under real-time or simulated real-time conditions, because such programs simply cannot afford to waste time revising previous conclusions.

Consider an example from traditional harmony: the leading tone. Leading tones often, but not always, resolve upward by step. A purely constraint-driven composing program would typically require leading tones to resolve upward by step, then qualify this constraint with a loophole such as "leading tones may move downward by a third if the normal degree of resolution appears in a different voice." A more flexible way of dealing with leading tones might be a heuristic of the form: "If the current note

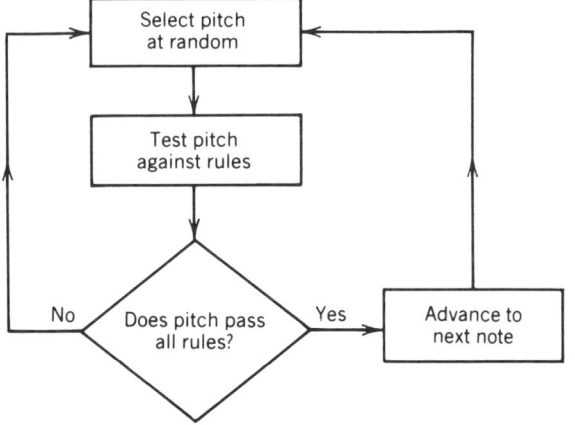

Figure 1. Decision mechanism of the *Illiac Suite* (Hiller and Isaacson, 1959).

is preceded in the same voice by a leading tone, then give priority to the upward resolution." Implementing heuristics thus becomes a matter of assigning each option a relative preference value, then scheduling options so that the most desirable options will be considered first. (For some problems it is more efficient to apply the constraints prior to scheduling.) Preference values can be derived either through black-and-white determinations, such as whether a particular condition is satisfied, or shades-of-gray determinations that admit ranges of values. For example, a program can figure out logically whether a chord contains any doublings, or it can explicitly tally up how many doublings actually occur. Efforts to quantify musical preference have no precedent in traditional music theoretic endeavors, indeed, they have yet to be acknowledged as a legitimate theoretical pursuit. Some efforts implementing preference in musical decisions have relied on concepts of musical magnitude and distance.

Concepts of musical magnitude cover musical evaluations driven by accent, stress, and strength. A program for emulating jazz improvisation has been described (Levitt, 1981); among other things, this program decides which phrases in the head melody are most suitable for thematic variation. Phrases receive point scores for unexpected features such as large leaps, chromatic tones, and syncopations. Maxwell's harmonic-analysis program considers metric stresses both in parsing harmonic rhythms and in locating and evaluating cadences. A quantitative value indicated whether a cadence was real, deceptive, or merely suggestive. Likewise, harmonic functions are graded: tonic and dominant chords are strongest, subdominant and submediant chords are less strong, mediant chords and secondary dominants are weak, borrowed and altered chords are weaker still. The program nominates key interpretations by considering which cadences are strongest; it confirms these interpretations by assessing the overall strengths of harmonic functions so analyzed.

Concepts of musical distance embrace both separation and contrast. They are not limited to concrete note attributes such as pitch, rhythmic placement, dynamics, and timbre (Martens, 1985). The need to quantify perceptual separations in the pitch-time plane for Tenney and Polansky's phrase-parsing program led these researchers to develop an analogy with geometric distances on the $x-y$ plane. Scarborough and co-workers' phrase-parsing heuristics take the form of grouping rules "based on proximity of note onsets or offsets and on significant differences in such attributes as pitch, duration, and articulation" (Jones, Scarborough, and Miller, in press b). The separation and contrast between two consecutive notes in a melody is quantified simply by counting how many of these grouping rules are violated. Short-term phrase boundaries are marked where the number of violations slightly exceeds the norm; long-term boundaries are marked at more dramatic contrasts. The results obtained by these researchers compare poorly to Maxwell's extractions of harmonic rhythms (a different, but probably similar, problem), especially when it is considered that existing phrase parsers deal only with one-voice melodies, whereas the relevant component of Maxwell's program processes polyphonic music by rote.

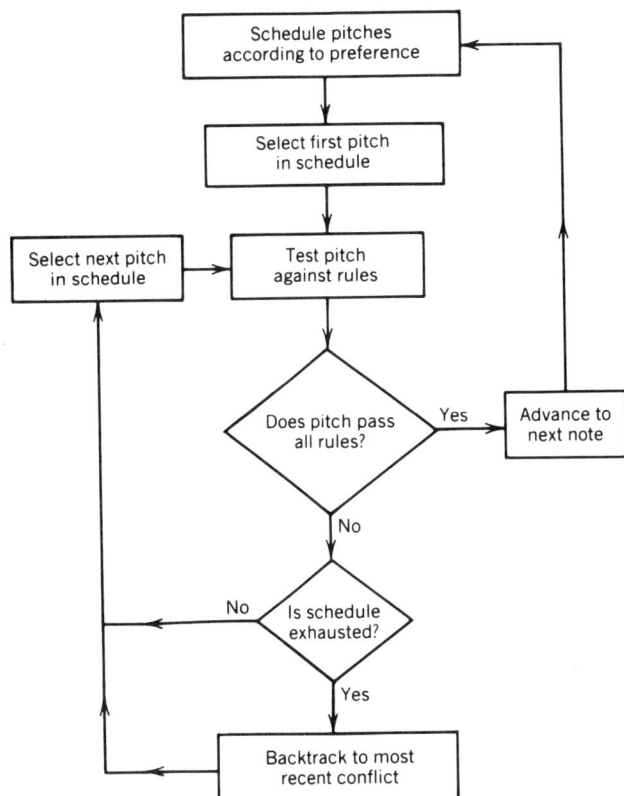

Figure 2. Heuristic scheduling with backtracking.

The notion of musical distance has been generated to deal quantitatively with the question of whether two motives are similar or contrasting (Polansky, 1987). Pitch-contour distances are quantified by calculating the root mean square of the difference between interval 1 of motive 1 and interval 1 of motive 2, difference between interval 2 of motive 1 and interval 2 of motive 2, etc. Motivic distance in this model has been a means to a compositional end, developing a model of musical variation that transcends rote inversions, retrogrades, and transpositions. Techniques of measuring motivic distance are also a necessary underpinning for programs that analyze the motivic structure of existing compositions, where literal imitations are more the exception than the rule. The analytic portion of Cope's EMI, for example, acquires stylistic signatures by matching intervallic and durational sequences in two or more source pieces.

The distance formulations described thus far do not accommodate ambivalences arising when two musical entities are close (similar) according to one criterion but distant (contrasting) according to another. Although ambivalences (as opposed to ambiguities) are not necessarily common in music, they tend to occur at important liaison points in compositional structures, eg, pivot chords in modulations. The role of ambivalence has been dealt only in a few specialized quantitative models. Maxwell's program at least accommodates pivot chords in modulations, and one approach (Levitt, 1984) prevents ambivalent mo-

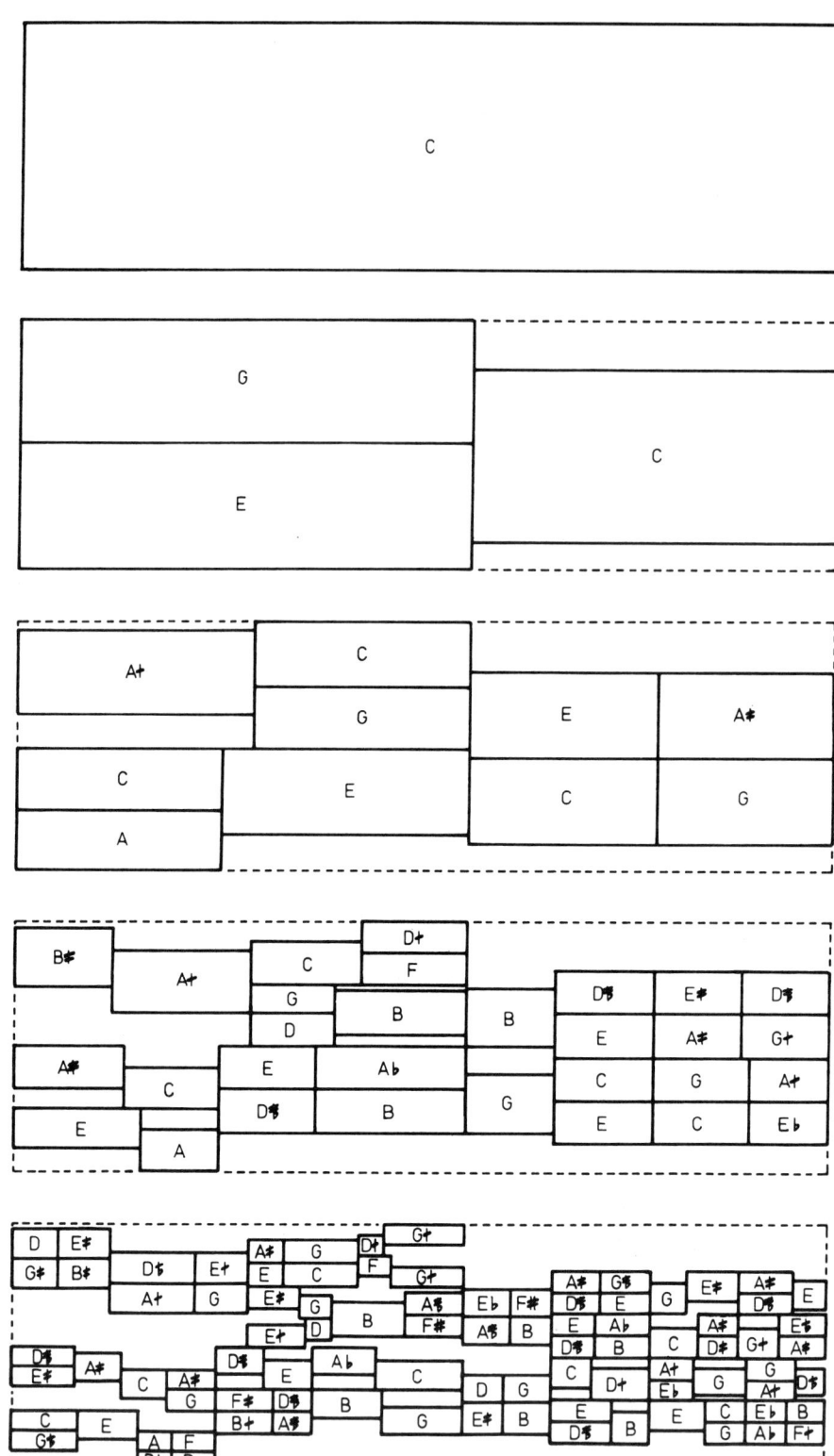

Figure 3. Hierarchic generation of a musical structure in Ames's *Crystals*. Each successive diagram describes the structure at an additional level of compositional detail. The horizontal dimension of each rectangle indicates duration, the vertical dimension indicates register, and the letters indicate degrees of a 36-tone scale (Ebcioglu, 1984).

tivic relationships from being misclassified as distant or contrasting. It has been proposed that motives should be judged similar or contrasting only when such a characterization applies uniformly over many viewpoints, eg, rhythm and pitch contour (Levitt, 1984).

Diverse heuristics are sometimes reconciled through prioritization. An early instance of this is a procedure developed for *Protocol* for solo piano (Ames, 1982b). By quantifying how strongly the members of a group of chords complemented one another, this procedure made it possible to evaluate many different groups of chords and select the most complementary among them. Pairs of chords were exhaustively compared, and tallies were compiled of the number of pairs sharing no common tones, sharing one common tone, and so on. These tallies were then packed into one long integer with tallies of less complementary chords (ie, pairs sharing more common tones) in the more significant bits. Prioritization has also been used to reconcile diverse considerations. For example, Ebcioglu's CHORAL evaluates an option by applying a variety of logical tests, then using a binary weighting scheme to pack these logical results into a single preference value.

Another issue of importance to musical AI has been statistical balance. The statistical implications of Schoenberg's serial technique of composition were pointed out decades ago by Xenakis. Despite this, musical theorists who do not use computers generally do not distinguish between random and statistical processes. Until the early 1980s, composing programs obtained statistical balances through ball-and-urn methods, which were limited in statistical reliability, resistant to constraints, and insensitive to contextual stress. The technique of statistical feedback (Ames, 1989b) eliminates these problems in compositional applications by maintaining statistics detailing how much each option has been used in the past and by assigning greater preference to less used options. Mixed, but encouraging, success has been attained in applying connectionist methodologies to the converse problem: deriving statistical inferences from existing scores (Jones and co-workers, 1989). This model employs "a network of interconnections . . . as a simple method for counting notes and weighing the evidence for one key versus another" (Jones and co-workers, 1989), in effect tabulating statistics on how much each degree of the chromatic scale has been used up to a particular point in a melody. Node activations decay with time so that conclusions made by the network are most strongly influenced by recent events.

EXHAUSTIVE SEARCHES

Of the two decision-making strategies discussed so far, constraint-based selection yields only acceptable solutions, whereas purely heuristic selection yields solutions that tend to have desirable qualities, but that are not guaranteed to meet any minimum standard. Blending constraints and heuristics increases quality control, but in no way insures an optimal solution. Optimality can only be ensured by exhaustively enumerating solutions and by keeping track of the best solution encountered along the way. However, such an approach is practical only when the number of solutions is manageable. Although rare exceptions have been documented, exhaustive searches do not provide a reasonable model of how composers make decisions. Most researchers shun them despite their optimality. Yet if the number of solutions is in fact manageable (a condition increasingly easy to satisfy as computer time becomes less and less precious a commodity), then the question comes to what is trying to be achieved: good modeling or good results.

Such were the considerations in mind when computer programs were devised to generate *Protocol*. This compositional effort employed searches for a variety of tasks: generating material, organizing this material into larger constructs, distributing the material around the form, and selecting the actual notes. Material was generated by a program that exhaustively enumerated chords, subject only to registral tolerances limiting where pitches could be placed. Preference values were derived by prioritizing a variety of considerations affecting the sonority of a chord; because the style of the work was dissonant, this included admonitions against adjacent pitches forming major or minor triads, etc. The chords, once generated, were passed along to a program that gathered chords into groups while maximizing tonal complementarity (see above). Complementarity was also a primary consideration in determining the actual progression of chords. A final program elaborated this progression into arpeggios, choosing the best notes to play at each point in the piece.

REPRESENTATION

Many computer-music applications today represent musical information according to the MIDI standards established by the synthesizer industry (*MIDI*, 1983; Yavelow, 1986). MIDI enables precise and detailed encoding of performance gestures such as keydown and keyup events, program changes (high-tech organ stops), and continuous pitch modulations. The MIDI standard was developed for a specific purpose—and has served that purpose well, but it hardly begins to address the needs of AI applications. Notes, specifically note durations, are represented only indirectly: a performer who pushes down a key must inevitably release the key at some later time. The MIDI standard provides no means for indicating how a note functions or how it relates compositionally to the rest of the score. By contrast, representation schemes for musical AI reflect a score's compositional genesis. They map out which decisions follow which, they indicate the nature of each decision, and they specify which decisions should conform and which should complement (Leman, 1985). Because AI programs spend much time evaluating the consequences of each decision, such programs rely on their representations both of product and of material (options) to structure information so that pertinent facts can be easily acquired.

Experience with early composing programs showed that strict left-to-right decision-making often gropes along blindly because choices are conditioned entirely by past origins, not future goals. Backtracking imparted limited prescience to the extent that programs could retreat from impasses and seek out alternative solutions, but it is clearly much more efficient to avoid bad choices in the first place. This might mean organizing decisions from the top down so that primary origins and goals are selected prior to working out the transitions between them (see "Grammars," below). It also might mean reordering decisions on the fly so that most urgent tendencies receive first attention; for example, a pitch-selection process might deal first with voices containing dissonances, second with voices containing leading tones, and third with voices containing stable chord tones. Such a process was implemented to write a six-part microtonal counterpoint for *Transitions* (Hiller and Ames, 1985; Ames, 1985).

Often a problem involves many different kinds of decisions, each with peculiar options, preferences, and constraints. In music these often translate into differences in function. For example, the CYBERNETIC COMPOSER used one set of methods to select main melody notes and a different set of methods to select passing tones, reaching tones, and other ornamental notes.

Decisions are also strongly influenced by context. Contextual relationships can be intricate in musical polyphony, where decisions pertaining to one voice are influenced not just by the voice's own history, but also by what the other voices have been doing and by the harmonic underpinning. To implement thematic imitation, it helps if the copy can be linked directly to the original on a note-by-note basis and if the characteristics of each linkage can be detailed: transposition, tolerance (is the imitation real or modal or is it enough simply to follow the original contour?), and so on. Questions of musical form have been approached on a higher level using similarity–contrast networks to specify how various decisions relate to one another. The programs used to generate the compositions *Transitions* and *Concurrence* (Ames, 1988) represented forms as small segments (eg, measures, short phrases, or single chords) with links indicating which segments were similar and which were contrasting. When these network representations had been assembled, heuristically driven searches could then be used to flesh out these abstract descriptions by selecting appropriate tonalities, rhythms, registers, dynamics, and timbres.

A variety of representations has proven helpful in helping a program decide efficiently whether the material it is considering is suitable or not. For example, a program devised for the composition *Excursion* (Ames, 1986) accepted proposed chords only if they were listed within a lexicon of approved sonorities. For *Concurrence*, the task of fleshing out a similarity–contrast network was greatly simplified by carrying out judgments of similarity and contrast in advance; material could then be organized into a thesaurus-like knowledge base linking each entry to its closest variants.

GRAMMARS

Recursive theories of musical structure have been around since well before computers. For example, Schenker's (1979) widely respected theories of chordal "prolongation" treat musical form as a structure of nested cadences, whereas Lorenz's analyses of the late Wagner operas reveal archetectonic ABA and AAB structures (Abraham, 1964). Any student of harmony knows that compositions often digress through many different key areas along the way to the final cadence and that these key areas may in turn draw secondary harmonies from yet more remote keys. It is, therefore, not surprising that writers as early as Winograd have sought to model compositional processes using Chomsky's generative grammars.

Roads (1978) suggested that composers might use terminal tokens to represent sound objects (such as notes, chords, motives, or textures) and nonterminal tokens to represent Chomsky-style context-free productions. Abbreviated descriptions of musical forms (axioms) might then be expanded automatically into detailed compositions. Roads's proposal was quickly implemented by Holtzman (1980) who added context-sensitive productions and rudimentary musical transformations, including transposition and retrograde. Representing sound objects abstractly, as tokens, has since proved unwieldy in practice. Approaches have been described that incorporate compositional attributes such as duration, register, and tonality directly in the axiom and the production mechanisms (Jones, 1981; Ames, 1982a, 1987; Langston, 1986; Kippen and Bell, in press). The CYBERNETIC COMPOSER uses grammars to refine the harmonic rhythm into solo, background, and bass rhythms. Each stylistic genre or subgenre has its own grammar. The end result describes when notes start, how long they last, how they function (cadence tone, chord tone, ornament, etc), and what they imitate; a second pass with backtracking is required to select pitches. Levitt (1985) takes a transformational approach toward the specification of musical dialects and toward motivic variation.

Researchers favoring generative models have often stood at odds with those who have pursued the Hiller-Isaacson model of constrained selection. However, experience has shown that attempts to generate rhythms and pitches using top-down productions often run afoul of stylistic conventions. These conventions become particularly troublesome in polyphonic applications, where each voice must keep constant tabs on what the other voices are doing.

In at least one instance, the realities of stringing notes together have forced reassessment of conventional wisdom. After struggling to incorporate Schenkerian prolongation as one viewpoint guiding CHORAL's harmonization procedures, Ebcioglu ultimately discarded prolongation as a conceptual hindrance. Whereas other writers (Rosen, 1971) had earlier argued that Schenker's theories were insufficient to explain the language of classical music, Ebcioglu's reluctant conclusion is the first indication that Schenkerism is unnecessary. Despite the shortcomings of Schenker's theories, Winograd, Maxwell, Tenney and Polansky, Scarborough and co-workers, and Cope have achieved varying degrees of success at parsing out elaborate grammatical structures in music. These successes seem to confirm that composers take great pains to make their structures readily apparent to a listener. Still, analysis alone reveals only the final product of a creative effort, providing little insight into what composers leave out and why. Such insight as cannot be gleaned by musicologists (through the composer's own writings or preliminary sketches) can only be gained through active simulation.

The conflict between constraint-oriented and generative approaches has lately given way to a realization that Chomsky-style rewrite rules are simply another variety of heuristic and that, like any other heuristic selection process, generative grammars can be constrained. A limited composing program employs grammars with backtracking to generate melodies with nested thematic structures (Marsella and co-workers, 1988). A different approach employed for the *Transitions* uses grammars to generate a similarity–contrast network (see above). Later passes fill in specific compositional details using top-down searches.

MUSIC-PROCESSING NETWORKS

An alternative stream of research has attempted to break creative musical processes down into simple, self-contained operations or primitives. Interrelationships between primitives are then represented as music-processing networks. Although most of today's efforts have been prompted by the recent surge in object-oriented programming, object instantiation was itself anticipated in two early music-processing utilities: MUSICV and PROJECT2. Object-oriented methodologies have been applied to real-time performance processing in HOOKUP (Yavelow, 1986) and PATCHER (Puckette, 1988) and to non-real-time score processing in LOCO (Desain and Honing, 1988), DOUBLETALK (Pope, 1986; Camurri and co-workers, 1986), and COMPOSE (Ames, in press). HMSL combines real-time and nonreal-time capabilities (Polansky and co-workers, 1987).

Some researchers regard these programs as intelligent, but the programs' actual decision-making capabilities fall far short of other approaches discussed in this article. Representations of musical data have to date excluded functional and relational information. Decision-making primitives have been limited for the most part to rote serial manipulations, random or chaotic generation, statistical transforms, and conditional mechanisms such as Markov chains and Chomsky grammars. In the last instance, the modularity of the primitives imposes a token-oriented implementation, which earlier was shown to be unwieldy (see above). No existing utility has backtracking, because constraints cannot be reliably enforced under real-time conditions. A few efforts have been made to develop decision-making primitives driven heuristically (by preference): Polansky has developed HMSL-based primitives for choosing close and distant thematic variants; Ames's COMPOSE includes a variety of selection modules guided by statistical feedback. Such efforts are severely hampered by the lack of representation of musical function and relationship.

PROCEDURAL KNOWLEDGE ACQUISITION

Although many programs analyze compositional structure, none can reduce the syntax of a work to a manageable set of constraints and heuristics. The OBSERVER program (Laske and Truax, 1979) gleaned procedural information by monitoring compositional activity but left the data to be interpreted by hand. MUSE (Schwanauer, 1986) infers compositional heuristics by solving elementary harmony exercises and by learning from its failures. Initially, solutions are proposed by a generate and test method. Learning is both success based and failure based. If a certain musical context consistently yields the same solution, then MUSE infers a heuristic. If a solution violates basic constraints (eg, parallel fifths or octaves), MUSE backtracks.

CONNECTIONISM

An outgrowth of studies in musical cognition, connectionist approaches to musical AI were recently reported to the wider computer music community in two special issues of the *Computer Music Journal* (1989). An early partisan has been Bharucha (1988) who argues against symbolic approaches in the following terms:

> [Symbolic models] have been successful at describing the formal structure of musical compositions but fail as psychological theories and are cumbersome as models for artificial intelligence. They lack parsimony: a [constraint or heuristic] is postulated for every structural property and exception thereof. They do not account for interactive phenomena in a straightforward way. They seldom exhibit emergent properties and do not typically generate novel predictions. Most importantly, they fail to account for the acquisition of the rules they postulate.

The intrinsic predictive capabilities of connection nets seem well suited to musical expectations. Their capabilities for pattern recognition suggest that they might be good emulators for associative musical processes such as thematicism. Most important to Bharucha, connection nets infer their insights directly from real-world examples, not through idealized, hard-coded rules.

To date, however, the most reliable programs have treated connection nets simply as a way of dealing with many, heavily interdependent decisions. This is the case in Sayegh's (1989) program for fingering guitar music. (Such a capability might have significant implications for an intelligent performer's assistant or for a composing program that seeks to write idiomatic guitar music.) This is a straightforward problem of selecting a finger and a string for each note in the music; it could be solved by search, but Sayegh instead uses Viterbi networks to deduce optimum path fingerings. In Desain and Honing's (1989) technique of rhythmic quantization, nodes of the network store durations in a rhythmic sequence; successive iterations gradually nudge durational relationships toward an equilibrium of small-integer ratios. Because each duration might potentially take on a continuous range of values, discrete search-based strategies simply would not work.

The predictive capabilities of connection networks make them especially well suited to simulating a listener's expectations. Jones and co-workers (in press a) describe two connectionist approaches for extracting meter from a melody. In their stronger resonance technique, network nodes simulate metronomes ticking at different tempi and phases. A metronome is stimulated when a note onset coincides with a metronome tick; metronome ticks in turn excite or inhibit the remaining metronomes," depending on whether or not [the receiving metronome] is in phase, and on whether [the sender's and receiver's] periods form a simple integer ratio." This technique seems to model human metric expectations intuitively, although to date it has been tested only on monophonic melodies. (Melodies in ensemble music often play heavily against a meter stated explicitly in other voices.) Also, Jones and co-workers (in press a) present techniques take no account of obvious factors such as accentuation and harmonic rhythm.

Connectionist pitch-processing methods have thus far compared poorly with other approaches. The 95% success rate for chord qualities that has been reported (Laden and Keefe, 1989) is hardly impressive for a task that rote methods get right in all cases. The effectiveness of Jones and co-workers' (1989) key-determination methods would undoubtedly be greatly improved if they took into account even a small part of the domain-specific knowledge assumed by Maxwell, eg, by suppressing pitch-node activations by nonharmonic notes or by acknowledging the fact that downbeat chords function differently from upbeat chords. In defending their connectionist results against Maxwell's superior symbolic ones, Jones and co-workers (in press b) argue that they are not, at least directly, seeking the best possible key analysis, but instead the most accurate model of human musical cognition:

> Backtracking—going back and making a second pass through the music once one has heard the entire piece [?]—is not a reasonable model of how humans process music. All our algorithms are constrained by the limits of human memory.

It is likely that Jones, Scarborough, and Miller's assumptions will evolve into a reasonable quantitative model of naive cognition: how a musically naive listener perceives a composition over the course of one hearing. On the other hand, Maxwell's program already emulates a trained musician, who listens repeatedly with score in hand until all ambiguities have been resolved.

The most ambitious goal among connectionists is a system which, after intensive exposure to musical examples in a given style, could generate fresh examples bearing the same traits and signatures. Efforts toward this goal include a program (Gjerdingen, 1989) that recognizes voice-leading signatures in Mozart, one (Todd, 1989) that extrapolates JAM FACTORY-style from learned melodies, sequence-learning proposals (Leman, 1988), and the TSTRUCTURE feature of HMSL (Polansky and co-workers, 1987). Musical results obtained to date fall far short of results obtained by symbolic programs such as CHORAL and the CYBERNETIC COMPOSER. The amount of domain-specific information required for Gjerdingen's limited ends suggests that inputs to the envisaged connectionist composing system will hardly be parsimonious (if such a system should truly be workable).

Bharucha's assertion (1988) that existing symbolic methods fail in and of themselves "to account for the acquisition of the rules they postulate" neglects Schwanauer's MUSE. He could argue, however, that MUSE falls short by inferring only heuristics that facilitate conformity to MUSE's basic constraints and that the acquisition of these constraints is itself not explained. Bharucha also neglects to acknowledge that such an accounting is of professional concern primarily to cognitive scientists such as himself. The question is not relevant to a theorist who already has some rules in mind and who simply wants to verify them, nor is it of great concern to a composer who wishes to find the most effective means of realizing inspirations as a concrete piece of music.

BIBLIOGRAPHY

G. Abraham, *100 Years of Music*, Duckworth, London, 1964, pp. 121–129; "AI in Music" issues of *Comput. Music J.* **4**(2–3) (1980).

C. Ames, "Automated Composition in Retrospect 1956–1986." *LEONARDO* **20**(2), 169 (1987).

C. Ames, "*Crystals*: Recursive Structures in Automated Composition," *Comput. Music J.* **6**(3), 46 (1982a).

C. Ames, "*Protocol*: Motivation, Design, and Production of a Composition for Solo Piano," *Interface* **11**(4), 213 (1982b).

C. Ames, "Stylistic Automata in *Gradient*," *Comput. Music J.* **7**(4), 45 (1983).

C. Ames, "Applications of Linked Data Structures to Automated Composition," in *Proceedings of the ICMC*, 1985, p. 251.

C. Ames, "Two Pieces for Amplified Guitar," *Interface* **15**(1), 25 (1986).

C. Ames, "Tutorial on Automated Composition," in *Proceedings of the ICMC*, 1987.

C. Ames, "Concurrence," *Interface* **17**(1), 3 (1988).

C. Ames, "Statistics and Compositional Balance," *Perspect. New Music* **28**(1), 80 (1989a).

C. Ames, "The Markov Process as a Musical Model," *LEONARDO* **22**(2), 175 (1989b).

C. Ames, "COMPOSE: A Modular Approach to Automated Score Generation and Score Processing," *Interface*, in press.

C. Ames and M. Domino, "A Cybernetic Composer Overview," in Conklin and Cleary, 1988, p. 46.

A. Andronico and A. Ciampa, "On Automatic Pattern Recognition and Acquisition of Printed Music," in *Proceedings of the ICMC*, Venice, 1982, p. 245.

J. J. Bharucha, "Neural Net Modeling of Music," in *Proceedings of the First AAAI Workshop on AI and Music*, 1988, p. 173.

D. Byrd, "An Integrated Computer Music Software System," *Comput. Music J.* **1**(2), 55 (1977).

A. Camurri, G. Haus, and R. Zaccaria, "Describing and Performing Musical Processes by Means of Petri Nets," *Interface* **15**(1), 1 (1986).

C. Chafe, B. Mont-Reynaud, and L. Rush, "Toward an Intelligent Editor of Digital Audio: Recognition of Musical Constructs," *Comput. Music J.* **6**(1), 30 (1982).

D. Conklin and J. Cleary, "Modeling and Generating Music Using Multiple Viewpoints," in *Proceedings of the First AAAI Workshop on AI and Music*, St. Paul, Minn., 1988, p. 125.

D. Cope, "An Expert System for Computer-Assisted Composition," *Comput. Music J.* **11**(4), 30 (1987).

R. Dannenberg, "An On-Line Algorithm for Real-Time Accompaniment," in *Proceedings of the ICMC,* Paris, 1984, p. 241.

R. Dannenberg and B. Mont-Reynaud, "Following an Improvisation in Real Time," in *Proceedings of the ICMC,* 1987, p. 241.

P. Desain and H. Honing, "LOCO: A Compositional Microworld in Logo," *Comput. Music J.* 12(3), 30 (1988).

P. Desain and H. Honing, "The Quantization of Musical Time: A Connectionist Approach," *Comput. Music J.* 13(3), 56 (1989).

K. Ebcioglu, "Computer Counterpoint," in *Proceedings of the ICMC,* Flushing, N.Y., 1980, p. 534.

K. Ebcioglu, "An Expert System for Harmonizing 4-Part Chorales," *Comput. Music J.* 12(3), 43 (1988).

B. Garton, "The ELTHAR Program," *Perspect. New Music* 27(1), 6 (1989).

S. Gill, "A Technique for the Composition of Music in a Computer," *Comput. J.* 6(2), 129 (1963).

R. O. Gjerdingen, "Using Connectionist Models to Explore Complex Musical Patterns," *Comput. Music J.* 13(3), 67 (1989).

L. Hiller, C. Ames, and R. Franki, "Automated Composition: An Installation at the 1985 International Exposition in Tsuduba, Japan," *Perspect. New Music* 23(2), 196 (1985).

L. Hiller and L. Isaacson, *Experimental Music,* McGraw-Hill Book Co., Inc., New York, 1959.

S. Holtzman, "A Generative Grammar Definitional Language for Music," *Interface* 9(1), 1 (1980).

J. A. Jones, D. L. Scarborough, and B. O. Miller, "Connectionist Models for Tonal Analysis," *Comput. Music J.* 13(3), 49 (1989).

J. A. Jones, D. L. Scarborough, and B. O. Miller, "PDP Models for Meter Perception," in *Proceedings of the Twelfth Annual Conference of the Cognitive Science Society,* Lawrence Erlbaum, Hillsdale, N.J., in press a.

J. A. Jones, D. L. Scarborough, and B. O. Miller, "Discovering Grouping Structure in Music," in *Proceedings of the Twelfth Annual Conference of the Cognitive Science Society,* Lawrence Erlbaum, Hillsdale, N.J., in press b.

K. Jones, "Compositional Applications of Stochastic Processes," *Comput. Music J.* 5(2), 45 (1981).

H. Katayose and co-workers, "Music Interpreter in the Kansei Music System," in *Proceedings of the ICMC,* Columbus, Ohio, 1989, p. 147.

J. Kippen and B. Bell, "Modeling Music with Grammars: Formal Language Representation in the BOL PROCESSER," in A. Marsden and A. Pople, eds., *Computer Representations and Models in Music,* Academic Press, Inc., New York, in press.

G. M. Koenig, "PROJECT2: A Programme for Musical Composition," *Electronic Music Rep.* 1(3), 1 (1969).

B. Laden and D. H. Keefe, "The Representation of Pitch in a Neural Net Model of Chord Classification," *Comput. Music J.* 13(4), 12 (1989).

P. S. Langston, "Eedie and Eddie on the Wire: An Experiment in Music Generation," in *Proceedings of the USENIX Summer Technical Conference and Exhibition,* 1986, p. 13.

O. Laske and B. Truax, "Goal Synthesis and Goal Pursuit in a Musical Transformation Task for Children between Seven and Twelve Years of Age," *Interface* 8, 207–235 (1979).

M. Leman, "Dynamical-Hierarchical Networks as Perceptual Memory Representations of Music," *Interface* 14(3–4), 125 (1985). No program is mentioned.

M. Leman, "Sequential (Musical) Information Processing with PDP Networks," in *Proceedings of the First AAAI Workshop on AI and Music,* 1988, p. 163.

D. Levitt, *A Melody Description System for Jazz Improvisation,* M.S. thesis, MIT, Cambridge, Mass., 1981.

D. Levitt, "Imitation of Musical Patterns," Boston, 1984 (lecture at the 1984 NEWCOMP Symposium).

D. Levitt, *A Representation for Musical Dialects,* Ph.D. dissertation, MIT, Cambridge, Mass., 1985.

S. C. Marsella, C. F. Schmidt, and J. L. Bresina, "A Problem-Reduction Approach to Automated Composition," in *Proceedings of the First AAAI Workshop on AI and Music,* 1988.

W. Martens, "PALETTE: An Environment for Developing an Individualized Set of Psychophysically Scaled Timbres," in *Proceedings of the ICMC,* 1985, p. 355.

M. V. Mathews and co-workers, *The Technology of Computer Music,* MIT Press, Cambridge, Mass., 1969.

H. J. Maxwell, "An Expert System for Harmonic Analysis of Tonal Music," in *Proceedings of the First AAAI Workshop on AI and Music,* 1988, p. 20.

J. Maxwell and S. Ornstein, *MOCKINGBIRD: A Composer's Amanuensis,* Xerox Corp., Palo Alto, Calif., 1981 (videotape).

MIDI: Musical Instrument Digital Interface Specification 1.0, International MIDI Assoc., North Hollywood, Calif., 1983.

B. Mont-Reynaud, "Problem Solving Strategies in a Music Transcription System," in *Proceedings of the Ninth IJCAI,* Los Angeles, Calif., Morgan-Kaufmann, San Mateo, Calif., 1985.

B. Mont-Reynaud and M. Goldstein, "On Finding Rhythmic Patterns in Musical Lines," in *Proceedings of the ICMC,* 1985, p. 391.

L. Polansky, "Morphological Metrics: An Introduction to a Theory of Formal Distances," in *Proceedings of the ICMC,* Urbana/Champaign, Ill., 1987, p. 197.

L. Polansky and co-workers, *Hierarchical Music Specification Language—Reference and User Manual,* Center for Contemporary Music, Mills College, Oakland, Calif., 1987.

S. T. Pope, "Music Notations and the Representation of Musical Structure and Knowledge," *Perspect. New Music* 24(2), 156 (1986).

M. Puckette, "Max Patcher, in *Proceedings of the ICMC,* Cologne, 1988.

C. Roads, *Composing Grammars,* Computer Music Assoc., San Francisco, Calif., 1978.

C. Roads, "Research in Music and Artificial Intelligence," *ACM Comput. Surv.* 17(2), 163 (1985). Much of this survey is devoted to Roads's IOS program for interactive orchestration.

C. Roads, "The Tsukuba Musical Robot," *Comput. Music J.* 10(2), 39 (1986).

C. Rosen, *The Classical Style,* W. W. Norton & Co., New York, 1971, pp. 33–36.

S. I. Sayegh, "Fingering for String Instrument with the Optimum Pat Paradigm," *Comput. Music J.* 13(3), 76 (1989).

H. Schenker, *Free Composition,* E. Oster, trans., Longman, New York, 1979. Originally published as *Der Freie Satz,* 1935.

J. Schillinger, *System of Musical Composition,* 2 vols., Carl Fisher, New York, 1941.

S. Schwanauer, *MUSE: A Learning System for Tonal Composition,* Ph.D. dissertation, Yale University, New Haven, Conn., 1986.

B. C. Schmidt, "Natural Language System for Music," *Comput. Music J.* 11(2), 25 (1986).

I. Stravinsky and R. Craft, *Expositions and Developments,* University of California Press, Berkeley, Calif., 1959, p. 99.

J. Sundberg, A. Askenfelt, and L. Fryden, "Musical Performance: A Synthesis-by-Rule Approach," *Comput. Music J.* 7(1) (1983).

J. Tenny and L. Polansky, "Temporal Gestalt Perception in Music," *J. Music Theor.* **24**(2), 205 (1980).

M. T. Thomas, "VIVACE: A Rule-Based AI System for Composition," in *Proceedings of the ICMC,* Vancouver, B.C., 1985, p. 267.

P. M. Todd, "A Connectionist Approach to Algorithmic Composition," *Comput. Music J.* **13**(4), 27 (1989).

B. Vercoe and M. Puckette, "Synthetic Rehearsal: Training the Synthetic Performer," in *Proceedings of the ICMC,* 1985, p. 275.

T. Winograd, "Linguistics and the Computer Analysis of Tonal Harmony," *J. Music Theor.* **12**(1), 2 (1968).

C. Yavelow, "MIDI and the Apple Macintosh," *Comput. Music J.* **10**(3), 11 (1986).

G. Zarlino, *The Art of Counterpoint,* G. Marco and C. Palisca, trans., W. W. Norton & Co., New York, 1968. Originally published in 1558.

D. Zicarelli, "*M* and *Jam Factory,*" *Comput. Music J.* **11**(4), 12 (1987).

CHARLES AMES
Eggertsville, New York

MYCIN

An early medical advice system to assist physicians in the antimicrobial treatment of patients with serious infections (bacteremia and meningitis). Developed by E. H. Shortliffe of Stanford University, MYCIN was one of the first expert systems to exploit the rule-based approach to knowledge representation (see E. H. Shortliffe, *Computer-Based Medical Consultations: MYCIN,* Elsevier, New York, 1976). Its underlying inferencing techniques were later generalized by W. vanMelle in the EMYCIN (qv) system, and it served as the foundation for many other research projects in the subsequent decade (see B. G. Buchanan and E. H. Shortliffe, *Rule-Based Expert Systems: The MYCIN Experiments of the Stanford Heuristic Programming Project,* Addison-Wesley, Reading, Mass., 1984).

E. H. SHORTLIFFE
Stanford University

NATURAL LANGUAGE GENERATION

Natural language generation is the process of deliberately constructing a natural-language text in order to meet specified communicative goals. The term "text" is intended as a general, recursive term that can apply to utterances or parts of utterances of any size, spoken or written. In people, whether a text is spoken or written has implications for the amount of deliberation and editing that may have gone on; if "spoken" language is identified with a lack of revision, most programs today "speak" even though nearly all only display words on a display screen. Since the choice of whether to revise, or whether to use print or voice, is usually not an option for a generation program today, these particulars are only mentioned when they are an issue in a program's design.

The goals come from another program, perhaps an expert reasoning system or an ICAI tutor, that is motivated to talk to a human user. The texts that are produced may range from a single phrase given in answer to a question, through multisentence remarks and questions within a dialogue to full-page explanations.

Generation is a different matter from simply having programs use English: programs have been printing natural language messages at their users for as long as there have been computers, yet one does not want to think of an error message from a FORTRAN compiler as either constructed or goal directed, however well written it may be. An error message does not "mean" anything to the program that prints it: any connection between the string of words and the program's situation is strictly within the mind of the programmer who wrote that preprogrammed, "canned" text. Even the use of parameterized "format" statements, where the canned word string can be augmented by names or simple descriptions by substituting for variables, is not really generation. These "fill-in-the-blank" or "template" techniques depend for their effectiveness on a tacit limitation in the number and complexity of the situations in which the program will need to use them; that they have been adequate up to now for expressing what programs have had to say is more of a comment on the simplicity of today's programs than on the capabilities of template-driven generation.

In contrast with such "engineering treatments," research on natural language generation, like the other areas of its parent field of computational linguistics (qv), has as its goal not just competent performance by a computer but the development of a computational theory of the human capacity for language and the processes that engage it. For generation, this focuses on the explanation of two key matters: versatility and creativity. What do people know about their language? What processes do they employ that enable them to be versatile, varying their texts in form and emphasis to fit an enormous range of speaking situations, and creative, with the potential to express any object or relation in their mind as a natural-language text? The need to accommodate these capabilities is the prime organizing force behind generation theories and is the basis of the special contributions that the people who work on generation make to the rest of computational linguistics and AI.

This article describes AI research on natural language generation with a historical perspective, emphasizing the special character of the problems to be solved. It begins by contrasting generation with language understanding in order to establish basic concepts about the breakdown of the process into components and the flow of information and decisions through it. A section of excerpts from the output of illustrative generation systems follows, showing what kinds of performance are possible and where the difficulties are. In the remainder of the entry the common approaches to generation are surveyed, including characteristic messages and the nature of a generator's lexicon. A separate section continues the survey with alternative approaches to the representation and uses of a grammar.

Character of the Generation Process

To understand why generation has the organization that it does, it helps to make a brief comparison with its more studied complementary process, natural language understanding (qv). In contrast with the organization of the understanding process—which to a first approximation can follow the traditional stages of a linguistic analysis: morphology (qv), syntax, semantics, pragmatics/discourse—the generation process has a fundamentally different character. This fact follows directly from the intrinsic differences in the information flow in the two processes. Understanding proceeds from texts to intentions; generation does the opposite. In understanding, the "known" is the wording of the text (and possibly its intonation). From the wording the process constructs and deduces the propositional content conveyed by the text and the probable intentions of the speaker in producing it. Its primary effort is to scan the words of the text in sequence, during which the form of the text gradually unfolds; the scanning requirement forces a process based on the management of multiple hypotheses and predictions that feed a representation that must be expanded dynamically. Major problems are caused by ambiguity—one form can convey a range of alternative meanings—and by underspecification—the audience receives more information from situationally motivated inferences than is conveyed by the actual text. In addition, mismatches in the speaker's and audience's model of the situation (and especially of each other) led to unintended inferences.

Generation has the opposite information flow. It proceeds from content to form, from intentions and perspectives to linearly arrayed words and syntactic markers. Its "known" is its awareness of its intentions, its plans, and the text it has already produced. Coupled with its model of the audience, the situation, and the discourse, they provide the basis for making choices among the alternative wordings and constructions that the language provides:

the primary effort in constructing a text deliberately. Most generation systems do produce the surface texts sequentially from left to right, but only after having made decisions top-down for the content and form of the text as a whole. Ambiguity in a generator's knowledge is not possible (indeed, one of its problems is to notice that it has inadvertently introduced an ambiguity into the text). Rather than underspecification, a generator's problem is to choose from its oversupplied sources how to adequately signal intended inferences to the audience and what information to omit from explicit mention in the text.

With its opposite flow of information, one might assume that a generation process could be organized like an understanding process but with the stages in opposite order. To a certain extent this is true: identification of intention (goals) largely precedes any detailing of the conceptual information the audience should be given; the planning of the rhetorical structure that will be imposed on the information largely precedes any construction of syntactic structures to realize it; and the syntactic context of a word must be fixed before the precise morphological and suprasegmental form it should take can be known. But to emphasize this ordering of linguistic representational levels would be to miss generation's special character, namely that generation is above all a planning (qv) process. It entails realizing goals in the presence of constraints and limitations on resources; its efforts consist of making decisions: decisions to use certain words or syntactic constructions and decisions to post constraints on later decisions. It is best organized as a process of progressive refinement.

This perspective on generation as planning permeates the views of the people who work on it. A language's syntax and lexicon become both resources and constraints, defining the elements available for the construction of the text and also the dependencies between them that determine their valid combinations. These dependencies, and the fact that they tacitly govern when the information on which each decision depends can become available are the fundamental reason why generation programs do largely follow the conventional stages identified by linguists. Goal identification precedes content selection and rhetorical planning, which precedes syntactic construction, only because that is a natural order in which to make decisions; it is simpler to go with the flow of the dependencies rather than jump ahead and take the chance that a premature decision will have to be undone because it later turns out to be inconsistent. Today's research concentrates on understanding how best to represent what decisions are possible and the dependencies among them, as well as on how to represent the constraints and opportunities earlier decisions place on later ones as the process proceeds.

The focus on planning and intention in generation research puts the underlying program in a pivotal position methodologically. Computational theories of processes must be implemented—embodied in a program that actually performs the behaviors under study—before they can be tested for coherence and procedural adequacy. One cannot test a theory of talking without having the underlying program talk about something—planning and realization must be in the service of some actual goals. One is therefore forced to generate "for" some underlying program or else run the risk of basing one's theory on an unrealistic, incoherent foundation. Unfortunately, underlying programs that one can pick up "off the shelf" have inevitably been designed without the concerns of generation in mind. They turn out to be lacking in conceptual support for subtleties of intention and representation that generation researchers need and to have structured their internal expressions in ways that make it difficult for a generation system to use alternative perspectives or groupings.

Faced with the potential problems of using underlying programs built to suit independent concerns, generation researchers have adopted various approaches. Some develop their generators as stand-alone facilities and concentrate on studying grammar or planning in isolation (Mann and Mathiessen, 1985; Appelt, 1985; Bates and Ingria, 1980). Others have dedicated a great deal of their own development effort to building a task-based conceptual program on their generator and give it something substantive to talk about (Davey, 1979; Clippinger, 1977; Kukich, 1983). Still others work from an independently developed program but have interposed some kind of independent "planning" system in between to patch over the differences (McDonald, 1985; McKeown, 1985). None of these approaches will lead soon to a general-purpose generation facility that can be attached freely to any underlying program, though some work has been directed that way (Goldman, 1975; McDonald, 1983; Mann and Moore, 1981).

Standard Components and Terminology

The natural language generation component does not stand by itself. It fits within a man–machine interface, which it shares with a component that does natural language understanding—the input to the system. In a good man–machine interface today one would also expect provisions for coordinated graphical input and output, complementing the natural language I/O. Bridging the two is a representation of the ongoing discourse, which they both add to and use for reference. The interface may end here, or it may extend further back with other shared components such as a discourse controller that directs the actions the generator takes and coordinates the interpretations made by the understander. Behind the interface is the nonlinguistic reasoning or database program that human users employ the interface to talk to. This program will be referred to here uniformly as the underlying program. It can be almost any type of AI system one can imagine: cooperative database, expert diagnostician, ICAI tutor, commentator, apprentice, advisor, mechanical translator. The nature of the underlying program presently has no significant influence on the generator's design.

Today most generation researchers work most often with underlying programs that are expert advisors (eg, McDonald, 1985; Wilensky and co-workers, 1984). With an advisor program the control of where the conversation goes is most likely to rest with the program rather than the person using it. In addition, advisor programs and intelligent machine tutors are likely to have a good understanding of what their human interlocutors are thinking. These features make them able to motivate fairly sophisticated texts, which makes them attractive to those generation researchers who are looking for already developed programs to work with.

The generation process starts within the underlying program when some event leads to a need for the program to speak. In the simplest case this may be the need to answer a question from the user; with a sophisticated discourse controller it may be the perception of a need to interrupt the user's activities in order to point out an impending problem. Once the process is initiated, three kinds of activities must be carried out:

1. Identifying the goals the utterance is to achieve
2. Planning how the goals may be achieved, including evaluating the situation and the available communicative resources
3. Realizing the plans as a text

Goals are typically to impart certain information to the audience or to prompt them to some action or reasoning. People, of course, talk for social and psychological reasons as well as practical ones; but as these needs are beyond the ken of today's computer programs, AI research on generation is forced to largely ignore them. Planning involves the selection (and deliberate omission) of the information units to appear in the text (eg, concepts, relations, individuals) and the adoption of a coordinating rhetorical framework or schema for the utterance as a whole (eg, temporal progression, compare and contrast). Particular perspectives may be imposed on the units to aid in the signaling of intended inferences.

Realization is the process of manifesting the planner's directives as actual text. It depends on a sophisticated knowledge of the language's grammar and rules of discourse coherency, and typically constructs a syntactic description of the text as an intermediate representation. The term "realization" is used technically within the field: For example, one speaks about choosing to "realize" a modification relationship as either an adjective or a relative clause. It emphasizes not only attention to linguistic form but also knowledge of the criteria that dictate how those forms are used. In many research projects the process that does grammatical realization is called the linguistic component (McDonald, 1983), and in some the planning and goal-identification processes are together called the *strategic component* (Thompson, 1977). Usually it is only the linguistic component that has any direct knowledge of the grammar of the language being produced. What form this grammar takes is one of the points of greatest difference between generation projects, though all projects largely agree on the function a grammar should serve in generation.

For the traditional linguist, a grammar is a body of statements in a notation. The content of the statements—the specific facts of a given natural language—is of less interest to the linguist, by and large, than the theoretical properties of the notation. These properties are measured by how expressive the notation is, what primitives it identifies, and what representations and principles it makes use of. The situation is not much different in theories of generation except that the notation—the procedural and representational framework—is designed to serve a very specific function with which the traditional linguist is not concerned, namely, to guide and constrain the process of generating a text with a specific content and goals in the presence of a specific audience. This has an overriding effect on the form grammars take; more importantly, it also strongly influences the information they must include. The grammar is now responsible for defining the choices that a language allows in form and vocabulary, and it must further include criteria of usage. Generation researchers must ask what circumstances lead to deciding on one alternative rather than another, as well as what functions the various constructions of the language serve that make them appropriate for fulfilling a certain goal. Only by including such information can a grammar serve as a resource defining the options available to the text planner. The other, more obvious, function of a grammar is to ensure that the texts that are produced follow the rules of the language, ie, that they are "grammatical." How exactly this is done is another point where the different schools of generation often part ways, but a common theme is that the grammar functions by defining dependencies and constraining decisions.

The nonlinguistic plan or specification that directs realization is typically called the message; some researchers talk about "realizing the message" and speak of the conceptual and rhetorical representations maintained by the planning and goal-identification processes as being at "the message level" (as opposed to realization activities at "the surface-structure level"). This is a convenient and commonsense terminology, but one must be careful not to presume too much from it. The typical mental image evoked by the term "message" is of written notes passed from one person to another, eg, as the result of a telephone conversation; however, this image does not fit the situation: Researchers who study both planning and realization continually make the point that there is no clean line between the two activities (see, eg, McDonald, 1985; Appelt, 1980; Danlos, 1984). Planning proceeds in layers of refinement and must appreciate the linguistic consequences of its decisions; the realization of units in early layers creates a grammatical context that imposes constraints on the range of realizations that can be planned for later. Goals may emerge or change in priority opportunistically as planning and even realization proceeds.

STATE OF THE ART

There is a firm consensus within the field (Mann and coworkers, 1982) that versatility and creativity in machine-generated text is possible only if all three of the following apply:

1. The generator incorporates a comprehensive linguistically principled grammar
2. The underlying program has a sophisticated, commonsensical, conceptual view

3. The text planner can make use of models of the audience and the discourse

Unfortunately, such generators are still only the subject of research today. When none of these conditions are met, the state of the art in generated text is still about the same as it was in 1970 in Winograd's SHRDLU program (1972). SHRDLU produced original sentences, which it constructed dynamically, as replies to the questions it was asked. It took program expressions out of its model of the state of the blocks on its table and the actions it had performed and applied what today would be called a "direct-replacement" procedure to make simple grammatical adjustments to the verbs and linearize the expressions to yield comfortably readable texts such as the one below.

When did you pick up [the green pyramid]?
While I was stacking up the red cube, a large red block, and a large green cube.

By the late 1970s generation systems of this simple but effective sort had become quite important in the early rule-based expert systems. They were needed to translate the large numbers of rules in these systems into an easily appreciated format in stylized English. A generator of some kind is required within these systems because the number of rules is large and their internal variation is too high to capture with a set of fixed, fill-in-the-blanks templates. It is a straightforward matter to provide a simple generation capability for any program where the objects in the knowledge base have a consistent structure, and there is only one situation—one communicative context—in which the text must appear. Such capabilities are developed quickly, typically on an ad hoc basis as the rule-based system is developed (Forbus and Stevens, 1981; Frank, 1980).

Generation researchers, however, are interested in more complex texts than the context-free presentation an expert system's rules can motivate. Today this almost invariably means that as well as working on their generator they must develop their own underlying programs to provide an adequate conceptual source to work from, but there are numerous technical problems in generation that can be profitably approached with only a minimal base. As an example, here is a simple description from a program by Sigurd (1984). Sigurd's point was to study how grouping is signaled though intonational effects; this text is actually spoken by a Votrax speech-production system.

The submarine is to the south of the port. It is approaching the port, but is not close to it. The destroyer is approaching the port too.

Although its content will not win it a place on the *New York Times* Best Seller List, its structure, especially its use of the inference-directing function words "but" and "too," represents an important contribution. The source propositions in the database of an expert system that reasoned about submarines and destroyers would not be "packaged" with the conceptual equivalents of such function words already in place and able to be read out by a simple template. This is because the inferences the words control are specific only to one particular choice of what facts are being mentioned and how they have been grouped, a planning decision that is not part of the reasoning system's job but cannot be omitted in generation.

A similar technical problem that is not yet well enough understood is "Subsequent Reference" (McDonald, 1978). What wording should be chosen when a reference to an object appears more than once in the text? Always using a pronoun may introduce ambiguities; in general, careful reasoning can be needed about how the audience will characterize the actors in a text in order to judge what phrasing to use. Below is an example text from a recent study of this problem by Granville (1984). He classifies the relations between a referent and its last point of mention and develops a set of structural rules for making subsequent references based on it.

Pogo cares for Hepzibah. Churchy likes her, too. Pogo gives a rose to her, which pleases her. She does not want Churchy's rose. He is jealous. He punches Pogo. He gives a rose to Hepzibah. The petals drop off. This upsets her. She cries.

The principal problem with that text as a piece of prose is that it is "choppy": No attempt has been made to group its individual propositions into larger units and the resulting sentences feel too short. Ultimately, such textural decisions require a linguistically sensitive analysis of text style; but they also require a conceptual basis for the grouping and an appreciation of what a grouping will signal to the audience. This information is not easy to come by in today's candidates for underlying programs.

It is no wonder then that the very best performances by generators have come from systems in which the generation researcher was also the person who developed the underlying program. That way one is sure that there will be a basis in the underlying representation for any rhetorical attitudes or distinctions that the subject matter calls for and will be a conceptual perspective by which to organize groupings. An important case in point is the program PROTEUS, developed by Davey (1979) in 1974. This program produced descriptions of games of tic-tac-toe (also called naughts and crosses) that are still among the most fluent texts ever produced by a machine.

The game started with my taking a corner, and you took an adjacent one. I threatened you by taking the middle of the edge opposite that and adjacent to the one which I had just taken but you blocked it and threatened me. I blocked your diagonal and forked you. If you had blocked mine, you would have forked me, but you took the middle of the edge opposite of the corner which I took first and the one which you had just taken and so I won by completing my diagonal.

The naturalness of PROTEUS's descriptions come largely from its appreciation of tic-tac-toe as a game: it has a rich model of how specific moves may be seen as threats or counters to threats, and it incorporates the rhetorical principle that one should put in a text only the most salient information in a situation, eg, missed opportunities or forks, while leaving the other information to be communicated implicitly by inference. PROTEUS has the equivalent of an underlying program in its routines for the analysis of the tic-tac-toe moves. These provide an annotation of the moves in terms of threats, blocks, etc, providing input to a planning facility that selects the best level of description for each move (eg, "block" vs "fork"). The planner then groups the moves two or three at a time into sentences according to what game-level relationship seems to provide the best description of their motivation (eg, "threat-but-block" or "although-threat-block-&-counter"). A grammar and realization facility than takes the described and grouped moves, works out the details of their form as English sentences, and produces the words of the text.

A rival to Davey's PROTEUS in fluency is Clippinger's 1974 program ERMA (1977). ERMA is the only program to date that has attempted to deal with the fact that people speak in real time and continue to think and plan as they do so. People reflect on what they are saying and notice, midsentence, omissions or unintended interpretations that they fix by dynamically replanning and restarting their speech in midutterance. To model this behavior, Clippinger, working with an undergraduate assistant, Brown (1974), analyzed 40 hours of transcripts of a patient in psychoanalysis in order to understand that patient's motivations and reasoning patterns sufficiently well to provide a computational account of one of the paragraphs in that transcript (shown below), which the program ERMA was able to reproduce in every detail. (Actually, the original transcribed paragraph included several additional "uhs" and a "you know;" there was also no attempt to account for the specific time delays that occurred or for some of the sentence-initial perseverations.) The text segments in parenthesis are what ERMA was planning to say before it cut itself off and restarted.

> You know for some reason I just thought about the bill and payment again. (You shouldn't give me a bill.) ⟨Uh⟩ I was thinking that I (shouldn't be given a bill) of asking you whether it wouldn't be all right for you not to give me a bill. That is, I usually by (the end of the month know the amount of the bill), well, I immediately thought of the objections to this, but my idea was that I would simply count up the number of hours and give you a check at the end of the month.

Clippinger and Brown developed an architecture of five major interlocking components that took a thought from its first appearance as an interpersonal goal, through a fleshing-out and lexicalization, evaluation for social acceptability, interjection of attenuating phrasings, and sometimes a complete reworking to soften harsh impacts, while all the time realizing and uttering whatever text plan was in force at that moment. This required something of a tour-de-force in terms of computer programming for 1974, and the project was not carried further.

HISTORICAL PERSPECTIVES ON THE PROBLEM

It is quite striking to realize that two of the most competent generation programs ever developed, Davey's PROTEUS and Clippinger's ERMA, are also among the oldest in the field. There are two reasons for this: first, until the early 1980s, comparatively few people had ever worked on the problem of generation and, second, the problem is very hard, harder in this writer's opinion than language understanding, the area where most of the AI work in natural-language processing has concentrated. These matters are not independent. A good deal of work on generation was in fact going on in the early 1970s, principally in the context of Ph.D. dissertations that built upon the first rush of significant results in language processing that had come a few years before with the work of Winograd (1972) on SHRDLU and of Woods (1970) with augmented transition networks (ATNs) (see GRAMMAR, AUGMENTED TRANSITION NETWORK). In addition to Davey and Clippinger, there was the work of Simmons and Slocum on the adaptation of ATNs to generation (Shapiro, 1982) and the thesis of Goldman (1975) focusing on how to organize word choice when generating from conceptual-dependency (qv) networks as well as other works (Brown, 1974; Halliday and Martin, 1981; McDonald, 1975; Shapiro, 1975; Wong, 1985). It is fair to say, however, that the initial reports of that generation work, principally at the important TINLAP meeting in 1975 (Bruce, 1975; Clippinger, 1975; Goldman, 1975), fell largely on deaf ears, and research on generation went into something of a hiatus for the last half of the decade. This is not to say that no work was done during those years; rather, generation was not perceived by the larger community as an important problem to be working on. By contrast, today there are entire sessions on generation at any large conference where natural language processing is included as a topic. There have also been three international workshops of generation specialists since 1983 with an ever-increasing number of participants.

Until the early 1980s generation was considered by most people in AI (those who did not work on it) to be a relatively simple problem. Indeed, it is a simple matter to take a statement in an internal representation of the sort people used in the middle 1970s, say, (#supports :block 6 :block 3), couple it with attributes stored separately for the individuals, and produce "The big red block supports a green one": Winograd's SHRDLU could do this in 1970. If this were all the competence one needed, generation would not be an important research problem. However, as soon as one begins to consider the various ways that simple sentence could be rewritten—the versatility the English language invites speakers to make use of—the difficulties begin to emerge. In that text, for example, should one always say "a green one" and not "a green block"; what kind of circumstances call for one but not the other? Suppose one wanted to use the Support assertion as an attribute of the green block, for example, as a way to distinguish it from the other green blocks: ". . . the green block that's supported by the big red one." How does one represent the grammatical knowledge that allows a generator to use its representation of the syntactic structure of the statement form of the text to produce the corresponding relative clause? How does the generator represent to itself in a general way the fact that the relative clause is even available or that such a use for the assertion is possible? Few people worked on generation in the later 1970s (or stayed with the problem for more than a year or two), either because they found the task too simple to be interesting (when working forward from the sorts of texts that reasoning programs needed at that time) or because they found it too difficult to make any headway (when working backward from the complexities of actual human texts).

COMMON APPROACHES

It is difficult to identify the common elements in the different research projects on generation. By contrast, in language-understanding research one can identify any number of primary approaches to the problem: using ATNs, semantic grammars (see GRAMMAR, SEMANTIC), demon-based systems grounded in conceptual-dependency representation, procedural semantics, and many more. These schools of thought have names, a body of literature, and a coherent historical development over decades or more. Generation research cannot yet be said to have any schools in this sense. This is partially because historically only a small number of individuals have made this their primary area of research (as just discussed); large research groups focused on generation have formed in only the last few years. A more significant reason is that the nature of generation research has made it difficult to see the commonalities among the different generation systems. The principal problem is the lack of a common starting point: unlike parsing research, where it is obvious that one must start by identifying and grouping the words of the text, independent research efforts in generation inevitably construct their messages using different internal representation languages, use differing amounts of planning, and focus on orthogonal technical problems. This lack of any immediate basis of comparison has made it hard for people to build on each other's work or even to test their own examples on another researcher's system. Nevertheless, the various generation projects have more in common with each other than not. There are common threads running through the projects: similar approaches, similar representations, similar grammars.

Two organizing questions are of common concern. The first is how to confront the diversity of forms in natural languages to develop functional accounts of them: to answer the question of why a person will use one form rather than another and to do so with a formal, computational account that a machine can use in dealing with people. Put another way, what is a person's model of the differences between syntactically or lexically similar versions of the same text and of the impact they will have on an audience? The second question is control of the generation process. What defines the choices that have to be made in a given speaking situation? What provides the basis for ordering them? How does one organize and represent the intermediate results? What awareness does the system have of the dependencies between choices? How are these dependencies represented and made to influence the control algorithms?

Alternative answers to these questions will be described throughout the rest of this entry. This section covers the nature of messages and approaches to the lexicon; the following section considers various treatments of grammar.

Control by Progressive Refinement of Message

All treatments of the diversity of forms have been bound together with accounts of control, making control the proper place to start in looking at the schools of thought as to how generation is actually done. Among generation systems that were built specifically to work from underlying systems, the predominant approach to control is to treat the message from the text planner as a kind of program, ie, to see it as an expression that one evaluates with a special kind of interpreter. Again a caution is in order. These "messages" are not simply expressions whose context and form are isomorphic to the target text that happen to be encoded in a non-natural computer language. They cannot just be translated. Of course, in the simplest treatments of generation, translation might be sufficient (as in most existing expert systems), but in treatments that focus on generation, the relations and arguments in a message are best viewed as instructions to achieve a certain effect by linguistic means. The evaluation proceeds by progressive refinement from outermost instructions to inner. This control technique is natural to the developers of the systems since it mimics the style of the programming languages that they use and takes advantage of the almost unconscious preference among practitioners of AI to follow a function-parameter, predicate-argument style of representation.

The most common messages today are not constructed by any planner but are simply data structures extracted from the underlying program and given a special interpretation by the generator. This is common practice in programs that need to explain their reasoning (Swartout, 1977; Clancey, 1979) (see EXPLANATION), with one of the clearest and earliest examples being to explain the reasoning embodied in simple natural deduction proofs in the predicate calculus. Below is such a proof, and the text produced is by an early version of McDonald's program MUMBLE (1983); the proof itself is taken from earlier generation work of Chester (1976).

Input

Line *1*: premis

$\quad$ Exists(x) [barber(x) and
$\qquad$ Forall(y).. shaves(x,y) iff not.shaves(y,y)]

Line *2*: existential instantiation (*1*)

$\quad$ barber(g) and Forall(y).. shaves(g,y) iff not.shaves(y,y)

Line *3*: conjunction reduction (*2*)

$\quad$ Forall(y).. shaves(g,y) iff not.shaves(y,y)

Line *4*: universal instantiation (*3*)

$\quad$ shaves(g,g) iff not.shaves(g,g)

Line *5*: tautology (*4*)

$\quad$ shaves(g,g) and not.shaves(g,g)

Line *6*: conditionalization (*5,1*)

$\quad$ (Exists(x) [barber(x) and
$\qquad$ Forall(y).. shaves (x,y) iff not.shaves(y,y)]
$\quad$ implies (shaves(g,g) and not.shaves(g,g))

Line 7: reductio-ad-absurdum (6)

not(Exists(x) barber(x) and
Forall(y).. shaves (x,y)
iff not.shaves(y,y))

Output

Assume that there is some barber who shaves everyone who doesn't shave himself (and no one else). Call him Giuseppe. Now, anyone who doesn't shave himself would be shaved by Giuseppe. This would include Giuseppe himself. That is, he would shave himself, if and only if he did not shave himself, which is a contradiction. This means that the assumption leads to a contradiction. Therefore it is false, there is no such barber.

The fluency of this text derives from an ad hoc model of the communicative force that accompanies a given instance of an inference rule of natural deduction (eg, "premis" or "universal instantiation"). The model provides an account of the motivations of the proof writer in selecting what rule to apply, eg, that the point of the right side of the biconditional in the first line is to place a restriction on the variable Y (". . . who doesn't shave himself"). These motivations license the decisions to realize the lines of the proof in specific ways. These motivations, however, do not appear anywhere in the proof (which was the sole input to the program). They are only presumed and so are valid only for a few example proofs written with that particular personal style of natural deduction.

The paucity of information or motives and perspectives in the messages of the underlying program is a perennial problem of work on generation: computational linguists are forced to read into the data structures of the underlying programs because they do not already include the kinds of rhetorical instructions the generator needs if it is to employ the syntactic constructions of the language in the way that a person would. Without such "extra" information, the coherency of what is said, especially for texts more than a few sentences in length, will depend on how consistent and how thorough the authors of the underlying programs have been in their representational conventions: a generator has no choice but to treat a symbol like "premis" or the biconditional in the same way each time it sees them in the same context. If consistency is maintained, the imaginative designer can make up for the deficiencies by embellishing the data structures once they are inside the linguistic component.

When a text planner is brought into the process, messages can be built from a combination of data structures from the underlying program and instructions about perspective and rhetorical effect that the planner introduces (McDonald, 1985). Below is an example of a complex message—a "generation program"—that leads to text of the quality a person would produce (taken from a design study reported in McDonald and Pustejovsky, 1985). Specification of effects to achieve are marked by colons in front of the symbols. The content information to be conveyed is given by reference to internal frame objects named in angle brackets. This content is to be put in specific perspectives (eg, main event and particulars), and the effect is to direct reasoning about linguistic alternatives in the presence of given rhetorical, and eventually grammatical, constraints. If the researcher's goal is to approximate the fluency and specificity of texts authored by people, messages will normally be as complex as this.

Specification

(the-day's-events-in-the-Gulf-tanker-war
:events-require-certification-as-to-source
(main-event#⟨same-event-type-varying-patient
#⟨hit-by-missiles Thorshavet⟩
#⟨hit-by-missiles Liberian⟩⟩
:unusual#⟨number-of-ships-hit 2⟩
:identify-the-ships)
(particulars #⟨damage-report Thorshavet Oslo-officials⟩
#⟨damage-report Liberian Lloyds⟩))

Output

Two oil tankers, the Norwegian-owned Thorshavet and a Liberian-registered vessel, were reported to have been hit by missiles Friday in the Gulf. The Thorshavet was ablaze and under tow to Bahrain, officials in Oslo said. Lloyds reported that two crewman were injured on the Liberian ship.

The goal of fluency and intentional specification of form motivates many of the more elaborate bits of computational machinery that constitute the common threads running through different research projects, particularly the use of phrasal lexicons and an intermediate linguistic representation. Stepping through a simple example will show why these are needed. Consider the logical formula below, given in the prenext notation that a program would typically use internally. (This example follows the treatments of Chester and McDonald described above.) This is the commonest kind of message one will find today: an expression straight from the model of an underlying program (the natural deduction proof system), now given a special interpretation because it is being used to specify a text.

(exists x
(and barber(x)
(forall y
(if-and-only-if shaves(x,y)
(not shaves(y,y))))))

In this formula, the generator is immediately confronted with choices of realization. Should the quantification be expressed literally ("There exists an X such that . . ."), or should it be folded within the body as determiner information on the realization of the variables (". . . some barber")? Should the biconditional if-and-only-if be realized literally as a subordinating conjunction or interpreted as a range restriction on the variable (yielding the modifying relative clause "anyone who doesn't shave himself")? A predication like barber(x) should presumably always be decoded and converted to a specification of how the variable is to be described since it reflects the logician's convention of expressing type restriction through initial conjunctions; the alternative of using an extra sentence ("X is a barber") would be too unnatural. The other choices are substantive, however, and need to be deliberated over.

In message-directed progressive refinement treatments, such deliberations are usually managed by grouping the alternatives according to the type of object involved. The objects that populate the "mind" of the underlying program, in this case logical connectives, predicates, and bound variables, are all linked to the words and grammatical constructs that are appropriate for realizing them through "specialist procedures" maintained within the generator. These procedures are the equivalent of the lexicon in an understanding system. The specialists build a realizing phrase by drawing on lexical information associated directly with the individual logical objects. They are able to look at properties of the objects such as when they were last mentioned or what kinds of objects they have as arguments. Each object typically has associated lexical items: A constant may have a name; a predicate may have an adjective or a verb. The specialist does its work by putting these into a phrasal context that will be completed by the recursive application of other specialists, eg, the two-place predicate "shaves(x,y)" becomes the clause template "x shaves y."

In this control regimen the execution of each of the specialists is compartmentalized and taken up in the order dictated by the hierarchical form of the controlling expression, in this case the formula. The quantifier "exists" would be dealt with first, then the "and," the "forall," etc. Consideration of how an element of the formula is to be interpreted is delayed until it is actually reached in the stepwise, incremental refinement process. Relations provide linguistic templates by which to order the realizations of their arguments, and the process proceeds recursively. This provides the benefits of the principle of least commitment, expediting the generation process as a whole by avoiding the possibility of having to "back up" out of prematurely made realization decisions that turn out to be incompatible with the grammatical context defined by a higher template.

Lexical Choice

Some approaches to machine reasoning emphasize the selection of a small set of primitives and the statement of a program's knowledge as a set of expressions over these primitives plus a set of constant terms for individuals. This has the advantage for reasoning of giving the commonalities among situations a structural prominence. This makes inferences easy to draw because they can be bundled into natural groups by the primitives. However, the reduction of the range of human actions to a set of, eg, only 13 conceptual primitives means that a great deal of the specificity that the words of the language carry, in this case the verbs, will have been distributed throughout the expressions and will have to be collected and discriminated during generation if specific verbs are to be used. Goldman pioneered this use of discrimination nets to determine the best words for realizing whole expressions in his thesis on generation from conceptual-dependency representation (Kay, 1984). He demonstrated how one would determine word choice by working outward from the core primitives, testing the other parts of an expression for certain properties. For example, from the action primitive "Ingest" one might get the verbs "drink," "eat," "inhale," "breath," "smoke," or "ingest" by testing whether, eg, the object ingested was a fluid or smoke.

Notice that one of the available words was "ingest," the least marked (most abstract) alternative the discrimination net allowed. It is inevitable in computer programs developed by people that the internal symbols will correspond to natural-language words, and indeed, there is invariably an intended correspondence in at least the back of an AI programmer's mind between the symbol and the word when they use it. Careful representation researchers point out that their conceptual terms have no real meaning in and of themselves: They could perfectly well be replaced with artificial print forms like G007 and the programs would continue to work perfectly well.

The fact that one is forced to make deliberate discriminations and word choices when working from expressions over neutral, underspecified primitives means that the problem will receive a good deal of attention. A discrimination net design invites the generation researcher to go beyond the base distinctions by object type and to include contextual factors like the speaker's emotional perspective in the decisions. Consequently, generation work based on underlying programs written using conceptual dependency has involved some of the most creative and interesting work on coordinated word choice of any in the field. Below is a sample from work by Hovy (1985). Hovy's aim is to bias the text to emphasize a desired point of view, in this case to report on this February primary in such a way that the results look good for Carter even though he lost.

> Kennedy only got a small number of delegates in the election on 20 February. Carter just lost by a small number of votes. He has several delegates more than Kennedy in total.

In contrast, representations based on frames, for whatever historical reason, tend to involve the use of a very large number of "primitive" terms, in principle at least one for every word sense in a natural language, with the commonalities among terms indicated by reference to an abstraction-generalization network. When working from such representations, lexical choice is often a nonissue since each term can be uniquely associated with a natural language word. This is not to say that choice of wording on the basis of affective perspective or degree of specificity for words cannot take place; rather, they are now seen as conceptual decisions rather than linguistic decisions. As a pragmatic matter, generation research that works off of such fine-grained representations tends to largely ignore the problem of lexical choice and put its energies elsewhere.

Phrasal Lexicons

What word to associate with simple conceptual terms like "barber" or "shaves" is obvious; however, for the objects in complex underlying programs, lexical choice can be more problematic. Representations based on "frame systems" employ structured objects that denote encapsulations of entire conceptual schema, whose "names" will consist of a single, highly hyphenated symbol, eg, "example-intrinsic-similarities-with-compeditive-product." Such conceptually uninterpreted "primitives" have a reasonable place in underlying programs, at least pragmatically, since an expert system can note qualitative properties of a phenomena without having the commonsense to understand it in enough detail to derive the term compositionally the way a person could. Technically these terms can be a considerable problem for generators since they may encode entire sentences at once yet will be used in rhetorical contexts where they may need to be modified with adverbs or adjectives or elaborated by subordinated clauses.

The natural recourse in this situation is to use a phrasal lexicon. This notion was identified by Becker (1975) and is an important tool of generation systems. Linguistically, a "phrasal" lexicon is a conceptual extension of a standard, word-based lexicon to include entire phrases as unanalyzed wholes on the same semantic basis as words. This provides a means of capturing in a natural way the open-ended idioms and manners of speech that people use every day. Since people appear to use these "fixed phrases" as undigested wholes, programs need to be able to do the same. This means that there need not be any internally represented expressions whose parts and relations are the direct source of the words and syntactic relations of the phrase: precisely what is needed to deal with heavily hyphenated symbols. Such texts can be quite good even though the underlying program understands little of what it is saying. The example below is from work by Kukich (1983); another notable effort specifically employing a phrasal lexicon is that of Jacobs (1985).

Wall Street securities markets meandered upward through most of the morning, before being pushed downhill late in the day yesterday. The stock market closed out the day with a small loss and turned in a mixed showing in moderate trading.

This information announcement was computed directly from an analysis of the data for the day's market behavior. Qualitative points in the results were paired directly with the stereotypical phrases of such announcements: "a small loss," "a mixed showing," "in moderate trading." Objects, actions, and time points were mapped directly into the appropriate word strings: "Wall Street securities markets," "meandered upward," "⟨be⟩ pushed downhill," "late in the day." The compositional template driving the assembly of these phrases into a text was based on clauses built out of the S–V–Advp phrase: ⟨market⟩ ⟨action⟩ ⟨time point⟩. The clauses were then grouped into sentences according to a few heuristics.

TREATMENTS OF GRAMMAR

In the study of generation, the choice of formalism for representing the language's grammar has always been bound up with the choice of control protocol. Broadly speaking, three approaches to this combined design decision can be identified:

1. Stating the grammar as an independent body of statements and filtering against it (with functional unification grammar as the prime example)
2. Using the grammar to specify all the valid surface structures that texts the language can have and then stating the planner's choices and the output of realization in terms of surface structure (message-driven approaches, TAG grammars)
3. Stating the grammar as a traversable graph structure and giving it control of the whole process once a text plan has been constructed (ATNs and most uses of systemic grammars)

There has yet to be any thorough comparative evaluation of these three alternative designs; individuals have adopted one or the other largely because of accidents of their own history; who they studied with, what was available locally, etc. This will maintain a studied neutrality. Each approach will be considered in turn from the perspective of the problems that have particularly motivated its use.

Some of the details that make a text "grammatical" arguably do not and should not have any counterparts in a message from an underlying program. Person and number agreement of subject and verb are an obvious case in English; relative pronouns (eg, "who" vs "whom"), the infinitive marker "to," and very large numbers of other linguistic phenomena are the same. This is not to say that these have no conceptual counterparts: agreement can be viewed as an expression of the semantic relation of predication, the lack of tense is often an indication of the action being generic, etc. The point is rather that this class of grammatically motivated information is not relevant to the text planner; it is not a natural part of the message and consequently should originate in the linguistics component. The question for the generation researcher is how to state this information and how to ensure that it is brought to bear at the appropriate moment.

Parsimony encourages the computational linguist to attempt to share as much of this information as possible between both generation and understanding systems. Given the radical differences in the intrinsic character of the control and information flow in the two processes, this leads researchers to declarative accounts of language rather than procedural ones, with elaborate derivational paradigms like generative grammar being ruled out of consideration quickly. When the purpose of the generation system is not to provide a communications facility for a mechanical actor, systems based literally on versions of transformational generative grammar have been quite appropriate. Two cases in point are the rule-testing facility developed by Friedman (1969) for the use of linguists to check the consistency of large sets of rules and the pedagogical ICAI system of Bates that has been used in the teaching of English as a foreign language (Bates and Ingria, 1980).

Among the long-standing linguistic traditions, about the most neutral paradigm that survives this criterion of being able to provide a declarative account is a system of rewrite rules. One of the very earliest mechanical generation systems of any sort was developed by Yngve in 1959 using a pushdown automata and a body of context-free phrase-structure rules with ad-lib lexical insertion (Yngve, 1960). Though it was not message-driven and generated text that was semantic nonsense which consequently would make it uninteresting as a generator today, it did establish the legitimacy of the enterprise of providing explanatory accounts of psycholinguistic phenomena through appeal to the computational properties of a virtual machine operating over representations of linguistic rules, a methodology that is becoming increasingly important to computational and noncomputational linguists alike.

There are, of course, new linguistic paradigms, many of them now put forward by people with computational backgrounds. One of these, functional unification grammar (FUG), developed by Kay (1979), has been employed in generators and is deliberately put forward as a "reversible" grammar, ie, able to serve equally well as a controlling description in generation and understanding.

Functional Unification Grammar in Generation

As presently used, functional unification grammars (FUGs) give a generator a modular, independent way of supplying the purely linguistic information that the process must have and do so without imposing specific demands on its control structure. The lack of demands to specify a control structure carries the entailment that one must be willing to live with whatever control structure is supplied. For Kay's FUG this is nondeterministic unification. If efficiency of execution is not relevant, this, of course, is no problem, however, there are indications that the generality of the FUG notation gives them undesirable computational complexity properties, ie, generating a structure from an arbitrary FUG appears to be NP-complete (Ritchie, 1986). Certainly, a specific individual grammar may not require this complexity to process; however, this result means that implementers of FUG generators must be especially careful in the construction of their algorithms since the formalism itself is not efficient.

The term "functional" in the name of the paradigm speaks to an intention on the part of its practitioners to go beyond description of the structure of linguistic forms to address the reasons why language is used. In contrast with the practice in systemic grammars, however, the functional elements in FUGs are thus far only a minimal extension beyond the standard categorical linguistic vocabulary used traditionally to describe syntactic form (eg, "clause," "noun phrase," "adjective") and are more in keeping with their paradigmatically close neighbor, "lexical-functional grammar" (Bresnan, 1984). In the FUGs actually employed in generators, ie, the Telegram grammar developed by Appelt (1985) and the realization component written by Bossie (1981) for the generation system of McKeown (1985), the extensions are just the addition of terms like "subject," "premodifier," or "head"—descriptions of the role a constituent plays within the category that dominates it. Classically functional concerns, such as the distinction between "given" and "new" information in a sentence studied by the Prague School (Danes, 1974) or the similar distinction between "theme" and "rheme" defined by the Firthian tradition (Firth, 1957), have not yet been incorporated into FUGs.

Figure 1 shows an example taken from Appelt (1980, p. 108). It describes the constituent roles that accompany the phrasal category of noun phrase. A full definition of the notation may be found in Kay (1979). Briefly, the brackets

$$\begin{bmatrix} \text{CAT} = \text{NP} \\ \text{PAT} = (...\langle\text{DET}\rangle\langle\text{PREMODS}\rangle\langle\text{HEAD}\rangle\langle\text{POSTMODS}\rangle...) \\ \text{AGR} = \langle\text{HEAD AGR}\rangle \\ \left\{\begin{bmatrix} \text{HEAD} = [\text{CAT} = \text{N}] \\ \left\{\begin{bmatrix} \text{TYPE} = \text{PROPER} \\ \text{DET} = \text{NONE} \end{bmatrix}\right\} \\ \text{TYPE} = \text{COMMON} \end{bmatrix}\right\} \\ \left\{\begin{matrix} \{\text{HEAD} = [\text{CAT} = \text{PRO}]\} \\ \{\text{HEAD} = [\text{CAT} = \text{SCOMP}]\} \end{matrix}\right\} \\ \text{DET} = \text{NONE} \\ \text{PREMODS} = \text{NONE} \\ \text{POSTMODS} = \text{NONE} \\ \{\text{PREMODS} = \text{NONE}\} \\ \{\text{PREMODS} = [\text{CAT} = \text{ADJP}]\} \\ \{\text{POSTMODS} = \text{NONE}\} \\ \{\text{POSTMODS} = [\text{CAT} = \text{PP}]\} \\ \{\text{POSTMODS} = [\text{CAT} = \text{SREL}]\} \end{bmatrix}$$

Figure 1. From Appelt (1980, p. 108).

define systems of features and values: square brackets define conjunctive sets, a description must specify all of the features within them; and curly brackets define disjunctive sets, where only one of the conditions defined by the feature-value pairs must be met.

FUGs are used to flesh out minimal, conceptually derived functional descriptions, eg, that the head of some noun phrase is to be the word "screwdriver." Recent work by Patten (Power, 1979) uses a systemic grammar in very much the same way. Operations at a semantic level of the kind performed in other approaches by planning level specialists specify a set of output features within the systemic grammar, the equivalent of the initial functional description that drives a FUG. A backward- and then forward-chaining sweep through the systemic grammar then determines what additional linguistic features must be added to the specification for a grammatical text to result.

FUGs are used in a process of successive mergers, constrained by the rules that govern how two descriptions may be unified. The key idea is that the planner first constructs a minimal description of a phrase, which it can do using specialists in the conventional way (eg, that it wants to produce a clause with a certain verb and two NPs whose heads are certain nouns). To flesh out the description to the points where it would be valid grammatically, it is then unified with the grammar. The description of the phrase and the specification of the grammar are progressively merged, with specified features in one being melded into unspecified or compatibly constrained features in the other. The instantiation of some of the description's previously unspecified features by grammar-supplied constants then brings about a ripple effect throughout the whole system: decisions that are dependent on a just-instantiated feature force further unifications cyclically until a grammatically complete description of the utterance has been formed. In addition, elements in planner's description will force selections among the disjunctive specifications in the grammar. For example, specifying a verb will force choice of grammatical subcategorization, which in turn will force a selection among the alternative clause-ordering patterns that the grammar defines since only one of them will have a compatible specification.

The complete descriptions will amount to a rooted tree of subdescriptions (constituents) as defined by the "pat" (pattern) feature, which dictates sequential order at each level. The actual production of the text is performed by scanning this tree and reading out the words in the lexical features of each constituent. Constraint has come about tacitly through the unification process; only compatible partial descriptions survive into the final result. This has the benefit that the planner need not be concerned with grammatical constraints and dependencies but also implies the corresponding potential deficit that the planner cannot make use of knowledge of the grammatical constraints should it want to.

From the point of view of grammar development, FUGs are a satisfying treatment because they allow one to state the facts of the language compactly, ie, interactions between statements need not be explicitly spelled out in the notation (as they would have to be in unaugmented treatments of phrase-structure grammar) since they will come about automatically through the action of unification.

Surface Structure as an Intermediate Level of Representation

Faced with the difficulties under a message-directed, direct-replacement approach of realizing conceptual relations directly as words, a number of generation researchers have independently chosen to interpose a level of explicitly linguistic representation between the levels of the message and the words of the text (McDonald, 1975, 1984; Kempen and Hoenkamp, 1982; Jacobs, 1985; Swartout, 1984). They believe that a syntactic description of the text under construction is the best means of dealing with the problems of grammatically motivated detail and the implementation of linguistically defined constraints and dependencies. The specifics of their individual treatments differ, but a common thread is clearly identifiable. The linguistic structures are produced as the output of realization, which tends to be organized as choices made by specialists. The representations consist of a phrase structure of one or another sort, ie, hierarchies of nodes and constituents. They incorporate functional concepts like "subject" and "focus." They are most aptly characterized as a kind of "surface structure" in the generative linguist's sense; ie, they undergo no derivation and are a proper description of the syntactic properties of the text that is produced.

Loosely speaking, this intermediate level of surface structure is used by the control structure in the same manner in all treatments. It is given as a tree, and its constituency pattern is used directly as the specification of a path, top-down and left to right through the tree, that controls the sequence and environment of realization and the order in which the words appear. The crucial consequence of this "folding together" of the process of realizing the elements of the message and traversing the surface structure is to provide an explicit, examinable representation of the grammatical context in which an element will appear and thus make it available to constrain the choices open to realization and the text planner.

The most elaborated theory of surface structure as an

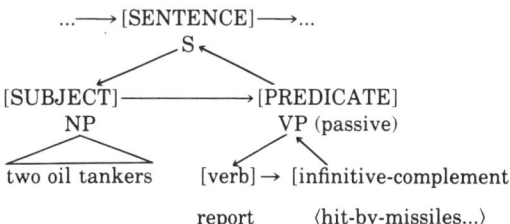

Figure 2. From McDonald and Pustejovsky (1985).

intermediate representation is McDonald's (Bossie, 1981). His design incorporates several points beyond the common elements of this approach. Figure 2 shows a surface structure as it would be in the middle of producing the text, "Two oil tankers were reported hit by missiles."

The traversal path through the structure is indicated by the arrows; the system is just about to select a realization for the underlying program predicate #⟨hit-by-missiles⟩. The realization is performed in the context of the constraints dictated by its position as a constituent within the sentence, which is represented by the labels in brackets above it. The labeled circle marks an "attachment point" where the surface structure may be extended by splicing in additional phrase structure, in this case the verb phrase and complement structure for the verb "report." This provides the capacity for producing texts whose hierarchical structures are different from that of the message that leads to them, the customary form of texts constructed under a message-driven control structure.

Direct Control of Realization by Grammar: Systemic Grammar and ATNs

The augmented transition network, or ATN, was adapted for use in generation almost from the moment of its definition. It was used first by Simmons and Slocum in 1970 (Simmons and Slocum, 1972; Slocum, 1973), whose system was then used by Goldman (1975). It was also independently adapted by Shapiro (1975, 1982) whose generator is the most elaborate of the group. All of the systems have a similar design. They scan a data structure provided by an underlying program, in effect "parsing" it. The networks follow the top-down format found in most ATN parsers, leading naturally to a progressive refinement process as the generator scans its governing data structure from the most important, widest scope relations on down. For the early ATNs this structure was a semantic net (see SEMANTIC NETWORKS) based on the concept of verb-centered case frames (another "functional" linguistic system). A special node in the network, a "modality vector," specified the root-level information such as tense and aspect or whether a sentence was to be active or passive. The primary function of the ATN in the early systems was to linearize a network structure that was for the most part already encoded in a linguistic vocabulary and to supplement the conceptual information in the semantic net with the purely linguistic information that all grammars must provide in generation.

As a linguistic formalism, ATNs are essentially a procedural encoding of a generative grammar (Woods, 1970). The registers that give them their "augmented" power are used as a deep-structure representation of grammatical relations, and the paths through the network encode all of the alternative surface-level constituent sequences. Constraints propagate from higher parts of the surface-structure tree to lower (ie, to recursive subnets of the ATN) through the values is designated registers, bringing the activity of those subnets under contextual control. Shapiro's ATN design is particularly enlightening, as his controlling data structure is the underlying program's entire computational state. [This state is encoded in a particularly sophisticated intensional network formalism known as SNePS (qv) (Shapiro, 1979).] The "parsing" his ATN performs amounts to the construction of an assessment, in terms appropriate for directing the generation of a text, of the steps that must be taken to satisfy the program's intended communicative goals, in effect, an implicit dynamic message.

A further aspect of the ATN design, the fact that the means of actually producing the words of the text is the execution of a side-effect action on the traversal of an arc, brings out the fact that this approach commits the generator to action almost at the very moment that a situation is perceived; eg, identification of the object that is to serve as the subject is followed directly by its realization and actual production. That this is possible is particularly striking when one appreciates that Shapiro's ATN never backs up (Swartout, 1984). This is quite unusual behavior for an ATN, given that they are usually thought of as expressly nondeterministic devices, and it serves to emphasize the fact that generation is in its essence a process of planning. Since modern planning processes are characteristically determinate, proceeding by incremental refinement and the posting of constraints rather than trial and error, the behavior of Shapiro's ATN is to be expected.

Viewed as a planner, the most significant deficit of the ATN designs is the difficulty of decoupling perception from action. Generators based on systemic grammar deal with this problem directly by introducing an intermediary representation in the form of a set of features, abstract symbols that serve as partial specifications of the text. To make a choice is to select a feature, which in turn creates a need to make certain other choices while rendering still others irrelevant. As was the case with surface structure, the use of an intermediary representation allows the specification of a text to be accumulated gradually, giving constraints an opportunity to propagate and influence later decisions. In this instance the abstract linguistic properties doing the constraining are not already bundled and formed as a phrase structure but are distributed as a feature space.

The overall specification of the text is determined in recursive layers top-down, as it is in nearly all of the approaches (the prime exception being systems that use phrasal lexicons). Features are accumulated at a given level, eg, the main clause of a sentence, until all of the aspects in which clauses can vary have been considered and the options settled. During this phase the issue is what functions are appropriate for the clause to carry out given the situation and the speaker's intentions; with those determined, the functional features are realized as a group and specify the clause's form. That form now creates an environment for the constituents of the clause. The determination of what functions each of them should serve is then carried out and, when completed, will lead to the realization of their forms, which in turn will lead to a functional analysis of their own constituents, and so on recursively until the constituents are words, at which point the text is read out as it would be from the description constructed with a FUG.

As a linguistic tradition, systemic grammar owes its form and perspective principally to one person, Halliday (1967), who was himself influenced by the London School of functionalism lead by Firth (1957). The influence of systemic grammar on generation research is considerably wider than just the systems that employ it directly since it is the sole well-known linguistic formalism that has as its very basis the identification of the choices implicit in a language. Choices form the notational basis of systemic grammars, which, like ATNs, are written as traversable graph structures that define the space of possible control flow for at least the linguistic portion of the generation process. The very small fragment of a grammar shown in Figure 3 illustrates how the graph is formed.

Choice systems are given either as AND paths (leading curled brace), where one choice must be made from each of the systems named on the right, or as OR paths (leading square brace), where only one of the alternative features listed may selected. The selection of a feature opens the system that it names (*note:* the feature will be the leftward "root node" of the tree on its side that constitutes a system within the network), which means that a choice from that system must now be made. Choices continue as the locus of control moves left to right through the network (usually simultaneously active in several choices at once due to the presence of the AND systems), until a rightmost system is reached that consists of a bare feature without an accompanying system. These rightmost nodes are the concrete elements from which specifications of form are built up. Leftward-pointing curled braces indicate path mergers in the control flow, where decisions in disjoint systems have a combined influence.

Two important generation systems have been based on systemic grammar, Davey's PROTEUS (1979) (discussed earlier) and Mann and Matthiessen's (1985) NIGEL (Mann, 1982). NIGEL is the largest systemic grammar in the world and very likely one of the largest machine grammars of any sort. Besides the quite important contribution simply of articulating a systemic grammar so thoroughly, Mann and Matthiessen have developed an original technique for formalizing the usage criteria that govern the choices the grammar defines (1983). A set of criterial predicates are defined for each choice system in the grammar, which act as functions from the internal state of the planner and underlying program to features. The generation process is carried out by starting at the leftmost entry system of the nextwork and applying successive "chooser" procedures to determine the path through the network (ie, the feature set) that best captures the speaker's intentions.

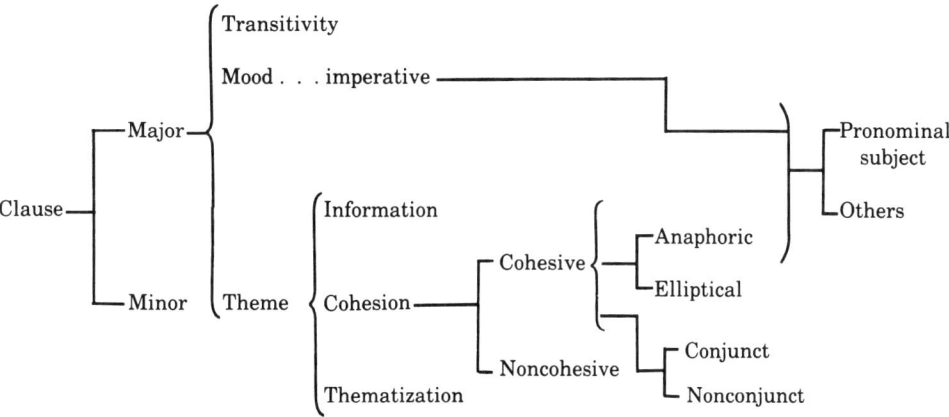

Figure 3. From Halliday and Martin (1981).

OTHER RESEARCH AREAS

The field of natural language generation, even as seen only by researchers in AI, is considerably larger than this article has been able to accommodate. Two areas must at least be mentioned in passing.

Planning. Pioneering work by Appelt (1980, 1985) supplied a rigorous logical framework by which to encode basic notions such as intention and reference. His planning technique, the progressive elaboration of goals through the use of Sacerdoti's procedural networks formalism (1977), builds on a tradition of viewing the articulation of a generator's goals by chaining backward from fundamental communications goals (Power, 1979; Cohen, 1978).

From a complementary direction, McKeown (1985) has presented a theory of the organization of paragraphs into groups of conversational moves, drawing on earlier work by Grimes (1975). She employs paragraph schemas as realizations of high-level moves such as "compare and contrast." The schemas act as templates to organize the content selection and rhetorical structuring that the planner does.

Psycholinguistic Theory. Once there are generation systems that have a significant capability, it becomes possible to consider deliberately chosen restrictions on the power of the virtual computational engine underlying the system's capacity. Such restrictions gain the possibility of providing an explanatory account of aspects of the human generation process by appealing to intrinsic properties of the machine that make it impossible for its behavior to be otherwise. There has been work toward this end by Kempen and Hoenkamp (1982) for restarting phenomena and by McDonald (1984) for an account of people's fluency and lack of grammatical error and certain classes of speech errors.

Generation is a young research area. It is populated by a vigorous, mutually identifying group of researchers that is growing at an ever-increasing rate. The intellectual climate within the generation community is not unlike that of the language-understanding community of about 1974, with a roughly similar number of players and a similar feeling in the air of significant things happening. There is every reason to believe that the further development and contributions of generation research to AI as a whole in the next 12 years will be every bit as large as the contribution of understanding research in the last 12.

BIBLIOGRAPHY

D. Appelt, "Problem Solving Applied to Language Generation," *Proceedings of the ACL,* Philadelphia, Pa., 1980, pp. 59–63.

D. Appelt, *Planning English Sentences,* Cambridge University Press, Cambridge, U.K., 1985.

M. Bates and R. Ingria, "Controlled Transformational Sentence Generation," *Proceedings of the ACL,* Stanford, Calif., 1980.

J. Becker, "The Phrasal Lexicon," *Proceedings of TINLAP-I,* ACM, pp. 60–64; also as Report 3081, Bolt Beranek and Newman, Cambridge, Mass., 1975.

S. Bossie, "A Tactical Component for Text Generation: Sentence Generation Using a Functional Grammar," TR MS-CIS-81-5, University of Pennsylvania, Philadelphia, 1981.

J. Bresnan, ed., *The Mental Representation of Grammatical Relations,* MIT Press, Cambridge, Mass., 1984.

G. Brown, *Some Problems in German to English Machine Translation,* MIT LCS TR 142, MIT, Cambridge, Mass., 1974.

R. Brown, *Use of Multiple-Body Interrupts in Discourse Generation,* Bachelor's thesis, MIT, Cambridge, Mass., 1974.

B. Bruce, "Generation as Social Action," *Proceedings of TINLAP-I,* ACM, 1975, pp. 74–78.

D. Chester, "The Translation of Formal Proofs Into English," *Artif. Intell.* 8(3), 261–278 (1976).

W. Clancey, "Tutoring Rules for Guiding a Case Method Dialog," *Proceedings of IJMMS II,* 1979, pp. 25–49.

J. Clippinger, "Speaking with Many Tongues: Some Problems in Modeling Speakers of Actual Discourse," *Proceedings of TINLAP-I,* ACM, 1975, pp. 68–73.

J. Clippinger, *Meaning and Discourse: A Computer Model of Psychoanalytic Speech and Cognition,* Johns Hopkins Press, Baltimore, MD, 1977.

P. Cohen, *On Knowing What to Say: Planning Speech Acts,* TR 118, University of Toronto, 1978.

F. Danes, *Papers on Functional Sentence Perspective,* Academia, Czechoslovakian Academy of Science, 1974.

L. Danlos, "Conceptual and Linguistic Decisions in Generation," *Proceedings of the COLING,* Stanford, Calif., 1984, pp. 501–504.

A. Davey, *Discourse Production,* Edinburgh University Press, Edinburgh, U.K., 1979.

J. R. Firth, *Papers in Linguistics 1934–1951,* Oxford University Press, Oxford, U.K., 1957.

K. Forbus and A. Stevens, "Using Qualitative Simulation to Generate Explanations," *Proceedings of the Third Annual Conference of the Cognitive Science Society,* Berkeley, Calif., August, 1981, pp. 219–221.

C. Frank, *A Step Towards Automatic Documentation,* WP-213, MIT AI Laboratory, 1980.

J. Friedman, "Directed Random Generation of Sentences," *CACM* **12**(6), 40–46 (1969).

N. Goldman, "The Boundaries of Language Generation," *Proceedings of TINLAP-I,* ACM, 1975, pp. 74–78.

N. Goldman, "Conceptual Generation," in R. Schank, ed., *Conceptual Information Processing,* North-Holland/Elsevier, Amsterdam, 1975, pp. 289–372.

R. Granville, "Controlling Lexical Substitution in Computer Text Generation," *Proceedings of COLING,* Stanford, Calif., 1984, pp. 381–384.

J. Grimes, *The Thread of Discourse,* Mouton, The Hague, 1975.

M. A. K. Halliday, "Notes on Transitivity and Theme in English," *J. Ling.* **3**(1), 37–81 (1967).

M. A. K. Halliday and J. Martin, eds., *Readings in Systemic Linguistics,* Batsford Academic, London, 1981.

E. Hovy, "Integrating Text Planning and Production in Generation," *Proceedings of the Ninth IJCAI,* Los Angeles, 1985, pp. 848–851.

P. Jacobs, "PHRED: A Generator for Natural Language Interfaces," TR 85/198, Berkeley Computer Science Department, Berkeley, Calif., 1985.

P. Jacobs, "A Knowledge-Based Approach to Language Production," TR 86/254, Berkeley Computer Science Department, Berkeley, Calif., 1985.

M. Kay, "Functional Grammar," *Proceedings of the Berkeley Linguistic Society,* Berkeley, Calif., 1979.

M. Kay, "Functional Unification Grammar: A Formalism for Machine Translation," *Proceedings of COLING,* Stanford, Calif., 1984, pp. 75–78.

G. Kempen and E. Hoenkamp, "Incremental Sentence Generation: Implications for the Structure of a Syntactic Processor," *Proceedings of COLING,* Prague, 1982.

K. Kukich, *Knowledge-Based Report Generation: A Knowledge Engineering Approach to Natural Language Report Generation,* Ph.D. dissertation, University of Pittsburgh, 1983.

D. McDonald, "A Preliminary Report on a Program for Generating Natural Language," *Proceedings of the Fourth IJCAI,* Tbilisi, USSR, 1975, pp. 401–405.

D. McDonald, "Subsequent Reference: Syntactic and Rhetorical Constraints," *Theoretical Issues in Natural Language Processing II,* Association of Computing Machinery, New York, 1978, pp. 38–47.

D. McDonald, "Natural Language Generation as a Computational Problem: An Introduction," in M. Brady and R. Berwick, eds., *Computational Models of Discourse,* MIT Press, Cambridge, Mass., 1983, pp. 209–266.

D. McDonald, "Description Directed Control: Its Implications for Natural Language Generation," in Cercone, ed., *Computational Linguistics,* Plenum, New York, 1984, pp. 403–424.

D. McDonald, "Description-Directed Natural Language Generation," *Proceedings of the Ninth IJCAI,* Los Angeles, 1985, pp. 799–805.

D. McDonald and J. Pustejovsky, "TAGs as a Grammatical Formalism for Generation," *Proceedings of the ACL,* Chicago, 1985, pp. 94–103.

K. McKeown, *Text Generation,* Cambridge University Press, Cambridge, U.K., 1985.

W. Mann, *The Anatomy of a Systemic Choice,* TR/RS-82-104, Information Sciences Institute, 1982.

W. Mann, *Inquiry Semantics: A Functional Semantics of Natural Language,* TR/RS-83-8, Information Sciences Institute, 1983.

W. Mann, M. Bates, B. Grosz, D. McDonald, K. McKeown, and W. Swartout, "Text Generation: The State of the Art and Literature," *JACL* **8**(2) (1982).

W. Mann and C. Matthiessen, "Nigel: A Systemic Grammar for Text Generation," in Freedle, ed., *Systemic Perspectives on Discourse: Selected Theoretical Papers of the Ninth International Systemic Workshop,* Ablex, Norwood, N.J., 1985.

W. Mann and J. Moore, "Computer Generation of Multi-Paragraph English Text," *JACL* **7**(1) (1981).

R. Power, "The Organisation of Purposeful Dialogues," *Linguistics* **17**, 107–151 (1979).

G. Ritchie, "The Computational Complexity of Sentence Generation using Functional Unification Grammar," *Proceedings of COLING,* Bonn, 1986.

E. Sacerdoti, *A Structure for Plans and Behavior,* Elsevier/North-Holland, Amsterdam, 1977.

S. Shapiro, "Generation as Parsing From a Network Into a Linear String," *JACL Fiche* **33**, 45–62 (1975).

S. C. Shapiro, "The SNePS Semantic Network Processing System," in Findler, ed., *Associative Networks,* Academic Press, New York, 1979.

S. C. Shapiro, "Generalized Augmented Transition Network Grammars for Generation From Semantic Networks," *JACL* **8**(1), 12–25 (1982).

B. Sigurd, "Computer Simulation of Spontaneous Speech Production," *Proceedings of COLING,* Stanford, Calif., 1984.

R. Simmons and J. Slocum, "Generating English Discourse From Semantic Networks," *CACM* **15**(10), 891–905 (1972).

J. Slocum, *Question Answering via Cannonical Verbs and Semantic Models: Generating English from the Model,* Department of Computer Science TR NL-23, University of Texas, 1973.

W. Swartout, *A Digitalis Therapy Advisor with Explanations,* MIT LCS Technical Report, MIT, Cambridge, Mass., 1977.

W. Swartout, personal communication, Information Sciences Institute, Los Angeles, July 1984.

H. Thompson, "Strategy and Tactics: A Model for Language Production," *Proceedings of the Chicago Linguistic Society,* 1977.

R. Wilensky, Y. Arens, and D. Chin, "Talking to UNIX in English: An Overview of UC," *CACM,* 577–593 (June 1984).

T. Winograd, *Understanding Natural Language,* Academic Press, New York, 1972.

H. K. T. Wong, *Generating English Sentences from Semantic Structures,* TR84, Department of Computer Science, University of Toronto, 1985.

W. Woods, "Transition Network Grammars for Natural Language Analysis," *CACM* **13**(10), 591–606 (1970).

V. H. A. Yngve, "A Model and a Hypothesis for Language Structure," *Proceedings of the American Philosophical Society,* 1960, pp. 444–466.

D. D. McDonald
University of Massachusetts

NATURAL LANGUAGE UNDERSTANDING

Natural language communication with computers has long been a major goal of AI both for the information it can give about intelligence in general and for its practical utility. Databases, software packages, and AI-based expert systems all require flexible interfaces to a growing community of users who are not able or do not wish to communicate with computers in formal, artificial command languages. Whereas many of the fundamental problems of general natural language processing (NLP) by machine remain to be solved, the area has matured in recent years to the point where practical natural language interfaces to software systems can be constructed in many restricted, but nevertheless useful, circumstances. This article is intended to survey the current state of natural language processing by presenting computationally effective NLP techniques, by exploring the range of capabilities these techniques provide for NLP systems, and by discussing their current limitations. This presentation is organized in two major sections: the first on language recognition strategies at the single-sentence level and the second on language processing issues that arise during interactive dialogues. In both cases the concentration is on those aspects of the problem appropriate for interactive natural language interfaces but relate the techniques and systems discussed to more general work on natural language, independent of application domain.

NATURE OF NATURAL LANGUAGE PROCESSING

Natural language processing (NLP) is the **formulation and investigation of computationally effective mechanisms for communication through natural language**. To take the bold face phrases in reverse order, first the subject area deals with naturally occurring human languages such as German, French, or English. Second, it is concerned with the use of these languages for communication, both communication between people, the purpose for which these languages evolved, and communication between a person and a computer. Third, NLP does not study natural language communication in an abstract way, but by devising mechanisms for performing such communication that are computationally effective, ie, can be turned into computer programs that perform or simulate the communication. It is this third characteristic that sets the NLP subarea of AI, itself a subarea of computer science, apart from traditional linguistics and other disciplines that study natural language. This article examines the relationship of NLP among two other closely related disciplines: linguistics and cognitive psychology (qv).

Linguistics is traditionally concerned with formal, general, structural models of natural language. Linguists, therefore, have tended to favor formal models that allow them to capture as much as possible the regularities of language and to make the most appropriate linguistic generalizations. Little or no attention was paid in the development of these models to their computational effectiveness. That is, linguistic models characterize the language itself, without regard to the mechanisms that produce it or decipher it. A good example, as shown below, is Chomskian transformational grammar perhaps the best known of all linguistic models, which turns out to be unsuitable as a basis for computationally practical language recognition (Chomsky, 1957, 1965; Petrick, 1965).

The goal of cognitive psychology (qv) on the other hand is not to model the structure of language but rather to model the use of language and to do it in a psychologically plausible way, where plausibility here is defined by correlation with experimental results, especially timing studies of language-understanding tasks (see Anderson (1976) for a good example of the flavor of this approach). This is somewhat closer to the spirit of AI-based NLP in its emphasis on the use of language in communication, but again it is not of primary importance to the cognitive psychologist whether the models are computationally effective. Moreover, the models produced are not often targeted at language understanding per se but at more general aspects of human cognition and memory organization, with natural language serving only as the vehicle through which these related phenomena are studied.

In addition to relating NLP to the study of language in other disciplines, a major division that arises within NLP itself should be pointed out. The distinction is between general and applied NLP. General NLP can be thought of as a way of tackling cognitive psychology from a computer science viewpoint. The goal is to make models of human language use and also to make them computationally effective. The vehicles for this kind of work are general story understanding, as in the work of Charniak (1972), Schank (1975), Cullingford (1978), Carbonell (1979), and others, and dialogue modeling, as in the work of Cohen and Perrault (1979), Allen (1979), Grosz (1977), Sidner (1979), and others. One of the most important lessons learned from this work is that general NLP requires a tremendous amount of real-world knowledge; most of the work just cited is mainly concerned with the representation of such real-world knowledge and its application to the understanding of natural language input. Unfortunately, AI has not yet reached the stage where it can routinely handle the amount of knowledge required for these tasks, with the result that systems constructed in this area tend to be pilot systems that demonstrate the feasibility of a concept or approach but do not contain a large enough knowledge base to make them work on more than a handful of carefully selected example natural language passages or dialogues.

Applied NLP, on the other hand, is not typically concerned with cognitive simulation but rather with allowing people to communicate with machines through natural language. The emphasis is pragmatic. It is less important in applied NLP whether the machine understands its natural language input in a cognitively plausible way than whether it responds to the input in a way helpful to the user and in accordance with the desires expressed in the input. Typical applications are database interfaces, as in the work of Hendrix (1977), Grosz (1983), Kaplan (1979), and others, and interfaces to expert systems (qv), as in the work of Brown and Burton (1975) and Carbonell (1971) and Carbonell and co-workers (1983). Because such systems must operate robustly with real users, in addition to actually processing well-formed natural language, they must be concerned with the detection and resolution of errors and misunderstandings by the user.

Basic Problem of NLP

If there were one word to describe why NLP is hard, it is *ambiguity*. It arises in natural language in many different forms including the following.

Syntactic (or Structural) Ambiguity.

John saw the Grand Canyon flying to New York.
Time flies like an arrow.

Is it John or the Grand Canyon doing the flying? The answer depends on the ambiguous syntactic role of the word *flying* in this example. Again, is time flying, or are we talking about a species of insect called time flies in the second example. It depends whether *flies* is a noun or a verb. (Actually, the second example here has at least six different parsings.)

Word Sense Ambiguity.

The man went to the bank to get some cash.
                              and jumped in.

Here the word *bank* refers either to a repository for money or the side of a river, depending on the two different continuations.

Case.

He ran the mile in four minutes
              the Olympics

Linguistically, a "case" refers to the relation between a central organizing concept, here an act of running, and a subsidiary concept, here time or location. In both examples the same preposition, *in*, indicates the two quite different relationships.

Referential.

I took the cake from the table and ate it.

What was eaten, the cake or the table? The answer is "obvious," but, independent of real-world knowledge, *it* could refer to either one. For instance, *it* would have a different referent in the example above if *ate* were replaced with *cleaned*.

Literalness.

Can you open the door?
I feel cold.

What are the correct interpretations here? There are some circumstances when the first question might be answered quite reasonably yes or no, eg, before setting off on a long journey to the place where the door is. On the other hand, it is easy to think of circumstances where the speaker might be very unhappy with such a reply. Again, the second example might be a statement of fact or a request to close a window. The ambiguities here lie in whether to interpret the utterance literally or whether to treat it as an indirect speech act (qv) (Searle, 1969), eg, an implicit request as in the examples above.

Because of these and other kinds of ambiguity, the central problem in NLP, and this is true for both the general and applied variety, is the translation of the potentially ambiguous natural language input into an unambiguous internal ie, internal to the program doing the processing, representation, as suggested by Figure 1.

The second layer of Figure 1 shows an example translation of a natural language database query into an expression in a database query language: the one used by the LADDER (Sacerdoti, 1977) system for access to its database of information about U.S. Navy ships. Note how a potentially ambiguous word such as *Kennedy* is resolved into the internal name, John F. Kennedy, of a specific ship, or *captain* is resolved into the name, Commander, of a field of the relational database conceptually underlying the LADDER system. The specific internal representation used here is, of course, highly specialized. In general, there is no standard commonly agreed upon for internal representations, and different types are useful for different purposes. A partial list includes:

Expressions in a database query language (for DB access).

Parse trees with word sense terminal nodes (for machine translation).

LISP expressions (most often for expert system requests).

Case frame instantiations (for a variety of applications).

Conceptual dependency (for story understanding).

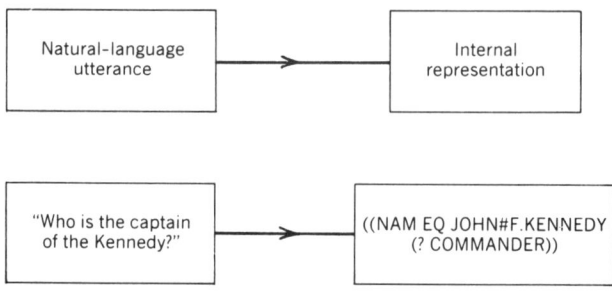

Figure 1. Translation from a natural language utterance to unambiguous internal representation.

In general NLP, translation of an utterance into an unambiguous internal representation can require inference based on a potentially unbounded set of real-world knowledge. Consider, for instance,

Jack took the bread from the supermarket shelf, paid for it, and left.

Coming up with an unambiguous representation for this requires answers to such questions as

What did Jack pay for? (the referent of *it*)
What did Jack leave?   (the ellipsed object of *left*)

and possibly even

Did Jack have the bread with him when he left?

To answer these questions, information on supermarkets, buying and selling, and other real-world topics is required. As mentioned above, AI knowledge representation (qv) techniques have not yet developed to the stage where they can handle at an acceptable level of efficiency the large quantities of such knowledge required to do a complete job of understanding a large variety of topics. Moreover, even if the knowledge could be represented, unresolved problems in inference techniques remain a barrier to applying the correct knowledge to the input in order to produce the desired unambiguous internal representation. The result is that current general NLP systems are demonstration systems that operate with a very small amount of carefully handcrafted knowledge, specifically designed to enable the processing of a small set of example inputs. The main point of such systems is to investigate the feasibility of certain inference or knowledge representation techniques rather than to achieve broad coverage in the NLP they perform.

Applied NLP systems potentially face exactly the same problem, but they finesse it by taking advantage of certain characteristics of the highly limited domains in which they operate. Suppose the input

How many terminals are there in the order?

was addressed to an expert system that acted as a computer salesman's assistant. Such a system need not consider many of the potential ambiguities lurking in this example. The word *terminals,* for instance, can be assumed to refer to computer terminals, rather than airport terminals, terminally ill patients, or terminal values of a mathematical series. Also, assuming the system processes one sales order at a time, *the order* can be assumed to refer to the current order without considering any others. In general, the technique is to premake as many inferences as possible in a way appropriate to the task at hand. For suitable tasks in many restricted domains, this has been used successfully to reduce the amount of knowledge that must be represented and the number of inferences that must be made to manageable proportions.

By restricting the natural language dealt with by an interface to that required to handle a limited task in a limited domain, it is thus possible to construct performance systems capable of useful natural language communication, and this represents the current state of the art in practical NLP. Clearly, this is far from satisfactory, because in particular, each task and domain that are tackled require careful preanalysis so that the required inferences can be preencoded in the system, thus making it difficult to transfer successful natural language interfaces from one task to another. Some research (Grosz, 1977) is being conducted to improve the portability of current interfaces, but until the problem of preencoding inferences is solved in a more general way, the portability issue will be the one that most hinders the widespread use of natural language interfaces. A practical alternative, however, is the Language Craft (Carnegie-Group Inc.) approach, where a development environment and grammar interpreter are provided to shorten drastically the development of new domain-specific interfaces.

NATURAL LANGUAGE ANALYSIS TECHNIQUES

In this section, several of the more common techniques for natural language analysis are examined in some detail, ie, for translating natural language utterances into a unique internal representation. Virtually all natural language analysis systems can be classified into one of the following categories:

Pattern matching [eg, ELIZA (qv) (Weizenbaum, 1986); PARRY (qv) (Parkinson and co-workers, 1977)].
Syntactically driven parsing (qv) [eg, ATNs (Woods, 1970)].
Semantic grammars (see GRAMMAR, SEMANTIC) [eg, LIFER (qv) (Hendrix, 1977); SOPHIE (qv) (Brown and Burton, 1975)].
Case frame instantiation [eg, ELI (qv) (see GRAMMAR, SEMANTIC) (Riesbeck and Schank, 1976)].
Wait and see (Marcus, 1980).
Word expert (Small and Kleger, 1982).
Connectionist (see CONNECTIONISM) (Small and co-workers, 1982).
Skimming [eg, FRUMP (qv) (Dejong, 1979) and IPP (Schank and co-workers, 1980)].

The examples provided with each category are the names of language analysis systems following that approach or the names of builders of such systems. Of these categories, the first four represent the bulk of the language analysis systems already constructed and are the only ones covered in detail. The reader is encouraged to follow up the references provided for further details of the other methods.

Pattern Matching

The essence of the pattern matching approach to natural language analysis is to interpret input utterances as a whole rather than building up their interpretation by combining the structure and meaning of words or other

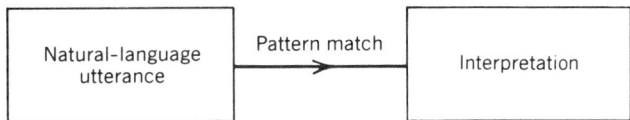

Figure 2. Parsing by pattern matching.

lower level constituents. The approach is thus holistic rather than constructive. With this approach, the interpretations are obtained by matching patterns of words against the input utterance. Associated with each pattern is an interpretation, so that the derived interpretation is the one attached to the pattern that matched. In the simplest case this arrangement is simply a list of correspondences between equivalence classes of utterances (the ones that match a given pattern) and interpretations (the ones associated with each pattern). In more sophisticated variations of the approach, patterns may involve higher level constituents or semantic elements so that some aspects of the interpretation may become constructive, but the basic flavor of the approach still remains to go as directly as possible from the input utterance to the interpretation, as suggested by Figure 2.

One of the simplest and earliest examples of pattern matching parsing was the ELIZA system (Weizenbaum, 1966). This system demonstrated how a very simple mechanism in the form of a computer program was able to mimic apparently intelligent behavior. The carefully selected task of ELIZA was to simulate a Rogerian psychologist interviewing a patient. The style of this school of psychology allowed ELIZA to understand virtually nothing of what was said and still, in many cases, come up with convincing replies. ELIZA did not construct an internal representation of its input as such but instead went directly from the input to its reply, which could therefore be thought of as the interpretation of the input. The input was matched by a small set of single-level patterns, each of which was associated with several replies. The first pattern found to match an input lead to a selected reply from the associated set; if a pattern matched again on a subsequent input, the next reply was given. Variables in the patterns that would match any sequence of words whatsoever allowed text from the input to be incorporated into the reply. Example patterns and corresponding replies with variables represented by X and Y include

X always Y	Can you think of a specific example? When? Really, always?
X and Y me	Why do you think I Y you? You like to think I Y you, don't you? Suppose that I did Y you? What would that mean?

These would allow ELIZA (E) to conduct the following dialogue with a patient (P):

P:	People always stare at me.	Matches first pattern
E:	Can you think of a specific example?	
P:	For instance you keep staring at me.	Matches second pattern with Y matching *keep staring at*
E:	Why do you think I keep staring at you?	First reply for second pattern with appropriate substitution for Y
P:	Because you hate me.	Second pattern again with Y matching *hate*
E:	You like to think I hate you, don't you?	Next (second) reply for second pattern

The simplicity of the matching and reply generation meant that most conversations with ELIZA did not go nearly as smoothly as this, but there are several anecdotes about people being fooled into thinking they were talking to a real person.

ELIZA could achieve its results with such a low level of analysis only by ignoring most of what was said. To make more complete analyses of the input using the same techniques would require far too many patterns: in the extreme, one pattern for every possible utterance. Moreover, many of these patterns would contain common subelements because they mentioned the same objects or had the same concepts arranged with slightly different syntax. In order to resolve these problems within the pattern matching approach, hierarchical pattern matching methods have been developed in which some patterns match only part of the input and replace that part by some canonical result. Other higher level patterns can then match on these canonical elements in a similar way, until a top-level pattern is able to match the canonicalized input as a whole according to the standard pattern matching paradigm. In this way similar parts of different utterances can be matched by the same patterns, and the total number of patterns is much reduced and made more manageable.

The best known example of hierarchical pattern matching is the PARRY system (Parkinson and co-workers, 1977; Colby, 1973). Like ELIZA, this program operates in a psychological domain but models a paranoid patient rather than a psychologist. Using the traditional pattern matching paradigm, PARRY interprets its input utterances as a whole by matching them against a set of about 2000 general patterns. The internal representation into which the input is transformed is a set of updates to a simple model of the paranoid patient's mental state plus a representation of any factual content of the input. Replies are generated from the updated paranoid model plus the factual content. However, before the general patterns are applied, PARRY massages its input through a series of eight canonicalizing steps, most of which are based on localized pattern matching. Examples of these steps include

Canonicalizing rigid idioms (eg, "have it in for" → "hate").

Noun phrase bracketing using an ATN (see below).

Canonicalizing flexible idioms (eg, "lend a hand" → "help").

Clause splitting (eg, "I think you need help" → "(I think) (you need help)").

Using rules of this form, an input such as

Do you have it in for me? I want to lend you a hand.

can be canonicalized into a form similar to

(YOU HATE ME) + INTERROGATIVE =?
(I WANT) (I HELP YOU)

An appropriate reply is generated by matching against PARRY's 2000 general patterns.

As well as matching patterns of words, it is also possible to analyze natural language input by matching patterns of semantic elements with potentially very powerful results as shown by the pilot machine translation (qv) system (Wilks, 1975). The goal of this system was to translate English input into French output. To do this, it first analyzed its English input into an internal semantic pattern from which it could generate the French. This analysis was performed by matching the input against a very general set of patterns such as

(MAN FORCE MAN)

which matches all events in which a person compels another person to do something. Other general patterns involved people doing things to objects, objects being in certain states, etc. To allow matches against these patterns, Wilks represented word senses as formulas of the same semantic primitives as appeared in the patterns, so for instance, *interrogate* was

((MAN SUB J) ((MAN OBJE) (TELL FORCE)))

ie, a person forcing another person to tell something, and *crook* was one of the following possibilities:

(((((NOTGOOD ACT) OBJE) DO) SUBJ MAN))
((((((THIS BEAST) OBJE) FORCE) SUBJ MAN)) POSS) LINE THING))

ie, a person who does bad things or a long thin thing that a person uses to force animals (normally sheep) to do something. As well as providing an interpretation of the input, the process of matching these formulas against the general patterns also allowed word senses to be disambiguated. So

The policeman interrogated the crook.

is analyzed by matching it against the (MAN FORCE MAN) pattern, and this also chooses the bad person sense of crook because it matches the second MAN of this pattern. There is also a (MAN FORCE THING) pattern, but this does not match as well because the formula for *interrogate* specifies MAN for its object. Note that the notion of degree of match is present in this system. As shown below, this idea makes parsing by pattern matching considerably more powerful, especially when the input contains grammatical errors.

To summarize this section on parsing by pattern matching, the basic paradigm is to recognize input utterances as a whole by matching them against patterns of words, wildcards, and semantic primitives. The result of the match is the interpretation of the utterance. Unless a very shallow level of analysis is acceptable, the number of patterns required is too large, even for restricted domains. This problem can be ameliorated by hierarchical pattern matching in which the input is gradually canonicalized through pattern matching against subphrases. The number of patterns can also be reduced by matching with semantic primitives instead of words.

Syntactically Driven Parsing

Syntax deals with the ways that words can fit together to form higher level units such as phrases, clauses, and sentences. Syntactically driven parsing (qv) is, therefore, naturally constructive, ie, the interpretations of larger groups of words are built up out of the interpretations of their syntactic constituent words or phrases. In this sense, it is just the opposite of pattern matching, in which the emphasis is on interpretation of the input as a whole. The most natural way for syntactically driven parsing to operate is to construct a complete syntactic analysis of the input utterance first and only then to construct the internal representation or interpretation. This leads to considerable inefficiency, and more recent syntactically driven approaches have tried to intermix parsing and interpretation.

Parse Trees and Context-Free Grammars. The most common form of syntactic analysis is known as a parse tree. Figure 3 shows a parse tree for the sentence

The rabbit nibbled the carrot.

The tree shows that the sentence is composed of a noun phrase (subject) and a verb phrase (predicate). The noun

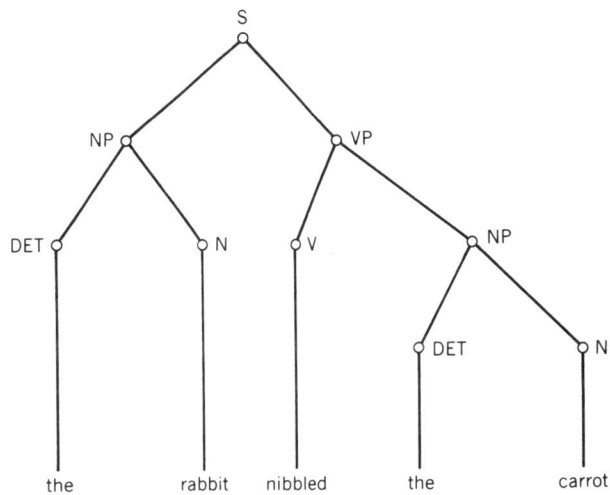

Figure 3. A parse tree for *the rabbit nibbled the carrot.*

phrase consists of a determiner (*the*) followed by a noun (*rabbit*), whereas the verb phrase consists of a verb (*nibbled*) followed by another noun phrase (the direct object), whose determiner is *the* and whose noun is *carrot*.

Syntactic analyses are obtained by application of a grammar that determines what sentences are legal in the language being parsed. The method of applying the grammar to the input is called a parsing (qv) mechanism or parsing algorithm. A very simple style of grammar is called a context-free grammar, which means that the symbol on the left side of a rewrite rule may be replaced by the symbol on the right side regardless of the context in which the left side symbol appears. The context-free grammar consists of rewrite rules of the following form:

$$S \to NP\ VP$$
$$NP \to DET\ N\ |\ DET\ ADJ\ N$$
$$VP \to V\ NP$$
$$DET \to the$$
$$ADJ \to big\ |\ green$$
$$N \to rabbit\ |\ rabbits\ |\ carrot$$
$$V \to nibbled\ |\ nibbled\ |\ nibble$$

As this example shows, context-free grammars have the advantage of being simple to define. They have been widely used for computer languages, and highly efficient parsing mechanisms (Earley, 1970; Tomita, 1986) have been developed to apply them to their input. However, they also suffer from some severe disadvantages. It should be clear that the above context-free grammar accounts for the parse shown in Figure 3; rewrite rules correspond directly to bifurcations in that tree. Although it accounts for that and several other good sentences, the grammar also allows several bad ones, such as

The rabbits nibbles the carrot.

The problem here is that the context-free nature of the grammar does not allow agreements such as the one required in English between subject and object. To enforce such an agreement, there would have to be two completely parallel grammars, one for singular sentences and the other for plural. Moreover, a grammar that also allowed passive sentences such as

The carrot was nibbled by the rabbit.

would have to have another completely different set of rules, even though the passive and the active forms of the same sentence have a clear syntactic relation, not to mention semantic equivalence. These duplications are multiplicative rather than additive, leading to exponential growth in the number of the grammar rules. Thus, in terms of the number of rules involved and in terms of being unable to capture related phenomena by related rules, context-free grammars turn out to be quite unsuitable for natural-language analysis. Recent work by Gazdar (1983) and others has shown that these problems of exponential rule growth can be masked using notational shorthand devices such as "metarules" plus relatively minor extensions to the context-free formalism and in particular without going to the transformational framework discussed below. However, the computational tractability of generalized phrase structure grammar (qv), as the extended formalism is called, has yet to be determined.

There is one more point to be made with this example, one not specific to context-free grammars, but a serious problem for all syntactically driven parsing. The above grammar also allows

The rabbit was nibbled by the carrot.

This is an example of a sentence that is perfectly good syntactically but makes no sense at all. For utterances that are ambiguous syntactically (and for more comprehensive grammars, syntactic ambiguity is very common), such acceptance of nonsensical interpretations can lead to the highly inefficient generation of multiple parses, only one of which has a reasonable translation into the final internal semantic representation.

Transformational Grammar. The problems mentioned above as specific to context-free grammars were tackled by linguists, in particular Chomsky (1957, 1965), through transformational grammar. As shown in Figure 4, their answer was to add another type of rule to a context-free grammar. The basic idea was to use the context-free grammar to generate a parse tree just as before but add onto it certain tags, such as one for a plural sentence. The set of transformations on the parse tree would then rearrange things so that the pluralness was transmitted to all parts of the tree concerned and the required agreements could be enforced. The transformations that enforced agreements were called obligatory transformations. A second class of optional transformations was used to capture the relations between, for instance, active and passive sentences; the active and passive versions of the same sentence had the same representation in the base component produced by the context-free grammar, but the passive version was the result of applying an extra optional transformation. Transformations are context-sensitive rules that map a parse tree into a related parse tree.

Although transformational grammar did a much better job of accounting for the regularities of natural language than context-free grammar, from the point of view of computational effectiveness, it was much worse. (However, significantly, a complete transformational grammar of English has never been produced.) As the above description implied, it was set up as a generative model, ie, it told you how to produce a sentence starting from the symbol S. Running the model in reverse to do sentence analysis turned out to be a computational nightmare, largely be-

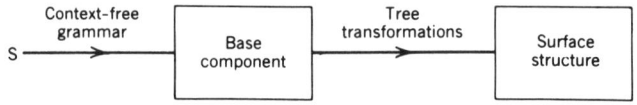

Figure 4. Transformational grammar.

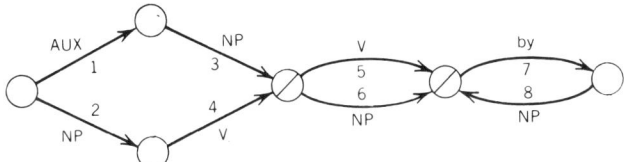

Figure 5. Example ATN.

Table 1. Tests and Actions for Traversing the Arc

Test		Predicate
1	T	(SETR V*)
		(SETR TYPE'QUESTION)
2	T	(SETR SUBJ*)
		(SETR TYPE'DECLARATIVE)
3	(agrees* V)	(SETR SUBJ*)
4	(agrees SUBJ*)	(SETR V*)
5	(AND (GETF PPRT) (= V'BE))	(SETR OBJ SUBJ)
		(SETR V*)
		(SETR AGFLAG T)
		(SETR SUBJ'SOMEONE)
6	(TRANS V)	(SETR OBJ*)
7	AGFLAG	(SETR AGFLAG FALSE)
8	T	(SETR SUBJ*)

cause transformations operate on trees, not strings of words, and so are highly nondeterministic when run backward. For instance, the "equi-NP deletion" transformation deletes without trace the second occurrence of a coreferential noun phrase in certain structures, and it is impossible to run a deletion backward if there is no clue as to what was deleted. Consequently, although some attempts have been made (Petrick, 1965), parsers based on transformational grammar have not played a major role in NLP.

Augmented Transition Networks. Largely in response to the problems of transformational grammar, Bobrow and Fraser (1969) proposed, and Woods (1970) subsequently developed, a method of expressing a syntactic grammar that was computationally tractable and yet still could capture linguistic generalizations in a concise way, in many cases more concisely than transformational grammar itself. The formalism Woods developed was known as an augmented transition network (ATN) (see GRAMMAR, AUGMENTED TRANSITION NETWORK). It consisted of a recursive transition network (formally equivalent in expressive power to a context-free grammar) augmented by a set of tests to be satisfied before an arc was traversed and a set of registers that could be used to save intermediate results or global state. An example ATN is shown in Figure 5. The network recognizes simple sentences with just a subject, verb, and direct object in all combinations of active, passive, declarative, and interrogative. The symbols attached to the arcs show what constituent must be recognized to traverse the arc; AUX is an auxiliary verb (like *is* or *have*); NP is a noun phrase, which is defined by another network in the same formalism as this one; V is a verb; and "by" is the word *by*. The numbers on the arcs serve as indices to Table 1, which list the tests that must be true to traverse the arcs and the action that must be performed as the arc is traversed.

In this LISP-like notation, the asterisk refers to the constituent just parsed, and SETR sets a register, whose name is specified by its first argument, to the value of its second argument. A concrete example of the network in operation will make this clearer. Suppose one wanted to parse

The rabbit nibbled the carrot.

One would start at the left-most node in the graph and at the left of the sentence. Two arcs lead from that node, but only arc 2 is applicable because in the input one is not looking at the auxiliary verb required by arc 1 but at a noun phrase, *the rabbit*, as required by arc 2. One can see from Table 1 that arc 2 has no additional test (indicated by T), so we traverse that link setting the SUBJ register to the thing just parsed, ie, *the rabbit,* and the TYPE register to DECLARATIVE. One is now at a node with only one arc, arc 3, and that arc requires a verb. Fortunately, one is now looking at *nibbled* in the input, so one can try to traverse it. Arc 3 has an additional test requiring that*, ie, the present word in the input (the verb), agree with the contents of the subject register; this is the way agreements are enforced in an ATN. In this case the agreement is correct, and one can traverse the arc, setting the V register to the verb. The node one gets to now has a line through it, indicating that this can be the end of the parse provided that there is no input left to consume, so *The rabbit nibbled* would be accepted here. In this example there is another noun phrase, *the carrot,* and so one follows arc 6, whose test requires that the verb in the V register be transitive, which *nibbled* is. So one ends up at another terminal node with no further input, and so the parse is completed successfully. The result of the parse is the setting of the four registers: SUBJ, TYPE, V, and OBJ, and these can be combined into a tree or whatever representation is desired.

A more interesting use of registers can be seen from the example

The carrot was nibbled by the rabbit.

To parse the first three words, we traverse arcs 2 and 3 much as before, with the difference that now *the carrot* is in SUBJ and *was* is in V. One cannot take arc 6 because one is only up to *nibbled* in the input, but one can take arc 5 because *nibbled* is a verb. The test on arc 5 also requires *nibbled* to be a past participle, which it is, and the contents of V to *be,* and because *was* is a form of the verb *to be,* the test is satisfied. The action on arc 5 is interesting; it puts the contents of the SUBJ register in the OBJ register, overwrites the verb register with the past participle verb, sets a flag to true, and puts a placeholder "someone" in the SUBJ register. This corresponds to recognizing that the sentence is in passive form, and in our case makes *the carrot* the object and *nibbled* the verb. One has reached "by" in the input and so can follow arc 7, which just requires the passive flag to be set; its only action is to turn this flag off, so that the arc cannot be traversed again. Finally, one gets back to their terminal node via arc 8, which puts *the rabbit* in the SUBJ register. Note that the result of this parse is the same as the result of the first example. Now try to follow the parses of

Did the rabbit nibble the carrot?
Was the carrot nibbled by the rabbit?

These brief examples should give some idea of the power of an ATN and of how its tests and registers can be used to capture the regularities of language in a concise and elegant way. Very large ATN grammars of several hundred nodes (Woods and co-workers, 1972) have been developed that capture large subjects of English. However, ATNs also have several disadvantages:

Complexity and Nonmodularity. As the coverage of an ATN increases, so does its structural complexity. It becomes extremely difficult to modify or augment an existing ATN without causing large numbers of unforeseen side effects. For instance, if another outgoing arc is added to a node with a large number of incoming arcs in order to handle an additional type of phrase that is a valid continuation of the parse represented by one of the incoming arcs, it could to lead to spurious and incorrect parses when the node is reached via a different incoming arc. (Fan-out and fan-in factors of 10 or 20 are not uncommon in large realistic grammars.)

Fragility. The current position in the network is a very important piece of state information for the operation of an ATN. If an input should be slightly ungrammatical, even by a single word, it is very hard to find the appropriate state to jump to that would enable the parse to continue, though see the work by Kwasny and Sondheimer (1981) and Weischedel and Black (1980) on dealing with such extragrammaticality and the work on island-driven ATN parsing for speech input by Woods and co-workers (1976).

Inefficiency through Backtracking Search. Although the above examples are not complex enough to show it, the task of traversing an ATN is in general nondeterministic and requires search. The natural way to search an ATN is through backtracking (qv). Because intermediate failures are not remembered in such a search, major inefficiencies can result through repetition of the same subparses arrived at through different paths through the network. Chart parsing techniques (Kaplan, 1973; Kay, 1973; Frederking, 1981) were designed as alternatives to ATNs precisely to avoid these inefficiencies.

Inefficiency through Meaningless Parses. Normally the grammar of an ATN is purely syntactic, and a complete syntactic parse is produced before any semantic interpretation is performed. In that situation many spurious meaningless parses can be produced, especially if the grammar is large and comprehensive. To combat this, recent parsers (Bobrow, 1978) in the ATN tradition have tried to interpret each constituent as it was produced, thus preventing complete parses based on constituents that could be predicted to be nonsensical.

More information on the relative advantages and disadvantages of ATNs is available (Hayes and Mouradian, 1981; Hayes and Reddy, 1983).

Semantic Grammars

Language analysis based on semantic grammars (qv) is similar to syntactically driven parsing except that in semantic grammars the categories used are defined semantically as well as syntactically. Thus instead of the category "noun phrase" in a syntactic grammar, a semantic grammar might have the category "description of a ship," which is syntactically always a noun phrase but has additional strong semantic constraints. Semantic grammars were introduced by Burton (1976) for use in SOPHIE (Brown and Burton, 1975), a computer-aided instruction system for electronic circuit debugging, to deal with the problems of inefficiency due to the generation of syntactically correct, but meaningless, parses mentioned above for ATN-based syntactic grammars. The goal was to eliminate the production of meaningless parses by setting up the grammar so that only meaningful parses could be produced. To do this, it was necessary to categorize all the objects and actions that the SOPHIE system needed to parse to conduct a conversation in its domain of electronic circuitry and then to construct the grammar so that, for instance, only a description of a switch could be the object of a "close" action. This technique, while retaining the fragility of an ATN, worked well to reduce parsing inefficiency. Because the relevant semantic categories were available at parse time, it also allowed semantic interpretation to proceed as the parse unfolded. However, the technique only works properly in restricted domains, like the one mentioned above, in which all objects and their relations can be categorized in advance, allowing a grammar to be built around the possible semantic relations. Semantic grammars are thus a technique useful only for applied natural language processing, not for general NLP.

For an example of how semantic grammars can be used, consider the following grammar definition in the formalism used by LIFER, a system for building semantic grammars developed by Hendrix (1977).

S → ⟨present⟩ the ⟨attribute⟩ of ⟨ship⟩

⟨present⟩ → what is | [can you] tell me

⟨attribute⟩ → length | beam | class

⟨ship⟩ → the ⟨shipname⟩ | ⟨classname⟩ class ship

⟨shipname⟩ → kennedy | enterprise

⟨classname⟩ → kitty hawk | lafayette

An expanded version of this grammar was used for access to a database of information about U.S. Navy ships in the

LADDER (Sacerdoti, 1977) system. Even the above miniversion is capable of recognizing such inputs as

What is the length of the *Kennedy*?
Can you tell me the class of the *Enterprise*?
What is the length of *Kitty Hawk* class ships?

Because the definitions used by LIFER are similar to those used for context-free grammars, the reader should have no difficulty in seeing how these inputs could be recognized by the above grammar. In addition to defining a grammar, LIFER also allowed an interface builder to specify the interpretations to be produced from rules that were used in the recognition of an input. In the above case this resulted in database query language statements corresponding to the inputs being produced as a direct result of the recognition. The database query language statements in effect took the place of a parse tree, and so no separate semantic interpretation stage was required.

Note in the example above that not all the categories are specializations of pure semantic categories; ⟨present⟩, for instance, will parse several phrases, none of which fits into any standard grammatical category. The phrases may differ from each other in their syntactic structure, including the number of verbs they contain. The ability to construct cross-grammatical categories like this allows a semantic grammar to incorporate some features of pattern matching. Also note how strongly directed the recognition is. The word *class* for instance occurs in two quite different ways in the grammar: once as a ship attribute and the other as part of the second type of ship description. Thus in the (rather silly) question

What is the class of *Lafayette* class ships?

the appropriate category for *class* would be used each time it appeared without considering its other role in the grammar. This directedness of recognition is also useful in building spelling correction into the recognition process. In an input like

What is the *legnth* of the *Kennedy*?

the spelling of *legnth* need only be checked against the list of ship attributes rather than the entire system vocabulary because a ship attribute is the only category that can appear at the place where the misspelling occurs. A final advantage of the strong top-down direction available through semantic grammars can be seen in LIFER's ellipsis mechanism, which was intended to deal with input sequences such as

What is the length of the *Kennedy*?
The beam?

Here the fact that *beam* and *length* are in the same semantic grammar category allows the second input to be interpreted as "What is the beam of the *Kennedy*?" rather than say "What is the length of the beam?" See below for discussion on ellipsis mechanisms in general.

In addition to their numerous advantages for limited domain applications, semantic grammars have several disadvantages, chief of which is the requirement that a new grammar be developed for each new domain, since the semantic categories for each domain will be quite different. However, if the applications are similar (eg, both include database access), there will be many parts of the grammar (eg, the basic framework for questions) that are the same. A related disadvantage is that semantic grammars tend to get large very quickly, partly because of the repetition of similar constructions in different semantic categories. This makes nontoy-semantic grammars quite hard to construct and can result in very "spotty" kind of coverage of syntactic variation. For instance, adding a rule that allows the possessive to be apostrophized in the description of a ship attribute (ie, you can say "the *Kennedy*'s length" as well as "the length of the *Kennedy*") does not also allow possessives to be apostrophized in the description of an attribute of a sailor (ie, you might not be able to say "officer's rank" even though you can say "rank of an officer") because the two categories are in different parts of the grammar, and their recognition is unrelated. A second rule would be required.

Three approaches have been tried to resolve these problems. One is to go back to recognition by a syntactic grammar before semantic interpretation, but to try to intermix the semantic and syntactic components much more closely, so that every syntactic constituent is interpreted as soon as it is constructed. The RUS system (Bobrow, 1978) is an example of this approach. It provides some improvement over a pure syntax first approach but is still not as efficient as pure semantic grammars; it is also difficult to incorporate semantic constraints, a process that requires writing different chunks of LISP code, called "I-rules," of each domain.

An alternative approach, as exemplified by the TEAM system (Grosz, 1983), is to focus in on a specific class of applications, access to relational databases, and to abstract out the linguistically common aspects of a semantic grammar for such a class. Building a specific interface, then, requires only instantiating a template, as it were, with the vocabulary and morphological variation required for a specific database. This approach has the potential to produce highly efficient natural language interfaces, but at the cost of some expressive power and inability to go beyond the class of applications without restarting from the ground up.

The third approach is to combine the strengths of several parsing strategies, such as semantic grammars, syntactic transformations, and pattern matching into a single system that maps structures into ore canonical forms before attempting to use the full semantic grammar, thus allowing many redundant and unnecessary constructions to be eliminated (Carbonell and Hayes, 1985; Carbonell, 1981a). This multistrategy approach has been implemented in the DYPAR system (Carbonell, 1985) and applied to database query, expert system command, and operating system command interfaces. Although richer in expressive power, this approach demands more sophistication of the grammar writer, requiring knowledge of how to write transformations, context-free rules, and patterns.

Case Frame Instantiation

A major development in computational linguistics (qv) was the inclusion of case frame instantiation (see GRAMMAR, CASE) in the repertoire of effective parsing techniques. Case frames were popularized by the linguist Fillmore (1968) in his seminal paper, and their computational import was quickly grasped by several researchers in natural language processing, including Simmons (1973), Schank (1975), and Riesbeck (1975). Case frame instantiation is one of the major parsing techniques under active research today. Its recursive nature, and its ability to combine bottom-up recognition of key constituents with top-down instantiation of less structured constituents, gives this method very useful computational properties (see also FRAMES).

What Are Case Frames? A case frame consists of a head concept and a set of roles, or subsidiary concepts, associated in a well-defined manner with the head concept. Initially, only sentential-level case frames were investigated, where the head consists of the main verb, and the cases include the agent that carries out the action, the object acted on, the location in which the action takes place, etc. For instance, consider the sentence

In Elm Street, John broke a window with a hammer for Billy.

In simplified generic notation, the case frame corresponding to this sentence is

[BREAK
  [case frame
    agent: JOHN
    object: WINDOW
    instrument: HAMMER
    recipient:
    directive:
    locative: ELM STREET
    benefactive: BILLY
    co-agent:]
  [modals
    time: past
    voice: active]]

In the notation above, cases, such as *agent*, are written in lowercase, and their fillers are in uppercase.

Case frames, as adopted in computational linguistics, differ markedly from simple, purely syntactic, parse trees. The relations between the head of the case frame and the individual cases are defined semantically, not syntactically. Hence, a noun in the subject position can fill the *agent* case, as in the example above, or it can fill an object case, as in *the window broke* (the window was not the agent that caused the breakage), or it can fill the *instrument* case, as in *the hammer broke the window*. These are different semantic roles played by the same syntactic constituent, "subject." Because the purpose of a nature language interface is to extract the semantics of the input it behooves the case frame representation to encode explicitly semantic differences in otherwise similar syntactic parse trees. Thus parsing into case frames requires semantic knowledge, as well as syntactic information, as shown below.

Consider some other properties of case frames. In the example above, only some of the cases were instantiated. What of the other cases, such as recipient and co-agent? There are examples that illustrate these shortly. First, consider the meaning of each case, as outlined below:

[⟨HEAD VERB⟩
  [case frame
    agent: ⟨the active causal agent instigating the action⟩
    object: ⟨the object on which the action is done⟩
    instrument: ⟨an instrument used to assist in the action⟩
    recipient: ⟨the receiver of an action, often the indirect object⟩
    directive: ⟨the target of an (usually physical) action⟩
    locative: ⟨the location where the action takes place⟩
    benefactive: ⟨the entity on whose behalf the action is taken⟩
    co-agent: ⟨a secondary or assistant active agent⟩
]]

If instead of saying *John broke the window with a hammer,* one were to say *John broke the window with Mary,* Mary would fill the co-agent case. Presumably John did not swing Mary over his head and use her as a battering ram to shatter the window, much as he would use an instrument like a hammer or a tree branch. Because Mary is taking part in causing the action to happen, regardless of whether her action is independent of, or in support of, John's action, she fills the co-agent case.

In order to illustrate the *directive* case, consider *John kicked the ball toward the goal* and *John flew the airplane to New York.* In the former example *the goal* fills the directive case, and in the latter *New York* fills the same case, because both express the direction in which each respective action was performed. In some early formulations of case frames no distinction was made between locative and directive, but the need to encode stative vs dynamic information explicitly (plus the need to represent sentences such as *In Yankee Stadium, John threw the ball at the catcher* that instantiate both cases) led to the acceptance of two semantically distinct cases, one encoding global location, the other a local change in location.

The recipient case is filled by *Mary* in both of the following: *John gave Mary a ball* and *John gave a ball to Mary.* Note that in this instance there are syntactically distinct sentences that map onto a unique semantic case frame representation, to wit:

[GIVE
  [case frame
    agent: JOHN

recipient: MARY
object: BALL]
. . .]

Required, Optional, and Forbidden Cases. Each case frame defines some required cases, some optional cases, and some forbidden cases. A required case is one that must be present in order for the verb to make sense. For instance, *break* requires the object case. A sentence is not complete without it, but no other case is required. *The window broke* is a complete, if not very informative, sentence. An optional case is one that, if present, provides more information to the case frame representation but, if absent, does not harm its semantic integrity. For instance agent, co-agent, and locative are optional cases of *break*. Forbidden cases are those that cannot be present with the head verb. The directive and recipient cases are forbidden for the *break* case frame.

Conceptual Dependency. It is often useful in natural language processing to employ a semantic representation that represents information in as canonical a manner as possible. In the ideal canonical representation, different ways of stating the same information would be represented identically, and propositions that encode similar information would map into semantic encodings that highlighted the similarities while retaining the differences in an explicit manner. The best known attempt at a canonical semantic representation is the conceptual dependency (CD) (qv) formalism (Schank, 1975; Shank and Abelson, 1977; Schank and Riesbeck, 1980) as a reductionistic case frame representation for common action verbs. Essentially, it attempts to represent every action as a composition of one or more primitive actions, plus intermediate states and causal relations.

To use Schank's example, suppose one wants to represent, in a case frame notation, *John gave Mary a ball* and *Mary took a ball from John*. These sentences differ syntactically, they differ in terms of verb selection, and they differ in how their cases are instantiated (eg, *John* is the agent of the first sentence and *Mary* of the second sentence). However, both sentences express the proposition that a ball was transferred from John to Mary, and in both cases one can infer that John had the ball before the action took place, that Mary has it after the action, and that John no longer has it after the action. The only significant difference is that in the first sentence, John performed the action, and in the latter Mary did so.

In CD there is a primitive action called ATRANS (for Abstract TRANSfer of possession, control, or ownership) that encodes the basic semantics of both of these verbs and many more. The CD representation of these sentences is

[ATRANS
  rel: POSSESSION
  actor: JOHN
  object: BALL
  source: JOHN
  recipient: MARY]
"John gave Mary a ball"

[ATRANS
  rel: POSSESSION
  actor: MARY
  object: BALL
  source: JOHN
  recipient: MARY]
"Mary took a ball from John"

(Some readers may be acquainted with Schank's complex notation of double and triple arrows. The direct simplified notation (shown above) is virtually isomorphic, somewhat clearer, and closer to the data structures used by most of the computer programs that parse into CD and other case frame representations.)

These two structures are very simple to match against each other to determine precisely in what aspects the two propositions differ and in what aspects they are identical. Moreover, inference rules associated with ATRANS can be invoked automatically when *give* and *take* are parsed into these structures. There are many more verbs that contain the ATRANS primitive (such as *bequeath, donate, steal, sell, buy, appropriate, expropriate*, etc). Sometimes ATRANS is used in conjunction with other CD primitives that capture other aspects of the meaning. The verb *sell*, for instance, involves two ATRANS primitives in mutual causation:

[ATRANS
  rel: OWNERSHIP   CAUSE
  actor: JOHN   ⟶
  object: APPLE   ⟵
  source: JOHN   CAUSE
  recipient: MARY]

[ATRANS
  rel: OWNERSHIP
  actor: MARY
  object: 24 CENTS
  source: MARY
  recipient: JOHN]

"John sold an apple to Mary for 25 cents"

The cases used in CD are similar but not identical to the set used originally in case grammars, although the basic ideas are the same. One refinement in CD was to separate *agent* into *actor* and *source,* as the two can be instantiated by different entities in the underlying semantic primitives. Other CD primitive actions include

PTRANS	Physical transfer of location.
MTRANS	Mental transfer of information.
MBUILD	Create a new idea or conclusion from other information.
INGEST	Bring any substance into the body.
PROPEL	Apply a force to an object.
ATTEND	Focus a sense organ (eg, eyes, ears).
SPEAK	Produce sounds of any sort.

Later work (Schank and Carbonell, 1979) has extended this list to include social and other interpersonal actions.

Parsing into Case Frames. The discussion of case frames thus far has focused on their structural properties, including parsimony and clarity of representation. Now the uses of case frames in parsing natural language are discussed, in particular certain parsing techniques available to parsers whose target representation is based on case frames. In essence, parsers built around case grammars help to combine bottom-up recognition of structuring constituents with more focused top-down instantiation of less structured, more complex constituents. This essential property is demonstrated in the example case frame recognition algorithm presented below (see also PARSING).

Thus far case frames have been mentioned that consist of a header and a collection of semantically defined cases. There is a bit more to it than that. Each case consists of a filler and a positional or a lexical marker. There have been examples of case fillers in the above sections. A positional case marker says that the filler of the case occurs in a predefined location in the surface string. A lexical case marker says that the case filler is preceded by one of a small set of marker words (usually prepositions) in the surface string. For instance, consider the following input to a natural-language interface to an operating system:

Copy the Fortran files from the system library to my directory.

Copy is the case header, the object case is marked positionally as the noun phrase occupying the simple direct object position (ie, the first noun phrase to the right of the verb that is not preceded by a preposition). The filler of the object case is constrained semantically to be some information structure in a computer. Hence, the parser knows where in the input to search for the filler of the object case and moreover knows what to expect in that position (a noun phrase denoting an information structure, like a file or directory in a computer). The source case is marked lexically by the preposition *from* and the recipient case is marked by the preposition *to*. Both case fillers are constrained to be noun phrases denoting information repositories in the computer (directories, tapes, etc). More explicitly, the case frame information available to the parser is:

[COPY ⟨header-pattern⟩
   [*object:*
      marker: (POSITIONAL DIRECT-OBJECT)
      filler: ⟨information-structure⟩]
   [*source:*
      marker: (LEXICAL ⟨from-marker⟩)
      filler: ⟨information-repiratory⟩|⟨input-device⟩]
   [*destination:*
      marker: (LEXICAL ⟨to-maker⟩)
      filler: ⟨information-respiratory⟩|⟨output-device⟩]
]

Where

⟨header-pattern⟩ → copy|transfer|move|...
⟨from-maker⟩ → from|in
⟨to-marker⟩ → to|into|onto
plus patterns or NP-level case frames to recognize output devices, input devices, information structures, and information repositories

A typical case frame parsing algorithm that operates on this case frame data structure could be summarized as follows:

1. For each case frame in the grammar, attempt an unanchored match of the header pattern against the input string. If none succeeds, the input is unparsable by the grammar. (An unanchored match is the process of searching for a particular pattern anywhere in the input, as opposed to an anchored match, where the match is attempted only starting at a predefined position in the input string.) If one or more matches are found, perform the following steps for frames where headers matched, and the ones that account for the entire input are the possible parses of the input string.

2. Retrieve the case frame indexed by the recognized case header.

3. Attempt to recognize each required case, as follows:

a. If the case is marked lexically, do an unanchored match for the case marker (a very simple one- or two-word pattern), and if that succeeds, perform the more complex recognition of the case filler by anchored match to the right of the case marker or by a more complex parsing strategy (such as recognizing an embedded case frame starting at that location in the input). *Source* and *destination* in the example above are marked lexically.

b. If the case is marked positionally, do an anchored match of the case filler (or again a more complex recognition strategy) starting at the designated point in the input string. *Object* in the example above is marked positionally.

c. If the case maker can be marked either way, search first for the lexical marker, and, failing that, attempt to recognize it positionally. For instance, the recipient case in GIVE can be marked by the word *to* (or *unto*, etc) or it can appear positionally in the indirect object location (*John gave an apple to Mary* vs *John gave Mary an apple*).

If one or more required cases are not recognized, return an error condition. This signifies a possible ellipsis, incorrect selection of the case frame, ill-formed user input, or insufficient grammatical coverage. The following sections address issues of robust recovery from ill-formed user input.

4. Attempt to recognize all the optional cases by applying the same method used to parse the required ones. If some are not recognized, however, do not generate error conditions.

5. If, after all, the required and optional cases have been processed and there is remaining input, generate a potential error condition denoting spurious input, insufficient coverage, or garbled or ill-formed input that may be recognized by more flexible parsing strategies.

As the case frame is parsed, the input segments recognized as case fillers are processed and stored as the value of the corresponding cases in the case frame. A partially instantiated case frame can serve to guide error-correction processes or to formulate focused queries to the user (Carbonell and Hayes, 1985; Hayes, 1981; Hayes and Carbonell, 1981a). The initial case frame selection phase can be speeded up by indexing the case header patterns by the words they contain and recognizing them in a pure bottom-up manner. This bottom-up index-based process is computationally effective if there are very many case frames, and each case header consists of a relatively simple pattern. Otherwise, the top-down unanchored pattern match is sufficiently efficient (few case frames), or both processes require substantial computation (large numbers of case frames with complex header patterns).

Case-frame instantiation can be applied recursively to parse relative clauses or any other linguistic structures that can be expressed as case frames. Noun phrases with postnominal modifiers (ie, trailing propositional phrases that modify the main noun phrase), for instance, can be encoded and recognized by an extension of the sentential-level case-frame instantiation algorithm presented above. Moreover, case frame instantiation works in concert with semantic grammars or patterns used to recognize any subconstituents such as case markers represented as nonterminal nodes in a grammar.

The advantages of case frame instantiation over other parsing techniques can be summarized as follows:

- Case frames combine bottom-up recognition of simple structuring constituents, such as case headers and case markers, with top-down recognition of semantically more complex, but syntactically less significant, case fillers. The differential treatment of different constituents provides more efficient parsing in general, allows for ellipsis resolution, and makes possible some forms of error recovery, as discussed below.
- Case frames combine syntax and semantics. Positional and case marker information is used in concert with semantic recognition of case fillers, thus reducing (though certainly not eliminating) structural and lexical ambiguity.
- Case frames are a fairly convenient representation for back-end systems to use. In contrast, parse trees must first be interpreted semantically and subsequently transformed into a representation more convenient for other modules in the system.

Robust Parsing

Any natural language interface that is used in a practical application with a multitude of users must be able to handle input that is outside its grammar or expectations in various ways. When people use language spontaneously, whether in spoken or written form, they inevitably make mistakes resulting in extragrammatical utterances that a natural language interface will receive. Given the present limited state of NLP, a natural language interface must also be prepared for input that is, as far as the user is concerned, perfectly correct but that the parser cannot recognize because of its own limited competence. Some types of extragrammatical utterances (Hayes and Mouradian, 1981; Hayes and Reddy, 1983) are listed below with example utterances that might be encountered by an interface to a college course registration system.

Spelling errors:

tarnsfer Jim Smith from *Econoics* 237 *too* Mathematics 156

Note that some spelling errors can result in different correctly spelled words (eg, *too*).

Novel words:

transfer Smith *out of* Economics 237 to *Basketwork* 100

Here one supposes that *out of* is not listed as a (multiword) preposition corresponding to the source case marker of transfer and that *Basketwork* is not in the interface's dictionary of department names.

Spurious phrases:

please enroll Smith *if that's possible* in *I think* Economics 237

Ellipsis or other fragmentary utterances:

also Physics 314

This might be a follow-up input to the previous one.

Unusual word order:

in Economics 237 Jim Smith enroll

Missing words:

enroll Smith Economics 237

Here the *in* is missing, but the meaning is still perfectly clear.

Unless a natural language interface can deal with problems in these classes easily, it will appear very uncooperative and stupid to its users, who will tend either not to use it if they have that choice or to use it with a high level of frustration. Examined below are techniques available to deal with some of the above deviations from grammaticality in more detail.

Spelling errors are the most common and normally the most easily corrected of all grammatical deviations. The usual basic approach when a word is found to be outside the vocabulary of a natural language interface is to compare the word against a set of known words and substitute the word (or words) from that list found to be closest to the unknown word according to some metric and subject to some threshold of closeness. There is not space here to go into the methods of comparison, but clearly the process will be made more efficient and less prone to error by shortening the list of words against which to compare the unknown word. For this reason, methods of language analysis, such as semantic grammars and case frame instantiation, that are able to apply strong top-down constraints to their recognition are at a significant advantage when it comes to spelling correction. For instance, in

tarnsfer Jim Smith from Econoics 237 too Mathematics 156

a system based on case frame instantiation such as that examined above need only compare *Econoics* against its list of department names rather than against its whole vocabulary. This ability is particularly important in the case of *too* in this example. *Too* is a real word that might well be in the system's vocabulary, and without the strong prediction that it should be a preposition marking a case of *transfer,* the system would be unable to correct it (a match against the whole vocabulary would make *too* the best match), or even notice that it is mispelled.

Whereas spelling correction can be dealt with at the lexical level, other forms of grammatical deviation require modification to a NLP system's grammatical expectations. The way in which this can be accomplished differs markedly by approach. In pattern matching, for instance, the obvious approach is partial pattern matching as attempted in the FlexP system (Hayes and Mouradian, 1981). Patterns are deemed to match partially if most, but not all, their elements actually do match the input. Clearly, this can be useful for missing or extra words, but is not useful in the case of unusual word order. Moreover, in practice, it turns out that some elements of a pattern are more important than others, and unless allowance is made for these differences, it is difficult to decide exactly how much of a pattern needs to match before the pattern as a whole can be declared to have matched.

Dealing with grammatical deviation in an ATN-based system turns out to be extremely difficult. The current position in the network is a very important piece of state information for the operation of an ATN. If an input should be slightly ungrammatical, even by a single word, it is very hard to find the appropriate state to jump to that would enable the parse to continue. This assumes, moreover, that it is possible to determine exactly where the input has departed from the grammar's expectations. The backtracking search used with most ATNs can make this difficult. Work by Weischedel and Black (1980) has dealt with extragrammaticality caused by incorrect agreements that can be resolved by relaxing the predicates on ATN arcs, and Kwasny and Sondheimer (1981) have looked into adding extra arcs to ATNs on a dynamic basis to make the grammar fit the input. Earlier work on speech parsing (Woods and co-workers, 1976) also tried to use ATNs in an island-driven mode.

A more recent development in robust parsing (Hayes and Carbonell, 1981a; Carbonell and Hayes, 1981) uses a construction-specific approach that fits in well with semantic grammars and case frame instantiation. The basic idea is to tailor parsing strategies to specific construction types; this not only results in efficient parsing of grammatical input but also permits built-in recovery strategies that exploit the characteristics of the particular construction type. For instance, the following simple recovery strategy works quite well for simple imperative case frames:

> Skip over unexpected input until a case marker is found; parse skipped segments against unfilled cases, using only semantic constraints.

If this strategy is applied to

transfer Economics 247 to Physics 317 Smith

Economics 247 and *Smith* will initially be skipped over, with *to Physics 317* being correctly parsed because *to* is a valid case marker. Then the skipped segments will be correctly parsed against the unfilled cases *source-course* and *student* respectively, leading to a parse identical to that for

transfer Smith from Economics 247 to Physics 317

Such methods of robust parsing are under active investigation at the moment with the chief outstanding problem being the coordination of multiple, independent, construction-specific parsing strategies on the same input.

DIALOGUE PHENOMENA

In addition to recognizing individual sentences, the problem of interactive communication through natural language, be it communication between man and machine or communication between two people, entails discourse phenomena that transcend individual sentences (see DISCOURSE UNDERSTANDING).

Anaphora. Pronouns and other anaphoric references (words like *it, that,* or *one*) refer to concepts described previously in a dialogue. Anaphoric resolution entails identifying the referents of these place holder words. Interactive dialogues invite the use of anaphora much more than simpler database query situations. Therefore, as natural language interfaces increase in complexity and expand their domain of application, anaphoric resolution becomes an increasingly important problem.

Definite Noun Phrases. Noun phrases often serve as another type of anaphoric reference by referring to previously mentioned concepts, much like the less specific anaphors do. Usually such phrases are flagged by a definite pronoun (eg, *the*). As Grosz (1977) noted, resolving the referent of definite noun phrases or any other anaphors often requires an understanding of the planning structure underlying cooperative discourse.

Ellipsis. People often use sentence fragments to express a complete proposition. These terse utterances must be filled out in the context of the dialogue. Sentential level ellipsis (qv) has long been recognized as ubiquitous in discourse. However, semantic ellipsis, where ellipsis occurs through semantically incomplete propositions rather than through syntactically incomplete structures, is also an important phenomenon. The ellipsis resolution method presented below addresses both kinds of ellipsis.

Extragrammatical Utterances. Interjections, dropped articles, false starts, misspellings, and other forms of grammatical deviance abound. Developing robust parsing techniques that tolerate errors has been the focus of much recent work (Weischedel and Black, 1980; Hayes and Carbonell, 1981a, 1981b; Carbonell and Hayes, 1981; Kwasny and Sondheimer, 1979), as discussed in the preceding section.

Metalinguistic Utterances. Intrasentential metalanguage has been investigated to some degree (Ross, 1970) but its more common intersentential counterpart has received little attention (Carbonell, 1982). However, utterances about other utterances (eg, corrections of previous commands, such as "I meant to type X instead" or "I should have said . . .") are not infrequent, and an initial stab is being made at this problem (Hayes and Carbonell, 1983). Note that it is a cognitively less demanding task for a user to correct a previous utterance than to repeat an explicit sequence of commands (or worse yet, to detect and undo explicitly each and every unwanted consequence of a mistaken command).

Indirect Speech Acts. Occasionally users of natural language interfaces will resort to indirect speech acts (qv) (Allen and Perrault, 1980; Perrault and co-workers, 1978; Searle, 1975), especially in connection with intersentential metalanguage or by stating a desired state of affairs and expecting the system to supply the sequence of actions necessary to achieve that state.

Empirical studies suggest that users of natural language interfaces avail themselves of discourse phenomena whenever such devices help in formulating short, succinct linguistic expressions over lengthier, more explicit ones. This observation is summarized as follows:

Terseness Principle: Users of natural-language interfaces insist on being as terse as possible, independent of task, communication media, typing ability, or instructions to the contrary, without sacrificing the flexibility of expression inherent in natural-language communication [This principle may be viewed as a surprisingly strong form of Grice's (1975) maxim of brevity].

Case Frame Ellipsis Resolution

In order to illustrate the ubiquity of ellipsis in interactive dialogues through a natural language interface, look at the XCALIBUR project, whose objective is to provide flexible natural language access (comprehension and generation) to the XSEL expert system (McDermott, 1982). XSEL, the Digital Equipment Corporation's automated salesman's assistant, advises on selection of appropriate VAX components and produces a sales order for automatic configuration by the R1 system (McDermott, 1980). Part of the XSEL task is to provide the user with information about DEC components, hence subsuming the database query task. However, unlike a pure database query system, an expert system interface must also interpret commands, understand assertions of new information, and carry out task-oriented dialogues (Grosz, 1977). XCALIBUR, in particular, deals with commands to modify an order, as well as information requests pertaining to its present task or its database of VAX component parts. In the following example dialogue, user inputs are preceded with a ">" prompt.

>What is the largest 11780 fixed disk under $40,000?
The rp07-aa is a 516 MB fixed pack disk that costs $38,000.
>The largest under $50,000?
The rp07-aa.
>Add two rp07-aa disks to my order.
Line item 1 added: (2 rp07-aa)
>Add a printer with graphics capability
fixed or changeable font?
>fixed font
lines per minute?
>make it at least 200, upper/lowercase.
OK. Line item 2 added: (1 lxy11-sy)
>Tell me about the lxy11
The lxy11 is a 240-l/m line printer with plotting capabilities.

Details of the XCALIBUR interface are available (Carbonell and co-workers, 1983, 1985; Carbonell, 1983). In this article, only illustrating the case frame ellipsis resolution method is discussed.

The XCALIBUR system handles ellipsis at the case frame level. Its coverage is a superset of the LIFER/LADDER system (Hendrix, 1977; Sacerdoti, 1977) and the PLANES (qv) ellipsis module (Waltz and Goodman, 1977). Although it handles most of the ellipsed utterances encountered, it is not meant to be a general linguistic solution to the ellipsis phenomenon. The following examples are illustrative of the kind of sentence fragments the current case frame method handles. For brevity, assume that each sentence fragment occurs immediately following the initial query below.

INITIAL QUERY: "What is the price of the three largest single port fixed media disks?"

"Speed?"
"Two smallest?"
"How about the price of the two smallest?"
"also the smallest with dual ports"
"Speed with two ports?"
"Disk with two ports?"

In the representative examples above, punctuation is of no help, and pure syntax is of very limited utility. For instance, the last three phrases are syntactically similar (indeed, the last two are indistinguishable), but each requires that a different substitution be made on the parse of the preceding query.

Ellipsis is resolved differently in the presence or absence of strong discourse expectations. In the former case the discourse expectation rules are tested first, and if they fail to resolve the sentence fragment, the contextual substitution rules are tried. If there are not strong discourse expectations, the contextual substitution rules are invoked directly.

An exemplary discourse expectation rule follows:

IF: The system generated a query for confirmation or disconfirmation of a proposed value of a filler of a case in a case frame in focus,

THEN: EXPECT one or more of the following:
1. A confirmation or disconfirmation pattern.
2. A different but semantically permissible filler of the case frame in question (optionally repeating the attribute or providing the case marker).
3. A comparative or evaluative pattern.
4. A query for possible fillers or constraints on possible fillers of the case in question. [If this expectation is confirmed, a subdialogue is entered, where previously focused entities remain in focus.]

The following dialogue fragment, presented without further commentary, illustrates how these expectations come into play in a focused dialogue:

>Add a line printer with graphics capabilities.
Is 150 lines per minute acceptable?
>No, 320 is better   Expectations 1, 2, & 3
(or) other options for the speed?   Expectation 4
(or) Too slow, try 300 or faster   Expectations 2 & 3

The utterance "try 300 or faster" is syntactically a complete sentence, but semantically it is just as fragmentary as the previous utterances. The strong discourse expectations, however, suggest that it be processed in the same manner as syntactically incomplete utterances since it satisfies the expectations of the interactive task. The terseness principle operates at all levels: syntactic, semantic, and pragmatic.

The contextual substitution rules exploit the case frame representation of queries and commands discussed in the previous section. The scope of these rules, however, is limited to the last user interaction of appropriate type in the dialogue focus, as illustrated below. The rules search the ellipsed fragment for case fillers (or case marker and filler pairs) to substitute for corresponding cases in the parse of the previous input. Substitution can occur at a top-level (sentential) case frame or in embedded (relative-clause or noun phrase) case frames.

>What is the size of the 3 largest single-port fixed-media disks?
>And the price and speed?

and

>What is the size of the 3 largest single-port fixed-media disks?
>disks with two ports?

Note that it is impossible to resolve this kind of ellipsis in a general manner if the previous query is stored verbatim or as a semantic-grammar parse tree. *Disks with two ports* would be best corresponded to some ⟨disk-descriptor⟩ nonterminal and hence, according to the LIFER algorithm (Hendrix, 1977; Sacerdoti, 1977), would replace the entire phrase *single-port fixed-media disks* that corresponded to ⟨disk-descriptor⟩ in the parse of the original query. However, an informal poll of potential users suggests that the preferred interpretation of the ellipsis retains the previous information in the original query. The ellipsis resolution process, therefore, requires a finer grain substitution method than simply inserting the highest level nonterminals in the ellipsed input in place of the matching nonterminals in the parse tree of the previous utterance.

Taking advantage of the fact that a case frame analysis of a sentence or object description captures the meaningful semantic relations among its constituents in a canonical manner, a partially instantiated nominal case frame can be merged with the previous case frame as follows:

Substitute any cases instantiated in the original query that the ellipsis specifically overrides. For instance *with two ports* overrides *single port* in our example, as both entail different values of the same case filler regardless of their different syntactic roles. (*Single port* in the original query is an adjectival construction, whereas *with two ports* is a postnominal modifier in the ellipsed fragment.)

Retain any cases in the original parse that are not explicitly contradicted by new information in the ellipsed fragment. For instance, *fixed media* is retained as part of the disk description, as are all the sentential-level cases in the original query, such as the quantity specifier and the projection attribute of the query (*size*).

Add cases of a case frame in the query that are not instantiated therein but are specified in the ellipsed fragment. For instance, the *fixed-head* descriptor is added as the media case of the disk nominal case frame in resolving the ellipsed fragment in the following example:

>Which disks are configurable on a VAX 11-780?
>Any configurable fixed-head disks?

In the event that a new case frame is mentioned in the ellipsed fragment, wholesale substitution occurs, much like in the semantic grammar approach. For instance, if after the last example one were to ask "How about tape drives?" the substitution would replace *fixed-head disks* with *tape drives* rather than replacing only *disks* and producing the phrase *fixed-head tape drives,* which is meaningless in the current domain. In these instances of wholesale context switch the semantic relations captured in a case frame representation and not in a semantic grammar parse tree prove immaterial.

The key to case frame ellipsis resolution is matching corresponding cases rather than surface strings, syntactic structures, or noncanonical representations. Although correctly instantiating a sentential or nominal case frame in the parsing process requires semantic knowledge, some of which can be rather domain specific, once the parse is attained, the resulting canonical representation, encoding appropriate semantic relations, can and should be exploited to provide the system with additional functionality such as the present ellipsis resolution method. More details and examples of the rules that perform case frame substitution are available (Carbonell and co-workers, 1985).

More Complex Phenomena

In addition to ellipsis and anaphora, there are more complex phenomena that must be addressed to understand and simulate human discourse. This type of deeper understanding has not yet been incorporated into practical natural language interfaces. However, as natural language interfaces increase in sophistication (as they surely will), these more complex phenomena require attention, so, as the final topic of this article, some examples of these more esoteric discourse phenomena are discussed.

Goal Determination Inference. The interpretation of an utterance may depend on the inferred conversational goals of the speaker. Consider the following set of examples, in which the same utterance spoken in somewhat different contexts elicits radically different responses. These responses depend on the interpretation of the initial utterance, in which the attribution of goals to the speaker plays a dominant role.

PASSER-BY: Do you know how to get to Elm Street?

PERSON ON THE STREET CORNER: Walk toward that tall building and Elm Street is the fifth or sixth on your left.

The passer-by's question was quite naturally interpreted as an indirect speech act, because the information sought (and given) was not whether the knowledge of getting to Elm Street was present but rather how actually to get there. Lest the mistaken impression be given that it is a simple matter to identify indirect speech acts computationally, consider the following variant to the example:

PASSER-BY: Do you know how to get to Elm Street?

PERSON READING A STREET MAP AND HOLDING AN ENVELOPE WITH AN ELM STREET ADDRESS ON IT: No, I haven't found it; could you help me?

In the second example, the listener infers that the goal of the passer-by is to render assistance, and therefore the initial utterance is interpreted as a direct query of the knowledge state of the listener in order to know whether assistance is required. Hence, the passer-by's question is not an indirect speech act in this example.

Nor is the task of the interpreter of such utterances only to extract a binary decision on the presence or absence of a speech act from goal expectations. The selection of which indirect speech act is meant often rests on contextual attribution of different goals to the speaker. Consider, for instance, the following contextual variant of our previous example:

PASSER-BY: Do you know how to get to Elm Street?

WAITING CABBIE: Sure, hop in. How far up Elm Street are you going?

In this example, the cabbie interpreted the goal of the passer-by as wanting a ride to an Elm Street location. Making sure the cabbie knows the destination is merely instrumental to the inferred goal. The social relation between a cabbie and a (potential) customer is largely responsible for triggering the goal attribution. Thus the passer-by's utterance in this example is also interpreted as an indirect speech act, but a different one from the first example (ie, wanting to be driven to the destination vs. wanting to know how to navigate to the destination). In summary, three totally different speech acts (qv) are attributed to identical utterances as a function of different goals inferred from contextual information [additional discussion of goal determination inferences in discourse comprehension is available (Frederking, 1981; Perrault and co-workers, 1978; Carbonell, 1981b)].

Example	Speech Act
Original example	Indirect information request
Map reader	Direct information request
Cabbie example	Indirect action request

Social Role Constraints. The relative social roles of the discourse participants affect their interpretation of utterances as illustrated below:

ARMY GENERAL: I want a juicy Hamburger.

AIDE: Yes sir!

CHILD: I want a juicy Hamburger.

MOTHER: Not today, perhaps tomorrow for lunch.

PRISONER 1: I want a juicy hamburger.

PRISONER 2: Yeah, me too. All the food here tastes like cardboard.

Clearly, the interpretation of the sentence "I want a juicy hamburger" differs in each example with no context present beyond the differing social roles of the participants and their consequent potential for action. In the first example a direct order is inferred, in the second a request, and in the third only a general assertion of a (presumably unattainable) goal. Therefore, comprehending a dialogue rests critically on knowledge of social roles (Carbonell, 1981b; Grosz, 1979). Moreover, social role constraints provide part of the setting essential in making goal attributions and therefore impinge (albeit indirectly) on goal determination inferences discussed in the previous section. In unconstrained discourse there is strong interaction between goal expectations, social role constraints, indirect speech acts, and metalanguage utterance interpretation.

CONCLUSION

This article has presented a brief overview of the current state of the art of NLP: the process of developing computer systems that communicate with their users through natural language. The computational approach to NLP differs from the more general open-ended approach to natural language in linguistics and cognitive psychology. As shown above, practical natural language interfaces can currently be constructed to perform limited tasks within restricted domains, and the various techniques that have been employed to construct such interfaces have been examined and compared. Further details on any of the systems or techniques described can, of course, be obtained by following the large set of references provided. Further general information has been published (Charniak and Wilks, 1976; Schank and Colby, 1973) and some implementation details of systems illustrative of the cognitive simulation approach are also available (Schank and Riesbeck, 1980; "Teaching Computers," 1986).

BIBLIOGRAPHY

J. F. Allen, *A Plan Based Approach to Speech Act Recognition,* Ph.D. dissertation, University of Toronto, 1979.

J. F. Allen and C. R. Perrault, "Analyzing Intention in Utterances," *Artif. Intell.* **15**(3), 143–178 (1980).

J. R. Anderson, *Language, Memory, and Thought,* Lawrence Erlbaum, Hillsdale, N.J., 1976.

R. J. Bobrow, *The RUS System,* BBN Report 3878, Bolt, Beranek, and Newman, Cambridge, Mass., 1978.

D. G. Bobrow and J. B. Fraser, "An Augmented State Transition Network Analysis Procedure," in *Proceedings of the First IJCAI,* Washington, D.C., Morgan-Kaufmann, San Mateo, Calif., 1969, pp. 557–567.

J. S. Brown and R. R. Burton, "Multiple Representations of Knowledge for Tutorial Reasoning," in D. G. Bobrow and A. Collins, eds., *Representation and Understanding,* Academic Press, Inc., New York, 1975, pp. 311–349.

R. R. Burton, *Semantic Grammar: An Engineering Technique for Constructing Natural Language Understanding Systems,* BBN Report 3453, Bolt, Beranek, and Newman, Cambridge, Mass., Dec. 1976.

J. G. Carbonell, *Subjective Understanding: Computer Models of Belief Systems,* Ph.D. dissertation, Yale University, New Haven, Conn., 1979.

J. G. Carbonell, "Towards a Robust, Task-Oriented Natural Language Interface," in *Workshop/Symposium on Human Computer Interaction,* Georgia Technical Information Sciences, Mar. 1981a.

J. Carbonell, *Subjective Understanding: Computer Models of Belief Systems,* UMI Research Ann Arbor, Mich., 1981b.

J. G. Carbonell, *Interpreting Meta-Language Utterances,* Preprints of the Workshop: L'Analyze du Language Naturel par L'Ordinateur, Cadarache, France, 1982.

J. G. Carbonell, "Discourse Pragmatics in Task-Oriented Natural Language Interfaces," *Proceedings of the Twenty-First Annual Meeting of the Association for Computational Linguistics,* Cambridge, Mass., 1983.

J. G. Carbonell, "Robust Man–Machine Communication, User Modelling and Natural Language Interface Design," in S. Andriole, ed., *Applications in Artificial Intelligence,* Petrocelli, Boston, 1985.

J. G. Carbonell, W. M. Boggs, M. L. Mauldin, and P. G. Anick, "The XCALIBUR Project, A Natural Language Interface to Expert Systems," in *Proceedings of the Eighth IJCAI,* Karlsrube, FRG, Morgan-Kaufmann, San Mateo, Calif., 1983, pp. 653–656.

J. G. Carbonell, W. M. Boggs, M. L. Mauldin, and P. G. Anick, "The XCALIBUR Project, A Natural Language Interface to Expert Systems and Data Bases," in S. Andriole, ed., *Applications in Artificial Intelligence,* Boston, Mass. 1985.

J. G. Carbonell and P. J. Hayes, "Dynamic Strategy Selection in Flexible Parsing," in *Proceedings of the Nineteenth Annual Meeting of the Association for Computational Linguistics,* Stanford University, Stanford, Calif., 1981, pp. 143–147.

J. G. Carbonell and P. H. Hayes, "Robust Parsing Using Multiple Construction-Specific Strategies," in L. Bolc, ed., *Natural Language Parsing Systems,* Springer-Verlag, New York, 1985.

J. G. Carbonell, J. H. Larkin, and F. Reif, *Towards a General Scientific Reasoning Engine,* CIP #445, Carnegie-Mellon University Computer Science Department, Pittsburgh, Pa., 1983.

J. R. Carbonell, *Mixed-Initiative Man-Computer Dialogues,* Bolt, Beranek, and Newman, Cambridge, Mass., 1971.

E. C. Charniak, *Toward a Model of Children's Story Comprehension,* TR-266, MIT AI, Cambridge, Mass., 1972.

E. Charniak and Y. Wilks, eds., *Computational Semantics,* North-Holland, Amsterdam, The Netherlands, 1976.

N. Chomsky, *Syntactic Structures,* Mouton, The Hague, 1957.

N. Chomsky, *Aspects of the Theory of Syntax,* MIT Press, Cambridge, Mass., 1965.

P. R. Cohen and C. R. Perrault, "Elements of a Plan-Based Theory of Speech Acts," *Cog. Sci.* **3,** 177–212 (1979).

K. M. Colby, "Simulations of Belief Systems," in R. C. Schank and K. M. Colby, eds., *Computer Models of Thought and Language,* W. H. Freeman, San Francisco, 1973, pp. 251–286.

R. Cullingford, *Script Application: Computer Understanding of Newspaper Stories,* Ph.D. dissertation, Yale University, New Haven, Conn., 1978.

G. Dejong, *Skimming Stories in Real-Time,* Ph.D. dissertation, Yale University, New Haven, Conn., 1979.

J. Earley, "An Efficient Context-Free Parsing Algorithm," *CACM* **13**(2), 94–102 (1970).

C. Fillmore, "The Case for Case," in E. Bach and R. Harms, eds., *Universals in Linguistic Theory,* Holt, Rinehart, and Winston, New York, 1968, pp. 1–90.

R. Frederking, "A Rule-Based Conversation Participant," in *Proceedings of the Nineteenth Annual Meeting of the ACL,* 1981.

G. Gazdar, "Phrase Structure Grammars and Natural Language," in *Proceedings of the Eighth IJCAI,* 1983, pp. 556–565.

H. P. Grice, "Conversational Postulates," in D. A. Norman and D. E. Rumelhart, eds., *Explorations in Cognition,* W. H. Freeman, San Francisco, 1975.

B. J. Grosz, "The Representation and Use of Focus in a System for Understanding Dialogues," in *Proceedings of the Fifth IJCAI,* Cambridge, Mass., Morgan-Kaufmann, San Mateo, Calif., 1977, pp. 67–76.

B. J. Grosz, "Utterance and Objective: Issues in Natural Language Communication," in *Proceedings of the Sixth IJCAI,* Tokyo, Morgan-Kaufmann, San Mateo, Calif., 1979, pp. 1067–1076.

B. J. Grosz, "TEAM: A Transportable Natural Language Interface System," in *Proceedings of the Conference on Applied Natural Language Processing,* Santa Monica, Calif., Feb. 1983.

P. J. Hayes, "A Construction Specific Approach to Focused Interaction in Flexible Parsing," in *Proceedings of the Nineteenth Annual Meeting of the ACL,* 1981, pp. 149–152.

P. J. Hayes and J. G. Carbonell, "Multi-Strategy Construction-Specific Parsing for Flexible Data Base Query and Update," in *Proceedings of the Seventh IJCAI,* Vancouver, B.C., Morgan-Kaufmann, San Mateo, Calif., 1981a, pp. 432–439.

P. J. Hayes and J. G. Carbonell, "Multi-Strategy Parsing and Its Role in Robust Man–Machine Communication," CMU-CS-81-118, Carnegie-Mellon University Computer Science Department, Pittsburgh, Pa., May 1981b.

P. J. Hayes and J. G. Carbonell, "A Framework for Processing Corrections in Task-Oriented Dialogs," in *Proceedings of the Eighth IJCAI,* 1983.

P. J. Hayes and G. V. Mouradian, "Flexible Parsing," *Am. J. Comput. Ling.* **7**(4), 232–241 (1981).

P. J. Hayes and D. R. Reddy, "Steps Toward Graceful Interaction in Spoken and Written man–machine Communication," *Int. J. Man-Machine Stud.* **19**(3), 211–284 (Sept. 1983).

G. G. Hendrix, "Human Engineering for Applied Natural Language Processing," in *Proceedings of the Fifth IJCAI*, 1977, pp. 183–191.

R. M. Kaplan, "A General Syntactic Processor, in R. Rustin, ed., *Natural Language Processing*, Algorithmics, New York, pp. 193–241, 1973.

S. J. Kaplan, *Cooperative Responses from a Portable Natural Language Data Base Query System*, Ph.D. dissertation, University of Pennsylvania, Philadelphia, 1979.

M. Kay, "The MIND System," in R. Rustin, ed., *Natural Language Processing*, Algorithmics, New York, 1973, pp. 155–188.

S. C. Kwasny and N. K. Sondheimer, "Ungrammaticality and Extragrammaticality in Natural Language Understanding Systems," in *Proceedings of the Seventeenth Meeting of the Association for Computational Linguistics*, San Diego, Calif., 1979, pp. 19–23.

S. C. Kwasny and N. K. Sondheimer, "Relaxation Techniques for parsing Grammatically Ill-Formed Input in Natural Language Understanding Systems," *Am. J. Comput. Ling.* **7**(2), 99–108 (1981).

J. McDermott, *R1:A Rule-Based Configurer of Computer Systems*, Carnegie-Mellon University, Pittsburgh, Pa., 1980.

J. McDermott, "XSEL: A Computer Salesperson's Assistant," in J. Hayes, D. Michie, and Y-H. Pao, eds., *Machine Intelligence*, Vol. 10, John Wiley & Sons, Inc., New York, 1982, pp. 325–337.

M. A. Marcus, *A Theory of Syntactic Recognition for Natural Language*, MIT Press, Cambridge, Mass., 1980.

R. C. Parkinson, K. M. Colby, and W. S. Faught, "Conversational Language Comprehension Using Integrated Pattern-Matching and Parsing," *Artif. Intell.* **9**, 111–134 (1977).

C. R. Perrault, J. F. Allen, and P. R. Cohen, "Speech Acts as a Basis for Understanding Dialog Coherence," in *Proceedings of the Second Conference on Theoretical Issues in Natural Language Processing*, Cambridge, Mass., 1978.

S. R. Petrick, *A Recognition Procedure for Transformational Grammars*. Ph.D. dissertation, MIT, Cambridge, Mass., 1965.

C. Riesbeck, "Conceptual Analysis," in R. C. Schank, ed., *Conceptual Information Processing*, North-Holland, Amsterdam, The Netherlands, 1975, pp. 83–156.

C. R. Riesbeck and R. C. Schank, *Comprehension by Computer: Expectation-Based Analysis of Sentences in Context*, Yale University, New Haven, Conn., 1976.

J. R. Ross, "Metalinguistic Anaphora," *Ling. Inq.* **1**(2), 273 (1970).

E. D. Sacerdoti, "Language Access to Distributed Data with Error Recovery," in *Proceedings of the Fifth IJCAI*, 1977, pp. 196–202.

R. C. Schank, *Conceptual Information Processing*, North-Holland, Amsterdam, The Netherlands, 1975.

R. G. Schank, and R. P. Abelson, *Scripts, Goals, Plans and Understanding*, Lawrence Erlbaum, Hillsdale, N.J., 1977.

R. C. Schank and J. G. Carbonell, "Re The Gettysburgh Address: Representing Social and Political Acts," in N. V. Findler, ed., *Associative Networks*, Academic Press, Inc., New York, 1979, pp. 327–362.

R. G. Schank and K. M. Colby, eds., *Computer Models of Thought and Language*, W. H. Freeman, San Francisco, 1973.

R. C. Schank, M. Lebowitz, and L. Birnbaum, "An Integrated Understander," *Am. J Comput. Ling.* **6**(1), 13–30 (1980).

R. Schank and C. Riesbeck, *Inside Computer Understanding*, Lawrence Erlbaum, Hillsdale, N.J., 1980.

J. R. Searle, *Speech Acts*, Cambridge University Press, Cambridge, UK, 1969.

J. R. Searle, "Indirect Speech Acts," in P. Cole and J. L. Morgan, eds., *Syntax and Semantics, Vol. 3, Speech Acts*, Academic Press, Inc., New York, 1975.

C. L. Sidner, *Towards a Computational Theory of Definite Anaphora Comprehension in English Discourse*, TR-537, MIT AI Laboratories, Cambridge, Mass., 1979.

R. F. Simmons, "Semantic Networks: Their Computation and Use for Understanding English Sentences," in R. C. Schank and K. M. Colby, eds., 1973, pp. 63–113.

S. Small, G. Cotrell, and L. Shastri, "Toward Connectionist Parsing" in *Proceedings of the Second National Conference on Artificial Intelligence*, Pittsburgh, Pa., AAAI, Menlo Park, Calif., 1982, pp. 247–250.

S. L. Small and C. Rieger, "Parsing and Comprehending with Word Experts (A Theory and its Realization)," in M. Ringle and W. Lehnert (eds., *Strategies for Natural Language Processing*, Lawrence Erlbaum, Hillsdale, N.J., 1982, pp. 89–147.

"Teaching Computers Plain English," *High Technol.*, 16 (May 1986).

M. Tomita, *Efficient Parsing for Natural Language*, Kluwer Academic Publishers, Boston, 1986.

D. L. Waltz and A. B. Goodman, "Writing a Natural Language Data Base System," in *Proceedings of the Fifth IJCAI*, 1977, pp. 144–150.

R. M. Weischedel and J. Black, "Responding to Potentially Unparseable Sentences," *Am. J. Comput. Ling.* **6**, 97–109 (1980).

J. Weizenbaum, "ELIZA—A Computer Program for the Study of Natural Language Communication Between Man and Machine," *CACM* **9**(1), 36–45 (Jan. 1966).

Y. A Wilks, "Preference Semantics," in Keenan, ed., *Formal Semantics of Natural Language*, Cambridge University Press, Cambridge, UK, 1975.

T. Winograd, *Language as a Cognitive Process, Vol. 1, Syntax*. Addison Wesley Publishing Co., Inc., Reading, Mass., 1982.

W. A. Woods, "Transition Network Grammars for Natural Language Analysis," *CACM* **13**(10), 591–606 (Oct. 1970).

W. A. Woods, W. M. Bates, G. Brown, B. Bruce, C. Cook, J. Klovstad, J. Makhoul, B. Nash-Webber, R. Schwartz, J. Wolf, and V. Zue, *Speech Understanding Systems*, Final Technical Report 3438, Bolt, Beranek, and Newman, Cambridge, Mass., 1976.

W. A. Woods, R. M. Kaplan, and B. Nash-Webber, *The Lunar Sciences Language System*, Final Report, 2378, Bolt, Beranek, and Newman, Cambridge, Mass., 1972.

JAIME G. CARBONELL
PHILIP J. HAYES
Carnegie Mellon University
and Carnegie Group Inc.

This research was sponsored in part by the Defense Advanced Research Projects Agency (DOD), ARPA Order No. 3597, monitored by the Air Force Avionics Laboratory under contract F33615-81-K-1539, and in part by the Air Force Office of Scientific Research under Contract F49620-79-C-0143. The views and conclusions contained in this document are those of the authors and should not be interpreted as representing the official policies, either expressed or implied, of DARPA, the Air Force Office of Scientific Research, or the U.S. Government.

NEAR-MISS ANALYSIS. See CONCEPT LEARNING; LEARNING, MACHINE.

NETtalk

A neural network model that was developed in 1985, NETtalk learns to read English aloud [see T. Sejnowski and C. Rosenberg, "Parallel Networks that Learn to Pronounce English Text," *Complex Systems* 1, 145–168, (1987)]. The input to the neural network is a string of letters and the output is a corresponding string of phonemes. When coupled to a speech synthesizer, a simulation of the network on a workstation can pronounce words at the rate of 10 letters per second. The network was trained using the backpropagation learning algorithm on a 20,000 word dictionary of aligned phonemes. The NETtalk database has become a benchmark for other learning systems and is available via FTP from nn-bench-Request@b.gp.cs.cmu.edu

TERRENCE J. SEJNOWSKI
University of California, San Diego

NEURAL NETWORKS

Historically, artificial intelligence grew out of work in neural networks, cybernetics (qv), information theory, and automata theory (as exemplified in, eg, Shannon and McCarthy, 1956). The serial symbol-manipulation approach dominated AI in the 60s and 70s, but the 80s saw a resurgence of interest in distributed computation and in neural networks in the AI community. [For a historical account, see Arbib (1987), and the collection of classical papers edited by Anderson and Rosenfeld (1988).] The term neural networks (NNs) may refer to the circuitry of real brains or to technological devices for a mode of parallel computation which complements approaches to AI based on serial processing and symbol manipulation. This mode of computation is known as neural computing, the study of artificial neural networks (ANNs); it is also referred to as connectionism (qv) or parallel distributed processing. While many people identify NNs with the training of layered NNs using techniques like back propagation (qv) to set the weights in such a net, a broader view is shown in this article, stressing the biological roots of the subject as well as theoretical approaches to networks based on optimization theory and statistical physics. Issues in learning and self-organization are emphasized, with applications to vision and motor control, and the importance of oscillations in NNs is stressed. (For a complementary view, see CONNECTIONISM.)

The language of force fields and energy landscapes provides a useful tool for the analysis of network properties, viewing a computer not in terms of programmed passage through a sequence of discrete states but rather in terms of the motion of a dynamic system towards some attractor set or in terms of oscillatory behavior described by limit cycles. Whereas time in sequential programs is a bookkeeping variable, so that the result of executing a program is not affected by the execution speed, the interaction between different subunits in massively parallel systems like NNs depends crucially on time. Neurons can change internal states of other neurons if particular messages are exchanged at the right time. The same messages might have no influence on the receiving neurons at other times. The additional degrees of freedom provided by the relative timing of neurons have to be taken into account when a program is designed and can be exploited for computation.

Thus, rather than thinking of computation as serial, the concern is with the new paradigm of *cooperative computation* (a shorthand for computation based on the competition and cooperation of concurrently active subsystems) in which local interactions yield an overall result through global self-organization without explicit executive control. Cooperation self-organizes a pattern of "strengthened alliances" between mutually consistent hypotheses about aspects of a problem; it is as a result of competition that hypotheses which do not meet the evolving (data-guided) consensus lose activity. A related theory is that of cooperative behavior in automata developed by Tsetlin (1973). Intriguingly, this work has roots in a classic but neglected study of the conduction of impulses in a network of connected excitable elements, specifically in cardiac muscle (Wiener and Rosenblueth, 1946; Selfridge, 1948) which has been suggested by Minsky (1969) as a possible theoretical basis for studies of epilepsy.

In one of the foundation papers for the study of cooperative computation, Kilmer and co-workers (1969) modeled the reticular formation of the brainstem as a series of interconnected modules, each receiving partial sensory input. They suggested a scheme whereby the modules (by continued interaction; not by executive fiat) could reach a consensus as to the correct global mode of activity for the organism. The modules cooperate while the modes compete. This approach to competition and cooperation can be placed in perspective by considering two early models, one a maximum selector and the other for stereo vision (qv), that also introduce themes to be developed in later sections. Didday (1976) modeled the frog tectum as a distributed network to convert a sensory input signaling a number of prey objects into an output array commanding a snap at one of them. This model embodies pure competition (the neuron that "wins" the competition determines which prey the frog will snap at), and is the earliest example of a "winner-take-all" network. Dev's (1975) model of stereopsis embodies both competition (between neurons encoding different depths in a given direction) and cooperation (so that neurons encoding similar depths in nearby directions will excite each other, thus favoring stable states that encode surfaces rather than rapid fluctuations in depth with changing visual direction). The Dev model may be considered a reticular formation which is so long that overall consensus is impossible; rather the length of regions that do reach consensus is maximized while relaxing to conditions imposed by attempting to match sensory cues from the two retinas. It is thus seen how concepts of short-range and long-range order may play a crucial role in understanding the global behavior of different NNs.

Although the study of distributed computation in AI is broader than that of NNs (it may focus on the interactions of several large subsystems), even where the ultimate analysis is in terms of neurons, it is unnecessary to go straight from some overall function to one vast neural net. First structural units (eg, anatomically defined brain regions like visual cortex) or functional units of intermediate complexity called *schemas* (such as the ability to recognize a house) are sought, and then these are mapped (perhaps again via intermediate structures) to actual NNs. Thus two grains of cooperative computation are used: a fine grain in which many neurons process patterns of information; and a coarse grain where relatively diverse schemas interact. This methodology does not restrict analysis to two levels. Schemas, like programs, may be defined recursively, with schemas becoming building blocks for schema assemblages that constitute schemas as units in yet greater assemblages. In the same way, a top-down analysis may decompose some overall behavior into a network of interacting subsystems, each of which may be further decomposed until the level is reached at which basic circuitry can be specified. Together, schemas and NNs define what has been characterized as the style of sixth generation computing (Arbib, 1989a). Within the biological realm itself, a hierarchy of descriptions from ionic channels to synapses to neurons to hypercolumns to brain regions may also be seen.

Much is to be learned from the explicit design of networks for cooperative computation, low level vision, perceptual robotics (qv), and other intelligent functions. Schemas provide the building blocks for a top-down specification language to complement the use of adaptive NNs in subsystems for visual preprocessing, speech recognition (qv), robot control, and so on. The coarse grain structure of schemas is the functional correspondent of the structural heterogeneity of the brain revealed in the diverse anatomy of different brain regions. Thus learning involves the complementary studies of how it affects the connections between a network of structured systems (a topic for distributed AI) and of how performance criteria can be met by changing the parameters of a single NN (a major topic of this article). While there are many technical applications where one stand-alone network can do the job, such as fingerprint or voice recognition, complex problems will still require people to program a network of interacting schemas, and to program the initial structure of those schemas which are built as neural nets. Such a view leads to the apparently paradoxical claim, "Neural computing is not restricted to neural networks" because system design must embrace both the coarse grain analysis of the overall system as a network of interacting schemas (see SCHEMA THEORY) as well as the fine grain neural analysis discussed in the present article.

NONADAPTIVE NEURAL NETWORKS

In the first half of the article a wide range of topics is considered in which NNs prove of value even when no learning is involved and their connections are fixed. The topics discussed include: the basic neural models; NNs and cooperative phenomena; attractor networks and other NN approaches to optimization; winner-take-all networks; neural models for low level vision; rhythm generating circuitry; and models of coupling of oscillators relevant both to motor control and to vision. The second half of the article will address issues in learning and self-organization.

The Basic Neural Models

There is no typical neuron, but the basic neuron of Figure 1 does schematize properties shared by many neurons. The *dendrites* comprise a major part of the input surface of the neuron; the *axon* provides the output channel. The tips of the axonal branches (*terminals* or *endbulbs*) impinge upon other neurons or effectors. Each endbulb forms a *synapse* on the cell on which it impinges (in fact, an axonal branch may make many synapses along its length). At present, NN theory is dominated by two models, the McCulloch-Pitts neuron and its variants, and the leaky integrator neuron (Arbib, 1989), each augmented by various rules for changing the strengths of synapses. Before presenting these models, it is stressed that real neurons are far more complex (Kandel and Schwartz, 1985), and that study of their complexities is not only essential for neuroscience but promises new insights for neural computing.

A change in the potential difference across the membrane encasing a neuron can propagate passively, decaying with distance, but if the change in potential difference exceeds a threshold, then a "spike" or "action potential"

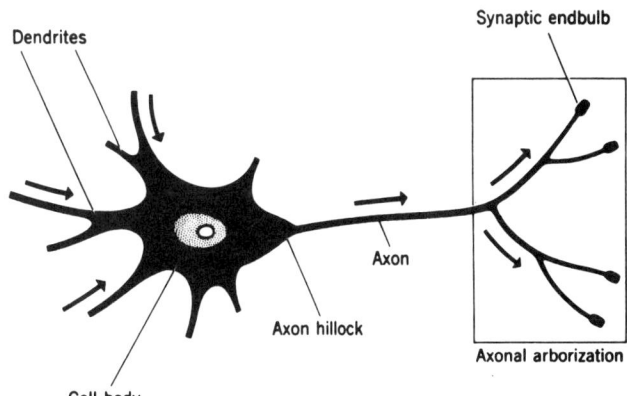

Figure 1. Schematic view of a neuron. Activity from receptors or other neurons modifies membrane potentials on the dendrites and cell body. The effects of these changes converge upon the axon hillock where, for appropriate spatiotemporal patterns of incoming activity, a pulse of membrane potential will be propagated along the axon, branching out into the axonal arborization to activate the synaptic endbulbs which modify the membrane potential of other neurons, or of muscle fibers, in turn.

can actively propagate down the axon without decrement. There is a short *refractory period* during which a new impulse cannot be propagated along the axon. When an impulse arrives at one of the endbulbs, after a slight delay it yields a change in membrane potential in the membrane of the cell on which it impinges. Most synapses are chemical; the electrical pulse reaching the endbulb causes the release of *transmitter* molecules which may have either *excitatory* effects, tending to move the postsynaptic neuron toward threshold, or *inhibitory* effects, tending to move the polarity away from threshold.

In the foundation paper for this subject, McCulloch and Pitts (1943) combined neurophysiology and mathematical logic to model the neuron as a binary discrete-time element. This tied neural nets to the idea of computation initiated by the study of effective procedures and mathematical logic in the 1930s, rather than stimulus-response properties and the formation of associations. The McCulloch-Pitts neuron (Fig. 2) operates on a discrete timescale, $t = 0,1,2,3, \ldots$ where the unit is comparable to a refractory period so that in each time period at most one spike can be generated in the axon of a given neuron. This is on the order of a millisecond in biology; in technology NNs may be used with switching times measured in nanoseconds, exchanging electronic speed for biological complexity.

Let w_i be the strength or weight of the ith synapse onto a given neuron. A synapse is called *excitatory* if $w_i > 0$, and *inhibitory* if $w_i < 0$. A threshold θ is also associated with each neuron, and exactly one unit of delay is assumed in the effect of all presynaptic inputs on the cell's output, so that a neuron "fires" (ie, has value 1 on its output line) at time $t + 1$ just in case the weighted values of its inputs at time t is at least θ. Formally, if at time t the value of the ith input to a neuron is $x_i(t)$ and the output one time step later is $y(t + 1)$, then

$$y(t + 1) = 1 \quad \text{if and only if} \quad \sum_i w_i x_i(t) \geq \theta \quad (1)$$

A slight generalization is to allow the state–output to vary continuously from 0 to 1, so that the next state is computed by passing the weighted input sum through some suitable (eg, sigmoid) function f to obtain the next state,

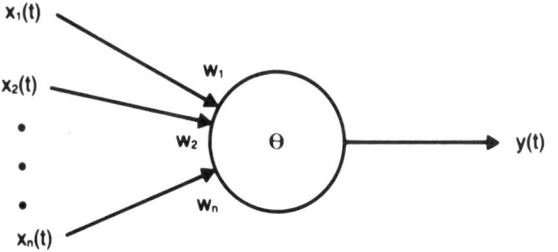

Figure 2. The McCulloch-Pitts neuron operates on a discrete time-scale. At each time step, an input or output is *on* (1) or *off* (0). Each connection or *synapse* has an attached *weight*. A neuron "fires" (ie, has value 1 on its output line) at time $t + 1$ just in case the weighted values of its inputs at time t is at least the neuron's threshold θ.

$$y(t + 1) = f\left(\sum_i w_i x_i(t)\right) \quad (2)$$

It is a standard exercise to choose weights and thresholds to obtain McCulloch-Pitts neurons which function as AND-gates, OR-gates, and NOT-gates, that can then be combined to form any Boolean function (possibly with some delay). McCulloch-Pitts neurons are thus sufficient to build networks that can function as the control circuitry for a computer carrying out computations of arbitrary complexity, ie, McCulloch and Pitts showed that the control box of any Turing machine (qv) can be replaced by one of their networks. Thus where Turing offered a "psychology" of the computable, McCulloch and Pitts offered a "physiology." This discovery played a crucial role in the development of automata theory (Arbib, 1987) and in the study of learning machines (discussed below).

Modern neuroscience no longer uses the binary model of the neuron, instead using continuous-time models that either represent the variation in the average firing rate of the neuron, or actually capture the time course of membrane potentials. It is only through such correlates of measurable brain activity that brain models can really feed back to biological experiments. Rather than offer an exhaustive analysis of such models (cf Koch and Segev, 1989), a model is presented that has long been used to help understand, for example, how large populations of neurons cooperate in vision (Amari and Arbib, 1977) and has been popularized by the work of Hopfield (1984). This *leaky integrator neuron* is a continuous-time model based on using the "firing rate" $M(t)$ (eg, the number of spikes traversing the axon in the most recent 20 msec) as a continuously varying output measure of the cell's activity, in which the internal state of the neuron is described by a single variable, the membrane potential at the axon hillock, $m(t)$. $M(t)$ is then approximated by a sigmoid function of the membrane potential, $M(t) = \sigma(m(t))$, where $\sigma(m)$ increases from 0 to some maximum as m increases from $-\infty$ to $+\infty$. The membrane potential of each cell is described by the differential equation

$$\tau_m \, dm(t)/dt = -m(t) + S_m(t)$$

where τ_m is the time constant for the rate of change of this potential and $S_m(t)$ is the total input the cell receives from other cells. If this input is 0, $m(t)$ exponentially decays toward 0 with time constant τ_m. If the total input $S_m(t)$ is positive, the equation will drive $m(t)$ toward a higher value; if negative, a lower value. NSL 2.0 (Weitzenfeld, 1990) is an object-oriented simulation system that allows the differential equations to be written in a model without reference to any numerical method, allowing the user to choose different numerical methods (trading off, eg, speed and accuracy) on different occasions without respecifying the model. NSL uses convolution with matrices of synaptic weights to simplify the specification of interactions between neural layers.

Neural Nets and Cooperative Phenomena

In many NNs, neighboring neurons encode similar information. Such nets can be modeled with "fields" that approximate a tissue of cells by functions that vary continuously over the tissue, except for a limited number of discontinuities. In, eg, a neural net which encodes a depth map, activity in neurons that code the depth in a given direction will be similar to that for nearby directions if they encode the depths of points on the same surface, but may differ discontinuously if an edge intervenes. Nonlinear analysis (and computer simulation) may be used to follow the unfolding of the pattern governed, say, by differential equations on some continuous manifold. This approach to pattern formation in biological systems goes back at least to Turing's (1952) paper on morphogenesis, which introduced the use of *reaction-diffusion* equations into the study of pattern formation. Turing considered a ring of cells, in each of which there are two chemical substances called morphogens. Within any one cell, these substances engage in chemical *reactions,* but the substances can also *diffuse* between cells. Turing showed that the system would eventually be structured with standing waves of chemical concentrations, thus providing a plausible substrate for the expression of biological pattern. He was once asked whether his model would explain the stripes of the zebra, and his reply was "The stripes are easy, it's the horse part that I have trouble with!" (Murray, 1989, offers a theory of zebra stripes and leopard spots.) The important point here is that local interactions give rise to global pattern.

Many current examples of local interactions that give rise to global patterns in NNs are based on analogies with the study of cooperative phenomena in physics, as when, in studying ferromagnets, understanding is sought on how atomic magnets can cooperate to yield global magnetic order through the mass effects of local interactions. But where classical work in physics emphasized *homogeneity*, this article studies how single neurons may be synthesized into heterogeneous cell assemblies that are meaningful for mediating action, perception, and memory.

In a ferromagnetic material, the individual atoms are submicroscopic magnets. The local interactions of the atoms tend to align their magnetic spin in the same direction; thermal motion tends to disturb the alignment and "randomize" the spins. If the magnet is not too hot, the local interactions can cooperate so that tracts of the material will have their spins oriented in the same direction. Such a tract is called a *domain*. If a strong enough external magnetic field is provided, it can bias the local interactions to get almost all the spins to align themselves with the field, and then there is one domain, and the material becomes what is called a magnet. Cragg and Temperley (1954) were perhaps the first to suggest a statistical mechanics of the brain by drawing analogies between cortical activity and domain formation in ferromagnets. For example, the visual cortex contains a great variety of cells tagged not only for visual direction but also for depth in the visual field (or, it may be that groups of cells encode depth, and thus provide the units of cooperativity). Thus we can imagine the process of recognizing regions in the visual input at different depths to be one of suppressing all neural activity except that corresponding to the depths within a given direction; segmentation thus has much in common with the process of domain formation in magnets (cf Julesz, 1971).

Stability in Dynamic Systems. Since the study of dynamic systems has become so important in the study of NNs, some basic concepts are reviewed. An *equilibrium* for a system is a state $q(t)$ in which the system can stay at rest for fixed values of the input, ie, an equilibrium state is one for which the time derivative $q(t)$ is 0. The study of *stability* is concerned with the issue of whether or not this rest point will be maintained in the face of slight disturbances. The image of a ball rolling on the "hillside" of Figure 3a is used to clarify the concepts involved. The point A atop the hillside is an *unstable* equilibrium because a slight displacement from A will tend to increase

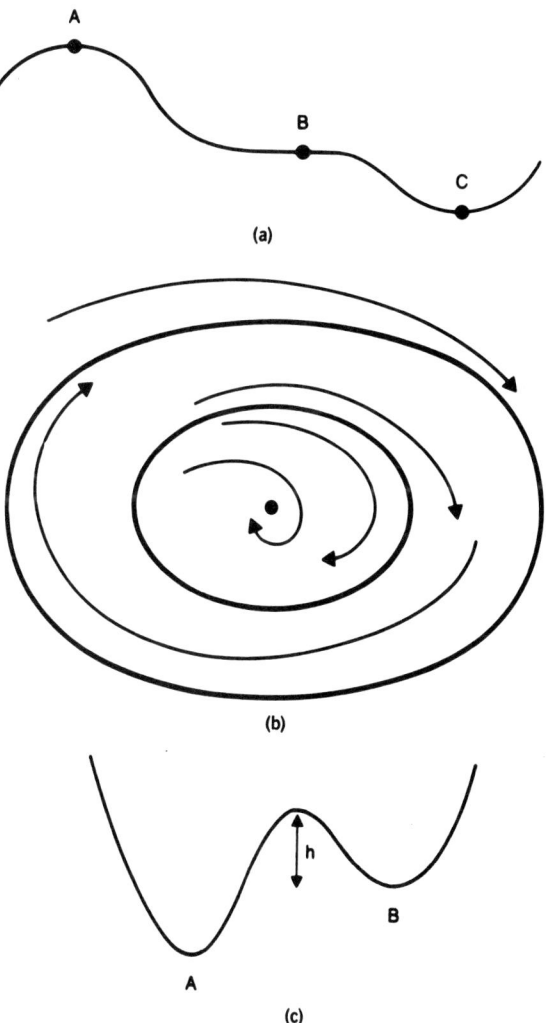

Figure 3. (a) For a ball rolling on this "hillside," A is a point of unstable equilibrium, B is a region of neutral equilibrium, and C is a point of stable equilibrium. (b) Nonlinear systems may exhibit limit cycles; closed trajectories in state space that may be thought of as "dynamic equilibria." In this example, the outer limit cycle is stable and the inner limit cycle is unstable. (c) An energy landscape in which energy increase h is required to escape from the valley of local minimum B to enter the attractor of the global minimum A.

over time; B, situated on a "plain," is called a region of *neutral* equilibrium because slight displacements will tend not to change further; while C, at the foot of the "valley," is a point of *stable* equilibrium, because small displacements will tend to disappear over time. Note the word "slight": in Figure 3a, a large displacement can move the ball "across a mountain range" from the *attractor* of one equilibrium to another.

A *linear system* is one of the form $q(t) = Aq(t) + \alpha(t)$ where A is a matrix, and $\alpha(t)$ is a general input vector. When A is invertible, the system has a unique equilibrium q_e for fixed $\alpha(t) = \alpha$, namely $q_e = -A^{-1}\alpha$. It turns out that the stability of this equilibrium can be characterized in terms of the eigenvalues of A: $q(t) \to q_e$ as $t \to \infty$ for each initial state $q(0)$ if all eigenvalues of A have negative real parts.

Nonlinear systems may exhibit *limit cycles* (Fig. 3b), closed trajectories in the state space that may be thought of as "dynamic equilibria." A limit cycle is stable if a small displacement will be reduced as the trajectory of the system approaches the original limit cycle, unstable if such excursions do not die out. Nonlinear systems may also exhibit *strange attractors* which, unlike simple limit cycles, describe such complex paths through the state space that, although the system is deterministic, a path which approaches the strange attractor gives every appearance of being random. Such a trajectory has become the accepted mathematical model of *chaos* (Gleick, 1987), used to describe such physical phenomena as the onset of turbulence.

To analyze the stability of a nonlinear system near an equilibrium the system may be approximated by either a linear system in that region, or by a "Lyapunov function" (Hirsch and Smale, 1974; Abraham and Shaw, 1983). Briefly, a differentiable map $V: Q \to R$ is a Lyapunov function for the system $\dot{q} = F(q)$ at the equilibrium q_e if there is a neighborhood Ω of q_e such that $V(q) > V(q_e)$ for all $q \in \Omega - \{q_e\}$ while $\dot{V}(q) \leq 0$ in Ω. If $\dot{V}(q) < 0$ for all $q \in \Omega - \{q_e\}$ then q_e is stable: $V(q)$ never increases, and it takes its minimum value at q_e. This provides the motivation for the notion of "energy" used in NNs.

Hopfield Networks and Optimization. Many authors have treated NNs as dynamical systems (an early example being Grossberg, 1967), employing notions of equilibrium, stability, energy, and so on, to classify their performance. However, much recent work has been motivated by the idea of a "spin glass" analogy. The notion of a spin as a binary variable can be traced back to the work of Ising (1925), who modeled magnets as a linear array of "Ising spins" which could be in one of two states, "up" or "down." The basic model associates with each point $k = (i,j)$ of a two-dimensional lattice a spin $s_k \in \{-1,1\}$. The dynamics of spins is stochastic. A spin tends to align with its neighbors, but the probability of doing so decreases toward .5 as the temperature T increases. The temperature dependence of the model reflects a basic discovery by Pierre Curie that there is a critical temperature, called the Curie temperature T_C, such that the global magnetization induced by an external magnetic field will be retained if the material is below this temperature, whereas the thermal fluctuations will dominate the local interactions to demagnetize a magnet hotter than T_C. The Curie temperature thus marks a critical point at which the material makes a *phase transition* from a phase in which it can hold magnetization to one in which it cannot—an order-disorder transition. One-dimensional physical systems in general cannot exhibit phase transitions, but Onsager (1944) showed that a two-dimensional Ising model can.

If spin k is allowed to be influenced by the spins in the set S_k of its four nearest neighbors in the lattice, spin k is set to 1 only if $h_k = \Sigma_{j \in S_k} s_j > 0$, and then only with probability

$$\text{prob}(s_k(t+1) = 1) = 1/(1 + e^{-h_k(t)/T})$$

which tends to .5 as T tends to infinity. In the deterministic case, $T = 0$, this reduces to $s_k(t+1) = 1$ if and only if $\Sigma_{j \in S_k} s_j > 0$, which looks suspiciously like a special case of the McCulloch-Pitts rule $y(t+1) = 1$ if and only if $\Sigma_i w_i x_i(t) \geq \theta$.

This analogy has been noted many times. For example, Little (1974) offered an Ising spin analogy of a NN which introduced the temperature or statistical fluctuations directly and crucially into the firing equations. The model gave both static and cyclic behavior, and had asymmetrical coefficients. However, Hopfield (1982) was the catalyst in attracting the attention of many physicists to this field of study. Amit (1989) presents the fruits of the first seven years of ensuing research by physicists studying NNs. The present section reviews Hopfield's idea of an energy function, and shows how it allows NNs to be used to solve optimization and constraint satisfaction problems. Hopfield presented a model similar to that of Little, but with symmetric connections, and without the statistical fluctuations. By introducing asynchronous firing, he obtained a dynamics which served to minimize a global energy measure. As a later section will show, learning may be used to adjust the potential surface so the minima will be placed in desired locations, using local minima to store different patterns.

The familiar McCulloch-Pitts neuron is used with an output that is 1 iff $h_i = \Sigma_{k=0}^{N} w_{ik} s_k \geq \theta_i$ and is otherwise 0, where s_k is the current value of the kth input and w_{ik} is the corresponding synaptic weight from unit k to unit i, with a threshold of θ_i. Classically, a McCulloch-Pitts net uses the *parallel synchronous update scheme* in which every neuron processes its inputs *synchronously* at each time step to determine a net output. By contrast, a *Hopfield net* (Hopfield, 1982) is a net of such units with *symmetric* weights ($w_{ij} = w_{ji}$) which uses the *random asynchronous update scheme*: "Pick a unit at random. If the sum of the weights on connections from other active units exceeds threshold, turn it on. Otherwise turn it off." The random choice of a neuron completely destroys all temporal correlations between neurons. Hopfield's contribution was to observe that, for a symmetric network with the random asynchronous update scheme, the function

$$E = -\frac{1}{2} \sum_{i,k=1}^{N} s_i w_{ik} s_k + \sum_{i=1}^{N} s_i \theta_i \qquad (3)$$

often called the *energy* of the neural system, decreases whenever the new activity state of a neuron differs from its previous state. This is not the physical energy of the neural net, it is rather a mathematical quantity that does for neural dynamics what potential energy does for a conservative Newtonian system. By exploiting the symmetry of w_{ik}, the decrease in energy ΔE can be rewritten as $|h_i - \theta_i|$ when neuron α changes its state. Since the function E is bounded from below for $N < \infty$ the network will reach a fixed point in finite time. Hence the dynamics of the net tends to move E toward a minimum. Different *local* minima may exist. Global minimization is not guaranteed!

The above expression for ΔE crucially depends on the symmetry condition. If $w_{ij} \neq w_{ji}$, the updating rule need not yield passage to a minimum of E, but might instead yield a limit cycle or chaotic motion. In most vision algorithms, constraints can be formulated in terms of symmetric weights, so that $w_{ij} = w_{ji}$ is appropriate. In a control problem, however, a link w_{ij} might express the likelihood that the action represented by activation of neuron i should precede that represented by activation of neuron j, in which case $w_{ij} = w_{ji}$ is normally inappropriate.

In the pages that follow, both deterministic networks and stochastic networks will be studied. For many phenomena, the deterministic model gives an excellent understanding of the average behavior of a biological NN or the useful behavior of an ANN. For other phenomena, the stochastic fluctuations generated by membrane noise and other phenomena play a crucial role in the biological system and offer the ability to extend the functionality of ANNs. The response of biological neurons, in fact, is influenced by fluctuations in the number of vesicles released and the amount of neurotransmitter per vesicle as well as by stochastic changes of membrane properties. With Gaussian fluctuations, the actual value of the local field h_i can be approximated by the probability distribution

$$P\{h_i = h\} = \frac{1}{\sqrt{2\pi\eta^2}} \exp\left[-\frac{(h - h_i)^2}{2\eta^2}\right]$$

The probability that neuron i will fire at time $t + 1$ is, therefore, determined by the probability that h_i exceeds θ_i, ie, by the integral

$$P\{h_i > \theta_i\} = \int_{\theta_i}^{\infty} \frac{dh}{\sqrt{2\pi\eta^2}} \exp\left[-\frac{(h - h_i)^2}{2\eta^2}\right]$$
$$\approx \frac{1}{1 + \exp[-\beta(h_i - \theta_i)]} \text{ with } \beta = 2\sqrt{2\eta} \quad (4)$$

The parameter $T = 1/\beta$ is often called computational or network temperature in analogy to magnetic systems, and controls the amount of noise in the neural dynamics. The connection between stochastic fluctuations of the local field h_i, which can be identified with the membrane potential for our purposes, and the firing probability parameterized by β was first studied by Little (1974).

The approximation of the error function in (4) with the logistic function $1/(1 + \exp(-\beta x))$ introduces a maximal error of one percent and allows us to study the dynamics of NNs with tools developed in statistical mechanics of magnetic systems. Using relation (4) the deterministic update rule must be modified to a probabilistic rule

$$V_i(t + 1) = 1 \quad \text{with probability}$$
$$\frac{1}{1 + \exp[-\beta(h_i(t) - \theta_i)]} \quad (5)$$

This establishes the connection of NNs to stochastic optimization. High noise levels often destabilize spurious attractors in associative memories, which proves the utility of a stochastic network dynamics. Consider how one might get a ball-bearing traveling along the curve in Figure 3c to avoid local minima and "probably end up" in the deepest minimum. The idea is to shake the box "about h hard"; then the ball is more likely to go from B to A than from A to B. So, on average, the ball should end up in A's valley. Kirkpatrick and co-workers (1983) developed the earlier work of Metropolis and co-workers (1953) on a Monte Carlo simulation to provide a general method called *simulated annealing* (qv) for making likely the escape from local minima by allowing jumps to higher energy states, in analogy with the annealing used by a craftsman forging a sword by alloying two metals while slowly cooling them.

The Boltzmann machine (qv) of Hinton and co-workers (1986) extends Hopfield nets by the use of simulated annealing, reintroducing fluctuations (Little, 1974) by adding a temperature-dependent stochastic element to avoid the problem of local minima. If the noise level of a *stochastic* attractor net with an energy function is specified, a search is made for the most likely distribution function compatible with the average energy constraint. The principle of maximum entropy (Jaynes, 1957), embodied in the formalism of statistical mechanics, allows one to determine this most likely distribution of network states. In particular, the principle postulates that the Boltzmann distribution from the theory of gases should also be used to describe neural interactions. An update rule for state transitions that goes back to Metropolis and co-workers (1953) comprises the following steps:

1. Pick a unit at random.
2. Compute $\Delta E = \Sigma s_j w_{ij} - \theta_i$. Then set s_i to 1 with probability

$$p_i(\Delta E) = 1/(1 + e^{-\Delta E/T}).$$

This converges to the old rule, a step function with the step at $\Delta E = 0$, as $T \to 0$. The "zero-temperature" dynamics chooses an element at random and flips its state if this will lower the energy of the net. Repeating this process (with $T = 0$) would eventually yield a local minimum. In general, for $T > 0$, the flips are random and yield a Markov process which is *regular,* ie, it has no absorbing barriers and no cycles and thus has a unique limiting distribution on the 2^n states of the n neurons. Annealing is the process whereby this passage to equilibrium is repeated for successively lower T. The resulting system can be implemented naturally in a parallel network. In the limit, if the process is slow enough, the system passes to its global minimum. However, the proof of this given by

Geman and Geman (1984) results in an annealing schedule that is hideously slow. Implemented algorithms relax faster, but are not guaranteed to reach the global minimum with probability one.

Elastic and Neural Optimization. A famous example of a hard optimization problem is the traveling salesman problem (TSP). A salesman wishes to find the shortest way to visit a set of cities only once and to return to his starting point (Fig. 4). The difficulty of this optimization problem originates from the huge number of legal solutions, ie, $N!/2N$, and from the fact that completely different tours may have almost the same tour length. In an influential paper, Hopfield and Tank (1986) suggested a network of leaky integrator neurons to solve this benchmark problem for optimization algorithms. Analysis of the scaling behavior of the network, however, revealed (Wilson and Pawley, 1988) that their network did not find good solutions of TSP on average, especially for instances with more than 30 cities. An alternative approach to solve TSP in a neural style was suggested by Durbin and Willshaw (1987). Their elastic net algorithm proved reliable even for larger (>100) instances of TSP. Both models will be introduced in this section and the reasons for such a different performance will be studied.

Hopfield and Tank mapped TSP to a constraint satisfaction network by letting the firing V_{Xi} of neuron X_i express the decision that city X is visited at stop i of a tour of N cities. The neural variables X_i represent a permutation matrix. Ideally, for each i there is a unique X such that V_{Xi} fires, and the aim is to design the energy function, then infer the appropriate weights, so that the network will be constrained to move towards states that meet this condition as well as expressing a minimum tour length. In general, however, the "tour" coded by the network includes many different segments for step i, each weighted by the current firing of the endpoint neurons (thus according with our intuition if there is a unique Y and $X \neq Y$ for which V_{Xi} and $V_{Y,i-1}$ equal 1). The move from city Y at stop $i - 1$ to the next city X costs

$$\sum_X \sum_{Y \neq X} d_{YX} V_{Xi} V_{Y,i-1}$$

where d_{YX} denotes the distance between cities X and Y, and so the cost of the complete "tour" is

$$\sum_i \sum_X \sum_{Y \neq X} d_{YX} V_{Xi} V_{Y,i-1} \quad (6)$$

The "visit a city only once" constraint can be enforced in a soft way by the penalty

$$\frac{\alpha}{2} \sum_X \sum_i \sum_{j \neq i} V_{Xi} V_{Xj} + \frac{\beta}{2} \sum_i \sum_X \sum_{Y \neq X} V_{Xi} V_{Yi} + \frac{\gamma}{2} \left(\sum_X \sum_i V_{Xi} - N \right)^2 \quad (7)$$

(The term *soft constraint* refers to the optimization strategy that add a cost for deviations from a legal solution, but is not rigidly excluded from such deviations.) The first term expresses the constraint that a city should not be visited more than once, the second forbids visiting two cities at the same time, while the third ensures that all N cities are visited. Combining (6) and (7) yields the total energy function

$$E_{\text{TSP}} = -\frac{1}{2} \sum_{Xi} \sum_{Yj} T_{Xi,Yj} V_{Xi} V_{Yj} - \gamma N \sum_{Xi} V_{Xi} \quad (8)$$

The variables $T_{Xi,Yj} = -\alpha \, \delta_{XY}(1 - \delta_{ij}) - \beta \, \delta_{ij}(1 - \delta_{XY}) - \gamma - d_{XY}(\delta_{ij} + 1 + \delta_{ij} - 1)$ define a connection matrix with inhibitory connections within each row and each column and a global inhibition of strength γ. To prevent complete inhibition of the NN resulting in a completely silent network state the neurons are excited from outside by an input of strength γN.

Hopfield and Tank used leaky integrator dynamics for graded response neurons to optimize the cost function E_{TSP}. Each neuron is characterized by an internal potential U_{Xi} and an output potential V_{Xi} (corresponding to the firing rate) which is a sigmoid function $\sigma(U_{Xi})$ of U_{Xi}. The U_{Xi} evolve according to the equations

$$\frac{dU_{Xi}}{dt} = -\frac{U_{Xi}}{\tau} + \sum_{Yj} T_{Xi,Yj} V_{Yj} + \gamma N. \quad (9)$$

These equations can also be interpreted as the time evolution of an electronic circuit with resistors $T_{Xi,Yj}$ and external currents γN. The equilibrium states of the NN for a step sigmoid function $\sigma(x)$ are supposed to have the form of a permutation matrix specifying the order in which the cities are visited on a tour. Hopfield and Tank published satisfactory simulation results of a 10 and a 30 city instance. They advocated the graded neuron approach as a fast optimization procedure since the kinetic equations of the neurons are deterministic. Another appealing feature of this approach is the prospect of implementing

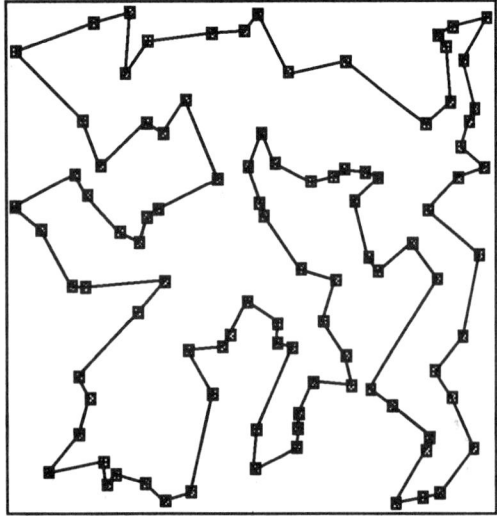

Figure 4. An instance of the traveling salesman problem with a good solution.

the network in analog VLSI, a natural choice if the form of the evolution equations is compared with electronic circuit equations. However, Wilson and Pawley (1988) did an extensive study on the scaling behavior of the Hopfield and Tank network and found that the promising results for small numbers of cities cannot be extended to larger TSP instances. The number of local minima in the cost function grows too fast with the problem size for this NN to find large tours with low costs.

Despite the limited success of this approach to TSP, it sparked a variety of more successful neural-style algorithms for optimization. Durbin and Willshaw (1987) put forward an alternative idea based on topology preserving algorithms studied in the context of self-organization of neural projections. Their elastic net algorithm maps neighboring points on a circular path to neighboring points (near to or, ideally, at cities) in the plane. This is a special case of a self-organizing, topology preserving map. Instead of characterizing TSP by the distance between cities, two-dimensional vectors x_i ($i = 1, \ldots, N$) are used to give the location of the cities in the plane. The tour is represented by a ring with points at positions $y_j (j = 1, \ldots, M \approx 3N)$ in the plane. The ring is considered "elastic" to express the constraint that tour length should be minimized. The position of the points j on the ring should be changed in such a way that the the ring relaxes to a legal traveling salesman solution. This suggests the update rule

$$\Delta y_j = \alpha(|x_{ji} - y_j|) + \beta K(|y_{j+1} - y_j| + |y_j - y_{j-1}|)$$

where x_{ji} is the city closest to y_j. These two terms may be described as "city matching" and "smoothness" conditions, akin to the "feature matching" and "smoothness" conditions used in the MATCH algorithm to be described below. However, instead of requiring the determination of x_{ji}, Durbin and Willshaw set

$$\Delta y_j = \alpha \sum_i w_{ij} (|x_i - y_j|)$$
$$+ \beta K(|y_{j+1} - y_j| + |y_j - y_{j-1}|) \quad (10)$$

where w_{ij} specifies the influence of city i on ring point j and is defined as

$$w_{ij} = \frac{\exp(-|x_i - y_j|^2/2K)}{\sum_k \exp(-|x_i - y_k|^2/2K)} \quad (11)$$

which decays with increasing distance $|x_i - y_j|$, so that y_j will try to move to a city near its current position. The update rule (10) always decreases the function

$$E = -\alpha K \sum_i \ln \sum_j \exp(-|x_i - y_j|^2/2K)$$
$$+ \beta \sum_j |y_{j+1} - y_j|^2 \quad (12)$$

and thus guarantees convergence to a legal solution. Actually, the update equation (10) is a dissipative dynamics with the energy (12), ie, $\Delta y_j = -K\partial E/\partial y_j$.

The constants α and βK determine the relative strength of the forces from cities and from neighboring points on the ring. βK plays the role of an elasticity constant in a rubber ring constraining y_j to move to reduce its distance from both y_{j-1} and y_{j+1}; K is reduced as relaxation proceeds to allow y_j's to converge to match an x_i exactly. Three snapshots of a typical simulation are shown in Figure 5. The number of ring points has to be larger (factor of 3) than the number of cities but the algorithm scales proportionally to the number of cities (order N) whereas the Hopfield-Tank approach scales as N^2 (one neuron for each city x and step i).

Why do these two analog, parallel algorithms perform so differently on large instances of TSP? Simic (1990) noted that they treat constraints differently. In the Hopfield and Tank approach, network states that correspond to tours with stops in different cities at the same time are penalized but are still possible solutions. In the same way, tours that do not pass through all cities can be local minima of the cost function in which the network might be trapped by its relaxation dynamics. The two corresponding constraints are strictly enforced in the Durbin and Willshaw algorithm with the obvious result that the network dynamics is not disturbed by unwanted, spurious minima. Observe the same influence of constraints on the performance of an algorithm when the winner-take-all system is discussed. Simic (1991) extended his analysis to the class of all quadratic assignment problems and derived a successful algorithm for elastic graph matching. Elastic graph matching seems to be related to the dynamic link architecture that will be discussed below.

Winner-Take-All Networks

Amari and Arbib (1977) studied a variant of Didday's model of prey-selection by frogs, the *primitive competition model*

$$\frac{du_i(t)}{dt} = -u_i + w_1 f(u_i) - w_2 g(v) - h_1 + s_i$$
$$\tau \frac{dv}{dt} = -v + \sum_{i=1}^{n} f(u_i) - h_2 \quad (13)$$

Here, there is an array of inputs s_i feeding an array of neurons with membrane potentials u_i and firing rates $f(u_i)$, where $f(u)$ is 0 for $u < 0$, and 1 for $u \geq 0$. Competition is mediated by a single inhibitory neuron with membrane potential v_i and firing rate $g(v)$, where $g(v)$ is 0 for $v < 0$, and v for $v \geq 0$. Clearly, a unit with larger u_i and larger s_i has a better chance of "riding through" the global inhibition $g(v)$ than its weaker brethren. In fact, on taking $h_1 \geq 0, 1 > h_2 \geq 0$, Amari and Arbib prove that the number K of elements excited in equilibrium cannot exceed

$$(s + w_1 - h)w_2^{-1} + h_2$$

where s is the smallest stimulus applied to any of the excited elements. As a result, if the maximum stimulus applied to the network satisfies

$$s_{\max} < h_1 - w_1 + (L + 1 - h_2)w_2$$

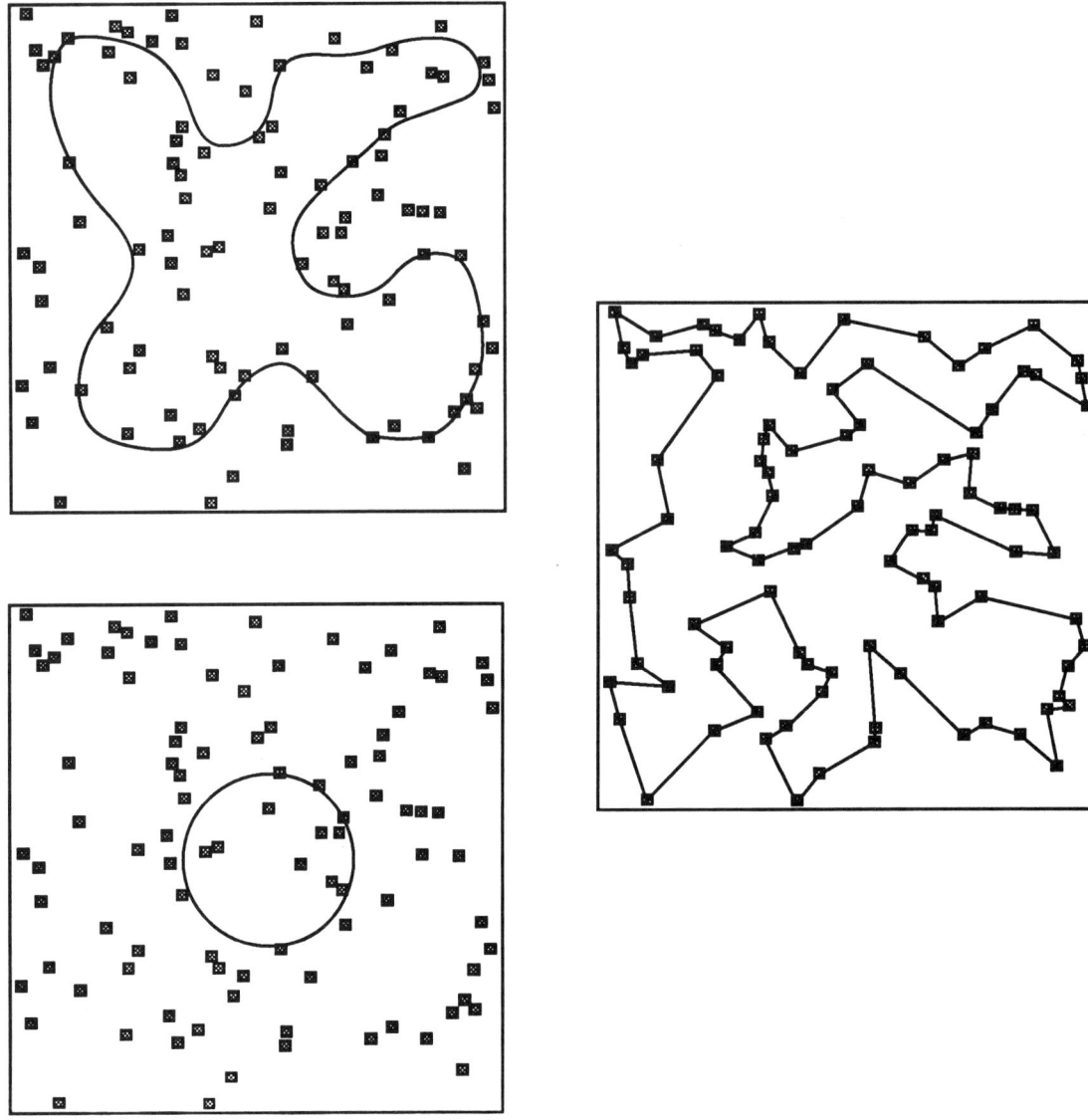

Figure 5. Three snapshots of a typical simulation of an elastic ring relaxing toward a solution of the traveling salesman problem according to the algorithm of Durbin and Willshaw (1987).

then, at most, L elements can be excited in equilibrium. Thus an equilibrium state selects one or more elements, and the number that can break through their neighbor's inhibition increases with the overall level of stimulation.

If the system starts from a state in which all u_i's are equal and reaches an equilibrium in which K elements are excited, it can be shown that they are those receiving the K largest stimuli. However, even in the case where s_{max} is so limited that $K = 1$, the theorem does not exclude the possibility that two or more elements are each activated prior to equilibrium.

We now concentrate on the *maximum selector* case ($K = 1$) and ask how the network responds to a change in the maintained stimulus pattern. Once in equilibrium, one may increase a nonmaximal stimulus s_2 so that it becomes larger than the previously largest stimulus s_1, yet not switch activity to the corresponding element. In other words there is *hysteresis*—the phenomenon, observed in many cooperative systems, in which the local interactions are such that the change in global state of the system occurs at a point dependent on the history of the system. For example, consider using an external magnetic field in a fixed left-right direction to reverse the magnetization of a bar magnet. Typically, a magnetic field $H_N > 0$ is required to shift the North pole from the left to the right end of the magnet, while a magnetic field $H_S < 0$ is required to reverse this. It is because the magnetic field does not simply have to flip each atomic magnet, but must do so against the cooperative effect of interaction with those that remain unflipped, that $H_N \neq H_S$. To avoid hysteresis in the Diday model, the threshold of all cells may be temporarily dropped so far that all cells are equally active (equivalently, strong global excitation may be provided), employing some "newness" mechanism to determine when to reset threshold. The above analysis uses stability theory to model cooperativity, including the phenomenon of hysteresis in NNs. As Amari (1982) makes clear, such methods have wide applicability for the analysis of information processing, development, and learning in NNs.

Statistical Mechanics of a Winner-Take-All System. The study of prey-selection motivated a deterministic approach to the design of a winner-take-all (WTA) system. Another approach motivated by statistical mechanics is described (Yuille, 1990). The system is simple enough to study the relationship between hard and soft constraints in detail. The restriction that is averaged only over legal configurations is called a *hard constraint* to distinguish it from an approach that would allow the system to assume illegal configurations at the expense of some penalty costs. Given a set of values $\{T_i, i = 1, \ldots, N\}$, we look for the maximum value. A NN could solve this problem by responding with exactly one neuron active, ie, $V_\alpha = 1$ and $V_i = 0$ for all $i \neq \alpha$. The usual procedure in statistical mechanics is as follows:

1. Define an energy (also called cost) function.
2. Derive equations for equilibrium values of the average neural activities $\langle V_i \rangle$.
3. After deriving the equilibrium properties of the system, design a NN composed of graded neurons with a dynamics.

$$\frac{\partial \langle V_i \rangle}{\partial t} = -\frac{\partial H^{\text{eff}}}{\partial \langle V_i \rangle} \quad (14)$$

The cost function for the WTA problem can be defined as

$$E = -\sum_{i=0}^{N} V_i T_i \quad (15)$$

where the variables V_i are restricted to the values $\{0,1\}$ indicating that T_i is the maximum ($V_i = 1$) or is not ($V_i = 0$). To impose the hard constraint that only one of the V_i can claim victory the additional constraint $\Sigma V_i = 1$ is introduced.

Just as Hinton and co-workers (1986) (recapturing the ideas of Little, and in the spirit of the maximum entropy principle) augmented McCulloch-Pitts neurons with a stochastic transition dependent on a temperature T, so Yuille assumes that the probability of a specific set of variables V_i is given by the Gibbs distribution of statistical mechanics that includes a parameter β playing the role of $1/T$. He shows that if averaging is only allowed over all legal combinations of V_i, ie, $\{V_i | V_i = 0,1; \Sigma_k V_k = 1\}$, as required by the hard constraint, then in the limit $\beta \to \infty$, only one $\langle V_i \rangle$ has a nonvanishing value. A network dynamics with the equilibrium solutions $\langle V_i \rangle$ found in this way is given by a system of differential equations whose only fixed point is the winner-take-all solution with $\langle V_i \rangle = 1$ if and only if T_i is the maximal value of the set $\{T_i\}$.

An alternative, "soft," approach is to enforce constraints only in an approximate way, allowing the system to deviate from the desired solutions at the expense of some additional cost. A suitable cost function for the winner-take-all system is

$$E = -\sum_{i=1}^{N} V_i T_i + \sum_{i=1}^{N} \left(\lambda \sum_{k=1; k \neq i}^{N} V_i V_k \right) \quad (16)$$

where the additional quadratic term ensures that too large deviations from legal winner-take-all solutions are unfavorable since the costs are increased whenever two different V_i assume nonvanishing values. The parameter λ weights the penalty term compared to the first cost term. Using the statistical mechanics technique of mean field approximation, Yuille shows that the average $\langle V_k \rangle$ corresponding to (16) can be determined by solving equations that can have several solutions, especially for very large β. In the limit of $\beta \to \infty$ the solutions correspond to minima of the energy function (16). In the simple case of $N = 2$, the energy will take values $-T_1$ and $-T_2$ for $(V_1, V_2) = (1,0)$ and $(V_1, V_2) = (0,1)$, respectively. The other two possible combinations $(V_1, V_2) = (1,1)$, $(V_1, V_2) = (0,0)$ yield corresponding energies $(-T_1 - T_2 + 2\lambda)$ and 0. If $\lambda > T_{\max}$ is chosen both states (1,0), (0,1) are minima, one being a local minimum and one being the global minimum. Enforcing constraints in a soft way has introduced spurious minima that do not correspond to a correct solution of the problem. (Compare the delicate interrelation of input activity and weight settings in the Amari-Arbib approach.)

The shift from stochastic, binary neuron models to graded neurons in applications was justified by the argument that additional degrees of freedom in the neural dynamics might destabilize local minima if a discrete optimization problem is embedded in a continuous space of approximate solutions and appropriate penalty terms enforce the admissibility of a solution. The prospect of implementing graded neurons with a deterministic dynamics on analog VLSI chips further stimulated the trend toward optimization networks with soft constraints. Yuille's analysis of the winner-take-all system and the earlier discussion of TSP, however, explain that it is advisable to search for algorithms that enforce constraints exactly.

Neural Models for Low Level Vision

Low level vision is the processing done to recode information prior to the application of knowledge about the objects being seen, and uses parallel array processing; high level vision comprises the "knowledge intensive processes" better modeled by distributed processing. Much research has been conducted on NNs for low level vision, both in analyzing biological systems and in developing "front ends" for visual systems. Such studies include the role of lateral inhibition in contrast enhancement (Ratliff, 1965), stereo vision (Nelson, 1975), optic flow, and, perhaps most importantly, the cooperation between different depth cues (House, 1989) or different cues for segmentation (Poggio, Gamble, and Little, 1988). This section briefly discusses feature extraction, offers an informal account of an algorithm for computing optic flow that stresses its evolutionary improvement through incorporation of edge-finding algorithms, and finally discusses a general mathematical framework for such cooperative algorithms which ties it firmly into our preceding discussion of constraint optimization.

Feature Detectors and Information Coding. Adopting Shannon's (1948) information theory, Attneave (1954) noted that whenever there is *a priori* information about an ensemble of "messages," this can be used to achieve an economy of description that would otherwise be unobtainable. For example, were arbitrary patterns of black and white dots to be equally meaningful patterns of visual stimulation in our everyday lives, there would be no way of representing a visual scene more economically than by giving the light intensity at every point of the scene. However, as the success of caricatures of political figures attests, much of the information about a visual scene can be given by a few contours. Further, these contours are usually made up of relatively few segments—the intricate wiggles due to the presence of fur that perturb the curve of a cat's back are irrelevant to our recognition of the outline of a cat, although our separate recognition of the texture of fur may add to our perception. Attneave thus suggested that the points of most importance in our recognition of form are those where a contour changes or comes to an end. For example, he constructed a caricature by finding the 38 points of maximum curvature from the contour of a picture of a sleeping cat and connecting appropriate points by straight lines. The result clearly recognizable as a sleeping cat. Barlow (1959) approached the problem of visual preprocessing in terms of more strictly neural considerations. Rather than simply reducing information, the goal of preprocessing is to make *explicit* the information that the organism/robot needs for its action-oriented perception. Preprocessing does not throw away the contour but rather recodes it in a form that is more compact and highlights data that may be useful in further interpretation.

In the earliest stages of visual processing, receptors extract local information about the light reflected from surfaces in the world. Even here, the nontrivial problem of separating surface reflectance from strength of illumination is confronted. Subsequent processes then collate information from some neighborhood to come up with useful image descriptors; early in the process, this information may be quite local (eg, small neighborhoods about a point); eventually, "high level vision" is to yield an overall action-oriented interpretation of the scene. Low level vision must provide an intermediate representation rich in explicit descriptors of edges and regions in the image. This representation encapsulates those aspects of the visual array best suited for interpretation of the image by processes of high level vision which can exploit the knowledge of objects and the tasks to which they are to be put. Much work has been done on how peripheral visual systems provide species-specific input (cf Lettvin and co-workers, 1959 for frog; Hubel and Wiesel, 1962, 1977 for the cat and monkey, respectively; Arbib, 1989, Sec. 3.3) but here the focus is on the frog work since it provides an early example of the influence of NN theory on neurophysiological experimentation.

Species-specific processing can be concentrated in the periphery to reduce the demands on central processing, but this then limits the generality of what can be achieved by later image processing stages. A frog does not normally move its eyes except to compensate for head or body movements to maintain a stabilized image on its retina. They prey only on moving worms or insects, and their attention is never attracted by stationary objects. A large moving object provokes an escape reaction. For them, a form deprived of movement cannot be recognized as predator or prey. Lettvin and co-workers (1959) sought "naturalistic" functions of the ganglion cells (the retina's output cells) by studying their response to objects. They were specifically motivated by Pitts and McCulloch (1947) who, in their study of "How We know Universals" presented a neural pattern recognition system structured as a stack of neural "manifolds," with each manifold, or layer, providing a retinotopic map (ie, an array codable in terms of places on the retina that yielded maximal stimulation) of the location of some specific feature in the stimulus array. Selfridge, whose paper on Pandemonium (1959) is a classic contribution to the literature of feature detectors, suggested to Lettvin and Maturana that they look in the frog for the structures hypothesized by McCulloch and Pitts. Actually, he hoped that more would be found, namely the group transformations that Pitts and McCulloch posited to underlie the recognition of invariant patterns. This was not to be, but the discovery of layered feature detectors in an actual brain was indeed a momentous discovery. Specifically, they found four groups defined functionally as four separate types of feature detector. Confirming the Pitts and McCulloch concept of a stack of feature arrays, they found that axons of the cells of each group end in a separate layer of the tectum, the main target of retinal projections in the frog midbrain. Each of these four layers of terminals in the tectum forms a "continuous" map of the retina with respect to the operation performed by the corresponding ganglion cells. The four layers are in registration in that points in different layers which are stacked atop each other in the tectum correspond to the same small region of the retina. The function of the frog retina is not to transmit information about the point-to-point pattern distribution of light upon it. On the contrary, it analyzes this image at every point in terms of four qualitative contexts (boundaries, moving curvatures, changing contrasts, and local dimming) and sends this information to the tectum where these functions are separated in four layers of terminals. Further, the encoding is such that it aids the frog in finding food and evading predators—in recognizing the universals prey and enemy.

There is a tension between what can be attributed to single cells and what functions must be delegated to networks. Then as now, researchers who emphasize the accomplishments of single cells seek to isolate their "essential characteristics," eg, as bug detectors, while network theorists are happier to note the multidimensionality of cells, whose output varies to encode changes in contrast, depth, orientation, etc, all at the same time. The Lettvin and co-workers findings remain a high point in the study of visual preprocessing but the above story is only the first approximation in unraveling the circuits which enable the frog to tell predator from prey. Such discrimination involves the cooperative computation of many neurons in retina, tectum, and pretectum, at the very least. It is the network view that plays the dominant role as it is seen how behaviorally significant properties of the environment are encoded in patterns distributed across one or more subnetworks (Arbib and Ewert, 1991).

The MATCH Algorithm for Optic Flow. The optic flow problem is to find the velocities of images of given visual features of the world, finding the vectors linking the corresponding points in successive frames of a movie. One constraint to help solve this correspondence problem follows the fact that nearby features in the world probably lie on the same object. Therefore, in the absence of contextual information to the contrary, the *local smoothness* condition that nearby features will move with roughly the same velocity is generally favored. However, this condition may fail on large regions of the image unless reinforced by other constraints. The MATCH algorithm (Prager and Arbib, 1983) combines the smoothness condition with the *stimulus matching* condition that a feature in Frame 1 should be displaced to match a similar feature in Frame 2. Thus let z_j be the position of feature j in Frame 1, and let y_j be the estimate of the displacement of this feature toward a matching feature in Frame 2. Then y_j is updated through repeated operations according to the rule

$$\Delta y_j = \alpha(|x_j - (z_j + y_j)|) + \beta \left(\frac{1}{n_j} \sum_{N_j} y_k - y_j \right)$$

where x_j is the Frame 2 feature closest to the current estimate $z_j + y_j$ of feature j's position in Frame 2 (and so varies from iteration to iteration), while the latter sum is over the n_j elements in some suitable neighborhood N_j of y_j. These two terms resemble the "city matching" and "smoothness" conditions of Durbin and Willshaw.

Computer simulation shows convergence within 20 iterations (one iteration involving a single update of each unit). Given a sequence of movie frames rather than just two, computer simulation shows that one can obtain an increasingly accurate estimate of the optic flow and yet use less iterations to handle each new frame as it is introduced. For example, if, having matched Frame n to Frame $n + 1$ we try to match Frame $n + 1$ to $n + 2$, it is reasonable to assume that, to a first approximation, the optic flow advances a feature by roughly the same amount in the two frames. If the repetition of the previous displacement, rather than a nearest neighbor match, is used to initialize the optic flow computation of the two new frames, it is found from simulations that only 4 or 5 iterations, rather than the original 20, are required, and that the quality of the match on real images is definitely improved.

To proceed (Fig. 6; Arbib, 1981), note that the MATCH algorithm runs into trouble if there are two objects moving in different relative directions so that points on opposite sides of the boundary have different motions. In this case the local smoothness condition breaks down, but in the present case it is fortunate because an "edge finding NN" can be built that looks for curves of rapid change in

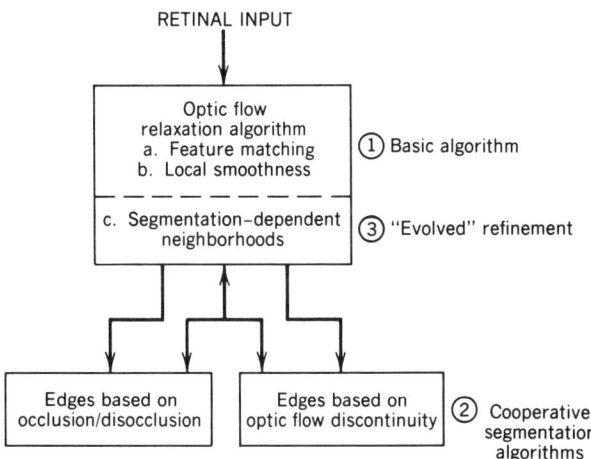

Figure 6. (1) The MATCH optic flow relaxation algorithm uses the consistency conditions of feature matching and local smoothness. (2) Optic flow estimates permit the hypothetization of edges on cues based on both occlusion–disocclusion and on optic flow discontinuity. (3) The resultant edge hypotheses can be used to refine the computation of optic flow by dynamically adjusting the neighborhoods used in employing the consistency conditions.

the optic flow estimates, and another NN can form edge hypotheses by linking features which are either all occluded or all disoccluded from one frame to the next. If both find evidence for the same edge, then the two together can proclaim quite confidently that there is indeed an edge on that locus. Combining these two cooperating edge-finding NNs with the original optic flow NN yields a more sophisticated machine which is not only able to compute optic flow, but is also able to separate the visual world into different objects. This provides a useful example of cooperative computation in which different NNs, each with its own inherent parallel activity, communicate concurrently to give an estimate not only of movement but also tools for decomposing the world into different objects. Moreover, Figure 6 shows an "evolutionary design process." The basic algorithm (1) provides new information that can be exploited in the design of the cooperative edge-finding algorithms (2), but once the edge information is available, the original algorithm can be refined by the introduction of segmentation-dependent neighborhoods (3), with the matching of features or the conformity with neighboring flow based mainly upon features on the same side of the currently hypothesized boundary.

Regularization Theory. It has been shown how such use of NNs for low level vision fits into a mathematical framework known as *regularization theory* (Poggio and co-workers, 1985). Just as for the other problems discussed above, the computational problem of extracting three-dimensional shape from two-dimensional projections possibly corrupted by noise is highly ambiguous with no unique solution. The ambiguity is exemplified in the stereo perception of random dot stereograms. Each pixel in one of the stereo pairs matches to many others in the corresponding image, each correspondence being a hypothesis about a particular disparity. Such problems with a high ambiguity are called *ill-posed*. The ambiguity in the matching problem can be removed by additional constraints on the interpretation of an image. As seen, objects in the world normally are composed of smooth surfaces, their boundaries are not rugged and the intensities vary gradually except at discontinuities. Introducing additional constraints, called stabilizers in the theory of ill-posed problems, to restrict the vast hypothesis space to a small region of meaningful image interpretations has emerged as one of the most powerful computational strategies in early vision (qv) which was applied to stereo matching, optical flow computation, surface reconstruction, color constancy, and other early vision problems.

A standard ill-posed problem (cf Tikhonov and Arsenin, 1977) is to compute the quantity z from the data y where $Az = y$. If the operator A is not invertible, the problem is ill-posed and so the problem is regularized by introducing a linear stabilizing functional Pz. The joint optimization of the functional

$$|Az - y|^2 + \lambda |Pz|^2 \qquad (17)$$

transforms the ill-posed problem into a well-posed minimization problem. λ is a suitable regularization parameter that controls the strength with which the additional constraint Pz is enforced. Minimizing (17) can be interpreted as a search for an estimation of z given the data y and a model A with the *a priori* regularization constraint Pz that should have a small norm.

There exist two main reasons why early vision problems are addressed in the mathematical framework of regularization theory: First, minimizing a functional like (18) permits insight into the structure of NNs that attempt to solve an early vision problem. There exists the hope that necessary constraints on the neural connectivity can be derived from knowledge of a regularization functional that solves an early vision problem with comparable performance as humans do. Psychophysical experiments can further bridge the gap between the mathematical formulation and a possible synaptic architecture that implements and optimizes the functional. The reproduction of optical illusions by an algorithm strongly enhances the confidence one can have in a specific regularization functional. The second reason for the outlined framework is its inherent parallelism. Algorithms of the form (17) can be implemented in analog VLSI (Mead, 1989) and, thereby, suggests why the human visual system processes information so fast compared to conventional computer vision techniques.

To put regularization theory into a concrete low level vision framework the stereo problem and its treatment are chosen as an ill-posed minimization problem. The left and right image are given by the intensity fields $L(x,y)$ and $R(x,y)$. A search for a disparity field $d(x,y)$ is made that describes the correct shift of each part of the right image compared with the left one. The functional minimized is

$$\int \{[\Delta G^*(L(x,y) - R(x + d(x,y),y))]^2 + \gamma(\nabla d)^2\} \, dx \, dy \qquad (18)$$

ΔG being the Laplacian of a Gaussian that is convolved with the difference between corresponding intensities in the two images. In the stereo example, the Tichonov stabilizer ∇d prevents a disparity field with steep gradients since such solutions would violate the smoothness property of real objects and their continuity in space. The stabilizer, however, performs quite poorly near an object discontinuity.

The problem of discontinuities, addressed by several authors (Geman and Geman, 1984; Koch, 1989) can be solved satisfactorily if an additional field for line processes is introduced, switching off the smoothness constraint in (18) whenever there exists an edge at position (x,y). (This is just the mathematical expression of the introduction of edge finding in Figure 6.) Replace $\gamma(\nabla d)^2$ by $\gamma(\nabla d)^2(1 - l(x,y))$ and add a cost term for each edge introduced, ie, the functional is

$$\int \{[DG^*(L(x,y) - R(x + d(x,y),y)]^2 \\ + \lambda(\nabla d)^2(1 - l(x,y)) + al(x,y)\} \, dx \, dy \qquad (19)$$

If all variables d are held fixed and $\lambda(\nabla d)^2 > a$ it pays to introduce an edge compared to the large costs for a steep gradient at position (x,y).

Oscillators and Neural Modulation

Much work has been done in computational neurobiology on the control of movement, going back at least to Merton's (1953) analysis of the role of feedback in spinal circuitry for control of limb movements. Another important area for interaction of theory and experiment has been the control of eye movements, such as the fast eye movements known as saccades (Fuchs, Kaneko, and Scudder, 1985; van Gisbergen, Robinson, and Gielen, 1981) and the vestibulo-ocular reflex, the VOR. Anastasio and Robinson (1989) have used back propagation to provide insights into the distributed coding of neurons in the vestibular nucleus, the brain region serving this reflex. However, rather than review the general body of literature on NNs for motor control, the following example of rhythm generating circuitry will be discussed, and a general perspective on oscillations in NNs will be offered which goes well beyond motor control to address issues in perception and memory that will be developed in later sections.

Rhythm Generating Circuitry. The NN of the lobster stomatogastric ganglion that controls rhythmic chewing is first examined to indicate the rich properties of biological neurons which have yet to be exploited in the technology of ANNs. As shown at the right of Figure 7a, lobsters have three teeth in their stomachs with attached muscles: two lateral teeth that move in and out, and medial teeth that move up and down. INT1 (interneuron 1) and the electrotonically coupled pair of cells LG/MG (the lateral gastric and medial gastric motoneurons) form a half-center oscillator that drives the whole system. INT1 and LG/MG are tonically active, but connected by reciprocal inhibition. The key is that each has post-inhibitory rebound. After firing for a while and inhibiting the other half of the pair, its level of inhibition decays to the point where the other cell becomes active. After inhibition is removed, each cell fires at above its tonic level. The tonic level is not enough to inhibit the other cell; the rebound level is. Thus firing of the cells alternates.

The interaction between LPG (the two lateral posterior gastric motoneurons) and LG/MG is probably too weak for them to function as a half-center oscillator. However, INT1 excites DG (the dorsal gastric motoneuron), and since INT1 inhibits LG/MG which in turn inhibits LPG the circuit may suffice to entrain the endogenous bursting of LPG. Thus INT1, DG, and LPG burst (almost) in phase. This ensures a phase coupling between the control of the lateral tooth (by DG and GM) and the control of the medial teeth (by LG, MG, and LPG) which yields the "squeeze mode" of chewing, in which the cusps of the three teeth move together simultaneously, with forward movement of the medial tooth following with only a small delay and a small backward movement of the lateral teeth.

To the class of synaptic transmitters that have an immediate excitatory or inhibitory effect on the postsynaptic membrane there has been added another class, the peptides, which act to change cellular properties on a timescale of seconds or more. Heinzel and Selverston (1988) have shown that the properties of the oscillator can be dramatically changed by bathing it in a peptide called proctolin. They showed that proctolin can change the gastric oscillator by targeting on LG and DG as follows (Fig. 7b): while DG is normally driven by strong excitatory input from INT1, it becomes an endogenous burster. LG shows plateauing (ie, it exhibits a new stable resting potential) and the DG to LPG plateauing becomes stronger, leading to disinhibition of LG from LPG. The plateauing LG inhibits its synergistic motoneuron MG more strongly than before, causing a delay of its burst. As a result of these proctolin-induced changes, the medial tooth subsystem (see the connections of DG and GM motoneurons in Fig. 7a) runs with a different phase in relation to the lateral tooth subsystem (LG, MG, LPG) from that in the normal situation described above. This corresponds to the "cut and grind" mode of chewing in which the serrated edges of the lateral teeth meet (cut) and the cusps of the lateral teeth rasp backward along the file of the medial tooth (grind), whereas in the squeeze mode only the three cusps are pressed against each other.

The model of Fig. 7a provides one of the three classes of models for generating rhythmic patterns in NNs (Cohen, Rossignol, and Grillner, 1988; Arbib, 1989, Sec. 6.1).

1. In a ring network, the rhythm is generated by the circulation of activity around a ring of neurons. Rhythmic activity can be tapped by suitable connections to flexors and extensors (Fig. 8a).
2. Alternating bursts may be explained by reciprocal inhibition (Fig. 8b), with fatigue of the inhibiting synapses with prolonged activation (cf the circuit in lobster stomatogastric ganglion).
3. The rhythm is driven by a pacemaker, which may be a single cell that generates an intrinsic oscillation (with or without spikes), or may be achieved by electrical coupling of an array serving to synchronize the cellular activity (Fig. 8c).

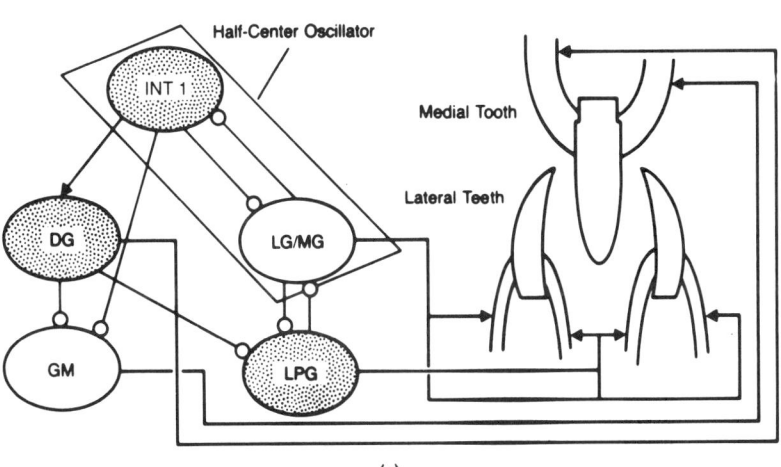

Figure 7. (a) The stomatogastric ganglion network controlling the teeth in the gut of the lobster. (b) Proctolin modulation of the gastric oscillator in the lobster stomatogastric ganglion turns the effective connectivity from that shown at the top to that shown at the bottom.

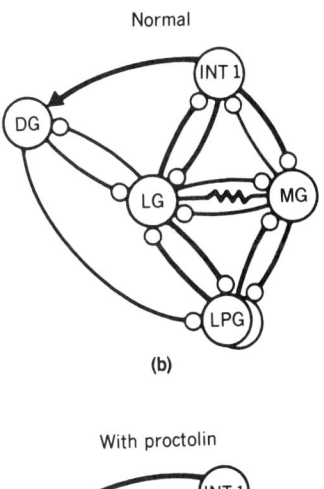
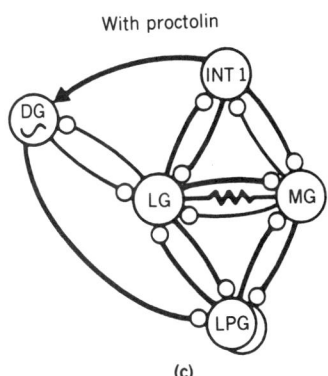

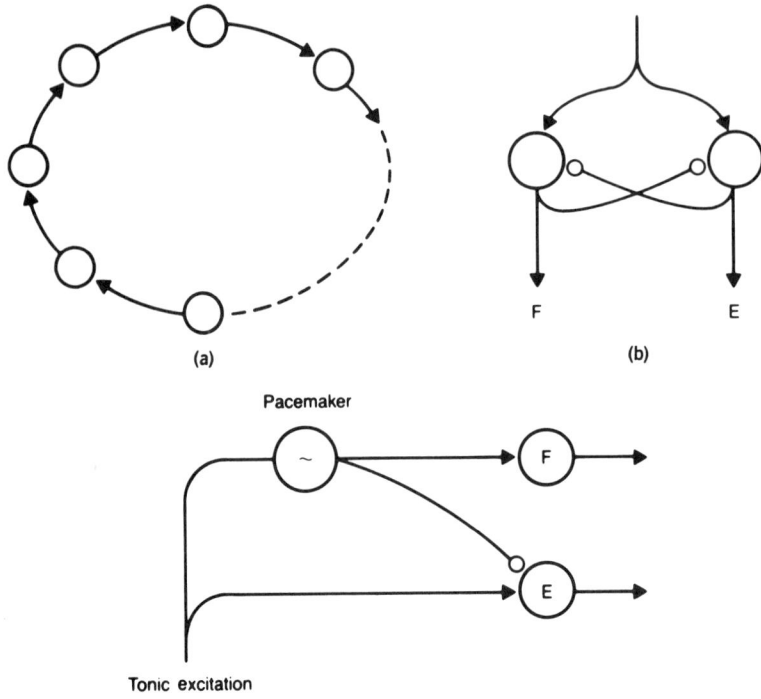

Figure 8. Three general schemes for neural networks controlling rhythmic behavior. (a) A ring network. (b) Alternating bursts are explained by reciprocal inhibition, with fatigue of the inhibiting synapses with prolonged activation. (c) The rhythm is driven by a pacemaker.

Rhythm generating networks may thus depend as much on pacemaker cells as on "reverberating loops" and real neurons are far more complex than McCulloch-Pitts neurons. In fact, a recurrent theme in brain theory is to choose the correct grain of detail at which to model neurons. Too much detail, and the model cannot reveal essential relationships; too little, and network properties cannot be explained. Similarly, the simplicity of a technological implementation may rest on the selection of the right form of neuron to serve as the unit for an ANN.

Three Examples of Oscillatory Neural Activity. It has been shown that the control of stereotypical rhythmic processes may involve interacting oscillators that work even when isolated from the rest of the circuit. Thus a key problem is the self-organization of correct phase relations in oscillating NNs. The desired relationship between phases is dependent on the functionality of a NN, as is shown in the following three examples:

1. In the spinal cord of lamprey, there is a sequence of about 100 ventral roots and one may observe 1 Hz bursts at each root, phase shifted along the cord by a phase proportional to distance. This constant phase lag indicates a constant propagation speed, to a first approximation. Some further constraints from the data are that the lamprey cord is a highly distributed system, because sufficiently long isolated sections of the cord can "swim." Fish can swim backward generating a wave which goes from tail to head. Faster swimming is accompanied by higher frequency and faster propagation speed, but the *same wavelength,* namely one body length, so the phase lag is not due to a delay line.

2. Oscillatory activity of pools of neurons has also been observed in the olfactory bulb and the olfactory cortex of rabbits. The correlations between the sniff cycle and the oscillatory activity patterns suggest that the oscillations are not merely a byproduct of a nonlinear neural dynamics with strong feedback, but carry functional information about odors and facilitate odor classification. Oscillations are viewed as a way to enhance associative recall in the olfactory cortex that is regarded as the prototype of a biological associative memory due to lack of topology in odor space.

3. Gray and co-workers (1989) discovered highly synchronized oscillations in the visual cortex of cats. Phase locked oscillations of field potentials as well as individual action potentials with zero phase shift have been observed when the animals were exposed to collinear bar stimuli. Phase-locking occurred between neurons with nonoverlapping receptive fields, a clear indication for cooperative phenomena in the cortex dynamics. The similarity of the stimuli, ie, collinearity of moving bars, turned out to be a necessary condition for synchronization; no synchronization or even weak antisynchronization was observed between neurons with quite different orientation specificity.

Oscillations are thus not restricted to low level processing tasks in motor control but occur also in odor classification and in visual segmentation. Different attempts to model, in a simplified way, the collective behavior of the coupled oscillators will be described, neglecting details of the individual oscillator dynamics inessential for the understanding of the oscillator network. Some of the models have not been specifically developed to describe NN dynamics but arise in theories of chemical reactions, solid state physics, and mathematical biology.

Synchronizing a Chain of Oscillators. The data from the spinal cord of lamprey motivate a mathematical study by Kopell and Ermentrout (Kopell, 1988; Rand, Cohen, and Holmes, 1988). The Kopell-Ermentrout model comprises a chain of oscillators with one oscillator near each ventral root, and the kth oscillator satisfying a dynamics $\dot{u}_k = F_k(u_k)$ that has a stable limit cycle. The real work is done by the coupling. The equations up to the nearest neighbor (there are other terms for other connections) are

$$\dot{u}_k = F(u_k) + s_k^+ G^+(u_{k+1}, u_k) + s_k^- G^-(u_{k-1}, u_k) \quad (20)$$

To provide a general analysis, some hypotheses on coupling are made: (1) Only *phase*, ie, the angle Φ between 0 and 2π which indicates progress around the limit cycle, is relevant (as is true for oscillators with limit cycles with attraction that is stronger than the connections). (2) One can replace point-by-point coupling signals by coupling *averaged* over each cycle. (This always works for weak coupling, but it is not true in general for strong coupling.) (3) Coupling is synaptic. (Electronic coupling, which plays an important role in some rhythm generators, has significantly different implications.) These assumptions reduce the equations to:

$$\dot{\Phi}_k = \omega_k + s_k^+ H_k^+(\Phi_{k+1} - \Phi_k) + s_k^- H_k^-(\Phi_{k-1} - \Phi_k)$$

They make the *synaptic coupling hypothesis*, $H^\pm(0) \neq 0$, to ensure that synchrony ($\theta_{k+1} \equiv \theta_k$) is not a solution even if the oscillators are identical. To solve the equations they work with the phase differences $\phi_k = \Phi_{k+1} - \Phi_k$ to get information about the spatial pattern of phases and frequency of the ensemble.

In another domain with a chain of oscillators, peristalsis, there is a gradient in the natural frequency of the oscillators. However, with a gradient in natural frequencies, the wave does not have constant speed. But with equal frequencies, and $H(0) \neq 0$, there is constant propagation, with the direction of the wave depending on the coupling. The theory leads to such physiological suggestions as "to go backwards, bias the coupling," and "to swim faster, increase frequencies uniformly but keep the same coupling and the wavelength will be unchanged," as well as to suggestions about the effects of lesion, split bath experiments, and development.

Homogeneously Coupled Oscillators. Kopell and Ermentrout reduced the complex dynamics of neurons in the spinal cord of lamprey to a chain of oscillators with constant amplitude and a cooperative dynamics in the phases. A family of different oscillator models will be presented that have been used to interpret the oscillations in *visual cortex*, attempting to explain the zero phase shift of oscillators that are several millimeters apart.

Computer simulations and theoretical analysis strongly favor long range connections over any local coupling scheme to support long range synchronization. Networks of limit cycle oscillators with local and long range coupling will be reviewed and then the models will be extended to networks of oscillators with phase and amplitude. In limit cycle oscillator networks, phase variables Φ_i describe the states of individual oscillators. Oscillator i is driven by a random internal frequency ω_i which is distributed as $g(\omega_i)$. The interaction between oscillators i, k is homogeneous and depends only on the phase difference $\Delta\Phi_{ik} = \Phi_i - \Phi_k$ of two oscillators. The interaction law $f(\Delta\Phi_{ik})$ should be continuous and periodic. To enable the system to synchronize itself $f(0) = 0$ must be chosen (contrary to the synaptic coupling hypothesis in the lamprey model), ie, two synchronized oscillators ($\Delta\Phi_{ik} = 0$) do not drive each other but follow their internal driving force ω_i. Note the difference to the objective of Kopell and Ermentrout's lamprey model where traveling waves and not a synchronized state of the oscillator chain is required to model the network behavior. Ermentrout (1985) and others have studied the following equations

$$\frac{d\Phi_i}{dt} = \omega_i - K \sum_{k \in \mathbf{N}_i} \sin(\Phi_i - \Phi_k) + \xi_i \quad (21)$$

a generic choice for a limit cycle system. Stochastic forces that act on the oscillator phases are described by the white noise term ξ_i. $\mathbf{N}_i$ is the set of all oscillators that are connected to oscillator i, ie, $\mathbf{N}_i = \{i - 1, i + 1\}$ for a one-dimensional chain of limit cycle oscillators or $\mathbf{N}_i = \{1, \ldots, N\}$ for a completely connected network. A completely connected oscillator network with dynamics (21) exhibits a strong tendency to synchronize phases if the noise and the width of the distribution $g(\omega_i)$ is not too large and the global coupling parameter K is sufficiently strong (Sakaguchi, 1988).

A special case of equation (21) is a network where all oscillators exhibit the same internal frequency ω_o. The coordinate transformation $\Psi_i = \Phi_i - \omega_o t$ reduces (21) to

$$\frac{d\Phi_i}{dt} = -\frac{\partial H}{\partial \Phi_i} + \xi_i$$

with the energy function $H = -K \sum_{i,k \in \mathbf{N}_i} \cos(\Phi_i - \Phi_k)$. This system with local nearest neighbor coupling in two dimensions has been extensively studied in solid state physics where it has been shown that phase synchronization is not a robust phenomenon. Any amount of noise, no matter how weak, will destroy a completely synchronized network state and create phase vortices. Such results indicate that the long range synchronization observed in Singer's experiments cannot be explained with a local connection scheme but require long range synapses. Such long intralayer connections have been discovered in the visual cortex of cats (Gilbert and Wiesel, 1983).

Let us briefly mention a model of linearly coupled oscillators that is more general than the limit cycle approach, with each oscillator characterized by amplitude as well as phase. The kinetics of the network is nonlinear, given by

$$\frac{dz_i}{dt} = z_i(1 - |z_i|^2 + i\omega_i) + \frac{K}{N} \sum_{k=1}^{N} (z_k - z_i) \quad (22)$$

$z_i(t)$ is the position of the ith oscillator in the complex plane. The oscillators have a stable limit cycle if interaction is switched off ($K = 0$). The dynamical behavior of interacting oscillators changes from the completely synchronized for strong interaction K to an incoherent behavior for small K and a not too narrow distribution of intrinsic frequencies. While lowering K and keeping the width of the distribution $g(\omega_i)$ fixed, the network traverses a region in parameter space where large oscillations, quasiperiodicity and chaos have been observed. An amazing phenomenon of oscillator death exists for strong coupling and a wide frequency distribution—all oscillators cease to oscillate and effectively stabilize the state $z_i = 0$, for all i. A detailed portrayal of the parameter space K, γ, and the respective network behavior has been presented by Matthews and Strogatz (1990).

LEARNING AND SELF-ORGANIZATION

In 1949, Hebb published *The Organization of Behavior*, providing the inspiration for many computational models of learning and adaptation in neural systems. He explained learning by the formation of cell assemblies in the brain. In Hebbian learning, the connection between two neurons (units akin to the formal neurons of McCulloch and Pitts) is strengthened if both neurons fire at the same time. Such a scheme tends to sharpen a neuron's predisposition "without a teacher," getting its firing to become better and better correlated with a cluster of stimulus patterns. Thus the final set of input weights to the neuron depends on both the initial setting of the weights and on the pattern of clustering of the set of stimuli to which it is exposed. By contrast, in the Perceptron scheme (Rosenblatt, 1958), a neuron's synapses are modified if the firing of the neuron does not match some pattern determined by a "teacher." The best known perceptron learning rule strengthens an active synapse if the efferent neuron fails to fire when it should have fired, and weakens an active synapse if the neuron fires when it should not have done so. Sutton and Barto (1981) reintroduced reinforcement into the study of adaptive networks, bringing out the interconnections between the literature of adaptive neurons and of conditioning by showing the similarity of the Perceptron learning rule not only to the Widrow-Hoff (1960) least mean squares model of adaptive control, but also to the Rescorla-Wagner (1972) model of Pavlovian (instrumental) conditioning. By contrast, Hebb's rule is a variant of classical conditioning. The extension of such rules to multilayer networks has been a key area of recent research, with "back propagation" becoming the most widely known such approach.

Thus, *unsupervised learning*, in which clustering is according to some built-in measure of similarity without explicit reference to any measure of performance (so that the measure of similarity acts as "a fixed built-in supervisor"), is distinguished from *supervised learning*, in which the environment/teacher specifies the correct classification. (It will be shown that associative nets use the desired recollection as the reference signal.)

Learning networks are valuable because it may be too hard to explicitly program the behavior that one sees in a black box, but one may be able to drive a network by the actual input-output behavior of that box, or by some description of its trajectories, to cause it to adapt itself into a network with (approximately) that given behavior. Such techniques are thus akin to the methods of "system identification" used in system theory, but with different assumptions about the underlying structure of the network (eg, a linear system or finite automaton rather than a NN; see Arbib (1987) for a comparison). However, a learning algorithm may not solve a problem within a reasonable period of time unless the initial structure of the network provides a suitable first approximation. This is part of the general question of whether the symbol-formation that is part and parcel of cognition and perception arises purely from regularities in the environment ("no teacher"), depends essentially on the (evolved) structural and functional architecture of the system (providing a "built-in teacher"), or relies primarily on explicit instruction. In this respect, it is interesting to note the studies on formation of feature detectors in visual cortex and the work of von der Malsburg and Willshaw (1977) on the formation of maps between retina and tectum (or between any two other retinotopic arrays), in both of which a key concern is the interaction of synaptic adaptation with genetically predetermined connection patterns or biases. Both clustering and supervised learning are important and work together.

There are now many techniques that can be used to make networks more adaptive. For much of the work, the emphasis is on neural computing, the building of neurally inspired devices, rather than biological modeling. These adaptive networks have created much excitement in the engineering community, but it must be realized that they have limited applicability. To this end, consider what methods for "learning with a teacher" achieve. A network N is given which, in response to the presentation of any x from some set X of input patterns, will eventually settle down to produce a corresponding y from the set Y of the network's output patterns. A training set is then a sequence of pairs (x_k, y_k) from $X \times Y$, $1 \le k \le n$. The results on ANNs say that in "many cases" (and the bounds are usually not yet well defined), if the net is trained with repeated presentations of the various (x_k, y_k), it will converge to a set of connections which cause it to compute a function $f: X \to Y$ with the property that each $f(x_k)$ "correlate fairly well" with the corresponding y_k. Of course, there are many other functions $g: X \to Y$ such that the $g(x_k)$ "correlate fairly well" with the y_k, and they may differ wildly on those x in X that do not equal an x_k in the training set. The view that one may simply present a trainable net with a few examples of solved problems, and it will adjust its connections to be able to solve all problems of a given class thus glosses over three main issues:

1. *Complexity.* Is the network complex enough to encode a solution?
2. *Practicality.* Can the net achieve such a solution within a feasible period of time?
3. *Efficacy.* How is it guaranteed that the generaliza-

tion achieved by the machine matches our conception of a useful solution?

At present, much research is underway to develop answers to these problems. Nonetheless, it is clear that these training techniques will work best for relatively restricted problems, and that future work in the neurally-inspired design of intelligent systems will still require many domain-specific techniques for system design. It is for this reason that Part I of this article is devoted to "Nonadaptive Neural Networks" and that, in the introduction, the need for a coarse grain of system analysis (schema theory) is stressed to complement the use of, possibly adaptive, NNs to implement specific subsystems. In particular, distributed AI will often employ hybrid solutions where some agents are implemented as adaptive nets, whereas others employ more traditional (for AI) means of symbol manipulation. The study of learning in such complex systems involves the *assignment of credit problem*. Suppose success is achieved by a complex mechanism after operating over a considerable period of time (for example, a chess (qv) playing program wins a game). To what particular decisions made by what particular components should the success be attributed? And, if failure results, what decisions deserve blame? The utility of making a certain action may depend on the sequence of actions of which it is a part, and an indication of improved performance may not occur until the entire sequence has been completed.

With this perspective established, this article now proceeds with the study of learning and self-organization. Even with the long list of topics to be covered below, the neural net literature is not exhausted, and so the article closes with a guide to further reading.

HEBBIAN PLASTICITY

Hubel and Wiesel (1965), moving beyond their discovery of cells in cat visual cortex tuned for orientation specificity, asked whether or not these orientations were genetically specified. They found that a cat raised with one eye closed lost the orientation specificity for input from that eye, whereas a cat with both eyes closed did acquire some specificity. This led initially to the hypothesis that the brain was genetically precoded, but that signals could lose their effectiveness through disuse. Subsequent research (Fregnac and Imbert, 1984) shows that the reality is in some sense a hybrid: there are populations of cells that are genetically pretuned, populations of cells that are somewhat modifiable, and other cells that are totally plastic in their wiring. A number of models of the formation of cortical feature detectors have been developed, but only one of the earliest, by von der Malsburg (1973) is presented to illustrate the ideas of Hebbian plasticity.

Hebb's idea was that learning would occur if synapses could automatically strengthen themselves to record associations. If s_i is the strength of the connection from the ith input to a neuron, with corresponding firing rates x_i and y, respectively, varying between 0 and 1, then a standard version of Hebb's rule increases the synaptic weight as:

$$\Delta s_i = k x_i y$$

ie, there is an increase if the input and output are simultaneously active. The trouble with this rule is that every synapse will eventually get stronger and stronger until they all saturate, thus destroying any selectivity of association. von der Malsburg's (1973) solution was to normalize the synapses impinging on a given neuron, replacing s_i by

$$\frac{s_i + \Delta s_i}{\Sigma_j (s_j + \Delta s_j)}$$

where the summation j extends over all inputs to the neuron. This new rule not only increases the strength of those synapses with inputs that were most strongly correlated with the cell's activity, it also decreases the strengths of other connections.

Another problem is that nearby cells might have initial random connectivity that makes them easily persuadable by the same stimulus or the same pattern might occur many times before a new pattern is experienced by the network. In either case, many cells would become tuned to the same pattern, with not enough cells left to learn important and distinctive patterns. This may be addressed using lateral inhibition (Fig. 9) whereby activity in any one cell is distributed laterally (ie, to all sides) to reduce (partially inhibit) the activity of nearby cells. This ensures that if one cell (A) were active, its connections to nearby cells would make them less active, and so make them less likely to learn, by Hebbian synaptic adjustment, those patterns that most excite A.

Initially, the inputs are randomly connected to the cells of the processing layer. As a result, none of these cells is particularly good at pattern recognition. However, by sheer statistical fluctuation of the synaptic connections, one will be slightly better at responding to a pattern than others were; it will thus slightly strengthen those synapses which allow it to fire for that pattern; through lateral inhibition, this will make it less easy for cells initially less well tuned for that pattern to become tuned to it. Thus, without any teacher, this network automatically organizes itself so that each cell becomes tuned for an important cluster of information in the sensory in-flow.

von der Malsburg used this scheme to model the formation of cortical feature detectors each tuned for edges of a

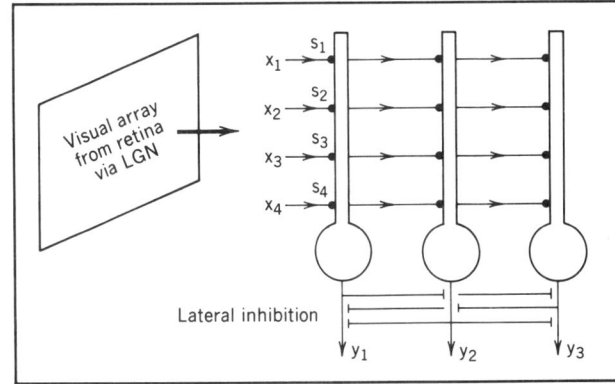

Figure 9. Hebbian synapses are augmented by normalization and lateral inhibition in the adaptive feature detectors of von der Malsburg (1973). (From Arbib and Robinson, 1990.) Courtesy of MIT Press.

specific orientation in their visual field. The cortical cells form a repertoire of feature detectors. The one that is initially the best (but still poor) detector for a cluster of patterns has its synapses tuned, through repeated exposure to these patterns, by a process of Hebbian learning plus normalization so that it becomes a finely-tuned feature detector responding vigorously to patterns in or near that cluster. Edelman (1987), in his theory of *Neural Darwinism,* would emphasize the initial predisposition and so speak of the learning process as one of selection; others would note that the process of synaptic adjustment changes the cell so much that we cannot think of a detector that is already adequate being simply selected from a pre-existing repertoire. Whatever the terminological choice, these ideas play an important role in our understanding of development and learning in natural and artificial networks. Rumelhart and Zipser (1985) give a useful overview of this topic.

HILL-CLIMBING AND LANDMARK LEARNING

The "robot," represented by an asterisk in Figure 10a can find its way toward the central goal, even without learning: Let z be a "payoff function," which is a smooth function of position in the "landscape" of Figure 10a, reaching its maximum at the central landmark. By thinking of z as "height on a hill" the robot's search for its goal is conceptualized as *hill-climbing,* in a process akin to a person climbing a hill in a fog. At time t the robot takes a single step in direction $i(t)$, moving from a position with payoff $z(t)$ to one with payoff $z(t + 1)$. If $z(t + 1) - z(t) > 0$, then the robot's next step is in the same direction, $i(t + 1) = i(t)$, with high probability. However, if $z(t + 1) - z(t) < 0$, then $i(t + 1)$ is chosen randomly. While hill-climbing alone can equip our "robot" to get to the top of the hill, its trajectory is, as seen from Figure 11a, inefficient. As an exercise in the theory of adaptive networks, it is now shown how to equip our robot with a simple nervous system (four neu-

rons!) which can be trained to use "olfactory cues" from the four landmarks to improve its direction-finding with experience (Barto and Sutton, 1981).

Each of the landmarks at the cardinal points also emits an "odor," decaying with distance, which does not act as an attractant but can serve as a cue to location in space. The "nervous system" is shown in Figure 10b. Inputs $x_i(t)$, for $i = N, S, E,$ and W, denote the signals at time t from the north, south, east, and west landmarks respectively, while a large $z(t) = \text{TREE}(t)$ signals proximity to the central goal–tree. Input $x_i(t)$ affects the jth "motor neuron" via a synaptic weight $w_{ji}(t)$ which encodes a degree of confidence that, when the asterisk is near landmark i, it should proceed in direction j to get nearer the tree. The four neurons control motions in the respective cardinal directions. Connection weights between input and output elements are shown as circles centered on the intersections of the input pathways with the element "dendrites." Positive weights appear as hollow circles and negative weights appear as shaded circles.

The interest of the present example is that the net can "learn" appropriate values for the weights. Hill-climbing is raised to a more abstract level: instead of hill-climbing in the physical space (choose a direction again if it takes the robot upward) hill-climbing is conducted in *weight space*. At each step, the weights are adjusted in such a way as to improve the performance of the network. The z input, with no associated weights of its own, is the "teacher" used to adjust the weights linking sensory inputs to motor outputs.

First it is shown how the current weight settings determine the next step of the robot. Let

$$s_j(t) = \Sigma_i w_{ji}(t) x_i(t) \qquad (22)$$

so that $s_j(t)$ sums up the degrees of confidence for a move in direction j on the basis of the current signals received from the four landmarks. Because the current weights w may not yet be correct, a noise term is added, setting the

Figure 10. (a) A spatial environment in which the attracting "tree" is surrounded by four other landmarks. The landmarks each possess a distinctive "odor" that can be sensed at a distance but that is not an attractant. Odor distributions decrease linearly from their associated landmarks and become undetectable at a certain distance (indicated for landmark W by the surrounding circle). (b) A network of goal-seeking adaptive elements. The five input pathways are labeled vertically on the left according to the landmarks to which they respond. The input pathway N indicates the extent to which the organism is near the north neutral landmark. The four output pathways controling actions are labeled horizontally at the bottom according to the direction of movement they cause. The shaded output elements indicate that a southeast movement is being made. The associative matrix weights are displayed as circles centered on the intersections of the horizontal input pathways and vertical output pathways. Positive weights are shown as hollow circles and negative weights are shown as solid circles (Barto and Sutton, 1981).

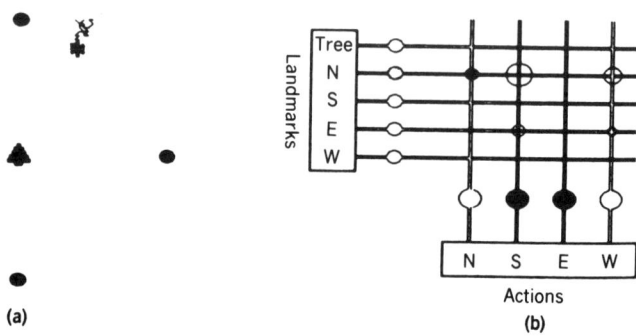

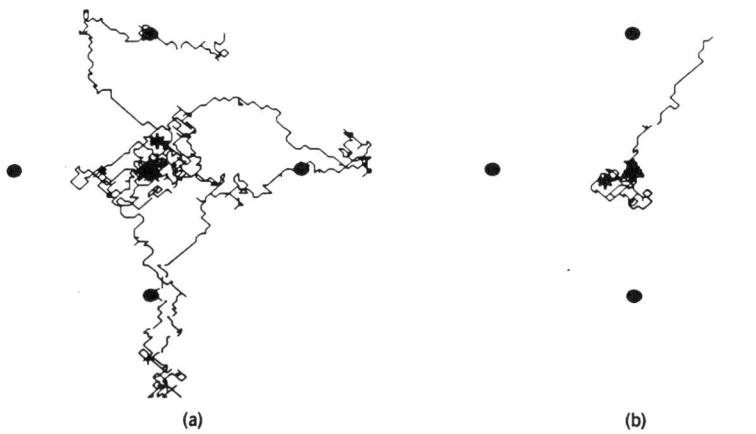

Figure 11. (a) The trail of an inexperienced organism that starts near the northern neutral landmark. Hill-climbing is difficult because noise has been added to the attractant level, but the organism eventually remains in the vicinity of the attractant peak. (b) The trail produced by an experienced organism. After the experience shown in (a), the organism is placed in its original starting position. It now proceeds directly to the tree, clearly benefiting from its previous experience (Barto and Sutton, 1981).

output of element j at time t to be

$$y_j(t) = 1 \text{ if } s(t) + \eta_j(t) > 0, \text{ else } 0 \quad (23)$$

where each $\eta_j(t)$ is a normally distributed random variable with zero mean (each with the same variance). The robot will run in direction j only if $s_j(t)$ is big enough to exceed threshold when noise is added. In case two elements fire simultaneously then the appropriate compound move is made, eg, northwest if N and W fire, no move if N and S fire. It is assumed that each move is a fixed distance and is always completed in one time step.

The weights change according to the following equation:

$$\Delta w_{ji}(t + 1) = c[z(t) - z(t - 1)]y_j(t - 1)x_i(t - 1) \quad (24)$$

where c is a positive constant determining the rate of learning which extends Hebbian learning by having the sign of Δw_{ji} depend on the direction in which the payoff changes. Hence w_{ji} will only change if a j movement takes place ($y_j(t - 1) > 0$) and the asterisk is near the i landmark ($x_i(t - 1) > 0$), but will change in the direction of $z(t) - z(t - 1)$. The weights can be evaluated globally by the extent to which they determine an uphill movement, associating with a particular vector w the sum

$$S(w) = \Sigma_x E\{[z(x + y(x,w)) - z(x)]\} \quad (25)$$

where $z(x)$ is the payoff value associated with position x in the plane, $z(x + y(x,w))$ is the payoff associated with the position that is reached by taking the step $y(x,w)$ determined by (22) and (23) using the weights w, and the expectation E averages over all the values of the noise terms in (23). We may think of S as defining height on a "metahill." The rule (24) tells how to change weights in a way which is likely (not guaranteed) to increase S using just local information based on the robot's current step in physical space. It is in this sense that the task of our learning rule is characterized as hill-climbing in weight space.

The matrix of weights forms an associative memory (motivating the more general account given later) that associates a movement with each vector of sensory data from the landmarks, but it need not be directly told what associations to store. Instead, it stores the successful results of hill-climbing in weight space. With sufficient experience, the system can learn to respond to the configuration of signals at each place with the action that is optimal for that place. Figure 11 illustrates the performance of this system. Figure 11a shows the trail of an inexperienced organism that starts near the northern neutral landmark. It eventually remains in the vicinity of the tree. Figure 11b shows the trail produced by replacing the organism at its original starting point after it has undergone the experience shown in Figure 11a. It now proceeds directly to the tree, clearly benefiting from its earlier experiences.

Figure 12a shows the network after learning. Nonzero weights have appeared so that, for example, proximity to the northern landmark causes a high probability of movement south since the "odor" of the northern landmark excites the element that causes movement south and inhibits the one that causes movement north. Figure 12b shows the results of learning as a vector field in which each vector shows the most likely direction that the organism will take on its first step from any place. The vector field is the organisms's map of its environment, and will be followed even if the tree and its attractant distribution are removed. Note, though, that unlike the retinotopic maps in the peripheral visual systems, this map is implicit—the vector field is not played out over a two-dimensional array of neurons with one for each position in the landscape; instead the vectors are implicitly encoded in terms of the 16 weights of our network.

FROM THE PERCEPTRON TO BACK PROPAGATION

To learn to recognize a letter A, a network must be shown many patterns and told by a "teacher" which is a letter A, and which is not. If a *preprocessor* extracts from the environment a set of d real numbers then any pattern x will be represented by a point $(x_1, x_2, \ldots, x_d)$ in a d-dimensional Euclidean space R^d called the *pattern space*. The pattern recognizer then takes the pattern and produces a response that may have one of N distinct values if there are N categories into which the patterns must be sorted. However, a category might be represented in more than

Figure 12. Associative memory contents after learning. (*a*) The network showing the weights. Nonzero weights have appeared so that, for example, proximity to the northern landmark causes a high probability of moving south since the "odor" of the northern landmark excites action S and inhibits action N. (*b*) A vector field representation of the associative memory's contents. Each vector shows the most likely direction that the organism will move on its first step from any place. Note the generalization to places it has never visited (Barto and Sutton, 1981).

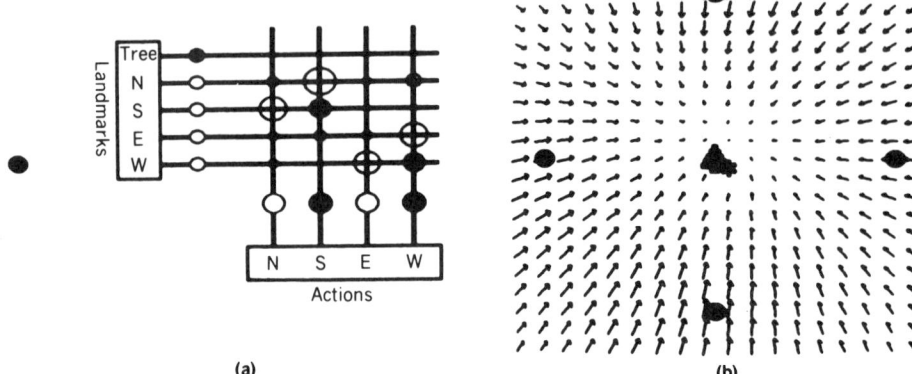

one region of R^d. To take an example from visual pattern recognition, *a*, *A*, **a**, and **A** are all members of the category of the first letter of the English alphabet, but they would probably be found in different regions of pattern space. In such cases it may be necessary to establish a hierarchical system involving a computer apparatus that recognizes the subsets, and a separate system that recognizes that the subsets all belong to the same set.

A function $f:R^d \to R^d$ is called a *discriminant function* if the equation $f(x) = 0$ gives the *decision surface* separating two regions of a pattern space. More subtle discriminations can be encoded by subdividing the pattern space with a whole set of decision functions. A basic problem of pattern recognition is the specification of such functions. Sklansky and Wassel (1981) give a textbook exposition of the classical contributions to this subject. It is virtually impossible for humans to "read out" the function they use (not to mention how they use it) to classify patterns. Thus a common strategy in pattern recognition is to provide a classification machine with an adjustable function and to "train" it with a set of patterns of known classification that are typical of those that the machine must ultimately classify. The function may be linear, quadratic, or polynomial depending on the complexity and shape of the pattern space and the necessary discriminations.

Perceptrons

Perceptrons (qv) (Rosenblatt, 1958, 1962) are neural nets that change with "experience," using an *error-correction rule* designed to change the weights of each response unit when it makes erroneous responses to stimuli that are presented to the network. Consider a twofold classification effected by using a threshold logic unit (ie, McCulloch-Pitts neuron) to process the output of a set of binary feature detectors. A set R of input lines (to be thought of as arranged in a rectangular "retina" onto which patterns may be projected) drive a network that consists of a single layer of preprocessors (associator units) whose outputs feeds into a threshold logic unit with adjustable weights. A *simple perceptron* (Fig. 13) is one in which the associator units are not interconnected, which means that it has no short-term memory. All that can be recognized by a simple perceptron is patterns that are *linearly separable* in terms of the preprocessing units. More formally, if a pattern on the retina is transformed into an array $(x_1, x_2, \ldots, x_d)$ of "feature values" by the array of preprocessing units, then a simple perceptron can only discriminate two sets of patterns if there exist weights $w_1, w_2, \ldots, w_d$ and threshold θ for the perceptron's output unit such that $w_1 x_1 + w_2 x_2 + \ldots + w_d x_d \geq \theta$ for patterns in the first class, and $w_1 x_1 + w_2 x_2 + \ldots + w_d x_d < \theta$ for patterns in the second class. A formal account of perceptron error-correction is outlined. First some notation: with each predicate ϕ, associate the binary function $\lceil \phi(x) \rceil$ which equals 1 if $\phi(x)$ is true, 0 if $\phi(x)$ is false. Let us augment x by adding a $(d + 1)$st component equal to 1 to obtain $y = (x_1, \ldots, x_d, 1)$. Then the scalar produce $\langle w | y \rangle = \Sigma_i w_i x_i - \theta$ if $w = (w_1, \ldots, w_d, -\theta)$, and so the equation for the response of the output unit can be abbreviated to the simple form

$$r = \lceil \langle w | y \rangle \geq 0 \rceil$$

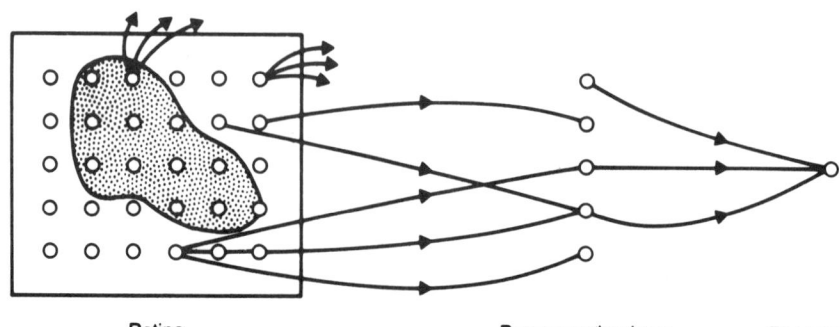

Figure 13. A simple perceptron. It is a feedforward network without loops, and the only adjustable connections are those feeding into the output layer (response units).

Consider a finite set $\mathbf{Y}_1$ of vectors corresponding to category 1, and a finite set $\mathbf{Y}_2$ corresponding to category 2 which are linearly separable, ie, there exists at least one weight vector w and threshold θ such that

$$\langle w|y\rangle \geq \theta \quad \text{if} \quad y \in \mathbf{Y}_1 \text{ while } \langle w|y\rangle < \theta \quad \text{if} \quad y \in \mathbf{Y}_2$$

An error-correction rule is specified which, if $\mathbf{Y}_1$ and $\mathbf{Y}_2$ are linearly separable, will with "sufficient experience" train the response unit to achieve separation. By starting with an arbitrary weight vector w, which presumably misclassifies many patterns, and trying to adjust it by working repeatedly through the patterns in $\mathbf{Y}_1$ and $\mathbf{Y}_2$, each is tested to see if the latest w classifies it correctly: if w classifies the current y correctly, leave w unchanged and move on to the next. If the classification is incorrect, however, change w to w' where

$$w' = w + y \quad \text{if} \quad y \in \mathbf{Y}_1; \text{ while } w' = w - y \quad \text{if} \quad y \in \mathbf{Y}_2$$

The idea is as follows: If y is in $\mathbf{Y}_1$ but w misclassified it, then we had $\langle w|y\rangle < 0$ where we should have had $\langle w|y\rangle \geq 0$. Since $\langle y|y\rangle > 0$ for any nonzero vector, we have that $\langle w+y|y\rangle = \langle w|y\rangle + \langle y|y\rangle$ which is greater than $\langle w|y\rangle$. Thus, even if we do not have $\langle w'|y\rangle > 0$, we at least have that w' classifies y "more nearly correctly" than w does. Similarly for the $\mathbf{Y}_2$ correction. Unfortunately, in classifying y "more correctly" the risk is run of classifying another pattern "less correctly." However, the *Perceptron convergence theorem* (Arbib, 1987, pp. 66–69) shows that Rosenblatt's procedure does not yield an endless seesaw, but will eventually converge to a correct set of weights if one exists, though perhaps after many iterations through the set of trial patterns.

The problem for many years was to extend the perceptron concept to multilayered networks to escape the restriction to linearly separable functions of a preassigned set of associator units. But the adjustment of connections deep within the network raises the question "How does a neuron deeply embedded within a network 'know' what aspect of the outcome of an overall action was 'its fault'?" This is the *structural credit assignment* problem. Given an "error" which is a global measure of overall system performance, what local changes can serve to reduce global error? In recent years, various techniques, such as the Boltzmann machine (qv) and the back propagation (qv) algorithm, have been devised for taking multilayered networks of perceptrons and finding ways of not only correcting the output units in terms of the observed error between their actual output and their desired output, but also of apportioning blame back into the network to train the hidden units. For example, back propagation (Rumelhart, Hinton, and Williams, 1986) is based on the discovery that gradient descent on an error function defined as a function of all the adjustable synaptic weights in the networks is essentially equivalent to having each neuron pass back to those that provide its input a message saying "If I'm wrong and you have a strong input to me, then you are greatly in error too; whereas, if I am wrong and you only have a weak input to me, then your error is so much the less." In this way, error messages propagate back to correct units further and further from the outputs. More of this scheme is seen below.

Network Complexity

The perceptron convergence theorem says that if there is a setting of the synaptic weights and threshold that will make a simple perceptron correctly classify a given training set of patterns, then the perceptron error correction rule will, after repeated presentation of all the patterns, finally converge on a setting of weights in which all the patterns in the training set are correctly classified. The catch was the "if." If the training set of patterns is linearly separable, a simple perceptron can be trained to classify the patterns correctly. Minsky and Papert (1969) revivified the study of perceptrons by responding to such convergence schemes with the question "Given a pattern-recognition problem, how much of the retina must each associator unit 'see' if the network is to do its job?" They gave a number of elegant theorems showing how complex the preprocessing layer would have to be if a simple perceptron were to linearly separate members of a class of patterns from nonmembers. Spira and Arbib (1967), on the other hand, following Winograd (1965), asked the complementary question "Given processing units of fixed size, how many layers of processing are required to achieve a given task?"

Minsky and Papert show how, if a predicate is unchanged by various permutations of its inputs, to use this fact to simplify the weights on the response unit, and then use this simplified form to place a lower bound on the complexity of the preprocessors. The basic idea of the approach will be conveyed by a simple example. Consider the simple Boolean operation of addition modulo 2 (also known as the exclusive or, XOR). If the vertices are labeled (0,0), (0,1), (1,1), and (1,0) in the Cartesian plane with $x_1 \oplus x_2$, 0's are at one diagonally opposite pair of vertices and 1's are at the other diagonally opposite pair of vertices (Fig. 14) and there is no way of interposing a straight line with the 1's on one side and the 0's on the other. While it is clear that no threshold element can perform addition modulo 2, it will be proved mathematically to exemplify the Minsky-Papert methodology. Consider the claim that we wish to prove wrong, that there exists a neuron with threshold θ and weights α and β such that $x_1 \oplus x_2 = 1$ if and only if $\alpha x_1 + \beta x_2 \geq \theta$. Since addition modulo 2 is symmetric we must also have $x_1 \oplus x_2 = 1$ if and only if $\beta x_1 + \alpha x_2 \geq \theta$, and, so, adding together the two terms, we have

$$x_1 \oplus x_2 = 1 \text{ iff } \tfrac{1}{2}(\alpha + \beta)(x_1 + x_2) > \theta \text{ iff } \tau(x_1 + x_2) > \theta$$

where $\tau = \tfrac{1}{2}(\alpha + \beta)$. Thus three putative parameters α, β, and θ have been reduced to just two, namely τ and θ. Now $t = x_1 + x_2$ is set and the polynomial $\tau t - \theta$ is observed. It is a degree 1 polynomial, but note: at $t = 0$, $\tau t - \theta$ must be less than zero ($0 \oplus 0 = 0$); at $t = 1$, it is greater than or equal to zero ($0 \oplus 1 = 1 \oplus 0 = 1$); and at $t = 2$, it is again less than zero ($1 \oplus 1 = 0$). This is a contradiction; a polynomial of degree 1 cannot change sign more than once.

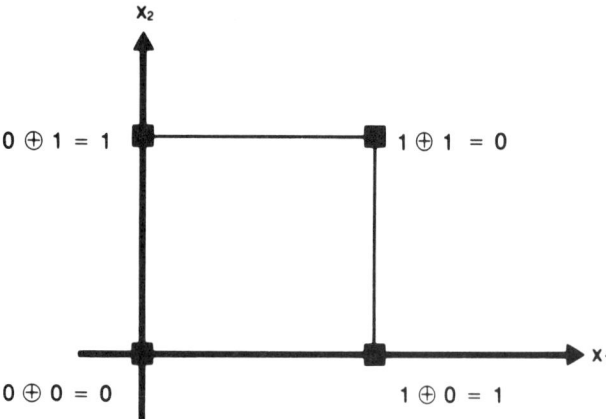

Figure 14. The graph shows clearly that the 0 and 1 values for $x_1 \oplus x_2$ are not linearly separable.

It is concluded, that there is no such polynomial, and thus that there is no threshold element which will add modulo 2.

A general method used by Minsky and Papert is now understood: start with a pattern-classification problem. Observe that certain symmetries leave it invariant, for instance, for the parity problem (Is the number of active elements even or odd?) which includes the case of addition modulo 2, any permutation of the points of the retina would leave the classification unchanged. Use this to reduce the number of parameters describing the circuit. Then lump items together to get a polynomial and examine actual patterns to put a lower bound on the degree of the polynomial, fixing things so that this degree bounds the number of inputs to the response unit of a simple perceptron.

Think of the retina R as having r elements, so that each preprocessor is defined by a Boolean (not necessarily linearly separable) function $\phi:\{0,1\}^r \to \{0,1\}$. Then, for any collection Φ of functions $\phi:\{0,1\}^r \to \{0,1\}$ define $L(\Phi)$, the class of functions linear with respect to Φ, to be precisely those functions ϕ such that $\phi(x) = 1$ iff it is true that $\Sigma \alpha_\phi \phi(x) > \theta$ for suitable choices of real numbers α_ϕ (the "weights") and θ (the "threshold"). Clearly, if Φ is the set of preprocessor functions for a simple perceptron, then the response $\{0,1\}^r \to \{0,1\}$ of the perceptron must belong to $L(\Phi)$. A function ϕ of Φ is of *degree* k if it may be associated with a neuron having k input lines from the retina R. The *order* of ϕ is then the smallest integer k for which $\phi \varepsilon L(\Phi)$ for some collection Φ of functions in which every ϕ is of degree $\leq k$. Thus, a linear threshold function is of order 1, and every function is of order $\leq |R|$, the size of the retina. Minsky and Papert ask how big an order is required for a function if the depth of the network is bounded by only allowing one level read out by a threshold element. They provide many interesting theorems. As just one example, note that they prove that the parity function $\phi_{\text{PAR}}(X) = [|X| \text{ is an odd number}]$ is of order $|R|$. To tell whether the number of inputs that are on is even requires neurons that are connected to all the retinal units. By contrast, to tell whether the number of on inputs reaches a certain threshold only requires two inputs per neuron in the first layer.

Other researchers tackled the complementary problem of how many layers of components are required if the number of inputs per component is bounded. Winograd (1965) and Spira and Arbib (1967) studied this question for algebraic functions (eg, multiplication) rather than for classifying patterns, with each module limited to having at most r input lines, and with a unit delay in the operation of each module. Their theory is based on the simple observation that if there are r inputs per module and if an output line of a circuit depends on r^m input lines, then it takes at least m time units for an input configuration to yield its corresponding output. A generalization of this observation is the basis for obtaining a lower bound on computation time for various functions and they provide for any group a network that is essentially time-optimal for its multiplication. There is thus an important result for any theory of NNs: for certain types of restricted components it can be shown how to build a network that is optimal with respect to the time required for computing a given function. However, a time optimal network may use an extremely redundant encoding for the input and output to ensure that "the right information would be in the right place at the right time." The flavor of this can be given by the observation that numbers can be multiplied far more quickly if they are given in prime decomposition, for example

$$(2^2 \cdot 3^4 \cdot 5^2 \cdot 7^1) \times (2^1 \cdot 3^0 \cdot 5^1 \cdot 7^2) = (2^3 \cdot 3^4 \cdot 5^3 \cdot 7^3)$$

than if they are given in decimal form. In the former case only exponents need to be added. The need for a critical investigation of the interplay between space and time in the design of networks is shown. It is also shown that the work of Minsky and Papert in no way proves (as some workers in AI believe) the superiority of serial processing over parallel and distributed computing, but simply provides a useful first chapter in the complexity theory of NNs. It is hardly surprising that limiting the complexity of a network limits its functionality; it is useful to have mathematical tools that delimit the order, say, of a set of interesting pattern functions.

Back Propagation

The task of back propagation is to train a loop-free network that has three types of unit: input units, "hidden units" carrying an internal representation, and output "visible" units (Fig. 15). Each unit has both input and output taking continuous values in some range $[a,b]$. The response is a sigmoidal function of the weighted sum. Thus if a unit has inputs x_k with corresponding weights w_{ik}, the output x_i is given by $x_i = f_i(\Sigma w_{ik} x_k)$, where f_i is the sigmoid function $f_i(x) = 1/1 + \exp\{-(x - \theta_i)\}$, with θ_i a bias or "threshold" for the unit.

The environment only evaluates the visible units. For each pattern p of a given set of input patterns, there corresponds a desired target pattern t_p for the output units. With o_p the actual output pattern elicited by input p, the aim is to adjust the weights in the network to minimize

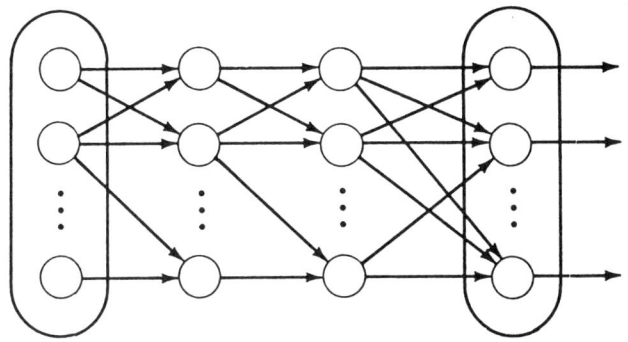

Figure 15. A typical feedforward network: the net is divided into layers with only forward connections (no loops), and with back propagation apportioning error from output units to hidden units so that a learning rule may be applied to adjust all the synaptic weights.

the error

$$E = \Sigma_{\text{patterns } p} \Sigma_{\text{output neurons } k}(t_{pk} - o_{pk})^2$$

Rumelhart and co-workers (1986) devised a formula for propagating back the gradient of this evaluation from a unit to its inputs, and this can continue by back propagation through the entire net. Robbins and Monro (1951), Bryson and Ho (1969), Werbos (1974), and Parker (1985) earlier devised related algorithms. Also, Rosenblatt (1962) by no means restricts himself to simple perceptrons but also discusses unsupervised learning rules and a form of back propagation. At each trial, the input pattern p is fixed and the corresponding "restricted error"

$$E = \Sigma_k(t_k - o_k)^2$$

is considered, where k ranges over the output units. The net has many units interconnected by weights w_{ij}. The learning rule is to change w_{ij} to reduce E by *gradient descent*:

$$\Delta w_{ij} = -\partial E/\partial w_{ij} = 2 \Sigma_k(t_k - o_k) \, \partial o_k/\partial w_{ij}$$

Consider a net divided into $m + 1$ layers, with nets in layer $g + 1$ receiving all their inputs from layer g; with layer 0 comprising the input units; and layer m comprising the output units. If i is an output unit (remember, w_{ij} connects from j to i) then

$$\Delta w_{ij} = 2(t_i - o_i) \, \partial f_i(\Sigma w_{il}o_l)/\partial w_{ij} = 2 \, (t_i - o_i) \, f'_i o_k$$

where f'_i is the derivative of the activation function evaluated at the activation level in $_i = \Sigma w_{il}o_l$ to unit i. It is thus concluded that Δw_{ij} is proportional to $\delta_i o_j$, where $\delta_i = (t_i - o_i)f'_i$ for an output unit.

Next, suppose that i is a hidden unit with an output that drives only output units. Then

$$\Delta w_{ij} = 2 \Sigma_k(t_k - o_k) \, \partial f_k(\Sigma w_{kl}o_l)/\partial w_{ij}$$

But the only o_l that depends on w_{ij} is o_i and so

$$\partial f_k(\Sigma w_{kl}o_l)/\partial w_{ij} = [\partial f_k(\Sigma w_{kl}o_l)/\partial o_i].[\partial o_i/\partial w_{ij}]$$
$$= [f'_k w_{ki}].[f'_i o_j]$$

so that

$$\Delta w_{ij} = 2 \Sigma_k(t_k - o_k) \, [f'_k w_{ki}].[f'_i o_j]$$

Recalling that $\delta_k = (t_k - o_k) f'_k$ for an output unit k, this may be rewritten as

$$\Delta w_{ij} = 2 \, (\Sigma_k \delta_k w_{ki}) \, f'_i o_j$$

Thus Δw_{ij} is proportional to $\delta_i o_j$, where $\delta_i = (\Sigma_k \delta_k w_{ki}) f'_i$, where k runs over all units which receive unit i's output. More generally, the following can be proved by induction on how many layers to go back to reach a unit:

Proposition: Consider a layered loop-free net with error $E = \Sigma_k(t_k - o_k)^2$, where k ranges over designated "output units," and let the weights w_{ij} be changed according to the gradient descent rule

$$\Delta w_{ij} = -\partial E/\partial w_{ij} = 2 \Sigma_k(t_k - o_k) \, \partial o_k/\partial w_{ij}$$

Then the weights may be changed inductively, working back from the output units, by the rule that Δw_{ij} is proportional to $\delta_i o_j$, where:
Basis Step: $\delta_i = (t_i - o_i)f'_i$ for an output unit.
Induction Step: If i is a hidden unit, and if δ_k is known for all units which receive unit i's output then

$$\delta_i = (\Sigma_k \delta_k w_{ki}) \, f'_i$$

where k runs over all units which receive unit i's output.

Thus the "error signal" δ_i *propagates* back by layer from the output units. In $\Sigma_k \delta_k w_{ki}$, unit i receives an error propagated back from a unit k to the extent to which i affects k. The above theorem tells how to compute Δw_{ij} for gradient descent. It does not guarantee that the above step-size is appropriate to reach the minimum, nor does it guarantee that the minimum, if reached, is global. The back propagation rule defined by this proposition is thus a heuristic rule, not one guaranteed to find a global minimum. Since it is heuristic, it may also be applied to neural nets which are not strictly layered. Although no formal proof is available, simulation shows that the scheme avoids many of the false minima that bedeviled other methods. However, there is still no convincing evidence that such a rule is implemented in biological tissue; nor a good hypothesis as to what a biologically plausible equivalent of back propagation might be.

Perhaps the most widely known example of the application of back propagation is a text-to-speech transformation network called NETTALK (Sejnowski and Rosenberg, 1987). It comprises 309 units with 18,629 connections. There is one output unit for each of the 55 phonemes pronounced by a speech synthesizer called

DECTALK. The job of the net is thus not to learn phonemes, but rather to learn to associate the correct phonemes with the successive letters of a word, each letter being coded by 29 input units, 29 being the number of different characters. Pronunciation of a letter depends on context—consider the different pronunciations of the underlined a in always, alw<u>a</u>ys, e<u>a</u>t (here it is silent) and b<u>a</u>t. To allow for this context, the input to the net represents a sequence of seven letters (including the blank), for which the output is to be the phoneme for the middle letter. NETTALK employs 80 hidden units, training them by back propagation. What makes this system so compelling is that the output of the net can be used to drive DECTALK, so one may hear the current phoneme sequence produced by the net. The effect is heightened by tuning the speech synthesizer to a child's high pitch instead of its usual deeper tones.

After training on 1000 words, NETTALK achieved 91% correct phonemes on the training set; when tested on a different 1000 words, it achieved 80% on the test set. With 15,000 words, the scores were 88% on the training set; 86% on the test set. Once the net has converged, the detective work begins. The idea is to look at hidden units in the trained net and try to describe their response properties. One sees a semidistributed representation; about 15% of the hidden units are highly active in each case. Sejnowski and Rosenberg averaged the activity of hidden units for each occurrence of a given vowel, a signal in 80-dimensional space. They did factor analysis for the 10 vowels, and got two-dimensional vectors with a position (with appropriate choice of axes) that correlates well with the position of the tongue in mouth. However, further tests need to be done to see if this "really" is the position in the mouth, or rather whether both the factor space and the tongue position correlate well with similarity, which then imposes a common distance metric on both two-dimensional spaces.

Another interesting application of back propagation is to sensorimotor learning. The intention to perform an act cannot be evaluated in terms of the motorneuron activity produced by the net, but rather by the sensory pattern produced by the movement. Let then X be the set of motorneuron patterns, and let Y be the set of sensory patterns produced by the actions they generate, with $f(x)$ the sensory pattern observed as a result of firing pattern x. How do we back propagate through the physics which produces $f(x)$ to go from a desired sensory pattern y to the firing pattern x which generates it? One answer (Jordan and Rumelhart, 1990) is to first build a mental model MM, a network which models the function f, predicting the sensory effects of every action (Fig. 16). In robotics, MM is equivalent to the kinematics of the motor controller. Once MM is built, its connections are fixed, or (since, in a growing organism, the analog of MM would need constant updating) slowly varying to provide a stable reference for MP, the network for generating motor programs that achieve a desired sensory situation. MP is adjusted by back propagation working back first through MM and then through MP, training MP to implement a function $g: Y \to X$ with the property that $f(g(y)) = y$ for each desired sensory situation y.

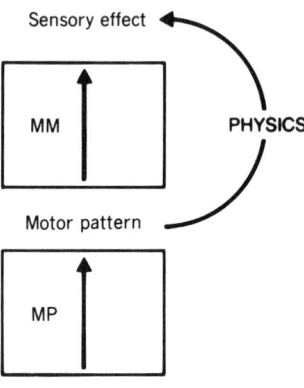

Figure 16. A two-stage back propagation scheme in which a mental model (MM) is first trained to represent the physics that transforms a motor command into the sensory consequences of an action. Back propagation can then proceed through the clamped connections of MM during the training of MP, the network for generating motor programs which achieve a desired sensory situation.

More specifically, consider the problem of learning to repeat words that have been heard. MP, the motor program, receives as input the "intention," a vector representing a word as heard, and is to yield a motor output which drives the articulators to reproduce that word. Since the teacher cannot specify the right motor activity to produce the word, MM is introduced to model the physics of the articulators and the ears, etc, that converts the motor output into sensory feedback:

Stage 1: This is a "babble phase" (or, in motor control: a "flailing phase"), using more or less random sounds and movements to build up MM. Here, with "Expectation" as the desired output of MM for a given input, training uses (Sensory Feedback − Expectation)^2 as the error to train MM by back propagation, using a sufficiently varied set of inputs from MP to "span" the motor space X.

Stage 2: MP repeatedly tries to utter a word and hear if it sounds the same as the instruction. MP is adjusted by applying back propagation to the combined network MP + MM, but with the connections in MM "clamped" as being already correct. Even though there will be error signals at the connections within MM, only the Δw_{ij} within MP are adjusted. It is again a heuristic device that suggests that the system will still converge to the desired "identity function" for MP + MM.

Statistical Mechanics of Learning

A learning procedure tries to minimize the error signal from a NN by changing the weights in an appropriate way. Looking at this minimization problem from a more abstract point of view yields the following picture of a learning algorithm like back propagation: A learning procedure searches through the space of all possible synaptic weights for those networks which fulfill the desired input–output relationship. This space shrinks more and more if one example after another is presented from the training set. Any theoretical result will, therefore, not yield one particular network but a distribution of networks which share the same functionality. The close analogy between training layered networks and optimizing a cost function enables us to analyze the learning problem as a statistical inference problem that is addressed with the maximum entropy principle. Questions like "How many training examples are necessary to achieve a certain generalization behavior?" and "How fast does learning and generalization occur?" can be studied using the powerful techniques of statistics.

In the following, a NN with M input nodes assuming the values S_i, $i = 1, \ldots, M$ and one output node is considered. The value of the output node σ depends on the synaptic weights w_i, $i = 1, \ldots, M$ and on the input pattern S_i, ie, $\sigma = \sigma(\mathbf{w};\mathbf{S})$. The network is trained to approximate or, if possible, to reproduce a target function $\sigma_o(\mathbf{S})$. The training procedure gathers information about the target function from a set of p training examples ($\mathbf{S}^l$, $\sigma_o(\mathbf{S}^l)$), $l = 1, \ldots, p$ that are chosen randomly from the entire input space. Presenting an input pattern $\mathbf{S}^l$ to an untrained network will result in a network response that differs by $\varepsilon(\mathbf{w};\mathbf{S}) = [\sigma(\mathbf{w};\mathbf{S}) - \sigma_0(\mathbf{S})]^2$ from the target function $\sigma_0(\mathbf{S})$. The sum over all p training examples constitutes the total training error or training energy $E(\mathbf{w}) = \sum_{l=1}^{p} \varepsilon(\mathbf{w};\mathbf{S}^l)$. Stochastic training algorithms are considered which, like back propagation, are gradient descent algorithms, but which differ by adding a noise term:

$$\frac{\partial w_i}{\partial t} = -\frac{\partial E}{\partial w_i}(w) + \eta_i(t)$$

with η_i being white noise with cross-correlation $\langle \eta_i(t)\eta_k(t')\rangle = 2T\delta_{ik}\delta(t - t')$. Such an algorithm arrives after long training at a Gibbs distribution of networks $P(\mathbf{w}) = Z^{-1}\exp[-E(\mathbf{w})/T]$ where Z is a normalization constant (it is, in fact, what is known as the partition function in statistical mechanics, cf Landau and Lifshitz (1980).

The stochastic learning algorithm relies on fluctuations in the training stage. What is the possible advantage of noisy learning? There are four main reasons why one wants to inject stochasticity in the network adaptation process:

1. A biologically plausible learning algorithm has to be able to cope with noise. Stochastic influences are abundant in nature and cannot be avoided, but might be exploited for information processing.

2. Stochastic learning can be considerably speeded up. The random fluctuations average out local minima and create a much smoother energy landscape than that for the deterministic case.

3. The noise in the training procedure might improve the generalization ability of the network.

4. A noisy learning algorithm produces a solution that does not rely on deterministic artifacts or on a favorable prewiring of the network. Noisy optimization reveals the average performance of an algorithm whereas other learning theories most often concentrate on the worst case performance.

Of particular interest in learning theory is the prediction of the generalization error of a network after it has seen p examples of the target function. The learning of the training set is of secondary importance because NNs are supposed to work as decision elements rather than lookup tables. The performance on not yet seen examples of one function determines the quality of a network. Two different types of behavior have been observed depending on the learning problem, ie, (1) incremental learning and (2) learning with a sharp transition to perfect generalization. The second case remotely resembles the popular observation in human learning that "a light went on" in a person's head.

A special example of a learning problem studied by Sompolinsky and co-workers (1990) is the contiguity problem. Imagine you have a bit string of 1's and −1's and you want to know if more than K groups of 1's are present in the string. One way to solve the problem is to use neurons with a localized receptive field in a second layer which fire whenever they detect an "intensity edge" in the input, ie, a $(1,-1)$ pair. Such an architecture for a contiguity counting network is depicted in Figure 17. Each cell in the second layer receives an excitatory synapse from a cell in the input layer just left to it and an inhibitory synapse from the next cell on the right in the previous layer. With a threshold slightly smaller than two, such a neuron will only respond if a $(1,-1)$ pair is presented in the input. The task of the cell in the third layer is then to fire if more than K of these edges occur, ie, if more than K cells in the second layer have fired.

Training a network to solve the contiguity problem is instructive for the study of the dynamics of the learning process. Since a solution for that problem is known, the performance of a partially trained network can always be compared with the perfectly trained network, and judged on how well it generalizes. The theoretical studies by Sompolinsky and co-workers demonstrated that the network typically generalizes very poorly if insufficient examples are shown. If the number of examples in the training set exceeds a threshold the network makes an abrupt transition to perfect generalization, as if it finally "understood" the concept behind the task. In cases where one

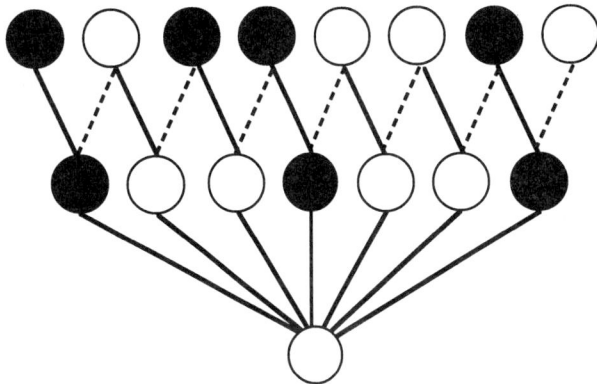

Figure 17. A network that is able to solve the contiguity problem (Sompolinsky and co-workers, 1990). Excitatory synapses are plotted as solid lines; inhibitory connections are shown as dashed lines.

asks not for a yes–no decision but for a gradual response the discontinuous transition to perfect generalization might be smeared out to an exponentially fast convergence.

However, there exist other tasks that are more challenging for NNs. Imagine there is a function that is not exactly implementable in the chosen architecture but can only be approximated. Such a target function is called a nonimplementable rule. The generalization error in these networks drops gradually if more and more examples are presented to the network. The training error remains zero as long as not too many examples are shown, but deviates from zero if the training set exceeds a critical value α_c and the architecture reveals its limitations. In the limit of many training examples the generalization error and the training error approach the same asymptotic value. The generalization error, however, does not necessarily decay in a monotonic fashion, thus making it a considerable problem to determine the optimal size of the training set. The different statistical mechanics approaches to these questions help to sharpen the intuition for deciding from one training situation to the next what size of training set is appropriate.

ASSOCIATIVE MEMORIES WITH FIXED POINT ATTRACTORS

Among the successful applications of NNs to information processing are associative memories, also known as content addressable memories, a topic which saw much activity even during the years in which AI was dominated by the serial computing paradigm. A number of authors, starting with Steinbuch (1961), studied *synaptic matrices*, NNs in which (just as in the landmark learning network) there are m input lines each forming synapses on the same n neurons, so that the "state of learning" of the net is completely described by the synaptic matrix $A = [w_{ij}]$ where w_{ij} is the strength of the synapse from input j to neuron i. Such workers as Steinbuch in the early 1960s and Anderson, Kohonen, and Trehub in the 1970s provided synaptic learning rules to adjust these connections so that the matrix forms an *associative memory* that is *distributed* and thus *resistant to localized damage*. When viewing a NN as an associative memory, the pattern on the input lines is known as the *key* and the pattern on the output lines (the outputs of the neurons), the *recollection*. In an *autoassociative* memory, learning is designed to make the key elicit the recollection of which it is a part, so that one has a content-addressable memory. In a *heteroassociative* memory, the key may be quite different from the recollection.

Although our main concern will be with nonlinear networks, here the linear case is shown to establish some basic ideas. Let $\langle x|y \rangle$ denote the scalar product of the two column vectors x and y; it equals the matrix product $x^T y$ of the transposed (row) vector x^T with the column vector y. Let f be a single key for which the recollection g is desired, and set $A = gf^T$. Then note that if the synaptic matrix A is supplied with key f, $Af = gf^T f$ is created which is just the desired recollection g scaled up by $\langle f|f \rangle = f^T f$; and thus will be precisely g if f is a unit vector, ie, if $\langle f|f \rangle = 1$. More generally, given a set f_k of keys and g_k of corresponding recollections, define the synaptic matrix to be

$$A = \Sigma\, g_k f_k^T \qquad (26)$$

which is obtained by adding up the "memory traces" $g_k f_k^T$ for each of the (f_k, g_k) pairings of key and recollection:

$$A(0) = 0;\ A(k) = A(k-1) + g_k f_k^T \qquad (27)$$

Assuming that each f_j is a unit vector, we have that

$$Af_j = g_j + \Sigma_{k \neq j} g_k \langle f_k, f_j \rangle \qquad (28)$$

This will equal g_j if the f_k's are orthonormal, ie, $\langle f_k, f_j \rangle = \delta_{kj}$, the Kronecker delta, which is just the identity matrix (1 on the diagonal, 0 off it).

Such synaptic matrices have no dynamics; each input yields a unique output. However, if loops are allowed within the connectivity of a network, it becomes a *dynamic system*. In particular, consider a network of N McCulloch and Pitts neurons, with no external input, described by binary variables $\{V_i\}_{i=1}^{N}$ (so that neuron i is either firing ($V_i = 1$) or quiet ($V_i = 0$)). It is a dynamic system with the vectors $(V_1, \ldots, V_N)$ as sates. The synaptic strengths w_{ik} determine the *local field* of neuron i in this state by $h_i = \Sigma_{k=0}^{N} w_{ik} V_k$. The state changes so that

$$V_i(t+1) = 1 \text{ iff } (h_i - \theta_i) \geq 0,$$
where θ_i is the threshold of neuron i \qquad (29)

The basic idea of associative memory is to design a system that receives incomplete information and that corrects and recalls stored information through its dynamics. Information is retrieved by its content and not by pointers to a particular memory address. An early example of the use of such dynamics in an associative memory is Anderson's BSB (brain states in a box) model, an autoassociative synaptic matrix with the output fed back to the input (Anderson and co-workers, 1977). The response is a continuous (not a binary) function of the input, but with lower and upper saturation levels. What is learned is a desired tuple of extreme values, the weights being adjusted each time equilibrium is reached with a given input in such a way as to reduce the discrepancy with the desired value. Anderson relates his model to human performance, with stabilization time being compared to human reaction times. The learning rule for this recurrent net is

$$A(t+1) = A(t) + ff^T$$

as in the nonrecurrent case (27), where f is now both key and recollection at time t. Note that if $A(0)$ is symmetric, then $A(t)$ is symmetric for all $t \geq 0$. Assume that $\{f_1, \ldots, f_k\}$ is an orthonormal set, and that f_i is presented k_i times as a forced firing pattern. Then

$$A = \sum_{1 \leq i \leq k} k_i f_i f_i^T$$

If A is real and symmetric, there is a basis $e_1, \ldots, e_N$ consisting of orthogonal eigenvectors of A: $Ae_i = \lambda_i e_i$ $i = 1, \ldots, N$ with each λ_i real. Now $Af_j = [\Sigma_{1 \leq i \leq k} k_i f_i f_i^T] f_j = k_j f_j$ since the $\{f_j\}$ are an orthonormal set and so the f_j are the eigenvectors. If $K < N$, the remaining eigenvalues are 0, their eigenvectors complete the basis. A is essentially a simple covariance matrix of the process generating the patterns. The eigenvectors of A correspond to "components," and those with the largest eigenvalues to "principal components" (cf factor analysis). In this, orthonormal, case, the eigenvalue is just a measure of the number of presentations. The general case involves a "weighted combination" of eigenvectors. The P which transforms A to its principal components is called the Karhunen-Loève transformation, and is frequently approximated by suboptimal transforms for which there exist fast algorithms (Kohonen, 1988). The use of eigenvalues allows one to discard the "infrequent" components to come up with vectors in a lower dimensional space which provides a reasonable approximation as "averaged over time."

Let $x(t)$ be the activity vector at time t, with $x(i,t)$ its ith component. Anderson posits no spontaneous decay in x, so that the current state $x(t)$ is augmented by the feedback term $Ax(t)$ to yield

$$x(t + 1) = x(t) + Ax(t) = (I + A)x(t)$$

If $x(t)$ is an eigenvector with eigenvalue λ, then

$$x(i, t + 1) = (1 + \lambda)x(t)$$

It can be shown that λ is positive and so $1 + \lambda > 1$. Thus $x(t)$ will increase exponentially as t increases. The system would thus be *unstable*. But Anderson puts the system "in a box" by having hard bounds $[-1, +1]$ on the components of $x(t)$ in the original coordinates. The hard bounds destroy linearity. The trajectory heads for an edge, then follows it to a corner. This breaks the space into *attractors* or *capture regions*. Inputs are thus *classified* by the corners of the box, ie, by amplifying the relative strengths of the original principal components. There are thus up to 2^n classifications in an n-element net—though, in general, not all corners will be stable attractors—and these classifications can be read by the "next net" which receives the output of the recurrent matrix.

Earlier it was established that the dynamics of a deterministic Hopfield network with symmetric coupling is governed by an energy function which yields a relaxation dynamics with fixed points as attractor states. Now it is studied how, in the same spirit as the above work, Hopfield (1982) specified the synapses w_{ik} in such a way that p predefined patterns $\{\xi^\nu = (\xi_1^\nu, \ldots, \xi_N^\nu); \nu = 1, \ldots, p\}$ are stable fixed points of the network. (There are two versions of the Hopfield model, one in which the states take value $V_i = 0$ or 1, and another in which the states take value $S_i = -1$ or $+1$. This apparently trivial change is accompanied by slight differences in other assumptions which yield subtle, and sometimes far-reaching, changes in the properties of the networks.) The novelty is that analysis does not build on looking at a specific set of patterns to be checked for, say, orthonormality, but rather is based on choosing random unbiased bit strings for the stored patterns, ie, $\xi_i^\nu = 1$ has the same probability as $\xi_i^\nu = 0$, and then analyzing network properties with methods from statistical mechanics. Hopfield adopted a slight variant of (26) for the synaptic matrix

$$w_{ik} = \frac{1}{N} \sum_{\nu=1}^{p} (2\xi_i^\nu - 1)(2\xi_i^\nu - 1) \qquad (30)$$

for connecting the neurons to form an associative memory. $(2\xi_k^\nu - 1)$ is called the presynaptic factor of the synaptic rule, $(2\xi_i^\nu - 1)$ the postsynaptic factor. The symmetric $N \times N$ matrix w_{ik} essentially stores the averaged correlations between neuron k and i with the average performed over all patterns.

If the NN is to work as an associative memory, all pattern states $\{\xi^\nu; \nu = 1, \ldots, p\}$ must be stable fixed points of the dynamics, or at least be located close to attractor states. Otherwise, the network will not relax to the correct pattern and would not perform an associative completion of a corrupted input. Stability of a network state requires that the local fields h_i exceed the threshold θ_i whenever $V_i = 1$ and that h_i is smaller than θ_i if $V_i = 0$. This condition can be reformulated as $(h_i - \theta_i)(2V_i - 1) \geq 0$. The stability of the pattern states of a network with the connectivity (30) is evaluated. Assume without loss of generality that the network is in the first pattern state ξ^1. Then, the local fields take on the values

$$h_i = \sum_{k=0}^{N} w_{ik} \xi_k^1 = \frac{1}{N} \sum_{k=0}^{N} \sum_{\nu=1}^{p} (2\xi_i^\nu - 1)(2\xi_k^\nu - 1)\xi_k^1$$

The sum over all patterns $\{\xi^\nu; \nu = 1, \ldots, p\}$ can be split into two parts, a signal part $(2\xi_i^1 - 1)(2\xi_k^1 - 1)\xi_k^1$ and a noise part $(2\xi_i^\nu - 1)(2\xi_k^\nu - 1)\xi_k^1$ with $\nu \neq 1$, ie,

$$h_i = h_i^s + h_i^n = \frac{1}{N}(2\xi_i^1 - 1)\sum_{k=0}^{N}(2\xi_k^1 - 1)\xi_k^1$$

$$+ \frac{1}{N}\sum_{k=0}^{N}\sum_{\nu=2}^{p}(2\xi_i^\nu - 1)(2\xi_k^\nu - 1)\xi_k^1 \qquad (31)$$

(compare the "deterministic decomposition" in (28)). The noise term h_i^n is zero on the average for a finite number of patterns stored since ξ_k^1 and $(2\xi_i^n - 1)$ are independent random variables. Its mean value is zero and its variance is of the order $\sqrt{p/N}$ which vanishes for finite p and very large numbers of neurons N. The noise part, however, limits the number of patterns that can be stored in a NN in the interesting region of p proportional to N. The signal part h_i^s (first term in (31)) stabilizes the pattern state ξ^1. In order to see that, the variables ξ_k^ν are averaged over to yield the expected value of

$$\left\langle \sum_{k=0}^{N}(2\xi_k^1 - 1)\xi_k^1 \right\rangle = \sum_{k=0}^{N}\langle(2\xi_k^1 - 1)\xi_k^1\rangle \approx N$$

Therefore, the signal term assumes the value 1 if $\xi_i^1 = 1$ and the value -1 if $\xi_i^1 = 0$. A threshold θ_i between these

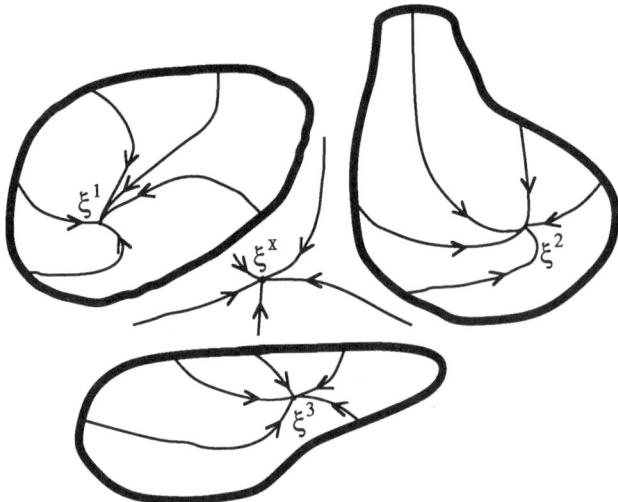

Figure 18. Schematic view of attractors with basins of attraction. The attractors ξ_i, $i \in \{1,2,3\}$, correspond to stored patterns, whereas ξ^x is a special network state to indicate failed association.

two bounds will stabilize the pattern x^1 as a fixed point attractor. $\theta_i = 0$ is a popular choice.

The dynamics of a Hopfield NN can be visualized as a relaxation flow to a set of fixed points, as shown in Figure 18. The different stored patterns $\{\xi^\nu; \nu = 1, \ldots, p\}$ are surrounded by basins of attraction (bold lines). A network with an initial state located inside a basin of attraction will relax to the corresponding fixed point. If the network is initialized in a state far away from a prespecified attractor ξ^x it will either flow to a dedicated state that indicates "failure of association" or it will relax to a spurious attractor. These spurious attractors are a nuisance for associative recall and can considerably degrade the capacity of an associative memory. The state ξ^x depicts the indicator state of failed association in Figure 18. For reliable associative recall it is desirable to design a network with equally shaped basins of attraction and with no spurious states.

The Spin Representation of the Hopfield Model

As seen in using the Ising model to motivate the analogy between magnets and neural networks in our earlier discussion of "Neural Nets and Cooperative Phenomena," models of magnetism usually postulate an ensemble of binary variables $S_i \in \{-1, 1\}$ that are analogous to the neural variables in the Hopfield model. The value of variable S_i is often interpreted as an upward or a downward direction, defined by an external magnetic field. These magnetic moments (or spins) with two states only can interact in a positive or a negative way. Positive (or excitatory) interaction favours alignment of two spins whereas negative (or inhibitory) interaction favours opposite directions. The dynamics of spin systems is controlled by the energy function

$$E = -\sum_{i=1}^{N} \sum_{k \in \mathbf{N}(i)} S_i J_{ik} S_k + \sum_{i=1}^{N} S_i H_i \quad (32)$$

where J_{ik} and H_i denote the interaction of spin i with spin k and the external magnetic field, respectively. $\mathbf{N}(i)$ determines the interaction radius of spin i which is usually quite short. The interactions are chosen to be symmetric to reflect the symmetry in the exchange forces in the physics of magnetic systems.

In analogy to the spin representation, one can transform the variables V_i of a NN to $S_i = 2V_i - 1$ and rewrite the connectivity matrix as

$$w_{ik} = \frac{1}{N} \sum_{\nu=1}^{p} \sigma_i^\nu \sigma_k^\nu \quad (33)$$

where σ_k^ν is a random number with elements $\sigma_k^\nu \in \{-1, 1\}$, while the local fields become

$$h_i = \sum_{k=0}^{N} w_{ik} V_k = \frac{1}{2} \sum_{k=0}^{N} w_{ik} S_k + \frac{1}{2} \sum_{k=0}^{N} w_{ik}$$

which completely determine the dynamics of the network. The V-representation corresponds to an S-representation with neural thresholds $\theta_i = \frac{1}{2} \sum_{k=0}^{N} w_{ik}$. Weisbuch and Fogelman-Soulie (1985) have optimized the number of stable attractors in the Hopfield network by varying the thresholds. They found that the choice $\theta_i = 0$ in the S-representation is optimal for patterns with an equal number of one and zero bits, ie, $\theta_o = 0$ is superior to $\theta_i = \frac{1}{2} \sum_{k=0}^{N} w_{ik}$. The S-representation has a higher storage capacity than the V-representation, however, the choice $\theta_i = 0$ for the thresholds does not yield optimal storage capacity for other coding schemes, ie, for the interesting sparse coding limit where the patterns are encoded by many zero bits and few one bits.

The previous section showed that all pattern states are stable network states if the synaptic connectivity matrix assumes the form $w_{ik} = 1/N \sum_{\nu=1}^{p} \sigma_i^\nu \sigma_k^\nu$. However, for reliable associative recall the pattern states should be the only stable fixed points of the NN. If the network has fixed points other than the pattern states, the recall dynamics could yield an answer which does not correspond to any pattern to be stored. *Spurious states,* as these additional fixed points are called, confuse the relaxation dynamics and are a nuisance for applications of associative memories in information processing.

Amit, Gutfreund, and Sompolinsky (1985) characterized all fixed points of a Hopfield NN with connectivity (33). They found that not only are the pattern states stable as designed, but so are all odd superpositions of patterns. The special case of a state $S_i = \text{sign}(\sigma_i^1 + \sigma_i^2 + \sigma_i^3)$ illustrates this finding which results from the superposition of the three different pattern states $\sigma_i^1, \sigma_i^2, \sigma_i^3$. The state S_i is called a symmetric three mixture because three pattern states with equal weight have been added and the majority rule to determine it has been used. The overlap between the mixture state S_i and the three pattern states is $m^\nu = 1/N \sum_{i=1}^{N} S_i \sigma_i^\nu = 0.5$. The stability of the mixture state can be checked in an analogous way to the previously demonstrated stability of pattern states. It is required that the product $S_i h_i$ between the neural states S_i and the respective local fields h_i is positive ($\theta_i = 0$ is assumed) and is decomposed into a signal part and a noise part. The noise part vanishes in the limit of infinitely many neurons and a finite number of patterns stored. The signal part takes the value

$$S_i \sum_{v=1}^{3} \sigma_i^v = 0.5(\sigma_i^1 + \sigma_i^2 + \sigma_i^3) \, \text{sign}(\sigma_i^1 + \sigma_i^2 + \sigma_i^3)$$

which is positive for all different choices of $\sigma_i^1, \sigma_i^2, \sigma_i^3 \in \{-1, 1\}$. The stabilizing factor $S_i h_i$ reaches a maximum for those neurons i, which have the same state in all three patterns 1,2,3, ie, $\sigma_i^1 = \sigma_i^2 = \sigma_i^3$. These S_i, by the way, are as stable as if the network is in a pure pattern state. All other S_i with two σ_i^v, $\nu = 1,2,3$, being the same and the third being different, are less stable. The overall stability of mixture states decreases if more complex mixture states are visited, ie, mixtures of five pattern states are less stable than mixtures of three pattern states.

Amit and co-workers (1985) proved that the approximate number of symmetric spurious states grows exponentially fast as $3^p/2$ where p is the number of "desired" patterns stored in the network. It has been speculated that this exponential number of stable states could be of advantage for information processing but it is more likely that spurious states are just a nuisance created indirectly by the specific synaptic rule (33).

Different magnetic systems have been extensively studied in the past. In models of ferromagnets, the simplest type of an interacting magnetic system, all J_{ik} are positive and of equal strength. If $\mathbf{N}(i)$ is chosen as the set of all nearest neighbors of spin i the famous Ising model is achieved. On the other hand, if $\mathbf{N}(i)$ is the set of all spins, equation (32) describes the energy of a long range ferromagnet. The preferred state of ferromagnets at zero temperature is a complete alignment of all spins in the same direction.

A novel class of disordered magnets with competing interactions, so-called *spin glasses* (because their disordered structure resembles ordinary glasses), has been studied experimentally and theoretically over the last 20 years. The spin interaction in these models assumes positive and negative values and is random. A simple model of a spin glass was proposed by Sherrington and Kirkpatrick (1975) who connected all spins with each other (long range spin glass) and chose the couplings J_{ik} as Gaussian normal distributed random numbers, ie, $P(J_{ik}) = \exp(-J_{ik}^2/2)/\sqrt{2\pi}$. This model played an important role in the understanding of disordered magnetic systems.

The connection between the Hopfield model and spin glasses becomes obvious if the number of neurons remains fixed and the number of stored patterns p goes to infinity. The sum in the Hebbian connection rule w_{ik} approaches a normal distribution as is found in the Sherrington-Kirkpatrick spin glass, ie, a Hopfield model where the ratio between stored patterns and neurons tends to infinity turns into a spin glass with long interaction range. Although spin glasses are quite simple to define, they show an extraordinary rich structure and a complicated dynamics. The number of local minima diverges exponentially with the number N of neurons. The search for the lowest energy state of a spin glass is an *NP*-hard problem which provides another connection between statistical physics and theoretical computer science.

Storage Capacity

One of the interesting questions from an engineering point of view is the efficiency of associative recall:

1. How many patterns can be stored in a NN with N neurons? How much storage capacity must be sacrificed for associative recall?
2. What is the average recall error? How many bits are not reproduced correctly by the neural net?

Both types of questions can be studied with methods of statistical mechanics. The analysis will be sketched and the key result summarized. The information content of an associative memory is the critical quantity to determine the efficiency of a NN compared to other storage methods. The maximal information content of the network must be compared with the number of synapses that are required to store the information reliably. If too many patterns are stored, the network will overload and the recall quality will deteriorate or, even worse, the attractors will no longer be located near the prototype patterns and the network will lose its associative abilities. Assume that there is a fully connected network with $N(N-1)/2$ different synapses (the network is symmetric and there is no self-coupling). The information stored in the network is expected to be at least proportional to N^2 bits. Therefore, since each pattern is encoded by N bits, at least $p = \alpha N$ patterns should be stored in the network.

What can happen if too many patterns are stored in the network? As demonstrated in the section on spin glasses, the Hopfield model becomes identical with the long range spin glass model in the limit $\alpha \to \infty$. The attractor states do not depend on the patterns σ_i^v that were used to generate the synaptic connections since they are completely randomized (Gaussian distributed) in the limit $\alpha \to \infty$. In the opposite limit $\alpha \to 0$, all pattern states are stable fixed points of the relaxation dynamics. There exists a critical value α_c for the storage capacity that divides the region of associative recall ($\alpha < \alpha_c$) from the spin glass region ($\alpha > \alpha_c$).

Amit and co-workers (1985) were the first to describe the dependence of α_c on the noise level in the network (recall Equation (5) from the section on "Hopfield Networks and Optimization"). The more noise injected into the dynamics of spinoidal neurons the lower the maximal storage capacity will be. This can be intuitively understood by studying a neuron with a very weak stabilizing local field. If that neuron is exposed to strong noise (which is larger than its local field) the neural state is no longer determined by the signal part of its local field and, therefore, by the pattern to be recalled, but by noise fluctuations. A complete phase diagram of the network properties depending on the network load α and the noise level measured by the temperature T has been calculated in Amit

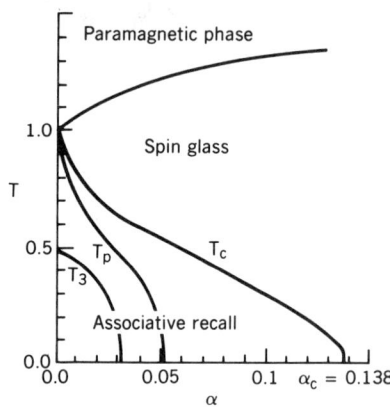

Figure 19. A complete phase diagram of the network properties depending on the network load α and the noise level measured by the temperature T (Amit and co-workers, 1985).

and co-workers (1985) and is reproduced in Figure 19. The different network phases are the following:

1. *Paramagnetic phase.* The noise level is too high and the network dynamics is controlled by noise and not by the connectivity.

2. *Spin glass phase.* Too many patterns have been stored in the network. The dynamics shows relaxation to attractor states but these fixed points are uncorrelated with stored patterns. The spin glass phase cannot be used for information processing.

3. *Associative recall phase.* For T and α not too high, the NN relaxes to fixed points that are highly correlated with prototype patterns. The critical storage capacity in the zero noise case is approximately $\alpha_c = 0.14$.

Let us now concentrate on the parameter region of the (T, α) plane where associative recall is observed. Below the line T_p the pattern states are the lowest energy states of the system. All spurious states have higher energy. Below T_3 the symmetric superpositions of three patterns become stable fixed points. When the memory is overloaded (passing the T_c-line) the network fails completely and forgets all patterns stored. This abrupt change of the network behavior is reflected in a first order phase transition comparable to the melting of ice.

Improvements on the Hopfield Network

A number of features of the Hopfield model have been criticized since its publication in 1982. The most serious criticisms and the publications which circumvent some of them are listed.

1. The neural dynamics in Hopfield-type models is reduced to a two state variable which completely neglects the dynamics of membrane potentials.

2. The connections are chosen symmetrically in contradiction to the asymmetric information flow across a chemical synapse.

3. The network is completely connected.

4. The synaptic values w_{ik} are not limited.

5. A given neuron may excite some neurons and inhibit others, violating Dale's law which states that a neuron is either excitatory or inhibitory (for further discussion see Shepherd, 1979).

6. The associative properties break down abruptly when the network is overloaded. Psychological studies, however, point to a more gradual loss of memory with a high probability of remembering the recently stored information.

Some of the criticism relates to technical simplifications introduced by Hopfield, eg, the symmetry of connections, the complete connectivity of the network, and the unlimited dynamical range of synapses, and can be dropped without jeopardizing the associative abilities. Peretto (1984) and Toulouse and co-workers (1986) limited the synaptic values in their models to a finite range but treated the synaptic bounds in a different way. Peretto showed that the network was able to learn a finite number of patterns using absorbing boundaries and did not memorize any new pattern when all synapses stuck either to the lower or the upper synaptic bound. The storage capacity was exhausted. If one endows a network with reflecting boundaries for the synapses, the neural net will learn patterns until its storage capacity is exhausted. After that it starts to forget the earlier learned patterns and retains only the latest information stored in the network. Both mechanisms might play a role in the brain since the error rate in psychological experiments is low for the earliest and the latest learned patterns and increases for the patterns in between.

The condition of all-to-all symmetric connections has been dropped by a number of authors. Derrida and co-workers (1987) cut almost all synapses so that each neuron was connected to only a finite number of other neurons as the total number goes to infinity. Computer simulations and analytical calculations confirmed that such "strongly diluted" networks exhibit qualitatively the same associative properties as completely connected networks. Other models composed of excitatory and inhibitory neurons but without neurons of mixed synaptic polarity have been proposed by a number of authors and are reviewed in the monograph of Amit (1989).

The high firing rate problem of the Hopfield model sparked research activities in two different directions. Several models have been proposed that generalize the coding prescription of the Hopfield model and encode the patterns by a percentage q of 1 bits and a percentage of $(1 - q)$ of 0 bits. In the case of q being small ($q < 0.01$) the patterns are encoded sparsely, referred to in the literature as low spatial activity. A simple Hebb rule in the low spatial activity limit yields very high storage capacity (compared to the Hopfield model) as will be discussed in the section on Gardner networks. The sparsely coded networks, however, are still attractor networks which means that qN neurons are firing all the time after the network relaxes to the fixed point attractor. Three different proposals to solve the high temporal firing rate problem for spin-like neurons are documented in the literature

(Treves and Amit, 1989; Rubin and Sompolinski, 1989; Buhmann, 1989) and the last suggestion will be discussed below in connection with oscillatory associative nets.

To do justice to the Hopfield model it must be emphasized that despite a long list of unbiological features and its relatively low storage capacity (0.14 bits per synapse) it played an important role in the understanding and the quantitative analysis of noisy associative memories and can be regarded as the harmonic oscillator of attractor NNs.

Gardner Networks

Amit, Gutfreund, and Sompolinski (1985) calculated the number of patterns that can be embedded as fixed points of a sequential asynchronous dynamics in a Hopfield model with a connection matrix $w_{ik} = 1/N \sum_{\nu=1}^{p} \sigma_i^\nu \sigma_k^\nu$, thus evaluating the efficiency of the Hopfield network as an associative storage medium. The more general issue of the optimal storage capacity of a network of threshold neurons is addressed. This question was first studied by Gardner (1988) who developed a technique to systematically explore the space of interactions w_{ik} (Toulouse, 1989), now sometimes called *inverse statistical mechanics*.

The task is to embed a set of p random N-bit patterns $\{\sigma_i^\mu | i = 1, \ldots, N, \mu = 1, \ldots, p\}$ such that they are stable fixed points. On the average each pattern is composed of $(1 + m)/2$ 1's and $(1 - m)/2$ -1's, $-1 \leq m \leq 1$, with the individual bits randomly drawn from the probability distribution

$$P\{\sigma_i^\mu\} = \frac{1+m}{2} \delta(\sigma_i^\mu - 1) + \frac{1-m}{2} \delta(\sigma_i^\mu + 1) \quad (34)$$

The dynamics of the network at zero temperature is defined by the update rule

$$S_i(t + 1) = \text{sign}(h_i(t) - \theta_i) \quad (35)$$

with the local fields $h_i = \sum_{k=1}^{N} w_{ik} S_k$. The configuration $\{S_i\}$ is a fixed point of the dynamics (35) provided the local fields point in the same direction as the spins at each site i, ie, the quantity

$$R_i(\{S_i\}) = S_i (h_i\{S_i\} - \theta_i) > 0 \text{ for all } i \quad (36)$$

Storing p patterns σ^μ as stable fixed points essentially requires a search for a set of $N(N - 1)$ synaptic strengths w_{ik} that fulfill the fixed point condition (36) for σ^μ. The synaptic strengths are normalized to

$$\sum_{k \neq i}^{N} (w_{ik})^2 = N \quad (37)$$

Gardner formulated the task of storing p patterns in an associative memory as the problem of measuring the volume of the space of w_{ik} that embed the patterns as stable fixed points of the network dynamics, ie, that observe the conditions (36) under the constraint (37). When the number of patterns to be stored is increased (the network filling factor α) the conditions (36) get more restrictive and the volume of w_{ik}-space, which is compatible with the stability condition (36), shrinks. The quantity

$$\Pi_{\mu,i} \Theta(R_i\{\sigma^\mu\}) \quad (38)$$

is one if and only if all fixed point conditions are fulfilled, $\Theta(x) = \begin{cases} 1, x \geq 0 \\ 0, x < 0 \end{cases}$ being the Heaviside step function. The fractional volume of w_{ik}-space, which satisfies all conditions (36) under constraint (37) is measured by

$$V_T = \frac{\int \prod_{k \neq i} dw_{ik} \prod_{\mu,i} \Theta(R_i\{\sigma^\mu\}) \delta\left(\sum_{k \neq i}^{N} (w_{ik})^2 - N\right)}{\int \prod_{k \neq i} dw_{ik} \prod_i \delta\left(\sum_{k \neq i}^{N} (w_{ik})^2 - N\right)} \quad (39)$$

Note that the volume V_T depends on the particular choice of the pattern set σ_i^μ. We are, therefore, interested in the typical value of the volume V_T in the limit of very large neural nets ($N \to \infty$) which is given by

$$V = \exp(\langle \ln V_T \rangle) \quad (40)$$

where the average is taken over all possible combinations of p random patterns σ^μ.

Gardner calculated the quantity V_T using methods developed in the theory of disordered magnets. The main result of these calculations is the functional dependence of the maximal possible storage capacity in threshold NNs on the parameter m, ie, how $\alpha_c(m)$ varies if m is changed. Approximations of the critical storage capacity in the limit of unbiased patterns, ie, patterns with an equal percentage of 1's and -1's ($m = 0$), and in the case of sparse coding, ie, $m \to 1$, are particularly simple. For $m \to 0$, the critical capacity is

$$\alpha_c = 2(1 + 2 m^2/\pi) \quad (41)$$

The result $\alpha_c(0) = 2$ for the case of unbiased patterns ($m = 0$) was established by Cover (1965) using a different method. In the opposite case of sparse coding a divergence of α_c is observed as

$$\alpha_c \sim \frac{1}{-(1-m)ln(1-m)} \quad (42)$$

This divergence is not very surprising since the information content per pattern drops to zero if m approaches 1. The total information content of the NN stays finite and scales proportionally to the number of synapses.

The results derived by measuring the volume of w_{ik}-space say something about the existence of a network which can store p patterns. Gardner's method does not provide a particular network structure that actually stores the patterns. We will now search for solutions of $\{w_{ik}\}$ that observe the conditions (36) and the constraint (37). In the limit of sparse coding a simple storage prescription for matrix associative memories that yields the critical capacity (42) was discovered by Willshaw and coworkers (1969). A generalization of the Willshaw model to recurrent associative memories was independently discovered by Buhmann and co-workers (1989) and by Tsodyks and Feigelman (1988).

No simple formula for a set $\{w_{ik}\}$ compatible with the stability condition (36) is known for the case of unbiased patterns. We, therefore, have to search for an iterative algorithm which converges towards a desired set $\{w_{ik}\}$. A gradient descent algorithm which converges towards a set $\{w_{ik}\}$ if it exists is defined as follows: let $\{w_{ik}\}$ be an arbitrary set of synaptic weights with vanishing diagonal terms $w_{ii} = 0$. A mask is defined as

$$\varepsilon_i^\mu = \Theta\left(\kappa \sqrt{\sum_{k \neq i}(w_{ik})^2} - R_i\{\sigma^\mu\}\right) \quad (43)$$

which is one if the stability condition for neuron i and pattern μ is violated. The parameter κ has been introduced to strengthen the stability of neuron i. The case $\kappa = 0$ corresponds to the discussion above. If the synaptic weights are updated according to the rule

$$\Delta w_{ik} = \varepsilon^\mu i \sigma^\mu i \sigma^\mu i \quad (44)$$

the perceptron convergence theorem will guarantee that, in finite time, a set $\{w_{ik}\}$ will be found that allows us to store all p patterns.

OSCILLATORY ASSOCIATIVE MEMORIES

NNs have been studied in which predefined pattern states are to be implemented as fixed points in the network dynamics. A nonergodic flow from an initial state inside a basin of attraction to the closest attractor state yields associative recall of stored information. However, such a recall principle is not limited to networks with fixed point attractors. Theoretically, one could imagine that a NN settles down in disjoint regions with a limit cycle or even a chaotic flow. These regions can be identified as stored patterns even without a stationary response of the network. The olfactory cortex, with a dynamics that is strongly dominated by an inhibitory feedback loop between pyramidal cells and inhibitory interneurons, is a brain region where pronounced oscillations have been found. It is often regarded as a simple associative memory (Haberly and Bower, 1989), while Freeman and co-workers (1988) argue that it functions as an oscillatory associative memory. How might oscillatory activity enhance the associative abilities of the network compared to associative memories with fixed point attractors? The role of oscillations in associative recall (according to Freeman's view) is to provide unbiased access to the memory traces and to facilitate transition from one pattern to another. His olfactory models even show deterministic chaotic behavior, stimulating speculation on the possible role of chaos in the brain (Skarda and Freeman, 1987).

Baird (1986) has proposed an oscillatory associative memory that models the oscillatory response of olfactory cortex in a simplified fashion. The model comprises excitatory neurons with long-range connections and local inhibitory neurons that are only connected to nearby excitatory cells. The excitatory layer of neurons implements the associative recall dynamics with its mutual cooperation among cells belonging to the same assembly and its competition between cells that represent different patterns. Inhibitory cells are connected to their excitatory counterparts and serve as the inhibitory feedback element to stabilize a limit cycle in the neural activity. The specific neural dynamics suggested by Baird is described by the leaky integrator equations

$$\frac{dx_i}{dt} = -\tau x_i - h y_i + \sum_{j=1}^{N/2} w_{ij} \sigma(x_i) + b_i \quad (45)$$

$$\frac{dy_i}{dt} = -\tau y_i + g x_i \quad (46)$$

where $\sigma(x) = \tanh(x)$ or some other sigmoid squashing function symmetric about zero. Baird has shown that the network is capable of storing Fourier components and suggested that complex motor patterns might be memorized in neural structures with oscillatory response like the one in olfactory cortex. This hypothesis still has to be substantiated by experimental results from motor cortex.

A different starting point for the study of oscillatory NNs has been chosen by Buhmann (1989). The straightforward (naive) interpretation of the activity state $V_i = 1$ as one action potential in attractor NNs poses the problem of unphysiologically high temporal firing rates. Neurons in neocortex which participate in associative memory tasks normally fire 30–50 times per second and rarely exceed an activity level of 100 Hz (Abeles, 1982). In spinlike NN models the typical time constant that can be identified with the average update time of a Boolean neuron is equivalent to a refractory period which totals not more than 5 msec. Using the naive interpretation for a spike yields a firing rate of around 200 Hz and beyond. To decrease the firing rates into a physiologically reasonable range it is necessary to drop the requirement that information be stored in networks with fixed point dynamics. A neuron representing a 1 bit should assume an increased temporal firing rate but should not settle down into a state of permanent hyperactivity. A neuron response with an alternation between the $V_i = 1$ state and the $V_i = 0$ state with a higher probability for the resting state would yield the temporally low firing rates and would reconcile two state neural nets with the physiology of neocortex. A sequentially asynchronous network of excitatory two state neurons with long-range connections and a second layer of short-range inhibitory neurons that connect to neighboring excitatory as well as inhibitory neurons shows the desired firing behavior (Buhmann, 1989). The excitatory neurons provide the synaptic structure for information storage and form the well known Hebbian assemblies that are responsible for the basins of attractions in fixed point attractors. Inhibitory neurons play a different role and are not directly involved in information storage but in activity control. A possible advantage for neural systems with controlled activity levels might be the larger sensitivity to incoming stimuli and the expanded dynamic range for a neural response. It has been shown that the proposed network is able to recall and associatively correct stored information and to exhibit the observed low firing rates. The neurons tend to stay for one time step in the activity state $V_i = 1$ and then rest for several time steps in the resting state $V_i = 0$. A 1 bit is identified by an enhanced temporal firing rate rather than by a high instantaneous activity. Readout of information has to be spread over several time steps and cannot be achieved instantly as in attractor neural nets with a static activity pattern. In addition to the low firing rates, the network exhibits strong oscillatory activity after an initial relaxation dynamics to a localized region in phase space which represents the stored information. These oscillations, although quite different in their origin, parallel the oscillations in the network of Baird and can be used for labeling information as well.

Obviously, the time domain endows the network with an additional degree of freedom that is not available to fixed point attractor networks. In the present section our emphasis is on the use of oscillations in pattern recognition even when the patterns do not themselves possess temporal order. Some relevant material is reviewed in the section on complex sequence recognition. Time can be used to label and segment patterns in NNs that are sensitive to synchronous neural events. Wang and co-workers (1990) demonstrated that such an oscillatory NN is able to separate two simultaneously presented patterns on a microscopic time scale of milliseconds but to keep the information about both patterns on a psychological time scale of a fraction of a second. A mechanism like this might be responsible for the ability of rats to discriminate different odors in a mixture without suppressing all fragrances except one. The network settled down near a limit cycle representing one pattern and switched to another limit cycle after a brief period of time. Wang and co-workers (1990) used a spatially averaged version of the low activity network. The stochastic asynchronous dynamics of the low activity network was replaced by population equations for pools of excitatory and inhibitory neurons.

Appropriate choices of the ratio of the time constants of the excitatory and inhibitory components relates the oscillator time to a physiological time scale. A nonlinearity in the inhibitory response to excitation proved to be useful in making oscillatory behavior a more robust phenomenon in the network, so that in spite of changes in excitatory gain (with varying numbers of groups in a pattern) the qualitative character of the phase portrait of the oscillators is invariant. They also use delayed self-inhibition, which is important to generate intermittent bursting. In addition to the interaction between excitatory units x_i and inhibitory units y_i, an x_i receives time-dependent external input $I_i(t)$ from a sensory area or from other networks, and internal input $S_i(t)$ from other oscillators.

Let us now study how the oscillatory network performs the segmentation task. They store p sparsely coded, random N bit words $\xi^\nu = \{\xi_i^\nu\}_{i=1}^N$ with pattern index $\nu = 1, \ldots, p$. The probability that a bit equals 1 is a, ie, $P(\xi_i^\nu) = a\,\delta(\xi_i^\nu - 1) + (1-a)\delta(\xi_i^\nu)$ with typically $a < 0.2$. The synapses are chosen according to the Hebbian rule

$$w_{ik} = \frac{1}{aN} \sum_\nu (\xi_i^\nu - a)(\xi_k^\nu - a)$$

With that connectivity, oscillator i receives input $S_i(t) = \sum_{k \neq i} w_{ik} x_k(t)$ from other oscillators.

In a simulation study, 50 oscillators were used and eight patterns (each of eight active units) were stored in the memory. The first three patterns presented to the network had the form

$$\xi^1 = (1,1,1,1,1,1,1,0,0,0,0,0,0,0,0,0,0,1,0,\ldots,0)$$
$$\xi^2 = (0,0,0,0,0,0,1,1,1,1,1,1,1,0,0,0,0,1,0,\ldots,0)$$
$$\xi^3 = (1,0,0,0,0,0,0,0,0,0,0,1,1,1,1,1,1,1,0,\ldots,0).$$

with a 25% mutual overlap among these three patterns and bits $\xi_{19}^\nu = 1$ for $\nu = 1, 2, 3$.

With this choice of stored patterns they tested pattern recall and pattern completion after presentation of just one incomplete pattern, the fundamental capability of associative memory. The network restored the information missing from the fragment within one or two cycles. A more intriguing dynamical behavior is shown by the network if all three patterns ξ^1, ξ^2, ξ^3 or parts of them are presented simultaneously. In all simulations external input was time-independent, but similar results can be expected for time-dependent input as used in Li and Hopfield (1989). The result of a simulation is shown in Figure 20 where the input is a superposition of patterns ξ^1, ξ^2, ξ^3 with one bit missing in each pattern. In this figure only the first 19 oscillators are monitored; the others stay silent due to lack of input and mutual inhibition among oscillators representing different patterns. All three patterns are recognized, completed, and recalled by the network.

In addition to the capabilities of conventional associative memory the network is able to segment patterns in time. The assembly of oscillators representing a single input pattern oscillates in a phase-locked way for several cycles. This period is followed by a state of very low activity, during which another assembly takes a turn to oscillate. Switching between one pattern and another can be produced either by noise, by delayed self-inhibition (the case shown here), or by a modulation of external input. A mixture of all three is likely to be biologically relevant. For conceptual reasons, only a limited number of states can be represented in response to a static input. A superposition of too many (more than perhaps 10) input states leads to ambiguity and the system responds with an irregular oscillation pattern. The exact number of entities that can be represented simultaneously depends on details of implementation, but a reasonable estimate seems to be the 7 ± 2 often cited in the psychophysical literature as the number of objects that can be held in the human attention span.

TEMPORAL-PATTERN ENCODING IN NEURAL NETS

NNs to store, recognize, and reproduce a temporal sequence of input stimuli have been studied by a number of investigators. Early models include the outstar avalanche (Grossberg, 1969) and the wave model (Stanley and Kilmer, 1975) that can reproduce a sequence of patterns

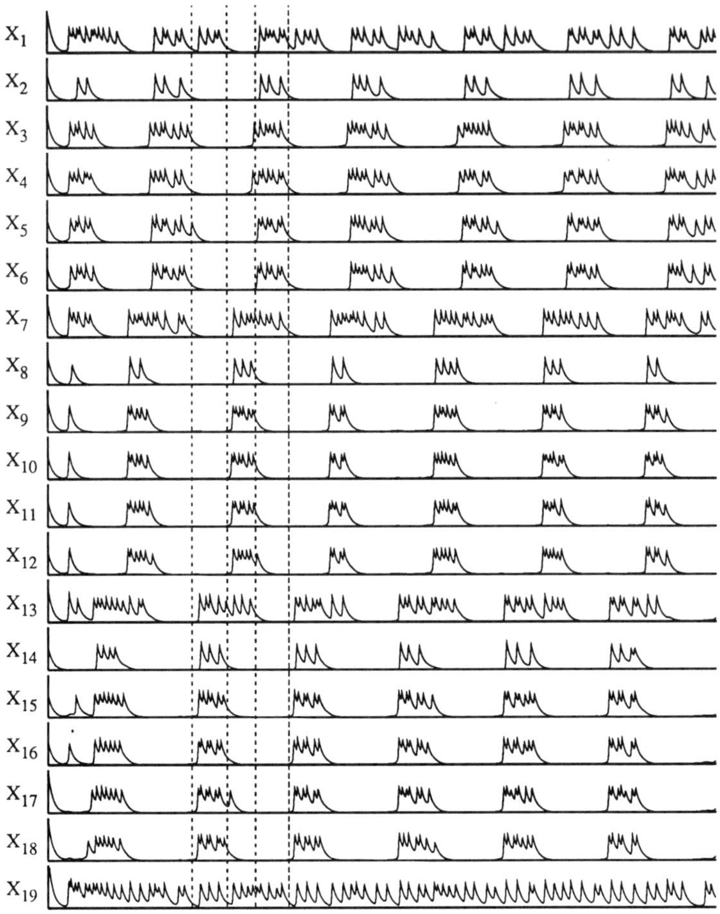

Figure 20. Performance of the first 19 oscillators (the others stay silent) of the oscillatory associative memory of Wang and co-workers (1990) when the input is a superposition of patterns ξ^1, ξ^2, ξ^3 with one bit missing in each pattern. All three patterns are recognized, completed, and recalled by the network.

based on learned associations between consecutive patterns. More recently, using synaptic triads each made up of three neurons as building blocks (high order synapses), Dehaene and co-workers (1987) proposed a layered NN, called the selection model, that can recognize temporal sequences. Kosko's (1988) bidirectional associative memory (qv) built from two neural fields can reproduce a sequence of patterns that alternates between the two fields.

Reproduction of a temporal sequence has also been explored using back propagation (Jordan, 1990; Elman, 1990; Doya and Yoshizawa, 1989). In the Jordan model and the Doya and Yoshizawa model, the basic idea is that the output layer associated to each component is fed back and blended with the input representing the next component, whereas in the Elman network, the hidden layer is fed back to influence the next pattern.

Storage of temporal sequences in the spinlike Hopfield network has been proposed recently by several authors (Amit, 1989). In this paradigm, each pattern is stable over some time period, at the end of which a sharp transition leading to the next pattern occurs due to stored transitions between consecutive patterns. Two different approaches to generating temporal sequences in the spinlike Hopfield network will be described, the delay synapse concept and the noise driven sequence recognizer, and then a different approach to complex sequence recognition will be studied.

Delay Synapse Networks

It was shown that spinlike associative memories exhibit exponentially many spurious minima composed of several patterns. If a network settles down into a pattern state and is pushed out of that fixed point attractor toward a second pattern, the structure of the configuration space may lead the network toward a superposition of three patterns instead of the second pattern. The activity of the network is spread out over different patterns and is no longer confined to individual pattern states. The recall of a sequence, therefore, breaks down. Sompolinsky and Kanter (1986) and, independently, Kleinfeld (1986) suggested an appealing solution to that spreading activation problem: they introduced two different types of synapses, one type with instantaneous response to stabilize the individual memory states and a second with a delayed response to trigger transitions between different pattern states. The excitation of neuron i, its local field, has the form

$$h_i(t + \delta t) = \sum_{\mu=1}^{p} \xi_i^\mu m^\mu(t) + \lambda \sum_{\mu=1}^{p} \xi_i^{\mu+1} m^\mu(t - \tau)$$

where $m^\mu(t)$ is the usual overlap between the network state and a pattern state. The network has stored random unbiased patterns (equal numbers of 1s and −1s). The first term stabilizes the individual patterns and endows the network with its associative abilities, ie, the ability to restore lost pattern information and to suppress noise. The second sum adds all the activity $m(t - \tau)$ delayed by τ. The combined effect of both terms drive the network out of pattern state μ into pattern state $\mu + 1$. Let us neglect all fluctuations ($p/N \ll 1$) to understand the mechanism of the second delay term in detail. At time $t = 0$ the network relaxed to pattern state μ coming from pattern $\mu - 1$. The overlap of the network with the different pattern states ideally assumes $m^\nu = \delta_{\nu\mu}$. The delayed activity $m^\nu(-\tau) = \delta_{\nu\mu-1}$ also favors the term ξ_i^μ which results in a total neuronal field

$$h_i(t + \delta t) = (1 + \lambda)\xi_i^\mu$$

At time $t = \tau$ the second term changes its form and projects strongly into the direction of the next pattern. The subsequent brief transient period will direct the network towards pattern state $\mu + 1$. A necessary condition to avoid the spread of activation between different patterns is the clear separation of the typical time scales for pattern transition and pattern recall, ie, $\tau \gg 1$.

This concept of storing temporal patterns in NNs with delayed synapses stimulated a lot of research among physicists since it combined the ideas of static recall with the time domain and since delay networks can be analyzed with statistical mechanics methods. Learning of time sequences using a form of a delayed Hebbian rule has been studied extensively by Herz and co-workers (1989). However, there are some drawbacks if one relies on this concept of temporal storage: (*1*) the temporal patterns are stored in a rigid way. There does not exist a simple mechanism to change the length of a sequence and the duration of individual patterns. (*2*) Individual synapses in vertebrates do not show the required long delays. Why should the brain distribute a melody all over the brain simply to acquire the necessary delay times for axonal propagation? (*3*) The scheme cannot handle complex sequences with patterns that are repeated several times.

Noise-Driven Sequence Recognizer

A different strategy for temporal recall of sequences has been suggested by Buhmann and Schulten (1987) that differs in two essential points from delay synapse networks: (*1*) The patterns stored in the network are coded in a sparse format, ie, with few 1's and many 0's. This destabilizes most of the spurious states that plagued Hopfield's preliminary simulations of sequence recall. (*2*) The transitions between succeeding states are triggered by fluctuations, ie, the computational temperature of the network. Special projections from pattern μ to pattern $\mu + 1$ guide the transition process that is driven by stochastic fluctuations. The authors have demonstrated that sequence recall is reliable and robust in that scheme. Furthermore, the noise level provides a control parameter to switch between static recall of an individual pattern in the sequence and the recall of the whole sequence. If a pattern sequence has to be recalled at different speeds, a modulation of the noise level in the network enables the network to change a pattern state at any time, which is a big advantage over the time delay model.

Complex Sequence Recognition

Complex sequences are those in which a letter occurs more than once, as in ABACD. Storage and retrieval of complex sequences is difficult since a letter need not provide a unique context for the next letter. The number of prior letters required to disambiguate the choice of each succeeding letter is referred to as the *degree* of the sequence. Wang and Arbib (1990) propose a mechanism for learning complex temporal sequences based on modeling short-term memory (STM) by units comprising recurrent excitatory connections between two local neuron populations. Each population is represented by a single quantity corresponding to local field potential. The activity induced by an input signal to a unit oscillates with damping, thus decaying over time. Using Hebbian learning at each synapse and a normalization rule among all synapses to a unit, the NNs with this model of STM are able to learn complex temporal sequences, recognize these sequences with tolerance to certain distortions in form, and reproduce them. What distinguishes this model from others are two basic hypotheses embodied in the model: (*1*) There is a common mechanism to process both complex sequences and simple sequences; and (*2*) reproduction of a component in a sequence is based on recognition of the context of the component.

Since STM is modeled by decay, it has a fixed temporal course, which makes the previous model unable to handle the time-warp problem. The time-warp problem poses different requirements for sequence recognition and reproduction. For sequence recognition, it is desirable for a network to recognize a time-warped sequence, whereas for reproduction a network should reproduce a sequence with the same temporal course as the learned sequence. In the previous model, all context recognizers use the same degree, which must not be less than the degree of an entire sequence to be recalled. The requirement is replaced in Wang and Arbib (1991) by a dynamic tuning mechanism whereby each recognizer learns during training its necessary degree for unambiguously producing the next symbol. They also propose a mechanism for hierarchical sequence recognition, similar to human information chunking. This mechanism seems both natural and necessary for processing long sequences, like a paragraph of sentences, a piece of music, and so forth.

In the back propagation approach to sequence learning (Jordan, 1990; Elman, 1990; Doya and Yoshizawa, 1989), when a state is fed back either from the output layer or the hidden layer, some history is preserved, and it was suggested that this feedback information be used for the disambiguation required in the complex sequence situation. Jordan uses the state, coded as temporal summation of a number of previous components in the sequence, as input to generate the next component. Since the entire previous subsequence is coded by a single state, different subsequences may not be uniquely recorded. In Wang and Arbib (1991), however, a previous history is distributed among different units, each of which maintains its own activation over a variable amount of time, depending on further inputs to the STM model.

SELF-ORGANIZATION OF FEATURE MAPS

It is known that fibers from the retina reach the tectum and there form an orderly, retinotopic map. Sperry (1944) showed that this orderly projection from retina to tectum would, at least in the frog, re-establish itself after section of the optic tract, even after rotation of the eyeball. After such rotation, nerve fibers growing out from the retina again find the "original" tectal locus, not the locus that corresponds to their new receptive field in the visual world, just as if the optic tract had not been severed. And this mapping, although it is no longer functional for the animal, is resistant to experience. (By contrast, a human can learn to adapt to the initially disorienting effects of wearing inverting prisms.) No matter how many times it snaps "up" at a worm that is really "down," the frog with the rotated eyeball will snap at the locus indicated by the original retinal coordinates, rather than that indicated by the new position of the eye in the orbit. This suggests that each fiber bears with it a unique "address" and goes directly to the target point on the tectum. However, experiments in the 1960s showed that if half a retina were allowed to innervate a tectum, then the map would expand to cover the whole tectum; while if a whole retina innervated half a tectum, then the map would be compressed. In other words, the fibers had in some sense to "sort out" their relative position in using available space, rather than simply going for a prespecified target.

There are now a number of models that explain this phenomenon not in terms of an overall global organization principle, but rather by local interactions of a few fibers and the portion of tectum upon which they find themselves, with global information restricted to the role of providing at most a "rough sketch." These models include the arrow model of Hope, Hammond, and Gaze (1976), the "marker" model of von der Malsburg and Willshaw (1977), and the branch-arrow marker model of Overton and Arbib (1982).

Kohonen (1982) offered a simplified version of this theory that was not restricted to topographical maps, but was applied to self-organization of maps of arbitrary features or attributes. His adaptive lookup tables find widespread applications whenever a nonlinear mapping has to be learned and an explicit formula for the map is hard to find. Among the successful applications are eye-hand coordination, learning of a lookup table for motor commands, and prediction of nonlinear time series (Martinetz and coworkers, 1990).

Kohonen's model comprises a feature space X with events $x_i \in X$ and a neuron space Γ with neurons $\rho \in \Gamma$. Greek symbols are used as indices (coordinates) in neuron space and roman letters are used as indices (coordinates) in feature space. The two spaces do not necessarily have the same dimension, ie, a two-dimensional neural layer might be mapped to a higher dimensional feature space. Each neuron ρ is characterized by a sensitivity vector $w(\rho)$, its receptive field. $w(\rho)$ defines that part in feature space for which neuron ρ is most sensitive. The excitation of a neuron ρ after stimulus x has been presented is postulated to be proportional to the norm of the difference vector $\|x - w(\rho)\|$. The goal of self-organization is to organize the set of neurons such that neighboring neurons in Γ are receptive to neighboring areas in feature space. An adaptive, unsupervised algorithm for that task is highly desirable since the stimuli are usually restricted to a low dimensional subspace of Γ and a complete coverage of the feature space is not feasible and would waste neuronal hardware. The essential ingredients of the self-organizing algorithm are:

1. Present a stimulus $x_i \in X$.
2. Determine that neuron ρ^* which is most sensitive to the presented stimulus x_i.
3. Update the sensitivity vectors of all neurons according to the update rule

$$\Delta w(\rho) = \varepsilon \, h(\rho - \rho^*(x))(x_i - w(\rho)) \quad (45)$$

4. Present the next stimulus $x_{i+1} \in X$ and iterate the update procedure.

The neighborhood function in neuron space is defined as

$$h(\rho - \rho^*(x)) = \exp\left(-\frac{(\rho - \rho^*(x))^2}{2\sigma^2}\right)$$

The neuron index ρ is usually two-dimensional to stress the analogy to NNs explicitly. It could, however, have another dimensionality, eg, one-dimensional neuron chains have been successfully employed in phoneme classification. The parameter ε controls the influence of stimulus x_i on the sensitivity vector $w(\rho)$. Large ε indicates fast learning which, unfortunately, also implies fast forgetting. At the end of the self-organization process the information should be preserved from the previously seen stimuli and, therefore, a small value for ε should be chosen. A widely used procedure to decrease ε is

$$\varepsilon(i) = \varepsilon_{\text{init}} \left(\frac{\varepsilon_{\text{init}}}{\varepsilon_{\text{final}}}\right)^{i/i_{\max}}. \quad (46)$$

The width of the neighborhood function σ is changed in the same way, ie,

$$\sigma(i) = \sigma_{\text{init}} \left(\frac{\sigma_{\text{init}}}{\sigma_{\text{final}}}\right)^{i/i_{\max}}. \quad (47)$$

To obtain good self-organization results σ_{init} should be half of the neuron population, eg, $N/2$ for a neural chain. At the end of the simulation the neurons are frozen at their actual positions choosing $\sigma_{\text{final}} = 1$.

The self-organization process can be intuitively understood if the unfolding of a one-dimensional chain in a two-dimensional stripe is studied. For a small width of the stripe the chain relaxes to the symmetric position along the midline. When the width of the stripe is increased a

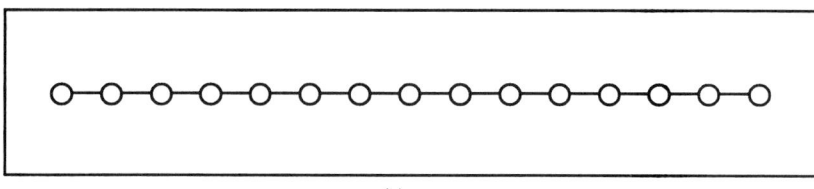

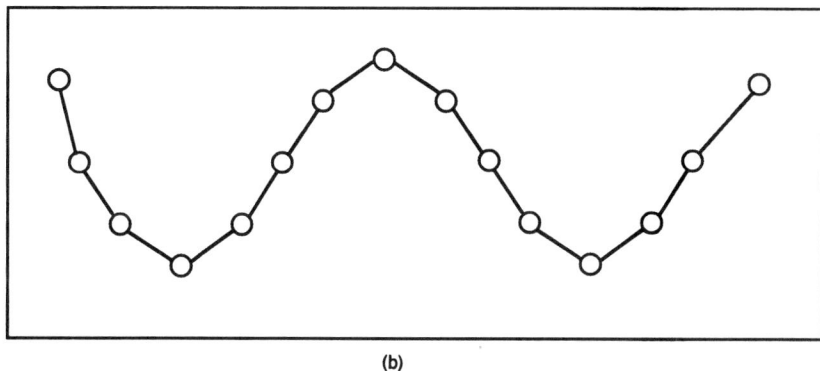

Figure 21. A neuron chain covers a rectangular input space with homogeneous data density. (a) The stretched chain is stable; (b) if the width of the input space exceeds a critical value the chain assumes a wavelike form to improve coverage of the input space.

critical width is passed above which the elongated chain is unstable to an oscillatory folding. The folded chain covers the area better than the stretched chain (Fig. 21). The critical stripe width and the type of solution above the transition width can be calculated using the theory of Markov processes (Ritter, 1989). An exhaustive discussion of self-organizing maps can be found in the monograph of Ritter and co-workers (1991).

THE DYNAMIC LINK ARCHITECTURE

To close this article, our study of synaptic plasticity goes back to the question of object recognition, by introducing the dynamic link architecture that uses connectivity as part of the NN state for real-time processing. Hebb's (1949) idea was to think of each neuron as an elementary symbol (though it could represent something quite complex), and then to have activity in an assembly of neurons constitute a higher level symbol. A major problem pointed out by Rosenblatt (1962) may be exemplified by exploring the hypothesis that the brain has a separate neuron or assembly for each of the four features, A, B, green, and red, and that a red A is represented by activating the A neuron and the red neuron, etc. But then a red A and a green B together activate all four neurons, the same neural encoding as for a green A with a red B. The classic solution to this ambiguity would be to introduce new neurons. One neuron would be permanently connected, or through learning has become permanently connected, to the red cell and the A cell so that it only fires when there is a red A; though even this would require some subsidiary wiring to ensure that the "red" and the "A" are at the same locus in the image. On this approach, every more and more complex situation would require a higher and higher level neuron that lights up for that combination of features in some location. If feature detectors are added for all possible relationships, the system will break down due to an exponential amount of feature detectors required.

von der Malsburg (1981) offered a new solution—to design NNs that can establish *dynamic links* between the A representation and the red representation to *transiently* couple A and red, and similarly to couple green and B when required. Psychologists have collected relevant data. If one flashes a visual pattern to a subject very quickly, such as the red A and the green B, the subject may recall the shapes and the colors but will not remember which shape was red, and which green. It appears that the brain does not have time to integrate the information in each "syntactic pair." The integration seems to require a form of selective attention, one needs time to pay attention to the various features of a pattern to make the necessary linkage. By contrast, if more and more complex concepts were encoded by a hierarchical set of neurons, it would take just a few milliseconds to trigger the next level of neurons.

This ability to dynamically link what is known in new ways allows us to make sense of a world that is continually changing. But how are the links formed in brains? von der Malsburg suggests that links will be formed between cells with similar temporal signatures. This is still far from proved but it provides a solution to the binding problem that is compatible with neural hardware, ie, with firing neurons. Data by people like Abeles (1982), Gray and co-workers (1989), and Opticon and Richmond (1987) show that there is much more to be learned about time patterns in the brain, but von der Malsburg's theory may work just as well with more general types of correlations serving to strengthen links whether there is a time signature to the correlation or not. In fact, the example given below for face recognition will involve correlations that do not have a temporal pattern underneath them.

The learning of new objects in the dynamic link architecture is handled as in conventional neural pattern recognition systems, eg, associative memories or multilayer perceptrons. A new object presented to the system triggers a learning mode in which a labeled graph is created in the memory area of the brain. The edges in that graph correspond to irreversibly strengthened or weakened synapses between activated neurons that represent the vertices. A sequential attention mechanism prevents a complete connectivity between all nodes belonging to the graph but strongly favors the growth of neighboring connections. The new graph might be embedded in already existing graphs.

How these concepts are exemplified in a face recognition system (Buhmann and co-workers, 1989a, 1990) will be shown. Consider recognizing the faces in an audience to which one has given several lectures. At a given lecture, some people will be sitting in the same places as before, some at different places, but what is clear is that as one looks around, each face stimulates a different part of the retina at different times. There is something in the brain that represents the new faces one has learned, but there is no "permanent hard-wired" link from every part of the retina that a given face could stimulate to the specific neurons in the brain that encode the long-term memory of a particular face. How do we connect a patch of retinal activity to an appropriate schema? A conventional AI approach would use explicit pointers to link schema instances down to regions in the output of low level processing and up to the permanently stored schemas. The new question here is "what could be a neural way of making these pointers–links?" The hypothesis is that visual recognition involves a short-term increase of synaptic strength between a patch of low level visual activity and the NN in the inferotemporal cortex that encodes the schema for recognizing the appropriate object or person. A model of direct linkages is presented even though there are many intermediate stages and many different linkages in the real brain.

The visual input is encoded as a graph of features. Edges connect nearby features so that there are not only features for eyes, nose, and hair but also the spatial relationship between them as encoded by a graph of connections. This is a flexible network rather than one of rigid geometric relationship because as the head turns, or the viewpoint moves further or closer, roughly the same features can be seen but the Euclidean relation between them changes. The memory contains a graph encoding a view of the face, with similar features in similar spatial relations. But, of course, there will be many other graphs representing other faces, other objects, and so the problem is to link the current visual inputs to just the right graph. The general idea is this: the process starts by building up connections from a peripheral feature to all the central features with which it is correlated, but those connections are strengthened if neighbors are also correlated. The result is a relaxation procedure, a pattern of self-organization whereby connections will only be stabilized if neighbors can make similar connections, whereas their neighbors can only be stabilized if their further neighbors can make stable connections, and so on, eventually yielding a stable pattern of connectivity from the periphery to the central graph that makes the best match.

What local features are suitable for this process and biologically feasible? Hubel and Wiesel (1962, 1977) found that, for each place on the retina, corresponding cells in the visual cortex of cats and monkeys encode detection of edges of different orientation. Work by psychophysicists established that there exist not only edge detectors but also bar detectors tuned for the width of the bar—the human visual system has "channels" tuned for different spatial frequencies. Daugman (1985) thus modeled the Hubel-Wiesel feature detectors not as responding to a single edge, but rather by using Gabor functions. Each function is like a sine-wave grating, with a given period and orientation, but with the strength of the mask falling off from the center as a Gaussian function of distance, ie,

$$\varphi_k(x) = n_{k,\sigma} \exp\left(-\frac{k^2 x^2}{2\sigma^2}\right) \exp(ikx) \quad (48)$$

A self-similar family of these functions is generated by dilation, rotation, and translation. The wavelength k is modified in half octaves, ie, $|k| = 2\pi/N\,(\sqrt{2})^\nu$, $\nu \in \{7, \ldots, 12\}$. The wave vector points in different directions, ie, $k = |k|\,(\cos\phi, \sin\phi)$ with $\phi = \tau\mu/8$, $\mu \in \{0, \ldots, 7\}$. The parameter $\sigma \approx 2\pi$ controls the relative width of the Gaussian envelope function compared to the wavelength of the oscillation. The $n_{k,\sigma}$ are normalization constants. $n_{k,\sigma} = 1$ is chosen to account for the decay of spectral power in natural images with increasing frequency. Fields (1987) discovered that the power spectrum scales like $1/k^2$, which is compensated by an increase of the filters in size proportional to k^2, resulting in a load balancing of the neural hardware.

The feature that is associated with a point x_0 of the image is a whole vector ($\mathbf{W}I\,(\cdot, x_0)$) of coefficients

$$(\mathbf{W}I)(k, x_0) = \int \varphi_k(x_0 - x)\,I(x)\,d^2x \quad (49)$$

showing how well Gabor functions for different spatial frequencies and different orientations correlate with the image as centered at that point. The different coefficients are indexed by the wave vector k. To avoid unnecessary local minima the coefficients that are actually used for matching are $J = |(\mathbf{W}I)|$ the magnitudes of the Gabor convolution (49). This vector is called a *Gabor jet* resembling the vector of derivatives given by Taylor's theorem.

If an image is reconstructed from the information extracted by the family of functions (48), what is achieved is not the complete image but rather a very informative description of the neighborhood of the given point x_o in the image. The reconstructions from Gabor jets centered at the eye and nose show a distinctive signature for different parts of the face. An "intelligent" system might use criteria to locate the eyes, nose, mouth, and so on, and quite economically, with just four or five jets, characterize each face distinctively. However, the study illustrated in Figure 22 just placed a rectangular grid over the face, and formed the Gabor jet for each point of this grid. This graph was then stored. If a new face is presented, dynamic linkage will find points with Gabor jets that can be matched with the Gabor jets in the stored image in a neighborhood-respecting way. The same face in a shifted viewing direc-

Figure 22. (a) A typical face out of a gallery of 65 faces. The grid and 45 feature vectors are stored per face. The unknown face (b) was compared with the gallery yielding prototype (a) as the best match. Topologically correct positions are found for nodes near the eyes and nose. The simulation (using the techniques of Buhmann and co-workers, 1989) clearly demonstrates distortion invariance due to facial expressions or to perspective changes.

tion (in plane rotation) will still yield a good match with the stored graph. A cost function **H** is optimized for link variables to find good correspondences between a stored graph and points in the new image introducing only minimal distortion of the spatial relationships of the nodes.

$$\mathbf{H}(x_i) = \frac{\lambda}{2} \sum_{\langle i,j \rangle} (\Delta x^I_{ij} - \Delta x^O_{ij})^2 - \sum_{i \in V} S(J^I(x_i), J^O_i) \quad (50)$$

with $\Delta x_{ij} = x_i - x_j$. Upper indices I and O refer to the image and to the stored object, respectively. $\langle i,j \rangle$ restricts summation to neighboring nodes. The first term in (50) evaluates the quality of local topology preservation. Deviations in difference vectors between two neighbouring nodes in I from those in O cause a cost penalty and thereby decrease the likelihood for the solution to be accepted. The second term measures the quality of a single match of jet $J^I(x_i)$ to J^O_i, $S(J_1, J_2) = J_1 J_2 / |J_1| |J_2|$.

In general, there will be other faces stored in memory and perhaps the input will be matched with other faces as well, but when the process of dynamic linkage is finished, one can measure the squared difference between the Gabor jets of the current image and the corresponding points in a candidate match. In pilot studies, a given face in different orientations gets a better match than two different faces seen from the same orientation.

The dynamic link architecture currently requires a different circuit to store each face. The algorithm makes connections from the image to the circuit that stores the face most similar to the present input. But does the brain use such separated storage, or does it distribute many faces over the same neural circuit, so that linkage is not with a specific circuit but perhaps a circuit in a particular state? Dynamical system theory studies resonances that depend on eigenvalues so that a circuit can behave in different ways depending on which mode of behavior is amplified. A future challenge, then, is to understand how many graphs might be stored in one circuit and then selectively called out.

This work does not yet make contact with current data on the role of cells in inferotemporal cortex for face recognition, nor does it make contact with the clinical data on prosopagnosia, data on how brain damage can affect the ability to recognize faces. But it does show us how a basic process of linkage between different parts of the visual system could take place if the notion of the neuron was extended from synapses that can only change slowly, to mediate long-term memory, to synapses that can also change rapidly. The formulation of the graph matching procedure is quite algorithmic in style but preserves some important ingredients of neural computation, eg, massive parallelism, some features of self-organization and adaptability. An important challenge to further research is the observation that in recognition of a complex scene several instances of the same schema may be "active" at the same time and that, to bring context into play, visual perception requires schema interaction as well as the activation of single schemas.

SUGGESTIONS FOR FURTHER READING

Despite the length of this article, it is still only a partial view of the burgeoning field of NNs, with the selection influenced in great part by our desire to emphasize nonadaptive as well as adaptive NNs, with special attention to approaches based on dynamical systems and statistical mechanics. For nonadaptive networks, optimization, winner-take-all networks, and low level vision have been stressed, and the importance of oscillations for both motor control and perception have been noted. This last point was continued in the analysis of learning and self-organization when the study of associative memories with fixed point attractors (with special attention to the statistical mechanics of Hopfield and related networks) was complemented with a study of oscillatory associative memories. The second part of the article also reviewed Hebbian plasticity, hill-climbing, and developments in learning with a teacher from the simple Perceptron to back propagation and the statistical mechanics of learning. Temporal-pattern encoding in neural nets, self-organization of feature maps, and the dynamic link architecture were also observed.

New books on NNs are published on at least a monthly basis (in 1990–1991), and so we close with a small sample to orient the reader. Perhaps the book that comes closest in scope to the present article, and is thus recommended as a first choice for continuing the study which it introduces, is that by Hertz, Krogh, and Palmer (1991). Amit (1989) takes the statistical mechanics of NNs even further, while Sompolinsky (1988) and Toulouse (1989) offer brief summaries of the subject. Arbib (1987) provides a historical perspective and places NNs in the perspective of theory of computation (finite automata, Turing machines, self-reproducing automata, and Gödel's incompleteness theorem), while his 1989 work looks at NNs and schemas for vision, action, and memory in the context of both brain theory and AI.

Anderson and Rosenfeld (1988) provide a valuable collection of classic papers in the field. Grossberg (1988) contains a number of influential papers by Grossberg and his colleagues. McClelland and Rumelhart (1986) provides a by now classic collection of papers in which the networks are inspired more by issues in distributed AI, such as constraint-satisfaction networks and by issues in cognitive psychology, than by neurophysiology. Such topics are treated in a number of places in this Encyclopedia.

Our emphasis has been on the generic properties of different classes of NNs rather than on the attempt to constrain such networks to explain the biological data on specific brain regions. One long-standing effort in the latter direction has been *Rana computatrix,* a set of models of the neural architectures and functions that underlie visually guided behavior in frogs and toads. Arrays of leaky integrator neurons provide the style of neural modeling most used in *Rana c.* to date, with the NNs "situated" using the methodology of schema theory, which integrates perception and action by decomposing an overall behavior into the interaction of functional, neurally explicable schemas. *Rana c.* includes models for depth perception, detour behavior, facilitation, pattern recognition, approach and avoidance, and habituation (Arbib and Ewert, 1991). Readers wishing to learn more of the biology of NNs may turn to Kandel and Schwartz (1985) or to Kuffler, Nichols, and Martin (1984) for the actual neurophysiology, and to Koch and Segev (1989), and McGregor (1987) for compendia of biologically-based neural models.

Finally, just two of the excellent symposium volumes that bring together workers in neuroscience with ANN researchers are mentioned: Schwartz (1990) and Zornetzer, Davis, and Lau (1990). Readers wishing to pursue the subject even further may turn not only to the references cited below but also to current research published in such journals as *Biological Cybernetics, IEEE Transactions on Neural Networks, Neural Computation, Networks,* and *Neural Networks.*

BIBLIOGRAPHY

M. Abeles, *Local Cortical Circuits,* Springer-Verlag, New York, 1982.

R. H. Abraham and C. D. Shaw, *Dynamics—The Geometry of Behavior: Part 2: Chaotic Behavior,* Ariel Press, Santa Cruz, Calif., 1983.

S. Amari, "Competitive and Cooperative Aspects of Dynamics of Neural Excitation and Self-Organization," in S. Amari and M. A. Arbib, eds., *Competition and Cooperation in Neural Nets,* Lecture Notes in Biomathematics 45, Springer-Verlag, New York, 1982, pp. 1–70.

S. Amari and M. A. Arbib, "Competition and Cooperation in Neural Nets," in J. Metzler, ed., *Systems Neuroscience,* Academic Press, Inc., New York, 1977, pp. 119–165.

D. J. Amit, *Models of Brain Function: The World of Attractor Neural Networks,* Cambridge University Press, Cambridge, 1989.

D. J. Amit, H. Gutfreund, and H. Sompolinsky, "Storing Infinite Number of Patterns in a Spin-Glass Model of Neural Networks," *Phys. Rev. Lett.* **55,** 1530–1533 (1985).

T. J. Anastasio and D. A. Robinson, "Distributed Parallel Processing in the Vestibulo-Oculomotor System," *Neural Comput.* **1,** 230–241 (1989).

J. A. Anderson and E. Rosenfeld, eds., *Neurocomputing: Foundations of Research,* MIT Press, Cambridge, Mass., 1988.

J. A. Anderson, J. W. Silverstein, S. A. Ritz, and R. S. Jones, "Distinctive Features, Categorical Perception, and Probability Learning: Some Applications of a Neural Model," *Psychol. Rev.* **84,** 413–451 (1977).

M. A. Arbib, "Visuomotor Coordination: From Neural Nets to Schema Theory," *Cogn. Brain Theory* **4,** 23–39 (1981).

M. A. Arbib, *Brains, Machines, and Mathematics,* 2nd ed., Springer-Verlag, New York, 1987.

M. A. Arbib, *The Metaphorical Brain 2: Neural Networks and Beyond,* Wiley-Interscience, New York, 1989.

M. A. Arbib, "Schemas and Neural Networks for Sixth Generation Computing," *J. Parallel Distribut. Comput.* **6,** 185–216 (1989a).

M. A. Arbib and J.-P. Ewert, eds., *Visual Structures and Integrated Functions,* Research Notes in Neural Computing, Springer-Verlag, New York, 1991.

F. Attneave, "Informational Aspects of Visual Perception," *Psych. Rev.* **61,** 183–193 (1954).

B. Baird, "Nonlinear Dynamics of Pattern Formation and Pattern Recognition in the Rabbit Olfactory Bulb, *Physica D* **22,** 150–175 (1986).

H. B. Barlow, "Sensory Mechanisms, the Reduction of Redundancy, and Intelligence," *Symp. on Mechanization of Thought Processes,* Her Majesty's Stationery Office, London, 1959, pp. 535–539.

A. G. Barto and R. S. Sutton, "Landmark Learning: An Illustration of Associative Search," *Biol. Cybern.* **42,** 1–8 (1981).

A. E. Bryson and Y.-C. Ho, *Applied Optimal Control,* Revised Printing, 1975, Hemisphere, New York, 1969.

J. Buhmann, "Oscillations and Low Firing Rates in Associative Memory Neural Networks," *Phys. Rev. A* **40,** 4145–4148 (1989).

J. Buhmann and K. Schulten, "Noise-Driven Temporal Association in Neural Networks," *Europhys. Lett.* **4**, 1205–1209 (1987).

J. Buhmann, R. Divko, and K. Schulten, "Associative Memory with High Information Content," *Phys. Rev. A* **39**, 2689–2692 (1989).

J. Buhmann, M. Lades, and C. von der Malsburg, "Size and Distortion Invariant Object Recognition by Hierarchical Graph Matching," *IJCNN International Conference on Neural Networks*, Vol. II, San Diego, Calif., 1990, pp. 411–416.

J. Buhmann, J. Lange, and C. von der Malsburg, "Distortion Invariant Object Recognition by Matching Hierarchically Labeled Graphs," *IJCNN International Conference on Neural Networks*, Vol. I, Washington, 1989a, pp. 155–159.

A. H. Cohen, S. Rossignol, and S. Grillner, eds., *Neural Control of Rhythmic Movements in Vertebrates*, Wiley-Interscience, New York, 1988.

T. M. Cover, "Geometrical and Statistical Properties of Systems of Linear Inequalities with Applications in Pattern Recognition," *IEEE Trans. Electronic Computers* **EC-14**, 326–334 (1965).

B. G. Cragg and H. N. V. Temperley, "The Organization of Neurones: A Cooperative Analogy," *EEG Clin. Neurophysiol.* **6**, 85–92 (1954).

J. Daugman, "Uncertainty Relation for Resolution in Space, Spatial Frequency, and Orientation Optimized by Two-Dimensional Visual Cortical Filters," *J. Opt. Soc. America A* **2**, 1160–1169 (1985).

T. Dahaene, J.-P. Changeux, and J. P. Nadal, "Neural Networks that Learn Temporal Sequences by Selection," *Proc. Natl. Acad. Sci. USA* **84**, 2727–2731 (1987).

B. Derrida, E. Gardner, and A. Zippelius, "An Exactly Soluble Asymmetric Neural Network Model," *Europhys. Lett.* **4**, 167–173 (1987).

P. Dev, "Perception of Depth Surfaces in Random-Dot Stereograms: A Neural Model," *Int. J. Man-Mach. Stud.* **7**, 511–528 (1975).

R. L. Didday, "A Model of Visuomotor Mechanisms in the Frog Optic Tectum," *Math. Biosci.* **30**, 169–180 (1976).

K. Doya and S. Yoshizawa, "Adaptive Neural Oscillator Using Continuous-Time Back-Propagation Learning," *Neural Networks* **2**, 375–385 (1989).

R. Durbin and D. Willshaw, "An Analogue Approach to the Travelling Salesman Problem Using an Elastic Net Method," *Nature* **326**, 689–691 (1987).

G. M. Edelman, *Neural Darwinism: The Theory of Neuronal Group Selection*, Basic Books, New York, 1987.

J. L. Elman, "Finding Structure in Time," *Cog. Sci.* **14**, 179–211 (1990).

G. B. Ermentrout, "Synchronization in a Pool of Mutually Coupled Oscillators with Random Frequencies," *J. Math. Biol.* **22**, 1–9 (1985).

D. Fields, "Relations between the Statistics of Natural Images and the Response Properties of Cortical Cells," *J. Opt. Soc. America A* **4**, 2379–2394 (1987).

W. J. Freeman, Y. Yao, and B. Burke, "Central Pattern Generating and Recognizing in Olfactory Bulb: A Correlation Learning Rule," *Neural Networks* **1**, 277–288 (1988).

Y. Fregnac and M. Imbert, "Development of Neuronal Selectivity in Primary Visual Cortex in Cat," *Physiol. Rev.* **64**, 325–434 (1984).

A. F. Fuchs, C. R. S. Kaneko, and C. A. Scudder, "Brainstem Control of Saccadic Eye Movements," *Ann. Rev. Neurosci.* **8**, 307–337 (1985).

E. Gardner, "The Space of Interactions in Neural Network Models," *J. Physics A* **21**, 257–270 (1988).

E. Gardner and B. Derrida, "Optimal Storage Properties of Neural Network Models," *J. Physics A* **21**, 271–284 (1988).

S. Geman and D. Geman, "Stochastic Relaxation, Gibbs Distributions, and the Bayesian Restoration of Images, *IEEE Trans. Pattern Anal. Mach. Intell.* **6**, 721–741 (1984).

C. D. Gilbert and T. N. Wiesel, "Clustered Intrinsic Connections in Cat Visual Cortex," *J. Neuroscience* **3**, 1116–1133 (1983).

J. Gleick, *Chaos: Making a New Science*, Viking, New York, 1987.

C. M. Gray, P. König, A. K. Engel, and W. Singer, "Oscillatory Responses in Cat Visual Cortex Exhibit Intercolumnar Synchronization which Reflects Global Stimulus Properties," *Nature* **338**, 334–337 (1989).

S. Grossberg, "Nonlinear Difference-Differential Equations in Prediction and Learning Theory," *Proc. Nat. Acad. Sci. USA* **58**, 1329–1334 (1967).

S. Grossberg, "Some Networks that Can Learn, Remember, and Reproduce Any Number of Complicated Space-Time Patterns, I," *J. Math. Mechan.* **19**, 53–91 (1969).

S. Grossberg, ed., *Neural Networks and Natural Intelligence*, MIT Press, Cambridge, Mass., 1988.

L. B. Haberly and J. M. Bower, "Olfactory Cortex: Model Circuit for Study of Associative Memory?" *Trends in Neurosciences* **12**, 258–264 (1989).

D. O. Hebb, *The Organization of Behavior*, John Wiley & Sons, Inc., New York, 1949.

H.-G. Heinzel and A. I. Selverston, "Gastric Mill Activity in the Lobster, III, Effects of Proctolin on the Isolated Central Pattern Generator," *J. Neurophysiol.* **59**, 566–585 (1988).

J. Hertz, A. Krogh, and R. G. Palmer, *Introduction to the Theory of Neural Computation*, Santa Fe Institute Studies in the Sciences of Complexity, Addison-Wesley Publishing Co., Inc., Reading, Mass., 1991.

A. V. M. Herz, B. Sulzer, R. Kühn, and J. L. van Hemmen, "Hebbian Learning Reconsidered: Representation of Static and Dynamic Objects in Associative Neural Nets," *Biol. Cybern.* **60**, 457–467 (1989).

G. E. Hinton, T. J. Sejnowski, and D. H. Ackley, "Boltzmann Machines: Constraint Satisfaction Networks that Learn," *Cog. Sci.* **9**, 147–169 (1986).

M. W. Hirsch and S. Smale, *Differential Equations, Dynamical Systems, and Linear Algebra*, Academic Press, Inc., New York, 1974.

R. A. Hope, B. J. Hammond, and R. M. Gaze, "The Arrow Model of Retino-Tectal Specificity and Map Formation in the Goldfish Visual System," *Proc. Roy. Soc. London B* **194**, 447–466 (1976).

J. J. Hopfield, "Neural Networks and Physical Systems with Emergent Collective Computational Properties," *Proc. Nat. Acad. Sci. USA* **79**, 2554–2558 (1982).

J. J. Hopfield, "Neurons with Graded Response have Collective Computational Properties like those of Two-State Neurons," *Proc. Nat. Acad. Sci. USA* **81**, 3088–3092 (1984).

J. J. Hopfield and D. W. Tank, "Computing with Neural Circuits: A Model," *Science* **233**, 625–633 (1986).

D. House, *Depth Perception in Frogs and Toads: A Study in Neural Computing*, Lecture Notes in Biomathematics **80**, Springer-Verlag, Berlin, 1989.

D. H. Hubel and T. N. Wiesel, "Receptive Fields, Binocular and Functional Architecture in the Cat's Visual Cortex," *J. Physiol.* **160**, 106–154 (1962).

D. H. Hubel and T. N. Wiesel, "Binocular Interaction in Striate Cortex of Kittens Reared with Artificial Squint," *J. Neurophysiol.* **28,** 1041–1059 (1965).

D. H. Hubel and T. N. Wiesel, "Functional Architecture of Macaque Monkey Cortex," *Proc. Royal Society of London B* **198,** 1–59 (1977).

E. Ising, *Z. Physik* **31,** 253 (1925).

E. T. Jaynes, "Information Theory and Statistical Mechanics," *Phys. Rev.* **106,** 620–630 (1957).

M. I. Jordan, "Motor Learning and the Degrees of Freedom Problem," in M. Jeannerod, ed., *Attention and Performance XIII,* Lawrence Erlbaum and Associates, Hillsdale, N.J., 1990, pp. 796–836.

M. I. Jordan and D. E. Rumelhart, "Forward Models: Supervised Learning with a Distal Teacher," *Cog. Sci.* (1990).

B. Julesz, *Foundation of Cyclopean Perception,* University of Chicago Press, Chicago, Ill., 1971.

E. R. Kandel and J. H. Schwartz, *Principles of Neural Science,* 2nd ed., Elsevier, New York, 1985.

W. L. Kilmer, W. S. McCulloch, and J. Blum, "A Model of the Vertebrate Central Command System," *Int. J. Man-Mach. Stud.* **1,** 279–309 (1969).

S. Kirkpatrick, C. D. Gelatt, Jr., and M. P. Vecchi, "Optimization by Simulated Annealing," *Science* **220,** 671–680 (1983).

D. Kleinfeld, "Sequential State Generation by Model Neural Networks," *Proc. Natl. Acad. Sci. USA* **83,** 9469–9473 (1986).

C. Koch, "Seeing Chips: Analog VLSI Circuits for Computer Vision," *Neural Comput.* **1,** 184–200 (1989).

C. Koch and I. Segev, eds., *Methods in Neuronal Modeling: From Synapses to Networks,* MIT Press, Cambridge, Mass., 1989.

T. Kohonen, "Self-Organized Formation of Topologically Correct Feature Maps," *Biol. Cybern.* **43,** 59–69 (1982).

T. Kohonen, *Self-Organization and Associative Memory,* 2nd ed., Springer-Verlag, New York, 1988.

N. Kopell, "Toward a Theory of Modelling Central Pattern Generators," in A. H. Cohen, S. Rossignol, and S. Grillner, eds., *Neural Control of Rhythmic Movements in Vertebrates,* Wiley-Interscience, New York, 1988.

B. Kosko, "Bidirectional Associative Memory," *IEEE. Trans. Sys. Man Cybern.* **18,** 49–60 (1988).

S. W. Kuffler, J. G. Nichols, and A. R. Martin, *From Neuron to Brain,* 2nd ed., Sinauer, Sunderland, Mass., 1984.

L. D. Landau and E. M. Lifshitz, *Course of Theoretical Physics,* Vol. 5, 3rd ed., Pergamon, Inc., Oxford, 1980.

J. Y. Lettvin, H. Maturana, W. S. McCulloch, and W. H. Pitts, "What the Frog's Eye Tells the Frog Brain," *Proc. IRE.* **47,** 1940–1951 (1959).

Z. Li and J. J. Hopfield, "Modeling the Olfactory Bulb and Its Neural Oscillatory Processing," *Biol. Cybern.* **61,** 379–392 (1989).

W. A. Little, "The Existence of Persistent States in the Brain," *Math. Biosci.* **19,** 101–120 (1974).

J. L. McClelland and D. E. Rumelhart, *Parallel Distributed Processing: Explorations in the Microstructure of Cognition,* 2 Volumes, MIT Press, Cambridge, Mass., 1986.

W. S. McCulloch and W. H. Pitts, "A Logical Calculus of the Ideas Immanent in Nervous Activity," *Bull. Math. Biophys.* **5,** 115–133 (1943).

R. J. McGregor, *Neural and Brain Modeling,* Academic Press, Inc., New York, 1987.

T. M. Martinetz, H. J. Ritter, and K. J. Schulten, "Three-Dimensional Neural Net for Learning Visuomotor Coordination of a Robot Arm," *IEEE Transact. Neural Networks* **1,** 127–136 (1990).

P. C. Matthews and S. H. Strogatz, "Phase Diagram for the Collective Behavior of Limit-Cycle Oscillators," *Phys. Rev. Lett.* **65,** 1701–1704 (1990).

C. Mead, *Analog VLSI and Neural Systems,* Addison-Wesley Publishing Co., Inc., Reading, Mass., 1989.

P. A. Merton, "Speculations on the Servo-Control of Movement," in *The Spinal Cord: A CIBA Foundation Symposium,* J. and A. Churchill Ltd., London, 1953, pp. 247–255 (Discussion, pp. 255–260).

N. Metropolis, A. W. Rosenbluth, A. H. Teller, and E. Teller, "Equation of State Calculations for Fast Computing Machines," *J. Chem. Phys.* **6,** 1087 (1953).

M. L. Minsky, "Theoretical Concepts of Synchrony," in H. H. Jasper, A. A. Ward, and A. Pope, eds., *Brain Mechanisms of the Epilepsies,* Little, Brown and Co., Boston, Mass., 1969, pp. 755–767.

M. L. Minsky and S. Papert, *Perceptrons, An Essay in Computational Geometry,* MIT Press, Cambridge, Mass., 1969.

M. L. Minsky and O. G. Selfridge, "Learning in Random Nets," in C. Cherry, ed., *Information Theory: Fourth London Symposium,* Butterworths, Kent, UK, 1961.

J. D. Murray, *Mathematical Biology,* Biomathematics Texts **19,** Springer-Verlag, New York, 1989.

J. I. Nelson, "Globality and Stereoscopic Fusion in Binocular Vision," *J. Theor. Biol.* **49,** 1–88 (1975).

L. Onsager, *Phys. Rev.* **65,** 117 (1944).

L. M. Opticon and B. J. Richmond, "Temporal Encoding of Two-Dimensional Patterns by Single Units in Primate Inferior Temporal Cortex, III, Information Theoretic Analysis," *J. Neurophysiol.* **57,** 162–178 (1987).

K. J. Overton and M. A. Arbib, "The Extended Branch-Arrow Model of Retino-Tectal Connections," *Biol. Cybern.* **45,** 157–175 (1982).

D. B. Parker, *Learning-Logic,* Technical Report **TR-47,** Center for Computational Research in Economics and Management Science, MIT Press, Cambridge, Mass., 1985.

P. Peretto, "Collective Properties of Neural Networks: A Statistical Physics Approach," *Biol. Cybern.* **50,** 51–62 (1984).

W. H. Pitts and W. S. McCulloch, "How We Know Universals, the Perception of Auditory and Visual Forms," *Bull. Math. Biophys.* **9,** 127–147 (1947).

T. Poggio, V. Torre, and C. Koch, "Computational Vision and Regularization Theory," *Nature* **317,** 314–319 (1985).

T. Poggio, E. B. Gamble, and J. J. Little, "Parallel Integration of Visual Modules," *Science* **242,** 436–440 (1988).

J. M. Prager and M. A. Arbib, "Computing the Optic Flow: The MATCH Algorithm and Prediction," *Comp. Vision, Graphics Im. Proc.* **24,** 271–304 (1983).

R. H. Rand, A. H. Cohen, and P. J. Holmes, "Systems of Coupled Oscillators as Models of Central Pattern Generators," in A. H. Cohen, S. Rossignol, and S. Grillner, eds., *Neural Control of Rhythmic Movements in Vertebrates,* Wiley-Interscience, New York, 1988.

F. Ratliff, *Mach Bands,* Holden-Day, San Francisco, Calif., 1965.

R. A. Rescorla and A. R. Wagner, "A Theory of Pavlovian Conditioning: Variations in the Effectiveness of Reinforcement and Nonreinforcement," in A. H. Black and W. F. Prokasy, eds., *Classical Conditioning II,* Appleton Century Crofts, New York, 1972, pp. 64–99.

G. Rinzel and B. Ermentrout, "Analysis of Neural Excitability and Oscillations," in C. Koch and I. Segev, eds., *Methods in*

Neuronal Modeling: From Synapses to Networks, MIT Press, Cambridge, Mass., 1989, pp. 135–169.

H. Ritter, T. Martinetz, and K. Schulten, *Neural Computation and Self-Organizing Maps,* Addison-Wesley Publishing Co., Inc., Reading, Mass., 1991.

H. Ritter and K. Schulten, "Convergence Properties of Kohonen's Topology Conserving Maps: Fluctuations, Stability, and Dimension Selection," *Biol. Cybern.* **60,** 59–71 (1988).

H. Robbins and S. Monro, "A Stochastic Approximation Method," *Ann. Math. Stat.* **22,** 400–407 (1951).

F. Rosenblatt, "The Perceptron: A Probabilistic Model for Information Storage and Organization in the Brain," *Psychol. Rev.* **65,** 386–408 (1958).

F. Rosenblatt, *Principles of Neurodynamics: Perceptrons and the Theory of Brain Mechanisms,* Spartan Books, 1962.

N. Rubin and H. Sompolinski, "Neural Network with Low Local Firing Rates," *Europhys. Lett.* **10,** 465–470 (1989).

D. E. Rumelhart and D. Zipser, "Feature Discovery by Competitive Learning," *Cog. Sci.* **9,** 75–112 (1985).

D. E. Rumelhart, G. E. Hinton, and R. J. Williams, "Learning Internal Representations by Error Propagation," in D. Rumelhart and J. McClelland, eds., *Parallel Distributed Processing: Explorations in the Microstructure of Cognition,* Vol. I, Cambridge, Mass., 1986, pp. 318–362.

H. Sakaguchi, "Cooperative Phenomena in Coupled Oscillator Systems under External Fields," *Prog. Theoret. Physics* **79,** 39–46 (1988).

E. L. Schwartz, ed., *Computational Neuroscience,* MIT Press, Cambridge, Mass., 1990.

T. J. Sejnowski and C. R. Rosenberg, "Parallel Networks that Learn to Pronounce English Text," *Complex Systems* **1,** 145–168 (1987).

O. G. Selfridge, "Some Notes on the Theory of Flutter," *Arch. Inst. Cardiol. Mex.* **18,** 177 (1948).

O. G. Selfridge, "Pandemonium: A Paradigm for Learning," in *Mechanisation of Thought Processes,* Her Majesty's Stationery Office, 1959, pp. 511–531.

C. E. Shannon, "The Mathematical Theory of Communication," *Bell System Tech. J.* **27,** 379–423, 623–656 (1948). (Reprinted with an introductory essay by W. Weaver as C. E. Shannon, and W. Weaver, *Mathematical Theory of Communication,* University of Illinois Press, Urbana, Ill., 1949.

C. E. Shannon and J. McCarthy, eds., *Automata Studies,* Princeton University Press, Princeton, N.J., 1956.

G. M. Shepherd, *The Synaptic Organization of the Brain,* Second Edition, Oxford University Press, New York, Oxford, 1979.

D. Sherrington and S. Kirkpatrick, "Solvable Model of a Spin Glass," *Phys. Rev. Lett.* **35,** 1792–1795 (1975).

P. D. Simic, "Statistical Mechanics as the Underlying Theory of "Elastic" and "Neural" Computation," *Network* **1,** 89–104 (1990).

P. D. Simic, "Constrained Nets for Graph Matching and Other Assignment Problems," *Neural Computation* **3,** 268–281 (1991).

C. A. Skarda and W. J. Freeman, "How the Brain Makes Chaos in Order to Make Sense of the World," *Behav. Brain Sci.* **10,** 161–195 (1987).

J. Sklansky and G. N. Wassel, *Pattern Classifiers and Trainable Machines,* Springer-Verlag, New York, 1981.

H. Sompolinsky, "Statistical Mechanics of Neural Networks," *Physics Today,* 2–12 (Dec. 1988).

H. Sompolinsky and I. Kanter, "Temporal Association in Asymmetric Neural Networks," *Phys. Rev. Lett.* **57,** 2861–2864 (1986).

H. Sompolinsky, D. Golomb, and D. Kleinfeld, "Global Processing of Visual Stimuli in a Neural Network of Coupled Oscillators," *Proc. Nat. Acad. Sci. USA* **87,** 7200–7204 (1990).

H. Sompolinsky, N. Tishby, and H. S. Seung, "Learning from Examples in Large Neural Networks," *Phys. Rev. Lett.* **65,** 1683–1686 (1990).

R. W. Sperry, "Optic Nerve Regeneration with Return of Vision in Anurans," *J. Neurophysiol.* **7,** 57–70 (1944).

D. N. Spinelli and F. E. Jensen, "Plasticity: The Mirror of Experience," *Science* **203,** 75–78 (1979).

P. M. Spira and M. A. Arbib, "Computation Times for Finite Groups, Semigroups and Automata," *Proceedings of the IEEE 8th Annual Symposium on Switching and Automata Theory,* New York, 1967, pp. 291–295.

J. C. Stanley and W. L. Kilmer, "A Wave Model of Temporal Sequence Learning," *Int. J. Man-Mach. Stud.* **7,** 397–412 (1975).

K. Steinbuch, "Die Lernmatrix," *Kybernetik* **1,** 36–45 (1961).

S. Sternberg, "High-Speed Scanning in Human Memory," *Science* **153,** 652–654 (1966).

R. S. Sutton and A. G. Barto, "Toward a Modern Theory of Adaptive Networks: Expectation and Prediction," *Psychol. Rev.* **88,** 135–170 (1981).

A. N. Tikhonov and V. Y. Arsenin, *Solutions of Ill-posed Problems,* Winston, Washington, DC, 1977.

G. Toulouse, "Perspectives on Neural Network Models and their Relevance to Neurobiology," *J. Phys. A* **22,** 1959–1968 (1989).

G. Toulouse, S. Dehaene, and J.-P. Changeux, "Spin Glass Model of Learning by Selection," *Proc. Nat. Acad. Sci. USA* **83,** 1695–1698 (1986).

A. Treves and D. J. Amit, "Low Firing Rates: An Effective Hamiltonian for Excitatory Neurons," *J. Phys. A* **22,** 2205 (1989).

M. L. Tsetlin, *Automaton Theory and Modelling of Biological Systems,* Academic Press, Inc., New York, 1973.

M. V. Tsodyks and M. V. Feigelman, "The Enhanced Storage Capacity in Neural Networks with Low Activity Level," *Europhys. Lett.* **6,** 101–105 (1988).

A. M. Turing, "The Chemical Basis of Morphogenesis," *Phil. Trans. Roy. Soc. London B* **237,** 37–72 (1952).

J. A. M. van Gisbergen, D. A. Robinson, and S. Gielen, "A Quantitative Analysis of Generation of Saccadic Eye Movements by Burst Neurons," *J. Neurophysiol.* **45,** 417–442 (1981).

G. von Békésy, *Sensory Inhibition,* Princeton University Press, Princeton, N.J., 1967.

C. von der Malsburg, "Self-Organization of Orientation-Sensitive Cells in the Striate Cortex," *Kybernetik* **14,** 85–100 (1973).

C. von der Malsburg, *The Correlation Theory of Brain Function,* Internal Report 81-2, Dept. of Neurobiologie, MPI Biophysikalische Chemie, Göttingen, 1981.

C. von der Marlsburg and D. J. Willshaw, "How to Label Nerve Cells so that they can Interconnect in an Orderly Fashion," *Proc. Nat. Acad. Sci. USA* **74,** 5176–5178 (1977).

D. L. Wang and M. A. Arbib, "Complex Temporal Sequence Learning Based on Short-Term Memory," *Proc. IEEE* **78,** 1536–1543 (1990).

D. L. Wang and M. A. Arbib, "Timing and Chunking in Temporal Order Processing," in press.

D. L. Wang, J. Buhmann, and C. von der Malsburg, "Pattern Segmentation in Associative Memory," *Neural Comput.* **2,** 94–106 (1990).

G. Weisbuch and F. Fogelman-Soulie, "Scaling Laws for the Attractors of Hopfield Networks," *J. Phys. Lett.* **46,** L623–L630 (1985).

A. Weitzenfeld, *NSL, Neural Simulation Language, Version 2.0,* Technical report 90-01, Center for Neural Engineering, University of Southern California, Los Angeles, Calif., 1990.

P. J. Werbos, "Beyond Regression: New Tools for Prediction and Analysis in the Behavioral Sciences," Ph.D. dissertation, Harvard University, Cambridge, Mass., 1974.

G. Widrow and M. E. Hoff, "Adaptive Switching Circuits, *1960 IRE WESCON Convention Record,* Part 4, 1960, pp. 96–104.

N. Wiener and A. Rosenblueth, "Conduction of Impulses in Cardiac Muscle," *Arch. Inst. Cardiol. Mex.* **16,** 205 (1946).

D. J. Willshaw, O. P. Buneman, and H. C. Longuet-Higgins, "Non-Holographic Associative Memory," *Nature* **222,** 960–962 (1969).

G. V. Wilson and G. S. Pawley, "On the Stability of the Travelling Salesman Problem Algorithms of Hopfield and Tank," *Biol. Cybern.* **58,** 63–70 (1988).

S. Winograd, "On the Time Required to Perform Addition," *J. Assoc. Comp. Mach.* **12,** 277 (1965).

A. Yuille, "Generalized Deformable Models, Statistical Physics, and Matching Problems," *Neural Comput.* **2,** 1–14 (1990).

S. F. Zornetzer, J. L. Davis, and C. Lau, eds., *An Introduction to Neural and Electronic Networks,* Academic Press, Inc., New York, 1990.

M. A. Arbib
J. Buhmann
University of Southern
California

NOAH

A hierarchical planner developed around 1975 by Earl Sacerdoti at SRI International, NOAH uses procedural nets to represent plans (see E. Sacerdoti, *A Structure for Plans and Behavior,* Technical Note 109, AI Center, SRI International, Menlo Park, Calif., 1975).

K. S. Arora
SUNY at Buffalo

NON-VON

The name NON-VON refers to a family of massively parallel "new generation" computer architectures (Shaw, 1985) developed at Columbia University for use in high performance AI applications. The NON-VON machine architecture is based on a very large number (many thousands and, ultimately, millions) of processing elements implemented using specially designed custom integrated circuit chips, each containing a number of processing elements.

NON-VON 1 became operational at Columbia in January 1985. Although the NON-VON project effort concluded in 1986, many similar architectural features are incorporated in certain machines now available commercially, such as The Connection Machine manufactured by Thinking Machines, Inc.

This article begins with a brief overview of the NON-VON architecture. Performance projections derived through detailed analysis and simulation are then summarized for applications in the areas of rule-based inferencing, computer vision, and knowledge base management. The results of these projections, most of which are based on benchmarks proposed by other researchers, suggest that a full-scale NON-VON machine could provide a performance improvement of as much as several orders of magnitude on such tasks by comparison with a conventional sequential machine of comparable hardware cost. The article concludes with a concise explanation of the basis for NON-VON's performance and cost/performance advantages in these superficially dissimilar AI task domains.

NON-VON Architecture

Central to all members of the NON-VON family is a massively parallel active memory. The active memory is composed of a very large number of simple, area-efficient small processing elements (SPEs) that are implemented using custom VLSI circuits. The final active memory chip contained eight 8-bit processing elements. Each SPE comprises a small local RAM, a modest amount of processing logic, and an I/O switch that permits the machine to be dynamically reconfigured to support various forms of interprocessor communication.

In the general NON-VON machine, the SPEs are configured as a complete binary tree whose leaves are also interconnected to form a two-dimensional orthogonal mesh. Each node of the active-memory tree, with the exception of the leaves and root, is thus connected to three neighboring SPEs, which are called the *parent, left child,* and *right child* of the node in question, and each leaf is connected to its parent and to its four mesh-adjacent SPEs, which are called its *north, south, east,* and *west* neighbors. In addition, the I/O switches may be dynamically configured in such a way as to support "linear neighbor" communication, in which all SPEs are capable of communicating in parallel with their left or right neighbors in a particular, predefined linear ordering.

NON-VON programs are not stored within the small RAM associated with each SPE but are instead broadcast to the active memory by one or more large processing elements (LPEs), each based on an off-the-shelf 32-bit microprocessor having a significant amount of local RAM. In the simplest NON-VON configuration, which was also the first to be implemented, the entire active memory operates under the control of a single LPE that broadcasts instructions through a high speed interface called the active memory controller for simultaneous execution by all enabled SPEs. This simple configuration thus restricts NON-VON's operation to what is often referred to as a *single instruction stream, multiple data stream* (SIMD) mode of execution.

The general NON-VON design, however, provides for a number of LPEs, each capable of broadcasting an independent stream of instructions to some subtree of the active memory tree, as first described in Stolfo and Shaw (1982). The LPEs in the general machine are interconnected using a high bandwidth, low latency interconnection network. The incorporation of a number of communicating LPEs gives the general NON-VON architecture the capacity for *multiple instruction stream, multiple data stream* (MIMD) and *multiple SIMD* execution, multitasking applications, and multiuser operation. The general NON-VON architecture also includes a *secondary processing subsystem* based on a bank of "intelligent" disk drives capable of high-bandwidth parallel transfers between primary and secondary storage and of the parallel execution of certain operators at the level of the individual disk heads.

Applications and Performance Evaluation

NON-VON's performance has been evaluated in three AI task areas:

1. Rule-based inferencing, implemented using the OPS5 production system language (see RULE-BASED SYSTEMS);
2. The performance of a number of low and intermediate-level image-understanding (qv) tasks; and
3. The execution of certain "difficult" relational algebraic operations having relevance to the manipulation of knowledge bases.

An experimental compiler and run time system for the execution of OPS5 on a one-LPE NON-VON has been written and tested on an instruction-level simulator (Hillyer and Shaw, 1982). In order to predict the algorithm's performance when executing real production systems, its running time has been calculated based on measurements obtained by Gupta and Forgy (1983) of the static and dynamic characteristics of six actual production systems, which had an average of 910 inference rules each. According to these calculations, a NON-VON configuration having approximately the same cost as a VAX 11/780 would execute approximately 903 productions per second. By way of comparison, a LISP-based OPS5 interpreter executing the sequential Rete Match algorithm on a VAX 11/780 typically fires between 1 and 5 rules per second, and a Bliss-based interpreter executes between 5 and 12 productions per second.

In the image-understandng domain, algorithms have been developed, simulated, and in some cases executed on the actual NON-VON 1 machine for image correlation, histograming, thresholding, union, intersection, set difference, connected component labeling, Euler number, area, perimeter, center of gravity, eccentricity, the Hough transform (qv), and the "moving light display" problem (Ibrahim, 1984). The results of these comparisons suggest that NON-VON would offer an increase in performance of between a factor of 100 and 1000 by comparison with a VAX 11/780 of approximately the same cost and should in a number of cases improve on the best results reported in the literature for special-purpose vision architectures and other highly parallel machines.

Algorithms for a number of database primitives have been developed for the NON-VON machine, including select, project, join, union, intersection, set difference, aggregation, and various statistical operations. To evaluate NON-VON's applicability to the kinds of database operations most relevant to AI applications, a detailed analysis was performed (Hillyer, Shaw, and Nigam, 1986) of the machine's projected performance on a set of benchmark queries formulated by Hawthorn and DeWitt (1982). This analysis predicted that NON-VON should provide higher performance than any of the five special-purpose database machines evaluated by Hawthorn and DeWitt at approximately the same hardware cost. Although NON-VON's relative cost/performance advantage over specialized database machines was modest in the case of relational selection, major advantages were found in the case of those computationally demanding operations that appear to be most relevant to AI applications.

Sources of NON-VON's Advantages

Different aspects of the NON-VON architecture appear to be responsible for the machine's advantages in different problem areas. It is nonetheless possible to identify a relatively small number of features, several of which are typically operative in the case of any single application, to which the machine's advantages may be attributed:

The effective exploitation of an unusually high degree of parallelism, which is made possible by the very fine granularity of the active memory.

The extensive use of broadcast communication, high speed content-addressable matching, and other associative processing techniques.

The use of the active memory tree to execute algebraically commutative and associative operations (such as sum and maximum) in logarithmic time.

The exploitation of other physical and logical interconnection topologies to support a number of problem-specific communication functions.

The capacity for SIMD, MIMD, and MSIMD execution and for a mixture of synchronous and asynchronous execution within a single algorithm.

The simplicity and cost-effectiveness with which the machine can be implemented using currently available technology.

NON-VON's strong performance on any given AI task is probably of less interest than the *range* of diverse AI tasks that would appear to be efficiently executable within a single machine. It must be noted that there is insufficient evidence to adequately evaluate the extent to which the NON-VON architecture might serve as the basis for a high performance "general AI machine." The diversity of AI applications for which NON-VON has been shown to offer significant potential performance and cost/performance advantages, however, suggests that some of the essential principles underlying this architecture might point the way toward one possible approach to the ultimate development of such machines (see also BOLTZMANN MACHINE; CONNECTION MACHINES; LISP).

BIBLIOGRAPHY

A. Gupta and C. L. Forgy, *Measurements on Production Systems*, Technical Report, Carnegie Mellon Computer Science Department, Pittsburgh, Pa., 1983.

P. B. Hawthorn and D. J. DeWitt, "Performance Analysis of Alternative Database Machine Architectures," *IEEE Trans. Software Eng.* **SE-8**(1), 61–75 (Jan. 1982).

B. K. Hillyer and D. E. Shaw, "Execution of OPS5 Production Systems on a Massively Parallel Machine," *J. Parall. Distr. Comput.* **3**(2), 236–268 (June 1986).

B. K. Hillyer, D. E. Shaw, and A. Nigam, "NON-VON's Performance on Certain Database Benchmarks," *IEEE Trans. Software Eng.* **SE-12**(4), 577–583 (April 1986).

H. A. H. Ibrahim, *Image Understanding Algorithms on Fine-Grained Tree-Structured SIMD Machines*, Ph.D. thesis, Department of Computer Science, Columbia University, New York, Oct. 1984.

D. E. Shaw, "Organization and Operation of a Massively Parallel Machine," in G. Rabbat, ed., *Computers and Technology*, Elsevier North-Holland, Amsterdam, 1985.

S. J. Stolfo and D. E. Shaw, "DADO: a Tree-Structured Machine Architecture for Production Systems," in *Proceedings of the Second National Conference on Artificial Intelligence*, Pittsburgh, Pa., AAAI, Menlo Park, Calif., 1982.

D. E. Shaw
D. E. Shaw & Co.

O

OBJECT-ORIENTED LANGUAGES. See LANGUAGES, OBJECT-ORIENTED.

OBJECT RECOGNITION

Object recognition is generally defined as the problem of identifying instances of known models from sensory data. It forms an integral part of many applications of intelligent vision, including hand-eye coordination systems, in which a system must locate objects in a cluttered environment in order to acquire and manipulate them; inspection and gauging tasks, in which a system must ensure that parts are properly sited and of appropriate dimensions; and mobile robot navigation, in which a system must locate itself relative to the world (see INSPECTION; ROBOT MANIPULATORS; ROBOTS, MOBILE).

Current approaches often separate object recognition into several related subproblems. Object detection refers to the problem of identifying a set of data features that correspond to a single object. Object identification refers to the problem of determining which model, from a library of known models, corresponds to a set of data features. Object localization (or pose estimation) refers to the problem of determining the position and orientation (or pose) of an instance of an object relative to the observer.

Clearly, these subproblems, and solutions to them, can interact with one another. For instance, object detection can be performed in a purely bottom up fashion, grouping data subsets together based on the likelihood that they have arisen from a single object, independent of the specifics of the object. On the other hand, knowing the identity of the object being sought can be used to guide the solution to the detection problem, by efficiently filtering data features that cannot possibly match the object. Similarly, while many applications require knowledge of the location of an object relative to the observer, identifying the existence of instances of an object often can be done without direct knowledge of the location of the instance. Because of this subdivision of the problem, it is often convenient to partition object recognition methods into three components:

Selection. How does the method select, or group, subsets of the sensory data into groups that are likely to have come from a single object? That is, how does the method deal with the object detection problem?

Indexing. How does the method find candidate models from its library that are likely to correspond to the data subsets? That is, how does the method deal with the object identification problem?

Correspondence. How does the method determine if there is a match between the data subsets and the candidate model? Further, how does the method deduce the pose of the object in the data? That is, how does the method deal with the object localization problem?

Most current approaches to object recognition focus on the selection and correspondence issues, usually in the context of finding and manipulating instances of a small number of known objects. Examples are shown in Figures 1 and 2, in which an object has correctly been identified and located, in the presence of other occluding objects.

Key Issues in Recognition

Why is object recognition a hard problem? Though simple variations of the object recognition problem exist, a number of key factors conspire to make efficient solutions to the general recognition problem elusive.

Representation. What information about an object should be represented to support recognition? Typically, object shape is used, but other attributes are possible, such as color or surface texture. A key issue is choosing attributes that are reliably detectable in the sensor data, since ultimately one must match object models to the data. How is an object's shape to be represented? Polyhedral representations have seen considerable attention, because of their simplicity, but other options are available, such as superquadrics and generalized cylinders. What class of object shapes is allowed? Typically, systems restrict attention to rigid objects, but more general problems involve articulated or even deformable objects. How does one build a model? For two-dimensional (2-D) recognition, a common practice is to use the sensor acquisition stage of the system on a canonical example of a model, thereby transforming the object into a form that will be comparable to instances seen later. For three-dimensional (3-D) recognition this has proved to be difficult, and more commonly systems rely on sources such as CAD systems to build object models.

Sensor Acquisition. While in some cases, such as with active ranging systems, one can directly measure object shape from a scene, in general this is not possible. In the case of recognizing objects from visible light images, a variety of factors conspire to create the brightnesses recorded in an image. These include complex interactions between the light sources and their positions, the object's surface shape and its position, and the reflective properties of the object's surface material. Because many of these factors are irrelevant to the object's intrinsic properties, unless one can explicitly control or measure these factors, direct matching of intensities between an image and a model is not possible. This means that the images must be processed to extract intrinsic measurements about an object (such as its shape). This transformation, however, introduces several confounding effects, including noise corruption of the measurements, extraneous measurements, and incomplete or missing measurements. Finally, the projection from the scene to the sensor can introduce additional difficulties. While active sensing devices provide 3-D measurements about 3-D objects directly, recognition from grey-level images of necessity involves a projection from the 3-D scene into the 2-D image. If the objects are known to lie in certain stable positions, this may not be a problem, but more general recognition tasks must deal with the distortion in perceived object shape inherent in this transformation. The class of projections allowed by a method also interacts with the representation used by a method. Examples include using full 3-D models, using sets of characteristic 2-D views of a model, or using parameterized 2-D models.

Scene Complexity. While some applications only require the identification of a single object isolated under a sensor, most recognition tasks deal with complex, cluttered scenes. This introduces two additional difficulties. First, the object of interest may be partially occluded by other objects in the scene. Second, most of the data extracted from a scene comes from other objects, and constitute confounding clutter that must be separated from the data due to the object of interest.

There are a range of problem variations within the context of these three factors. For example, optical character recognition systems have seen considerable success, in part because many of these confounding effects are removed, eg, the problem involves 2-D models and measurements, the object shape can be readily extracted from the image because light source, orientation, and albedo effects can be removed or measured, projection problems are removed, and there is generally no occlusion. More general recognition systems, such as those illustrated in Figures 1 and 2, do not have this luxury.

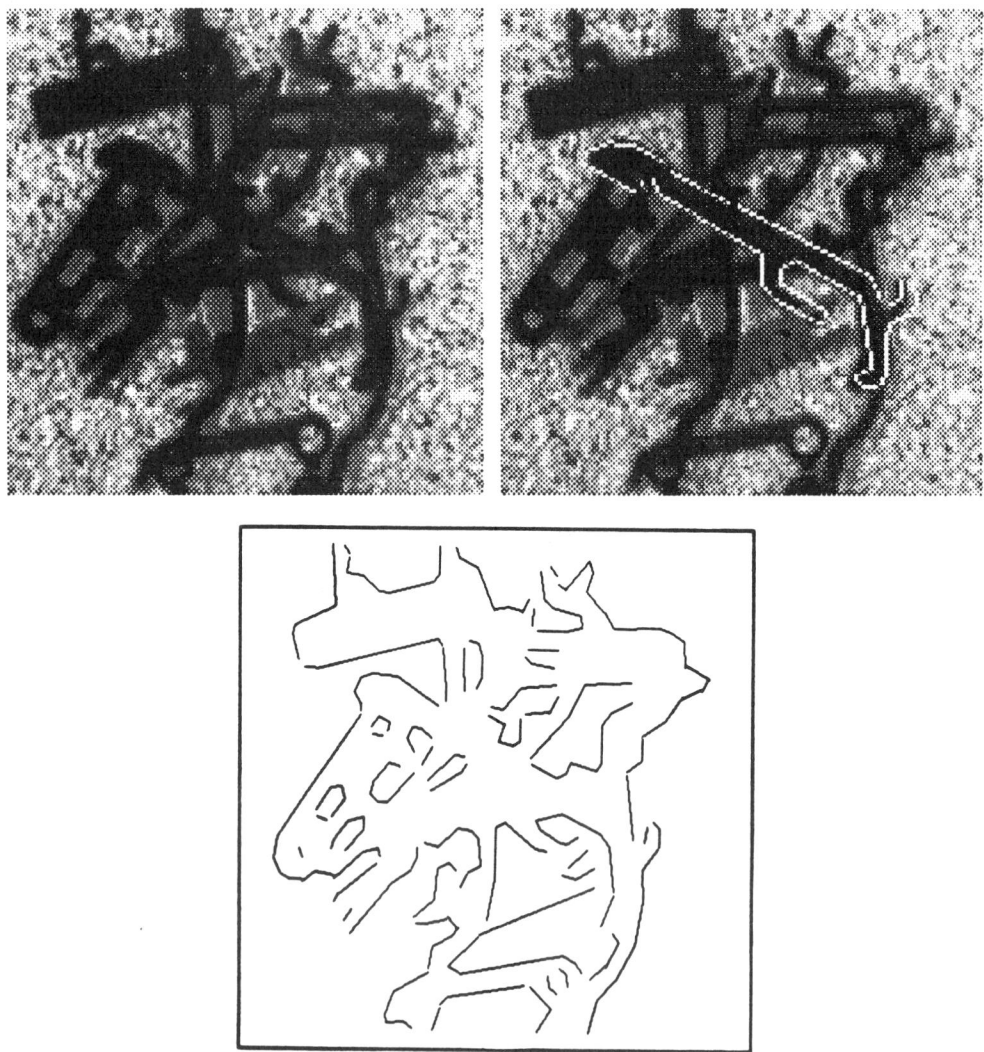

Figure 1. An example of 2-D recognition. From the grey level image on the top left, instances of objects as indicated on the top right must be found. The edge data on which this is done is shown at the bottom. Intensity variations, noise, and other imaging effects may cause the edges on which the matching is performed to be fragmented and incomplete. Nonetheless, good recognition systems can still succeed in this case. Courtesy of T. Cass.

Figure 2. An example of 3-D recognition. The top figure is the original image and the bottom figure is the overlayed solution. Courtesy of D. Huttenlocher.

The literature on object recognition is huge, and within the confines of this entry it is not feasible to survey all the approaches and their variations. Instead, representative examples of some of the major themes of object recognition are explored in sufficient depth to give the reader a sense of their strengths and weaknesses, as well as an indication of where research in the area is headed. These examples explore the spectrum of possible solutions. Key issues that are addressed include the trade off between global and local methods, the central role that search plays in solving the recognition problem, the factors that drive up the complexity of the problem, and approaches for reducing components of that complexity.

GLOBAL METHODS FOR RECOGNITION

Noncorrespondence, or global, recognition involves finding an instance of an object and its pose without first determining the correspondence between individual parts or features of the model and the data. Instead, recognition is based on global parameters of a model and an image, ie, parameters that depend on the entire object, such as its area or volume.

The general idea is to compute a vector of global parameters of a model, and a similar vector from the sensory data. Indexing is solved by comparing the image vector against candidate model vectors, looking for the best matching model. Properties of some of the parameters are then used to determine the pose of the object in the data. Clearly, there are many factors that can be adjusted in such systems, including what parameters to use, how to compare vectors of features, and how to compute the actual pose.

Several variations on this approach have appeared in the literature. Examples include systems based on simple geometric parameters such as area, perimeter, elongation, Euler number, systems based on moments of inertia, systems based on Fourier or other spatial frequency descriptions, and systems based on tensor measurements. Representative examples include Hu (1962), Zahn and Roskies (1972), Gleason and Agin (1979), Wallace and co-workers (1981), Tejwani and Jones (1985), Bamieh and De Figueiredo (1986), and Horn (1986).

Parameter Vectors

One of the simplest, and earliest, methods uses parameters based on simple geometric properties that are invariant to the object's pose. This is important since one wants to recognize instances of an object independent of their current pose. For example, in the restricted case of flat objects that can translate and rotate on a support plane oriented parallel to the camera's image plane, one can use properties such as area, perimeter, or Euler number. Notationally, the jth object in the library is represented by a vector

$$\mathbf{M}_j = (m_{1,j}, m_{2,j}, \ldots, m_{n,j})$$

where each m_i is a different property of the model.

To recognize an object, one must compute similar properties from the image data. One standard approach assumes that the image of the scene can be processed to yield a binary image, in which each pixel (picture element) of the image corresponding to a point on the object takes on the value 1 while all other pixels take on the value 0. If the object's reflectance properties are sufficiently different from the background's, one can histogram the image intensities, select a threshold sufficient to separate the two peaks associated with the object and background, and then set all pixels with intensities below the threshold to one value, and those with values above the threshold to the other. In more general imaging situations, such simple methods are insufficient, however, and more clever schemes for binarizing an image are needed. Such a binary image can be represented by a *characteristic function*:

$$b(x, y) = \begin{cases} 1, & \text{if the point } (x, y) \text{ is on the object,} \\ 0, & \text{otherwise.} \end{cases}$$

Once an image has been converted to this form, it is straightforward to compute the same set of global parameters, now associated with the data:

$$\mathbf{D} = (d_1, d_2, \ldots, d_n).$$

To recognize an object, one must now compare $\mathbf{D}$ against all model vectors $\mathbf{M}_j$. In the ideal case, there would be an exact match between $\mathbf{D}$ and the correct model vector $\mathbf{M}_j$, but in practice, sensor error will make this unlikely. This means that determining the best match is more problematic. One option is to use Euclidean distance, ie, and the $\mathbf{M}_j$ satisfying:

$$\min_j \|\mathbf{D} - \mathbf{M}_j\|^2 = \min_j \sum_{i=1}^{n} (d_i - m_{i,j})^2.$$

Since the individual parameters are measuring "apples and oranges," using this distance metric to find the best match makes sense only if one can normalize the individual dimensions of the vector space to "equally weight" each contribution. In practice, this can be difficult to do.

A second option is to count the number of parameters in agreement:

$$\max_j \sum_{i=1}^{n} \delta(d_i, m_{i,j}, \varepsilon_i)$$

where

$$\delta(d_i, m_{i,j}, \varepsilon_i) = \begin{cases} 1 & \text{if } |d_i - m_{i,j}| \leq \varepsilon_i. \\ 0 & \text{otherwise} \end{cases}$$

The ε_i's are error bounds associated with the individual parameters. This method basically counts the number of parameters of the data vector consistent, modulo error, with the associated model parameters. Provided one can find reasonable values for ε_i, and provided there are sufficient parameters to distinguish the library of objects, this method has good performance. Other options for determining the "best match" are possible.

Once the indexing problem has been solved, standard methods can be used to determine the object's pose. For example, the translation part of the pose is that needed to align the centers of mass of the object and the data. The rotation can be computed either by aligning distinctive points on the boundary, or by aligning associated axes of least inertia. Note that these methods assume that there is no selection problem; that is, that all of the data belongs to a single object, and that the object is completely visible.

Fourier Descriptors

A second example of the noncorrespondence approach is based on Fourier components (Zahn and Roskies 1972; Persoon and Fu, 1974). Fourier descriptors provide a way of representing the closed boundary of a 2-D region by treating it as a periodic function and applying Fourier series. The motivation is that typically the general shape of an object is captured by the first few low order terms, with higher terms providing fine detail. If the boundary is parameterized in terms of arclength, then the Fourier descriptors are independent of scale, translation, and rotation (ie, of pose) and hence can be used in a manner similar to the feature vectors above.

Moments of Inertia

A third example of the noncorrespondence approach to recognition, applicable to laminar objects and binary images, uses moments of inertia. Given a binary characteristic function b, one can compute the moments of inertia associated with both the object and the data.

$$M_{p,q} = \sum_x \sum_y x^p y^q b(x, y).$$

The idea is to compute some set of functions of such moments for each model, forming a vector of parameters, and then compute the same set of moments for the binarized image. To do this, attention is focused on determining combinations of moments that are pose invariant, since they can be directly compared to determine if the data matches an object (Hu, 1962; Bamieh and De Figueiredo, 1986). For instance, Bamieh and De Figueiredo list the following low order moments which form a complete system (ie, any other invariant combination of moments of this order can be expressed as a combination of the moments listed below):

$$J_1 = M_{02}M_{20} + M_{11}$$
$$J_2 = (M_{03}M_{30} - M_{21}M_{12})^2 - 4(M_{03}M_{12} - M_{21}^2)(M_{21}M_{30} - M_{12}^2)$$
$$J_3 = M_{40}M_{04} - 4 M_{31}M_{13} + 3 M_{22}^2$$
$$J_4 = M_{40}M_{22}M_{04} - 2 M_{31}M_{22}M_{13} - M_{40}M_{13}^2 - M_{04}M_{31}^2 - M_{22}^3.$$

By comparing the image vector of such combinations of moments against the set of stored model vectors of the same combinations of moments, the system can, in principle, choose the best match and use this to determine which object is present. Note that the issue of how to match these vectors is not entirely clear. Simple solutions again include measuring Euclidean distance between the vectors, or counting the number of parameters of an image vector within a bounded distance of the corresponding model vector.

Once a match is obtained, some of the moments can be used to determine the pose of the object (Horn, 1986). If an object has some elongation, then simple combinations of the zeroth, first, and second moments can be used to solve for the scale, translation, and rotation of the object.

Scope of Global Methods

What are the drawbacks of these approaches? There are several. It is assumed that the image can be binarized, separating object from background. If one has control over the illumination conditions under which the image was taken, eg, a backlit support plane, or a background plane with very different reflective properties from the objects, and the objects are of uniform reflectance, then it may be possible to reliably derive the binary image. In general, however, this will not be possible to guarantee. Thus, more sophisticated methods are needed for separating figure from ground (eg, applying an edge detector to the image, then using coloring algorithms to find connected regions). As one moves from controlled imaging situations to more general ones, however, the performance of such methods in separating object from background tends to degrade.

Of course, one can extend this method to deal with grey level images, for example, by computing moments of the actual intensities, rather than just the binary characteristic function. In principle, one could compare vectors of these moments with corresponding model vectors. Even here, however, there are problems with guaranteeing that the model moments are consistent with the image moments. In particular, the intensity recorded at a point in

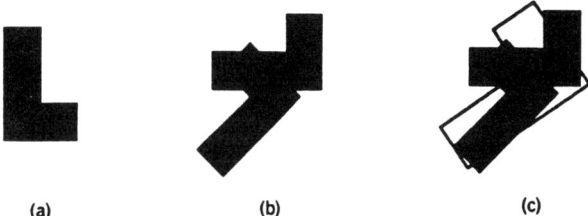

Figure 3. (a) Example of a binary object. (b) A binary image of a pair of overlapping objects. The moments associated with the left and right figures are not the same; hence, simple moment-based schemes would not be able to recognize the two instances of the left object in the right image. (c) Solution found by applying the moment-based method.

an image is dependent on a large number of factors, including the orientation of the patch of surface reflecting light into that image point, and the position and strength of the light sources themselves. Unless one can guarantee that all of those factors are known before computing the moments of the object models, the comparison of image moments and model moments may not be a well formed problem.

A more troublesome problem has to do with the scope of such methods. While the method described above can be implemented in an efficient manner and shows reasonable robustness in the presence of noise, it has difficulties in dealing with occlusion and clutter. Consider the example shown in Figure 3. Using the moments approach described above leads to the solution shown in the figure. Clearly, this is an unsatisfactory solution. Why does it occur? Since the described method computes global measurements, any overlapping objects will be treated as part of the same object. This can have deleterious effects on the computed moments and cause the system to misrecognize the object, since all of the moments and combinations of moments are affected by the overlapping object. It will cause such global methods to badly estimate the pose of an object, even in cases in which one can clearly identify the overlapping objects. In short, global methods often assume that there is no occlusion so that the selection problem can be solved by simple means, such as connected components. If this does not hold, the methods tend to degrade in performance.

FEATURE MATCHING METHODS FOR RECOGNITION

An alternative is to focus on establishing a correspondence between local features extracted from the sensory data and corresponding local features of the object model (see also EDGE AND LOCAL FEATURE DETECTION). By concentrating on local features, one expects to establish appropriate correspondences in the presence of occlusion of an object and in the presence of additional spurious data. Occlusion will simply remove some features from consideration, but will not affect other local features in the scene. Spurious features in the data will simply increase the set of possibilities to be considered, but again will not affect other local features in the scene.

While local features yield more robust matching in the presence of occlusion and spurious data, they are also less distinctive as matching components, ie, there may be many data features that could match an individual model feature. In order to find the correct correspondence one needs more information, and this is typically obtained by considering global aspects of an object's shape. As opposed to the noncorrespondence methods, however, one can use geometric relationships between local features, rather than global metrical properties, as the means of capturing information about an object's shape. In this way, one can ensure that aggregates of features match both individually and with respect to global relationships, while avoiding the difficulties of occlusion and spurious data.

To define the local feature matching approach to recognition, let

$\{F_i | 1 \leq i \leq m\}$ denote a set of model features

$\{f_i | 1 \leq i \leq s\}$ denote a set of sensory features

$\mathcal{T}$ denote a legal transformation

$\ell: \{1, \ldots, s\} \mapsto \{1, \ldots, m\} \cup \{\star\}$ denote a mapping.

Under this notation a possible solution to the recognition problem is to determine a mapping ℓ which assigns each data feature to a model feature such that there exists a legal transformation that maps the model features to within error ranges ε of their associated data features:

$$\rho(\mathcal{T}(F_{\ell(i)}), f_i) \leq \varepsilon \quad \forall i \text{ such that } \ell(i) \neq \star \quad (1)$$

where ρ is some suitable distance metric. The null character $\star$ indicates that the feature is not part of the object. For example, if the objects undergo only rigid transformations, then any legal transformation is represented by

$$\mathcal{T}(\mathbf{x}) = \Pi(R\mathbf{x} + \mathbf{t})$$

where R is a rotation matrix, $\mathbf{t}$ is a translation vector, and Π is a projection operation. Typically ρ would be selected as the Euclidean distance metric.

Because there may be several possible solutions to the problem, one usually adds the following condition. Let

$$g(\{(i, \ell(i)) | i = 1, \ldots, s\})$$

be a measure applied to a correspondence between data and model features (for example, g may simply be the counting measure). Then the solution to the recognition problem is to find the mapping ℓ that maximizes:

$$\max_{\ell} g(\{(i, \ell(i)) | i = 1, \ldots, s\}) \quad (2)$$

over the set of mappings $\{\ell\}$ that satisfy equation 1, where $\mathcal{T}$ is defined as the best transformation associated with ℓ.

For example, it is common to use polygonal approximations of an object's boundary to represent object models, and to use linear approximations to edges detected in an image of a scene as data features. Given a model and a scene as in Figure 4, if a recognition method can identify the mappings

$f_1 \mapsto F_4, f_2 \mapsto F_5, f_3 \mapsto F_6, f_9 \mapsto F_6, f_{10} \mapsto F_1,$
$f_{11} \mapsto F_2, f_{14} \mapsto F_2, f_{15} \mapsto F_3$ and $f_4 \mapsto F_5,$
$f_5 \mapsto F_6, f_6 \mapsto F_1, f_7 \mapsto F_2, f_8 \mapsto F_3, f_{12} \mapsto F_4,$
$f_{13} \mapsto F_5$

with all other data features mapped to $\star$, then such correspondences will yield two consistent assignments of model and data edges, the corresponding poses of which are shown in Figure 4. Clearly, this is a much more satisfying solution than that of Figure 3. The key is developing recognition methods that can efficiently deduce the above correspondences of features.

Components of Feature Matching Systems

For recognition and localization from local features, one must represent object models in terms of spatially localized features, such as distinguished points, edges or other distinctive curves on an object, patches of surfaces, or axes of simple shapes such as cylinders. Because these features are matched to data measurements, this implies that the sensory data from a scene must be processed to obtain similar local features.

Given such localized data and model features, recognition and localization now entails establishing a correspondence between them. Of the three problems of selection, indexing, and correspondence, most current recognition systems concentrate on the selection and correspondence problems, and assume that localization can be used implicitly to solve the indexing problem. A simple approach to indexing is to sequentially examine each model in turn,

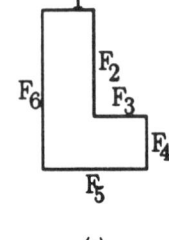
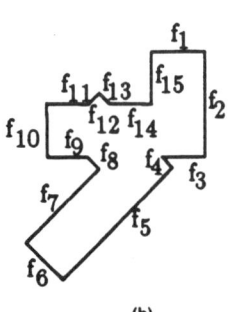

Figure 4. (a) The model of a simple object. (b) The boundary of a set of overlapping objects in an image. By matching local features, the two interpretations shown in (c) are found.

(a)   (b)   (c)

and accept as possible solutions only those models for which there exists a correspondence of data and model features consistent with a rigid transformation. This is sufficient when only a few models are involved, but is not computationally efficient for dealing with general recognition problems involving large libraries of objects.

Most current approaches to model-based localization cast it as a search (qv) problem, the search being for a consistent matching between model features and data features. The complexity of this search problem is the central contributor to the difficulty of the recognition problem, and most current approaches utilize a variety of techniques to control that complexity. Some approaches, especially those that focus on finding the correspondence between features, are inherently exponential, although under certain conditions the expected search can be reduced to low order polynomial. Other approaches, especially those that focus on finding the pose of an object, can be shown to be worst case polynomial, but even in this case much effort has focused on keeping the size of this polynomial cost small.

Searching the Correspondence Space

There are two main choices for the space of possibilities that must be searched to find correct interpretations of the data. One focuses on finding the mapping ℓ, the second focuses on finding the transformation $\mathcal{T}$.

The first possibility is to focus on the matching process, ie, on finding ℓ. One way to structure the search problem is to consider the space of all possible matches of data features to model features. If there are s sensory data features and m model features, one can visualize an s dimensional space, along each axis of which there are $m + 1$ discrete possible values. Thus, each point along an axis defines a possible matching for an individual data point: m different labels corresponding to each of the model features, plus an extra one for $\star$, to indicate the case where the data feature is not part of the object. A simple example of such a correspondence space is shown in Figure 5. This correspondence space consists of $(m + 1)^s$ different nodes. An alternative would be to use the axes of the space to represent the different model features, each of which has $s + 1$ possible values, leading to a space of $(s + 1)^m$ nodes. Although this second option gives rise to a smaller space of possibilities, it prohibits the possibility of letting a given extended model feature match more than one fragmented data feature. Since such cases often occur in practice, one is usually forced to use the larger $(m + 1)^s$ space to represent the search.

Each point in this discrete space defines an interpretation (or mapping ℓ) of all the data points, because the projection of a point onto each axis defines a pairing of a model feature (the point on the axis) and a data feature (the axis itself), or in the case of the extra label, indicates that the data feature is not part of the object and is to be excluded from the interpretation.

In this space, the focus is on finding consistent data interpretations, ie, nodes with an associated interpretation that satisfies equations 1 and 2. Note that in this case finding the object's pose $\mathcal{T}$ is secondary to finding consis-

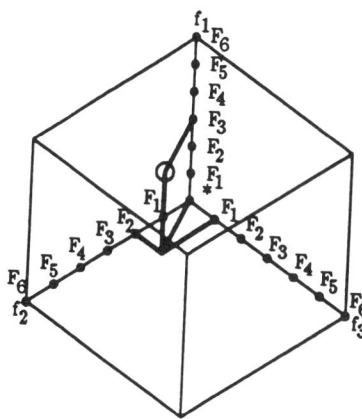

Figure 5. A simple example of a correspondence search space. Each axis represents a different data feature, f_i. Along each axis there is a discrete set of possible corresponding values, one for each model feature, F_j, plus a special character $\star$ indicating that the data feature is spurious. The open circle indicates the node in this search space corresponding to the matching of f_1 with F_3, f_2 with F_2, and f_3 with F_1.

tent nodes in the search space, although one must ultimately deduce that pose.

Search Alternatives

To find good nodes in the correspondence space, one has several alternatives which are discussed in turn. The main choices are between exhaustive search, complete constrained search, and heuristic search.

Exhaustive Search. One very straightforward way of finding consistent nodes in the correspondence space is simply to test all of them in some orderly manner, with the guarantee of finding the best possible interpretations of the data. Note that in this case, testing a node means determining if the node satisfies equation 1. If there is such a legal transformation, then this defines the pose of the object as well as verifying that one has a consistent interpretation. If there is not, then one can ignore the interpretation associated with this node.

The problem with this simple approach is that for most realistic situations, the space is far too large for the approach to be practical. There are $(m + 1)^s$ nodes in this space, and even with implementations on parallel machines, this number is generally far too large to be searched in reasonable time (it is common for m to be on the order of 100 and s to be on the order of 1,000 or larger). The inefficiency of this approach is compounded by the fact that, in general, solving for and testing a legal transformation from a set of data-model pairings is a relatively expensive operation, and must be performed for all $(m + 1)^s$ matches.

Complete Constrained Search. To avoid considering all the nodes in the correspondence space, one needs methods for ignoring most of them without performing much work and without overlooking correct interpretations. Fortunately, most of the nodes in the space either will be inconsistent, (ie, no legal transformation $\mathcal{T}$ exists) or the nodes are uninteresting, (ie, most of the data features are matched to ★). The key is to find methods for identifying such nodes as ones that can be ignored, without explicitly testing them all. This means constraints on the correspondence process are needed.

To obtain such constraints, one must consider attributes associated with each model feature and data feature, and the conditions under which those attributes can be considered in agreement with one another. In general, the attributes associated with a feature are not selective enough to identify a unique match. The idea is to look for measurements on both the data and the model that can be used to rule out some, if not all, of the infeasible pairings. Common examples are to use aspects of the shape of an object. For example, suppose one is considering 2-D objects, represented by sets of edges, and that the image data is processed to extract intensity edges. Then possible geometric constraints include:

- The length of a data edge must be less than the length of an associated model edge, modulo error and scale factors.
- The relative angle between a pair of data edges must agree with the relative angle between an associated pair of model edges, modulo error.
- The range of distances between a pair of data edges must be contained with the range of distances of an associated pair of model edges, modulo error.
- The range of values for components of a vector separating two data edges must be contained within the associated range of values for components of a vector between model edges.

Very similar constraints relating features of 3-D objects are also possible. All of these constraints capture aspects of the relative shape of an object, and as a consequence are independent of the specific pose of the object. Each constraint will not rule out all incorrect pairings of model features to data features, but each can remove many inconsistent pairings. Thus each local feature cannot be uniquely identified with a model feature, but it can serve to remove many possible matches for a feature. The point of these constraints is to reduce the search process. In order for a node to be consistent, it must be the case that each data-model pairing specified by the node satisfy all applicable constraints. More importantly, however, the constraints can rule out entire subspaces of the correspondence space, without explicitly exploring them.

Typically, recognition systems use combinations of such unary and binary constraints on the matching process. Unary constraints apply to a single pairing of a data feature and a model feature. Such constraints could involve geometric measurements such as the length of an edge, or the angle of a corner, or the area of a surface patch, etc. Unary constraints could also involve other sensory measurements, for example, the color associated with a feature, or the texture of a feature, or surface reflectance properties of a feature. Binary constraints apply to a pair of pairings of data features and model features. Examples include the relative angle between two edges, or the range of distances between two edges, as well as nongeometric measurements.

For example, consider the axis of the space corresponding to the first data feature. Any point along this axis that does not satisfy some unary constraint is inconsistent, and hence the entire subspace spanned by the remaining axes of the correspondence space associated with this point are also inconsistent. If one is careful about the manner in which to explore the correspondence space, this entire subspace can be ignored. Figure 6a shows this, by using dots to indicate the nodes examined, and darker planes to indicate those subspaces still under consideration.

For each of these subspaces, one can turn to the second data point. Again one can apply unary constraints to nodes along this axis, and ignore subspaces corresponding to inconsistent nodes, as shown in Figure 6b.

At this stage, one need only consider nodes in the correspondence space along the subspaces shown in bold in Figure 6c. Note that any appropriate binary constraints can be applied to the node shown as the open circle. If any such binary constraints are inconsistent, the associated subspace can be ignored. Similarly, for any of the nodes along the remaining subspaces, one can continue to apply unary and binary constraints, dropping subspaces whenever an inconsistency is found.

By applying these constraints in a judicious manner, the hope is to reduce the number of nodes in the correspondence space that actually must be examined. Note that any node in the space that is deemed consistent must still be tested for the existence of a rigid transformation that maps the model features correctly into their associated data features.

Figure 6. (a) By applying unary constraints to pairings of model features with the first data feature, entire subspaces can be removed from consideration. The dots indicate the nodes examined, and the darker planes indicate those subspaces corresponding to consistent assignments of the first data point. (b) Repeat the process for the second data feature, applying unary constraints to pairings of model features with that data feature. (c) After the first two stages, only nodes in the intersection of consistent subspaces from the previous constraints need to be considered.

 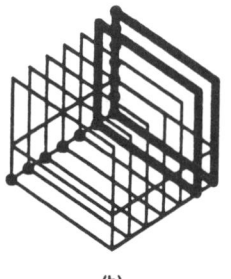 

(a)   (b)   (c)

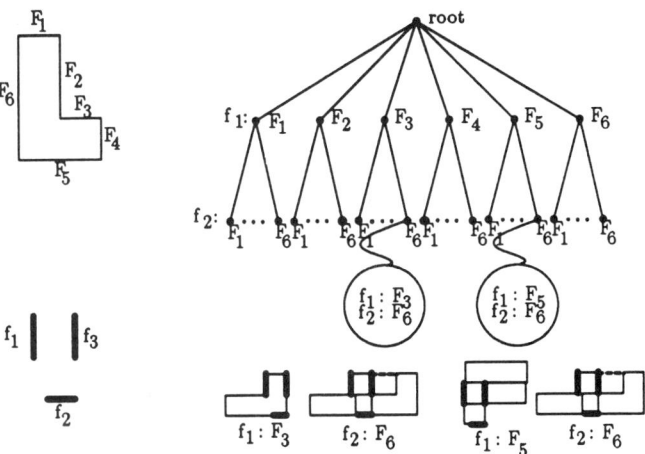

Figure 7. Each node in the second level of the tree defines a pairing for the first two data features, found by tracing up the tree to the root. The left example is consistent with a single rigid transformation, since the two ranges of poses specified by each of the data-model feature pairings have a common pose. The right example is not consistent with a single transformation, as its two ranges of poses do not have a common pose.

Searching the Interpretation Tree. The correspondence space characterizes all the possible matchings of data and model features. The key is to find points in that space that identify correct interpretations, without explicitly having to explore the entire space, since the full space is of large exponential size $(m + 1)^s$. One method for completely accounting for the correspondence space (ie, the method is guaranteed to find the best solutions) while avoiding the cost of exhaustive search, is to transform the space into an equivalent representation better suited to a directed search, for example, by using a tree of interpretations (Grimson and Lozano-Pérez, 1987; Baird, 1985; Murray and Buxton, 1990).

The interpretation tree provides a means of systematically searching the correspondence space in a depth-first manner. The idea is to select a data feature, and hypothesize in turn that it is in correspondence with a different model feature. This essentially selects each point on the first axis of the search space, each of which can be represented as a node at the first level of a tree. Given each one of these hypothesized assignments of f_1 to F_j, $1 \leq j \leq m$, one can consider all possible assignments of the second data feature f_2 to model features, relative to the assignment of the first data feature. This is shown in Figure 7. Note that below each node of the first level of the tree, the points along the second axis of the search space are replicated, and the entire set of nodes in the second level of the tree corresponds to the set of points in the search space spanned by the first two axes.

Figure 7 also shows examples of the pairings of the first two data features (in this case image edges) with model features. The example on the left is consistent with a single rigid transformation of the object, while the example on the right is not, as indicated by the fact that the two ranges of possible poses do not have a pose in common.

This process is continued, adding new levels to the tree, one for each data feature. Each such level represents the choices described by a new dimension of the search space. A node at level n of the interpretation tree describes a partial n-interpretation, in that the nodes lying directly between the current node and the root of the tree identify an assignment of model features to the first n data features. Any leaf of the tree defines a complete s-interpretation, where s is the number of sensor features.

One advantage of using a tree of interpretations is that the search of the space of possible solutions can be focused in a coherent manner. For example, one can use backtracking depth-first search (see SEARCH, DEPTH-FIRST) of the tree. Starting at the root one tracks down the left most branch, testing each node for consistency. If a node is consistent, the search continues downward. If a node is inconsistent, ie, no legal transformation will correctly align model and data feature, the search can terminate any further downward exploration below this node, as adding new data-model pairings to the interpretation defined at that node will not turn an inconsistent interpretation into a consistent one. The search then backtracks to the previous level and takes the next branch. If there are no further branches at this node, one recursively backtracks further up the tree and repeats the process.

There are several choices for testing for consistency at a node. One could explicitly solve for the best legal transformation, and test that all of the model features do in fact get mapped into agreement with their corresponding data features. This is implied by the examples shown in Figure 7. One drawback with explicitly solving for a transform at each node is the associated computational expense. There are some methods for incrementally computing the transformation (Ayache and Faugeras, 1986; Faugeras and Hebert, 1987) to reduce this expense. A second complication is that if noise and occlusion are present in the data, then the pairings of data and model features define ranges of possible transformations rather than a unique solution. This complicates the issue of deciding what constitutes the best legal transformation, or even if a single transformation consistently maps a set of model features onto a set of data features.

A second choice is to seek less complete methods for testing consistency, for example finding constraints that can be applied at any node of the interpretation tree, with the property that while no single constraint can uniquely guarantee the consistency of an interpretation, each constraint can rule out some interpretations. The hope is that if enough independent constraints can be combined together, their aggregation will prove powerful in determining consistency, while at a lower cost than full consistency constraints. For example, in Figure 7 one would like some simple method of deducing that the second example is not consistent, without directly solving for the best transformation mapping the two identified model features onto their matched data features.

Typically, recognition systems apply geometric constraints, based on the relative shapes of features, to accomplish this. If a constraint is true, then this implies that that data-model pairings to which it was applied may be part of a consistent interpretation. If it is false, however, then that pairing cannot possibly be part of such an interpretation. The advantages of these kinds of constraints are that they can be computationally quite simple, while retaining considerable power to separate consistent from inconsistent interpretations, and that they can be applied at virtually any node in the interpretation tree. Note that at each new node, there is a new data-model pairing that must be subjected to the unary constraints. There are also several new binary constraints, since each new node at the nth level of the tree allows for $n - 1$ new pairs of data-model pairings that can be checked for constraint consistency. Thus, the lower one goes in the tree, the more constraints that that must hold true, and hence the stronger the likelihood that the interpretation is in fact globally consistent.

If the search reaches a leaf of the tree, this defines a possible interpretation of the data relative to the model. One can either terminate the search at this point, or accumulate that possible interpretation, backtrack and continue until the entire tree has been explored and all the possible interpretations have been found.

Formulated in this way, this approach to recognition can be considered as a problem of constraint satisfaction (qv), or consistent labeling, a problem that has received considerable attention in AI literature. Although backtracking search is one simple way of exploring the space of solutions, there are other methods available for finding solutions to a consistent labeling problem. These include best first search, beam search, full and partial look-ahead, forward checking, back checking, and back marking.

Model Tests to Verify Hypotheses. Once the search reaches a leaf of the tree, the associated correspondence between data and model features can be checked for global validity. To do this, one solves for a legal transformation mapping points $\mathbf{V}$ in model coordinates into points $\mathbf{v}$ in sensor coordinates, given by

$$\mathbf{v} = sR\mathbf{V} + \mathbf{v}_0$$

where R is a rotation matrix, $\mathbf{v}_0$ is a translation vector, and s is a scale factor, if this is a free parameter.

Typically, recognition methods use a least-squares method to find the transformation minimizing the error between the transformed model features and the data features. To ensure that this transformation is correct, the methods test that the application of it causes each model feature to be mapped to a position in the sensor coordinate frame that is in agreement (to within the bounds of error) with the corresponding data feature.

To summarize, the interpretation tree approach performs a depth-first, backtracking search of a tree of interpretations. At each node, it applies unary and binary constraints on the relative shapes of data and model features to cut off fruitless paths in the tree. Any leaf of the tree reached by the process essentially defines an hypothesis for a feasible interpretation. Each such hypotheses is tested by solving for the pose of the object based on that interpretation, and verifying that such a pose is consistent with the components of the interpretation.

Dealing with Spurious Data. If all the data is known to have come from a single object, one can use search methods such as the interpretation tree without the null character. Although the search in principle involves m^s nodes, in practice, only a quadratic amount of search is needed to solve the correspondence (Grimson, 1991).

When confronted with situations such as the simple example in Figure 8, one must include a method for selecting subsets of the data corresponding to a single object. One method is to use the null character ($\star$) to separate out relevant subsets. At each node of the interpretation tree, an extra branch corresponding to this feature is added as a last resort. This feature indicates that the data feature to which it is matched is to be excluded from the interpretation, and treated as spurious data. To complete this addition to the matching scheme, one must define the consistency relationships between data-model pairings involving a null character match. Since the data feature is to be excluded, it cannot affect the current interpretation, and hence any constraint involving a data feature matched to the null character is deemed to be consistent.

With this addition, it is possible for the constrained search method to deal with spurious data. For example, given the model and data in Figure 8, one valid path through the corresponding interpretation tree is shown in

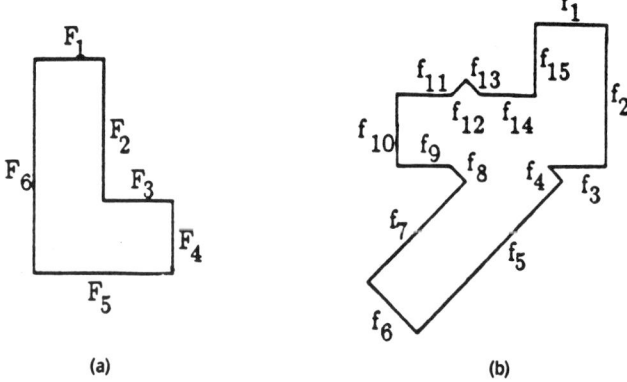

Figure 8. A simple example of a scene with occlusion and spurious data. Since there is no legal rotation of the object model on the left that will align it with all of the data features, the basic constrained tree search method will not find any interpretations of the data. Note that the example data on the right does not include the effects of error, but does include occlusion.

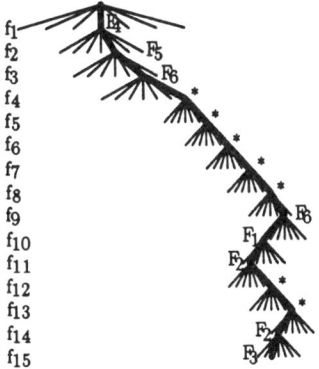

Figure 9. An example of a valid path through the interpretation tree. Shown is a portion of the interpretation tree for the example of Figure 8. The path corresponds to the interpretation that identifies the top version of the object in Figure 8. Of course, more of the interpretation tree than that shown here would actually be explored. Note the branches of the tree corresponding to the null character, which exclude some data features from the interpretation.

Figure 9. Here valid means that all the nodes, including the identified leaf, are consistent with available geometric constraints, and hence the nodes identify a legal pairing of model features and data features. Of course, more of the interpretation tree than that shown here would actually be explored. Note the branches of the tree corresponding to the null character, which exclude some data features from the interpretation.

The only changes to the previous method are that any constraint involving the null character is automatically consistent, and in applying a model test to hypothesized interpretations, only pairings involving real model features are used both in the computation of the transformation and in checking that model features are mapped onto corresponding data features.

The cost, however, is that the expected search for such cases is again exponential (Grimson, 1991).

Heuristic Search. An alternative to the above method is to forego the notion of a complete search, at the cost of possibly making an error in identification but at the gain of considerably reducing the expense of the search. A number of different methods have been explored for shortening the search cost in this way.

Selection, or Grouping, Methods

The null character helps select groups of data features corresponding to a single object, but it does so at the expense of considerable extra search of the correspondence space. One alternative is to use the object model to guide the selection of data subsets corresponding to a single object, as outlined below in discussing alignment methods. A second alternative is to use data-driven selection methods, ie, to select subsets of the data features likely to have come from a single object, independent of the specific object involved. Intuitively, such methods can select out small portions of the full correspondence space to search.

The goal is to isolate fruitful subspaces, likely to contain a correct solution, while reducing the likelihood that a correct solution is not contained in any of the selected subspaces.

One approach is to use saliency methods, (Sha'ashua and Ullman, 1988). In this method, some particular local feature, such as curvature of a contour, is selected and all data features are clustered and ranked on the basis of this measure, to select those clusters of features (eg, connected contours) that are most salient. If the saliency feature is selected appropriately, such mechanisms can be used to group together subsets of features likely to have come from a single object.

A similar method is to use perceptual grouping (Witkin and Tenenbaum, 1983; Lowe, 1985). The motivation is again to extract features from an image likely to have come from a single object. For example, one can look for collections of features in the image that give rise to special inferences about the 3-D structure from which they come, and which are unlikely to occur at random. Examples would include finding parallel lines, lines with proximal endpoints, and lines that are collinear (Lowe, 1985). One extension to this idea, which has been shown to dramatically reduce the cost of searching for solutions, is to find convex sets of edges, then rank order pairs of sets on the basis of proximity and relative angle of support (Jacobs, 1989).

Termination of Search

Because of the expense of searching the correspondence space, especially when spurious data is present, many search methods incorporate selection methods to reduce the problem size. As well, many search methods utilize a second method for reducing search costs, namely the termination of the search once a "sufficiently good" interpretation is found. The motivation is that if one can set a threshold on some measure of the "goodness" of an interpretation, eg, the number of data features assigned to an actual model feature, or the total linear extent of the matched data features, then the search through the correspondence space can be terminated as soon as a solution surpassing this threshold is found. This can drastically reduce the computational expense associated with the search. Typically, the threshold is set based on empirical evidence. There are more formal methods for selecting the threshold, however. Grimson and Huttenlocher (1990) show that one can automatically set the threshold as a function of the desired probability of a false positive identification, as the number of sensor and model features, and as a bound on the noise in the measurements.

Using termination of the search can reduce the associated cost of finding solutions. In particular, (Grimson, 1991), if the ratio of data features to model features is sufficiently small, the expected search is reduced to a cubic polynomial, whereas if too many data features are included, the expected search is still exponential. This suggests that for these kinds of search methods, the selection problem is critical to successful solutions, and thus it is useful to consider other means of solving this problem.

Termination is particularly effective when coupled with other variations for guiding the search through correspondence space.

Ordering the Features. Since the goal is to find a correct interpretation as quickly as possible, one way to improve the search is to arrange the data features and the model features in an order optimal for finding correct interpretations with minimal search. There are several ways to approximate an optimal ordering. For example, one can order the data features by saliency or significance. One simple way to do this is to take the largest features first, such as the longest edges or the surface patches with the largest area (Grimson and Lozano-Pérez, 1987; Ayache and Faugeras, 1986). The motivation is that such features are likely to provide more constraint on the possible interpretations of an object, thereby reducing the search involved with incorrect but locally consistent partial interpretations. Another option is to look for distinctive groupings of features, eg, Lowe (1985) looks for collections of edges that are parallel, coterminate, or collinear.

Using Proximity. One can use other geometric constraints to order the data features. For example, suppose the first data feature, perhaps chosen on the basis of size, is matched to some model feature. Then proximity or connectivity of the data features can be used to select the next one to consider (Ayache and Faugeras, 1986). The motivation for this is that features connected to or close to previously matched features are more likely to have come from the same object than are distal features. One can similarly order the model features.

Visibility Conditions. Additional geometric constraints can be used to remove some model features from consideration before any matching takes place. Consider the problem of matching 3-D objects to sensory data. As part of the compile-time process of building a model representation, one can compute the set of model features that will be visible to the sensor, as a function of the pose of the model, where the pose is sampled at some resolution. Due to the opacity of the object, not all features will be visible at the same time, so for each pose only a limited set of model features needs to be considered. This geometric constraint can be used at run time to automatically remove some model features for consideration at each node of the search tree. In particular, the search method can be extended by computing the actual pose associated with a current interpretation, using it to index into a precomputed table of visible model features, and consider only those features as possible matches for the next data feature, thus reducing the set of branches to be considered for each node in the search tree. For details on this method, see Goad (1986) and Ikeuchi (1987).

Alignment, or Hypothesize and Test, Methods

All of the approaches described above focus on reducing the complexity of the search process. One of the most effective methods is selection or grouping, in which the data features are grouped in a data-driven manner to find subsets likely to have come from a single object. If this is done sufficiently, the expected cost of finding a correct solution is reduced from exponential to cubic. An alternative to data-driven selection is to use the object model to help select subspaces of the correspondence space.

This idea forms the basis for alignment methods for recognition (Bolles and Cain, 1982; Bolles and Horaud, 1986; Huttenlocher and Ullman, 1990; Ayache and Faugeras, 1986, Dhome and co-workers, 1989; Horaud, 1987; Lowe, 1985). Here one considers correspondences of data and model features, but only of a size sufficient to compute a complete transformation. For example, for recognition of 2-D objects from linear edge data, a single pairing of a data edge to a model edge is sufficient to deduce the three parameters of the transformation. For recognition of 2-D objects from point data, two pairs of data and model points, or a point and its orientation, are sufficient to deduce the three parameters of the transformation. For recognition of 3-D objects from 2-D images, then three pairs of data and model points are sufficient to deduce the six parameters of the transformation, in the case of affine transformations.

For each such point in the correspondence space, one can apply any appropriate unary and binary constraints, as before, and compute the associated transformation for all consistent nodes. Note that one need only search a small number of small dimensional subspaces of the correspondence space rather than the entire space.

Each transformation constitutes an hypothesis about the pose of the object, which must be verified. Verification means that additional evidence, either supporting or refuting the hypothesis, must be accumulated in the image, and the set of hypotheses must be weighted according to that evidence, so that the best interpretations can be selected. Typically, this is done by can be selected aligning the model with the data, that is, applying the hypothesized transformation to the model and using the transformed model to predict additional model features that might be evident in the data. This guides the search for additional supporting matches, which are used to refine the pose.

To be more concrete, consider the example shown in Figure 10. Suppose the primitive features include corners as well as edges. In this example, the search method might select the highlighted corner in Figure 10 as an initial feature to match. Given the image data in the example, there are only a small number of possible matching corners. Since a corner can include unary information, such as the angle subtended, and the side on which the object lies, not all corners in the image are possible matches. If the bounds on permissible error are small enough, then only the two candidate corners shown as darker circles would be selected as matches (both of which will lead to correct solutions). Even if considerable error is allowed in the data features so that a greater deviation in subtended angle is allowed, there are only six possible matches of focal features, shown as circles in Figure 10.

Consider the match of the model feature corner to the image corner formed by the junction of edge F_{14} and edge F_{15}. For this match, one can concentrate on the image features shown in Figure 11 as features for further match-

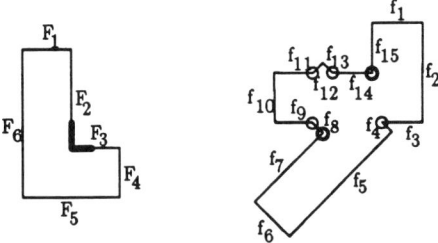

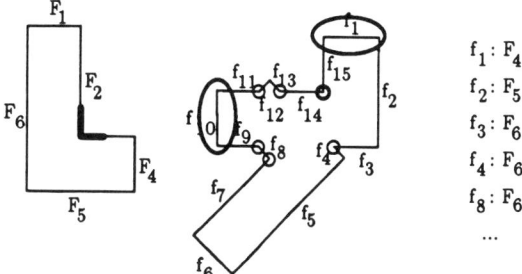

Figure 10. Focused search. Suppose corners are used as basic features, then the search process can focus on matching the highlighted model corner to candidate image corners. If the bounds on permissible error are small enough only the two candidate solutions shown in darker circles need to be considered. Even if significant noise is included, only the six candidate corners need to be matched.

Figure 12. Given a match of the focal model corner to the indicated image corner, where the orientation of the corner is included, an even more restrictive set of possible matches are defined for further matching. For example, possible matches for model feature F_1 are restricted to the region shown at the left, and possible matches for model feature F_4 are restricted to the region shown at the top. This reduces the partial list of possible matches to that shown at the right.

ing, since they are the only ones close enough to the focal feature. For each image feature, one can collect possible matching model features, and this set of model-data feature pairings can be used to define a graph to be searched, using the unary and binary constraints as outlined above.

One can see that this method can very quickly reduce the size of the search space. By concentrating on focal features, one need only do a small amount of search to find possible poses of the object. For each such candidate, one can restrict attention to a potentially smaller number of features. In Figure 11, the search for possible matching focal features considers only the small number of corners in the data. Given a candidate match as shown, one can immediately exclude some data features from any further consideration.

Note that in this simple case, a single feature is used as a focal feature, and its position is simply used to define a region in which to focus the search. This means that any data edge within an appropriate distance of the matched focal corner would be considered in the second stage of matching, and that all model edges would be considered as possible matches for each such edge, as indicated in Figure 11. One could also use the rough orientation of the feature (eg, the orientation of the bisector of the corner) together with the position of the feature to both translate and rotate the model relative to the image. This means that the set of possible data-model feature matches can be considerably reduced, to include only those pairings that roughly agree with the alignment of the model implied by the focal feature match, as shown in Figure 12. That is,

one not only reduces the set of data features to be considered, but one also reduces the set of model features to be considered. While this simple example results in only a single possible model feature as a candidate match for the nearby data features, in more realistic examples there may still be several (though not all) model features as candidate matches for a data feature.

As suggested by the examples above, there are several alternatives for how to search the subspaces isolated by alignment methods. One possibility is to incrementally refine the transformation associated with a partial interpretation as each new pairing of a data feature and a model feature is added (Ayache and Faugeras, 1986), and to use the updated pose to select a single new pairing as the best to add to the interpretation. A second is to use the alignment of the model together with bounds on the error associated with the data to restrict the set of possible matches to each feature. This effectively defines a very small search space which can then be explored to find correct interpretations, either using interpretation tree methods, or maximal clique approaches (Bolles and Cain, 1982).

To generate the hypotheses, one can simply exhaustively explore all pairings of data and model features, up to size d sufficient to compute a coordinate-frame transformation. One can be more efficient by utilizing methods that choose optimal features for initiating the alignment (Bolles and Cain, 1982).

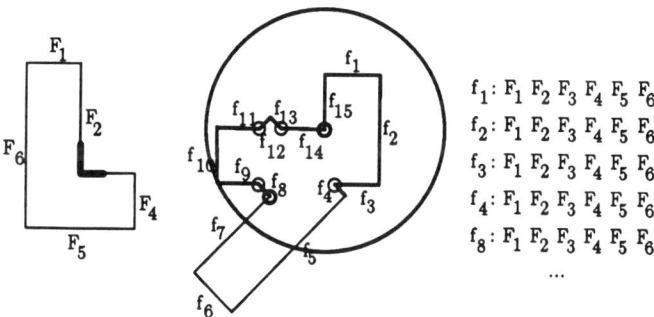

Figure 11. Given a match of the focal model corner to the indicated image corner, only those edges and corners that are nearby need be considered for further matching. A partial list of possible matches is shown on the right.

3-D from 2-D Recognition Using Alignment

One of the key advantages of alignment methods is that they easily extend to deal with 3-D recognition from 2-D data. Earlier methods are better suited to recognize 2-D models from single images, or 3-D models from 3-D data. The alignment techniques can directly incorporate the effects of projection from the scene into the image, along with the rotation and translation need to align a model and an image, so they can more easily deal with 3-D from 2-D recognition.

While the actual verification of the aligned model is done in the 2-D domain of the image, the actual alignment process can use a variety of different representations of the model. These include full 3-D models (Huttenlocher and Ullman, 1990), sets of characteristic 2-D views of an object (Freeman and Chakravarty, 1980; Gigus and coworkers, 1988; Koenderink and van Doorn, 1979; Kriegmann and Ponce, 1989; Plantinga and Dyer, 1986) or canonical models together with a method for automatically generating any other view by linear combinations of those canonical views (Ullman and Basri, 1989; Edelman and Poggio, 1990).

Parallel Relaxation

Central to all of these methods is the issue of searching for correspondences between model and data features, especially in the presence of spurious data. The search may be attacked as a problem of constraint satisfaction, as a subgraph matching problem, or by other means. Another means of reducing that search is to use relaxation, an approximation technique that uses a local function to iteratively approximate a global function. Because the computation in such methods is local, all the work of one iterative step can be performed in parallel, suggesting that such techniques may be well suited to parallel architectures. Relaxation methods have a large number of applications, but in the case of recognition (Rosenfeld and coworkers, 1976), relaxation is generally used as a suboptimal graph search algorithm (Bhanu and Faugeras, 1984; Faugeras and Berthod, 1981).

Such methods proceed as follows. A graph is constructed with nodes representing pairs of model and image features, and with arcs connecting pairs of nodes. The arcs are weighted according to the degree to which two nodes specify a consistent match of model and data features. A highly consistent set of model and image features corresponds to a subgraph with high weights connecting all the nodes in the subgraph. A good method of determining the weights is to use the inverse of the amount of stretching needed for the two image features to match the two model features (Davis, 1979). Other methods for choosing weights are given in Bhanu and Faugeras (1984).

The parallel relaxation algorithm works by removing those nodes for which some local evaluation function is below threshold and iterating until no node falls below the threshold. The remaining connected components of the graph are subgraphs with relatively high weights connecting the nodes and correspond to highly consistent sets of features pairs. Such methods can be considered as finding approximations to the maximal clique method of local feature focus.

Searching the Pose Space

All of the preceding discussion focused on searching the correspondence space for consistent interpretations of the data. The primary goal of such methods is to find the association of data features and model features; determining the pose of the object is secondary. An alternative is to directly search for consistent poses of an object model relative to the data. In this case, the search is focused in a *pose space*, that is a parameter space with axes that represent possible values for the parameters that determine a transformation. For example, for 2-D problems the pose space is either three- or four-dimensional, having two axes for each of two independent translation components, one axis for the rotational component and possibly one axis for a scale factor. 3-D problems have six- or seven-dimensional pose spaces, consisting of three translational parameters, three rotational parameters, and possibly a scale parameter.

Each point in the pose space represents a different possible pose or transformation of the model, and the problem is to determine which poses best fit the data. One straightforward method for doing this is to sample points in the pose space at some regular spacing, and use the associated transformation to map the model into image coordinates. Then, one can measure the amount of data accounted for by that transformation and use that to score the consistency of the pose. If one does that for all points (at some spacing) in the pose space, one can simply use the pose with the highest score as the solution. Such methods have been proposed in the past and basically are equivalent to correlating the object model with the sensor data over all possible poses and finding the best correlation.

The problem with this approach is that in order to have reasonable accuracy in the computed pose, and in order to correctly identify poses, one must sample the pose space quite finely, and this means that one is testing an enormous number of possibilities. For example, if one requires rotational accuracy to within a degree and translational accuracy to within a pixel, then on a standard size image, one must test 90,000,000 different poses. As with correspondence space methods, one needs more intelligent ways of avoiding useless testing.

Generalized Hough Transforms

One standard method for reducing the search of the pose space is to use voting schemes, such as the generalized Hough transform (qv) (Ballard, 1981). The generalized Hough transform finds possible solutions to the object pose problem by searching for large clusters of evidence in a discrete version of a parameter space. A parameter vector, **p**, represents a point in an n-dimensional space, $\mathcal{P}$. Each point in $\mathcal{P}$ maps to a point in the n-dimensional discrete Hough space, $\mathcal{H}$, that is specified by quantizing each of the n components of **p**. The Hough transform method is often referred to as parameter hashing because each quantized parameter value is a hash key. Implementations of Hough generally use an n-dimensional table to represent $\mathcal{H}$, and refer to table entries as buckets.

When the generalized Hough method is used for transformation clustering, each dimension of the parameter space, $\mathcal{P}$, corresponds to a component of the transformation from model to image. If the coordinate system of the image is denoted by $\mathcal{I}$, and the model coordinate system is denoted by $\mathcal{M}$, then $\mathcal{P}$ is a space of mappings from $\mathcal{M}$ to $\mathcal{I}$.

For each pair of model and image features, the range of possible transformations is computed. This set of transformations defines a region, $T \subseteq \mathcal{P}$. The quantized values of this n-dimensional volume, T, are used to enter the model-image pairing into all the buckets in $\mathcal{H}$ that intersect the range of possible transformations. Those model-image pairings that fall into the same quantization bucket define a cluster of similar transformations. It is assumed that the large clusters will identify correct transformations from a model to an image. Thus recognition consists of searching the n-dimensional discrete table (the space $\mathcal{H}$) for those buckets with a large number of entries.

Note that the Hough transform is actually performing a search over both the correspondence space and the pose space. The method must consider all pairings of data and model features, and this implies the method examines at least all nodes along each of the axes of the correspondence space. The results of examining each such node are transformed into pose space, where a second search for large clusters takes place. If several pairings of data and model features are needed to compute a set of feasible transforms, then larger portions of the correspondence space are first searched, before looking for clusters in pose space.

As an example, suppose that a model consists of linear segments, and the sensory data has been processed to produce comparable linear segments. Suppose there are m different model segments, and s sensory segments. Each sensory measurement taken from $\mathcal{I}$ is matched in turn with each model segment, for a total of ms model-data pairings. Consider the pairing of data edge f_j with model edge F_J. One can compute the transformation required to brig the model segment into correspondence with the data segment. In 2-D this transformation can be defined as the angle of rotation θ_{jJ} needed to align the tangents of the two segments, and the 2-D translation $\mathbf{t}_{jJ}$ needed to then align the rotated model edge with the data edge.

In the case of no uncertainty, $(\theta_{jJ}, \mathbf{t}_{jJ})$ exactly defines the transformation associated with the data-model pair, jJ. This transformation $(\theta_{jJ}, \mathbf{t}_{jJ})$ is represented by a point in the 3-D transform space $\mathcal{P}$. If there is sensor error or partial occlusion, then the pairing $f_j F_J$ defines a range of a possible transformations, represented by a volume in $\mathcal{P}$. The corresponding parameters θ_{jJ} and $\mathbf{t}_{jJ}$ are quantized, and used to enter the pairing $f_j F_J$ into those buckets of the 3-D Hough table that intersect the volume in $\mathcal{P}$.

The Hough transform must still examine all the points in the pose space (at some sampling) and test the score associated with that point against other scores. The advantage is that the work required to compute that score is much reduced compared to the straightforward method.

The Hough transform has both advantages and disadvantages when applied to the recognition problem. It can be implemented very efficiently. In cases of limited scene clutter and low noise, it is generally very robust in finding correct interpretations. With increased spurious, noisy data, however, the number of false peaks detected in the Hough space can increase dramatically and may force the recognition system to expend considerable extra effort in verifying the hypothesized peaks in the Hough space.

Note that similar to the previously described methods, the Hough transform also relies on geometric constraints, In this case, the constraint arises from considering the set of transformations consistent with a pairing of a model and data feature. The rigidity of an object implies that such a set of transformations is considerably smaller than the whole space of possible transformations, and hence, each such pairing strongly constrains the possible interpretations consistent with it. By combining these constraints as a voting scheme in pose space, the search needed to find feasible interpretations of the data is greatly restricted.

Sampling the Pose Space

There are other methods for exploring the pose space. Suppose the set of transformations consistent, modulo error, are computed with a pairing of a particular data and model features. This defines a volume of pose space and a vote can be cast on behalf of the data-model feature pairing for all of the transforms in that volume. By repeating this for all pairings of features, and summing the votes cast by different pairs for the same spot in pose space, a mapping f on pose space in which $f(\mathbf{p})$ is the number of volumes containing the point $\mathbf{p}$ can be created. This mapping is piecewise constant, and ideally it would be ideal to find the region in transform space over which f takes on a maximal value. The Hough transform approaches this by integrating f over equal sized regions (the buckets) and finding the maximum such value (note that here integration means adding the contributions from different pairings that intersect the same bucket). This integration may cause nonoverlapping volumes that happen to intersect the same bucket to add up to an amount that is larger than the best value for $f(\mathbf{p})$. A more correct method is to actually sample the pose space at points at which f changes value. One can approximate this by sampling the pose space at some regular spacing (Cass, 1988). A better method (Cass, 1990) is to find a set of points in pose space such that all transitions in value f are sampled. By computing the value of f at all such points, one can find maximal matchings between data and model features.

Recognizing Parameterized Objects

Most of the current work in recognition focuses on rigid objects, as is evident from the preceding discussion. More general recognition should deal with parts that are deformable, or objects that are characterized by general families of parts. The constrained search methods outlined above can be generalized to handle some simple kinds of deformable objects (Grimson, 1991; Ettinger, 1988).

Other alternatives for dealing with the recognition of parameterized objects include generalized cylinders, elastically deformable models, and superquadrics. Generalized cylinders, originally proposed by Binford (1971), were the first major attempt at devising a parameterized volume representation for vision. A generalized cylinder can be defined by four constituent parts (Shafer, 1985):

- A space curve, called the *axis*.
- A *cross-sectional plane*, defined for each point on the axis by some fixed angle relative to the tangent to the axis.
- A planar curve for each cross-section plane, called a *cross-section*.
- A *transformation rule* (or sweeping rule) that specifies the transformation of the cross-section as the plane is swept along the axis.

Representative examples of generalized cylinder-based recognition include Agin and Binford (1976), Nevatia and Binford (1977), and Marr and Nishihara (1978). Most of these approaches focus on generative aspects of generalized cylinders, or look at recognition when all of the data is known to come from a single object, thereby ignoring the segmentation problem. An exception to this is the work of Rao and Nevatia (1988), which specifically applies generalized cylinder methods to noisy cluttered stereo data. Probably the best known system based on generalized cylinders is ACRONYM (Brooks, 1981), which attacks the recognition problem by applying geometric constraints to reduce ranges of parameterized variables associated with a deformable model. Brooks' system dealt with both rigid subparts and constraints that incorporated free parameters at run time.

A second alternative, similar to generalized cylinders, is to use physical models of elastically deformable objects (Terzopoulos and co-workers, 1987). Although complicated in form, the deformable models method shows considerable power in modeling complicated shapes. Its ability to extract such descriptions from cluttered data is less clear however, as current approaches often require some initial human intervention.

A third alternative is to use superquadrics, discovered by Hein (Gardiner, 1965), and developed for vision problems by a variety of researchers, eg, Barr (1981), Pentland (1986), and Bajcsy and Solina (1987). It can be represented as a parameterized volume, by the vector

$$\mathbf{x}(\eta, \omega) = \begin{bmatrix} a_1 \cos^{\varepsilon_1} \eta \cos^{\varepsilon_2} \omega \\ a_2 \cos^{\varepsilon_1} \eta \sin^{\varepsilon_2} \omega \\ a_3 \sin^{\varepsilon_1} \eta \end{bmatrix}.$$

By changing the angles η, ω the squareness parameters $\varepsilon_1, \varepsilon_2$ and the size parameters a_1, a_2, a_3, a superquad can take on a variety of volumetric shapes. As in the previous cases, much of the work on superquadrics has focused on generative uses, or on inducing shapes from isolated objects, although some work has considered the segmentation issue as well.

SUMMARY

Object recognition involves identifying instances of known objects in sensory data. Key factors contributing to the difficulty of the problem include choosing good representations of objects, extracting reliable corresponding measurements from the data, and handling occlusion and clutter in the data. Much of the work has focused on effective methods for structuring the search for correspondences between model features and data features. Current methods can deal reasonably well with rigid polyhedral objects, in moderately complex scenes. Extensions to deal with more general object shapes and to deal with large libraries of objects remain an open problem.

BIBLIOGRAPHY

G. J. Agin and T. O. Binford, "Computer Description of Curved Objects," *IEEE Trans. Comput.* **25,** 439–449 (1976).

N. Ayache and O. D. Faugeras, "HYPER: A New Approach for the Recognition and Positioning of 2D Objects," *IEEE Trans. Pattern Anal. Mach. Intell.* **8**(1), 44–54 (1986).

H. S. Baird, *Model-Based Image Matching Using Location*, MIT Press, Cambridge, Mass., 1985.

D. H. Ballard, "Generalizing the Hough Transform to Detect Arbitrary Patterns," *Pattern Recognition* **13**(2), 111–122 (1981).

B. Bamieh and R. J. P. De Figueiredo, "A General Moment Invariants/Attributed-Graph Method for 3D Object Recognition from a Single Image," *IEEE J. Rob. Autom.* **2**(1), 31–41 (1986).

R. Bajcsy and F. Solina, "Three Dimensional Object Representation Revisited," *First Int. Conf. Comp. Vision*, London, UK, 231–240 (1987).

A. Barr, "Superquadrics and Angle-Preserving Transformations," *IEEE Comput. Graphics Appl.* **1,** 11–23 (1981).

B. Bhanu and O. D. Faugeras, "Shape Matching of 2D Objects," *IEEE Trans. Pattern Anal. Mach. Intell.* **6**(2), 137–156 (1984).

T. O. Binford, "Visual Perception by Computer," *Proceedings of the IEEE Conference on Systems and Control*, Miami, Fla., 1971.

R. C. Bolles and R. A. Cain, "Recognizing and Locating Partially Visible Objects: The Local Feature Focus Method," *Int. J. Robot. Res.* **1**(3), 57–82 (1982).

R. C. Bolles and P. Horaud, "3DPO: A 3D Part Orientation System," *Int. J. Robots. Res.* **5**(3), 3–26 (1986).

R. Brooks, "Symbolic Reasoning Among 3D Models and 2D Images," *Artif. Intell.* **17,** 285–349 (1981).

T. A. Cass, "A Robust Parallel Implementation of 2D Model-Based Recognition," *IEEE Conf. Comp. Vision, Patt. Recog.*, Ann Arbor, Mich., 879–884 (1988).

T. A. Cass, *Feature Matching for Object Localization in the Presence of Uncertainty*, MIT AI Lab Memo 1133, 1990.

L. S. Davis, "Shape Matching Using Relaxation Techniques," *IEEE Trans. Pattern Anal. Mach. Intell.* **1**(1), 60–72 (1979).

M. Dhome, M. Richetin, J.-T. Lapreste, and G. Rives, "Determination of the Attitude of 3-d Objects from a Single Perspective View," *IEEE Trans. Pattern Anal. Mach. Intell.* **11**(12), 1265–1278 (1989).

S. Edelman and T. Poggio, *Bringing the Grandmother Back Into the Picture: A Memory-Based View of Object Recognition*, MIT AI Lab Memo 1181, 1990.

G. J. Ettinger, "Large Hierarchical Object Recognition Using Libraries of Parameterized Model Sub-Parts," *IEEE Conf. Comp. Vision, Patt. Recog.*, 32–41 (1988).

O. D. Faugeras and M. Berthod, "Improving Consistency and Reducing Ambiguity in Stochastic Labeling: An Optimization Approach," *IEEE Trans. Pattern Anal. Mach. Intell.* **3,** 412–424 (1981).

O. D. Faugeras and M. Hebert, "The Representation, Recognition and Locating of 3-D Objects," *Int. J. Robot. Res.* **5**(3), 27–52 (1986).

H. Freeman and I. Chakravarty, "The Use of Characteristic Views in the Recognition of 3D Objects," in E. Gelsema and L. Kanal, eds., *Pattern Recognition in Practice*, North-Holland Publishers, Amsterdam, 1980, pp. 277–288.

M. Gardiner, "The Superellipse: A Curve that Lies Between the Ellipse and the Rectangle," *Sci. Amer.* **213**, 222–234 (1965).

Z. Gigus, J. Canny, and R. Seidel, "Efficiently Computing and Representing Aspect Graphs of Polyhedral Objects," *Proceedings of the 2nd International Conference on Computer Vision*, Tampa, Fla., 1988, pp. 30–39.

G. Gleason and G. J. Agin, "A Modular Vision System for Sensor-Controlled Manipulation and Inspection," *Proceedings of the 9th International Symposium on Industrial Robots*, 1979, pp. 57–70.

C. Goad, "Fast 3D Model-Based Vision," in A. P. Pentland, ed., *From Pixels to Predicates*, Ablex, Norwood, N.J., 1986, pp. 317–391.

W. E. L. Grimson, *Object Recognition by Computer: The Role of Geometric Constraints*, MIT Press, Cambridge, Mass., 1991.

W. E. L. Grimson and D. P. Huttenlocher, "On the Verification of Hypothesized Matches in Model-Based Recognition," *First European Conference on Computer Vision*, 1990, pp. 489–498.

W. E. L. Grimson and T. Lozano-Pérez, "Localizing Overlapping Parts by Searching the Interpretation Tree," *IEEE Trans. Pattern Anal. Mach. Intell.* **9**(4), 469–482 (1987).

R. Horaud, "New Methods for Matching 3-D Objects with Single Perspective Views," *IEEE Trans. Pattern Anal. Mach. Intell.* **9**(3), 401–412 (1987).

B. K. P. Horn, *Robot Vision*, MIT Press, Cambridge, Mass., 1986.

M. K. Hu, "Visual Pattern Recognition by Moment Invariants," *IRE Trans. Inform. Theory* **8**, 179–187 (1962).

D. P. Huttenlocher and S. Ullman, "Recognizing Solid Objects by Alignment with an Image," *Int. J. Comp. Vision* **5**(2), 195–212 (1990).

K. Ikeuchi, "Generating an Interpretation Tree from a CAD Model for 3D-Object Recognition in Bin-Picking Tasks," *Int. J. Comp. Vision* **1**(2), 145–165 (1987).

D. W. Jacobs, *Grouping for Recognition*, MIT AI Lab Memo 1177, 1989.

J. K. Koenderink and A. J. van Doorn, "The Internal Representation of Solid Shape with Respect to Vision," *Biol. Cybern.* **32**, 211–215 (1979).

D. Kriegman and J. Ponce, "Computing Exact Aspect Graphs of Curved Objects: Solids of Revolution," *Proceedings of the IEEE Workshop on Interpretation of 3D Scenes*, Austin, Tex., 1989.

D. G. Lowe, *Perceptual Organization and Visual Recognition*, Kluwer Academic Publishers, Boston, Mass., 1985.

D. Marr and H. K. Nishihara, "Representation and Recognition of the Spatial Organization of 3D Shapes," *Proc. R. Soc. London B* **200**, 269–294 (1978).

D. W. Murray and B. F. Buxton, *Experiments in the Machine Interpretation of Visual Motion*, MIT Press, Cambridge, Mass., 1990.

R. Nevatia and T. O. Binford, "Description and Recognition of Curved Objects," *Artif. Intell.* **8**, 77–98 (1977).

A. Pentland, "Perceptual Organization and the Representation of Natural Form," *Artif. Intell.* **28**(3), 293–331 (1986).

E. Persoon and K. S. Fu, "Shape Discrimination Using Fourier Descriptors," *IEEE Trans. Sys. Man. Cybern.* **7**, 170–179 (1977).

W. H. Plantinga and C. R. Dyer, "An Algorithm for Constructing the Aspect Graph," *Proceedings of the 27th Annual Symposium on Foundations of Computer Science*, 1986, pp. 123–131.

K. Rao and R. Nevatia, "Computing Volume Descriptions from Sparse 3-D Data," *Int. J. Comp. Vision* **2**(1), 33–50 (1988).

A. Rosenfeld, R. Hummel, and S. Zucker, "Scene Labeling by Relaxation Operations," *IEEE Trans. Sys. Man Cybern.* **7**, 420–433 (1976).

A. Sha'ashua and S. Ullman, "Structural Saliency: The Detection of Globally Salient Structures Using a Locally Connected Network," *Second International Conference on Computer Vision*, Tarpon Springs, Fla., 1988, pp. 321–327.

S. A. Shafer, *Shadows and Silhouettes in Computer Vision*, Kluwer Academic Publishers, Boston, Mass., 1985.

Y. J. Tejwani and R. A. Jones, "Machine Recognition of Partial Shapes Using Feature Vectors," *IEEE Trans. Sys. Man Cybern.* **15**, 504–516 (1985).

D. Terzopoulos, A. Witkin, and M. Kass, "Symmetry-Seeking Models and 3D Object Reconstruction," *Int. J. Comp. Vision* **1**(3), 211–221 (1987).

S. Ullman and R. Basri, *Recognition by Linear Combinations of Models*, MIT AI Lab Memo 1152, 1989.

T. P. Wallace, O. R. Mitchell, and K. Fukunaga, "3D Shape Analysis Using Local Shape Descriptors," *IEEE Trans. Pattern Anal. Mach. Intell.* **3**, 310–323 (1981).

A. P. Witkin and M. Tenenbaum, "On the Role of Structure in Vision," in Rosenfeld and Beck, eds., *Human and Machine Vision*, Academic Press, Inc., New York, 1983, pp. 481–543.

C. T. Zahn and R. Z. Roskies, "Fourier Descriptors for Plane Closed Curves," *IEEE Trans. Computers* **21**(3), 269–281 (1972).

W. E. L. GRIMSON
Massachusetts Institute of Technology

ONCOCIN

A large medical-advice system that has adapted the skeletal-plan refinement methodology for application to the management of cancer patients who receive episodic treatments with chemotherapeutic agents. Important for its emphasis on temporal reasoning, integration of an expert system with its related medical-database system, and its use of advanced graphical techniques to enhance the interface for physician users [see S. W. Tu and co-workers, "Episodic Skeletal-Plan Refinement Based on Temporal Data," *Communications ACM* **32**, 1439–1455 (1989)].

L. M. FAGAN
E. H. SHORTLIFFE
Stanford University

OPAL

OPAL is a graphical knowledge-acquisition tool for the ONCOCIN cancer-chemotherapy advisor (see S. W. Tu and co-workers, "Episodic Skeletal-Plan Refinement Based on Temporal Data," *CACM* **32**(12), 1439–1455, Dec. 1989). The OPAL program incorporates an explicit model of the task of administering cancer chemotherapy, and allows cancer specialists to create new knowledge bases for ONCOCIN automatically by filling out graphical forms and by drawing flow chart diagrams on a workstation display. OPAL translates the visual representations of cancer-therapy plans entered by physician-users into the rules and frames required by ONCOCIN to generate recommendations for patient management. The PROTÉGÉ system (qv) allows knowledge-acquisition tools like OPAL themselves to be generated automatically from metalevel specifications. OPAL was developed at Stanford University in 1985 [see M. A. Musen, L. M. Fagan, D. M. Combs, and E. H. Shortliffe, "Use of a Domain Model to Drive an Interactive Knowledge-Editing Tool," *Int. J. Man-Machine Stud.* **26**, 105–121 (1987)].

M. A. MUSEN
Stanford University

OpEd

OpEd (Opinions to/from the Editor) is a prototype editorial comprehension and question answering system in the politico-economic domain. OpEd is designed to take editorial text as input and answer subsequent questions concerning the beliefs/arguments of the editorial writer and of others whom the writer may criticize. The process of editorial comprehension is viewed as one of managing many different knowledge sources, which include scripts, social acts, affects, causal chains of reasoning, economic entities, goals, plans, actions, characters, beliefs, and belief relationships. OpEd's central organizing constructs of abstract knowledge of argumentation are termed Argument Units (AUs). AUs consist of configurations of support and attack relationships among beliefs, where the content of each belief refers to goal/plan situations. Knowledge of AUs allows OpEd to recognize and interpret arguments in the politico-economic domain, as long as the system has sufficient planning skill and domain knowledge to build up instances of the particular goals, plans, and beliefs occurring within that domain. (See S. J. Alvarado, *Understanding Editorial Text: A Computer Model of Argument Comprehension,* Kluwer Academic Publishers, Boston, Mass., 1990; see ARGUMENT COMPREHENSION.)

SERGIO J. ALVARADO
University of California at Davis

OPS5

OPS5 is a high performance, forward-chaining, rule-based programming language. OPS5 was the final in a series of domain-independent production systems conceived of at Carnegie Mellon University (see C. L. Forgy and J. McDermott, "OPS, a Domain-Independent Production System," *Proceedings of the Fifth International Joint Conference on Artificial Intelligence,* Cambridge, Mass., Morgan-Kaufmann, San Mateo, Calif., 1977, pp. 933–939). A public domain lisp-based OPS5 (see C. L. Forgy, *OPS5 User's Manual, Technical Report, CMS-CS-81-135,* Carnegie Mellon University, July 1981) was used to implement the final version of the first commercial expert system, R1, written for Digital Equipment Corporation by John McDermott. R1 was later evolved into XCON using Digital's Bliss-based implementation of OPS5, VAX OPS5.

OPS5 was the first production system with sufficient performance to explore the potential of nonprocedural programming approaches. Unlike procedural languages (like C), rules are not executed in the sequence defined. Rules are "fired" in the recognize-act cycle. In each cycle, the set of rules that could execute, based on the current global state, are identified. A single rule is selected according to the "conflict resolution strategy" being used. This rule is then "fired"; that is, its right-hand side (RHS) or action side is executed, making a change to the global state. The recognize-act cycle is continued until there is an explicit halt, or no rules can fire.

The high performance of OPS5 comes from the RETE algorithm (see C. L. Forgy, *On the Efficient Implementation of Production Systems,* Ph.D. thesis, Carnegie Mellon University, 1979). Based on the premise that the amount of change is small relative to the total amount of data, RETE uses caching and compilation techniques to reduce significantly the amount of data that must be referenced for each rule firing.

KEN GILBERT
JOHN MCDERMOTT
Digital Equipment Corp.

ORDER-SORTED LOGIC. See LOGIC, ORDER-SORTED.

OTTER

A resolution/paramodulation automated deduction system (see RESOLUTION, BINARY) for first-order logic with equality, OTTER has assisted with the solution of several open problems in logic and mathematics. OTTER's strong point is the ability to quickly explore very large search spaces. (See W. W. McCune, *OTTER 2.0 Users Guide,* Technical Report ANL 90/9, Mathematics and Computer Science Division, Argonne National Laboratory, Argonne, Ill., 1990.)

W. W. MCCUNE
Argonne National Laboratory

P

PAM

A goal-based story-understanding system (see STORY ANALYSIS) PAM was written in 1978 by Wilensky at Yale University (see R. Wilensky, "PAM," in R. C. Shank and C. K. Riesbeck, eds., *Inside Computer Understanding: Five Programs Plus Miniatures*, Lawrence Erlbaum, Hillsdale, N.J., 1981, pp. 136–179).

M. R. TAIE
AT&T Bell Laboratories

PANDEMONIUM

Pandemonium is a conceptual architecture for certain kinds of learning; it was one of the earliest attempts, and appeared in the late 1950s. It stresses the importance of features in recognition of patterns, and suggests that features form a hierarchy that has a dominant and natural hierarchy. The layers of the hierarchy exhibit much of the structural properties and functions proposed for multilayer neural nets or connectionist systems. Selfridge and Samuel were the first to discuss the generation of new features from modifications or combinations of old ones. [See O. G. Selfridge, "Pandemonium: A Paradigm for Learning," *The Mechanisation of Thought Processes*, H. M. Stationery Office, London, 2 vols., 1959, reprinted in L. Uhr, ed., *Pattern Recognition; Theory, Experiment, Computer Simulations, and Dynamic Models of Form Perception and Discovery*, John Wiley and Sons, Inc., New York, 1966; A. L. Samuel, "Some Studies in Machine Learning Using the Game of Checkers," *IBM J. Res. Dev.* **3**, 210–299 (1959), reprinted in E. A. Feigenbaum and J. Feldman, eds., *Computers and Thought*, McGraw-Hill, New York, 1963.]

OLIVER G. SELFRIDGE
GTE Laboratories

PARALLEL LOGIC PROGRAMMING LANGUAGES

Logic programming languages are based on predicate logic and characterized by the fact that logical inference corresponds to computation. Thus a program can be written declaratively and can be executed procedurally by computer (Kowalski, 1974). Many logic programming languages can be imagined. The one based on Horn logic is the most successful and has been extensively studied.

A logic program is represented by a finite set of universally quantified Horn clauses. A goal statement is used to invoke computation that can be regarded as refutation of the goal statement under the given set of clauses. PROLOG was the first language to realize this idea (Roussel, 1975). Its computation rule corresponds to left-to-right and depth-first traversal of an AND–OR tree.

Given a set of Horn clauses, there are many strategies for refutation other than the one adopted in PROLOG. Among these, parallel strategies are of great interest. These correspond to the parallel interpretation of logic programs. Conery and Kibler (1981) classified them into four models: OR-parallelism, independent AND-parallelism, AND-parallelism, and search-parallelism (some use the terms AND-parallelism and Stream-parallelism, instead of the terms independent AND-parallelism and AND-parallelism, respectively). AND-parallelism has received much attention because of its expressive power suitable for systems programming and other applications. Several parallel logic programming languages based on AND-parallelism have been proposed. They include Relational Language (Clark and Gregory, 1981). Concurrent Prolog (Shapiro, 1983, 1986), PARLOG (Clark and Gregory, 1986; Gregory, 1987; Ringwood, 1988), Guarded Horn Clauses (Ueda, 1985b, 1986a, 1986b), Oc (Hirata, 1985), and FLENG (Nilsson and Tanaka, 1986).

The following ideas and requirements seem to be what spurred creation of these languages. The first was to create a parallel execution model for logic programs to fully utilize new parallel computer architecture. As hardware technology evolves, highly parallel computers become realizable using VLSI technology. However, to write a program for a parallel computer is a complicated task and involves new problems quite different from those in programming on a sequential computer. The gap between hardware and software seems to increase. It is believed that the success of the parallel computer depends on the software technology. Choosing languages for parallel programming is the most important decision in parallel software technology. In order for a programmer to avoid various problems and extract parallelism easily, languages should have clear semantics and be inherently parallel themselves. Because of their semantic clarity and high level constructs useful for programming and debugging, logic programs are being regarded as a candidate to fully utilize the power of parallel architectures.

The second issue is the extension of control of logic programming languages. Control facilities of PROLOG are similar to those of conventional procedural languages, although the model for logic programming languages includes no specific control mechanism. There have been several proposals for more flexible computation. They augment PROLOG by introducing new control primitives such as coroutines. Languages based on AND-parallelism can be regarded as an alternative attempt to extend control. These languages abandoned the rules of sequential execution and thus first introduced parallelism. A great deal of effort was devoted to finding a reasonable set of control primitives for managing the parallelism obtained as a result.

The third point is to exploit new programming styles in logic programming and thus exploit new applications of logic programming. Logic programming languages such as PROLOG are suitable for database applications and natural language processing but were suspected of being inadequate for applications such as operating systems. Parallel logic programming languages with control primitives managing parallelism aim at covering such applications as systems programming, object-oriented programming, and simulation and thus enlarging the applications of logic programming.

The development of parallel logic programming languages began in the early 1980s. In this short time, research has been intensive around the world, and many fruitful results have been obtained. One book (Shapiro, 1987) includes many papers on this research area from theoretical foundation to advanced applications. For more analytical language comparison and related programming techniques, readers should refer to Shapiro's survey (1989).

AND-PARALLEL COMPUTATION MODEL

AND-parallel computation models were studied by Clark and co-workers (1982) and van Emden and de Lucena (1982) independently as extended interpretation models of logic programs. Without introducing specific languages, this section will informally review AND-parallel computation models. Consider the following logic program [syntax similar to that of Edinburgh PROLOG (Clocksin and Mellish, 1984) is used]:

    quicksort(List,Sorted) :- qsort(List,Sorted,[ ]). (1)
    qsort([ ],H,H). (2)
    qsort([A|B],H,T) :-
        partition(B,A,S,L),
        qsort(S,H,[A|T1]),
        qsort(L,T1,T). (3)
    partition([ ],X,[ ],[ ]). (4)
    partition([A|B],X,[A|S],L) :- A < X, partition(B,X,S,L). (5)
    partition([A|B],X,S,[A|L]) :- A >= X, partition(B,X,S,L). (6)

The predicate **quicksort(List,Sorted)**, expresses the relation that **Sorted** is the sorted list of the list **List**. **qsort(List,H,T)** represents the fact that the difference list **H-T** is the sorted list of the list **List**. **partition(List,E,S,L)** says that **S** is a sublist of **List**, each element of which is less than **E** and **L** is a sublist each element of which is greater than or equal to **E**. Given the above program and the following goal statement:

    ?- quicksort([2,1,3],X).

the PROLOG interpreter will return the following answer substitution:

    X = [1,2,3].

The algorithm used in the above logic program is *divide and conquer*. Given a list, the CDR is divided into two lists, one consisting of elements less than CAR and the other of elements greater than or equal to CAR. Both lists are sorted independently and combined to construct the sorted list of the original list. The algorithm is typically embodied in clause 3. The clause can be read procedurally in the following way: To sort a list [A|B], partition B into S and L with respect to A, and sort S and L. According to the sequential computation rule of PROLOG, these subgoals are executed from left to right, that is, first the list **B** is partitioned, then **S** is sorted, and finally **L** is sorted.

There are two possibilities for exploiting parallelism in the above program, especially in clause (3). One is cooperative parallelism. Since the lists **S** and **L** can be sorted independently, execution of two qsorts can be done in parallel. Although they share a variable, **T1**, they can cooperate in the construction of a list **H-T** by constructing nonoverlapping sublists, **H-T1** and **T1-T**, of **H-T** in parallel. The other is pipelining parallelism. Note that both lists, **S** and **L**, are constructed incrementally from the heads by partition, and these two lists are consumed from their heads by two separate qsorts. Therefore, it is possible to start execution of the two qsorts with available parts of the lists before partition completes the lists. The parallelism of partition and the two separate qsorts resembles so-called pipelining parallelism. Both parallelisms, processed by a parallel computer, are expected to be effective at reducing computation time.

Cooperative parallelism and pipelining parallelism are typical kinds of parallelism that AND-parallel interpretation can extract from logic programs by parallel interpretation of conjunctive goals. Goals sharing variables are not independent and can interact with each other. AND-parallelism involves cooperation of goals executed in parallel through shared variables. This is in clear contrast to independent AND-parallelism, where no collaboration among goals is considered. In independent AND-parallel interpretation, conjunctive goals are solved independently and consistent solutions are extracted from their solutions. Independent AND-parallel interpretation is in danger of generating an excessive amount of irrelevant computation, since unnecessary computation is proved to be irrelevant only when it terminates.

AND-parallel interpretation avoids this problem in the following way. First, bindings created in the course of computation are transported to other computations as soon as possible. This helps parallel computations to exchange bindings of shared variables in order to maintain consistency. Second, it provides new control primitives which can restrict access modes to shared variables. There can be two modes in access to a variable, although the mode is implicit and multiple in logic programming. These modes are input (read) and output (write). New primitives can be used to restrict the access mode to a shared variable to either input or output. Appropriate restriction of access modes to a shared variable enables the variable to be used as an asynchronous communication channel between parallel computations. Using such asynchronous communication channels, programmers can coordinate parallel goals and suppress irrelevant computation. In sum, the parallelism explored in AND-parallelism is controlled parallelism, and the languages based on AND-parallelism can extract maximum parallelism while reducing irrelevant parallel computation.

COMMON LANGUAGE FEATURES

Several parallel logic programming languages have been proposed. They are Relational Language, Concurrent Prolog, PARLOG, Guarded Horn Clauses (hereafter called

GHC), Oc, and FLENG. (Real PARLOG provides many higher-level constructs such as sequential AND and all solution predicates; however, since these features can be reduced to kernel features they are not treated here.) The common features of these languages, which will be defined, were first proposed in Relational Language.

Syntax

For notational convenience, the common syntax is defined. A program is a finite set of guarded clauses. A guarded clause is a universally quantified Horn clause of the form

$$H :- G_1, \ldots, G_n | B_1, \ldots, B_m. \quad n, m \geq 0$$

where "|" is called a commitment operator or commit; $G_1, \ldots, G_n$ is called the guard part; $B_1, \ldots, B_m$, the body part. H is called the head of the clause. A set of clauses sharing the same predicate symbol with the same arity is defined as the definition of that predicate. A goal statement is a conjunction of goals of the form

$$:-P_1, \ldots, P_n. \quad n > 0.$$

Declarative Semantics

The declarative meanings of "," and "|" are *and* ("$\wedge$"). ":-" declaratively means implication ($\subset$). The clause can be read declaratively as follows: For all term values of the variables in the clause, H is true if both $G_1, \ldots, G_n$ and $B_1, \ldots, B_m$ are true. Thus

$$H \subset G_1 \wedge \cdots \wedge G_n \wedge B_1 \wedge \cdots \wedge B_m$$

Process Reading

Logic programming was founded on the dual readings of definite clauses: declarative and procedural readings. Parallel logic programming languages employ a third reading of logic programs: process reading. In process reading, a solution process of a goal is regarded as a process initiated by that goal. A process terminates when the goal is solved. In general, a process forms a tree with an initial goal at the root node, since a goal may invoke several subgoals in parallel. A unit goal is analogous to a process snapshot, a conjunctive goal is analogous to a set of process snapshots, and variables shared between goals function similarly to communication channels. The guarded clause above is read behaviorally. A process with snapshot H can change to the system of subprocesses whose snapshots are B_1 and B_2 and ... and B_m if G_1 and G_2 and ... and G_n successfully terminate. A process terminates by changing to the empty system.

In the process reading, the actions a process can take are specified by a set of guarded clauses; all a process can do is change itself to other states using one of them. The guarded clause is similar to Dijkstra's guarded-command in its effect. In the course of this change, variables shared with other processes may get instantiated via unification, thus achieving the effect of process communication. To achieve process synchronization, parallel logic programming languages provide various primitives.

Sketch of Operational Semantics

Roughly speaking, "," procedurally means fork. Namely, a conjunction, "P,Q," indicates that goals, P and Q, are to be solved in different processes. The procedural meaning of a commitment operator is to cut off alternative clauses. A sketch of operational semantics using two kinds of processes, an AND-process and an OR-process, following the method used in (Miyazaki and co-workers, 1985) is given below.

The goal statement is fed to a root-process, a special case of an OR-process. Given a conjunction of goals, a root-process creates one AND-process for each goal. When all these AND-processes succeed, the root-process succeeds; when one fails, the root-process fails.

Given a goal G with the predicate symbol P, an AND-process creates one OR-process for each clause defining the predicate P and passes the goal to each process. When all of these OR-processes fail, the AND-process fails. Otherwise some OR-process C succeeds and attempts to be selected for subsequent execution of G. To be selected, C must first confirm that no other brother OR-processes have been selected for G. If confirmed, C is selected indivisibly, and the execution of G is said to be committed to the clause C. Then for each goal in the body part of the clause kept by C, it creates an AND-process and replaces itself by these AND-processes. Choice of a clause is not backtrackable. In this sense, it is called committed choice.

Given a goal and a clause, an OR-process unifies the goal with the head of the clause and solves the guard part of the clause by creating an AND-process for each goal in the guard. When all these AND-processes succeed, it succeeds. When one of these fails, it fails.

There are some remarks. First, conjunctive goals are solved in parallel by AND-processes. A clause such that the head can be unified with the goal and the guard can successfully terminate is searched for in parallel by OR-processes, but only one is selected by commitment. Parallel search is similar to OR-parallelism but is not the same because it is bounded in the evaluation of guard parts. A commitment operator selects one clause, cuts off the rest, and terminates OR-parallelism.

Second, computation is organized hierarchically as an AND- and OR-process tree. Each OR-process may be associated with a local environment storing bindings that would influence other competing OR-processes if they were revealed.

Third, in general, if access to a variable is restricted to input mode, then no unification that instantiates the variable to a nonvariable term is allowed and such unification is forced to suspend until the variable is instantiated. This kind of synchronization mechanism is useful for delaying commitment until enough information is obtained. Languages proposed so far have different syntactic primitives for specification of restriction of access mode.

RESTRICTION OF ACCESS MODE

Different primitives for restricting access mode are adopted by different languages. In fact, the method of representing this restriction characterizes each language.

Mode Declaration

PARLOG and its predecessor, Relational Language, take this approach. Restriction of access mode is specified by mode declaration. In PARLOG, each predicate definition must be associated with one mode declaration. It has the form

mode $R(m_1, \ldots, m_k)$.

where R is a predicate symbol with arity k. Each m_i is "?" or "^". "?" indicates that access to a variable at this position in a goal is restricted to input mode; "^" indicates output mode. Note that there is no neutral (multiple) mode. During head unification, any attempt to instantiate a variable appearing in an argument specified as input in a goal to a nonvariable term is forced to suspend. Output mode indicates that a term pattern at the corresponding argument position in the head will be issued from the clause. Unification between such output patterns and corresponding variables in the goal could be performed after the clause is selected. Implementation of synchronization using one-way unification is presented in (Clark and Gregory, 1985).

A merge operator merging two lists into one in arbitrary order can be defined in PARLOG as follows:

mode merge(?,?,^).

merge([A|X],Y,[A|Z]) :− true | merge(X,Y,Z).
merge(X,[A|Y],[A|Z]) :− true | merge(X,Y,Z).
merge([ ],Y,Y) :− true | true.
merge(X,[ ],X) :− true | true.

Read-Only Annotation

Concurrent Prolog adopts this primitive. Read-only annotation is denoted by "?". It can be attached to any variable. A variable with read-only annotation is called a read-only variable. Read-only annotation restricts access to the variable to read mode only. Any attempt to instantiate an unbound variable with read-only annotation to a nonvariable term is forced to suspend until the variable is instantiated. Read-only annotation must be handled in unification procedure, since read-only variables can appear anywhere in a term. More rigorous treatment of read-only annotation is described in (Shapiro, 1986). Using this annotation, the merge operator can be defined as follows:

merge([A|X],Y,[A|Z]) :− true | merge(X?,Y,Z).
merge(X,[A|Y],[A|Z]) :− true | merge(X,Y?,Z).
merge([ ],Y,Y) :− true | true.
merge(X,[ ],X) :− true | true.

Invocation of the goal takes the form:

merge(X?,Y?,Z).

Input Guard

This is adopted in GHC, Oc, and FLENG. Restriction of access mode to variables in a goal is subsumed in the definition of a guard part. In GHC, given a goal G and a clause C, during head unification and computation of the guard part of C, any attempt to instantiate a goal is forced to suspend. Oc and FLENG have no guard condition, in other words, a guard part is always "true." Hence, their specifications of synchronization are simpler than that of GHC. In Oc and FLENG, any attempt to instantiate a goal in head unification is forced to suspend. Intuitively, a head and a guard part of these languages specify conditions to be satisfied by input data received from a goal. The definition of merge is

merge([A|X],Y,Oz) :− true | Oz=[A|Z], merge(X,Y,Z).
merge(X,[A|Y],Oz) :− true | Oz=[A|Z], merge(X,Y,Z).
merge([ ],Y,Oz) :− true | Oz=Y.
merge(X,[ ],Oz) :− true | Oz=X.

Note that output unification must be put in the body part of each clause. Otherwise it will cause suspension, since the output pattern will be regarded as the input pattern.

Comparison

The primitives for restricting access mode are basically divided into two classes: procedure-level representation and data-level representation. The fact that procedures and data are complementary objects in a programming language indicates the clear contrast between these two approaches.

Relational Language, PARLOG, GHC, Oc, and FLENG belong to the procedure-level representation. Relational Language and PARLOG adopt mode declaration for specification of input and output. GHC, Oc, and FLENG utilize a guard part for the specification of input. One mode is given for each predicate definition. On the other hand, an input guard can include input specifications for each clause. Although they put input specifications at different levels, a predicate definition and a clause, both approaches associate input specification with a procedure.

Concurrent Prolog belongs to the data-level representation and adopted read-only annotation to restrict access mode. A variable with read-only annotation cannot be instantiated (written), but can be read. In general, a variable with read-only annotation can be regarded as a protected term (Hellerstein and Shapiro, 1984; Takeuchi and Furukawa, 1985) since it is protected from instantiation. Only a process that has access to the variable without read-only annotation can instantiate it. Since input synchronization is embedded in a data object, it becomes difficult to predict where and when synchronization will occur. This may impair transparency of control flow of the program. On the other hand, embedding control in a data object will enable novel control abstraction. This is investigated in the implementation of bounded buffer communication using protected terms in (Takeuchi and Furukawa, 1985).

OR-PARALLEL MULTIPLE ENVIRONMENTS AND GUARD SAFETY

Multiple Environments

Given a goal and a clause, an OR-process evaluates head unification and the guard part. Since there are competing OR-processes, bindings made for variables in the goal must be hidden from processes other than descendants of the OR-process. Therefore, conceptually, each OR-process has a local environment where these bindings are stored. Local environments associated with OR-processes form a tree, since AND-processes and OR-processes are hierarchically organized. The tree can dynamically expand and contract as computation proceeds. There is no need to manage this dynamic tree if no local binding is made, but otherwise it is an unavoidable task.

Safety

A clause is defined to be safe if and only if, for any goal, evaluation of head unification and the guard part never instantiates the goal. The definition is due to Clark and Gregory (1985). A few definitions are added. A program is defined to be safe, if and only if each clause in the program is safe. A language is defined to be safe if and only if any program written in it is safe. If a language is safe, then it does not need to manage local environments. The concept of safety clarifies the difference between the languages.

Safe Languages. PARLOG, GHC, Oc, and FLENG are safe. The design philosophy of PARLOG excludes any program that requires multiple environments. In PARLOG, a program that may be unsafe is excluded as a dangerous program at compile-time mode analysis. GHC, Oc, and FLENG also do not need multiple environments. In fact, the rule of suspension in GHC, Oc, and FLENG can be paraphrased so that any attempt to form bindings that should be stored in the local environment is forced to suspend. Thus, safety is guaranteed at run-time by the suspension mechanism.

Unsafe Languages. Concurrent Prolog is not safe. Thus, the tree of local environments has to be managed. Several attempts to implement Concurrent Prolog have been reported. Levy proposed a lazy copying scheme for implementation of multiple environments (Levy, 1984). Miyazaki and co-workers (1985) proposed a shallow binding scheme for this purpose. Implementation of Concurrent Prolog must solve two complicated problems associated with multiple environments: value access control and detection of inconsistency between local environments.

Local environments are organized as a tree structure. An environment in a node must be accessible from nodes under the node, but must be hidden from others until the OR-process associated with the environment succeeds in being selected. Once the OR-process successfully terminates and is selected, its local environment is merged with the local environment of the parent AND-process (the local environment associated with the parent OR-process of the AND-process). Controlling the scope of variable access in this way is called value access control. On commitment, however, it may happen that these two environments contain inconsistent bindings. When should the inconsistency be detected? This is called the problem of detection of inconsistency of local bindings. Ueda (1985a) presents two possible solutions: early detection, which seeks to detect inconsistency as soon as possible (if inconsistency exists, the clause fails before commitment and is never selected) and late detection, which seeks to detect inconsistency immediately after commitment. In this case, the clause succeeds in being selected, but fails immediately after commitment. Programmers may prefer early detection, but it requires a complicated locking mechanism for variables when implemented on a distributed memory machine. Ueda examined the semantics of Concurrent Prolog from the point of view of parallel execution and highlighted several subtle issues that become crucial problems in distributed implementation of the languages (Ueda, 1985a).

Codish (1985) defines a concept of safety in Concurrent Prolog that is different from the one stated here. He introduced output annotation into Concurrent Prolog. Output annotation is used to declare which terms will be issued to a goal in head unification. In his model, a clause is defined to be safe if, for any goal, no binding for variables in the goal is made except those declared by output annotation during head unification and guard computation. Management of local binding becomes simple in execution of a program ensured to be safe, since such bindings are syntactically predictable.

HIERARCHICAL COMPUTATION STRUCTURE AND FLATNESS

Generally, computation is organized as an AND- and OR-process tree. The depth of the tree corresponds to the depth of nesting of guard computations. Some parallel logic programming languages have a flat computation structure.

Flat Languages

Flat Concurrent Prolog is a subset of Concurrent Prolog in which guard parts are restricted to specify system predicates (Mierowsky and co-workers, 1985). Since no general computation is allowed in a guard, computation structure is always flat. No tree-structured multiple local environments exist. This greatly reduces the complexity of implementation of the language, but it does not eliminate the problem of detecting inconsistency. Flat Concurrent Prolog seems to adopt late detection.

PARLOG can be flattened. Owing to the safe property of a clause, OR-parallel search for a clause can be translated into AND-parallel goals. In the course of translation, clauses defining a predicate are collected into one clause. In this clause, OR-parallel evaluation of guards is expressed by AND-parallel evaluation of conjunction of meta-calls, each of which calls the guard of each clause. The commitment operator is also expressed by a goal, which receives results from meta-calls, selects one and aborts the other meta-calls. Thus, there exists simple hierarchy of AND-processes in PARLOG.

The languages Oc, FLENG, and Flat GHC are flat. Flat GHC is a subset of GHC. In Flat GHC, as well as Flat Concurrent Prolog, a guard part is restricted to being a set of system predicates. Oc, FLENG, and Flat GHC have no computation hierarchy, since no general computation is allowed in a guard, and this makes implementation of suspension simpler than in GHC. In fact, it can be implemented by one-way unification primitives similar to those of PARLOG.

Nonflat Languages

Clearly, Concurrent Prolog and GHC are not flat. In GHC, AND- and OR-process tree is essential. Unification suspends if and only if binding made by the unification has to be stored in a local environment. In order to know whether a binding of a variable has to be stored in a local environment, the birthplace of the variable in the hierarchy must be identified. If it is the location where the binding is about to be made, then the binding can be made. Otherwise the attempt to bind is forced to suspend. This is why the hierarchical computation structure has to be managed with appropriate information on variables in GHC.

SUMMARY COMPARISON OF LANGUAGES

Safety and flatness help reduce the complexity of implementation. Safety makes the management of multiple local environments quite simple. Flatness excludes the hierarchical structure of computation.

The suspension mechanism is independent of the other mechanisms in Concurrent Prolog. However, management of hierarchy of computation and multiple environments is complicated. Safe Concurrent Prolog is an attempt to revise the language to reduce the complexity of managing multiple environments. Flat Concurrent Prolog has neither hierarchy of computation nor multiple environments.

Owing to compile-time mode analysis, at run-time a PARLOG program has a simple computation model in which suspension is realized by one-way unification primitives, computation hierarchy management is simple and no multiple environments exist. What PARLOG compiler does at compile-time can be regarded as detection of multiple environments over the hierarchical structure inferred from a program with mode declaration for possible data flow. One flaw of PARLOG is that one cannot write a meta-interpreter for the language in itself, while in other languages this is possible. The ability to write a meta-interpreter for the language in itself is an important property of a language for the self-contained development of its programming system.

In GHC, the suspension mechanism and computation hierarchy are closely coupled, although GHC needs no multiple environments. Oc, FLENG, and Flat GHC are similar to Kernel PARLOG (Clark and Gregory, 1985). In fact, any program written in Oc and Flat GHC can be translated into a Kernel PARLOG program. If we can imagine Flat Kernel PARLOG that prohibits general goals and meta-calls in a guard, then Oc, Flat GHC, and Flat Kernel PARLOG are equivalent to each other and constitute the simplest parallel logic programming language.

Other important language classes not discussed above include the CP family, P-Prolog, and ALPS. CP is a family of parallel logic programming languages (Saraswat, 1985, 1987a, 1987b, 1989) which has many control primitive options. These include

	don't care commit
&	don't know commit
↓	wait
[...]	a block
;	sequential-AND
;;	sequential-OR
&&	sequential don't know commit
>	salience

A CP family language is denoted by CP(...) if it does not have a block, and CP[...] if it does have a glock, where ... is a list of options. Any CP language must have at least one commit operator. As the name indicates, CP was influenced by and is close to Concurrent Prolog.

Yang proposed a language P-Prolog that subsumes both AND- and OR-parallelism and achieves true mixture of both parallelism (Yang and Aiso, 1986). In P-Prolog, clauses are divided into single- and double-neck clauses. For single-neck clauses the notion of deterministic reduction (commitment) plays a central role in synchronization.

Maher (1987) proposed ALPS, a class of flat committed choice logic programming languages. A unique feature of ALPS is that the expressiveness of constraints is allowed to appear in guards. ALPS uses constraints in the style of Prolog II (Colmerauer, 1982, 1984), Prolog III, and CLP($\mathcal{R}$) (Heintze and co-workers, 1986). ALPS has the unique commitment law. The closest is that of P-Prolog. In ALPS, computation commits to a clause if it is the only clause satisfied by the current constraint, or if it is validated by the current constraint.

SEMANTICS ISSUES

The semantics of logic programs has been extensively investigated (van Emden and Kowalski, 1976; Clark, 1979; Apt and van Emden, 1982; Lloyd, 1984). These investigators provide a rigid basis for various mathematical manipulations of logic programs such as program verification, equivalent program transformation and declarative debugging. Logical foundations for parallel logic programming languages are also indispensable for the development of the theory of parallel logic programming including verification, transformation, and debugging. However, the results for pure logic programs are not directly applicable to parallel logic programming languages because of the new control primitives.

Suppose that a goal failed. This implies neither that the result is not in the success set, nor that the result is always in the finite-failure set, since the goal may fail even if there is a possibility of success because of commitment to an incorrect clause. The declarative semantics becomes insufficient also if two programs with different input/output behaviors need to be distinguished.

Parallel logic programming languages have two control primitives not appearing in pure logic programs. These are a commitment operator and a synchronization primitive. Parallel logic programming relies heavily on these control primitives. A commitment operator changes the semantics of failure and a synchronization primitive introduces procedural flavor. It is now obvious that declarative semantics for pure logic programs cannot characterize such aspects of parallel logic programs as failure and input/output behavior. There have been many attempts to build operational semantics of parallel logic programs (Saraswat, 1985, 1987a, 1987b, 1989; Ueda and Furukawa, 1988; Maher, 1987; Falaschi and Levi, 1988; Gerth and co-workers, 1988). There have also been attempts to adapt the declarative semantics of logic programs to that of parallel logic programs (Levi, 1988; Murakami, 1988). Levi (1988) introduced the concept of a guarded atom, which is a guarded clause such that all atoms in the guard part and the body part are unification atoms. A guarded atom can be regarded as a unit clause in a parallel logic program. It can be also viewed as an atom with explicit representation of input/output history. With guarded atoms, Levi discussed the construction of model theoretic semantics of a parallel logic program, which is analogous to that of a logic program.

BIBLIOGRAPHY

K. R. Apt and M. H. van Emden, "Contributions to the Theory of Logic Programming," *J. ACM,* **29**(3), 841–862 (1982).

K. L. Clark, *Predicate Logic as a Computational Formalism*, Research Report 79/59, Department of Computing, Imperial College, London, 1979.

K. L. Clark and S. Gregory, "A Relational Language for Parallel Programming," in *Proceedings of the ACM Conference on Functional Programming Languages and Computer Architecture*, ACM, New York, 1981, pp. 171–178.

K. L. Clark and S. Gregory, "Notes on the Implementation of PARLOG," *J. Log. Prog.* **2**(1), 17–42 (1985).

K. L. Clark and S. Gregory, "PARLOG: Parallel Programming in Logic," *ACM Trans. Prog. Lang. Syst.* **8**(1), 1–49 (1986).

K. L. Clark, F. McCabe, and S. Gregory, "IC-Prolog Language Features," in K. L. Clark and S.-Å. Tärnlund, eds., *Logic Programming*, Academic Press, Orlando, Fla., 1982, pp. 253–266.

W. F. Clocksin and C. S. Mellish, *Programming in Prolog*, 2nd ed., Springer-Verlag, New York, 1984.

M. Codish, *Compiling OR-Parallelism into AND-Parallelism*, master's thesis, Computer Science, Feinberg Graduate School of the Weizmann Institute of Science, Rehovot, Israel, 1985.

A. Colmerauer, *Prolog II: Reference Manual and Theoretical Model*, Internal Report, Groupe Intelligence Artificielle, Université Aix-Marseille II, Marseille, France, 1982.

A. Colmerauer, "Equations and Inequations on Finite and Infinite Trees," in *Proceedings of the International Conference on Fifth Generation Computer Systems 1984*, Institute for New Generation Computer Technology, OHMSHA, Ltd., Tokyo, 1984, pp. 85–99.

J. S. Conery and D. F. Kibler, "Parallel Interpretation of Logic Programs," in *Proceedings of the ACM Conference on Functional Programming Languages and Computer Architecture*, ACM, New York, 1981, pp. 163–170.

M. Falaschi and G. Levi, "Finite Failures and Partial Computations in Concurrent Logic Languages," in Institute for New Generation Computer Technology, ed., *Proceedings of the International Conference on Fifth Generation Computer Systems 1988*, Institute for New Generation Computer Technology, OHMSHA, Ltd., Tokyo, 1988, pp. 364–373.

R. Gerth, M. Codish, Y. Lichtenstein, and E. Shapiro, "Fully Abstract Denotational Semantics for Flat Concurrent Prolog," in *Proceedings of the IEEE Symposium on Logic in Computer Science*, IEEE, Washington, D.C., 1988, pp. 320–333.

S. Gregory, *Parallel Logic Programming in PARLOG*, Addison-Wesley, Reading, Mass., 1987.

N. C. Heintze and co-workers, *The CLP Programmer's Manual*, Department of Computer Science, Monash University, Melbourne, Australia, June 1986.

L. Hellerstein and E. Shapiro, "Implementing Parallel Algorithms in Concurrent Prolog: The MAXFLOW Experience," *J. Log. Prog.* **3**(2), 157–184 (1984).

M. Hirata, "Self-Description of Oc and Its Applications," in *Proceedings of the 2nd National Conference of Japan Society for Software Science and Technology*, Japan Society for Software Science and Technology, Tokyo, 1985, pp. 153–156 (in Japanese).

R. A. Kowalski, "Predicate Logic as Programming Language," in *Proceedings of IFIP Congress 74*, North-Holland, Amsterdam, 1974, pp. 569–574.

G. Levi, *A New Declarative Semantics of Flat Guarded Horn Clauses*, Technical Report, Institute for New Generation Computer Technology, Tokyo, 1988.

J. Levy, "A Unification Algorithm for Concurrent Prolog," in *Proceedings of the 2nd International Conference on Logic Programming*, Uppsala University, Uppsala, Sweden, 1984, pp. 331–342.

J. W. Lloyd, *Foundations of Logic Programming*, Springer-Verlag, New York, 1984.

M. J. Maher, "Logic Semantics for a Class of Committed Choice Programs," in J.-L. Lassez, ed., *Logic Programming, Proceedings of the Fourth International Conference*, MIT Press, Cambridge, Mass., 1987, pp. 858–876.

C. Mierowsky, S. Taylor, E. Shapiro, and S. Safra, *The Design and Implementation of Flat Concurrent Prolog*, Technical Report CS85-09, The Weizmann Institute of Science, Rehovot, Israel, 1985.

T. Miyazaki, A. Takeuchi, and T. Chikayama, "A Sequential Implementation of Concurrent Prolog Based on the Shallow Binding Scheme," in *Proceedings of 1985 Symposium on Logic Programming*, The Computer Society of IEEE, IEEE Computer Society Press, Washington, D.C., 1985, pp. 110–118.

M. Murakami, "A Declarative Semantics of Parallel Logic Programs with Perpetual Processes," in Institute for New Generation Computer Technology, ed., *Proceedings of the International Conference on Fifth Generation Computer Systems 1988*, Institute for New Generation Computer Technology, OHMSHA, Ltd., Tokyo, 1988, pp. 374–381.

M. Nilsson and H. Tanaka, "Fleng Prolog—the Language Which Turns Supercomputers into Prolog Machines," in E. Wada, ed., *LNCS-264, Logic Programming '86*, Springer-Verlag, New York, 1986.

G. A. Ringwood, "PARLOG86 and the Dining Logician," *CACM* **31**(1), 10–25 (1988).

P. Roussel, *Prolog: Manuel reference et d'utilisation*, Technical Report, Groupe d'Intelligence Artificielle, Marseille-Luminy, France, 1975.

V. A. Saraswat, "Partial Correctness Semantics for CP[!,|,&]," in *LNCS-206, Proceedings of the Foundation of Software Technology and Theoretical Computer Sciences Conference*, Springer-Verlag, New York, 1985, pp. 347–368.

V. A. Saraswat, "The Concurrent Logic Programming Language CP: Definition and Operational Semantics," in *Proceedings of the Symposium on Principles of Programming Languages*, ACM, New York, 1987a, pp. 49–62.

V. A. Saraswat, "GHC: Operational Semantics, Problems and Relationship with CP(↓,|)," in *Proceedings of 1987 Symposium on Logic Programming*, The Computer Society of IEEE, IEEE Computer Society Press, Los Alamitos, California, 1987b, pp. 347–358.

V. A. Saraswat, *Concurrent Constraint Programming Languages*, Ph.D. thesis, Carnegie Mellon University, Pittsburgh, Pa., 1989.

E. Shapiro, *A Subset of Concurrent Prolog and Its Interpreter*, Technical Report TR-003, Institute for New Generation Computer Technology, Tokyo, 1983.

E. Shapiro, "Concurrent Prolog: A Progress Report," *IEEE Computer,* **19**(8), 44–58 (1986).

E. Shapiro, ed., *Concurrent Prolog, Collected Papers*, The MIT Press, Cambridge, Mass., 1987.

E. Shapiro, "The Family of Concurrent Logic Programming Languages," *Comput. Surv.* **21**(3), 412–510 (1989).

A. Takeuchi and K. Furukawa, "Bounded Buffer Communication in Concurrent Prolog," *New Generation Comput.* **3**(2), 145–155 (1985).

K. Ueda, *Concurrent Prolog Re-examined*, Technical Report TR-102, Institute for New Generation Computer Technology, Tokyo, 1985a.

K. Ueda, *Guarded Horn Clauses*, Technical Report TR-103, Institute for New Generation Computer Technology, Tokyo, 1985b.

K. Ueda, *Guarded Horn Clauses*, Ph.D. thesis, The University of Tokyo, Tokyo, 1986a.

K. Ueda, *Guarded Horn Clauses: A Parallel Logic Programming Language with the Concept of a Guard*, Technical Report TR-208, Institute for New Generation Computer Technology, Tokyo, 1986b.

K. Ueda and K. Furukawa, "Transformation Rules for GHC Programs," in Institute for New Generation Computer Technology, ed., *Proceedings of the International Conference on Fifth Generation Computer Systems 1988*, Institute for New Generation Computer Technology, OHMSHA, Ltd., Tokyo, 1988, pp. 582–591.

M. H. van Emden and G. J. de Lucena, "Predicate Logic as a Programming Language for Parallel Programming," in K. L. Clark and S.-Å. Tärnlund, eds., *Logic Programming*, Academic Press, Orlando, Fla., 1982, pp. 189–198.

M. H. van Emden and R. Kowalski, "The Semantics of Predicate Logic as a Programming Language," *J. ACM,* **23**(4), 733–742 (1976).

R. Yang and H. Aiso, "P-Prolog: A Parallel Logic Language Based on Exclusive Relation," in E. Shapiro, ed., *LNCS-225, Third International Conference on Logic Programming*, Springer-Verlag, New York, 1986, pp. 255–269.

AKIKAZU TAKEUCHI
SONY Computer Science
Laboratory Inc.

This article is based on the following paper: A. Takeuchi and K. Furukawa, "Parallel Logic Programming Languages," in E. Shapiro, ed., *LNCS-225, Third International Conference on Logic Programming*, Springer-Verlag, New York, 1986, pp. 242–254.

PARALLEL MACHINE ARCHITECTURE

Parallel machine architectures for AI applications have been a flourishing subject of research and development since 1980. There are many good reasons for the meeting of AI applications and parallel computer architectures, among which two are most significant:

1. AI applications are deemed to be extremely hungry in terms of MIPS and megabytes. This is often the case, because nonexact reasoning, graph search algorithms, nondeterminism, and huge data sets are commonly used to represent typical AI problems. A realistic case solved by an AI program often saturates any sequential computer, which is bad for the response time and for AI in general, hence the many attempts to devise parallel dedicated architectures or parallel implementations of AI systems on commercial multiprocessors.

2. Programming languages used for implementation of AI problems lend themselves to parallelization more naturally than do conventional languages. They are declarative in essence, and exhibit many potential parallelizations.

To exhaustively list people and organizations dealing with this subject would be impossible here, since most universities in the U.S., Japan, and Europe do research in this area. The Institute for New Generation Computer Technology (ICOT), a research center sponsored by the Japanese government (MITI), is composed of six laboratories and concentrates on systems based on parallel logic programming in a 10-year global project started in 1983. The European Computer-Industry Research Center (ECRC) in Munich, was created in 1984 by three European IT companies (BULL, ICL, and Siemens) to address research themes related to AI and logic programming. The Swedish Institute of Computer Science (SICS) in Stockholm has a large research program which focuses on parallel AI systems and is sponsored by the Swedish administration and private companies (IBM Sweden and Ericsson). The Microelectronics and Computer Technology Corp. (MCC) in Austin, Texas, has conducted several projects on logic and knowledge base parallel systems. The ESPRIT I and ESPRIT II programs of the Commission of the European Communities have been launching several large-scale projects involving hundreds of partners. In the U.S., DARPA and the NSF are funding more and more large-scale projects in this area. Besides these large organizations, virtually all computer manufacturers have projects on parallel AI systems (eg, DEC, IBM, TI, BBN, Thinking Machines Corporation, NEC, Mitsubishi, and OKI), and most universities worldwide have research programs related to this area (eg, Berkeley, Stanford, CMU, MIT, Technical University of Munich, and the Universities of Illinois, California, Wisconsin, Bristol, Manchester, Pisa, Karlsruhe, and Bratislava).

This article does not follow the usual taxonomy of parallel computers, but rather the broad application areas and systems for which parallel computer architectures have been designed. The next section summarizes the unique features of symbolic and AI processing in order to better understand the motivations and justifications for parallel AI systems. Then four sections describe major results corresponding to four areas: PROLOG and logic programming systems, LISP and functional programming systems, object-oriented systems, and knowledge base systems. The final section attempts to define the trends in parallel machine architectures for the future. Space does not permit mention of all valuable work underway, thus, the article concentrates on AI computer architectures rather than on AI systems or software (see Kowalik (1988); Reeve (1989); Uhr (1987) for the latter). However, to convey the peculiarities of these architectures, a few projects having sufficient achievements and available documentation are described in more detail, but in no case should this be considered a complete catalogue. This article deliberately does not cover other important aspects of parallelism in AI applications such as vision (see VISUAL PERCEPTION), robotics (qv), or neural networks (qv).

FEATURES OF AI SYSTEMS

Innovative Parallel Architectures are Required

AI systems (ie, applications and languages) tend to require innovative parallel architectures because they differ from conventional numerical or data management processing in various ways.

Symbolic Processing. AI systems mainly involve computations on symbolic information, ie, not only character or string operations but also more complex operations, such as pattern matching, composition, sorting, and extraction.

Complex Data Structures. Lists, trees, stacks, and other arbitrary data structures are often used to represent and manage information. Creation, access, and modification operations are heavily used in the program, leading to a temptation to make them basic atomic operations in a CPU design dedicated to AI. Moreover, dynamic typing and pattern matching or unification call for a special internal representation using tagging techniques. In general, data structures in an AI program are accessed in a nonregular manner, making any pipelining or arraylike access methods impossible.

Unusual Primitive Control Operations. Intermediate levels for AI languages resort to primitives not found in conventional CPU instruction sets: unification, dereferencing, list operations (car, cdr), backtracking, trailing, and environment creation and deletion. Complex stack operations are common, and hardwiring them into a VLSI chip is of immediate and great benefit.

Executable Code. AI systems may generate or modify the executable code, a feature not taken into account in conventional computers (where the code cache, for example, is often read only and never written back). Moreover, debugging parallel AI programs is more complex and requires *ad hoc* tools that can be supported by the hardware.

Nondeterminism. AI programs may generate several answers to a given problem statement. They may support several kinds of nondeterminisms and lead to combinatorial searches through huge search spaces generating lots of parallel activities.

Parallelism and Concurrent Processing. Contrary to conventional procedural languages, the declarative nature of AI languages naturally provides several kinds of potential parallelisms and/or concurrency. These parallelisms are mainly of the MIMD type and do not naturally match a pipeline or vector architecture.

Why Some Architectures May Not Fit AI Systems

The features of AI systems obviously ask for new computer architectures; however, there are also many reasons why AI programs may not (or not yet) perform well on parallel systems.

Parallelisms and Nondeterminisms. Paradoxically, there are still open issues there. Problems associated with them range from the exact types of parallelisms to be dealt with or their usefulness ("wild" parallelism may be disastrous in some cases) to the granularity, which should be carefully and dynamically controlled. Other problems relate to the debugging and monitoring tools, or the user interface necessary to provide the adequate ease of use.

System Issues. Even if an AI program generates enough parallelism with the right granularity, the architecture and the system will be under high pressure trying to manage concurrent tasks. Dedicated dynamic memory management, adapted load balancing techniques, and innovative task scheduling strategies are all vital to the efficiency and effectiveness of the parallel AI program. Further, the capability to run several applications and to handle multiple users raises another dimension of complexity that current AI systems hardly address yet.

Links to Conventional Processing. An AI application will often resort to other information or programs written in conventional code (user interface, database administrator, distributed directory, etc). These quasi-necessary links to other programs and databases do not favor a special-purpose architecture for the AI part of the application.

PROLOG AND LOGIC PROGRAMMING SYSTEMS

Parallel Prolog systems fall into two major families: committed choice systems, employing don't care nondeterminism, and pure parallelism systems, implementing various combinations of OR- and AND-parallelisms (see PARALLEL LOGIC PROGRAMMING LANGUAGES). In committed choice systems, the exploitable concurrency is expressed by the data dependences between the arguments of goals in the selected clause, which are activated in a producer–consumer way. Additional parallelism is found in the determination of the single elected clause in a multiple clause predicate by performing the guard parts of all candidate clauses in parallel. After the commit point, however, all clauses are killed and forgotten forever except the successful one, which is allowed to proceed. Problems posed by committed choice systems are the nonlogical nature of programs (in some cases), the creation and management of processes, and the efficiency of the resulting system. "Safe" and "flat" versions of these systems greatly improve the clarity of their semantics and also the processing complexity.

In pure parallelism systems, OR-parallelism correspond to launching several clauses (corresponding to one predicate) in parallel, each leading to a new branch in the search tree, while AND-parallelism involves the parallel execution of goals within the same clause. Combining both parallelisms does not raise conceptual problems but tends to make run time data management more complex. OR-parallelism introduces the issue of managing several bindings for the same variables whereas in sequential PROLOG, this does not occur because the many bindings are performed one after the other by backtracking. Several solutions have been invented that either minimize the dependences among subtrees (eg, the Kabu Wake method, in which the environment is copied to the newly created son, so that brothers may proceed independently), or minimize the data space used by sharing as much data as possible (eg, the SRI model of Warren, or the PEPSys model derived from Borgward's Hash Windows). AND-parallelism, apart from the way it is expressed in the source language, automatically by the compiler or the run-time system, raises the problem of producing the complete answer by forming the cross product of all subsolutions until all parallel goals exhaust their search space. An incremental production of the answers is always better in principle but may create complex management issues at run time, especially when OR-parallelism is integrated with AND-parallelism. The nature and status of the numerous projects and products in this area are so different that a structured presentation is impossible. First, some of the committed choice systems are outlined, starting with ICOT's FGCS project. Then, pure parallelism projects are presented, with some emphasis on three of them and an illustration of their capabilities.

The Parallel Inference Machine

Founded in 1983, ICOT has since concentrated the resources of nearly 60 people on parallel logic systems. Based on KL-0 (a sequential committed choice language), the concurrent language GHC, then called KC-ONE, has been defined and chosen as the principal input for the design and implementation of the parallel inference machine (PIM) multiprocessor system to support AI applications. Figure 1 summarizes phases of the project. The first stage comprised studies of KL-0, and of sequential PROLOG machines (PSI-1, CHI), as well as initial investigations of parallel machine architectures suitable for parallel logic languages (PIM-D, a data flow system, and PIM-R, a reduction based system). The intermediate stage of FGCS, started in 1985, defines several directions (Taki, 1990):

Consolidation of the KL-ONE language.

Implementation of Multi-PSI V1 and Multi-PSI V2 multiprocessor test vehicles.

Design and implementation of the PIM/p system and its variations.

Implementation of the PIMOS operating system for the Multi-PSI and PIM machines.

Multi-PSI V1 is a six-PE system, where each PE is a PSI-1 sequential PROLOG machine with a tagged architecture, a microprogrammed PROLOG interpreter, and a CPU architecture using conventional technology to imple-

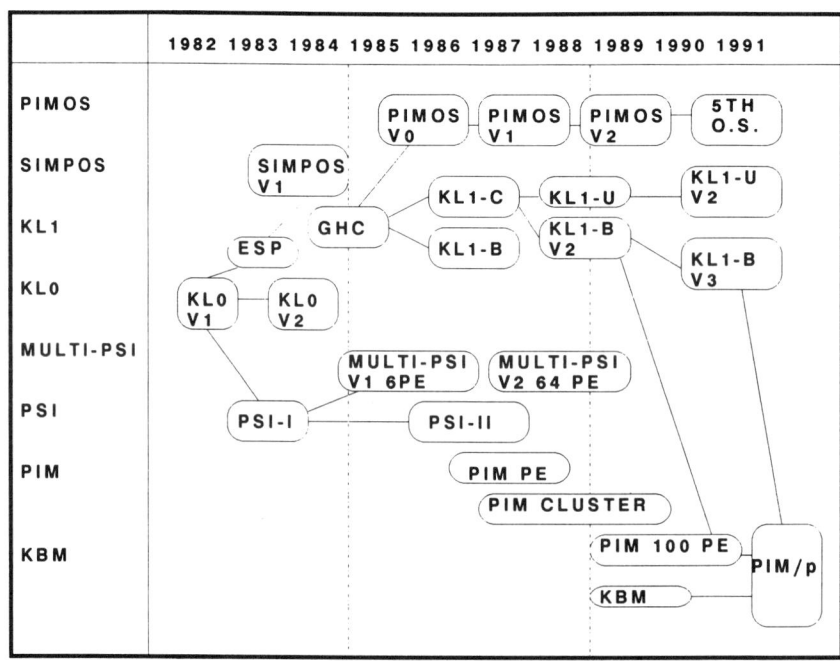

Figure 1. Overview of main FGCS project items.

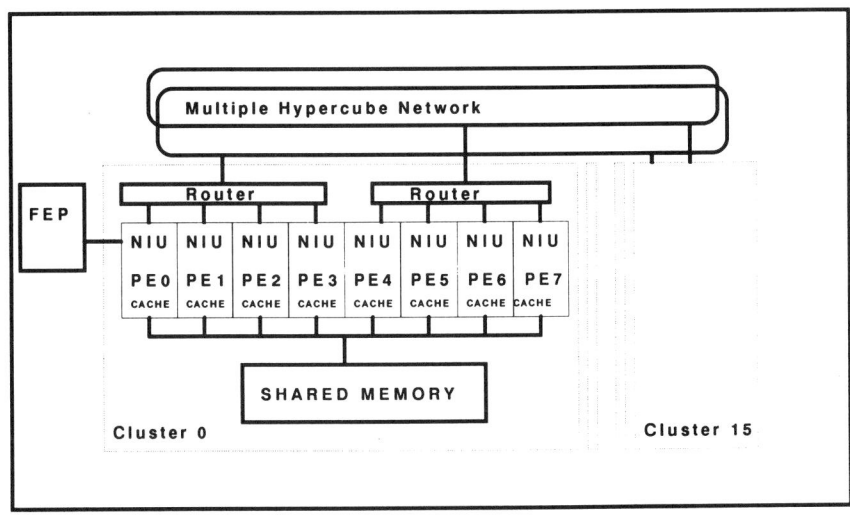

Figure 2. Configuration of PIM/p.

ment PROLOG primitives directly in hardware. The performance of PSI-1 is around 30 Klips. Multi-PSI V1 interconnects its processors by a two-dimensional mesh network to initially evaluate the real needs in load balancing and operating system capabilities.

Multi-PSI V2 contains 64 PEs, where each PE is a PSI-2 CPU, based on a modified WAM language (300 Klips). The network is identical to Multi-PSI V1, and the resulting hardware system integrated into eight large cabinets housing a total of 512 printed boards (out of them 5 GB of main memory). Up to eight front-end processors can be connected. More than 10 Multi-PSI V2 systems have been fabricated and distributed to ICOT and cooperating companies.

The final stage of FGCS aims to build a 1000 PE system based on the intermediate stage results. ICOT is currently building five different versions of the PIM system, all running a version of the PIMOS operating system. The PIM/p system (Fig. 2) corresponds to the first small-scale version of what should be the final PIM system to be delivered at the end of the final third stage of FGCS. Its main characteristics are as follows:

1. A 128 PE system, composed of 16 clusters of eight processors each, hosted in two cabinets (with provision for a configuration with 64 clusters to reach 512 processors). In a cluster, however, each processor is independently equipped with a network interface.
2. The RISC-based processing element, housed in five 80K gate VLSI chips, will sit on one printed board. Its 60-ns cycle is expected to give a performance of 600 Klips. Two caches, each of 64 KB, with write back strategy and Illinois invalidation-based coherence system, are used for data and code.

PIM/c differs from PIM/p in that it adopts a crossbar interconnection network to connect 32 clusters of 8 processors. The intracluster processors are connected to a single bus, and each cluster possesses one network interface A microprogrammed CISC processor (50-ns cycle time, 0.8-μm gate array) is used for the processing element.

PIM/i resembles the PIM/c architecture (eight PE clusters on a bus and one network interface per cluster) but is composed of two clusters only (the network is reduced to a single bus). The processing element is a RISC-based architecture employing a 1.2-μm standard cell technology. PIM/i uses a broadcast cache coherence protocol (where PIM/c and PIM/m use a write back, invalidation-based strategy).

PIM/k is a vehicle for testing hierarchical caches. It is composed of two clusters and a cluster is composed of 16 processors. A processor is a RISC-based, custom VLSI chip, with an on-chip first-level cache. A group of four processors share a second level cache, and the four groups of four processors share the common main memory. Finally, PIM/m follows a radically different architecture since it has no shared memory: PIM/m is a mesh of 256 processors, each with its own private main memory. The processor, a CISC-like structure, uses a 0.8-μm standard cell technology. As of the beginning of 1991, an experimental PIM/p system is in assembly and testing at ICOT. Plans call for a refined prototype cluster of eight processors to be operational as of March 1991, and for PIM/m clusters to be ready for power in April 1991. The three other systems are under fabrication at the different manufacturers' plants.

Other Implementations of Committed Choice Systems

Strand (Foster and Taylor, 1989) is a parallel programming tool comprising a language, development environment, and parallel programming libraries. Designed to be easily portable, it runs on SUN workstations and several multiprocessor systems, including Intel iPSC, NCube, SEQUENT, ENCORE, and Butterfly. Performance on a SUN 3/75 gives 23.5K reductions per second for Naive Reverse, and 9.8 for quicksort.

LOGIX is the environment for an implementation of Flat Concurrent Prolog (Houri, 1986), implemented among others on SUN and Intel iPSC systems. Coarse-grain parallel applications do well, but fine-grain parallel show a high overhead of process creation and synchronization. The performance is lower than Strand (on a SUN 3/

50, 6K reductions per second for Naive Reverse compared to 17.7K with Strand, and 1.9K for quicksort compared to 8.2K).

PARLOG has been implemented on various systems (Crammond, 1988), and runs at 7.9K reductions/s for Naive Reverse (compared to 23.5 K with Strand on the same Sun3/75 machine).

Pure Parallelism Systems on Shared Memory Multiprocessors

Existing commercial shared bus multiprocessors have been extensively used to implement parallel logic systems. They are worth being mentioned here because they consist of complete implementations that locate and solve the actual problems raised by parallel processing of AI applications in several areas: parallel execution models, shared and private data structures, and parallel run time system.

The SRI Model and AURORA System. Based on SICSTUS Prolog, a WAM-based Prolog system, AURORA (Warren, 1987) extends it with OR parallelism. Conflicts in multiple bindings are resolved by "binding arrays," which guarantee a constant access time to a variable, but not a constant time for process creation, and imposes some sequentiality in the allocation of memory space (hence the need for a shared memory multiprocessor). The importance of scheduling strategies led to the implementation of several alternatives:

Argonne Scheduler. The workers in the system are "attracted" by available work.
Manchester Scheduler. The matching of worker to available work is performed before the migration.
Wavefront Scheduler. The wavefront represents the set of processes and information considered public (global) in the current search tree. Below it are processes having their private information and working on it.

These systems have been implemented and evaluated on SEQUENT Balance, SEQUENT Symmetry (Fig. 3a), and ENCORE Multimax multiprocessors. Results indicate that the wavefront scheduler performs slightly better than the others. The overhead of work installation (ie, updating the binding arrays for a new task) is about 14% more than the sequential Sicstus system.

Aurora has been compared to KL-ONE (ICOT) on the same eight-PE symmetry testbed. Results show that Aurora performs from two to nine times better and has better memory behavior than KL-ONE. However, OR-parallel systems cannot exploit parallelism as efficiently as dependent AND parallel systems like KL-ONE.

The BC-Machine and the MUSE System. Developed at SICS, the BC machine uses a broadcast protocol to update global variable cells in all processors participating in the program execution. The MUSE system (Ali, 1990) is an evolution of the BC machine with the main new feature of sharable frames avoiding the multiple copy mechanism used in the BC machine. Further refinements in MUSE include partial copying by incrementally copying only the different parts of the states of P and Q. MUSE assumes that processors access a private local memory space and a global shared space. A hardware prototype of a MUSE machine has been implemented and tested and is composed of seven processors (MC 68020) with local memory (2.5 MB), a common VME bus, and a shared memory (4 MB). The MUSE system has also been implemented on a SEQUENT symmetry system (Fig. 3b) and actually performs better than any other OR parallel system ever implemented on this class of machine. The overhead for managing parallelism and data sharing has been reduced to only 5% compared with SICSTUS sequential Prolog, as compared to 14% in Aurora.

The PEPSys Model at ECRC. PEPSys (Chassin, 1988; Baron, 1988) handles combined OR- and independent AND-parallelisms, as well as backtracking and retroactive parallelization. Binding conflicts are resolved by local Hash windows, and a date stamp, leading to minimal overhead at work installation time (no copy or update is necessary). PEPSys can be implemented on nonshared memory systems. On a SEQUENT multiprocessor, each PE runs a PEPSys process, which takes work from a

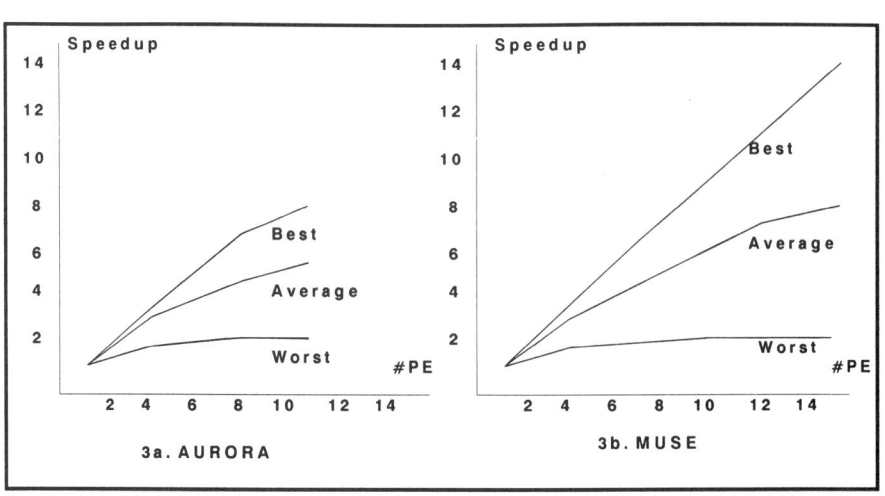

Figure 3. Performance of AURORA and MUSE (Symmetry).

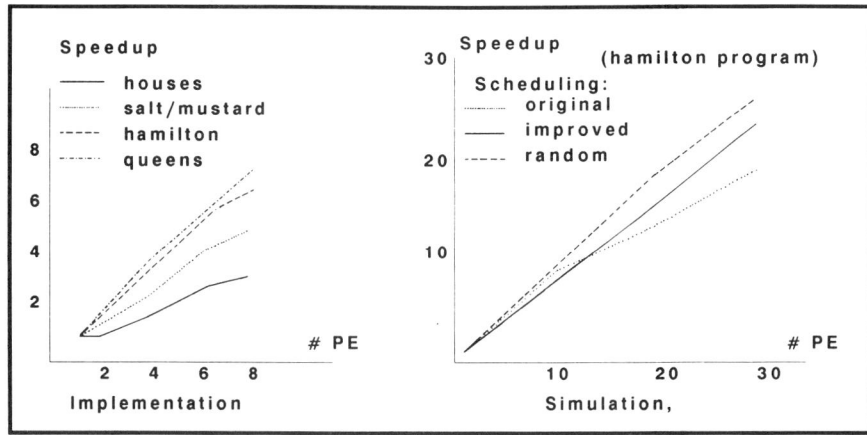

Figure 4. Experimental results on PEPSys.

shared workpool. No new work is created if resources are saturated, instead the parallel branch point is treated sequentially by conventional Prolog backtracking. If resources become available, the parallel node can be restored to the workpool, allowing other processors to take remaining branches. OR parallelism is implemented by creating OR branch points in the work tree. An idle worker will take one alternative branch and start processing. It shares all possible information with its father, and creates a local hash window to store and update variables shared with its brothers. Independent AND-parallelism is treated by forming cross product solutions incrementally with special "join cell" pointers.

The results of an implementation on SEQUENT Balance and Symmetry systems (Fig. 4) show a performance equal to Aurora. Several scheduling strategies have been tried ("help worker," "higher in the tree," and random) as well as a complete simulator system allowing execution of PEPSys programs on a distributed multiprocessor system. Latest versions include a parallel constraint propagation subsystem providing superlinear speedups in most cases.

Other Implementations of Pure Parallelism Systems

Aurora was implemented on the BBN Butterfly machine and shows significant speedups: 40 on a 40-PE configuration for a semigroup computation problem, corresponding to 56 s instead of 20 min on a SUN 4 machine. However, speedup tends to be limited if task size is not large (overheads in the scheduler become important).

ANDORRA Prolog (Haridi, 1990), developed by the GIGALIPS group, implements OR parallelism combined with dependent AND parallelism. Goals are executed in AND-parallel as soon as they become determinate. A prototype of ANDORRA on SEQUENT has been running and shows linear speedups. Parallel NU-Prolog is a Prolog system combining stream AND-parallelism and "don't know" nondeterminism. Its implementation on an ENCORE Multimax shows a 12-Klips performance for each PE, and a quasi-linear speedup with up to 12 processors. ROPM (Reduce Or Process Model), from the University of Illinois, has been implemented on various multiprocessor systems (ALLIANT, iPSC/2, SEQUENT, ENCORE).

The Parallel Inference Machine PIE64 (Tanaka, 1986), a large project at Tanaka Labs of the University of Tokyo, implements an extended committed choice language called FLENG Prolog. PIE 64 consists of 64 inference units connected by two high speed interconnection networks with an automatic load balancing facility. Each inference unit consists of a Sparc processor with local memory modules, an inference coprocessor, and network interface coprocessors. The coprocessor for PROLOG, called UNIRED, is a hardware interpreter of parallel logic programs executing several goal rewriting rules using pipelines. One network deals with process allocation while a second network supports the data allocation and access primitives.

The Data Diffusion Machine (Warren, 1988) is a scalable shared virtual memory multiprocessor, consisting in a hierarchy of buses and data controllers linking an arbitrary number of processors each having a large set associative memory. Each data controller has a set associative directory containing status bits for data under its control, and it supports remote data access by snooping on the buses below and above it. The data access protocol provides for the automatic migration, duplication, and replacement of data while maintaining data coherency. The design of the system, intended for parallel logic programs but not dedicated to them, is under way at Bristol University and SICS.

n-Parallel PROLOG (a trademark of Paralogic, Inc.) is an interpreter of PROLOG programs that uses OR- and AND-parallelism to generate parallel tasks on a multiprocessor composed of transputers connected in an array-like fashion (Paralogic, 1990). This product implements a proprietary model of parallel PROLOG with the strict conventional Edinburgh syntax (hence the portability of programs is guaranteed from a sequential system to the transputer array), from which are extracted some restricted forms of OR-parallelism and AND-parallelism. When a task may generate parallelism, the running transputer invokes its neighbors through the four possible hardware links, and if any neighbor is idle, a portion of the parallel activity is passed to that neighbor (otherwise the parallel task is treated sequentially using backtracking). The speedups reported for n-parallel Prolog with five transputers, relative to a sequential execution on one transputer, are 2.50 for an AND-parallel benchmark (Quicksort) or three for a database search benchmark.

LISP AND FUNCTIONAL PROGRAMMING SYSTEMS

Although apparently not so well parallelizable as Prolog, LISP has received considerable attention for its parallel implementation on multiprocessors. (Itoh and Halstead, 1990) give a comprehensive overview of parallel LISP implementations on multiprocessors. Agarwal (1990) introduces LISP futures in the APRIL processor. Futures allow the creation of a parallel activity corresponding to a LISP expression while the caller proceeds. However, it may only proceed until an operation involving the value of the LISP expression is invoked: In that case the operation is suspended until the value is made available by the concurrent task evaluating this expression. Futures provide an elegant abstraction for the synchronization of producers and consumers of LISP values.

NTT Data Flow Machine (DFM)

The NTT data flow machine, developed at NTT (Amamiya, 1986) supports a functional language called VALID. DFM supports extensions to the basic functional execution model such as the lenient cons operator and lazy evaluation. The architecture of DFM is composed of clusters linked to a common bus, where each cluster hosts eight processors and eight original structure memories, interconnected by various buses. An elementary PE is a dataflow processor with a circular pipeline structure. A special operand memory unit, implemented in a semicontent addressable memory, performs all matching operations. The structure memories perform high level functional primitives such as car, cdr, or cons, as well as garbage collection. In DFM a unique load-balancing system allows function calls to be executed in the least loaded processor, due to a special structure called RPQ (result packet queue), which is maintained by the cluster control unit. Other functional parallel architectures have been or are under development in Japan, such as EM-3 and IXM of ETL Laboratories (Ohbuchi, 1988).

LISP On the Butterfly Machine

The Butterfly computer (Allen, 1988) consists of up to 256 nodes connected through a proprietary, high performance switch network (Fig. 5). Each PE is a MC 68020 CPU and 68881 FPU and has a memory expandable to 4 MB. Butterfly is a shared memory system and belongs to the NUMA (nonuniform memory access) class of multiprocessors. The operating system Chrysalis provides the execution environment where the tasks are distributed among the nodes without concern for the physical location of processed data. Each node is equipped with a processor node controller (PNC), which manages all memory references, and performs, by microcode, all atomic memory operations necessary in a parallel environment. The Butterfly network uses packet switching networking techniques to implement processors to memory operations. It represents a compromise between the expensive crossbar switch and the common bus. In Butterfly the cost of the switch grows proportionally to $N*\log4 N$, and the bandwidth grows slightly less than linearly. Among other AI application tools developed on Butterfly, a LISP environment is available. It includes support for both the Common LISP and Scheme languages, with parallel extensions. A user interface with program development facilities is implemented on a Symbolics 3600.

Butterfly LISP is a shared memory, multiple-interpreter system. It supports memory sharing by providing a single LISP heap, mapped identically by all interpreters. It uses the future mechanism as its basic task creation primitive. Butterfly LISP uses a stop-and-copy garbage collector, which does not penalize the main processing stream too much (around 15%).

MaRS: A Combinator Graph Reduction Multiprocessor

The MaRS machine (Contessa, 1989) is an experimental modular distributed control multiprocessor employing the graph reduction paradigm. It runs MaRS LISP, a pure functional parallel language with call-by-need, higher order functions, and a parallel mechanisms similar to futures. A prototype has been built and evaluated. Specific VLSI chips were designed to handle reduction, memory operations, and communication based on an Omega net-

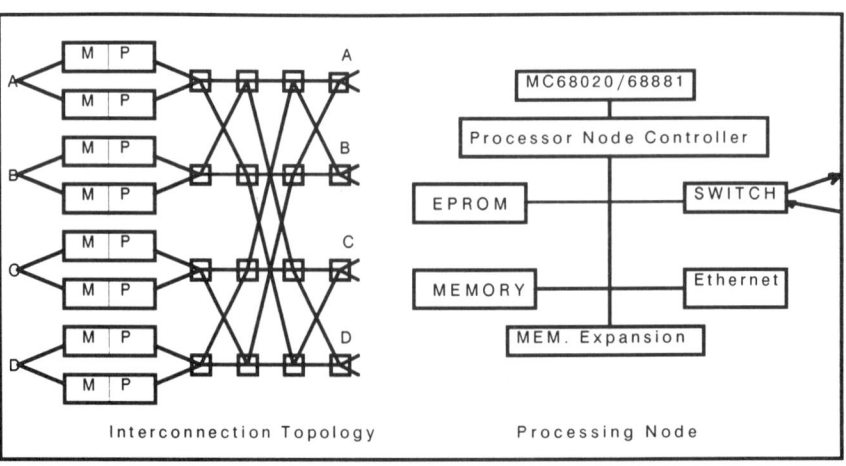

Figure 5. The BBN Butterfly Multiprocessor (here, an 8-PE configuration).

work. The communication network provides automatic load balancing by using the load information propagated through the network. A reduction processor (running up to eight processes) performs node reduction in the combinatory graph representing the program, and memory processors (1 million cells of 38 bits each) perform all node management (allocation, recovery, synchronization). The network is made of two Omega subnetworks of 2×2 switches. Each subnetwork contains four stages of eight switches each, the whole net supporting 64 communication processors.

Top Level Common LISP is a fully supported, production-quality implementation of Common LISP extended for parallel programming, derived from research at the University of Massachusetts at Amherst. This system uses the concept of futures, just like most others, and provides multiple grain sizes: fine-grained threads, mid-sized-grain tasks and processes, and large-grained nodes. Along with the LISP product developed by Top Level, Inc. (1990), utilities such as a parallel compiler, a parallel debugger which runs on EXPLORER or SYMBOLICS LISP machine, are provided to ease program development. Top Level Common LISP runs on the ENCORE and SEQUENT computers.

PARALLEL OBJECT-ORIENTED SYSTEMS

As part of ESPRIT I, Project 415, Subproject A, headed by Philips Research Labs in Eindhoven, the Netherlands, addressed the parallel object-oriented paradigm. This comprehensive subproject led to the definition of two high level programming languages, POOL and POOL2, an abstract machine called APM, and several prototypes of loosely coupled multiprocessor systems called DOOM and POOMA (Odijk, 1989).

Object-oriented programming, where objects and messages exchanged between them are the sole data and processing primitive mechanisms, lends itself to a natural parallel decomposition of program execution very suitable for execution in a loosely coupled environment. The core of the POOMA architecture consists of a loosely coupled network of computing nodes with a distributed memory. Communication between the nodes is performed by means of a packet switching point-to-point network, such that the available communication bandwidth is scalable to several hundreds of nodes without requiring high speed elementary interconnection links. Each node can support several (10–100) processes simultaneously via multitasking.

The communication processor has been designed with the following characteristics: absence of deadlocks and starvation, independence from network topology, free routing (possibility to select alternate routes), independent operation, and VLSI implementability. The routing tables are downloaded at initialization time. A packet comprises 256 bits of information and defines the destination processor. Memory management in POOMA must deal with special requirements for object orientation: small memory blocks that may be allocated and released (thus memory fragmentation problems), and high rates of block demands. It uses memory management units adapted to small page sizes.

The latest hardware implementation of POOMA is composed of 100 nodes. A node uses a MC 68020 processor at 16 MHz, a MC68851 MMU, a MC 68881 floating point unit, 4 MB of local memory, and a prototype communication processor sitting on two boards. The communication processor does not actually implement all the intended features, but the VLSI version being developed will provide all the required features. Some nodes possess an Ethernet board to connect to the host machine, and some nodes are equipped with 300-MB disks for secondary storage. The interconnection network in POOMA was deliberately left open for experiments, and allows three different topologies to be evaluated: torus (10×10), chordal rings (on 100 nodes with chordal distance = 18), and extended chordal rings. First results indicate that the network is extremely robust to high throughput (up to 80% of link occupation), as well as to hot spots. The current hop time with the prototype communication processor is around 50 μs, but will be reduced to 16 μs with the VLSI version, thereby increasing the scalability and throughput without major problems.

KNOWLEDGE BASE SYSTEMS

Data and knowledge base multiprocessors handle operations specific to retrieval and manipulation of relations and data in potentially large databases. The main topics addressed so far fall into several categories:

1. Loosely coupled versus tightly coupled systems. Lakshmi (1989) analyzes join operations in a loosely coupled system of many microprocessors in a network (DBMC) and in a shared memory system (TCMP) and concludes that TCMP is more advantageous.
2. Multiuser querying, where interquery parallelism is looked for. Such a parallelism is found in existing commercial relational systems but also in specialized architectures (Bergsten, 1988).
3. Distributed query evaluation with intraquery parallelism, as exemplified by the EDS machine (see below) or other systems such as BUBBA, GRACE, DDC, and SABRE (Bueltzingsloewen, 1988).
   a. Parallelization of SQL primitives (select, join, ordered by, etc).
   b. Data partitioning with parallel disk access (GAMMA, MDBS, SABRE, etc).
   c. Hardwired filtering techniques.
   d. Interconnection network for database systems (Hsiao, 1988).

Multiuser Parallelism in RDBMS on Commercial Multiprocessors

ENCORE Multimax and SEQUENT Symmetry machines have parallel implementations of more and more relational database products. Table 1 summarizes some experiments performed on a SEQUENT Symmetry

Table 1. Audited Performance Results

Informix on SEQUENT *Symmetry*

Model	#PE	Memory	Disks (264 MB)	TPS	Percentage of Responses under 1 s
S27	2	16	5	30	99.13
S27	4	16	6	40	97.30
S81	6	32	8	60	96.88
S81	8	40	11	80	95.38

Ingres on SEQUENT *Symmetry*

Model	#PE	Memory	Disks (264 MB)	TPS	Percentage of Responses under 1 s
S81	4	80	16	36.8	99.4
S81	8	80	16	67.8	97
S81	12	80	16	88	97
S81	16	80	16	104.4	95

(SEQUENT, 1989). Figures given in the table correspond to those from 1989 and illustrate the speed-up obtained by adding more processors. It is likely that performance will dramatically increase with tuning and optimizations of the core database engine. As of March 1991, SEQUENT and ORACLE have demonstrated an on-line transaction-processing system rated at more than 400 TPS (transactions per second). In the near future, a 20-processor system may well break the 1000 TPS barrier.

The figures in Table 1 correspond to multiuser processing with no use of AI tools and may be seen as a first step of RDBMS parallelization. However, it is worth mentioning here that the parallelization of some heavily used SQL operators such as "group by," "order by," and joins, is near completion at most major vendors, constituting the second step. The third step will be intraquery parallelization (see following section on EDS) and introduction of AI techniques and tools.

European Declarative System

EDS (Syre, 1990; Haworth and co-workers, 1990) is ESPRIT II TIP project 2025. It involves Bull, ICL, Siemens, ECRC, and a number of small companies and European universities, aiming at the design and implementation of a large-scale, multiparadigm multiprocessor system, with special emphasis on database applications. This four-year project started in 1989 and involves more than 110 researchers. Configurable from 4 to 256 processors, the EDS architecture is based on a distributed memory and a powerful interconnection network (of the delta family). Each processing element consists of a high speed processing unit (SPARC CPU), a system support unit implemented with a low cost SPARC, a network interface unit implemented by ASICs, and a store unit of up to 64 MB of DRAM. The system architecture of EDS is based on a common process control language (PCL), used by all application components: the relational component, the functional component, and the logic programming component. All components are parallel subsystems. PCL is built on top of a parallel operation system such as MACH or CHORUS.

The relational component, developed by Bull and its associates (Bergsten and co-workers, 1991), is a parallel database system and consists of several managers (request, data, session, catalogue, object managers, which are all different processes running concurrently and possibly with many instances). A request manager accepts queries in an extended SQL language and compiles them into runnable code through several levels of optimization (logical optimization, physical optimization, parallelization). A data manager accepts runnable queries for execution, distributes data across the object memories, manages all transactions and concurrency, navigates to the data, accesses the base relations, and returns the results. All managers in the parallel database system use PCL tasks and use PCL message-passing facilities.

The functional component of EDS, under Siemens responsibility, consists of a parallel common LISP system augmented with mechanisms similar to futures. LISP sessions can interact with database sessions. The logic programming component of EDS has its roots in the work developed at ECRC (PEPSys) and will be extended with several features matching the goals of EDS: connection to the database system, allowing both large-scale logic programming applications and database processing with deductive capabilities, parallel constraint satisfaction techniques, and a new type of parallelism well suited to problems with large databases. A 64-PE prototype system is being built by ICL and will serve as a test vehicle to assess the fundamental ideas of EDS.

Parallel Blackboard Systems

The blackboard model may be thought of as a collection of experts or knowledge sources (KSs) doing computations using a blackboard as a communication medium (Bisiani and Forin, 1989), and as such, inherently contains several potentialities for concurrent and parallel processing. In effect, multiprocessing may take place within each KS, among KS instances (KSIs), within the blackboard machinery itself, or in the control process. However, despite a promising inclination to parallelization, the potential parallelism provided by each of these sources looks rather small. Some reasons for this are that a KS can only see a portion of the blackboard at any time (otherwise the system performance would degrade too much), and that the experts are dependent on each other (they generally wait for other agents to produce tangible results before proceeding safely) (Rice, 1989).

Experiments with CAGE and POLIGON. In the framework of the Advanced Architectures Project at Stanford, two experiments have been undertaken by Rice, Aiello, and Nii to exercise the CAGE and POLIGON systems on a parallel simulator, using the Elint application of interpretation of radar emissions. The simulator was an adaptation of the CARE system to a shared memory multiprocessor organization. The concurrency of CAGE was expressed in a variation of QLisp, while POLIGON made use of a form of distributed object-oriented system supported by the CARE simulator. The experiments are described in Rice (1989); their conclusions are summarized here:

1. Speedups vary considerably depending on the synchronization mode: with serial control and parallel KSs in CAGE, 8 or 16 processors achieve a speedup of 2. Without synchronization among KSs, the speedup amounts to 4 with 8 processors. Introducing finer granularity in the program gives 4.5 and 5.6 for speedups with 8 and 16 processors, respectively. As far as POLIGON is concerned, the same order of speedups was observed for a number of processors varying from 2 to 16 as in CAGE experiments. By varying the size of data sets, speedups of 3.6 for small data sets, and of 8 for large data sets were achieved with 32 processors. The maximum speedup obtained is 11.5 with 128 processors (there is doubt about the bus saturation).

2. Despite a great potential for parallelization, blackboard systems suffer from inherent serial control sequences, which limit the overall gain on multiprocessors. Moreover, large data sets, needed to avoid too much communication, also reduce the parallelism.

3. Blackboard nodes are generally long-lived processes, and load balancing happens to become a major factor of efficiency, which in this particular case looks fairly difficult to solve.

ANGEL: A Parallel Blackboard System under AGORA. ANGEL is a speech recognition system, decomposing the utterance in levels similar to those used in Hearsay II. It is structured as four loosely coupled blackboard subsystems (Bisiani and Forin, 1989), and their interconnection is also implemented as a blackboard. Each subsystem is activated by the data produced by the subsystem preceding it in the pipeline. The first component is basically a signal extractor module with five knowledge sources. The second component, the phonetic/acoustic analyzer, has four knowledge sources cooperating to build sets of coherent hypotheses. The word hypothesizer is the third component, with the search knowledge source being possibly duplicated a number of times. The last component is the sentence hypothesizer, interacting with the word hypothesizer by putting messages on each others' blackboard. The sentence hypothesizer can be implemented by multiple versions using different paradigms or algorithms to discover the sentence. ANGEL requires about 600 mips to be operational and therefore is a good candidate for parallelization. The Agora system was defined and implemented to assist in the design on ANGEL. Agora supports a programming style called shared data types (SDTs), where the system provided operations for an SDT automatically synchronize (the user does not need to explicitly use locks). Agora provides a set of basic access functions for the creation, destruction, and access to shared data structures. The KSs of the ANGEL system are implemented as independent processes or as independent threads (the system is programmed in C and LISP). Agora uses the shared memory abstraction of the mach kernel.

ANGEL delivers a speedup of 8 on 12 processors by making use of parallelism and pipelining.

Knowledge Base Applications on the Connection Machine

Waltz (1988) gives an overview of AI related research on the Connection Machine, which has been used to experiment several paradigms for knowledge base systems. First, an ATMS (Assumption-Based Truth Maintenance System) has been implemented. In the ATMS formalism, problem solutions consist of a set of variables that have been assigned specific values. The full set of assumptions for all variables represents the search space of the ATMS. The program must then apply constraints, which allow the ATMS system to eliminate sets of assumptions that are inconsistent. On a 16K CM2 machine, a 13-queens benchmark program provided all solutions in 60 s (against 4235 s on the fastest implementation on a SYMBOLICS machine).

Another field of experimentation on the Connection Machine is the memory-based reasoning (qv) paradigm, where everything the system experiences is kept stored in the memory, so that identical situations may make use of the past computations to derive the answer. Other applications run on the connection machine include parallel retrieval, neural net modeling, vision, chess endgames, and natural language systems.

Parallel Architectures for Production Systems

Production or rule-based systems are widely used to express AI problems, where basically each step of the computation consists in firing "best rules" from the current knowledge (extensional database plus facts already derived) in order to obtain the desired result. They are used in many areas of AI such computer configurations, VLSI routing, and medical consultation. Gupta (1986) gives a comprehensive overview of the sources of parallelism in production systems based on OPS-5 (qv) and a comparison of a shared memory multiprocessor architecture adapted to parallel processing of rule firing in OPS-5 with other dedicated systems like DADO (qv), NON-VON (qv) (Gupta, 1986). The main results obtained by this study can be summarized as follows:

1. Although at first sight production rules are excellent candidates for parallel processing, there are a number of limitations: the number of candidate rules at each step is rather small, and the amount of processing for each rule may vary considerably. This leads to the need to exploit parallellism at much finer granularity (the parallelization of the RETE algorithm, the heart of the OPS-5 system). The observed parallelism was less than 10.

2. This finer granularity imposes communication and synchronization requirements that can be best achieved by a shared memory multiprocessor with outstanding performance at the bus and memory levels. It is reported that DADO and NON-VON, two highly parallel tree-structured machines using thousands of processors, perform significantly worse than the proposed shared memory multiprocessor.

CONCLUSION AND TRENDS

Parallel computer architectures for AI processing are a fast moving area of computer architecture. Existing conventional multiprocessors are now commonly used for parallel database environments and for experiments in parallel logic and functional systems. Special-purpose systems have been devised to address the specific problems of the new types of parallelism and concurrency raised by AI languages. More general but specific multiprocessors, such as the Monarch multiprocessor (Rettberg, 1990), DADO, NYU, RP-3, NON-VON, FAIM, or the Connection Machine (Waltz, 1988), are excellent vehicles to investigate new methods and algorithms for parallel AI systems.

Parallel machine architectures for AI (Shrobe, 1988; Wah, 1988) are currently in their infancy, and despite extraordinary progress made during the past 5 years, they need more time to become mature enough for large-scale commercial exploitation, for several reasons:

1. Far from all issues have been resolved at levels other than pure computer architecture: high level languages, operating systems, and even applications have a dramatic impact on the architecture. In the language area object-oriented systems are creating a demand for distributed systems, more scalable but at the same time more difficult to program, tune, and still slower than tightly coupled multiprocessors. Logic and relational systems are giving rise to new computer architectures such as the PIM or EDS machine. These depart from usual systems and much work still remains to provide a comfortable user environment or an easy connection to existing databases. The history of dedicated sequential LISP systems is an example of semi-failure of innovative implementation of AI computers.

2. There are still many quasi-unsolved issues with unsatisfactory answers, in both conventional or dedicated multiprocessors running AI systems: granularity and control of parallelism, scheduling strategies and their connections to the OS own scheduling, time sharing and multiuser systems, load balancing, etc. Though much has been achieved in the past few years, a lot remains to do to get efficient marketable products.

3. The battle between conventional multiprocessors capable of supporting more conventional data processing and specialized architectures dedicated to a limited class of algorithms is not at its end. Every year, new computer architectures are designed, with more processors, more efficiency, and more elaborate programming environments, but at the same time, shared bus multiprocessors are becoming commercially viable and always provide better performance or better tools. In the near future radically new systems with numbers of processors in the range of 10,000–1,000,000 will compete with commercial computers made of 1–20 clusters of 1–8 100–500 mips processors running C and C++.

The best evidence for these rather conservative statements is left to the reader by letting him or her compare the systems presented here with those mentioned in the January 1987 issue of *IEEE Computer*. Most of them have disappeared and only a few have survived; even these have yet to prove viable. Nonetheless, this area is still certainly one of the most exciting and is a major point for the success of AI applications, always more and more hungry for megabytes and mips.

BIBLIOGRAPHY

A. Agarwal and co-workers, "APRIL: A Processor Architecture for Multiprocessing," in *Proceedings of the 17th International Symposium on Computer Architecture,* Seattle, May 1990; ACM SIGARCH, Vol. 18, no. 2; IEEE Computer Society Press 90CH2887-8, 1990, pp. 104–112.

K. A. M. Ali and R. Karlsson, "The Muse Approach to Or-Parallel Prolog," *Int. J. Parallel Program.*, **19**(2), 129–162 (Feb. 1990).

D. C. Allen and N. S. Sridharan, "Application of the Butterfly Parallel Processor in Artificial Intelligence," in J. Kowalik, ed., *Parallel Computation and Computers for Artificial Intelligence,* Kluwer Academic Publishers, Norwell, Mass., 1988, pp. 153–164.

M. Amamiya, M. Takesue, R. Hasegawa, and H. Mikami, "Implementation and Evaluation of a List-Processing Oriented Data Flow Machine," in *Proceedings of the 13th International Symposium on Computer Architecture,* Tokyo, June 2–5, 1986, IEEE and ACM, IEEE Computer Society Press, June 1986, pp. 10–19.

U. Baron, J. Chassin de Kergommeaux, M. Hailperin, M. Ratcliffe, P. Robert, J. C. Syre, and H. Westphal, "The Parallel ECRC Prolog System PEPSys: An Overview and Evaluation Results," in *Proceedings of FGCS 88, International Conference on Fifth Generation Computer Systems,* Tokyo, Nov. 1988, pp. 841–850.

B. Bergsten, M. Coupry, P. Valduriez, "DBS3: An Implementation of the EDS DBMs on a Shared Memory Multiprocessor," to appear in *Proceedings of the ESPRIT 1991 Conference,* Brussels, (Nov. 1991).

B. Bergsten, R. Gonzalez-Rubio, B. Kerherve, and J. Rohmer, "An Advanced Database Accelerator," *IEEE Micro,* **8**(5), 47–63 (Oct. 1988).

R. Bisiani and A. Forin, "Parallelization of Blackboard Architectures and the Agora System," in V. Jagannathan, R. Dodhiawala, and L. S. Baum, eds., *Blackboard Architectures and Their Applications,* Academic Press, Inc., 1989, Chapt. 7, pp. 137–152.

G. von Buetzlingsloewen, C. Iochpe, R. P. Liedtke, K. Dittrich, and P. L. Lockeman, "A Two-Level Transaction Management in a Multiprocessor Database Machine," in *Proceedings of the 3rd International Conference on Data and Knowledge Bases,* Jerusalem, Morgan-Kaufman Publishers, San Mateo, Calif., June 1988, pp. 374–386.

J. Chassin de Kergommeaux, J. C. Syre, and H. Westphal, "Implementation of a Parallel Prolog System on a Commercial Multiprocessor," in *Proceedings of the European Conference on Artificial Intelligence,* Munich, Aug. 1988.

A. Contessa, E. Cousin, C. Coustet, M. Cubero-Castan, G. Durrieu, B. Lecussan, M. Lemaitre, and P. Ng, "MaRS, A Combinator Graph Reduction Machine," in E. Odijk, M. Rem, and J. C. Syre, eds., *PARLE '89: Parallel Architectures and Languages Europe,* Lecture notes in Computer Science, Springer-Verlag, New York, 1989, pp. 176–192.

J. Crammond, *Implementation of Committed Choice Languages on Shared Memory Systems,* Ph.D. dissertation, Heriot Watt University, Edinburgh, 1988.

I. Foster and S. Taylor, "Strand: A Practical Parallel Programming Tool," in *Proceedings of the North American Conference on Logic Programming,* MIT Press, Cambridge, Mass., 1989.

A. Gupta, C. Forgy, A. Newell, and R. Wedig, "Parallel Algorithms and Architectures for Rule-Based Systems," in *Proceedings of the 13th International Symposium on Computer Architecture,* IEEE Computer Society Press, Tokyo, June 1986, pp. 28–37.

S. Haridi and S. Janson, "Kernel Andorra Prolog and its Computational Model," in *Proceedings of the 7th International Conference on Logic Programming,* MIT Press, Cambridge, Mass., 1990.

B. Hart, S. Danforth, and P. Valduriez, "Parallelizing a Database Programming Language," in *Proceedings of the 4th International Conference on Databases in Parallel and Distributed Systems,* Austin, Tex., IEEE Computer society and ACM SIGARCH, Dec. 1988, pp. 72–79.

G. Haworth, S. Leunig, C. Hammer, and M. Reeve, "The European Declarative System, Database, and Languages," *IEEE Micro* 10, pp. 20–23 (Dec. 1990).

A. Houri and E. Shapiro, *A Sequential Abstract Machine for Concurrent Prolog,* Report TR-CS 86-20, The Weizmann Institute, Rehovot, Israel, 1986.

D. K. Hsiao, "The Impact of the Interconnecting Network on Parallel Database Computers," in M. Kitsuregawa and H. Tanaka, eds., *Data Base Machines and Knowledge Base Machines,* Kluwer Academic Publishers, 1988, pp. 216–224.

T. Itoh and R. H. Halstead, Jr., ed., *Parallel LISP: Languages and Systems, Proceedings of the US/Japan Workshop on Parallel Lisp,* Sendai, Japan, June 1989, Lecture notes in Computer Science, Vol. 441, Springer-Verlag, New York, 1990.

J. S. Kowalik, ed., *Parallel Computation and Computers for Artificial Intelligence,* Kluwer Academic Publishers, Norwell, Mass., 1988.

M. S. Lakshmi and P. S. Yu, "Analysis of Parallel Processing Architectures for Database Systems," in K. McAuliffe and P. Kogge, eds., *Proceedings of the 1989 International Conference on Parallel Processing,* Vol. 1, Pennsylvania State University Press, University Park, Pa., Aug. 1989, pp. 83–90.

Odijk, "Parallel Computers for Advanced Information Processing: The Achievements of ESPRIT Project 415," in *Conference Proceedings, ESPRIT Week 1989,* Kluwer Academic Publishers, 1989, pp. 345–360.

R. Ohbuchi, "Overview of AI Application-Oriented Parallel Processing in Japan," in J. Kowalik, ed., *Parallel Computation and Computers for Artificial Intelligence,* Kluwer Academic Publishers, 1988, pp. 247–259.

Paralogic, "Parallel Prolog On Your Desktop," in *AI Review,* Paralogic, Inc., Bethlehem, Pa., 1990, pp. 39–42.

M. Reeve and S. E. Zenith, eds., *Parallel Processing and Artificial Intelligence,* John Wiley and Sons, Inc., New York, 1989.

R. D. Rettberg, W. R. Crowther, P. P. Carvey, and R. S. Tomlinson, "The Monarch Parallel Processor System," *IEEE COMPUTER,* 23(4), 18–30 (Apr. 1990).

J. Rice, N. Aiello, and H. P. Nii, "See How They Run . . . The Architecture and Performance of Two Concurrent Blackboard Systems," in V. Jagannathan, R. Dodhiawala, and L. S. Baum, eds., *Blackboard Architectures and Their Applications,* Academic Press, Inc., 1989, Chapt. 8, pp. 153–176.

SEQUENT, SEQUENT Computer Systems, Inc., SEQUENT/INGRES Performance Report (DB1008), and SEQUENT/INFORMIX Performance Report, DB 1012, 1989.

H. E. Shrobe, "Symbolic Computer Architectures," in E. Shrobe and the American Association for Artificial Intelligence, eds., *Exploring Artificial Intelligence, Survey Talks from the National Conferences on Artificial Intelligence,* Morgan-Kaufmann Publishers, San Mateo, Calif., 1988, pp. 545–618.

J. C. Syre, "EDS, European Declarative System," in M. Vanneschi, ed., *CRAI Summer School on Highly Parallel Systems,* Capri, 1990.

K. Taki, "The Parallel Inference Machine System in the Intermediate Stage of the FGCS Project," in ICOT ed., *Proceedings of the International Conference on Fifth Generation Computer Systems,* 1988, pp. 16–36.

H. Tanaka, "PIE, A Parallel Inference Machine," *IEEE Computer,* 19(5), (1986); *Proc. FGCS 1986,* ICOT, 1988, pp. 970–977.

Top Level, "Introducing Top Level Common Lisp," Top Level, Inc., Amherst, Mass., 1990.

L. M. Uhr, *Multi-Computer Architectures for Artificial Intelligence,* John Wiley and Sons, Inc., New York, 1987.

B. W. Wah and G. J. Li, "A Survey of Special Purpose Computer Architectures for AI," in J. S. Kowalik, ed., *Parallel Computation and Computers for Artificial Intelligence,* Kluwer Academic Publishers, 1988, pp. 263–291.

D. L. Waltz, "Artificial Intelligence Related Research on the Connection Machine," in *Proceedings of the Fifth Generation Computer Systems,* Tokyo, Vol. 2, ICOT, 1988, pp. 1010–1024.

D. H. D. Warren, "The SRI Model of OR-parallelism, Abstract Design and Implementation Issues," in *4th Symposium on Logic Programming,* San Francisco, Sept. 1987, pp. 46–53.

D. H. D. Warren, "Data Diffusion Machine, a Scalable Shared Virtual Memory Multiprocessor," in ICOT ed., *Proceedings of the International Conference on Fifth Generation Computer Systems,* 1988, pp. 943–952.

J. C. SYRE
Bull S.A. EDPS

PARRY

PARRY was one of the earliest attempts at belief modeling (see BELIEF REPRESENTATION SYSTEMS). Designed by Colby around 1971 at Stanford University, PARRY simulated the conversational behavior of a paranoid person. The system integrates inferences with affects and intentions to produce behavior that has been classified as paranoid by several psychologists who conversed with the program (see K. Colby, *Artificial Paranoia,* Pergamon, New York, 1975).

K. S. ARORA
SUNY at Buffalo

PARSING

Parsing a sentence of a natural language such as English is the process of determining if it is syntactically well formed (grammatical) and, if so, of finding one or more structures (structural descriptions) that encode useful information of some kind about it. The word is derived from the Latin *pars orationis* (part of speech) and reflects a process that has been carried out by human beings from medieval times to the present. This activity traditionally took the form of assigning a part of speech to every word in a given sentence, of determining the grammatical categories of words and phrases, and of enumerating the grammatical relations between words. Its purpose was pedagogical, to help students of a language increase their mastery of it.

In modern times developments in linguistics and computer science have led to a somewhat different set of activities being associated with the term parsing. The availability of computers was one of the factors that led to the replacement of vague, partially specified procedures that were carried out by humans by well-specified algorithms that were carried out by machines. Also, the change in purpose of the activity led to a corresponding change in the nature of the structural descriptions produced. Pedagogical concerns were replaced by a requirement that structural descriptions reflect the meaning(s) of the sentences. This is of special importance in AI applications, in which the intent of input sentences must be understood and acted on in an appropriate manner.

Still another change stemmed from the use of formal systems to model aspects of natural languages. In particular, many different types of formal, generative grammar have been devised to specify the sentences of a language and to pair each sentence with a corresponding set of structural descriptions. The nature of these grammars, however, usually does not provide an obvious algorithm for computing structural descriptions from sentences. In this respect they are similar to systems of logic, which implicitly specify a set of provable theorems but do not explicitly tell how a particular theorem is to be proved. Just as proof procedures must be devised for systems of logic, so must parsing procedures be devised for formal grammars of natural languages. Parsing a given sentence with respect to a given grammar, then, is the process of determining whether the sentence belongs to the language specified by the grammar and, if so, finding all the structures that the grammar pairs with the sentence.

The most common type of grammar used within computer science to syntactically specify the sentences of a particular programming language and to assign structure to them is the BNF (Backus-Naur form) grammar. This is a notational variant of a class of grammars called context-free (CF) grammars, which play a prominent role in many computational and AI models of natural language. It is worth remarking, however, that there is a central difference between the use of CF grammars in computer science and in computational linguistics. In the former, subclasses of CF grammars are used that are both unambiguous (ie, they assign at most one structural description to a sentence) and parsable in time linearly proportional to the length of the sentence parsed. In the latter, however, use is made of a parsing algorithm either for the general class of (ambiguous) CF grammars or for an even more general class of grammars, which often makes some use of CF grammars. For this reason the parsing of CF grammars shall be treated in some detail. The next section contains introductory material on phrase-structure grammars. The subsequent sections return to the central problem of parsing.

PHRASE-STRUCTURE GRAMMARS

The four components of a phrase-structure grammar are a set of symbols from a terminal vocabulary V_T (terminals), another disjoint set of symbols from a nonterminal vocabulary V_N (nonterminals), a distinguished element of V_N called the start symbol, and a set of rules or productions P. By suitably replacing restrictions on the allowable productions, different types of phrase-structure grammar may be specified. The previously mentioned CF grammar is one such type. All of its rules are of the form $A \to A_1 A_2 \ldots A_n$ where A belongs to V_N, and the A_i belong either to V_T or V_N. The CF right member of a production is the empty string, and such a production is called an erasing rule.

A derivation with respect to a CF grammar (V_N, V_T, S, P) is a sequence of strings, the first of which is the start symbol S, and each subsequent member (sentential form) is producible from its predecessor by replacing one nonterminal symbol A by a string of terminal and nonterminal symbols $A_1 A_2 \ldots A_n$ where $A \to A_1 A_2 \ldots A_n$ is a production of P. Sentential forms consisting entirely of terminal symbols can have no successors in a derivation, and the set of all such terminal sentential forms is said to constitute the language specified by the given grammar (V_N, V_T, S, P).

By way of illustration, consider the CF grammar G1 = (V_N, V_T, S, P) where V_N = (S, NP, VP, DET, N, V, PP, PREP); V_T = (I, the, a, man, park, telescope, saw, in, with) terminals such as *telescope* and nonterminals such as PREP are to be regarded as atomic symbols; and P is the set of productions:

S → NP VP   N → man/park/telescope
VP → V NP/VP PP   DET → the/a
NP → I/NP PP/DET N   V → saw
PP → PREP NP   PREP → in/with

The BNF abbreviatory convention is used for writing

VP → V NP/VP PP

to indicate the two productions VP → V NP and VP → VP PP. A sample derivation is the sequence of sentential forms:

S, NP VP, I VP, I VP PP, I V NP PP, I saw NP PP.

I saw DET N PP, I saw the N PP.

I saw the man PP, I saw the man PREP NP.

I saw the man in NP, I saw the man in DET N.

I saw the man in the N, I saw the man in the park.

The final sentential form, "I saw the man in the park," is one of the sentences in the language generated by G1.

G1 has been made simple to aid in illustrating certain parsing algorithms, but it is deficient in generating such sentences as "a park in I saw I." A much more complicated set of productions is required to produce reasonable coverage of a natural language without generating such unwanted strings of terminals.

Requiring that the structural descriptions reflect meaning makes the task of producing adequate grammars much more difficult. The use of derivations can be extended to provide for structural descriptions by replacing each production $A \rightarrow A_1 A_2 \ldots A_n$ by a corresponding production $A \rightarrow (_A A_1 A_2 \ldots A_n)$ where $(_A$ and $)$ are two new terminal symbols.

The result of such systematic replacement of productions P and augmentation of V_T for G1 is another CF grammar, G2. For every derivation of G1 there is a derivation of G2 in which corresponding productions are invoked. The structural description of a sentence generated by G1 is the sentence generated by the corresponding derivation with respect to G2. For the example, that derivation is

S, $(_S \text{NP VP})$, $(_S(_{NP}\text{I}) \text{ VP})$, . . . ,
$(_S(_{NP}\text{I}) (_{VP}(_{VP}(_V\text{saw}) (_{NP}(_{DET}\text{the}) (_N\text{man})))$
$(_{PP}(_{PREP}\text{in}) (_{NP}(_{DET}\text{the}) (_N\text{park})))))$

This last sentential form of the derivation with respect to G2 is the structural description of "I saw the man in the park." It is a labeled bracketing that is one notation for expressing the tree structure shown in Figure 1.

This representation is easier for humans to assimilate but takes more space, and henceforth the labeled bracketing format will be used to represent trees, further simplifying it to

(S (NP I) (VP (VP (V saw) (NP (DET the) (N man)))
(PP (PREP in) (NP (DET the) (N park)))))

Note that there is a second structural description of "I saw the man in the park:"

(S (NP I) (VP (V saw) (NP (NP (DET the) (N man))
(PP (PREP in) (NP (DET the) (N park))))))

that groups the words in such a way that the string "the man in the park" is a single constituent, an NP, leading naturally to the interpretation that the man was in the park when he was seen. The first structural description, however, does not group the string "the man in the park" as a single constituent. Instead, the VP "saw the man" is a sister to the PP "in the park," indicating the interpretation that the location of the seeing of the man was in the park.

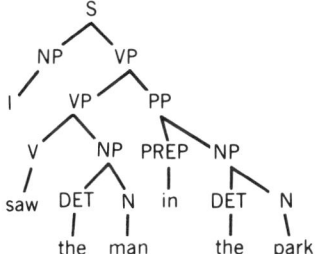

Figure 1.

Other types of phrase structures such as finite-state grammars, context-sensitive grammars, and unrestricted rewriting systems (Aho and Ullman, 1972, 1977; Hopcroft and Ullman, 1979) are definable by placing suitable restrictions on the type of productions allowed. They play a lesser role in specifying natural languages and hence are not treated here.

A topic of some importance in parsing is that of equivalence between two grammars. Grammars that generate the same language are said to be weakly equivalent. The term *strong equivalence* has been used to imply at least the existence of a 1:1 correspondence between the structural descriptions of two grammars, and in some definitions of strong equivalence, the existence of a trivial homeomorphism from the structures of one grammar to those of another has been required. The importance of equivalent grammars to parsing is that there are several circumstances in which it is preferable not to parse a given grammar directly but rather to construct from it an equivalent grammar and to parse with respect to it instead. In certain cases the structural descriptions assigned by the equivalent grammar are just as useful as those assigned by the given grammar. In other cases structural descriptions with respect to the given grammar are needed, but it still may be more efficient to obtain an equivalent grammar, parse with respect to it, and convert the resulting structural descriptions to those of the given grammar than to parse directly with respect to that given grammar. There is another reason for using equivalent grammars in parsing. Sometimes a particular parsing algorithm is only valid for grammars with productions satisfying some restrictions, and it can be shown that for an arbitrary grammar, an equivalent grammar that satisfies those restrictions can be constructed. Often such restrictions are not essential for a particular parsing algorithm but greatly simplify its exposition and hence are useful for pedagogical purposes.

Three types of equivalent grammar for CF grammars much used in parsing are those with no erasing rules, Chomsky normal-form grammars, and Greibach normal-form grammars (Aho and Ullman, 1972; Hopcroft and Ullman, 1979). Using capital letters to denote nonterminals and lowercase letters to denote terminals, Chomsky normal-form grammars are those with rules $A \rightarrow BC$ or $A \rightarrow a$, and Greibach normal-form grammars are those with rules $A \rightarrow a A_1 A_2 \ldots A_n$ where $A_1 A_2 \ldots A_n$ is a string of zero or more nonterminals.

Another topic to be considered in this section relates to the encoding of complex information in the nodes of structural description trees and to generalizing productions so as to require that the nodes they involve have prescribed information. This information usually takes the form of features and their values. Feature names are atomic entities such as ANIMATE, NUMBER, and GENDER; feature values are sometimes binary (+ or −), sometimes n-valued but atomic such as MASCULINE, FEMININE, and NEUTER, and sometimes complex such as a set of recursively used feature-value pairs. Often, the use of such features can enormously simplify the complexity of the set of productions required to specify a particular language. Also, it can be shown that such use of features can be made in ways that do not affect the class of languages definable. Thus, for example, it is possible to extend CF grammars with feature restrictions in such ways that the languages definable are precisely those definable by ordinary CF grammars. This use of features has played an important role in restoring to favor the use of CF languages in natural language specification and parsing. They are discussed further in a subsequent section.

The final subject to be discussed in this section involves the equivalence between phrase-structure grammars and corresponding automata. All of the types of phrase-structure grammars mentioned have as counterparts corresponding types of automata. Finite-state automata correspond to finite-state grammars; pushdown automata correspond to CF grammars; linear bounded automata, to CS grammars; and Turing machines, to unrestricted rewriting systems. By correspondence is meant the existence of constructions from grammars to automata and vice versa that preserve the languages specified and the structural descriptions assigned to their sentences.

There are several ways in which this correspondence can be exploited; the one of most concern regards the use of automata to model particular parsing algorithms and to model ways of implementing those algorithms. Space allows only informally describing parsing algorithms rather than specifying them precisely by means of automata, but other sources for instances of such usage of equivalent automata are available (Hopcroft and Ullman, 1972; Griffiths and Petrick, 1965). In the next three sections, three of the most commonly used CF parsing algorithms are examined: recursive descent, left corner, and chart.

RECURSIVE-DESCENT PARSING

Recursive-descent parsing, sometimes called top-to-bottom CF parsing (Aho and Ullman, 1972, 1977; Griffiths and Petrick, 1965), systematically pieces together structural description trees from top to bottom and from left to right. At each stage of parsing the left-most unexpanded nonterminal is identified, and its daughter nodes are attached using one of the productions that rewrite that nonterminal. If there is more than one such production, the parser tries them all, following a separate continuation path in each case. Such a process is called nondeterministic. Its implementation is often achieved by using a pushdown list to store continuations that are subsequently retrieved and followed.

Terminal symbols thus incorporated into a structural description are matched against the next symbols of the string being parsed. Failure to match causes the continuation in question to fail or block. A continuation also fails if there are remaining input string symbols after the last nonterminal has been expanded.

One successful parse path is given by:

S
(*S* NP VP)
(*S* (NP I) VP)
(*S* (NP I) (VP V NP))
(*S* (NP I) (VP (V saw) NP))
(*S* (NP I) (VP (V saw) (NP NP PP)))
(*S* (NP I) (VP (V saw) (NP (NP DET N) PP)))
(*S* (NP I) (VP (V saw) (NP (NP (DET the) N) PP)))
(*S* (NP I) (VP (V saw) (NP (NP (DET the) (N man)) PP)))
(*S* (NP I) (VP (V saw) (NP (NP (DET the) (N man)) (PP PREP NP))))
(*S* (NP I)(VP (V saw)(NP (NP (DET the) (N man)) (PP (PREP in) NP))))
(*S* (NP I) (VP (V saw) (NP (NP (DET the) (N man)) (PP (PREP in) (NP DET N)))))
(*S* (NP I) (VP (V saw) (NP (NP (DET the) (N man)) (PP (PREP in) (NP (DET the) N)))))
(*S* (NP I) (VP (V saw) (NP (NP (DET the) (N man)) (PP (PREP in) (NP (DET the) (N park))))))

Another successful parse path leads to the structural description

(*S* (NP I) (VP (VP (V saw) (NP (DET the) (N man))) (PP (PREP in) (NP (DET the) (N park)))))

whose structure indicates the sequence of continuations involved in producing it.

Note that whenever the production NP → NP PP is used to expand a left-most nonterminal, the resulting structure continues to have NP as its leftmost unexpanded nonterminal. Hence, expansion via this rule takes place indefinitely, and it is seen that the algorithm does not terminate. More generally, it is observed that nontermination of the recursive descent algorithm will occur whenever it is applied to a grammar that admits recursive left branching, ie, a left-most derivation from some nonterminal A to a string beginning with A.

There are several ways of ensuring termination of this algorithm. First, the grammar to be parsed can be required to disallow recursive left branching. This is not as serious a limitation as might at first be expected because it has been shown that there are constructions that map a given CF grammar into an equivalent CF grammar that is not left recursive. Constructions to Greibach normal form can be used for this purpose. One such construction was proposed by Rosenkrantz (1967). A second way of ensuring termination of the algorithm is applicable to grammars that contain no erasing rules. For such grammars a continuation can be blocked whenever the number of nonterminals that remain to be expanded exceeds the number of still unmatched terminal symbols in the input string.

An obvious improvement that can be made to recursive-descent parsing involves the use of a left-branching reachability matrix $\mathbf{R}$ with elements $\mathbf{R}(A,B)$ whose arguments A and B range over the union of V_T and V_N. $\mathbf{R}(A,B)$ is T (true) or F (false) depending, if B belongs to V_N, on whether it is possible to left branch down from B to A, and, if B belongs to V_T, depending on whether $A = B$. That is, $\mathbf{R}(A,B)$ is T if the grammar in question has a derivation from B to a string beginning with A or if $A = B$. Note that **R** depends only on a given CF grammar, not on any particular string to be parsed with respect to it. Thus **R** can be computed once and for all for a given grammar of interest. Warshall's (1962) algorithm for computing **R** has been proved optimal and is, therefore, recommended.

Use of matrix **R** is illustrated by the following continuation:

S
$(S\ NP\ VP)$
$(S\ (NP\ DET\ N)\ VP)$

The left-most unexpanded nonterminal DET cannot left branch down to the next input string terminal "I" because $\mathbf{R}(I,DET) = F$. Hence, this continuation can be blocked at this point without having to consider further continuations that result from expanding DET.

LEFT-CORNER PARSING

As the name implies, left-corner parsing [also called SBT parsing (Griffiths and Petrick, 1965)] builds sentence structures in a left-to-right, bottom-to-top fashion, piecing together the left corner of a structural description tree first. It is not the only parsing algorithm that builds structure from bottom to top. Shift-and-reduce parsing is one of the more commonly encountered cases in point (Aho and Ullman, 1972, 1977; Griffiths and Petrick, 1965). At each step in left-corner parsing, having determined a left-corner subtree of a structural description tree, it attempts to extend that subtree by scanning the productions for those whose right members begin with the root node of the left-corner subtree. Substituting that subtree for the first constituent of the right member of such a production gives a larger left-corner subtree; all of the daughter nodes of its root node except the first remain to be replaced by appropriate structure, this being accomplished in left-to-right order, recursively using this same left-corner parsing algorithm.

Once again, this algorithm is nondeterministic. There can be more than one production with a right member beginning with a given constituent, leading to one type of nondeterminism. Another source of nondeterminism arises whenever a subtree is successfully built up to replace a constituent other than the first one in the right member of some production. In addition to making the replacement, it is also necessary to attempt to build the subtree up to a larger subtree with the same root node.

As with recursive-descent parsing, the recursive left-branching matrix $\mathbf{R}(A,B)$ can be used to curtail continuations that must eventually fail. At each point where a left-corner subtree has been built up, one knows the nonterminal that one is next attempting to satisfy (ie, to replace). If that subtree has root A, and B is the nonterminal to be satisfied, then it is necessary to block if $\mathbf{R}(A,B) = F$ without attempting further left-corner building of this subtree.

The first few steps in one successful path for the left-corner parsing of the sentence "I saw the man in the park" with respect to the grammar G1 are the following: The only production whose right member begins with the first word in the sentence to be parsed, "I," is NP → I This gives the left-corner subtree (NP I), and one of the productions whose right member begins with the root of this subtree is S → NP VP. Letting the left-corner subtree satisfy the NP node of this production gives the new (partially determined) subtree (S (NP I) VP). It is still necessary to parse the remaining string "saw the man in the park" up to a tree with root VP to satisfy the VP node in (S (NP I) VP). Proceeding in the same way, the left-corner subtree (V saw) and then the partially determined subtree (VP (V saw) NP) are obtained. The remaining input string at this point is "the man in the park." An initial substring of it must be left-corner parsed up to a subtree with root NP. Suppressing the details of this, it turns out to be (NP (DET the) (N man)), with "in the park" left as the remaining portion of the input string. This subtree is used to replace the NP node in the previous structure (VP (V saw) NP), giving the new left-corner subtree (VP (V saw) (NP (DET the) (N man))). Next one of the productions is chosen whose right member begins with VP, VP → VP PP, and it is combined with the previously determined left-corner subtree to obtain (VP (VP (V saw) (NP (DET the) (N man))) PP). Finally, the remaining input string "in the park" is left-corner parsed up to a subtree with root node PP, and this subtree is used to replace the PP in the previous structure. The result is one of the required structural descriptions, (S (NP I) (VP (VP (V saw) (NP (DET the) (N man))) (PP (PREP in) (NP (DET the) (N park))))).

The Rosenkrantz equivalent grammar construction was previously mentioned as a means of eliminating left branching. It is also of value in relating recursive-descent parsing and left-corner parsing. Griffiths and Petrick (1969a) have shown that the left-corner parsing of a given CF grammar is mimicked by the recursive-descent parsing of the corresponding Rosenkrantz equivalent grammar. This has been exploited in parsing efforts making use of the PROLOG programming language. The productions of a CF grammar can be directly transcribed into a PROLOG form that permits parsing without programming any parsing algorithm. PROLOG itself provides a top-down, depth-first search procedure, which has the effect of performing recursive-descent parsing (see RECURSION). Although PROLOG does permit the easy implementation of a CF parser, its value is limited by the limitations of recursive-descent parsing, namely that it does not allow recursive left branching, and it is slower than such alternatives as left-corner parsing and chart parsing for most grammars of practical interest. To avoid both of these problems, the Rosenkrantz equivalent grammar construction (programmed in PROLOG) has been used to obtain a grammar that can be parsed via the PROLOG recursive-descent procedure, thus mimicking left-corner parsing of the original grammar. Griffiths and Petrick (1969b) also used the Rosenkrantz construction to prove that the time required for left-corner parsing is, at worst, a constant (depending on the grammar) multiple of the time required to parse the sentence with respect to the same grammar by recursive descent.

CHART PARSING

All of the parsing algorithms described to this point have worst-case exponential upper bounds. That is, there exist grammars and sentences whose parsing requires a number of steps proportional to a constant raised to the power of the number of words in the input string of words. The reason for this is that when two or more nondeterministic continuations arise, each of them can lead to the identical determination of some substructure common to them all. To avoid this, it is possible to store information as to which subtrees have been found to span substrings of the input string. This information can then be looked up to avoid computing it more than once.

There are a number of different chart-parsing algorithms. One variant, separately discovered by Cocke, Kasami, and Younger, is now usually referred to as CKY parsing (Younger, 1967). Like most of the other chart-parsing algorithms, it has a worst-case upper bound proportional to the cube of the length of the input string. Other chart-parsing algorithms of note were proposed by Kay (1967), Earley (1970), Kaplan (1973), and Ruzzo and co-workers (1980). The latter is both especially simple and efficient, having a worst-case upper bound proportional to the cube of the input string length with an attractively small constant of proportionality.

Ruzzo's parsing algorithm makes use of a chart or matrix whose elements $t_{i,j}$ ($0 \leq i \leq j \leq n$) are determined during the course of parsing a string of length n. Each element $t_{i,j}$ consists of a set of items each of which is a production of the given grammar with a single dot located somewhere among the constituents of the right member. For example, PP $\rightarrow$ PREP DOT NP is a typical item. The positions between the terminals of the input string are numbered as in (0 I 1 saw 2 the 3 man 4 in 5 the 6 park 7). If element $t_{i,j}$ contains the item $A \rightarrow A_0 \ldots A_k$ DOT $A_{k+1} \ldots A_m$, this indicates that the input string between points i and j has been parsed up to a string of trees whose roots are $A_0 A_1 \ldots A_k$, and if some string beginning at point j can be parsed up to a string of trees with roots $A_{k+1} \ldots A_m$ the concatenation of both those strings of trees can be parsed up to the parent node A to obtain a tree with root A.

For grammar G1 the items of $t_{0,0}$ are ($S \rightarrow$ DOT NP VP, NP $\rightarrow$ DOT I, NP $\rightarrow$ DOT NP PP, NP $\rightarrow$ DOT DET N, DET $\rightarrow$ DOT the, and DET $\rightarrow$ DOT a). They are obtained by taking the productions that begin with a constituent A such that $\mathbf{R}(A,S) = T$, where $\mathbf{R}$ is the left-branching reachability matrix, and forming items in which the dot is located in front of the first constituent. These items indicate the initial possibilities. Three types of action fill in the elements of the matrix $t_{i,j}$. Elements $t_{j,j}$ are filled in by generating items of the type that was seen for $t_{0,0}$ in much the same manner that has already been illustrated. Some of the items of elements $t_{i,j}$ are formed from those of $t_{i,j-1}$ by hopping the dot one position to the right if the constituent hopped over is either the input string terminal located between points $j - 1$ and j or else a nonterminal from which there is a derivation to that input terminal. The remaining items are filled in by considering, in the proper sequence, pairs of items, the first of which is of the form $A \rightarrow A_0 \ldots A_p$ DOT $A_{p+1} \ldots A_q$ and the second of which is the form $A_{p+1} \rightarrow \ldots$ DOT. If such a pair comes from corresponding elements $t_{i,j}$ and $t_{j,k}$, this indicates that the substring of terminals from points i to j has been parsed up to the string $A_0 \ldots A_p$ with a possible continuation of A_{p+1}, and the substring from points j to k has been parsed up to A_{p+1}, realizing that possibility. Hence, the dot is hopped over the constituent to its right in the first item, and the resulting item is included among the items of $t_{i,k}$.

Acceptance is indicated by the presence of an item of the form $S \rightarrow \ldots$ DOT in $t_{0,n}$. Structural descriptions are easily obtained by modifying the form of items described above to indicate the tree structure of the constituents to the left of the dot. Whenever the dot is hopped over a constituent, that constituent is replaced by any structure it dominates. The necessary information about this structure comes either from the other item involved or from information supplied by the grammar about a derivation of the next terminal symbol from the hopped-over nonterminal.

COMPLEX FEATURE-BASED GRAMMARS

There are a number of types of grammar of current interest for specifying natural languages that make some central use of complex feature-augmented rules and structures. To various degrees, they also incorporate other formal devices in addition to their central phrase-structure components. They share a common requirement for matching, in a certain way, rules containing complex features with structural description trees or tree fragments containing complex features, and hence they are sometimes referred to as unification-based grammars. Examples of such grammars are generalized phrase-structure grammars (see GRAMMAR, GENERALIZED PHRASE STRUCTURE) (Gazdar and co-workers, 1985), definite clause grammars (Pereira and Warren, 1980), functional unification grammars (Kay, 1985), head grammars and head-driven grammars (Proudian and Pollard, 1985), lexical functional grammars (Bresnan, 1982), and PATR-II-type grammars (Shieber and co-workers, 1983).

It is beyond the scope of this article to describe these formalisms sufficiently to describe their parsers. Note that they all incorporate the use of a suitably modified phrase-structure grammar parser (see GRAMMAR, PHRASE-STRUCTURE), usually one of the more common types of parsers.

Two other types of grammar might also be included among those of this section because their rules and structures also make essential use of complex features. These two, transformational grammars and augmented transition network grammars, however, are treated separately in the subsequent sections.

TRANSFORMATIONAL GRAMMAR PARSING

It should first be noted that there is no single theory that is agreed on by all who use the term transformational grammar (TG) (qv) to label the syntactic theory they advocate. This is so because TG has evolved, splitting on occasion into distinct formal models of language with significant differences in the type of rules that are allowed, on the constraints imposed on rule application, and on the type of structural descriptions and intermediate structures that are advocated. It is beyond the scope of this article to discuss these diverse types of grammars and their parsers. Some of them are discussed in transformational grammar. A few general remarks are given below.

TG makes central use of a base phrase-structure-grammar component (usually a CFG) to specify a set of base trees (deep structures) and a transformational component to map those trees into a set of surface-structure trees. A simple operation (usually just extracting the terminals) on a surface-structure tree yields one of the sentences in the language thus specified. The meaning of a sentence is encoded in either the base structures, the surface structures, or some combination of both, depending on the type of TG in question.

The transformational component consists of a set of one or more transformations, usually ordered in their application in a rather complex way. A transformation maps each of a class of trees that satisfies certain conditions into a corresponding tree.

Note that the normal direction in which transformations are formulated to operate is from deep structure to surface structure. In transformational parsing, however, it is required to find the corresponding deep and surface structures in a sentence. For some applications and some variants of TG it is sufficient to find only the surface structure or only the deep structure, but it is in general only possible to know one of them has been correctly determined if the other has also been determined and the transformational mapping between them has been verified.

One way to determine the deep and surface structures assigned by some TG to a given sentence is to limit the possible phrase-structure and transformational rules that might be applicable to the derivation of that sentence and then to try all combinations of these rules in the forward direction to see which paths terminate with the given sentence. This is called analysis by synthesis. It was suggested by Matthews (1961) but was never implemented. It appears to be prohibitively inefficient.

Another way to determine deep and surface structure is to reverse the forward generative procedure, going from a sentence to its surface structures. Unfortunately, the machinery for forward generation is not directly convertible to a corresponding system for going in the other direction. The first step, determination of the surface structure corresponding to a given sentence, is complicated by the fact that it includes structure reflecting base phrase-structure productions as well as other structure of transformational origin. Petrick (1965) has shown that it is possible to compute from a given TG meeting certain requirements a new CF grammar whose productions are a superset of the TG's base component productions and that generates a set of structural description trees that include all of those surface structures assigned to sentences of length not exceeding n by the TG. This augmented base-component CF grammar can be used to determine all of the surface structures a TG assigns to any sentence of length n or less, together with some possible spurious ones (given a particular sentence of some length, the augmented CF grammar valid for sentences up to that length can be found if one has not already been determined).

Petrick also presents several ways of inverting the effect of transformations. True inverse transformations are, in general, not computable, but pseudoinverse transforms can be mechanically computed from a given set of forward transforms, and they can be applied, together with some additional CF parsing, to obtain a set of structures that includes all of the deep structures assigned by the TG. These must be checked to ensure that they contain only bse-component phrase structure and to ensure that they may be mapped into the previously determined surface structure using the transformational component of the TG in question.

This parsing algorithm is dependent on certain restrictions being placed on the class of TGs to which it is applied. Without such restrictions, classes of grammars such as those of Chomsky's aspects model have been proved to be equivalent to Turing machines (qv) (Peters and Ritchie, 1973) and hence it is known that no parser valid for the entire class is possible.

A final point to note with respect to transformational parsing is that most parsers labeled transformational are not constructed from a given TG in such a way as to guarantee their correctness. Neither are they usually constructed by hand and then proved to be valid parsers of normally formulated TGs. Rather, they are usually mechanisms of some kind that directly produce structures of the type thought to be correct at some time by the advocates of some variant of TG. Examples of this type that make use of inverse transformations include parsers developed at MITRE (Zwicky and co-workers, 1965) and IBM (Petrick, 1973; Loveman and co-workers, 1971). Examples that do not make any use of transformations but do attempt to produce "transformational" structure include certain ATN parsers and Marcus (1980) parsers.

AUGMENTED-TRANSITION-NETWORK PARSING

Augmented transition networks (ATNs) have played a major role in computational linguistics (qv), since the early 1970s, providing syntactic analysis for many systems with natural language understanding capabilities (see GRAMMAR, AUGMENTED TRANSITION NETWORK). They are a natural extension of finite-state automata, the automata equivalent of finite-state grammars.

A finite-state automaton (FSA) is a finite set of states connected by directed arcs, each labeled with a symbol from a terminal vocabulary V_T. One state is designated as the initial state, and some subset of the states are designated as final states. In following a path from the initial state to any of the final states, a sequence of arcs is traversed, and the corresponding string of labels from V_T is said to constitute a sentence specified by the FSA. The set of sentences so specified is the language generated by the FSA. The automaton is said to be a deterministic finite-state automaton (DFA) if no node has two or more outgoing arcs bearing the same label. Otherwise, the automaton is said to be a nondeterministic finite-state automaton

(NFA). There is an effective procedure for constructing from an NFA an equivalent minimal state DFA, ie, a DFA that generates the same language and does so with the use of the smallest possible number of states.

One improvement of this model of language is the replacement of specific natural language words as members of V_T by categories and use of a conventional lexicon to assign specific words to these categories. A further improvement is a generalization of the NFA, namely the basic transition network IBTN), which is weakly equivalent to CF grammars. BTNs contain several different kinds of arcs, most of which are not of major concern. Two of note, however, are the CAT (category) arc and the PUSH arc. CAT arcs are merely ones with labels denoting word categories, parts of speech to be augmented by a lexicon as already discussed above. PUSH arcs are the basic recursion mechanism that extends finite-state grammar equivalency to context-free grammar equivalency. PUSH arcs contain the name of another basic transition network. To traverse a PUSH arc labeled A, control is transferred to the transition network named A (the convention generally used has a transition network named by its initial state), and when it reaches one of its final states, control is transferred back to the state pointed to by the push arc labeled A. Corresponding to the previously given grammar G1 is the BTN shown in Figure 2.

To illustrate the manner in which BTN parsing proceeds, consider the parsing of the sentence "I saw a man in the park" with respect to this BTN: Beginning in state $S/$ it is necessary to traverse the arc labeled PUSH NP/. Beginning at state NP/ of the subnetwork with initial state NP/, there are three choices. In this exposition one set of correct choices are made, but exhaustive nondeterministic following of all paths is required to guarantee finding all structural descriptions. The arc labeled CAT PRO can be taken because the next input-string word "I" is of category PRO. This leads to the final state NP/N, completing the traversal of this network and returning control back to state S/NP, the state pointed to by the arc labeled PUSH NP/. Now the arc labeled PUSH VP/ is traversed. Thus control is transferred to the subnetwork with initial state VP/. Both arcs out of this state lead to acceptance, but only the PUSH VP/ arc will be followed. If once again in state VP/ the CAT V arc is followed, the next input symbol "saw" is consumed, and movement is to state VP/V. The arc out of this state is labeled PUSH NP/, and this leads to state NP/. From there it is possible to traverse through state NP/DET to the final state NP/N, consuming in the process the next two input symbols, "the" and "man." From this final state NP/N, control is passed back to state VP/NP, which is also a final state. This, in turn, transfers control back to state VP/VP because the PUSH VP/ condition has been satisfied. Next encountered is the arc PUSH PP/ and then the push to the subnetwork with initial state PP/. The arc labeled CAT PREP is traversed, consuming the next input string symbol "in," resulting state PP/PREP. The only arc out of this state is labeled PUSH NP/, and it is possible to satisfy this arc by successfully traversing the subnetwork named NP/, consuming in the process the last two input string symbols "the" and "park." This lead to the final state PP/NP, which satisfies the PUSH PP/ arc and moves to state VP/NP. It is also a final state, so control is transferred back to state S/VP because the arc labeled PUSH VP/ has been satisfied. The sentence is accepted because it ended in a final state of the top-level subnetwork and consumed in the process the entire input string of words.

It is seen that the BTN formalism is one means of specifying a context-free parser. By adding the use of a set of registers and extending the types of arcs to include register testing and setting, by allowing other types of conditions and actions to be associated with arc traversal, and by providing for sentence structure to be built up and stored in registers, the popular ATN formalism, proposed by Woods (1970), is defined.

ATNs are equivalent in their generative power to unrestricted rewriting systems or Turing machines, a circumstance that indicates that further restrictions are needed to obtain a model appropriate for the specification of natural languages. Without such restrictions, ATNs are not even guaranteed to terminate.

Note in the illustration using the BTN parser for the language of grammar GI that parsing was performed in a top-down, left-to-right fashion. This is the natural way to parse using an ATN, but with its Turing machine power, it is not the only way. Note also that, as formulated here, recursive left branching would lead to a nonterminating sequence of actions being taken. To rectify this, it is necessary either to disallow networks that reflect recursive left branching or to restrict the PUSH and POP mechanism to limit the depth of PUSHing.

The popularity of ATNs in computational linguistic circles has already been noted (Waltz, 1977), and it is reasonable to ask why this is so. The choice does not appear to be motivated from linguistic considerations. A discussion of

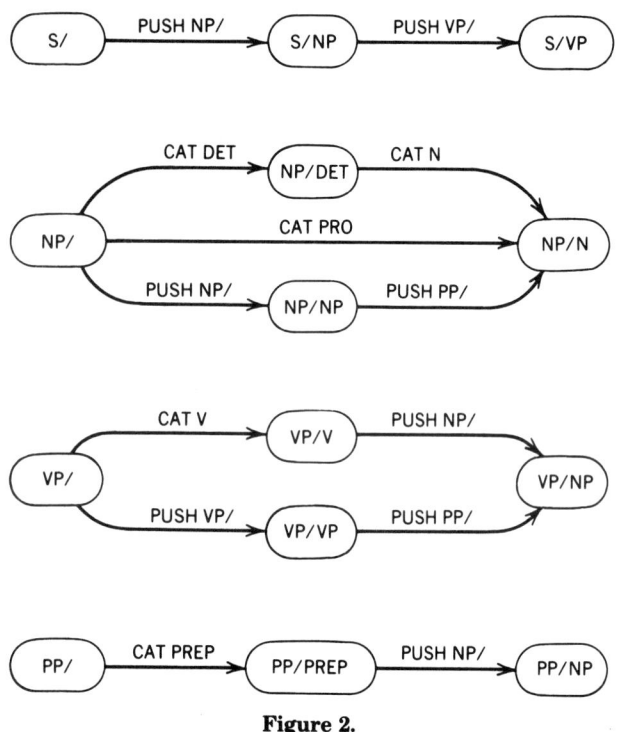

Figure 2.

this has been published (Dresher and Hornstein, 1976). ATN parsers are, however, easier to implement than transformational parsers. The often made, but unsupported, claims of greater speed, which are discussed in the next section, are also probably responsible for the choice of an ATN in many applications. One advantage that TG might have been expected to have over ATNs was the existence of many grammars or grammar fragments, especially in the early days of ATN development. This advantage was not important, however, because very few transformational grammars of any size have been produced. Linguists have been more concerned with refining the type of transformations and the conditions on their usage allowed than with writing and testing large, coherent grammars. Similarly, it is possible to ask why the ATN formalism is being replaced in large measure by the phrase-structure grammar-based models of language and parsing — cited above. Linguistic arguments for some of these models have been made, earlier criticism of them has been refuted, and some success in making practical application of them has been achieved. Also, progress in semantics has made the semantic interpretation of the structural descriptions they assign more tenable. Most important, at least some of them are basically simpler models and, as such, will remain of interest until they can be shown to have inherent defects or until another unquestionably superior model emerges.

EMPIRICAL COMPARISONS OF PARSING SPEED

A few results relating to known mathematical bounds on some of the parsing methods described have been cited above. Results relative to the worst-case performance of the parser for a class of grammars, however, are of less importance than the performance of a particular parsing algorithm on specific grammars of actual interest for some application. Hence, empirical results of parsing efficiency are, for some purposes, more important than theoretical results.

There are, however, difficulties in making empirical comparisons of parsing speed. Allowance must be made for differences in computer speed, for differences in efficiency of implementation (programming), for differences in direct parsing time vs indirect time requirements (paging, I/O, garbage collection, etc), and for differences in coverage of a natural language provided by the grammars with respect to which parsing is performed. Nevertheless, a few results are cited to illustrate the disparity often encountered between theoretical and empirical comparisons of efficiency.

One study of this type (Slocum, 1981) gives experimental results comparing the efficiency of a CKY CF grammar parsing-algorithm implementation with that of a left-corner parsing-algorithm implementation. These results were obtained using a large CF grammar for a subset of German. He considered a number of factors, some of which relate to the use of complex feature restrictions, but his basic conclusion was that the left-corner parser was 7% faster than the CKY parser for the sentences considered, even though the former had a worst-case exponential bound and the latter only an n-cubed bound. Slocum cited another study in which a recursive left-descent parser was compared to two different versions of CKY parsers, two different database-query grammars being used in this study. Both of the CKY parsers proved faster than the top-down parser, by factors of roughly two to five, depending on the grammar and parser.

A similar study made by Petrick compared the left-corner parser used in the TQA system with the Ruzzo chart parser described above. The two LISP implementations in question were comparable with respect to their care in choosing and manipulating appropriate data structures, and the same computer and LISP system were used for both. In this study 45 sentences from a database-retrieval application were chosen for comparison. These were sentences that had been submitted to the TQA system by city employees while the system had been installed at the city hall of a local municipality. The grammar in question was a large CF grammar used to assign surface structure to sentences as one step in transformational parsing. For 78% of these sentences the left-corner algorithm was faster by an average factor of more than two, and for the remaining 22% the Ruzzo parser was faster. The latter sentences, however, were the ones with significantly greater parsing times, resulting in overall lower average parsing time for the Ruzzo parser (0.78 s/sentence) than the left-corner parser (1.15 s/sentence).

Finally, another empirical study of parsing efficiency is a comparison of parsing efficiency for an ATN parser and a TG parser. Petrick compared the ATN LUNAR system parser to that of the TQA system and concluded that although the former's syntactic component was faster, it achieved this by assigning structural descriptions that were less satisfactory for subsequent semantic processing (translation to a formal query language) (Kuno, 1963). Prepositional phrases, for example, were simply attached to the nearest noun phrase rather than to the noun phrase they actually modified. TQA system structural descriptions, on the other hand, contain no prepositional phrases. They are reduced to noun-phrase arguments of abstract verbs. For this reason, the LUNAR system required more extensive and time-consuming semantic processing to translate structural descriptions to machine-interpretable form, and the resulting overall syntactic plus semantic processing times of the two systems were found to be comparable.

This study illustrates some of the difficulties that must be faced in making empirical comparisons. Different grammars were involved, and the differences in coverage of English they offered had to be estimated. The quality of the structural descriptions they assigned also had to be taken into consideration because simplifying the work of the syntactic component as found to complicate that of the semantic component. And finally, different computers and programs were used. Unfortunately, such disparities are all too often encountered in making empirical comparisons of diverse methods of parsing.

DISCUSSION

As has been indicated, there are a host of parsers based on almost as many different linguistic theories and their associated grammars. The requirement of an efficient parser is just one of the demands placed on a class of grammars, so the popularity of particular parsers at different times has to some extent reflected the favored theories of language at those points but has often deviated. In recent years, computational linguistics (qv) in general and parsing in particular have exerted more influence on the development of theoretical linguistic models than was previously the case.

The sequence of events in the development of parsing has been something like the following: early efforts in machine translation were based on no syntactic theory beyond part of speech classification and the identification of a few strings of words and word categories. In the 1960s, efforts were made to develop CP natural language grammars and their associated parsers. This gradually fell into disfavor because the CF model was generally discredited by linguists, the semantic interpretation of structural descriptions assigned by CF grammars presented problems that seemed to limit the value of the CF model, and empirical results involving the parsing of sentences with respect to large CF grammars indicated it was not possible to achieve wide coverage of a natural language without assigning a very large (more than 100 in many cases) number of structural descriptions, whose indications of sentence meanings were, at best, tenuous (Kuno, 1963).

For these reasons, efforts were made beginning in the mid-1960s to develop transformational grammar parsers to complement the dominant linguistic theory, TG. ATNs, beginning in the early 1970s, were motivated in large part by the desire for an efficient natural language parser and subsequently have been espoused and modified by some theoretical linguists. Both ATN and TG parsers continue in usage to date.

In the 1980s, there was a resurgence of interest in phrase-structure grammars, usually augmented with complex features and other extensions. It is natural to ask why this happened. Returning to the reasons cited above for the earlier demise of the CF model, many of the previously given theoretical arguments against CF grammars were successfully refuted (particularly those involving subsets of natural languages that are not CF), and much progress was made on the semantic interpretation of CF grammar-assigned structural descriptions. The remaining objection, wide coverage without wild ambiguity of structural description assignment, remains to be satisfied. No comprehensive grammars of large natural language subsets have yet been produced and subjected to parsing experiments designed to determine whether this objection has been overcome. Clearly, it is the hope of the developers of phrase-structure—based systems that their augmentations of CF theory and their newly developed innovations in writing grammars for those systems will prove adequate in providing just those structural descriptions that reflect all required meanings and no others.

BIBLIOGRAPHY

A. V. Aho and J. D. Ullman, *Theory of Parsing, Translation and Compiling, Vol. 1, Parsing,* Prentice-Hall, Inc., Englewood Cliffs, N.J., 1972.

A. V. Aho and J.D. Ullman, *Principles of Compiler Design,* Addison-Wesley, Publishing Co., Inc., Reading, Mass., 1977.

J. Bresnan, ed., *The Mental Representation of Grammatical Relations,* MIT Press, Cambridge, Mass., 1982.

B. E. Dresher and N. Hornstein, "On Some Supposed Contributions of Artificial Intelligence to the Scientific Study of Language," *Cognition* **4,** 321–398 (1976).

J. Earley, "An Efficient Context-Free Parsing Algorithm," *CACM* **13**(2), 94–102 (Feb. 1970).

G. Gazdar, E. Klein, G. K. Pullum, and I. A. Sag, *Generalized Phrase Structure Grammar,* Blackwell, Oxford, UK, 1985.

T. V. Griffiths and S. R. Petrick, "On the Relative Efficiencies of Context-Free Grammar Recognizers," *CACM* **8**(5), 289–300 (May 1965).

T. V. Griffiths and S. R. Petrick, "Top-Down Versus Bottom-Up Analysis," in *Proceedings of the IFIP Congress 68,* Edinburgh, UK, *Information Processing 68,* North-Holland, Amsterdam, The Netherlands, 1969a, pp. 437–443.

T. V. Griffiths and S. R. Petrick, *Reactive Bounds for Two Methods of Context-Free Grammar Parsing,* IBM RC 2699, Nov. 1969b.

J. Hopcroft and J. Ullman, *Introduction to Automata Theory, Languages, and Computation,* Addison-Wesley Publishing Co., Inc., Reading, Mass., 1979.

R. M. Kaplan, *A General Syntactic Processor,* Algorithmics, New York, 1973.

M. Kay, "Experiments with a Powerful Parser," in *Proceedings of the Second International Conference on Computational Linguistics,* Grenoble, Aug. 1967.

M. Kay, "Parsing in Functional Unification Grammar," in *Studies in Natural Language Processing,* Cambridge University Press, Cambridge, UK, 1985, pp. 251–278.

S. Kuno, "The Current Grammar for the Multiple Path English Analyzer," in *Mathematical Linguistics and Automatic Translation,* Report No. NSF 8, Computation Laboratory, Harvard University, Cambridge, Mass., 1963.

D. G. Loveman, J. A. Moyne, and R. G. Tobey, "CUE: A Preprocessor System for Restricted Natural English," in J. Minker and S. Rosenfeld, eds., *Proceedings of the Symposium on Information Science and Retrieval,* University of Maryland, College Park, April 1971.

M. Marcus, *A Theory of Syntactic Recognition for Natural Language,* MIT Press, Cambridge, Mass., 1980.

G. H. Matthews, "Analysis by Synthesis of Sentences of Natural Languages," in *Proceedings of the 1961 International Congress on Machine Translation of Languages and Applied Language Analysis,* National Physical Laboratory, Teddington, UK, 1961.

F. C. N. Pereira and D. H. D. Warren, "Definite Clause Grammars for Language Analysis: A Survey of the Formalism and a Comparison with Augmented Transition Networks," *Artif. Intell.* **13,** 231–278 (1980).

P. S. Peters and R. W. Ritchie, "On the Generative Power of Transformational Grammars," *Inf. Sci.* **6,** 49–83 (1973).

S. R. Petrick, *A Recognition Procedure for Transformational Grammars,* Ph.D. dissertation, MIT, Cambridge, Mass., 1965.

S. R. Petrick, "Transformational Analysis," in R. Rustin, ed., *Natural Language Processing,* Algorithmics, New York, pp. 27–41, 1973.

E. Proudian and C. Pollard. "Parsing Head-Driven Phrase Structure Grammar," in *Proceedings of the Twenty-Third Annual Meeting of the Association for Computational Linguistics,* University of Chicago, Chicago, Ill., July 1985, pp. 8–12.

D. J Rosenkrantz, "Matrix Equations and Normal Forms for Context-Free Grammars," *JACM* **14**(3), 501–507 (1967).

W. L. Ruzzo, S. L. Graham, and M. A. Harrison, "An Improved Context-Free Recognizer," *ACM Trans. Progr. Lang. Sys.* **3**, 415–462 (July 1980).

S. M. Shieber, H. Uszkoreit, F. C. N. Pereira, J. J. Robinson, and M. Tyson, "The Formalism and Implementation of PATR-II," in *Research on Interactive Acquisition and Use of Knowledge*, Artificial Intelligence Center, SRI International, Menlo Park, Calif., 1983.

J. Slocum, "A Practical Comparison of Parsing Strategies," in *Proceedings of the Nineteenth Annual Meeting of the ACL*, Stanford University, Stanford, Calif., June 29–July 1, 1981, pp. 1–6.

D. L. Waltz, ed., "Natural Language Interfaces," *ACM SIGART Newslett.* (61), 16–64 (Feb. 1977).

S. Warshall, "A Theorem on Boolean Matrices," *JACM* **9**, 11 (Jan. 1962).

W. A. Woods, "Transition Network Grammars for Natural Language Analysis," *CACM* **13**(10), 591–606 (Oct. 1970).

D. H. Younger, "Recognition and Parsing of Context-Free Languages in Time n^3," *Inf. Ctrl.* **10**, 189–208 (1967).

A. Zwicky, J. Friedman, B. Hall, and D. Walker, "The MITRE Syntactic Analysis Procedure for Transformational Grammars," in *Proceedings of the 1965 Fall Joint Computer Conference*, Thompson, Washington, D.C., 1965.

S. PETRICK
University of Wyoming

PARSING, CHART. See PARSING.

PARSING, WORD-EXPERT

The theory of word-expert parsing (WEP) treats the individual words of language as the organizational elements of the human knowledge of language interpretation. Each word has a different effect on the understanding process by its range of possible meanings and the discrimination among them and by its interrelationships with other words with which it combines to form larger meaning fragments. Word-expert parsing does not represent a semantic theory (see SEMANTIC NETWORKS) but rather a theory of language analysis (see NATURAL LANGUAGE UNDERSTANDING). As such, it describes the representation and use of syntactic, semantic, and real-world knowledge for approximating the cognitive mechanisms of language interpretation.

Word-expert parsing views individual words of language as the fundamental carriers of knowledge about the parsing process. It is crucial to realize the implications of this view to understand the WEP perspective. Individual words to not constitute the input to some mechanism that analyzes sentences from above according to some general external principles about language. Rather, the words themselves form the mechanism. Each word of language is seen as an active lexical agent called a "word expert," which participates in the overall control of the parsing process by its internal actions and its interactions with other such agents. The meaning of a particular word in some context is dictated by its interrelationships with other words in the text, by the meaning of existing pieces of the text, and by general commonsense knowledge (see REASONING, COMMONSENSE).

The interrelationships among words in a fragment of text ought not to be viewed statically, from some point above where all such associations are perceived as schematic juxtapositions. Words themselves are active agents, idiosyncratically controlling the parsing process. The procedural, distributed way of looking at language leads to the WEP notion of active lexical interaction. From this vantage point, the theory of syntax describes stereotypic patterns of lexical interactions, which, because of the rich semantic particularities of individual words, cannot be used to model comprehension. The process of WEP for a particular fragment of text consists of the active lexical interactions among the individual agents representing the words of that fragment and the interactions between those agents and the other mechanisms of comprehension. The nature and scope of these interactions, and not any particular declarative structure, represent the analysis of the fragment.

The theory of WEP not only provides a different way of looking at language through comprehension but also suggests that such classical problems as word-sense ambiguity and idiom be made the framework of such a theory. Almost every common word of language has many different contextual meanings, Furthermore, the ways in which certain meanings are preferred over others seem to be idiosyncratic to the individual words themselves. The original English dictionary by Johnson (1755) clearly makes this point in describing over a hundred word senses for the word "take" and using each one in a separate example sentence. Certain words can pair up with others in certain ways, with no substitutions possible. Two words meaning similar things can be interchanged in all but a few exceptional cases. Certain sentences can be put in the passive voice and have the same meanings as before, and others cannot. The theory of WEP places the explanatory burden on mechanisms associated with individual words. The exceptional cases are thus promoted to a central place in the theory of comprehension.

The ability for an idiomatic expression to retain its special meaning when manipulated in certain ways has been described as its "degree of tightness." The wide variation in the tightness of particular expressions leads Bolinger (1975) to an extreme statement:

> The question arises whether everything we say may be in some degree idiomatic—that is, whether there are affinities among words that continue to reflect the attachments the words had when we learned them, within larger groups. This is not a welcome view to most American linguists.

The perspective of WEP does not deviate much from the radical postulate suggested here. The individual words of language are perceived as the carriers of parsing knowledge and actively interact with other words, based on idiosyncratic criteria, to create meaningful fragments. Such criteria include notions about particular lexical attachments, general syntax and semantics, and beliefs about the nature of the real world. These criteria are clearly not universal. A single sentence could easily mean two different things to two different people and likewise to the same person at two different times (in the same context). The process of language analysis depends on the knowledge and perspectives of the analyzer.

Principles

The control structure of the word-expert parser is intended to suggest some new ideas about the mechanisms of language understanding. Several principles regarding the nature of the understanding process have influenced the organization of the model. Seven of them are described below.

1. Parsing knowledge is organized around individual word experts.
2. Parsing consists of nonuniform word-sense discrimination and active lexical interaction among the distributed word experts.
3. Parsing takes place from left to right, except when directed to do differently by the word experts themselves.
4. Parsing takes place without backtracking, proceeding in a wait-and-see manner (deterministically) toward a meaning interpretation.
5. The reader expectations triggered by particular words in the context of discourse and real-world knowledge comprise an important source of dynamic parsing knowledge.
6. Parsing is principally data-driven, in that these high-level expectations assist, but do not direct, the process.
7. The syntax of language provides structural cues for the interpretation of word meanings and can be viewed as the active lexical interactions among word experts.

These principles combine some new perspectives of the word-based distributed framework with certain perspectives found in previous work, in particular, the works on word-sense selection (Wilks, 1973) conceptual analysis and the view of parsing as a memory process (Riesbeck, 1974), and analysis in a data-driven and deterministic manner (Marcus, 1980).

THE WORD-EXPERT PARSER

The word-expert parser is a working computer program that analyzes fragments of English text, producing symbolic data structures to represent their unambiguous meaning content in context. The parser successfully analyzes input fragments rich in word-sense ambiguity and idiom and also handles a range of interesting syntactic constructions. The program works by having the individual words of language themselves direct the process. Each word is modeled by a separate computer program (a coroutine) and parsing takes place through the successive execution of the expert programs corresponding to the words of the input.

The effect of these programs is to augment the overall meaning representation and to alter the control flow of the overall process. One problem in reading from left to right is that sometimes the meaning (or role) of a word does not become clear until later in the sentence, after a few more words have been seen. Since each word expert is responsible for fitting its word onto the overall interpretation of the sentence, it sometimes needs to wait a while in just this way, only to continue later. The individual word expert thus affects the high-order processing of the model by waiting for what it needs and then forcing itself back into the action, obviously disrupting the normal left-to-right flow of things.

The parser was developed in Maryland LISP (qv) on the Univac 1100/42 at the University of Maryland and was converted to run in VLISP on the DEC-10 at IRCAM in Paris and in Franz LISP on the VAX/780 at the University of Rochester. It operates with a small vocabulary of 40 implemented word experts, illustrating an interesting variety of different word-expert functions and interaction requirements. The existing collection of experts is sufficient to analyze sentences containing many different contextual usages of the content words "eat," "deep," "throw," "pit," "case," "by," "in," and "out." The analysis of a sentence containing such a word entails the determination of exactly what it means in context. The parser correctly determines the meanings of fragments such as "throw in the towel," "throw the ball in the pit," "throw out the garbage," "throw out the court case," and "throw a party." The following complete sentences have been analyzed by WEP:

(S.1) The deep philosopher throws in the towel.
(S.2) The man throws a peach pit in the deep pit.
(S.3) The judge throws out a case.
(S.4) The man throws out a pit.

The current WEP easily analyzes sentences similar to these examples, and interprets them as having the particular meanings intended. In addition, a version of WEP at the University of Leuven has been shown (Adrianes, 1986) to analyze Dutch sentences with multiple lexical ambiguities particular to that language.

Word experts do not only model content words, however. In fact, they are not even restricted to words but also represent affixes, punctuation marks, sets of items, and nonlexical cues. The collection of implemented experts includes experts for function words "the" and "a," for suffixes "en," "s," and "ing," for the set of all integers, for the punctuation mark ".", and for capital letters. Unimplemented experts that have been studied include the expert for the relative "who," for unknown words, for the conjunctions "while" and "and," and for the dollar sign.

The word expert for the verb suffix "en" has two implemented usages, as the following analyzed sentences show:

(S.5) The case was thrown out by the court.
(S.6) The man has thrown a party.

In passive sentences, the "en" expert has a central responsibility to coordinate the analysis, as in sentence S.5, and in other contexts (eg, sentence S.6) makes little contribution at all. The "ing" expert coordinates the different analyses that WEP performs for the following examples:

(S.7) The man eating tiger growls.
(S.8) The man eating spaghetti growls.
(S.9) The man eating shrimp growls.
(S.10) The spaghetti eating shrimp growls.

The "ing" expert is the one that figures out who eats whom (or what) in these cases. The final "." on all these sentences indicates a sentence break, and the "." expert is responsible for relating that fact to the model.

The word-expert parser analyzes fragments of text through a distributed word-based control structure. The organization of the system around the individual word-expert programs leads to interesting parsing behaviors. The parsing of passive sentences through the actions of expert programs modeling "en," "by," and "was," for example, suggests various things about parsing knowledge, One of the most provocative word experts for future research is the expert for unknown words. What does it mean for this expert to "fit its word into the overall interpretation" of some fragment? This entry suggests how WEP addresses such interesting topics, but the reading list should be consulted for more detailed articles.

FORMALIZING WORD-EXPERT PARSING

The representation of word experts has been the principal focus of attention during the course of the WEP model development. Recall the dual responsibility of each word expert to discriminate the intended role of its word in context and at the same time to provide useful information to its neighbors.

Word experts are represented as graphs composed of designated subgraphs that have no cycles, as shown symbolically in Figure 1. Each subnetwork consists of nodes that ask questions and perform side-effect actions. The focus of the WEP research has been the constant development, refinement, and redevelopment of these questions and actions, which comprise a taxonomy of knowledge for WEP. Although this epistemology does not yet satisfy strict adequacy criteria, it has nevertheless taken shape enough to be provocative (Small, 1980).

The representation language for word experts makes up a formal theory of word-based parsing founded on the

```
⟨expert ⟨name⟩
        [entry0
            (node0 ⟨node type⟩ ⟨node body⟩)
            (node1 ⟨node type⟩ ⟨node body⟩)
            ...
            (noden ⟨node type⟩ ⟨node body⟩)    ]
        [entry1 ...]
        ...
        [entry_m ...]⟩
```

Figure 1. Word-expert structure.

underlying notions of word-sense discrimination and active lexical interaction. The parsing process has been conceptually divided into these two fundamental aspects, and although the word-expert representation language comprises a single formalism, the natural separation between these two facets has been maintained. The word-expert formalism consists of the lexical-interaction language (LIL) and the sense-discrimination language (SDL). The syntax of the languages, presented formally in Small (1980), specifies only the organization of word experts and not the semantics of the individual nodes comprising them. This section briefly describes their semantics, a more complete description of which appears in Small (1980, 1985) and Small and Reiger (1982).

The word-expert representation languages describe the context-probing questions asked by word experts and the actions they perform to build concept structures and to interact with the other experts representing the words of the input sentence. The statements of the LIL include one causing the expert to AWAIT data from another expert, one to transmit a control SIGNAL to another expert, and the other to REPORT a conceptual entity to other experts and to the model as a whole. The statements of the SDL serve to build and refine concept representations, post expectations and constraints, and carry out similar operations aimed at determining the meaning and role of the particular word in the text at large. The questions and actions of word experts serve to analyze context and assemble structures (sense discrimination) and to communicate this information outside (active lexical interaction). These word-expert functions are summarized in Figure 2.

Word-Expert Structure

The "deep" expert shown in Figure 3 illustrates the basic structure of word experts and includes certain of the im-

Side-Effect Actions

Ask that the next word be read and its expert initialized.
Build a concept structure to represent some meaning or to use as a filter.
Change the global state of the system (a description of the syntactic focus of the system).

Multiple-Choice Questions

Ask about the system state description.
Ask about the word represented by a particular expert.
Ask about the lexical origins of some concept structure.

Lexical Interactions

Report new information to the model at large or to a particular word expert making a request.
Post a timed demon to await some piece of needed information.
Suspend execution until some information arrives (or relevant demons time themselves out).
Terminate execution after completing its diagnosis as to its role.

Memory Interactions

Request information from a discourse tracking process.
Request an inference from a general semantic-memory mechanism.
Request a constrained pattern-matching operation.

Figure 2. Word-expert functions.

```
[word-expert deep
    [entry0 (node0:q  signal signal0
                      [entity-construction node1]
                      [* node2])
            (node1:a  (declareg)
                      (continue entry1))
            (node2:a) (openg entity-construction)
                      (declareg)
                      (pause entry1))]
    [entry2 (node0:q  view concept1
                      [=c#anything node4]
                      [=c#person node1]
                      [=c#artistic-object node2]
                      [=c#volume node3])
            (node4:a  (refinec concept1 =c#deep-entity)
                      (report concept1))
            (node1:a  (refinec concept1 =c#deep-intellectual)
                      report concept1))
            (node2:a  (refinec concept1 =c#deep-art-object)
                      (report concept1))
            (node3:a  (refinec concept1 =c#deep-volume)
                      (report concept1))]
    [entry1 (node0:a  (createc concept2 entity)
                      (refinec concept2 =c#1#deep)
                      (refinec concept2 =c#deep-entity)
                      (buildc concept3 entity
                        (one of =c#person
                                =c#artistic-object
                                =c#volume
                                =c#anything))
                      (await concept entity
                        (bindconcept con-
                          cept1)
                        (filter concept3)
                        (report here)
                        (wait group 1)
                        (continue entry 2)
                        (else entry3)))]
    [entry3 (node0:a  (link concept2)
                      (report concept2))]]
```

Figure 3. The deep expert.

portant statements of LIL and SDL. The body of a word expert consists of a collection of tree structures, each of which is called a continuation or entry point (entry) of the word expert. Each entry point is made up of action nodes and question nodes. An action node contains a number of structure-building or interaction statements with at most one successor node. A question node consists of a single context-probing question and a number of successor nodes corresponding to its possible answers. The individual entry points are connected together into a large network by an expert action causing a branch from one continuation to another and by expert resumption after suspension, which always takes place at an entrypoint. A word expert is a network of nodes organized modularly into tree structures called entry points, each a distinguished subgraph of the expert.

Each time a word expert gains execution control, four items are provided to it by the parser. One of these is the entry point where processing should continue. The first time the expert runs, it receives the designated starting point ENTRY0 as its incoming entry variable. Wake-up demons provide the continuation for subsequent reentries. The three other input messages to the expert are a concept structure, a control signal, and the expert sending them (ie, its internal name). On the initial execution, the parser always provides the expert with a control signal, whether it is one sent explicitly by some other expert or the special signal posted as the current control state of the parser. Every expert's signal variable SIGNAL0 Note that the root node of the deep expert asks about the value of this signal.

The deep expert of Figure 3 contains four distinct entry points, the initial entry ENTRY0, a continuation from ENTRY0 called ENTRY1, and two restart entry points, ENTRY2 and ENTRY3. The AWAIT statement of ENTRY1 creates a restart demon to resume execution later at ENTRY2. If the awaited data does not arrive in time, however, the time-out condition of that demon resumes deep at ENTRY3. The entry points of word experts represent modular subexperts to perform well-contained functions for their overall sense-discrimination processing.

The two kinds of nodes within entry points ask questions and perform actions. Note in Figure 3 that each entry point contains several nodes, each node indicating its type as A (action) or Q (question). The root node of the deep expert asks a SIGNAL question, and the root node of ENTRY2 asks a VIEW question. All other nodes in the word expert perform side-effect actions. The sole node of ENTRY1 performs five such actions, the BUILDC action creates a new concept, REFINEC refines its conceptual value, the second BUILDC constructs a concept for use as a filter and expectation, and the AWAIT mechanism creates and posts a restart demon. Any node having no explicit successor represents an expert suspension or termination node. If the expert has any outstanding restart demons, it suspends at such nodes; otherwise, it terminates. In the deep expert, for example, the node of ENTRY1 always suspends the expert because of the AWAIT contained there, while all action nodes of ENTRY2 cause expert termination.

Model Organization

The decentralized representation of parsing knowledge in word experts leads to an overall model organization to support exchange of information and distributed decision-making (ie, agreement on overall meaning). The executing word expert is temporarily the coordinator of the entire parsing process, changing structures and invoking procedures in its environment. The control structure of the parser is a lexical-interaction control structure. The basic aspects of this distributed control for a particular word expert include suspending execution while waiting for needed information and resuming execution when that information becomes available. When word-sense discrimination requires some word expert to ask a question of another expert, it must wait to receive the answer before proceeding. When the information arrives, the word expert continues processing where it left off. Eventually, the word expert completes its sense discrimination and determines the intended meaning of its word in context.

The control flow that results from this coroutine control

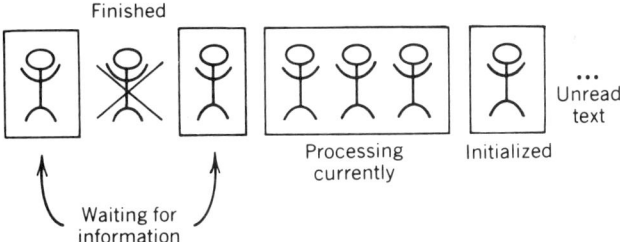

Figure 4. Word-expert parser control flow.

environment can be viewed as the movement of a window across the input stream. Inside the window control passes from word expert to word expert and back again, but the hearing of new words and the termination of old experts causes the overall processing window to move ahead. Figure 4 illustrates the control structure of the model in terms of this metaphor. The hearing of new words expands the right side of the window as the termination of word experts contracts the left side. Eventually, the window includes the last word of the input text, and the process terminates.

Control Mechanisms: Expert Suspension and Resumption

Any word expert that desires some piece of information through interaction with one of its neighbors specifies the nature of that information in a data structure called a restart demon. The demon has the responsibility of monitoring the data transmissions on the two central pathways in the model. When the requested datum appears, the restart demon provides it to its associated word expert, which continues where it left off. The execution of the statement does not cause the suspension of the expert. The expert continues its processing as if nothing had happened. Of course, it cannot make use of the needed data until it arrives, and thus often it must choose to suspend its execution at the time of demon creation. Note, however, that the expert might simultaneously create several restart demons, all awaiting different information.

As a procedural distributed model, the word-expert parser does not contain some finite fixed-length buffer to represent a working memory but models memory limitation with processes that have a strictly limited life span. The human understander does not wait indefinitely for information that could aid his or her understanding, and the model cannot either. When a word expert posts a restart demon to await some piece of information from another expert, a companion time-out demon is initiated to monitor the duration of the wait. In the ideal case the desired information quickly becomes available in the model, and the awaiting expert promptly receives it. If the information does not appear within a certain time, however, the special time-out demon must command the awaiting process to go on without it. The time-out demon specifies both how long the expert is willing to wait for the information it desires and the name of an entry point within the awaiting expert where processing should continue if the associated restart demon "times out" instead. The units of measurement for time-outs are based on certain model events, including the number of syntactic groups created, the number of words read, the number of sentence breaks encountered, and the termination (as opposed to suspension) of particular word experts.

Message and Memory Objects: Expert Interaction Data

The restart demons and time-outs of WEP coordinate the interaction among cooperating word experts. This interaction involves sending and receiving messages of only two (well-defined) types: concept structures and control signals. Concept structures represent the meaning of fragments of text, referents, relations, conceptual expectations, and all other conceptual knowledge in the system and can be thought of as case frames, such as those of Fillmore, 1968 (see also GRAMMAR, CASE). Control signals represent syntactic and idiosyncratic lexical cues, query–reply handshaking among experts, cues to accompany concept structures and to indicate their significance, and similar kinds of stereotypic information. Controls signals are currently just unstructured atomic symbols. Every interaction in the parser involves the transmission of a single message, which includes one concept structure and one control signal.

Example Analysis

The WEP is a distributed system in which the bulk of knowledge centers on individual words of language, and thus the main memory requirements of the parser are not great. The word experts are recalled from mass storage as needed by the WEP interpreter and purged from core by the LISP garbage collector when no longer active. The parser requires about 120 kbyte of memory for its functions and about 40 kbyte for the control work space and active memory. With the interpreter, a total of about 256,000 LISP nodes are needed. A word expert of average size requires between 2000 and 4000 cells of random-access memory on file, with expert size directly related to the richness of contextual meaning of the represented word.

Word-expert parsing consists of determining the contextual meanings of those words making up each sentence to be interpreted and figuring out how they combine to form larger conceptual conglomerates. The process involves word-sense discrimination by the word experts representing the individual words of language carried out through the distributed control of active lexical interaction. Each word in a sentence contributes to the understanding of that sentence by some hearer in its own idiosyncratic way. Content words usually require significant processing of the local sense-discrimination variety, while function words and inflectional morphemes usually provide cues on how to combine meanings into larger structures. Those words playing syntactic roles are thus the control coordinators of distributed WEP.

Example Sentence. The following sentence has been chosen as our example because it combines in an interesting way the requirements for word-sense discrimination and active lexical interaction:

(S.11) The man eating peaches throws out a pit.

The analysis of the subject of this sentence requires complex word-expert interactions coordinated by the "ing" expert and knowledge of the real world to discriminate between a "man eating peaches" and the similar case of "man eating tigers." The "throw" expert must interact with the word expert for the particle "out" to determine its word sense. The man "throwing out a pit" must be distinguished from the man "throwing out a suggestion" or even "throwing out the window" something. The word expert for "pit" must decide, without benefit of a modification such as "peach" or "deep," whether it represents a fruit pit, a hole in the ground, a place for race cars to refuel, or some other concept.

The important aspects of a word-expert execution (note that each expert runs and suspends a number of times before terminating) consist of the input values to the expert, the entry points and nodes traversed, and the actions taken at each node. Since these elements cannot be fully elaborated for the present example due to space limitations, the reader is referred to Small (1980, 1982) and Small and Reiger (1982) for completely annotated program traces. Program traces for Dutch are in Adrianes (1986).

Abbreviated Execution Trace. Summarized below are all of the word-expert activations required to analyze the example sentence S.11. Note particularly the sequence in which the particular experts are activated and reactivated in order to process the input sentence.

the. The "the" expert initiates a new lexical group.

man. The "man" expert participates in the ongoing lexical group, reacting to the incoming signal from "the," and excludes the verbal meanings of "man." The "man" expert signals the end of the group and sends its concept representation back to "the."

the. The "the" expert had been awaiting the signal for the end of a group, so that it could report the concept to the system at large.

ing. The "ing" expert initiates a new lexical group and awaits a verb.

eat. The "eat" expert constructs a concept structure to represent "eating." Not enough information is available yet to refine the contextual meaning, so "eat" awaits it with a restart demon.

ing. The "ing" expert resumes and notes the name of its associated verb.

s. The "s" group (s1) initiates a new lexical group, which it knows from incoming context signals to be a noun group.

ing. The "ing" expert closes its lexical group and suspends again.

s. The "s" expert (s1) now prepares to await a signal indicating the end of a group and an accompanying concept structure.

peach. The "peach" expert receives a signal indicating the prior execution of "s" an thus rules out a modifier role in favor of a nominal role. Further, it begins the development of a concept structure to represent its meaning.

s. A new instantiation of the "s" expert (s2) opens a new lexical group, which it knows from incoming context signals to be a verb group.

peach. The "peach" expert ends the noun group and sends its concept structure to the awaiting "s" expert (s1).

s. The "s" expert (s1) grabs the concept structure and reports it to the model at large.

ing. The "ing" expert now resumes with the concept representing the meaning of the group to the right of "eating" in the sentence. Next it builds up two action concepts representing "man eats peaches" and "peaches eat man," determines that the former is plausible and the latter not, and sends the concepts to the model at large.

eat. The "eat" expert receives the concept representing its agent and refines its representation to reflect a person eating.

eat. The "eat" expert receives the concept representing its object.

ing. The "ing" expert resumes for the last time and cleans up.

throw. The "throw" expert receives a signal from "s" (s2) indicating a verb group and a concept representing its agent. Before determining its meaning, it must examine the word to its right.

out. The "out" expert begins executing with a signal indicating that a verb expert believes it to be a verb particle. The "out" expert awaits evidence either way.

a. The "a" expert begins a new lexical sequence.

out. The "out" expert posts a restart demon to await the upcoming nominal.

pit. The "pit" expert participates in the current group. It looks to its right for pairing words (eg, "pit stop," "pit boss") and, not finding any, begins sense discrimination. This leads to the discourse expectations of something viewable as garbage, and a fruit pit fills the expectation.

out. The "out" expert resumes knowing that it pairs with "throw," and it sends "throw" a signal to that effect along with the object concept.

throw. The "throw" expert resumes with acceptance by "out" of its offer to pair up. Thus, "throw" completes its sense discrimination and terminates.

***per*.** The "." expert forces certain restart demons to time out, eg, the demons awaiting the temporal or spatial indices for the action. It terminates after sending a special sentence-break signal to the model.

Working Memory after Analysis

A number of concept structures are stored in the working memory of the model as a result of the analysis. These concepts represent the throwing away of garbage by a human adult male. The nature of the garbage is a fruit pit, and the man getting rid of it happens to be eating peaches. Although certain information deriving from the meaning of the input sentence must still be inferred in higher-order mechanisms, the parser has made significant progress toward getting at the full contextual meaning of the sentence.

SUMMARY AND CONCLUSIONS

The word-expert parser is a theory of natural-language understanding by computer and a program to implement partially that theory. The theory is based on the idea that the individual words of language are the primary sources of parsing knowledge and must be treated as such in a computer model. These word-expert knowledge sources coordinate the parsing process through active lexical interaction and the resulting patterns of behavior-model understanding.

Word-expert parsing has been motivated by observations about both human-language processing and existing computational efforts to engineer the process. People have an incredible facility for organizing and selecting word senses in arriving at the intended meaning of sentences in context. This takes place with such unnoticed and subconscious ease that it has been often overlooked. To those building language-parsing systems, however, this phenomenon represents a central problem that has been difficult to address. The reason for this lies in the inherent nature of the sense-selection problem, which can be viewed in terms of the rule-based problem-solving method (see RULE-BASED SYSTEMS) as one of conflict resolution. Systems of rules capture similarities; they work best when there is a single choice at each decision point in the solution of a problem or when the process of choosing can be performed in a uniform way for all data. This situation is precisely opposite that involved in word-sense discrimination, in which the conflicts among applicable rules dominate the process. For accurately choosing the intended meaning of a word in context, the decision process must be tuned to the idiosyncrasies of that particular word. Uniform word-sense discrimination cannot succeed because each word interacts with its environment in particular knowledge-dependent ways to form meaning.

How can a language-understanding program account for all the meanings of individual words? The answer lies in focusing on the differences rather than the similarities of word usage in language. That means that instead of organizing the parsing system around rewrite rules, the system focuses on the individual word and on its idiosyncratic interaction with its context. The word-expert parser has done precisely that. Each word is represented as an active agent in its own right having the responsibility to fit itself into the overall meaning of the larger discourse structure in which it plays a part (see DISCOURSE UNDERSTANDING).

The underlying framework for the organization and construction of word-based agents derives from discrimination networks. The nodes of a word-sense discrimination network comprise the context-probing questions of one word trying to determine its contextual usage. The arcs from the nodes represent the multiple choice of possible answers to the questions. The traversal of the network corresponds to the discrimination of the appropriate sense of the word in context. Each question probes one part of the context, and the answer chooses one path down the network, eliminating others. Eventually, the network traversal arrives at a terminal node, and the discrimination process has converged. Since the word-sense discrimination process is done on a word-by-word basis, the nature and order of the context-probing questions are different for each individual word.

The development of a parsing system based on sense nets has depended on determining the nature of the questions they ask and devising methods for providing the answers. This question–answer process requires that the networks modeling individual words be able to communicate with each other to gain the contextual information that each one needs in determining its meaning. Besides interacting with each other the word-expert questions must probe other higher-order aspects of context, such as the meaning of an overall discourse or the individual beliefs of the reader. Finally, each lexical agent must be able to postpone the answering of particular questions until enough information is available to do it correctly.

This entry has described WEP from two perspectives, that of the individual word, in which sense discrimination is primary, and that of the overall behavior of the distributed system, in which the pattern of lexical interactions is emphasized. The focus of research has been the representation of word experts and the development of a support environment for their processing. Word experts are represented with the LIL and the SDL. The statements of LIL permit an expert to ask questions of other experts and wait for the answers and to provide data to the system as a whole, often for use as answers to questions. The statements of SDL ask questions about discourse and real-world knowledge, build concept and signal structures, and coordinate internal network traversal. The patterns of behavior that arise during WEP are complex and provocative and suggest a new viewpoint on the nature of natural-language comprehension.

BIBLIOGRAPHY

G. Adrianes, "Process Linguistics: The Theory and Practice of a Cognitive-Scientific Approach to Natural Language Understanding," Ph.D. Dissertation, University of Leuven, Belgium, 1986.

D. Bolinger, *Aspects of Language*, Harcourt Brace Jovanovich, New York, 1975.

C. J. Fillmore, "The Case for Case," in Bach and Harms, eds., *Universals in Linguistic Theory*, Holt, Rinehart and Winston, New York, 1968.

S. Johnson, *Dictionary of English*, W. Strahan, London, 1755.

M. P. Marcus, *A Theory of Syntactic Recognition for Natural Language*, MIT Press, Cambridge, Mass., 1980.

C. K. Riesbeck, "Computational Understanding: Analysis of Sentences and Context," Ph.D. Dissertation, Department of Computer Science, Stanford University, Palo Alto, Calif., 1974.

S. L. Small, "Word Expert Parsing: A Theory of Distributed Word-Based Natural Language Understanding," Ph.D. Dissertation, Department of Computer Science, University of Maryland, College Park, Md., 1980.

S. L. Small, "Parsing as Cooperative Distributed Inference: Understanding through Memory Interactions," in King, ed., *Parsing Natural Language*, Academic Press, New York, 1982.

S. L. Small, "A Word-Based Approach to Natural Language Understanding," in Bolc, ed., *Natural Language Processing,* Springer-Verlag, Berlin, 1985.

S. L. Small and C. J. Rieger, "Parsing and Comprehending with Word Experts (A Theory and its Realization)," in Lehnert and Ringle, eds., *Strategies for Natural Language Processing,* Lawrence Erlbaum, Englewood Cliffs, N.J., 1982.

Y. Wilks, *Preference Semantics,* Technical Memo No. 206, Stanford Artificial Intelligence Laboratory, Palo Alto, Calif., 1973.

General References

R. Berwick, "Transformational Grammar and Artificial Intelligence: A Contemporary View," *Cog. Brain Theor.* **6**(4), 383–416 (1983).

G. W. Cottrell and S. L. Small, "A Connectionist Scheme for Word Sense Disambiguation," *Cog. Brain Theor.* **6**(1), 89–120 (1983).

J. A. Feldman and D. H. Ballard, "Connectionist Models and Their Properties," *Cog. Sci.* **6**(3), 205–254 (1982).

M. P. Marcus, *Wait and See Strategies for Parsing Natural Language, Working Paper No. 36,* MIT Artificial Intelligence Laboratory, Cambridge, Mass., 1974.

D. C. Marr, *Artificial Intelligence—A Personal View/Technical Memo No. 355,* MIT Artificial Intelligence Laboratory, Cambridge, Mass., 1976.

D. McDermott and G. Sussman, *The Conniver Reference Manual, Technical Memo No. 259a,* MIT Artificial Intelligence Laboratory, Cambridge, Mass., 1974.

C. J. Rieger, "Viewing Parsing as Word Sense Discrimination," in W. O. Dingwall, ed., *A Survey of Linguistic Science,* Greylock, Stamford, Conn., 1977.

C. J. Rieger, "The Importance of Multiple Choice," *Proceedings on Theoretical Issues in Natural Language Processing,* Urbana, Ill., 1978: also TR-656, Computer Science Department, University of Maryland, College Park, Md., 1978.

C. J. Rieger, "Spontaneous Computation in Cognitive Models," *Cog. Sci.* **1**(3), 315–354 (1977).

C. J. Rieger and S. L. Small, "Toward a Theory of Distributed Word Expert Natural Language Parsing," *IEEE Trans. Sys. Man Cybernet.* **11**(1), 43–51 (1981).

C. K. Riesbeck and R. C. Schank, *Comprehension by Computer: Expectation-Based Analysis of Sentences in Context, Research Report No. 78,* Department of Computer Science, Yale University, New Haven, Conn., 1976.

R. C. Schank, "Conceptual Dependency: A Theory of Natural Language Understanding," *Cog. Psychol.* **3**(4), 552–631 (1972).

S. L. Small, "Viewing Word Expert Parsing as Linguistic Theory," *Proceedings of the Seventh International Joint Conference on Artificial Intelligence,* Vancouver, B.C., 1981.

S. L. Small, "Demon Timeouts: Limiting the Life Spans of Spontaneous Computations in Cognitive Models," *Proceedings of the Cognitive Science Society,* Berkeley, Calif., 1981.

S. L. Small, G. W. Cottrell, and L. Shastri, "Towards Connectionist Parsing," *Proceedings of the American Association for Artificial Intelligence,* Pittsburgh, Pa., 1982.

S. L. Small and M. Lucas, "A Computer Model of Sentence Comprehension," *Richerche di Psicologia* **25** (1983). Also appeared as Technical Report No. 1, Cognitive Science Program, University of Rochester, Rochester, N.Y., 1983.

D. Waltz and J. Pollack, "Massively Parallel Parsing: A Strongly Interactive Model of Natural Language Interpretation," *Cog. Sci.* **9**(1), 51–74 (1985).

S. L. SMALL
University of Rochester

PATTERN RECOGNITION

Automatic pattern recognition attempts to automate a class of perceptual and cognitive processes. These processes include extraction, identification, classification, and description of patterns in data gathered from real and simulated environments. Extraction is the task of processing raw data to derive intermediate results more representative of patterns of interest for the problem at hand. The design of a classifier involves analysis of sample data, modeling the variability among patterns belonging to the same class, determining the subset from an available set of measurements that adequately characterizes distinct categories, specification of techniques for extracting the measurement subset, and the design of the classification algorithm itself. At a more fundamental level the task of identifying whether or not patterns exhibit distinct characteristics for categorization and, if they do, which are those categories, are cognitive processes of concern in automatic pattern recognition. Complex patterns may be generated by specific interconnections of several primitive patterns; the generation of descriptions of these interconnections is the main problem in syntactic and structural pattern recognition. The understanding and exploitation of both the statistical and structural aspects of patterns have been pursued using techniques and ideas from many fields including formal linguistic theory and parsing (qv) methodology, geometry, physics, and other classical sciences and problem-solving (qv) methods of AI.

Pattern-recognition systems usually form parts of complex information-processing systems. A hypothetical advanced automation system is examined below to help understand how pattern-recognition problems arise in practice as well as how several practical problems may be formulated in this manner. The scenario consists of a robot in a manufacturing plant. The robot looks around and moves in the environment. It receives parts from a conveyor, examines them for defects, determines the type of a part among those it expects to receive, decides where parts should be fitted, and assembles them. Occasionally, it takes instructions from a human supervisor and might also ask for help. The robot is a general-purpose machine in the sense that it can be assigned to one of several shop floors supervised by many people. The following are some of the pattern-recognition problems that need to be solved for the successful operation of these robots:

Training the robot to follow the speech of the assigned supervisor: limited-vocabulary speech recognition (qv) problem.

Clustering (qv) to separate different types of parts using measurements on the sample or on its image.

Rejecting defective parts.

Generating descriptions of the assembly sequence.

Detecting situations requiring human intervention.

Generating descriptions to synthesize appropriate speech signals to ask for help.

Understanding speech instructions given by human operators.

A considerable amount of literature was generated on the application of statistical decision theory and discriminant analysis to the automatic classification of patterns. Subsequent criticism for focusing attention entirely on the statistical relationships among measurements and ignoring other structural properties led to proposals based on modeling patterns as sentences generated by a formal grammar. Today, in order to apply pattern-recognition techniques to solve problems such as those mentioned above, it is necessary to identify the fundamental mathematical problem that most closely resembles a practical problem at hand, make engineering approximations to the underlying functions, implement the scheme on an experimental basis, and test its performance before using it in a real-life situation. This entry presents a brief overview of the existing literature, techniques, and applications of pattern recognition.

Until recently, textbooks on pattern recognition covered mostly statistical or syntactic methods. Some of them cover both in distinct parts. Now some textbooks with titles including words such as adaptive pattern recognition and neurocomputing have also been published. Related books useful for pattern recognition are those on exploratory data analysis. Duda and Hart (1973), Fukunaga (1972), Tou and Gonzalez (1974), Sklansky and Wassel (1981), Devijver and Kittler (1982), and Bow (1984) are some of the textbooks on statistical pattern recognition. A popular way of organizing the material on statistical techniques is in the decreasing order of *a priori* information available to design recognition systems.

Bayesian decision theory is directly applicable when complete information about *a priori* class probabilities, multivariate class conditional probability density functions over the feature (measurement) space, and the loss function of classification are available. At the next lower level of prior information, the exact class conditional probability functions are not known; but their functional forms and a set of training samples from each class are available. The problem then reduces to the estimation of the parameters of the density functions. When it is not reasonable to assume any particular form for a density function, estimation of the entire density function is carried out by nonparametric methods. On the other hand, it is possible to assume forms of the discriminant functions (as against density functions) for classification and determine the parameters of these functions from training samples. Linear discriminant functions are simple to design and implement. Finally, the lowest level of *a priori* information that can be made available for training a classifier is in a set of unlabeled training pattern samples. A common method of classifying them is by clustering. Anderberg (1973), Hartigan (1975), and Jain and Dubes (1988) are excellent books on clustering algorithms, their analyses, and their applications. An alternative to clustering is unsupervised learning. This treats the problem as one of mixture density estimation. Whereas unsupervised learning trains a classifier, clustering yields a classification of a given set of unlabeled samples. The classified samples may then be used in a second stage to train a classifier. Bezdek (1981) and Kandel (1982) present fuzzyset based decision-making models as compatible but distinct companions to other statistical pattern-recognition models. Possible advantages claimed for fuzzy-set approaches are simpler decision functions, the ability to handle lack of multivariate statistics, and soft clustering with varying memberships of a pattern sample to all the categories.

Textbooks on syntactic pattern recognition include Fu (1982), Pavlidis (1977), and Gonzalez and Thomason (1978). Syntactic pattern recognition views patterns as sentences or other higher level interconnections of primitives. The structure of interconnections decides the pattern category. Thus, techniques for syntactic recognition depend heavily on the theory of formal languages and the concatenation relationships. String and higher dimensional languages, syntax analysis, error-correcting parsing for strings, and error-correcting tree automata are treated in detail in Fu (1982). Gramatical inference is the syntactic pattern-recognition analog of learning in statistical pattern recognizers. State-space and problem-reduction models of artificial intelligence are discussed in most AI textbooks, eg, Nilsson (1980). Such models have been used by Kanal and his associates in both statistical and structural pattern recognition. Search strategies for these and other models are presented in Kanal and Kumar (1988). The 1971 book by Nilsson on learning machines, which covered work on perceptron learning algorithms and statistical classification procedures has been recently reissued. New textbooks on adaptive pattern recognition and neurocomputing include Hecht-Nielsen (1990) and Pao (1989). Several additional textbooks on artificial neural systems are expected to be published soon. Goldberg (1988) is an excellent text on Genetic Algorithms which have been recently used in the design of classifiers and neural networks.

Exploratory data analysis is a topic of importance to the successful design of pattern classifiers. Display of scatter plots, analysis of variance, factor analysis, and determination of linear transformations to lower dimensions retaining most of the variations in the data are crucial to feature selection, choice of a good technique for classification, and a preliminary assessment of the achievable performance. Many excellent books have been published on data analysis due to its wide applicability in engineering, sociology, psychology, and economics. Mosteller and Tukey (1977), Wolff and Parsons (1983), McNeil (1977), and Chien (1978) are some of the books on data analysis applicable to pattern recognition.

Research papers on the theory and applications of pattern recognition appear in many international journals, including the following which are prominent in the United States:

IEEE Transactions on Pattern Analysis and Machine Intelligence
IEEE Transactions on Systems, Man and Cybernetics
IEEE Transactions on Information Theory
IEEE Transactions on Acoustics, Speech, and Signal Processing
IEEE Transactions on Geoscience and Remote Sensing
IEEE Transactions on Biomedial Engineering
IEEE Transactions on Neural Networks
Pattern Recognition
Pattern Recognition Letters
Journal of Classification
Information Sciences
International Journal of Neural Networks
Neural Computation
Biological Cybernetics
Applied Optics
Journal of Photogrammetry & Remote Sensing

Important survey papers are Nagy (1968), Ho and Agrawla (1968), Kanal (1972, 1974), Toussaint (1974), and Fu and Rosenfeld (1984). The International Joint Conference on Pattern Recognition, the International Joint Conferences on Neural Networks, and other conferences on pattern recognition and applications are held periodically and their proceedings are a valuable source of material on recent research developments. Important handbooks that include a wealth of information on pattern-recognition theory and applications include Krishnaiah and Kanal (1982) and Young and Fu (1985). Continuing developments are reported in a series of edited books entitled *Machine Intelligence and Pattern Recognition* published by North-Holland/Elsevier. Books published to date in the series include two volumes edited by Kanal and Rosenfeld (1981, 1985), three by Gelsema and Kanal (1980, 1985, 1989), two by Toussaint (1985, 1988), one by Rosenfeld (1985), and six volumes on Uncertainty in AI starting with Kanal and Lemmer (1986). Excellent tutorial surveys on nonlinear dynamical systems, neural networks, genetic algorithms, and adaptive nonlinear networks of some relevance to pattern classification are to be found in a 1989 volume titled Lectures in the Sciences of Complexity, edited by D. Stein. Articles on parallel algorithms for machine intelligence and vision appear in a recent volume edited by Kumar, Gopalakrishnan, and Kanal (1990). This list of books, journals, and surveys barely scratches the surface of the voluminous literature being generated in pattern recognition.

MODELS AND METHODOLOGIES

Many pattern recognition methodologies and design techniques have been developed over the years and new approaches continue to emerge. Earlier methodologies include: signal processing techniques, single and multilayer learning networks (Rosenblatt 1962; Kanal, 1962; Nilsson, 1965; Sklansky and Wassel, 1981; Barron and coworkers, 1984), "one-level" statistical classifiers (Duda and Hart, 1973; Fukunaga, 1972), hierarchical statistical classifiers (Kanal, 1972; 1974), and structural or syntactic pattern recognition techniques (Fu, 1974; Gonzales and Thomason, 1978). Interactive exploratory pattern analysis and statistical classification systems were developed in response to the reality that the varying characteristics and capabilities of the different methodologies for different types of data and objectives made it difficult, if not impossible, to automatically match techniques to problems or to try all the potentially applicable techniques in a batch mode (Sammon, 1970; Kanal, 1972; Gelsema, 1980; Kanal and Gelsema, 1980). In recent years artificial intelligence expert systems, genetic algorithms, and a new generation of multilayer connectionist and artificial neural systems (ANS), have appeared (Shapiro, 1987; Rumelhart and McClelland, 1986; Goldberg, 1988; Hecht-Nielsen, 1990). These provide additional tools for our pattern recognition tool kit.

Figure 1 shows that highly iterative process of the development of a pattern-recognition system. Each task within the developmental process can be accomplished by well-established and/or new innovative techniques. This section outlines some of the existing methodologies and their specific techniques, and the situations in which they are useful.

Signal Processing

Signal processing transforms one sequence of data to another to produce information in a form suitable for processing by pattern-recognition techniques. Such transformations are very useful for a variety of reasons including dimensionality reduction. Signals such as speech, sonar, and textured images, which are required to be classified into a number of categories, are inherently high dimensional. A straightaway modeling of the inter- and intraclass variability fails for several reasons, including the effect of insufficient training samples. The signal-processing approach represents these signals as functions of a few parameters and a long sequence of random numbers. The random numbers are from the same distribution for all the pattern classes. Therefore, distinct classes are modeled by the relatively small set of remaining parameters. For classification, we first pass the pattern through the signal processor to estimate the parameters. Examples of other uses of signal processing in pattern recognition are noise removal by filtering and curve fitting for detection of primitives in syntactic pattern recognition. Srinath and Rajasekharan (1979) is a useful book for pattern-recognition applications of signal processing.

Decision Theoretic Model

One of the earliest pattern-recognition models used statistical decision theory. In this model each pattern is represented by a vector of measurements $u = [u_1, \ldots, u_N]^t$ *(also known as features, observations,* attributes). The statistical distributions of these features given that a pattern

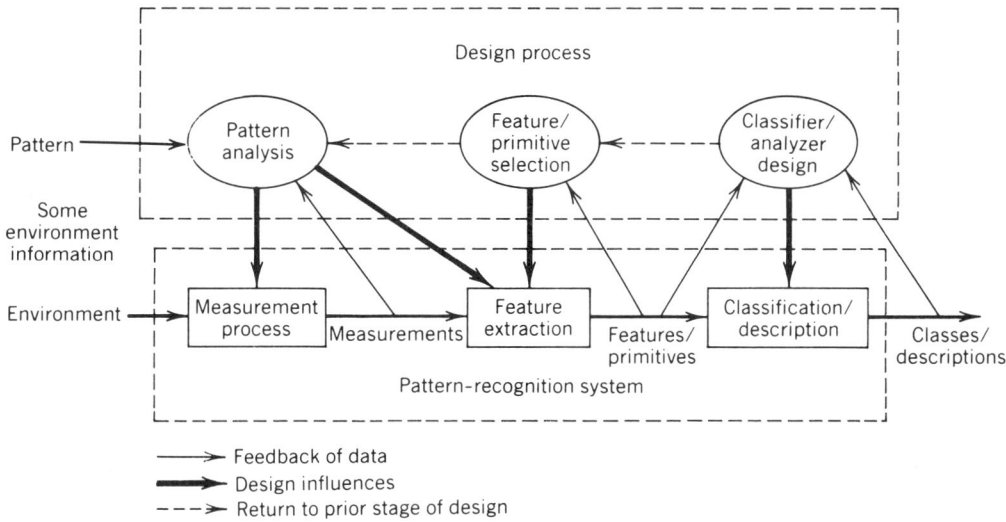

Figure 1. Iterative development of a pattern-recognition system.

belongs to a known category $\omega_i \in \{\omega, \ldots, \omega_M\}$ is a known function $p(u|\omega_i)$. The decision theoretic problem is given u, decide the category, ω_i. Many approaches are possible depending on the criterion of optimality. Bayesian decision theory assumes that the categories occur with a priori probabilities $P(\omega_i)$ and decides the category with the maximum a posteriori probability. Thus, for an observation u, the class decision is ω_k such that

$$P(\omega_k|u) = \max_{i \in \{1,\ldots,M\}} \frac{p(u|\omega_i)P(\omega_i)}{\sum_{l=1}^{M} p(u|\omega_l)P(\omega_l)} \quad (1)$$

The performance of such a classifier is represented by the probability of correct classification given by

$$P_c = \int_u \left\{ \max_{i \in \{1,\ldots,M\}} p(u|\omega_i)P(\omega_i) \right\} du \quad (2)$$

In many applications, different combinations of classifications and misclassifications are associated with different quantities of loss. Let a pattern belonging to class ω_i incur a cost λ_{ij} if it is classified as ω_j. The above Bayesian theory is extended to minimum-risk classification by minimizing the expected loss conditioned on observations:

$$\min_{j \in \{1,\ldots,M\}} \sum_{i=1}^{M} \lambda_{ij} \frac{p(u|\omega_i)P(\omega_i)}{\sum_{l=1}^{M} p(u|\omega_l)P(\omega_l)} \quad (3)$$

The problem is complicated if the a priori probabilities are not known. A simple solution is to assume that all the classes are equally likely. The resulting maximum a posteriori probability decision is known as the maximum-likelihood decision. A conservative approach is to express the minimum risk as a function of variable a priori probabilities and then maximize the minimum risk with respect to the a priori probabilities. The resulting classifier is known as the minimax classifier. Many two-class pattern-recognition problems are detection of a hazardous event (warranting an alarm) against a null event in the presence of noise. Often, the user specifies a tolerable false-alarm rate. The scheme of minimizing the rate of miss constrained to a specified false-alarm rate is called the Neyman–Pearson scheme.

The above techniques devise decision mechanisms under the assumption that the class conditional distributions of the features are available. When such information is not available, the distribution functions need to be estimated from training samples. Estimation of characteristics of pattern classes is an essential part of the design of decision theoretic pattern classifiers. In supervised estimation sets of patterns, each set drawn from one class, are available. If the functional forms of underlying class conditional distributions are known or can be assumed, the problem reduces to the estimation of a finite number of parameters. Gaussian distribution forms are very popular for many reasons. An N-dimensional Gaussian distribution is completely represented by an N-dimensional mean vector and an $N \times N$ covariance matrix. Estimation of these quantities is simple. The distribution functions are smooth and are defined over the entire N-dimensional vector space. Resulting decisions turn out to be at most quadratic functions of the observation vector u. The central-limit theorem in the theory of random variables justifies Gaussian approximations when a random variable is a result of a combination of several physically independent effects.

Techniques for parameter estimation fall into three broad categories: point, interval, and Bayesian estimation. In point estimation the parameters are taken to be unknown constants. An explicit function of the observation is used as the estimate of the parameter. Maximum-likelihood estimation is one such technique. This substitutes a dummy variable (or dummy variables in the case of a vector parameter) for the unknown parameter and expresses the probability of observing the given sample set as a function of the dummy variable. The value of the dummy variable at which this probability is maximum is the maximum-likelihood estimate. In interval estimation the interest is in computing an interval that contains the parameter (being estimated) with a specified probability (confidence level). Bayesian estimation is appropriate if we can assume that the parameter is a random variable with an *a priori* density. The density is updated as more samples are given for estimation. Updated densities get sharper with the number of samples. The value of the parameter is taken to be the one at which the updated density peaks. A class of density functions known as the exponential family have the reproducing property in that the *a priori* and the updated densities are all of the same functional form, differing only in the values of some parameters. Another desirable property for both point and Bayesian estimation is the existence of a low-dimensional sufficient statistic. The sufficient statistic (if available) allows us to represent a large set of independent samples from the same distribution by a small number of numbers from which the estimate can be computed. This is very helpful in recursive estimation.

Nonparametric Techniques

Nonparametric techniques in pattern recognition are concerned with density estimation and classifier design using a set of labeled samples when there is insufficient information to assume forms of class conditional density functions. Nonparametric density estimation deals with pattern samples from one class and attempts to fit a density function spanning the entire feature space. In the Parzen window and the potential function method, the value of the density function at a point in the feature space is expressed as the cumulative contribution from individual samples used for estimation. A sample contributes to the density function through a window or a density kernel function. Examples of these kernel functions are rectangular functions and truncated squared-cosine functions. The potential function method treats a contributing sample as an electrically charged particle; the contribution to the density function is proportional to the potential at the point of interest due to the contributing sample. The k-nearest-neighbor density-estimation procedure computes the value of the density function at a point by a fraction that depends inversely on the volume of the region in the feature space enclosing the k nearest neighbors of the point in question.

Whereas nonparametric density estimation is one approach to overcome the lack of knowledge of functional forms for class conditional densities, the other approach is to directly design a classifier from labeled design samples, bypassing issues of individual density functions. Chief among such classifiers are the k-nearest-neighbor, linear and piecewise linear classifiers. The nearest-neighbor classifier assigns that category to a test pattern sample that is the class label of the geometrically closest design sample (a test sample is one whose category is to be decided by classification; a design sample is one from the set of labeled samples used to train a classifier). The technique is easily extended to k nearest neighbors. An interesting property of the nearest-neighbor classifier is that as the number of design samples tends to infinity, the error rate of the classifier is bounded by twice the Bayesian error rate (Bayesian error is the minimum achievable error). Linear classifiers designed from labeled samples are popular due to their simplicity of operation and the availability of optimization techniques applicable in their design. In the two-class problem, when the design samples are known to be separable into respective classes by a hyperplane, design techniques include the perceptron learning algorithm, the gradient descent, and the Ho-Kashyap (1973) procedures. The general approach is to solve for a set of linear inequalities if the design set is linearly separable or to minimize the mean square distance of misclassified design samples from the discriminating plane if they are not.

Unsupervised Methods

Unsupervised methods are useful when the design data consist of unlabeled samples. It is then necessary to determine whether or not patterns exhibit distinct characteristics in order to categorize them. In unsupervised classification the given sample set is clustered into a number of groups. An important criterion for clustering is the minimization of the sum of squared error from the cluster means. If c is the number of clusters, u_{ij} the jth sample in the ith cluster, and μ_i the centroid of the ith cluster, the sum of squared error is given by

$$J_e = \sum_{i=1}^{c} \sum_{j} |u_{ij} - \mu_i|^2 \qquad (4)$$

Therefore, given a set of samples u_k and the number of clusters c, the clustering problem is to group them into c sets such that J_e is a minimum. A related criterion for minimization is the ratio of the sum of the intracluster squared distances to the sum of the intercluster squared distances. The sum of intracluster squared distance is the sum of the squared distances of each sample from the centroids of the respective clusters. The sum of the intercluster squared distances is the sum of the squared distances from cluster centroids to the mean of all the cluster centroids. A variety of other criteria using scatter matrices is also used. All these criteria lead to the same final cluster configurations provided the samples are well separated. A set of samples forming c clusters is well separated if the distance between any pair of samples within any cluster is less than the distance between any sample in one cluster to any sample in any other cluster. Algorithms for clustering based on the above criteria usually use iterative optimization techniques that guarantee only a local minimum starting from an initial partition of the sample set. Some of the other clustering methodologies are the hierarchical clustering schemes that successively merge the nearest pair of distinct clusters starting from as many clusters as the number of samples, graph-theoretic clustering, and the k-means procedure (Anderberg 1973; Hartigan, 1975). Unsupervised learning differs from clustering in that unsupervised learning schemes attempt to learn the characteristics of the individual categories from unlabeled samples for use in training a classifier. The standard formulation is the estimation of the parameters of a mixture density. However, analytical solutions do not exist even for very simple forms of densities, and numerical solutions require nonlinear programming.

Multistage Classification

Any mathematical transformation from the feature space (u) to the pattern category space $(\omega_1, \ldots, \omega_M)$ is a pattern classifier. The distinction between types of classifiers rests on the way the transformation is designed and/or implemented. All the classification techniques described above are the so called one-shot methods. In contrast, multistage methods take several partial decisions in a sequence. Each decision can be viewed as a transformation from a subfeature space to an intermediate decision set (the intermediate decision set is not necessarily a subset of classes). The transformation at a stage depends on the previous decision. The resulting phased decision structure is often referred to as a decision tree. There are many advantages in using multistage decision-making structures: In many instances design of partial decisions is conceptually simpler as they are required to examine the information relevant to the present stage only. This would also save the expense of gathering information not required for the sequence of decisions a pattern sample may encounter. The flexibility of the multistage decision-making model enhances its applicability in a wide range of problems. However, this less restrictive representation opens up so many possibilities in tailoring a multistage scheme that there is no straightforward method to design a decision tree. Theoretically, when the *a priori* class probabilities, class conditional feature distributions, and misclassification cost function are known, the optimal pattern classifier turns out to be a decision tree only if feature measurements have costs associated with them (Dattatreya and Sarma, 1981). In practice, the optimal tree can be computed only for discrete features with moderate dimensionality and a small number of outcomes per feature. Figure 2 shows such a decision tree designed for spoken vowel recognition after a feature reduction transformation and discretization of the resulting eight normalized autocorrelation coefficients into three levels each. The three branches emanating from every intermediate node are the three decisions for low, medium, and high autocorrelation coefficients in the left-to-right order.

Other methods for decision tree design usually define frameworks for classification schemes to take advantage of the peculiarities in the data. Independent subrecognition systems design several classification systems, each to distinguish one class from the rest. A combination of decisions at the second stage yields the final decision. Such schemes are useful when it is possible to identify different feature subsets each of which highlights one class. Hierarchical classifiers reject classes in successive stages until one class remains. They are useful if groups of classes form a hierarchy and different groups can be distinguished by different features and/or decision functions. Dynamic tree-development methods are usually data analytic, and they successively split features to separate data sets belonging to different classes. A detailed review of decision-tree approaches to pattern recognition appears in Dattatreya and Kanal (1985).

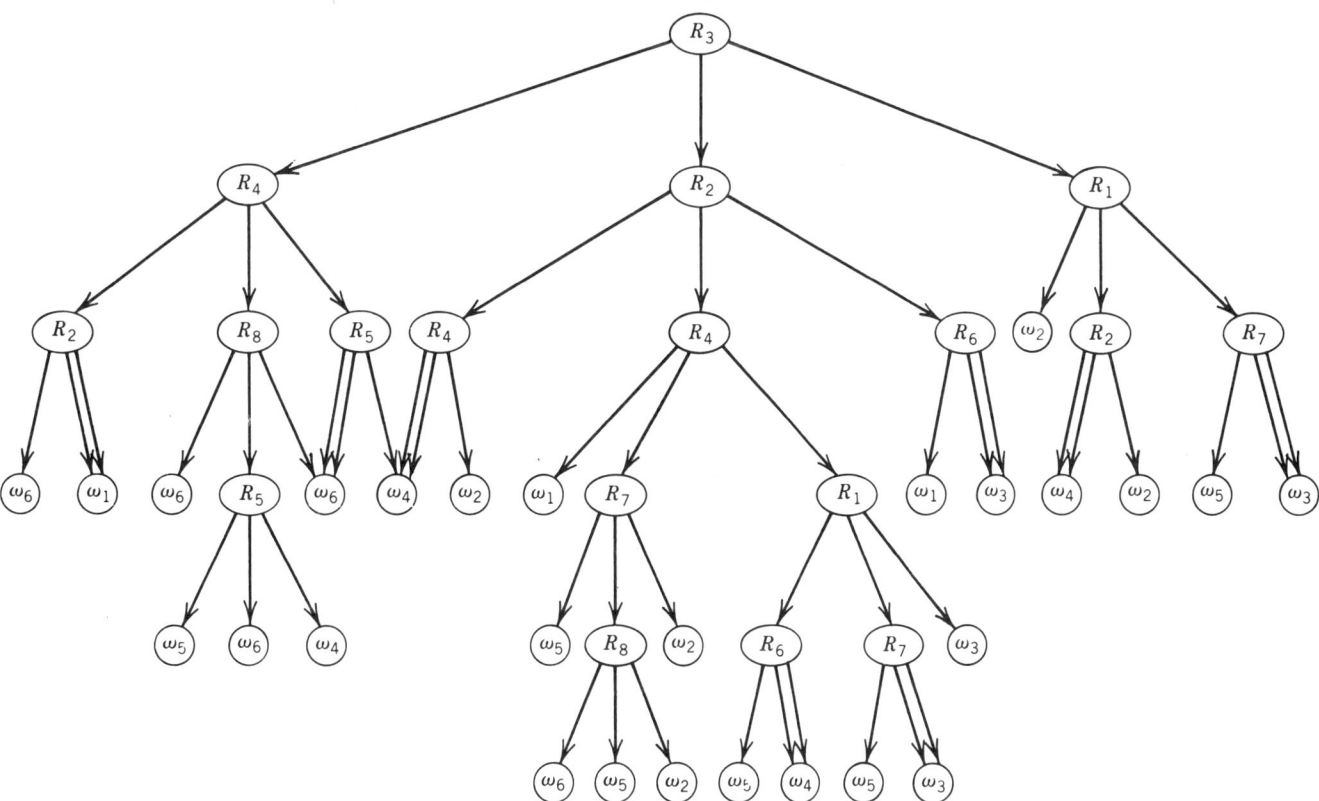

Figure 2. Decision tree designed for spoken-vowel recognition.

State-Space Models

In many practical problems it is possible to arrive at a partial structure of multistage classifiers. The class hierarchy and the features best suited for discrimination among the subgroups of classes may be available from *a priori* problem knowledge or data analysis. But such a structure is not a complete classifier since no decision rules are available. Concepts and search procedures from AI help to work out decision strategies. These strategies view classification as a search for a goal node in a state-space graph in which terminal nodes are class labels and other nodes specify features to be measured. The costs associated with the classification process are the measurement cost at every measurement node and classification risk at goal nodes. Two search strategies have been used. The S-admissible search strategy minimizes the total cost up to and inclusive of the decided goal node when the risk of classification is not influenced by measurements at nodes not along the path to the optimal goal node. If a good state-space graph is worked out in an interactive design phase, this property would hold approximately. If not, the B-admissible strategy allows for risk to be dependent on all measurements. Further details can be found in Kulkarni and Kanal (1978).

Syntactic Pattern Recognition

The structural information about the interconnections in a complex pattern cannot be handled very well by statistical pattern recognition. Since a large number of distinct interconnections occur in practical pattern environments, it was found necessary to devise techniques to describe a large number of similar structures by the same category while allowing distinct descriptions among categorically different patterns. As an example, consider a single pictorial pattern in Figure 3. The accompanying description is shown in Figure 4. A slight movement in the objects would not change the description, but an interchange of the positions of the two objects would. Notice the similarity of the description to the syntactic parsing of sentences in a language. Figure 5 shows the development of a syntactic pattern-recognition system. The analog of the conventional feature extractor is the primitive detector in syntactic pattern recognition; that of the classifier is the syntax analyzer The training or the learning procedure in statistical pattern recognition corresponds to grammatical or structural inference in syntactic pattern recognition. Segmentation, decomposition, and detection of primitives in a syntactic pattern are usually carried out by signal processing, curve fitting, or other conventional

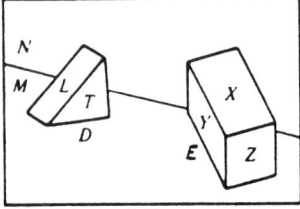

Figure 3. Pictorial pattern.

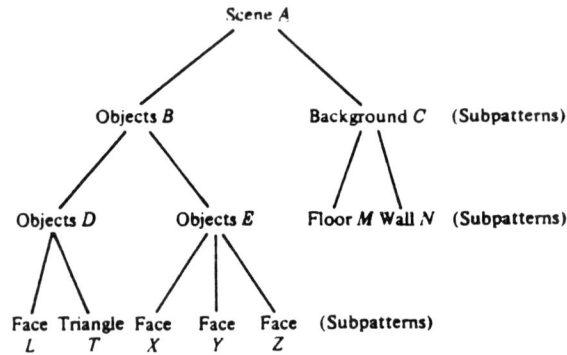

Figure 4. Description of pictorial pattern of Figure 3.

techniques. The type of primitives used for representing pattern samples varies with application areas, The primitives should serve as basic building blocks to provide a compact but adequate description of the patterns in terms of the specified structural relations. They should be easily extracted or recognized by nonsyntactic techniques with good accuracy. Patterns (or images of patterns) that are inherently line drawings are well represented by cursive strokes as primitives. Character recognition, chromosome classification, and waveform representation fall in this category. Examples of other primitives are polygonal regions. Representations of patterns and pattern categories rely on the theory of formal languages. A phrase-structure grammar G is a four-tuple; $G = (V_N, V_T, P, S)$ in which V_N and V_T are nonterminal and terminal symbols of the vocabulary, respectively, of G. $V_N \cap V_T = \emptyset$ and $V_N \cup V_T = V$; P is a finite set of production rules, each rule denoted by $\alpha \rightarrow \beta$, where α and β are strings over V, with α involving at least one symbol from V_N. $S \in V_N$ is the start symbol. Grammars are classified by restrictions on the types of production rules, which in turn restrict the sets of sentences that can be generated. No restrictions on P implies an unrestricted grammar and the set of sentences generated by an unrestricted grammar is called the unrestricted language. Context-sensitive grammars allow production rules of the form $\gamma_1 \alpha \gamma_2 \rightarrow \gamma_1 \beta \gamma_2$, where $\alpha \in V_N$, γ_1, γ_2, and β are strings formed from the total vocabulary. The interpretation of such a production rule is that α can be replaced by β in the context of γ_1 and γ_2. Context-free grammars have production rules in which a nonterminal symbol may be replaced by a non-null string.

Consider the patterns generated from four primitives corresponding to unit-length arrows in the north, east, south, and west directions (Fig. 6). It may be of interest to recognize square patterns against other polygons generated by the same set of primitives. Sentences of the form $a^n b^n c^n d^n$ represent a set of such squares, although there are other sentences representing squares in the same model (α^n is the short-form notation for the concatenation of n symbols of α). Further, such patterns may be generated by context-free as well as context-sensitive grammars. Therefore, primitive selection and grammar construction should be carried out in an interactive, iterative development. Recognition that a syntactic pattern belongs to a particular language (class) is performed by syntax

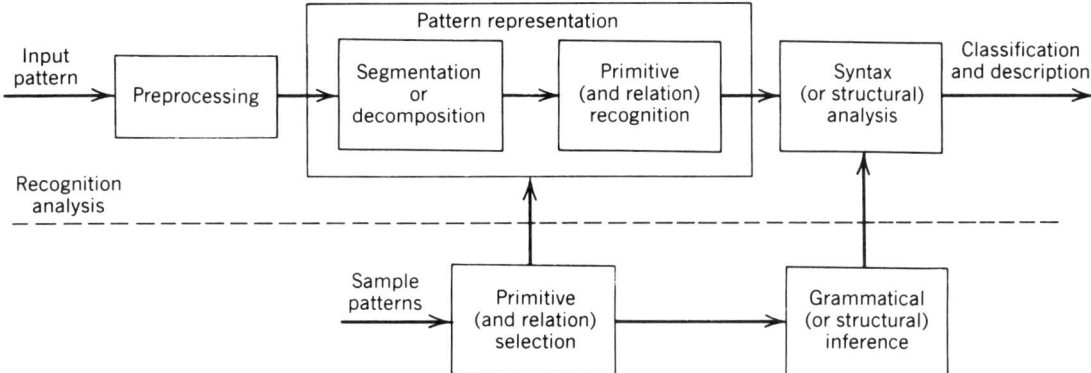

Figure 5. Development of syntactic pattern-recognition system.

analysis or parsing. The parser will also derive the process through which the syntax of the pattern is generated, thus giving us the description of the pattern. The top-down parsing (qv) method starts with the start symbol S and applies production rules of grammars of different categories to attempt generation of the given sentence (see PROCESSING, BOTTOM-UP AND TOP-DOWN). This goal-oriented approach sets intermediate goals and changes them when they fail to be satisfied. In the bottom-up parsing procedure production rules are applied backward to reduce the sentence to the start symbol. At any stage the string is searched for existence of substrings that are right parts of allowed production rules. Several efficient parsing algorithms have been developed for the many kinds of grammars used in syntactic pattern recognition. In practical situations in which possible sentences in a grammar category overlap with those in another category, stochastic grammars are useful to model the associated uncertainty. They are also useful when a grammar constructed to generate desired patterns is able to generate unwanted patterns in addition. A probability is associated with every string in a language. Multiple productions are handled by randomizing the productions and the state transitions in the recognition procedures. Another way of handling such ambiguities is by defining similarity measures over pairs of sentences and deciding the category with the maximum similarity.

Whereas strings of primitives are powerful in representing many syntactic patterns, there are operations on primitives more general than simple concatenation. For example, if one wants to indicate the topographic relation between three or more primitives, concatenation will not suffice. Web and graph grammars are important high dimensional grammars. Tree grammars are a very important class of graph grammar and are naturally applicable whenever patterns can be described by trees. An application of tree grammars is in representing patterns of electrical networks constructed from elemental building blocks of two-port networks. The syntax analysis or the recognition procedure for patterns generated by tree grammars is carried out by tree automata (Fu, 1982).

Grammatical inference is the process by which training data are analyzed to work out the grammars that generate the required patterns. Care is required to limit the number of unwanted patterns generated by an inferred grammar as well as to avoid generating the same sentence by grammars of two or more categories (unless the training data itself had identical patterns belonging to different categories). The mathematical problem is to infer syntactic rules of a unknown grammar G based on a finite set of sentences from a language. Another set of sentences generated from grammars of other categories may also be given. In most cases there is no unique grammar as the solution and hence no unique technique for inference. Inference techniques are simplified by making extra assumptions. Some of these techniques are grammatical inference via a lattice structure, by using structural information sequence, and through inductive inference. These are discussed in Fu (1982).

Problem-Reduction Representations

The state-space search methods outlined earlier are an application of an AI approach to pattern recognition. Another AI model found useful for pattern recognition is the problem-reduction representation (PRR). This approach establishes subproblems and sub-subproblems until, finally, the original problem is reduced to a set of primitive solvable problems. The overall problem to be solved (the recognition of a pattern to a constituent category in this case) has several (possibly only one) versions initially, only one of which is to be solved. A successor function allows us to break up the problem into several subproblems, known as AND successors (or AND problems), all of which need to be solved before it can be claimed that the original problem is solved. Any problem can also have several versions, called the OR successors, such that the solution of any of these successors guarantees the solution

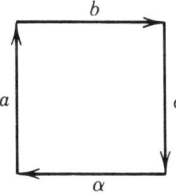

Figure 6. Set of primitives to generate class of polygons.

of the subproblem under consideration. Possible problem reductions of an overall problem are depicted by an AND/OR graph (qv). Any AND/OR graph can be modified so that a node that is an AND problem has only OR successors and vice versa. Given the problem-reduction representations of pattern categories, the task of pattern recognition is to find the solution tree of an AND/OR graph. The tip nodes in the PRR denote primitive problems of the structural pattern recognition. It is known that context-free grammars and AND/OR trees (with a specified ordering among each set of AND successors) are equivalent. Thus, syntactic pattern-recognition problems involving context-free grammars are amenable to solution by the AI problem-reduction approach.

It is useful to take this approach when solutions of primitive problems (recognition of primitives in the environment) are computationally complex. Furthermore, the AI approach brings in interaction between the detection of primitives and the description of structure. The solution tree of the AND/OR graph is searched for by a state-space search procedure called the *SSS** algorithm, which produces a rank-ordered set of solution graphs representing alternative structural descriptions of the pattern being analyzed. By using both top-down and bottom-up state-space operators, the algorithm allows a model-directed, data-confirmed and data-directed, model-confirmed approach to pattern analysis such that the occurrence of a piece of information in the data triggers the generation of model-based hypotheses. These hypotheses are then used to intelligently localize and direct the search for more information in the data space. The hypothesize-and-detect process is continued until the original problem of getting structural descriptions of the pattern is solved. In this way several lines of competing reasoning are simultaneously developed leading to multiple merit-ordered solutions. Also, data primitives can be searched for in a non left–right manner, different from that represented by the scan order. Thus, the top-down, bottom-up, non left-right implementation of the *SSS** algorithm permits treatment of pattern analysis in terms of searching two spaces—a model space and a data space with feedback between the two. It also allows the use of simultaneous statistical and structural information. Mathematical details are found in Kanal (1979), Stockman and Kanal (1983), and Kanal and Dattatreya (1985).

In Stockman and Kanal (1983), this model was applied to the recognition of waveforms among different categories based on the morphs made up of constrained mathematical curves. A shortcoming of the AND/OR model is the requirement that all AND subproblems be solved in order to solve the parent problem. In many applications, such as ship classification using inverse synthetic aperture radar, it became evident that because of missing data not all AND subproblems would be solvable. B. A. Lambird and D. Lavine proposed the SOME/OR graph model in which only some of the subproblems need be solved until sufficient evidence is accumulated to declare the parent solved. Modification of the *SSS** search algorithm to work on SOME/OR graphs and analytical and experimental results on its operation have appeared in a report (L.N.K. Corporation, 1989). Figure 7 shows a hypothetical SOME/OR tree for a ship.

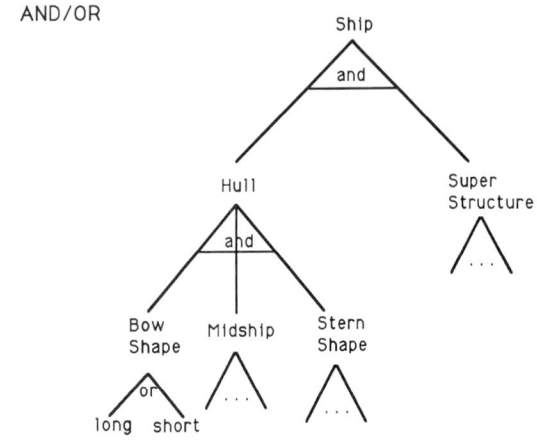

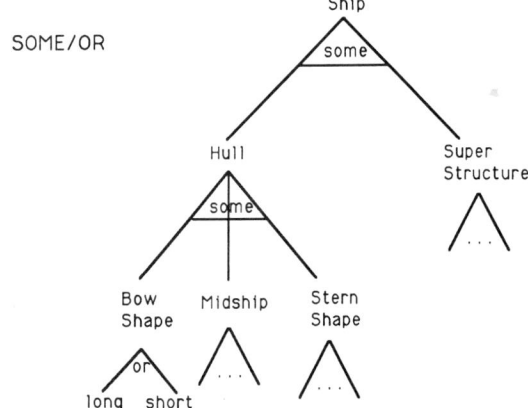

Figure 7. Simplified AND/OR tree and SOME/OR tree example for a ship.

Artificial Neural Networks

Perceptrons (qv) (Rosenblatt, 1962) and other 1960s vintage learning or self-organizing networks are examples of models that, at least initially, were biologically motivated. Although excitement about them was greatly dampened by the publication of Minsky and Papert's attack showing the limited pattern classification and function approximating capabilities of single layer perceptrons (1969), the Proceedings of a 1974 conference showed a revival of interest in biologically motivated automata, neural models, and learning networks (Conference on Biologically motivated Automata, 1974). Researchers such as Albus (1971), Amari (1972), Fukushima (1969), Grossberg (1982), and Kohonen (1988), continued working without attracting a lot of attention. Minsky and Papert's proof that the single layer perceptron could not implement the EXCLUSIVE OR logical function and several other predicates, did not apply to multilayer perceptrons. Although Rosenblatt (1962) proposed a "back-propagating error correction" procedure for perceptrons which used error from the output units to propagate correction back to the sensory end, neither he nor others were able at that time to demonstrate a convergent procedure for training multilayer perceptrons.

The resurgence of artificial neural systems in the 1980s was due to: (1) the development and popularization of convergent error back-propagation (EBP) algorithms for training multilayer neural networks (Werbos, 1974; Rumelhart and McClelland, 1986); and (2) the popularization of the energy function minimization technique by Hopfield and others (Hopfield, 1984; Hopfield and Tank, 1986). Figure 8 shows some of the currently popular neural network paradigms, and lists some of the learning algorithms in use. Textbooks by Hecht-Nielsen (1990) and others have now appeared providing much information on a wide spectrum of neural networks and training procedures. Recently it has been shown that multilayer feedforward networks with a sufficient number of intermediate or "hidden units" between the input and output layers of processing elements, have a "universal approximation" property: they can "approximate virtually any function of interest to any desired degree of accuracy" (Hornik and co-workers, 1989). It has also been shown that EBP is essentially an application of a special stochastic approximation procedure, well developed in statistics, to solving the first order conditions for a nonlinear least-squares regression problem (White, 1989).

Genetic Algorithms

Genetic algorithms (GA) are search procedures modeled on "natural selection." Possible solutions are represented by chromosomes made up of a number of genes. Each gene represents an attribute in the problem domain. Collections of chromosomes are grouped into populations known as generations. Selective and combinative functions are used to produce subsequent generations. Each individual chromosome's potential as a solution is determined by a fitness function. The fitness functions map individual chromosomes into real numbers and are used to determine which chromosomes will be used, and how frequently, to produce the next generation. Fitness functions typically make use of heuristic information due to the fact that precise judgments of suitability of a chromosome are often unattainable. For example, in a scene labeling procedure

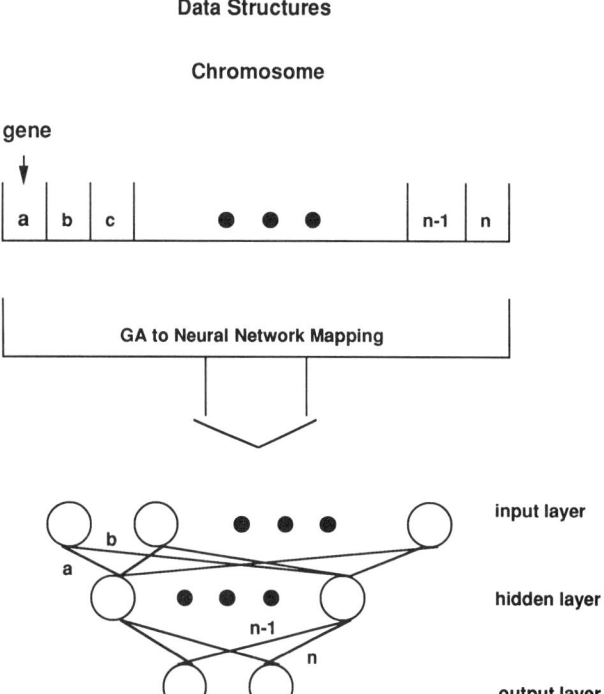

Figure 9. Adaptive learning algorithm for neural networks.

for image understanding, the exact spatial relationship of objects is imprecise. Therefore, a fitness function for a GA approach to segment recognition would need to take into account a tolerance measure for spatial relationships (Ankenbrandt, 1990).

Throughout the history of GA research, the central theme has been robustness. That is, the balance between efficiency and efficacy. It is obvious from observing nature that robustness and adaptation go hand in hand. The goal of GA research is to produce artificial systems (both hardware and software) with the robustness, efficiency, and flexibility of natural systems. There has been substantial work done, both theoretical and empirical, to prove and demonstrate the robustness of the GA in complex search spaces. Holland's seminal work "Adaptation in Natural and Artificial Systems" provides a very good theoretical basis for ongoing work. Examples of applications of GA are numerous, ranging from gas pipe flow optimization (Goldberg, 1988) to scene recognition (Ankenbrandt, 1990). Currently researchers are working on combining the effectiveness of the GA to search complex spaces with the adaptability of neural networks to learn generalizations of data. Using the weights between neurons as the genes of a GA has proved very fruitful, giving convergence in an order of magnitude less than error back propagation. Figure 9 shows this architecture called ALANN for Adaptive Learning Algorithm for Neural Networks.

Performance Assessment and Feature Selection

Evaluation of performance of pattern classifiers is a thorny problem. If the pattern-recognition problem is posed as an optimization problem, as it is in Bayesian decision theory, the expected performance may be com-

---

EXAMPLES OF NEURAL NETWORK TOPOLOGIES

Feedforward Networks
  Backpropagation, Perceptrons, Associative Memory, Adaline, Madaline
Resonating or Feedback Networks
  Hopfield, ART 1, ART 2
Stochastic Models
  Boltzmann Machines
Hierarchical Models
  Cognitron, Neocognitron, ART 3
Hybrid Models
  Counterpropagation, ART + BP, ART 3

EXAMPLES OF LEARNING RULES

Supervised
  Perception, Delta, Error-Backpropogation, Hebbian, Least-Mean-Squares
Unsupervised
  Competitive Learning, Grossberg Learning Rules

Figure 8. Some neural network topologies and learning rules.

puted either by analytical or by numerical techniques. However, such a measure is representative of the actual performance only if the underlying assumptions, such as forms of distributions, are true. The discrepancy between the calculated and the actual performance depends on the accuracy of the values of the parameters used. Performance of a classifier designed using a finite set of labeled samples is harder to evaluate. It is possible to design a classifier to correctly classify all the available training samples. But then there is no way to evaluate the performance simply because there are no more labeled samples to test the classifier. Therefore, designers split an available labeled sample set into a design set and a test set. However, the total sample set itself is somewhat inadequate in practice to design a good classifier, and the designer prefers not to sacrifice a sizable portion of it. Another technique that yields a performance closer to the true value is the leave-one-out method. This requires the design of a classifier as many times as the size of the sample set, each time leaving one sample as a test sample. The average of the performance of all these classifiers, each tested with one sample, is taken as the performance. Obviously, the procedure requires excessive computation. The leave-one-out method can be generalized to the rotation method in which different numbers of samples are left out from the design set to be used for testing. Several classifiers with different combinations of design and test samples are used to obtain the average rotation method performance.

The variation of performance of a classifier with respect to the number of features used is another important concern. Again, if the model, the forms of distributions, and the values of parameters are correct, addition of a feature cannot worsen the performance of a classifier and in general improves it. However. due to the discrepancy between the model and reality and due to the effect of finite design samples, addition of a feature can worsen the performance of a practical classifier (Foley, 1972).

Selection of features for use in a pattern classifier is therefore a nontrivial problem. Even in the absence of any finite design samples' effect, a union of individually good features is not necessarily a good choice for a proper subset of features of a specified size. Thus, to select the best set of n features from a larger set of N, the only guaranteed technique is the exhaustive search involving the enumeration of the performance of all classifiers each designed with one subset of n features. The problem of optimal classifier design is compounded by the above-mentioned effect of finite design samples. However, in practice, it is being increasingly recognized that globally optimal pattern classifiers are neither necessary nor beneficial for applications of short duration. The user is willing to sacrifice optimality in favor of easier design and operation. Nevertheless, an understanding of theoretical issues in feature selection, dimensionality, and finite sample effects helps in better design. Toussaint (1974) is a good review on error estimation. More recent work on error estimation and effects of dimensionality and sample size can be found in a number of articles in Krishnaiah and Kanal (1982). See especially the articles by van Campenhout and by Jain and Chandrasekharan in Krishnaiah and Kanal (1982) and also the recent articles by Fukunaga and Hayes (1989a,b).

APPLICATIONS

Pattern recognition has been applied to real-life problems in a wide variety of areas including medical information processing, speech processing, character recognition, fingerprint identification, earth and space sciences, particle physics, and chemistry. A brief mention of some specific problems and dominant approaches to them follows.

Medical Information Processing

Identification of diseases and affected areas from chest X-rays and CAT (computer-aided tomography) scans have been attempted by pattern-recognition techniques. Clustering is a common approach to these problems. Automatic recognition of white blood cells from their images is an active area. The requirement is in computing the percentages of various types of white blood cells present in a sample of peripheral blood. Several tens of features are formulated with images in two color bands. Interactive and decision-tree approaches are used in addition to conventional methods. Often, 85–90% correct recognition rates are reported (Gelsema and Landweerd, 1982). Syntactic pattern recognition has been successfully applied to the classification of chromosomes from their images using cursive strokes as primitives. Medical waveforms processed by pattern recognition are electrocardiograms (ECGs), electroencephalograms (EEGs), carotid pulse waves, and head murmurs. Syntactic techniques have been used to classify ECGs into normal and different kinds of abnormality. A signal-processing technique, deconvolution, has been attempted to separate the excitation waveform and the effect of filtering it goes through before being sensed by electrodes. Together the two help in better identification of the state of the vascular system. Statistical techniques for ECG analysis are reviewed in van Bemmel (1982). The theory of random processes applied to EEGs has helped in classifying different stages of sleep. Carotid pulse waves are sensed by noninvasive techniques and are known to help in identifying the state of cardiac activity. Studies on structural representations of carotid pulse waves using the PRR approach appear in Kanal (1979), Stackman and Kanal (1983), and Kanal and Dattatreya (1985).

Speech Processing

Recognition and understanding of spoken information initially received wide attention but is now limited to specific problems within the general area (White, 1976). The most widely used speech recognizers are limited vocabulary recognizers of vocabulary sizes as large as a thousand words (see SPEECH UNDERSTANDING). The main approach continues to be segmentation (intervals of a specified size; 10–20 ms each), computation of a distance value and template matching of the sequence with those of stored templates by dynamic warping. Continuous speech-recognition techniques are reviewed in Jelinek and co-workers

(1982). Speaker recognition received some attention with possible applications in security checks. But practically achievable accuracies fall below acceptable levels. However, the techniques are useful in speaker normalization, a training procedure to tune speech-recognition systems to one of several speakers.

Earth and Space Science

Classification of remotely sensed data (from airborne and spaceborne platforms) is useful in forest and crop inventory, monitoring seasonal changes, water pollution, and in detection of earth resources. Typically, a scanner senses intensities of electromagnetic waves radiated/reflected from the earth's surface in several spectral bands. Bayesian approaches require ground truth. Parameter selection, feature selection, design of discriminant functions, and performance evaluation are the steps in the iterative development of these classifiers. Clustering and decision-tree approaches have also been widely used. There have also been attempts to use syntactic pattern recognition using textural features. A review of pattern-recognition techniques for remote-sensing applications appears in Swain (1982).

Other earth sciences' areas for application of pattern recognition are meteorology, oil exploration through geophysical signal processing, and oil-spill identification. In meteorology, data gathered from satellites as well as wind speeds and directions, pressure, humidity, etc, are correlated to predict weather patterns by statistical methods. In geophysics, acoustic waves (usually impulses) are generated by an artificial explosion under the earth's surface. As the waves propagate, their shapes get modified; they are also reflected at junctions of two different kinds of materials. Reflected data are gathered by several sensors. Statistical time-series and pattern-recognition techniques are used to locate the desired junctions within the earth. The problem in oil-spill identification is the matching of spilled oil samples from coastal water with one or more suspect oil samples to detect the spiller. Matching is usually accomplished by interactive pattern recognition and graphical displays of multidimensional data extracted from the oil sample by infrared and fluorescent spectroscopy (Chien and Killeen, 1982).

Fingerprint and Character Recognition

Fingerprints are powerful in identifying a human being. The need for automatic fingerprint recognition in security applications arises due to the large number of templates with which a sample should be compared. Syntactic techniques with tree grammars have been applied to this problem (Fu, 1982). Primitives used are directional strokes (in several directions) merging and branch points, loops, segment, and abrupt ending. In character recognition the typical requirement is the classification into the alphabet of a binary matrix obtained by digitizing a character. Recognition of machine-printed or typewritten text is much simpler once the font is known. Handprinted character recognition (qv) has applications in the post office. Both statistical and syntactic techniques have been used for this purpose. The simplest technique assumes as many binary features as the number of pixels in the matrix and class conditional independence among features. Sequential and decision-tree approaches have also been formulated (Nagy, 1982). The syntactic method is especially suited for Chinese character recognition as they are made up of stroke segments. An overall system described in Fu (1982) consists of a contour tracing program to determine the boundary of each character component. A search is then conducted to find a stroke segment to be used as a starting point. The algorithm then crawls along the stroke until the end of the stroke or a junction of strokes is encountered. The graph of the component is then built in terms of the stroke segments. The graph is traversed in a specific order, and a sequence of primitives is generated. Final recognition is achieved by matching the pattern with syntactic representations of characters.

Radar and Sonar

The most common pattern-recognition problem in radar and sonar is the two-class problem of deciding the presence or absence of a target based on noisy signals received from target areas. Radar radiates electromagnetic waves and processes the reflected signal. Radars are used to detect aircraft and ship targets from sensors stationed on ground, ships, and aircraft. Sonars use acoustic waves and are only useful underwater. Passive sonars rely on acoustic noise generated by ships' machinery for target detection. The set of features used for classification by a radar is known as a radar signature, a vector sequence of temporally ordered returns from the target. Parametric classification using estimated parameters and nonparametric and sequential schemes are widely used. In the sequential technique decisions are defined on successive signatures. An example of a multiclass radar problem is the classification of ship types. Radar applications of pattern recognition are reviewed in Grometstein and Schoendorf (1982).

Other examples of applications of pattern recognition are analysis of photographic plates exposed in particle cloud chambers, detection of materials through nuclear magnetic resonance, identification of compounds by chemical means, and classification of rocks.

CONCLUSION

Automatic pattern recognition has been attracting the attention of investigators from engineering, science, the humanities, and the arts. The methodologies and applications briefly discussed here touch upon earlier and more recent developments, with the earlier methods generally better understood. Desktop workstation hardware together with flexible software implementing interactive pattern classification, search of graph representations of structures, expert system shells, and neural net and genetic algorithms, make for much easier exploration of alternative pattern recognition techniques than ever before. The current resurgence of artificial neural systems has led to a level of excitement about pattern recognition that was present in the early 1960s. Many exciting developments can be expected because of the interdisciplinary interest in pattern recognition.

BIBLIOGRAPHY

J. S. Albus, "A Theory of Cerebellar Function," *Math. Biosci.* **10,** 25–61 (1971).

S. I. Amari, "Learning Patterns and Pattern Sequences by Self-Organizing Nets of Threshold Elements," *IEEE Trans. Comput.* **C-21,** 1197–1206 (Nov. 1972).

M. R. Anderberg, *Cluster Analysis for Applications,* Academic Press, New York, 1973.

C. A. Ankenbrandt, B. P. Buckles, and F. E. Petry, "Scene Recognition Using Genetic Algorithms with Semantic Nets," *Pattern Recognition Letters* **2,** 285–293 (1990).

R. L. Barron, A. N. Mucciardi, F. J. Cook, J. N. Craig, and A. R. Barron, "Adaptive Learning Networks: Development and Application in the United States of Algorithm Related to GMDH," in S. J. Farlow, ed., *Self-Organizing Methods in Modeling–GMDH Type Algorithms,* Marcel Dekker, Inc., 1984, pp. 25–65.

J. C. Bezdek, *Pattern Recognition with Fuzzy Objective Function Algorithms,* Plenum Press, New York, 1981.

S. T. Bow, *Pattern Recognition,* Marcel Dekker, New York, 1984.

Y. T. Chien, *Interactive Pattern Recognition,* Marcel Dekker, New York, 1978.

Y. T. Chien and T. J. Killeen, "Computer and Statistical Considerations for Oil Spill Identification," in P. R. Krishnaiah and L. N. Kanal, eds., *Handbook of Statistics,* North-Holland, Amsterdam, 1982, pp. 651–672.

G. R. Dattatreya and L. N. Kanal, "Decision Trees in Pattern Recognition," in L. N. Kanal and A. Rosenfeld, eds., *Progress in Pattern Recognition 2,* North-Holland, Amsterdam, 1985.

G. R. Dattatreya and V. V. S. Sarma, "Bayesian and Decision Tree Approaches for Pattern Recognition Including Feature Measurement Costs," *IEEE Trans. Pattern Anal. Mach. Intell.* **PAMI-3,** 293–298 (May 1981).

P. A. Devijver and J. Kittler, *Pattern Recognition: A Statistical Approach,* Prentice-Hall, Englewood Cliffs, N.J., 1982.

R. O. Duda and P. E. Hart, *Pattern Classification and Scene Analysis,* John Wiley and Sons, Inc., New York, 1973.

D. H. Foley, "Considerations of Sample and Feature Size," *IEEE Trans. Inf. Theory* **IT-18,** 618–626 (Sept. 1972).

K. S. Fu, *Syntactic Methods in Pattern Recognition,* Academic Press, New York, 1974.

K. S. Fu, *Syntactic Pattern Recognition and Applications,* Prentice-Hall, Englewood Cliffs, N.J., 1982.

K. S. Fu and A. Rosenfeld, "Pattern Recognition and Computer Vision," *Computer* **17,** 274–282 (Oct. 1984).

K. Fukanaga, *Introduction to Statistical Pattern Recognition,* Academic Press, New York, 1972.

K. Fukunaga and R. R. Hayes, "Effects of sample Size in Classifier Design," *IEEE Trans. Pattern Anal. Mach. Intell.* **PAMI-2**(8), 873–885 (Aug. 1989a).

K. Fukunaga and R. R. Hayes, "Estimation of Classifier Performance," *IEEE Trans. Pattern Anal. Mach. Intell.* **PAMI-2**(10), 1087–1101 (Oct. 1989b).

K. Fukushima, "Visual Feature Extraction by a Multilayered Network of Analog Threshold Elements," *IEEE Trans. Syst. Sci. Cybern.* **SSC-5,** 322–333 (Oct. 1969).

E. S. Gelsema, "ISPAHAN, An Interactive System for Pattern Analysis: Structure and Capabilities," in E. S. Gelsema and L. N. Kanal, eds., *Pattern Recognition in Practice,* Amsterdam, North-Holland, 1980, pp. 481–491.

E. S. Gelsema and L. N. Kanal, *Pattern Recognition in Practice,* Vols. 1 and 2, North-Holland, Amsterdam, 1980 and 1985.

E. S. Gelsema and G. H. Landweerd, "White Blood Cell Recognition," in P. R. Krishnaiah and L. N. Kanal, eds., *Handbook of Statistics,* North Holland, Amsterdam, 1982, pp. 595–608.

D. E. Goldberg, *Genetic Algorithms in Search, Optimization, and Machine Learning,* Addison-Wesley, Reading, Mass., 1988.

R. C. Gonzales and M. G. Thomason, *Syntactic Pattern Recognition,* Addison-Wesley, Reading, Mass., 1978.

A. A. Grometstein and W. H. Schoendorf, "Applications of Pattern Recognition in Radar," in P. R. Krishnaiah and L. N. Kanal, eds., *Handbook of Statistics,* North-Holland, Amsterdam, 1982, pp. 575–594.

S. Grossberg, *Studies of Mind and Brain,* Reidel Press, Boston, 1982.

I. A. Hartigan, *Clustering Algorithms,* John Wiley and Sons, Inc., New York, 1975.

R. Hecht–Nielsen, *Neurocomputing,* Addison-Wesley, Reading, Mass., 1990.

Y. C. Ho and A. K. Agrawala, "On Pattern Classification Algorithms: Introduction and Survey," *Proc. IEEE* **56,** 2101–2114 (Dec. 1968).

J. J. Hopfield, "Neurons with Graded Responses have Collective Computational Properties like those of Two-State Neurons," *Proc. Natl. Acad. Sci. USA* **81,** 3088–3092 (1984).

J. J. Hopfield and D. W. Tank, "Neural Computation of Decisions in Optimization Problems," *Biol. Cybern.* **52,** 141–152 (1985).

K. Hornik, M. Stinchcome, and H. White, "Multilayer Feedforward Networks are Universal Approximators," *Neural Networks* **2,** 359–366 (1989).

A. K. Jain and R. C. Dubes, *Algorithms for Clustering Data,* Prentice-Hall, Englewood Cliffs, N.J., 1988.

F. Jelinek, R. L. Mercer, and L. R. Bahl, "Continuous Speech Recognition: Statistical Methods," in P. R. Krishnaiah and L. N. Kanal, eds., *Handbook of Statistics,* North-Holland, Amsterdam, 1982, pp. 549–574.

L. N. Kanal, "Evaluation of a Class of Pattern-Recognition Networks," in E. E. Bernard and M. R. Kare, eds., *Biological Prototypes and Synthetic Systems, Vol. 1,* Plenum Press, New York, 1962, pp. 261–269.

L. N. Kanal, "Interactive Pattern Analysis & Classification Systems: A Survey & Commentary," *Proc. IEEE* **60,** 1200–1215 (Oct. 1972).

L. N. Kanal, "Patterns in Pattern Recognition: 1968–1974," *IEEE Trans. Inf. Theory,* **IT-20**(6), 697–722 (Nov. 1974).

L. N. Kanal, "Problem-Solving Methods and Search Strategies for Pattern Recognition," *IEEE Trans. Pattern Anal. Mach. Intell.* **PAMI-1,** 193–201 (Apr. 1979).

L. N. Kanal and B. Chandrasekaran, "Recognition, Machine 'Recognition', and Statistical Approaches," in M. S. Watanabe, ed., *Methodologies of Pattern Recognition,* Academic Press, New York, 1969, pp. 317–332.

L. N. Kanal and G. R. Dattatreya, "Problem Solving Methods for Pattern Recognition," in T. Y. Young and K. S. Fu, eds., *Handbook of Pattern Recognition and Image Processing,* Academic Press, New York, 1986, pp. 143–165.

L. N. Kanal and E. S. Gelsema, "ISPAHAN; An Interactive System for Pattern Analysis & Classification," *Am. Stat.* **34**(3), 185 (Aug. 1980).

L. N. Kanal and V. Kumar, *Search in Artificial Intelligence,* Springer-Verlag, 1988.

L. N. Kanal and J. F. Lemmer, eds., *Uncertainty in Artificial Intelligence,* North-Holland, Amsterdam, 1986.

L. N. Kanal and A. Rosenfeld, *Machine Intelligence and Pattern Recognition* (formerly titled *Progress in Pattern Recognition*), Vols. 1 and 2, North-Holland, Amsterdam, 1981 and 1985.

A. Kandel, *Fuzzy Techniques in Pattern Recognition*, John Wiley and Sons, Inc., New York, 1982.

T. Kohonen, *Self-Organization and Associative Memory*, 2nd ed., Springer-Verlag, 1988.

P. R. Krishnaiah and L. N. Kanal, *Handbook of Statistics, Vol. 2, Classification, Pattern Recognition, and Reduction of Dimensionality*, North-Holland, Amsterdam, 1982.

A. V. Kulkarni and L. N. Kanal, "Admissable Search Strategies for Parametric and Nonparametric Hierarchical Classifiers," *Proceedings of the Fourth International Joint Conference on Pattern Recognition*, Kyoto, Japan, IEEE, New York, 1978, pp. 238–248.

V. Kumar, P. S. Gopalakrishnan, and L. N. Kanal, *Parallel Algorithms for Machine Intelligence and Vision*, Springer-Verlag, 1990.

L. N. K. Corp. Report (1989), *Novel Graph Searching Methods for Image Analysis*, Final Report, Contract N00014-87-C-0689, Office of Naval Research, Aug. 1989.

D. R. McNeil, *Interactive Data Analysis*, John Wiley and Sons, Inc., New York, 1977.

M. Minsky and S. Papert, *Perceptrons: An Introduction to Computational Geometry*, M.I.T. Press, Cambridge, Mass., 1969.

F. Mosteller and J. W. Tukey, *Data Analysis and Regression*, Addison-Wesley, Reading, Mass., 1977.

G. Nagy, "State of the Art in Pattern Recognition," *Proc. IEEE* **56**, 836–862 (May 1968).

G. Nagy, "Optical Character Recognition: Theory and Practice," in P. R. Krishnaiah and L. N. Kanal, eds., *Handbook of Statistics*, North-Holland, Amsterdam, 1982, pp. 621–650.

U. Neisser, "Recognizing Patterns: Studies in Living and Automatic Systems," *Am. Sci.* **56**(4), 464A–465A (1968).

N. J. Nilsson, *Learning Machines*, McGraw-Hill, New York, 1965.

N. J. Nilsson, *Principles of Artificial Intelligence*, Tioga, Palo Alto, Calif., 1980.

Y. Pao, *Adaptive Pattern Recognition and Neural Nets*, Addison-Wesley, Reading, Mass., 1989.

T. Pavlidis, *Structural Pattern Recognition*, Springer-Verlag, Berlin, 1977.

F. Rosenblatt, *Principles of Neurodynamics*, Spartan Books, New York, 1962.

A. Rosenfeld, *Techniques for 3-D Machine Perception*, North-Holland, Amsterdam, 1985.

D. E. Rumelhart and J. L. McClelland, *Parallel Distributed Processing: Explorations in the Microstructure of Cognition, I and II*, MIT Press, Cambridge, Mass. 1986.

J. W. Sammon, Jr., "An Optimal Discriminant Plane," *IEEE Trans. Comput.* (Short Notes) **C-19**, 826–829 (Sept. 1970).

J. Sklansky and G. N. Wassel, *Pattern Classifiers and Trainable Machines*, Springer-Verlag, New York, 1981.

M. D. Srinath and P. K. Rajasekharan, *An Introduction to Statistical Signal Processing with Applications*, John Wiley and Sons, Inc., New York, 1979.

G. C. Stockman and L. N. Kanal, "Problem Reduction Representation for the Linguistic Analysis of Waveforms," *IEEE Trans. Pattern Anal. Mach. Intell.* **PAMI-5**, 287–298 (May 1983).

P. H. Swain, "Pattern Recognition Techniques for Remote Sensing Applications," in P. R. Krishnaiah and L. N. Kanal, eds., *Handbook of Statistics*, North-Holland, Amsterdam, 1982, pp. 609–620.

J. T. Tou and R. C. Gonzalez, *Pattern Recognition Principles*, Addison-Wesley, Reading, Mass., 1974.

G. T. Toussaint, "Bibliography on Estimation of Misclassification," *IEEE Trans. Inf. Theory* **IT-20**, 472–479 (July 1974).

G. T. Toussaint, *Computational Geometry*, North-Holland, Amsterdam, 1985 and 1988.

J. H. van Bemmel, "Recognition of Electrocardiographic Patterns," in P. R. Krishnaiah and L. N. Kanal, eds., *Handbook of Statistics*, North-Holland, Amsterdam, 1982, pp. 501–526.

P. Werbos, "Beyond Regression: New Tools for Prediction & Analysis in the Behavioral Sciences," Ph.D. dissertation, Harvard University, 1974.

P. Werbos, "Backpropagation: Past & Future," *Proc. IEEE Int. Conf. Neural Networks* **1**, IEEE Press, New York, 343–353 (1988).

G. M. White, "Speech Recognition: A Tutorial Review," *Computer* **9**, 40–53 (May 1976).

H. White, "Learning in Artificial Neural Networks: A Statistical Perspective," *Neural Computation* **1**, 425–464 (1989).

D. D. Wolff and M. L. Parsons, *Pattern Recognition Approaches to Data Interpretation*, Plenum Press, New York, 1983.

T. Y. Young and K. S. Fu, *Handbook of Pattern Recognition and Image Processing*, Academic Press, New York, 1985.

L. N. Kanal
University of Maryland

G. R. Dattatreya
University of Texas at Dallas

PEPSys

PEPSys is a Parallel Logic Programming System implementing combined OR-parallelism and independent AND-parallelism. PEPSys includes a parallel PROLOG language, an implementation on Sequent Symmetry systems, and a distributed MIMD system simulator. Results show quasi-linear speedups up to 30 PEs. PEPSys is used in the logic component of the EDS ESPRIT II Project, and extended with data parallelism, constraint satisfaction techniques, and RDBMS connection (see U. Baron, J. Chassin de Kergommeaux, M. Hailperin, M. Ratcliffe, P. Robert, J. C. Syre, and H. Westphal, "The Parallel ECRC Prolog System: an Overview and Evaluation Results," in *Proceedings of the Conference on Fifth Generation Computer Systems*, Tokyo, Nov. 1988, pp. 841–850).

J. C. Syre
BULL EDPS

PERCEPTRONS

Perceptrons are a fairly typical chapter in the early history of AI but deserve special attention because the issues were eventually tied up and elucidated in a particularly tidy way. In the late 1950s it was quite common to think of self-organizing, randomly connected networks as a basis for intelligence. (The perceptron is a device that weighs evidence obtained from many small experiments in order to decide whether an event fits a certain pattern.) Learning could take place by some kind of feedback that would eventually produce systematic and adaptive behavior in the network.

This idea was often pursued in a fuzzy, somewhat romantic spirit. One of those who turned it into a different form was Rosenblatt (1962). He began to construct machines using a very specific concept of randomly connected networks as a mechanism for a particular kind of intelligence. His machines used very small networks and learned to discriminate among extremely simple classes of visual stimuli by a process of repeated exposure. Nevertheless, the fact that such simple machines could do anything at all gave rise to a sense of excited hope that a complex machine could do very much more. There was little awareness of the possibility that the difficulties of more complex machines might grow faster than their increase in power. Thus, the early experiments excited hopes, skepticism, and debates.

PRACTICAL LIMITATIONS

What is exceptional about the history of the perceptron is that simultaneously with the excitement and a certain amount of funding for construction, a mathematical theory was being developed that would lead to a particularly clear understanding of exactly what perceptrons could and could not do (Minsky and Papert, 1969). This theory has a number of different facets that lend it interest. Most directly relevant to the hopes aroused by early perceptrons was a very clear-cut demonstration that the particular cases in which the perceptron worked were very particular cases. There was no hope that they would generalize to a method that could, in principle, carry out all interesting visual discriminations. So, in one sense, the mathematical theory tied up the concept of the perceptron and put it to rest.

THEORETICAL ISSUES

However, the mathematical theory led to much more than proving something to be impossible. It also led to insights about why the perceptron succeeded where it did and why it could not succeed in general. These particular insights happen to connect with some very general principles of applied mathematics. Stated in the simplest form, the perceptron can be regarded as the linear case of a much larger class of algorithms. Extensive history in physics and engineering demonstrates that the linear case works very simply and by methods that do not generalize to the greater number of nonlinear cases.

The analogy with applied mathematics and the physical sciences is very straightforward; when a problem is linear, one can mobilize very powerful methods for solving it. In the case of the perceptron, when a problem can be solved in a linear way, one can generate some extremely powerful algorithms whose results seem totally counterintuitive. An example is the design of a perceptron to count the number of "blobs" in a picture.

No perceptron can tell whether there is more than one object in a given topological scene. On the other hand, if one knows that the only kind of object that exists has a reasonably simple shape, like a circle, ellipse, octagon, or any other shape that does not have too many concavities, it is possible for a perceptron to count them. The fact that a perceptron can do this is not at all obvious. Indeed, it is quite counterintuitive for someone who has general knowledge of what perceptrons can and cannot do.

The method of designing a perceptron to do this is rooted in some quite deep and not at all obvious mathematics—as are many of the uses of linear methods in physics. In fact, the possibility of these blob-counting perceptrons is another way of expressing one of the fundamental theorems of topology: Euler's theorem on the invariance of a number. This has become known as the Euler number: "Diameter-limited perceptrons cannot recognize any nontrivial topological properties except the Eulerian predicates" (Minsky and Papert, 1969, p. 134).

AS CONTEXT FOR OTHER ISSUES

The perceptron can also be used as a context for discussing general methodological issues. A few years ago, Piaget and Chomsky (Piattelli-Palmarini, 1980) were brought together at a conference in Royeaumont, France. Not surprisingly, the question came up concerning what kinds of knowledge could be innate. The position elaborated by Chomsky (1975) and Fodor (1979) essentially insists that the basic structure of mental abilities must be innate, that there cannot be any significant learning of basic structures. Piaget's view is that most of what we observe in intelligence develops through an interaction between the organism and its environment; although certain innate qualities obviously exist, they do not have any kind of one-to-one correspondence to the abilities of grown-up, developed, intelligent individuals.

Perceptrons entered this debate in the following way. Suppose one has an automaton organized as a perceptron and asks if the ability to do arithmetic, the idea of number, is innate to this machine. Clearly, there is an obvious sense in which the idea of number is not innate. One could very carefully examine the specifications of the machine for a long time without finding any representation of number there. Yet the Euler theorem tells us that something structured in this particular, linear way is matched in a rather specific way with the ability to count. That is, the machine is able to learn to count because it has this structure, even though the structure itself is very far removed from the structure of numbers. This understanding of the perceptron challenged both parties to clarify what they meant by *innate*.

Thus, the perceptron can be seen as valuable in three ways. First, the theoretical understanding of the perceptron had practical consequences. Pattern-recognizing devices (see PATTERN RECOGNITION) of any significant size simply cannot be built that way, so new generations of AI researchers are pursuing other possibilities. Second, certain theoretical issues emerged from these efforts to carry out functions such as vision, thinking, or learning. The perceptron turned out to be the linear case of a much more general process. Third, the perceptron can be used to sharpen understanding of quite different issues. Because it is clear what the perceptron can and cannot do, other issues can be crystallized by posing them in this context—one in which divergent positions must be stated more rigorously.

BIBLIOGRAPHY

N. Chomsky, *Reflections on Language,* Pantheon Books, New York, 1975.

J. A. Fodor, *The Language of Thought,* Harvard University Press, Cambridge, Mass., 1979.

M. Minsky and S. Papert, *Perceptrons: An Introduction to Computational Geometry,* MIT Press, Cambridge, Mass., 1969.

M. Piattelli-Palmarini, ed., *Language and Learning: Debate Between Piaget and Chromsky,* Harvard University Press, Cambridge, Mass., 1980.

I. F. Rosenblatt, "The Perceptron: A Perceiving and Recognizing Automaton," Rep. 85-460-1, Project Para, Cornell Aeronautical Laboratory, Ithaca, NY, 1957; *Principles of Neurodynamics: Perceptrons and the Theory of Brain Mechanisms,* Spartan Books, Washington, D.C., 1962.

S. PAPERT
MIT

PERSUADER

The PERSUADER is a computer program that automates the behavior of a labor mediator in contract negotiations. The system consists of three agents: a company, its union, and the mediator whose task is to help the other two agents reach an acceptable compromise. Emulating the behavior of human mediators, it engages in parallel negotiations with each of the disputants to arrive at a mutually satisfying settlement. The PERSUADER embodies a general negotiation model that handles multi-agent, multi-issue, single or repeated negotiations based on an integration of case-based reasoning (qv) and multi-attribute utility theory. The PERSUADER incorporates an ontology for goals and characteristics of negotiation. It generates a negotiated agreement by proposing settlements, producing evaluations and justification of the proposed settlements, restructuring the problem to make progress in difficult situations, generating counterproposals that narrow the parties' differences, and generating persuasive arguments to influence the parties' beliefs and negotiating behavior. The PERSUADER's input is the set of conflicting goals of the company and union, and the dispute context. Its final output is either a single plan in the form of an agreed upon compromise, or an indication of failure if the parties to the dispute did not reach agreement within a particular number of negotiation cycles. The PERSUADER's high level tasks are (1) propose an initial compromise, (2) repair and improve a rejected compromise, and (3) persuade the parties to change their evaluation of a compromise. [See K. Sycara, "Resolving Goal Conflicts via Negotiation," in *Proceedings of the Seventh National Conference on Artificial Intelligence,* St. Paul, Minn., 1988, AAAI, Menlo Park, Calif., pp. 245–250; K. Sycara, "Argumentation: Planning Other Agents' Plans," in *Proceedings of the Eleventh International Joint Conference on Artificial Intelligence,* Detroit, Mich., Aug. 1989, Morgan-Kaufmann, San Mateo, Calif., pp. 517–523; K. Sycara, "Negotiation Planning: An AI Approach," *Eur. J. Operational Res.* 46(2), 216–234 (May 1990)].

KATIA P. SYCARA
Carnegie Mellon University

PHENOMENOLOGY

As an approach to philosophical issues and problems, phenomenology splits into two very different and opposed points of view. It will be useful to identify these, at least briefly, because both have been brought to bear, though in very different ways, on the philosophical analysis of recent work in AI.

Both branches of phenomenology share a common philosophical ancestor, Husserl (1972). Husserl's aim was to turn philosophy into a strict science by identifying its proper subject matter and method. Husserl believed that philosophy was essentially concerned with the understanding of intentionality. This notion is notoriously slippery, but for present purposes only the roughest idea of what is involved is needed. Intentionality includes such things as having meaning, being about or representing something. For Husserl, following Brentano (1966), intentionality was not primarily a property of signs or symbols but of conscious thought. The intentionality of signs and symbols was to be construed as secondary, derived from the intentionality of the conscious acts in which they figured. And intentionality was not just one property of consciousness among others, according to Husserl, but was its defining characteristic. On this view conscious acts are by their very nature of or directed toward some represented objective.

Husserl's theory of intentionality may be thought of as a response to certain problems faced by Brentano. Brentano accounted for the directedness of conscious acts by means of their objects. For Brentano, to say that conscious acts are intentional is to say that they always have an object. But it is difficult to account in this way for acts that do not seem to reach their objectives, eg, illusory perceptions or hallucinations of nonexistent entities. For Husserl, the directedness of consciousness is not a matter of the objects of its acts, which may or may not exist in any particular case, but rather of the internal content that makes them the kind of act they are and determines the sort of object required to fulfill them.

Brentano's thesis that every mental act has an object thus became, for Husserl, the thesis that every act has a meaning, or *noema.* The directedness of mental acts is a function of their internal sense whether or not they have any external reference. And Husserl devoted the remainder of his philosophical career to the investigation of experience in terms of this model of conscious acts.

TRANSCENDENTAL AND EXISTENTIAL PHENOMENOLOGY

The split in phenomenology began during Husserl's lifetime with the publication of Heidegger's (1962) *Being and Time* in 1927. Heidegger disagreed with Husserl over the fundamental nature of intentionality and, consequently, over the appropriate analysis of human experience. The philosophical legacy of this division is orthodox Husserlian (sometimes called transcendental) phenomenology on the one hand and existential phenomenology on the other; both versions are alive and well today.

Husserl believed that intentionality was to be understood in terms of the necessary structures by means of which consciousness organizes experience. He was convinced that these structures were determined by the nature of consciousness itself, so that from the appropriate standpoint it was possible to see not just how things happened to be but how they must be in terms of the conditions governing the possibility of conscious experience of the relevant sort. So Husserl sought the laws determining the experience of objects as objects in general, as perceptual objects, as objects with cultural significance or instrumental value, etc. Because these laws are implicit in individual conscious experience, the individual could gain reflective access to them if certain elaborate methodological precautions were taken.

The distinguishing features of this theory of intentionality vis-à-vis Heidegger's are the following. Individual consciousness is the primary subject of intentionality. Meaning or intentional content consists of a number of layers arranged in a natural hierarchy. The more fundamental levels of meaning represent objects simply as objects of perception or conscious apprehension. Higher layers of meaning add more complicated characteristics such as those objects have as practically useful or valuable things.

For Heidegger the primary subject of intentionality is social rather than individual. Human existence is culturally conditioned, and meaning is a function of a public network of norms and practices rather than a matter of private mental contents. As a result, the most basic level of meaning includes essentially the practical utility and value of things, and things as mere objects of perception or conscious apprehension emerge only as the result of a special effort to strip away their more fundamental characteristics for legitimate practical purposes (as in science) or perverted philosophical ones (as in traditional metaphysics). In short, Husserl's hierarchy of meaning is turned upside down and his theory of intentionality inverted.

PHENOMENOLOGY AND AI

What bearing has any of this on work in AI? More than two decades ago philosophical critics of cognitivism in general and AI in particular began to appeal to the work of Heidegger, Merleau-Ponty (1962) and other existential phenomenologists in support of their positions (Taylor, 1972; Dreyfus, 1972). This led to a closer look at Husserl in terms of the current philosophical debate over the foundations of cognitive science (qv). The result was a number of surprising and still controversial claims (Dreyfus, 1982), including the following:

- Husserl should be viewed as an interesting precursor of modern cognitive science.
- The problems with which Husserl wrestled are essentially the problems plaguing current researchers in AI.
- The debate between Husserl and Heidegger over the nature of intentionality is virtually identical to the current debate over the possibility of AI.

Rather than examining arguments for or against these claims, the consequences they have been taken to have will be followed, from the standpoint of orthodox Husserlian phenomenology, in terms of the prospects for AI. These are as follows:

- Husserl's defense of his method and fundamental assumptions demonstrates that the entire enterprise of modern cognitive science rests on a firm foundation.
- Husserl's successful solutions of the problems encountered in applying his method to various forms of human experience show that the present problems facing AI have solutions within the framework in which they are currently posed.
- Husserl's successful integration of the everyday world (the "lifeworld") into the framework of transcendental phenomenology in his last works shows that the phenomena associated with practical activity and everyday life require no radical Heideggerian or anticognitivist interpretations of the sort that would be fatal to the AI program.

Of course, from the standpoint of contemporary existential phenomenology, Husserl's failure in each of these areas carries the appropriate negative forecast for the future of AI along with an explanation of several past and present impasses.

The plausibility of the above positions, both pro and con, emerges from a closer look at Husserl and his philosophical quarrel with Heidegger. Husserl's phenomenology hooks up with modern cognitive science in the following way. Husserl's meanings, or *noemata*, are remarkably similar both in content and function to the representations of contemporary functionalist accounts of the mental. Husserl's meanings consist of layers of "predicate-senses" with hierarchical relations of dependence among them and further components that connect them with other closely related meanings. They function as strict rules for organizing and unifying experience. And Husserl's technique for studying these meanings or representations, his famous phenomenological reduction, places essentially the same constraints on the study of the mental as does what Putnam and Fodor (1981) have labeled "methodological solipsism." (Of course, the motives are somewhat different. Husserl is afraid of the adverse effects of naturalism in philosophy, whereas Fodor is convinced that in the absence of a complete physical theory and an adequate theory of reference in the foreseeable future, this constraint is unavoidable.)

The very close connection between Husserl and AI becomes apparent on closer inspection of the meanings or representational structures that give each conscious act its identity. For each object of consciousness there must be such a representational structure functioning as a rule for organizing the experience of it (Husserl, 1960):

> Any object whatever . . . points to a structure . . . that is governed by a rule, . . . a universal rule governing possible other consciousnesses of it as identical. . . . And naturally the same is true of any "imaginable" object, anything conceivable as something intended.

So all conscious activity is a function of representations, and that functioning is strictly rule-governed. Husserlian phenomenology, like AI, is committed to capturing the representational structures and mental operations involved in all forms of intelligent behavior.

Early attempts by AI researchers to model the human ability to cope with a world of objects made no use of expectations. Intelligence was thought of as a passive receiver of context-free facts. Husserl, on the other hand, viewed intelligent experience as a context-determined, goal-directed activity, a kind of search for anticipated facts. For Husserl, the representational structure for each object contains components that provide a context, or horizon, of predelineations for interpreting incoming data. These expectations are of several kinds: those features that must remain "inviolably the same as long as the objectivity remains intended as this one and of this kind," further features that are possible or likely but not necessary for this type of object, and somewhat open indications of further related objects typically encountered along with this particular one (Husserl, 1960, 1973). In 1973 Minsky (1983a), in a paper described by Winston (1975) as "the ancestor of a wave of progress in AI," introduced a new data structure for representing knowledge that is unmistakably Husserlian in character (see FRAMES):

> A frame is a data-structure for representing a stereotyped situation. . . . We can think of a frame as a network of nodes and relations. The top levels of a frame are fixed, and represent things that are always true about the supposed situation. The lower level have terminals . . . (which can specify conditions (their) assignments must meet. . . .
>
> Much of the phenomenological power of the theory hinges on the inclusion of expectations and other kinds of presumptions. A frame's terminals are normally already filled with "default" assignments.

HUSSERL, HEIDEGGER, AND AI

Husserl's attempt to give a complete account of the mental in terms of explicit rules and representations encountered serious problems. What Husserl came to see, in part through Heidegger's "help," was that the significance of any part of the mental involved other parts and eventually opened onto the entire world of everyday life. Husserl saw this as a difficulty of size and complexity, with which he wrestled for the remainder of his life. Heidegger saw it as a much more fundamental difficulty, indicating the incorrectness of Husserl's basic assumptions about the nature of human intentionality. So Husserl (1970) spent much of his last writings, especially the posthumously published *Crisis of European Sciences and Transcendental Phenomenology*, (1970) attempting to bring the world of daily life into his phenomenology by describing the representational structures through which everyday objects acquire their significance. Heidegger's early writings were devoted to showing how the nonrepresentable background of everyday life gives things a significance that cannot be understood in terms of mental representations.

Heidegger's alleged insight is that one's understanding of things is rooted in one's practical activity of coping with them in the everyday world, and that this everyday world is essentially a context of socially organized purposes and human roles that cannot be represented as a set of facts. This context and the everyday ways of functioning in it are not something human beings know but, through socialization, form what human beings are. Using the term *clearing* for this background of practical life, Heidegger (1971) wrote, "the clearing in which present beings as such . . . can be discerned by man . . . is not an object of mental representation, but is the dominance of usage."

Dreyfus, probably the leading phenomenological critic of AI, has long been arguing for this same insight and its negative implications for the future of AI research. He claims that the failure of every attempt to generalize the techniques of the impressive microworld successes of the early 1970s [eg, Winograd's SHRDLU (qv), Evans's Analogy Problem Program, and Waltz's Scene Analysis Program] is a result of running head-on into Heidegger's nonrepresentable background of norms and practices that determines the significance of things in the everyday world (Dreyfus, 1979). Impressive in the artificial domains for which they were invented, each of these programs proved incapable of yielding anything similar to human understanding or problem solving in the absence of their initial artificial restrictions. The truth, according to Dreyfus, is that microworlds are not worlds at all or, from the other side, that the various domains or regions of the everyday human world are not anything like microworlds. This insight emerged most clearly in the attempt to program children's story understanding. It was soon discovered that the "world" of even a single children's story, unlike a microworld, is not a self-contained domain and cannot be treated independently of the larger everyday world onto which it opens. Everyday understanding seems to be presupposed in every real domain, no matter how small. The everyday world is not composed of smaller independent worlds at all, is not like a building made of tiny bricks, but is rather a whole somehow present in each of its parts.

Husserl's response to Heidegger was to accept as much of the new perspective as possible without abandoning any of his traditional assumptions. Husserl was willing to grant that each meaning functions only against the practical horizon of the "life-world." But he was convinced that the background practices themselves must consist essentially of a system of "sedimented beliefs," each with its own meaning content, which could be reactivated by phenomenological investigation and analyzed in the orthodox Husserlian manner. AI has responded to Dreyfus's attack and the relevant research impasses in much the same manner. Surely the everyday background, the commonsense world, must be a belief system, a set of implicit assumptions that differ from explicit ones only by being more easily overlooked by the cognitive scientist and more difficult for the ordinary person to recall. This cognitivist conviction has become more difficult to maintain in the light of increasing estimates of the necessary size and complexity of the required system of beliefs as well as by the lack of progress in dealing with the frame problem. Intelligent guesses at the number of beliefs involved in everyday knowledge have grown from Minsky's (1968) estimate:

> I therefore feel that a machine will quite critically need to acquire the order of a hundred thousand elements of knowledge in order to behave with reasonable sensibility in ordinary situations. A million, if properly organized, should be enough for a very great intelligence.

to Dennett's (1984) estimate, "We know trillions of things," and his likening of the cognitive scientist's reaction to any exercise of commonsense knowledge to "the unsettling but familiar 'discovery' that so far as armchair thought can determine, a certain trick we have just observed is flat impossible."

The frame problem is the problem of updating the massive belief system involved in everyday knowledge to take account of changes as time passes and actions are performed. Somehow effortless and automatic for human beings, it adds another dimension to the already unmanageable problem of programming a computer to display common sense and has led Fodor (1983) to make the following comment:

> If someone—a Dreyfus, for example—were to ask us why we should even suppose that the digital computer is a plausible mechanism for the simulation of global cognitive processes, the answering silence would be deafening.

AI AND HUMAN EXPERTISE

The newest challenge to the working assumptions of AI draws more heavily on the existential phenomenology of Merleau-Ponty than on that of Heidegger. Merleau-Ponty (1962) held that all human behavior, including cognitive behavior, could best be understood in terms of the development and employment of habitual skills and that all such skills, from the motor or sensory-motor to the purely intellectual, had the same basic structure. In terms of this view, Heidegger's everyday background is to be understood as the world of the ensemble of skills of a human being, and those skills range from the most basic perceptual and motor skills to the most sophisticated social and intellectual ones. As was the case for Heidegger, these skills cannot be captured in terms of representations and rules, and the world of a skill or ensemble of skills is not equivalent to a belief system of any sort.

The principal assailant bringing such a view to bear on work in AI is, to borrow Fodor's phrase, "a Dreyfus," not Hubert this time, but his brother Stuart. The principal target is the branch of AI known as "expert-systems" research, but the criticism strikes at the foundations of the whole AI enterprise. Research in expert systems (qv) attempts to endow computers with human expertise in very specific domains [eg, medical diagnosis, spectrograph analysis, and various areas of management]; Samuels checkers-playing program is a well-known example of this type of approach (Minsky, 1966, 1983b) in the following way. Human experts in the domain are interviewed to ascertain the rules or principles they employ. These are then programmed into the computer. Human experts and computers then work from the same facts using the same inference rules. Because the computer cannot forget or overlook any of the facts, cannot make any faulty inferences, and can make correct inferences much more swiftly than the human expert, the expertise of the computer should be superior. And yet in study after study the computer proves inferior to the human experts who provide its working principles. Dreyfus claims that these results can be understood if one follows Merleau-Ponty's advice and pays careful attention to the actual process of skill acquisition and employment rather than forcing expertise into the currently popular information-processing mold. The following account of the stages of skill acquisition emerged from his study of that process among airplane pilots, chess players, automobile drivers, and adult learners of a second language (Dreyfus and Dreyfus, 1986). It was later found to fit almost perfectly data that had been gathered independently on the acquisition of clinical nursing skills (Benner, 1984). For the sake of brevity, the following summary of this account refers only to the chess players (see COMPUTER CHESS AND SEARCH).

Stage 1: Novice. During this first stage of skill acquisition through instruction, the novice is taught to recognize various objective facts and features relevant to the skill and acquires rules for determining what to do based on these facts and features. Relevant elements of the situation are defined so clearly and objectively for the novice that recognition of them requires no reference to the overall situation in which they occur. Such elements are, in this sense, context free. The novice's rules are also context free in the sense that they are simply to be applied to these context-free elements regardless of anything else that may be going on in the overall situation. For example, the novice chess player is given a formula for assigning point values to pieces independent of their position and the rule "always exchange your pieces for the opponent's if the total value of pieces captured exceeds that of pieces lost." The novice is generally not taught that there are situations in which this rule should be violated.

The novice typically lacks a coherent sense of the overall task and judges performance primarily in terms of how well the rules that were learned were followed. After acquiring more than just a few such rules, the exercise of this skill requires such concentration that the capacity to talk or listen to advice becomes very limited.

The mental processes of the novice are easily imitated by the digital computer. Because it can use more rules and consider more context-free elements in a given amount of time, the computer typically outperforms the novice.

Stage 2: Advanced Beginner. Performance reaches a barely acceptable level only after the novice has considerable experience in coping with real situations. In addition to the ability to handle more context-free facts and more sophisticated rules for dealing with them, this experience has the more important effect of enlarging the learner's conception of the world of the skill. Through practical experience in concrete situations with elements neither instructor nor learner can define in terms of objectively recognizable context-free features, the advanced beginner learns to recognize when these elements are present. This recognition is based entirely on perceived similarity to previously experienced examples. These new features are situational rather than context-free. Rules for acting may now refer to situational as well as context-free elements. For example, the advanced chess beginner learns to recognize and avoid overextended positions and to respond to such situational aspects of board positions as a weakened king's side or a strong pawn structure even though he lacks precise objective definitional rules for their identification.

Because the advanced beginner has no context-free rules for identifying situational elements, this ability can be communicated to others only by the use of examples. Thus the capacity to identify such features, as well as the ability to use rules that refer to them, is beyond the reach of the computer. The use of concrete examples and the ability to learn context-determined features from them, easy for humans but impossible for the computer, represents a severe limitation on computer intelligence.

Stage 3: Competence. As a result of increased experience, the number of recognizable elements present in concrete situations, both context free and situational, eventually becomes overwhelming. To cope with this, the competent performer learns or is taught to view the process of decision making in a hierarchical manner. By choosing a plan and examining only the relatively small number of facts and features that are most important, given that choice, the performance can be simplified and improved. A competent chess player (such a player would have a rating of approximately class A, which is a rank in the top 20% of tournament players), for example, may decide, after studying the position and weighing alternatives that the opponent's king can be attacked. The player would then ignore certain weaknesses in his or her own position and personal losses created by the attack, and the removal of pieces defending the enemy king would become salient.

The choice of a plan, although necessary, is no simple matter for the competent performer. It is not governed by an objective procedure like the context-free feature recognition of the novice. But performance at this level requires the choice of an organizing plan. And this choice radically alters the relation between the performer and the environment. For the novice and the advanced beginner, performance is entirely a matter of recognizing learned facts and features and then applying learned rules and procedures for dealing with them. Success and failure can be viewed as products of these learned elements and principles, of their adequacy or inadequacy. But the competent performer, after wrestling with the choice of a plan, feels personally responsible for, and thus emotionally involved in, the outcome of that choice. Although the player both understands the initial situation and decides on a particular plan in a detached manner, the player is involved in what transpires thereafter. A successful outcome will be very satisfying and leave a vivid memory of the chosen plan and the situation as organized in terms of that plan. Failure, also, will not be easily forgotten.

Stage 4: Proficiency. The novice and advanced beginner simply follow rules. The competent performer makes conscious choices of goals and plans for achieving them after reflecting on various alternatives. This actual decision making is detached and deliberative in nature, even though the competent performer may agonize over the selection because of involvement in its outcome.

The proficient performer is usually very involved in the task and experiences it from a particular perspective as a result of recent previous events. As a result of having this perspective, certain features of the situation will stand out as salient, and others will recede into the background and be ignored. As further events modify these salient features, there will be a gradual change in plans, expectations, and even which features stand out as salient or important. No detached choice or deliberation is involved in this process. It seems to just happen, presumably because the proficient performer has been in similar situations in the past, and memory of them triggers plans similar to those that worked in the past and expectations of further events similar to those that occurred previously.

The proficient performer's understanding and organizing of the task is intuitive, triggered naturally and without explicit thought of prior experience. But the player will still think analytically about what to do. During this reasoning elements that present themselves as salient due to the performer's intuitive understanding will be evaluated and combined by rule to yield decisions about the best way to manipulate the environment. The spell of involvement in the world of the skill is temporarily broken by this detached and rule-governed thinking. For example, the proficient chess player (such players are termed masters, and the roughly 400 American masters rank in the top 1% of all serious players) can recognize a very large repertoire of types of positions. Recognizing almost immediately and without conscious effort the sense of a position, the player sets about calculating a move that best achieves the intuitively recognized plan. For example, the player may know that an attack is in order, but it is necessary to deliberate about how best to do so.

Stage 5: Expertise. The expert performer knows how to proceed without any detached deliberation about the situation or actions and without any conscious contemplation of alternatives. While deeply involved in coping with the environment, the expert does not see problems in a detached way, does not work at solving them, and does not worry about the future or devise plans. The expert's skill has become so much a part of the individual that there need be no more awareness of it than the individual is of his or her own body in ordinary motor activity. In fact, tools or instruments become like extensions of the expert's body. Chess grandmasters (there are about two dozen players holding this rank in the United States, and they, along with about four dozen slightly weaker players called International Masters, qualify as what are here referred to as experts), for example, when engrossed in a game, can lose entirely the awareness that they are manipulating pieces on a board and see themselves instead as involved participants in a world of opportunities, threats, strengths, weaknesses, hopes, and fears. When playing rapidly, they sidestep dangers in the same automatic way that a child, also an expert, avoids missiles in a familiar video game. In general, experts neither solve problems nor make decisions; they simply do what works. The performance of the expert is fluid, and involvement in the task is unbroken by detached deliberation or analysis.

This fluid performance of the expert is a natural extension of the skill of the proficient performer. The proficient performer, as a result of concrete experience, develops an intuitive understanding of a large number of situations. The expert recognizes an even larger number along with the associated successful tactic or decision. When a situation is recognized, the associated course of action simultaneously presents itself to the mind of the expert performer. It has been estimated that a master chess player can distinguish roughly 50,000 types of positions. Humans doubtless store far more typical situations in their memories than words in their vocabularies. Consequently, these reference situations, unlike the situational elements learned by the advanced beginner, bear no names and defy complete verbal description.

The grandmaster chess player recognizes a vast repertoire of types of position for which the desirable tactic or move becomes immediately obvious. Expert chess players can play at a rate of speed at which they must depend almost entirely on intuition and hardly at all on analysis and the comparison of alternatives without any serious degradation in their performance. In a recent experiment International Master Julio Kaplan was required to add numbers presented to him audibly at the rate of about one number per second while at the same time playing five-second-a-move chess against a slightly weaker, but master-level, player. Even with his analytical mind completely occupied with the addition, Kaplan more than held his own against the master in a series of games. Deprived of the time necessary to see problems or construct plans, Kaplan still produced fluid and coordinated play.

CONCLUSIONS

What emerges from Dreyfus's account of human skill acquisition is a progression from the analytic, rule-governed behavior of a detached subject who consciously breaks down his environment into recognizable elements to the skilled behavior of an involved subject based on an accumulation of concrete experiences and the unconscious recognition of new situations as similar to remembered ones. The innate human ability to recognize whole current situations as similar to past ones facilitates the individual's acquisition of high levels of skill and seems to separate humans dramatically from the artificially intelligent digital computer endowed only with context-free fact- and feature-recognition devices and with inference-making power.

The reason that the expert-systems programs fail to perform like human experts is implicit in the above account. When the interviewer elicits rules and principles from the human expert, the expert is forced, in effect, to revert to a much lower skill level at which rules were actually operative in determining actions and decisions. This is why experts frequently have a great deal of trouble "recalling" the rules they use even when pressed by the interviewer. They seem more naturally to think of their field of expertise as a huge set of special cases (Feigenbaum and McCorduck, 1983). It is not surprising that systems based on principles of this sort do not capture the experts' expertise. In terms of skill level, the computer is stuck somewhere between the novice and advanced beginner and has no way of advancing beyond this stage. What has obscured this fact for so long is the tremendous memory of the computer in terms of numbers of facts and features that can be stored and the tremendous number of rules and principles it can utilize with superhuman speed and accuracy. Although its skill is of a kind that would place it below the level of the advanced beginner, its computing power makes its performance vastly superior to that of a human being at the same skill level. But power of this kind alone is not sufficient to duplicate the intuitive ability of the human expert.

This way of looking at skilled behavior and its development does more than explain the failure of expert-systems research to achieve its intended goals. It also helps to explain the more general failure of AI to duplicate everyday knowledge or common sense which, as Heidegger argued, plays an essential role in all experience. As Heidegger also maintained, everyday knowledge is not a knowing *that*, not primarily a matter of explicit beliefs or relations between the mind and propositions, but is much more a matter of knowing *how*, of being able to cope with a world of implicit social norms, human purposes, and instrumental objects. And know-how and skill are virtually synonymous. In the central areas of everyday cognitive life an individual is, for the most part, an expert. Humans are expert perceivers, speakers, hearers, and readers of the native language and expert problem solvers for a wide range of everyday problems. This expertise does not mean that individuals do not make mistakes, but it does mean, if the Dreyfus account of skills is correct, that a human's performance is entirely different in kind from that of the programmed digital computer. In each of these areas the computer is, at best, a very powerful and sophisticated beginner, competent in artificial microworlds where situational understanding and intuition have no part to play but incompetent in the real world of human expertise.

That is the present state of the interface between AI and phenomenology. The lines are clearly drawn, but the battle that is likely to ensue as a result of this latest attack has scarcely begun. The challenge to AI is to account not just for everyday knowledge but for human expertise in general, solely in terms of explicit rules and representations (see also PHILOSOPHICAL QUESTIONS; REASONING, COMMONSENSE; KNOWLEDGE REPRESENTATION).

BIBLIOGRAPHY

P. Benner, *From Novice to Expert: Excellence and Power in Clinical Nursing Practice,* Addison-Wesley Publishing Co., Inc., Reading, Mass., 1984.

F. Brentano, *The True and the Evident,* Routledge & Kegan Paul, London, 1966.

D. Dennett, "Cognitive Wheels: The Frame Problem of AI," in C. Hookway, ed., *Minds, Machines and Evolution,* Cambridge University Press, New York, 1984, pp. 134–136.

H. Dreyfus, *What Computers Can't Do,* Harper & Row, New York, 1972.

H. Dreyfus, *What Computers Can't Do,* rev. ed., Harper & Row, New York, 1979.

H. Dreyfus, *Husserl, Intentionality and Cognitive Science,* MIT Press, Cambridge, Mass., 1982, pp. 1–27.

H. Dreyfus and S. Dreyfus, *Mind over Machine,* Macmillan, New York, 1986, Chapt. 1.

E. Feigenbaum and P. McCorduck, *The Fifth Generation, Artificial Intelligence and Japan's Computer Challenge to the World,* Addison-Wesley Publishing Co., Inc., Reading, Mass., 1983, p. 82.

J. Fodor, "Methodological Solipsism Considered as a Research Strategy in Cognitive Psychology," in J. Haugeland, ed., *Mind Design,* Bradford, Montgomery, Vt., 1981.

J. Fodor, *The Modularity of Mind,* MIT Press, Cambridge, Mass., 1983, p. 129.

M. Heidegger, *Being and Time,* Harper & Row, New York, 1962.

M. Heidegger, *On the Way to Language,* Harper & Row, New York, 1971, p. 33.

E. Husserl, *Cartesian Meditations,* Nijhoff, The Hague, 1960, pp. 53–54.

E. Husserl, *The Crisis of European Sciences and Transcendental Phenomenology,* Northwestern University Press, Evanston, Il., 1970.

E. Husserl, *Ideas: General Introduction to Pure Phenomenology,* Collier, New York, 1972.

E. Husserl, *Experience and Judgment,* North-western University Press, Evanston, Ill., 1973, pp. 125, 331.

M. Merleau-Ponty, *Phenomenology of Perception,* Routledge & Kegan Paul, London, 1962.

M. Minsky, "Artificial Intelligence," *Scientif. Am.* 215(4), 247–260 (Oct. 1966).

M. Minsky, *Semantic Information Processing,* MIT Press, Cambridge, Mass., 1968, p. 26.

M. Minsky, "A Framework for Representing Knowledge," in J. Fodor, ed., *The Modularity of Mind,* MIT Press, Cambridge, Mass., 1983a, p. 96.

M. Minsky, interview with Arthur Samuel, Stanford University News Office press release, Apr. 28, 1983b.

C. Taylor, *The Explanation of Behavior,* Routledge and Kegan Paul, London, 1964.

P. Winston, *The Psychology of Computer Vision,* McGraw-Hill Book Co., Inc., New York, 1975, p. 16.

H. HALL
University of Delaware

PHILOSOPHICAL QUESTIONS

The interests of philosophers and workers in AI intersect and overlap in many ways. Some philosophers have tried to use the resources of AI to shed new light on long-standing philosophical problems, and others have been vocal critics of the philosophical claims made by AI researchers. There has also been convergence. In carrying out specific projects, AI researchers have frequently been led into areas traditionally discussed and investigated by philosophers, providing new opportunities for collaborative exploration.

The philosophical impact of AI has been greatest on the philosophy of mind. AI has suggested new answers to long-standing questions about the nature of mind, led to the reformulation of traditional problems, and given birth to new controversies of its own. The mind–body problem, the mechanism of free-will debate, and disputes regarding the nature of understanding, intentionality, and intelligence have all been transformed in substantial ways by the advent of AI.

There are also important connections between AI and other areas of philosophy as diverse as the philosophy of science, the philosophy of language, metaphysics, and epistemology (qv). (The relevance of logic is almost too obvious to mention.) AI issues in these other areas have not generated the sort of emotion-laden controversy associated with issues in the philosophy of mind, but in the opinion of some philosophers they may turn out to be of greater importance in the long run (Glymour, 1985).

PHILOSOPHY OF MIND

At least since the seventeenth century and the rise of modern mechanistic theories of the physical world, philosophers have debated the place of mental phenomena within the mechanistic scheme. The development of modern computers and AI programs gave new impetus to these debates. For the first time it seemed possible to actually construct machines that were both undeniably mechanistic in their operations and possessed characteristics and abilities uniquely associated with minds. The possibility of computing machines able to play chess, prove theorems, and perhaps engage in conversation gave the mind–mechanism dispute a timely urgency.

The Turing Test

The mechanism question has been posed in a variety of related but independent forms, including "Can machines think?" "Do computers have minds?" "Is artificial intelligence really intelligence?" In his seminal 1950 paper "Computing Machinery and Intelligence," Turing (1950) considered the first of these questions and found it too meaningless to deserve discussion. He proposed, therefore, to replace it with another question that was more precise and decidable but that captured the essential issues raised by the more familiar popular formulation.

Turing proposed an imitation game to be played by a human interrogator and two unseen participants X and Y, one a human and the other a machine (see TURING TEST). The interrogator is able to address any questions to X and Y and they are to respond by typewritten messages. Both the machine and the unseen human have the same objective in the game: each tries to convince the interrogator that it is the human respondent. Turing's replacement question was posed in terms of this game, "Are there imaginable digital computers which would do well in the imitation game?" He answered the question in the affirmative and predicted that within 50 years digital computers would be able to play the imitation game well enough that an interrogator would have no more than a 70% success rate in identification of the machine respondent after a five-minute conversation.

Objections to Test's Criteria. The truth value of Turing's prediction about machine success at the imitation game is obviously an empirical and not a philosophical matter. However, philosophers have challenged its adequacy as a substitute for the original "Can machines think?" query. Criticism has focused on the behavioral evidence that forms the basis of the text. The sample of behavior may seem too limited; a 5-minute conversation appears an inadequate basis for a judgment of mentality. Such objections are not really very serious. Although the conversation is brief, interrogators are not limited in their range of discussion topics. They may make inquiries about poetry, sports, music, or cuisine, and in all these areas the machine must produce plausible humanlike responses. The test could also be modified to allow for longer conversations without altering its rationale.

The behavioral evidence has been challenged in a more substantial way by philosophers who have argued that behavioral criteria alone cannot suffice for the applicability of mental predicates. They argue that having a mind is not merely a matter of exhibiting certain patterns of verbal or nonverbal behavior but also requires that the right sort of internal processes produce the relevant behavior. Sometimes the objection is raised as a denial that the machine does exhibit the same behavior as a human (Gunderson, 1964). The machine and the human respondent may produce the same end result, a given sequence of words on the printer's output, such as "I do not have much taste for Mexican cooking," but it does not follow that they are exhibiting the same behavior. In the human case, causing those words to be printed is the making of an assertion. It is a significant linguistic act produced as the result of a prior communicative intention. The machine respondent's printing of those same words would count as an assertion only if it were also produced by a similar communicative intention: Since interrogators have access only to the physically indistinguishable end products, they cannot determine which instances of seemingly communicative behavior are genuine assertions. Their inability to identify genuine assertions on the basis of limited available evidence in no way implies that the two respondents are both engaging in the same sorts of behaviors.

A General Antibehaviorist Objection to the Test. Another way of making the antibehaviorist point is by imagining a system that simulates human behavior well enough to pass the Turing test but does so as the result of internal processes that obviously involve no genuine thought or intelligence. One such example has been provided by Block (1981). Block imagines a device that consists primarily of an enormous memory that stores a very large but finite list of all English-language conversational exchanges up to a given length (with a further limit on the length of each utterance in the exchange). The list must be ordered in some way that allows rapid access. Confronted with an interrogator in a Turing test, the machine searches its memory to find a conversation whose first segment corresponds to the interrogator's initial question. It then prints the next utterance from that conversation. Following the interrogator's reply, it again searches for a conversation whose first three segments correspond to those in its present dialogue and prints the fourth utterance from that conversation. It continues this process up to the length of the test, which is no greater than the length of its stored conversations.

One may object that such a machine is wildly impractical and argue that no such machine could ever be built, but to do so would be to miss the philosophical point of the example. The machine is in practice an impossibility; indeed, the number of items it would have to store if the conversation length were increased might soon outstrip the number of elementary particles in the universe (Churchland and Churchland, 1981). As a thought experiment, the example is not intended as a practical suggestion for building conversation machines. It is intended to make a conceptual point about the notions of intelligence and having a mind by showing that they require more than the satisfaction of the sorts of behavioral criteria employed by the Turing test. Being intelligent or having a mind is also a matter of the internal processes that produce behavior. Such conceptual connections may be obscured by the fact that in normal human intercourse, judgments about another person's mental state are normally made on purely behavioral evidence. Someone who can paraphrase a story and answer a suitable range of questions about it is considered to have understood that story. But in such cases the other person's status as a rational thinking understanding agent is not in question, only that person's mastery of the particular story at hand. As philosophers have noted, the criteria that suffice in these specific cases cannot simply be extended to other cases where the basic issue of having a mind at all is in question (Scriven, 1953).

Some may object that the Block (1981) example shows only that the internal processes underlying genuine intelligence must satisfy real-time constraints. However, Block's example is intended to make a stronger point and is taken by many to have done so. The existence of such a machine operating in real time is at least a logical (if not an engineering) possibility, and there is a strong intuition that such a device would have no genuine understanding of language.

Functionalism and AI

Philosophical dissatisfaction with the Turing test reflected a general rejection of behaviorism as a theory of mind. Few philosophers any longer believe that mental predicates can be defined or explicated in purely behavioral terms. However, the functionalist theory of mind (Block, 1980; Dennett, 1978) that dominates present philosophical thinking, preserves some elements of the earlier behaviorism, especially in its claim that many commonsense or folk-psychological mental concepts are to be explicated at least partially in terms of their behavior-causing roles. The functionalist program has been strongly influenced by analogies drawn from computer science and AI, both in its general outlook and in several of its specific applications to problems about the nature of mind.

Functionalism as a distinctive position was developed in the 1960s (Fodor, 1968; Putnam, 1967; Lewis, 1972) as an attempt to avoid the shortcomings of the two then most popular philosophical views of mind, behaviorism and physicalist identity theory, while retaining the strengths of each. Its central idea is that psychological states, such as desiring to be famous, believing that it will rain tomorrow, feeling a pain, or being angry, are type-individuated on the basis of their causal functional roles in mediating an organism's or system's interaction with its environment. Being in pain or having a belief that chalk is white is a matter of bearing appropriate causal relations to sensory inputs, behavioral outputs, and other internal states mediating the system's connections between perception and action. Items with radically different intrinsic natures can all count as instances of the same psychological kind as long as they play the same causal roles within their respective containing systems.

Functionalism thus rejects the Cartesian intuition that a mental state's psychological kind is fixed by its intrinsic, directly introspectible properties. For the functionalist it is the state's causal relations within the system that are relevant. Functionalism differs from behaviorism primarily in two respects (Block, 1978). First, it treats mental states as genuine causes, as actual internal states that play a role in the production of behavior. Many behaviorists regarded mental predicates simply as abbreviated ways of talking about behavioral patterns or regularities. Attributing to someone a desire to be wealthy was, for the behaviorist, only a way of describing the agent's behavior, not explaining the production of that behavior by reference to an inner cause. Functionalism's realism about inner causes also accounts for its second difference from behaviorism. Functional states are defined by their relations not only to input and output but also to one another. Functionalism can thus deal with the holism of the mental and the fact that mental states normally produce behavior only in joint operation. A desire for a cold beer will produce little behavior in the absence of suitable beliefs, and some mental states, such as a belief in a law of logic, will have functional roles that almost exclusively concern their influence on internal processes, such as patterns of inferential reasoning.

Functionalism and Physicalism. Functionalism departs from its other philosophic ancestor, type-identity theory, in its emphasis on function as opposed to structure. Type-identity theorists had proposed to identify mental kinds with specific physical kinds (normally neurophysiological kinds) empirically found to be correlated with their occurrence (Smart, 1959). The property of being in pain might, for example, be identified with the property of having one's C fibers firing. Functionalists, with the aid of insights drawn from computer science, have argued that even if as a matter of fact a given functional role is normally filled by a specific physical structure, other physical structures might in other contexts fill that same causal role (Putnam, 1967). Type-identity theorists have erred in identifying mental states with the narrow range of physical states that fill the relevant causal roles in human brains, thus unreasonably excluding organisms with different physiologies as well as robots and AI devices from the realm of the mental (Block, 1980). This functionalist critique of the identity theory, which is known as the multiple-realization argument, was directly inspired by computer and AI analogies. The philosophical presentations of the argument allude to the fact that the same algorithm may be carried out on a wide range of physically dissimilar devices (Putnam, 1967). The claim is also often explained by appeal to the software–hardware distinction, where again multiple realizations are possible and common.

Intentional Stance. AI has also had a strong influence in leading functionalists to distinguish among various levels of abstraction at which organized systems can be described and explained. Perhaps best known is Dennett's (1987) scheme, which is introduced in application to a chess-playing computer and includes three stances from which one may attempt to explain its behavior: the physical stance, the design stance, and the intentional stance. They involve descriptions and predictions based, respectively, on structure and physical causation, teleological function, and rational belief–desire explanation. They correspond in a rough way to what in AI might be called hardware, software, and knowledge-level descriptions. Dennett's account of the intentional stance should be of interest to AI researchers as well as philosophers since it separates the notion of having intentional states such as beliefs and desires from any metaphysical commitments about the system's underlying substance (spiritual, organic, or electronic) and provides a practical method for determining when descriptions of a system's (or subcomponent's) behavior involve implicit attributions of rationality and mentality. Although Dennett's intentional-systems theory has been subjected to much philosophical criticism (Stich, 1981), it is a clear improvement over the casual and unregimented use of intentional terminology in AI by which it is partly inspired.

Dennett's work also provides the best example of another major application of AI resources to the functionalist program in dealing with the problem of hidden theoretical homunculi (Dennett, 1975). Mentalistic psychology has often been faulted for implicitly relying on covert internal agents who account for regularities in external behavior by reproducing within a subpersonal component the cognitive abilities of the person that are supposedly being explained. The threat of vacuity or vicious infinite regress looms large when explanations of visual perception rely on a mind's eye to perceive an internal object or explanations of rational action refer to an inner decider who ranks alternative courses of action. Dennett has drawn directly on work in AI to resolve this centuries-old problem. The first part of his solution is to apply the AI strategy of decomposing a complex task or function into a set of organized subtasks and then subjecting those second-level tasks to the same sort of decomposition, repeating the process until the whole organized hierarchy comes to rest on interacting components whose behavior is straightforwardly mechanizable. Using the intentional system's method for keeping track of implicit attributions of rationality and mentality, the descriptions at each level become progressively less mental as one descends the hierarchy. Dennett (1975) describes the procedure as decomposing homunculi at each level into a committee of individually dumber homunculi at the next level down until the process terminates at an "army of idiots." Dennett's use of AI techniques thus answers philosophical criticism of homunculi by showing that their theoretical use need involve neither vacuity nor infinite regress.

Computational Theory of Mind

A third application of AI to functionalism involves the computational theory of mind (CTM). Functionalist philosophers have carried the analogy between AI programs and the organization of the mind one step further in suggesting not only that the mind decomposes into a hierarchical series of levels but also that the operations of the subcomponents at the underlying levels consist entirely in the computational manipulation of representational structures or formal symbols. The operations are computational in that they are governed by rules that can be completely and explicitly formulated in terms of the formal and syntactic properties of the representations (Fodor, 1980). As representations, such structures also have semantic content, but the underlying processors that manipulate them do so solely on the basis of their forms and syntax. The CTM is intended to resolve (or dissolve) the philosophical problem of explaining how intentional content can have a causal impact on the physical world. According to the CTM, content can have causal consequences only insofar as it is mirrored in formal structure. Differences in representational content that are not reflected in formal differences detectable by internal processors can have no impact on behavior. The CTM thus employs an entirely syntactic taxonomy of internal representations and individuates psychological states solely on the basis of the formal objects to which they are related. Since facts about the social, cultural, historical, or physical environment play no direct role in the determination of computational content, the CTM is said to be methodologically solipsistic in its approach to psychology (Fodor, 1980).

Anticomputationalist Critique. To those philosophers who accept the CTM, it represents perhaps the most important application of AI theory to the philosophy of mind. However, it has provoked other philosophers to the strongest and most widely discussed criticisms of recent work in AI. The outstanding critic in this regard has been Searle, who in his influential article "Minds, Brains and Programs" (1980) attempts to refute the claims made by Roger Schank and others that their script-based story-understanding programs literally "understand" the stories on which they comment and answer questions (see Scripts; Story analysis). Searle has a larger goal than merely challenging some perhaps exaggerated or premature claims about the level of present AI success. His aim is to refute the CTM and all work in AI that relies on it. His examples and arguments are meant to demonstrate that understanding (or having any other intentional state) can never be simply a matter of having the right sort of internal formal structure or being an instantiation of the right sort of computer program.

The central focus of Searle's argument is a thought experiment that has come to be known as the "Chinese room." Searle imagines himself locked in a room with three batches of Chinese writing and some sets of instructions for manipulating Chinese symbols. The rules are given in English, and Searle can carry them out although he does not understand Chinese since they specify the operations to be carried out purely in virtue of the shapes of the Chinese symbols and do not allude to their meanings. Searle carries out the instructions and passes back strings of Chinese symbols produced as the result of his operations. The reader is asked to imagine that the three batches of Chinese symbols correspond to what Schank and his colleagues would call a script, a story and questions, that the instructions correspond to a program, and that the strings of symbols Searle produces represent conversationally appropriate answers to the questions about the story. Searle's contention is that in such a case he would satisfy all the conditions on the basis of which a computer running Schank's program is said to understand Chinese, and yet it is intuitively obvious that in such a case he (Searle) would not understand a word of Chinese; thus, he infers that Schank's computer is equally lacking in understanding of Chinese. Although Searle's argument bears some similarities to earlier criticisms of the Turing test, it has relevance to a far wider class of theories. It is directed not only against behaviorist views, which equate understanding with performance, but also against the CTM and all those versions of functionalism and AI that attempt to account for the mental production of behavior purely in terms of formal structures and computational rules.

Replies to Anticomputationalist Argument. Searle's argument has provoked a great deal of vigorous criticism, but he has displayed considerable dialectical skill in replying to his critics. It has been argued that although Searle alone would not understand Chinese, the ensemble of Searle plus instructions and batches of symbols does understand Chinese. In reply, Searle has offered a modified example in which he memorizes the batches of symbols and rules, although continuing to treat the symbols as mere uninterpreted shapes. In such a case every part of the ensemble would be internal to Searle, and yet intuitively he would not seem to understand Chinese. Some critics have conceded genuine understanding requires more than the formal ability to manipulate symbols since understanding a symbol's meaning requires the ability to relate the symbol to the nonsymbolic external world. Thus, genuine understanding would require a robot capable of perception and action as well as of merely "conversational" performance.

Such AI proposals are in keeping with the functionalist view that mental kinds are determined by the causal role that a state plays in regulating purposeful interaction with the environment. Searle has also varied his example to answer these robot proposals, albeit perhaps with less convincing success. He imagines himself in the robot's control room, where in addition to his earlier symbolic inputs, various formal symbols appear on a screen. Those unknown to Searle are perceptual inputs; to him they are just further uninterpreted shapes to be manipulated according to rules governing only formal operations. Unknown to him, his activity produces appropriate external responses by the robot. Searle argues that he still would not understand Chinese although the robot's behavior might seem to show an understanding of how Chinese symbols relate to real-world items. Many functionalists do not share Searle's intuitions about the robot case, especially if the entire organized robot, rather than merely its Searle "component," is considered as the potential understander of Chinese. Searle's intuitions seem to rest on the absence of any subjective or experiential elements in the robot's internal processes, but it is a theoretically open question whether such processes are essential for genuine understanding. Thus, the controversy surrounding Searle's argument turns in the end on a basic conflict of fundamental intuitions.

Semantics and the Problem of Original Intentionality. The problem raised by Searle is closely related to what Haugeland has called the problem of original intentionality (Haugeland, 1985). Some symbols, such as the words of a natural public language like English, may borrow or derive their meaning from other symbols, such as ideas or other inner mental symbols, through a process of association. But if a vicious and infinite regress is to be avoided, there must be some symbols that have their meaning in a nonderivative or primary sense. The problem of original meaning is that of explaining how such nonderivative symbols come to have the semantics or meanings that they do. Haugeland's own solution is a form of interpretational semantics; he requires that a way of interpreting the symbols of an automatic symbol manipulating system (whether a brain or a computer) be found so that its inputs and outputs make sense, a notion that he admittedly leaves less than precisely defined. However, anticomputationalists like Searle would say that such an interpretational theory can provide at best an account of what it is to treat something as if it had semantics or meaning, but not an account of what it is to have original meaning in the literal sense.

A wide variety of other theories have been offered to solve the problem of original semantics. Following Cummins (1989), these theories can be classified into five main categories which respectively account for semantics or representational content in terms of similarity (Locke, 1959), covariance (Fodor, 1987; Dretske, 1981), adaptational role (Millikan, 1984), functional role (Block, 1986), or interpretational semantics (Haugeland, 1985). Each position has supporters and merits along with critics and weaknesses, and as yet no consensus view has emerged. The problem remains one of the most active and exciting areas of current philosophical research.

Connectionism and the Philosophy of Mind. The advent of connectionism (qv) and the development of parallel distributed processing architectures for AI tasks has provoked considerable discussion. Some philosophers have appealed to connectionism to attack more traditional versions of the computational theory of mind (Churchland, 1986); in particular they have tried to diminish the plausibility of the language-of-thought hypothesis, which attempts to explain mental states in terms of computational relations to inner symbolic structures with both syntactic and semantic properties (Smolensky, 1988). The impressive initial successes of connectionist architectures in simulating at least some cognitive abilities has lent support to the claim that a computational explanation of mentality need involve no commitment to inner sentences or any type of computationally manipulated inner symbols.

The proponents of the language-of-thought hypothesis have defended their position vigorously and argued that connectionist models are incapable of accounting for certain features of our psychological makeup, such as the systematicity of mental representation, ie, the fact that one cannot, for example, acquire the ability to believe that Tom loves Mary without also acquiring the ability to believe that Mary loves Tom (Fodor and Pylyshyn, 1988). A third group of philosophers has suggested that the traditional language-of-thought (or rules and representations) view is in fact compatible with connectionism and the two models need not be regarded as competitive or mutually exclusive models of the mind (Bechtel, 1987). A further issue has concerned the compatibility of connectionism with our common sense or folk theory of mind. Some supporters of connectionism have argued that if connectionism turns out to be the correct computational model of human cognition, it will follow that humans do not actually have beliefs, desires, or any of the other common mental states referred to by our fold psychology (Ramsey and co-workers, 1990). At this point connectionism is too new and developing too rapidly for there to be much clarity about its philosophical implications.

The Problem of Machine Consciousness. A number of philosophers have argued that problem of subjective consciousness is the real core of the mind–machine question.

They argue that when concerned about whether a computer can have a mind, the real question is, in Thomas Nagel's words, "Whether there is anything that it is like to be such a computer?" in the sense that there is something that it is like to be a human being, a dog, or a bat (Nagel, 1974). Nagel has claimed that most current theories of mind are inadequate because of their neglect of the subjective aspect of mentality and that current attempts to understand the mind by analogy with computers will eventually be recognized as a gigantic waste of time (1986). Searle has also argued for the thesis that the notion of mentality is essentially connected with that of consciousness and that there can be no such thing as a genuinely mental and intentional state that is in principle inaccessible to consciousness (Searle, 1990).

Defenders of the computational theory of mind have responded in a twofold way. They have attempted to reconstruct some aspects of the traditional notion of consciousness within a computational or functionalist framework, and rejected those aspects of the traditional notion of consciousness that resist such treatment as the confused and reactionary residue of discredited Cartesianism (Van Gulick, 1988).

The debate remains undecided. The arguments offered in support of the centrality of consciousness seem intuitively appealing but less than logically compelling. On the other hand, the computational theories of consciousness offered to date are far from adequate, and the success of future theory construction remains an open question.

Antimechanism and the Gödel Argument

The possibility of AI and the computational modeling of mind has also been attacked with philosophical arguments of quite a different sort based on rigorous results in mathematical logic. It has been argued that Kurt Gödel's theorems concerning the imcompleteness of arithmetic and the limits of formal systems show that no machine or computational device can be a completely adequate model of the human mind and that human minds are fundamentally different from machines (see COMPLETENESS). Although these arguments have generated extensive philosophical discussion and debate, many of the central issues remain obscure, and it is often difficult to understand just what claims are being made or denied. The logical results are quite clear, precise, and beyond question. However, their application to questions about mechanism and the human mind remain far from obvious.

In his seminal article "Minds, Machines and Gödel" Lucas (1961) appealed to the Gödel results in an attempt to show that no machine can duplicate the abilities of the human mind. Given any machine that might be thought to do so, Lucas argued that there will always be some sentence the machine cannot show to be true that he (Lucas) can recognize and show to be true. The Gödel results figure in the following way. Gödel's first theorem states that any consistent formal system S containing an adequate axiomatization of arithmetic will be incomplete, ie, there will be a sentence G of S such that neither it nor its negation is a theorem of S. Gödel proved this by showing that if S is an adequate axiomatization of arithmetic, S is adequate to express arithmetic statements that encode statements about its own syntax and proof relation. Thus, it is possible to construct within S a sentence G that encodes the statement that it, G, is not a theorem of S, ie, that it is not provable in S. He also showed that if a sentence K is a theorem of S, there is another sentence of S that says or encodes that K is provable in S, and that the latter sentence will also be provable in S. Thus, if G were provable in S, the sentence that says G is provable in S would also be a theorem of S. But that sentence would be logically equivalent to the negation of G. So both G and its negation would be theorems of S, and S would not be consistent. So if S is consistent, G cannot be proved in S. It is this Gödel sentence G that plays the crucial role in Lucas's argument. He claims that any machine M_i is the concrete instantiation of a formal system S_i such that the sequence of states through which M_i passes in producing a sentence F as output corresponds to a proof of F in S_i. Thus, he argues that for any machine M_i proposed as a candidate model of the human mind there will be a Gödel sentence G_i that M_i cannot produce as true. This is the sentence that says of itself that it is not provable by M_i (or not provable in the formal system S_i that M_i instantiates). But Lucas asserts that he, standing outside of M_i, can see that G_i is true. Thus, there is something he can do that M_i is not able to do, and M_i has failed to duplicate his abilities. Since the argument presented is fully general and applies to any machine, Lucas concludes that no machine can duplicate the abilities of the human mind.

Replies to Gödel's Argument. The replies to Lucas's argument have been numerous and diverse. His claim that any machine is the instantiation of a formal system has been questioned since it is not clear just what counts as a machine in Lucas's sense. A more precise Lucas-style argument can be given if the well-defined notion of a Turing machine (qv) is substituted for Lucas's inexact intuitive notion of a machine. The revised claim is that no Turing machine can be an adequate model of the human mind. It is easy to link formal systems with Turing machines since for any given formal system S_i there is a Turing machine T_i whose output consists exactly of the theorems of S_i. For any such Turing machine T_i there will be a Gödel sentence G_i that it cannot prove, a sentence that says of itself that it is not provable by T_i. Although shifting to a claim about Turing machines provides a clear connection with Gödel's results regarding axiomatized formal systems, it leaves unclear the implications concerning actual concrete machines.

A Turing machine is an abstract device exhaustively specified by its machine table, which is a function from ordered pairs of machine state and input to ordered pairs of subsequent machine state and output. Any actual concrete physical device will be an instantiation of many different Turing machines. As Dennett (1978, pp. 256–266) has argued, the limits that apply to a concrete device under one of its Turing-machine descriptions need not restrict absolutely what it can do as a physical machine or under one of its other descriptions. If an actual device X is an instantiation of Turing machine T_i, it cannot under that description prove G_i, the Gödel sentence of T_i, but X

may well do so under one of its other descriptions. Thus, the Turing-machine version of Lucas's claim might well prove inadequate to establish his larger antimechanist conclusion. Nonetheless, if the Turing-machine claim could be established, it might be sufficient to refute the computational theory of mind and undermine AI hopes to duplicate or fully explain human mental abilities since any modern digital computer is in principle equivalent to some Turing machine (leaving aside the fact that the computer as physical device might never produce its total output).

However, the Turing-machine version of Lucas's argument is also open to objection. Benacerraf (1967) has pressed the question of just what it is that Lucas supposes himself able to do in besting an alleged Turing machine duplicate T_i. As Benacerraf notes, it cannot be proving T_i's Gödel sentence G_i as a theorem of S_i, that is, proving G_i using S_i's axioms and inference rules. Lucas is no more able to do this than is T_i. But if the sense of "prove" is left vague and informal, it no longer remains certain that T_i cannot in this informal sense "prove" G_i.

Another major line of criticism has focused on the fact that the Gödel result applies only to consistent formal systems. Thus, in order to establish the truth of G_i for any Turing machine T_i, Lucas must be able to show that T_i or its corresponding formal system S_i is consistent. How can Lucas know this? Given the dialectical manner in which he presents his imagined contest with the mechanist, Lucas (1961) does have a response that he can and does make on this point. Lucas assumes that humans are consistent. Thus, if a candidate machine is inconsistent, it cannot be an adequate model of the human mind. If it is consistent, the Gödel result applies to it, and it can be shown inadequate by the original argument. The assumption that humans are consistent, on which Lucas's response depends, would seem to be falsified by ordinary facts and observations. Human beings are far from perfectly consistent. Lucas has tried to deny the relevance of familiar human inconsistency by distinguishing between different ways of being inconsistent: as the result of malfunctioning misuse of consistent principles and as the result of the proper use of inconsistent principles. However, Lucas's claim that humans are inconsistent only in the former sense and thus consistent in the sense needed for his argument has been found less than convincing and been regarded as one of his argument's weakest links (Benacerraf, 1967). The consistency assumption is especially problematic since it is not independent of the central point at issue: if humans are Turing machines, it follows by Gödel's second theorem that they cannot prove their own consistency (at least in the sense of proving it within the formal systems corresponding to the machines they instantiate). Thus, for Lucas to assume that he can prove his own consistency might seem to beg the question against his mechanist opponent.

Although Lucas's arguments fail to establish his antimechanist conclusions, the relevance of the Gödel results to AI remains an unresolved but intriguing issue of potentially great philosophical importance. Benacerraf has suggested that perhaps the Gödel theorems show that if humans are Turing machines, they cannot know which machines they are (Benacerraf, 1967), and Hofstadter (1979) has conjectured that they may provide a fundamental key to understanding consciousness and the nature of mind.

EPISTEMOLOGY AND AI

The nature of knowledge has been a central question of philosophical investigation since the birth of philosophy. The problem originally posed by Plato of how to distinguish knowledge (episteme) from true opinion (doxa) remains a subject of debate. Although it is generally accepted today that knowledge cannot be analyzed merely as justified true belief (Gettier, 1963), most philosophers do accept the necessity for including some sort of justification condition in the analysis of knowledge. Knowledge differs from mere true belief at least in part in the rational justification the knower has for his belief. Thus, the theory of knowledge has a greater interest in the nature of human reasoning. Its concerns here naturally overlap with those of AI researchers attempting to formalize systems of rational inference for use in cognitive problem-solving programs and knowledge engineering. Philosophical assessments of the prospects for machine rationality have differed widely and tended to reflect the affinities or divergences between competing philosophical views of rationality and the methods employed by AI. On the whole, philosophers of a phenomenological orientation have been less sympathetic and more pessimistic about AI attempts at programming rationality, and philosophers in the logical empiricist tradition have been more optimistic.

Phenomenological Critique

Critique of Early AI. The phenomenological critique of AI's attempt to formalize human reasoning can be best understood through the work of its most prominent proponent, Dreyfus (see PHENOMENOLOGY). In the two editions of his book "What Computers Can't Do," Dreyfus (1979) aimed to expose the weaknesses and shortcomings of a variety of then existing AI programs. His larger intent was to show that these defects were not merely incidental to the programs he considered nor remediable by further use of the basic techniques originally employed. Dreyfus argued that the programs were flawed in principle and failed to take account of essential features of creative human problem solving and relied on fundamentally mistaken underlying assumptions. Dreyfus examined early AI work in game playing, language comprehension, problem solving, and pattern recognition and found that the programs in each area lacked important abilities possessed by humans.

The chess-playing programs Dreyfus considered rely on heuristically guided searches and examine a large number of possible moves. Human expert players are able to zero in on a small number of promising moves as the result of fringe consciousness, the phenomenon by which implicit background understanding focuses attention and transforms the object of attention. In the chess-playing case (see COMPUTER CHESS AND SEARCH) the fringe consciousness embodies the expert player's implicit understanding of global patterns of board organization acquired through experience. In problem-solving (qv) programs Dreyfus focused on human insight and the ability to discriminate the essential from the nonessential features of a task situation. Understanding the deep structure of the problem is a necessary first step in human problem solving. Dreyfus noted that in many AI programs this process was carried out not by the program but by the programmer in setting up the problem task and in the choice of factors from which the program was required to fashion a solution.

A similar point applies to computer learning in which the Piercean process of abduction is performed largely by the programmer. The human ability to learn is as much a matter of figuring out what factors are likely to yield regularities and how they must be categorized in order to reveal them as it is of inductively discovering the connections among those variables. However, in the AI learning programs considered by Dreyfus, such as Winston's (1976) arch-learning program, the range of potentially relevant factors was already greatly constrained and categorized by the programmer. Thus, such learning programs at best simulate one component of the human ability to learn, and perhaps the less interesting component. In the area of language comprehension Dreyfus emphasized the human ability to tolerate a high degree of ambiguity in linguistic expressions and to disambiguate them in context on the basis of extralinguistic information relevant to the communication situation. Moreover, he argued that this human ability did not depend on the use of any underlying fully determinate rules. In contrast, the early language-comprehension programs he considered relied on determinate rules sensitive to only a much narrower range of variables actually present in the text.

Context and Holism. Two major themes run through these specific objections, both of which are inspired by the history of the phenomenological movement and the later work of Wittgenstein. One is the global nature of human understanding and the crucial role played by context in comprehension. Facts are not understood in isolation but always as parts of a large-scale structure of meaning. To grasp the significance of any given event, problem, or assertion, one must be able to appreciate its place within a larger context of meanings. Using a notion employed by Husserl (1931), the founder of the phenomenological movement, every object and event is perceived within an "outer horizon." It is the outer horizon that, although not itself explicitly perceived, structures and organizes that of which one is aware. In chess it is the human player's overall understanding of the game or board position that implicitly provides the outer horizon within which the player perceives a given piece or move.

The second major theme is the claim that the implicit organizing background cannot be made explicit. In particular, it cannot be articulated by a system of relations between context-free elements or as an exhaustive set of determinate rules. This view derives not from the work of Husserl but from that of the later phenomenologists Heidegger (1962) and Merleau-Ponty (1962) as well as Wittgenstein's *Philosophical Investigations* (1953). Husserl, who set out to make the organizing framework of meaning explicit, found the project incompletable as the outer horizon of meaning always receded at his approach. Heidegger went further and argued that Husserl had failed to complete his program, not because he had undertaken an enormous or infinite task, but because the very conception of the project was mistaken. Heidegger stressed that the surrounding context of meaning did not consist just of further beliefs, expectations, and rules. Rather, it included the context of social and cultural practices, physical artifacts, tools, and equipment as well as the physical, biological, and historical situation within which human beings live, perceive, and use language. According to Heidegger, it is the actual situations within which human beings live that provide the background for the structure of human meaning, and these situations are not to be confused with a set of beliefs about one's situation or an internalized representation of the situation. It is the situations themselves that provide the boundaries, the limits, and the organizing structure for meaningful behavior. On this view it is simply mistaken to suppose that all of this structure must somehow be internalized in the mind of the agent in order for that person's action to fit within and derive its significance from the larger context.

This second theme is related as well to Wittgenstein's (1953) claim that any attempt to analyze meaningful behavior as acting in accordance with a rule must always require sooner or later the existence of a meaning-giving context that is not itself to be explicated in terms of rule following. Wittgenstein argued that a behavior could be counted as following a given rule only relative to a context. The physical actions of pointing and uttering a sound count as actions of demonstrative reference and naming only relative to a social context that connects these behaviors with a variety of others. And using a word according to a rule to refer on each occasion to the same sort of thing can only make sense relative to a context that determines what is to count as the same kind of thing. If this context were itself to be analyzed in terms of rule following, it would, in turn, presuppose yet a further context within which the social behaviors would count as rule following. If an infinite and vicious regress is to be avoided, at some point there must be a meaning giving social context that is not itself a matter of following rules.

Critique of More Recent AI

It is these two major claims about the global role of context and the impossibility of making the context fully explicit as a system of beliefs or rules that constitute the basis for the continuing phenomenological critique of AI. Given the rapidly changing nature of AI research, Dreyfus's criticisms of early AI programs would be only of historical interest. Indeed, more recent work in AI has sought to remedy many of the defects Dreyfus noted. Chess-playing programs employ descriptions of larger organizational patterns, and language-comprehension programs include a large store of information about the nonlinguistic world. AI programmers have become especially aware of the need to include a great deal of background information about ordinary commonsense matters in their programs, as in Minsky's (1975) Frames (qv) or Schank's Scripts (qv) (Schank and Abelson, 1977). But phenomenological critics like Dreyfus argue that although these more recent attempts are improvements over early AI programs, they are nonetheless certain to fall short of achieving genuine intelligence or understanding. These critics see the attempt to program the background context of everyday knowledge as a repetition of Husserl's unsuccessful program of phenomenology and fated to fail for the same reasons.

Current AI researchers could be said to have responded to one of the two themes of the phenomenological critique (the importance of context) but to have not accepted the other theme: the claim that the global context should not be thought of as a structure of beliefs, rules, or representations but rather as an actual situation or form of life within which the understander lives. To accept this second claim would be to abandon the project of AI, at least in anything like its current form, and so it is not likely to be acknowledged as was the role of context. As the phenomenological critics admit, the claim that meaning and understanding presuppose a nonrepresentational context is not the sort of claim that can be proved by demonstrative argument. Its force derives rather from an overall picture of meaningful human behavior. In the absence of conclusive argument, AI researchers are not likely to abandon their own competing picture, which treats the background or context of meaning as capable of explicit and determinate formalization. The conflict between AI and its phenomenological critics will have to be settled on the basis of AI's subsequent success or failure rather than on the basis of *a priori* arguments.

Logical Empiricism and AI

Many of the problems faced by AI were also addressed by the philosophical movement known as logical positivism and its successor logical empiricism (Ayer, 1959). Since the methodological assumptions of the positivists were much closer to those of present-day workers in AI than were those of the phenomenologists, philosophers sympathetic to the positivist program are more likely than are phenomenologists to be optimistic about the prospects of AI. The philosopher of science, Glymour (1985), has argued that AI, or at least those areas of AI concerned with machine learning, should be viewed as continuous with the logical empiricist philosophy of science in their goals and approach despite their minimal direct historical connection. The positivist and logical empiricist programs were aimed at a rational reconstruction of scientific method. The result was intended not only to be descriptive in rendering explicit the methods and reasoning that underlay the success of modern science but also to provide an idealized account of scientific method, which might diverge from and improve on some of the practices of actual scientists. Glymour (1985) has pointed out that the goals of the positivist program were similar in many respects to current work in AI. The positivists aimed to formulate precise rules to specify such central scientific notions as the empirical or observational content of a theory, the degree of confirmation of a hypothesis by a body of evidence, and the explanation of an event by the appeal to scientific laws. In each case the positivists demanded a high degree of specificity in any rules that were to count as solutions to these or other problems in their program.

As Glymour has stressed, it is this demand for specificity as much as the problems addressed that marks the similarity between logical positivism and AI. The AI demand for precise and fully determinate rules, which has drawn criticism from phenomenologists, is what most closely links AI with positivism. The positivist's demand grew out of their epistemological commitment to a strong form of foundationalism; semantic properties were attributed only to a limited class of statements concerning the simple immediate objects of sense experience, sense data. All other meaningful statements were to be constructed in terms of logical relations defined over sense-data statements. In consequence, the method allowed for virtually no undefined semantic relations. One could not take as understood such notions as being a positive instance of a hypothesis or being an observation consequence of a theory. All such relations had to be spelled out by precise and largely syntactic rules. Even ordinary commonsense notions such as being a physical object or remaining rigid in motion had to be defined precisely by reference to the restricted class of sense-data statements. AI's demand for specificity has a different source. AI rules must be computable if they are to be implemented, and they must not rely on undefined semantic notions since the machine has no prior knowledge of what has not been programmed into it. Thus, Glymour argues, the different methodological constraints of AI and logical positivism impose a common demand for spelling out crucial semantic notions by specific precise syntactic rules. The formal tools employed also differ since logical positivists relied primarily on the predicate calculus, but the goal of formalization remains the same.

Logical Empiricism and Machine Learning. The fact that logical positivism is generally regarded as having failed to achieve its goals, need not, Glymour contends, reflect unfavorably on AI. The weakness in the positivistic program lay in its commitment to a sense-data foundationalism, which is not shared by AI. One can hope that positivist goals with respect to such problems as formalizing the process of hypothesis confirmation will still be solved by AI. Glymour argues that greater communication between those working on machine learning and those who wish to continue the logical empiricist program would be mutually beneficial. He notes that the AI attempt by Shapiro (1983) to model a logic of confirmation on Popper's logic of scientific discovery (1959) makes clear just what needs to be done to employ Popper's method of conjecture and refutation. In particular, machine implementation requires specific rules to determine which hypothesis to blame or refute when a negative result is obtained with respect to the prediction entailed by a conjunction of hypotheses. Without solving the problem of assessing blame, the general method cannot be programmed. In the absence of the demands for specificity imposed by machine implementation, the importance of the problem can be overlooked in philosophical discussion. Conversely, as the AI application of Popper's method illustrates, AI has much to gain from research done in the philosophy of science on topics that have naturally and independently arisen in AI.

OTHER AREAS OF PHILOSOPHY

Although epistemology and the philosophy of mind are the two subfields of philosophy with the most direct connection to AI, other areas such as metaphysics, the philosophy of action, and the philosophy of language also have relevance to AI. As McCarthy and Hayes (1969) have noted, this is especially true when one wishes to program general understanding, which requires building into the program a great deal of background knowledge about such common but metaphysically central notions as probability, causality, action, intention, and personhood. Such concepts have long been the subjects of intense philosophical investigation within diverse philosophical traditions and with varying degrees of formal rigor. Although no general philosophical consensus has developed on most of these issues, progress has been made and many promising suggestions, which might tempt uninformed workers in AI, have been explored by philosophers and found unacceptable. Among the many particular topics on which the philosophical literature might be of interest to AI researchers would be causation (see REASONING, CAUSAL) (Sosa, 1975), counterfactuals (Lewis, 1973), conditionals (Harper, 1980), practical reasoning (Jeffrey, 1965), intentional action (Goldman, 1970), the structure of events (Bennett, 1988), speech acts (qv) (Searle, 1969), and conversational implications (Grice, 1975).

BIBLIOGRAPHY

A. J. Ayer, ed., *Logical Positivism*, Macmillan, New York, 1959.

W. Bechtel, "Connectionism and the Philosophy of Mind," *South. J. Philos.* supplement 17–41 (1987).

P. Benacerraf, "God, the Devil, and Gödel," *Monist* 51, 9–32 (1967).

J. Bennett, *Events and their Names*, Hackett, Indianapolis, Ind., 1988.

N. Block, "Troubles with Functionalism," in C. W. Savage, ed., *Perception and Cognition, Issues in the Foundations of Psychology, Minnesota Studies in the Philosophy of Science*, Vol. 9, University of Minnesota Press, Minneapolis, Minn., 1978, pp. 261–325.

N. Block, "What is Functionalism?" in N. Block, ed., *Readings in the Philosophy of Psychology*, Vol. 1, Harvard University Press, Cambridge, Mass., 1980, pp. 171–184.

N. Block, "Psychologism and Behaviorism," *Philos. Rev.* 90, 5–43 (1981).

N. Block, "Advertisement for a Semantics for Psychology," in *Midwest Studies in Philosophy*, Vol. 10, University of Minnesota Press, Minneapolis, Minn., 1986.

P. Churchland, *Neurophilosophy*, MIT Press, Cambridge, Mass., 1986.

P. M. Churchland and P. S. Churchland, "Functionalism, Qualia, and Intentionality," *Philos. Top.* 12, 121–145 (1981).

R. Cummins, *Meaning and Mental Representation*, MIT Press, Cambridge, Mass., 1989.

D. C. Dennett, "Why the Law of Effect Won't Go Away," *J. Theor. Soc. Behav.* 2, 169–187 (1975); reprinted in Dennett, 1978.

D. C. Dennett, *Brainstorms*, MIT Press, Cambridge, Mass., 1978.

D. C. Dennett, *The Intentional Stance*, MIT Press, Cambridge, Mass., 1987.

F. Dretske, *Knowledge and the Flow of Information*, MIT Press, Cambridge, Mass., 1981.

H. Dreyfus, *What Computers Can't Do*, 2nd ed., Harper & Row, New York, 1979.

J. Fodor, *Psychological Explanation*, Random House, New York, 1968.

J. Fodor, "Methodological Solipsism Considered as a Research Strategy for Cognitive Science," *Behav. Brain Sci.* 3, 63–109 (1980).

J. Fodor, *Psychosemantics*, MIT Press, Cambridge, Mass., 1987.

J. Fodor and Z. Pylyshyn, "Connectionism and Cognitive Architecture: A Critical Analysis," *Cognition* 28, 2–71 (1988).

E. Gettier, "Is Justified True Belief Knowledge," *Analysis* 23, 121–123 (1963).

C. Glymour, "Android Epistemology: Reflections on Artificial Intelligence and the Philosophy of Science," paper presented at Pacific Division Meeting of the American Philosophical Association, San Francisco, Calif., Mar. 1985.

Goldman, *A Theory of Human Action*, Prentice-Hall, Englewood Cliffs, N.J., 1970.

H. P. Grice, "Logic and Conversation," in D. Davidson and G. Harman, eds., *The Logic of Grammar*, Dickenson, Encino, Calif., pp. 64–74, 1975.

K. Gunderson, "The Imitation Game," *Mind* 73, 234–245 (1964).

W. Harper, *Ifs: Conditionals, Belief, Decision, Chance and Time*, Reidel, Dordrecht, The Netherlands, 1980.

J. Haugeland, *AI, The Very Idea*, MIT Press, Cambridge, Mass., 1985.

M. H. Heidegger, in J. Macquarrie and E. Robinson, eds., *Being and Time*, p. 45; reprinted in M. Merleau-Ponty, *Phenomenology of Perception*, Routledge and Kegan Paul, London, 1962.

D. Hofstadter, *Gödel, Escher, Bach: An Eternal Golden Braid*, Basic Books, New York, 1979.

E. Husserl, *Ideas General Introduction to Pure Phenomenology*, Macmillan, New York, 1931.

D. Jeffrey, *The Logic of Decision*, McGraw-Hill, New York, 1965.

D. Lewis, "Psychophysical and Theoretical Identification," *Austral. J. Philos.* 50, 249–258 (1972).

D. Lewis, *Counterfactuals*, Harvard University Press, Cambridge, Mass., 1973.

J. Locke, *An Essay Concerning Human Understanding*, edition of A. Fraser, Dover, New York, 1959.

J. R. Lucas, "Minds, Machines and Gödel," *Philosophy* 36, 112–127 (1961).

J. McCarthy and P. J. Hayes, "Some Philosophical Problems from the Standpoint of Artificial Intelligence," in B. Meltzer and D. Michie, eds., *Mach. Intell.*, Vol. 4, Halstead, New York, 1969, pp. 463–502.

M. Merleau-Ponty, *Phenomenology of Perception*, Routledge and Kegan Paul, London, 1962.

R. Millikan, *Language, Thought and Other Biological Categories*, MIT Press, Cambridge, Mass., 1984.

M. Minsky, "A Framework for Representing Knowledge," Memo 306, MIT Artificial Intelligence Laboratory, Cambridge, Mass., excerpts published in P. H. Winston, ed., *The Psychology of Computer Vision*, McGraw-Hill, New York, 1975, pp. 211–277.

T. Nagel, "What Is It Like to Be a Bat?" *Philos. Rev.* **83,** 435–450 (1974).

T. Nagel, *The View from Nowhere,* Oxford University Press, New York, 1986.

K. R. Popper, *The Logic of Scientific Discovery,* Hutchinson, London, 1959.

H. Putnam, "The Nature of Mental States," in W. H. Capitan and D. D. Merrill, eds., *Art, Mind, and Religion,* University of Pittsburgh Press, Pittsburgh, Pa., 1967, pp. 37–48.

W. Ramsey, S. Stich, and J. Garon, "Connectionism, Eliminativism, and the Future of Folk Psychology," in J. Tomberlin, ed., *Philosophical Perspectives 4: Action Theory and the Philosophy of Mind,* Ridgeview Publishing, Atascadero, Calif., 1990.

R. Schank and R. Abelson, *Scripts, Plans, Goals and Understanding,* Lawrence Erlbaum, Hillsdale, N.J., 1977.

M. Scriven, "The Mechanical Concept of Mind," *Mind* **62,** 230–240 (1953).

J. Searle, *Speech Acts,* Cambridge University Press, Cambridge, 1969.

J. Searle, "Minds, Brains and Programs," *Behav. Brain Sci.* **3,** 417–457 (1980).

J. Searle, "Consciousness, Explanatory Inversion, and Cognitive Science," *Behav. Brain Sci.* **13,** 585–642 (1990).

E. Shapiro, *Algorithmic Program Debugging,* MIT Press, Cambridge, Mass., 1983.

J. J. C. Smart, "Sensations are Brain Processes," *Philos. Rev.* **68,** 141–156 (1959).

P. Smolensky, "On the Proper Treatment of Connectionism," *Behav. Brain Sci.* **11,** 1–74 (1988).

E. Sosa, *Causation and Conditionals,* Oxford University Press, London, 1975.

S. Stich, "Dennett on Intentional Systems," *Philos. Top.* **12,** 39–62 (1981).

A. Turing, "Computing Machinery and Intelligence," *Mind* **59,** 433–460 (1950).

R. Van Gulick, "A Functionalist Plea for Self-Consciousness," *Philos. Rev.* **97,** 149–188 (1988).

P. Winston and staff of MIT AI Laboratory, Proposal to ARPA, MIT AI Memo 336, Cambridge, Mass., 1976.

L. Wittgenstein, *Philosophical Investigations,* Blackwell, Oxford, 1953.

General References

A. R. Anderson, *Minds and Machines,* Prentice-Hall, Englewood Cliffs, N.J., 1964 (an anthology of important articles from the early period of the mind–machine debate).

P. M. Churchland, *Matter and Consciousness: A Contemporary Introduction to the Philosophy of Mind,* MIT Press, Cambridge, Mass., 1984.

H. Dreyfus, ed., *Husserl, Intentionality and Cognitive Science,* MIT Press, Cambridge, Mass., 1982 (a collection of essays bringing the phenomenological perspective to bear on work in AI and cognitive science).

C. Glymour, *Theory and Evidence,* Princeton University Press, Princeton, N.J., 1980 (a detailed account of confirmation).

J. Haugeland, *Mind Design Philosophy, Psychology, and Artificial Intelligence,* MIT Press, Cambridge, Mass., 1982 (an excellent anthology of recent philosophical and theoretical work on AI).

J. Lucas, *The Freedom of the Will,* Oxford University Press, Oxford, 1970 (includes further discussion of the Gödel argument with bibliography).

A. Newell, "Intellectual Issues in the History of Artificial Intelligence," in F. Machlup and U. Mansfield, eds., *The Study of Information Interdisciplinary Messages,* John Wiley and Sons, Inc., New York, 1983, pp. 187–228.

F. Suppe, ed., *The Structure of Scientific Theories,* 2nd ed., University of Illinois Press, Urbana, Ill., 1979 (includes a critical introduction that provides an overview of recent work in the philosophy of science that would be of relevance to AI).

R. Van Gulick
Syracuse University

PHRAN AND PHRED

A natural-language analyzer and a natural-language generator that have been developed around 1980 and used at the University of California at Berkeley in Robert Wilensky's research group, these two programs have served as the front-end and back-end, respectively, of planning systems like PAM (qv) and UC. PHRAN was written by Yigal Arens, and PHRED was written by Steve Upstill and Paul Jacobs (see R. Wilensky, *Planning and Understanding,* Addison-Wesley, Reading Mass., 1983, and F. Rose, *Into the Heart of the Mind,* Harper & Row, New York, 1984, pp. 98–115).

K. S. Arora
SUNY at Buffalo

PHYSICS, NAIVE

Naive physics is the body of knowledge that people have about the surrounding physical world. The main enterprises of naive physics are explaining, describing, and predicting changes in the physical world. There is an important distinction between classic physics and naive physics. Classical physics is based on the presupposition that there is a shared unstated common sense prephysical knowledge rooted in experience. Naive physics is this prephysical knowledge rooted in experience. It is important to notice that in classical physics, concepts such as state, law, cause equilibrium, oscillation, momentum, feedback, etc are qualitative in nature. However, they have been embedded in a complex framework established by the mathematics of real numbers and differential equations. The relationship between qualitative (commonsense) models and mathematical models can be shown as in Figure 1. Qualitative simulation captures less detail and, therefore, may produce partial behavioral descriptions. Also, the quantitative precision of these descriptions is reduced whereas crucial distinctions are retained.

A research directed at understanding and modeling naive physics reasoning concentrates mainly on deriving the qualitative concepts used in naive physics from formal models and identifying the core knowledge underlying physical intuition (Hobbs and Moore, 1985). The main conjectures guiding the research are that naive physics knowledge, to a large degree, can be derived from commonsense observation and that quantitative laws can be mapped to qualitative ones.

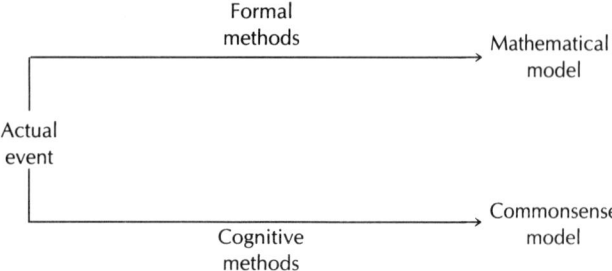

Figure 1. Relationship between commonsense and mathematical models.

Reasoning about physical changes is the main motivation behind acquiring naive physics knowledge. Because by their nature, these changes involve physical (dynamic) systems that undergo some transformation over time, they can be viewed from two perspectives: a device-centered perspective and a process-centered perspective. Each perspective generates its own conceptual vocabulary and its own set of relations between concepts. A brief review of current research on the representation of naive physics knowledge from the above two perspectives is given in this article. In addition, a brief discussion on the issue of the organization of knowledge in mental models and their cognitive validity will follow. A detailed state-of-the-art account of the research on naive physics can be found in recently edited collections of papers (Bobrow and Hayes, 1984; Gentner and Stevens, 1983; Hayes, 1985).

In the device-centered ontology developed by De Kleer and Brown (1983, 1984), the function of a dynamic system is derived from its structure (see PHYSICS, QUALITATIVE). However, it is of crucial importance that in the knowledge representation used to model the reasoning, the function must not be encoded in the structure. The main concern here is the general form of the physical law and the calculi for deriving the inferences from this law. Causality gets central treatment: how the systems achieve their behavior is as important as what the behavior is. Consequently, in this ontology the world is viewed as a complex machine with interacting components. The laws for a component of a dynamic system do not influence other parts. Classwide assumptions are made for the generic systems distinguishing them from idiosyncratic assumptions for a particular system. The approach to modeling is reductionist, and the types of physical constituents considered are materials, components, and conduits. Graph topology is used for modeling devices with nodes as components and edges as conduits. The laws in the system must be time invariant. Laws describing behavior over time require explicit integrals in their formulation. Relations are stated as confluences that are qualitative differential equations, where time is made discrete by states, and the physical parameter values are made discrete by a mapping to quantity space. The states determine the operating range of the confluences. The program ENVISION, which models some aspects of the theory, takes as input a set of components and their allowable paths of interaction, an input signal to the system, and a set of boundary conditions that constrain the system. Because qualitativeness may sometimes underdetermine behavior, the output of the program consists of a set of possible behaviors of the system and not a single unique solution.

The qualitative process theory developed by Forbus (1983, 1984) is a process-centered ontology and is not equational in nature. The main enterprise of the theory is reasoning about processes, their effects, and their limits. Quantity space separates magnitudes of equations from their signs: $[-1, 0, 1]$. Here, changes in physical situation perceived as causal due to one's interpretation of them are corresponding either to direct changes caused by processes or propagation of those direct effects through functional dependencies. Also histories, which consist of episodes, are used as descriptions of objects that are extended through time but are always spatially bound.

Kuipers (1984) makes the jump from differential equations directly to qualitative constraints among state variables of a system (structural description → behavioral description → functional description). The components in this framework are only state variables, and the connections are the constraints. This simulation assumes that causality is identical to value propagation with constraints.

Gentner (1983) observes that the analogical models used in science can be characterized as structure mapping between complex systems. Such an analogy conveys that similar relational systems hold within two different domains. The predicates of the base domain (the known domain), particularly the relations that hold among the objects, can be applied in the target domain. Thus a structure-mapping analogy asserts that identical operations and relationships hold among nonidentical things. The relational structure is preserved but not the objects.

It seems that naive physics reasoning has two characteristics that make its scientific inquiry very hard: size (very large amounts of knowledge are involved) and specialized structures (the knowledge structures that are apparently used by humans for naive physics reasoning are a product of many years of experience interacting with the physical world and hence are compiled to a great extent). This makes it difficult to extract their content.

Naive physics is not bad physics. It is different from classical physics both in scope and in power, and its value is measured by its practical validity. For example, consider an everyday life event in which soup is too hot to eat and the time required for the soup to reach a comfortable temperature must be estimated. Classical physics, given the current knowledge in fluid mechanics and transport processes and the current computer technology, is unable to give a meaningful answer within the natural time constraints imposed by the situation. However, naive physics has a practical solution and almost anyone can use common sense to figure out what to do.

Undoubtedly, naive physics knowledge about the dynamic and the static nature of the everyday physical world is vital to any agent who plans to act successfully. Furthermore, understanding the way this knowledge is acquired and modified through use can shed light on the nature of human information processing.

BIBLIOGRAPHY

D. G. Bobrow and P. J. Hayes, eds., *Artif. Intell.* 24(1–3) (1984).

J. de Kleer and J. S. Brown, "Assumptions and Ambiguities in Mechanistic Mental Models," in Gentner and Stevens, 1983, pp. 155–190.

J. de Kleer and J. S. Brown "A Qualitative Physics Based on Confluences," in Bobrow and Hayes, 1984, pp. 7–83.

K. D. Forbus, "Qualitative Reasoning about Space and Motion," in Gentner and Stevens, 1983, pp. 53–73.

K. D. Forbus, "Qualitative Process Theory," in Bobrow and Hayes, 1984, pp. 87–168.

D. Gentner, "Flowing Waters or Teaming Crowds: Mental Models of Electricity," in Gentner and Stevens, 1983, pp. 99–129.

D. Gentner and A. L. Stevens, eds., *Mental Models,* Lawrence Erlbaum, Hillsdale, N.J., 1983.

P. Hayes, "The Naive Physics Manifesto," in Hobbs and Moore, 1985, pp. 1–36.

J. R. Hobbs and R. C. Moore, eds., *Formal Theories of the Commonsense World,* Ablex, Norwood, N.J., 1985.

B. Kuipers, "Commonsense Reasoning about Causality: Deriving Behavior from Structure," in Bobrow and Hayes, 1984, pp. 169–203.

S. L. HARDT
Bellcore

PHYSICS, QUALITATIVE

Qualitative physics, like conventional physics, provides an account of behavior in the physical world. The vision of qualitative physics is to provide, in conjunction with conventional physics, a broad integrated and formal account of behavior—an account rich enough to enable intelligent systems to perform tasks such as design, diagnosis, analysis, explanation and simulation (the emphasis of this article). However, unlike conventional physics, qualitative physics predicts and explains behavior in qualitative terms.

The behavior of a physical system can be described by the exact quantitative values of its variables (forces, velocities, positions, pressures, etc) at each time instant. Such a description, although complete, fails to provide much insight into how the system functions. The insightful concepts and distinctions are usually qualitative, but they are embedded within the much more complex framework established by continuous real-valued variables and differential equations. Qualitative physics is an alternative physics in which these concepts are defined within a far simpler, but nevertheless formal, symbolic qualitative basis.

It is important to note that qualitative physics yields qualitative descriptions of behavior based on qualitative descriptions of the physical situation and physical laws. The key contribution that makes qualitative physics useful and possible is that moving to the qualitative level preserves many of the important behavioral distinctions. For example, important concepts and distinctions underlying behavior include state, cause, law, equilibrium, oscillation, momentum, quasistatic approximation, contact force, and feedback. These terms are qualitative and can be intuitively understood.

Qualitative physics is, perhaps more than anything, a long-term research program. A great deal of further research is required before qualitative physics can even come close to explaining the range of physical phenomena accounted for by conventional physics. Much of the research on qualitative physics recapitulates fundamental physical and mathematical investigations that took place centuries ago. Driven by the necessity to formalize common sense and enabled by the idea of computation and the modeling techniques of artificial intelligence, these new theories characterize what these investigations took for granted.

Qualitative physics is an active area of artificial intelligence research. Although this research is unified in its goal to account for physical behavior qualitatively, this goal is addressed with a great deal of technical, notational and methodological diversity. For conciseness this article adopts the point of view of de Kleer and Brown (1984) and explains the alternative proposals in its terms.

QUANTITATIVE VS QUALITATIVE

Figure 1 illustrates the approach of qualitative physics contrasted with conventional physics. Both start by modeling physical situation, both end with a qualitative commonsense description of the behavior. The first step in the conventional approach is to formulate and solve the differential equations to obtain a solution. The second step is to interpret this solution to obtain a commonsense description of the behavior. The qualitative analysis begins by formulating qualitative differential equations and then solves these. The result is a similar commonsense description of the behavior that is obtained more simply, and a causal explanation for that behavior.

Unlike quantitative variables, qualitative variables can only take on one of a small number of values. Each qualitative value corresponds to some (disjoint) interval on the real number line. *Landmark values* demarcate the boundaries between qualitatively distinguishable intervals. The most common landmark is zero, in which case the three important qualitative values are positive, negative, and zero or, for a derivative, whether a quantity is increasing, decreasing, or constant. This simple, but most important, quantity space with respect to the landmark zero consists of only three values: $+$, $-$, and 0.

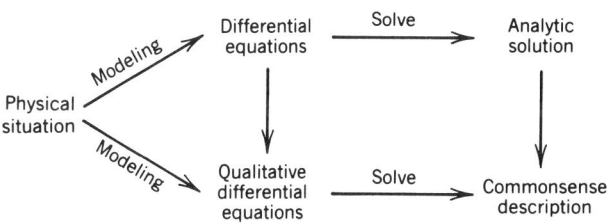

Figure 1. Qualitative vs quantitative.

Why Do Qualitative Reasoning?

The motivations for developing a qualitative physics stem from outstanding problems in psychology, education, artificial intelligence, and physics. Qualitative physics research wants to identify the core knowledge that underlies physical intuition. Humans appear to use a qualitative causal calculus in reasoning about the behavior of their physical environment. Judging from the kinds of explanations humans give, this calculus is quite different from the classic physics taught in classrooms. This raises questions as to what this (naive) physics is like and how it helps with reasoning about the physical world.

In classic physics, the crucial distinctions for characterizing physical change are defined within a nonmechanistic framework, and thus they are difficult to ground in the commonsense knowledge derived from interaction with the world. Qualitative physics provides an alternative and simpler way of arriving at the same conceptions and distinctions and thus provides a simpler pedagogical basis for educating students about physical mechanisms.

Artificial intelligence and (especially) its subfield of expert systems are producing very sophisticated computer programs capable of performing tasks that require extensive human expertise. A commonly recognized failing of such systems is their extremely narrow range of expertise and their inability to recognize when a problem posed to them is outside this range of expertise. In fact, expert systems usually cannot solve simpler versions of the problems they are designed to solve. The missing common sense can be supplied, in part, by qualitative reasoning. Some of the advantages of qualitative reasoning are described below.

- *It Identifies All Modes of System Functioning.* The qualitative analysis of a system can identify all its possible behaviors. This is crucial in many applications because it highlights undesirable modes to be avoided and this information is almost impossible to obtain with a conventional numerical simulation.
- *It Functions with Incomplete Models.* A qualitative physics analysis does not require a detailed quantitative model of the system's components—information that may not be readily available.
- *It Functions with Incomplete Data.* Similarly, a qualitative analysis requires only a qualitative description of the initial conditions and system inputs (if any).
- *It Is More Efficient.* Qualitative analysis can be implemented with simple constraint satisfaction that (unless there are a large number of qualitative ambiguities) is much more efficient than symbolic equation manipulation or numerical simulation.
- *It Provides Explanations.* Qualitative analysis provides direct, often causal, explanations for its predictions; this information can be conveyed to a user or can be examined by programs to determine what could cause the undesirable behavior (eg, in design and diagnosis tasks).
- *It Simplifies Subsequent Quantitative Analysis.* Qualitative analysis helps identify which component's function is critical and which is secondary; this advice can then be used to guide the selection of quantitative models for components. Also, the solutions to the qualitative equations indicate the regions within which the quantitative solutions are to be found.

Relationship to Psychology and Physics

Running throughout qualitative physics is a fundamental tension concerning whether the goal is to model the world or human behavior. The basic question concerns what gold standard(s) the predictions of a qualitative physics theory are to be judged by. Here are some of the points of view (note that, no qualitative physics solely adopts one of these views) (Weld and de Kleer, 1990).

Predictions of Physics. The goal is to model the world as it is characterized (and idealized) by physics. Here, qualitative physics piggybacks on the development of modern science (eg, by comparing the qualitative predictions with the "gold standard" quantitative predictions). Because qualitative physics uses a coarser granularity, this comparison raises many difficulties that have been discussed at length (Kuipers, 1986; Struss, 1989).

Observations of human performance are used as guidance; there is no interest in empirical verification or modeling human foibles. This approach seeks to understand the physical common sense of an ideal expert; this article tends toward this view.

Physical Predictions. There are many common aspects of the physical world for which physics does not have a very good model. For example, consider the act of throwing a ball onto a carpet—try to find a physics text that explains how the ball stops bouncing and starts rolling. Qualitative physics can help handle such nonideal real-world situations by piecing together models of different fragments of the situation that may use different levels of granularity and that make different approximations.

Modeling Human Thinking. The goal of these approaches is to develop languages that allow the expression of a variety of physical theories and the reasoning of experts and neophytes to be modeled with these theories. For example, examples of Newtonian, Aristotelian, and Impetus theories of mechanics have been used to demonstrate the power of qualitative process theory (Forbus, 1984). Another example of the psychological approach is one that bases its conclusions on protocols taken from human subjects (Collins and Gentner, 1983).

Composability

A goal of qualitative physics is to draw inferences about composite device solely from laws governing the behaviors of their parts. This requires that the models used in qualitative physics be composable. Given a description of a device in terms of models of its constituents, the composition of component models must accurately characterize the composite device. This requirement is crucial for most applications. For example, if the designer of a troubleshooting program erroneously introduces assumptions of the function of a device into its constituent components, then the program will miss faults and symptoms or incorrectly identify components as being faulted.

This view raises a difficult question: where do the laws and the descriptions of the device being studied come from? Unless some conditions are placed on the laws and the descriptions, the inferences that can be made may be (implicitly) preencoded in the structural description or the component model library.

The no-function-in-structure principle is central: the laws of the parts of the device may not presume the functioning of the whole. Take as a simple example a light switch. The model of a switch that states, "if the switch is off, no current flows; and if the switch is on, current flows," violates the no-function-in-structure principle. Although this model correctly describes the behavior of the switches in some offices, it is false because there are many closed switches through which current does not necessarily flow (such as two switches in series). Current flows in the switch only if it is closed and there is a potential for current flow.

Without this principle, qualitative physics would be an architecture for building handcrafted (and thus *ad hoc*) theories for specific devices and situations. It would provide no systematic way of ensuring that a particular class of laws did not already have built into them the answers to the questions that the laws were intended to answer. Therefore, there would be no guarantee that the same models would accurately describe the behavior the same constituents in new systems.

QUALITATIVE PHYSICS ANALYSIS

Structure

To do a qualitative physics analysis a program must be provided with a description of the physical situation about which it must draw inferences. There are three main approaches: constraint based, component based, and process based.

The constraint-based approach (Kuipers, 1984) describes the physical situation directly in terms of a set of variables and constraints relating those variables. For example, Figure 2 presents the constraint structure description for a simple heat-flow system. The description contains three constraints: a qualitative adder, a qualitative proportionality, and a qualitative differential. These constraints relate three variables: T the temperature of the material, T_s the temperature of the source of heat, ΔT the temperature difference, and inflow the resulting rate of heat flow into the material.

The process-based approach (Forbus, 1984) describes the physical situation in terms of the physical processes that are potentially present. Intuitively, a process is something that causes changes in objects over time. For example, flowing, bending, heating, cooling, stretching, compressing, and boiling are all processes in qualitative process theory.

The component-based approach (de Kleer and Brown, 1984; Williams, 1984a; Weld, 1986) is reductionist: the

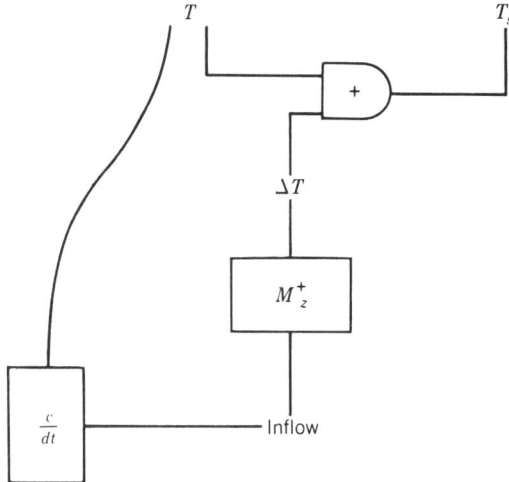

Figure 2. A qualitative constraint structure.

behavior of a physical structure is accounted for by the behaviors of its physical constituents. The situation has been described in terms of the organic molecules present (Weld, 1986). Other authors distinguish three kinds of constituents: materials, components, and conduits (de Kleer and Brown, 1984; Williams, 1984a). Physical behavior is accomplished by operating on and transporting materials such as water, air, electrons, etc. The components are constituents that can change the form and characteristics of material. Conduits are simple constituents that transport material from one component to another and cannot change any aspect of the material within them. Some examples of conduits are pipes, wires, and cables. The physical structure of a device can be represented by a topology in which nodes represent components and edges represent conduits. Figure 3a illustrates the device topology of the pressure regulator diagramed in Figure 3b. In this device topology, the conduits IN and OUT transport material of type fluid and conduit FP transports material of type force. The control on valve VV adjusts the area available for flow, and SNS senses the output pressure to control the value inversely (so that if pressure rises, area available for flow decreases).

Each modeling approach has its advantages and disadvantages. The constraint-based approach makes it possible to sidestep the modeling constituents at the cost of ignoring the no-function-in-structure principle. The process-based approach is extremely general, including the capability for creating and destroying constituents as well as rearranging objects. This capability introduces a large amount of inefficiency, particularly for systems with large numbers of interconnections (eg, electrical and fluid circuits). The component-based approach is efficient, more easily obeys no-function-in-structure, and is ideally suited for systems with a fixed interconnect topology.

The naive physics approach (Hayes, 1979) does not really fit into the classifications of this article. It advocates the large-scale axiomatizations of commonsense domains in predicate calculus. Although the spirit of this proposal guides much of the research, most qualitative

1152   PHYSICS, QUALITATIVE

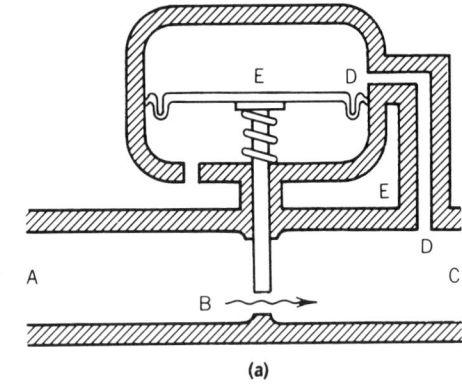

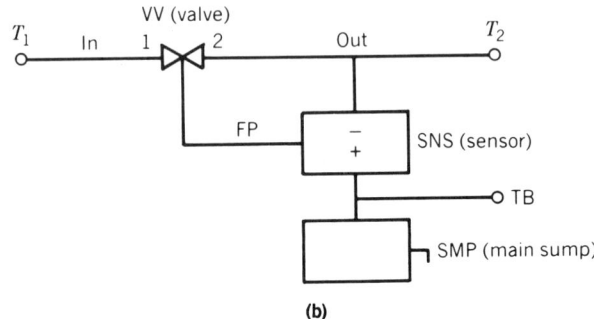

Figure 3. Pressure regulator.

Table 1. $[X] + [Y]$

[Y]	[X]		
	−	0	+
−	−	−	
0	−	0	+
+		+	+

physics research deviates from its suggestions. A central focus of qualitative physics is the study of behaviors of systems over time and, in particular, the determination of function from structure, issues about which Hayes (1979) is unconcerned. Nevertheless, the goal of formalizing much of the commonsense world is central to the Cyc project (Lenat and Guha, 1990).

Qualitative Arithmetic with +, −, and 0

The qualitative value of x is denoted $[x]$; $[x] = +$ if and only if $x > 0$, $[x] = 0$ if and only if $x = 0$, and $[x] = −$ if and only if $x < 0$. Addition and multiplication are defined in a straightforward manner (Tables 1 and 2). Note that although $[xy] = [x][y]$, $[x] + [y]$ is not always defined. This +, 0, − value set is surprisingly versatile. For example, to distinguish x with respect to landmark value a, a new variable is defined $y = x − a$. Then $[y] = +$ corresponds to $x > a$, $[y] = 0$ corresponds to $x = a$, and $[y] = −$ corresponds to $x < a$.

Qualitative Derivatives

In the formalism "x is increasing" is $\left[\dfrac{dx}{dt}\right] = +$. This notation tends to be cumbersome both for typography and computer input–output. Thus ∂x is used as an abbreviation for $\left[\dfrac{dx}{dt}\right]$, and more generally $\partial^n x$ for $\left[\dfrac{d^n x}{dt^n}\right]$. Note that unlike quantitative calculus, $\partial^{n+1} x$ cannot be obtained by differentiating $\partial^n x$ (eg, consider $x = 2 + \sin t$, $[x] = +$ everywhere but ∂x varies between +, 0, and −). It is always necessary to go back to the quantitative definition $\partial^{n+1} x = \left[\dfrac{d^{n+1} x}{dt^{n+1}}\right]$.

There is little notational agreement in qualitative physics research. Although some authors (de Kleer and Brown, 1984; Williams, 1984a; de Kleer and Bobrow, 1984) use the conventions in this article, de Kleer and Brown (1983) use $[x] = + \equiv X = +$, Forbus (1984) uses $[x] \equiv A_s x$ and $\partial x \equiv D_s x$, Kuipers (1984) uses $\partial x = + \equiv$ increasing (x), and Kuipers (1985) uses $[x] = +$ and $\partial x = −$ is represented as $\langle (0, \infty), \text{dec} \rangle$.

Qualitative Equations

A confluence, is an expression in terms of qualitative values, variables, and operators. A set of qualitative values satisfies a confluence if either the qualitative equality strictly holds using the arithmetic of Tables 1 and 2, or one side of the confluence cannot be evaluated because the addition operation is not closed. Consider the confluence $\partial P + [P]\partial A − \partial Q = 0$. Usually if all but one of the variables of a confluence are known, the last one can be determined. If $\partial P = +$, $[P] = +$, and $\partial A = +$, then ∂Q must be +. However, this is not always the case. If $\partial P = −$, $[P] = +$, and $\partial A = +$, then the confluence is satisfied for any value of ∂Q. A set of values contradicts a confluence if both sides evaluate to a distinct qualitative value and the confluence is not satisfied. Thus $\partial P = +$, $[P] = +$, $\partial A = +$, and $\partial Q = −$ are contradictory. Note that by this definition a confluence need neither be satisfied nor contradicted if some of the variables do not have assigned values.

Qualitative equations cannot be manipulated as conventional quantitative ones. The conventional manipulations rely on the mathematical field axioms; however, Table 1 does not even describe an algebraic group. For example, it is not possible to subtract $[y] + [z] = 0$ from $[x] + [y] + [z] = 0$ to obtain $[x] = 0$ because the assignment $[x] = +$, $[y] = +$, $[z] = −$ also satisfies the two original confluences. Nevertheless, a number of qualitative algebras have been developed that define the legal manipulations on qualitative equations (Williams, 1991; Dormoy and Raiman, 1988).

Neither Forbus (1984) nor Kuipers (1985) employ confluences for qualitative modeling. Both extend the conventional arithmetic operators with an explicit qualitative proportionality operator. Kuipers calls this operator

Table 2. $[X] \times [Y]$

[Y]	[X]		
	−	0	+
−	+	0	−
0	0	0	0
+	−	0	+

Process heat-flow

Individuals:
   src an object, Has-Quantity(src, heat)
   dst an object, Has-Quantity(dst, heat)
   path a Heat-Path, Heat-Connection(path, src, dst)

Preconditions:
   Heat-Aligned(path)

Quantity conditions:
   A[temperature(src)] > A[temperature(dst)]

Relations:
   Let flow-rate be a quantity
   A[flow-rate] > ZERO
   flow-rate $\propto_{Q^-}$ (temperature(src) − temperature(dst))

Influences:
   1−(heat(src), A[flow-rate])
   1+(heat(dst), A[flow-rate])

Figure 4. Heat flow process.

M. For example, the inflow = $M_z^+(\Delta T)$ of Figure 2 indicates that inflow is a strictly monotonically increasing function (indicated by the superscript +) of ΔT and that this function passes through zero (indicated by the subscript z). This proportionality corresponds to [inflow] = [ΔT] and ∂inflow = $\partial \Delta T$ in confluence notation. The analogous operator of Forbus (1984) is $\propto_{Q^+}$ (Fig. 4).

Quantity Spaces

The +, −, 0 value space is insufficient for many applications. Often some variable has multiple landmarks above or below which a component's behavior is governed by differing confluences. For example, water temperature has two landmarks 0°C and 100°C. Water is a liquid between these two landmarks, a solid below them, and a vapor above them. Thus a network of inequalities may exist among the variables.

The choice of landmarks for variables is a serious problem. Clearly, zero is an important landmark for derivatives, but what is the origin of the landmarks for other variables? The phase transition temperatures for water are obvious landmarks. Landmarks should either be defined by the component models themselves (as is the case with water temperature) or inferred by the qualitative physics analysis. The seductive scheme of choosing simple symbolic vocabularies (eg, hot, very hot, etc) is problematic. Such arbitrarily chosen schemes are based on the particular situation being analyzed. It is always possible to choose just the right symbolic vocabulary for each variable *after* analyzing the situation. What is very hot for some task may be just hot for another. Choosing a vocabulary arbitrarily produces a model, a solution, and an interpretation that have the appearance of cogency, but are, in fact, vacuous because the appearance of success depends on knowing the answer beforehand. Most implementations require extensive computation with inequalities. Forbus (1984) utilizes a general quantity space representation to reason with inequalities in qualitative process theory.

Ambiguities

Qualitative reasoning is inherently ambiguous and thus may make multiple behavioral predictions (called interpretations). At a minimum for a prediction to be correct, one of the interpretations must correspond to the actual behavior of the real system. A stronger criterion follows from observing that the structural description of a particular device implicitly characterizes a wide class of physically realizable devices with the same topology. Ideally, the behavior of each device in the class is described by one of the interpretations, and every interpretation describes the behavior of some device in the class. For example, every possible interpretation of the pressure regulator (Fig. 3a) corresponds to some physically possible regulator behavior, and every physically possible regulator behavior is described by some interpretation.

Unfortunately, this criterion is too strong (Kuipers, 1986). There are devices that have interpretations that are not physically realizable. For example, if the quantitative model was $x + y + z = 0$ and $y + z = 0$, the confluences would be $[x] + [y] + [z] = 0$ and $[y] + [z] = 0$. The qualitative operations of Tables 1 and 2 place no constraints on the value of $[x]$. The original quantitative model indicates that $x = 0$, but this cannot be inferred from the confluences alone. The same two confluences also describe the quantitative equations $x + 2y + z = 0$ and $y + z = 0$ from which it is not possible to infer $x = 0$.

Modeling

In the process- or component-based approach qualitative analysis must construct a qualitative model consisting of constraints from the structural description. (This step is avoided in constraint-based approaches in which the physical situation is initially described in terms of constraints.) In the component-based approach each type of physical constituent has a distinct model. The component model characterizes all the potential behaviors that the component can manifest. The lawful behavior of a component is expressed by a set of possible states and their associated specifications and confluences. For example, a valve could be modeled by A the area available for flow, P the pressure across the valve, and Q the flow through the valve. In state OPEN, the valve functions as a simple conduit, there is no pressure drop across it, and the flow through it is unconstrained. Neither can the pressure across it change; that can only be caused by a change in position of the valve. The state CLOSED is the dual to state OPEN. In it the valve completely disconnects the input from the output. There is no flow through the valve and the pressure across it is unconstrained. The flow through it cannot change without changing the area available for flow. In the WORKING state, the valve acts like a fluid resistance; its resistance controlled by A. For example, if $\partial A = 0$, then $\partial P = \partial Q$. This can be encoded as:

OPEN: $[A = A_{max}]$, $[P] = 0$, $\partial P = 0$

WORKING: $[0 < A < A_{max}]$, $[P] = [Q]$,
    $\partial P + [P]\partial A - \partial Q = 0$

CLOSED: $[A = 0]$, $[Q] = 0$, $\partial Q = 0$.

A state specification consists of a set of inequalities that define different component operating regions whose behavior is governed by distinct confluence sets. These inequalities play a fundamental role in reasoning with time, because values will change enough to cause components to change state.

The component models for a given composite device state (ie, a selection of operating regions for all the device's components) define a set of confluences that govern the behavior of the device in each composite state. Any complete set of variable values that satisfies all confluences for all the components of the system, specifies a possible behavior.

The laws for flowlike variables are based on the assumption that conduits are always completely full of material and incompressible; therefore, any material added through one terminal must result in material leaving by some other terminal. In other words, material is instantaneously conserved. This rule is called the continuity condition and is from system dynamics (Shearer and co-workers, 1971). For electrical circuits, it is called Kirchoff's current law; for fluid systems, the law of conservation of matter; and for thermal systems, the law of conservation of energy. The continuity condition requires that the sum of the current, forces, heat flows, etc, into a conduit (and most components) be zero. Because these rules are simple sums they also apply to the derivatives of attributes. These can all be expressed as confluences.

Because the value of the pressurelike variable in a conduit is the same everywhere in the conduit, there are no pressure laws for individual conduits or components. No matter which path the material takes from component A to B, the sum of the individual pressure drops along each path must be equal. This is called the compatibility condition (also from system dynamics). For example, if the pressure between conduits A and B is x and the pressure between conduits B and C is y, then the pressure between conduits A and C is $x + y$ (and thus qualitatively $[x] + [y]$). Compatibility requires equal voltages, velocities etc at points where the components are connected.

The process-based approach takes a mirror-image approach to modeling. Instead of modeling the lawful behavior of objects, a process describes possible interactions among a collection objects. For example, Figure 4 is the specification of a heat flow process: In qualitative process theory a process is specified by five parts: the individuals, preconditions, quantity conditions, relations, and influences. Heat flow applies to three individuals: src, which is the source of the heat; dst, which is the destination of the heat; and path, which is the path through which the heat flows. The preconditions and quantity conditions must hold for the process to be active. The preconditions are intended to reflect external conditions (affected by an external agent). A precondition for heat flow is that the heat path must be aligned so that heat can flow. Quantity conditions differ from preconditions in that quantity conditions only test internally affected quantities. A quantity condition for heat flow is that the temperature of the source be higher than the temperature of the destination. The relations impose constraints among the parameters of the individuals. For example, the amount of the flow rate is greater than zero and proportional to the difference between the source and destination temperature (an indirect influence). The direct influences specify the root causes that change parameters. I^-(heat(src), A[flow rate]) specifies that the flow rate negatively influences the amount of heat in the source. In the terminology of this article, this formula asserts that there is a qualitative sum of the form ∂heat(src) = ... - $[A$[flow-rate]] + ..., where heat(src) and A[flow-rate] are qualitative variables. The development and clarification of this language is a major contribution of Forbus (1984).

At any particular time a quantity must be directly influenced, indirectly influenced, or not influenced at all. If a quantity is both directly and indirectly influenced, then the physical theory is incorrect. This condition is intended to capture a notion of causality. All directly influenced quantities are independent, acted on directly by active processes. All other quantities must be changed indirectly as a consequence of changes processes make on the directly influenced quantities.

The value of a directly influenced quantity is the sum of its direct influences in all processes:

$$\frac{dx}{dt} = \sum_{I^+(x,q_i)} q_i - \sum_{I^-(x,q_i)} q_i$$

In most cases this sum is equivalent to the confluence:

$$\partial x = \sum_{I^+(x,q_i)} [q_i] - \sum_{I^-(x,q_i)} [q_i]$$

using the qualitative arithmetic of Tables 1 and 2. If the sum is ambiguous, then inequality information is used to resolve influence. For example, ∂x is ambiguous if the direct influences on x are $I^-(x, a)$ and $I^+(x, b)$ (where $a > 0$, and $b > 0$). However, if $a > b$, then $\partial x = -$. The indirect influences are resolved in an analogous manner, except qualitative proportionality ($\propto_Q$) is a weaker operator (and thus inequality information cannot be used):

$$[x] = \sum_{x \propto_{Q+} q_i} [q_i] - \sum_{x \propto_{Q-} q_i} [q_i]$$

By definition, qualitative process theory requires that there be no loops in the confluence structure, so all influences can be resolved by simple local propagations.

The process-based and component-based approaches are similar in that both rely on an underlying formulation in terms of constraints and conditions. However, information that is locally available in one theory is distributed in the other. In qualitative process theory, the influences of diverse processes must be gathered to determine a constraint on a variable. In the component-based approach, each confluence of a component model places a necessary constraint on all the variables it references.

Processes can become active and inactive as quantities change. This feature is used to great advantage in developing physical theories. For example, the three behavioral states of the pressure regulator would be modeled by three different processes. However, sometimes differing processes are required in the process-based approach when one component suffices in the component-based approach. For example, an additional instance of the heat flow process is required if heat could flow in either direction, while the same component set models heat flow in both directions.

Constructing models for larger systems can be quite difficult. There may be multiple models available for system components each making its own approximations. In this case the goal of the modeler is to construct a composite model of the device that is adequate to correctly solve the task at hand but yet simple enough to be solvable with the information and techniques available. These issues have been examined (Addanki and co-workers, 1991; Falkenhainer and Forbus, 1991).

Qualitative Calculus

As time passes, variables change toward landmarks causing transitions to other operating regions and component states (equivalently, processes become active and inactive). At any given time, many variables may be approaching their respective landmarks, and the analysis must determine which variable(s) reach their landmarks first. This process is sometimes called limit analysis (Forbus, 1984) or transition analysis (Williams, 1984a).

A theory of change presumes a theory of time. Roughly speaking, three models of time have been used in qualitative physics. Forbus (1984) and Weld (1986) model time as a sequence of intervals as suggested by Allen (1983). de Kleer and Brown (1984) model time by intervals separated by any number of instants. Williams (1984a), Kuipers (1984), and de Kleer and Bobrow (1984) model time as intervals separated by single instants. This latter approach is used in the remainder of the article.

The rules necessary to reason about change over time derive directly from the conventional calculus (Williams, 1984a, 1984b), particularly the mean value theorem. These rules, in essence, solve the qualitative differential equations constructed by the modeling. If variables are differentiable, then the rules for determining time behavior are remarkably simple, The following five rules apply to all derivative orders:

A. *Instant to Interval.* Any nonzero quantity, must remain nonzero during the following interval; if a quantity $[x]$ is zero at the instant, then on the following interval it must obey the integration constraint $[x] = \partial x$.

B. *Interval to Instant.* A nonzero quantity may become zero on the following interval if and only if $[x] = -\partial x \neq 0$.

C. *Continuity.* Variables change continuously; continuous changes are between 0 and + or − (in either direction), but not between + and −.

D. *Contradiction Avoidance.* A transition is only possible if the resulting state satisfies the qualitative equations for that state.

E. *Analyticity.* A quantity that is zero for any interval, is zero for all time; conversely, a quantity that is nonzero at some time cannot become identically zero.

Envisioning

Envisioning is a reasoning process that uses the modeled device to produce a description of the behaviors of the device over time. An attainable envisionment describes all possible behaviors given some initial state. A total envisionment describes all possible behaviors for each possible initial state.

The envisioning process can be illustrated by examining the diaphragm–spring–stem fragment of the pressure regulator. If the input pressure increases, the output pressure increases, producing a force on the diaphragm. This force acts against the spring force and friction. The valve slowly gains velocity as it closes; however, by the time it reaches the position where the force exerted by the pressure balances the restoring force of the spring, the valve has built up a momentum causing it to move past its equilibrium position, thus reducing the pressure below what it should be. As it has overshot its equilibrium the spring pushes it back, but by the same reasoning, the valve overshoots again, thereby producing ringing or oscillation. Figure 5 illustrates the essential details: a mass situated on a spring and shock absorber (ie, friction).

The envisioning process of (de Kleer and Bobrow, 1984) is based on the five rules of the qualitative differential calculus:

1. Start with some initial state(s) (usually at an instant).
2. Identify those quantities that are moving to their landmarks.
3. Construct partial descriptions of tentative next states using rule A or B.
4. Using rules C, D and E expand and prune the possible next states.
5. For each state not yet analyzed, go to step 2.

Note that envisioning can proceed in parallel. The resultant state diagram is the envisionment for the system.

The behavior of the mass is described by Newton's law $F_m = ma$, or qualitatively $[F_m] = \partial v$ (more generally, $\partial^n F_m = \partial^{n+1} v$). Hooke's law for the spring $F_s = -kx$ becomes $\partial^{n+1} F_s = -\partial^n v$. The resistance of the shock absorber is modeled by $\partial^n F_f = -\partial^n v$. For simplicity sake, define $x = 0$ as the mass position with the spring at equilibrium, and $x > 0$ to be to the right. The net force on the mass is provided by the spring and shock absorber: $F_m = F_s + F_f$, or qualitatively $\partial^n F_m = \partial^n F_s + \partial^n F_f$.

Suppose the system is started by stretching the mass to the right. At this instant the velocity is zero, but the mass

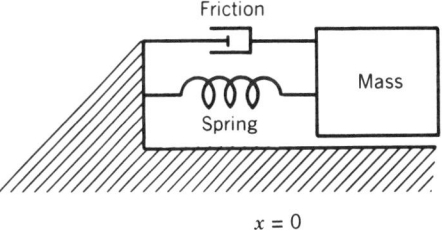

Figure 5. Mass–spring–friction system.

is pulled to the right. Thus the initial instant is

	[x]	∂x	$\partial^2 x$	$[F_m]$	∂F_m	$[F_f]$	∂F_f	$[F_s]$	∂F_s
Instant 1	+	0	−	−	+	0	+	−	0

By rule A (instant to interval), all nonzero quantities remain nonzero on the following interval:

	[x]	∂x	$\partial^2 x$	$[F_m]$	∂F_m	$[F_f]$	∂F_f	$[F_s]$	∂F_s
Instant 1	+	0	−	−	+	0	+	−	0
Interval 2	+	?	−	−	+	?	+	−	?

In addition by rule A (instant to interval), the instantaneously zero quantities, particularly $[F_f]$ and ∂x must obey the integration constraints on the interval, and as their respective derivatives are known: $[F_f] = \partial F_f = +$ and $\partial x = \partial^2 x = −$. If no further derivatives are computed, then rule A (instant to interval) places no constraint on ∂F_s. Superficially it looks as if the initial state could change to one of three possible subsequent states, corresponding to $\partial F_s = +, −,$ or 0. However, by rule D (contradiction avoidance), the only consistent value for ∂F_s is +, because $\partial F_s = −\partial x$. Therefore, the transition is unambiguous:

	[x]	∂x	$\partial^2 x$	$[F_m]$	∂F_m	$[F_f]$	∂F_f	$[F_s]$	∂F_s
Instant 1	+	0	−	−	+	0	+	−	0
Interval 2	+	−	−	−	+	+	+	−	+

The analysis for the transition to the subsequent instant is more complex, but nevertheless unambiguous as well. By rule B the only variables guaranteed not to change are $\partial x = −$ and $[F_f] = +$. However, those quantities determine the values of the remaining variables. By Hooke's law, $\partial F_s = +$. Using rule D, consider the possibility that $[F_s]$ becomes zero. Then $[F_m] = [F_f] + [F_s] = +$. However, $[F_m]$ cannot change from − to + without violating rule C. Thus $[F_s] = −$. Following this style of argument, the next state is unambiguous:

	[x]	∂x	$\partial^2 x$	$[F_m]$	∂F_m	$[F_f]$	∂F_f	$[F_s]$	∂F_s
Instant 1	+	0	−	−	+	0	+	−	0
Interval 2	+	−	−	−	+	+	+	−	+
Instant 3	+	−	0	0	+	+	0	−	+

Applying rules A, C and D produces a single unambiguous subsequent interval:

	[x]	∂x	$\partial^2 x$	$[F_m]$	∂F_m	$[F_f]$	∂F_f	$[F_s]$	∂F_s
Instant 1	+	0	−	−	+	0	+	−	0
Interval 2	+	−	−	−	+	+	+	−	+
Instant 3	+	−	0	0	+	+	0	−	+
Interval 4	+	−	+	+	+	+	−	−	+

This generation process continues for many steps until the initial situation is reencountered. The resulting envisionment shows that changes in forces cause changes in acceleration that cause changes in velocity that cause changes in position that cause changes in position that in turn causes changes in forces, producing an endless oscillation. The qualitative physics analysis has provided an accurate description of the behavior of the mass–spring system without invoking the classic differential calculus.

CAUSALITY AND FEEDBACK

Many tasks require characterizing behavior in more abstract and functional terminology (Rieger and Grinberg, 1977). Qualitative physics aspires to describe how the predicted behavior arises, not just what this behavior is. Thus an underlying theme of much of qualitative physics research is causality. Developing a notion of causality is important for pedagogy, cognitive modeling, analogical reasoning, theory formation, diagnosis, and, perhaps most important, as a step toward gaining access to more abstract functional knowledge of behavior. Progress toward a workable theory of causality in qualitative physics has been slow, perhaps because there is no widely agreed on formal notion of causality in science.

The starting point for the various notions of causality in qualitative physics is the underlying constraint model of a device. At a minimum, for A to be caused by B, then A must depend on B using the constraints of the model (where A and B are assignments of qualitative values to variables). However, causality is more restrictive than simple dependence: just because A depends on B does not imply A is caused by B. The varying notions of causality in qualitative physics differ on which additional desiderata are imposed on simple dependence. The difficulty with using simple dependence alone for defining causality is that it permits many explanations for the same behavior, many of which do not meet the intuitive notion of causality.

Two central criteria often imposed to define causality are locality and temporal order. Locality requires that only physically adjacent components can interact, thus for A to cause B, A and B must describe behaviors of physically adjacent components. Temporal ordering requires for A to cause B, A must immediately precede [by perhaps an infinitesimal amount, the *mythical time* of de Kleer and Brown (1984)] B. These criteria usually isolate a single causal description of a device's behavior. Having obtained the canonical causal process by which the device functions, it can be parsed to describe the physical mechanisms by which it operates. This physical mechanism can then be used as an index into other knowledge about general device behavior. For example, knowing that a particular transistor is operating as an emitter follower, immediately suggests (from previous experience) how it should be modeled for analysis, what approximations are applicable, and what kinds of failure modes it is susceptible to (de Kleer, 1985).

Feedback presents difficulties for determining causality. Mathematically, as every quantity in a feedback loop depends on every other, there is no simple dependence among these quantities. Some researchers (Simon, 1977; Iwasaki and Simon, 1986) argue that as a consequence there is no causality in feedback loops. Others (de Kleer and Brown, 1984; Williams, 1984a) introduce additional heuristics that identify the causality in feedback loops approximating conventional engineering intuitions (ie, causality goes through the signal path from input to output and then back through the error path).

Causality is an ontological commitment. There is an, often implicit, presupposition in much of qualitative physics research: by developing a notion of causality that is in close alignment with how the physical system actually functions, the resulting explanations will be more powerful. However, this is an unnecessarily extreme position. It is sufficient that present society embodies a notion called *causality*. By formalizing that notion, qualitative physical analysis can describe device functioning in familiar terms and access society's accumulated knowledge of device behavior.

CURRENT AND FUTURE RESEARCH

Compared to conventional physics, qualitative physics represents a research direction that has only just started. Although significant progress has been made, relatively few physical phenomena have been accounted for. The following are a few of the current directions of qualitative physics research.

Most of the qualitative physics research presumes that the physical structure can be modeled by a relatively small number of distinct objects and interactions. However, many physical situations are, in fact, modeled by a large number of identical objects: water flow in a river, heat flow along a slab, molecules in a pipe, etc. Such systems cannot be accounted for in current qualitative physics. More formally, qualitative physics has [with few exceptions (Weld, 1986)] thus far focused on lumped-parameter systems that are described by ordinary differential equations. Little progress has been made on distributed systems whose behavior is described by partial differential equations with respect to spatial variables.

Qualitative physics has tended to focus on dynamics. Reasoning about spatial movement of objects and shapes of objects and their interactions is extremely difficult and less progress has been made (de Kleer, 1975; Forbus, 1983). Examples of recent progress (Nielsen, 1983; Gelsey, 1987) and discussion of some of the difficulties inherent in spatial reasoning (Davis, 1987) have been published.

A much more sophisticated notion of time is required. Thus far time has been an implicit, not explicit, variable, making it difficult to express certain laws (delays) and to reason about the consequences of the events without analyzing every intermediate event as well. Systems oscillate, approach asymptotes, and become unstable. Most qualitative physics cannot account for such long-term behavioral effects. Most qualitative physics has assumed that the underlying functions are well behaved, continuous, and differentiable. Often systems go through discontinuous transitions that are produced or produce impulses. A qualitative theory of such generalized functions is required and a start has been made (Nishida and Doshita, 1987).

Humans must learn commonsense physics from interactions with the world. Some suggestions about learning qualitative laws have been published (Forbus and Genter, 1983). Complex system can be described at many levels of abstraction. Currently, qualitative physics does not include any notion of hierarchy or when it is necessary to move to other levels of abstraction.

BIBLIOGRAPHY

S. Addanki, R. Cremonini, and J. S. Penberthy, "Graph of Models," in de Kleer and Williams, 1991.

A. Collins and D. Gentner, "Multiple Models of Evaporation Processes," in *Proceedings of the Fifth Annual Meeting of the Cognitive Science Society,* Rochester, N.Y., 1983.

E. Davis, "A Framework for Qualitative Reasoning about Solid Objects," in G. Rodriquez, ed., *Proceedings of the Workshop on Space Telerobotics,* NASA and the Jet Propulsion Laboratory, 1987, pp. 369–375.

J. de Kleer, *Qualitative and Quantitative Knowledge in Classical Mechanics,* TR-352, AI Laboratory, MIT, Cambridge, Mass., 1975.

J. de Kleer, "How Circuits Work," in D. G. Bobrow, ed., *Qualitative Reasoning about Physical Systems,* MIT Press, Cambridge, Mass., 1985.

J. de Kleer and D. G. Bobrow, "Higher-Order Qualitative Derivatives," in *Proceedings of the Fourth National Conference on Artificial Intelligence,* Austin, Tex., AAAI, Menlo Park, Calif., 1984, pp. 86–91.

J. de Kleer and J. S. Brown, "The Origin, Form, and Logic of Qualitative Physical Laws," in *Proceedings of the Eighth IJCAI,* Karlsruhe, FRG, Morgan-Kaufmann, San Mateo, Calif., 1983a, pp. 1158–1169 [ambiguity].

J. de Kleer and J. S. Brown, "Assumptions and Ambiguities in Mechanistic Mental Models," in D. Gentner and A. L. Stevens, eds., *Mental Models,* Lawrence Erlbaum, Hillsdale, N.J., 1983b, pp. 155–190.

J. de Kleer and J. S. Brown, "A Qualitative Physics Based on Confluences," *Artif. Intel.* **24,** 7–83 (1984).

J. de Kleer and J. S. Brown, "Theories of Causal Ordering," *Artif. Intell.* **29,** 33–62 (1986).

J. de Kleer and B. C. Williams, eds., *Qualitative Reasoning about Physical Systems II, Special Issue, Artificial Intelligence* **51,** MIT Press, Cambridge, Mass., (1991).

J. Dormoy and O. Raiman, "Assembling a Device," in *Proceedings of the Seventh National Conference on Artificial Intelligence,* St. Paul, Minn., AAAI, Menlo Park, Calif., 1988.

B. Falkenhainer and K. D. Forbus, "Compositional Modeling," in de Kleer and Williams, 1991.

B. Faltings and P. Struss, *Recent Advances in Qualitative Physics,* MIT Press, Cambridge, Mass., 1991.

K. D. Forbus, "Qualitative Reasoning about Space and Motion," in D. Gentner and A. L. Stevens, eds., *Mental Models,* Lawrence Erlbaum, Hillsdale, N.J., 1983, pp. 53–73.

K. D. Forbus, "Qualitative Process Theory," *Artif. Intell.* **24,** 85–168 (1984).

K. D. Forbus, "The Qualitative Process Engine," in Weld and de Kleer, 1990.

K. D. Forbus and S. Gentner, "Learning Physical Domains: Towards a Theoretical Framework," in *Proceedings of the Second International Machine Learning Workshop,* Urbana, Ill., 1983, pp. 198–202.

A. Gelsey, "Automated Reasoning about Machine Geometry and Kinematics," in *Proceedings of the Third IEEE Conference on AI Applications,* Orlando, Fla., 1987, pp. 182–187.

P. J. Hayes, "The Naive Physics Manifesto," in D. Michie, *Expert Systems in the Microelectronic Age,* Edinburgh University Press, Edinburgh, UK, 1979, pp. 242–270.

Y. Iwasaki and H. A. Simon, "Causality in Device Behavior," *Artif. Intell.* **29,** 3–32 (1986).

B. J. Kuipers, "Commonsense Reasoning about Causality: Deriving Behavior from Structure," *Artif. Intell.* **24,** 169–203 (1984) [on creating new landmarks dynamically].

B. J. Kuipers, "The Limits of Qualitative Analysis," in *Proceedings of the Ninth IJCAI,* Los Angeles, Calif., Morgan-Kaufmann, San Mateo, Calif., 1985, pp. 128–136.

B. J. Kuipers, "Qualitative Simulation," *Artif. Intell.* **29,** 289–338 (1986).

B. J. Kuipers and J. P. Kassirer, "Causal Reasoning in Medicine: Analysis of a Protocol," *Cogn. Sci.* **8,** 363–385 (1984).

D. B. Lenat and R. V. Guha, *Building Large Knowledge-Based Systems: Representation and Inference in the Cyc Project,* Addison-Wesley Publishing Co., Inc., Reading, Mass., 1990.

P. Nielsen, "A Qualitative Approach to Mechanical Constraint," in *Proceedings of the Seventh National Conference on Artificial Intelligence,* St. Paul, Minn., AAAI, Menlo Park, Calif., 1988, pp. 270–275.

T. Nishida and S. Doshita, "Reasoning about Discontinuous Change," in *Proceedings of the Sixth National Conference on Artificial Intelligence,* Seattle, Wash., AAAI, Menlo Park, Calif., 1987, pp. 643–648.

C. Rieger and M. Grinberg, "The Declarative Representation and Procedural Simulation of Causality in Physical Mechanisms," in *Proceedings of the Fifth IJCAI,* Cambridge, Mass., Morgan-Kaufmann, San Mateo, Calif., 1977, pp. 250–256.

J. L. Shearer, A. T. Murphy, and H. H. Richardson, *Introduction to System Synamics,* Addison-Wesley Publishing Co., Inc., Reading, Mass., 1971.

H. A. Simon, "Causal Ordering and Identifiability," in W. C. Hood and T. C. Koopmans, eds., *Studies in Econometric Models,* John Wiley & Sons, Inc., New York, 1953, pp. 49–74.

P. Struss, "Problems of Interval-Based Qualitative Reasoning," in Weld and de Kleer, 1990.

D. S. Weld, "The Use of Aggregation in Causal Simulation," *Artif. Intell.* **30,** 1–34 (1986).

D. S. Weld and J. de Kleer, eds., *Readings in Qualitative Reasoning about Physical Systems,* Morgan-Kaufmann, San Mateo, Calif., 1990. [Includes most of papers in this bibliography and a general introduction to the field].

B. C. Williams, "Qualitative Analysis of MOS Circuits," *Artif. Intell.* **24,** 281–346 (1984a).

B. C. Williams, "The Use of Continuity in a Qualitative Physics," in *Proceedings of the Fourth National Conference on Artificial Intelligence,* Austin, Tex., AAAI, Menlo Park, Calif., 1984b, pp. 350–354.

B. C. Williams, "Doing Time: Putting Qualitative Reasoning on Firmer Ground," in *Proceedings of the Fifth National Conference on Artificial Intelligence,* Philadelphia, Pa., AAAI, Menlo Park, Calif., 1986, pp. 105–112.

B. C. Williams, "Minima: Integrating Qualitative and Quantitative Algebraic Reasoning," in Weld and de Kleer, 1990.

General References

J. F. Allen, "Maintaining Knowledge about Temporal Intervals," *Commun. ACM* **26**(6), 832–843 (1983).

D. G. Bobrow, ed., *Qualitative Reasoning about Physical Systems,* MIT Press, Cambridge, Mass., 1985.

P. Dague, O. Raiman, and P. Deves, "Troubleshooting: When Modeling Is the Trouble," in *Proceedings of the Sixth National Conference on Artificial Intelligence,* Seattle, Wash., AAAI, Menlo Park, Calif., 1987, pp. 590–595.

D. DeCoste, "Interpreting Measurements of Physical Systems," in de Kleer and Williams, 1991 [inferring the changing hidden internal state of a physical system].

J. de Kleer, *Causal and Teleological Reasoning in Circuit Recognition,* TR-529, AI Laboratory, MIT, Cambridge, Mass., 1979.

K. D. Forbus and B. Falkenhainer, "Self-Explanatory Simutations: An Integration of Qualitative and Quantitative Knowledge," in *Proceedings of the Ninth National Conference on Artificial Intelligence,* Boston, Mass., AAAI, Menlo Park, Calif., 1990, pp. 380–387.

P. E. Hart, A. Barzilay, and R. O. Duda, "Qualitative Reasoning for Financial Assessments—A Prospectus," *AI Mag.* **7,** 62–68 (1986).

J. R. Hobbs and R. C. Moore, *Formal Theories of the Commonsense World,* Ablex, 1985 [on common sense and naive physics].

B. J. Kuipers, C. Chiu, D. T. Dalle Molle, and D. Throop, "Higher-Order Derivative Constraints in Qualitative Simulation," in de Kleer and Williams, 1991 [sophisticated uses of higher order derivatives].

W. W. Lee and B. J. Kuipers, "Non-Intersection of Trajectories in Qualitative Phase Space: A Global Constraint for Qualitative Simulation," in *Proceedings of the Seventh National Conference on Artificial Intelligence,* St. Paul, Minn., AAAI, Menlo Park, Calif., 1988, pp. 286–291.

J. Mohammed and R. Simmons, "Qualitative Simulation of Semiconductor Fabrication," in *Proceedings of the Fifth National Conference on Artificial Intelligence,* Philadelphia, Pa., AAAI, Menlo Park, Calif., 1986, pp. 794–799.

O. Raiman, "Order of Magnitude Reasoning," in de Kleer and Williams, 1991.

R. Rajagopalan, "Qualitative Modeling in the Turbojet Domain," in *Proceedings of the Fourth National Conference on Artificial Intelligence,* Austin, Tex., AAAI, Menlo Park, Calif., 1984, pp. 283–287.

R. G. Simmons, *Representing and Reasoning about Change in Geologic Interpretation,* TR-749, AI Laboratory, MIT, Cambridge, Mass., 1983.

R. G. Simmons, " 'Commonsense' Arithmetic Reasoning," in Mohammed and Simmons, 1986, pp. 118–124. (A general system for reasoning about inequalities is described).

P. Struss, "Global Filters for Qualitative Behaviors," in *Proceedings of the Seventh National Conference on Artificial Intelligence,* St. Paul, Minn. AAAI, Menlo Park, Calif., 1988, pp. 275–280 [use of qualitative dynamics to reduce ambiguity].

B. C. Williams, "Interaction-Based Invention: Designing Novel Devices from First Principles," in *Proceedings of the Ninth National Conference on Artificial Intelligence,* Boston, Mass.

AAAI, Menlo Park, Calif., 1990, pp. 349–356 [relation to conventional calculus; transition ordering].

M. K. Yip, "Understanding Complex Dynamics by Visual and Symbolic Reasoning," in de Kleer and Williams, 1991 [describes the KAM system].

JOHAN DE KLEER
Xerox Palo Alto Research Center

PLANES

PLANES was a natural language front-end developed at the University of Illinois for accessing a relational database of Navy flight and maintenance data. PLANES used a semantic grammar (see GRAMMAR, SEMANTIC); it matched processed inputs against a set of framelike templates (corresponding to well-formed queries) and filled in the templates to generate database queries. PLANES could handle some nongrammatical inputs. [See D. Waltz, "An English Language Question Answering System for a Large Relational Database," *CACM* 21 (7), 526–539 (1978), for an overview of the system; and H. Tennant, "Experience With the Evaluation of Natural Language Question Answerers," *Proceedings of the Sixth IJCAI*, Tokyo, Aug. 1979, pp. 874–876, for user evaluations of PLANES.]

DAVID WALTZ
Thinking Machines Corp. and Brandeis University

PLANLOG

A proposal for a logic programming language that incorporates "procedural" features to cope with destructive change (see B. Fronhöfer, "PLANLOG: A Language Framework for the Integration of Logical and Procedural Programming," in J. McDermott, ed., *Proceedings of the 10th International Joint Conference on Artificial Intelligence*, Milan, Aug. 1987, Morgan-Kaufmann Inc., San Mateo, Calif., 1987, pp. 15–17). It is based on a logical plan generation calculus called linear proofs which avoids the frame problem (see W. Bibel, "A Deductive Solution for Plan Generation," *New Generation Computing* 4, 115–132 (1986)).

BERTRAM FRONHÖFER
Technical University of Munich

PLANNER

A LISP-based AI programming language for inference control, PLANNER was designed in 1972 at the MIT AI Lab by Hewitt and extensively demonstrated by Winograd in his SHRDLU (qv) project [see G. Sussman, T. Winograd, and E. Charniak, "MICRO-PLANNER Reference Manual," AI Memo 203, AI Laboratory, MIT, Cambridge, Mass., 1970, and C. Hewitt, "Description and Theoretical Analysis (Using Schemata) of PLANNER, a Language for Providing Theorems and Manipulating Models in a Robot," Report No. TR-258, AI Laboratory, MIT, Cambridge, Mass., 1972].

A. HANYONG YUHAN
AT&T Bell Laboratories

PLANNING

Planning is the generation of an action sequence or action program for an agent, such as a robot, that can change its environment. The purpose of a plan is to achieve one or more explicit goals. The essential inputs for planning are an initial world state, a repertoire of actions for changing that world, and a set of goals. The form of the plan is commonly just a linear sequence or acyclic directed graph of actions, although the full range of programming control structures are potentially relevant. For planning to be effective, the environment in which the plan will be executed must be largely predictable, but need not be completely deterministic. However, planning will be ineffective for chaotic domains, and an agent can only react to events.

Planning is probably the most reliable method for controlling the behavior of living and artificial agents, but it is not the only method, and not necessarily the fastest. A person certainly does not synthesize a plan to remove his hand from a hot dish. It seems a reasonable hypothesis that people normally plan their behavior only in novel or critical situations. In familiar situations, people probably merely retrieve and apply stored behavior programs. Artificial systems can adopt the same approach. However, application of stored routines, while faster than planning, can lead to inappropriate or unsuccessful behavior. An illustration is the situation where a person enters a darkened room during a power failure and automatically turns on a wall switch even when he knows perfectly well that the power is off.

Planning may require a search through an enormous space of possible plans, and so search control is an important consideration. Other key planning topics are the representation of actions, goal protection, management and modeling of time (see REASONING, TEMPORAL), and the ordering of goals and subgoals for achievement. Dynamic situations present additional challenges, including the detection of plan violations during execution of a plan, replanning in response to changing goals or unexpected events, actions and events with uncertain consequences, and the presence of other agents or physical processes in the environment. Areas of application for planning include automated manufacturing (qv), autonomous vehicles, the control of unmanned spacecraft, and robotics (qv). Planners are large, complex AI artifacts. A state-of-the-art planner requires many years of work to perfect, although a simple planner with numerous limitations can be written in a couple of months. This article emphasizes task planning with logical world models, rather than the

THE BLOCKS WORLD

Many of the basic principles of planning can be illustrated on a simple model called the blocks world. This is a two-dimensional world consisting of a table of unbounded size and a number of square blocks, labeled with distinct letters, that can be arranged to form stacks. Figure 1 shows a typical blocks world planning problem. Blocks world states are described by four kinds of literals:

(CLEAR x)   There is no block on top of x. (This representation became common because early planners were unable to handle negations and existential quantifiers).
(HOLDING x) A hand of an agent is holding block x.
(ON x y)   Block x rests directly on block y.
(ONTABLE x) Block x rests directly on the table.

The initial state description for a completely known world consists of a conjunction of such literals. Using these literals, the initial state in Figure 1 is represented by the following conjunction: (CLEAR C) (ON C A) (ONTABLE A) (CLEAR B) (ONTABLE B).

REPRESENTATIONS OF ACTIONS

An action is any change in the world state caused by an agent executing a plan. Actions may conveniently be partitioned into primitive and macro actions. This is a relative distinction, and depends on the purposes of the planning. A primitive action is one whose finer details are not of interest. A macro action is an aggregate of primitive actions and other macro actions, and is analogous to a subroutine in algorithmic programming languages. For example, for a travel agent planning an itinerary "flying from major city x to major city y" may be a convenient primitive action; for an airline pilot, on the other hand, this is a large macro action with primitive actions such as "set flaps for takeoff" and "taxi to runway." All of the normal control mechanisms potentially apply in forming macro actions: sequencing, conditionals, concurrency, looping, etc. However, most contemporary planners do not provide for loops or conditionals, and the final plan is commonly a partially ordered network of primitive actions. Macro actions are also known by a variety of synonyms, such as "skeletal plans," "plan schemas," and "scripts."

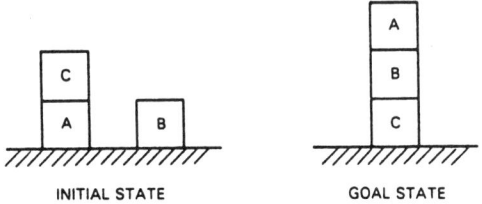

Figure 1. A blocks world planning problem.

```
(PICKUP (block)
    (ONTABLE block)
    (CLEAR block))
  ⟶
  ((HOLDING block)
    (NOT (CLEAR block))
    (NOT (ONTABLE block))))

(PUTDOWN (block)
    ((HOLDING block))
  ⟶
  ((CLEAR block)
    (ONTABLE block)
    (NOT (HOLDING block))))

(STACK (top-block under-block)
    ((CLEAR under-block)
    (HOLDING top-block))
  ⟶
  ((CLEAR top-block)
    (ON top-block under-block)
    (NOT (HOLDING top-block))
    (NOT (CLEAR under-block))))

(UNSTACK (top-block under-block)
    ((ON top-block under-block)
    (CLEAR top-block))
  ⟶
  ((HOLDING top-block)
    (CLEAR under-block)
    (NOT (CLEAR top-block))
    (NOT (ON top-block under-block))))
```

Figure 2. The Four Blocks World Actions.

It is often important to distinguish an event from an action. An event is a spontaneous change in world state. An event is triggered automatically because of natural or artificial mechanisms, whereas an action occurs only if an agent elects to perform it. A person can set a clock radio by moving the alarm control button. This is an action. The next morning the radio switches on and the person wakes up. These changes are events. If the causes and effects of events are known, it is possible to generate plans in which events play a role in achieving goals. However, the agent cannot directly "execute" an event but can only take actions leading to a world state that triggers the desired event.

Primitive actions may be modeled by specifying their preconditions and postconditions, both of which are conjunctions of literals. Preconditions are conditions that must be true in the world for an action to take place. Postconditions are conditions that hold after the action has occurred. (If it is important to model changes in world state *during* the action, then the action is not a primitive, but a macro action, and should be further decomposed). Figure 2 presents the action definitions for the four blocks world primitives: PICKUP, PUTDOWN, STACK, and UNSTACK. The definitions are given in the form

⟨⟨action-name⟩ ⟨action-variable-list⟩
  ⟨preconditions⟩
  →
  ⟨postconditions⟩)

As defined, PICKUP is the change from a single block resting directly on the table to the state in which a hand is holding the block. Postconditions routinely contradict preconditions, as in this example. Inclusion of the literal (NOT (CLEAR block)) as a postcondition is a somewhat arbitrary, subtle decision that prevents a planner from attempting to stack a block on another one that is being held. Preconditions could be augmented to include negations of positive literals in the postcondition. For example, (NOT (HOLDING block)) could be added to the preconditions of PICKUP. However, this is usually regarded as redundant. This particular formulation of the blocks world permits unbounded concurrency since any number of hands are assumed available for the PICKUP and UNSTACK actions. In these action descriptions the variable name "block" is purely mnemonic and does not formally convey any type information.

Primitive events can be modeled in exactly the same way as actions, and may be inserted into plans by the same backward-chaining process of node expansion as that described later. The causes of an event are listed as preconditions and the effects as postconditions. The difference is that event rules must also be allowed to chain forward whenever their preconditions are accidently satisfied. The action-event distinction will not be mentioned again; in most of the remaining discussions actions can be taken to include events as well.

Logical inferences can also be written in the same format as action and event rules. For example, a global "ABOVE" literal in the blocks world might be inferred with the following rule:

(ABOVE INFERENCE (block1 block2 block3)
 ((ON block 1 block2)
  (ON block 2 block3))
 →
 ((ABOVE block1 block3))).

The literals in the postcondition of an inference rule (in the context of planning) are sometimes called derived assertions. It is permissible to write derived-assertion literals as preconditions in other action, event, or inferences rules and to achieve these subgoals by backward chaining with inference rules. However, derived assertions have the unique property that, unlike action and event postconditions, they remain true exactly as long as their preconditions remain true. This has important implications for the way a planner protects derived-assertion preconditions, and will be explained later after the topic of goal protection has been properly introduced.

It should be emphasized that an action description in precondition–postcondition form is *not* a logical implication in the first-order predicate calculus (see Logic, Predicate). However, one early approach to planning, called the situation calculus, did model actions with first-order logic (Green, 1969; McCarthy and Hayes, 1969). In the situation calculus all domain literals are augmented with a state variable. For example, if s1 and s2 are distinct state variables, then (CLEAR block s1) does not contradict (NOT (CLEAR block s2)). If (PUTDOWN block s1) represents the new state reached by applying PUTDOWN to s1, then the putdown action in Figure 2 could be written as the following first-order axiom:

Forall s1 (HOLDING block s1) →
 (CLEAR block (PUTDOWN block s1))
 (ONTABLE block (PUTDOWN block s1))
 (NOT (HOLDING block (PUTDOWN block s1)))

The problem with this approach is that a typical action changes only a few of the many assertions describing a complete world, and says nothing about whether other assertions are still true in the new state. A separate "frame axiom" is required for each action and assertion type to allow a theorem prover to infer that the rest of the world is unchanged in the new state. For example, the following axiom is required to propagate ON literals across a PUTDOWN action:

Forall x, y, s, block (ON x y s) → (ON x y (PUTDOWN block s))

Frame axioms are tedious to write and a crushing computation load for any theorem prover that must apply them. This "frame problem" (there are others) was the subject of some concern and debate in the early 1970s. While discussion continues among theoreticians, it is now clear that there is no fundamental impediment to the generation, with acceptable computation times, of plans for real problems. The proper conclusion is that feeding first-order action and frame axioms into a general-purpose theorem prover is not an efficient way to generate plans.

In the NOAH-NONLIN class planners described later, world states are distributed over a partially ordered network of nodes, and no explicit state updating is necessary. Every literal is identified with a specific node in the network that "asserts" that literal. Ordered nodes may assert contradictory literals. Propagation of assertions across actions is implicit in these planners, and is justified by two higher-order frame axioms:

Forall literal, node
 (ASSERTS node literal) → (TRUE.AT node literal)

Forall literal, node1, node2
 (TRUE.AT node1 literal)
 (ORDERED node1 node2)
 (NOT (ASSERTS node2 (NOT literal))) → (TRUE.AT node2 literal)

A PLANNER IN OPERATION

Many of the basic planning issues and procedures can be illustrated by following through the major steps of a planner as it solves the problem of Figure 1. The planner to be illustrated is a slightly generalized version of NONLIN (Tate, 1977). Control is straightforward: The planner keeps its goals on a stack and does an ordered depth-first search (see Search, depth-first) through the space of possible plans. It synthesizes a plan from the primitive blocks world actions defined earlier.

The state of the planner is largely summarized by the plan diagrams shown in Figures 3 to 9. The final plan is shown in Figure 10. In these diagrams, unordered actions

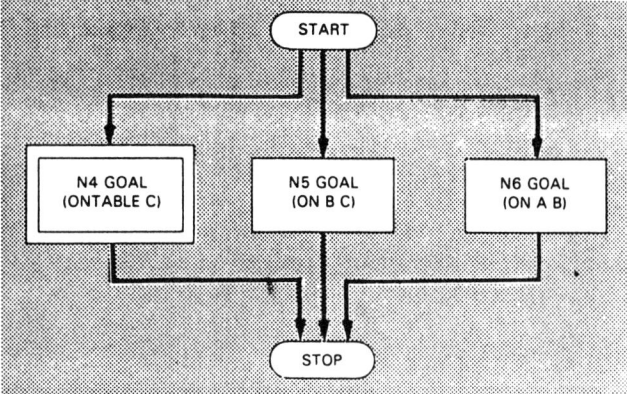

Figure 3. Initial plan diagram for the blocks world problem.

are concurrent. Each node in the diagrams, except the stop node, has associated with it a set of assertions. For the start node these assertions are the set of literals describing the initial state. For action nodes the assertions are the instantiated postconditions of the action. The top goal on the planner's goal stack is denoted by a double-outlined box. Figure 3 shows the initial plan diagram. Three goal nodes are shown in parallel; (ONTABLE C) will be attempted first. Not shown, to avoid cluttering the plan diagrams, are the node assertions and the goal protections (Tate, 1976) (also called collectively the "goal structure"), which govern the protection of goals within a plan.

Goal protection is recorded by meta-level assertions of the form (PROTECTED ⟨literal⟩ ⟨node1⟩ ⟨node2⟩), which signify that ⟨literal⟩ must not be contradicted in the region of the plan between the termination of ⟨node1⟩ and the termination of ⟨node2⟩, where ⟨node1⟩ asserts ⟨literal⟩ and ⟨node1⟩ preceeds ⟨node2⟩ in the plan diagram. In con-

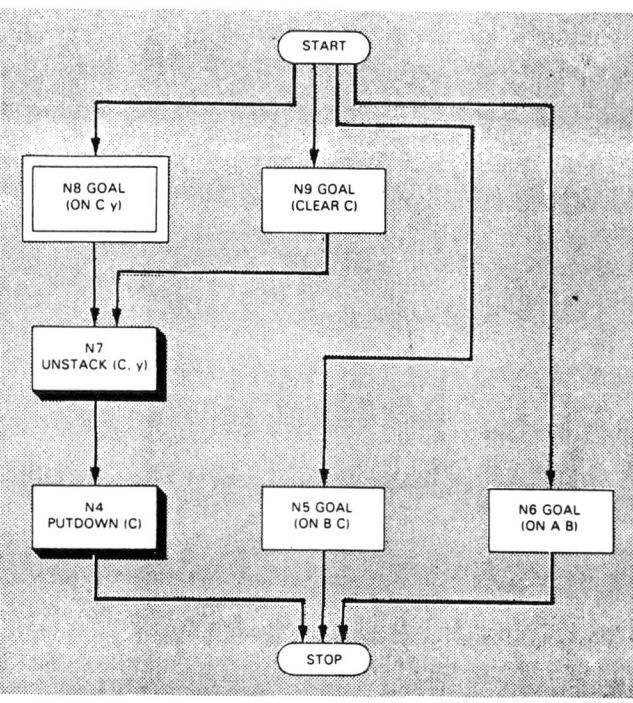

Figure 5. Plan diagram after step 2.

structing the initial diagram in Figure 3, the planner records the following goal protections:

(PROTECTED (ONTABLE C) N4 STOP)
(PROTECTED (ON B C) N5 STOP)
(PROTECTED (ON A B) N6 STOP)

Goal protections are the sinews that bind together the elements of a plan and ensure its coherence. In this exam-

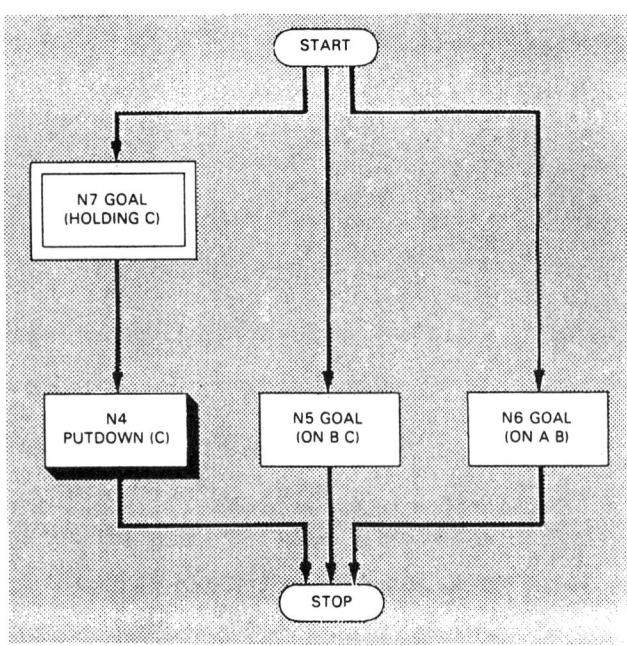

Figure 4. Plan diagram after step 1.

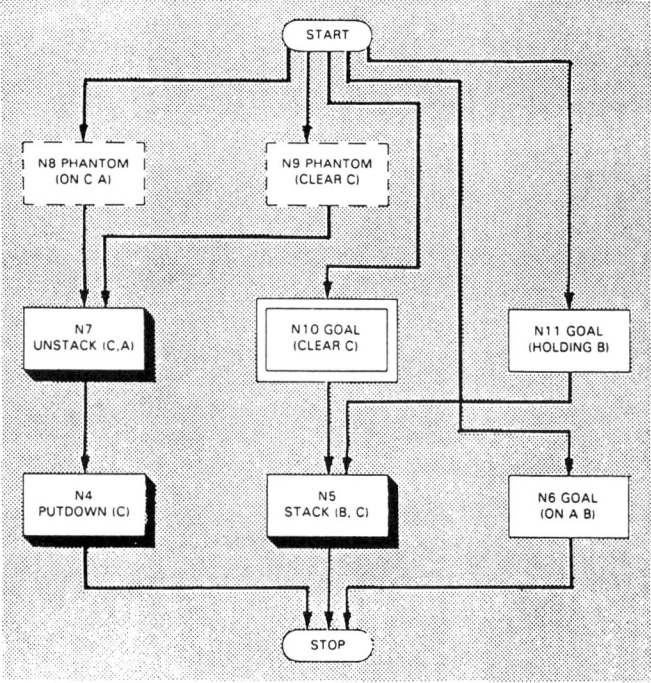

Figure 6. Plan diagram after step 5.

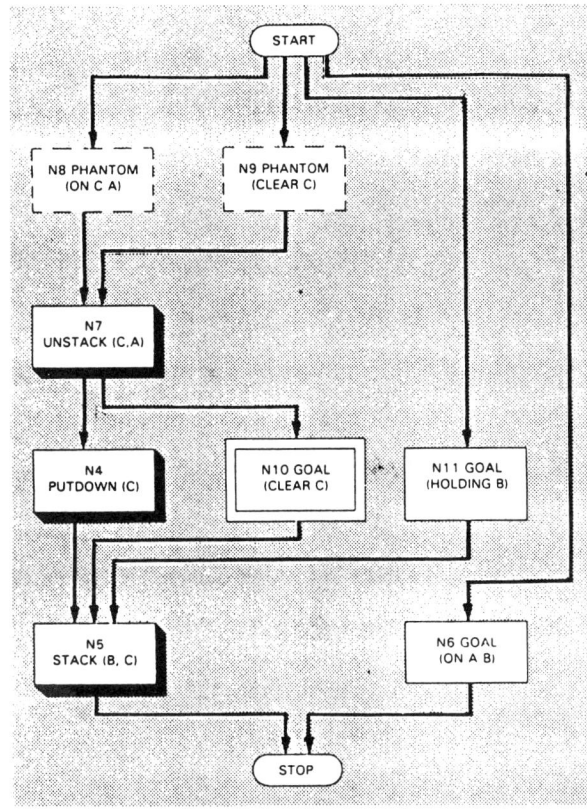

Figure 7. Plan diagram after step 7.

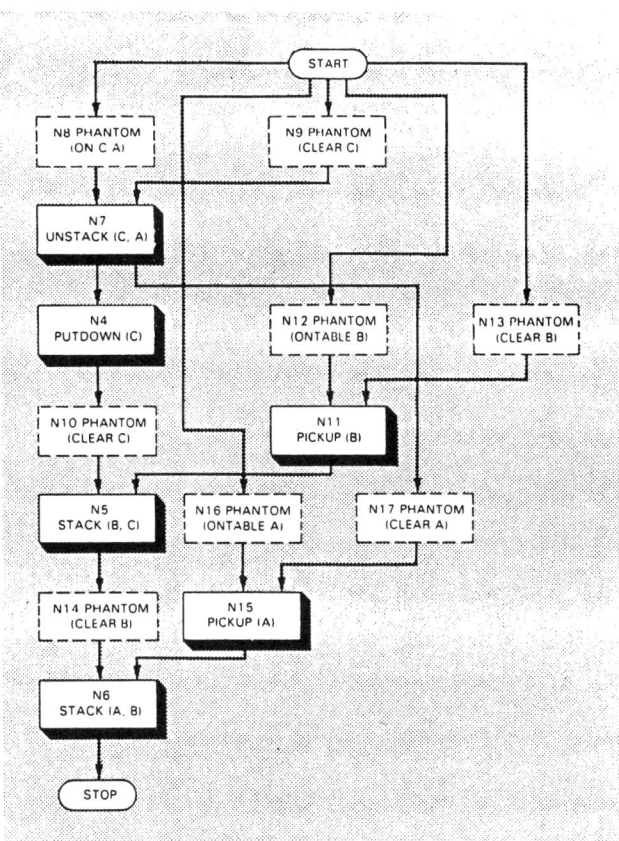

Figure 9. Final plan diagram.

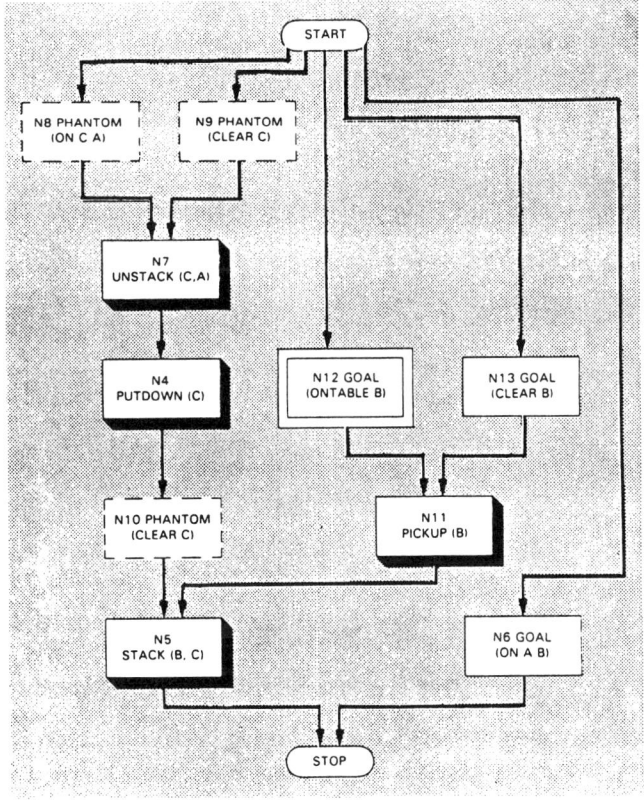

Figure 8. Plan diagram after step 9.

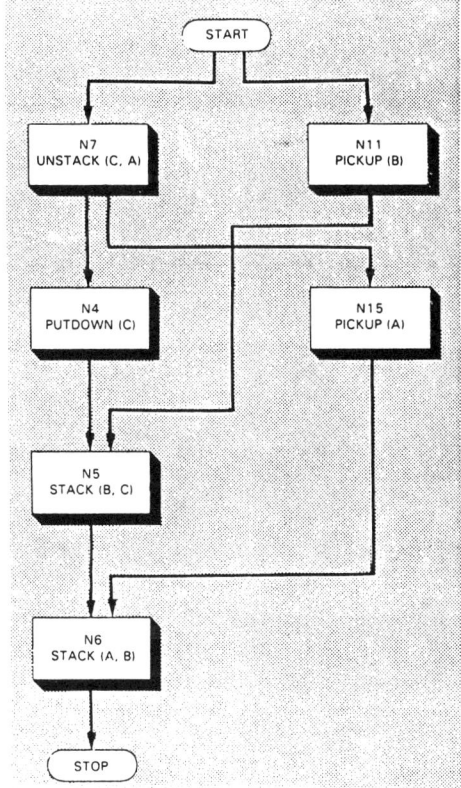

Figure 10. Final blocks world plan (without phantoms).

ple they ensure that the three goal conditions hold simultaneously when the plan terminates. Without observing goal protections a planner may merely achieve one goal at the expense of another, like the crow in Aesop's fable who drops the cheese when she opens her mouth to sing.

If a goal is not already true, the planner must insert an action in the plan to make it true. It selects an action with a postcondition literal that matches the goal, and the preconditions of that action become new goals. Placing the new goals on top of the goal stack results in a depth-first search. In the blocks world only a PUTDOWN action asserts an ONTABLE literal, and so there is no choice. This process is called node expansion, and the result is shown in Figure 4. (The generic term for node expansion, backward chaining, applies to a broader range of AI systems than just planners). A protection relation is established between the new goal node, N7, and the parent node N4. The instantiated postconditions of PUTDOWN become the three assertions of N4: (ONTABLE C) (NOT (HOLDING C)) (CLEAR C). The last two assertions, (NOT (HOLDING C)) and (CLEAR C) are "side effects" that are not protected because they are incidental to the purpose of N4. If there are several actions that can achieve the goal, this amounts to an OR branch in the search tree. One action must be selected for expansion and the others remembered for backtracking (qv). Expanding goal node N7 with an UNSTACK action yields Figure 5. Note that the lower block is still an uninstantiated variable at this point.

If every goal required a node expansion, planning would never terminate. Fortunately, there is another process, called linking, that also achieves a goal. Linking is performed when the goal is "already true" somewhere in the plan, ie, when the goal matches an assertion of another node in the plan. That other node must not be ordered below the goal, however. In this case (ON C y) will match (ON C A) in the start node, giving a value for y. N8 becomes a "phantom node" and is ordered below the start node. In addition, the goal protection (PROTECTED (ON C A) START N7) is recorded. In practice, the planner always first tries to achieve a goal by linking and does a node expansion only when linking is impossible. Why should an agent have to work for the goal when it has already been achieved? In general, there may be several possible linking alternatives, just as there may be several possible expansions. After linking N8 and N9 and expanding N5 with a STACK action, the diagram is as shown in Figure 6. Implied by the linking process is the ability to retrieve literals asserted by any node in the plan that match a given pattern and that are not below a given node.

At this point in plan synthesis a conflict is detected. A conflict is the situation where two unordered nodes assert contradictory literals. Here N4 asserts (CLEAR C) and N5 asserts (NOT (CLEAR C)). (Recall that the assertions of an action node are the instantiated action postconditions.) A conflict is symptomatic of a contradictory or inconsistent world state. It can be resolved by ordering the two nodes while respecting the protection relations of the upper node. If the planner does not resolve conflicts as soon as they come into existence, it becomes indeterminate

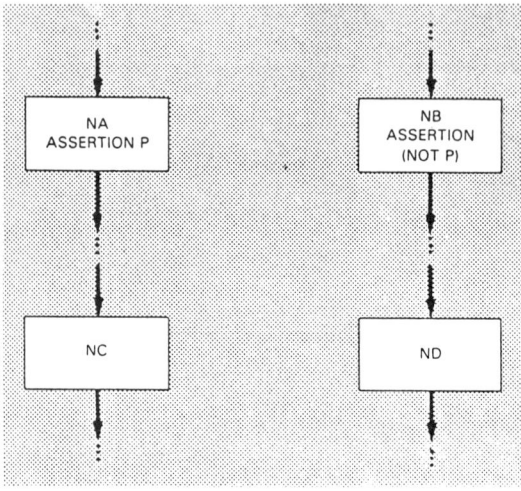

Figure 11. A conflict situation.

whether an assertion is true at a particular point in the plan. Linking then becomes impossible and the selection of a "best" node expansion (described later) is unreliable. The general conflict situation is illustrated in Figure 11. Here P and (NOT P) are the contradictory assertions of unordered nodes, with P being protected between NA and NC and (NOT P) being protected between NB and ND. There are two possible resolutions of the conflict: order NC above NB or order ND above NA. Simply ordering NA directly above NB or NB directly above NA would violate the goal protections and invalidate the plan. Of course, if there are no protections on the contradicting literals, as is the case at this point in the blocks world example, a simple ordering of the contradicting nodes is satisfactory. The planner orders N4 above N5. There is also a second conflict at this point: (CLEAR C) in N10 and (NOT (CLEAR C)) in N7. This is resolved by ordering N7 above N10. The plan diagram now looks like Figure 7.

The three fundamental operations of a basic planner have now been illustrated: linking, node expansion, and conflict resolution by ordering. To reach a complete solution merely requires a repetition of these moves. The complete sequence of planning steps is given in Table 1. The plan is complete when the goal stack has been emptied and all conflicts are resolved. This state is reached in Figure 9. Removing the phantom node scaffolding from this diagram yields Figure 10, the actual plan.

Although this blocks world problem does not illustrate expansion with inference rules or linking to derived assertions, these will now be briefly described. Recall that derived assertions cease to be true at the moment when one of their preconditions is contradicted, whereas assertions of actions continue to hold until they are explicitly contradicted. This means that goal protections involving derived assertions must be iteratively "extended" during planning using the following protection transitivity rule:

If (PROTECTED literal1 node1 node2) and
   (PROTECTED derived.literal node2 node3) Then
  Record (PROTECTED literal1 node1 node3)

Table 1. Major Steps in Generating a Blocks World Plan

1. Expand goal N4, (ONTABLE C), into PUTDOWN (C).	See Fig. 4.
2. Expand goal N7, (HOLDING C), into UNSTACK(C, y).	See Fig. 5.
3. Link goal N8, (ON C y), to the Start node by applying substitution [A/y].	
4. Link goal N9, (CLEAR C), to the Start node.	
5. Expand goal N5, (ON B C), into STACK(B, C).	See Fig. 6
6. Order N4 above N5 to resolve the conflict over (CLEAR C) in N4 and (NOT (CLEAR C)) in N5.	
7. Order N7 above N10 to resolve the conflict over (CLEAR C) in N10 and (NOT (CLEAR C)) in N7.	See Fig. 7.
8. Link goal N10, (CLEAR C) to N4.	
9. Expand goal N11, (HOLDING B), into PICKUP(B).	See Fig. 8.
10. Link goal N12, (ONTABLE B), to the Start node.	
11. Link goal N13, (CLEAR B), to the Start node.	
12. Expand goal N6, (ON A B), into STACK(A, B).	
13. Order N5 above N6 to resolve the conflict over (CLEAR B) in N5 and (NOT CLEAR B)) in N6.	
14. Order N11 above N14 to resolve the conflict over (CLEAR B) in N14 and (NOT (CLEAR B)) in N11.	
15. Link goal N14, (CLEAR B), to N5.	
16. Expand goal N15, (HOLDING A), into PICKUP(A).	
17. Order N7 above N15 to resolve the conflict over (CLEAR A) in N7 and (NOT (CLEAR A)) in N15.	
18. Link goal N16, (ONTABLE A), to the Start node.	
19. Link goal N17, (CLEAR A), to the Start node.	See Fig. 9

Whenever a new protection relation is recorded, the planner must attempt to extend it using this rule. The net result is that nonderived preconditions of inference rules are protected over the region of the plan in which a derived assertion must hold. Also, inferences must be allowed to chain forward spontaneously, like event rules, so that all conflicts involving derived assertions can be detected. These conflicts are resolved like any other. Because it is relatively expensive to monitor the triggering of forward-chaining rules in a distributed network of assertions, it is computationally advantageous to minimize the use of inferences and derived assertions in planning.

Finally, backtracking must be mentioned. If no linking is possible for a particular goal and no expansion exists, the goal cannot be satisfied. The planner has reached an impasse and must backtrack up the search tree and reconsider one of its earlier decisions. In this blocks world example no backtracking is required, but it is routine in planning for real-world applications.

ACTION SELECTION

It is frequently the case that more than one action is a candidate for expanding a goal node. How does the planner decide which to try first? There are two general categories: domain-independent criteria and domain-specific advice.

Useful domain-independent criteria for rating candidate actions are the number of nonlinkable preconditions, the number of "bonus goals" (described later), and resource consumption. In the blocks world planning example there were two expansions for N7: UNSTACK(C) and PICKUP(C). At step 2, both the preconditions of UNSTACK can be linked, and for PICKUP the precondition (ONTABLE C) would need to be expanded. This extra expansion would mean more work for both the planner and the agent executing the plan. Thus UNSTACK looks like the better choice.

Every node expansion is undertaken to satisfy the current top goal on the goal stack. Sometimes the new action will, by virtue of its other consequences, serendipitously achieve additional goals in the stack. These are bonus goals, which the planner will be able to satisfy merely by linking. If two expansion candidates have the same number of nonlinkable preconditions, the one that achieves more bonus goals will likely result in a simpler plan. A reasonable heuristic static evaluation function for rating expansion candidates is

(F * bonus-goal-count - nonlinkable-precondition-count)

Here F is a factor greater than 1. It is desirable that F approximate the average number of nonlinkable preconditions expected for actions in a particular domain. This domain-independent evaluation function quantifies the doctrine that the best action is one that maximally reduces the difference between the desired state, represented by the unsatisfied goals, and the present planning state, represented by the start node assertions plus the assertions of actions already planned. It favors actions that achieve several goals at once over those that achieve just one.

A third measure of the relative desirability of alternative actions is their "cost," that is, the consumption of valuable resources, such as time and money. For example, in a temporal planner (discussed later) where action durations are available, the quicker action will be preferable, all else being equal. When known, and when they differ significantly, resource consumption considerations may in fact dominate over the linking and bonus goal count evaluation in the selection of alternative actions. Nontemporal cost will be domain-specific but once computed can be factored into a general evaluation function.

Domain-dependent criteria for action selection may be implemented by adding additional preconditions to the action description. For example, if there are two competitive actions, PICKUP-BY-HAND and PICKUP-WITH-

FORKLIFT, for lifting objects, it might be appropriate to "advise" the planner to discriminate on the basis of weight. PICKUP-BY-HAND could be given two additional preconditions (WEIGHT-IN-LBS object w) and (LESSP w 40). PICKUP-WITH-FORKLIFT would be given a similar condition requiring a weight of at least 40 lb. The second precondition is actually an example of an action constraint, which is discussed later. This approach has the advantage of not requiring additional machinery in the planner beyond that needed for ordinary preconditions. However, for logical clarity in complex domains it may be preferable to factor out the control preconditions into distinct "metarules" for managing such control decisions (Davis, 1980).

An alternative to mechanical decision making in selecting an action is for the planner to ask a human operator to make the choice. This is the interactive approach to planning exemplified by SIPE (Wilkins, 1984). By keeping a person in the loop, the possibility of the planner getting lost in search is greatly reduced. SIPE also provides a number of other custom features such as a constraint language for constraining the value of uninstantiated variables and nonconsumable resource management procedures that allow action resources to be specially declared in the action description. A more recent version also has sophisticated procedures for recovering from execution errors (Wilkins, 1985).

CONSTRAINTS

As seen in the PICKUP example, it is highly desirable to be able to place constraints on the variables of an action rule. What exactly is a constraint? For present purposes it may be defined as any EVALuable LISP form having action variables among its arguments. Normally evaluation of a constraint is delayed until all variables have been instantiated. If evaluation returns a non-NIL value, the constraint is satisfied. Such a feature bridges between the logic-based planner and conventional algorithmic computation and allows the planner to carry along partial descriptions of uninstantiated variables without a premature commitment (Stefik, 1981). Constraints that are not completely instantiated in the course of plan generation may require a special constraint satisfaction (qv) package to select values for remaining variables.

In some planning problems it may be desirable to allow selected constraints to be violated. A recent version of GARI (Descotte and Latombe, 1985) provides for both "hard" and "soft" constraints. These are invoked by advice rules rated with a numerical priority. The rules are applied in order of decreasing priority. If an inconsistent plan results, the system backtracks to the most recent lowest-priority constraint application and discards it. The procedure is shown to satisfy an optimality property, and feasibility has been demonstrated on plans for the machining of mechanical parts.

INHIBITING BACKWARD CHAINING

Not all preconditions of an action should be expanded if not already true. For example, in the UNSTACK action the precondition (ON upper-block lower-block) should already be true when the unstacking occurs since it is pointless to stack two blocks just so they can be unstacked. Such preconditions should be achieved only by linking. Tate called these "hold" conditions (Tate, 1976). Contemporary planners commonly have syntactic conventions for indicating in an action description when backward chaining of a precondition should be inhibited. This helps to reduce the number of candidate node expansions (since a candidate may be eliminated if the condition is not already true), and reduces aimless search during backtracking. Otherwise, even if the condition can be achieved initially by linking, on backtracking over the linking operation the planner may try a node expansion when this would be inappropriate.

HIERARCHICAL PLANNING WITH MACRO ACTIONS

Programmers writing in algorithmic languages find it convenient to group statements into subroutines and functions. For similar reasons the author of an action knowledge base for a planner may find it convenient to "program" primitive actions into macro actions. As with subroutines, the elements of a macro action may themselves be macro actions. The analogy to LISP macros is even better since macro actions are usually completely expanded prior to execution. In addition to organizational convenience, planning with macro actions may help to reduce search. In the case where each macro action has just one expansion, search is eliminated entirely, and the task of writing the action descriptions takes on the character of conventional programming. NOAH, NONLIN, SIPE, and MOLGEN are examples of planners that can synthesize plans from macro actions.

Goal protections are necessary to tie together the structure of macro actions. Allowing embedded goals (in addition to preconditions at the "top" of the macro) gives added power. Figure 12 shows a diagram for the macro action DECORATE in the domain of home construction (Tate, 1976). The dotted lines signify protection relations. The top-level action in this domain is BUILD-HOUSE, which expands into ten intermediate-level actions such as LAY-BRICKWORK, FINISH-GRADING, and DECORATE. All the components of DECORATE happen to be primitive actions. For example, the primitive action FINISH-CARPENTRY is defined:

(FINISH-CARPENTRY()
   () → ((CARPENTRY-FINISHED)))

By writing macro actions, the author of the action knowledge base is able to control the sequence of actions as well as suppress much of the state description detail in modeling the construction world. This can be a convenience in stereotyped circumstances, but there are also disadvantages, which are discussed later.

In a system that constructs plans from macro actions, both goal nodes and action nodes may be expanded into either primitive actions or macro actions. In expansion with a macro action, successors of the expanded node generally become successors of the bottom node(s) of the macro action, in this example C8. [However, SIPE (Wilkins, 1984) allows more options here.] Predecessors of

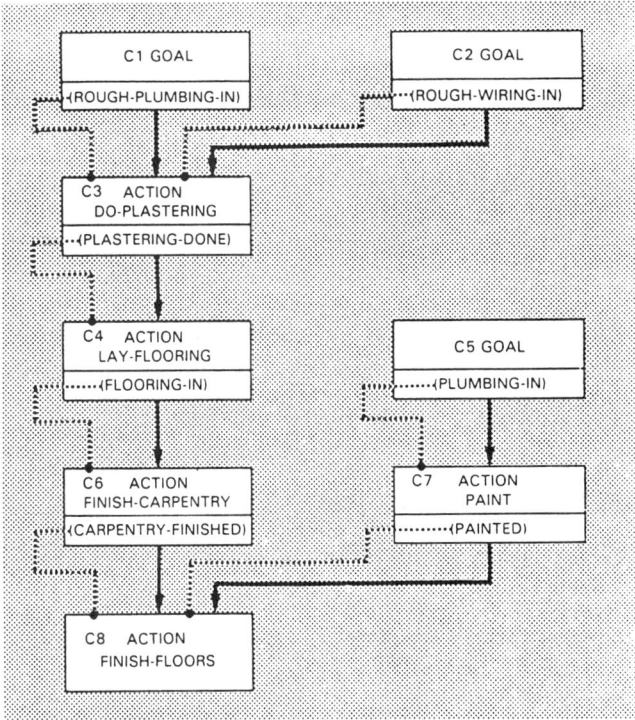

Figure 12. The DECORATE macro action.

the expanded node become predecessors of the "top" nongoal nodes in the expansion, in this example C3 and C7.

The subject of hierarchical "actions" brings out an issue in planning philosophy. A planner knowledge base that merely specifies alternative expansions of high level actions into lower level ones, without reference to underlying state changes, is effectively a hierarchical set of recipes. For example, the rule base might specify an expansion for the action "reseed lawn" as the sequence: mow grass very short, rake up loose debris, distribute seed, cover with topping mulch, distribute fertilizer, roll with a lawn roller, and water frequently. Although this plan suffices for the amateur gardener, it is not based on a deep understanding of plant physiology and soil chemistry. If the knowledge base author provides for several levels, with alternatives and metalevel control, the rote nature of this style of "planning" may not be apparent or harmful. In fact, if the underlying domain theory is poorly understood or unnecessarily complex, as in this gardening example, empirical expansions are the method of choice. Also, plan generation with preprogrammed sequences is much faster than synthesis from scratch because little or no search is required. However, it is important to realize that the person is the one who is actually doing the planning, by writing behavior procedures to be executed. On the other hand plans constructed in this way may exhibit less flexibility and novelty because the planner can only assemble and play back action patterns that have been programmed into the knowledge base. And if during execution a sequence goes awry (eg, you run out of topping mulch on New Year's day) empirical expansions offer little guidance in attempting to repair (replan) the programmed sequence. Thus the general issue of deep knowledge vs shallow knowledge applies to planners as well as to other knowledge-based systems.

Hierarchical planning with macro actions normally proceeds in a top-down manner. Another planning control paradigm has been proposed, opportunistic planning, in which control jumps about between levels, sometimes working bottom-up and sometimes top-down as the plan is assembled (Hayes-Roth and co-workers, 1979). These ideas were derived from studying verbal protocols of human subjects planning multiple-goal errand-running problems ("stop at the vet," "visit the bookstore," etc) in a hypothetical town. Using a sophisticated blackboard control architecture (see BLACKBOARD SYSTEMS), pattern-invoked *knowledge sources* were written that successfully simulated the planning behavior of a human subject on an errand-planning problem. The order of achieving goals is decided dynamically, for example, to take advantage of the physical proximity of two places to be visited.

PROCEDURAL SUBPLANNERS

For certain specialized planning tasks, such as route planning (see ROBOT PATH PLANNING AND OBSTACLE AVOIDANCE), it may be much more efficient to invoke a procedural subplanner (Fikes, 1977). This is a domain-specific subsystem that aids in planning the achievement of a specific class of goals. For example, in the robot domain the goal (INROOM ROBOT x) would be associated with a procedural route-generating subplanner that could apply special search algorithms and geometric knowledge. When an INROOM goal is encountered that is not linkable, the subplanner is invoked to generate a primitive or macro action into which the goal is expanded. A macro action might specify a sequence of traveling actions or intermediate location goals that would achieve the original INROOM goal.

GOAL HIERARCHIES AND GOAL ORDERING

Planning is inherently sensitive to the order in which goals are attempted because earlier actions may change the world state for later actions. This applies both to the original goal set as well as to action preconditions, which become subgoals upon node expansion. An adverse ordering can dramatically increase the amount of search required to find an acceptable plan or even prevent a solution from being found.

To understand the problem, consider a domain with a midget household robot that must stand on a chair to reach a light switch. Assume that chairs are too heavy for the robot to move. Suppose the robot's turn-off-light action has the preconditions (ON ROBOT chair) and (NEXTTO chair LIGHTSWITCH). Suppose further that there are many chairs, only one of which is near the switch. With this ordering of preconditions the planner will probably arbitrarily pick the wrong chair to stand on and have to backtrack many times until it finds the one that is near the switch. If the order of the goals is reversed, the correct instantiation for "chair" is immediately obtained, and the planner does not have to backtrack at all. Analogous phenomena are also seen in constraint satisfaction (qv) and database retrieval problems. The incorrect ordering can cause backtracking over large segments of a plan. To see how an adverse ordering can prevent a solution entirely, suppose now that the robot is stronger and *can* push chairs about, and in the initial state there is only one chair, which is not near the switch. The planner achieves the first goal by standing on the chair, and then protects (ON ROBOT CHAIR). To achieve the second goal, not already true, the robot must be on the floor to push the chair. However, protection of the first goal pins the robot on the chair, preventing the second goal from being achieved. Again, reversing the order of the goals enables a solution.

Several remedies exist for this class of problem. One, already suggested, is for the planner to permute the order of all its goals (and subgoals) if it fails to find a solution. However, except in small, toy domains, this will lead to intolerable computation times. A better idea is to establish a hierarchy or priority scheme on the literals of a domain (Siklossy and Dreussi, 1973; Sacerdoti, 1974). At the top level are literals that are most difficult to achieve, determine the essential structure of the domain's state space, or are not affected by any plannable action. At the bottom of the hierarchy are the easy, detail-level literals. The planner's goal stack is segregated according to this hierarchy, just as the job queue of an operating system is ordered by job priority. All goals at level n are achieved before going to work on level $n + 1$ goals. In this way the planner is able to generate a broad-brush plan at an abstract level and then progressively refine the plan as goals at the lower levels are achieved. In a mobile robot domain Sacerdoti defined the following hierarchy:

Level 1: TYPE, COLOR.
Level 2: INROOM.
Level 3: PLUGGED-IN, UNPLUGGED.
Level 4: NEXTTO.

The type and color of an object cannot be changed by an action and so are the most critical. NEXTTO is the easiest, requiring only a movement within a room.

Some permutation of goal ordering within a given level may still be required to ensure a thorough search for an acceptable plan. Thus goal hierarchies can greatly reduce but in general cannot eliminate the need to permute goals. Although most domains are probably amenable to the hierarchic approach, the process of sorting the literals of a domain into classes is at present an art, and no algorithmic procedure is known. The penalty for a poorly chosen hierarchy may be unnecessary search or overlooked solutions.

Assuming goals are protected after achievement, it has been shown that there exist nonpathological goal sets for which *no* ordering of the goals will admit a solution (Joslin and Roach, 1989). To find a solution in such cases, goals already achieved must be violated knowingly by the planner and then reachieved. This can be accomplished with procedure called *plan splicing* (Vere, 1985), which also provides a more efficient alternative to goal permutation upon failure. Splicing may be viewed as an additional option (besides node ordering) in conflict resolution. To resolve the conflict, goal protections are intentionally violated, and the violated nodes are "demoted." Demotion may involve anything from changing a phantom back to a goal to the recursive erasure of large sections of the plan already generated. Splicing allows a planner to do a thorough search much faster than by permuting goals, but the performance improvement has not been determined analytically. The subplan erasure procedures of splicing also enable efficient replanning at plan execution time in response to unexpected events. If an unexpected event occurs that contradicts a protected condition in a plan, the same demolition procedures erase the affected portion of the plan, recreate goals, and then reinvoke the planner to mend the plan in accordance with the new world state (Vere and Bickmore, 1990).

TEMPORAL PLANNING

The planners previously discussed know nothing of numerical time. Actions are assumed to be instantaneous, and there is no way to impose time constraints on actions or goals. A temporal planner called DEVISER (Vere, 1983), an extension of NONLIN, overcomes some of these limitations. In the DEVISER system every action has a duration, which may be zero, and a start time interval called the window, which bounds the point in time when the action may begin. The default window is $(0\ \infty)$. As the plan develops, these windows are compressed as necessary so that time constraints are observed. Other features of DEVISER include external events scheduled to occur at future times, forward chaining spontaneous events, the free mixture of inferences and events in the plan structure, and packaged goals that may have time constraints on their achievement (including ideal achievement times) and a protected achievement duration. When planning terminates, the system schedules each action by selecting a start time from within the final window.

The following action description illustrates the specification and integration of durations:

(FILL-CYLINDER (capacity cylinder old-level rate duration)
 ((FLOW-RATE rate)
  (CAPACITY cylinder capacity)
  (LEVEL cylinder old-level)
  (duration = rate * (capacity - old-level)))
 —→
 ((LEVEL cylinder capacity)
  (NOT (LEVEL cylinder old-level)))

(DURATION duration))

When two actions are ordered, their windows may need to be compressed. Each compression may induce a ripple of compressions of neighboring nodes in the plan diagram, spreading out from the point of the ordering. Suppose (EST1 LST1) and (EST2 LST2) are, respectively, the windows of action nodes N1 and N2, and D1 is the duration of N1. If NI is ordered above N2, it may be necessary to decrease LST1 and increase EST2 in order to maintain the inequalities EST1 + D1 ≤ EST2 and LST1 + D1 ≤ LST2. Figure 13 shows how the duration D1 acts to compress the two windows when ordering occurs. Of course, if D1 is too long, LST1' may become less than EST1, indicating a time constraint violation, and forcing backtracking.

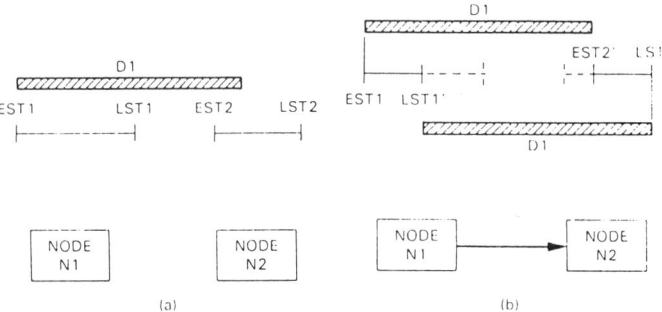

Figure 13. Window compression before and after ordering N1 and N2.

Consecutivity is another temporal constraint even stronger than ordering. Two actions N1 and N2 are *consecutive* if N2 begins immediately on termination of N1, ie, EST1 + D1 = EST2 and LST1 + DI = LST2. Operationally, this means that if the window of one node is adjusted by delta t, the window of the other must move by the same amount. Allen and Koomen (1983) have formulated a exhaustive set of seven temporal relationships that may exist between actions: before (ordered), equal, meets (consecutive), overlaps, during, starts, and finishes. See also Bell and Tate (1985), on the utilization of time constraints in planning.

PRACTICAL APPLICATIONS OF PLANNING

AI planning methods have reached sufficient maturity to support useful practical applications. Quite a few systems have achieved convincing demonstrations of planning in a variety of real-world domains. These include DEVISER in planning activities for unmanned spacecraft, GARI in the machining of mechanical parts (Descotte and Latombe, 1981), ISIS in manufacturing (Fox, 1983), MOLGEN in genetic experiments (Stefik, 1981), NONLIN in turbine overhaul and naval resupply missions (Tate and Whiter, 1984), SIPE (Wilkins, 1984) in aircraft-carrier deck operations, and Spar (Hutchinson and Kak, 1990) in robotic assembly. A very impressive domain-specific system was Wesson's air traffic control planner (Wesson, 1977), which in 1977 rivaled human controller performance.

ADVANCED TOPICS AND RESEARCH QUESTIONS IN PLANNING

There remain many open problems in planning where present understanding is weak or nonexistent. This section presents some speculative, partially overlapping advanced topics and questions for future research in planning. Their scope ranges from the level of a master's thesis upward to the completely unexplored. The general trend of planning research in recent years is toward planning in dynamic situations, since planning in static, deterministic situations is now relatively well understood.

1. What is the best way to plan with stochastic or nondeterministic actions in partially unknown environments? A closely related problem is planning with information gathering actions. The outcome of such an action is by definition unknown until the action is executed. Is it sufficient to provide the planner with the ability to generate conditional plans (Warren, 1976)?

2. Static planners do not learn and improve with practice. People do not plan anew each morning how they are going to get to work. The problem is planned once or twice, and thereafter they merely access and execute the same stored plan. How can a planner be made to improve its performance and reduce its search time with practice in a particular domain? Triangle tables (Fikes and co-workers, 1972) were an early approach to this problem, in which a linear sequence of actions is stored in flexible form so that subsequences may be applied to some new problem (see also Kibler and Porter, 1983). However, the crucial problem of efficient retrieval and screening of stored plans has not been solved. In the absence of efficient retrieval and screening, it may well be faster for a planner simply to synthesize plans from scratch rather than search through a large library of old plans every time a new goal or subgoal is encountered. How can previously successful plans and subplans be stored, retrieved, and screened for applicability to new planning problems (Hammond, 1989a)?

3. Wesson's domain-specific planner dealt with a dynamic world of aircraft flying through three-dimensional space (Wesson, 1977). How can domain-independent planners deal with dynamic external worlds (Hendrix, 1973)? For example, given a knowledge of the laws of physics, how could a planner synthesize the series of rocket engine and thruster firings that would enable a spacecraft in Earth orbit to intercept a passing comet of known trajectory?

4. Protracted (or maintenance) goals are those that must be preserved for a span of time. DEVISER could achieve protracted goals when a single action would suffice for the desired duration. How can protracted goals be planned when a series of actions are required, each action only maintaining the goal for part of the desired duration?

5. Avoidance goals (McDermott, 1982) are negative protracted goals in the above terminology. It is insufficient merely to backtrack the planner whenever an avoidance goal is violated. The planner must be able to intentionally insert actions into the plan that will contradict the preconditions of all possible spontaneous event chains leading to an avoidance goal. How can planners be extended to handle general avoidance goals?

6. Discrete event simulation is a mature technology for modeling complex domains with remarkable precision.

But simulations are passive and do not synthesize actions to achieve goals. It is possible to envision a "planulator," blending the capabilities of a planner and discrete event simulator. How can the world-modeling power of simulation be combined with the logical reasoning and plan synthesis capabilities of an AI planner?

7. One of the weaknesses afflicting contemporary planners is uncontrolled chronological backtracking. The doctrine of dependency-directed backtracking (qv) (De Kleer and co-workers, 1979) offers guidance, but the computationally efficient adaptation of this idea to planners is still a difficult research problem. In fact, an inordinate fear of backtracking probably impels much of the research on elaborate control architectures. A really efficient selective backtracking method for planners would greatly reduce the cost of bad decisions and lessen the imperative for infallible first-time decision processes.

8. Program synthesis and plan synthesis show striking parallels, and over the years concepts from algorithmic programming have been a source of inspiration to planning researchers. In fact, program synthesis may be viewed as the planning of action sequences for agents called computers. Synthesizing plans for a robot to fetch the longest piece of straight lumber in a pile and for a microprocessor to return the largest positive integer in a list are very similar problems. This is a sobering perspective because program synthesis is appreciated to be immensely difficult, and yet programming is evidently only a special case of the general planning problem. Is there a useful theoretical framework in which planning, program synthesis, and program verification can be unified? (see AUTOMATIC PROGRAMMING).

9. There is talk of generating "plans" that would, in fact, consist of sets of production rules for controlling the behavior of a system. How can such plans be generated, and for what class of problems would this kind of plan be advantageous?

10. Suppose a planner fails to generate a successful plan. Under what circumstances should it try again later, as the state of the world changes (Hammond, 1989b)?

11. Another immensely difficult topic is the generation of plans for multiple sentient agents that may have to communicate and negotiate to achieve and preserve mutual and conflicting goals (Georgeff, 1984; Appelt, 1985; Schank and Abelson, 1977; Wilensky, 1983; Power, 1979; Houghton and Isard, 1987). How can contemporary AI planning methods be extended into an operational theory of "computational politics?" Will it be possible to automate the U.S. House of Representatives?

HISTORICAL NOTES

Planning and problem solving began as a common topic with GPS (Newell and Simon, 1963), and in some circles these two terms are still synonymous. In GPS, differences between the present and desired state guided the selection of operators. STRIPS (Fikes and Nilsson, 1971) was an influential early planner that in 1969 generated linear plans for SRI's robot SHAKEY (qv). It introduced the notions of add- and delete-lists, which have evolved only slightly into the present precondition and postcondition style rules for primitive actions. STRIPS MACROPS were an early form of macro action limited to a sequence of primitive actions. Hacker (Sussman, 1975) was constructed in 1973 to explore the problem of improving performance with experience. As an incidental feature, it introduced the notion of goal protection. In 1975 NOAH (Sacerdoti, 1977) introduced concurrency into plans and extended the notion of macro actions. It originated the ideas of conflict detection and resolution by ordering. NONLIN (Tate 1976, 1977) improved on the NOAH model by adding goal structure, backtracking, and linking. NOAH did not do linking but rather planned each goal back to the initial state, and then applied heuristic "critics" to simplify the plan. More recent functional planners have used linking.

BIBLIOGRAPHY

J. Allen and J. Koomen, "Planning Using a Temporal World Model," *Proceedings of the Eighth IJCAI*, Karlsruhe, FRG, Morgan-Kaufmann, San Mateo, Calif., 1983, pp. 741–747.

D. E. Appelt, *Planning English Sentences*, Cambridge University Press, Cambridge, 1985.

C. Bell and A. Tate, "Using Temporal Constraints to Restrict Search in a Planner," *Proceedings of the Third Alvey IKBS SIG Workshop*, Sunningdale, Oxfordshire, UK, 1985.

M. Brady and co-workers, *Robot Motion: Planning and Control*, MIT Press, Cambridge, Mass., 1982.

D. Chapman, "Planning for Conjunctive Goals," *Artif. Intell.* **32**, 333–377 (July 1987).

R. Davis, "Meta-Rules: Reasoning About Control," *Artif. Intell.* **15**, 179–222 (Dec. 1980).

J. de Kleer and co-workers, "Explicit Control of Reasoning," in P. H. Winston and R. H. Brown, eds., *Artificial Intelligence: An AI Perspective*, Vol. 1, MIT Press, Cambridge, Mass., 1979, pp. 93–116.

Y. Descotte and J. C. Latombe, "GARI: A Problem Solver that Plans How to Machine Mechanical Parts," *Proceedings of the Seventh IJCAI*, Vancouver, B.C., Morgan-Kaufmann, San Mateo, Calif., 1981, pp. 766–772.

Y. Descotte and J. C. Latombe, "Making Compromises Among Antagonist Constraints in a Planner," *Artif. Intell.* **27**, 183–217 (Nov. 1985).

R. E. Fikes, "Knowledge Representation in Automatic Planning Systems," in J. K. Jones, ed., *Perspectives in Computer Science*, 1977, pp. 63–75.

R. E. Fikes and N. J. Nilsson. "STRIPS: a New Approach to the Application of Theorem Proving," *Artif. Intell.* **2**, 189–208 (Winter 1971).

R. E. Fikes and co-workers, "Learning and Executing Generalized Robot Plans," *Artif. Intell.* **3**, 251–288 (1972).

M. S. Fox, *Constraint-Directed Search: A Case Study of Job-Shop Scheduling*, Ph.D. dissertation, Computer Science Dept., Carnegie Mellon University, Pittsburgh, Pa., Oct. 1983.

M. Georgeff, "A Theory of Action for MultiAgent Planning," *Proceedings of the Fourth National Conference on Artificial Intelligence*, Austin, Tex., AAAI, Menlo Park, Calif., 1984, pp. 121–125.

C. Green, "Theorem-Proving by Resolution as a Basis for Question-Answering Systems," in B. Meltzer and D. Michie, eds., *Machine Intelligence*, Vol. 4, Halsted, Wiley, New York, 1969, pp. 183–205.

K. J. Hammond, *Case-Based Planning: Viewing Planning as a Memory Task*, Academic Press, Cambridge, Mass., 1989a.

K. J. Hammond, "Opportunistic Memory," *Proceedings of the 11th IJCAI*, Detroit, Mich., Morgan-Kaufmann, San Mateo, Calif., 1989, pp. 504–510.

B. Hayes-Roth and co-workers, "Modelling Planning as an Incremental, Opportunistic Process," *Proceedings of the Sixth IJCAI*, Tokyo, Japan, Morgan-Kaufmann, San Mateo, Calif., 1979, pp. 375–383.

G. G. Hendrix, "Modelling Simultaneous Actions and Continuous Processes," *Artif. Intell.* **4,** 145–180 (1973).

G. Houghton and Stephen Isard, "Why to Speak, What to Say and How to Say It: Modelling Language Production in Discourse," in P. Morris, ed., *Modelling Cognition*, John Wiley & Sons, Inc., Chichester, 1987.

S. A. Hutchinson and A. C. Kak, "Spar: A Planner that Satisfies Operational and Geometric Goals in Uncertain Environments," *AI Magazine* 30–61 (Spring 1990).

D. Joslin and J. Roach, "A Theoretical Analysis of Conjunctive-Goal Problems," *Artif. Intell.* **41,** 97–106 (Nov. 1989).

D. Kibler and B. Porter, "Episodic Learning," *Proceedings of the Third National Conference on Artificial Intelligence*, Washington, D.C., AAAI, Menlo Park, Calif., 1983, pp. 191–196.

J. McCarthy and P. J. Hayes, "Some Philosophical Problems from the Standpoint of Artificial Intelligence," in B. Meltzer and D. Michie, eds., *Machine Intelligence*, Vol. 4, Halsted, John Wiley & Sons, Inc., New York, 1969, pp. 463–501.

D. A. McDermott, "A Temporal Logic for Reasoning about Processes and Plans," *Cog. Sci.* **6,** 101–155 (1982).

A. Newell and H. A. Simon, "GPS, a Program that Simulates Human Thought," in E. A. Feigenbaum and J. Feldman, eds., *Computers and Thought*, McGraw-Hill, New York, 1963, pp. 279–293.

R. Power, "The Organization of Purposeful Dialogues," *Linguistics* **17,** 107–152 (1979).

E. D. Sacerdoti, "Planning in a Hierarchy of Abstraction Spaces," *Artif. Intell.* **5,** 115–135 (1974).

E. D. Sacerdoti, *A Structure for Plans and Behavior*, Elsevier/North-Holland, New York, 1977.

R. C. Schank and R. P. Abelson, *Scripts, Plans, Goals, and Understanding*, Erlbaum, Hillsdale, N.J., 1977.

L. Siklossy and J. Dreussi, "An Efficient Robot Planner Which Generates Its Own Procedures," *Proceedings of the Third IJCAI*, Stanford, Calif., Morgan-Kaufmann, San Mateo, Calif., 1973, pp. 423–430.

M. Stefik, "Planning with Constraints (MOLGEN: Part I)," *Artif. Intell.* **16,** 111–139 (May 1981).

G. J. Sussman, *A Computer Model of Skill Acquisition*, American Elsevier, New York, 1975.

A. Tate, *Project Planning Using a Hierarchic Non-Linear Planner*, Report No. 25, Artificial Intelligence Dept., University of Edinburgh, Aug. 1976.

A. Tate, "Generating Project Networks," *Proceedings of the Fifth IJCAI*, Cambridge, Mass., Morgan-Kaufmann, San Mateo, Calif., 1977, pp. 888–893.

A. Tate and A. M. Whiter, "Planning with Multiple Resource Constraints and an Application to a Naval Planning Problem," *Proceedings of the First Conference on AI Applications*, Denver, Colo., 1984, pp. 410–416.

S. A. Vere, "Planning in Time: Windows and Durations for Activities and Goals," *IEEE Trans. Pattern Anal. Mach. Intell.* **PAMI-5,** 246–267 (May 1983).

S. A. Vere, "Splicing Plans to Achieve Misordered Goals," *Proceedings of the Ninth IJCAI*, Los Angeles, Calif., Morgan-Kaufmann, San Mateo, Calif., 1985, pp. 1016–1021.

S. A. Vere and T. W. Bickmore, "A Basic Agent," *Comp. Intell.*, 41–60 (May 1990).

D. H. D. Warren, "Generating Conditional Plans and Programs," *Proceedings of the AISB Conference*, University of Edinburgh, 1976, pp. 344–354.

R. B. Wesson, "Planning in the World of the Air Traffic Controller," *Proceedings of the Fifth IJCAI*, Cambridge, Mass., Morgan-Kaufmann, San Mateo, Calif., 1977, pp. 473–479.

R. Wilensky, *Planning and Understanding*, Addison-Wesley, Reading, Mass., 1983.

D. E. Wilkins, "Domain-Independent Planning: Representation and Plan Generation," *Artif. Intell.* **22,** 269–301 (April 1984).

D. E. Wilkins, *Recovering from Execution Errors in SIPE*, Technical Note 346, AI Center, SRI International, Menlo Park, Calif., Jan. 1985.

General References

L. Daniel, "Planning and Operations Research," in T. O'Shea and M. Eisenstadt, eds. *Artificial Intelligence: Tools, Techniques, and Applications*, Harper & Row, New York, 1984, pp. 423–452. Reviews STRIPS, NOAH, and NONLIN in detail, and discusses their limitations.

M. Drummond and A. Tate, *AI Planning: a Tutorial and Review*, Technical Report AIAI-TR-30, AI Applications Institute, Edinburgh, Scotland, Jan. 1989. A recent survey that compares 15 major planners.

M. Georgeff, "Planning," in *Annual Review of Computer Science*, Vol. 2, 1987, pp. 359–400. A survey of planning from a theoretical perspective.

E. D. Sacerdoti, "Problem Solving Tactics," *Proceedings of the Sixth IJCAI*, Tokyo, Japan, Morgan-Kaufmann, San Mateo, Calif., 1979, pp. 1077–1085. Discusses methods for improving the efficiency of planners.

W. Swartout, and co-workers, "Summary Report," *Proceedings of Knowledge-Based Planning Workshop*, DARPA, Austin, Tex., Dec. 1987, A1-A23. Summary of a workshop to identify and explore new directions for planning research.

D. E. Wilkins, *Practical Planning*, Morgan-Kaufmann, San Mateo, Calif., 1988. An in-depth exposition of the SIPE planner.

S. VERE
Lockheed AI Center

PLANNING, REACTIVE

Planning, in AI, refers to a body of techniques used to automate the process of selecting and carrying out actions to bring an environment to some desired state. In *Classical Planning* [eg, STRIPS (Fikes and Nilsson, 1971), NONLIN (Tate, 1975), DEVISER (Vere, 1983), TWEAK (Chapman, 1987), an application domain is encoded in terms of a set of primitive actions and their preconditions and effects characterized as state predicates. A planning problem consists of this domain description plus an initial and final (or goal) state. Planning in this framework consists of searching through the space of action orderings to find one which takes the initial state to the goal state. This set of ordered actions is called the plan. The 'blocks world' is the archetypical domain for classical planning: a world consisting of a number of blocks which the agent (usually thought of as a robot) can stack upon each other. The agent is the only entity active in the environment, and the configurations of the blocks are precisely known at all times.

Many real-world application domains, particularly robotic applications, do not have the static characteristics of blocks world. Schoppers (1988) describes an example domain that contrasts strongly with the blocks world: his 'baby world.' This domain is similar to the blocks world, except it is inhabited by a "mischievous baby who will flatten block towers, snatch blocks out of the robot's hand, and even throw blocks at the robot." The crucial new ingredients in this problem domain are that the agent (1) cannot be certain of the effects of its actions, (2) cannot make the assumption that the world remains static and unchanging except when it carries out an action, and (3) cannot assume that it knows everything about the world. This is exactly the problem faced by a robotic machine operating in the "real-world," the same uncertain (see 1, 3) and dynamic (see 2) environment that humans inhabit in everyday life.

Classical planning becomes too brittle in these application domains (Kaelbling, 1986; Chapman, 1987; Brooks, 1986; Agre and Chapman, 1987) for two main reasons: because the world can change while planning is in progress, partial plans may be, thus, rendered useless; and, because of the uncertain effects of actions, "correct" plans actually may fail to achieve their goal. Chapman (1987) summarizes the state-of-the-art in classical planning. He shows that classical planning, in the general case, is undecidable, and even in its simpler forms can be computationally intractable. Furthermore, Arbib (1981) (see also SCHEMA THEORY) has maintained for some time that behavior should not be produced as the result of symbolic reasoning from axioms, but rather as the result of cooperation and competition between concurrent, active agents called *schema instances*. His schema theory is a bridge between Cognitive Science, Brain Theory, and Artificial Intelligence, and implementations of it have been made by Lyons (1989), Ankin (1989), and Draper and coworkers (1989), among others.

Work in building planning systems that can operate well in application domains such as Schoppers' "baby-world" has shown up recently in a number of workshops and conferences, eg, the 1986 Timberline Lodge workshop, the 1988 Rochester Planning Workshop, the 1990 and 1991 AAAI Spring Symposia, and the 1990 Workshop on Innovative Approaches to Planning, Scheduling, and Control. This work has been grouped together under the name *Reactive Planning*. It has been noted that reactive planning is dangerously near a contradiction in terms, because reaction is usually considered acting *without* planning. The term reactive planning is used here to refer to techniques developed to cope with the selection and execution of actions to achieve objectives in an uncertain and dynamic environment. In one sense, the goal of this field is to combine the advantages of a reactive system, robustness, and time–critical response, with the advantages of a planning system, look–ahead and global optimality. However, it can be argued that such integration may lead to a redefinition of the meaning of both planning and reaction.

In the next section, the characteristics of the reactive planning domain are described via a running example of an automated tour guide. Subsequently, a selection of the key reactive planning techniques and a description of how they can be used to address the tour guide example is presented. Finally, there is a summary of the state of the field, and a discussion of what problems remain open.

CHARACTERISTICS OF THE REACTIVE PLANNING DOMAIN

This section introduces the characteristics of the reactive planning problem domain via a running example: an automated New York City tour guide. Basically, the duty of a tour guide is to take the tour to a set of landmarks, explain each one, and answer any questions. However, in practice, there is more than this to being a good tour guide. A tour guide must fulfill one of the most stringent aspects of a reactive planning problem—he/she must be prepared to act and interact *at any time*.

Reactivity

Continual vigilance is essential to a reactive system. For example, a tour guide is continuously on duty once the tour starts. The audience can ask questions about almost anything at anytime, and the guide should be prepared to respond. There are also a host of other tasks, such as making sure everyone is back on the bus before going to the next location, working around the changing weather, considering the preferences of the audience, guarding the general safety of the tourists, etc. The classical planning approach involves the *a priori* complete or incremental generation of a plan, which is then sent to a plan executer to be carried out. A plan executer can do nothing without a plan to execute. A reactive system needs to be able to respond to the environment without necessary recourse to plans.

Timely Activity

Coordination with externally imposed time constraints is unavoidable in a reactive domain. For example, the tour guide must deal with the fact that the timeliness of actions is important. Specific opening hours of parks, museums, zoos, etc, must be considered if the tour is to remain on time, and in the rescheduling of events if there are any disturbances to the tour. The tour can only stop for a limited time at each location, and the next location needs to be given to the bus driver in advance. Time constraints are involved in reactive planning in three ways: (1) the agent must carry out actions in a timely fashion, (2) the agent must consider the effects of time in choosing which actions are appropriate, and (3) the strategy for choosing the next action must also abide by time constraints. As an example of this third constraint, note that the strategy for deciding where to go next can only occupy some fraction of the time allocated to visit a location.

Uncertainty

Dealing with uncertainty is a fact of life for a reactive system. A tour guide has *a priori* information at his or her disposal. Nonetheless, making a tour plan in the sense of the classical planning approach, *a priori* production of set of actions and some ordering information, is out of the question because the state of the environment and the actions of other entities during plan execution time (ie, the duration of the tour) are uncertain. Weather forecasts tend to be imperfect, and the preferences and humors of tour group members are notoriously fickle, not to mention the traffic patterns of New York City! For example, a good tour guide will visit outdoor locations, such as Central Park, when it is dry. Indoor activities will be scheduled for times when it rains. In New York City, this will occasionally demand hasty improvisations. Improvising the completion of a tour will require that the guide think about timely coordination with entities such as museums, parks, and restaurants, as well as maintain an on-going interaction with the audience. In such a case, it is better to keep the audience dry and interested than to spend time deriving an optimal perturbed tour!

Improvisation and Interaction

Effective behavior in a reactive planning domain is the result of the close interaction of agent and environment. For example, special events, such as parades or street theater, can be both a nuisance (for routes might have to be changed) and an opportunity (to expose tourists to those events) for a tour guide. A good tour guide should take advantage of unexpected opportunities when possible. This may mean adding new locations to the tour or selecting different paths between locations. With a human tour guide, the description and emphasis of the talks delivered at each location would also change. As another example, a good guide asks the tourists for their preferences before and during the tour, and may adapt the tour accordingly. Thus, a good tour is not a sequence of actions carried out by the guide on a passive audience, but rather a continual interaction between guide and audience. It is less successful to carry out a predetermined tour, hear the complaints afterwards, and try to convince the complainers to take another tour which will incorporate their wishes (ie, a "recovery from error" paradigm).

Actually building an "automated" tour guide would require the application of many other areas of AI in addition to reactive planning: speech-understanding, computer vision, tutorial-systems, cooperative problem-solving, user-modeling, path-planning, redundant kinematics, etc. In this example, the reactive planning component concerns the selection and execution of actions appropriate to the situation.

TECHNIQUES FOR REACTIVE PLANNING

This section discusses the techniques that have been developed for dealing with reactive planning problems. The first work in this area dates from about 1986 (though the inspiration could indeed be traced back to the STRIPS Triangle Table work from the 1970s); and the field is still far from solved. The techniques developed in this field can be effectively classified into three groups, based on their objectives:

1. *Architectures for Reactive Machines.* A reactive machine is a system in which the choice of the next action is based on hardwired response to sensory input and built-in goals. It differs from a classical plan executer in that it is always ready to carry out actions; it is not waiting for a plan to be loaded. Work in this area is in developing architectures, representations, and algorithms that can be used in building reactive machines that exhibit intelligent and robust behavior. This was one of the first areas of the field to be explored. It produced the unexpected results that it is possible to build a reactive agent that produces behavior that an observer would classify as intelligent, despite the lack of classical planning and reasoning in the agent.

2. *Design of Reactive Machines.* One of the first criticisms of reactive machines was that their robustness and intelligence really depended on the skills of the programmer who built them. This second area of reactive planning responded by designing tools which automatically build reactive systems to fulfill a set of desired criteria. The machine generation stage is assumed to be off-line; a specification of the machine and its environment is written and then input to the generation tool, which produces a detailed description of the reactive machine.

3. *Planning for Reaction.* Another major criticism of reactive machines is that they were "myopic"—unable to rise above local responses to the environment. This third area of reactive planning responded by trying to integrate the concept of planning-ahead with that of reaction to the environment.

Architectures for Reactive Machines

Chapman finished his TWEAK (Chapman, 1987) paper by suggesting that improvisation might be a better paradigm than planning. Agre and Chapman (1987) carried out the first step on the road to building systems that can exhibit intelligent behavior in uncertain and dynamic domains. They argued that "before and beneath any activity of plan following, life is a continual improvisation, a matter of deciding what to do *now* based on how the world is *now*." They built a program, *Pengi,* based on these concepts. Pengi played a video arcade game called Pengo. In a typical Pengo game, the computer appeared to hunt down targets, build traps, escape ambushes, take advantage of opportunities, and act in a timely fashion. However, the intelligent behavior of Pengi was the result of the interaction of relatively simple opportunistic strategies with a complex, structured environment. Two key ideas developed for Pengi were the concept of *routines* and the concept of *indexical-functional* representation.

Routines. A routine is a pattern of interaction between agent and environment. A routine need not be explicitly represented by the agent. It can simply be a property of the regularity in the interaction between the environment and the agent. For example, tour groups exhibit certain behavioral regularity: they may listen to the guide, they ask questions, they wander off, etc. The tour guide will typically explain some landmark, accepting and responding to questions as they arise. This highly interactive pattern is an example of a routine. Internally, the tour guide may simply have rules that say "answer any question asked" and "describe current landmark". The routine is created by the interleaved effects of these rules driven off the behavior of the environment (tour group). Recognizing and exploiting regularity in the environment allows for the construction of simpler and more robust agents that can effectively cope with uncertainty.

Indexical-Functional Representation. In an indexical-functional representation [called *deictic representation* in the more systematic exposition in Agre (in press)], properties of the immediate environment are only represented in terms of the impact they have on the objectives of the agent. For instance, a tour guide may have to deal with many people and many tours in any day. A classical planning approach would involve uniquely naming each individual encountered, eg, PERSON-23. This introduces combinatorics, since the space of persons must now be searched for appropriate instances. A Pengi-like tour guide would not uniquely name every person it encountered, but would only represent people in terms of their impact on its objectives, eg, person-now-asking-question, or person-in-danger-of-being-lost. The perceptual system directly matches the environment with such indexical-functional entities, and no search is required. Pengi used a similar mechanism to measure directly from the environment clues as to which actions to take next; these are called indexical-functional aspects. A Pengi tour guide might have such aspects as tour-becoming-bored (and hence should be livened up), or street-theater-in-view (consider diverting to look at it), etc.

Behaviors and Subsumption. Brooks (1986) noted that the standard view of intelligent robot-control architectures as pipe-lined collections of functional modules caused problems with robustness, buildability, and testability. He suggested a novel architecture, called the subsumption architecture, that emphasized building intelligent control from layers of task–achieving behaviors (see Figure 1) much in the spirit of Braitenberg (1984). He built a number of robot systems (Brooks 1986, 1987, 1989) that exhibited behavior similar to Pengi: they appeared to act in a robust intelligent way in complex environments. And like Pengi, they consisted internally of simple opportunistic control rules.

Brooks built his systems as networks of augmented fine state machine modules. Each module can accept input, has internal state, and can produce output. In addition, the output of a module can be inhibited or the input suppressed and replaced. (Brooks associates a time interval with the inhibition and suppression, which will be omitted in the simple examples here). For example, a particularly simple tour guide could be described by two connected modules: Local-Wander, which produces random heading signals, connected to a Move which when given a heading will move in that direction. A subsumption architecture is a hierarchy of such behaviors. High-level behaviors subsume the behaviors of lower levels but add in some extra behavior where appropriate. If we consider the "wander-move" behavior as a level zero subsumption architecture, we can build a level one architecture that "directs" the lower level when appropriate, but otherwise remains silent (see Fig. 2).

Level 1 consists of a counter (Up Counter) that indexes through the list of landmarks, suppresses the local wander behavior to force the guide to each location, and then triggers a speech at that location. While the guide is at a location, the local wander behavior becomes unsuppressed and the guide wanders around the landmark. This is a more useful tour guide, but it is still rather inflexible. We can add a third level that allows for reorganization of the schedule should the weather turn nasty, eg, Figure 3. If bad weather is seen by the Weather module, it inhibits the counter output and replaces it with the index to a landmark that is known to be indoors.

Goals and Beliefs. Nilsson (1988) has put forward an action network structure for teleoactive agents. These agents take changing environmental and goal conditions into account before acting. A strong motivation for this work was the dissatisfaction with conventional action control methods, where higher level units surrender control when they activate a lower-level unit and have to suspend until control is explicitly returned. This scheme can cause low level units to continue to operate in situations for which they are no longer relevant, since changes in situation go unnoticed by the suspended higher levels. To overcome this, Nilsson proposed a new scheme for organizing behavior based on networks of combinatorial circuits in

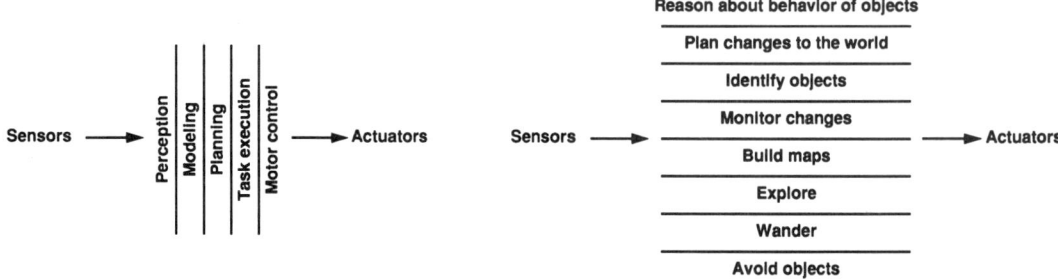

Figure 1. The traditional architecture vs the subsumption architecture.

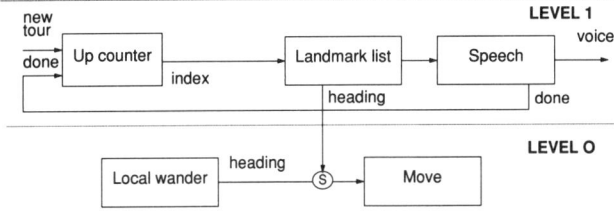

Figure 2. Levels 0 and 1 of a Subsumption tour guide.

which higher level routines enable lower level ones but do *not* surrender control. In addition, he developed a language, ACTNET, that allows a user to specify these control networks as networks of combinatorial circuits. The goals and beliefs of an agent are explicitly represented in this network. The planning component of a network is 'built-in' in the sense that goals are hard-wired to fire particular actions.

The basic unit in Nilsson's network is an action unit (see Fig. 4). An action unit is a logical gate that decides whether to fire a particular action based on the goal request G, the absence of goal establishment (the purpose P) and the preconditions P_i of the action. An action unit continually monitors its input, and fires the action as soon as it is applicable and executable. Goals, as well as preconditions, can be dynamic in nature ("talk so loud that all the tourists can hear it" is dependent on the background noise level). Networks are constructed by tying together the signals representing the goals, preconditions, etc, in an appropriate fashion. Higher level networks can enable lower level ones by turning on their purpose input.

As an example of network, consider the case of a tour guide trying to show the Empire State Building (ESB) to the group (see Fig. 5). This goal fires two primitive goals, ie, at_ESB and present_ESB_speech via action-unit Show_ESB. These establish the goals for the units move_to_ESB and present_ESB_speech. Since present_ESB_speech has as its precondition at_ESB, it has to wait until the other action unit move_to_ESB has established that precondition.

In later work Nilsson (in press) generalizes the notion of action networks to structures that reactively execute sequences of goal-seeking actions, and develops a language for programming such structures. Whereas action units achieve their goals single-handedly, teleo-reactive

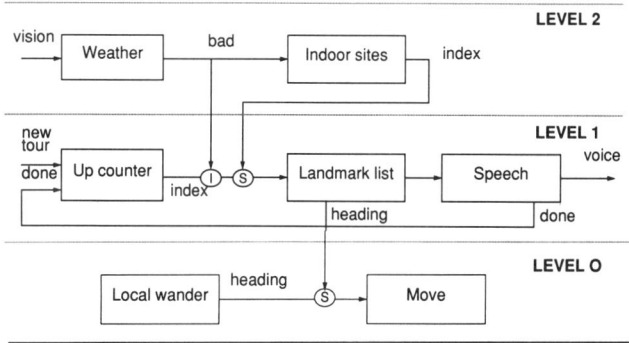

Figure 3. Levels 0, 1, and 2 of a Subsumption tour guide.

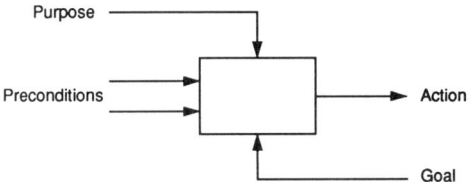

Figure 4. Nilsson's Action Unit.

structures eventually achieve their effects by conditionally enlisting other teleo-reactive structures or actions to achieve necessary subgoals.

Monitoring Change. In dynamic worlds, change proceeds regardless of the agent's state. Therefore, keeping track of the state of affairs is a nontrivial task in such domains. Hendler's DR [Hendler (1989), Sanborn and Hendler (1988)] is an approach to managing observations and actions in dynamic domains. In DR, monitors are employed to keep track of the environmental situation. A monitor is an independent information gathering component of the overall reasoning system that maintains the world model. The duty of a monitor is to report significant events.

Monitoring is coupled to reaction via constraints reporting. Every action has a set of constraints on its execution state. Constraints are divided into inhibitory constraints that prevent an applicable action from executing, and enabling constraints that allow an applicable action to execute. Action selection is based on the active constraints. If an enabling constraint is found on an action, then that action is performed. If an inhibitory constraint is found on an action, then the action is suspended and another applicable action is pursued until the constraint is removed.

Design of Reactive Machines

Reactive machines produce intelligent, but improvised, behavior, and were a major step forward in addressing the problem of acting in uncertain and dynamic environments. They respond quickly and robustly, and can be surprisingly intelligent given their lack of internal models. However, much of the power of a Brooks-style

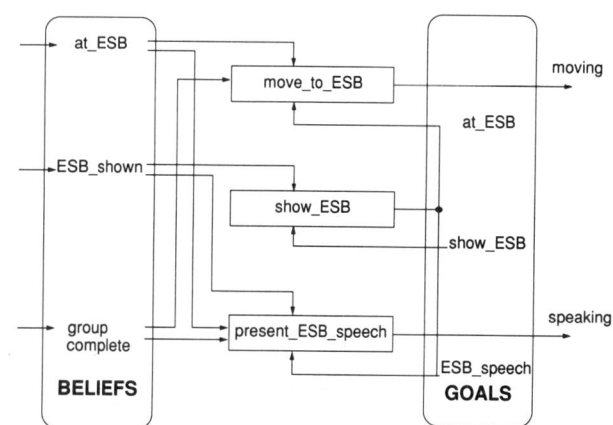

Figure 5. Part of a Tour Guide Action Network.

1176 PLANNING, REACTIVE

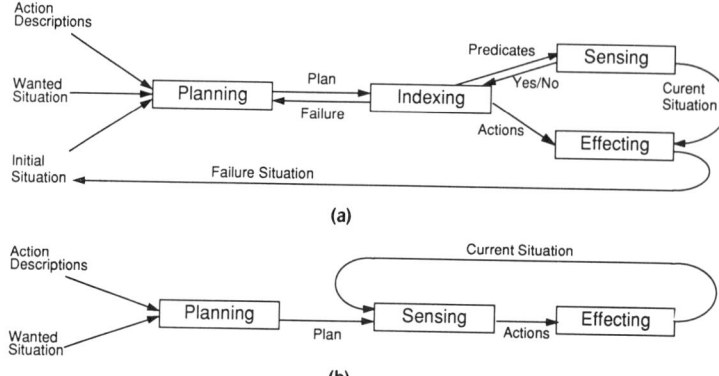

Figure 6. (a) The Classical vs (b) the Universal Plan approach.

robot, for example, comes from the skill with which the behaviors have been designed and composed together in the subsumption architecture. A major portion of work in reactive planning tries to develop techniques to design formally correct machines, and provide tools for automatically generating a reactive machine to suit a set of design criteria.

Universal Plans: The Autogeneration of Reactive Machines. The Universal Plan (Schoppers, 1987) is an approach to building reactive machines as highly conditional plans. It is a plan that can achieve a goal given any possible initial state of the environment. In this approach, actions are selected through the classifications of the actual situation encountered at execution time, as opposed to the classical approach of selecting actions based on a single initial situation at planning time. In a universal plan, the failure of an action to achieve its predicted effects does not require replanning, only the selection of a new initial point from which to execute the plan. (See Fig. 6.) Therefore, the task of a planner has changed from generating a sequence of actions, to anticipating all possible situations and the concomitant appropriate responses. At execution time, a sensing module recognizes the actual situation and selects the appropriate action to perform.

For example, a (simplified) universal plan for a tour guide showing the Empire State Building (ESB) is shown in Figure 7. The goal, to have the landmark shown to the tour, initiates the two subgoals at_ESB and ESB_speech (by the action SHOW_ESB). Carrying out the universal plan consists of examining the truth values of these two goals. If either goal is not true, then an appropriate universal plan is employed to achieve that goal (in order). For instance the universal plan for at_ESB is to move to the location (MOVE_TO_ESB), but only on the condition that the group is already complete. If this condition does not hold, then the group must first be assembled. Notice that failure of the action MOVE_TO_ESB, for any reason, results in the predicate at_ESB remaining false. This allows the action to be attempted again without replanning. Once the group is at the location, the guide can then pursue the other goal of actually presenting the history of the building.

Situated Automata: Formally Correct Reactive Machines. The *situated automata* model of Rosenschien and Kaelbling (1986, 1987, 1988) has influenced many workers in the field of reactive planning. This model addresses the issues of real-time performance and provably correct behavior. A program in this model is a finite machine with internal state that transforms inputs to outputs within a small time period. It therefore provides a good base on which to build reactive systems. A Lisp-like language, called Rex, was developed to specify such machines. The output of a Rex program is a description of a digital circuit for a machine that meets the Rex specification.

A key characteristic of the situated automata model is the correctness with which the machine's potential behavior is addressed by considering the *knowledge* that the machine contains, where knowledge is analyzed in terms of the relationship between a machine and its environment. A machine is defined to know a proposition ϕ in machine state s, if in all states s, ϕ is satisfied. Given a Rex program, a background theory describing facts about the environment, and a description of the epistemic meaning of the machine inputs, the situated automata model provides a methodology for attacking the problem of verifying the meaning of the machine outputs.

Kaelbling (1988) describes a compiler, Gapps, that maps a goal specification and set of goal reduction rules, to a Rex program, for a machine to achieve these goals. The goal reduction rules capture domain specific information. In this fashion, a correct reactive system can be automatically generated off-line.

Planning for Reaction

A crucial problem with any reactive machine is that should the environment diverge from that in which the machine was designed to operate, then the machine may produce inappropriate behavior. The best a reactive ma-

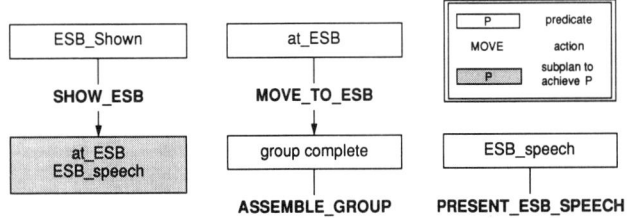

Figure 7. A Universal Tour Guide.

chine can do in the face of such a change is to degrade gracefully; that is, its responses may not be as efficient or appropriate in the new environment, however, these responses will not result in self-destruction. To address this problem completely, it is necessary to integrate the concept of the reactive machine with the concept of *a priori* planning. Note that these two concepts have some complementary characteristics: a reactive machine is not able to look ahead and plan, while an on-line, time-constrained planner cannot react quickly enough to deal with unexpected hazards. In this section we look at some approaches to integrating a planning component with a reactive machine.

Time Constraints on Planning. Interaction with a dynamic world forces time-constraints onto both planning and reaction. Reactive systems can usually cope with these constraints, however, it is more difficult for planners. Dean and Boddy (1987) introduced the class of ANYTIME algorithms to deal with time-dependent planning. An algorithm has the ANYTIME property if it can handle preemption, will return a sensible answer at any time when terminated, and, most importantly, will return answers which improve monotonically over time. The design of ANYTIME algorithms plays a key role in many approaches to reactive planning.

Integrating Planning and Reaction in a Hierarchy. Hendler (1990) notes the conflicting needs of reactors and planners: the reactors need input that closely matches the external world and need to respond on a very short timescale, the planners need to abstract away from the details of the external world and may need to work for some time on a problem. The solution suggested is a hierarchy as shown in Figure 8, based on the DR model discussed earlier. A scheduler chooses planner or reaction agents on a time permitting basis.

To investigate this scheduling approach, Spector and Hendler (1988) propose a model in which planning and reaction interact across five different levels: sensory/motor, spatial, temporal, causal, and conventional (ie, general world knowledge). This multilevel reasoning is realized in a parallel, blackboard-based planner called APE (Abstraction Partitioned Evaluator). As an example of

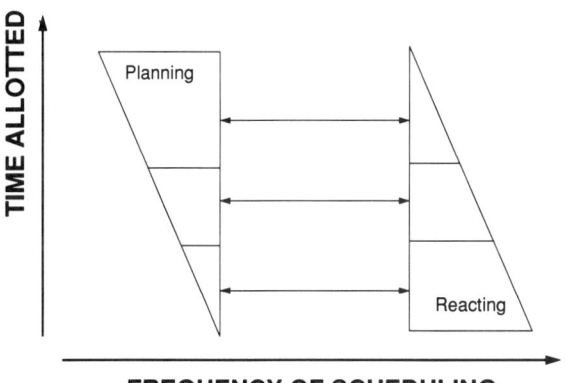

Figure 8. Hendler's Planning-Reaction hierarchy.

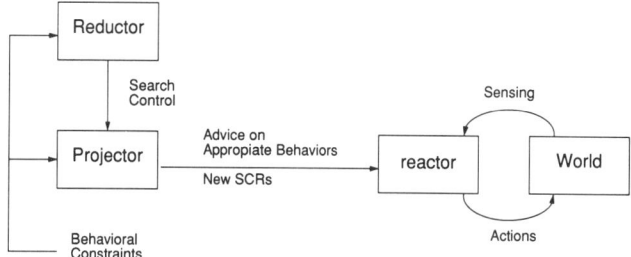

Figure 9. ERE Reductor-Projector-Reactor architecture.

how APE would reason, suppose that the tour guide has a plan for conducting a tour that includes visiting the Empire State Building. Upon arrival however, the tour guide sees an excessive line for entrance to the Empire State Building. This would first be reported as a problem at the spatial level. Replanning at that level is then immediately attempted (eg, find another, shorter line), but if that fails, then the problem is passed to the next highest level for solution and so on. During higher level reasoning, the tour guide would be using more of its resources on those levels, and would be less able to react to change in the environment, thus the propagation of information to higher levels only occurs when time (and the environment) permits.

Planning to Guide Reaction. Bresina and Drummond (1990) introduce an alternative approach to systems that produce intelligent action under time constraints. Their domain of application is photoelectric telescope scheduling problems. They suggest an architecture, called ERE, that combines the ability to react to the current environment with the ability to plan ahead. Their system consists of three independent and concurrent components (see Fig. 9): a *reactor,* based on Drummonds plan-net formalism, that reacts to the current environment; a *projector,* that determines the future effect of possible next actions, and advises the reactor on which ones best satisfy the systems objectives; and a *reductor* that advises the projector about which possible next actions are the appropriate ones to explore given the systems objectives (ie, the Reductor provides search control to the Projector).

The ERE architecture evolved from Drummond's work on the plan-net formalism (Drummond (1986)). This formalism is based on net theory (Peterson, 1981), and was designed to provide the ability to represent iterated actions and the sensory effects of actions. For example, the fact that a tour guide can deliver a speech about some landmark only if he/she is at that landmark and he has not delivered the speech before on that tour is represented by the plan–net of Figure 10. Circles represent conditions that must exist. Boxes represent events. When arcs join conditions and events, this denotes that the conditions enable the events. When arcs join events to conditions, this denotes that the events cause the conditions. There is much more to plan-nets than this condition-event theory, but this is sufficient for our examples. The net in Figure 10 demands that the tour guide be at a landmark x, at which a speech has not previously been given, $\neg done(x)$, before the action-event speech can occur. Once the action

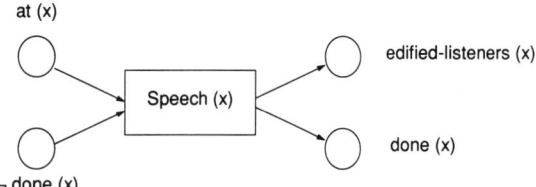

Figure 10. Example Plan-Net.

occurs, a physical change to the world occurs because the speech has happened, and the internal representation of the tour guide is updated to include done(x).

An ERE Reactor component for a tour guide that presents landmarks at random is given by the set of one instance of each of the three nets in Figure 11 for each landmark location x ∈ Landmarks. The first net is simply the speech net of Figure 10. The second net 'motivates' the tour guide to visit new landmarks. The third net models the fact that a tour will get wet if it visits an outdoor landmark while it is raining. In any given situation s, the Reactor derives the set of actions that can be carried out by the tour guide. These are simply the set of actions that are enabled in the plan-net by the situation s, enabled(s). One of these is chosen nondeterministically and carried out.

This Reactor is capable of exhibiting all tour behaviors. However, it does so in a myopic fashion, since its only criterion for selecting actions is that they be enabled. The objective of the Projector component is to use a description of the Reactor's plan-net to determine, in this case, which tours are acceptable given the current environment and a set of desired behavior constraints.

For example, consider an automated tour guide which has explicit instructions not to get the tour wet. For all worlds in which it doesn't rain, the Reactor is capable of fulfilling this constraint. However, should the world change and it starts to rain, then the Reactor will not obey this constraint on its own. This constraint, expressed in ERE's behavioral constraint language, would be (prevent tour-is-wet tour-start-time tour-end-time). Using estimates of the probability of conditions and the utility of actions, the Projector component projects forward in time the effects of action sequences that could be selected from the Reactor's plan-net (Drummond and Bresina (1990) describe a theory of temporal projection based on these plannets). When it finds the first sequence that obeys the behavioral constraint, it compiles a set of *Situated Control Rules* (SCRs) and sends them to the Reactor. These are if-then rules that offer the Reactor advice on the best subset of *enabled*(s) to carry out to keep in line with the behavioral constraint. In our example, the SCRs would advise the next acceptable place to go, ie, that subset of *enabled*(s) where *indoors*(s) is true. Once the Projector has found one good sequence, it continues by inspecting other less likely conditions and again updating the Reactor with SCRs when available. The nature of Projector-Reactor interaction is as follows: Without any planning, the Reactor should be able to give some sort of a tour; with some planning, the Reactor should be able to give, say, a single acceptable tour; and with lots of planning, the Reactor should be able to give many different acceptable tours (one tour being selected over another depending on various environmental circumstances).

Planner and Reactor as a Coupled System. Lyons and Hendriks and co-workers (1990, 1991) address the problem of planning for reaction by considering a Planner and a Reactor as two elements of a concurrent, cooperating system. The Planner interacts with, and is influenced by, the Reactor, in the same fashion that the Reactor interacts with, and is influenced by, the World. This architecture is shown in Figure 12. This reactor component is based on a special purpose model of computation developed for representing highly conditional robot plans. The model, called $\mathcal{RS}$, is an extension of the *Robot Schemas* model of Lyons and Arbib (1989) and inherits the philosophy of Arbib's schema theory (Arbib, 1992). It sees behavior as the result of the cooperation and competition of a set of interacting schema instances. The model is process-based, and process–algebra methods (Hoare, 1985) are used to analyze the process network behaviors. Processes can be defined in terms of networks of other processes, grounding out with a set of atomic, pre-defined, processes. This provides a powerful mechanism for specifying flexible, hierarchical structures. They make the point that to analyze the behavior of reactive machines it is very necessary to know in what sort of environment the machine will be situated. Thus, in reactive machine analysis, the $\mathcal{RS}$ model is used to represent both the plan (or controller) and the environment in which the plan will be carried out (Lyons, 1990).

An $\mathcal{RS}$ Reactor is specified by a set of recursive process equations, where processes can be coupled in networks in two ways: (1) they can communicate messages to each other via *communication ports*, or (2) they can be composed together using several kinds of *process composition operators*. An $\mathcal{RS}$ tour guide reactor, TourGuide, that

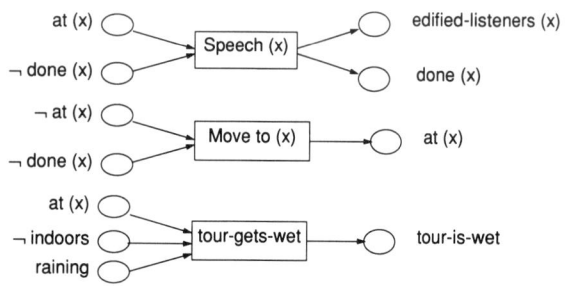

Figure 11. ERE Tour Guide.

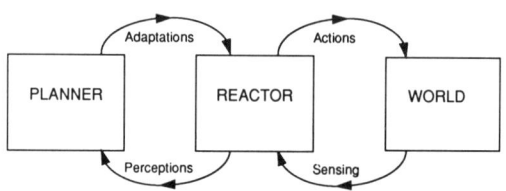

Figure 12. Planner-Reactor-World system.

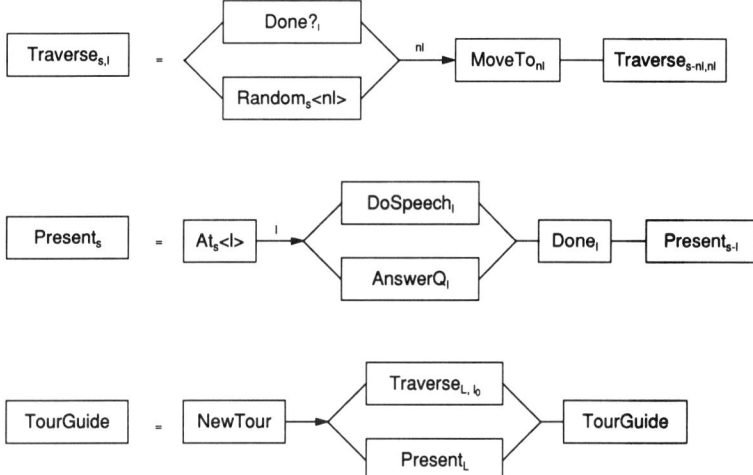

Figure 13. $\mathcal{RS}$ Tour Guide Reactor.

tours landmarks in some arbitrary order is illustrated in Figure 13, and defined algebraically as follows:

$\text{Traverse}_{S,l} = (\text{Done?}_l, \text{Random}_S\langle nl \rangle) : (\text{MoveTo}_{nl} ; \text{Traverse}_{S-nl,nl})$

$\text{Present}_S = \text{At}_S\langle l \rangle : (\text{Dospeech}_l, \text{AnswerQ}) ; \text{Done}_l ; \text{Present}_{S-l})$

$\text{TourGuide} = \text{NewTour} : (\text{Traverse}_{L,l_0}, \text{Present}_L) ; \text{TourGuide}$

The Traverse network consists of the concurrent network that selects the next landmark to visit, nl, from the set of landmarks, S, while monitoring for when the current landmark has been completed; it then signals a move to the new position, after which it recurses. The Present network consists of a monitor process that reports when the tour guide is first at landmark l and then concurrently interleaves delivering the landmark speech, Dospeech_l and question answering, AnswerQ. When these are finished it signals the landmark is done, and recurses. (The interaction between Done? and Done is a typical application of $\mathcal{RS}$ message passing.) The reactor network, TourGuide, recursively activates a concurrent combination of Traverse and Present for each new tour. Recursion of Traverse and Present is bounded using the conditional composition operator (denoted ':'). (Conditional composition is special kind of sequential composition in which the second process is only created if and when the first process terminates successfully; if it aborts, then the composition aborts. If Random and At abort when given an empty argument, then the above reactor recursion is bounded).

The Planner "tunes" the Reactor so that the concurrent composition of Reactor and the world model, World, continue to produce appropriate behavior. The full system is then a concurrent composition of the Planner and the Reactor-World system: (Planner,(Reactor,World)). By considering a Reactor to be a set of concurrent situation-labeled actions, Lyons and Hendriks formally define what it means for the Planner to *improve* the behavior of the Reactor over time. The Planner cycles continuously, making changes to the Reactor in accordance with the definition of Reactor improvement. The Planner does not have access to the complete internals of the Reactor; its observations are restricted to the output of *perception processes* that it can embed into the Reactor. Thus, the Planner can ignore the bulk of the sensing carried out by the Reactor, and concentrate on a few important pieces of information. Perception processes are used to (1) determine when some part of the Reactor is in danger of failing, (2) reflect ongoing resource usage, and (3) determine whether certain goals or subgoals have been met.

For example, if during a tour, clouds start moving in, a perception process may signal this to the planner. From this information, the Planner deduces the possibility for rain and therefore the possibility of the tour getting wet if it is at an outdoor location. Therefore, it reasons to adapt the Reactor by changing the Traverse network to restrict the selection of landmarks to only indoor ones when it is raining, while retaining the full choice otherwise. After sending down this adaptation to the Reactor, the latter has become self-sufficient to deal with rain or sun shine, and the Planner doesn't need to worry about weather changes again. In this fashion, the Planner can use the Reactor to focus its reasoning, and in turn the Reactor is guided by the Planner to improve its behavior.

DISCUSSION AND REMAINING PROBLEMS

Reactive planning is still a young field. It has established alternatives to classical planning when operating in an uncertain and dynamic environment; however, no single reactive-planning paradigm has emerged yet. What has emerged is a number of themes that will be important to this field.

1. Reactive machines can behave intelligently and robustly. They work best when they can be designed to exploit an environment. This results in what Agre and Chapman call *routines*, patterns of behavior that are goal directed, but which are not represented explicitly in the agent, rather they are brought about as a consequence of the interaction between agent and environment. The terms *situated activity* and *emergent behavior* refer to similar phenomena.

2. A number of concepts have been developed to help build reactive machines: indexical-functional representation, behaviors and subsumption; decentralized, concurrent decision making; and formal analysis of agent and world as a coupled system.
3. The main critique on the approach of achieving reactive behavior by the *a priori* design of reactive machines (as voiced by Ginsberg, 1989) is that of the enormous computational complexity, both at design time (as the machine should have an appropriate action for every possible situation) and execution time (as the sensing system must be able to identify all aspects of the world that distinguish situations). The latter, however, can be partially remedied by a decision-tree approach to the determination of the actual situation in which the agent finds itself (Schoppers, 1987). From an efficiency viewpoint, however, there is a problem in that large parts of the plan are irrelevant (as most situations are very unlikely to occur), yet all achieve equal attention during the design phase.
4. The weaknesses of reactive machines are clear: they can be very myopic and there are limits to their robustness. Some form of additional, longer-term reasoning is necessary. However, it is an open question as to how to integrate reactive machines and longer-term reasoning. The importance of having planning and reaction as concurrent, interacting activities has become evident.

There are still a lot of open questions in this area, and of course, much work in other fields of planning, nonmonotonic reasoning, robotics, etc, also impacts reactive planning. We list here just a few of the open areas:

1. There has been little work in integrating the reactive machine work with the extensive real-time computation field.
2. Resources play a key role in many reactive domains—the concept of 'making do' with what is available—but as yet there is no unique reactive viewpoint on resources.
3. There are a number of suggestions, but no definitive answers yet, on an appropriate way to view long-term 'planning' so as to integrate it with reaction.
4. Learning can play a key role in increasing the scope in which a reactive planning system can operate. There appears to be a synergy between reaction and learning (Sutton, 1990; Mitchel, 1990). For example, the learning component of Sutton's Dyna occupies a similar place in his architecture to the planning component in Bresina and Drummond's ERE.

BIBLIOGRAPHY

P. E. Agre, *The Dynamic Structure of Everyday Life,* Cambridge University Press, Cambridge, U.K., in press.

P. E. Agre and D. Chapman, "Pengi: An Implementation of a Theory of Action," in *Proceedings of the 6th National Conference on Artificial Intelligence,* Santa Cruz, Calif., AAAI, Menlo Park, Calif., 1987, pp. 123–154.

M. A. Arbib, "Perceptual Structures and Distributed Motor Control," in V. B. Brooks, ed., *Handbook of Physiology—The Nervous System II. Motor Control,* Amer. Physiological Society, Bethesda, Md., 1981, pp. 1449–1480.

R. C. Arkin, "Motor Schema-Based Mobile Robot Navigation," *Int. J. Rob. Res.* **8**(4), 92–112 (Aug. 1989).

V. Braitenberg, *Vehicles,* MIT Press, Cambridge, Mass. and London, U.K., 1984.

J. Bresina and M. Drummond, "Integrating Planning and Reaction," in J. Hendler, ed., *AAAI Spring Workshop on Planning in Uncertain, Unpredictable or Changing Environments,* Stanford Calif., Mar. 27–29, 1990, Systems Research Center, University of Maryland, College Park, Md.

R. Brooks, "A Robust Layered Control System for a Mobile Robot," *IEEE J. Rob. Aut.* **RA-2**(1): 14–23 (Mar. 1986).

R. Brooks, "A Hardware Retargetable Distributed Layered Architecture for Mobile Robot Control," in IEEE International Conference of Robotics and Automation, Raleigh, N.C., 1987.

R. Brooks, "A Robot that Walks; Emergent Behaviors from a Carefully Evolved Network," *Neural Computation,* 1(1) (1989).

R. Brooks, "Intelligence without Representation," *Artific. Intell.* **47**(1–3), 139–160 (Jan. 1991).

D. Chapman, "Planning for Conjunctive Goals," *Artific. Intell.* **32**, 333–377 (1987).

T. Dean and M. Boddy, "An Analysis of Time-Dependent Planning," in *Proceedings of the 10th International Joint Conference on Artificial Intelligence,* Morgan Kaufman, San Mateo, Calif., 1987, pp. 49–54.

B. A. Draper, R. T. Collins, J. Brolio, A. R. Hanson, and E. M. Riseman, "The Schema System," *Int. J. Comp. Vis.* **2**(3), 209–250 (1989).

M. Drummond, "A Representation of Action and Belief for Automatic Planning Systems," in *Workshop on Planning & Reasoning about Action,* Timberline, Oreg., 1986, pp. 267–289.

M. Drummond and J. Bresina, "Anytime Synthetic Projection: Maximizing the Probability of Goal Satisfaction," in *Proceedings of the 9th National Conference on Artificial Intelligence,* July 29–Aug. 3, 1990, AAAI, Menlo Park, Calif., 1990.

R. E. Fikes and N. J. Nilsson, "Strips: A New Approach to the Application of Theorem Proving to Problem Solving," *Artific. Intell.* **2**, 189–208 (1971).

M. Ginsberg, "Universal Planning: An (Almost) Universally Bad Idea," *AI Mag.,* 40–44 (Winter 1989).

J. Hendler, "Real-time Reaction for Planning Systems," in *AAAI Spring Symposium on Planning and Search,* March 1989, AAAI, Menlo Park, Calif., 1989, pp. 24–26.

J. Hendler, "Abstraction and Reaction," in J. Hendler, ed., *AAAI Spring Workshop on Planning in Uncertain, Unpredictable or Changing Environments,* Stanford, Calif., Mar. 27–29, 1990, Systems Research Center, University of Maryland, College Park, Md., 1990.

C. A. R. Hoare, *Communicating Sequential Processes,* International Series in Computer Science, Prentice-Hall, New York, 1985.

L. P. Kaelbling, "An Architecture for Intelligent Reactive Systems," in *Workshop on Planning & Reasoning about Action,* Timberline, Oreg., 1986, pp. 235–250.

L. P. Kaelbling, "Goals as Parallel Program Specifications," in

Proceedings of the 7th National Conference on Artificial Intelligence, St. Paul, Minn., 1988, AAAI, Menlo Park, Calif., 1988, pp. 60–65.

D. M. Lyons, "A Formal Model for Reactive Robot Plans," in *2nd International Conference on Computer Integrated Manufacturing,* RPI, Troy, N.Y., May 21–23, 1990.

D. M. Lyons and M. A. Arbib, "A Formal Model of Computation for Sensory-Based Robotics," *IEEE Trans. on Robotics Automation* 5(3), 280–293 (June 1989).

D. M. Lyons, A. J. Hendriks, and S. Mehta, "Achieving Robustness by Casting Planning as Adaptation of a Reactive System, in *IEEE International Conference on Robotics and Automation,* Apr. 7–12, 1991, IEEE, New York, 1991.

D. M. Lyons, R. Pelavin, A. Hendriks, and P. Benjamin, "RS: A Formal Model for Reactive Robot Plans," in J. Hendler, ed., *AAAI Spring Symposium on Planning in Uncertain and Changing Environments,* Stanford, Calif., Mar. 27–29, 1990, Systems Research Center, University of Maryland, College Park, Md., 1990.

T. Mitchell, "Becoming Increasingly Reactive," in *Proceedings of the 9th National Conference on Artificial Intelligence,* Boston, Mass., July 29–Aug. 3, 1990, AAAI, Menlo, Calif., 1990, pp. 1051–1058.

N. J. Nilsson, "Action Networks," in J. Weber, J. Tenenberg, and J. Allen, eds., *From Formal Systems to Practical Systems,* Dept. of Computer Science, University of Rochester, Rochester, N.Y., 1988, pp. 21–52.

N. J. Nilsson, "Toward Agent Programs with Circuit Semantics," unpublished.

J. L. Peterson, *Petri-Net Theory and the Modelling of Systems,* Prentice-Hall, New York, 1981.

S. Rosenschein, "Synthesizing Information-Tracking Automata from Environmental Descriptions," in R. Brachman, H. Levesque, and R. Reiter, eds., *Proceedings of 1st International Conference on Principles of Knowledge Rep and Reasoning,* May 1989, Toronto, Canada, Morgan Kaufman, San Mateo, Calif., pp. 386–393.

S. J. Rosenschein and L. P. Kaelbling, *The Synthesis of Digital Machines with Provable Epistemic Properties,* Technical Note 412, SRI International, Menlo Park, Calif., April 1987.

J. Sanborn and J. Hendler, "A Model of Reaction for Planning in Dynamic Environments," *AI in Eng.* 3(2), 95–102 (1988).

M. J. Schoppers, "Universal Plans for Reactive Robots in Unpredictable Environments," in *Proceedings of the 10th International Joint Conference on Artificial Intelligence,* 1987, Morgan Kaufman, San Mateo, Calif., 1987, pp. 1039–1046.

M. Schoppers, *Representation and Automatic Synthesis of Reaction Plans,* Report, Dept. of Computer Science, University of Illinois, Urbana-Champaign, Ill., 1989.

L. Spector and J. Hendler, "An Abstraction-Partitioned Model for Reactive Planning," in Y. Wilks and P. McKevitt, eds., *Fifth Rocky Mountain Conference on AI,* Computing Research Laboratory, New Mexico State University, Las Cruces, N.M., June 1990.

M. Stefik, "Planning with Constraints (Molgen: Part 1); and Planning and Meta-Planning (Molgen: Part 2)." *Artific. Intell.* **6**, 111–170 (1981).

R. Sutton, "First Results with Dyna," in J. Hendler, ed., *AAAI Spring Symposium on Planning in Uncertain and Changing Environments,* Stanford, Calif., Mar. 27–29, 1990, Systems Research Center, University of Maryland, College Park, Md., 1990.

A. Tate, "Generating Project Networks," in *Proceedings of the 5th International Joint Conference on Artificial Intelligence,* Cambridge, Mass., 1977, Morgan Kaufman, San Mateo, Calif., 1977, pp. 888–893.

S. Vere, "Planning in Time: Windows and Durations for Activities and Goals," *IEEE PAMI,* 5(3), 246–267 (1983).

D. E. Wilkins, "Domain-Independent Planning: Representation and Plan Generation," *Artific. Intell.* **22**(3), 269–301, 1984.

D. M. Lyons
A. J. Hendriks
North American Philips Corp.

A synopsis of the diverse work in this field would not have been possible without the cooperation of other researchers. The authors thank the following people for their insightful comments and helpful discussions: Phil Agre, Michael Arbib, Marc Drummond, Jim Hendler, Nils Nilsson and Marcel Schoppers.

PLAUSIBLE REASONING. See Reasoning, plausible.

POLITICS

A system that simulates human ideological understanding of international political events, POLITICS was written in 1979 by Carbonell at Yale University and is a successor to MARGIE and a predecessor to BORIS (qv) (see J. Carbonell, "POLITICS," in R. C. Schank and C. K. Riesbeck, eds., *Inside Computer Understanding: Five Programs Plus Miniatures,* Lawrence Erlbaum, Hillsdale, N.J., 1981, pp. 259–307).

M. R. Taie
AT&T Bell Laboratories

POPLOG

POPLOG is an AI environment for teaching, research, and product development. It provides a vehicle for implementation of multiple languages based on a common virtual machine from which machine-code for target machines is generated, and which provides a "compiler toolkit" for further language development. It is designed to realize AI technology on standard hardware. Its hardware requirements are moderate; it needs no special-purpose architecture and has an executable image that can be below 1 MB. Yet unlike most LISP systems, it is capable of exploiting the full addressing capability of 32-bit machines. POPLOG is used to "rescue" AI applications that have "run out of steam" on a restricted vehicle, such as an expert systems shell.

The system was developed at Sussex University and incorporates fundamental work by Edinburgh University on languages for AI. It provides the following integrated capabilities:

1. POP-II. The system implementation language is derived from Burtstall and Popplestone's POP-2 (see R. M. Burstall, J. S. Collins, and R. J. Popplestone,

POP-2 Papers, Edinburgh University Press, 1968). (See POP-11.) It provides symbolic processing.

2. PROLOG. The POPLOG Virtual Machine was developed by Gibson and Hardy and is descended from the Elliott 4130 designed by Hoare and co-workers (which was the target machine for the first implementation of POP-2). As a result of a collaboration with Mellish, POP-11 and Prolog were implemented as intercallable languages, sharing one environment on the VAX computer.

3. Common LISP. The implementation by Williams was originally oriented toward providing a secure and convenient implementation of the language; it has subsequently been tuned to exploit the code-generating capabilities of the Virtual Machine.

4. ML. This strongly typed functional language has a stylistic relationship to POP-2 and PROLOG, and is based on the work of Darlington, who developed the use of recursion equations as a functional equivalent to the logic clauses embodied in PROLOG. The type inference system, due to Milner, supports polymorphism and thus obviates much of the straitjacket that earlier type-systems (such as that of Pascal) placed on expressivity. The Poplog implementation is by Nichols and Duncan.

5. VED. An integrated editor compiles selected code incrementally and supports the online documentation. Operating in either native or EMACS mode, this operating system interface implements a range of system calls interactively and uniformly and allows access to significant Unix and VMS capabilities.

6. Compiler toolkit. Supports the implementation of new languages within the environment and allows the user to create efficient code by calling a standardized set of code-planting procedures. The planted code operates on a POPLOG virtual machine, which provides the capabilities required for POP-11, Common Lisp, and PROLOG.

The anticipated market role of X-windows has effected the recent evolution of POPLOG. The product has evolved to align itself with a C-based approach to X. While CLX is supported, it is not seen as primary, and the major emphasis has been in supporting OpenLook and Motif in addition to a native POPLOG widget set. This in turn has had an impact on the virtual machine architecture, in order to enhance compatibility with C. In order to support callback from C to the POPLOG languages, data-structures managed by the garbage collector can be orthogonally given a "fixed" attribute which causes them to be nonrelocatable, thus avoiding one of the notorious pitfalls of interworking. POPLOG pointers and C-pointers are now identical, since the "dope" information required for the AI languages is placed before the location pointed to. Moreover, a capability of describing structures in POP-11 that are fully compatible with C-structures has been provided. [See also C. Mellish and S. Hardy, "Integrating Prolog into the POPLOG Environment," in *Proceedings of the Eighth IJCAI,* Karlsruhe, FRG, 1983.

ROBIN POPPLESTONE
University of Massachusetts

POP-11

This language is derived from Burstell and Popplestone's POP-2 (see POPLOG). It provides symbolic processing and is the system implementation language. The original POP-2, although owing most to the early work on LISP by McCarthy and co-workers, was influenced syntactically by Algol 60 and semantically by Strachey's CPL and Landin's ISWIM. It provided a uniform name-space encompassing both functions and data, closures by lambda-lifting, and (in 1971) continuations. It was the original implementation language of the Boyer-Moore theorem prover (see R. S. Boyer and Moore J. Strother, *A Computational Logic,* Academic Press, New York, 1979). POP-2 supported work on structure-sharing in implementations of Robinson's resolution and a pioneering study in the integration of vision and touch in robotics. Another aspect, due to Michie [D. Michie, Memo Functions and Machine Learning, *Nature* **218**, 19–22 (1968)] was memoization of functions, permitting flexible, user controlled trade-offs between space and time.

Technological developments underlying POP-2 included incremental compilation supporting interactive computing, a uniform space for atoms and lists under the control of a generalized relocating garbage collector, and a restricted form of lightweight process, which supported the use of POP-2 as a command language for the Multipop time sharing system. Modernized as POP-11 by Sloman and Hardy, the language has taken on board lexical variables (from Scheme) and the representation of numbers of Common LISP. The syntax was made more redundant as a means of catching errors earlier in the program development process, and an on-line help system provides hundreds of help files covering langue features and various aspects of AI, with hypertext-like cross-linking.

ROBIN POPPLESTONE
University of Massachusetts

PREDICATE LOGIC. See LOGIC, PREDICATE.

PREFERENCE SEMANTICS

Preference semantics (PS) had its philosophical origins in Wilks (1971, 1972) who argued that

1. To have a meaning is to have one from among a set of possible meanings.
2. Giving meaning is the process of choosing or preferring among those.

3. Meanings are, if anything, only other symbols, usually the words of the explanations given to convey meanings to others.
4. Referential accounts of meaning receive too much attention, because adults hardly ever point at anything to give, or clarify, meaning.

The first and second assumptions have a procedural flavor and only the third a representational one: PS is primarily a procedural theory but it has, nonetheless, been strongly associated with a particular kind of network representation.

PS was developed as a computational semantic theory of natural language. The main topic addressed has always been semantic ambiguity (lexical ambiguity, case ambiguity, and anaphoric ambiguity) in line with the first and second assumptions above. Special attention has also been paid to interpreting metaphor, learning new word senses (sense extension), and producing a robust theory that can always produce some interpretation of a sentence.

PS is a theory of language in which the meaning of a text is represented by a complex semantic structure that is built up out of components; this compositionality is a typical feature of semantic theories. The principal difference between PS and other semantic theories is in the explicit and computational treatment of ambiguous, metaphorical, and nonstandard language use. It is an assumption of PS that these features of natural language use are standard and endemic and no theory of language can ignore them. The original application of PS in the mid-1960s was to the semantic analysis of philosophical texts (Wilks, 1968a, 1968b). In the early 1970s, Wilks developed an English–French machine translation system (Wilks, 1973). Because the theory is procedural, rather than representational, it has been possible to provide some fairly simple empirical tests of its claims and the results have been encouraging (Whittemore and co-workers, 1990; Grishman and Sterling, 1989a, 1989b).

MAIN PRINCIPLES

The main principles of PS (Wilks, 1968a, 1973, 1975a, 1978) are as follows:

Computational Semantics. Some of the following principles are part of a general trend within artificial intelligence and computational linguistics that can be called computational semantics (Wilks and co-workers, 1989), a trend opposed not only to independent syntactic processing and to model-theoretic semantics, but also to a central theme in artificial intelligence that could be styled naive knowledge-based processing or, in its extreme form, expert systems. That extreme form could be identified with the claim that, if adequate knowledge structures are available to a parser, then practical problems of language semantics (lexical ambiguity, etc) do not arise. The answer to which is that the claim is false, unless (1) the domain chosen is trivial or (2) the domain chosen includes language itself. Computational semantics is not marked off from knowledge realms and their formal expression: on the contrary, knowledge of language and the world are not separable, just as they are not separable into databases called, respectively, dictionaries and encyclopedias.

Procedural Semantics. Procedures in some sense give the meaning of quantifiers and other symbols (Wilks, 1982). In PS, the description of the representation and the mechanisms that generate it should, ideally, all be procedural and the representation should be the product of a few, general and autonomous (not content-dependent) procedures. The procedural semantics idea goes back to the "meaning as use" slogan of Wittgenstein (1953) and the operationalist explanations of symbols of Bridgman (1936) and appears in the work of Winograd (1972) and Woods (1973).

Least Effort Principle. Procedures should be consistent with a least effort principle of language understanding (Wilks, 1975a, 1975b) of doing the minimum amount of analysis necessary, a consequence of which is that linguistic forms, however well formed on other grounds, that require excessive processing cannot, and should not, be understood.

Preference. This principle is that the best, most internally coherent, representation is chosen from among competing representations. Representational structures can be seen as preferring other associated representations, and an overall representation for a text is produced by allowing maximal satisfaction or best fit of all such preferences, which will mean (as in the political analogy on which the notion is based) that some constituent representations do not have their local preferences satisfied consider:

1. My car drinks gasoline.
2. John ran a mile.

In the PS view, the violation of preferences, such as the preference of *drinks* for an animate agent in sentence 1 and the preference of *ran* for zero object in sentence 2, is the norm and must not be treated as an exceptional matter outside the core of English. Such locutions are statistically so normal and understood even when wholly novel that their representation and processing must be performed as part of the central processes of a language understander.

Semantic Parsing. This principle, also held by the conceptual dependency (CD) group at Yale (Schank, 1975; Schank and Abelson, 1977; Schank and Riesbeck, 1981) among others, is that English can be parsed to a semantic representation without a module devoted explicitly to syntactic analysis and without traditional syntactic classification of words or sentence components (eg, N, NP, and VP). The necessary generalizations for parsing can all be expressed in the terms needed for the semantic representation. Moreover, these need not result in any kind of text skimming that misses essential features of the text and its content.

Beliefs. Analysis of the relationships found in text and the representation of that text is a function of the beliefs (Wilks and Ballim, 1987) of the analysis system. Thus the analysis of sentence 1 depends on what the system believes about drinking and about cars (thus crossing what would be, for many, a semantic–pragmatic boundary) and, likewise, the analysis of sentence 2 depends on beliefs about running and distance (and so similarly for the so-called syntax–semantics distinction and the class of intransitive verbs.

Level of Representation. The level of representation required for natural language understanding is not fixed, but can be at any appropriate level that the representational scheme allows. However, there need be no assumption that all knowledge of the world must be in such a representation: much shallower levels will serve for many purposes.

Semantic Primitives. The representation is based on a set of semantic primitives, of differing types (actions, substantives, qualities, etc) but no claims are made that the set is universal: there could be many alternative sets for special tasks, domains, or cultures. All that is required is there be some privileged set to generate a representation, even though these primitives may in the end be no different in type from (nonprivileged) words of the language (Wilks, 1977).

Linear Boundaries of Language. The representation emphasizes the linear, rather than the recursive properties of language; its structure, therefore, emphasizes the linear boundaries of clauses and phrases (with no special role for sentences) as a basis for a surface representation from which progressively deeper representations can be obtained by inference. The representational item corresponding to the piece of language between two such boundaries (whether a word or a sentence) is called a template, which is a complex structure (see below) having no associations with the term as used to denote a string of surface items, as in vision analysis.

Not Model Theoretic. The representation need not be of the model theoretic type, and the classic problems of, for example, quantification, can be dealt with by special procedures. From the PS point of view, the errors of model theoretic semantics were that it ignored the fact that language always reached other symbols as referents, not unambiguous objects [a criticism made most forcefully by Quine (1960)], and that it ignored an essential feature of natural languages: their constant sense extensibility (Wilks, 1989).

BASES OF THE THEORY

PS contains a number of types of knowledge representation and process. The following types of knowledge representation are used for language analysis in the theory:

1. 80–100 semantic elements or primitives.
2. Semantic formulas, which represent word senses.
3. Bare templates, which represent basic messages.
4. Templates, which represent clauses.
5. Paraplates, which represent the senses of prepositions.
6. Commonsense inference rules, which are used for resolving anaphora.
7. Semantic blocks, which represent whole texts.
8. Thesaurus structure, which provides hierarchical structure (post-1975).
9. Pseudo-texts, which represent both text structure and the contingent, factual aspect of frame structures (post-1975).

Five different kinds of process were used for language analysis:

1. Template expansion, which evaluates selection restrictions.
2. Preference, which chooses the semantically densest semantic reading.
3. TIE routines, which apply paraplates to correct structures corresponding to prepositional phrases.
4. Extractions, which deepen templates by expanding their case subparts and applying commonsense inference rules.
5. Projection rules, which attempt to interpret metaphor (post-1975).

Semantic Primitives. The semantic primitives used in the Preference Semantics System were originally derived from a system of biological classification (Richens, 1958). There are 19 case primitives, including SUBJ (the agent case), OBJE (the object case), and *DIRE (the general direction case). There are 34 action primitives, including GET (obtaining some thing or substance) and GIVE (yielding up some thing or substance). There are 31 nominal primitives (19 plus 12 class elements, classifying the 19), including *HUM (any human entity) and *PHYSOB (any physical object). There are 16 qualifier elements, including GOOD (morally correct or approved), MAL (indicates the sex of the entity qualified is male), and FEM (indicates the sex of the entity qualified is female). A complete list is available (Wilks, 1977).

The case, nominal, and action primitives are organized into small semantic networks in which the primitives appear as nodes. The network for nominal primitives, which is much more complex than those for the others, is given in Figure 1. The arcs of the network, which are unlabeled, denote class inclusion, eg, MAN (the class of human beings) belongs to *ANI (the class of animate entities).

Semantic Formulas. These are constructed out of semantic primitives and represent individual senses of words. Formulas are constructed from subformulas using a form of dependency syntax. A subformula is any left–right pair whose two members are either a primitive or another subformula. The right-hand element is the gover-

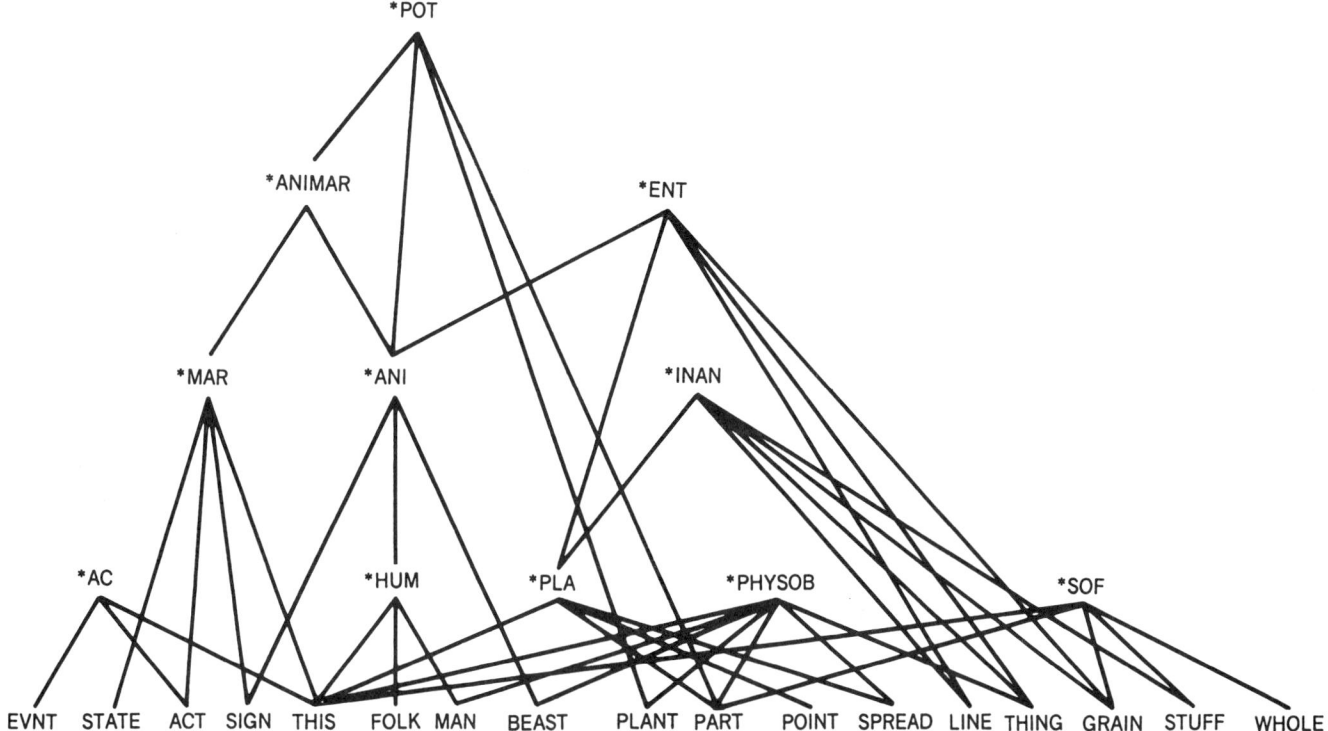

Figure 1. Semantic network of nominal primitives in preference semantics (Fass, 1988a).

nor and the left-hand element the dependent. The very rightmost element of a semantic formula is its head, which represents the main element, for example, whether a noun refers to a man or a thing, or whether a verb denotes an act of thinking or of doing. In a semantic formula, the top-level subformulas are usually case subformulas that have as their principal (rightmost) elements the case primitives SUBJ, OBJE, GOAL (Purpose), and INST (Instrument). The following is a simplified semantic formula for the action *drink*:

((*ANISUBJ)(((FLOWSTUFF)OBJE)(MOVECAUSE)))))

Reading the formula for *drink*: it is an action, preferably done by animate things (*ANI SUBJ) to liquids ((FLOW STUFF) OBJE). The SUBJ case displays the preferred agent of an action; and the OBJE case, the preferred object or patient. Below is the semantic formula for the action *fire at*:

((*HUM SUBJ) ((*ANI OBJE) ((STRIK GOAL)
    ((THING INST) ((THING MOVE) CAUSE)))))

It is an action, preferably done by human things, which uses an instrument (a gun) to cause a thing (a bullet) to move, with the goal of striking an animate thing.

It has been argued that because no real distinction existed between primitives and words (the former being just a privileged subset of the latter) there could be mixed-type representations in which English words were inserted into semantic formulas (Wilks, 1975c). For example, the words *gun* and *bullet* were inserted into the semantic formula for *fire at* to give

((*HUM SUBJ) ((*ANI OBJE) ((STRIK GOAL)
    ((gun INST) ((bullet MOVE) CAUSE)))))

These formulas were described as reentrant because formulas are mentioned inside each other, ie, *gun* and *bullet* have their own semantic formulas elsewhere in the system. These mixed-type formulas were seen as a notational convenience (Wilks, 1975d):

> in that "gun" in a formula for "shoot" is now just a shorthand form for the formula for "gun" existing elsewhere in the system. This makes the formulas easier to read for a human user by avoiding the insertion of too much material in terms of primitives into the body of the formula itself.

Bare Templates. A bare template is a structure containing the gist of a message. Each bare template contains three primitives, an agent–action–object triple (once again, a caselike structure). There is a list of these bare templates, corresponding to numerous basic message forms.

3. The crook drank some beer.

In analyzing sentence 3, the heads are obtained for the semantic formulas of *crook, drink,* and *beer*. Suppose *crook* has two senses, the less probable one being a shepherd's crook or staff, with the heads [crook (MAN)] and [crook

(THING)]. *Drink* has the head CAUSE and *beer* has the head (FLOW STUFF). Two candidate interpretations are produced:

[MAN CAUSE]
[THING CAUSE STUFF]

These are compared against the list of bare templates, and if one does not match, it is rejected. Those structures that remain are expanded into templates. The origin of such gist structures is found in Masterman (1961).

Template. A template is a structure, based on slots for three semantic formulas that can themselves have dependent formulas, such that the whole structure represents a possible message, and can contain any number of formulas. Each fragment of a sentence (clause or phrase) has a corresponding template; the existence of more than one template per fragment is representational ambiguity. That ambiguity is reduced by examining the internal fit of templates and the ties between templates for successive fragments of text.

The template expansion algorithm (process 1) seeks to resolve this. It consults the formulas in each template and looks at their case subparts to see if their preferences are satisfied. In what follows, square brackets denote the semantic formula for a word sense. For example, [crook (MAN)] denotes the formula for the human sense of the word *crook* where MAN is the head primitive. [drink] prefers an animate thing as agent. [crook (MAN)] can satisfy this preference but [crook (THING)] cannot. [drink] prefers a liquid as object; this is available in both representations. The following is obtained:

[crook (MAN)] → [drink] ← [beer (FLOW STUFF)]

[crook (THING)]   [drink] ← [beer (FLOW STUFF)]

where → or ← represents satisfied preferences. The first of these has the largest number of satisfied preferences, or greater semantic density, so it is chosen because the process of preference chooses the template with the most satisfied preferences, ie, the semantically densest semantic reading available.

A template, therefore, is a simple graph of three nodes, where any number of other nodes can depend on each of the three. Each node (original or dependent) can be expanded as a formula tree. A certain amount of ingenuity was required to force clauses and phrases of English, say, into this format: prepositional phrases by convention had the sense of the preposition functioning at the central, action node accompanied by a dummy agent. In a sense, the underlying triple structure of the template is just another notational variant on predicates, semantic networks, frames, etc, as shown in Figure 2. In the notations, the relational primitive (ISA, COLOR, LEGS) occupies, respectively, the middle element of the triple, the function name of the predicate, the arc label of the network, and the slot value of the frame.

Paraplates. Paraplates are used to represent the case ambiguity of prepositions. Paraplates are essentially patterns that span two templates, ordered from specific to general.

4. He left Comano by the autostrada.
5. He left Comano by car.
6. He left Comano by following the arrows.

For example, the preposition *by* expresses three different case relations in the examples above. In sentence 4 *by* is direction; in sentence 5, the instrument case; and in sentence 6, the direction case.

(*ANI) (MOVE) (WHERE POINT) →
 [ ] [ ] (WHERE LINE)

(*ANI) (MOVE) (WHERE POINT) → [ ] [ ] (*REAL)

(*ANI) (MOVE) (WHERE POINT) →
 [ ] (*DO) (WHERE SIGN)

Sentences 4–6 have the above paraplates mapped to them, where [ ] represents a dummy agent. For each paraplate, the three elements before the arrow are mapped onto the template representing a clause preceding the preposition and all the paraplate match the first clause of each of sentence 4–6. The three elements following the arrow are mapped onto the template representing the clause following the preposition and here the three paraplates each make one of the borders of sentences 4–6. Each paraplate can be thought of as expressing a case (those given) and the match of a paraplate (applied as a stack ordered in application as shown, the top one always being applied first) determining the application of the corresponding case between main clause and prepositional phrase.

TIE routines (process 3) use paraplates as above to bind templates together. The routines attempt to match the templates for clauses surrounding a preposition against the ordered stack of paraplates for that preposition until a paraplate is found that is general enough to match.

7. The soldiers fired at the women, and I saw several of them fall.

The problem in sentence 7 is to resolve the ambiguity of *them* as women rather than soldiers.

Triples Notation	Predicate Notation
(CLYDE, ISA, ELEPHANT)	isa(clyde, elephant)
(CLYDE, COLOR, GRAY)	color(clyde, gray)
(CLYDE, LEGS, 4)	legs(clyde, 4)
Network Notation	**Frame Notation**
clyde ----isa--- elephant clyde ----color--- gray clyde ----legs---- 4	[clyde, [[isa, elephant], [color, gray], [legs, 4]]]

Figure 2. Identical information represented in triples, predicate, network, and frame notation.

Commonsense Inference Rules. In such cases, where the tie routines will not resolve the anaphora, commonsense inference rules are used. The one needed here is

[1 strikes animate2] → [animate2 falls].

The process of extraction (process 4) is used here. It operates on template representations and infers new template forms from the case subparts of formulas. For sentence 7 a template form [soldiers strike women] is produced by deepening the formula for *fire at*: women being the object of the firing action. [soldiers strike women] matches the left-hand side of the commonsense inference rule above, hence the inference that the women fell.

Semantic Blocks. A semantic block represents a paragraph (or even a whole text). It consists of templates bound together by paraplates and commonsense inferences.

Thesauruses. After 1975, a thesaurus structure was added because it "provides the lexical specificity that primitive representations lack" (Wilks, 1975d). Wilks (1978) describes the idea of a thesaurus in some detail. A thesaurus, like *Roget's*, is a grouping of words into semi-synonymous rows, usually having the same part of speech type. These rows are grouped under 1 of about 1000 heads, which in turn are grouped under about 10 general sections. These general Roget heads could be identified with such primitives as MAN, THING, and perhaps other primitives corresponding to the section names from *Roget's Thesaurus*, eg, #Abstract Relations (GRAIN), #Space (WHERE), #Matter (STUFF), #Intellect (THINK), #Volition (GOAL), etc. Under the general section #volition the head #22 propulsion may be found, and under that a subhead #221 firer, attached to some row of "firer" words would be found:

#221 firer: gun, bow, rifle, howitzer.

Heads, subheads, and row members all have associated semantic formulas. Row comembers, eg, *gun* and *bow* should have common parts to their formulas, eg, all are THINGS, all have a GOAL of hitting something. This common part should be the simpler, more general formula for that row's subhead, #firer. This progressive generalization should extend right up the thesaurus to the general section names (Wilks, 1978). The thesaurus imposes a hierarchy of formulas and pseudo-texts, where row members will have structurally similar pseudo-texts.

Pseudo-texts. The pseudo-text is a conception of a frame. "A pseudo-text is a structure of factual and functional information about a concept or item" (Wilks, 1978). A pseudo-text is composed of templates linked by case ties, exactly the case ties that the TIE routines above would impose. Hence a pseudo-text is not only a framelike knowledge structure but is also identical to the representational that a PS parser would output. On this view, as noted at the beginning, knowledge structures and those derived for texts are of the same type. A pseudo-text for *car* has been shown (Wilks, 1978). Its first two lines refer to the insertion of fuel, the next three to the fact that the gasoline-using engine moves the car, and the last four to the way the driver turning the wheel changes the direction of the car. This entity is pointed to by the token *car*, which also points to the semantic formula [car].

The pseudo-texts for general primitives such as MAN (which could then be equated to general heads at the top of the thesaurus, in this case Humanity) would consist of general assertional forms such as:

MAN HAVE THING
MAN THINK SIGN
MAN WANT THING

which are also exactly the forms of bare templates (see above).

> Readers will have remarked that the whole formula/pseudo-text distinction rests on some intuitive meaning/factual distinction that cannot be formally justified. . . . I think one can only say that the meaning/factual distinction, even if not philosophically sound, does have some role in out understanding (Wilks, 1978).

By contrast, Charniak's (1977) frames put both formula-like and factlike information in the name formalism, although the reader can easily detect which is which. The notion of connecting the generality expressed by the primitives with the generality of taxonomy to be found in the upper heads of a thesaurus has also been discussed by Masterman (1957).

The process of projection (process 5) operates on pseudo-texts. A brief example of projection is given for sentence 1. Projection operates only on preference violations. The best representation of sentence 1 contains a preference violation, so projection is used. The algorithm compares the template representation

[my+car drink gasoline]

for sentence 1 against templates from the pseudo-text of *car*, seeking the closest match, and selects [ICengine (USE) #liquid] because a car has an IC (internal combustion) engine and gasoline is a liquid. (USE) is then projected onto *drink* in the sentence representation, which becomes

[my+car use gasoline].

In a later development of PS, pseudo-texts were used as the representational basis for a theory of beliefs (Wilks and Bien, 1979, 1983; Wilks and Ballim, 1987): they became structures (renamed environments) that were to be considered as the set of beliefs of an individual about a topic, which might in turn be another believer. An algorithm was given for nesting such belief environments so as to produce default structures for the beliefs of believers by inference, ie, not known directly. The only real connection to PS was an argument that, because such nested belief structures were required for understanding the utterances and texts of others, only some such default projection would be plausible as a least-effort realization of what would, otherwise, be an overmassive computational enterprise. It has been argued at this stage that belief was essentially involved in natural language understanding and that many of the phenomena discussed above (eg, metaphoricity, prepositional phrase attachment, differences in meanings, and anaphorical reference across individuals) could properly be seen as differences of belief (Ballim and co-workers, 1991).

In another later development (Wilks and co-workers, 1985) an algorithm was given that established the ties binding templates for prepositional phrases into the semantic block, but based not on paraplates but on the preferences of the principal words of the sentence: nouns, verbs, and prepositions. PS was never properly extended to handle phrase attachment until this 1985 "walk through" algorithm. The algorithm located the best structure by a two-pass processing of a sentence, once leftward and once rightward. That alone showed that it was not intended as a plausible psychological process, but that has never been a principal aim of PS. In a test against other methods of attachment (Whittemore and co-workers, 1990) this algorithm performed the best.

Meanings of 'Preference'

In the preceding description of PS, the term *preference* had several different but related meanings. Fass and Wilks (1983) noted two different meanings of *preference*. The first meaning is as a selection restriction in the manner of Katz and Postal (1964). These preferences are found in semantic formulas, paraplates, and, in a weak form, bare templates. Hence, in the semantic formula for *drink,* shown earlier, its agent preference is the primitive *ANI and the object preference is (FLOW STUFF).

The second meaning of *preference* is as a Boolean value, either satisfied or violated. In the Preference Semantics System preferences are evaluated by the template expansion algorithm, which checks to see if preferences are satisfied by constructing paths on the semantic networks of nominal, action, and case primitives. It was suggested earlier that the arcs of these networks denoted class inclusion, hence satisfied preferences are those paths through the semantic networks of primitives that denote instances of class inclusion. Correspondingly, violated preferences are network paths that denote class exclusion.

To illustrate this, consider the preceding analysis of sentence 3 and the satisfied preference found between the agent preference of *drink* and the human sense of *crook*. The agent preference for [drink] is for *ANI, the class of animate things, and the head primitive of the thief sense of *crook* is MAN. These two primitives, *ANI and MAN, are shown in Figure 3 which is part of the semantic network of nominal primitives shown in Figure 1. The network path between *ANI and MAN is highlighted in bold. The path denotes inclusion, ie, men are animate things, hence the preference *ANI is satisfied.

A third meaning of *preference* is selecting the representation with the greatest semantic density, which in PS is the representation with the greatest sum of satisfied preferences. The process of preference embodies this notion of preference, which is the one meant by the term preference semantics and the one discussed earlier.

A fourth meaning of *preference* is selecting the most specific representation: alternatives are ranked from specific to general and each one is tried in turn until a match is found. In PS, paraplates are ordered and tried in this way by the TIE routines: "paraplates, for a given preposition, are ordered and 'more preferred template' simply means 'the paraplate applied earlier'" (Wilks, 1976).

EXTENSIONS OF PREFERENCE SEMANTICS

The theory of preference semantics has been developed in a number of directions. Boguraev's work (1979) and his analyzer has had a strong influence on research (Alshawi, 1987; Carter, 1986, 1987; Cater, 1981, 1983, 1986; Fass, 1988a; Huang, 1988a, 1988b; Tait, 1982, 1983, 1985) although, by adding an explicit syntactic analysis component and depth-first syntax-driven semantic interpretation, all of this work departs from Wilks's views on semantic parsing (qv). Slator's (1988a, 1988b) PREMO analysis system, which was less influenced by Boguraev, is most in the spirit of the original PS program. Grishman and Sterling's (1989b) implementation of PS will also be described here.

Boguraev (1979) focused on paraphrase, lexical case, and structural ambiguity. He simplified some of the representations and processes, introduced obligatory cases into semantic formulas, removed bare templates, and simplified paraplates into preplates. Moreover, he put in a depth-first syntax-driven (ATN) semantic analyzer in

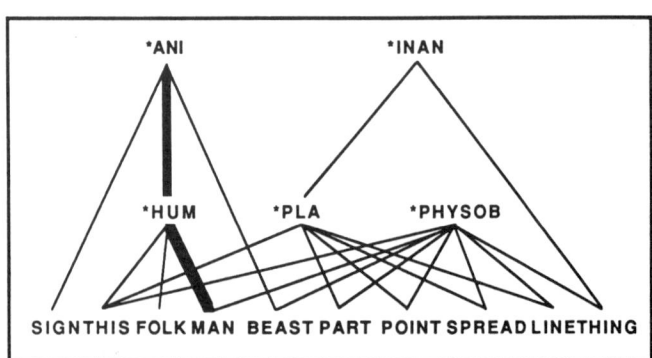

Figure 3. A satisfied preference, ie, a semantic network path denoting inclusion in preference semantics (Fass, 1988a).

which PS was used to check the internal semantic consistency within syntactic constituents.

Boguraev's semantic analyzer was integrated into a natural language interface to a database (Boguraev and Jones, 1981, 1982, 1983a, 1983b, 1984). The same analyzer was also the basis of a series of parsers that used modified versions of PS and that addressed a subset of the semantic problems tackled by PS. All of these parsers followed Boguraev's lead in being syntax-driven. Alshawi (1987) used Boguraev's parser and focused on lexical ambiguity resolution and inference. Carter's (1986, 1987) contributions were in the areas of improved anaphor resolution and more systematic semantic formulas, including a better form of self-reference than Wilks's use of the primitive SELF. Cater (1981, 1983, 1986) developed an ATN-based semantic analyzer that used a CD-style of semantic representation together with semantic interpretation based on the use of preferences. Huang (1988a, 1988b) developed XTRA, a large English-to-Chinese machine translation system. Semantic interpretation in XTRA was based on simple type checking. Metaphor handling was done using relaxation techniques. Special attention was paid to the resolution of structural ambiguity (Huang, 1984a) and language generation (Huang, 1984b). Huang and Guthrie (1986) explored implementing a parallel processing version of XTRA.

Fass's collative semantics (CS) is modeled on PS and aims to provide a deeper semantic analysis of metaphor, metonymy, and other related semantic problems. The focus of the theory is on lexical ambiguity and seven kinds of semantic relation: literal, metonymic, metaphorical, anomalous, redundant, inconsistent, and novel relations.

8. The *kettle* is boiling (= the liquid in the kettle)
9. Denise drank the *bottle* (= the liquid in the bottle).

In a metonymy, the name of one thing is substituted for that of another related to it. Sentences 8 and 9 contain examples of metonymy in which the name of a container (kettle, bottle) is substituted for its contents. Both of these are CONTAINER FOR CONTENTS metonymies. These examples can be contrasted with sentence 1, which contains a metaphor. The difference between metaphor and metonymy, according to CS, is that the core of a metaphor is a relevant analogy whereas the core of a metonymy is a chain of one or more metonymic concepts (Lakoff and Johnson, 1980) like CONTAINER FOR CONTENTS or PART FOR WHOLE (Fass, 1988b, 1991).

CS has four components, consisting of two representations, sense frames and semantic vectors, and two processes, collation and screening. Sense frames are the knowledge representation scheme and represent individual word senses. Collation matches the sense frames of two word senses and discriminates the semantic relations between the word senses as a complex system of mappings between their sense frames. Semantic vectors represent the systems of mappings produced by collation and hence the semantic relations encoded in those mappings (except for metonymic relations). Screening chooses between two semantic vectors by applying rank orderings among semantic relations and a measure of conceptual similarity, thereby resolving lexical ambiguity. CS has been implemented in a computer program called meta5, which analyzes sentences, discriminates the seven kinds of semantic relation between pairs of word senses in those sentences, and resolves any lexical ambiguity. The meta5 program consists of a lexicon containing the sense frames of about 500 word senses, a small grammar, and semantic routines that contain the collation and screening processes.

Sense frames are an extension of Wilks's mixed-type, reentrant semantic formulas but, instead of containing a mixture of primitives and words, sense frames are composed of word senses that perform the function of the semantic primitives in PS. These word senses are reentrant because they have their own sense frames, much like Quillian's (1967) planes and much like the circular organization of a real dictionary. Sense frames contain preferences and assertions, which distinguish two uses of semantic information. A preference contains semantic information expressing a restriction on the local context (Wilks, 1975a; Fass and Wilks, 1983); an assertion contains semantic information to be imposed onto the local context. For example, the adjective *female* has a preference for an animate thing (eg, an animal or plant), but its assertion is that the same animate thing is female, hence a *female person* is a person (an animate thing) that is female.

Slator's (1988a, 1988b) PREMO, short for preference machine organization, is a robust knowledge-based parser for natural language. Parsing is robust in that some structure is returned for every input, no matter how ill-formed or "garden-pathological" it is. PREMO contains a phrase grammar and a machine-readable lexicon derived from the *Longman Dictionary of Contemporary English* (Procter and co-workers, 1978). The derivation of the lexicon is described elsewhere (Slator and Wilks, 1987; Wilks and co-workers, 1988, 1989; Slator, 1989a, 1989b). PREMO deliberately uses everything on offer in LDOCE, notably its grammatical predictions, the TYPE hierarchy as given, and the PRAGMATIC hierarchy as restructured. This contrasts with the original PS system, which used a hand-coded lexicon and which had very little other knowledge of either grammar or pragmatics.

PREMO is organized like the stack model of a standard operating system. Partial parses are represented in process control block structures called language objects. The control structure is a priority queue of these language objects. The language object at the front of the queue has the highest score as computed by a preference metric that weighs grammatical predictions, semantic type matching, and pragmatic coherence. Each parse is a process operating on a private copy of the current sentence. The first process to emerge from the queue with its sentence buffer empty is declared the winner and is saved.

Every language object receives a preliminary preference score when first created. The initial score depends on the word's sense number (the lower the word sense number, the higher the score, thereby giving an advantage to the lower numbered and more commonly used word senses). Immediately thereafter, various attributes of the language object are evaluated and the initial score is adjusted. Adjustments to scores are either minor (2%), standard (10%), or major (50%), and can be in either direction. Attributes that cause preliminary scores to be decreased include an LDOCE time-and-frequency code of archaic or rare. Preliminary scores are slightly increased if, for example, the language object is for a phrasal definition (such as alternating current), if it makes a grammatical prediction, or if it is a word with only a single sense definition. Finally, scores are strongly influenced, in either direction, by the position of the word with respect to a restructured pragmatic hierarchy computed for the text. For example, if the text has a scientific orientation then the scientific senses of words are given increased scores (such as the scientific senses of measure), and the scores of other senses of those words are decreased (such as the political and musical senses of measure).

The input to PREMO is unconstrained text; the output is a collection of lexical semantic objects, one for every sense of every word in the text. Each lexical semantic object contains grammatical and subcategorization information, often with general (and sometimes specific) grammatical predictions. Content word objects also have semantic selection codes; many have contextual (pragmatic) knowledge with a score for comparing word senses for their contextual coherence and the text of selected dictionary definitions.

PREMO employs a uniform representation at the word, phrase, and sentence levels. Furthermore, at every step in the process there is a dominating language object visible, that is, there is always a well-formed partial parse extant. This gives an appealing processing model (of a language understander that stands ready to accept the next word, whatever it may be), and a real-time flavor, where the next word is understood in the context of existing structure. One of the PREMO design principles is "always return something" and that policy is guaranteed by keeping every possibility open, if unexplored (this is the PREMO approximation to back-tracking).

By exploiting the operating system metaphor for control, PREMO inherits some very attractive features. First, PREMO avoids combinatorial explosion by ordering the potential parse paths and only pursuing the one that seems the best. This is antithetical to the operating system principle of "fairness," a point where the metaphor is intentionally abandoned in favor of a scheme that has some faint traces of psychological plausibility. Second, the operating system metaphor is an extendible one; that is, it is possible to conceive of PREMO actually being implemented on a dedicated machine. Furthermore, because the multiplication factor at each cycle through the algorithm is small (in the 40–60 range for the near worst case of 10–12 word senses times 4–5 applicable grammar rules) and because each of these pairings is independent, it is easy to imagine PREMO implemented on a shared memory parallel processor (like a Sequent). Each of the pairs would be dispatched to a different processing element.

10. Fred licked his rifle all over and found that the stock tasted good.

Slator's work can be viewed as dealing with a criticism of PS best put by Hayes (1976), who argued that in sentence 10 the local preferences of PS would always resolve *stock* to *soup* rather than the (correct) *gun part*. Slator's PREMO has shown how to meld local and global preferences so as to tackle precisely such examples.

Grishman and Sterling (1989b) have recently implemented a version of PS as part of the PROTEUS message understanding system, which processes U.S. Navy OPREP (operation report) messages concerning sightings and engagements at sea. Using PS, PROTEUS correctly analyzed 74% of a corpus of 105 messages; without PS, only 54% were correctly analyzed.

Relationship to Other Work

Computational Semantics. Among approaches to computational semantics, PS has been most closely associated, and confused, with CD. There has certainly been cross-influence with CD work. Lehnert (1978) added noun representations to CD, which had until then (and unlike PS) been wholly verb based. The PHRAN parser (Wilensky and Arens, 1980) explicitly added templatelike triples of atoms to its parsing recognition system. Work on anaphora resolution (Carbonell and Brown, 1988) and robust parsing (Lehman and Carbonell, 1989) used an explicit preference measuring algorithm. In the other direction, the addition of the commonsense inference rules to PS in 1974 was almost certainly under the influence of inference rules in Rieger's (1975) work.

Schank and his associates always took a much less relativistic view of primitives, believing that there really was a correct set and that this had a hardware implementation in human brains. On that view, the primitives were not special words at all, as on the PS view they plainly were. This was an attempt within CD to achieve successful extralinguistic reference (even if only to bits of the brain), an idea that makes little sense within PS. A remaining difference has been the importance of psychological claims in the CD school and their absence in PS, as witnessed in the two-pass attachment algorithm (Wilks and co-workers, 1985), which could hardly be psychologically valid but which is effective, and the claimed symmetry of analysis and generation in PS (Wilks, 1991). CD researchers have always strongly emphasized any connection between their representations and psycholinguistic evidence.

The emphasis in the CD group shifted in the 1980s from describing the work as natural language processing to describing it as human memory research, but the change was largely cosmetic, because at Yale the approach was still applied to machine translation and database front ends. Lehnert's (1987) work, is a return to early CD concerns and is certainly computational semantics; in fact, it is a fusion of the PS and CD approaches. That phase of Lehnert's work is connectionist as well, by which is meant the current cluster of artificial intelligence theories around the notion of small computing units (connected in very large numbers) learning from experience by means of shifting aggregated weights in a network (Smolensky, 1988; Waltz and Pollack, 1985). That development shares many of the views of PS: an emphasis on nonsyntactic methods, a continuity with other forms of world knowledge, and some difficulty in reconciling its claims with those of logic-based approaches.

Preference. Preference-like notions have been stressed in connectionism, such as competition between representational structures where the stronger, more connected, ones win out. Connectionism, however, seeks a more general algorithm than the simple counting relativity by which PS establishes the densest network. Sparck Jones (1984) has made the point that preference counting was less plausible if it was 7 over 6 (as opposed to 10 over 1). This ties directly to the concerns of connectionists who are concerned with generating "a big enough gap" over the representations.

Preference notions can also be seen in the general idea of optimizing numerical values for lexical ambiguity resolution in the marker passing approaches of Charniak (1983) and Hirst (1987), as well as connectionist approaches to lexical ambiguity resolution such as Waltz and Pollack (1985). Grishman and Sterling's (1989b) version of PS included a longest parse mechanism that was built into the original scoring scheme. The notion of partial model is a key one here: a formal technique that leads to algorithms of exactly this type (selecting the largest partial model). In the belief area this is not far from Gaspar's (1990) notion of preferred model of belief (which tends to be the largest set although the method of choosing it is unclear).

Other related notions of preference have appeared over the years in natural language processing, often used for ambiguity resolution, including Petitpierre and co-workers (1987), Tsujii and co-workers (1988), Virkar and Roach (1988), Inagaki and co-workers (1990), Malnati and Paggio (1990), and Fawcett (in press). Preference-like notions also appear in robust parsing techniques, for example, least-deviant first parsing (Lehman and Carbonell, 1989) resembles the most preferred first parsing used in PS.

A notion of syntactic preference has been used by Pereira (1985), Hobbs and Bear (1989), and others from the Frazier and Fodor (1978) tradition of minimal attachment and Kimball's (1973) ideas about right association. This tradition has now adopted the notion of lexical preference, possibly stemming from PS (Schubert 1984, 1986). Pereira (1985) proposed what he claimed is a simple, precise, falsifiable, general framework "in which improved versions of Right Association and Minimal Attachment can be formulated." Within the framework, the two principles RA and MA "correspond to two precise rules on how to choose between alternative parsing actions. It was also claimed that principles such as RA and MA could be described "starting from very few assumptions about grammar and parsing mechanisms." The parsing mechanism proposed is bottom-up using the shift-reduced method. Hobbs and Bear's (1989) approach within their dialogic is generalized to "pick the reading with the most restrictive context."

Semantic Parsing. There has always been confusion about semantic parsing as a part of PS. It was certainly never claimed that syntactic information was not used in parsing: it is only necessary to note that a parser of English must know that adjectives normally follow determiners to show that semantic parsing proponents could hardly have denied that. What semantic parsing argued was that all such information could be expressed in semantic terms, whether or not it was more efficient to do so and so no separate syntactic analysis module was required. What semantic parsing is certainly inconsistent with is any syntactic parsing theory that claims (Marcus, 1980) that the constraints of Chomsky's universal grammar can be given procedural form and that there are important generalizations, having nothing whatever to do with meaning, that any parsing system must take account of, and that cannot be expressed at all in a semantic parsing approach.

11. The lecture was believed to have been given yesterday.

The work of Marcus and others has marvelously sharpened what it is semantic parsing has to show to stay in business. Consider the Marcus account of sentence 11 in terms of traces. Any semantic parsing account can deal with this, given plausible assumptions about the semantic preferences for filling the slots involved, eg, that *believe* prefers a clause to an entity as object, if it can get one, taken together with general heuristics about what kinds of slot (eg, subjects) hold or cede their contents during any reorganization of the structure of the sentence.

Semantic Primitives. There has been much misunderstanding about the claims of primitives in PS and their relativistic nature (as opposed to the CD claims). Criticisms of the notion of primitives from Hayes (1974) and Winograd (1978) have missed this point, as did the architects of KRL (Bobrow and Winograd, 1977) when attacking PS. This issue was clarified in Lehnert and Wilks (1979).

BIBLIOGRAPHY

H. Alshawi, *Memory and Context for Language Interpretation*, Cambridge University Press, Cambridge, UK, 1987.

A. Ballim, Y. A. Wilks, and J. A. Barnden, "Belief Ascription, Metaphor, and Intensional Identification," *Cogn. Sci.* (1991).

D. G. Bobrow and T. Winograd, "An Overview of KRL, A Knowledge Representation Language," *Cogn. Sci.* **1**, 3–46 (1977).

B. K. Boguraev, *Automatic Resolution of Linguistic Ambiguities*, Technical Report No. 11, Cambridge University Computer Laboratory, Cambridge, UK, 1979.

B. K. Boguraev and K. Sparck Jones, "A General Semantic Analyzer for Data Base Access," in *Proceedings of the Seventh IJCAI*, Vancouver, B.C., Morgan-Kaufmann, San Mateo, Calif., 1981, pp. 443–445.

B. K. Boguraev and K. Sparck Jones, "Steps Towards Natural Language to Data Language Translation Using General Semantic Information," in *Proceedings of the Fifth European Conference on AI*, Paris, 1982, pp. 232–233.

B. K. Boguraev and K. Sparck Jones, "How to Drive a Database Front End Using General Semantic Information," in *Proceed-*

ings of the First Conference on Applied Natural Language Processing, Santa Monica, Calif., 1983a, pp. 81–89.

B. K. Boguraev and K. Sparck Jones, *A Framework for Inference in Natural Language Front Ends to Databases.* Technical Report No. **64,** Cambridge University Computer Laboratory, Cambridge, UK, 1983b.

B. K. Boguraev and K. Sparck Jones, "A Natural Language Front End to Databases with Evaluative Feedback," in G. Gardarin and E. Gelenbe, eds., *New Applications of Databases,* Academic Press, Inc., New York, 1984, pp. 159–183.

P. Bridgman, *The Nature of Physical Theory,* Princeton University Press, Princeton, N.J., 1936.

J. G. Carbonell and R. Brown, "Anaphora Resolution: A Multi-Strategy Approach," in *Proceedings of the Twelfth International Conference on Computational Linguistics,* Budapest, Hungary, 1988, pp. 96–101.

D. M. Carter, "Common-Sense Inference in a Focus-Guided Anaphora Solver," *J. Semant.* **4,** 237–246 (1986).

D. M. Carter, *Interpreting Anaphors in Natural Language Texts,* Ellis Horwood, Chichester, UK, 1987.

A. W. S. Cater, *Analysis and Inference for English,* Technical Report No. **19,** Cambridge University Computer Laboratory, Cambridge, UK, 1981.

A. W. S. Cater, "Request-Based Parsing with Low-Level Syntactic Recognition," in K. Sparck Jones and Y. A. Wilks, eds., *Automatic Natural Language Parsing,* Ellis Horwood, Chichester, UK, 1983, pp. 141–147.

A. W. S. Cater, "Preference-Directed Use of ATN's," in *Proceedings of the Seventh European Conference on AI,* Munich, 1986, pp. 23–28.

E. Charniak, "A Framed PAINTING: On the Representation of a Common Sense Knowledge Fragment," *Cogn. Sci.* **1**(4), 355–394 (1977).

E. Charniak, "Passing Markers: A Theory of Contextual Influence in Language Comprehension," *Cogn. Sci.* **7,** 171–190 (1983).

D. C. Fass, *Collative Semantics: A Semantics for Natural Language Processing,* Memorandum in Computer and Cognitive Science, MCCS-**88-118,** Computing Research Laboratory, New Mexico State University, 1988a.

D. C. Fass, "Metonymy and Metaphor: What's the Difference?," in *Proceedings of the Twelfth International Conference on Computational Linguistics,* Budapest, Hungary, 1988b, pp. 177–181.

D. C. Fass, "Met*: A Method for Discriminating Metonymy and Metaphor by Computer," *Computat. Ling.* **17**(1), 49–90, 1991.

D. C. Fass and Y. A. Wilks, "Preference Semantics, Ill-Formedness and Metaphor," *Computat. Ling.* **9**(3–4), 178–187 (1983).

R. P. Fawcett, "A Systemic Functional Approach to Selectional Restrictions, Roles and Semantic Preferences," *J. Machine Translat.,* in press.

L. Frazier and J. D. Fodor, "The Sausage Machine: A New Two-Stage Parsing Model," *Cognition* **6**(4), 291–325 (1978).

G. Gaspar, "Communication and Belief Changes in a Society of Agents," in *Proceedings of the Fifth Rocky Mountain Conference on Artificial Intelligence,* Las Cruces, N. Mex., 1990, pp. 319–325.

R. Grishman and J. Sterling, "Analyzing Telegraphic Messages," in *Proceedings of the DARPA Speech and Natural Language Workshop,* Los Altos, Calif., Morgan-Kaufmann, 1989a, San Mateo, Calif., pp. 204–208.

R. Grishman and J. Sterling, "Preference Semantics for Message Understanding," in *Proceedings of DARPA Workshop on Speech and Natural Language,* Cape Cod, Mass., 1989b.

P. J. Hayes, "Some Problems and Non-Problems in Representation Theory," in *Proceedings of the AISB Conference,* University of Sussex, UK, 1974, pp. 63–78.

P. J. Hayes, "Semantic Markers and Selectional Restrictions," in E. Charniak and Y. A. Wilks, eds., *Computational Semantics,* North-Holland, Amsterdam, The Netherlands, 1976, pp. 41–54.

G. J. Hirst, *Semantic Interpretation and the Resolution of Ambiguity,* Cambridge University Press, Cambridge, UK, 1987.

J. Hobbs and J. Bear, "Two Principles of Parse Preference," in *DARPA Workshop Fall 89,* Morgan-Kaufmann, San Mateo, Calif., 1989.

X. Huang, "A Computational Treatment of Gapping, Right Node Raising and Reduced Conjunction," in *Proceedings of the Tenth International Conference on Computational Linguistics,* Stanford, Calif., 1984, pp. 243–246.

X. Huang, "The Generation of Chinese Sentences from the Semantic Representations of English Sentences," in *Proceedings of International Conference on Machine Translation,* Cranfield, UK, 1984b.

X. Huang, *XTRA: The Design and Implementation of a Fully Automatic Machine Translation System,* Memoranda in Computer and Cognitive Science MCCS-**88-121,** Computing Research Laboratory, New Mexico State University, 1988a.

X. Huang, "Semantic Analysis in XTRA, An English-Chinese Machine Translation System," *Comput. Translat.* **3,** 101–120 (1988b).

X. Huang and L. Guthrie, "Parsing in Parallel," in *Proceedings of the Eleventh International Conference on Computational Linguistics,* Bonn, FRG, 1986, pp. 140–145.

H. Inagaki and co-workers, "Sentence Disambiguation by Domain Oriented Preference Sets," in *Proceedings of the Thirteenth International Conference on Computational Linguistics,* Helsinki, Finland, 1990.

J. Kimball, "Seven Principles of Surface Structure Parsing in Natural Language," *Cognition* **2**(1), 15–47 (1973).

G. Lakoff and M. Johnson, *Metaphors We Live By,* Chicago University Press, Chicago, Ill., 1980.

J. F. Lehman and J. G. Carbonell, "Learning the User's Language: A Step Towards Automated Creation of User Models," in A. Kobsa and W. Wahlster, eds., *User Models in Dialog Systems,* Springer-Verlag, New York, 1989, pp. 163–194.

W. G. Lehnert, *The Process of Question Answering,* Lawrence Erlbaum, Hillsdale, N.J., 1978.

W. G. Lehnert, "Learning to Integrate Syntax and Semantics," in *Proceedings of the Fourth International Workshop on Machine Learning,* Irvine, Calif., 1987.

W. G. Lehnert and Y. A. Wilks, "A Critical Perspective on KRL," *Cogn. Sci.* **3,** 1–28 (1979).

G. Malnati and P. Paggio, "A Preference Mechanism Based on Multiple Criteria Resolution," in Inagaki and co-workers, 1990.

M. P. Marcus, *A Theory of Syntactic Recognition for Natural Language,* MIT Press, Cambridge, Mass., 1980.

M. Masterman, "The Thesaurus in Syntax and Semantics," *Mechanical Translat.* **4**(1–2) (1957).

M. Masterman, "Semantic Message Detection for Machine Translation, Using an Interlingua," in *Proceedings of the 1961 International Conference on Machine Translation of Languages and Applied Language Analysis,* National Physical Laboratory, Her Majesty's Stationery Office, Teddington, Middlesex, UK, 1961, pp. 437–475.

F. C. N. Pereira, "A New Characterization of Attachment Preferences," in D. R. Dowty, L. Karttunen, and A. M. Zwicky, eds.,

Natural Language Parsing, Cambridge University Press, Cambridge, UK, 1985, pp. 307-319.

D. Petitpierre, S. Krauwer, D. Arnold, and G. B. Varile, "A Model for Preference," in *Proceedings of the Third Conference of the European Chapter of the Association for Computational Linguistics,* Copenhagen, Denmark, 1987.

P. Procter and co-workers, *Longman Dictionary of Contemporary English,* Longman Group Limited, Harlow, UK, 1978.

M. R. Quillian, "Word Concepts: A Theory and Simulation of Some Basic Semantic Capabilities," *Behav. Sci.* **12,** 410-430 (1967).

W. V. O. Quine, *Word and Object,* MIT Press, Cambridge, Mass., 1960.

R. H. Richens, "Tigris and Euphrates," in *Proceedings of the Symposium on the Mechanisation of Thought Processes,* National Physical Laboratory, Her Majesty's Stationery Office, Teddington, UK, 1958.

C. Reiger, "Conceptual Memory," in R. C. Schank, ed., *Conceptual Information Processing,* North-Holland, Amsterdam, The Netherlands, 1975, pp. 157-288.

R. C. Schank, *Conceptual Information Processing,* North-Holland, Amsterdam, The Netherlands, 1975.

R. C. Schank and R. P. Abelson, *Scripts, Plans, Goals and Understanding,* Lawrence Erlbaum, Hillsdale, N.J., 1977.

R. C. Schank and C. K. Riesbeck, *Inside Computer Understanding: Five Programs Plus Miniatures,* Lawrence Erlbaum, Hillsdale, N.J., 1981.

L. K. Schubert, "On Parsing Preferences," in *Proceedings of the Tenth International Conference on Computational Linguistics,* Stanford, Calif., 1984, pp. 247-250.

L. K. Schubert, "Are There Preference Trade-Offs in Attachment Decisions?" in *Proceedings of the Fifth National Conference on Artificial Intelligence,* Philadelphia, Pa., AAAI, Menlo Park, Calif., 1986, pp. 601-605.

B. M. Slator, *Lexical Semantics, Preference Semantics, and the Machine Analysis of Text,* Memoranda in Computer and Cognitive Science MCCS-88-143, Computing Research Laboratory, New Mexico State University, 1988a.

B. M. Slator, "PREMO: The PREference Machine Organization," in *Proceedings of the Third Annual Rocky Mountain Conference on Artificial Intelligence,* Denver, Colo., 1988b, pp. 258-265.

B. M. Slator, "Extracting Lexical Knowledge from Dictionary Text," *Knowledge Acquisition* **1**(1), 89-112 (1989a).

B. M. Slator, "Extracting Lexical Knowledge from Dictionary Text," *SIGART Newslett.* **108,** 173-174 (1989b).

B. M. Slator and Y. A. Wilks, *Toward Semantic Structures from Dictionary Entries,* Memorandum in Computer and Cognitive Science, MCCS-87-96, Computing Research Laboratory, New Mexico State University, 1987.

P. Smolensky, "On the Proper Treatment of Connectionism," *Behav. Brain Sci.* **11** (1988).

K. Sparck Jones, Personal communication, 1984.

J. I. Tait, *Automatic Summarising of English Texts,* Ph.D. dissertation, Cambridge University, Cambridge, UK, 1982.

J. I. Tait, "Semantic Parsing and Syntactic Constraints (Mark IV)," in Cater, 1983, pp. 169-177.

J. I. Tait, "An English Generator for a Case-Labelled Dependency Representation," in *Proceedings of the Second Conference of the European Chapter of the Association for Computational Linguistics,* Geneva, Switzerland, 1985, pp. 194-197.

J. Tsujii, Y. Muto, Y. Ikeda, and M. Nagao, "How to Get Preferred Readings in Natural Language Analysis," in *Proceedings of the Twelfth International Conference on Computational Linguistics,* Budapest, Hungary, 1988, pp. 683-687.

R. S. Virkar and J. W. Roach, "Pattern-Based Parsing for Word-Sense Disambiguation," in *Proceedings of the Tenth Annual Cognitive Science Society Conference,* Montreal, Que., Canada, 1988, pp. 688-694.

D. L. Waltz and J. B. Pollack, "Massively Parallel Parsing: A Strongly Interactive Model of Natural Language Interpretation," *Cogn. Sci.* **9,** 51-74 (1985).

G. Whittemore, K. Ferrara, and H. Brunner, "An Empirical Study of the Predictive Powers of Simple Attachment Schemes for Post-Modifier Prepositional Phrases," in *Proceedings of the Twenth-Eighth Annual Meeting of the ACL,* Pittsburgh, Pa., 1990, pp. 23-30.

R. Wilensky and Y. Arens, "PHRAN: A Knowledge-Based Natural Language Understander," in *Proceedings of the Eighteenth Annual Meeting of the ACL,* Philadelphia, 1980, pp. 117-121.

Y. A. Wilks, *Argument and Proof in Metaphysics, from an Empirical Point of View,* Ph.D. dissertation, Cambridge, UK, 1968a.

Y. A. Wilks, "On-Line Semantic Analysis of English Texts," *Machine Translat.* **11**(3-4), 59-72 (1968b).

Y. A. Wilks, "Decidability and Natural Language," *Mind* **80,** 497-520 (1971).

Y. A. Wilks, *Grammar, Meaning and the Machine Analysis of Language,* Routledge and Kegan Paul, London, 1972.

Y. A. Wilks, "An Artificial Intelligence Approach to Machine Translation," in R. Schank and K. M. Colby, eds., *Computer Models of Thought and Language,* W. H. Freeman, San Francisco, 1973, pp. 114-151.

Y. A. Wilks, "An Intelligent Analyzer and Understander for English," in B. J. Grosz, K. S. Jones, and B. L. Webber, eds., *Readings in Natural Language Processing,* Morgan-Kaufmann, San Mateo, Calif., 1975a, pp. 193-203.

Y. A. Wilks, "A Preferential Pattern-Seeking Semantics for Natural Language Inference," *Artif. Intell.* **6,** 53-74 (1975b).

Y. A. Wilks, "Primitives and Words," in *Proceedings of the First Workshop on Theoretical Issues in Natural Language Processing,* Cambridge, Mass., 1975c, pp. 38-41.

Y. A. Wilks, *Seven Theses on Artificial Intelligence and Natural Language,* Working Paper No. **17,** Institut Pour Les Etudes Semantiques et Cognitives, Universite de Genève, Switzerland, 1975d.

Y. A. Wilks, "Parsing English II," in Hayes, 1976, pp. 155-184.

Y. A. Wilks, "Good and Bad Arguments about Semantic Primitives," *Commun. Cogn.* **10,** 181-221 (1977).

Y. A. Wilks, "Making Preferences More Active," *Artif. Intell.* **11,** 197-223 (1978).

Y. A. Wilks, "Some Thoughts on Procedural Semantics," in W. G. Lehnert and M. H. Ringle, eds., *Strategies for Natural Language Processing,* Lawrence Erlbaum, Hillsdale, N.J., 1982, pp. 495-516.

Y. A. Wilks, "On Keeping Logic in its Place," in Y. A. Wilks, ed., *Theoretical Issues in Natural Language Processing,* Lawrence Erlbaum, Hillsdale, N.J., 1989.

Y. A. Wilks, *One the Claimed Symmetry of Analysis and Generation,* Memoranda in Computer and Cognitive Science, Computing Research Laboratory, Las Cruces, N. Mex., 1991.

Y. A. Wilks and A. Ballim, "Multiple Agents and the Heuristic Ascription of Belief," in *Proceedings of the Tenth IJCAI,* Milan, Italy, Morgan-Kaufmann, San Mateo, Calif., 1987, pp. 118-124.

Y. A. Wilks and J. Bien, "Speech Acts and Multiple Environ-

ments," in *Proceedings of the Sixth IJCAI,* Tokyo, Japan, Morgan-Kaufmann, San Mateo, Calif., 1979, pp. 968–970.
- Y. A. Wilks and J. Bien, "Beliefs, Points of View, and Multiple Environments," *Cogn. Sci.* **7**, 95–116 (1983).
- Y. A. Wilks, D. C. Fass, C. M. Guo, J. E. McDonald, T. Plate, and B. M. Slator, "Machine Tractable Dictionaries as Tools and Resources for Natural Language Processing," in Tsujii and coworkers, 1988, pp. 750–755.
- Y. A. Wilks, D. C. Fass, C. M. Guo, J. E. McDonald, T. Plate, and B. M. Slator, "A Tractable Machine Dictionary as a Resource for Computational Semantics," in B. K. Boguraev and T. Briscoe, eds., *Computational Lexicography for Natural Language Processing,* Longman, Harlow, UK, 1989, pp. 193–228.
- Y. A. Wilks, X. Huang, and D. C. Fass, "Syntax, Preference and Right Attachment," in *Proceedings of the Ninth IJCAI,* Los Angeles, Calif., Morgan-Kaufmann, San Mateo, Calif., 1985, pp. 779–784.
- T. Winograd, *Understanding Natural Language,* Academic Press, New York, 1972.
- T. Winograd, "On Primitives, Prototypes, and Other Semantic Anomalies," in *Proceedings of the Second Workshop on Theoretical Issues in Natural Language Processing,* University of Illinois at Urbana-Champaign, 1978, pp. 25–32.
- L. Wittgenstein, *Philosophical Investigations,* Blackwell, Oxford, UK, 1953.
- W. A. Woods, "An Experimental Parsing System for Transition Network Grammars," in R. Rustin, ed., *Natural Language Processing,* Algorithmics Press, New York, 1973, pp. 112–154.

YORICK WILKS
New Mexico State University

DAN FASS
Simon Fraser University

PRESUPPOSITION

If someone says to a friend, "I'm sorry that I wasn't at home when you called," he is not, in the ordinary sense, telling his friend that he was not at home. That would in any event be superfluous: presumably the friend already knows. The clause *that I wasn't at home when you called* needs to be spelled out to make clear what it is that the speaker is sorry about; but its truth is not put on the line, it is assumed to be common knowledge shared by both participants in the conversation. This is a typical case of presupposition: the speaker presupposes that he was not at home when his friend called and states that he is sorry about that fact. Presupposition has been a lively topic of debate in linguistics and philosophy for some time, yet its nature is still controversial; a great many relevant facts are now known, but there is still no consensus on the best way of understanding the phenomenon.

In order to highlight the peculiar nature of presupposition consider sentence 1, immortalized by Russell (1905):

1. The present king of France is bald.

This presupposes sentence 2:

2. There is a king of France.

There are two fundamental intuitions concerning sentence 1. The first is that not only does it in some sense imply 2, but so does its ordinary negation, sentence 3:

3. The present king of France is not bald.

(Similarly, *I'm sorry that I wasn't at home when you called* and *I'm not sorry I wasn't at home when you called* both imply *I wasn't at home when you called.*) The second intuition concerns the consequences of falsity in a presupposition. Suppose that sentence 2 is false at the time sentence 1 is uttered (as, indeed, it is at the time of writing). What can be said about the logical status of sentence 1? It certainly cannot be true, but on the other hand, it is not really false, either. Furthermore, the same thing could be said about sentence 3. For the moment, these two intuitions may be regarded as basic to the notion of presupposition. By way of contrast, consider sentence 4:

4. Lesley is a woman.

This implies sentence 5:

5. Lesley is female.

Notice, however, that sentence 6, the negation of sentence 4, does not imply sentence 5:

6. Lesley is not a woman.

Furthermore, the falsity of sentence 5 does not lead to a lack of truth value in sentences 4 and 6; on the contrary, both would have clear truth values: sentence 4 would be false and sentence 6 would be true. It is clear, therefore, that sentence 5 is not a presupposition of sentence 4.

The technical linguistic–philosophical notion of presupposition needs to be sharply delimited from what might be termed everyday presupposing. There are many occasions when something is assumed to be the case as a basis for proceeding with some action or drawing some inference. For instance, when a light switch is turned to the on position on entering a dark room, it is taken for granted that there has not been a power failure, otherwise there would be no point in operating the switch. Or when someone writes a letter, it is normally assumed that the addressee is literate in the language in which the letter is written; and when the letter is posted it is taken for granted that the letter will be picked up and subsequently delivered. All these cases may be loosely described as presuppositions. But they are not presuppositions in the technical sense. The presuppositions under discussion here are in some sense characteristic properties of certain linguistic forms, or so as not to prejudice later discussion, it should perhaps be said that the potential to exhibit particular presuppositions in appropriate circumstances is characteristic of certain linguistic forms or expressions. Such forms are often referred to as presupposition inducers or presupposition triggers.

Presupposition is by no means a rare phenomenon and appears in association with quite a wide variety of linguistic forms and expressions. The following is a summary of the main types that are currently recognized; the classification broadly follows that of Levinson (1983). In each of the following, the "a" sentence exemplifies a carrier sentence, and the "b" sentence expresses one of its presuppositions.

Definite Descriptions
7a. Take me to your leader.
7b. You have a leader.
8a. I want to meet the winner of yesterday's egg-and-spoon race.
8b. There was an egg-and-spoon race yesterday.

Presuppositions like sentences 7b and 8b are known as existential presuppositions.

Factive Verbs
9a. I am sorry that I was not at home.
9b. I was not at home.
10a. He was surprised to see me.
10b. He saw me.

Implicative Verbs
11a. He succeeded in convincing me.
11b. He acted with the intention of convincing me.
12a. They managed to collect £2,000 for charity.
12b. They acted with the intention of collecting money for charity.

Aspectual Verbs
13a. He finished loading the wagon.
13b. He had been loading the wagon.
14a. He reloaded the wagon.
14b. The wagon had already been loaded previously.

Certain Temporal Clauses
15a. While you were asleep, we were working.
15b. You were asleep.
16a. When you see him, give him my regards.
16b. You will see him.

Cleft and PseudoCleft Sentences
17a. It wasn't John who told her.
17b. Somebody told her.
18a. What she does play is the bassoon.
18b. She plays something.

Stressed Constituents
19a. He doesn't play the BASSOON.
19b. He plays something.
20a. HE doesn't play the bassoon.
20b. Somebody plays the bassoon.

Comparisons
21a. John swims better than Bill does.
21b. Bill swims.

22a. I have more money than you.
22b. You have some money.

Counterfactual Conditionals
23a. If only he played the bassoon, we could take him on.
23b. He doesn't play the bassoon.
24a. If I had spoken to her, I could have prevented the accident.
24b. I did not speak to her.

Questions
25a. Does she play the bassoon, or does she play the cornet?
25b. She plays either the bassoon or the cornet.
26a. Who drank the vodka?
26b. Somebody drank the vodka.

Manner Adverbs
27a. She plays the bassoon well.
27b. She plays the bassoon.

This example is perhaps less obvious than some of the others, but notice that *She doesn't play the bassoon well* does not normally negate sentence 27b. To the above examples may be added what Seuren (1985) calls categorial presuppositions. These are induced by certain lexical items, and the presupposition is that something belongs to an appropriate category:

28a. X died.
28b. X was at one time alive.
29a. John drank it.
29b. It was a liquid.

More technical aspects of description and explanation are discussed next.

PHILOSOPHICAL ASPECTS: FREGE, RUSSELL, AND STRAWSON

Presupposition was first studied by philosophers and logicians in connection with reference and referring expressions. The first was Frege (1952). Although his remarks were few and informal, they were influential in drawing attention to basic properties of presuppositions. For Frege, a presupposition is not to be considered part of the meaning of a sentence that presupposes it. He also mentions the fact that an assertion and its denial both carry the same presuppositions, and suggests that the truth of a presupposition can be regarded as a precondition for the possession of a truth value by the presupposing assertion. Frege was not explicit in regard to the nature of the presupposing entity, that is to say, whether it is a sentence, an assertion, or the speaker.

Russell formulated his views at least partly in opposition to Frege, whom he believed to be incorrect in holding that the meaning of a presupposition is not part of the meaning of the presupposing sentence. Russell's suggestion for the logical form of a sentence like sentence 1 incorporated the existential presupposition as a component proposition:

30. *The king of France is bald* = $\exists x \, (\text{king}(x) \, \& \sim \exists y \, ((y \neq x) \, \& \, \text{king}(y)) \, \& \, \text{bald}(x))$

This translates roughly as "There exists an entity x such that x is the king of France and there does not exist any entity y such that y is the king of France and x is not y, and x is bald." This formulation has the merit of being explicit. It also provides a natural explanation for something that has not been mentioned so far, namely, the existence of two distinct interpretations of negative sentences like sentence 3. It has been seen that in normal use, a sentence like sentence 3 leaves the existential presupposition intact; but there is another interpretation, usually marked by special intonation and stress, in which the presupposition is also negated:

31. The king of France is *not* bald, because there *is* no king of France.

Russell's formulation can account for these two readings in terms of the scope of the negative operator. There are two possibilities for the scope of the negative. The first is the whole compound proposition:

32. $\sim (\exists x \, (\text{king}(x) \, \& \sim \exists y \, (\text{king}(y) \, \& \, (y \neq x)) \, \& \, \text{bald}(x))$

This translates as "It is not the case that there exists an entity x such that x is the king of France and there does not exist any entity y such that y is the king of France and y is not x, and x is bald." This is called wide-scope negation and makes it possible to deny that the king of France exists. It is therefore equivalent (logically) to sentence 31. The scope of the negative can also, however, be restricted to the proposition that the king of France is bald:

33. $\exists x \, (\text{king}(x) \, \& \sim \exists y \, (\text{king}(y) \, \& \, (y \neq x)) \, \& \sim \text{bald}(x))$

The negative here is said to have narrow scope, and sentence 33 can, therefore, be seen as a representation of the logical form of sentence 3 in its normal interpretation.

Russell's formulation, however, does have shortcomings as a model of the intuitive notion of presupposition. First of all, it gives the existential presupposition exactly the same status as what is intuitively the main point of the utterance, namely, the attribution of baldness. Second, if the existential presupposition is false, then the whole compound proposition is predicted to be necessarily false.

The matter was next taken up by Strawson (1952), who essentially went back to the Fregean understanding of presupposition, but made it more explicit. In Strawson's view, presupposition is a relation between statements, not sentences [statements are described by Lyons (1977) as propositions uttered with epistemic commitment]:

34. A statement P presupposes another statement Q if and only if:
    i. if P is true, then Q is true
    ii. if P is false, then Q is true

Notice that it follows from this that if Q is false, then P can neither be true nor false, or to put it another way, the truth of Q is a precondition for P having a truth value.

Strawson's proposal captures the basic facts mentioned in the introduction: constancy of presupposition under negation and the absence of a truth value when the presupposition is false. However, it is unable to account for the presupposition-canceling negation illustrated in sentence 31 (or, indeed, any type of presupposition cancellation). It has frequently been claimed that the only way to accommodate cases like sentence 31 within a logical account of presupposition is to have two distinct negative operators, a development that most logicians and formal linguists have fiercely resisted. Among the reasons for this resistance are, first, a deep suspicion of any departure from classic logic; second, the difficulty of demonstrating ambiguity in natural language negation; and third, the fact that no natural language has lexically distinct negative operators corresponding to presupposition-preserving and presupposition-canceling negation.

SEMANTIC THEORIES OF PRESUPPOSITION

The notion of presupposition entered linguistics proper in a largely Strawsonian form, except that it was regarded as a relation between sentences rather than between statements. It was assumed that the major properties of presuppositions should be directly represented in the definition, and that the latter should have a logical form like that suggested by Strawson (Levinson, 1983):

35. Sentence A presupposes another sentence B if and only if:
    i. in all situations where A is true, B is true
    ii. in all situations where A is false, B is true.

Theories of presupposition, like that embodied in sentence 35, in which presuppositions are held to be part of the inherent meaning of certain sentences, are known as semantic theories of presupposition. They stand in contradistinction to pragmatic theories, in which presuppositions are seen as arising from interaction between inherent meaning and context, or as not being truth-conditional in nature.

Semantic theories have been subject to criticism on a number of counts. One of the consequences of a definition like that in sentence 35 is that analytic sentences such as *All bachelors are unmarried* and *Tall men are tall* are presuppositions of all other sentences; because they are always true, they will be true whether some arbitrary sentence S is true or false. They are sometimes called trivial presuppositions and are regarded by most linguists as a drawback of logical definitions of presupposition. At least one linguist, however (Burton-Roberts, 1989), welcomes them as a desirable consequence, on the grounds that they are to be interpreted as indicating that the truth or falsity of a sentence presupposes that the normal rules of language are in operation.

There are, however, more serious drawbacks to semantic definitions of presupposition like that in sentence 35. Such definitions imply that the truth of a presupposition is an ineluctable consequence of the truth (or falsity) of the presupposing sentence. But it can easily be shown that presuppositions are susceptible to suppression or cancellation in certain circumstances; they are, as the technical term has it, defeasible. An example of this is sentence 31. But there are other examples. Consider sentences 36a, 36b and 36c:

36a. Charles doesn't know that Jane is the best player.
36b. Jane is the best player.
36c. I don't know that Jane is the best player.

Normally, sentence 36a presupposes sentence 36b: *know* triggers a factive presupposition in the same way that *regret* and *be sorry* do. But sentence 36c does not presuppose sentence 36b: obviously the main point of sentence 36c is to contradict what would otherwise be a presupposition of the embedded clause. But there is no contradiction here: the presupposition is merely suppressed. (Notice that sentence 36a also has a reading analogous to that of sentence 36c.) Similar examples can be constructed with temporal clauses containing *before* and *until*:

37. A: Did you finish *War and Peace?*
    B: No, I got fed up long before I got to the end.
38. John sensibly didn't stay until his money ran out completely; he came back while he still had enough for the fare home.

Much has been written about what is called the projection problem for presuppositions. This concerns what happens to the presuppositions of simple sentences when they are combined to form more complex ones. The first explicit proposal (Langendoen and Savin, 1971) was that the presuppositions of any simple sentence will be inherited by any complex sentence containing it. However, this proposal has turned out to be untenable, and it has proved extremely difficult to predict in a systematic way what will happen when simple sentences are combined. This has generally been viewed as a shortcoming of the logical-semantic approach to presupposition; sentence 35 does not seem to lend itself to incorporation in any predictive algorithm. Levinson (1983) draws attention to two aspects of the projection problem: first, presuppositions survive in certain circumstances where entailments do not and, second, presuppositions fail to survive in some contexts where entailments do. Let us consider an example of the first type. Notice, first, that sentence 39a entails sentence 39b but presupposes sentence 39c:

39a. The president of the Farmers' Union killed a rabbit.
39b. A rabbit died.
39c. There is a president of the Farmers' Union.

Sentences 40a and 40b, however, although still presupposing sentence 39c, do not entail sentence 39b:

40a. It is possible that the president of the Farmers' Union killed a rabbit.
40b. If the president of the Farmers' Union killed a rabbit he will be asked to resign.

Predicates like modals and conditionals, which block entailments but allow presuppositions to pass, are described by Karttunen (1973) as holes. The opposite case is illustrated by sentence 31 (repeated here for convenience):

31. The king of France is *not* bald, because there *is* no king of France.

Here we have suppressed the presupposition that the king of France exists. However, it is not possible to suppress entailments in this way: all that results is a contradiction:

41. *The president of the Farmers' Union killed a rabbit, although the rabbit did not, in fact, die.

In some contexts, presuppositions can be suspended, whereas entailments cannot. Thus sentences 42a and 42b both presuppose sentence 42c, but in sentence 42d the presupposition is suspended:

42a. The president of the Farmers' Union killed another rabbit.
42b. The president of the Farmers' Union did not kill another rabbit.
42c. A rabbit was killed previously.
42d. The president of the Farmers' Union did not kill another rabbit, if, indeed, he ever killed one in the first place.

The picture is further complicated by the existence of "plugs" and "filters." Plugs are predicates, such as *dream, tell, say, report,* and *claim*, which are claimed to block both presuppositions and entailments [but Levinson (1983) gave a dissenting opinion]. For instance, sentence 43a presupposes sentence 43b and entails sentence 43c, but sentence 43c does neither:

43a. The president of the Farmers' Union kissed John.
43b. There is a president of the Farmers' Union.
43c. The president of the Farmers' Union did something to John.
43d. John dreamed that the president of the Farmers' Union kissed him.

Filters are predicates that allow some types of presupposition to be inherited by complex sentences, but will block others. Thus both sentences 44a and 44b presuppose sentence 44c, but only sentence 44b presupposes sentence 44d:

44a. If the president of the Farmers' Union kills the rabbit, he will regret it.
44b. The president of the Farmers' Union will regret killing the rabbit.
44c. The rabbit exists.
44d. The president of the Farmers' Union will kill the rabbit.

In recent years, the weight of scholarly opinion has swung behind the pragmatic approach to presupposition, mainly because of the apparent failure of the semantic approaches to provide satisfactory accounts of defeasibility and the projection phenomena. Before pragmatic approaches are considered in greater detail, however, some account should be taken of the views of two linguists who have maintained, in rather different ways, and against the prevailing trend, that a semantic account of presupposition is not only possible, but desirable.

Burton-Roberts: A Revised Logical Definition

Burton-Roberts assumes a pretheoretical distinction between presupposition and assertion that runs as follows:

Presupposition. To presuppose a proposition consists in being committed to that proposition while *not* countenancing the possibility that it might be false.

Assertion. To assert a proposition consists in being committed to that proposition while countenancing the possibility that it might be false.

To put it another way, asserting a proposition exposes it to possible contradiction; presupposing it keeps it, as it were, protected from possible contradiction. Burton-Roberts accepts all the well-known facts about presuppositions as forming part of what a theory of presupposition must explain, but questions the widely held assumption that a satisfactory logical definition must necessarily incorporate all the facts directly. He vigorously repudiates the notion of a three-valued logic with two negative operators, adopting instead a classic two-valued logic with gaps; that is to say, he allows the possibility that some sentences will lack a truth value.

Burton-Roberts's (1989) definition of presupposition hinges on definitions of strong and weak entailment.

45a. $S2$ is a weak entailment of $S1$ if and only if wherever $S1$ is true, $S2$ is true.
45b. $S2$ is a strong entailment of $S1$ if and only if
  i. $S2$ is a weak entailment of $S1$.
  ii. wherever $S2$ is false, $S1$ is false.
45c. $S2$ is a presupposition of $S1$ if and only if
  i. $S2$ is a weak entailment of $S1$
  ii. $S2$ is not a strong entailment of $S1$

It will be noticed that this definition does not specifically incorporate any mention of the presuppositions of a negative sentence. These, in fact, follow from the definition in sentence 45 as what Burton-Roberts calls default implications. The negation of $S1$ entails that at least one of the strong entailments of $S1$ is false, but, according to Burton-Roberts, says nothing about the weak entailments. Under these circumstances, there is a default implication that the weak entailments of $S1$ are still true. This is not unlike the implication in sentence 46 that B has not washed the dishes:

46a. Have you cleared the table and washed the dishes?
46b. I've cleared the table.

However, the presuppositional default implication of not-$S1$, according to Burton-Roberts, differs from the conversational variety illustrated in sentences 46 in being (*1*) context independent and (*2*) not subject to cancellation. The apparent cancellation of presuppositions in cases like sentence 47

47. He *hasn't* stopped beating his wife because he never *did* beat her.

is explained, following Horn (1985) as pragmatic and metalinguistic in nature; it usually follows an explicit statement to the contrary, and constitutes an objection to the speaker's use of certain expressions. A possible gloss of sentence 47 might, therefore, be "It's not appropriate to say 'He's stopped beating his wife,' because he never did beat her." Sentence 47 is thus not a logical negation at all (the only true logical negation is the one that generates the default implication) and, therefore, does not need to be accommodated by the logical definition.

One advantage of the formulation in sentence 45 is that the falsity of $S2$ does not automatically entail a lack of truth value in $S1$. Hence this account can accommodate examples like sentence 48:

48. The king of France visited me yesterday.

which is intuitively false rather than truth valueless and constitutes an embarrassment for definitions like sentence 35. Burton-Roberts claims, too, that his definition does not suffer from a projection problem: the presuppositions of conditionals, modals, and coordinations can be correctly derived from the definition on standard logical principles. However, it must be pointed out that Burton-Roberts does not address all the projection problems mentioned by, say, Levinson. It remains to be seen how well this undoubtedly ingenious account survives the scrutiny of formal linguists.

Seuren: Presupposition As a Discourse Phenomenon

Like Burton-Roberts, Seuren believes that the notion of presupposition both can and should be treated semantically, rather than as part of pragmatics. But unlike Burton-Roberts, he rejects a specifically logical definition and regards presuppositions rather as a matter of discourse semantics. (It is worth noting that most linguists regard discourse phenomena as belonging to pragmatics.) Seuren gives two main reasons why any logical definition is bound to be inadequate. First, there can be no account within logic of the semantic nature of presupposition. Seuren distinguishes two types of entailment: semantic entailment, where the entailed sentence is intuitively a valid inference from the entailing sentence, as with *It's a dog* and *It's an animal*; and mere logical entailment, where the entailment arises from the mathematical properties of the system and is intuitively unnatural as an inference, as with *They all liked the performance* and *Whoever is alive is not dead*. That is to say, the fact that a logical definition necessarily admits trivial presuppositions is for Seuren a serious drawback, because it means that no account is given of the semantic nature of nontrivial presuppositions and makes it impossible to frame any sort of diagnostic test for presuppositions. The second reason for the inadequacy of logical definitions, according to Seuren, is that presuppositions are carried not only by statements (the domain of logic) but also by questions and commands. There is, according to Seuren, no satisfactory logical construal of entailment that is applicable to nonassertive speech acts.

For Seuren, presuppositions are fundamentally a discourse-related phenomenon. They are defined as semantic entailments that are also projections. A projection of S is a proposition whose presence in preceding discourse is required for S to be interpretable. If P is a projection of S, then P (and/but) S will be an acceptable piece of discourse. Hence, *It's an animal* is an entailment, but not a presupposition of *It's a dog*, because *It's a dog and it's an animal* is not an acceptable piece of discourse; *There is a king of France* is a presupposition of *The king of France is bald* because (1) it is a nontrivial entailment and (2) *There is a king of France and (he) is bald* is an acceptable piece of discourse.

Seuren's account has further distinguishing features. He adopts a fully worked out three-valued logic, with two negations; radical negation, which negates everything including presuppositions; and minimal negation, which leaves presuppositions intact. A number of what are usually considered to be presuppositions are classified by Seuren as mere projections. These are not full-fledged presuppositions because they do not have the status of entailments, appearing merely as suggestions or invited inferences. The category of mere projections includes, for instance, *There is a king of France* in relation to *The king of France is not wise*. Seuren distinguishes the latter case from that of *The king of France is unwise*, which entails, prejects and hence presupposes *There is a king of France* in the full sense. The distinction between, for instance, *The king of France is* not *wise, because there* is *no king of France*, which exhibits radical negation, and *The king of France is unwise*, which exhibits minimal negation, is cited by Seuren to counter one of the most common arguments against having two negative operators, namely, that the distinction between them is never overtly signaled in natural language.

PRAGMATIC APPROACHES TO PRESUPPOSITION

Assume for present purposes that semantics deals with aspects of meaning that are (1) context independent and (2) truth conditional in nature and that pragmatics deals with all other aspects of meaning. A number of different pragmatic accounts of presupposition have been proposed; the principle ones will be reviewed here. (It is worth noting that Burton-Roberts's default implications and metalinguistic negation and Seuren's invited inferences have more than a hint of pragmatics about them. The division between semantic and pragmatic accounts of presupposition is, therefore, not absolutely clear-cut.)

Karttunen and Peters: Presuppositions As Conventional Implicatures

Those who reject semantic accounts of presupposition (probably the majority), do so, according to Levinson, principally because presuppositions do not have the kind of invariant character that seems to be required by semantic theory. The same criticism applies to some pragmatic accounts, in particular, that of Karttunen and Peters (1975, 1979). They treat presuppositions as conventional implicatures associated with certain linguistic forms. Conventional implicatures, unlike the conversational variety, are not tied to the propositional content of a sentence, but to particular surface elements or constructions. They are regarded as part of the conventional meaning of expressions, but they are not truth conditional in nature. They are unlike conversational implicatures also in that they are not susceptible to suppression by contextual factors. The theory of Karttunen and Peters is formulated within the framework of Montague grammar. Presuppositions are generated in parallel to, and by a similar mechanism to, the normal truth conditionally relevant semantic representation. Karttunen's classification of embedding constructions into plugs, filters, and holes is adopted to handle the projection problem. This theory, although strictly speaking not semantic because it is not truth conditional, suffers from at least some of the same sorts of weakness as semantic theories do; in particular, it makes presuppositions seem much more robust than they actually are.

Gazdar: Presuppositions as Conventional But Cancelable

Another theory that treats presuppositions as part of the conventional meaning of expressions is Gazdar's (1979a, 1979b). However, Gazdar's presuppositions differ from those of Karttunen and Peters in that they are cancelable by contextual factors, and Gazdar provides an explicit mechanism for this. Put at its simplest, what happens is as follows. First, the set of potential presuppositions of a sentence is generated; if the sentence is complex, this set contains the presuppositions that each of the constituent clauses would have on its own in a minimum context. In order subsequently to become actual presuppositions of an utterance of the sentence, potential presuppositions must be compatible with the current context: those that are not are canceled. However, for this simple principle to work, the context must be construed in a particular way. The initial context comprises propositions mutually accepted by speaker and hearer. When either of them speaks, propositions are added to this initial set. The context is, however, not incremented all in one go: there are various sources within the meaning of a sentence, and there is a specific order of addition to the context:

49a. The entailments of the uttered sentence S.
49b. The clausal implicatures of S.
49c. The scalar implicatures of S.
49d. The presuppositions of S.

At each stage, additions not compatible with current context are canceled. Both conversational implicatures (sentences 49b and 49c) and presuppositions are, therefore, susceptible to cancellation. A few examples will illustrate the process of cancellation. Consider sentence 50:

50. If there is a king of France, the king of France is not wise.

The consequence clause on its own would presuppose sentence 51:

51. There is a king of France.

But it is a clausal implicature of the conditional clause that the speaker believes it possible that there is no king of France. Because this is added to the context before sentence 51, the latter, being inconsistent with the now current context, is canceled. Another example is sentence 52:

52. I was not surprised that John had bought a Mercedes, because in fact he hadn't.

This entails sentence 53:

53. John did not buy a Mercedes.

which is, therefore, the first to be added to the context. The first conjunct on its own would presuppose that John did buy a Mercedes, but this is canceled because it is inconsistent with sentence 53. Finally, consider sentence 54:

54. The prisoner was executed before he managed to escape.

The temporal clause in sentence 54 presupposes that the prisoner managed to escape. However, this is inconsistent with what presumably forms part of the initial context, namely, the assumption that people do not carry out actions like escaping after they have been executed.

Gazdar's theory shows a clear superiority over that of Karttunen and Peters, particularly in regard to defeasibility and the projection problem. However, in spite of this, it shares with the latter theory a fundamental weakness: as Levinson points out, no explanation is offered for the association of any presupposition with a particular propositional meaning: all such associations are presented as arbitrary facts about particular items in particular languages, on a par with the association of a phonetic form with a meaning at the morphemic level. Some presuppositions are certainly like this: they cause a lexical item to have arbitrary collocational restrictions. But many presuppositions are intuitively fully motivated. The difference between the two types of presupposition can be illustrated in connection with *kick the bucket* and *die* (Cruse, 1986). *X kicked the bucket* (in its idiomatic sense) presupposes *X is human*. But this fact cannot be predicted from the propositional content of the former. This is to be contrasted with the fact that *X died* presupposes *X was alive*. In this case, however, the presupposition is an essential precondition for the propositional content to have any coherence; if something is not alive, then logically it cannot die. Most of the presuppositions discussed in the literature are of the nonarbitrary sort exemplified by *X was alive* in relation to *X died*.

The Entailment Analysis

Probably the most influential theory within which phenomena usually considered to be presuppositional are shown to be nonarbitrary is what is known as the entailment analysis. In a way this is not really a theory of presupposition at all, because the facts that other theories consider to be presuppositional are all reanalyzed as something else, namely, entailment, or entailment together with some pragmatic process such as conversational implicature.

One approach (Kempson, 1975; Wilson, 1975), claims that the so-called presuppositions of affirmative sentences are in fact straightforward entailments, whereas the so-called presuppositions of negative sentences are conversational implicatures. Consider the case of sentences 55a and 55b, which are usually considered to presuppose sentence 55c:

55a. John has stopped drinking.
55b. John has not stopped drinking.
55c. John was in the habit of drinking.

On the entailment analysis, sentence 55a simply entails sentence 55c, because in any world in which sentence 55a is true, sentence 55c is also true. However, to explain the fact that sentence 55b normally implies sentence 55c it is possible to appeal to the notion of conversational implicature as expounded by Grice (1975, 1978). If the information the speaker wishes to convey is that John does not drink and never has done, then mention of John's stopping drinking is inadequately motivated; it is irrelevant. Because the speaker may be assumed to be trying to communicate something as efficiently as he can, it can be assumed that he has good reason for bringing up the topic of John's stopping drinking. The most obvious reason is that John had in fact been drinking at the time of utterance. A drawback of this approach noted by Levinson (1983) is that a fully motivating and fully predictive account is difficult to achieve for many presuppositions and, in any case, must be constructed *ad hoc* for each presupposition. An alternative approach (Wilson and Sperber, 1979) is to work entirely in terms of entailments and to treat presuppositions merely as entailments that are not currently relevant. Entailments can be calculated on general principles, and form well-defined logically ordered chains. General principles can also be suggested that relate foregrounding and backgrounding (current relevance or lack of it) to linguistic form. This account holds out the promise of a more coherent account, but runs into the familiar problems of defeasibility, and the survival of presuppositions in some contexts where entailments do not survive.

CONCLUSION

It is difficult to disagree with Levinson's (1983) comment: "We conclude that presupposition remains, ninety years after Frege's remarks on the subject, still only partially understood." Perhaps part of the problem is the assumption that presuppositions constitute a coherent conceptual category of the classic type for which it should, in principle, be possible to draw up necessary and sufficient criteria. It is not easy to justify this apparently widely held assumption. In some ways, presuppositions can just as convincingly be pictured as a rather disparate set of nonprototypical members of another category, something like natural inferences, whose prototypical members would be highly reliable and have high current relevance. An understanding of factors affecting degree of reliability and degree of relevance would then generate an ill-defined periphery to the category, where what are now called presuppositions would find their home.

BIBLIOGRAPHY

N. Burton-Roberts, *The Limits to Debate: A Revised Theory of Semantic Presupposition,* Cambridge University Press, Cambridge, UK, 1989.

D. A. Cruse, *Lexical Semantics,* Cambridge University Press, Cambridge, UK, 1986.

G. Frege, "On Sense and Reference," in P. T. Geach and M. Black, eds., *Translations from the Philosophical Writings of Gotlob Frege,* Blackwell, Oxford, UK, 1952.

G. Gazdar, *Pragmatics: Implicature, Presupposition and Logical Form,* Academic Press, Inc., New York, 1979a.

G. Gazdar, "A Solution to the Projection Problem," in C.-K. Oh and D. A. Dineen, eds., *Syntax and Semantics II: Presupposition,* Academic Press, Inc., New York, 1979b, pp. 57–89.

H. P. Grice, "Logic and Conversation," in P. Cole and J. L. Morgan, eds., *Syntax and Semantics 3: Speech Acts,* Academic Press, Inc., New York, 1975, pp. 41–58.

H. P. Grice, "Further Notes on Logic and Conversation," in P. Cole, ed., *Syntax and Semantics 9: Pragmatics,* Academic Press, Inc., New York, 1978, pp. 113–128.

L. Horn, "Metalinguistic Negation and Pragmatic Ambiguity," *Language* **61**(1), 121–174 (1985).

L. Karttunen, "Presuppositions of Compound Sentences," *Ling. Inquiry* **4**, 169–193 (1973).

L. Karttunen and S. Peters, "Conventional Implicature in Montague Grammar," in *Proceedings of the First Annual Meeting of the Berkeley Linguistics Society,* 1975, pp. 266–278.

L. Karttunen and S. Peters, "Conventional Implicature," in C.-K. Oh and D. A. Dineen, eds., *Syntax and Semantics II: Presupposition,* Academic Press, Inc., 1979, pp. 360–371.

R. M. Kempson, *Presupposition and the Delimitation of Semantics,* Cambridge University Press, Cambridge, UK, 1975.

D. T. Langendoen and H. B. Savin, "The Projection Problem for Presuppositions," in C. J. Fillmore and D. T. Langendoen, eds., *Studies in Linguistic Semantics,* Rinehart and Winston, New York, 1971, pp. 55–62.

S. C. Levinson, *Pragmatics,* Cambridge University Press, Cambridge, UK, 1983.

J. Lyons, *Semantics,* Cambridge University Press, Cambridge, UK, 1977.

B. Russell, "On Denoting," *Mind,* **14,** 385–389 (1905).

P. A. M. Seuren, *Discourse Semantics,* Blackwell, Oxford, UK, 1985.

P. F. Strawson, "On Referring," *Mind,* **59,** 320–344 (1952).

D. Wilson, *Presupposition and Non-Truth Conditional Semantics,* Academic Press, Inc., New York, 1975.

D. Wilson and D. Sperber, "Ordered Entailments: An Alternative to Presuppositional Theories," in Oh and Dineen, 1979, pp. 229–324.

General References

P. Cole, ed., *Syntax and Semantics 9: Pragmatics,* Academic Press, Inc. New York, 1978.

P. Cole and J. L. Morgan, eds., *Syntax and Semantics 3: Speech Acts,* Academic Press, Inc., New York, 1975.

G. M. Green, Pragmatics and Natural Language Understanding, Lawrence Erlbaum, Hillsdale, N.J., 1989.

C.-K. Oh and D. A. Dineen, eds., *Syntax and Semantics II: Presupposition,* Academic Press, Inc., New York, 1979.

D. A. Cruse
University of Manchester

PROBABILISTIC NETWORKS

PROBABILISTIC REASONING

Probability theory provides powerful mechanisms for expressing and drawing plausible conclusions from uncertain premises. The theory can be used in reasoning tasks whenever relationships between entities of interest are uncertain, either because some necessary information is lacking or because describing them in detail is computationally infeasible. For example, relationships between diseases and symptoms in medical diagnosis, between messages sent and the ones received along communication channels, and between objects and features in classification tasks are more naturally described probabilistically rather than categorically.

Traditional approaches to these reasoning tasks face a critical choice: either specify precise relationships between all interacting variables or make uniform independence assumptions throughout. The first choice is computationally infeasible except in very small domains, whereas the second, which is rarely justified, often yields inadequate conclusions.

Probabilistic networks are graphical models that offer a compromise between these two extremes by encoding independence when possible and dependence when necessary. They allow a wide spectrum of independence assertions to be considered by a model builder so that a practical balance can be established between computational needs and adequacy of conclusions. This article describes the principles underlying probabilistic networks. It focuses on Bayesian networks, a salient subclass of probabilistic networks suitable for causal modeling. In particular, the next section discusses the definition of Bayesian networks (alternate names in the literature include belief networks, causal networks, knowledge maps and probabilistic influence diagrams). Subsequent sections explore inference algorithms associated with Bayesian networks, the relationships between causation and probabilistic dependencies, and alternative network formulations.

BAYESIAN NETWORKS

Among the various types of probabilistic networks, Bayesian networks have attracted most attention in artificial intelligence because they provide a convenient language for expressing domain knowledge about causal relationships and a computational scheme for drawing quantitative and qualitative inferences (see BAYESIAN INFERENCE METHODS).

Informal Description

The Bayesian network formulation is best explained via a simple example. Consider the following description. Age and weather are factors influencing whether a human gets a sore throat. There are five mutually exclusive and exhaustive types of a sore throat: viral pharyngitis, strep throat, mononucleosis, tonsillar cellulitis, and peritonsillar abscess. Several symptoms are associated with a sore throat, including fever, toxic appearance, abdominal pain, tonsillar pus, and palatal spots. Most symptoms occur independently of each other in patients having a sore throat, except toxic appearance, which depends on having fever or abdominal pain.

A Bayesian network representing this description is given in Figure 1 (Heckerman, 1990b). The network is constructed from cause-and-effect relationships by placing links from each cause to its direct consequences, eg, fever is a cause for toxic appearance. For each variable u, the distribution $P(u|\pi(u))$ is estimated, where $\pi(u)$ is the set of parents of u in the network. When u has no parents, ie, $\pi(u) = \emptyset$, then $p(u)$ is estimated. Continuous variables such as age and fever are made discrete. For example, the values of age can be partitioned into infant, child, and adult and the values of fever can be partitioned into normal, medium, and high. Consequently, $P(fever|disease)$ is specified by 15 numbers one for each combination of disease and fever values, and $P(age)$ is specified by three numbers, depending on the relative proportion of infants, children, and adults among the intended users. Such conditional distributions are assigned for each node in the network. The product of these conditional distributions, one per each node in the network constitutes a probability distribution

$$P(u_1, \ldots, u_n) = \prod_{u_i} P(u_i|\pi(u_i)) \qquad (1)$$

that represents numerically the qualitative dependencies among variables in the domain, as depicted in the network.

If statistical data are available, the validity of the network (and of the product form) can be ascertained by testing whether independence assertions implied by this product approximate the reality to a reasonable extent. If such data are not available, then the independence assertions

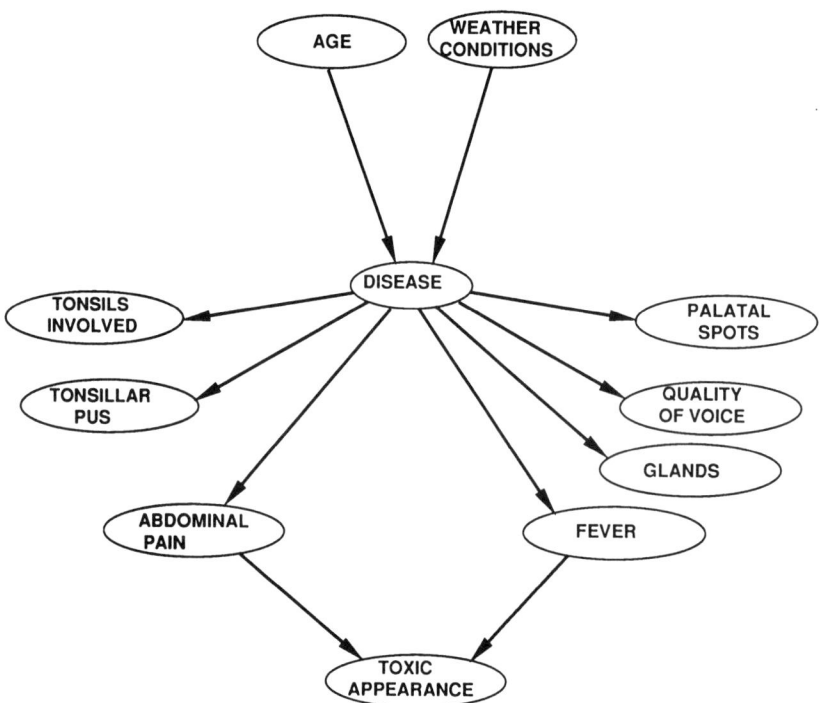

Figure 1. A Bayesian network for a sore throat.

embodied in the product form represent a probabilistic encoding of the judgments according to which some variables are identified as the direct causes of others. An independence assertion is, loosely, a statement that given some conditions, the values of one set of variables are irrelevant for reasoning about values of another set of variables (a precise definition is given below). In particular, the product form above is equivalent to stating that given its parent's values, each variable is independent of all variables that are not its descendants (Howard and Matheson, 1984; Olmsted, 1983).

Consequently, the builder of the network of Figure 1 must judge whether age and weather conditions are independent, which in this case is quite realistic. However, if this assertion, or any other assertion encoded in the network, does not reflect reality to a reasonable extent, then additional nodes or links should be drawn until a reasonable model is at hand. For example, it may be argued that the life span on the north pole is generally shorter than that in, say, California where weather conditions are more benign. This dependency between age and weather conditions could be modeled by adding a new node called climate and making it the parent of both weather conditions and age. Such weak dependencies are ignored in practice.

Another independence assertion that is implied by the network in Figure 1 is that toxic appearance is independent of disease, given that it is known whether the patient has fever and abdominal pain. This assertion reflects a view that fever and pain are the only intervening mechanisms by which a sore throat causes toxic appearance. If there are other intervening mechanisms beside pain and fever, then these can either be specified explicitly by additional nodes, or a direct link can be added between disease and toxic appearance to summarize the impact of these mechanisms while keeping them implicit.

The network and the probability distribution that result from this judgmental process provide an approximate model of the domain as conceived by an expert and can be used to draw diagnostic and predictive inferences. Statistical samples obtained from measurements are an alternative source of information for constructing Bayesian networks. Such construction methods, however, are not practical yet because tests for conditional independence are laborious and require many samples.

Formal Definition

Before the definition of Bayesian networks can be stated, some notational conventions must be established. Throughout this article a finite set of variables $U = \{u_1, \ldots, u_n\}$ each having a finite domain, denoted $domain(u_i)$, and a probability distribution P over U having the Cartesian product $\times_{u_i \in U} domain(u_i)$ as its sample space are considered.

Definition. Let P be a probability distribution over a finite set of variables U. A directed acyclic graph (ie, a graph with no directed cycles) D is a Bayesian network representing P if D is constructed from P by the following steps: assign a construction order $u_1, u_2, \ldots, u_n$ to the variables of U and designate a node, denoted u_i, for each variable u_i. For each variable u_i in U, identify a minimal set of predecessors $\pi(u_i) \subseteq \{u_1, \ldots, u_{i-1}\}$ such that

$$P(u_i|\pi(u_i)) = P(u_i|u_1, \ldots, u_{i-1})$$

for all values of $u_1, \ldots, u_i$ ($\pi(u)$ is minimal with respect to set inclusion ie, no proper subset of $\pi(u)$ satisfies the equation above). Assign a direct link from every node in $\pi(u_i)$ to node u_i.

This definition does not dictate the choice of the construction order, which has a crucial effect on the complexity of the resulting structure and the number of parameters it requires. In practice, cause-and-effect and time-order relationships are used to determine a tentative network and then the definition above is employed for validating the network obtained.

Multicausal Interactions

The formulation of Bayesian networks presented thus far requires a model builder to specify the conditional distribution of each variable given any combination of its parents' values. Such a requirement is sometimes overwhelming because the number of such combinations grows exponentially with the cardinality of the parent set. Even worse, experts encounter difficulties imagining how complex combinations of causal factors influence a given manifestation and, so, the estimates elicited are unreliable.

For example, while a medical doctor may estimate the probability of having a toxic appearance given a fever and the probability of having a toxic appearance given abdominal pain, difficulty will be encountered when estimating the probability of having a toxic appearance given every combination of fever and abdominal pain. Consequently, a generic rule must be formulated for combining causal influences, a rule that in the example above will mechanically infer $P(toxic\ appearance|fever, abdominal\ pain)$ from the estimates of $P(toxic\ appearance|fever)$ and $P(toxic\ appearance|abdominal\ pain)$.

A disjunctive combination rule for variables having exactly two values (ie, binary variables) was used by Good (1961) and has been further developed within the framework of Bayesian networks by Pearl (1988). Suppose node u has n binary parents $c_1, \ldots, c_n$ each being active (true) or inactive (false). Each active parent c_i alone has a probability p_i of rendering u active and a probability $q_i = 1 - p_i$ of leaving it inactive, ie, $q_i = P(u = false|only\ c_i\ is\ active)$. The combination rule, often called a noisy or-gate, dictates that u is inactive if and only if none of its active parents renders it active and that the activation mechanisms are independent:

$$P(u = \text{false}|c_1, \ldots, c_k) = \prod_{i:\ c_i\ \text{is active}} q_i$$

This rule can be generalized to the case where both u and its parents are multivalued as in the example of fever and toxic appearance (Henrion, 1989b). Other combination rules representing enabling and inhibitory interactions can also be used to model multicausal interactions (Pearl,

1988). These use different logical gates but enjoy similar computational benefits as long as exceptions are assumed to act independently from each other.

Experts' Judgments and Subjective Probability

The parameterization of Bayesian networks using experts' judgments is founded on a subjective interpretation of probabilities by which probabilities stand for the degree of belief of an individual regarding the truth of propositions. Under this interpretation, the ratio rule for conditional probabilities, $P(H|E) = P(H, E)/P(E)$, as well as Bayes's rule

$$P(H|E) = P(H) \cdot P(E|H)/P(E)$$

which are tautological when probabilities are interpreted as frequencies, constitute a theory for plausible updating of beliefs. In particular, the ratio rule provides a formal interpretation of the conditional phrase "given that we know E," and Bayes's rule dictates a way of changing the degree of belief about an hypothesis H after evidence E has been observed.

These formulas were given an axiomatic justification by Cox (1946), who postulated that degrees of belief can be summarized with a single number between zero and one, where zero signifies total disbelief and one signifies belief with certainty. He defined desirata, ie, axioms that degrees of belief ought to satisfy, and proved that these axioms imply the ratio rule for conditional probabilities as well as Kolmogorov's axioms of probability. Consequently, Bayes's rule follows.

Finally, a suitable interpretation of probabilities, whether frequency based, subjective, or other has been the subject of debate among researchers for decades (for example, Savage and De Finetti). The relevance of this debate to artificial intelligence is the realization that probability theory multifacets can be used legitimately both when judgments are subjective as well as when statistical data are available. Historical accounts of these developments have been published (Kyburg and Smokler, 1980; Shafer and Pearl, 1990).

SEMANTICS AND INFERENCE

To be useful for reasoning, Bayesian networks must be coupled with inference algorithms, ie, algorithms that compute the posterior probability of a hypothesis h_i given some findings (ie, $P(h_i|f_1, \ldots, f_n)$) and identify the most likely explanation, ie, a set of hypotheses most likely to explain a given collection of findings. In principle, these computations are straight forward because each Bayesian network defines a full probability distribution over the relevant variables (eq. 1). However, any computation would be inefficient in both time and space unless it uses conditional independence assertions encoded in the network.

Semantics

The semantics of a Bayesian network associates conditional independence assertions with each of its missing links. This semantics is used both for verifying that a network faithfully represents a domain and for devising efficient inference algorithms.

Definition. Let $U = \{u_1, \ldots, u_n\}$ be a finite set of variables with finite domains and let P be a joint distribution over U. Let X, Y, and Z be three disjoint subsets of U. Then X is conditionally independent of Y given Z, if the following equation holds for every value of X, Y, and Z.

$$P(X = \mathbf{X}|Z = \mathbf{Z}, Y = \mathbf{Y}) = P(X = \mathbf{X}|Z = \mathbf{Z}) \quad (2)$$

whenever $P(Y = \mathbf{Y}, Z = \mathbf{Z}) > 0$. When $Z = \emptyset$, then X and Y are marginally independent.

Definition. A trail in a Bayesian network is a sequence of edges that form a path in the underlying undirected graph, ie, in the graph obtained from the network by ignoring the directionality of its links. A node b is called a head-to-head node with respect to a trail t if there exist two consecutive edges $a \to b$ and $b \leftarrow c$ on t. A trail t is active given Z if (1) every head-to-head node with respect to t either is in Z or has a descendant in Z and (2) every other node along t is outside Z. Otherwise, the trail is said to be blocked (or d-separated) by Z (Pearl, 1988).

In Figure 2, for example, both trails between $X = \{2\}$ and $Y = \{3\}$ are d-separated by $Z = \{1\}$; the trail $2 \leftarrow 1 \to 3$ is d-separated by $\{1\}$ because node 1, which is not a head-to-head node with respect to that trail is in Z while the trail $2 \to 4 \leftarrow 3$ is d-separated by $\{1\}$ because node 4 (a head-to-head node) and all its descendants are outside Z. However, the later trail is not d-separated by $Z = \{1,5\}$ because 5 is a descendent of a head-to-head node on that trail.

> *Theorem 1.* Let D be a Bayesian network representing a probability distribution P over a finite set of variables U and let X, Y, and Z be three disjoint subsets of U.
>
> *Soundness.* If all trails between a node in X and a node in Y are blocked by Z, then X and Y are conditionally independent given Z in P (Verma, 1986).
>
> *Completeness.* The criterion above lists all independence assertions that can be identified from the topology of D (Geiger and Pearl, 1990).

This is an important theorem. It implies, for example, that each variable is independent of all its nondescendants, conditioned on its parents, because the parents of each node block all trails between a node and its nondescendants. It also implies that all root nodes (nodes having no parents) are marginally independent of each other and that each variable is independent, given its parents, children, and its children's parents, of all other variables in the network. Such assertions are the cornerstone of any efficient inference algorithm. Theorem 1 has been generalized to networks that include deterministic nodes, ie, nodes whose value is a function of their parents values (Geiger and co-workers, 1990). Related algorithmic work has been published (Shachter, 1990).

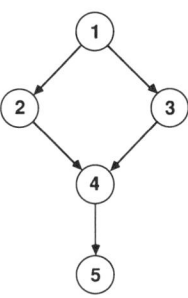

Figure 2. An abstract example of a Bayesian network.

Exact Inference Algorithms

Several inference algorithms for computing posterior probabilities have been developed that rely on independence relationships encoded in the network.

Pearl (1982) and Kim and Pearl (1983) developed remarkable distributed algorithms for trees and singly connected networks, ie, networks in which every two nodes are connected with at most one trail. Each node is viewed as a processor that repeatedly sends messages to each of its neighbors. The computations reach equilibrium regardless of the order of execution in time proportional to the length of the longest trail in the network. The algorithm is easily implementable by parallel architectures. Pearl (1986) extended the algorithm to general graphs: first a set of nodes S is found that cuts all loops in a given network (a loop is a cycle in the underlying unidirected graph). Then the tree algorithm is applied once for each combination of values of the nodes in S and, finally, the results are combined. The complexity of this method grows exponentially with the size of S.

Another important inference algorithm is that of Lauritzen and Spiegelhalter (1988), which initially compiles a given network into a tree in which each node represents a cluster of variables. This tree represents a modified version of the original probability distribution in which groups of variables, called cliques, are collapsed into single variables whose domain is the Cartesian product of their constituents. Whereas every network can trivially be collapsed into a single node, this would amount to storing a table of exponentially many entries, one for each combination of values. Instead, the algorithm minimizes as much as possible the size of the largest clique. Inference is done using message propagation in the clique tree, in time exponential in the size of the largest clique.

Shachter (1986) developed an inference algorithm based on two types of transformation: node removal and arc reversal. To compute $P(x|Y)$ the algorithm picks a node z (a parent of x that is not in Y) reorients all z's adjacent links into z using the transformation of arc reversal and then, when z has no children, it is removed using the node-removal transformation. These transformations are applied until only nodes in Y remain parents of node x, in which case the distribution $P(x|Y)$ is explicitly stored in the network. In each step, changes in the parameters of the transformed network are computed via a simple closed-form formula. An algorithm for computing the most likely explanation for a collection of findings is available (Pearl, 1988).

Alternative Inference Algorithms

The time complexity of the above algorithms when applied to arbitrary networks is exponential in the number of variables, a fact that is not surprising because inference in Bayesian networks is NP-hard (Rosenthal, 1975; Cooper, 1990). Consequently, research has focused on developing inference algorithms that are tailored for specific network topologies and developing inference algorithms that use approximate computations.

A topology for which efficient inference algorithms have been devised is depicted in Figure 3. It is used in medical applications. Each node d_i represents a disease and is associated with the marginal distribution $P(d_i)$, and each node f_j represents a finding and is associated with the conditional probability $p(f_j|d_{j_1}, \ldots, d_{j_k})$ where $d_{j_1}, \ldots, d_{j_k}$ are disease variables that correspond to the direct parents of node f_j. These conditional distributions are formed using noisy or-gates and their product represents the relationship between symptoms and diseases. Note that in this network any combination of diseases is feasible; diseases are not assumed mutually exclusive.

Heckerman (1990a) found a closed-form formula for computing the probability of a disease given positive and negative findings. The algorithm is exponential only in the number of positive findings, which is typically low. Henrion (1989a) provided a branch and bound algorithm for finding the most likely explanation, ie, a set of diseases most likely to explain the symptoms.

Several algorithms that approximate posterior probabilities have been developed. One method is stochastic simulation (Pearl, 1987). Each node computes the conditional distribution of its values given its parents, children, and its children's parents. It flips a coin using this distribution and updates its value. Each node performs this operation repeatedly and counts the proportion of time the coin has entered any of its states. These counts converge to the corresponding posterior probabilities; however, when probabilities are close to zero, the convergence rate deteriorates.

Another approximation method is probabilistic logic sampling (Henrion, 1988). Random scenarios of events are generated according to the probabilities encoded in the network. Scenarios that disagree with the findings are discarded. Posterior probabilities are computed based on the frequency in which a certain value is present relative to the number of scenarios in which it is not present. These frequencies converge to the corresponding posterior probabilities; however, when findings are rare, this method is slow because many scenarios must be discarded.

CORRELATION AND CAUSATION

Cause-and-effect relationships play a key role in the construction of Bayesian networks from human judgments, because it is causal knowledge that is normally consulted in putting these networks together, from which dependence information can be inferred. The converse task, that of inferring causal relationships from probabilistic dependencies, is far less understood; almost every textbook on statistics alerts its readers that correlation is no proof of causation. Bayesian networks offer criteria for determining when an inference from correlation to causation is sound.

One approach to this problem is to view the task of inferring causal relationships as an identification game that scientists play against nature (Geiger and co-workers, 1990). First, it is assumed that nature possesses true cause-and-effect relationships and that these relationships form a causal schema, namely, a directed acyclic graph (dag) where each node represents a variable in the domain and the parents of that node correspond to its direct causes, as designated by nature. Next it is assumed that nature annotates the causal schema by assigning probabilistic parameters to its links, in precisely the same way as Bayesian networks are interpreted, that is, direct causes of each variable render that variable conditionally independent of all other variables except its consequences.

Definition. A causal schema is a directed acyclic graph D where each link $a \to b$ corresponds to a direct causal influence of a on b. A joint probability distribution P is said to be generated by D if P can be factored as follows:

$$P(u_1, \ldots, u_n) = \prod_{u_i} P(u_i | \pi(u_i))$$

where the $\pi(u_i)$ are the variables corresponding to the parents of node u_i and P cannot be factored this way if any link of D is deleted. (This factorization is equivalent to the requirement that given its parents each variable be independent of all other variables except its consequences.)

Nature permits scientists to observe the resulting distribution and to ask questions about its properties, but hides the underlying causal schema. Several workers have investigated the feasibility of recovering the schema's topology from features of the joint distribution (Glymour and co-workers, 1987; Pearl, 1988; Geiger and co-workers, 1990; Verma and Pearl, 1990; Spirtes and co-workers, in press).

This formulation contains several simplifications of the actual task of scientific discovery. It assumes, for example, that scientists obtain the distribution, rather than events sampled from that distribution. This assumption is justified when a large sample is available, sufficient to reveal all the dependencies embedded in the distribution. It also assumes that the scientist can observe all relevant variables in the schema. (A way to relax this assumption is found in Verma and Pearl, 1990.) Relevant variables that cannot be measured often prevent scientists from distinguishing between spurious correlations (Simon, 1954) and genuine causes; a causal relation $a \to b$ may in fact result from a chain $a \leftarrow c \to b$ where c is an unmeasured variable. Another assumption is that the scientist has access to the variables that participate in the causal schema, not to some aggregate thereof. Aggregation might result in feedback loops that are excluded from the language of Bayesian networks.

Clearly, if nature wishes to confuse the scientist, it could choose a distribution that hides some of the causal links. For example, if nature makes two causal paths have precisely equal strengths and opposite signs the scientist would have no way of distinguishing this incidental cancellation from a permanent absence of a causal connection in the underlying schema. As a consequence, to allow for such cancellations, the scientist would never be able to rule out the possibility that the underlying schema is a complete graph; a structure that with a clever choice of parameters can mimic the behavior of any other schema, regardless of the variable ordering. Thus structural identifiability requires that some reasonable restrictions be imposed on the manner in which the causal schema is annotated to yield the observed distribution.

One convenient restriction is that of total faithfulness (also called dag isomorphism), assuming that all observed independencies be structural and not result from numerical cancellations. Algorithms for the recovery of causal schema under the assumption of faithfulness have been described (Verma and Pearl, 1990; Spirtes and co-workers, in press). A somewhat less restrictive assumption is that of minimality, ie, that the observed distribution be compatible with no other causal schema except those capable of emulating the underlying schema. Using this notion of minimality, Verma and Pearl (1990) showed that an operational distinction can be devised between genuine and spurious causes, allowing for the existence of latent variables.

A less restrictive assumption on the distribution function has been reported (Geiger and co-workers, 1990). For example, in the causal schema of Figure 3 many of the links can be identified and oriented, provided the following requirements are met:

- Every combination of diseases and symptoms has some positive probability of occurring (ie, exceptions are always present).
- Each link represents a genuine causal influence of a disease on a symptom, ie, $P(s|d) \neq P(s|\bar{d})$ where d is a parent of s and $\mathbf{d}$ and $\bar{\mathbf{d}}$ are its values.
- Two symptoms of the same disease are dependent unless it is known whether the disease has or has not occurred (ie, no accidental cancellations).
- All diseases are mutually independent.

Notably, the directionality of some links can never be recovered from the joint distribution because these directionalities do not constrain the distribution. For example, identical probability distributions are generated by alternative causal schemas in which the link between d_1 and f_1 is reversed. However, whenever the conditions above are met, the remaining links can be uniquely oriented (Geiger and co-workers, 1990).

This transition from symmetric probabilistic associations to asymmetric directed relationships is an essential

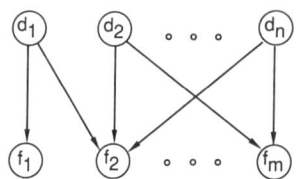

Figure 3. A graphical representation of symptoms and diseases.

prerequisite for attributing a causal interpretation to these associations. The theory of Bayesian networks provides the tools for deciding which directionalities (in a proposed causal model) could potentially be substantiated by observational studies and which can only be determined by controlled manipulative experiments.

OTHER NETWORK FORMULATIONS

Probabilistic networks have evolved independently in various fields such as decision analysis, econometrics, image recovery, statistics, and social sciences. Each field created its own terminology and adapted a suitable graphical model. Three of these formulations are outlined below.

Influence Diagrams

Influence diagrams are important extensions of Bayesian networks used for decision analysis. An influence diagram consists of decision nodes, which represent possible actions; chance nodes, which represent uncertain variables; deterministic nodes, which represent functional relationships between variables; and a single value node, which represents preferences. Like Bayesian networks, influence diagrams possess precise semantics that are used to compute the most suitable action based on the principle of maximum expected utility (see BAYESIAN INFERENCE METHODS). Influence diagrams were conceived as representation schemes that help a decision maker express information regarding a decision. The diagrams were then converted to a decision tree for the actual computation of the preferred action (Howard and Matheson, 1984). Later, Shachter (1986) developed an algorithm for computing the preferred action directly from the diagram without producing a decision tree. Whereas decision tree techniques enumerate all possible strategies, this algorithm prunes the search by consulting independence relationship embodied in the network.

Markov Networks

Markov networks are probabilistic networks based on undirected graphs. A Markov network of a probability distribution P is an undirected graph in which each node represents a variable, and for every three disjoint sets of nodes X, Y, and Z, if Z intercepts all paths between X and Y, then X and Y are conditionally independent given Z in P, and no edge can be deleted from the graph without destroying this property. If P is strictly positive, then it has a unique Markov network that can be constructed by a simple procedure; connect any pair of variables that are dependent given the values of all other variables.

Markov networks are used to represent symmetric probabilistic association, such as those between adjacent cells of digitized images. Every node represents a pixel and is connected to the nodes representing adjacent pixels. This forms a grid. A probability distribution for the intensity of all pixels is assigned such that the intensity of each pixel conditioned on the intensity of its adjacent pixels is independent of the intensity of all other pixels. Markov networks are also used as an internal representation scheme in Lauritzen and Spiegelhalter's algorithm for updating Bayesian networks. Markov networks and their applications have been discussed (Geman and Geman, 1984; Isham, 1981; Lauritzen, 1982; Pearl, 1988).

Gaussian Networks

Gaussian networks are probabilistic networks in which each node represents a variable v, which is the sum of its parents values, plus a noise term, which is normally distributed and independent of all ancestors of v. These networks, which form the basis for path analysis, are used for causal modeling in economics, social sciences, psychology, and genetics (Pearl, 1988). Notably, the foundation of Bayesian networks can be traced to the early work of geneticist Wright (1921) on path diagrams.

FURTHER READINGS

The topic of probabilistic networks is covered by a handful of books. The most comprehensive book is Pearl (1988), which contains most of the relevant material, historical background, and many citations. Neapolitan (1990) wrote a textbook concentrating on inference in Bayesian networks. A statistical viewpoint on probabilistic networks concentrating on parameter estimation techniques has been provided (Whittaker, 1990). Most of the research work on this subject has been reported in the proceedings of the *Uncertainty in AI* conferences published by Elsevier (Kanal and Rosenfeld, 1986–1990). Shafer and Pearl (1990) edited a valuable collection of key articles. Other useful collections are Howard and Matheson (1984) and Oliver and Smith (1989). Additional articles on probabilistic networks can be found in *Artificial Intelligence*, the proceedings of the International Joint Conferences on Artificial Intelligence (IJCAI), *IEEE Systems Man and Cybernetics*, *International Journal of Approximate Reasoning*, *Annals of Statistics*, and *Operations Research*. *Networks* published a special issue on this topic (Shachter, 1990).

Many issues regarding Bayesian networks have not been covered here. The abstract concept of conditional independence rests on an axiomatization called graphoids (qv) (Pearl and Paz, 1989; Geiger, 1990). Bayesian networks can be employed for evidential reasoning using formalisms other than probability (Hunter, 1990; Shenoy, 1990). A comparison between Mycin's certainty factors and Bayesian networks provides insights on the advantages of the latter (Heckerman, 1986). The requirement of specifying conditional distributions for each node can be relaxed to that of specifying intervals instead (Fertig and Breese, 1990) or by qualitatively specifying positive and negative influences (Wellman, 1990). The construction of Bayesian networks from experts judgments is studied by Heckerman (1990b). Munin is a large expert system based on Bayesian networks (Andreassen and co-workers, 1987). Finally, much work has been devoted to practical problems such as knowledge organization, user interfaces, explanation facilities, and systems integration (Kanal and Rosenfeld, 1986–1990).

SUMMARY

Probabilistic networks provide a tool for balancing computational efficiency and description refinement. The network provides an efficient language for encoding independence assertions and for making them readily available for inference. The intuitive interpretation of their structure, together with their solid theoretical foundation, renders probabilistic networks a flexible tool for encoding imprecise knowledge and drawing inference in a wide variety of domains.

BIBLIOGRAPHY

S. Andreassen, M. Woldbye, B. Falc, and S. K. Andersen, "MUNIN—A Causal Probabilistic Network for Interpretation of Electromyographic Findings," in *Proceedings of the Tenth IJCAI,* Milan, Italy, Morgan-Kaufmann, San Mateo, Calif., 1987, pp. 366–372.

G. F. Cooper, "Computational Complexity of Probabilistic Inference Using Bayesian Belief Networks (Research note)," *Artif. Intell.* **42**(2), 393–405 (1990).

R. T. Cox, "Probability, Frequency and Reasonable Expectations," *Am. J. Physics* **14**, 1–13 (1946).

K. W. Fertig and J. S. Breese, "Interval Influence Diagrams," in M. Henrion, R. D. Shachter, T. S. Levitt, L. N. Kanal, and J. F. Lemmer, eds., *Uncertainty in Artificial Intelligence,* Vol. 5, Elsevier, Amsterdam, The Netherlands, 1990, pp. 149–161.

D. Geiger, *Graphoids: A Qualitative Framework for Probabilistic Inference,* Ph.D. dissertation, University of California, Los Angeles, 1990.

D. Geiger, A. Paz, and J. Pearl, "Learning Causal Trees from Dependence Information," in *Proceedings of the Eighth National Conference on Artificial Intelligence,* Boston, Mass., 1990, pp. 770–776.

D. Geiger and J. Pearl, "On the Logic of Causal Models," in R. D. Shachter, T. S. Levitt, L. N. Kanal, and J. F. Lemmer, eds., *Uncertainty in Artificial Intelligence,* Vol. 4, Elsevier, Amsterdam, The Netherlands, 1990, pp. 3–12.

D. Geiger, T. S. Verma, and J. Pearl, "Identifying Independence in Bayesian Networks," *Networks* **20**, 507–534 (1990).

S. Geman and D. Geman, "Stochastic Relaxation, Gibbs Distributions and the Bayesian Restoration of Images," *IEEE Trans. Patt. Anal. Machine Intell.* **6**, 721–742 (1984).

C. Glymour, R. Scheines, P. Spirtes, and K. Kelly, *Discovering Causal Structure,* Academic Press, Inc., New York, 1987.

I. J. Good, "A Causal Calculus," *Philos. Sci.* **11**, 305–318 (1961).

D. Heckerman, "Probabilistic Interpretations for Mycin's Uncertainty Factors," in J. F. Lemmer and L. N. Kanal, eds., *Uncertainty in Artificial Intelligence,* Elsevier, Amsterdam, The Netherlands, 1986, pp. 167–196.

D. Heckerman, "A Tractable Inference Algorithm for Diagnosing Multiple Diseases, in R. D. Shachter, T. S. Levitt, L. N. Kanal, and J. F. Lemmer, eds., *Uncertainty in Artificial Intelligence,* Vol. 5, Elsevier, Amsterdam, The Netherlands, 1990a, pp. 163–171.

D. Heckerman, "Probabilistic Similarity Networks," *Networks* **20**, 607–636 (1990b).

M. Henrion, "Propagation of Uncertainty by Probabilistic Logic Sampling in Bayes' Networks," in J. F. Lemmer and L. N. Kanal, eds., *Uncertainty in Artificial Intelligence,* Vol. 2, Elsevier, Amsterdam, The Netherlands, 1988, pp. 149–164.

M. Henrion, "Towards Efficient Probabilistic Diagnosis in Multiply Connected Belief Networks," in R. M. Oliver and J. Q. Smith, eds., *Influence Diagrams, Beliefnets and Decision Analysis,* John Wiley & Sons, Inc., New York, 1989a, pp. 385–407.

M. Henrion, "Some Practical Issues in Constructing Belief Networks," in L. N. Kanal, T. S. Levitt, and J. F. Lemmer, *Uncertainty in Artificial Intelligence,* Vol. 3, Elsevier, Amsterdam, The Netherlands, 1989b, pp. 161–173.

R. A. Howard and J. E. Matheson, "Influence Diagrams," in R. A. Howard and J. E. Matheson, eds., *The Principles and Applications of Decision Analysis,* Vol. 2, Strategic Decisions Group, Menlo Park, Calif., 1984.

D. Hunter, "Parallel Belief Revision," in R. D. Shachter, T. S. Levitt, L. N. Kanal, and J. F. Lemmer, eds., *Uncertainty in Artificial Intelligence,* Vol. 4, Elsevier, Amsterdam, The Netherlands, 1990, pp. 241–251.

V. Isham, "An Introduction to Spatial Point Processes and Markov Random Fields," *Int. Stat. Rev.* **49**, 21–43 (1981).

L. N. Kanal and A. Rosenfeld, eds., *Uncertainty in Artificial Intelligence,* 5 vols., Elsevier, Amsterdam, The Netherlands, 1986–1990.

J. H. Kim and J. Pearl, "A Computational Model for Combined Causal and Diagnostic Reasoning in Inference Systems," in *Proceedings of the Eighth IJCAI,* Morgan-Kaufmann, San Mateo, Calif., 1983, pp. 190–193.

H. E. Kyburg and H. E. Smokler, eds., *Studies in Subjective Probability,* Krieger, New York, 1980.

S. L. Lauritzen, *Lectures on Contingency Tables,* 2nd ed., University of Aalborg Press, Denmark, 1982.

S. L. Lauritzen and D. J. Spiegelhalter, "Local Computations with Probabilities on Graphical Structures and Their Application to Expert Systems (with discussion)," *J. R. Stat. Soc. B,* **50**(2), 1 –224 (1988).

R. E. Neapolitan, *Probabilistic Reasoning in Expert Systems: Theory and Algorithms,* John Wiley & Sons, Inc., New York, 1990.

R. M. Oliver and J. Q. Smith, eds., *Influence Diagrams, Beliefnets and Decision Analysis,* John Wiley & Sons, New York, 1989.

S. M. Olmsted, *On Representing and Solving Decision Problems,* Ph.D. dissertation, Stanford University, Stanford, Calif., 1983.

J. Pearl, "Reverend Bayes on Inference Engines: A Distributed Hierarchical Approach," in *Proceedings of the National Conference on Artificial Intelligence,* Pittsburgh, Pa., 1982, pp. 130–136.

J. Pearl, "Fusion, Propagation, and Structuring in Belief Networks," *Artif. Intell.* **29**, 241–288 (1986).

J. Pearl, "Evidential Reasoning Using Stochastic Simulation of Causal Models," *Artif. Intell.* **32**, 247–257 (1987).

J. Pearl, *Probabilistic Reasoning in Intelligent Systems: Networks of Plausible Inference,* Morgan-Kaufmann, San Mateo, Calif., 1988.

J. Pearl and A. Paz, "Graphoids: A Graph-Based Logic for Reasoning about Relevance Relations," in B. Du Boulay and co-workers, eds., *Advances in Artificial Intelligence-II,* North-Holland, Amsterdam, The Netherlands, 1989, pp. 357–363.

A. Rosenthal, "A Computer Scientist Looks at Reliability Computations," in Barlow and co-workers, eds., *Reliability and Fault Tree Analysis,* SIAM, Philadelphia, 1975, pp. 133–152.

R. D. Shachter, "Evaluating Influence Diagrams," *Operat. Res.* **34**, 871–882 (1986).

R. D. Shachter, ed., "Special Issue on Influence Diagrams," *Networks* **20** (1990).

G. Shafer and J. Pearl, eds., *Readings in Uncertain Reasoning*, Morgan-Kaufman, San Mateo, Calif., 1990.

P. Shenoy and G. Shafer, "Axioms for Probability and Belief Function Propagation," in R. D. Shachter, T. S. Levitt, L. N. Kanal, and J. F. Lemmer, eds., *Uncertainty in Artificial Intelligence* Vol. 4, Elsevier, Amsterdam, The Netherlands, 1990, pp. 169–198.

E. H. Shortliffe, *Computer-Based Medical Consultation: MYCIN*, Elsevier Science Publishing Co., Inc., New York, 1976.

H. Simon, "Spurious Correlations: A Causal Interpretation," *J. Am. Stat. Assoc.* **49**, 469–492 (1954).

P. Spirtes, C. Glymour, and R. Scheines, *Inferring Causality from Statistical Data*, in press.

T. S. Verma, *Causal Networks: Semantics and Expressiveness*, Technical Report R-65, Cognitive Systems Laboratory, University of California, Los Angeles, 1986.

T. S. Verma and J. Pearl, "Equivalence and Synthesis of Causal Models," in *Proceedings of the Sixth Conference on Uncertainty in AI*, North-Holland, Amsterdam, 1991, pp. 220–227.

M. Wellman, "Fundamental Concepts of Qualitative Probabilistic Networks," *Artif. Intell.* **44**(3), 257–304 (1990).

J. Whittaker, *Graphical Models in Applied Multivariate Statistics*, John Wiley & Sons., Inc., New York, 1990.

S. Wright, "Correlation and Causation," *J. Agri. Res.* **20**, 557–585 (1921).

DAN GEIGER
Technion IIT

The author thanks Judea Pearl for his comments and Northrop Research and Technology Center for providing the ideal environment for preparing this article.

PROBLEM REDUCTION

Problem reduction is a problem-solving approach that tries to solve a problem by transforming it into subproblems that have known solutions. In this approach an initial problem description, a set of operators, and a set of primitive problems are given.

The problem-solving process proceeds from the initial problem until it is transformed into primitive problems. A primitive problem is a problem whose solution is known. An operator transforms a problem into a set of subproblems. For any given problem there may be many operators that are applicable. Each of them produces an alternative transformation of the problem into subproblems; to produce a set of problems that are all solvable, several operators might have to be tried. Solving a problem can be equated with finding an appropriate finite set of applicable operators that transform the problem into primitive problems.

For example, the problem of going from Minneapolis to New York can be represented as a combination of getting to the airport, taking a flight, and getting to downtown New York from the airport. Each of those three subproblems can be transformed into other subproblems. For instance, to get to the airport one could either drive or take a cab. To get to downtown New York one could take a cab, take the subway, or get a ride from a friend living there. The original problem is transformed into a conjunction of subproblems (all of which have to be solved to solve the problem) and alternative subproblems (only one of them has to be solved to solve the problem). In AI, problem reduction has always meant a general method of representing and solving problems that are described by an AND/OR graph. This is the interpretation given in this article.

REPRESENTATION

Traditionally in AI, a problem reduction representation is based on the use of an AND/OR graph (qv). An AND/OR graph provides a convenient means for keeping track of which subproblems have been attempted and which combinations of subproblems are sufficient to solve the original problem. Suppose that a problem P is represented graphically by a node. This problem may be transformed into one or more subproblems P_i that may be related to the original problem in many ways.

A relationship is shown by a directed arc connecting two nodes. If an arc is directed from node n_i to node n_j, then the node n_j is called a child of n_i, and the node n_i is called a parent of n_j. A node n_k is an ancestor of node n_i if n_k is a parent of n_i or is an ancestor of a parent of n_i. A node n_k is a descendant of node n_i if n_i is an ancestor of n_k. A node having no children is called a tip node. It can be either a node that corresponds to a primitive problem or a node to which no operators can be applied. A node representing a primitive problem is called a primitive node and a node representing a nontransformable problem a dead end node. The start node of the AND/OR graph corresponds to the initial problem. A tree is a special case of a graph in which each node has only one parent. There is a node having no parent that is called the root of the tree. It corresponds to the initial problem.

Two common relationships between a problem and its subproblems are AND and OR. An AND relationship between a problem and at least two subproblems exists when the solution of all subproblems implies the solution of the problem. An AND relationship means that all the subproblems have to be solved in order for the problem to be solved. Graphically an AND relationship is shown by a circular mark connecting all the arcs that are part of the AND relationship An OR relationship between a problem and its subproblems exists when the solution of any one of its subproblems implies the solution of the problem. An OR relationship means that the solution of one of the subproblems suffices to solve the problem. When there are no AND relationships, the AND/OR graph is an OR graph.

Each arc in an AND relationship is called an AND link. Analogously each arc in an OR relationship is called an OR link. In an AND/OR graph, the same node may be pointed to by an AND link and an OR link. Instead of defining AND and OR links, many authors prefer to define AND and OR nodes. Different definitions have been used in the literature. In earlier work a node of an AND/OR graph was defined as either an AND node or an OR node depending on the relationship that it has with its parent node (Nilsson, 1971; Slagle, 1963). An OR node represents an alternative subproblem; an AND node represents a problem that is a member of a conjunction of problems. This definition of AND and OR nodes is appropriate when the problem is represented by an AND/OR tree. In the general case of an AND/OR graph things are more complex because a node can be an AND node with respect to one of its parents and an OR node with respect to another parent. The more commonly used definition (Nilsson, 1980; Pearl, 1984) defines the type of a node depending on the type of links that the node issues. When a node has both AND and OR relationships with its subproblems, dummy nodes are added to the graph to maintain the purity of node types. Dummy nodes have to be taken into account when searching for an optimal solution because they increase the number of links to be traversed to obtain a solution.

Since in general AND/OR graphs are more interesting than AND/OR trees, a different definition is more appropriate even though less intuitive (Nilsson, 1980; Martelli and Montanari, 1978). An AND/OR graph could be defined as a hypergraph. Instead of arcs it has hyperarcs connecting a parent node with a set of child nodes. The hyperarcs are called connectors. Formally, an AND/OR graph G is a pair (N,C) where N is a set of nodes and C a set of connectors $C \subseteq \cup_{k=1}^{m} N^{k+1}$ where N^{k+1} is a Cartesian product. Each k connector is an ordered $(k+1)$ tuple where the first element of the tuple is the parent and the other elements are the children. The parent node of a connector is called the input node of the connector; the children are called the output nodes. A 1 connector corresponds to an OR link. A k connector, with $k > 1$ corresponds to k AND links from one node.

An example of an AND/OR graph is shown in Figure 1. The connector (n_0, n_1) is a 1 connector; the connector (n_0, n_3, n_4) is a 2 connector. An important assumption made when using an AND/OR graph is that the order in which the problems are solved does not matter. This limits the applicability of this problem-solving method to decomposable problems (Nilsson, 1980).

AND/OR graphs have been shown (Hall, 1973) to be equivalent to context-free grammars. Methods to transform state-space representation into problem reduction and vice versa have been described (Barr and Feigenbaum, 1982; Amarel, 1968). Unfortunately, transforming one representation into another does not help in finding a better representation for the given problem. This is largely an unexplored area (VanderBrug and Minker, 1975; Amarel, 1983).

PROBLEMS REPRESENTABLE USING PROBLEM REDUCTION

The problem reduction approach is especially suited to problems for which the solution can be conveniently represented as a tree or a graph. Pearl (1984) describes these problems as good candidates for problem reduction:

1. Strategy seeking problems.
2. Problems whose solution is an unordered or partially ordered sequence of actions. Typical examples are symbolic integration and chemical structures generation.
3. Logical reasoning and theorem proving.
4. Problems in which the set of subproblems has a unique linear hierarchy so that once a set of subproblems is solved another set can be solved without undoing the former. The classical example is the Tower of Hanoi (Amarel, 1983).

Nilsson (1980) classified problems according to the type of production system necessary to describe them. In his definition, problem reduction can be used on problems that are described by a commutative and decomposable production system. Unfortunately, most interesting problems do not fall into this class because they share variables and because the ordering in which the subproblems are solved affects the solution.

When problems are nearly decomposable (Simon, 1981), it is possible to work on each subproblem separately and then handle potential interactions between subproblems with appropriate techniques. Waldinger (1977) describes a technique for achieving several goals simultaneously in which a plan is developed to achieve one goal and then the plan is modified to achieve the others as well. An appropriate ordering of the subgoals could reduce the search for the solution in a substantial way. Many theorem provers use the generate-and-test method to prove conjunctive goals that share variables. The difficulty with the generate-and-test approach is that an arbitrary choice of the subgoal to solve next may result in inefficiency or may even make the problem impossible to solve. Kowalsky (1979) introduced the cheapest-first heuristic in which the subgoal that is cheapest to achieve is tried first. Pereira (1982) showed how to take advantage of independence of subproblems to do selective backtracking (qv). Smith and Genesereth (1985) introduced the notion of cost of a given sequence of conjuncts, and they showed how to use cost information to order conjuncts effectively. Similar techniques have been in use in the database community to optimize conjunctive queries to databases.

Horn clauses can be related to problem reduction (Kowalsky, 1979). Horn clauses are the basis of logic programming, as done, for instance, in PROLOG. A Horn clause can transform a problem into a conjunction of subproblems. The procedural interpretation of Horn clauses

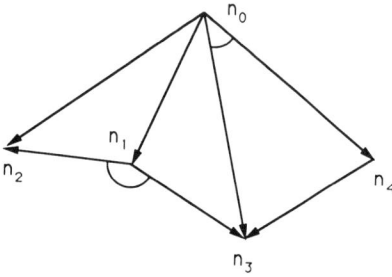

Figure 1. An AND/OR graph.

done in PROLOG is a top-down interpretation in which a problem is transformed into subproblems until primitive problems (called assertions) are found. Note that in this interpretation each clause is seen as a procedure in which the name of the procedure identifies the form of the problems that the procedure can solve. The body of the procedure is a set of procedure calls. Note the use of "set" instead of "sequence." Procedure calls can be executed in any order or in parallel. A procedure call corresponds to invoking one of the procedures with the desired name. The solution to the problem is obtained by doing depth-first search with backtracking. Unification unifies terms with variables. This allows subproblems to share variables. When conjunctive goals share variables, the binding for variables found by the unification algorithm is used as long as it allows solution of successive problems. When the solution cannot proceed any further, the system backtracks and tries a different unification.

Problem reduction has been related to recursive formulation of problems (Amarel, 1983). To solve a problem recursively, it is important to recognize what are the primitive problems whose solution is known and to find ways of transforming the original problem into subproblems of the same type but easier to solve than the original problem. This is the well-known divide-and-conquer approach. The main difference is that in divide-and-conquer the order in which subproblems are solved is important and that subproblems are not independent as they are in problem reduction.

The antecedent–consequent production rules used in an expert system can be represented as an AND/OR graph (Winston, 1984). A known fact is a primitive node. The consequent of a rule is a problem. The antecedents of a rule are the subproblems. This allows a simple graphical representation of rules. The elementary explanation mechanism of rule-based systems (the famous "how" and "why" questions) is simply obtained by identifying the children or the parent of a node.

SEARCH

A solution to a problem represented by an AND/OR graph can be found by searching the graph. To simplify the search process, most of the algorithms make the assumption that the AND/OR graph is acyclic. This means that no node is its own ancestor. This assumption is not too restrictive, because a cycle represents a circular reasoning chain that is undesirable.

There is a distinction between the graph to be searched and the graph or tree that is constructed as the search proceeds. The graph to be searched is ordinarily not explicit. It is called the search space. It can be large or even infinite. The graph that is constructed as the search proceeds is called the search graph. It is explicit. A node is included in the search graph only if a path has been discovered from the start node to it. The search graph grows as the search proceeds.

Before describing the search process with AND/OR graphs some additional definitions are useful. A sequence of nodes $n_i, n_{i+1}, \ldots n_{i+k}$ with each n_j a child of n_{j-1} is called a path of length k from node n_i to n_{i+k}. A node is solved if one of the following conditions holds:

1. It is a primitive node.
2. It is a nontip node and at least one of its outgoing connectors is connected to nodes that are all solved.

A node is unsolvable if one of the following conditions holds:

1. It is a dead end node.
2. It is a nontip node and all its outgoing connectors are connected to at least one unsolvable node.

A solution graph is a hyperpath between the start node and the set of primitive nodes. It could be defined recursively:

1. If the start node is a primitive node, the solution graph consists of that single node.
2. Otherwise, there should be one outgoing connector from the start node that connects the start node to nodes, each of which has a solution graph. The solution graph consists of the start node, the outgoing connector, and the solution graphs for all nodes connected by that outgoing connector.

Informally, a solution graph of an AND/OR graph is analogous to a path of an ordinary graph. It can be obtained by starting with the start node and by selecting exactly one outgoing connector for each node. Because the solution graph is a subgraph containing only solved nodes, the start node is solved. Figure 2 shows two solution graphs of the graph of Figure 1.

It is important to compute the cost of a solution graph. Nilsson (1971) proposes two different ways of computing the cost of a solution graph. The first is called "sum cost" because the cost is the sum of the arc costs in the solution graph. The second is called "max cost" because the cost is the cost of the path in the solution graph having maximum path cost. The most used method is the sum cost (Martelli and Montanari, 1973), and that is the method used in the following. A precise definition of the properties needed in a cost function is given in Mahanti and Bagchi (1985). In computing the cost of a solution graph, only one outgoing connector from each node is considered. Let n be

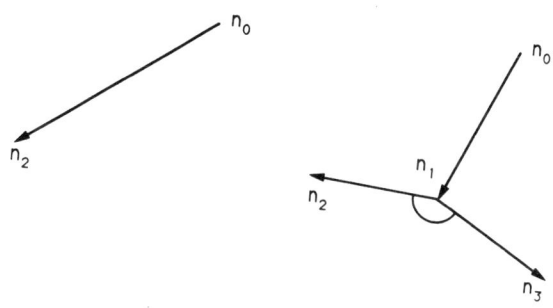

Figure 2. Two solution graphs of the graph shown in Figure 1.

the standing node. The following cost is associated with the node n:

1. If n is a primitive node, then $c(n) = 0$.
2. Otherwise, the cost of n is obtained by adding the cost of the connector c_n to the sum of the costs of the solution graphs of all nodes n_i connected by that connector. If the connector is a k connector, $c(n) = c_n + \sum_{i=1}^{k} c(n_i)$. We assume that the cost of a connector is a positive number.

A solution graph having minimum cost is called an optimal solution graph. The cost of an optimal solution graph is defined recursively as the minimum cost of the solution graph rooted at all the children of the node n. Let the cost of an optimal solution graph rooted at n be denoted by $h(n)$.

1. If n is a primitive node, then $h(n) = 0$.
2. If n is a dead end node, $hn = \infty$ (or a very large number).
3. If n is a nontip node having j outgoing connectors, then $h(n)$ is the minimum over the j connectors of the costs $c(n)$ computed for each of the j connectors.

Search Algorithms

The basic operation in all search algorithms is to construct a search graph by expanding nodes. Generating all children of a node through all its outgoing connectors is called expanding the node. When a child node is generated that is the same as a node generated before, an arc to the original node is created instead of creating a new node. A tip node is never expanded. A node that is not a tip node and that is not yet expanded is called an unexpanded node. Most of the algorithms differ only in the way in which the nodes to be expanded are selected. An algorithm that is guaranteed to find a solution graph with minimum cost, if one exists, is called admissible.

Uninformed Search. Algorithms for breadth-first and depth-first search in AND/OR graphs are similar to the breadth-first and depth-first search algorithms for state-space search. The main difference lies in the computation of the termination conditions. Every time a new node or a group of nodes is generated, the algorithm has to check whether the start node can be marked "solved" or "unsolvable." Nilsson (1971) describes the algorithms for breadth-first and depth-first search for AND/OR trees and provides suggestions for their extensions to AND/OR graphs.

Heuristic Search. Heuristic search can be performed with different objectives. Typically, an optimal solution (a solution with minimum cost) is desirable. Sometimes a solution that can be found with the minimum search effort (a solution that reduces the number of nodes explored) is more desirable. Often the interest is in minimizing some combination of the cost of the path and the cost of the search required to obtain the path or in minimizing the cost averaged over the problem domain. Some task-dependent information can be used to reduce the search effort.

This type of information is usually called heuristic information.

During the process of search in the AND/OR graph, there are nodes whose children have not yet been generated by the search process. The cost of such nodes cannot be computed, but it can be estimated using the heuristic information. The estimated cost of a node is then used to select which node to expand. Assume that for each node n there is an estimate $h^*(n)$ of the cost of an optimal solution graph starting at n. The estimated cost is computed in much the same way as the cost:

1. If n is a primitive node, then $h^*(n) = 0$.
2. If n is a dead end node, then $h^*(n) = \infty$.
3. If n is a nontip node whose children have not yet been generated, then $h^*(n) =$ the value of the heuristic estimate.
4. If n is a nontip node having j outgoing connectors, $h^*(n)$ is the minimum of the estimated costs of all potential solution graphs starting at n and going through each of the j connectors. The estimated cost of each potential solution graph is obtained by adding the cost of the connector c_n to the sum of the estimated costs of all the nodes connected by that connector.

The heuristic search algorithm is a top-down algorithm that starts at the start node and, at each step, selects one node and expands it by generating all of its children.

Top-Down Algorithm for Heuristic Search.
1. Create an initial graph G consisting of only the root n. Associate with n its cost $h^*(n)$.
2. Repeat until n is solved or until its cost becomes ∞:
   a. Select any unexpanded node n_i of the possible partial solution graph that is obtained by tracing down the marked connectors from n.
   b. Expand n_i by generating all its children. If there are none, the cost of n_i becomes ∞. This means that n_i is a dead end node. Associate with each newly generated node its cost. Label "solved" the nodes that are primitive nodes.
   c. Create a set of nodes S containing only n_i.
   d. Repeat until S is empty:
      i. Remove from S a node n_j that has no known descendants in S.
      ii. Update the cost of n_j as follows: Compute the estimated cost of a solution graph starting at n_j through each outgoing connector. Set the cost of n_j to be the minimum of those costs over all the outgoing connectors. Mark a connector through which the minimum is achieved, erasing the previous marking if different. If all the output nodes of the marked connector are labeled "solved," label n_j as "solved."
      iii. If n_j has been marked "solved" or if its cost has been changed, add to the set S all the ancestors of n_j.

The algorithm first expands one node selected by tracing down through the marked connectors. The marks indicate a tentative optimal partial solution graph from each node. The next operation is to update the cost of the selected node and to mark the connector through which the minimum is achieved. The new updated cost is propagated backward. An optimal solution graph is obtained by tracing down from n a hyperpath through the marked connectors. The cost of the solution is the value of $h^*(n)$ at the end of the search.

The cost revision in the algorithm becomes simpler by making the additional assumption that the estimate of the cost is consistent. This means that for each node n and for each outgoing connector the estimated cost associated with the node n cannot be larger than the sum of the estimated costs of all the children of n through that connector plus the cost of the connector itself. With this assumption step (iii) of the algorithm can be modified because the cost of a node cannot decrease. Not all ancestors of node n_j need a cost revision, but only those that are connected through a marked connector to a node whose cost has been revised. Step (iii) of the top-down algorithm for heutistic search can be modified as follows:

If n_j has been marked "solved" or if its cost has been changed, add to the set S all those parents of n_j such that n_j is one of their output nodes through a marked connector.

The top-down algorithm presented here with the consistency assumption is called AO*. The name was given by Nilsson (1980). The algorithm AO* is admissible if the estimates of the cost are admissible. In other words the algorithm is guaranteed to find an optimal solution if one exists, whenever the estimated cost of each node is a lower bound of the cost of an optimal solution graph rooted at the node. The proof is given in Bagchi and Mahanti (1983). The condition that the heuristic estimates are admissible is less stringent than the condition that they are consistent. AO* has been proved admissible when the cost function underestimates the cost of the solution graph but does not underestimate cost at every node (Chakrabarti and co-workers, 1988). Bounds on the cost of the solution when the admissibility condition does not hold are given in Chakrabarti and co-workers (1988).

Additional algorithms based on heuristic search are described in Pearl (1984) and Mahanti and Bagchi (1985). The algorithm AO* and other search algorithms have been shown to be a special case of an improved version of the branch-and-bound algorithm (Kumar and co-workers, 1988; Nau and co-workers, 1984). How to effectively parallelize branch-and-bound algorithms remains a challenging and open problem (Ferguson and Korf, 1988).

THE USE OF PROBLEM REDUCTION METHODS

Some of the early work in artificial intelligence used problem reduction techniques. For instance, the logic-theory machine of Newell and co-workers (1963) proved theorems in propositional calculus by working backward from the theorem to be proved and by keeping track of alternative paths with an OR tree of subproblems.

Gelernter (1963) worked on a geometry theorem prover that was based on problem reduction techniques. Each problem to solve is transformed into subproblems; every primitive problem is either an axiom or a "given" hypothesis. His program is considered the first program that was able to handle conjunctive subgoals.

Slagle (1963) used trees and graphs in his work on symbolic integration. He was the first to call these trees AND/OR trees. Symbolic integration problems are transformed into subproblems by observing that the integral of a sum can be transformed into the sum of integrals. Since all the expressions have to be integrated, this transformation generates AND links. Each expression that can be integrated in alternative ways generates OR links. Chang and Slagle (1971) describe a method of using AND/OR graphs that is much more similar to the state-space approach.

Martelli and Montanari (1973, 1978) show that dynamic programming can be formulated as AND/OR search. The algorithim for heuristic search in AND/OR graphs that we have illustrated is the same as the algorithm that they describe.

Levi and Sirovich (1976) introduce the definition of generalized AND/OR graphs to model subproblem interdependence. The main difference with conventional AND/OR graphs is that they allow reduction operators to reduce simultaneously a set of input problems to a set of output problems. Because of problem interdependence, the search algorithm must be able to find different solutions to the same subproblem. This capability is not needed when all subproblems are independent because a particular solution to a subproblem can never prevent finding a solution to another subproblem. They give an admissible algorithm, and they prove that generalized AND/OR graphs are equivalent to type 0 grammars. They show that they can handle problems requiring consistent binding of variables and problems involving the use of scarce resources. However, they do not address the much more important issue of subproblems that share variables.

AND/OR graphs are important in theorem proving. A theorem prover starts with a set of axioms and a set of inference rules. At each step new statements can be deduced from a subset of axioms and previously deduced statements. When a conclusion is obtained, the internal order in which the statements were derived is not important as long as they are available at the appropriate time. An AND/OR graph is appropriate to describe the search space. Kowalsky (1972) discusses AND/OR graphs in the context of theorem proving. Loveland and Stickel (1976) show how to use AND/OR trees to represent deduction and search space instead of using resolution.

BIBLIOGRAPHY

S. Amarel, "On Representations of Problems of Reasoning about Actions," in D. Michie, ed., *Machine Intelligence 3,* American Elsevier, New York, pp. 131–171, 1968.

S. Amarel, "Problems of Representation in Heuristic Problem Solving: Related Issues in the Development of Expert Systems," in M. Groner, R. Groner, and W. Bischof, eds., *Methods*

- of Heuristics, Lawrence Erlbaum, Hillsdale, NJ, pp. 245–349, 1983.
- A. Bagchi and A. Mahanti, "Admissible Heuristic Search in AND/OR Graphs," Theoretical Computer Science, 24, 207–219 (1983).
- A. Barr and E. Feigenbaum, The Handbook of Artificial Intelligence, Vol. 1, Kaufman, Los Altos, Calif., 1982.
- P. P. Chakrabarti, S. Ghose, and S. C. DeSarkar, "Admissibility of AO* when Heuristics Overestimate," Artif. Intell. 34, 97–113 (1988).
- C. L. Chang and J. R. Slagle, "An Admissible and Optimal Algorithm for Searching AND/OR Graphs," Artif. Intell. 2, 117–128 (1971).
- C. Ferguson and R. E. Korf, Distributed Tree Search and its Application to Alpha-Beta Pruning, Proc. of the National Conference on Artificial Intelligence (AAAI-88), St. Paul, Minn. 128–132, 1988.
- H. Gelernter, "Realization of a Geometry Theorem Proving Machine," in E. A. Feigenbaum and J. Feldman, eds., Computers and Thought, McGraw-Hill, New York, pp. 134–152, 1963.
- P. A. Hall, "Equivalence Between AND/OR Graphs and Context Free Grammars," CACM 16, 444–445 (1973).
- R. Kowalski, "AND/OR Graphs, Theorem Proving Graphs, and Bidirectional Search," in B. Meltzer and D. Michie, eds., Machine Intelligence 7, Edinburgh University Press, Edinburgh, UK, pp. 167–194, 1972.
- R. Kowalsky, "Algorithm = Logic + Control," CACM 22, 424–436 (1979).
- V. Kumar, D. Nau, and L. Kanal, "A General Branch-and-Bound Formulation for AND/OR Graph and Game Tree Search," in L. Kanal and V. Kumar, eds., Search in Artificial Intelligence, Springer-Verlag, New York, pp. 91–130, 1988.
- G. Levi and F. Sirovich, "Generalized AND/OR Graphs," Artif. Intell. 7, 243–259 (1976).
- D. W. Loveland and M. E. Stickel, "A Hole in Goal Trees: Some Guidance from Resolution Theory," IEEE Trans Comput. C-25, 335–341 (1976).
- A. Mahanti and A. Bagchi, "AND/OR Graph Heuristic Search Methods," JACM 32, 28–51 (1985).
- A. Martelli and U. Montanari, "Additive AND/OR Graphs," Proc. Third IJCAI, Stanford, Calif., 1973.
- A. Martelli and U. Montanari, "Optimizing Decision Trees through Heuristically Guided Search," CACM 21, 1025–1039 (1978).
- D. S. Nau, V. Kumar, and L. N. Kanal, "General Branch-and-Bound and its Relation to A* and AO*," Artif. Intell. 23, 29–58 (1984).
- A. Newell, J. Shaw, and H. Simon, "Empirical Explorations of the Logic Theory Machine," in E. A. Feigenbaum and J. Feldman, eds., Computers and Thought, McGraw-Hill, New York, pp. 109–133, 1963.
- N. J. Nilsson, Problem-Solving Methods in Artificial Intelligence, McGraw Hill, New York, 1971.
- N. J. Nilsson, Principles of Artificial Intelligence, Tioga, Palo Alto, Calif., 1980.
- J. Pearl, Heuristics: Intelligent Search Strategies for Computer Problem Solving, Addison-Wesley, Reading, Mass., 1984.
- L. M. Pereira, "Selective Backtracking," in K. Clark and S. Tarnlund, eds., Logic Programming, Academic Press, New York, pp. 107–114, 1982.
- H. A. Simon, The Sciences of the Artificial, 2nd ed., The MIT Press, Cambridge, Mass., 1981.
- J. R. Slagle, "A Heuristic Program that Solves Symbolic Integration Problems in Freshman Calculus," in E. A. Feigenbaum and J. Feldman, eds., Computers and Thought, McGraw-Hill, New York, pp. 191–203, 1963; also in JACM, 10, 507–520 (1963).
- D. E. Smith and M. R. Genesereth, "Ordering Conjunctive Queries," Artif. Intell. 26, 171–215 (1985).
- G. VanderBrug and J. Minker, "State-Space, Problem-Reduction, and Theorem Proving," CACM 18, 107–115 (1975).
- R. Waldinger, "Achieving Several Goals Simultaneously," in E. Elcock and D. Michie, eds., Machine Intelligence 8, Ellis Horwood, Chichester, UK, 1977, pp. 94–136.
- P. H. Winston, Artificial Intelligence, Addison-Wesley, Reading, Mass., 1984.

JAMES SLAGLE
MARIA GINI
University of Minnesota

PROBLEM SOLVING

Problem solving is the central phenomenon studied in AI. It is a process that involves finding, or constructing, a solution to a problem. Such a process is carried out by a problem solver executing a problem-solving procedure. A major goal of AI is to develop and study problem-solving systems that are computationally efficient and effective over a broad range of problems. In this article, the notion of a problem and its formulations for a problem-solving system will be presented, and issues of choosing a problem representation will be discussed. A broad operational classification of problems will be given, and procedural schemas for problem solving will be described. Special categories of problems studied in AI, including problems of planning, learning, theory formation, and analogical reasoning, will be discussed, and comments will be made about the state of research in this area.

DECLARATIVE PROBLEM FORMULATIONS

Posing a problem to a problem-solving system amounts to communicating to the system a problem statement in the following general form:

> Given a domain specification D, find a solution x such that x is a member of a set of possible solutions X and it satisfies the problem conditions C.

In such a statement, it is assumed that both the set X and the conditions C are expressed in terms of concepts in D. The problem-solving system can "understand" the problem statement, and it can then proceed to perform a solution seeking process in response to the statement, if it has means of interpreting and of effectively using the information in D, X, and C. This type of problem statement is very close to the concept of a declarative formulation of a problem; it is discussed in detail in Amarel (1969, 1981). Also, it is closely related to the notion of a set representation of a problem, introduced by Newell and Simon (1972).

The nature of a solution x depends on the problem at hand. It can be a number, a truth value, a proof, a transportation schedule, a computer program, a theory within a formal system, etc. The specification of the set X amounts to a characterization of the possible (candidate) solutions for the problem. Typically, such a characterization is given in terms of necessary conditions for the *internal structure* of solutions or in terms of rules for constructing legal solutions by aggregating available solution elements in the domain. In many cases of interest to AI, the set X is specified in the form of a *generator* for members of the set. The problem conditions C specify further constraints that a member of X (a candidate solution) must satisfy in order for it to be accepted as a solution for the problem under consideration.

The domain specification D is a body of basic knowledge about the problem domain: types of objects and predicates that enter in the specification of the problem, relationships among them, and special characteristics of the problem environment under consideration. In general, D includes a description of a *system of concepts* in terms of which specific problems in the domain can be expressed, understood, and processed.

In essence, a problem statement contains a description of the solution object in one form and a request to find a description of the object in another, specified, form. The second form is more directly useful to the poser of the problem. In most cases it consists of an explicit specification of the internal structure of the solution object, while the first form provides an implicit characterization of the object.

A problem statement represents a well-defined problem for a given problem-solving system if there exists an effective procedure, performable by the system, that will determine if an object proposed as a solution is in fact a solution (Newell and Simon, 1972). *Performable* is used to mean that a reasonable amount of computational effort is needed to perform the test. The notion of a well-defined problem was proposed by McCarthy (1956). Related notions of well-structured and ill-structured problems are discussed by Simon (1973). For a problem to be well-defined it is required that its associated X and C be made known to the problem-solving system that will handle it and that the system should have effective and relatively efficient procedures for determining whether a proposed solution object is a member of X and whether it satisfies the conditions C. In general, the problem-solving processes that are developed and studied in AI are concerned with well-defined problems.

Frequently, not all the information needed to state a well-defined problem is explicitly communicated to a problem-solving system. Often, the relevant D and the set X may not be given explicitly, or they may be presented in incomplete form during an initial specification of the problem. The problem solver must then complete its "conceptualization" of the problem by inferring the missing information from context or in some other way. This act of selecting, or completing, a domain description for a problem, ie, of placing the problem in some conceptual frame of reference, represents a crucial decision that can greatly influence the ease with which a solution to the problem can be found. Indeed, under certain conditions, as some relevant psychological studies suggest (Tversky and Kahneman, 1981), the selection of alternative frames within which a problem is cast may result in radically different solutions to the problem. It has been well known that the process of "mobilizing" relevant information to complete a problem specification is an important part of the problem-solving process (Polya, 1957). In some cases this *problem acquisition* phase, which can be regarded as a "problem understanding" task, is the central part of the problem solving-effort. Within AI there has been relatively little work on "problem understanding" problems (Hayes and Simon, 1974). So far, the emphasis of research in this area has been on how to construct some valid problem statement in response to input information about a problem that is presented in natural language and is not guaranteed to be complete. This is an area in which much more work is needed.

Regardless of the specific way in which a problem statement comes about—whether it is formulated all at once or is assembled from fragments, some externally communicated and some mobilized internally—it is conceptually useful to assume that there exists such a statement (or its equivalent, from the point of view of information content and access) at the starting point of any problem-solving process. If the problem-solving activity requires a problem acquisition stage whose end point is a problem statement that will govern the next stage of solution construction, it is useful to conceive of the situation as consisting of two well-defined problems: a problem acquisition problem and a solution construction problem. To date, work in machine problem solving has concentrated mainly on the second part, while the problem acquisition part was left largely to humans.

In many cases where a problem solver interacts with a changing outside world, the problem conditions C can be seen as changing in the course of the problem-solving activity. In such cases the problem solver can be seen as responding to a sequence of problem formulations. Typically, the changes between successive formulations are relatively small, and this permits the problem solver to move incrementally between successive stages of problem-solving activity, which means that much of the work done in response to a previous formulation can be used in connection with the current (changed) formulation. Problems of interpreting or controlling in real time a dynamic process (eg, understanding speech, controlling a power plant), of generating plans in a dynamic world environment (eg, planning the path of a vehicle in a world where not all obstacles are known *a priori*, but they become known as the path is executed), and of game playing (eg, playing chess), are illustrative of situations of this type. In these situations, problem solving can be seen as proceeding in a succession of cycles, each responding to a well-defined problem acquisition problem followed by a well-defined solution construction problem. During problem acquisition, the problem solver updates the problem conditions; typically, this involves updating its current "model of the world." The updated conditions are used in the solution construction phase that follows. One of the interesting problems in this area, which requires more research, is how to organize the sequence of problem acquisition and solution construction activities, so that the computational complexity of the overall process is as small as possible.

It is useful to abstract the main components of a problem statement and to define in their terms the concept of a *declarative problem representation* (or *declarative problem formulation*). Thus, the declarative representation of a problem P can be defined as

$$\text{Rep}_d(P) = (D, X, C)$$

Usually, a problem is formulated as a member of a problem class. Such a formulation requires a specification of the class and additional information for distinguishing the given problem from all the others in the class. The importance of the notion of a class of problems lies in the fact that problem-solving systems are commonly designed for problem classes.

The specification of a class of problems p can be given in terms of a schema of problem conditions (SC) and of a problem data domain (PD). The schema SC specifies the type of problem conditions that enter in the formulation of problems that are members of the class, and the domain PD is a set of parameter values, each associated with an individual problem in the class. A problem P in p has an associated parameter value d, which is an element of the domain PD. The condition schema for a problem class has variables (or slots) that can be assigned values (can be instantiated) from the domain PD. The problem conditions C of a problem P in class p are obtained by assigning the parameter value d associated with P to the variables (slots) of the condition schema for the class. Thus, given the schema SC and the parameter value d associated with P, the conditions C of the problem P can be uniquely specified. In other words the conditions that define an individual problem can be expressed as a specialization of the condition schema of a class in which the problem is assumed to belong. In view of these notions, the declarative representation of a problem class p can be defined as

$$\text{Rep}_d(p) = (D, X, \text{SC}, \text{PD})$$

and the declarative representation of a problem P in terms of a class p can be defined as

$$\text{Rep}_d(P, p) = (D, X, \text{SC}, \text{PD}, d)$$

To date, the formulation of a problem in terms of a class is mainly done by people. Research on problem understanding (Hayes and Simon, 1974) and on problem solving by analogy (Carbonell, 1981) is relevant to the mechanization of this task. Much more work is needed in this area.

PROCEDURAL PROBLEM FORMULATIONS

For a problem-solving system to proceed with a solution-seeking activity in response to a problem, it must have available a formulation of the problem in procedural form; ie, the formulation must be in a form that can be readily assimilated/accepted by a procedural schema for problem solving that is available to the system. The assimilation of a problem formulation into a procedural schema amounts to defining a specific problem-solving procedure. Such a procedure is an instantiation of the schema in accordance with the contents of the procedural formulation.

In order to understand the nature of problem-solving procedures, it is helpful to focus on ways in which solutions are constructed and, more specifically, on ways in which elements of a problem formulation are used to control the solution construction process. In many AI tasks the desired solution is an object with considerable internal structure that is assembled from smaller parts during the problem-solving process. For example, in a problem of reasoning about actions, a solution has the form of a structured plan made of a sequence of actions that are suitably combined to ensure that the plan satisfies desired goals; in a problem of program synthesis, a solution has the form of a program made of statements in a programming language that are appropriately articulated to achieve the desired program characteristics. In these types of situations, the set of candidate solutions X can be regarded as a solution language; and the language can be specified by a solution grammar $G(X)$ (see Amarel, 1981). Candidate solutions can be represented as graphs of special types. These graphs can be viewed as analogs of strings in ordinary language.

Solution graphs are made of *terminal* and *nonterminal* elements. Terminal elements represent well-specified solution fragments. An example of a terminal element is a proposed action to be taken at a particular situation in a planning problem. Nonterminals represent parts of solutions that are incompletely specified; they can be regarded as "gaps" in a solution structure. Typically, the rules of replacement of solution grammars are *nondeterministic*. This reflects a common situation encountered in AI problem solving: at any one point in the construction of a solution, there are several alternative ways of proceeding with the construction process. In other words, to start filling an "open gap" in a candidate solution, one has the option of using several alternative solution fragments. This element of *a priori* uncertainty about how to proceed in building a structured object from a given set of building blocks is fundamental to the processes studied in AI. It is also responsible for the combinatorial growth of computational effort needed to explore the construction of solution alternatives.

As in the case of ordinary grammars, solution grammars need a designated nonterminal element as a starting element for the generation, (or parsing), of solution graphs. Now, a solution graph can be defined constructively in terms of a process of generation that starts with the starting element of the grammar and proceeds by applying a sequence of grammar rules until the solution graph is obtained.

For example, in a problem of finding a minimal sequence of actions that can transform a situation s_i to another situation s_t in some domain, the set of candidate solutions X consists of all "legal" action sequences, ie, sequences in which a component action satisfies all the sequencing constraints imposed on actions in the domain.

This set of "legal" action sequences can be regarded as the language of solutions in the domain, and it can be specified by a grammar $G(X)$. A specific problem in this domain can be seen as a member of a class of problems whose condition schema SC stipulates that the action sequence that transforms a situation s_i to a situation s_t should be minimal. Furthermore, the data domain PD for the class consists of all the possible values for pairs of situations (s_i, s_t). The schema SC, together with a specific value d for a pair of situations, define the conditions C for a specific problem in the class. Solutions and partly specified solutions to problems in this class can be represented by special solution graphs. For example, the following graph GR_1 represents a partly specified solution, with only the first two actions A_1, A_2 specified.

$$GR_1 \quad \underset{s_i}{\circ} \xrightarrow{A_1} \underset{s_a}{\circ} \xrightarrow{A_2} \underset{s_b}{\circ} \rightarrow - \underset{s_t}{\circ}$$

The two segments of the graph from the left represent terminal elements, and the right segment represents a nonterminal. The nodes s_a, s_b represent intermediate situations obtained from s_i by applying the actions A_1, A_2 in succession. Further specification (construction) of the solution can proceed by applying a rule of replacement of the grammar to the graph.

A grammar rule is typically specified in terms of a transition, which has the form

$$\underset{s_1}{\circ} \rightarrow \underset{s_2}{\circ} \quad \longrightarrow \quad \underset{s_1}{\circ} \xrightarrow{A_3} \underset{s_{1,1}}{\circ} \rightarrow - \underset{s_2}{\circ}$$

and a set of applicability conditions AC. The rule is applicable to a partially specified solution, such as the one represented by GR_1, if the left side of its transition matches the nonterminal in GR_1 (ie, if s_b matches s_1 and if s_t matches s_2), and if the conditions AC are satisfied by GR_1. If the rule is found to be applicable, then it can be applied, thus producing a new graph GR_2:

$$GR_1 \quad \underset{s_i}{\circ} \xrightarrow{A_1} \underset{s_a}{\circ} \xrightarrow{A_2} \underset{s_b}{\circ} \xrightarrow{A_3} \underset{s_c}{\circ} \rightarrow - \underset{s_t}{\circ}$$

which represents an extension of the previous partly specified solution. The new node s_c in GR_2 represents the situation resulting when action A_3 is applied at s_b; it corresponds to $s_{1,1}$ in the right side of the rule's transition, with appropriate bindings of variables. Note that the applicability conditions AC that enter in the specification of the solution grammar embody the conditions that govern the composition of individual actions into sequences. These can be viewed as local structural conditions that solutions must satisfy, and they are distinct from the problem class conditions SC (or the problem conditions C) that impose more global constraints on solutions.

A solution grammar provides a model for a generator of candidate solutions that can be used in a problem-solving system. At any intermediate stage of its problem-solving activity, a system with such a generator will have under consideration several alternative solution candidates in different stages of construction. In order to decide what solution candidate the activity of the generator should focus attention on next, and what generation action (grammar rule) to select in continuing the construction of a solution candidate, the system must have an appropriate controller. Such a controller would operate under the guidance of control knowledge (CK). One part of CK would consist of domain-dependent heuristic rules for attention control and action selection, and another part would consist of more general, domain independent, procedural knowledge that is relevant to the operation of the problem-solving system.

The conditions C that enter in the formulation of a problem can be used to influence solution construction activities in two ways: (1) by *a posteriori* testing whether a candidate solution satisfies the problem conditions (and possibly evaluating a candidate in terms of the degree to which it satisfies the conditions, and (2) by *a priori* constraining the generator (and possibly influencing the controller), to minimize the chances of working on solution candidates that do not satisfy the problem conditions. Thus, C can be used to test candidates proposed by $G(X)$, and also to influence the generation of candidates via constraints imposed on $G(X)$ and CK. Let POST(C) be a procedure for *a posteriori* testing whether a solution candidate satisfies C, and let PRIOR(C) be a procedure for *a priori* constraining the solution generator, and possibly the controller, in a manner that minimizes the production of solution candidates that are inconsistent with C. In general, given C, it is fairly straightforward to specify POST(C), but specifying a good procedure PRIOR(C) can be a demanding task for certain types of problems.

The procedural schemas used in AI specify solution construction processes that involve generators and controllers in various combinations, as well as procedures PRIOR(C) and POST(C), for using problem conditions in *a priori* and *a posteriori* modes. The most general, and weakest, procedural schema is the generate-and-test schema. More specialized and refined schemas that are in the general mold of generate-and-test but that are each "best suited" to handle different types of problems have been developed in AI, and will be discussed later.

Consider a problem P, with a declarative formulation (D, X, C), that is being solved in accordance with the generate-and-test schema. A system operating in accordance with this schema proceeds in a sequence of cycles, and it involves the following information entities:

1. A domain database that implements D.
2. A generator based on some grammar $G(X)$.
3. A controller governed by control knowledge CK (which may depend on C).

4. A procedure PRIOR(C) for using the problem conditions C in an *a priori* mode to control $G(X)$ and CK.
5. A procedure POST(C) for using C in an *a posteriori* mode to test and/or evaluate generated solution candidates.
6. A working database where a record of solution construction activities is kept.

The basic operation of the generate-and-test schema is as follows:

Initialize
Set the characteristics of $G(X)$ and CK that depend on PRIOR(C); direct $G(X)$ to perform an initial solution construction action.

Test
Examine, via POST(C), whether the working database contains a desired solution; if yes, exit with success; else, continue.

Generate
Direct $G(X)$ to perform a solution construction action, based on the current state of the working database and in view of CK; if no action is possible, or if available computational resources are exhausted, then exit with failure; else, go back to the test step.

Various other procedural schemas differ in several ways from generate-and-test; however, they all involve the same types of information entities in their operation. Thus, the procedural representation (or procedural formulation) of a problem P can be defined as follows:

$$\text{Rep}_p(P) = (D, G(X), \text{PRIOR}(C), \text{POST}(C), \text{CK})$$

By using information in $\text{Rep}_p(P)$ to specify parameters (or slots) of a problem-solving schema, the schema can be transformed into a specific procedure for solving P. The procedural representation of a problem P in terms of a class p can be defined as:

$$\text{Rep}_p(P, p) = (D, G(X), \text{PRIOR}'(\text{SC}, d), \text{POST}'(\text{SC}, d), \\ \text{CK}, \text{PD}, d)$$

where PD stands for the problem data domain of the class, d is the specific problem data associated with P, and SC represents the schema of problem conditions for the class p. The problem conditions C of an individual problem P are defined as the instantiation of SC by the problem data d. The procedure PRIOR′ (SC, d) is functionally equivalent to PRIOR(C); similarly, POST′(SC, d) is functionally equivalent to POST(C).

Currently, the procedural formulation of a problem for a problem-solving system that is organized in accordance with a given schema is done almost exclusively by people. This activity can be seen as programming the problem for an AI system at a very high level of specification.

THE PROBLEM OF REPRESENTATION IN PROBLEM SOLVING

The choice of a problem formulation for a given problem-solving schema strongly affects the ease (complexity) of constructing a solution for the problem. Understanding principles for making such a choice, and finding ways of mechanizing (parts of) the choice, are at the heart of the problem of representation in problem solving (Amarel, 1967, 1968, 1969, 1970, 1971, 1981). One of the issues in this area is how to transform a declarative problem formulation into a procedural formulation that would be appropriate for a given problem-solving schema.

The choice of a specific representational framework for D is a significant component of the problem of representation. Not only should such a framework provide sufficient linguistic and control facilities for expressing and processing domain knowledge of relevance to the problem on hand, it must also do so in an efficient manner. Essentially, here is the problem of choosing an appropriate "view of the world" in the form of a theory of some sort or of a model, within which a given problem is to be handled, where appropriateness refers to questions of problem-solving efficiency.

There is no clear *a priori* basis for partitioning knowledge between D and $G(X)$. It is conceivable that rules for generating (or for characterizing) solutions in a domain might be included in a single body of knowledge about the domain. This has been the practice in many of the AI systems developed in recent years, where general information about a domain and about possible solution–construction actions in the domain are embodied in a single knowledge base of the system. However, the distinction between D and the specification of X is conceptually useful in the context of problem representation choices. It permits us to consider separately the choice of a view of the world (ie, of a domain conceptualization), and the choice of specific rules for constructing solutions to classes of problems within that world. The rules that are used to characterize the set of candidate solutions embody knowledge about a specific class of problems in the domain; and the capturing and expressing of such knowledge depends heavily on the domain conceptualization. For a given domain of discourse represented by a given D, there may be several classes of problems, each having its own grammar for solutions of problems in the class. A central issue in the problem of representation is how to choose the most appropriate solution grammar for a specific class of problems in a domain.

Experience in the area of problem representations shows that mechanizing the process of choosing a "good" initial problem formulation is a very difficult task. Recent work shows that a more promising approach is to assume that one or more problem formulations are somehow available, and to explore processes of reformulation, in particular those that lead to reformulations that result in increased efficiency of problem solving (Amarel, 1981). In order to achieve good reformulations, it is essential to have methods for acquiring additional domain-specific knowledge and of using it appropriately in the restructuring of key components of a formulation; in particular, of the solution grammar rules, which determine ways of articulating solution structures from substructures, and of the procedures PRIOR and POST, which determine how problem conditions influence solution construction. To mechanize processes of reformulation, progress is needed in theory formation (and related issues of machine learning) and program synthesis.

In recent years considerable progress was made in the area of knowledge representation (qv). Work in this area is relevant to issues of problem representation. Typical questions of knowledge representation are how to encode various objects, facts, rules, and concepts of a domain in appropriate data structures, ie, in data structures that can be created and/or updated and accessed in ways that are computationally efficient. Propositional representations, production rules, and various types of structured objects, are examples of approaches that have been developed and studied in this area. The availability of good knowledge representations is a necessary condition for good problem representations; however, it is not a sufficient condition. What is needed in addition is good choices of a grain of description and of knowledge distribution over the various parts of a problem solving system, where good is meant in the sense of leading to effective and efficient ways of handling problems, in a given class, by the system.

Research on problem formulation (problem representation), and reformulation, has intensified in the past few years. This is partly due to a renewed interest (and progress) in machine learning. The proceedings of two recent workshops on problem reformulation provide a good account of current developments in this area (Benjamin, 1990; Van Baalen, 1990).

SOLUTION METHODS. PROBLEM-SOLVING PROCEDURES

In general, a computer-based problem-solving procedure is designed to handle a given class of problems. The input domain of the procedure corresponds to the data domain of the problem class, and a specific element of the input domain is representative of a specific problem in the class. If a procedure is executed for an element of its input domain, which stands for a given problem, then a process is carried out that either terminates with success and returns a solution to the problem or with failure, due, for example, to errors or to exhaustion of available computational resources. A procedure expresses a method of solution for a problem class in terms of statements that are interpretable and executable by the system according to a well-defined plan. The procedure can be seen as embodying a specific way of utilizing knowledge about a problem class (which is contained in the problem class formulation) that results in a transformation of the initial problem class into a configuration of simpler problem classes that the system knows how to solve.

The success of conventional problem solving by computer in many areas of science, engineering, and data processing owes a great deal to the large amounts of systematic knowledge that exists in these areas and to the availability of strong methods of solution finding that use the available knowledge in a highly effective manner. Under these conditions efficient problem-solving procedures, whose correctness and optimality can be often justified on formal grounds, can be custom produced. The situation is quite different in AI, where the emphasis is on problems with limited amounts of systematic knowledge, and where solution-finding processes rely primarily on weak methods (Newell and Simon, 1972; Rich, 1983; Laird and Newell, 1983). These are general solution-seeking methods, such as generate-and-test, that are widely applicable over families of problem classes. Under the guidance of heuristic knowledge, the weak methods use available knowledge about a problem in certain generic ways in their attempt to search for a solution. The concept of heuristically guided search is central to the problem-solving processes studied in AI. In general, there is no sharp dividing line between the problem-solving procedures of AI and the procedures used in conventional computing. The distinctions are based on the relative amounts of systematic versus heuristic knowledge available to the procedures and on the form in which the available knowledge is used (Amarel, 1969; Newell, 1969).

THE DERIVATION-FORMATION SPECTRUM OF PROBLEMS

Experience shows that problem-solving power depends on the degree to which problem conditions can be made to influence directly the process of solution construction. Furthermore, the amount of influence exerted by problem conditions depends on their relative use in an *a priori* or an *a posteriori* mode. The more dominant the *a priori* mode, the more powerful (more selective, more sure) the problem-solving process. By focusing on the different ways in which problem conditions can be used to control solution construction processes, we are led to a broad classification of problems along a spectrum. Problems are ordered in this spectrum by the degree to which their problem conditions can be used to control directly the solution generation process. At the two ends of the spectrum we have derivation problems and formation problems (Amarel, 1969; 1970). These two families of problems correspond respectively to the "problems to prove" and "problems to find" discussed by Polya (1957).

Derivation Problems

In derivation-type problems the situation can be viewed as follows: the problem conditions are given as parts of the desired solution structure, and the task of the problem solver is to complete this partially specified structure by using rules for solution construction that are specified by a given solution grammar, in such a manner that the initially given parts are well integrated in the structure. Usually, the problem conditions specify boundary parts of the solution structure, and the problem-solving process consists of finding a "connecting bridge" between the given boundaries by piecing together solution elements in accordance with the rules of the grammar. It is characteristic of a derivation problem that the solution construction process is strongly controlled by the problem conditions. Problem conditions are primarily used in an *a priori* mode in the process of solution construction. This can be seen by examining the way in which procedures PRIOR(*C*) and POST(*C*) appear in procedural formulations of derivation problems. In these problems a procedure PRIOR(*C*) can be seen as specifying the starting element of the solution grammar for the problem; thus, the problem conditions *C* enter directly in this specification. For example, in a problem of finding a sequence of actions that can take us from a situation s_i to another situation s_t, the starting element of the grammar is set [by PRIOR(*C*)], as follows:

$s_i \qquad s_t$

A procedure POST(*C*) can be seen as testing whether a candidate solution is completely specified, ie, if the solution graph is made exclusively of terminal elements; if yes, it is an acceptable solution, else, the procedure (if appropriately "informed") assigns to the incomplete solution some estimate of distance to completion.

A typical example of a derivation problem is the task of constructing a proof to a theorem in a formal system. Other examples are problems of path finding (between well-specified points) and problems of plan generation (to satisfy explicit goals).

Formation Problems

In formation-type problems, the relationship between problem conditions and the structure of a solution is more complex than in derivation problems. Here the problem conditions are given in the form of properties, that the solution as a whole must satisfy, and the problem solver is to generate a solution description within a language of solution structures that satisfies the required properties. Typically, no choice of solution elements can be determined directly from the given problem conditions. The solution process cannot proceed by reasoning from the problem conditions to specific parts of the solution, as is possible in derivation problems. The general approach here is to generate candidate solutions in the language of solutions, and to test them against the problem conditions. The problem solver must have an effective procedure that can take as input the description of a candidate solution and can decide whether (or how well) the candidate satisfies the given solution properties. In general, an entire solution candidate must be assembled before it can be tested. Problem conditions are primarily used in an *a posteriori* mode in solution construction. This can be seen by examining the way in which procedures PRIOR(*C*) and POST(*C*) enter in procedural formulations of formation problems.

As in the case of derivation problems, PRIOR(*C*) can be regarded as specifying the starting element of a solution grammar *G*(*X*) for the problem. However, in the present case the problem conditions *C* enter indirectly and weakly in the specification. Consider, for example, the problem of synthesizing a program in a given language *L* to satisfy a set of input–output correspondences, where the inputs are of data type T_1 and the outputs of data type T_2. Here, the desired solution is a program in the language *L*; and *L* is specified in terms of a program grammar *G*(*L*). The set of input–output correspondences define the problem conditions *C*. In the present problem, PRIOR(*C*) may simply specify the starting element of *G*(*L*) in the form of a program schema that satisfies certain properties of the set of correspondences, eg, the starting schema has inputs of type T_1 and outputs of type T_2. By successively applying rules of replacement from *G*(*L*) to the starting element, the starting program schema becomes increasingly better specified until a completely specified candidate program is generated. This type of problem, and various approaches to its solution, are described in Amarel (1971, 1986).

A procedure POST(*C*) in the formulation of a formation problem can be seen as doing the following: It takes a completely specified candidate solution, and it tests whether it satisfies the problem conditions *C*; if yes, it is an acceptable solution, else, the procedure (if appropriately informed) assigns to the candidate solution an estimate of "degree of success" in satisfying *C*. Testing whether a candidate satisfies the given problem conditions involves computing properties of the candidate so that a direct assessment can be made, via comparison, of whether the candidate satisfies the conditions. In some cases this process of testing can be a complex problem-solving effort by itself. In the program synthesis example, a candidate program is tested by running it over all the given inputs and by comparing the computed outputs with the given outputs. Many problems in theory formation, and in the interpretation of experimental data, are of formation type. In these types of situations, testing a candidate theory may involve deducing consequences of the theory and comparing them with experimental data. Often, these processes are highly demanding in computational resources.

MAJOR PROBLEM-SOLVING SCHEMAS

The bulk of work on problem-solving processes in AI has been done in the area of derivation problems. Two problem-solving schemas have been extensively used and studied in this area: the production schema (or state-space search method) and the reduction schema (Amarel, 1969; Nilsson, 1971). A third schema, called relaxed reduction (Amarel, 1981) which is especially appropriate for goal-directed reasoning in planning problems, has received increased attention in recent years. Each of these schemas represents a different approach to constructing a solution for a problem of derivation type, and it has different ways of utilizing knowledge about a problem in controlling the solution construction process.

Production Schema

The main concepts that enter in the specification of a production schema are states, moves, an evaluation function for states, a move selection function, and a state selection function. A state represents the current state of a solution candidate, from the point of view of the problem-solving process. More specifically, the state must provide a description of the current status of the solution candidate under construction that is sufficient for determining whether the candidate is already a solution or, if not, for deciding what move to apply on the candidate in order to continue the solution construction process. Applying a move represents a solution construction action. A move is characterized by its effect on a (partly specified) solution candidate and by its applicability conditions. The effect of a move can be represented by a transition between a "from" state and a "to" state. The applicability conditions of a move specify under what conditions the move can be applied from a state. A move selection function chooses one or more of the applicable moves for actual application. A state evaluation function assigns to a state (which represents an incompletely specified solution candidate) a heuristic estimate of "effort" needed to reach a completely specified solution from the state. Such an estimate may be in the form of a number of moves needed to complete a solution from the given state. This can be seen as the distance between the current state and the nearest state representing a completely specified solution. Alternatively, the estimate may be interpreted as a measure of computational effort needed to obtain a solution from the state. A state selection function chooses the state on which the problem-solving process must focus attention next, on the basis of the values assigned to states by the evaluation function.

Commonly, a solution has the form of a sequence of situations starting from a given initial situation and ending with a given terminal situation (or with a situation that belongs to a given set of terminal situations); each of the situations in the sequence (except the first) is obtainable from the previous one by application of a permissible action (or operator) in the domain. The notion of a situation is different from the notion of a state, but it is closely related to it. While a situation portrays a "state of the world," a state represents a "state of reasoning about states of the world." For example, in a problem of reasoning about actions, where the task is to find a sequence of actions that can transform a situation s_i into a situation s_t, there may be a partly specified solution candidate in the following form:

$$\underset{s_i}{\bigcirc} \xrightarrow{A_1} \underset{s_a}{\bigcirc} \longrightarrow \underset{s_t}{\bigcirc}$$

The state (of solution) S in this case may be defined as the pair (s_a, s_t). This concept of state is chosen with the intent of providing all the information necessary for deciding about the next step of solution construction from the state.

There is a close correspondence between the main components of a production procedure and the components of a procedural formulation of a problem. The solution grammar $G(X)$ together with PRIOR(C) determine the set of states $\{S\}$, the set of moves $\{M\}$, and the initial state S_0. The procedure POST(C) determines the state evaluation function. The move selection and state selection functions are major parts of the control knowledge CK that define the controller. Thus, it is straightforward to go from a procedural formulation of a problem to the specification of a production procedure for solving it. The value of a procedural formulation lies in the convenience that it offers in specifying key elements of a procedure at an "appropriately high" level of description, without having to go into implementation details.

The set of all situations in a domain, together with the set of all permissible actions (operators) define a space of situations. This is commonly called a state space under an interpretation of state to mean "state of the world." The problem-solving activity carried out by a production procedure can be seen as search in this space. The "search paradigm" involving a space of objects that are interpreted as possible "states of the world" of a problem domain has been dominant in much AI work on problem solving since the early days of the field (Newell and Simon, 1972; Newell, 1980).

For a given problem the production procedure can be seen as searching for a solution, starting from a boundary situation (typically, the initial situation) and piecing together in an incremental manner a sequence of actions (operators) until the second boundary is reached. Typically, several actions are applicable to a situation, and this gives rise to a search tree (more generally to a search graph) in situation space. The nodes of the tree represent situations, and the branches represent action applications that transform a situation into another. Different approaches to search may be represented by different ways of moving in situation space. It is possible to initiate the search from the terminal situation and to proceed (by inverse application of actions) in the direction of the initial situation. It is also possible to proceed with bidirectional search, where search proceeds simultaneously from both boundary situations toward the middle.

A production procedure "grows" a tree in its working database that is isomorphic with the search tree in situation space; it can be seen as a search tree in state space. The notion of state is used here in the sense of "solution state," ie, as a state of the problem-solving activity. The nodes of the search tree in state space are solution states, and the branches represent move applications that take a solution state into another. This tree represents the alternative solution construction activities and their relationships during a problem-solving process. An example of search trees in situation space and state space for a simple problem of reasoning about actions is shown in Figure 1. The problem is to find a sequence of actions that takes a situation s_i to a situation s_t.

The basic operation of a production schema is as follows:

Initialize. Set the initial state S_0 from the problem data; make it the root node of the search tree; apply move selection function on S_0 and generate descendant states.

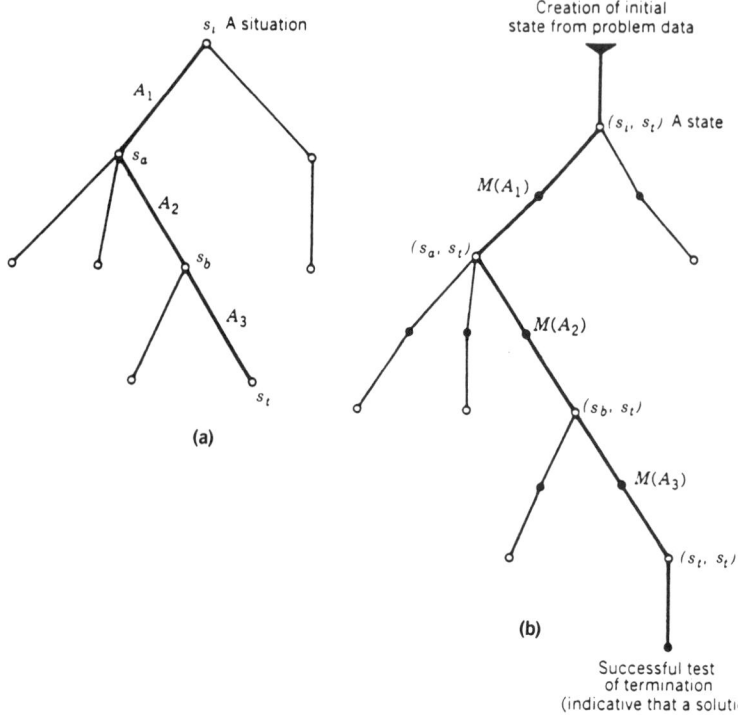

Figure 1. Search trees associated with a production scheme. (a) Search tree in situation space (solution is the darkened path from s_i to s_t). (b) Search tree in state space [solution construction trace is represented by the darkened path, dark nodes represent move applications, $M(A)$ stands for a move corresponding to application of action A].

Test. Examine if the search tree contains a solution; if yes, exit with success; else, assign evaluation function to new states.

Generate.
  a. If computational resources are exhausted or if there are no unprocessed states in the search tree, exit with failure; else, continue.
  b. Apply state selection function on states of search tree.
  c. Apply move selection function on selected state.
  d. Generate new states by applying the selected moves.
  e. Go to the test step.

By choosing different state selection and move selection functions, it is possible to implement different search disciplines. "Breadth-first" search, "Depth-first" search, and "Best-first" search are disciplines that have been widely used in AI. To each of these disciplines there corresponds a procedure from the class of production procedures. Best-first search procedures choose a state (on which attention is to focus next) on the basis of the best value of a heuristic estimate of "distance to solution" that is associated with states in the search tree. Several algorithms, including A*, have been developed and analyzed in this area (Nilsson, 1971, 1980; Pearl, 1984). The performance of these algorithms depends strongly on the quality of the state evaluation function, ie, on the accuracy of heuristic estimates of "distance." One of the important problems in this area is how to choose and improve the evaluation function via acquisition and proper use of domain knowledge. A promising approach is to focus on a simplified version of the problem on hand, to extract relevant properties of solutions to the simplified problem (eg, solution length), and to use these properties in the formulation of a heuristic evaluation function for the original problem (Pearl, 1984).

Reduction Schema

The main concepts that enter in the specification of a procedure organized in accordance with a reduction schema are very close to those that enter in the specification of a production procedure. The main distinction is in the specification of moves. In a reduction procedure there are two kinds of moves: a set of reduction moves (at least some of) which transform a state into two or more states that are presumed easier to handle than the original, and a set of terminal moves that completely resolve whatever is problematic in a state, ie, they recognize that a state is solved or they assign an appropriate (known) solution to the state. As in the case of production procedures, the notion of state refers to "state of solution," but it is more circumscribed and local. Suppose that a solution candidate is being constructed and there are two or more "gaps" in the solution structure that need attention. Suppose further that the gap can be attended independently, and solution construction can proceed for each gap on the basis of characteristic information about the gap. The information about a gap in a solution structure, which permits decisions to be made about "how to fill the gap," is precisely the information that enters in the definition of a state of a reduction procedure. The state can be seen as representing such a gap; more generally, it can be seen as representing a problematic situation. Commonly, a state S has the form of a pair (s_1, s_2), where each element of the pair can be seen as describing one side of the gap, which is represented by S. Often, the elements of the pair can be interpreted as situations, or "states of the world," in the sense used in production procedures. Other interpretations are possible according to the nature of solutions and their gaps. There is a logical interpretation of the concept of state that associates with the state $S = (s_1, s_2)$ a proposition $(s_1 \Rightarrow s_2)$, which means that "s_2 is attainable from s_1 (in the space where s_1, s_2 are defined)." This is equivalent to the proposition that "the (problematic) state S is solvable." These logical interpretations are useful for clarifying the nature of reduction procedures. The principal activity of these procedures can be seen as reasoning about problematic situations.

A reduction procedure starts by setting an initial state, or problematic situation, and its goal is to resolve it by building a nested sequence of reductions, obtained by the application of reduction moves, that will lead to "simpler" problematic situations, all of which are directly resolvable by terminal moves. The reduction schema reflects a "*divide-and-conquer*" method of handling a problem. A problem is decomposed into parts, each part is handled separately, and the results of the individual processes are combined appropriately. This can be seen also as representing an approach to constructing a solution that is different from the approach taken in the production schema where a solution is built incrementally and sequentially from one boundary toward the other. In the reduction approach, different parts of the solution can be built simultaneously and independently of each other, and then combined in an appropriate manner. If good reduction moves can be found in a domain, then it is possible to increase appreciably the power of problem solving in the domain.

A reduction move that transforms a state S_0 into a set of reduced states $S_1, S_2, \ldots, S_m$, (for $m > 1$) must satisfy at least the logical condition that if $S_1, S_2, \ldots, S_m$ are all solvable, then S_0 is also solvable. In addition, a good reduction move must reduce the amount of effort needed to solve the original problem. Usually, such a move incorporates a considerable amount of knowledge about the space in which a search for solution takes place. This knowledge is needed in order to determine decompositions of problematic situations into noninteracting, independent parts.

A reduction procedure "grows" a search tree in its working database with two types of nodes: state nodes and move nodes. Since several moves may be applicable at a state, there may be several descendants below a state node. Since each reduction move is characterized by a specific number of descendant states, a reduction move node will have its characteristic number of descendants in the search tree. A solution is represented in the search tree as a subtree rooted at the initial state and ending with terminal move nodes, where each state node in the tree has exactly one descendant and each move node has its characteristic number of descendants. The state nodes in the search tree are considered to be OR nodes, and the move nodes with more than one descendant are AND nodes. This comes from the fact that a state is solvable if any of its descendant moves lead to a solution, and a reduction move establishes that its parent state in the search tree is solvable only if all its descendant states are solvable. Thus, search trees "grown" by reduction procedures are

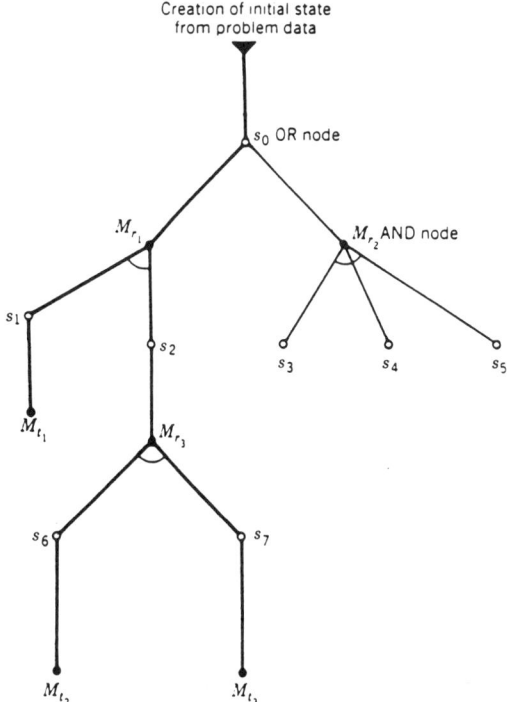

Figure 2. Search tree in state space of a reduction procedure.

usually AND/OR trees. An example of a search tree associated with a reduction procedure is shown in Figure 2.

The basic operation of a reduction schema (ie, the overall control structure) is basically the same as that of a production schema. However, because of the different nature of states and moves in the two schemas, the specification of state evaluation functions and of state selection and move selection functions must be based on different considerations. There has not been as much work on the design and analysis of these functions in reduction procedures as in production procedures.

An interesting historical perspective on production and reduction approaches to problem solving is presented in Groner and co-workers (1983). The reduction approach is close to the concept of analysis developed by the ancient Greeks, while the production approach is related to the ancients' concept of synthesis. In a solution by analysis, work concentrates on conditions of a problem; the conditions are manipulated until one or more points are reached that are known or can be proved to be true. In a solution by synthesis, work moves systematically from a given body of knowledge toward a desired result.

Reduction processes are often used in problems where one or more goals are to be achieved, or where the problem conditions can be seen as requiring the achievement of a set of explicit goals. In these problems, states have the form $(s \Rightarrow g_1, g_2, \ldots, g_n)$, where each g represents a goal, and s represents a "state of affairs" from which the goals are to be achieved. The nature and interdependence between the goals are of crucial importance for the choice of problem-solving method. In certain relatively simple situations it is possible to specify reduction processes for solving such problems. One of the earliest systems for solving such goal attainment problems via reduction processes was GPS (Ernst and Newell, 1969).

A key method used in GPS was *means–ends analysis*. To each "end," which was defined as a difference between a given state of affairs and a desired goal, there was associated a "means" in the form of an operator whose application was expected to reduce the difference. A GPS formulation of a problem included the specification of a "table of differences," which defined these associations for the problem domain. The main approach was to focus on the most difficult difference of the current problematic situation and to reduce the problematic situation into the following sequence of (hopefully simpler) problematic situations: Starting from the present state of affairs, achieve the preconditions needed for applying an operator that would remove the difference; apply the operator and work on the remaining problematic situation, which consists of the previous situation with the most difficult difference removed. GPS could handle a problem provided that an appropriate ordering of the goals was provided. Recently, the GPS approach was generalized to handle more complex goal configurations via the introduction of certain types of macro-operators (Korf, 1985). A macro-operator is a structured aggregate of (elementary) operators in the problem domain (eg, a sequence of operators), which can be seen as an extension of the notion of an operator; it can be applied as a single entity from a "from" state if its applicability conditions are satisfied at that state, and it can transform it then into a "to" state by a systematic application of its component operators. The introduction of macro-operators can reduce the complexity of search for solutions in a problem class. It is therefore an important approach to problem reformulation for increased problem-solving efficiency (Amarel, 1968, 1981).

PLANNING PROBLEMS, RELAXED REDUCTION

It is typical of planning problems that they require the attainment of multiple goals. Many of these problems have as their objective to find a structured assembly of actions (usually, a sequence) that obey certain local constraints and that bring about the attainment of a set of goals. In many cases these problems are approached by a GPS-like system. More generally, they are approached by goal-directed reasoning that attempts, to the extent possible, to proceed via reduction of a problem into subproblems. If a reduction into independent subproblems is possible, then the conventional reduction schema can be used. However, sets of goals that are interdependent are frequently faced here. In these types of situations, it is difficult to reason about the choice of a solution construction move from the analysis of an individual goal in the set. A promising approach in this area is offered by the relaxed reduction schema, which is exemplified by the NOAH system (Sacerdoti, 1977). In this approach work on the problem starts by relaxing interactions between goals, focusing attention on the individual goals, and working on each of them to a certain depth, as if they were independent. This initial stage is followed by a second stage where the neglected dependencies are taken into consideration in an attempt to combine the component solution fragments that were developed for each goal in the first stage. The problem-solving activity is made of consecutive cycles, each consisting of this two-stage sequence. Clearly, different types of dependencies between goals require different processes of critique/adjustment in the second stage of a problem-solving cycle. This is an area where much more work is needed.

Many problems of design have similar characteristics with planning problems. In the case of design a functional requirement of a structure to be designed from given structural elements can be seen as the analog of a goal to be attained by a plan that is made by a sequence of actions. Thus relaxed reduction schemas provide promising approaches to the solution of design problems with several interdependent goals and constraints (Amarel, 1989). Problems of concurrent design, which are receiving increased attention in recent years, are of this type. Again, the specific characteristics of each design problem have a substantial bearing on the definition of the adjustment stage of relaxed reduction, where dependencies that are initially neglected have to be taken into consideration.

GPS was an early attempt by AI researchers at Carnegie Mellon University to develop a general architecture for problem-solving procedures. Interest in this area has grown again at CMU in recent years in connection with the SOAR project (Laird and Newell, 1983). The general objective of SOAR is to define a broad schema of problem solving that could be made to specialize to appropriate procedures of different types in response to various problem formulations. Aside from its utility as a system development tool/environment, such a schema has great value for a better understanding of problem-solving processes and of problem formulations.

PROBLEMS WITH HYBRID DERIVATION AND FORMATION

Most real-life problems that are being studied in AI can be placed in some intermediate position between derivation and formation problems. The position in the spectrum depends on the amount of knowledge available about the relationship between solution structures and problem conditions, and on the form of this knowledge. A high proportion of knowledge in the form of links (rules, mappings) from problem conditions to solution structures brings us closer to derivation problems. When the available knowledge is mainly in the form of links from candidate solutions to problem conditions to formation problems are close.

Interpretation Problems

An important example of a family of real-life problems that is spread over the derivation–formation spectrum, depending on the ways in which their problem conditions can be used, is the problem of interpretation. These problems have received considerable attention in the 1980s in the context of work on AI applications. Typically, a problem of interpretation involves the following kind of reasoning. Given input observations (data) about an individual case in some domain and a body of domain knowledge in terms of which the case is to be interpreted (understood, explained), the problem is to construct a hypothesis about the input case in terms of the given body of knowledge. The input data is presented in a language of observations that is not necessarily the same as the language of hypotheses. Problems that lie close to the "formation" end of the problem spectrum include in their formulation a set of rules (or a procedure) that can be used to compute consequences of a candidate hypothesis in the language of observations (ie, expected manifestations of the hypothesis in the world of the observables). Usually, the formulation of an interpretation problem includes, in addition, another set of rules that can be used to reason from input data to candidate hypotheses. Such rules can be used either to evoke the generation of promising hypotheses or to block consideration of unpromising hypotheses. Depending on the strength (selectivity) of this inferential link from data to hypotheses, interpretation problems occupy different positions in the derivation–formation spectrum. The stronger this link, the closer is the problem to the derivation end of the spectrum. Examples of AI systems that have been developed to handle interpretation problems are Heuristic DENDRAL (qv) (Buchanan and Feigenbaum, 1978; Lindsay and co-workers, 1980) and various expert systems for medical diagnosis (Szolovits, 1982). While the problems handled by DENDRAL have been close to the formation end of the problem spectrum, most of the medical diagnosis systems have been close to the derivation end.

The task of Heuristic DENDRAL is to find plausible structures for organic molecules, given analytic instrument data from a mass spectrometer and a nuclear magnetic resonance spectrometer, and user-supplied constraints on the answers derived from any other source of knowledge available to the user. The system has a generator for producing all the topologically legal candidate structures; this defines a set of possible hypotheses, ie, the set of possible solutions. A planning process analyzes the data and produces constraints that are used to control hypothesis generation so that only candidates that satisfy all the constraints are produced. These candidates are then tested by computing for each of them (on the basis of the model of the analytical instruments) the instrument data that would result if they were analyzed by these instruments, and by comparing the computed data with the actual input data. The output of the system consists of the set of candidate hypotheses that score high in this test.

In DENDRAL, the generator of legal candidate structures corresponds to the grammar of solutions in a procedural formulation of the task, and the instrument data augmented by user-supplied constraints correspond to the problem conditions. The component POST(C) in such a formulation corresponds to the process of computing the instrument data that would be obtained from a candidate structure and comparing it to the given instrument data. One of the most interesting parts of the system is the planning process, which corresponds to the component PRIOR(C) of the procedural formulation. This process consists of analyzing/manipulating the instrument data in accordance with a set of rules and obtaining constraints on the structures, and tailoring the structure generating process to be consistent with the constraints. The problem-solving scheme used in DENDRAL is a modified generate-and-test. A key part is played by the planning process that controls the characteristics of the generator. All candidate solutions up to a given level of complexity that are consistent with the constraints of the "planner," are generated and tested against the instrument data. There is no feedback from test results to the generation process. Finally, all candidates that satisfy the test within given bounds of accuracy are considered to be possible solutions.

Constraint Satisfaction Problems

An important class of problems that is conceptually close to DENDRAL (from the viewpoint of the problem-solving method) is the class of constraint satisfaction (qv) problems. Problems of this class have the following form: Given a set of variables, each to be instantiated in a finite domain, and a set of predicates to be satisfied by values of the variables, find an assignment of values to variables. *Cryptoarithmetic problems* (Newell and Simon, 1972; Simon, 1969) are of this type, and so are problems of assigning interpretations (in terms of edge types, etc) to features of visual scenes. Work on Vision has resulted in procedures for solving constraint satisfaction problems that are based on the notion of eliminating candidate solutions via a method of successive refinements of value sets of the variables (Waltz, 1975; Montanari, 1974; Mackworth, 1977). The elimination is achieved by reasoning with the constraints of the problem and by identifying subsets of the set of candidate solutions that are inconsistent with the constraints. The stronger the dependencies between the constraints, the more complex (and more exhaustive) the process of *a priori* elimination of solution candidates. Following the candidate elimination stage, the problem solver can proceed with the process of finding a solution by searching in the reduced set of candidates, using a generate-and-test schema or one of its variants. An analysis of processes for solving constraint satisfaction problems shows that these processes involve simultaneous work in two spaces, ie, in the space of solution structures (sets of assignments of values to variables) and the space of problem conditions (specified by the predicates and their relationships) (Mackworth, 1977). One of the important problems in this area is how to coordinate work in these two spaces, ie, how to control the focus of attention between analysis of problem conditions that lead to restrictions on the space of solution candidates (and possibly to the identification of promising solution candidates), and generation of (parts of) solution candidates and testing them in light of problem conditions.

In DENDRAL, the basic generate-and-test schema was modified and augmented to yield remarkably high performance in a task that is essentially of formation type. The main device used in this case was to constrain the generation of solution candidates *a priori* by suitable analysis of problem conditions. There are several other variants of generate-and-test that are extensively used in AI, each based on a different device for limiting the explosive generation of solution alternatives. An important such variant is the Hill-Climbing schema. In this schema, feedback from the "test" step is used to guide the generator in its selection of the next solution construction action. More specifically, the test step is not used only to establish whether a (completely specified) candidate solution satisfies the desired problem conditions, but it also assesses how close the candidate is to the goal of attaining the conditions. The generator focuses attention on the candidate with the strongest closeness assessment, and it performs solution construction actions that amount to relatively small modifications of the candidate. In the subsequent cycle, attention focuses on the modified candidate with the strongest closeness assessment, and so on. The choice of a solution grammar (which characterizes the ways in which solutions can be modified), and an assessment function have a strong impact on the performance of Hill-Climbing procedures. Some of the difficulties encountered in these procedures are due to "local maxima," "plateaus," and "ridges" in assessment functions defined over the set of candidate solutions. These "topographical" features of assessment functions make it hard for a procedure to move toward a desired solution. Various techniques have been developed for alleviating (but not for eliminating) these difficulties.

Optimization Problems

A class of problems in which variants of Hill-Climbing are frequently used is optimization problems, exemplified by the Traveling Salesman problem. In these problems, in addition to various structural constraints imposed on the solution, there is also a minimality (or maximality) condition on a feature of the solution; for example, the desired tour in the Traveling Salesman problem must be of minimum length. An interesting approach to these problems is that developed to obtain k optimal tours for the Traveling Salesman problem via a process of successive approximations (Lin, 1973). Here, processing takes place mainly in the space of solution structures, and movements in this space are in the form of local deformations of entire solutions. Up to k segments of a given candidate solution (a tour) are changed in a disciplined way so that no structural constraints are violated, and eventually a new candidate solution is reached that cannot be improved by any modification in up to k of its segments. Thus, the thrust of reasoning is from possible solution structures to problem conditions. Problem conditions have little *a priori* influence on the generation of solution candidates. Representations of solutions and their possible deformations, and a disciplined handling of the process of successive approximations, are of key importance.

Shifts in Problem Formulation Viewed as Movement over the Derivation–Formation Spectrum

It is a common phenomenon in human problem solving that the formulation of a problem in a given domain changes as experience accumulates and as more knowledge about handling problems in the domain becomes available. Often, this can be seen as movement of the problem over the derivation–formation spectrum in the direction of the derivation end. This type of movement represents an important mode of shift in problem representation, which may result in a significant improvement in problem-solving performance. In general, growth in problem-solving expertise seems to involve the acquisition of more knowledge in a form that permits increased direct control of the solution construction process by the problem conditions.

A good example of this type of representational shift can be seen in DENDRAL (Buchanan and Feigenbaum, 1978). Experience of work with DENDRAL has shown that as more knowledge became available in a form suitable to exert *a priori* control over the process of generating candidate solutions, via strengthening of the planning process, the system acquired additional selectivity and power. Furthermore, it became clear that the appropriate approach for strengthening the planning process was not through specification of a single general procedure for going from a broad data domain to a corresponding very large space of hypotheses. What was needed was to partition the data domain into appropriate subdomains and to develop for each of the subdomains specialized data analysis processes for constraining the set of hypotheses. Thus, expert high performance behavior was obtained in the present case via the development of several strong reasoning links from data to hypotheses, each specialized to a subdomain of the problem. This type of approach has been extensively used in the design of expert systems that followed DENDRAL.

PROBLEMS OF LEARNING, THEORY FORMATION, ANALOGY, AND ABSTRACTION

The issue of expertise acquisition, ie, the transition from less expert or relatively weak to more expert or stronger problem-solving performance, has received increased attention in recent years. In particular, the problem of mechanizing certain aspects of expertise acquisition (or of strategy improvement) is being explored by several AI workers. One of the approaches studied is learning applicability conditions of problem-solving moves; that is, using problem-solving experience to redefine the applicability conditions of moves in a way that increases the selectivity of their application. For example, the LEX project has concentrated on this problem in the context of a symbolic integration task (Mitchell, 1983). The key problem here is to learn a good definition for the domain of a move, ie, to form a concept of the move's domain in terms of features of problem states. This is an instance of concept formation of the kind that received considerable attention in machine learning research.

The area of machine learning has received "pulses of attention" by the research community since the early stages of work in AI. More recently, from about the mid-1980s, there has been a new surge of interest in this area. Learning tasks have different forms depending on the nature of the body of information that constitutes input to the task, the language in which the output of learning is expressed, and the rules and biases that control the learning process. Several researchers have pointed out that learning is an instance of problem solving (Simon and Lea, 1974; Mitchell, 1983). This is a fruitful conceptual view that permits ideas from other areas of problem solving to be transferred to learning tasks. For example, in a concept formation problem, the problem conditions have the form of given instances of the concept (positive and negative) and these instances must be consistent with the concept definition that the system is asked to find. Furthermore, the concept definition (ie, the desired solution) must be constructed in a given language, and it must satisfy certain other global conditions, such as simplicity. Depending on how instances are used in the process of constructing a concept definition, the concept formation problem has characteristics of a derivation or a formation problem. If the instances are used directly, together with rules of generalization, to come up with hypotheses about concept definitions, then the problem is close to the derivation end of the derivation–formation spectrum. If the main thrust of reasoning can be seen as search in the space of concept definitions, with the instances used mainly for testing candidate concepts (hypotheses), then the problem is close to the formation end of the spectrum. Concept learning problems of the latter type are closely related to an important class of theory formation problems, where a substantial part of the problem-solving effort involves search in the space of hypotheses/theories. What distinguishes the concept learning problems from the theory formation problems is that the latter use a language of hypotheses/theories that is generally richer than the language used in the former.

Learning and theory formation are problem-solving processes that are needed to extract knowledge from problem-solving experience in a task domain, so that problem-solving performance (expertise) in the domain can be strengthened. A good understanding of properties of various problem-solving schemas—and in particular of "points of leverage" in these schemas where augmentation of knowledge can improve performance—is also needed in order to take advantage of the added knowledge. One aspect of theory formation that did not receive much attention as of yet, but is clearly important for processes of strategy improvement (as well as for many areas of scientific work) is concept discovery. This activity can be regarded as selecting an interesting subdomain of phenomena for which it is deemed desirable to find a theoretical characterization/explanation. In general, theoretical studies of a "piece of the world" involve both the choice of a circumscribed domain of phenomena in the world that are to be expressed in some conceptual framework and also the finding of expressions within the framework for defining/explaining the domain of phenomena. The interplay between domain choice and the formulation of a theory for the domain is an interesting and complex process which is difficult to capture at present. A promising study in this area is Lenat's work on AM, where the task is to discover interesting concepts in elementary number theory (Davis and Lenat, 1982). The AM system starts with a small set of mathematical concepts and with rules for modifying definitions of existing concepts and for combining concepts. This defines a space of concepts, which is searched selectively via a generate-and-test schema. The generator is guided by a body of heuristic rules, and the test stage is guided by rules of "interestingness" that act as a filter for candidate concepts that are produced by the generator.

One of the important approaches to problem solving involves finding a "similar problem" for which a solution is known, and proceeding to find a solution to the original problem "in analogy to" the solution of the similar problem. This is a powerful approach, which is receiving increased attention in AI (Carbonell, 1981). Much more work is needed in this area. A related approach is to solve a simplified version of the original problem and to use the solution of the simplified problem as a guide for solving the original. An attempt to mechanize this approach goes back to the early days of AI, where the logic theorist, whose task was to find proofs in elementary symbolic logic, used a planning stage that produced a skeletal proof, which then guided the construction of the final proof (Newell and co-workers, 1963). In the early 1970s the ABSTRIPS system was developed to facilitate the solution of complex planning problems by creating a simplified problem where some of the preconditions of actions were stripped out, and by using its solution to find a complete solution for the original problem (Sacerdoti, 1973). More recently, methods are being developed for synthesis of good heuristic evaluation functions in derivation (state-space search) procedures on the basis of properties of simplified versions of the problem that is being solved (Pearl, 1984; Mostow and Prieditis, 1989). This general approach, of finding and solving a simplified version of the original problem and then using its solution as a guide for solving the original, has conceptual similarities with the relaxed reduction approach. In both approaches more work is needed, especially in identifying ways of effectively using the relaxed or simplified solutions in the process of constructing the full solutions.

CONCLUDING COMMENTS

Problem solving is the art of using relevant knowledge in the attainment of desired goals. Within AI, work on problem solving focuses on techniques for solving exponentially hard problems in polynomial time by exploiting knowledge about the problem in a relatively small number of generic ways. Of key importance are mechanisms for acquiring, representing, and using knowledge. Problem-solving systems in AI are slowly acquiring capabilities of changing (improving) their performance in a domain on the basis of their experience in the domain. These capabilities are mediated by learning and theory formation processes, which are themselves problem-solving processes. To mechanize and coordinate this variety of processes it is essential to have a broad conceptual framework in which to clearly see properties and relationships of various problem formulations, of problem-solving methods, and of procedures for constructing solutions.

BIBLIOGRAPHY

S. Amarel, "An Approach to Heuristic Problem Solving and Theorem Proving in the Propositional Calculus," in J. Hart and S. Takasu, eds., *Systems and Computer Science,* University of Toronto Press, Toronto, Canada, 1967, pp. 125–220.

S. Amarel, "On Representations of Problems of Reasoning About Actions," in D. Michie, ed., *Machine Intelligence 3,* Edinburgh University Press, Edinburgh, UK, 1968, pp. 131–171.

S. Amarel, "On the Representation of Problems and Goal-Directed Procedures for Computers," in R. Banerji and M. Mesarovic, eds., *Theoretical Approaches to Non-Numerical Problem Solving,* Springer-Verlag, Heidelberg, 1970, pp. 179–244; also appears in *Communications of the American Society for Cybernetics,* 1(2) (July 1969).

S. Amarel, "Problem Solving and Decision Making by Computer: An Overview," in P. Garvin, ed., *Cognition: A Multiple View,* Spartan Books, New York, 1970, pp. 279–329.

S. Amarel, "Representations and Modeling in Problems of Program Formation," in B. Meltzer and D. Michie, eds., *Machine Intelligence 6,* University of Edinburgh Press, UK, 1971, pp. 411–466.

S. Amarel, "Problems of Representation in Heuristic Problem Solving; Related Issues in the Development of Expert Systems," in R. Groner, M. Groner, and M. W. Bischof, eds., *Methods of Heuristics,* Lawrence Erlbaum Associates, Publishers, Hillsdale, N.J., pp. 245–349; also appears as Technical Report CBM-TR-118, LCSR, Rutgers University, New Brunswick, N.J., Feb. 1981.

S. Amarel, "Program Synthesis as a Theory Formation Task: Problem Representations and Solution Methods," in R. S. Michalski, J. G. Carbonell, and T. M. Mitchell, Eds., *Machine Learning: an Artificial Intelligence Approach, Vol II,* Morgan-Kaufmann, San Mateo, Calif., 1986, pp. 499–571.

S. Amarel, "Artificial Intelligence and Design: Opportunities, Research Problems and Directions," in M. Bloom, ed., *High Level Vision and Planning Workshop Proceedings,* IDA Doc. D-649, IDA, Alexandria, Va., Aug. 1989, pp. 47–78; available as Technical Report LCSR-124, LCSR, Rutgers University, June 1989.

D. Paul Benjamin, ed., *Change of Representation and Inductive Bias,* Kluwer Academic Publishers, Boston, Mass., 1990.

B. G. Buchanan and E. A. Feigenbaum, "DENDRAL and Meta-DENDRAL: Their Applications Dimension," *Artif. Intell.* Special Issue on Applications to Science and Medicine, **11**(1,2) (Aug. 1978).

J. G. Carbonell, Jr., "A Computational Model of Analogical Problem Solving," in *Proceedings of the Seventh IJCAI,* Vancouver, B.C., Morgan-Kaufmann, San Mateo, Calif., 1981.

R. Davis and D. Lenat, "AM: Discovery in Mathematics as Heuristic Search," in *Knowledge-Based Systems in Artificial Intelligence,* Pt. 1, McGraw-Hill, New York, 1982.

G. W. Ernst and A. Newell, *GPS: A Case Study in Generality and Problem Solving,* Academic Press, New York, 1969.

M. Groner, R. Groner, and W. F. Bischof, "Approaches to Heuristics: A Historical Review," in R. Groner, M. Groner, and W. F. Bischof, eds., *Methods of Heuristics,* Lawrence Erlbaum Associates, Hillsdale, N.J., 1983.

J. R. Hayes and H. A. Simon, "Understanding Written Problem Instructions," in L. W. Gregg, ed., *Knowledge and Cognition,* Lawrence Erlbaum, Associates, Potomac, Md., 1974.

R. Korf, *Learning to Solve Problems by Searching for Macro-Operators,* Pitman Publishing, Marshfield, Mass., 1985.

J. E. Laird and A. Newell, *A Universal Weak Method,* Technical Report #83-141, Computer Science Department, Carnegie Mellon University, Pittsburgh, Pa., June 1983; also appears in summary form in *Proceedings of the Eighth IJCAI,* Karlsruhe, FRG, Morgan-Kaufmann, San Mateo, Calif., 1983.

S. Lin, "An Effective Heuristic Algorithm for the Traveling Salesman Problem," *Oper. Res.* **21**(2) (Mar.–Apr. 1973).

R. K. Lindsay, B. G. Buchanan, E. A. Feigenbaum, and J. Lederberg, *Applications of Artificial Intelligence for Organic Chemistry: The DENDRAL Project,* McGraw-Hill, New York, 1980.

A. K. Mackworth, "Consistency of Networks of Relations," *Artif. Intell.* **8**(1), 1977.

J. McCarthy, "The Inversion of Functions Defined by Turing Machines," in C. E. Shannon and J. McCarthy, eds., *Automata Studies,* Annals of Mathematical Studies, 34, Princeton University Press, Princeton, N.J., pp. 177–181, 1956.

T. M. Mitchell, "Learning and Problem Solving," *Proceedings of the Eighth IJCAI,* Karlsruhe, FRG, Morgan-Kaufmann, San Mateo, Calif., 1983, pp. 1139–1151.

U. Montanari, "Networks of Constraints: Fundamental Properties and Applications to Picture Processing," *Info. Sci.* **7,** (1974).

J. Mostow and A. E. Prieditis, "Discovering Admissible Search Heuristics by Abstracting and Optimizing," *Proceedings of the Eleventh IJCAI,* Detroit, Mich., Aug. 1989; available as Rutgers AI/Design Project Working Paper No. 114-1, LCSR, Rutgers University, 1989.

A. Newell, "Heuristic Programming: III Structured Problems," in J. Aronofsky, ed., *Progress in Operations Research,* Vol. 3., Wiley, New York, 1969, pp. 360–414.

A. Newell, "Reasoning, Problem Solving and Decision Processes: The Problem Space as Fundamental Category," in R. Nickerson, ed., *Attention and Performance VIII,* Lawrence Erlbaum Associates, Hillsdale, N.J., 1980.

A. Newell and H. A. Simon, *Human Problem Solving,* Prentice-Hall, Englewood Cliffs., N.J., 1972.

A. Newell, J. C. Shaw, and H. A. Simon, "Empirical Exploration of the Logic Theory Machine: A Case Study in Heuristics," *Proceedings of the 1957 Western Computer Conference,* Western Computer Conference, 1957; also appears in E. A. Feigenbaum and J. Feldman, eds., *Computers and Thought,* McGraw-Hill, New York, 1963.

N. J. Nilsson, *Problem-Solving Methods in Artificial Intelligence,* McGraw-Hill, New York, 1971.

N. J. Nilsson, *Principles of Artificial Intelligence,* Tioga Publishing Co., Palo Alto, Calif., 1980.

J. Pearl, *Heuristics: Intelligent Search Strategies for Computer Problem Solving,* Addison-Wesley, Publishing Co., Reading, Mass., 1984.

G. Polya, *How To Solve It,* 2nd ed., Doubleday & Co., Garden City, N.Y., 1957.

E. Rich, *Artificial Intelligence,* McGraw-Hill, New York, 1983.

E. Sacerdoti, "Planning in a Hierarchy of Abstraction Spaces, *Proc. of the Third IJCAI,* Stanford, Morgan-Kaufmann, San Mateo, Calif., Aug. 1973.

E. D. Sacerdoti, *A Structure for Plans and Behavior,* Elsevier Science Publishing Co., Inc., New York, 1977.

H. A. Simon, *The Sciences of the Artificial,* MIT Press, Cambridge, Mass., 1969.

H. A. Simon, "The Structure of III Structured Problems," *Artif. Intell.* **4,** 181–201 (1973).

H. A. Simon and G. Lea, "Problem Solving and Rule Induction: A Unified View," in L. W. Gregg, Ed., *Knowledge and Cognition,* Lawrence Erlbaum Associates, Potomac, Md., 1974, pp. 105–127.

P. Szolovits, ed., *Artificial Intelligence in Medicine,* Westview Press, Boulder, Col., 1982.

A. Tversky and D. Kahneman, "The Framing of Decisions and the Psychology of Choice," *Science* **211** (Jan. 30, 1981).

J. Van Baalen, "Change of Representation and Problem Reformulation Workshop," *Inf. Proc.,* Price Waterhouse Technology Center, Menlo Park, Calif., 1990.

D. Waltz, "Understanding Line Drawings of Scenes with Shadows," in P. Winston, ed., *The Psychology of Computer Vision*, McGraw-Hill, New York, 1975.

S. AMAREL
Rutgers University

PROCESSING, BOTTOM-UP AND TOP-DOWN

Bottom-up vs. top-down, forward vs. backward, and data-driven vs. goal-directed are three pairs of modifiers for terms such as *chaining, inference, parsing, processing, reasoning,* and *search*. They express essentially the same distinction, their difference lying in different metaphors drawn from different subareas of computer science and AI. The bottom-up–top-down distinction comes from parsing (see NATURAL LANGUAGE PROCESSING); the forward–backward chaining distinction comes from rule-based systems (qv); goal-directed comes from problem solving (qv) and search (qv); and data-directed comes from discussions of control structures (qv). Now, however, they are virtually interchangeable.

One general way to consider the distinction is from within the paradigm of search. The basic issue of all search is to find a way to get from where you are to where you want to be. If you organize this by starting from where you are and search until you find yourself where you want to be, you are doing forward, data-directed, or bottom-up search. If you think about where you want to be, and plan how to get there by working backward to where you are now, you are doing backward, goal-directed, or top-down search. Notice that, having found the route during backward search, you still have to get to your goal. Although you are now moving in the forward direction, this is not forward search because all the search was already done in the backward direction.

Another general way to consider the distinction is from within the paradigm of rule-based systems (qv). A generic rule can be thought of as having a set of antecedents and a set of consequents. When the rule-based system notices that all the antecedents of a rule are satisfied, the rule is triggered and may fire (whether all triggered rules actually fire depends on the specifics of the rule-based system). When the rule fires, the consequent propositions are added to the knowledge base and the consequent actions are performed. These steps of triggering and firing happen as just described regardless of whether the rule-based system is using forward (or data-directed or bottom-up) reasoning or backward (or goal-directed or top-down) reasoning. To make the distinction, it is useful to isolate the step of rule activation. Only activated rules are subject to being triggered. In forward (or data-directed, or bottom-up) reasoning, whenever new data is added to the system, the data is matched against all antecedents of all rules (actual systems are more efficient than this sounds). If the data matches an antecedent of a rule, that rule is activated (if it is not already activated), and if all antecedents of the rule are now satisfied, the rule triggers. When a rule fires, the consequent propositions that are added to the knowledge base are treated like new data, matched against antecedents, and may cause additional rules to be activated and to be triggered. In backward (or goal-directed, or top-down) reasoning, rules are not activated when data is added. Rather, when a query is asked of the system, or the system is asked to do something, the query (or goal) is matched against all consequents of all rules (again, actual systems are more efficient than this sounds). If the query matches a consequent of a rule, the rule is activated, all its antecedents are treated as new queries or goals (now called subqueries, or subgoals), and may activate additional rules. Whenever a query or subquery matches an unconditional proposition in the knowledge base, it is answered, and if it came from an antecedent, the antecedent is now known to be satisfied. As soon as all antecedents of some rule are known to be satisfied, the rule triggers and may fire. When a rule fires, the queries that activated it are answered, and now other antecedents may be known to be satisfied, and their rules might be triggered. Notice that the triggering and firing of a rule always seems to happen in a "forward" direction, due to the significance of antecedents vs. consequents, but what distinguishes forward from backward chaining is when the rule is activated.

Some of the history of these terms will be discussed later, followed by explanations of the distinctions via examples of parsing, rule-based systems, and search. Then there will be some comparative comments and, finally, some discussion of mixed strategies.

HISTORY OF TERMS

Bottom-Up vs. Top-Down

The earliest published occurrence of the phrase "top-down vs. bottom-up" seems to have been in a paper by Cheatham and Sattley (1964), although the term "top-down," at least, seems to already have been in use:

> The Analyzer described in this paper is of the sort known as "top down," the appellation referring to the order in which the Analyzer sets its goals. . . . The order in which a "bottom up" Analyzer sets its goals is much more difficult to describe. (Cheatham and Sattley, 1964, p. 55)

It took a while, however, for these terms to become fully accepted. In 1965 Griffiths and Petrick (1965) used the terms "bottom-to-top" and "top-to-bottom":

> There are many ways by which the typology of recognition algorithms for [Context Free] grammars can be approached. For example, one means of classification is related to the general directions in which creation of a structural description tree proceeds: top-to-bottom, bottom-to-top, left-to-right and right-to-left.

However, in 1968, they use the terms "bottom-up" and "top-down" in a title (Griffiths and Petrick, 1969).

Also in 1968, Knuth (1968) used the term "bottom-up" to describe a function "which should be evaluated at the sons of a node before it is evaluated at the node" and "top-down" to describe a function f as "one in which the value of

f at node x depends only on x and the value of f at the *father* of x." Knuth encloses these terms in quotes.

By 1970 Early (1970) used the phrase "the familiar top-down algorithm" without attribution in the abstract of an article, and by 1973 "The Top-down Parse" and "The Bottom-up Parse" appear as section titles in a text (Weingarten, 1973).

Bottom-up and top-down parsing are referred to as the "morsel" and the "target" strategies, respectively, in Sparck Jones and Kay (1973, p. 87), where the Predictive Analyzer of Kuno and Oettinger (1963) is cited as an early example of the target strategy, and "the algorithm due to John Cocke and used in Robinson's PARSE program (Robinson and Marks, 1965) was the earliest published example of a program using a morsel strategy." Calingaert (1979) cites Lucas (1961) as the first described use of recursive descent parsing, which is a form of top-down parsing.

Forward vs. Backward Chaining

The terms "forward chaining" and "backward chaining" almost surely come from Newell, Shaw, and Simon's Logic Theory Machine (LT) paper, first published in 1957 (Newell and co-workers, 1957). They discuss four methods used by LT to help find a proof of a formula in propositional logic (qv). The last two methods discussed are called "the chaining methods":

> These methods use the transitivity of the relation of implication to create a new subproblem which, if solved, will provide a proof for the problem expression. Thus, if the problem expression is "a implies c," the method of forward chaining searches for an axiom or theorem of the form "a implies b." If one is found, "b implies c" is set up as a new subproblem. Chaining backward works analogously: it seeks a theorem of the form "b implies c," and if one is found, "a implies b" is set up as a new subproblem. (Newell and co-workers, 1963, pp. 117–118)

This is not exactly the characterization of forward and backward chaining given earlier, but the essential idea is there. In both methods if a certain theorem is found, an appropriate subproblem is set up. In forward chaining the theorem is found by matching its antecedent, and its consequent is involved in the new subproblem, whereas in backward chaining the theorem is found by matching its consequent, and its antecedent is involved in the new subproblem. Finding a theorem is analogous to activating a rule in the characterization described at the beginning of this article.

The rule-based system version of forward and backward chaining grew out of the LT version via the production system architecture of problem-solving systems promulgated by Newell and Simon (1972).

Goal-Directed Processing

The notion of goal-directed behavior surely comes from psychology. In a 1958 psychology text the following description of problem solving occurs:

> We may have a choice between starting with where we wish to end, or starting with where we are at the moment. In the first instance we start by analyzing the *goal*. We ask, "Suppose we did achieve the goal, how would things be different—what subproblems would we have solved, etc.?" This in turn would determine the sequence of problems, and we would work back to the beginning. In the second instance we start by analyzing the *present situation*, see the implications of the given conditions and lay-out, and attack the various subproblems in a "forward direction." (Krech and Crutchfield, 1958, p. 383)

Also, goals and subgoals are discussed in the section on motivation:

> The person perceives in his surroundings *goals* capable of removing his needs and fulfilling his desires. . . . And there is the important phenomenon of emergence of *subgoals*. The pathways to goals are often perceived as organized into a number of subparts, each of which constitutes an intermediate subgoal to be attained on the way to the ultimate goal. (Krech and Crutchfield, 1958, pp. 218–219)

Cheatham and Sattley, who are mentioned earlier as publishing probably the first use of "bottom up vs. top down," also compared top-down parsing to goal-directed behavior:

> In our opinion, the fundamental idea—perhaps "germinal" would be a better word—which makes syntax-directed analysis by computer possible is that of *goals*: A Syntactic Type is construed as a goal for the Analyzer to achieve, and the Definiens of a Defined Type is construed as a recipe for achieving the goal of the type it defines. . . . Needless to say, this use of the term "goal" is not to be confused with the "goal-seeking behavior" of "artificial intelligence" programs or "self-organizing systems." (Cheatham and Sattley, 1964, p. 33)

Needless to say, the several uses of "goal" indeed have much in common.

Data-Driven Processing

The term "data-driven" seems to have been introduced by Bobrow and Norman in a paper on the processing of memory schemata:

> Consider the human information processing system. Sensory data arrive through the sense organs to be processed. Low-level computational structures perform the first stages of analysis and then the results are passed to other processing structures. . . . *The processing system can be driven either conceptually or by events*. Conceptually driven processing tends to be top-down, driven by motives and goals, and fitting input to expectations; event driven processing tends to be bottom-up, finding structures in which to embed the input. (Bobrow and Norman, 1975, pp. 138–140)

They go on to use "conceptually driven" and "top-down" as synonymous and "event-driven," and "data-driven" interchangeably and synonymously with "bottom-up."

EXAMPLES

Parsing

The simple grammar of Figure 1 and the sentence "They are flying planes" will be used to illustrate and explain

1. S → NP VP
2. NP → N
3. NP → PRO
4. NP → ADJ N
5. VP → VT NP
6. VT → V
7. VT → AUX V
8. N → planes
9. PRO → they
10. ADJ → flying
11. AUX → are
12. V → are
13. V → flying

the difference between top-down and bottom-up parsing. The grammar is presented as a set of rules, numbered for the purposes of this discussion. The direction of the arrows is traditionally shown as if the grammar were being used for generation of sentences. For parsing, the rules are backward—the antecedents on the right side and the consequent on the left side, as in PROLOG (see LOGIC PROGRAMMING). For example, rule 1 can be read "If a string consists of a noun phrase (NP) followed by a verb phrase (VP), then the string is a sentence (S)."

Top-down parsing begins with S, the initial symbol, which will be the root of the parse tree. This is equivalent to establishing the goal of finding that the string of words is a sentence. Rule 1 says that every sentence will consist of a noun phrase (NP) followed by a verb phrase (VP). Whenever there is a choice, the lowest numbered rule is tried first, and the rule is expanded left to right. Therefore, the next subgoal generated is that of finding an initial string of the sentence that is a NP. Rule 2 is activated, followed by rule 8. This situation is shown in Figure 2a. Since "planes" does not match "they," the algorithm backs up, and in place of rule 2, rule 3 is activated followed by rule 9, which succeeds. Next, the algorithm returns to rule 1 and generates the subgoal of finding a VP. Rules 5, 6, and 12 are activated, and rule 12 succeeds. This stage is shown in Figure 2b. The rest of the top-down parse is shown in stages in the rest of Figure 2.

Bottom-up parsing begins with the words in the sentence. Again, additional ordering decisions must be made, so the leftmost possibility is tried first, as is the lowest numbered rule when there is a choice. So, the first thing that happens is that the first word of the sentence, "they," matches the antecedent of rule 9, which fires, analyzing "they" as a pronoun (PRO). Then rule 3 fires, analyzing "they" as a NP. NP matches antecedents in rules 1 and 5, but neither of these is triggered yet, and the parse moves on to "are." This causes rule 11 to fire. (Although rule 12 is also triggered, it does not fire due to the ordering rules.) Then rule 10 fires, followed by rules 8 and 2. This stage is shown in Figure 3a. At this point, nothing more can be done with the string NP+AUX+ADJ+NP, so there is backtracking (qv) to the most recently triggered but unfired rule, which is rule 4. Nothing can be done with the string NP+AUX+NP, so again the most recently triggered unfired rule fires, which now is rule 13, which analyzes "flying" as a V. Then rule 6 fires, followed by rule 5. This is shown in Figure 3c. Nothing can be done with the string NP+AUX+VP, so rule 7 fires, analyzing "are flying" as a single VT. Then rule 5 fires again, followed by rule 1, and the parse, shown in Figure 3d, is complete.

The purpose of this example was to compare top-down with bottom-up parsing. The use of left-to-right order, numerical order of the rules, and chronological backtracking

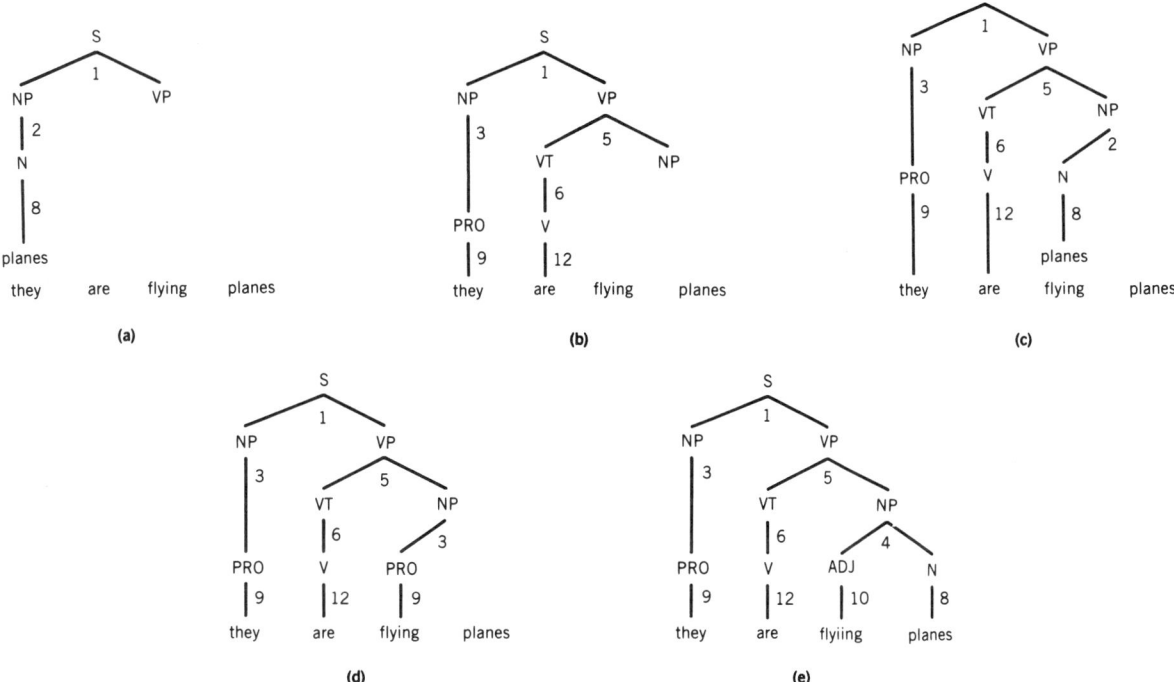

Figure 2. Top-down parsing.

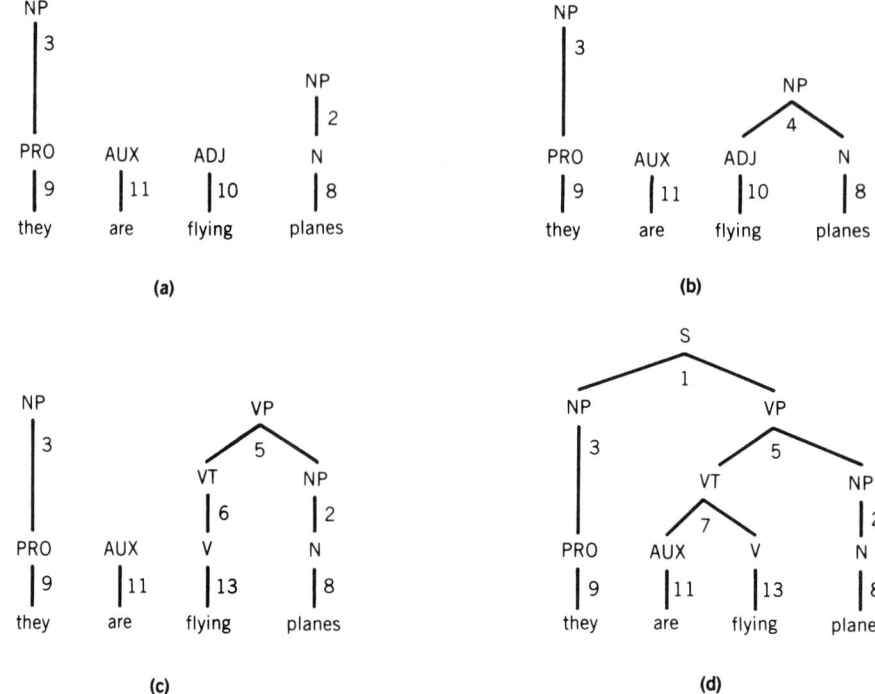

Figure 3. Bottom-up parsing.

was merely to keep the two algorithms as similar as possible although causing them to result in different parses.

Rule-Based Systems

Forward vs. backward chaining and data-directed vs. goal-directed processing will be compared using some made-up rules for how to spend the evening. These are shown in Figure 4 in the usual rule order, with the antecedents to the left of the arrow and the consequent to the right. For example, rule 1 says that if there is a good movie on TV and I have no early appointment the next morning, then I enter "Late-Movie-Mode."

For the examples of forward and backward chaining, it is assumed that all triggered rules fire and that processing is in parallel.

Suppose a forward-chaining system with these rules is first told that I have no early appointment. Rules 1 and 2 are activated. Suppose the system is then told that I need to work. Rule 3 is activated, and rule 2 is triggered and fired, concluding that I am in Late-Work-Mode. This activates, triggers, and fires rules 5 and 6, concluding that I should return to the office and stay up late.

To do the same problem using backward chaining, suppose that the system was first told that I had no early appointment and had work to do and then was asked whether I should return to the office. This query would activate rules 6 and 7, which would generate the subgoals Late-Work-Mode? and Work-at-Office-Mode? These would activate rules 2 and 3, generating the subgoals No-Early-Appointment?, Need-to-Work?, and Need-References? The first two would be satisfied, resulting in rule 2 triggering and firing. This would cause Late-Work-Mode to be satisfied, triggering and firing rule 6, and concluding that I should return to the office.

Notice that in forward inference more conclusions are generated, whereas in backward inference more subgoals are generated. Since the data were the same for the two examples, the same rules were fired, but different rules were activated.

Search

Forward and backward search can be illustrated with a water-jug problem. For this problem there are two jugs, one capable of holding 3 gallons and one capable of holding 4 gallons. The legal operations (see Figure 5) are filling the 3-gallon jug from a water tap (symbolized as f3); filling the 4-gallon jug from the water tap (f4); emptying the 3-gallon jug by pouring out all its contents (e3); emptying the 4-gallon jug by pouring out all its contents (e4); pouring the contents of the 3-gallon jug into the 4-gallon jug until either the 3-gallon jug is empty or the 4-gallon jug is full, whichever happens first (p34); or pouring the contents of the 4-gallon jug into the 3-gallon jug until either the 4-gallon jug is empty or the 3-gallon jug is full, whichever happens first (p43). Each state of the problem is represented by a pair of integers showing the contents of the 3-gallon jug and then the contents of the 4-gallon jug. For example, ⟨1, 4⟩ represents the state in which there is 1

1. Good-Movie-on-TV & No-Early-Appointment → Late-Movie-Mode
2. No-Early-Appointment & Need-to-Work → Late-Work-Mode
3. Need-to-Work & Need-References → Work-at-Office-Mode
4. Late-Movie-Mode → Stay-Up-Late
5. Late-Work-Mode → Stay-Up-Late
6. Late-Work-Mode → Return-to-Office
7. Work-at-Office-Mode → Return-to-Office

Figure 4. Rules for the evening.

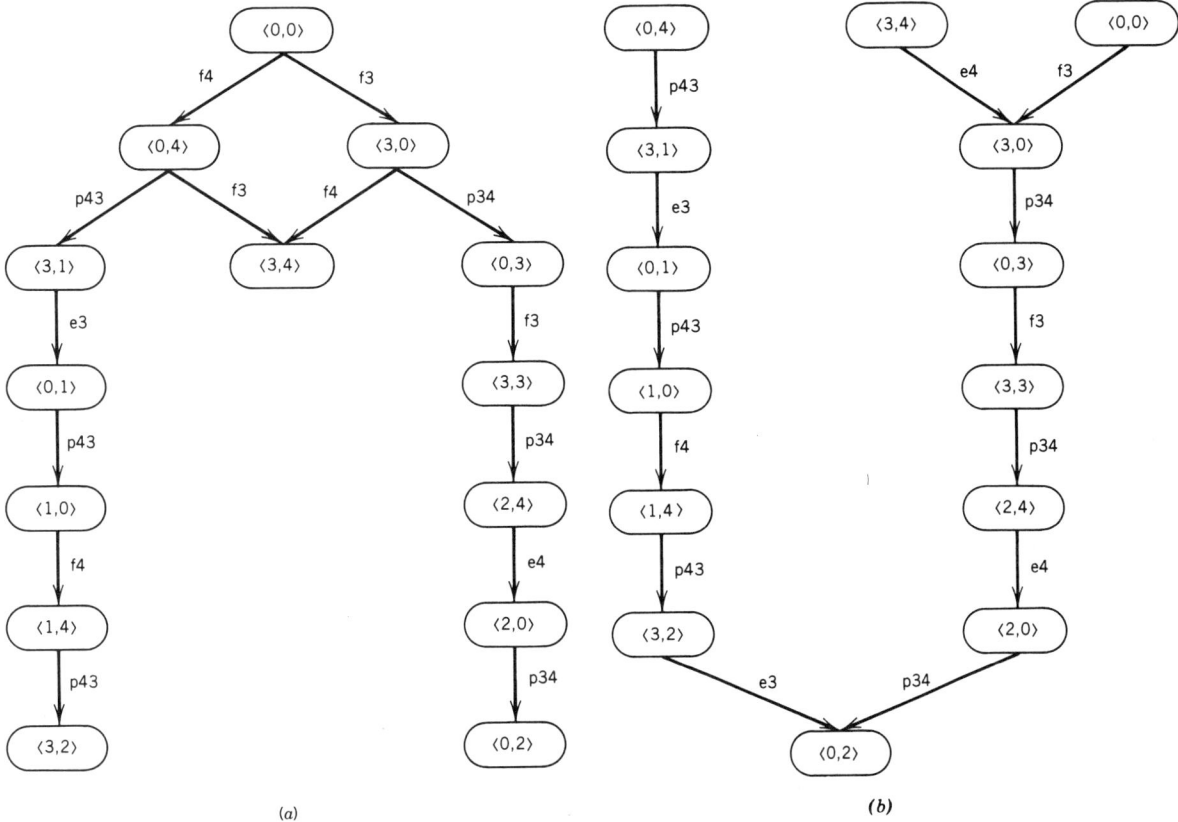

Figure 5. (a) Forward search. (b) Backward search.

gallon in the 3-gallon jug and 4 gallons in the 4-gallon jug. If operator p43 is applied to this state, the resulting state is ⟨3, 2⟩. The particular problem under consideration is that of getting from state ⟨0, 0⟩ to state ⟨0, 2⟩.

Figure 5 shows the state-space representation of this problem, assuming a parallel breadth-first search that stops as soon as the goal is found. No operator is shown that would move from a state to a state at the same or an earlier level of the search tree. For example, from state ⟨3, 1⟩ operator f4 would go to state ⟨3, 4⟩, but that is on the same level as ⟨3, 1⟩, and operator e4 would go to state ⟨3, 0⟩, but that is on an earlier level. What level a state is on, of course, depends on where the search started.

Figure 5a shows a forward search from ⟨0, 0⟩ until ⟨0, 2⟩ is found. Figure 5b shows a backward search from ⟨0, 2⟩ to ⟨0, 0⟩. Notice that, in this example, the same states are explored, but in a slightly different order. Notice also the difference between searching backward to find a way of getting from ⟨0, 0⟩ to ⟨0. 2⟩ and searching forward to find a way of getting from ⟨0, 2⟩ to ⟨0, 0⟩. In the latter case, one operator, namely e4, would suffice.

COMPARISONS

Efficiency

Whether bottom-up (or forward, or data-driven) processing is more efficient than top-down (or backward, or goal-directed) processing depends on the way the search space branches. If the average state has more successors than predecessors, backward search will be more efficient. If it has more predecessors than successors, forward search will be more efficient. To consider an extreme, if the search space forms a tree rooted in the start state, a forward search will have to search a large part of the tree, whereas a backward search will only have to search up a linear branch.

Pattern Matching and Unification

In rule-based systems or reasoning systems, the choice of forward vs. backward chaining affects the difficulty of the required pattern-matching routines. In forward chaining, or data-driven reasoning, one is always asserting new facts to the system, and these have no free variables. Similarly, when rules fire, the newly inferred facts have no free variables. Therefore, one is always matching antecedents that may have variables against facts with no variables. Pattern matching two symbol structures when only one might have variables is a fairly simple routine.

On the other hand, in backward-chaining systems one often asks "wh" questions, such as "What shall I do this evening?" or "What organism is infecting this patient?" If the rules are represented in predicate logic rather than in propositional logic (see LOGIC, PREDICATE; LOGIC, PROPOSITIONAL), this involves matching a question with a variable against consequents with variables. Subgoals may also have variables, so in general, back-chaining systems must be written to match two symbol structures, both of which may have variables, and this requires the unification algorithm (see UNIFICATION), which is considerably more involved than simple pattern matching.

MIXED STRATEGIES

Bidirectional Search

If it is not clear whether forward or backward search would be better for a particular application, bidirectional search (qv) is probably appropriate. Essentially, bidirectional search starts from both the start state and the goal state and searches from both ends toward the middle.

"Predictive syntactic analysis" is described by Bobrow (1967), where the first computer implementation is ascribed to Rhodes (1961). The bidirectional nature of this technique may be inferred from Bobrow's description that "an initial prediction is made that the string to be scanned is a sentence. From this prediction and the initial word in the sentence . . . more detailed predictions are made of the expected sentence structure" (Bobrow, 1967, p. 235).

Bidirectional Inference

Another kind of bidirectional processing uses the initial data to activate rules that then trigger backward chaining through their other antecedents (Shapiro and co-workers, 1982). Subgoals that match neither consequents nor data can remain as demons to be satisfied by new, later data. The system can be designed so that data that satisfy demons (antecedents of activated rules) do not activate additional inactive rules, thus focusing future forward inference on rules that take previous context into account.

Left-Corner and Expectation-Based Parsing

When the bidirectional style of inference is applied to parsing, one gets what is called left-corner parsing. In terms of the parsing example discussed earlier, the system would first look at "they," find rule 9 as the only rule to account for it, then find rule 3 to be the only way to account for a PRO, and then find rule 1 as the only rule with a consequent side that starts with a NP. Next the system would try to parse "are flying planes" as a VP top-down. This is also very similar to expectation-driven parsing since the rules activated top-down form expectations of what will be in the rest of the sentence based on what actually occurred earlier in the sentence.

CONCLUSIONS

The control structure of an AI system that does reasoning, parsing, problem solving, or search is often organized into one of two basic approaches. One approach is called bottom-up, forward, or data-driven. The other is called top-down, backward, or goal-directed. The distinction is most easily understood as whether search is from goal to start or if rules are activated by their consequents or their antecedents.

Issues of efficiency or ease of implementation may decide which approach to take in a particular application, but mixed strategies are also possible.

BIBLIOGRAPHY

D. G. Bobrow, "Syntactic Theories in Computer Implementations," in H. Borko, Ed., *Automated Language Processing*, Wiley, New York, pp. 215–251, 1967.

D. G. Bobrow and D. A. Norman, "Some Principles of Memory Schemata," in D. G. Bobrow and A. Collins, Eds., *Representation and Understanding: Studies in Cognitive Science*, Academic Press, New York, pp. 138–140, 1975.

P. Calingaert, *Assemblers, Compilers, and Program Translation*, Computer Science Press, Rockville, Md., 1979.

T. E. Cheatham and K. Sattley, "Syntax-Directed Compiling," *Proceedings of the Spring Joint Computer Conference Washington, DC*, Spartan Books, Baltimore, Md., 31–57, 1964.

J. Early, "An Efficient Context-Free Parsing Algorithm," *CACM* **13**(2), 94–102 (February 1970).

T. V. Griffiths and S. R. Petrick, "On the Relative Efficiencies of Context-Free Grammar Recognizers," *CACM* **8**(5), 289–300 (May 1965).

T. V. Griffiths and S. R. Petrick, "Top-Down Versus Bottom-Up Analysis," in A. J. H. Morrell, Ed., *Information Processing 68: Proceedings of IFIP Congress 1968*, North-Holland, Amsterdam, pp. 437–442, 1969.

D. E. Knuth, *The Art of Computer Programming*, Vol. 1, *Fundamental Algorithms*. Addison-Wesley, Reading, Mass., p. 362, 1968.

D. Krech and R. S. Crutchfield, *Elements of Psychology*, Knopf, NY, p. 383, 1958.

S. Kuno and A. G. Oettinger, "Multiple-Path Syntactic Analyzer," in C. M. Popplewell, Ed., *Information Processing-1962*, North-Holland, Amsterdam, pp. 306–312, 1963.

P. Lucas, "Die Strukturanalyse von Formeluebersetzern," *Elektron. Rechenanl.* **3**, 159–167 (1961).

A. Newell and H. A. Simon, *Human Problem Solving*, Prentice-Hall, Englewood Cliffs, NJ, 1972.

A. Newell, J. C. Shaw, and H. A. Simon, "Empirical Explorations with the Logic Theory Machine: A Case Study in Heuristics," *Proceedings of the Western Joint Computer Conference*, Los Angeles, 218–239, 1957. Reprinted in E. A. Feigenbaum and J. Feldman, Eds., *Computers and Thought*, McGraw-Hill, New York, pp. 109–133, 1963.

I. Rhodes, "A New Approach to the Mechanical Syntactic Analysis of Russian," *Mechan. Transl.* **6**, 33–50 (1961).

J. J. Robinson and S. Marks, "PARSE: A System for Automatic Analysis of English Text," RM-4564-PR, Rand Corporation, Santa Monica, Calif., 1965.

S. C. Shapiro, J. Martins, and D. McKay, "Bidirectional Inference," *Proceedings of the Fourth Annual Conference of the Cognitive Science Society*, Ann Arbor, Mich., 90–93, 1982.

K. Sparck Jones and M. Kay, *Linguistics and Information Science*, Academic Press, New York, 1973.

F. W. Weingarten, *Translation of Computer Languages*, Holden-Day, San Francisco, 1973.

S. C. SHAPIRO
SUNY at Buffalo

PROGRAMMING STYLES

Programming languages offer various ways for expressing similar intentions. The decision of preferring some constructions to others is dependent on how one thinks the computer works. Various researchers in mainstream computer science have developed checklists for "good" programming style. Proposals in that direction are, for example, "One should not use too many GOTOs." This is based on the assumption that programs using too many GOTOs are not readable. However, readability and understanding are hard to define. The instruction style can be checked in the written program. One could count the GOTOs and, if there are more than one per five statements say: "This is bad style."

Programming styles such as functional programming (function-oriented programming) or object-oriented programming should not be classified as good or bad. No programming styles are superior to others; some are more appropriate than others for certain applications. Concepts of programming styles should be usable to classify written programs much in the same way as buildings are classified. That means style criteria are necessary to classify existing programs. This does not help to characterize the process of program design and program development. For this purpose programming methodology exists that develops methods. It might be (and there is some support for this) that some programming styles are more convenient than others for various stages of program development. For example, a function-oriented style is more convenient in the early phases of programming than the instruction-oriented style, which may be used at the end for the sake of efficiency.

It should be possible to check which style the programmer has chosen by looking into the programs. One can use languages such as Pascal or FORTRAN by writing chains of instructions, planning a future process step by step. The instructions should have very simple arguments only: constants and variables. The result is a machine program in terms of the higher programming language. In contrast, one could try to define hierarchies of functions and write complicated expressions as arguments. As an extreme case the entire program could be written as one expression. This *gedanken experiment* proves that a programming language can be used to program in different styles. It seems that a style of programming is, at least to some extent, independent of the programming language used. It is possible to design a programming language that conveniently supports a given programming style. However, formalisms usually are interpretable in more than one way: a language once defined might be used (or misused) for more than one programming style.

Why do programmers follow a style? Or, what assumptions are to be used while programming according to a style? The following is a good explanation: a programming style is based on imagining how the computer will execute the programs written for it, ie, an execution model or an abstract machine model. It should be taken into account that this may be directed at a completely theoretical (or even, in principle, unrealizable or noneffective) device, which cannot serve as the basis for a working computer (or the main idea of a theory of algorithms). One may quickly imagine such devices, which have been proven impossible by theoretical research: for example, a computer that could prove each theorem formulated in the predicate calculus within a short time, or a computer that instantly maps a given object into a value object if a func-

tion name is also presented. The more abstract the model, the more the programs, written in the related style, are independent of concrete computers—and, alas, the more inefficient they will be. At the same time, they will win in transportability.

To sum up, a *computational model* (execution model) is associated with a *programming style* which is used for programming in a *programming language*. The three concepts together characterize AI programming. There are various programming styles already known: for example, function-oriented, instruction-oriented, and object-oriented styles. Because new models of computation will be invented in the future (Banatre and LeMetayer, 1986), the list of programming styles is open. In fact a good AI application methodology includes the step of inventing a new programming style.

The following application method has been approved for solving AI application problems:

1. Study the problem for the inherent computational model.
2. Invent a corresponding programming style.
3. Design a programming language.
4. Implement the programming language (by embedding in LISP).
5. Use the programming language to formulate the application problem. Experiment in order to study the power and weakness of the implementation, the language design, and the computational model.

Style and Language Names

In general, the one element of a programming language that plays the main role in all programs written in that style is used for the purpose of naming as in "functional programming" or "predicative programming." The following language elements have been used to date: *instruction, function, rule, object, relation*. *Logic* is not within this system. This article refers to the programming styles by using the suffix "-oriented" in expressing the tendency of a programming style; a style is generally realized only to some extent. Using this, a list of known programming styles might include:

- *Instruction-oriented* (conventional).
- *Function-oriented* programming (also called functional, applicative). (Henderson, 1980).
- *Rule-oriented* programming. (eg, R1) (Davis and King, 1977).
- *Object-oriented* programming.
- *Relation-oriented* programming (by constraints).
- *Logic-oriented* programming (predicative) (Kowalski, 1979).
- *Operator-oriented* programming (Ernst and Newell, 1969).
- *Plan-oriented* programming (Stoyan, 1990).

Programming languages are named by using the suffix "-based" if they have a close affinity to a programming style. The reason is that a programming language is generally constructed around an element that is used most if the programmer follows the style intended. A short list of some programming languages follows:

- FORTRAN is an instruction-based programming language.
- ML is function-based (Gordon and co-workers, 1984).
- OPS-5 is rule-based (Brownston and co-workers, 1985).
- Smalltalk is object-based (Goldberg and Robson, 1983).
- PROLOG is logic-based (Clocksin and Mellish, 1985).
- GPS is operator-based (Ernst and Newell, 1969).
- XFRAME is plan-based (Stoyan, 1990).

An unnamed *relation-based* programming language was introduced by Sussman and Steele (1980) and further developed and implemented by Steele (1980).

Wegner (1987) proposed a terminology for object-based languages that is quite different from this one.

Overview

The function-oriented programmer is not very interested in the possible course of evaluation. He or she constructs mountains of forms (terms, applications) for describing values. His or her main activity is the economical representation of goal–subgoal structures where the arguments of a form are the subgoals required for the value creation. The tool for abstraction is function definition, which helps to rule the complexity (Stoyan and Görz, 1984).

Logic-oriented programmers should not develop an interest in the steps of evaluation, which, in this context, means steps of proof. Their duty is the reconstruction of real or conceptual relations by logical means. Abstraction is realized by implicit definition of predicates in systems of axioms (facts, implications)—a challenging intellectual activity that cannot be exercised by the conventional programmer because of the work load.

Object-oriented programmers must bring order into two worlds. The first of these is the macroscopic world of objects that need ruling by division into classes. The genuine problem of abstraction shows up in this context. The counterpart is the microscopic world within the objects, where the inner structure is to be defined and the possible activities should be prescribed.

The rule-oriented programmer concentrates on reacting to situations. Diverse situations must be mastered, mainly without having to enforce a possible sequence of situations during execution. It is more helpful to make an abstraction step and disentangle the possibilities for reaction out of the whole system context. This would enable a step forward in AI programming software engineering. Rule-based languages have a definite weakness here at the abstraction point.

The relation-oriented programmer systemizes the subject by describing facts using connected relations. Situations are symbolized by sets of tuples (ie, sequences of symbols for objects that are seen to be in a relation). The change of situation is modeled by computation of new relations. At present the relation is used as data model (a statical object to be manipulated) mostly in computer science instead of a means for computation. AI is working on introducing a computational model based on relations (or constraints, as it is called).

Plan-oriented programming is the realization of the vision of a computer that is intended to follow concurrent plans. Plans in this sense are not sequences of instructions but formalisms for structuring goals. Minsky (1975) thought more in the direction of plans for situation diagnosis than in the direction of generalized Pascal records when developing the concept of frames.

Operator-oriented programming is done by describing problems. The problem description languages developed to date permit the formulation of problem situations by data structures and the notation of operators by rule-, instruction-, or functionlike constructions. Abstraction by focusing on typical components of such problems was not possible. This is the reason for only singular (play) problems being formalized.

In current AI literature, the concept of a *programming paradigm* is usually taken to describe the subject discussed (Bobrow, 1985). By doing so, authors try to refer to Kuhn (1969) and his theory of scientific revolutions. The reason may be to express the feeling that the new programming styles initiate fundamental changes in computer science. However, the word usage is very misleading. Of course, a new programming style does initiate a new way of thinking in computer science, but this will not be a revolution in the sense of Kuhn. Most programming styles may be followed simultaneously: in the left window one might use function-oriented programming; in the right, object-oriented; and on paper, instruction-oriented. Many people can never master a style other than the instruction-oriented style, while others can switch from one style to another. "Programming paradigm" is one of those phrases that sounds impressive but does not transport very much. A good example of its inflationary use can be studied by reading Floyd's Turing Lecture (1979). The concept of a paradigm is not explanatory and does not enhance our understanding, but our three related concepts—execution model, programming language, and programming style—not only are explanatory but even lead to reflected usage. They also enable us to search for new groups of execution models, programming languages, and programming styles that are impossible for a paradigm.

Since the early 70s, it has become common usage to call new programming languages "knowledge representation formalisms." This was done first in the tradition of mapping a psychology into moving and computing machines in which a computer state is named by concepts of psychology in an unreflected manner. Many statements can be found (and not only among AI scientists) that contain sentences such as: "The program knows . . ." An author without this colorful fantasy would have written: "The program has computed . . ." (the word "compute" seems to be harmless). Minsky has introduced the concept of "knowledge representation" (1968) by intending to form a concept for the description of all the data an automated problem solver collects during the course of its activities.

Minsky saw the danger of intermixing psychology and computer science, but he believed that computer-based definitions of concepts such as "knowledge" could make psychology more exact. At least he expressed the opinion that misusing undefined or badly defined concepts of psychology is harmless. Psychologists who try to develop models of human memory and human knowledge processing may use computer models to describe their subject. However, to believe that a computer knows something because it has a storage slot where a symbol (to be interpreted by a human brain!) is stored, is something else.

A second source of "knowledge representation" probably results from the fact that programming by rules, objects, messages, or logical formulas is of a better quality than the instruction-oriented programming generally used. The desire to have a complete new name may have developed this way. AI experts are aware of this! For a long time, they did know about the function-oriented programming style with its orientation toward value description instead of execution organization, and this was introduced within their own ranks! [In opposition to this, the idea existed for some time that "procedural knowledge representation" exists (Winograd, 1975).]

A third source of the word "knowledge representation" seems to be the field of natural language processing, which appears to make some sense—but would the concept "semantic representation" not be more realistic?

Additionally, the misleading idea of understanding logic as the "theory of thought" (instead of a structural theory of reality) makes people believe that if a computer can execute the *modus ponens,* it can think. There is no principal difference between computing with numbers and computing with strings (structures) that represent logical formulas. A computer creates "new knowledge" in the same way it adds two numbers or substitutes a formula into the variable of a logical axiom. There is only the difference of the basic domain—the permitted operations, nothing else!

Calling the formalisms "knowledge representation formalisms" was a rather bad idea. There are many scientists who literally believe that computers know something simply because they store some rules or data structures. This hinders the development of AI because it is believed that we have reached a goal that is, in fact, still far away. (Simply calling a state that is not very advanced the same as the goal state does not solve a problem.) This confuses the reality, because human knowledge is not simply "represented" if reflected in a formal notation. Using a "knowledge representation language" means, in fact, a complete construction of something new. This is related to knowledge, of course, and in much the same way is a description in a natural language, and therefore, "knowledge reconstruction" (Schefe, 1982) is more precise.

Wedekind (1987) insisted on the *knowledge reconstruction* character of programming. As a result of the experience with function-oriented programming, this direction was taken. Therefore, one should understand "knowledge representation formalisms" to be programming languages. This is possible because a general programming concept is necessary to cover both instruction- and function-oriented programming.

BIBLIOGRAPHY

J-P. Banatre and D. LeMetayer, *A New Computational Model and Its Discipline of Programming,* INRIA, TR 566, Paris, 1986.

D. G. Bobrow, "If Prolog Is the Answer, What Was the Question? Or, What it Takes to Support AI Programming Paradigms," *IEEE Trans. Software Eng.,* SE-11(11), S.1401–1408 (1985).

L. Brownston, R. Farrell, E. Kant, and N. Martin, *Programming Expert Systems in OPS5,* Addison-Wesley, Reading, Mass., 1985.

W. F. Clocksin and C. B. Mellish, *Programming in PROLOG,* 2nd ed., Springer, Berlin, 1985.

R. Davis and J. King, "An Overview on Production Systems," in E. W. Elcock and D. Michie, eds., *Machine Intelligence,* Vol. 8, Wiley, New York, 1977.

G. W. Ernst and A. Newell, *GPS—A Case Study in Generality and Problem Solving,* Academic Press, New York, 1969.

R. Floyd, "The Paradigms of Programming," *Comm. ACM,* **22** (8) (1979).

A. Goldberg and D. Robson, *Smalltalk80—The Language and its Implementation,* Addison-Wesley, Reading, Mass., 1983.

M. Gordon, R. Milner, C. Wadsworth, G. Cosineau, G. Huet, and L. Paulson, *The ML-Handbook, Version 5.1,* INRIA, Paris, 1984.

P. Henderson, *Functional Programming—Application and Implementation,* Prentice-Hall, Englewood Cliffs, NJ, 1980

R. Kowalski, *Logic for Problem Solving,* Elsevier, New York, 1979.

T. Kuhn, *Theory of Scientific Revolutions,* New York, 1969.

M. L. Minsky, "Introduction," in M. L. Minsky, ed., *Semantic Information Processing,* MIT Press, Cambridge, Mass., 1968.

M. L. Minsky, "A Framework for Representing Knowledge, in P. Winston," ed., *The Psychology of Computer Vision,* McGraw-Hill, New York, 1975.

P. Schefe, "Some Fundamental Issues in Knowledge Representation," *GWAI-82,* Informatik-Fachberichte, Springer, Berlin, 1982.

G. L. Steele, *The Definition and Implementation of a Computer Programming Language Based on Constraints,* MIT AI-TR 595, Cambridge, Mass., 1980.

H. Stoyan and G. Görz, *LISP, Eine Einführung in die Programmierung,* Springer, Berlin, 1984

H. Stoyan, "Programming Styles in Artificial Intelligence," in J. Laubsch, ed., *GWAI-84,* Informatik-Fachberichte, Springer, Berlin, 1985.

H. Stoyan, *Programmiermethoden der Künstlichen Intelligenz,* Springer, Berlin, 1988, 1990.

G. J. Sussman and G. L. Steele, "Constraints—A Language for Expressing Almost Hierarchical Descriptions," *Artif. Intell.* **14,** 1–39 (1980).

H. Wedekind, *Datenbanksysteme I,* BI Wissenschaftsverlag, Mannheim, FRG, 1981.

P. Wegner, Dimensions of Object-Based Language Design, *Proceedings of the OOPSLA Conference, SIGPLAN* **22**(12), 168–182 (1987).

T. Winograd, "Frame Representation and the Declarative-Procedural Controversy," in D. G. Bobrow and A. Collins, eds., *Representation and Understanding,* Academic Press, New York, 1975.

HERBERT STOYAN
University of Erlangen

PROLOG. See Logic programming; Parallel logic programming languages.

PROOF TRANSFORMATION

The MKRP (qv) system delivers the proofs of mathematical theorems as resolution proofs represented as abstract refutation graphs that are often difficult to read. The object of this part of the MKRP project is to translate such a proof into a more human-oriented representation. In a first step, a refutation graph is transformed into a natural deduction proof (Gentzen style calculus). Current work concentrates on the simplification of the natural deduction proofs by deleting obvious steps, by grouping small numbers of steps, and by adding new rules to the basic calculus with the final goal, to transform these proofs into natural language, ie, into proofs as they might appear in a mathematics text book.

J. H. Siekmann
Universität Kaiserlautern

PROPOSITIONAL LOGIC. See Logic, propositional.

PROSPECTOR

An early expert system (qv) that interprets geological, geochemical, and geophysical data, thereby helping mineral explorationists discover deeply buried ore deposits. PROSPECTOR was developed in 1975–1980 by Duda, Hart, Reboh and others at SRI International, Menlo Park, Calif. Among other contributions, PROSPECTOR was the first expert system to use inference networks for explicitly representing links between evidence and conclusions, and the first to employ formal Bayesian methods for managing uncertainty. [See R. O. Duda, J. G. Gaschnig, and P. E. Hart, "Model Design in the PROSPECTOR Consultant System for Mineral Exploration," in D. Michie, ed., *Expert Systems in the Micro-Electronic Age*, Edinburgh University Press, Edinburgh, U.K., 1979, pp. 153–167; see also A. N. Campell, V. F. Hollister, R. O. Duda, and P. E. Hart, "Recognition of a Hidden Mineral Deposit by an Artificial Intelligence Program," *Science,* **217**(4563), 927–929 (Sept. 3, 1982.)]

P. E. Hart
Syntelligence, Inc.

PROTÉGÉ

An interactive program developed in 1987 at Stanford University, PROTÉGÉ creates graphical, task-oriented knowledge-acquisition tools. The tools that PROTÉGÉ generates are much like the OPAL knowledge-acquisition system (qv). Whereas OPAL was hand-programmed to allow physicians to enter knowledge bases for the ONCOCIN cancer-chemotherapy advisor [see S. W. Tu, M. G. Kahn, M. A. Musen, J. C. Ferguson, E. H. Shortliffe, and L. M. Fagan, "Episodic Skeletal-Plan Refinement Based on Temporal Data," *CACM* **32**(12), 1439–1455 (Dec. 1989)], the tools produced by PROTÉGÉ are created automatically from metalevel specifications. Knowledge-engineering teams use PROTÉGÉ to custom-tailor knowledge-acquisition tools for specific application areas; the domain experts who interact with the tools that PROTÉGÉ generates then fill out graphical forms and draw diagrams on the workstation screen to describe individual tasks within the relevant application area. These graphical specifications are in turn translated into the knowledge representations required by a domain-independent version of the ONCOCIN inference engine. The PROTÉGÉ approach separates the problem of creating a model of a task area (at the PROTÉGÉ level) from that of entering the content knowledge for a knowledge base (at the level of the PROTÉGÉ-generated tool) (see M. A. Musen, *Automated Generation of Model-Based Knowledge-Acquisition Tools*, Pitman Artificial Intelligence Research Notes Series, London, 1989).

M. A. Musen
Stanford University

PROTEIN STRUCTURE PREDICTION

In many domains of scientific investigation, data has been accumulated at an increasing speed. However, often adequate computational tools are not yet available to organize, analyze, and extract knowledge from the data, and to help researchers better understand their scientific domains. It is a misconception that solving scientific problems is just "number crunching." It has been proven that brute-force approaches are not plausible for many scientific problems; they must be approached intelligently. Domain knowledge (qv) and heuristics (qv) are necessary. Representation is often a crucial issue, and examining and learning from a large number of existing cases is often important. One such scientific domain is the study of protein sequences and structures in molecular biology. Proteins are fundamental molecules for all living organisms. Their amino acid sequence determines their structure, which in turn determines their function. It is now fairly easy to determine a protein's amino acid sequence, but extremely difficult to determine its three-dimensional structure (conformation) by biological technology (through X-ray crystallography, which is, at best, time consuming—typically about ten man years per structure—and sometimes impossible, because of unsuitable or unavailable crystals (Sternberg, 1986)). Presently, the number of known protein structures is about 400, and the number of known protein sequences is above 15,000. The known protein sequences–structures ratio is getting larger and larger. Thus, the development of computational approaches to determine (predict) a protein's conformation from its amino acid sequence is both necessary and important. It is of great scientific and practical significance. For example:

- *Understanding Existing Proteins.* The function of a protein is closely related to its structure. Once the structure is known, it helps greatly in understanding its functions.
- *Modification of Existing Proteins and Design of New Proteins.* Once it is known which (sub)structure is responsible for what function, certain functions can be added or removed from existing proteins by modifying their structures, or a new protein can be synthesized to obtain desired functions.
- *Drug Design.* Once the structures of proteins in a virus are known, drugs can be designed to target the specific virus.

Simply stated, the goal of research on protein structure prediction is to compute a protein structure, such as the one displayed in Figure 1a, from its components—an amino acid sequence as shown in Figure 1b. It is poorly understood how such a one-dimensional sequence folds into the three-dimensional structure. The main source of information available right now is a database of known protein structures; that is, a set of examples of how some amino acid sequences fold into certain structures. Thus, it is also an interesting computational problem: how do we use such examples to solve a new problem?

A Great Challenge. Problem solving is a central theme in AI research. Protein structure prediction suggests itself as a good domain to work on: it is from the real world; it is well defined; there is a fairly large data set to work on; and it is of great scientific significance. How can AI contribute to solving this scientific problem? On the one hand is a set of examples of known protein structures plus bits and pieces of knowledge about protein folding from molecular biologists; on the other hand is a set of AI techniques that has been accumulated since the 1960s. A great challenge is how to put the two together. Biology can benefit from this "marriage" because solving the protein structure prediction problem is of great scientific significance itself. There are many other important problems in biology that are similar to this problem and can be approached in similar ways. AI can also benefit from this marriage. The intrinsically complex problem will stimulate new techniques to emerge that have general applicability.

(a)

V-A-S-Y-D-Y-L-V-I-G-G-G-S-G-G-L-A-S-A-R-R-A-A-E-L-G-A-R-A-A-V-V-E-S-H-K-L-G-G-T-A-
V-N-V-G-A-V-P-K-K-V-M-W-N-T-A-V-H-S-E-F-M-H-D-H-A-D-Y-G-F-P-S-C-E-G-K-F-N-W-R-
V-I-K-E-K-R-D-A-Y-V-S-R-L-N-A-I-Y-Q-N-N-L-T-K-S-H-I-E-I-I-R-G-H-A-A-F-T-S-D-P-K-P-T-
I-E-V-S-G-K-K-Y-T-A-P-H-I-L-I-A-T-G-G-M-P-S-T-P-H-E-S-Q-I-P-G-A-S-L-G-I-T-S-D-G-F-F-
Q-L-E-E-L-P-G-R-S-V-I-V-G-A-G-Y-I-A-V-E-M-A-G-I-L-S-A-L-G-S-K-T-S-L-M-I-R-H-D-K-V-L-
R-S-F-D-S-M-I-S-T-N-C-T-E-E-L-E-N-A-G-V-E-V-L-K-F-S-Q-V-K-E-V-K-K-T-L-S-G-L-E-V-S-
M-V-T-A-V-P-G-R-L-P-V-M-T-M-I-P-D-V-D-C-L-L-W-A-I-G-R-V-P-N-T-K-D-L-S-L-N-K-L-G-I-
Q-T-D-D-K-H-I-I-V-D-E-F-Q-N-T-N-V-K-G-I-Y-A-V-G-D-V-C-G-K-A-L-L-T-P-V-A-I-A-A-G-
R-K-L-A-H-R-L-F-E-Y-K-E-D-S-K-L-D-Y-N-N-I-P-T-V-V-F-S-H-P-P-I-G-T-V-G-L-T-E-D-E-A-I-
H-K-Y-G-I-E-N-V-K-T-Y-S-T-S-F-T-P-M-Y-H-A-V-T-K-R-K-T-K-C-V-M-K-M-V-C-A-N-K-E-E-
K-V-V-G-I-H-M-Q-G-L-G-C-D-E-M-L-Q-G-F-A-V-A-V-K-M-G-A-T-K-A-D-F-D-N-T-V-A-I-H-P-
T-S-S-E-E-L-V-T-L-R

(b)

Figure 1. (a) The three-dimensional structure of a protein. An α helix and a β sheet are highlighted. (b) The corresponding amino acid sequence.

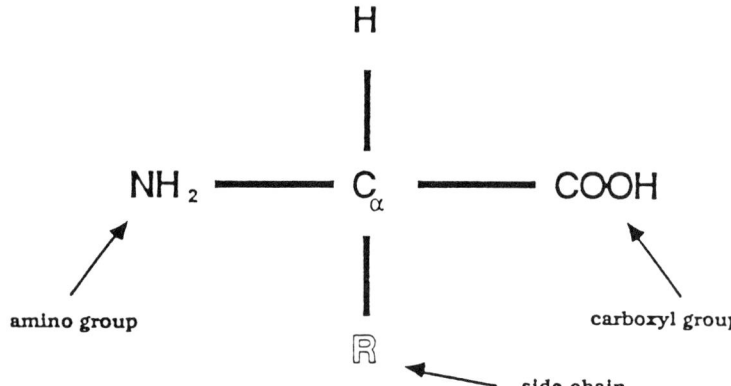

Figure 2. The chemical structure of the un-ionized form of an amino acid.

This article provides brief background information on biology necessary for readers to understand the problem of protein structure prediction, reviews the important work in this field of research, and points out some future directions.

BACKGROUND: MOLECULAR BIOLOGY

Proteins play crucial roles in virtually all biological processes. (The word "protein," coined by Berzelius in 1838 to emphasize the importance of a class of macromolecules, was derived from the Greek word *proteios*, meaning "of the first rank.") Nearly all chemical reactions in biological systems are catalyzed by enzymes, which are a class of protein. Many small molecules and ions (eg, oxygen) are transported by specific proteins. Proteins are also the major component of muscle. Antibodies are highly specific proteins for immune protection. The response of nerve cells to specific stimuli is mediated by receptor proteins. Thus, to understand the properties and functions of proteins is an important step in our scientific pursuit to understand human beings and any living creatures.

Amino Acids

Amino acids are the basic structural units of proteins. There are twenty different amino acids. An amino acid consists of an amino group (NH_2), a carboxyl group (COOH), a hydrogen atom (H), and a distinctive R group (often referred to as side chain) that are all bonded to a carbon atom, called the α-carbon (C_α) (Fig. 2). Figure 3 shows the three-dimensional structure of an amino acid.

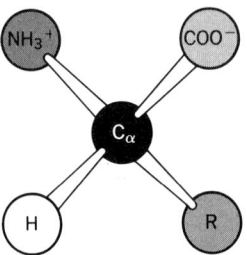

Figure 3. The three-dimensional structure of an amino acid (Stryer, 1988). Courtesy of W. H. Freeman and Company.

Table 1 lists the names of all twenty amino acids and their abbreviations.

Each of the twenty amino acids has the same structure except for its side chain, which determines all that is unique about a particular amino acid. Figure 4 displays the side-chains for the twenty amino acids. The twenty kinds of side chains vary in size, shape, charge, chemical reactivity, and hydrogen-bonding capacity (the property that determines whether an amino acid tends to bind with water or not; also referred to as hydrophobicity or hydrophilicity.) Amino acids can be classified according to these properties. All proteins in all species, from bacteria to humans, are constructed from the same set of twenty amino acids. This fundamental alphabet of proteins is at least two billion years old. The remarkable range of functions mediated by proteins results from the diversity and versatility of these twenty building blocks.

Polypeptide Chains

In proteins, the carboxyl group of one amino acid is joined to the amino group of another amino acid by a *peptide*

Table 1. The Names and Abbreviations of the Twenty Amino Acids.

Amino Acid	Abbreviation (3-letter)	Abbreviation (1-letter)
Alanine	Ala	A
Arginine	Arg	R
Asparagine	Asn	N
Aspartic acid	Asp	D
Cysteine	Cys	C
Glutamine	Gln	Q
Glutamic acid	Glu	E
Glycine	Gly	G
Histidine	His	H
Isoleucine	Ile	I
Leucine	Leu	L
Lysine	Lys	K
Methionine	Met	M
Phenylalanine	Phe	F
Proline	Pro	P
Serine	Ser	S
Threonine	Thr	T
Tryptophan	Trp	W
Tyrosine	Tyr	Y
Valine	Val	V

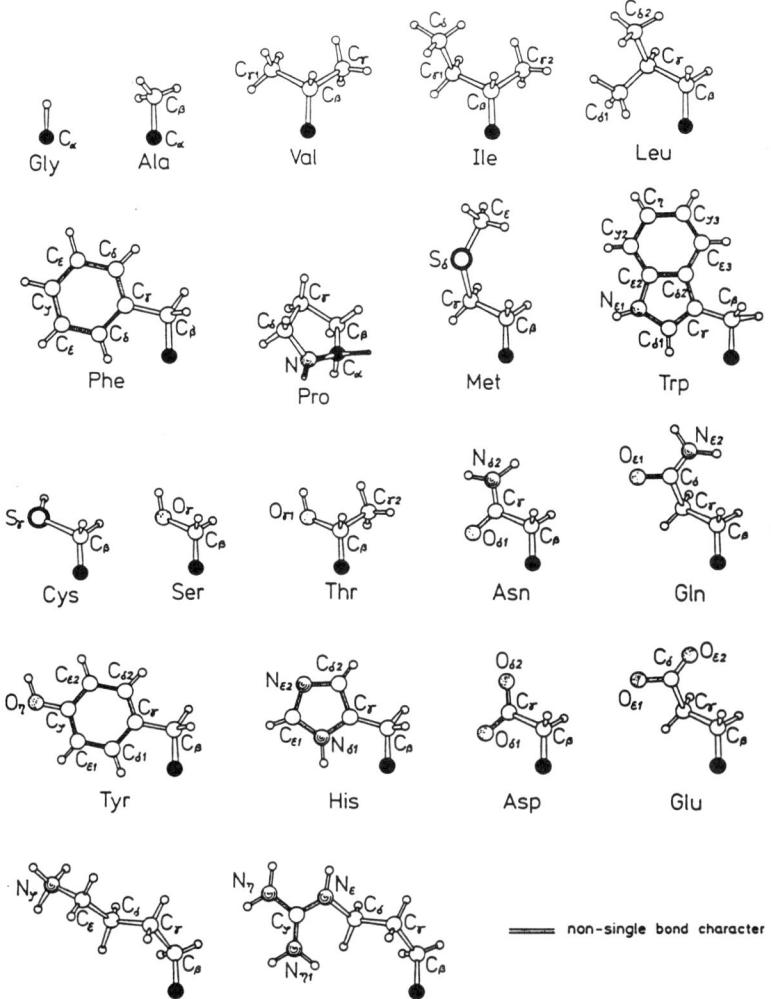

Figure 4. The side chains of the twenty different amino acids (Shulz and Schirmer, 1979). Courtesy of Springer-Verlag.

bond. Many amino acids, usually more than a hundred, are joined by peptide bonds to form a polypeptide chain, which is an unbranched structure (Fig. 5). An amino acid unit in a polypeptide chain is called a residue. By convention, the amino end is taken to be the beginning of a polypeptide chain.

Each protein has a unique, precisely defined amino acid sequence. In proteins, the peptide unit is rigid and planar (Fig. 6) and all of the bond lengths are invariant. However, there is considerable freedom of rotation around the bonds joining the peptide units to the α-carbon atom (the ϕ and ψ angles in Figure 6). The parameters ϕ and ψ are the determining factors for conformation. A very useful device for studying protein conformation is the Ramachandran plot (Schulz and Schirmer, 1979), which plots ϕ against ψ distributions for all the residues in the known protein structures (Fig. 7). The angles are obviously not evenly distributed. There are two dense regions that correspond to specific structures called α helix and β sheet, respectively, which are discussed below.

Levels of Structure in Proteins

In discussing the structure of proteins, it is convenient to refer to four levels. Primary structure is simply the sequence of amino acids. Secondary structure refers to the spatial (steric) relationship of amino acid residues that are close to one another in the linear sequence. Some of these steric relationships are of a regular kind, giving rise to a periodic structure. Tertiary structure refers to the steric relationship of residues that are far apart in the linear sequence. (It should be noted that the dividing line between secondary and tertiary structures is somewhat arbitrary, eg, the residues in different strands in a β sheet

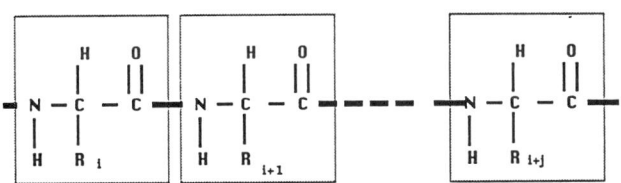

Figure 5. A polypeptide chain. The chain starts at the amino end (*left*).

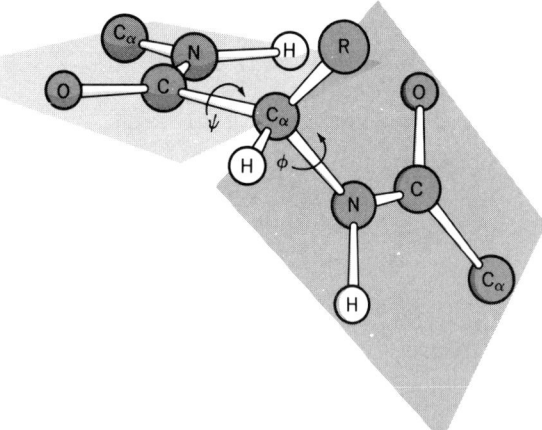

Figure 6. The peptide unit is a rigid planar unit. There is considerable freedom of rotation about the bonds joining the peptide groups to the α-carbon atoms (Stryer, 1988). Courtesy of W. H. Freeman and Company.

Secondary Structures. Secondary structures are the common substructures that occur across different proteins, which include α helix, β sheet, and β turn. They are the most regular part of the proteins, and they have been studied the most. They deserve a more detailed discussion here. The term "coil" is often used to denote any part of a protein that is not in one of the preceding secondary structures.

An α helix is a rodlike structure (Fig. 8). The tightly coiled polypeptide main chain forms the inner part of the rod, and the side chains extend outward in a helical array. In an α helix, each residue is related to the next one by a translation of 1.5Å along the helix axis and a rotation of 100°, which gives 3.6 amino acid residues per turn of the helix. The pitch of the α helix is 5.4Å (the product of the translation and the number of residues per turn), with a hydrogen bond between the NH of residue n and the CO of residue $n + 3$, which stabilizes the helix. The intervening stretch of backbone contains 13 atoms (including the hydrogen). In certain proteins, as much as 80% of their structure can be helical (Richardson, 1981).

The polypeptide chain in a β sheet is almost fully extended rather than being tightly coiled as in the α helix. The axial distance between adjacent amino acids is 3.5Å. The β sheet is stabilized by hydrogen bonds between NH and CO groups in different polypeptide strands, whereas in the α helix the hydrogen bonds are between NH and CO groups in the same polypeptide strand. β strands can interact in either parallel or antiparallel orientation. Figure 9 shows an antiparallel β sheet. β strands can combine into either a pure parallel sheet, a pure antiparallel sheet, or a mixed sheet with some strand pairs parallel and some antiparallel. However, there is a strong bias against mixed sheets. Only about 20% of the strands inside β sheets have parallel bonding on one side and antiparallel

may not be close to each other along the sequence.) Proteins that contain more than one polypeptide chain display an additional level of structural organization, namely quaternary structure, which refers to the way in which the chains are packed together. These chains are also called "subunits," each of which can form a stable folded structure by itself. The amino acid sequences can be identical, similar, or completely different for each subunit. Within a single subunit, contiguous portions of the polypeptide chain frequently fold into compact, local, semi-independent units called domains. The most common domain size is between 100 and 200 residues (Richardson, 1981).

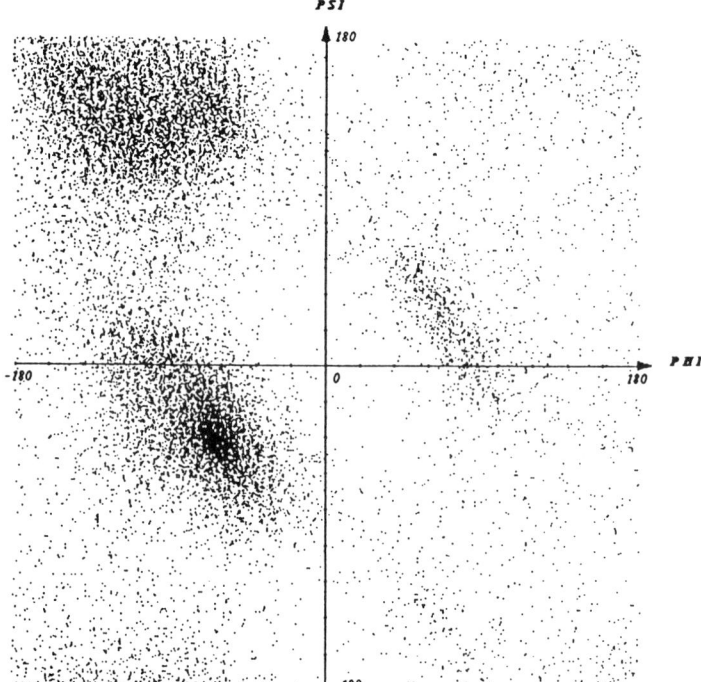

Figure 7. Plot of main chain dihedral angles ϕ and ψ for residues in the known protein structures.

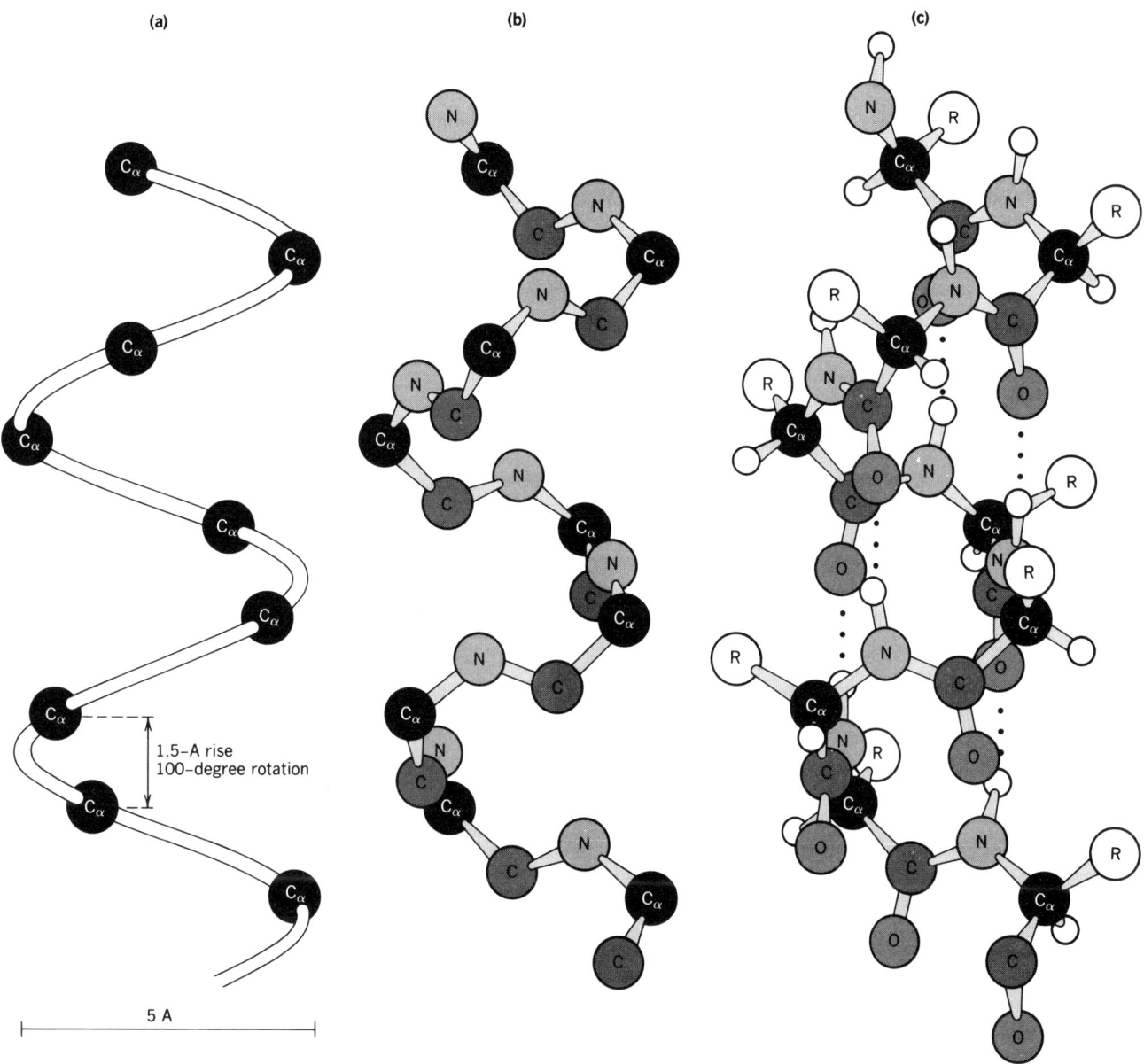

Figure 8. Models of α helix: (a) only the α-carbon atoms are shown on a helical thread; (b) only the backbone nitrogen (N), α-carbon, and carbonyl carbon (C) atoms are shown; (c) the entire helix (Stryer, 1988). Courtesy of W. H. Freeman and Company.

on the other. Parallel β structure almost never occurs in sheets of less than five total strands, whereas antiparallel β structure often occurs as a twisted ribbon of just two strands. A single α helix can have as many as 35 residues, whereas the longest β strands include only about 15 residues.

Most proteins have compact, globular shapes due to frequent reversals of the direction of their polypeptide chains. Many of these chain reversals are accomplished by a common structural element called the β turn. A typical example of β turn is that the CO group of residue $n + 1$ of a polypeptide chain is hydrogen bonded to the NH group of residue $(n + 4)$ (Fig. 10). However, unlike α helix and β sheet, there is less agreement about the definition of β turns among researchers, eg, how many residues should be in a turn. By any sort of definition β turns are an important feature of protein structure. Kuntz (1972) found 45% of protein backbone in turns. Chou and Fasman (1974) found 32% of protein chain in turns (counting four residues per turn). Richardson (1981) found eight different kinds of turns.

Renaturation Experiments

In renaturation experiments, a folded active protein is denatured and unfolded to a random, high free energy state (such as by raising the temperature, or by certain solvent; the covalent bonds between amino acids are pre-

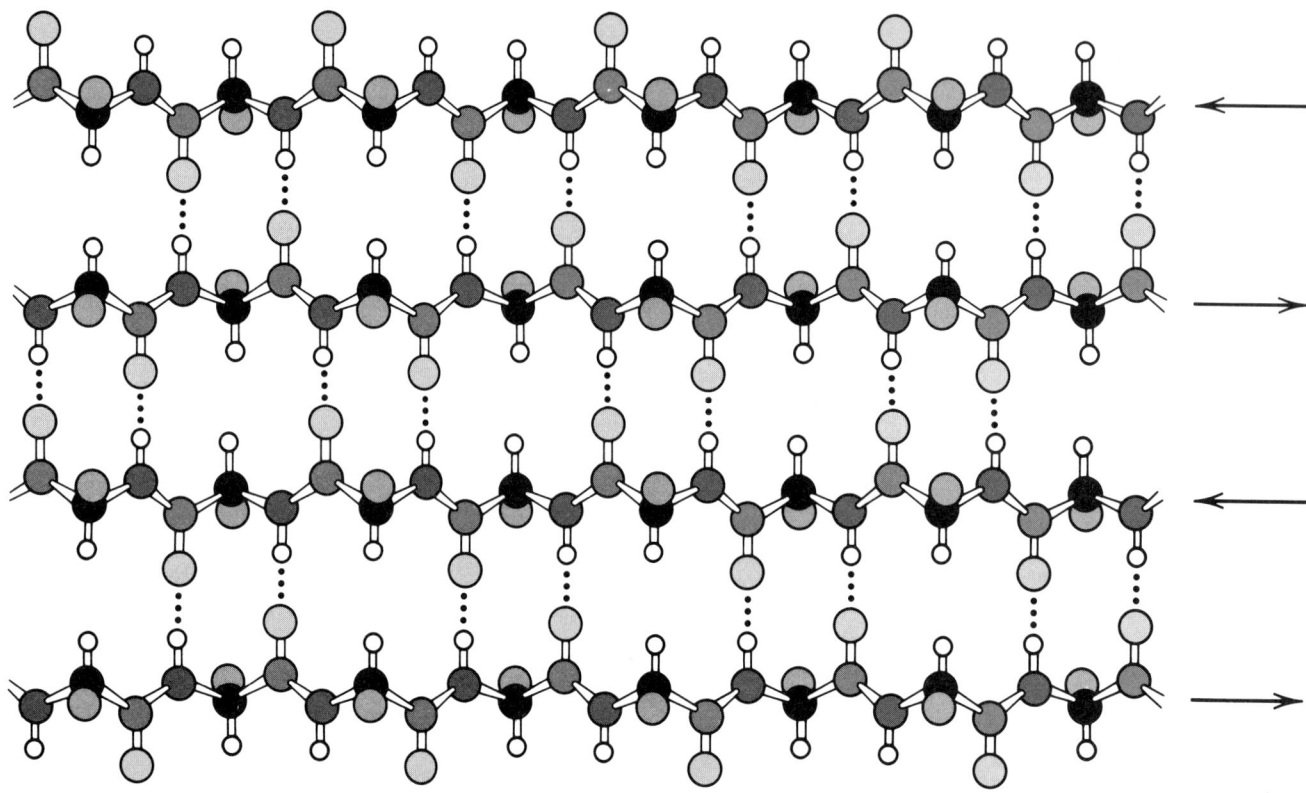

Figure 9. Antiparallel β sheet. Adjacent strands run in opposite directions. Hydrogen bonds between NH and CO groups of adjacent strands stabilize the structure. The size chains are above and below the plane of the sheet (Stryer, 1988). Courtesy of W. H. Freeman and Company.

served). However, the removal of the denaturation factors always causes the protein to fold back to the same native structure of low free energy. This result demonstrates that a protein sequence can independently fold into a unique structure, and suggests that there is a one-to-one correspondence between the sequence and the structure for proteins in nature (Schulz and Schirmer, 1979). This does not mean that any amino acid sequence corresponds to a unique structure. Many "artificial sequences," sequences synthesized in the laboratory, cannot fold into a stable structure at all; thus, evolution has selected those amino acid sequences that have specific structures and functions to be what are called proteins.

Homologous Proteins

Homologous proteins are proteins that evolved from a common ancestor. They usually have similar amino acid sequences and three-dimensional structures; thus, they often have similar properties and functions. Once a protein's structure is known, it is much easier to determine the structures of proteins that are homologous to it (eg, the condition to crystallize the proteins are generally similar.) Because of this, many proteins in the Brookhaven Protein Databank (the major databank for the known protein structures worldwide) have homologous proteins in the same databank. It is an interesting research topic to examine how small changes in an amino acid sequence affect the protein's structure and function. However, the high concentration of homologous proteins in the databank is an artifact, and does not reflect the real situation in nature. Thus, when selecting protein structures from the databank for structure prediction research, it is a common practice to use nonhomologous proteins as working data.

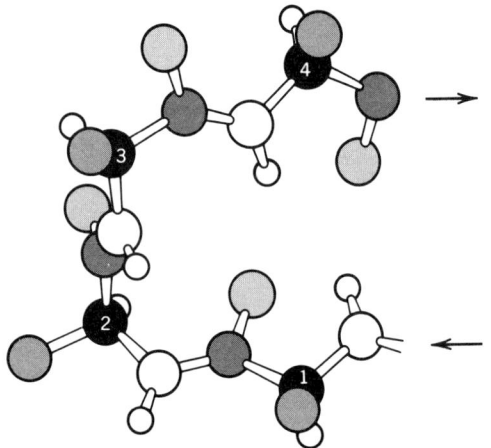

Figure 10. Structure of a β-turn. Here the CO group of residue $i + 1$ is hydrogen bonded to the NH group of residue $i + 4$, which results in a turn (Stryer, 1988). Courtesy of W. H. Freeman and Company.

Summary

In summary, proteins have unique amino acid sequences which specify their three-dimensional structures. It is easy to determine a protein's amino acid sequence, or chemically synthesize an arbitrary amino acid sequence, but extremely difficult to determine its conformation. To be able to determine the structure of proteins automatically and quickly is extremely important.

PREDICTION OF PROTEIN SECONDARY STRUCTURES

Since the 1970s, secondary structures have been the focus in protein structure prediction research. Many algorithms have been developed, which generally adopt the "local strategy" of moving a "window" (typically 7–19 residues wide) along an amino acid sequence and making predictions based on the residues inside each window (Fig. 11). To evaluate an algorithm, the known protein structure data are divided into two sets: the "training data set" is used to adjust the parameters of the algorithm, and the "test data set" is used to test its prediction accuracy.

From the 15 amino acid sequences and the corresponding conformations known at the time, Chou and Fasman (1974) computed the frequencies with which each amino acid appears in α helices, β sheets, and β turns, and in their boundaries. For an α helix, for example, each amino acid was classified as either helix-former, or helix-neutral, or helix-breaker based on the computed frequencies. The same was done for β turns and sheets. This information was then used to predict the secondary structures in other proteins given their primary sequences. Their prediction accuracy is between 50% and 60% correct for the three categories (α helix, β sheet, and coil).

The prediction of secondary structures can be seen as a way of assigning each residue in the primary sequence into one of three (or four) states: α helix, β sheet (β turn), or coil, and it is completely determined by the residues within the same primary sequence. Let $S_j \in \{\alpha\text{–helix}, \beta\text{–sheet}, (\beta\text{–turn}), \text{coil}\}$. The likelihood that residue j is in state S_j can be expressed as $I(S_j; R_1, R_2, \ldots R_n)$, where R_i is the ith residue, and assuming there are n residues in the primary sequence. It was suggested that the influence was essentially local, and that the state of a residue had a strong effect on other residues up to eight residues distant. Based on this, Garnier and co-workers (1978) used the following approximation:

$$I(S_j; R_1, R_2, \ldots R_n) \simeq \sum_{m=-8}^{m=+8} I(S_j; R_{j+m}).$$

where $I(S_j; R_{j+m})$ represents the influence that residue at position $j + m$ plays on the conformational state of the jth residue. This algorithm was reported giving a better prediction than Chou and Fasman's method. It was further improved (Gibrat, 1987) by considering correlation between residues R_j and R_{j+m} in addition to correlation between S_j and R_{j+m}, ie,

$$I(S_j; R_1, R_2, \ldots R_n) \simeq \sum_{m=-8}^{m=+8} I(S_j; R_{j+m}, R_j).$$

This improved algorithm was 63% accurate on a set of test cases for three-state (helix, sheet, coil) prediction. Biou and co-workers (1988) further improved this algorithm by combining its result with that of two other algorithms, the "homology" method and the "bit pattern" method, to achieve a reported accuracy of 65.5%.

Another method for predicting secondary structures is to compute amino acid patterns for each secondary structure, and match these patterns against a new sequence to locate the corresponding secondary structures there (Cohen and co-workers, 1983). In order to find the patterns that are general enough, the twenty amino acids were categorized based on their properties. A pattern is something like "$A_1 ** A_2 * A_1$", where A_1 and A_2 are subcategories of amino acids and $*$ means "anything." One difficulty here was to choose the right amino acid categorization. Rooman and Wodak (1988) took a similar approach. They developed a set of "sequence motifs" (amino acid patterns) for predicting the secondary structures, and their conclusion was that the identification of predictive sequence motifs is limited by the size of the currently available data set. Here, no amino acid categorization is precomputed. Rather, they are formed along with the patterns. For example, if both $X_1X_2X_3$ and $X_1X_4X_3$ occur frequently in α helix (X_i is an amino acid), then pattern $X_1\{X_2, X_4\}X_3$ is formed; that is, the second position of this pattern can be either X_2 or X_4. However, X_2 and X_4 may not be interchangeable in other places.

Qian and Sejnowski (1988) used the back-propagation artificial neural net algorithm to predict the α helix and β sheet of 15 test proteins. The first network they used had three layers and was fully connected. Different numbers of hidden units and different numbers of input residues for the neural network were tested. The optimal numbers they found were 40 hidden units and 13 input residues. The best result of this network was 62.7% accurate. A second network was added with inputs that were sequences of outputs from the first network. These two "cascaded networks" generated 64.3% prediction accuracy on their test data set of 15 proteins. Qian and Sejnowski also tested other network architectures and different representations of amino acids, which did not improve the prediction.

Though many algorithms exist, their highest prediction accuracy has always been around 60%, and often quite different prediction accuracies have been reported for the same algorithm by different people. To determine the key factors that influence the secondary structure prediction accuracy, Zhang and co-workers (1990) analyzed the results of different algorithms. Error and statistical significance measures were developed and great care was taken in redoing previous experiments in order to make fair comparisons.

To evaluate the progress of this field, it is important to

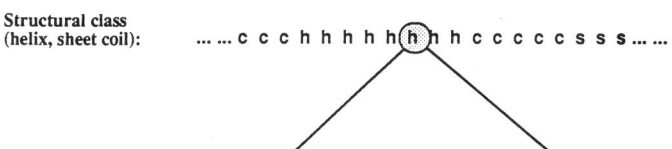

Figure 11. Residues in a "window" and the structural class of the center residue.

have a rigorous procedure to objectively estimate the prediction accuracy of an algorithm and to have a criteria to measure the significance of the difference between two algorithms' prediction accuracies. Statistical theory provides a method to compute the "significance interval" for the difference between two population proportions. In the case of secondary structure prediction, the "proportion" is the percentage of residues in a set of test data with secondary structure that has been correctly predicted. Assume the prediction accuracy of two algorithms are p_1 and p_2 for two test data sets of r_1 and r_2 residues, respectively, then we say that we are $a\%$ confident that the true difference between the two predictions is within $|p_1 - p_2| \pm d$, where d depends on p_1, p_2, r_1, r_2, and a: (Daniel, 1987)

$$d = Z\left(\frac{1+a}{2}\right) \cdot \sqrt{\frac{p_1(1-p_1)}{r_1} + \frac{p_2(1-p_2)}{r_2}} \quad (1)$$

where z follows the unit normal distribution; eg at confidence level $a = 95\%$, $Z\left(\frac{1+a}{2}\right) = 1.96$. The difference between p_1 and p_2 is said to be statistically significant (at confidence level $a\%$) only when $d < |p_1 - p_2|$. For example, in Qian and Sejnowski's work, there were 3520 residues in their test set of 15 proteins; the significant difference interval with confidence level of 95% is 2.2%. Thus the improvement of the cascaded networks over a single network, 64.3% − 62.7% = 1.6% was not statistically significant by this criteria.

Though it is a usual practice that some known protein structures are used as test data to estimate what the prediction accuracy of an algorithm will be for a protein sequence whose structure is really unknown, there are often two sources of erroneous biases in this estimate: (1) the same protein sequence or homologous protein sequences are used in both training and test data set; (2) more subtly, the performance of the algorithm on the test data set is observed and used to adjust the parameters in the algorithm, ie, the parameters are optimized for the particular set(s) of test data. To avoid both kinds of biases and objectively estimate the prediction accuracy of an algorithm, the following testing procedure was used by Zhang and co-workers (1990).

1. There were 113 protein sequences in their database, which were randomly grouped into 7 groups (16 sequences in each group).
2. One group was used as test data and the others as training data.
3. All the parameters of the algorithm were computed and set based solely on the training data (this includes, for example, the weights for each structural class in statistical methods, and the "learning rate" and the number of training cycles for neural nets).
4. Predictions were made on the test data.
5. Steps 2–4 were repeated using every group as test data.

This test was repeated three times, thus, there are $7 \times 3 = 21$ sets of test data. This testing procedure not only shows the average prediction accuracy of an algorithm, but also how much the accuracy varies for different test groups and what the factors are that affect the prediction accuracy (such as the α helix and β sheet contents in the test data, or the training data used). Each protein will be in three different test groups, each time with a different training set.

Zhang and co-workers obtained a statistically better prediction on secondary structures than all known previous methods by combining three different algorithms, which are representatives of many previous systems. The three algorithms are (1) a statistical method to compute statistical correlations between amino acids and the secondary structure they form according to the training data and apply them to the test data; (2) memory-based reasoning (Stanfill and Waltz, 1986) to compare sequences in the test data set to those in the training data set, and to make predictions based on closely matched segments of sequences; (3) an artificial neural net to use the training data to train an artificial neural network, and apply the network to the test data. Another neural net was used to take the outputs of the three algorithms as inputs, and produce final predictions.

They found that:

1. For a given set of test data, the predictions generated by each of the three algorithms were different in certain cases, and no one algorithm was always correct. Thus each algorithm captures some information that other algorithms cannot, and a combination of the different algorithms generated better results.
2. With the same test data set, the maximum differences in prediction accuracy among different algorithms tested was about 4%, whereas the maximum difference for each individual algorithm on different test data sets was about 7%. Thus the known protein structure data used was the most determinant factor on the accuracy of protein secondary structure prediction.
3. Each algorithm can give different predictions for the same protein when the algorithm is trained with different training data and this difference is statistically significant.
4. All three methods agreed on about 80% of all their residues in the 21 test sets of 57,954 residues, which is much higher than their agreement with the real structure (ie, their prediction accuracy). This suggests that the "local rules" (the rules mapping segments of amino acid sequences to secondary structures) obtained by the seemingly quite different methods from the training data were actually very similar. In places where all methods have the same but wrong prediction, the structures might be influenced by nonlocal interactions.

With the same training and test data sets, and through the same rigorous, extensive testing procedure as described previously, the following secondary structure prediction accuracies were obtained: Zhang's combined algorithm was 66.4%, and Qian and Sejnowski's was 64.0%. Biou's program, tested with 39 proteins nonhomologous to its training data set, was 62.4% accurate.

REPRESENTATION AND PREDICTION OF GLOBAL STRUCTURES

Representations

Since there has not been a complete theory of how amino acid sequences fold into proteins, one way to approach the protein structure prediction is to learn from the known protein structures, to find out correlations between amino acids and the structures they form. A key step in this process is then to represent the protein structures in such a way that it can, on the one hand, reflect the enormous complexity and variety of different protein structures, and yet, on the other hand, facilitate the identification of similar substructures across different proteins. No such representations are available yet. The representations commonly used are unsatisfactory.

- The known protein structures with atomic resolution can be represented by the three-dimensional coordinates of every atom in it. This representation carries all the details of the structure, but it is difficult to identify similar substructures in different proteins and to abstract high level descriptions.
- In most secondary structure prediction researches, the structure is represented by a linear sequence of structural category labels, ie, α helix, β sheet, and sometimes β turn. This is a great simplification of the real structure. Even if all the secondary structures of a protein are known, there is still a long way to go to determine the full 3-D structure. Also, different people have different criteria for assigning the secondary structures to a protein given its residue coordinates.
- Another representation occasionally used is the distance matrix, a matrix of distances between all pairs of residues in a protein. It contains more information than that of the secondary structures and less information than the 3-D coordinates. It is still not obvious how common substructure can be abstracted.

There have been several efforts to develop new representations of protein structures, often using each residue's C_α positions as the main information. Unger and co-workers (1989) analyzed hexamers (six consecutive residues in a protein sequence) and showed that their structure tends to concentrate in specific clusters rather than vary continuously. A limited set of basic "building blocks" were taken from these clusters to replace about 76% of all hexamers in high resolution known protein structures with an error of less than 1Å, and could be joined together to cover 99% of the residues. Richards and Kundrot (1988) first defined different types of "secondary elements" as the conformation of contiguous segments of a protein sequence. Then α helices and β strands were idealized as straight line segments and the axial directions and locations were compiled from the C_α coordinate list of the known structures. The geometric relations between these line segments are then calculated and output as the first level of supersecondary structure. A maximum of six parameters are required for a complete description of the relations between each pair. Sklenar and co-workers (1989), Hunter and States (1991), and Rooman and co-workers (1990) have also developed new descriptions/classifications of protein local structures, either including more atoms than just C_α as input, or using more complicated geometric representation, or considering different number of residues.

Zhang and co-workers (1989) took an incremental, bottom-up learning approach in developing representations for protein structures using machine learning techniques, with the known protein structure as training data.

1. First a structural state vector of a residue is defined, which depends on its spatial position relative to its neighbor residues along the amino acid sequence, ie, its ϕ, ψ angles (see above section on Molecular Biology) and whether the residue is on the surface or inside a protein. Then a "canonical" form (called a "feature vector") of these residue state vectors is computed by training an auto-association back-propagation (McClelland and Rumelhart, 1986) network to make useful information explicit and remove redundancies.

2. A classification of residue structural states is made based on their feature vectors. An induction algorithm is then used to find common patterns of residue structural classes along the protein sequences of known structures, and produces a set of regular expressions as the structure representation, which can easily represent periodical local structures such as α helix and β sheet. The substructures represented by these regular expressions are at the secondary structure level.

3. Adjacent secondary structures are grouped to form higher level structures based on their geometric relations, which correspond to what have been called "super secondary structures."

The residue structural classes were found to have strong amino acid preference, ie, some amino acids occur frequently or rarely in certain classes. Correlations were found among some of the structural classes, ie, when structural class X occurs in one place, another class Y tends to occur in some other place along the amino acid sequence. This information is very important for structure prediction.

Two important advantages of these new approaches for structure representations are: (1) given a protein's residue coordinates a hierarchy of structural representation can be built with different levels of abstraction; higher level representations are built upon lower level ones, (2) these representations are grounded on a few objective, observable structural parameters whose accuracy depends only on the accuracy of the crystal data, rather than some subjective judgment.

Prediction of Protein Global Structures

There is still a long way to go before a protein's three-dimensional structure can automatically be determined based only on its amino acid sequence. However, efforts have already been made in computing certain structural properties of proteins beyond the secondary structure level.

Prediction of Super-Secondary Structures. Pattern-matching methods have been used to predict higher order structures. Taylor and Thornton (1984) used a technique similar to that of Cohen and co-workers (1983) to predict a super-secondary structure $\beta\alpha\beta$ (two β strands with an α helix in between). The essence of their method is the use of a $\beta\alpha\beta$ template, derived from an analysis of all known $\beta\alpha\beta$ units, to locate probable $\beta\alpha\beta$ units in a new primary sequence.

Prediction of Surface Residues. The folding process of an amino acid sequence is strongly influenced by the hydrophobicity of the amino acid side chains. It is generally accepted that, to a rough approximation, two opposing tendencies are reflected in the final structure of a protein when it folds. The resulting compromise allows hydrophilic side chains access to the aqueous solvent while at the same time minimizing contact between hydrophobic side chains and the water in the solvent. Kyte and Doolittle (1982) used an experimentally obtained amino acid hydrophobicity–hydrophilicity value (called hydropathy) of each side chain and a window moving along a protein sequence to compute the hydropathy of each segment of the sequence, so they could predict whether each segment would appear on the surface or inside the protein, which is very important conformational information.

Prediction of Protein Classes. The secondary structure prediction algorithms can be adjusted to have a much higher accuracy if the class of the protein to be analyzed is known, such as whether it is α-helix rich, β-sheet rich, mixed, or non-$\alpha\beta$. Klein and Delisi (1986) attempted to allocate amino acid sequences to one of the preceding secondary structural classes, based on estimates of percentages of α and β structures, and on regular variations in the hydrophobic values of residues along the sequence, occurring with periods of 2 and 3.6 residues, and reported classification accuracy of 84% for this allocation. Cohen and co-workers (1983) tried to divide protein sequences into $\alpha\beta$ and non-$\alpha\beta$ types. Hiroshi and co-workers (1986) found that the class of a protein is closely related to its composition, the percentage of each amino acid in the protein. The information obtained from these algorithms can help predict protein structures.

Prediction of Tertiary Structures. Relatively fewer efforts have been made to predict the tertiary structure of proteins. Blundell and co-workers (1987) observed that the 3-D structures of homologous proteins are conserved in evolution more than their amino acid sequences, and proposed using the known structure of homologous proteins as a "framework" for a new protein. The requirement that there must exist one or more homologous proteins for each new protein restricts the applicability of this method.

Free Energy Minimization Method. The results of renaturation experiments (see section in Molecular Biology) suggest that the native structure is at the conformation of lowest free energy, thus, one way to predict the protein structure might be to compute the lowest free energy state for a primary sequence. However, at present an incomplete understanding of adequate constraints on the range of configurations that need to be considered, and the exponentially growing amount of computation required (even the smallest protein with 50 residues can adopt some 10^{50} conformations (Sternberg, 1986) preclude structural determinations based on this method for all but the most special cases, and then only for very short sequences.

Simplified Models. Recently several efforts have been made to simulate the protein folding process with simplified representation of protein structures. Often a single atom is used to approximate the effect of each amino acid. Some researchers assumed that a protein is a freely rotating rigid chain (Wilson and Doniach, 1989); others constrained each residue to be on the grids of some lattice (Skolnick and Kolinski, 1990). Energy functions describing the attraction and repulsion between different types of amio acids, and the preference for certain local (secondary) structures can be determined directly from the distribution of amino acids in the database of known protein structures. Simulated annealing (qv) has usually been used as the optimization technique to search in the conformation space for the "low energy" states. Some specific small proteins were reported to have been folded from random starting states to native-like structures.

AI Efforts. Several AI researchers have worked on the protein structure prediction problem. Hayes-Roth and co-workers (1986) used multiple sources of information, including information from a Nuclear Magnetic Resonance (NMR) device, and the blackboard control architecture, to identify legal positions for each of a protein's constituent structures (atoms, amino acids, helices, etc), which usually correspond to a large number of possible conformations. The NMR technique currently can only be applied to small proteins (with less than 150 residues). The ARIADNE system (Lathrop and co-workers, 1987) is another interesting effort. It is essentially a recognition system that uses hierarchical representation to decide whether a primary sequence can fold into a given 3-D structure.

SUMMARY

Molecular biology is an exciting field. Its advance not only satisfies our scientific curiosity and understanding of the world, but also affects our daily lives (eg, medicine, diet). There are growing demands for information processing techniques to deal with fast-increasing amounts of data. For example, the proposed "human genome project" plans to map and sequence the whole human gene, which contains about three billion DNA bases. What do they encode? What are the relations among different parts of the gene? What proteins does each part encode? What are the structures and functions of these proteins? How do these proteins interact with one another? The many complex problems in molecular biology pose great challenges to all disciplines of computational sciences. AI should make its contribution.

BIBLIOGRAPHY

V. Biou, J. F. Gibrat, J. M. Levin, B. Robson, and J. Garnier, "Secondary Structure Prediction: Combination of Three Different Methods," *Protein Eng.* **2**(3), 183–191 (1988).

T. L. Blundell, B. L. Sibanda, M. J. E. Sternberg, and J. M. Thornton, "Knowledge-based Prediction of Protein Structures and the Design of Novel Molecules," *Nature (London)* **326**(26) (March 1987).

P. Y. Chou and G. D. Fasman, "Prediction of Protein Conformation," *Biochemistry* **13**(2) (1974).

F. E. Cohen, R. M. Abarbanel, I. D. Kuntz, and R. J. Fletterick, "Secondary Structure Assignment for a α/β Proteins by a Combinatorial Approach," *Biochemistry* **22** (1983).

W. W. Daniel, *Biostatistics: A Foundation for Analysis in the Health Sciences,* 4th ed., Wiley, New York, 1987.

J. Garnier, D. J. Osguthorpe, and B. Robson, "Analysis of the Accuracy and Implications of Simple Methods for Predicting the Secondary Structure of Globular Proteins," *J. Mol. Biol.* **120** (1978).

J. F. Gibrat, J. Garnier, and B. Robson, "Further Developments of Protein Secondary Structure Using Information Theory," *J. Mol. Biol.* **198**, 425–443 (1987).

B. Hayes-Roth and co-workers, "Protean: Deriving Protein Structure from Constraints," *Proceedings of the Fifth National Conference on AI,* AAAI, Menlo Park, Calif., 1986.

L. Hunter and D. States, "Bayesian Classification of Protein Structural Elements," *Proceedings of the Hawaiian International Conference on System Science 24, Emerging Technologies and Applications Track, Biotechnology Computing Minitrack,* 1991.

D. G. Kneller, F. E. Cohen, and R. Langridge, "Improvements in Protein Secondary Structure Prediction by an Enhanced Neural Network," *J. Mol. Biol.* **214**, 171–182 (1990).

J. Kyte and R. F. Doolittle, "A Simple Method for Displaying the Hydropathic Character of a Protein," *J. Mol. Biol.* **157**, (1982).

R. H. Lathrop, T. A. Webster, and T. F. Smith, "Ariadne: Pattern-directed Inference and Hierarchical Abstraction in Protein Structure Recognition," *CACM* **30**(11) (1987).

J. L. McClelland and D. E. Rumelhart, eds., *Parallel Distributed Processing,* MIT Press, Cambridge, Mass., 1986.

H. Nakashima, K. Nishikawa, and T. Ooi, "The Folding Type of a Protein is Relevant to the Amino Acid Composition," *J. Biochem.* **99**(1), 153–1620 (1986).

N. Qian and T. J. Sejnowski, "Predicting the Secondary Structure of Globular Proteins Using Neural Network Models," *J. Mol. Biol.* **202** (1988).

F. Richards and C. Kundrot, "Identification of Structural Motifs from Protein Coordinate Data: Secondary Structure and First-Level Supersecondary Structure," *Proteins,* **3**, 71–84 (1988).

J. S. Richardson, "The Anatomy and Taxonomy of Protein Structure," *Adv. in Protein Chem.* **34**, 167–339 (1981).

M. J. Rooman and S. Wodak, "Identification of Predictive Sequence motifs limited by Protein Structure Data Base Size," *Nature (London)* **335**(1), 45–49 (Sept. 1988).

M. J. Rooman, J. Rodriguez, and S. Wodak, "Automatic Definition of Recurrent Local Structure Motifs in Proteins," *J. Mol. Biol.* **213**, 327–336 (1990).

G. E. Shulz and R. H. Schirmer, *Principles of Protein Structure,* Springer-Verlag, New York, 1979.

H. Sklenar, C. Etchebest, and R. Lavery, "Describing Protein Structure: A General Algorithm Yielding Complete Helicoidal Parameters and a Unique Overall Axis," *Proteins* **6**, 46–60 (1989).

J. Skolnick and A. Kolinski, "Simulations of the Folding of A Globular Protein," *Science* **250**, 1121–1125 (1990).

C. Stanfill and D. Waltz, "Toward Memory-based Reasoning," *CACM* **29**(12) (1986).

M. J. E. Sternberg, "Prediction of Protein Structure from Amino Acid Sequence," *Anti-Cancer Drug Design* **1**, 169–178 (1986).

L. Stryer, *Biochemistry,* 3rd ed., W. H. Freeman and Co., New York, 1988.

W. R. Taylor and J. M. Thornton, "Recognition of Super-Secondary Structure in Proteins," *J. Mol. Biol.* **173** (1984).

R. Unger, D. Harel, S. Wherland, and J. L. Sussman, "A 3D Building Blocks Approach to Analyzing and Predicting Structure of Proteins," *Proteins* **5**, 355–373 (1989).

C. Wison and S. Doniach, "A Computer Model to Dynamically Simulate Protein Folding: Studies with Crambin," *PROTEINS: Structure, Function, and Genetics* **6**, 193–209 (1989).

X. Zhang and D. Waltz, "Developing Hierarchical Representations for Protein Structures: An Incremental Approach," *AAAI Symposium on Artificial Intelligence and Molecular Biology,* March 1989.

X. Zhang, D. Waltz, and J. Mesirov, "Determinant Factors in Protein Secondary Structure Prediction," 1990.

XIRU ZHANG
Thinking Machines Corp.

PROTOS

Protos is an automated knowledge acquisition system that embodies a unified approach to concept representation, classification, and learning. Because of the variability inherent in instances of real-world concepts, Protos employs a case-based knowledge representation, augmented with general domain knowledge. When a new case is presented, Protos attempts to assign a classification by locating a similar case in its memory and to provide an explanation of how the case's features determine its classification. If the classification is incorrect or the explanation is inadequate, the case is retained, and additional knowledge is gleaned from interaction with a human teacher. Protos was developed by Ray Bareiss and Bruce Porter in 1987 [see R. Bareiss, *Exemplar-Based Knowledge Acquisition,* Academic Press, San Diego, Calif., 1989 and B. Porter, R. Bareiss, and R. Holte, "Concept Learning and Heuristic Classification in Weak-Theory Domains," *Artif. Intell.* **45**(1–2), 229–263 (1990)].

RAY BAREISS
Northwestern University

PTTP

PTTP is an extension of PROLOG that is a complete theorem prover for the full first-order predicate calculus. It augments PROLOG with sound unification, depth-first iterative deepening search, and the ancestor-resolution rule of the model-elimination theorem-proving procedure. PTTP has a high inference rate because its input can be compiled in the same manner as PROLOG clauses [see M. E. Stickel, "A PROLOG Technology Theorem Prover: Implementation by an Extended PROLOG Compiler," *Journal of Automated Reasoning* **4**, 353–380 (1988)].

MARK E. STICKEL
SRI International

R1. See XCON.

RANGE DATA ANALYSIS

The purpose of analyzing range data is to extract pertinent features that will yield an interpretation of the environment being sensed. The information garnered should be sufficient to describe what is being seen and how sensed objects are related to each other in space. The concept of usefulness immediately casts the problem within the framework of task performance (a system to recognize and understand paint defects on an automobile may not be able to solve the problem of the orbital docking of spacecraft). When one uses ranging systems, the prevailing task is to obtain the description of a scene in three-dimensional space.

Range data analysis ultimately involves the determination of subsets of the data which are accounted for by certain features. This is generally known as the *segmentation problem* in computer vision literature. Here, we use the term feature loosely to include such entities as edges, three-dimensional surface descriptors like polynomial and curvature patches, and constructed geometric forms like cylinders and spheres. The recognition of objects in a scene, which we shall not address in this article, usually involves reasoning with the juxtaposition of these feature primitives. We shall restrict ourselves to the extraction of feature primitives from range data.

SOURCES OF RANGE DATA

Three-dimensional range data is obtained in two ways. The first is from explicit range encoding sensors which produce *three-dimensional points* (x, y, z) in a known reference coordinate system with the possible inclusion of the point properties, such as local surface reflectance, surface roughness, point velocity, vibration, polarization, temperature, X-ray attenuation, or magnetic properties. The second infers range information from imaging constraints and depth cues in intensity images.

A wide variety of physical principles have been used in three-dimensional sensing, including radar and sonar (range from time, phase, or beat frequency); triangulation (range from disparity angles and baseline); structured light (range from light triangulation of pattern projection); lens focusing (range from blur); moire methods (range from grating phase modulation); holographic inferometry (range from optical phase modulation); fresnel diffraction (range from local contrast); tactile and proximity sensing (position information from touch); computerized tomography (structure from x-ray or ultrasound attenuation); positron and single-photon emission computerized tomography; and nuclear magnetic resonance imaging (structure from magnetic dipoles). The first seven are discussed in detail in (Besl, 1988b). Tactile sensors were surveyed by Harmon (1982). The last three, used primarily in medical applications, have been described in Bates and co-workers (1983) CT; Roth and co-workers (1983) X-ray CT; Greenleaf (1983) Ultrasound CT; Knoll (1983) SPECT; Rogers and co-workers (1987) PET; and Hinshaw and Lent (1983) MRI.

Explicit range sensors usually produce dense image arrays, each pixel of which is a measurement of the distance of the corresponding surface point in three-dimensional space to the sensor's coordinate system. Most sensors do not produce Cartesian coordinates directly. For example, many range imaging sensors output distance measurements that indicate range along 3–D direction vectors indexed by two integers (i, j), Such a range is said to be in raster, or r_{ij}, form. Given an ideal orthographic range image where r_{ij} is the pixel value at the i-th row and the j-th column of the image, the 3–D coordinates (x_i, y_j, z_{ij}) in the sensor's coordinate frame would be given as

$$x_i = a_x + s_x i$$
$$y_j = a_y + s_y j$$
$$z_{ij} = a_z + s_z r_{ij} \quad (1)$$

where the s_x, s_y, s_z values are scale factors and the a_x, a_y, a_z values are coordinate offsets. One often also encounters a spherical coordinate system, shown in Figure 1, where the (i, j) indices correspond to elevation (latitude) angles and azimuth (longitude) angles respectively. The spherical to Cartesian transformation is the following:

$$x_{ij} = a_x + s_r r_{ij} \cos(i s_\phi) \sin(j s_\theta)$$
$$y_{ij} = a_y + s_r r_{ij} \sin(i s_\phi)$$
$$z_{ij} = a_z + s_r r_{ij} \cos(i s_\phi) \cos(j s_\theta) \quad (2)$$

where the s_r, s_ϕ, s_θ values are the scale factors in range, elevation, and azimuth and the a_x, a_y, a_z values are again offsets.

Most range image analysis algorithms must include provisions for such transformations to be performed on raw sensor data at some point to yield the (x, y, z) coordinates used by most applications. The exact stage of signal processing where one should introduce the transformation, if needed, depends on the application and the sensor and is often not easy to determine. Performing the transformation too early may unnecessarily complicate certain types of processing for some applications wheres other applications, such as a vehicle that is rolling and pitching significantly during range image acquisition, require immediate transformation to Cartesian form with inertial guidance information in order to make sense out of the data.

Range image analysis algorithms should include provisions for handling various types of noise models that will depend in general on the sensor and the application. Ideally, algorithms could be structured so that an application's sensor could be queried for a standardized description of its geometric and noise properties before geometric

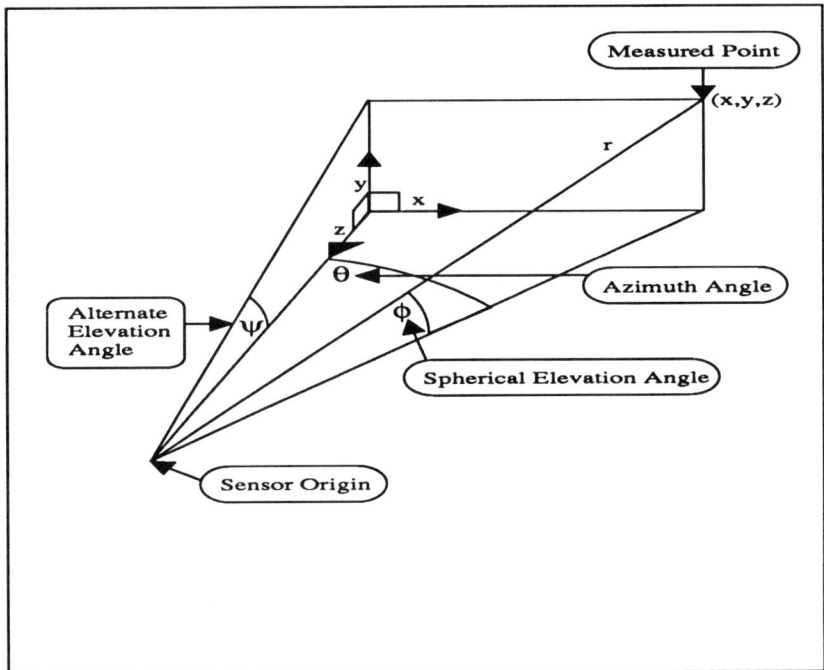

Figure 1. Cartesian, spherical, and orthogonal-axis coordinates.

signals are processed so that appropriate operations could be performed automatically given the idiosyncrasies of a given sensor.

The other methods of obtaining range data extract distance information from image data, which does not explicitly contain range information. Each pixel of these images contains information (eg, intensity) about the corresponding point in three-dimensional space. Since information about the three-dimensional configuration of the scene is extracted by the application of certain cues, such techniques are called *shape-from-x* techniques (where x is the cue applied). Examples of these techniques are: shape from shading (Enab and Luh, 1988; Ikeuchi and Horn, 1981; Pentland, 1988); shape from texture (Aloimonos, 1988; Kender, 1981; Witkin, 1981); shape from binocular stereo (Baker and Binford, 1981; Barnard, 1986; Bolles and co-workers, 1987; Marr and Poggio, 1976); and shape from contour (Barrow and Tenenbaum, 1981; Brady and Yuille, 1983; 1984; Horaud and Brady, 1987; Kanode, 1981). Extensive discussions on these techniques can be found in Aloimonas (1988) and Besl and Jain (1985).

It is not our purpose here to survey in detail the various techniques for generating range or depth data. We do need, however, to have a cursory understanding of such data before we can proceed to determine the processes necessary for their analysis. With the availability of range information from the data, one may easily be lulled into believing that the bulk of the problem in three-dimensional image understanding is solved. We do, after all, have information about where everything is. This is far from the truth. The only information explicitly available in the data is how far particular opaque surface points are from the sensor's coordinate system. There are no organized shape structures in the data. For this reason, *shape-from-x* is usually a misnomer. What these techniques provide are either depth points (typically sparse) or estimates of local surface normals at, or intrinsic to, each point in the image. One often thinks of shape as such extrinsic descriptors as circular arcs, straight lines, etc in two-dimensions, and cylinders, spheres, planes, etc in three-dimensions. At best, *shape-from-x* techniques generate data equivalent to that available from explicit range sensors. To emphasize this lack of structure in range imagery, Barrow and Tenenbaum (1981) called such data *intrinsic images*.

What is lacking in general is an organizational structure other than pixel (point) adjacency. (For some range sensors, even point adjacency information is totally lacking and must be computed.) Most higher-level application-specific algorithms require range information to be framed into subgroupings of meaningful units, or features.

RANGE DATA NOISE MODELING

Sensor noise may be caused by several different phenomena depending on the type of sensor and the type of scene geometry being sensed. Nonetheless, noise in geometric signals may be broken down into different contributions: randomly uncorrelated normally distributed sensor noise $\vec{n}_n$; quantization noise $\vec{n}_q$; systematic noise introduced by sensor imperfections $\vec{n}_s$, and other types of random non-normal noise $\vec{n}_r$ that might be analyzable. Even if most of the geometric sensor data can be explained by the above types of noise, it is common to have small amounts of the geometric data be completely corrupted. We use the term "outlier noise" $\vec{n}_o$ to represent any noise sources that have a large effect on a small percentage of the data. In range imaging for example, specular reflections, multiple reflections, steep relative surface angles, depth discontinuities, and other effects can produce wrong measurements not explainable by simple probabilistic models.

Given the above observations, the additive noise contribution at the i, j-th pixel in a range image may be decomposed into the following form:

$$\vec{n}(i,j) = \vec{n}_n(i,j) + \vec{n}_q(i,j) + \vec{n}_s(i,j) + \vec{n}_r(i,j) + \vec{n}_o(i,j). \tag{3}$$

The choices for handling this model are the following: (1) pretend that the other terms besides the normally distributed noise do not exist, (2) try to analyze the noise process as thoroughly as possible using probabilistic techniques, or (3) use methods that are insensitive to the exact form of the noise probability distributions. The first option is the usual approach and it works surprisingly well in many cases. However, for accurate geometry extraction, there are definite problems that arise. The second option usually gets bogged down in either analysis or computation at some point. The third option involves the application of a branch of statistics known as *robust statistics*. Robust statisticians have developed methods that are *distributionally robust* in the sense that they are fairly insensitive to the actual probabilistic nature of the noise. There is a huge body of useful literature that has remained untapped by computer vision researchers until recently. The methods are usually computationally intensive and beyond our given scope, but by judicious application to portions of the data where it is needed, practical techniques for real applications may be feasible. See Besl and co-workers (1989) for an example of robust surface fitting.

REPRESENTATIONS OF RANGE DATA

One may conceive of the analysis of range images as the extraction of certain features from the data. The features extracted are obviously dependent upon the type of analysis to be performed. Pertinent to the analysis of range images, though, is that visible smooth surfaces and edges (discontinuities in range) are the most natural representation and immediately computable since these are the entities "seen" in the data. The bulk of our treatment will center on visible surfaces since there are more data points on these as opposed to edges. Indeed, distance estimation errors are greater at points of discontinuity in many range sensing techniques owing to local averaging and high spatial frequency effects within the sensor. Therefore, we focus our attention on surfaces.

What is a surface? A reasonable first approximation may be that a surface is a smooth three-dimensional manifold where smoothness is defined as the lack of discontinuities in the normals to the surface. This, is however, not always the case. The hood of an automobile is often considered a single surface although there may be an ornamental ridge-like protrusion down the middle of the hood. Two planes melding at an obtuse angle via a smooth fillet surface may not possess any abrupt surface discontinuities, but we have just said that they are two planar surfaces. A more general definition has to take into account the kind of surface one expects to find. This being said, smooth surfaces as defined in our first approximation above are of great interest in range image analysis.

Surface description schemes may be divided into two classes. The first class represents the absolute-three dimensional location of the surface in space and the second details how the surface bends in space. The task of describing the location of a surface in three-dimensional space is essentially that of fitting one or more surface functions to the range data by applying either linear or non-linear regression techniques. These surfaces may be bivariate polynomials (planes being the most prominent class), splines, quadrics, finite element grids, etc. The second class of surface description involves the computation of differential geometry based surface curvatures. Curvature-based representations have many attractive qualities such as rotational and translational invariance.

Surface Representations

In this section, we describe several representations which permit a pointwise evaluation of the surface.

Algebraic Surfaces. An algebraic polynomial surface of degree m (an integer) is defined implicitly by the polynomial

$$g(x, y, z) = \sum_{i+j+k \leq m} a_{ijk} x^i y^j z^k = 0 \tag{4}$$

where i, j, k are non-negative. Quadrics are general second degree algebraic surfaces, which include spheres, ellipsoids, elliptic paraboloids, hyperbolic paraboloids, hyperboloids of one sheet, hyperboloids of two sheets, cones, cylinders (elliptic, parabolic, and hyperbolic), and planes depending on the coefficients. Approximating range data with quadrics can be done using the three different methods in (Hall and co-workers, 1982; Fan and co-workers, 1989; Taubin, 1988). The ten coefficients of a quadric can be then used to form a symmetric 4×4 matrix and various surface shapes can be recognized by the matrix invariants (Hall and co-workers, 1982). Quadrics do allow rational polynomial parameterizations. Sederberg (1987, 1986) has studied cubic piecewise algebraic surfaces. One should probably use Taubin's method (1988) for any cubic or higher order algebraic approximations.

Supertori and Superellipsoids. The implicit form of a supertorus of degree l, m centered at the origin is given by (Barr, 1981):

$$g(x, y, z) = \left| \left(\frac{|x|^m}{a^m} + \frac{|y|^m}{b^m} \right)^{1/m} - d \right|^l + \frac{|z|^l}{c^l} - 1 = 0. \tag{5}$$

The parametric form of the supertorus is given by

$$x(u, v) = a(d + \cos^p(u)) \cos^q(v) \tag{6}$$
$$y(u, v) = b(d + \cos^p(u)) \sin^q(v) \tag{7}$$
$$z(u, v) = c \sin^p(u) \tag{8}$$

where $p = 2/l$ and $q = 2/m$, not necessarily integers. A supertorus is the generalization of the torus, a special case where $l = m = 2$. The class of superellipsoids is the special case where $d = 0$. The torus and the sphere are special cases of cyclides (Knapman, 1987), a class of surfaces whose lines of curvature are circular arcs. Supertori, superellipsoids, and superhyperbola (known collectively as superquadrics) possess interesting duality relationships (eg $\vec{n} \cdot \vec{x} = 1$) between the center point to surface point vector $\vec{x}$ and a *non-unit-length normal vector* at the surface point $\vec{n}$ as discussed in (Barr, 1981; Pentland, 1986). Two example superellipsoid shapes are shown in Figure 2. For an example of recovering and matching bent and tapered superquadrics, see Bajcsy and Solina (1987).

Parametric Polynomial and Spline Surfaces. In the power basis form, a parametric polynomial surface of degree m is given by

$$\vec{x}(u, v) = \sum_{i,j=0}^{m} \vec{a}_{ij} u^i v^j \qquad \vec{a}_{ij} \in \mathcal{R}^3 \qquad (9)$$

After a change of basis to Bernstein polynomials, the *Bezier surface patch* form is

$$\vec{x}(u, v) = \sum_{i,j=0}^{m} \vec{p}_{ij} b_{ij}^m(u, v) \qquad \vec{p}_{ij} \in \mathcal{R}^3 \qquad (10)$$

where $b_{ij}^m(u, v) = b_i^m(u) b_j^m(v)$ (a separable tensor-product form), where the Bernstein polynomials are given by

$$b_i^m(t) = \frac{m!}{i!(m-i)!} t^i (1 - t)^{m-i}, \qquad (11)$$

and where the control points are given by a transformation of the form $P = MAM^T$ where P is the matrix of control points $\{\vec{p}_{ij}\}$, A is the matrix of vector coefficients $\{\vec{a}_{ij}\}$, and the coefficients in M depend only on m and are derivable from the Bernstein polynomial definition above. Bezier surface patches (and polynomial surfaces) are efficiently derived from range data via regular tensor-product approximation techniques:

$$P = (V^T W_V V)^{-1} V^T W_V X W_U U (U^T W_U U)^{-1} \qquad (12)$$

where P is the $(m + 1) \times (m + 1)$ matrix of control points, X is a rectangular matrix of data points, $U_{ki} = b_i^m(u_k)$ and $V_{lj} = b_j^m(v_l)$, and W_U and W_V are diagonal weight matrices containing the separable weight vectors for the u and v directions. Tensor-product methods do not require exactly equally spaced points (in the u-v parameter domain), but the sampling in the u-direction must be consistent for all v and vice versa. Individual parametric surface patches can be compared and matched in a stable manner using the Bezier control points as a feature vector and using 3-D point set matching, but this does not help most applications because one seldom obtains the exact same rectangular region from image segmentation algorithms. Use of vector polynomial coefficients for comparing shapes is strongly discouraged for almost all purposes.

A tensor-product piece-wise polynomial (spline) surface $\vec{x}(u, v)$ of order (m, n) (degree $(m - 1, n - 1)$) is defined over a rectangle $[u_{m-1}, u_{K_v-m}] \times [v_{n-1}, v_{K_v-n}]$ partitioned by (non-decreasing sequence) knot vectors $T_u = [t_0, t_1, \ldots, t_{K_u}]$ and T_v. A total of $N_u N_v$ control points are used where $K_u = N_u + m$ and $K_v = N_v + n$ if no interior knots are duplicated. The spline surface is a linear combination of control points weighted by separable bivariate tensor-product B-splines $B_{i,j}^{m,n}(u, v; T_u, T_v) = B_i^m(u; T_u) B_j^n(v; T_v)$:

$$\vec{x}(u, v) = \sum_{i=0}^{N_u-1} \sum_{j=0}^{N_v-1} \vec{p}_{ij} B_{i,j}^{m,n}(u, v; T_u, T_v) \qquad (13)$$

where the ith univariate B-spline of order m for N_u control points may be defined recursively as

$$B_i^m(u; T_u) = \frac{u - t_i}{u_{i+m-1} - t_i} B_i^{m-1}(u; T)$$

$$+ \frac{u - t_{i+m}}{t_{i+1} - t_{i+m}} B_{i+1}^{m-1}(u; T) \qquad (14)$$

$$B_i^1(u; T) = \begin{cases} 1 & \text{if } t_i \leq u < t_{i+1} \\ 0 & \text{otherwise.} \end{cases} \qquad (15)$$

where $0/0 = 0$ by convention. Tensor-product splines (piecewise-polynomial) may be approximated using the same weighted least-squares tensor-product formalism above. If the data matrix X as defined above is very noisy

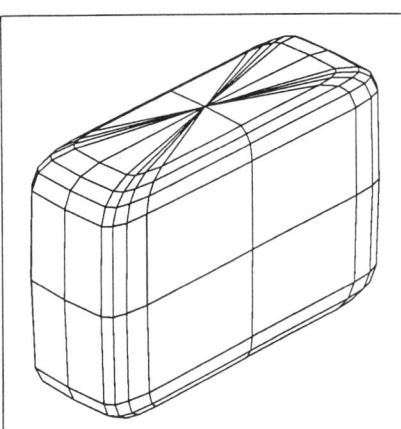
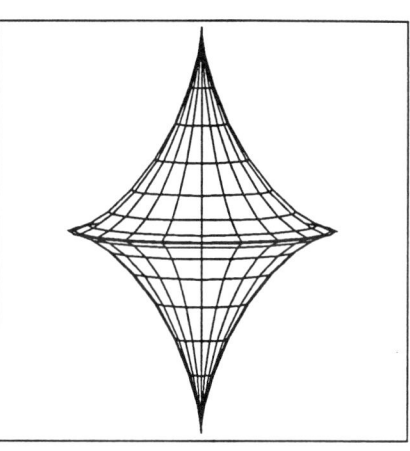

Figure 2. Two superellipsoids (1, m = 8), (m = 2, 1 = .6).

or if a step edge or crease edge is present in the data, the reader should be aware that the resulting least-squares spline approximation will contain significant undesirable oscillations. Such oscillations can be controlled with a variety of techniques, including tensioning, smoothing, ripping, and convexity preservation. However, almost every other method besides the simple tensor-product least squares involves orders of magnitude more computation and memory. For example, a 1000×1000 data grid can be approximated with a 100×100 control point grid essentially for the cost of two 100×100 matrix inversions and some 100×100 matrix multiplications. Most other methods that can provide better results require $10,000 \times 10,000$ matrix manipulations. Inoue (1986) has an interesting variation of smoothing splines based on B-spline basis functions which uses a successive over-relaxation (SOR) multi-resolution technique.

Rational Polynomial and Spline Surfaces. A rational 3–D Bezier (polynomial) surface patch of degree m is represented in 4–D homogeneous coordinates as

$$\vec{x}^r(u, v) = \sum_{i,j=0}^{m} w_{ij} \vec{p}_{ij}^r b_{ij}^m(u, v)$$

$$\vec{p}_{ij}^r = [\vec{p}_{ij} \ 1] \in \Re^4 \qquad (16)$$

where $0 < w_{ij} \leq 1$ are scalar weights, where the $\vec{p}_{ij}$s are the usual 3–D control points, and where it is implied that the first three evaluated components of the homogeneous vector should each be divided by the fourth component to yield three dimensional coordinates. The important unifying advantage of rational polynomial surfaces is that common quadric surfaces can be represented exactly as degree-2 rational polynomials. Unfortunately, there are no inexpensive (eg, linear least squares) computational methods for approximating discrete data with these rational functions since rational polynomials do not form a linear space. Therefore, this mathematical form is of less utility for extracting feature shapes from range data since the algebraic form allows the use of linear methods.

Rational B-splines (often called NURBs for Non-Uniform [knot vector] Rational B-splines) are represented as

$$\vec{x}^r(u, v) = \sum_{i=0}^{N_u-1} \sum_{j=0}^{N_v-1} w_{ij} \vec{p}_{ij}^r B_{i,j}^{m,n}(u, v; T_u, T_v) \qquad (17)$$

using the same notation as above. NURBs have been an IGES standard for industrial CAD systems since 1983 (IGES). A trimmed NURB is a surface whose boundary curves have been modified using planar curve(s) to define closed region(s) and hole(s) in the parameter domain of an untrimmed NURB. Trimmed NURBs are very general, but complex mathematical entities, and can be used to exactly represent (1) all polyhedral shapes, (2) all quadrics, and (3) all piecewise-polynomial (spline) free-form surfaces as well as other (rationally parameterized) shapes that do not fall into these three categories. This allows very general purpose algorithms to be written to handle an extremely general class of 3–D object shapes.

The tradeoff is mathematical and computational complexity and certain difficulties that may be encountered in modeling some physical objects. Fortunately, most 3–D graphic workstation vendors now supply software and/or hardware to perform the tedious chore of displaying these surfaces.

Surface Smoothing Splines. The B-spline formalism does not generalize well to non-tensor product multivariate splines and is not well suited to interpolating irregularly spaced data. If arbitrarily space data points are given, the preferred method outside the computer vision field is to use triangular domain surface patches on a Delaunay surface triangulation of the points. Multivariate smoothing splines also allow surfaces to be defined over arbitrarily spaced points and they generalize the properties of univariate "thin rod" cubic smoothing splines, which can be analyzed in the context of B-splines (De Boor, 1978). Smoothing splines are often called "thin plate" splines because they can approximately model a thin plate that bends under the influence of springs with spring constants β_i attached to "control" points (x_i, y_i, z_i). The thin-plate assumes a shape that minimizes the sum of its bending energy and the potential energy in the springs.

$$\varepsilon(f) = \lambda \int_\Omega Q(f) dx dy + \sum_{i=1}^{N} \beta_i (z_i - f(x_i, y_i))^2 \qquad (18)$$

where $Q(f) = f_{xx}^2 + 2f_{xy}^2 + f_{yy}^2$ is the smoothness or "bending energy" measure. The term λ is an adjustable parameter that weights the relative importance of surface smoothness and the closeness to the data.

The C^2 smoothing spline $z = g(x, y)$ for N arbitrarily spaced points is computed in terms of $N + 3$ coefficients $\vec{a} = \{a_i\}$ and basis functions ϕ_i:

$$z = g(x, y) = \sum_{i=-2}^{N} a_i \phi_i(x, y). \qquad (19)$$

The radial basis functions for positive indices i are $\phi_i(x, y) = r_i^2(x, y) \log(r_i^2(x, y))$ where $r_i^2(x, y) = (x - x_i)^2 + (y - y_i)^2$. The three other basis functions are $\phi_0(x, y) = 1$, $\phi_{-1}(x, y) = x$, and $\phi_{-2}(x, y) = y$. For a chosen value of the smoothing parameter λ, the following set of linear equations must be solved:

$$(\Phi_p + N\lambda \mathbf{I}_N)\vec{a}_p + \Phi_n \vec{a}_n = \vec{z}_p \qquad \vec{z}_p \in \Re^N \qquad (20)$$

$$\Phi_n^T \vec{a}_p = (0, 0, 0)$$

where $\vec{a}_p = \{a_i\}$ $(i > 0)$ and $\vec{a}_n$ are the remaining three coefficients. Φ_p is the symmetric $N \times N$ matrix of all $\phi_i(x_j, y_j)$ $(i, j > 0)$ and Φ_n is the $3 \times N$ matrix of all $\phi_i(x_j, y_j)$ with $i \leq 0$ $(j > 0)$. This set of $N + 3$ equations in $N + 3$ unknowns may be written as a single matrix equation: $\Phi \vec{a} = \vec{z}$. When $\lambda \to \infty$, $\vec{a}_p \to \vec{0}$ and the smoothing spline surface becomes the best fit plane to the (x, y, z) data. When $\lambda = 0$, the smoothing spline surface is a purely interpolating surface. For more on visual surface reconstruction using smoothing splines, see (Terzopoulos, 1983, 1986;

Grimson, 1982; Kerder and co-workers, 1985; Blake and Zisserman, 1985; Craven and Wahba, 1979; Wendelberger, 1982).

Smoothing splines have not received much attention in the computer aided geometric design literature because of the following problems: (a) the surface is defined globally so a change in a single point causes the entire surface definition to change even though most of the surface changes are primarily local, (b) if a surface approximating N data points is needed, the surface evaluation procedure requires $N + 3$ coefficients in addition to the N data points and requires the computation of N logarithms, and (c) one cannot easily reduce smoothness requirements by duplicating knot values as in tensor-product B-splines.

The 2-D smoothing spline is one type of surface interpolation method based on radial basis functions. Hardy multiquadrics $\psi(r) = \sqrt{r^2 + d^2}$ and shifted logarithm functions $\psi(r) = \log(r^2 + d^2)$ have been compared to smoothing splines by Dyn and co-workers (1986).

Range data analysis generally requires more in the way of approximation than interpolation, and smoothing splines have therefore received less attention in dense range data analysis than in the sparse range data literature (binocular stereo, etc).

Boolean Sum of Curves. Gordon surfaces (1971) interpolate a network of compatible, intersecting control curves. Given a U family of $N_u + 1$ curves $\vec{x}_i(u)$ where $u \in [0, 1]$, and a V family of $N_v + 1$ curves $\vec{y}_j(v)$ where $v \in [0, 1]$ that intersect at a set of points $\{(u_j, v_i)\}$ (denoted $\vec{z}_{ij} = \vec{x}_i(u_j) = \vec{y}_j(v_i)$), then the Gordon surface $\vec{z}(u, v)$ that interpolates the U and V curve network is given by

$$\vec{z}(u, v) = \sum_{i=0}^{N_u} \vec{x}_i(u)\psi_i(v) + \sum_{j=0}^{N_v} \vec{y}_j(v)\phi_j(u)$$
$$- \sum_{i=0}^{N_u}\sum_{j=0}^{N_v} \psi_i(v)z_{ij}\phi_j(u). \qquad (21)$$

where $\psi_i(v)$ and $\phi_j(u)$ are any two sets of basis functions such that $\psi_i(v_k) = \delta_{ik}$ and $\phi_j(u_k) = \delta_{jk}$ where δ_{ij} is the Kronecker delta (1 when subscripts are equal and 0 otherwise). If $N_u = 1$ and $N_v = 1$, the Gordon surface reduces to the better known Coon's surface patch, which defines a surface that interpolates four compatible boundary curves. This is a *boolean sum* method because the surface defined by the U and V curve families is the sum of the surfaces defined by each family alone minus the surface defined by their intersection points, which can be denoted as

$$S(U \cup V) = S(U) + S(V) - S(U \cap V). \qquad (22)$$

Boolean sum surfaces are quite different than other surface representations in that the mathematical form of the individual curves or basis functions is not really involved and can be varied from application to application. For example, the Gordon mechanism can be used to reduce the total number of control points that need to be stored in order to represent certain shapes. Consider a quadrilat-

Table 1. Parameter Requirements for Some Common Surface Types

Geometric Surface Entity	Parameters
Plane	4
Sphere	4
Ellipsoid	9
General Quadric	10
Superellipsoid	11
Supertorus	12
Cubic Algebraic Surface	22
Quartic Algebraic Surface	37
Tensor-Product Parameteric Quadratic	27
Tensor-Product Parametric Cubic	48
Tensor-Product Parametric Quartic	75
Degree-m Tensor-Product Parametric	$3(m + 1)^2$
B-Spline (Order-m,MxN-pts,Uniform)	3MN
B-Spline (Order-m,MxN-pts,K-knots)	3MN + K

eral shape where three of the four boundary curves are straight lines representable by four points while the fourth boundary curve could be arbitrarily complicated with N (eg, 100s) of control points. A NURBs representation of the same shape would require double the control points.

Range data analysis is also not likely to make use of this mathematical form for low-level image processing and feature extraction although there is potential for basic data reduction while preserving shape.

Parameter Requirement Comparison. Table 1 summarizes the number of parameters needed to describe several common algebraic surfaces. The simpler mathematical forms have received the greatest attention in the computer vision literature since such shapes are easier to deal with. It is still not clear how machine perception systems will be able to use the more expressive, more general shape representations to provide more intelligent automated functions based on range data input, but it is likely that systems will be moving in that direction.

Curvature-Based Surface Description

There are two basic mathematical entities that are considered in the differential geometry of smooth surfaces. In the classical mathematics of partial derivatives, they are known as the first and second fundamental forms of a surface. Modern mathematics uses differential forms and favors an equivalent formulation of these quantities in terms of the metric tensor and the Weingarten mapping (or "shape operator" (O'Neill, 1966)). Complete knowledge of either of these forms at every surface point uniquely characterizes and quantifies general smooth surface shape so it is natural to investigate this method of describing shape when processing range data.

It is generally recognized that it is very difficult to compute differential quantities accurately from raw noisy range data. For example, the 3×3 and 5×5 operators often used in intensity (video) image processing for smoothing or edge detection are virtually useless when trying to compute second order properties such as surface curvature in the presence of noise or surface texture. One may use large window operators (bigger than 11×11), which tends to disturb shapes near transition regions and virtually eliminates any fine details, or one may perform various type of iterative relaxation methods as in Sander (1988).

An alternative to pixel level processing is to somehow extract larger primitives first and then compute curvature properties from the intermediate primitives if they are a faithful representation of the raw data. One should be very careful when approximating raw range data with any type of curved surface because most commonly used surface approximation methods (linear least squares) are only trying to approximate the zeroth-order behavior (ie, the position) of most of the data points. Explicit constraints for raw-data surface-normal preservation and perhaps even raw-data surface-curvature preservation may be necessary in order to insure that the extracted primitives are useful to a given application.

It is also important to note that meaningful curvature values are "exponentially" more difficult to compute in very noisy range data as compared to high quality range data. Whereas it is possible today to get 6–bit to 8–bit accurate range data at rates up to 10 million points per second (480×512 at video rates!), it is also possible to get 0.1 mm (0.004 inches) accuracy data at rates of 10,000 points per second from commercial sources. Processing high-quality 10–bit range data is radically different in many ways than processing the type of data (4–bit to 6–bit consistency) found in the earlier days of range data analysis.

Definitions. The first fundamental form I of a parametric surface $\vec{x}(u, v)$ evaluated at the point (u, v) in the direction (u_s, v_s) is given by

$$I(u, v, u_s, v_s) = \vec{x}_s \cdot \vec{x}_s \quad (23)$$

$$= (\vec{x}_u u_s + \vec{x}_v v_s) \cdot (\vec{x}_u u_s + \vec{x}_v v_s) \quad (24)$$

$$= \vec{x}_u \cdot \vec{x}_u u_s^2 + 2\vec{x}_u \cdot \vec{x}_v u_s v_s + \vec{x}_v \cdot \vec{x}_v v_s^2$$

$$= E u_s^2 + 2F u_s v_s + G v_s^2$$

$$= [u_s \ v_s] \begin{bmatrix} g_{11} & g_{12} \\ g_{21} & g_{22} \end{bmatrix} \begin{bmatrix} u_s \\ v_s \end{bmatrix}$$

$$= \vec{u}_s^T [\mathbf{g}] \vec{u}_s$$

where $\vec{u}_s = (u_s, v_s)$, where the [**g**] matrix elements are defined as

$$g_{11} = E = \vec{x}_u \cdot \vec{x}_u$$
$$g_{22} = G = \vec{x}_v \cdot \vec{x}_v$$
$$g_{12} = g_{21} = F = \vec{x}_u \cdot \vec{x}_v, \quad (25)$$

and where the subscripts denote the partial derivatives $\vec{x}_u(u, v) = \partial \vec{x}/\partial u$; $\vec{x}_v(u, v) = \partial \vec{x}/\partial v$. The vectors $\vec{x}_u$ and $\vec{x}_v$ are the *u-tangent vector* and the *v-tangent vector* functions respectively, and they may or may not be orthogonal to each other. These two tangent vectors are said to lie in and form a basis for the tangent plane $T(u, v)$ (or tangent space) of the surface at the point $\vec{x}(u, v)$: $T(u, v) = \{\vec{x} \in \mathcal{R}^3 : \vec{x} = a\vec{x}_u(u, v) + b\vec{x}_v(u, v), (a, b) \in \mathcal{R}^2\}$. The [**g**] matrix is known as the first fundamental form matrix or the metric tensor of the surface. Since the vector dot product is commutative, this [**g**] matrix is symmetric and has only three independent components. The E,F,G notation of Gauss is used along with the matrix element subscript notation because both are useful in different circumstances, and both have occurred often in the differential geometry literature.

The first fundamental form I measures the small amount of movement $\|\vec{x}_s\|^2$ on the surface at a point (u, v) for a given small movement ds in the parameter plane direction (u_s, v_s). This form is invariant to surface parameterization changes and to translations and rotations of the surface. I is an intrinsic property of a surface in that it depends only on the surface itself, and now on how the surface is embedded in 3–D space. In fact, the functions E,F,G determine all intrinsic properties of a surface.

In contrast, the second fundamental form of a surface is dependent on the embedding of the surface in 3–D space and is therefore known as an extrinsic property of the surface. The second fundamental form II is given by

$$II(u, v, u_s, v_s) = \vec{x}_{ss} \cdot \vec{n} \quad (26)$$

$$= (\vec{x}_{uu} u_s^2 + 2\vec{x}_{uv} u_s v_s + \vec{x}_{vv} v_s s) \cdot \vec{n}$$

$$= L u_s^2 + 2M u_s v_s + N v_s^2$$

$$= [u_s \ v_s] \begin{bmatrix} b_{11} & b_{12} \\ b_{21} & b_{22} \end{bmatrix} \begin{bmatrix} u_s \\ v_s \end{bmatrix}$$

$$= \vec{u}_s^T [\mathbf{b}] \vec{u}_s \quad (27)$$

where the [**b**] matrix elements may be defined as

$$b_{11} = L = \vec{x}_{uu} \cdot \vec{n}$$
$$b_{22} = N = \vec{x}_{vv} \cdot \vec{n}$$
$$b_{12} = b_{21} = M = \vec{x}_{uv} \cdot \vec{n} \quad (28)$$

where $\vec{n}(u, v) = \vec{x}_u \times \vec{x}_v / \|\vec{x}_u \times \vec{x}_v\|$ is the *Unit Surface Normal Vector,* and where the double subscripts denote the second partial derivatives. The [**b**] matrix is the second fundamental form matrix and is also symmetric if the surface is well-behaved in the sense that the mixed partial derivatives $\vec{x}_{uv} = \vec{x}_{vu}$ are equal. The Gauss-like L,M,N notation is introduced again as above. The second fundamental form is also invariant to changes in the parameterization, orientation, or position of the surface.

Since $\vec{n}$ is defined to be orthogonal to both $\vec{x}_u$ and $\vec{x}_v$, we have

$$0 = (\vec{n} \cdot \vec{x}_s)_s = \vec{n}_s \cdot \vec{x}_s + \vec{n} \cdot \vec{x}_{ss} = 0 \quad (29)$$

which implies that

$$II(u, v, u_s, v_s) = -\vec{n}_s \cdot \vec{x}_s. \quad (30)$$

The second fundamental form therefore measures the negative correlation between the change in the normal vector $\vec{n}_s$ and the change in the surface position $\vec{x}_s$ at a surface point (u, v) as a function of a small movement ds in the direction (u_s, v_s) in the parameter space. Since $\vec{n} \cdot \vec{n} = 1$, $\vec{n}_s \cdot \vec{n} = 0$, the normal vector derivative $\vec{n}_s$ always lies in the tangent plane $T(u, v)$.

Mean and Gaussian Curvature. The shape operator (Weingarten mapping) matrix [S] is defined by the matrix product $[\mathbf{S}] = [\mathbf{g}^{-1}][\mathbf{b}]$. Hence, the [S] matrix combines the first and second fundamental form matrices into a single matrix.

$$[\mathbf{S}] = \begin{bmatrix} E & F \\ F & G \end{bmatrix}^{-1} \begin{bmatrix} L & M \\ M & N \end{bmatrix}$$

$$= \frac{1}{EG - F^2} \begin{bmatrix} GL - FM & GM - FN \\ EM - FL & EN - FM \end{bmatrix} \quad (31)$$

This matrix is a linear operator that maps vectors in the tangent plane to other vectors in the tangent plane at each point on a surface. The metric [g] is the generalization of the speed of a planar curve whereas the shape operator [S] is a generalization of the curvature of a planar curve. The concept of torsion is not relevant to surfaces since the dimension of the space orthogonal to the tangent space is only one just as it was in the case of planar curves. The *Gaussian curvature* function K of a surface can be defined from the first and second fundamental form matrices s the determinant of the shape operator matrix function as follows:

$$K = \det[\mathbf{S}] = \det\left(\begin{bmatrix} E & F \\ F & G \end{bmatrix}^{-1}\right) \det\left(\begin{bmatrix} L & M \\ M & N \end{bmatrix}\right)$$

$$= \frac{LN - M^2}{EG - F^2}. \quad (32)$$

The *mean curvature* function of a surface can be defined similarly as half the trace of the shape operator matrix function as follows:

$$H = \frac{1}{2}\text{tr}[\mathbf{S}] = \frac{1}{2}\text{tr}\left(\frac{1}{EG - F^2}\begin{bmatrix} GL - FM & GM - FN \\ EM - FL & EN - FM \end{bmatrix}\right)$$

$$= \frac{EN + GL - 2FM}{2(EG - F^2)}. \quad (33)$$

The surface curvature functions H and K are the two "natural" algebraic invariants of the 2×2 shape operator matrix (coefficients of the characteristic polynomial) and are independent of surface parameterization unlike the E,F,G,L,M,N functions themselves. In addition, Gaussian curvature uniquely determines the shape of convex surfaces (Minkowski, 1897; Chern, 1957; Horn, 1984), and the mean curvature uniquely determines the shape of graph surfaces under various auxiliary conditions (Gilbarg and Trudinger, 1983; Guisti, 1978; Besl, 1988). The eigenvalues of [S] are the *principal curvatures* and the eigenvectors are the *principal direction vectors*.

Normal and Principal Curvatures. There are other ways of looking at surface curvature based on curves that lie in the surface. If $\vec{x}(s)$ is a parameterization of a curve that lies in a parametric surface $\vec{x}(u, v)$, then we can write down the derivatives of $\vec{x}$ as a space curve and as a part of the surface:

$$\vec{x}_s(s) = \nu(s)\vec{t}(s)$$

$$\vec{x}_{ss}(s) = \nu_s(s)\vec{t}(s) + \kappa(s)\nu^2(s)\vec{n}(s)$$

$$\vec{x}_s(u(s), v(s)) = u_s\vec{x}_u + v_s\vec{x}_v$$

$$\vec{x}_{ss}(u(s), v(s)) = u_{ss}\vec{x}_u + v_{ss}\vec{x}_v + u_s^2\vec{x}_{uu}$$

$$+ 2u_s v_s \vec{x}_u \cdot \vec{x}_v + v_s^2 \vec{x}_{vv} \quad (34)$$

where ν is the speed along the curve, $\vec{t}$ is the curve tangent vector, and κ the scalar curvature of the curve. If the unit surface normal $\vec{n}(u(s), v(s))$ is aligned with the unit normal to the curve $\vec{n}(s)$, then taking the dot product of the expressions above with the surface/curve normal vector yields the *normal curvature* function

$$\kappa_n(u, v, u_s, v_s) = \frac{II(u, v, u_s, v_s)}{I(u, v, u_s, v_s)} \quad (35)$$

where the speed of the curve in the surface ν is specified by the first fundamental form: $\nu^2(u(s), v(s)) = \|\vec{x}_s(u(s), v(s))\|^2 = I(u, v, u_s, v_s)$. Rewriting this ratio using the quadratic form notation and $\vec{u} = (u, v)$ and $\vec{u}_s = (u_s, v_s)$, we get a *Rayleigh quotient form*:

$$\kappa_n(\vec{u}, \vec{u}_s) = \frac{\vec{u}_s^T[\mathbf{b}(\vec{u})]\vec{u}_s}{\vec{u}_s^T[\mathbf{g}(\vec{u})]\vec{u}_s} \quad (36)$$

The maximum and minimum normal curvature values at the point (u, v) must satisfy the condition $\partial \kappa_n / \partial \vec{u}_s = 0$. Applying the quotient derivative rule, we obtain

$$\partial \kappa_n / \partial \vec{u}_s = (\vec{u}_s^T[\mathbf{g}(\vec{u})]\vec{u}_s) \cdot 2[\mathbf{b}(\vec{u})]\vec{u}_s$$

$$- (\vec{u}_s^T[\mathbf{b}(\vec{u})]\vec{u}_s) \cdot 2[\mathbf{g}(\vec{u})]\vec{u}_s = 0 \quad (37)$$

which implies that

$$[\mathbf{b}(\vec{u})]\vec{u}_s = \kappa_n[\mathbf{g}(\vec{u})]\vec{u}_s. \quad (38)$$

Solving for the minimum and maximum values of κ_n is an example of solving the generalized eigenvalue problem $Ax = \lambda Bx$. Since $[\mathbf{g}(\vec{u})]$ is always nonsingular for any nondegenerate surface parameterization and since matrices commute with scalars, the problem easily converts into the standard eigenvalue problem:

$$[\mathbf{S}(\vec{u})]\vec{u}_s = \kappa_n \vec{u}_s. \quad (39)$$

Given $H = \mathbf{tr}(\mathbf{S})/2$ and $K = \det(\mathbf{S})$ as defined above, the problem is easily solved using simple quadratic formula algebra to obtain the eigenvalues, which are the maximum and minimum principal curvatures:

$$\kappa_1 = H + \sqrt{H^2 - K} \quad \text{(maximum principal curvature)} \quad (40)$$

$$\kappa_2 = H - \sqrt{H^2 - K} \quad \text{(minimum principal curvature)}. \quad (41)$$

The eigenvectors of [S] are the directions in the (u, v) parameter plane such that the normal curvature function achieves its maximum and minimum values. The *unnormalized* principal direction vectors $\vec{u}_1$ and $\vec{u}_2$ in the u–v plane for the corresponding principal curvatures κ_1 and κ_2 are given in a symmetric form by

$$\vec{u}_1 = \begin{bmatrix} u_1 \\ v_1 \end{bmatrix} = \begin{bmatrix} \kappa_1 + M(F + G) - N(F + E) \\ \kappa_1 + M(F + E) - L(F + G) \end{bmatrix} \quad (42)$$

$$\vec{u}_2 = \begin{bmatrix} u_2 \\ v_2 \end{bmatrix} = \begin{bmatrix} \kappa_2 + M(F + G) - N(F + E) \\ \kappa_2 + M(F + E) - L(F + G) \end{bmatrix}. \quad (43)$$

These directions are not in general orthogonal in the (u, v) parameter plane since the 2×2 Weingarten mapping matrix is not symmetric with respect to the surface parameterization. However, the Weingarten mapping itself is a symmetric linear operator on 3–D vectors in the 3–D tangent plane and the 3–D principal direction vectors of surface points are orthogonal in the tangent plane. This orthogonality property is seen directly by proving that $\vec{x}_1 \cdot \vec{x}_2 = 0$ where the *unnormalized* maximum and minimum principal direction vectors in 3–D space are given by

$$\vec{x}_1 = (u_1 \vec{x}_u + v_1 \vec{x}_v) \qquad \vec{x}_2 = (u_2 \vec{x}_u + v_2 \vec{x}_v). \quad (44)$$

The principal frame field of a surface is given by

$$(\vec{n}(u, v), \vec{e}_1(u, v), \vec{e}_2(u, v)) = \text{Principal Frame Field} \quad (45)$$

where $\vec{e}_i = \vec{x}_i / \|\vec{x}_i\|$ for $i = 1, 2$.

If $\vec{v} = \cos\theta \vec{e}_1 + \sin\theta \vec{e}_2$ is any unit direction vector in the tangent plane at a point, then the normal curvature $\kappa_n(\cdot)$ at (u, v) in the direction of $\vec{v}$ is a function of θ and the principal curvatures:

$$\kappa_n(u, v, \theta) = \kappa_1(u, v) \cos^2\theta + \kappa_2(u, v) \sin^2\theta \quad (46)$$

If principal curvatures are given, one can easily compute the Gaussian and mean curvature in terms of the principal curvatures:

$$K = \kappa_1 \kappa_2 \qquad H = \frac{(\kappa_1 + \kappa_2)}{2}. \quad (47)$$

The underlying relationship is that the principal curvatures κ_1 and κ_2 are the two roots of the quadratic equation:

$$\kappa^2 - 2H\kappa + K = 0. \quad (48)$$

If $H^2 = K$ or $\kappa_1 = \kappa_2$ at a surface point, the point is known as an *umbilic* point to denote that the principal curvatures are equal and every direction is a principal direction. In other terms, the normal curvature function κ_n at an umbilic point is a constant function independent of direction since $\cos^2\theta + \sin^2\theta = 1$. A surface must be either locally flat or spherical in the neighborhood of an umbilic point. Saddle shaped (hyperbolic) surface patches are necessarily free of umbilic points. In cases where noisy surface data is covered with umbilic points, they are not of much use for range data analysis. However, if larger, faithful surface primitives can be extracted, isolated umbilic points can be a useful feature for various applications.

	$\kappa_1 < 0$	$\kappa_1 = 0$	$\kappa_1 > 0$
$\kappa_2 < 0$	peak	ridge	saddle
$\kappa_2 = 0$	ridge	flat	valley
$\kappa_2 > 0$	saddle	valley	pit

(a)

	$K < 0$	$K = 0$	$K > 0$
$H < 0$	peak	ridge	saddle ridge
$H = 0$	(none)	flat	minimal
$H > 0$	pit	valley	saddle valley

(b)

Figure 3. Surface types determined by surface curvature signs: (a) Surface types from principle curvature signs; (b) Surface types from mean and Gaussian curvature signs.

Alternative Surface Curvature Quantities. Surface curvature has been viewed in principal curvature coordinates and in mean and Gaussian curvature coordinates. If only the sign of these quantities is considered, principal curvature sign allows one to identify points as peaks, pits, ridges, valleys, planes, and saddles as shown in Figure 3a whereas mean and Gaussian curvature sign allows one to subdivide saddle shapes into saddle ridges, saddle valleys, and minimal surfaces as shown in Figure 3b.

Other surface curvature coordinates also provide a useful way to look at surface curvature. In Figure 4, four different sets of surface coordinates are shown. The eight fundamental types of surfaces (see Fig. 5) are denoted for each pair of coordinates. Note that in principal curvature coordinates (or the $\kappa_1\kappa_2$-plane), umbilic points lie on the unit slope line whereas they lie on a parabola in the right half plane of the mean and Gaussian curvature space (or HK-plane). A forbidden region lies inside this parabola in the HK-plane which corresponds to the forbidden half-plane below the unit slope line in the principal curvature plane.

As a first alternative, a polar coordinate transformation is used to define (ρ, ψ) surface curvature similar to the space curve case:

$$\rho^2(u, v) = \tfrac{1}{2}(\kappa_1^2(u, v) + \kappa_2^2(u, v))$$

$$\psi(u, v) = \tan^{-1}(\kappa_2(u, v)/\kappa_1(u, v)) - \frac{\pi}{4}. \quad (49)$$

The ρ function measures the total "bending energy" of the surface in both directions. In other terms, it is the distance of the curvature coordinates from the origin, ie ideal planarity. The ψ function indicates the angle in principal curvature plane; it is 0 for umbilic points and 90 degrees for minimal points.

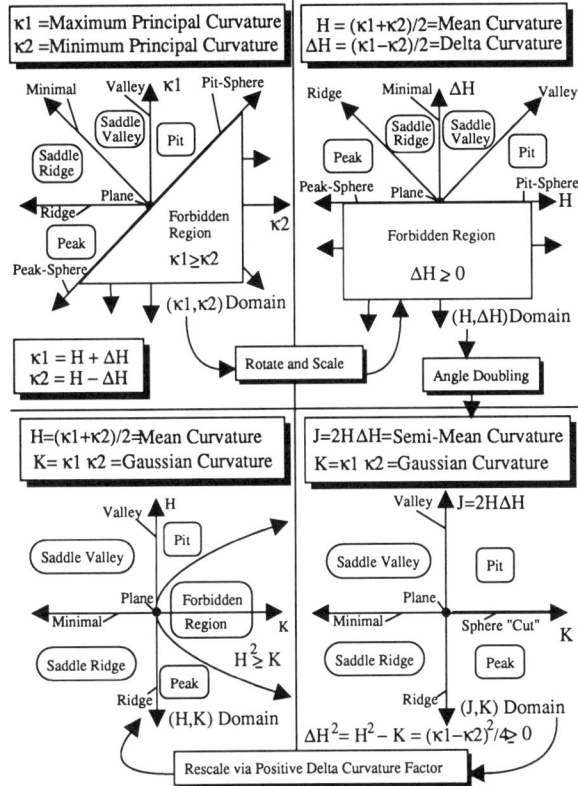

Figure 4. Four surface curvature coordinate systems.

As a second alternative, a simple rotation and scale transformation is performed on the principal curvature coordinates to obtain $(H, \Delta H)$ coordinates:

$$H = \tfrac{1}{2}(\kappa_1 + \kappa_2)$$
$$\Delta H = \tfrac{1}{2}(\kappa_1 - \kappa_2) \qquad (50)$$

where $\Delta H(u, v) \geq 0$ always by definition of maximum and minimum principal curvatures. The inverse transformation is

$$\kappa_1 = H + \Delta H$$
$$\kappa_2 = H - \Delta H. \qquad (51)$$

Note that $\Delta H = \sqrt{H^2 - K}$ using previous relationships. The same polar curvature coordinates (ρ, ψ) given above can also be defined in terms of the $(H, \Delta H)$ coordinates:

$$\rho^2 = H^2 + \Delta H^2 \qquad \psi = \tan^{-1}(\Delta H/H). \qquad (52)$$

The $(H, \Delta H)$ coordinates provide perhaps the most convenient description of the forbidden region, the lower half plane $\Delta H < 0$, and the most convenient domain for defining "curvature probability densities" and computing surface curvature histograms (the upper half plane).

As a third alternative, suppose an angle doubling transformation is used to map the upper half plane to the whole plane such that the forbidden region disappears. In complex numbers, recall that if $z = \rho e^{i\psi} = H + i\Delta H$, then $z^2 = \rho^2 e^{2i\psi} = (H^2 - \Delta H^2) + 2iH\Delta H$. Hence, the complex squaring operation is a convenient angle doubling transformation. The transformed surface curvatures are denoted (J, K) where

$$K = H^2 - \Delta H^2 = \text{Gaussian Curvature}$$
$$J = 2H\Delta H. \qquad (53)$$

The JK-plane is interesting in that each generic surface type (peak, pit, saddle ridge, saddle valley) corresponds to a separate quadrant. (Generic means type is not changed by small perturbations in surface curvature values.) The $K = 0$ axis corresponds to the non-generic ridges and valleys whereas the $J = 0$ axis corresponds to non-generic

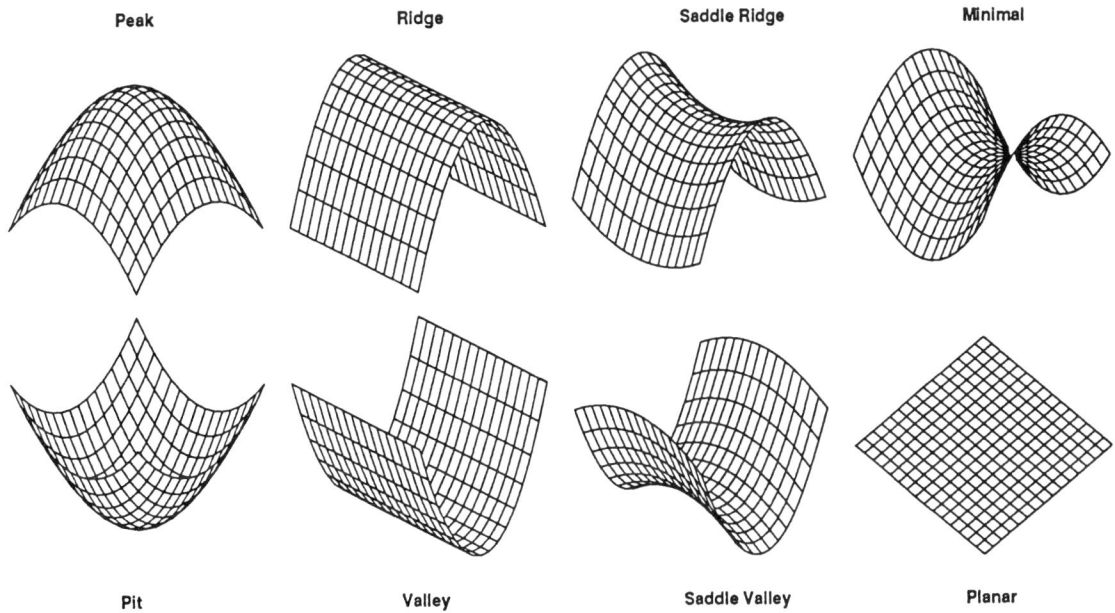

Figure 5. The eight fundamental surface types.

minimal and umbilic points. A subtle point of this representation is that there is a "cut" on the $J = 0$, K positive axis such that elliptic points near the axis cannot be perturbed to cross the axis by small surface changes. The polar surface coordinates are obtained via

$$\rho^4 = K^2 + J^2 \qquad \psi = \tfrac{1}{2}(\tan^{-1}(J/K)). \qquad (54)$$

In summary, surface curvature has many alternative representations for different analysis purposes: (κ_1, κ_2), (H, K), $(H, \Delta H)$, (J, K), (ρ, ψ). In particular, the three surface-curvature histograms of $(H, \Delta H)$, (J, K), (ρ, ψ) each provide different advantages depending on noise levels in the range data and on what an application is looking for.

Numerical Estimation of Differential Properties

Local Surface Approximation Methods. Differential geometry provides us with useful invariant geometric quantities if we can accurately estimate the necessary first and second partial derivatives. Such derivative estimation may be based on local or global approximation techniques, or on local approximations followed by global relaxation. We consider the most basic local approximation technique here.

Given a point and its neighboring points, one can estimate derivatives at the given point by taking the appropriate differences in the point neighborhood. The appropriate differences can be determined using a local surface fitting model. The basic idea (whether working locally or globally) is to fit the point neighborhood with a function and estimate the derivatives at the point with the derivatives of the fitted function. Almost any useful finite difference scheme can be derived using this approach. In general, the results one gets depend on the order of the function being fitted to the data, the relative weights one places on the importance of the points in the neighborhood, and the type of error measure that is used to compare the estimated function to the data points. The speed of an implementation depends on the factors above as well as the separability of the weights and the function model, the spacings of the parameter values (if any are given), the number of points in each neighborhood, and the efficiency with which surfaces are fitted.

For our discussion, only equally spaced parameter values, the sum of squares error measure, square neighborhoods, and equal weights for all points are considered. The method is based on a local least squares surface model using discrete orthogonal polynomials. This method has been discussed in (Allen, 1935; Anderson and Houseman, 1942; Davis, 1963; Prewitt, 1970; Hueckel, 1973; Beaudet, 1978; Haralick and Watson, 1981; Powell, 1981; Bolle and Cooper, 1984; Haralick and co-workers, 1983; Bartels and Jezioranski, 1985; Besl and Jain, 1986).

Each data point in an $N \times N$ window (neighborhood) is associated with a position (u, v) from the set $U \times U$, where for convenience N is assumed odd:

$$U = \{-(N-1)/2, \ldots, -1, 0, 1, \ldots, (N-1)/2\}. \qquad (55)$$

The following discrete orthogonal polynomials (for odd size windows) provide the basic second order fit necessary for estimating first and second partial derivatives necessary for differential geometric descriptions:

$$\phi_0(u) = 1, \qquad \phi_1(u) = u,$$
$$\phi_2(u) = (u^2 - M(M+1)/3) \qquad (56)$$

where $M = (N-1)/2$. A corresponding set of $b_i(u)$ functions are the normalized versions of the orthogonal polynomials $\phi_i(u)$ given by $b_i(u) = \phi_i(u)/P_i(M)$ where the $P_i(M)$ are normalizing constants (polynomials in M), which are defined as $P_i(M) = \Sigma_u \phi_i^2(u)$. The three normalization constants are given by

$$P_0(M) = N \qquad P_1(M) = \tfrac{2}{3}M^3 + M^2 + \tfrac{1}{3}M$$
$$P_2(M) = \tfrac{8}{45}M^5 + \tfrac{4}{9}M^4 + \tfrac{2}{9}M^3 - \tfrac{1}{9}M^2 - \tfrac{1}{15}M. \qquad (57)$$

The normalized $b_i(u)$ basis functions and the $\phi_i(u)$ basis functions satisfy the orthogonality relationship

$$\sum_{u \in U} \phi_i(u) b_j(u) = \delta_{ij} \qquad (58)$$

where $\delta_{ij} = 1$ if $i = j$ and $\delta_{ij} = 0$ otherwise (the Kronecker delta). There is nothing unique about the way these functions are defined with respect to the normalization constants. The normalization constants of the $b_i(u)$ functions could just as well have been grouped with the $\phi_i(u)$ functions, or the square root of the normalization constants could have been grouped with both functions so that there would be no distinction between them. The latter is perhaps the most common practice, but in image processing, it is convenient to have normalization constants with no square roots so that faster integer arithmetic can be used after appropriate scaling of quantities by the denominator.

The recipe for computing derivatives at a sample point using odd size data windows is simple since the $b_i(u)$ vectors may be precomputed for any given window size, and convolved with the image data to provide derivative estimates. A surface function estimate $\hat{f}(u, v)$ is obtained in the form

$$\hat{f}(u, v) = \sum_{i+j \leq 2} a_{ij} \phi_i(u) \phi_j(v) \qquad (59)$$

that minimizes the total equally weighted square error term

$$\varepsilon^2 = \sum_{(u,v) \in U^2} (f(u, v) - \hat{f}(u, v))^2. \qquad (60)$$

The solution for the unknown coefficients is given by

$$a_{ij} = \sum_{(u,v) \in U^2} f(u, v) b_i(u) b_j(v). \qquad (61)$$

This simple (inner product) summation is obtained only because of the orthogonality of the basis functions. If we were not using orthogonal basis functions, the solution would have to be expressed using matrix inverses and the corresponding computations would be more involved than a simple summation. The first and second partial derivative estimates are then given by

$$f_u = a_{10} \quad f_v = a_{01} \quad f_{uv} = a_{11} \quad f_{uu} = 2a_{20} \quad f_{vv} = 2a_{02}. \quad (62)$$

The total fit error can be efficiently computed after the a_{ij} coefficients are determined:

$$\varepsilon^2 = \sum_{(u,v) \in U^2} f^2(u, v) - \sum_{i,j} P_i(M) P_j(M) a_{ij}^2. \quad (63)$$

Since the discrete orthogonal quadratic polynomials over the 2–D window are separable in u and v as shown in the above equations, partial derivative estimates can be computed for an entire image using a separable convolution operator. This is much more efficient than nonseparable convolution operations for large window sizes on general purpose computers.

Surface Normals from Covariance Matrix. If $S = \{\vec{x}_i\}$ is a discrete set of (x, y, z) surface points in the neighborhood $N(k, r)$ of radius r of a point $\vec{x}_k$:

$$N(k, r) = \{\vec{x}_i \in S : \|\vec{x}_i - \vec{x}_k\| \le r\}, \quad (64)$$

then covariance matrix $C(k, r)$ of the neighborhood $N(k, r)$ is defined as the expectation of the outer product of the difference vectors in the neighborhood:

$$C(k, r) = \frac{1}{|N|} \sum_{\vec{x}_i \in N(k,r)} (\vec{x}_i - \vec{x}_k)(\vec{x}_i - \vec{x}_k)^T$$

$$= \left(\frac{1}{|N|} \sum_{\vec{x}_i \in N(k,r)} \vec{x}_i \vec{x}_i^T \right) - \vec{x}_k \vec{x}_k^T \quad (65)$$

where $|N|$ is the number of points in the neighborhood $N(k, r)$. The covariance matrix is a symmetric 3×3 matrix. It is typically of full rank for all neighborhoods with more than three data points from a real sensor. Let $\sigma_1 \le \sigma_2 \le \sigma_3$ be the eigenvalues for the matrix $C(k, r)$ and let $\vec{v}_1$, $\vec{v}_2$, and $\vec{v}_3$ be the corresponding unit eigenvectors. If the data points are noisy samples from a flat or gently curving smooth surface, then the surface normal at the k-th point is given by

$$\vec{n}_k = \vec{v}_1 \quad (66)$$

and the principal directions are given by the other two eigenvectors. The value σ_1 is a measure of planar fit error in the direction specified by the surface normal $\vec{v}_1$. The advantages of this technique is that there is no preferred direction, there is no assumed parameterization, and the data need not lie on a grid. The disadvantage is that the results tend to be noisier than the local approximation method above.

Surface Curvature from Surface Normals. If a surface normal is assigned to every surface point in a neighborhood, then surface curvature properties can be computed as in Hoffman and Jain (1987). The normal curvature for a curve passing through the points $\vec{x}_j$ and $\vec{x}_k$ is given by

$$\kappa_n(k, j) = \frac{\|\vec{n}_k - \vec{n}_j\|}{\|\vec{x}_k - \vec{x}_j\|}. \quad (67)$$

The minimum and maximum principal curvatures are determined by comparing the normal curvatures of all points $\vec{x}_j$ in the neighborhood. The mean and Gaussian curvatures are computed as the average and the product of the principal curvatures.

Iterative Relaxation Methods. Since there are no compatibility conditions between adjacent pixels for the local methods, noisy data causes curvature values to vary wildly. However, by considering the sign-of-curvature types and imposing a smooth surface constraint, it is possible to eliminate many bad results at individual pixels that lie amidst predominantly correct results (Boulanger, 1988). For example, pit pixels should not be directly adjacent to pit pixels; a plane or other intermediate pixel types should lie between. By imposing such constraints and iteratively reprocessing the image results, one can clean up local approximation labeling results. Based on the corrected labels, the curvature values themselves can also be adjusted to be more reasonable. Also, robust least-median-squares averaging in suitably sized windows will also provide helpful adjustment of curvature values.

Global Approximation Methods. An alternative estimation scheme which avoids the problems of local approximation is to somehow compute a parametric surface representation for all the smooth surfaces in a range image. The chief criterion for the parametric model is that it must be twice differentiable (C^2 continuous). These yield a closed form mathematical description of the surfaces. Assuming that the model represents accurately the surface, surface curvatures can be computed for each point (x, y) in the surface from the close form parametric description. This process has the following advantages:

- Since the parametric model is fitted to an entire smooth region, the surface description at each point on the surface is based upon a greater amount of data than the points in a local window.
- The curvature computation is valid to the degree that the entire parametric surface is faithful to the data in position and surface slope.

Global estimation using polynomial surfaces fitted to the data as in Besl and Jain (1988) has been shown to yield good results (Quek, 1990).

The disadvantages of global approximation are that the range image must first be segmented to obtain smooth surfaces.

SEGMENTATION OF RANGE DATA

Up to this point, it has been assumed that the mathematical models are applied to subsets of (x, y, z) points in a range image. The determination of which data points belong to particular sets is the segmentation problem. Unfortunately, this is a problem with no general solution. One has to know the primitives present to determine the region it occupies in an image.

One approach to the problem is to detect the first and second order discontinuities (or edges) in an image and use these as boundaries for the regions (Fan and co-workers, 1980; Liou and co-workers, 1990). This is possible only under certain conditions. Consider the instance of geometric surfaces which merge smoothly in such a way that there is no local zeroth or first order discontinuity anywhere along the seam. Examples of these are bending pipes elbows, cylinders filleted into planes, any surfaces meeting in smooth fillets, etc. Simple methods, such as applying global quadric models to regions separated by edges, invariably fail in these cases.

A second approach is the *region growing* approach adopted by Besl and Jain (1988). The approach applies a set of functions (bivariate polynomials) to seed regions and grows these regions until they can no longer be modeled by polynomials. This effectively segments the image into regions of coherent surfaces by applying the model (the polynomial function) to determine which data points belong to the region. The drawback to this approach is its relatively high cost in computation.

Neither method is able to reliably segment and reliably separate smoothly merging surfaces. Local image operators like edge detectors will not separate the components, and neither will region growing approaches in all cases depending upon noise levels. There is nothing intrinsic to the raw data that warrants the segmentation of smoothly merging surfaces. The information needed to make such separation lies in the observers understanding and expectation of the forms. This problem was addressed by Quek (1990) by a combination of region splitting and growing.

Let a smooth region described by a surface function $\mathcal{S}(u, v)$ in a range image be a representation of one or more smoothly merging surfaces. The purpose of splitting the surface into subregions is to obtain a set of subregions each member of which is in one and only one constructed surface.

Let $(c_i \in \mathcal{C})$ be the set of N constructed surfaces represented by an overarching surface $\mathcal{S}(u, v)$. $\mathcal{C}$ is by definition a disjoint set such that $\{(c_i \cap c_j = \emptyset) | \forall i \neq j\}$. Let $(r_j \in \mathcal{R})$ be the set of M subregions obtained by the splitting of the surface $\mathcal{S}$. Again, $\mathcal{R}$ is a disjoint set such that $\{(r_i \cap r_j = \emptyset) | \forall i \neq j\}$. The criterion for splitting the region is given by:

$$(r_i \subset c_j) \text{ and } (r_i \subset c_k) \text{ iff } (j = k)$$
$$\forall (1 \leq i \leq M) \text{ and } (1 \leq j, k \leq N) \quad (68)$$

To perform such a split, one must operate on a hypothesis of the forms that are present in the image. To detect merging planes, for example, the image may be divided into regions of similar surface normals. Equation 68 specifies that the splitting must be aggressive. Over splitting is a recoverable error by merging while under splitting is fatal. In our example, the threshold of similarity of the surface normals may be over sensitive, splitting potential planes rather than under sensitive to accept planes merging at an obtuse angle.

Let $(r_j \in \mathcal{R})$ be the set of M subregions obtained by a splitting operation which satisfies the *splitting criterion* of equation 68:

$$(r_i \subset c_j) \text{ and } (r_i \subset c_k) \text{ iff } (j = k)$$
$$\forall (1 \leq i \leq M) \text{ and } (1 \leq j, k \leq N)$$

The purpose of region merging is to recover the desired $\{c_i \in \mathcal{C} | (1 \leq i \leq N)\}$ (N being the number of desired surfaces constituted of $\mathcal{R}$).

Define *form-set* $\{\mathcal{O}_i \in | (1 \leq i \leq K)\}$ as the set of K forms or classifications into which the splitted regions may be grouped. Define the *merging predicate* $\mathcal{M}_i$ which determines if a subset of adjacent splitted regions $[r_j]$ belongs to the same instance of class $\mathcal{O}_i$, ie,

$$\mathcal{M}_i([r_j]) \rightarrow ([r_j] \subseteq \mathcal{F}_k) \quad (69)$$

where $\mathcal{F}_k$ is an instance of class $\mathcal{O}_i$. The requirement of adjacency may be relaxed to allow the reconstruction of surfaces which are fragmented by occlusion, but such a relaxation is usually employed to merge the larger regions which result from the coalescing of all adjacent splitted regions. The selection of the merging predicate $\mathcal{M}_i$ in any coalescing operation to uncover component surfaces has to be guided by the hypothesis of the identity of the surface. In our example, the merging predicate may take the form of the fitting error of adjacent regions to a planar function.

USES OF RANGE DATA

Range data is not analysed as a goal in itself, but rather serves as a means to an end. For lack of a better categorization, we shall establish four broad categories for discussion: inspection, modeling, recognition, and navigation. Inspection techniques take sets of range data, provide for alignment with a known model geometry if needed, and compare sensed data with the expected shape via pointwise operators and perhaps feature-based post processing. Modeling or reconstruction techniques describe subsets of data points in such a way as to allow the data to be recreated from the extracted feature information within a given tolerance. Recognition techniques segment the range data into units which constitute features that facilitate the recognition of the objects in the scene responsible for the observed data. Navigation techniques do not require inspection, modeling, or recognition per se, but rather allow an autonomous agent to move through an unknown environment without being able or having time to build elaborate models or recognize exact object descriptions. Certain component algorithms of these applications may be identical, but the overall application goals and required knowledge are generally quite different.

Inspection

Describing range data as a point set $S = \{x_i, y_i, z_i | 0 < i \leq N\}$ and given a geometric model M, determine the registration transformation to bring S into alignment with M if such a transformation is not given, and then determine the distance between all the points of S and the model M. Given the alignment transformation, distance determination is computationally intensive for most surfaces models discussed in the surface representation section, but there are generally straightforward, known techniques for computing the inspection distances. Many applications require post-processing of the distance data to look for trends or features in the comparison results. If the alignment is not given, it is generally quite difficult to do, eg, a least squares fit between a point set and a nonpoint set geometric surface model (eg, a trimmed NURB model). Nonlinear optimization techniques are necessary, but the iterations are often trapped in local minima. No good general techniques exist for complicated models, but simple shapes such as (super)quadrics or polyhedral objects can be handled well.

Modeling

Describing range data as a set $S = \{x_i, y_i, z_i | 0 < i \leq N\}$, modeling or reconstruction techniques are used to compute a geometric model M, usually some set of surface or volume representations to provide a good approximation of the data as the model's surface points. There are a wide variety of techniques that could fall into this category depending on what one is willing to call a model and what one is going to use the model for. The most critical need for modeling from a machine perception point of view is that data/knowledge is needed as input for object recognition systems. Where will this data/knowledge come from? Will people have to spoon-feed computers forever with carefully and laboriously created geometric models and other information so that they, the computers, will be able to understand their environment? Machine perception systems must eventually be able to build their own geometric models and acquire their own information by sensing physical examples of shapes that they encounter. Therefore, the ability to automatically learn about shape is one goal of modeling.

In the meantime, automated modeling systems could provide greater immediate services than limited capability recognition systems by assisting the people who operate computer-aided geometric design systems to create geometric models for manufacturing or other purposes. Consider the fact that for a machine perception system to assist or replace a person doing an inspection or recognition or navigation task, the machine perception system must provide a human-like response to the sensed environment in a very short time frame; generally less than a second is highly desirable. Otherwise, the machine provides little added value to many tasks at hand. In contrast, consider the CAD system operator who may require two weeks to build a CAD model from input specifications or as is still often done from measurements of a physical prototype part. Any worthwhile automated geometric modeling capability could remove days from the process.

Many schemes for building mathematical models from sensed data have appeared in the computer vision literature since Baumgart's work (1974). Range data is a much better source of information than intensity (video) imagery, and so range data analysis is a key component of such modeling approaches. However, aside from polyhedral, (super)quadric, and oct-tree models, very little in the way of automatic approaches has been accomplished in this area.

Recognition

If the purpose is recognition, the data analysis need not extract features or surface models that allow a pointwise surface reconstruction. Although surface reconstruction techniques alone are adequate for recognition in the case of simple (super)quadric or polyhedral primitives, creating a complex reconstructed CAD surface representation of a part still requires a lot of high-level processing to identify the part. In order for recognition to be fast, a machine perception system should probably not waste time building elaborate geometric descriptions to take up to the model library, but rather it should use a few select hypotheses generated from as many low-level features as can be quickly recovered in order to compare a few likely models to the range data. Today's computer hardware support this basic direction: all geometric surface models can be decomposed into connected meshes of triangle surface facets and can be rendered into range image format (a z-buffer) at rates of up to one million triangles per second, or 33,000 triangles per video frame. Since 16–bit image subtraction can also be accomplished in a frame time, it is easy to see that generating the few reasonable hypotheses from whatever range data features can be quickly computed is the hard part of a feasible recognition strategy for complex objects. Indeed, object recognition has already been achieved for polyhedral and (super)quadric primitives, yet many of these methods do not provide the upward path for many real world problems.

Navigation

When range data is available at fast enough rates over large enough depths of field, what types of range data analysis algorithms will support the less well defined needs of navigation applications? Navigation techniques have the luxury of not having to worry about being too precise, but they also have the curse of extremely high cost for most mistakes. If an inspection system fails, or a modeling system generates a shoddy model, or a recognition system did not recognize a given part in some orientation, the machine perception systems will continue to exist so they can be debugged and perhaps provide better capability in the future. If a navigation perception subsystem fails, the entire system will probably need to be replaced or else the environment and other entities in the environment may be damaged. The autonomous vehicle may drive off a cliff because of unforeseen circumstances, or it may cross the yellow line on the highway owing to an unexpected condition, or some other unfortunate circumstance may occur. Therefore, navigation via range data requires fast, high-reliability, qualitative, geometric reasoning about the range data. For this reason, simple planes, polyhedra, and (super)quadric primitives are probably adequate geometric abstractions for many applications, but the interpretations regarding these abstractions must have a very low probability of error in the given environment.

BIBLIOGRAPHY

F. E. Allan, "The General Form of the Orthogonal Polynomials for Simple Series with Proofs of Their Simple Properties," *Proc. R. Soc. Edinburgh* **50**, 310–320 (1935).

J. Aloimonos, "Shape from Texture," *Biol. Cybernetics* **58**, 345–360 (1988).

J. Y. Aloimonos, "Visual Shape Computation," *Proc. IEEE* **76**(8), 899–916 (Aug. 1988).

R. L. Anderson and E. E. Houseman, *Tables of Orthogonal Polynomial Values Extended to N=104.* Research Bulletin 297, Iowa State College of Agriculture and Mechanic Arts, Ames, Iowa, April, 1942.

R. Bajcsy and F. Solina, "Three Dimensional Object Representation Revisited," *Proceedings of the International Conference on Computer Vision,* London, U.K., IEEE-CS, 1987, pp. 231–240.

H. H. Baker and T. O. Binford, "Depth from Edge and Intensity Based Stereo," *Proceedings of the Seventh International Joint Conference on Artificial Intelligence,* Vancouver, B.C., Morgan-Kaufmann, San Mateo, Calif., 1981, pp. 349–387.

S. T. Barnard, "A Stochastic Approach to Stereo Vision," *American Association of Artificial Intelligence*, 1986, pp. 676–680.

R. E. Barnhill, "A Survey of the Representation and Design of Surfaces," *IEEE Comput. Graphics Applications* **3**(7), 9–16 (Oct. 1983).

A. H. Barr, "Superquadrics and Angle-preserving Transformations," *IEEE Comput. Graphics Applications* **1**(1), 11–23 (Jan. 1981).

H. G. Barrow and J. M. Tennenbaum, "Computational Vision," *Proc. IEEE* **69**(5), 572–595 (May 1981).

R. H. Bartels and J. J. Jezioranski, "Least-squares Fitting Using Orthogonal Multinomial," *ACM Trans. Mathematical Software* **11**(3), 201–217 (Sept. 1985).

R. H. T. Bates, K. L. Garden, and T. M. Peters, "Overview of Computerized Tomography with Emphasis on Future Developments," *Proc. IEEE* **71**(3), 356–372 (Mar. 1983).

B. G. Baumgart, *Geometric Modeling for Computer Vision,* Ph.D. dissertation, Computer Science Dept., Stanford University, Stanford, Calif., 1974.

P. R. Beaudet, "Rotationally Invariant Image Operators," in *Proceedings of the 4th International Conference on Pattern Recognition,* Kyoto, Japan, 1978, pp. 579–583.

P. J. Besl, "Active Optical Range Imaging Sensors," *Mach. Vision Applications J.* **1** (April 1988). See also (1) *Advances in Machine Vision: Architectures and Applications,* J. Sanz, ed., Springer-Verlag, New York; (2) *Range Imaging Sensors,* Research Report GMR-6090, General Motors Research Laboratories, Warren, Mich.

P. J. Besl, *Surfaces in Range Image Understanding,* Springer-Verlag, New York, 1988.

P. J. Besl, and R. Jain, "Three-dimensional Object Recognition," *Comput. Surv.* **17**(1) (Mar. 1985).

P. J. Besl and R. C. Jain, "Invariant Surface Characteristics for Three-dimensional Object Recognition in Range Images," *Comput. Vision, Gr. Im. Process.* **33**(1), 33–80 (1986).

P. J. Besl and R. Jain, "Segmentation Through Variable-order Surface Fitting," *IEEE Trans. PAMI* **PAMI-10**(2), 167–192 (Mar. 1988).

P. J. Besl, J. B. Birch, and L. T. Watson, "Robust Window Operators," *Mach. Vision Applications J.* **2**, 179–191 (1989).

A. Blake, "Reconstructing a Visible Surface," in *Proceedings of the Fourth National Conference on Artificial Intelligence,* Austin, Tex., AAAI, Menlo Park, Calif., 1984, pp. 23–26.

A. Blake and A. Zisserman, *Visual Reconstruction,* MIT Press, 1987.

W. Boehm, G. Farin, and J. Kahmann, "A Survey of Curve and Surface Methods in CAGD," *Comput. Aided Geometric Des.* **1**(1), 1–60, (July 1984).

R. M. Bolle and D. B. Cooper, "Bayesian Recognition of Local 3–D Shape by Approximating Image Intensity Functions with Quadric Polynomials," *IEEE Trans. PAMI* **PAMI-6**(4), 418–429 (July 1984).

R. C. Bolles, H. H. Baker, and D. H. Marimont, "Epipolar Plane Image Analysis: An Approach to Determining Structure," *Int. J. Comput. Vision* **1**, 7–55 (1987).

P. Boulanger, "Label Relaxation Applied to the Topographic Primal Sketch," *Proceedings of Vision Interface '88,* Edmonton, Alberta, Canadian Image Processing and Pattern Recognition Society, 1988, pp. 10–15.

M. Brady and A. Yuille, "An Extremum Principle for Shape from Contour," *Proceedings of the Eighth International Joint Conference of Artificial Intelligence,* Karlsruhe, FRG, Morgan Kaufmann, San Mateo, Calif., Aug. 1983, pp. 969–972.

M. Brady and A. Yuille, "An Extremum Principle for Shape from Contour," *IEEE Trans. PAMI* **PAMI-6**(3), 288–301 (1984).

S. S. Chern, "A Proof of the Uniqueness of Minkowski's Problem for Convex Surfaces," *Am. J. Math.* **79**, 949–950 (1957).

P. Craven and G. Wahba, "Smoothing Noisy Data with Spline Functions: Estimating the Correct Degree of Smoothing by the Method of Generalized Cross Validation (GCV)," *Numerische Mathematik* **31**, 377–403 (1979).

P. J. Davis, *Interpolation and Approximation.* Dover, New York, 1963, Chp. 10.

C. DeBoor, *A Practical Guide to Splines,* Springer-Verlag, New York, 1978.

N. Dyn, D. Levin, and S. Rippa, "Numeric Procedures for Surface Fitting of Scattered Data by Radial Functions," *SIAM J. Sci. Stat. Computing* **7**(2), 639–659 (Apr. 1986).

Y. M. Enab and J. Y. S. Luh, "Shape from a Single View Using Matching Method," *Pattern Recognition* **21**(4), 313–318 (1988).

T. Fan, G. Medioni, and R. Nevatia, "Recognizing 3–D Objects Using Surface Descriptions," *IEEE Trans. PAMI* **PAMI-11**(11), 1140–1157 (Nov. 1989).

D. Gilbarg and N. Trudinger, *Elliptic Partial Differential Equations of Second Order.* 2nd ed., Springer-Verlag, New York, 1983.

W. Gordon, "Blending Functions of Bivariate and Multivariate Interpolation and Approximation," *SIAM J. Numerical Analysis* **8**, 158–177 (1971).

J. F. Greenleaf, "Computerized Tomography with Ultrasound," *Proc. IEEE* **71**(3), 330–337 (Mar. 1983).

W. E. L. Grimson, "A Visual Theory of Visual Surface Interpolation," *Phil. Trans. R. Soc. London B* **298**, 395–427 (1982).

E. Guisti, "On the Equation of Surfaces of Prescribed Mean Curvature: Existence and Uniqueness Without Boundary Conditions," *Inventiones Mathematicae* **46**, 111–137 (1978).

E. L. Hall, J. B. K. Tio, C. A. McPherson, and F. A. Sadjadi, "Measuring Curved Surfaces for Robot Vision," *Comput.* **15**(12), 42–54 (Dec. 1982).

R. M. Haralick and L. Watson, "A Facet Model for Image Data," *Comput. Gr. Im. Process.* **15,** 113–129 (1981).

R. M. Haralick, L. T. Watson, and T. J. Laffey, "The Topographic Primal Sketch," *Int. J. Robotics Res.* **2**(1) 50–72 (Spring 1983).

L. D. Harmon, "Automated Tactile Sensing," *Int. J. Robotics Res.* **1**(2), 3–32 (Summer 1982).

W. S. Hinshaw and A. H. Lent, "An Introduction to NMR Imaging: From the Bloch Equation to the Imaging Equation," *Proc. IEEE* **71**(3), 338–350 (Mar. 1983).

R. Hoffman and A. K. Jain, "Segmentation and Classification of Range Images," *IEEE Trans. PAMI* **PAMI-9**(5), 608–620 (1987).

R. Horaud and M. Brady, "On the Geometric Interpretation of Image Contours," *Proceedings of the First International Conference on Computer Vision,* London, U.K., 1987, pp. 374–382.

B. K. P. Horn, "Extended Gaussian Images," *Proc. IEEE* **72**(12), 1656–1678 (Dec. 1984).

M. Hueckel, "A Local Operator Which Recognizes Edges and Lines," *J. Assoc. Comp. Mach.* **20,** 634–647 (1973).

IGES, *Initial Graphics Exchange Specification,* Document No. PB83-137448, National Information Services (NTIS), 5285 Port Royal Rd., Springfield, Va., 20161.

K. Ikeuchi and B. K. P. Horn, "Numerical Shape from Shading and Occluding Boundaries," *Artif. Intell.* **17,** 141–184 (Aug. 1981).

H. Inoue, "A Least Squares Smooth Fitting for Irregularly Spaced Data: Finite Element Approach Using the Cubic B-spline Basis," *Geophysics* **51**(11), 2051–2066 (1986).

T. Kanade, "Recovery of the Three-Dimensional Shape of an Object from a Single View," *Artif. Intell.* **17,** 409–460 (Aug. 1981).

J. R. Kender, "Shape from Texture: An Aggregation Transform that Maps a Class of Textures into Surface Orientation," *Proceedings of the Seventh International Joint Conference on Artificial Intelligence,* Morgan-Kaufmann, San Mateo, Calif., 1981, pp. 475–480.

J. R. Kender, D. Lee, and T. Boult, "Information Based Complexity Applied to Optimal Recovery of the 2.5-D Sketch," *Proceedings of the Third Workshop on Computer Vision: Representation and Control,* Bellaire, Mich., IEEE-CS, 1985, pp. 157–167.

J. Knapman, "Dupin's Cyclide and Cyclide Patch," *Image and Vision Computing* **5**(2), 167–173 (1987).

G. F. Knoll, "Single Photon Emission Computed Tomography (SPECT)," *Proc. IEEE* **71**(3), 320–329 (Mar. 1983).

D. Lee and T. Pavlidis, "One-dimensional Regularization with Discontinuities," *Proceedings of the International Conference on Computer Vision,* London, U.K., IEEE-CS, 1987, pp. 572–577.

S. Liou, A. H. Chiu, and R. C. Jain, "A Parallel Technique for Signal-level Perceptual Organization," Accepted for publication—*PAMI,* 1990.

D. Marr and D. Poggio, "Cooperative Computation of Stereo Disparity," *Science* **194,** 283–287 (1976).

H. Minkowski, "Allgemeine Lehrsatze Uber Die Konvexen Polyeder," *Nachrichten von der Koniglichen Gesellschaft der Wissenschaften,* Mathematisch-Physikalische Klasse, Gottingen, 1897, pp. 198–219.

B. O'Neill, *Elementary Differential Geometry,* Academic Press, New York, 1966.

A. Pentland, "Perceptual Organization and the Representation of Natural Form," *Artif. Intell.* **28,** 293–331 (1986).

A. Pentland, "On the Extraction of Shape Information from Shading," *MIT Media Lab Vision Sciences Group,* Cambridge, Mass., Tech. Report 102, Mar. 1988, pp. 1–11.

M. J. D. Powell, *Approximation Theory and Methods,* Cambridge University Press, Cambridge, U.K., 1981.

J. Prewitt, "Object Enhancement and Extraction," in *Picture Processing and Psychopictorics,* B. Lipkin and A. Rosenfeld, eds., Academic Press, New York, 1970, pp. 75–149.

F. K. H. Quek, *On Three-Dimensional Object Recognition and Pose Determination: An Abstraction Based Approach,* Ph.D. dissertation, Electr. Eng. Comp. Sci. Dept. University of Michigan, Ann Arbor, Mich., Mar. 1990.

R. A. Robb, E. A. Hoffman, L. J. Sinak, L. D. Harris, and E. L. Ritman, "High Speed Three-dimensional X-ray Computed Tomography," *Proc. IEEE* **71**(3), 308–319 (Mar. 1983).

J. G. Rogers, R. Harrop, and P. E. Kinahan, "The Theory of Three-Dimensional Image Reconstruction for PET (Positron Emission Tomography)," *IEEE Trans. Medical Imaging* **MI-6**(3), 239–243 (Sept. 1987).

P. Sander, *On Reliably Inferring Differential Structure from Three-dimensional Images,* Ph.D. dissertation, Dept. of Electrical Eng., McGill University, Montreal, Queb., 1988.

T. W. Sederberg, "Algebraic Geometry for Surface and Solid Modeling," *Geometric Modeling: Algorithms and New Trends SIAM,* 29–42 (1987).

T. W. Sederberg and S. R. Parry, "Free Form Deformations of Solid Geometric Models," *Comput. Graphics* **20**(4), 151–160 (1986).

G. Taubin, *Algebraic Nonplanar Curve and Surface Estimation in 3-space with Applications to Position Estimation,* Tech. Report LEMS-43, Div. of Eng., Brown University, Providence, R.I., 1988.

D. Terzopoulos, "Multilevel Computational Processes for Visual Surface Reconstruction," *Comput. Vision, Gr., Im. Process.* **24,** 52–96 (1983).

D. Terzopoulos, "Regularization of Inverse Visual Problems Involving Discontinuities," *IEEE Trans. PAMI* **PAMI-8**(4), 413–424 (July 1986).

J. G. Wendelberger, *Smoothing Noisy Data with Multidimensional Splines and Generalized Cross Validation,* Ph.D. thesis, Department of Statistics, University of Wisconsin, Madison, Wis., 1982.

A. P. Witkin, "Recovering Surface Shape and Orientation from Texture," *Artif. Intell.* **17,** 17–47 (1981).

RAMESH JAIN
PAUL BESL
FRANCIS QUEK
University of Michigan

REASONING, CASE-BASED

Case-based reasoning is the technique of solving new problems by adapting solutions that were used to solve old problems. This reliance on previous experiences (or cases) is a hallmark of case-based reasoning. Each case can contain a great deal of information including a description of the situation that was encountered, ways in which the situation differed from similar situations, and how the system reacted to the situation.

There are many examples of people using case-based

reasoning in their daily lives. A caterer who remembers a meal served at a previous banquet and adapts it to fit the demands of a new client is using case-based reasoning. So is a car mechanic who suspects the problem when a car is brought into the shop with symptoms similar to a previous one that has been fixed. A business executive uses case-based reasoning by remembering past experiences when doing long range planning for the future.

In particular, case-based reasoning can mean adapting old solutions to meet new demands, using old cases to explain new situations, using old cases to critique new solutions, or reasoning from precedents to interpret a new situation (much like lawyers do) or create an equitable solution to a new problem (much like labor mediators do).

Case-based reasoning is used extensively by people in both expert and commonsense situations. It provides a wide range of advantages.

- Case-based reasoning allows the reasoner to propose solutions to problems quickly, avoiding the time necessary to derive those answers from scratch.
- Case-based reasoning allows a reasoner to propose solutions in domains that are not completely understood.
- Case-based reasoning gives a reasoner a means of evaluating solutions when no algorithmic method is available for evaluation.
- Cases are particularly useful for use in interpreting open-ended and ill-defined concepts.
- Remembering previous experiences is particularly useful in warning of the potential for problems that have occurred in the past, alerting a reasoner to take actions to avoid repeating past mistakes.
- Cases help a reasoner to focus on important parts of a problem by pointing out what features of a problem are the important ones.

Below, the development of the case-based reasoning (CBR) paradigm is traced and the advantages of CBR as a problem-solving methodology are discussed in more detail. The general CBR algorithm and some of the fundamental issues that must be dealt with in any CBR system is described. Next, a survey of CBR systems that have been built to perform various tasks along with pointers for further reading is presented, and finally, a short discussion of the implications of CBR as a cognitive model and some pointers on how to go about building a CBR system are included.

EVOLUTION OF THE CBR PARADIGM

Case-based reasoning differs markedly from other types of reasoning and problem-solving techniques and is, in some instances, a direct reaction to the problems of these other techniques. Two important factors have contributed to the evolution of the CBR paradigm.

Theories of Memory

CBR evolved in part from research on human memory, particularly the theory of Dynamic Memory (qv) developed by Schank (1982). This theory introduced the memory organization packet (MOP) memory structures which can be considered the intellectual precursor to cases. MOPs are used to store not only general information about the world, but specific experiences as well. The theory of dynamic memory provided a framework for describing how these individual experiences can be stored in memory, how they may be combined and abstracted, and how they can be retrieved and used when the need arises. Specifying the content and process of memory in this way provided the groundwork for some of the ideas of CBR.

Problems with Rule-based Reasoning

A second driving force in the evolutionary history of CBR was dissatisfaction with rule-based reasoning (expert systems (qv)), the predominant problem-solving technique at the time. Three problems with rule-based systems which prompted a search for an alternative paradigm for problem-solving concern knowledge acquisition, memory, and robustness.

Knowledge Acquisition. Under the rule-based problem solving paradigm, collecting knowledge to encode into the systems was a very difficult endeavor. Knowledge engineers found it hard to uncover the hundreds of rules that the "expert" used to solve problems, mainly because the expert often had a hard time trying to articulate his or her problem-solving skill in the form of IF-THEN rules. This problem became known as the knowledge acquisition bottleneck (Hayes-Roth and co-workers, 1983). Furthermore, it became unclear whether experts were actually using rules at all; often experts will say that it is their experience that makes them experts. In addition, while rules seemed like nice compact representations to collect, it is often the case that rules have many exceptions, making the knowledge acquisition problem that much harder. To complicate matters even further, it was necessary to trace the interactions between rules to ensure that they could chain together properly, and that contradictions were eliminated.

No Memory. A second major criticism of rule-based reasoning systems is that most did not have any memory; that is, the system would not remember previous encounters with the same problem, and would have to solve them again from scratch. This, of course, is terribly inefficient, but even dismissing efficiency issues for a moment, an even more important point is that a system with no memory will not be able to remember past mistakes. Without this ability, the system is surely condemned to repeat those mistakes again and again. This type of stupidity is not tolerated in human problem solvers, and many people were dissatisfied with rule-based systems' inability to learn from their mistakes.

Robustness. A third serious criticism of rule-based systems is that they were brittle. Since all their knowledge was recorded in terms of rules, if a problem did not match any of the rules, the system could not solve it. In other words, rule-based systems had little or no ability to work beyond their rule base; they could not adapt to handle novel situations very well, if at all.

ADVANTAGES OF THE CBR APPROACH

CBR has many advantages as a theory and methodology of reasoning and problem-solving. Many of these advantages are in direct response to the factors, outlined above, that led to the development of the CBR paradigm.

Psychological Plausibility

Given that it grew out of research on human memory, it is not surprising that one of the things that makes CBR appealing as a model of reasoning and problem solving is that it is based on the way in which humans reason and solve problems. Reasoning from past cases, as opposed to a (large) set of rules, has been thought to be a more psychologically plausible model of how people reason (Holyoak and Koh, 1987).

There is much evidence that people use case-based reasoning in their daily reasoning. Ross (1989a, 1989b), for example, has shown that people learning a new skill often refer back to previous problems to refresh their memories on how to do the task. Other research has shown that both novice and experienced car mechanics use their own experiences and those of others to help them generate hypotheses about what is wrong with a car, recognize problems (eg, a testing instrument not working), and remember how to test for different diagnoses (Lancaster and Kolodner, 1988; Redmond, 1989). In an unpublished study, Kolodner found that physicians use previous cases extensively to generate hypotheses about what is wrong with a patient, to help them interpret test results, and to select therapies when several are available and none are understood very well. Goel and Pirolli (1989) observed architects and mechanical engineers recalling, merging, and adapting old design plans to create new ones. Klein and Calderwood (1988) have observed routine use of case-based reasoning among experts making decisions in dynamically-changing situations. Read and Cesa (1991) observed people using old cases to construct explanations of social situations.

Cases vs Rules

As discussed above, the ideas of CBR developed, in part, as a reaction to the problems of rule-based reasoning. Case-based reasoning offers advantages over rule-based systems in the following ways:

Knowledge Acquisition. Cases are more memorable than abstract rules. It is often easier for experts to remember and articulate specific examples of the problems they have encountered and their solutions to those problems (ie, their "war stories"), than it is for them to describe their problem-solving technique in terms of potentially large numbers of rules. In fact, several people building expert systems that know how to reason using cases have found it easier to build case-based expert systems than traditional ones (Barletta and Hennessy, 1989; Goodman, 1989).

Learning from Experience. Case-based reasoning systems, by definition, are built on a memory of prior cases. Each time the system solves a problem, that problem and its solution are stored in memory as a case. In this way CBR systems can easily learn from experience; they don't have to waste effort re-solving a problem that is just like one they have seen before, nor will they repeat the mistakes they may have made solving the problem the first time around. While systems that do problem-solving from first-principles spend large amounts of time solving their problems from scratch, case-based systems have been found to be several orders of magnitude faster (Koton, 1988a). This ability to learn from experience is discussed in greater detail in the next section.

Adaptivity. While rule-based systems are brittle, CBR systems display more robustness upon encountering new situations. This robustness derives from the techniques of case adaptation. When trying to solve a new problem, a CBR system can search its memory for previously seen problems with similar features and adapt the solutions to those problems so that they are useful in solving the new problem (Kass, 1989).

Natural Learning Mechanism

Learning from experience, as mentioned above, is one of the advantages that CBR has over rule-based systems. The CBR paradigm provides a natural mechanism for learning. A case-based reasoner learns in two basic ways. First, it can become a more efficient reasoner by remembering old solutions and and adapting them rather than having to derive answers from scratch each time. If a case was adapted in a novel way, if it was solved using some novel method, or if it was solved by combining the solutions to several cases, then when it is recalled during later reasoning, the steps required to solve it won't need to be repeated for the new problem. Second, a case-based reasoner becomes more competent over time, deriving better answers that it could with less experience. One of case-based reasoning's fortes is its ability to help a reasoner anticipate and thus avoid past mistakes.

Case-based learning offers many advantages as a learning paradigm, including:

- **Easier knowledge acquisition.** Because knowledge is stored primarily in the form of cases, the start-up threshold is smaller. That is, learning processes can begin with much less "data" than rule-based systems typically require. Debugging the knowledge base is also easier because there tend to be far fewer interactions between cases than between rules. Finally, many domains already have information encoded in case format, prime examples being the law, mathematics, and design domains.
- **Performance enhancements.** Because CBR systems store previous encounters with problems, they can reuse old solutions instead of having to derive new solutions from scratch. In addition, by remembering past mistakes, a CBR problem-solving system can avoid making the same mistakes again. Both of

these factors contribute to improved performance (efficiency) of CBR systems.

- **Straightforward learning.** In general, learning in a CBR system does not require a complex causal model of the domain or detailed domain knowledge. Of course, the addition of either or both of these items can enhance the performance and power of a case-based system.
- **Cases can serve as explanations.** One feature that is often desired in problem solving systems is the ability to offer an explanation for the solution obtained. In a CBR system, such explanations are simply the case (or cases) that were used, making them easy (or even trivial) to generate. In fact, because CBR solves problems like people do, an explanation based on a concrete past case may be more satisfying then explanations constructed out of chains of rules, the primary method of explanation in rule-based systems.
- **Scalability.** The common problem encountered when scaling up a system, that of massive search, is in some ways avoided in CBR by the use of indexing (discussed in the section on the Indexing Problem). With the development of parallel algorithms for retrieval, it appears that large CBR systems may be able to approach, or even achieve, real-time performance.

THE BASIC CBR ALGORITHM

The basic processing cycle of CBR is "input a problem, retrieve relevant past solutions, adapt them to the current problem, store the new case along with its solution." In this section we elaborate on this cycle, spelling out the various steps in a typical case-based reasoning algorithm. While different CBR systems may emphasize different parts of the cycle, all systems address the following steps in some way.

1. *Accept and Analyze.* Upon input of a new problem, the first step of processing is known as the analysis phase. In this step, the input is analyzed to extract features to use in retrieving cases with similar features. These features, which are given special status in CBR, are called indexes. Thus, the main task in this step is index extraction. Index extraction is a very complex problem, discussed in more detail in the following section.

2. *Retrieve Cases from Memory.* The indexes computed in Step 1 are used to retrieve cases from memory. The goal here is not to retrieve just any set of cases. Those cases that can be used in the reasoning to be done in the next steps and that have the potential to make useful predictions about the current problem are the kinds of cases that should be retrieved. Various techniques for retrieving cases exist, including iterative, parallel, and constraint-satisfaction models (see section on retrieval algorithms following).

3. *Select Most Relevant Case(s).* The (potentially large) set of relevant cases obtained in Step 2 often needs to be narrowed down to just a few "most relevant" cases. These cases will be the ones considered most worthy of intensive processing in forming the basis for the new solution. The problem in this step is assessing how relevant each case really is. Typical techniques for this include a variety of ranking schemes and similarity metrics, overlap of salient features, and importance of shared features being two examples. Some of the problems of assessing similarity are discussed in the section on similarity metrics below.

4. *Construct Solution.* This step uses the cases selected in Step 3 to create a solution or interpretation (depending on the task) for the input case. Along with the solution, many CBR systems will also construct the justifications or supporting arguments for the solution at this point. The retrieved cases are used in constructing the solution in at least two important ways. First, the actual solution is constructed by adapting the solutions to the previously seen cases so that they are relevant to the current case. Second, the retrieved cases can be used to warn of potential snags in solution construction, allowing the system to anticipate and thus avoid making the same kinds of mistakes encountered in previous problems.

5. *Evaluate Solution.* After a potential solution has been constructed, it is subjected to testing, evaluation, and criticism. The goal in this step is to assess the utility, strengths, and weaknesses of the proposed solution. Several methods for doing this exist, including testing the solution against counterexamples (real or hypothetical), using the solution as an index into memory to see if there are any examples of this solution that have been known to fail in similar circumstances, or simulating the results of the proposed solution. Examples of systems which use these methods are HYPO (Ashley, 1987, 1988; Rissland, 1986), which provides guidelines for creating and using hypotheticals, and CHEF (qv) (Hammond, 1986, 1989a), which used a simulation to test its solutions. Employing internal testing mechanisms like these is especially critical in domains where the cost of an incorrect or inefficient solution is high (eg, medical diagnosis).

6. *Execute Solution and Analyze Results.* In this step the solution is tried out in the real world and the system obtains feedback about what happened. This feedback is then subjected to careful analysis to see if the results were as expected. This process of obtaining and analyzing feedback is crucial if a CBR system is to learn from its mistakes and avoid repeating them. If something unexpected occurred the system attempts to explain the anomalous events. The problem of trying to decide which parts of the solution caused the problems, known throughout the machine-learning field as the credit/blame assignment problem, comes into play here. One technique that can be used to partially avoid this notoriously hard problem is to recall similar failures encountered in the past and to use the explanations of those failures in explaining the current failure (Rissland and Ashley, 1988). This process is simply another version of a case-based reasoning problem and can often be done by a recursive call to the CBR system.

7. *Update Memory.* After the results of testing the solution in the real world have been analyzed, the next step is to update memory by storing the new case. The new

case is composed of not only the solution arrived at, but also the justifications and supporting arguments constructed in Step 4. The most important aspect of this step is where to put this case in memory, or, in CBR terminology, how to index it. One common technique is to index a case by the problems or failures that were encountered (in Steps 5 and 6) so that these same mistakes can be avoided when a similar situation is encountered in the future (see section below for more detail on other indexing techniques). The success or failure of a CBR system depends heavily on this step. Good indexing strategies will cause the relevant cases to be recalled when they can best be used, resulting in good performance, while a poor indexing scheme will not cause the most relevant cases to be retrieved and system performance will be degraded.

This section was an attempt to give a brief overview of the general CBR algorithm. For more detail on CBR basics, particularly implementation details, an excellent starting point is Riesbeck and Schank's (1989), *Inside Case-Based Reasoning*. Good general introductions for the lay reader can be found in Slade (1991) and Kolodner (1990, 1991).

FUNDAMENTAL ISSUES IN CBR

Because the heart of any case-based reasoning system involves case retrieval and selection, the fundamental issues of CBR revolve around these issues. Below are presented some of the major areas of current research, the questions that each is trying to address, and some of the proposed solutions.

The Indexing Problem

Retrieval of relevant cases from memory being a cornerstone of the CBR algorithm, it follows that an extremely important issue is how to label cases so that they may be recalled when needed. The assignment of labels to cases is called indexing, the labels themselves are called indexes.

The Nature of Indexes. What are indexes comprised of? This question has long plagued CBR researchers. In general, an index can be any feature used in the representation of a case or computed from that representation. But which features should be used as indexes? One option is to use concrete features, ie, those features which are either included in the description of the case, or can be easily computed. These kinds of features, also known as low level, or surface features, have the advantage that they are simple to represent and do not require much (if any) effort to extract from the input. The simplicity and ease of computation of these kinds of features tend to make them favored for use in parallel retrieval algorithms (see section below). The problem with low level features, however, is that they may not be adequate to index cases so that only the most relevant cases are recalled. Combinations of simple features are often insufficient in describing the type of case being looked for with sufficient specificity, resulting in a large set of cases, only a few of which are relevant, being retrieved from memory. If this happens, the CBR system must then devote additional effort in weeding out the less relevant cases.

A second option is to use as indexes more complex, abstract features which are computed from the input. These high level features have the advantage of being able to more accurately represent the type of case being searched for, resulting in fewer, but more relevant cases being retrieved from memory. The two main problems with using high level features as indexes are deciding which high level features to compute and, of course, the cost of computing them. The former problem, that of deciding which high level features to compute (out of a potentially infinite set of possibilities) is such a notoriously hard problem in CBR that it has been given a special name. The indexing problem is the problem of determining what other nonobvious features, aside from those directly provided in the input, should be used as indexes in a particular domain.

Once a decision to use high level features has been made, however, there are still several issues that must be dealt with. First, it must be decided which high level features are more likely to help retrieve relevant cases in a given domain. A second, related issue that must be addressed is whether the end justifies the means. That is, will the improvement in system performance due to better case selection outweigh the extra cost of computing the high level features? CASEY (qv) (Koton, 1988a), JUDGE (Bain, 1986), CHEF (Hammond, 1986, 1989a), and ANON (Owens, 1989a, 1989b) each provide different initial approaches to this problem.

There has been a great deal of debate among CBR researchers about the relative merits of using low level vs high level features as indexes. Arguments for low level features include Thagard and Holyoak (1989b) and Waltz (1989), while endorsements for the use of high level features (like goal and plan interactions) include Collins' (1987) COACH, other recent work by Collins and Birnbaum (1989; 1990), as well as Schank (1982), Martin (1989a, 1989b), Owens (1989a), and Pazzani (1989) among others. More recently, however, the debate over the level of indexes used has waned as it has become clear that no one kind of index is appropriate for all systems. This has been paralleled by investigations of human analogical reasoning that have found both surface and deep features are used for retrieval (Gentner, 1989). Researchers are now arguing for a more functional approach in which index selection would be based on an analysis of the task the system is to perform. Those features, both surface and deep, which are best suited to the particular task facing the system would be selected as indexes (Hammond, 1989c).

One final trend in addressing the indexing problem has been to investigate whether there is any way of describing a general framework for the content of indexes. If such a method could be developed, it would be a first step towards automating the choice of indexes for a given domain. This would at least partially obviate the need for the programmer of a CBR system to make this difficult decision. A first attempt at describing a general content theory of indexes has resulted in the formulation of the Universal Indexing Frame (UIF), a representational system whose utility is currently being investigated (Schank and co-workers, 1990).

Guidelines for Addressing the Indexing Problem. The indexes of a case are those features that distinguish it from other cases, because they are predictive of something important in the case. Guidelines for addressing the indexing problem include the following:

- Feature combinations used as indexes should be predictive of something important for later reasoning.
- Indexes should be abstract enough to be generally applicable but concrete enough to be easily recognizable without a great deal of inference.
- Cases should be indexed in ways that support reasoning that a system has to do. For example:
    To choose plans that achieve goals according to the details of a situation, index by goal, constraint, and feature combinations that led to solving a problem in a particular way.
    To anticipate potential problems, to help explain problem solving errors, and to help recover from problem solving errors, index by the combinations of features responsible for failures.
    To evaluate proposed solutions, index by combinations of features that were responsible for unexpected outcomes and by descriptions of those unusual outcomes.

Guidelines for choosing indexes are still ahead of the technology for automating index selection. Nevertheless, several methodologies for choosing indexes automatically do exist or have been suggested. (See Table 1 for information about the CBR systems mentioned throughout this article).

- Keep track of norms and index by features different from the norm (CYRUS (qv), MEDIATOR (qv), PERSUADER (qv)).
- Index by a fixed and well-known set of features known to be predictive (CYRUS (qv), HYPO).
- Index by differences between what is already in memory and the case being indexed (CYRUS, MEDIATOR, PERSUADER).
- Index on features that predict failure or unexpected success as follows: After receiving feedback and explaining a failure or unexpected success, use explanation-based learning (EBL) techniques to generalize the explanation. Index by the combination of features that go into the generalized explanation (CHEF (qv), JULIA (qv)).
- Index on features found to be useful in achieving some goal or doing some task as follows: Use EBL techniques to generalize the reasoning that went into making decisions while solving a problem. Index by the combination of features that make up that general reasoning chain (Lockheed AI Project, JULIA).

Memory Organization

Choosing good indexes is not the only factor that contributes to a CBR system's ability to retrieve relevant cases in an efficient manner. A critical factor, especially for large CBR systems containing hundreds or even thousands of cases, is how the system's memory is organized. Traditional approaches have used discrimination networks (cf Feigenbaum, 1963), typical examples being the earlier work of Kolodner (1983a, 1983b) and Lebowitz (1983). More recently, work has concentrated on memory organizations that support parallel retrieval methods, eg, Kolodner (1986, 1988). (See the following section for more discussion on retrieval methods.)

Intrinsically bound up with the question of how memory is organized is the question of how individual cases are represented. Should cases be stored in one place or should they be broken into pieces? The advantage of the former approach is that by storing the entire case in one place, it may be retrieved and used to solve a new problem in just "one shot." A disadvantage is that it is harder to create solutions that are based on pieces of several cases. To do this it would be necessary to go through memory finding and "collecting" the appropriate pieces from the various cases. Systems that use a unitary representation for cases include CASEY, CHEF, and HYPO (see Table 1 for more information on these and other CBR systems).

An alternative is to use a more piecemeal representational scheme for cases, that is, breaking cases into parts which are located in different areas of memory and connected by pointers. This technique makes it easier to create solutions based on partial solutions from several different cases because it is easier to identify and access the parts that are needed. Many feel that this type of solution construction results in more creative solutions to problems. The cost incurred by this approach, however, is that extra work needs to be done to put a single case "back together" before it can be used as a whole. JULIA and CELIA (Redmond, 1990) are examples of CBR systems that use this approach to case representation.

In addition to questions about how memory is organized and how cases are represented, another issue that needs to be considered is forgetting. Should case-based systems ever "throw out" cases? If so, when should this be done? This issue has received very little attention (but see, eg, Hunter, 1989), and much work still needs to be done.

Retrieval Algorithms

Because the CBR paradigm relies on a large memory of cases to give it problem-solving power, a major issue that needs to be considered is how to retrieve cases from memory quickly and efficiently. The larger the memory, the more important this question becomes.

The two main strategies that are used for retrieval are based on the two types of memory organizations discussed above. Memories organized in discrimination nets typically use a concept-refinement search that takes advantage of the generalization–specialization hierarchy built into the net. In this technique search starts at the top of

Table 1. Summary of CBR Systems*

Program	Reference	Domain	Task
ABE	Kass (1990)	Anomalous events	Adaptating explanations
ANON	Owens (1989a)	Proverbs	Indexing prototypical cases
CASEY	Koton (1988a, 1988b)	Heart failures	Explanation of anomalies
CELIA	Redmond (1990)	Automobile troubleshooting	Diagnosis
CHEF	Hammond (1986, 1989a); Riesbeck & Schank (1989)	Recipes	Goal-driven design, plan-repair
CLAVIER	Barletta & Hennessey (1989)	Autoclave layout	Layout design
COACH	Collins (1987); Riesbeck & Schank (1989)	Football strategy	Plan repair, counterplanning
CSI BATTLE PLANNER	Goodman (1989)	Military	Plan critique and repair
CYCLOPS	Navinchandra (1988)	Landscaping	Design
CYRUS	Kolodner (1984)	Political events	Memory organization
DMAP	Riesbeck & Martin (1985); Riesbeck & Schank (1989)	Natural language parsing	Classification, recognition
HYPO	Ashley (1987, 1988); Rissland (1986); Rissland & Ashley (1986, 1988)	Patent law	Evaluation by comparison
JUDGE	Bain (1986); Riesbeck & Schank (1989)	Criminal sentencing	Evaluation by comparison
JULIA	Hinrichs (1988, 1989)	Catering	Goal-driven design
KRITIK	Goal (1989); Goel & Chandrasekaran (1989)	Mechanical assemblies	Design
MEDIATOR	Simpson (1985); Kolodner & Simpson (1989)	Common-sense disputes	Goal-driven design
MEDIC	Turner (1989)	Medicine	Multiple diagnostic goals
PARADYME	Kolodner (1988)	Cooking	Parallel retrieval
PERSUADER	Sycara (1987)	Labor contracts	Goal-driven design
PLEXUS	Alterman (1986, 1988)	Subway riding	Execution time plan repair
PROTOS	Bareiss (1989)	Hearing disorders	Diagnosis, learning
EXPEDITOR	Robinson & Kolodner (1991)	Daily errands	Planning for multiple goals
SWALE	Kass and co-workers (1986); Kass & Leake (1988); Leake & Owens (1986)	Death and destruction	Explanation of anomalies
TRUCKER	Hammond (1989b)	Scheduling	Opportunistic planning

* After Slade (1991).

the net and progresses downward only when a match can be made at the current level. In this way, large portions of the memory can be eliminated from the search almost immediately. When the search terminates, the set of cases grouped below the current node can be returned. This set will have increasing similarity to the probe to the extent that the search progresses further down the net. Thus, the set of cases returned will all, in some sense, be "close" to the probe (Kolodner, 1983a, 1983b; Lebowitz, 1983).

The second major class of retrieval algorithms are parallel algorithms. These derive their power by examining all (or many) cases at once. Generally what is done is that each match is given a rating of its goodness (using some metric) and those cases with the highest ratings are the ones returned by the search. Kolodner's (1984) CYRUS was the first to investigate the use of parallelism in CBR. Her solution used a combination of shared feature networks and redundant discrimination networks that could be searched in parallel. Other types of parallel algorithms that have been developed for use in CBR systems include parallel search of a flat memory (as in MBR (Stanfill and Waltz, 1988)), and parallel search of a hierarchical memory (as in PARADYME (Kolodner, 1988)). Further discussion of parallel retrieval techniques can be found in Owens (1989b), Thagard and Holyoak (1989b), Domeshek (1989), and Waltz (1989).

Similarity Metrics

If a CBR system is to solve new problems by adapting solutions to old problems, immediately one must face the question of how to recognize one situation as being similar to another. In trying to choose the best cases to reason with, the system must first match the input to cases in memory to retrieve a set of candidate cases and then narrow down this set to include only the most relevant cases (Steps 2 and 3 in the CBR Algorithm section above). Since it is unlikely that a new case will always match a case in memory exactly, a system must be able to do partial matching in order to accomplish the first step of retrieving relevant cases. The system must also have the ability to compare the goodness-of-match of the retrieved cases in order to do the second step of narrowing down the set of relevant cases to a smaller set of "best" cases. Both of these processes entail the need to have similarity metrics, or ways of judging how alike two cases are (along various dimensions).

A naive method of assessing similarity between two cases would be to count the number of matching features that the two cases have. This technique is of limited usefulness though, since the relative importance of features often changes depending on the context. More sophisticated methods use the cases already in memory, along with various decision heuristics, in deciding which features are important for matching (Ashley and Rissland, 1988; Kolodner, 1988; Owens, 1989a; Rissland and Ashley, 1988; Stanfill, 1987).

The advantage of the naive approach, however, is that comparison of simple features is computationally less expensive than matching complex structures. The issue of efficiency becomes quite important in deciding on a similarity metric, since assessing similarity between cases plays a role in many of the steps in the CBR algorithm. Recent efforts at reducing the complexity of matching cases have used the UIF to implement flat-matching, that is, eliminating the use of variable binding in the matching algorithm by Domeshek (in press).

There remain a number of open issues in similarity assessment. Bareiss and King (1989) mention the following:

- How can similarity be computed when cases are represented in a uniform manner?
- How does general domain knowledge come into play in similarity assessment?
- How can the context of the problem solving situation affect the determination of similarity?
- Can similarity indeed be assessed independent of the items being compared? In other words, is similarity computed from first principles each time a judgment must be made, or is it recalled from past experiences? Work on judgments of similarity is relevant here (cf Holyoak and Koh (1987)).

See Bareiss and King (1989) for an overview of current work on similarity assessment, other relevant work being Ashley (1989), Kolodner (1989), Porter (1989), Thagard and Holyoak (1989a), and Whitaker and co-workers (1989).

Case Adaptation

Once the case or cases which are to be used in the construction of a solution have been selected, the next step is to adapt the solutions from the selected cases to the problem at hand. If the current problem is nearly the same as one that has already been solved, then the old solution can be used directly and no adaptation is needed. This, however, is an unusual occurrence and general strategies for adapting cases are needed to handle the more frequently occurring situation in which the solution cannot be used unaltered. The search for case adaptation strategies is basically an attempt to find ways to adapt a case to make it relevant to a new situation.

Techniques for adapting cases vary according to the type of task being performed by the CBR system and to the extent that they are dependent on the particular domain that the system is operating in. CBR systems that do planning or problem solving often have strict criteria that a potential solution must meet. This emphasis on evaluation places limits on the kinds of adaptations that are permitted. Systems that come up with designs or explanations often place more emphasis on creative solutions, encouraging a wider variety of adaptation techniques which, while they may yield many "bad" solutions, may often come up with interesting or creative ones.

Another trend in research on case adaptation strategies has been to try to discover very general, domain-independent rules for modifying cases. If such rules could be discovered, they could be "plugged in" to any CBR system, regardless of whether its task was designing recipes or diagnosing heart conditions. In addition, these general rules might also be able to form the basis for the learning of more specific, domain-dependent rules by the system itself. Several methods of adaptation have been identified to date.

Substitution methods are used to substitute an object, value, or set of objects or values in an old solution for one or a set that better fit the new situation.

> *Reinstantiation* means instantiating the framework for the old solution with new arguments.
>
> *Parameter adjustment* is a method of adjusting a solution parameter from the old case based on differences between the old and new case descriptions.
>
> *Local search* is a search in semantic hierarchies for a substitute for some object in an old solution that must be replaced.
>
> *Query memory* is a broader search for a substitute.
>
> *Specialized search* directs search to portions of the knowledge base where a substitution is likely to be found.

Transformation methods transform a piece of an old solution to fit the new situation.

> *Commonsense transformation* makes use of commonsense knowledge about what kinds of things can be transformed.
>
> *Model-guided repair* uses a qualitative model to guide transformation.

Critic application is a methodology for implementing several of the types of adaptation listed above. It also provides a way of implementing ad-hoc adaptation heuristics, especially those that do insertions, deletions, and reorderings.

Derivational replay replays the method used in the old case for deriving some piece of the solution rather than taking the solution itself.

The area of case adaptation is currently a topic of active research. Some early examples of work that used adaptation are CHEF (Hammond, 1986, 1989a), and SWALE (Kass, 1986; Kass and co-workers, 1986). More recent work on adaptation includes Collins (1989), Goel and Chandrasekaran (1989), Hinrichs (1989), and Kass (1989). ABE (Kass, 1990) investigates adaptation techniques in the domain of explaining anomalous events.

REASONING USING CASES: APPLICATIONS OF CBR

There are two main styles of case-based reasoning: problem solving and interpretive. In the problem solving style of case-based reasoning, solutions to new problems are derived using old solutions as a guide. This style of CBR is characterized by heavy use of adaptation processes to generate solutions and interpretive processes to evaluate derived solutions.

In the interpretive style, new situations are evaluated in the context of old situations. A lawyer, for example, uses interpretive case-based reasoning when he or she uses a series of old cases to justify an argument in a new case. The interpretive style of case-based reasoning uses cases to provide justifications for solutions, allowing evaluation of solutions when no clear-cut methods are available and interpretation of situations when definitions of the situation's boundaries are open-ended or fuzzy.

This section presents a survey of the various tasks to which CBR systems have been applied, classified by the kind of CBR being done by each system. A summary of the CBR systems is presented in Table 1.

CBR and Problem Solving

Case-based reasoning is useful for a wide variety of problem solving tasks, including planning, diagnosis, and design. In each of these, cases are useful in both suggesting solutions and in warning of possible problems that might arise. There are additional advantages for each problem solving task.

CBR for Design. In design, problems are defined as a set of constraints, and the problem solver is required to provide a concrete artifact that solves the constraint problem. Usually the given constraints underspecify the problem (ie, there are many possible solutions). Sometimes, however, the constraints overconstrain the problem (ie, there is no solution if all constraints must be fulfilled). In addition, in design, a solution to one piece of a design problem is often tightly coupled to the solution of other pieces. While constraints can be used to maintain the connections between pieces, methodologies that require backtracking are too tedious for complex problems. Case-based reasoning addresses all of these issues.

- Cases suggest solutions to underconstrained problems. The solutions might not be exactly right, but since many different solutions might be appropriate, adaptation heuristics can generally create a satisfactory solution easily.
- When problems are over-constrained, cases suggest an alternative set of constraints that has worked in the past. While some adaptation might still have to be done, the full application of constraint relaxation can be avoided.
- When problem subparts are tightly coupled, cases can provide the glue that holds a solution together. Rather than solving the subparts by decomposing, recomposing, and fixing discrepancies, as is done in solving nearly-decomposable problems, a case suggests an entire solution, and the pieces that don't fit the new situation are adapted in place.

Several problem solvers have been built to do case-based design. JULIA (Kolodner, 1987; Hinrichs, 1988, 1989) plans meals; CYCLOPS (Navinchandra, 1988) uses case-based reasoning for landscape design; and KRITIK (Goel, 1989; Goel and Chandrasekaran, 1989) combines case-based with model-based reasoning for design of small mechanical assemblies. It uses case-based reasoning to propose solutions and uses the model to verify its proposed solutions, to point out where adaptation is needed, and to suggest adaptations. MEDIATOR (Kolodner and Simpson, 1989; Simpson, 1985), the earliest case-based problem solver, solved simple resource disputes, eg, two children wanting the same candy bar or two faculty members wanting to use the copy machine at the same time. PERSUADER (Sycara, 1987) solved labor management disputes.

At least one design problem solver is being put to use in the real world. CLAVIER (Barletta and Hennessy, 1989) is being used at Lockheed to lay out pieces made of composite materials in an oven to bake. The task is apparently a black art, ie, there is no known complete causal model of what works and why. Pieces of different sizes need to be in particular parts of the oven, but the size of some pieces and density of a layout might keep other pieces from heating correctly. The person in charge of layout kept a card file of the experiences, both those that worked and those that did not. Based on those experiences, CLAVIER can place pieces in appropriate parts of the oven and avoid putting pieces in the wrong places. It works as well as the expert whose experiences it uses, and is thus useful to Lockheed when the expert is unavailable. CLAVIER almost always uses several cases to do its design. One provides an overall layout, which is adapted appropriately. The others are used to fill in holes in the layout that adaptation rules by themselves cannot cover.

In almost all design problems, more than one case is necessary to solve the problem. Design problems tend to be large, and while one case can be used to solve some of it, it is usually not sufficient for solving the whole thing. In general, one case provides a framework for a solution and other cases are used to fill in missing details. In this way, decomposition and recomposition are avoided, as are large constraint satisfaction (qv) and relaxation problems.

CBR for Planning. Planning involves a number of complexities. Charniak and McDermott (1985) provide an excellent overview. Good plans must be sequenced appropriately so that late steps in a plan do not undo the intended results of earlier steps, preconditions of late steps in a plan are not violated by the results of earlier ones, and preconditions of later plan steps are fulfilled before the step is scheduled. As the number of plan steps increases, the computational complexity of projecting effects and comparing preconditions increases exponentially. In addition, a planner that must interact with the real world must deal with the real world's complexity, including the fact that it is in many ways unpredictable and that time is not limitless. Streams of goals might need to be achieved almost simultaneously. Time used for planning can take away from the time available for execution. Because conditions in the world can change between developing a plan and carrying it out, a plan might fail at execution time and require replanning, recovery, or repair. A planner with little time might miss opportunities during planning that can be better noticed and taken advantage of during execution. See Marks and co-workers (1988) for better explanations of these problems. Case-based reasoning can address many of these planning issues.

- Cases provide already worked-out plans in which sequencing, protection maintenance, and scheduling of preconditions have already been worked out. Rather than reasoning from scratch, the planner is required only to make repairs in old plans.
- If cases are indexed by the conjunctions of goals they achieve, they can be used to suggest ways of achieving several goals simultaneously or in conjunction with each other.
- Warnings provided by cases can help a planner anticipate and avoid problems, decreasing the likelihood of failure at execution time.
- Adaptation strategies used to adapt old plans to new situations can be used for execution-time recovery and repair.
- Suggestions made by cases shortcut the planning process, providing relatively more time for execution.
- Suggestions made by cases allow the reasoner to notice some opportunities (eg, to achieve goals simultaneously) more easily during planning.
- A case-based plan executor can notice opportunities during execution and use its adaptation strategies to update its plan accordingly.

Case-based reasoners are addressing many of these issues. PLEXUS (Alterman, 1986, 1988), a program that knows how to ride a subway, is able to do execution-time repairs by adapting and substituting semantically similar steps for those that have failed.

CHEF (Hammond, 1986, 1989a), one of the earliest case-based planners, addresses the problem of anticipating problems before execution time by learning from its problematic experiences. When problems happen at execution time, CHEF attempts to explain them and then to figure out how they could be repaired. It stores its hypothesized repair in memory and indexes the case by features that are likely to predict that the problem will recur. Before it begins plan derivation, it looks for failure situations and uses any it finds to anticipate the problems they point out. Later, it uses the repaired failure situations to suggest a plan that will avoid the problem it has anticipated.

Case-based planners that address some of the other problems mentioned above have also been built. TRUCKER (Hammond, 1989b) is an errand-running program that keeps track of its pending goals and is able to take advantage of opportunities that arise that allow it to achieve goals earlier than expected. MEDIC (qv) (Turner, 1989) is a diagnosis program. It is able to reuse previous plans for diagnosis but is flexible enough in its reuse to be able to follow up on unexpected turns of events. EXPEDITOR (Robinson and Kolodner, 1991) plans the events in the life of a single parent who must deal with kids and work. It caches its experiences achieving multiple goals by interleaving them. While it is slow in its initial planning, it gains competence over time as it is able to reuse its plans. The CSI BATTLE PLANNER (Goodman, 1989) shows how cases can be used to criticize and repair plans before they are executed.

CBR for Diagnosis. In diagnosis, a problem solver is given a set of symptoms and asked to explain them. A case-based diagnostician can use cases to suggest explanations for symptoms and to warn of explanations that have been found to be inappropriate in the past. Of course, one cannot expect a previous diagnosis to apply intact to the new case. Just as in planning and design, it is often necessary to adapt an old diagnosis to fit a new situation. CASEY (Koton, 1988a) was able to diagnose heart problems by adapting the diagnoses of previous heart patients to new patients. CASEY is a relatively simple program built on top of an existing model-based diagnostic program. When a new case is similar to one it has seen previously, it is several orders of magnitude more efficient at generating a diagnosis than is the model-based program (Koton, 1988a). CASEY's adaptations are based on a valid causal model (CASEY uses model-guided repair as its method of adaptation). Thus, its diagnoses are as accurate as those made from scratch based on the same causal model.

Cases are also useful in diagnosis in pointing the way out of previously-experienced reasoning quagmires. PROTOS (qv) (Bareiss, 1989) is designed to ensure that this happens in an efficient way. PROTOS diagnoses hearing disorders. In this domain, many of the diagnoses manifest themselves in similar ways and are difficult to differentiate. While novices are not aware of these subtle differences, experts are. PROTOS begins as a novice, and when it makes mistakes, a "teacher" explains its mistakes to it. As a result, PROTOS learns these subtle differences. As it does, it leaves difference pointers in its memory that allow it to move easily from the obvious diagnosis to the correct one.

Generating a diagnosis from scratch is a time-consuming task. In almost all diagnostic domains, however, there is sufficient regularity for a case-based approach to diagnosis generation to provide efficiency. Of course, no person or program can assume that a case-based suggestion is correct. The case-based suggestion must be validated. Often, however, validation is much easier than generation. In those kinds of domains, case-based reasoning can provide big wins.

Interpretive CBR

Interpretive case-based reasoning is a process of evaluating situations or solutions in the context of previous experience. It takes a situation or solution as input, and its output is a classification of the situation, an argument supporting the classification or solution, and/or justifications supporting the argument or solution. It is useful for situation classification, evaluation of a solution, argumentation, justification of a solution, interpretation, or plan, and projection of the effects of a decision or plan.

Interpretive case-based reasoning is most useful for evaluation when there are no computational methods available to evaluate a solution or position. Often, in these situations, there are so many unknowns that even if computational methods were available, the knowledge necessary to run them would usually be absent. A reasoner who uses cases to help evaluate and justify decisions or interpretations is making up for his lack of knowledge by assuming that the world is consistent.

Justification and Adversarial Reasoning. Adversarial reasoning means making persuasive arguments to convince others that we or our positions are right. A persuasive argument states a position and supports it, sometimes with hard facts and sometimes with valid inferences. But often the only way to justify a position is by citing relevant previous experiences or cases. Law thus provides a good domain for the study of adversarial reasoning and case-based justification for this reason, and much research in this area uses the legal domain (Ashley, 1987, 1988; Bain, 1986; Branting, 1989; Rissland, 1983).

HYPO (Ashley, 1987, 1988; Rissland, 1986) is the earliest and most sophisticated of the case-based legal reasoners. HYPO's method's for creating an argument and justifying a solution or position has several steps. First, the new situation is analyzed for relevant factors. Based on these factors, similar cases are retrieved. They are positioned with respect to the new situation. Some support it and some are against it. The most on-point cases of both sets are selected. The most on-point case supporting the new situation is used to create an argument for the proposed solution. Those in the nonsupport set are used to pose counter-arguments. Cases in the support set are then used to counter the counter-arguments. The result of this is a set of three-ply arguments in support of the solution, each of which is justified with cases. An important side effect of creating such arguments is that potential problem areas get highlighted.

In general, cases are useful in constructing arguments and justifying positions when there are no concrete principles or only a few of them, if principles are inconsistent, or if their meanings are not well-specified.

Classification and Interpretation. Interpretation in the context of case-based reasoning means deciding whether a concept fits some open-ended or fuzzy-bordered classification. The classification might be derived on the fly based on the task at hand or it might be well known but not well-defined in terms of necessary and sufficient conditions. Many of the classifications assumed to be defined are classifications of the open-ended variety. For example, it is assumed that a vehicle means a thing with wheels used for transportation, but when a sign says "No vehicles in the park," it is probably not referring to a wheelchair or a baby stroller, both of which fit our simple definition.

One way a case-based classifier works is to ask whether the new concept is enough like another one known to have the target classification. PROTOS (Bareiss, 1989), which diagnoses hearing disorders, works like this. Rather than classifying new cases using necessary and sufficient conditions, PROTOS does classification by trying to find the closest matching case in its case base to the new situation. It classifies the new situation by that case's classification.

To do this, PROTOS keeps track of how prototypical each of its cases is and what differentiates cases within one classification from each other. It first chooses a most likely classification, then chooses a most likely matching case in that class. Based on differences between the case it is attempting to match and the new situation, it eventually zeros in on a case that matches its new one well.

When no case matches well enough, it is sometimes necessary to consider hypothetical situations. Much of the work on this type of interpretation also comes from the study of legal reasoning. HYPO (Ashley, 1987, 1988; Rissland, 1986) uses hypotheticals for a variety of tasks necessary for good interpretation: to redefine old situations in terms of new dimensions, to create new standard cases when a necessary one does not exist, to explore and test the limits of reasonableness of a concept, to refocus a case by excluding some issues, to tease out hidden assumptions, and to organize or cluster cases. HYPO creates hypotheticals by making "copies" of a current situation that are stronger or weaker than the real situation for one side or the other. This work is guided by a set of modification heuristics that propose useful directions for hypothetical case creation based on current reasoning needs. HYPO's strategies for argumentation guide selection of modification heuristics. For example, to counter a counterexample, one might propose variations on a new situation that make it more like the counterexample.

Projecting Effects. Projection, the process of predicting the effects of a decision or plan, is an important part of the evaluative component of any planning or decision making scheme. When everything about a situation is known, projection is merely a process of running known inferences forward from a solution to see where it leads. More often, however, in real-world problems, everything is not known and effects cannot be predicted with accuracy based on any simple set of inference rules.

Cases provide a way of projecting effects based on what has been true in the past. Cases with similar plans that were failures can point to potential plan problems. Cases with similar plans that were successes give credence to the current plan. In addition, when parts of a plan are targeted for evaluation, cases can help with that.

Automated use of cases for projection has not been a focus of case-based reasoning research, but aid to a person doing projection is being addressed. CSI's BATTLE PLANNER (Goodman, 1989) is a case-retrieval system whose interface is set up to allow a person to use cases to project effects. A student commander can propose a solution plan to the system. The BATTLE PLANNER retrieves the best-matching cases that use a similar plan and divides them into success and failure situations. The person can examine the cases, use them to fix a plan, and then attempt a similar evaluation of the repaired plan. Or, the person can use the system to do a sensitivity analysis. By manipulating the details of the situation and looking at the changes in numbers of wins and losses (in effect, asking a series of "what-if" questions), he or she can determine which factors of the current situation are the crucial ones to repair and which should be left unchanged.

Interpretive Case-Based Reasoning and Problem Solving. Much work on interpretation has centered on the law domain and has looked at justifying an argument for or against some interpretation of the law. Case-based interpretation is not merely for interpretive problems, however. It is very useful as part of the evaluative or critical component of problem solving and decision making whenever strong causal models are missing. Though there has been little work in this area, the processes involved in interpretive case-based reasoning have the potential to play several important roles for a problem solver. First, if the framework for a solution is known, or if constraints governing it are known, these methods could be used to choose cases that would provide such a solution. Second, argument creation and justification result in knowledge of what features are the important ones to focus on. Knowing where to focus is important in problem solving also. Third, a side effect of HYPO's methods is that it can point out which features, if they were present, would yield a better solution. It does this by keeping track of near-miss dimensions and creation of hypothetical cases. A problem solver could use such information to inform its adaptation processes. Finally, interpretive methods can be used to predict the usefulness, quality, or results of a solution.

IMPLICATIONS OF CBR AS A COGNITIVE MODEL

One goal of building CBR systems is to attempt to understand the processes involved in reasoning in a case-based way. Psychologists who study analogical reasoning are investigating similar processes. There are several important potential applications of an understanding of the way people solve problems in a natural way.

- Decision support systems. This understanding can be used to help build decision aiding systems for people that can help them retrieve cases better. Psychologists have found that people are comfortable using cases to make decisions but do not always remember the right ones. The computer could be used as a retrieval tool to augment people's memories. (See the following section for further discussion on this application of CBR.)
- Teaching as providing cases. An understanding of human case-based reasoning might allow us to create teaching strategies and build teaching tools that teach based on good examples. If people are comfortable using examples to solve problems and know how to do it well, then one of our responsibilities as teachers might be to teach them the right ones. Systems that teach in a case-based way have recently begun to be developed (Burke and Ohmaye, 1990; Schank, 1991).
- Teaching the process of CBR. If it is understood which parts of this natural process are difficult to do well, people can be taught how to do case-based reasoning better. One criticism of using cases to make decisions, for example, is that it puts unsound bias into the reasoning system, because people tend to assume an answer from a previous case is right without justifying it in the new case. This says that people should be taught how to justify case-based suggestions and that justification or evaluation is crucial to good decision making. If other problems people have in solving problems in a case-based way can be isolated, then people can be taught to do those things better.

BUILDING CBR SYSTEMS

There are many reasons one might want to build a CBR system. It might be needed to solve problems, to suggest concrete answers to problems, to be suggestive without providing answers (ie, to give abstract advice), or to just act as a database that can retrieve partially-matching cases. This suggests several different kinds of case-based reasoning systems that might be built. At the two extremes are fully-automated systems and retrieval-only systems. Fully automated systems are those that solve problems completely by themselves and have some means of interacting with the world to receive feedback on their decisions. Retrieval-only systems work interactively with a person to solve a problem. The role of such systems is just to augment a person's memory, providing cases for consideration that he or she might not have been aware of; the user is left responsible for doing the reasoning and making the hard decisions. The CSI BATTLE PLANNER (Goodman, 1989) provides this type of capability now for battle planning. Then there is the whole range of systems in between, some requiring more on the part of the person using the system, some less.

How might one go about building a CBR system? What is required for the simplest of systems is a library of cases that coarsely cover the set of problems that come up in a domain. Both success stories and failures must be included and the cases must be appropriately indexed. This library, along with a friendly and useful interface, can act as an "expert assistant" by augmenting the memory of a human user. Once a system consisting of the case library and user interface has been built, automated reasoning and problem-solving processes can then be added incrementally.

SUMMARY

The case-based reasoning paradigm grew out of research on human memory and a growing dissatisfaction with rule-based systems. CBR has several advantages as a theory and methodology of problem-solving, including psychological plausibility, easier knowledge acquisition, and robustness. In addition, CBR provides a natural mechanism for incorporating learning, offering such advantages as performance enhancements and scalability.

The basic method of CBR is to adapt past solutions to solve a current problem. This involves extracting indexes from the input and using these indexes to retrieve relevant cases from memory. After narrowing down the set of retrieved cases to a few most worthy of consideration, a CBR system adapts these cases to form a solution to the current problem. This solution is evaluated and, if acceptable, it is executed in the real world. The system then receives feedback about the success or failure of its solution and may modify the solution in response to an analysis of this feedback. Once the solution is acceptable, it is added to memory to be used to solve similar problems in the future.

This basic algorithm gives rise to many interesting issues which are currently being researched in the CBR community. Some of the issues discussed here are indexing vocabularies, memory organization, retrieval algorithms, similarity metrics, and case adaptation. While much progress has been made, a great deal more work remains to be done, making it likely that the CBR paradigm will continue to be an active area of research in the years to come.

CBR systems have been designed to perform a wide variety of both problem-solving and interpretive tasks. Design, planning, and diagnosis are three areas where problem-solving CBR has been applied. Systems doing interpretive CBR have been built to do justification and adversarial reasoning, classification, and interpretation tasks, as well as projecting the effects of plans. Given its success in such a diverse set of domains and tasks, it is not surprising that case-based reasoning continues to enjoy a great deal of popularity as a reasoning and problem solving paradigm.

BIBLIOGRAPHY

R. Alterman, "An Adaptive Planner," *Proceedings Fifth National Conference on Artificial Intelligence*, Philadelphia, Pa., AAAI, Menlo Park, Calif., 1986, pp. 65–69.

R. Alterman, "Adaptive Planning," *Cogn. Sci.* **12**, 393–422 (1988).

K. D. Ashley, "Distinguishing—A Reasoner's Wedge," *Proceedings of the 1987 Conference of the Cognitive Science Society*, Lawrence Erlbaum, Hillsdale, N.J., 1987, pp. 737–747.

K. D. Ashley, *Modeling Legal Argument: Reasoning with Cases and Hypotheticals*, Ph.D. dissertation, COINS Technical Report No. 88–01, Department of Computer and Information Science, University of Massachusetts, Amherst, Mass., 1988.

K. Ashley, "Assessing Similarities Among Cases: A Position Paper," *Proceedings: Case-Based Reasoning Workshop (DARPA), II*, Morgan-Kaufmann, San Mateo, Calif., 1989, pp. 72–75.

K. Ashley and E. Rissland, "Waiting on Weighting: A Symbolic Least Commitment Approach," in *Proceedings of the Seventh National Conference on Artificial Intelligence*, St. Paul, Minn., AAAI, Menlo Park, Calif., 1988, pp. 239–244.

W. Bain, *Case-Based Reasoning: A Computer Model of Subjective Assessment*, Ph.D. dissertation, Yale University, New Haven, Conn., 1986.

E. R. Bareiss, *Exemplar-Based Knowledge Acquisition: A Unified Approach to Concept Representation, Classification, and Learning*, Academic Press, Inc., Boston, Mass., 1989.

R. Bareiss and J. King, "Similarity Assessment in Case-Based Reasoning," *Proceedings: Case-Based Reasoning Workshop (DARPA), II*, Morgan-Kaufmann, San Mateo, Calif., 1989, pp. 67–71.

R. Barletta and D. Hennessy, "Case Adaptation in Autoclave Layout Design," *Proceedings: Case-Based Reasoning Workshop (DARPA), II*, Morgan-Kaufmann, San Mateo, Calif., 1989, pp. 203–207.

L. Birnbaum and G. Collins, "Remindings and Engineering Design Themes: A Case Study in Indexing Vocabulary," *Proceedings: Case-Based Reasoning Workshop (DARPA), II*, Morgan-Kaufmann, San Mateo, Calif., 1989, pp. 47–51.

L. K. Branting, "Integrating Generalizations with Exemplar-Based Reasoning," *Proceedings of the Eleventh Annual Conference of the Cognitive Science Society*, Lawrence Erlbaum, Hillsdale, N.J., 1989, pp. 139–146.

R. Burke and E. Ohmaye, "Case-Based Environments for Learning," in B. Woolf and E. Soloway, eds., *Knowledge-based Environments for Learning and Teaching*, Symposium conducted at AAAI Spring Symposium Series, Stanford University, Stanford, Calif., 1990.

E. Charniak and D. McDermott, *Introduction to Artificial Intelligence*, Addison-Wesley, Reading, Mass., 1985.

G. Collins, *Plan Creation: Using Strategies as Blueprints*, Ph.D. dissertation, Yale University, New Haven, Conn., 1987.

G. Collins, "Plan Adaptation: A Transformational Approach," *Proceedings: Case-Based Reasoning Workshop (DARPA), II*, Morgan-Kaufmann, San Mateo, Calif., 1989, pp. 47–51.

G. Collins and L. Birnbaum, "Problem-Solver State Descriptions as Abstract Indices for Case Retrieval," in *Working Notes of the 1990 AAAI Spring Symposium on Case-Based Reasoning*, Stanford, Calif., March 1990.

E. Domeshek, "Parallelism for Index Generation and Reminding," *Proceedings: Case-Based Reasoning Workshop (DARPA), II*, Morgan-Kaufmann, San Mateo, Calif., 1989, pp. 244–247.

E. Domeshek, *Case-Based Advising in the Social Domain: Representation, Indexing and Retrieval*, Ph.D. dissertation, Yale University, New Haven, Conn., (in preparation).

E. Feigenbaum, "The Simulation of Verbal Learning Behavior," in E. Feigenbaum and J. Feldman, eds., *Computers and Thought*, McGraw-Hill, New York, 1963, pp. 297–309.

D. Gentner, "Finding the Needle: Accessing and Reasoning from Prior Cases," *Proceedings: Case-Based Reasoning Workshop (DARPA), II*, Morgan-Kaufmann, San Mateo, Calif., 1989, pp. 137–143.

A. Goel, *Integration of Case-Based Reasoning and Model-Based Reasoning for Adaptive Design Problem Solving*, Ph.D. dissertation, Ohio State University, Columbus, Ohio, 1989.

A. Goel and B. Chandrasekaran, "Use of Device Models in Adaptation of Design Cases," *Proceedings: Case-Based Reasoning Workshop (DARPA), II*, Morgan-Kaufmann, San Mateo, Calif., 1989, pp. 100–109.

V. Goel and P. Pirolli, "Motivating the Notion of Generic Design within Information-Processing Theory: The Design Problem Space," *AI Mag.* **10**(1), 18–36 (1989).

M. Goodman, "CBR in Battle Planning," *Proceedings: Case-Based Reasoning Workshop (DARPA), II*, Morgan-Kaufmann, San Mateo, Calif., 1989, pp. 264–269.

K. Hammond, "CHEF: A Model of Case-Based Planning," *Proceedings of the Fifth National Conference on Artificial Intelligence*, Philadelphia, Pa., AAAI, Menlo Park, Calif., 1986, pp. 267–271.

K. J. Hammond, *Case-Based Planning: Viewing Planning as a Memory Task*, Academic Press, Inc., Boston, Mass., 1989a.

K. Hammond, "Opportunistic Memory," *Proceedings of the Eleventh International Joint Conference on Artificial Intelligence*, Detroit, Mich., Morgan-Kaufmann, San Mateo, Calif., 1989b, pp. 504–510.

K. Hammond, "On Functionally Motivated Vocabularies: An Apologia," *Proceedings: Case-Based Reasoning Workshop (DARPA), II*, Morgan-Kaufmann, San Mateo, Calif., 1989c, pp. 52–56.

F. Hayes-Roth, D. A. Waterman, and D. B. Lenat, eds., *Building Expert Systems*, Addison-Wesley, Reading, Mass., 1983.

T. R. Hinrichs, "Towards an Architecture for Open World Problem Solving," in J. Kolodner, ed., *Proceedings: Case-Based Reasoning Workshop (DARPA)*, Morgan-Kaufmann, San Mateo, Calif., 1988, pp. 182–189.

T. Hinrichs, "Strategies for Adaptation and Recovery in a Design Problem Solver," *Proceedings: Case-Based Reasoning Workshop (DARPA), II*, Morgan-Kaufmann, San Mateo, Calif., 1989, pp. 115–118.

K. Holyoak and K. Koh, "Surface and Structural Similarity in Analogical Transfer," *Memory & Cognition* 15, 332–340 (1987).

L. Hunter, "Finding Paradigm Cases or When is a Case Worth Remembering?" *Proceedings: Case-Based Reasoning Workshop (DARPA), II*, Morgan-Kaufmann, San Mateo, Calif., 1989, pp. 57–61.

A. Kass, "Modifying Explanations to Understand Stories," *Proceedings of the Eighth Annual Conference of the Cognitive Science Society*, Lawrence Erlbaum, Hillsdale, N.J., 1986, pp. 691–696.

A. Kass, "Adaptation-Based Explanation: Extending Script/Frame Theory to Handle Novel Input," in *Proceedings of the Eleventh International Joint Conference on Artificial Intelligence*, Detroit, Mich., Morgan-Kaufmann, San Mateo, Calif., 1989, pp. 141–147.

A. Kass, *Developing Creative Hypothesis by Adapting Explanations*, Ph.D. dissertation, Yale University, New Haven, Conn., 1990. Reprinted as Technical Report 6, Institute for the Learning Sciences, Northwestern University, Evanston, Ill.

A. M. Kass and D. B. Leake, "Case-Based Reasoning Applied to Constructing Explanations," in J. Kolodner, ed., *Proceedings: Case-Based Reasoning Workshop (DARPA)*, Morgan-Kaufmann, San Mateo, Calif., 1988, pp. 190–208.

A. M. Kass, D. B. Leake, and C. C. Owens, "Swale: A Program That Explains," in R. C. Schank, ed., *Explanation Patterns: Understanding Mechanically and Creatively*, Lawrence Erlbaum, Hillsdale, N.J., 1986, pp. 232–254.

G. A. Klein and R. Calderwood, "How Do People Use Analogues to Make Decisions?" in J. Kolodner, ed., *Proceedings: Case-Based Reasoning Workshop (DARPA)*, Morgan-Kaufmann, San Mateo, Calif., 1988, pp. 209–218.

J. L. Kolodner, "Reconstructive Memory: A Computer Model," *Cogn. Sci.* 7, 281–328 (1983a).

J. Kolodner, "Towards an Understanding of the Role of Experience in the Evolution from Novice to Expert," *Int. J. Man Machine Studies* 19, 497–518 (1983b).

J. L. Kolodner, *Retrieval and Organization Strategies in Conceptual Memory: A Computer Model*, Lawrence Erlbaum, Hillsdale, N.J., 1984.

J. Kolodner, "Towards a Memory Architecture That Supports Reminding," *Proceedings of the Eighth Annual Conference of the Cognitive Science Society*, Lawrence Erlbaum, Hillsdale, N.J., 1986, pp. 467–477.

J. L. Kolodner, "Capitalizing on Failure Through Case-Base Inference," *Proceedings of the Ninth Annual Conference of the Cognitive Science Society*, Lawrence Erlbaum, Hillsdale, N.J., pp. 715–726, 1987.

J. L. Kolodner, "Retrieving Events from a Case Memory: A Parallel Implementation," in J. Kolodner, ed., *Proceedings: Case-Based Reasoning Workshop (DARPA)*, Morgan-Kaufmann, San Mateo, Calif., 1988, pp. 233–240.

J. Kolodner, "Judging Which is the Best Case for a Case-based Reasoner," *Proceedings: Case-Based Reasoning Workshop (DARPA), II*, Morgan-Kaufmann, San Mateo, Calif., 1989, pp. 77–81.

J. Kolodner, *An Introduction to Case-based Reasoning*, Technical Report No. GIT-ICS-90/19, College of Computing, Georgia Institute of Technology, Atlanta, Ga., 1990.

J. Kolodner, "Improving Human Decision Making Through Case-based Decision Aiding," *AI Mag.* 12(2), 52–68 (1991).

J. L. Kolodner and R. L. Simpson, "The MEDIATOR: Analysis of an Early Case-based Problem Solver," *Cog. Sci.* 13, 507–549 (1989).

P. Koton, *Using Experience in Learning and Problem Solving*, Ph.D. dissertation, Massachusetts Institute of Technology, Cambridge, Mass., 1988a.

P. Koton, "Reasoning about Evidence in Causal Explanations," *Proceedings of the Seventh National Conference on Artificial Intelligence*, St. Paul, Minn., AAAI, Menlo Park, Calif., 1988b, pp. 256–261.

J. S. Lancaster and J. L. Kolodner, "Varieties of Learning from Problem Solving Experience," in *Proceedings of the Tenth Annual Conference of the Cognitive Science Society*, Lawrence Erlbaum, Hillsdale, N.J., 1988, pp. 447–453.

D. Leake and C. Owens, "Organizing Memory for Explanations," in *Proceedings of the Eighth Annual Conference of the Cognitive Science Society*, Lawrence Erlbaum, Hillsdale, N.J., 1986, pp. 710–715.

M. Lebowitz, "Generalization from Natural Language Text," *Cog. Sci.* 7, 1–40 (1983).

M. Marks, K. J. Hammond, and T. Converse, "Planning in an Open World: A Pluralistic Approach," in J. Kolodner, ed., *Proceedings: Case-Based Reasoning Workshop (DARPA)*, Morgan-Kaufmann, San Mateo, Calif., 1988, pp. 271–285.

C. Martin, "Indexing Using Complex Features," *Proceedings: Case-Based Reasoning Workshop (DARPA), II*, Morgan-Kaufmann, San Mateo, Calif., 1989a, pp. 26–30.

C. Martin, "Complex Indices: A Metaphorical Example," *Proceedings: Case-Based Reasoning Workshop (DARPA), II*, Morgan-Kaufmann, San Mateo, Calif., 1989b, pp. 295–299.

D. Navinchandra, "Case-Based Reasoning in CYCLOPS, a Design Problem Solver," in J. Kolodner, ed., *Proceedings: Case-Based Reasoning Workshop (DARPA)*, Morgan-Kaufmann, San Mateo, Calif., 1988, pp. 286–301.

C. Owens, "Domain-Independent Prototype Cases for Planning in J. Kolodner, ed., *Proceedings: Case-Based Reasoning Workshop (DARPA)*, Morgan-Kaufmann, San Mateo, Calif., 1988, pp. 302–311.

C. Owens, "Plan Transformations as Abstract Indices," *Proceedings: Case-Based Reasoning Workshop (DARPA), II*, Morgan-Kaufmann, San Mateo, Calif., 1989a, pp. 62–65.

C. Owens, "Integrating Feature Extraction and Memory Search," *Proceedings of the Eleventh Annual Conference of the Cognitive Science Society*, Lawrence Erlbaum, Hillsdale, N.J., 1989b, pp. 163–170.

M. Pazzani, "Indexing Strategies for Goal Specific Retrieval of Cases," *Proceedings: Case-Based Reasoning Workshop (DARPA), II*, Morgan-Kaufmann, San Mateo, Calif., 1989, pp. 52–56.

B. Porter, "Similarity Assessment: Computation vs Representation," *Proceedings: Case-Based Reasoning Workshop (DARPA), II*, Morgan-Kaufmann, San Mateo, Calif., 1989, pp. 82–84.

S. Read and I. Cesa, "This Reminds Me of the Time When . . . : Expectation Failures in Reminding and Explanation," *J. Experimental Social Psych.* **27**, 1–25, (1991).

M. Redmond, "Combining Explanation Types for Learning by Understanding Instructional Examples," *Proceedings of the Eleventh Annual Conference of the Cognitive Science Society*, Lawrence Erlbaum, Hillsdale, N.J., 1989, pp. 147–154.

M. Redmond, "Distributed Cases for Case-Based Reasoning; Facilitating Uses of Multiple Cases," *Proceedings of the Eighth National Conference on Artificial Intelligence*, AAAI, Menlo Park, Calif., 1990, pp. 304–309.

C. Riesbeck and C. Martin, *Direct Memory Access Parsing*, Technical Report YALEU/CSD/RR 354, Yale University, New Haven, Conn., 1985.

C. K. Reisbeck and R. S. Schank, *Inside Case-Based Reasoning*, Lawrence Erlbaum, Hillsdale, N.J., 1989.

E. L. Rissland, "Examples in Legal Reasoning: Legal Hypotheticals," *Proceedings of the Eighth International Joint Conference on Artificial Intelligence*, Karlsruhe, FRG, Morgan-Kaufmann, San Mateo, Calif., 1983, pp. 90–93.

E. L. Rissland, "Learning How to Argue: Using Hypotheticals," in J. L. Kolodner and C. K. Riesbeck, eds., *Experience, Memory, and Reasoning*, Lawrence Erlbaum, Hillsdale, N.J., 1986, pp. 115–126.

E. L. Rissland and K. D. Ashley, "Hypotheticals as a Heuristic Device," *Proceedings of the Fifth National Conference on Artificial Intelligence*, Philadelphia, Pa., AAAI, Menlo Park, Calif., 1986, pp. 289–297.

E. Rissland and K. Ashley, "Credit Assignment and the Problem of Competing Factors in Case-Based Reasoning," in J. Kolodner, ed., *Proceedings: Case-Based Reasoning Workshop (DARPA)*, Morgan-Kaufmann, San Mateo, Calif., 1988, pp. 327–344.

S. M. Robinson and J. L. Kolodner, "Indexing Cases for Planning and Acting in Dynamic Environments: Exploiting Hierarchical Goal Structures," *Proceedings of the Thirteenth Annual Conference of the Cognitive Science Society*, Lawrence Erlbaum, Hillsdale, N.J., 1991.

B. H. Ross, "Remindings in Learning and Instruction," in S. Vosniadou and A. Ortony, eds., *Similarity and Analogical Reasoning*. Cambridge University Press, New York, 1989a, pp. 438–469.

B. H. Ross, "Some Psychological Results on Case-based Reasoning," *Proceedings: Case-Based Reasoning Workshop (DARPA), II*, Morgan-Kaufmann, San Mateo, Calif., 1989b, pp. 144–147.

R. Schank, *Dynamic Memory: A Theory of Learning in Computers and People*, Cambridge University Press, New York, 1982.

R. C. Schank, *Case-Based Teaching: Four Experiences in Educational Software Design*, Technical Report No. 7, Institute for the Learning Sciences, Northwestern University, Evanston, Ill., 1991.

R. Schank and co-workers, "Towards a General Content Theory of Indices," in *Working Notes of the AAAI Spring Symposium on Case-Based Reasoning*, American Association for Artificial Intelligence, Stanford, Calif., 1990, pp. 36–40.

R. L. Simpson, *A Computer Model of Case-Based Reasoning in Problem Solving: An Investigation in the Domain of Dispute Mediation*, Ph.D. dissertation, Technical Report No. GIT-ICS-85/18, School of Information and Computer Science, Georgia Institute of Technology, Atlanta, Ga., 1985.

S. Slade, "Case-Based Reasoning: A Research Paradigm," *AI Mag.* **12**(1), 42–55 (1991).

C. Stanfill, "Memory-Based Reasoning Applied to English Pronunciation," in *Proceedings of the Sixth National Conference on Artificial Intelligence*, AAAI, Menlo Park, Calif., 1987, pp. 577–581.

C. Stanfill, and D. L. Waltz, "The Memory-Based Reasoning Paradigm," in J. Kolodner, ed., *Proceedings: Case-Based Reasoning Workshop (DARPA)*, Morgan-Kaufmann, San Mateo, Calif., 1988, pp. 414–424.

E. P. Sycara, *Resolving Adversarial Conflicts: An Approach to Integrating Case-based and Analytic Methods*, Ph.D. dissertation, Technical Report No. GIT-ICS-87/26, School of Information and Computer Science, Georgia Institute of Technology, Atlanta, Ga., 1987.

P. Thagard and K. Holyoak, "How to Compute Semantic Similarity," *Proceedings: Case-Based Reasoning Workshop (DARPA), II*, Morgan-Kaufmann, San Mateo, Calif., 1989a, pp. 85–86.

P. Thagard and K. Holyoak, "Why Indexing is the Wrong Way to Think About Analog Retrieval," *Proceedings: Case-Based Reasoning Workshop (DARPA), II*, Morgan-Kaufmann, San Mateo, Calif., 1989b, pp. 36–40.

R. M. Turner, *A Schema-based Model of Adaptive Problem Solving*, Ph.D. dissertation, Technical Report No. GIT-ICS-89/42. School of Information and Computer Science, Georgia Institute of Technology, Atlanta, Ga., 1989.

D. Waltz, "Is Indexing Used for Retrieval?" *Proceedings: Case-Based Reasoning Workshop (DARPA), II*, Morgan-Kaufmann, San Mateo, Calif., 1989, pp. 41–44.

L. Whitaker, S. Wiggins, and G. Klein, "Using Qualitative or Multi-Attribute Similarity to Retrieve Useful Cases from a Case Base," *Proceedings: Case-Based Reasoning Workshop (DARPA), II*, Morgan-Kaufmann, San Mateo, Calif., 1989, pp. 345–347.

MENACHEM Y. JONA
Northwestern University

JANET L. KOLODNER
Georgia Institute of Technology

This work was supported in part by the Defense Advanced Research Projects Agency, monitored by the Air Force Office of Scientific Research under contract F49620-88-C-005; by the NSF under grant IST-8608362; and by ARI under contracts MDA-903-86-C-173 and MDA-903-90-K-0112. The Institute for the Learning Sciences was established in 1989 with the support of Andersen Consulting, part of The Arthur Andersen Worldwide Organization. The authors thank Marie Paro for helpful comments on a draft of this article.

REASONING, CAUSAL

A cause is something that produces or results in an effect. Causal reasoning applies knowledge of such connective relationships in order to predict future events from present conditions and to explain the sequencing of events observed in the past. In AI, causal reasoning automates these kinds of inferences to describe the behavior of symbolic models of systems, mechanisms, or people.

Research involving causal reasoning in AI and related disciplines is very diverse. One approach to organizing this work is to distinguish broadly between causal models and theories of causation. *Causal models* apply specialized types of causal reasoning to predict or explain behavior in particular domains. Examples include diagnosing medical problems or circuit faults, simulating physical systems, understanding stories, and planning robotic tasks. Most AI research involving causal reasoning falls into this "applied" category. In contrast, *theories of causation* focus on understanding the nature of causal relations and causal reasoning per se. Traditionally, such analyses have been the concern of philosophers of science, statisticians, and cognitive scientists. Recently, AI researchers have developed computational theories of causation, typically cast as formal logics. These formalisms define domain-independent logical representations for causal relationships in the world and automated deduction algorithms that capture causal inferences.

Causal models can be partitioned into two subclasses based on how they depict causation: explicitly or implicitly. Explicit causal models draw behavioral inferences in terms of structures that are specifically and uniquely interpreted as causal relations. Typically, causal links (eg, "causes," "possibly causes," or "causes with probability x"), are used to connect states or events in a chain or network. Causal reasoning in these systems hinges on tracing the links signifying causal relations from known states to other states that represent either future behavior (prediction) or elaborations of already observed situations (explanation).

In contrast, causal knowledge in implicit models is either: (1) not represented explicitly; or (2) modeled using explicit structures that do not have uniquely causal interpretations. Approach 1 is typified by symbolic simulators of mechanical or electronic devices: the algorithms that generate model system behaviors implicitly reflect causal structure in the world, but the simulators make no essential reference to causation at all. Most logic-based planning systems exemplify approach 2: axioms, called causal or projection rules, specify the behavioral consequences of basic model actions such as picking up and moving blocks about a table. Planning systems apply these predictive axioms to determine whether a given action will help to achieve desired goals. However, reasoning based on such "causal" axioms is not explicitly distinguished from inferences derived from noncausal axioms (eg, that prohibit simultaneous actions or two objects cooccupying a single location.)

This categorization captures important distinctions in the field although, like most organizing frameworks, it is somewhat broad. Causal modelers frequently make important observations about the nature of causation, while causal theorists sometimes apply their accounts to construct causal models in particular domains. The following sections review AI and related literature on causal models and theories. A brief critical assessment of the field and future research directions concludes the entry.

EXPLICIT CAUSAL MODELS

Explicit causal models often depict causal relationships as links between nodes in a network that represent states, state changes, events, or actions. These models have been explored most extensively in two quite different contexts: diagnosis of medical problems or circuit faults and story understanding. In both domains, the goals of causal inference are to (1) map available observations onto network nodes and (2) activate additional nodes as necessary to construct a subnetwork of states and events linked in a causally coherent pattern. This subnetwork constitutes a causal explanation or prediction for the observed situation.

Rieger and Grinberg (1977) introduced the first extensive causal-link representation. Their goal was to express causal knowledge of the operation of a complex mechanism sufficient to simulate its behavior. Their model encompasses types of nodes that represent actions, tendencies, states, and state changes, together with link types that depict primitive causal relations among these nodes. Connective link types include causality, enablement, and concurrency. Each node and causal link in a mechanism description is implemented as an independent computational agent. Activation percolates through the network according to the semantics of each type of link, in a temporal sequence intended to correspond to the sequence of states, actions, or state changes in the behavior of the mechanism. The simulator can, however, introduce spurious temporal ordering relations among events on independent causal paths; no provisions were made for detecting or correcting these anomalies. Rieger and Grinberg demonstrated this apparatus by building structural models and behavioral simulations for several nontrivial mechanisms, including the forced hot-air furnace and the flushing toilet.

Research on story understanding (see STORY ANALYSIS) employs causal reasoning to reconstruct complete and coherent scenarios from narrative fragments such as "Joe burned his hand because he forgot the stove was on." Schank parses stories into complex symbolic networks of acts and their participants (Schank and Abelson, 1977). An elaborate grammar specifies legal constructions of objects, actors, and primitive "act" types such as PROPEL, GRASP, and PTRANS (physical transfer of objects). Stereotypic activities such as dining at a restaurant are captured in predefined network templates called scripts (qv). Scripts establish an expected sequencing of acts, including nominal and exceptional "branching" situations, and their relationships to actors' plans and goals. Shank's program extends parsed story networks through a set of inference patterns, enabling causal questions (eg, how and why), to be answered about elements unmentioned in the input narrative. In particular, causality inference patterns generate explicit causal links from conjoined sequences of acts such as "John hit Bob and he fell." Similarly, belief and intention patterns ground reasoning about the mental states and causal motivations of actors in the story. Subsequent research has explored various alternative modeling frameworks and inference techniques (Dyer, 1983); however, reasoning about the causal content of stories remains a central issue.

As in story understanding, the purpose of causal reasoning in medical diagnosis (see MEDICINE, AI IN) is to determine a causally coherent set of events that has taken place and that matches the available observations. The explicit causal models embodied in diagnostic systems typically employ simpler models consisting of a single type of node representing partial descriptions of patients' states and a single type of causal link.

The CASNET program (Weiss, 1978) diagnoses various forms of the eye disease glaucoma. Causal relationships in CASNET are represented as links weighted with confidence factors, scaled from 1 (rarely causes) to 5 (almost always causes). A disease process is modeled as a causal chain of anomalous "pathophysiological" states, whose partial ordering depicts the progression of the disease over time. An example causal chain is that angle closure (if prolonged and untreated) Causes elevated intraocular pressure, which Causes optical-disk cupping, which Causes glaucomatous visual field loss. CASNET incorporates two other levels of description, one for disease categories such as open-angle glaucoma, and one for clinical observations such as patient symptoms and test results. Support for diagnostic hypotheses is propagated by associational links from clinical evidence to pathophysiological states, across causal links among pathophysiological states, and by classification links from anomalous states to disease categories. Diagnostic inferencing in CASNET treats the weighted causal links simply as conditional probabilities. However, the links reflect actual connections in the glaucoma domain and therefore can be activated in orderly chains with causally meaningful relations to disease hypotheses. Thus, the causal interpretation of links is relevant for constructing and validating the medical knowledge base, but not for the internal operation of the program per se.

The ABEL program (Patil, 1981) uses weighted causal links between anomalous states to reason about acid-base and electrolyte disturbances in patients. ABEL's links are more complex than CASNET's, consisting of multivariate relations between multiple cause and effect states that can also reflect diagnostic context and default assumptions. ABEL's causal links, while homogeneous, can also be decomposed hierarchically. For example, "{Coleostomy, Diarrhea, Fistula} Cause Lower-GI-Fluid-Loss, which Consists-of {Water-loss, Sodium-Loss, . . .} and which Causes {Dehydration, Acute-Renal-Failure, Hypotension, . . .}." Finally, ABEL interprets link weights as measures of magnitudes rather than as probabilities. This allows ABEL to reason about interactions between multiple diseases by deciding whether a known cause is sufficient to account for the observed magnitude of the disorder. If not, a second disturbance may be interacting with the first to cause the observed problem. ABEL relies on numeric calculations to generate disease-interaction hypotheses and to test whether a given cause is sufficient to account for an observed effect, which restricts the applicability of this technique to domains where adequate numerical theories exist. CADUCEUS (qv) (Pople, 1982) is the successor to INTERNIST-1, a general diagnostic program for internal medicine. CADUCEUS develops a pattern of interactions between causal and taxonomic links among disease hypotheses and pathophysiological states, focusing on the search for appropriate intermediate states. The causal network portion of the model features a single kind of link, meaning "may be caused by," to connect nodes that represent patient states. During diagnosis, the causal network is used to focus search on a small set of possible causes for an observed finding or inferred intermediate states. Simultaneously, the independent taxonomic network is navigated to isolate a parallel set of differential diagnosis problems. CADUCEUS then combines the two analyses to determine the diagnostic test that best refines the set of candidate diagnostic hypotheses at lowest cost.

Causal-link models generally depend on networks made up of behavioral fragments, state/event/action nodes, connected by causal relation arcs. Such models have been criticized on the grounds that they cannot represent the structure of mechanisms, nor derive behavioral predictions from structure. Without this capability, interactions between processes are difficult to reason about since they interact by having simultaneous influences on structural parameters. As noted above, ABEL (Patil, 1981) addresses this issue by assigning numeric strengths to causal links and performing substantial calculations with those numbers. In contrast, Pipitone (1984) *combines* causal and structural knowledge to troubleshoot electronic circuits: causal knowledge is incorporated as rules that depict the propagation of abnormal behavior through structural models. Most rules take the form "Given Test-Precondition-X, Parameter-1 Abnormality-1 at Terminal-1 always/sometimes causes Parameter-2 Abnormality-2 at Terminal-2." Abnormalities can be quantitative or qualitative, such as "DC-voltage-HIGH." The structural model specifies connections between terminals of relevant device modules. The rules and structural model are applied to find combinations of component faults consistent with test results reported by a technician. Given test costs and a priori probabilities of component failures, Pipitone's system computes the probability of a given fault combination and the most cost-effective test to perform next to further isolate device faults. Causal rules can also represent explicit fault models, such as "Faulty module-X sometimes causes Abnormality-Y," considerably enhancing diagnostic efficiency.

IMPLICIT CAUSAL MODELS

Symbolic simulation is a type of causal reasoning in which the behaviors of individual components of complex physical or biological systems are described; the global behavior of the system is then deduced from the interactions of the components. Fundamentally different approaches for describing component behavior have been developed for discrete and continuous process models of systems.

Symbolic simulation of a continuous system derives a qualitative description of that system's possible behaviors from a qualitative description of its structure. The structural description, which represents an abstraction of the exact differential equations that model the system, is based on a set of continuous state variables and constraints that must be satisfied by the values of those variables at each instant in time. Consider, for example, a system consisting of two containers filled with liquid connection by a uniform pipe with a valve. State variables would include flow, rate of flow, the relative heights and fluid levels of the containers, and valve position. Values can be landmark points in a continuous space (eg, 0, Min-X, ∞), intervals between landmark points, (eg, partially full), or points from a discrete space (eg, open, closed). System constraints, following simple fluid mechanics, would be that the total volume of fluid remain constant, that the rate of flow into one container is equal to the rate of flow out of the other, and so on. Biophysical systems can be characterized similarly, by combining qualitative physics and chemistry.

A single behavior of a mechanism is represented as a sequence of qualitative values of the state variables, together with directions of value changes. For example, both flow and rate of flow can increase, decrease, or remain constant. Qualitative simulation propagates changes of state through the structural description (eg, opening the pipe valve), by cycling through the following steps: (1) propagating a partial set of variable values across constraints to construct a complete system description at given instants; (2) examining variables with changing values in a given state to determine whether they are approaching limiting landmark values; and (3) determining the next qualitatively distinct state by analyzing the possible transitions of individual variables to determine which transitions can occur next. Different researchers use transition-ordering decision procedures (Williams, 1984a, 1984b; Forbus, 1984; Kuipers, 1984) or constraint-based transition filtering rules (Kuipers, 1985; de Kleer, 1984; de Kleer and Brown, 1984; de Kleer, 1979) to accomplish this step. Structural descriptions may not provide sufficient information to specify the next qualitative state uniquely, so qualitative simulators create a branching tree or directed graph of state descriptions that represent possible behaviors (and alternative solutions to the abstracted differential equations). Variations in qualitative structural models and simulation algorithms are described more fully in Bobrow (1985) (see PHYSICS, QUALITATIVE).

Reasoning in qualitative simulation is based on structural models devoid of explicit causal structures. Causal knowledge is nonetheless both implicitly present and important. For example, process-based structural descriptions (Forbus, 1984) depend on the concept of spatially and temporally localized histories (Hayes, 1979) to infer restrictions on the set of possible causal interactions. More significantly, simulation algorithms for propagating disturbances through a network of constraint equations presuppose notions of "causal flow." Intuitively, causal flow depicts the movement of "information" through a system, such as fluid, current, or applied force. Flow serves to identify which state variables are dependent and independent with respect to one another; these relationships, in turn, determine the order for solving the simultaneous constraint equations. Iwasaki and Simon (1986) offer an insightful critique of the "mythical causality" flow model underlying de Kleer and Brown's (1984) qualitative simulator as compared with Simon's (1977) earlier theory of causal ordering for solving exact differential equations. By virtue of this latent causal content and the ordering of model events generated by a simulation, qualitative behavioral descriptions can be used to answer causal questions about the systems they depict. Thus, while qualitative simulation fails to model or explicate causation per se, it clearly provides an important vehicle for understanding and predicting the behavior of complex physical and biological systems.

Symbolic simulation of continuous systems maps continuous value spaces into discrete spaces of qualitative descriptions. In digital electronic systems, on the other hand, state variables already have discrete values. The set of permissible state changes is constrained not by continuity but by the Boolean semantics of digital circuit components (eg, AND and OR logic gates). Digital simulators thus rely on catalogs of device descriptions rather than a fixed set of qualitative state-transition rules; both structure and behavior of circuit modules are modeled as equations relating input, output, and state variables. Symbolic descriptions of variable values are still needed to handle abstractions of values and disjunctions of possible values; such symbolic data must be propagated forward through the simulation model when sufficient information is not available to specify exact values uniquely.

Discrete symbolic simulation has been extensively investigated for automatically: verifying designs for digital circuits; generating tests for manufactured circuits (Shirley, 1986) and diagnosing malfunctioning circuits. For example, VERIFY (Barrow, 1984) simulates the behavior of a complex digital circuit and compares this prediction to the device specification. Hierarchical decomposition of system descriptions into modules allows different levels to operate in different value domains: voltage levels, logic values, integers. Diagnosis is required when the behavior of an actual circuit fails to satisfy a correctly specified design. A hypothesized fault in the circuit can be tested by simulating the circuit forward from the suspect component(s) with the given set of test inputs to see whether the prediction matches the observed anomalous outputs. The space of possible fault hypotheses in nontrivial digital circuits is generally very large, so that intelligent search (qv) is crucial. Davis's (1983) troubleshooting system controls search through a set of assumptions about the nature of the fault, which are progressively suspended as search is completed in the most likely portions of fault space. Research continues very actively on alternative, more efficient search algorithms for fault diagnosis. Most simulators for circuit diagnosis only reason about faults involving topological adjacency: logical connectivity between gates or modules spelled out in the design schematic. Davis (1984) investigated faults related to physical adjacency (eg, bridging short circuits caused by wire or solder fragments connecting adjoining traces, faults induced by electromagnetic field or thermal proximity). Discrete simulators that reason about the spatial arrangement of the actual fabricated circuit elements can uncover fault candidates through potential causal pathways of interaction that are not revealed in logical schematics.

Discrete simulation is a very useful application of behavioral modeling in the specialized domain of digital circits. As with continuous qualitative reasoning, causal information such as "Fault-X explains Behavior-Y" can be derived from simulations that are not explicitly causal in character. However, the extension or applicability of discrete simulation research results to the general study of causal reasoning appears to be limited.

The third major class of implicit causal models consists of logic-based systems for planning (qv) and other forms of commonsense reasoning (qv) (Davis, 1990). Causal structure in these models is captured implicitly in so-called "causal" or projection axioms (Dean, 1987). Such axioms specify the behavioral consequences of applying a domain-specific operator or being in a particular state in a dynamic physical system. An example blocks-world axiom would be "IF (On ?x ?z ?t1) & (Kind-of ?x block) & (Kind-of ?z block) & (Clear ?x ?t1) & Move (?x table ?t1) & (= ?t2 (+ 1 ?t1)) THEN (On ?x table ?t2) & (Clear ?x ?t2) & (Clear ?z ?t2)." Intelligent "look-ahead" planners use such axioms to predict the utility of possible alternative actions in achieving goals. As in other implicit models, neither the causal nature nor content of projection axioms play any explicit, distinguished role in problem-solving reasoning.

THEORIES OF CAUSATION

Explicit causal models take as primitive the notion that one event can cause another, and derive implications from this relationship without defining the meaning of causation; causal links simply stand in for deeper, "first principles" theories or "compiled" bodies of statistical (eg, diagnostic) knowledge. Implicit causal models supply deep behavioral theories (eg, qualitative physics, Boolean logic of digital circuits), but their reasoning lacks any essential reference to causation, either scientific or commonsensical. In contrast, theories of causation focus directly on the meaning of causation and the criteria for legitimately asserting causal relationships given observed regularities in the world. This section discusses research on causal theories in AI, statistics, cognitive science, and the philosophy of science.

Much of what we take to be "causal" knowledge of the commonsensical physical world is not easily captured in simple causal links or other causal models. For example, we know that water poured from a canteen might splash off a rock, wetting both the rock and one's legs, and then soak into the ground. Hayes (1979) notes that a critical prerequisite for automating reasoning about such phenomena is a representational model that is sufficiently expressive to state the simple facts and relationships that constitute commonsense knowledge. He also argues that causation, as such, is not a self-contained category that can support independent axiomatization; rather, it is a type of knowledge that must be represented separately for different physical domains: causal knowledge about liquids is knowledge about liquids, not about causality. Subsequent research by Hayes and others to codify causal knowledge in this piecemeal manner is collected in (Hobbs and Moore, 1985).

CYC, an intelligent encyclopedia project (Lenat and coworkers, 1990), is an ambitious attempt to construct a massive knowledge base that captures and reasons about the body of commonsense facts and concepts about the world that we know and assume others to know. Like most AI researchers, Lenat subscribes to a linguistic rather than an ontological view of causation: causal relations hold between propositions describing events rather than between events per se. His theory of causation can be summarized via the following set of axioms: (1) causation entails (and is stronger than) material implication [ie, if P Causes Q then $(P \supset Q)$]; (2) causing events occur before the start of caused events; (3) propositions describing events are true either because they were asserted or by virtue of a deduction involving a causal rule (eg, $P(e_1)$ Causes $Q(e_2)$ and $P(e_1)$ is true; (4) Causes is a general class relation that has numerous specializations; and (5) in statements of the form "$P(e_1)$ Causes $Q(e_2)$," Causes is either a primitive relation or decomposable such that "$P(e_1)$ Causes$_3$ $P_3(e_3)$ . . . $P_n(e_n)$ Causes$_n$ $Q(e_2)$." Axioms 4 and 5 are of particular interest. CYC supports a diversity of specialized causal relations, such as electricalConductingCauses, a specialization of physicallyCauses that holds among ElectricalEvents. Lenat also holds that complex causal relations are decomposable into temporally extended sequences chains of different, more specific types of causal links. [In contrast, ABEL (Patil, 1981) allows only for hierarchies of a single type of causal link.] Together, these features allow CYC to (1) systematically address problems concerning alternative causal explanations and (2) provide different levels of explanation in terms of causal relations of varying levels of complexity or granularity. Lenat holds that causal relations are nonprimitive in the sense that causal statements constitute a distinguished subset of implications [ie, P Causes Q is defined as $(P \supset Q)$ & Causal $'(P \supset Q)$]; however, he has not yet proposed a precise definition for the metalogical predicate "Causal."

The RX program (Blum, 1982) is an "automated statistician" that examines medical evidence stored in a time-oriented database and determines whether causal relationships can be inferred. RX follows accepted procedures in statistical data analysis and uses an operational definition of causality: A is said to cause B if, over repeated observations (1) A is generally followed by B, (2) the intensity of A is correlated with the intensity of B, and (3) no known third variable C is responsible for the correlation. RX's causal links incorporate multiple attributes, including numeric ones such as intensity and frequency. The central concern of RX lies with the third test of causality, for nonspuriousness, and is responsible for the bulk of its domain-specific knowledge of causal relations.

Pearl (1986) defines a type of belief network based on a probabilistic causal theory (see BAYESIAN INFERENCE METHODS). Causal networks are directed, acyclic graphs of nodes representing propositions about multivalued observations or mutually exclusive hypotheses (eg, Test-result is low medium, high, Patient-diagnosis is disease A, B, or C). Causal relations are represented by directed links connecting pairs of nodes X and Y; each link is quantified by a matrix $(M(Y|X)$. A matrix element $M(Y|X)i,j$ is the conditional probability of Y_i given X_j, whose value is a constant between 0 and 1. Matrix values are static and fixed. The influence of new evidence on belief nodes in the causal network is propagated through links using an updating algorithm based on Bayes's theorem for manipulating conditional probabilities. Pearl demonstrates evidence fusion and belief propagation for binary causal trees, in which exactly one variable can be the cause of another. For example, the patient having disease Xj causes "Test-Result-k" to be Zj. Extension to multiply connected networks is based on the use of auxiliary dummy variables, called "hidden causes," to flatten out the network.

Pearl argues that his causal belief networks reflect the cognitive structure of human causal model formation. For example, we posit unifying, centralized causal variables, such as standard time, to account for observed correlations in the world, such as the agreement of personal watches and public clocks. The common "causal" mechanism also enables us to treat individual observations as being independent of one another. Pearl's Bayesian model is cognitively attractive because of its modularity and computational efficiency, but unintuitive in its purely quantitative measure of (the strength of) causal links. Suppes (1970) also defines causation via conditional probabilities but specifies conditions to qualify causal relations as genuine, spurious, direct, indirect, supplementary, sufficient, or negative.

Most of the recent theories of causation by AI researchers extend formal logics developed for temporal reasoning. This trend reflects the intimate relationship between theories of time, which are necessary to describe change, and theories of causation, which constrain possible changes to conform to some restricted set of regular patterns. The primary goal of causal logics in AI is to address the classic frame problem (see FRAMES), which Shoham (1988b) reformulates into two issues: the *qualification* problem—how to specify projection rules that characterize the "physics" of change in a domain without endless assumptions that qualify relevant background conditions; and the *extended prediction* problem—how to make predictions over significant intervals of time without having to worry about possible intervening events (eg, a gun becoming unloaded before it is fired). To solve these problems, formal logics attempt to establish (1) the unique syntactic forms that causal-temporal assertions take in a body of knowledge, (2) a precise semantics for interpreting such statements, and (3) algorithms for propagating causal knowledge forward in time. These logics are called nonmonotonic (see REASONING, NONMONOTONIC), because statements true at one time can subsequently become false as the world changes.

Hayes's (1979) concept of histories is an important precursor to causal logics in addressing the prediction problem. Objects and events are taken to have four-dimensional spatiotemporal extents, called histories. We generally have definite intuitions about such boundaries in both space and time. Two objects can interact only if their histories intersect. For example, moving a block on a tabletop cannot affect a block that is now in the other room because the histories of the two blocks do not intersect and because the history of a move action does not have a sufficient radius to affect both blocks. On the other hand, the move action could potentially affect other blocks on the same table, so a more careful check for collisions is warranted. Thus, histories constrain the types of causal interactions that need to be considered in a given situation.

Causal-temporal logics in AI establish a logical representation of events, continuous change, and primitive causal relations. Various axioms ground inferences about temporal and causal assertions. Allen (1984) takes for his primitives properties, events, processes, and temporal intervals. ECauses is a primitive causal relation on events and intervals that is transitive, antisymmetric, and antireflexive. Two of Allen's deductive axioms are (1) if ECause(e,t,e',t') and e occurs, then e' occurs; and (2) if ECause(e,t,e',t') then interval t' precedes, meets, overlaps, or lies within interval t. ACause, Allen's other primitive relation, holds between human agents and their actions. McDermott (1982) posits primitive facts, events, and instants; intervals are defined as sets of instants. His axioms are similar to Allen's. McDermott models time as a branching set of chronicles, with a single past and multiple possible futures. A chronicle is a global history of the entire universe, in contrast to Hayes's bounded histories of individual objects. McDermott posits two primitive causal predicates, ECause, where one event causes another, possibly with an intervening interval of delay (eg, setting a timer in the morning to switch on lights at night), and PCause, where an event causes a persisting fact. Persistent facts address the problem of extended prediction; once known, facts can be assumed to remain true over some specified, extended interval in the absence of information to the contrary. McDermott also analyzes the causal notion of a current action preventing a future event from taking place, in terms of alternative future chronicles.

Shoham's (1988a, 1990) causal-temporal logic is the most comprehensive AI theory of causation to date, complete with a rigorous semantic interpretation. Unlike other causal theorists, Shoham adopts an epistemic modal logic (see LOGIC, MODAL). Base axioms take the form □(t1,t2,P), where the modal operator "□," read "It is necessary that," applied to the temporal proposition is interpreted as "an agent *believes that* P is true during interval [t1,t2]." Shoham defines "A Causes B" as "If whenever one believes $A(t_i)$, and one does not believe that some set of background conditions $C(t_j)$ are false, then one believes $B(t_k)$" for i,j < k. C represents a set of plausible default assumptions, which, if known to be violated would force the "effect" belief to be retracted. For example, □(t5, t5, turn-key) Causes □(t6, t6, car-starts) given that □(t5, t5, battery-OK & plugs-clean, . . .}). A *theory* is a collection of causal statements (as defined above) and base axioms. *Chronological ignorance* is a criterion for selecting theories in which as little as possible that runs contrary to the defaults is known for as long as possible. For example, prefer the theory in which □(t6, t6, car-starts) over one in which □(t5, t5, battery-dead). Shoham proves that there is a unique and effectively computable causal theory that is maximally chronologically ignorant, thus addressing the qualification problem. Similarly, Shoham deals with extended prediction by selecting a (unique, computable) subset of causal theories, called inertial theories. Potential histories, a variant of McDermott's persistent facts, form the basis of the inertial preference criterion. Intuitively, a potential history picks out a "natural" course of events that persists unless there is explicit information to the contrary about intervening causal influences. Shoham also offers formal definitions of causal notions such as prevention and enablement.

An important feature of Shoham's account is that causal statements have a unique logical form. Moreover, causal and lawlike statements are distinct, both syntactically and in meaning: causal statements are contingently true (ie, "defeasible"), whereas laws are universally and necessarily true. An important disadvantage is that causal reasoning in Shoham's logic is exclusively predictive; no uniqueness theorems exist in his logic for projecting theories backward in time. This precludes abduction, which explains why things are the way they are by reasoning from effects to their likely causes. [Note: Pearl (1988) deals with this problem of "retrodictive" explanation by adding a separate class of probabilistic links to his belief networks. These links reflect accrued evidential support (eg, if smoke, then fire), where causal links, directed oppositely, reflect accrued causal support (eg, if fire, then smoke).] Finally, Shoham argues that his logic represents an attractive cognitive model with its low memory overhead, computational efficiency, and modularity; background conditions are isolated from causal principles and maintained as default or statistically most likely assumptions relative to a given environment.

Lifshitz (1987) proposed a theory of action based on a nontemporal causal logic to address the problems of qualification and prediction. He takes causation as a primitive relational predicate on actions, states and fluents, which are functions on situations (eg, The current U.S. President). Explicit causal axioms of the form Causes(action old-state new-state) depict the effects of successfully performed actions, such as Cause(toggle-switch on off) and Cause(shoot-gun loaded false). The preconditions for actions to be successful are declared in separate axioms, such as Precond(loaded-gun, shoot-gun). Lifschitz demonstrates that changes occur in his models only if they conform to the causal axioms, without explicit reference to time.

AI research on causal reasoning benefits greatly by considering the constraints on human causal knowledge discovered by cognitive scientists. Cognitive theories attempt to accommodate the kinds of variation observed in the human population (individual, developmental, and historical) within general models of causal relations and problem-solving performance. Such models provide valuable resources for AI-based causal knowledge representations and automated reasoning methods in both commonsensical and technical domains. As in many areas of developmental psychology, Piaget (1966) provides the earliest systematic studies of causal knowledge, looking at the types of early theories children create to explain phenomena such as the wind blowing, clouds moving, boats floating, shadows, bicycles, and airplanes. He identifies three distinct classes of causal explanations—psychological–magical, animistic, and rational–mechanical; only the third encompasses what we normally consider as "causation." Piaget argues that evolution through these classes is driven by three processes of cognitive development: the progression from a subjective to an objective view of causality as external to the self, from the view of causality as an almost immediate cooccurrence of events to an ordered sequence of intermediate steps, and from causal relations seen as irreversible changes to reversible mechanical connections.

Empirical cognitive studies collecting and analyzing verbal protocols have been used to construct explicit causal computational models of the behavior of heat engines (Williams and co-workers, 1983) and to build a qualitative simulation of the physiological mechanisms underlying a kidney disease (Kuipers and Kaissirer, 1984). Other researchers have investigated the influence of causal knowledge on other kinds of reasoning. For example, Tversky and Kahneman (1980) demonstrated that schemas of causal relations strongly dominate the process of estimating relative and absolute probabilities in situations where exact knowledge is unavailable. Cognitive research has been particularly active in education, studying the differences between naive causal models of mechanical systems used by novice students and lay adults as contrasted with those of expert physicists. Related studies have explored analogies between the historical evolution of physical theories (eg, from pre-Galilean to Newton dynamics) and the progression of causal models adopted by science students. Gentner and Stevens (1983) have collected important research papers in this area.

A third important class of cognitively oriented studies of causation consists of recent computational models for acquiring or learning causal knowledge. Anderson (1989) incorporates "inate knowledge" of causal inferences into his cognitive model PUPS to demonstrate rationalistic learning, which he defines as the extraction of problem-solving operators from experience. His store of causal induction principles include heuristics involving identity, previous action, and minimal contrast. For example, on typing (lis) into a computer that responds (lis: unknown function object), the recurring token "lis" can be inferred to have a causal role in the occurrence of the second event. The second heuristic stipulates that if an event has no discernible cause, ascribe as its cause an immediately preceding action. Finally, if pairs of antecedent and consequent events are identical except in one point, infer that the difference between the first pair of events causes the difference in the second pair.

The machine learning program OCCAM (Pazzani, 1987) acquires simple causal models for predicting the outcomes of everyday phenomena such as dropping cups or opening heavy doors. Models are comprised of roles (actors, objects), actions (move, decide), and descriptive attributes (material, age). Causal elements in these models consist of domain-specific "dispositions" (eg, fragility, strength), of objects or agents that effect actions. For example, by virtue of their strength, adults applying force to heavy objects such as doors induce state changes, namely, door motions. OCCAM forms a "current best causal hypothesis" by differential analysis of current observations and events recalled from memory. Preference is given to hypotheses that involve minimal sets of previously useful distinctions. For example, the program prefers age over hair color in selecting between "When a person (who is an adult/who has brown hair) pulls on a door, it opens" because of its previous utility in successfully predicting outcomes of household activities. Generalization rules ground example-based learning of new causal regularities or dispositions. An example rule schema is that differences in actors performing similar actions cause differences in results. OCCAM's rules are structured to reflect the causal factors of (1) covariation (effects always accompany causes), (2) temporal order (causes precede effects), and (3) mechanism (physical mediators link cause and effect).

Causation has been analyzed most extensively by philosophers of science. A comprehensive review of this literature is well beyond the scope of this entry; Mackie (1974) provides an excellent general introduction, while Sosa (1975) collects important contemporary papers (eg, Lewis, 1973). Most accounts derive from the work of Hume, the eighteenth-century empiricist philosopher. Modern Humean "regularity" accounts hold events to be causally connected just in case an ordered sequence of those events instantiates an observed regular succession of events belonging to appropriate event categories or classes. For example, let C and E stand for the propositions that events c and e exist or occur. Let L stand for some nonempty set of true lawlike propositions (eg, all metallic objects expand when heated), F denote some set of true propositions of particular fact, and $\supset$ stand for the relation of material implication. Then c causes e if and only if (1) C and E are true; and (2) L and F jointly imply $C \supset E$, although L and F jointly do not imply E, and F alone does not imply $C \supset E$. Here, causation does not connect events per se; rather, it is defined in terms of logical relations among *propositions* that describe the relevant events (C,E), environmental context or background conditions (F), and lawlike regularities (L). In accordance with intuition, causal relations are asymmetric and irreversible: expanding metallic objects do not cause them to be heated; nor is it the case that not heating metallic objects cause them not to expand (ie, the contrapositive).

Regularity accounts engender several difficulties. First, events characterized in some ways may give rise to causal relations as per definition, while events that we intuitively take to be identical, specified by different descriptions, may turn out to be causally *un*related on the very same analysis. For example, consider the events c (Y's firing of a bullet at time t), e (X's death from a bullet wound in the heart suffered shortly after t, and e' (X's death from a bullet wound in the heart suffered shortly after t, where that bullet was fired by Y at time t). c and e are causally related by the definition presented above, but not c and e', since F alone implies $C \supset E'$ when $C \supset E'$ is a tautology.

Second, there are misfits between the notions of lawful and causal dependence. Regularities having no apparent relevance to our notions of direct causal dependence can be cast into (universal or statistical) lawlike form, ostensibly suitable for supporting causal relations as per definition. Consider, for example, the semantic regularity that a woman inevitably becomes a widow on the death of her husband. Another (noncausal) psychological regularity is that conscientious programmers who discover bugs in their code invariably try to correct their errors. A third illustration (McDermott, 1982) is the physical regularity that the arrival of one's shadow always precedes one's own arrival.

Finally, uniform definitions of causal relations invariably tend to be both stronger and weaker than our intuitions in unusual circumstances. Here, stronger means that causal relations obtain by definition but counter to intuition; weaker corresponds to the reverse situation. These tensions arise because our commonsense causal intuitions are simply not uniformly consistent across age, education, or history. Our individual intuitions are particularly divergent when faced with novel or complex situations, such as physical systems containing feedback loops (Iwasaki and Simon, 1986).

Any theory of causation, whether proposed by philosophers, cognitive scientists, or AI researchers, must provide answers to these three problems, in the form of (1) a comprehensive ontology of events (or states) that specifies criteria for event identity and individuation; (2) a general account of "significant" lawhood, which must be free of presuppositions concerning causal relations to avoid circularity; and (3) a precise specification of whose commonsense or scientific causal intuitions are being analyzed. These issues are as profound and difficult as the concept of causation itself, which means that a fully adequate theory of causation is not imminent. Nevertheless, research on these fundamental questions is indispensible for continued advances in causal reasoning, as the concluding section will suggest.

DISCUSSION

AI research on causal models has achieved important successes in representing and reasoning about behavior in complex systems and commonsensical causal relationships. However, these models display some serious shortcomings, both individually and collectively. First, causal models employ diverse, typically incompatible patterns of causal inference and representations for causal relations (eg, network links, rule connectives, projection axioms). The clear utility of these models strongly suggests that they all capture important aspects of causal knowledge. Deep theories of causation are needed to provide (1) an analytic framework for unifying heterogeneous causal models across scientific domains and commonsense knowledge and (2) rigorous foundations for causal reasoning. Lenat's taxonomy of causal relations and Shoham's causal logic represent important steps in this direction.

Second, in general, current causal models cannot be constructed mechanically. Causal structures in explicit causal models are primitive and unanalyzable; thus, designers and domain experts must build, verify, and extend causal knowledge bases manually. Excepting component-based simulators, similar limitations hold for AI systems that represent causal structures or inference implicitly. Automated tools for developing causal models will depend on theories of causation that specify explicit definitional grounds for causal relations: knowledge acquisition and maintenance tools can then be constructed that exploit these truth conditions to mechanically confirm or deny the assertion of causal relations in particular domains and problem contexts.

Third, current causal models cannot discover new kinds of causal structures, nor recognize and react to causally interesting aspects of observed situations. Such adaptive capacities presuppose (1) generalized principles of causal induction and (2) a capacity for meta-level reasoning, such as reflection about ongoing inferences. The causal theories embodied in PUPS and OCCAM represent a strong start on research into the first topic. Important early investigations in the second area include Davis's research on relaxing causal assumptions in digital circuit diagnosis and Weld's (1986) algorithm for causal "aggregation," which recognizes recurring (discrete) cycles in qualitative simulations and abstracts them into a continuous repetitive process. In sum, significant research challenges remain in understanding the nature of causation itself. The theories of causation that result from this research will provide solid foundations for a new generation of causal models that truly automate causal reasoning in AI.

BIBLIOGRAPHY

J. F. Allen, "Towards a General Theory of Action and Time," *Artif. Intell.* **23**, 123–154 (1984).

J. R. Anderson, "Theory of the Origins of Human Knowledge," *Artif. Intell.* **40**, 347–410 (1989).

H. G. Barrow, "VERIFY: A Program for Proving Correctness of Digital Hardware Designs," *Artif. Intell.* **24**, 437–491 (1984).

R. L. Blum, "Discovery and Representation of Causal Relationships from a Large Time-Oriented Clinical Database: The RX Project," *Lecture Notes in Medical Informatics*, Vol. 19, Springer, New York, 1982.

D. G. Bobrow, ed., *Qualitative Reasoning about Physical Systems*, MIT Press, Cambridge, Mass., 1985, reprinted in *Artif. Intell.* **24**, 1984 (which collects important papers on implicit causal models; qualitative and discrete simulation).

E. Davis, *Representations of Commonsense Knowledge*, Morgan-Kaufmann, Palo Alto, Calif., 1990.

R. Davis, "Diagnosis via Causal Reasoning: Paths of Interaction and the Locality Principle," *Proceedings of the Third National Conference on Artificial Intelligence*, Washington, D.C., AAAI, Menlo Park, Calif., 1983.

R. Davis, "Diagnostic Reasoning Based on Structure and Behavior," *Artif. Intell.* **24**, 347–410 (1984).

T. L. Dean and M. Boddy, "Incremental Causal Reasoning," *Proceedings of the 6th National Conference on Artificial Intelligence*, Seattle, Wash., AAAI, Menlo Park, Calif., 1987.

M. G. Dyer, *In-Depth Understanding: A Computer Model of Intelligent Processing for Narrative Comprehension*, MIT Press, Cambridge, Mass., 1983.

K. D. Forbus, "Qualitative Process Theory," *Artif. Intell.* **24**, 85–168 (1984).

D. Genter and A. Stevens, eds., *Mental Models*, Erlbaum, Hillsdale, N.J., 1983 (an excellent overview collection of papers on cognitive science research on causal reasoning).

P. J. Hayes, "The Naive Physics Manifesto," in D. Michie, ed., *Expert Systems in the Micro-Electronic Age*, Edinburgh University Press, Edinburgh, 1979.

J. R. Hobbs and R. C. Moore, eds., *Formal Theories of the Commonsense World*, Ablex Publishing, Norwood, N.J., 1985.

Y. Iwasaki and H. A. Simon, "Causality in Device Behavior," *Artif. Intell.* **29**, 3–32 (1986).

J. de Kleer, "The Origin and Resolution of Ambiguities in Causal Arguments," *Proceedings of the Sixth IJCAI*, Tokyo, Morgan-Kaufmann, San Mateo, Calif., 1979.

J. de Kleer and J. S. Brown, "A Qualitative Physics Based on Confluences," *Artif. Intell.* **24**, 7–83 (1984).

B. J. Kuipers, "Commonsense Reasoning about Causality: Deriving Behavior from Structure," *Artif. Intell.* **24**, 169–204 (1984).

B. J. Kuipers, "The Limits of Qualitative Simulation," *Proceedings of the Ninth IJCAI*, Los Angeles, Calif., Morgan-Kaufmann, San Mateo, Calif., 1985.

B. J. Kuipers and J. P. Kassirer, "Causal Reasoning in Medicine: Analysis of a Protocol," *Cog. Sci.* **8**, 363–385 (1984).

D. B. Lenat, R. V. Guha, K. Pittman, D. Pratt, and M. Shepherd, "CYC: Toward Programs with Common Sense," *Commun. ACM* **33**, 30–49 (1990).

D. Lewis, "Causation," *J. Philos.* **70**, 556–567 (1973); reprinted in E. Sosa, ed., *Causation and Conditions*, Oxford University Press, London, 1975.

V. Lifshitz, "Formal Theories of Action (Preliminary Report)," *Proceedings of the Tenth IJCAI*, Milan, Italy, Morgan-Kaufmann, San Mateo, Calif., 1987.

J. L. Mackie, *The Cement of the Universe: A Study of Causation*, Oxford University Press, London, 1974 [reviews both historical (Hume, Kant) and more contemporary philosophical theories of causation].

D. McDermott, "A Temporal Logic for Reasoning about Processes and Plans," *Cog. Sci.* **6**, (1982).

R. S. Patil, P. Szolovits, and W. B. Schwartz, "Causal Understanding of Patient Illness in Medical Diagnosis," *Proceedings of the Seventh IJCAI*, Vancouver, B.C., Morgan-Kaufmann, San Mateo, Calif., 893–899, 1981.

M. Pazzani, M. Dyer, and M. Flowers, "Using Prior Learning to Facilitate the Learning of New Causal Theories," *Proceedings of the Tenth IJCAI*, Milan, Italy, Morgan-Kaufmann, San Mateo, Calif., 1987.

J. Pearl, "Fusion, Propagation, and Structuring in Belief Networks," *Artif. Intell.* **29**, 241–288 (1986).

J. Pearl, "Embracing Causality in Default Reasoning," *Artif. Intell.* **35**, 259–271 (1988).

J. Piaget, *The Child's Conception of Physical Causality*, Routledge and Kegan Paul, London, 1930; reprinted by Littlefield, Adams & Co., Totowa, N.J., 1966.

F. Pipitone, "An Expert System for Electronics Troubleshooting Based on Function and Connectivity," *Proceedings of the First IEEE Conference on AI Applications*, Boulder, Colo., IEEE Computer Society Press, Washington, D.C., 1984.

H. E. Pople, Jr., "Heuristic Methods for Imposing Structure on Ill Structured Problems: The Structuring of Medical Diagnostics," in P. Szolovits, ed., *Artificial Intelligence in Medicine*, AAAS/Westview, Boulder, Colo., 1982.

C. Rieger and M. Grinberg, "The Declarative Representation and Procedural Simulation of Causality in Physical Mechanisms," *Proceedings of the Fifth IJCAI*, Cambridge, Mass., Morgan-Kaufmann, San Mateo, Calif., 1977.

R. C. Schank and R. P. Abelson, *Scripts, Plans, Goals, and Understanding*, Erlbaum, Hillsdale, N.J., 1977.

M. H. Shirley, "Generating Tests by Exploiting Designed Behavior," *Proceedings of the Fifth National Conference on Artificial Ingelligence*, Philadelphia, AAAI, Menlo Park, Calif., 1986.

Y. Shoham, "Nonmonotonic Reasoning and Causation," *Cog. Sci.* **14**, 213–252 (1990).

Y. Shoham, "Chronological Ignorance: Experiments in Nonmonotonic Temporal Reasoning," *Artif. Intell.* **36**, 279–331 (1988a).

Y. Shoham, *Reasoning about Change: Time and Causation from the Standpoint of Artificial Intelligence*, MIT Press, Cambridge, Mass., 1988b.

H. A. Simon, *Models of Discovery*, D. Reidel, Boston, 1977.

E. Sosa, ed., *Causation and Conditions*, Oxford University Press, London, 1975 (a collection of articles on causation, including counterfactual theories).

P. Suppes, *A Probabilistic Theory of Causation*, North Holland, Amsterdam, 1970.

A. Tversky and D. Kahneman, "Causal Schema in Judgments under Uncertainty," in M. Fishbein, ed., *Progress in Social Psychology, 1*. Erlbaum, Hillsdale, N.J., 1980.

S. M. Weiss, C. A. Kulikowski, S. Amarel, and A. Safir, "A Model-Based Method for Computer-Aided Medical Decision-Making," *Artif. Intell.* **11**, 145–172 (1978).

D. S. Weld, "The Use of Aggregation in Causal Simulation," *Artif. Intell.* **30**, 1–34 (1986).

B. Williams, "The Use of Continuity in a Qualitative Physics," *Proceedings of the Fourth IJCAI*, Austin, Tex., Morgan-Kaufmann, San Mateo, Calif., 1984a.

B. Williams, "Qualitative Analysis of MOS Circuits," *Artif. Intell.* **24**, 281–346 (1984b).

M. D. Williams, J. D. Hollan, and A. L. Stevens, "Human Reasoning about a Simple Physical System," in D. Genter and A. Stevens, eds., *Mental Models*, Erlbaum, Hillsdale, N.J., 1983.

RICHARD M. ADLER
Symbiotics, Inc.

REASONING, COMMONSENSE

For an artificial system to act sensibly in the real world, it must know about that world and it must be able to use its knowledge effectively. The common knowledge about the world that is possessed by every schoolchild and the methods for making obvious inferences from this knowledge are called common sense in both humans and computers. Almost every type of intelligent task (natural language processing, planning, learning, high level vision, expert-level reasoning) requires some degree of commonsense reasoning to carry out. The encoding of commonsense knowledge has been recognized as one of the central issues of AI since the inception of the field (McCarthy, 1959).

Endowing a program with common sense, however, is a very difficult task. Common sense involves many subtle modes of reasoning and a vast body of knowledge with complex interactions. Consider the following quotation from *The Tale of Benjamin Bunny*, by Beatrix Potter:

> Peter did not eat anything; he said he should like to go home. Presently he dropped half the onions.

Except that Peter is a rabbit, there is nothing subtle or strange here, and the passage is easily understood by five-year-old children. Yet these three clauses involve, implicitly or explicitly, concepts of quantity, space, time, physics, goals, plans, and speech acts. An intelligent system cannot, therefore, understand this passage unless it possesses a theory of each of these domains and the ability to connect this theory in a useful way to the story.

Many of the central issues in the automation of commonsense reasoning appear in all types of AI reasoning, particularly the development of domain-independent knowledge structures and inference techniques, and the analysis and implementation of plausible reasoning. Because these issues are common throughout AI, they will not be studied in this article. (See KNOWLEDGE REPRESENTATION; REASONING, DEFAULT; REASONING, NONMONOTONIC; REASONING, PLAUSIBLE). Here, the focus will be on issues that arise in the study of specific commonsense domains.

GENERAL ISSUES AND METHODOLOGY

The analysis of reasoning in a commonsense domain has three major parts:

1. *Representation*. The development of knowledge structures that can express facts in the domain.
2. *Domain Theory*. The characterization of the fundamental properties of the domain and the rules that govern it.
3. *Inference Techniques*. The construction of algorithms or heuristics that can be used to automate useful types of reasoning.

A popular methodology for carrying out these kinds of analysis runs along the following lines (McCarthy, 1968; McCarthy and Hayes, 1969; Hayes, 1977, 1978; McDermott, 1978; Davis, 1990; Minsky, 1975; McDermott, 1987). The researcher begins by defining a microworld, a small, coherent domain of study. Aspects of the real world that lie outside the microworld will either be ignored in the work, or will be represented in some very coarse, *ad hoc* manner. Next, a coherent collection of commonsensically obvious inferences in the microworld are assembled. The researcher determines what problem-specific information and general domain knowledge (qv) is needed, explicitly, or implicitly, to justify these inferences. A language is developed in which these facts can be expressed and these inferences can be validated; typically, this language is written in some known logic (qv). Having categorized the types of information and rules that are needed, the researcher can work on developing data structures and procedures that allow the efficient solution to some significant classes of problems.

A knowledge representation for a commonsense domain must satisfy three requirements. First, the representation must be able to describe the relevant aspects of the domain involved. Second, it must be possible to use the representation to express the kinds of partial knowledge typically available; the design of the language must take account of likely kinds of ignorance. Third, it must be possible to implement useful inferences as computations using the representation. These requirements are called ontological adequacy, expressivity or epistemic adequacy, and effectiveness or heuristic adequacy (McCarthy and Hayes, 1969). Each of these requirements is defined relative to a certain set of problems; a representation may be adequate for one kind of problem but not for another.

The greatest difference between representations for commonsense reasoning and representations used in other areas of computer science lies in the expressivity requirement. Most computer science representations assume either complete information, or information that is partial only along some limited dimensions. By contrast, commonsense reasoning requires dealing with a wide range of possible types of partial information, and degrading gracefully as the quality and quantity of information declines. Reasoning from partial information is important for three reasons: (1) it may be expensive, time-consuming, or impossible to get complete information; (2) computing with exact information may be too complex; (3) reasoning with partial information allows the inference of general rules that apply across a wide class of cases. For instance, suppose a person is driving a car at the top of a cliff, and the driver wishes to determine whether it would be better to take the winding road to the bottom or to drive down the cliff. Given exact specifications of the car and the exact topography of the cliff, it may be possible to predict exactly what would happen if the car was driven off the cliff. But the driver may not have this information or any way to get it; even if the driver had the information, the computation would be horrendous; the conclusion would apply only to a specific car and a specific cliff. The calculation would have to be redone for each new car and each new cliff.

TIME

Temporal reasoning is probably the most central issue in commonsense reasoning. Almost every application involves reasoning about time and change; few microworlds of interest are purely static.

The first task of a temporal representation is to express changes over time; for example, to represent such facts as "At one time, the light was off; later, it was on." Such a representation is often based on the concepts of situations and fluents. A situation is an instantaneous snapshot of the world at an instant. A fluent is a description that changes its value from one situation to another, such as "the light being on" or "the president of the United States." A fluent like "the light being on" that has possible values "true" and "false" is called a Boolean fluent or state.

A first-order language (see LOGIC, PREDICATE) for describing situations and fluents can be defined using the following nonlogical symbols:

- True_in(S,A), predicate: state A is true in situation S.
- Value_in(S,F), function: the value of fluent F in situation S.
- Precedes($S1$,$S2$), predicate: situation $S1$ precedes $S2$.

For example, the sentence "At one time the light was off; later it was on," can be expressed in the formula

$$\exists_{S1,S2} \text{precedes}(S1,S2) \land \neg\text{true\_in}(S1,\text{on}(\text{light1})) \\ \land \text{true\_in}(S2,\text{on}(\text{light1}))$$

Most events do not occur instantaneously; they occur over finite stretches of time. To incorporate events into representations, the concept of a time interval, a set of successive situations, is introduced. The following symbols are added to the language:

- $S \in I$, predicate: situation S is in interval I.
- [$S1$,$S2$], function: the closed interval from $S1$ to $S2$.
- Occurs(I,E), predicate: event E occurs during interval I.

Using this language, a variety of dynamic microworlds can be described. For instance, the blocks world rule "If X and Z are clear, then the result of putting X onto Z will be that X is on Z" can be expressed as follows:

$$\forall_{S1,S2,X,Y} [\text{true\_in}(S1,\text{clear}(X)) \land \text{true\_in}(S1,\text{clear}(Y)) \\ \land \text{occurs}([S1,S2],\text{puton}(X,Y))] \Rightarrow \text{true\_in}(S2,\text{on}(X,Y))$$

In developing such a theory of a microworld, where the occurrence of an event changes the state of the world, the following problem is encountered: the theory must specify, not only the fluents that change as a result of an event but also the fluents that remain the same. For example, in the blocks world, it is necessary to infer that, when the robot puts X on Y, the only "on" states affected are those involving X. The problem of expressing or deriving such rules efficiently is known as the "frame" problem (McCarthy and Hayes, 1969); it has been the focus of much recent research (Hanks and McDermott, 1987; Shoham, 1988; Brown, 1987; Pylyshyn, 1987).

The language described above follows McDermott (1982). Many other types of temporal languages have been devised, including languages that use only intervals but no individual situations (Allen 1983, 1984), languages that distinguish sections of space–time (Hayes, 1978), and modal temporal languages (Prior, 1967; van Benthem, 1983).

SPACE

Commonsense spatial reasoning (see REASONING, SPATIAL) serves three major functions:

- *High Level Vision.* The interpretation of visual information in terms of world knowledge and the integration of information gained through vision into a general knowledge base.
- *Cognitive Map Maintenance.* The formation, maintenance, and use of a knowledge base describing the spatial layout of the environment. In particular, the use of a cognitive map for navigation, planning a route to a destination.

- *Physical Reasoning.* Spatial characteristics of physical systems are generally critical in understanding its behavior. The behavior of many physical systems consists largely of spatial motions. Spatial reasoning is, therefore, a vital component of physical reasoning.

Finding a language for spatial knowledge that is both expressive and computationally tractable is difficult. Ideally, a spatial language would allow the description of any physically meaningful spatial layout and spatial behavior, including specifications of shapes, positions, and motions; it would allow the expression of all types of information that are relevant to commonsense reasoning; it would allow a wide range of partial specifications, corresponding to the types of information that may be obtained from perception, natural language text, or physical inference; and it would do all this in a way that supports efficient algorithms for commonsense reasoning. No such language has yet been found.

The following are some of the more extensively studied spatial representations (Requicha, 1980; Ballard and Brown, 1982; Hoffmann, 1989):

1. *Occupancy Array.* The space is divided up into a rectangular grid, and each cell of the grid is associated with one element of an array. Each element of the array holds the name of the object(s) that intersect the corresponding rectangle in space. One disadvantage of this representation is that it is costly in terms of memory. This can be mitigated by the use of quad-trees or oct-trees, which merge adjacent array elements with identical labels.

2. *Constructive Solid Geometry.* A shape is characterized as the union and difference of a small class of primitive shapes.

3. *Boundary Representations.* A shape is characterized in terms of its boundary. For example, the representation might approximate a two-dimensional shape as a polygon, which is defined by listing its edges, its vertices, and the coordinates of the vertices.

4. *Topological Representations.* A spatial layout is characterized by describing topological relations between objects. For instance, the TOUR program (Kuipers, 1978) describes a road map by stating the order in which places appear on a path and the cyclic order in which paths meet at a place. Randell and Cohn (1989) characterize the spatial relations between objects in terms of such relations as abutment and overlapping.

PHYSICAL REASONING

Unlike the sciences, which aim at a simple description of the underlying structure of physical reality, the commonsense theory of physics must try to describe and systematize physical phenomena as they appear and as they may most effectively be thought about for everyday purposes. The problems addressed in physical reasoning include predicting the future history of a physical system, planning physical actions to carry out a task, and designing tools to serve a given purpose.

Commonsense physical reasoning characteristically avoids the use of exact numerical values. Rather, it relies on qualitative characterization of the physical parameters involved, such as "If a kettle of water is placed on a flame, it will heat up; the higher the flame, the faster the water will heat." This rule does not specify the exact rate at which the temperature changes; it specifies that the change is positive, and that the rate is an increasing function of the height of the flame. Accordingly, the mathematical structure of such constraints has been extensively studied (see QUALITATIVE PHYSICS) (de Kleer and Brown, 1985; Kuipers, 1986).

Complex physical systems, particularly artificial devices, can often be effectively analyzed by viewing them as a collections of connected components. In simple cases, the connections between the components remain constant over time; what varies are the values of various one-dimensional parameters of the system. Components are connected at ports; each parameter is associated with one port. The laws that govern these systems are component characteristics, which constrain the values of the parameters at the ports of the component, and connection characteristics, which constrain the values of parameters at ports that meet in a connection. For example, in electronics, the component characteristics are rules such as "The difference between the voltages at the two ends of a resistor is equal to the current through it times its resistance." The connection characteristics are the rules, "At a connection, the voltages of all the ports is equal, and sum of all the current flows into the ports is zero." The particular device is specified by describing the components it contains, and the connections between their ports (de Kleer and Brown, 1985).

An alternative way to decompose physical systems (Forbus, 1985) focuses on the processes that occur. Consider, for example, a closed can of water above a flame. A process-based description of the behavior of this system would say that there is first a heating process, in which the temperature of the water rises to its boiling point; then a boiling process, in which the water turns from a liquid to a gas; then another heating process, in which the temperature and pressure of the gas rise steadily, and finally a bursting event, when the pressure of the gas exceeds the strength of the can. The central elements of such a representation are process types, such as heating and boiling, and parameters, such as temperature and pressure. The laws that govern the system describe how a process influences a parameter, such as "A boiling process tends to reduce the quantity of liquid and increase the quantity of gas"; they describe influences of one parameter on another, such as "The pressure of a gas tends to rise with its temperature"; and they describe the circumstances under which a process can take place, such as "Boiling occurs just if there were a heat flow into a body of water that is at its boiling point."

Reasoning about systems of solid objects involves techniques of a different kind. The central problem here is the geometric reasoning required, which can be very complicated, particularly with three-dimensional objects of complex shapes. However, the physical laws describing such systems are fairly straightforward. Many mechanisms, particularly synthetic devices where the parts are tightly constrained can be analyzed using only the physical laws that solid objects are rigid and cannot overlap. Such an analysis is known as a kinematic analysis (Faltings 1987; Joskowicz, 1987). For loosely constrained systems of solid objects, such as a bouncing ball, it is generally necessary to use dynamic analysis, invoking the concepts of Newtonian mechanics. Liquids are still more complicated to represent and reason about, because they are not divided into discrete objects; they continually combine and separate. Hayes (1985) discusses a logical analysis of a commonsense theory of liquids.

One final issue in physical reasoning is causality. Ordinary discourse about physical events is often framed in terms of one event causing another; however, none of the theories mentioned above make any use of causality as a concept. Extracting a causal account from such theories has proven to be difficult, particularly as there is no consensus on exactly what purpose a causal account should serve (de Kleer and Brown, 1985; Iwasaki and Simon, 1986; Shoham, 1988; Pearl, 1988).

KNOWLEDGE AND BELIEF

To reason about other agents, or even about oneself at other times, it is necessary to have a theory describing their mental life. AI studies of commonsense theories of cognitions have primarily focused on agents' knowledge and beliefs, discussed in this section, and their plans and goals, discussed in the next.

Representations of knowledge and belief must necessarily be quite different in structure from the representations that were considered above for temporal, spatial, and physical information. The relation, "A knows ϕ" takes as its argument a proposition, which may contain Boolean operators, quantifiers, or imbedded statements about knowledge. (Consider, for example, "John knows that Mary knows that all Libras were born in either September or October.") Operators in first-order languages, by contrast, can take as arguments only terms that denote entities. Moreover, first-order operators are referentially transparent; if two terms τ and ω denote the same entity then ω can be substituted for τ in any sentence without changing the truth of the sentence. By contrast, psychological relations, such as "A knows ϕ," are referentially opaque; substitution of equal terms may change the truth of a sentence. For example, given that Sacramento is the capital of California, it follows that "John is in Sacramento" is true if "John is in the capital of California" is true. However, it is possible for "John knows that he is in Sacramento" to be true but "John knows that he is in the capital of California" to be false, if John believes that Los Angeles is the capital of California.

Three general types of representations have been developed for these kinds of relations:

1. *Know* and *believe* can be represented as operators in a modal logic (see LOGIC, MODAL), a logic that extends first-order logic by allowing additional operators on sentences. In such a theory, the sentence mentioned above could be represented

know(john, know(mary, $\forall_x$ libra(X) $\Rightarrow$ born_in(X,sept) $\lor$ born_(X,oct)))

2. *Know* and *believe* can be represented as first-order predicates that take as arguments a string of characters that spell out the sentence known or believed. The above sentence would be represented

know(john, {know(mary, {$\forall_x$ libra(X) $\Rightarrow$ born_in(X,sept) $\lor$ born_in(X,oct)})})

where { and } are string delimiters. In this example, the difference between the two theories appears trivial; in fact, there are deep differences in their logical characteristics.

3. Facts about knowledge and belief can be expressed in terms of accessibility relations among possible worlds. A possible world is one conceivable way that the world could be; a fact may be true in one possible world and false in another. A world $W1$ is accessible from world $W0$ relative to the knowledge of agent A if nothing in $W1$ contradicts something that A knows in $W0$. Then the fact that A knows ϕ in world W can be expressed by saying that ϕ is true in every world accessible from W. Thus the statement "John knows in world $W0$ that he is in Sacramento" can be represented

$\forall_{W1}$ know_acc(john, $W0$, $W1$) $\Rightarrow$ true_in($W1$,in(john,scaramento))

where the predicate "know_acc(A,$W0$,$W1$)" means that world $W1$ is accessible from world $W0$ relative to the knowledge of A, and "true_in" means the same as in the section on temporal reasoning. The other sample sentence can be represented

$\forall_{W1,W2}$ [know_acc(john,$W0$,$W1$) $\land$ know_acc(mary,$W1$,$W2$)] $\Rightarrow$ $\forall_x$ true_in($W2$,libra(X)) $\Rightarrow$ [true_in($W2$,born_in(X,sept)) $\lor$ true_in($W2$,born_in(X,oct))]

Extensive discussions of these representations and their relative merits have been published (Moore, 1985a; Halpern and Moses, 1985; Morgenstern, 1988).

The next problem is to characterize what agents know and believe in a way that supports reasonable commonsense inferences. Most theories to date have been modeled on implicit knowledge and belief. An agent implicitly knows ϕ if, in principle, he has enough information to determine ϕ; that is, if ϕ is a logical consequence of facts that he knows. However, in many situations, such as teaching, implicit knowledge is not a reasonable theory; a teacher who assumes that the students can immediately perceive all the consequences of what is said will be disappointed. It has been difficult to find more psychologically plausible theories of knowledge and belief that accommodate the fact that reasoners are limited in the speed and power of their inferential abilities (Konolige, 1985; Levesque, 1984).

Other issues that have been studied in AI theories of knowledge include the gaining of knowledge through perception (Davis, 1988) and the auto-epistemic inference, which allows an agent to infer that ϕ is false from the fact that he does not know ϕ (Moore, 1985b).

PLANS AND GOALS

The second major focus of AI commonsense psychological theories has been in representing and reasoning about plans and goals. Plans and goals have been studied primarily in connection with two high level tasks: plan construction, the problem of finding actions that an agent can perform to accomplish the goal; and motivation analysis, the problem of explaining an agent's actions in terms of plans and goals. The chief problems in analyzing plans and goals are the following:

- Constructing a language to describe plans and goals and defining what it means to carry out a plan or to accomplish a goal described in the language.
- Characterizing the feasibility of a plan, the validity of a plan for achieving a given goal, and the cost of a plan.
- Characterizing the typical high level goals of human actors.
- Giving criteria for evaluating alternative explanations of actions in terms of plans and goals.
- The problem of searching for the best plan in plan construction or the best explanation in motivation analysis.

Most of the planning literature in AI has assumed a particularly simple model of plans and goals. A goal is taken to be a desired state of the world, such as "Block C is on block B" or "John is home." A plan is taken to be a sequence of primitive actions, actions that can be directly carried out by a low level robotic controller. For example, in the blocks world, the action, "Put X on Y" could be taken to be primitive. Plans would then be sequences of "put on" instructions such as "First put A on the table; then put C on B." Furthermore, it is assumed that the planner is omniscient and knows everything that can possibly be relevant. Under these assumptions, the definitions of feasibility and correctness are straightforward: a plan is feasible if the preconditions of each successive action hold at the time that the action is scheduled to be performed; a plan accomplishes a goal if the goal holds after all the actions have been performed. The main problem is then one of search: finding a correct plan, given a starting situation and a goal. More sophisticated theories generalize this basic notion of plans and goals in a number of different ways:

1. A plan may only partially specify the actions to be taken, leaving details to be completed at execution time. Consider, for example, a plan to mail a letter consisting of five steps: (1) Insert the letter in an envelope, (2) address the envelope, (3) attach a stamp to the envelope, (4) seal the envelope, and (5) put the envelope in a mail box. When forming the plan, it is probably not necessary to identify exactly which envelope, stamp, and mail box should be used; when the plan is executed, the most convenient objects of these types may be chosen. Moreover, the steps need not be totally ordered at planning time. As long as step 4 follows 1, and 5 is the last operation, other ordering relations among the steps may be chosen at execution time (Sacerdoti, 1975; Chapman, 1987).

2. If it will be necessary for an agent to achieve goals of a similar form repeatedly, it may be worthwhile constructing a generic plan, that will accomplish these goals in all circumstances, rather than planning each case individually. For example, in the blocks world, it is possible to construct the generic plan "Clear block X; clear block Y; put X on Y" for achieving the goal "X on Y." (Sussman, 1975; Manna and Waldinger, 1987.)

3. If planners that are not omniscient, but have only partial knowledge of the environment are considered, then the analysis of plans becomes more complicated in several respects. First, in this context, plans and goals become referentially opaque operators, like knowledge and belief. John may plan or wish to go to the capital of California and yet not plan or wish to go to Sacramento, if he does not know that they are the same place. It is, therefore, necessary to use one of the techniques described in the previous section (modal logic, syntactic operators, or possible worlds) to represent the plans and goals of agents who are not omniscient.

Planners with partial knowledge must also deal with circumstances in which the planner must gain information to achieve the goal. For example, if John wants to call Mary, but does not know her phone number, he may construct the plan, "First look up Mary's number in the phone book; then dial that number." The analysis of this kind of plan is known as the knowledge preconditions problem (Moore, 1985a; Morgenstern, 1988).

4. For either generic plans or planning with partial knowledge, it may be useful to augment the planning language so that a plan can specify actions that depend on the state of the world. For this purpose, it may be useful to introduce operators similar to those of programming languages, such as conditionals, loops, variable binding, interrupts, and so on.

In order to carry out motivation analysis (the explanation of an agent's actions in terms of goals and plans) it is necessary to have a theory that describes characteristic goals. Otherwise, it would be possible to explain any action as done for the fun of it. Schank and Abelson (1977) suggest five general categories of top-level goals:

Satisfaction Goals. Basic physical needs, such as hunger, thirst, and fatigue, that arise periodically.

Preservation Goals. The desire to preserve certain key personal states, such as preservation of life, health, and possessions.

Achievement Goals. Large-scale ambitions accomplished over a long term, such as raising a family or success in a career.

Entertainment Goals. The short-term enjoyment of some activity, such as seeing a movie.

Delta Goals. The acquisition of certain goods, particularly wealth and knowledge.

OTHER ISSUES

Other commonsense domains that have been studied in the AI literature include emotions (Dyer, 1983; Sanders, 1989), interactions among agents (Wilensky, 1983; Bond and Gasser, 1988), communication (Perrault and Allen, 1980), and thematic relations between people (Schank and Abelson, 1977).

BIBLIOGRAPHY

J. Allen, "Maintaining Knowledge about Temporal Intervals," *Comm. ACM* **28,** 832–843 (1983).

J. Allen, "Towards a General Theory of Action and Time," *Artif. Intell.* **23,** 123–154 (1984).

D. Ballard and C. Brown, *Computer Vision,* Prentice Hall, Inc., Englewood Cliffs, N.J., 1982.

A. Bond and L. Gasser, *Readings in Distributed Artificial Intelligence,* Morgan-Kaufmann, San Mateo, Calif., 1988.

F. Brown, ed., *The Frame Problem in Artificial Intelligence: Proceedings of the 1987 Workshop,* Morgan-Kaufmann, San Mateo, Calif., 1987.

D. Chapman, "Planning for Conjunctive Goals," *Artif. Intell.* **32,** 333–378 (1987).

E. Davis, "Inferring Ignorance from the Locality of Visual Perception," in *Proceedings of the Seventh National Conference on Artificial Intelligence,* St. Paul, Minn., AAAI, Menlo Park, Calif., 1988, pp. 786–790.

J. de Kleer and J. S. Brown, "A Qualitative Physics Based on Confluences," in D. Bobrow, ed., *Qualitative Reasoning about Physical Systems,* MIT Press, Cambridge, Mass., 1985, pp. 7–84.

M. Dyer, *In-Depth Understanding—A Computer Model of Integrated Processing for Narrative Comprehension,* MIT Press, Cambridge, Mass., 1983.

B. Faltings, "Qualitative Kinematics in Mechanisms," *Proceedings of the Tenth IJCAI,* Milan, Italy, Morgan-Kaufmann, San Mateo, Calif., 1987, pp. 1331–1336.

K. Forbus, "Qualitative Process Theory," in D. Bobrow, ed., *Qualitative Reasoning about Physical Systems,* MIT Press, Cambridge, Mass., 1985, pp. 85–168.

J. Halpern and Y. Moses, "A Guide to the Modal Logics of Knowledge and Belief," in *Proceedings of the Ninth IJCAI,* Los Angeles, Morgan-Kaufmann, San Mateo, Calif., 1985, pp. 480–490.

S. Hanks and D. McDermott, "Nonmonotonic Logic and Temporal Projection," *Artif. Intell.* **33,** 379–412 (1987).

P. Hayes, "In Defense of Logic," in *Proceedings of the Fifth IJCAI,* Cambridge, Mass., Morgan-Kaufmann, San Mateo, Calif., 1977, pp. 559–565.

P. Hayes, "The Naive Physics Manifesto," in D. Michie, ed., *Expert Systems in the Micro-Electronic Age,* Edinburgh University Press, Edinburgh, UK, 1978.

P. Hayes, "Naive Physics 1: Ontology for Liquids," in J. Hobbs and R. Moore, eds., *Formal Theories of the Commonsense World,* Ablex, Norwood, N.J., 1985, pp. 71–108.

C. Hoffmann, *Geometric and Solid Modeling: An Introduction,* Morgan-Kaufmann, San Mateo, Calif., 1989.

Y. Iwasaki and H. Simon, "Causality in Device Behavior," *Artif. Intell.* **29,** 3–32 (1986).

L. Joskowicz, "Shape and function in Mechanical Devices," in *Proceedings of the Sixth National Conference on Artificial Intelligence,* Seattle, Wash., AAAI, Menlo Park, Calif., 1987, pp. 611–618.

K. Konolige, "Belief and Incompleteness," in J. Hobbs and R. Moore, eds., *Formal Theories of the Commonsense World,* Ablex, Norwood, N.J., 1985, pp. 71–108.

B. Kuipers, "Modeling Spatial Knowledge," *Cogn. Sci.* **2**(2), 129–154 (1978).

B. Kuipers, "Qualitative Simulation," *Artif. Intell.* **29,** 289–338 (1986).

H. Levesque, "A Logic of Explicit and Implicit Belief," in *Proceedings of the Fourth National Conference on Artificial Intelligence,* Austin, Tex., AAAI, Menlo Park, Calif., 1984.

J. McCarthy, "Programs with Common Sense," in *Proceedings of the Symposium on Mechanisation of Thought Processes,* Vol. 1, London, 1959.

J. McCarthy, "Programs with Common Sense," in M. Minsky, ed., *Semantic Information Processing,* MIT Press, Cambridge, Mass., 1968, pp. 403–418.

J. McCarthy and P. Hayes, "Some Philosophical Problems from the Standpoint of Artificial Intelligence," in B. Meltzer and D. Michie, eds., *Machine Intelligence,* Vol. 4, Edinburgh University Press, Edinburgh, UK, 1969, pp. 463–502.

D. McDermott, "Tarskian Semantics, or No Notation Without Denotation!" *Cogn. Sci.* **2**(3), 277–282 (1978).

D. McDermott, "A Temporal Logic for Reasoning about Processes and Plans," *Cogn. Sci.* **6,** 101–155 (1982).

D. McDermott, "A Critique of Pure Reason," *Computat. Intell.* **3,** 151–160 (1987).

Z. Manna and R. Waldinger, "A Theory of Plans," in M. Georgeff and A. Lansky, eds., *Reasoning about Actions and Plans,* Morgan-Kaufmann, San Mateo, Calif., 1987.

M. Minsky, "A Framework for Representing Knowledge," in P. Winston, ed., *The Psychology of Computer Vision,* McGraw-Hill Book Co., Inc., New York, 1975.

R. Moore, "A Formal Theory of Knowledge and Action," in J. Hobbs and R. Moore, eds., *Formal Theories of the Commonsense World,* Ablex, Norwood, N.J., 1985a, pp. 319–358.

R. Moore, "Semantical Considerations on Nonmonotonic Logic," *Artif. Intell.* **25,** 75–94 (1985b).

L. Morgenstern, *Foundations of a Logic of Knowledge, Action, and Communication,* Ph.D. dissertation, New York University, 1988.

J. Pearl, *Probabilistic Reasoning in Intelligent Systems; Networks of Plausible Inference,* Morgan-Kaufmann, San Mateo, Calif., 1988.

C. Perrault and J. Allen, "A Plan-Based Analysis of Indirect Speech Acts," *Am. J. Computat. Ling.* **6,** 167–182 (1980).

A. N. Prior, *Past, Present, and Future,* Clarendon Press, Oxford, UK, 1967.

Z. Pylyshyn, *The Frame Problem and Other Problems of Holism in Artificial Intelligence,* Ablex, Norwood, N.J., 1987.

D. A. Randell and A. G. Cohn, "Modeling Topological and Metrical Properties in Physical Process," in *Proceedings of the Firt International Conference on Principles of Knowledge Representations and Reasoning,* Toronto, 1989.

A. A. G. Requicha, "Representations for Rigid Solids: Theory,

Methods, and Systems," *ACM Comput. Surv.* **12**(4), 437–464 (1980).

E. Sacerdoti, *A Structure for Plans and Behaviors,* Elsevier Science Publishing Co., Inc., New York, 1975.

K. Sanders, "A Logic for Emotion," in *Proceedings of the Conference for Cognitive Science,* Ann Arbor, Mich., 1989, pp. 357–363.

R. Schank and R. Abelson, *Scripts, Plans, Goals, and Understanding,* Lawrence Erlbaum, Hillsdale, N.J., 1977.

Y. Shoham, *Reasoning about Change,* MIT Press, Cambridge, Mass., 1988.

G. Sussman, *A Computer Model of Skill Acquisition,* Science Publishing Co., Inc., New York, 1975.

J. van Bethem, *The Logic of Time,* Reidel, Dordrecht, 1983.

R. Wilensky, *Planning and Understanding,* Addison-Wesley Publishing Co., Inc., Reading, Mass., 1983.

General References

R. Brachman and H. Levesque, eds., *Readings in Knowledge Representation,* Morgan-Kaufman, San Mateo, Calif., 1985. Reprints of many classic articles and extensive bibliography.

E. Charniak and D. McDermott, *Introduction to Artificial Intelligence,* Addison-Wesley Publishing Co., Inc., Reading, Mass., 1985. Chapters 1, 6, and 7 give an excellent introduction to knowledge representation and commonsense reasoning.

E. Davis, *Representations of Commonsense Knowledge,* Morgan-Kaufmann, San Mateo, Calif., 1990. Comprehensive textbook.

M. Genesereth and N. Nilsson, *Logical Foundations of Artificial Intelligence,* Morgan-Kaufmann, San Mateo, Calif., 1988. Extensive discussion of logic, nonmonotonic inference, and knowledge representation.

J. Hobbs and R. Moore, *Formal Theories of the Commonsense World,* Ablex, Norwood, N.J., 1985. Collection of research papers.

D. Lenat and R. Guha, *Building Large Knowledge-Based Systems: Representation and Inference in the CYC Project,* Addison-Wesley Publishing Co., Inc., Reading, Mass., 1990. Description of the CYC program, a large knowledge base for commonsense knowledge.

D. Weld and J. de Kleer, *Qualitative Reasoning about Physical Systems,* Morgan-Kaufmann, San Mateo, Calif., 1989. Extensive collection of research papers on physical reasoning.

Ernest Davis
Courant Institute

REASONING, DEFAULT

A main goal of AI research is the construction of programs capable of displaying commonsense behavior. The work on default reasoning purports to contribute to this goal in two ways: by developing frameworks for understanding the nature and form of inference patterns that rely on assumptions, and by developing representation languages and inference procedures for capturing such patterns in AI programs.

What is a default inference? It is an inference that relies on hidden assumptions. For example, the expectations that the car is now where it was last parked and that the car is going to start when the ignition key is turned are default inferences. Both presume that certain facts, like the car being stolen or the battery being dead, are not true. Because these assumptions usually hold, the expectations they support will hold as well, permitting appropriate action plans to be adopted. On the other hand, if the assumptions are found to be wrong, the expectations will be revised and new plans of actions will be considered.

In order to capture this type of behavior in systems that encode knowledge declaratively, two issues need to be addressed. First, a language is needed in which to express both categorical and default knowledge. For example, it is desirable to be able to express things such as "normally, if the ignition key is turned, the car will start," "the car will not start if the battery is dead," and so on. Second, it is necessary to have a semantics for the language, ie, a specification of the legitimate expectations that default gives rise to. The language and the semantics must also provide meaningful primitives with an interpretation that must correspond with the intuitions of the knowledge base builder. As will be noted later, the failure of a number of nonmonotonic logics to accomplish this goal has been a main driving force of much of the recent work in the area.

Among the knowledge representational languages proposed to accommodate some form of default inference, two groups can be distinguished. On the one hand, are special-purpose systems that evolved from the experimental work in AI. These include inheritance networks, truth-maintenance (qv) systems, and logics programs with negation as failure. On the other hand are formalisms derived from classical logic which aim to capture default inference as classical logic captures deductive inference. The special-purpose systems will be reviewed first, and then the more general formalisms, which draw their main intuitions from the former.

SYSTEMS THAT REASON BY DEFAULT

A number of systems in AI involve forms of default inference. These systems point to the type of inferences that an adequate formal account of default inference must accommodate and illustrate that even without a complete understanding of defaults a lot is already known about how they are used in commonsense reasoning. In this section some of these systems will be considered, focusing on databases, inheritance hierarchies (qv), general logic programs, and truth-maintenance systems.

Databases

Databases are systems designed for the efficient storage and retrieval of information about objects and their relations. A departmental database, for example, may contain a relation *teach* with two tuples ⟨*gray, c*⟩ and ⟨*kay, lisp*⟩, indicating that Professor Gray teaches C and Professor Kay, LISP. Relations and tuples are understood as encoding ground atoms in classical first-order logic; in this case, the atoms *teach*(*gray, c*) and *teach*(*kay, lisp*). Thus if queried about who teaches C or PASCAL, the answer *gray* can be understood from the fact that the atomic encoding of the database sanctions the sentence *teach*(*gray, c*) $\vee$ *teach*(*gray, pascal*) as a theorem.

The logic of databases, however, involves more than atoms. For example, conclusions such as "*kay* does not teach *c*" and "only *gray* teaches *c*," do not follow from the atoms contained in the database. To account for such conclusions, the atomic encoding of the database must be augmented with certain assumptions about both the names of the objects and the world that the database is supposed to represent. These are the unique names assumption, by which individuals with distinct names are assumed distinct, the domain closure assumption, by which all individuals are assumed named, and the closed world assumption, by which it is assumed that there are no more instances of a relation than those deducible from the database (Reiter, 1984). Provided with these assumptions, the conclusions supported by the database will now be theorems of its logical encoding. This logical encoding, however, is not incremental; more information in the database (eg, a new class on C taught by Kay) will render some of the former assumptions false. This is not surprising though; the behavior of the database changes nonmonotonically (ie, more information sometimes implies fewer conclusions), whereas the behavior of its logical encoding can only change monotonically.

Inheritance Hierarchies

Inheritance hierarchies (qv) are directed acyclic graphs used to represent subsumption relations among classes of objects (Touretzky, 1986). Nodes in the hierarchy stand for individual objects or classes, and links stand for class membership (if they connect an individual to a class) or class subsumption (if they connect a class to another class). The concept of inheritance hierarchies originated in the work on semantic networks and in recent years has found applications in both programming and knowledge representation languages.

Figure 1 depicts a simple inheritance network. The network involves two types of link: positive links ($\rightarrow$), which assert that one class is a (not necessarily strict) subclass of another (eg, birds are flying things), and negative links ($\nrightarrow$), which assert that one class is a (not necessarily strict) subclass of the complement of another (eg, penguins are not flying things). Classes are assumed to inherit the properties of their superclasses unless otherwise specified. In the net depicted in Figure 1, for example, canaries are assumed to inherit the property "fly" from birds, just as penguins are assumed to inherit the property "animal." On the other hand, penguins do not inherit the property "fly" from birds, because the link from penguins to the complement of "fly" is more specific than the link from birds to "fly" and overrides the default inheritance path "penguin $\rightarrow$ bird $\rightarrow$ fly." This preference for more specific information in cases of conflict is at the core of inheritance algorithms and points to an important aspect of default inference that an adequate account of defaults must be able to capture.

Negation as Failure

Logic programs are collections of implicitly universally quantified rules of the form $A \leftarrow L_1, L_2, \ldots, L_n$, where A is an atom called the head of the rule and each L_i, $i = 1, \ldots, n$, $n \geq 0$ is positive or negative literal in the rule's body. When the rules only involve positive literals, logic programs can be given both a procedural and a declarative reading: a rule $A \leftarrow L_1, L_2, \ldots, L_n$ can be understood as stating either that A is true when the literals L_i, $i = 1, \ldots, n$ are true, or that the goal A can be derived by deriving each of the subgoals L_i, $i = 1, \ldots, n$. When some of the literals L_i are negative, however, things are not so simple, and the declarative reading of logic programs is usually dropped. Such programs are commonly understood in procedural terms, with negative literals $\neg A_i$ assumed to be derivable when the derivation for the atom A_i finitely fails (Clark, 1978). Such form of negation as failure has turned out to be particularly useful in programming and follows a tradition that goes back to PLANNER-like languages (Hewitt, 1972). The effect of negation as failure is to assume that negative literals hold by default. Logical accounts of such a behavior have been recently developed, and will be discussed in the next section.

Truth Maintenance Systems

Truth maintenance systems (qv) (TMSs) keep track of dependencies among propositions and often perform some type of inference (Doyle, 1979; de Kleer, 1986). See also the bibliography in Martins (1991). In Doyle's TMS, a user expresses justifications among propositions in a restricted propositional language and the TMS generates a labeling where each proposition is believed (IN) or not (OUT), according to whether or not the proposition has a valid justification. Each justification is made up of two lists of propositions, an IN list and an OUT list, and is valid when each proposition in the IN list and no proposition in the OUT list has a valid justification. To avoid circularities, admissible labelings are also required to be well founded, or what amounts the same, to be minimal in the set of propositions that are believed.

As an example, consider the following justifications (syntax is IN list|OUT list $\rightarrow$ prop):

$$J_1 : D | H \rightarrow W$$
$$J_2 : C | \rightarrow H$$
$$J_3 : \rightarrow D$$

stating that (1) "if today is a working day and it is not believed that John is at home, then John is at work"; (2) "if John's car is parked in front of his home, then John is at home"; and (3) "today is a working day." The TMS algorithm will then label both D and W as IN, and H as OUT. If a new justification $\rightarrow C$ ("John's car is parked in front of his home") is added, however, H will become IN,

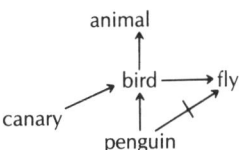

Figure 1. A simple inheritance hierarchy.

defeating the default justification for W and thus forcing W to go OUT.

Although long understood in procedural terms, some formal accounts of the TMS belief revision process have been recently advanced (Elkan, 1988; Reinfrank and co-workers, 1989). More interestingly, such accounts reveal that Doyle's TMS is not very different from a propositional logic program and that admissible TMS labeling are nothing else but stable models (Gelfond and Lifschitz, 1988) of the logic program that results from mapping each TMS justification $p_1, \ldots, p_n | q_1, \ldots, q_m \to p$ into a logic programming rule $p \leftarrow p_1, \ldots, p_n, \neg q_1, \ldots, \neg q_m$.

NONMONOTONIC LOGICS

The systems reviewed in the previous section all embed a default component. Still, such a component is the result of well-crafted algorithms tailored to specific languages and tasks. Nonmonotonic logics, on the other hand, were developed with the aim of providing general-purpose languages for representing and reasoning with defaults (see LOGIC, NONMONOTONIC). For that they need to address mathematical as well as epistemological issues. The mathematical issues arise because default reasoning, unlike deductive reasoning, is nonmonotonic; namely, conclusions sometimes need to be retracted in the light of new information. This implies for instance that proofs, if there are such things in the context of nonmonotonic logics, will be quite different from proofs in classic logic: they will not only depend on the information which is present in the knowledge base, but on information which is absent as well. The epistemological issues, on the other hand, arise because defaults, much like the standard logical connectives, possess a meaning to the builder of the knowledge base that an adequate logical account must be able to reflect. Logical accounts of defaults that predict conclusions that bear no relation to those intended by the user could have some mathematical interest, but will certainly have little value for knowledge representation.

In this section some of the standard nonmonotonic formalisms will be reviewed, and how they relate to one another and to the systems reviewed in the previous section will be discussed.

Default Logic

Reiter's (1980) default logic extends classic first-order logic with tentative rules of inference of the form:

$$\frac{\alpha(x) : \beta(x)}{\gamma(x)}$$

where $\alpha(x)$, $\beta(x)$, and $\gamma(x)$ are formulas with free variables among those of $x = \{x_1, x_2, \ldots\}$, called the precondition, the test condition and the consequent of the default, respectively. For a tuple a of ground terms, such a default permits $\gamma(a)$ to be derived from $\alpha(a)$, provided that $\neg\beta(a)$ is not derivable. For instance, a default

$$\frac{bird(x) : flies(x)}{flies(x)}$$

yields the conclusion $flies(Tim)$ from $bird(Tim)$. However, if the negation of $flies(Tim)$ is observed, the default gets blocked and the former conclusion is no longer supported.

The appeal to nonderivability in the body of defaults together with their use to extend the set of derivable sentences lead, in certain cases, to conflicts among defaults. For instance, given a second default:

$$\frac{injured(x) : \neg flies(x)}{\neg flies(x)}$$

and that Tim is injured, two defaults become applicable. However, if the first one is applied, the second one becomes blocked, and vise versa. Reiter deals with those situations by introducing the notion of extensions of a default theory $T = \langle W, D \rangle$, for a set of wffs W and a set of defaults D.

Formally, if it is assumed that $\Gamma(S)$ expands a set of wffs S according to T when $\Gamma(S)$ stands for the minimal deductively closed set of wffs that includes W and every consequent γ of defaults $\alpha : \beta/\gamma$ in D for which $\alpha \in \Gamma(S)$ and $\beta \notin S$, then an extension of T is a set E of wffs that expands into itself, ie, $E = \Gamma(E)$. A default theory $T = \langle W, D \rangle$ may give rise to one, none, or many extensions, and each one reflects a possible "completion" of the classic theory W, according to the defaults in D. In the example above, two different extensions arise, one in which Tim flies and one in which he does not. Default logic has been used for specifying the behavior of inheritance hierarchies with exceptions (Etherington and Reiter, 1983) and logic programs with negation (Bidoit and Fridevaux, 1987). The complexity of reasoning in default logic has been recently studied (Kautz and Selman, 1989).

Circumscription

Circumscription (qv) is a formal device for asserting that the objects that can be shown to satisfy a certain predicate P in a given first-order theory are the only objects that do (McCarthy, 1980, 1986). For instance, from a database only containing the fact $Q(a)$, the circumscription of Q yields the formula $\forall x. Q(x) \Rightarrow x = a$. Thus if b is an object different from a, the circumscription of Q sanctions $\neg Q(b)$ as a conclusion. If $Q(b)$ is learned, however, $\neg Q(b)$ goes away and the new conclusions turn out to be those derivable from the formula $\forall x. Q(x) \Leftrightarrow x = a \lor x = b$. Circumscription thus behaves as a powerful, adaptable, closed-world assumption, capable of dealing with theories that are richer than those expressible in databases.

Formally, if $A(P)$ stands for a first-order sentence containing the predicate P, and $A(\Phi)$ denotes the sentence that results from replacing all the occurrences of P by a predicate Φ with the same arity as P, the circumscription $Circ[A(P); P]$ of P in $A(P)$ is given by the second-order schema:

$$A(P) \land A(\Phi) \land \forall x. [\Phi(x) \Rightarrow P(x)] \Rightarrow \forall x. (P(x) \Rightarrow \Phi(x))$$

that asserts that among the predicates Φ satisfying the constraint $A(\Phi)$, P is the strongest. Thus if $A(Q)$ is the sentence $Q(a)$, for example, the substitution of $\Phi(x)$ by the predicate $\Phi^*(x):\lambda x. (x = a)$ in the schema renders the formula

$$Q(a) \wedge a = a \wedge \forall x. [x = a \Rightarrow Q(x)] \Rightarrow \forall x. Q(x) \Rightarrow x = a$$

which simplifies to $\forall x. Q(x) \Leftrightarrow x = a$. The predicate $\Phi^*(x)$ is indeed the strongest predicate that satisfies $A(\Phi)$, and thus the effect of circumscribing Q in $A(Q)$ is to set Q to Φ^*.

Circumscription accommodates nonmonotonic forms of reasoning but does not uniquely specify how defaults should be encoded. For that purpose McCarthy (1986) introduced a convention by which defaults such as "birds fly" are encoded in the circumscriptive framework as formulas

$$\forall x. \, bird(x) \wedge \neg ab_i(x) \Rightarrow flies(x)$$

read as "every nonabnormal bird flies." Once defaults are so expressed, the expected behavior is obtained by circumscribing the ab_i predicates or, as McCarthy prefers to say, by "minimizing abnormality." However, before that can be done effectively, a more powerful form of circumscription is needed in which certain predicates can be minimized at the expense of others.

The circumscription Circ$[A(P, \mathbf{Z}); P, \mathbf{Z}]$ of the predicate P in the sentence $A(P, \mathbf{Z})$, where $\mathbf{Z}$ stands for a tuple of predicates allowed to vary in the minimization of P, is defined by the following second-order formula (McCarthy, 1986):

$$A(P, \mathbf{Z}) \wedge \forall \Phi, \Psi \, A(\Phi, \Psi) \wedge \forall x. [\Phi(x) \Rightarrow P(x)] \\ \Rightarrow \forall x. [P(x) \Rightarrow \Phi(x)]$$

This formula permits us to minimize the extension of P at the expense of the extension of the predicates in $\mathbf{Z}$. Indeed, the formula Circ$[A(P, \mathbf{Z}); P, \mathbf{Z}]$ can be shown to sanction as theorems the sentences that hold in all models of the sentence $A(P, \mathbf{Z})$, which are minimal in P with respect to $\mathbf{Z}$ (Lifschitz, 1985; Etherington, 1988). A model M of $A(P, \mathbf{Z})$ is minimal in P with respect to $\mathbf{Z}$ if there are no other models M' of $A(P, \mathbf{Z})$, which assign a smaller extension to P and which preserve from M the same domain and the same interpretation of symbols other than P and those in $\mathbf{Z}$.

The generalization of circumscription for dealing with multiple predicates, known as parallel circumscription, is straightforward. More interesting is the case of prioritized circumscription in which the user is allowed to specify a priority ordering among the circumscribed predicates (McCarthy, 1986; Lifschitz, 1985). For instance, the circumscription Circ$[A; P_1 > P_2 > \ldots > P_n; \mathbf{Z}]$ of predicates $P_1, P_2, \ldots, P_n$ in decreasing order of priority, translates into the conjunction of $n - 1$ circumscriptions of the form Circ$[A; P_i; \mathbf{Z} \cup \{P_{i+1}, \ldots, P_n\}]$ together with Circ$[A; P_n; \mathbf{Z}]$. Predicates of higher priority are thus circumscribed at the expense of predicates of lower priority. Although it is not clear in general how priorities among predicates are to be selected, general guidelines for the domains of logic programs and inheritance hierarchies have been proposed (Lifschitz, 1988; Krishnaprasad and co-workers, 1989). A proof theory for prioritized circumscription has also been developed (Baker and Ginsberg, 1989; Geffner, 1990).

Autoepistemic Logic

Autoepistemic logic is a nonmonotonic extension of classic logic proposed by Moore (1985) as a reconstruction of McDermott and Doyle's (1980) nonmonotonic logic. Since then, autoepistemic logic has received growing attention and has been studied by a number of researchers. Autoepistemic logic deals with autoepistemic theories: propositional theories augmented by a belief operator L, where sentences of the form $L\alpha$ are read as "α is believed." The stable expansions of an autoepistemic theory T are defined as the sets of formulas $S(T)$, which satisfy the equation

$$S(T) = \text{Th}(T + \{Lp : p \in S(T)\} + \{\neg Lp : p \notin S(T)\})$$

where Th(X) stands for the set of tautological consequence of X. Stable expansions are supposed to reflect possible states of belief of an ideal rational agent, closed both under positive and negative introspection. A default such as "if it is a bird, it flies" can be encoded in autoepistemic logic as a sentence $bird \wedge \neg Lab_i \Rightarrow flies$. Then, given $bird$, the only autoepistemic expansion will contain the autoepistemic sentence $\neg Lab_i$ and, therefore, the target sentence $flies$.

An autoepistemic theory may have one, none, or many stable expansions. For instance, a theory such as $T = \{\neg Lp \Rightarrow p\}$ has no stable expansions, whereas a theory $T' = \{\neg Lp \Rightarrow q, \neg Lq \Rightarrow p\}$ has two. Autoepistemic logic has been successfully applied to characterize the semantics of general logic programs (Gelfond and Lifschitz, 1988) and truth maintenance systems (Elkan, 1988; Reinfrank and co-workers, 1989). Both characterizations are natural and simple, requiring in essence the replacement of logic negation ($\neg p$) by autoepistemic negation ($\neg Lp$). They also suggest how to compute with certain classes of autoepistemic theories, and due to the close relation between autoepistemic and default logic (Konolige, 1988; Marek and Truszczynski, 1989), how to compute with certain class of default theories as well.

RECENT DEVELOPMENTS

Each of the formalisms reviewed in the last section, circumscription, default logic, and autoepistemic logic, extends classic logic with some formal device that permits nonmonotonic forms of reasoning. These formalisms generalize and provide a logical basis to the mechanisms discussed earlier and take us closer to the goal of a general-purpose language for representing and reasoning with defaults. Defaults, however, exhibit features other than nonmonotonicity, which are not always captured by these formalisms. In this section some of these features will be examined and some recent proposals for dealing with them will be discussed.

Model Preference

A source of difficulties for capturing default inference in the standard formalisms was noticed by Hanks and McDermott (1987) who noted that the encoding of theories involving causal relations in the standard formalisms often failed to legitimize conclusions that were otherwise obvious to the user. Their example, known as the "Yale shooting" problem, deals with a person who is alive in a given situation but who is shot with a gun that was loaded an instant earlier. The intuition is that the gun stays loaded and that the person dies as a result of the shooting. However, the encoding in the formalisms analyzed by Hanks and McDermott also accommodates a different outcome in which the fluent "loaded" changes, and the fluent "alive" stays the same. Many proposals have been advanced since then to account for the distinction between intuitive and counterintuitive behavior in the presence of actions and persistences. Some involve variations of the formalisms and encodings used by Hanks and McDermott [eg, Morris (1989) uses nonnormal defaults and stable closures]. Others, such as chronological minimization (Shoham, 1988) have led to alternative ways of specifying nonmonotonic inference relations.

Chronological minimization is a semantic criterion for interpreting theories for reasoning about change in which a preference is established for models that give rise to minimal sets of changes that occur as late as possible. This preference relation is used to define a nonmonotonic entailment relation that unlike classic entailment only considers the overall preferred models of the target theory. In the Yale shooting problem, for example, the class of models in which the person dies turns out to be preferred to the class of models in which the gun gets unloaded, as the change sanctioned by the first class of models occurs later. As a result, the right behavior in the Yale shooting problem is captured.

As discussed above, the idea of a preference relation on models is not foreign to the semantics of circumscription which establishes a preference for models that minimize certain predicates. The difference, however, it that chronological minimization bypasses the circumscriptive axiom altogether, appealing directly to a model-preference criterion. This move has resulted in a more powerful way of specifying nonmonotonic behavior and no significant loss: the circumscriptive axion is not a particular source of insight and it has not been found of general use for computing circumscription (Przymusinski, 1989; Ginsberg, 1989). Model preference, on the other hand, has been found to be a flexible device for specifying nonmonotonic inference in a variety of domains (Morgenstern and Stein, 1988; Selman and Kautz, 1989).

Conditional Logics

Another feature of default reasoning that is not explicitly accounted by standard nonmonotonic formalisms is specificity: when two defaults are in conflict there is usually a preference to accept the conclusion supported by the most specific one. Inheritance hierarchies (Fig. 1) provide plenty of examples. To account for such a behavior in a framework such as circumscription, priorities must be introduced (Krishnaprasad and co-workers, 1989). What is the origin of these priorities or why they are needed, however, are not questions that circumscription addresses. Something similar happens with default and autoepistemic logic that do not provide devices as clean as priorities for capturing specificity preferences.

Some answers to these questions have recently emerged from the field of conditional logic as the similarities between defaults and conditionals have become increasingly apparent (Nute, 1984) (see LOGIC, CONDITIONAL). For example, both conditionals and defaults appear to violate principles such as chaining (from $p \to q$ and $q \to r$ derive $p \to q$), contraposition (from $p \to q$ derive $\neg q \to \neg p$), and strengthening the antecedent (from $p \to r$ derive $p \land q \to r$), all of which are corner stones of classic logic. Similarly, they both seem to obey principles like augmentation (from $p \to q$ and $p \to r$ derive $p \land q \to r$), reduction (from $p \to q$ and $p \land q \to r$ derive $p \to r$), and cases (from $p \to r$ and $q \to r$ derive $p \lor q \to r$).

In AI, two types of conditional interpretation of defaults have recently been studied. In one, defaults $p \to q$ are regarded as stating that the conditional probability $P(q|p)$ is arbitrarily high, short of being one (Geffner and Pearl, 1990); in the other $p \to q$ is regarded as a constraint on model-preference orders, stating that q must be true in all preferred models of p (Delgrande, 1987; Kraus and co-workers, 1988). The benefit of the conditional interpretation of defaults is that they account for certain preferences among conflicting defaults without having to explicate exceptions or priorities. The shortcoming, on the other hand, is that patterns of inference involving independence assumptions are no longer captured. Some recent proposals attempt to combine the benefits of standard nonmonotonic logics and conditional interpretations (Lehmann, 1989; Pearl, 1989). An interesting result is that the conditional aspects of defaults can be captured in the framework of prioritized circumscription by a careful selection of the default priorities (Geffner, 1990).

Architectures for Default Reasoning

Most of the work in default reasoning has been focused on the mathematical and semantic aspects of default inference: how to analyze default inference in logical terms and how to capture the intended meaning of defaults. For default reasoning to be useful in building AI programs, however, there is an additional need for reasoning with defaults: namely computing the valid default consequences as opposed to just specifying what makes them valid. The latter is what the formalisms for default reasoning do; the former is the task of default reasoning architectures. Because of the results that relate inheritance hierarchies, truth maintenance systems, and logic programs with negation to specialized circumscriptive, default, and autoepistemic theories, the former systems can be regarded as specialized default reasoning architectures. More recent work has attempted to use or extend these architectures to cope with more expressive languages. Gelfond and Lifshitz (1989), for example, investigate the compilation of circumscriptive theories into logic programs and Junker and Konolige (1990), the computation of extensions of default and autoepistemic theories by means of a TMS. Similarly, argument-based systems have extended the language of inheritance hierarchies to accommodate both conjunctions and negation and, in certain cases, the full power of first-order classical logic. Default inference is viewed in argument-based systems as the result of the interaction between supporting and rebutting arguments, in analogy to the interaction between positive and negative paths in inheritance-based systems. Most argument-based systems have also addressed the problem of the specificity of arguments (Nute, 1986; Poole, 1985; Loui, 1987). Recent results also show a great resemblance between argument-based systems and the proof theory of prioritized circumscription (Baker and Ginsberg, 1989; Geffner, 1990).

CONCLUSIONS

The first decade of work in default reasoning has witnessed an enormous growth in the understanding of the mathematics of nonmonotonic inference and a significant, although less dramatic, growth in the understanding of the epistemological issues involved. A handful of formal devices are now available for extending classical logic with nonmonotonic features, and there is a much better grasp of their power and limitations. Mechanisms such as truth maintenance, negation as failure, and inheritance are understood in logical terms, and new and more powerful architectures seem forthcoming. The gap between intuitions and formalizations has also gotten narrower, as a better understanding of the standard and new formalisms and a better appreciation of the causal and conditional aspects of defaults have developed.

An area where progress has been scant is applications. Except for a few attempts to deal with theories involving actions and persistences, no default formalism has been tried in realistic domains. This has been, in part, due to the emphasis on getting the theory right first as well as the lack of adequate algorithms. As progress along both dimensions continues, however, it is expected that more interesting applications will follow. The work by Grosof (1988) and Loui (1990), using defaults for reasoning about partially specified probabilities and utilities, are an indication of such a trend.

BIBLIOGRAPHY

A. Baker and M. Ginsberg, "A Theorem Prover For Prioritized Circumscription," in *Proceedings of the Eleventh IJCAI*, Detroit, Mich., Morgan-Kaufmann, San Mateo, Calif., 1989, pp. 463–467.

N. Bidoit and C. Froidevaux, "Minimalism Subsumes Default Logic and Circumscription in Stratified Logic Programming," in *Proceedings of the Symposium on Principles of Database Systems*, 1987.

K. Clark, "Negation as Failure," in H. Gallaire and J. Minker, eds., *Logic and Data Bases*, Plenum Press, New York, 1978, pp. 293–322.

J. de Kleer, "An Assumption-Based Truth Maintenance System," *Artif. Intell.* **28**, 280–297 (1986).

J. Delgrande, "An Approach to Default Reasoning Based on a First-Order Conditional Logic," in *Proceedings in the Sixth National Conference on Artificial Intelligence*, Seattle, Wash., AAAI, Menlo Park, Calif., 1987, pp. 340–345.

J. Doyle, "A Truth Maintenance System," *Artif. Intell.* **12**, 231–272 (1979).

C. Elkan, *A Rational Reconstruction of Nonmonotonic TMSs*, Technical Report, Cornell University, Ithaca, N.Y., 1988.

D. Etherington and R. Reiter, "On Inheritance Hierarchies with Exceptions," in *Proceedings of the Intelligence*, Washington, D.C., AAAI, Menlo Park, Calif., 1983, pp. 104–108.

D. Etherington, *Reasoning with Incomplete Information*, Pitman, London, 1988.

H. Geffner, "Conditional Entailment: Closing the Gap between Defaults and Conditionals," in *Proceedings of the Third International Workshop on Non-Monotonic Reasoning*, South Lake Tahoe, Calif., 1990, pp. 58–72.

H. Geffner and J. Pearl, "A Framework for Reasoning with Defaults," in H. Kyburg, R. Loui, and G. Carlson, eds., *Knowledge Representation and Defeasible Inference*, Kluwer, The Netherlands, 1990.

M. Gelfond and V. Lifschitz, "The Stable Model Semantics for Logic Programming," in *Proceedings 1988 Symposium on Logic Programming*, MIT Press, Cambridge, Mass., 1988, pp. 1070–1080.

M. Gelfond and V. Lifschitz, "Compiling Circumscriptive Theories into Logic Programs," in M. Reinfrank and co-workers, eds., *Proceedings of the Second International Workshop on Non-Monotonic Reasoning*, Berlin, Germany, 1989, pp. 74–99.

M. Ginsberg, "A Circumscriptive Theorem Prover," *Artif. Intell.* **39**, 209–230 (1989).

B. Grosof, "Non-Monotonicity in Probabilistic Reasoning," in J. Lemmer and L. Kanal, eds., *Uncertainty in Artificial Intelligence*, Vol. 2, Elsevier Science Publishing Co., Inc., New York, 1988, pp. 237–249.

S. Hanks and D. McDermott, "Non-Monotonic Logics and Temporal Projection," *Artif. Intell.* **33**, 379–412 (1987).

C. Hewitt, *Description and Theoretical Analysis of Planner: A Language for Proving Theorems and Manipulating Models in a Robot*, Technical Report TR-258, MIT, AI Laboratory, Cambridge, Mass., 1972.

U. Junker and K. Konolige, "Computing the Extensions of Autoepistemic and Default Logic with a Truth Maintenance System," in *Proceedings of the Ninth National Conference on Artificial Intelligence*, Boston, AAAI, Menlo Park, Calif., 1990.

H. Kautz and B. Selman, "Hard Problems for Simple Default Logics," in *Proceedings of the First International Conference on Principles of Knowledge Representation and Reasoning*, Toronto, Ont., 1989, pp. 189–197.

K. Konolige, "On the Relation between Default Logic and Autoepistemic Logic," *Artif. Intell.* **35**, 343–382 (1988).

S. Kraus, D. Lehmann, and M. Magidor, *Preferential Models and Cumulative Logics*, Technical Report, Hebrew University, Jerusalem, Israel, Aug. 1988.

T. Krishnaprasad, M. Kiefer, and D. Warren, "On the Circumscriptive Semantics of Inheritance Networks," in Z. Ras and L. Saitta, eds., *Methodologies for Intelligent Systems*, Vol. 4, North-Holland, Amsterdam, The Netherlands, 1989.

D. Lehmann, "What Does a Conditional Knowledge Base Entail?" in *Proceedings of the First International Conference on Principles of Knowledge Representation and Reasoning*, Toronto, 1989, pp. 212–222.

V. Lifschitz, "Computing Circumscription," in *Proceedings of the*

Ninth IJCAI, Los Angeles, Calif., Morgan-Kaufmann, San Mateo, Calif., 1985.

V. Lifschitz, "On the Declarative Semantics of Logic Programs," in J. Minker, ed., *Foundations of Deductive Databases and Logic Programming,* Morgan-Kaufmann, San Mateo, Calif., 1988, pp. 177–192.

R. Loui, "Defeat among Arguments: A System of Defeasible Inference," *Comput. Intell.* **3**(3), 100–106 (1987).

R. Loui, "Defeasible Specification of Utilities," in H. Kyburg, R. Loui, and G. Carlson, eds., *Knowledge Representation and Defeasible Inference,* Kluwer, The Netherlands, 1990.

W. Marek and M. Truszczynski, "Relating Autoepistemic and Default Logics," *Proceedings of the First International Conference on Principles of Knowledge Representation and Reasoning,* Toronto, 1989, pp. 276–288.

J. Martins, "The Truth, the Whole Truth, and Nothing But the Truth," *AI Mag.* **11**(5) (1991).

J. McCarthy, "Circumscription—A Form of Non-Monotonic Reasoning," *Artif. Intell.* **13**, 27–39 (1980).

J. McCarthy, "Applications of Circumscription to Formalizing Commonsense Knowledge," *Artif. Intell.* **28**, 89–116 (1986).

D. McDermott and J. Doyle, "Non-Monotonic Logic I," *Artif. Intell.* **13**, 41–72 (1980).

R. Moore, "Semantical Considerations on Non-Monotonic Logics," *Artif. Intell.* **25**, 75–94 (1985).

L. Morgenstern and L. Stein, "Why Things Go Wrong: A Formal Theory of Causal Reasoning," in *Proceedings of the Seventh National Conference on Artificial Intelligence,* St. Paul, Minn., AAAI, Menlo Park, Calif., 1988.

P. Morris, "Autepistemic Stable Closures and Contradiction Resolution," in M. Reinfrank and co-workers, eds., *Proceedings of the Second International Workshop on Nonmonotonic Reasoning,* Berlin, 1989, pp. 60–73.

D. Nute, "Conditional Logic," in D. Gabbay and F. Guenthner, eds., *Handbook of Philosophical Logic,* D. Reidel, Dordrecht, 1984, pp. 387–439.

D. Nuto, *LDR: A Logic for Defeasible Reasoning,* Technical Report ACMC Research Report **01-0013**, University of Georgia, Athens, 1986.

J. Pearl, *System Z: A Natural Ordering of Defaults with Tractable Applications to Non-Monotonic Reasoning,* Technical Report, UCLA, Los Angeles, 1989.

D. Poole, "On the Comparison of Theories: Preferring the Most Specific Explanation," in *Proceedings of the Ninth IJCAI,* Morgan-Kaufmann, San Mateo, Calif., 1985, pp. 144–147.

T. Przymusinski, "An Algorithm for Circumscription," *Artif. Intell.* **38**, 49–73 (1989).

M. Reinfrank, O. Dressler, and G. Brewka, "On the Relation between Truth Maintenance and Autoepistemic Logic," in *Proceedings of the Eleventh IJCAI,* Morgan-Kaufmann, San Mateo, Calif., 1989, pp. 1206–1212.

R. Reiter, "A Logic for Default Reasoning," *Artif. Intell.* **12**, 81–132 (1980).

R. Reiter, "Towards a Logical Reconstruction of Relational Database Theory," in M. Brodie, J. Mylopoulos, and J. W. Schmidt, eds., *On Conceptual Modelling,* Springer-Verlag, New York, 1984, pp. 163–189.

B. Selman and H. Kautz, "The Complexity of Model Preference Default Theories," in M. Reinfrank and co-workers, eds., *Proceedings of the Second International Workshop on Nonmonotonic Reasoning,* Berlin, 1989, pp. 115–130.

Y. Shoham, *Reasoning about Change: Time and Causation from the Standpoint of Artificial Intelligence,* MIT Press, Cambridge, Mass., 1988.

D. Touretzky, *The Mathematics of Inheritance Systems,* Pitman, London, 1986.

HECTOR GEFFNER
IBM T. J. Watson Research Center

REASONING, MEMORY-BASED

Memory-based reasoning (MBR) is a technique in which artificial intelligence is realized by direct reference to memory (Stanfill and Waltz, 1986, 1988). In MBR, there is no fundamental distinction among learning, reasoning, and remembering. Most forms of AI that benefit from experience use experiences to create an intermediate abstraction, such as a set of rules or a set of weights in a network; MBR retains the actual events. Most memory models use knowledge available at the time of an experience to decide how to store and index it; MBR depends instead on intensive computation at the time an experience is required (Waltz, 1989).

The simplest, best studied form of MBR is as a solution to the classification problem. This problem may be represented as follows: a system is given two sets of objects, a training set and a performance set. Each object is represented by a vector of features (attributes), and each object is assigned to a class. The system has access to all features of all objects, and to the classes of objects in the training set. The task of the system is to assign classes to the objects in the performance set, minimizing the number of incorrect class assignments. The memory-based approach to this problem is to iteratively (1) choose a target object from the performance set, (2) find its nearest neighbor in the training set (the training set object that is most similar to the target), and (3) assign the class of the nearest neighbor to the target. Alternatively, it is possible to (2) find the k nearest neighbors and (3) assign the target's class according to the majority of the neighbors. The key issue in such a system is a computational realization of similarity, usually represented as a distance function that, given a pair of objects, returns a nonnegative number measuring the distance between the objects, subject to the constraint that the distance between an object and itself is zero. If there are n objects in the training set and m objects in the performance set, then it is necessary (in general) to evaluate the distance function for $O(mn)$ object pairs, which usually requires a very fast (parallel) machine. For some similarity measures, there may be efficient algorithms requiring fewer than $O(mn)$ such computations.

Many distance measures are possible. The simplest is *Hamming distance,* which is the number of attributes in which two objects differ. A simple variant is the weighted Hamming distance, in which each attribute is assigned a weight measuring its importance in determining the class of the object. An attribute that was very important would have a weight of 1, whereas an attribute that was totally unimportant would have a weight of 0. Importance can be determined by a variety of statistical measures. If the attributes are numeric, then distance can be measured by the Euclidean distance metric, treating each attribute as an axis in a vector space. The above forms of MBR have been well known in the fields of nonparametric statistics and pattern recognition as the nearest-neighbor and k nearest-neighbor classification methods (Atkeson, 1990). Until the advent of parallel computing, such methods were generally considered computationally too expensive for practical use, but their application may now be considered possible. All these methods use a simple global distance measure: the weight given to each feature is uniform across the entire set of objects. It is possible, however, to use a nonglobal weighting scheme. For example, it is possible to (1) determine the importance of each feature, (2) find the 100 nearest neighbors, (3) determine the importance of each feature in that neighborhood, and (4) recompute the nearest neighbors. In effect, every time a new object is to be classified, a new metric that is appropriate to that object's neighborhood will be created. This ability to dynamically create metrics is an important difference between MBR and the traditional statistical methods. The application of MBR to classification has been studied for the pronunciation of English words (Stanfill and Waltz, 1986; Stanfill, 1987), optical character recognition, the interpretation of job category description on census forms (Creecy and co-workers, 1991), and protein secondary structure prediction (Zhang, Waltz, and Mesirov, 1988).

MBR has also been applied to the task of approximating continuous functions (Atkeson, 1990). In this problem, each object in the training and performance sets is associated with a numeric value. Furthermore, it is known that this numeric value is a continuous function of the features used to describe the objects. Values of this function are known for data in the training set, but not for data in the performance set. The task is to predict, as accurately as possible, the values for the performance set. The simplest application of MBR to this task would be to (1) choose an object from the performance set as the target object, (2) find its nearest neighbor in the training set, and (3) assign the value of the nearest neighbor to the target. The problem with this method is that it can only produce target values that are present in the training set. The resulting function will thus have discontinuities. The solution is to introduce some method of interpolating the results. The best approach at this point appears to be (1) assign each object in the training set a weight depending on its distance from the target object, with the nearer objects receiving higher weights; (2) perform a *weighted quadratic regression,* which produces a quadratic function from the object features to the object values that minimized error in the neighborhood of the target point; and (3) apply the quadratic function to the target point, producing a predicted value. This method has been demonstrated on robotic kinematic problems (Atkeson, 1989). For example, the state of a robot arm can be characterized at any point in time by a set of numbers measuring the angles, angular velocities, torques, and angular accelerations of each of its joints. The function to be approximated would be the state of the arm at a time t milliseconds in the future. The training set then consists of a set of snapshots of the state of the arm at various points in time. Locally weighted quadratic regression, as described above, is then employed.

It is possible to combine primitive MBR units into systems exhibiting fairly complex behavior. One such system modeled a first-grade child learning to read (Stanfill, 1988). The system had an auditory memory (a set of words known by sound, represented phonetically), an initially empty set of words known by spelling, and a set of simple pronunciation rules. When confronted with a new word, the system would first check its spelling memory to see whether the word was already known. If not, it would try to sound out the word by remembering pronunciation rules or by remembering words with similar spellings. It would then check its auditory memory for a word that sounded like its pronunciation and, if one was found, create a new item in its spelling memory linked with the corresponding entry in the auditory memory.

MBR can be thought of as occupying one extreme of a continuum of learning and reasoning methods, varying from abstraction-based to memory-based. At the abstraction-based extremes are traditional rule-based systems, where a human translates knowledge of a domain into an abstraction (a set of rules). Slightly less abstraction-based is machine learning, in which a set of rules are inferred from a set of data; the data themselves are not used at run time. Traditional (parametric) statistics plus nontraditional methods (such as back-propagation learning) produce numerical functions rather than symbolic rules, but are at approximately the same point in the abstraction- to memory-based scale. Radial basis functions use points in a training set in forming the basis of a vector space and are yet more memory based. Nearest-neighbor techniques using global metrics are the next steps in the continuum, because the data themselves are used in conjunction with a precomputed abstraction (the global metric). Finally, nearest-neighbor techniques with metrics constructed on the fly are the most extremely memory based. MBR may be considered a subclass of case-based reasoning. However, many case-based reasoning systems employ significant amounts of domain-specific (abstract) knowledge to organize memory, to retrieve items from memory, and to adapt memories to the specific purposes at hand. It may be possible to consider case-based reasoning as a high level architecture and memory-based reasoning as a low level inference technique.

BIBLIOGRAPHY

C. Atkeson, *Memory-Based Approaches to Approximating Continuous Functions,* in *Proceedings of the Sixth Yale Workshop on Adaptive and Learning Systems,* New Haven, Conn., 1990.

C. Atkeson, "Learning Arm Kinematics and Dynamics," *Ann. Rev. Neurosci.* **12,** 157–183 (1989).

R. H. Creecy, B. Masand, S. Smith, and D. Waltz, "Trading MIPS and Memory for Knowledge Engineering: Automatic Classification of Census Returns on a Massively Parallel Computer,"

Technical Report TMC-192, Thinking Machines Corp., Cambridge, Mass., 1991.

C. Stanfill, "Memory-Based Reasoning Applied to English Pronunciation," in *Proceedings of the Sixth National Conference on Artificial Intelligence,* Seattle, Wash., AAAI, Menlo Park, Calif., 1987.

C. Stanfill and D. L. Waltz, "Toward Memory-Based Reasoning," *Commun. ACM* **29**(12), 1213–1228 (1986).

C. Stanfill and D. L. Waltz, "Learning to Read: A Memory-Based Model," in *Proceedings of the Case-Based Reasoning Workshop,* Clearwater Beach, Fla., May 1988.

D. L. Waltz, "Is Indexing Used for Retrieval?" in *Proceedings of the Case-Based Reasoning Workshop,* Pensacola Beach, Fla., 1989.

X. Zhang, D. L. Waltz, and J. Mesirov, "Protein Structure Prediction Using Memory-Based Reasoning: A Case Study of Data Exploration," Technical Report RL 88-3, Thinking Machines Corporation, 1988.

CRAIG STANFILL
Thinking Machines Corporation

REASONING, NONMONOTONIC

In many situations, appropriate reasoning involves drawing default conclusions based on incomplete data. The results of such reasoning are in general unsound, ie, they are not necessarily true even though the data on which they are based may be true. Nonetheless, such reasoning can be important. For instance, a robot may assume that in the absence of information to the contrary its arms may be used to transport objects in the normal manner. Similarly, in normal conversation, the appropriate response to "Did you understand that article?" is not "I understood 90% of it," if in fact the latter speaker understood it all. Even though the indicated response is not strictly false, it is misleading because it encourages the questioner to conclude (unsoundly) that only 90% of the article was understood. That is, in the absence of information to the contrary, the questioner might normally and usefully assume that the respondent is being cooperative rather than misleading. These and other examples strongly suggest that reasoning by default is prevalent throughout commonsense reasoning.

Minsky (1975) coined the term nonmonotonic logic in developing an argument that tools of formal logic are inadequate to the task of representing commonsense reasoning. His argument involved an analysis of the use of defaults. As indicated above, these are conclusions based on the absence of contrary information. Consider the example of concluding from the knowledge that Tweety is a bird that Tweety can fly. Such a conclusion is not necessarily true, although it certainly can be very useful in some situations. It is possible to try to specify precisely those situations in which such a conclusion is sound, but any effort to do so quickly leads to despair. The possible circumstances in which any presumed correct line of reasoning can be defeated astounds: Tweety may be an ostrich, may have a broken wing, may be chained to a perch, may be too weak, etc. Indeed, the problem is virtually the same as that of the well-known qualification problem: the special conditions relevant to determining what may be the case in a complex environment defies precise specification. Although there appears to be a meaningful sense of certain typical situations (such as typical birds being ones which, among other things, can fly), it is notoriously hard to define typicality.

However, Minsky's claim was more than this: he argued that, first, conclusions of the sort given in the Tweety example are contingent on what else is known (eg, if it is already known that Tweety cannot fly, than the opposite conclusion is not made) and that, second, such conclusions do not obey the customary phenomenon of monotonicity of formal systems of logic. That is, a standard logic L has the property that if ϕ is a theorem of L and if L is augmented to L^* by additional axioms, then ϕ remains a theorem of L^*. Indeed the same proof of ϕ in L is a proof of ϕ in L^*. However, commonsense reasoning seems to allow a proof (at least in the form of a tentative supposition) that Tweety can fly, given only that Tweety is a bird, whereas in the augmented state in which it is known also that Tweety cannot fly, no such proof is forthcoming. In effect, account seems to be taken of what the reasoner does not know, an issue already much studied in the area of databases in the context of the closed-world assumption (Reiter, 1978a), in which any atomic formula not explicitly present in the database is intended (or assumed) to be false. Similarly, inheritance hierarchies provide mimicked traits (eg, flying) for subclasses (eg, robins) of other classes (eg, birds) unless made exceptional (eg, ostriches).

It is true that any straightforward attempt to represent such reasoning in terms of sentences in a traditional monotonic logic (in which the stated conclusions are theorems) will fail for the simple reason that these logics will necessarily have the original theorem (Tweety can fly) carried over to the augmented theories by virtue of their monotonicity. Several questions then arise:

1. Are there other formal logics that can represent such reasoning?
2. Has commonsense reasoning been fairly portrayed here or are there other factors involved that might change the assessment of the role of nonmonotonicity?
3. Might not a clever use of monotonic logic allow the effect of nonmonotonic deductions?

Minsky seems to have concluded that formal methods per se are inappropriate to capture such reasoning, whereas others have taken his ideas as a challenge by which to find more powerful formal methods. Out of this challenge has arisen a substantial field of research in nonmonotonic reasoning.

In fact, vigorous efforts have been made toward answering each of the three questions above, and the terrain has by now shown itself to be a rich and varied one involving ideas from divers parts of artificial intelligence, logic, natural language, and philosophy. One theme that seems to have emerged is that a key element in commonsense reasoning dealing with uncertainty (due to the abundance of special conditions defying specification) is self-reference: the reasoning entity uses information about the extent of its own knowledge. Indeed, answers suggested to the above three questions can be viewed in terms of their approach to representing such self-reference. This will be explored in what follows.

The topic of nonmonotonic reasoning has undergone an explosion of new material in recent years, so that it will not be possible to do justice to it in this brief survey. More information is available (Ginsberg, 1987; Reinfrank and co-workers, eds., 1988; Brachman and co-workers, 1989; Genesereth and Nilsson, 1987).

NONMONOTONIC FORMALISMS

Two distinct formalisms emerged around 1980 that attempted to capture the essence of nonmonotonic reasoning by providing a new kind of logical framework. One (McDermott and Doyle, 1980) simply bears the name nonmonotonic logic, and the other (Reiter, 1980) is called default logic. Both employ inferential tools making explicit use of information about what information the formalism itself has available to it. In both cases new syntactic and inferential constructs are developed. Each of these will be discussed in turn.

Nonmonotonic Logic

Nonmonotonic logic (NML) (McDermott and Doyle, 1980) takes as point of departure the desire to represent axiomatically such notions as "If an animal is a bird then, unless proven otherwise, it can fly." To do this a modal operator M is introduced into the language (initially a first-order language) so that if p is a formula then so is Mp (read "p is consistent"). Now in this language it is possible to write formulas that seem to express the kind of reasoning given earlier. For instance, the formula

$$(x)[\text{Bird}(x) \;\&\; M \,\text{Flies}(x) \;.\to \text{Flies}(x)]$$

appears to convey information appropriate to concluding of typical birds that they can fly. A means is needed to characterize deductions with formulas containing the operator M, however, and McDermott and Doyle (1980) went to some length to develop this. As it is essential to their treatment, some time will be spent examining it. To provide an example for the following discussion, let A be the theory $\{\text{Bird}(x) \;\&\; M\,\text{Flies}(x) \to \text{Flies}(x), \text{Bird(Tweety)}\}$.

At first blush, it would appear easy to state what is wanted. For if indeed the formula p is consistent (with the rest of the axioms of the particular instance of NML that is to be used) and if in typical situations (ie, ones in which p is consistent) the formula q happens to be true, then a rule such as "from Mp deduce q" seems appropriate. However, McDermott and Doyle chose M to be a part of the language itself, ie, Mp is a formula as well as p. This means that a mechanism is needed to make it possible to prove formulas such as Mp, and this is problematic because proofs of consistency are not only notoriously hard in general but in fact are usually impossible within the same axiomatic system with respect to which consistency is sought. To deal with this problem, McDermott and Doyle extended the notion of proof to allow a kind of consistency test, at the expense of effectiveness. In fact, all formal approaches to nonmonotonic reasoning seem to run into this same issue. Their notion of proof is as follows: If L is a first-order language modified by the addition of a modal operator M, A is a theory in the language L, and S is a set of formulas in the language L of A, let

$$NM_A(S) = Th(A \cup As_A(S))$$

where

$$As_A(S) = \{Mq : q \in L \text{ and } \neg q \notin S\} - Th(A)$$

Here $Th(A)$ is the usual set of first-order consequences of A, and $As_A(S)$, the so-called set of assumptions from S, consists of those formulas Mq not in $Th(A)$ for which $\neg q$ is not in S. Intuitively, an Mq that is not already proven is to be considered an assumption on the basis of S if S does not rule q out, ie, Q is considered to be possible. The idea is to adjoin assumptions to A and find all (usual) consequences, this producing the set $NM_A(S)$. S, of course, could be A itself, or even empty. However, when NM_A is formed, new formulas are thereby available for use (ie, they are considered proven) and these may themselves provide the basis for another round of assumptions. So S plays the role of a recursion variable, and a fixed point of $NM_A(S)$ is sought. It is desired then to consider as theorems precisely those formulas contained in all fixed points S. However, some theories A have no such fixed points, and for these such a definition will not do. McDermott and Doyle settled on the entire language L in such cases, thereby defining the set of theorems nonmonotonically derivable from A as

$$TH(A) = \cap(\{L\} \cup \{S : NM_A(S) = S\})$$

In terms of the example theory $\{\text{Birds}(x) \;\&\; M\text{Flies}(x) \to \text{Flies}(x), \text{Bird(Tweety)}\}$, every fixed point S will contain the sentence Flies(Tweety). Intuitively, because ¬Flies(Tweety) is not initially in the theory, and each stage of generating new assumptions will produce only additional sentences such as MFlies(Tweety) as well as their ordinary consequences (such as Flies(Tweety)), then Flies(Tweety) will be remain present in all iterations of the assumption process. Thus Flies(Tweety) will be a nonmonotonic theorem of A.

Note that any attempt to calculate $TH(A)$ leads to consistency tests. For in iterating $NM_A(S)$ for S initially empty, it is immediately necessary to determine whether, for any given q, Mq is in $Th(A)$. This is in general undecidable and amounts precisely to determining whether $A \cup \{\neg Mq\}$ is inconsistent. McDermott and Doyle acknowledged this difficulty and showed that in very restricted cases, essentially propositional logic, there is a remedy. [They also defined a notion of model for NML; however, there is some dispute as to the completeness of their definition (Davis, 1980).]

McDermott (1982) tried to strengthen NML to overcome certain weaknesses in the original version, in particular the fact that Mp and $\neg p$ are not contradictory. The newer effort makes fuller use of the modal character of the language, but the case he explores most collapses into equivalence with an ordinary monotonic logic. More recent work suggests, however, that in other cases this collapse need not occur (Marek and Truszczynski, 1989b).

A Distinction: Semantic Approaches

Moore (1983) reexamined the underlying goals of NML and concluded that two ideas were being conflated: typicality on the one hand and beliefs about beliefs on the other. He distinguished between concluding Tweety can fly on the basis that it is not known that Tweety cannot fly and that typically birds can fly, and concluding Tweety can fly on the basis that it is not known that Tweety cannot fly and that "I would know it if Tweety could not fly." Moore argued that the former is intended to be approximate and error prone, whereas the latter (which he called autoepistemic reasoning) is intended to be sound. He devised a logical semantics (usually denoted AEL) for the latter form of reasoning.

It does appear that autoepistemic reasoning forms a part of commonsense reasoning. The example above is not as striking as one given by Moore: "I would know it if I had an elder brother." Here he is presumably not merely stating a belief about typicality (that people typically know their older brothers, although that seems true enough) but rather a belief that "I" specifically do know of all "my" brothers. Admittedly this is arguable, because situations exist in which an older brother may be unknown, but they are not likely to be taken seriously, so that again a kind of typicality may be present here.

Moore pointed out that in autoepistemic beliefs there is a possibility of failure, ie, the belief can be false (I may have an elder brother after all) in which case I must alter that belief, whereas in the case of typicality I may merely conclude that I am atypical regarding knowledge of brothers and yet preserve the belief that typically elder brothers are known. Still, if I do discover to my surprise that such a brother exists, it would seem likely that I would conclude immediately that I was wrong about my autoepistemic belief but that the belief still applies to most people, ie, there seems a very fine and tenuous line between the two forms of beliefs. It seems possible to move back and forth between explicit typicality beliefs in which uncertainty is acknowledged and more stubborn autoepistemic ones, for the same assertions, depending on context, and the willingness of people to alter their position when challenged may attest to an implicit default character even in autoepistemic cases.

It is of interest that both forms of reasoning, however, like all nonmonotonic formalisms, depend at least implicitly on a determination that in fact certain formulas are not theorems of the formalism in question. Note that in Moore's example it must somehow be determined that in fact an elder brother is not known before using the autoepistemic belief and *modus ponens* to conclude there is no such brother. Again, this self-referential or consistency aspect of the reasoning seems the most striking characteristic, and the one presenting the greatest formal difficulty. Related approaches have been published (Halpern and Moses, 1984; Shoham, 1988; Bell, 1990).

Default Logic

Reiter (1980) introduced a logic for default reasoning (DL). In specifically singling out default reasoning, Reiter identified his concern as that of studying typicality rather than other possible nonmonotonic forms of reasoning. His formalism in fact bears close resemblance to NML, the most obvious difference being that the language is strictly first order, with the operator M playing a role only in rules of inference rather than in axioms. Specifically, Reiter allowed inference rules (default rules) such as

$$\text{Bird}(x): M\,\text{Flies}(x)$$
$$\text{Flies}(x)$$

where $M\,\text{Flies}(x)$ is intended not as an antecedent theorem to the consequent $\text{Flies}(x)$ but instead as a condition that must be met before $\text{Flies}(x)$ can be concluded from $\text{Bird}(x)$. The condition is, roughly (and as in all nonmonotonic formalisms) that $\text{Flies}(x)$ be consistent with the rest of the axiomatic framework. Thus if the above rule and the axiom Bird(Tweety) are employed, the conclusion Flies(Tweety) results. As with NML, formalizing the notion of consistency for the indicated purpose requires care. Making this precise and showing it to be useful is the bulk of the task Reiter undertook. He employed a hierarchy of iterations along lines similar to that of NML, also arriving at a fixed point, in determining a notion of proof for default rules.

Reiter and Criscuolo (1981) also considered what they called interacting defaults, ie, default rules that separately might lead to opposed conclusions, such as in "Richard Nixon is a Quaker and a Republican" where it is known, say, that typically Quakers are pacifists and Republicans are not. This appears to be a substantial difficulty for any form of nonmonotonic reasoning that pretends to deal with typicality. Along the lines of interacting defaults, yet another approach has gotten much attention: inheritance hierarchies (Horty, 1990; Horty and co-workers, 1987; Selman and Levesque, 1989; Touretzky, 1984a, 1984b; Touretzky and co-workers, 1987; Etherington and Reiter, 1983).

REMAINING WITHIN FIRST-ORDER LOGIC

McCarthy (1980) has devised an ingenious means for representing and calculating knowledge about situations involving minimization of particular notions. He called this technique circumscription (which we will denote CL). It is noteworthy in the present context because it seems able to handle many of the kinds of reasoning with self-reference found in nonmonotonic approaches and yet stays within first-order logic. McCarthy managed this by use of an axiom schema that partially captures the notion of a model of a set of sentences, similar to (and in fact generalizing) the familiar manner of defining the natural numbers by a minimizing schema applied to the successor operation. Much work has followed his original paper. In particular, by introducing a predicate for abnormal McCarthy (1986) has been able to capture some of the intuitions about reasoning about typicality, that is, circumscribing that predicate can lead to conclusions to the effect that Tweety can fly, because it is abnormal for a bird not to fly and because abnormality is (intended to be) minimized by circumscription. Some positive and negative results on this have been published (Etherington and co-workers, 1985; Perlis and Minker, 1986).

PROBLEMATIC ASPECTS UNDERLYING NONMONOTONIC REASONING

Kowalski (1979) and Israel (1980) suggested that something was missing from Minsky's account of commonsense reasoning under uncertainty: the reasoning entity creating the "proof" (say that Tweety flies) must know that it does not know certain facts (such as that Tweety is an ostrich), and furthermore, that when this knowledge of self is properly represented, the reasoning is no longer nonmonotonic, thereby rendering unnecessary the development of new (nonmonotonic) logics. Their argument is as follows: a default rule such as "if X is not known then Y" (eg, if Tweety doesn't fly is not known then Tweety flies) is at least implicit in nonmonotonic proofs, and so the reasoning must make use, in some fashion, of X not being known, before concluding Y. This means there must be an additional mechanism M to determine that in fact X is not known. But then if the system is augmented by coming to know X (Tweety is an ostrich and, therefore, cannot fly, say) then the system can no longer derive "X is not known" as long as the mechanism M for such derivations is faithful to the facts. That is, not only has the system been augmented by now knowing X, it has had an old piece of knowledge removed (and properly so, for it no longer is true), namely that "X is not known," and that piece of information was precisely what previously allowed the now inadmissable conclusion Y.

What has happened in such a scenario is that one logic has been replaced by another that contains additional information but also has lost some information (namely information that no longer is true because of the very presence of the new information). In effect, a reasoning system that is to know about its own reasoning would appear to require temporal changes reflecting the fact that its previous states obeyed different truths. If a system first does not know X and then later does, it was true at first that "X is not known" and later this is false. If the system itself is to have this knowledge represented (as Kowalski and Israel argued) then Minsky's argument for nonmonotonicity fails, because there is no longer a strict augmentation of the original axioms. Israel, in particular, argued that a sequence of logics is a better way to view the situation, in which axioms are constantly added and subtracted as new facts become known and that this process is not one of deduction but of interaction with the happenstance environment. To a certain extent this acknowledges Minsky's point that logic is not (entirely) what is involved here. However, the insight provided by making explicit the default knowledge and mechanism M that utilizes it suggests that logic still may do all, and that other processes invoke the necessary self-referential inspections to determine whether or not X is still known. In fact, just such an approach has been undertaken in experimental reasoning systems (Perlis, 1984; Elgot-Drapkin, 1988).

Israel also argued that a sufficiently perceptive agent that uses nonmonotonic reasoning will necessarily entertain (at least occasional) inconsistencies. Perlis (1987) formalized this into specific challenges for the three formalisms DL, NML, and CL. In particular, the presence of beliefs to the effect that some of the nonmonotonic conclusions are false can lead to inconsistency or to the blocking of desired default conclusions. This has been investigated and partial solutions have been found (Etherington and co-workers, in press).

The issue of determining "what is not known" to a reasoner, as indicated above, appears to be central to all current formalizations of nonmonotonic reasoning. This is subject to computability constraints (undecidability in the general case) but also others. For instance, Perlis (1987) has shown that if a first-order reasoner is able to introspect both positively and negatively (Known(P) is inferred whenever P is itself known, and not-Known(P) is inferred whenever P is not known) and also has even fairly mundane arithmetical knowledge, then the reasoner is inconsistent. This also obtains if *known* is treated as a modality.

INTERCONNECTIONS

Given that there are three or four principal formalisms already in the literature aimed at capturing the informal notion of nonmonotonic reasoning, it is natural to ask about comparisons between them. Some results have been established along these lines, relating AEL, DL, circumscription, and logic programming (Reiter, 1982; Konolige, 1989, 1987; Marek and Subrahmanian, in press; Marek and Truszczynski, 1989a, in press; Przymusinski, 1989).

APPLICATIONS AND RELATED WORK

As with much of commonsense reasoning techniques, formal nonmonotonic modes of reasoning naturally present themselves as candidates for a reasoning mechanism that could in principle be used in an intelligent robot, for instance, in conjunction with a theorem prover. So far, little has been done in a concrete way to address these issues. Some preliminary work has been presented (Perlis, 1984).

One rather specific application of nonmonotonic reasoning that has received much attention is temporal persistence in the presence of conflicting defaults. This problem was most vividly noted in connection with the Yale Shooting Problem (Hanks and McDermott, 1986). Here each of two states of affairs (a person's being alive and a gun's being loaded) alone tends to persist. But together it is possible to negate the other (if at some point the gun is aimed at the person and the trigger is pulled). Has the gun remained loaded up to that point? Has the person remained alive up to that point? What general principles lead to intuitive conclusions here? Hanks and McDermott showed that the problem is nontrivial, indeed, they further argued that the problem illustrates a fundamental inappropriateness of any formal techniques to commonsense reasoning, thereby aligning themselves with Minsky's original position. But, not surprisingly, many proposals were forthcoming that provided various formalisms designed to solve this sort of problem. A survey of this entire area has been published (Haugh, 1989).

BIBLIOGRAPHY

J. Bell, "The Logic of Non-Monotonicity," *Artif. Intell.* **41**, 365–374 (1990).

R. Brachman, H. Levesque, and R. Reiter, eds., *Proceedings of the First International Conference on Principles of Knowledge Representation and Reasoning*, 1989.

M. Davis, "The Mathematics of Non-Monotonic Reasoning," *Artif. Intell.* **13**(1–2), 73–80 (1980).

J. Elgot-Drapkin, *Step-Logic: Reasoning Situated in Time*, Ph.D. dissertation, University of Maryland, College Park, 1988.

D. Etherington, S. Kraus, and D. Perlis, "Limited Scope and Circumscriptive Reasoning," in K. Ford and P. Hayes, eds., *Advances in Human and Machine Cognition*, Vol. 1, JAI Press, in press.

D. Etherington, R. Mercer, and R. Reiter, "On the Adequacy of Predicate Circumscription for Closed-World Reasoning," *J. Comput. Intell.* **1**, 11–15 (1985).

M. Genesereth and N. Nilsson, *Logical Foundations of Artificial Intelligence*, Morgan-Kaufmann, San Mateo, Calif., 1987.

M. Ginsberg, *Readings in Non-Monotonic Reasoning*, Morgan-Kaufmann, San Mateo, Calif, 1987.

J. Halpern and Y. Moses, "Towards a Theory of Knowledge and Ignorance: Preliminary Report in *Proceedings of the Workshop on Nonmonotonic Reasoning*, New Paltz, N.Y., 1984, pp. 125–143.

S. Hanks and D. McDermott, "Default Reasoning, Nonmonotonic Logics and the Frame Problem," in *Proceedings of the Fifth National Conference on Artificial Intelligence*, Philadelphia, AAAI, Menlo Park, Calif., 1986, pp. 328–333.

B. Haugh, *Nonmonotonic Formalisms for Commonsense Temporal Causal Reasoning*, Ph.D. dissertation, University of Maryland, College Park, 1989.

J. Horty, *Some Direct Theories of Nonmonotonic Inheritance*, Technical Report, University of Maryland Institute for Advanced Computer Studies, College Park, 1990.

J. Horty, R. Thomason, and D. Touretzky, "A Skeptical Theory of Inheritance in Nonmonotonic Semantic Networks, in *Proceedings of the Sixth National Conference of Artificial Intelligence*, Seattle, Wash., AAAI, Menlo Park, Calif., 1987, pp. 358–363.

D. Israel, "What's Wrong with Non-Monotonic Logic," in *Proceedings of the First National Conference on Artificial Intelligence*," Stanford, Calif., AAAI, Menlo Park, Calif., 1980, pp. 99–101.

K. Konolige, "On the Relation between Default Theories and Autoepistemic Logic," in *Proceedings of the Tenth IJCAI*, Milan, Italy, Morgan-Kaufmann, San Mateo, Calif., 1987.

K. Konolige, "On the Relation between Autoepistemic Logic and Circumscription," in *Proceedings of the Eleventh IJCAI*, Detroit, Mich., Morgan-Kaufmann, San Mateo, Calif., 1989.

R. Kowalski, *Logic for Problem Solving*, North-Holland, Amsterdam, The Netherlands, 1979.

J. McCarthy, "Circumscription—A Form of Non-Monotonic Reasoning," *Artif. Intell.* **13**(1–2), 27–39 (1980).

J. McCarthy, "Applications of Circumscription to Formalizing Commonsense Knowledge," *Artif. Intell.* **28**, 89–116 (1986).

D. McDermott, "Nonmonotonic Logic II: Non-Monotonic Modal Theories," *JACM*, **29**(1), 33–57 (1982).

D. McDermott and J. Doyle, "Non-Monotonic Logic I," *Artif. Intell.* **13**(1–2), 41–72 (1980).

W. Marek and V. S. Subrahmanian, "The Relationship between Stable, Supported, Default and Auto-Epistemic Semantics for General Logic Problems," *Theor. Comput. Sci.*, in press.

W. Marek and M. Truszczynski, "Relating Autoepistemic and Default Logics," in R. Brachman, H. Levesque, and R. Reiter, *Proceedings of the First International Conference on Principles of Knowledge Representation and Reasoning*, 1989a, pp. 276–288.

W. Marek and M. Truszczynski, "Stable Semantics for Logic Programming and Default Logic," in *Proceedings of the North American Conference on Logic Programming*, Cleveland, Ohio, 1989b.

W. Marek and M. Truszczynski, "Autoepistemic Logic," *JACM*, in press.

M. Minsky, "A Frameword for Representing Knowledge," in P. Winston, ed., *The Psychology of Computer Vision*, McGraw-Hill Book Co., Inc., New York, 1975.

R. Moore, "Semantical Considerations on Non-Monotonic Logic," in *Proceedings of the Eighth IJCAI*, Karlsruhe, FRG, Morgan-Kaufmann, San Mateo, Calif., 1983, pp. 272–279.

D. Perlis, "Non-Monotonicity and Real-Time Reasoning," in Halpern and Moses, 1984.

D. Perlis, "On the Consistency of Commonsense Reasoning," *Comput. Intell.* **2**, 180–190 (1987).

D. Perlis and J. Minker, "Completeness Results for Circumscription," *Artif. Intell.* **28**, 29–42 (1986).

T. Przymusinski, "Three-Valued Formalizations of Non-Monotonic Reasoning and Logic Programming," in Brachman and co-workers, 1989, pp. 341–348.

M. Reinfrank, J. de Kleer, M. Ginsberg, and E. Sandewall, eds., *Non-Monotonic Reasoning, Proceedings of the Second International Workshop*, Grassau, Springer-Verlag, New York, 1988.

R. Reiter, "A Logic for Default Reasoning," *Artif. Intell.* **13**(1–2), 81–132 (1980).

R. Reiter, "On Closed World Databases," in H. Gallaire and J. Minker, eds., *Logic and Databases*, Plenum, New York, 1987a, pp. 55–76.

R. Reiter, "On Reasoning by Default," in the *Proceedings of the Second TINLAP*, Urbana, Ill., 1987b.

R. Reiter and G. Criscuolo, "On Interacting Defaults," in *Proceedings of the Seventh IJCAI*, Vancouver, B.C., Morgan-Kaufmann, San Mateo, Calif., 1981.

B. Selman and H. Levesque, "The Tractability of Path-Based Inheritance," in *Proceedings of the Eleventh IJCAI*, 1989.

Y. Shoham, *Reasoning about Change*, MIT Press, Cambridge, Mass., 1988.

D. Touretzky, "Implicit Ordering of Defaults in Inheritance Systems," in *Proceedings of the Fourth National Conference on Artificial Intelligence*, Austin, Tex., Morgan-Kaufmann, San Mateo, Calif., 1984a.

D. Touretzky, *The Mathematics of Inheritance Systems*, Ph.D. dissertation, Carnegie Mellon University, Pittsburgh, Pa., 1984b.

D. Touretzky, H. Horty, and R. A. Thomason, "A Clash of Intuitions: The Current State of Non-Monotonic Multiple Inheritance Systems," in *Proceedings of the Tenth IJCAI*, 1987.

General References

K. Clark, "Negation as Failure," in H. Gallaire and J. Minker, eds., *Logic and Databases*, Plenum Press, New York, 1978, pp. 293–322.

J. Doyle, "A Truth Maintenance System," *Artif. Intell.* **12**, 231–272 (1979).

D. Etherington, *Reasoning with Incomplete Information*, Morgan-Kaufmann, San Mateo, Calif., 1988.

B. Grosof, "Default Reasoning as Circumspection," in *Proceedings of the Workshop on Nonmonotonic Reasoning*, New Paltz, N.Y., 1984.

K. Konolige, "Circumscriptive Ignorance," in *Proceedings of the Second International Conference on Artificial Intelligence*, Pittsburgh, Pa., AAAI, Menlo Park, Calif., 1982, pp. 202–204.

K. Konolige, *Belief and Incompleteness*, SRI Technical Note 319, SRI International, Menlo Park, Calif., 1984.

I. Kramosil, "A Note on Deduction Rules with Negative Premises," in *Proceedings of the Fourth IJCAI*, Tbilisi, USSR, Morgan-Kaufmann, San Mateo, Calif., 1975, pp. 53–56.

S. Kraus, D. Lehmann, and M. Magidor, "Nonmonotonic Reasoning, Preferential Models and Cumulative Logics," *AIJ*, in press.

D. Kueker, "Another Failure of Completeness for Circumspection," paper presented at Week on Logic and Artificial Intelligence, University of Maryland, College Park, 1984.

H. Levesque, "Incompleteness in Knowledge Bases," *SIGART Newslett.* **74**, 150 (1981a).

H. Levesque, "The Interaction with Incomplete Knowledge Bases: A Formal Treatment," in *Proceedings of the Seventh IJCAI*, Vancouver, B.C., Morgan-Kaufmann, San Mateo, Calif., 1981b.

H. Levesque, *A Formal Treatment of Incomplete Knowledge Bases*, Ph.D. dissertation, University of Toronto, Toronto, Canada, 1981.

V. Lifschitz, "Some Results on Circumscription," in *Proceedings of the Workshop on Nonmonotonic Reasoning*, New Paltz, N.Y., 1984.

W. Lipski, "On the Logic of Incomplete Information," in *Lecture Notes in Computer Science*, Vol. 53, Springer-Verlag, New York, 1977, pp. 374–381.

W. Lukaszewicz, "General Approach to Nonmonotonic Logics," in *Proceedings of the Eighth IJCAI*, Karlsruhe, FRG, Morgan-Kaufmann, San Mateo, Calif., 1983, pp. 352–354.

J. McCarthy, "Applications of Circumscription to Formalizing Common Sense Knowledge," in *Proceedings of the Workshop on Nonmonotonic Reasoning*, New Paltz, N.Y., 1984.

J. Minker, "On Indefinite Databases and the Closed-World Assumption," in *Lecture Notes in Computer Science*, Vol. 138, Springer-Verlag, New York, 1982, pp. 292–308.

J. Minker and D. Perlis, "Protracted Circumscription," in *Proceedings of the Workshop on Nonmonotonic Reasoning*, New Paltz, N.Y., 1984a.

J. Minker and D. Perlis, "Applications of Protected Circumscription," in *Lecture Notes in Computer Science*, Vol. 170, Springer-Verlag, New York, 1984b, pp. 414–425.

R. Moore, *Reasoning from Incomplete Knowledge in Procedural Deduction System*, Memo **347**, MIT Artificial Intelligence Laboratory, Cambridge, Mass., 1975.

D. Nute, "Conditional Logic," in D. M. Gabbay and F. Guenthner, eds., *Handbook of Philosophical Logic*, Reidel, Dordrecht, 1984, pp. 387–439.

J. Nutter, *Default Reasoning in AI Systems*, M.Sc. thesis, SUNY at Buffalo, 1983a.

J. Nutter, "What Else Is Wrong with Nonmonotonic Logics? Representational and Informational Shortcomings," in *Proceedings of the Fifth Cognitive Science Conference*, Rochester, N.Y., 1983b.

M. A. Papalaskaris and A. Bundy, "Topics for Circumscription," in *Proceedings of the Workshop on Nonmonotonic Reasoning*, New Paltz, N.Y., 1984.

D. Perlis, "Languages with Self-Reference II: Knowledge, Belief, and Modality," *Artif. Intell.* **34**, 179–212 (1988).

J. Pollack, "A Refined Theory of Counterfactuals," *J. Philosph. Logic* **10**, 239–266 (1981).

R. Reiter, "Equality and Domain Closure in First-Order Databases," *JACM* **27**(2), 235–249 (1980).

R. Reiter and G. Criscuolo, "Some Representational Issues in Default Reasoning," *J. Comput. and Maths. with Applications*, (special issue on computational linguistics) **9**, 1–13 (1983).

E. Rich, "Default Reasoning as Likelihood Reasoning," in *Proceedings of the Third National Conference on Artificial Intelligence*, Washington, D.C., AAAI, Menlo Park, Calif., 1983.

E. Sandewall, *Partial Models, Attribute Propagation Systems, and Non-Monotonic Semantics*, LITH-IDA-R-83-01, Linkoping University, Linkoping, Sweden.

R. Stalnaker, *A Note on Non-Monotonic Modal Logic*, Department of Philosophy, Cornell University, Ithaca, N.Y., 1980.

D. PERLIS
University of Maryland

REASONING, PLAUSIBLE

In the past, the management of uncertainty in expert systems (qv) has usually been left to *ad hoc* representations and combining rules lacking either a sound theory or clear semantics. However, the aggregation of uncertain information (facts) is a recurrent need in the reasoning process of an expert system. Facts must be aggregated to determine the degree to which the premise of a given rule has been satisfied, to verify the extent to which external constraints have been met, to propagate the amount of uncertainty through the triggering of a given rule, to summarize the findings provided by various rules or knowledge sources or experts, to detect possible inconsistencies among the various sources, and to rank different alternatives or different goals.

COPING WITH UNCERTAINTY IN EXPERT SYSTEMS

Over the past few years, uncertainty management has received a vast amount of attention from the researchers in the field, leading to the establishment of two well-defined approaches based on probability and possibility theory, respectively. In this article these approaches will be illustrated and compared.

Sources of Uncertainty

In a survey of reasoning with uncertainty (Bonissone and Tong, 1985), it was noted that there are two major types of uncertainty: randomness and fuzziness. Randomness deals with the uncertainty of whether a given element belongs or does not belong to a well-defined set (event). Fuzziness deals with the uncertainty derived from the partial membership of a given element to a set whose boundaries are not sharply defined.

These two types of uncertainty can be introduced in reasoning systems by a variety of sources: the reliability of the information, the inherent imprecision of the representation language in which the information is conveyed, the incompleteness of the information, and the aggregation or summarization of information from multiple sources.

The first source type is related to the reliability of information: uncertainty can be present in the factual knowledge (ie, the set of assertions or facts) due to inaccuracy and poor reliability of the instruments used to make the observations. Uncertainty can also occur in the knowledge base (ie, the rule set) as a result of using weak implications. Unlike categorical rules (describing set subsumption relationships) weak implications or plausible rules are typically used to describe likely interpretations of situations. By their very nature, these rules are less reliable than categorical rules and are used when the expert or model builder is unable to establish an exact correlation between premise and conclusion. In most expert systems the degree of implication is expressed as a scalar value on an interval (certainty factor, conditional probability, degree of sufficiency, etc). This value represents the change from the strict implication for all x, $A(x) \to B(x)$, to the weaker statement for most x, or usually, for all x, $A(x) \to B(x)$. The latter statement is not categorical and allows the possibility of exceptions to the rule. Thus the logical implication has now been changed into a plausible implication or disposition (Zadeh, 1985a, 1988). A natural way to express such a degree of implication is achieved by using fuzzy quantifiers such as *most, almost all,* etc (Zadeh, 1983a, 1984a). A fuzzy quantifier is a fuzzy number representing the relative cardinality of the subset of elements in the universe of discourse that usually satisfy the given property, ie, the implication. Uncertainty in the data can be compounded by aggregating uncertain data in the premise, by propagating certainty measures to the conclusion, and by consolidating the final certainty measure of conclusions derived from different rules. Triangular norms and conorms (Schweizer and Sklar, 1963; Dubois and Prade, 1984) can be used to generalize the conjunction and disjunction operators that provide the required aggregation capabilities. A description of their characteristics is provided under "Triangular Norm Based Reasoning Systems," below.

The second type of uncertainty is caused by the inherent imprecision of the facts and rules representation language. Observations can contain ill-defined concepts. Rules can contain vague predicates describing tests that cannot be expressed by Boolean expressions (eg, a great change in heading). As a result, these rules cannot be interpreted exactly. This problem has been partially addressed by the possibilistic theory of approximate reasoning that, in light of imprecise fact and rule descriptions, allows weaker inferences to be made based on a generalized *modus ponens* (Zadeh, 1975).

The third type of uncertainty is caused by the incompleteness of the information. This type of uncertainty has generally been modeled by nonnumerical characterizations, such as Doyle's (1983) reasoned assumptions.

The fourth type of uncertainty arises from the aggregation of information from different knowledge sources or experts. When unconditional statements (facts) are aggregated, three potential problems can occur: the closure of the representation may no longer be preserved when the facts to be aggregated have different granularity (the single-valued certainty measures of the facts may change into an interval-valued certainty measure of the aggregated fact), the aggregation of conflicting statements may generate a contradiction that should be detected, and the rule of evidence combination may create an overestimated certainty measure of the aggregated fact, if a normalization is used to eliminate or hide a contradiction (Zadeh, 1984b, 1985b). The first two problems are typical of single-valued numerical approaches, whereas the last problem is found in the two-valued approach (Dempster, 1967).

All these approaches will be discussed in the following section. The state of the art of techniques for reasoning with uncertainty will be reviewed. The numerical approaches will be emphasized, and probabilistic and possibilistic methods will be compared and evaluated against a list of requirements.

State of the Art of Reasoning with Uncertainty

The existing approaches to representing uncertainty can be subdivided into two basic categories according to their quantitative or qualitative characterizations of uncertainty.

Among the quantitative approaches, are two types of reasoning that differ in the semantics of their numerical representation. One is the probabilistic reasoning approach, based on probability theory. The other one is the possibilistic reasoning approach, based on the semantics of many-valued logics. Some of the more traditional techniques found among the approaches derived from probability are based on single-valued representations. These techniques include Bayes rule (Peark, 1982, 1985, 1988a), modified Bayesian rule (Duda and co-workers, 1976), and confirmation theory (Shortliffe and Buchanan, 1975). A more recent trend among the probabilistic approaches is represented by approaches based on interval-valued representations such as Dempster (1967) and Shafer (1976) theory; evidential reasoning (Lowrance and co-workers, 1986); probability bounds, ie, consistency and plausibility (Quinlan, 1983); and evidence space (Rollinger, 1983).

Over the last five years, considerable efforts have been devoted to improve the computational efficiency of Bayesian belief networks for trees and small polytrees (Pearl, 1988b) and for directed acyclic graphs (influence diagrams) (Howard and Matheson, 1984; Schachter, 1986; Agogino and Rege, 1987). Problem decomposition techniques (eg, loopcuts and cliques) (Lauritzen and Spiegelhalter, 1988) and approximate methods (eg, conditioning, clustering, bounding interval, and simulations) (Henrion, 1989) have been derived to handle multiconnected Bayesian belief networks (Pearl, 1988b).

Among the approaches anchored on many-valued logics, the most notable are based on a fuzzy-valued representation of uncertainty. These include necessity and possibility theory (Zadeh, 1978, 1979a), the linguistic variable approach (Zadeh, 1979b, 1983b), and the triangular-norm based approach (Bonissone, 1987a, 1990; Bonissone and Decker, 1986; Bonissone and co-workers, 1987).

With numerical representations, it is possible to define a calculus that provides a mechanism for propagating uncertainty through the reasoning process. Similarly, the use of aggregation operators provides summaries that can then be ranked to perform rational decisions. Such a numerical representation, however, cannot provide a clear explanation of the reasons that led to a given conclusion. The typical available explanations are usually annotated traces of the reasoning paths followed by the inference engine.

Models based on qualitative approaches, on the other hand, are usually designed to handle the aspect of uncertainty derived from the incompleteness of the information, such as reasoned assumptions (Doyle, 1983) and default reasoning (Reiter, 1980). With a few exceptions, they are generally inadequate to handle the case of imprecise information, as they lack any measure to quantify confidence levels (Doyle, 1983). A few approaches in this group have addressed the representation of uncertainty, using either a formal representation, such as knowledge and belief (Halpern and Moses, 1985), or a heuristic representation, such as the theory of endorsements (Cohen, 1985; Cohen and Grinberg, 1983a).

The formal approach has a corresponding (modal) logic theory that determines the mechanism by which inferences (theorems) can be proven or believed to be true. The heuristic approach has a set of context-dependent rules to define the ways by which framelike structures (endorsements) can be combined, added, or removed. The symbolic representations are more suitable for providing a trace from the sources of the information through the various inference paths to the final conclusions. However, no calculus can be defined for the propagation, aggregation, and ranking of such uncertain information. The only available partial solution is the use of context-dependent rules to determine how each piece of evidence can be compared or summarized.

In this article, the qualitative approaches will be briefly covered. However, most of the discussion will be focused on describing and comparing quantitative approaches. In particular the probabilistic and possibilistic reasoning systems will be analyzed.

APPROXIMATE REASONING SYSTEMS

Reasoning systems must attach a truth value to statements about the state or the behavior of a real world system. When this hypothesis evaluation is not possible due to the lack of complete and certain information, approximate reasoning techniques are used to determine a set of possibilities (possible worlds) that are logically consistent with the available information. These possible worlds are characterized by a set of propositional variables and their associated values. Because it is generally impractical to describe these possible worlds to an acceptable level of detail, approximate reasoning techniques seek to determine some properties of the set of possible solutions or some constraints on the values of such properties (Ruspini, 1987, 1989a, 1989b).

A large number of approximate reasoning techniques have been developed over the past decade to provide these solutions, and a survey has been published (Pearl, 1988a). The similarities and differences between the two most common approximate reasoning techniques, probabilistic and possibilistic reasoning, will be highlighted.

Probabilistic Reasoning

Probability-based, or probabilistic, reasoning seeks to describe the constraints on the variables that characterize the possible worlds by indentifying their conditional probability distributions given the evidence in hand. Its supporting formalisms are based on the concept of set measures, additive real functions defined over certain subsets of some space. Probabilistic methods seldom make categorical assertions about the actual state of the system being investigated. Rather, they indicate that there is an experimentally determined (or believed) tendency or propensity for the system to be in some specified state. Thus they are oriented primarily toward decisions that are optimal in the long run, describing the tendency or propensity of truth of a proposition without assuring its actual validity. Depending on the nature of the information, probabilistic reasoning estimates the frequency of the truth of a hypothesis as determined by prior observation (objectivist interpretation) or a degree of gamble based on the actual truth of the hypothesis (subjectivist interpretation).

From a practical computational viewpoint, probabilistic methods suffer from problems associated with the reliable determination of all required joint and conditional probabilities. In complex systems, many variables interrelate in ways that cannot be expressed in terms of simpler interactions. In these cases, the complexity of probabilistic inference is exponential in the size of the largest subgraph into which the system can be decomposed.

Possibilistic Reasoning

Conversely, possibilistic reasoning, which is rooted in fuzzy set theory (Zadeh, 1965) and many-valued logics, seeks to describe the constraints on the values of the variables of the possible worlds in terms of their similarity to other sets of possible worlds. The supporting formalisms are based on the mathematical concept of metrics instead of set measure. These methods focus on single situations and cases. Rather than measuring the tendency of the given proposition to be valid, they seek to find another related, similar proposition that is valid. This proposition is usually less specific and resembles (according to some measure of similarity) the original hypothesis of interest.

The notion of similarity is based on the concept of metric or distance. Distances are functions that assign a number greater than zero to pairs of elements of some set (for sake of simplicity, it will be assumed that the range of this function is the interval [0,1]). Distances are reflexive, commutative, and transitive. Similarity can be defined as the complement of distance, ie,

$$S(A,B) = 1 - d(A,B) \qquad (1)$$

The basic structural characteristics of the similarity functions is an extended notion of transitivity that allows the computation of bounds on the similarity between two objects A and B on the basis of knowledge of their similarities to a third object C:

$$S(A,B) \geq T(S(A,C),S(B,C)) \qquad (2)$$

where T is a triangular norm (Bonissone and Decker, 1986; Bonissone, 1987a). Any continuous triangular norm $T(A,B)$ falls in the interval $\text{Max}(0, A + B - 1) \leq T(A,B) \leq \text{Min}(A,B)$. Thus it can be observed that if the lower bound of the range of T norms is used in the expression describing the transitivity of similarity (eq. 2), the triangular inequality for distances is obtained. If the upper bound is used, the ultrametric inequality is obtained.

This similarity notion is a direct extension of the notion of accessibility relation that is of fundamental importance in modal logics. This notion is further described by Ruspini (1990). In summarizing Ruspini's results, it can be observed that the notion of accessibility captures the idea that whatever is true in some world w, is true, but in a modified sense, in another w' that is accessible from it. When considering multiple levels of accessibility (indexed by a number between 0 and 1), this relation, measuring the resemblance between two worlds, may be used to express the extent by which considerations applicable in one world may be extended to another world.

The basic inferential mechanism, underlying the generalized *modus ponens* (Zadeh, 1979b), makes use of inferential chains and the properties of a similarity function to relate the state of affairs in the two worlds that are at the extremes of an inferential chain.

Given the duality of purpose and characteristics between probabilistic and possibilistic methods, it can be concluded that these technologies ought to be regarded as being complementary rather than competitive.

PROBABILISTIC APPROACHES

Having contrasted probabilistic and possibilistic reasoning techniques, selected representative approaches will now be examined. Among the probabilistic techniques to be analyzed are the Bayesian approaches (Bayesian, modified Bayesian, and Bayesian belief networks), confirmation theory (certainty factors), and the Dempster-Shafer (belief) theory.

Bayes Rule

Given a set of hypotheses $H = \{h_1, h_2, \ldots, h_n\}$ and a sequence of pieces of evidence $\{e_1, e_2, \ldots, e_m\}$, Bayes rule (see BAYESIAN INFERENCE METHODS), derived from the formula of conditional probability, states that the posterior probability $P(h_i \mid e_1, e_2, \ldots, e_m)$ can be derived as a function of the conditional probabilities $P(e_1, e_2, \ldots, e_m \mid h_i)$ and the prior probability $P(h_i)$:

$$P(h_i \mid e_1, e_2, \ldots, e_m) = \frac{P(e_1, e_2, \ldots, e_m \mid h_i) P(h_i)}{\sum_{i=1}^{n} P(e_1, e_2, \ldots, e_m \mid h_i) P(h_i)} \qquad (3)$$

The Bayesian approach is based on two fundamental assumptions. Each hypothesis h_i is mutually exclusive with any other hypothesis in the set **H** and the set of hypotheses **H** is exhaustive, ie,

$$P(h_i, h_j) = 0 \quad \text{for } i \neq j \qquad (4)$$

$$\sum_{i=1}^{n} P(h_i) = 1 \qquad (5)$$

Second, each piece of evidence e_j is conditionally independent under each hypothesis, ie,

$$P(e_1, e_2, \ldots, e_m \mid h_i) = \prod_{j=1}^{m} P(e_j \mid h_i) \qquad (6)$$

Note that equations 4 and 5 are required to derive Bayes rule from the formula of conditional probability. Equation 6, on the other hand, is an assumption usually made to alleviate the difficulty of determining the conditional joint probability required by equation 3. Thus under equation 6, equation 3 becomes computationally feasible.

This method requires a large amount of data to determine the estimates for the prior and conditional probabilities. Such a requirement becomes manageable when the problem can be represented as a sparse Bayesian network that is formed by a hierarchy of small cluster of nodes. In this case the dependencies among variables (nodes in the network) are known and only the explicitly required conditional probabilities must be obtained (Pearl, 1985).

Modified Bayes Rule

In addition to equations 4 and 5 (for derivational needs) and equation 6 (for operational convenience) needed by the original Bayes rule, the modified Bayesian approach, used in PROSPECTOR, also requires that each piece of evidence e_j be conditionally independent under the negation of each hypothesis, ie,

$$P(e_1, e_2, \ldots, e_m \mid \neg h_i) = \prod_{j=1}^{m} P(e_j \mid \neg h_i) \qquad (7)$$

The modified Bayesian approach is based on a variation of the odds–likelihood formulation of Bayes rule. When all the pieces of evidence are certainly true, this formulation defines the posterior odds as:

$$O(h_i|e_1, e_2, \ldots, e_m) = \frac{P(e_1|h_i)}{P(e_1|\neg h_i)} \frac{P(e_2|h_i)}{P(e_2|\neg h_i)} \cdots$$
$$\frac{P(e_n|h_i)}{P(e_n|\neg h_i)} \frac{P(h_i)}{P(\neg h_i)} \quad (8)$$
$$= \lambda_{1,i}\lambda_{2,i}O(h_i)$$

where

$$\lambda_{j,i} = \frac{P(e_j|h_i)}{P(e_j|\neg h_i)}$$

is the likelihood ratio of e_j for hypothesis h_i and

$$O(h_i) = \frac{P(h_i)}{P(\neg h_i)}$$

is the odds on hypothesis h_i. An analogous odds–likelihood formulation is derived for the case when all the pieces of evidence are certainly false:

$$O(h_i|\neg e_1, \neg e_2, \ldots, \neg e_m) = \frac{P(\neg e_1|h_i)}{P(\neg e_1|\neg h_i)} \frac{P(\neg e_2|h_i)}{P(\neg e_2|\neg h_i)}$$
$$\cdots \frac{P(\neg e_n|h_i)}{P(\neg e_n|\neg h_i)} \frac{P(h_i)}{P(\neg h_i)} \quad (9)$$
$$= \lambda_{1,i}^*\lambda_{2,i}^* \cdots \lambda_{n,i}^*O(h_i)$$

The likelihood ratio $\lambda_{j,i}$ measures the sufficiency of a piece of evidence e_j to prove hypothesis h_i. Similarly, $\lambda_{j,i}^*$ measures the necessity of such a piece of evidence to prove the given hypothesis (Pearl, 1982).

Equations 8 and 9 assume that evidence e_j is precise (ie, $P(e_j) \in \{0,1\}$). This is not the case in most expert system applications. Therefore, the above equations must be modified to accommodate uncertain evidence. This is accomplished by using a linear interpolation formula. For the case of single evidence, the posterior probability $P(h_i|e_j')$ is computed as:

$$P(h_i|e_j') = P(h_i|e_j)P(e_j|e_j') + P(h_i|\neg e_j)P(\neg e_j|e_j') \quad (10)$$

where $P(e_j|e_j')$ is the user's assessment of the probability that the evidence e_j is true, given the relevant observation e_j'. An effective likelihood ratio, $\lambda_{j,i}'$, is calculated from the posterior odds:

$$\lambda_{j,i}' = \frac{O(h_i|e_j')}{O(h_i)} \quad (11)$$

The posterior odds for all the evidence is then computed as:

$$O(h_i|e_1', e_2', \ldots, e_m') = O(h_i) \prod_{j=1}^{m} \lambda_{j,i}' \quad (12)$$

Equation 10, however, requires a modification, because it overconstrains the input requested from the user. In fact, the user must specify: $O(h_i)$, the prior odds on h_i from which $P(h_i)$ can be derived; $\lambda_{j,i}$, the measure of sufficiency from which $P(h_i|e_j)$ can be derived; $\lambda_{j,i}^*$, the measure of necessity from which $P(h_i|\neg e_j)$ can be derived; and $O(e_j)$, the prior odds on e_j from which $P(e_j)$ can be derived. These requirements are equivalent to specifying a line in the space $[P(e|e'), P(h_i|e')]$ by specifying three points:

$$(0, P(h_i|\neg e_j))$$
$$(P(e_j), P(h_i))$$
$$(1, P(h_i|e_j))$$

The modification adopted in this approach to prevent the user's inconsistencies is to change equation 10 into a piecewise linear function defined by two line segments passing through the above three points (Duda and co-workers, 1976).

In an analysis of this approach (Pednault and co-workers, 1981), it was concluded that for the cases of more than two hypotheses, equations 6 and 7, requiring conditional independence of the evidence both under the hypotheses and their negation, were inconsistent with equations 4 and 5, requiring an exhaustive and mutually exclusive space of hypotheses. Specifically, it was proved that, under these assumptions, no probabilistic update could take place, ie,

$$P(e_j|h_i) = P(e_j|\neg h_i) = P(e_j) \,\forall i,j \quad (13)$$

However, a pathological counterexample to equation 13 was obtained (Glymour, 1985), and a fault was found in the original proof of Hussain's theorem that constituted the basis for Pednault and co-workers' results. Johnson (1986) extended this analysis by first showing that there are also nonpathological counterexamples that refute Pednault's results. However, Johnson proved that under the same assumptions used in Pednault's work, for every hypothesis h_i there is at most one piece of evidence e_j that produces updating for h_i. Further studies (Cheng and Kashyap, 1986) have also indicated that there are at least max $[0, (m - [n/2])]$ pieces of evidence that are irrelevant to all the hypotheses in the system. An evidence e_j is said to be irrelevant to the hypothesis h_i if $P(h_i|e_j) = P(h_i)$. This lower bound is for a system satisfying equations 4 and 5, in which n is the number of mutually exclusive exhaustive hypotheses ($n > 2$), and m is the number of evidence. The conclusion was that equation 7 should be dropped.

Pearl (1985) has argued that equation 7, requiring the conditional independence of the evidence under the negation of the hypotheses, is overrestrictive. By discarding this assumption, Pearl has derived new, more promising results. However, equation 6, requiring the conditional independence of the evidence under the hypotheses, is still required for computational efficiency.

The Bayesian approach has various shortcomings. The assumptions on which it is based are not easily satisfied, eg, if the network contains multiple paths linking a given evidence to the same hypothesis, the independence equations 6 and 7 are violated. Similarly, equations 4 and 5, requiring the mutually exclusiveness and exhaustiveness of the hypotheses, are not very realistic; equation 4 would not hold if more than one hypothesis could occur simultaneously and is as restrictive as the single-fault assumption of the simplest diagnosing systems. Equation 5 implies that every possible hypothesis is *a priori* known, and it would be violated if the problem domain were not suitable to a closed-world assumption. Perhaps the most restrictive limitation of the Bayesian approach is its inability to represent ignorance (ie, noncommitment) as illustrated by its two-way betting interpretation (Giles, 1982). The two-way betting interpretation of the Bayesian approach consists of regarding the assignment of probability p to event A as the willingness of a rational agent to accept any of the two following bets:

1. If you pay me $\$p$ then I agree to pay you $\$1$ if A is true (for $p \in [0,1]$).
2. If you pay me $\$(1 - p)$ then I agree to pay you $\$1$ if A is false.

The first bet represents the belief that the probability of A is not larger than p, the second bet represents the belief that the probability of A is not smaller than p.

Instead of being explicitly represented, ignorance is hidden in prior probabilities. Further shortcomings are represented by the fact that it is impossible to assign any probability to disjunctions, ie, to nonsingletons, which implies the requirement for a uniform granularity of evidence. This problem is usually solved with an approximation, using the maximum entropy principle (MEP). According to MEP, the probability assigned to the disjunct (a subset of singletons in the sample space) is equally divided among the singletons in the subset. This approximation, however, creates an interpretation of the original information, which may not always been appropriate. Finally, as has been pointed out (Quinlan, 1983), in this approach conflictive information is not detected but simply propagated through the network.

Confirmation Theory (Certainty Factors)

The certainty factor (qv) (CF) approach (Shortliffe and Buchanan, 1975), used in MYCIN, is based on confirmation theory. The certainty factor $CF(h,e)$ of a given hypothesis h is the difference between a measure of belief $MB(h,e)$ representing the degree of support of a (favorable) evidence e, and a measure of disbelief $MD(h,e)$ representing the degree of refutation of an (unfavorable) evidence e. MB and MD are monotonically increasing functions that are respectively updated when the new evidence supports or refutes the hypothesis under consideration. The certainty factor $CF(h,e)$ is defined as:

$$CF(h,e) = \begin{cases} 1 & \text{if } P(h) = 1 \\ MB(h,e) & \text{if } P(h|e) > P(h) \\ 0 & \text{if } P(h|e) = P(h) \\ -MD(h,e) & \text{if } P(h|e) < P(h) \\ -1 & \text{if } P(h) = 0 \end{cases} \quad (14)$$

The measures of belief MB and measure of disbelief MD could be interpreted as a relative distance on a bounded interval. Given an interval $[A,B]$ and a reference point R within the interval, the relative distance $d(X,R)$ between any arbitrary point X within the interval and the reference R can be defined as:

$$d(X,R) = \begin{cases} \dfrac{(X - R)}{(B - R)} & \text{if } X > R \\ 0 & \text{if } X = R \\ \dfrac{(R - X)}{(R - A)} & \text{if } X < R \end{cases} \quad (15)$$

By making the following substitutions in equation 15

$$A = 0$$
$$B = 1$$
$$R = P(h)$$
$$X = P(h|e)$$

the definition of the measure of belief (MB) and measure of disbelief (MD) can be obtained.

$$MB(h,e) = \begin{cases} \dfrac{P(h|e) - P(h)}{1 - P(h)} & \text{if } P(h|e) > P(h) \\ 0 & \text{otherwise} \end{cases} \quad (16)$$

$$MD(h,e) = \begin{cases} \dfrac{P(h) - P(h|e)}{P(h)} & \text{if } P(h|e) < P(h) \\ 0 & \text{otherwise} \end{cases} \quad (17)$$

The CF was originally interpreted as the relative increase or decrease of probabilities. In fact, from equations 14, 16, and 17, it can be shown that

$$P(h|e) = P(h) + CF(h,e)[1 - P(h)] \quad \text{for } CF(h,e) \geq 0 \quad (18)$$

$$P(h|e) = P(h) - |CF(h,e)|P(h) \quad \text{for } CF(h,e) \leq 0 \quad (19)$$

Too often the CF paradigm has been incorrectly used in reasoning systems, interpreting the CF as absolute rather than incremental probability values. The original interpretation of the CF as a probability ratio, however, can no longer be preserved after the CF have been aggregated using the heuristic combining functions provided in MYCIN (Shortliffe and Buchanan, 1975).

Ishizuka and co-workers (1982) have shown that these combining functions were an approximation of the classical Bayesian updating procedure in which a term had been neglected (Ishizuka, 1982). In their analysis it was concluded that the assumption of mutual independence of evidence was required for the correct use of this approach. The original definition of certainty factor is asymmetric and prevents commutativity. Another source of concern in the use of CF is caused by the normalization of MB and MD before their arithmetic difference is computed. This normalization hides the difference between the cardinality of the set of supporting evidence and that of the set of refuting evidence.

Buchanan and Shortliffe (1984) have proposed a change to the definition of CF and its rules of combination:

$$\text{CF}(h,e) = \frac{MB(h,e) - MD(h,e)}{1 - \min(MB(h,e), MD(h,e))} \quad (20)$$

$$\text{CF}_{\text{combine}}(x,y) = \begin{cases} x + y - xy & \text{for } x > 0, y > 0 \\ \dfrac{x+y}{1-\min(|x|,|y|)} & \text{for } x < 0, y > 0 \\ & \text{or } x > 0, y < 0 \\ -\text{CF}_{\text{combine}}(-x,-y) & \text{for } x < 0, y < 0 \end{cases}$$
$$(21)$$

where $CF(h,e_1) = x$ and $\text{CF}(h,e_2) = y$. This new definition avoids the problem of allowing a single piece of negative (positive) evidence to overwhelm several pieces of positive (negative) evidence. However, it has even less theoretical justification or interpretation than the original formulas.

Recently, Heckerman (1986) has derived a new definition for the CF that does allow commutativity and has a consistent probabilistic interpretation. The new definition is

$$\text{CF}(h,e) = \frac{P(h|e) - P(h)}{P(h|e)[1 - P(h)] + P(h)[1 - P(h|e)]} \quad (22)$$

There are still numerous serious problems that characterize this approach: the semantics of the CF, ie, the interpretation of the number (ratio of probability, combination of utility values and probability); the assumptions of independence of the evidence; and the inability of distinguishing between ignorance and conflict, both of which are represented by the assignment CF = 0.

This type of representation of uncertainty has also been advocated by Rich (1983), as an alternative to default reasoning. Rich claims that default reasoning could actually better be interpreted as likelihood reasoning, providing a uniform representation for statistical, prototypical, and definitional facts.

Bayesian Belief Networks

An efficient propagation of belief on Bayesian networks was originally proposed by Pearl (1982). Pearl described an efficient updating scheme for trees and, to a lesser extent, for polytrees (1988b). However, as the complexity of the graph increases from trees to polytrees to general graphs, so does the computational complexity. The complexity for trees is $O(n^2)$, where n is the number of values per node in the tree. The complexity for polytrees is $O(K^m)$, where K is the number of values per parent node and m is the number of parents per child. This number is the size of the table attached to each node. Because the table must be constructed manually (and updated automatically), it is reasonable to assume that it is small. The complexity for multiconnected graphs is $O(K^n)$, where K is the number of values per node and n is the size of the largest nondecomposable subgraph. To handle such complexity, techniques such as moralization and propagation in a tree of cliques (Lauritzen and Spiegelhalter, 1988) and loop cutset conditioning (Suermondt and co-workers, 1990; Stillman, 1990) are typically used to decompose the original problem (graph) into a set of smaller problems (subgraphs). When this problem decomposition process is not possible, exact methods must be abandoned in favor of approximate methods. Among these methods the most common are clustering, bounding conditioning (Horvitz and co-workers, 1989), and simulation techniques (logic samplings and Markov simulations). Figure 1 illustrates a taxonomy of these Bayesian inference mechanisms.

Dempster-Shafer (Belief Theory)

The belief theory (Shafer 1976) was developed within the framework of Dempster's work on upper and lower probabilities induced by a multivalued mapping (see DEMPSTER-SHAFER METHOD). The one-to-many nature of the mapping is the fundamental reason for the inability of applying the well-known theorem of probability that determines the probability density of the image of one-to-one mappings. In fact, given a differentiable strictly increasing or strictly decreasing function ϕ on an interval I, and a continuous random variable X with a density f, such that $f(x) = 0$ for any x outside I, then the density function g can be computed as:

$$g(y) = f(x) \left|\frac{dx}{dy}\right|$$
$$y \in \phi(I)$$
$$x = \phi^{-1}(y)$$

In this context, the lower probabilities have been identified as epistemic probabilities and associated with a degree of belief. This formalism defines certainty as a function that maps subsets of a space of propositions θ on the [0,1] scale. The sets of partial beliefs are represented by mass distributions of a unit of belief across the propositions in θ. This distribution is called basic probability assignment (BPA). The total certainty over the space is 1. A non-zero BPA can be given to the entire space θ to represent the degree of ignorance. Given a space of propositions θ, referred to as frame of discernment, a function $m: 2^\theta \rightarrow$

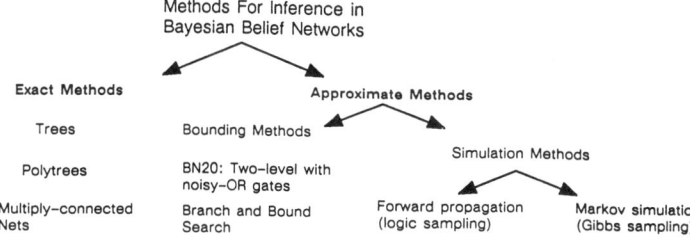

Figure 1. Taxonomy of inference mechanisms for Bayesian belief networks. Courtesy of M. Henrion.

[0,1] is called a basic probability assignment if it satisfies the following three conditions:

$$m(\phi) = 0 \qquad (23)$$

where ϕ is the empty set

$$0 < m(A) < 1 \qquad (24)$$

$$\sum_{A \subseteq \theta} m(A) = 1 \qquad (25)$$

The certainty of any proposition B is then represented by the interval $[Bel(B), P^*(B)]$, where $Bel(B)$ and $P^*(B)$ are defined as:

$$Bel(B) = \sum_{x \subseteq B} m(x) \qquad (26)$$

$$P^*(B) = \sum_{x \cap B \neq \phi} m(x) \qquad (27)$$

From the above definitions the following relation can be derived

$$Bel(B) = 1 - P^*(\neg B) \qquad (28)$$

If m_1 and m_2 are two BPA induced from two independent sources, a third BPA, $m(C)$, expressing the pooling of the evidence from the two sources, can be computed by using Dempster's rule of combination:

$$m(C) = \frac{\sum_{A_i \cap B_j = C} m_1(A_i) m_2(B_j)}{1 - \sum_{A_i \cap B_j = \phi} m_1(A_i) m_2(B_j)} \qquad (29)$$

Dempster's rule of combination normalizes the intersection of the bodies of evidence from the two sources by the amount of nonconflictive evidence between the sources. This amount is represented by the denominator of the formula.

There are two problems with the belief theory approach. The first problem stems from computational complexity: in the general case, the evaluation of the degree of belief and upper probability requires time exponential in $|\theta|$, the cardinality of the hypothesis set (frame of discernment). This is caused by the need of (possibly) enumerating all the subsets and supersets of a given set. Barnett (1981) showed that, when the frame of discernment is discrete (and simple support functions are used), the computational time complexity could be reduced from exponential to linear by combining the belief functions in a simplifying order. Strat (1984) proved that the complexity could be reduced to $O(n^2)$, where n is the number of atomic propositions, ie, intervals of unit length, when the frame of discernment is continuous. In both cases, however, these results were achieved by introducing various assumptions about the type and structure of the evidence to be combined and about the hypotheses to be supported. As a result, in addition to the requirements of mutual exclusive hypotheses and independent evidence that are needed by this approach, the following constraints must be included. For the case of discrete frame of discernment, each piece of evidence is assumed to support only a singleton proposition or its negation rather than disjunctions of propositions (ie, propositions with larger granularity), and for the case of continuous frame of discernment, only contiguous intervals along the number line can be included in the frame of discernment and thus receive support from the evidence.

The second problem in this approach results from the normalization process present in both Dempster's and Shafer's work. Zadeh (1984b, 1985b) has argued that this normalization process can lead to incorrect and counterintuitive results. By removing the conflictive parts of the evidence and normalizing the remaining parts, important information is discarded rather than being dealt with adequately. A proposed solution to this problem is to avoid completely the normalization process by maintaining an explicit measure of the amount of conflict and by allowing the remaining information to be subnormal (ie, $Bel(\theta) < 1$). Zadeh (1985b) has proposed a test to determine the conditions of applicability of Dempster's rule of combination. Dubois and Prade (1985) have also shown that the normalization process in the rule of evidence combination creates a sensitivity problem, where assigning a zero value or a very small value to a BPA causes very different results. It should be noted that this behavior also occurs in other probabilistic schemes, where the assignment of a value of zero to a prior probability would prevent any subsequent updating.

Ginsberg (1984) has proposed the use of the Dempster-Shafer approach as an alternative to nonmonotonic logic. This suggestion is an extension to Rich's (1983) idea of interpreting default reasoning as likelihood reasoning. Ginsberg provides a rule for propagating the lower and upper bounds through a reasoning chain or graph. The result is based on the interpretation of a production rule as a conditional probability rather than as a material implication. Smets (1981, 1988) has further explained the relations between belief functions, plausibilities, necessities, and possibilities and has extended Dempster's concepts to handle the case when the evidence is a fuzzy set (Zadeh, 1965).

Evidential Reasoning

Evidential reasoning (Garvey and co-workers, 1981; Lowrance and Garvey, 1983; Lowrance and co-workers, 1986) adopts the evidential interpretation of the degrees of belief and upper probabilities. Fundamentally based on Dempster-Shafer's theory, this approach defines the likelihood of a proposition A as a subinterval of the unit interval [0,1]. The lower bound of this interval is the degree of support of the proposition $S(A)$, and the upper bound is its degree of plausibility $Pl(A)$. The likelihood of a proposition A is written as $A_{[S(A),Pl(A)]}$. Table 1 illustrates a sample of interval-valued likelihoods and their interpretation.

Given two statements $A_{[S(A),Pl(A)]}$ and $B_{[S(B),Pl(B)]}$, the set of inference rules corresponding to the logical operations on these statements are defined (Garvey and co-workers, 1981) as follows.

Table 1. Sample of Interval-Valued Likelihoods and Their Interpretations

$A_{[0,1]}$	No knowledge at all about A
$A_{[0,0]}$	A is false
$A_{[1,1]}$	A is true
$A_{[0.3,1]}$	The evidence partially supports A
$A_{[0,0.7]}$	The evidence partially supports $\neg A$
$A_{[0.3,0.7]}$	The evidence simultaneously provides partial support for A and $\neg A$
$A_{[0.3,0.3]}$	The probability of A is exactly 0.3

$$\text{Intersection: } AND(A,B)_{[\max(0,S(A)+S(B)-1),\min(Pl(A),Pl(B))]} \quad (30)$$

$$\text{Union: } OR(A,B)_{[\max(S(A),S(B)),\min(1,Pl(A)+Pl(B))]} \quad (31)$$

$$\text{Negation: } NOT(A)_{[1-Pl(A),1-S(A)]} \quad (32)$$

This approach, embodied in GISTER (Lowrance and co-workers, 1986), implements Dempster-Shafer theory. When distinct bodies of evidence must be pooled, this approach uses the same Dempster-Shafer techniques, requiring the same normalization process that was criticized by Zadeh.

Evidence Space

Evidence space (Rollinger, 1983) represents the uncertainty of a statement as a point in a two-dimensional space. The (X,Y) coordinates of this space represent the positive or supporting evidence $(E+)$ and the negative or disconfirming evidence $(E-)$ available for any given proposition, respectively. The evidence space is a $[0,1]\times[0,1]$ square whose four vertices represent ignorance (0,0), absolute certainty in the support (1,0), absolute certainty in the refutation (0,1), and maximum conflictive evidence (1,1). The diagonal line defined by the equation $x + y - 1 = 0$ represents the locus of probability points, the sum of whose coordinates is 1.

It is interesting to note that if the dimensions of the evidence space $(E+, E-)$ represent the necessary evidence, ie, the lower bounds of the degree of support and refutation $(S(E), S(-E))$, the evidence space is reduced to the lower left triangle. Its three vertices (0,0), (1,0), and (0,1) represent ignorance, absolute support, and absolute refutation, respectively. The maximum amount of conflict is given by the point (0.5, 0.5). On the other hand, if the dimensions of the evidence space $(E+, E-)$ represent the possible evidence, ie, the upper bounds of the degree of support and refutation $(Pl(E),Pl(\neg E))$, the evidence space is reduced to the upper right triangle. Its three vertices (1,1), (1,0), and (0,1) represent ignorance, absolute support, and absolute refutation, respectively. The maximum amount of conflict is again given by the point (0.5,0.5). If the lower bounds are equated to the upper bounds, ie, $(S(E),S(\neg E)) = (Pl(E),Pl(\neg E))$, a new set of coordinates $(P(E),P(\neg E))$, representing Bayesian probability, can be obtained. In this new set of coordinates, the evidence space collapses to the diagonal line $x + y - 1 = 0$ that is the intersection of the two triangles and that indeed represents the probability line.

Rollinger suggests the use of a distance to verify the validity of any given premise in a rule. This approach, however, does not suggest any way of aggregating evidence, propagating uncertainty through an inference chain, selecting an appropriate metric of similarity between patterns and data, etc.

POSSIBILISTIC APPROACHES

Among the possibilistic reasoning techniques, the ones based on many-valued logic operators (triangular norms, or T-norms) and the generalized *modulus ponens* will be discussed.

Triangular Norm Based Reasoning Systems

These possibilistic techniques have been implemented in a reasoning with uncertainty module (RUM) (Bonissone and Decker, 1986; Bonissone and Wood, 1989).

Uncertainty in RUM is represented in both facts and rules. A fact represents the assignment of a value to a variable. A rule represents the deduction of a new fact (conclusion) from a set of given facts (premises). Facts are qualified by a degree of confirmation and a degree of refutation. For a fact A, the lower bound of the confirmation and the lower bound of the refutation are denoted by $L(A)$ and $L(\neg A)$, respectively. As in the case of Dempster's (1967) lower and upper probability bounds, the following identity holds: $L(\neg A) = 1 - U(A)$, where $U(A)$ denotes the upper bound of the uncertainty in A and is interpreted as the amount of failure to refute A. Note that $L(A) + L(\neg A)$, need not necessarily be equal to 1, as there may be some ignorance about A, that is given by $(1 - L(A) - L(A))$. The degree of confirmation and refutation for the proposition A can be written as the interval $[L(A),U(A)]$.

RUM provides a natural representation for plausible rules. Rules are discounted by sufficiency (s), indicating the strength with which the antecedent implies the consequent, and necessity (n), indicating the degree to which a failed antecedent implies a negated consequent. Note that conventional strict implication rules are special cases of plausible rules with $s = 1$ and $n = 0$. RUM's inference layer is built on a set of five triangular norms (T-norms) based calculi (Bonissone and Decker, 1986; Bonissone, 1987a). T-norms and T-conorms are two-place functions from $[0,1]\times[0,1]$ to $[0,1]$ that are monotonic, commutative and associative. They are the most general families of binary functions that satisfy the requirements of the conjunction and disjunction operators, respectively. Their corresponding boundary conditions satisfy the truth tables of the logical AND and OR operators. Five uncertainty calculi based on the following five T-norms are used in RUM:

$$T_1(a,b) = \max(0, a + b - 1)$$

$$T_{1.5}(a,b) = (a^{0.5} + b^{0.5} - 1)^2 \quad \text{if } (a^{0.5} + b^{0.5}) \geq 1$$
$$= 0 \quad \text{otherwise}$$

$$T_2(a,b) = ab$$

$$T_{2.5}(a,b) = (a^{-1} + b^{-1} - 1)^{-1}$$

$$T_3(a,b) = \min(a,b)$$

Their corresponding DeMorgan dual T-conorms, denoted by $S_i(a,b)$, are defined as

$$S_i(a,b) = 1 = T_i(1 - a, 1 - b)$$

These five calculi provide the user with an ability to choose the desired uncertainty calculus starting from the most conservative (T_1) to the most liberal (T_3). T_1 (T_3) is the most conservative (liberal) T-norm in the sense that for the same input certainty ranges of facts and rule sufficiency and necessity measures, T_1 (T_3) shall yield the minimum (maximum) degree of confirmation of the conclusion. For each calculus (represented by the above five T-norms), the following four operations have been defined in RUM.

Antecedent Evaluation. To determine the aggregated certainty range $[b,B]$ of the n clauses in the antecedent of a rule, when the certainty range of the ith clause is given by $[b_i,B_i]$:

$$[b,B] = [T_i(b_1,b_2, \ldots ,b_n), T_i(B_1,B_2, \ldots ,B_n)]$$

Conclusion Detachment: Modus Ponens. To determine the certainty range, $[c,C]$ of the conclusion of a rule, given the aggregated certainty range, $[b,B]$ of the rule premise and the rule sufficiency s and rule necessity n:

$$[c,C] = [T_i(s,b), 1 - (T_i(n,(1 - B)))]$$

Conclusion Aggregation. To determine the consolidated certainty range $[d,D]$, of a conclusion when it is supported by m ($m > 1$) paths in the rule deduction graph, ie, by m rule instances, each with the same conclusion aggregation T-conorm operator. If $[c_i,C_i]$ represents the certainty range of the same conclusion inferred by the ith proof path (rule instance), then

$$[d,D] = [S_i(c_1 c_2, \ldots ,c_m), S_i(C_1,C_2, \ldots ,C_m)]$$

Source Consensus. To determine the certainty range, $[L_{\text{tot}}(A),U_{\text{tot}}(A)]$ of the same evidence, A, obtained by fusing the certainty ranges, $[L_i(A),U_i(A)]$, of the ith information source out of a total of n different possible information sources:

$$[L_{\text{tot}}(A),U_{\text{tot}}(A)] = [\max_{i=1,\ldots,n} L_i(A), \min_{i=1,\ldots,n} U_i(A)]$$

The theory of possibilistic reasoning has been embedded in the reasoning with uncertainty module (Bonissone and co-workers, 1987) and the plausible reasoning modules (PRIMO) (Bonissone and co-workers, 1990).

Possibilistic Reasoning System: RUM

RUM's rule-based system integrates both procedural and declarative knowledge in its representation. This integration is essential for solving situation assessment problems, which involve both heuristic and procedural knowledge.

The expressiveness of RUM is further enhanced by two other functionalities: the context mechanism and belief revision. The context represents the set of preconditions determining the rule's applicability to a given situation. This mechanism provides an efficient screening of the knowledge base by focusing the inference process on small rule subsets. For instance, in SA, selected rules describe the behavior of friendly planes, whereas others should only be applied to unfriendly or unidentified ones. The rule's context provides this filtering mechanism.

RUM's belief revision is essential to the dynamic aspect of the classification problem. The belief revision mechanism detects changes in the input, keeps track of the dependency of intermediate and final conclusions on these inputs, and maintains the validity of these inferences. For any conclusion made by a rule, the mechanism monitors the changes in the certainty measures that constitute the conclusion's support. Validity flags are used to reflect the state of the certainty. For example, a flag can indicate that the uncertainty measure is valid, unreliable (because of a change in the support), too ignorant to be useful, or inconsistent with respect to the other evidence. These AI capabilities are used to develop a knowledge base, in conjunction with RUM's software engineering facilities, such as flexible editing, error checking, and debugging.

Possibilistic Reasoning System: PRIMO

The most recently developed technology embodying possibilistic reasoning techniques is the plausible reasoning module (PRIMO) (Bonissone and co-workers, 1990). PRIMO is a reasoning system that integrates the theories of plausible reasoning (based on monotonic rules with degrees of uncertainty) and defeasible reasoning (based on default values supported by nonmonotonic rules). The PRIMO system consists of a representation language that includes declarative specifications of uncertainty and default knowledge, reasoning algorithms, and an application development environment.

PRIMO, like its predecssor RUM, handles uncertain information by qualifying each possible value assignment to any given propositional variable with an uncertainty interval. The interval's lower bound represents the minimal degree of confirmation for the value assignment. The upper bound represents the degree to which the evidence failed to refute the value assignment. The interval's width represents the amount of ignorance attached to the value assignment. The uncertainty intervals are propagated and aggregated by triangular-norm–based uncertainty calculi (Bonissone and Decker, 1986; Bonissone, 1987a; Schweizer and Sklar, 1983, 1963). The uncertainty interval constrains intervals of subsequent dependent values.

PRIMO handles incomplete information by evaluating nonmonotonic justified (NMJ) rules. These rules are used to express the knowledge engineer's preference in cases of total or partial ignorance regarding the value assignment of a given propositional variable. The NMJ rules are used when there is no plausible evidence (to a given numerical threshold of belief or certainty) to infer that a given value assignment is either true or false. The conclusions of NMJ rules can be retracted by the belief revision system, when enough plausible evidence is available.

PRIMO uses the numerical certainty values generated by plausible reasoning techniques to quantitatively distinguish the admissible extensions generated by defeasible reasoning techniques. The method selects a maximally consistent extension (Bonissone and co-workers, 1990) given all currently available information.

For efficiency considerations some restrictions are placed on the language in which PRIMO rules can be expressed. The monotonic rules are noncyclic Horn clauses and are maintained by a linear belief revision algorithm operating on a rule graph. The NMJ rules can have cycles, but cannot have disjunctions in their conclusions.

By identifying sets of NMJ rules as strongly connected components (SCCs), the rule graph can be decomposed into a directed acyclic graph (DAG) of nodes, some of which are SCC with several input edges and output edges. PRIMO contains algorithms to efficiently propagate uncertain and incomplete information through these structures at run time. Treating the SCC independently can result in a significant performance improvement over processing the entire graph. However, this heuristic may result in loss of correctness in the worst case. These algorithms require finding satisfying assignments for nodes in each SCC, and are thus NP-hard in the unrestricted case. Tractability can be achieved by restricting the size and complexity of the SCCS, precomputing their structural information, and using run-time evaluated certainty measures to select the most likely extension.

Necessity and Possibility Theory

Necessity and possibility (Zadeh, 1979a, 1978) measure the degree of entailment and intersection of two fuzzy propositions represented by their normalized possibility distributions. Normal necessity and possibilities correspond to consonant belief and plausibility functions, respectively. Given two fuzzy propositions P and $D \subset U$, characterized by their possibility distributions $\mu_P(x)$ and $\mu_D(x)$, their degree of matching is represented by the interval $[\text{Nec}(P|D), \text{Poss}(P|D)]$, where

$$N(P|D) = \bigwedge_x (\mu_D(x) \to \mu_P(x))$$
$$= \bigwedge_x (\max[(1 - \mu_D(x)), \mu_P(x)])$$
$$= 1 - \bigvee_x (\min[(1 - \mu_P(x)), \mu_D(x)]) \quad (33)$$

$$\Pi(P|D) = \bigvee_x (\min[\mu_P(x), \mu_D(x)]) \quad (34)$$

From the above definition, it is possible to derive for necessity and possibility the same duality observed between belief functions and upper probabilities (eq. 22)

$$\text{Nec}(P|D) = 1 - \text{Poss}(\neg P|D) \quad (35)$$

The intersection of necessity measures and the union of possibility measures provide tighter bounds than those obtained by the intersection of belief functions and the union of plausibility functions (Prade, 1985).

QUALITATIVE REPRESENTATION

Among the nonnumerical representations of uncertainty, two approaches typify the characterization of uncertain information in a purely symbolic manner: reasoned assumptions and theory of endorsements.

Reasoned Assumptions

In the reasoned assumption approach (Doyle, 1983) the uncertainty embedded in an implication is (partially) removed by listing all the exceptions to that rule. When this is not possible, assumptions are used to show typicality of a value (default values) and defeasibility of a rule (liability to defeat of a reason). When an assumption used in the deductive process is found to be false, nonmonotonic mechanisms are used to keep the integrity of the data base of statements. Assumption based systems can cope with the case of incomplete information, but they are inadequate to handle the case of imprecise information. In particular, they cannot integrate probabilistic information with reasoned assumptions. Furthermore, these systems rely on the precision of the defaulted value. On the other hand, when specific information is missing, the system should be able to use analogous or relevant information inherited from some higher level concept. This surrogate for the missing information is generally fuzzy or imprecise and only provides some elastic constraints on the value of the missing information. Doyle (1983) recognized that assumptions based systems lack facilities for computing degrees of belief, which "may be necessary for summarizing the structure of large sets of admissible extensions as well as for quantifying confidence levels."

Theory of Endorsements

A different approach to uncertainty representation was recently proposed (Cohen and Grinberg, 1983a, 1983b), and is based on a purely qualitative Theory of Endorsements. Endorsements are based on the explicit recording of the justifications for a statement, as in a truth maintenance system. In addition, endorsements classify the justification according to the type of evidence (for and against a proposition), the possible actions required to solve the uncertainty of that evidence, and other related features. Endorsements provide a good mechanism for explanations, because they create and maintain the entire history of justifications (reasons for believing or disbelieving a proposition) and the relevance of any proposition with respect to a given goal. Endorsements are divided into five classes: rules, data, tasks, conclusions, and resolution endorsements. However, combination of endorsements in a premise, propagation of endorsements to a conclusion, and ranking of endorsements must be explicitly specified for each particular context, creating potential combinatorial problems.

COMPARISON OF APPROACHES FOR REASONING WITH UNCERTAINTY

From previous reviews of the state of the art of reasoning systems (Bonissone and Brown, 1986) and from previous analysis of applications (Bonissone, 1987a, 1987b; Bonissone and Wood, 1988), a desiderata (ie, a list of requirements to be satisfied by the ideal formalism for representing uncertainty and making inference with uncertainty) has been derived. In this section, the approximate reasoning technologies described above will be compared to the desiderata. This idea was first proposed by Quinlan (1983), who suggested a list of four requirements to illustrate the shortcomings of the Bayesian and confirmation theory approaches and to compare them with INFERNO, his proposed approach to uncertain inference. The requirements proposed by Quinlan are

- "An inference system should not depend on any assumptions about the probability distributions of the propositions."
- "It should be possible to assert common relationships between propositions . . . when the relationships are indeed known."
- "It should be possible to posit information about any set of propositions and observe the consequences for the system as a whole."
- "If the information provided to the system is inconsistent, this fact should be made evident along with some notion of alternative ways that the information could be made consistent."

Quinlan's work has been inspirational in the development of the following desiderata, which subsumes and extends Quinlan's initial list. As noted above, the proposed desiderata describes the requirements to be satisfied by the ideal formalism for representing uncertainty and making inference with uncertain information. To be consistent with the organizing principle typical of automated reasoning systems, the desiderata is subdivided into the same three layers of representation, inference, and control.

Representation Layer

1. There should be an explicit representation for the amount of evidence for supporting and for refuting any given hypothesis.
2. There should be an explicit representation of the information about the evidence, ie, meta-information, such as evidence source and credibility, logical dependencies, etc.
3. The representation should allow the user to describe the uncertainty of information at the available level of detail, ranging from singletons to any subset of the universe of discourse. This property will be referred to as heterogeneous information granularity.
4. There should be an explicit representation of consistency. Some measure of consistency or compatibility should be available to detect trends of potential conflicts and to identify essential contributing factors in the conflict.
5. There should be an explicit representation of ignorance to allow the user to make noncommitting statements, ie, to express the user's lack of conviction about the certainty of any of the available choices or events.
6. The representation should be natural to the user to enable the description of uncertain input and to interpret uncertain output. The representation should also be natural to the expert to enable the elicitation of consistent weights representing the strength of the implication of each rule.

Inference Layer

7. The combining rules should not be based on global assumptions of evidence independence.
8. The combining rules should not be based on global assumptions of hypotheses exhaustiveness and exclusiveness.
9. The combining rules should maintain the closure of the syntax and semantics of the representation of uncertainty.
10. Any function used to propagate and summarize uncertainty should have clear semantics. This is needed both to maintain the semantic closure of the representation and to allow the control layer to select the most appropriate combining rules.

Control Layer

11. There should be a clear distinction between a conflict in the information (ie, violation of consistency), and ignorance about the information. To solve the conflict, the controller (meta-reasoner) must retract one or more elements of the conflicting set of evidence. To remove the ignorance, the controller must select a (retractable) default value or tag the information with an assumption.
12. The traceability of the aggregation and propagation of uncertainty through the reasoning process should be available to resolve conflicts, to explain the support of conclusions, and to perform meta-reasoning for control.
13. It should be possible to make pairwise comparisons of uncertainty because the induced ordinal or cardinal ranking is needed for performing any kind of decision-making activities.
14. It should be possible to select the most appropriate combination rule by using a declarative form of control (ie, by using a set of context-dependent rules that specify the selection policies).

EVALUATION OF THE APPROACHES

The above desiderata was used to guide the development of RUM and PRIMO. Table 2 summarizes the evaluation of the formalisms discussed in the previous section against this desiderata. The order in which the formal-

Table 2. Evaluation of Uncertainty Approaches against the Desiderata

	Representation						Inference				Control			
Approach	1	2	3	4	5	6	7	8	9	10	11	12	13	14
Modified Bayesian	N	N	N	N	N	Y	N	N	Y	Y	N	N	Y	N
Confirmation	N	N	N	N	Y	N	N	Y	N	N	N	N	N	N
Dempster-Shafer	Y	N	Y	Y	Y	Y	N	N	Y	Y	Y	N	Y	N
Probability bounds	Y	N	Y	Y	Y	Y	Y	Y	Y	Y	Y	N	Y	Y
Fuzzy necessity–possibility	Y	N	Y	Y	Y	Y	Y	Y	Y	Y	Y	N	Y	N
Evidence space	Y	N	N	Y	Y	Y	Y	Y	Y	Y	Y	N	Y	N
RUM–PRIMO	Y	Y	N	Y	Y	Y	Y	Y	Y	Y	Y	Y	Y	Y
Reasoned assumptions	N	Y	N	Y	N	Y	Y	Y	Y	Y	N	Y	N	Y
Endorsements	N	Y	N	Y	N	Y	Y	Y	Y	Y	N	Y	N	Y

isms appear in the table reflects their numeric or nonnumeric nature: the numeric formalisms are listed above RUM–PRIMO, the nonnumeric ones are shown below it. RUM–PRIMO is considered a hybrid, because it uses both numeric and symbolic information.

REAL-TIME APPROXIMATE REASONING SYSTEMS

This survey will conclude with a few remarks on the applicability of approximate reasoning systems (probabilistic and possibilistic) to many real-world problems requiring real-time performance. To achieve real-time performance levels, probabilistic reasoning systems need an efficient updating algorithm. The main problem consists in conditioning the existing information with respect to the new evidence: the computation of the new posterior probabilities in general belief networks is NP-hard (Cooper, 1990). A variety of solutions have been proposed, ranging from compilation techniques (to shift the burden from run time to compile time) to the determination of bounds of the posterior probabilities.

Horvitz (1988) and Breese and Frehling (1990) have established the applicability of decision–theoretic principles in defining bounded rationality for reasoning with limited resources. Heckerman and co-workers (1989) have provided a decision–theoretic based analysis of computation versus compilation. Given a description of the nature of evidential relationships in the domain, the utilities attached to alternative actions, the cost of run-time delay, and the cost of memory, their analysis determines the subset of evidence that is more cost-effective to compile. The analysis also determines the conditions under which run-time computation is preferable to look-up tables (generated at compile time).

Horvitz and co-workers (1989) have proposed a method to approximate the posterior probabilities of the variables in each subgraph of a belief network. This method, called bounded conditioning, defines the upper and lower bounds of these probabilities and, if given enough resources, converges on the final point probabilities.

A rather different approach has been suggested by D'Ambrosio. In contrast with the anytime algorithms discussed above (Dean and Boddy, 1988; Horvitz and co-workers, 1989), D'Ambrosio has proposed a design-to-time algorithm. Whereas the anytime algorithms try to yield a result any time they are interrupted, the design-to-time algorithms seek to "dynamically construct and execute a problem solving procedure which will [probably] produce a reasonable answer within [approximately] the time available" (D'Ambrosio, 1989). D'Ambrosio's (1988, 1990) initial development of the hybrid uncertainty management (HUM) seeks to provide an incremental and defeasible model, using an assumption-based truth maintenance system (ATMS) to maintain a mapping between symbolic structures (assumptions, logical support, and environments) and measures (numeric values for ranking and decision making). These ideas have been extended and integrated with a dynamic schema instantiation (DSI), which, given a time bound, dynamically instantiates a qualitative probabilistic model of the problem.

Due to its different underlying theory, possibilistic reasoning does not exhibit the same complexity problems as probabilistic reasoning. Most of the efforts aimed at achieving real-time performance from possibilistic reasoning systems have been based on translation–compilation techniques (Pfau, 1987; Bonissone and Halverson, 1990) or hardware solutions (Corder, 1989; Watanabe and Dettloff, 1987).

Among the compilation techniques, a notable effort is RUMrunner, RUM's run-time system. The objective of RUMrunner is to provide a software tool that transforms the customized knowledge base generated during the development phase into a fast and efficient real-time application.

This goal is achieved by a combination of efforts: the translation of RUM's (development system) complex data structure into simpler and more efficient ones (to reduce overhead), the compilation of the rule set into a compiled network (to avoid run-time search), the load-time estimation of each rule's execution cost (to determine, at run-time, the execution cost of any given deductive path), and the planning mechanism for model selection (to determine the largest relevant rule subset that could be executed within a given time-budget).

An agenda mechanism is used to asynchronously receive any number of input tasks (such as backward-chaining on a goal or forward-chaining on a given piece of evidence) from various sources. Each task in the agenda receives a (static) priority number, determining the relative importance of the task with respect to the others. A time deadline, expressed in absolute time, is attached to the task to indicate its urgency (ie, its expiration time), which is used by the planning mechanisms described below.

A scheduler sorts the tasks by priority and, within the same priority level, by the shortest deadline. The highest priority task is then scheduled for execution by the forward or backward chainer (Durfee and Lesser, 1987). The results of these tasks are in turn isolated from external connecting systems via buffers or streams and a layer of interface functions.

External or internal interrupts, with reentrant reasoning, can supersede the current task. Because the state of the current knowledge base is dynamically maintained in the knowledge base nodes themselves, any changes to the knowledge base by the interrupting task will be automatically taken into account when the preempted task is resumed.

Among the hardware solutions to the problem of realtime performance for possibilistic reasoning systems, the most notable are the fuzzy chips (Corder, 1989; Watanabe and Dettloff, 1987). These chips are used in the application of approximate reasoning systems to industrial control. Fuzzy process controllers (Sugeno, 1985) represent one of the earliest instances of simple, but effective, knowledge-based systems successfully deployed in the field. Their main use has been the replacement of the human operator in the feedback control loop of industrial processes. Their applications range from the development of the controller of a subway train system (Yasunobu and Miyamoto, 1985) to the use of a predictive fuzzy controller for container crane operation (Yasunobu and Hasegawa, 1986) to their application in the control of a continuously variable automobile transmission (Kasia and Morimoto, 1988).

BIBLIOGRAPHY

A. Agogino and A. Rege, "Ides: Influence Diagram Based Expert System," *Math. Model.* **8,** 227–233 (1987).

J. Barnett, "Computational Methods for a Mathematical Theory of Evidence," in *Proceedings of the Seventh IJCAI*, Morgan-Kaufmann, San Mateo, Calif., Vancouver, B.C., 1981.

P. P. Bonissone, "Summarizing and Propagating Uncertain Information with Triangular Norms," *Int. J. Approx. Reas.* **1**(1), 71–101 (Jan. 1987a).

P. P. Bonissone, "Using T-Norm Based Uncertainty Calculi in a Naval Situation Assessment Application," in *Proceedings of the Third AAAI Workshop on Uncertainty in Artificial Intelligence*, AAAI, Menlo Park, Calif., July 1987b, pp. 250–261.

P. P. Bonissone, "Now that I Have a Good Theory of Uncertainty, What Else Do I Need?" in M. Henrion, R. Shachter, L. Kanal, and J. Lemmer, eds., *Uncertainty in Artificial Intelligence*, Vol. 5, North-Holland, Amsterdam, The Netherlands, 1990, pp. 237–253.

P. P. Bonissone and A. L. Brown, "Expanding the Horizons of Expert Systems," in T. Bernold, ed., *Expert Systems and Knowledge Engineering*, North-Holland, Amsterdam, The Netherlands, 1986, pp. 267–288.

P. P. Bonissone, D. Cyrluk, J. Goodwin, and J. Stillman, "Uncertainty and Incompleteness: Breaking the Symmetry of Defeasible Reasoning," in Bonissone, 1990, pp. 67–85.

P. P. Bonissone and K. S. Decker, "Selecting Uncertainty Calculi and Granularity: An Experiment in Trading-off Precision and Complexity," in L. Kanal and J. Lemmer, eds., *Uncertainty in Artificial Intelligence*, North-Holland, Amsterdam, The Netherlands, 1986, pp. 217–247.

P. P. Bonissone, S. Gans, and K. S. Decker, "RUM: A Layered Architecture for Reasoning with Uncertainty," *Proceedings of the Tenth IJCAI*, Milan, Italy, Morgan-Kaufmann, San Mateo, Calif., 1987, pp. 891–898.

P. P. Bonissone and P. C. Halverson, "Time-Constrained Reasoning Under Uncertainty," *J. Real Time Sys.* **2**(1–2), 22–45 (May 1990).

P. P. Bonissone and R. M. Tong, "Editorial: Reasoning with Uncertainty in Expert Systems," *Int. J. Man-Machine Stud.* **22**(3), 241–250 (Mar. 1985).

P. P. Bonissone and N. C. Wood, "Plausible Reasoning in Dynamic Classification Problems," in *Proceedings of the Validation and Testing of Knowledge-Based Systems Workshop*, AAAI, Menlo Park, Calif., Aug. 1988.

P. P. Bonissone and N. C. Wood, "T-Norm Based Reasoning in Situation Assessment Applications," in L. Kanal, T. Levitt, and J. Lemmer, eds., *Uncertainty in Artificial Intelligence*, Vol. 3, North-Holland, Amsterdam, The Netherlands, 1989, pp. 241–256.

J. S. Breese and M. R. Fehling, "Control of Problem Solving: Principles and Architecture," in R. Shachter, T. Levitt, L. Kanal, and J. Lemmer, eds., *Uncertainty in Artificial Intelligence*, Vol. 4, North-Holland, Amsterdam, The Netherlands, 1990, pp. 59–68.

B. Buchanan and E. Shortliffe, *"Rule-Based Expert Systems,"* Addison-Wesley Publishing Co., Inc., Reading, Mass., 1984.

Y. Cheng and R. Kashyap, *Irrelevancy of Evidence Caused by Independence Assumptions*. Technical Report TR-EE-86-17, School of Electrical Engineering, Purdue University, West Lafayette, Ind., 1986.

P. Cohen, *Heuristic Reasoning about Uncertainty: An Artificial Intelligence Approach*. Pittman, Boston, 1985.

P. Cohen and M. Grinberg, "A Framework for Heuristics Reasoning about Uncertainty," In *Proceedings of the Eighth IJCAI*, Karlsruhe, FRG, Morgan-Kaufmann, San Mateo, Calif., 1983a, pp. 355–357.

P. Cohen and M. Grinberg, "A Theory of Heuristics Reasoning about Uncertainty," *AI Mag.*, 17–23 (1983b).

G. Cooper, "The Computational Complexity of Probabilistic Inference Using Bayesian Belief Networks," *Artif. Intell.* **42**(2–3), 393–405 (1990).

R. Corder, "A High Speed Fuzzy Processor," in *Proceedings of the Third International Fuzzy Systems Association*, IFSA, Seattle, Wash., Aug. 1989, pp. 379–389.

B. D'Ambrosio, "A Hybrid Approach to Reasoning Under Uncertainty," *Int. J. Approx. Reas.* **2**(1), 29–45 (Jan. 1988).

B. D'Ambrosio, "Resource Bounded-Agents in an Uncertain World," in *Proceedings of the AAAI Workshop on Real-Time Artificial Intelligence Problems*, AAAI, Menlo Park, Calif., Aug. 1989.

B. D'Ambrosio, "Process Structure, and Modularity in Reasoning with Uncertainty," in R. Shachter, T. Levitt, L. Kanal, and J. Lemmer, eds., *Uncertainty in Artificial Intelligence*, Vol. 4, North-Holland, Amsterdam, 1990, pp. 15–25.

T. Dean and M. Boddy, "An Analysis of Time Dependent Planning," in *Proceedings of the Seventh National Conference on Artificial Intelligence*, St. Paul, Minn., AAAI, Menlo Park, Calif., 1988, pp. 49–54.

A. Dempster, "Upper and Lower Probabilities Induced by a Multivalued Mapping," *Ann. Math. Stat.* **38**, 325–339 (1967).

J. Doyle, "Methodological Simplicity in Expert System Construction: The Case of Judgements and Reasoned Assumptions, *AI Mag.* **4**(2), 39–43 (1983).

D. Dubois and H. Prade, "Criteria Aggregation and Ranking of Alternatives in the Framework of Fuzzy Set Theory," in H. Zimmerman, L. Zadeh, and B. Gaines, eds., *TIMS/Studies in the Management Science,* Vol. 20, Elsevier Science Publishing Co., Inc., New York, 1984, pp. 209–240.

D. Dubois and H. Prade, "Combination and Propagation of Uncertainty with Belief Functions—A Reexamination," in *Proceedings of the Ninth IJCAI,* Los Angeles, Calif., Morgan-Kaufmann, San Mateo, Calif., 1985, pp. 111–113.

R. Duda, P. Hart, and N. Nilsson, "Subjective Bayesian Methods for Rule-Based Inference Systems," *Proc. AFIPS* **45**, 1075–1082 (1976).

E. H. Durfee and V. R. Lesser, *Planning to Meet Deadlines in a Blackboard-Based Problem Solver,* Technical Report COINS-87-07, COINS, University of Massachusetts, Amherst, 1987.

T. Garvey, J. Lowrance, and M. Fischler, "An Inference Technique for Integrating Knowledge from Disparate Sources," in Barnett, 1981, 319–325.

R. Giles, "Semantics for Fuzzy Reasoning," *Int. J. Man-Machine Stud.* **17**(4), 401–415 (1982).

M. Ginsberg, "Non-Monotonic Reasoning Using Dempster's Rule," in *Proceedings of the Fourth National Conference on Artificial Intelligence,* Austin, Tex., AAAI, Menlo Park, Calif., 1984, pp. 126–129.

C. Glymour, "Independence Assumptions and Bayesian Updating," *J. Artif. Intell.* **25**, 95–99 (1985).

J. Y. Halpern and Y. Moses, "A Guide to Modal Logics of Knowledge and Belief," in *Proceedings of the Ninth International Conference on Artificial Intelligence,* AAAI, Menlo Park, Calif., 1985, pp. 480–490.

D. Heckerman, "Probabilistic Interpretations for MYCIN Certainty Factors," in Bonissone and Decker, 1986, pp. 167–196.

D. E. Heckerman, J. S. Breese, and E. J. Horvitz, "The Compilation of Decision Models," in *Proceedings of the Fifth AAAI Workshop on Uncertainty in Artificial Intelligence,* AAAI, Menlo Park, Calif., Aug. 1989, pp. 162–173.

M. Henrion, "Practical Issues in Constructing a Bayes' Belief Network," in Bonissone and Wood, 1989, pp. 161–173.

E. J. Horvitz, "Reasoning under Varying and Uncertain Resource Constraints," in Dean and Boddy, 1988, pp. 111–116.

E. J. Horvitz, H. J. Suermondt, and G. F. Cooper, "Bounded Conditioning Flexible Inference for Decisions under Scarce Resources," in Heckerman and co-workers, 1989, pp. 182–193.

R. Howard and J. Matheson, "Influence Diagrams," in R. Howard and J. Matheson, eds., *The Principles and Applications of Decision Analysis,* Vol. 2, Strategic Decisions Group, Menlo Park, Calif., 1984, pp. 719–762.

M. Ishizuka, "An Extension of Dempster-Shafer Theory to Fuzzy Sets for Constructing Expert Systems," *Seisan-Kenkyu* **34**, 312–315 (1982).

M. Ishizuka, K. Fu, and J. Yao, "A Rule-Based Inference with Fuzzy Set for Structural Damage Assessment," in M. Gupta and E. Sanchez, eds., *Fuzzy Information and Decision Processes,* North-Holland, Amsterdam, The Netherlands, 1982.

R. Johnson, "Independence and Bayesian Updating Methods," *J. Artif. Intell.* **29**, 217–222 (1986).

Y. Kasai and Y. Morimoti, "Electronically Controlled Continuously Variable Transmission," in *Proceedings of the International Congress on Transportation Electronics,* IEEE, 1988, pp. 33–42.

S. Lauritzen and D. Spiegelhalter, "Local Computations with Probabilities on Graphical Structures and Their Application to Expert Systems," *J. R. Stat. Soc. Ser. B* **50**, 157–224 (1988).

J. Lowrance and T. Garvey, *Evidential Reasoning: An Implementation for Multisensor Integration,* "Technical Report Note 307, SRI International, Artificial Intelligence Center, Menlo Park, Calif., 1983.

J. Lowrance, T. Garvey, and T. Strat, "A Framework for Evidential-Reasoning Systems," in *Proceedings of the Fifth National Conference on Artificial Intelligence,* Philadelphia, Pa., AAAI, Menlo Park, Calif., 1986, pp. 896–903.

J. Pearl, "Reverend Bayes on Inference Engines: A Distributed Hierarchical Approach," in *Proceedings of the Second National Conference on Artificial Intelligence,* Pittsburgh, Pa., AAAI, Menlo Park, Calif., August 1982, pp. 133–136.

J. Pearl, "How to Do with Probabilities What People Say You Can't," in *Proceedings of the Second Conference on Artificial Intelligence Applications,* IEEE, Dec. 1985, pp. 1–12.

J. Pearl, "Evidential Reasoning under Uncertainty," In H. E. Shrobe, ed., *Exploring Artificial Intelligence,* Morgan-Kaufmann, San Mateo, Calif., 1988a, pp. 381–418.

J. Pearl, *Probabilistic Reasoning in Intelligent Systems: Networks of Plausible Inference,* Morgan-Kaufmann, San Mateo, Calif., 1988b.

E. Pednault, S. Zucker, and L. Muresan, "On the Independence Assumption Underlying Subjective Bayesian Updating, *J. Artif. Intell.* **16**, 213–222 (1981).

L. M. Pfau, *RUMrunner: Real-Time Reasoning with Uncertainty,* Master's thesis, Rensselaer Polytechnic Institute, Troy, N.Y., Dec. 1987.

H. Prade, "A Computational Approach to Approximate Reasoning and Plausible Reasoning with Applications to Expert Systems," *IEEE Trans. Pattern Anal. Machine Intell.* **7**(3), 260–283 (1985).

J. Quinlan, "Consistency and Plausible Reasoning," in *Proceedings of the Eighth IJCAI,* Karlsruhe, FRG, Morgan-Kaufmann, San Mateo, Calif., 1983, pp. 137–144.

R. Reiter, "A Logic for Default Reasoning," *Artif. Intell.* **13**, 81–132 (1980).

E. Rich, "Default Reasoning as Likelihood Reasoning," in *Proceedings of the Third National Conference on Artificial Intelligence,* AAAI, Menlo Park, Calif., 1983, pp. 348–351.

C. Rollinger, "How to Represent Evidence—Aspects of Uncertainty Reasoning, in Quinlan, 1983, pp. 358–361.

E. Ruspini, *The Logical Foundations of Evidential Reasoning,* Technical Note 408, Artificial Intelligence Center, SRI International, Menlo Park, Calif., 1987.

E. Ruspini, *On the Semantics of Fuzzy Logic,* Technical Note 475, Artificial Intelligence Center, SRI International, Menlo Park, Calif., 1989a.

E. Ruspini, "The Semantics of Vague Knowledge," *Rev. Syst.* **3**(4), 387–420 (1989b).

E. Ruspini, "Possibility as Similarity: The Semantics of Fuzzy Logic," in *Proceedings of the Sixth Conference on Uncertainty in Artificial Intelligence,* Cambridge, Mass., 1990, pp. 281–289.

R. Schachter, "Evaluating Influence Diagrams," *Operations Res.* **34,** 871–882 (1986).

B. Schweizer and A. Sklar, "Associative Functions and Abstract Semi-Groups," *Publicationes Mathematicae Debrecen* **10,** 69–81 (1963).

B. Schweizer and A. Sklar, *Probabilistic Metric Spaces.* North-Holland, Amsterdam, The Netherlands, 1983.

G. Shafer, *A Mathematical Theory of Evidence,* Princeton University Press, Princeton, N.J., 1976.

E. Shortliffe and B. Buchanan, "A Model of Inexact Reasoning in Medicine," *Math. Biosci.* **23,** 351–379 (1975).

P. Smets, "The Degree of Belief in a Fuzzy Set," *Inform. Sci.* **25,** 1–19 (1981).

P. Smets, "Belief Functions," in P. Smets, A. Mamdani, D. Dubois, and H. Prade, eds., *Non-Standard Logics for Automated Reasoning,* Academic Press, Inc., New York, 1988.

J. Stillman, "On Heuristics for Finding Loop Cutsets in Multiply-Connected Belief Networks," in *Proceedings of the Sixth Conference on Uncertainty in AI,* 1990, pp. 265–272.

T. Strat, "Continuous Belief Functions for Evidential Reasoning," in Ginsberg, 1984, pp. 308–313.

J. Suermondt, G. Cooper, and D. Heckerman, "A Combination of Cutset Conditioning with Clique-Tree Propagation in the Pathfinder System," in *Proceedings of the Sixth Conference on Uncertainty in AI,* 1990, pp. 273–279.

M. Sugeno, ed., *Industrial Applications of Fuzzy Control,* North-Holland, Amsterdam, The Netherlands, 1985.

H. Watanabe and W. Dettloff, "Fuzzy Logic Inference Processor for Real Time Control: A Second Generation Full Custom Design," in *Proceedings of the Twenty-first Asilomar Conference on Signal, Systems & Computers,* IEEE, Nov. 1987, pp. 729–735.

S. Yasunobu and G. Hasegawa, "Evaluation of an Automatic Crane Operation System Based on Predictive Fuzzy Control," *Contr. Theor. Adv. Technol.* **2,** 419–432 (1986).

S. Yasunobu and S. Miyamoto, "Automatic Train Operation by Predictive Fuzzy Control," in Sugeno, 1985, pp. 1–8.

L Zadeh, "Fuzzy Sets," *Inform. Contr.* **8,** 338–353 (1965).

L. Zadeh, "Fuzzy Logic and Approximate Reasoning (in Memory of Grigor Moisil)," *Synthese* **30,** 407–428 (1975).

L. Zadeh, "Fuzzy Sets as a Basis for a Theory of Possibility," *Fuzzy Sets Sys.* **1,** 3–28 (1978).

L. Zadeh, "Fuzzy Sets and Information Granularity," In M. Gupta, R. Ragade, and R. Yager, eds., *Advances in Fuzzy Set Theory and Applications,* Elsevier Science Publishing Co., Inc., New York, 1979, pp. 3–18.

L. Zadeh, "A Theory of Approximate Reasoning," in P. Hayes, D. Michie, and L. Mikulich, eds., *Machine Intelligence,* Halstead Press, New York, 1979, pp. 149–194.

L. Zadeh, "A Computational Approach to Fuzzy Quantifiers in Natural Language," *Comput. Math.* **9,** 149–184 (1983).

L. Zadeh, "Linguistic Variables, Approximate Reasoning, and Dispositions," *Med. Inform.* **8,** 173–186 (1983b).

L. Zadeh, "A Computational Theory of Disposition," in *Proceedings of the International Conference of Computational Linguistics,* 1984a, pp. 312–318.

L. Zadeh, "Review of Books: A Mathematical Theory of Evidence," *AI Mag.* **5**(3), 81–83 (1984b).

L. Zadeh, "Syllogistic Reasoning in Fuzzy Logic and Its Application to Usuality and Reasoning with Dispositions," *IEEE Trans. Syst. Man Cybernet.* **15,** 754–765 (1985a).

L. Zadeh, *A Simple View of the Dempster-Shafer Theory of Evidence and Its Implications for the Rule of Combinations,* Technical Report 33, Institute of Cognitive Science, University of California, Berkeley, 1985b.

L. Zadeh, "Dispositional Logic," *Appl. Math. Lett.* **1**(1), 95–99 (1988).

P. BONISSONE
General Electric

REASONING, SPATIAL

Human beings and other creatures spend much of their time solving spatial problems, such as finding their way around. Furthermore, people often seem to use spatial methods for solving problems analogically, as when they reason about graphs by drawing or imaging pictures. Research in this area tries to duplicate or mimic some of these abilities. Tentatively, it can be divided into these subheadings:

Visual object recognition.
Cognitive maps and path finding.
Simulations of human imagery.
Visualization for qualitative physical reasoning.

It seems a good guess that all of these problem areas share representations and algorithms. However, to date most of them have evolved in different directions. Not all of these areas are covered here. In particular, visual object recognition is omitted entirely. Surveys of research in this area have been published (Kak, 1988; Chen, 1990).

A key issue in spatial reasoning is qualitative shape representation. Most humans have little trouble visualizing objects and reasoning about them without precise knowledge about their dimensions. For instance, suppose a balloon landed on a pincushion. What might happen? Although the pins might puncture the balloon, it is quickly realized that they are unlikely to in this case because they are head side up. When most people solve a problem like this, they are obviously unaware of the exact shape of the pincushion or the detailed distribution of the pins. Yet they imagine a "picture" of the situation. Controversy has raged about what is really going on in the mind when this picturelike entity is experienced (see below). Fortunately for AI, the computational question can be asked how the knowledge about the shapes of objects like pins and pincushions is represented and used without an *a priori* commitment to any answer to questions about human visual imagery.

Various proposals have been made about representation of spatial information. Many of them limit themselves to two dimensions instead of three, either as a research tactic or because of a belief that it is desirable for efficiency to reduce three-dimensional problems to two dimensions when possible. Shape representations tend to fall into various categories: part whole, volumetric, and surface descriptions. Overviews are available (Ballard and Brown, 1982; Davis, 1990).

Part-Whole Descriptions

Objects are described in terms of the parts that make them up. Typically these descriptions employ some kind of associative network. There is nothing special about this use of associative networks; the resulting descriptions would be similar to those in nonspatial domains, such as descriptions of corporate organizations. So the pincushion description might mention the presence of zero or more pins as parts.

The representations becomes more spatial when coordinates and other parameters are added to it. For instance, with each pin might be stored its approximate length and position with respect to the pincushion. It is often useful to invert the resulting data structure. For instance, given a table of cities and their locations, it might be desirable to find a city near some location. Rather than search all the cities, it is possible to use a discrimination tree(2), in which objects are sorted by discriminating on their X and Y coordinates (Fig. 1). Other quantitative and symbolic discriminators can be introduced, such as the population or shape of each object. [The term "k-d tree" has been used by Bentley and Friedman (1979) for a tree discriminated on several numerical coordinates.] To find an object in such a tree, given as a key an X interval and a Y interval, the computer can start at the top and follow only branches compatible with the key intervals, so only a subset of the cities are ultimately compared with the key interval.

Volumetric Descriptions

Objects are described as combinations of volumes. The volumes are often overlapping and often do not necessarily designate distinct parts of the overall shape. For example, a milk bottle might be described as a cylinder topped by truncated cone. The dimensions and relative locations and orientations of the volumes must be specified (Marr and Nishihara, 1978; Brooks, 1981). The component volumes may be drawn from a vocabulary of primitives or constructed by sweeping surfaces along axes (so-called generalized cylinders) (Agin and Binford, 1976). In some systems volumes may be subtracted as well as added. For example, a spool might be described as a solid cylinder with a small parallel cylinder subtracted from its axis. This approach is often called constructive solid geometry (Requicha, 1980).

One of the simplest ways of describing volumes (or, in two dimensions, areas) is with arrays representing space (up to some grain), whose cells are labeled with the object filling the part of space. These are often called *occupancy arrays* and their cells are called *pixels* in two dimensions (a term borrowed from computer graphics), or *voxels* in three dimensions. In Figure 2a the shape of a house is represented by putting an H in every cell the house fills. This is a two-dimensional projection; a three-dimensional array could be used if required. However, even the two-dimensional version is costly. The quadtree device allows the information to be compressed in an elegant way (Klinger and Rhodes, 1979; Samet, 1984). The grid is represented as a tree whose nodes are square areas of the picture. The top node represents the entire picture. Each node has zero or four children. If the square region corresponding to a node lies entirely inside or outside the house, it is a leaf of the tree and is labeled with an H or E (for empty). Otherwise, it has four children representing the four quadrants of its square. The division stops at some convenient grain (Fig. 2b). The same ideas applied to three dimensions yields the octree. A natural extension of the occupancy-array idea is to store a more complex vector of data at each pixel. For example, in a military application, the elevation, slope, and vegetation might be stored at each pixel (Antony, 1990; Thorpe and co-workers, 1988).

Another interesting generalization was proposed by Moravec (1988). Instead of classifying each pixel as occu-

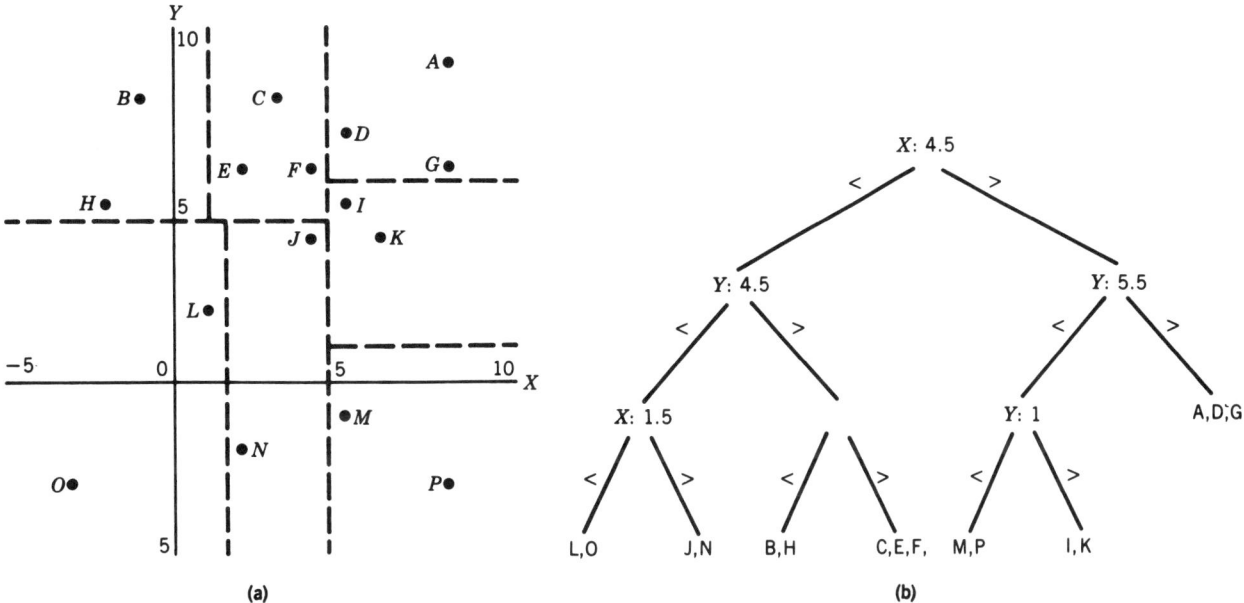

Figure 1. An $X-Y$ discrimination tree: (*a*) cities; (*b*) discrimination tree.

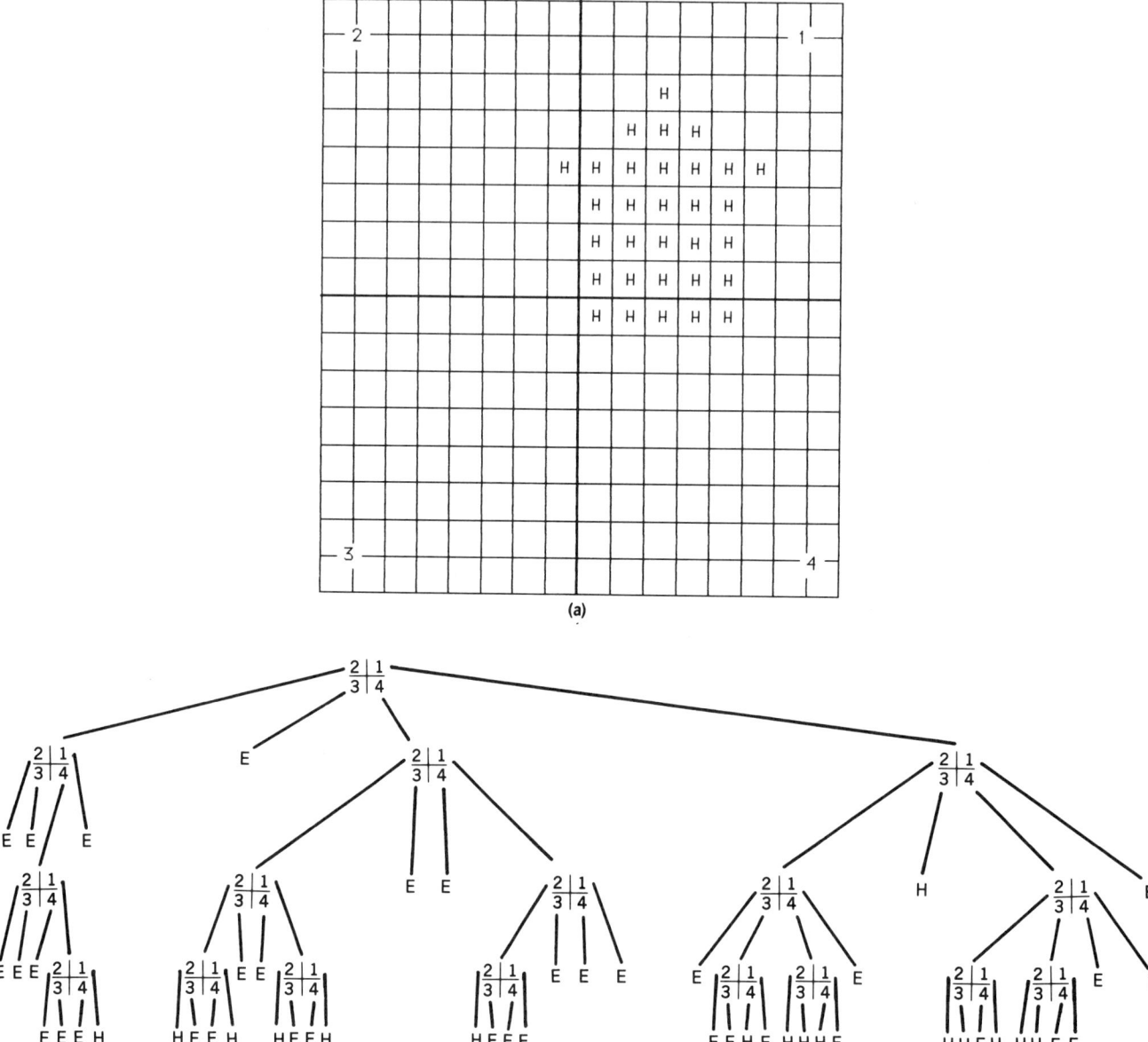

Figure 2. Grid representation and quadtree: (a) occupancy array; (b) corresponding quadtree.

pied or not, the probability of its being occupied is stored. The resulting representation is called a certainty grid. The probabilities are derived from sensor data. New sensor readings are combined with old using Bayesian techniques. Data obtained at different levels of resolution can be stored using different pixel densities. For example, areas farther from the sensor would normally be broken into a few large pixels, whereas areas nearby could be broken into many small ones.

Boundary Description

Objects are described by their bounding surfaces. The bounding surfaces are often planar, which limits the description to polyhedral objects or to polyhedral approximations of curved objects (Baumgart, 1975). In two dimensions the bounds are curves, often approximated as polygons or "polylines" (chains of lines, not necessarily closed curves) (Davis, 1985).

Many of these shape-representation ideas are borrowed from machine vision and graphics. If the goal is to draw a picture of an object, the application of these representations is well understood. Unfortunately, for the kind of qualitative spatial reasoning discussed above, much of the information provided in these formats is useless, and ideas have been lacking on what is needed instead. For instance, devices such as cubic splines are excellent for parameterizing a curve or surface with just a few numbers. However, the resulting data compression is of little use in spatial reasoning because the numbers say little about the way the surface behaves. In spatial reasoning it is more likely that information such as *can be used as a conduit* or *is almost horizontal* is desired. It is often necessary or desirable to approximate spatial knowledge. If a wall is almost flat, for many purposes there is no need to keep its slight deviations from flatness in mind, even if they are known. Hence the model used by the system for reasoning will usually be a simplified version of the truth. There may be multiple models for different purposes.

The most common approach to this problem is to use a simple symbolic vocabulary. If an object is known to be a cylinder, and nothing else is known about it, then it is described by the symbol *cylinder*. Usually the machine knows something about the dimensions of the object (Brooks, 1981), so it might be represented as

cylinder
   length > width
   axis-curvature = 0

This idea can be thought of as sorting objects into qualitative "bins" with labels like *cylinder*. Within each bin, objects are distinguished by different values of parameters such as length and axis curvature. This approach is by far the most common; for specialized applications, such bins are usually easy to find. For instance, in a route-finding application objects might be classified as streets, buildings, regions, rivers, etc, each with its own set of parameters. The boundaries between classes would seldom be crossed. The classes are useful because there is a large set of inferences that pertain to just the objects belonging to a given class. For instance, an object classified as a street can be used to get somewhere; an object classified as a river requires finding a bridge, etc.

The difficulty with this scheme is generalizing it to handle more than one application area. In the general case, the following problems are encountered.

1. The qualitative-bin notation has trouble with detailed descriptions of objects. Once an object has been classified as a cylinder, it may be necessary to describe it further as "slightly flattened on one side" or "peppered with thousands of holes." Little is known about how to turn such natural language descriptions into something more formal.

2. An object may fall into more than one bin. The big advantage of the qualitative-bin idea is that similar objects have similar representations. The two objects in Figures 3a and 3b are obviously similar because they are both classed as cylinders with different axis curvatures. But if the sequence of similar objects is continued, this ultimately leads to Figure 3d, which would have been classed as a torus (with a gap represented somehow). Such qualitative discontinuities may make it necessary to maintain multiple descriptions of objects.

3. An object may fall into no bins. For any given application it is usually easy to find qualitative classes that include every object of interest. It is much harder to find a set of classes that works just as well for every application. If you simply take all the classes that have ever been

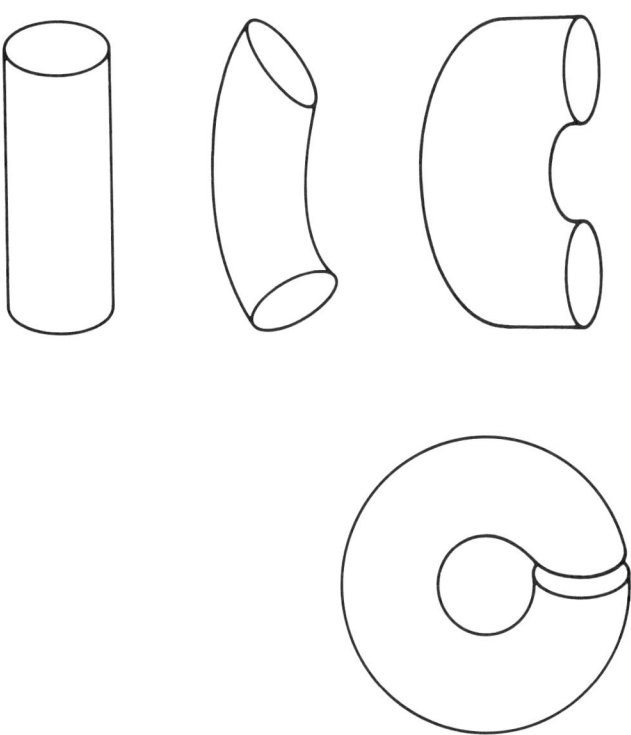

Figure 3. Object with multiple descriptions.

proposed, many objects will fall into more than one or none at all.

All these problems may be evidence that there is no solution to the general spatial-reasoning problem. As elsewhere in AI, the mere ability to discern a problem may not mean it actually has a solution. Still, it is hard on introspective grounds to believe that humans have a collection of independent task-oriented spatial representations in their heads, and this is reason to keep looking for a solution to the general case.

In what follows, various specialized problem areas are examined, keeping some of these problems in mind.

ROUTE FINDING AND EXPLORATION

The route-finding problem is planning a route from one place to another and then following it. It assumed that the planner (henceforth referred to as the robot) has a cognitive map of its surroundings that it can consult for this purpose. This map is incomplete, so that the planner may need to ask directions or explore as it goes. In this section it is assumed that the robot is small compared to the spaces through which it is navigating. A somewhat different line of research assumes that the robot is large but that the shapes and positions of all obstacles in the space are known so that intricate reasoning is required to squeeze it through. This is called the robot motion-planning problem (see VISUAL MOTION ANALYSIS). The assumption is also made that the robot is moving on a two-dimensional surface. The objects it sees are assumed to approximately prismatic and perpendicular to this surface, so that they can be described by specifying their cross sections and heights.

There are several approaches to the route-finding problem, based on quite different assumptions about what the problem is. There is no obvious definition of what a *place* is; it cannot be taken to be a point in Cartesian space. The coordinate system for such a point would be underdetermined, although in many applications there is an obvious choice. A more basic problem is that a place must be bigger than a single point, both because space is intuitively divided up that way and because otherwise it would be impossible for a robot to visit the same place twice. Another problem, usually simply neglected, is that some places, such as the interiors of airplanes and elevators, do not correspond to a fixed location with respect to a larger coordinate frame.

One solution to these conundrums is to define places in terms of stable perceptions (Kuipers and Byun, 1988; Kuipers and Levitt, 1988). A place is an area within which some perceptual invariant is preserved, such as "I see four corridors at 90° angles." This definition requires some refinement, because two places can look identical and because the same point in space can change its appearance over time. Another solution is to impose a grid on a coordinate system, so that a place is defined as an arbitrary square region (Moravec, 1988). This approach is related to the occupancy-array representation described above. A third approach is to put places aside and focus on the locations and orientations of identifiable objects in the region of interest (Chatila and Laumond, 1985; Smith and Cheeseman, 1986). Places can then be picked out if necessary by relating them to these objects. A place might be defined as "the region between two known walls."

A fourth "approach" is to let places be whatever humans find natural to designate as places, such as "Apartment 3G at 200 York Street," "The vacant lot on my block," or even "Highway 61." ("Abe said, Where you want this killing done? God said, Out on Highway 61," Bob Dylan.) This idea says little about how to carve up space into places, but it does raise the issue of why carve it up at all. If the task is to have a robot get orders from humans to go somewhere and do something, then at some point the robot must have matched up human labels with its own percepts. The alternative is to assume that the robot has its own goals that require it to know its way around, but so far the only goal studied is simply to learn the map, which leaves the choice of one definition of place versus another somewhat unjustified. In the remainder of this section, navigation methods will be examined using the various representations and then methods for learning maps.

Grid-based navigation methods are the most straightforward. Here it is assumed that the robot has methods for getting its approximate global position and orientation before it examines its surroundings perceptually. For example, in a military application, it can be assumed that satellites or airplanes can provide a rover with information about where it is in a terrain that is already well mapped to some resolution. It can further be assumed that the robot's objective is given with respect to the same global coordinate frame.

The route-finding problem in a grid-oriented representation is to plot a path from one pixel in the grid to another. A natural approach is to use the A*, or best-first search, algorithm (Hart and co-workers, 1968), treating a single-pixel move as an operator, and straight-line distance as a heuristic estimator (see A* ALGORITHM; SEARCH, BEST-FIRST). Figure 4 shows an example somewhat schematically. Occupied, untraversable pixels are shaded. A line from the center of one pixel to the center of an adjacent pixel indicates a single-pixel operator application. There are several little detours branching off the final path found, but the straight-line distance estimate keeps the algorithm on track fairly well. It does worse when it has to back out of cul de sacs, because the estimator is least accurate in those situations. The A* approach has the advantage of being simple and adaptable to a variety of situations. In any particular context, a more efficient algorithm can be found. A survey of a wide variety of such algorithms has been published (Mitchell, 1988).

Usually other criteria are added to the estimator so that something other than the shortest path is found. Moravec (1988) describes an algorithm for finding such a route in a certainty grid, where the criteria include minimizing the probability of encountering an obstacle. In a military context, the occupancy grid can be used to store information about roads and vegetation, and a path can be sought that minimizes opportunities for interdiction by the enemy.

Another context in which good positional information is known is a stored street or highway map. In this case, places are taken to be addresses or intersections, and it is assumed that the map has been completely inputted before route finding begins. Elliot and Lesk (1982) describe an A*-style algorithm that provides automatic directions to places in a city. The heuristic evaluation function favors large streets and penalizes routes containing many left turns so that the directions it finds tend to be the sort humans like to follow.

The frequent use of best-first-search algorithms in metric domains is no accident, because the estimated straight-

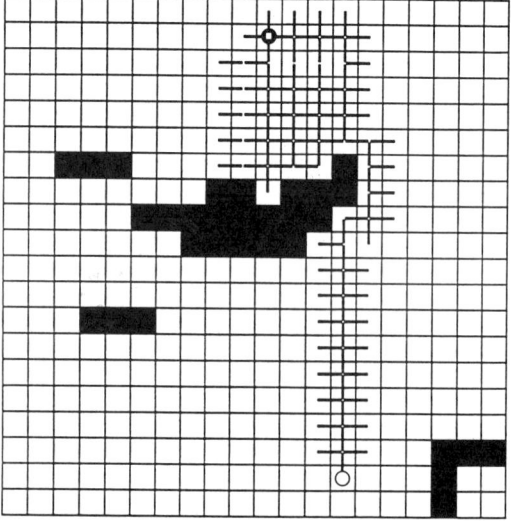

Figure 4. $A*$ search applied to route finding.

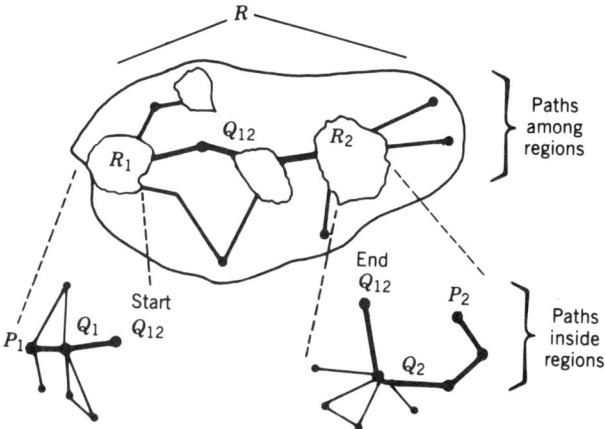

Figure 5. Finding routes between points in different regions.

line distance to a destination is such a good heuristic path-cost estimator, except in mazes (Lumelsky and Stepanov, 1987). This assertion remains true even when only approximate metric information is available (McDermott and Davis, 1984). However, in cases where metric information is assumed to be almost completely absent, other search strategies come to the fore, including searching through hierarchically organized graphs. The TOUR program (Kuipers, 1978) operates in the context of a city street network. The network is incomplete, and there are no global coordinates stored for anything. It maintains a hierarchical structure of regions. Paths are located inside regions and can run between regions. This structure makes it natural to find hierarchical plans for getting from one place to another (a hierarchical plan for a task consists of a short sequence of large steps, each of which is broken down into smaller plans if necessary). Here is a sketch of an algorithm for finding such plans (Fig. 5):

To find a path between two points P_1 and P_2:
    Find the smallest region R including both points.
    Find the regions R_1 and R_2 just below R that contain P_1 and P_2, respectively.
    Find a route Q_{12} from R_1 to R_2 (by some search process).
    Recursively find a route Q_1 from P_1 to Q_{12} in R_1 and a route Q_2 from P_2 to Q_{12} in R_2.
    Return result $Q_1 - Q_{12} - Q_2$.

This algorithm is not guaranteed to return optimal routes, but it works without requiring any sort of global coordinates. All it requires is that the area actually be organizable into appropriate hierarchical structure of major routes between fairly well-defined regions.

Attention is now turned to the problem of exploring and learning an unknown area. As mentioned, it is possible to distinguish between perceptual approaches, in which the goal is to discern and relate places defined by perceptual invariants, and metric approaches, in which the goal is to discover objects and learn their shapes, positions, and orientations.

A survey of the first kind of approach is available (Kuipers and Levitt, 1988). The perceptual technique is often coupled with the assumption that the overall structure of the cognitive map is a graph whose edges correspond to paths and whose nodes correspond to places (Kuipers and Byun, 1988). Sometimes the paths are given by a road network, but in less structured domains paths can be defined in terms of robot control strategies. For example, if a robot can follow a wall, then a large open room might be organized as a set of paths around its walls, punctuated by places at the corners and doors. This picture makes the most sense when the robot's sensors and effectors are assumed to be reliable only over short distances, so that it has little hope of being able to make sense of its location after launching itself through the interior of the room.

Under such short-range assumptions, which are reasonable with today's robots, places can be defined as areas satisfying some distinctiveness criterion. For example, a cul de sac might be defined as a place where most of the viewing angles around the robot are occupied by solid material. A corridor would debouch on a room at a place where there is a 180° open area on one side and two nearby solid peaks on the other. If this distinctiveness criterion can be quantified, as a distinctiveness measure, then the center of a distinctive neighborhood can be reached by moving until a local maximum of distinctiveness is reached. Doing this hill climbing allows the robot to attain a canonical location from which to launch subsequent explorations.

In one model (Kuipers and Byun, 1988) exploration requires moving out into open space from the current place, then adopting an appropriate control strategy to move along a path to the next place. Eventually, in a closed world, the robot will come back to a place it has already visited, which will satisfy the same distinctiveness criterion as before. However, it is entirely possible that two places could look very similar, so some care must be taken in deciding whether to identify the current place with one seen earlier. Kuipers and Byun use the following heuristic for deciding whether two places, P_{old} and P_{new}, are the same. Because the robot has been to P_{old} and left, it knows what some neighboring places look like. Hence it can attempt to traverse a path to those neighbors. If it gets to places that look right, it assumes P_{old} and P_{new} are the same place, and builds the graph accordingly. If it gets to places that don't match, it treats P_{old} and P_{new} as unrelated places. This strategy requires being able to identify directions out of P_{new} with those out of P_{old}, which depends on either a global compass or an asymmetrical distinctiveness criterion. The procedure is not foolproof, both because the directions might fail to match up properly, and because two similar places might have neighboring places that look similar. The first problem would lead to failure to realize that P_{old} and P_{new} were the same; the second problem would lead to the opposite error. The term *identification problem* is used to refer to the possibility of these kinds of error.

Another perceptual technique has been developed (Levitt and co-workers, 1987) that is based on the assumption that a robot can reliably track landmarks at a distance. Over a given time interval, a stable set of such landmarks (towers, tall buildings, mountains) will be perceivable around the robot, in a stable order. Whenever two landmarks are simultaneously visible, the robot can know when it has crossed the line between them, called a *landmark pair boundary* (LPB). It can tell which side it is on by whether, in panning clockwise, it sees landmark 1 before landmark 2. Places can be defined as minimal polygons bounded by LPB, and routes can be plotted by running an A* algorithm through the resulting tesselation of the plane. Currently the theory does not specify how landmarks are first noticed or how they are reliably tracked.

With metric approaches to route finding and exploration, the map-learning problem is to sort the world into objects and locate the objects in space. In special cases, today's sensors allow very impressive performance simply by sensing a scene repeatedly from a moving robot, generating a series of overlapping models, and matching up successive models. The NavLab project (Thorpe and coworkers, 1988), can create a map hundreds of meters long and a hundred meters wide by this method. The map is represented as a grid giving the elevation at discrete x, y coordinates over a wide area, and marking some pixels as containing obstacles. The method depends on using a laser range finder to generate high quality elevation maps and an inertial guidance system to help match up successive scenes.

A more general solution to the metric map-learning problem would rely more on passive vision, and would have to cope with uncertainty of robot position. It would also have to solve the problem of recognizing a familiar group of objects when they are approached from a new direction. First, it is necessary to represent the shapes of the objects. The usual approach is to classify each object as a standard shape (eg, a rectangle) with uncertain numerical attributes (eg, its length and width). A more ambitious representation has been used (Davis, 1985), which allowed objects to be approximated by arbitrary polygons whose sides were of uncertain length and joined at uncertain angles. Second, it is necessary to manage all this uncertainty. Typically, the task is to keep track of the intervals within which quantities lie (McDermott and Davis, 1984) or of probability distributions for those quantities (Smith and Cheeseman, 1986; Chatila and Laumond, 1985; Moutarlier and Chatila, 1989). As new information is gathered, the probability distributions become sharper (Fig. 6).

A fundamental question is what coordinate system to use for quantities like the x coordinate of an object. Even when there is an obvious coordinate system to use, there is the problem of capturing precise local information. For instance, the robot might know that objects A and B are close together without knowing much about their location in the global coordinate system. The approach taken by most probabilists is to store the probability distributions as means and variances (ie, to assume that they are Gaussian) and then to store a covariance matrix for all pairs of quantities in order to capture local relationships. Estimation theory supplies methods for updating these matrices as new observations occur. The alternative (McDermott and Davis, 1984) is to maintain many local coordinate systems, so that B's position could be stored with respect to A's frame. Obtaining B's position with respect to the

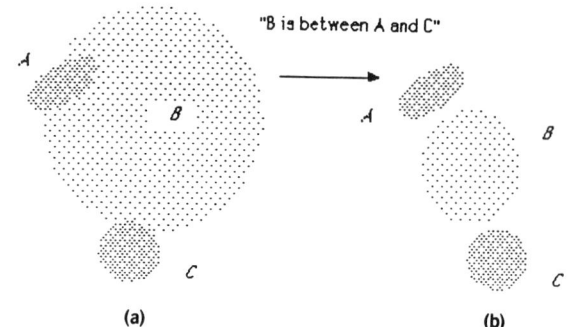

Figure 6. New information sharpens probability distributions on coordinates: (*a*) before new information; (*b*) after.

global frame might then require composing the information about its position with respect to A and information about A's position with respect to the global frame. The fact that all these quantities are stored as intervals make the computations rather messy.

It is possible to accumulate information about the parameters of an object only if the object can be reliably recognized when encountered. This is just the identification problem again, which arose with perceptual approaches in connection with deciding when to equate perceptually similar places and landmarks. Many workers in the field assume that recognizing previously seen objects is a job for the vision module. Others assume that the current scene can be converted into a local map, which can then be merged into a global map, by searching for the piece of the global map that matches it best. Elfes (1989) described algorithms for matching certainty grids. Davis (1985) described an algorithm for matching polygonal maps, where the polygons are required only to approximate underlying shapes. Lavin (1979) developed one for a more specialized representation of Gaussian hills.

One issue that has received remarkably little attention is how to correct errors in learned maps. Once a distortion gets introduced, future attempts to make new information consistent with it tend to introduce worse and worse distortions. A discussion of some of the problems is available (Davis, 1988). It is hoped that probabilistic representations could tolerate errors by having later observations overwhelm them, pushing parameters back toward correct values, but that hope runs into the problem that parameter-value errors can make matching errors more likely, causing the system's map to get further and further from the truth.

PHYSICAL REASONING

An active area of AI research is the study of reasoning about the structure and function of physical systems. Structure inevitably includes spatial structure. A key problem type for algorithms developed in this area is: given a mechanism, what will it do? In many cases, physical-reasoning algorithms are expected to take qualitative descriptions of systems and draw qualitative conclusions about their behavior. For example, given the signs of initial values of quantities, infer whether the values ever become zero (de Kleer and Brown, 1984; Forbus, 1984) (see PHYSICS, QUALITATIVE).

Unfortunately, when spatial structure is important, it is hard to find cases where it is possible to infer much without knowing the details of the initial layout of a system. Hence, especially in recent research, it has been conceded that detailed quantitative knowledge of the shape and initial configuration of a mechanism are needed, even if all that is wanted is a qualitative description of its behavior over time.

When people solve spatial-reasoning problems in their heads, they often have a subjective feeling of seeing a picture. For example, if asked to name all 50 states, almost everyone reports visualizing a path through which the attention wanders. There is a controversy about what these reports are reports of. On one side are researchers such as Shepard and Metzler (1971) and Kosslyn (1980, 1983) who believe that there is an actual picturelike entity in the brain performing useful computations. On the other are critics such as Pylyshyn (1985) who believe that pictures are poor computing devices and that subjective impressions are misleading.

The first issue to settle in building a computational model of imagery is what the underlying picture medium is. It is possible to begin by assuming that a map of the United States was stored as a hierarchical pointer structure, with nodes representing large areas (like New England) pointing to smaller component areas (like states) and other, less familiar, areas pointing to a sparser set of subareas. Such a model might explain many facts [eg, certain distortions in subjects' memories of maps (Stevens and Coupe, 1978)], but would not itself explain why the data structure is experienced as a picture when it is traversed. Researchers who believe that this is one of the prime facts to be explained make their models pictorial from the start. A dangerous pitfall here is to assume that a mental image is nothing but a picture, so that some homunculus must "look" at it. To avoid the need for the homunculus, image theorists usually assume that the pictorial medium is active, capable of computation on its own.

There have been several attempts to avoid the need for detailed quantitative knowledge of spatial layouts, notably the work of Hayes (1985a, 1985b) on naive physics (See PHYSICS, NAIVE), the effort to formalize what "everyone knows" about the way objects in the world behave and interact. He presents axioms about the behavior of liquids in containers, where the containers are described in terms of their bounding surfaces. The notation omits most of the details of where these surfaces are located or how they are shaped and instead focuses on qualitative description of them as separating volumes into different functional parts. An open container, for instance, is described as a volume with just one free face, the top. The brim of the container is the "face of its top face," that is, the edge bounding its top face. Hayes argues that the way to bring time and change into this formalism is to analyze activity as four-dimensional histories of objects. For example, if an open container full of liquid is tilted, there will be a "leaving" history at the brim of the container that interfaces to a "falling" history in the free space nearby. A more recent attempt to axiomatize knowledge about space and change is available (Davis, 1990).

In practical programs, more specialized solutions often obviate a detailed representation. Figure 7 shows a problem solved by deKleer's (1979) program NEWTON. The program reasons about the qualitative shape of the roller coaster in order to realize that the object cannot get to point X. Other physics-problem solvers reason about situations of similar complexity (Novak, 1977; Bundy, 1978).

None of these programs rely on a general-purpose shape representation. All of them use some version of the qualitative-bin representation. For example, Novak's program accepts physics-problem statements in natural language. It turns a sentence like "a man stands on a ladder" into an internal representation in which a man modeled as a point mass is located on a ladder represented as a line. Each such internal entity has various parameters associated with it, such as the man's mass. In different problem statements the man would get modeled as some other kind of entity, with different parameters. Equations involving these parameters are set up and solved to produce the solution to the overall problem. The concern about these representations is that they presuppose so much about the problem class. At no point does the program possess a neutral statement of the geometric setup, which is independent of the question type to be asked. It is hard to imagine a purely qualitative representation of this kind.

The difficulty of finding an effective qualitative spatial representation has led researchers to assume that good quantitative information is available about the shapes and positions of objects. The problem then is to extract reasonable predictions about behavior from these initial conditions, where "reasonable" is hard to define, but tends to mean "concise and symbolic," as opposed to voluminous and numerical.

One way to get a quantitative representation of spatial change over time is to use a changing spatial-occupancy array. Each pixel now records its current state, and can change to a new state after communicating with its neighbors. Interesting inferences then occur by the combined action of all the pixels. This model is quite attractive to imagery theorists, because in the brain a natural imple-

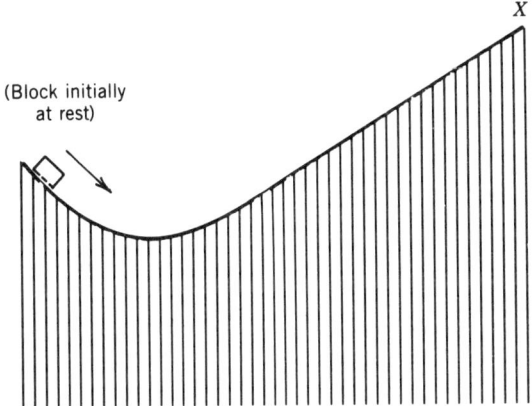

Figure 7. Problem solved by NEWTON: "Will the block reach point X?" (de Kleer, 1975).

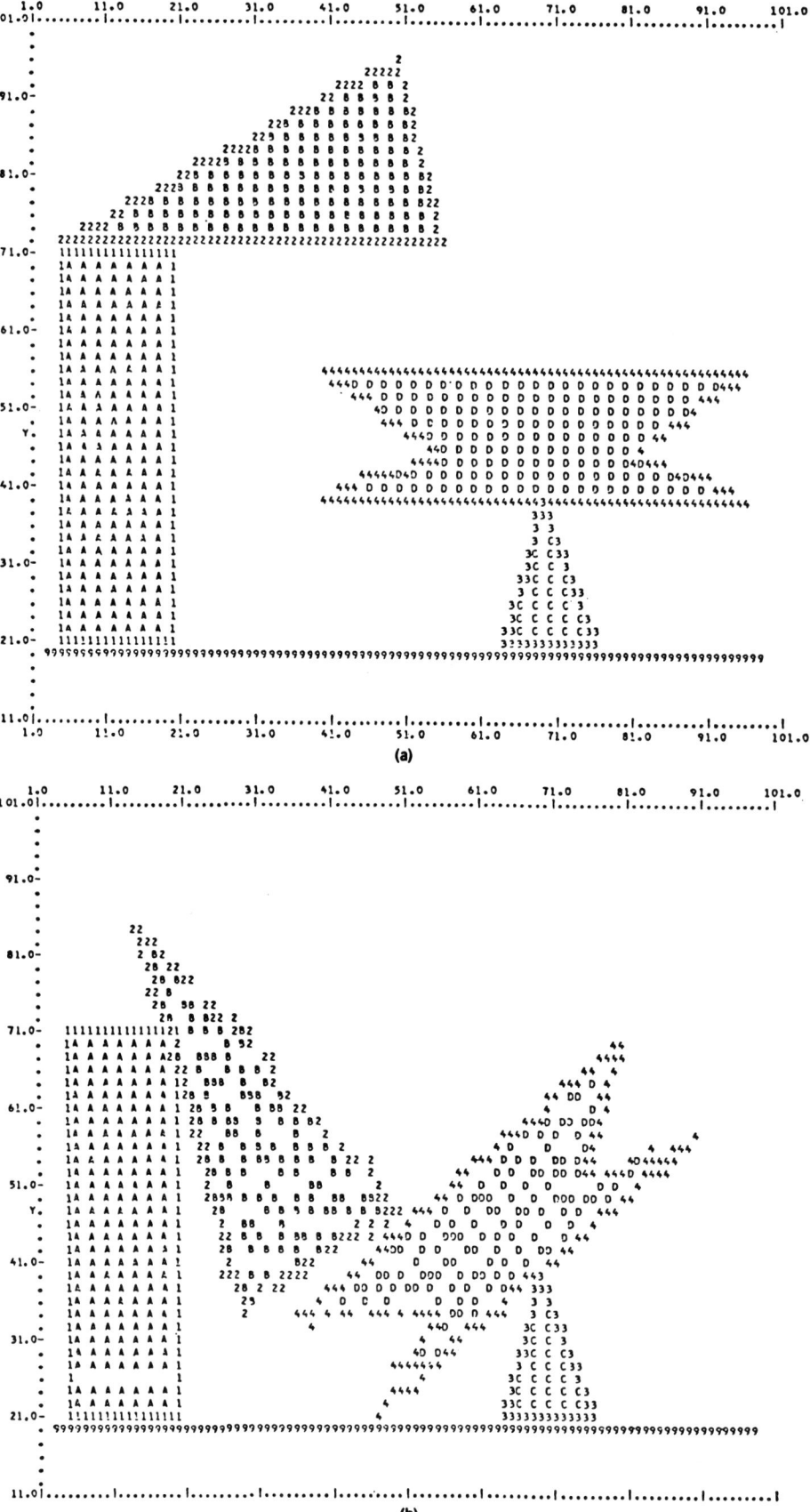

Figure 8. Use of blocks-world image to reason about stability: (a) initial snapshot; (b) final snapshot.

mentation would involve groups of neurons, probably laid out in an actual two-dimensional field. In a digital computer each pixel is a data structure arranged in an array, and a sequential algorithm simulates each in turn; but a special-purpose computer could be built that implemented the pixels as separate pieces of silicon, all running in parallel. If this could be made to work, it might be very fast.

An example of this kind of system is Funt's (1976, 1987) program WHISPER, which solves problems in the "blocks world," (Fig. 8). Block A is indicated by labeling the pixels it occupies with an A for pixels in A's interior, or a 1 for pixels on A's boundary. In that figure the program decides that block B is unstable and will cause D to fall when it does. The image machine helps in several ways. First, the center of gravity of B must be found, by having each pixel labeled B or 2 report its location to a central processor, which adds the coordinates and averages. The processor notes that the center of gravity of B is not above A, so B will fall. Then it simulates the fall by instructing each pixel of B to rotate around the upper right corner of A. This rotation occurs step by step [actually, two arrays of pixels are used (Funt, 1987)]. The collision between B and D is noticed when a 2-labeled pixel attempts to transfer its contents into one already labeled with a 4. The advantage of this approach to thinking about colliding blocks is that no intricate calculation about intersecting lines is required to detect a collision. A more recent example, involving simulating a wider array of physical phenomena is that of Gardin and Meltzer (1989).

Other spatial representations can be set in motion besides occupancy arrays. An active area of research is in modeling mechanisms, where the ubiquity of curved surfaces make volume and boundary descriptions more appropriate than occupancy arrays. The mechanism-envisioning problem involves starting with a detailed description of, say, a clock, and producing a "qualitative" description of its behavior. Because this work is still in an exploratory phase, it has encountered a common obstacle in AI: not being able to say exactly what the output is to be used for. Some researchers (Faltings, 1990) attempt to produce a classification of the possible positions the mechanism can be in. Others (Gelsey and McDermott, 1990) produce a symbolic description of some traces of machine behavior for typical initial conditions, without attempting an exhaustive analysis of the machine's possible configurations in advance.

The study of possible configurations is called *machine kinematics*, and, of course, has been carried out by human engineers for decades (Reuleaux, 1876). An important idea in this study is the configuration space of the machine, an abstract space with one dimension for each degree of freedom of the machine. For example, a machine with a single wheel rotating on an axle has one degree of freedom, and a single number (the angle the wheel makes with the axle) suffices to describe its state completely. A complex machine can have a configuration space with many dimensions, which can be expensive to analyze. However, the fact that the focus is on machines makes things better than they could be. In the abstract, a simple wheel has six degrees of freedom (three coordinates in space, plus three rotations to specify its orientation), and that is neglecting deformations. When it is stipulated that the wheel is a rigid body that makes permanent contact with a fixed axle, all but one of the degrees of freedom go away.

The configuration space for a machine can be divided into two regions: states of the machine in which parts would overlap and states where they would not. The second region consists of the states the machine can actually be in. The boundary between the two regions are the states in which parts are in contact, and it is here that most of the interesting behavior of the machine occurs, because forces are transmitted only during contacts.

A frequently studied example is the clock escapement. An example appears in Figure 9 (Faltings, 1990). The odd-shaped part at the top is called the lever. Its two ends catch the teeth of the escape wheel at the bottom, allowing it to turn only when the lever is disengaged, and hence synchronizing its turning rate to the period of the lever (which is connected to an oscillating balance wheel, not shown). This mechanism has two degrees of freedom, characterized by the angles of rotation of the lever and escape wheel around their axes. The configuration space of the mechanism is shown in Figure 10 (Faltings, 1990). It has two dimensions, reflecting the two degrees of freedom. Most of the space is gray, because it is impossible for the two angles to take on most of their possible values

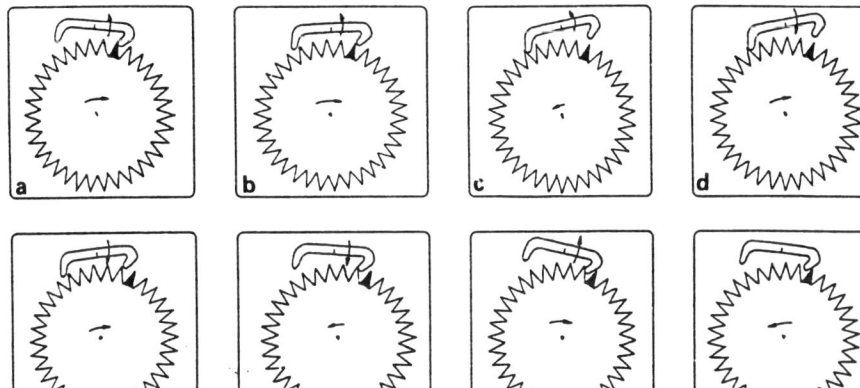

Figure 9. The behavior of a simple clock escapement (Faltings, 1990; courtesy of *Artificial Intelligence*).

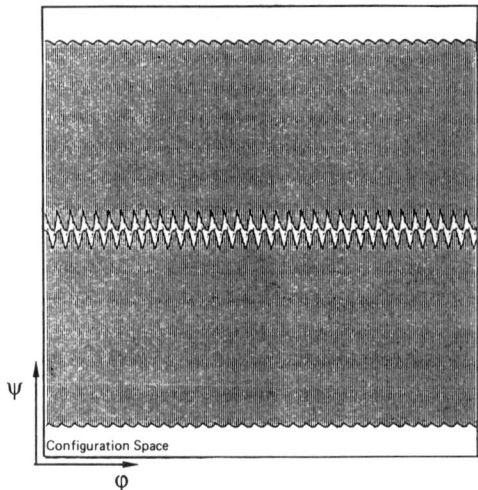

Figure 10. Configuration space for the mechanism of Figure 9 (Faltings, 1990; courtesy of *Artificial Intelligence*).

simultaneously without causing the lever and the escape wheel to overlap. The jagged white stripe in the middle is the escapement's normal region of operation. The open white space at the top and bottom is a normally unreachable region in which the lever is turned over, and never engages the escape wheel.

A variety of algorithms have been developed for making inferences about mechanisms like this, starting from a geometrical description. Joskowicz's (1987, 1988) algorithm finds a complete description of the boundary of the configuration space starting from a description of the boundaries of the parts. Faltings's (1990) algorithm divides the free region of configuration space into "places" in which the behavior of the machine has a simple qualitative description. This place vocabulary can then be used to support qualitative envisioning of the mechanism (Nielsen, 1988). The algorithms of Hoffman and Hopcroft (1987), Cremer (1989), and Gelsey (1990) avoid computing the configuration space at all, but go directly to quantitative simulation. Figure 11 shows a trace of the evolution of an escapement found by Gelsey's algorithm. This output is then analyzed to find repetitions of configurations, yielding a concise description of the basic loop the mechanism evolves through. Simulated experiments are then performed to determine how and when the loop comes to an end and a new regime begins, characterized by a change in the contacts responsible for the system's behavior. In the case of the escapement, the description says merely that the mechanism will oscillate at a constant period until the spring runs down.

BIBLIOGRAPHY

G. J. Agin and T. O. Binford, "Computer Descriptions of Curved Objects," *IEEE Trans. Comput.* **25**(4), 439–449 (1976).

R. T. Antony, "A Hybrid Spatial/Object-Oriented DBMS to Support Automated Spatial, Hierarchical, and Temporal Reasoning," in Chen, 1990, pp. 63–132.

D. Ballard and C. Brown, *Computer Vision*, Prentice-Hall, Englewood Cliffs, N.J., 1982.

B. G. Baumgart, *Geometric Modeling for Computer Vision*, Stanford Artificial Intelligence Lab Report STAN-CS-74-463, Stanford, Calif., 1975.

J. Bentley and J. H. Friedman, "Data Structures for Range Searching," *Comput. Surv.* **11**(4), 397–409 (1979).

R. A. Brooks, "Symbolic Reasoning Among 3-D Models and 2-D Images," *Artif. Intell.* **7**(1–3), 285–348 (1981).

A. Bundy, "Will It Reach the Top? Prediction in the Mechanics World," *Artif. Intell.* **10**(2), 129–146 (1978).

R. Chatila and J. Laumond, "Position Referencing and Consistent World Modeling for Mobile Robots," in *Proceedings of the*

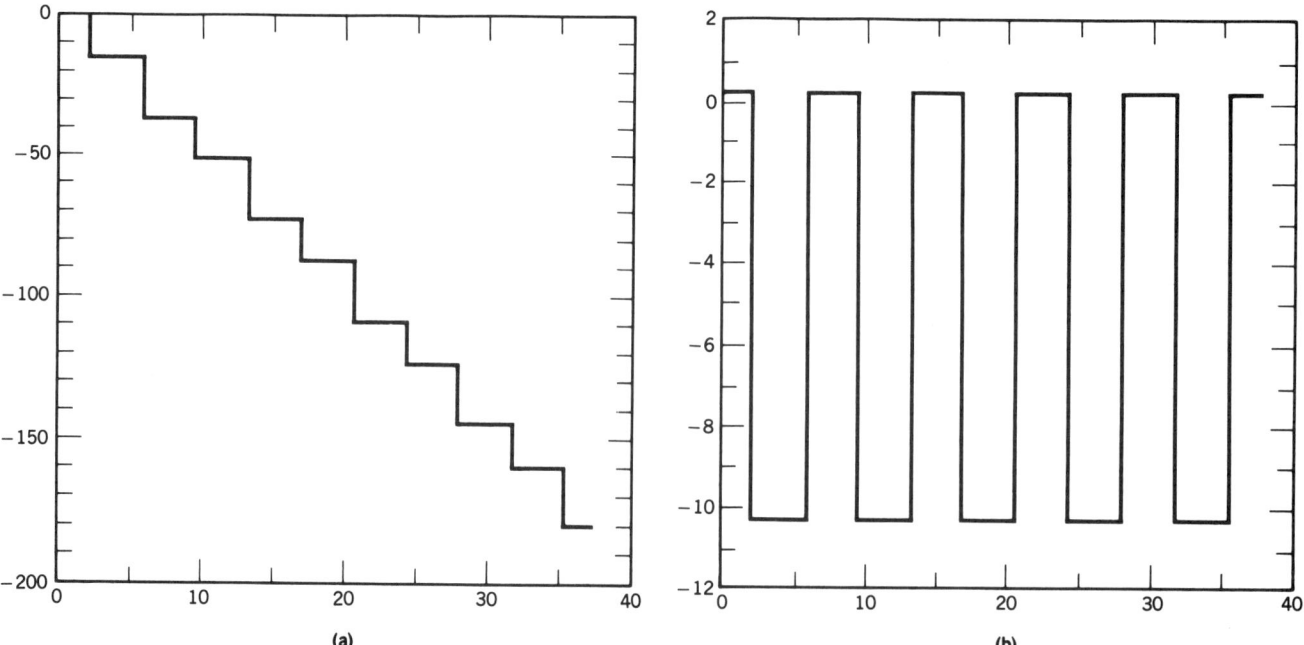

Figure 11. Simulated behavior of the escapement over time: (*a*) lever; (*b*) escape wheel.

IEEE International Conference on Robotics and Automation, IEEE Computer Society, Washington, D.C., 1985, pp. 138–170.

S. Chen, *Advances in Spatial Reasoning,* Vol. 1, Ablex Publishing Corp., Norwood, N.J., 1990.

J. F. Cremer, *An Architecture for General Purpose Physical System Simulation—Integrating Geometry, Dynamics, and Control,* Ph.D. dissertation, Cornell University, Ithaca, N.Y., 1989.

E. Davis, *Representing and Acquiring Geographic Knowledge,* Pitman Publishing, New York, 1985.

E. Davis, "Error Correction in Large-Scale Cognitive Maps," in *Proceedings of the SPIE Workshop on Sensor Fusion: Spatial Reasoning and Scene Interpretation,* Boston, Mass., 1988, pp. 332–337.

E. Davis, *Representations of Commonsense Knowledge,* Morgan-Kaufmann, San Mateo, Calif., 1990.

J. de Kleer, "Qualitative and Quantitative Reasoning in Classical Mechanics," in P. H. Winston and R. H. Brown, eds., *Artificial Intelligence: An MIT Perspective,* Vol. 1, MIT Press, Cambridge, Mass., 1979, pp. 11–30.

J. de Kleer and J. S. Brown, "A Qualitative Physics Based on Confluences," *Artif. Intell.* **24,** 7–83 (1984).

A. Elfes, "Using Occupancy Grids for Mobile Robot Perception and Navigation," *IEEE Comput.* (special issue), 46–58 (June 1989).

R. J. Elliot and M. E. Lesk, "Route Finding in Street Maps by Computers and People," in *Proceedings of the Second National Conference on Artificial Intelligence,* Pittsburgh, Pa., AAAI, Menlo Park, Calif., 1982, pp. 258–261.

B. Faltings, "Qualitative Kinematics in Mechanisms," *Artif. Intell.* **44**(1–2), 89–119 (1990).

K. Forbus, "Qualitative Process Theory," *Artif. Intell.* **24,** 85–168 (1984).

B. V. Funt, *WHISPER: A Computer Implementation Using Analogues in Reasoning,* Technical Report 76-09, University of British Columbia, Vancouver, 1976.

B. V. Funt, "Analogical Modes of Reasoning and Process Modelling," in N. Cercone and G. McCalla, eds., *The Knowledge Frontier,* Springer-Verlag, New York, 1987, pp. 414–428.

F. Gardin and B. Meltzer, "Analogical Representations of Naive Physics," *Artif. Intell.* **38**(2), 139–159 (1989).

A. Gelsey, *Automated Reasoning About Machines,* Report **785,** Yale University, New Haven, Conn., 1990.

A. Gelsey and D. McDermott, "Spatial Reasoning About Mechanisms," in Chen, 1990, pp. 1–33.

P. E. Hart, N. J. Nilsson, and B. Raphael," A Formal Basis for the Heuristic Determination of Minimum Cost Paths," *IEEE Trans. Sys. Sci. Cybernet.* **4**(2), 100–107 (1968).

P. Hayes, "The Second Naive Physics Manifesto," in J. Hobbs and R. C. Moore, eds., *Formal Theories of the Commonsense World,* Ablex Publishing Corp., Norwood, N.J., 1985a, pp. 1–36.

P. Hayes, "Naive Physics I: Ontology for Liquids," in J. Hobbs and R. C. Moore, eds., *Formal Theories of the Commonsense World,* Albex Publishing Corp., Norwood, N.J., 1985b, pp. 71–107.

C. M. Hoffman and J. E. Hopcroft, "Simulation of Physical Systems from Geometric Models," *IEEE J. Robot. Automat.* **3**(3), 194–206 (1987).

L. Joskowicz, "Shape and Function in Mechanical Devices," in *Proceedings of the Sixth National Conference on Artificial Intelligence,* Seattle, Wash., AAAI, Menlo Park, Calif., 1987, pp. 611–615.

L. Joskowicz, *Reasoning About Shape and Kinematic Function in Mechanical Devices,* Courant Institute of Mathematical Sciences Report 402, New York, 1988.

A. Kak, ed., Special Issue, *AI Mag.* **9** (Summer 1988).

A. Klinger and M. L. Rhodes, "Organization and Access of Image Data by Areas," *IEEE Trans. Patt. Anal. Machine Intell.* **1,** 50–60 (1979).

S. Kosslyn, *Image and Mind,* Harvard University Press, Cambridge, Mass., 1980.

S. Kosslyn, *Ghosts in the Mind's Machine: Creating and Using Images,* W. W. Norton, New York, 1983.

B. Kuipers, "Modeling Spatial Knowledge," *Cogn. Sci.* **2**(2), 129–154 (1978).

B. Kuipers and Y. Byun, "A Robust, Qualitative Method for Robot Spatial Reasoning," in *Proceedings of the Seventh National Conference on Artificial Intelligence,* St. Paul, Minn., AAAI, Menlo Park, Calif., 1988, pp. 774–779.

B. Kuipers and T. S. Levitt, "Navigation and Mapping in Large-Scale Space," *AI Mag.,* 25–43 (Summer 1988).

M. Lavin, "Analysis of Scenes from a Moving Viewpoint," in de Kleer, 1979, pp. 185–208.

T. S. Levitt, D. T. Lawton, D. M. Chelberg, and P. C. Nelson, "Qualitative Landmark-Based Path Planning and Following," in *Proceedings of the Sixth National Conference on AI,* AAAI, Menlo Park, Calif., 1987, pp. 689–694.

V. Lumelsky and A. Stepanov, "Path Planning Strategies for a Point Mobile Automaton Moving Amidst Unknown Obstacles of Arbitrary Shape," *Algorithmica* **3**(4), 403–430 (1987).

D. Marr and H. K. Nishihara, "Representation and Recognition of the Spatial Organization of Three-Dimensional Shapes," *Proc. R. Soc. B* **200,** 269–294 (1978).

D. McDermott and E. Davis, "Planning Routes Through Uncertain Territory," *Artif. Intell.* **22,** 107–156 (1984).

J. S. B. Mitchell, "An Algorithmic Approach to Some Problems in Terrain Navigation," *Artif. Intell.* **37**(1–3), 171–201 (1988).

H. P. Moravec, "Sensor Fusion in Certainty Grids for Mobile Robots," *AI Mag.,* 61–74 (Summer 1988).

P. Moutarlier and R. Chatila, "Stochastic Multisensory Data Fusion for Mobile Robot Location and Environment Modelling," *Proc. Int. Symp. Robot. Res.* **5,** 207–216 (1989).

P. Nielsen, *A Qualitative Approach to Rigid Body Mechanics,* Ph.D. dissertation, University of Illinois, 1988.

G. Novak, "Representations of Knowledge in a Program for Solving Physics Problems," in *Proceedings of the Fifth IJCAI,* Morgan-Kaufmann, San Mateo, Calif., 1977, pp. 286–291.

Z. Pylyshyn, *Computation and Cognition: Toward a Foundation for Cognitive Science,* MIT Press, Cambridge, Mass., 1985.

A. A. G. Requicha, "Representations for Rigid Solids: Theory, Methods, and Systems," *ACM Comput. Surv.* **12,** 437–464 (1980).

F. Reuleaux, *The Kinematics of Machinery,* Macmillan and Co., London, 1876.

H. Samet, "The Quadtree and Related Hierarchical Data Structures," *Comput. Surv.* **16**(2), 187–260 (1984).

R. C. Smith and P. Cheeseman, "On the Representation and Estimation of Spatial Uncertainty," *Int. J. Robot. Res.* **5**(4), 56–68 (1986).

R. N. Shepard and J. Metzler, "Mental Rotation of Three-Dimensional Objects," *Science* **171,** 701–703 (1971).

A. Stevens and P. Coupe, "Distortions in Judged Spatial Relations," *Cogn. Psychol.* **10,** 422–437 (1978).

C. Thorpe, M. H. Hebert, T. Kanade, and S. Shafer, "Vision and

Navigation for the Carnegie Mellon Navlab," *IEEE Trans. Patt. Anal. Machine Intell.* **10**(3), 362–373 (1988).

General References

N. Cercone and G. McCalla, eds., *The Knowledge Frontier,* Springer-Verlag, New York, 1987.

J. Hobbs and R. C. Moore, eds., *Formal Theories of the Commonsense World,* Ablex Publishing Corp., Norwood, N.J., 1985.

P. H. Winston and R. H. Brown, eds., *Artificial Intelligence: An MIT Perspective,* Vol. 1, MIT Press, Cambridge, Mass., 1979.

D. McDermott
Yale University

REASONING, TEMPORAL

It is hard to think of a research area within AI that does not involve reasoning about time in one way or another: medical-diagnosis systems try to determine the time at which the virus infected the blood system, circuit-debugging programs must reason about the period over which the charge in the capacitor increased, automatic programmers and program synthesizers must deduce that after procedure P is executed the value of variable X is zero, and robot programmers must make sure that the robot meets various deadlines when carrying out a set of tasks. One particular subfield of AI, which has become known as the area of temporal reasoning (TR), acknowledges this central role. Although most subfields merely employ temporal terminology, the very goal of TR is a general theory of time.

Of course, the passage of time is important only because changes are possible. In a world where no changes were possible (no viruses infecting blood systems, no electrical charges changing, no changes in program counters, not even changes in the position of the sun in the sky or the position of the hands on wristwatches) not only would there be no computational justification for keeping track of time but the very concept of time would become meaningless. Therefore, the ideal theory of time must meet two requirements. The first is that it provide a language for describing what is true and what is false over time. The second is that it provide a criterion of lawful change.

The work that is described here is mostly in the form of various formalisms, which usually means a logic with more or less well worked out syntax and semantics. The first section reviews the work done within AI, describing a somewhat idealized progression of such formalisms. The last section describes related work from philosophy and theoretical computer science.

How is temporal information represented? Suppose the task is to represent in logic the fact that the color of a particular house is red at time t. There are several options:

> Time can simply be included as an argument to the predicate: COLOR(HOUSE,RED,T), where T is a time argument (a point, an interval, or otherwise).
>
> The proposition can be "reified" (or, as McCarthy once proposed, "thingified"): HOLD(T,COLOR(HOUSE, RED); here COLOR serves as a function symbol rather than a relation symbol.
>
> Time need not be mentioned at all! Instead, the interpretation of formulas is complicated. If in classic logic a formula φ is either true (written $\models \varphi$) or false (and in this article the discussion is confined to the propositional case), now a formula is either true at a given time t (written $t \models \varphi$) or false at that time. (Here again there is a choice of choosing t to be a point, an interval, or some other temporal entity.)

The first option is not acceptable from the standpoint of TR. If time is represented as an argument (or several arguments) so predicates, there is nothing general that can be said about it. For example, it cannot be said that "effects cannot precede their causes"; at most it can be said about specific causes and effects. Indeed, this first option accords no special status to time, neither conceptual nor notational, which goes against the grain of the TR spirit.

The second option fares better in this respect, and in one guise or another has been widely accepted in TR. Taking this approach seriously requires paying special attention to the meaning of the terms in the language, which now also serve the function of what otherwise would be relation symbols.

The third option, favored in modern philosophy and theoretical computer science, has for the most part been ignored in AI until very recently.

TEMPORAL REASONING IN AI

Situation Calculus, STRIPS, Histories, Intervals, and Chronicles

McCarthy and Hayes (1981) introduced the situation calculus (SC), a temporal formalism that to this day is the basis for many temporal representations. A situation is a snapshot of the universe at given moment. Actions are the means of transforming one situation into another. For example, by performing the action PICKUP(A) in the situation where ON(A, B) and ISCLEAR(A) are true, a new situation is arrived at where ISCLEAR(B) is true. The actual formal construction uses the function RESULT that accepts a situation and an action as arguments and returns a new situation. If in the above example the first situation is S1 and the second S2, then S2 = RESULT(S1,PICKUP(A)). It is possible, of course, to construct longer chains of action, as in S3 = RESULT(RESULT(S1,PICKUP(B)),PUTDOWN(B)).

SC makes several strong commitments. The first is about discreteness of time, which precludes discussion of continuous processes such as water flowing into a container and gradually filling it. The second is about contiguity of cause and effect, so to speak; the effects of an action are manifested at the very next situation. A further limitation of SC was that it did not allow concurrent actions, even in the framework of discrete time. The best known problem introduced by SC is the frame problem. Consider the same situations S1 and S2 as described above with the additional information that in S1 COLOR

(A,GREEN) is true. Is COLOR(A,GREEN) still true in S2? It is hoped that the answer is affirmative, but in fact this conclusion is not warranted by the theory. The RESULT function specifies only what changes as a consequence of taking an action but not what is true by virtue of having not changed. In order to be able to make those inferences, it is possible to add numerous frame axioms, specifying for each action what it does not affect. The first problem with this solution is that such axioms are numerous: Picking up a block does not change its color, does not affect any other block, does not change the president of the United States, etc. It is obviously impossible to explicitly list what is unaffected by an action. A further complication arises if concurrent actions are introduced. In this case frame axioms are simply wrong: Someone might paint the block as it is being PICKUPed.

As was mentioned before, despite these limitations SC has proved very influential. For example, it has been the basis for several planning (qv) systems. One of the first of such systems was STRIPS (Fikes and Nilsson, 1971), which embodied a natural solution to the frame problem. STRIPS is a name for both a formalism and a planner based on that formalism. This article is concerned primarily with the former. The STRIPS framework adopted the same view of time as SC but made the following addition. With each action STRIPS associated two lists. The addlist specified what becomes true as a result of the action, and the deletelist specified what ceases to be true after the action. The STRIPS assumption was that if action A transformed state S1 into state S2, then a proposition P was true in state S2 if and only if either P was in the addlist of A or P was true in S1 and was not in the deletelist of A. This assumption was the basis for the regression operator in the STRIPS planner (see PLANNING).

One of the strong advocates of formal reasoning about the commonsense world has been Hayes. Hayes (1984a, 1984b) offered a general justification of his approach as well as an actual formalism to describe the behavior of liquids (see PHYSICS, NAIVE). (These are slightly revised versions; the original papers were written in the 1970s.) In the latter paper Hayes introduced the notion of histories, which has had a strong influence on TR. A history is a connected piece of four-dimensional space–time. For example, a falling history is the space occupied by a liquid for the duration of its freefall. This view of the world is a radical departure from the SC paradigm. It acknowledges the continuous nature of time (and space, although that is not directly relevant to this discussion) and allows the representation of gradual change. There is no restriction to snapshots of the universe and a method for stringing them together. Instead an entire interval of time is described. Of course, it is possible to describe a snapshot of the universe by taking a slice through a history (which is the projection of the history onto the three-dimensional space at a given point in time). The theory of histories was partially applied by Forbus (1984) to reasoning about qualitative physics.

The spatial nature of Hayes's histories has drawn some criticism. For one thing, some occurrences do not have a well-defined spatial extent: What are the spatial boundaries of a conversation? Of an election? Of a confusion? Furthermore, histories are extensional in that the space–time of the history completely determines the history. But this cannot possibly be right, due to the fusion problem: more than one history can take place at the same space–time, eg, a concert history and a stale-air history. Nevertheless, Hayes's bold transition from states to interval inspired much of the later work, including Allen's interval calculus and McDermott's temporal logic.

Retaining the interval-based view of time, Allen (1984) proposed a theory of action and time and identified the 13 possible relations between two intervals (identity, the one totally preceding the other, overlapping, etc). The ontology proposed by Allen associates with an interval one of three objects: a property, an event, or a process. A property is something that is statically true or false, eg, "the pen is red." Allen represented this assertion by the formula HOLD(I, COLOR(PEN, RED)). Properties hold uniformly throughout an interval; a proposition holds for an interval exactly when it holds for all subintervals: $\forall I, P$ HOLD(I, P) $\equiv \forall I' \in I$ HOLD(I', P) (and in fact Allen required a slightly stronger axiom). Because properties are reified propositions, to retain their intuitive meaning, Allen simulated the logical connectives. For example, HOLDS(I, AND(P, Q)) $\equiv$ HOLDS(I, P) $\wedge$ HOLDS(I, Q) is an axiom in Allen's system.

Contrary to properties, events are holistic entities. If an event occurred over an interval, it did not occur over any subinterval. An example of an event is "I went to the shop"; such an event is repeatable but not divisible. The predicate denoting occurrence of events is OCCUR(I, EVENT). Processes are a hybrid case. An example of a statement describing a process is "I am walking"; if it is true for an interval, it must be true for some subinterval but need not be true for all of subintervals (I may rest during my hour-long walk).

Allen's proposal also included an account of causation. Event causation describes a relation between events (and associated intervals). The properties of this relation are exactly the following: the occurrence of causes entails the occurrence of effects, effects may not precede their causes, and the relation is transitive and antisymmetric. Other parts of Allen's proposal include the notions of agents, actions, level generation (Goldman, 1970), intentions, plans, commitment, knowledge, and belief.

McDermott (1978) began exploring the connection between problem solving (qv) and theories of time and action. He proposed a temporal logic to be used in the process of planning (McDermott, 1982a), in which he introduced the notion of chronicles. McDermott's construction takes as primitive the notion of a state, which is a point in time in some set of possible worlds. A fact type is a reified proposition that may be instantiated as a fact token. For example, "I am walking" is a fact type, and "I am walking on 1.1.2000 from 1:00 to 1:45" is a fact token. The construction is set theoretic: the assertion $T(S, P)$, denoting the existence of a particular fact token, is shorthand for $S \in P$. Similarly for an event type E, the assertion OCC(S1, S2, E), denoting the existence of an event token, is merely shorthand for $\langle S1, S2 \rangle \in E$. The assertion TT(S1, S2, P) ("p is true throughout the interval [s1, s2]") is shorthand for [S1, S2] $\subset P$.

McDermott assumes that time, as well as being a partial order, is dense. He furthermore arranges time in chronicles, which are linear timelines that form a treelike structure: chronicles may branch into the future, and once they do, the different branches do not meet again. When taking an action is contemplated, it is necessary to compare the world (or chronicle) in which the action is taken to the world in which it is not. McDermott's formulation was the first one to provide a mechanism for such a comparison within the logic; different worlds are simply separate paths in the chronicle tree. In particular, he managed to give meaning to the notion of preventing.

McDermott also devotes a large part of the discussion to causation as a representation of rules governing change. The notion he considers are ECAUSE, for one event causing another, and PCAUSE, for an event causing a fact. The former allow for a delay between the cause and the effect. The latter are particularly interesting, because they introduce the notion of persistences. The idea is that the effect of a PCAUSE is a defeasible prediction. For example, the predicted effect of a boulder rolling to a particular location is that the boulder will be there for the next 50 years. This prediction will be violated if a construction company decides to erect a building on that particular site at an earlier time. Persistences, whose semantics are loosely based on nonmonotonic logic (see REASONING, NONMONOTONIC) are McDermott's (1982b) solution to the frame problem. Other topics covered by McDermott are continuous change, qualitative physics and potrans (potential transfer), planning, and the notion of a subtask. Further applications of temporal reasoning to planning have been published (McDermott, 1984).

Application to Qualitative Physics

Much of physical reasoning involves time for obvious reasons. It is possible to reason about what a physical system will do starting from initial conditions, or contrariwise it is possible to reason backward from final conditions to an explanation in terms of previous behavior. Most of the work has focused on the former process, which is called envisioning (de Kleer, 1975) or projection (Wilenskey, 1983; Simmons, 1983).

Envisioning is not the same as simulation. It is desired that the reasoner see interesting patterns in the behavior, that it recognize an oscillator, not just become one. Furthermore, it is important that the reasoning be able to proceed in the absence of the detailed quantitative information that a simulator would require. The resulting paradigm is called qualitative reasoning about physical systems. It has been pursued by de Kleer and Brown (1984), Forbus (1984), and Kuipers (1984) (see PHYSICS, NAIVE; REASONING, CAUSAL; REASONING, COMMONSENSE).

There are two phases to the reasoning in this paradigm. First the program must produce an abstract version of the structure of the system, then it must use this structure to reason. In almost every case, the abstract structure is analyzed as a set of devices with connections to each other. Causality flows through the connections from one device to another. The state of a device is represented by the values of a set of quantities. A device can have differ-

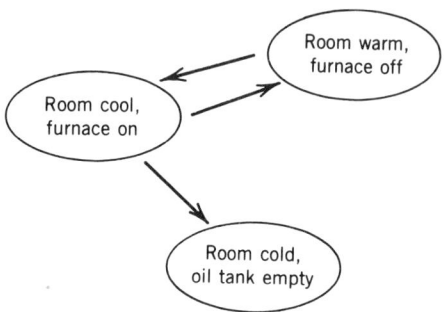

Figure 1. A simple state diagram.

ent behaviors depending on what ranges various quantities lie in. For instance, a thermostat-controlled heating system will be characterized by quantities such as room temperature and heat flow out of room. The furnace will be in state OPERATIVE or OFF depending on whether the room temperature is greater than the thermostat setting. If it is OPERATIVE and the tank is NONEMPTY, there will be a constant value of furnace heat flow into the room. And so forth.

Devices connect quantities together; they enforce certain relationships among them. Hence, from an initial set of quantity relationships, the temporal reasoner can deduce how the quantities will change. If the furnace is on, and it is not too cold outside, the room temperature will increase. Any such change, if allowed to continue, will eventually drive some quantity out of its current range, thus changing the behavior of some device. The reasoner must, therefore, reproject the behavior of the system under the altered circumstances. The new analysis will result in a different pattern of changes, leading to new behavior shifts, and so forth. The final analysis may be displayed as a graph, as in Figure 1. States of the system are shown as ovals. An arrow joins two states if the first may evolve into the second through quantity changes. A loop in the graph indicates that the system may oscillate between the two given states. If the analysis is correct and useful, it can be expected that a finite number of significantly different states will be found, and hence it is expected that every system to enter one state and will stay there or loop among some set of states. Note that the "furnace on" state has two potential successors: either the room becomes warm or the oil runs out. Both possibilities appear because the qualitative analysis shows two quantities changing: the room temperature is increasing and the oil level is decreasing. Without further information about the magnitudes of the quantities, the reasoner cannot decide which will reach its threshold first and cause the system to change state.

The early work by Hendrix (1973) anticipated much of current research in planning and qualitative physics. Hendrix's extension of the STRIPS formalism includes representation of continuous change (using real values for quantities) and concurrent actions. The central component of the system (which is a set of data structures and a skeleton of a simulation program rather than a logical formalism) is the process monitor. This module continuously attempts to identify "active processes" and compute their effects.

Rieger (1976) also addressed the issue of continuous change in his proposal of commonsense algorithms (1976). Among the many notions he considered are continuous causality and gated causal rules. His system too is couched in terms of data structures and algorithms, and McDermott (1982a) pointed out some of the difficulties in assigning meaning to the symbols in Rieger's system.

Another system that is primarily a serious attempt at incorporating one of the more sophisticated logics into a computer program is Dean's (1986) Time Map Managing System. The system, which can be viewed as a temporal reason-maintenance system, was designed to be used as part of an automated planner. It is loosely constructed around McDermott's temporal logic. A earlier attempt along similar, although more modest, lines is Vilain's (1982) system, a time-maintenance system based on a formalism that is similar to Allen's.

It is worth pointing out that the more "applied" work on TR has not been based to any great extent on the representational research described earlier. This can be viewed as evidence that the foundations of the applied work are shaky, or that the logic-level research has not yet become sophisticated enough to be of real value, or both.

WORK OUTSIDE AI

Both AI and theoretical computer science owe an intellectual debt to philosophy, where time, action, and causation have been studied for many years. Although it is not possible here to properly cover the relevant philosophical literature, two good expositions of the work done on causation are available (Mackey, 1974; Sosa, 1975). Other investigations into the nature of actions have been published (Goldman, 1970; Davidson, 1967).

Work done in formal philosophy on the logic of time is particularly relevant. It was mentioned in the introduction that one possibility for representing temporal information is to have time implicit in the interpretation of the formulas. The way this option is exercised is through modal logic, to which a modern introduction is Chellas (1980). The formulas of the logic are augmented by one or more modal operators; if P is a wff and $\bigcirc$ is a (unary) modal operator, then $\bigcirc P$ is a wff too. In the basic modal logic there is a single modal operator $\square$, called "box" and pronounced "necessarily." Its dual operator $\diamond$, called "diamond" and pronounced "possibly," is defined by $\diamond P \equiv \neg \square \neg P$. The widely accepted semantics for the resulting logic are possible world semantics introduced by Kripke (1963). When applied to temporal logic, possible worlds are equated with time points, and the modal operators are usually some variant of the following.

FP: p is true in some future time point.
GP: p is true in all future time points.
PP: p is true in some past time point.
HP: p is true in all past time points.

The outstanding feature of these systems is the indexicality of time: formulas are interpreted with respect to a time point (usually called now) and may contain reference to other time points through use of the modal operators. Thus if p is taken to mean "it is raining," the formula $\neg p \supset G \neg p$ means "if it isn't raining now then it never will." From this logic a more traditional modal logic can be derived such as S4, for example by defining $\square p$ to be $p \wedge Gp$. (The other well-known construction is define $\square p$ to be H$p \wedge p \wedge Gp$.)

Prior (1967) is the philosopher widely credited for first applying the principles of modal logic to temporal logic. He explored various possible properties of time (linearity, future branching, circularity, additivity, having a metric defined on it) and related the resulting logics to known modal systems. Rescher and Urquhart (1971) did the same, employing more conventional notation and using more recent results from logic. In particular, they discussed decision procedures based on the semantic tableau method. The most recent comprehensive study of temporal logics appears in a book by van Benthem (1983). He conveniently divides the discussion into the structure of time on the one hand and the nature of temporal assertions on the other. In each part he considers two cases: basing the logic on points and basing the logic on intervals, the latter possibility having recently gained currency in philosophy. As was said earlier, the philosophical literature on time is very rich; these references are merely initial pointers to it.

In theoretical computer science there has been considerable interest in TR, although until recently there was no overlap between that work and TR in AI. Pnueli (1977, 1979) was the first in computer science to apply modal temporal logic to program verification. There are several variants of modal temporal logic, stemming from different models of time (discrete or continuous, linear or branching) and different choices of modal operators (Emerson and Halpern, 1983). Discreteness is usually assumed, and "time points" correspond to the instants when the program interpreter is about to execute the next command. The modal operator $\bigcirc$ is the "next-state" operator: $\bigcirc P$ is true if and only if P is true the next time the interpreter is about to execute a command. Using the logic, various properties can be expressed very concisely, such as termination, freedom from deadlock, fair execution, and more (Manna and Pnueli, 1981). Temporal logic has been the framework in which much research on concurrent computation was done (Gabbay and co-workers, 1980).

Dynamic logic, first introduced by Pratt (1976) in conjunction with Moore, is the other major area of TR in theoretical computer science, and it too is geared toward reasoning about computer programs and digital devices. Rather than the usual modal operator of temporal logic, dynamic logic associates modal operators with each program. If α is a (nondeterministic) program, then $\langle \alpha \rangle P$ means that P holds after some possible execution of α. Similarly, $[\alpha]P$ means that P holds after all possible executions of α. For a systematic treatment of dynamic logic, from so-called simple dynamic logic to the full-fledged first-order one, see Harel (1979).

Both dynamic logic and temporal logic interpret statements over time points. Because in AI statements are often encountered that refer to time intervals rather than time points ("the robot performed the task," "I solved the problem"), neither formalism is completely adequate for AI. There have been several extensions of these formalisms to time intervals. For example, dynamic logic was generalized to process logic (Pratt, 1979; Harel and co-workers, 1982). In process logic formulas are interpreted over paths, or sequences of discrete time points. In Harel and co-workers' (1982) version, the two modal operators (in addition to the ones introduced by dynamic logic) are F ("first") and SUF (roughly, "until"). $S_1, \ldots, S_n \models F\ p$ iff $S_1 \models p$. $S_1, \ldots, S_n \models p$ SUF q iff, for some j, $S_i, \ldots, S_n \models p$ for all i, $0 < i < j$, and $S_j, \ldots, S_n \models q$.

Interval temporal logic is a similar formalism, introduced by Moszkowski (1983) in conjunction with Halpern and Manna, which was applied to reasoning about digital devices. There are several other logics of time intervals, including a proposal by Halpern and Shoham (1986). This logic, which extends point-based temporal logic in a way that is analogous to the way process logic generalizes dynamic logic, is one of few temporal logics in computer science (whether point-based or interval-based) that are not committed to the discrete view of time.

It was mentioned at the beginning that to date neither temporal logic nor dynamic logic have had much influence on AI. Some exceptions, however, can be found (Fusaoka and co-workers, 1983; Moszkowski, 1985; Shoham, 1986; Mays, 1983; Georgeff and Lansky, 1985).

BIBLIOGRAPHY

J. F. Allen, "Towards a General Theory of Action and Time," *Artif. Intell.* **23**(2), 123–154 (July 1984).

B. F. Chellas, *Modal Logic,* Cambridge University Press, Cambridge, UK, 1980.

D. Davidson, "The Logical Form of Action Sentences," in N. Rescher, ed., *The Logic of Decision and Action,* Pittsburgh University Press, Pittsburgh, Pa., 1967.

T. Dean, *Temporal Imagery: An Approach to Reasoning about Time for Planning and Problem Solving,* Ph.D. dissertation, Yale University, New Haven, Conn., 1986.

J. de Kleer, *Qualitative and Quantitative Reasoning in Classical Mechanics,* Technical Report 352, MIT Artificial Intelligence Lab, Cambridge, Mass., 1975.

J. de Kleer and L. Seely Brown, *A Qualitative Physics Based on Confluences,* Technical Report, Xerox PARC Intelligent Systems Laboratory, Palo Alto, Calif., Jan. 1984.

E. A. Emerson and J. Y. Halpern, "'Sometimes' and 'Not Never' Revisited: on Branching versus Linear Time," in *Proceedings of the Tenth ACM Symposium on Principles of Programming Languages,* 1983, pp. 127–140.

R. Fikes and N. J. Nilsson, "STRIPS: A New Approach to Application of Theorem Proving to Problem Solving," *Artif. Intell.* **2**, 189–208 (1971).

K. D. Forbus, *Qualitative Process Theory,* Ph.D. dissertation, Artificial Intelligence Laboratory, MIT, Cambridge, Mass., 1984.

A. Fusaoka, H. Seki, and K. Takahashi, "A Description and Reasoning of Plant Controllers in Temporal Logic," in *Proceedings of the Eighth IJCAI,* Karlsruhe, FRG, Morgan-Kaufmann, San Mateo, Calif., 1983, pp. 405–408.

D. Gabbay and co-workers, "On the Temporal Analysis of Fairness" in *Proceedings of the Seventh ACM Symposium on Principles of Programming Languages,* 1980, pp. 163–173.

M. P. Georgeff and A. L. Lansky, "A Procedural Logic," in *Proceedings of the Ninth IJCAI,* Los Angeles, Calif., Morgan-Kaufmann, San Mateo, Calif., 1985, pp. 516–523.

A. Goldman, A *Theory of Human Action,* Princeton University Press, Princeton, N.J., 1970.

J. Y. Halpern and Y. Shoham, *A Propositional Modal Logic of Time Intervals, Logic in Computer Science,* Springer-Verlag, New York, June 1986.

D. Harel, "First-Order Dynamic Logic," in Goos and Hartmanis, eds., *Lecture Notes in Computer Science,* Vol. 68, Springer-Verlag, New York, 1979.

D. Harel, D. Kozen, and R. Parikh, "Process Logic: Expressiveness, Decidability, Completeness," *JCSS* **25**(2), 145–180 (Oct. 1982).

P. J. Hayes, "The Naive Physics Manifesto," in J. R. Hobbs and R. C. Moore, eds., *Formal Theories of the Commonsense World,* Ablex, Norwood, N.J., 1984.

P. J. Hayes, "Naive Physics 11: Ontology for Liquids," in J. R. Hobbs and R. C. Moore, eds., *Formal Theories of the Commonsense World,* Ablex, Norwood, N.J., 1984b.

G. G. Hendrix, "Modeling Simultaneous Actions and Continuous Processes," *Artif. Intell.* **4**, 145–180 (1973).

S. Kripke, "Semantical Considerations on Modal Logic," *Acta Philos. Fenn.* **16**, 83–94 (1963).

B. Kuipers, "Commonsense Reasoning about Causality: Deriving Behavior from Structure," *Artif. Intell.* **24**(1), 169–203 (1984).

J. M. McCarthy and P. J. Hayes, "Some Philosophical Problems from the Standpoint of Artificial Intelligence," in *Readings in Artificial Intelligence,* Tioga, Palo Alto, Calif., 1981, pp. 431–450.

D. V. McDermott, "Planning and Acting," *Cogn. Sci.* **2**(2), 71–109 (1978).

D. V. McDermott, "A Temporal Logic for Reasoning about Processes and Plans," *Cogn. Sci.* **6**, 101–155 (1982a).

D. V. McDermott, "Nonmonotonic Logic II: Nonmonotonic Modal Theories," *JACM,* **29**(1), 33–57 (1982b).

D. V. McDermott, "Reasoning about Plans," in J. R. Hobbs and R. C. Moore, eds., *Formal Theories of the Commonsense World,* Ablex, Norwood, N.J., 1984.

J. L. Mackey, *The Cement of the Universe: a Study of Causation,* Oxford University Press, Oxford, UK, 1974.

Z. Manna and A. Pneuli, *Verification of Concurrent Programs: Temporal Proof Principles,* Technical Report, Weizmann Institute, Department of Applied Mathematics, Rehovot, Israel, Sept. 1981.

E. Mays, "A Modal Temporal Logic for Reasoning about Change," in *Proceedings of the Annual Conference of the Association for Computational Linguistics,* Cambridge, Mass., June 1983.

B. C. Moszkowski, *Reasoning about Digital Circuits,* Ph.D. dissertation, Stanford, University, Stanford, Calif., July 1983.

B. C. Moszkowski, *Executing Temporal Logic Programs,* Technical Report **71**, University of Cambridge, Cambridge, UK, Aug. 1985.

A. Pneuli, "A Temporal Logic of Programs," in *Proceedings of the Eighteenth FOCS,* IEEE, Oct. 1977, pp. 46–57.

A. Pneuli, "The Temporal Semantics of Programs," *Theor. Comput. Sci.* **13**, 45–60 (1979).

V. R. Pratt, "Semantical Considerations on Floyd-Hoare Logic," in *Proceedings of the Seventeenth FOCS,* IEEE, Oct. 1976, pp. 109–121.

V. R. Pratt, "Process Logic," *Proceedings of the Sixth POPL,* ACM, Jan. 1979, pp. 93–100.

A. N. Prior, *Past, Present, and Future*, Clarendon Press, Oxford, UK, 1967.

N. Rescher and A. Urquhart, *Temporal Logic*, Springer-Verlag, New York, 1971.

C. Rieger, "An Organization of Knowledge for Problem Solving and Language Comprehension," *Artif. Intell.* **7** (1976).

Y. Shoham, *Reasoning about Change: Time and Causation from the Standpoint of Artificial Intelligence*, Ph.D. dissertation, Yale University, New Haven, Conn., 1986.

R. Simmons, "The Use of Qualitative and Quantitative Simulations," in *Proceedings of the Third National Conference on Artificial Intelligence,* Washington, D.C., AAAI, Menlo Park, Calif., 1983.

E. Sosa, *Causation and Conditionals*, Oxford University Press, Oxford, UK, 1975.

J. F. A. K. van Benthem, *The Logic of Time*, Reidel, Dordrecht, 1983.

M. B. Vilain, "A System for Reasoning about Time," in *Proceedings of the Second National Conference on Artificial Intelligence,* Pittsburgh, Pa., AAAI, Menlo Park, Calif., 1982, pp. 197–201.

R. Wilenskey, *Planning and Understanding*, Addison-Wesley Publishing Co., Inc., Reading, Mass., 1983.

Y. SHOHAM
D. V. MCDERMOTT
Yale University

RECOVERY. See VISUAL RECOVERY.

RECURSION

In this entry recursion is just a self-referential feature for procedures (and similar constructs) in certain programming languages. It was first available in LISP (qv) (McCarthy and co-workers, 1962), the principal systems implementation language for AI, and is available in most modern programming languages; for example, Pascal (Wirth, 1976), Logo (qv) (Harvey, 1985), Ada (Wiener and Sincovec, 1983), and Modula 2 (Ogilvie, 1985). Rogers (1987) and Manna (1974) contain fine mathematical treatments of recursion's connections to mathematical recursive (or inductive) definitions, the subtleties of assigning formal semantics to recursion, and the use of proofs by mathematical induction to verify correctness of recursive procedures. Shapiro (1986) is an excellent introduction to programming in LISP that effectively teaches one how to think recursively.

Essentially, recursion simply allows the instructions of a computer procedure to invoke the procedure itself. This brings up questions as to how it is possible to implement a thing like that and why anyone would want to use it. Suppose such a feature is allowed in computer procedures; the entry sketches how it is actually implemented. First, the usefulness of recursion is motivated by presentation of a simple, but illustrative example.

Some programming tasks create headaches for the programmer by ostensibly requiring that he or she devise methods to handle tedious "bookkeeping" subtasks that are subsidiary to the main tasks. Many times in such situations recursion can be used to free the programmer's mind of such unpleasant details; the details are handled instead by the computer implementation of recursion. Recursion in these cases enables the human programmer to produce succinct, conceptually clean programs that are easy to understand and verify as being correct.

Sometimes in solving problems the intelligent thing to do, artificially or otherwise, is to systematically consider all the possibilities in a given situation. This can take the form of exhaustively and systematically searching some, perhaps complicated, structure (see SEARCH). Two examples are searching a maze for desirable objects and searching a game tree (qv) for good moves. It is difficult in programming such searches to devise correct, clear strategies for the program to keep track of where it has already searched and where it still needs to go.

Here is an example. Imagine wanting to employ a programmable, electronic monkey to collect all the bananas in any "tree" of a certain type. A picture of the type of tree is presented in the tree-shaped diagram of Figure 1. This figure consists of dots and lines. The dots are called nodes. The bottom node in such a tree is called the root. For example, node 1 is the root of the tree pictured in Figure 1. Branching upward from each node are either two lines leading to two respective nodes or no lines leading to nodes. The entire tree is finite. The tree pictured in Figure 1 has 15 nodes that are numbered to facilitate some of the exposition. Assume that any such tree has bananas only at its nodes. These assumptions as to the type of tree to be considered are merely to simplify the problem. The monkey is initially placed on the root of a tree and is capable of understanding and performing the following primitive tests and instructions that have obvious corresponding meanings. The tests are: "bananas_present_at_current_node" and "there_is_a_node_above." The instructions are: "pick_up_bananas_present_at_current_node," "climb_up_one_node_to_the_left," "climb_up_one_node_to_the_right," and "climb_down_one_node." Assume the monkey can be programmed with a block-structured lan-

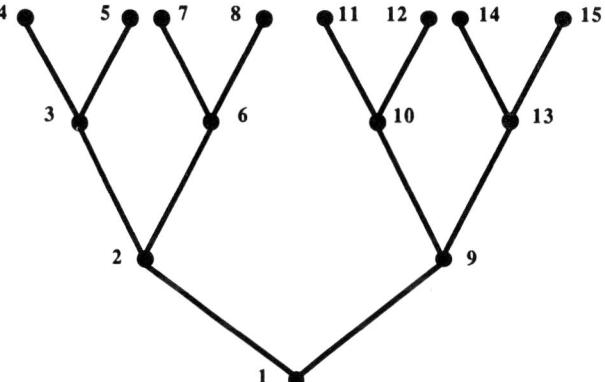

Figure 1. A tree is comprised of a root (*1*), nodes, and branches, and is finite.

guage (as in the procedure "collect_bananas" given later) that allows recursion in procedures. The task is to program the monkey to gather all the bananas in any tree (of the type desired) if it is placed on the root of that tree. The monkey must also return to the root of the tree when it has finished gathering bananas. The problem is to make sure the monkey systematically traverses the tree without getting lost or missing any nodes.

Here is a crucial observation about the trees that makes a solution using recursion possible. Pick any node in one of the trees. That node together with the nodes and lines connected above it constitutes a tree itself. For example, if node 2 in the tree pictured in Figure 1 is selected, the connected substructure of the tree having nodes 2, 3, 4, 5, 6, 7, and 8 is itself another tree with root node 2. So is the substructure having nodes 6, 7, and 8 (the root is 6), as is the substructure consisting only of node 8 (the root is 8). Hence, from the point of view of the monkey, if it is sitting at node 6, it is ready to explore the subtree with nodes 6, 7, and 8. The following procedure, called "collect_bananas," accomplishes the programming task. The instruction "climb_down_one_node," used twice, is to reposition the monkey after it has completed a subtree and ensure that the monkey finishes an invoking of "collect_bananas" at whatever node it was on when that invoking began.

```
procedure collect_bananas:
    begin
        if bananas_present_at_current_node
            then pick_up_bananas_present_at_current_node;
        if there_is_a_node_above
            then
                begin
                    climb_up_one_node_to_the_left;
                    collect_bananas;
                    climb_down_one_node;
                    climb_up_one_node_to_the_right;
                    collect_bananas;
                    climb_down_one_node
                end
    end
```

This procedure is recursive because it invokes itself at two points inside the then part of the second if–then. It is a problem for the monkey's computer to keep track of which invoking of the procedure it is currently working on and which it needs to get back to; with recursion this keeping-track is done by the computer, not the programmer. This computer bookkeeping of invokings prevents the programmer from having to devise an intricate bookkeeping algorithm for the task being programmed. Essentially, bookkeeping is handled once to implement recursion in the programming language, and then it does not have to be handled for other tasks.

If the sequence of invokings of "collect_bananas" is carefully traced for the example tree pictured in Figure 1, it will be seen that the instruction

if bananas_present_at_current_node
    then pick_up_bananas_present_at_current_node

is executed at the nodes of that tree in the numbered order of its nodes.

Recursion is nice for the programmer, but there is a cost of computational resources in its execution, ie, the cost of the computer's bookkeeping to keep track of the invokings. On the one hand, for some tasks it is hard to see how to proceed without recursion. For example, it is difficult to produce and verify the correctness of an algorithmic solution to the famous Tower of Hanoi Puzzle (Cooper and Clancy, 1985) that does not employ recursion; however, the standard recursive solution is exquisite in its simplicity (Cooper and Clancy, 1985). On the other hand, the extra cost can be essentially eliminated in some commonly occurring special cases of recursion such as tail recursion. Tail recursion occurs when the recursive calls always occur at the end (or tail) of the procedure and can always be implemented with ordinary iterative loops. Wirth (1976) has a nice discussion of these cases and advice on when to use iteration rather than recursion.

A data structure called the stack is usually employed to implement the general cases of recursion for a programming language. The nitty-gritty details of how to do this for Algol, eg, may be found in Randell and Russell (1964). The general idea of how to do it by hand is sketched for simple cases; the computer implementations merely code an efficient, fleshed out version of the description.

To keep track by hand of recursive calls when executing a procedure such as "collect_bananas," it suffices to do the following:

1. Each time an invoking of the procedure recursively calls the procedure itself, put a blank sheet of paper on a stack of sheets on a table (the first sheet just goes directly on the table) and write on that sheet a succinct description of exactly where you were in the invoking of the procedure that made that self-call.
2. Invoke the self-call.
3. When any procedure call is finished, pull the sheet (if any) that is on the top of the stack and use that sheet to figure out what to do next in the execution of the procedure call that invoked the just-finished procedure call.
4. If an invoking finishes and there are no sheets on the stack, you are done.

The general case is more complicated. For example, some recursive procedures call other procedures that in turn call them; many recursive procedures have parameters whose values also have to be kept account of in the stack.

BIBLIOGRAPHY

D. Cooper and M. Clancy, *Oh! Pascal!,* 2nd ed., Norton, New York, 1985.

B. Harvey, *Computer Science Logo Style,* Vol. 1, *Intermediate Programming,* MIT Press, Cambridge, Mass., 1985.

Z. Manna, *Mathematical Theory of Computation,* McGraw-Hill, New York, 1974.

M. McCarthy and co-workers, *Lisp 1.5 Programmers Manual,* MIT Press, Cambridge, Mass., 1962.

J. Ogilvie, *Modula-2 Programming,* McGraw-Hill, New York, 1985.

H. Rogers, *Theory of Recursive Functions and Effective Computability,* McGraw-Hill, New York, 1967; reprinted, MIT Press, Cambridge, Mass., 1987.

B. Randell and L. Russell, *Algol 60 Implementation: Translation and Use of Algol 60 Programs by Computers,* Academic Press, New York, 1964.

S. Shapiro, *Lisp: An Interactive Approach,* Computer Science Press, Rockville, Md., 1986.

R. Wiener and R. Sincovec, *Programming in Ada,* Wiley, New York, 1983.

N. Wirth, *Algorithms + Data Structures = Programs,* Prentice Hall, Englewood Cliffs, NJ, 1976.

J. CASE
University of Delaware

REDUCE 3

REDUCE 3 is an interactive software system designed for general mathematical computations of interest to physicists, mathematicians and engineers. It is described in several books, including G. Rayna, *REDUCE Software for Algebraic Computation,* Springer-Verlag, New York, 1987. The present version includes facilities for exact integer and arbitrary precision real arithmetic, and the evaluation, substitution, expansion, simplification, factorization, differentiation and integration of polynomials, rational functions and general algebraic expressions. Built-in matrix algebra includes evaluation of determinants and inverses, resultants and eigenvalues. The solution of equations with algebraic coefficients is also supported. Facilities for calculations of interest to high energy physicists, including Dirac gamma matrix algebra, are also provided.

A number of user-programmable switches control the simplification process (for example, permitting or inhibiting full expansion of expressions, and the cancellation of greatest common divisors), and provide a variety of output formats, by grouping or separating parts of expressions. Of special interest is an option to output expressions in a FORTRAN format for direct use in floating-point computations. In addition to these specific capabilities, the program contains a powerful general-purpose pattern matching facility to permit the introduction of user-defined simplification rules and side relations, and to perform algebraic computations not provided by the built-in routines.

The REDUCE language provides block structures, control structures such as FOR and WHILE, and procedure definition, and a variety of algebraic and symbolic data types. The symbolic capability of the language is complete enough to enable the entire program to be written in its own source language. The program currently uses Standard LISP as an intermediate language.

The system has been applied to a variety of problems in many different research areas, including quantum electrodynamics and quantum chromodynamics, electrical network analysis, plasma physics, celestial mechanics, general relativity, numerical analysis and a variety of engineering problems such as turbine and ship hull design.

A. C. HEARN
RAND

REF-ARF

REF-ARF is a heuristic problem-solving system completed in 1970 by Fikes at Carnegie Mellon University. The system accepts problems stated in REF, a nondeterministic programming language, and invokes ARF, a heuristic problem solver, to find solutions. ARF contains a symbolic interpreter for nondeterministic programs that conducts a heuristic search through the space defined by the choice points in the program. The interpreter discovers constraints that must hold on paths through the program and employs constraint satisfaction techniques to find paths that are solutions and to eliminate those that are inconsistent. [See R. E. Fikes, "REF-ARF: A System for Solving Problems Stated as Procedures," *Artif. Intell.* **1,** 27–120 (1970).]

RICHARD FIKES
Stanford University

RESOLUTION, BINARY

Binary resolution (J. Robinson, 1965b), often referred to as resolution, is a formal inference rule whose use permits computer programs to "reason logically". Specifically, as the examples in the next sections show, a computer program relying on resolution and related inference rules can find new facts and new relationships that follow logically from given facts and relationships. The introduction of binary resolution (in 1963 at Argonne National Laboratory)—although preceded by a number of approaches to the automation of deductive reasoning—initiated a significant broadening of computer science and the use of computers. Indeed, the research stemming from a study of binary resolution eventually culminated in the formulation of far more powerful inference rules and sophisticated strategies to control their application (Wos, 1991, 1987). These inference rules and strategies form the basis of computer programs, called "automated reasoning programs", that now (in 1991) provide valuable assistance for various types of research and diverse applications. Of the reasoning programs currently in use, the program OTTER (Organized Techniques for Theorem-proving and Effective Research) is of particular interest (McCune, 1990). Its attractiveness rests with its portability, power, generality, and availability; near the end of this article, the focus is on OTTER and how one can obtain (without cost) this most interesting program.

Automated reasoning programs (Lusk and Overbeek, 1984; Smith, 1988; McCune, 1990) can be used to answer open questions from mathematics (Winker and Wos, 1978; Winker and co-workers, 1981; Winker, 1982) and logic

(Wos and co-workers, 1983; Wos and co-workers, 1984a; McCune and Wos, 1987; Wos and McCune, 1988), to design superior logic circuits (Wojciechowski and Wojcik, 1983), to validate existing circuit designs (Wojcik, 1983), and to verify various properties claimed for existing computer programs (Boyer and Moore, 1985). Were it not for the formulation of binary resolution and the research it spawned, such programs—and even the field of automated reasoning itself—might not exist today.

To provide a complete picture, the article begins with an informal treatment of how resolution works, followed by the formal definitions and properties of resolution and related inference rules. Since automated reasoning programs are not effective without the use of mechanisms to control the application of the inference rules, the focus then turns to strategy to restrict the reasoning and strategy to direct it. Various reasoning programs, with OTTER as the feature, and current applications are reviewed. However, before addressing the various topics, a comparison of a resolution-based approach with the approach that preceded it is presented.

INTRODUCTION AND HISTORICAL SIGNIFICANCE

By 1960, various logicians and mathematicians had expressed interest in the objective of using the computer to prove theorems from diverse areas of mathematics. Computer programs (Davis and Putnam, 1960; Gilmore, 1960; Prawitz and co-workers, 1960; Wang, 1960) had been implemented that could prove extremely simple theorems. The most popular approach at the time was to use a particular language of logic (discussed later) and rely on Herbrand instantiation (discussed later). Rather than deducing new facts and relationships from given statements, the Herbrand instantiation approach draws conclusions by merely substituting for the variables in the given statements to yield trivial consequences of them. In contrast, applications of resolution can yield new information, and hence the reasoning it affords is more substantial. With both Herbrand instantiation and resolution, the object is to consider some given statement corresponding to a purported theorem of the form "if P, then Q" and attempt to prove that the statement is in fact a theorem. With either approach, rather than the given statement, the statement actually considered corresponds to assuming P true and Q false. This choice is made because the approach seeks a "proof by contradiction".

For a brief illustration of the instantiation approach, a simple theorem from abstract algebra will suffice—an example, incidentally, that is beyond the power of those early theorem-proving programs that depend on instantiation. A favorite example from 1965 until this writing (in 1991) is the theorem "in a group, if the square of every element is the identity, then the group is commutative". Let the theorem be represented symbolically as "if P, then Q", where P consists of the set of axioms for a group together with the special hypothesis that the square of every element is the identity, and where Q is the conclusion that states that the group is commutative. The instantiation procedure begins by assuming the conclusion Q false, and therefore replaces Q with the denial or negation of the conclusion. In particular, it is assumed that (at least) two elements a and b exist such that the product ab is not equal to the product ba. The procedure next calls for the statements of P and those resulting from assuming Q false all to be represented in the "clause language" (Chang and Lee, 1973; Wos and co-workers, 1991). For example, the clause

$$\text{EQUAL}(\text{prod}(\text{prod}(x,y),z),\text{prod}(x,\text{prod}(y,z)))$$

is an acceptable way to express the associativity of product, $(xy)z = x(yz)$ for all x, y, and z. Let S denote the set of clauses that is thus produced. Then, by substituting (Herbrand) terms (discussed later) for the variables in the clauses in S, the procedure generates ever-expanding sets of variable-free clauses in search of a set that can be proved truth-functionally unsatisfiable. A set of variable-free clauses is "truth-functionally unsatisfiable" if the set evaluates to **false** for every consistent assignment of **true** or **false** to the elements that make up the clauses in the set. The basic result from logic (Herbrand, 1930, 1967) on which the procedure rests says that if the starting set S of clauses does in fact correspond to assuming an actual theorem false, then one of the variable-free sets of clauses considered by the instantiation procedure will be truth-functionally unsatisfiable, and conversely. (As shown later, resolution also relies on the same basic result.)

As it turns out, this procedure of considering ever-expanding sets obtained by Herbrand instantiation and then testing for truth-functional unsatisfiability has two undesirable properties. First, the sets of variable-free clauses become very large very early in the consideration, which in turn causes the test for unsatisfiability to become very cumbersome. Second, the generality that often contributes to efficiency in searching for a proof is lacking. In particular, the procedure must cope with many instances of a fact rather than coping with the fact itself. For example, if the purported theorem under investigation were about arithmetic, then the procedure under discussion might be forced to consider

$$0 + a = a$$
$$0 + (a + a) = (a + a)$$
$$0 + -a = -a$$
$$\cdot$$
$$\cdot$$
$$\cdot$$

rather than coping with $0 + x = x$ (for all x) which captures the preceding instances as trivial corollaries.

Computer programs employing this Herbrand instantiation procedure are not able to prove very interesting theorems. In addition to offering only the most elementary type of reasoning, they typically suffer from employing a level-saturation search for the desired unsatisfiable set. (The search is called level saturation because all Herbrand terms of level 1 are first considered for substitution, then those of level 2, and so on.)

By formulating the inference rule of binary resolution, Robinson (J. 1965b) provided an important advance over the Herbrand instantiation approach. What he did, directly and indirectly, was provide a means for computers to reason far more effectively than was previously possible. Resolution focuses on general statements rather than on trivial instances of them. In addition, its use avoids truth-functional analysis. Finally, and perhaps most important, Robinson's work led to the formulation of more effective inference rules (J. Robinson, 1965a; Slagle, 1967; G. Robinson and Wos, 1969; Loveland, 1970; Luckham, 1970; Boyer, 1971; Kuehner, 1972; Henschen and Wos, 1974; McCharen and co-workers, 1976a; Wos and co-workers, 1984b) and to the discovery of powerful strategies (Wos and co-workers, 1964a, 1965; McCharen and co-workers, 1976a) to control the application of inference rules. Such research was prompted by the observation that an approach relying solely on binary resolution is simply not effective for solving most problems. Its application yields too many conclusions, each representing too small a step of reasoning. The need for inference rules that take larger reasoning steps and for strategies to control the reasoning can easily be established with experimentation (McCharen and co-workers, 1976b). The significance of the research triggered by the formulation of resolution is amply demonstrated by the successes achieved with a number of automated reasoning programs (Wos and co-workers, 1964a; Guard and co-workers, 1969; Allen and Luckham, 1970; Bledsoe and Bruell, 1974; Lusk and Overbeek, 1984; Smith, 1988; McCune, 1990) which are based on the results of that research. (Logic programming, and especially Prolog, can be traced to the formulation of resolution; see LOGIC PROGRAMMING.) The fact that the successes range from answering previously open questions (Winker and Wos, 1978; Winker and co-workers, 1981; Winker, 1982; Wos and co-workers, 1983, 1991; McCune and Wos, 1987; Wos and McCune, 1988) to designing superior logic circuits (Wojciechowski and Wojcik, 1983) establishes that resolution-based reasoning programs are useful in a number of unrelated areas.

From the historical perspective, the research that was well under way by 1960 caused an entire field to come into existence. Robinson's contribution of resolution represented an important step forward for that field. (Although the actual paper on resolution was not published until 1965, Robinson formulated the rule in 1963.) The objective of "proving theorems" with a computer program gave the name to the field at the time. It was first called "mechanical theorem proving", then "automatic theorem proving", and finally by 1968 "automated theorem proving" (see THEOREM PROVING). In 1980, noting that, in addition to finding proofs, the uses of such computer programs include finding models and counterexamples (Winker, 1982), testing hypotheses, and designing circuits, the name "automated reasoning" (Wos and co-workers, 1991) was introduced for the expanded field. Because of the excitement and interest engendered by this new field of automated reasoning, and because resolution plays such a vital role, resolution-based reasoning programs will continue to be the focus of attention for the foreseeable future.

INFORMAL TREATMENT OF BINARY RESOLUTION

To gain a feeling for the actions of binary resolution, recall how both modus ponens and syllogism work. Modus ponens applied to the (variable-free) statements

Nan is female

and

Nan is **not** female **or** Nan is **not** male

yields

Nan is **not** male

as the conclusion. Syllogism applied to the (variable-free) statements

Nan is French **or** Nan is Irish

and

Nan is **not** Irish **or** Nan is Spanish

yields

Nan is French **or** Nan is Spanish

as the conclusion. If binary resolution is applied to either of the two examples, where the examples are expressed in the clause language, then the conclusions just cited will also be drawn. For example, if the clauses

FEMALE(Nan)
¬FEMALE(Nan) | ¬MALE(Nan)

are considered simultaneously by resolution, then the clause

¬MALE(Nan)

is obtained as the logical conclusion, where "¬" is read as **not** and "|" is read as **or**. The conclusion is obtained by "canceling" FEMALE(Nan) in the first clause with ¬FEMALE(Nan) in the second.

In addition to "canceling" part of one clause against part of another, binary resolution relies on "substituting" expressions for variables within a clause. For example, where the symbol x is a variable, the clause

¬FEMALE(x) | ¬MALE(x)

says that "x is **not** female **or** x is **not** male" for (implicitly) all x. If binary resolution considers this clause simultaneously with the earlier clause

FEMALE(Nan)

again the conclusion is

¬MALE(Nan)

stating that Nan is **not** male. In effect, the conclusion is obtained by first substituting Nan for the variable x to obtain the temporary clause

¬FEMALE(Nan) | ¬MALE(Nan)

and then canceling as before.

Although the actions of binary resolution for this last example have been explained as a two-step process, in reality the inference rule has the useful property of drawing conclusions in one step without generating such temporary clauses. (The name "binary resolution" suggests the nature of the inference rule. First, the rule always simultaneously considers two clauses from which to attempt to draw a conclusion, hence "binary". Second, the rule attempts to resolve the question of what is the maximum common ground covered by obvious consequences of the two clauses, hence "resolution".) In the first of the two examples of applying binary resolution, no effort is required to find the common ground; no substitution for variables is necessary to permit an obvious cancellation. In the second example, however, to find the common ground requires substituting Nan for the variable x in the second clause.

A more important property of resolution is the generality of the conclusions yielded by its application. For example, from the clauses

¬HASAJOB(x,nurse) | MALE(x)
(for all x, x is **not** a nurse **or** x is male)
¬FEMALE(y) | ¬MALE(y)
(for all y, y is **not** female **or** y is **not** male)

binary resolution yields the clause

¬HASAJOB(x,nurse) | ¬FEMALE(x)
(for all x, x is **not** a nurse **or** x is **not** female)

as the conclusion. It does not yield

¬HASAJOB(Kim,nurse) | ¬FEMALE(Kim)
(Kim is **not** a nurse **or** Kim is **not** female)

which also follows logically from the two given clauses. This last conclusion simply lacks the generality that is so vital to the effectiveness of the various automated reasoning programs now in use.

In addition to the "generality" property, binary resolution has a vital logical property. The inference rule is "sound"—the conclusions drawn with it follow inevitably from the two statements to which it is applied. Thus the arguments produced by relying solely on resolution are flawless; any flawed piece of information must come from a faulty hypothesis. To complement the property of soundness, a desirable property possessed by some inference rules (or some sets of inference rules) is that of "refutation completeness". If an inference rule is refutation complete, then, for any set of clauses corresponding to the denial (or negation) of a theorem, there exists a procedure employing that inference rule that guarantees to find a proof of the inconsistency of that set eventually. Binary resolution, if augmented by the inference rule of "factoring" (discussed later), has that property.

Unfortunately, possession of the properties of soundness and refutation completeness does not imply that the inference rule (or set of inference rules) is effective. In fact, binary resolution (even if augmented with factoring) is not effective in most problem domains. The inference rule usually yields too many conclusions, each representing too small a step of reasoning. Nevertheless, programs employing binary resolution and factoring as their sole inference rules are far superior to those relying on Herbrand instantiation. Resolution-based programs do actually "reason" rather than merely drawing trivial conclusions by instantiating (substituting for variables) the given information. In particular, they deduce new facts and new relationships from existing ones. Since the information deduced with resolution exhibits the generality property discussed earlier, the formulation of resolution represents an important step forward in the quest for computer programs that could and would find proofs of purported theorems. That quest in fact culminated in the implementation of very useful programs (discussed later). Those programs rely on research that can be directly traced to the discovery of binary resolution. In particular, the study of binary resolution led to the formulation of far more effective inference rules and the discovery of powerful strategies for controlling the inference rules.

FORMAL TREATMENT OF BINARY RESOLUTION AND RELATED INFERENCE RULES

Binary resolution and related inference rules possess important logical properties. These properties contribute to the impetus for using such formal rules. Not only are the arguments produced with such rules logically sound, but, when certain conditions are met, their use guarantees that a "proof by contradiction" can be found. In order to give the precise conditions and discuss "proof by contradiction", certain theorems from logic and various formal definitions are required. Since inference rules are designed to draw conclusions—to operate on statements to produce other statements—a discussion of a language sufficient for representing many problems is also needed.

Representation

The most commonly used language for representing information when using binary resolution and related inference rules is the "clause language" (Chang and Lee, 1973; Wos and co-workers, 1991), a language directly descended from the pure first-order predicate calculus. The following definitions briefly formalize the clause language.

Definitions. A "term" is a constant, a variable, or an n-ary function symbol followed by n arguments all of which are terms.

Definition. An "atom" is an n-ary predicate symbol followed by n arguments all of which are terms.

Definition. A "literal" is an atom or the negation of an atom.

Definition. A "clause" is a finite disjunction of zero or more distinct literals. All variables in a clause are (implicitly) universally quantified, and their scope is just the clause in which they occur.

Definition. A "clause set" is the (implicit) conjunction of a set of clauses.

For example, a clause set might consist of the following three clauses.

¬FEMALE(x) | ¬MALE(x)
FEMALE(x) | MALE(x)
¬HASAJOB(x,nurse) | MALE(x)

An implicit logical **and** exists between the first and second clauses and also between the second and third. Although the variable x occurs in all three clauses, replacing x by the variable y in the second and replacing x by the variable z in the third produces a logically equivalent set of clauses. (Clauses are treated as having no variables in common.) The literal ¬MALE(x) is the negation of the atom MALE(x), which itself is a literal.

Statements can be represented in the clause language by first representing them (where possible) with a formula in the first-order predicate calculus and then transforming them with a well-known procedure (Chang and Lee, 1973). The procedure first transforms a formula to prenex normal form and then to conjunctive normal form and finally removes each existentially quantified variable by instead employing an appropriate function or constant. The functions and constants that are employed are called "Skolem functions" (Davis and Putnam, 1960). The remaining quantifiers are then dropped to yield the set of clauses. Although the procedure does not necessarily produce a logically equivalent formula, the needed logical properties for proof finding are preserved (discussed later). For example, the clause

$$\text{EQUAL}(\text{sum}(y,\text{minus}(y)),0)$$

is an acceptable translation of the statement "there exists z such that for all y there exists x such that the sum of y and x equals z". This clause employs the Skolem function minus and the Skolem constant (function of no variables) 0, and, although not logically equivalent to the formula from which it is obtained, it conveys the required meaning. The clause language does not accept statements employing such logical operators as **if-then** and **equivalent**, but instead relies on transformations that replace such statements with others that are logically equivalent to them and that use **not**, **or**, and (implicitly) **and**.

Proof Finding

The most common use of a resolution-based computer program is to find a proof of some purported theorem. The typical proof found by such a program is a "proof by contradiction". To seek such a proof, a formula in the first-order predicate calculus is written (if possible) that corresponds to assuming the purported theorem false. As discussed earlier, the formula is then transformed into a corresponding set of clauses. The definitions and theorems of this section establish that, if the first-order formula does in fact represent the denial (or negation) of a theorem, then the resulting set of clauses possesses the needed logical properties to permit a proof by contradiction to be found. Before turning to the precise formalism, a trivial example given earlier will serve as an illustration.

The specific fact that Nan is female and the general fact that everyone is **not** female or **not** male together obviously imply that Nan is **not** male. If the goal were to have a reasoning program find a proof of this obvious conclusion, the approach calls for assuming the conclusion false. From the corresponding clauses

1. FEMALE(Nan)
2. ¬FEMALE(x) | ¬MALE(x)
3. MALE(Nan)

a one-step proof can easily be obtained. By applying binary resolution to clauses 2 and 3, clause 4

4. ¬FEMALE(Nan)

is deduced, which obviously contradicts clause 1. Clause 1 is the special hypothesis, clause 2 the only axiom, and clause 3 the denial (or negation) of the conclusion. With this simple example of a proof by contradiction in view, the formalism that justifies the underlying approach can now be given.

Definition. An "interpretation" of a variable-free set of clauses is a uniform assignment of either **true** or **false** to each of the literals in the clause set. The assignment must be consistent; if literal L is assigned the value **true**, then the negation of L must be assigned the value **false**.

Definition. A set of variable-free clauses is "truth-functionally satisfiable" if there exists an interpretation such that the conjunction of the clauses evaluates to **true**. A set of variable-free clauses is "truth-functionally unsatisfiable" if no interpretation exists that establishes the set to be truth-functionally satisfiable.

Definition. The "Herbrand universe" for a set S of clauses consists of all well-formed terms that can be composed from the function symbols and individual constants that are present in S. When no constants are present, the constant c is supplied.

Definition. An "Herbrand interpretation" of a set S of clauses is a consistent assignment of either **true** or **false** to each of the well-formed expressions that can be composed from the predicates of S and the terms from the Herbrand universe.

For the next definition, note that a set S of clauses, some of which may contain variables, can be evaluated to **true** or to **false** for a given Herbrand interpretation. Such an evaluation can be made by considering the full set of variable-free clauses obtainable by substituting terms from the Herbrand universe into the clauses in S. The full set is considered, for recall that the variables in a clause are (implicitly) assumed to mean "for all".

Definition. A set S of clauses is "satisfiable" if there exists an Herbrand interpretation of S for which S evaluates to **true**. A set S of clauses is "unsatisfiable" if no Herbrand interpretation exists that establishes the set to be satisfiable; in other words, S evaluates to **false** for every Herbrand interpretation.

The following definitions and theorem establish a much simpler criterion for determining the unsatisfiability of a set of clauses.

Definition. A "substitution" is a set of ordered pairs t_i/v_i, where the t_i are terms and the v_i are distinct variables. A substitution is applied to a clause by simultaneously replacing each v_i with the corresponding t_i.

Definition. The clause C' is an "instance" of the clause C if C' can be obtained from C by applying a substitution.

Definition. An instance C' of the clause C is "ground" if C' is variable-free.

Theorem. A set S of clauses is unsatisfiable if and only if there exists a finite set of (Herbrand) ground instances of S that is truth-functionally unsatisfiable (Herbrand, 1930, 1967; Chang and Lee, 1973; Wos and co-workers, 1991).

For example, the unsatisfiability of the set consisting of the clauses

$P(a,y) \mid P(b,y)$
$\neg P(x,c)$

can be established by considering the clauses

$P(a,c) \mid P(b,c)$
$\neg P(a,c)$
$\neg P(b,c)$

which are a truth-functionally unsatisfiable set of ground instances of the preceding set of two clauses. Note that there are two distinct instances of the second clause.

One final theorem is needed to justify the approach for finding proofs by relying on the use of the language of clauses.

Theorem. A formula of the first-order predicate calculus is unsatisfiable if and only if its representation in clause form is unsatisfiable (Chang and Lee, 1973).

Binary Resolution and Related Inference Rules

To define binary resolution, the following definitions are needed.

Definition. A "most general common instance" (MGCI), if one exists, of expressions E_1 and E_2 is an expression E such that E is an instance of both E_1 and E_2 and such that, if E' is an instance of both E_1 and E_2, then E' is an instance of E.

Definition. The literals L_1 and L_2 are said to "unify" if there exists a substitution that, when applied to both L_1 and L_2, produces L_1' and L_2' respectively such that $L_1' = L_2'$. The literals are then said to be "unifiable". A substitution that, when applied, yields an MGCI of two unifiable literals is called a "most general unifier" (MGU).

Definition. The inference rule "binary resolution" (J. Robinson, 1965b) yields the clause C from the clauses A and B (implicitly assumed to have no variables in common) when A contains the literal L_1, B contains the literal L_2, one of L_1 and L_2 is a positive and the other a negative literal, and (ignoring sign) L_1 and L_2 are unifiable. The clause C is obtained by finding an MGU of L_1 and L_2 (ignoring sign), applying the MGU to both A and B to yield A' and B' respectively, and forming the disjunction (without duplicate literals) of $A' - L_1'$ (A' minus a single occurrence of the literal L_1') and $B' - L_2'$. The clause C is termed a "resolvent" of A and B, and A and B are termed the "parents" of C.

For example, binary resolution applied to the two clauses

$\neg P(x) \mid Q(x,y)$
$P(a) \mid P(f(b,z))$

yields two clauses

$Q(a,y) \mid P(f(b,z))$
$Q(f(b,z),y) \mid P(a)$

as binary resolvents, depending on which literals are chosen in the parents, the first pair of clauses. On the other hand, binary resolution applied to the clauses

$Q(y,y)$
$\neg Q(x,f(x))$

yields no clauses. The two literals (ignoring sign) cannot be unified.

In order to be useful for proof finding, an inference rule should possess the logical properties of "soundness" and "refutation completeness".

Definition. An inference rule is "sound" if any clause deduced by applying the rule is a logical consequence of the clauses to which the rule is applied.

Theorem. Binary resolution is a sound inference rule (J. Robinson, 1965b).

To establish the unsatisfiability of a set of clauses, it is sufficient to deduce a contradiction from that set, which is why the property of refutation completeness is relevant. The following definitions characterize the notion of contradiction in the context of clause sets.

Definition. A clause with exactly one literal is called a "unit clause" (or simply a "unit").

Definition. Two clauses are termed "contradictory unit clauses" if each of the two clauses contains a single literal, if the two are opposite in sign, and if the two literals (ignoring sign) can be unified. When two such clauses have been obtained, "unit conflict" has been found.

Contradiction can also be defined in terms of the "empty clause", where the empty clause is the empty set of literals. The empty clause can be interpreted as having the value **false**. The connection between the two notions of contradiction is established by noting that the resolution of two conflicting units yields the empty clause. Given a set of clauses, a deduction of unit conflict (or of the empty clause) with sound rules of inference completes a proof by contradiction of the unsatisfiability of that set of clauses.

Definition. An inference rule (or set of inference rules) is "refutation complete" if for every unsatisfiable set of clauses there exists a procedure relying solely on that inference rule (or set of inference rules) such that a proof by contradiction can be obtained by using the procedure.

Although binary resolution is a sound inference rule, it is not by itself refutation complete. The following unsatisfiable set of two clauses is a counterexample to its refutation completeness.

$P(x) \mid P(y)$
$\neg P(x) \mid \neg P(y)$

All clauses that can be obtained by repeatedly applying binary resolution, starting with the two given clauses, contain exactly two literals. However, if binary resolution is employed together with the inference rule "factoring" (Wos and co-workers, 1964b), then the resulting set of inference rules is refutation complete.

Definition. The inference rule "factoring" yields the clause C' from the clause C when C contains two literals L_1 and L_2 that have the same sign and that can be unified. The clause C', called a "factor", is obtained by applying to C a most general unifier that unifies L_1 and L_2. In addition, all factors of factors of C are themselves factors of C and are said to be obtained by factoring.

For example, the previous two clauses have factors

$P(x)$

and

$\neg P(x)$

respectively, which conflict as units.

For another example, the clause

$P(f(y)) \mid \neg Q(f(y))$

is a factor of the clause

$P(x) \mid P(f(y)) \mid \neg Q(x)$

which can be seen by unifying the first two literals of the second clause.

Theorem. Factoring is a sound inference rule.

Theorem. The combination of binary resolution and factoring is refutation complete (J. Robinson, 1965b; Chang and Lee, 1973).

This theorem might suggest that there exists a decision procedure employing binary resolution and factoring—a procedure that will always correctly identify unsatisfiable and satisfiable sets of clauses. Unfortunately, such is not the case. In fact, no such procedure exists, regardless of which inference rules and strategies are employed. This deep and complex result is based on theorems of Church (1936) and Turing (1936). In particular, for any given algorithm, finite sets of clauses exist that are satisfiable, but for which the algorithm will be unable to establish that fact in a finite amount of time. This lack of a decision procedure is not critical, however, when the objective is to prove theorems (in contrast to *deciding* whether some statement *is* or *is not* a theorem). Indeed, since the corresponding objective is to prove that some given set of clauses is in fact unsatisfiable, the important considerations for an inference rule (or set of inference rules) are soundness, refutation completeness, and effectiveness.

Although using binary resolution is not effective for solving most problems, its formulation did lead to the discovery of other closely related and more effective inference rules.

Definition. The inference rule "hyperresolution" (J. Robinson, 1965a) yields the clause C by considering simultaneously the clause N and the clauses A_i. The clauses N and A_i are assumed pairwise to have no variables in common. For hyperresolution to apply, the clause N must contain at least one negative literal, and the clauses A_i must each contain only positive literals. If successful, hyperresolution yields a clause C containing only positive literals. The clause C is obtained by finding an MGU that (ignoring sign) simultaneously unifies one positive literal in each of the A_i with a distinct negative literal in N, applying the MGU to yield N' and A_i', and taking the disjunction of all literals in the A_i' and in N' that do not participate in the unification. The clause N is termed the "nucleus" and the clauses A_i the "satellites" for that application of hyperresolution. The clause C is termed a "hyperresolvent".

Hyperresolution applied to the 4 clauses

1. $\neg P(x,y) \mid \neg P(y,z) \mid \neg Q(z) \mid R(x,z)$
2. $P(a,x)$
3. $P(b,c)$
4. $Q(x) \mid S(x)$

yields

$R(a,c) \mid S(c)$

as a hyperresolvent by resolving clause 2 with the first literal of clause 1, clause 3 with the second literal, and clause 4 with the third literal.

Where the inference rule of hyperresolution focuses on the signs of the literals to be present in the conclusion,

"UR-resolution" (McCharen and co-workers, 1976a) focuses on the number of literals to be present. Similar to the definition of hyperresolution, the definition of UR-resolution (unit-resulting resolution) can be obtained by observing the following constraints. When the satellites are required to be (positive or negative) unit clauses and the nucleus is constrained to have exactly one more literal than the number of satellites and the conclusion is required to be a unit clause (positive or negative), the definition of UR-resolution is obtained. Other variations of binary resolution include unit resolution (Kuehner, 1972; Henschen and Wos, 1974), semantic resolution (Slagle, 1967), linear resolution (Loveland, 1970; Luckham, 1970), and lock resolution (Boyer, 1971).

None of the cited inference rules applies to that case in which the intention is to treat equality as "built in". To address that case, the inference rule "paramodulation" (G. Robinson and Wos, 1969) was formulated.

Definition. An "equality literal" is a literal whose predicate is to be interpreted as "equal". The inference rule "paramodulation" yields the clause C from the clauses A and B (implicitly assumed to have no variables in common) when A contains a positive equality literal K and B contains a term t that unifies with one of the arguments of K. Assume without loss of generality that the chosen equality literal K has the form EQUAL(r,s) for terms r and s, and that the first argument is that which is being unified with the chosen term t in B. The clause C is obtained from A and B with the following procedure. First, find an MGU for the argument r and the term t. Second, apply the MGU to A and B, yielding A', B', K', and t' as the respective correspondents of A, B, K, and t. Third, generate B'' from B' by replacing t' by s', where K' is of the form EQUAL(r',s'). Finally, form the disjunction of B'' and $A' - K'$ (A' minus a single occurrence of K'). Clause A is called the "from clause", clause B the "into clause", and clause C a "paramodulant".

For a trivial example, paramodulation applied to the equation "$a + -a = 0$" and the statement "$a + -a$ is congruent to b" yields in a single step "0 is congruent to b". In clause form, from

EQUAL(sum(a,minus(a)),0)

into

CONGRUENT(sum(a,minus(a)),b)

the clause

CONGRUENT(0,b)

is obtained by paramodulation. For a slightly more interesting example, recalling that variables such as x mean "for all x", paramodulation applied to the equation "$a + -a = 0$" and the statement "$x + -a$ is congruent to x" yields in a single step "0 is congruent to a". In clause form, from

EQUAL(sum(a,minus(a)),0)

into

CONGRUENT(sum(x,minus(a)),x)

the clause

CONGRUENT(0,a)

is obtained. Finally, for a complex and surprising example, paramodulation applied to the equations "$x + -x = 0$" and "$y + (-y + z) = z$" yields in a single step "$y + 0 = -(-y)$". In clause form, from

EQUAL(sum(x,minus(x)),0)

into

EQUAL(sum(y,sum(minus(y),z)),z)

the clause

EQUAL(sum(y,0),minus(minus(y)))

is obtained by paramodulation. To see that this last clause is in fact a logical consequence of its two parents, unify the argument sum(x,minus(x)) with the term sum(minus(y),z), apply the corresponding MGU to both the "from" and "into" clauses, and then make the appropriate term replacement.

Where resolution combines in a single step the operations of substitution for variables and cancellation of literals, paramodulation combines in a single step the operations of substitution for variables and replacement of (equal) terms. In contrast to binary resolution, paramodulation operates at the term level rather than at the literal level. Consequently, the use of paramodulation often yields shorter and more natural proofs than the use of binary resolution does. In particular, when a proof calls for the substitution of one term for its equal, the use of binary resolution usually requires several deductions to arrive at the desired conclusion. The use of paramodulation, on the other hand, requires but one deduction to perform the substitution. The difference in the number of deductions is explained in part by the fact that resolution treats each predicate syntactically in contrast to paramodulation which treats certain predicates semantically. Specifically, if a predicate is used to mean equality, then paramodulation treats that predicate as if it were "understood" ("built in"). In fact, as is especially evident in the third example of how paramodulation works, this inference rule generalizes the usual notion of equality substitution.

Although the use of paramodulation has many advantages, because of operating at the term level rather than at the literal level, uncontrolled application can yield far too many clauses. In particular, if the rule is applied to a pair of clauses where the "into clause" contains many terms, many conclusions may be drawn from that single pair of clauses alone. Binary resolution, on the other hand, if applied to that pair will usually yield far fewer conclusions. Simply put, clauses usually contain far fewer literals than terms. Even when all clauses contain only a few terms, uncontrolled application of paramodulation—and, for that matter, of any known inference rule — has the potential of causing a reasoning program to be extremely ineffective. The potential ineffectiveness results from two causes. First, a reasoning program can easily get lost, spending its time focusing on one unwisely chosen clause after another. Second, a reasoning program can easily draw many conclusions that are irrelevant to the question under investigation. What is needed to cope with this potential ineffectiveness is strategy— strategy to direct the reasoning, and strategy to restrict the reasoning.

STRATEGY

With the formal treatment of inference rules completed, the focus of attention shifts to strategies to control the various inference rules. Although the inference rules of hyperresolution (J. Robinson, 1965a), UR-resolution (McCharen, 1976a), and paramodulation (G. Robinson, 1969) each give reasoning programs potentially far more reasoning power than is available with binary resolution, their (uncontrolled) individual or collective use is not effective for solving most problems. In most cases, effectiveness is sharply increased with the use of strategy—strategy to direct the reasoning, and strategy to restrict the reasoning.

The first strategy—in fact, the notion of strategy in the context of automated theorem proving—was introduced by researchers at Argonne National Laboratory in 1964 (Wos and co-workers, 1964b). That strategy, called "unit preference", directs theorem-proving and reasoning programs to prefer applications of binary resolution to some pair of clauses in which at least one of the clauses is a unit clause—a clause that contains one literal. The intuitive justification for the value of this approach is the intention of increasing the probability of producing unit clauses. (Resolving two clauses, one of which is a unit clause and one of which is not, produces a resolvent with at least one less literal than the nonunit clause.) Unit clauses in part derive their importance from the fact that almost all proofs by contradiction can be completed by finding two "conflicting units". (A natural extension of the unit preference strategy can be applied to inference rules other than binary resolution.)

Although the introduction in 1964 of the unit preference strategy enabled theorem-proving programs to prove simple theorems that had not previously been proved with such programs, the strategy was discovered to be inadequate for most proof searches. The inadequacy stems from the potential size of the clause set that the program might be forced to search. Even for simple problems, the number of clauses that might be considered can be enormous. Since the unit preference and similar strategies are designed to direct the reasoning, a need also exists for strategies that restrict the reasoning. In general, strategies that restrict the application of inference rules are far more powerful than strategies that direct their application.

In response to the need for restriction strategies, the "set of support strategy" (Wos and co-workers, 1965) was formulated in 1965. (Although the strategy was originally formulated to restrict the application of binary resolution, it is currently used to effectively control other inference rules employed by automated reasoning programs.) For binary resolution, certain clauses are in effect marked as inadmissible for consideration pairwise by the reasoning program. In particular, the marked clauses are not allowed to act together to deduce additional clauses. Any marked clause can, however, participate in a deduction step if the other clause is not marked. Formally, to employ the set of support strategy, the user chooses a (not necessarily proper) subset T of the set S of clauses that represents the theorem to be proved or problem to be solved. For a pair of clauses in S to be considered for the application of resolution, at least one of the two clauses must be in T. When a clause deduced with resolution is added to the set of clauses, with respect to the set of support strategy, the clause is treated as if it were an element of the set T. Such clauses can then be considered with any clause from S for possible applications of resolution. The pairs of clauses that are not admissible are those clauses A and B where both A and B are in $S - T$.

From one viewpoint, the intent of using the set of support strategy is to block the reasoning program from drawing conclusions that may have nothing to do with the task at hand. From the opposite viewpoint, the object of using the set of support strategy is to cause the reasoning program to focus on certain clauses, using the other clauses merely to complete some deduction step. If the focal clauses are well chosen, then the conclusions that are drawn will be relevant to the problem under study. In effect, the set of support strategy permits the user to designate certain clauses as key to the study being made.

For example, if $S - T$ consists of the basic axioms for the theory from which the problem under study is taken, then the program is prohibited from exploring the underlying theory. One effective choice for T consists of the clauses corresponding to the special hypothesis of the theorem to be proved together with the clauses resulting from assuming the purported theorem false. For the group theory problem cited earlier, T would then consist of the clause

EQUAL(prod(x,x)e)

stating that the square of every element is the identity e, and the clause

¬EQUAL(prod(a,b),prod(b,a))

stating that (at least) two elements exist that do not commute. A second effective choice for T consists of just those clauses resulting from the assumption that the purported theorem is false. For the example from group theory, the clause

¬EQUAL(prod(a,b),prod(b,a))

would be the only element of T. An analysis of either of the two generally described choices for T shows that the strategy is designed to force a reasoning program to draw conclusions that are relevant to some proof of the theorem under consideration. From a more general viewpoint, recalling that a proof by contradiction is the usual goal, the strategy seeks to take advantage of the known consistency of that set of clauses corresponding to the axioms—those clauses that characterize the underlying theory from which the problem has been selected. After all, applying sound inference rules to a consistent set will yield additional consistent information, but a proof of inconsistency is the goal. The set of support strategy is still considered to be the most powerful strategy available to reasoning programs. The strategy is "refutation complete", as established with the following theorem.

Set of Support Theorem. If S is an unsatisfiable set of clauses, and if T is a subset of S such that $S - T$ is satisfiable, then the imposition of the set of support strategy on the combination of binary resolution and factoring preserves the property of refutation completeness for that combination (Wos and co-workers, 1965).

A third strategy, known as the "weighting strategy" (McCharen and co-workers, 1976a), enables the user to direct the reasoning of the computer program according to the user's knowledge and intuition. The user assigns values to the various concepts and symbols in the problem to be solved, and the program chooses where to focus its attention according to priorities based on those values. The program also purges information from its database when that information has a computed value larger than some preassigned limit for retained information. The weighting strategy has proved very useful and in general more effective than the unit preference strategy for directing the reasoning.

Two other procedures, "subsumption" (J. Robinson, 1965b) and "demodulation" (Wos and co-workers, 1967), are in many cases indispensable when using a reasoning program. With subsumption, the clause B is discarded in the presence of the clause A when there exists a substitution for the variables in A such that, when applied to A, the result is a subclause of B. For example, the clause

$P(x)$

subsumes the clause

$P(a)$

in view of the admissible replacement of x by a. Subsumption can be termed a "deletion" strategy although, when it was formulated, the notion of strategy had not yet been introduced to the field of automated theorem proving. Its use purges the database of trivial consequences of existing information. In the cited example, an instance of a clause is subsumed by the clause itself. A more interesting example is provided by the pair of clauses

$P(x)$
$P(a) \mid Q(b)$

in which the first clause subsumes the second. Ironically, subsumption acts in opposition to the earlier procedure based on Herbrand instantiation; the former purges instances, and the latter generates them.

Demodulation, on the other hand, rather than removing or adding information to the database, rewrites information by simplifying and canonicalizing it. The corresponding procedure attempts to apply various equality unit clauses, called "demodulators" (Wos and co-workers, 1967), that have been designated for that purpose. As an example of simplification, the clause

EQUAL(sum(0,a),b)

is immediately rewritten to

EQUAL(a,b)

in the presence of

EQUAL(sum(0,x),x)

if the last of the three clauses has been designated a demodulator. As an example of canonicalization, the clause

EQUAL(prod(prod(a,x),b),c)

is immediately rewritten to

EQUAL(prod(a,prod(x,b)),c)

in the presence of

EQUAL(prod(prod(x,y),z),prod(x,prod(y,z)))

if the last of these three has been designated a demodulator. The formulation of demodulation and paramodulation eventually led to the study of complete sets of reductions (Knuth and Bendix, 1970) and rewrite rules.

REASONING PROGRAMS

The first resolution-based computer program was designed and implemented by D. Carson (Wos and co-workers, 1964a), and, until 1973, it was considered the most powerful theorem-proving program available. The program was designed to prove theorems, most of which were taken from abstract algebra. It relied heavily on the use of strategy. Experiments with Carson's program led to the discovery of the set of support strategy (Wos and co-workers, 1965) and the concept of demodulation (Wos and co-workers, 1967).

In contrast to that first resolution-based program, which was usable only in batch mode, Allen and Luckham (1970) designed and implemented a program that could be used in batch or interactive mode. Their program, also relying on resolution, proved a number of theorems from mathematics. Other useful programs extant in the late 1960s include Green's question-answering program (Green, 1969), Bledsoe's program (Bledsoe and Bruell, 1974), and Guard's program (Guard and co-workers, 1969). Guard's program deserves special mention, for—in addition to offering interactive capability—its use led to finding a new result in mathematics, the lemma from lattice theory known as SAM's lemma.

The use of an automated reasoning program to find new results in mathematics would not occur again until 1978 when the program AURA (Smith, 1988) was used to answer a previously open question in algebra (Winker and Wos, 1978). AURA, written in IBM assembly language, was designed and implemented by Overbeek with contributions from Smith, Winker, and Lusk. Although the use of AURA led to a number of useful results in mathematics and logic, its lack of portability proved to be a serious disadvantage. Therefore, LMA (Lusk and co-workers, 1982a, 1982b), which is a collection of subroutines written in Pascal for the purpose of implementing automated reasoning programs tailored to the user's specification, was designed and implemented in 1980 by Overbeek, Lusk, and McCune. LMA was used to produce the program ITP (Lusk and Overbeek, 1984) now used by more than 100 institutions for various types of research and diverse applications.

Despite the interest shown in ITP, McCune—correctly recognizing that substantial changes could be made to produce an even better program—designed and implemented the program OTTER (McCune, 1990). OTTER (written in C) runs with impressive speed on a wide variety of computers, including personal computers. Evidence shows that its performance does *not* deteriorate with time or with the number of kept clauses; OTTER continuously deduces approximately 2000 conclusions per CPU-second on a SPARCstation 1+. Among its inference rules, OTTER offers binary resolution, hyperresolution, UR-resolution, paramodulation, and various linked inference rules (Wos and co-workers, 1984b). To restrict the actions of the inference rules with the object of increasing the likelihood of drawing relevant conclusions, OTTER offers the set of support strategy. For focusing its reasoning according to the user's dictates, OTTER relies on the weighting strategy. It uses demodulation to automatically simplify and canonicalize information, and uses subsumption to purge its database of certain types of logically weaker information.

Potential users of OTTER might find it interesting to note that certain tasks that had required 4 CPU hours (on a SPARCstation 1+) to complete now require approximately 2 CPU minutes (Wos, 1990). The most efficient means to obtain a copy of OTTER (without cost) is electronically. The details can be obtained from its designer, Dr. William McCune, either by electronic mail,

mccune@mcs.anl.gov,

or by surface mail,

Dr. William McCune
Mathematics and Computer Science Division
Argonne National Laboratory
Argonne, IL 60439-4844.

CURRENT APPLICATIONS

The current applications (in 1991) of resolution-based reasoning programs include research in mathematics and formal logic (Winker and Wos, 1978; Winker and co-workers, 1981; Winker, 1982; Wos and co-workers, 1983, 1984a; McCune and Wos, 1987; Wos and McCune, 1988), design and validation of logic circuits (Wojciechowski and Wojcik, 1979, 1983; Wojcik, 1983; Kabat and Wojcik, 1985), verification of claims made for computer programs, database inquiry, and the reasoning required by various expert systems. A number of successes in these diverse areas have been achieved with the assembly-language program AURA (Smith, 1988), which, before the design and implementation of the program OTTER (McCune, 1990), was considered to be the most powerful reasoning program available. With the assistance of AURA, open questions were solved in ternary Boolean algebra (Winker and Wos, 1978), in finite semigroup theory (Winker and co-workers, 1981), and in equivalential calculus (Wos and co-workers, 1983, 1984b). Some of the circuits designed (Wojciechowski and Wojcik, 1983) by relying on this program are superior (with respect to transistor count) to those previously known. The design of a 16-bit adder was validated (Wojcik, 1983) with AURA.

Two recent successes merit particular attention, each achieved with the new program OTTER. The first success focuses on the formulation of the first systematic strategy for finding (when they exist) fixed point combinators. With this strategy, known as the *kernel strategy,* OTTER was used to answer a series of open questions (McCune and Wos, 1987; Wos and McCune, 1988). As evidence of the effectiveness of the new strategy and the power of this new program, we note that some of the questions were answered in less than 1 CPU second on a Sun 3 workstation.

The second recent success focuses on a general approach to finding shorter proofs. Using the feature in OTTER that permits the program to compare the lengths of different deductions of the same conclusion, shorter proofs of various theorems of equivalential calculus have been obtained (Wos, 1990).

SUMMARY

The formulation in 1963 of the inference rule binary resolution by J. A. Robinson (J. Robinson, 1965b) changed the course of automated theorem proving and, eventually, had a dramatic impact on the use of computers. Briefly, binary resolution is a way of reasoning that considers two statements in the clause language and attempts to deduce some new fact or new relationship. Since the reasoning programs under study before 1963 (Davis and Putnam, 1960; Gilmore, 1960) merely substituted terms for the variables in a statement to deduce trivial consequences, Robinson's formulation of resolution represented a promising development.

In one sense, that promise was not fulfilled since, for most problems, application of resolution yields too many steps, each representing too small a reasoning step. On the other hand, the promise was more than fulfilled, for the formulation of binary resolution did in fact lead to the discovery of other, more effective inference rules (J. Robinson, 1965a; Slagle, 1967; G. Robinson and Wos, 1969; Loveland, 1970; Luckham, 1970; Boyer, 1971; Kuehner, 1972; Henschen and Wos, 1974; McCharen and co-workers, 1976a; Wos and co-workers, 1984b) and to the discovery of powerful strategies (Wos and co-workers, 1964b, 1965; McCharen and co-workers, 1976a) to control those rules. For resolution—as well as for all other currently available inference rules—to be effective, strategy to restrict and strategy to direct its application are required.

An accurate evaluation of the full significance of the discoveries that can be directly traced to the formulation of resolution cannot be made until various objectives have been attained. However, one important goal has already been reached. Now (in 1991) computers can be used to assist in the reasoning required in many areas of research and for many applications. To be able to instruct a single computer program to "reason" from given facts and relationships and have it obey the instructions sufficiently well that desired proofs and models and counterexamples are found gives individuals primarily interested in research access to a valuable assistant. Equally, to have that same program reason sufficiently well that important information is provided for solving problems in design, validation, control, and testing gives individuals primarily interested in some specific application that same advantage.

The effectiveness of a computer program that functions as an automated reasoning assistant is proportional to the types of inference rule and strategy it offers and to the excellence of its design and implementation. Excellent resolution-based reasoning programs (Lusk and Overbeek, 1984; Smith, 1988; McCune, 1990) are in fact now being used for various kinds of research and diverse applications.

The evidence of the preceding few years already shows that the work begun more than 30 years ago has in fact culminated in success. The previously open questions that were answered (Winker and Wos, 1978; Winker and co-workers, 1981; Winker, 1982; Wos and co-workers, 1983, 1984a; Wos and Winker, 1984; Wos and McCune, 1988; McCune and Wos, 1987), the superior circuits that were designed (Wojciechowski and Wojcik, 1983), and the existing circuit designs that were validated (Wojcik, 1983) are examples of what has been achieved with the assistance of a resolution-based reasoning program. The goal pursued by mathematicians and logicians and (eventually) by various other scientists has been reached. Computer programs are now available that function effectively as automated reasoning assistants.

The future of automated theorem proving and automated reasoning is by far brighter than at any other time in its history. There now exists (in 1991) the excellent program OTTER, which is easily obtained and which runs with impressive speed on a variety of computers including personal computers. In addition, to complement the book (Wos and co-workers, 1991) which provides a complete introduction to the subject with detailed discussions of various applications, there now exists a book (Wos, 1987) presenting in detail research problems to solve. This second book also includes test problems for evaluating research ideas and program performance, and the clauses needed to study various areas including set theory. In an important sense, the excellent state of automated reasoning today can be traced to J. A. Robinson's formulation of binary resolution (J. Robinson, 1965b).

BIBLIOGRAPHY

J. Allen and D. Luckham, "An Interactive Theorem-Proving Program", in B. Meltzer and D. Michie, eds., *Machine Intelligence,* Vol. 5, American Elsevier, New York, 1970, pp. 321–336.

W. Bledsoe and P. Bruell, "A Man-Machine Theorem-Proving System", *Artif. Intell.* **5,** 51–72 (1974).

R. Boyer, *Locking: A Restriction on Resolution,* Ph.D. Thesis, University of Texas, Austin, Texas, 1971.

R. Boyer and J Moore, "Program Verification", *J. Autom. Reas.* **1,** 17–23 (1985).

C. Chang and R. Lee, *Symbolic Logic and Mechanical Theorem Proving,* Academic Press, New York, 1973.

A. Church, "An Unsolvable Problem of Number Theory", *Am. J. Math.* **58,** 345–363 (1936).

M. Davis and H. Putnam, "A Computing Procedure for Quantification Theory", *JACM* **7,** 201–215 (1960).

P. Gilmore, "A Proof Method for Quantification Theory: Its Justification and Realization", *IBM J. Res. Devel.* **4,** 28–35 (1960).

C. Green, "Theorem Proving by Resolution as a Basis for Question-Answering Systems", in B. Meltzer and D. Michie, eds., *Machine Intelligence,* Vol. 4, American Elsevier, New York, 1969, pp. 183–205.

J. Guard, F. Oglesby, J. Bennett, and L. Settle, "Semi-Automated Mathematics", *JACM* **16,** 49–62 (1969).

L. Henschen and L. Wos, "Unit Refutations and Horn Sets", *JACM* **21,** 590–605 (1974).

J. Herbrand, "Recherches sur la Théorie de la Démonstration", *Travaux de la Société des Sciences et des Lettres de Varsovie,* Classe III Science Mathematique et Physiques, University of Paris, 1930.

J. Herbrand, "Investigations in Proof Theory: The Properties of Propositions", in J. van Heijenoort, ed., *From Frege to Gödel: A Source Book in Mathematical Logic,* Harvard University Press, Cambridge, Mass., 1967, pp. 525–581.

W. Kabat and A. Wojcik, "Automated Synthesis of Combinational Logic Using Theorem Proving Techniques", *IEEE Trans. Comput.* **C-34,** 610–628 (1985).

D. E. Knuth and P. B. Bendix, "Simple Word Problems in Universal Algebras", in J. Leech, ed., *Computational Problems in Abstract Algebra,* Pergamon Press, New York, 1970, pp. 263–297.

D. Kuehner, "Some Special Purpose Resolution Systems", in B. Meltzer and D. Michie eds., *Machine Intelligence,* Vol. 7, American Elsevier, New York, 1972, pp. 117–128.

D. W. Loveland, "A Linear Format for Resolution", *Proceedings of the 1968 IRIA Symposium on Automatic Demonstration,* Springer-Verlag, New York, 1970, pp. 147–162.

D. Luckham, "Refinements in Resolution Theory", *Proceedings of the 1968 IRIA Symposium on Automatic Demonstration,* Springer-Verlag, New York, 1970, pp. 163–190.

E. Lusk, W. McCune, and R. Overbeek, "Logic Machine Architecture: Kernel Functions", in D. W. Loveland, ed., *Lecture Notes in Computer Science,* Vol. 138, Springer-Verlag, New York, 1982a, pp. 70–84.

E. Lusk, W. McCune, and R. Overbeek, "Logic Machine Architecture: Inference Mechanisms", in D. W. Loveland, ed., *Lecture Notes in Computer Science,* Vol. 138, Springer-Verlag, New York, 1982b, pp. 85–108.

E. Lusk and R. Overbeek, *The Automated Reasoning System ITP*, Technical Report ANL-84-27, Mathematics and Computer Science Division, Argonne National Laboratory, Argonne, Ill., 1984.

J. McCharen, R. Overbeek, and L. Wos, "Complexity and Related Enhancements for Automated Theorem-Proving Programs", *Comput. Math. Appl.* **2**, 1–16 (1976a).

J. McCharen, R. Overbeek, and L. Wos, "Problems and Experiments for and with Automated Theorem Proving Programs", *IEEE Trans. Comput.* **C-25**, 773–782 (1976b).

W. McCune, *OTTER 2.0 Users Guide*, Technical Report ANL-90/9, Mathematics and Computer Science Division, Argonne National Laboratory, Argonne, Ill., 1990.

W. McCune and L. Wos, "A Case Study in Automated Theorem Proving: Finding Sages in Combinatory Logic", *J. Autom. Reas.* **3**, 91–107 (1987).

D. Prawitz, H. Prawitz, and N. Voghera, "A Mechanical Proof Procedure and Its Realization in an Electronic Computer", *JACM* **7**, 102–128 (1960).

G. Robinson and L. Wos, "Paramodulation and Theorem Proving in First-Order Theories with Equality", in B. Meltzer and D. Michie, eds., *Machine Intelligence*, Vol. 4, American Elsevier, New York, 1969, pp. 135–150.

J. Robinson, "Automatic Deduction with Hyper-Resolution", *Int. J. Comput. Math.* **1**, 227–234 (1965a).

J. Robinson, "A Machine-Oriented Logic Based on the Resolution Principle", *JACM* **12**, 23–41 (1965b).

J. Slagle, "Automatic Theorem Proving with Renamable and Semantic Resolution", *JACM* **14**, 687–697 (1967).

B. Smith, *Reference Manual for the Environmental Theorem Prover, An Incarnation of AURA*, Technical Report ANL-88-2, Mathematics and Computer Science Division, Argonne National Laboratory, Argonne, Ill., 1988.

A. Turing, "On Computable Numbers, with an Application to the Entscheindungs Problem", *Proc. Lond. Math. Soc.* **42**, 230–265 (1936).

H. Wang, "Towards Mechanical Mathematics", *IBM J. Res. Devel.* **4**, 224–268 (1960).

S. Winker, "Generation and Verification of Finite Models and Counterexamples Using an Automated Theorem Power Answering Two Open Questions", *JACM* **29**, 273–284 (1982).

S. Winker and L. Wos, "Automated Generation of Models and Counterexamples and Its Application to Open Questions in Ternary Boolean Algebra", *Proceedings of the Eighth International Symposium on Multiple-Valued Logic*, IEEE, Rosemont, Ill., 1978, pp. 251–256.

S. Winker, L. Wos, and E. Lusk, "Semigroups, Antiautomorphisms, and Involutions: A Computer Solution to an Open Problem, I", *Math. Computat.* **37**, 533–545 (1981).

W. Wojciechowski and A. Wojcik, "Multiple-Valued Logic Design by Theorem Proving", *Proceedings of the Ninth International Symposium on Multiple-Valued Logic*, IEEE, New York, 1979, pp. 196–199.

W. Wojciechowski and A. Wojcik, "Automated Design of Multiple-Valued Logic Circuits by Automatic Theorem Proving Techniques", *IEEE Trans. Comput.* **C-32**, 785–798 (1983).

A. Wojcik, "Formal Design Verification of Digital Systems", *Proceedings of the Twentieth Design Automation Conference*, Miami Beach, Fla., 1983, pp. 228–234.

L. Wos, *Automated Reasoning: 33 Basic Research Problems*, Prentice-Hall, Englewood Cliffs, N.J., 1987.

L. Wos, "Meeting the Challenge of Fifty Years of Logic", *J. Autom. Reas.* **6**, 213–232 (1990).

L. Wos and W. McCune, *Searching for Fixed Point Combinators by Using Automated Theorem Proving: A Preliminary Report*, Technical Report ANL-88-10, Mathematics and Computer Science Division, Argonne National Laboratory, Argonne, Ill., 1988.

L. Wos and S. Winker, "Open Questions Solved with the Assistance of AURA", in W. W. Bledsoe and D. Loveland, eds., *Automated Theorem Proving: After 25 Years*, American Mathematical Society, Providence, R.I., 1984, pp. 73–88.

L. Wos, G. Robinson, and D. Carson, *Some Theorem-Proving Strategies and Their Implementation*, Technical Memo 72, Mathematics and Computer Science Division, Argonne National Laboratory, Argonne, Ill., 1964a.

L. Wos, D. Carson, and G. Robinson, "The Unit Preference Strategy in Theorem Proving", *Proceedings of the Fall Joint Computer Conference, 1964*, Thompson Book Co., New York, 1964b, pp. 615–621.

L. Wos, D. Carson, and G. Robinson, "Efficiency and Completeness of the Set of Support Strategy in Theorem Proving", *JACM* **12**, 536–541 (1965).

L. Wos, G. Robinson, D. Carson, and L. Shalla, "The Concept of Demodulation in Theorem Proving", *JACM* **14**, 698–704 (1967).

L. Wos, S. Winker, R. Veroff, B. Smith, and L. Henschen, "Questions Concerning Possible Shortest Single Axioms in Equivalential Calculus: An Application of Automated Theorem Proving to Infinite Domains", *Notre Dame J. Form. Log.* **24**, 205–223 (1983).

L. Wos, S. Winker, R. Veroff, B. Smith, and L. Henschen, "A New Use of an Automated Reasoning Assistant: Open Questions in Equivalential Calculus and the Study of Infinite Domains", *Artif. Intell.* **22**, 303–356 (1984a).

L. Wos, R. Veroff, B. Smith, and W. McCune, "The Linked Inference Principle, II: The User's Viewpoint", in R. E. Shostak, ed., *Lecture Notes in Computer Science*, Vol. 170, Springer-Verlag, New York, 1984b, pp. 316–332.

L. Wos, R. Overbeek, E. Lusk, and J. Boyle, *Automated Reasoning: Introduction and Applications*, 2nd ed., McGraw-Hill, New York, 1991.

General References

R. Boyer and J Moore, *A Computational Logic*, Academic Press, New York, 1979.

R. Boyer and J Moore, *Proof Checking the RSA Public Key Encryption Algorithm*, Technical Report 33, The Institute for Computing Science, University of Texas, Austin, Texas, 1982.

R. Boyer and J Moore, *A Computational Logic Handbook*, Academic Press, San Diego, Calif., 1988.

D. Loveland, *Automated Theorem Proving: A Logical Basis*, North-Holland, New York, 1978.

L. Wos
Argonne National Laboratory
R. Veroff
University of New Mexico

RESOLUTION, GRAPH-BASED

Automated deduction and especially its subfields automated theorem proving and logic programming have grown up around Robinson's resolution principle (Robinson, 1965). Most of today's theorem-proving systems and all logic programming languages use this deduction rule. Its main idea lies in the following rule of inference:

From $(A \vee B)$ and $(\neg A \vee C)$ infer the resolvent $(B \vee C)$

Robinson shows the (refutation) completeness of a calculus based essentially on this rule and its heart, the unification procedure, for first-order predicate logic. Thus with this single rule we are able to derive an elementary contradiction from any unsatisfiable set of first-order formulas. To put it a little bit more precisely, this works only for universal formulas that are in conjunctive normal form, ie, for sets of clauses. Here clauses are sets (ie, disjunctions) of literals, which in turn are positive and negative atoms. However, it is well known that every set of first-order formulas can be transformed into a set of clauses without affecting its (un)satisfiability.

The resolution rule takes two clauses with complementary literals, ie, with literals that have the same predicate symbol but opposite signs. The unification procedure is used to decide whether the arguments of the two complementary literals can be made equal by substituting variables with suitable terms. If such a unifying substitution, or unifier, can be found, a new clause is generated that contains all the other literals of the two parent clauses. The clause is then instantiated with the unifier, and this resulting resolvent is added to the clause set. If the iterated application of the resolution rule produces two singleton clauses with complementary literals, a final application of resolution to them terminates with an empty clause that indicates an elementary contradiction.

With an unrestricted application of the resolution rule, this procedure obviously spans a highly redundant search space. A lot of control strategies have been developed in order to avoid this redundancy (cf Chang and Lee, 1973; Bläsius and Bürckert, 1989). One of the most famous ones is SLD-resolution, the basic procedure of logic programming (Lloyd, 1984). However, as early as 1974, Kowalski proposed a graphical representation of clause sets, the *connection graphs*, both as a data structure and an indexing device for a resolution-based proof procedure (Kowalski, 1974). The connection graph of a set C of clauses is defined as a set of nodes labeled with sets of literals, the clauses of C, and a set of links between literals of the nodes (see Figure 1a). The original definition of Kowalski allowed only for resolution links between different clauses connecting exactly the complementary literals with unifiable arguments, and the links are labeled with their unifiers. His connection graph procedure now starts with an initial connection graph of the input clause set. It processes the graph by repeatedly applying the following steps:

1. As long as there are unlinked literals in the graph, delete *all* clauses that contain unlinked literals and all their links. [By Robinson's purity rule, such unlinked clauses can be deleted from the clause set without affecting its (un)satisfiability.]

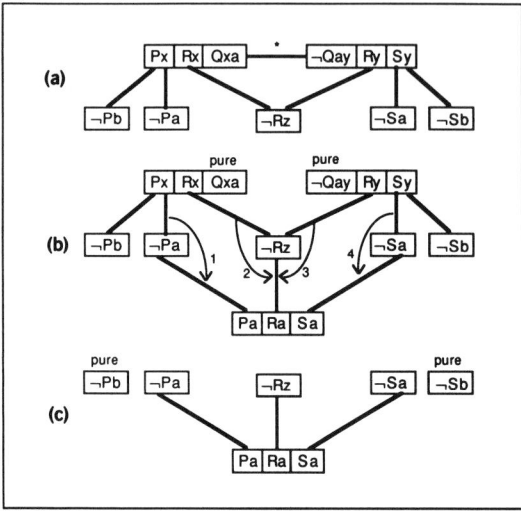

Figure 1. (a) Connection graph of the unsatisfiable clause set $\{\{\neg Pa\}, \{\neg Pb\}, \{\neg Rz\}, \{\neg Sa\}, \{\neg Sb\}, \{Px, Rx, Qxa\}, \{\neg Qay, Ry, Sy\}\}$ with all resolution links; the unifiers are dropped. Resolution on the marked link (∗) and removal of this link results in graph (b). Arrows (1–4) show link inheritance (2 and 3 with a merge of the two inherited links). Deleting the two clauses with the pure literal and all links connected to them results in graph (c). It has again two pure (unit) clauses that are deleted (notice that they do not contribute to the refutation). Resolution on the remaining three links ends with an empty clause. Thus, the clause set was, in fact, unsatisfiable.

2. Select a link, delete it from the graph, and add the resolvent of the corresponding two clauses to the graph together with its associated new links.

This last step is not as complex as it may look at first glance. It can be shown that those new links can be inherited from the links that are associated with the parent nodes of the resolvent. This means that if we start with a complete connection graph of an unsatisfiable input clause set designating all possible resolution steps on this initial clause set, then the links of a resolvent are instantiated copies of exactly those original links of the parents' literals that are compatible with the unifier of the resolvent. Each new link gets as a label the combination of the resolvent's unifier with that of its own parent link.

Although it has been known (and used) since the mid-1970s, the connection graph procedure was proven complete only recently by Eisinger (1988). Of course, Kowalski's original procedure was not complete, as it did not take into account factorization and self-resolution, ie, resolution between complementary literals in different copies of the same clause. However, this required just an extension of connection graphs by additional links. One of the main remaining problems was the question of whether deletion of the link resolution takes place in step 2 and its effects destroys completeness (Eisinger, 1988). Notice that now further application of rule 1 is possible (see Figure 1 again for the snowball effect to which this may lead).

Eisinger also gives some further extensions of the procedure with deletion rules for clauses and links, generalizing the purity rule and some other well-known deletion rules for clauses, such as the tautology and subsumption rules (Chang and Lee, 1973). These extensions, however, required some very sophisticated completeness proofs, and worse some turned out to destroy completeness. On the other hand, this combination with new deletion rules for both clauses and links may still increase the snowball effect mentioned before in its combination with deletion rule 1 such that after some resolution steps the whole connection graph collapses to a trivial graph. These reduction rules are supported by additional links indexing the possibilities for their application. Such a *clause graph* has several different kinds of (colored) links, representing possibilities for resolution, tautology deletion, subsumption deletion, etc, with respect to both clauses and links. The latter represent cases, where the derived resolvent will be tautological or subsumed, ie, they allow for looking one step ahead.

Siekmann and Wrightson (1980) extended clause graphs for equality handling by integrating paramodulation links. Based on their "paramodulized" clause graph procedure, Bläsius (1987) developed a further extension with *equality graphs*. Here links may be replaced by equality graphs designating how the arguments of the literals can be made equal, not syntactically as above, however, but with respect to some equalities between the terms that are given with the input clause set.

Still further extension came up with realizations of Stickel's theory resolution rule (1985). Here resolution between two clauses with complementary literals is extended with resolution between sets of clauses with "theory complementary" parts. That means that each clause has a subclause such that they together are unsatisfiable with respect to some built-in theory. In order to extend the connection graph procedure for theory resolution, Ohlbach (1987) generalized clause graphs in allowing for multilinks between the theory complementary parts of sets of clauses. In addition, generalizations of the colored links mentioned before, eg, theory tautology or theory subsumption, become necessary as well as new colored links.

A special form of clause graphs are refutation graphs. In order to represent factorization steps, too, the resolution links of refutation graphs may fan out at their two ends into more than one literal of the connected two clauses with same predicate symbol and same sign. Refutation graphs can be seen as a representation of a whole class of refutation proofs of an unsatisfiable set of clauses. Shostak (1976) showed that a clause set is unsatisfiable if and only if (iff) for sufficiently many copies of the clauses there exists a refutation graph such that every literal node is connected with exactly one (fanning-out) resolution link and its unifier unifies the corresponding arguments of every pair of literals connected by that link.

Most of these extensions and techniques and some others are implemented in the Markgraf Karl Refutation Procedure (MKRP), a connection graph theorem-proving system that has been implemented at the universities of Karlsruhe and Kaiserslautern, Germany (cf Eisinger and Ohlbach, 1989). It also supports theory unification and sort unification. The first is a special case of equality handling with built-in equational theories specifying properties of function symbols like associativity or commutativity. The second uses type hierarchies for the arguments of function and predicate symbols in order to treat distinguished unary predicate symbols, the sorts. In both cases unification has to be extended as there may now be more than one (most general) unifiers that identify argument terms of complementary literals. Therefore, similar as in the case of theory resolution, the links of a clause graph may be labeled not only by single unifiers but also by sets of unifiers.

Two other realizations of the connection graph procedure have been described (eg, McKay and Shapiro, 1981; Powers and co-workers, 1988). Both of these approaches make use of connection graphs in order to avoid termination problems with recursive rules, the first for the inference system of a semantic network processing system (SNePS), the other, for a concurrent logic programming system (CONG). For more details about connection graph procedures and extensions, see Kowalski (1979) or Bläsius and Bürckert (1989). The latter also provides a comparison with the tableau calculus and the matrix (or connection) method.

BIBLIOGRAPHY

K. H. Bläsius, *Equality Reasoning Based on Graphs,* dissertation, Universität Kaiserslautern, Germany, 1987; SEKI-Report SR-87-01.

K. H. Bläsius and H.-J. Bürckert, *Deduction Systems in Artificial Intelligence,* Ellis Horwood, 1989.

C.-L. Chang and R. C. Lee, *Symbolic Logic and Mechanical Theorem Proving,* Academic Press, New York, 1973.

N. Eisinger, *Completeness, Confluence, and Related Properties of Clause Graphs,* dissertation, Universität Kaiserslautern, Germany, 1988; SEKI-Report SR-88-07.

N. Eisinger and H. J. Ohlbach, "Chapter II: The Foundations," in K. H. Bläsius and H.-J. Bürckert, eds., *Deduction Systems in Artificial Intelligence,* Ellis Horwood Publishers, Chichester, UK, 1989, pp. 37–115.

J. W. Lloyd, *Foundations of Logic Programming,* Springer, 1984.

R. Kowalski, "A Proof Procedure Using Connection Graphs," *J.ACM* **22**, 572–595 (1975).

R. Kowalski, *Logic for Problem Solving,* North-Holland, 1979.

D. P. McKay and S. C. Shapiro, "Using Active Connection Graphs for Reasoning With Recursive Rules," in *Proceedings of the Seventh IJCAI,* Morgan-Kaufmann, San Mateo, Calif., 1981, pp. 368–374.

H. J. Ohlbach, "Link Inheritance in Abstract Clause Graphs," *J. of Automated Reasoning* **3**(1), 1–34 (1987).

D. M. W. Powers, L. Davila, and G. Wrightson, "Implementing Connection Graphs for Logic Programming", in R. Trappl, ed., *Cybernetics and Systems' 88,* Kluwer Academic Publishers, 1988, pp. 957–964.

J. A. Robinson, "A Machine Oriented Logic Based on the Resolution Principle," *J. ACM* **12**, 23–41 (1965).

R. E. Shostak, "Refutation Graphs," *Artifical Intelligence* **7**(1), 51–64 (1976).

J. H. Siekmann and G. Wrightson, "Paramodulated Connectiongraphs," *Acta Informatica* **13**, 67–86 (1980).

M. E. Stickel, "Automated Deduction by Theory Resolution," *J. of Automated Reasoning* **1**(4), 333–356 (1985).

Hans-Jürgen Bürckert
Deutsches Forschungszentrum
für Künstliche Intelligenz
GmbH (DFKI)

The author would like to thank David Powers for carefully reading an early draft. The author's current work is supported by the German Bundesministerium für Forschung und Technologie under grant ITW 89030.

RESOLUTION, THEORY

Theory resolution (Stickel, 1985) is a method for constructing hybrid reasoning systems by incorporating specialized reasoning procedures into a resolution theorem prover. The reasoning task can then be effectively divided into two parts. Special cases, such as reasoning about inequalities or taxonomic information, can be handled efficiently by specialized reasoning procedures, whereas more general reasoning is handled by resolution. The two reasoning components are connected by the resolution procedure, which resolves on sets of literals whose conjunctions are determined to be contradictory by the specialized reasoning procedure.

Binary resolution (see Resolution, binary) allows the derivation of the clause $A|B$ from the clauses $\neg P|A$ and $P|B$:

$$\frac{\neg P|A \\ P|B}{A|B}$$

This is justified by $\neg P$ and P being contradictory or, equivalently, the clause $P|\neg P$ being valid. Binary resolution resolves on pairs of literals such as $\neg P$ and P that are syntactically contradictory. Theory resolution extends resolution to resolve on sets of literals that are semantically contradictory.

When $<$ is interpreted as a total ordering relation, the clause $x < y|x = y|x > y$ is valid. This justifies the inference:

$$\frac{\begin{array}{ll} 1. & \neg(a<b)|A \\ 2. & \neg(a=b)|B \\ 3. & \neg(a>b)|C \end{array}}{A|B|C} \qquad (1)$$

Because it would be a contradiction for all of $a < b$, $a = b$, and $a > b$ to be false, at least one must be true. That plus the truth of clauses 1–3 in equation 1 implies at least one of A or B or C must be true. The result can be obtained in three binary resolution steps from the clauses in equation 1 and the clause $x < y|x = y|x > y$. Alternatively, it can be obtained in a single theory resolution step if the theory of $<$ as a total ordering is built in. Clauses of built-in theories, such as $x < y|x = y|x > y$, need not be present. Theory resolution is arguably better than binary resolution because its inference steps are larger and the clauses that define the theory can be omitted.

Theory resolution operations can operate on an arbitrarily large number of clauses. The cycle $a < b < c < d < a$ is contradictory in the theory of $<$ as a total ordering and justifies the theory resolution operation:

$$\frac{\begin{array}{l} a < b|A \\ b < c|B \\ c < d|C \\ d < a|D \end{array}}{A|B|C|D}$$

Partial theory resolution can be used to reduce the number of clauses needed by allowing resolution on sets of literals that are only partially semantically contradictory. For example, $a < b$ and $b < c$ would be contradictory if $\neg(a < c)$ were also present. The complements of the conditions (if any) that are necessary to complete the contradiction are added to the resolvent. The result of a total theory resolution operation can be obtained incrementally by a sequence of partial theory resolution operations. Thus the total theory resolvent $A|B|C|D$ could be obtained instead by three partial theory resolution operations:

$$\frac{a < b|A \\ b < c|B}{a < c|A|B}$$

$$\frac{a < c|A|B \\ c < d|C}{a < d|A|B|C}$$

$$\frac{a < d|A|B|C \\ d < a|D}{A|B|C|D}$$

The literals in a partial theory resolvent that were not present in the parent clauses are called the residue of the partial theory resolution operation.

Theory resolution can be used to incorporate efficient taxonomic or terminological reasoning into a resolution theorem prover. Building in a taxonomic theory can allow theory resolution operations such as:

$$\frac{elephant(Clyde)|A \\ \neg mammal(x)|B(x)}{A|B(Clyde)}$$

$$\frac{car(a)|A \\ powered\text{-}by(a,b)|B}{engine(b)|A|B}$$

The KRYPTON knowledge representation system (Brachman and co-workers, 1985) allows such inferences. It contains a terminological reasoning component (the TBox) and an assertional reasoning component (the ABox, a resolution theorem prover). The TBox is used to implement a terminological theory that is used in theory resolution operations in the ABox.

Theory resolution is an alternative to *many-sorted resolution* (Walther, 1987), which also incorporates taxonomic inference without taxonomic axioms. Theory resolution may also be used in richer sorted logics that retain characteristic literals for sorts (Cohn, 1987) and resolve on them. The linked inference principle (Wos and co-workers, 1984) can also be used to build in theories. Theories are built in by linking clauses, which are used in hidden resolution operations. Theory resolution instead allows a theory to be incorporated as a black box that identifies contradictory sets of literals in an unspecified manner. The idea of using semantic contradiction instead of syntactic contradiction as the basis for inference can be applied to other logical calculi besides resolution (Bibel, 1987; Murray and Rosenthal, 1988).

BIBLIOGRAPHY

W. Bibel, *Automated Theorem Proving*, 2nd ed., Vieweg, Braunschweig, 1987.

R. J. Brachman, V. P. Gilbert, and H. J. Levesque, "An Essential Hybrid Reasoning System: Knowledge and Symbol Level Accounts of KRYPTON," in *Proceedings of the Ninth IJCAI*, Los Angeles, Calif., Morgan-Kaufmann, San Mateo, Calif., 1985, pp. 532–539.

A. G. Cohn, "A More Expressive Formulation of Many Sorted Logic," *J. Automat. Reas.* **3**, 113–200 (1987).

N. V. Murray and E. Rosenthal, "Theory Links in Semantic Graphs," in *Proceedings of the Eighth International Conference on Automated Deduction*, Oxford, UK, 1988, pp. 353–364.

M. E. Stickel, "Automated Deduction by Theory Resolution," *J. Automat. Reas.* **1**, 333–355 (1985).

C. Walther, *A Many-Sorted Calculus Based on Resolution and Paramodulation*, Pitman, London, 1987.

L. Wos, R. Veroff, B. Smith, and W. McCune, "The Linked Inference Principle, II: The User's Viewpoint," in *Proceedings of the Seventh International Conference on Automated Deduction*, Napa, Calif., 1984, pp. 316–332.

MARK STICKEL
SRI International

REVE

In artificial intelligence and software engineering, there are many situations where one needs to reason on logical universes described by equations. This need led to the construction of a software called REVE. REVE knows how to manipulate equations, how to solve them, and how to deduce nontrivial facts from them. Therefore, REVE should be seen as a computer environment that performs automated deduction in equational theories. Actually in some exercises it surpasses professional mathematicians. For instance, it has solved difficult properties in group theory. Created to prove properties related to software specifications, REVE has since been applied to mathematics, parallelisms and data basis problems. REVE is also a tool for experimentation in new methods in automated deduction, logic programming, and functional programming.

The principle on which REVE is based is rewriting. This is a technique that consists in orienting equations to get first efficiency, but this orientation also allows the computer to make new inferences easily. When the equations have been oriented one can use them to simplify expressions and find *irreducible forms,* also called *normal forms.* The main procedure used in REVE is completion.

REVE was created as a cooperation between the Centre de Recherche en Informatique de Nancy and the Laboratory for Computer Science at the Massachusetts Institute of Technology. It has been distributed to more than 50 laboratories. REVE-2 is the version that is usually distributed. It was followed by other versions for equational (REVEUR-3) and conditional (REVEUR-4) rewriting. Among its followers, LP (Larch Prover) can handle real life applications, and ORME insists mostly on the internal design.

PIERRE LESCANNE
Centre de Recherche en
Informatique de Nancy
INRIA

ROBOT

A natural language database interface program written by Harris in 1977, ROBOT was the research prototype for the commercial INTELLECT (qv) product. It explored the linguistic aspects of providing a "portable" natural language interface, ie, one that could be applied across a variety of discourse domains. The primary design goal of ROBOT was to provide maximal fluency subject to the constraint that the all application specific definitions be made in conventional DP terminology.

The application builder was not required to have computational linguistic skills. (See L. Harris, in L. Bolc, ed., *Natural Language Based Computer Systems,* Hansen Press, Munich, 1980, p. 285).

LARRY R. HARRIS
AICorp, Inc.

ROBOT HANDS AND END-EFFECTORS

Like animals, robots interact with their environments using end-effectors. In animals, the end-effectors take a wide array of forms including mouths, pincers, hands, and tentacles, each designed for a set of grasping and manipulation tasks. Many animals use their end-effectors not only as organs of action, but also as exploratory organs, relaying information about the outside world. The end-effector therefore establishes a bidirectional connection between the animal and the world around it.

For robots, too, the end-effector is a connection through which the robot learns about, and modifies, its environment. As such, the end-effector is potentially among the most important elements of a robotic application. Despite this fact, there was a tendency in early robotic applications to view end-effectors as "accessories" to the robot and to leave their selection or design as a last-minute decision, after the robot and associated materials-handling or processing equipment were chosen. This was unfortunate, since the end-effector is an integral part of the overall tooling, fixturing, and sensing strategy. The end-effector, and the tools and fixtures it interacts with, can represent a substantial capital investment and can be responsible for the ultimate success or failure of the application. Today, as robots grow more sophisticated and begin to work in more demanding applications, the importance of end-effector design is increasingly recognized.

This article discusses issues in end-effector design, from the standpoint of grasp choice, actuation, and sensing, and also from the standpoint of design methodology. It begins with a look at the human hand, for inspiration and for clarification of the issues involved in grasping and hand control. Next, the basic categories of robotic end-effectors in use today are examined and their characteristics are discussed using several examples. The promise, and limitations, of dextrous multifingered hands that are being developed in a number of research institutions are examined. The article then turns to underlying issues in end-effector design, including the specification and use of sensors, actuators, and transmission systems. The final sections return to the broader view of end-effector design as part of an overall solution in which trade-offs among the end-effector, robot, and environment are made in order to accomplish a task.

THE HUMAN HAND: A SOURCE OF INSPIRATION

Although today's industrial robot end-effectors are often little more than tongs or clamps, some appreciation of the potential importance of end-effectors can be obtained by considering their human counterpart. In large measure, the hand is responsible for our own versatility and capability. The importance of the hand can be seen in the proportion of our tactile sensors, information processing, and motor control capabilities that are devoted to it (as large as those of the arms, legs and trunk combined (Rabischong, 1981)). When it is used as an end-effector, the hand becomes Aristotle's "instrument of instruments," remarkably well adapted to acquiring and working with a wide variety of object shapes and sizes. Indeed, it has been suggested that human hands and tool-holding capabilities have undergone a mutual evolution. The first hominids manufactured very crude flint tools using hands considerably less flexible than those of Homo sapiens (Napier, 1962).

It is significant that humans often use different grasps for acquiring tools or parts and working with them. For example, consider picking up a screwdriver and then using it to turn a screw. The hand first adopts a "preshape" (Iberall and MacKenzie, 1990) for grasping the handle and lifting it from a flat surface. The grasp is with the fingertips to avoid interference with the table. When ready to turn the screw, the hand shifts to a more powerful "wrap" grasp in which the fingers encompass the handle so that a substantial torque and thrust force can be applied. The choice of grasp depends on the task to be performed. If little torque but considerable precision of motion is required (as when using a small screwdriver to turn an adjusting screw), then the fingertips may be used throughout. If the screwdriver is used for prying open a paint can, a slightly different wrap grasp is used which facilitates the exertion of bending moments and rotations with the wrist.

More generally, it has been recognized that human grasps used in manufacturing can be organized into a taxonomy which relates grasp choices to task and object shape requirements (Cutkosky, 1989). An abbreviated version of the human grasp taxonomy is shown in Figure 1. Each of the numbered grasps in the abridged taxonomy represents a family of closely related grasps.

Like the human hand, robot end-effectors must address the separate requirements of acquiring an object, gripping it, and performing a task. Increasingly, robot end-effectors are also equipped with sensors for measuring and controlling grasp forces, imparting motions or identifying object attributes. The requirements of different tasks lead to different grasp choices and end-effector designs. From a design standpoint it is therefore instructive to refer to the human grasp taxonomy and to understand the relationships among preferred grasp choices and task and object shape requirements.

At the top of the taxonomy of human grasps for manufacturing the distinction is made between "power" and "precision" grasps. The former are used for holding parts and tools securely while the latter permit manipulation with the fingertips. Once the basic choice between a power grasp and a precision grasp has been made, a combination of task-related and geometric considerations comes into play. Starting at the top of Figure 1, let us suppose that a power grasp has been chosen. The first question is: does the object need to be clamped to sustain forces from a variety of directions, or does it merely need to be supported? If it merely needs to be supported, then a *non-prehensile* hook grasp (as used in carrying a suitcase) or a palmar platform (as used by a waiter carrying a tray) may be adequate. If the object must be clamped, a prehensile grip is chosen in which the fingers and palm confine the object. At this stage some basic geometric considerations become important: Is the object large? small? flat? thin? For example, if a power grip is needed, and the object is small and flat (as in turning a key in a lock) then a lateral pinch (grasp 5 in Figure 1) will probably be used. If the object has a compact or approximately spherical shape then grasp 3 is most likely. If the object is prismatic (ie, a long shape with nearly constant cross section, such as a cylinder or a hexagonal prism), then a wrap is chosen. Since many objects, including the handles of most tools, have prismatic shapes, the power wrap represents a large family of manufacturing grips.

The precision branch of the taxonomy shows several fingertip grasps used in working with small tools and assembling light components. While the different precision grasps appear to be motivated by part geometry, the deci-

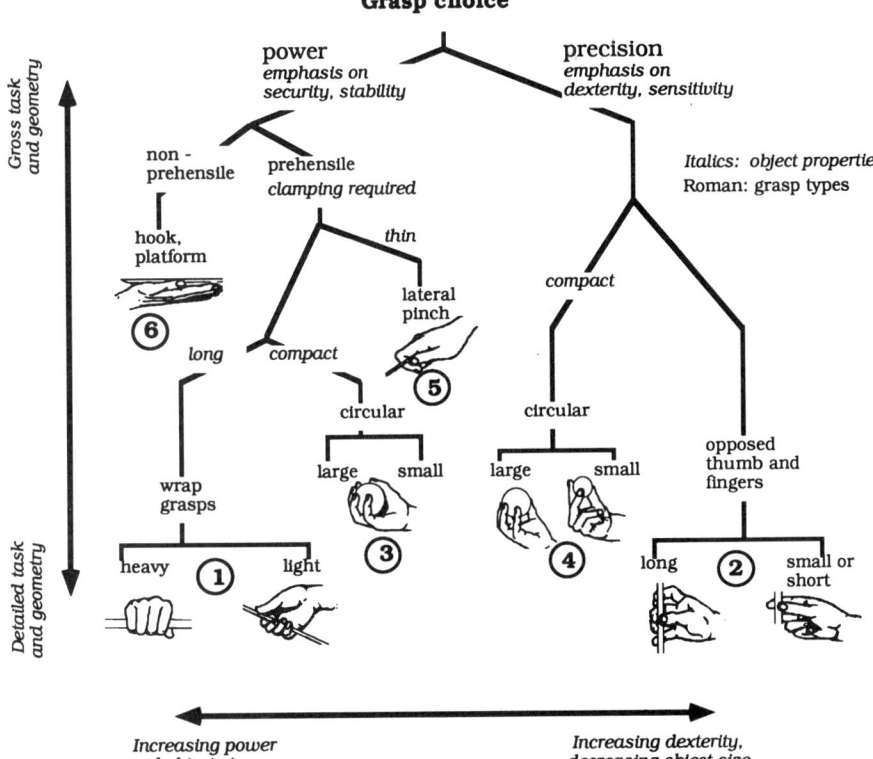

Figure 1. An abbreviated taxonomy of human grasps used in manufacturing (adapted from Cutkosky, 1989; reprinted with permission of the Robotics Institute, Carnegie Mellon University).

sion to use one precision grasp instead of another may be task-related, as many objects have several gripping surfaces with different shapes. For example, a light cylindrical object can be gripped either using the thumb and four fingers as in grasp 2, or it can be gripped by one end, using grasp 4. The role of task forces and torques on grip choice is most apparent when the hand shifts between grips during a task. For example, in unscrewing a jar lid the hand shifts from grasp 3 to grasp 4. Similarly, when holding a tool, as in grasp 1, the hand shifts from a heavy wrap grasp to a light wrap as the forces decrease and may adopt a precision grasp, grasp 2, if the forces become still smaller.

Applying Taxonomy to Design

For designing robot hands, we need to turn from the details of human grasp choice to a general consideration of how grasps satisfy geometric and task requirements. For this purpose, the taxonomy is useful, because it allows one to see where a set of grasps lies in the space of all possible grasps and to see how a specific grasp descends from the generic grasp types.

One way to generalize on the taxonomy is to consider grasps in terms of "virtual fingers" that do not necessarily have a one-to-one correspondence with fingers of the human hand. Iberall and MacKenzie (1990) argue that in most grasps the object is held between two virtual fingers and that the type of opposition (eg, trapping an object between the fingers and the palm, or between the thumb and the index finger) is of central importance. Iberall therefore recognizes three basic types of grasps:

1. *Encompassing grasps (grasps with palm opposition).* Grasps 1 and 3 are the most obvious examples of encompassing grasps.
2. *Lateral grasps (grasps with side opposition).* Grasp 5 is a grasp with side opposition.
3. *Precision grasps (grasps with pad opposition).* The precision grasps, 2 and 4 on the right hand side of the taxonomy, display pad opposition.

It is also possible to examine industrial gripper design in light of the taxonomy in Figure 1. For the most part, today's commercial grippers achieve instances of the power grasps on the left hand side of the taxonomy. For example, a two-fingered parallel-jaw gripper, such as the one shown in Figure 2, is capable of pushing objects (a sub-category under grasp 6) and of a grasp that resembles grasp 5, in which a small object is clamped securely between two strong fingers. As another example, the commercial gripper of Figure 3 is capable of wrap grasps (grasp 1).

Increasingly, however, such general-purpose industrial grippers are inadequate for the variety of object shapes and tasks encountered in robotic applications. As discussed in the section on Achieving Greater Versatility, a common solution is to provide an array of special-purpose grippers for each part style. Although this method leads to difficulty in routing power and sensory information from the fingers through connections into the robot arm, and increases cycle times as grippers are swapped, it is attractive to manufacturing engineers since the grippers can be much less complicated than a universal hand. The taxon-

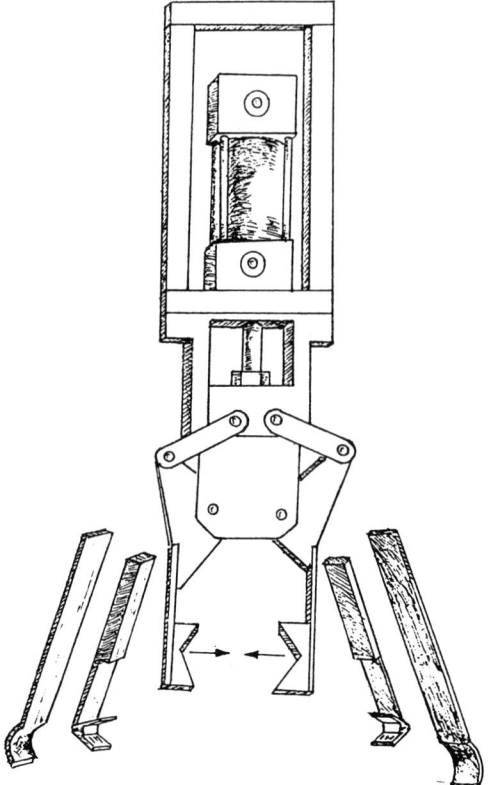

Figure 2. An angular-jaw industrial end-effector with changeable fingertips (Wright and Cutkosky, 1985).

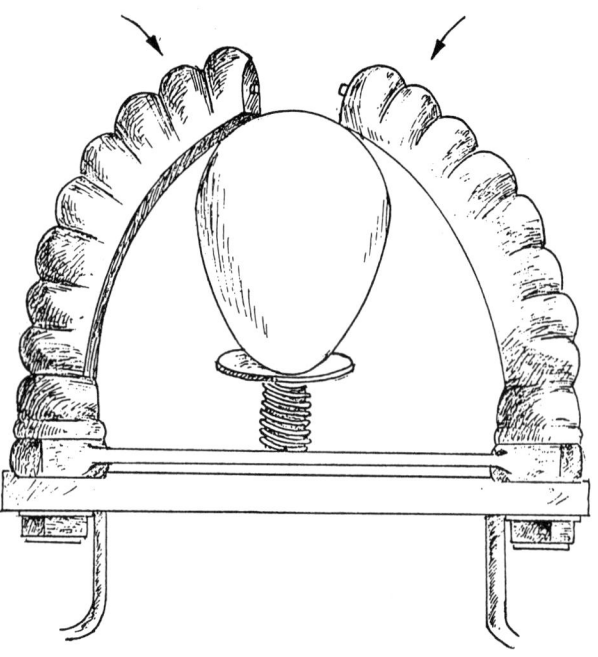

Figure 3. A soft pneumatic end-effector that achieves a wrap grasp (Simrit, 1984).

omy in Figure 1 suggests, however, that if several grippers are to be used, they should be designed for classes of grasps and tasks, not for different part styles. To design a gripper for individual part styles is to design a tool, not a hand. Thus, like a Phillips-head screwdriver which can only be used with Phillips-head screws, such a gripper is a special-purpose device.

A better approach is to start with basic task requirements and let those requirements dictate the design. For example, one might construct a three-fingered gripper for precision grasps and a second gripper for wrap grasps. Note also that while it suits the machinist with his human hand to bring out a full repertoire of grasps, some of these may be unnecessary for a robot. For example, a task that humans perform with grasp 4 might acceptably be performed with grasp 3.

Finally, we observe that although the human hand is an excellent source of inspiration for the end-effector designer, it would be a mistake to assume that the ultimate or ideal robotic end-effector would necessarily resemble a human hand. For one thing, the tasks and environments that even the most sophisticated robots have to contend with are very restricted compared to those that humans encounter every day. Simpler and more specialized designs can therefore be expected to perform equally well. Indeed, it is useful to look at the specialized designs found in nature, where sensing and control capabilities are limited and where there is a premium on compact and simple solutions. In particular, insect physiology reveals numerous ways of reducing the size and complexity of muscular and neuronal systems for a gripper. For example, grasping requires strength and control only in closing the gripper; very rarely is power or precision needed in opening. Consequently, certain insects and arthropods have large muscles for closing their grippers but none for opening. Opening is accomplished by the elasticity of the cuticle and by blood pressure within the limb.

A second point is that the hand is "designed" for many activities besides manipulation (eg, communication and thermoregulation). This suggests that in limited situations, robotic end-effectors should even be able to improve on human performance. Indeed, when working on a car, the first thing a mechanic reaches for is his toolbox with "hand adaptor" tools such as needle-nose pliers, tweezers, and work gloves to help him finish the job.

In summary, the human hand and grasp taxonomy provide insights for end-effector design, construction, and control. By appropriately generalizing from the details of the human solution, it is possible to develop robotic hands that are capable of a specified and necessary subset of tasks, but are not over designed and hence overly expensive.

TYPES OF ROBOTIC END-EFFECTORS

Robotic end-effectors today include everything from the simple two-fingered grippers and vacuum attachments that are ubiquitous in industrial applications to elaborate multi-fingered hands in research laboratories. Perhaps the best way to become familiar with end-effector design issues is to first review a few end-effector types. For those interested in designing their own end-effectors, a number of texts (eg, Lundstrom and co-workers, 1977; Kato, 1982; Wright and Cutkosky, 1985; Tanie, 1985) provide a wider range of examples.

Passive End-Effectors

Most end-effectors in use today are passive. As such, they emulate the power grasps in Figure 1 that people use for holding an object securely, without manipulating it or controlling the forces applied. However, a passive end-effector may (and generally should) be equipped with sensors, and the information from these sensors may be used in controlling the robot. For many manufacturing tasks (eg, assembling machined parts, pick-and-place operations) this combination of a passive end-effector and an actively controlled arm or wrist is perfectly adequate. In other applications, when parts are light and where delicate forces must be applied, an active end-effector is in order.

Two-Fingered Angular- and Parallel-Jaw Grippers. The most common end-effectors by far are two-fingered grippers and vacuum attachments. This is not surprising when we consider that such grippers, equipped with appropriate fingertips, can be made to handle a large fraction of the small components found in industrial assemblies. In terms of the taxonomy, these grippers execute the equivalent of grasp 5, or perhaps a variation on grasp 1 if jaws are shaped to surround the part.

Figure 2 shows a typical pneumatic end-effector, with some fingertips that have been designed to grasp different parts. The most inexpensive two-fingered grippers are generally angular-contact grippers, like the one in Figure 2, in which the jaws pivot about an axis. The disadvantage to this approach is that the fingertips do not remain parallel and, therefore, planar contact with flat shapes is not assured. This results in somewhat less stable and precise grasping than can be obtained with parallel-jaw grippers, such as the gripper in Figure 4.

Figure 4 illustrates a parallel-jaw gripper. This gripper is used on a semi-autonomous mobile robot to assist severely handicapped individuals. The hand needs to be able to pick up items from a cluttered countertop and present them to the disabled individual (Leifer, 1981). The robot is programmed by simple voice commands and the position information is therefore often imprecise. To overcome this difficulty, the fingertips of the end-effector are equipped with short-range (0–4 mm) and long-range (100 mm) optical proximity sensors to help it locate objects and close upon them automatically when they are centered between the fingers.

The fingers are actuated by a DC motor through a ball screw mechanism and a pair of four-bar parallel linkages. The motor runs off the same batteries as the mobile robot. An interesting feature of the design is that the links of the four-bar mechanism are offset at 45 degrees from horizontal. This offset places the fingertips below the plane of the drive motor and robot wrist. Since the robot wrist and drive motor are bulky, it is advantageous to keep them up and out of the way of possible obstacles in the vicinity of the fingertips. In addition, the 45 degree angle makes better use of the kinematic workspace of the robot arm, when working at countertop height.

Whether angular- or parallel-jawed, two-finger grippers have a number of common characteristics that may determine whether they can be used in a particular application:

- Two-fingered grippers are sold in many shapes and sizes, and typically come without fingertips, since these are the most product-specific part of the design. Indeed, it is likely that each new application will require custom fingertips. The fingertips are adjusted

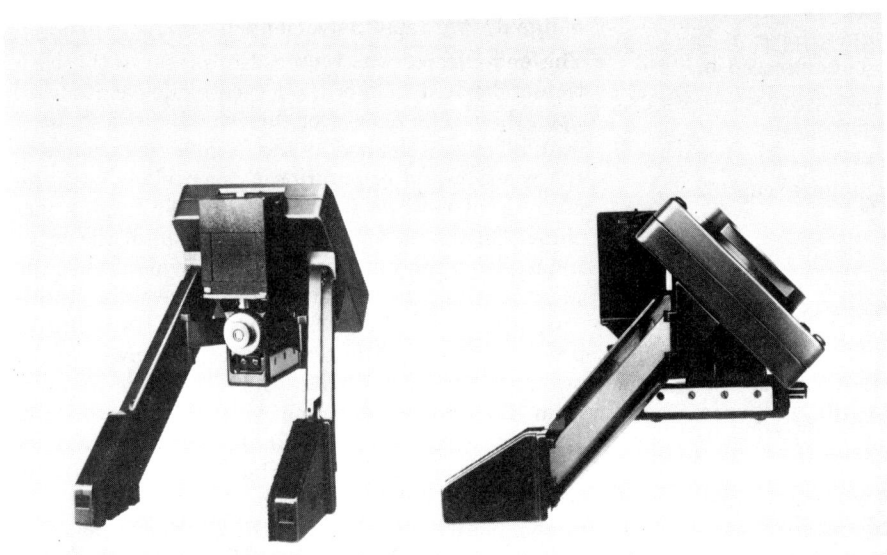

Figure 4. A parallel-jaw gripper with proximity sensors for a mobile robot that works in cluttered environments.

to match the size of components (most grippers have a short open-close stroke and therefore cannot accommodate a wide range of part sizes without fingertips that provide the correct gap size) and also the shape of components (flat, or V-grooved for cylindrical parts) and material (eg, rubber or plastic to avoid damaging fragile objects).

- The actuation of two-fingered end-effectors is most commonly pneumatic, due to the availability of compressed air in most applications and the high power-to-weight ratio that can be obtained with pneumatic cylinders. The grasp force can be controlled by regulating the air pressure. Electric motors are also fairly common, and the grasp force can be regulated by controlling the motor current. A wide variety of drive mechanisms can be employed between the motor or cylinder and the gripper jaws, including worm gears, rack and pinion, toggle linkages, and cams. Actuation and transmission issues are discussed further in the sections on Sensing, Actuation Methods, Force Analysis, and Transmission Systems.
- Since two-fingered end-effectors typically use a single cylinder or motor that operates both fingers in unison, they will tend to center parts that they grasp. This means that when they grasp parts that are not free to slide sideways (for example, when removing pegs that have been set into holes, or when removing parts from fixtures) some compliance must be added, as discussed in the sections on Soft Grippers and Grippers for Irregular Shapes, and Achieving Greater Versatility.

Vacuum and Magnetic Grippers. Vacuum grippers are commonly used in electronics assembly applications. They can be supplied with a variety of vacuum cup attachments to handle large or small parts with more or less smooth surfaces. Unlike two-fingered grippers, they do not tend to center parts and therefore make it easier to program the robot when working with constrained parts (eg, when extracting components from fixtures). If difficulties are encountered in grasping parts with a vacuum gripper, it is helpful to remember that problems can be addressed in any of several ways including:

Increasing the vacuum pressure

Increasing the suction cup area through larger cups or multiple cups

Using a softer cup material for a better seal

Redesigning the parts to be grasped so that they present a smoother surface (perhaps by affixing smooth tape to the surface)

Augmenting suction with conformal grasping, as employed in end-effectors for soft or irregular shapes in the following section.

Soft Grippers and Grippers for Irregular Shapes. A number of applications are not well handled either by two-finger parallel end-effectors or vacuum grippers. These include applications involving parts with rough or irregular shapes and applications in which large forces must be applied, while at the same time avoiding high contact pressures between the end-effector and the part. Examples of such applications include handling rough forgings or delicate items such as fruit. In such applications, humans use wrap and spherical power grasps. The fingers envelop part, and a nearly uniform pressure is maintained so that friction is used to maximum advantage in resisting task-related loads.

For such applications it is usually necessary to design new grippers, although a few commercial possibilities exist, such as the soft pneumatic gripper shown in Figure 3. This gripper consists of two rubber fingers that respond to pneumatic pressure by curling around a component and holding it against the "palm" that is centered between them. The analogy to the human heavy wrap grasp (grasp 1 in Fig. 1) is obvious.

Another solution is to employ a combination of fingers that can settle upon a component. For a passive gripper, the fingers need not be independently actuated but can be driven through a common linkage. An example of this approach is shown in Figure 5, which illustrates a gripper designed to retrieve turbine blade forgings from an open-die forging machine, present them to a visual inspection station, and then hold them securely during stamping and marking operations. The main requirements of this end-effector design problem were:

- The blades represented a family of irregular shapes, so that a flexible gripper was required. In addition, the blades were rough, hot (over 500°C), and nonmagnetic ruling out the use of magnetic or vacuum grippers.
- Some blades were heavy (up to 50 kg) and long (up to 1 m) with a large moment of inertia about the center of mass. As a result it was important to assure multi-point contact between the gripper and the blades. This point is illustrated graphically in Figure 6. Without multi-point contact, it would be difficult to prevent the blades from pivoting about their midpoints during rapid movements of the robot arm.
- The end-effector was required to preserve the position and orientation of the forged blades as it closed upon them. The reason for this was that the shape of each blade was defined by the forging operation, and the position and orientation of each blade was precisely known while it remained in the forging machine. On the other hand, the position of the large industrial robot was imprecisely known because the robot was not particularly accurate over large distances. Reestablishing alignment is always a difficult process and it therefore made sense to preserve the orientation of the blades when transferring them from the forging machine to the inspection and stamping operations. A similar criterion applies whenever machined or assembled components are retrieved from fixtures. The location of the parts is known more accurately than the location of the robot arm and it is therefore desirable for the robot end-effector to adapt to the parts' position and orientation rather than trying to center the parts.

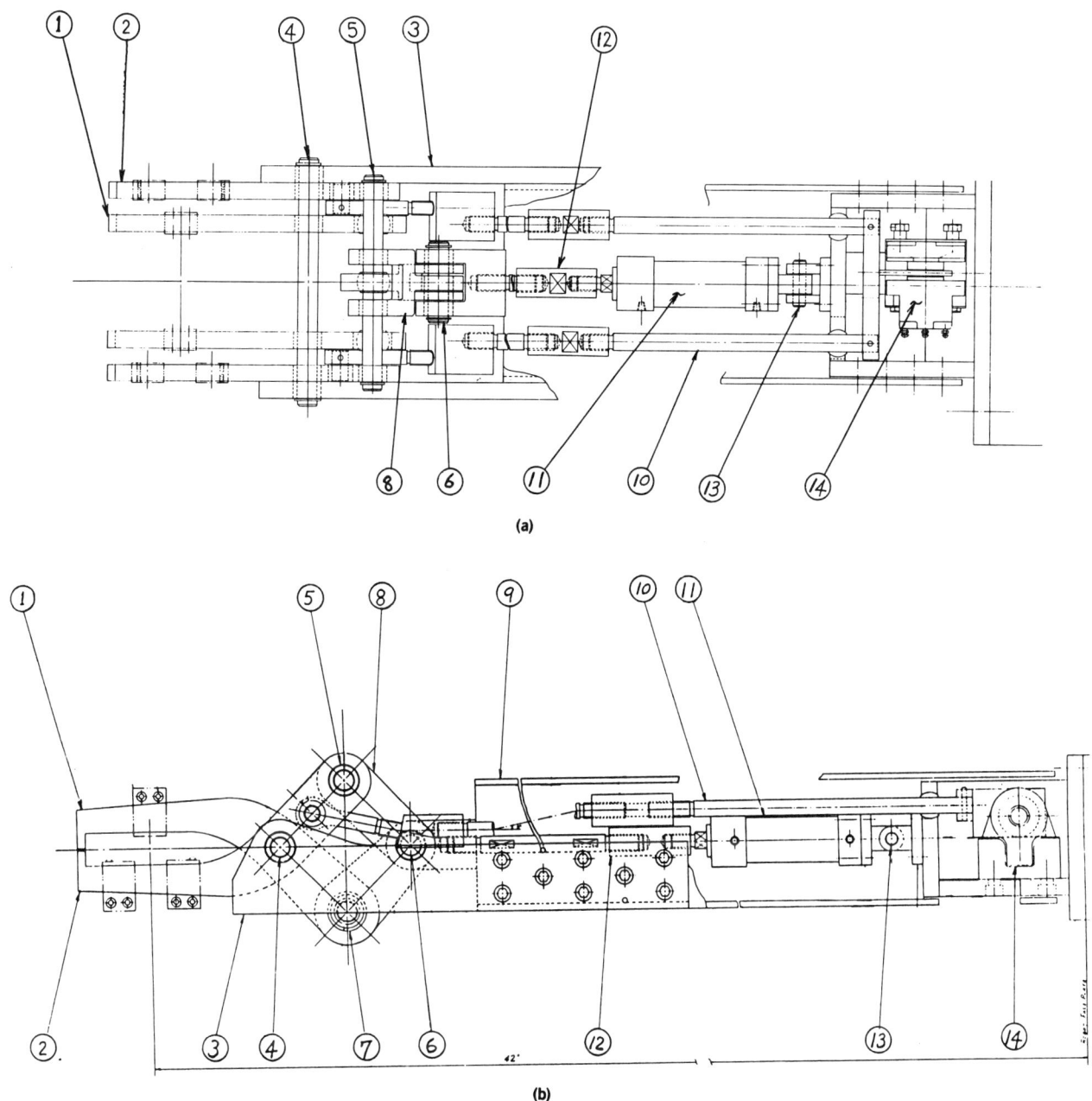

Figure 5. A flexible gripper that conforms to the shapes and orientations of irregular forged workpieces. (a) Top view; (b) side view. Key: (1) upper finger (articulated), (2) lower finger, (3) frame, (4) fixed shaft, (5) floating shaft, (6) floating shaft, (7) shaft with ball joints, (8) link, (9) structural tube, (10) linkage for disc brake, (11) cylinder, (12) adjustment, (13) cylinder pivot, (14) disc brake. (Cutkosky and Kurokawa, 1985.)

The adopted solution consists of four fingers made of a heat-resistant alloy. The two upper fingers are connected to a linkage with ball-joint pivots. The linkage allows the upper fingers to settle independently against the twisted and uneven shapes of the blades. The lower fingers move in unison, but they are hinged so that all four fingers can rotate approximately +/− 10 degrees about a common axis, even while the gripper is holding a part. The upper and lower fingers are actuated by a single hydraulic cylinder which is located remotely to protect it from radiant heat. As the cylinder rod retracts, the fingers settle against the blade. The cylinder rod continues to retract until all fingers are pressing firmly against the part and any play in the linkage has been taken up so that no further motion is possible. Once the cylinder has stopped, it becomes necessary to eliminate the extra degree of freedom provided by the hinged lower fingers. Otherwise the part could pivot with respect to the robot even while all

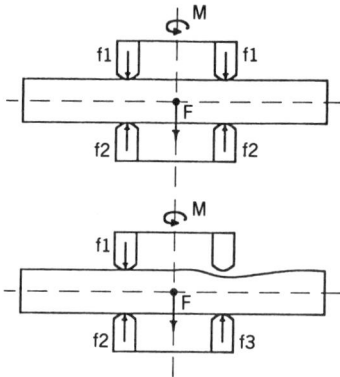

Figure 6. Holding a long workpiece with three and four points of contact (Wright and Cutkosky, 1985).

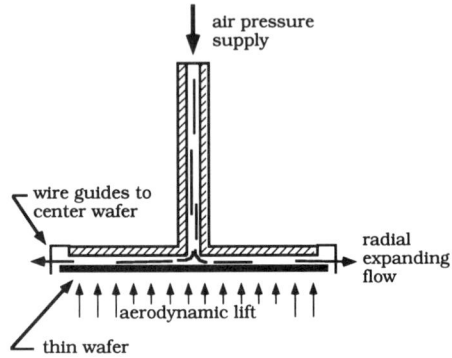

Figure 8. A noncontact end-effector for acquiring and transporting delicate wafers.

fingers continued to press against it. The extra degree of freedom is eliminated using a standard industrial disc brake that locks up part of the linkage so that the original orientation of the blade is preserved.

Carrying the concept of fingers with multiple contacts to its extreme leads us to the design in Figure 7. In this design each finger is a chain of links connected to a single cable. Pulling on the cable causes the chains to wrap around objects of arbitrary shape, exerting a gentle pressure against them (Hirose and Umetani, 1978). A large version of this gripper was tested as a device for rescuing people.

Still another approach to handling irregular or soft objects is to augment a vacuum or magnetic gripper with a bladder containing particles or a fluid. Lundstrom, Glemme, and Rooks (1977) describe a technique for fabricating conformal vacuum grippers for objects with irregular, but smooth surfaces. Magnetic grippers employing bladders filled with iron particles have also been developed (Warnecke and Schmidt, 1979). Still another approach is to use fingertips filled with an electrorheological fluid. The fingertips conform easily to irregular surfaces when unenergized and lock up when an electrostatic potential is applied (Kenaley and Cutkosky, 1989).

Perhaps the ultimate approach to "soft" grasping is the noncontact end-effector illustrated in Figure 8. This end-effector is designed to lift and transport delicate silicon wafers. It lifts the wafers by blowing gently on them from above so that aerodynamic lift is created via the Bernoulli effect. Thin guides around the periphery of the wafers keep them centered beneath the air source.

Active Hands

Two-Fingered-Servo Grippers. For many manufacturing tasks the combination of an active robot arm and wrist with a passive end-effector provides sufficient dexterity. However, the increasing sophistication of robot applications has motivated the development of a number of active end-effectors. These end-effectors have servocontrolled fingers or jaws, and sensors to measure applied forces and motions. For example, Figure 9 shows a relatively simple two-fingered servo gripper for assembling light components. This end-effector is the active counterpart of the passive two-fingered end-effectors discussed in the above section on this subject. The fingers slide back and forth on linear guideways, so this is a parallel-jaw gripper. Each finger is driven by a high-torque DC servo motor. The motors drive the fingers through timing belts in an arrangement that resembles (and was inspired by) mechanisms for moving the printer heads on dot matrix printers. A two-stage pulley transmission provides a two-to-one mechanical advantage.

The positions of the fingers are measured by potentiometers and the forces at the fingertips are measured by 3–axis load cells. As a result, each finger can be operated as either a position or a force servo. The gripper is therefore capable of three primary modes of operation:

1. *Both Fingers under Position Control.* In this mode a bias force maintains the grasp while the object is

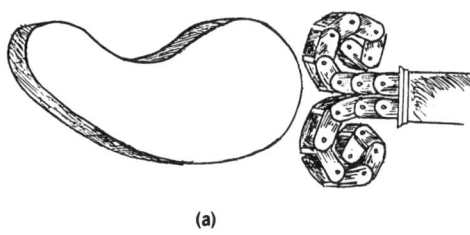

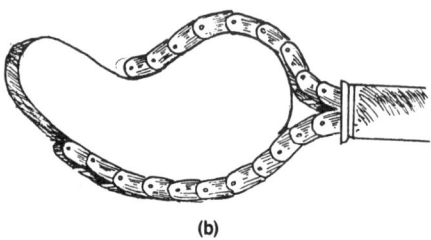

Figure 7. (a) Top and (b) side views of an articulated conformal gripper that exerts uniform pressure (Wright and Cutkosky, 1985), adapted from design in Hirose and Umetani (1978).

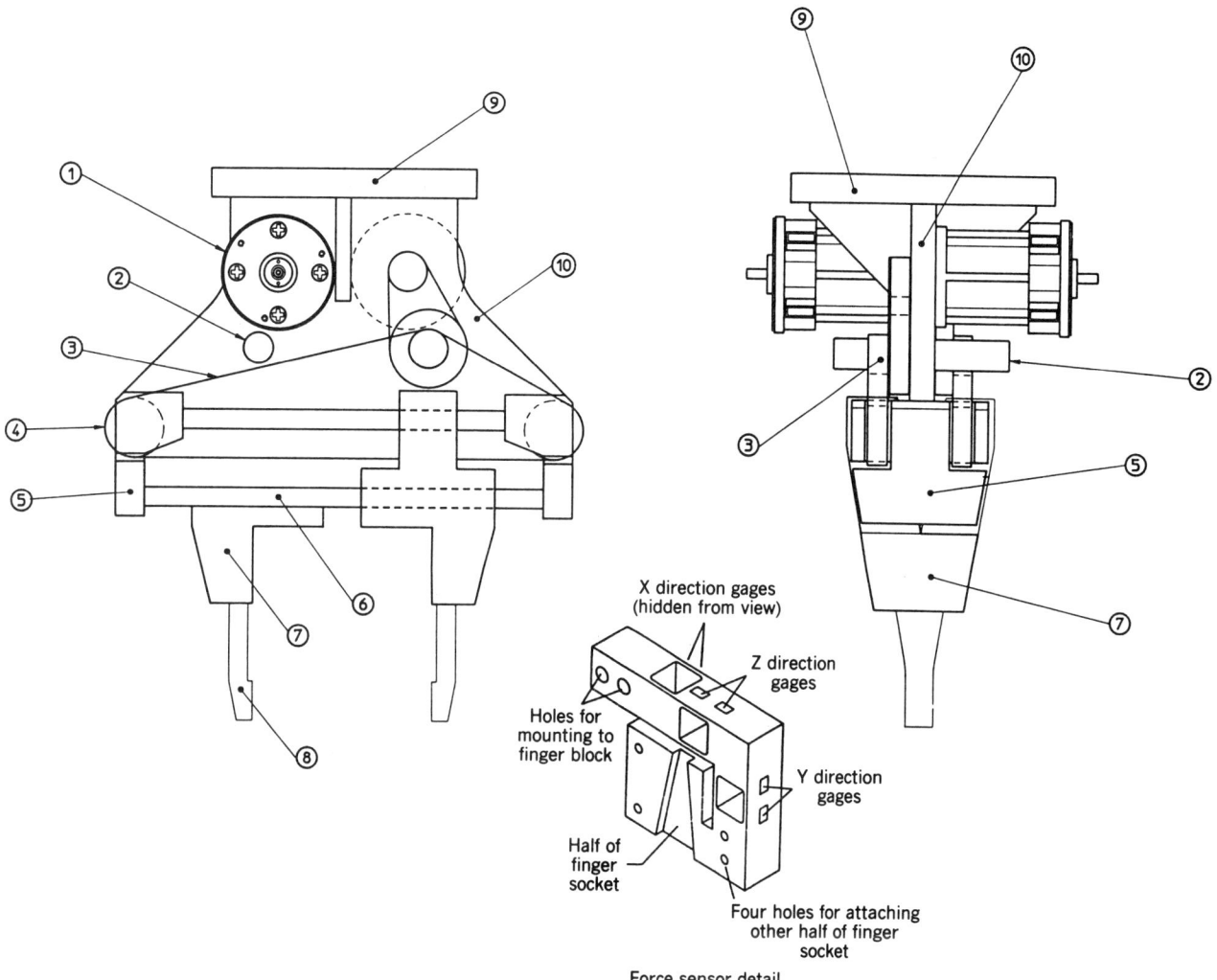

Figure 9. A two-finger servo gripper with force sensing and changeable fingertips. *Key:* (1) DC motor, (2) potentiometers, (3) timing belt, (4) pulley, (5) end plate, (6) guide rod, (7) finger base, (8) finger tip, (9) mounting flange, (10) side plate (Pearce and co-workers, 1986).

manipulated back and forth. The fingers will tend to center an object as they grasp it, much like the simple two-fingered grippers of the above section on this subject. This mode of operation is useful when correcting for position errors of the robot arm and when precise grasp force control is not required.

2. *Object Position and Grasp Force Control.* In this mode the grasp force between the two fingers is controlled while also controlling the position of the midpoint between the fingers (ie, controlling the average position of the fingers). If the grasp force is too low, both fingers press harder in unison. If the midpoint position is incorrect, one finger pushes harder while the other finger relaxes until the object moves the desired amount. This mode of operation is useful when grasping parts that are not precisely located and for which the grasp force must be controlled.

3. *Both Fingers under Force Control.* In this mode each finger pushes until a specified force level is attained. This mode of operation is useful when the fingers should accommodate themselves to the position of a part that is constrained. Thus, the active gripper in this mode emulates the passive gripper of Figure 5.

In addition to providing input to the control system, the sensors of a servo gripper provide useful information for robot programming. For example, the position sensors can be used to measure the width of the grasped component, thereby providing a check that the correct component has been grasped. Similarly, the force sensors are useful for weighing grasped objects and monitoring task-related forces.

Dextrous Hands. For tasks requiring a combination of dexterity and versatility for grasping a wide range objects, a dextrous multifingered hand is the ultimate solution. The advantages of a dextrous hand include:

- More versatility for fine motions. A dextrous hand permits the robot to attempt the tiny movements that people make in threading a bolt into a tapped hole or when using a small screwdriver to turn an adjusting screw. This is particularly true when the axis of the grasped object does not coincide with the final axis of the wrist. Since the wrist is separated by some distance from the object, it must both rotate and translate to produce a rotation about the tip of the object—which is inconvenient. In fact, when the turning force on a screwdriver becomes too large to apply with the fingertips, people change their grip so that the screwdriver handle points along the central axis of the wrist, permitting them to twist the screwdriver without translational motions.
- A wide range of grasps. One of the chief advantages to dextrous hands is their ability to accommodate a wide range of grasps and part shapes. Indeed, it can be argued that fingers are more important for grasping than for manipulation. For example, a parallel-jaw hand has been built (Datseris and Palm, 1984) that can manipulate objects with up to five degrees of freedom, perhaps more precisely than a multi-fingered hand. However, it has just the same grasping capabilities as any other parallel-jaw gripper. By contrast, a multifingered hand has a large workspace due to the serial-chain kinematics of the fingers.
- Sensors in direct contact. With sensors in intimate proximity to the object and task, a dextrous hand is particularly sensitive to dynamic changes in loads upon the object and can rapidly adjust the gripping force and rigidity as required. In addition, a dextrous hand permits tactile sensors to be used for characterizing the properties of an object (eg, surface texture, coefficient of friction).
- More complete loading information. Forces measured at the robot wrist can only determine the resultant force and torque at a point. Forces measured in the fingers, which touch the object in several places, provide additional information about the distributions of loads on the object.
- Higher possible bandwidth. Since there are no intermediate masses between the hand and the part, the control system of the hand can have a higher dynamic bandwidth (for quicker responses) than the robot arm or wrist.
- Control of gripping forces. By placing the fingertips judiciously and controlling the grasp forces, the dextrous hand can keep grasp forces as low as possible without allowing the object to slip. This prevents damage to fragile objects and makes the robot safer in operations involving contact between the grasped object and external fixtures. It is often desirable for a part to slip out of the hand when a large, unexpected force occurs (as during a collision) so that the hand and arm do not sustain the brunt of the load.

A number of multifingered hands have been described in the literature, of which the best known are those by Okada (1979), Salisbury (1985), and Jacobsen and co-workers (1984). Most of these hands are frankly anthropomorphic in design, although kinematic criteria such as workspace and grasp isotropy (basically a measure of how accurately motions and forces can be controlled in different directions) have also been used (Salisbury, 1985). Other "quality measures" that account for friction, compliance and kinematics have been proposed in the literature. A summary of these analytic measures is provided in Cutkosky, (1989).

Despite their practical advantages, dextrous hands have thus far been confined to a few research laboratories. One reason for this is that the design and control of such hands presents numerous difficult trade-offs among cost, size, power, flexibility, and ease of control. For example, the desire to reduce the dimensions of the hand, while providing adequate power, leads to the use of cables that run through the wrist to drive the fingers. These cables bring attendant control problems due to elasticity and friction. A discussion of these issues is provided in Jacobsen and co-workers (1984).

A second reason for the slow progress in applying dextrous hands to manipulation tasks has been the formidable difficulties in programming and controlling them. For one thing, the equations associated with several fingertips sliding and rolling on a grasped object are complex. The problem amounts to coordinating the control of several little robots at the end of a robot. In addition, the mechanics of the hand/object system are very sensitive to variations in the contact conditions between the fingertips and object (eg, variations in the object profile and the local coefficient of friction) (Cutkosky and Wright, 1986a). Moreover, the fingers are continually making and breaking contact with the object, and starting to slide, or ceasing to slide, with attendant changes in their dynamic behavior which must be accounted for in the controller. As a result of these difficulties, dextrous hands are time-consuming to program and their operations are susceptible to minor errors in the coefficient of friction, etc.

The difficulties involved in programming and controlling dextrous hands have underscored the importance of tactile sensing in manipulation. Tactile sensing is essential for monitoring the state of the hand/object system and for announcing changes in the coefficient of friction, contact forces, contact geometries, etc. Indeed, when people manipulate objects they rely heavily on dynamic tactile sensors to tell them just how hard to squeeze to prevent slipping (Johansson and Westling, 1984). Recently there has been considerable interest in robotic tactile sensing, and summaries of tactile sensing developments can be found in Hollerbach (1987), Nicholls and Lee (1989), and Howe and Cutkosky (1990). However, the application of such sensors is still in a very early phase.

Recognizing that the advantage of having fingers is at least as much for grasping as for manipulation, some multifingered hands have recently been designed that are not intended for active fingertip manipulation. Examples include the Skinner Hand (Skinner, 1975), the Pennsylvania Hand (Abramowitz and co-workers, 1983) and a three-fingered industrial hand from Odetics Inc.

Some intermediate approaches between fully servoed fingers and passive multifingered hands also suggest themselves. For example, the hand could be simplified by servoing only those joints that contribute importantly to finger manipulation. The joints used primarily for grasping, or for preshaping the hand for a class of grasps, need not be servoed. Thus, one might servo the last two joints of the fingers, while leaving the base joints nonservoed but able to shift between different positions so that the hand could shift among grasps 1, 2, and 3 in Figure 1. A second way to simplify the hand might be to emphasize only those motions that are performed least well by the robot arm or wrist for example, rolling about an axis perpendicular to the wrist axis.

Summary of End-Effector Types

Figure 10 provides a summary of the basic categories of end-effectors, and helps to clarify the applications of each. The taxonomy is roughly analogous to the taxonomy of human grasps in Figure 1. The left side includes passive end-effectors, that are capable of executing certain power grasps, while the right side consists of active hands. Under the passive side, the left-most branch includes vacuum, electromagnetic, and Bernoulli-effect end-effectors. As these end-effectors neither confine parts nor apply grasp forces across them, they are kinematically closest to the non prehensile platform grip that people use (albeit, with the important advantage of being able to pull as well as push). The second branch includes wrap grippers such as those in Figures 3 and 5. Like the human wrap and power spherical grasps, these end-effectors envelop the part, and distribute the grasp forces. The next branch includes passive pinch grippers such as the grippers in Figures 2 and 4. These grippers typically have small contact areas and apply a strong grasp force between two fingers, like the human Lateral Pinch grasp in Figure 1.

The right side of the taxonomy includes both the two-fingered servo gripper of Figure 9 and dextrous multi-fingered hands. Here the distinctions depend largely on the number of fingers and the number of joints per finger. For example, the comparatively simple two-fingered gripper of Figure 9 is confined to opposed-thumb/index-finger grasps (shown at the extreme lower right of Figure 1). The multifingered dextrous hands are capable of a wider repertoire of precision grasps, although they tend to be specialized for specific sub classes. For example, the Stanford/JPL hand (Salisbury, 1985) is best suited for grasp 4 of the human grasp taxonomy.

DESIGN ISSUES

Design Approach

Good end-effector design is in many ways the same as good design of any mechanical device. Foremost, it requires:

- A formal understanding of the functional specifications and relevant constraints. In the author's experience, most end-effector design "failures" occurred not through faulty engineering but through incompletely articulated requirements and constraints. In other words, the end-effector solved the wrong problem.
- A "concurrent engineering" approach in which such issues as ease of maintenance, as well as related problems in fixturing, robot programming, etc, are addressed in parallel with end-effector design.
- An attention to details in which issues such as power requirements, impact resistance, and sensor signal routing are not left as an afterthought.

Constraints on End-Effector Design

As discussed in the first section, the end-effector is a bridge connecting the robot to the world around it. End-effector design is therefore influenced almost equally by three sets of constraints arising from the task, the environment, and the robot itself. While the presence of these constraints means that the end-effector cannot be designed independently from the robot or the working environment, it also provides opportunities, as shown in Figure 11. Thus, a difficult end-effector design task can often be made easier by redesigning the robot and vice-versa. This theme will be returned to in the final section of this chapter, after exploring a number of design issues in more detail.

Table 1 lists suggested end-effector design solutions for various classes of parts. These suggestions should, however, be tempered by the characteristics of the task to be performed and the robot itself. In particular, Tables 2 and 3 summarize the main issues involved in arriving at an end-effector design solution for a particular task and robot.

Sensing

Although sensors are vital for some applications, and useful in many others for detecting unexpected situations (eg, if a part is missing or has been dropped) they are surprisingly scarce in many industrial applications. This condition is beginning to be reversed, however, as robot controllers become more sophisticated and better able to respond to sensory information. The sensors used in end-effectors

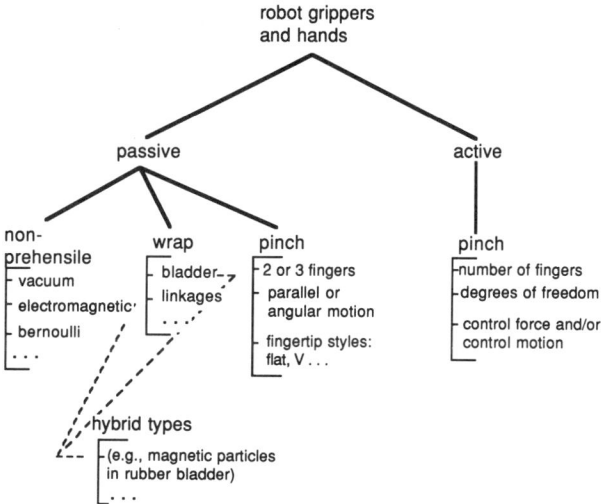

Figure 10. A taxonomy of the basic end-effector types.

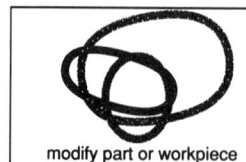

Figure 11. Constraints on end-effector design and alternative strategies.

can be grouped broadly into three categories: binary, analog and vector/matrix.

- Binary sensors include on/off devices such as microswitches and magnetic or optical proximity sensors. They are typically inexpensive, reliable, and easy to interface to industrial robot controllers. They are the sensor of choice whenever a "go/no-go" decision is required. In many cases, the threshold for triggering a binary sensor can be manually adjusted, which allows them to be used to detect excessive contact forces, etc. Typical applications of binary sensors include checking for part presence in the gripper, gripper status (jaws open or closed), force overload, and confirming that a part is correctly registered in a gripper (ie, that all contact surfaces have established solid contact).
- Analog sensors include linear-variable-differential-transformers (LVDTs), thermocouples, strain gauges, piezo-electric sensors. They are more expensive than binary sensors, especially since they typically require power supplies, amplification, and A/D conversion for use with a robot controller. They are used when the magnitude of a quantity is required. Examples of applications include the measurement of grasp forces, part weight, or the dimension of an object grasped by the fingers.
- Vector and matrix sensors include multi-axis load cells and tactile arrays. These sensors typically require local signal processing and multiplexing. The rate at which information can be relayed to the robot controller is consequently slower than with binary or simple analog sensors. Examples of applications include the measurement of contact forces between the grasped object and the environment (eg, for contour tracking) and the measurement of surface shapes or features on a grasped object. The use of such sensors for exploration and manipulation with active end-effectors is an emerging field. Reviews of sensor technologies and discussions of the potential applications of these sensors to manipulation can be found in Hollerbach (1987), Nicholls and Lee (1989), and Howe and Cutkosky (1990).

Actuation Methods

The power source for most industrial end-effectors continues to be compressed air. The advantages to pneumatic actuation include high speeds and large forces from compact actuators. In addition, it is easy to adjust the grasp force by regulating the air pressure. The chief drawbacks of pneumatic actuation are the difficulties in achieving precise position control for active hands (due primarily to the compressibility of air) and the need to run air lines down what is otherwise usually an all-electric robot arm.

Electric actuation remains the method of choice for servo grippers since it is easy to achieve precise force and position control with DC servo motors. A danger with electric actuation is that the motor(s) can overheat. Solutions to this problem include designing the motors for prolonged stall loads (the motor is stalled when the gripper has closed upon an object and the fingers are not moving), and equipping the gripper with a brake or using a non-backdrivable transmission (see the section on Transmission Systems) which would allow the motor current to be reduced after the fingers have settled on the part. The latter two solutions are preferable if motor size and weight must be minimized.

Hydraulic power is most commonly used where large forces are needed and/or the robot is hydraulic so that a hydraulic supply is readily available. Advantages to hydraulic power include the ability to achieve very large clamping forces with small actuators and the ability to precisely control finger motions using conventional servovalves. Disadvantages may include slower actuation (unless the gripper is designed accordingly) and the inevitable tendency of hydraulic systems to leak small amounts of fluid.

Force Analysis

Force analysis is a standard exercise in engineering statics and will not be covered here. For details we refer the reader to engineering textbooks and to articles by Kato (1982), Tanie (1985) and Chen (1982) which provide a number of useful worked examples for industrial grippers.

The actuator, acting through the fingers, applies forces to the object or tool being held. These forces must resist

Table 1. Part Characteristics and Associated Solutions for End-Effector Grasping

Part Characteristics	Grasping Solutions
Size, Weight	
Large, heavy	Grippers using wrap grips, taking advantage of friction, vacuum, or electromagnetic holding.
Small, light	Two-fingered gripper; vacuum cup if smooth surface; electromagnet if ferrous alloy.
Shape	
Prismatic	Two fingered parallel-jaw gripper; angular motion if all parts have approximately same dimensions.
Cylindrical	Parallel or angular motion two-finger gripper with V-jaw fingertips if light; wrap gripper if heavy; consider gripping on end with three-finger gripper if task or fixtures permit.
Flat	Parallel or angular motion gripper or vacuum attachment.
Irregular	Wrap grasp using linkages or bladder; consider augmenting grasp with vacuum or electromagnetic holding for heavy parts.
Surface	
Smooth	Good for vacuum attachments, simple electromagnets, two-fingered grippers with flat fingertips.
Rough	Compliant material (eg, low durometer rubber) on fingertips or compliant membrane filled with powder or magnetic particles. Grippers that use a wrap grasp are less sensitive to variations in surface quality.
Slippery	Consider electromagnet or vacuum to help hold onto slippery material. Grippers that use a wrap grasp are less sensitive to variations in friction.
Material	
Ferrous	Electromagnet (provided that other concerns do not rule out the presence of strong magnetic fields).
Soft	Consider vacuum or soft gripping materials.
Very delicate	Soft wrap grippers and vacuum grippers such as those in Figure 3 can grip very gently. Compliant fingertips with foam rubber or a membrane covering a powder can also be used to distribute the contact pressure. If the part is very light and fragile, consider lifting it using the Bernoulli effect.

Table 2. Task Considerations in End-Effector Design

Initial Accuracy

Is the initial accuracy of the part high (as when retrieving a part from a fixture or lathe chuck) or low (as when picking unfixtured components off a conveyor)? If the former case, design the gripper so that it will conform to the part position and orientation (as do the grippers in Figures 5 and 9). In the latter, make the gripper center the part (as will most parallel-jaw grippers and the gripper in Figure 2).

Final Accuracy

Is the final accuracy of the part high or low? In the former case (as when putting a precisely machined peg into a chamfered hole) the gripper and/or robot arm will need compliance. In the latter case, use an end-effector that centers the part.

Anticipated Forces

What are the magnitudes of expected task forces and from what directions will they come? Are these forces resisted directly by the gripper jaws, or indirectly, through friction? For example, vertical forces are resisted directly by the gripper jaws in Figure 6, but forces along the cylinder are resisted only by friction.

Speed, Cycle-Time

Are speeds and accelerations large enough that inertial forces and moments should be considered in computing the required grip force?

---

the externally applied forces and moments arising from gravity, robot accelerations, and contact with objects in the environment. Estimation of dynamic loads requires information about the maximum accelerations that should be expected. The maximum acceleration of a robot arm is usually known (typically at least 4.2 m/s^2 or about one half the acceleration of gravity). These accelerations, however, are small compared to those that occur when a robot comes into contact with a fixture (frequently four times the acceleration of gravity). As a result, some designers recommend an additional safety factor of 1.2 to 2.0 for dynamic loads.

Once the forces on the object are known it becomes possible to estimate the required gripping forces. These will depend on the coefficient of friction in addition to the geometry of the gripper. For a gripper with steel fingers holding a steel part the coefficient of friction will usually be 0.3 or greater. For a gripper with rubber fingertips the coefficient is often 1.0 or greater, although this will depend greatly on whether the surfaces are clean or dirty (Cutkosky and co-workers, 1987). If the required gripping force seems excessive it will be necessary to look for more compliant fingertip materials and/or a grasp that more effectively envelops the part. Table 4 illustrates typical grasp and actuator force calculations for an industrial end-effector such as that in Figure 2.

For multifingered hands, the force balance between the fingers and the object is usually statically indeterminate, in which case equilibrium equations constrain, but do not uniquely determine, the fingertip forces. In these cases it

Table 3. Robot Consideration in End-Effector Design

Accuracy

What is the robot accuracy? In particular, is it better or worse than the initial part presentation accuracy? In the former case, consider having the gripper locate or center the part. In the latter, use compliance and/or let the gripper conform to the part's location while gripping. Similar arguments apply to the final (eg, as assembled) accuracy of the part. If the robot accuracy is poorer than the final accuracy, compliance in the robot and/or gripper will be necessary. If the robot accuracy is better than the final accuracy, compliance in unconstrained directions is generally undesirable as it can degrade the accuracy of part placement.

Degrees of Freedom

How many degrees of freedom does the robot have? If it has four or less then the range of possible gripping positions and orientations will be severely restricted and will have a strong influence on the gripper design.

Actuation Power

What is the robot power source? (All things being equal, a hydraulic gripper clearly makes more sense on a hydraulic robot than an electric one.)

Ease of Modifying Robot Program Dynamically

If the robot is a simple one, for which it is difficult to update the robot program to account for minor variations in part placement etc, consider providing the ability to make some adjustments with the gripper. For example, the gripper in Figure 5 has the ability to passively adjust the orientation of a workpiece and the gripper in Figure 9 has controllable fingertips that simplify robot programming.

Provisions for Sensor Input

What provisions does the robot controller have for responding to sensor input? Most controllers accept binary inputs, but analog and array sensors usually require an additional microprocessor for interpreting the data and communicating with the robot over a serial or parallel line.

Provisions for Additional Servos

Does the robot have provisions for controlling extra axes? If so, this may simplify active hand control and coordination with the robot. However, hand control is very different from robot joint control (small motions, low speeds, emphasis on forces) so that standard robot joint controllers are usually not suited for end-effectors.

---

is convenient to decompose the force balance into external and internal grasp forces. The former are used to match external forces and moments on the object while the latter work in combination with friction to prevent slipping. For a more detailed discussion of internal and external grasp force specification see Kerr and Roth (1986), and Li and co-workers (1989).

Finally, it is important to ensure that the number of contact points assumed in the force balance is really achieved. As discussed in the section on Soft Grippers this was an important consideration in the design of the end-effector in Figure 5.

Transmission Systems

Once the grip force is established, the actuator force or torque can be computed for a given gripper and transmission design. Numerous transmissions systems using linkages, gears, cables, cams, and power screws are available for transmitting forces between the actuator and the fingers. The relative merits and drawbacks of each will not be explored here; however there are a couple of questions that must always be addressed:

- What is the desired mechanical advantage or gear ratio? Depending on the type of actuator, range of motion required, and desired grasp forces the transmission ratio may be anything from 1/1 to over 100/1. Often it is easiest to experiment with different ratios by using the virtual work relationship:

$$\eta V_a P = 2 V_f F$$

where V_a and V_f are the actuator and fingertip velocities, respectively, P and F are the actuator and fingertip forces respectively, and η is a factor representing the efficiency of the transmission system. For a first pass, η can often be set to one (although this underestimates the required actuator force). The ratio of V_a/V_f can usually be easily established from a scale drawing of the gripper. For example, if the fingertips move 2 mm for 1 mm of actuator travel the ratio is 1/2, in which case (assuming no transmission losses) the required actuator force is $4F$. In Table 4 this method is used to compute the gripping and actuator forces for the end-effectors in Figure 2. For many grippers, the transmission ratio varies as a function of how far the gripper is closed. If the gripper is to handle a range of objects, this ratio must be determined for each size. This effect can also be used to advantage in designing a linkage that provides the largest grasping force for a given actuator when the fingers are closing on the heaviest object.

- Should the mechanism be back-drivable? That is, should a sufficiently large force applied to the jaws be able to force them apart by driving the actuator backwards? Most pneumatic designs are back-driveable, provided the air pressure is not too high. This makes the gripper more forgiving of programming errors; if a part held in the gripper unexpectedly encounters an obstacle in the environment, the resulting forces will pry open the gripper jaws, causing the gripper to release the part instead of transmitting the full load of the collision to the robot. On the other hand, electrically actuated end-effectors are commonly designed not to be back-driveable so that the motor can be turned off, or the motor torque at least reduced, after gripping to prevent overheating the motor. The most common transmissions for this purpose include worm gear and screw drives, as employed in the gripper of Figure 4.

Table 4. Typical Gripping and Actuator Force Values for a Two-Fingered End-Effector such as that in Figure 2 (adapted from Wright and Cutkosky (1985))

	Velocity Ratio[1] (V_a/V_f)	Friction Coefficient[2] (μ)	Grip Force[3] (2 F)	Actuator Force[4] (P)	Pneumatic Cylinder Diameter[5] (D)
Gripper in Figure 2: With Steel Fingers	3.0	0.3	333 N (75 lbf)	111 N (25 lbf)	2.0 cm (0.8 inch)
With Rubber-Surfaced Fingers	3.0	1.0	100 N (22.5 lbf)	33 N (7.5 lbf)	1.1 cm (0.4 inch)

1. As discussed in the section, Design Issues, the ratio, (V_a/V_f), is equal to the velocity of the actuator divided by the velocity at which the fingertips move together. The ratios in the table are typical values for when the grippers are nearly closed. The ratio for the design in Figure 2 becomes considerably smaller when the gripper is only partly closed (as in gripping an over-sized object).
2. The coefficient of friction, μ, will depend on the materials used and on how clean and smooth the surfaces are. The numbers used in the table are conservative values for steel against steel and rubber against steel.
3. The grip force, 2 F, is calculated for a compact metal object weighing approximately 25 N. The object is picked up with a high speed robot, capable of accelerating 9.8 m/sec^2, about equal to the acceleration of gravity. The maximum acceleration the part could experience is therefore 2 g, corresponding to a force of 50 N. A dynamic safety factor of 2 is used so the required grip force is given by: $2 \mu F \geq 100$ N.
4. The actuator force, P, is a function of the grip force and the velocity ratio: $2 F = P(V_a/V_f)$.
5. The pneumatic cylinder diameter is chosen so that the required actuator force will be achieved as long as the air supply pressure remains above 35 N/cm^2 (50 psi).

DESIGN GUIDELINES

Achieving Greater Versatility

As robots are applied to more demanding tasks and expected to work with a wider range of parts, there is a need to extend the versatility of their end-effectors. The basic approaches to increasing the versatility include arrays of interchangeable grippers, "universal" grippers, and compound grippers.

- Interchangeable grippers are perhaps the most common solution to allowing a robot to grasp a wider array of part sizes and shapes. The usual approach is to provide a magazine of different end-effectors and a quick-change wrist so the robot can easily mount and dismount them as required. A similar strategy, and a simpler one if sensory information is to be routed from the end-effector down the robot arm, is to provide changeable fingertips for a single gripper. This is the approach adopted in the servo gripper of Figure 9. The signals from the force and position sensors (10 in all) would have to be routed through contacts at a quick-change wrist if the gripper were to be dismounted. Therefore, it was easier to provide an array of specialized snap-on fingertips that could be exchanged by the robot using a special tool.
- Universal grippers include dextrous hands such as those discussed in the section on Dextrous Hands and passive versions of multifingered hands that can adopt a variety of grasp styles. The advantages of a universal gripper (no need to pause while changing end-effectors and the ability to hold an extremely wide range of part shapes) must be weighed against their cost and complexity and the likelihood that they will never grasp particular components as precisely as single-purpose grippers with custom-designed fingertips can.
- Compound grippers are a "Swiss army knife" approach that consists of putting a variety of different fingertips onto a single pair of gripper jaws. Provided that the different fingertips do not interfere with each other, this solution combines the advantages of not having to pause to change end-effectors with the advantages of custom-designed fingertips for special parts. In addition, this approach is typically far less expensive than designing universal hands. Figure 12 illustrates the design of some compound fingertips for a parallel-jaw gripper. The inner surfaces permit the gripper to close on small cylindrical and rectangular components while the rounded outer surfaces grasp by expanding against the inside diameters of large tubes.

Stepping back from the design of the end-effector itself, it is useful to recall that the design of the end-effector is coupled with the the design of fixtures, parts and the robot. Thus when trying to increase the versatility of an end-effector it is worth considering whether the problem might be more economically addressed by redesigning any of these.

Integrate the Design of End-effectors and Fixturing. The designs of end-effectors, fixtures and materials handling components (eg, feeders, pallets) tend to be thought of as separate problems but are in fact highly coupled. For example, consider the relationship between an end-effector and the fixtures it interacts with. If the fixtures are well designed, the task of loading and unloading them becomes much easier. For example, the fixtures may have cut-outs that make it easy for the gripper jaws to get around the part before closing.

In some applications, it is possible for an end-effector to become a fixture. For example, the end-effector in Figure 5 is used as a fixture while the forgings are inspected and

Gripper with compound fingertips

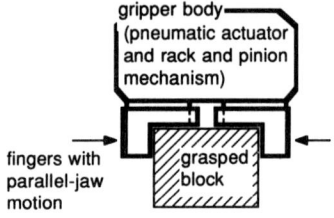

Fingers detail:

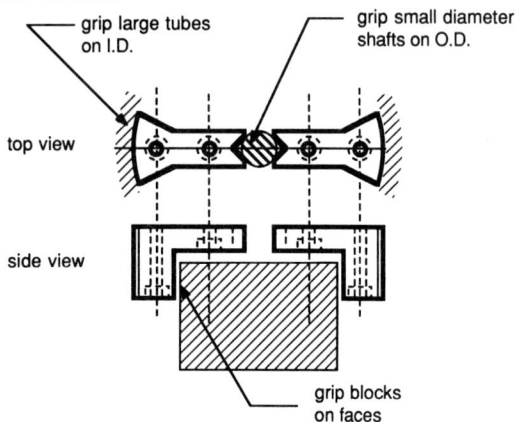

Figure 12. Compound fingertips with multiple gripping abilities.

stamped. Similarly, one robot may hold a part while another robot works on the part or adds components to it. Going a step further, consider using a gripper which is detached at the wrist, while still holding a part, so that it becomes a kind of portable vise. In a recent application, clamplike end-effectors for machined turbine blades were developed which remained attached to the blades, rather than the robot, so that accuracy was maintained during machining and inspection (Cutkosky and co-workers, 1982). Instead of repeatedly grasping and ungrasping the complex turbine blades, the robot simply mounted and dismounted the end-effectors at the wrist.

Integrate the Design of End-Effectors and Parts. One solution to the problem of grasping a variety of parts is to standardize the design of the parts themselves, using Group Technology principles (Eckert, 1984) to reduce the variability in sizes and geometries. This approach is very much in the spirit of the grasp taxonomy of Figure 1, which advocates designing grippers for families or classes of parts. When it is difficult to reduce the range of parts to a few standard families (or when the parts are simply hard to grip) consider adding special non-functional features such as tabs or handles so that a simple gripper can work with them. An example of this approach is shown in Figure 13. The application was to study the design of grippers and fixtures for storing and retrieving tools for astronauts. After some exploration, it was determined that it would be easier and more reliable to provide special tool palettes with standard gripping holes, which the robot arm could grasp using an expanding pin, than to try to design an end-effector capable of handling all the tools and instruments that people might use.

Integrate Design of End-effectors and the Robot or Robot Wrist. In many applications, an active servo gripper is undesirably complicated, fragile, and expensive, and yet, it is desirable to obtain some of the compliant force/motion characteristics that an actively controlled gripper can provide. For example, when assembling close-fitting parts, compliance at the end-effector can prevent large contact forces from arising due to minor position errors of the robot or manufacturing tolerances in the parts themselves. For such applications a compliant wrist, mounted between the gripper and the robot arm may be the solution. In particular, remote center of compliance (RCC) wrists allow the force/deflection properties of the end-effector to be tailored to suit a task (Whitney, 1982; Cutkosky and Wright, 1986b). Specifically, the stiffness matrix of a part held in the end-effector is made to be diagonal at or near its tip, where it first contacts a mating part. This ensures that the contact forces will guide the parts together and minimizes the likelihood of jamming. Active wrists have also been developed for use with end-effectors for precise, high-bandwidth control of forces and fine motions (Glassman and co-workers, 1984; Hollis and co-workers, 1988).

SUMMARY

As the illustrations of end-effectors and the design guidelines in the section Design Guidelines should suggest, there are many ways of solving end-effector design problems. It is also a truism of design methodology that for every design solution, there is a more general problem statement for which a wider array of solutions could be found. A useful design methodology for ensuring that such opportunities are not missed is to construct "how/why" diagrams like those in Figures 14 and 15. "How to" solutions are obtained by traversing the tree from top to bottom. The rationale (why) is found at the node just above each solution.

For example, Figure 14 illustrates a how/why diagram for a hypothetical design problem in which the designer has been asked to redesign an end-effector so that it can pick up thin components from a flat work surface and grasp them. This statement of the problem initially leads to solutions such as those in the lower left corner of Figure 14, including special fingertips for scooping up thin parts, magnetic grippers if the parts are ferromagnetic, or vacuum grippers if the parts have smooth surfaces and are not too heavy. But end-effector redesign is just one solution to picking up parts from a flat surface. Another solution is to redesign the parts themselves so that an existing end-effector could be retained. Perhaps the parts can be made thicker without making them less functional or more expensive to produce. If not, perhaps gripping tabs or holes can be provided to the parts. (This was essentially

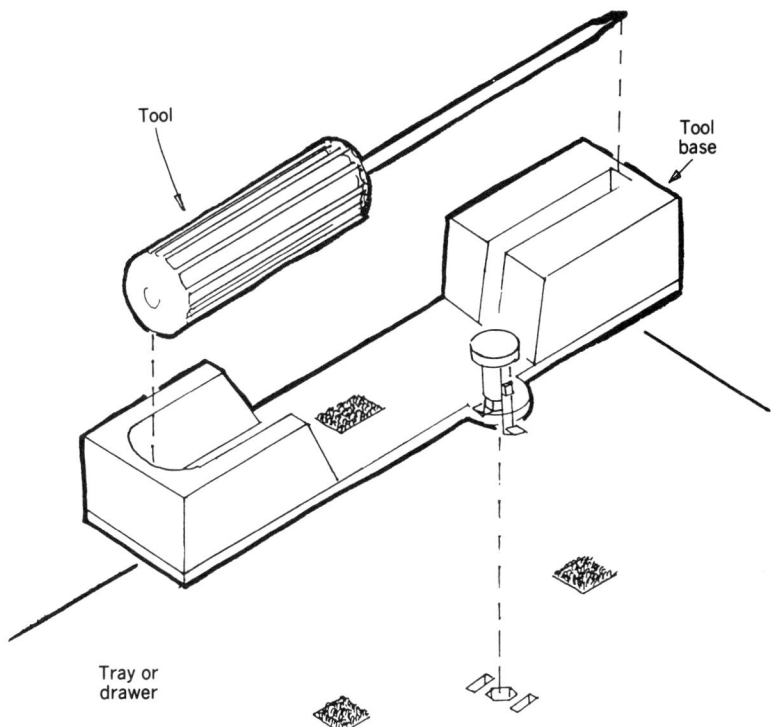

Figure 13. A proposed solution for "palletizing" parts and tools for a robotic storage/retrieval system for use in space (Vaska and co-workers, 1989).

the solution adopted in the example concerning a robot to retrieve tools for astronauts). Moving up another level, one asks, "Why is it necessary to acquire thin parts from a table?" This leads to other solutions. Perhaps the table can be redesigned turning it into a rack from which parts are easily picked up, or perhaps holes can be cut in the table surface to prevent interference with the gripper. Moving up still another level, one asks, "Why do we need to acquire the parts at all?" In this example, the answer is that they need to be picked up after they have been placed on a flat surface for visual inspection. Thus, another solution might be to inspect the parts without setting them down in the first place. Still another solution might be to design an end-effector that travels with the part (like the clamp end-effectors used with machined turbine blades discussed in the last section).

Figure 15 shows a similar how/why diagram for enabling an end-effector to grasp a wider range of part shapes. Perhaps the most obvious solution is to design a more versatile end-effector—something like a dextrous hand. However, there are many other solutions, some of which have been explored in the preceding sections, including magazines of interchangeable grippers or fingertips and the use of compound fingers. One level up, one asks "Why do we need to grasp a wider range of parts?" Perhaps the parts can be redesigned to make them more standard, or perhaps special pallets or adaptors can be designed for the parts that make them simpler to grasp.

As these examples illustrate, there are numerous solutions to end-effector design problems and it is always worthwhile to consider end-effector design in the context of the broader problem of acquiring and manipulating

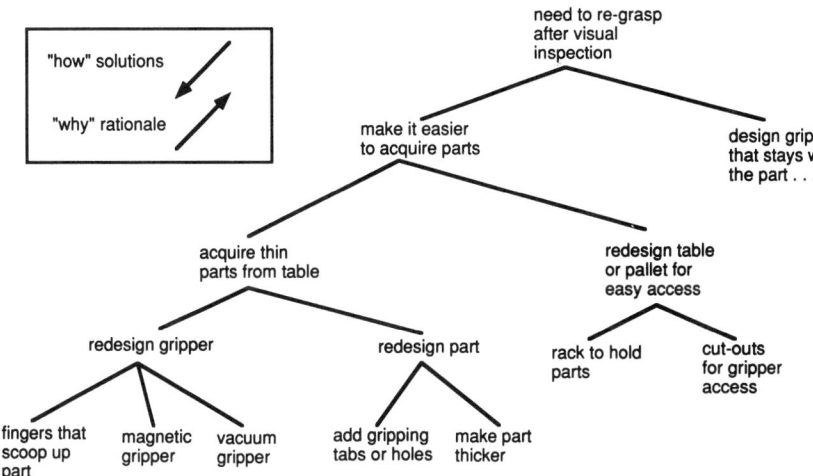

Figure 14. A "how/why" diagram of design solutions and rationale for a problem involving picking up thin components from a flat surface.

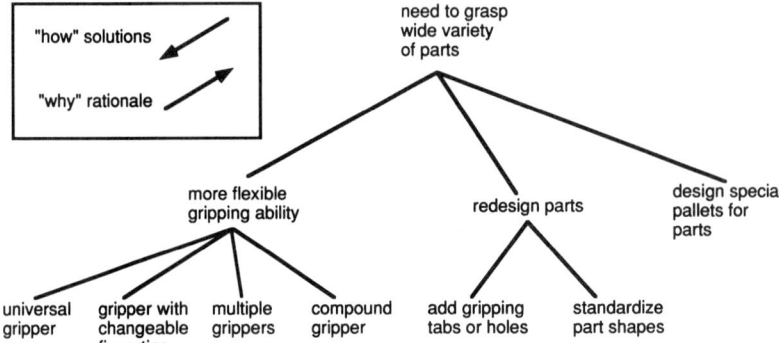

Figure 15. A "how/why" diagram of solutions and rationale for a design problem involving a need to grasp a wide range of parts.

parts, in which the robot, the parts, the end-effector, and the environment are all candidates for redesign.

BIBLIOGRAPHY

J. D. Abramowitz, J. W. Goodnow, and B. Paul, "Pennsylvania Articulated Mechanical Hand," *International Conference on Computers in Engineering,* ASME, Chicago, Ill., Aug. 1983.

F. Y. Chen, "Force Analysis and Design Consideration of Grippers," *Industrial Robot* (UK) **9,** 243–249 (Dec. 1982).

M. R. Cutkosky, "On Grasp Choice, Grasp Models, and the Design of Hands for Manufacturing Tasks," *IEEE Trans. Robotics Autom.* **5,** 269–279 (June 1989).

M. R. Cutkosky and P. K. Wright, "Friction Stability and the Design of Robotic Fingers," *Int. J. Robotics Res.* **5,** 20–37 (1986a).

M. R. Cutkosky and P. K. Wright, "Active Control of a Compliant Wrist in Manufacturing Tasks," *ASME J. Eng. Indust.* **108,** 36–43 (1986b).

M. R. Cutkosky, J. M. Jourdain, and P. K. Wright, "Skin Materials for Robotic Fingers," *Proceedings of the IEEE Conference on Robotics and Automation,* Raleigh, N.C., Mar. 1987, pp. 1649–1654.

M. R. Cutkosky, E. Kurokawa, and P. K. Wright, "Programmable Comformable Clamps," *Autofact 4,* Philadelphia, Pa., 11.51–11.58 (Nov. 1982).

P. Datseris and W. Palm, "Principals on the Development of Mechanical Hands Which Can Manipulate Objects by Means of Active Control," *Paper 84–DET–37,* ASME, 1984.

R. L. Eckert, "Codes and Classification Systems," in N. L. Hyer, ed., *Group Technology at Work,* Society of Manufacturing Engineers, Dearborn, Mich., 1984, pp. 43–51.

E. Glassman, R. L. Hollis, and R. H. Taylor, "Compliant Gripper," *IBM Tech. Discl. Bull.* **27**(1B), 772–773 (June 1984).

S. Hirose and Y. Umetani, "The Development of Soft Gripper for the Versatile Robot Hand," *Mech. Mach. Theory* (GB), 351–358 (1978).

J. M. Hollerbach, "Robot Hands and Tactile Sensing," in Grimson and Patil, eds., *AI in the 1980's and Beyond,* MIT Press, Cambridge, Mass., 1987, pp. 317–342.

R. L. Hollis, A. P. Allan, and S. Salcudeanm, "A Six Degree-of-Freedom Magnetically Levitated Variable Compliance Fine Motion Wrist," in R. Bolles and B. Roth, eds., *Robotics Research, the Fourth International Symposium,* MIT Press, Cambridge, Mass., 1988, pp. 65–73.

R. Howe and M. R. Cutkosky, "Touch Sensing for Robotic Manipulation and Recognition," submitted to *Robotic Review* (May 1990).

T. Iberall and C. MacKenzie, "Opposition Space and Human Prehension," in *Dextrous Robot Hands,* Springer-Verlag, New York, 1990, Chapt. 2.

S. Jacobsen, J. Wood, D. F. Knutti, and K. B. Biggers, "The Utah/M.I.T. Dextrous Hand: Work in Progress," *Int. J. Robotics Res.* 3(4) (Winter 1984).

R. S. Johansson and G. Westling, "Roles of Glabrous Skin Receptors and Sensorimotor Memory in Automatic Control of Precision Grip when Lifting Rougher or More Slippery Objects," *Exp. Brain Res.* **56,** 550–564 (1984).

I. Kato, *Mechanical Hands Illustrated,* Hemisphere Publishing Corporation, New York, 1982.

G. M. Kenaley and M. R. Cutkosky, Electrorheological Fluid-Based Robotic Fingers with Tactile Sensing," *Proceedings of the IEEE Conference on Robotics and Automation,* Scottsdale, Ariz., May 14–19, 1989, pp. 132–136.

J. Kerr and B. Roth, "Analysis of Multifingered Hands," *Int. J. Robotics Res.* **4,** 3–17 (1986).

L. Leifer, "Rehabilitative Robots," *Robotics Age,* 4–15 (May/June 1981).

Z. Li, P. Hsu, and S. Sastry, "Grasping and Coordinated Manipulated by a Multifingered Hand," *Int. J. Robotics Res.* **8,** 33–50 (1989).

G. Lundstrom, B. Glemme, and B. W. Rooks, *Industrial Robots—Gripper Review,* International Fluidics Services Ltd., 35–39 High Street, Kempston, Bedford, England, 1977.

J. Napier, "The Evolution of the Hand," *Sci. Am.* **207,** 56–62 (Dec. 1962).

H. R. Nicholls and M. H. Lee, "A Survey of Robot Tactile Sensing Technology," *Int. J. Robotics Res.* **8,** 3–30 (June 1989).

T. Okada, "Object Handling System for Manual Industry," *IEEE Trans. Syst. Man Cybern.* **SMC-9,** 79–89 (Feb. 1979).

E. Pearce, E. Pfaff, J. McManus, and A. Yee, *Flexible Robotic Servo Gripper,* Final report, Master's engineering design project, Mechanical Engineering Dept., Stanford University, 1986.

P. Rabischong, "Phylogeny of the Hand," in R. Tubiana, ed., *The Hand,* W. B. Saunders Co., Philadelphia, Penn., 1981, Chapt. 4.

J. K. Salisbury, "Kinematic and Force Analysis of Articulated Hands," in M. T. Mason and J. K. Salisbury, eds., *Robot Hands and the Mechanics of Manipulation,* MIT Press, Cambridge, Mass., 1985, section I.

Simrit Corp., *Pneumatically Operating Gripping and Clamping Elements,* Arlington Hts., Ill., 1984.

F. Skinner, "Designing a Multiple Prehension Manipulator," *J. Mech. Eng.* **97**, 30–37 (Sept. 1975).

K. Tanie, "Design of Robot Hands," in S. Y. Nof, ed., *The Handbook of Industrial Robotics,* Wiley, New York, 1985, Chapt. 8.

U.S. Pat. 4,545,722 (Oct. 1985), M. R. Cutkosky and E. Kurokawa.

Vaska and co-workers, *Automatic Tool Storage and Retrieval System,* Senior engineering design project, Mechanical Engineering Dept., Stanford University, 1989.

H. J. Warnecke and I. I. Schmidt, "Flexible Grippers For Handling Systems—Design Possibilities and Experiences," *Fifth I.C.P.R.,* Chicago, Ill., Aug. 1979, pp. 320–324.

D. E. Whitney, "Quasi-Static Assembly of Compliantly Supported Parts," *ASME Trans. Dyn. Syst., Measur. Control* **104**, 65–77 (Mar. 1982).

P. K. Wright and M. R. Cutkosky, "Design of Grippers," in S. Nof, ed., *The Handbook of Industrial Robotics,* John Wiley and Sons, Inc., New York, 1985, Chapt. 2.4.

M. R. CUTKOSKY
Stanford University

ROBOTICS

The objective of this article is to survey the state of the art of intelligent robots. By way of introduction, the terms robot and artificial intelligence are defined, intelligent robots are classified according to their level of intelligence, social and technoeconomic incentives for the development of intelligent robots are discussed, and the article touches on the socioeconomic impacts of this development. Past accomplishments and present issues in major robotics research areas are covered.

ROBOT CHARACTERISTICS

Capability, Components, and Intelligence

Several definitions for the term robot have been proposed (Jablonowski and Posey, 1985). None of these definitions are adequate because they exclude robot intelligence of any kind. Hence, the following definition is proposed (Nitzan and co-workers, 1983):

> A robot is a general-purpose machine system that, like a human, can perform a variety of different tasks under conditions that may not be known a priori.

Being a general-purpose machine system, the terms robot and robot system are regarded as synonymous. A robot system may include any of the following major functional components:

Effectors. "Arms," "hands," "legs," and "feet" (see ROBOT HANDS AND END EFFECTORS; ROBOTS, LEGGED).

Sensors. Contact and noncontact (see SENSORS AND SENSOR FUSION).

Computers. Top-level controller and lower level controllers (including communication channels).

Auxiliary Equipment. Tools, jigs, fixtures, tables, pallets, conveyors, part feeders, etc.

A robot (or robot system) is controlled by a single top-level computer (or controller). A group of such systems, which may or may not interact, are regarded as separate robots if they are not controlled by the same top-level computer; adding a single computer above them will merge these systems into a single robot.

Although a robot performs some human tasks and there is a similarity between the functional components of a robot and those of a human (or a human team), a robot is not required to act or look like a human. It should, however, be able to perform tasks that require flexibility and artificial intelligence. Flexibility means the ability to perform a class of different tasks; artificial intelligence means the ability of a machine system to perceive conditions that may not have been known *a priori,* to decide what actions should then be performed, and to plan those actions accordingly. Some of the potential robot tasks can be performed by humans; others cannot (eg, in a high radiation environment).

Classification

Like human intelligence, robot intelligence is variable. This observation is compatible with the Japanese classification of industrial robots into five categories (Sadamoto, 1981):

> A slave manipulator teleoperated by a human master.
> A limited-sequence manipulator (further classified into hard-to-adjust and easy-to-adjust categories).
> A teach-replay robot.
> A computer-controlled robot.
> An intelligent robot.

Learning from Biological Systems

Current robot capabilities to act, sense, and think are in many respects inferior to those of animals, in general, and humans, in particular. By studying biological systems, principles may be discovered that can be used, perhaps by analogy, to improve the functional components of a robot as well as their cooperation. Using such a bionic approach may lead to improvements in robot effectors (eg, the automatic feedback control of cooperative flexible arms, fingers, and legs or the dexterity of multifinger hands), sensors (eg, integration of several sensors in parallel) (see SENSORS AND SENSOR FUSION), and computer processing, eg, representation of knowledge (see KNOWLEDGE REPRESENTATION) and reasoning (qv). These improved capabilities will advance sensor-guided manipulation (eg, picking one of jumbled objects in a bin), perception (eg, recognizing, locating, and inspecting objects in cluttered environments or outdoor scenes), and other activities in which these components are integrated.

Incentives for Intelligent Robot Development

The important incentives for the developments of intelligent robots are social and technoeconomic.

Social Incentives. The most important incentive for developing robots should be social, replacing humans who perform undesired jobs by machines. Japan, for example, is planning to embark on a large-scale program for the development of robots operating in hazardous environments (Umetani and Yonemoto, 1983). The ranking of robot development should thus be ordered according to job undesirability, ie, jobs that are

Lethal (eg, in a high radiation environment).
Harmful (eg, paint spraying, handling toxic chemicals).
Hazardous (eg, combat, fire fighting).
Strenuous (eg, lifting heavy loads or visual inspection).
Noisy (eg, forging, riveting)
Dull (eg, sorting, assembling).

Technoeconomic Incentives. The second most important incentive for robot development is technoeconomic: reducing the cost of manufacturing products and improving their quality.

Current Limitations. In spite of the strong social and economic incentives mentioned above, only a very small fraction of the entire human workforce in the world has been replaced by industrial robots. Furthermore, Engleberger (1980) estimates that the growth rate of the total number of industrial robots (excluding teleoperators (qv) and limited-sequence manipulators) will rise from 2,000 per year in 1980 to 40,000 per year in 1990; these figures correspond to a yearly replacement of about 0.003–0.06% of the total blue-collar workforce in the industrialized countries. Such a low rate of growth of robot population has resulted primarily from the following limitations of today's industrial robots (Nitzan and co-workers, 1983).

Insufficient Material-Handling Flexibility. Workpieces and other objects can be handled only if they are indexed within tolerances that match the accuracy of the robot manipulator. Such restriction limits the flexibility of manufacturing, especially in batch production of a mix of products.

Open-Loop Control. Jobs that require closed-loop feedback control to correct local errors cannot be performed. For example, today's arc-welding robots cannot track a joint of randomly variable shape and gap in one pass and adjust the torch movement and welding parameters accordingly; this limitation excludes these robots from a large market.

Inability to Detect and Correct Errors. Detection of unexpected errors and the recovery from them cannot be done; a robot system cannot verify that all the robot actions have been executed as planned. The resulting penalty may be costly. For example, the cost of debugging and repairing a final assembly may be several orders of magnitude higher than the cost of correcting that error in process, whereas subassemblies are easily accessible.

Restricted Mobility. The locomotion of today's robotic carts is restricted to fixed guidance (eg, by buried cables or painted lines). These carts cannot navigate freely, avoid obstacles, or find their targets in an unstructured environment. Such a restriction limits the flexibility of material handling in batch production (see ROBOTS, MOBILE).

Future Capabilities. The best way to overcome the limitations of today's muscle-only robots is to provide them with intelligence, ie, adaptive sensing and thinking capabilities. Such intelligent robots will be able to compete more effectively with not only blue-collar workers but also white-collar workers. Most industrial companies have not yet agreed with this observation but they will, eventually, when the threat of worldwide market competition becomes unbearable.

Socioeconomic Problems. Development of intelligent robots may raise many problems, the major one of which is unemployment (Ayres and Miller, 1983). Obstructing development of intelligent robots by the labor unions will only worsen the unemployment problem because other countries, especially Japan, will proceed with such development and, as a result, foreign competition will become stronger. This complex problem will probably be mitigated by three factors (Nitzan and co-workers, 1976).

New Related Jobs. An increased demand for skills related to intelligent robots directly (eg, engineering, computer programming, and manufacturing) and indirectly (eg, professional training, marketing, shipping, and servicing).
New Unrelated Jobs. A shift to other jobs, especially in the service industry (thus raising the standard of living).
Fewer Working Hours. Reducing the working hours per week with no reduction in the standard of living.

Whether these factors will be able to solve the unemployment problem remains to be seen. In the meantime, the current rate of intelligent-robot development is low, amounting to robot evolution rather than robot revolution. Such evolution will enable society to adjust gradually, without adverse repercussions, to the advent of the intelligent robot.

Technical Approach. The technical approach to intelligent robot development should be based on the application of AI techniques to robotics under four engineering constraints:

High Reliability. The robot must be robust; if it fails, it should be able to detect the error and recover from it or call for help.
High Speed. The robot should be able to perform its functions as fast as necessary.
Programmability. The robot should be flexible (able to perform a class of different functions for a variety of tasks), easily trainable (for new tasks or modification of old ones), and intelligent (able to perceive problems and solve them).
Low Cost. The cost of the robot should be low enough to justify its application.

Clearly, these constraints may conflict with each other. For example, increasing the robot speed or lowering its cost may also lower its reliability. A trade-off, therefore, must be engineered for different applications according to the significance of each constraint.

RESEARCH AND DEVELOPMENT TOPICS

As shown above, a robot system may be divided into effectors, sensors, computers, and auxiliary equipment. Robotics research and development topics associated with these major functional components include manipulation (of arms), end effectors, and mobility; sensing (in general), noncontact sensing, and contact sensing; adaptive control (which utilizes sensors to monitor and guide effector actions); and robot programming and manufacturing process planning (which generate task-specific computer programs that are executed by the top-level and lower level controllers). Past achievements and research issues related to each of these topics are described briefly in the following sections.

Manipulation

Robot manipulation entails the kinematics, motion trajectories, dynamics, and control of a robot arm.

Kinematics. The location (position and orientation) of a robot wrist in a frame attached to the base of the robot arm is described in two ways:

Joint Coordinates. The angles of the rotary joints and the lengths of the sliding joints of the arm.

World Coordinates. The Cartesian coordinates of the wrist position and the direction cosines defining the wrist orientation.

Joint coordinates must be used to command the robot arm to arrive at a given wrist location. On the other hand, humans prefer to describe the wrist location in terms of world coordinates. Hence, means are provided for transforming from one set of coordinates to another.

Joint-to-World Coordinate Transformation. A frame of Cartesian coordinates (x, y, z) is attached to every arm joint according to a set of rules proposed by Denavit and Hartenberg (1955). The homogeneous coordinates $(x, y, z, 1)$ of a given point in each joint frame are converted to those of a neighboring one by means of a transform: a 4×4 homogeneous coordinate-transformation matrix. Multiplying the transforms of all the arm joints results in the arm-to-wrist transform whose elements, expressed in terms of the joint coordinates, describe the position and orientation (direction cosines) of the arm wrist (Rosen and co-workers, 1974; Paul, 1981).

World-to-Joint Coordinate Transformation. Given the position and orientation of the wrist of an arm, solving for the corresponding joint coordinates is less systematic and more difficult than vice versa. Each arm has a unique solution in which joint coordinates are computed sequentially in a fixed order (Rosen and co-workers, 1974).

Motion Trajectories. *Workstation Transforms.* Denoting the homogeneous coordinates $(x, y, z, 1)$ of a point P in a frame F by $P(F)$, then $P(F_1) = [F_1/F_2] * P(F_2)$, where $[F_1/F_2]$ is the 4×4 transform from frame F_1 to frame F_2 (Fig. 1a). Note that $P(F_2) = [F_2/F_1] * P(F_1)$, where $[F_2/F_1]$ is the inverse of $[F_1/F_2]$.

Consider a robot arm with an end effector mounted on its wrist moving in a workstation, and let A, W, E, and C denote frames attached to the arm, the wrist, the end effector, and the current (instantaneous) action target of the robot, respectively. Given transforms $[A/C]$, $[C/E]$, and $[W/E]$, the unknown transform $[A/W]$ is computed from the relation $[A/W] = [A/C] * [C/E] * [E/W]$, where $[E/W]$ is the inverse of $[W/E]$ (Fig. 1b). Knowing $[A/W]$, the corresponding joint coordinates are then computed using the world-to-joint arm solution.

Smooth Path. Paul (1975) developed a technique for moving the robot end effector along a path consisting of straight segments and smooth transitions between them (Paul, 1981; Rosen and co-workers, 1976; Taylor, 1979). A straight segment is obtained by interpolating world and joint coordinates between its end locations while maintaining a constant linear velocity. A smooth transition between two straight segments is obtained by bypassing their intersection point along a parabolic curve tangent to both segments. Each pair of straight segments may be defined in either a single frame or in two frames, each of which may be moving with a constant velocity relative to the arm frame. For example, a robot spot-welding gun may move with velocity V_1 along a straight line in the arm frame toward a moving conveyor, veer and change its velocity smoothly, and continue to move with velocity V_2 along a second straight line in the conveyor frame toward a welding spot. Training for a task to be performed on a moving line is done while the workpiece is stationary.

Dynamics. The dynamics of a manipulator relate the applied forces–torques to the joint motion (positions, velocities, and accelerations as functions of time). Two dynamics problems are distinguished (Featherstone, 1983):

The Forward Problem. Given the applied forces and torques, solve for the resulting joint motions.

The Inverse Problem. Given the joint motions, solve for the required forces–torques.

The inverse problem is more important for real-time arm control and, fortunately, easier than the forward problem.

Different numerical methods have been proposed for solving the equations of motion of an n-joint manipulator. These methods are assessed on the basis of their computational complexity (the number of additions and multiplications required). The methods are based on either the Lagrangian formulation (Paul, 1981; Hollerbach, 1980) or the Newton-Euler formulation (Luh and co-workers, 1980). The Lagrangian formulation is less efficient, but Silver (1982) showed that the two formulations are essen-

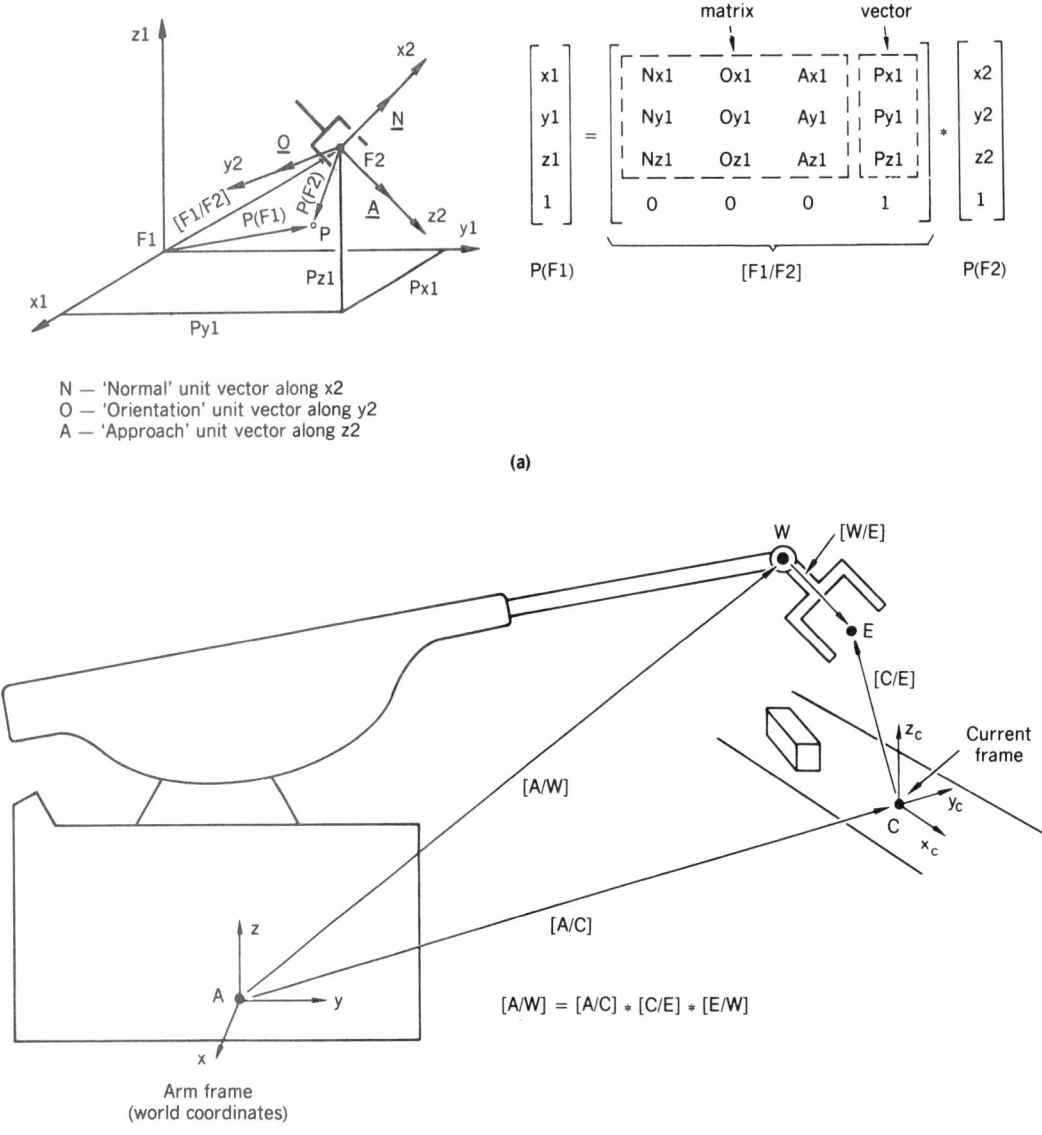

Figure 1. Arm-transformation matrices: (*a*) Transformation matrix: N = normal unit vector along $x2$, O = orientation unit vector along $y2$, A = approach unit vector along $z2$. (*b*) Matrix description of arm system.

tially equivalent and that the complexity of computation depends on its structure and the representation of the rotational dynamics. Kane and Levinson (1983) proposed another approach that uses explicit dynamic equations without the unnecessary computations entailed in either of the above formulations and, hence, should be more efficient.

Control. The motion of a manipulator in a free space is usually controlled by means of a position servo in each joint. If the manipulator is required to move while exerting a specified force/torque on an object, appropriate force/torque servo and position servo must be executed simultaneously (Paul, 1981). Such a hybrid control can be achieved by replacing the position servos of selected joints by force/torque servos so that the manipulator is free to move in the specified direction while the prescribed forces/torques are applied to the object-surface normals. For example, grinding a horizontal surface requires simultaneous control of the position of the grinding wheel and the vertical force it exerts. As another example, inserting a peg into a hole requires motion along their common axis while exerting zero forces along two directions normal to it. Stopping the motion of a manipulator can be controlled by specifying a given force/torque condition.

End-Effectors

An end-effector is a functional device attached to the wrist of a robot arm (see ROBOT HANDS AND END-EFFECTORS). Four types of end-effector are distinguished: hand, tool, hand/tool holder, and micromanipulator. Each of these should be small, light, fast, accurate, multifunctional, and inexpensive.

Hand. A hand, the major function of which is to grasp objects, includes a number (eg, two or three) of fingers attached to its palm. Each finger should have humanlike structural dexterity and rigidity (bone), object-grasping compliance (flesh), surface tactile sensors (skin), and proximity sensors for collision avoidance (no human equivalence). The hand may be equipped with a wrist force sensor, a visual sensor (eye), a range sensor, or any other sensor. To minimize the number of wires between the hand and the robot controller, local signals and hand functions should be processed by microprocessors mounted on the hand itself (resulting in a smart hand).

Three-finger hands have been built at the Electrotechnical Laboratory (Okada and Tsuchiya, 1977) and at Stanford University (Salisbury and Craig, 1982). The Salisbury hand is shown in Figure 2. A kinematic analysis of the latter hand yields a large number (373) of different ways the hand can grasp an object. Hand control is very complex; it is equivalent to the control of three cooperating three-joint arms with force sensors.

Tool. A tool may be a spot-welding gun, an arc-welding torch, a wrench, or any other device that performs a certain task. If a sensor is mounted on or near the tool, it must be ensured that neither one will prevent the other from access to its target. For example, using visual sensing to guide a robot to arc weld workpieces with corners may require that the sensor and the welding torch be free to move relative to each other.

Hand/Tool Holder. A hand/tool holder is a device mounted between the arm wrist and a hand or a tool for one of two purposes:

- Quick hand/tool changing and mounting for different tasks, which may be achieved by a standard latch–unlatch device or a hand.
- Local accommodation, which may be implemented passively by a remote center compliance (RCC) device, developed at Draper Laboratories (Drake, 1977), or

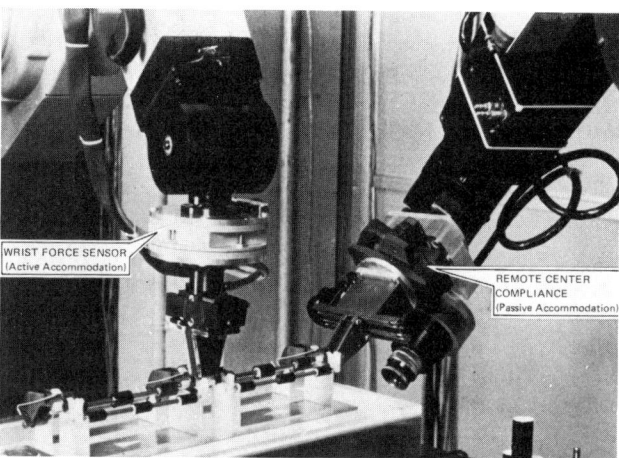

Figure 3. PUMA hands with passive and active accommodation devices.

actively by a force/torque sensor. For example, in Figure 3 plastic parts are assembled by two two-finger PUMA (Unimation, Inc.) hands, one mounted on an RCC (made by Lord Corp.) and guided locally by its eye and the other mounted on an xyz force/torque sensor.

Micromanipulator. The function of a micromanipulator is to correct a locational error that is measured by a robot sensor and is smaller than the spatial resolution of the arm wrist. Having a much smaller inertia, the micromanipulator is also much faster than the arm. A micromanipulator may be an xyz device or a multifinger hand.

Mobility

Most industrial robots today are anchored to fixed locations; a few have a limited mobility on tracks mounted on the factory floor or on a gantry (see ROBOTS, MOBILE). There are also mobile carts that transport workpieces, but these carts can move only in a structured environment, eg, by following buried cables or painted lines. Robot mobility, however, is also needed for a wide variety of robot functions in unstructured environments, such as mining, military operations, and aid to the handicapped. Some robot-mobility issues follow.

Surfaces and Locomotion. The mechanism for the robot locomotion depends strongly on the type of surface the robot must be able to move on. Indoor surfaces include floors, ramps, stairs, and cluttered environments. Outdoor surfaces include roads, smooth ground (flat and slanted), terrain with holes and ditches, and terrain with large obstacles.

Robot locomotion is realized with wheels, tracks, and legs. Wheels perform well if the terrain is not rough and the traction is sufficient. Tracks perform well if the terrain slope is not too high or no major obstacles are encountered. In a recent development at Hitachi (Iwamoto and co-workers, 1983) the loop of each track forms a triangle whose shape is adjusted according to the terrain, thus enabling the vehicle to pass over different obstacles and climb up and down stairways.

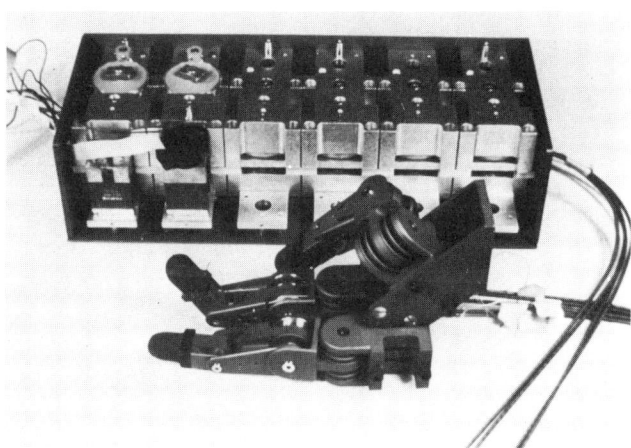

Figure 2. Three-finger hand. Courtesy of Salisbury, MIT.

Legged vehicles have been developed for robot mobility in rough terrain, where wheels and tracks are useless (see ROBOTS, LEGGED). The major issues are stability, gait, strength, speed, and control. Static stability is achieved if the vertical projection of the center of gravity is within the polygon formed by the vehicle's feet on the ground. A six-legged vehicle with at least three legs always on the ground is inherently stable. Six-legged vehicles have been built at Ohio State University (McGhee, 1983), Carnegie Mellon University (Raibert and Sutherland, 1983), and Odetics (Bartholet, 1983). The Odetics vehicle (Fig. 4) is characterized by high strength-to-weight ratio and agility.

Control. A major research issue in robot mobility is autonomous control, which includes motor control, sensing, navigation, communication, obstacle avoidance, and task performance. SRI's Shakey the Robot (qv) (Nitzan, 1981) was developed in the 1960s as an intelligent mobile robot with these properties. Shakey (Fig. 5) had autonomous wheel-drive control and visual, range, and binary tactile sensors; navigated through laboratory rooms; communicated with its brain (a DEC PDP-10 computer) via a radio link; avoided obstacles; and pushed boxes according to the plan of a task it was assigned to do. Since then other

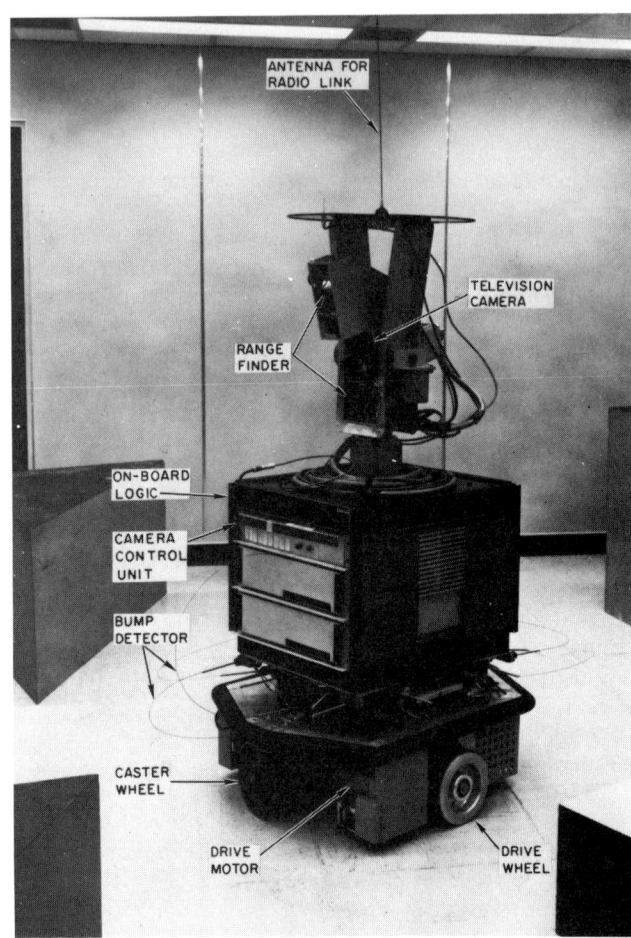

Figure 5. SRI's Shakey, a mobile robot.

similar robots have been developed in the United States (eg, at Carnegie Mellon University and MIT), France (eg, LAAS in Toulouse), and Japan (eg, Mechanical Engineering Laboratory in Tsukuba). These robots use wheels to move on laboratory floors and shaft encoders to sense their two-dimensional positions. To correct for random locational errors, some of them use infrared beacons, a directable laser range finder, and visual perception. Sonar sensors (which are inexpensive) are commonly used to avoid obstacles, but they are not adequate for navigation because of their poor resolution, short range, and vulnerability to specular reflection.

The primary research issues in planning for and execution of robot mobility along long-range paths are representation and mapping of a three-dimensional world, noncontact sensing, outdoor visual perception, navigation, and communication, and those along short-range paths are noncontact and contact sensing, obstacle avoidance, foothold location (to avoid holes, ditches, and the like), and recovery from accidental falls (see ROBOTS, MOBILE).

ROBOT SENSING

Sensing Sequence

Robot sensing is defined as perception: translation of relevant characteristic or relational object properties into the

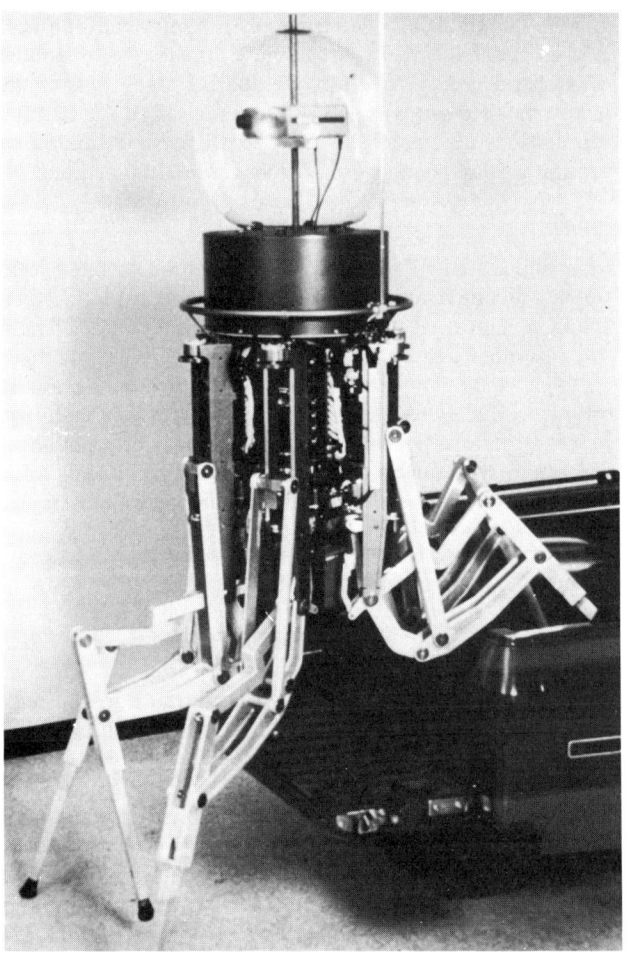

Figure 4. Six-legged walking vehicle. Courtesy of Odetics, Inc. (Anaheim, Calif.)

information required to control the robot in performing a given robot function (Nitzan and co-workers, 1983) (see also SENSORS AND SENSOR FUSION). The object properties may be geometric, mechanical, optical, acoustic, material, electric, magnetic, chemical, and the like. Robot functions may be passive (eg, RECOGNIZE, LOCATE, and INSPECT) or active (eg, GRASP, TRANSPORT, and WELD). Each of these functions may be expanded by lower level robot functions (eg, RECOGNIZE = (TAKE-PICTURE, FIND-EDGE, EXTRACT-FEATURES, INTERPRET-FEATURES)), or be used to define higher level ones (eg, using the functions FIND, ACQUIRE, HOLD, MOVE, ALIGN, INSERT, and VERIFY to define ASSEMBLE). As shown in Figure 6, a robot sensing sequence is performed in the following steps.

1. *Transducing.* Converting (in hardware) the relevant object properties into a signal.
2. *Processing.* Transforming the signal into the required information, usually in two substeps: preprocessing, improving the signal (usually in hardware), eg, filtering out noise, and interpreting, analyzing the improved signal and extracting the required information (usually in software).

The above steps probably cannot be implemented by a general-purpose system. Instead, each step or substep should be performed by effective hardware–software schemes, regarded as tools, that depend on the environmental conditions and the specified robot functions. To be able to carry out a wide variety of sensing tasks, the sensing system will consist of sets of tools, or toolboxes, and a knowledge-based supervisor that can select the best tools for each given task.

Sensing Strategy

If the extracted information is not sufficient, the sensing sequence is modified and repeated in order to obtain complementary information. Three cases are distinguished as follows.

1. *Supplementary Images.* Imaging additional surfaces, which are hidden from a fixed sensor in the previous sensing sequence(s), by means of a sensor mounted on the robot end effector or multiple sensors at different viewpoints.
2. *Sensing Efficiency.* Achieving efficient sensing by first using coarse resolution and then fine resolution, such as, recognizing an object, then locating it precisely; and recognizing and locating an object approximately, then inspecting some of its windows, where distinctive features or defects may be found, with fine resolution.
3. *Multisensing.* Utilizing different sensors to supplement a sensor output, such as recognizing and locating an object with vision and then locating it precisely and verifying its grasp with tactile sensing, ie, verifying the sensing of one sensor by another.

Sensor Signals

A given object property may be measured by different sensor signals, such as light intensity, range, acoustic, tactile, force, and temperature (Table 1). A point signal is distinguished from an array (one- or two-dimensional) of point signals. As shown in Table 2, each of these signals may be generated by different sensor transducers, eg, a point light intensity may be transduced by a photocell, a photomultiplier, a 1-dimensional array, or a two-dimensional array.

Research Issues

Robot sensing could be advanced by developing

Sensor transducers that have a higher resolution, higher speed, smaller size, and lower cost.

Faster hardware–software processors that can process a larger amount of sensor signals and extract more information.

Sensor modeling and planning, including sensor selection, for a given task and off-line signal prediction.

NONCONTACT SENSING

Noncontact sensing is based on a signal generated by a transducer that is not in physical contact with the object it senses. Noncontact sensing is classified according to the type of signal, ie, light intensity (or, briefly, intensity), range, acoustic, temperature, chemical, etc. Noncontact sensing for robot applications has so far been based primarily on intensity and range signals; future robot applications should also utilize the other types of signals.

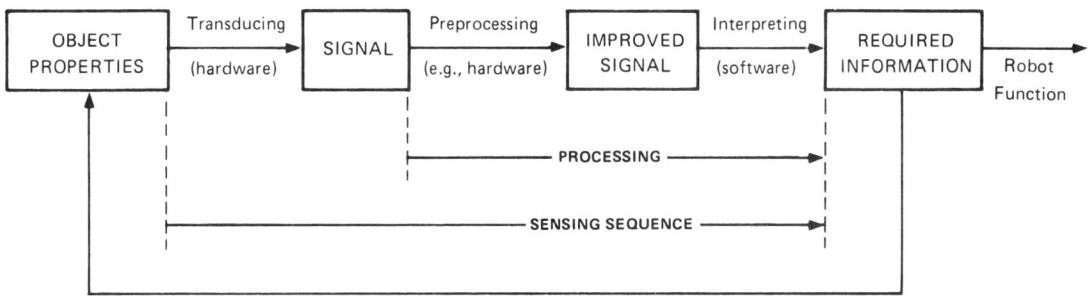

Figure 6. Robot sensing diagram.

Table 1. Measurement of Object Properties: Possible Signals for Each Object Property

Object Property	Intensity (Point/Array)		Range (Point/Array)		Acoustic (Point/Array)		Tactile (Point/Array)		Force (Point)	Temperature (Point/Array)	
Geometric											
Centroid	×		×				×				
Edge, corner	×		×		×		×				
Surface	×		×		×		×				
Volume			×				×				
Width	×		×		×		×	×			
Texture	×		×		×		×				
Shape	×		×		×		×				
Proximity			×	×	×	×	×	×			
Mechanical											
Weight									×		
Force–torque									×		
Pressure							×	×	×		
Optical											
Reflectance	×	×									
Color	×	×									
Acoustic											
Reflectance					×	×					
Material											
Hardness							×	×	×	×	×
Temperature										×	×

The output of the signal-transduction step is an image if it consists of a two-dimensional array of sensory data values. Thus it is possible to distinguish between an intensity image, which consists of $N \times M$ picture elements, or pixels, and a range image, which consists of $N \times M$ range elements, or rangels, where N and M are resolution integers. An intensity image provides information about the reflectance of object surfaces in the scene, but it may be ambiguous geometrically because of the loss of one-dimensional information in the process of transforming a three-dimensional world into a two-dimensional gray-level image. A range image, on the other hand, provides three-dimensional information directly but no reflectance information. Intensity and range images are thus complementary and should, therefore, be in exact registration to simplify the analysis of their integrated information.

Intensity transducers include a photocell, a photomultiplier, a one-dimensional array camera, and a two-dimensional array camera. Intensity transducers require the following improvements (Nitzan, 1981).

- Chips with higher precision, improved quality, color discrimination, higher resolution (eg, 1024×1024 or even 2048×2048 pixels).
- Lenses with lower distortion and better focus in the infrared region.
- Fast, computer-controlled adaptive lens opening and focusing as well as intensity thresholding.

Indirect measurement of range or surface orientation may be inferred from molecular two-dimensional images under certain conditions (Mundy, 1975; Jarvis, 1983; Nitzan and co-workers, 1986; Horn, 1975); but this subject is beyond the scope of this article. The following section focuses on direct range measurement and its current problems.

Direct Range Measurement

Two basically different techniques can be used to measure range directly: triangulation and time of flight.

Triangulation Techniques. Triangulation is based on elementary geometry (Fig. 7a): given the baseline of a triangle, ie, the distance between two of its vertices, and the angles at these vertices, the range from one of the vertices

Table 2. Measurement of Object Properties: Possible Sensor Transducers for Each Signal

Signal	Transducers
Intensity	
Point	Photocell, photomultiplier, array (1-D, 2-D)
Array	Array or equivalent (lower dimensional array scanning)
Range	
Point	Projector (laser, planar light)/receiver (photomultiplier, array, two arrays), acoustic
Array	Scanning projector (laser, planar light)/receiver (photomultiplier, array), two 2-D arrays or equivalent
Acoustic	
Point	Acoustic transducer
Array	Array of acoustic transducers or equivalent
Tactile	
Point	Microswitch, array of tactile transducers
Array	Array of tactile transducers or equivalent
Force (point)	Force transducer
Temperature	
Point	Thermocouple, infrared transducer
Array	Array of infrared transducers or equivalent

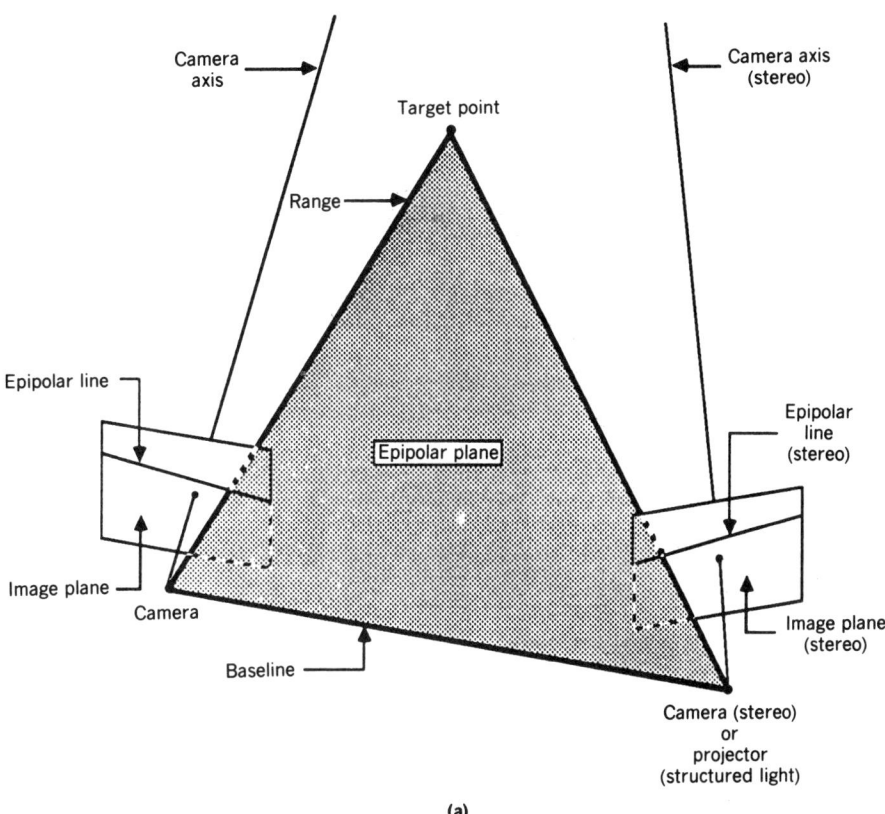

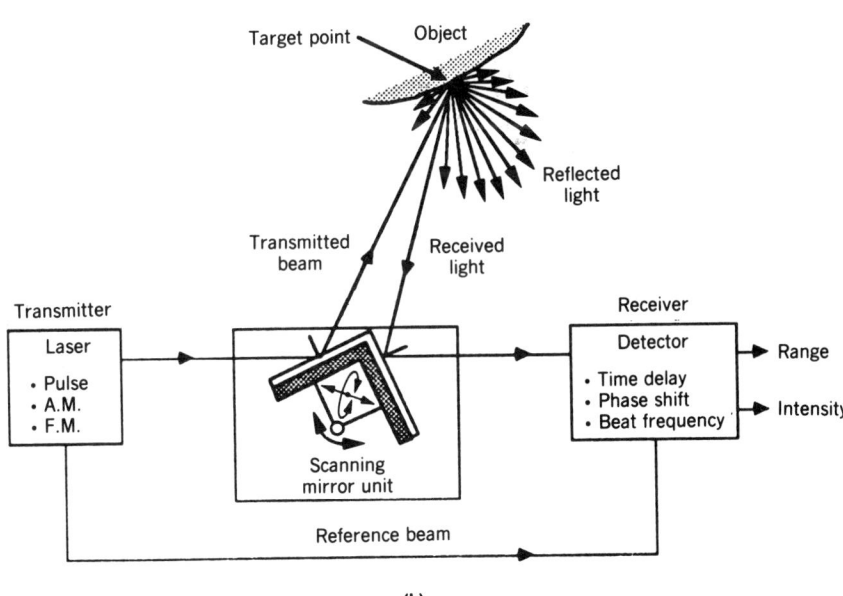

Figure 7. Direct range-sensing schemes: (a) Triangulation range sensing (Nitzan and co-workers, 1977). (b) Time-of-flight laser range sensing. Courtesy of Bolles, SRI International.

to the third one is computed as the corresponding triangle side. Triangulation techniques are subdivided into two schemes: stereo, using ambient light and two cameras (a passive scheme), and structured light, using a projector of controlled light and camera (an active scheme). The plane in which the triangle lies is called the epipolar plane, and its line of intersection with a camera image plane is called the epipolar line.

The main drawbacks of any triangulation technique are missing data for points in the scene that are not seen from both vertices of the triangle. This problem can be partially solved in two ways:

- Decreasing the baseline (this remedy, however, will increase the measurement errors).
- Using multiple cameras for the stereo scheme or multiple projectors and cameras for the structured light scheme (this provision will also reduce the measurement errors and mitigate the problem of occlusion, including self-occlusion, in machine vision, but it

will increase the cost, complexity, and measurement time of the system).

Stereo. Relying on passive ambient light, triangulation stereo techniques use an image sensor (in particular, a TV camera) at each of two triangle vertices. A stereo pair of images can be obtained either from two static cameras (at different locations) or from one camera that is moved between two locations.

In addition to the missing-data problem, the main issue in stereo vision is the correspondence problem: how to match corresponding points in stereo images reliably and quickly. This problem has no solution if the two images have uniform reflectance. Conversely, the correspondence problem becomes easier as the stereo images include more intensity features, such as edges, especially if they are perpendicular to the epipolar line. These features should be extracted on the basis of microconstraints as well as macroconstraints. For example, local intensity changes imply edge points, but if these points are too isolated to be linked into a continuous edge, they should be disregarded. The effect of the correspondence problem is an increase in the measurement time.

Structured Light. One way to dispose of the correspondence problem is to use active light: a scheme in which one of the stereo cameras is replaced by a source of specially controlled illumination, called structured light. The structured light may be projected serially, by scanning a collimated light beam (usually a laser), or in parallel, either by diverging a laser beam with a cylindrical lens or by using a slit or a slide projector. The structured light may consist of single or multiple light patterns, each of which may be a straight line (a beam), planar, or nonplanar.

In addition to the missing-data problem, the structured light scheme entails two issues:

Specular Reflection. Reflection from a mirrorlike surface may result in no range measurement if the reflected light does not reach the camera and false (larger or smaller) measured range values if the reflected light is subsequently reflected by other surfaces before part of it reaches the camera.

Slow Measurement.. Serial projection of multiple light planes requires too much time for data acquisition.

The latter problem can be mitigated by projecting the light planes in parallel, but this entails determination of the correspondence between each light plane and the image of its intersection with the target. As a trade-off between serial vs parallel projection, the following time-coded light pattern projection method was proposed (Altschuler and co-workers, 1981): each plane among a set of different light planes is turned on or off during each of a sequence of time slots according to a given code, and the resulting images are decoded to determine the correspondence between each plane and its image.

Time-of-Flight Techniques. A time-of-flight range sensor (Fig. 7b) includes a signal transmitter and a signal receiver consisting of a collector of part of the signal reflected by the target and the electronics for measuring the round-trip travel time of the returning signal and its intensity. Two types of signal are practical: ultrasound (such as used by the Polaroid range sensor) and laser light. Ultrasound is much more adversely affected by surface specularity and has a much poorer spatial resolution than laser light; hence, let us consider only laser light.

Time-of-flight laser range sensors use a scanning mirror to direct the transmitted laser beam along pan-and-tilt orientations with equal angular increments in order to obtain a range image consisting of $N \times M$ rangels. Like with triangulation range sensing, by also measuring the intensity of the reflected light, we obtain an intensity image consisting of $N \times M$ pixels in complete registration with the range image. On the other hand, the missing-data problem that is inherent in triangulation range sensing is eliminated by mounting the laser transmitter coaxially with the receiver's reflected light collector.

Three schemes can be distinguished for measuring the length of the transmitter–target–receiver optical path in time-of-flight laser range sensing (Fig. 7b):

1. *Pulse Time Delay.* Using a pulsed laser and measuring the time of flight directly (Johston, 1973); this scheme requires advanced electronics.
2. *AM Phase Shift.* Using an amplitude-modulated laser and measuring the phase shift, which is proportional to the time of flight (Nitzan and co-workers, 1977).
3. *FM Beat.* Using "chirps" of laser waves that are frequency modulated as a linear function of time and measuring the beat frequency, which is proportional to the time of flight (Goodwin, 1985).

Time-of-flight laser range sensors have the following problems:

Specular Reflection. Reflection from a mirrorlike surface may result in no range measurement if the reflected light does not reach the receiver and larger measured range values if the reflected light is subsequently reflected by other surfaces before part of it reaches the receiver.

Slow Measurement. A long integration time is required to reduce the photon noise (and other types of noise) to an acceptable level, especially if the target is dark. For given values of target reflectance, incidence angle, range, and measurement error, the integration time is inversely proportional to the product of the transmitted laser power and the area of the receiver's collector (Nitzan and co-workers, 1977).

Ambiguity in AM Phase Shift. If the phase shift ϕ between the transmitted light and the received light in an amplitude-modulated scheme may exceed 2π, the (true) range r is ambiguous: $r = n\lambda + r(\phi)$, where $n = 0, 1, 2, \ldots$, λ is the wavelength of the modulation frequency, and $r(\phi)$ is the measured range assuming that $0 \leq \phi \leq 2\pi$; detection of range discontinuities, which are unexpected based on the world knowledge, may be used to determine the value(s) of n.

Processing of light-intensity images and range images are discussed separately in the following two sections.

Intensity Image Processing

Light-intensity image processing in robotic applications is intended primarily to recognize, locate, and inspect objects from an intensity range. Assuming that the image of an object in a given stable state is invariant to its location (position and orientation), processing of three types of intensity image are distinguished below: a complete and isolated outline, a partial or connected (not isolated) outline, and a gray-level image of an object. Processing the intensity images of three-dimensional objects in general is a more difficult task.

Complete and Isolated Outline. The complete outline of an isolated two- or three-dimensional object in a given stable state is the boundary between the top-view image (viewed from infinity) of the object and its background. An object outline can be sensed in two ways:

- *By Detecting the Black-to-White and White-to-Black Transitions in a Binary Image (Silhouette).* The main problems here are obtaining a high black–white contrast when using front illumination (it is relatively easy with back illumination) and adjusting the threshold that converts the image into binary pixels dynamically as the task and lighting conditions vary.
- *By Detecting the Edges between Dark and Bright Regions in a Gray-Level Image.* Edges may be detected by using several methods, such as the Sobel operator (Duda and Hart, 1973) and thinning the resulting "thick edges" or by applying the MIT zero-crossing operator (Hildreth, 1982) which extracts chains of zero-valued pixels from the convolution of the gray levels with the Laplacian of a bivariate Gaussian distribution function. The main problems here are lack of robustness (obtaining false edge points and missing true ones), linking the edge points into expected outlines, and relatively lengthy computation time.

The SRI vision module (Gleason and Agin, 1979) implements the outline interpretation (recognition, location, and inspection) by matching the features of each "blob," or connected region, of the measured outline with those of a model (prototype). The vision module utilizes many global features, such as the outline's area, perimeter, area–perimeter-squared ratio, radius vectors (minimum, maximum, and average) from the centroid to the perimeter, first and second moments, and number and area of holes. Two recognition schemes are distinguished.

Nearest Neighbor Classifier. Selection of the nearest object prototypes in a multifeature space.

Decision Tree. Sequentially divides object prototypes into two groups along tree branches according to the largest gap between the values of the most distinctive feature until reaching a leaf.

The SRI vision module (Fig. 8) consists of three components: one to four TV cameras, a hardware preprocessor, and vision software stored in a microcomputer. Several companies (eg, Machine Intelligence Corp. and Automatix Inc.) have been manufacturing industrial vision systems based on the SRI vision module.

Partial or Connected Outline. Consider two- or three-dimensional objects that may be partially viewed, overlapping without altering their top views substantially or touching. Object outlines are extracted from binary or gray-level images using the same techniques as for an isolated object. The observable outline of any one of these objects may be partial, complete, or connected with another outline; hence, matching cannot be based on global features.

Object recognition and location based on any of these outlines was achieved at SRI (Bulles and Cain, 1982) by focusing on local features, such as small holes, convex corners, and concave corners, which are much smaller than the image of the entire object. As a local feature is detected, the shape and location of its closest local features are extracted and compared with those of a model until there is sufficient match to hypothesize the object's identity and location. The hypothesis is then verified by comparing the observable-object outline, excluding the local features matched previously, with the model outline. For example, local features extracted from the silhouette of four overlapping or touching door hinges were analyzed by this match–verify system and the resulting outlines, shown in Figure 9, were as expected. The system is robust, but further research is needed to explain (by reasoning about object outlines) why portions of some objects are not visible.

Gray-Level Image. Techniques for matching the gray-level image of an object with that of a model are covered in several textbooks (Duda and Hart, 1973; Rosenfeld and

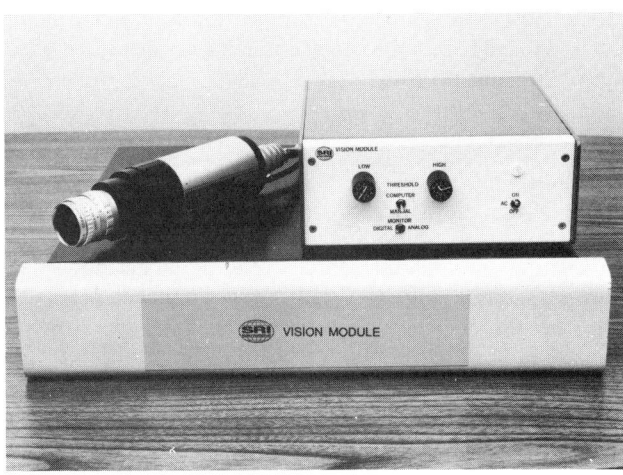

Figure 8. The SRI vision module.

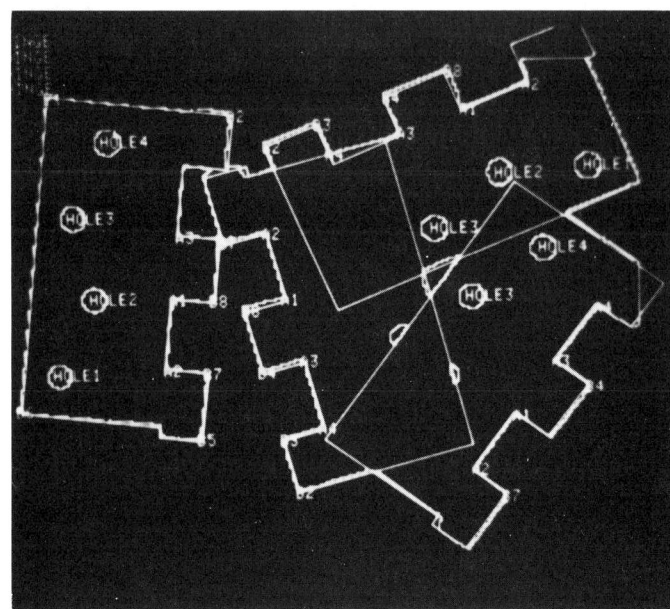

Figure 9. Using local features to locate overlapping or touching door hinges. Courtesy of Bolles, SRI International.

Kak, 1976; Ballard and Brown, 1982; Horn, 1986). These techniques vary over a wide range of complexity, depending on the tasks. One technique, explained previously, is to detect expected edges between dark and bright regions and match the global or local features of these edges with those of an object model. Two other matching techniques are as follows.

- *Average Gray-Level Matching.* The average gray level of a windowed (partial) or the entire image of an indexed object (ie, placed in a known location) is compared with that of a model to determine if there is an acceptable match; simple and fast, this technique is used in commercial visual inspection systems (Miyagawa and co-workers, 1983).
- *Statistical Gray-Level Matching.* A gray-level histogram (a function showing, for each gray-level increment, the number of pixels in the image whose gray-levels lie within that increment) of an image of an indexed object is compared with that of a model to detect missing or severely damaged parts, and a gray-level joint distribution of the object and its model are used to detect missing or misplaced parts (Barnard, 1980).

Range Image Processing

Range image processing is intended primarily to recognize, locate, and inspect three-dimensional objects (see also RANGE DATA ANALYSIS). Basically, such processing is implemented by extracting three-dimensional geometric features and matching them with those of a model. Matching the three-dimensional features of an isolated object whose image is variable is much more difficult than matching the two-dimensional features of an isolated object whose image is invariable. Matching the features of three-dimensional objects that are piled on a tray or jumbled in a bin is even more difficult because each object may have infinite possible orientations and may be partially occluded by other objects. Compared with visual image processing, range image processing has barely scratched the surface; much research is still needed in this area.

Because range data describe the surface of a solid object (not its interior), the object should be represented by its surface (not its volume). Three useful representations of three-dimensional surfaces are considered below: faces, generalized cylinder surfaces, and volumetric.

Faces. Object faces are usually represented mathematically by a number of unbounded planar or curved surfaces (eg, cylindrical, conic, or spherical) that confine the object. These surfaces may intersect along edges that, in turn, may intersect at vertices. Geometric modeling in most computer-aided design (qv) (CAD) systems is based on this representation.

Geometric features (surfaces, edges, and vertices) seen by a range sensor can be extracted from its range image. The challenge here is to extract these features reliably and quickly from range data that may be incomplete and noisy. Previous range image processing (Nitzan and co-workers, 1977; Nitzan, 1972; Duda and co-workers, 1979) has extracted the following features:

- Jump edges, the boundaries between occluding and occluded surfaces (as seen by the range sensor), which are characterized by range discontinuities; jump edges constitute the portion of the occluding object outline where no contact is made with any other object.
- Convex or concave edges, which are characterized by discontinuity in the range gradient.
- Planar surfaces, classified into horizontal, vertical, and slanted ones (an example is shown in Fig. 10).

More recently, Bolles and Horaud (1986) developed a system for determining the location (position and orientation) of each visible part in a bin of jumbled pads of the

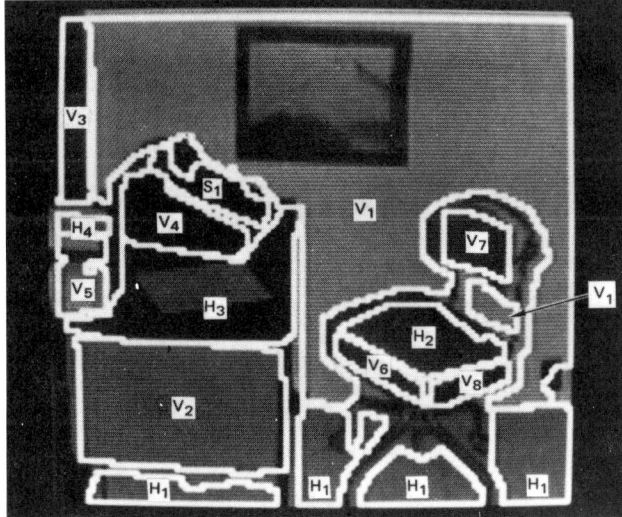

Figure 10. Office scene partitioned into planar surfaces. H = horizontal, V = vertical, S = slanted (Duda and co-workers, 1979).

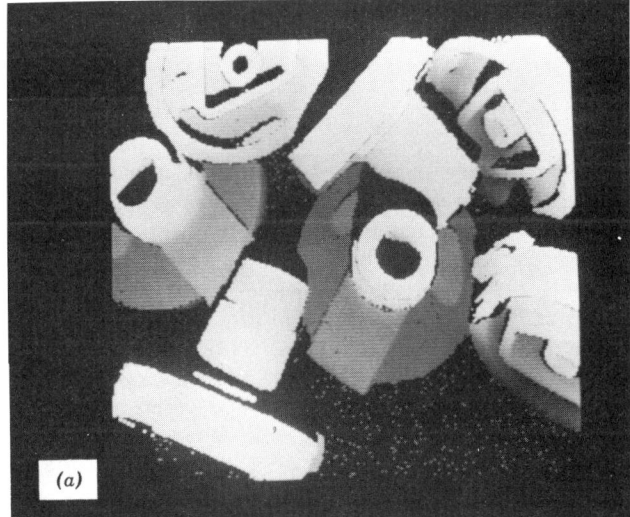

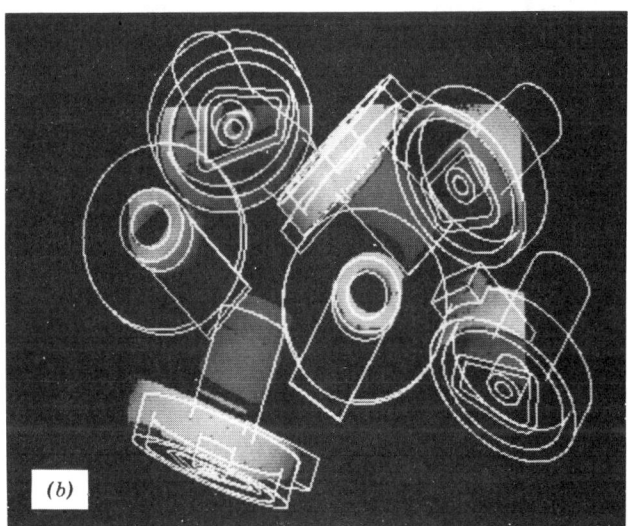

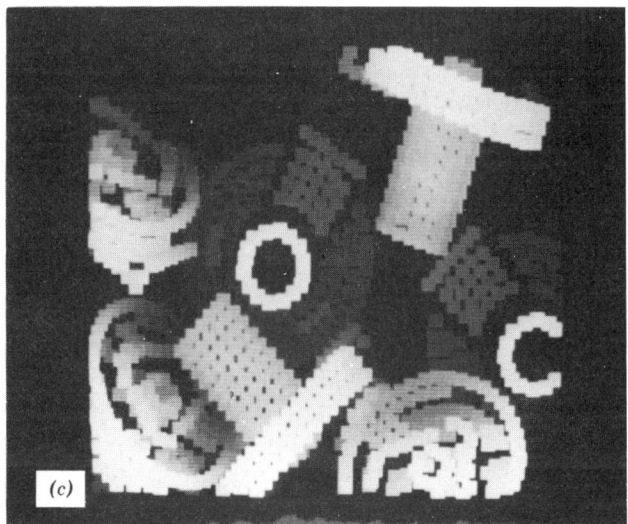

Figure 11. Locating castings in a bin. (*a*) Measured height data (higher points are brighter). (*b*) Hypothesized castings. (*c*) Hypothesis verification. Courtesy of Bolles and Horaud, SRI International.

same type. The system generates a hypothesis about the location of each part by extracting three-dimensional edge features of three types (straight dihedral, circular dihedral, and straight tangential) from range data and matching a sufficient number of distinctive features to those in the part's model. For example, Figure 11a depicts the measured height of seven castings; higher points are brighter. The system analyzes these range data, extracts three-dimensional edge features, and hypothesizes the casting locations, as shown in Figure 11b. Next, the resulting hypothesis of patches is verified by predicting the range values on the object's surface and comparing them to the measured data (Fig. 11c). Furthermore, the system locates the pads on top of the pile so that a robot hand can pick them up.

Generalized Cylinder Surfaces. A generalized cylinder is the volume swept by a two-dimensional region moving along and normal to an axis (straight or curved) in a three-dimensional space.

Surfaces of generalized cylinders were used to represent a manufactured doll (Agin and Binford, 1973) and other complex objects (Nevatia and Binford, 1973). Generalized cylinder surfaces were extracted from range data (obtained by using planar light slices) and matched with their models.

Contour lines are the intersections of a set of known planes with a three-dimensional object of an arbitrary shape. The planes may be parallel and equidistant (as in topographical maps), radial with equal angular increments, and the like. Contour lines may be viewed as an extended representation of a generalized cylinder surface formed by sweeping a region of arbitrary shape along an axis that may branch into separate axes. The intersections of a set of light planes with an arbitrary object, used to measure its range image, constitute the visible portions of its contour lines. As such, contour-line representation is compatible with range measurement based on structured light and can be used to inspect the shape and dimensions of three-dimensional objects (Mulgaonkar and co-workers, 1985).

Volumetric Representations

Volumetric representations can be used to compute the mass properties of objects as well as their surfaces. Three volumetric representations are distinguished: spatial occupancy, cell decomposition, and constructive solid geometry (Ballard and Brown, 1982).

A spatial occupancy representation (voxels) of a solid object is a three-dimensional array of cells (eg, cubes); the higher the resolution the larger the required memory space. A cell decomposition representation is obtained by subdividing a solid object into solid cells (no holes). One such representation is the "Oct-tree," which is obtained by recursive subdivision of the solid until all the cells have elementary shapes. A solid object may be represented by combining primitive solids, eg, construction of animals using cylinders.

Research Issues

Although impressive progress has been made in edge & local feature detection (qv) and relational optical flow (Hildreth, 1983), and three-dimensional vision, these areas require further research. Other research issues in noncontact sensing include parallel computation, object representation, extraction of intrinsic and relational features from surface images, and strategies for matching these features to object models. Different applications have required different sensor types and different object representations. The question is how much of these differences is economical and how much is inherent.

CONTACT SENSING

As the name implies, contact sensing requires physical contact with an object whose properties are measured. Contact-sensor signals include tactile, force/torque, temperature, and position. Of these, tactile and force/torque sensors are more general.

Tactile Sensors

Classification. Tactile sensors may be classified according to the following criteria:

- *Resolution.* A single element (eg, a microswitch) vs an array of elements.
- *Dynamic Range.* Binary (contact or no contact) vs gray-level (continuous) contact force.
- *Directionality.* Normal vs tangential force measurement.

Applications. A binary microswitch may be used in various move-till-touch applications (Nitzan, 1981), such as reaching a target, preventing collision damage, robot training, object grasping, and dimensional measurement.

Arrays of tactile transducers (binary or gray-scale) mounted on compliant fingers of a robot hand are applicable to object recognition (Hillis, 1982), grasping, locating, inspection, and slip detection. Rather than being detected, a slip may be prevented by increasing the normal force, N, just before the sensed tangential force reaches $\mu_0 N$, where μ_0 is the coefficient of static friction between the object and the tactile transducers. Some tactile sensors may also be used to measure the hardness and thermal properties of materials (Dario and De Rossi, 1985); these properties may supplement three-dimensional features in object recognition.

In a survey conducted by Harmon (1982) the following applications for tactile sensing were identified: bin picking, adaptive grasping, assembly, dimensional inspection, shape detection, temperature measurement, tight-part mating, electronic-component insertion, wire-harness construction, limp-material handling, fruit picking, and cow milking.

Transducers. Tactile transducers may be based on the following technologies (Dario and De Rossi, 1985; Harmon, 1982).

- *Pressure-Sensitive Resistivity.* Simple, inexpensive, and heat resistant but lacking sensitivity.
- *Semiconductors.* Small and sensitive but fragile and sensitive to the environment.
- *Piezoelectric Transduction.* Potentially useful but lacking dc response.
- *Capacitive Transduction.* Potentially useful but too sensitive to external fields.
- *Optoelectronic Transduction.* Highly sensitive detection of light whose intensity varies by force-sensitive mechanical means, which are bulky.
- *Piezoelectric and Pyroelectric Transduction.* Potentially useful for sensing pressure and thermal properties, but sensing them separately is electronically difficult.

A few examples follow.

Hillis (1982) developed a 16 × 16-element tactile sensor consisting of two 16-conductor sheets aligned perpendicularly to each other and separated by a thin elastic medium. The local resistance between each pair of crossing conductors decreases (nonlinearly) as the applied pressure increases. A tactile-pressure image is obtained by applying a voltage to one column conductor at a time and measuring the current flowing in each of the row conductors as they are grounded one at a time. Hillis realized one conductor sheet by an etched flexible printed-circuit board, the other by an anisotropically conductive silicon rubber, and the elastic medium by a nylon woven mesh. Further development of this sensor was terminated due to problems with material manufacturing and robustness (Hollerbach, 1985).

Boi (1984) developed a 6 × 6-element tactile sensor consisting of six conductors etched on an elastic/dielectric layer and six conductors etched normally to the ones above on a flexible printed-circuit board (Fig. 12). The local capacitance between each pair of crossing conductors increases as the applied pressure increases because the

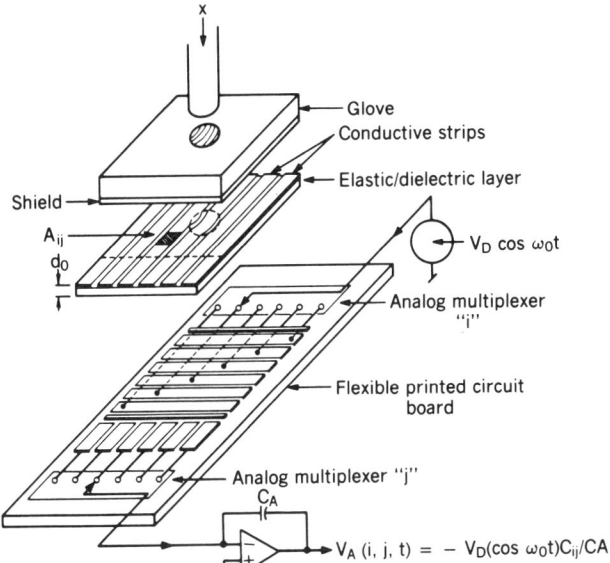

Figure 12. Exploded view of capacitive tactile sensor (Boie, 1984).

distance between them decreases. This sensor scheme appears encouraging and is being pursued further at MIT (Hollerbach, 1985).

A 3 × 6-element tactile sensor combining a transducer (pressure-sensitive conductive elastomer) and a VLSI signal processor has been designed and built by Raibert and Tanner (Raibert, 1982) (Fig. 13). The quality of the transduced data was not good because of the hysteresis and poor mechanical ruggedness of available elastomers and because of the difficulties in placing analog electronics on a chip (Raibert, 1984). Raibert (1984) has attempted to overcome these problems by developing a scheme for measuring local pressure digitally.

A survey of tactile transducers by Dario and De Rossi (1985) includes the following ones: optoelectronic transducers using optical fibers (the Jet Propulsion Laboratory in Pasadena, Calif., and MIT in Cambridge, Mass.) and LED–photo detectors (developed at SRI International and manufactured by Lord Corp.), piezoresistive transducers (Carnegie Mellon University in Pittsburgh, Pittsburgh, Pa., and LAAS in Toulouse, France), piezoelectric–pyroelectric transducers using polyvinylidene fluoride polymers (PVF2) (University of Pisa, Italy).

Desired performance specifications for tactile sensing depend on the application but, on the average, are as follows (Harmon, 1982):

Resolution (5 × 10 to 10 × 20 elements with 1–2 mm spacing, matching the human fingertip).
Sensitivity (1–10 g).
Dynamic range (1000:1).
Response Time (1–10 ms).
Nonlinearity is acceptable but hysteresis is not.
Robust sensing skin on a compliant material (flesh) that covers each finger of a robot hand.
Local data processing (resulting in a smart hand).

Tactile sensors that meet all of these specifications are yet to be developed. Such development could perhaps be helped by studying the mechanisms entailed in human sensing. Most attempts to develop humanlike tactile sensors have failed so far, primarily due to material problems.

Tactile Image Processing. A tactile image generated by a set of transducer elements that have been activated by contacting an object may be binary or gray-level. Hence, binary or gray-level vision-processing techniques are applicable directly to tactile image processing (Hillis, 1982).

Grimson and Lozano-Perez (1984) developed a method for recognition and location of an isolated polyhedral three-dimensional object with three degrees of freedom based on a set of surface-point positions and normals measured by tactile sensors. The large number of possible interpretations in matching the measured points with modeled object surfaces is reduced considerably by using constraints on the distances between faces, the angles between face normals, and the angles between sensed-point vectors and face normals. This object-matching method was later extended (Grimson and Lozano-Perez, 1985) to cases in which the position and orientation of planar-surface patches (or linear segments) are measured by a sensor (eg, gray-level visual sensor).

A research issue is how to perform image interpretation that is unique to contact sensing. For example, interpreting tactile data associated with object grasping entails friction (which is hard to model) and grasp location. Another issue is dynamic vs static tactile sensing, how to interpret dynamic tactile data, how the information it provides differs from that of static tactile data, and what the analogy with dynamic and static vision is.

Applicability of Tactile versus Noncontact Sensing. Tactile sensing is applicable to object grasping, but its applicability to object recognition, location, and inspection is questionable because these tasks can be done today much more effectively by visual sensing.

Compared with noncontact (vision and range) sensing of a three-dimensional object, today's tactile sensing has inferior performance specifications, has insufficient techniques for image interpretation, must entail manipula-

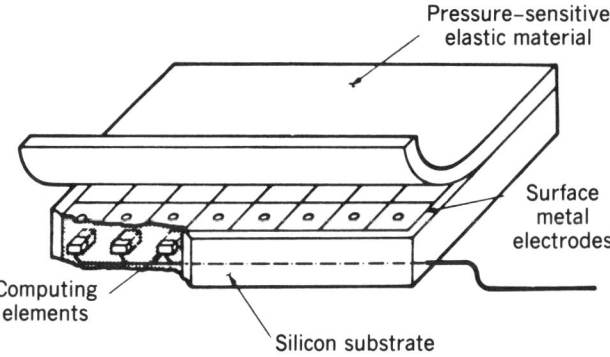

Figure 13. VLSI tactile array sensor (Raibert and Tanner, 1982).

tion (eg, by a robot arm and hand), and may cause some object displacement. On the other hand, tactile sensing is direct, requires no illumination, and can provide information about the object grasping, including slip detection or prevention. In addition, noncontact sensing is inferior if the surface of the object is occluded (eg, during object grasping), is either too dark (eg, in deep sea) or too specular (causing transducer blooming or misleading multiple reflections), or is characterized by uniform reflectance despite range variations.

In conclusion, tactile sensing should complement noncontact sensing, not compete with it. Before such sensor integration can be achieved, however, tactile sensing needs to be advanced to a level comparable to that of noncontact sensing.

Force Sensors

A six-axis wrist force sensor measures the three components of force and three components of torque acting between the wrist of a robot arm and its end effector which, in turn, exerts the measured force or torque on an object.

Force transduction is achieved by measuring the deflection of compliant sections as a result of the applied force and torque. Force transducers include piezoelectric material and semiconductor strain gauges. The accuracy of force transducers may be increased by mounting them directly on the end effector fingers rather than on the wrist. Figure 14 shows a strain-gauge wrist sensor developed at SRI (Rosen and co-workers, 1974).

Research Issues

Research issues include improving the performance of tactile transducers (see above specifications), analysis of tactile gray-level images (for object handling, recognition, location, and inspection), friction modeling (for slip detection or prevention), and the applicability of tactile sensing with and without noncontact sensing.

Other research issues are effective discrete and continuous sensing, contact location and friction, applicability of contact sensing, combined force–position control, force control of cooperating arms or fingers, performance prediction, and pattern recognition.

ADAPTIVE CONTROL

Overview

The dynamic behavior and positioning accuracy of a robot arm under fixed control vary with the arm configuration and load. An arm with unknown or time-varying parameters could, in principle, be controlled dynamically using adaptive control (see ROBOT CONTROL SYSTEMS) by adjusting the parameters according to the position, velocity, and acceleration servo errors. The problem is that the theory

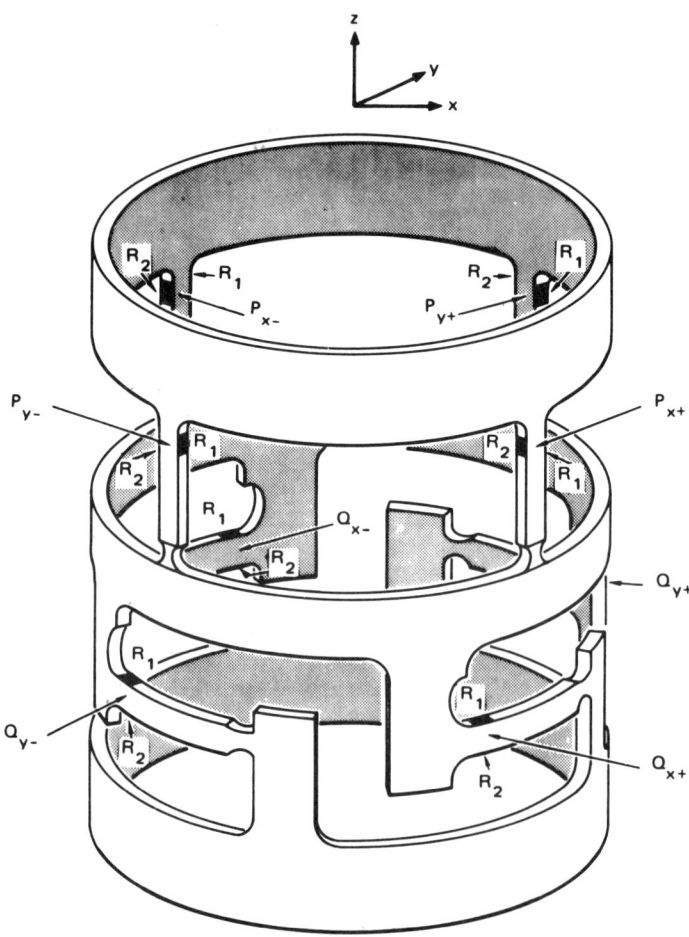

Figure 14. Strain-gauge wrist force sensor.

for adaptive control of nonlinear, stochastic systems is inadequate (Sanderson and Weiss, 1985). Craig (1985) divided the dynamic model into two parts: one with known parameters (eg, link inertia) and the other with a known structure but unknown parameters (eg, friction and load inertia) that may vary in time. He proposed a scheme using an adaptation law that adjusts the estimated values of the unknown parameters in a closed loop until they converge to values resulting in zero servo errors. The scheme is based on nonlinear equations of motion and uses Liapunov (Hahn, 1963) function to guarantee stability but is not fast. Controlling a robot arm dynamically by evaluating its unknown and time-varying parameters in order to minimize the servo errors is a research issue.

Adaptive control of a robot arm may be implemented by using sensors, in particular visual and range sensors, to measure the location (position and orientation) of its end effector relative to a target object, despite measurement delay and noise. Sanderson and Weiss (1983) distinguished between two visual feedback representations: a position-based feedback, whose parameters are relative locations, and an image-based feedback, whose parameters are image features. The latter is inherently faster (because it entails no feature-to-space computation delay) but its feedback is nonlinear. They also distinguished between two types of joint-control structures: look-and-move and visual tracking.

Examples

Adaptive control demonstrations at SRI included the following.

Compressor-Cover Assembly. Using global and local features, a compressor housing and its cover were located by a vision subsystem, picked up by a Unimate arm, and placed on an xy table (Fig. 15). Guided by the vision subsystem, the xy table moved to each of eight positions where an Auto-Place limited-sequence manipulator bolted the cover while the table was free to move slightly to accommodate locational errors. Visual and positional sensing were used to verify this operation (McGhie and Hill, 1978).

Figure 15. Compressor-cover assembly

Figure 16. Visually guided arc-welding robot. Courtesy of Kremers and co-workers, SRI International.

Tracking. Visual–range servoing techniques were developed using a projector of a light plane and a TV camera mounted on the end effector of a Unimate arm and applied to simulated spot welding on a moving line and tracking a cornered path in three dimensions (Agin, 1979).

Arc Welding. Using a laser scanner range sensor mounted on its wrist, a Cincinnati-Milacron T3 arm was guided by the vision subsystem in one-pass arc welding of different workpiece joints (Fig. 16) (Kremers and co-workers, 1983).

Modular Printer-Carriage Assembly. A nine-part printer carriage was assembled by a modular-assembly station consisting of two PUMA arms with visual and force sensors, respectively, attached to their wrists, a binary vision module, and general-purpose part feeder and assembly fixture on two tables, respectively (Fig. 17). Binary visual sensing was used to locate plastic rockers and, subsequently, force and click sensing were used to verify that they have been snapped properly into a shaft (Smith and Nitzan, 1983).

Issues

Some issues entailed in adaptive robot control are as follows.

> *Basic Theory.* Developing a general analysis that guarantees stability and high speed in controlling nonlinear, stochastic systems with unknown and varying parameters.

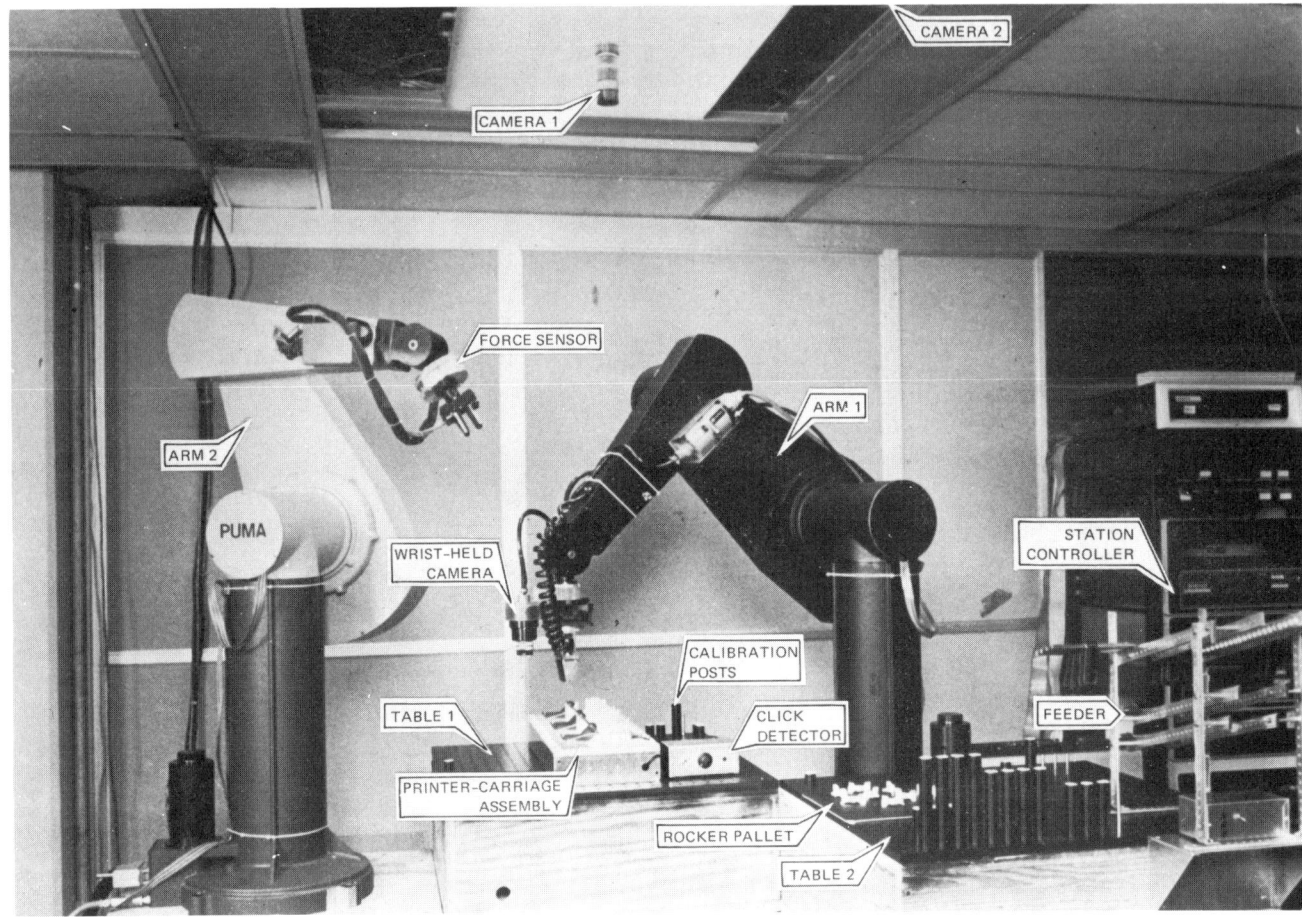

Figure 17. Modular assembly station.

Sensor Integration. Selecting the best sensors for a given task and integrating their outputs into the robot control system.

Branching. Planning cost-effective conditional branches for robot actions, depending on the sensor signals.

Execution Speed. Obtaining and matching high speed sensory data processing, arm motion, and arm control.

ROBOT PROGRAMMING

Training today's industrial robot arm is usually done by a human operator who, using a teach box with push buttons, leads that arm through its task steps and records the location or action of each step. Although popular, this teaching-by-doing method may be wasteful (eg, no useful work during training for batch production), tedious (eg, training for many computable locations), or inadequate (eg, training for sensor-guided task steps). These limitations can be partially overcome by using a computer-based textual robot-programming language. Furthermore, a robot-programming language (or an equivalent computer program) is essential for programming a robot system, working alone or with other machines, that consists of manipulators, sensors, and auxiliary devices and is controlled by a hierarchy of distributed computers.

A robot programming-language is applicable in two programming modes: on-line programming and off-line programming. On-line programming is performed by a programmer who, although sensing and handling real equipment and workpieces, generates a program text that may include manipulator locations (either taught by doing or typed in), robot sensing (to overcome uncertainties), and logic or control statements (which usually constitute the bulk of the program). Off-line programming is similar to on-line programming except that the programmer deals with simulated objects (workpieces, sensors, manipulators, and other equipment) rather than real objects.

Robot-Programming Languages

The main goal of using a robot-programming language is to facilitate the programming of a robot system for a new task or modification of an old one. To achieve this goal, a robot-programming language provides the user with high level programming capabilities. These capabilities are implemented by means of a language processor and a robot controller: the processor accepts and checks the user statements and translates them into commands for the controller, the controller then generates lower level commands for the corresponding device (eg, the trajectories, joint values, and servo commands for the arm joints).

Current Robot-Programming-Language Capabilities. Eight commercially available U.S. robot-programming languages have been compared by Gruver and co-workers (1983).

- AL, Stanford University (Mujtaba and co-workers, 1981).
- AML, IBM Corp. (Taylor and co-workers, 1982).
- HELP, General Electric Co. (1982).
- JARS, Jet Propulsion Laboratory (Craig, 1980).
- MCL, McDonnell Douglas Corp. (Wood and Fugelso, 1983).
- RAIL, Automatix, Inc. (1982).
- RPS, SRI International (Parks, 1983).
- VAL, Unimation, Inc. (1980, 1981).

The combined features of these robot languages are classified below into general and robotic programming capabilities (see the above references for individual robot-language capabilities).

General Programming Capabilities. General programming capabilities include the following high level language features:

- *Data Types.* Integer, real, character string, label, and aggregate (an ordered set of data types) (Taylor and co-workers, 1982).
- *Operations.* Arithmetic, relational, logical, assignment, etc.
- *Control Expressions.* Block structure (BEGIN_END), branching (GOTO), conditional branching (IF_THEN; IF_THEN_ELSE_), continuing (WHILE_DO_), and looping (DO_UNTIL_).
- *Subroutines and Functions.* Library (compiled) and user-generated (interpreted).
- *Interactive Support Modules.* Text editing, hot editing (run, stop, edit, and continue to run a program), compiling, interpreting, graphic simulation, etc.
- *Debugging Features.* Break points, tracing, and single-stepping.

Robotic Programming Capabilities. Robotic programming capabilities, invoked by declarations or commands, are usually built into the robot language; in a few cases, however, they are incorporated into the language by interfacing with external modules (eg, RPS interfaces with the PUMA VAL (Unimation, Inc.) controller and the SRI and MIC vision modules). These capabilities are classified below according to the nature of the robot functions:

- *Geometric Data Types.* Vector, displacement, rotation, frame, transform, and path of points.
- *Motion of Arm End Effector.* Specified joint(s), interpolated joints (between two points), straight line (to a given destination), straight line via a given point, continuous path (through given points), sawtooth weaving superimposed on a continuous path, specification of speed and acceleration or deceleration, departure and approach, etc.
- *Vision.* Picture taking, binary feature extraction, silhouette-based object recognition and location, adjustment of thresholds and windows, and gray-level feature extraction (eg, histograms).
- *Servoing with Sensory Feedback.* Visual sensing, limit switch, and force/torque sensing.
- *Multiprocessing.* Simultaneous control of multiple arms, sensors, machines, and other devices in a manufacturing cell.

Limitations and Issues. Current robot-programming languages are handicapped by the following limitations and issues (Soroka, 1983; Goldman, 1985).

System Integration. Robot-programming languages, currently capable of controlling a single arm, should be able to concurrently control a flexible workcell comprised of two or more arms, machines, vision modules, other sensors, and auxiliary equipment, and be integrable into the factory CAD–CAM system.

Task-Level Commands. Robot-programming languages, currently including only manipulator-level commands, should also include higher, task-level commands to simplify workcell programming for more complex tasks.

Flexibility and Intelligence. Robot-programming languages should be flexible and intelligent enough to handle unpredictable situations, eg, be able to verify that specified trajectories are collision-free.

Hardware Dependency. Robot-programming-language software is closely tied to specific computer hardware; although achieving higher speed, this dependency hinders computer portability.

Language Standardization. A commercial robot-programming language is proprietary with its vendor and depends heavily on the kinematics of the arm it controls; hence, users of different arms must program them in several languages. This problem could be solved by having a standard, arm-independent language processor that interfaces with each arm-specific controller that servos the arm joints.

Marketing Considerations. Robot-arm marketing appears to be the major incentive for developing a robot programming language. This factor may oppose efforts to standardize robot programming languages unless one robot manufacturer dominates the market.

User–Language Compatibility. The spectrum of users who match the complexity of a given robot-programming language is narrow. Developing robot-programming languages that match a wide spectrum of users, from a factory worker to a computer scientist, is an issue. Along this line, the utility of a robot-programming language that is restrictive when used by a sophisticated programmer who requires programming flexibility may be questioned. An alternative approach is to utilize the general programming capabilities of a high level language (such as C, Pascal, or Ada) and, with an appropriate computer operating system, develop hierarchies of robot-function subroutines that constitute robot-programming capabilities. This approach could reduce the cost and enhance the portability of the robot software as well as improve programming flexibility.

Off-Line Programming

Off-line programming is performed by a programmer who generates a program text that may include simulated manipulator locations, simulated robot sensing, and logic or control statements.

Advantages and Disadvantages. Compared with on-line programming, off-line programming has the following advantages.

No Production Stoppage. Production need not be stopped to make real robotic equipment available for programming. This is a major cost-reduction factor.

Safety. The danger of harm to the programmer, the equipment, and the workpieces during programming is eliminated.

Early Programming. Programming can begin before workpieces, robots, machines, fixtures, and other equipment arrive and, hence, is not susceptible to delays caused by late deliveries.

Product Redesign. Any mistake in the design of a workpiece or a product can be detected and corrected before it is produced.

Sensitivity Verification. The generated program can be verified under exhaustive conditions that can be simulated but not realized experimentally. For the same reason, determining the sensitivity of operation to variation of parameters must be based on simulation.

On the other hand, the disadvantages of off-line programming are described below.

Model Limitations. The accuracy of simulating a robot system depends on the authenticity of its model; complex phenomena that are hard to model precisely will result in simulation errors.

Modeling Cost. Unlike on-line programming, simulation in off-line programming entails modeling cost.

Three-Dimensional Geometric Models. Three types of geometric model of three-dimensional objects are distinguished:

1. *Wire-Frame Models.* Represent objects by their vertices and edges; these models are simple and fast but are hard to visualize (especially if hidden lines are not eliminated) are useless for collision detection, and may be ambiguous.
2. *Surface Models.* Represent objects by their surfaces; the above wire-frame model drawbacks are eliminated by using surface models, but they are slow and provide no information about the mass, inertia, and stability of objects.
3. *Solid Models.* Represent objects by their volumes (including surfaces); most of the above drawbacks are eliminated by using solid models, but they are slow.

Simulation. A graphic simulation system uses a three-dimensional model to generate static or dynamic displays of objects and workcell layout. Such a system enables a programmer to view workcell objects from different directions (using perspective transformations) with variable magnification (eg, zooming), as if the programmer were a "flying eye" observing a real workcell. Using this facility, an off-line programmer interactively writes and debugs the program steps for a given task, observes the animation of the operation, and when satisfied with the results, downloads the program on to the (real) workcell controller and runs it. For example, Figure 18 shows a display (generated on a Silicon Graphics IRIS 2400 system) of a simulated PUMA arm with a two-finger hand mounted on a wrist force sensor, a table, and a cylindrical part on it. A simple task was programmed off-line and executed by a real, calibrated workcell: a vision module (simulated but not shown in Fig. 18) located the part and the arm, guided by this information, picked up the part and moved it to its destination.

CAD–CAM Database. Ultimately, the geometric and nongeometric representations of all the equipment and workpieces in a factory will be stored in a computer, and these databases will be applied to CAD and computer-aided manufacturing (CAM) (see MANUFACTURING, AI IN). Currently, however, a limited amount of such a database

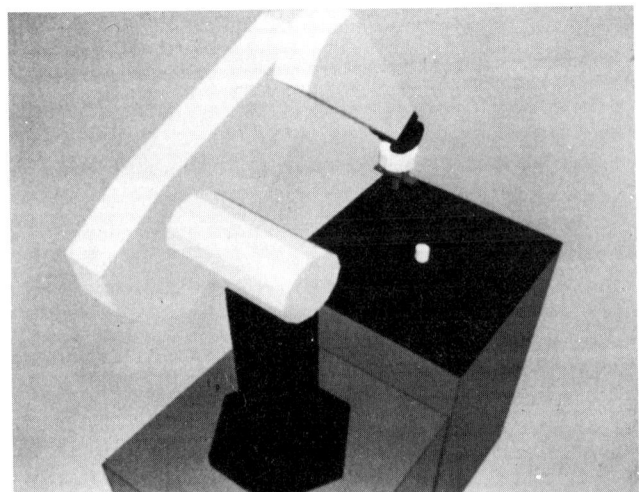

Figure 18. Graphic simulation in off-line programming of a robot system. Courtesy of Smith, SRI International.

exists in certain industries (eg, some aerospace and automotive industries), and its use is limited to static and dynamic graphic display in the design stage and to programming numerically controlled (NC) part machining in the manufacturing stage.

Research Issues. Among the research issues related to off-line programming are the following ones:

- *Three-Dimensional Object Modeling.* Increasing the speed of processing surface and solid models both algorithmically and by hardware, modeling flexible objects, locational uncertainty.
- *CAD–CAM.* Tolerances, path planning and collision avoidance, task-level robot functions acting on workpieces under a range of constraints, near optimal robot selection and workcell-layout design, nongeometric workpiece and equipment representations, standardizing robot tools and types, rules for manufacturing processes (fabrication, handling inspection, and assembly), integration of different CAD–CAM systems.
- *Simulation.* Efficient user interface: robot sensing simulation, robot reach, robot dynamics, static and dynamic process simulation.

MANUFACTURING PROCESS PLANNING

Manual robot-system programming entails a major effort even if facilitated by a robot-programming language or done off-line. Graphic simulation may help specify robot locations, but not logic or control statements, which usually constitute most of the program. Developing a task-oriented programming language will mitigate this problem, but a long-term solution is automatic robot-system planning and programming.

Consider a programmable assembly workcell that is controlled by a hierarchy of distributed computers and includes manipulators, sensors, part feeders, and auxiliary devices. If instructed to assemble a particular product, the workcell must be provided with a workable plan for the assembly process. Consider how such a plan can be generated cost-effectively in a future factory equipped with robotic CAD–CAM systems.

The output of the CAD system for a given product will include two major components: the design of the product parts and their attachment sequence. This information is used to plan the robotic assembly operations, each of which includes actions and verifications of equipment, parts, and the actions themselves. The CAD output can be generated interactively by a human designer without much difficulty. In contrast, planning the details of the actions and, especially, the verification of each assembly operation is very tedious and prone to human errors. Hence, there is a need to automate planning of robotic assembly processes (and, for similar reasons, other manufacturing processes).

Process planning (qv) depends on the state of the process world, which describes the equipment, workpieces, and actions vs time, and is part of the process knowledge base. Few automatic planners using AI techniques have been developed to date, and these planners [eg, DEVISER (Vere, 1981)] are based on the assumption that the state of the process world is known exactly at the planning time. In an unstructured world, where this assumption is invalid, the state of the process world should be determined by robot sensors.

Development of a sensor-based planner and execution monitor using AI techniques was begun by Cheeseman at SRI (Nitzan, 1983). The planner will include a knowledge base ("expert system"), which consists of a world model (effectors, sensors, and other devices), process rules, and sensor-selection rules, as well as a plan generator which plans the action and checking steps for a given robot process. The generated plan will be sent to the execution controller, which will command and coordinate the process execution. As the process world changes, its state will be updated by the robot sensors; this information is required to execute and monitor the plan actions. The highlights of the sensor-based planner are described below.

The plan will call for the use of sensors at run time to fill in unknown information of two types: enabling execution of actions in the plan, eg, visually servoing an arm, and monitoring the plan execution, ie, verifying its actions. The planner will select the best sensor(s) for a given task on the basis of rules and estimated locational errors of objects, effectors, and sensors. Conditional planning will provide alternative branches for all possible sensor outputs, followed by immediate rejoining of the branches to simplify the plan (ie, prevent branch bushiness).

Multiple sensors will be used to combine sensory information if a single sensor is not sufficient. Fixed sensors (eg, mounted on the ceiling) will be distinguished from manipulated ones (eg, mounted on robot end effectors) because the latter entail actions, in addition to information gathering, which must be planned. Error detection and correction will be implemented. If a failure is detected, the process will be halted and, if possible, replanned locally to minimize production down time.

Research issues in planning include the following: a formal theory and representation of knowledge (eg, geometry, uncertainty, temporal relationships, and condition monitoring); planning collision-free paths, fine-motion sensing, part mating, error detection and correction, and multiple robot cooperation; real-time planning and replanning; planning for multiple agents (distributed AI); and planner learning. These research issues are extremely difficult to solve. Despite the importance of automatic planning, its implementation will take many years. Eventually, however, automatic robot-system planning will be an essential component of the factory.

BIBLIOGRAPHY

G. J. Agin, "Real Time Control of a Robot with a Mobile Camera," in *Proceedings of the Ninth International Symposium and Exposition on Industrial Robots,* Washington, D.C., Mar. 1979, pp. 233–246.

G. J. Agin and T. O. Binford. "Computer Description of Curved

Objects," in *Proceedings of the Third IJCAI,* Stanford, Calif., Morgan-Kaufmann, San Mateo, Calif., 1973, pp. 629–640.

M. D. Altschuler and co-workers, "The Numerical Stereo Camera," in *Proceedings of the Society for Photo-Optical Instrumentation Engineers Conference on 3-D Machine Perception,* Vol. 283, SPIE, Bellingham, Wash., 1981, pp. 15–24.

Automatix, *RAIL Software Reference Manual (ROBOVISION and CYBERVISION),* Rev. 3.0, MN-RB-07, Automatix, Burlington, Mass., Jan. 1982.

R. U. Ayres and S. M. Miller, *Robotics: Applications and Social Implications,* Ballinger Publishing Co., Cambridge, Mass., 1983.

D. H. Ballard and C. M. Brown, *Computer Vision,* Prentice-Hall., Inc., Englewood Cliffs, N.J., 1982.

S. Barnard, "Automated Inspection Using Gray-Scale Statistics," in *Proceedings of the First National Conference on Artificial Intelligence,* Stanford, Calif., AAAI, Menlo Park, Calif., 1980, pp. 49–52.

T. G. Bartholet, "The First 'Functionoid' Developed by Odetics, Inc.," in *Proceedings of the IEEE International Conference on Advanced Robotics,* Tokyo, Japan, Sept. 12–13, 1983, pp. 293–298.

R. A. Boie, "Capacitive Impedance Readout Tactile Image Sensor," in *Proceedings of the IEEE International Conference on Robotics,* Atlanta, Ga., Mar. 13–15, 1984, pp. 370–378.

R. C. Bolles and R. A. Cain, "Recognizing and Locating Partially Visible Objects: The Local-Feature-Focus-Method," *Int. J. Robot. Res.* **1**(3), 57–82 (Fall 1982).

R. C. Bolles and P. Horaud, "3DPO: A Three-Dimensional Part Orientation System," *Int. J. Robot. Res.* **5**(3) (1986).

J. J. Craig, *JARS: JPL Autonomous Robot System,* Jet Propulsion Laboratory, Pasadena, Calif., 1980.

J. J. Craig, "An Adaptive Algorithm for the Computed Torque Method of Manipulator Control," in D. Nitzan and R. C. Bolles, eds., *Workshop on Intelligent Robots: Achievements and Issues,* SRI International, Menlo Park, Calif., 1985, pp. 171–184.

P. Dario and D. De Rossi, "Tactile Sensors and the Gripping Challenge," *Proc. IEEE Spectr.* **22**(8), 46–52 (Aug. 1985).

J. Denavit and R. S. Hartenberg, "A Kinematic Notation for Lower-Pair Mechanisms Based on Matrices," *J. Appl. Mechan. (ASME),* 215–221 (June 1955).

S. Drake, *Using Compliance in Lieu of Sensory Feedback for Automatic Assembly,* Report T-657, Charles Stark Draper Laboratory, Cambridge, Mass., Sept. 1977.

R. O. Duda and P. E. Hart, *Pattern Classification and Scene Analysis,* John Wiley & Sons, Inc., New York, 1973.

R. O. Duda, D. Nitzan, and P. Barret, "Use of Range and Reflectance Data to Find Planar Surface Regions," *IEEE Trans. Pattern Anal. Mach. Intell.* **PAMI-1**(3), 259–271 (July 1979),

J. F. Engelberger, *Robotics in Practice,* Kogan Page, London, 1980.

R. Featherstone, "The Calculation of Robot Dynamics Using Articulated-Body Inertias," *Int. J. Robot. Res.* **2**(1), 13–30 (Spring 1983).

General Electric, *Allegro Operator's Manual, A12 Assembly Robot,* General Electric Co., Bridgeport, Conn., 1982.

G. J. Gleason and G. J. Agin, "A Modular Vision System for Sensor-Controlled Manipulation and Inspection," in *Proceedings of the Ninth International Symposium and Exposition on Industrial Robots,* Washington, D.C., 1979, pp. 57–70.

R. Goldman, "Programming Languages for Robots," in D. Nitzan and R. C. Bolles, eds., *Workshop on Intelligent Robots: Achievements and Issues,* SRI International, Menlo Park, Calif., 1985, pp. 231–236.

F. E. Goodwin, *Coherent Laser Radar 3-D Vision Sensor,* SME Technical Paper MS85-1005, Society of Manufacturing Engineers, Dearborn, Mich., 1985.

W. E. L. Grimson and T. Lozano-Perez, "Model-Based Recognition and Location from Tactile Data," in *Proceedings of the 1984 IEEE International Conference on Robotics,* Atlanta, GA, 1984, pp. 248–255.

W. E. L. Grimson and T. Lozano-Perez, "Recognition and Location of Overlapping Parts from Sparse Data in Two and Three Dimensions," in *Proceedings of the IEEE International Conference on Robotics and Automation,* St. Louis, Mo., Mar. 25–28, 1985, pp. 61–66.

W. A. Gruver, B. I. Soroka, J. J. Craig, and T. L. Turner, "Evaluation of Commercially Available Robot Programming Languages," *Proceedings of the Thirteenth International Symposium on Industrial Robots and Robots,* Vol. 7, Chicago, Ill., Apr. 18–21, 1983, pp. 12.58–12.68.

W. Hahn, *Theory and Application of Liapunov's Direct Method,* Prentice-Hall, Inc., Englewood Cliffs, N.J., 1963.

L. D. Harmon, "Automated Tactile Sensing," *Int. J. Robot. Res.* **1**(2), 3–32 (Summer 1982).

E. C. Hildreth, "Edge Detection for Computer Vision System," *Mechan. Eng.,* 48–53 (Aug. 1982).

E. C. Hildreth, *The Measurement of Visual Motion,* MIT Press, Cambridge, Mass., 1983.

W. D. Hillis, "A High-Resolution Image Touch Sensor," *Int. J. Robot. Res.* **1**(2), 33–44 (Summer 1982).

J. M. Hollerbach, "A Recursive Lagrangian Formulation of Manipulator Dynamics and a Comparative Study of Dynamics Formulation Complexity," *IEEE Trans. System Man Cybernetics* **10**(11), 730–736 (1980).

J. M. Hollerbach, "Tactile Sensors and Interpretation of Contact Features," in D. Nitzan and R. C. Bolles, eds., *Workshop on Intelligent Robots: Achievements and Issues,* SRI International, Menlo Park, Calif., 1985, pp. 143–152.

B. K. P. Horn, "Shape from Shading," in P. H. Winston, ed., *The Psychology of Computer Vision,* McGraw-Hill Book Co., Inc., New York, 1975.

B. K. P. Horn, *Robot Vision,* MIT Press, Cambridge, Mass., 1986.

T. Iwamoto, H. Yamamoto, and K. Honma, "Transformable Crawler Mechanism with Adaptability to Terrain Variations," in Bartholet, 1983, pp. 285–291.

J. Jablonowski and J. W. Posey, "Robotics Terminology," in S. Y. Nof, ed., *Handbook of Industrial Robotics,* John Wiley & Sons, Inc., New York, pp. 1271–1303, 1985.

R. A. Jarvis, "A Perspective on Range Finding Techniques for Computer Vision," *IEEE Trans. Pattern Anal. Mach. Intell.* **PAMI-2**, 122–139 (Mar. 1983).

A. R. Johnston, *Infrared Laser Rangefinder,* Report NPO-13460, Jet Propulsion Laboratory, Pasadena, Calif., Aug. 1973.

T. R. Kane and D. A. Levinson, "The Use of Kane's Dynamical Equations in Robotics," *Int. J. Robot. Res.* **2**(3), 3–21 (Fall 1983).

J. H. Kremers and co-workers, "Development of a Machine-Vision Based Robotic Arc-Welding System," in *Proceedings of the Thirteenth International Symposium on Industrial Robots and Robots,* Vol. 7, Chicago, 1983, pp. 14.19–14.33.

J. Y. S. Luh and co-workers, "On-Line Computational Scheme for Mechanical Manipulators," *Trans. ASME, J. Dyn. Sys. Meas. Contr.* **102**(2), 69–76 (1980).

R. B. McGhee, "Vehicular Legged Locomotion," in G. N. Saridis, ed., *Advances in Automation and Robotics,* JAI, Greenwich, Conn., 1983.

D. F. McGhie and J. W. Hill, "Vision Controlled MS78-685 Subassembly Station," in *SME Robots III Conference,* Technical Paper MS78-685, Chicago, Ill., Nov. 7–9, 1978.

M. Miyagawa and co-workers, "Flexible Vision System "Multi-Window" and This Application," in *Proceedings of the IEEE International Conference on Advanced Robotics,* Tokyo, Japan, 1983, pp. 171–178.

S. Mujtaba and R. Goldman, *AL User's Manual,* 3rd ed., Report No. STAN-CS-81-889, Stanford University, Stanford, Calif., Dec. 1981.

P. G. Mulgaonkar, D. Nitzan, C. K. Cowan, and A. Bavarsky, Inspection of Three-Dimensional Objects," *Proceedings of the Twelfth NSF Conference on Production Research and Technology,* University of Wisconsin, Madison, Wis., May 1985, pp. 431–435.

J. L. Mundy, "The Limits of Accuracy for Range Sensing," in D. Nitzan and R. C. Bolles, eds., *Workshop on Intelligent Robots: Achievements and Issues,* SRI International, Menlo Park, Calif., 1985, pp. 109–133.

D. Nitzan, *Scene Analysis Using Range Data,* AI Center Technical Note 69, Stanford Research Institute, Menlo Park, Calif., Aug. 1972.

D. Nitzan, "Assessment of Robotic Sensors," in *Proceedings of the First International Conference on Robot Vision and Sensory Controls,* Stratford-Upon-Avon, UK, Apr. 1981, pp. 1–11.

D. Nitzan, C. Bavrouil, P. C. Cheeseman, and R. C. Smith, "Use of Sensors in Robot Systems," in *Proceedings of the IEEE International Conference on Advanced Robotics,* Tokyo, Japan, 1983, pp. 123–132.

D. Nitzan, A. Brain, and R. Duda, "The Measurement and Use of Registered Reflectance and Range Data in Scene Analysis," *Proc. IEEE* 65(2), 206–220 (Feb. 1977).

R. Nevatia and T. O. Binford, "Structured Descriptions of Complex Objects," in *Proceedings of the Third International Joint Conference on Artificial Intelligence,* Morgan-Kaufmann, San Mateo, Calif., 1973, pp. 641–647.

D. Nitzan, R. C. Bolles, J. H. Kremers, and P. G. Mulgaonkar, "3-D Vision for Robot Applications," in *Proceedings of the NATO Workshop on Knowledge Engineering for Robotic Applications,* Maratea, Italy, May 12–16, 1986.

D. Nitzan and C. A. Rosen, "Programmable Industrial Automation," *IEEE Trans. Comput.* 25(10), 1259–1270 (Dec. 1976).

T. Okada and S. Tsuchiya, "On a Versatile Finger System," in *Proceedings of the Seventh International Symposium on Industrial Robots,* Tokyo, Japan, Oct. 19–21, 1977, pp. 345–352.

W. T. Parks, "The SRI Robot Programming System (RPS)," in *Proceedings of the Thirteenth International Symposium on Industrial Robots and Robots,* Vol. 7, Chicago, 1983, pp. 12.21–12.41.

R. P. Paul, "Manipulator Path Control," in *Proceedings of the International Conference on Cybernetics and Society,* San Francisco, Calif., Sept. 1975, pp. 147–152.

R. P. Paul, *Robot Manipulation: Mathematics, Programming, and Control,* MIT Press, Cambridge, Mass., 1981.

M. H. Raibert, "An All Digital VLSI Tactile Array Sensor," in *Proceedings of the IEEE International Conference on Robotics,* Atlanta, Ga., 1984, pp. 314–319.

M. H. Raibert and I. E. Sutherland, "Machines That Walk," *Sci. Am.* 248(2), 44–53 (Jan. 1983).

M. H. Raibert and J. E. Tanner, "Design and Implementation of a VLSI Tactile Sensing Computer," *Int. J. Robot. Res.* 1(3), 3–18 (Fall 1982).

B. Raphael, *The Thinking Computer: Mind Insider Matter,* W. H. Freeman, San Francisco, Calif., 1976.

C. A. Rosen and co-workers, *Exploratory Research in Advanced Automation,* 2nd report, NSF Grant GI-38100X1, Stanford Research Institute, Menlo Park, Calif., Aug. 1974.

C. A. Rosen and co-workers, *Machine Intelligence Research Applied to Industrial Automation,* 6th report, NSF Grant APR75-13074, Stanford Research Institute, Menlo Park, Calif., Nov. 1976.

A. Rosenfeld and A. C. Kak, *Digital Picture Processing,* Academic Press, Inc., New York, 1976.

K. Sadamoto, *Robots in the Japanese Economy,* Survey Japan, Tokyo, 1981.

J. K. Salisbury and J. J. Craig, "Articulated Hands: Force Control and Kinematic Issues," *Int. J. Robot. Res.* 1(1), 4–17 (Spring 1982).

A. C. Sanderson and L. E. Weiss, "Adaptive Visual Servo Control of Robots," in A. Pugh, ed., *Robot Vision,* IFS Publications, UK, 1983.

A. C. Sanderson and L. E. Weiss, "Adaptive Control of Sensor-Based Robotic Systems," in D. Nitzan and R. C. Bolles, eds., *Workshop on Intelligent Robots: Achievements and Issues,* SRI International, Menlo Park, Calif., 1985, pp. 185–205.

W. M. Silver, "On the Equivalence of Lagrangian and Newton-Euler Dynamics for Manipulators," *Int. J. Robot. Res.* 1(2), 60–70 (Summer 1982).

R. C. Smith and D. Nitzan, "A Modular Programmable Assembly Station," in *Proceedings of the Thirteenth International Symposium on Industrial Robots and Robots,* Vol. 7, Chicago, 1983, pp. 5.53–5.75.

B. I. Soroka, "What Can't Robot Languages Do?" in *Proceedings of the Thirteenth International Symposium on Industrial Robots and Robots,* Vol. 7, Chicago, 1983, pp. 12.1–12.8.

R. H. Taylor, "Planning and Execution of Straight Line Manipulator Trajectories," *IBM J. Res. Dev.* 23(4), 253–264 (July 1979).

R. H. Taylor, P. D. Summers, and J. M. Meyer, "AML: A Manufacturing Language," *Int. J. Robot. Res.* 1(3), 19–41 (Fall 1982).

Y. Umetani and K. Yonemoto, "Japan Robotics Research for the Next Generation," in *Proceedings of the IEEE International Conference on Advanced Robotics,* Tokyo, 1983, pp. 3–20.

Unimation, *User's Guide to VAL,* Version 12, No. 398-H2A, Unimation Inc., Danbury, Conn., June 1980.

Unimation, *VAL Univision Supplement,* Version 13 (VSN), 2nd ed., Unimation Inc., Danbury, Conn., July 1981.

S. A. Vere, *Planning in Time: Windows and Durations for Activities and Goals,* Jet Propulsion Laboratory Report, California Institute of Technology, Pasadena, Calif., Nov. 1981.

B. O. Wood and M. A. Fugelso, "MCL, The Manufacturing Control Language," in *Proceedings of the Thirteenth International Symposium on Industrial Robots and Robots,* Vol. 7, Chicago, 1983, pp. 12.84–12.96.

General References

Books

J. K. Aggarwal, R. O. Duda, and A. Rosenfeld, eds., *Computer Methods in Image Analysis,* IEEE Press, New York, 1977.

I. Aleksander, *Artificial Vision for Robots,* Chapman & Hall, New York, 1984.

I. Aleksander, ed., *The World Yearbook of Robotics Research and Development,* Kogan Page, London, 1985.

B. G. Batchelor and co-workers, eds., *Automated Visual Inspection,* IFS Publications, UK, 1985.

G. Beni and S. Hackwood, eds., *Recent Advances in Robotics,* John Wiley & Sons, Inc., New York, 1985.

J. M. Brady, ed., *Computer Vision,* North-Holland, Amsterdam, The Netherlands, 1981.

J. M. Brady and co-workers, eds., *Robot Motion: Planning and Control,* MIT Press, Cambridge, Mass., 1982.

J. M. Brady and R. Paul, *Robotics Research: The First International Symposium,* MIT Press, Cambridge, Mass., 1984.

P. Coiffet, *Robot Technology,* 7 vols., Prentice-Hall, Inc., Englewood Cliffs, N.J. 1981.

J. J. Craig, *Introduction to Robotics: Mechanics and Control,* Addison-Wesley Publishing Co., Inc., Reading, Mass., 1986.

A. J. Critchlow, *Introduction to Robotics,* Macmillan, New York, 1985.

G. G. Dodd and L. Rossol, eds., *Computer Vision and Sensor-Based Robots,* Plenum Press, New York, 1979.

R. C. Dorf, *Robotics and Automated Manufacturing,* Reston Publishing Co., Reston, Va., 1983.

W. B. Gevartner, *Intelligent Machines—An Introductory Perspective of Artificial Intelligence and Robotics,* Prentice-Hall, Inc., Englewood Cliffs, N.J., 1985.

M. P. Groover and E. W. Zimmers, Jr., *CAD/CAM—Computer-Aided Design and Manufacturing,* Prentice-Hall, Inc., Englewood Cliffs, N.J., 1984.

A. R. Hansen and E. M. Riseman, *Computer Vision Systems,* Academic Press, Inc., New York, 1978.

W. B. Heginbotham, ed., *Programmable Assembly,* IFS Publications, UK, 1984.

V. D. Hunt, *Smart Robots,* Chapman & Hall, New York, 1985.

C. G. S. Lee, R. C. Gonzales, and K. S. Fu, *Tutorial on Robotics,* 2nd ed., Computer Society Press, Silver Springs, Md., 1986.

M. D. Levine, *Vision in Man and Machine,* McGraw-Hill Book Co., Inc., New York, 1985.

D. Marr, *Vision,* W. H. Freeman, San Francisco, 1982.

M. E. Mortenson, *Geometric Modeling,* John Wiley & Sons, Inc., New York, 1985.

R. Nevatia, *Machine Perception,* Prentice-Hall, Inc., Englewood Cliffs, N.J., 1982.

W. M. Newman and R. F. Sproull, *Principles of Interactive Computer Graphics,* McGraw-Hill Book Co., Inc., New York, 1979.

S. Y. Nof, ed., *Handbook of Industrial Robots,* John Wiley & Sons, Inc., New York, 1985.

Y. C. Pao, *Elements of Computer-Aided Design and Manufacturing,* John Wiley & Sons, Inc., New York, 1984.

T. Pavlidis, *Structural Pattern Recognition,* Springer-Verlag, New York, 1977.

W. Pratt, *Digital Image Processing,* John Wiley & Sons, Inc., New York, 1978.

A. Pugh, *Robot Vision,* IFS Publications, UK, 1983.

A. Pugh, *Robot Sensors, Vol. 1-Vision; Vol. 2-Tactile and Non-Vision,* IFS Publications, UK, 1986.

P. Ranky, *The Design and Operation of Flexible Manufacturing Systems,* IFS Publications, UK, 1983.

W. G. Rohm, "A Remote Promise," *Infosystems,* 52–56 (Sept. 1986).

A. Rosenfeld and A. C. Kak, *Digital Picture Processing,* Academic Press, New York, 1976.

W. E. Snyder, *Industrial Robots: Computer Interfacing and Control,* Prentice-Hall, Inc., Englewood Cliffs, N.J., 1985.

D. J. Todd, *Walking Machines—An Introduction to Legged Robots,* Chapman & Hall, New York, 1985.

J. T. Tou and R. C. Gonzalez, *Pattern Recognition Principles,* Addison-Wesley Publishing Co., Inc., Reading, Mass., 1974.

M. W. Thring, *Robots and Telechirs,* Halstead Press, a Division of John Wiley & Sons, Inc., New York, 1983.

Conference Proceedings

Proceedings of the International Symposium on Industrial Robots (ISIR), nos. 1–15, 1970–1985, Robotics International of the Society of Manufacturing Engineers, Dearborn, Mich.

Proceedings of the Annual Robots Conferences, Nos. 1–10, 1976–1986, Robotics International of the Society of Manufacturing Engineers, Dearborn, Mich.

Proceedings of the Annual IEEE International Conference on Robotics and Automation, 1984, 1985, 1986, IEEE Computer Society Press, Washington, D.C.

Proceedings of the First International Symposium on Robotics Research, J. M. Brady and R. Paul, eds., MIT Press, Cambridge, Mass., 1984.

Proceedings of the Second International Symposium on Robotics Research, H. Hanafusa and H. Inoue, eds., Kyoto, Japan, MIT Press, Cambridge, Mass., 1985.

Proceedings of the Annual IEEE Conferences on Computer Vision and Pattern Recognition, IEEE Computer Society Press, Washington, D.C.

Proceedings of the First World Conference on Robotics Research, Bethlehem, Pa., Robotics International of SME, Dearborn, Mich., 1984.

Proceedings of the Second World Conference on Robotics Research, Scottsdale, Ariz., Robotics International of SME, Dearborn, Mich., Aug. 1986.

Digital Image Proceedings and Analysis, Vols. 1–2, R. Chellappa and A. W. Sawchuck, eds., IEEE Computer Society Press, Washington, D.C., 1985.

Journals

IEEE Journal of Robotics and Automation.
International Journal of Robotics Research.
International Journal of Robotics and Computer Integrated Manufacturing.
Robotics Today.
Robotics World.
The Industrial Robot.
Sensor Review.
International Journal of Advanced Manufacturing Technology.
International Journal of Robotics.
Journal of Robotic Systems.

D. Nitzan
SRI International

ROBOTS, LEGGED

Legged robots offer the possibility of vehicular travel where only animals can now go. They also offer a tool for the scientific study of legged locomotion in people and animals. This article surveys research on legged robots, starting with work in the nineteenth century and proceeding to 1990. Attention is given to the distinction between statically stable and actively balanced machines, and rough-terrain locomotion is discussed.

WHY STUDY LEGGED MACHINES?

Aside from the sheer thrill of creating machines that actually run and walk, there are two serious reasons for exploring legged robots. One reason is mobility: there is a need for vehicles that can travel on difficult terrain, where existing vehicles cannot go. Wheels excel on prepared surfaces such as rails and roads, but perform poorly where the terrain is soft or uneven. Only about half the earth's landmass is accessible to existing wheeled and tracked vehicles, whereas a much greater area can be reached by animals on foot. It should be possible to build legged vehicles that can go to the places that only animals can now reach. Such vehicles may be useful in industrial, agricultural, military, and space applications.

One reason legs provide better mobility than wheels on rough terrain is that they can use isolated footholds that optimize support and traction, whereas a wheel requires a continuous path of support. As a consequence, a legged system is free to choose among the best footholds in the reachable terrain wheres a wheel is forced to negotiate the worst terrain along the chosen path. A ladder illustrates this point: rungs provide footholds that enable legged systems to climb, but the spaces between the rungs would prevent a wheeled system from making progress. Another advantage of legs is that they provide an active suspension that decouples the path of the body from the paths of the feet. The payload is free to travel smoothly despite pronounced variations in the terrain. A legged system can also step or leap over obstacles. The performance of legged vehicles can, to a great extent, be independent of the detailed roughness of the ground.

A second reason for exploring legged machines is to understand how humans and animals use their legs for locomotion. People use a diverse and rich set of motions to carry, swing, toss, glide, and otherwise propel their bodies through space, maintaining orientation, balance, and speed as they go. Animals also demonstrate great mobility and agility. They use their legs to move quickly and reliably through forest, swamp, marsh, and jungle and from tree to tree. They move with great speed and efficiency. These systems, people and animals, are impressive from a mechanical engineering, sensory-motor integration, and computational point of view.

Despite skill in using limbs for locomotion, humans are still at a primitive stage in understanding the principles that underlie walking and running. What control mechanisms do animals use? The development of legged machines can lead to new ideas about animal locomotion. To the extent that an animal and a machine perform similar locomotion tasks, their control systems and mechanical structures must solve similar problems. Results in biology have already helped with the progress of legged robots. Perhaps results in robotic legged locomotion can provide insight into the principles and control algorithms underlying animal locomotion.

HISTORY OF LEGGED MACHINES

The scientific study of legged locomotion began just over a century ago when Leland Stanford, then governor of California, commissioned Eadward Muybridge to find out whether or not a trotting horse left the ground with all four feet at the same time. Stanford had wagered that it never did. After Muybridge proved him wrong with a set of stop-motion photographs that appeared in *Scientific American* in 1878, Muybridge went on to document the walking and running behavior of more than 40 mammals, including humans (Muybridge, 1955, 1957). Even after 100 years, his photographic data are of considerable value and beauty, and survive as a landmark in locomotion research.

The study of machines that walk also had its origin in Muybridge's time. An early walking model appeared in about 1870 (Lucas, 1894). It used a linkage to move the body along a straight horizontal path while the feet moved up and down to exchange support during stepping. The linkage was based on a design by Chebeyshev, the famous Russian mathematician, made some years earlier. During the 80 or 90 years that followed, workers viewed the task of building walking machines as the task of designing linkages that would generate stepping patterns when driven by a source of power. Many designs were proposed (U.S. Pat., 1893, 1926, 1928, 1928, 1947, 1949, 1958, 1959; Shigley, 1957; Morrison, 1968) (Fig. 1). The performance of such machines was limited by their fixed patterns of motion, since they could not adjust to variations in the terrain. By the late 1950s it had become clear that linkages providing fixed motion would not do the trick and that useful walking machines would need a more versatile form of control (Liston, 1970).

A second approach to providing control for legged locomotion was to harness a human. Mosher used this approach in a four-legged walking truck at General Electric in the mid-1960s (Liston and Mosher, 1968). The project was part of a decade-long campaign to build advanced teleoperators capable of providing better dexterity through high fidelity force feedback. The walking machine Mosher built stood 11 ft tall, weighed 3,000 lb, and was powered hydraulically (Fig. 2). A human driver controlled the motion. Each of the driver's limbs was connected to a handle or pedal that controlled one of the truck's four legs. Whenever the driver caused a truck leg to push against an obstacle, force feedback would cause the handle or pedal to push back on the human, letting the driver feel the obstacle as though it were his or her own arm or leg doing the pushing. After about 20 hours of training, Mosher was able to handle the machine with surprising agility. Films of the machine operating under his control show it ambling along at about 5 mph, climbing a stack of railroad ties, pushing a foundered jeep out of the mud, and maneuvering a large drum onto some hooks. Despite its dependence on a well-trained human for control, the GE Walking Truck was a milestone in legged technology.

A third approach to controlling legged locomotion became feasible in the 1970s: using a digital computer. McGhee (1983) and co-workers at the Ohio State University were the first to do so. In 1977, they built an insectlike hexapod that would walk with a number of gaits, turn, walk sideways, and negotiate simple obstacles. The computer's primary task was to solve kinematic equations in

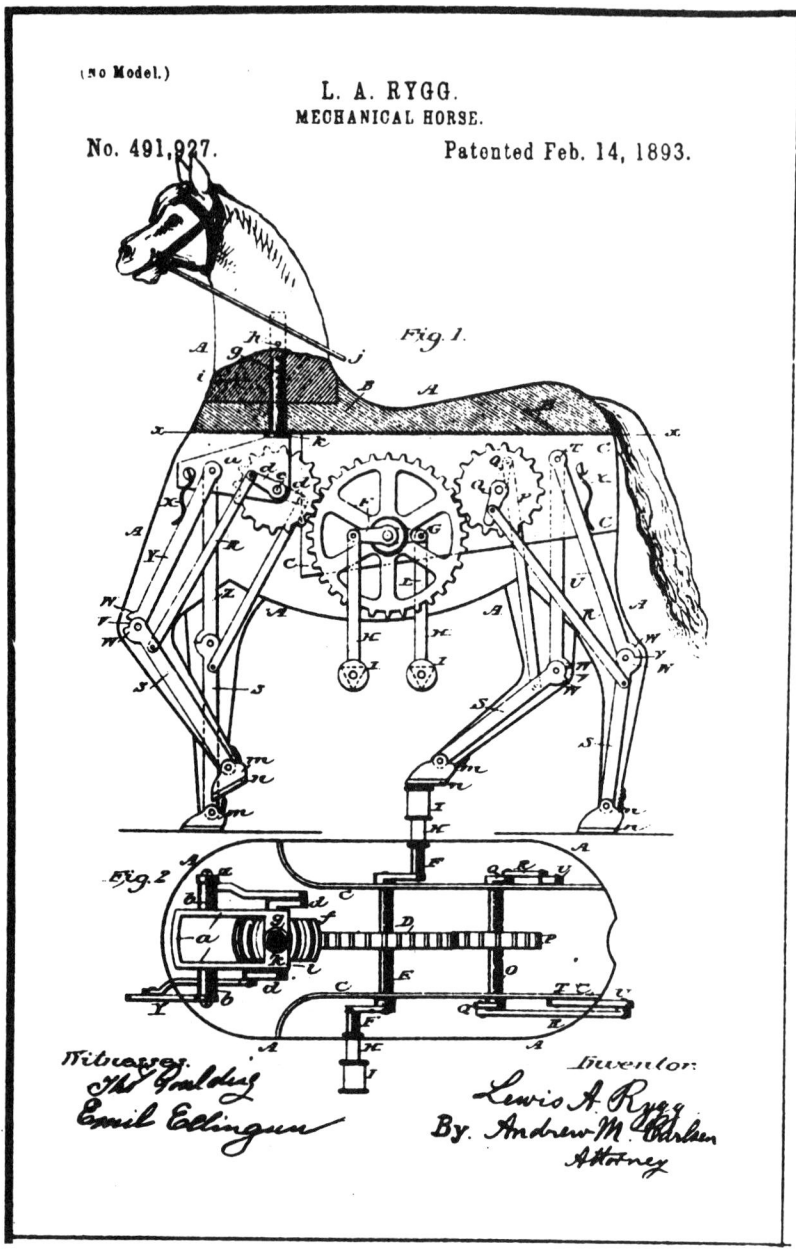

Figure 1. Mechanical horse (U.S. Pat., 1983). The stirrups double as pedals so the rider can power the stepping motions. The reins move the head and forelegs from side to side for steering.

order to coordinate the 18 electric motors driving the legs. The coordination ensured that the machine's center of mass stayed over the polygon of support provided by the supporting feet while allowing the legs to sequence through a gait (Fig. 3). The machine traveled quite slowly, covering several yards per minute. The hexapod provided McGee with an experimental means of pursuing his earlier theoretical findings on the combinatorics and selection of gait (McGhee, 1968; McGhee and Jain, 1972; Koozekanani and McGhee, 1973).

At about the same time, Gurfinkel and co-workers (1981) in the USSR built a machine with characteristics and performance quite similar to McGhee's (Okhotsimski and co-workers, 1977; Devjanin and co-workers, 1983). It used a hybrid computer for control, with analog computation aiding in kinematic calculations. The group at Ohio State subsequently built a much larger hexapod, called the Adaptive Suspension Vehicle (Fig. 4). It was designed for self-contained operation on natural terrain (Waldron and co-workers, 1984; Pugh and co-workers, 1990). It carries a gasoline engine for power, several computers and a human operator for control, and a laser range sensor for terrain preview. This machine walked at about 5 mph, negotiated simple obstacles on rough terrain, and pulled heavy loads.

Hirose realized that the three basic approaches to controlling legged locomotion, mechanical linkage, human teleoperation, and computer control, are not mutually exclusive. His experience with clever and unusual mechanisms (he had built seven kinds of mechanical snake) led to a leg with special mechanical structure that simplified the control of locomotion and could improve efficiency (Hirose and Umetani, 1980; Hirose and co-workers, 1984). The leg was a three-dimensional pantograph that trans-

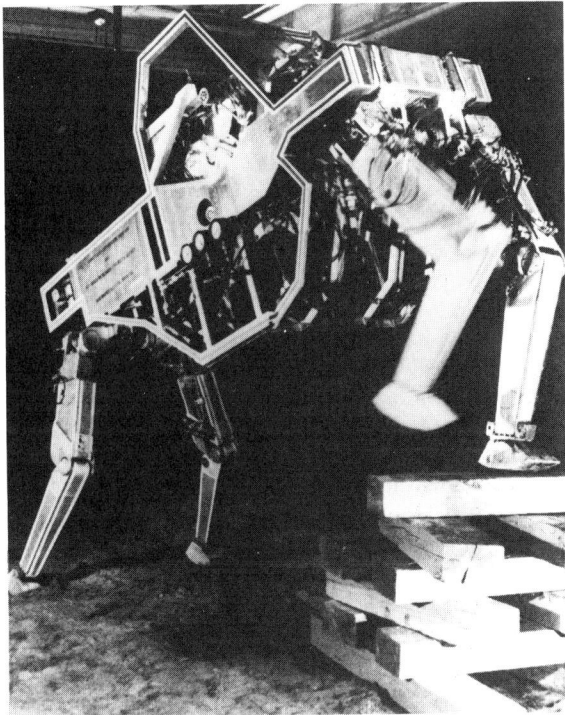

Figure 2. Walking truck developed by Mosher at General Electric in about 1968. The human driver controlled the machine with four handles and pedals that were connected to the four legs hydraulically. Courtesy of General Electric Research and Development Center.

Figure 4. The hexapod walking machine developed at Ohio State University. It stands about 10 ft tall and 15 ft long and weighs 3 t. A 90 hp motorcycle engine provides power to 18 variable displacement hydraulic pumps that drive the joints. The legs use pantograph linkages to improve energy efficiency. The operator normally provides steering and speed commands while computers control the stepping motions of the legs.

lated the motion of each actuator into a pure Cartesian translation of the foot. With the ability to generate x, y, and z translations of each foot by merely choosing an actuator, the control computer was freed from the task of performing kinematic solutions. The mechanical linkage helped to perform the calculations needed for locomotion. The linkage was efficient because the actuators performed only positive work in moving the body forward and no work was done against gravity when moving on the level. Hirose used the pantograph leg in a small quadruped, about 3 ft long.

These three walking machines, McGhee's, Gurfinkel's, and Hirose's, represent a class called static crawlers. Each differs in the details of construction and in the computing technology used for control, but shares a common approach to balance and stability. They all keep enough feet on the ground to guarantee a broad base of support at all times, and the body and legs move to keep the center of mass over this broad support base. The forward velocity is kept low enough so that kinetic energy can be ignored in the stability calculation. Other machines in this class have also been studied (Russell, 1983; Sutherland and Ullner, 1984; Ooka and co-workers, 1985; Carlton and Bartholet, 1987; Bares and Whittaker, 1990).

DYNAMICS AND BALANCE

The study of dynamic legged machines that balance actively will now be considered. These systems operate in a regime where the velocities and kinetic energies of the

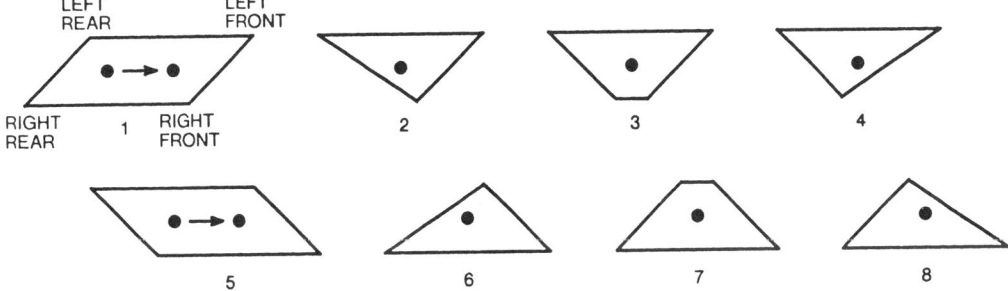

Figure 3. Statically stable gait. The diagram shows the sequence of support patterns provided by the feet of a quadruped walking with a crawling gait. The body and legs move to keep the projection of the center of mass within the polygon defined by the feet. A supporting foot is located at each vertex. The dot indicates the projection of the center of the mass. Adapted from McGhee and Frank (1968).

masses are important to the behavior. Geometry and configuration are not adequate in themselves to model such systems that move with substantial speed. Consider, for example, a fast-moving vehicle that might tip over if stopped suddenly with its center of mass too close to the front feet.

In order to predict and influence the behavior of a dynamic system, the energy stored in the velocity of each mass, in the elevation of each mass, and in the deflection of each complaint element must be considered. The exchange of energy among its various forms is also important in dynamic legged systems. For example, in running the body's potential energy of elevation changes into kinetic energy during falling, then into strain energy when parts of the leg deform elastically during rebound with the ground, then into kinetic energy again as the body accelerates upward, and finally back into potential energy of elevation. Energy is also exchanged in dynamic walking: the kinetic and gravitational potential energies oscillate out of phase throughout the cycle. Because these energies are out of phase, strain energy storage is modest during walking. This sort of dynamic exchange is central to legged locomotion.

Dynamics play a role in giving legged systems the ability to balance actively. A statically balanced system avoids tipping and the ensuing horizontal accelerations by keeping its center of mass over the polygon of support formed by the feet. In contrast, a dynamic legged system is always tipping. The control system avoids tipping too far by manipulating body and leg motions to ensure that each tipping interval is brief and that each tipping motion in one direction is compensated by a tipping motion in the opposite direction. An effective base of support is thus maintained over time. The ability of an actively balanced system to depart from static equilibrium relaxes the rules governing how legs can be used for support. For example, if a legged system can tolerate tipping, then it can position its feet away from the center of mass in order to use footholds that are widely separated or erratically placed. On the other hand, by keeping the feet near the centerline the system can travel where there is only a narrow path of good support. If a legged system can tolerate intermittent support, then it can move all its legs to new footholds at one time, to jump onto or over obstacles, and to use short periods of ballistic flight for increased speed. Animals routinely exploit active balance to travel on difficult terrain; legged vehicles must balance actively, too, if they are to move with animallike mobility and speed.

RESEARCH ON ACTIVE BALANCE

The first machines that balanced actively were automatically controlled inverted pendulums. A person can balance a broom on his or her finger with relative ease. Why not use automatic control to build a broom that can balance itself? Claude Shannon was probably the first to do so. In 1951 he used the parts from an erector set to build a machine that balanced an inverted pendulum atop a small powered truck. The truck drove back and forth in response to the tipping movements of the pendulum, as sensed by a pair of switches at its base. In order to move from one place to another, the truck first had to drive away from the destination to unbalance the pendulum, then proceeded toward the destination. In order to balance again at the destination, the truck moved past the destination until the pendulum was again upright with no forward velocity, then moved back to the destination.

At Shannon's urging, Cannon and his students at Stanford University set about demonstrating controllers that balanced two pendulums at once. In one case the pendulums were mounted side by side on the cart, and in the other they were mounted one on top of the other (Fig. 5). They also demonstrated balance for a flexible inverted pendulum (Schaefer, 1965; Schaefer and Cannon, 1966). Cannon's group was interested in the single-input multiple-output problem and in the limitations of achievable balance: how could the cart's motor be used to control the angles of two pendulums as well as the position of the cart? How far from balance could the system deviate before it was impossible to return to equilibrium, given such parameters of the mechanical system as the cart motor's

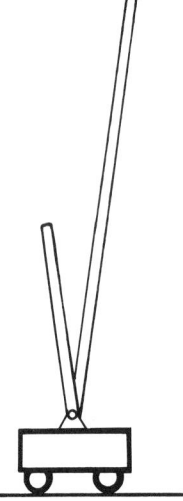
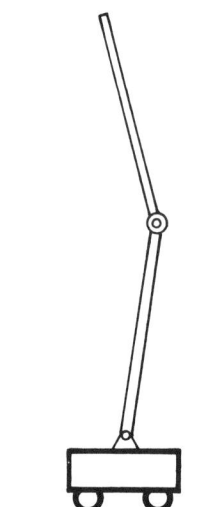
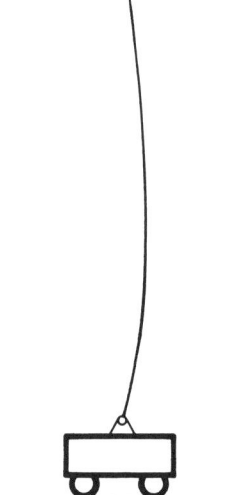

Figure 5. Cannon and co-workers built machines that balanced inverted pendulums on a moving cart. They balanced two pendulums side by side, one pendulum on top of another, and a long, limber inverted pendulum. Only one input, the force driving the cart horizontally, was available for control. Adapted from Schaefer and Canon (1966).

strength and the pendula lengths? These studies of balance for inverted pendulums were important precursors to later work on locomotion. The inverted pendulum model for walking would become a primary tool for studying balance in legged systems (Hemami and Weimer, 1974; Vukobratovic and Stepaneko, 1972; Vukobratovic, 1973; Hemami and Golliday, 1977; Kato and co-workers, 1983; Miura and Shimoyama, 1984).

The importance of active balance in legged locomotion was recognized for some years (Manter, 1938; McGhee and Kuhner, 1969; Frank, 1970; Vukobratovic, 1973; Gubina and co-workers, 1974), but the first dynamic legged systems did not appear until about 1980. Kato and co-workers (1983) built a biped that walked with a quasi-dynamic gait (Ogo and co-workers, 1980). The machine had 10 hydraulically powered degrees of freedom and two large feet. This machine was usually a static crawler, moving along a preplanned trajectory to keep the center of mass over the base of support provided by the large supporting foot. Once during each step, however, the machine temporarily destabilized itself to tip forward so that support would be transferred quickly from one foot to the other. Before the transfer took place on each step, the catching foot was positioned to return the machine to equilibrium passively. No active response was required. The inverted pendulum model was used to plan the tipping and catching motions. This machine walked with a quasi-dynamic gait, taking about a dozen 0.5-m steps per minute. Kato's approach represents an interesting way to achieve dynamic behavior. The system was not dynamic in the sense of reacting at run time to the progress of the motion. Instead, an off-line analysis of the dynamics of the system specified how to position the catching foot statically to get run-time dynamic behavior. Knowledge of dynamics of the system was "compiled" into a simple run-time strategy.

Miura and Shimoyama (1984) built a walking machine that may have been the first to balance itself actively. Their stilt biped was patterned after a human walking on stilts. Each foot provided only a point of support, and the machine had three actuators: one for each leg that moved the leg sideways and a third that separated the legs fore and aft. Because the legs did not change length, the hips were used to pick up the feet. This gave the machine a pronounced shuffling gait reminiscent of Charlie Chaplin's stiff-kneed walk. Control for the stilt biped relied, once again, on the inverted pendulum model of its behavior. Each time a foot was placed on the floor, its position was chosen according to the tipping behavior expected from an inverted pendulum. Actually, the problem was broken down as though there were two planar pendulums, one in the pitching plane and one in the rolling plane. The choice of foot position along each axis took the current and desired state of the system into account. The control system used tabulated descriptions of planned leg motions together with linear feedback to perform the necessary calculations. Unlike Kato's machine, which came to static equilibrium before and after each dynamic transfer, the stilt biped tipped all the time.

Furusho and Masubuchi (1987a, 1987b) used an inverted pendulum model in conjunction with an hierarchical control scheme. A low level servo moved each joint toward a desired position. An inverted pendulum model was derived from the dominant modes of the closed-loop system. The set points for the closed-loop system were selected to produce a walking motion. Their five-link planar biped started from standing, walked at 0.8 m/s, then returned to a standing position. Later machines built by Furusho and Sano (1990) with seven and nine links walked in three dimensions and used ankle torques to control forward speed.

Later work in Kato's laboratory (Takanishi and co-workers, 1985, 1989, 1990b) resulted in a series of actively balanced walking bipeds. They modeled the electric motors as point masses and the links as massless. Because the electric motors are so much heavier than the links of the robots, this simplified model yielded useful results. One of these machines has a large upper trunk that moves back and forth and side to side to stabilize the walking motion and to balance when pushed (Fig. 6).

McGeer (1989, 1990) took an unusual and elegant approach to dynamic walking, called passive dynamic walking. He was motivated by the stable behavior of toy animals that walk downhill by waddling from side to side and by work on ballistic walking, which suggested that humans swing their legs passively during the swing phase of walking (McMahon and Mochon, 1980, 1981). McGeer designed machines that travel downhill using no sensors, actuators, or computers. They rely on appropriate choices

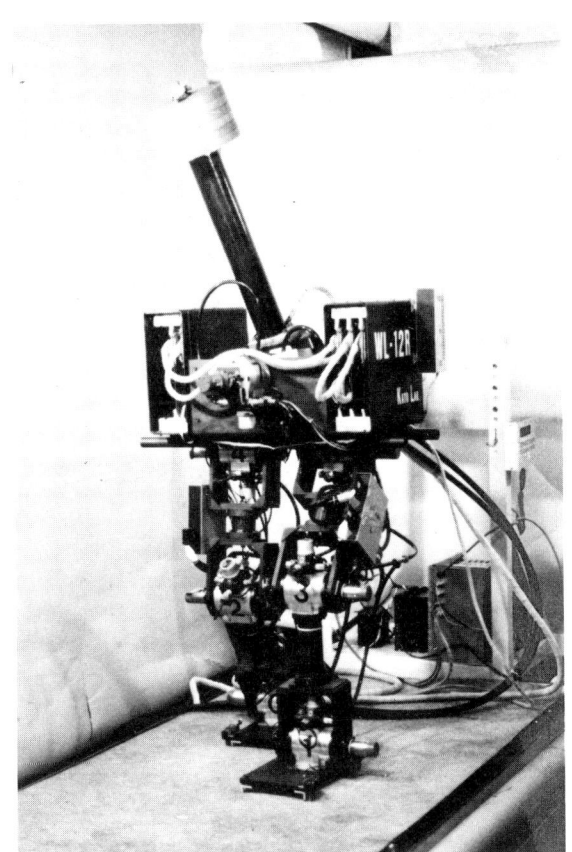

Figure 6. Dynamic walking biped built by Takinishi. The control system stabilizes the walking motion by moving the upper trunk back and forth.

of machine geometry (link lengths, link masses, joint damping, walking surface slope, and foot shape) to do the computing. McGeer's machines can be thought of as mechanical computers whose algorithms are embedded in the form of the structure. These machines are remarkable because they obtained stable dynamic walking from such a parsimonious design. Future legged machines will probably combine the passive characteristics of McGeer's design with the active control found in most other robots.

RUNNING MACHINES

Running is a form of legged locomotion in which all feet leave the ground at some point in the cycle. In animals, running is usually associated with travel at high speed. Matsuoka (1980) was the first to build a machine that ran; the goal was to model repetitive hopping in humans. He formulated a model with a body and one massless leg and simplified the problem by assuming that the duration of the support phase was short compared with the ballistic flight phase. This extreme form of running, in which nearly the entire cycle is spent in flight, minimizes the influence of tipping during support. This model permitted Matsuoka to derive a time-optimal state feedback controller that provided stability for hopping in place and for low speed translations.

To test the method for control, Matsuoka built a planar one-legged hopping machine. The machine operated at low gravity by rolling on ball bearings on a table that was inclined 10° from the horizontal in an effective gravity field of 0.17 g. An electric solenoid provided a rapid thrust at the foot. The machine hopped in place at about 1 hop per second and balanced itself as it traveled back and forth on the table.

Other running machines were built by Raibert and coworkers. They started by building one-legged machines that hopped like a kangaroo, using a series of leaps (Raibert and co-workers, 1984; Raibert, 1986a, 1986b) (Fig. 7). The study of machines with only one leg let them concentrate on active balance and dynamics, while avoiding the difficult task of coordinating many legs. The control algorithms for the hopping machines were based on a three-part decomposition of the problem: the forward travel, hopping motion, and posture of the body were controlled independently. Each part of the control system acted as though it influenced just one component of the behavior, while interactions due to imperfect decoupling were treated as disturbances. This decoupling resulted in a particularly simple control implementation. Raibert's group extended the control algorithms used for one-legged hopping to machines that ran on two legs and trotted, paced, and bounded on four. These machines traveled at specified speeds, changed gait during running, ran fast (13 mph), jumped, maintained balance when disturbed, climbed stairs, and performed rudimentary gymnastic maneuvers (Hodgins and co-workers, 1985; Raibert and co-workers, 1986; Koechling and Raibert, 1988; Hodgins and Raibert, 1990; Raibert, 1990).

An important aspect of these running machines was the mechanical springiness built into their legs. To a large

(a)

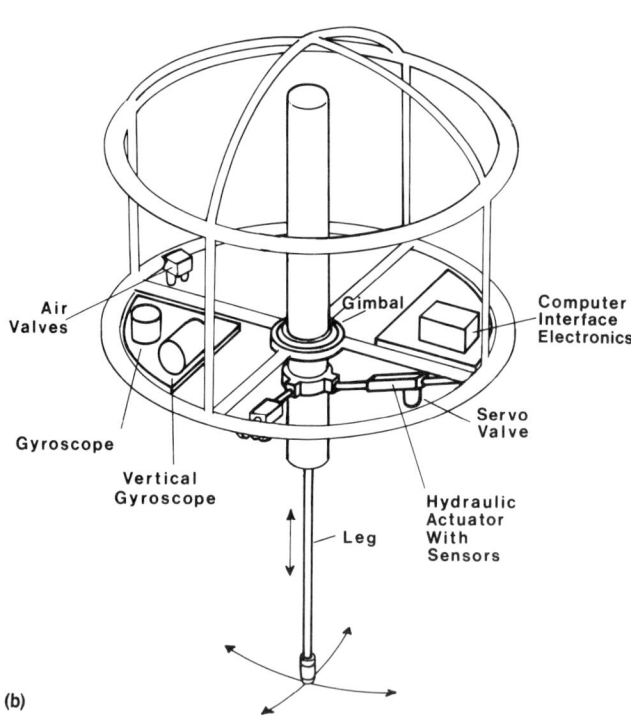

(b)

Figure 7. Three dimensional hopping machine used for experiments. The control system operates to regulated hopping height, forward velocity, and body posture. Top recorded running speed was about 2.2 m/s (4.8 mph).

degree, the hopping motion was a passive elastic rebound that occurred when the downward motion of the body was reversed by the springy leg. The control algorithm responsible for hopping excited and modulated these bouncing motion, but did not specify the details of the trajectory. The control system and the mechanical system worked together to produce the hopping behavior. Synergy between mechanism and control is a theme gaining importance in robotics.

LOCOMOTION ON ROUGH TERRAIN

The practical value of legged machines is tied to the promise of mobility on rough terrain. Static and dynamic locomotion systems can both play useful roles in this context. Because they generally move slowly, statically stable systems can acquire data from terrain sensors before they move, interpret the sensor information, and find sequences of feasible footholds. Dynamically stable systems can use their kinetic energy to bridge large gaps that may separate one foothold from the next, or to jump over obstacles. These approaches to rough terrain are discussed in this section.

There are several ways that characteristics can make terrain rough and, therefore, difficult to negotiate.

- The terrain may not be level.
- Traction may be limited (slippery).
- There may be areas of poor or nonexistent support (holes).
- Vertical variations may cause uneven altitude of footholds; or may include large obstacles between footholds (poles).
- The terrain may offer only intricate footholds (eg, rungs of a ladder).

For a statically stable system to travel on rough terrain, the control must decide which locations on the terrain provide suitable footholds and then place the feet on the chosen footholds. A suitable foothold is one that provides adequate support, allows the system to keep its balance, and permits progress toward the goal. It is assumed that the task of placing a foot on a desired foothold, once chosen, is easy for a statically stable system. Okhotsimski and Platonov (1973, 1975) devised such an algorithm for a simulated six-legged walker. Information from a range finder provided terrain information to identify feasible footholds. Their algorithm took the physical structure of the walking machine into account so as to choose footholds that minimized the maximum force exerted by any leg and to keep each foot's reaction force as nearly vertical as possible. Their simulations traveled on three-dimensional poles and holes terrain using the sequence of support polygons found by the foothold selection algorithms.

Several workers have developed algorithms for statically stable rough terrain locomotion. These algorithms first choose a desired path along which the body is to move, followed by heuristic selection of reachable footholds along the path. This approach is called the bodymotion-then-footholds paradigm. McGhee and Iswandhi (1979) used such a paradigm for six-legged walking. After specifying the body motion, their algorithm lifted the legs with the least kinematic travel available in the direction of travel, while putting legs into support with the largest available travel. This heuristic extended each support state to increase the probability that it would overlap with the next support state. Avoidance of deadlock was emphasized over stability by maximizing the number of legs in the air.

Hirose (1984) applied the bodymotion-then-footholds paradigm to quadruped rough-terrain locomotion. He developed an hierarchical algorithm with one level providing gait control and another level providing basic motion regulation. The motion regulation performed such functions as controlling the pitch and height of the body and preventing collisions between the legs. In Hirose's computer simulations, a quadruped walked across terrain with holes, crossed a river, and made local modifications to the motion trace to avoid a large hole.

Okhotsimski and co-workers built a six-legged walking machine that could climb up onto a small ledge (Devjanin and co-workers, 1983). The machine climbed by raising its body and then placing each foot up on the ledge. Care was taken to keep the body level during climbing. They also implemented algorithms to control the forces in the legs during locomotion on soft soil (Gorinevsky and Shneider, 1990).

The work on rough-terrain locomotion described above assumes that global knowledge of the terrain is available, such as would be provided by computer vision or scanning range data. Such information is called terrain preview information, and the assumption of its availability and interpretability is common. It is possible, however, for rough terrain locomotion to be accomplished without global information. Sensors in each foot can inform the control computer whether the foot is pressing on anything, and if so how hard. In this case, the legs can act like sensing probes. Two machines, discussed earlier in this article, used this approach. Hirose and Umetani's (1980) quadruped used switches on the feet to probe the terrain directly in the path of the robot. If a foot switch signaled contact as the foot advanced forward, a reflexlike algorithm caused the foot to be pulled back, lifted, then advanced forward again. Another reflexlike algorithm caused support legs to push downward if a load cell in the foot indicated that it was not bearing an adequate vertical load. A third reflex caused the relative altitude of the feet to be adjusted so the body remained level, as indicated by an oil-damped pendulum. Hirose's quadruped used these reflexes to climb up and down steps without a model of the terrain and without human intervention. The Ohio State University Adaptive Suspension Vehicle could also travel on rough terrain without global terrain information (Pugh and co-workers, 1990). It used force sensors in the leg actuators and a force distribution control algorithm to accomodate variations in the terrain, without foothold selection or planning. They made convincing demonstrations of their machine's ability to travel on gentle slopes, through a muddy cornfield, and over railroad ties, all without a visual sensor or human foothold selection.

So far, we have considered rough terrain in the context of static slow-moving systems. Dynamic legged systems should be able to traverse more difficult terrain than static systems of comparable size and reach. In principle, dynamic legged systems should be able to use balance to travel where available footholds provide only a narrow base of support, to use kinetic energy to travel where the available footholds form an erratic pattern of support, and to use ballistic flight phases to leap over regions of terrain that offer no good support at all. Generally, a dynamic legged system can use its kinetic energy as a bridge from one foothold to the next. These potential advantages of dynamic legged systems are obtained at the expense of more complicated control for placing the feet. Foot placement is straightforward in statically stable systems, once a reachable foothold has been chosen. In dynamic legged systems, however, the act of positioning the feet with respect to available footholds interacts with the need for stability. Each placement of a foot on the ground causes the body to accelerate, and influences the forward speed and direction of travel. The algorithm responsible for placing the feet must manipulate the dynamic parameters of the system to simultaneously balance the machine and keep it moving as desired.

Takanishi and co-workers (1990a) built several robots that walk dynamically on simple rough terrain. Their most recent machine walks up and down 0.1 m stairs and on ±10° slopes. The control algorithms are based on a generalization of zero moment point control, as introduced by Vukobratovic and Stepaneko (1972). When the terrain is not smooth the zero moment point moves along a surface connecting the point of contact of the feet rather than along the surface of the ground. Given knowledge of the terrain, trajectories for the feet, and the zero moment point, the control system precomputes trunk and waist motions that execute the planned trajectories and cause the machine to walk.

Hodgins studied algorithms for running on rough terrain (Hodgins and Raibert, 1991). Three methods were implemented for adjusting the robot's stride to place the feet on desired footholds while maintaining balance. Each method adjusted a different parameter of the running cycle, the forward running speed, the running height, and the duration of ground contact. All three control methods were successful in manipulating step length in laboratory experiments on a planar biped running machine, but the method that adjusted forward speed provided the widest range of step lengths with accurate control of step length. Hodgins used these control methods to demonstrate a robot placing its feet on a target, leaping over an obstacle, and running up and down a short flight of stairs (Fig. 8).

DEVELOPMENT OF USEFUL LEGGED ROBOTS

Most of the legged machines that have been built are not yet useful vehicles or even prototypes for such vehicles. They are experimental apparatus used in the laboratory to explore ideas about legged locomotion. Each was designed to isolate and examine a few specific locomotion problems, while postponing or ignoring many other prob-

Figure 8. Planar biped running up and down a flight of three stairs. The control system adjusts the length of the machine's steps so that the feet land approximately in the center of each stair. The machine is shown running from right to left at about 0.5 m/s. Light sources indicate the paths of the feet. Each stair is 0.18 m high and 0.3 m deep.

lems. A summary of the development of legged robots is given in Table 1. It is important to ask what problems remain to be solved before legged robots are transformed into practical machines that do useful work.

Terrain Sensing

Perhaps the most severe problem limiting current walking machines as well as other forms of autonomous vehicle, is their inability to perceive the shape and structure of their immediate surroundings. Humans and animals use their eyes to locate good footholds, to avoid obstacles, to measure their own rate and direction of progress, and to navigate with respect to visible landmarks. The problem of giving machines the ability to see has received intensive and consistent attention for the last 25 or 30 years. There has been steady progress during that period. Current machines can see well enough to operate in well-structured and partially structured environments, but it is difficult to predict when legged machines will be able to see well enough to operate autonomously in rough outdoor terrain. Such autonomous machine behavior will probably not be seen for at least ten years.

Sensors simpler than vision may be able to provide solutions to certain parts of the problem under certain circumstances. For instance, sonar and laser range data may be used to detect and avoid nearby obstacles. Motion data may be used for measuring speed and direction of travel with techniques that are substantially simpler than those needed to perceive shape in three dimensions.

Travel on Rough Terrain

Complete knowledge of the geometry of the terrain, as might be supplied by vision or other senses would not in itself solve the problem of locomotion on rough terrain. A system traveling on rough terrain needs to know or figure out what terrain shapes provide good footholds, which sequence of footholds would permit traversal of the terrain, and how to move so as to place the feet on the available

Table 1. Milestones in the Development of Legged Robots

1836	Weber and Weber	Measurements in human corpses show that natural frequency of leg as compound pendulum is similar to cadence in walking
1850	Chebyshev	Designs linkage used in early walking mechanism (Lucas, 1894)
1872	Muybridge	Develops stop-motion photography to document running animals
1893	Rygg	Patents human-powered mechanical horse
1945	Wallace	Patents hopping tank with reaction wheels that provide stability
1961	Space General	Eight-legged linkage machine walks in outdoor terrain (Morrison, 1968)
1963	Cannon, Higdon and Schaefer	Control system balances single, double, and limber inverted pendulums
1968	Frank and McGhee	Simple digital logic controls walking of Phony Pony
1968	Mosher	GE quadruped truck climbs railroad ties under control of human driver
1969	Bucyrus-Erie Co.	Big Muskie, a 15,000 t walking dragline is used for strip mining; it moves in soft terrain at a speed of 900 ft/h (Sitek, 1976)
1977	McGhee	Hexapod robot walks with wave gait using digital computer to coordinate leg motion
1977	Gurfinkel	Hybrid computer controls hexapod walker in USSR
1977	McMahon and Greene	Human runners set new speed records on tuned track at Harvard; its compliance is adjusted to mechanics of human leg
1980	Hirose and Umetani	Quadruped machine climbs stairs and climbs over obstacles using simple sensors and reflexlike control; the leg mechanism simplifies control
1980	Kato	Hydraulic biped walks with quasidynamic gait
1980	Matsuoka	Mechanism balances in the plane while hopping on one leg
1981	Miura and Shimoyama	Biped balances actively while walking in three-dimensional space
1983	Sutherland	Self-contained hexapod carries human rider; computer, hydraulics, and human share computing task
1983	Odetics	Self-contained hexapod lifts and moves back end of pickup truck (Russell, 1983)
1983	Raibert	One-legged machine hops in place, travels at a specified rate, keeps its balance when disturbed, and jumps over small obstacles
1984	Furusho	Planar five-link biped starts walking from a standing position, and travels at 0.8 m/s
1987	Waldron and McGhee	Three-ton self-contained hexapod carrying human driver travels at 5 mph, travels in irregular terrain, and pulls a load
1988	Hodgins and Koechling	Planar biped climbs short stairway, jumps over obstacles, and runs with top speed of 13.1 mph.
1989	Raibert	Quadruped runs with trotting, pacing, and bounding gaits, and changes between gaits
1990	McGeer	Planar biped with knees walks passively down sloping surface

footholds. It will be necessary to coordinate the dynamics of the vehicle with the dynamics of the terrain.

The techniques that will allow legged systems to operate on rough terrain will involve the mechanics of locomotion, kinematics, dynamics, geometric representation, spatial reasoning, and planning. Although course- and medium-grain knowledge of the terrain will be important, it is expected that techniques that make legged systems inherently insensitive to fine-grain terrain variations will play an important role too. Ignoring the hard sensing issues mentioned earlier, it is believed that the perception and control mechanisms required for legged systems to travel on rough terrain will require a substantial research effort, but can be solved within the next 10 years if they are pursued vigorously.

Mechanical Design and System Integration

When these sensing and control problems are solved, it will remain to develop mechanical designs that function with efficiency and reliability. Useful vehicles must carry their own power, control computers, and a payload. A host of interesting problems present themselves including such matters as energy efficiency, structural design, strength and weight of materials, and efficient control. For instance, the development of materials and structures for efficient storage and recovery of elastic energy will be particularly important for legged vehicles. It is expected that initial useful legged vehicles can be built with existing mechanical and aerospace techniques.

BIBLIOGRAPHY

J. E. Bares and W. L. Whittaker, "Walking Robot with a Circulating Gait," in *IEEE International Workshop on Intelligent Robots and Systems,* 1990, pp. 809–816.

V. V. Biletskii, "Biped Locomotion Dynamics I," *Izv. AN SSSR Mekhanika Tverdogo Tela* **10**(3), 3–14 (1975).

R. E. Carlton and S. J. Bartholet, "The Evolution of the Application of Mobile Robotics to Nuclear Facility Operations and Maintenance," in *Proceedings of the IEEE International Conference on Robotics and Automation,* Raleigh, N.C., 1987, pp. 720–726.

E. A. Devjanin, V. S. Gurfinkel, E. V. Gurfinkel, V. A. Kartashev, A. V. Lensky, A. Y. Schneider, and L. G. Shtilman, "The Six-Legged Walking Robot Capable of Terrain Adaptation," *Mechanisms Machine Theory* **18**, 257–260 (1983).

A. A. Frank, "An Approach to the Dynamic Analysis and Synthesis of Biped Locomotion Machines," *Med. Bio. Eng.* **8**, 465–476 (1970).

J. Furusho and M. Masubuchi, "A Theoretically Motivated Reduced Order Model for the Control of Synamic Biped Locomotion," *J. Dynam. Sys. Contr.* **109**, 155–163 (1987a).

J. Furusho and M. Masubuchi, "Control of a Dynamical Biped

Locomotion System for Steady Walking," in H. Miura and Shimoyama, eds., *Study on Mechanisms and Control of Bipeds,* University of Tokyo, Tokyo, 1987b, pp. 116–127.

J. Furusho and A. Sano, "Sensor-Based Control of a Nine-Link Biped," *Int. J. Robot. Res.* **9**(2), 83–98 (1990).

D. M. Gorinevsky and A. Y. Shneider, "Force Control in Locomotion of Legged Vehicles over Rigid and Soft Surfaces," *Int. J. Robot. Res.* **9**(2), 4–23 (1990).

F. Gubina, H. Hemami, and R. B. McGhee, "On the Dynamic Stability of Biped Locomotion," *IEEE Trans. Biomed. Eng.* **21**, 102–108 (1974).

V. S. Gurfinkel, E. V. Gurfinkel, A. Y. Shneider, E. A. Devjanin, A. V. Lensky, and L. A. Shitilman, "Walking Robot with Supervisory Control," *Mechanism Machine Theory* **16**, 31–36 (1981).

H. Hemami and C. L. Golliday, Jr., "The Inverted Pendulum and Biped Stability," *Math Biosci.* **14**, 95–110 (1977).

H. Hemami and F. C. Weimer, "Further Considerations of the Inverted Pendulum," in *Proceedings of the Fourth Iranian Conference on Electrical Engineering,* Shiraz, Iran, 1974, pp. 697–708.

S. Hirose, "A Study of Design and Control of a Quadruped Walking Vehicle," *Int. J. Robot. Res.* **3**, 113–133 (1984).

S. Hirose, M. Nose, H. Kikuchi, and Y. Umentani, "Adaptive Gait Control of a Quadruped Walking Vehicle," *Int. J. Robot. Res.* **1**, 253–277 (1984).

S. Hirose and Y. Umetani, "The Basic Motion Regulation System for a Quadruped Walking Vehicle," in *ASME Conference on Mechanisms,* 1980.

J. Hodgins, J. Koechling, and M. H. Raibert, "Running Experiments with a Planar Biped," in *Third International Symposium on Robotics Research,* MIT Press, Cambridge, Mass., 1985.

J. Hodgins and M. H. Railbert, "Biped Gymnastics," *Int. J. Robot. Res.* **9**(2), 115–132 (1990).

J. Hodgins and M. H. Railbert, "Adjusting Step Length for Rough Terrain Locomotion," *IEEE J. Robot. Automat.* **7**(3), 289–298 (1991).

T. Kato, A. Takanishi, H. Jichikawa, and I. Kato, "The Realization of the Quasi-Dynamic Walking by the Biped Walking Machine," in A. Morecki, G. Bianchi, and K. Kedzior, eds., *Fourth Symposium on Theory and Practice of Robots and Manipulators,* Polish Scientific Publishers, Warsaw, 1983, pp. 341–351.

J. Koechling and M. H. Raibert, "How Fast Can a Legged Robot Run?" in K. Youcef-Toumi and H. Kazerooni, eds., *Symposium in Robotics,* DSC Vol. 11, American Society of Mechanical Engineers, Boston, 1988.

S. H. Koozekanani and R. B. McGhee, "Occupancy Problems with Pairwise Exclusion Constraints—An Aspect of Gait Enumeration," *J. Cybernet.* **2**, 14–26 (1973).

R. A. Liston and R. S. Mosher, "A Versatile Walking Truck," in *Proceedings of the Transportation Engineering Conference,* Institution of Civil Engineers, London, 1968.

E. Lucas, "Huitieme recreation—La machine a marcher," *Recreat. Math.* **4**, 198–204 (1894).

T. McGeer, "Powered Flight, Child's Play, Silly Wheels, and Walking Machines," in *IEEE Conference on Robotics and Automation,* Scottsdale, Ariz., 1989.

T. McGeer, "Passive Dynamic Walking," *Int. J. Robot. Res.* **9**(2), 62–82 (1990).

R. B. McGhee, "Some Finite State Aspects of Legged Locomotion," *Math. Biosci.* **2**, 67–84 (1968).

R. B. McGhee, "Vehicular Legged Locomotion," in G. N. Saridis, ed., *Advances in Automation and Robotics,* JAI Press, 1983.

R. B. McGhee and A. A. Frank, "On the Stability Properties of Quadruped Creeping Gairs," *Math. Biosci.* **3**, 331–351 (1968).

R. B. McGhee and G. I. Iswandhi, "Adaptive Locomotion of a Multilegged Robot over Rough Terrain," *IEEE Trans. Sys. Man Cybernet.* **9**, 176–182 (1979).

R. B. McGhee and A. K. Jain, "Some Properties of Regularly Realizable Gait Matrices," *Math. Biosci.* **13**, 179–193 (1972).

R. B. McGhee and M. B. Kuhner, "On the Dynamic Stability of Legged Locomotion Systems," in M. M. Gavrilovic and A. B. Wilson, Jr., eds., *Advances in External Control of Human Extremities,* Yugoslav Committee for Electronics and Automation, Belgrade, Yugoslavia, 1969, pp. 431–442.

J. Manter, "Dynamics of Quadrrupedal Walking," *J. Exper. Biol.* **15**, 522–539 (1938).

K. Matsuoka, "A Mechanical Model of Repetitive Hopping Movements," *Biomechan.* **5**, 251–258 (1980).

H. Miura and I. Shimoyama, "Dynamic Walk of a Biped," *Int. J. Robot. Res.* **3**, 60–74 (1984).

S. Mochon and T. A. McMahon, "Ballistic Walking," *J. Biomechan.* **13**, 49–57 (1980).

S. Mochon and T. A. McMahon, "Ballistic Walking: An Improved Model," *Math. Biosci.* **52**, 241–260 (1981).

E. Muybridge, *The Human Figure in Motion,* Dover Publications, New York, 1955. Originally published by Chapman and Hall, Ltd., London, 1901.

E. Muybridge, *Animals in Motion,* Dover Publications, New York, 1957. Originally published by Chapman and Hall, Ltd., London, 1899.

K. Ogo, A. Ganse, and I. Kato, "Dynamic Walking of Biped Walking Machine Aiming at Completion of Steady Walking," in A. Morecki, G. Bianchi, and K. Kedior, eds., *Third Symposium on Theory and Practice of Robots and Manipulators,* Elsevier, Amsterdam, The Netherlands, 1980.

D. E. Okjotsimski, V. A. Gurfinkel, E. A. Devyanin, and A. K. Platonoc, "Integrated Walking Robot Development," in *Conference on Cybernetic Models of the Human Neuromuscular System,* Engineering Foundation, 1977.

D. E. Okjotsimski and A. K. Platonov, "Control Algorithm of the Walker Climbing over Obstacles," in *Proceedings of the Third IJCAI,* Stanford, Calif., Morgan-Kaufmann, San Mateo, Calif., 1973.

D. E. Okjotsimski and A. K. Platonov, "Perceptive Robot Moving in 3D World," in *Proceedings of the Fourth IJCAI,* Tbilisi, Ga., Morgan-Kaufmann, San Mateo, Calif., 1975.

A. Ooka, K., Agi, Y. Wada, Y. Kida, A. Takemoto, K. Okamoto, and K. Yoshida, "Intelligent Robot System II," in *Second International Symposium on Robotics Research,* MIT Press, Cambridge, Mass., 1985, pp. 341–347.

D. R. Pugh, E. A. Ribble, V. J. Vohnout, T. E. Bihari, T. M. Walliser, M. R. Patterson, and K. J. Waldron, "A Technical Description of the Adaptive Suspension Vehicle," *Int. J. Robot. Res.* **9**, 24–42 (1990).

M. H. Raibert, *Legged Robots That Balance,* MIT Press, Cambridge, Mass., 1986a.

M. H. Raibert, "Symmetry in Running," *Science* **231**, 1292–1294 (1986b).

M. H. Raibert, "Trotting, Pacing, and Bounding by a Quadruped Robot," *J. Biomechan.* **23** (Suppl. 1), 79–98 (1990).

M. H. Raibert, H. B. Brown, Jr., and M. Chepponis, "Experiments in Balance with a 3D One-Legged Hopping Machine," *Int. J. Robot. Res.* **3**, 75–92 (1984).

M. H. Raibert, M. Chepponis, and H. B. Brown, Jr., "Running on Four Legs as Though They Were One," *IEEE J. Robot. Automat.* **2**, 70–82 (1986).

M. Russell, Jr., "Odex I: The First Functionoid," *Robot. Age* **5**, 12–18 (1983).

J. F. Schaefer, *On the Bounded Control of Some Unstable Mechanical Systems*, Ph.D. dissertation, Stanford University, Stanford, Calif., 1965.

J. F. Schaefer and R. H. Cannon, Jr., "On the Control of Unstable Mechanical Systems," in *International Federation of Automatic Control*, London, 1966, pp. 6c.1–6c.13.

R. Shigley, *The Mechanics of Walking Vehicles*, Report **7**, Land Locomotion Laboratory, Detroit, Mich., 1957.

G. Sitek, "Big Muskie," *Heavy Duty Equipment Maintenance* **4**, 16–13 (1976).

I. E. Sutherland and M. K. Ullner, "Footprints in the Asphalt," *Int. J. Robot. Res.* **3**, 29–36 (1984).

A. Takanishi, H. Lim, M. Tsuda, and I. Kato, "Realization of Dynamic Biped Walking Stabilized by Trunk Motion on a Sagittally Uneven Surface," in *IEEE International Workshop on Intelligent Robots and Systems*, 1990a, pp. 323–330.

A. Takanishi, G. Naito, M. Ishida, and I. Kato, "Realization of Plane Walking by a Biped Walking Robot WL-10R," in A. Morecki, G. Bianchi, and K. Kedzior, eds., *Fifth Symposium on Theory and Practice of Robots and Manipulators*, MIT Press, Cambridge, Mass., 1985, pp. 383–394.

A. Takanishi, T. Takeya, H. Karaki, and I. Kato, "A Control Method for Dynamic Biped Walking under Known External Force," *IEEE International Workshop on Intelligent Robots and Systems*, 1990b, pp. 795–801.

A. Takanishi, M. Tochizawa, H. Karaki, and I. Kato, "Dynamic Biped Walking Stabilized with Optimal Trunk and Waist Motion," in *IEEE/RSJ International Workshop on Intelligent Robots and Systems*, 1989, pp. 187–192.

U.S. Pat. 491,927 (1893), L. A. Rygg.

U.S. Pat. 1,574,679 (1926), F. A. Nilson.

U.S. Pat. 1,691,233 (1928), A. Ehrlich.

U.S. Pat. 2,430,537 (1947), E. Snell.

U.S. Pat. 2,491,064 (1949), W. E. Urschel.

U.S. Pat. 2,822,878 (1958), P. E. Corson.

U.S. Pat. 2,918,738 (1959), I. R. Bair.

M. Vukobratovic, "Dynamics and Control of Anthropomorphic Active Mechanisms," in A. Morecki, G. Bianchi, and K. Kedzior, eds., *Theory and Practice of Robots and Manipulator Systems, Proceedings of RoManSy'73*, Elsevier, Amsterdam, The Netherlands, 1973, pp. 313–332.

M. Vukobratovic and Y. Stepaneko, "On the Stability of Anthropomorphic Systems," *Math. Biosci.* **14**, 1–38 (1972).

K. J. Waldron, V. J. Vohnout, A. Pery, and R. B. McGhee, "Configuration Design of the Adaptive Suspension Vehicle," *Int. J. Robot. Res.* **3**, 37–48 (1984).

General References

M. G. Bekker, "Is the Wheel the Last Word in Land Locomotion?" *New Sci.* **17**, 406–410 (1961).

D. T. Higdon, *Automatic Control of Inherently Unstable Systems with Bounded Control Inputs*, Ph.D. dissertation, Stanford University, Stanford, Calif., 1963.

D. T. Higdon and R. H. Cannon, Jr., "On the Control of Unstable Multiple-Output Mechanical Systems," in *ASME Winter Annual Meeting*, 1963.

R. A. Liston, "Walking Machine," *J. Terramechanics* **3**, 18–31 (1964).

R. A. Liston, "Increasing Vehicle Agility by Legs: The Quadruped Transporter," paper presented at the Thirty-eighth National Meeting of the Operations Research Society of America, 1970.

R. B. McGhee, "Robot Locomotion with Active Terrain Accommodation," in *Proceedings of the National Science Foundation Robotics Research Workshop*, University of Rhode Island, Providence, 1980.

S. Song and K. J. Waldron, *Machines That Walk*, MIT Press, Cambridge, Mass., 1989.

U.S. Pat. 1,669,906 (1928), E. A. Kinch.

U.S. Pat. 2,371,368 (1942), H. W. Wallace.

W. Weber, *Mechanik der Menschlichen Gehwerkzeuge*, Dieterich'sche Buchhandlung, Goettingen, German, 1836.

MARC H. RAIBERT
MIT

JESSICA K. HODGINS
IBM T. J. Watson Research Center

This research was supported by a grant from the System Development Foundation and a contract from the Defense Advanced Research Projects Agency.

ROBOTS, MOBILE

Mobile robots are vehicles that move autonomously through an unstructured environment, performing a useful mission. Related devices share some of these capabilities, but each differs in at least one important aspect. Teleoperated vehicles perform similar tasks in similar environments, but replace autonomous operation with direct human control. Automatic guided vehicles (AGV), operating in factories, typically follow guide wires embedded in the floor and thus do not work in an unstructured world. Even wind-up toys (or Simon's famous ant on the beach) can move autonomously in unstructured environments and can generate an appearance of sophistication, but they usually do not accomplish anything useful or purposeful. In contrast, real mobile robots operate in buildings with unmapped clutter and unpredictable moving objects or in the rugged outdoor world. They operate for extended periods without direct human supervision. They are designed to perform tasks requiring purposeful mobility, ranging from planetary exploration to materials transport to excavation to planting and harvesting.

The research challenge in building autonomous mobile robots is focused on handling unstructured environments. There are several approaches:

- Impose structure on the environment, such as deploying beacons for positioning.
- Sense the environment, and build internal structures, by image understanding techniques.
- Plan and react to the environment, both before and during moving, to bypass obstacles.

- Engineer mechanical solutions to overcome limitations of the environment.
- Integrate a robot architecture that combines several of the above approaches into a capable system.

POSITION SENSING

Mobile robots need to measure their position and motion. Relative position measurement, which tells how far the vehicle has moved from a previous vehicle position, is important for local maneuvering (has that obstacle been cleared yet?) and for perception (what is the effective baseline for motion stereo?). Absolute positioning, in a global coordinate framework, is often important for mission execution (dig at position X) and for reporting results (unexpected obstacle detected at position Y). Inferring positions from landmarks or motion from visual tracking is still, in general, a difficult problem, although sensing offers some solutions. It is increasingly possible and desirable to find technological solutions for direct position measurement.

Beacons. Both acoustic and electromagnetic beacons are available in a large variety of forms. The simplest beacons are continuously active and are used by the vehicle to measure bearing to the beacon. A single beacon is only useful for homing to that beacon. If the vehicle has a compass, then knowing its bearing to a beacon constrains its position to a line in space. Measuring the angle between two visible beacons constrains the vehicle position to lie on a circle (or sphere, in three dimensions). Three beacons, or two beacons and a compass, will give the exact vehicle location and heading.

Transponders are beacons that require active transmission both by the vehicle and by the beacons. The vehicle emits a pulse, which is received by the transponder. The transponder responds with another pulse, often at a different frequency to reduce confusion. By knowing the speed of sound or light and knowing the delay in the transponder, the total time until the vehicle hears the return pulse gives the range to the beacon. A single transponder, used for range and bearing, plus an onboard compass, is sufficient to give position on the plane.

Passive beacons are reflectors, often used with a laser on the vehicle. Typically the reflectors are all mounted at the same height above a flat floor, with the laser spinning in the same plane. When a vehicle-mounted sensor sees a bright reflection, the angle of the laser gives the bearing to the beacon.

Global positioning system (GPS) is an increasingly popular beacon system based on satellites. Each satellite continuously broadcasts an accurate time reference signal. The receiver compares the time skew between signals from pairs of satellites, which, multiplied by the speed of light, gives the difference in distance from the vehicle to each satellite. Observing four satellites is sufficient to give three-dimensional position. Certain noise effects of GPS are randomly distributed with zero mean, so filtering the position estimates over time will improve accuracy. Other effects, including ionospheric disturbances, introduce a bias into the measurement. Differential GPS uses a second receiver at a known, fixed, nearby location to calculate the current systematic errors and correct for them.

Inertial. Inertial navigation in its pure form uses three single-axis gyros and three accelerometers, mounted orthogonally, to measure three degrees of freedom of orientation and acceleration. Integrating acceleration gives velocity; a second integration gives position. Sources of error range from thermal drift of the gyros to local variation in the earth's gravitational field, which corrupts the accelerometer readings. Because the raw data are doubly integrated, inertial navigation position errors can build up rapidly over time. There are several commonly used solutions for error reduction. If the vehicle can periodically come to a complete stop, the accelerometers can be reset and any accumulated error can be reduced. Other schemes use external measurements, from beacons, landmarks, or shaft encoders, for long-term stability and use inertial sensing for short-term accuracy. The best methods use filtering schemes to combine the various sources of information (Maybeck, 1979).

Dead Reckoning. Dead reackoning is the simplest and least expensive means of position sensing, but also the least accurate. The robot senses its motion by shaft encoders on its wheels and integrates its motion to estimate position. Vehicle heading may be sensed directly by compass, or inferred by the difference in distance traveled between right and left wheels, or calculated by distance traveled and angle of steered wheels. Dead reckoning errors come from the assumption that a revolution of the axle means a fixed distance traveled by the wheel. Several factors make this assumption inaccurate: wheel slip on the ground; low tire pressure, which reduces effective wheel radius; tire squirm when concerning, which causes the vehicle to move slightly tangentially to the tire direction; etc. Approaches to reducing dead reckoning error include instrumenting nondriven wheels to reduce the likelihood of slip or measuring the motion of all wheels and trying to infer actual vehicle motion.

SENSING

Sensing for mobile robots subsumes most of image understanding (qv). Many of the tasks for mobile robots involve straightforward applications of techniques developed for other purposes, such as object recognition. The distinctive sensor processing required for mobile robots involves obstacle detection, map building, and object tracking. Typical sensors include both active (sonar and laser range finders) and passive (video cameras) (see SENSORS AND SENSOR FUSION; see also VISUAL MOTION ANALYSIS; NEURAL NETWORKS).

Sonar

The most common sensor for indoor mobile robots is sonar, due to its low cost and compact size. Typical sonars have a range of about 30 ft, a coverage of approximately 30°, and an accuracy of approximately 2 in. For each pulse, only the distance to the first echo is reported, which could be anywhere within the 30° cone of sensitivity. For use as a soft bumper, this wide scan has the great advantage of low data rate and thus fast and cheap processing. If the sonar is to be used for building maps, however, it requires much more detailed processing to localize the source of the echo. One approach (Elfes, 1987) models the sonar return statistically. Each distance measurement is used to update occupancy probabilities in the sensed area. The area inside the wedge scanned by the sonar does not generate an echo and is, therefore, most likely unoccupied. Occupancy probabilities for that area are reduced. Somewhere along the rim of the wedge, at a distance given by the reading, some object must have generated the echo. The region along the rim is more likely to be occupied, and can have its probability increased. During an actual run, the world is tiled with cells, each initially unknown. As the vehicle moves, takes sonar readings, and updates the occupancy probability of each cell, the outlines of objects gradually emerge and the free space around the robot becomes better defined.

Another set of approaches to sonar interpretation model the geometry of the objects that caused the echo (Leonard and co-workers, 1990; Kuc and Siegel, 1987). Sound waves reflect specularly (ie, at a mirrorlike angle), so echos must come either from a perpendicular surface, from a rounded object, or from the interior of a corner where sound reflects off of both walls. These different geometries will have different effects as the vehicle moves. If the reflection comes from a wall, for instance, the echo location will appear to move with the vehicle, whereas reflections from a corner remain fixed. This sort of reasoning about geometries and physics of the sonar can provide an accurate map, especially from an uncluttered environment where corners and curved objects are relatively rare.

Laser Range Finders

Mobile robots often need much more accurate range data than are available from sonar, especially for terrain mapping outdoors. The current state of the art is scanning laser range finders, (Besl and Jain, 1985; Besl, 1988). For a typical amplitude-modulated system, the output of a laser is modulated with a sine wave, the laser is pointed at an object, and the returned energy is measured. The phase shift between outgoing and returned signals gives the elapsed time for the laser, which is used to measure the distance to the object. The beam is typically directed at a pair of mirrors, first a multifaceted spinning mirror that generates horizontal scans, followed by a nodding mirror that moves those scans vertically down the scene. The resulting "image" is an array of range values. The performance of these systems is limited by a low laser power for eye safety and requires balancing range resolution, number of pixels, scanning time, and maximum range. The performances of a typical first-generation scanner (built by ERIM) and a second-generation scanner (from Perceptron) are given in Table 1. Other range sensing technology uses pulsed lasers and directly measures time of flight or separates the source and the detector and measures range from triangulation.

Range data can be used at several levels of detail. If the robot's surroundings are flat, with only isolated vertical obstacles, thresholding the elevation value is adequate for obstacle detection. In rolling terrain, it is necessary to look through the elevation data for areas that are too steep, too rough, or unreachable from the current vehicle location, and treat those as obstacles. In really rough terrain, it is necessary to reason about vehicle geometry, and search for paths for individual wheels, in order to find feasible paths.

Individual frames of range data do not always provide adequate information. Data from multiple frames must often be combined to fill in gaps in coverage and to provide increased resolution. If the vehicle has a very accurate inertial navigation system, fusing range data can be as simple as averaging the elevations reported at each location from the different scans. For vehicles with less precise relative positioning, the elevation data from different view points must be matched to find the most likely vehicle motion before combining the data. If the range data contains easily identifiable features, such as isolated objects or clean range edges, it is easy to do symbolic feature matching from frame to frame. In more chaotic terrain, it is necessary to do iconic matches, comparing elevation data in the various frames or to use variants of optical

Table 1. Relative Performance of Example Range Scanners

Characteristic	ERIM	Perceptron
Eye safe	yes (?)	yes
Field of view (h × v)	80 × 30	60 × 60 (programmable tilt)
Pixels	256 × 64	256 × 256
Ambiguity interval	20 m	40 m
Depth	8 bits (8 cm)	12 bits (1 cm)
Intensity	8 bits	8 bits
Max range	40 m (?)	50 m
Scan rate	2 frames/s	2 frames/s
Scan direction	top to bottom	programmable
Interface	VME to Sun	VME to Sun
Temperature	narrow range	"Pittsburgh"
Construction	wire wrap	printed circuit
Components	all custom	most off the shelf
Size (w × h × d)	90 × 35 × 45 (cm)	45 × 35 × 35 (cm)
Weight	50 kg	<25 kg
Power	26 VDC	110 VAC

flow tailored for range data (Herbert and co-workers, 1990; Olin and co-workers, 1987). A particularly interesting variation is the TraX system (Bobick and Bolles, 1989), which tracks objects as they are approached by the vehicle. As the object's size in the image increases, TraX generates more detailed segmentations and interpretations. A bush, for instance, might start out as a spherical blob and end up segmented into individual branches.

Passive Ranging

Instead of sensing range directly with range finders, range can also be inferred from images, using stereo or motion processing. Shape from motion methods are particularly popular on mobile robots (Bhanu, 1989; Dutta and Snyder, 1990; Graefe, 1990; Matthies and Shafer, 1987; Matthies and co-workers, 1988). In feature matching methods, individual points or lines are tracked from image to image, and their ranges are calculated by triangulation based on vehicle motion between frames. In optical flow methods, the apparent brightness "flow" of the image is used to directly calculate a depth field, without going through the intermediate step of finding and tracking features. Shape from motion is limited by not being able to calculate depth directly ahead of the vehicle. The point toward which the camera is moving is the focus of expansion (FOE), the image point from which objects seem to expand in optical flow. Objects directly at the FOE will not appear to move as the vehicle approaches, and shape from motion cannot calculate their depth. This is obviously a disadvantage for obstacle detection algorithms. Objects near the FOE will have inaccurate calculated depths, depending on how accurately the true vehicle motion is known. Several methods have been used to increase accuracy of motion methods, including tracking the FOE from the images, or using Kalman filters to update depth estimates.

Monocular Vision

If the environment in which a robot operates is mapped, the vehicle can use visual cues as landmarks to determine its location and motion (Faugeras, 1987; Fennema and co-workers, 1989). This is particularly useful in man-made environments, where many objects have sharp edges and other easy to track features. Systems for indoor navigation typically look for vertical edges, fit lines to the detected edge points, and match those lines to wire-frame models of the building interior. Once lines have been matched, triangulation gives the vehicle's current location. Variations on this method track the lines over many frames to filter the position estimates, or find features in outdoor images, or track horizontal as well as vertical edges.

Example: Road Following

A common task for outdoor mobile robots is following roads using video data, either color or monochrome. There are three general types of system: feature tracking, pattern classification, and neural networks. Feature tracking systems follow the lines, edges, and stripes of main roads (Dickmanns and Zapp, 1986; Kenue, 1989a, 1989b; Kluge and Thorpe, 1990). They usually consist of simple image processing operators, such as edge detectors or template matching systems, managed by a controller process. The controller examines the output of the image processing feature trackers, decides which detected points and lines are valid and which are outliers, updates its model of the current road geometry and passes it off to the steering program, and positions windows for the feature trackers in the next image. Controllers are based on control theory, on robust statistics, or on Hough transforms, all looking for consistent data. More sophisticated programs can examine the discarded features, decide the reason for failure, and update road models or image processing parameters as the road shape changes (eg, at an intersection) or illumination conditions vary.

Unimproved roads, which do not have lines or clean edges to track, are usually followed by pattern classification methods (Crisman and Thorpe, 1990; Turk and co-workers, 1988). These methods examine all the pixels in an image, classify each one according to color (sometimes adding texture or other features), and create an output image with each pixel labeled road or nonroad, perhaps with a confidence value. They then search the image for the most likely road location, fit a road model to the detected location, and update their color models for the next round of classification. Using the entire image, instead of isolated features, and using probabilities, instead of binary classifications, add to the ability of these algorithms to follow roads even in ill-structured conditions of shadows, dirt, broken edges, and changing road appearance.

Recent research in applying neural networks to road following has achieved some impressive results. The Autonomous land vehicle in a neural net (ALVINN) (Pomerleau, 1990) is a fully connected three-layer back-propagation network. It is trained by driving the robot by hand, giving the network the video images as input, and the human driver's steering wheel position as model output. After seeing approximately 200 training images, the network settles and is ready to take control. Typically, running on an unimproved road, ALVINN's hidden units learn large matched filters that look for the entire road or for road edges. Running on roads with lines and stripes, the network tends to settle on representations that look for those features. The advantage of this kind of system is that it is easy to retrain for many different kinds of road. The main disadvantage is that it has no symbolic representation of what it is looking for, so it is difficult to modify its representation without retraining. There is no clean way, for instance, to modify the network to run on a road that is twice as wide as the one for which it has been trained.

PLANNING

The most difficult aspects of robot planning (qv) arise in the lowest levels. High level planning for robots includes all the usual AI planning problems, including scheduling, partitioning plans among multiple intelligent agents, constraint satisfaction, and so forth. Although some of these are difficult problems, they are not unique to mobile robots, they involve symbolic reasoning, and they can often be solved off-line. Most problems of planning routes at large scales are pure geometric problems and, again, can be solved off-line, often by overlaying a grid on the world map and searching for suitable paths along the grid. But at the lowest level, the reasoning has to involve the interface with the real world. Robot trajectory planners, which plan how the vehicle should negotiate the next few meters of terrain, must get beyond symbolic and geometric planning to consider issues of precision and control.

Graphs. Indoor robots typically abstract space into occupied regions (often represented by sets of convex polygons) and free space (Brooks, 1986; Lozano-Perez and Wesley, 1979). This representation is further abstracted into a graph of possible robot paths, either skirting the edge of obstacles (for obstacle-based representations) or running down the middle of corridors of free space (for free-space methods). Additional nodes are added to the graph for the current vehicle position and the goal position, and paths are added to link the start and goal nodes into the graph. The graph is then searched by $A*$ or similar search methods to find the shortest path to the goal.

Potentials. A different abstraction for the path-planning problem is to use potential field models. Obstacles near the robot generate repulsive forces, whereas the goal attracts the vehicle. Repulsive potentials increase as the robot nears an object, guaranteeing safe clearance. Variants on potential field methods add potentials toward subgoals (Pauton, 1986) or make the obstacle potentials dependent not just on distance but also on closing speed (Krugh, 1984). Potential field methods have the advantage of quick, local calculations and are, therefore, suitable for reflexes during a robot run. Their local evaluation functions, however, allow them to be trapped in local minima, such as inside a U-shaped object, without reaching the goal. Hybrid methods use initial global search to find and eliminate local minima, or to select a rough global path, then use potential methods for fine-scale adjustment (Thorpe, 1984).

Vehicle Models. Typical cross-country trajectory planners cannot classify the world into obstacles and free space, but must instead examine the paths followed by individual wheels, and their interactions with the terrain, to determine traversability. Simple planners look for areas that are too steep, have too large a vertical step, or have vertical spikes that would entrap the vehicle's undercarriage (Kiersey and co-workers, 1988). More advanced cross country planners, in addition consider accuracy constraints (for both perception and vehicle motion) and sensor positioning (Stentz, 1990). Two distant objects may appear to be far enough apart to allow safe passage, but the planner may not be able to guarantee that the vehicle can move to and past the objects accurately enough to miss them. In that case, the planner must generate a path that moves closer to the objects, orient the vehicle so that sensors can see the objects and update their relative positions, and then replan to go through. The planner must also reason about nonholonomic motion constraints (limited turning radius) and variation of traversibility with vehicle orientation (both because of wheel orientation and vehicle shape). So, for instance, a particular ditch may be traversable if the vehicle approaches perpendicularly, but would entrap a wheel if the vehicle's path were nearly parallel to the ditch.

Example: Navlab Planner

The cross-country trajectory planner developed for the Navlab mobile robot incorporates the above concerns (Stentz, 1990). The search starts at the current vehicle configuration and expands, following the constraints of turning radius, to reach the goal. Each path is fattened by maximum expected error, which turns a planned ray in configuration space into a cone of possible trajectories. In order for a path to succeed, all paths within that cone must arrive within the goal configuration envelope without encountering obstacles. If that is impossible, the planner must select an intermediate goal and replan. The search is made efficient by an oct-tree representation of obstacles and free space, and by considering various pruning strategies.

MECHANISMS

Specialized mechanical designs, some specific to robots, facilitate navigation in difficult circumstances. The main designs serve two functions: increasing maneuverability, to help in tight situations with limited clearance, and increasing terrainability, to navigate rugged terrain. (See ROBOTS, LEGGED.)

Steering. Maneuvering in tight locations with a conventionally steered vehicle requires detailed sensing and planning. Even humans occasionally have a difficult time parallel parking. Many indoor robots avoid this problem by using omnidirectional steering. A commonly used design has three wheels, all steered and driven together, to keep the body orientation constant while the vehicle moves in any direction. Most such platforms have a circular cross section, which simplifies path planning, and a rotating turret, so cameras and other sensors can be pointed independently of the direction of the motion.

More complex omnidirectional vehicles allow independent steering of each wheel. This requires careful attention to coordination. A four-wheeled vehicle has eight control parameters (steering angle and wheel velocity for each wheel), but only three degrees of freedom in motion. In order to move without actuator conflict, all wheels must instantaneously be moving along concentric circles, with their axles pointed toward the center of the circle and their speeds proportional to their effective radii.

Rugged Terrain. Designs for rugged terrain range from tracks and wheels to multisegment bodies to walking machines. Many of these have been inspired by planetary exploration, especially the soft sands and rugged, eroded terrain of Mars. Bulldozer-style tracks provide great ter-

Figure 1. An assortment of mobile robots, real and fanciful. Rear left: the JPL loop-wheel vehicle, designed for planetary exploration. Rear center: Shakey, the pioneering AI-based robot, from SRI. Rear right: a Denning Sentry commercial mobile robot. On steps: Omnibot, a toy robot. Left in front of steps: Sea Rover, a highly mobile underwater vehicle, used primarily as a flying eyeball. Right in front of steps: RB5X, designed for educational use. Foreground: a robot prop from the movie *Runaway*. Courtesy of the Computer Museum, Boston.

rainability, but require impractical amounts of power, both for skid steering and because small rocks get caught and crushed between track segments. An improved design, the JPL loop-wheel vehicle, uses four stiff circular bands that deflect more than a tire but are not as flexible as treads. Using four smaller bands makes conventional steering feasible, and using one-piece loops instead of steel segments decreases rock entrapment.

A different approach is to build multisegment vehicles, with each segment having one or two pairs of wheels. Designs include segments connected with a flexible backbone, segments connected with active articulation that can lift the body over steep steps, and even robots with passive wheels and active articulation that move like a snake. Specialized mechanisms include a family of pipe climbers (Fukuda and co-workers, 1990) and a family of wall climbers (Nishi and co-workers, 1990). The first of the wall robots at Waseda University used a suction fan to hold the robot body to the wall and used wheels for propulsion. The second is a biped walker, with suction cup feet, that is more capable of surmounting ridges and ledges. The latest in the series uses a small aircraft propeller to hold the robot against the wall and to propel it at speeds up to 5 m/s.

Legs. Several families of walking machines have been developed, including dynamically stable hoppers (Raibert, 1989) and the Ohio State Adaptive Suspension Vehicle (Song and Waldron, 1989). Walking robots provide high terrainability and are much more efficient than wheeled vehicles in rough and soft terrain (see ROBOTS, LEGGED).

Example: AMBLER

The largest and perhaps most unusual walking land robot today is the AMBLER (Bares and co-workers, 1989). It has six orthogonal legs, each with a rotational shoulder and prismatic elbow operating in the horizontal plane, and a prismatic vertical outer link. On rough terrain, the AMBLER adjusts its vertical axes to keep the body horizontal, allowing efficient translational motion. Whenever possible, the body is kept at a constant elevation, saving the energy that a wheeled vehicle would expend climbing over every rock it encountered. The AMBLER's legs are arranged in two sets, with the three legs on each side sharing a common shoulder axis. The legs move in a novel "circulating" gait. Each leg in turn is placed ahead of the body, then moves past the outer edge of the body during its propulsion phase. Legs are recovered (brought forward to begin the walking cycle) by swinging them through a cavity in the middle of the body. This continuous rotation of the shoulders allows each leg to be placed only once while the body moves up to three meters, rather than requiring each leg to pick up and shuffle forward several times to follow the leg ahead of it, as in most walking machines.

Walking machines pose special planning problems. High speed walking machines must first select an appropriate gait, which defines the order in which legs should be recovered and the number of legs in the air at any one time. Slower machines, such as the AMBLER, move only a single leg at a time. Deciding which leg to move, and where to place it, requires considering terrain, body advance, and vehicle stability constraints. The center of gravity of a statically stable walking machine must be kept over its support polygon, the bounding polygon of the contact points of all feet touching the ground. The ABMLER uses a further constraint, the conservative support polygon (CSP). The CSP is formed by intersecting all of the support polygons formed by considering each set of $N-1$ supporting feet. If the center of gravity of the AMBLER is held above the CSP, any single foot can fail without the vehicle tipping over. Part of the planning problem, then, consists of placing feet so that the sequence of CSP lines up with the desired direction of motion and allows continuous safe body advances (Wettergreen, 1990).

ARCHITECTURES

The separate parts of a mobile robot's software (sensing, thinking, and acting) must be organized by an architectural framework. An architecture for a complex robot must handle multiple sensors, potentially conflicting subgoals, planning at different levels, and execution monitoring. The architecture must also define interfaces and provide tools to allow many programmers to build the system and to allow multiprocessor execution.

Centralized. The most conventional architectures separate robot software into separate modules for sensing, thinking, and control. This has the advantage of giving one module control of the vehicle, another control of all sensors, and a third control of modeling and planning. This decomposition groups design tasks in the likely areas of expertise of separate research groups. The drawback of this approach is that it does not allow for high speed special-purpose reflexes, that must do sensing, thinking, and control all in one tightly integrated module.

Subsumption. The opposite approach is typified by Brooks (1986) in his subsumption architecture. In his robots, each module covers the complete range from sensory input to control output. He divides his modules into a hierarchy of functions, each subsuming the lower levels. The first module watches sensor data and moves the vehicle away from obstacles. The next layer moves the vehicle randomly, unless the lowest layer takes over to avoid hitting an object. Higher layers add purpose to the wandering (eg, toward open doorways), look for objects of interest, and so forth. Each layer is relatively simple to build, and at least in principle mostly decoupled from adjacent layers. But with no central world model, it takes careful design to ensure that various modules are not working at cross purposes. Related ideas include reactive or reflexive planning, which emphasize quick response rather than careful preplanning, and behaviors, which package sensing and control modes appropriate for specific situations (Payton, 1986).

Hybrid. Several attempts have been made to build architectures that combine the best of both approaches. These systems typically propose a hierarchy, in which sensor interpretation at each level feeds into both planning at the same level and higher level sensor interpretation (Albus and co-workers, 1987). Plans at each level are decomposed into lower level steps, and given to the next lower level for execution. The hierarchies are often structured by time (quick reflexes at the low level, through slower processes at higher levels), data abstraction (raw signals to symbolic reasoning), and space (local effects to global databases). In trying to encompass all possible systems, these general-purpose architectures lose their prescriptive power. Their main contribution may instead be descriptive, providing a common vocabulary in which to discuss the differences between architectures.

Trade-Offs

For current robot systems, there appears to be no single best architecture. A robot such as the AMBLER, which moves very slowly to conserve energy, may be best served by an architecture that centralizes all decision making. The task control architecture (Bares and co-workers, 1989) on the AMBLER collects all control information in a central module, so the best choice can be made before spending energy on moving. Smaller robots with limited computing may be better off with subsumption-style architectures. These robots do not have central world models based on sensor fusion and may not always make optimal decisions, but can react quickly. In a sense they substitute physical search and backtracking, moving through the environment, for the computer-based exploration of search spaces typical of an AI system.

SUMMARY

Mobile robots have evolved extensively from early systems such as Shakey (qv) (Nilsson, 1984) and the Stanford Cart (Moravec, 1983). VaMoRs now drives the autobahn at 100 km/h (Dickmanns and Zapps, 1986). Denning Sentries patrol warehouses at night. Raibert's (1989) machines hop, skip, and jump. EAVE-East looks for underwater objects (Blidberg, 1989). Yet very few truly autonomous vehicles are actually at work. This is partly due to issues of cost and hardware reliability. But it is still largely because of the remaining challenges in dealing with unstructured environments. Developing general-purpose practical robots will require further advances in position sensing, image understanding, planning, mechanical design, and system architectures. Additional open issues remain in coordinating multiple vehicles, sensing and handling moving obstacles, error detection and recovery, integrating vehicle motion and manipulation, and human interfaces.

But even though there are still deep research issues in each of those areas, there is beginning to be more emphasis on bringing together the components that already do work, in the limited domains in which they are reliable, to build complete prototype systems. New robot development and application initiatives, from hazardous waste cleanup to cooperating reconnaissance vehicles to intelligent vehicle highway systems, are all just getting under way. Mobile robots have already made the transition from science fiction to laboratory research. They are now poised for the next transition, to becoming practical working machines.

BIBLIOGRAPHY

J. Albus, H. McCain, and R. Lumia, *NASA/NBS Standard Reference Model for Telerobot Control System Architecture (NASREM)*, Technical Report Technical Note 1235, National Bureau of Standards, Gaithersburg, Md., 1987.

J. Bares, M. Hebert, T. Kanabe, E. Krotkov, T. Mitchell, R. Simmons, and W. Whittaker, "An Autonomous Rover for Exploring Mars," *IEEE Comput. Mag.* **22**(6) (June 1989).

P. Besl, *Range Imaging Sensors*, Technical Report GMR-6090, General Motors Research Laboratory, Warren, Mich., Mar. 1988.

P. Besl and R. Jain, "Three-Dimensional Object Recognition," *ACM Comput. Surveys* **17**(1) (Mar. 1985).

B. Bhanu, "Understanding Scene Dynamics," in *Proceedings of the Image Understanding Workshop*, Morgan-Kaufmann, San Mateo, Calif., 1989.

D. R. Bildberg, "Autonomous Underwater Vehicles: Current Activities and Research Opportunities," in *Proceedings of IAS-2*. IOS, Amsterdam, The Netherlands, Dec. 1989.

A. F. Bobick and R. C. Bolles, "Representation Space: An Approach to the Integration of Visual Information," in *Proceedings of CVPR*, IEEE, June 1989.

R. Brooks, "A Robust Layered Control System for a Mobile Robot," *IEEE J. Robot. Automat.* **2**(1) (1986).

J. D. Crisman and C. E. Thorpe, "Color Vision for Road Following," in C. E. Thorpe, ed., *Vision and Navigation: The Carnegie Mellon Navlab,* Kluwer Academic Publishers, Boston, 1990, Chapt. 2.

E. Dickmanns and A. Zapp, "A Curvature-Based Scheme for Improving Road Vehicle Guidance by Computer Vision," in *Proceedings of the SPIE Conference 727 on Mobile Robots,* Cambridge, Mass., 1986.

R. Dutta and M. A. Snyder, "Robustness of Correspondence-Based Structure from Motion," in *DARPA Image Understanding Workshop,* Morgan-Kaufmann, san Mateo, Calif., Sept. 1990.

A. Elfes, "Sonar-Based Real-World Mapping and Navigation," *J. Robot. Automat.* **3** (1987).

O. Faugeras, F. Lustman, and G. Toscani, "Motion and Structure from Motion from Point and Line Matches," in *Proceedings of ICCV'87*, 1987.

C. Fennema, A. Hanson, and E. Riseman, "Towards Autonomous Mobile Robot Navigation," in *DARPA Image Understanding Workshop,* Morgan-Kaufmann, San Mateo, Calif., May 1989.

T. Fukuda, H. Hosokai, and N. Shimasaka, "Autonomous Plant Maintenance Robot," in *Proceedings of IROS 90,* IEEE Industrial Electronics Society, July 1990.

V. Graefe, "An Approach to Obstacle Recognition for Autonomous Mobile Robots, in *Proceedings of IROS 90,* IEEE Industrial Electronics Society, July 1990.

M. Hebert, I. Kweon, and T. Kanade, "3-D Vision Techniques for Autonomous Vehicles, in C. Thorpe, ed., *Vision and Navigation: The Carnegie Mellon Navlab,* Kluwer, Boston, 1990, Chapt. 8.

D. M. Keirsey, D. W. Payton, J. K. Rosenblatt, "Autonomous Navigation in Cross Country Terrain," in *Proceedings of the Image Understanding Workshop,* Morgan-Kaufmann, San Mateo, Calif., 1988.

S. K. Kenue, "Lanelok: Detection of Land Boundaries and Vehicle Tracking Using Image-Processing Techniques. Part I: Hough-Transform, Region-Tracing, and Correlation Algorithms," in *Mobile Robots IV,* SPIE, Nov. 1989a.

S. K. Kenue, "Lanelok: Detection of Land Boundaries and Vehicle Tracking Using Image-Processing Techniques. Part II: Template Matching Algorithms," in *Mobile Robots IV,* SPIE, Nov. 1989b.

K. Kluge and C. E. Thorpe, "Explicit Models for Robot Road Following," in C. Thorpe, ed., *Vision and Navigation: The Carnegie Mellon Navlab,* Kluwer, Boston, 1990, Chapt. 3.

B. Krogh, "A Generalized Potential Approach to Obstacle Avoidance Control," in *Robotics Research Conference Proceedings,* Bethlehem, Pa., Aug. 1984.

R. Kuc and M. W. Siegel, "Physically Based Simulation Model for Acoustic Sensor Robot Navigation," *PAMI* **9**(6) (Nov. 1987).

J. Leonard, H. Durrant-Whyte, and I. J. Cox, "Dynamic Map Building for an Autonomous Mobile Robot," in *Proceedings of IROS 90,* IEEE Industrial Electronics Society, July 1990.

T. Lozano-Perez and M. A. Wesley, "An Algorithm for Planning Collision-Free Paths among Polyhedral Obstacles," *CACM* **22**(10) (Oct. 1979).

L. Matthies and S. Shafer, "Error Modeling in Stereo Navigation," *J. Robot. Automat.* **3** (1987).

L. Matthies, R. Szeliski, and T. Kanade, "Kalman Filter-Based Algorithms for Estimating Depth from Image Sequences," in *Proceedings of the Image Understanding Workshop,* Cambridge, Mass., 1988.

P. S. Maybeck, *Mathematics in Science and Engineering: Stochastic Models, Estimation, and Control,* Academic Press, Inc., New York, 1979.

H. P. Moravec, "The Stanford Cart and the CMU Rover," *Proc. IEEE* **71**(7) (July 1983).

N. J. Nilsson, *Shakey the Robot,* Artificial Intelligence Center Technical Note **323**, SRI International, Menlo Park, Calif., Apr. 1984.

A. Nishi, M. Ohkura, and H. Miyagi, "A Robot Capable of Moving on a Vertical Wall Using Thrust Force," in *Proceedings of IROS 90,* IEEE Industrial Electronics Society, July 1990.

K. Olin, F. Vilnrotter, M. Daily, and K. Reiser, "Developments in Knowledge-Based Vision for Obstacle Detection and Avoidance," in *Image Understanding Workshop,* Los Angeles, 1987.

D. W. Payton, "An Architecture For Reflexive Autonomous Vehicle Control," in *Proceedings of the IEEE International Conference on Robotics and Automation,* IEEE, 1986.

D. A. Pomerleau, "Neural Network Based Autonomous Navigation," in C. Thorpe, ed., *Vision and Navigation: The Carnegie Mellon Navlab,* Kluwer, Boston, 1990, Chapt. 5.

M. H. Raibert, *Legged Robots That Balance,* The MIT Press, Cambridge, Mass., 1989.

S. Song and K. J. Waldron, *Machines That Walk: The Adaptive Suspension Vehicle,* The MIT Press, Cambridge, Mass., 1989.

A. Stentz, "Multi-Resolution Constraint Modeling for Mobile Robot Planning," in C. Thorpe, ed., *Vision and Navigation: The Carnegie Mellon Navlab,* Kluwer, Boston, 1990, Chapt. 11.

C. E. Thorpe, "Path Relaxation: Path Planning for a Mobile Robot," in *Proceedings of the Fourth National Conference for Artificial Intelligence,* Austin, Tex., AAAI, Menlo Park, Calif., 1984.

M. Turk, D. Morgenthaler, K. Gremban, and M. Marra, "VITS — A Vision System for Autonomous Land Vehicle Navigation," *IEEE PAMI* **10**(3) (May 1988).

D. S. Wettergreen, H. J. Thomas, and C. Thorpe, "Planning Strategies for the AMBLER Walking Robot," in *Proceedings of the IEEE International Conference on Systems Engineering,* Aug. 1990.

CHARLES E. THORPE
Carnegie Mellon University

ROSIE

A software tool to facilitate the building of expert systems (qv), ROSIE is a general-purpose, rule-based, procedure-oriented system. The system, when provided with a knowledge base, will become an expert system for the domain embodied by the knowledge base. It was developed around 1981 at Rand Corporation (see J. Fain and co-workers, The Rosie Language Reference Manual, Technical Note N-1647-ARPA, Rand Corp., 1981, and F. Hayes-Roth and co-workers, Rationale and Motivation for Rosie, Technical Note N-1648-ARPA, Rand Corp., 1981).

K. S. ARORA
SUNY at Buffalo

RULE-BASED SYSTEMS

Rule-based systems (RBSs) constitute the best means available today for codifying the problem-solving know-how of the human expert. Empirically, it seems that experts can express most of their problem-solving techniques simply as a set of situation—action rules. This makes RBSs the method of choice for building knowledge-intensive expert systems. Although many different techniques have emerged to organize collections of rules into automated experts, RBSs share many key properties:

- An RBS incorporates practical human knowledge expressed in terms of conditional if–then rules.
- An RBS grows in skill as its collection of rules is incrementally expanded.
- The RBS can solve a wide range of possibly complex problems by selecting relevant rules and combining their results in appropriate ways.
- The RBS determines dynamically the best rules to execute.
- The RBS explains its conclusions by retracing its actual line of reasoning and translating to English the logic of each rule employed (see EXPLANATION).

Rule-based systems address the need to capture, represent, store, distribute, reason about, and apply human knowledge electronically. Within the current state of the art they provide a practical means of building automated experts in application areas where job excellence requires consistent reasoning and rewards practical experience. Table 1 lists some application areas addressed by current RBS technology.

RBSs take their name from the way they represent knowledge about plausible inferences and preferred problem-solving tactics. Some of them are listed in Table 2. Typically, they represent both sorts of know-how in terms of conditional rules. The examples below illustrate rules taken from a variety of applications, employing varying syntactic conventions.

Table 1. Rule-Based System Applications

Problem	System Functions
Equipment maintenance	Diagnose faults and recommend repairs
Component selection	Elicit requirements and match parts catalog
Computer operation	Analyze requirements; select and operate software
Product configuration	Elicit preferences and identify parts that satisfy constraints
Troubleshooting	Analyze situation, suggest treatments, and prescribe preventative measures
Process control	Spot problematic data and remedy irregularities
Quality assurance	Assess task, propose practices, and enforce requirements

Table 2. Some Rule-Based Expert Systems

ACTOR	M.1
AGE	MAC
AGE-PUFF	Meta-DENDRAL
AMORD	MRS
BB1	MYCIN
BIP	NEOMYCIN
CASNET	NESTOR
CLOT	NUDGE
CRYSALIS	OCEAN
DART	OPS
DENDRAL	PLANNER
Diagnosis I	PROLOG
Diagnosis II	PROSPECTOR
EMYCIN	PUFF
EXPERT	RITA
FRL	ROGET
HASP	ROSIE
HEARSAY II	S.1
INTERNIST-1	SACON
IRIS	SOPHIE
KRL	TEIRESIAS
LITHO	XCON

Example 1. Automotive troubleshooting rules represented in an S.1 program. As cars incorporate more electronic subsystems, they become more difficult for average technicians to repair. S.1 provides a structural framework for organizing and applying thousands of rules. General Motors plans to aid its service technicians with several large-scale RBSs.

Rule408:

C is a car.

If: the pattern observed by attaching an oscilloscope to the charging circuit of the car C is fluctuating arches, and

the alternator of the car C responds properly to different loads.

then: there is strongly suggestive evidence $\langle 0.9 \rangle$ that the cause of the problem with the car C is voltage-regulator bad.

Rule428:

C is a car.

If: the pattern obtained by attaching an oscilloscope to the charging circuit of the car C is straight line.

the result pulling out the field connector is no.flash.

the field connector does not have a voltage.

the input of the voltage regulator does not have a voltage.

the dashboard's lights do not glow when their ground circuit is completed.

the fusable link is getting voltage.

the fusable link is not conducting power.

then: it is definite $\langle 1.0 \rangle$ that the cause of the problem with the car C is fusable.link.bad.

Example 2. Legal heuristics for product liability represented in a ROSIE (qv) program. Each rule expresses an independent chunk of know-how. ROSIE provides a stylized English-like syntax for expressing conditions and actions.

> If the plaintiff did receive an eye injury
> > and there was just one eye that was injured
> > and the treatment for the eye did require surgery
> > and the recovery from the injury was almost complete
> > and visual acuity was slightly reduced by the injury
> > and the condition is fixed,
>
> increase the injury trauma factor by $10,000.
>
> If the plaintiff's injury did cause (a temporary disability of an important function)
> > and the plaintiff's doctors were not certain about the disability being temporary
> > and the plaintiff's recovery was almost complete.
> > and the condition is fixed,
>
> increase the fear factor by $1000 per day.
>
> If the plaintiff did not wear glasses before the injury
> > and the plaintiff's injury does requires (the plaintiff to wear glasses),
>
> increase the faculty loss factor by $1500
> and increase the inconvenience factor by $1500.

Rule-based systems may be defined as modularized know-how systems. Know-how refers to practical problem-solving knowledge. It consists of a variety of kinds of information, including inferences that follow from observations; abstractions, generalizations, and categorizations of given data; necessary and sufficient conditions for achieving some goal; suggested places to look for information that might be needed: preferred strategies for eliminating uncertainty or minimizing other risks; likely consequences of hypothetical situations; and probable causes of symptoms.

Today's RBS technology provides the first practical methodology and notation for developing systems capable of knowledge-intensive automated performance. Although AI researchers have developed several alternatives, only the RBS approach consistently produces expert problem solvers. This reflects a feature of the current state of the art in automatic reasoning, namely that RBSs can incorporate directly rules that emulate the effective special-case reasoning characteristic of highly experienced professionals. On the other hand, general-purpose deductive schemes lack the efficiency required to solve complex practical tasks. Because each rule approximates an independent nugget of know-how, RBS development has two key characteristic features: the systems improve performance incrementally as system builders refine the existing and add new knowledge and the ability of the systems to explain their reasoning makes their logic practically transparent, which meets a widely recognized need for understandability of computer systems.

By incorporating know-how, acquired in an incremental and transparent manner, RBSs open up key computing applications not readily addressable by alternative techniques. These include tasks where the demands for quality performance by humans exceed the supply. Such demands may arise from a variety of causes, including workers in the same job may differ significantly in job abilities, expert job performance produces significantly better results than average, and conventional means of training and automation prove inadequate to produce expert performance. Automating expertise in specialized tasks generally requires a few hundred to a few thousand heuristic rules. With existing technology, this makes good economic sense in hundreds of application areas.

RBSs embody an operating concept that differs radically from von Neumann architectures. In this concept intelligent problem-solving means an iterative cycle of identifying from experience those heuristic rules that bear on a problem at hand and applying one of those rules to solve or simplify the problem. The technology for building RBSs supports this cycle by providing a dynamic working memory for partial results, a device to identify relevant rules, and selective means for applying desirable rules. Many people conjecture that human problem-solving activity follows the RBS model. Whether that proves true, human experts generally find it easy to express methods for solving problems in their application areas using a rule formation.

Today rule-oriented components are becoming central in many advanced computing applications. This article surveys the state of RBS technology. The goal is to help readers determine whether this technology can contribute significantly in their own areas of interest. The following sections present an overview of RBS techniques, discuss the RBS niche in the larger field of computing, look at the structure of a rule and the architecture of an entire RBS, review the conceptual and historical development of RBSs, and evaluate the current state of the art.

THE RBS IN OVERVIEW

A simplified form of the rule-based system consists of storage and processing elements, often loosely labeled as the knowledge base plus inference engine (Fig. 1) The basic cycle of a rule-based system consists of select and execute phases. In the select phase the system determines which rules can apply and chooses one in particular to execute. In the execute phase the system interprets the selected rule to draw inferences that alters the system's dynamic memory. System storage includes components for long-term static data and short-term dynamic data. The long-term store, called the knowledge base, contains rules and facts. Rules specify actions the system should initiate when certain triggering conditions occur. The conditions define important patterns of data that can arise within the working memory. The system represents data in terms of relations, propositions, or equivalent logical expressions. Facts define static, true propositions. In contrast with conventional DP systems, the basic RBS distributes its logic over numerous independent condition–action rules, moni-

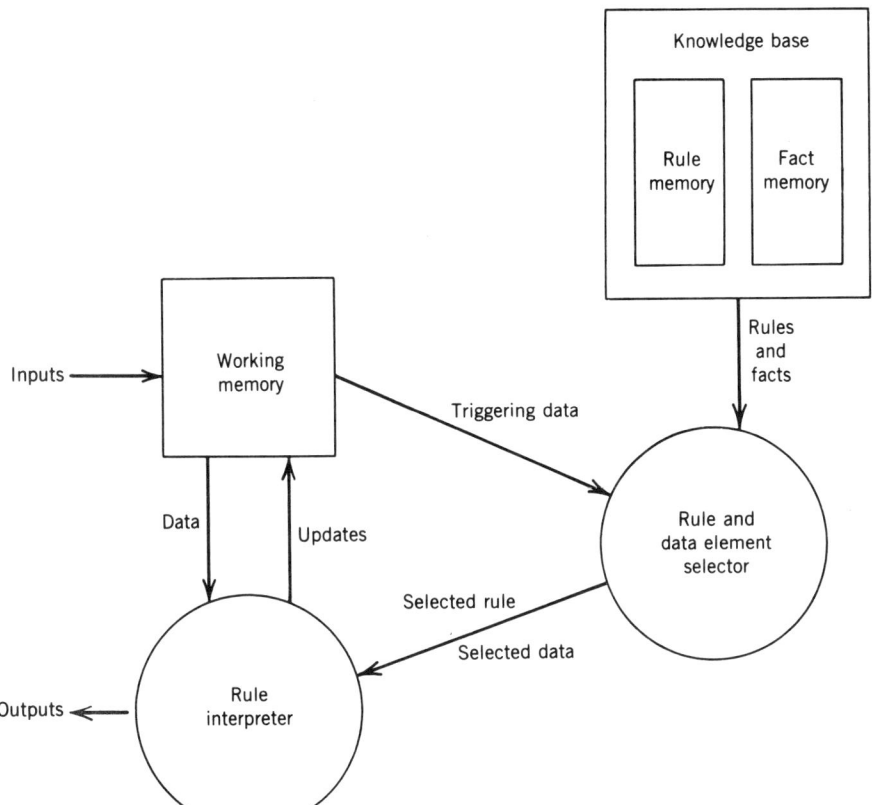

Figure 1. Basic features of rule-based systems.

tors dynamic results for triggering patterns of data, determines its sequential behavior by selecting its next activity from a set of candidate triggered rules, and stores its intermediate results exclusively in a global working memory.

Roughly speaking, an RBS consists of a knowledge base plus an inference engine. A knowledge base consists of rules and facts. Rules always express a conditional, with an antecedent and a consequent component. The interpretation of a rule is that if the antecedent condition can be satisfied, the consequent can be too. When the consequent defines an action, the effect of satisfying the antecedent is to schedule the action for execution. When the consequent defines a conclusion, the effect is to infer the conclusion.

Because the behavior of the RBS derives from this simple regimen, given particular problem-solving data, the rules completely specify the actual behavior of the system. As a means of specifying behavior, rules perform a variety of distinctive functions. First, the rules decompose the overall state-transition behavior into parallel actions that respond independently to distinct properties of a system state. This in turn simplifies the tasks of auditing and explaining system behavior. Every result is traceable to its antecedent data and intermediate rule-based inferences. Second, because rules can express logical relationships (conditionals) and definitional equivalences, they provide a means to simulate deduction and reasoning. Third, when the rules translate low level signal data into higher level pattern classes, they can simulate human perception. Finally, by using conditional rules to express rules of thumb, often called heuristics (qv), the RBS simulates subjective decision making.

Several major ways have emerged for organizing RBSs. For example, rules may express deductive knowledge, such as logical relationships. This knowledge can support inference, verifications, or evaluation tasks. On the other hand, rules may express goal-oriented knowledge, which an RBS applies to seek a problem solution and cites to justify its own goal-seeking behavior. Finally, rules may express causal relationships, which an RBS can use to answer "what if" questions or to determine possible causes for specified events (see REASONING, CAUSAL).

An RBS can only solve problems when it incorporates effective rules. The rules use symbolic descriptions to characterize relevant situations and corresponding actions. The language employed for these descriptions imposes a conceptual framework on the problem and its solution. The rules may be precise or gross; the intermediate partial solutions may be abstract or detailed. Efforts to solve the problem may proceed top-down, bottom-up, or in some other way (see PROCESSING, BOTTOM-UP AND TOP-DOWN). The meaning, importance, and contribution of each rule depends on its effectiveness as a contributor within the entire set of rules available for solving a problem.

Facts constitute the other kind of data in a knowledge base. Facts express assertions about properties, relations, propositions, etc. Where each RBS gives an imperative interpretation to rule-based knowledge, the RBS typically views the fact as static and inactive. Implicitly, a fact is silent regarding the pragmatic value and dynamic utilization of its knowledge. Thus although in many cases facts and rules may be logically interchangeable, RBS distinguish facts and rules for performance reasons. Rules specify in a conditional form potential inferences that the RBS must consider as a basis for its next action.

In addition to its static memory for facts and rules, the RBS employs a working memory for storing temporary assertions These assertions record earlier rule-based inferences. The contents of working memory can be interpreted as problem-solving state information. Ordinarily, the data in working memory adhere to the syntactic convention of facts. The temporary assertions thus correspond to dynamic facts.

The computing environment for interpreting rules consists of the current facts and the inference engine itself. Together these provide a context for interpreting the current state, understanding what the rules mean, and applying relevant rules appropriately. In the examples given in the first section hints of this implicit frame of reference can be detected. The legal rules specify changes to make to various "factors," and the auto-repair rules assert conclusions about causes of problems. These rules are not universally valid. They each depend on many unstated assumptions that characterize the implicit frame of reference where they express valid relationships. The validity of these rules depends critically on their being interpreted in the right context. Generally, RBSs cannot obviate all concerns of conventional computer programming (such as representation of state, control of sequencing, and variable scoping) because someone has to ensure that as a computer program the RBS applies rules appropriately in their meaningful contexts. Many people mistakenly assume that RBSs turn unstructured heaps of universally valid, independent rules into effective problem solvers. That is a serious misinterpretation of the current state of technology. So, the rule writer must consider the rule-interpretation environment when the rule is written. By employing knowledge of this context, many RBS can translate a rule or its applications to produce explanations using convenient notations or excellent English.

The basic function of the RBS is to produce results. The primary output may be a problem solution, an answer to a question, or an analysis of data. Whatever the case, the RBS will employ several key processes in determining its overall activity. A "world" manager maintains information in working memory. A built-in control procedure will define the basic, high level loop. And if the built-in control provides for programmable specialized control, an additional process will manage branching to and returning from special control blocks.

THE RBS NICHE IN COMPUTING

RBSs combine a variety of techniques and address numerous shortcomings apparent in conventional technology. Some of the needs RBSs address are:

Prescribing how complex programs should behave.

Adapting rapidly to requirements changes arising during development.

Involving users and experts in specifying program operation.

Developing computer-based competence experimentally.

Capturing and distributing the expertise needed to exploit existing computer capabilities.

The features of RBSs that address these problems include:

Modularity of know-how.

Knowledge bases for storing rules and facts that directly determine decisions.

Incremental development, with steady performance improvements.

Explanation of results, lines of reasoning, and questions asked.

Intelligibility of encoded beliefs and problem-solving techniques.

Dynamic assembly of inference chains, within the context of a built-in control procedure.

Given the importance of the problems for which these techniques seem appropriate, it should be expected that the RBS niche would expand over time. Rules as a basis for representing knowledge can provide the right solution to some of these problems.

THE RULE AS OBJECT

Rules may contain much information beyond their simple conditional if–then component (Fig. 2). Whereas the antecedent and consequent of a rule specify data sufficient for inferring a conclusion or performing another action, other parts of a rule serve additional important roles. Many large RBSs benefit from hierarchical structuring, in which each rule may belong to one or more higher order collections. These collections, called rulesets, aggregate and differentiate rules according to their function within the system. An RBS may ignore all rules in rulesets momentarily deemed irrelevant to a problem. Data about the rule, such as who wrote it and when, can support testing, evaluation, explanation, and maintenance, Typically,

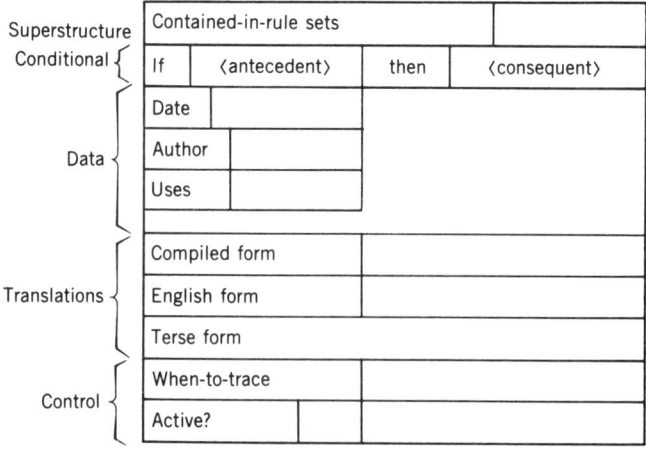

Figure 2. Rule components support multiple functions.

each rule exists in several alternative representations derived by translation. One machine-oriented translation serves the need for high performance at run time; one human-oriented form uses English to support publication and explanation, and another exploits terseness to improve reading and editing. Yet other facets of the rule structure determine how the inference engine should treat the rule. The system may need to trace rule evaluations and applications, justify the rule's relevance, or selectively ignore the rule under various conditions.

The rule is spoken of as a relatively independent piece or chunk of know-how. Psychologists, for some time, have emphasized the subjective reality of chunks. Chunks correspond to the elementary patterns people perceive and manipulate in thinking. They differ from person to person. They reflect the learned, appropriate, effective distinctions in each person's skill areas. A rule corresponds to a chunk of problem-solving know-how.

As used by most RBSs, the rule specifies analytic problem-solving knowledge. The rule is a datum employed by an inference engine to infer a solution to its goal problem. Thus, when the rule writer expresses know-how in rule format, one possible path is offered to reduce a goal to subgoals or draw a plausible inference from plausible data or transform an expression. This information about the rule typically comprises its familiar if–then components. However, as the number of rules in an RBS grows, maintainers need additional assistance to extend and maintain the knowledge base. For this reason, many additional facets or attributes are introduced. These generally represent data about the rule's analytic knowledge and its preferred manner of use.

RBS ARCHITECTURE

An RBS generally is a complete computing system: it takes inputs, uses memory and processing, and produces outputs. The key elements of RBS technology include rules, interpreters, translations, and explanations.

From the architectural perspective, rules constitute data. Generally these data conform to highly specialized grammars capable of using symbolic expressions to define conditions and actions. Current systems differ primarily in the generality and notational convenience their symbologies support.

The rule interpreter matches a rule component to working-memory data. Generally, this requires pattern matching (qv) that finds constants in working memory that match identical constants or unbound variables in rule patterns. Existing systems differ primarily in the methods they use to simplify rule definition and pattern matching. The action of the rule is produced by another part of the rule interpreter. Actions generally consist of two sorts: changes to working memory or external actions such as I–O.

Some RBSs employ multiple representations of rules, such as one for data entry, another for interpretation, and another for explanations. Typically, all rules are maintained in one preferred representation and translated as needed for other purposes.

The hallmark of RBSs has been their ability to explain their conclusions. Explanations have been generated by translating to English the rules used in reaching the result of interest. This requires maintaining a history of working memory changes and their causes. This history can be searched as needed for explanation.

RBSs have been organized in a variety of ways. An RBS organization consists of a set of decisions about what meaning to give rules and how and when to interpret them. Two organizations are most common: stimulus-driven, often called forward-chaining, and goal-directed, usually called back-chaining. In the former case a rule is triggered when changes in working-memory data produce a situation that matches its antecedent component. Some RBSs allow rules to fire repeatedly as long as the working data still match the rule, but most process a specific working-memory data configuration only once for each rule. In back-chaining, the RBS begins with a goal and successively examines rules whose consequent components match it. One at a time these candidate rules are considered. From each such rule whose applicability remains plausible, the unmet conditions of the antecedent are extracted. Each such condition, in turn, is defined to be a new goal. And the back-chaining control procedure shifts attention toward the new goal, recursively. This effort terminates whenever the top goal has been reduced to a set of satisfied subgoals.

From the point of view of computer architecture, two kernel facilities distinguish RBSs from conventional systems. First, the RBS makes heavy use of pattern matching between rule components and working memory. Second, RBSs must quickly identify rules that become relevant as working memory changes. This requires a means of accessing rules by pattern-matched values. Most RBSs support these requirements today in software, although some current hardware efforts aim at improving performance on these tasks.

The simple model of the RBS, consisting merely of a knowledge base and inference engine, undergoes substantial modification as the RBS advances in complexity (Fig. 3). Two primary objectives motivate these elaborations: clarity of the knowledge and run-time performance. Knowledge clarity meets many of the key requirements for RBS development. These include expressibility of know-how by experts; intelligibility of the knowledge and related reasoning to experts, their peers, and users; and modifiability and extensibility. Many of the differentiated features evident in the advanced system address the concern for enhanced knowledge clarity. These include the elaboration of a multidimensional working memory and the separation among rules, metarules, and control procedures. The goal of performance also motivates many of the embellishments the advanced system incorporates. A rule compiler converts the triggering data conditions into a data-flow network that optimizes the computing required to identify executable rules. The advanced system introduces three additional data sources to aid in the selection of the one rule to execute next. Higher level rules called metarules express preferences and priorities that differentially favor specific candidates (see META-KNOWLEDGE, METARULES, AND META-REASONING). The prioritized list of rules

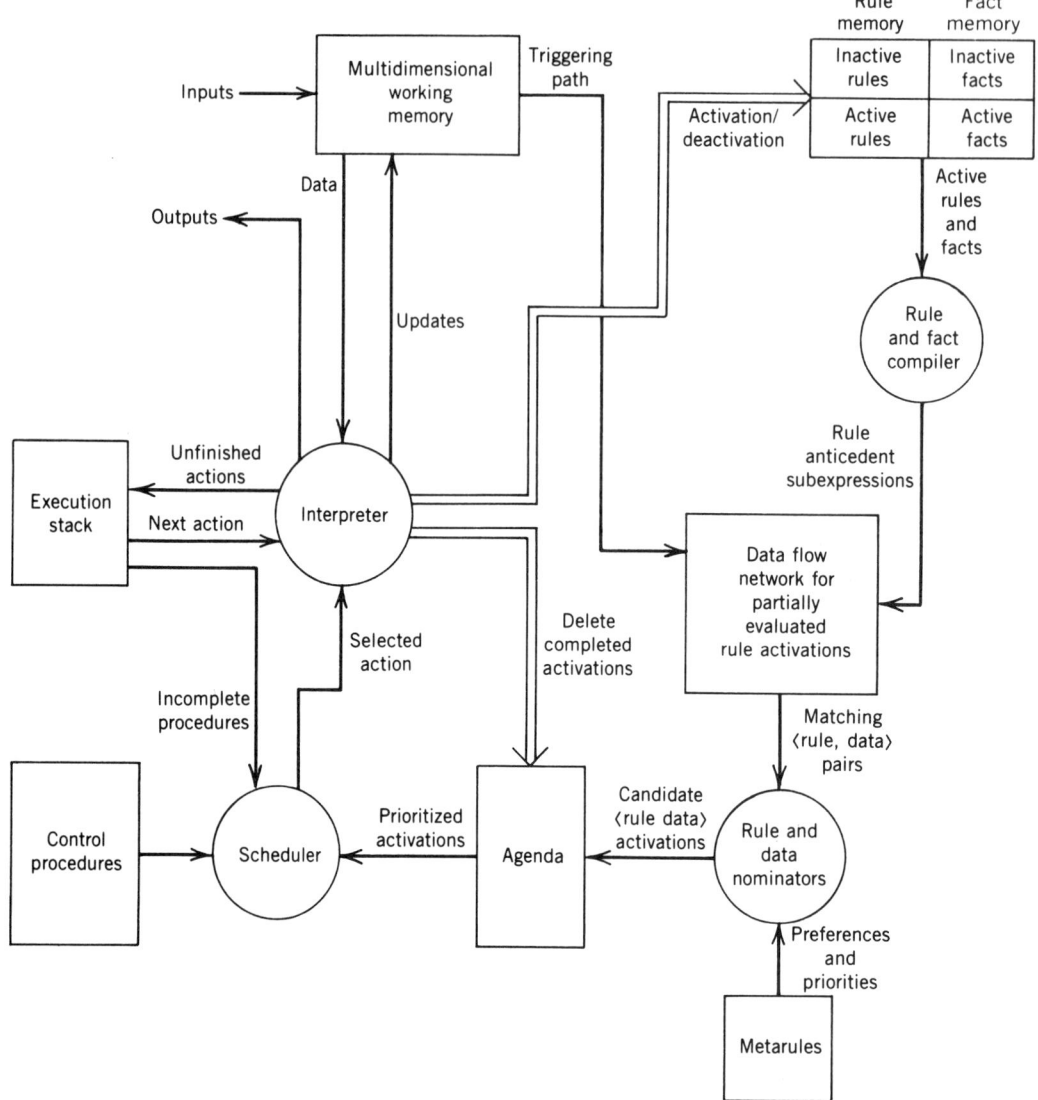

Figure 3. Representative advanced rule-based system.

awaiting execution constitutes the agenda (see AGENDA-BASED SYSTEMS). The process examines the agenda of waiting rules and whatever specialized control procedures the system includes. The scheduler selects for execution next either a new procedure, a procedure continuation, or the action of a high priority rule.

ROLE IN EVOLUTIONARY SYSTEM DEVELOPMENT

RBSs have proved invaluable as a practical means for evolving poorly understood knowledge. Although today's RBSs cannot substitute for the full range of mature DP application-building technology, they offer a unique advantage missing from the conventional toolkit. It should be anticipated that as the technology matures, the essential ingredients of RBSs will migrate into DP technology as a basis for rapid prototyping, improving extensibility, and enhancing software maintenance and support.

RELATIONSHIP TO SEARCH

The focus on knowledge in applied AI systems represents a reaction to the abortive attempts to solve important problems using general-purpose or weak methods. As the importance of knowledge became clear, many AI researchers became knowledge engineers. They emphasized picking high value problems with symbolic solutions, identifying corresponding human experts, and debriefing the experts to find out what they knew.

In many cases the power of expertise corresponded to hints and tricks for obviating work that a less experienced person might need to perform. Often, this meant reducing what would be a big search space for a general problem-solving program to a small search space for a specialized, knowledge-intensive program. So although some RBSs perform search (qv), they generally incorporate a representation of the problem and chunks of the solution that greatly simplify the task. Search is a last resort for problem solvers. Most rule-based systems perform little or no search.

RELATIONSHIP TO PROGRAMMING

As suggested earlier, today's RBS technology requires the rule writer to consider and understand the organization and operation of the target RBS. That means writing rules is a special kind of programming. Like conventional programming, effective rule programming requires mental modeling of state changes, syntactic and semantic checking of rule conditions and execution effects, and heuristic methods to validate and verify the proposed system. In contrast with conventional (procedural) programming, however, rule-based programming requires the author to think more analytically than procedurally. Most programmers have some difficulty with this for a few weeks. Conventional programming requires the programmer first to appreciate the relevant goals and heuristic methods and then to implement a corresponding customized problem-solving program. Rule-based programming, in contrast, requires the programmer first to understand the general method of rule-based problem solving and then to express the current problem description and related heuristic methods in a form consistent with the available knowledge base and inference engine. This requires different skills. Beyond what is normally required, the rule programmer must formulate explicitly the heuristics and problem features. However, the RBS automates nearly everything else required for solving the problem. It should be anticipated that the complimentary strengths of conventional programming and RBS will motivate research efforts to marry the two technologies so that applications can exploit the advantages of both.

CONCEPTUAL EVOLUTION OF RBS

Rule-based systems incorporate many ideas derived from both theory and experience. Figure 4 depicts the evolution of rule-based systems technology resulting from efforts to apply general concepts that originated in the academic disciplines of psychology and computing theory. The discipline of AI does not appear explicitly in the figure because the entire circle depicts a major portion of the field.

The figure portrays the field's evolution in the spiral form of a nautilus, where each new development phase derives from those just prior and rests on previous generations of related developments. Many different paths through the spiral make interesting histories. By following the spiral clockwise, the successive cycles of concurrent activities in the four sectors can be retraced. By traversing a radial spoke outward from the center, the successive changes in concept and *zeitgeist* within a discipline are quickly passed over. Following a ray within the RBS sector, the major developments in RBS technology are retraced.

At the outset Markov rules provided a simple technique for defining stochastic processes via probabilistic rules that mapped any current state into its possible successors. Postproductions showed that machines following simple string-matching condition–action rules could perform all computations. Subsequently, theorem provers emerged that automated deduction. The dual goals of performing human problem-solving tasks and avoiding some gross inefficiencies of general-purpose deduction led to condition–action production–rule systems. These often emphasized low level and detailed activities so they soon gave way to knowledge rules. Knowledge rules embody chunks of expert know-how. After the initial success of knowledge rules for expert systems, many people began developing general-purpose rule-based programming systems. Often a single rule in these systems combined analytical knowledge about the problem domain and control knowledge about ways to achieve problem-solving efficiency. Subsequently these forms were distinguished. Control blocks expressed imperative knowledge in a procedural form, and metarules emerged to represent other forms of knowledge about knowledge in a rule-based format.

The cognate areas have both supported and adapted to the developments in RBS technology. Developments in computing theory have provided a foundation in automata, grammars, theorem proving, relational algebra, applicative programming styles, executable specifications, and distributed control. Developments in psychology have evolved from extremely general and simple views of intelligent functions as in Markov models, EPAM, and GPS to successively more knowledge-intensive and elaborated views of cognition. These later conceptual generations distinguish what is known from how it can be applied, taught, or made more efficient. The primary foci of applications have shifted over time from general-purpose simulation, string processing, and automated deduction to address more pressing, higher value, and knowledge-intensive concerns. Successively, these tasks have reflected needs for heuristic solutions, specialized expert systems for problem solving, autonomous intelligent agents, knowledge systems for storing and distributing in electronic forms large quantities of institutional knowledge, and heuristic systems for adaptive control and other management tasks.

The RBS of today incorporates numerous influences and has engendered many related technology developments. The essence of the RBS derives from the production-system model used in automata theory and psychology. The basic model was the stimulus–response (S–R) association presumed by some to underlie all animal behavior. In a similar manner theorists sometimes have found it convenient to describe all computational behavior in terms of state-transition tables that define rules for moving between states. An early model of perception called PANDEMONIUM (qv) viewed human-signal-interpretation activity in terms of the actions of independent pattern–action modules called demons.

Many researchers have gravitated toward rule-based representations of knowledge for two other reasons. First, rules seem a natural way to express the situation–action heuristics evident in experts' thinking-aloud problem-solving protocols. Second, perhaps more than for any other form of knowledge, researchers have developed learning

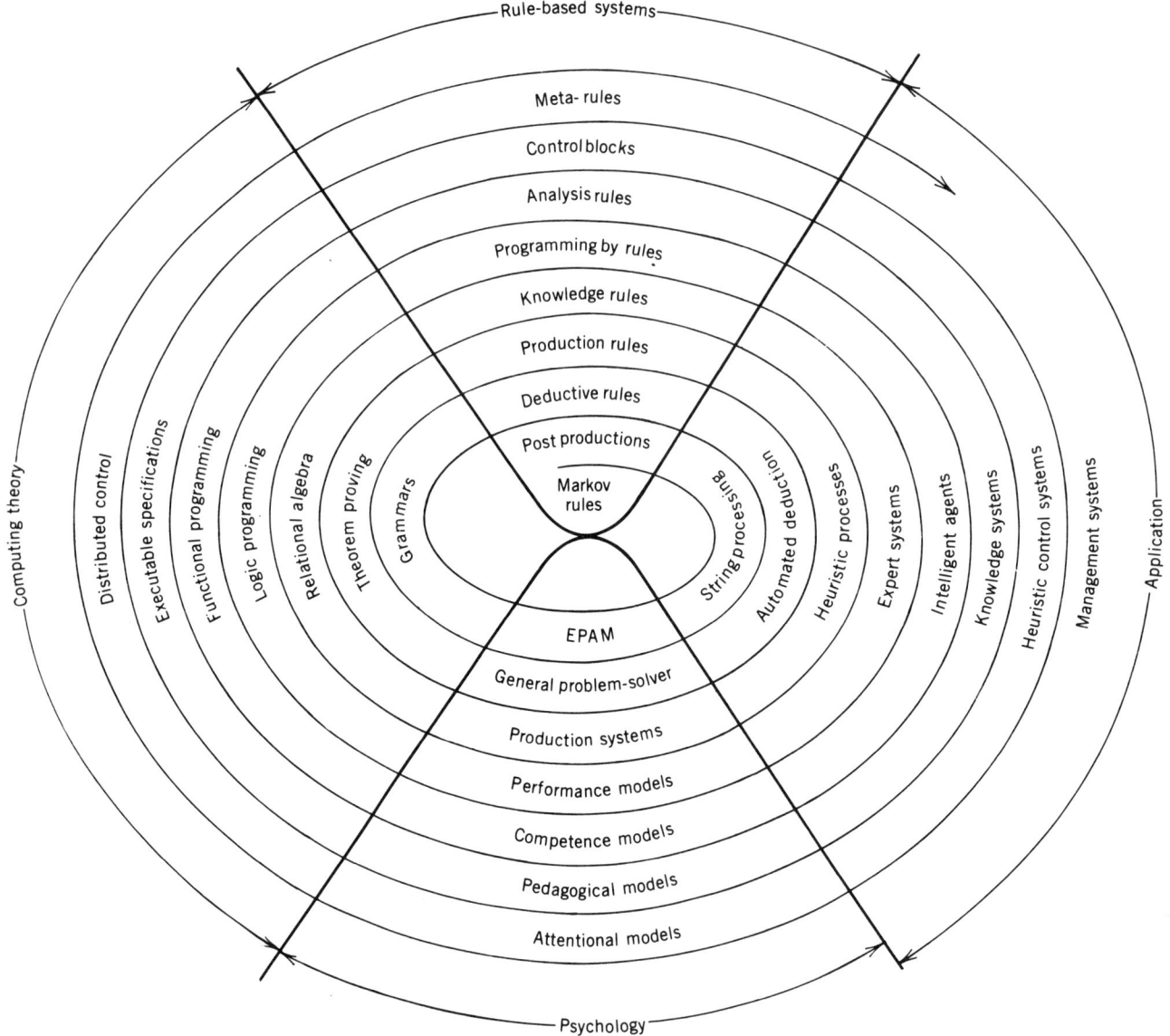

Figure 4. Evolution of rule-based system concepts.

procedures capable of inferring rules from experience. In addition, RBSs often can accept and assimilate a newly learned rule merely by incorporating it into the knowledge base.

Specialized RBS architectures have evolved to address different target applications. Each specialty seems to benefit from slightly different emphases. Today, special formalisms and supporting systems have been developed in each of these areas: rule-based programming systems, rule-based signal-understanding systems, rule-based cognitive simulations; teachable and learnable rule-based systems; systems for learning rules, and systems for building commercial rule-based expert systems.

By now the key ideas of RBSs have infected many other areas of computing. Chief among these are rule-based subsystems for communications architectures; rule formalisms for representing military doctrine, standard policies, and historical precedents; rules for deduction and programming as rule-based controlled deduction; macrorules in the form of pattern-directed modules for distributed architectures and systems of cooperating experts; metarules for heuristic adaptive control of resource-limited systems; and rules as a basis for enforcing constraints. Although many of these new uses are experimental today, many should mature in the years ahead.

TECHNOLOGY EVOLUTION OF RBS

The technology of RBSs has incorporated many ideas from diverse sources. A brief and highly simplified recounting of this development follows. This account focuses on the principal developments in computer science that have most advanced the RBS field.

The story begins with decision tables and compilers. This technology emerged about 20 years ago. It provides a representation of decision logic for transaction processing and report generation. A decision-table entry defines a condition–action rule. Rules execute sequentially on the current input data. The context effects are immediate because there are no working data. The only knowledge-base entries are the rules, which must represent simple Boolean conditions. Large rule tables prove quite complex, the rigid order of rule evaluation often proves unsatisfactory, and an ability to describe complex symbolic patterns and to combine intermediate results dynamically limits the range of applications.

Early AI problem-solving languages such as PLANNER (qv) from MIT, provided means for representing rules within the context of programmable theorem provers. Workers at Carnegie Mellon University were the first to build RBSs with thousands of rules and to develop efficient compilers and translators. One RBS initiated at CMU, called XCON, became the first to earn a multimillion-dollar profit, when it was used to eliminate errors in Digital Equipment Corp. VAX orders. The general rule-based programming system called OPS, used for XCON, has been used for several other RBS applications.

Workers at Stanford developed the MYCIN (qv) family of RBSs. MYCIN was the first to achieve acceptance by experts, perform expert-level subjective reasoning with uncertain data and knowledge, and explain its reasoning in English. A similar system called PROSPECTOR (qv), developed by SRI, automated knowledge of mineral deposits and is retrospectively credited with identifying a major source for at least one mine operation. (It coincidentally identified the mine source with several human prospectors.) Subsequent work on TEIRESIAS and MRS emphasized metarules for expressing explicit knowledge about control.

Systems at Stanford and CMU for reasoning about signal data have evolved to handle larger macrorules called specialists, knowledge sources, or pattern-directed modules. These systems include HEARSAY-II (qv), HASP, AGE, and BB1. These systems often pack a great deal of knowledge into a single module. Each module has a condition and an action, and the overall system behaves like the RBS that have been considered. These systems differ from the more typical RBS by using local memory in its computations. In this regard these systems have much in common with object-oriented architectures (such as Smalltalk or Intel's S-432).

PROLOG was the first general-purpose logic-based programming language. It is an RBS that uses stored facts and rules to deduce solutions to goal patterns. It was designed for theorem proving but has proved attractive for a wider range of AI tasks.

The RITA and ROSIE (qv) systems, developed at Rand, advanced the concept of using RBS methods for conventional programming. These programming systems blend a rule-based representation for programs with flexible I–O. These capabilities make these research languages very attractive for building automated intelligent assistants for computer-based communication tasks.

The programming system M.1, developed at Teknowledge, incorporates techniques for tolerating uncertainty and combining evidence within a general-purpose rule-based programming system that operates on an IBM personal computer. M.1 marries the rule-based programming capabilities of PROLOG, RITA, and ROSIE to the evidence-combining capabilities of MYCIN. This combination, plus the ability to run on personal computers, has made M.1 the most popular tool for building small-to-medium expert systems. Several other vendors offer tools with some of these features.

The expert-system building tool S.1, also developed at Teknowledge, advanced previous RBS technology by differentiating representations for analytic and imperative knowledge. S.1 employs rules for analytic knowledge and procedural control blocks for imperative knowledge. It provides a built-in back-chaining control mechanism with points of escape for user-supplied control blocks. By separating these two forms of knowledge, users create more intelligible knowledge bases that permit much improved automated explanations. The following example illustrates a control block that defines an approach to organizing rule-based reasoning to diagnose a car. It would employ the earlier car diagnose rules shown in Example 3.

Example 3. A control block expressing procedural know-how in a sophisticated RBS. S.1 provides a procedural syntax for expressing imperative knowledge by distinguishing control blocks and rules; the sophisticated RBS enhances intelligibility and produces improved explanations of its lines of reasoning.

High level.problem-solving.approach.

In order to diagnose and repair a car, follow this procedure:

C is a car.

Display the following.

Welcome to the car-charging diagnosis and repair advisor.

Find out about a car called C.

Determine the initial symptoms of the car C.

Determine the cause of the problem with the car C.

Determine the recommendations for fixing the problem with the car C.

Show the recommendations to fix the problem with the car C.

IMPLEMENTATION AND AVAILABILITY

A partial list of supported tools available for building RBSs appears in Table 3. Current efforts in RBS-related research and development, within, the DOD-sponsored Strategic Computing Initiative focus on the following ob-

Table 3. A Representative Set of RBS Software Products

Product	Host	Vendor
M.1	IBM PC compatibles	Cimflex Teknowledge
PC Expert	IBM PC compatibles	Texas Instruments
OPS	DEC VAX	Digital Equipment Corp.
ART	LISP machines	Inferences
ROSIE	Sun workstations	Rand
Copernicus	Tandem	Cimflex Teknowledge

jectives: increase the size of practical rule bases to 10,000 rules or more, increase the speed by two orders of magnitude or more, broaden the set of inference techniques used by the interpreters, improve the methods for reasoning with uncertainty, simplify the requirements for creating and extending knowledge bases, and exploit parallel computing in RBS execution.

ASSESSMENT: REPUTATION VS REALITY

Because RBSs have played an important role in demonstrating the importance and practicality of knowledge systems, they have received much attention. The reputation of the RBS should now be clarified. The RBS is not a panacea either for DP or AI problems. It represents a technology of broad and important applicability. RBSs differ from conventional programs in several important ways. Compared to many of the techniques of conventional data processing, the younger RBS technology possesses distinct advantages that will advance and improve for years to come.

RBSs have attracted attention because they have important strengths:

- RBSs address a largely unmet area of opportunity by representing problem-solving know-how in a manner suitable for application by computers.
- RBSs modularize chunks of knowledge.
- RBSs support incremental development.
- RBSs make decision making more intelligible and explainable.
- Specialized RBS architectures have emerged that constrain and simplify application methods.
- Recent advances in RBS technology distinguish imperative and analytic know-how but integrate both to produce more effective, cogent, and maintainable knowledge bases.
- Rule-based reasoning can provide a conceptual basis for the analytic formulation of imperative know-how.
- RBSs provide a fertile framework for conceptualizing computation in general.
- RBSs open new opportunities by providing a non–von Neumann schema for computing systems that can exploit parallelism.

However, RBSs lack several qualities that would make them more suitable as a general computing approach. What are lacking are a precise analytic foundation for the problems solvable by RBSs, a suitable verification methodology or a technique to test the consistency and completeness of a rule set, a theory of knowledge organization that would enable RBSs to be scaled up without loss of intelligibility or performance, high grade rule compilers and specialized hardware accelerators, and methods for integrating RBSs easily and seamlessly with conventional DP systems.

The near-term research objectives in RBS technology include integration of RBSs with conventional software systems, modularization and reuse of RBS components, and sharability of RBS knowledge bases among several related applications. Beyond these near-term objectives, long-range goals in RBS research focus on improved hardware for RBS storage and execution tasks, improved standard software and algorithms for common RBS functions, improved architectures that use metaknowledge efficiently, automatic translation of diverse forms of knowledge into rule form, and optimizing compilers for RBSs that perform global data-flow optimizations and exploit multiprocessor opportunities.

BIBLIOGRAPHY

General References

The suggested readings span a range from introductory to state of the art. Brownston and co-workers (1985) extensively review techniques for using OPS5 (qv), a relatively simple but mature rule-based programming system. The Duda and Gaschnig (1981) article is a readable, simple introduction. Erman and co-workers (1984) describe the motivations behind S.1 and the techniques used to distinguish analytical rules from imperative prescriptions. *Building Expert Systems* (Hayes-Roth and co-workers, 1983) surveys a variety of issues in representing and implementing know-how, including but not limited to RBSs. Shortliffe (1976) describes one of the seminal projects in RBS technology. Waterman and Hayes-Roth's book (1978) surveys the field of RBSs and the closely related but more general pattern-directed inference systems.

L. Brownston, R. Farrell, E. Kant, and N. Martin, *Programming Expert Systems in OPS5*, Addison-Wesley Publishing Co., Inc., Reading, Mass., 1985.

R. O. Duda and J. G. Gaschnig, "Knowledge-Based Expert Systems Coming of Age," *Byte* **6**(9), 238–278 (1981).

L. E. Erman, A. C. Scott, and P. E. London, "Separating and Integrating Control in a Rule-Based Tool," in *Proceedings of the IEEE Workshop on Principles of Knowledge-Based Systems,* Denver, Colo., 1984.

F. Hayes-Roth, D. A. Waterman, and D. B. Lenat, *Building Expert Systems*, Addison-Wesley Publishing Co., Inc., Reading, Mass., 1983.

F. Hayes-Roth, "Rule-Based Systems," *CACM* **28**, 921–932 (Sept. 1985).

E. H. Shortliffe, *Computer Based Medical Consultations: MYCIN*, Elsevier Science Publishing Co., Inc., New York, 1976.

D. A. Waterman, and F. Hayes-Roth, *Pattern-Directed Inference Systems*, Academic Press, Inc., New York, 1978.

F. HAYES-ROTH
Cimflex Teknowledge Corp.

S

SAINT

SAINT is a symbolic automatic integrator written by Slagle in 1961 at MIT using the technique of heuristic search in an AND/OR graph (qv) of goals [see J. Slagle, *A Heuristic Program that Solves Symbolic Integration Problems in Freshman Calculus: Symbolic Automatic Integrator (SAINT)*, Report No. 5G-0001, Lincoln Laboratory, MIT, Cambridge, Mass., 1961, and J. Slagle, "A Heuristic Program that Solves Symbolic Integration Problems in Freshman Calculus," *JACM* **10**, 507–520 (1963)].

A. Hanyong Yuhan
AT&T Bell Laboratories

SAM

A script-based (see Scripts) story understander, SAM was written at Yale in 1978 by a team headed by Cullingford. SAM used scripts descriptive of stereotyped activities such as are seen, for example, in many kinds of newspaper stories to form a knowledge structure representing adult-level understanding. It demonstrated that understanding by answering questions about the story, summarizing or paraphrasing it, and generating its responses in several natural languages. SAM constitutes the earliest complete knowledge-based story understander. [See Lehnert, *The Process of Question Answering*, Lawrence Erlbaum, Hillsdale, N.J., 1978; J. G. Carbonell, R. E. Cullingford, and A. V. Gershman, "Steps Toward Knowledge-Based Machine Translation," *IEEE Trans. Patt. Anal. Mach. Intell.* **PAMI-3**(4), 376–392 (July 1978); R. E. Cullingford, "SAM," in R. C. Schank and C. K. Riesbeck, eds., *Inside Computer Understanding*, Erlbaum, Hillsdale, N.J. (1981).]

R. E. Cullingford
Intelligent Business Systems

SCHEMA THEORY

Schema theory provides a way to tame the complexity of very large systems that are to function in the real world, offering an approach to knowledge representation that is explicitly designed to contribute to distributed artificial intelligence (DAI), as well as to serve as a bridge between cognitive science and brain theory (BT). Speaking loosely, a schema is an active modular entity, involving data structures and (goal- or task-oriented) control in each entity. More rigorously, the schema itself is the description of this integration of data and control, and it is instances of the schema that give this integration its active, dynamic expression. In characterizing schemas below, items 1 through 6 list those defining properties that are shared by schemas whether or not their relation to the brain is under discussion, whereas items 7 through 9 distinguish the characteristics of schemas used as part of an artificial system from those used to define a brain model, where schemas for a given behavior must pass the extra test of being mappable onto neural circuitry.

1. Where conventional computers store data passively, to be retrieved and processed by some central processing unit, schema theory explains behavior in terms of the interaction of many concurrent activities for recognition of different objects, and the planning and control of different activities. Schemas are ultimately defined by the execution of tasks within a physical environment rather than (as in most AI systems) by a closed network of cross-references in some logical formalism. Schema theory sees behavior as based not on inferences from axioms, but rather as the result of competition and cooperation between schema instances that, due to the limitations of experience, cannot constitute a completely consistent axiom-based logical system.

2. A schema is both a store of knowledge and the description of a process for applying that knowledge. As such, a schema may be instantiated to form multiple schema instances as active copies of the process to apply that knowledge. For example, given a schema that represents generic knowledge about some object, several active instances of the schema, each suitably tuned to subserve the perception of a different instance of that object, may be needed. Schemas are thus modular entities whose instances can become activated in response to certain patterns of input from sensory stimuli or other schema instances that are already active.

3. Schema theory provides a distributed model of computation, supporting many concurrent activities for recognition of objects and the planning and control of different activities. The use, representation, and recall of knowledge is mediated through the activity of a network of interacting computing agents, the *schema instances,* which between them provide processes for going from a particular situation and a particular structure of goals and tasks to a suitable course of action (which may be overt or covert, as when learning occurs without action or the animal changes its state of readiness). This activity may involve passing of messages, changes of state (including activity level), instantiation to add new schema instances to the network, and deinstantiation to remove instances. Moreover (as in 6, below), such activity may involve self-modification and self-organization.

4. Schema theory provides *inter alia* a language for the study of action-oriented perception (Arbib, 1972; Neisser, 1976). A set of *basic motor schemas* is hypothesized to provide simple, prototypical patterns of movement. These combine with *perceptual schemas* to form *coordinated control programs* which interweave their activations in accordance with the current task and sensory environment to

mediate more complex behaviors. Thus motor schemas in general may be either basic or built up from other schemas as coordinated control programs. Schema activations are largely task driven, reflecting the goals of the animal and the physical and functional requirements of the task. Schema theory can also express models of language and other cognitive functions. There is a tendency (although not a necessity) to root such models in action and perception.

5. The *activity level* of an instance of a perceptual schema represents a confidence level that the object represented by the schema is indeed present; whereas that of a motor schema may signal its degree of readiness to control some course of action. A schema network does not, in general, need a top-level executor because schema instances can combine their effects by distributed processes of competition and cooperation (ie, interactions that, respectively, decrease and increase the activity levels of these instances), rather than the operation of an inference engine on a passive store of knowledge. This may lead to apparently emergent behavior, due to the absence of global control.

The activity level of a schema may be but one of many parameters that characterize it. Thus a schema for *ball* might include parameters for its size, color, and velocity. (If a schema is implemented as a neural network then all the schema parameters could be implemented via patterns of neural activity. It is thus important to distinguish activity level as a particular parameter of a schema from the neural activity that will vary with different neural implementations of the schema.)

6. Schema theory is a learning theory too. In a general setting, there is no fixed repertoire of basic schemas. Rather, new schemas may be formed as assemblages of old schemas; but once formed a schema may be tuned by some adaptive mechanism. This tunability of schema-assemblages allows them to start as composite but emerge as primitive, much as a skill is honed into a unified whole from constituent pieces. [For this reason, a model expressed in a schema-level formalism may only approximate the behavior of a model expressed in a neural net formalism (cf the discussion of program synthesis and visuomotor coordination in Arbib, 1981a). When used in conjunction with neural networks, schema theory provides a means of providing a functional–structural decomposition and is to be contrasted with models that employ some learning rule to train an otherwise undifferentiated network to respond as specified by some training set.]

The key question for analyzing the brain, with its many different regions active at the same time, is also crucial to the design of large, complex systems, namely to understand how local interactions can integrate themselves to yield some overall result without explicit executive control. This represents a change from the domain of serial computation to a concern with complex functions distributed over a set of cooperating modules. Schema theory seeks to develop this paradigm, with schemas as the programs, and *cooperative computation* (a shorthand for computation based on the competition and cooperation of concurrently active agents) as their style of interaction.

Cooperation yields a pattern of strengthened alliances between mutually consistent schema instances that allows them to achieve high activity levels to constitute the overall solution of a problem (as perceptual schemas become part of the current short-term model of the environment or motor schemas contribute to the current course of action). It is as a result of competition that instances that do not meet the evolving (data-guided) consensus lose activity, and thus are not part of this solution (although their continuing subthreshold activity may well affect later behavior). The following sections will provide a number of examples. The section on the RS approach offers a message passing formalism that can (but need not) involve activity levels, and that on schema modulation and evolution shows how schemas may modulate one another to compensate for the incompleteness of information available to each one. It will be shown how motor schemas may cooperate by summing their effects on the motor apparatus, while a discussion of schemas and vision demonstrates both the competition between schema instances offering discordant interpretations of a region of an image and the cooperation between instances of perceptual schemas that provide contextual cues for one another.

Note that in (1) through (6), apart from parenthetical remarks, the words "brain" and "neural" do not appear. Neural schema theory may thus be regarded as a specialized branch of schema theory, just as neuropsychology is a specialized branch of psychology. An analogy might be that just as thermodynamics is a freestanding branch of physics but statistical mechanics relates it to the more microscopic dynamics of atoms and molecules, so is schema theory a freestanding branch of AI but brain theory relates it to the more microscopic dynamics of neurons and neural networks. In points 7 to 9 just what makes a schema-theoretic model part of brain theory or distributed artificial intelligence will be discussed. But first it is worth stressing that a schema is, as the name suggests, schematic. Initially, in the development of a model of some intelligent behavior, it may be very schematic indeed, but, as more knowledge is gained, the description can be refined. It is possible to go from simply specifying how the schema responds to a single sensory stimulus to specifying how the schema responds to a spatial pattern on a sensory array. It is then the disposition of activity in an array that constitutes the inputs or outputs of the various schemas that can be related by some overall specification, which may then be further refined as the system is implemented, as it adapts, or as its range of applicability is extended.

7. In BT, a given schema, defined functionally, may be distributed across more than one brain region; conversely, a given brain region may be involved in many schemas. A top-down analysis may advance specific hypotheses about the localization of (sub)schemas in the brain, and these may be tested by lesion experiments, with possible modification of the model (eg, replacing one schema by several interacting schemas with different localizations) and further testing. In DAI, schema instances must be allocated to a limited set of processors, thus raising issues of (distributed) scheduling.

8. A given schema may have many different implementations, either biologically or technologically. In BT, once a schema-theoretic model of some animal behavior has been refined to the point of hypotheses about the localization of schemas, it is possible then to model a brain region by seeing if its known neural circuitry can indeed be shown to implement the posited schema. In some cases the model will involve properties of the circuitry that have not yet been tested, thus laying the ground for new experiments. A neuron may participate in the implementation of multiple schemas. For example, in the toad brain it has been found that certain neurons whose activity correlates with that of the perceptual schema for predators will also, via an inhibitory pathway, contribute to the perceptual schema for prey. In DAI, individual schemas may be implemented by artificial neural networks, or in some programming language on a standard (possibly distributed) computer. In the former case, the development of schema theory for DAI is much influenced by BT; in the latter case, schema theory converges with work on concurrent object-oriented programming (Yonezawa, 1990).

9. For BT, the analysis of interacting computing agents called schema instances is intermediate between the overall specification of some behavior and the neural networks that subserve it. For DAI, schemas provide a form of knowledge representation that differs from frames and scripts by being of a finer granularity. A schema is more like a molecule than an atom in that schemas may well be linked to others to provide yet more comprehensive schemas. As the name *frame* suggests, frames tend to build in from the overall framework, whereas schema theory is more generative. Rather than represent a birthday party by a single frame or script with specific slots to be filled in, schema theory would form such a representation as an assemblage of schemas for salient objects and actions.

This article proceeds as follows: a brief history of the idea of a schema is offered, and schema theory is compared with other approaches to AI. A formalism that uses port automata to model particular schemas is offered, with pointers to how it may be extended for those cases in which schemas are to be implemented by neural networks. It is shown that a complete schema system need not be formally programmed but may be evolved as new schemas are added to modulate, and extend the utility of, existing schema networks. A comparison with connectionism is noted, followed by a very brief view of how schema theory leads the cognitive scientist to view memory, perception, and action.

Although the bulk of this article presents schema theory in a form suitable for AI and cognitive science in their (nonneural) generality, a number of models that relate schemas for visuomotor coordination to data on their localization in the brains of frog and toads are reviewed. Then it is shown how one such model has inspired a novel approach to reactive planning in the control of a mobile robot. A conceptual analysis of the role of schema assemblages in representing a visual scene is offered and a particular computer implementation that uses schemas for scene interpretation is presented. These two sections between them serve as background for a brief discussion of explicit versus implicit planning. Finally, a discussion of distributed mechanisms of schema change is presented, illustrating this theme with a model of language acquisition that demonstrates how schema theory, rooted in the study of action and perception, may be extended to handle higher mental functions.

HISTORY AND COMPARISONS

The twentieth-century history of schemas starts with the work of Head and Holmes (1911) who localized a body schema in the parietal lobe to explain why a person with damage to that brain lobe on one side might lose awareness that the body on the opposite side actually belonged to her. Bartlett (1932), who had been a student of Head, carried this idea of the schema into the realm of psychology. He found that when people try to recall a story they have heard, they reconstitute the story in their own terms, relating what they experience to a familiar set of schemas, rather than by rote memorization of arbitrary details. Instead of thinking of ideas as impressions of sense data, schema theory posits an active and selective process of schema formation that in some sense constructs reality as much as it embodies it. Craik (1943) furthered these ideas with his observation that the brain creates a model of the world, forming expectations on which actions could be based adaptively.

Although this British tradition was quite separate from the Continental tradition, resonances here with Piaget's use of schemas (Piaget, 1971; Beth and Piaget, 1966) in his study of cognitive development in terms of assimilation (making sense of the situation in terms of the available stock of schemas) and accommodation (developing new schemas to the extent that mismatches arise) can be seen. This provides a point of contact between schema theory and that part of neural networks research that centers on the learning rules that allow a network of neurons to adapt itself automatically to conform to some specification of its input–output behavior. Because behaviors are in general subserved by networks of schemas rather than a single network of neurons, a coarse-grain analysis of how a network of schemas may come to subserve the overall behavior (the study of AI learning, as modified to conform with a schema architecture) must be offered to complement a fine-grain analysis of how a particular schema can change (whether or not this is done using adaptive neural networks).

Schema theory provides a knowledge representation protocol that is related to frames (Minsky, 1975) and scripts (Schank and Abelson, 1977), but is distinguished by the criteria listed in the introduction. In particular, schema theory has a grain size smaller than frames and scripts, but larger than neural models (but see below). In its emphasis on the interaction of active computing agents (the schema instances), schema theory is related to studies in distributed artificial intelligence rooted in work on actors (Hewitt, 1977), the HEARSAY speech understanding system (Erman and co-workers, 1980), and distributed problem solving (Davis and Smith, 1983). Because each schema combines knowledge with the processes for using it, schemas are more like actors than like frames or systems with unitary blackboards.

As a point of comparison, consider the original form of the HEARSAY (qv) system for speech understanding, where various hypotheses generated as the interpretation of the input proceeds are placed on a single data structure called the blackboard. The blackboard has various levels to hold the hypotheses, starting from the raw spectrogram, to the phonemic level, the lexical level (the word level) and the phrasal level (binding words together into phrases with some specified grammatical and semantic structure). Each hypothesis represents the spoken input during a specific time interval, and for any time interval there may be more than one hypothesis in a level. Each hypothesis is linked to the other hypotheses that support it, and each hypothesis has a confidence level associated with it, giving a rough measure of how strong the support had so far been shown to be. Computing agents called knowledge sources act on hypotheses at one level to try to come up with a hypothesis at another level. Knowledge sources in HEARSAY include the lexicon, various processes embodying grammatical knowledge, and so on. The lexicon is like a dictionary, so that the knowledge of an individual word would have much finer granularity, more like that of schemas. Knowledge sources were brought in one at a time by a serial scheduler in HEARSAY. By contrast, schemas describe units in a network of active processes communicating with each other. Nonetheless, it is possible to use distributed blackboards in implementing schemas (see below).

Working within the perspective of schema theory, Arbib (1989a) offers an account of action and perception, Arbib and Hesse (1986) developed philosophical analyses linking the schemas of the individual to the social construction of reality (including an account of consciousness and free will), and Arbib and co-workers (1987) study language perception, acquisition, and generation. Moreover, much work in BT and AI contributes to schema theory, even though the scientists involved do not use this term. For example, Minsky (1985), in a theory that seems to subsume rather than replace his frame theory of 1977, espouses a society-of-mind analogy in which members of society, the agents, are analogous to schemas. Brooks (1986) controls robots with layers made up of asynchronous modules that can be considered as a version of schemas. This work shares with schema theory, with its mediation of action through a network of schemas, the point that no single, central, logical representation of the world need link perception and action (Arbib, 1972), while sharing with Walter (1953) and Braitenberg (1965, 1984) the study of the evolution of simple creatures with increasingly sophisticated sensorimotor capacities.

There is no consensus view as to what constitutes schema theory. The schema theory presented here owes much to the work of McCulloch. McCulloch and Pitts's (1943) formal theory of neural networks laid the basis for automata theory and, via such papers as those in Shannon and McCarthy (1956), artificial intelligence. Pitts and McCulloch (1947) gave a study of neural networks for pattern recognition that showed how visual input could control motor output via the distributed activity of a layered neural network without the intervention of executive control, perhaps the earliest example of cooperative computation. Kilmer and co-workers (1969) foreshadowed the schema level of analysis by showing how to analyze activity in a brain region that could set the organism's overall mode of behavior through the cooperative computation (again, no executive control) of modules that aggregate the activity of many neurons. Arbib and Didday (1971) developed the slide-box metaphor for visual perception and started the work on *Rana computatrix* (Arbib, 1989b), which models data on visuomotor coordination in the frog and toad to study the integration of action and perception in distributed systems in such a way as to contribute both to brain theory and perceptual robotics. This, plus the work of Bernstein (1967) on synergies as units of motor control, led to the analysis of visual perception and motor control in terms of slides and output feature clusters (Arbib, 1972), which was then refined and renamed perceptual schemas and motor schemas, respectively (Arbib, 1975, 1981a).

THE RS APPROACH

There is no formalism that captures all aspects of current and future work in schema theory (any more than Turing machines provide a good formal model of Pascal-like programs, let alone recursive or concurrent object-oriented programs). Nonetheless, it may be useful to outline one formal approach to schemas that embodies many of the criteria listed above for schemas for DAI. The Robot Schema language (RS) (Lyons and Arbib, 1989) is a language designed to facilitate sensory-based task-level robot programming. Computation is performed in a distributed manner by the interaction of a number of concurrent computing agents, known as schema instances. A schema constitutes the long-term memory of a perceptual or motor skill or the structure coordinating such skills, whereas the process of perception or action is controlled by active copies of schemas, called *schema instances*. For certain behaviors, there may be no distinction between schema and instance, a single neural network may embody the skill memory and provide the processor that implements it. However, in more complex behaviors, the different mobilizations of a given skill-unit must be carefully distinguished.

In the RS formalism, each schema instance (SI) has a set of input and output ports through which it can communicate with other schema instances. The behavioral description of a schema defines how an instance of that schema will behave in response to communication. An assemblage is a network of schema instances, and its characteristics are similar to that of a single schema. Instantiation and deinstantiation operations capture the notion that, as action and perception progress, certain schema instances need no longer be active (they are deinstantiated), while new ones are added as new objects are perceived and new plans of action are elaborated (schemas are instantiated as new schema instances). Two more points in preparation for what follows: a schema assemblage formed as a network of schema instances may itself be considered a schema for further processes of assemblage formation and the schema instance network will, in general, be dynamic, growing and shrinking as various instantiations and deinstantiations occur. In RS, then, a schema may be either a basic schema or a schema assemblage.

The RS syntax of a basic schema definition is [N (ip) (op) (v) (b)] where:

N is the identifying name for the schema,
ip is the list of input port names,
op is the list of output port names,
v is the list of internal variable names, and
b is a specification of behavior.

The behavior specification makes explicit how an instance of the schema will read inputs, write outputs, change internal state, and execute (de)instantiations. In RS, it is a sequence of statements forming a C-like program augmented by instantiation and deinstantiation operations and "Forall" statements. The C-like program comprises assignments that either evaluate an expression based on internal variables or values read in on input ports to update an internal variable or evaluates such an expression to write a value to an output port. It also contains conventional conditional statements to link the assignments via appropriate tests. *Instantiation* creates and names a new instance of a schema and couples certain input ports of the instance to output ports of the schema instance calling for the instantiation and vice versa. *Deinstantiation* removes the specified schema instance from the schema instance network.

The above definition establishes a basic schema in terms of an explicitly programmed behavior specification. Schemas may also be formed hierarchically, forming instances of given schemas into a new assemblage. A schema assemblage may itself be considered a schema for further processes of assemblage formation; and the network itself will be dynamic, growing and shrinking as various instantiations and deinstantiations occur. Like a basic schema, an assemblage also has communication ports, but its behavior is defined through the interactions of a network of schema instances. An assemblage, then, is a schema whose behavior is defined in terms of a network of communicating schema instances. The syntax of an assemblage definition is [N (ip) (op)(v) (s)(ib)(p)(n)] where

N is the identifying name for the assemblage
ip is the list of input port names
op is the list of output port names
v is the list of internal variable names
s is a list of component schemas
ib lists the commands to form instances
p renames the ports of the component schema instances as ports of the assemblage
n defines the port connection mappings between component schema instances

Because several copies of a given schema in the list s may be used in defining the network that constitutes N, ib is required to provide distinct names for these instances. p names the ports used in communication with the assemblage, names that may differ from their original names in the constituent schemas (this is especially important when distinguishing corresponding ports from different instances of a given schema). Finally, n specifies how the output port of one instance must be connected to an input port of another in forming N.

The RS syntax for an assemblage does not depend on how the behavior specification is given, whether directly as in a basic schema, or indirectly, as when the schemas constituting an assemblage are themselves schema assemblages. It is thus simple, where appropriate, to extend RS to include neural net specifications by making it possible, in the basic schemas, to define the behavior directly in terms of a neural network as well as by a C-like program.

Detail Hiding: Toward More Schematic Schemas. In the RS approach to schemas, each schema is completely specified as a basic schema or an explicit assemblage. A major shortcoming with this approach is that, in RS, each schema is concrete. RS uses port automata to provide the semantics of schemas. Each RS schema is either a basic schema represented by a particular port automaton, or it is an assemblage (of assemblages of assemblages . . .) whose semantics is again given by a specific port automaton. However, the intent of schema theory in general is to use schema assemblages to hide their details when they are unnecessary. The idea of detail hiding is also important for specification and programming of software systems and has led to the concept of abstract data types and modules. The theory of programming modules (Ehrig and Mahr, 1990) encapsulates the body of a composite module by offering a restricted export interface (the data and operations that are not hidden by the encapsulation, these are *not* analogous to the output ports of a schema), and specifies each module at an abstract level independent of concrete realization. There are several mechanisms for interconnecting module specifications to yield module specifications on a higher level, and each module specification also has a designated import interface (analogous to the set of schemas used to build a schema assemblage, not to the input ports of a schema). Ehrig and Mahr show how the semantics and correctness of a composite module specification can be obtained from that of the basic units. Arbib and Ehrig (1990) have started to show how to move schema theory in this direction by distinguishing a schema as a pattern of behavior from the concrete network that yields that behavior. In a somewhat different direction, Lyons (1990) has introduced a new set of composition operations to provide a richer language for forming schema networks and has added some formal structure to aid reasoning about the behavior of networks so formed.

SCHEMA MODULATION AND EVOLUTION

The cooperative computation of schemas makes possible an evolutionary design process, in which schemas that perform a task fairly well can be modulated by new schemas to perform the task even better (Arbib 1981b). This is illustrated with the evolution of the MATCH algorithm (Prager and Arbib 1983), which uses two cues to update estimates of optic flow between two frames (in the sense of successive images in a movie). One cue is the smoothness condition, betting that nearby features are on the same surface and thus move similar amounts. The other is the stimulus matching criterion that tries to pair a feature in Frame 1 with a similar feature in Frame 2. In one iteration of the MATCH algorithm, the current estimate of the optic flow (the posited displacement in Frame 2 of a Frame 1 feature) is a weighted combination of two: one estimate formed by feature matching, adjusting the optic flow estimate for a Frame 1 feature, A say, to the Frame 2 feature nearest to B (the current estimate of A's Frame 2 position); and the other estimate formed by local smoothness, which seeks to align A's estimate with that of its neighbors (Fig. 1a).

The feature matching update will work well if the real world feature is visible in both frames, but if the feature either becomes occluded or disoccluded in the change of viewpoint from Frame 1 to Frame 2 then a correct feature match will not be possible. Similarly, the local smoothness update is successful when the neighbors of a particular feature lie on the same surface, but this neighborhood constraint will be inappropriate if the neighbors lie on opposite sides of an edge separating two distinct objects. However, these problems provide an evolutionary opportunity to create an edge finding schema (2 in Fig. 1b), and if it can be estimated where the edges are, MATCH can be made to work better, dynamically changing the neighborhood of each point (3 in Fig. 1b) so that the matching of features or the conformity with neighboring flow can be based more on features on the same side of the currently hypothesized boundary than on features that appear to be separated. Such evolution of the algorithm yields markedly improved performances, for instead of blurring the optic flow near an edge, it allows both the confident estimation of the position of edges and the sharpening of the estimate of optic flow for points that appear to lie on the same object. The evolutionarily more primitive system provides the basis for the evolution of higher level systems, the cooperative edge-finding algorithms. But these new systems then provide an environment in which return pathways can evolve that enable the lower level system to evolve in turn into a more effective form, by the introduction of segmentation-dependent neighborhoods, yielding adaptive behavior in a wider set of circumstances.

This model also gives insight into how the brain evolves, not just by adding more and more new schemas but also by adapting older systems to take advantage of the new information environment in the brain. The evolution of new circuitry enlarges the information environment for the earlier circuitry, which may then evolve in turn to exploit these new patterns. There is no longer a simple one-way flow of information, but rather a dynamic equilibrium of multiple systems continually adjusting to significant changes in the world. Evolution not only yields new brain regions connected to the old, but yields reciprocal connections that modify those older regions. This observation is reminiscent of the subsumption architecture

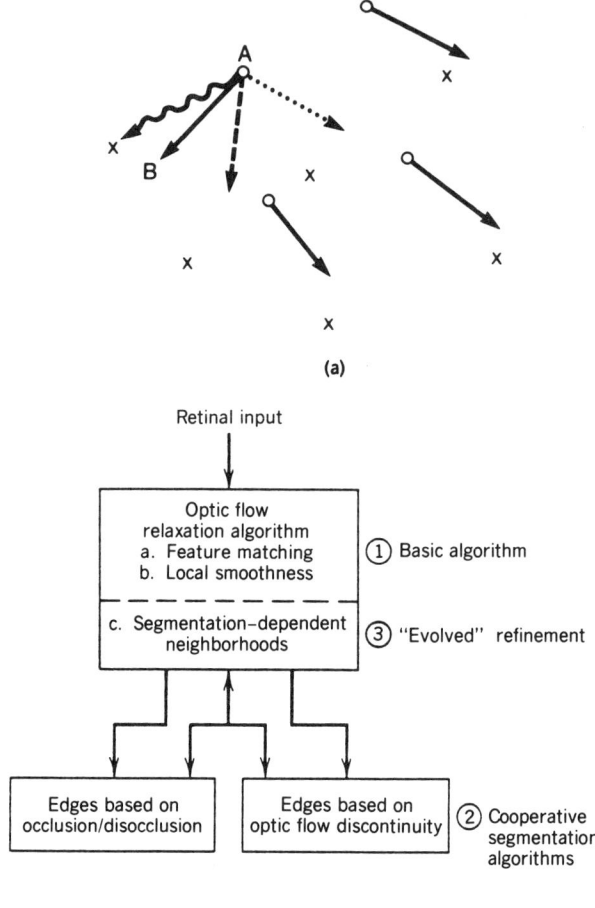

Figure 1. (a) One iteration of the MATCH algorithm. The solid arrows show the current estimate of the optic flow; the head of the arrow shows the posited displacement in Frame 2 of the Frame 1 feature at the tail of the arrow. Feature matching alone would adjust A's optic flow to the wavy arrow pointing to the Frame 2 feature nearest to B (the current estimate of A's Frame 2 position); local smoothness would yield the dotted arrow, the average of the optic flow of the neighbors, and the MATCH relaxation algorithm yields the dashed arrow as a weighted combination of these two estimates. (b) The basic optic flow algorithm **1** uses the consistency conditions of feature matching and local smoothness. The resultant optic flow estimates permits the hypothetization of edges on cues based on both occlusion/disocclusion and an optic flow discontinuity **2**. The resultant edge hypotheses can then be used to refine the computation of optic flow **3** by dynamically adjusting the neighborhoods used in employing the consistency conditions (Arbib, 1981b).

of Brooks (1986), in which a control system is structured in layers, with layers 0 through $n - 1$ providing a limited functionality that is extended and refined by adding a new layer n, which can provide inhibitory and suppressive control of the lower levels. However, Brooks makes an assumption that was rejected in the above example, namely that lower levels are unmodified (except for this suppression and inhibition) in the process of subsumption. In other terms, schema theory lends itself to heterarchical structures in which the flow of control may be multidirectional rather than hierarchical. Minsky (1985) provides many examples of such patterns when he shows how a multiplicity of agents (≈ schemas) interact. For example,

> To start to see how minds are like societies, try this: pick up a cup of tea! Your grasping agents want to keep hold of the cup; your balancing agents want to keep the tea from spilling out; your thirst agents want you to drink the tea; your moving agents want to get the cup to your lips. Yet none of these consume your mind as you roam about the room talking to your friends. You scarcely think at all about Balance; Balance has no concern with Grasp; Grasp has no interest in Thirst; and Thirst is not involved with your social problems. Why not? Because they can depend on one another. If each does its own little job, the really big job will get done by all of them together: drinking tea.

This style of coarse-grained cooperative computation is far removed from serial computation and the symbol-based ideas that have dominated conventional AI. The representation of the world is the pattern of relationships between all its partial representations. There is no executive center. Rather, the brain (or a DAI system designed according to schema theory) has different subsystems whose states constitute a distributed representation of the world, and this representation mediates the competition and cooperation whereby the subsystems find the appropriate pattern of interaction with the world.

A COMPARISON WITH CONNECTIONISM

In connectionism, each node (artificial neuron), has an activity level, and problems are solved by processes of competition and cooperation based on spreading activation and inhibition (cf CONNECTIONISM; NEURAL NETWORKS; the subsection on schema assemblages below). However, in a connectionist network, the units are small, each doing a small part of the computation in parallel, and communicating via activation levels. The nodes have no internal structure, just a single scalar state that either equals or (eg, via a sigmoid function) determines the activity level. By contrast (as the assemblage construct, or the previous evolutionary example makes clear), a schema may be a highly structured object with a subtle internal dynamics. Thus a node in a connectionist network can only bear a representation in terms of the way in which its activity rises or falls as a function of network inputs, whereas the state of a schema instance can indeed carry a (partial) representation of articulated structures and relationships. Similarly, schema instances can interact by passing structured messages in addition to the activity levels that are the primary medium of their distributed control.

Many studies in AI now advocate hybrid system architectures that combine low-level connectionist models with high level symbolic reasoning. Such systems typically use symbolic terms, which might be called schemas, to guide functioning of the lower level. Though they use a variant of schema theory, they almost never explicitly label it as such. Barnden and Pollack (1990) offer a useful compendium of such models. Pollack offers a connectionist model of language and learning that generates a partial interpretation of sentences through simple processors that fight among themselves for superiority. The model is said to be psychologically driven in that understanding of language emerges as the collection of cooperating partial interpretations that survive, whereas Lehnert (1990) describes a top-down semantic parser (built from a symbolic parser based on conceptual dependency), which drives a bottom-up syntactic parser (built from a connection network that uses numerical relaxation with lateral inhibition). The architecture is reminiscent of the schema-theoretic approach to language of Arbib and co-workers (1987).

MEMORY, PERCEPTION, AND ACTION

How schema theory views human memory, perception, and action is charted to set the stage for the more formal accounts in the following sections. Long-term memory (LTM) is seen as a network encoding a lifetime of experience in a personal encyclopedia of hundreds of thousands of schemas, ranging from perceptual schemas for words and objects through memories of many specific episodes, to skills and belief systems, which themselves weave together a multitude of other schemas. But humans do not have a different schema for every different object of every different size or position in space, because each schema may be tuned by parameters (size, speed, color, etc) that adapt its generalities to the specifics of the current situation. Human knowledge is neither certain nor neatly compartmentalized. Schemas do not correspond to isolated facts but may be linked to subsidiary schemas, as when the skill of riding a bike incorporates the ability to judge distances to potential obstacles, and one schema may generalize another, as in the relationship between the ability to recognize houses in general and the ability to recognize one house in particular. Thus knowledge forms a tangled skeinwork. The schema theorist seeks to understand it by looking at some subnetwork in isolation, but always aware that this is an approximation to an incredibly complex whole. The theorist's explicit analysis of schemas does not imply that in the normal course of activities humans have explicit, conscious access to all, or even most, of the schemas that direct behavior. Recall Minsky's example of the knowledge (society of agents/schemas) involved in drinking a cup of tea.

Perception involves a continual updating of initial comprehension of the more salient aspects of the current environment–situation by noting discrepancies between what is expected and what the senses now relate. Short-term memory (STM) is thus viewed as a short-term model that is constructed as a dynamic network of perhaps tens or hundreds of schema instances suitably connected and parameterized to represent knowledge of current relevance to the subject. However, this usage runs counter to that in the psychology of learning, where the distinction is rather between information encoded in the brain in a manner that may be permanently disrupted by distraction (STM) and that which may resist distraction, or even such insults as electroconvulsive therapy (LTM) (Squire, 1987). From an AI point of view, it seemed more important to stress the importance of information of current relevance.

Exciting recent research on the brain has revealed such memory, exemplified in delayed reaction tasks in monkeys, where activity in specific brain regions correlated with the desired response persists precisely from the period from the presentation of the cue that specifies the response to the emission of the response on presentation of a neutral trigger stimulus (Fuster and co-workers, 1982; Goldman-Rakic, 1991). This form of memory is now referred to as *working memory,* and this term could in the future be used for what this article, in conformity with the prior literature of schema theory, refers to as STM.

To relate this to LTM, consider that each time a schema is instantiated in STM, it can be annotated with information about actions taken at that time and the consequences of such action. Such data can be consolidated over time to provide useful guides to action, helping update LTM by editing existing schemas and adding new schemas. A schema provides abilities for recognition and guides to action but must also provide expectations about what will happen so that actions may be chosen appropriately. These expectations may be wrong, and so it is that humans sometimes learn from their mistakes. Learning is necessary because schemas are fallible. Schemas, and their connections within the schema network, change through the processes of accommodation (Piaget's term), adjusting the network of schemas so that over time they may well be able to handle a certain range of situations in a more adaptive way. This is reminiscent of the way in which a scientific community modifies and develops its theories on the basis of the pragmatic criterion of successful prediction and control (Hesse, 1980), and in fact the scientific community metaphor has been developed by Kornfeld and Hewitt (1981) in the context of the actor model of computation.

Therefore, in STM (working memory) a schema assemblage combines an estimate of environmental state with a representation of goals and needs. New sensory input as well as internal processes update the schema assemblage. The internal state is also updated by knowledge of the state of execution of current plans made up of motor schemas. Perceptual schemas allow recognition of some class of objects, and motor schemas guide some class of actions. But pure perception and action are but two points on a continuum, and most schemas intermesh perceptual and motor skills with more abstract forms of knowledge.

Animal perception has evolved so as to estimate the parameters needed for control of movement. Nothing guarantees that the estimate is correct, but survival depends on schemas that are correct enough, often enough, as when the time until collision parameter of oncoming traffic is estimated to decide whether or not to cross the road. The parameters required by each schema must then be specified to tune the movement, filling in the details. The notion of parameterized motor schemas is closely related to the view of motor control in terms of selecting and coordinating from a relatively short list of synergies of groups of muscles (Bernstein 1967). These motor schemas are akin to control systems but distinguished in that they can be combined to form coordinated control programs that control the phasing in and out of patterns of coactivation, with the passing of control parameters from perceptual to motor schemas. The term coordinated control program (Arbib, 1982) emphasizes that it has some of the properties of a computer program in that activation can be passed from one part of the program to another, but also some of the properties of a control system in that many of the boxes can be active at the same time, passing data back and forth. The language of coordinated control programs abstracts from the coordinated phasing in and out of the brain's manifold control systems. While certain basic programs are hard-wired, most are generated as the result of a planning process. (The issue of to what extent planning should be viewed as an explicit process is of great current concern, and will be discussed below) (cf PLANNING, REACTIVE).

The coordinated control program for reaching and grasping of Figure 2 illustrates the high level channeling of pertinent sensory information to the control structures responsible for different submovements. Subschemas for finger adjustment and hand rotation, movements that precede the actual grasping of the object, receive visual and proprioceptive information necessary for their respective sensorimotor transformations. The spoken instructions given to the subject drive the planning process that leads to the creation of the appropriate plan of action/activation of the appropriate coordinated control program, in which perceptual schemas coordinate the interwoven activation of motor schemas for reaching and grasping. Several schema instances may be active at the same time, but not all need be concurrently active. In addition to its own internal changes, the activity of a particular instance may serve both to pass messages as indicated by the solid lines to other activated subsystems, and also to instantiate (call for the activation of instances of) other schemas, as indicated by the dashed lines. There can just as well be deactivation (deinstantiation) of schema instances.

SCHEMAS FOR RANA COMPUTATRIX

A perspective on how schemas may be used to model the brain is offered by a few examples from *Rana computatrix,* a set of models of visuomotor coordination in frog and toad. The first example shows how lesion experiments can test schema models of behavior. Frogs and toads snap at small moving objects and jump away from large moving objects. Thus a simple schema-model of the frog brain might simply postulate four schemas, two perceptual schemas (processes for recognizing objects or situations) and two motor schemas (controlling some structured behavior). One perceptual schema recognizes small moving objects and activates a motor schema for approaching the prey; the other recognizes large moving objects and activates a motor schema for avoiding the predator. Lesion experiments can put such a model to the test. It was thought that the tectum (a key visual region in the animal's midbrain) was the locus for recognizing small moving objects, while the pretectum (a region just in front of the tectum) was the locus for recognizing large moving objects. With these hypotheses on localization of schemas in the brain, the above model would predict that an animal with lesioned pretectum would be unresponsive to

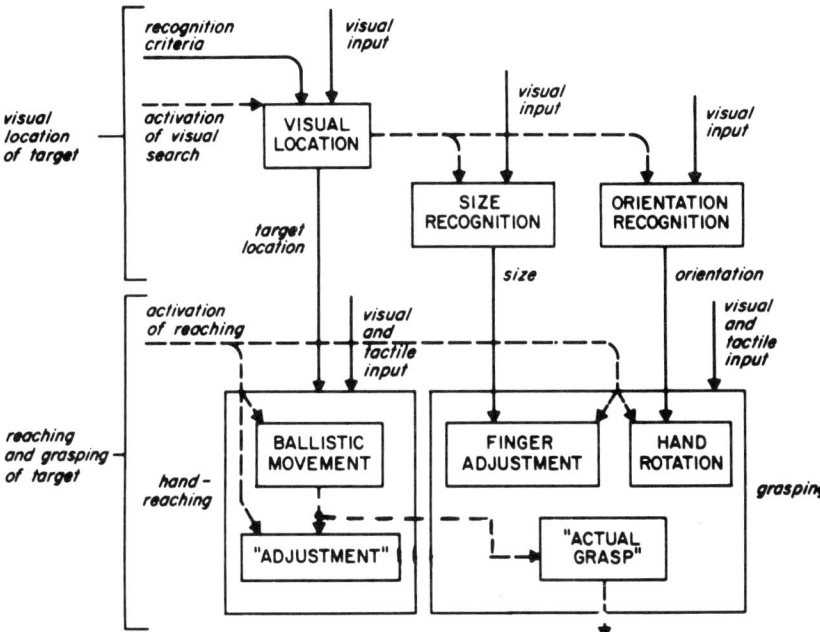

Figure 2. Control of the movements for grasping an object can be described by a coordinated control program of interacting perceptual and motor schemas, where solid lines convey data between concurrently active schemas and dashed lines convey activation signals. Visual location and parameterization of the target are performed by three perceptual schemas (the top half of the figure). Arm movements are controlled by two motor schemas (on the bottom left) whereas finger and wrist movements are controlled by an assemblage of three motor schemas (bottom right) (Arbib, 1981a).

large objects, but would respond normally to small objects. However, the facts are quite different. A pretectum-lesioned toad will approach moving objects large and small, and does not exhibit avoidance behavior. This leads to a new schema model in which a perceptual schema to recognize large moving objects is still localized in the pretectum but the tectum now contains a perceptual schema for all moving objects. This model is essentially that of Ewert and von Seelen (1974), but theirs is refined to give a more precise account of what stimuli excite the perceptual and motor schemas and to what extent they excite them. Furthermore, that activity of the pretectal schema not only triggers the avoid motor schema but also inhibits approach. This new schema model still yields the normal behavior to large and small moving objects, but also fits the lesion data, because removal of the pretectum removes inhibition, and so the animal will now approach any moving object. In related studies, Ewert (1989) relates perceptual and motor schemas to the (not necessarily neural) innate releasing mechanisms (IRM) and fixed action patterns (FAPs), respectively, of the ethologists (students of animal behavior), and then notes that neuroethology has the additional task of finding the neural mechanisms for these units. For example, his command releasing systems provide a neural equivalent for the coordinated control programs of schema theory.

In such studies of *Rana computatrix*, each basic schema may be thought of as having its own dedicated neural circuitry, with more complex schemas being realized by patterns of activity across the circuits that realize the schemas of the coordinated control program that defines it. In particular, if the same basic schema occurs more than once in some coordinated control program, then it is implied that the program will require the activity of only one of these instances at any one time. For example although the overall schema for "prey-capture and predator avoidance" (Arbib and Cobas, 1991) contains the "orient"

motor schema in the subschemas for both prey-capture and predator avoidance, the overall schema is so structured that at most one of those subschemas is active at any one time, and so the circuitry for the orient schema will be activated either with parameters for orienting toward the prey, or with parameters for orienting away from the predator. Moreover, should the competition between the prey-capture and predator avoidance subschemas be unsuccessful in such a way that both activate the orient schema, it will simply mean that the same circuitry receives simultaneous, conflicting, commands, in which case it might, for example, orient the animal to the average direction. Arbib and Cobas model prey-catching and predator avoidance at the level of maps and schemas, which is the right level to capture and extend data from lesion and behavioral experiments (they do not offer neural network models). The motor schemas are driven by specific internal maps that between them constitute a distributed internal representation of the world. These maps collectively provide the transition from topographically coded sensory information to population-coded inputs to the diverse motor schemas that drive muscle activity. However, whereas stimulus and response direction are the same for prey, different maps are involved for predator location and escape direction. Arbib and Cobas thus distinguish between the positional heading hypothesis (heading codes the position of the object) and the motor heading hypothesis (each system has a separate projection pathway converging in a different way onto a heading map coding the required motor response). They follow the latter hypothesis, with motor actions constructed through the interaction of different motor schemas via competition and cooperation. It is not necessary for control of action to devolve to a single motor schema. Two or more schemas (eg, Approach and Orient) may cooperate to yield the final motor pattern. The model generates different motor zones for prey-catching behavior that match those observed in normal conditions and in studies of lesioned animals, and offers predictions for experiments on both approach and avoidance behaviors.

It is seen that a schema may be incomplete. Arbib and Cobas specified how the orient schema will generate a motor command when given a single heading parameter as input, yet said nothing about how it will react to multiple inputs. However, a more detailed specification in terms of, say, a neural network receiving an array of headings as input, might well predict responses in aberrant situations, predictions that could then be put to experimental test. The results may or may not require refinement of the neural network model, but will certainly allow the extension of the original schema-level specification to encompass a wider range of situations.

Two models are presented as schemas for the insight they offer into the processes of competition and cooperation at the level of neural nets (see NEURAL NETWORKS). The Didday (1976) model of prey-selection embodies pure competition (the neuron that wins the competition determines which prey the frog will snap at); the Dev (1975) model of stereopsis embodies both competition (between neurons encoding different depths in a given direction) and cooperation (so that neurons encoding similar depths in nearby directions will excite each other, thus favoring stable states that encode surfaces rather than rapid fluctuations in depth with changing visual direction). Each of these models presents a single neural network. The point for the present consideration is that they define schemas that are used in later studies, but are not themselves constituted by an assemblage of schemas. For example, the Cue Interaction Model (House, 1989) couples two copies of the Dev schema, one driven by disparity and the other by accommodation, giving an example of cooperation between schemas to yield a form of sensor fusion. An accommodation-driven field M receives information about accommodation (the sharper the image at a particular depth in a given direction, the greater the activity of the neuron corresponding to that spatial position), while a system S uses disparity information as input. The initial state of the accommodation field is blurred, representing the lack of fine tuning offered by accommodation. Targets are better tuned in the stereopsis field, but they offer ghost images in addition to the correct images. However, the systems are so intercoupled that a point in the M field will excite the corresponding point in S, and vice versa. As a result, ghost targets are suppressed while accommodation information is sharpened. Localization is now precise and unambiguous, and can be used to guide the behavior of the animal. This shows how the binocular cue of disparity and the monocular cue of accommodation may be used to complement each other to yield a system that achieves more accurate depth estimates than could a system relying on a single cue. (Recall the earlier slogan that "the representation of the world is the pattern of relationships between all its partial representations," which is certainly embodied here and in the work of Arbib and Cobas.) The Path-Planning Model (see the next section) then shows how a toad, confronted by a worm behind a semitransparent barrier, can "choose" whether to approach the worm directly or to make a detour. The important methodological point here is that the model demands separate schemas for mapping the location of barriers and for locating a prey, but does not depend on the use of a neural network to implement them. Lara and co-workers (1984) have provided schemas for a wider range of toad behavior that shows how the toad's response to prey is modified by intervening chasms as well as barriers.

While the brain may be considered as a network of interacting boxes, namely anatomically distinguishable structures, there is no reason to expect each such box to mediate a single function that is well-defined from a behavioral standpoint. An experimentalist might, for example, approach the cerebellum by postulating that it serves for learning elemental movements or mediating feed-forward or rendering movement more graceful. It may do just one of these things, but it is more likely that it does none of them by itself, but rather participates in each of them and more besides. The language of schemas lets us express hypotheses about the various functions that the brain performs that are separated from a commitment to localization of any one function in any one region, but that can nonetheless allow us to express the way in which many regions participate in a given function, while a given region may participate in many functions. More generally, schema theory requires the ability to maintain several different instances, each suitably tuned, of a schema simultaneously. As a result the linkage of schema instances in an assemblage cannot be thought of as always corresponding to fixed anatomical connections between the circuitry implementing the given schemas. This latter point is related to Lashley's (1951) discussion of the problem of repetition of action in a sequence of behaviors, and is taken up by Arbib (1990) in the context of motor set.

PATH-PLANNING AND DETOUR BEHAVIOR

It has been seen that work on *Rana computatrix*, modeling brain mechanisms of frog and toad, has contributed to the development of schema theory. As a specific example of how work in BT contributes concepts to AI as well, the motor schemas involved in detour behavior will be briefly considered. A toad, viewing a vertical paling fence through which it can see a worm, may either snap directly at the worm, or may detour around the barrier. However, it will not move when it sees a barrier if there is no worm behind it. Thus it is the worm that triggers the animal's response, but there is a complex trajectory dependent on the relative spatial position of worm and barrier. Study of the toad's brain led Arbib and House (1987) to posit separate schemas to provide the depth maps for prey and barriers, and to ask how their output is used to guide the animal's behavior. Their Path-Planning Model associates with each point of the two depth maps (for prey and barriers) a two-dimensional vector to indicate the preferred direction of the animal were it to follow a path through that corresponding position. The set of all these arrows forms a "potential field" showing the potential movement of the animal at each location represented in the depth map. A single prey will set up an attractant field in which, from every point in the animal's representation of space, there is an arrow suggesting a choice of movement toward the prey. Fenceposts have a local repulsive field. A fence post has no effect on the toad's behavior unless it is within a body width of the toad. By summing up all the vectors corresponding to objects the toad senses in its environment, the model forms a potential field from which it may compute the appropriate course of action. This model provides a parallel computation scheme for converting the perception of prey and barriers into the parameters that characterize an appropriate trajectory.

Application of the neural technology of this model to a mobile robot (Arkin 1989) provides a case study of how thinking about schemas for brain modeling may help develop the AI study of perceptual robotics. The robot, which can plan its way around a building or across a given space, has hierarchical control provided by AURA, an AUtonomous Robot Architecture. A subsystem called the Navigator conducts off-line path planning on the basis of a terrain map using relatively conventional AI techniques. Another subsystem, called the Pilot, extracts more specific features, eg, landmarks, to elaborate the plan into motor schemas, with perceptual schemas embedded within the motor schemas. Such schemas include stay-on-path, move-to-goal, move-ahead, find-landmark, and avoid-obstacles and are each defined by a potential field. The path along which the robot is going is represented by a flow field. The vector field defines what the dynamics will be if the world remains constant as the animal moves. However, the whole field need not be computed in advance, but only the field for the locale of the robot at the time of sensing. If an obstacle appears as the robot moves along its path, then, by integrating the repulsive potential field from the obstacle, the robot will detour around the obstacle, but the potential field for the planned path will then recapture it to move it along its way.

SCHEMAS AND HIGH LEVEL VISION

Recognition of the location, size, and orientation of an object can set the parameters that motor schemas need to successfully guide an action. Moreover, in everyday life, our behavior depends on the recognition of many different objects, and an appreciation of their changing positions. Consider walking across a street, where the recognition of cars, pedestrians, and shops enter into determining the pattern of movement. In this section, the general properties of schema assemblages, which represent such complex situations, will be discussed and a specific computer system for schemas for scene interpretation will be analyzed.

Schema Assemblages

A simple connectionist account of interpreting a scene with multiple objects might assign a neuron to each schema for a type of object that might occur in the environment, where these neuronlike elements have weighted links between them and each has an output value that can vary continuously between 0 and 1 (no claim is made that this corresponds to a single neuron in the brain). The neurons would be so connected with each other and the retinal network that a schema will be more active (its neuron will have an output value nearer 1) to the extent that the object that it represents appears to be present in the input pattern. The connections would be like those in a constraint satisfaction network. Consider a blurred view of two regions, with the top region green and the bottom brown, so that it could be pistachio-ice-cream-and-cone or foliage-and-trunk of a tree (Fig. 3a). The input from the top region would activate the neurons for recognizing foliage and pistachio ice cream. Perceptual schemas that are candidates for interpreting the lower region are those for trunk and for cone. As shown in Fig. 3b, excitatory links (cooperation) would couple the matched interpretations whereas inhibitory links (competition) between schemas for the same region would ensure that normally only one interpretation is valid for any particular region: as one schema of the pair gets more active, it will inhibit the activity of the other schema until one suppresses the other to provide the final interpretation. In this example, competition indicates a general processing constraint. An ob-

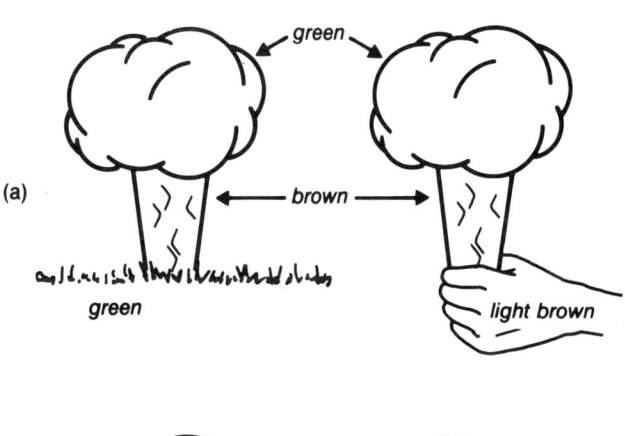

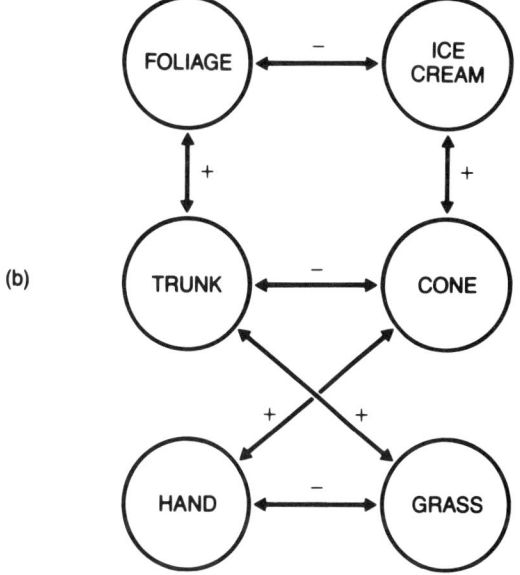

Figure 3. (a) A figure that could be either an ice-cream cone or a tree. (b) The schema network that is to interpret the figure. Schemas for ice cream and cone cooperate, as do those for foliage and tree trunk (+ signs), whereas different schemas compete to interpret a given region (− signs) (Arbib, 1989a).

ject cannot have two incompatible interpretations, so there is no reason to store explicitly the knowledge that "A is not equal to B" when A and B have no common relationship, as in ice cream cone vs tree. In other cases, competition could encode specific knowledge that two particular objects cannot occur together, as in linking the schemas for fire and ice, or in discriminating fine differences between objects that might easily be confused, as in "O" vs "Q". Note that such knowledge sets expectations rather than setting absolute conditions on what might be seen. A fire blazing in front of an igloo can be imagined, but a view of an ice cube in the fire is expected to be evanescent at best.

There are various strategies that are used in visual perception beyond simply letting the schemas battle it out, if there is a real scene, rather than a limited caricature. It is possible to move closer to see the detailed texture that would tip the balance between foliage and ice cream, without further inspection of trunk and cone. Or the figure could be disambiguated by looking at the context. For example, if the object is being held in a hand, it is far likelier to be an ice cream cone than a tree.

Even with such refinements, the simple example raises more problems than it answers. How does a schema recognize a particular object no matter where it is in the scene and despite various distortions? Answers, which involve explicit group transformations, run from "How we know universals" (Pitts and McCulloch, 1947) to the neocognitron (Fukushima, 1980) and the dynamic link architecture (see NEURAL NETWORKS). Cues from depth, size, motion, and so on may constrain both the interpretation and the possible transformations. Moreover, once a schema is activated, how is it linked to the appropriate region so that a winner-take-all process occurs only between schemas for the same region? Again, cooperation depends on spatial relationships (among others), the contextual relations that have been offered depend on the ice cream being above the cone, the foliage above the trunk. Cooperation must be made dependent on such relationships.

This is part of the general issue of how schemas can organize themselves to represent a visual scene. It is not quite true that only one schema can win the competition to interpret a given region of a scene. One important class of examples is given by the PART-OF hierarchy; it is possible to see simultaneously a region as a wall and as part of a house. This raises the issue of how knowledge that two interpretations are compatible can be encoded so as to override the general processing constraint that an object cannot have two incompatible interpretations. One further subtlety addresses the fact that, for example, two or three windows can be seen along the wall of a house. Humans see through a sequence of eye movements that allows the fovea to be directed at any part of the visual field. The brain can create a new instance of the schema the first time the fovea provides input to activate it; it must then create an assemblage of these instances, keeping track of the relative location and other parameters of the objects these instances represent (and so updating an extant instance, rather than creating a new one, when an object is foveated again), to form the current internal model (STM in the sense of working memory) of the world.

Note here the departure from the simplest connectionist formulation of one schema, one neuron, because it is necessary to provide multiple instances, each linked to the appropriate region of the image and parameterized accordingly. This raises the issue of real time changes in effective connectivity (see NEURAL NETWORKS).

Schemas for Scene Interpretation

The approach to schema-based interpretation in the VISIONS computer vision (Riseman and Hanson, 1987; Draper and co-workers, 1989) system is an important exemplification of the above ideas within AI. It employs active, independent schema instances, and the schemas encode mechanisms for using features in multiple representations and conducting information fusion and sensor fusion in a knowledge-directed manner. The main idea is that an object's characteristics determine the best way to recognize it (although schema theory in general would go further to stress the extraction of parameters relevant to a current task, rather than mere recognition), and so a schema for an object class has an object-specific control strategy for efficient context-dependent object and scene recognition.

As in most computer vision systems, low-level vision takes an image (eg, a color photograph) and, working independently of object-specific knowledge, extracts multiple representations, including regions, lines, surfaces, and vertices, tagged with features such as color, texture, shape, size, and location. Given a pair or sequence of images, other processes can yield further information such as depth and motion. The result is an intermediate representation (a set of partial representations) of the image that may be updated as interpretation proceeds. The interacting schemas that encode recognition routines for houses and walls and trees provide the processes to grab different features of the intermediate representation and come up with the overall interpretation of the image.

In the VISIONS system, the knowledge required for interpretation is stored in LTM (long-term memory) as a network of schemas whereas the state of interpretation of the particular scene unfolds in STM (working memory) in the form of a network of schema instances. The user starts the interpretation process by invoking an arbitrary number of initial schemas. These may reflect general visual goals, such as "interpret this image as a road scene," or more specific needs, such as "find the sidewalk in this image." Each schema instance has an associated activity level (or confidence level) that changes on the basis of interactions with other units in the (dynamically reconfigurable) STM network. The STM network makes context explicit: each object represents a context for further processing, using to advantage the relations among objects. When a schema instance is activated, it is with an associated area of the image and an associated set of local variables. Multiple instances of a given schema are normally associated with separate portions of the image. The structure of STM is further constrained in part by relationships encoded within LTM, both those between schemas for inter-object relations and those within a schema for geometric relations of parts.

In addition to schema instances, the STM contains hypotheses and goals. A hypothesis asserts that a particular object provides the interpretation of a portion of the image. The hypothesis is registered when the relevant schema instance achieves a threshold in its confidence level and will then include parameters descriptive of the object so recognized; contrast schema activation (when an instance starts to process) with schema firing or propagation (when an instance posts a hypothesis that can affect the activity of other schemas). A schema instance may set as a goal the confirmation that a certain context applies; and posting the goal may in turn lead to the forming of a schema instance to check whether a posited object occurs in a certain portion of the image (in the example below, recognizing a roof sets the goal of finding a wall region beneath it in the image).

Active schema instances set out to accomplish their goals as independently acting agents. As part of recognizing their particular scene or object, schemas may invoke other schemas to recognize subparts of their objects, or to recognize spatially, functionally, or contextually related objects. The set of schemas that another schema invokes is flexible. A schema for recognizing houses, for example, may only invoke a schema for recognizing a wall if one of its hypotheses needs additional support. Otherwise, it may never invoke the wall schema. Thus the network of schema instances changes dynamically in response to the viewer's needs (through schema instances activated by the user) and the image (which dictates which schemas another schema will activate). It should also be noted that, once activated, the wall schema (or any schema) becomes an independent process that can outlast the schema that invoked it or even contradict that schema's hypotheses.

Instantiation of a schema may thus be either data driven or goal driven, ie, on the basis of data extracted from the image or on the basis of goals set by the context of other hypotheses and instances. In a data-driven interpretation routine for the sky (other routines can use contextual cues to determine that a region is skylike), measures of goodness of fit m_i are calculated for a region for such features as location, color, shape, and texture. Then a region r is adjudged more skylike the greater is some linear combination $m_{sky}(r)$ of the $m_i(r)$. Such measures have proved effective in assigning a confidence level to an initial data-driven classification of a region on the basis of local cues (Riseman and Hanson, 1987). In general, this will only be the first step and in no way forces the final interpretation.

To see how the system works, imagine how schemas might process an image of an outdoor scene in which a house is set against a wintry sky, and is such that a lack of contrast leads low level vision to overlook a crucial edge separating wall and sky. The sky schema runs on the segmented image and finds a region reasonably high in the image and with a high value for m_{sky}. However, because the segmentation left out a crucial edge, the "sky" in fact includes one of the walls of the house. The roof region, of a slate color, also has sky-like properties, but because it is lower in the image, the color is not quite sky, and it has more texture, its $m_{sky}(r)$ is much lower. Meanwhile, an instance of the roof schema finds that the roof region has just the right geometrical characteristics and is in the right position of the image to yield a high value of m_{roof} and thus posts the hypothesis that it is indeed the roof. As a result, the low confidence hypothesis that it might be sky does not play any further part in the computation. The roof hypothesis leads to formation of a house hypothesis, and this, in turn, leads to the goal of finding confirming context, invoking an instance of the wall schema to search underneath the posited roof to see if the criteria for a wall are met, as indeed they are. But because of the missing edge in the roofline, there is now a big region that is interpreted both as wall and sky. As was seen in the case of the roof, if one confidence level were much stronger than another, further interactions would tend to ignore the low confidence schema instance. But here the two hypotheses are both too strong to be ignored. One solution is to reprocess the sensory data to extract missing details, for example, to resegment the offending region with a lower threshold for edges. Instances of the sky and wall schemas can now compete over just these regions to quickly yield their contribution to the final interpretation. Other schemas can then continue their competition and cooperation to yield the overall interpretation.

Schema instances are concurrently acting, independent agents. Thus where HEARSAY uses a single blackboard and serial scheduler, each schema instance in the VISIONS schema system (Draper and co-workers, 1989) has its own local blackboard, which serves as its own working memory. Hypotheses are the objects that a recognition process reasons about, such as regions, line segments, and objects. Knowledge sources are the actions that a schema can take to reason about a hypothesis. Hence interpretation is a process of applying knowledge sources to hypotheses that live on the local blackboard. Schema instances cooperate by exchanging information across a global blackboard, but there is no global scheduler. Thus the house schema mentioned above, having invoked a wall schema instance, can then monitor the process of the wall's hypotheses by watching the global blackboard, and the wall can get information about current house hypotheses in the same manner.

The distinction between the global and local blackboards is both for efficiency and clean semantics. Schemas only post their top-level object hypotheses to the global blackboard. All other information is restricted to the local blackboard. This greatly reduces traffic across the global blackboard, removing a major bottleneck for concurrent blackboard systems. Just as important, it keeps the system modular. When interpreting an image, the house schema may extract much information that is meaningful only to itself. For example, it might decide that line segments ought to be grouped in a certain way. This grouping may not coincide with the optimal grouping strategy for finding a different object. The local blackboards allow each schema to reason in its own, object-specific space.

Whether a huge knowledge source is brought to bear by a serial scheduler as in HEARSAY, or whether schemas activate themselves in various combinations, nothing ensures that the "knowledge" they encode is correct. Their processing can create errors and ambiguities. The problem is to ensure that the schema interactions will usually sort themselves out into a useful interpretation so that what may be wrong to start with will be removed and replaced by better hypotheses en route to the final analysis. The VISIONS schema system shares the common weakness of all knowledge-directed vision programs: its knowledge base is difficult and costly to develop. One focus of current work is thus on the problem of automatically learning recognition schemas from an object description and a set of training images (Draper and Riseman, 1990).

Action-Oriented Perception

In the VISIONS system, it is the user who starts the interpretation process by invoking general goals such as "interpret this image as a road scene" or such specific goals as "find the sidewalk in this image." It is thus worth stressing that the above considerations still have much to offer when applied to analyzing the vision of a robot or an animal. However, in such systems, it is the current goals of the autonomous system, not the demands of some user, that guide the process of action-oriented perception. The way in which such goals change the perceptual demands as action proceeds is illustrated by the example (Arkin, 1990) of the strategies used by someone instructed to turn right at the flashing traffic light. At first the person walks along looking for some long distance perceptual event (something flashing), after which the perceptual schema for traffic lights is brought to bear. Once a flashing traffic light is identified, the emphasis shifts from identification of the light per se to recognition of spatial relations appropriate to executing a right turn "at" the light.

EXPLICIT VS IMPLICIT PLANNING

In classic AI, explicit planning precedes execution, taking the form of a centralized sequential deliberation based on goals and a world model to yield a sequence of actions. Such an approach may impose unrealistic requirements for modeling and perception because all relevant information must be available before planning begins. This makes it hard to adapt the plan to events not predicted by the model. In reaction to this, some critics have advocated reactive planning (qv), in which selection and execution of actions are inextricably intertwined. Such reactive systems (eg, Brooks's subsumption architecture) are parallel and distributed, with a hard-wired priority scheme that is fixed at compile time. There is no deliberation and no model. Inhibition–suppression rules determine which modules will control action, on the basis of current input.

However, such reactive systems are hard-wired, difficult to design, and completely data oriented, and their goals are implicit and thus cannot be referred to in decision making. Maes (1991) models selection of behavior by extending the notion of reactive systems to control by networks that have explicit nodes for motivation and goals as well as actions. The network operates by a combination of external and internal spreading activation. In external spreading activation, sensor data activate partial matches, goal nodes activate nodes for actions that can achieve them, and protected goals (those already achieved that must remain achieved) inhibit destroyers (those action nodes with inhibitory links to the protected goal nodes). In the internal spreading activation, executable behavior activates successors (ie, a goal that has the given behavior as a precondition) with a portion of its energy, nonexecutable behavior spreads energy back to its predecessors, to help activate subgoals, and every behavior inhibits its connectors. The result is a dynamic intertwining of planning and execution. However, note that this is still a case of using goals and motivation to bias activity within a given network, as is the case in *Rana computatrix*, where the animal can use its hard-wired schemas to react in situations in which there are prey, predators, barriers, and other obstacles to be taken into account in finding a path to food or safety, and where motivation can shift activation between the prey and predator subsystems.

All this is a form of planning (as the result of activity emerging in a flexible network) that is compatible with schema theory. The analysis of the VISIONS system makes it clear that schema theory embraces a more general form of planning involving generativity to form novel sequences of schema activation that may involve creation of novel networks. However, it still retains the crucial notions that planning is intertwined with execution, that the plan may be updated as action proceeds, and that planning is a process emerging from the cooperative computation of multiple agents rather than being imposed by a separate executive planning system. As such, this approach to planning falls squarely within the paradigm of cooperative, distributed problem solving (Durfee and co-workers, 1989).

SCHEMAS AND LEARNING

One of the major sources of ideas for schemas has been the work of Piaget, who developed an informal theory of the cognitive development of the child. Thus the notion of learning is a crucial part of schema theory in the general literature of cognitive science, but has played rather little part in the development of the computational theory, linked to both BT and DAI, reviewed here. An early exception is the work of Cunningham (1972), while more recent work includes that of Hill (1983) and Drescher (1989). In a related vein, Rumelhart and co-workers (1986) suggest how schemas may be seen as emergent properties of adaptive, connectionist networks. In the present section, human learning in a schema-theoretic context is reviewed and then Hill's computational model will be examined. Clearly, a major effort is required to assess the relation of these efforts to the current broad sweep of work in machine learning.

Not only do humans form new assemblages in short-term memory, but the stock of schemas in long-term memory changes with maturity. Although new schemas may initially enter long-term memory as assemblages of old schemas, they may, once formed, be tuned to form a new integral schema, much as a skill is honed into a unified whole from constituent pieces. In the initial stage of driving a car, the foot pedals, steering wheel, and passing scene all seem to require minute and conflicting attention to fit into an ill-learned assemblage specified by verbal rules that only outline what is necessary to survive in traffic. Practice yields schemas for an integrated skill that can operate in tandem with conversation in all but the most trying of traffic situations. Not only have separate schemas for eyes, hands, and feet been acquired and combined, but the new composite, the coordinated control program, has been tuned to form a whole in which each part is so adapted to the others that their integration no longer engages our conscious effort. While the coordinated control program can spell out how the pieces are put together, learning processes can smoothly meld the pieces; like a carpenter planing, sanding, and varnishing an assemblage of blocks of wood to achieve a single smooth unity in a piece of furniture. In some BT and AI studies, the task may be to explain learning in terms of the plasticity of neural networks, but this is not a necessary form of specification of schema change—schema theory and neural network theory are complementary disciplines.

Piaget sees the child starting with schemas for basic survival like breathing, eating, digesting, and excreting, as well as such basic sensorimotor schemas as suckling, grasping, and rudimentary eye–hand coordination. Objects are secondary to these primary schemas, and such schemas pave the way for more global concepts such as the schema for object permanence, the recognition that when an object disappears from view, the object still exists and is there to be searched for. This schema develops to allow the use of extrapolation to infer where a moving object that has passed from sight is likely to reappear. Piaget argues that such schemas lead to further development until the child has schemas for abstract thought that are no longer rooted in the sensorimotor particularities.

Through assimilation and accommodation, a complex schema network arises that can mediate first the child's, and then the adult's, reality. Through being rooted in such a network, schemas are interdependent, so that each finds meaning only in relation to others. For example, a house is defined in terms of parts such as a roof, yet a roof may be recognized because it is part of a house recognized on the basis of other criteria such as "people live there," each enrich and are defined by the others (and may change when a formal linguistic system allows explicit, though partial, definition). Although processes of schema change may affect only a few schemas at any time, such changes may cohere to yield dramatic changes in the overall pattern of mental organization. There is change yet continuity, with many schemas held in common, yet changed because they must now be used in the context of the new network.

Acquiring a Language

To provide a concrete example of learning at the schema theory level, consider a schema-based approach to language acquisition (Hill, 1983) that models both how the two year old responds to adult utterances, usually with a truncated form of that utterance, and how the child's linguistic and conceptual structures change with each such repetition. Each adult utterance can serve to modify the child's evolving representation without enforcing the exact structure of that utterance, and thus this model of schema-based sampling is not vitiated by the observation that children seem resistant to admonitions on how to speak properly. Where Chomskian linguists would argue that the initial structure of the brain gives to the child certain universals concerning grammatical rules, this neo-Piagetian theory sees grammar as acquired on the basis of the ability to abstract sound patterns, to associate sound patterns with visual stimulation or patterns of action (the link into the sensorimotor domain of much schema theory), etc. Hill's model shows that innate patterns of schema change can yield an increasing richness of language without building on language universals, so long as the child has schemas for, and talks about, relations; can employ word order; can apply concatenation and deletion rules; and can form classes of concepts and classes of words, with the classifying process causing successive reorganizations of the information stored. The lexical classes of adult grammar are not given to the model. Rather, a process of "classification through word use" ensures that words that are used in similar ways will come to be assigned to the same class, thus extending from members of the class to further members of the class certain patterns (templates) of word use. The initial grammar is given by a set of templates, consisting of a "relation" and a "slot." The grammar exhibits simple patterns the child had already broken out of experience, and it is the dynamics of schema change that enables the child to use language that comes more and more to be describable by, but is not generated by, general rules that increasingly approximate the grammarian's description of adult language.

CONCLUSION: THE TWO FACETS OF SCHEMA THEORY

There are two facets to schema theory, as a language and as a theory of intelligent behavior. In, for example, RS and the VISIONS schema system, the beginnings of a language for distributed systems are seen at a level abstract enough to convey some real understanding of complex problem-solving behaviors and yet precise enough that the specification can be refined to some concrete implementation. Yet when brain models are discussed and a class of designs for AI systems that is inspired by them is advocated, the other facet of schema theory, a model of intelligence, which uses schema theory *qua* language for expressing such models, is seen. In the language sense, schema theory is more like group theory than relativity theory. Relativity theory is a model of the physical world; it can be falsified or revised on the basis of physical experiments. However, group theory stands or falls for the scientist seeking to explain the world (as distinct from the mathematician proving theorems) not by any criterion of whether it is true or false, but rather on whether its terminology and theorems aid the expression of successful models. Schema theory as an abstract model of computation does not yet have the rigor or stock of theorems of group theory, but the success of models using the language of instantiation, modulation, activity levels, etc, strengthens its claim to be a valuable tool in the development of artificial intelligence as well as brain theory. However, the language of schema theory has developed in tandem with a schema-based theory of human and artificial intelligence, such as that discussed here. It is in the latter sense that it is possible to make such statements as that in schema-theoretic models of language and other cognitive functions "there is a tendency (although not a necessity) to root such models in action and perception." In either sense, the paradigm of schema theory is indeed evolving in a fashion well suited to contribute to distributed artificial intelligence as well as to bridge between cognitive science and brain theory.

BIBLIOGRAPHY

M. A. Arbib, *The Metaphorical Brain: An Introduction to Cybernetics as Artificial Intelligence and Brain Theory.* Wiley-Interscience, New York, 1972.

M. A. Arbib, "Artificial Intelligence and Brain Theory: Unities and Diversities," *Ann. Biomed. Eng.* **3**, 238–274 (1975).

M. A. Arbib, "Perceptual Structures and Distributed Motor Control," in V. B. Brooks, ed., *Handbook of Physiology—The Nervous System II. Motor Control,* American Physiological Society, Bethesda, Md., 1981a, pp. 1449–1480.

M. A. Arbib, "Visuomotor Coordination: From Neural Nets to Schema Theory," *Cogn. Brain Theory* **4**, 23–39 (1981b).

M. A. Arbib, *The Metaphorical Brain 2: Neural Networks and Beyond,* Wiley-Interscience, New York, 1989a.

M. A. Arbib, "Visuomotor Coordination: Neural Models and Perceptual Robotics," in J.-P. Ewert and M. A. Arbib, eds., *Visuomotor Coordination: Amphibians, Comparisons, Models, and Robots,* Plenum Press, New York, 1989b, pp. 121–171.

M. A. Arbib, "Programs, Schemas, and Neural Networks for Control of Hand Movements: Beyond the RS Framework," in M. Jeannerod, ed., *Attention and Performance XIII. Motor Representation and Control,* Lawrence Erlbaum, Hillsdale, N.J., 1990, pp. 111–138.

M. A. Arbib and A. Cobas, "Schemas for Prey-Catching in Frog and Toad," in S. Wilson and J.-A. Meyers, eds., *Simulation of Animal Behavior: From Animals to Animats,* The MIT Press, Cambridge, Mass., 1991.

M. A. Arbib, E. J. Conklin, and J. C. Hill, *From Schema Theory to Language,* Oxford University Press, Oxford, UK, 1987.

M. A. Arbib and R. L. Didday, "The Organization of Action-Oriented Memory for a Perceiving System. I. The Basic Model," *J. Cybernet.* **1**, 3–18 (1971).

M. A. Arbib and H. Ehrig, "Linking Schemas and Module Specifications for Distributed Systems," in *Proceedings of the Workshop on Distributed Computing Systems,* Cairo, 1990.

M. A. Arbib and M. B. Hesse, *The Construction of Reality,* Cambridge University Press, Cambridge, Mass., 1986.

M. A. Arbib and D. H. House, Depth and Detours: An Essay on Visually-Guided Behavior," in M. A. Arbib and A. R. Hanson, eds., *Vision, Brain, and Cooperation Computation,* MIT Press, Cambridge, Mass., 1987, pp. 129–163.

R. C. Arkin, "Neuroscience in Motion: The Application of Schema Theory to Mobile Robotics," in J.-P. Ewert and M. A. Arbib, eds., *Visuomotor Coordination: Amphibians, Comparisons, Models, and Robots,* Plenum Press, New York, 1989, pp. 649–671.

J. A. Barnden and J. B. Pollack, eds., *Advances in Connectionist and Neural Computation Theory, Vol. 1: High-Level Connectionist Models,* Ablex, Norwood, N.J., 1990.

F. C. Bartlett, *Remembering,* Cambridge University Press, Cambridge, UK, 1932.

N. A. Bernstein, *The Coordination and Regulation of Movement,* Pergamon Press, Oxford, UK, 1967.

E. W. Beth and J. Piaget, *Mathematical Epistemology and Psychology,* W. Mays, trans., Reidel, Dordrecht, 1966.

V. Braitenberg, "Taxis, Kinesis, Decussation," *Prog. Brain Res.* **17**, 210–222 (1965).

V. Braitenberg, *Vehicles: Experiments in Synthetic Psychology,* MIT Press, Cambridge, Mass., 1984.

R. A. Brooks, "A Robust Layered Control System for a Mobile Robot," *IEEE J. Robotics Automat.* **RA-2**, 14–23 (1986).

K. J. W. Craik, *The Nature of Explanation,* Cambridge University Press, Cambridge, UK, 1943.

M. Cunningham, *Intelligence: Its Origins and Development,* Academic Press, Inc., New York, 1972.

R. Davis and R. G. Smith, "Negotiation as a Metaphor for Distributed Problem Solving," *Artif. Intell.* **20**, 63–109 (1983).

P. Dev, "Perception of Depth Surfaces in Random-Dot Stereograms: A Neural Model," *Int. J. Man Machine Studies* **7**, 511–528 (1975).

R. Didday, "A Model of Visuomotor Mechanisms in the Frog Optic Tectum," *Math. Biosc.* **30**, 169–180 (1976).

B. A. Draper, R. T. Collins, J. Brolio, A. R. Hanson, and E. M. Riseman, "The Schema System," *Int. J. Comput. Vision* **2**, 209–250 (1989).

B. A. Draper and E. R. Riseman, "Learning 3D Object Recognition Strategies," in *Third International Conference on Computer Vision,* Osaka, Japan, 1990.

G. L. Drescher, "A Mechanism for Early Piagetian Learning," in *Proceedings of the Eleventh IJCAI,* Detroit, Mich., Morgan-Kaufmann, San Mateo, Calif., 1989, pp. 290–294.

E. H. Durfee, V. R. Lesser, and D. D. Corkill, "Cooperative Distributed Problem Solving," in A. Barr, P. R. Cohen, and E. A. Feigenbaum, eds., *The Handbook of Artificial Intelligence,* Vol. 4, Addison-Wesley Publishing Co., Inc., Reading, Mass., 1989, pp. 83–147.

H. Ehrig and B. Mahr, *Fundamentals of Algebraic Specification 2: Module Specifications and Constraints,* EATCS Monographs on Theoretical Computer Science **21**, Springer-Verlag, New York, 1990.

L. D. Erman, F. A. Hayes-Roth, V. R. Lesser, and D. R. Reddy, "The Hearsay-II Speech Understanding System: Integrating Knowledge to Resolve Uncertainty," *Comput. Surv.* **12**, 213–253 (1980).

J.-P. Ewert, "The Release of Visual Behavior in Toads: Stages of Parallel/Hierarchical Information Processing," in J.-P. Ewert and M. A. Arbib, eds., *Visuomotor Coordination: Amphibians, Comparisons, Models, and Robots,* Plenum Press, New York, 1989, pp. 39–120.

J.-P. Ewert and W. von Seelen, "Neurobiologie und System-Theorie eines Visuellen Muster-Erkennungsmechanismus bei Kröte," *Kybernetik* **14**, 167–183 (1974).

N. Fukushima, "Neocognitron: A Self-Organizing Neural Network Model for a Mechanism of Pattern Recognition Unaffected by Shift in Position," *Biol. Cybernet.* **36**, 193–202 (1980).

J. M. Fuster, R. H. Bauer, and J. P. Jervey, "Cellular Discharge in the Dorsolateral Prefrontal Cortex of the Monkey in Cognitive Tasks," *Exp. Neurol.* **77**, 679–694 (1982).

P. Goldman-Rakic, "Parallel Systems in the Cerebral Cortex: The Topography of Cognition," in M. A. Arbib and J. A. Robinson, eds., *Natural and Artificial Parallel Computation*, MIT Press, Cambridge, Mass., 1991, pp. 155–176.

H. Head and G. Holmes, "Sensory Disturbances from Cerebral Lesions," *Brain* **34**, 102–254 (1911).

M. B. Hesse, "Theory and Value in the Social Sciences," in *Revolutions and Reconstructions in the Philosophy of Science*, Indiana University Press, Bloomington, 1980, pp. 187–205.

C. E. Hewitt, "Viewing Control Structures as Patterns of Passing Messages," *Artif. Intell.* **8**, 323–364 (1977).

J. C. Hill, "A Computational Model of Language Acquisition in the Two-Year-Old," *Cogn. Brain Theory* **6**, 287–317 (1983).

D. House, *Depth Perception in Frogs and Toads: A Study in Neural Computing*, Lecture Notes in Biomathematics, **80**, Springer-Verlag, New York, 1989.

W. L. Kilmer, W. S. McCulloch, and J. Blum, "A Model of the Vertebrate Central Command System," *Int. J. Man Machine Studies* **1**, 279–309 (1969).

W. A. Kornfeld and C. Hewitt, "The Scientific Community Metaphor," *IEEE Trans. Sys. Man Cybernet.* **11**, 23–33 (1981).

R. Lara, M. Carmona, F. Daza, and A. Cruz, "A Global Model of the Neural Mechanisms Responsible for Visuomotor Coordination in Toads," *J. Theoret. Bio.* **110**, 587–618 (1984).

K. S. Lashley, "The Problem of Serial Order in Behavior," in L. Jeffress, ed., *Cerebral Mechanisms in Behavior: The Hixon Symposium*, John Wiley & Sons, Inc., New York, 1951, pp. 112–136.

W. Lehnert, "Symbolic–Subsymbolic Sentence Analyses: Exploiting the Best of Two Worlds," in J. A. Barnden and J. B. Pollack, eds., *Advances in Connectionist and Neural Computation Theory, Vol. 1: High-Level Connectionist Models*, Ablex, Norwood, N.J., 1990.

D. M. Lyons, "A Formal Model for Reactive Robot Plans," in *Second International Conference on Computer Integrated Manufacturing*, Troy, N.Y., 1990.

P. Maes, "A Bottom-Up Mechanism for Behavior Selection in an Artificial Creature," in S. Wilson and J.-A. Meyers, eds., *Simulation of Animal Behavior: From Animals to Animats*, MIT Press, Cambridge, Mass., 1991.

W. S. McCulloch and W. H. Pitts, "A Logical Calculus of the Ideas Immanent in Nervous Activity," *Bull. Math. Biophys.* **5**, 115–133 (1943).

M. L. Minsky, "A Framework for Representing Knowledge," in P. H. Winston, ed., *The Psychology of Computer Vision*, McGraw-Hill, Book Co., Inc., New York, 1975, pp. 211–277.

M. L. Minsky, *The Society of Mind*, Simon & Schuster, New York, 1985.

U. Neisser, *Cognition and Reality: Principles and Implications of Cognitive Psychology*, W. H. Freeman Co., San Francisco, 1976.

J. Piaget, *Biology and Knowledge*, Edinburgh University Press, Edinburgh, UK, 1971.

W. H. Pitts and W. S. McCulloch, "How We Know Universals, The Perception of Auditory and Visual Forms," *Bull. Math. Biophys.* **9**, 127–147 (1947).

J. M. Prager and M. A. Arbib, "Computing the Optic Flow: The MATCH Algorithm and Prediction," *Comp. Vision Graphics Image Proc.* **24**, 271–304 (1983).

E. M. Riseman and A. R. Hanson, "A Methodology for the Development of General Knowledge-Based Vision Systems," in M. A. Arbib and A. R. Hanson, eds., *Vision, Brain and Cooperative Computation*, MIT Press, Cambridge, Mass., 1987, pp. 285–328.

D. E. Rumelhart, P. Smolensky, J. L. McClelland, and G. E. Hinton, "Schemata and Sequential Thought Processes in PDP Models," in J. L. McClelland and D. E. Rumelhart, eds., *Parallel Distributed Processing: Explorations in the Microstructure of Cognition*, Vol. 2, MIT Press, Cambridge, Mass., 1986, Chapt. 14.

R. Schank and R. Abelson, *Scripts, Plans, Goals and Understanding: An Inquiry into Human Knowledge Structures*, Lawrence Erlbaum, Hillsdale, N.J., 1977.

C. E. Shannon and J. McCarthy, eds., *Automata Studies*, Princeton University Press, Princeton, N.J., 1956.

L. R. Squire, *Memory and Brain*, Oxford University Press, Oxford, UK, 1987.

W. G. Walter, *The Living Brain*, Penguin Books, Harmondsworth, UK, 1953.

A. Yonezawa, ed., *ABCL: An Object-Oriented Concurrent System*, MIT Press, Cambridge, Mass., 1990.

MICHAEL A. ARBIB
University of Southern
California

SCHOLAR

The SCHOLAR system is a set of programs written by Carbonell (J. R. Carbonell, *Mixed-Initiative Man–Computer Instructional Dialogues*, Ph.D. dissertation, MIT, Cambridge, Mass., June 1970). SCHOLAR, like older CAI (computer-assisted instruction) programs, simulates a teacher, but it permits the student to ask questions and in that sense is a mixed-initiative system. SCHOLAR acts as a geography teacher; however, its network-based knowledge representation (qv) makes it possible to change the teaching subject with only minor changes to the executive program (see J. R. Carbonell "AI in CAI: An Artificial Intelligence Approach to Computer-Assisted Instruction," *IEEE Trans. Man–Machine Syst.* **MMS-11**(4), 190–202 (Nov. 1970)).

J. GELLER
New Jersey Institute of
Technology

SCRIPTS

In this article the notion of script (Schank and Abelson, 1977) is discussed as a memory structure that organizes knowledge about stereotypical situations, such as dining at a restaurant, going to the movies, or shopping for groceries. The entry focuses on the structure of scripts, script application, problems with scripts, psychological validity of the script notion, and issues in script acquisition. The process of script application is discussed from the perspective for four story-understanding computer programs.

A script (Schank and Abelson, 1977) is a knowledge structure containing a stereotypic sequence of actions.

Scripts encode culturally shared knowledge of stereotyped actions that occur in socially ritualized activities, such as: going to stores, restaurants, and museums; riding trains and subways; attending plays and banquets; and playing games or driving cars. Scripts are intended to capture situations in which the behavior is so stylized that the need for complex goal and planning analysis rarely arises. People probably acquire scripts through repeated exposure to stereotypic situations. Scripts are knowledge constructs that tell people what can happen in a situation, what events follow, and what roles various people are expected to play in a given social setting. In addition to guiding behavior, scripts are of value in directing cognitive processes, eg, while reading narratives that involve social activities.

An example of a prototypical script is $RESTAURANT, which captures the activities involved in eating in a restaurant. The $ distinguishes the script from the word "restaurant," which refers to the physical setting in which the scriptal activities occur. It is important to realize that the notion of a script is independent of any natural language used to describe it. For example, the event of being seated in a restaurant is described using different words or phrases in Spanish, but the events themselves are the same. Of course, the content of a script will vary by subculture since different social groups have distinct forms of ritualized behavior. For example, the events in $WEDDING will differ in African cultures. However, all people probably access and apply knowledge constructs that serve the function of scripts. From this point of view, the notion of a script is a cultural universal.

In $RESTAURANT, eg, the ordinary course of affairs is that the patron enters, is seated, and orders a meal. The meal is then prepared and served, and the patron eats it. Finally, the patron pays the bill and leaves. Each of these activities is described by a stereotyped sequence of events, which prescribes the order in which things happen and the people and objects participating in the action. Entering the restaurant, looking for a table, walking over to one, and sitting down comprise one such event chain. Each event has resulting states that in turn become the enabling conditions for further events to occur. For example, one must be physically inside the restaurant before one can look for a table. Seeing an empty table enables walking over to it. As a result of walking to a table, one can sit down at it.

Scripts help both humans and computers process text involving stereotypical situations. Consider the following script-based story:

> Mary went to a restaurant. She ordered lobster. She left a large tip.

$RESTAURANT provides the context necessary for inferring events not explicitly mentioned in the story (eg, eating lobster and paying the check) and for recognizing the causal relationships among events explicitly mentioned in the story (eg, the relationship between ordering lobster and eating it).

In this entry the concept of script and its application in natural-language processing is discussed with emphasis on the structure of a script; use of, and problems with, scripts; psychological validity of scripts; and the script-acquisition process. In addition, the uses of the notion of script by the computer system SAM (qv), FRUMP (qv), BORIS (qv), and OpEd (qv) are described.

Structure of a Script

What does a script look like internally (Cullingford, 1978, 1981)? Consider the subway script (eg, in New York). A patron enters the station and goes to a turnstile. Next the patron puts a token in, passes through, and goes to the appropriate platform. Eventually, the train comes. The patron enters and finds a seat. After a number of stops the destination is reached, and the patron leaves the train and exits the station.

This stereotyped sequence of events in the "backbone" of the subway script is understood and used by millions of commuters in New York and, with minor variations, in other cities as well. In each case, there is an organization (the subway company or authority) providing a certain kind of transportation to a member of the public in return for money. In $SUBWAY there is a cast of characters (roles), the objects they use while going about their business (props), and the places (setting) where the script's activities happen. The roles, props, and setting of a script taken together make up the script variables, which are matched up against real-world (or fictitious) people, places, and objects. For instance, the roles of the subway script are:

&PATGRP	A group of subway riders
&CASHIER	The cashier
&CONDUCTOR	The conductor
&DRIVER	The person controlling the train
&SUBORG	The subway organization

For example, the patron role (&PATGRP) in $SUBWAY must be filled by the class PERSON or GROUP since both "John Smith" and "Mr. and Mrs. Smith" are accepted as role fillers. The subway company providing the service, eg, "the BMT," must belong to the class ORGANIZATION.

The settings of the script are the places where the script's events happen. Settings belong to the class LOCALE. In $SUBWAY the three most important settings are the originating station, the inside of the car the patron selects, and the destination station.

The props of a script are associated either with the script's roles or its settings. Role-based props include such small objects as tokens and coins. Setting-based props function as "furniture" in a script. For example, the cashier's booth and the turnstile are props in the subway concourse; seats and bubble gum machines are props on a platform. A special prop in $SUBWAY is the train itself. This is an example of "structured" physical object whose parts, the cars, are important locations for script activity in their own right. The props of $SUBWAY include:

&TOKEN	A token
&FARE	Money paid for a token

&TURNSTILE	A turnstile
&PLATSEAT	A seat on the platform
&SUBWAY	The train itself
&SUBWAYCAR	One of the cars
&CARSEAT	A seat on the car
&STRAP	A strap for the patron to grasp
&EXITGATE	The gate leading from the platform at the destination station

The most important components of $SUBWAY are its events, involving the roles, props, and settings. Scriptal events are represented in terms of conceptual-dependency (qv) (CD) structures (Schank, 1973, 1975). For example, the patron's giving money to the cashier at the cashier's cage is represented as:

(ATRANS
    ACTOR   &PATGRP
    OBJECT &FARE
    FROM   &PATGRP
    TO   &CASHIER)

where ATRANS represents, in CD notation, an abstract transfer of possession or control.

As with scripts in general, the representation of events in CD are language-free. The CD representation of an event provides a canonical form for mapping many surface strings or inputs that are conceptually equivalent. For instance, the same CD form would be used no matter if the sentence were "John gave a dollar to the cashier," "The cashier got a dollar from John," or "a dollar was received from John by the cashier." The use of CD representation thus cuts down tremendously on the size of the script since only the conceptual content (and not the surface form) of the sentences need be considered. It also reduces the amount of processing since needed inferences can be tied together via conceptual events rather than having to be duplicated for each distinct surface string with an equivalent meaning. For instance, if x ATRANS object o from x to y, then one can conclude that x no longer controls o and y now does. By representing and factoring out the transfer of control aspect of "give," "get," "buy," "loan," "steal," etc, in terms of an ATRANS predication, one acquires access immediately to those inferences associated with ATRANS. For instance, although "steal" maps to more than ATRANS alone (eg, stealing implies that it is against the owner's will), that aspect of its representation in terms of ATRANS allows natural-language analyzers to conclude automatically from, say, "John stole the car from Bill" that Bill has lost physical control of the car and John now has control of it.

Script events contain both "constant" parts (eg, ACTOR and ATRANS in the example given above) and "variable" parts, ie, they are patterns designed to match an arbitrary range of real-world events. For example, any member of the public can ride on the subway, so the corresponding slot in the script's events cannot be fixed but must accept any person or group that comes along in the story. In the "paying the cashier in the subway" activity, one needs a way to specify the things that are always true. For example, this event has a person handing over an amount of money to another person who is an agent of the subway organization. One also has to provide for things that can vary in small details. The fare may be expressed as "a dollar" or "four quarters." "John" may pay the cashier or "John and Mary" may pay.

The basic idea in defining a pattern is to include the minimum amount of information needed to uniquely identify the event. Consider, for example, the pattern for:

Patron enters the station

(PTRANS
    ACTOR   &PATGRP
    OBJECT &PATGRP
    TO   (INSIDE
                PART &STATION))

where PTRANS is a CD predicate that organizes inferences involving transfer of physical location. This pattern can match conceptualizations that correspond to inputs such as:

1. John and Mary went into a subway station.
2. John walked into a subway station.
3. John strolled out of a restaurant up the street into a subway station.
4. John went into the BMT (Brooklyn-Manhattan Transit).

Example 1 would instantiate the pattern because John and Mary form a group. In example 2 the pattern would consider the fact that John "walked" to the subway as insignificant; it would create the same conceptualization if John had "sauntered," "rambled," "ran," or even "came in on rollerskates." In 3 where John came from is of no interest to $SUBWAY. (It would constitute a signal that the activated $RESTAURANT be closed before $SUBWAY is opened.) Finally, 4 would instantiate the pattern because BMT is a subway organization.

Script Invocation with Script Headers. An important class of patterns are called script headers, which act to "invoke" or "instantiate" a script. The basic rule in defining a script header is that a complete event is needed to bring the script into play. For example, $RESTAURANT should not be invoked just because "a restaurant" is mentioned. This is not to say that script information should be completely suppressed because it may be used in later stages of understanding. For example, in "I met a truck driver in a restaurant," remembering that in $RESTAURANT the person had a &DRIVER role in $TRUCKING may be crucial to understanding what he might say or do later.

Conceptualizations can be produced not only by surface clauses but also by certain kinds of prepositional phrases. Such phrases can act as complete thoughts by modifying the time or place setting of the main event. Consider the following sentence:

Mary was killed in an auto accident.

The above phrase can be paraphrased roughly as "When an accident occurred, Mary was killed." The top-level event of Mary's being killed is placed into some temporal relation to the "accident." Thus, just the prepositional phrase "in an auto accident" is sufficient to create a conceptualization that can invoke the entire $VEHICLE-ACCIDENT script.

Script headers come in four varieties and are ranked on the basis of how strongly they predict that the associated context will be instantiated. The first type is called a precondition header (PH) because it triggers a script on the basis of a main script precondition being mentioned in the text. As an example, the sentence "John was hungry" is a PH for $RESTAURANT because it is enabling the condition for the main conceptualization (INGEST food) of the script. A story understander having access to both scripts and plans would make the (relatively weak) prediction that $RESTAURANT might come up because this is known to be a common means (ie, a plan) of getting fed. A related PH would be an actual statement of the specific goal that the script is normally assumed to achieve or one from which that goal could easily be inferred. In "John wanted to eat a hamburger" or "John wanted some Italian food," the inference chain to the script precondition is relatively straightforward.

A second type of header, which makes stronger predictions than a PH about the associated context, is the instrumental header (IH). An IH comes up in inputs that refer to two or more scripts, at least one of which can be interpreted as an "instrument" for the others. For example, in "John took the subway to the restaurant," both $SUBWAY and $RESTAURANT would be predicted, since subsequent inputs about either would make perfectly good sense. Here, the reference to $RESTAURANT is anticipatory, and $SUBWAY is a recognized instrumental means of reaching locales in which more important script goals can be expected to be accomplished.

The notion of a time–place setting for a script leads to the third and most strongly predictive type of header, the locale header (LH). Many organizations have a "residence" or "place of business" in which they characteristically carry on their activities. They may have distinctively designed ornaments or buildings (eg, a pawn shop's sign, a barber's pole, or McDonald's Golden Arches) that signal their scripts in the world. When an understander reads that an actor is in the proximity of the residence, or, better yet, inside the residence, its expectations about the occurrence of the script are correspondingly reinforced. Examples of LHs are "John went to the soccer field" and "John went into the Museum of Modern Art."

The final type of header is a flat assertion that the script occurred. Examples include:

There was a car accident.
An earthquake struck.
John went on vacation.
Mary went sailing.

Such a direct header (DH) is the top-level pattern in a script. DHs are always the first pattern to be checked in a context, since they have the maximum predictive power.

Here are the headers of the subway script:

DIRECT HEADER:

```
($SUBWAY
   MAIN     &PATGRP
   PTRORG   &SUBORG
   ORIG     &ORIG
   DEST     &DEST)
```

LOCALE HEADER:

```
(PTRANS
   ACTOR    &PATGRP
   OBJECT   &PATGRP
   TO       (INSIDE
              PART &STATION))
```

INSTRUMENTAL HEADER:

```
(PTRANS
   ACTOR    &SUBORG
   OBJECT   &PATGRP
   TO       (PROX
              PART &DEST))
```

PRECONDITION HEADER:

```
(GOAL
   PART     &PATGRP
   OBJECT   (PTRANS
              ACTOR    &PARTORG
              OBJECT   &PARTORG
              TO       (PROX
                         PART &DEST)))
```

The DH is intended to handle conceptualizations corresponding to input such as "John took a subway ride to Coney Island." The LH takes care of sentences such as "John walked into the Boro Hall subway station." The IH will handle conceptualizations such as "The IRT (Interborough Rapid Transit) took John to Shea Stadium." Finally, the PH would match conceptualizations for sentences such as "John wanted to go downtown."

Script Events, Episodes, and Scenes. Activities in scripts are stereotyped. Events follow one another in one of a small set of recognized ways. On entering the subway, eg, the patron may either proceed directly to the turnstile or stop to buy a token. A chain of event patterns describing one of these well-understood activities is called an episode. "Buying a token" is an episode consisting of the events "enter the station," "see the cashier's cage," "go to it," "ask for a token," "be told the fare," and "pay the fare." Each of these events is represented in a language-independent way using conceptual dependency. Note that the script demands that the fare be paid before the token is handed over. This is how the episode is always structured in the subway script, although the actions can be reversed in other scripts, such as when a person is buying an ice cream cone.

Every episode has a main conceptualization, or Maincon, which is the goal or point of the episode. The episodes (marked with "E") and Maincons (marked with "M") of $SUBWAY are shown in the Figure 1.

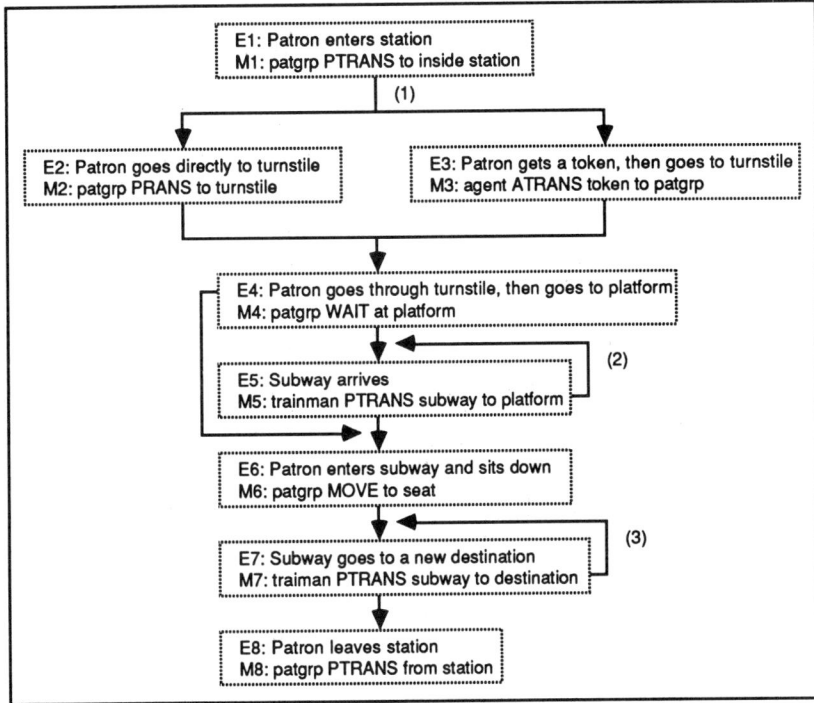

Figure 1. Episodes of subway script.

In Figure 1 the branching paths at 1 lead to the subsequent episodes E2 and E3, which describe alternative ways of arranging to get through the turnstile. The "loops" at point 2 and 3 are for the cyclic episodes E5 and E7, ie, for episodes that may happen several times in succession. At 2 several trains may arrive before the one the patron wants, and so the patron must continue to wait.

One could make a single episode out of all the events from entering the subway to leaving the destination station. However, one would clearly be ignoring important facts about the structure of $SUBWAY. Some parts of the subway ride are more important, more central to the situation, than others. Getting a token, eg, is an important activity in $SUBWAY because without one a patron cannot get through the turnstile to get his ride. Taking a seat on the platform, on the other hand, is not so important because it does not really have any effect on whether the patron can get on the train. Also, sometimes different ways of doing the same thing may be available. Having a token before the ride, asking for one at the counter, or showing the cashier a special pass are all possible ways of procuring a ride. In this case one has a set of episodes that seem to go together.

The activities of a script that always have to occur in order to recognize that the script has in fact been instantiated are called scenes. The scenes of $SUBWAY are:

$SUBWAYENTER   Enter the station and wait at the platform
$SUBWAYRIDE   Enter the train and ride to destination
$SUBWAYEXIT   Leave the station at destination

"Entering," including buying and using a token, is a scene of the subway script because it is necessary to procure a ride. "Riding" is a scene because this transporting activity is what the script is all about. "Leaving" is a scene because one cannot be sure that the ride is over until the patron exits the station (ie, the patron might just otherwise be transferring between subway lines). Each scene of a script is defined by a set of episodes that describes the different ways in which an important activity of the scene can happen and other, less important actions, such as sitting down on the platform, that can be interlinked with the main episodes but do not contribute directly to their accomplishment. Scenes commonly organize events that occur within the same sublocale. For example, all the events in the SUBWAYRIDE scene occur in the train locale.

Why Scripts are Useful

Early attempts to program computers to understand natural language (see NATURAL LANGUAGE UNDERSTANDING), despite the initial optimism of the researchers, met with only limited success. For example, the problem of machine translation (qv) between languages was viewed as being essentially one of supplying the computer with dictionaries and grammars of sufficient high quality. The ultimate failure of the translation projects of the 1950s, as described, eg, by Bar-Hillel (1964), can be directly attributed to the reliance on formal, syntactic methods. Knowledge of the world was completely lacking in the systems actually built at that time.

Two of the earliest semantics-based approaches to natural language processing were represented by the SHRDLU (qv) (Winograd, 1972) and MARGIE (Schank, 1975; Schank and co-workers, 1975) systems. SHRDLU engaged in an interactive dialogue concerning a microworld of blocks. It could answer questions about blocks and carry out simple commands, such as "Pick up the red pyramid on a blue block." SHRDLU represented the meaning of a sentence in terms of a procedure to carry out a set of actions within the blocks microworld. For instance, "the pyramid red on a blue block" would be translated into a program to examine each block until a blue one was found and then check to see if a red pyramid was on top of it and, if not, continue searching for another blue block, etc. Unfortunately, this approach of procedural representation made it difficult to represent the meaning of a sentence outside the context of a prespecified microworld.

In contrast, MARGIE was based on a representational system intended to be independent of any particular microworld. MARGIE's representational system was based on a fixed set of CD primitives (Schank, 1973, 1975) and was composed of three modules: ELI (Riesbeck, 1975), MEMORY (Rieger, 1975), and BABEL (Goldman, 1975). ELI parsed English sentences, producing CD representations. MEMORY then generated all the inferences that arouse from the conceptual representations produced by ELI. These inferences were themselves represented in CD. Finally, BABEL generated paraphrases by expressing each CD conceptualization in English.

However, MARGIE had great difficulty handling more than one sentence at a time. This occurred because MEMORY generated every possible inference it could. Since each inference would generate a CD and since that CD had many potential inferences associated with it, very quickly MEMORY would be overcome by a combinatorial explosion of inferences. There seemed to be no way of constraining inferences to those that were relevant to the text at hand.

The combinatorial problem was partially solved by the notion of a script. Although independently developed, the notion of the script takes the same standpoint as the more general notion of a frame (Charniak, 1977, 1978), (see FRAMES) which was developed originally to handle problems in vision (Minsky, 1975, 1977). Like frames, scripts seek to represent a variety of knowledge domains in terms of a hierarchical data structure containing slots that describe what features of the input can bind to these slots and how to construct default values if these features are missing from the input.

Scripts are useful in supplying expectations during text processing. These expectations represent an active context and help in such tasks as:

1. *Pronoun Resolution.* In a $RESTAURANT context, clearly the "he" in "he left him a big tip" is the customer while "him" must be the waiter.
2. *Word-Sense Disambiguation.* The expressions "ordered" and "to go" have different meanings in a restaurant ("John ordered a pizza to go") than in the military ("The general ordered a private to go").
3. *Supplying Inferences.* Once a script is chosen, processing can proceed very efficiently since missing information is automatically provided by the script. For example, the reader can infer that a waiter or waitress brought the food to the diner even if the text only states "When the food came, he ate it and left a big tip."

Scripts also contain one or more paths (Cullingford, 1978), each supplying a possible alternative sequence of actions to the "ghost" (or default) path (Lehnert, 1978). An alternative path in $RESTAURANT includes leaving without paying because the food was improperly cooked. This path information is used to answer questions, such as:

Q: Why didn't John eat the hamburger?

In this case the search heuristic starts with the "ghost path" in which the food would have been eaten. The retrieval heuristic backs up along this path until a branch point is found. Here resides the reason perhaps:

A: The hamburger was burnt.

that an alternative path was taken.

Problems with Scripts

A strictly script-based approach to natural-language processing has serious limitations for three reasons:

1. Scripts were conceived as self-contained "chunks" of knowledge. As a result, it is difficult to share knowledge across scripts. For example, a restaurant serves meals, but people also eat meals in nonrestaurant situations (eg, home and picnics). This meal knowledge should be shared with restaurant knowledge even though the meal server in a restaurant differs from the meal server at home.
2. Experiences occurring within one script cannot be generalized to other relevant situations because scripts are self-contained (Schank, 1982a). For example, the knowledge that one can refuse to pay for burnt food in a restaurant should be available in other scriptal contexts. If a mechanic fails to properly fix one's car engine, refusing to pay should come to mind as a potential course of action (Dyer, 1981a). But this is impossible with scripts since refusing payment is firmly attached to $RESTAURANT (and not to $AUTO-REPAIR).
3. Scripts lack intentionality. From a scriptal point of view, each event occurs next simply because it is the next event in the script. Although script-based programs know that characters initiate $RESTAURANT to satisfy hunger, they do not know why any specific event within $RESTAURANT occurs. This is analogous to answering:

Q: Why does the diner tip the waitress?
A: I do not know. That is just what he does in a restaurant after he has eaten.

Lack of intentionality has both advantages and disadvantages. It is certainly more efficient, since goals and plans do not have to be processed in order to predict what a character will do next. However, it is difficult to handle novel situations, where a character's reaction might be explainable if the underlying goals and motivations (for the expected event) were known (Wilensky, 1978, 1983).

In response to limitations 1 and 2 above, and to experiments (Bower and co-workers, 1979) regarding memory confusions not predicted by scripts, Schank (1982b) developed a theory of MOPs (memory-organization packets) (qv). Aspects of this theory were subsequently implemented in a number of text-processing systems. MOPs are memory-structures that, like scripts, encode expectations, but unlike scripts, MOPs are not isolated chunks of knowledge. Instead each MOP has strands that indicate how the MOP has been constructed from other knowledge sources. Each strand connects an event in one MOP to some event in another MOP. In this way, MOPs are overlaid on one another. Consider Figure 2, which shows how restaurant knowledge is encoded as MOPs in the BORIS understanding system (Dyer, 1983).

Events in M-RESTAURANT are overlaid with their corresponding events in M-MEAL and M-SERVICE. In this way M-RESTAURANT can be viewed from different perspectives. From the perspective of M-MEAL, a restaurant is simply a setting in which people have meals. From the perspective of M-SERVICE, the diner in M-RESTAURANT is engaged in a service contract with the restaurant owner. The restaurant must serve food to the diner and, in return, the diner is expected to pay for this service.

As stated earlier, script-based systems represent scriptal deviations in terms of alternative "paths." Thus, $RESTAURANT contains BURNT-FOOD→LEAVE-WITHOUT-PAYING path. But this approach causes a proliferation of paths for two reasons:

1. Every possible deviation has to be anticipated and "canned" into the script; otherwise the script would not be able to handle the deviation.
2. Each service-related script ends up copying the same path. For example, in $AUTO-REPAIR there has to be a BAD-REPAIR→LEAVE-WITHOUT-PAYING path. By overlaying these scripts with M-SERVICE, a single deviation path, POOR-SERVICE→REFUSE-TO-PAY, in M-SERVICE can represent deviation knowledge at a more general level. Likewise, "payment for service" occurs in many situations, not just in $RESTAURANT. Therefore, tipping should be understood at a more general level than $RESTAURANT.

When stereotypic situations are first encountered, people let their scriptal knowledge handle the situation until a violation occurs. At this point they become aware of other perspectives associated with the script, each potentially useful in understanding the violation.

For instance, one rarely thinks about the contractual aspects of restaurants when eating in one of them. Restaurants are usually "taken for granted" as a place where one can have a meal and socialize. Only when something goes wrong does one think of the contract one is implicitly engaged in. If the service is bad, one considers the amount of the tip and what it is for.

More important, a deviation that has never before been encountered may be handled as long as some strand exists from the script to a knowledge structure with information about this type of deviation. For instance, if $MOVIE has strands to M-SERVICE, the very first time the movie projector breaks, one can use the deviation path in M-SERVICE to think of demanding a refund even if the projector breaking down is a novel experience.

Natural-Language-Understanding Systems Using Scripts

The notion of script has been used by several natural-language understanding (qv) systems, which include SAM, FRUMP, BORIS, and OpEd. How these systems apply the notion of script during text understanding is described below.

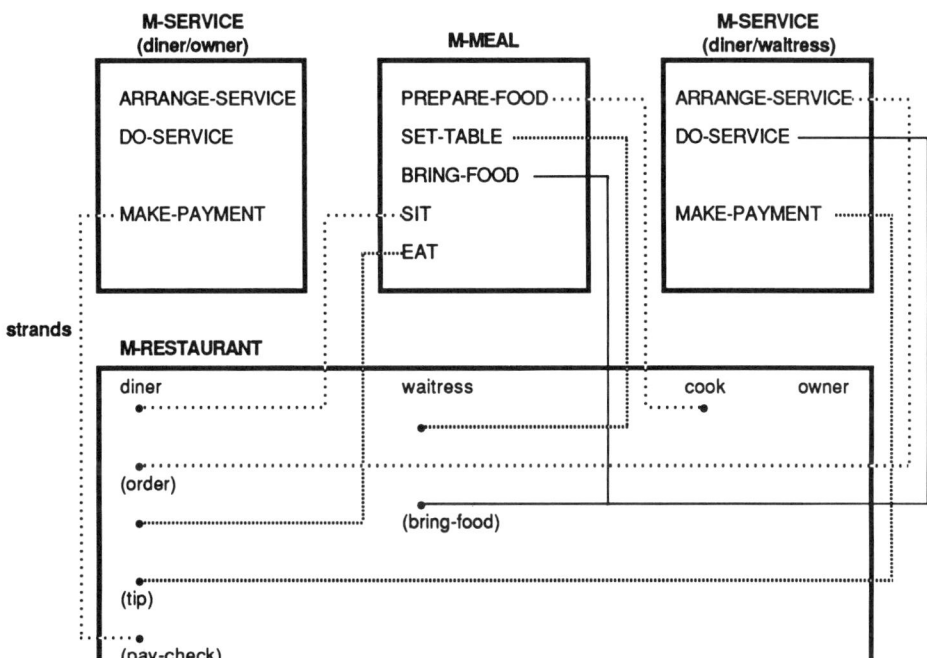

Figure 2. Example of MOP overlay scheme is BORIS.

Script Application in SAM. SAM (Script-Applier Mechanism) (Cullingford, 1975, 1976, 1978, 1981) is a system of computer programs written to investigate how knowledge of context can be used to aid in understanding stories. The basic knowledge source SAM applies is the script. Using scripts of various degrees of complexity, SAM can read (by the process of script application) not only simple stories but also newspaper articles referring to domains as diverse as car accidents and VIP (very important person) state visits. Each of these types of text involves certain invariant components, such as what can happen, the order in which things happen, and who is involved. This consistency of form and content enables the script-based model of reading to be used.

SAM can also answer questions about stories that have been read. The theory underlying SAM's question-answering (Q/A) capability is provided by QUALM (Lehnert, 1978). In addition, SAM can summarize and paraphrase a story by accessing the story representation and picking out the important or interesting events recorded there. SAM's internal CD structures are converted to natural-language output by a generator, described in Goldman (1975).

The following example of SAM's input and output illustrates the level of story understanding SAM achieved.

Input text:

John went to a restaurant. He ordered a hot dog. The waiter said they didn't have any. He asked for a hamburger. When the hamburger came, it was burnt. He left the restaurant.

Question-answering output:

Q1: Did John sit down at the restaurant?
A1: PROBABLY.
Q2: Did John order a hot dog?
A2: YES.
Q3: Did John eat a hot dog?
A3: NO, THE WAITER TOLD JOHN THE MANAGEMENT WAS UNABLE TO GIVE IT TO HIM.
Q4: What did the waiter serve John?
A4: THE WAITER SERVED JOHN A HAMBURGER.
Q5: Why didn't John eat the hamburger?
A5: BECAUSE THE HAMBURGER WAS OVERDONE.
Q6: Did John pay the check?
A6: NO, JOHN WAS ANGRY BECAUSE THE HAMBURGER WAS OVERDONE AND SO HE LEFT THE RESTAURANT.

SAM's inferences are accomplished through application of $RESTAURANT, where unstated events are instantiated via script application. An example of a causal-chain completion inference is to be seen in the answer to question 1, which asks about an implicit, yet normative, event.

Question 4 also shows SAM's ability to analyze in context. The story input "when the hamburger came" has been identified as referring to the "serving" event. Here a role-merging inference has identified "the waiter" as the active entity in this event, given that hamburgers obviously cannot move by themselves.

In addition to inferring what happened while reading the story, SAM is also capable of making inferences at the time of question answering. This arises with questions about events that did not happen. In question 3 the nonoccurrence of the highly expected "eating" event is attributed to an "interfering" condition, ie, the restaurant was out of hot dogs. Similarly, in questions 5 and 6 SAM infers that the reason for the second nonoccurrence of "eating," followed by the customer's refusal to pay the check, is a second "interfering" condition, ie, the hamburger was burnt.

Basically, SAM is configured as a set of three modules: ELI (qv) (Riesbeck, 1975), which analyzes the text into a conceptual-dependency (CD) meaning representation; PP-MEMORY, which tags and identifies references to physical objects; and APPLIER, which applies scripts. PP here stands for "picture producer," ie, anything that is concrete enough to create an image in one's mind. ELI is the only module of SAM that is concerned with linguistic knowledge, and it is the only one that worries about the particular ways that English-speaking people indicate meaning via the choice of word senses, the order of words, the inflection of words, etc. ELI's job in SAM is to extract from an English sentence only the conceptual elements that are there explicitly, avoiding inference as far as possible. In SAM the task of inferring the things an input leaves out is reserved for the "memory" routines (PP-MEMORY and the script applier). This is because making inferences of this type depends on the use of world knowledge rather than on the superficial semantic information ELI possesses as part of its knowledge of English.

When PP-MEMORY is finished processing ELI's output, it sends the result to the script applier. This program has three fundamental problems to solve as it processes a new conceptualization: locating a new input in its database of scripts; setting up predictors about likely inputs to follow; and instantiating the appropriate segment of the script up to the point referred by the input. Of these three problems, the first one, called the script-management problem, is the most important.

The script applier controls the comprehension process by consulting its collection of scripts. Each script has several important parts. First, there are the script's characteristic event chains or episodes. Since an event in a script may be realized in the world in many ways, the events in script episodes are patterns.

A special set of patterns is found in the script "preconditions," or those global facts SAM assumes to be true when a script is entered for the first time unless it reads something to the contrary. When $RESTAURANT is activated, eg, the script applier will assert that the patron is hungry and has money to pay for the meal. If the text has indicated that the patron does not have any money (if, eg, he left his wallet at home), the violation of the precondition will trigger a prediction that the patron will have trouble when it comes time to pay the bill.

An important part of each script is the information that is always active in memory. This includes static data such as: an initial list of those patterns that activate the script (the headers); how related episodes are combined into chunks or "scenes," time and place-setting data for the script; and how other, simpler scripts may be used as units in the main script.

The script applier's three main procedures are a pattern matcher, a predictor, and an instantiator. All three procedures run under an executive, and all have access to script data. The pattern matcher consists of a routine that sets up desired script contexts one at a time, the matcher proper, and a set of auxiliary inference processes. The predictor adds and removes event patterns based on the pattern currently active and what has gone before.

The script applier attempts to understand a story by introducing the most inclusive script it possesses that is initiated by the first conceptualization in the story. As each input conceptualization is recognized in the script, predictions are made by the script applier about future inputs. This cycle continues until the system receives an input that does not refer to a predicted event. At this point it again brings in the largest script the input initiates, matches roles and props across the script interfaces, checks the preconditions, if any, for the new script, and starts matching inputs in the new context.

In the course of story understanding the script applier maintains data structures that describe the state of each script present in the system. This information forms a script context which, if the script is active, is updated whenever a new conceptualization is found to fit within the context. Each script context is defined by the list of patterns from that script that are currently in memory; an association list of tokens bound to script variables; the name of the last pattern matched in the script; the list of script episodes currently in memory; the header for this incarnation of the script; and a script-global inference-strength indicator the applier uses to flag how probable its inferences appear to be.

The most important data structure is the conceptual story representation being constructed by the script applier for the current text. This structure provides access to the final record of the story and is used by the question-answering routines.

The script applier's basic cycle is to call the script contexts one at a time and to attempt to locate an input in the context invoked. Candidate scripts are brought into active memory in the following order: first are those script contexts explicitly referred by the input or indirectly accessed via a PP or a subconceptualization in the input; next are the currently active scripts; last are the scripts the system possesses but that have not been invoked.

Once an input has been located in a script context, the Instantiator links it up with what has gone before in that context and then checks on the effect this may have on other active contexts. If the script is being referenced for the first time, the applier checks on the script preconditions to see whether the script is being entered normally or if some unusual events are to be expected in the new context because of previous events. If more than one context is current, the applier may be able to update the story representation on the basis of the static information that is always available for the scripts. For example, $TRAIN contains the information that a reference to the $RESTAURANT context via "dining car" in an existing $TRAIN context defines a "parallel-nested" relationship. Inputs to follow may refer to either script, but $RESTAURANT should be completed before $TRAIN.

Many transitions between component scripts are handled by the more complex scripts that define the "global" context of the story. For example, $BUS, $TRAIN, $PLANE, etc, are known to be "instrumental" means of reaching or leaving a place where the "goal" activity of the trip takes place. The global $TRIP script may be explicitly introduced, as in "John went to Miami on a business trip," or implicitly referenced by one of its instruments, as in "John took a train to Miami." Script situations, as these scripts are called, provide the most important machinery for the solution of what is called the script-management problem.

Skimming in FRUMP. FRUMP (Fast Reading, Understanding, and Memory Program) (DeJong, 1979a, 1979b, 1982a) is a text-understanding program that skims and extracts sparse summaries of news articles. FRUMP displays its understanding by generating a summary that represents the "gist" of a story. Unlike SAM, FRUMP ignores many words in the text. The resulting memory of a story often misses events and situations that occur within the story.

FRUMP reads numerous stories on the UPI (United Press International) news wire. FRUMP contains over 50 "sketchy" scripts concerning such things as earthquakes, kidnappings, visiting dignitaries, labor strikes, and breaking diplomatic relations.

Unlike SAM, analysis in FRUMP is integrated with other processes to the extent that "sketchy" scripts direct it in a "top-down" manner (see PROCESSING, BOTTOM-UP AND TOP-DOWN). Once a knowledge structure is referred to in the text, this structure directs subsequent parsing strategies. When FRUMP finds a story that involves one of its scripts, it uses that single script to guide its analysis of the text. In SAM the ELI parser would first analyze a sentence and produce a CD representation for the conceptual content of that sentence. Then the current active script would be applied to the input CD. For instance, in "he ate it," the "he" would be bound to the diner since it is the role of the diner to eat the food. In contrast, FRUMP is organized around a predictor and a substantiator. Once a sketchy script has been selected, the predictor actually directs the substantiator to find in the text what the predictor is looking for. Thus, there is no prior parse phase (ie, mapping text to CDs) once a sketchy script is active. For instance, assume the $FIGHTING sketchy script is already active and the predictor has predicted that SHOOTING will occur. At this point the predictor tells the substantiator to try to find an instance of shooting (ie, PROPEL object = bullets). The substantiator knows about English and searches in the appropriate place in the text for words that have this PROPEL CD conceptualization associated with them. For example, if the substantiator encounters the word "fire" with the appropriate actors (eg, "the soldiers did fire at the enemy"), it automatically selects the PROPEL-bullets meaning of "fire" rather than the "flame/combustion" meaning of "fire." Thus, the parser is under the control of memory rather than parsing independently and then presenting the results for script application. The advantage of this integrated approach is that the context can direct the comprehension process.

The following I/O example illustrates the level of comprehension that FRUMP attains.

> MOUNT VERNON, ILL. (UPI)—A small earthquake shook several Southern Illinois counties Monday night, the National Earthquake Information Service in Golden, CO, reported.
> Spokeman Don Finley said the earthquake measured 3.2 on the Richter scale, "probably not enough to do any damage or cause any injuries." The quake occurred about 7:48 P.M. CST [Central Standard Time] and was centered about 30 miles east of Mount Vernon, Finley said. It was felt in Richland, Clay, Jasper, Effington, and Marion counties.
> Small earthquakes are common in the area, Finley said.
>
> SELECTED SKETCHY SCRIPT $EARTHQUAKE.
> CPU TIME FOR UNDERSTANDING = 3040 MILLISECONDS
> ENGLISH SUMMARY:
>   THERE WAS AN EARTHQUAKE IN ILLINOIS WITH A 3.2 RICHTER SCALE READER.

To process the story above, FRUMP uses an earthquake "sketchy" script and extracts the place and magnitude of the quake. Everything else, however, is ignored.

The top-down approach fulfilling prior expectations and selectively ignoring information not conforming to these expectations gives FRUMP a great deal of robustness. The main negative consequence is that unusual or unexpected information is often missed since it does not conform to the predictor's script-based expectations. As a result, unusual (and interesting) events in the text fail to be incorporated into a final memory representation of the story. This approach is adequate, however, for the task of extracting sparse summaries for stories via skimming.

Integrated In-Depth Parsing in BORIS. BORIS (Dyer, 1981a, 1981b, 1983; Dyer and Lehnert, 1982; Lehnert and co-workers, 1983) is an in-depth story-understanding and question-answering system that deals with the specification and interaction of many sources of knowledge. In contrast to text skimmers, BORIS attempts to understand narratives as deeply as possible. For BORIS understanding a narrative "in depth" means the following: reading in a careful mode rather than skimming; handling narratives that involve multiple interacting knowledge sources; parsing text in an integrated fashion, where memory search and construction processes are evoked on a word-by-word basis; and recognizing the key thematic patterns that characterize a narrative at very abstract levels.

BORIS attempts to construct a complete representation of a narrative, including all physical events and mental states, along with the causal connections between them. As a result, BORIS operates in a very bottom-up manner. Processing is directed more from information arising in the input than from predetermined expectations as in FRUMP. Expectations in BORIS are encoded in the episodic memory of the narrative read thus far and are activated by search processes. This bottom-up approach gives BORIS the capability of noticing unusual events, which are often missed by exclusively top-down processing approaches. It is the unusual and unexpected events, including the mistakes and failures of the characters, that often make a story memorable. By their very nature, such events cannot be predicted in a top-down manner.

BORIS is a highly integrated system. All memory search, instantiation, and inference tasks occur as side effects of a single, unified parsing process that occurs on a word-by-word basis. That is, BORIS neither parses a complete sentence before calling a script applier nor relies on an active script to tell the parser completely how to map text into conceptualizations. Instead, BORIS associates parsing and memory-search processes with each word (phrase) in its lexicon. As a word or phrase is encountered, these processes (called "demons") knit together CD fragments from the input, perform inferences, call upon script appliers, and search memory for a number of different knowledge constructs. Furthermore, narrative questions are parsed by the same processes that handle the narratives themselves. One natural consequence is that BORIS often knows the answer to a question before it has completely understood the question. Another natural consequence is a "Loftus Effect" (Loftus, 1979, 1975). That is, asking a question about a narrative may cause the memory of the narrative to be altered (Dyer, 1983).

In contrast to early script-based systems that operate within restricted knowledge-source domains and deal poorly with script interactions, BORIS uses a MOP overlay scheme to achieve a much higher level of generality, which is especially useful in processing norm violations when they occur within scriptal contexts. For example, consider how BORIS processes the following fragment of DIVORCE-2 (Dyer, 1983), a complicated narrative concerning marital infidelity:

> George was having lunch . . . when the waitress accidentally knocked a glass of coke on him. George was very annoyed and left refusing to pay the check.
>
> *Q1:* Where did George have lunch?
> *A1:* AT THE RESTAURANT.
> *Q2:* What happened at the restaurant?
> *A2:* THE WAITRESS SPILLED THE COKE ON GEORGE AND HE REFUSED TO PAY THE CHECK.
> *Q3:* How did George feel at the restaurant?
> *A3:* GEORGE WAS ANGRY BECAUSE THE WAITRESS SPILLED COKE ON HIM.

In order to understand this fragment, BORIS uses the MOP overlay scheme shown in Figure 2. Briefly, an analysis of "having lunch" activates M-MEAL. When "waitress" occurs, the MOPs associated with this role are examined. If a MOP being examined has a strand to an active MOP, it is also activated. As stated earlier, there are strands from M-RESTAURANT to M-MEAL. Thus, since M-MEAL is already active, M-RESTAURANT is activated also. (This approach avoids the problem of invoking the restaurant script simply at the mention of a waitress, as in "John is in love with a waitress.")

An interpretation of "accidentally" indicates that a violation may follow. This heuristic is based on the assumption that unintended actions usually violate scriptal expectations.

"Knocked a glass of coke on him" is analyzed in terms of the CD primitive PROPEL with Object=Liquid. Given this event, BORIS tries to match it against the event expected in M-RESTAURANT. This match would normally fail since M-RESTAURANT does not expect waitresses to PROPEL foodstuffs. However, "accidentally" has warned BORIS of a possible violation, so a violation match is attempted and succeeds. At this point BORIS realizes that the PROPEL event is a violation of the event BRING-FOOD in M-RESTAURANT rather than some event totally unrelated to M-RESTAURANT.

Now what is BORIS to do? In previous systems there would be a prespecified path in the script for such a deviation. However, this is not the case here. When BORIS encounters a deviation, it searches the strands connected to the event where the deviation occurred. This leads to DO-SERVICE in M-SERVICE (Fig. 2).

Associated with M-SERVICE is general knowledge about how things may "go wrong" for each event in M-SERVICE. There are several events, such as ARRANGE-SERVICE, DO-SERVICE, INFORM-BILL, MAKE-PAYMENT, etc. For example, the sentence

The waitress overcharged George

constitutes a violation of INFORM-BILL.

In addition, there is knowledge about how violations may be related to each other. This knowledge is represented by rules, such as:

IF SERVER has done SERVICE badly (or not at all), THEN SERVER should either not BILL CONTRACTOR or BILL for amount less than NORM.

IF SERVER has done service badly or BILLs CONTRACTOR for amount greater than NORM, THEN contractor may refuse PAYMENT.

BORIS uses this knowledge to recognize the connection between the waitress PROPEL LIQUID and George's refusal to pay a check.

Finally, consider how BORIS realizes that the violation of BRING-FOOD actually constitutes POOR-SERVICE. This is accomplished by tracking the goals of the characters. The PROPEL LIQUID on George is understood to cause a PRESERVE-COMFORT goal for George. This goal is examined by M-SERVICE, which applies the following heuristic:

IF SERVER causes a PRESERVATION GOAL for CONTRACTOR while performing SERVICE, THEN it is probably POOR-SERVICE.

Thus, BORIS uses several sources of knowledge to understand what has happened. M-RESTAURANT supplies expectations for what the waitress should have done. Knowledge about PROPEL and LIQUIDs supplies goal information, and M-SERVICE (between waitress and diner) provides general knowledge about how contractors will respond to poor service.

The overlay scheme used in BORIS causes equivalences to be set up among component structures in different MOPs and has three major advantages:

1. Each knowledge structure needs to know only what is directly relevant to it. For example, what a waitress does is captured in M-RESTAURANT, although her reasons for doing her job are represented at the M-SERVICE level (which handles any type of service); thus M-SERVICE need not be repeated for janitors, salespersons, etc. This supports economy of storage, but more important, it means that any augmentation of the knowledge in M-SERVICE will automatically improve the processing ability of any MOP with strands to it.

2. Related knowledge sources need not be activated unless something goes wrong during process. For instance, people do not normally think of the contract between themselves and the restaurant manager unless they are having trouble with the service.

3. A given event can be understood from several perspectives. For example, a "business lunch" involves M-MEAL, M-SERVICE, M-RESTAURANT, and M-BUSINESS-DEAL simultaneously.

Reasoning Scripts in OpEd. OpEd (Opinions to/from the Editor) (Alvarado, 1990; Alvarado and co-workers, 1985, 1986, 1990a, 1990b, 1990c) is a prototype editorial comprehension and question answering system. OpEd is designed to take editorial text as input and answer subsequent questions about the beliefs or arguments of the editorial writer and of others whom the writer may criticize. The editorials read by OpEd are in the politico-economic domain and contain arguments for or against protectionist policies used to resolve conflicts in international trade. OpEd's design is based on the conceptual parser implemented in BORIS (qv), the question-answering theory developed by Dyer and Lehnert (1982) as an extension of previous work by Lehnert (1978), the argument-graph technique developed by Flowers and co-workers (1982), and the theory of argument units (AUs) developed by Alvarado (1990) to deal with the organization and application of abstract knowledge of argumentation (see ARGUMENT COMPREHENSION).

Editorial segments used as input to OpEd are in English and contain essential issues and arguments of the original editorials. The memory representation built while parsing (qv) an editorial forms a graph of conceptual constructs instantiated during editorial comprehension. Within this argument graph, instantiated constructs are connected by memory links that indicate knowledge dependencies such as causal relationships, support or attack relationships, containment relationships, and indexing relationships. Five major classes of instantiated constructs compose the editorial's argument graph: (1) domain-specific constructs, which include goals, plans, events, and states underlying the issues addressed in the editorial, (2) argument participants, which include the editorial writer and his or her implicit opponents, (3) beliefs, which involve the argument participants' evaluations about plans and expectations about the success or failure of goals, (4) belief relationships, which include support and attack structures that represent relationships among evaluative and causal beliefs, and (5) argument units, which organize configurations of support and attack structures, and represent the editorial writer's one-sided arguments. Initial entry to the editorial's argument graph is provided by indexing structures associated with argument participants, plans, and goals. These indexing structures allow search and retrieval processes access to the argument graph during question answering.

Like BORIS, OpEd is a highly integrated system. Memory and inference tasks are performed on a word-by-word basis by active processes called demons. These tasks include disambiguating word senses, resolving pronoun and concept references, matching and binding conceptualizations, recognizing beliefs, belief relationships, and argument units, tracking causal chains of reasoning, determining the conceptual category of input questions, and retrieving answers from editorial memory.

Part of OpEd's politico-economic knowledge is represented by reasoning scripts (Flowers and Dyer, 1984), which organize causal domain knowledge (qv) in the form of prespecified reasoning-chain sequences. Each of OpEd's reasoning scripts (prefixed by "$R-") holds a chain of cause-effect relationships involving economic quantities associated with the activity of international trade. Such a causal chain shows why economic goals become active as a result of changes in import prices and consumer spending, or why economic-protection plans result in changes in the level of earnings and employment in domestic industries. For example, the script $R-ECON-PROTECTION→FEWER-EXPORT-JOBS represents a causal chain that leads from the use of import restrictions to a decrease in the number of jobs in export industries of the countries implementing the restrictions (Fig. 3). There are four major reasons underlying the causal chain in $R-ECON-PROTECTION→FEWER-EXPORT-JOBS:

1. Import restrictions cause a decrease in sales by exporting countries and, consequently, a decrease in their level of export earnings.
2. Countries play two different roles in international trade: as producers, they export their products to other countries; and as consumers, they import products from other countries. These roles depend on one another because the level of spending on imports is directly proportional to the level of export earnings.
3. The level of earnings of export industries is directly proportional to the industries' sales to importing countries.
4. The level of employment in export industries is directly proportional to the industries' level of earnings.

Clearly, $R-ECON-PROTECTION→FEWER-EXPORT-JOBS allows OpEd to encode knowledge about a negative side effect of applying restrictions to international trade.

During editorial comprehension, OpEd recognizes and instantiates reasoning scripts in order to follow belief justifications that contain sequences of causal effects. The occurrence of reasoning scripts is signaled by beliefs involving a goal-achievement or a goal-failure relationship between a plan P and a goal G, or a negative spiral in which a plan P causes goal failures that require repeated applications of the same plan P. That is, beliefs of the form P—achieve→G, P—thwart→G, and P1—thwart→G2—intend→P2 (where P1 and P2 are instances of the same plan P) act as headers of reasoning scripts. When one such belief is recognized, OpEd accesses the reasoning scripts organized by the given plan P and searches for the script associated with the type of plan-goal relationship contained in that belief.

Once the script has been selected, OpEd attempts to understand the next input sentence from the context of that script. The representation of the sentence is matched against the conceptualizations in the script's causal chain and, if the match succeeds, the chain is instantiated up to the point referred to by the input. This process is repeated with successive input sentences until OpEd reads one that does not refer to any of the uninstantiated components of the script. At this point, it is assumed that the references to those components are implicitly stated in the editorial. As a result, OpEd instantiates the entire script and builds a support link from the instantiated script to the causal belief that triggered the application of the script in the first place.

To illustrate the use of the script-application algorithm, consider how OpEd processes the following fragment of ED-JOBS (Alvarado, 1990), a segment from an editorial by Friedman (1982):

Recent protectionist measures by the Reagan administration . . . will cost jobs. If we import less, foreign countries will earn fewer dollars. They will have less to spend on American exports. The result will be fewer jobs in export industries.

\$R-ECON-PROTECTION→FEWER-EXPORT-JOBS	
ROLES:	C1: Country imposing import restrictions C2: Country affected by import restrictions G1: Government of C1 I1: Export industry from C1 P1: Product by I1 P2: Import from C2
HEADER:	P-ECON-PROTECTION by G1 on P2 —thwart→ G-PRESERVING-JOBS in C1 by G1
CAUSAL CHAIN:	P-ECON-PROTECTION by G1 on P2 —cause→ decrease in SPENDING by C1 on P2 —cause→ decrease in SALES of P2 by C2 —cause→ decrease in EARNINGS of C2 —cause→ decrease in SPENDING by C2 on P1 —cause→ decrease in SALES of P1 by I1 —cause→ decrease in EARNINGS of I1 —cause→ decrease in EMPLOYMENT in I1 —thwart→ G-PRESERVING-JOBS in C1 by G1

Figure 3. Reasoning script $R-ECON-PROTECTION→FEWER-EXPORT-JOBS.

Q: Why does Milton Friedman believe that the limitations on imports will cost jobs?

A: Milton Friedman believes that protectionist policies by the Reagan administration will thwart the preservation of jobs for U.S. because Milton Friedman believes that as a consequence of protectionist policies by the Reagan administration, U.S. imports fewer products; and if U.S. imports fewer products, then there is a decrease in profits of foreign countries; and if there is a decrease in profits of foreign countries, then foreign countries buy fewer American exports; and if foreign countries buy fewer American exports, then there is a decrease in profits of export industries; and if there is a decrease in profits of export industries, then there is a decrease in jobs in export industries; and a decrease in jobs in export industries thwarts the preservation of jobs for U.S.

In the above excerpt, the word "cost" stands for a goal-failure relationship between a plan and a preservation goal. Giving this relationship, the sentence "protectionist measures . . . cost jobs" gets mapped into the following belief:

BELIEF1: Friedman believes
P-ECON-PROTECTION1—thwart→ G-PRESERVING-JOBS1

where P-ECON-PROTECTION1 is an instance of the planning structure P-ECON-PROTECTION, which represents the courses of action that a government can take to protect industries. Once BELIEF1 has been recognized, OpEd accesses the reasoning scripts organized by P-ECON-PROTECTION in order to find the script that fully expands BELIEF1 into a causal chain of effects. In OpEd, P-ECON-PROTECTION organizes reasoning scripts in terms of the achievement and thwarting effects that import restrictions have on economic goals associated with international trade. Those scripts show how import restrictions achieve the goals of preserving earnings and attaining profitability for industries being protected, thwart the goal of preserving earnings for consumers and industries that use imports, thwart the goal of preserving jobs for workers in export industries, and trigger protectionist spirals and economic retaliation. In the case of Friedman's editorial, the applicable script is $R-ECON-PROTECTION→FEWER-EXPORTS-JOBS, which provides OpEd with the context for understanding why import restrictions will cause a decrease in U.S. exports and, consequently, a decrease in U.S. jobs. The process of applying this script is shown in Figure 4.

As Figure 4 indicates, the use of reasoning scripts allows OpEd to follow belief justifications that contain structural gaps, ie, justifications involving causal chains with implicit cause-effect relationships. Those relationships are inferred as a side effect of the process of mapping input sentences into a reasoning script and instantiating the script with the information provided in those sentences. When processing Friedman's editorial, the use of $R-ECON-PROTECTION→FEWER-EXPORT-JOBS allows OpEd to infer the relationship between import restrictions and the level of U.S. spending on imports, between U.S. spending and the level of earnings by foreign countries, between foreign earnings and the level of foreign spending on U.S. exports, and between foreign spending and the number of jobs in U.S. export industries. For example, the connection between foreign spending and U.S. export jobs corresponds to the following fragment of the instantiated chain in $R-ECON-PROTECTION→FEWER-EXPORT-JOBS:

decrease in SPENDING by foreign countries on U.S. exports—causes→
decrease in SALES of U.S. exports by U.S. export industries—causes→
decrease in EARNINGS of U.S. export industries—causes→
decrease in EMPLOYMENT in U.S. export industries

In Friedman's editorial, the process of applying $R-ECON-PROTECTION→FEWER-EXPORT-JOBS finishes

Input Sentence	Representation of Input Sentence	Instantiation of $R-ECON-PROTECTION→FEWER-EXPORT-JOBS After Processing Input Sentence
If we import less, foreign countries will earn fewer dollars	decrease SPENDING U.S. —cause—> decrease EARNINGS foreign country	P-ECON-PROTECTION U.S. —cause—> decrease SPENDING U.S. —cause—> decrease SALES foreign exports —cause—> decrease EARNINGS foreign country
They will have less to spend on American exports	decrease SPENDING foreign country	P-ECON-PROTECTION U.S. —cause—> decrease SPENDING U.S. —cause—> decrease SALES foreign exports —cause—> decrease EARNINGS foreign country —cause—> decrease SPENDING foreign country
The result will be fewer jobs in export industries	decrease EMPLOYMENT U.S.	P-ECON-PROTECTION U.S. —cause—> decrease SPENDING U.S. —cause—> decrease SALES foreign exports —cause—> decrease EARNINGS foreign country —cause—> decrease SPENDING foreign country —cause—> decrease SALES U.S. exports —cause—> decrease EARNINGS U.S. industry —cause—> decrease EMPLOYMENT U.S. —thwart—> G-PRESERVING-JOBS U.S.

Figure 4. Example of script application in OpEd.

after OpEd reads the sentence referring to the decrease in export jobs. At that point, OpEd builds two belief structures:

BELIEF2: Friedman believes
$R-ECON-PROTECTION→FEWER-EXPORT-JOBS1

S-POSSIBLE-FAILURE: BELIEF2—support→BELIEF1

where S-POSSIBLE-FAILURE is a support structure that represents Friedman's plan-based reasoning. This support structure is later retrieved by OpEd as the answer to the question "Why does Milton Friedman believe that the limitations on imports will cost jobs?" As such, OpEd's answer gives a detailed account of all the steps in Friedman's reasoning chain. For example, the inferred relationship between foreign spending and U.S. export jobs corresponds to the following fragment of OpEd's answer:

If foreign countries buy fewer American exports, then there is a decrease in profits of export industries; and if there is a decrease in profits of export industries, then there is a decrease in jobs in export industries.

Thus, the use of reasoning scripts allows OpEd to infer missing steps in a chain of reasoning that justifies a particular belief in the editorial.

Psychological Validity of Scripts

The script notion has generated much interest among psychologists. Scripts help computer programs represent and organize their knowledge of stereotypical events. In addition, it seems reasonable to believe that humans use their stereotypical knowledge of the world to understand and behave appropriately in everyday situations, such as going to a supermarket or a restaurant. At this point, consider whether humans organize their stereotypical knowledge in scripts, ie, whether the concept of script is psychologically valid.

First, it is clear that children acquire cognitive structures exhibiting the major features of scripts very early in their development. In a series of open-ended interviews, eg, Nelson and Gruendel (1981) found that preschool children up to the age of three can reliably report on the ordering of activities and the characteristic roles in common activities such as going to McDonald's or to a birthday party. In fact, children also learn these structures very rapidly. Within a week or so after entering a new situation, such as preschool, they have formed a clear notion of their expected roles, settings, and sequences of activities.

As reported in Abelson (1981), a great many experiments have been carried out to investigate basic properties of scripts. For instance, Bower and co-workers (1979) and Graesser and co-workers (1980) have demonstrated that people tend to infer and recognize unmentioned script events when presented with stories about scripted activities. In these experiments subjects were first asked to read script-based stories that contained only some of the normative events of the evoked scripts. Later, they were asked to write down all actions they could remember from the stories read. Results showed that people cited actions from the scripts that were not explicitly mentioned in the stores but that could be inferred from the script.

Bower and co-workers (1979) have also found that when people are asked to remember script-based stories that present some events displaced from their usual positions, they tend to recall the stories with those events shifted toward their normative positions. Abelson (1981) believes that this can be explained as a compromise in reconstructive memory between the known event ordering and the presented ordering, since, in general, subjects can agree on event ordering in scripts (Galambos and Rips, 1979).

Other experiments by Bower and co-workers (1979) have further shown that understanding a given event in terms of a recognized script does not require searching through a sequential list of the script events until the given event is found. For example, understanding the eating event after processing the ordering event within $RESTAURANT does not require instantiating the low level events (eg, holding the fork) that follow the ordering event and precede the eating event. According to Abelson (1981), this can be explained because some script events are more central than others to the script and flow of action within the script and central events summarize script scenes containing low level events. Moreover, Galambos and Rips (1979) have demonstrated that it is faster to verify central events as belonging to the script than low level events. This "centrality" concept was originally proposed in Schank and Abelson (1977) and implemented as script main conceptualizations, or MAINCONs, in Cullingford (1978, 1981).

A number of experiments have also been done to investigate how knowledge of scriptal activities is used during question answering. Galambos and Black (1985) have shown that when answering questions about the reasons for actions in scriptal activities, the most frequently used strategy is to answer with a subsequent action in the script. For example, if within the activity MAKING-A-CAMPFIRE a person is asked for the reason of the action GETTING-MATCHES, the most common answer is the next action in that activity, ie, LIGHTING-THE-FIRE. In addition to this causality, it has also been shown in Galambos (1983), Galambos and Black (1983), Galambos and Rips (1982), and Reiser and co-workers (1982) that the time to answer questions about stereotypical activities is influenced by four other features:

1. distinctiveness, a measure of whether the action occurs in one or many activities;
2. centrality, the importance of the event to the backbone of the script;
3. standardness, a measure of the frequency with which the action is performed within a given activity; and
4. sequential position of the action within the activity.

For example, people do not have difficulty answering that $RESTAURANT is the activity in which the action SEE-

HEAD-WAITER can be performed since this action appears in few (if any) other activities, ie, SEE-HEAD-WAITER is highly distinctive to $RESTAURANT.

Bower and co-workers (1979) have also demonstrated that memories for script episodes are not necessarily stored with the representation for the particular script, but rather they are represented as scenes that can be shared among scripts. This sharedness results in confusions at recall time. For example, the waiting-room scene is shared by the doctor's and dentist's office scripts. Thus, memories of events indexed by the waiting-room scene may not preserve distinction between the doctor's and dentist's offices.

These memory-confusion results demonstrated that the original notion of a SAM-style script as a self-contained unit of knowledge is too restrictive. In fact, the development of MOPs by Schank and his colleagues (1982a, 1982b) came about as a response to these experimental results.

Finally, Reiser and co-workers (1985) have performed experiments that give evidence for a memory organization based on general actions, ie, memory structures that encode generalizations about actions common to stereotypical activities. For instance, the general action MAKE-RESERVATIONS is common to the activities GOING-ON-VACATIONS and PLAYING-INDOOR-TENNIS. These general actions correspond to the generalized scenes (Schank, 1982a, 1982b) around which MOPs are organized.

Script Acquisition

It has been shown how scripts allow people to recognize and understand events they have encountered many times. Being able to use scripts provides an efficient way to act in stereotypical situations without having to explain them repeatedly in terms of the plans and goals of the events' characters. One faces many situations that are highly scriptal in nature. If scripts do not already exist to handle them, they must be learned. How new scripts are learned and how they organize episodes already existing in memory are still open-ended problems.

Schank and Abelson (1977) believe that children learn about stereotypical activities, such as going to restaurants and department stores, by going through those experiences enough times. Dyer (1983) pointed out that children (and adults) can learn how to behave in these situations without having to understand the intentional structures underlying their behavior. For example, suppose a child goes to a restaurant for the first time. Although events relating to HAVING-A-MEAL (ie, SET-TABLE, BRING-FOOD, SIT, and EAT) would be familiar, he would notice many novel events and would try to process them in terms of HAVING-A-MEAL. For instance, he would notice that it is the waitress who sets the table and brings the food in a restaurant (rather than one of his parents). Furthermore, he would also see his parents leaving money at the table and paying at the cashier. However, his understanding of these last events would simply be "that's what one does" after eating in a restaurant. These events are harder to understand in terms of HAVING-A-MEAL because they do not have analogous counterparts. It might be years before he realizes the full contractual significance of tipping and paying the bill. For instance, a friend admitted to Dyer that as a child, she enjoyed pocketing the coins people left on restaurant tables. One day she was caught by her parents, who informed her that these coins were to reward the waitress for her service. Until this moment, in which this child grasped the intentional significance of tipping, it had just been a "scriptal action" for her.

DeJong (1982b) has outlined an approach to learning schemas (ie, any knowledge chunks, such as a script, frame, or MOP) called explanatory schema acquisition. In this approach understanding an event for which there is no previous schema requires generalizing the new event into a new schema. This generalization process constructs an explanation of relationships among components of the new events by applying knowledge about the underlying goals and plans involved in the event. The generalization process distinguishes four types of situations.

1. schema composition, connecting known schemas in a novel way;
2. schema alteration, modifying a nearly correct schema so that it fits the requirements of a new situation;
3. secondary-effect elevation, acquiring a new schema that is nearly the same as an existing schema but whose main effect is only a side effect in the original schema; and
4. volitionalization, transforming a schema for which there is no planner into a schema which can be used by a planner to attain a specific goal.

For example, learning about kidnapping, ie, building a KIDNAP schema, involves combining two previous known schemas: THEFT (in this case of a person) followed by BARGAIN (in this case the paying for the well-being of the victim). An example of schema alteration involves the case in which $RESTAURANT is modified to account for new situations in which the typical scene ordering is altered, such as the first visit to a fast-food restaurant where the patron has to pay before eating the food (Schank, 1982a).

Schema acquisition can also be accomplished by specializing previously learned schemas. This approach has been used in IPP (Lebowitz, 1980, 1983), CYRUS (Kolodner, 1983a, 1983b, 1984), and OCCAM (Pazzani, 1985, 1988). IPP (Integrated Partial Parser) is a computer system designed to read and form generalizations from a large number of news stories about terrorism. IPP's knowledge about terrorism is organized by two specific types of knowledge structures (Lebowitz, 1980): action units, which describe events, such as shootings, deaths, and bombings; and simple MOPs (S-MOPs), which organize abstract levels of actions, such as extortions and attacks on people. IPP maintains a long-term episodic memory of stories it has read and uses this memory as a basis for making generalizations about terrorism. New generalizations are indexed by new S-MOPs that are specializations of existing ones. For instance, if IPP reads several stories about attacks against the British by the IRA, IPP will make the generalization that terrorist attacks in Britain are normally caused by the IRA. IPP can use this generalization to infer terrorists' affiliation if it is not mentioned in later stories involving terrorism in Britain.

CYRUS (Computerized Yale Retrieval and Updating System) is a computer program that organizes and searches a model of dynamic memory based on episodes from the lives of former Secretaries of State Cyrus Vance and Edmund Muskie. Episodes in CYRUS are organized by Episodic MOPs (E-MOPs) (Kolodner, 1983a, 1983b). E-MOPs organize similar events with respect to each other by indexing them according to their differences. For example, the "diplomatic meeting" E-MOP indexes each of Vance's or Muskie's diplomatic meetings. In CYRUS creation of new E-MOPs that hold generalizations about events is triggered by remindings (Schank, 1982a). Remindings occur when CYRUS indexes a second event where a first is already indexed. In this case similarities between the two events are extracted, and a new E-MOP with generalized information based on those occurrences is created. For example, the first time CYRUS hears about a meeting in which Vance discusses military aid with a foreign defense minister, it indexes that meeting uniquely in the "diplomatic meetings" E-MOP under the property "underlying topic is military aid." The second time Vance meets about military aid, CYRUS is reminded of the first episode because both have the same topic. It checks the descriptions of both, and if the second one involves a defense minister, CYRUS concludes that "meetings about military aid are usually with defense ministers." Then CYRUS creates a new "meetings about military aid" E-MOP and indexes the two meetings within that E-MOP. Although the memory-organization and -generalization processes in IPP and CYRUS are similar, IPP's emphasis is on memory-based parsing whereas CYRUS's is on episodic memory retrieval and reconstruction.

OCCAM is a computer program that organizes memories of events and learns by creating explanatory and tentative generalized events. OCCAM distinguishes three types of generalized events (Pazzani, 1985): explanatory generalized events, MOPs created as specialization of a more general MOP; tentative generalized events, MOPs inductively generalized from examples without an appropriate general MOP; and organizational generalized events, which correspond to the factual generalizations of IPP involving S-MOPs. In contrast to DeJong's explanatory schema acquisition (DeJong, 1982b), OCCAM can learn incrementally since there are cases in which a specialized new schema cannot be created from the first example encountered. For instance, the motivation for kidnapping infants (ie, they cannot testify against the kidnapper) cannot be learned from the first example of a kidnapping since the explanation process can find an explanation for kidnapping any person. In OCCAM, after the basic KIDNAP schema is learned, later examples direct OCCAM to explain coincidences about the age of the victims and make the appropriate generalization.

Conclusions

The authors have discussed the notion of a script, a memory structure that organizes chunks of stereotypical cultural knowledge. The script concept has created much interest among natural-language researchers in both psychology and AI. This construct has proved useful:

- in theories of representation and organization of knowledge, where scripts capture the stereotypic, cultural knowledge needed by natural-language-understanding systems to process script-based texts;
- in control of inferences, where scripts reduce combinatorial problems by containing the most relevant, normative event sequences as a memory structure rather than having to rederive event relationships through general problem solving and planning each time;
- in psychological models of human narrative comprehension, where scripts explain human behavior in stereotypical situations (Abelson, 1981); and
- in language analysis, where scripts help resolve pronoun references and perform word-sense disambiguation when dealing with script-based text.

The notion of script has probably shed light on some of the basic problems any intelligent system must address: knowledge representation, organization, acquisition, and application. Furthermore, the notion of script has contributed to bringing together researchers from AI and psychology in their quest for efficient and accurate models of human cognition.

BIBLIOGRAPHY

R. P. Abelson, "The Psychological Status of Script," *Am. Psychol.* **36**, 715–729 (1981).

S. J. Alvarado, *Understanding Editorial Text: A Computer Model of Argument Comprehension,* Kluwer Academic Publishers, Boston, Mass., 1990.

S. J. Alvarado, M. G. Dyer, and M. Flowers, "Memory Representation and Retrieval for Editorial Comprehension," *Proceedings of the Seventh Annual Conference of the Cognitive Science Society,* Irvine, Calif., 1985, pp. 228–235.

S. J. Alvarado, M. G. Dyer, and M. Flowers, "Editorial Comprehension in OpEd Through Argument Units," *Proceedings of the Fifth National Conference on Artificial Intelligence,* Philadelphia, Pa., AAAI, Menlo Park, Calif., 1986, pp. 250–256.

S. J. Alvarado, M. G. Dyer, and M. Flowers, "Natural Language Processing: Computer Comprehension of Editorial Text," in H. Adeli, ed., *Knowledge Engineering,* McGraw-Hill, New York, 1990a.

S. J. Alvarado, M. G. Dyer, and M. Flowers, "Argument Representation for Editorial Text," *Knowledge-Based Systems,* **3**, 87–107 (1990b).

S. J. Alvarado, M. G. Dyer, and M. Flowers, "Argument Comprehension and Retrieval for Editorial Text," *Knowledge-Based Systems,* **3**, 139–162 (1990c).

J. Bar-Hillel, *Language and Information,* Addison-Wesley, Reading, Mass., 1964.

G. H. Bower, J. B. Black, and T. J. Turner, "Scripts in Memory for Text," *Cog. Psychol.* **11**, 177–220 (1979).

E. Charniak, "A Framed Painting: Representation of a Commonsense Knowledge Fragment," *Cog. Sci.* **1**(4), 355–394 (1977).

E. Charniak, "On the Use of Framed Knowledge in Language Comprehension," *Artif. Intell.* **11**(3), 225–265 (1978).

R. E. Cullingford, "An Approach to the Representation of Mundane World Knowledge: The Generation and Managements of Situational Scripts," *Am. J. Computat. Ling.*, Microfiche **44** (1975).

R. E. Cullingford, "The Uses of World Knowledge in Text Understanding," *Proceedings of the Sixth International Conference on Computational Linguistics*, Ottawa, Canada, 1976.

R. E. Cullingford, *Script Application: Computer Understanding of Newspaper Stories*, Ph.D. thesis, Research Report No. 116, Department of Computer Science, Yale University, New Haven, Conn., 1978

R. E. Cullingford, "SAM," in R. C. Schank and C. K. Reisbeck, eds., *Inside Computer Understanding: Five Programs Plus Miniatures*, Erlbaum, Hillsdale, N.J., 1981, pp. 75–119.

G. F. DeJong II, "Prediction and Substantiation: A New Approach to Natural Language Processing," *Cog. Sci.* **3**, 251–273 (1979a).

G. F. DeJong II, *Skimming Stories in Real Time: An Experiment in Integrated Understanding*, Ph.D. thesis, Research Report No. 158, Department of Computer Science, Yale University, New Haven, Conn., 1979b.

G. F. DeJong II, "An Overview of the FRUMP System," in W. G. Lehnert and M. H. Ringle, eds., *Strategies for Natural Language Understanding*, Erlbaum, Hillsdale, N.J., 1982a, pp. 149–176.

G. F. DeJong II, "Automatic Schema Acquisition in a Natural Language Environment," *Proceedings of the Second National Conference on Artificial Intelligence*, Pittsburgh, Pa., 1982b, pp. 410–413.

M. G. Dyer, "$RESTAURANT Revisited or "Lunch with BORIS," *Proceedings of the Seventh International Joint Conference on Artificial Intelligence*, Vancouver, B.C., Morgan-Kaufmann, San Mateo, Calif., 1981a.

M. G. Dyer, "Integration, Unification, Reconstruction, Modification: An External Parsing Braid," *Proceedings of the Seventh International Joint Conference on Artificial Intelligence*, Vancouver, B.C., Morgan-Kaufmann, San Mateo, Calif., 1981b.

M. G. Dyer, *In-Depth Understanding: A Computer Model of Integrated Processing for Narrative Comprehension*, MIT Press, Cambridge, Mass., 1983.

M. G. Dyer and W. G. Lehnert, "Question Answering for Narrative Memory," in J. F. Le Ny and W. Kintsch, eds., *Language and Comprehension*, North-Holland, Amsterdam, 1982, pp. 339–358.

M. Flowers and M. G. Dyer, "Really Arguing with your Computer in Natural Language," *Proceedings of the National Computer Conference*, 1984.

M. Flowers, R. McGuire, and L. Birnbaum, "Adversary Arguments and the Logic of Personal Attacks," in W. G. Lehnert and M. G. Ringle, eds., *Strategies for Natural Language Understanding*, Erlbaum, Hillsdale, N.J., 1982, pp. 275–294.

M. Friedman, "Protection that Hurts," *Newsweek* 90 (Nov. 15, 1982).

J. A. Galambos, "Normative Studies of Six Characteristics of Our Knowledge of Common Activities," *Behav. Meth. Instru.* **15**, 327–340 (1983).

J. A. Galambos and J. B. Black, "Getting and Using Context: Functional Constraints on the Organization of Knowledge," *Proceedings of the Fourth Conference of the Cognitive Science Society*, Ann Arbor, Mich., pp. 44–46, 1982.

J. A. Galambos and J. B. Black, "Using Knowledge of Activities to Understand and Answer Questions," in A. C. Graesser and J. B. Black, eds., *The Psychology of Questions*, Erlbaum, Hillsdale, N.J., 1985.

J. A. Galambos and L. J. Rips, "The Representation of Events in Memory," Paper presented to the Midwestern Psychological Association, 1979.

J. A. Galambos and L. J. Rips, "Memory for Routines," *J. Verb. Learn. Verb. Behav.* **21**, 260–281 (1982).

N. Goldman, "Conceptual Generation," in R. C. Schank, ed., *Conceptual Information Processing*, North-Holland, New York, 1975, pp. 289–371.

A. C. Graesser, S. B. Woll, D. J. Kowalski, and D. A. Smith, "Memory for Typical and Atypical Actions in Scripted Activities," *J. Exper. Psychol. Hum. Learn. Mem.* **6**, 503–515 (1980).

J. L. Kolodner, "Maintaining Organization in a Dynamic Long-Term Memory," *Cog. Sci.* **7**(4), 243–280 (1983a).

J. L. Kolodner, "Reconstructive Memory: A Computer Model," *Cog. Sci.* **7**(4), 281–328 (1983b).

J. L. Kolodner, *Retrieval and Organizational Strategies in Conceptual Memory: A Computer Model*, Erlbaum, Hillsdale, N.J., 1984.

M. Lebowitz, *Generalization and Memory in an Integrated Understanding System*, Ph.D. thesis, Research Report No. 186, Department of Computer Science, Yale University, New Haven, Conn., 1980.

M. Lebowitz, "Memory-Based Parsing," *Artif. Intell.* **21**(4), 363–404 (1983).

W. G. Lehnert, *The Process of Question Answering*, Erlbaum, Hillsdale, N.J., 1978.

W. G. Lehnert, M. G. Dyer, P. N. Johnson, C. J. Yang, and S. Harley, "BORIS: An In-Depth Understander of Narratives," *Artif. Intell.* **20**(1), 15–62 (1983).

E. F. Loftus, "Leading Questions and the Eyewitness Report," *Cog. Psychol.* **7**, 560–572 (1975).

E. F. Loftus, *Eyewitness Testimony*, Harvard University Press, Cambridge, Mass., 1979.

M. A. Minsky, "Framework for Representing Knowledge," in P. Winston, ed., *The Psychology of Computer Vision*, McGraw-Hill, New York, 1975.

M. A. Minsky, "Frame-System Theory," in P. Johnson-Laird and P. Wason, eds., *Thinking: Readings in Cognitive Science*, MIT Press, Cambridge Mass., 1977.

K. Nelson and J. Gruendel, "Generalized Event Representations: Basic Building Blocks of Cognitive Development," in A. Brown and M. Lamb, eds., *Advances in Developmental Psychology*, Vol. 1, Erlbaum, Hillsdale, N.J., 1981.

M. J. Pazzani, "Explanation and Generalization Based Memory," *Proceedings of the Seventh Annual Conference of the Cognitive Science Society*, Irvine, Calif., 1985, pp. 323–328.

M. J. Pazzani, *Learning Causal Relationships: An Integration of Empirical and Explanation-Based Learning Methods*, Ph.D. dissertation, Technical Report UCLA-AI-88-10, Computer Science Department, University of California, Los Angeles, 1988.

C. J. Rieger III, "Conceptual Memory and Inference," in R. C. Schank, ed., *Conceptual Information Processing*, North-Holland, New York, 1975, pp. 157–288.

C. K. Riesbeck, "Conceptual Analysis," in R. C. Schank, ed., *Conceptual Information Processing,* North-Holland, New York, 1975, pp. 83–156.

B. J. Reiser, J. B. Black, and R. P. Abelson, "Knowledge Structures in the Organization and Retrieval of Autobiographical Memories," *Cog. Psychol.* **17**(1), 89–137 (1985).

B. J. Reiser, J. A. Galambos, and J. B. Black, "Retrieval from Semantic and Autobiographic Memories," Paper presented at the Twenty-third Annual Meeting of the Psychonomic Society, 1982.

R. C. Schank, "Identification of Conceptualizations Underlying Natural Language," in R. C. Schank and K. M. Colby, eds., *Computer Models of Thought and Language,* W. H. Freeman, San Francisco, Calif., 1973, pp. 184–247.

R. C. Schank, ed., *Conceptual Information Processing,* North-Holland, New York, 1975.

R. C. Schank, *Dynamic Memory: A Theory of Reminding and Learning in Computers and People,* Cambridge University Press, New York, 1982a.

R. C. Schank, "Reminding and Memory Organization: An Introduction to MOPs," in W. G. Lehnert and M. H. Ringle, eds., *Strategies for Natural Language Understanding,* Erlbaum, Hillsdale, N.J., 1982b, pp. 455–493.

R. C. Schank and R. P. Abelson, *Scripts, Plans, Goals, and Understanding,* Erlbaum, Hillsdale, N.J., 1977.

R. C. Schank, N. Goldman, C. J. Rieger III, and C. K. Riesbeck, "Inference and Paraphrase by Computer," *J. Assoc. Comput. Mach.* **22**(3), 309–328 (1975).

R. Wilensky, *Understanding Goal-Based Stories,* Ph.D. thesis, Research Report No. 140, Department of Computer Science, Yale University, New Haven, Conn., 1978.

R. Wilensky, *Planning and Understanding: A Computational Approach to Human Reasoning,* Addison-Wesley, Reading, Mass., 1983.

T. Winograd, *Understanding Natural Language,* Academic Press, Inc., New York, 1972.

MICHAEL G. DYER
UCLA

RICHARD E. CULLINGFORD
Intelligent Business Systems

SERGIO J. ALVARADO
University of California at Davis

SEARCH

Search is a universal problem-solving mechanism in artificial intelligence. In AI problems, the sequence of actions required for solution are not known *a priori*, but must be determined by a systematic trial-and-error exploration of alternatives. The problems that have been addressed by search algorithms fall into three general classes: single-agent path-finding problems, two-player games, and constraint-satisfaction problems.

Classic examples in the AI literature of path-finding problems include the Eight Puzzle (Fig. 1) and its larger relative the 4 × 4 Fifteen Puzzle. The Eight Puzzle consists of a 3 × 3 square frame containing eight numbered square tiles and an empty position called the blank. The

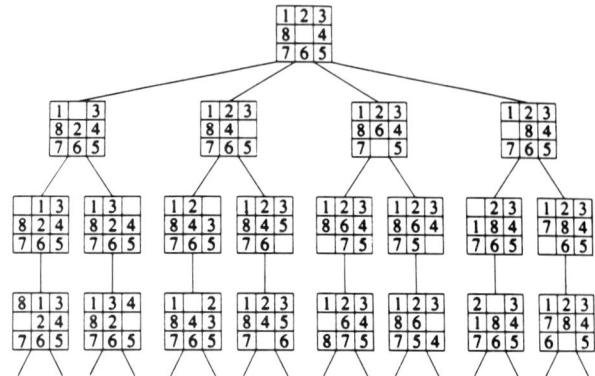

Figure 1. Eight Puzzle search tree.

legal operators are to slide any tile that is horizontally or vertically adjacent to the blank into the blank position. The problem is to rearrange the tiles from some random initial configuration into a particular desired goal configuration. The sliding-tile puzzles are a common testbed for research in search algorithms because they are extremely simple to represent and manipulate, yet finding optimal solutions is extremely difficult, in fact NP-complete (Ratner and Warmuth, 1986). Other examples include Rubik's Cube, the Traveling Salesman Problem, and theorem proving. All these are called path-finding problems because the task is to find a sequence of operations that map an initial state to a goal state.

The other classes of search problems are two-player games, such as chess, and constraint-satisfaction problems, such as the Eight Queens Problem. The task is to place eight queens on a chessboard, such that no two queens are attacking each other along the same row, column, or diagonal. Because these problem areas are covered by their own overview articles (see GAME PLAYING; CONSTRAINT SATISFACTION), this article is limited to single-agent path-finding algorithms. However, many of the concepts introduced here are equally applicable to these other domains as well. In addition, many of the algorithms described here are covered in more detail in separate articles.

The problem space model on which search algorithms are based is discussed first. Brute-force searches are then considered including breadth-first, uniform-cost, depth-first, depth-first iterative-deepening, and bidirectional search. Next, various heuristic searches are examined including pure heuristic search, the A* algorithm, iterative-deepening-A*, and the heuristic path algorithm. Then algorithms for interleaving search and execution will be considered, including minimin lookahead search, alpha pruning, and real-time-A*. Finally, searching with other sources of knowledge, such as probabilities of success, subgoals, macro-operators, and abstraction hierarchies will be examined. The efficiency of these algorithms, in terms of the costs of the solutions they generate, the amount of time the algorithms take to execute, and the amount of computer memory they require are of central concern throughout. The reason is that search is a universal problem-solving method, but what limits its applicability is the efficiency with which it can be performed.

Search algorithms represent one end of a spectrum of problem-solving methods. At the other end are deterministic procedures, such as sorting algorithms. The points along the spectrum vary in generality, efficiency, and amount of domain-specific knowledge. Brute-force search uses no knowledge, and hence is very general but very inefficient. Heuristic search incorporates some domain-specific knowledge and thus gains efficiency at the expense of some generality. A deterministic algorithm, at the other extreme, uses enough knowledge to determine which action to take next at each point, and hence is very efficient, but not very general. Most AI problem solvers fall somewhere along this spectrum of power vs generality, depending on the amount of domain-specific knowledge they employ.

PROBLEM SPACE MODEL

A problem space is the environment in which a search takes place (Newell and Simon, 1972). A problem space consists of a set of states of the problem and a set of operators that change the state of the problem. For example, in the Eight Puzzle, the states are the different possible permutations of the tiles, and the operators are to slide a tile into the blank position. A problem instance is a problem space together with an initial state and a goal state. In the case of the Eight Puzzle the initial state would be whatever (eg, random) initial permutation the puzzle starts out in, and the goal state is a particular desired permutation. The problem-solving task is to find a sequence of operators that map the initial state to a goal state. In the Eight Puzzle, the goal state is given explicitly. In other problems, such as the Eight Queens Problem, the goal state is not given explicitly, but rather implicitly specified by certain properties that must be satisfied by any goal state.

Graphs are often used to represent problem spaces. The states of the space are represented by nodes of the graph, and the operators by edges between nodes. Edges may be undirected or directed, depending on whether their corresponding operators are invertible or not. The task then is to find a path in the graph from the initial node to a goal node. Figure 1 shows a small part of an Eight Puzzle problem space graph.

Figure 1 is an example of the simplest type of problem space, the state space. In a state space the nodes represent states of the world, and the operators represent primitive actions in the problem domain. This graph is also called an OR graph because the problem represented by any given node can be solved if any one of its child nodes can be solved. Other important problem spaces include AND/OR graphs (qv) and game trees (qv).

Although most problem spaces correspond to graphs with more than one path between a pair of nodes, for simplicity they are often represented as trees where the initial state is the root of the tree. The cost of this simplification is that if the same state can be reached by two different paths, it will be represented by duplicate nodes in the tree, increasing the size of the tree. The benefit of a tree is that the absence of cycles greatly simplifies many search algorithms.

The two parameters of a search tree that determine the efficiency of various search algorithms are its branching factor and its depth. The branching factor is the average number of children of a given node. For example, in the Eight Puzzle the average branching factor is about 1.7. The depth of a problem instance is the length of a shortest path from the initial state to a goal state, or the length of a shortest sequence of operators that solves the problem. If the goal were in the bottom row of Figure 1, the depth of the problem instance represented by the initial state at the root would be three moves.

BRUTE-FORCE SEARCH

The most general search algorithms are brute-force searches, because they do not require any domain-specific knowledge. All that is required for a brute-force search is a state description, the set of legal operators, the initial state, and a description of the goal state. The most important brute-force techniques are breadth-first, uniform-cost, depth-first, depth-first iterative-deepening, and bidirectional search. In the descriptions of the algorithms below, to generate a node means to create the data structure corresponding to that node, whereas to expand a node means to generate all the children of that node.

Breadth-First Search

Breadth-first search expands nodes in order of their distance from the root, generating one level of the tree at a time until a solution is found (Fig. 2). Because it never generates a node in the tree until all the nodes at shallower levels have been generated, breadth-first search always finds a shortest path to the goal.

The amount of time used by breadth-first search is proportional to the number of nodes generated, because each node can be generated in constant time, and is a function of the branching factor b and the solution depth d. Because the number of nodes at level d is b^d, the total number of nodes generated is $b + b^2 + b^3 + \cdots + b^d$ in the worst case. For large values of d, this sum can be approximated by b^d, and hence the asymptotic time complexity of breadth-first search is of order b^d or $O(b^d)$.

The main drawback of breadth-first search is its memory requirement. Because each level of the tree must be saved in order to generate the next level, and the amount of memory is proportional to the number of nodes stored, the space complexity of breadth-first search is also $O(b^d)$. As a result, breadth-first search is severely space-bound in practice, and may exhaust the available memory in a matter of minutes on typical computer configurations.

Uniform-Cost Search

If all edges do not have the same cost, then breadth-first search generalizes to uniform-cost search. Instead of expanding nodes in order of their depth from the root, uniform-cost search expands nodes in order of their total cost from the root. At each step the next node n to be expanded is one whose total cost $g(n)$ is lowest, where $g(n)$ is the

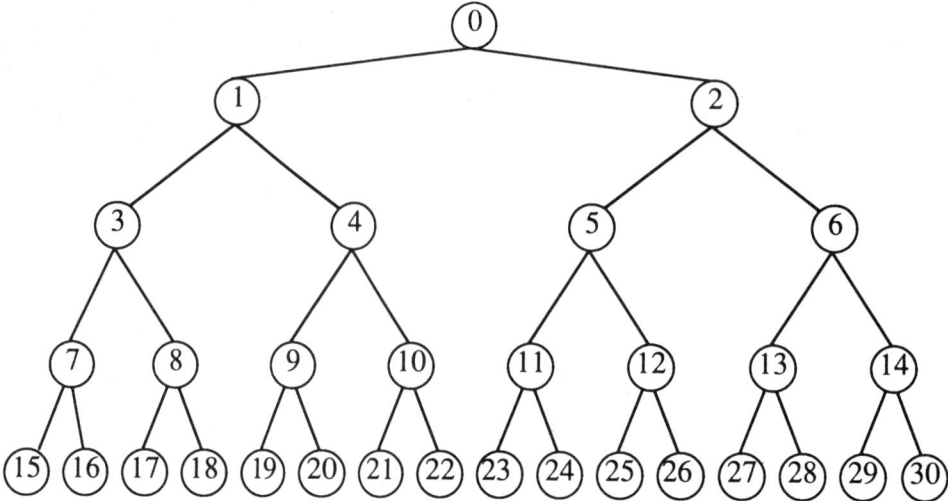

Figure 2. Order of node generation for breadth-first search.

sum of the edge costs from the root to node n. This algorithm is better known as Dijkstra's (1959) single-source shortest-path algorithm.

When a node is chosen for expansion by uniform-cost search, a lowest cost path to that node has been found. The worst-case time complexity of uniform-cost search is $O(b^{c/m})$, where c is the cost of an optimal solution, and m is the minimum edge cost. Unfortunately, it also suffers the same memory limitation as breadth-first search.

Depth-First Search

Depth-first search (see SEARCH, DEPTH-FIRST) remedies the space limitations of breadth-first search by always generating next a child of the deepest unexpanded node (Fig. 3). Both algorithms can be implemented using a list of unexpanded nodes, with the difference that breadth-first search manages the list as a first-in, first-out queue, whereas depth-first search treats the list as a last-in, first-out stack.

The advantage of depth-first search is that its space requirement is only linear in the search depth, as opposed to exponential for breadth-first search. The reason is that the algorithm only needs to store a stack of the nodes on the path from the root to the current node. The time complexity of depth-first search is still $O(b^d)$, because it generates the same set of nodes as breadth-first search, but simply in a different order. As a practical matter, depth-first search is time-limited rather than space-limited on current machines.

The disadvantage of depth-first search, however, is that in general it requires a cutoff depth to prevent it from going down the leftmost path forever. Although the ideal cutoff is the solution depth d, this value is rarely known in advance of actually solving the problem. If the chosen cutoff depth is less than the solution depth d, the algorithm will fail to find a solution, whereas if the cutoff depth is greater than d, a large price is paid in execution time, and the first solution found may not be an optimal one.

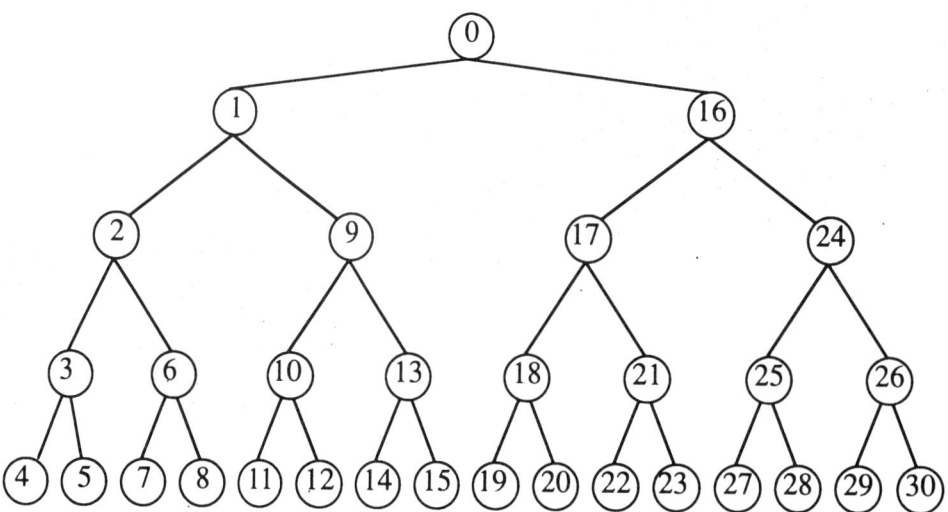

Figure 3. Order of node generation for depth-first search.

Depth-First Iterative-Deepening

Depth-first iterative-deepening (DFID) combines the best features of breadth-first and depth-first search (Stickel and Tyson, 1985; Korf, 1985a). DFID first performs a depth-first search to depth one, then a depth-first search to depth two, continuing to execute depth-first searches to successively greater depths, until a solution is found (Fig. 4). If the edge costs differ, then DFID is modified by replacing depth thresholds with cost thresholds.

Because it never generates a node until all shallower nodes have been generated, the first solution found by DFID is guaranteed to be a shortest path. Because at any given point it is executing a depth-first search, saving only a stack of nodes, and the algorithm terminates when it finds a solution at depth d, the space complexity of DFID is $O(d)$.

Although it appears that DFID wastes a great deal of time in the iterations prior to the one that finds a solution, this extra work is usually insignificant. To see this, note that the number of nodes at depth d is b^d, and each of these nodes are generated once, during the final iteration. The number of nodes at depth $d - 1$ is b^{d-1}, but each of these are generated twice, once during the final iteration, and once during the penultimate iteration. In general, the number of nodes generated by DFID is $b^d + 2b^{d-1} + 3b^{d-2} + \cdots + db^d$. This is asymptotically $O(b^d)$ if b is strictly greater than 1, because for large values of d the lower order terms become insignificant. In other words, most of the work goes into the final iteration, and the cost of the previous iterations is relatively small. The ratio of the number of nodes generated by DFID to the number of nodes generated by breadth-first search is approximately $b/(b - 1)$. In fact, DFID is asymptotically optimal in terms of time and space among all brute-force shortest-path algorithms on a tree (Korf, 1985a).

On a graph with cycles, however, breadth-first search may be much more efficient than any depth-first search. The reason is that a breadth-first search can check for duplicate nodes whereas a depth-first search cannot. Thus the complexity of breadth-first search grows only as the number of nodes at a given depth, while the complexity of depth-first search depends on the number of paths of a given length. For example, in a square grid, the number of nodes within a radius r of the origin is $O(r^2)$, whereas the number of paths of length r is $O(3^r)$, because there are three children of every node, not counting its parent. Thus in a graph with a large number of short cycles, breadth-first search is preferable to depth-first search, if sufficient memory is available.

Bidirectional Search

Bidirectional search is a brute-force algorithm that requires an explicit goal state in addition to the basic problem space (Pohl, 1971) (see SEARCH, BIDIRECTIONAL). The main idea of bidirectional search is to simultaneously search forward from the initial state, and backward from the goal state until the two searches meet in the middle. The path from the initial state is then concatenated with the inverse of the path from the goal state to form the complete solution path.

Bidirectional search still guarantees optimal solutions. Assuming that the comparisons for identifying common states can be done in constant time per node, by hashing for example, the time complexity of bidirectional search is $O(b^{d/2})$, because each search need only proceed to half the solution depth. Because at least one of the searches must be breadth-first in order to find a common state, the space complexity of bidirectional search is also $O(b^{d/2})$. Multiplying the time and the space requirements of bidirectional search results in $O(b^d)$, which is the time requirement of unidirectional search.

Combinatorial Explosion

The problem with all brute-force search algorithms is that their time complexities grow exponentially with problem size. This is called combinatorial explosion, and its effect is that the size of problems that can be solved with these

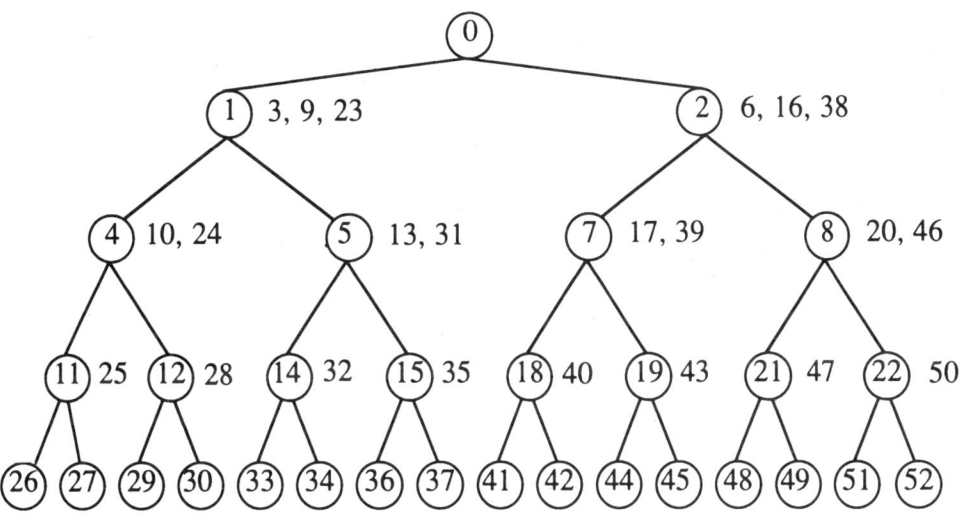

Figure 4. Order of node generation for depth-first iterative-deepening search.

techniques is quite limited. For example, while the Eight Puzzle, with about 10^5 states, is easily solved by brute-force search, the Fifteen Puzzle contains over 10^{13} states, and hence cannot be solved with brute-force techniques on current machines. Faster machines will not have a significant impact on this problem, because the 5×5 Twenty-Four Puzzle contains almost 10^{25} states.

HEURISTIC SEARCH

To solve larger problems, some domain-specific knowledge must be added to improve search efficiency. In AI, heuristic search has a general meaning and a more specialized technical meaning. In a general sense, the term heuristic is used for any advice that is often effective, but isn't guaranteed to work in every case (see HEURISTICS). Within the heuristic search literature, however, the term heuristic usually refers to the special case of a heuristic evaluation function.

Heuristic Evaluation Functions

In a single-agent problem, a heuristic evaluation function estimates the cost of a shortest path between a pair of states. For example, Euclidean or airline distance estimates the highway distance between a pair of locations. A common heuristic function for the sliding-tile puzzles is called Manhattan distance. It is computed by counting, for each tile not in its goal position, the number of moves along the grid it is away from its goal position, and summing these values over all tiles. If the goal state is fixed as the second argument, then a heuristic evaluation becomes a function of one state, $h(n)$, estimating the distance from node n to a given goal state.

The key properties of a heuristic evaluation function are that it estimates actual cost, and that it is inexpensive to compute. For example, the Euclidean distance between a pair of points can be computed in constant time. The Manhattan distance between a pair of states can be computed in time proportional to the number of tiles. In addition, most naturally occurring heuristic functions are lower bounds on actual cost. Airline distance is a lower bound on road distance between two points, because the shortest path between a pair of points is a straight line. Similarly, Manhattan distance is a lower bound on the actual number of moves necessary to solve an instance of the Eight Puzzle, because every tile must be moved at least as many times as its distance in grid units from its final position.

A number of algorithms make use of heuristic functions, including pure heuristic search, the A^* algorithm, iterative-deepening A^*, and the heuristic path algorithm. In addition, heuristic information can be employed in bidirectional search as well (see SEARCH, BIDIRECTIONAL).

Pure Heuristic Search

The simplest algorithm, pure heuristic search, expands nodes in order of their heuristic values $h(n)$ (Doran and Michie, 1966). It maintains a *Closed* list of those nodes that have been expanded, and an *Open* list of those nodes that have been generated but not yet expanded. The algorithm begins with the initial state on the Open list. At each cycle, a node on the Open list minimum $h(n)$ value is expanded, generating all of its children, and is placed on the Closed list. The heuristic function is applied to the children, and they are placed on the Open list in order of their heuristic values. The algorithm continues until a goal state is chosen for expansion.

In a graph with cycles, multiple paths will be found to the same node, and the first path found may not be the shortest. When a shorter path is found to an Open node, the shorter path is saved and the longer one discarded. When a shorter path to a Closed node is found, the node is placed on Open with the shorter path.

The main drawback of pure heuristic search is that because it ignores the cost of the path so far to node n, it does not find optimal solutions. Both pure heuristic search and uniform cost search are special cases of a more general algorithm called best-first search (qv). They differ only in that uniform-cost search uses $g(n)$ as the cost function, and pure heuristic search uses $h(n)$.

A* Algorithm

The A* algorithm (Hart and co-workers, 1968) combines uniform-cost search with pure heuristic search to efficiently compute optimal solutions. A* is a best-first search in which the figure of merit associated with a node is $f(n) = g(n) + h(n)$, where $g(n)$ is the cost of the path from the initial state to node n, and $h(n)$ is the heuristic estimate of the cost of a path from node n to a goal. Thus $f(n)$ is an estimate of the total cost of the cheapest solution path going through node n. At each point a node of lowest f value is chosen for expansion. The algorithm terminates when a goal node is chosen for expansion.

A* finds an optimal path to a goal if the heuristic function $h(n)$ never overestimates actual cost (Hart and co-workers, 1968). For example, because airline distance never overestimates actual highway distance, and Manhattan distance never overestimates actual moves in the Eight Puzzle, A* using these evaluation functions will find optimal solutions to these problems. In addition, A* makes the most efficient use of a given heuristic function in the following sense: among all shortest-path algorithms using a given heuristic function $h(n)$, A* expands the fewest number of nodes (Dechter and Pearl, 1985).

The main drawback of A*, and indeed of any best-first search, is its memory requirement. Because at least the entire Open list must be saved, A* is severely space-limited in practice and is no more practical than breadth-first search on current machines. For example, although it can be run successfully on the Eight Puzzle, it exhausts available memory very quickly on the Fifteen Puzzle.

Iterative-Deepening A*

Just as depth-first iterative-deepening solved the space problem of breadth-first search, iterative-deepening A* (IDA*) drastically reduces the memory requirement of A* without sacrificing solution optimality (Korf, 1985a). Each iteration of the algorithm is a complete depth-first search that keeps track of the cost, $f(n) = g(n) + h(n)$, of each node generated. As soon as this cost exceeds the threshold for that iteration, the branch is cut off and the search continues. The cost threshold starts with the heuristic estimate of the initial state, and in each successive iteration is increased to the minimum value that exceeded the previous threshold.

Because IDA* performs a sequence of depth-first searches, its memory requirement is linear in the solution depth. In addition, if the heuristic function never overestimates actual cost, the first solution found by IDA* is an optimal one. Finally, by an argument similar to that presented for DFID, IDA* expands the same number of nodes, asymptotically, as A* on a tree, provided that the number of nodes grows exponentially with cost. An additional benefit of IDA* is that it is easier to implement and often runs faster than A*. This is because it does not incur the overhead of managing the Open and Closed lists.

Complexity of Finding Optimal Solutions

The time complexity of a heuristic search algorithm depends on the accuracy of the heuristic function. For example, if the heuristic evaluation function is exact, then A* runs in linear time, expanding only those nodes on an optimal solution path. Conversely, with a heuristic that returns zero everywhere, A* degenerates to uniform-cost search, which has exponential complexity.

In general, the time complexity of A* and IDA* is an exponential function of the error in the heuristic function (Pearl, 1984). Thus if the heuristic has constant absolute error, meaning that it never underestimates by more than a constant amount regardless of the magnitude of the estimate, then the running time of A* is linear in the solution depth (Gaschnig, 1979). A more realistic assumption is constant relative error, which means that the error is a fixed percentage of the quantity being estimated. In that case, the running times of A* and IDA* are exponential (Pohl, 1970a). The base of the exponent, however, is smaller than the brute-force branching factor, reducing the asymptotic complexity and allowing somewhat larger problems to be solved. For example, using the Manhattan Distance heuristic, IDA* can optimally solve random instances of the Fifteen Puzzle (Korf, 1985a).

Heuristic Path Algorithm

Because the complexity of finding optimal solutions to these problems is generally exponential, in order to solve significantly larger problems, the optimality requirement must be relaxed. An early approach to this problem is the heuristic path algorithm (HPA) proposed by Pohl (1970b). HPA is a generalization of several best-first search algorithms, where the figure of merit of a node n is $f(n) = (1 - w) * g(n) + w * h(n)$. Varying w produces a range of algorithms from uniform-cost search ($w = 0$), through A* ($w = 0.5$), to pure heuristic search ($w = 1$). Increasing w beyond 0.5 generally decreases the amount of computation while increasing the cost of the solutions generated. Often, this trade-off is quite favorable, with small increases in solution cost yielding huge savings in computation. Furthermore, it can be shown that the solutions found by this algorithm are guaranteed to be no more than a factor of $w/(1 - w)$ greater than optimal (Davis and co-workers, 1989). The memory limitation of this best-first algorithm can be overcome simply by replacing A* with IDA* using the same weighted evaluation function.

INTERLEAVING SEARCH AND EXECUTION

In the discussion above, it is assumed that a complete solution can be found before even the first step need be executed. This is in contrast to the situation in two-player games, where because of computational limits and uncertainty due to the opponent's moves, search and execution are interleaved, with each search determining only the next move to be made. This paradigm is also applicable to single-agent problems. In the case of autonomous vehicle navigation, for example, information is limited by the horizon of the vehicle's sensors, and it must physically move to acquire more information. Thus one move must be calculated at a time, and that move executed before calculating the next.

Minimin Search with Alpha Pruning

Minimin search is designed to determine individual single-agent moves in constant time per move (Korf, 1990). The algorithm searches forward from the current state to a fixed depth determined by the information or computational resources available. At the search horizon, the A* evaluation function, $f(n) = g(n) + h(n)$, is applied to the frontier nodes. Because all decisions are made by a single agent, the value of the root is the minimum of the frontier values. A single move is then made to the neighbor of the current state with the minimum value.

Alpha pruning is a branch-and-bound technique that improves the efficiency of minimin search by evaluating interior nodes as well as frontier nodes (Korf, 1990). It is based on the fact that most heuristic functions obey the triangle inequality characteristic of distance measures. In that case, $f(n) = g(n) + h(n)$ is guaranteed to be monotonically nondecreasing along a path. Given a monotonic cost function, it is possible to keep track of the minimum-cost frontier node encountered so far, and prune any branch when its cost equals or exceeds the best so far. The performance improvement due to alpha pruning is quite dramatic, in some cases extending the achievable search horizon by a factor of five relative to brute-force minimin search (Korf, 1990).

Minimin search with alpha pruning is an algorithm for evaluating the immediate children of the current node. As such, it is run as a simulation until the best child is identified, at which point the chosen move is executed in the real world. The static evaluation function combined with lookahead search and alpha pruning can be viewed as simply a more accurate, but computationally expensive, heuristic function. In fact, it provides an entire spectrum of heuristic functions differing in accuracy and cost, depending on the search horizon.

Real-Time-A*

Simply repeating minimin search for each move ignores information from previous searches and thus results in infinite loops. In addition, because actions are committed based on limited information, often the best move may be to undo the previous move. The principle of rationality is that backtracking should occur when the estimated cost of continuing the current path exceeds the cost of going back to a previous state, plus the estimated cost of reaching the goal from the previous state. Real-time-A* implements this policy in constant time per move (Korf, 1990).

For each move, the $f(n) = g(n) + h(n)$ value of each neighbor of the current state is computed, where $g(n)$ is now the cost of the edge from the current state to the neighbor, instead of from the initial state. The problem solver moves to a neighbor with the minimum $f(n)$ value, and stores with the previous state the second-best $f(n)$ value, which is the best value among the remaining alternatives. This represents the $h(n)$ value of the previous state from the perspective of the new current state. This is repeated until a goal is reached. To determine the $h(n)$ value of a neighboring state, if it has previously been visited, then the stored value is used, and otherwise the heuristic evaluator is called. Note that the heuristic evaluator may employ minimin search with alpha pruning in addition to the heuristic function itself.

In a finite problem space in which there exists a path to a goal from every state, RTA* is guaranteed to eventually find a solution, regardless of the initial heuristic values (Korf, 1990). Furthermore, on a tree, RTA* makes locally optimal decisions given the information it has seen so far.

OTHER KNOWLEDGE SOURCES

In addition to heuristic evaluation functions, other sources of knowledge can be used to improve the performance of search algorithms. Such knowledge can take many different forms, including probabilities of success, subgoals, macro-operators, and abstraction spaces.

Probabilities. Consider, for example, the situation of deciding where to drill for oil. There is likely to be information on the *a priori* probabilities of finding oil in various places, as well as information on the cost of drilling in each place. Both Slagle (1964) and Simon and Kadane (1975) have shown that in this case a best-first search should be performed where the figure of merit is the ratio of the probability of success to the cost of finding out.

Subgoaling. A ubiquitous technique for solving a complex problem is to break it down into a sequence of subgoals (Korf, 1987; Chakrabarti, 1986). For example, the problem of driving from Los Angeles to New York can be decomposed into two subproblems of driving from Los Angeles to St. Louis, and driving from St. Louis to New York. In general, however, the combination of optimal subproblem solutions will not be an optimal solution to the original problem. On the other hand, because search complexity is often an exponential function of search depth, dividing the search into a set of searches to shallower depths greatly improves efficiency. The greater the number of subgoals, the less the search, but the greater the cost of the resulting solutions.

Macro-Operators. A macro-operator is a sequence of primitive operators that are stored and applied as if they were a single operator (Korf, 1985b; Laird and co-workers, 1987). For example, in order to navigate home, normally a stored path is simply replayed from memory. The route may involve a fairly complex sequence of turns and use many different roads, but is stored and executed as if it were a single operator. As an area becomes more familiar, a large number of these different macro-operators are learned and stored, greatly reducing the amount of search that is required.

Abstraction. Given a complex problem, the idea of abstraction is to at first ignore the low-level details of the problem, concentrating on the essential features, and then fill in the details later. In navigating from Los Angeles to New York, for example, a map of the interstate highway system may first be consulted. Because this is a much sparser problem space, a route in the interstate system from the Los Angeles area to the New York area can be quickly found. Then, a route from the origin in Los Angeles to the interstate, and finally a route from the interstate in New York to the destination must be found. These problems are also relatively easy because the distance that must be covered in each case is quite small. Thus by ignoring the detail of all the roads in the country, and first focusing only on the interstate system, and then solving the relatively small problems of getting to and from the interstate, the overall complexity of the problem is greatly reduced. By extending this technique to multiple hierarchical levels of abstraction, the complexity of some problems can be reduced from exponential to linear (Korf, 1987).

The most complete reference for the state of the art in this area as of 1984 is Pearl (1984). Short survey articles are available (Pearl and Korf, 1987; Korf, 1988) and an edited volume has been published (Kanal and Kumar, 1988).

BIBLIOGRAPHY

P. P. Chakrabarti, S. Ghose, and S. C. Desarkar, "Heuristic Search Through Islands," *Artif. Intell.* **29**(3), 339–347 (1986).

H. W. Davis, A. Bramanti-Gregor, and J. Wang, "The Advantages of Using Depth and Breadth Components in Heuristic Search," in Z. W. Ras and L. Saitta, eds., *Methodologies for Intelligent Systems,* Vol. 3, North-Holland, Amsterdam, The Netherlands, 1989, pp. 19–28.

R. Dechter and J. Pearl, "Generalized Best-First Search Strategies and the Optimality of A*," *J. Assoc. Comput. Machinery* **32**(3), 505–536 (July 1985).

E. W. Dijkstra, "A Note on Two Problems in Connexion with Graphs," *Numerische Mathematik,* **1,** 269–71 (1959).

J. E. Doran and D. Michie, "Experiments with the Graph Traverser Program," *Proc. R. Soc. A* **294,** 235–259 (1966).

J. Gaschnig, *Performance Measurement and Analysis of Certain Search Algorithms,* Ph.D. dissertation, Carnegie-Mellon University, Pittsburgh, Pa., 1979.

P. E. Hart, N. J. Nilsson, and B. Raphael, "A Formal Basis for the Heuristic Determination of Minimum Cost Paths," *IEEE Trans. Sys. Sci. Cybernet.* **4**(2), 100–107 (1968).

L. Kanal and V. Kumar, eds., *Search in Artificial Intelligence,* Springer-Verlag, New York, 1988.

R. E. Korf, "Depth-First Iterative-Deepening: An Optimal Admissible Tree Search," *Artif. Intell.* **27**(1), 97–109 (1985a).

R. E. Korf, "Macro-Operators: A Weak Method for Learning," *Artif. Intell.* **26**(1), 35–77 (1985b).

R. E. Korf, "Planning as Search: A Quantitative Approach," *Artif. Intell.* **33**(1), 65–88 (1987).

R. E. Korf, Search in AI: A Survey of Recent Results," in H. E. Shrobe, ed., *Exploring Artificial Intelligence,* Morgan-Kaufmann, San Mateo, Calif., 1988.

R. E. Korf, "Real-Time Heuristic Search," *Artif. Intell.* **42**(2–3), 189–211 (Mar. 1990).

J. E. Laird, A. Newell, and P. S. Rosenbloom, "SOAR: An Architecture for General Intelligence," *Artif. Intell.* **33**(1), 1–64 (1987).

A. Newell and H. A. Simon, *Human Problem Solving,* Prentice-Hall, Inc. Englewood Cliffs, N.J., 1972.

J. Pearl, *Heuristics,* Addison-Wesley Publishing Co., Inc., Reading, Mass., 1984.

J. Pearl and R. E. Korf, "Search Techniques," in *Annual Review of Computer Science,* Vol. 2, Annual Reviews Inc., Palo Alto, Calif., 1987, pp. 451–467.

I. Pohl, "First Results on the Effect of Error in Heuristic Search," in B. Meltzer and D. Michie, eds., *Machine Intelligence* Vol. 5, Elsevier Science Publishing Co., Inc., New York, 1970a, pp. 219–236.

I. Pohl, "Heuristic Search Viewed as Path Finding in a Graph," *Artif. Intell.* **1**, 193–204 (1970b).

I. Pohl, "Bi-Directional Search," in B. Meltzer and D. Michie, eds., *Machine Intelligence* Vol. 6, Elsevier Science Publishing Co., Inc., New York, 1971, pp. 127–140.

D. Ratner and M. Warmuth, "Finding a shortest solution for the $N \times N$ extension of the 15-Puzzle is intractable," in *Proceedings of the Fifth National Conference on Artificial Intelligence* Philadelphia, Pa., AAAI, Menlo Park, Calif., 1986.

H. A. Simon and J. B. Kadane, "Optimal Problem-Solving Search: All-or-None Solutions," *Artif. Intell.* **6**(3), 235–247 (1975).

J. R. Slagle, "An Efficient Algorithm for Finding Certain Minimum-Cost Procedures for Making Binary Decisions," *J. Assoc. Comput. Machinery* **11**(3), 253–264 (July 1964).

M. E. Stickel and W. M. Tyson, "An Analysis of Consecutively Bounded Depth-First Search with Applications in Automated Deduction," in *Proceedings of the Ninth IJCAI,* Los Angeles, Calif., Morgan-Kaufmann, San Mateo, Calif., 1985.

RICHARD E. KORF
University of California at
Los Angeles

This work was supported in part by NSF Grant IRI-8801939, by an NSF Presidential Young Investigator Award, and by a grant from Rockwell International. The author would like to thank Judea Pearl for his comments on an earlier draft of this article.

SEARCH, BEAM

Beam search is a heuristic search technique in which a number of nearly optimal alternatives (the *beam*) are examined in parallel. Beam search is a heuristic technique because heuristic rules are used to discard nonpromising alternatives in order to keep the size of the beam as small as possible. The use of heuristic rules to *prune* the set of alternatives is what sets beam search apart from other search techniques. Some of the successful applications of beam search include speech recognition (Lee, 1988), job-shop scheduling (Fox, 1983), vision (Rubin, 1978), learning (Dietterich and Michalski, 1981), and planning (Muscettola and co-workers, 1989).

Beam search can be easily explained by using a search state space described by a directed graph in which each node is a state and each arc represents the application of an operator that transforms a state into a successor state. A solution is a path from an initial state to a goal state. A few operators are necessary: an operator (NEXT) to expand the set of states, ie, generate all the successor nodes; an operator (SCORE) to evaluate the states, ie, generate the likelihood that each node belongs to the optimal solution; an operator (PRUNE) to select the alternatives that are most promising, ie, choose the best nodes; and an operator (FOUND) to check if the goal has been reached. The operation implemented by PRUNE is often called forward pruning. Beam search also requires two data structures: one that contains the set of states that are being extended (called CURRENT.STATES) and one that contains the set of new states that is being created (called CANDIDATE.STATES). At each iteration of the algorithm a new set of states is generated and becomes the current set of states for the next iteration.

Given these operators and data structures, beam search can be expressed by this simple program:

```
Start: CURRENT.STATES := initial.state
    while (not FOUND (CURRENT.STATES)) do
        CANDIDATE.STATES := NEXT
            (CURRENT.STATES)
        SCORE (CANDIDATE.STATES)
        CURRENT.STATES := PRUNE
            (CANDIDATE.STATES)
```

The algorithm is started by providing an initial state (eg, the initial node of the graph to be searched). Then the NEXT and SCORE operators are applied to generate all the possible new states and give them a score. When all the new states have been generated, the PRUNE operator is applied to the set of new states and the unpromising alternatives are discarded. The algorithm iterates until the goal has been reached.

EXAMPLE

Beam search is used in the Sphinx speech recognition system (Lee, 1988) to search a graph that embodies the syntactic and vocabulary constraints of the language as a sequence of fixed length acoustic events (frames). This is a graph in which any path from the initial state to the final state represents a pronunciation of a legal sentence. Given an unknown utterance, Sphinx divides the utterance into a sequence of frames and computes the likelihood that each frame represents a given acoustic event. The sequence of frames is then compared against each of the alternative paths in the graph that represent acceptable sequences in the language. The operator NEXT extracts from the graph all the nodes that can follow the nodes in CURRENT.STATES. The operator SCORE returns a value that indicates how well they match. The PRUNE operator computes a threshold score as a function of the best score and then discards all the nodes that have a score that is worse than the threshold. Therefore, in the Sphinx system, the pruning is anchored to the best path and all the nodes are kept that are close enough to the best node to have a chance of being on the best path. The FOUND operator simply triggers when all the input speech data have been evaluated. At this point, if the search was successful, the set CANDIDATE.STATES contains the last node in the network and the correct utterance can be retrieved by tracing the best path backward (a simple lookup operation if the pointers for each path in the beam are kept until the end of the search). Note that the best node at each segment during the search is not necessarily on the globally best path discovered at the end of the search. Thus local errors, eg, errors due to errorful acoustic data, are recovered by delaying commitment to a particular path until the end.

PERFORMANCE

As one can see from the Sphinx system example, the NEXT and SCORE operators depend on the problem being searched and do not directly influence the performance of the search. The PRUNE operator instead influences the performance both in terms of how expensive the search is and in terms of the algorithm being able to reach the goal. In general, a "permissive" PRUNE will reach the goal most of the time with the expense of examining many unpromising paths (in the extreme case, beam search simply becomes a breadth-first search).

On the contrary, a very "strict" PRUNE will limit the amount of computation but will increase the risk of pruning the path that leads to the goal. Therefore, one would like to use the strictest PRUNE that does not prevent the algorithm from finding the optimal solution. How well (if at all) such a compromise can be reached is a function of the domain being searched and of the quality of the scoring function. For example, in a speech system, if the SCORE operator generates high scores for only a few nodes (including the correct one) and low scores for the other nodes, the algorithm will tolerate a very narrow beam without losing accuracy. In general, the pruning function is no substitute for the quality of the scores, since poor and confused scores will generate sets of nodes for which the score does not truly reflect the likelihood that a node is on the correct path. Finally, it should be noted that, although beam search is a very cost-effective search method, because it examines only some of the alternatives, it does not guarantee that the optimal solution will be found.

One of the reasons that makes beam search attractive is that it reduces computation by reducing the number of states that have to be examined. The amount of saving depends on the specific search domain. Experiments with speech recognition programs showed an improvement of a factor of ten over an exhaustive search. Nevertheless, the large size of some search spaces requires even higher performance. To this end, the design of parallel beam search algorithms has been investigated. Although it would appear that parallelism could be readily exploited by performing the NEXT and SCORE operations in parallel, beam search needs to be partitioned into such small components that their synchronization, using the primitives available on general purpose multiprocessors, results in too much overhead. This problem can be solved by designing special architectures for beam search (Bisiani, 1988).

BIBLIOGRAPHY

R. Bisiani, "BEAM: An Accelerator for Speech Recognition," *International Conference on Acoustics, Speech and Signal Processing*," IEEE, May 1989.

T. G. Dietterich and R. S. Michalski, "Inductive Learning of Structural Descriptions: Evaluation Criteria and Comparative Review of Selected Methods," *Artif. Intell.* **16,** 257–294 (Nov. 1981).

M. S. Fox, "Constraint Directed Search: A Case Study of Job-Shop Scheduling," Ph.D. Dissertation, Carnegie Mellon University, Pittsburgh, Penn., Dec. 1983.

K.-F. Lee, "Large-Vocabulary Speaker-Dependent Continuous Recognition: The Sphinx System," Ph.D. dissertation, Carnegie-Mellon University, Pittsburgh, Penn., May 1988.

S. Rubin, "The ARGOS Image Understanding System," Ph.D. dissertation, Carnegie Mellon University, Pittsburgh, Penn., Nov. 1978.

N. Muscettola, S. F. Smith, G. Amiri, and D. Patak, *Generating Space Telescope Observation Schedules, Technical Report No. CMU-RI-TR-89-28*, The Robotics Institute, Carnegie Mellon University, Pittsburgh, Penn., Nov. 1989.

Roberto Bisiani
Carnegie Mellon University

SEARCH, BRANCH-AND-BOUND

Branch and bound (B&B) is a problem-solving technique that has been usefully employed in various problems encountered in operations research and combinatorial mathematics. Many heuristic search (qv) procedures used in AI can be viewed as B&B procedures. The class of problems solved by B&B procedures can be abstractly stated as: given a (possibly infinite) discrete set X and a real-valued cost function f whose domain is X, find an optimal element x^* of X such that $f(x^*) = \min\{f(x)|x \in X\}$. Discussion in this article is also applicable (with appropriate modifications) to the case when a largest cost element is desired, ie, an optimal element is defined as an element x^* of X such that $f(x^*) = \max\{f(x)|x \in X\}$. Unless there is enough problem-specific knowledge available to obtain an optimum element of the set in some straightforward manner, the only available alternative may be to implicitly enumerate the set X. For practical problems, the size of the set X is quite large, which makes exhaustive enumeration prohibitively time consuming.

Using the available knowledge about the problem, B&B procedures decompose the original set into sets of smaller and smaller sizes. The decomposition of each generated set S is continued until tests reveal either that S is a singleton (in which case its value is measured directly and compared with the currently best member's cost) or that there is an optimum element x^* not in S (in which case the set is pruned or eliminated from further consideration). If the decomposition process is continued (and satisfies some properties), an optimum element will eventually be found. The utility of this approach derives from the fact that, in general, most of X will be pruned, whence only a small fraction of X need be enumerated. B&B is commonly used to solve such important problems as integer programming, scheduling problems, network problems, the traveling salesman problem, the knapsack problem, and the shortest path problem.

B&B, techniques appear to have been conceptualized in the early 1960s to tackle integer programming and nonlinear-assignment problems. Later similar techniques, with some modifications, were found to be applicable in many other problem domains. As more and more applications were discovered, the B&B methodology evolved. Various formal models of B&B were presented and later superseded by more general models (Balas, 1968; Mitten, 1970, 1971; Ibaraki, 1977, 1978; Kohler and Steiglitz, 1974; Kumar, 1982). In the earlier formulations of B&B (Balas, 1968; Mitten, 1970, 1971), only the lower and upper bounds on the costs of the elements of (sub)sets (of X) were used for pruning. If two sets X_1 and X_2 are in the collection of sets under consideration, and the lower bound on the costs of elements in X_1 is no smaller than the upper bound on the costs of elements in X_2, X_1 can be pruned. The use of bounds for pruning gave the procedure its name branch and bound. The concept of pruning by bounds was later generalized to include pruning by dominance (Ibaraki, 1977, 1978; Kohler and Steiglitz, 1974; Kumar, 1982). Dominance may be used to perform pruning even when adequate lower bound information is not available. Pruning by dominance provides a powerful mechanism for using problem-specific knowledge for efficient search of an optimum element of the set X.

A GENERAL B&B FORMULATION

Here the basic elements of a B&B formulation are briefly described. The formulation presented here is very similar to Kumar and Kanal (1983). The dominance relation in the formulation is used for pruning in a manner somewhat different than in other studies (Ibaraki, 1977, 1978; Kohler and Steiglitz, 1974).

Basic Definitions

Let Y be the set of all subsets of X, ie, $Y = 2^X$. X_i denotes a subset of X, and A denotes a collection of subsets of X (ie, $A \subseteq Y$). For brevity, A is sometimes referred to simply as a collection. For notational convenience, the union of all subsets in any collection A is denoted by $\cup(A)$, ie, $\cup(A) = \cup\{X_i | X_i \in A\}$. The quantity $f^*(X_i)$ is defined to be the minimum of the costs of the elements in X_i. Any element $x^* \in X_i$ such that $f(x^*) = f^*(X_i)$ is called an optimum element of X_i.

A branching function BRANCH is any function that divides the members of the collection A into subsets that collectively include precisely the same elements of X as the original collection A. Mathematically, it is any function mapping collections into collections such that:

1. $X_i \in \text{BRANCH}(A) \Rightarrow X_i \subseteq X_j$ for some $X_j \in A$
2. $\cup(\text{BRANCH}(A)) = \cup(A)$

Often the function BRANCH is defined as a composition of selection and splitting functions. A selection function is any function SELECT mapping collections into collections such that $\text{SELECT}(A) \subseteq A$. A splitting function SPLIT is any function satisfying the properties of a branching function. BRANCH is then defined as

$$\text{BRANCH}(A) = (A - \{\text{SELECT}(A)\}) \cup \text{SPLIT}(\text{SELECT}(A))$$

Although this definition of BRANCH is mathematically equivalent to the one given above, it emphasizes the characteristic that only the elements from a certain selected subset of the collection A are divided, and the rest are returned unchanged. In fact, in many implementations of BRANCH, only one selected element from the collection A is divided, and the rest are returned unchanged.

The dominance relation D is the binary relation between subsets X_i, X_j of X such that $X_i D X_j$ if and only if $f^*(X_i) \leq f^*(X_j)$. Clearly, if X_i and X_j are present in a collection A and X_i dominates X_j, then X_j can be pruned.

The pruning function PRUNE prunes a dominated subset of A. It is defined as $\text{PRUNE}(A) = A - A^D$, where A^D is a subset of A such that for all $X_i \in A^D$ there exists some $X_j \in A - A^D$ such that $X_j D X_i$. From the definition of dominance, it follows that $A - A^D$ will contain at least one optimal element of $\cup(A)$.

An Abstract B&B Procedure

The procedure BB given below represents the essence of many B&B procedures. Here, A denotes the collection of subsets of X on which the branching and pruning operations are performed in each iteration of BB, and $|S|$ denotes the cardinality of a set S.

procedure BB (* B&B procedure to search for an optimum element of a set X *)

begin

    $A := \{X\}$; (* initialize the collection A *)

    while $|\cup(A)| \neq 1$ do (* loop until A contains only one element of X *)

        $A := \text{BRANCH}(A)$; (* branch on the collection A *)

        $A := \text{PRUNE}(A)$ (* eliminate the dominated subsets

    end

end

No element of X is lost from A in the branching operation, and at least one optimal element of $\cup(A)$ is there in PRUNE(A). Hence, if the procedure BB terminates, A contains only an optimal element of X. Note that the termination of BB is not guaranteed. In order to guarantee the termination of BB, BRANCH, and PRUNE must satisfy certain additional properties.

Best-First B&B

In many problem domains it is possible to define a function lb on the subsets X_i of X such that

1. For all $x \in X_i$, $lb(X_i) \leq f(x)$, ie, $lb(X_i)$ is a lower bound on the costs of the elements of X_i.
2. For all $x \in X$, $lb(\{x\}) = f(x)$, ie, the lower bounds for singleton sets are not unnecessarily loose.

This lower bound information can be fruitfully used in selecting an element for branching. If in every cycle of BB's loop an element of A is chosen for branching that has the least lower bound of all the elements of A, the selection rule is called best-first, and the B&B procedure using this strategy is called best-first B&B (see SEARCH, BEST-FIRST). An interesting feature of best-first B&B is that whenever a singleton set $\{x\}$ is selected for branching, the procedure can terminate. This is because $f^*(\{x\}) = f(x) = lb(\{x\}) \leq lb(X_i) \leq f^*(X_i)$ for all $X_i \in A$, and thus $\{x\}$ dominates all the other elements in A. If more than one element of A is selected for branching, the selection rule is still called best-first as long as at least one of the selected elements (eg, X_1) has the least lower bound of all the elements of A. In such cases B&B can successfully terminate if X_1 is a singleton.

If the bounds $lb(X_i)$ are good approximations of $f^*(X_i)$, best-first B&B can be very efficient. In the extreme case, if $lb(X_i) = f^*(X_i)$ for all $X_i \subseteq X$, the B&B procedure finds an optimal element of X by splitting only those sets that contain optimal elements. On the other hand, if the bounds $lb(X_i)$ are not good approximations of $f^*(X_i)$, best-first B&B can be very inefficient and may require a lot of storage.

Depth-First B&B

Another way of selecting a set for branching from the active collection A is to select a set from those sets that have been generated most recently as a result of branching (Lawler and Wood, 1966). This selection rule is called depth-first, and the B&B procedure using such a rule is called depth-first B&B (see SEARCH, DEPTH-FIRST). The major advantage of the depth-first selection rule over the best-first selection rule is that, in general, it requires less storage. But the depth-first search, being a uninformed search, can be much slower than the best-first search. A theoretical comparison of various search strategies used in B&B procedures has been published (Ibaraki, 1976).

More on Branching and Pruning

In this abstract formulation a number of details have been left out. For example, only the basic properties of a branching function have been defined. In a practical implementation of a B&B procedure, a branching function is chosen that is natural for the problem domain in question and satisfies the properties given here. The splitting function is usually suggested by the problem. But sometimes, a problem may have many natural splitting functions [eg, the traveling salesman problem has many natural splitting functions (Papadimitriou and Steiglitz, 1982)]. The selection function can be depth-first, best-first, or some other function suitable for the problem at hand.

For pruning, in each cycle of BB, a dominated subset A^D of the collection A needs to be constructed. Note that for any two subsets X_1, X_2 of X, at least one of them dominates the other [either $f^*(X_1) \geq f^*(X_2)$ or $f^*(X_2) \geq f^*(X_1)$]. Hence, in theory, A^D could be constructed to have all but one set of the collection A. This would make the procedure BB terminate in a very few cycles because in every cycle of BB all but one of the generated sets is eliminated. In practice, it may not be known which sets in A dominate which other sets in A without exhaustively enumerating the elements in the sets that are members of A. However, partial knowledge from the problem domain is often available to reveal that certain sets in A dominate certain other sets in A. This partial knowledge of the dominance relation can be used to construct a dominated subset A^D of A.

Next a practical B&B procedure is presented that finds a shortest path in a directed graph. This also illustrates how domain knowledge about directed graphs can be used to devise practical branching and pruning functions. B&B can be used in other applications (Lawler and Wood, 1966; Papadimitriou and Steiglitz, 1982; Horowitz and Sahni, 1978).

Examples

Finding a Shortest Path in a Graph. A directed graph G is given. Each arc (n,m) in G has a cost $c(n,m) \geq 0$, and for every path P in G, $\text{cost}(P)$ is defined as the sum of the arc costs of P. The problem is to find a least-cost directed path from a source node s in G to a terminal node t in G. For this problem X is the set containing each path from s to t. For $x \in X$, $f(x) = \text{cost}(x)$.

If (m,n) is an arc in G, n is called a successor of m. Suppose $P = (n_1, n_2, \ldots, n_j)$ is a path in G, then Pn is the path $(n_1, n_2, \ldots, n_j, n)$. A path P from s to a node n is used to represent the set of paths in X that are extensions of P. [In actual implementations of B&B, the set X and its subsets are not represented explicitly. Instead, some problem-specific data structure is used that implicitly represents X and its subsets (Nau and co-workers, 1984).] Let $n_1, \ldots, n_k$ be successors of n in G; then a natural splitting function on P is $\text{SPLIT}(P) = \{Pn_i | 1 \leq i \leq k\}$. For a path P from s to a node n, a lower bound function lb is defined as $lb(P) = \text{cost}(P)$.

Pruning Based on Lower Bounds. Let P' be a path from s to t, and $\text{cost}(P') \leq lb(P'')$, where P'' is some path between s and a node n. Clearly, P' is no worse than any path represented by P'', ie, P' dominates P''. Hence if P' and P'' are present in the collection A in BB, P'' can be pruned. Figure 1 shows the operation of a best-first B&B procedure using this kind of pruning on the graph of Figure 2.

Figure 2a shows a path (s) that represents X, the set of all paths between s and t. At the beginning of BB, A is initialized to s. Figure 2b shows A after a branching oper-

SEARCH, BRANCH-AND-BOUND 1471

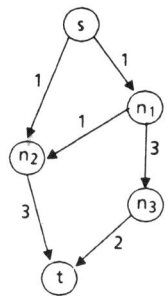

Figure 1. Steps of a best-first B&B search procedure using bounds for pruning.

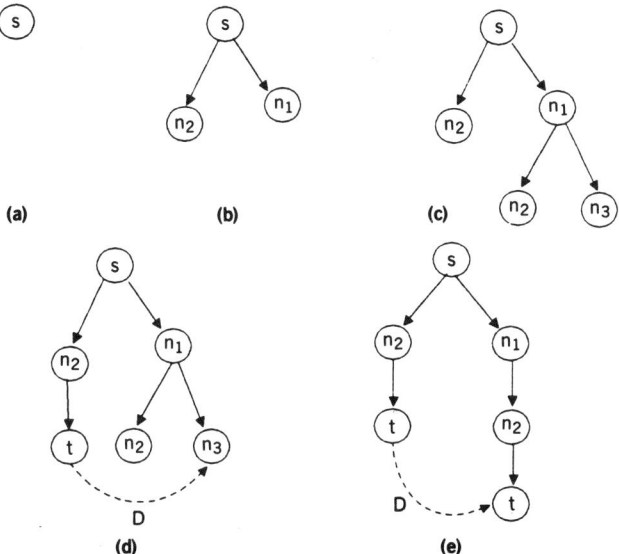

Figure 2. A directed graph G. Arc costs are given next to the arcs.

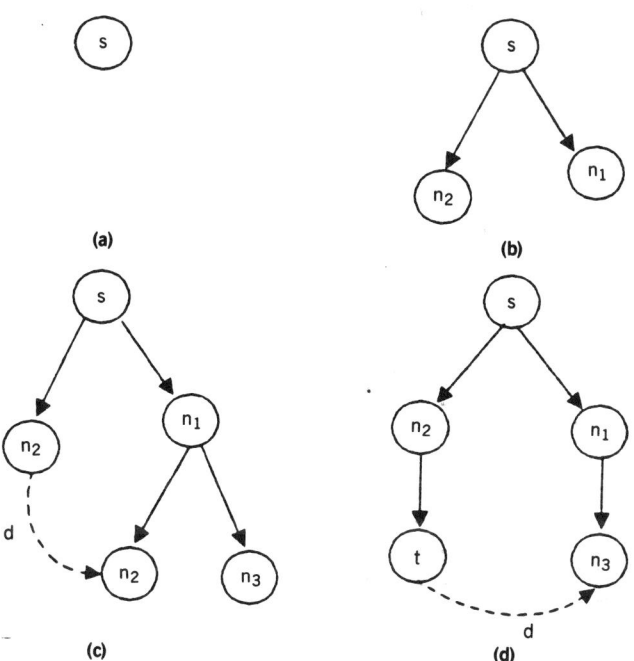

Figure 3. Steps of a best-first B&B search procedure using dominance for pruning.

ation is performed on s, which results in paths (s,n_1) and (s,n_2). No pruning is performed in this cycle of BB. In the next cycle of BB the splitting operation is performed on (s,n_1) [because $lb(s,n_1)) \le lb((s,n_2))$], which results in (s,n_1,n_2) and (s,n_1,n_3). Figure 2c shows A $[= \{(s,n_2), (s,n_1,n_2), (s,n_1,n_3)\}]$ at this point. In the next cycle of BB, (s,n_2) is selected for splitting. The resulting path (s,n_2,t) dominates (s,n_1,n_3) because $f(s,n_2,t) \le lb(s,n_1,n_3)$. Therefore, (s,n_1,n_3) is pruned (Fig. 2d). In the next cycle of BB, (s,n_1,n_2) is selected for splitting, which results in (s,n_1,n_2t). As shown in Figure 2e, (s,n_2,t) dominates (s,n_1,n_2,t); hence (s,n_1,n_2,t) is pruned. Now A contains only (s,n_2,t), which is a singleton set. Therefore, BB terminates with (s,n_2,t) as a shortest path between s and t.

Pruning Based on Dominance. If P' and P'' are two paths between s and a node n, and $\text{cost}(P') \le \text{cost}(P'')$, $P'DP''$ because for any extension of P'' there exists an extension of P' that has no larger cost than the extension of P''. Thus the structure of the graph reveals dominance between two paths even when adequate bound information is not available. Note that the lower bound information may be used to conclude $P'DP''$ (or $P''DP'$) only if n is the terminal node. Figure 3 shows the operation of a best-first B&B using dominance for pruning on the graph of Figure 2.

The first two steps, as shown in Figures 3a and 3b, are identical to the ones shown in Figures 2a and 2b. Figure 3c shows A after splitting (s,n_1). The path (s,n_2) dominates (s,n_1,n_2) because they both end at n_2 and $\text{cost}((s,n_2)) \le \text{cost}((s,n_1,n_2))$; hence, (s,n_1,n_2) is pruned. In the next step (s,n_2) is chosen for splitting. As shown in Figure 3d, the resulting path (s,n_2,t) dominates (s,n_1,n_3); hence (s,n_1,n_3) is pruned. Now A contains only (s,n_2,t), which is a singleton set. Therefore BB terminates with (s,n_2,t) as a shortest path between s and t.

Complexity of B&B Search

The complexity of a B&B search procedure depends on the problem being solved and the branching and pruning functions used. For NP-hard problems, the worst case complexity of any B&B procedure has to be exponential (assuming P ≠ NP), even though the B&B technique is usually much better than the exhaustive search. For example, for the n-city traveling salesman problem, the worst-case complexity of a B&B procedure (Papadimitriou and Steiglitz, 1982) is $O(2^n)$, whereas the complexity of the exhaustive search procedure is $O(n^n)$. But even for NP-hard problems the average case complexity of a B&B procedure can be subexponential. Many researchers have tried to analyze the average complexity of the B&B procedures for specific abstract problem models. Dechter (1981) developed a tree-based model of B&B and used it to investigate the relationships of the characteristics of the problem, the lower bound function, and the branching function to the average time complexity of the B&B procedure. Smith (1984) analyzed the average time-and-space complexities for different search strategies used by special kinds of B&B procedures called relaxation-guided procedures. The complexity results of Huyn and co-workers (1980) derived in the context of A^* (qv) are also applicable to B&B, as A^* can be viewed as a B&B procedure.

RELATIONSHIP WITH AI SEARCH ALGORITHMS

The central idea of branching and pruning to discover an optimal element of a set is at the heart of many AI search algorithms. For example, the A* algorithm (Nilsson, 1980) for state-space search can be viewed as a best-first B&B procedure (Nau and co-workers, 1984). A* differs only slightly from the best-first B&B procedure for finding a shortest path presented in this article, as A* uses a more informed lower bound. The nodes on the OPEN list in A* represent the active set of paths on which branching and pruning is performed. The process of node selection and expansion corresponds to branching. Node elimination corresponds to pruning-dominated paths. Many other heuristic procedures for searching state-space graphs can be viewed as B&B procedures using different selection and pruning functions. The AND/OR graph search algorithm AO* (Nilsson, 1980) and the game-tree (qv) search procedures $\alpha-\beta$ (Nilsson, 1980), SSS* (Stockman, 1979), and B* (Berliner, 1979) can also be viewed as B&B procedures (Kumar and Kanal, 1983). It has been shown that all these procedures can be viewed as instantiations of a general B&B procedure for searching AND/OR graphs (qv) (Kumar and co-workers, 1988).

RELATIONSHIP WITH DYNAMIC PROGRAMMING

B&B procedures are closely related to dynamic programming. Historically, the earlier dynamic programming procedures used structural dominance for pruning but did not use bounds. Selection was essentially breadth-first. Whereas, as noted before, the earlier formulations of B&B used bounds for selection and pruning but did not use dominance (in its general form) for pruning. In the recent formulations of dynamic programming (Morin and Marsten, 1976; Kumar, 1984) and B&B, both dominance and bounds are used. Nevertheless, B&B and dynamic programming are different techniques for solving optimization problems. As has been discussed (Kumar, 1982; Kumar and Kanal, 1988), dynamic programming can be viewed as a bottom-up search, whereas B&B can be viewed as a top-down search (see PROCESSING, BOTTOM-UP AND TOP-DOWN). In the context of state-space graphs, the difference between them vanishes, as for every state-space graph, it is possible to construct a dual state-space graph such that the top-down search of one is equivalent to the bottom-up search of the other (Kumar and Kanal, 1988). That is why Dijkstra's (1959) algorithm for finding the shortest path in a graph could be classified both as B&B (Hall, 1971) and as dynamic programming (Dreyfus and Law, 1977).

BIBLIOGRAPHY

E. Balas, "A Note on the Branch-and-Bound Principle," *Operat. Res.* **16**, 442–444, 886 (1968).

H. Berliner, "The B* Tree Search Algorithm: A Best-First Proof Procedure," *Artif. Intell.* **12**, 23–40 (1979).

A. Dechter, A Probabilistic Analysis of Branch-and-Bound Search, Technical Report UCLA-ENG-CSL-**8139**, Cognitive Systems Laboratory, UCLA, Los Angeles, Oct. 1981.

E. W. Dijkstra, "A Note on Two Problems in Connection with Graphs," *Numer. Math.* **1**, 269–271 (1959).

S. E. Dreyfus and A. M. Law, *The Art and Theory of Dynamic Programming*, Academic Press, Inc. New York, 1977.

P. A. V. Hall, "Branch-and-Bound and Beyond," in *Proceedings of the Second IJCAI*, London, Morgan-Kaufmann, San Mateo, Calif., 1971, pp. 641–658.

E. Horowitz and S. Sahni, *Fundamentals of Computer Algorithms*, Computer Science Press, Potomac, Md., 1978.

N. Huyn, R. Dechter, and J. Pearl, "Probabilistic Analysis of the Complexity of A*," *Artif. Intell.* **15**, 241–254 (1980).

T. Ibaraki, "Theoretical Comparison of Search Strategies in Branch and Bound," *Inter. J. Comput. Inform. Sci.* **5**, 315–344 (1976).

T. Ibaraki, "The Power of Dominance Relations in Branch and Bound Algorithms," *JACM* **24**, 264–279 (1977).

T. Ibaraki, "Branch-and-Bound Procedure and State-Space Representation of Combinatorial Optimization Problems," *Inform. Ctrl.* **36**, 1–27 (1978).

W. H. Kohler and K. Steiglitz, "Characterization and Theoretical Comparison of Branch and Bound Algorithms for Permutation Problems," *JACM* **21**, 140–156 (1974).

V. Kumar, *A Unified Approach to Problem Solving Search Procedures*, Ph.D. dissertation, University of Maryland, College Park, 1982.

V. Kumar, "A General Bottom-up Procedure for Searching AND/OR Graphs," in *Proceedings of the Fourth National Conference on Artificial Intelligence*, Austin, Tex., AAAI, Menlo Park, Calif., 1984.

V. Kumar and L. Kanal "A General Branch and Bound Formulation for Understanding and Synthesizing and/or Tree Search Procedures," *Artif. Intell.* **21**(1), 179–198 (1983).

V. Kumar and L. Kanal, "The CDP: A Unifying Formulation for Heuristic Search, Dynamic Programming, and Branch-and-Bound," in L. Kanal and V. Kumar, eds., *Search in Artificial Intelligence*, Springer-Verlag, New York, 1988, pp. 1–28.

V. Kumar, D. Nau, and L. Kanal, "General Branch-and-Bound Formulation for AND/OR Graph and Game Tree Search," in Kumar and Kanal, 1988, pp. 91–130.

E. L. Lawler and D. E. Wood, "Branch-and-Bound Methods: A Survey," *Operat. Res.* **14**, 699–719 (1966).

L. G. Mitten, "Branch and Bound Methods: General Formulations and Properties," *Operat. Res.* **18**, 23–34 (1970).

L. G. Mitten, "Errata," Operat. Res. **19**, 550 (1971).

T. L. Morin and R. D. Marsten, "Branch and Bound Strategies for Dynamic Programming," *Operat. Res.* **24**, 611–627 (1976).

D. S. Nau, V. Kumar, and L. N. Kanal, "General Branch-and-Bound and Its Relation to A* and AO*," *Artif. Intell.* **23**, 29–58 (1984).

N. Nilsson, *Principles of Artificial Intelligence*, Tioga, Palo Alto, Calif., 1980.

Papadimitriou and Steiglitz, *Combinatorial Optimization: Algorithms and Complexity*, Prentice-Hall, Inc., Englewood Cliffs, N.J., 1982.

D. R. Smith, "Random Trees and the Analysis of Branch and Bound Procedures," *JACM*, 163–188 (Jan. 1984).

G. C. Stockman, "A Minimax Algorithm Better than Alpha-Beta?" *Artif. Intell.* **12**, 179–196 (1979).

V. KUMAR
University of Minnesota

SEARCH, DEPTH-FIRST

State-space search methods are useful when a problem can be formulated in terms of finding a solution path in a directed graph from an initial node to a goal node. State-space graphs are implicitly represented. They are generated on the fly with the aid of a successor-generator function; given a node of the graph, this function generates its successors. Depth-first search is a name commonly used for various search methods that perform search as follows. The search begins by expanding the initial node, ie, by generating its successors. At each later step, one of the most recently generated nodes is expanded. (In some problems, heuristic information is used to order the successors of an expanded node. This determines the order in which these successors will be visited by the depth-first search method.) If this most recently generated node does not have any successors or if it can be determined that the node will not lead to any solutions, then backtracking (qv) is done, and a most recently generated node from the remaining as yet unexpanded nodes is selected for expansion.

A depth-first search method can be used to find a solution in the search space by simply terminating the algorithm when the first solution is found. It can also be used to find a least-cost solution (by letting the algorithm run until the whole search space is exhausted, and also by keeping track of the best solution seen so far). Following are three search methods that use the depth-first search strategy.

1. Simple backtracking is a depth-first search method that is used to find any one solution and that uses no heuristics for ordering the successors of an expanded node. Heuristics may be used to prune nodes of the search space so that search can be avoided under these nodes.

2. Ordered depth-first search is a depth-first search method that is used to find any one solution and that uses heuristics for ordering the successors of an expanded node. Heuristics may also be used to prune nodes of the search space so that search can be avoided under these nodes.

3. Depth-first branch-and-bound (DFBB) is a depth-first search method that is used to find an optimal solution. These search methods use a lower bound function (defined over the nodes of the search space) to prune those nodes that cannot lead to a solution that is better than the one already found. They also often use a heuristic to order the successors of an expanded node.

There is a considerable confusion regarding the names that are used by various researchers to label different search techniques. For example, the names depth-first branch-and-bound and backtracking are used by some researchers to refer to the class of algorithms that here are called ordered depth-first search.

If the search space to the left of the first goal node is infinite (or very large), then search would never terminate (or take a very long time). This problem can be corrected by having a bound L on the depth of the space searched. This kind of search is called depth-bounded depth-first search. If there is no goal node at a depth L or earlier, then the search would fail even if there is a goal node at a depth greater than L. In such cases the search will have to be restarted with a larger depth bound.

Usually, a depth-first search procedure has lower storage requirement than a best-first search procedure. If every node has k successors, then the storage requirement of a depth-first procedure for searching to a depth of n is $O(n \times k)$. In best-first search, if the heuristic evaluation function is bad, then the storage requirement can be as much as $O(k^n)$. Furthermore, depth-first search has very little overhead as compared to best-first search in which a priority queue must be rearranged after every node expansion.

BIBLIOGRAPHY

General References

E. Horowitz and S. Sahni, *Fundamentals of Computer Algorithms,* Computer Science Press, Rockville, Md., 1978.

L. Kanal and V. Kumar, eds., *Search in Artificial Intelligence.* Springer-Verlag, New York, 1988.

N. J. Nilsson, *Principles of Artificial Intelligence,* Tioga Press, Palo Alto, Calif., 1980.

J. Pearl. *Heuristics—Intelligent Search Strategies for Computer Problem Solving.* Addison-Wesley, Reading, Mass., 1984.

V. KUMAR
University of Minnesota

SEGMENTATION

Image segmentation is the partition of an image into a set of nonoverlapping regions whose union is the entire image. The purpose of image segmentation is to decompose the image into parts that are meaningful with respect to a particular application. For example, in two-dimensional part recognition, a segmentation might be performed to separate the two-dimensional object from the background. Figure 1a shows a gray-level image of an industrial part, and Figure 1b shows its segmentation into object and background. In this figure, the object is shown in white and the background in black. In simple segmentations, this article will use gray levels to illustrate the separate regions. In more complex segmentation examples where there are many regions, white lines on a black background will be used to show the separation of the image into its parts.

It is very difficult to tell a computer program what constitutes a meaningful segmentation. Instead, general segmentation procedures tend to obey the following rules.

1. Regions of an image segmentation should be uniform and homogenous with respect to some characteristic such as gray level or texture.
2. Region interiors should be simple and without many small holes.
3. Adjacent regions of a segmentation should have significantly different values with respect to the characteristic on which they are uniform.
4. Boundaries of each segment should be simple, not ragged, and must be spatially accurate.

(a)

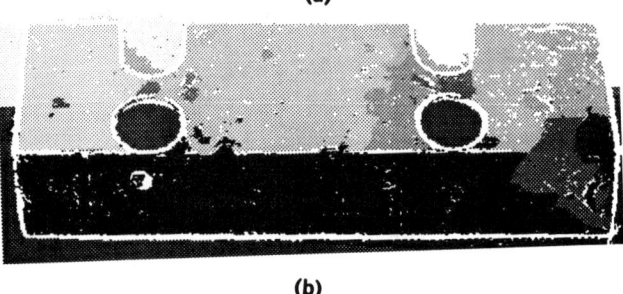

(b)

Figure 1. (a) A gray-level image of an industrial part and (b) a segmentation of the image into object (white) and background (black).

Achieving all these desired properties is difficult because strictly uniform and homogeneous regions are typically full of small holes and have ragged boundaries. Insisting that adjacent regions have large differences in values can cause regions to merge and boundaries to be lost.

Clustering in pattern recognition (qv) is the process of partitioning a set of pattern vectors into subsets called clusters (Young and Calvert, 1974). For example, if the pattern vectors are pairs of real numbers illustrated by the point plot of Figure 2, clustering consists of finding subsets of points that are close to each other in Euclidean two-space. As there is no full theory of clustering, there is no full theory of image segmentation. Image segmentation techniques are basically *ad hoc* and differ precisely in the way they emphasize one or more of the desired properties and in the way they balance and compromise one desired property against another. The difference between image segmentation and clustering is that in clustering, the grouping is done in measurement space. In image segmentation, the grouping is done on the spatial domain of the image and there is an interplay in the clustering between the (possibly overlapping) groups in measurement space and the mutually exclusive groups of the image segmentation.

This article describes the main ideas behind the major image segmentation techniques and gives example results for a number of them. Additional image segmentation surveys have been published (Zucker, 1976; Riseman and Arbib, 1977; Kanade, 1980; Fu and Mui, 1981). This article will view segmentation with respect to the gray-level characteristic. Segmentation on the basis of some other characteristic, such as texture, can be achieved by first applying an operator that transforms local texture to a texture feature value (see also TEXTURE). Texture segmentation can then be accomplished by applying segmentation with respect to the texture pattern value characteristic exactly as if it were a gray-level characteristic.

MEASUREMENT–SPACE GUIDED SPATIAL CLUSTERING

This technique for image segmentation uses the measurement–space clustering process to define a partition in measurement–space. Then each pixel is assigned the label of the cell in the measurement–space partition to which it belongs. The image segments are defined as the connected components of the pixels having the same label.

The segmentation process is, in general, an unsupervised clustering, because no *a priori* knowledge about the number and type of regions present in the image is available. The accuracy of the measurement–space clustering image segmentation process depends directly on how well the objects of interest on the image separate into distinct measurement–space clusters. Typically, the process works well in situations where there are a few kinds of distinct objects having widely different gray-level intensities (or gray-level intensity vectors, for multiband images) and these objects appear on a near uniform background.

Clustering procedures that use the pixel as a unit and compare each pixel value with every other pixel value can require excessively large computation time because of the large number of pixels in an image. Iterative partition rearrangement schemes must go through the image data set many times and if done without sampling can also take excessive computation time. Histogram mode seeking, because it requires only one pass through the data, probably involves the least computation time of the measurement–space clustering techniques, and it is the approach discussed here.

Histogram mode seeking is a measurement–space clustering process in which it is assumed that homogeneous objects on the image manifest themselves as the clusters in measurement–space. Image segmentation is accomplished by mapping the clusters back to the image domain where the maximal connected components of the mapped back clusters constitute the image segments. For images that are single band images, calculation of this histogram in an array is direct. The measurement–space clustering can be accomplished by determining the valleys in this histogram and declaring the clusters to be the interval of values between valleys. A pixel whose value is in the ith interval is labeled with index i and the segment it belongs to is one of the connected components of all pixels whose label is i. Thresholding techniques are examples of histogram mode seeking with bimodal histograms.

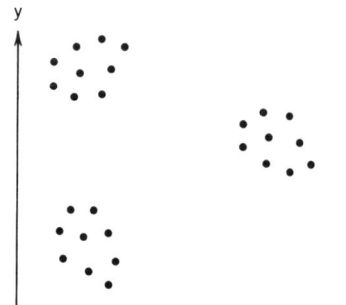

Figure 2. A set of points in a Euclidean measurement space that can be separated into three clusters of points. Each cluster consists of points that are in some sense close to each other.

Figure 3 illustrates an example image that is the right kind of image for the measurement–space clustering image segmentation process. It is an enlarged image of a polished mineral ore section. The width of the field is about 1 mm. The ore is from Ducktown, Tennessee, and shows subhedral to enhedral pyrite porophyroblests (white) in a matrix of pyrorhotite (gray). The black areas are holes. Figure 4 shows the histogram of this image. The valleys are no trouble to find. The first cluster is from the left end to the first valley. The second cluster is from the first valley to the second valley. The third cluster is from the second valley to the right end. Assigning to each pixel the cluster index of the cluster to which it belongs and then assigning a unique gray level to each cluster label yields the segmentation shown in Figure 5. This is a virtually perfect (meaningful) segmentation.

Figure 6 shows an example image that is not ideal for measurement–space clustering image segmentation. Figure 7 shows its histogram, which has three modes and two

Figure 5. The segmentation of the image of Figure 3, produced by clustering the histogram of Figure 4.

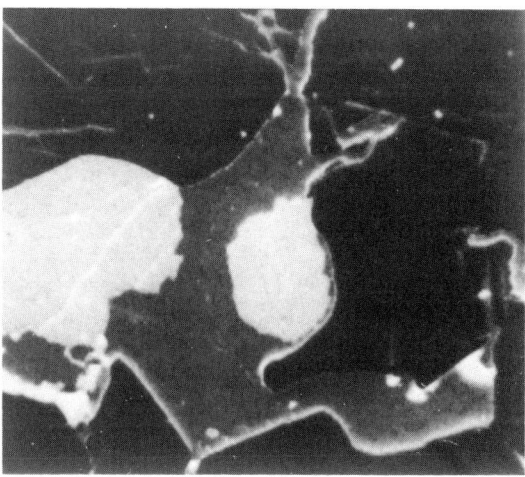

Figure 3. An enlarged raw mineral ore section. The bright areas are grains of pyrite; the gray areas constitute a matrix of pyrorhotite; the black areas are holes.

Figure 6. An image similar in some respects to the image of Figure 3. Because some of the boundaries between regions are shadowed, homogeneous region segmentation may not produce the desired segmentation.

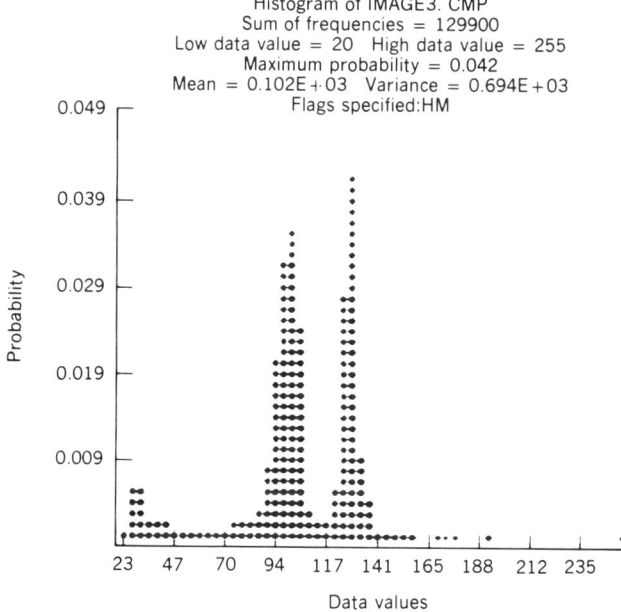

Figure 4. The histogram of the image in Figure 3. The three nonoverlapping modes correspond to the black holes, the pyrorhotite, and the pyrite.

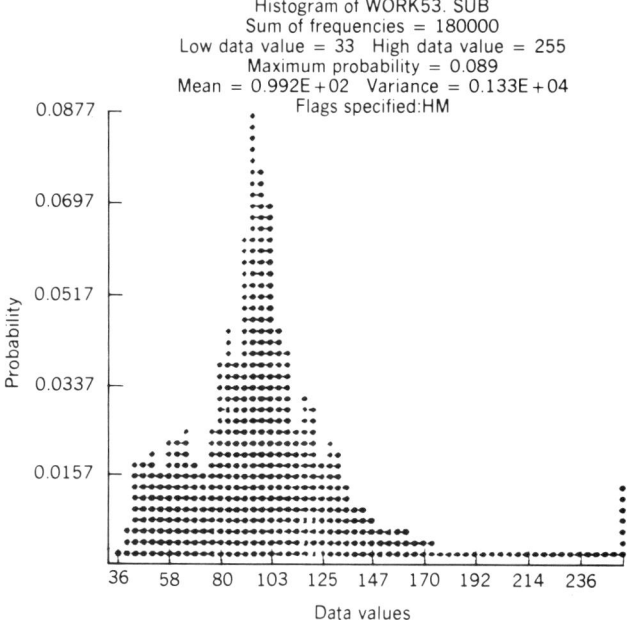

Figure 7. A histogram of the image of Figure 6.

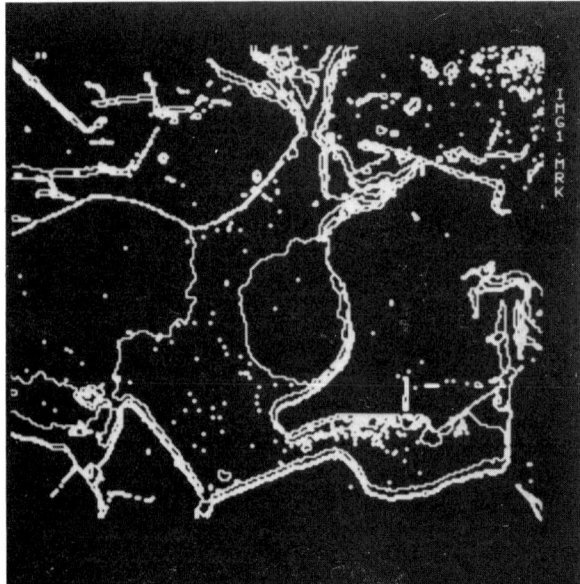

Figure 8. The segmentation of the image of Figure 6, produced by clustering the histogram of Figure 7.

Figure 9. An F-15 bulkhead.

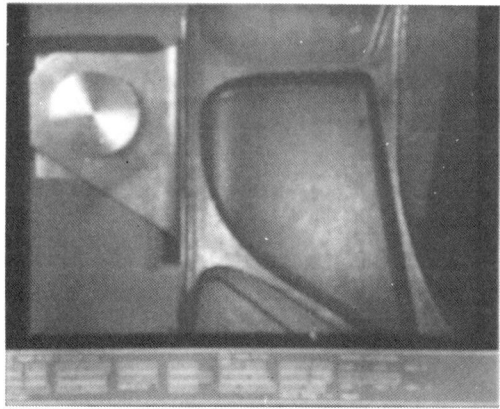

Figure 10. A section of the F-15 bulkhead.

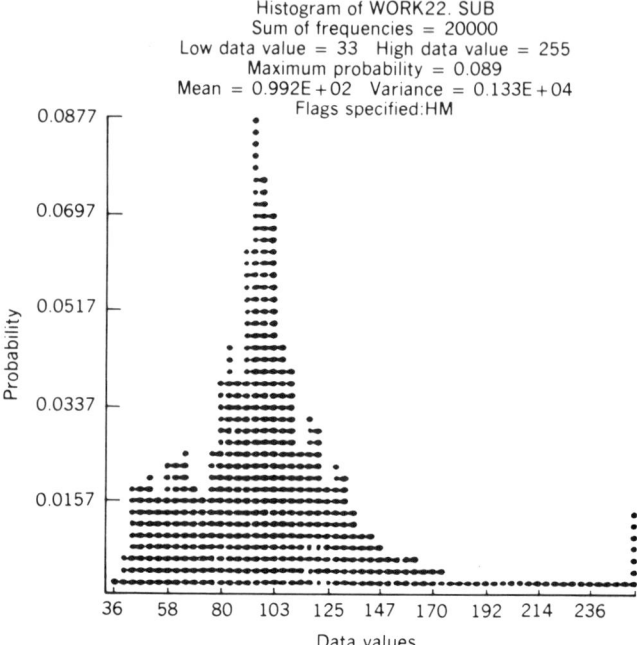

Figure 11. A histogram of the bulkhead image of Figure 10.

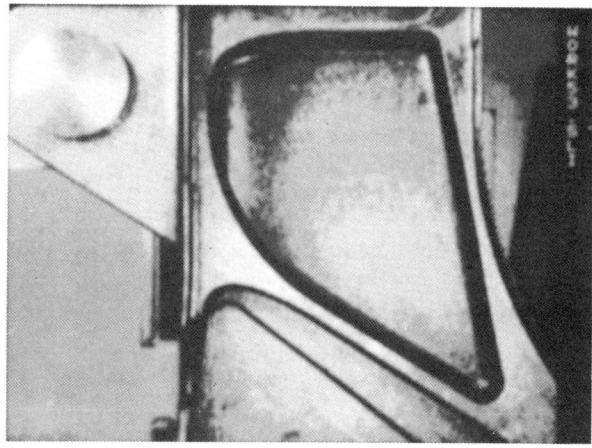

Figure 12. The segmentation of the bulkhead by a measurement–space clustering into five clusters.

valleys, and Figure 8 shows the corresponding segmentation. Notice the multiple boundary area. It is apparent that the boundary between the grain and background is in fact shaded dark, and there are many such border regions that show up as dark segments. In this case, it is not desired that the edge borders be separate regions, and although the segmentation procedure did exactly as it should have done, the results are not what was desired. This illustrates that segmentation into homogeneous regions is not necessarily a good solution to a segmentation problem.

The next example further illustrates the fallacies of measurement–space clustering. Figure 9 is a diagram of an F-15 bulkhead. Images of portions of the bulkhead, which were used as test data for an experimental robot guidance–inspection system, will be used as examples throughout the rest of this article. Figure 10 illustrates an image of a section of the F-15 bulkhead. It is clear that the image has distinct parts such as webs and ribs. Figure 11 shows the histogram of this image. It has two well-separated modes. The narrow one on the right, with a long left tail, corresponds to specular reflection points. The main mode has three valleys on its left side and two valleys on its right side. Defining the depth of a valley to be the probability difference between the valley bottom and the lowest valley side and eliminating the two shallowest valleys produces the segmentation shown in Figure 12. The problem in the segmentation is apparent. Because the clustering was done in measurement space, there was no requirement for good spatial continuation and the resulting boundaries are very noisy and busy. Separating the main mode into its two most dominant submodes produces the segmentation of Figure 13. Here the boundary noise is less, the resulting regions more satisfactory, but the detail provided is much less.

Ohlander and co-workers (1978) refine the clustering idea in a recursive way. They begin by defining a mask selecting all pixels on the image. Given any mask, a histogram of the masked image is computed. Measurement–space clustering enables the separation of one mode of the histogram set from another mode. Pixels on the image are then identified with the cluster to which they belong. If there is only one measurement–space cluster, then the mask is terminated. If there is more than one cluster, then each connected component of all pixels with the same cluster is, in turn, used to generate a mask that is placed on a mask stack. During successive iterations the next mask in the stack selects pixels in the histogram computation process. Clustering is repeated for each new mask until the stack is empty.

Figure 14 illustrates this process, which is called a recursive histogram-directed spatial clustering. Figure 15 illustrates a recursive histogram-directed spatial clustering technique applied to the bulkhead image of Figure 10. It produces a result with boundaries being somewhat busy and many small regions in areas of specular reflectance. Figure 16 illustrates the results of performing a morphological opening with a 3 × 3 square structuring element on the segmentation of Figure 15. The tiny regions are

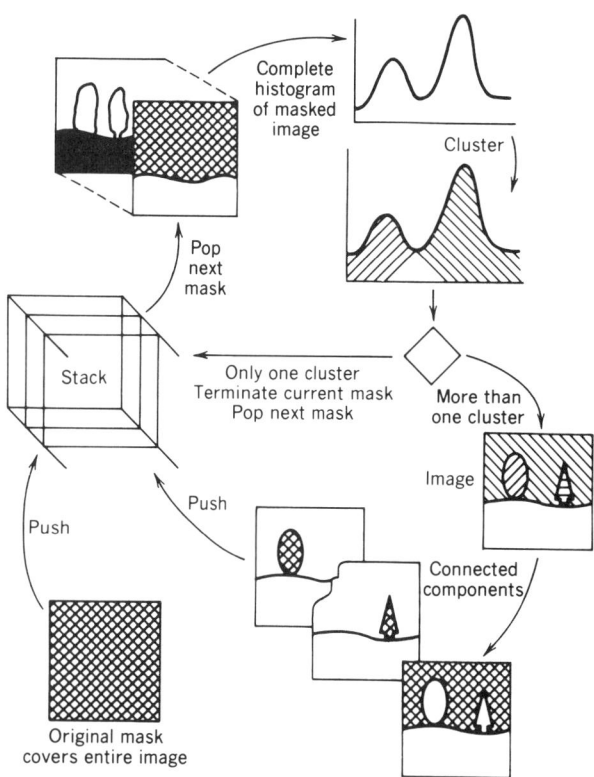

Figure 14. The recursive histogram-directed spatial clustering scheme of Ohlander and co-workers (1978).

removed in this manner, but several important long, thin regions are also lost.

For ordinary color images, Ohta and co-workers (1980) suggest that histograms not be computed individually on the red, green, and blue (RGB) color variables, but on a set of variables closer to what the Karhunen-Loeve (principal components) transform would suggest. They suggest $(R + G + B)/3$, $(R - B)/2$, and $(2G - R - B)/4$. Figure 17 illustrates a color image. Figure 18 shows two segmentations of the color image: one by recursive histogram-

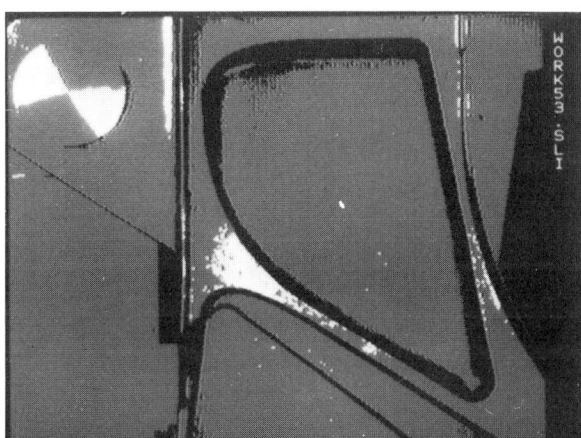

Figure 13. The segmentation of the bulkhead, induced by a measurement–space clustering into three clusters.

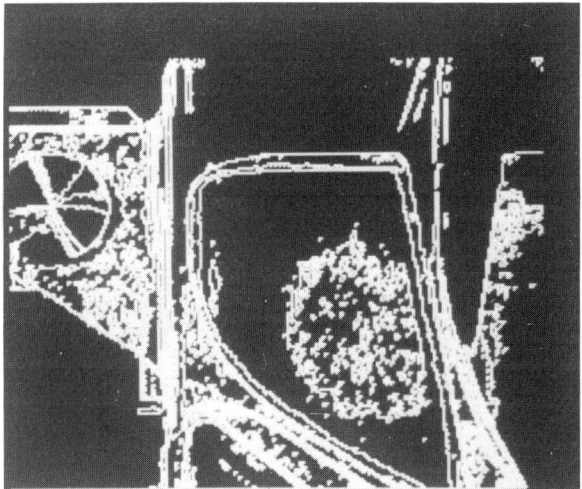

Figure 15. The results of the histogram-directed spatial clustering when applied to the bulkhead image.

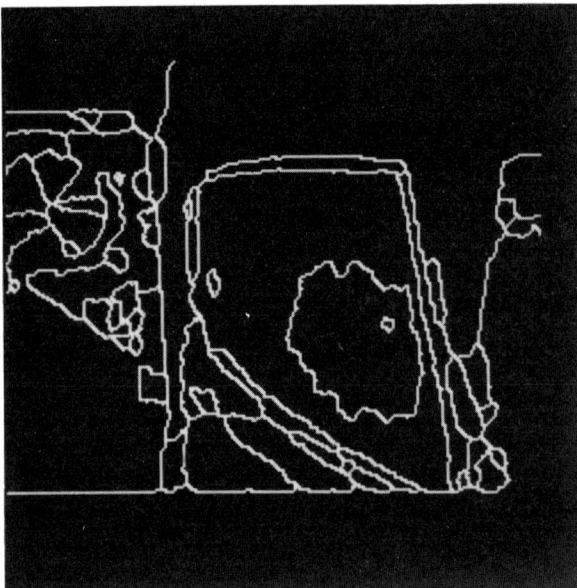

Figure 16. The results of performing a morphological opening with a 3 × 3 square structuring element on the segmentation of Figure 15.

Figure 17. A color image.

directed spatial clustering using the R, G, and B bands and the second by the same method, but using the transformed bands suggested by Ohta and co-workers (1980).

Thresholding

If the image contains a bright object against a dark background and the measurement-space is one-dimensional, measurement-space clustering amounts to determining a threshold such that all points smaller than or equal to the threshold are assigned to one cluster and the remaining points are assigned to the second cluster. In the easiest cases, a procedure to determine the threshold need only examine the histogram and place the threshold in the valley between the two modes. Unfortunately, it is not always the case that the two modes are nicely separated by a valley. To handle this kind of situation a variety of techniques can be used to combine the spatial information on the image with the gray-level intensity information to help in threshold determination.

Chow and Kaneko (1972) suggest using a threshold that depends on the histogram determined from the spatially local area around the pixel to which the threshold applies. Thus, for example, a neighborhood size of 33 × 33 or 65 × 65 can be used to compute the local histogram. Chow and Kaneko avoided the local histogram computation for each pixel's neighborhood by dividing the image into mutually exclusive blocks, computing the histogram for each block, and determining an appropriate threshold for each histogram. This threshold value can be considered to apply to the center pixel of each block. To obtain thresholds for the remaining pixels, they spatially interpolated the block center pixel thresholds to obtain a spatially adaptive threshold for each pixel.

Weszka and co-workers (1974) suggest determining a histogram for only those pixels having a high Laplacian magnitude. They reason that there will be a shoulder of the gray-level intensity function at each side of the boundary. The shoulder has high Laplacian magnitude. A histo-

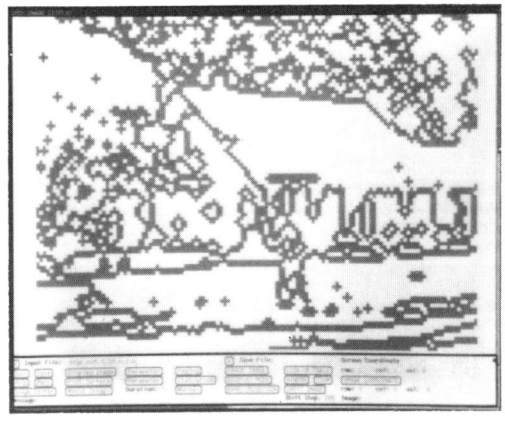

(a)

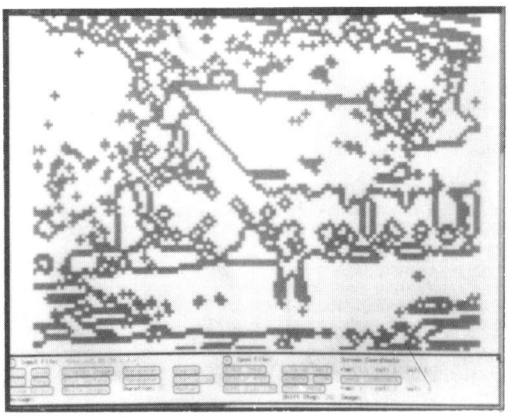

(b)

Figure 18. Two segments of the color image. The left segmentation was achieved by recursive histogram-directed spatial clustering using R, G, and B bands. The right segment was achieved by the same method, but using the transformed bands $(R + G + B)/3$, $(R - B)/2$, and $(2G - R - B)/4$ suggested by Ohta and co-workers (1980).

gram of all shoulder pixels will be a histogram of all interior pixels just next to the interior border of the region. It will not involve those pixels in between regions that help make the histogram valley shallow. It will also have a tendency to involve equal numbers of pixels from the object and from the background. This makes the two histogram modes about the same size. Thus the valley-seeking method for threshold selection has a chance of working on the new histogram.

Weszka and Rosenfeld (1978) describe one method for segmenting white blobs against a dark background by a threshold selection based on busyness. For any threshold, busyness is the percentage of pixels having a neighbor whose thresholded value is different from their own thresholded value. A good threshold is that point near the histogram valley between the two peaks that minimizes the busyness.

Watanabe (1974) suggests choosing a threshold value that maximizes the sum of gradients taken over all pixels whose gray level equals the threshold value. Kohler (1981) suggests a modification of the Watanabe idea. Instead of choosing a threshold that maximizes the sum of gradient magnitudes taken over all pixels whose gray-level intensity equals the threshold value, Kohler suggests choosing that threshold that detects more high contrast edges and fewer low contrast edges than any other threshold.

Kohler defines the set $E(T)$ of edges detected by a threshold T to be the set of all pairs of neighboring pixels one of whose gray-level intensity is less than or equal to T and one of whose gray level intensity is greater than T:

$$E(T) = \{(i, j), (k, l))| \quad (1)$$

where pixels (i, j) and (k, l) are neighbors and

$$\min\{I(i, j), I(k, l)\} \leq T < \max\{I(i, j), I(k, l)\}\}$$

The total contrast $C(T)$ of edges detected by threshold T is given by

$$C(T) = \sum_{((i,j),(k,l))\in E(T)} \min\{|I(i, j) - T|, |I(k, l) - T|\} \quad (2)$$

The average contrast of all edges detected by threshold T is then given by $C(T)/\#E(T)$. The best threshold T_b is determined by that value that maximizes $C(T_b)/\#E(T_b)$.

Milgram and Herman (1979) reason that pixels that are in between regions probably have in between gray-level intensities. If it is these pixels that are the cause of the shallow valleys, then it should be possible to eliminate their effect by only considering pixels having small gradients. They take this idea further and suggest that by examining clusters in the two-dimensional measurement space consisting of gray-level intensity and gradient magnitude, it is even possible to determine multiple thresholds when more than one kind of object is present.

Panda and Rosenfeld (1978) suggest a related approach for segmenting a white blob against a dark background. Consider the histogram of gray levels for all pixels that have small gradients. If a pixel has a small gradient, then it is not likely for it to be an edge. If it is not an edge, then it is either a dark background pixel or a bright blob pixel. Hence, the histogram of all pixels having small gradients will be bimodal and for pixels with small gradients, the valley between the two modes of the histogram is an appropriate threshold point. Next consider the histogram of gray levels for all pixels that have high gradients. If a pixel has a high gradient, then it is likely for it to be an edge. If it is an edge separating a bright blob against a dark background and if the separating boundary is not sharp but somewhat diffuse, then the histogram will be unimodal, the mean being a good threshold separating the dark background pixels from the bright blob pixels. Thus Panda and Rosenfeld suggest determining two thresholds: one for low gradient pixels and one for high gradient pixels. By this means they perform the clustering in the two-dimensional measurement–space consisting of gray-level intensity and gradient. A survey of threshold techniques can be found in Weszka (1978).

Multidimensional Measurement–Space Clustering

A LANDSAT image comes from a satellite and consists of seven separate images called bands. The bands are registered so that pixel (i, j) in one band corresponds to pixel (i, j) in each of the other bands. Each band represents a particular range of wavelengths. For multiband images such as LANDSAT or Thematic Mapper, determining the histogram in a multidimensional array is not feasible. For example, in a six-band image where each band has intensities between 0 and 99, the array would have to have $100^6 = 10^{12}$ locations. A large image might be 10,000 pixels per row by 10,000 rows. This only constitutes 10^8 pixels, a sample too small to estimate probabilities in a space of 10^{12} values were it not for some constraints of reality: (1) there is typically a high correlation between the band-to-band pixel values and (2) there is a large amount of spatial redundancy in image data. Both these factors create a situation in which the 10^8 pixels can be expected to contain only between 10^4 and 10^5 distinct 6-tuples. Based on this fact, the counting required for the histogram is easily done by mapping the 6-tuples into array indexes. The programming technique known as *hashing*, which is described in most data structures texts, can be used for this purpose.

Clustering using the multidimensional histogram is more difficult than univariate histogram clustering, because peaks fall in different places in the different histograms. Goldberg and Shlien (1977, 1978) threshold the multidimensional histogram to select all N-tuples situated on the most prominent modes. Then they perform a measurement–space connected components on these N-tuples to collect together all the N-tuples in the top of the most prominent modes. These measurement–space connected sets form the cluster cores. The clusters are defined as the set of all N-tuples closest to each cluster core.

An alternate possibility (Narendra and Goldberg, 1977) is to locate peaks in the multidimensional measurement space and region grow around them, constantly descending from each peak. The region growing includes all successive neighboring N-tuples whose probability is no higher than the N-tuple from which it is growing. Adjacent mountains meet in their common valleys.

Rather than accomplish the clustering in the full measurement–space, it is possible to work in multiple lower order projection spaces and then reflect these clusters back to the full measurement–space. Suppose, for example, that the clustering is done on a four-band image. If the clustering done in bands 1 and 2 yields clusters c_1, c_2, c_3 and the clustering done in bands 3 and 4 yields clusters c_4 and c_5 then each possible 4-tuple from a pixel can be given a cluster label from the set $\{(c_1, c_4), (c_1, c_5), (c_2, c_4), (c_2, c_5), (c_3, c_4), (c_3, c_5)\}$. A 4-tuple (x_1, x_2, x_3, x_4) gets the cluster label (c_2, c_4) if (x_1, x_2) is in cluster c_2 and (x_3, x_4) is in cluster c_4.

REGION GROWING

Single Linkage Region Growing

Single linkage region growing schemes regard each pixel as a node in a graph. Neighboring pixels whose properties are similar enough are joined by an arc. The image segments are maximal sets of pixels all belonging to the same connected component. Figure 19 illustrates this idea with a simple image and the corresponding graph with the connected components circled. In this example, two pixels are connected by an edge if their values differ by less than five and they are 4-neighbors. Single linkage image segmentation schemes are attractive for their simplicity. They do, however, have a problem with chaining, because it takes only one arc leaking from one region to a neighboring one to cause the regions to merge.

As illustrated in Figure 19, the simplest single linkage scheme defines "similar enough" by pixel difference. Two neighboring pixels are similar enough if the absolute value of the difference between their gray-level intensity values is small enough. Bryant (1979) defines similar enough by normalizing the difference by the quantity (square root of 2) times the root mean square value of neighboring pixel differences taken over the entire image. For the image of Figure 19, the normalization factor is 99.22. The random variable that is the difference of two neighboring pixels normalized by the factor $1/99.22$ has a normal distribution with mean 0 and standard deviation 99.22. A threshold can now be chosen in terms of the standard deviation instead of as an absolute value. For pixels having vector values, the obvious generalization is to use a vector norm of the pixel difference vector.

Hybrid Linkage Region Growing

Hybrid single linkage techniques are more powerful than the simple single linkage technique. The hybrid techniques seek to assign a property vector to each pixel where the property vector depends on the $K \times K$ neighborhood of the pixel. Pixels that are similar are so because their neighborhoods in some special sense are similar. Similarity is thus established as a function of neighboring pixel values and this makes the technique better behaved on noisy data.

One hybrid single linkage scheme relies on an edge operator to establish whether two pixels are joined with an arc. Here an edge operator is applied to the image labeling each pixel as edge or nonedge. Neighboring pixels, neither of which are edges, are joined by an arc. The initial segments are the connected components of the nonedge labeled pixels. The edge pixels can either be left assigned edges and be considered as background or they can be assigned to the spatially nearest region having a label.

The quality of this technique is highly dependent on the edge operator used. Simple operators such as the Roberts and Sobel operators may provide too much region linkage, for a region cannot be declared as a segment unless it is completely surrounded by edge pixels. Haralick and Dinstein (1975), however, do report some success using this technique on LANDSAT data. They perform a dilation of the edge pixels in order to close gaps before performing the connected components operator. Perkins (1980) uses a similar technique.

Haralick (1982, 1984) discusses a very sensitive zero-crossing of second directional derivative edge operator. In this technique, each neighborhood is least squares fitted with a cubic polynomial in two variables. The first and second partial derivatives are easily determined from the polynomial. The first partial derivatives at the center pixel determine the gradient direction. With the direction fixed to be the gradient direction, the second partials determine the second directional derivative. If the gradient is high enough and if in the gradient direction, the second directional derivative has a negatively sloped zero-crossing inside the pixel's area, then an edge is declared in the neighborhood's center pixel.

Figure 20 shows the edges resulting from the second directional derivative zero-crossing operator using a gradient threshold of 4, a 9×9 neighborhood, and a zero-crossing radius of 0.85. The edges are well placed and a careful examination of pixels on perceived boundaries that are not classified as edge pixels will indicate the step edge pattern to be either nonexistent or weak. A connected components of the nonedge pixels accomplishes the initial segmentation. After the connected components operation, the edge pixels are assigned to their spatially closest component by a region filling operation. Figure 21 shows the boundaries from the region filled image. Obvi-

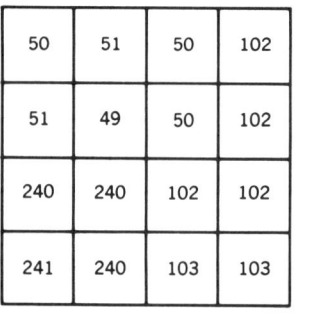 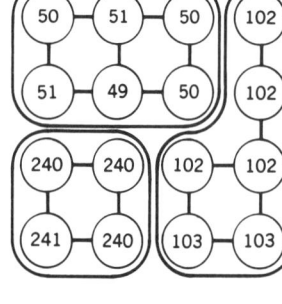

(a)   (b)

Figure 19. A simple gray-level image and the graph resulting from defining "similar enough" to be differing in gray level by less than five and using the 4-neighborhood to determine connected components.

Figure 20. The second directional derivative zero-crossing operator using a gradient threshold of 4, a 9 × 9 neighborhood, and a zero-crossing radius of 0.85 applied to the bulkhead image of Figure 10.

ously, there are some regions that have been merged together. However, those boundaries that are present are placed correctly and they are reasonably smooth. Lowering the gradient threshold of the edge operator could produce an image with more edges and thereby reduce the edge gap problem. But this solution does not really solve the gap problem in general.

Yakimovsky (1976) assumes regions are normally distributed and uses a maximum likelihood test to determine edges. Edges are declared to exist between pairs of contiguous and exclusive neighborhoods if the hypothesis that their means are equal and their variances are equal has to be rejected. For any pair of adjacent pixels with mutually exclusive neighborhoods R_1 and R_2 having N_1 and N_2 pixels, respectively, the maximum likelihood technique computes the mean

$$\overline{X}_i = \frac{1}{N_i} \sum_{X \in R_i} X \qquad (3)$$

and the scatter

$$S_i = \sum_{X \in R_i} (X - \overline{X}_i)^2 \qquad (4)$$

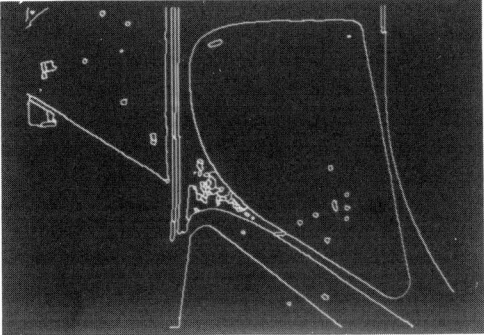

Figure 21. A hybrid linkage region growing scheme in which any pair of neighboring pixels, neither of which are edge pixels, can link together. The resulting segmentation consists of the connected components of the nonedge pixels and where edge pixels are assigned to their nearest connected component. This result was obtained from the edge image of Figure 20.

as well as the grand mean

$$\overline{X} = \frac{1}{N_1 + N_2} \sum_{X \in R_1 \cup R_2} X \qquad (5)$$

and grand scatter

$$S = \sum_{X \in R_1 \cup R_2} (X - \overline{X})^2 \qquad (6)$$

The likelihood ratio test statistic T is given by

$$T = \frac{[S^2/(N_1 + N_2)]^{N_1 + N_2}}{[S_1^2/N_1]^{N_1}[S_2^2/N_2]^{N_2}} \qquad (7)$$

Edges are declared between any pair of adjacent pixels when the T statistic from their neighborhoods is high enough. As N_1 and N_2 get large, $2 \log T$ is asymptotically distributed as a chi-squared variate with 2 degrees of freedom.

If it can be assumed that the variances of the two regions are identical, then the statistic

$$F = \frac{(N_1 + N_2 - 2)N_1 N_2}{N_1 + N_2} \frac{(\overline{X}_1 - \overline{X}_2)^2}{S_1^2 + S_2^2} \qquad (8)$$

has an F distribution with 1 and $N_1 + N_2 - 2$ degrees of freedom under the hypothesis that the means of the regions are equal. For an F value that is sufficiently large, the hypothesis can be rejected and an edge declared to exist between the regions.

Haralick (1981) suggests fitting a plane to the neighborhood around the pixel, and testing the hypothesis that the slope of the plane is zero. Edge pixels correspond to pixels between neighborhoods in which the zero slope hypothesis must be rejected. To determine a roof or V-shaped edge, Haralick suggests fitting a plane to the neighborhoods on either side of the pixel and testing the hypothesis that the coefficients of fit, referenced to a common framework, are identical.

Another hybrid technique first used by Levine and Leemet (1976) is based on the Jarvis and Patrick (1973) shared nearest neighbor idea. Using any kind of reasonable notion for similarity, each pixel examines its $K \times K$ neighborhood and makes a list of the N pixels in the neighborhood most similar to it. Call this list the similar neighbor list, where it is understood that a neighbor is any pixel in the $K \times K$ neighborhood. An arc joins any pair of immediately neighboring pixels if each pixel is in the other's shared neighbor list and if there are enough pixels common to their shared neighbor lists, that is, if the number of shared neighbors is high enough.

To make the shared neighbor technique work well, each pixel can be associated with a property vector consisting of its own gray-level intensity and a suitable average of the gray level intensity of pixels in its $K \times K$ neighborhood. For example, (x, a) and (y, b) can denote the property vectors for two pixels if x is the gray-level intensity value, a is the average gray-level intensity value in the neighborhood of the first pixel, y is the gray-level intensity value, and b is the average gray-level intensity value in the neighborhood of the second pixel. Similarity can be established by computing

$$S = w_1(x - y)^2 + w_2(x - b)^2 + w_3(y - a)^2 \qquad (9)$$

where w_1, w_2, and w_3 are nonnegative weights. Thus the quantity S takes into account the difference between the gray levels of the two pixels in question and the difference between the gray level of each pixel and the average gray level of the neighborhood of the other pixel. The weights w_1, w_2, and w_3 can be learned from training data for a particular class of images. The pixels are called similar enough for small enough values of S.

Pong and co-workers (1984) suggest an approach to segmentation based on the facet model of images. The procedure starts with an initial segmentation of the image into small regions. The initial segmentations used by Pong group together pixels that have similar facet fitting parameters, but any initial segmentation can be used. For each region of the initial segmentation, a property vector, which is a list of values of a set of predefined attributes, is computed. The attributes consist of such properties of a region as its area, its mean gray level, its elongation, and so on. Each region with associated property vector is considered a unit. In a series of iterations, the property vector of a region is replaced by a property vector that is a function of its neighboring regions. (The function that worked best in Pong's experiments replaced the property vector of a region with the property vector of the best-fitting neighborhood of that region.) Then adjacent regions having simlar final property vectors are merged. This gives a new segmentation that can then be used as input to the algorithm. Thus a sequence of coarser and coarser segmentations are produced. Useful variations are to prohibit merging across strong edge boundaries or when the variance of the combined region becomes too large. Figures 22, 23, and 24 illustrate the results of the Pong approach on the image of Figure 10 for one, two, and three iterations, respectively. Figure 25 illustrates the result of removing regions of size 25 or fewer pixels from the segmentation of Figure 24.

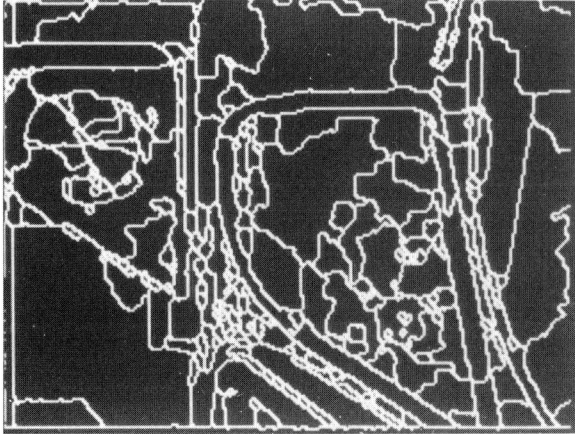

Figure 22. One iteration of the Pong algorithm on the bulkhead image of Figure 10.

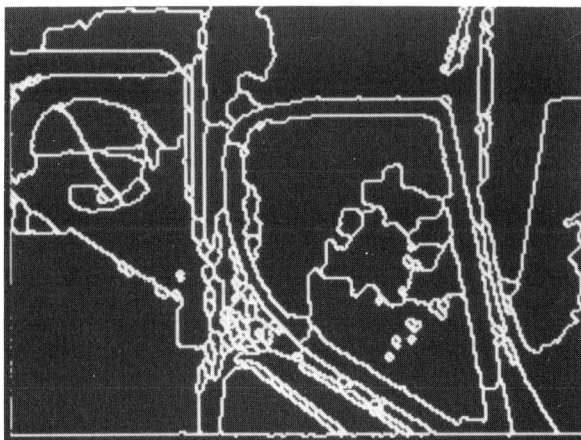

Figure 23. The second iteration of the Pong algorithm.

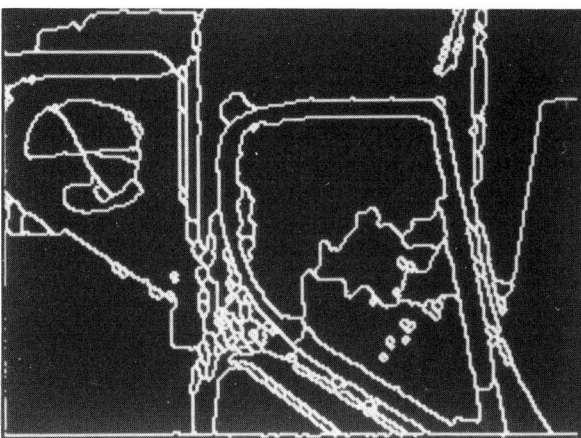

Figure 24. The third iteration of the Pong algorithm.

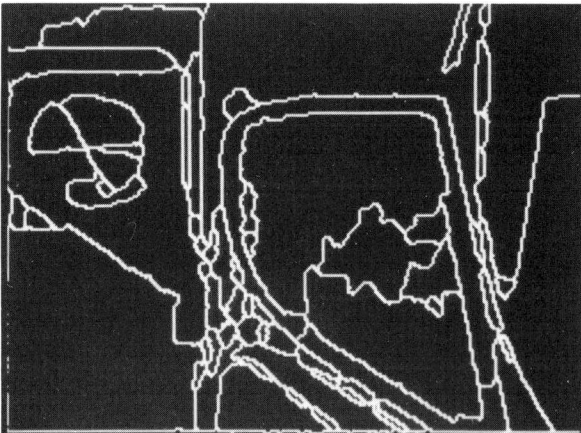

Figure 25. The segmentation obtained by removing regions smaller than size 25 from the segmentation of Figure 24.

Centroid Linkage Region Growing

In centroid linkage region growing, in contrast with single linkage region growing, pairs of neighboring pixels are not compared for similarity. Rather, the image is scanned in some predetermined manner such as left-right top-bottom. A pixel's value is compared to the mean of an already existing but not necessarily completed neighboring segment. If its value and the segment's mean value are close enough, then the pixel is added to the segment and the segment's mean is updated. If there is more than one region that is close enough, then it is added to the closest region. However, if the means of the two competing regions are close enough, the two regions are merged and the pixel is added to the merged region. If no neighboring region has its mean close enough, then a new segment is established having the given pixel's value as its first member. Figure 26 illustrates the geometry of this scheme.

Keeping track of the means annd scatters for all regions as they are being determined does not require large amounts of memory space. There cannot be more regions active at one time than the number of pixels in a row of the image. Hence, a hash table mechanism with the space of a small multiple of the number of pixels in a row can work well.

Another possibility is a single band region growing technique using the T-test. Let R be a segment of N pixels neighboring a pixel with gray-level intensity y. Define the mean $\overline{X}$ and scatter S^2 by

$$\overline{X} = \frac{1}{N} \sum_{(r,c) \in R} I(r, c) \qquad (10)$$

and

$$S^2 = \sum_{(r,c) \in R} (I(r, c) - X)^2 \qquad (11)$$

Under the assumption that all the pixels in R and the test pixel y are independent and have identically distributed normals, the statistic

$$T = \left[\frac{(N-1)N}{(N+1)} (y - \overline{X})^2/S^2 \right]^{\frac{1}{2}} \qquad (12)$$

has a T_{N-1} distribution. If T is small enough y is added to region R and the mean and scatter are updated using y. The new mean and scatter are given by

$$\overline{X}_{\text{new}} \leftarrow (N\overline{X}_{\text{old}} + y)/(N + 1) \qquad (13)$$

and

$$S^2_{\text{new}} \leftarrow S^2_{\text{old}} + (y - \overline{X}_{\text{new}})^2 + N(\overline{X}_{\text{new}} - \overline{X}_{\text{old}})^2 \qquad (14)$$

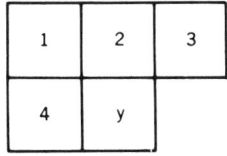

Figure 26. The region growing geometry for one-pass scan, left-right, top-bottom region growing. Pixel i belongs to region R_i whose mean is X_i, $i = 1, 2, 3$, and 4. Pixel y is added to a region R_j if by a T-test the difference between y and $\overline{X}_j$ is small enough. If for two regions R_i and R_j the difference is small enough, and if the difference between $\overline{X}_i$ and $\overline{X}_j$ is small enough, regions R_i and R_j are merged and y is added to the merged region. If the difference between $\overline{X}_i$ and $\overline{X}_j$ is significantly different, then y is added to the closest region.

If T is too high the value y is not likely to have arisen from the population of pixels in R. If y is different from all of its neighboring regions then it begins its own region. A slightly stricter linking criterion can require that not only must y be close enough to the mean of the neighboring regions, but that a neighboring pixel in that region must have a close enough value to y. This combines a centroid linkage and single linkage criterion. The next section discusses a more powerful combination technique, but first it is necessary to develop the concept of "significantly high."

To give a precise meaning to the notion of too high a difference, an α-level statistical significance test is used. The fraction α represents the probability that a T statistic with $N - 1$ degrees of freedom will exceed the value $t_{N-1}(\alpha)$. If the observed T is larger than $t_{N-1}(\alpha)$, then the difference is declared to be significant. If the pixel and the segment really come from the same population, the probability that the test provides an incorrect answer is α.

The significance level α is a user-provided parameter. The value of $t_{N-1}(\alpha)$ is higher for small degrees of freedom and lower for larger degrees of freedom. Thus, for region scatters considered to be equal, the larger a region is, the closer a pixel's value must be to the region's mean to merge into the region. This behavior tends to prevent already large regions from attracting to it many other additional pixels and tends to prevent the drift of the region mean as the region gets larger.

Note that all regions initially begin as one pixel in size. To avoid the problem of division by 0 (for S^2 is necessarily 0 for one pixel regions as well as for regions having identically valued pixels) a small positive constant can be added to S^2. One convenient way of determining the constant is to decide on a prior variance $V > 0$ and an initial segment size N. The initial scatter for a new one-pixel region is then given by NV and the new initial region size is given by N. This mechanism keeps the degrees of freedom of the T-statistic high enough so that a significant difference is not the huge difference required for a T-statistic with a small number of degrees of freedom. Figure 27 illustrates a second image of the F-15 bulkhead. Figure 28 illustrates the resulting segmentation of the bulkhead image for a 0.2% significance level test after all region smaller than 25 pixels have been removed.

Pavlidis (1972) suggests a more general version of this idea. Given an initial segmentation where the regions are

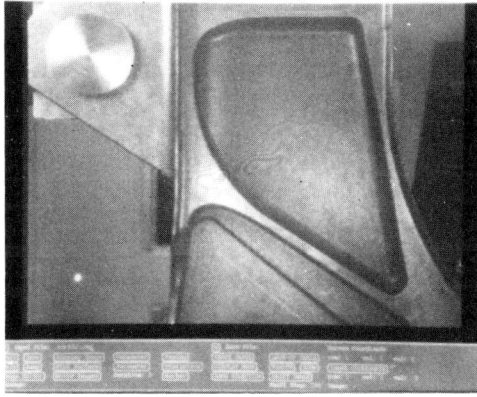

Figure 27. A second image of the F-15 bulkhead.

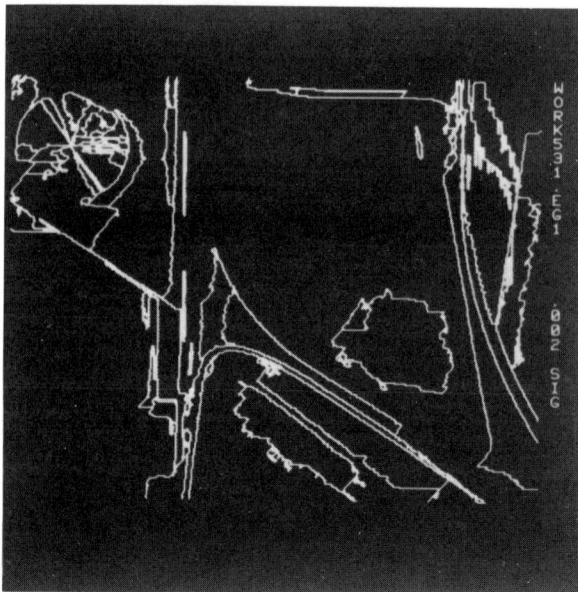

Figure 28. The one-pass centroid linkage segmentation of the bulkhead image of Figure 27. A significance level of 0.2% was used.

approximated by some functional fit guaranteed to have a small enough error, pairs of neighboring regions can be merged, if for each region the sum of the squares of the differences between the fitted coefficients for this region and the corresponding averaged coefficients, averaged over both regions, is small enough. Pavlidis gets his initial segmentation by finding the best way to divide each row of the image into segments with a sufficiently good fit. He also describes a combinatorial tree search algorithm to accomplish the merging that guarantees the best result. Kettig and Landgrebe (1975) successively merge small image blocks using a statistical test, They avoid much of the problem of zero scatter by considering only cells containing a 2 × 2 block of pixels.

Gupta and co-workers (1973) suggest using a T-test based on the absolute value of the difference between the pixel and the nearest region as the measure of dissimilarity. Kettig and Landgrebe (1975) discuss the multiband situation leading to the F-test and report good success with LANDSAT data.

Nagy and Tolaba (1972) just examine the absolute value between the pixel's value and the mean of a neighboring region formed already. If this distance is small enough, the pixel is added to the region. If there is more than one region, then the pixel is added to that region with the smallest distance.

The Levine and Shaheen scheme (1981) is simlar. The difference is that Levine and Shaheen attempt to keep regions more homogeneous and try to keep the region scatter from getting too high. They do this by requiring the differences to be more significant before a merge takes place if the region scatter is high. For a user-specified value θ, they define a test statistic T where

$$T = |y - \overline{X}_{\text{new}}| - (1 - S/\overline{X}_{\text{new}})\theta \qquad (15)$$

If $T < 0$ for the neighboring region R in which $|y - \overline{X}|$ is the smallest, then y is added to R. If $T > 0$ for the neighboring region in which $|y - \overline{X}|$ is the smallest, then y begins a new region. It should be noted that there are misprints in the formulas given for region scatter and region scatter updating in the Levine and Shaheen (1981) paper.

Brice and Fennema (1970) accomplish the region growing by partitioning the image into initial segments of pixels having identical intensity. They then sequentially merge all pairs of adjacent regions if a significant fraction of their common border has a small enough intensity difference across it.

Simple single-pass approaches that scan the image in a left-right, top-down manner are, of course, unable to make the left and right sides of a V-shaped region belong to the same segment. To be more effective, the single pass must be followed by some kind of connected components merging algorithm in which pairs of neighboring regions having means that are close enough are combined into the same segment. This is easily accomplished by using the two-pass label propagation logic of the Lumia and co-workers (1983) connected components algorithm.

After the top-bottom, left-right scan, each pixel has already been assigned a region label. In the bottom-up, right-left scan, the means and scatters of each region can be recomputed and can be kept in a hash table. Whenever a pair of pixels from different regions neighbor one another, a T-test can check for the significance of the difference between the region means. If the means are not significant, then they can be merged. A slightly stricter criterion would insist not only that the region means be similar, but also that the neighboring pixels from the different regions must be similar enough. Figure 29 shows the resulting segmentation of the bulkhead image for a 0.2% significance level after one bottom-up, right-left merging pass and after all regions smaller than 25 pixels have been removed.

One potential problem with region growing schemes is their inherent dependence on the order in which pixels and regions are examined. A left-right, top-down scan does not yield the same initial regions as a right-left, bottom-up scan or for that matter a column major scan. Usually, however, differences caused by scan order are minor.

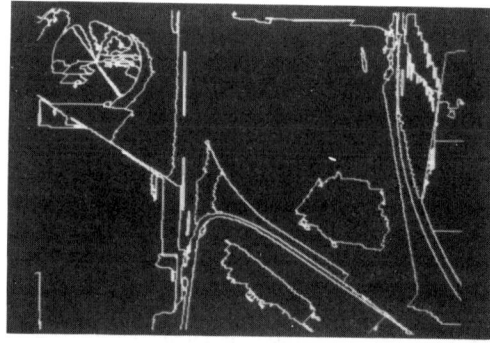

Figure 29. The two-pass centroid segmentation of the bulkhead image of Figure 27. A significance level of 0.2% was used on both passes.

HYBRID LINKAGE COMBINATIONS

The previous section mentioned the simple combination of centroid linkage and single linkage region growing. In this section the more powerful hybrid linkage combination techniques are discussed.

The centroid linkage and the hybrid linkage can be combined in a way that takes advantage of their relative strengths. The strength of the single linkage is that boundaries are placed in a spatially accurate way. Its weakness is that edge gaps result in excessive merging. The strength of centroid linkage is its ability to place boundaries in weak gradient areas. it can do this because it does not depend on a large difference between the pixel and its neighbor to declare a boundary. It depends on a large difference between the pixel and the mean of the neighboring region to declare a boundary.

The combined centroid hybrid linkage technique does the obvious thing. Centroid linkage is only done for non-edge pixels; that is, region growing is not permitted across edge pixels. Thus if the parameters of centroid linkage were set so that any difference, however large, between pixel value and region mean was considered small enough to permit merging, the two-pass hybrid combination technique would produce a connected components of the non-edge pixels. As the difference criterion is made more strict, the centroid linkage will produce boundaries in addition to those produced by the edges.

Figure 30 illustrates a one-pass scan combined centroid and hydrid linkage segmentation scheme using a significance level test of 0.2%. Edge pixels are assigned to their closest labeled neighbor, and regions having fewer than 25 pixels are eliminated. Notice that the resulting segmentation is much finer than that shown in Figures 28 and 29. Also the dominant boundaries are nicely curved and smooth. Figure 31 illustrates the two-pass scan combined centroid and hybrid linkage region growing scheme using a significance level test of 0.2%. The regions are somewhat simpler because of the merging done in the second pass.

SPATIAL CLUSTERING

It is possible to determine the image segments by simultaneously combining clustering in measurement–space

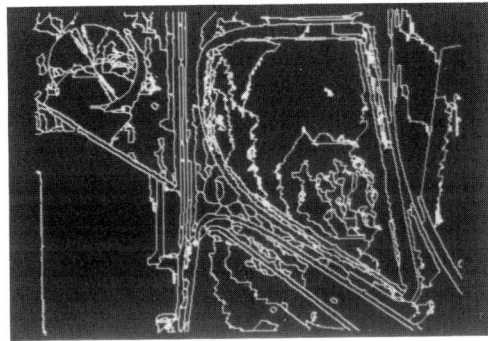

Figure 30. One-pass combined centroid and hybrid linkage segmentation of the bulkhead image of Figure 27. A significance level of 0.2% was used.

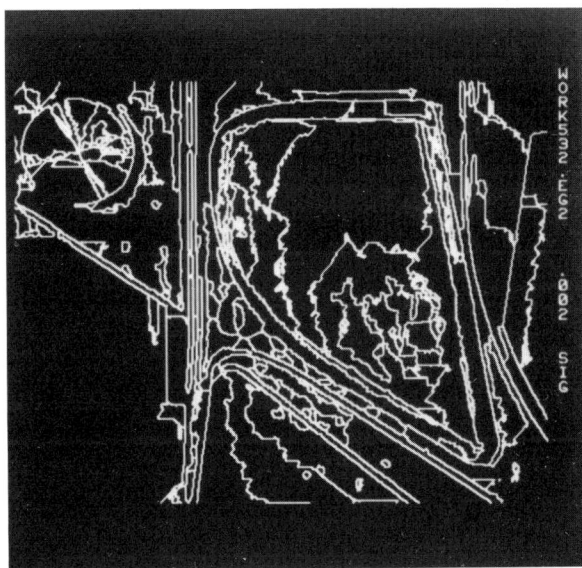

Figure 31. The two-pass combined centroid and hybrid linkage segmentation of the bulkhead image of Figure 27. A significance level of 0.2% was used on both passes.

with a spatial region growing. Such a technique is called spatial clustering. In essence, spatial clustering schemes combine the histogram mode seeking technique with a region growing or a spatial linkage technique.

Haralick and Kelly (1969) suggest that segmentation be done by first locating, in turn, all the peaks in the measurement–space histogram, and then determining all pixel locations having a measurement on the peak. Next, beginning with a pixel corresponding to the highest peak not yet processed, both spatial and measurement–space region growing are simultaneously performed in the following manner. Initially, each segment is the pixel whose value is on the current peak. Consider for possible inclusion into this segment a neighbor of this pixel (in general, the neighbors of the pixel that is being grown from) if the neighbor's value (an N-tuple for an N band image) is close enough in measurement–space to the pixel's value and if its probability is not larger than the probaiblity of the value of the pixel that is being grown from. Matsumoto and co-workers (1981) discuss a variation of this idea. Milgram (1979) defines a segment for a single band image to be any connected component of pixels, all of whose values lie in some interval I and whose border has a higher coincidence with the border created by an edge operator than for any other interval I. The technique has the advantage over the Haralick and Kelly technique in that it does not require the difficult measurement space exploring done in climbing down a mountain. However, it must try many different intervals for each segment. Extending it to efficient computation in multiband images appears difficult. However, Milgram does report good results of segmenting white blobs against a black background. Milgram and Kahl (1979) discuss embedding this technique into the Ohlander and co-workers (1978) recursive control structure.

Minor and Sklansky (1981) make more active use of the gradient edge image than Milgram, but restrict themselves to the more constrained situation of small convex-like segments. They begin with an edge image in which each edge pixel contains the direction of the edge. The orientation is so that the higher valued gray level is to the right of the edge. Then each edge sends out for a limited distance a message to nearby pixels and in a direction orthogonal to the edge direction. The message indicates what is the sender's edge direction. Pixels that pick up these messages from enough different directions must be interior to a segment.

The spoke filter of Minor and Sklansky counts the number of distinct directions appearing in each 3×3 neighborhood. If the count is high enough they mark the center pixel as belonging to an interior of a region. Then the connected components of all marked pixels is obtained. The gradient-guided segmentation is then completed by performing a region growing of the components. The region growing must stop at the high gradient pixels, thereby ensuring that no undesired boundary placements are made.

Burt and co-workers (1981) describe a spatial clustering scheme that is a spatial pyramid constrained ISODATA kind of clustering. The bottom layer of the pyramid is the original image. Each successive higher layer of the pyramid is an image having half the number of pixels per row and half the number of rows of the image below it. Initial links between layers are established by linking each parent pixel to the spatially corresponding 4×4 block of child pixels. Each pair of adjacent parent pixels has 8 child pixels in common. Each child pixel is linked to a 2×2 block of parent pixels. The iterations proceed by assigning to each parent pixel the average of its child pixels. Then each child pixel compares its value with each of its parent's values and links itself to its closest parent. Each parent's new value is the average of the children to which it is linked, etc. The iterations converge reasonably quickly for the same reason the ISODATA iterations converge. If the top layer of the pyramid is a 2×2 block of great grandparents, then these are at most 4 segments that are the respective great grandchildren of these 4 great grandparents. Pietikainen and Rosenfeld (1981) extend this technique to segment an image using textural features.

SPLIT AND MERGE

A splitting method for segmentation begins with the entire image as the initial segment. Then it successively splits each of its current segments into quarters if the segment is not homogeneous enough; that is, if the difference between the largest and smallest gray-level intensities is large. A merging method starts with an initial segmentation and successively merges regions that are similar enough.

Splitting algorithms were first suggested by Robertson (1973) and Klinger (1973). Kettig and Landgrebe (1975) try to split all nonuniform 2×2 neighborhoods before beginning the region merging. Fukada (1980) suggests successively splitting a region into quarters until the sample variance is small enough. Efficiency of the split and merge method can be increased by arbitrarily partitioning the image into square regions of a user selected size and then splitting these further if they are not homogeneous.

Because segments are successively divided into quarters, the boundaries produced by the split technique tend to be squarish and slightly artificial. Sometimes adjacent quarters coming from adjacent split segments need to be joined rather than remain separate. Horowitz and Pavlidis (1976) suggest the split-and-merge strategy to take care of this problem. They begin with an initial segmentation achieved by splitting into rectangular blocks of a prespecified size. The image is represented by a segmentation tree, which is a quadtree data structure (a tree whose nonleaf nodes each have four children). The entire image is represented by the root node. The children of the root are the regions obtained by splitting the root into four equal pieces, and so on. A segmentation is represented by a cutset, a minimal set of nodes separating the root from all of the leaves. In the tree structure, the merging process consists of removing four nodes from the cutset and replacing them with their parent. Splitting consists of removing a node from the cutset and replacing it with its four children. The two processes are mutually exclusive; all of the merging operations are followed by all of the splitting operations. The splitting and merging in the tree structure is followed by a final grouping procedure that can merge adjacent unrelated blocks found in the final cutset. Figure 32 illustrates the result of a Horowitz and Pavlidis type split-and-merge segmentation of the bulkhead image. Muerle and Allen (1968) suggest merging a pair of adjacent regions if a statistical test determines that their gray-level intensity distributions are similar enough. They recommend the Kolmogorov-Smirnov test.

Chen and Pavlidis (1980) suggest using statistical tests for uniformity rather than a simple examination of the difference between the largest and smallest gray-level intensities in the region under consideration for splitting. The uniformity test requires that there be no significant difference between the mean of the region and each of its

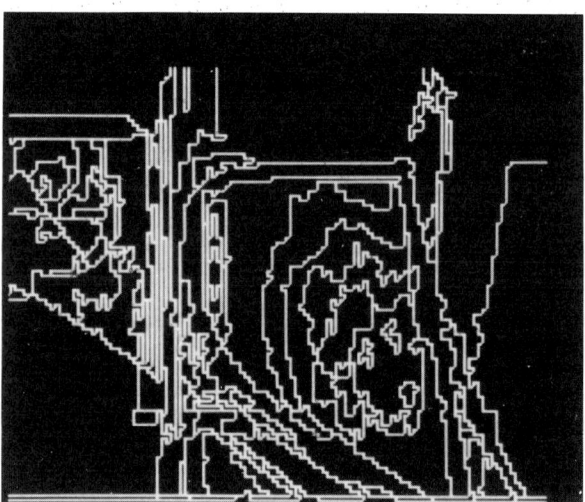

Figure 32. A split-and-merge segmentation of the bulkhead image of Figure 10.

quarters. The Chen and Pavlidis tests assume that the variances are equal and known.

Let each quarter have K pixels, X_{ij} be the jth pixel in the ith region, X_i be the mean of the ith quarter and $X..$ be the grand mean of all the pixels in the four quarters. Then in order for a region to be considered homogeneous, Chen and Pavlidis require that

$$|X_i - X..| \le \varepsilon, \quad i = 1, 2, 3, 4 \quad (16)$$

where ε is a given threshold parameter.

The F-test for testing the hypothesis that the mean and variances of the quarters are identical is given here. This is the optimal test when the randomness can be modeled as arising from additive Gaussian-distributed variates. The value of variance is not assumed known. Under the assumption that the regions are independent and have identically distributed normals, the optimal test is given by the statistic F which is defined by

$$F = \frac{K \sum_{i=1}^{4} (X_i. - X..)^2/3}{\sum_{i=1}^{4} \sum_{k=1}^{K} (X_{ik} - X_i.)^2/4(K-1)} \quad (17)$$

It has a $F_{3,4(K-1)}$ distribution. If F is too high the region is declared not uniform.

The data structures required to do a split-and-merge on images larger than 512×512 are extremely large. Execution of the algorithm on virtual memory computers results in so much paging that the dominant activity may be paging rather than segmentation. Browning and Tanimoto (1982) give a description of a space-efficient version of the split-and-merge scheme that can handle large images, using only a small amount of main memory.

RULE-BASED SEGMENTATION

The rules behind each of the methods discussed so far are encoded in the procedures of the method. Thus it is not easy to try different concepts without complete reprogramming. Nazif and Levine (1984) solve this problem with a rule-based expert system for segmentation. The knowledge in the system is not application domain specific, but includes general-purpose, scene-independent knowledge about images and grouping criteria.

The Nazif and Levine system contains a set of processes, the initializer, the line analyzer, the region analyzer, the area analyzer, the focus of attention, and the scheduler, plus two associate memories, the short-term memory (STM) and the long-term memory (LTM). The short-term memory holds the input image, the segmentation data, and the output. The long-term memory contains the model representing the system knowledge about low level segmentation and control strategies. A system process matches rules in the LTM against the data stored in the STM. When a match occurs, the rule fires, and an action, usually involving data modification, is performed.

The model stored in the LTM has three levels of rules. At level 1 are knowledge rules that encode information about the properties of regions, lines, and areas in the form of situation–action pairs. The specific actions include splitting a region; merging two regions; adding, deleting, or extending a line; merging two lines; and creating or modifying a focus of attention area. Knowledge rules are classified by their actions. At level 2 are the control rules that are divided into two categories: focus-of-attention rules and inference rules. Focus-of-attention rules find the next data entry to be considered: a region, a line, or an entire area. These rules control the focus-of-attention strategy. The inference rules are metarules in that their actions do not modify the data in the STM. Instead, they alter the matching order of different knowledge rule sets. Thus they control which process will be activated next. At level 3, the highest rule level, are strategy rules that select the set of control rules that executes the most appropriate control strategy for a given set of data.

The conditions of the rules in the rule base are made up of (1) a symbolic qualifier depicting a logical operation to be performed on the data, (2) a symbol denoting the data entry on which the condition is to be matched, (3) a feature of this data entry, (4) an optional NOT qualifier, and (5) an optional DIFFERENCE qualifier that applies the operation to differences in feature values. Table 1 shows the different types of data entries allowed. Table 2 shows the different kinds of features, and Table 3 shows the possible actions that can be associated with a rule. Table 4 illustrates several rules from the system.

The Nazif and Levine approach to segmentation is useful because it is general, but allows more specific strategies to be incorporated without changing the code. Other rule-based segmentation systems tend to use high level knowledge models of the expected scene instead of general rules. The work of McKeown takes this approach for aerial images of airport scenes.

MOTION-BASED SEGMENTATION

In time-varying image analysis the data are a sequence of images instead of a single image. One paradigm under which such a sequence can arise is with a stationary camera viewing a scene containing moving objects. In each frame of the sequence after the first frame, the moving objects appear in different positions of the image than in

Table 1. Allowable Data-Entry Types in the Nazif and Levine Rule-Based Segmentation System

Data Entry	Symbol
Current region	REG
Current line	LINE
Current area	AREA
Region *adjacent* to current region	REGA
Region to the *left* of current line	REGL
Region to the *right* of current line	REGR
Line *near* the current line	LINEN
Line in *front* of current line	LINEF
Line *behind* current line	LINEB
Line *parallel to* current line	LINEP
Line *intersecting* current region	LINEI

Table 2. The Different Kinds of Features That Can Be Associated with the Condition Part of a Rule

Numerical Descriptive Features

Feature 1	Feature 2	Feature 3
Variance 1	Variance 2	Variance 3
Intensity	Intensity variance	Gradient
Gradient variance	X-centroid	Y-centroid
Minimum X	Minimum Y	Maximum X
Maximum Y	Starting X	Starting Y
Ending X	Ending Y	Starting direction
Ending direction	Average direction	Length
Start-End distance	Size	Perimeter
Histogram bimodality	Circularity	Aspect ratio
Uniformity 1	Uniformity 2	Uniformity 3
Region contrast 1	Region contrast 2	Region contrast 3
Line contrast 1	Line contrast 2	Line contrast 3
Line connectivity	Number of regions	Number of lines
Number of areas		

Numerical Spatial Features

Number of *adjacent* regions	Adjacency values
Number of *intersecting* regions	Line content between regions
Distance to line in *front*	Nearest point on line in *front*
Distance to line *behind*	Nearest point of line *behind*
Distance to *parallel* line	Number of *parallel* points
Adjacency of *left* region	Adjacency of *right* region
Number of lines in *front*	Number of lines *behind*
Number of *parallel* lines	Number of regions to the *left*
Number of regions to the *right*	

Logical Features

Histogram is bimodal	Region is bisected by line
Line is open	Line is closed
Line is loop	Line end is open
Line start is open	Line is clockwise
Area is smooth	Area is textured
Area is bounded	Area is new
One region to the *left*	One region to the *right*
Same region to the *left* and *right* of line	
Same region *left* of line 1 and line 2	
Same region *right* of line 1 and line 2	
Same region to the *left* of line 1 and *right* of line 2	
Same region to the *right* of line 1 and *left* of line 2	
Two lines are touching (8-connected)	
Areas are absent	Regions are absent
Lines are absent	System is starting
Process was regions	Process was lines
Process was areas	Process was focus
Process was generate areas	Process was active

the previous frame. Thus the motion of the objects creates a change in the images that can be used to help locate the objects and thus to segment the images.

Jain and co-workers (1979) used differencing operations to identify areas containing moving objects. The images of the moving objects were obtained by focusing the segmentation processes on these restricted areas. In this way, motion was used as a cue to the segmentation process. Thompson (1980) developed a method for partitioning a scene into regions corresponding to surfaces with distinct velocities. He first computed velocity estimates for each point of the scene and then performed the seg-

mentation by a region-merging procedure that combined regions based on similarities in both intensity and motion.

Jain (1984) handled the more complex problem of segmenting dynamic scenes using a moving camera. He used the known location of the focus of expansion to transform the original frame sequence into another camera-centered sequence. The ego-motion polar transform (EMP) works as follows.

Suppose that A is a point in three space having coordinates (x, y, z), and the camera at time 0 is located at (x_0, y_0, z_0). During the time interval between frames, the camera undergoes displacement (dx_0, dy_0, dz_0), and the point

Table 3. The Different Kinds of Actions That Can Be Associated with a Rule

Area Analyzer Actions

Create smooth area	Add to smooth area	Save smooth area
Create texture area	Add to texture area	Save texture area
Create bounded area	Add to bounded area	Save bounded area
	Relabel area to smooth	Relabel area to texture
	Relabel area to bounded	Delete area

Region Analyzer Actions

Slit a region by histogram   Merge two regions
Split region at lines

Line Analyzer Actions

Extend line forward	Extend line backward
Join lines forward	Join lines backward
Insert line forward	Insert line backward
Merge lines forward	Merge lines backward
Delete line	

Focus of Attention Actions

Region with highest adjacency	Largest *adjacent* region
Region with lowest adjacency	Smallest *adjacent* region
Region with higher label	Next scanned region
Region to the *left* of line	Region to the *right* of line
Closest line in front	Closest line *behind*
Closest *parallel* line	Shortest line that is near
Longest line that is near	Strongest line that is near
Weakest line that is near	Line with higher label
Next scanned line	Line *intersecting* region
Defocus (focus on whole image)	Focus on areas
Clear region list	Clear line list
Freeze area	Next area (any)
Next smooth area	Next texture area
Next bounded area	

Supervisor Actions

Initialize regions	Initialize lines	Generate areas
Match region rules	Match line rules	Match area rules
Match focus rules	Start	Stop

A undergoes displacement (dx, dy, dz). When the projection plane is at $z = 1$, the focus of expansion is at $(dx_0/dz_0, dy_0/dz_0)$. The projection A' of point A after the displacements is at (X, Y) in the image plane where

$$X = \frac{(x + dx - x_0 - dx_0)}{(z + dz - z_0 - dz_0)}$$

and

$$Y = \frac{(y + dy - y_0 - dy_0)}{(z + dz - z_0 - dz_0)}$$

The point A' is converted into its polar coordinates (r, θ) with the focus of expansion being the origin in the image plane. The polar coordinates are given by

$$\theta = \tan^{-1}\left(\frac{dz_0(y + dy - y_0) - dy_0(z + dz - z_0)}{dz_0(x + dx - x_0) - dx_0(z + dz - z_0)}\right)$$

and

$$r = ((X - dx_0)^2 + (Y - dy_0)^2)^{\frac{1}{2}}$$

In (r, θ) space, the segmentation is simplified. Assume that the transformed picture is represented as a two-dimensional image have θ along the vertical axis and r along the horizontal axis. If the camera continues its motion in the same direction, then the focus of expansion remains the same, and θ remains constant. Thus the radial motion of the stationary point A' in the image plane due to the motion of the camera is converted to horizontal motion in (r, θ) space. If the camera has only a translational component to its motion, then all the regions that show only horizontal velocity in the (r, θ) space can be classified as due to stationary surfaces. The regions having a vertical velocity component are due to nonstationary surfaces. The segmentation algorithm first separates the stationary and nonstationary components on the basis of

Table 4. Several Examples of Rules from the Nazif and Levine System

A Region Merging Rule

IF: 1. The REGION SIZE is VERY LOW
2. The ADJACENCY with another REGION is HIGH
3. The DIFFERENCE in REGION FEATURE 1 is NOT HIGH
4. The DIFFERENCE in REGION FEATURE 2 is NOT HIGH
5. The DIFFERENCE in REGION FEATURE 3 is NOT HIGH

THEN: 1. MERGE the two REGIONS

A Region-Splitting Rule

IF: 1. The REGION SIZE is NOT LOW
2. The REGION AVERAGE GRADIENT is HIGH
3. The REGION HISTOGRAM is BIMODAL

THEN: 1. SPLIT the REGION according to the HISTOGRAM

A Line-Merging Rule

IF: 1. The LINE END point is OPEN
2. The LINE GRADIENT is NOT VERY LOW
3. The DISTANCE to the LINE IN FRONT is NOT VERY HIGH
4. The two LINES have the SAME REGION to the LEFT
5. The two LINES have the SAME REGION to the RIGHT

THEN: 1. JOIN the LINES by FORWARD expansion

A Control Rule

IF: 1. The LINE GRADIENT is HIGH
2. The LINE LENGTH is HIGH
3. SAME REGION LEFT and RIGHT of the LINE

THEN: 1. GET the REGION to the LEFT of the LINE

---

their velocity components in (r, θ) space. The stationary components are then further segmented into distinct surfaces by using the motion to assign relative depths to the surfaces.

SUMMARY

The place of segmentation in vision algorithms has been surveyed as well as common techniques of measurement-space clustering, single linkage, hybrid linkage, region growing, spatial clustering, and split and merge used in image segmentation. The single linkage region growing schemes are the simplest and most prone to the unwanted region merge errors. The hybrid and centroid region growing schemes are better in this regard. The split-and-merge technique is not as subject to the unwanted region merge error. However, it suffers from large memory usage and excessively blocky region boundaries. The measurement-space guided spatial clustering tends to avoid both the region merge errors and the blocky boundary problems because of its primary reliance on measurement space. But the regions produced are not smoothly bounded, and they often have holes, giving the effect of salt-and-pepper noise. The spatial clustering schemes may be better in this regard, but they have not been well enough tested. The hybrid linkage schemes appear to offer the best compromise between having smooth boundaries and few unwanted region merges. When the data form a time sequence of images, instead of a single image, motion-based segmentation techniques can be used. All the techniques can be made to be more powerful if they are based on some kind of statistical test for equality of means and more flexible if part of a rule-based system.

Not discussed as part of image segmentation is the fact that it might be appropriate for some segments to remain apart or to be merged not on the basis of the gray-level distributions, but on the basis of the object sections that they represent. The use of this kind of semantic information in the image segmentation process is essential for the higher level image understanding work. The work of McKeown describes a system that uses domain-specific knowledge in this manner.

BIBLIOGRAPHY

C. Brice and C. Fennema, "Scene Analysis Using Regions," *Artif. Intell.* **1**, 205–226 (1970).

J. D. Browning and S. L. Tanimoto, "Segmentation of Pictures into Regions with a Tile by Tile Method," *Patt. Recogn.* **15**, 1–10 (1982).

J. Bryant, "On the Clustering of Multidimensional Pictorial Data," *Patt. Recogn.* **11**, 115–125 (1979).

P. J. Burt, T. H. Hong, and A. Rosenfeld, "Segmentation and Estimation of Image Region Properties through Cooperative Hierarchical Computation," *IEEE Trans. Sys. Man Cybernet.* **11**, 802–809 (1981).

P. C. Chen and T. Pavlidis, "Image Segmentation as an Estimation Problem," *Comput. Graphics Image Process.* **12**, 153–172 (1980).

C. K. Chow and T. Kaneko, "Boundary Detection of Radiographic Images by a Thresholding Method," in S. Wanatabe, ed., *Frontiers of Pattern Recognition*, Academic Press, Inc., New York, 1972, pp. 61–82.

K. S. Fu and J. K. Mui, "A Survey on Image Segmentation," *Patt. Recogn.* **13**, 3–16 (1981).

Y. Fukada, "Spatial Clustering Procedures for Region Analysis," *Patt. Recogn.* **12**, 395–403 (1980).

M. Goldberg and S. Shlien, "A Four-Dimensional Histogram Approach to the Clustering of LAND-SAT Data," in *Machine Processing of Remotely Sensed Data*, IEEE CH 1218-7 MPRSD, Purdue University, West Lafayette, Ind., 1977, pp. 250–259.

M. Goldberg and S. Shlien, "A Clustering Scheme for a Multispectral Image," *IEEE Trans. Sys. Man Cybernet.* **8**, 86–92 (1978).

J. N. Gupta, R. L. Kettig, D. A. Landgrebe, and P. A. Wintz, "Machine Boundary Finding and Sample Classification of Remotely Sensed Agricultural Data," in *Machine Processing of Remotely Sensed Data*, IEEE 73 CHO 834-2GE, Purdue University, West Lafayette, Ind., 1973, pp. 4B-25–4B-35.

R. M. Haralick, "Edge and Region Analysis for Digital Image Data," *Comput. Graphics Image Process.* **12**, 60–73 (1980).

R. M. Haralick, "Zero-Crossing of Second Directional Derivative Edge Operator," in *Proceedings of the Society of Photo-Optical Instrumentation Engineers Technical Symposium East*, Arlington, Va., Vol. 336, 1982.

R. M. Haralick, "Digital Step Edges from Zero Crossing of Second

Directional Derivative," *IEEE Trans. Patt. Anal. Machine Intell.* **6**, 58–68 (1984).

R. M. Haralick and I. Dinstein, "A Spatial Clustering Procedure for Multi-Image Data," *IEEE Trans. Circuits Sys.* **22**, 440–450 (1975).

R. M. Haralick and G. L. Kelly, "Pattern Recognition with Measurement-Space and Spatial Clustering for Multiple Images," *Proc. IEEE* **57**, 654–665 (1969).

S. L. Horowitz and T. Pavlidis, "Picture Segmentation by a Tree Traversal Algorithm," *J. ACM* **23**, 368–388 (1976).

R. C. Jain, "Segmentation of Frame Sequences Obtained by a Moving Observer," *IEEE Trans. Patt. Anal. Machine Intell.* **6**, 624–629 (1984).

R. Jain, W. N. Martin, and J. K. Aggarwal, "Extraction of Moving Object Images through Change Detection," in *Proceedings of the Sixth IJCAI*, Tokyo, Morgan-Kaufmann, San Mateo, Calif., 1979, pp. 425–428.

R. A. Jarvis and E. A. Patrick, "Clustering Using a Similarity Measure Based on Shared Near Neighbors," *IEEE Trans. Comput.* **22**, 1025–1034 (1973).

T. Kanade, "Region Segmentation: Signal vs. Semantics," *Comput. Graphics Image Process.* **13**, 279–297 (1980).

R. L. Kettig and D. A. Landgrebe, "Computer Classification of Multispectral Image Data by Extraction and Classification of Homogeneous Objects," LARS Information Note 050975, Purdue University, West Lafayette, Ind., 1975.

K. Klinger, "Data Structures and Pattern Recognition," in *Proceedings of the First International Joint Conference on Pattern Recognition*, Washington, D.C., 1973, pp. 497–498.

R. Kohler, "A Segmentation System Based on Thresholding," *Comput. Graphics Image Process.* **15**, 319–338 (1981).

M. D. Levine and J. Leemet, "A Method for Non-Purposive Picture Segmentation," *Proceedings of the Third International Joint Conference on Pattern Recognition*, 1976, pp. 494–497.

M. D. Levine and S. I. Shaheen, "A Modular Computer Vision System for Picture Segmentation and Interpretation," *IEEE Trans. Patt. Anal. Machine Intell.* **3**, 540–556 (1981).

R. Lumia, L. G. Shapiro, and O. Zemiga, "A New Connected Components Algorithm for Virtual Memory Computers," *Comput. Vision Graphics Image Process.* **22**, 287–300 (1983).

K. Matsumoto, M. Naka, and H. Yanamoto, "A New Clustering Method for LANDSAT Images Using Local Maximums of a Multidimensional Histogram," in *Machine Processing of Remotely Sensed Data*, IEEE CH 1637-8 MPRSD, Purdue University, West Lafayette, Ind., 1981, pp. 321–325.

D. L. Milgram and M. Herman, "Clustering Edge Values for Threshold Selection," *Comput. Graphics Image Process.* **10**, 272–280 (1979).

D. L. Milgram and D. J. Kahl, "Recursive Region Extraction," *Comput. Graphics and Image Process.* **9**, 82–88 (1979).

L. G. Minor and J. Sklansky, "The Detection and Segmentation of Blobs in Infrared Images," *IEEE Trans. Sys. Man Cybernet.* **11**, 194–201 (1981).

J. Muerle and D. Allen, "Experimental Evaluation of Techniques for Automatic Segmentation of Objects in a Complex Scene," in G. Cheng and co-workers, eds., *Pictorial Pattern Recognition*, Thompson, Washington, D.C., 1968, pp. 3–13.

G. Nagy and J. Tolaba, "Nonsupervised Crop Classification Through Airborne Multispectral Observations," *IBM J. Res. Develop.* **16**, 138–153 (1972).

P. M. Narendra and M. Goldberg, "A Non-Parametric Clustering Scheme, for LANDSAT," *Patt. Recogn.* **9**, 207–215 (1977).

A. M. Nazif and M. D. Levine, "Low-Level Image Segmentation: An Expert System," *IEEE Trans. Patt. Anal. Machine Intell.* **6**(5), 555–557 (1984).

R. Ohlander, K. Price, and D. R. Reddy, "Picture Segmentation Using a Recursive Region Splitting Method," *Comput. Graphics Image Process.* **8**, 313–333 (1978).

Y. Ohta, T. Kanade, and T. Sakai, "Color Information for Region Segmentation," *Comput. Graphics Image Process.* **13**, 222–241 (1980).

D. P. Panda and A. Rosenfeld, "Image Segmentation by Pixel Classification in (Gray Level, Edge Value) Space," *IEEE Trans. Comput.* **27**, 875–879 (1978).

T. Pavlidis, "Segmentation of Pictures and Maps through Functional Approximation," *Comput. Graphics Image Process.* **1**, 360–372 (1972).

W. A. Perkins, "Area Segmentation of Images Using Edge Points," *IEEE Trans. Patt. Anal. Machine Intell.* **2**, 8–15 (1980).

M. Pietikainen and A. Rosenfeld, "Image Segmentation by Texture Using Pyramid Node Linking," *IEEE Trans. Sys. Man Cybernt.* **11**, 822–825 (1981).

T. C. Pong, L. G. Shapiro, L. T. Watson, and R. M. Haralick, "Experiments in Segmentation Using a Facet Model Region Grower," *Comput. Vision Graphics Image Process.* **25**, 1–23 (1984).

E. Riseman and M. Arbib, "Segmentation of Static Scenes," *Comput. Graphics Image Process.* **6**, 221–276 (1977).

T. V. Robertson, "Extraction and Classification of Objects in Multispectral Images," *Machine Processing of Remotely Sensed Data*, IEEE 73 CHO 837-2GE, Purdue University, West Lafayette, Ind., 1973, pp. 3B-27–3B-34.

W. B. Thompson, "Combining Motion and Contrast for Segmentation," *IEEE Trans. Patt. Anal. Machine Intell.* **2**(6), 543–549 (1980).

S. Wanatabe and the CYBEST Group, "An Automated Apparatus for Cancer Prescreening: CYBEST," *Comput. Graphics Image Process.* **3**, 350–358 (1974).

J. S. Weszka, "A Survey of Threshold Selection Techniques," *Comput. Graphics Image Process.* **7**, 259–265 (1978).

J. S. Weszka, R. N. Nagel, and A. Rosenfeld, "A Threshold Selection Technique," *IEEE Trans. Comput.* **23**, 1322–1326 (1974).

J. S. Weszka and A. Rosenfeld, "Threshold Evaluation Techniques," *IEEE Trans. Sys. Man Cybernet.* **8**, 622–629 (1978).

Y. Yakimovsky, Y. "Boundary and Object Detection in Real World Image," *J. ACM* **23**, 599–618 (1976).

T. Y. Young, and T. W. Calvert, *Classification, Estimation, and Pattern Recognition*, Elsevier Science Publishing Co., Inc., New York, 1974.

S. Zucker, "Region Growing: Childhood and Adolescence," *Comput. Graphics Image Process.* **5**, 382–399 (1976).

General References

Y. G. Leclerc, "Constructing Simple Stable Descriptions of Image Partitioning," *Int. J. Comput. Vision* **3**, 73–102 (1989).

D. L. Milgram, "Region Extraction Using Convergent Evidence," *Comput. Graphics Image Process.* **11**, 1–12 (1979).

ROBERT HARALICK
University of Washington

SELF-REPLICATION

In machine self-reproduction, an instruction-obeying device (such as a general-purpose computer) is augmented with physical manipulation capability (as in an industrial robot), supplied with raw materials, and programmed to produce a duplicate of itself. A theoretical model of this process was proposed by von Neumann (1951) in which the initial machine resides in an environment of spare parts (switching, sensing, cutting, fusing elements, etc). The parent machine plucks parts at random from its surroundings, identifies them, and following stored instructions, assembles the parts into a duplicate of itself.

This informally described kinematic model was superseded by von Neumann's (1951, 1966) cell-space model (Burks, 1970; Thatcher, 1970). [Conway's "Game of Life" is an example of an extremely simple cell-space system (Gardner, 1983; Berlekamp and co-workers, 1982).] In von Neumann's cell-space model machine reproduction takes place in an indefinitely extended, two-dimensional rectangular array, each square of which contains an identical automaton in direct communication with its four cardinal-direction neighbors. Each cell automaton is capable of being in any one of 29 different states. These states determine the way in which a cell automaton interacts with its neighbors. Depending on its state and the state of its neighbors, a cell automaton can transmit, switch, or store information or can undergo a change of state. Configurations of cell automata can be designed to form higher order information-processing devices, such as pulsers (units that when stimulated emit a stream of pulses) and decoders (units activated only on receipt of particular patterns of pulses). These and other higher order units can be combined to form a self-reproducing machine consisting of a general-purpose computer with an indefinitely expandable memory unit and a constructor (a device containing banks of pulsers that can emit signals that cause a cell automaton to assume any one of the 29 states).

The self-reproducing process proceeds as follows: the parent machine, reading instructions from memory, first directs the constructor to produce trains of pulses that transform cell automata at the periphery of the original machine, so that a constructing-arm pathway of newly activated cells is created and extended out into an undifferentiated region of the cell space. Then the parent machine, making use of a stored description of itself, directs the arm to move and to emit pulses so as to produce a configuration of cells that is identical to that of the original machine (although as yet lacking the memory contents of the original). The parent machine then reads its memory a second time and loads a copy of the contents into the memory of the offspring machine, turns on the new machine, and withdraws the constructing arm. This completes the self-reproduction.

This process of self-reproduction thus has two principal phases: first, the memory unit contents are read and interpreted as instructions for construction; next, the memory is read a second time in order to load a copy into the new memory. This action parallels the biological process of reading nucleic acids twice, once to carry out protein synthesis and again to replicate the genetic message.

Theoretical research since von Neumann has taken several directions. Alternative (usually simpler) cell spaces have been shown capable of supporting the reproductive process (Codd, 1968; Banks, 1970). Hybrid cellular-kinematic systems have been devised that make machine movement a more direct process (Arbib, 1966) (in the original von Neumann cell space, a machine movement is implemented by erasing a configuration of cells in one location and recreating it in another).

Other hybrid systems emphasize machine capacity for identifying system componentry (Laing, 1975). In such systems a machine may initially possess less than complete knowledge of itself but may still be able to reproduce itself because the deficiency can be made up by self-inspection (Laing, 1977). This also means that a machine can undertake partial self-repair: the machine compares its present configuration (obtained through self-inspection) with what its configuration should be (as contained in a stored description of itself) and uses its constructor to reduce the discrepancy. This strategy can be generalized to enable robotic machines to exhibit intentional goal seeking and evolution (Burks, 1984).

In a machine evolutionary process successive offspring machines cannot be mere exact duplicates of parents but must in some respect come to be both different and superior. One approach to machine evolution is to mimic the natural evolutionary processes of random variation of type and subsequent selection of better adapted types, but Myhill (1974) has shown that an indefinitely continued sequence of reproducing machines, each offspring superior to its parent, can be produced in an entirely deterministic fashion.

Machines that accept inputs and produce outputs can be viewed as implementing mathematical functions. In self-reproduction machines read or otherwise refer to or act on themselves to produce their outputs. Recursive-function theory is the abstract and general study of such self-reference computations and is thus an important tool for the precise investigation of self-reproducing systems. For example, the results and techniques of recursive-function theory were employed in the Myhill result cited above and also in establishing the conditions under which a reproducing machine system will eventually have a sterile descendant, will continue to produce descendants indefinitely in a periodic manner, or will produce descendants indefinitely but aperiodically (Case, 1974).

The processes by which artificial machines can exhibit various forms of reproduction, self-inspection, repair, and evolution can serve as explanatory models of similar processes in natural biological systems as well as contributing to the development of a broad theoretical biology of the possible organisms of possible universes.

Although complete physical artificial-machine self-reproduction has not yet been achieved, automation in which computer-controlled machines carry out the manufacture of other machines (including computing machines) has been moving steadily in that direction. Full exploitation of the concept will take advantage of the exponential nature of the reproductive process. Environmental concerns and the cost of energy and raw materials severely constrain Earth-based manufacturing of such an explosive nature. The lunar surface has been proposed as a suitable environment for the first economically practicable general-purpose self-reproducing factory (Cliff and co-workers, 1980). An extensive bibliography of machine replication and other biological-like processes has been published (Langton, 1988).

BIBLIOGRAPHY

M. Arbib, "Simple Self-Reproducing Universal Automata," *Inform. Contr.* **9**, 177–189 (1966).

E. R. Banks, "Universality in Cellular Automata," in *Proceedings of the Eleventh Switching and Automata Theory Conference,* 1970, pp. 194–215.

G. E. Berlekamp, J. Conway, and R. Guy, *Winning Ways,* Academic Press, Inc., New York, 1982, pp. 817–850.

A. W. Burks, "Computers, Control, and Intentionality," in D. Kerr and co-workers, eds., *Science, Computers, and the Information Onslaught,* Academic Press, Inc., New York, 1984, pp. 29–55.

A. W. Burks, "Von Neumann's Self-Reproducing Automata," in A. W. Burks, ed., *Essays on Cellular Automata,* University of Illinois Press, Urbana, 1970, pp. 3–64.

J. Case, "Periodicity in Generations of Automata," *Math. Syst. Theor.* **8**, 15–32 (1974).

R. Cliff, R. Freitas, R. Laing, and G. von Tiesenhausen, "Replicating Systems Concepts: Self-Replicating Lunar Factory and Demonstration," in R. Freitas and W. P. Gilbreath, eds., *Advanced Automation for Space Missions,* Publication 2255, NASA/ASEE Conference, Santa Clara, Calif., 1980, pp. 189–335.

E. Codd, *Cellular Automata,* Academic Press, Inc., New York, 1968.

M. Gardner, *Wheels, Life, and Other Mathematical Amusements,* W. H. Freeman, New York, 1983, pp. 214–257.

R. Laing, "Some Alternative Reproductive Strategies in Artificial Molecular Machines," *J. Theoret. Biol.* **54**, 63–84 (1975).

R. Laing, "Automaton Models of Reproduction by Self-Inspection," *J. Theoret. Biol.* **66**, 437–456 (1977).

C. Langton, ed., *Artificial Life,* Addison-Wesley Publishing Co., Inc., Reading, Mass., 1988, pp. 567–643.

J. Myhill, "The Abstract Theory of Self-Reproduction," in A. W. Burks, ed., *Essays in Cellular Automata,* University of Illinois Press, Urbana, 1974, pp. 206–218.

J. Thatcher, "Universality in the von Neumann Cellular Model," in A. W. Burks, ed., *Essays on Cellular Automata,* University of Illinois Press, Urbana, 1970, pp. 132–186.

J. von Neumann, "The General and Logical Theory of Automata," in L. A. Jeffress, ed., *Cerebral Mechanisms in Behavior,* John Wiley & Sons, Inc., New York, 1951, pp. 1–31.

J. von Neumann, *Theory of Self-Reproducing Automata,* edited and completed by A. W. Burks, University of Illinois Press, Urbana, 1966.

RICHARD LAING
Logical Mechanisms

SEMANTIC NETWORKS

A semantic network or net is a structure for representing knowledge as a pattern of interconnected nodes and arcs. The earliest semantic networks used in AI were designed as intermediate languages for machine translation (qv), and many of them are still strongly oriented toward the features of natural languages. But the more recent versions have grown in power and flexibility to compete with frame systems (see FRAMES) and logic programming (qv) systems as general knowledge representation languages.

Since the late 1950s, dozens of different versions of semantic networks have been proposed and implemented. Because of the diversity, the terminology and notations vary widely. Certain themes, however, are common to most versions:

1. Nodes in the net represent concepts of entities, attributes, events, and states.
2. Different nodes of the same concept type refer to different individuals of that type unless they are marked with a name, variable, or coreference link to indicate the same individual.
3. Arcs in the net, called conceptual relations, represent relationships that hold between the concept nodes. Labels on the arcs specify the relation types.
4. Some conceptual relations represent linguistic cases, such as, agent, patient, recipient, or instrument. Others represent spatial, temporal, causal, and logical connectives.
5. Concept types are organized in a hierarchy according to levels of generality, such as ENTITY, LIVING-THING, ANIMAL, CARNIVORE, FELINE, CAT.
6. Relationships that hold for all concepts of a given type are inherited through the hierarchy by all subtypes.

Besides these commonalities, the various networks diverge on a number of issues: philosophical questions of meaning; methods for representing all the quantifiers and operators of symbolic logic; techniques for manipulating the networks and performing inferences; and stylistic conventions for drawing the nodes and arcs and labeling them with words or other symbols. Some systems emphasize the ability to assert propositions and reason with them, and others place more emphasis on the mechanisms for defining new concepts in the type hierarchy. Despite the differences, all the versions are based on some common assumptions: network notations are easy for people to read, efficient for computers to process, and powerful enough to represent the semantics of natural languages.

HISTORICAL SURVEY

The Greek philosopher Porphyry began the practice of drawing type hierarchies as trees with their roots at the top. In the third century A.D., he wrote an introduction to Aristotle's categories (Porphyry, 1887), which was widely circulated by the medieval Scholastics. Figure 1 shows the *tree of Porphyry* as it still appears in textbooks on Aristotle's categories and syllogisms. At the top of the tree is SUBSTANCE, the supreme genus or most general concept type. The differentiate *material* and *immaterial* are attributes of SUBSTANCE that distinguish the two major sub-

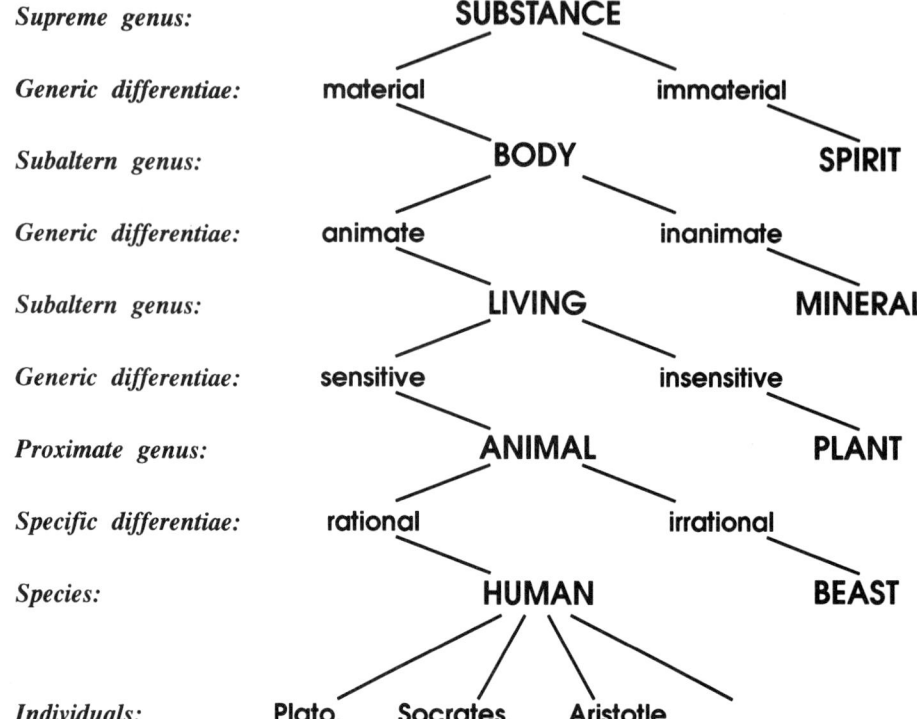

Figure 1. The tree of Porphyry.

types, BODY and SPIRIT. Below BODY are the more specialized subtypes LIVING, ANIMAL, and HUMAN. Below HUMAN are instances of individual humans, such as Socrates, Plato, and Aristotle. All the features of Porphyry's tree are still important aspects of the semantic networks in AI.

Porphyry's tree was a taxonomy for classifying concepts rather than an assertional system for stating propositions. In 1879, Frege developed the first assertional network, his *Begriffsschrift,* or *concept writing* (Frege, 1967), which represented propositions as trees. Frege's networks formed the first complete system of predicate logic (see LOGIC, PREDICATE). Independently of Frege, the philosopher Charles S. Peirce experimented with various notations for logic. In 1882, he developed relational graphs, which had strong similarities to modern semantic nets but could not express all of first-order logic (Peirce, 1986). Then in 1883, Peirce developed the first complete linear notation for predicate logic; but in 1897, he abandoned it for his system of existential graphs, which he called "the logic of future" (Peirce, 1960; Roberts, 1913). Figure 2 shows a relational graph for the sentence A *farmer owns and beats a donkey.*

In Figure 2, a linked set of bars, which Peirce called a *line of identity,* represent an existential quantifier ∃. The

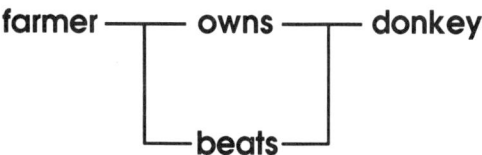

Figure 2. A relational graph in Peirce's notation.

bars on the left represent (∃x), and the ones on the right represent (∃y). The graph corresponds to following formula in the modern linear notation:

(∃x)(∃y)(farmer(x) ∧ donkey(y) ∧ owns(x, y)
∧ beats(x, y))

Peirce's original graphs could represent existential quantifiers and conjunction, but he was frustrated by the difficulty of showing the scope and interactions between different kinds of quantifiers and Boolean operators. He tried to mark the nodes and arcs with symbols for the universal quantifier, negation, and disjunction, but none of his attempts could represent all of first-order logic Meanwhile, his linear notation was complete, and he continued to use it for most of his research in logic. Then in 1896, he made a simple but brilliant discovery that solved all the problems at once: Instead of marking single nodes and arcs with negations, he introduced an oval that could enclose and negate an arbitrarily large graph or subgraph. That innovation enabled him to show the scope of quantifiers and to define all the operators and quantifiers in terms of the existential ∃, conjunction ∧, and negation ⌐. The implication ⊃, for example, could be represented with a nest of two ovals, since (p ⊃ q) is equivalent to ~(p ∧ q). Figure 3 shows one of Peirce's existential graphs for the sentence *If a farmer owns a donkey, then he beats it.*

The outer oval of Figure 3 is the antecedent, or if part, which contains *farmer,* linked by a line representing (∃x) to *owns,* which is linked by a line representing (∃y) to *donkey.* The subgraph in the outer oval may be read *If a farmer x owns a donkey y.* The lines x and y are extended into the inner oval, which represents the consequent *then*

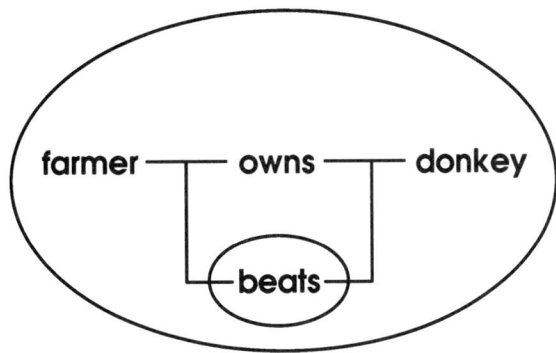

Figure 3. Existential graph.

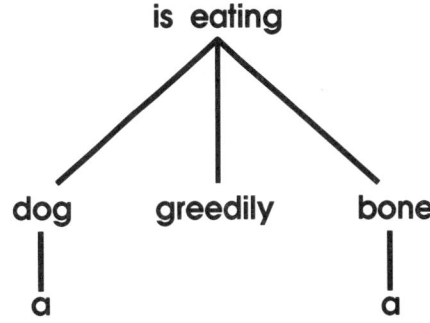

Figure 4. A dependency graph in Tesnière's notation.

x beats y. Figure 3 may be translated to the following formula in linear notation:

$$\neg(\exists x)(\exists y)(\text{farmer}(x) \land \text{donkey}(y) \land \text{owns}(x, y) \land \sim\text{beats}(x, y))$$

This formula is equivalent to

$$(\forall x)(\forall y)((\text{farmer}(x) \land \text{donkey}(y) \land \text{owns}(x, y)) \supset \text{beats}(x, y))$$

Peirce's struggles with relational graphs were repeated 80 years later by AI researchers who were unaware of his work. Like Peirce, they tried notations that marked a single node or arc at a time. Not until the propositional semantic networks of the 1970s did they rediscover ways of negating entire graphs and subgraphs.

In psychology, Otto Selz (1913, 1922) used graphs to represent patterns of concepts and the inheritance of properties in a concept hierarchy. His theory of schematic anticipation had strong similarities to AI theories of frames and pattern-directed invocation of procedures. Selz's theories had a strong influence on de Groot's (1965) studies of chess playing. De Groot, in turn, influenced Newell and Simon's work on problem solving. Their student Ross Quillian developed a network system for semantic memory (qv) and cited Selz in his dissertation (Quillian, 1968) Frijda and de Groot (1981) present a summary of Selz's work. See Norman and Rumelhart (1975) and Anderson and Bower (1980) for later applications of semantic networks in psychology.

In linguistics, Tesnière was developing graph notations in the 1930s for his system of dependency grammar (Tesnière, 1965). Figure 4 shows a dependency graph for the sentence *A dog is greedily eating a bone*. The verb *is eating* is drawn at the top, and the constituents that depend on it—subject, object, and adverb—hang underneath. Beneath nouns are the adjectives and determiners that depend on them. In the United States, Hays (1964) and Klein and Simmons (1963) adopted dependency theory for computational linguistics. They influenced Roger Schank, who shifted the emphasis from syntactic dependencies to conceptual dependencies (Schank, 1975; Schank and Tesler, 1969). Tesnière has had a major influence on European linguistics. Valency theory (Allerton, 1982), which is used in some machine translation systems (Vauquois and Boitet, 1985), is also derived from his work. Tesnière's posthumously published book (1965) is still used as a textbook in courses on linguistics.

The first implementations of semantic networks were developed for machine translation in the late 1950s and early 1960s. Margaret Masterman's system at Cambridge University (1961) was the first one to be called a semantic network. She had developed a set of 100 primitive concept types, such as FOLK, STUFF, THING, DO, and BE. In terms of these primitives, her group defined a conceptual dictionary of 15,000 entries. She organized the concept types into a lattice and had a mechanism for inheriting properties from supertypes to subtypes. Yorick Wilks (1962, 1975) continued to use Masterman's primitives as a basis for his system of preference semantics (qv). Another system for machine translation was based on Silvio Ceccato's (1961, 1964) correlational nets. Ceccato defined a list of 56 different relations, which included case relations, subtype, member, part-whole, and miscellaneous relations such as kinship. He used the nets of concepts and relations as patterns for guiding a parser and resolving syntactic ambiguities. At a major conference on machine translation in 1961, Ceccato, Hays, and Masterman presented papers on their networks, and other early researchers, such as Ross Quillian, were on the attendance list (National Physical Laboratory, 1961).

Although Quillian's (1968) networks were not the first, they were highly influential. His most significant innovation was the marker passing algorithm for spreading activations, which influenced later systems such as Fahlman's NETL (1979), Waltz and Pollack's massively parallel parser (1985), and many versions of neural networks. His method of representing types and tokens (terms that were first introduced by C. S. Peirce) has had a strong influence on taxonomic systems such as KL-ONE (qv) (Brachman, 1979). And his technique of language generation by following an utterance path through the network influenced Goldman (1975) and McNeill (1979).

In other AI systems, semantic nets were used for question answering, automatic programming, and studies of learning, memory, and reasoning. Besides the groups mentioned before, other early implementers include Raphael (1964), Reitman (1965), Simmons (1966), and Shapiro and Woodmansee (1969). During the 1970s, network systems proliferated and attained a considerable degree of power and sophistication. The most complete reference for that decade is the collection by Findler (1979);

many of those systems are also discussed in the remaining sections of this entry. During the 1980s, the boundary lines between network, framelike, and linear forms of logic tended to disappear. Expressive power is no longer a significant argument in favor of network vs linear forms, since new ideas stated in one notation can usually be adapted to other notations. Instead, the arguments are over secondary issues, such as readability, efficiency, naturalness, theoretical elegance, and ease of typing, editing, and printing.

Besides implementations, theoretical studies that analyze the underlying assumptions have made major contributions to the field. In his classic paper, "What's in a Link," Woods (1975) systematically analyzed and criticized the foundations of semantic networks and pointed out weaknesses that subsequent researchers have tried to correct. In a lighter style but with equally serious intent, McDermott (1976) wrote a critique with the unforgettable title "Artificial Intelligence Meets Natural Stupidity." Other important analyses were written by Israel and Brachman (1981), Maida and Shapiro (1982), Israel (1983), Sowa (194), Touretzky (1986), and Shastri (1988). The field is still growing, with many new implementations and theoretical refinements (Sowa, 1991; Lehmann, 1991).

RELATIONAL GRAPHS

The simplest networks used in AI are relational graphs consisting of interconnected nodes and arcs with no partitioning into separate contexts. Their structure is similar to Peirce's original relational graphs (Figure 2) or Tesnière's dependency graphs (Figure 4). Many of the people who developed semantic networks, including Masterman, Ceccato, Quillian, and Schank, shifted the emphasis from words to the deeper concepts and relations. Figure 5 shows a Schankian graph for the sentence *A dog is greedily eating a bone*. Instead of Tesnière's unlabeled arcs, Schank used different kinds of arrows for different relations, such as ⇔ for the agent-verb relation or an arrow marked with *o* for object; he replaced the verb *eat* with one of his primitive acts *ingest;* he replaced adverbs like *greedily* with adjective forms like *greedy;* and he added the linked arrows marked with *d* for direction to show that the bone goes from some unspecified place into the dog (the subscript 1 indicates that the bone went into the same dog who ingested it). Even while he was adding more conceptual detail, Schank ignored many of the linguistic details. The progressive aspect of *is eating* is not represented, and the indefinite articles in the phrases *a dog* and *a bone* are missing.

In translating sentences to conceptual primitives, the researchers in AI and machine translation were searching for a language-independent *interlingua*. Yet none of them have succeeded in developing a universal system of primitive concepts. In later work, Schank and Carbonell (1979) used high-level concept types such as AUTHORIZE without requiring them all to be translated to primitives. Sowa (in press) argued for a surface level like Figure 6 with concept types that are close to the words in the original sentence and with definitional mechanisms for translating the surface level to a deeper conceptual level only when needed. Instead of special arrows, labeled circles allow an open-ended number of conceptual relations, including AGNT for agent, PTNT for patient, and MANR for manner. In this approach, some concepts and relations are more primitive than others, but there are no ultimate primitives; any level could be transformed into another level to emphasize some details or to hide others.

Figure 6 uses the conceptual graph notation with boxes around the concept nodes and circles around the relation nodes (Sowa, 1984). The styles of drawing graphs or networks vary from one author to another. Some use ovals instead of boxes; some write labels next to the arcs instead of enclosing them in circles; some abbreviate the labels with single letters like *A* for agent and *O* for object; and others use many different styles of arrows. Since diagrams are hard to type and take a lot of space on the printed page, many authors type their graphs in a more compact notation. Figure 1 could also be written in a linear form with square brackets for the boxes and rounded parentheses for the circles:

[EAT]-
    (AGNT)→[DOG]
    (PNT)→[BONE]
    (MANR)→[GREED]

When each node has only one or two arcs attached to it, a graph can be drawn in a straight line. But since the [EAT] node in Figure 6 is linked to three relations, it is followed by a hyphen to show that its relations are continued on subsequent lines. In this notation, the graph looks very much like a frame. When a graph has cycles, cross references must be shown with variables or subscripts (such as the subscripts on DOG in Figure 5).

The concepts corresponding to verbs are typically linked to complex patterns of relations. They include the case relations or thematic roles like AGNT and PTNT.

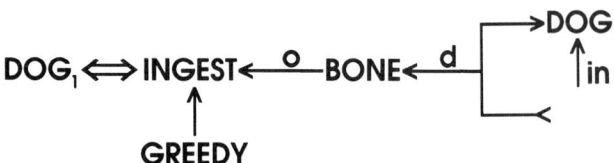

Figure 5. A Schankian conceptual dependency graph.

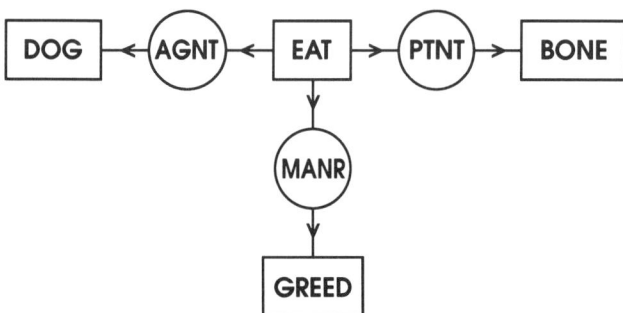

Figure 6. A conceptual graph with surface level concept types.

Other relations include prepositions, conjunctions, and relations like MANR for linking verbs to manner adverbs. Tenses and aspects, which are ignored in some systems, are represented by relations attached to verbs in other systems. Since the verb is such an important part of a sentence, many systems make it the centerpiece of the representation, as Tesnière did in his dependency graphs. Such notations may be called verb-centered relational graphs. As an example, Figure 7 shows a graph for the sentence *While a dog was eating a bone, a cat passed by unnoticed*. It has three concepts derived from verbs: [EAT], [PASS-BY], and [¬NOTICE]. Each one is linked to a monadic relation (PAST) to indicate the tense. The relation (WHL) indicates that [PASS-BY] occurred while [EAT] was in progress. In the original sentence, the subject of the participle *unnoticed* was left unspecified; the same ambiguity could have been preserved in the graph by omitting the (AGNT) relation that links [¬NOTICE] to [DOG].

Although verb-centered graphs are highly flexible, they have some serious limitations. Like other forms of relational graphs, they cannot express the scope of quantifiers, tenses, and modal operators. Although many AI researchers have used them extensively, they never developed a general method for handling contexts. Figure 7 illustrates the difficulty: the relation (PAST) is attached to [EAT] but not to [BONE], which probably ceased to exist after the act of eating. The graph also shows (WHL) linking [PASS-BY] to [EAT], but it does not show that the cat's passing by and the dog's not noticing occurred at the same time. A notation for showing context is necessary: (PAST) should modify the entire context of the dog eating the bone, and (WHL) should link that context to another context where the cat is passing by unnoticed.

As a system of logic, relational graphs can only represent a subset of first-order logic, usually with only conjunctions and existential quantifiers. Conjunction is shown implicitly by adding more nodes and arcs to a graph or by drawing another graph next to the first one. Existence is shown by concept nodes, which implicitly assert the existence of some entity, action, or state. Although some notations can show negations, disjunctions, and universal quantification, they do not clearly show their scope. Figure 7, for example, represented *unnoticed* with the negation sign (¬) in front of NOTICE. That is the kind of local negation that Peirce had in his relational graphs of 1882. Not until Peirce introduced contexts in 1896 did he finally have a complete graphical system of logic with a general way of showing the scope of quantifiers and Boolean operators (Roberts, 1973).

PROPOSITIONAL NETWORKS

Propositional networks express global relations between sentences, unlike the relational networks that can only express local relations such as AGNT and PTNT that hold within a sentence. To serve as the point of attachment for those global relations, propositional networks have nodes that represent phrases, clauses, sentences, paragraphs, or even entire stories. Relations between those nodes are used to express the following features of natural languages:

1. *Conjunctions*. The most direct way of putting two sentences together is by joining them with a conjunction. Some conjunctions, like *and, or*, and *if*, express logical connectives; others, like *after, when, while, since,* and *because*, express time and causality.

2. *Verb Complements*. Many verbs take an infinitive or embedded clause as one of their complements. Such verbs include *say, believe, think, know, persuade, threaten, attempt, try, help,* and *prevent*.

3. *Sentential Modifiers*. Many adverbs and prepositional phrases directly modify the verb, but others modify the entire sentence. Such adverbs, like *possibly* or *usually*, are often placed at the beginning of a sentence. The phrase *once upon a time* may modify an entire story.

4. *Modes and Tenses*. The auxiliary verbs *may, can, must, should, would,* and *could* express modal operators that govern the entire clause in which they occur. Tenses may be expressed by endings on verbs or by separate adverbs, such as *now, later, once,* or *tomorrow*.

5. *Connected Discourse*. Besides the local relations expressed in a single sentence, there are global relations between the sentences of a story, discussion, or explanation. Some of them are not stated explicitly; time sequence and the steps of an argument are often implied by the order in which sentences are stated.

As an example of a propositional network, Figure 8 shows a conceptual graph for the sentence *Sue thinks that Bob believes that a dog is eating a bone*. The concepts [THINK] and [BELIEVE] take propositions as patients: what Bob believes is the proposition *A dog is eating a*

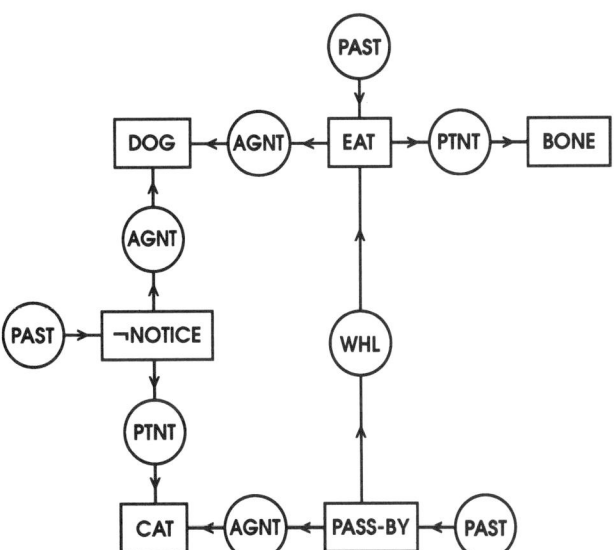

Figure 7. A verb-centered relational graph.

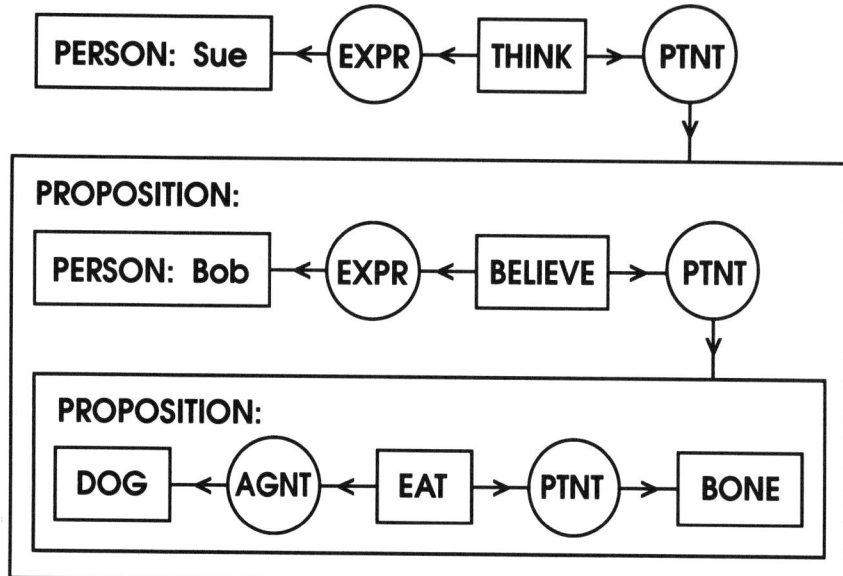

Figure 8. A conceptual graph with nested propositions.

bone; what Sue thinks is the more complex proposition *Bob believes that a dog is eating a bone.* Such nesting of propositions within propositions can be iterated any number of times. Note that the experiencer relation (EXPR) is [THINK] to Sue and [BELIEVE] to Bob, but the agent relation (AGNT) links [EAT] to [DOG]. The reason for the different relations is that thinking and believing are states that people experience, but eating is an act performed by an agent.

Figure 8 uses the conceptual graph notation (Sowa, 1984) for expressing propositions. The graph that states each proposition is nested inside a concept node labeled PROPOSITION, and the proposition nodes may be linked to other concepts by conceptual relations. Instead of nesting graphs within proposition nodes, some systems attach the constituents of a proposition to the outside of the node. A system with separate proposition nodes is Shapiro's MIND system (Shapiro, 1971), which was the first propositional semantic network to be implemented; it later evolved into SNePS (Semantic Network Processing System) (Shapiro, 1979). For comparison, Figure 9 shows the SNePS equivalent of Figure 8. The nodes M1, M2, M3, M4, and M5 are proposition nodes: Proposition M1 corresponds to the outermost context in Figure 8, which asserts the entire proposition about Sue thinking something; the object of Sue's thought is the proposition M2, which asserts that Bob believes M3; and M3 is the proposition about a dog eating a bone. The propositions M2 and M3 correspond to the two boxes of type PROPOSITION in Figure 8.

Besides the stylistic conventions for representing propositions, Figures 8 and 9 illustrate deeper issues concerning the referents of each node. In Figure 8, the box [PERSON: Sue] refers to an individual named Sue of type PERSON; the box [DOG] refers to an unnamed individual of type DOG. In Figure 9, the nodes SUE and BOB do not show that those individuals are persons; if necessary, that

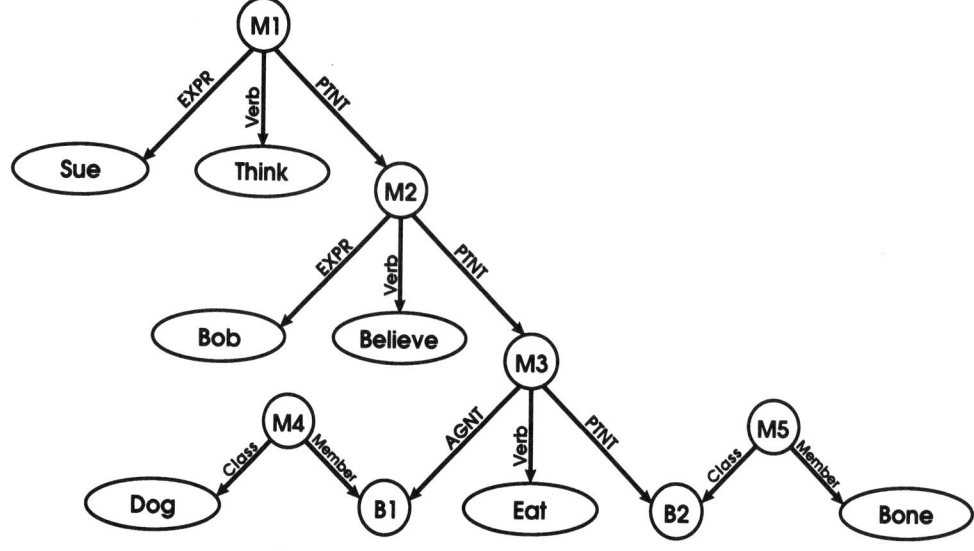

Figure 9. SNePS equivalent of Figure 8.

information could be stated by separate propositions. The nodes B1 and B2 represent the unnamed dog and bone; the proposition nodes M4 and M5 state that B1 is a member of the DOG class, and B2 is a member of the BONE class. Another difference between these two diagrams is in the treatment of verbs. In Figure 9, the concepts that represent verbs are linked only to the proposition nodes, and the case relations AGNT, PTNT, and EXPR are linked to the proposition nodes instead of the verb nodes.

Except for the details of drawing concept nodes as boxes or ovals, most relational graphs have strong similarities. Propositional networks, however, differ in several design considerations:

1. *Enclosing the Context.* Some systems, such as Peirce's existential graphs, Hendrix's partitioned nets (1975, 1979), and Sowa's conceptual graphs enclose the components of a proposition inside a context box (Figure 8). Others such as Shapiro's SNePS attach the constituents to the outside of a proposition node (Figure 9).

2. *Strict Nesting.* Some systems enforce a strict nesting of contexts: the existential graphs by Peirce, the hierarchical graphs by Janas and Schwind (1979), and the conceptual graphs by Sowa. For partitioned nets, Hendrix allowed overlapping contexts: A concept could occur in two different contexts, neither of which was nested in the other.

3. *Coreference Links.* With strictly nested contexts, coreference links, variables, or indices are necessary to show that two concepts in different contexts refer to the same individual. With overlapping contexts, the same concept may occur in both contexts, and coreference links may be unnecessary.

4. *Optional Proposition Nodes.* A sentence like *A happy dog jumped* may be considered a single proposition or it may be broken down into two propositions: *A dog jumped* and *The dog was happy*. In some systems, two separate proposition nodes are required for this sentence, and in others, they may be optional.

These differences are stylistic conventions that do not affect the logical expressive power, but they may affect readability and the ease of mapping to and from natural languages. Both Hendrix and Sowa, who enclose their contexts in boxes, implement them with special nodes to which they attach the enclosed graphs. If they had chosen to do so, they could have drawn them without the enclosing boxes. The choice of nested vs overlapping contexts is also a stylistic choice: Strictly nested contexts can always be drawn on a plane, but complex networks, can become unreadable or undrawable with overlapping contexts. As an example, Figure 10 shows a partitioned net that corresponds to Peirce's Figure 3 for the sentence *If a farmer owns a donkey, then he beats it*.

The two boxes in Figure 10 represent partitions that enclose the propositions for the antecedent and consequent of the implication. The antecedent, or if partition, encloses a node for FARMER, who is in a state (STAT) of OWNS, and a DONKEY, which is the patient of OWNS. Because of the overlap, the consequent, or then partition, encloses the same FARMER and DONKEY nodes but shows the farmer as the agent of BEATS and the donkey as the patient of BEATS. Figure 11 shows the equivalent in a conceptual graph. Since conceptual graphs are strictly nested (no overlapping), the farmer and donkey nodes may only occur in one of the contexts, in this case, the antecedent, or if context. To represent them in the consequent, or then context, there are two additional concepts represented as [⊤], where ⊤ is the most general type or the top of the type hierarchy. The dotted lines are coreference links that show that the two concepts of type ⊤ are coreferent with the farmer and donkey nodes.

Conceptual graphs require the extra nodes and coreference links because they do not permit overlapping contexts. But the extra nodes tend to occur in the same

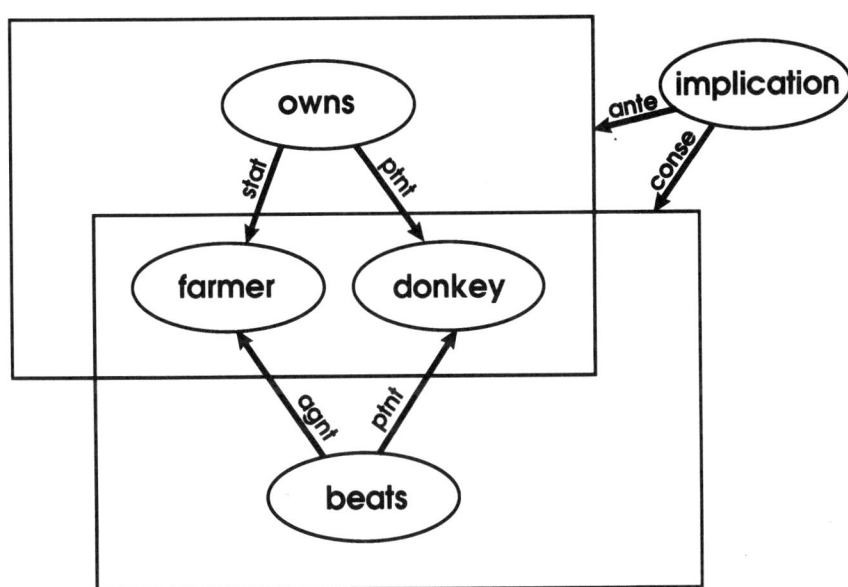

Figure 10. A partitioned net corresponding to Figure 3.

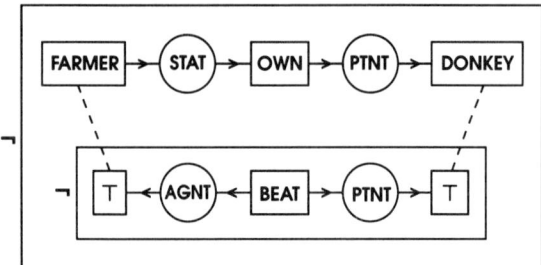

Figure 11. A conceptual graph corresponding to Figures 3 and 10.

places as pronouns and other anaphoric references in natural language. In Figure 11, for example, the two concepts of type ⊤ correspond to the pronouns *he* and *it* in the English sentence. The partitioned net in Figure 10 has no explicit nodes that correspond to the pronouns. Remarkably, the discourse representation structures independently developed by Hans Kamp (1981) have nested contexts that are isomorphic to the contexts in Peirce's existential graphs and Sowa's conceptual graphs. Whereas Peirce's goals were to represent logic in as simple a form as possible, Kamp's goals were to find a representation that had the most direct mapping to natural language. Their convergence on a common form for nested contexts suggests that there is something fundamental about the nesting.

The various forms of propositional networks have been implemented efficiently and used in many practical applications. Shapiro was the first to implement all the operators and quantifiers of first-order logic in a general network notation. As a theorem prover, his SNePS is comparable in efficiency to systems that use a linear notation for logic. In fact, one of his students wrote a translator from standard logic to SNePS: input and output were in linear formulas, but the proofs were carried out on the network forms. To demonstrate its use for expert systems, Shapiro (1981) used SNePS to implement a microbiology system called COCCI. Tranchell (1982) demonstrated its generality by implementing another network system, KL-ONE, completely in SNePS. Several other researchers have developed highly flexible versions of propositional networks and applied them to a wide variety of AI problems. Schubert (Schubert, 1975; Schubert and co-workers, 1979) extended propositional networks to handle essentially every feature that could be expressed in a linear logic. Hendrix's partitioned nets were used in the LADDER system for question answering and the PROSPECTOR system for mineral exploration (Hendrix, 1979; Duda and co-workers, 1979). Sowa's conceptual graphs (1976, 1984), have been used in a number of applications: an expert system for financial auditing (Garner and Tsui, 1985); a tool for knowledge acquisition from natural language (Farques and co-workers, 1986); an Italian question-answering system (Velardi and co-workers, 1988); a product configurator at Reuters (Smith, 1990); and a system used for applications ranging from robot control to DNA sequence analysis (Coombs and Hartley, 1987).

TYPE HIERARCHY

A type hierarchy is an ordering of concepts by levels of generality, but it is only a *partial ordering* because many types are not comparable: neither DOG < HOUSE, nor HOUSE < DOG. All hierarchies include entities: BEAGLE < DOG < CARNIVORE < ANIMAL < LIVING-THING < PHYS-OBJECT < ENTITY. They may also include events: DONATE < GIVE < ACT < EVENT. And they may include states: ECSTASY < HAPPINESS < EMOTIONAL-STATE < STATE. Aristotle's hierarchy had ten general categories at the top: SUBSTANCE, QUANTITY, QUALITY, RELATION, PLACE, TIME, POSITION, STATE, ACTIVITY, and PASSIVITY. For completeness, most systems have a universal type above all the others. It is often represented by the symbol ⊤, commonly used for the top of a lattice.

There is no universally accepted terminology for the type hierarchy. The symbol < between a more specialized type and a more general type may be read *is a subtype of, is a subset of, is a subclass of, is a subsort of, is a kind of, is a flavor of,* or simply *isa.* Unfortunately, there are objections to all of these terms:

1. Russel used the word *type* in a more restricted sense in logic. This is one reason why logicians use the word *sort* in the sense that programmers use the word *type*.
2. The term *isa* is ambiguous, since it could mean either subtype in the sense *A beagle is a dog* or instance in the sense *Snoopy is a beagle.*
3. The terms *set* and *subset* confuse intensions with extensions: the types in a conceptual system are categories of thought, which may or may not correspond to sets of existing entities in the real world.
4. The term *class* is used in procedural object-oriented languages like Smalltalk, C++, and Simula. But it can cause confusion, since the word *class*, like *set*, is used in logic in an extensional sense.
5. The term *sort* can cause confusion with the keys used by sorting programs.
6. The terms *kind* and *flavor* are not widely used.

Of all these terms, *type* and *subtype* are the most common. The fact that Bertrand Russell used the term in a narrower sense is not a serious objection, since the AI usage includes Russell's meaning as a special case.

The simplest hierarchies are trees, where each type except the top has only one immediate supertype. But the limitations of trees were recognized even in ancient times: Aristotle and his followers observed that dividing ANIMAL into subtypes SEA-ANIMAL and LAND-ANIMAL would conflict with a division into BIRD, MAMMAL, and FISH. A simple tree could not accommodate a type like SEA-BIRD, since it would have two immediate supertypes, BIRD and SEA-ANIMAL. To allow types with more than one immediate supertype, a more general hierarchy is needed. Figure 12 shows three kinds of hierarchies: a lattice, a tree, and an arbitrary acyclic graph.

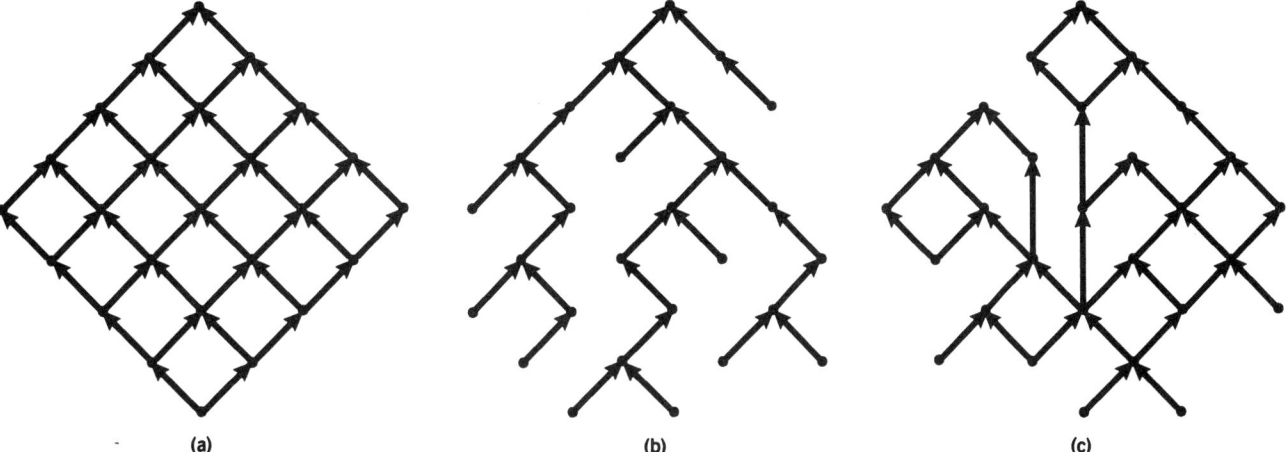

Figure 12. Three kinds of hierarchies: (a) lattice; (b) tree; and (c) arbitrary.

In Figure 12, the arrows extend from subtypes to supertypes. Unlike trees, a lattice allows types to have multiple immediate supertypes. An arbitrary acyclic graph like the one on the right is not a lattice because some pairs of nodes have no common supertype, some pairs have no common subtype, and some pairs have more than one minimal common supertype. Following are the characteristics of these kinds of hierarchies:

1. *Acyclic Graph.* Every partial ordering can be drawn as an acyclic graph, a graph with no cycles. Although an acyclic graph has no cycles, it may have branches that separate and come back together again, permitting some nodes to have more than one parent. Such graphs are sometimes called tangled hierarchies.
2. *Tree.* The simplest hierarchy is a *rooted tree*. It is an acyclic graph with further constraints that untangle the hierarchy: There is a single general type at the top, and every other type has exactly one immediate supertype.
3. *Lattice.* Unlike trees, lattices may have nodes with multiple parents. But they impose other constraints: every pair of types x and y must have a unique minimal common supertype $x \cup y$ and a unique maximal common subtype $x \cap y$. These constraints cause a lattice to look like a tree from both ends. At the top, it has a maximal node $\top$ that is a supertype of all others, and at the bottom, it has a minimal node $\bot$ that is a subtype of all others. (It is also possible to have infinite lattices with no top or bottom.)

Lattices are general enough to solve Aristotle's problem, since they allow different subdivisions to coexist. The type ANIMAL, for example, could have subtypes SEA-ANIMAL and LAND-ANIMAL as well as subtypes BIRD, MAMMAL, and FISH. Then SEA-BIRD would be an immediate subtype of both BIRD and SEA-ANIMAL.

The first mechanized type lattice was Leibniz's universal characteristic (1903). He assigned integers to each type: the number 1 would represent $\top$ or the supreme genus; each property or *differentia,* that distinguishes a subtype from its immediate supertype would be represented by a prime number. Then each type below $\top$ would be represented by the product of the primes for each of its differentiae. The set of all these numbers forms a lattice: For any types x and y, x is a subtype of y if y divides x; the minimal common supertype $x \cup y$ is the greatest common divisor of x and y; and the maximal common subtype $x \cap y$ is the least common multiple. One of Leibniz's reasons for designing the first calculator to do multiplication and division was to automate this system of reasoning. Masterman's original semantic network (1961) was also organized as a lattice. Since then, lattices have been widely used to support multiple inheritance through different paths in the type hierarchy.

INHERITANCE

A major use for a type hierarchy is to allow properties to be inherited from supertypes to subtypes: Whatever is true for any ANIMAL is true for any subtype such as MAMMAL, BIRD, or FISH. The original inheritance system is Aristotle's theory of syllogisms. According to Lukasiewicz (1957), the basic form of an Aristotelian syllogism is a conditional:

If A is predicated of all B,
and B is predicated of all C,
then A is predicated of all C.

This is the pattern of the first *mood*, which the medieval Scholastics named Barbara (the three *a*'s in "Barbara" indicate three universal affirmative clauses). Aristotle systematically analyzed all 24 valid moods with four kinds of clauses: universal affirmative (A); particular affirmative (I); universal negative (E); and particular negative (O). The syllogism Celarent for example, has three clauses of type E, A, and E:

If A is predicated of no B,
and B is predicated of all C,
then A is predicated of no C.

Aristotle showed that all 24 moods could be derived by transformations from Barbara and Celarent. Barbara is the most important mood and the most widely implemented in modern AI systems.

With the rise of symbolic logic, the syllogism went into a decline. Logicians tended to ignore it as merely a variant of quantification theory limited to monadic predicates. Yet the type hierarchy and inheritance remain important for several reasons:

1. Monadic predicates, represented by common nouns and adjectives, pervade natural languages.
2. The type hierarchy provides a good structure for indexing a knowledge base and organizing it efficiently.
3. Following a path through a hierarchy can be much faster than general theorem proving.
4. Selectional constraints used in a parsing program depend primarily on inheritance, not on general proof procedures.
5. Procedures as well as properties can be inherited through a type hierarchy. Such an inheritance method has been implemented in the procedural semantic networks of the TAXIS project (Levesque and Mylopoulos, 1979).
6. Finally, the syllogism could not have dominated logic for over two millennia if it had not been a vital and natural form of reasoning.

Because of its importance, inheritance methods have been widely used in AI since its earliest days. Raphael's SIR (1964) was one of the most influential of the early systems.

An important modern system that emphasizes inheritance through the type hierarchy is KL-ONE (qv) (Brachman, 1979; Brachman and Schmolze, 1985). Figure 13 shows a definition of DOG-HOUSE in a KL-ONE network. The three concepts marked with asterisks (HOUSE, ANIMAL, and DOG) are primitives that have no definition. The circle with a box in it shows a role: The concept HOUSE has a role named Inhabitant. The notation (1, NIL) indicates one or more inhabitants; and the notation v/r shows that ANIMAL is a value restriction on the kinds of entities that may fill the inhabitant role. The double arrow shows that the newly defined concept DOG-HOUSE is a subtype of HOUSE. The single arrow marked Restricts shows that DOG further restricts the inhabitant role for the subtype DOG-HOUSE. Subtypes inherit the roles of their supertypes, but they may have more roles and tighter constraints on the roles they inherit.

During the 1980s, the KL-ONE system was widely circulated throughout the AI community, and many groups adopted it as a basis for further research and development. That work led to guidelines for defining concept types, efficient methods for implementing inheritance, and programming techniques for practical applications. The FAME system for financial applications (Mays and co-workers, 1987, 1988) is a large, robust system that combines a KL-ONE-like inheritance system with procedural methods for computation; an important innovation is its partitioning into subhierarchies that enable multiple knowledge engineers to develop different aspects of a knowledge base simultaneously. MacGregor (1991) wrote a history of the KL-ONE family of systems, and Brachman and his colleagues (1991) developed a successor called CLASSIC.

One problem with inheritance is the proper treatment of defaults. The concept type BIRD, for example, might have a default property *can-fly*. Exceptions such as PENGUIN, OSTRICH, or KIWI could be marked by a canceling operator that would block that default. But Brachman (1985) raised some criticisms of operators for negating or canceling inheritance: a rock, for example, could be defined as an elephant except that it does not have a trunk, it is not alive, it has no feet, etc. With unrestricted use of canceling, inheritance becomes a vacuous theory that offers no guidelines for organizing a knowledge base. Conflicting defaults raise another problem, as in the Nixon diamond (Figure 14): Richard Nixon is both a Quaker and a Republican; Quakers are normally pacifists, and Republicans are normally not pacifists. Does Nixon inherit pacifism along the Quaker path, or is it blocked by the negation on the Republican path? Despite these problems, defaults and partial inheritance have been widely implemented in practical systems and have stimulated a great deal of fruitful research (Touretzky 1986; Thomason and Touretzky, 1991).

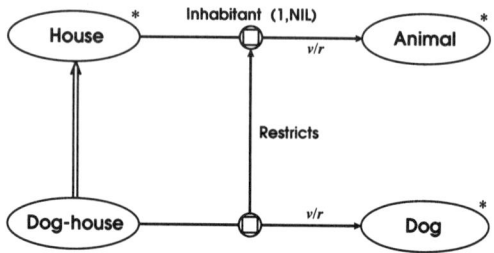

Figure 13. A KL-ONE definition for DOG-HOUSE.

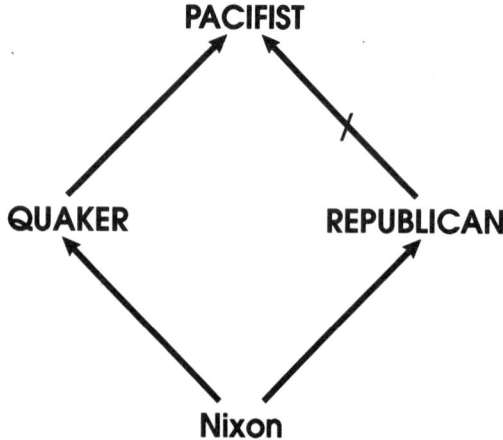

Figure 14. The Nixon diamond.

LOGIC

Since anything that can be expressed in logic can be said in any natural language, a semantic representation must contain all of logic as a subset. But the first implementations of semantic nets had to handle so many complexities of language that logic was not one of their first priorities. After some of the problems of syntax and semantics were solved, network theorists turned to logic. Shapiro (1971) built the first system that handled full first-order logic. Hendrix (1975) implemented partitioned nets (Figure 10) with many similarities to Peirce's graphs. Schubert (1975) implemented modal operators and definite and indefinite descriptions in his graphs. Since then, semantic networks have evolved into versatile systems that can express anything expressible in any other form of logic.

Logicians sometimes criticize AI researchers for inventing new notations "when standard logic is just as good and much more familiar." But the common notation for predicate calculus is not "just as good." From the earliest days, Frege (1967) and Russell (1905) emphasized the structural differences between their systems and natural language. Linguists such as Keenan (1972), Lakoff (1972), and Jackendoff (1983) criticized those differences in their search for a more natural logical form. To illustrate those criticisms, consider the sentence *A cat chased a mouse*, which might be represented by the formula,

$$(\exists x)(\exists y)(\text{cat}(x) \wedge \text{mouse}(y) \wedge \text{chased}(x, y))$$

The most unnatural feature is the way this formula splits a noun phrase such as *a cat* into discontinuous constituents: a quantifier $(\exists x)$ and a predicate $\text{cat}(x)$, which are associated by the variable symbol x. Another weakness is the treatment of tense on *chased*. To represent the past tense, the next formula adds a variable t:

$$(\exists x)(\exists y)(\exists t)(\text{cat}(x) \wedge \text{mouse}(y) \wedge \text{time}(t) \\ \wedge \text{chase}(x, y, t) \wedge \text{before}(t, \text{now}))$$

This notation is still inadequate because it shows the time t as governing only the verb and not the cat or the mouse (which may have ceased to exist after the chase). A more general notation would require the quantifiers that govern x and y to be nested inside a context indexed by the time t:

$$(\exists t)(\text{time}(t) \wedge \text{before}(t, \text{now}) \wedge \\ \text{at}(t, (\exists x)(\exists y)(\text{cat}(x) \wedge \text{mouse}(y) \wedge \text{chase}(x, y))))$$

This formula is no longer first order, since it has a formula nested as an argument of the *at* predicate. It also has an asymmetry between nouns and verbs: the variables x and y refer to the cat and the mouse, but the act of chasing has no variable of its own. Such variables would be needed to express anaphoric references in subsequent sentences, such as *The chase lasted 39 seconds*. Therefore, the next formula adds another variable z for the act itself:

$$(\exists t)(\text{time}(t) \wedge \text{before}(t, \text{now}) \wedge \\ \text{at}(t, (\exists x)(\exists y)(\exists z)(\text{cat}(x) \wedge \text{mouse}(y) \wedge \text{chase}(z, x, y))))$$

But this formula is still asymmetric, since the predicates have only one argument for nouns but three for the verb. Furthermore, the relationships between the nouns and verbs are expressed only by the position of the arguments of $\text{chase}(z, x, y)$. A more explicit notation would introduce predicates to express case relations: $\text{agnt}(z, x)$ to show that the agent of chase z is cat x and $\text{ptnt}(z, y)$ to show that the patient of chase z is mouse y:

$$(\exists t)(\text{time}(t) \wedge \text{before}(t, \text{now}) \wedge \\ \text{at}(t, (\exists x)(\exists y)(\exists z)(\text{cat}(x) \wedge \text{mouse}(y) \wedge \text{chase}(z) \\ \wedge \text{agnt}(z, x) \wedge \text{ptnt}(z, y))))$$

As this example shows, the linear notation requires many more symbols to express the common distinctions underlying ordinary English. Logicians developed it as a tool for analyzing the foundations of mathematics. It is well suited to that purpose, but it is awkward as a logical form for natural language.

To illustrate the readability of the network notations, Figure 15 shows a conceptual graph for the sentence *A cat chased a mouse*. Every concept implicitly asserts the existence of something of the corresponding type. This graph asserts the existence of a cat, an instance of chasing, and a mouse. It further asserts that the cat is the agent of chasing and the mouse is the object of chasing. To represent the past occurrence of this situation, the monadic relation PAST is attached to a context box that encloses the entire graph. To save space on the printed page, Figure 15 can also be written in the linear form with square brackets to represent concepts and rounded parentheses to represent conceptual relations:

(PAST)→[[CAT]←(AGNT)←[CHASE]→
(PTNT)→[MOUSE]]

The relation PAST is not a primitive. In the next section, it will be defined in terms of other relations, PTIM (point in time) and SUCC (successor). Whether the relation PAST or its definition is used, the conceptual graph is shorter, simpler, and more readable than the linear notation, but it captures the same semantic distinctions. There are other semantic distinctions in the notation that could be made explicit if necessary: The context box is actually a concept of type SITUATION, and the nested graph states a proposition that describes the situation. These details are explained in a later section on situations.

Besides readability, graphs have an important computational advantage: They can keep all the information

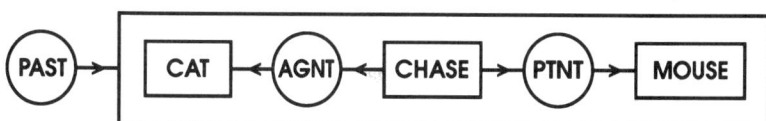

Figure 15. A conceptual graph.

about an entity at a single node and show related information by arcs connected directly to that node. Network systems take advantage of that connectivity in algorithms for scanning the graphs to generate language or perform inferences. By contrast, linear notations tend to scatter related pieces of information throughout a formula or collection of formulas. That scattering of information not only destroys the readability of the formula but also obscures the semantic structure of the sentence from which the formula was derived.

TAXONOMIC AND ASSERTIONAL SYSTEMS

The arcs in an assertional system may resemble the type–subtype links in a type hierarchy, but their nature is totally different. As an example, consider the agent relation in a Schankian graph (Figure 5), a conceptual graph (Figure 6), a SNePS network (Figure 9), or a partitioned net (Figure 10). In each of those graphs, the relation links an instance of an act, such as EAT, to an instance of an actor, such as a DOG. It makes a first-order assertion about individuals. In the tree of Porphyry (Figure 1) or the KL-ONE diagram (Figure 13), however, a type–subtype link makes a second-order assertion about types: It implies that everything of type HUMAN is also of type ANIMAL or everything of type DOG-HOUSE is also of type HOUSE. The difference in nature between those two kinds of links has led to a great deal of confusion in the AI literature. Depending on which kinds of links they emphasize, semantic networks have diverged in two directions:

1. *Assertional systems* emphasize the ability to make statements, but they sometimes neglect the type hierarchy. Roger Schank's (1975) conceptual dependency graphs, for example, were designed to represent the meaning of sentences in natural languages. Yet Schank did not emphasize the type hierarchy, and he even denied that his system should be called a semantic net.
2. *Taxonomic systems* emphasize the type hierarchy and methods for defining new types, but they tend to neglect the propositional aspects. Masterman's (1961) original semantic networks, Quillian's (1968) semantic memory, Martin's (1979) OWL, and Brachman's (1979) KL-ONE emphasized definitional mechanisms, but they were all weak in asserting propositions.

The divergence between assertional and taxonomic systems began with the earliest systems of logic. Aristotle was a taxonomist who developed the method of definition by genus and differentiae: Each new type is defined by stating its genus or supertype and its differentiae or properties that distinguish it from other subtypes (cf the tree of Porphyry in Figure 1). Symbolic logic takes the opposite approach of emphasizing assertions while ignoring the taxonomy of terms. Boole, Frege, and their followers emphasized the ability to assert propositions but did not develop mechanisms for defining the predicates that make up those propositions.

To distinguish these two kinds of systems, Brachman and co-workers (1983, 1985) introduced the terms T-box for the taxonomic system and A-box for the assertional system. In the *hybrid systems* KRYPTON (Brachman and co-workers, 1983) and KL-TWO (Vilain, 1985), the KL-ONE component becomes T-box for defining new types, and a system of logic is grafted onto it as the A-box. KRYPTON uses a version of first-order predicate calculus as the A-box, and KL-TWO uses a quantifier-free predicate calculus with equality. In effect, they combine an Aristotelian style of syllogistic with a resolution theorem prover.

C. S. Peirce was keenly aware of the importance of definitions, since he wrote most of the mathematical and philosophical definitions for the *New Century Dictionary*. But he did not develop a formal mechanism for definitions in his logic. With the λ-calculus, Alonzo Church finally developed a fully general method for building a definitional stucture on top of an assertional system. The λ-calculus was first adapted to propositional networks by Schubert (1975) and to conceptual graphs by Sowa (1979, 1984). With such techniques, a certain number of types may be taken as primitive, and new ones can then be introduced by definition. The following linear graph, for example, asserts the proposition *A dog lives in a house* (STAT is the state relation and IN represents the preposition *in*):

[DOG]→(STAT)→[LIVE]→(IN)→[HOUSE]

By parametrizing this proposition, one can define predicates for new types. The symbol (λx) is used to designate some concept node flagged by *x as the formal parameter. By designating the HOUSE node as the formal parameter, the following λ-abstraction defines a new type DOG-HOUSE as a subtype of HOUSE in which a DOG lives:

DOG-HOUSE = (λx) [DOG]→(STAT)→
 [LIVE]→(IN)→[HOUSE: *x]

By designating DOG as the parameter, the next λ-abstraction defines HOUSE-DOG as a type of DOG that lives in a house:

HOUSE-DOG = (λx) [DOG: *x]→
 (STAT)→[LIVE]→(IN)→[HOUSE]

The use of λ-expressions eliminates the need for a hybrid language, since it permits the same underlying language to be used for both assertions and definitions.

New relations can also be introduced by λ-abstractions. The past tense relation, for example, marks a SITUATION whose point in time (PTIM) is a time that has a successor (SUCC), which is the context-dependent speech time, designated by #s-time:

PAST = (λx) [SITUATION: *x]→(PTIM)→
 [TIME]→(SUCC)→[TIME: #s-time]

Similar definitions could be used to represent various theories of tense and aspect. Each tense could be represented by a monadic relation like PAST for the past tense or PPRT for the past perfect tense. Then those relations could be defined in terms of the context-dependent reference times.

The λ-abstraction that defines a type is a synonym for the type label. As an example, the type HOUSE-DOG and its defining λ-expression can be used interchangeably in any conceptual graph, as in the next linear graph for the sentence *Every house dog is pampered:*

[HOUSE-DOG: ∀]←(PTNT)←[PAMPER]

Instead of defining the special type HOUSE-DOG to assert this proposition, the corresponding λ-expression could be inserted in place of the type label:

[(λx) [DOG: *x]→(STAT)→[LIVE]→(IN)→
            [HOUSE]: ∀]←(PTNT)←[PAMPER]

This graph represents the sentence *Every dog that lives in a house is pampered.* The domain of the quantifier ∀ can be specified either by a type label or by a λ-expression that defines the type. This use of λ-expressions with quantifiers provides a powerful mechanism for representing the generalized quantifiers needed for natural language semantics.

GENERIC AND INDIVIDUAL CONCEPTS

In mapping language to logic, common nouns like *cat* map into monadic predicates like $CAT(x)$. But proper names like *Felix* map into individual constants. The term *isa* tends to blur this distinction: one says *Felix is a cat* in the same form as *A cat is an animal.* Consequently, many AI systems label their nodes with *cat* or *Felix* in the same format. One of the first network implementations, Ceccato's correlational nets (1961), had distinct relations for the two, but many later systems confused them. The confusion is compounded by terminology that differs from one author to another. Several different notions must be distinguished:

1. *Particular Individuals.* In logic, constants designate individuals in the real world or some possible world. The fictional cat Felix, for example, does not exist in the real world, but it is a well-defined character in a comic strip. Many systems have special nodes or notations for individuals. Sowa (1991), for example, writes a name or identifier after the type in a concept node: [CAT: Felix] represents an individual concept of a cat named Felix.
2. *Indefinite References.* The English phrase *a cat* refers to some individual of type CAT but does not say which one. Hilbert introduced his *epsilon operator* to express such terms: the notation $\varepsilon x CAT(x)$ represents an arbitrary x for which the predicate $CAT(x)$ is true (Leisenring, 1969). Sowa uses the notation [CAT], called a generic concept, to represent an arbitrary individual of type CAT. Its referent is the epsilon term $\varepsilon x CAT(x)$.
3. *Anaphoric References.* After an individual has been mentioned, a later pronoun or noun phrase may refer back to it. In semantic nets, it is common to join all the nodes in a context that refer to the same individual. Yet when a parser finds an anaphoric reference, such as *the cat,* it may not be clear which cat is meant. The parser may therefore flag the concept node with a marker such as # to indicate a reference to be resolved later: the concept [CAT: #] would later be linked to some other cat node in the current context or an enclosing context.
4. *Definite Descriptions.* Besides being used for anaphoric references, the definite article *the* is also used to introduce a unique individual that has a given property. For example, *the fourteenth president of the United States* denotes a unique person, but most people would not be able to identify that person without checking a history book. Definite descriptions can be handled as special cases of anaphoric references: if a referent cannot be found, a new individual concept may be introduced into the context and marked with the specified properties.
5. *Types.* The nodes that represent types should be distinguished from the nodes that represent individuals. In relating semantic networks to logic, Sowa maps concept types to predicates; referents of concepts to individual expressions; and concepts and conceptual graphs to formulas. For the generic concept [CAT], the type predicate is $CAT(x)$; the referent is the epsilon term $\varepsilon x CAT(x)$; and the formula is the result of applying the predicate to the referent, $CAT(\varepsilon x CAT(x))$, which is equivalent to the formula $\exists x CAT(x)$.

Not all versions of semantic networks distinguish these five different notions. Schubert (1975) was the first to introduce definite and indefinite descriptions into his version of semantic networks. Brachman (1979) emphasized the distinction between generic and individual concepts. Some systems still lack a general method for handling definite, indefinite, and anaphoric references.

INTENSIONS AND EXTENSIONS

To say that a semantic network represents semantics is circular: A graph notation is just another kind of syntax. To give it some semantic content, there must be an independent basis for determining the meaning of its nodes and arcs. In talking about meaning, philosophers have drawn a distinction between the *intension* of a word (its basic meaning in itself) and its *extension* (the set of things to which it refers). Frege gave the example of the *evening star* vs the *morning star.* These two terms have different intensions: one means a star that is seen in the morning, and the other means a star that is seen in the evening. Yet both of them have the same extension, namely the planet

Venus. In defining a semantic basis, one must decide whether it is extensional (a definition that lists the individuals a term refers to) or intensional (a definition by properties or criteria without any concern for the existence of things that have those properties).

In logic, first-order predicate calculus is purely extensional. For a given model, the meaning of any predicate is completely determined by listing the set of individuals for which it is true. Modal logic, however, is intensional: it deals with possibilities that do not exist and may never exist. Its model theory requires infinite families of infinite worlds together with an accessibility relation that shows how the worlds are related (Kripke, 1963). In such a system, extensional definitions are impossible because there is no way to list an infinite number of possibilities.

Although some people working with semantic networks have tended to ignore the logical and philosophical foundations, others have explicitly analyzed the nature of the networks as intensional systems. Woods (1975) explicitly noted that taxonomic systems are intensional systems where the meaning of a concept type is independent of the existence of the corresponding individuals: the nonexistence of unicorns is irrelevant to the definition of UNICORN as a subtype of MAMMAL. Janas and Schwind (1979) gave explicit rules for relating intensions to extensions. Their networks are intensional: They specify the meaning of a sentence independent of any interpretation. But they also defined a method of evaluating the extensions: Given sets of individuals and relations between individuals, the extension of a network is determined by rules that project the networks into the sets. Shapiro and his colleagues (1982, 1987) also emphasized the intensional nature of SNePS as a system for representing meaning. Sowa (1984) used conceptual graphs to represent both extensional models of the world and intensional propositions about the world. To determine the truth or falsity of a proposition, he defined projection rules similar to Janas and Schwind's to map the propositional graphs into the model graphs. For graphs without nested intensional contexts, the semantics is equivalent to first-order model theory. When modal and intensional relations are attached to the contexts, different versions of modal and intensional semantics can be represented.

SITUATIONS

Situation semantics, introduced by Barwise (1989) and Barwise and Perry (1983), has become one of the most important theories of meaning in natural language. It follows the model-theoretic tradition, but it explicates meaning in terms of finite situations, instead of the potentially infinite possible worlds in Montague semantics. But a great deal of work is necessary to relate Barwise and Perry's philosophical analysis to a workable system for semantics and knowledge representation. As an example of a representation in their original notation, the following event type represents the meaning of the sentence *A dog is eating a bone*:

$$E := \text{at } l: \quad \text{dog}, a; \text{ yes}$$
$$\text{bone}, b; \text{ yes}$$
$$\text{eating}, a, b; \text{ yes}$$

This notation represents an event type E at location l, where there exists a dog a and a bone b and a is eating b. Each yes indicates that the preceding assertion is true in the situation. Recently, Barwise (1989) has simplified the notation slightly by replacing yes and no with 1 and 0. To add linguistic features, some linguists and logicians (Fenstad and co-workers, 1987 have collaborated to develop *situation schemata*, which use the formalism of lexical-functional grammar (LFG) to represent both the syntactic features and the logical relationships. The LFG formalism is fine for syntax but is rather unwieldy as a form of knowledge representation; the situation schema to represent the sentence *A dog is eating a bone* would take about half a page.

The detailed notation of situation semantics may be useful for Barwise's original purpose of making the philosophical assumptions explicit. But as a semantic representation, its verbosity makes it worse than the predicate calculus in obscuring the linguistic structure; for knowledge representation, it becomes unreadable for anything larger than a toy example. Sowa (1991) and Wilensky (1991) have argued that semantic networks can be adapted to situation semantics to provide a theoretically sound representation that can clarify the semantic relationships without excessive verbosity. To illustrate a situation-semantic analysis in conceptual graphs, consider the next two sentences:

A dog is greedily eating a bone.
Greedily, a dog is eating a bone.

In the first sentence, the manner of eating was greedy; this sentence was represented by the relational graphs in Figures 5 and 6. In the second sentence, however, the situation as a whole was greedy; the manner of eating might actually have been quite refined. Relational graphs cannot distinguish these two cases, since they only provide one point of attachment for the adverb *greedily*. Figure 16 shows a conceptual graph for this sentence: greed is the manner (MANR) of a situation, which has a description (DSCR), which is the proposition that a dog is eating a bone. Compare this graph to Figure 6, where the concept EAT is the point of attachment for the manner relation.

Situation semantics makes a sharp distinction between a situation, a proposition that describes the situation, and a sentence that states the proposition. The DSCR relation explicitly shows how the situation and the proposition are related. A graph of this form is useful for making the relationships explicit, but it has too many nodes that have no direct correspondence to the words of the sentence. To simplify the notation, Figure 17 shows a *contraction* of Figure 16 with the conceptual graph in the referent field of the concept of type SITUATION.

A representation that respects the linguistic structure should avoid a needless proliferation of nodes that have no direct mapping to words in the sentence. The contraction

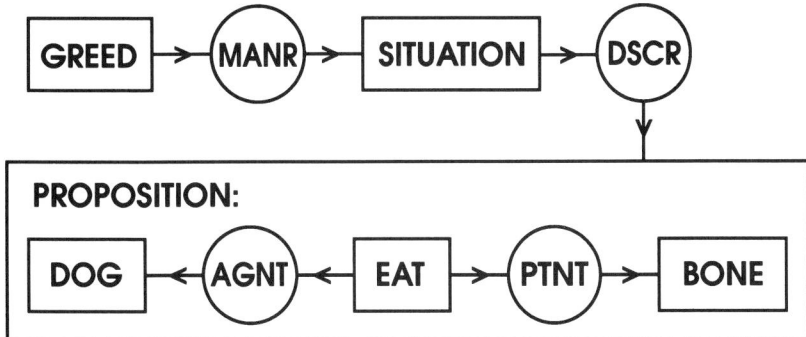

Figure 16. A manner relation that modifies a situation.

in Figure 17 contributes to that goal by simplifying the notation without losing information. The contracted information can always be recovered from the type labels on the nodes: When a conceptual graph occurs in the referent field of a concept of type GRAPH, it serves as a literal that represents itself. When it occurs in a concept of type PROPOSITION, it does not represent a proposition; it states the proposition. And when it occurs in a concept of type SITUATION, it states a proposition that describes the situation. These contractions resemble the type coercions in programming languages. They enable the graphs to encode many subtle distinctions in a compact form.

LANGUAGE PARSING AND GENERATION

Without a semantic representation, language analysis depends on syntactic rules supplemented with tests of semantic features. The structure of a semantic net can guide a parser by showing the normal ways that concepts link together. When the parser finds an ambiguity, it can use the net as a guide in selecting one option or another. Several different parsing techniques have been used with them:

1. *Syntax-directed Parsing.* The parser is controlled by a phrase-structure grammar augmented with structure-building and testing operators. As the input is analyzed, the structure-building operators construct a semantic net, and the testing operators check constraints on the partially built net. If the constraints are not met, the current grammar rule is rejected, and the parser tries another option. This approach is one of the most common.

2. *Semantic Parsing.* A semantic parser runs like a syntax-directed parser, but its categories are high-level concept types like SHIP and TRANSPORT instead of syntactic categories like Noun-Phrase or Verb-Phrase. The LADDER system (Hendrix and co-workers, 1978) was one of the best known systems that used a semantic parser to generate a semantic net.

3. *Conceptual Parsing.* The semantic network itself shows expected constraints on the way words may be related and leads to expectations for other words that may occur in the sentence. The verb *give*, for example, requires an animate subject and raises expectations for a recipient and an object given. Schank (1975) has been one of the strongest advocates of conceptual parsing.

4. *Word-expert Parsing.* Because of all the irregularities in natural languages, some people have abandoned the search for universal generalizations and have implemented their dictionaries as collections of independent procedures called (word experts) (Rieger and Small, 1981; see also PARSING, WORD EXPERT). The analysis of a sentence is treated as a cooperative process between word experts, each of which may be as arbitrary and irregular as necessary to handle special cases and exceptions.

Arguments over parsing techniques are usually debated with more religious fervor than hard facts. One of the few projects that has experimented with all of these techniques is the Semantic Representation Language (SRL) Project at the Technical University of Berlin (Habel and co-workers, 1980; Rollinger, 1984). Over the years,

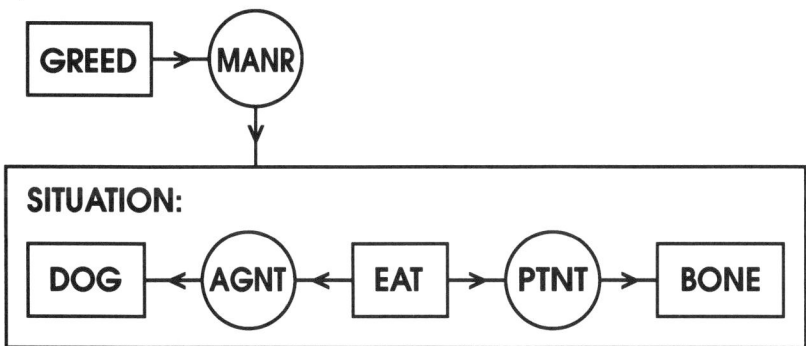

Figure 17. Contraction of Figure 16.

they have written four different parsers for analyzing German and mapping it into the SRL network form:

1. The first parser was a Schankian-style conceptual parser. Adding new words to its lexicon was easy, but it could only parse simple sentences and relative clauses. Broadening its syntactic coverage was difficult.
2. Their second parser was a semantic-oriented augmented transition net (qv). Making the syntax more general was easy, but it ran slower than the first parser.
3. Next, they implemented a word-expert parser. Handling special cases was easy, but the distribution of the grammar among many separate procedures made it difficult to understand, modify, and maintain.
4. The most recent parser is a syntax-directed one based on a generalized phrase-structure grammar (GPSG). It is the most general and systematic, and it is also reasonably fast.

These results are similar to the experiences of many other computational linguists: syntax-directed parsers are usually the most general, but a good set of network operators is necessary for a smooth interface between the grammar and the semantic net.

Generating language from a semantic network is the inverse of parsing: Instead of parsing a linear string to generate a network, the language generator parses a network to generate a linear string. In fact, Shapiro (1982) developed a highly symmetric version of an ATN that used exactly the same kinds of rules to generate or to parse. In one of the early systems, Quillian (1968) generated English from a network simply by tracing a path, mapping concepts along the path into words and relations into prepositions and other syntactic markers. Although Quillian's method was highly restricted, McNeill (1979) and Sowa (1983) elaborated it into a general theory of the *utterance path*. Instead of focusing on the utterance path, syntax-directed approaches control the generation by grammar rules that use the network to determine which rule to apply next. Yet in practice, both methods have an underlying similarity: The utterance path may be regarded as the sequence of nodes that are visited by a syntax-directed generator.

One language that is specifically designed for mapping natural languages to and from a network form is Heidorn's PLNLP (Programming Language for Natural Language Processing). An earlier version, called NLP, was used to implement verb-centered relational graphs for an automatic programming system (Heidorn, 1972, 1975). The PLNLP version has been used to implement a broad coverage grammar of English (Jensen and co-workers, 1984), which has been used in machine translation and in a semantic interpreter that generates conceptual graphs from the PLNLP parse trees (Sowa and Way, 1986). PLNLP supports two basic kinds of rules: Decoding rules parse a linear language and build a network; encoding rules scan a network and generate either linear strings or a transformed network. The semantic interpreter, for example, used encoding rules to map parse trees into conceptual graphs. Following is an example of an encoding rule for generating a sentence S consisting of a noun phrase NP followed by a verb phrase VP:

$$S \rightarrow NP(\%AGNT(S)) \; VP(\%S, NUMB = NUMB(AGNT), -AGNT)$$

The basic form is a phrase-structure rule (S → NP VP) augmented with structure-building and testing operations in parentheses. If the current node is S, this rule constructs a new node of type NP, which is a copy (indicated by the symbol %) of the node linked via AGNT to the S node; then it constructs a node of type VP, which is a copy of the S node (indicated by %S), but with the NUMB attribute (indicating singular or plural) set to the NUMB attribute of the node linked via AGNT and with the AGNT link deleted (−AGNT). Following is a decoding rule for parsing a verb phrase with a direct object:

$$VP(TRANS, \neg OBJ) \; NP \rightarrow VP(OBJ = NP)$$

This rule says that if a verb phrase VP has a transitive attribute (TRANS) and no object (OBJ) and it is followed by a noun phrase NP, then construct a VP node, which is the same as the previous VP node but with its OBJ set to point to the NP node. As these examples show, the graph-building and following operations are nestled among the syntactic rules for language parsing and generation.

MACHINE LEARNING

Graphs and networks are good notations for programs that try to learn new structures. A convenient feature is their ease of adding, deleting, and comparing nodes and arcs. Such operations are usually easier to perform on graphs than on linear notations. Following are some learning programs that used versions of semantic networks:

1. Winston (1970) used a form of relational graphs to describe structures, such as arches and towers. When given positive and negative examples of various structures, his program would derive graphs for the necessary and sufficient conditions for each type of structure.
2. Salveter (1979) used verb-centered relational graphs to represent the case relations associated with verbs. For each type of verb, her program MORAN would infer the expected case relations by comparing descriptions of scenes before and after the actions described by those verbs.
3. Schank (1982) developed his theory of MOPs (memory organization packets) to explain how people learned general information from particular experiences. A MOP is a highly general graph structure that contains the essential relationships abstracted from many specific graphs that describe particular experiences.

4. Haas and Hendrix (1983) developed the NANOKLAUS system that would learn type hierarchies by being told. Instead of requiring a person to give detailed definitions of each concept type, NANOKLAUS would carry on a dialog to determine the necessary and sufficient conditions.
5. Lendaris (1988, 1990) developed a hybrid system that combined conceptual graphs with neural networks. Instead of using a neural network to match inputs directly to outputs, he used concepts as an intermediate representation. In the first stage, his system would match inputs to concepts; in the second stage, it would match conceptual graphs formed from those concepts to the outputs. The hybrid system had a significantly reduced error rate and a faster learning rate than a system that matched inputs to outputs directly.

PROCEDURAL ATTACHMENTS

Semantic networks are a declarative form of knowledge representation. In that respect, they resemble logic and frame systems. Yet many declarative systems provide an escape mechanism for attaching procedures, either as a set of built-in primitives or as some form of subroutine calls to programs written in another language. Such procedural attachments serve several purposes:

1. *Efficiency.* When a well-defined algorithm exists, compiled code is usually faster than a more general AI system. An extreme case is a call to built-in arithmetic operators instead of a theorem prover that reduces everything to Peano's axioms.
2. *External Interfaces.* An AI program may be one component of a larger system. It may have to interact with programs in other languages, external databases, the operating system, or a network of other computers.
3. *Unsolved Problems.* A purely declarative system requires an axiom for every aspect of a problem. When a problem is not completely understood, it may be possible to write a "quick and dirty" procedure that handles an important aspect of it.

The TAXIS project at the University of Toronto has concentrated on procedural semantic networks (PSNs) that emphasize programming aspects (Levesque and Mylopoulos, 1979). Unlike propositional networks, which are based on logic, PSNs have an operationally defined semantics. They are especially useful for modeling systems that are changing and evolving through time. The PSNs do have some declarative aspects: they support a type hierarchy that allows procedures to be inherited from supertypes to subtypes.

Hybrid approaches that combine procedural and declarative networks have also been designed. Roussopoulos (1976) had two interconnected networks: a propositional network that was purely declarative and a network of procedural nodes that supported computation. Concept nodes (but not relation nodes) could be shared by both networks. Sowa (1976, 1984) developed a similar system of data flow graphs bound to conceptual graphs; he called the computational nodes *actors* to emphasize the parallels with other AI systems.

BIBLIOGRAPHY

D. J. Allerton, *Valency and the English Verb,* Academic Press, New York, 1982.

J. R. Anderson and G. H. Bower, *Human Associative Memory: A Brief Edition,* Lawrence Erlbaum Associates, Hillsdale, NJ, 1980.

J. Barwise, *The Situation in Logic,* CSLI, Stanford, Calif., 1989.

J. Barwise and J. Perry, *Situations and Attitudes,* MIT Press, Cambridge, Mass., 1983.

R. J. Brachman, "On the Epistemological Status of Semantic Networks," in Findler, 1979, pp. 3–50.

R. J. Brachman, "'I Lied abut the Trees' or, Defaults and Definitions in Knowledge Representation," *AI Mag.* 6(3), 80–93 (1985).

R. J. Brachman and J. G. Schmolze, "An Overview of the KL-ONE Knowledge Representation System," *Cogn. Sci.* 9(2), 171–216 (1985).

R. J. Brachman, R. E. Fikes, and H. J. Levesque, "Krypton: A Functional Approach to Knowledge Representation," *Computer* 16(10), 67–73 (1983).

R. J. Brachman, V. P. Gilbert, and H. J. Levesque, "An Essential Hybrid Reasoning System," *Proceedings of IJCAI* 1985, pp. 532–539.

R. J. Brachman, D. L. McGuinness, P. F. Patel-Schneider, L. A. Resnick, and A. Borgida, "Living with CLASSIC: When and How to Use a KL-ONE-Like Language," in Sowa, 1991.

S. Ceccato, *Linguistic Analysis and Programming for Mechanical Translation,* Gordon and Breach, New York, 1961.

S. Ceccato, "Automatic Translation of Languages," *Infor. Storage Retrieval* 2(3), 105–158 (1964).

M. J. Coombs and R. T. Hartley, "The MGR Algorithm and Its Application to the Generation of Explanations for Novel Events," *Int. J. Man-Machine Stud.* 27, 679–708 (1987).

A. D. de Groot, *Thought and Choice in Chess,* Mouton, The Hague, 1965.

R. Duda, J. Gaschnig, and P. Hart, "Model Design in the PROSPECTOR Consultant System for Mineral Exploration," in D. Michie, ed., *Expert Systems in the Micro-Electronic Age,* Edinburgh University Press, Edinburgh, 1979, pp. 153–167.

S. E. Fahlman, *NETL: A System for Representing and Using Real-World Knowledge,* MIT Press, Cambridge, Mass., 1979.

J. Fargues, M. C. Landau, A. Dugourd, and L. Catach, "Conceptual Graphs for Semantics and Knowledge Processing," *IBM J. of Res. Dev.* 30(1) (1986).

J. E. Fenstad, P. K. Halvorsen, T. Langholm, and J. van Benthem, *Situations, Language, and Logic,* Reidel, Dordrecht, The Netherlands, 1987.

N. V. Findler, ed., *Associative Networks: Representation and Use of Knowledge by Computers,* Academic Press, New York, 1979.

G. Frege, "Begriffsschrift," in *From Frege to Gödel, 1879–1931,* J. van Heijenoort, ed., Harvard University Press, Cambridge, Mass., 1967, pp. 1–82.

N. H. Frijda and A. D. de Groot, *Otto Selz: His Contribution to Psychology,* Mouton, The Hague, 1981.

B. J. Garner and E. Tsui, "Knowledge Representation for an Audit Office," *Austral. Comput. J.* 17(3), 106–112 (1985).

N. M. Goldman, "Conceptual Generation," in Schank, 1975, pp. 289–371.

N. Haas and G. G. Hendrix, "Learning by Being Told," in R. S. Michalski, J. G. Carbonell, and T. M. Mitchell, eds., *Machine Learning*, Tioga Publishing, Palo Alto, Calif., 1983, pp. 405–427.

C. Habel, C. R. Rollinger, A. Schmidt, and H. J. Schneider, "A Logic Oriented Approach to Automatic Text Understanding," in L. Bolc, ed., *Natural Language Based Computer Systems*, Hanser/Macmillan, New York, 1980.

D. G. Hays, "Dependency Theory: A Formalism and Some Observations," *Language*, **40**(4), 511–525 (1964).

G. E. Heidorn, Natural Language Inputs to a Simulation Programming System, Report NPS-55HD72101A, Naval Postgraduate School, Monterey, Calif., 1972.

G. E. Heidorn, "Augmented Phrase Structure Grammar," in R. C. Schank and B. L. Nash-Webber, eds., *Theoretical Issues in Natural Language Processing*, ACL, 1975, pp. 1–5.

G. G. Hendrix, "Encoding Knowledge in Partitioned Networks," in Findler, 1979, pp. 51–92.

G. G. Hendrix, "Expanding the Utility of Semantic Networks through Partitioning," in *Proceedings of the Fourth IJCAI*, 1975, pp. 115–121.

G. G. Hendrix, E. D. Sacerdoti, D. Sagalowicz, and J. Slocum, "Developing a Natural Language Interface to Complex Data," *ACM Trans. Database Syst.* **3**, 105–147 (1978).

D. J. Israel, "Interpreting Network Formalisms," *Comput. Math. With Applications*, **9**(1), 1–13 (1983).

D. J. Israel and R. J. Brachman, "Distinctions and Confusions," *Proceedings of the Seventh IJCAI*, 1981, pp. 452–458.

R. Jackendoff, *Semantics and Cognition*, MIT Press, Cambridge, Mass., 1983.

J. M. Janas and C. B. Schwind, "Extensional Semantic Networks," in Findler, 1979, pp. 267–302.

K. Jensen, G. Heidorn, L. Miller, and Y. Ravin, "Parse Fitting and Prose Fixing: Getting a Hold on Ill-Formedness," *Amer. J. Comput. Ling.* **9**(3–4), 147–160 (1984).

H. Kamp, "A Theory of Truth and Semantic Representation," in J. A. G. Groenendijk, T. M. V. Janssen, and M. B. J. Stokhof, eds., *Formal Methods in the Study of Language*, Mathematical Centre Tracts, Amsterdam, 1981, pp. 277–322.

E. L. Keenan, "On Semantically Based Grammar," *Ling. Inq.* **3**, 413–462 (1972).

S. Klein and R. F. Simmons, "Syntactic Dependence and the Computer Generation of Coherent Discourse," *Mechan. Transl.* **7** (1963).

S. A. Kripke, "Semantical Analysis of Modal Logic I," *Zeitschrift Für Mathe. Logik Grund. der Mathematik*, **9**, 67–96 (1963).

G. Lakoff, "Linguistics and Natural Logic," in G. Harman and D. Davidson, eds., *Semantics for Natural Language*, Reidel, Dordrecht, The Netherlands, 1972.

F. Lehmann, ed., *Computers & Mathematics with Applications*, [Special issue on semantic networks in AI] (1991).

G. W. Leibniz, "Elementa Characteristica Universalis," in L. Couturat, Ed., *Opuscules et Fragments Inédits de Leibniz*, Ancienne Librairie Germer Bailliere, Paris, 1903, pp. 42–92.

A. C. Leisenring, *Mathematical Logic and Hilbert's ε-Symbol*, Gordon and Breach, New York, 1969.

G. G. Lendaris, "Neural Networks, Potential Assistants to Knowledge Engineers," *Heuristics*, **1**(2) (1988).

G. G. Lendaris, "Conceptual Graphs as a Vehicle for Improved Generalization in a Neural Network Pattern Recognition Task," *Proceedings of the Fifth Annual Workshop on Conceptual Structures*, Boston, AAAI, Menlo Park, Calif., 1990, pp. 90–91.

H. Levesque and J. Mylopoulos, "A Procedural Semantics for Semantic Networks," in Findler, 1979, pp. 93–120.

J. Lukasiewicz, *Aristotle's Syllogistic from the Standpoint of Modern Formal Logic*, Clarendon Press, Oxford, U.K., 1957.

R. MacGregor, "The Evolving Technology of Classification Based Knowledge Representation Systems," in J. F. Sowa, ed., *Principles of Semantic Networks: Explorations in the Representation of Knowledge*, Morgan Kaufmann Publishers, San Mateo, Calif., 1991.

A. S. Maida and S. C. Shapiro, "Intensional Concepts in Propositional Semantic Networks," *Cogn. Sci.* **6**, 291–330 (1982).

W. A. Martin, "Descriptions and the Specialization of Concepts," in P. H. Winston and R. H. Brown, eds., *Artificial Intelligence: An MIT Perspective*, MIT Press, Cambridge, Mass., 1979, pp. 375–419.

M. Masterman, "Semantic Message Detection for Machine Translation, Using an Interlingua," *Proceedings of the International Conference on Machine Translation*, 1961, pp. 438–475.

E. Mays, C. Apté, J. Griesmer, and J. Kastner, "Organizing Knowledge in a Complex Financial Domain," *IEEE Expert* **2**(3), 61–70 (1987).

E. Mays, C. Apté, J. Griesmer, and J. Kastner, "Experience with K-Rep: An Object Centered Knowledge Representation Language," *Proceedings of the Fourth Conference on AI Applications*, San Diego, 1988, pp. 62–67.

D. V. McDermott, "Artificial Intelligence Meets Natural Stupidity," *SIGART Newsletter*, no. 57, April 1976; reprinted in J. Haugeland, ed., *Mind Design*, MIT Press, Cambridge, Mass., 1976, pp. 143–160.

D. McNeill, *The Conceptual Basis of Language*, Lawrence Erlbaum Associates, Hillsdale, NJ, 1979.

R. Montague, *Formal Philosophy*, Yale University Press, New Haven, Conn.

National Physical Laboratory, *International Conference on Machine Translation of Languages and Applied Language Analysis*, Her Majesty's Stationery Office, London, 1961.

D. A. Norman, D. E. Rumelhart, and the LNR Research Group, *Explorations in Cognition*, Freeman, San Francisco, 1975.

C. S. Peirce, "Manuscripts on Existential Graphs, in A. W. Burks, ed., *Collected Papers of Charles Sanders Peirce*, Vol. 4, Harvard University Press, Cambridge, Mass., 1960, pp. 320–410.

C. S. Peirce, "Letter to O. H. Mitchell," *Writings of Charles S. Peirce*, Vol. 4, Indiana University Press, Bloomington, 1986, pp. 394–399.

Porphyry, *Isagoge et in Aristotelis Categorias Commentarium*, in A. Busse, ed., *Commentaria in Aristotelem Graeca*, 4(1), (1887).

M. R. Quillian, *Semantic Memory*, Report AD-641671, Clearinghouse for Federal Scientific and Technical Information, 1966; abridged version in M. Minsky, ed., *Semantic Information Processing*, MIT Press, Cambridge, Mass., 1968, pp. 227–270.

B. Raphael, SIR: A Computer Program for Semantic Information Retrieval, Ph.D. dissertation, MIT, Cambridge, Mass., 1964.

W. R. Reitman, *Cognition and Thought*, Wiley, New York, 1965.

C. J. Rieger and S. L. Small, "Toward a Theory of Distributed Word Expert Natural Language Parsing," *IEEE Trans. Syst. Man Cyber.* **11**(1), 43–51 (1981).

D. D. Roberts, *The Existential Graphs of Charles S. Peirce*, Mouton, The Hague, 1973.

C. R. Rollinger, ed., *Probleme des (Text-) Verstehens, Ansätze der Künstlichen Intelligenz,* Max Niemeyer Verlag, Tübingen, FRG, 1984.

N. D. Roussopoulos, A Semantic Network Model of Data Bases, Ph.D. dissertation, University of Toronto, 1976.

B. Russell, "On Denoting," *Mind,* 14, 479–493 (1905).

S. C. Salveter, "Inferring Conceptual Graphs," *Cogn. Sci.* 3, 141–166 (1979).

R. C. Schank, ed., *Conceptual Information Processing,* North-Holland, Amsterdam, 1975.

R. C. Schank, *Dynamic Memory,* Cambridge University Press, New York, 1982.

R. C. Schank and J. G. Carbonell, Jr., "Re: The Gettysburg Address," in N. V. Findler, ed., *Associative Networks: Representation and Use of Knowledge by Computers,* Academic Press, New York, 1979, pp. 327–362.

R. C. Schank and L. G. Tesler, "A Conceptual Parser for Natural Language," *Proceedings of the First IJCAI,* 1969, pp. 569–578.

L. K. Schubert, "Extending the Expressive Power of Semantic Networks," *Proceedings of the Fourth IJCAI,* 1975, pp. 158–164.

L. K. Schubert, R. G. Goebel, and N. J. Cercone, "The Structure and Organization of a Semantic Net for Comprehension and Inference," in Findler, 1979, pp. 121–175.

O. Selz, *Über die Gesetze des geordneten Denkverlaufs,* Spemann, Stuttgart, Germany, 1913.

O. Selz, *Zur Psychologie des produktiven Denkens und des Irrtums,* Friedrich Cohen, Bonn, 1922.

S. C. Shapiro, "A Net Structure for Semantic Information Storage, Deduction and Retrieval," *Proceedings of the Second IJCAI,* 1971, pp. 512–523.

S. C. Shapiro, "The SNePS Semantic Network Processing System, in Findler, 1979, pp. 179–203.

S. C. Shapiro, COCCI: A Deductive Network Program for Solving Microbiology Unknowns, Technical Report 173, Dept. of Computer Science, SUNY at Buffalo, New York, 1981.

S. C. Shapiro, "Generalized Augmented Transition Network Grammars for Generation from Semantic Networks," *Amer. J. Comput. Ling.* 8(1), 12–25 (1982).

S. C. Shapiro and W. J. Rapaport, "SNePS Considered as a Fully Intensional Propositional Semantic Network," in N. Cercone and G. McCalla, eds., *The Knowledge Frontier,* Springer-Verlag, New York, 1987, pp. 263–315.

S. C. Shapiro and G. H. Woodmansee, "A Net Structure Based Relational Question Answerer," *Proceedings of the First IJCAI,* 1969, pp. 325–346.

L. Shastri, *Semantic Networks: An Evidential Formulation and its Connectionist Realization,* Morgan-Kaufmann Publishers, San Mateo, Calif., 1988.

R. F. Simmons, "Storage and Retrieval of Aspects of Meaning in Directed Graph Structures," *ACM* 9, 211–215 (1966).

B. Smith, "The Client Admin Expert System Based on Conceptual Graphs," *Proceedings of the Fifth Annual Workshop on Conceptual Graphs,* Stockholm, 1990.

J. F. Sowa, "Conceptual Graphs for a Database Interface," *IBM J. Res. Dev.* 20(4), 336–357 (1976).

J. F. Sowa, "Definitional Mechanisms for Conceptual Graphs," in V. Claus, H. Ehrig, and G. Rozenberg, eds., *Graph Grammars and Their Application to Computer Science and Biology,* Springer-Verlag, Berlin, 1979, pp. 426–439.

J. F. Sowa, "Generating Language from Conceptual Graphs," *Computers and Mathematics with Applications* 9(1), 29–43 (1983).

J. F. Sowa, *Conceptual Structures: Information Processing in Mind and Machine,* Addison-Wesley, Reading, Mass., 1984.

J. F. Sowa, ed., *Principles of Semantic Networks: Explorations in the Representation of Knowledge,* Morgan-Kaufmann Publishers, San Mateo, Calif., 1991.

J. F. Sowa, "Towards the Expressive Power of Natural Language," in Sowa, 1991.

J. F. Sowa, "Lexical Structures and Conceptual Structures," in J. Pustejovsky, ed., *Lexical Semantics,* MIT Press, Cambridge, Mass., in press.

J. F. Sowa and E. C. Way, "Implementing a Semantic Interpreter Using Conceptual Graphs," *IBM J. Res. Dev.* 30(1) (1986).

L. Tesnière, *Éléments de Syntaxe Structurale,* 2nd ed., Librairie C. Klincksieck, Paris, 1965.

R. H. Thomason and D. S. Touretzky, "Inheritance Theory and Networks with Roles," in Sowa, 1991.

D. S. Touretzky, *The Mathematics of Inheritance Systems,* Morgan-Kaufmann, San Mateo, Calif., 1986.

L. M. Tranchell, *A SNePS Implementation of KL-ONE,* Technical Report 198, Dept. of Computer Science, SUNY at Buffalo, 1982.

B. Vauquois and C. Boitet, "Automated Translation at Grenoble University," *Comput. Ling.* 11(1), 28–36 (1985).

P. Velardi, M. T. Pazienza, and M. DeGiovanetti, "Conceptual Graphs for the Analysis and Generation of Sentences," *IBM J. Res. Dev.* 32(2), 251–267 (1988).

M. Vilain, "An Approach to Hybrid Knowledge Representation," *Proceedings of the Ninth IJCAI,* 1985.

D. L. Waltz and J. B. Pollack, "Massively Parallel Parsing," *Cogn. Sci.,* 9, 51–74 (1985).

R. Wilensky, "Sentences, Situations, and Propositions," in Sowa, 1991.

Y. A. Wilks, *Grammar, Meaning, and the Machine Analysis of Language,* Routledge & Kegan Paul, London, 1972.

Y. A. Wilks, "An Intelligent Analyzer and Understander of English," *CACM* 18(5), 264–274 (1975).

P. Winston, "Learning Structural Descriptions from Examples," Ph.D. dissertation, Report MAC-TR-76, MIT, Cambridge, Mass., 1970.

W. A. Woods, "What's in a Link: Foundations for Semantic Networks," in D. G. Bobrow and A. Collins, eds., *Representation and Understanding,* Academic Press, New York, 1975, pp. 35–82.

JOHN F. SOWA
IBM Systems Research

SENSORS AND SENSOR FUSION

Sensors are detectors, or transducers, that record the radiant energy, temperature, density, content, and composition of a scene and convert the recorded information into appropriate electrical signals. Such detectors emulate human senses and can be based on acoustic, optical, or tactile sensing. Computer vision, in large part, deals with the design and operation of such sensors and with the interpretation of sensor data. This article provides an overview of several sensing modalities: visual, thermal, and tactile

SENSOR DESIGN PRINCIPLES

Optical Sensors

The operational principle of an optical sensor is the detection of *optical energy,* which is the energy that falls in the optical spectrum. The *optical spectrum* is a subset of the electromagnetic spectrum that spans the optical wavelengths. The range of wavelengths in the optical spectrum is not universally agreed on. The optical spectrum spans the wavelengths from 0.01 to 1000 μm (Stimson, 1974). The visible portion of the optical spectrum spans the wavelengths from approximately 0.38 to 0.76 μm. Other labeled regions in the optical spectrum are the ultraviolet and the near, middle, and far infrared regions. All have somewhat arbitrary boundaries. Figure 1 shows the electromagnetic spectrum, the optical spectrum, and the labeled regions in the optical spectrum.

Optical energy is emitted, absorbed, reflected, and transmitted by objects in the environment. An object emits or absorbs optical energy due to the internal activity of the atoms composing the object. As the electrons that orbit an atom change energy levels, they absorb or emit (or both) quanta of energy in the form of electromagnetic radiation (or photons). Such transitions of electrons can be induced by internal energy, chemical reactions, or the absorption of external energy. An object can also reflect or transmit optical energy emitted or reflected from other objects in the environment.

When an optical sensor is designed to detect optical energy, the amount of energy detected by the sensor is determined by the radiant flux of the source, the attenuation and scattering by the intervening medium, the emission geometry, the size of the sensor, and the efficiency of the sensor in detecting and converting optical energy.

The amount of optical energy an emitting source radiates is usually not uniform across the optical spectrum. For an incandescent source, such as a blackbody, the spectral characteristics of the emitted energy are primarily determined by the source's temperature. For light produced by electrical excitation (such as neon light), the spectral distribution of optical energy shows unique characteristic lines. Figures 2 and 3 show the relative spectral energy distribution of blackbodies and of certain gaseous sources, respectively.

If the spectral energy distribution of a source is denoted as $\Phi(\lambda)$, where λ denotes the wavelength, then the total power emitted by a radiant source is given by the integral of the spectral energy distribution

$$F = \int_0^\infty \Phi(\lambda) d\lambda$$

where F is called the radiant flux of the source and is normally expressed in watts or photons/s.

The amount of radiant flux incident on a sensor's surface is determined by the attenuation and scattering by the intervening medium, the emission geometry, and the size of the sensor. The effect of the emission geometry on the response of a sensor can best be illustrated by a simple example using a point source of light. Consider a point of light emitting photon flux in all directions. The incremen-

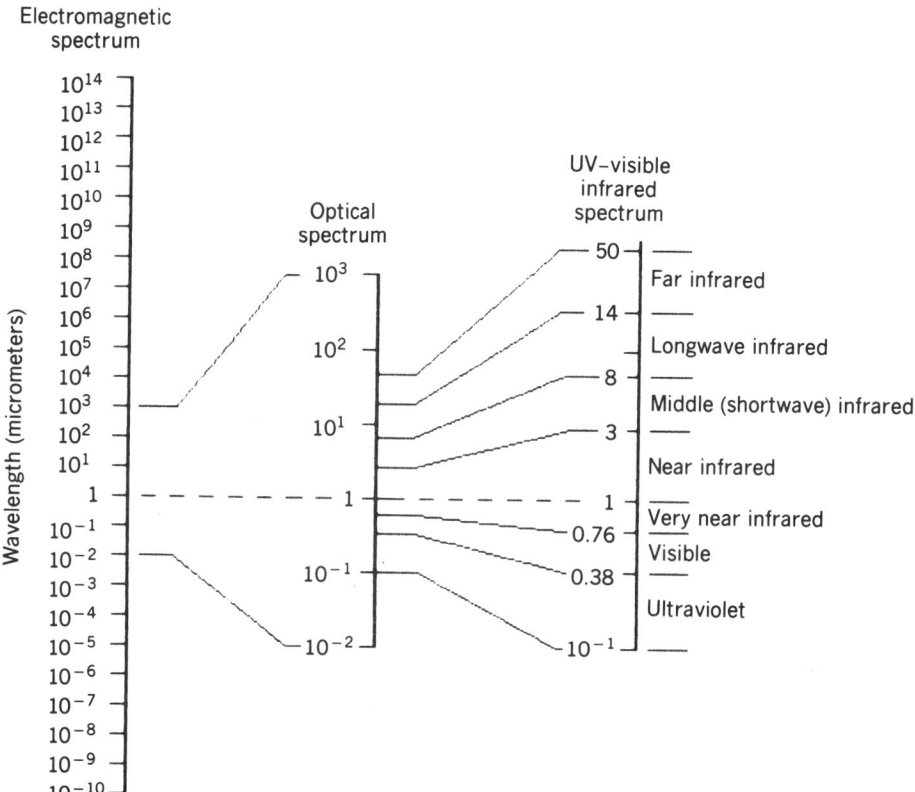

Figure 1. The electromagnetic spectrum, the optical spectrum, and the labeled regions in the optical spectrum (Pinson, 1984).

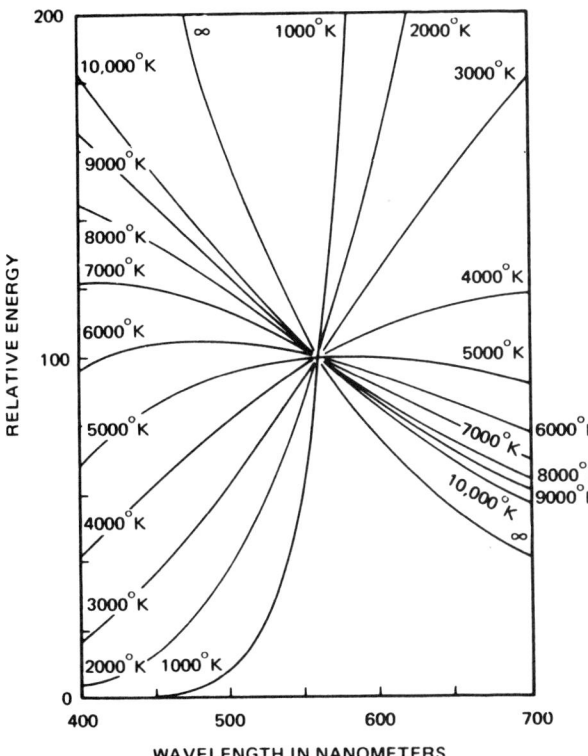

Figure 2. Relative spectral energy distribution curves for blackbodies of different temperatures (Hunter, 1975).

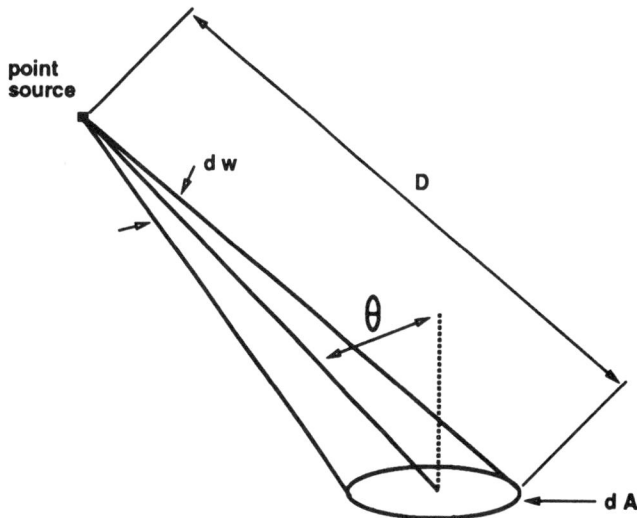

Figure 4. The emission geometry for single point source of light.

tal amount of flux dF that is radiated into a unit solid angle $d\omega$ is

$$I = \frac{dF}{d\omega}$$

which is measured in watts per steradian. The angle $d\omega$ subtends an area dA on the sensor's surface, and the incremental amount of photon flux incident on the area is

$$E = \frac{dF}{dA} = \frac{dF}{d\omega}\frac{d\omega}{dA} = \frac{I \cos \theta}{D^2}$$

where D denotes the distance from the point source to the sensor's surface and θ is the angle between the normal of the sensor's surface and the direction of the point source (Fig. 4).

An extended light source can be considered to be composed of many tiny point light sources distributed all over the surface of the extended source. The incident photon flux from an extended source on a point in a sensor's surface is thus the integration over all point light sources composing the extended source using the above equation. Such integration can be carried out over the whole surface of the optical sensor to generate a profile of the incident energy from the extended source.

It becomes extremely difficult to characterize analytically the incident energy distribution when possible secondary reflections and the attenuation and scattering of optical energy by the intervening medium are considered. If a sensor operates in a controlled environment, the attenuation and scattering of optical energy by the intervening medium can usually be neglected (such is not the case if the sensor operates over a long range or across the atmosphere). However, to follow the journey of every photon through all possible reflections in the environment is infeasible unless very few sources and reflecting objects are present. Conceptually, it is possible to imagine photon flux incident on the surface of a sensor from all directions through direct emission as well as through secondary reflection. Let $\phi(x, y, t, \lambda)$ denote the spatial energy distribution at spatial coordinates (x, y) at time t and at wavelength λ on the surface of a sensor.

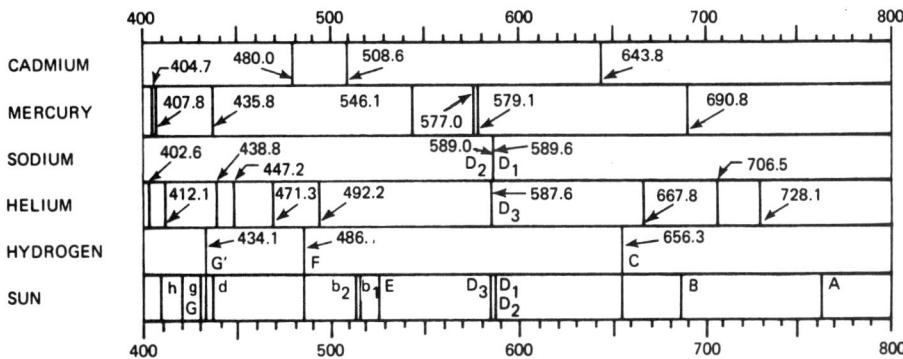

Figure 3. Spectral lines of certain gaseous sources (Hunter, 1975).

Different sensors respond differently to the incident optical energy ϕ. Similar to the way that a source is characterized by its efficiency in emitting optical energy across the optical spectrum, a sensor is characterized by its efficiency in detecting optical energy at different spectral bands. For example, a standard observer (ie, an average young healthy human) responds differently to the optical energy emitted in different spectral bands. The response differs under strong light (photopic response) and weak light (scotopic response). Photopic response is typical of daylight vision and scotopic response is typical of night vision. From Figure 5, which shows the photopic and scotopic responses of a standard observer, it is clear that the human eye response is more sensitive and shifts to shorter wavelengths at reduced levels of radiant energy. The photopic response represents the response of the cones in the eye, and the scotopic response is for the rods. The rods are more sensitive to light than the cones, which explains the eye's increased sensitivity at night. Color vision is a function of the cones so that the increased sensitivity of night vision lacks the ability to discriminate colors well.

Depending on the material and technology used in constructing an optical sensor, the sensor will respond differently to the incident optical energy in different spectral bands. The relative spectral luminous efficiency of a sensor is represented by $\Psi(\lambda)$, which ranges from 0 (no response) to 1 (full response). The perceptual brightness B at a point (x, y) on the sensor's surface at time t is thus

$$B = \int_0^\infty \phi(x, y, t, \lambda)\Psi(\lambda)d\lambda$$

An optical sensor then converts B into appropriate electrical signals by a suitable readout method.

Optical sensors can be classified into two general classes based on their design principles: quantum detectors and thermal detectors (Pinson, 1984). Figure 6 illustrates the fundamental design principle of quantum detectors. As the optical energy of the incident photons is transferred to the charge carriers, the charge carriers are alleviated from the valence band to the conduction band and made available for conduction. These free charge carriers thus change the electrical properties of the semiconductor material in a measurable way.

To alleviate a charge carrier into the conduction band requires a minimum energy (ie, $Q_c - Q_v$). Because photon

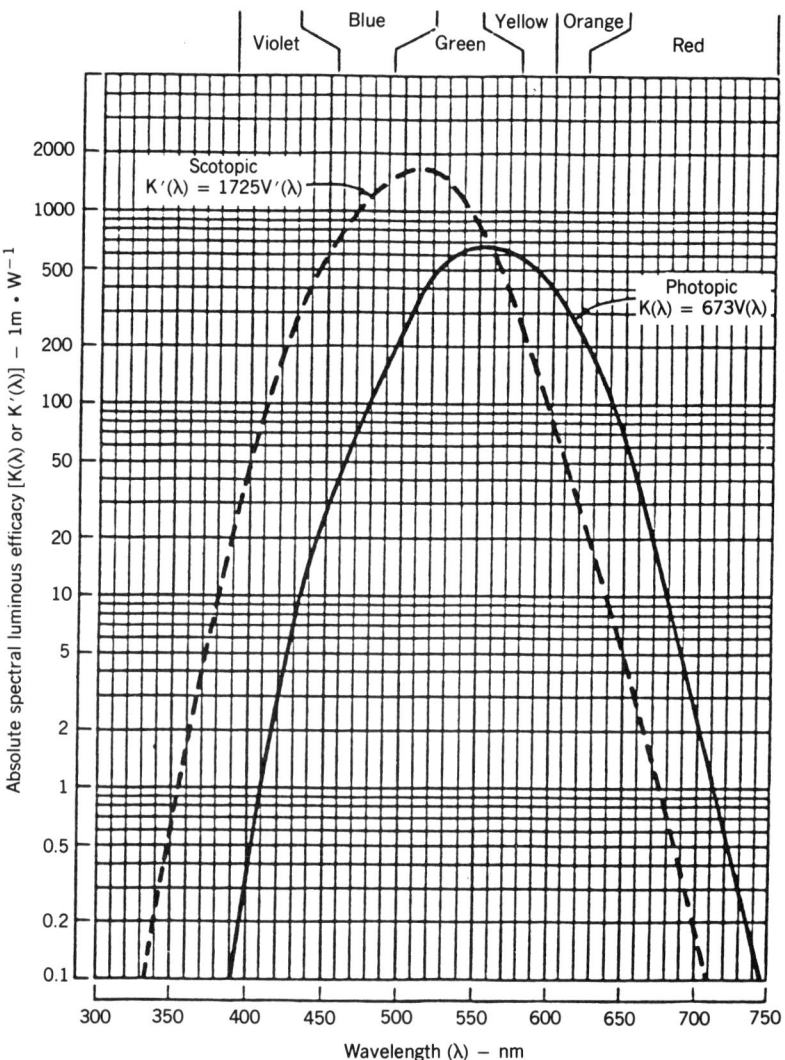

Figure 5. Spectral response curves for the human eye for photopic and scotopic vision (Pinson, 1984).

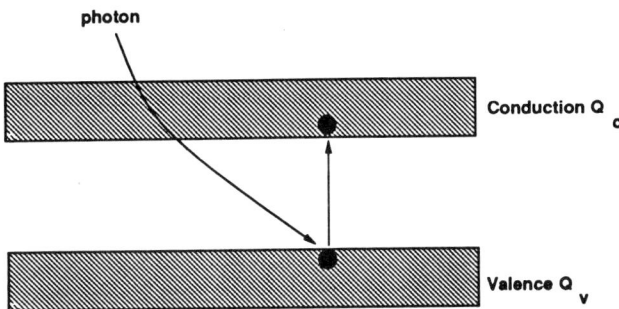

Figure 6. Fundamental principle of quantum detection.

energy is hc/λ, where h is Planck's constant and c is the speed of light, the wavelength $hc/(Q_c - Q_v)$ is the longest one to which a quantum detector will respond. The response to shorter wavelengths (higher energy photons) is limited by the ability of the detector material to stop and absorb photons. In general, absorption efficiency decreases as photon energy increases. Hence, a quantum detector will respond only to a relatively narrow range of wavelengths (ie, the Ψ-function has a narrow nonzero region).

In quantum detectors, the change of the electrical properties of the semiconductor material can be measured by a number of readout methods classified into photoemissive, photoconductive, photovoltaic, photojunction, and photon drag (Pinson, 1984). Photoemissive material has a propensity to release free electrons when excited by incident photons. Thus, detection consists of measuring the number of released electrons from the detector's surface. Photoconductive detection is based on the change of the conductance of a semiconductor material through the absorption of photons. An external bias voltage is applied across the detector, and the change in the amount of current flowing through the detector is measured.

Photons absorbed at a $p - n$ junction produce hole-electron pairs that change the junction barrier potential. Thus the change in the open-circuit output voltage of a $p - n$ junction is a measure of the optical radiation in photovoltaic detectors, which do not require an external bias voltage. The heating of a detector by current flowing through the detector is thus avoided.

Thermal detectors absorb photons or radiant energy over a relatively broad band of optical wavelengths. The absorbed energy causes a rise in the temperature of the detector material. The rising temperature affects the electrical properties of the material in a measurable way. For a thermistor, the resistance is temperature sensitive. The detector readout is thus measured as the voltage across a load resistor in series with the thermistor and a bias voltage. For a pyroelectric detector, the capacitance is temperature sensitive. Hence, a pyroelectric detector produces an output voltage that is proportional to the time rate of change of the temperature or

$$v = Ri = dq/dt = Ap\frac{dT}{dt}$$

where v denotes the voltage, i denotes the current, R denotes the load resistance, q denotes the stored charge on a pyroelectric detector, p denotes the pyroelectric coefficient, A denotes the surface area of the detector, T denotes the temperature, and t denotes the time.

The performance of an optical sensor is usually characterized by its responsivity, detectivity, time lag, and sensitivity to noise and temperature variation. Responsivity is a measure of the detector's ability to convert the incident optical energy into a measurable output parameter (typically volts or amperes). The responsivity R can be defined as

$$R = k\frac{\int_0^\infty \Phi(\lambda)\Psi(\lambda)d\lambda}{\int_0^\infty \Phi(\lambda)d\lambda}$$

where k is a conversion constant (eg, from photons/s to volts or amperes). It can be seen that the responsivity of a sensor is a function of the spectral luminous efficiency, which depends on the material and design principle of the sensor, as well as of the spectral energy distribution $\Phi(\lambda)$ of the energy source. Thus responsivity stated as a measurement for a particular detector must be accompanied by the source used for that measurement. Usually, a blackbody at a given temperature is used as the source for such measurements to establish a common ground for comparison.

The detectivity is defined as the inverse of the noise equivalent power, which is the level of the incident radiant energy that produces an output signal-to-noise ratio of unity. The limiting noise factor is typically thermal noise in thermal detectors and fluctuation in the number of charge carriers in quantum detectors. Because the noise equivalent power is a function of the wavelength and the operating temperature of the sensor, detectivity is also affected by these limiting factors.

The conversion of radiant flux to an electrical signal shows a time lag because of several limiting factors, such as the charge carrier lifetime, the transport time, the thermal capacitance, and the finite rise and fall times of the electronics. Finally, the performance of an optical detector is affected by the operating temperature of the detector. For thermal detectors, heat energy cannot be easily distinguished from the optically induced heat. Hence, cooling is required to reduce thermal noise. A detailed discussion and evaluation of sensor performance is available (Pinson, 1984).

Thermal Sensors

A thermal camera senses the irradiation of the environment in the infrared spectrum (for example, from 8 μm to 12 μm). The registered irradiation is then used to compute the temperature of the imaged radiating source using Planck's equation:

$$\int_{\lambda_1}^{\lambda_2}\frac{C_1}{\lambda^5(e^{C_2/\lambda T} - 1)}d\lambda = K_a L_t + K_b$$

where L_t is the thermal camera voltage output directly proportional to the net radiation absorbed by the detector. Furthermore, in the above model, the secondary reflection from sources and other scene objects are neglected; hence, registered irradiation in the 8–12 μm is primarily from the direction emission by the imaged object. K_a and K_b are calibrated by imaging at least two objects of known thermal properties (ie, the emissivity and temperature).

Thermal sensors can also be designed by emulating the human sense of touch. Russel (1985) introduced such a method to provide tactile feedback using a sensed material's thermal property. Basically, the blood supply heats the fingers above room temperature. Contact with an object causes heat to be conducted from the finger to the object at a rate depending on the material property of the object. The skin's resulting temperature drop provides information on the material's thermal properties.

The sensor is constructed with a source of heat (a power transistor), a layer of elastic material of known thermal conductivity to couple the heat source to the touched object (silicone rubber), and a temperature transducer to measure the contact-point temperature. Successful qualitative discrimination between aluminum, wax, cork, and polystyrene foam has been reported. As expected, aluminum feels cold because of a large temperature drop through heat conduction. Paraffin wax, cork, and plastic foam feel progressively warmer due to a small heat conduction.

Tactile Sensors

Tactile sensing is a relatively new sensing mechanism that obtains surface measurements by making physical contact. Tactile feedback is important in object grasping and manipulation and can be used to adjust grasping forces to prevent slippage. Tactile sensors can also be used to locate the corners and edges of an object, which are usually feasible grasping locations.

Contact force induces a change in material properties that affects sensor readings. For example, the resistance of piezoresistive material, such as thick-film polymer (Tise, 1988), varies as a function of the mechanical load. The thick-film polymer has been used to construct a force sensing resistor (FSR) in a voltage divider circuit (Tise, 1988). The output voltage (V_{out}) of the divider circuitry is related to the applied force F by a simple formula:

$$V_{out} = \frac{V_{EE} R_{FSR}}{R_{FSR} + R_{fixed}} = \frac{V_{EE} k F^{-1}}{k F^{-1} + R_{fixed}}$$

where V_{EE} is the applied voltage to the voltage divider circuitry, and R_{FSR} and R_{fixed} are the resistance (in ohms) of the force sensing resistor and the fixed by-pass resistor, respectively. For typical piezoresistive material, k is approximately $8.98 \times 10^6 \, \Omega \cdot lb$.

A prototype sensor is constructed using force sensing resistors in VLSI fabrication. The sensing area is 0.5×0.5 in. with a 16×16 (or 0.031 in.) spatial resolution. The overall package measures $0.8 \times 0.8 \times 0.25$ in., which is small enough to be located on a fingertip. It has been reported that the sensor is sensitive at low loads yet is still useful for large loads.

Hillis (1982) designed a high resolution tactile sensor. The sensor uses two layers of conductive material to form a cross-bar architecture with pressure sensors built at junctions. One of the layers is made of anisotropically conductive silicone rubber (ACS), which conducts only along one axis in the plane of a sheet. The other layer is a printed circuit board etched to conduct perpendicularly to the ACS layer. A separator is inserted between these two layers to pull the conducting layers apart when pressure is released. When pressure is applied, the conductive rubber presses through the separator. The area of contact and the contact resistance vary with the applied pressure. The sensor array can be scanned by applying a voltage to one column at a time. The output voltage of a divider circuitry is used to estimate the contact resistance and the contact force.

An experimental tactile sensor design that uses optical fibers, a type of dielectric waveguide, has been presented (Winger and Lee, 1988). These waveguides channel light energy by trapping it between layers of dielectric materials. In an ideal straight fiber, light propagates in a finite number of modes (ray paths) with virtually no energy loss. If force is applied to bend a fiber, such modes are lost in the bent section. A light ray trapped in the bent fiber must radiate part of its energy. The amount of energy lost depends on fiber parameters as well as on the radius of curvature and the spatial frequency of the bend. Such energy loss is detected by a sensing circuitry placed at the end of the optic fiber. Fibers of graded index, multimodes, and profiles that are approximately parabolic have been used because they are much more sensitive to microbending. Experiments have been conducted to study the relationship between bending and energy loss. It has been reported that for deflections up to 0.102 mm (0.004 in.), the sensor output exhibits unrepeatable, nonlinear behavior; for larger deflections, it has been observed that light attenuation is proportional to the bending in a linear manner (Winger and Lee, 1988).

Other principles in designing tactile sensors include VLSI fabrication (Raibert and Tanner, 1982) capacitive sensing (Fearing, 1987), and strain–stress tensor analysis (Fearing and Hollerbach, 1984). Raibert and Tanner (1982) reported a tactile sensor using a pressure sensitive VLSI design similar to that of Hillis (1982). Sensors were placed under windows in the overglass (an insulating layer of SiO_2 normally placed on integrated circuits for protection). Simple computing elements were placed in the VLSI chip, where no windows were present, to allow parallel filtering and convolution with programmable masks. Fearing (1987) used a design where the voltage across variable-distance capacitor plates was related to the applied force, which altered the spacing between plates. Fearing and Hollerbach (1984) conducted an analysis using solid mechanics models and contact theory for tactile sensing.

Radars and Ladars

Radar is an active sensing device for target detection and ranging. It has become an indispensable tool in modern warfare and in many civilian applications, such as commercial aircraft traffic control, communication satellite location, and speed monitoring on highways. Radar has two primary functions: detecting and tracking targets. To detect the presence of moving targets in a region surrounding a radar site, a continuous-wave system or a pulse system may be used. A continuous-wave radar employs a high-power oscillator. Detection is accomplished by means of a bank of Doppler filters matched to all possible radial target velocities (DiFranco and Rubin, 1980). Stationary targets (or very slow-moving targets) cannot be detected, because their reflected signals show little or no Doppler shift in the frequency domain.

A pulse system permits the detection of stationary (or very slow-moving) targets. In a pulse radar system, pulses of energy are transmitted. The transmitted energy waves bounce off objects in the environment and the returned echos are detected by the radar. The time-of-flight principle is used to detect the reflecting object's range:

$$v\Delta t = 2D$$

where v is the speed of signal propagation, Δt is the time between when the signal is transmitted and the echo is received, and D is the distance between the sensor and the reflecting object. The radar pulse can be shaped like a wedge (such as the fan beam used in a ground surveillance radar) or like a narrowly focused cone (a pencil beam). The aiming direction of a radar can be mechanically steered to cover a wide range.

The detection range of a pulse system is limited by the energy of the transmitted signal, the gains of the transmitter and receiver, the background noise, the effective size of the reflecting object, and the noise in the electrical components. A good approximation of the maximum range R at which a radar can successfully detect or track a target is provided by the classic radar range equation (Bachman, 1982)

$$R = \left[\frac{EG_t G_r \lambda^2 \sigma_t F^4}{(4\pi)^3 (S/N) KT_{Nl} L}\right]^{1/4}$$

where E is transmitted waveform energy; G_t and G_r are the power gains of the transmitter and receiver, respectively; λ is the wavelength; σ_t is the effective cross section of the target; and K is Boltzmann constant (1.38×10^{-23} J/K). L is the total radar loss that takes into account loss in the transmitter and receiver circuitry and loss due to weather conditions. The propagation factor F represents the actual electrical field strength existing at the target divided by that which would exist if only direct-path radiation were present. F has a typical range of values from 0 to about 2, with values greater than 2 possible but rare (Bachman, 1982). Basically, the F model takes into consideration possible earth reflection and atmospheric refraction. S/N is the minimum ratio of waveform energy to noise-power density that provides the specified probability of detection. Such a probability of detection, in turn, depends on a number of other factors.

Once the presence of targets is established, a radar can be used to measure target range, direction, velocity, and size. Furthermore, these capabilities are available under conditions that normally impair optical vision, such as night, rain, fog, smoke, snow, and clouds. The measurement capabilities of a radar are hampered at low frequencies (less than 100 MHz) by restrictions on antenna aperture size and at high frequencies (greater than 15,000 MHz) by attenuation (DiFranco and Rubin, 1980). Hence, traditional radar technology has achieved its greatest growth in the microwave spectrum. Information about radar technology is available (Bachman, 1979, 1982; DiFranco and Rubin, 1980; Farina and Studer, 1985).

With the invention of laser, radar technology readily extends to the optical portion of the electromagnetic spectrum. Laser radar is a radar system operating in the optical spectrum. Due to its short wavelength, laser radar can be pinpointed to a very narrow field of view. Thus details of targets in the scene can be discerned, and the Doppler shifts in the returned signal allow the measurement of the velocity of moving objects. Laser radar overcomes the disadvantage of poor resolution in conventional microwave band radar systems. In recent years, the available power from laser devices and the capacity of detectors have been greatly improved. This makes laser radar feasible for many kinds of ground-to-ground sensing applications.

Range Sensors

Range sensors collect three-dimensional distance information from the surfaces of imaged objects. Such sensors can be designed based on a wide variety of principles, which are loosely classified into six categories (Table 1). The taxonomy is based on the sensing techniques, which may be either passive or active, and the sensing configurations, which may be monocular, binocular, or more complicated than binocular.

Passive range sensors compute range information from ambient light reflection while active sensors usually employ an energy source of some kind to actively probe the environment. In general, passive sensors have a wider range of applicability because they do not use an artificial energy source. However, the freedom of using an artificial source to manipulate the sensing configuration can greatly facilitate the computation of range information and provides more accurate range readings than those obtained in passive methods. In fact, some passive range detection methods do not provide quantitative range information of the imaged objects. Such is the case with shape from occlusion, which only indicates that more "complete" (or less occluded) objects are usually nearer to the viewer. Some passive techniques provide an orienta-

Table 1. Range Sensor Design Principles

Configuration	Passive	Active
Monocular	Shape from X (shading, texture, gradient, occlusion, line drawing, etc), lens focusing	Time of flight, amplitude, modulation, phase modulation
Binocular	Stereopsis	Structured light, moire, holographic interferometry
Others	Motion analysis, optical flow	

tion map (eg, shape from shading and shape from texture gradient) instead of a range map. Relative depth (or the structure) of the imaged surfaces can be computed by integrating the orientation map; however, the absolute distance of the surface to the viewer cannot be determined. Such descriptions are usually called the $2\frac{1}{2} - D$ (two and a half dimensions) descriptions (Marr, 1982).

In a monocular sensing configuration, the source (if used) and the detector assume coaxial positions, whereas in a binocular sensing configuration, the detectors or the source-detector pairs are separated by a nonzero baseline. Multiple viewing positions can occur if the sensors and the imaged objects move relative to each other. In general, binocular techniques suffer from a potential problem of missing parts. That is, the description of the portion of the imaged surfaces, which are not visible in either view, cannot be inferred. Monocular sensors are not subject to this malady.

Passive monocular ranging techniques are mostly shape-from-X techniques. It is well documented in the psychological literature that humans use a great variety of depth cues to perceive the three dimensionality embedded in a single image frame. For instance, shape-from-shading techniques infer the shape of a three-dimensional surface by exploiting the photometric constraints imposed by the image formation process (Barrow and Tenenbaum, 1981; Brady, 1982). The change in the size and appearance of surface markings (ie, texture) has also been used to infer surface orientation.

Passive binocular techniques (or stereopsis) emulate the human visual perception in computing depth. Two image frames, separated by a nonzero baseline of length B, are used to record the scene (Fig. 7). A point $P(X,Y,Z)$ in space projects onto P_r and P_l in the right and left image frames, respectively. The discrepancy in the projected locations of P_r and P_l is usually called the disparity, $d = |P_l - P_r|$. It can be shown (Barnard and Fishler, 1982) that the disparity d is related to the depth Z of the point P by

$$Z = \frac{fB}{d}$$

where f is the focal length of the imaging system. Stereo analysis is accomplished by extracting features from both left and right images, matching features to establish their correspondence, computing depth according to the above equation, and, finally, interpolating feature positions in space to obtain a surface description.

When the imaging system and the imaged objects move relative to each other (eg, a camera is mounted on a mobile platform to explore an unknown environment), a sequence of changing descriptions results. The goal is to recover not only the range map at each viewing position, but also the motion of the object and camera, or both, between image frames. Many motion analysis and flow analysis techniques have been developed to compute range information from a sequence of image frames (Cappellini and Marconi, 1987; Huang, 1981, 1983, 1987; Martin and Aggarwal, 1988). Most of the reported approaches follow these steps: (1) compute the observables in the images and (2) relate these observables to the object structure and motion in space. Various observables have been considered: points, lines, and optical flow.

In principle, the observation of a number of points in two or more image frames yields the position of these points in space and the relative displacement between the vantage locations. The consensus is that the observation of five points in two views yields both structure and motion. Tsai and Huang (1984) prove that seven points in a general configuration are required to obtain a linear formulation in solving the structure and motion parameters. Optical flow is the field of instantaneous apparent velocities of points on the surfaces of moving objects in space, which can be used to recover the relative depth of points.

Active monocular range sensors can be based on three possible principles: time of flight, amplitude modulation, and phase modulation. It is well known that bats and porpoises navigate by emitting ultrasonic waves and detecting echos from the transmitted waves. The basic equation of the time-of-flight technique (which is the same as that used in radars) is $v\Delta t = 2D$.

Instead of sending out a short pulse, waiting for an echo, and measuring the transit time, it is also possible to send out continuous waves that are modulated in either the amplitude or the phase. Nitzan and co-workers (1977) described such a system based on amplitude modulation. A laser beam was split into a reference beam and an object beam. The object beam was used to probe three-dimensional objects in the environment. Due to the different path lengths these two laser beams traveled, a phase difference (ψ) resulted. Nitzan and co-workers showed that the phase difference is related to the extra optical path traveled by the object beam

$$\psi = \omega_{AM} 2D/c$$

where ω_{AM} is the modulation frequency, D is the distance from the sensor to the reflecting object, and c is the speed of light. The continuous waves can also be modulated in the phase angle; the reflected signal is then mixed with

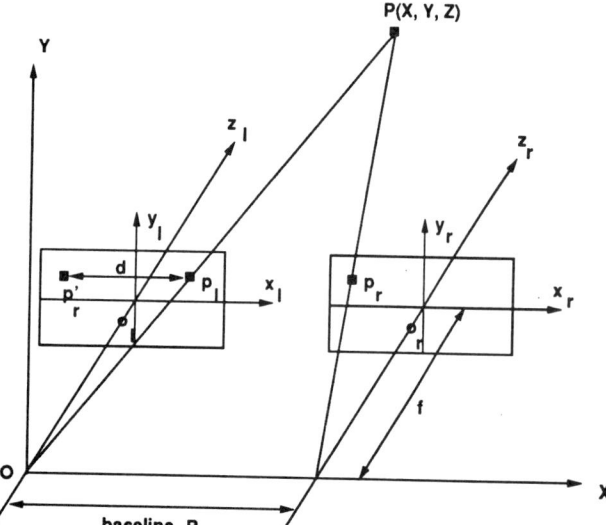

Figure 7. The configuration of a passive binocular imaging system.

the reference signal to create a frequency that depends on the range to the reflecting object (Besl, 1989).

Active binocular techniques use the same triangulation principle to compute depth as that used in stereopsis. Instead of using a pair of passive detectors, one of the detectors is replaced by an energy source (laser, infrared led, slide projector, etc). The energy source projects a light pattern to encode the objects in the scene for analysis. If the relative position of the sensor and the emitting source has been calibrated, the depth of the illuminated object surface can be inferred from the positions of the emitted pattern and the perceived pattern through triangulation. Various patterns have been used, such as a single point, multiple points, a single line, multiple lines, a cross pattern, a circle, and a grid pattern (Besl, 1989). In general, to obtain a dense depth map, the scene objects are scanned or the sensor is scanned if a simple pattern is used. A complicated pattern (such as a grid) does not need scanning; however, it is more difficult to establish the correspondence relationship between the projected and the perceived patterns (Aggarwal and Wang, 1988; Besl, 1989; Wang and Aggarwal, 1988).

Both moire technology and holographic interferometry are based on the interference of waves. In moire techniques, an amplitude-modulated pattern is projected onto the scene, and the reflected pattern is viewed through another amplitude-modulated grating positioned in front of the recording camera. The output signal is thus the multiplication of these two waveforms:

$$A(x) = A_o(1 + m_o \cos(\omega_o x + \phi_o(x))) \cdot A_c(1 + m_c \cos(\omega_c x + \phi_c(x)))$$

where A_o represents the object waveform and A_c represents the camera grating. The recorded signal consists of four spatial frequency components of frequency $\omega_o - \omega_c$, ω_o, ω_c, and $\omega_o + \omega_c$. By passing the recorded signal through a low pass filter to remove frequencies above $\omega_o - \omega_c$, the a phase difference term $\phi_o(x) - \phi_c(x)$ can be extracted. Such phase difference encodes the distance information.

SENSOR DATA FUSION

Many types of sensor may be used to gather information on the surrounding environment, for example, visual sensors, visual sensors augmented with structured lighting, thermal (infrared) sensors, proximity sensors, tactile sensors, ultrasonic range finders, and laser range finders. It should be noted that different sensors possess distinct characteristics, are designed based on differing physical principles, operate in a wide range of the electromagnetic spectrum, and are geared toward a variety of applications. A single sensor operating alone provides a limited sensing range and is inherently unreliable due to operational errors. However, a synergistic operation of many sensors provides a rich body of information on the sensed environment from a wide range of the electromagnetic spectrum.

Research on fusing data from a multitude of sensors has started to gain attention for the following reasons:

- Much effort has been expended to study the design and operation of visual, acoustic, laser ranging, infrared, and tactile sensors; the analysis of visual (Barrow and Tanenbaum, 1981; Brady, 1982), acoustic (Borenstein and Koren, 1988; Jarvis, 1983), laser ranging (Besl and Jain, 1985; Jarvis, 1983), infrared (Burton and Benning, 1981; Nandhakumar and Aggarwal, 1987, 1988), and tactile (Cameron and coworkers, 1988; Fearing and Hollerbach, 1984; Fearing, 1987; Hillis, 1982; Tise, 1988) sensor's images provides a better understanding of the strengths and limitations of these sensors and facilitates their integration.

- Due to significant advances in sensing, storing, and processing technologies, the acquisition and storage of large amounts of data from multiple sensors are becoming feasible.

- The quest for industrial automation provides the thrust to develop intelligent autonomous robots that replace humans in many assembly and manufacturing tasks. An intelligent robot often operates in an unstructured environment; therefore, it must react to sudden, unexpected events and changes in the environment. To achieve a desirable degree of autonomy and to be able to make intelligent decisions, it is crucial that a robot understand and react to the environment; sensors provide the basic means to accomplish such interactions.

Fusing sensor data involves more than choosing the right sensors and averaging sensor output. As has been pointed out (Brady, 1988), the simple averaging of sensor measurements is prone to distortion by individual noisy measurements and makes the overall variance of measurements worse. Furthermore, sensor data may be used in such a way that data from one sensor guide the operation and exploration of another sensor. Such is the case in using a visual sensor with a tactile sensor (Allen, 1988; Allen and Bajcsy, 1986; Allen and Michelman, 1989; Stansfield, 1988) and in intensity guided range sensing (Aggarwal and Magee, 1986). As mentioned before, the key issue in tactile sensing is that blind groping on a surface with a tactile sensor is a poor and inefficient way to understand three-dimensional structure. Touch must be guided, and vision data provide guidance to an active tactile sensor. To improve the efficiency in gathering range data, intensity images may be analyzed first to locate corners, edges, and regions with large variations in the perceived depth. Range data are then acquired for a much smaller set of image points (Aggarwal and Magee, 1986) to speed up the data acquisition process.

The following sections present a brief survey of the techniques and systems for multisensor data fusion. The survey covers techniques for fusing data from a variety of sensors and several general frameworks for sensor data fusion.

Thermal and Visual Sensing

Traditionally, thermal images have been used in many military applications for target detection and in civilian applications for home energy audits, fault detection in components, and medical diagnoses. Most existing techniques for analyzing thermal images rely on statistical pattern recognition techniques with features that are computed directly from image pixel values (Burton and Benning, 1981; Kim and co-workers, 1984; Sevigny and co-workers, 1983). The techniques are simple and straightforward; however, the performance is sensitive to scene radiance, occlusion, and viewing direction. It is desirable to establish a correct mathematical model of thermal sensing.

A new technique has been proposed to integrate information from both thermal (infrared) and visual images (Nandhakumar and Aggarwal, 1987, 1988). A model for thermal sensing in outdoor environments under bright sunlight was developed, and extensive calibration and experiments were conducted to verify the correctness of the model. As was pointed out, temperature alone is not a good indicator for the region classification (under the sun, everything feels hot). Instead, for classification the ratio between the heat fluxes conducted from an imaged surface to the interior of the object to the total absorbed heat fluxes (W_{cd}/W_{abs}) was used. Concrete walls, brick walls, pavements, cars, and vegetation all have quite distinct W_{cd}/W_{abs} ratios (Nandhakumar and Aggarwal, 1988).

It was observed that under thermal equilibrium, the total heat fluxes absorbed by a surface (W_{abs}) equals those lost to the environment. Heat fluxes might leave a surface in three possible ways: through radiation, convection, and conduction,

$$W_{abs} = W_{cd} + W_{cv} + W_{rad}$$

Radiation and convection heat transfer depend on the difference between the surface temperature and the temperature of the environment, as well as on the emissivity and the convection heat transfer coefficient of the imaged surface, which can be estimated empirically. The temperature of an imaged surface is reported by the thermal sensor and is used to compute W_{cv} and W_{rad}. Hence, if W_{abs} can be estimated, W_{cd} and W_{cd}/W_{abs} can be computed from the above equation to classify imaged surfaces.

The total absorbed heat fluxes W_{abs} are determined by the solar absorptivity of the surface (α_s) and by the orientation of the surface toward the sun (θ_i). Information on α_s and θ_i is not readily available from a thermal image. However, many shape-from techniques have been developed in computer vision research to compute the surface orientation from visual images (Aggarwal and Chien, 1989; Barrow and Tanenbaum, 1981; Brady, 1982). A simple shape-from-shading technique was used to estimate θ_i (Nandhakumar and Aggarwal, 1987, 1988). Assuming that the viewed surface is opaque and Lambertian, a simple reflection model is constructed that relates the perceived brightness to the incident angle θ_i and to the reflectivity of the surface $\rho (= 1 - \alpha_s)$:

$$L_v = K_\rho \cos \theta_i + C_v = \rho K_v \cos \theta_i + C_v$$

where L_v is the digitized value of the intensity of the visual image, and K_v and C_v are the overall gain and offset of the visual imaging system given through calibration.

For each image region, the θ_i of one pixel is computed from either stereopsis or other shape-from techniques. This angle is used to compute the solar absorptivity of the whole surface. Once the solar absorptivity of the surface is known, the orientation of the remaining pixels can be estimated. Nandhakumar and Aggarwal (1987, 1988) reported experimental results using the W_{cd}/W_{abs} ratio to classify outdoor scenes with cars, pavement, buildings, and vegetation.

Tactile and Visual Sensing

Allen (1988) and Allen and Bajcsy (1986) reported a method for combining stereo vision with touch sensing. Visual sensing is used to construct low and medium level descriptions to guide further tactile exploration. It was pointed out that stereo vision cannot handle many candidate match points, is unable to match horizontally oriented zero-crossings, and is subject to image quantization error. Hence, the best that can be expected from stereopsis is a sparse set of matched points on the contours of regions isolated from visual sensing. It was suggested that touch sensing could be used to collect data on objects where no stereo analysis is performed or where views are occluded in visual images.

Visual images were analyzed by stereo matching using zero-crossings as features (Allen, 1988; Allen and Bajcsy, 1986). Epipolar constraint is used to limit the search for matching zero-crossing pairs. To eliminate multiple matches, the sign and orientation of matches zero crossings need to be consistent. Furthermore, local neighborhoods around matched zero crossings need to show a good pattern correlation. The experimental objects are common kitchen items such as mugs, plates, bowls, pitchers, and utensils homogeneous in color with no discernible textures. The lack of surface detail on the test object limits the number of features that can be used in the stereo matching process. Hence, stereo vision provides only sparse depth measurements of points along contours.

To build a more accurate surface description, a multilevel Coon's patch description is constructed by specifying positions, tangents in each of the parametric directions, and the twist vectors (cross derivatives) of the surface patch at knot points. A stereo depth map provides information to construct a level 0 description using a 2 × 2 rectangular knot set located on the surface boundary. To refine the description, more knot points are needed. Positions, tangents, and twist vectors at new knot points are obtained by a tactile sensor. The tactile sensor traces in the direction of the midpoints of the level 0 boundary curves using the surface contacts from the tactile sensor to control the robot arm motion. The level 1 surface is then formed by adding tactile traces onto the level 0 surface constructed from the vision. The level 2 surface is formed by adding tactile traces to each of the four patches defined by the level 1 surface. Hence, a hierarchical surface description is constructed using this successive refinement process.

Stansfield (1988) proposed another method for combining vision and touch. He studied a vision–guide–touch strategy similar to Allen (1988) and Allen and Bajcsy (1986). His method involved first performing a stereo analysis on edge pixels along contours and simple region segmentation based on thresholding and grouping. A tactile sensor was used to further exploit the properties of the edges and regions detected in the visual images.

The tactile sensor detected several simple haptic primitives. Seven haptic primitives for touch sensing were suggested: elasticity, compliance, roughness, the normal contact position of a surface, and three types of contact (point, edge, and extended). For example, the compliance of a surface could be measured by first bringing the tactile sensor into contact with the surface, next applying successively greater forces, and finally recording the position of the sensed surface under different external pressures. The greater the deformation, the higher the compliance measurement. Elasticity could be measured by pushing the surface at the contact point, releasing the pressure, and observing whether the surface bounces back to its original shape. The normal contact position was established by groping the surface from many different directions and measuring the contact area. Because the sensor has a planar shape, when the maximum area is attained, the sensor is approximately tangent to the surface, and the surface normal direction could be estimated. Contacts were classified into extended, point, and edge contacts, depending on their shape and size. Simple routines (called specialists) were implemented for these haptic primitives, which form the lowest level of the tactile perceptual system.

Several knowledge-based modules were designed that employ the specialists to determine surface shape, part (small shape), contour, edge, and corner. For example, the edge expert does simple active edge following. It is triggered by an edge contact reported by the low level specialists. Once triggered, the edge expert is primarily data driven by keeping contact with the object edge and by determining whether it has encountered more edge contacts. The contour expert is triggered by the detection of an edge contact. It invokes the edge expert to follow the edge until an edge termination condition is met. The contour expert may then signal a closed contour or invoke a corner expert for corner detection.

An object is divided into components. Each component is further divided into a set of features (surface patch, contour, and part). Visual sensing provides a rough segmentation and localization of features. The active stage explores each of the visible components from several different views (top, front, left, and right). Various haptic specialists and knowledge-based modules are used to measure the material properties and the shape of the contact surface. Information is stored in a set of feature frames generated for the object. Sensor fusion occurs at the beginning of the exploration, when visual data are used to determine how active touch exploration is to proceed, and at the intermediate levels, when visual information is used for the motor guidance of the arm–sensor system during its active feature extraction.

Ladar and Visual Sensing

Chu and co-workers (1988) developed a method for segmenting outdoor scenes using ladar range and ladar intensity data. The goal was to separate man-made objects from the background. It was observed that in an intensity image, background regions show large degrees of intensity variation whereas regions representing man-made objects are relatively smooth. In a range image, man-made objects with clearly defined structures usually have smooth variations in depth; such is not true with natural objects, eg, bushes and trees. An intensity image was segmented into regions based on the mean and standard deviation of pixel intensities. An input image was smoothed and convolved with a Laplacian operator. A threshold was selected so that points of relatively low values in the convolved image were labeled and grouped into segments. To compute the deviation of image intensities, the difference image between the smoothed image and the original input image was found. The mean and standard deviation of pixel values of the difference image were computed. Pixels were grouped if they were adjacent and their intensities fell in a small range. A man-made object was located in a range image if it had a significant area (more than a fixed percent of the image area) and could be approximated by a planar surface patch within a reasonable error threshold. The segmentation maps from intensity and range images were intersected to generate a combined result.

Chu and co-workers (1989) subsequently developed a knowledge-based system to assign semantic meanings to the segmented regions located in their 1988 paper. The goal was to identify military vehicles in a natural scene. A rule-based strategy was used to interpret segmented regions. Knowledge from both input images and the specific application domain (ie, outdoor scene analysis) was used to construct rules. Knowledge extracted from input images included numerical parameters, such as region size, contour length, surface fitting result, mean and deviation of pixel intensity values, etc, and neighborhood relationships. Domain-dependent knowledge included target dimension and shape and commonsense knowledge about the outdoor environs. Rules were applied in a fixed order. Low level attributes obtained through the segmentation process were used to determine whether a region represents man-made objects or background. The neighborhood relationship of regions was examined to group regions into objects. The attributes of objects were computed and objects were classified. For example, a typical rule stated that if a region were classified as representing man-made objects, had a size no wider than 4 m and no taller than 2 m, and had a small surface fitting error, then it was determined with high confidence that the region might be a jeep.

Range and Visual Sensing

An algorithm has been introduced for inferring the surface structure of three-dimensional (3-D) objects from multiple viewing directions using the integration of structured light and visual sensing (Wang and Aggarwal, 1987, 1989). Construction of the surface description of a 3-D object was decomposed into two stages: (*1*) the surface orientation and partial structure were first inferred from a set of single views using structured light sensing, and (*2*) the surface structures inferred from different viewpoints were integrated to complete the 3-D description using both the structured light and visual sensing. In the first stage, an active structured light technique was used to recover the visible surface orientation and partial structure. The structured light technique projected a spatially modulated pattern (eg, a rectangular grid pattern) to encode object surfaces for analysis. When a regular grid pattern was projected onto an object surface, the perceived pattern showed many forms of distortion. Intuitively speaking, the way the pattern was distorted was affected by the imaged surface structure. A constraint satisfaction algorithm was developed that used the orientation of the perceived pattern to infer the visible surface orientation using the following equations:

$$A \sin \Psi_o + B \sin \Theta_o \cos \Psi_o = 0$$
$$C \cos \Theta_o \cos \Psi_o + D \sin \Theta_o \cos \Psi_o + E \sin \Psi_o = 0$$

where Θ_o and Ψ_o are the pan and elevation angles of the surface normal vector. A, B, C, D, and E are functions of (ρ_1, ρ_2), which are the image orientations of the two stripes in the projected grid pattern. The visible surface structure was recovered by integrating the orientation map inferred from the structured light.

To integrate the surface structure from multiple viewpoints, two sources of information were used, namely the occluding contours extracted from the visual images and the surface structure inferred from the structured light. Occluding contours or silhouettes could be readily obtained by a simple thresholding operation on intensity images. They present an estimate of the projective range of the surface structures. The bounding volume description of the object was constructed by intersecting the occluding contours from multiple viewing directions in space. The bounding volume description presented a first approximation to the true object surface structure.

As mentioned earlier, a structured light technique was used to infer the detailed surface structure from multiple viewpoints, and the inferred structure presented strong surface constraints. This structure was used to further refine the 3-D surface description. To position such a partial structure with respect to the bounding volume, its position along the line of sight must be determined. It can be shown that unique positions exist to place a structure without violating the geometrical constraints imposed by the occluding contours and the bounding volume. Intuitively speaking, a partial surface structure cannot be positioned outside the bounding volume. Otherwise, its projection along a certain viewing direction will be outside the region delineated by the silhouette of the object in that particular direction. Furthermore, when positioning a partial surface structure against the bounding volume, extremal points exit on the structure that must make contact with the bounding volume. Such contact relations uniquely determine the position of a partial structure with respect to the bounding volume.

General Sensor Data Fusion Schemes

In this section, several algorithms and systems that were designed for the general purpose of manipulating and interpreting data from multiple sensors are presented. Grimson and Lozano-Perez (1980) presented a technique for locating and recognizing partially occluded objects using data gathered from a variety of sensing modules including sonar, laser, tactile, and visual sensors. It was assumed that the object to be recognized could be modeled as a set of planar faces. Only sparse surface position and orientation measurements were available, and these measurements could be from many different sensors.

The essence of the recognition process was to construct a tree of interpretations. Each level of the tree corresponded to a measured planar patch from sensor data. Each node had the same number of fan outs as the number of faces in the model. Each leaf node was an interpretation, which consisted of pairing every sensed patch with a model surface. If there were m sensed patches and n faces in the model, then a tree of interpretations had m levels, with n^m nodes at the leaf level. To efficiently find the correct interpretation from the n^m possibilities, it was important to prune infeasible interpretations as soon as they were identified.

Pruning was achieved by testing the consistency of various inner product measurements that are coordinate independent. For example, suppose two sensed patches P_i and P_j are matched with two model faces P_k and P_l, then the inner product of the two sensed surface normals (ie, $n_i \cdot n_j$) should be similar to the inner product of the two model surface normals (ie, $n_k \cdot n_l$). If the two products do not agree, then no interpretation that assigns those patches to these model faces must be considered. This corresponds to pruning the entire subtree below the considered node.

If occlusion is allowed, extraneous points and surface patches that may not correspond to any model points and faces might be presented in the sensor data. One more branch that represents the possibility of discarding the sensed patch, called the null face, is included. Furthermore, when traversing the tree of interpretations, the length of the current longest match is kept. At any node in the tree, a null face interpretation is allowed only if the sum of the number of nonnull faces in the partial match and the number of remaining data points is at least as large as that of the longest match. In this way, a path that contains many null (but still consistent) interpretations is not futilely explored.

Ayache and Faugeras (1988) presented a method for fusing multiple 3-D descriptions from stereo data taken at different positions. Sensor data were gathered by a pair of stereo cameras positioned on a mobile platform. Stereo data were first analyzed to build a 3-D local map. Local maps constructed at different locations were registered to provide a better estimate of the movement of the mobile platform between various viewpoint positions. Finally, the estimated movements of the mobile robot were used to further reduce the positional uncertainty of the geometric primitives found in local maps. The extended Kalman filtering was suggested for building, registering, and updating visual maps.

It was pointed out that the tasks of building, registering, and updating visual maps could be put into a common abstract framework that optimizes a certain parameter based on a certain observation. For example, in a stereo reconstruction process, the observation is the location of a feature in the pair of stereo images, and the parameter to be estimated is the 3-D position of the observed feature. In fusing local 3-D maps from different locations, the observation is the 3-D location of a feature from different viewpoints, and the parameters are the translation and rotation between viewpoints. Finally, to update the description of the geometry and the uncertainty of a particular feature visible from a certain viewpoint F_i (a parameter), the feature position from another viewpoint, say F_j, and the translation and rotation between F_i and F_j are used as the observations. In all these tasks, the observation ($\mathbf{x}$) is corrupted by noise, which is modeled as an additive zero mean Gaussian noise. Given a number of observations $\mathbf{x}_i$, the task is to best estimate the parameter vector $\mathbf{a}$, given that $\mathbf{x}_i$ and $\mathbf{a}$ are related by

$$f_i(\mathbf{x}_i, \mathbf{a}) = 0$$

It was suggested that Kalman filtering, which is an optimal linear recursive estimator, be used for the tasks. The Kalman filter propagates a conditional probability density function, $f_{\mathbf{a}|\mathbf{x}_1,\mathbf{x}_2,\cdots\mathbf{x}_i}$, by incorporating observations $\mathbf{x}_i$ recursively without recomputing a global optimization at each iteration. Under the assumptions that the system is linear and that the noise in the observations is white (noise values are not correlated) and Gaussian, then it can be proven that all reasonable choices for an optimal estimate (mean, mode, median, etc) coincide. The Kalman filter can also be shown to be the best filter of any conceivable form. Hence, the Kalman filter provides an optimal way to fuse multiple sensor data.

By linearizing the relation $\mathbf{f}_i(\mathbf{x}_i, \mathbf{a}) = \mathbf{0}$, the following is obtained:

$$\mathbf{y}_i = \mathbf{M}_i \mathbf{a} + \mathbf{u}_i$$

where $\mathbf{y}_i$ involves observation $\mathbf{x}_i$ and $\mathbf{u}_i$ represents a noise term. Starting with an initial estimate, $\hat{\mathbf{a}}_0$ of $\mathbf{a}$, and its associated covariance matrix, $\mathbf{S}_0 = E((\hat{\mathbf{a}}_0 - \mathbf{a})(\hat{\mathbf{a}}_0 - \mathbf{a})^t)$, Kalman filtering provides a mechanism to deduce an estimate $\hat{\mathbf{a}}_n$ of $\mathbf{a}$ and its covariance matrix $\mathbf{S}_n = E((\hat{\mathbf{a}}_n - \mathbf{a})(\hat{\mathbf{a}}_n - \mathbf{a})^t)$ by taking into account n observations recursively in a statistically optimal way (Ayache and Faugeras, 1988).

Henderson and co-workers (1984) proposed a sensor data integration system. A multisensor kernel system was configured by defining the low level and high level representations and the logical sensor specification. At low level processing, the system coordinated the operations of several sensors such as turning a sensor on and off, aiming and focusing a camera, etc. To integrate data from various sensors, it was assumed that the raw data from a sensor were in the form of two pieces of information, namely a feature (point, line, surface, etc) and a location of that feature. A 3-D structure called the spatial proximity graph was used as the low level data organizational tool. The nodes of the spatial proximity graph corresponded to the positions in space of the features extracted from raw sensory data. Nodes were linked by an edge if they were within some prespecified distance in space.

The high level object model was assumed to be either a feature model or a structure model. Feature models involved mapping sensed data onto a single number or onto a vector that represented the data. For example, many industrial vision systems model objects in terms of the surface area, the number of corners, the number of holes, the size of the holes, etc. Structural models provide a description of the components of an object and the relations between the components.

To bridge the gap between the sensor data represented in a proximity graph and 3-D objects represented in either a feature or a structure model, the concept of logical sensor was introduced. Physical sensors were defined by parameters associated with each individual sensor (eg, spatial resolution and the aspect ratio of a CCD camera). A logical sensor, in contrast, was defined in terms of physical devices and algorithms on the data. For example, an edge image sensor was defined by a physical sensor, which acquired images, and by an algorithm, which extracted edges from the image. The notion of a logical sensor thus allowed a flexible hardware–software mix in terms of sensors and processing algorithms on sensed data. Logical sensors could be designed to construct a spatial proximity graph from raw sensor data or to map low level sensor data into high level models.

Henderson and co-workers (1988) further developed the multisensor integration idea and described a system to model the structure and behavior of multisensor systems. This multisensor knowledge system was used to describe both the parameters and characteristics of the individual components of a multisensor system and to deduce the global properties of the complete system. The system supported the description of various components in a multisensor system, such as sensors, analysis algorithms, processes, actuators, and interconnection schemes. The multisensor knowledge system was also capable of simulating and monitoring the behavior of such a system to evaluate the system's performance.

CONCLUSIONS

This article presented a brief survey of the design and analysis techniques of five types of sensor and discussed several algorithms and systems for sensor data fusion. It should become apparent from the discussion that the sensor data fusion capacity will become an indispensable ingredient in many intelligent robotic applications.

The analysis and interpretation of sensor data are still confronted by several unsolved issues: how can the behavior of a sensor be best modeled, what is a suitable strategy to match sensors with the task at hand, how can a suitable data structure for sensor data fusion be designed, what is an ideal strategy to use sensor data synergistically, and how can sensing activities be best organized? It is believed that more research is needed to provide answers to the above questions and to develop feasible sensor data fusion techniques–systems. It should be mentioned that it was not the intent (or was it possible) to include all research work in the area of sensor design and sensor data fusion.

BIBLIOGRAPHY

J. K. Aggarwal and C. H. Chien, "3-D Structures from 2-D Images," in J. Sanz, ed., *Advances in Machine Vision,* Springer-Verlag, 1989, pp. 64–121.

J. K. Aggarwal and M. J. Magee, "Determining Motion Parameters Using Intensity Guided Range Sensing," *Patt. Recogn.* **19**(2), 169–180 (1986).

J. K. Aggarwal and Y. F. Wang, "Inference of Object Surface Structure from Structured Lighting—An Overview," in H. Freeman, ed., *Machine Vision Algorithms, Architectures, and Systems,* Academic Press, Inc., San Diego, Calif., 1988, pp. 193–220.

P. Allen, "Integrating Vision and Touch for Object Recognition Tasks," *Int. J. Robot.* **7**(6), 15–33 (1988).

P. Allen and R. Bajcsy, "Two Sensor Are Better Than One: Example of Integration of Vision and Touch," in *Proceedings of the Third International Symposium on Robotics Research,* Gouvieux, France, 1986, pp. 59–64.

P. Allen and P. Michelman, "Acquisition and Interpretation of 3-D Sensor Data from Touch," in *Proceedings of the Workshop on Interpretation of 3-D Scene,* Austin, Tex., no. 27–29, 1989, pp. 33–40.

N. Ayache and O. D. Faugeras, "Building, Registering and Fusing Noisy Visual Maps," *Int. J. Robot. Res.* **7**(6), 45–65 (Dec. 1988).

C. G. Bachman, *Laser Radar Systems and Techniques,* Artech House, Dedham, Mass., 1979.

C. G. Bachman, *Radar Sensor Engineering,* Lexington Books, Lexington, Mass., 1982.

S. T. Barnard and M. A. Fishler, "Computational Stereo," *ACM Comput. Surv.* **14**(4), 553–572 (Dec. 1982).

H. G. Barrow and J. M. Tenenbaum, "Computational Vision," *Proc. IEEE,* **69**, 572–595 (1981).

P. J. Besl, "Active Optical Range Imaging Sensors," in J. Sanz, ed., *Advances in Machine Vision,* Springer-Verlag, 1989, pp. 3–63.

P. Besl and R. Jain, "Range Image Understanding," in *Proceedings of CVPR,* San Francisco, 1985, pp. 430–449.

J. Borenstein and Y. Koren, "Obstacle Avoidance with Ultrasonic Sensors," *IEEE J. Robot. Automat.* **4**(2), 213–218 (1988).

M. Brady, "Computational Approaches to Image Understanding," *ACM Comput. Surv.* **14**(1), 3–71 (1982).

M. Brady, "Foreword, Special Issue on Sensor Data Fusion," *Int. J. Robot. Res.* **7**(6), 2–4 (1988).

M. Burton and C. Benning, "Comparison of Imaging Infrared Detection Algorithms," *Proc. SPIE,* **302,** 26–32 (1981).

A. Cameron, R. Daniel, and H. Durrant-Whyte, "Touch and Motion," in *Proceedings of the IEEE International Conference on Robotics and Automation,* Vol. 2, Philadelphia, Pa., 1988, pp. 1062–1067.

V. Cappellini and R. Marconi, eds., *Time-Varying Image Processing and Moving Object Recognition,* Elsevier, Amsterdam, The Netherlands, 1987.

C. C. Chu, N. Nandhakumar, and J. K. Aggarwal, "Scene Segmentation and Information Integration from Laser Radar Range and Intensity Data," in *Proceedings of the Pattern Recognition for Advanced Missile Systems Conference,* 1988, pp. 93–105.

C. C. Chu, N. Nandhakumar, and J. K. Aggarwal, "Interpretating Segmented Laser Radar Images Using a Knowledge-Based Systems," in *Proceedings of the SPIE Sensor Fusion Workshop: Human and Machine Strategies,* 1989, pp. 314–323.

J. V. DiFranco and W. L. Rubin, *Radar Detection,* Artech House, Inc., Dedham, Mass., 1980.

A. Farina and F. A. Studer, *Radar Data Processing,* Research Studies Press, Letchworth, UK, 1985.

R. S. Fearing, "Some Experiments with Tactile Sensing during Grasping," in *Proceedings of the IEEE International Conference on Robotics and Automation,* Vol. 3, Raleigh, N.C., 1987, pp. 1637–1643.

R. S. Fearing and J. M. Hollerbach, "Basic Solid Mechanics for Tactile Sensing," *Int. J. Robot. Res.* **4**(3), 40–54 (1984).

W. E. L. Grimson and T. Lozano-Perez, "Search and Sensing Strategies for Recognition and Localization of Two- and Three-Dimensional Objects," in *Proceedings of the Third International Symposium on Robotics Research,* Gouvieux, France, 1986, pp. 59–64.

T. C. Henderson, W. Fi, and C. Hansen, "MKS: A Multisensor Kernel System," *IEEE Trans. Sys. Man Cybernet.* **14**(5), 784–791 (1984).

T. Henderson, E. Wetz, C. Hansen, and A. Mitiche, "Multisensor Knowledge Systems: Interpreting 3D Structure," *Int. J. Robot. Res.* **7**(6), 114–137 (Dec. 1988).

W. D. Hillis, "A High Resolution Imaging Touch Sensor," *Int. J. Robot.* **1**(2), 33–44 (1982).

T. S. Huang, ed., *Image Sequence Analysis,* Springer, Berlin, 1981.

T. S. Huang, ed., *Image Sequence Processing and Dynamic Scene Analysis,* Springer, Berlin, 1983.

T. S. Huang, ed., *Time-Varying Image Analysis,* JAI Press, Greenwich, Conn., 1987.

R. S. Hunter, *The Measurement of Appearance,* John Wiley & Sons, Inc., New York, 1975.

R. A. Jarvis, "A Perspective on Range Finding Techniques for Computer Vision," *IEEE Trans. PAMI* **5**(2), 122–139 (Mar. 1983).

J. H. Kim, D. W. Payton, and K. E. Olin, "An Expert System for Object Recognition in Natural Scenes," in *Proceedings of the First Conference on AI Applications,* Denver, Colo., 1984, pp. 170–175.

D. Marr, *Vision,* W. H. Freeman, San Francisco, 1982.

W. N. Martin and J. K. Aggarwal, eds., *Motion Understanding: Robot and Human Vision,* Kluwer Academic Publisher, Nowell, Mass., 1988.

N. Nandhakumar and J. K. Aggarwal, "Multisensor Integration—Experiments in Integrating Thermal and Visual Sensors," in *Proceedings of the First International Conference on Computer Vision,* London, UK, 1987, pp. 83–92.

N. Nandhakumar and J. K. Aggarwal, "Integrated Analysis of Thermal and Visual Images for Scene Interpretation," *IEEE Trans. PAMI* **10**(4), 469–481 (1988).

D. Nitzan, A. E. Brain, and R. O. Duda, "The Measurement and Use of Registered Reflectance and Range Data in Scene Analysis," *Proc. IEEE* **65**(2), 206–220 (1977).

L. J. Pinson, "Robot Vision: An Evaluation of Imaging Sensors," *J. Robot. Sys.* **1**(3), 263–314 (1984).

M. H. Raibert and J. E. Tanner, "Design and Implementation of a VLSI Tactile Sensing Computer," *Int. J. Robot.* **1**(3), 3–18 (1982).

R. A. Russell, "A Thermal Sensor Array to Provide Tactile Feedback for Robots," *Int. J. Robot.* **1**(3), 35–40 (1985).

L. Sevigny, G. Hvedstrup-Jensen, M. Bohner, E. Ostevold, and S.

Grinaker, "Discrimination and Classification of Vehicles in Natural Scenes from Thermal Imagery," *Comput. Vision Graphics Image Processing* **25,** 229–243 (1983).

S. A. Stansfield, "A Robotic Perceptual System Utilizing Passive Vision and Active Touch," *Int. J. Robot.* **7**(6), 138–161 (1988).

A. Stimson, *Photometry and Radiometry for Engineers,* John Wiley & Sons, Inc., New York, 1974.

B. Tise, "A Compact High Resolution Piezoresistive Digital Tactile Sensor," in *Proceedings of the IEEE International Conference on Robotics and Automation,* Vol. 2, Philadelphia, Pa., 1988, pp. 760–764.

R. Y. Tsai and T. S. Huang, "Uniqueness and Estimation of Three-Dimensional Motion Parameters of Rigid Objects with Curved Surfaces," *IEEE Trans. PAMI* **6,** 13–26 (1984).

Y. F. Wang and J. K. Aggarwal, "On Modeling 3-D Objects Using Multiple Sensory Data," in *Proceedings of The IEEE International Conference on Robotics and Automation,* Vol. 2, Raleigh, N.C., 1987, pp. 1098–1103.

Y. F. Wang and J. K. Aggarwal, "Geometric Modeling Using Active Sensing—An Overview," *IEEE Contr. Sys. Mag.* **3**(2), 7–13 (1988).

Y. F. Wang and J. K. Aggarwal, "Integration of Active and Passive Sensing Techniques for Representing Three-Dimensional Objects," *IEEE J. Robot. Automat.* **5**(4), 460–471 (1989).

J. G. Winger and K-M Lee, "Experimental Investigation of a Tactile Sensor Based on Bending Losses in Fiber Optics," in *Proceedings of the IEEE International Conference on Robotics and Automation,* Vol. 2, Philadelphia, Pa., 1988, pp. 754–759.

General References

J. K. Aggarwal, "Segmentation and Analysis of Multi-Sensor Images," in *Machine Vision for Three-Dimensional Scenes,* Academic Press, 1990, pp. 267–299.

N. Ahuja and B. J. Schachter, "Image Models," *ACM Comput. Surv.* **13**(4), 373–397 (Dec. 1981).

A. Ahuja and B. J. Schachter, *Pattern Models,* John Wiley & Sons, Inc., New York, 1983.

M. Asada, "Building a 3-D World Model for a Mobile Robot from Sensory Data," in *Proceedings of the IEEE International Conference on Robotics and Automation,* Vol. 2, Philadelphia, Pa., 1988, pp. 918–923.

S. Begej, "Planar and Finger-Shaped Optical Tactile Sensors for Robotic Applications," *IEEE J. Robot. Automat.* **4**(5), 472–484 (1988).

P. J. Besl and R. C. Jain, "Three-Dimensional Object Recognition," *Comput. Surv.* **17,** 75–145 (1985).

T. O. Binford, "Survey of Model-Based Image Analysis Systems," *Int. J. Robot.* **1**(1), 18–64 (1982).

J. M. Brady, ed., *Computer Vision,* North-Holland, Amsterdam, The Netherlands, 1981.

B. L. Burks, G. de Suassure, C. R. Weisbin, J. P. Jones, and W. R. Hamel, "Autonomous Navigation, Exploration, and Recognition Using the HERMIES-IIB Robot," *IEEE Expert* **2** 18–27 (Winter 1987).

E. Cheung and V. Lumelsky, "Motion Planning for Robot Arm Manipulators with Proximity Sensing," in *Proceedings of the IEEE International Conference on Robotics and Automation,* Vol. 2, Philadelphia, Pa., 1988, pp. 740–745.

R. T. Chin and C. R. Dyer, "Model-Based Recognition in Robot Vision," *ACM Comput. Surv.* **18,** 67–108 (1986).

C. C. Chu and J. K. Aggarwal, "The Integration of Region and Edge-Based Segmentation," *Proceedings of the Third International Conference on Computer Vision,* Osaka, Japan, Dec. 4–7, 1990, pp. 117–120.

C. C. Chu and J. K. Aggarwal, "Multi-Sensor Image Interpretation Using Laser Radar and Thermal Images," *Proceedings of The Seventh Conference on Artificial Intelligence Applications,* Miami Beach, Florida, Feb. 24–28, 1991, pp. 190–196.

C. C. Chu, N. Nandhakumar, and J. K. Aggarwal, "Image Segmentation Using Laser Radar Data," *Patt. Recogn.* **23**(6), 569–581 (1990).

J. L. Crowley, "World Modeling and Position Estimation for a Mobile Robot Using Ultrasonic Ranging," in *Proceedings of the IEEE International Conference on Robotics and Automation,* Vol. 2, 1989, pp. 674–680.

M. Daily, J. Harris, D. Keirsey, K. Olin, D. Payton, K. Reiser, J. Rosenblatt, D. Tseng, and V. Wong, "Autonomous Cross-Country Navigation with the ALV."

M. J. Daily, J. G. Harris, and K. Reiser, "An Operational Perception System for Cross-Country Navigation," in *Proceedings of the IEEE CVPR Conference,* Ann Arbor, Mich., 1988, pp. 794–820.

S. J. Dickinson and L. S. Davis, "An Expert Vision System for Autonomous Land Vehicle Road Following," in *Proceedings of the IEEE CVPR Conference,* Ann Arbor, Mich., 1988, pp. 826–831.

W. K. Pratt, *Digital Image Processing,* Wiley, New York, 1978.

M. Drumheller, "Mobile Robot Localization Using Sonar," *IEEE Trans. PAMI* **9**(2), 325–332 (1987).

R. T. Dunlay, "Obstacle Avoidance Perception Processing for the Autonomous Land Vehicle," in *Proceedings of the IEEE International Conference on Robotics and Automation,* Vol. 2, Philadelphia, Pa., 1988, pp. 912–917.

A. Elfes, "Sonar-Based Real-World Mapping and Navigation," *IEEE J. Robot. Automat.* **3**(3), 249–265 (1987).

A. M. Flynn, "Combining Sonar and Infrared Sensors for Mobile Robot Navigation," *Int. J. Robot. Res.* **7**(6), 5–14 (1988).

Herbert Freeman, ed., *Machine Vision: Algorithms, Architectures and Systems,* Academic Press, Inc., New York, 1988.

D. B. Gennery, T. Litwin, B. Wilcox, and B. Bon, "Sensing and Perception Research for Space Telerobotics at JPL," in *Proceedings of the IEEE International Conference on Robotics and Automation,* Vol. 1, Raleigh, N.C., 1987, pp. 311–317.

Y. Goto and A. Stentz, "The CMU System for Mobile Robot Navigation," in *Proceedings of the IEEE International Conference on Robotics and Automation,* Vol. 1, Raleigh, N.C., 1987, pp. 99–105.

Y. Goto and A. Stentz, "Mobile Robot Navigation: The CMU System," *IEEE Expert* **2**(4), 44–54 (Winter 1987).

W. E. L. Grimson, and T. Lozano-Perez, "Model-Based Recognition from Sparse Range or Tactile Data," *Int. J. Robot.* **3**(3), 3–35 (1984).

L. D. Harmon, "Automated Tactile Sensing," *Int. J. Robot.* **1**(2), 3–32 (1982).

S. Y. Harmon, "The Ground Surveillance Robot (GSR): An Autonomous Vehicle Designed to Transit Unknown Terrain," *IEEE J. Robot. Automat.* **3**(3), 266–279 (1987).

G. Hager and M. Mintz, "Task-Directed Multi-Sensor Fusion," in *Proceedings of the IEEE International Conference on Robotics and Automation,* Vol. 2, 1989, pp. 662–667.

R. M. Haralick, "Statistical and Structural Approaches to Texture," *Proc. IEEE* **67,** 786–804 (1979).

R. M. Haralick and L. G. Shapiro, "Image Segmentation Techniques," *CVGIP* **29,** 100–132 (1985).

T. Henderson and E. Shilcrat, "Logical Sensor Systems," *J. Robot. Sys.* **1**(2), 169–193 (1984).

M. Hebert, and C. Caillas, E. Krotkov, I. S. Kewon, and T. Kanade, "Terrain Mapping for a Roving Planetary Explorer," in *Proceedings of the IEEE International Conference on Robotics and Automation*, Vol. 2, 1989, pp. 997–1002.

B. K. P. Horn, "Understanding Image Intensities," *Artif. Intell.* **8**(2), 201–231 (1977).

K. Ikeuchi, *Shape from Regular Pattern*, Technical Report A. I. Memo **567**, MIT AI Laboratory, Cambridge, Mass., 1980.

A. K. Jain, "Advances in Mathematical Models for Image Processing," *Proc. IEEE* **69**(5), 502–528 (May 1981).

A. K. Jain, *Fundamentals of Digital Image Processing*, Prentice Hall, Inc., Englewood Cliffs, N.J., 1989.

T. Kanade, "Region Segmentation: Signal vs. Semantics," *CGIP* **13**, 279–297 (1980).

T. Kanade, ed., *Three-Dimensional Machine Vision*, Kluwer Academic Publisher, Norwell, Mass., 1987.

D. J. Kriegman, E. Triendl, and T. O. Binford, "A Mobile Robot: Sensing, Planning and Locomotion," in *Proceedings of the IEEE International Conference on Robotics and Automation*, Vol. 1, Raleigh, N.C., 1987, pp. 402–408.

D. Kuan, G. Phipps, and A-C Hsueh, "Autonomous Robotic Vehicle Road Following," *IEEE Trans. PAMI* **10**(5), 648–658 (1988).

D. Kuan and U. K. Sharma, "Model-Based Geometric Reasoning for Autonomous Road Following," in *Proceedings of the IEEE International Conference on Robotics and Automation*, Vol. 1, Raleigh, N.C., 1987, pp. 416–423.

E. N. Lund and C. B. Wilson, *The Mathematical Description of Shape and Form*, Ellis Horwood, Chichester, UK, 1984.

R. L. Madarasz, L. C. Heiny, R. F. Cromp, and N. M. Mazur, "The Design of an Autonomous Vehicle for the Disabled," *IEEE J. Robot. Automat.* **2**(3), 117–125 (1986).

L. Matthies and A. Elfes, "Integration of Sonar and Stereo Range Data Using a Grid-Based Representation," in *Proceedings of the IEEE International Conference on Robotics and Automation*, Vol. 2, Philadelphia, Pa., 1988, pp. 727–733.

T. Pavlidis, "Algorithms for Shape Analysis of Contours and Waveform," *IEEE Trans. PAMI* **2**, 301–312 (1980).

A. Pentland, "A New Sense for Depth of Field," *IEEE Trans. PAMI* **9**(4), 523–531 (1987).

F. P. Preparata and M. I. Shamo, *Computational Geometry—An Introduction*, Springer, Berlin, 1985.

A. A. G. Riquicha, "Representation for Rigid Solids: Theory, Methods and Systems," *ACM Comput. Surv.* **12**, 437–464 (1980).

E. M. Riseman and M. A. Arbib, "Computational Techniques in Visual Segmentation of Static Scenes," *CGIP* **6**, 221–276 (1977).

A. Rosenfeld, ed., *Image Modeling*, Academic Press, Inc., New York, 1981.

A. Rosenfeld, ed., *Techniques for 3-D Machine Perception*, North-Holland, Amsterdam, The Netherlands, 1986.

A. Rosenfeld and L. S. Davis, "Image Segmentation and Image Models," *Proc. IEEE* **67**, 764–772 (1979).

A. Rosenfeld and A. C. Kak, *Digital Picture Processing*, Academic Press, Inc., New York, 1976.

R. E. Sampson, "3D Range Sensor via Phase Shift Detection," *IEEE Comput. Mag.* **20**(8), 23–24 (Aug. 1987).

J. Serra, *Image Analysis and Mathematical Morphology*, Academic Press, Inc., New York, 1982.

S. N. Srihari, "Representation of Three-Dimensional Digital Images," *ACM Comput. Surv.* **13**(4), 399–424 (1981).

D. Terzopoulos, A. Witkin, and M. Kass, "Constraints on Deformable Models: Recovering 3D shape and Nonrigid Motion," *Artif. Intell.* **36**, 91–123 (1988).

C. Thorpe, T. Kanade, M. Hebert, and A. Shafer, "Vision and Navigation for the Carnegie Mellon Navilab," *IEEE Trans. Patt. Anal. Mach. Intell* **PAMI-10**, 362–373.

G. T. Toussaint, "Pattern Recognition and Geometrical Complexity," *Proceedings of ICPR*, 1324–1347 (1980).

J. K. Tsotsos, "Knowledge and the Visual Process: Content, Form and Use," *Patt. Recogn.* **17**, 13–27 (1984).

T. Tsujimura and T. Yabuta, "Object Detection by Tactile Sensing Method Employing Force/Torque Information," *IEEE J. Robot. Automat.* **5**(4), 444–450 (1989).

M. A. Turk, D. G. Morgenthaler, K. D. Gremban, and M. Marra, "Video Road-Following for the Autonomous Land Vehicle," in *Proceedings of the IEEE International Conference on Robotics and Automation*, Vol. 1, Raleigh, N.C., 1987, pp. 273–280.

M. A. Turk, D. G. Morgenthaler, K. D. Gremban, and M. Marra, "VITS—A Vision System for Autonomous Land Vehicle Navigation," *IEEE Trans. PAMI* **10**(3), 342–361 (1988).

L. Van Gool, P. Dewaele, and A. Oosterlinck, "Texture Analysis Anno 1983," *CVGIP* **29**, 336–357 (1985).

A. M. Waxman, J. J. LeMoigne, L. S. Davis, B. Srinivasan, T. R. Kushner, E. Liang, and T. Siddalingaiah, "A Visual Navigation System for Autonomous Land Vehicle," *IEEE J. Robot. Automat.* **3**(2), 124–141 (1987).

W. M. Wells III, "Visual Estimation of 3-D Line Segments from Motion—A Mobile Robot Vision System," *IEEE J. Robot. Automat.* **5**(6), 820–825 (1989).

A. P. Witkin, "Recovering Surface Shape and Orientation from Texture," *Artif. Intell.* **17**, 17–45 (1981).

S. Yalamanchili and J. K. Aggarwal, "Analysis of a Model for Parallel Image Processing," *Patt. Recogn.* **18**(1), 1–16 (1985).

D. M. Zuk and M. L. Dell'eva, *Three-dimensional Vision System for the Adaptive Suspension Vehicle*, Final Report No. 170400-3-F, ERIM, DARPA 4468, Defense Supply Service, Washington, D.C.

J. K. AGGARWAL
University of Texas at Austin
Y. F. WANG
University of California at Santa Barbara

This research was supported in part by a contract from the Army Research Office, DAAL 03-87-K0089, and by a grant from the National Science Foundation, IRI-8908627.

SETHEO

SETHEO (SEquential THEOrem prover) is a high-performance theorem prover for first-order predicate logic. The inference machine of the system is based on the model elimination calculus, which is realized using PROLOG technology. SETHEO incorporates a preprocessing module for a size reduction of the input formula. The main proof procedure is implemented as a variant of Warren's abstract machine. SETHEO also permits factorization and the application of lemmata. The entire system is implemented in portable C, with a peak performance of 70,000 lips (logical inferences per second) on a Sun SPARC 1. [See R. Letz, J. Schumann, S. Bayerl, and W. Bibel, "SETHEO: A High-Performance Theorem Prover," *Journal of Automated Reasoning* (in press).]

R. Letz
Technische Universität
München

SHAKEY THE ROBOT

For a period of about five years in the late 1960s, a group of researchers at the Artificial Intelligence Center of SRI International constructed and experimented with a collection of computer programs and hardware known as Shakey the Robot. The hardware consisted of a mobile cart, about the size of a small refrigerator, with touch-sensitive "feelers," a television camera, and an optical range-finder. The cart was capable of rolling around an environment consisting of large boxes in rooms separated by walls and doorways; it could push the boxes from one place to another in its world. Its suite of programs consisted of those needed for visual scene analysis (it could recognize boxes, doorways, and room corners), for planning (it could plan sequences of actions to achieve goals), and for converting its plans into intermediate-level and low-level actions in its world. Several advances in artificial intelligence were stimulated by the research on Shakey. The most prominent of these were the A* search algorithm, the STRIPS and ABSTRIPS planning systems, programs for generalizing and learning macro-operators (MACROPS), "triangle-tables" for plan execution, and region-finding scene analysis programs.

Nils J. Nilsson
Stanford University

SHAPE

Shape representations are mathematical tools used to build geometric models. This survey of shape representation relies on mathematical intuition and motivation. Mathematical details can be found in various excellent books and research papers; here, it is possible only to review results, issues, and problems in geometric modeling.

Effective geometric models of complex objects are structural, built by "divide and conquer;" they subdivide objects into simple parts, build models of simple parts, and then build up complex objects from simple parts by a local to global process. Parts are still too complex; parts are decomposed into primitive local surface patches that are modeled and pieced together. Surface patches are modeled by parametric polynomials or by implicit algebraic surfaces. Surface patches are pieced together into parts in the form of spline surfaces, ie, piecewise smooth surfaces. They most difficult part is joining surface patches. This article first describes curve segments and surface patches, and then describes joining them into coherent compound curves or surfaces. Finally it describes volume modeling.

Utility is beauty. Shape representation is elegant if it makes geometric computations computationally efficient and simple to program. Many people think of geometric modeling as a solved problem, as a static, mature field. The successes of graphics and B-spline surfaces hide difficult, unsolved mathematical problems in building practical systems for manufacturing, graphics, and other uses. As computation cost drops and geometric modeling capability increases while computation power increases, geometric modeling is becoming a core technology across many disciplines.

Sketching of 3-D objects is not really quick and simple now. On the other extreme, detailed input of surfaces like turbine blades, derived from mathematical analysis, is also difficult. Manual building of models is difficult and tedious. Automated building of models from data is quite limited. Researchers are motivated to develop shape representations to aid model input, geometric computations, and geometric reasoning for important applications.

Concepts of shape and form are important in natural language. Most mathematical concepts of surface geometry don't express our intuitive sense of shape well. Intuitive concepts of shape appear to be concepts from a part/whole decomposition and dimensions of parts. We will consider concepts of the geometry of volumes that reflect human intuition somewhat.

LOCAL GEOMETRY

Topology introduces a few general concepts of shape such as dimension and connectedness. Topology defines the dimension of a space and dimensions of geometric entities embedded in a space. *Dimension* is defined recursively: a space has dimension zero at point p if its boundary is empty at p. The dimension of isolated points is zero. A space has dimension $n + 1$ at point p if its boundary has dimension n at p (Hurewicz, 1941). The boundary of a curve is a set of points; they have dimension zero. A curve has dimension 1. The boundary of a surface is a set of curves; a surface has dimension 2. The boundary of a volume is a set of surfaces; the volume has dimension 3. In 3-space, volumes are 3-D, surfaces are 2-D, curves are 1-D, and points are 0-D. In 2-space, areas are 2-D, curves are 1-D, and points are 0-D. In 4-D space/time, hypervolumes are 4-D, hypersurfaces are 3-D, etc.

Topology also defines the connectedness and genus of a space, ie, the number of components and handles or holes. Topology says little about shape; wildly different shapes have the same dimension, connectedness, and genus. For example, only a through hole is a hole in topology, ie, it changes genus; but a blind hole is a hole in natural language and engineering use. A protrusion does not matter in topology unless it changes genus, ie, forms a handle in the topological sense. A topologist is one who cannot tell a man from a woman or a cup from a saucer if the cup does not have a handle. The term topology of a shape is widely misused to refer to metric properties.

Geometry is defined in metric spaces. Local geometry is differential geometry, the geometry of curve segments and surface patches chosen small enough to be described adequately by low order differentials. *Surface patches* are simple by assumption, ie, they are C^n continuous, continuous with continuous derivatives through order n. A C^0 patch has continuous value, a C^1 patch has continuous value and first derivatives. A first-order patch is a first differential, eg, the tangent plane to the surface at a point. The normal is defined by the tangent plane. A second-order surface patch is a second differential, represented by a point, tangent plane, and curvatures. *Curvatures* are derivatives of the normal, ie, second derivatives. The curvature tensor has maximum and minimum curvatures, called principal curvatures. Maximum and minimum curvatures are orthogonal, defined by a single direction. Curves along which curvature is everywhere maximum or minimum are called *lines of curvature*. A curve is 1-D, indexed by one parameter, ie, defined as a map from R^1 into R^n. A surface is 2-D, indexed by two parameters, defined by a map from R^2 into R^n. A volume is 3-D. A directed surface patch may represent a patch of the boundary of a volume with its outward normal, but the directed surface patch is 2-D. It is usual to represent a volume by its boundary, a surface. They are not equivalent. In CT or MRI images, there are data about the nonuniform interior. In finite element problems in fluid flow, thermal, and viscoelastic behavior, the interior is also nonuniform.

Second-order patches are called ellipsoidal or hyperbolic. For ellipsoidal patches, both principal curvatures have the same sign. Hyperbolic patches are saddle-shaped; principal curvatures have opposite signs. Special cases of both ellipsoidal and hyperbolic patches include zero curvature, a plane; equal curvatures, a sphere; one principal curvature equal to zero, parabolic.

Surface normal, tangent plane, curvature, and max and min curvatures can be defined inherent to the surface patch, independent of a coordinate system. These definitions are usually made by choosing a local coordinate system from among many possible local coordinate systems. Surfaces are not typically single-valued for a single fixed coordinate system.

Differential geometry of curves is like that of surfaces, defined by a point and derivatives. The first derivative is the tangent; the second derivative defines the principal normal and the curvature; the third derivative, the derivative of the normal, defines the torsion.

Differential geometry rests on properties that are not observable, ie, derivatives and continuity. That raises a challenge to formulation in science and engineering. In mathematics, patches can be arbitrarily small to avoid overlapping discontinuities. In science and engineering, discrete samples are used. It is not possible to subdivide arbitrarily: eg, in analyzing images in vision or synthesizing images in graphics, an image has limited resolution; cameras and displays have physical limitations to resolution. Pixels are weighted averages over an image area. Differential operators have diameters ranging from a few pixels to many or infinite. Even the smallest areas overlap discontinuities, boundaries of surface patches; ie, a covering by pixels or operators overlaps boundaries. Those patches that overlap discontinuities are not C^n patches as above. The utility of surface patches and differential geometry can be extended by including surface patches with discontinuities, eg, patches that overlap two or more continuous patches. Extended surface patches may have discontinuities at points or along boundary curves between patches. They may be discontinuities in value D^0 (zeroth order) as a delta or step, in tangent plane D^1 (first order), or in curvature D^2 (second order). Three or more patches may intersect in a point. Discontinuities are defined in terms of two-sided derivatives. Extended surface patches with discontinuities are useful for image analysis. More patches will satisfy assumptions of extended patches than continuous patches and thus approximate accurately the local surface. Edge elements in computer vision are surface patches with discontinuities.

Local to Global Geometry

Local geometry is chosen for simplicity and is thus limited to describing simple surface patches but not complex objects. Complex surfaces are described using compound or composite surfaces, chopping surfaces into pieces small enough to be simple, then joining the pieces with continuous joints where the surface is continuous, and finally trimming pieces at intersections of surface elements. A compound surface is a piecewise mesh of surface elements with piecewise C^n continuity. Surface elements join with C^n continuity or intersect at edges. Usually surface elements have parametric polynomials as basis functions. A large family of compound surfaces is formed by choosing among options for basis functions for surface elements, and options for continuity conditions and boundary conditions. A compound curve is a piecewise mesh of curve elements with C^n continuity in joining elements.

A compound surface or curve is called a *spline*, with some choice of basis functions, eg, implicit polynomials. Numerical analysts restrict the term spline to meshes with parametric polynomial bases. Splines go beyond differential geometry in offering a global mesh of patches that are coherent in preserving C^n continuity relations between neighboring patches. These are weak but important relations between surfaces. Splines are very important.

Surface elements are surface patches from differential geometry. The only reason surface elements are large enough to cover a surface in a few pieces is that the objects we consider are simple, describable by large surfaces with low curvatures. Mathematics considers a zoo of ferocious monsters, a much broader, more complex class of surfaces than those we consider in the physical world. Differential geometry constructs are too weak to restrict analysis to physically reasonable shapes.

One use of modeling is interactive approximation of a design surface maintaining continuity of order n or discontinuity. Piecewise decomposition replaces high order surfaces with simple surface elements having complex joints. High order surfaces are difficult to control, with unwanted oscillations and unnecessary high curvatures. Piecewise surfaces give a net gain in fidelity at the cost of difficulty of analysis and programming and computational complexity of algorithms. Another use of modeling is interpolation or approximation of data, point samples, or points with normals. Discontinuities are more difficult to maintain than continuity; most methods smooth over discontinuities or are inefficient at detecting and preserving discontinuities of an underlying piecewise continuous representation of sampled, discrete data.

COMPOUND CURVES

Compound curves will be considered first. Compound surface meshes are built with similar techniques. Most curves and most surfaces are not functions $y = f(x)$, ie, they are singular and not single-valued. Surfaces and curves are implicit forms $f(x, y) = 0$ or parametric polynomials $\vec{r}(t)$. A straight line is:

$$ax + by + c = 0 \qquad a^2 + b^2 = 1$$

A circle is:

$$(x - x_0)^2 + (y - y_0)^2 - r^2 = 0$$

There are also implicit surfaces, eg, a sphere:

$$(x - x_0)^2 + (y - y_0)^2 + (z - z_0)^2 - r^2$$

Parametric polynomial curves are widely used, eg, a straight line in the parameter u:

$$\vec{p} = \vec{p}_1 + u(\vec{p}_2 - \vec{p}_1) \qquad (1a)$$

A curve is one-dimensional with a single parameter. A parametric cubic curve has the form:

$$\begin{pmatrix} x(u) = a_{10} + a_{11}u + a_{12}u^2 + a_{13}u^3 \\ y(u) = a_{20} + a_{21}u + a_{22}u^2 + a_{23}u^3 \\ z(u) = a_{30} + a_{31}u + a_{32}u^2 + a_{33}u^3 \end{pmatrix} \qquad (1b)$$

Any curve can be approximated by a parametric polynomial with sufficiently high degree. High degree polynomials are difficult to control; they have spurious oscillations between points, poor approximation at discontinuities, and wild behavior extrapolating beyond endpoints. Instead, a piecewise mesh of parametric polynomials with low degree is better behaved. It is useful to break curves at discontinuities. The resulting smooth curves may still require high degree polynomials; they can be broken into a few low order curves at knots where curve elements join to preserve C^n continuity. Interactive segmentation is simple, but automated segmentation is very difficult.

A curve may interpolate a set of points, ie, pass through the points; otherwise it approximates the points. A polynomial of degree $n - 1$ can interpolate n points. A polygon is a mesh of first-degree segments, straight lines; at knots it can be made C^0, ie, continuous; but obviously, it cannot be C^1, with continuous tangent vector. A mesh of quadratic parametric segments can be made C^1 at knots.

Continuity here is parametric continuity, ie, continuity of derivatives with respect to the parameter. A mesh of cubic parametric segments can be made C^2 at knots, ie, with continuous second derivative. Parametric polynomial and implicit polynomial segments themselves are C^∞ between knots.

Splines have a form of completeness; splines can approximate any curve and its n derivatives arbitrarily well. Choose the basis functions of degree $n + 1$, as simple as possible to satisfy C^n continuous derivatives. Make the pieces as small as necessary to satisfy the criterion for approximation; use as many pieces as necessary. Straight line segments can approximate position, but they cannot approximate curvature at all. Second-degree curves are used to approximate tangent vectors with fewer pieces or to approximate curvature.

In 3-vector form, a parametric cube is:

$$\vec{p}(u) = \begin{pmatrix} x(u) \\ y(u) \\ z(u) \end{pmatrix} = \begin{pmatrix} a_{10} & a_{11} & a_{12} & a_{13} \\ a_{20} & a_{21} & a_{22} & a_{23} \\ a_{30} & a_{31} & a_{32} & a_{33} \end{pmatrix} \begin{pmatrix} 1 \\ u \\ u^2 \\ u^3 \end{pmatrix} \qquad (1)$$

$$\vec{p}(u) = \vec{a}_0 + \vec{a}_1 u + \vec{a}_2 u^2 + \vec{a}_3 u^3 \equiv A\vec{U}$$

This system of linear equations with four vector coefficients has 12 parameters. A parametric cubic interpolates four points which have 12 constraints. Standard solutions for linear systems fix the curve uniquely. There are two other free parameters, ie, uniform parameter intervals between points are assumed: $u_1 = 0$, $u_2 = 1/3$, $u_3 = 2/3$ and $u_4 = 1$. Uniform parameter intervals are the typical choice. Nonuniform intervals give additional freedom and additional difficulty in solving for spline parameters. As an example, an approximation to arc length can be estimated by assigning parameter intervals to Euclidean distance between data points.

A Bezier cubic approximates four points but does not interpolate them; it passes through two points with tangents along the vectors between endpoints and intermediate points. It does not pass through intermediate points. Parameter intervals may be uniform or nonuniform for Bezier curves.

A Hermite cubic interpolates a pair of points and derivatives; each endpoint and each parametric derivative has three constraints. The curve is determined only by endpoints and derivatives; their 12 constraints fix the curve. There are no free parameter intervals here. Measurement of points with tangent vectors is frequently convenient. Unit tangent vectors have physical meaning, but parametric derivatives are arbitrary. Unit tangents of 3-vectors have two components; specifying unit tangents at endpoints imposes only two constraints at each endpoint, leaving two free parameters. Magnitudes of parametric derivatives are two arbitrary parameters that are free to control segment shape.

Those examples of parametric cubics were single curve elements defined by differential data (two points with tangents or four points) and different constraints (interpolation of points or interpolation of points with tangents). Considering compound curves made up of these basic functions, for three points with derivatives, one Hermite cubic interpolates the first and second points and their derivatives. A second Hermite cubic interpolates the second and third points with derivatives. The two curve segments join at the second point where they have the same position and derivatives, ie, they are C^1. By induction, the mesh can be extended to an arbitrary number of points k and their derivatives with $k-1$ segments. This mesh is an interpolating curve, ie, the curve passes through all sample points and interpolates between them. The mesh is also local since moving any point affects only two segments of the mesh. If parametric derivatives are supplies, the curve is determined uniquely, but if unit tangent vectors are supplied, there are k free parameters.

This is a spline curve made up of cubic segments between sample points. Splines may have segments from linear, quadratic, cubic or higher degree parametric polynomials and may have different continuity conditions at knots and different boundary conditions at endpoints. The different choices generate a family of splines. A spline curve with linear parametric segments is a polygon. A spline made up of parametric cubic elements that interpolate four points as above can be C^0 but not C^1. A cubic spline that interpolates points with C^2 continuity at joints and zero second derivative at endpoints is a *natural spline*. Each segment between points is a cubic with 12 parameters of uniform parameter intervals; there are $12m$ parameters for m segments. At each of $(m-1)$ knots, there are 12 constraints of continuity of first and second parametric derivative:

$$\vec{p}_{i-1}(1) = \vec{p}_i(0)$$
$$\vec{p}_{i-1}u(1) = \vec{p}_iu(0)$$
$$\frac{d^2}{du^2}\vec{p}_{i-1}(1) = \frac{d^2}{du^2}\vec{p}_i(0)$$

That leaves 12 free parameters. In addition there are six constraints at two endpoints. That leaves six free parameters supplied by boundary conditions that second derivatives at endpoints be zero. Splines are also solutions to variational problems, determining minimum bending energy in a thin plate (de Boor, 1978).

A natural spline is global, ie, moving one point affects all segments. Bezier curves are also global. Bezier curves were defined above for four points; they are defined for more points by approximation with Bernstein polynomials. A Bezier curve with m points has $m-1$ degree. B-splines are defined to be local. A cubic B-spline segment is a linear weighted sum of four points (Bartels, 1987). Moving one point of a cubic B-spline affects only four segments. A cubic B-spline is defined C^2 at joints. While a natural spline interpolates sample points, a B-spline approximates sample points rather than interpolating them, ie, a B-spline cannot pass through sample points in general. B-splines trade interpolation for locality. Locality aids in controlling approximation of curves or data by changing control points.

A rational parametric polynomial is the ratio of two parametric polynomials, eg, given parametric cubics $x(u)$, $y(u)$, $z(u)$, $w(u)$, define rational cubics:

$$x'(u) = \frac{x(u)}{w(u)}; \quad y'(u) = \frac{y(u)}{w(u)}; \quad z'(u) = \frac{z(u)}{w(u)}$$

This example is the perspective transformation that is fundamental in image formation. Rational parametrics are a superset of nonrational parametrics, ie, they are more powerful than nonrational parametrics; eg, conics are included in rational quadratic parametrics but not in nonrational quadratic parametrics. However, rational quadratics require more than two pieces to generate a single circle.

A B-spline curve can have uniform or nonuniform parameter intervals. As above, parameter intervals between knots are arbitrary. B-splines with rational parametric segments and nonuniform parameter intervals are nonuniform rational B-splines (NURBs). The splines discussed here are linear in their parameters, the coefficients. Splines are linear sums of powers of the parameter. Solution for spline coefficients is solution of a linear system of equations. Effective machinery is available and efficient. B-splines have parametric continuity constraints at knots, ie, continuity of first and second parametric derivatives of curves. Typically we are interested in geometric continuity, ie, continuity of unit tangent vector and curvature (Barsky, 1981). B-splines defined with geometric continuity are β-splines. Geometric continuity imposes two fewer constraints than parametric continuity. Thus, there are two free parameters to adjust the global shape of β-splines.

COMPOUND SURFACES

A surface is two-dimensional, ie, a parametric surface has two parameters. Consider first single surface patches. A plane is defined by three points, $\vec{p}_0$, $\vec{p}_1$ and $\vec{p}_2$:

$$\vec{p}(u, v) = \vec{p}_0 + u(\vec{p}_1 - \vec{p}_0) + v(\vec{p}_2 - \vec{p}_0)$$

A bilinear surface patch is not a plane; it has a second degree term in uv:

$$\vec{p}(u, v) = \sum_{i=0}^{1}\sum_{j=0}^{1} \vec{a}_{ij}u^iv^j \quad \text{for } u, v \in [0, 1]$$

A bicubic surface patch has the form

$$\vec{p}(u, v) = \sum_{i=0}^{3}\sum_{j=0}^{3} \vec{a}_{ij}u^iv^j \quad \text{for } u, v \in [0, 1]$$

A bicubic has $4 \times 4 = 16$ vector parameters, ie, 48 scalar parameters. Four curves $u = 0, 1$; $v = 0, 1$ bound the patch. Any fixed value of u or v defines an isoparameter curve.

Hermite curves interpolate a pair of endpoints with tangent vectors. A Hermite surface patch interpolates four corner points and eight tangent vectors of a 2×2 surface patch, but they define only 12 vector constraints. Four additional vector constraints are necessary, four twist vectors. Corner points with tangent vectors define four boundary curves. The surface interpolates the boundary curves. As above, Hermite surface patches obviously extend to meshes with C^1 continuity. Because adjacent surface patches share endpoints and tangents, thus sharing boundary curves, surfaces are C^1 continuous across boundaries. These are Coons patches (Mortenson, 1985). Surface patches are much more complex in analysis than Hermite curve segments. Specifying data is much more difficult, with eight derivatives and four twist vectors. As above, it is natural to specify unit tangent vectors, but twist vectors are not intuitively clear. The large number of parameters in bicubics makes them difficult to control. Intersections of bicubics are difficult to calculate.

A different bicubic patch can interpolate a 4 × 4 mesh, ie, 16 points determine 16 vector constraints. Again, parameter intervals in u, v are arbitrary; they may be uniform or nonuniform, eg, by approximating arc length. A mesh of such elements can be made C^0 but not C^1. A class of surfaces is generated by interpolating four cross-section curves in one of the parameters. It is common in design to specify cross-section curves. Again, continuity is only C^0.

Bezier surface patches on a 4 × 4 grid pass through the four corner points with slopes determined by nearest neighbors. A Bezier surface is a tensor product of Bezier curves. Control points in u, v space form a rectangular grid. Bezier surfaces can be extended to larger meshes. Bezier surfaces are nonlocal as are Bezier curves. Changing one control point on a Bezier surface changes the whole surface. Bezier patches and Coons patches (Hermite interpolation) can be defined over triangular meshes (Barnhill, 1985). Although formulation is more complex over triangular meshes, triangulation has greater flexibility, eg, in boundaries of surfaces that are not isoparameter curves.

For surface meshes, the issue is joining surface patches with C^n continuity at joints. Compound surface meshes with planar basis functions are polyhedra. But bilinear surface patches are not planar. Polyhedra can be made C^0 at joints for a triangular mesh. A rectangular mesh cannot have planar elements except in special cases, but can have bilinear elements. Four points are not coplanar in general. Triangular meshes and rectangular meshes are motivated by different concerns.

A B-spline surface is a tensor product of B-spline curves. Control points form a rectangular grid. B-spline surfaces are chosen to be local and to preserve C^n continuity. Changing one control point affects only a few surface elements of the B-spline. A B-spline of degree k has C^{k-1} continuity. A bicubic B-spline is defined to be C^2. A bicubic B-spline is a linear weighted sum over a 4 × 4 local submesh of control points. Moving any point affects only 4 × 4 bicubic surface elements that overlap the point. B-spline surfaces approximate control points; they do not pass through control points. Parameter intervals can be chosen as uniform or nonuniform. Rational B-splines have rational parametric polynomials. In imaging, bicubic B-splines project to rational bicubic B-splines, not to bicubic B-splines. NURBS are particularly important. Rational B-splines can be defined as 4-D splines with 4-D control points:

$$x(u, v), y(u, v), z(u, v), w(u, v)$$

$$\frac{x}{w}, \frac{y}{w}, \frac{z}{w}$$

Various classes of splines with parametric polynomials and rational parametrics were developed to solve practical problems. They were defined to satisfy locality, continuity conditions, and boundary conditions. The next section will consider criteria for representation from the viewpoint of problems they are meant to solve.

CRITERIA FOR REPRESENTATION

Criteria for representation come from practical uses of geometric modeling. Building models is a major effort in computer graphics. Underlying all uses of geometric models discussed below are the problems of joining surfaces to make composite surfaces, ie, calculating intersections of surfaces and calculating C^n continuous joining of surface patches to make composite surfaces. Building models from 3-D range data is important. Building models requires fitting surface patches to data, and determining discontinuities at intersections from data.

Advances in geometric modeling aided by low-cost, powerful computing hardware and improved software tools make geometric modeling widely available on microcomputers and workstations, increasingly capable, faster, lower in cost, and easier to use. The impact of geometric modeling will accelerate in graphics, manufacturing, space, education, entertainment, medical and military applications. Here we aim to gain intuition about which geometric operations are important in uses of geometric modeling. These geometric operations motivate requirements for shape representation. Computer graphics, rendering, and visualization dominate uses of geometric modeling, requiring a particular set of geometric operations and geometric representations. Other uses of geometric modeling require other geometric operations and other geometric representations.

Photorealism in graphics is achieved through simulation of physics by ray tracing, enabling valuable physical effects, eg, anti-aliasing, texture, transparency, and shadows. The central operation in ray tracing is intersection of a ray with surfaces of object model, backward rays from the corners of an image pixel, with a computation cost of $(m + 1)(n + 1)$ for an $m \times n$ image. Ray tracing is brute force and thus extremely computationally expensive. Rendering of curved surfaces is usually done by approximating the surface by polygons and rendering polygons. Polygons dominate in ray tracing; quadric surfaces also appear. Low computational cost of ray intersections with polygons wins over higher quality and higher cost of rendering by computing ray intersections with curved surfaces, eg, bicubic splines. Ray intersections with curved surfaces have been achieved by algebraic elimination and by iterative methods, eg, for parametric splines, NURBS, and algebraic surfaces. Anti-aliasing in space and time is achieved approximately by averaging over multiple rays.

The dominant method of display used in workstations in software or special hardware is z-buffer rendering of polygons. Many polygons are necessary to avoid stairstepping at boundaries. Polygons are typically bilinear; they need not be planar. The z-buffer display scan converts the polygon, computing range at each image pixel in the polygon. If the surface is nearer than that in the z-buffer, the z value for the pixel replaces the value in the z-buffer, and the color is put into the display pixel. Workstations quote rendering power in polygons per second. For entertainment films or conference quality examples, many polygons are used, eg, half a million, with computation cost in days.

Photorealism imposes geometric requirements on algorithms and representation. First, images of curved surfaces approximated by polygons have unpleasant stairstepping at silhouettes, the jaggies. Second, image shading must be C^1 to appear smooth, ie, to avoid false edges, Mach bands. From the image intensity equation, the surface must be C^2. The image intensity is given by

$$I = I_0 \rho \hat{i} \cdot \hat{n}$$

where I is image intensity, I_0 is surface incident illumination, ρ is surface reflectivity, $\hat{i}$ is a unit vector from the source, and $\hat{n}$ is the unit surface normal. In other words, image intensity is determined by surface orientation; the derivative of image intensity is determined by the derivative of orientation, ie, curvature. As an approximation, Gouraud shading interpolates intensities between polygon vertices. At vertices, normals are calculated from a curved surface model, if available, or by interpolating normals of polygons that meet at the vertex. Gouraud shading makes great improvements, though problems are still noticeable. Phong shading interpolates surface normals and intensities and calculates intensities from normal values. Phong shading makes a major difference at highlights where shading changes rapidly with surface orientation.

Mutual illumination adds to realism, ie, light reflected from one surface illuminates others. Radiosity computations approximate mutual illumination by computing the illumination of polygons by polygons.

Computer-aided design, engineering, and manufacturing (CAD, CAE, and CAM, respectively) are evolving rapidly. CAD is evolving from drafting and archiving (including part input, documentation, and display) to dimension and tolerancing, integrating design with manufacturing in concurrent engineering. A broader range of geometric computations are in use, including parametric design and research on constraints and geometric reasoning. Esthetic design requires interactive input. Numerical control and splines had strong motivation from free-form surfaces in manufacturing, especially aircraft. Free-form surface manufacturing has evolved with splines; simple discrete parts manufacturing has evolved with solid modeling (computational solid geometry). In engineering, parts models are translated into finite element meshes (FEM) for analysis of kinematics and dynamics, simulation with mode analysis, stress/strain, and electrical and thermal analysis. FEM and other tools are being incorporated in automating design for injection molding. In CAM, process planning, interference testing, and numerical control help to automate machine tool programming. Research is moving to automate inspection and robotic manipulation. In discrete part manufacturing, continuity of second derivatives is often not required; eg, in fillets and blends. C^1 continuity is required. Functional surface design requires C^2 continuity along with fidelity of surface topology and geometry, eg, for hydrodynamics in turbine blades, airfoils, and cams for which surface design is based on physical equations. *Fidelity* is important; small variations in aerodynamic surfaces degrade performance. *Fidelity* is important; small variations in aerodynamic surfaces degrade performance. Fidelity of topology refers to preserving intersection of surfaces and suppression of spurious intersection of surfaces, especially tangent surfaces, by controlling spurious surface oscillations. Fidelity of geometry means controlling surface position and derivatives within design specifications. Building models of functional surfaces is tedious, especially maintaining topological and geometric fidelity.

In computer vision, many of the same geometric operations are important: building models from data, preserving C^2 continuity in shading and specularity computation, and symbolic methods for parameterized models. Specularities are important in predicting radar images. Accurate prediction of discontinuities implies avoiding false discontinuities which cause false specularities, eg, false concave corners. In medicine and biology, reconstruction from serial sections raises issues of compensation for distortions, continuity among connected components, dealing singularities, and segmentation at discontinuities.

In summary, building models motivates low computation cost for computing surface–surface intersection and joining of surfaces with specified continuity, for surface fitting from data, and for estimating surface intersections in data. Computer graphics adds requirements on these geometric operations: low computation cost for intersection of rays with surfaces, for computing silhouettes, and for z-buffer operations; low cost for radiosity computations; C^2 continuous surfaces; triangulation and polygonal approximation of surfaces. CAD/CAM adds requirements for geometric operations: smooth joins between surfaces, ie, fillets, blends, and offsets; fidelity of topology and geometry; volume representation for finite-element analysis; and symbolic models for constraint resolution.

GEOMETRIC OPERATIONS

Geometric representations are designed to make geometric operations efficient computationally. The initial section discussed composite surfaces built from parametric polynomial surface patches, especially B-splines and NURBS. By definition, splines preserve continuity at joints. Surface–surface intersections have been computed for piecewise parametric surfaces (Barnhill, 1987). Intersection computations are very difficult with parametric polynomials. Piecewise parametric surfaces are attractive, and there is a large body of work with parametric surfaces. There are deep unsolved problems with parametric polynomials because they have high degree. A parametric surface with degree m in u and degree n in v has implicit degree $2mn$, eg, a biquadratic rational polynomial has implicit degree 8; a bicubic surface has degree 18. The intersection of bicubic splines has degree 324. The intersection of surfaces with degree m has degree m. An intersection with degree 324 is extremely complex, for either analytic or iterative numerical solutions. Difficulty grows very rapidly with degree. There are problems with finding all solutions and accounting for all singularities and exceptions. Intersections for high degree surfaces can be very sensitive to uncertainties in coefficients, ultimately data points. Intersections break up into separate connected components, potentially many for bicubics. Also because bicubic splines have high implicit degree, they are difficult to control to maintain fidelity of topology and geometry, ie, intersections and derivatives.

Some investigate implicit algebraic surfaces that have lower degree than biquadratic or bicubic parametrics (Sederberg, 1988; Bajaj, 1988), eg, degree 3 implicit vs degree 8 or 18 parametric. Extensive early work in modeling dealt with quadric surfaces. All parametric curves and surfaces have implicit forms. Only a few implicit curves and surfaces have rational forms. Only a small subset of cubic plane curves and only a small subset of fourth degree surfaces are parameterizable; ie, rational forms are a small subset of implicit forms. Almost all quadratic implicit curves and cubic surfaces have implicit forms (Bajaj, 1988). Finding implicit forms is done with algebraic elimination. Researchers seek to use both implicit and parametric forms for a single surface. Testing whether a point lies on a curve or surface is simple for parametric forms. Many problems remain with implicit algebraic forms.

VOLUMES: SOLID GEOMETRY

The term *solid modeling* is usually used for surface modeling, ie, modeling the boundaries of volumes. Modeling the boundary of a volume is not modeling the interior of the volume. Modeling the surface shell has particular importance for computer graphics of opaque objects, the dominant use of geometric modeling. Now that surface and volume visualization replace rendering as a theme, there is greater awareness of modeling volumes. Modeling the boundary of a volume gives no information about its interior. The interior is nonuniform for CT and MRI images in medicine and for FEM mesh analysis for stress/strain, temperature, etc. A similar relation holds in 2-D: modeling an area by its bounding curve is not equivalent to modeling its interior.

A volume element is 3-D; a surface element is 2-D. Examples of surface elements are an infinitesimal disc in parameter space (u, v) or a square in parameter space bounded by isoparameter curves $u \pm d/2$, $v \pm d/2$. Any "smooth" surface can be parameterized locally (not uniquely). It is natural to think of surface elements in terms of a parameter space of the surface, not of an embedding space (not unique), because an arbitrary simple surface element in parameter space satisfies the constraint that it lie on the surface. Most people carry the particular intuition of a uniform embedding Cartesian space, of uniform, empty space with a surface embedded in it. A surface element corresponds to a deformed area in an embedding Cartesian space. By contrast, it is usual to think of an element of the interior as an infinitesimal cube in a uniform embedding Cartesian space, except for a nuisance near the volume boundary where a volume element intersects the boundary and is not in the interior. It is natural but not usual to think of a volume element in parameter space (u, v, w). That intuition is powerful if the parameter space defines iso-contours of the interior and if boundaries are chosen simple in parameter space, eg, iso-parameter surfaces. This intuition corresponds to typical physics problems, eg, motion on a sphere, the earth; motion in a gravitational field; flow with a finite element mesh oriented along streamlines. The notion of integrating parameter space in a global Cartesian space can be hazardous to one's health. In a river, on a mountain, or near earth, it does not make sense to move in straight lines. In many cases, the parameter space is implicit, ie, the iso-parameter surfaces are not known but are part of a solution to a mathematical problem.

Thus, one natural volume element is the *voxel*, a cube in a uniform embedding Cartesian space. The boundary surface of a volume is a complicated constraint in the Cartesian space. A dual notion is a cube volume element in uniform parameter space that is a deformed volume in a warped embedding space.

Voxels

The voxel representation is a volume representation by a grid of volume cells (voxels) with uniform resolution in an embedding Cartesian space. Visualization by voxels has been common, especially for voxel data in MRI and CT, and for uniform grids of data from FEM analysis. There is an equivalent cell decomposition for areas in 2-D. Multigrid algorithms have been found with much lower computational complexity than methods with a single grid. Pyramids are multi-grids with a range of scales, typically logarithmic scales from finest to coarsest, eg, scales a power of 2: 1, 2, 4, ... The number of cells in a 2-D pyramid is: $n^2(1 + 1/4 + 1/16 + 1/64 + \cdots = 1.33n^2$. Clearly, there is little extra cost in computing the pyramid; most of the cells are in the lowest scale. Any place in the grid has the same set of cells of all scales. A pyramid with discrete property labels in cells can be simplified without loss of information by dropping any subtree of cells that is uniform in the property. The result is called a *quadtree* for areas in 2-D, or an *octree* for volumes in 3-D (Samet, 1984). Quadtrees can be effective in grids with large uniform areas because most cells are at the lowest scale.

Quadtrees are natural for data with a few discrete labels over discrete pixels. They are also natural for associating neighbors of points. Likewise, octrees are natural for voxel data with a few discrete labels, and for associating neighbors of points. If quadtrees are used with line drawings, infinite subdivision is required at edges and vertices. A quadtree can be defined for line drawings by identifying three kinds of cells: interior cells, those that cross a single edge, and those that cover a single vertex (Samet, 1986). Quadtree computations are difficult for line drawings with curves for which it is difficult to determine whether a curve crosses a cell, equivalent to intersecting a line with a curve. Use of octrees with curved surfaces in 3-D requires intersections of planes with surfaces, ie, it is difficult to decide whether voxel cubes are interior or exterior to the volume, or on its boundary. A voxel grid is conceptually simple and does represent the interior of a volume. However, a voxel grid does not preserve C^n continuity of the surface. Finding neighbors of any point can also be done with K-D trees.

Voxel representations are discrete grids in a Cartesian embedding space. A natural extension to surface patches is parametric volume patches, sometimes called *hyperpatches*, defined in parameter space and defining a warped space in an embedding Cartesian space. A parametric polynomial volume element is 3-D; hence it is defined by three parameters:

$$\vec{p} = \begin{pmatrix} x(u, v, w) \\ y(u, v, w) \\ z(u, v, w) \end{pmatrix} \quad u, v, w \in [0, 1]$$

Very little is done with parametric polynomial volume patches in computer graphics because surfaces are dominant, but they are important in numerical analysis.

The sense of uniform space makes it seem natural to represent a volume by its boundary. The only action is at the boundary. In a grid decomposition, all interior cells are cubes and hence, uninteresting. In a parameterized volume, however, "natural" volume elements may be strongly distorted by boundaries. In a finite element problem, it may be natural to consider warping. Natural interior elements defined by a parameterization may be distinctly not cubes. There is a sense of representing space vs representing shape. In one view, space is simple; objects are complex. Space is Euclidean or remotely Riemannian, not intensely warped. In the geometric physical model, space is strongly warped around objects (black holes or nuclei).

In the simple view of space, 2-space is represented by a hierarchical family of grids of disjoint squares or spheres with different scales. The hierarchical family may be uniform, eg, a pyramid, or nonuniform, a quadtree in 2-space. A K-D tree may be defined on points in the plane. Representing complex objects in terms of quadtrees and pyramids is not easy. They are usually meant for points, not extended objects. Samet (1986) describes a quadtree representation for polygon figures. It is difficult to extend to curved planar figures.

Voxel representations have limited use with respect to problems other than voxel data. Voxel CAD models are of very little use. CAD models are composite parametric or implicit algebraic surfaces. Voxels are not used in much of graphics. Splines are piecewise smooth composites of surface elements joined at discontinuities. Actually splines are concerned with C^n continuous joints and essentially ignore intersection. Volumes are modeled by their bounding surfaces. Computational Solid Geometry models (CSG) define volumes in a similar way and ignore piecewise smooth joints.

CSG Models

Computational solid geometry (CSG) models combine volumes by regularized Boolean set operations, ie, union, intersection, and set difference of volumes. A regular solid is the closure of its interior; solids are defined as regular in order to have no dangling surfaces or edges. CSG traditionally uses simple volumes or simple half-spaces, ie, volumes bounded by infinite surfaces with one side of the oriented surface labeled interior. These volumes are simple closed solid primitives, eg, blocks, cylinders, spheres, and cones; or interior half-spaces bounded by oriented, infinite simple surfaces, typically quadric surfaces, eg, planes. For example, a volume A is formed from a block B by milling two block-shaped cuts C_1 and C_2 and drilling a hole H:

$$A = B - C_1 - C_2 - H$$

CSG models are implicit in the sense that boundaries of surfaces are specified only by the intersections of surfaces. It is often difficult to compute interior volumes, boundary surfaces, and intersection curves explicitly. Typically, CSG models have been chosen to have simple bounding surfaces that make computing intersections tractable. Note that these are half-spaces bounded by quadric surfaces, not piecewise smooth quadric composite surfaces. Quadric surfaces are quite limited.

Composite spline models are explicit in the sense that boundaries of surfaces are specified by parameter ranges. However, discontinuities in composite surface splines are intersections of spline surfaces; intersections of biquadratics or bicubics are very difficult to compute. While surfaces are typically infinite in CSG, splines are bounded surface patches. There are efforts to extend CSG by extending the class of half-spaces used, to include semi-algebraic surfaces, splines, and implicit polynomial surfaces. Other research is devoted to using bounded surface patches, called *trimmed surfaces,* that are defined by explicit computation of intersection curves that bound surfaces. It may be useful to think of CSG models as a solid modeling hierarchy over parametric and implicit algebraic surfaces. Like splines, CSG models define volumes by their bounding surfaces. They are not volume models in the sense that we have used here of modeling the interior of a volume explicitly.

Trimmed surfaces are a form of *boundary representation* (BREP). A BREP is a model of a solid as a graph of surfaces, edges, and vertices. Each surface node has bounding edges and neighbor surfaces. Each edge node has two surfaces that intersect at the edge and two end vertices. Surfaces are directed, bounded explicitly by edges bounded by vertices (*trimmed surfaces*). The plague of geometric computation and graphics is singular cases. Even with planar bounding surfaces, degenerate cases require detailed treatment (Laidlaw, 1986). CSG and BREP are complementary; researchers work to combine them naturally, eg, in combining complex free-form surfaces in CSG models. Other work defines BREP as a VSCP graph in which nodes are volumes, surfaces, curves, and points with boundary and neighbor arcs.

Winged-edge representations define a data structure with fixed size: an edge has two region neighbors and two end vertices. At each end, there are clockwise and counter-clockwise edges. Using edge structures, it is simple to traverse the ordered edges of a surface or the ordered edges at a vertex (Baumgart, 1972). Fixed size winged-edge structures simplify memory management, which is a consideration in languages without automatic memory management.

Wireframe models are a type of BREP. Polyhedra have planar faces that can be represented completely by their edges. Many old and simple geometric modeling systems are wireframe modelers with hidden line rendering instead of hidden, shaded surface rendering. For curved surfaces, edges are not enough to specify surfaces completely. It is necessary to specify a parametric or implicit form for each surface. Wireframe information is incomplete, ie, ambiguous. An algorithm exists that computers polyhedra corresponding to a wireframe (Markowsky, 1980).

Generalized Cylinders

Parametric forms determine points $p(u)$ on a curve, $p(u, v)$ on a surface, and $p(u, v, w)$ in a volume. Implicit forms also determine points on a curve or surface. Some intuitive descriptions used by humans correspond to volume representations rather than surface representations; eg, a part/whole decomposition is a decomposition into volume parts. Also, one thinks of the thickness of a snake, or the length, width, and height of most objects, concepts that reflect relations among surfaces.

In physical problems, iso-parameter curves provided a natural coordinate system for volumes, a warped space intrinsic to the problem. In the same way, distances provide a natural coordinate system for volumes. In the plane, the distance from any point in the interior of a region to the boundary of a region can be calculated. The same can be done in 3-space. This distance transform, ie, computing a distance for any interior point, defines a canonical body-centered coordinate system that is invariant under rigid body transformations. The Blum transform defined a distance on plane curves and volumes, by a prairie fire in grass. The curves of local maximum distance in the plane, and surfaces of local maximum distance in 3-space define a medial axis. The transform is invertible from the axis with distances. The Blum transform is equivalent to the minimal set of maximal circular neighborhoods; ie, at every point, the maximal circular neighborhood, one that first touches a boundary, is defined. Any maximal neighborhood contained in another neighborhood is eliminated. The Blum transform establishes relations between points equidistant from the medial axis and can be computed reasonably efficiently on a grid.

The medial axis transform has recently been called a Voronoi diagram. Voronoi diagrams were defined on sets of sample points in the plane and in n-space. The edges of the Voronoi diagram are straight lines equidistant between two points. Collectively, edges define cells of the plane for which one sample point is the nearest sample point. The Voronoi diagram can be extended to curves in the plane and to curved surfaces in 3-space. There are algorithms to compute the Voronoi diagram for circular arcs in the plane with complexity $n \: logn$ where n is the number of arcs in the plane. The distance transform or Blum transform or Voronoi diagram is very useful as an area representation in the plane or as a volume representation in 3-space. It is unique and invertible. That is an advantage and a disadvantage. There are other distance transforms that have other advantages. Surprisingly, being unique is a disadvantage rather than an advantage.

Consider the medial axis of a circle and a semi-circle. The medial axis does give an idea of the shape of the semi-circle, but there is little similarity between the medial axis of the circle and semi-circle, although there is a common shape element. A "better" representation for a semi-circle is a CSG representation, a circle intersected with a half-plane. Both have simple representations, the circle by a point with radius. The CSG representation is better because it allows a similarity relation to the circle and because it is "simpler," again an ill-defined concept. Capturing this notion of similarity is an aim for computer vision and other purposes, eg, design. The improved representation is possible because it is piecewise, ie, it depends on a segmentation of the plane figure into a semi-circle and a straight line, or segmentation of its transform into a point at the center of the circle and a point at infinity.

In spite of its limitations, the medial axis has been used to define an important class of primitive shape elements. These elements are known as generalized ribbons in 2-D, and as generalized cylinders in 3-D. Complete shapes are then represented as part–whole graphs of joined primitive shapes (Binford, 1971). Complete shapes are like splines, ie, piecewise smooth combinations of generalized cylinders with continuity conditions or discontinuities at joints.

An ordinary cylinder is the volume swept out by translating an arbitrary cross section along an infinite straight line. A cylinder is translationally invariant along its axis of rotational symmetry. It may be truncated at either end. A circular cylinder has circular cross section, and a prism has polygonal cross section. Both are special cases of cylinders.

A cylinder may be generalized in two ways, by sweeping along a space curve called the spine or axis, instead of a straight line, and by transforming the cross section as it is swept. Sweeping a circle along a circle generates a torus. Sweeping a circle along a helix generates a helicoid, eg, a coiled spring. A cone is the volume swept out by a circle as it is translated and scaled linearly along a straight line. The cross section can be transformed by rotation, scaling, or distortion. A screw is a circle with a notch that is rotated while it is swept along a straight line. A screw is also the set difference between a cylinder and a helicoid. If the sweep function is not constant, a generalized cone (GC) is generated. The terms *generalized cylinder* and *generalized cone* are often used interchangeably. GCs may be expressed by generalized translational invariance in which one cross section is mapped into another by a translation followed by a congruence operation. The spine is often not unique.

GC primitives are segmented at discontinuities in cross section. They may be truncated by a surface, eg, a plane face or hemisphere. Primitives may be formed by smooth joining of elements, as in splines. A GC primitive is related to a complete shape by a rotation and translation, which may be parameterized by an articulation, eg, a ball-

and-socket joint. This has long been standard in many disciplines, especially computer graphics and physics.

In the following paragraphs, we discuss some of the issues involved in representation of volumes by GCs.

Complete Specification. Specifying the cross section, sweep function, and spine determines a generalized cylinder. A complete specification is locally generative, ie, it approximates local forms and pieces them together globally to cover a large class of primitives (Binford, 1971). A GC may be specified by sample cross sections and interpolating functions, ie, as a spline. It resembles a load of sliced bread. It may be thought of as a mapping between cross-sections. The spine is represented as a spline space curve. The cross-section is a compound of primitive cross-sections, each of which is a generalized cylinder in a lower dimension.

Generalized cylinders combine surface and volume representations. A volume GC primitive is generated by sweeping a surface cross section that may be planar. A surface GC primitive is generated by sweeping a curve cross section that may be planar. A surface cross section is made from surface GC primitives, a part–whole graph. A cross section primitive is specified as a generalized cylinder, ie, by sweeping. The same issues are relevant for cross sections and plane figures as for volumes. Implementations to date have used a weaker representation of cross sections by their boundary segments (eg, Brooks, 1981; Brooks and co-workers, 1978).

Continuity. Primitives are defined by continuity of cross section. Intuitively, a block is a physical part; its faces are not parts. GCs attempt to capture this sense of volume continuity. Surface continuity determines surface primitives, ie, faces.

Product Decomposition. GCs are specified as a product of spine and cross section. A surface cross section is itself a product. This parameterization of three-dimensional shape along a curve is especially simple for simple shapes and may define small, additive complexity in typical cases of branching objects.

Interior. GCs combine interior (volume) and boundary (surface) representation of three-dimensional shape in three-space and interior (area) and boundary (curve) representations of two-dimensional shape in the plane. GCs are composed of cross-sectional slices, elements that have the same dimension as the shape represented. A finite number of volume elements cover a well-behaved volume.

Structure. GCs define a boundary representation different from typical surface representations. GCs define a volume relation between "opposing surfaces" whereas typical surface representations relate adjacent surfaces across edges. The issue is not only interior vs boundary representations but whether volume adjacency or surface adjacency relations are specified. Surfaces that are close in a volume sense can be very far apart in boundary order. The volume elements thus defined are convenient for important physical operations. GC volumes provide relations among surface elements in the sense of two-finger experiments, grasping, as contrasted with one-finger experiments, surface tracing. GCs are locally realizable, ie, cross-sectional slices are closed and nonintersecting. This issue is equally important for representing areas.

Similarity and Object Class. A key problem in computational vision is identification of object classes composed of objects that are not identical but are "similar." Object classes more resemble functional classes than shape classes; shape is an indicator of function (Winston and co-workers, 1985). A representation of shape enables a similarity classification. Generalized cylinders provide a structure of similar shapes. Shapes are similar if they have the same part–whole structure and approximately similar proportions of parts. Spine, cross section, and sweeping rule form the basis for a taxonomy of primitives (Nevatia, 1974; Hollerbach, 1975; Shafer and Kanade, 1983).

Disjoint. Primitives should be constructed of disjoint elements. Fourier eigenfunctions and Blum transform neighborhoods are not disjoint (Blum, 1967). Cross-sectional slices of generalized cylinders are disjoint. This criterion has intuitive value because it leads to local representation, not because decomposition into orthogonal functions is difficult.

Formalization. A generalized cylinder maps one cross section into another, as discussed above. The map can be singular and crossing, as at the apex of a cone. The map must be continuous along the spine and within a cross section. To avoid "kinking," the axis of any rotation should not lie within a cross section. An effective definition of maps of cross sections is to transform the axis of a cross section into a new axis and to transform its cross section.

Adequacy. It is often stated that generalized cylinders are adequate for elongated objects. They are also adequate for short, wide objects that are not elongated at all, eg, coins, but that have a direction of generalized translational invariance. Generalized cylinders are not apt for spheres for which there is no such direction. The correspondence of "opposite" surface elements, which is central to generalized cylinders, is useful for spheres or quasispheres. GCs are not apt for crumpled pieces of paper or rocks, which may not have compact representations. There may be no systematic representation, which is better. The opposite relation among surfaces is still useful in these cases. One theme of representation is to model fabrication. That is, a heart may be represented by a volume model. However, a better model is to represent individual muscles as generalized cylinders and to represent volume relations between them to the extent that they are coordinated. To the extent that independent objects are unaligned or have different shapes, volumes of free space are often complex and not easily represented by generalized cylinders. Free space in architecture is often well described by generalized cylinders, however.

Levels of Detail. Typical objects have branching structure. The importance of parts is not entirely related to their size, ie, fingers are important in a model of a human, but they are small compared to the torso. It is useful to include in one description small detail, down to the level of cells if necessary, along with gross detail. Branching structures have exponential detail; typical joints preserve area and branch sizes decrease exponential. More generally, a discrete structure of fabrication gives a natural level of detail, like the human body built of muscles, organs, etc, each built of layers.

Generalized cylinders were invented in 1971 (Binford, 1971) with strong influence from the Blum transform (Blum, 1967). They were intended for use in computer vision for symbolic description of object classes. Agin (1972) used them in describing primitive curved objects in depth data. Nevatia (1974) used them in segmenting depth data into complex objects, in structuring a visual memory, in indexing into the visual memory, and in recognition. They were used in the ACRONYM model-based system (Brooks, 1978; Brooks and co-workers, 1981). A subclass of generalized cylinders was considered by Marr (1978, 1982).

For vision, it is essential to compute descriptions by feasible algorithms. An original motivation was that much of the part–whole structure and shapes of parts were recoverable from images, ie, quasi-invariant. Levels of detail could be accommodated in the part–whole graph. Two-dimensional projections of generalized cylinders have been called ribbons. Extracting generalized cylinders from depth data and from images has primarily depended on the opposite relation between curve boundary elements (Nevatia, 1974; Brady and Asada, 1984). This has been called "smoothed local symmetries" (Brady and Asada, 1984). In dealing with depth data, much current activity is concerned with surface representations, eg, lines of curvature. Volume representations provide more global structure.

BIBLIOGRAPHY

G. J. Agin, *Representation and Description of Curved Objects*, Stanford Artificial Intelligence Memo AIM-173, Stanford, Calif., 1972.

C. Bajaj, *Geometric Modeling With Algebraic Surfaces*, Technical report CSD-TR-825, Purdue University, West Lafayette, Ind., 1988.

R. E. Barnhill, "Surfaces in Computer-Aided Geometric Design: A Survey With New Results," *Computer Aided Geometric Design* **2**, 1–17 (1985).

R. E. Barnhill, G. Farin, M. Jordan, and B. R. Piper, "Surface/Surface Intersection," *Computer-Aided Geometric Design* **4**, 3–16 (1987).

B. Barsky, "The Beta-Spline: A Local Representation Based on Shape Parameters and Fundamental Geometric Measures," Ph.D. dissertation, University of Utah, 1981.

R. H. Bartels, J. C. Beatty, and B. Barsky, "An Introduction to Splines for Use in Computer Graphics and Geometric Modeling," Morgan-Kaufmann, San Mateo, Calif., 1987.

B. Baumgart, "Winged-Edge Polyhedron Representation," Report CS-320, Computer Science Dept., Stanford University, Stanford, Calif., 1972.

T. O. Binford, "Visual Perception by Computer," invited paper at the IEEE Conference on Systems, Man and Cybernetics, Miami, Fla., 1971.

H. Blum, "A Transformation for Extracting New Descriptors of Shape," in W. Dunn, ed., *Models for Perception of Speech and Visual Form*, MIT Press, Cambridge, Mass., 1967, pp. 362–380.

M. Brady and H. Asada, *Smoothed Local Symmetries and Their Implementation*, MIT AI Memo 757, Cambridge, Mass., 1984.

R. A. Brooks, "Symbolic Reasoning Among 3-D Models and 2-D Images," *Artif. Intell.* (Aug. 1981).

R. A. Brooks, R. Greiner, and T. O. Binford, "A Model-Based Vision System," *Proceedings of the Image Understanding Workshop*, Boston, May 1978.

C. de Boor, *A Practical Guide to Splines*, Springer-Verlag, New York, 1978.

G. Farin, *Curves and Surfaces for Computer-Aided Geometric Design*, Academic Press, New York, 1990.

R. T. Farouki, "Trimmed-Surface Algorithms for the Evaluation and Interrogation of Solid Boundary Representations," *IBM J. Res. Develop.* **31**, 314–333 (1987).

C. M. Hoffman, "Geometric and Solid Modeling: An Introduction," Morgan-Kaufmann, San Mateo, Calif., 1989.

J. Hollerbach, Technical Report AI-TR-346, MIT, Cambridge, Mass., Nov. 1975.

W. Hurewicz, H. Wallman, *Dimension Theory*, Princeton University Press, Princeton, N.J., 1941.

D. H. Laidlaw, W. B. Turmbore, and J. F. Hughes, "Constructive Solid Geometry for Polyhedral Objects," *ACM SIGGRAPH* (1986).

G. Markowsky and M. A. Wesley, "Fleshing Out Wire Frames," *IBM J. Res. Dev.* **24**, 582–597 (1980).

D. Marr, *Vision*, W. H. Freeman, San Francisco, Calif., 1982.

D. Marr and K. Nishihara, *R. Soc. Lond. B* **200**, 269–294 (1978).

M. E. Mortenson, *Geometric Modeling*, Wiley, New York, 1985.

R. Nevatia, *Structured Descriptions of Complex Curved Objects for Recognition and Visual Memory*, Stanford Artificial Intelligence Memo AIM-250, Stanford, Calif., 1974.

H. Samet, "The Quadtree and Related Hierarchical Data Structures," *Comput. Surv.* **16**, 187–260 (1984).

H. Samet, "Quadtree for Line Drawings," IEEE CG&A, 1986.

T. W. Sederberg, "A Tutorial on Modeling With Cubic Algebraic Surfaces," *ACM SIGGRAPH* (1988).

S. Shafer and T. Kanade, *The Theory of Straight Homogeneous Generalized Cylinders and A Taxonomy of Generalized Cylinders*, Carnegie Mellon University CMU-CS-83-105, Pittsburgh, Pa., 1983.

P. H. Winston, T. O. Binford, B. T. Katz, and M. Lowry, *Learning Physical Descriptions from Functional Definitions, Examples and Precedents*, AIM-349 Report STAN-CS-82-950, Stanford University, Stanford, Calif., 1983; MIT AI Memo 679, Cambridge, Mass., 1983.

T. O. BINFORD
Stanford University

SHRDLU

SHRDLU is a natural language understanding (qv) program that was developed by Winograd for his dissertation (T. Winograd, *Understanding Natural Language,* Academic Press, New York, 1972). SHRDLU understands sentences limited to the blocks-world domain. Knowledge is represented in procedural form using two special extensions of LISP, PROGRAMMAR, and PLANNER (qv). PROGRAMMAR was written by Winograd to deal with syntactic parsing (qv). Meanings are represented in Hewitt's PLANNER (C. Hewitt, PLANNER: A Language for Proving Theorems in Robots, *Proceedings of the First International Joint Conference on Artificial Intelligence,* Washington, D.C., 1969, pp. 295–301). Winograd's treatment of syntax is based on Halliday's systemic grammar [see M. A. K. Halliday, "Categories of the Theory of Grammar," *Word* **17,** 241–292 (1961); and "Language Structure and Language Function," in J. Lyons, ed., *New Horizons in Linguistics,* Penguin Books, Harmondsworth, UK, 1970, pp. 140–165.] SHRDLU reached at its time an unprecedented level of performance in language understanding.

Terry Winograd
Stanford University

SIMULA

SIMULA (SIMUlation LAnguage) was developed as an extension of ALGOL-60. It permits the definition of processes that can be executed quasi-parallel. Every process has its own data set and a set of instructions. SIMULA introduced the concept of "class" into programming languages. Single processes are instances of a possibly user-defined class. SIMULA had a big impact on many modern programming languages, eg, SMALLTALK (qv) and ADA. An introduction to the process aspects of SIMULA is given by O-J. Dahl and K. Nygaard, "SIMULA an ALGOL-Based Simulation Language," *CACM* **9,** 671–678 (Sept. 1966). Information about SIMULA67 can be found in O-J. Dahl, B. Myhrhaug, and K. Nygaard, *The SIMULA67 Common Base Language,* Publication no. S-2, Norwegian Computing Center, Forskningsveien 1B, Oslo, 1968.

J. Geller
New Jersey Institute of Technology

SIMULATED ANNEALING

Simulated annealing is a good example of carrying over an analogy from one field of science and making use of it in another. In metallurgy, one anneals a metal to ensure that it has transformed to a state that is primarily crystalline while avoiding the possibility of quenching, which leaves the metal in an amorphous, or glasslike, state. A many-particle system, in equilibrium, will have a distribution of energies. This distribution allows the system to crystallize completely from an unordered state by allowing occasional uphill energetic moves of the particles so that they can find a local state that minimizes global energy of the structure. Annealing is the careful control of temperature to allow the process of crystallization while avoiding the possibility of quenching. The key analogy was realized by researchers who were trying to simulate the transition to minimum energy states in idealized models called spin glasses. They realized that their method could be applicable to general optimization problems that possessed local minima. Applied to general optimization problems, the simulated annealing algorithm samples a corresponding energy distribution and simulates the phase transition of a system from an unordered to an ordered minimum-energy state. In general optimization problems, the spatial configuration is replaced with a general configuration in parameter space. For a detailed description of simulated annealing and its applications, see van Laarhoven and Aarts (1987), Aarts and Korst (1989), and Otten and van Ginneken (1989).

HISTORY

Simulated annealing makes use of a Monte Carlo algorithm that was first developed for hard-to-solve problems in statistical physics (Metropolis and co-workers, 1953). Kirkpatrick and co-workers (1983) at IBM and independently Černý (1985) of Comenius University, Czechoslovakia, applied this Metropolis Monte Carlo algorithm to hard combinatorial optimization problems. The hope was that drawing parallels between the collective dynamics of many-body systems and hard optimization problems would have both practical and theoretical benefit. This Monte Carlo algorithm is extremely effective and manifold in computational physics. It is used to simulate the states and dynamics of matter in high-energy physics (lattice gauge simulations), quantum chemistry, molecular dynamics, and statistical physics (spin glasses). The origins of simulated annealing brought an influx of people trained in physics to research in combinatorial optimization, neural networks, and artificial intelligence and along with them a certain jargon and insight on the nature of hard optimization problems.

THE SIMULATED ANNEALING ALGORITHM

There are actually two similar methods for obtaining the minimum-energy configuration of a many-body system and both have been used in simulated annealing. One is the original Metropolis method [used by Kirkpatrick and co-workers (1983)] and the other is the heat bath method [used by Geman and co-workers (1984)]. We will present the Metropolis method and describe how to modify it for the heat bath variant.

The Metropolis method consists of generating a random walk to estimate (via sampling) the energy distribution of a many-body system at equilibrium. This distribution is called the Gibbs or Boltzmann distribution. The

Gibbs distribution is the probability at a fixed temperature T of finding the system in state j with energy E_j:

$$p_j = \frac{\exp(-E_j/T)}{Z}$$

where Z is a normalization, called the *partition function* or *sum over states* (in German, *Zustandssumme*) and is a sum over all possible states of the system at a given temperature:

$$Z = \sum_i \exp\left(-\frac{E_i}{T}\right)$$

Pseudocode for the general annealing algorithm is shown in Figure 1.

To anneal an optimization problem, a domain-specific energy function must be developed. For example, in the traveling salesman problem, the length of the tour can be the energy (Bonomi and Lutton, 1984). (The system temperature T is a control parameter of the annealing algorithm. The domain-dependent energy is not a function of temperature). The outermost loop represents the cooling of the system according to a cooling schedule. For each system temperature T, we accept or reject trial perturbations of the system in parameter space according to the Metropolis criterion:

$$\text{Probability of accepting trial} = \begin{cases} 1 & \text{if } \Delta E \leq 0 \\ e^{-\Delta E/T} & \text{otherwise} \end{cases}$$

where ΔE is the difference in energy between the trial state and the present state.

For a derivation of why this criterion induces a random walk that estimates the Gibbs distribution, see Binder (1984), Hammersly and Handscomb (1964), and Kalos and Witlock (1986). The trials at a given temperature are repeated until the system has reached equilibrium. In past work, the typical number of trials at a given temperature are a few hundred. Equilibrium criteria that have been used include the following:

- A constant number of trials (often a function of the size of the problem).
- A given number of accepted trials (often modified so that cool temperatures, where acceptance is low, do not create extremely large iterations).
- Other measures of equilibrium, such as looking at fluctuations in average energy over the trials.
- Combinations of the preceding.

The initial temperature for annealing is set at a point where most trials are being accepted. One procedure for finding a good initial temperature is to start with a small initial value of the temperature and increase it on a schedule by multiplying the temperature by a factor greater than 1. A measure for when the system is frozen in its lowest state is when successive lowering of temperature result in no new accepted trials or when the downward movement in energy effectively halts. A domain-dependent method of generating new trial configurations (see the next section) for the accept–reject test must also be specified. One principle carried over from experience with the Metropolis method in statistical physics is to keep the ratio of accepted to proposed trials about 50% (Kalos and Witlock, 1986). In Greene and Supowit (1984), a method of annealing without rejected moves is described that is too complicated to elaborate here.

There has been a great deal of theoretical work on cooling schedules; see Hajek (1988), Geman and Geman (1984), and Otten and van Ginneken (1989) for elaboration. The theoretical schedules, however, are much too slow in practice. One simple conservative schedule is to decrease the current temperature by a multiplicative factor less than 1—typically between 0.8 and 0.99. One method for accelerating the schedule is to focus the trials around temperatures where there are phase transitions (Basu and Frazer, 1990). One can find these temperatures, called *critical temperatures*, by doing initial trial runs of the problem using a conservative schedule. These critical temperatures are associated with peaks in the *specific heat curve* given by

$$\frac{\partial}{\partial T}\langle E(T)\rangle = \frac{\sigma^2(T)}{T^2}$$

where

$$\sigma^2(T) = \langle E^2(T)\rangle - \langle E(T)\rangle^2$$

and

$$\langle E(T)\rangle \approx \frac{1}{N}\sum_{k=1}^N E(\text{Trial}_k)$$

and

$$\langle E^2(T)\rangle \approx \frac{1}{N}\sum_{k=1}^N E^2(\text{Trial}_k)$$

where N is the number of trials at a fixed temperature T, $\langle E(T)\rangle$ is the expectation value for the energy, $\langle E^2(T)\rangle$ is the expectation value of the square of the energy, and

```
Given Schedule list of T
Calculate Initial Previous-Energy (Initial Parameters)
Loop for Next T in schedule and not end criterion
    Loop until Equilibrium
        Loop for each Parameter of Optimization Problem
            Trial-Parameter = Parameter + Random-Variation
            ΔEnergy = Energy(Parameters) − Previous-Energy
            If ΔEnergy < 0 or
                Uniform-Random-Variable(0,1) ≤ exp(−ΔEnergy/T) then
                Previous-Energy = Energy
                Parameter = Trial-Parameter
            Endif
        Endloop
    Endloop
Endloop
```

Figure 1. The Metropolis Method.

Trial$_k$ represents the kth trial (van Laarhoven and Aarts, 1987). Peaks in the specific heat represent when the system is about to undergo a sudden phase transition to a more ordered state. This notion of a sudden transition in the amount of order a solution possesses is an important insight carried over from statistical physics. The exact number and nature of these phase transitions are domain dependent. Once these peak(s) are found, a schedule that decreases rapidly to the highest temperature peak, then cools slowly around the peak(s), followed by slow cooling thereafter is implemented (Basu and Frazer, 1990).

For an implementation of the annealing algorithm for the traveling salesman problem, see Section 10.9 in Press and co-workers (1988) and supplied software. Due to the domain-specific nature of annealing and the fact that annealing is normally applied to hard problems where simple descent methods fail, a hands-on approach for specifying the initial temperature, stopping criteria (temperature), temperature decrease schedule, and criteria for equilibrium at a given temperature is necessary.

In the heat bath version of annealing, the estimation of the Gibbs distribution by the Metropolis accept–reject random walk is replaced by a direct generation of the distribution. Then, for a fixed temperature, one random draw is taken from this distribution. There may be domain- or implementation-specific efficiencies to be gained in generating the Gibbs distribution directly instead of using the Metropolis method to estimate it (Basu and Frazer, 1990). Simulated annealing has been formally analyzed as Markov chains and Markov random fields to derive convergence for different classes of annealing schedules (Otten and van Ginneken, 1989; van Laarhoven and Aarts, 1987; Geman and Geman, 1984; Hajek, 1988; Gelfand, 1987).

APPLICATIONS

The first applications of simulated annealing were for hard combinatorial optimization problems; the traveling salesman problem is a canonical and often-used example (Černý, 1985; Kovacs and Goodin, 1985; Bonomi and Lutton, 1984; Aarts and co-workers, 1988; Press and co-workers, 1988). One of the first practical uses of simulated annealing, and perhaps one of the most successful, is in VLSI design for placement and routing (Kirkpatrick and co-workers, 1983). It is currently used in the TimberWolf VLSI design package (Sechen and Sangiovanni-Vincentelli, 1985). See Wong and co-workers (1988) for an overview of simulated annealing in VLSI design applications. Simulated annealing is also at the core of an unsupervised training method for neural network architectures, called Boltzmann machines (Aarts and Korst, 1989; Ackley and co-workers, 1985).

It has been shown that simulated annealing also works for general optimization problems with continuous variables, such as function minimization (Corana and co-workers, 1987; Vanderbilt and Louie, 1984; van Laarhoven and Aarts, 1987) and the solution of ill-posed inverse problems like those in vision and seismic inversion (Geman and Geman, 1984; Carnevali and co-workers, 1985; Basu and Frazer, 1990; Jeffrey and Rosner, 1986).

One view of simulated annealing is that it allows for *greedy* methods (ie, local-in-time-or-space-optimal) to find globally optimal solutions. For example, with the traveling salesman problem, Lin's 2-opt, a greedy method, is used to generate the set of possible trials. This demonstrates that a successful application of simulated annealing to combinatorial optimization often requires the use of some greedy method (possibly already existing as an established heuristic) to generate the trial set.

When simulated annealing is applied to image processing problems such as image restoration and segmentation, there is an associated spatial neighborhood involved in the trial set, and there are special considerations and analysis for this case. Simulated annealing in vision applications is a kind of stochastic relaxation method and is formally tied to the theory of Markov random fields (Geman and Geman, 1984) and spin glasses (Carnevali and co-workers, 1985). In particular, mean-field approximations and renormalization are possible methods to accelerate or supplant the annealing procedure.

BIBLIOGRAPHY

E. H. L. Aarts and J. Korst, *Simulated Annealing and Boltzmann Machines: A Stochastic Approach to Combinatorial Optimization and Neural Computing,* Wiley, Chichester, 1989.

E. H. L. Aarts, J. H. M. Korst, and Peter J. M. van Laarhoven, "A Quantitative Analysis of the Simulated Annealing Algorithm: A Case Study for the Traveling Salesman Problem," *J. Stat. Phys.* **50**(1/2), 187–206 (Jan. 1988).

D. H. Ackley, G. E. Hinton, and T. J. Sejnowski, "A Learning Algorithm for Boltzmann Machines," *Cogn. Sci.* **9**(1), 147–169 (Jan.–March 1985).

A. Basu and L. N. Frazer, "Rapid Determination of the Critical Temperature in Simulated Annealing Inversion," *Science* **249**, 1409–1412 (Sept. 21, 1990).

K. Binder, *Applications of the Monte Carlo Method in Statistical Physics,* Springer-Verlag, New York, 1984.

E. Bonomi and J.-L. Lutton, "The N-city Travelling Salesman Problem: Statistical Mechanics and the Metropolis Algorithm," *SIAM Review* **26**(4), 551–568 (Oct. 1984).

P. Carnevali, L. Coletti, and S. Patarnello, "Image Processing by Simulated Annealing," *IBM J. Res. Dev.* **29**(6), 569–579 (Nov. 1985).

V. Černý, "Thermodynamical Approach to the Traveling Salesman Problem: An Efficient Simulation Algorithm," *J. Optimization Theory Applic.* **45**(1), 41–51 (Jan. 1985).

A. Corana, M. Marchesi, C. Martini, and S. Ridella, "Minimizing Multimodal Functions of Continuous Variables with the Simulated Annealing Algorithm," *ACM Trans. Math. Software* **13**(3), 262–280 (Sept. 1987).

S. B. Gelfand, Analysis of Simulated Annealing Type Algorithms, Technical Report CICS-TH-3, MIT Laboratory for Information and Decision Systems, MIT, Cambridge, Mass., May 1987.

S. Geman and D. Geman, "Stochastic Relaxation, Gibbs Distributions, and the Bayesian Restoration of Images," *IEEE Trans. Patt. Anal. Mach. Intell.* **PAMI-6**, 721–741 (Nov. 1984).

J. W. Greene and K. J. Supowit, "Simulated Annealing Without Rejected Moves," *IEEE Trans. Computer-Aided Design.* **CAD-5**, 221–228, 1986.

B. Hajek, "Cooling Schedules for Optimal Annealing," *Math Op. Res.* **13**(2), 311–329 (May 1988).

J. M. Hammersley and D. C. Handscomb, *Monte Carlo Methods,* Chapman & Hall, London, 1964.

W. Jeffrey and R. Rosner, "Optimization Algorithms: Simulated Annealing and Neural Network Processing," *Astrophysical J.* **310**, 473–481 (Nov. 1, 1986).

M. H. Kalos and P. A. Witlock, *Monte Carlo Methods, Vol. 1: Basics,* Wiley, New York, 1986.

S. Kirkpatrick, C. D. Gelatt, Jr., and M. P. Vecchi, "Optimization by Simulated Annealing," *Science* **220**(4598), 671–680 (May 13, 1983).

W. J. Kovacs and D. T. Goodin, "A Statistical Approach to the Traveling Salesman Problem," *Transpn. Res.-B* **19B**(3), 239–252 (1985).

N. Metropolis, A. W. Rosenbluth, M. N. Rosenbluth, A. H. Teller, and E. Teller, "Equations of State Calculations by Fast Computing Machines," *J. Chem. Phys.* **21**(6), 1087–1091 (June 1953).

R. H. J. M. Otten and L. P. P. P van Ginneken, *The Annealing Algorithm,* Kluwer Academic Publishers, Boston, 1989.

W. H. Press, B. P. Flannery, S. A. Teokolosky, and W. T. Vetterling, *Numerical Recipies in C: The Art of Scientific Computing,* Cambridge University Press, New York, 1988.

C. Sechen and A. L. Sangiovanni-Vincentelli, "The TimberWolf Placement and Routing Package," *IEEE J. Solid State Circuits* **SC-20**, 510–522 (1985).

P. J. M. van Laarhoven and E. H. L. Aarts, *Simulated Annealing: Theory and Applications,* D. Reidel Publishing Company, Boston, 1987.

D. Vanderbilt and S. G. Louie, "A Monte Carlo Simulated Annealing to Optimization over Continuous Variables," *J. Comput. Phys.* **36**, 258–271 (1984).

D. F. Wong, H. W. Leong, and C. L. Liu, *Simulated Annealing for VLSI Design,* Kluwer Academic Publishers, Boston, 1988.

ALBERT BOULANGER
Bolt, Beranek, and Newman

SIR

SIR was an early experimental system implemented at the MIT AI Laboratory to explore ways of representing knowledge in computers. The SIR program demonstrated some of the properties later called *inheritance* in object-oriented languages, *rule-based knowledge* in expert systems, and *inference* in logic programming. With a pseudo natural language front-end, the entire LISP-based system ran in a 144 KByte mainframe computer of the early 1960s. (See B. Raphael, "SIR: A Computer Program for Semantic Information Retrieval," in M. Minsky, ed., *Semantic Information Processing,* MIT Press, Cambridge, Mass., 1968.)

B. RAPHAEL
Compass Point Travel, Inc.

SITUATION THEORY AND SITUATION SEMANTICS

Situation theory grew out of the development by Barwise and Perry in the early 1980s of a semantic theory for natural language known as situation semantics. It became widely known with the publication of the book *Situations and Attitudes* (Barwise and Perry, 1983). Since the appearance of that early work, the subject has changed considerably. The most comprehensive up-to-date treatment of situation theory and situation semantics is to be found in the book *Logic and Information* (Devlin, 1991) (see also Barwise, 1989; Cooper, Mukai, and Perry, 1990).

Situation theory should not be confused with the *situation calculus* of McCarthy, Hayes, and co-workers, [see, eg, Chap. 11, Gensereth and Nilsson, 1987). The "situations" considered in the latter can be regarded as examples of the situations in situation theory, with situation theory being a far more general and less AI-driven theory than the situation calculus, but the connections between the two are not strong.

As the name suggests, situation semantics is a semantic theory in that it tries to come to grips with the nature of "meaning"; but in terms of the traditional linguistic distinctions between syntax, semantics, and pragmatics, situation semantics takes on board many of the issues that would normally be classified as pragmatics.

SITUATION THEORY

Although originally developed to provide an ontological framework for situation semantics, situation theory provides a very general framework for a qualitative study of information. The situation-theoretic approach to the study of information starts from the consideration of an agent situated in the world and interacting with its environment. The ontology depends upon (or reflects) the behavior of the agent.

The critical notion that gives the theory its name is that of a *situation*. Situations are limited parts of the world, either concrete or abstract, that the agent either cognitively individuates or else behaviorally discriminates. Examples of situations are regions of space–time, human activities going on in a certain region of space–time, conversations (including long-distance telephone conversations), certain actions taking place in a computer system, visual scenes, databases, Unix directories, background conditions for the constraints that underpin reasoning, and fictional worlds such as those described in novels.

The theory regards situations in an intensional manner; indeed, they generally defy a precise extensional description. Situations are on the same ontological footing as individuals such as tables, chairs, apples, people, pencils, etc. The distinction is that situations have an internal structure that plays a significant role in the theory in a way that the structure of an individual does not. It is possible for the same object to be classified as both an individual and a situation.

Situations may be categorized by means of formal objects called *situation types*. More generally, types are similarity categories across individuals, situations, and other objects in the ontology.

An agent can extract from one situation information about another situation by means of a *constraint,* an abstract linkage between situation types. For example, an agent who encounters a smokey situation may infer that there is a fire by virtue of the constraint that links the type of those situations in which there is smoke to the type of those situations in which there is fire.

In the case where the first situation type is that of an utterance, the relevant constraints include the meaning of the sentence uttered, and this is how situation semantics becomes a special case of a general theory of information flow. This leads to one of the basic ideas of situation semantics, namely the relational theory of meaning, where the meaning of an expression ϕ, denoted by $\|\phi\|$, is viewed as providing a relation between pairs of situations, the one in which the expression is uttered and the one it describes. The relational theory thus provides a conceptual scheme to express the way the agent may utilize information in the circumstances of utterance. Clearly, this view of meaning is quite different from that given by semantic theories that view the meanings of expressions as mathematical objects that can be described independently of the uses of the expression.

Situation theory treats information as a discrete commodity, independent of representation. This allows both for the study of the manner in which information can be represented and for an investigation of reasoning involving different forms of representation, such as text, pictures, and sound. Information is regarded as consisting of discrete "items" called *infons,* of which more will be said presently.

One of the early successes of situation theory was the development of mathematical models of information systems involving self-reference or circularity. The book (Barwise and Etchemendy, 1987) provides a situation-theoretic treatment of self-referential statements and includes a resolution of the famous liar paradox; Chapter 9 of Barwise (1989) develops a situation-theoretic treatment of common knowledge that avoids infinite regress or fixed points. Such mathematical modeling makes use of the theory of non-well-founded sets developed by Aczel (1988). Israel and Perry (1989) use situation theory as a basis for a detailed investigation of the nature of information and the representation of information. Barwise and Etchemendy (1990a) shows how situation theory can be used to study mathematical reasoning involving two distinct forms of representation, text and pictures. An extension of this study is their current development of Hyperproof, a computer system to help the user perform such "heterogeneous" mathematical reasoning. This system is described in Barwise and Etchemendy (1990b). A logic programming language based upon situation theory is currently under development. Known as PROSIT (for "programming in situation theory"), this language is described in Nakashima and co-workers (1988).

ONTOLOGY

The objects (or uniformities) in the ontology include the following:

- Individuals: objects such as tables, chairs, tetrahedra, cubes, people, hands, fingers, etc, that the agent either individuates or at least discriminates (by its behavior) as single, essentially unitary items.
- Relations: uniformities individuated or discriminated by the agent that hold of, or link together specific numbers of, certain other uniformities.
- Spatial locations: these are not necessarily like the "points" of mathematical spaces (though they may be so) but can have spatial extension.
- Temporal locations: as with spatial locations, temporal locations may be either points in time or regions of time.
- Situations: structured parts of the world (concrete or abstract) discriminated by (or perhaps individuated by) the agent.
- Types: higher order uniformities (see presently) discriminated (and possibly individuated) by the agent.
- Parameters: indeterminates that range over objects of the various types.

The intuition is that the activity (both physical and cognitive) of a particular agent or species of agent is systematically affected by certain regularities, or uniformities, that the agent either individuates or else discriminates in its behavior. For instance, people individuate certain parts of reality as objects (individuals in the theory), and their behavior can vary in a systematic way according to spatial location, time, and the nature of the immediate environment (situation types in the theory).

INFONS

If P is an n-place relation in the ontology and $x_1, \ldots, x_n$ are objects (in the ontology) that are appropriate for the respective argument roles of P, then

$$\langle\!\langle P, x_1, \ldots, x_n, 1 \rangle\!\rangle$$

denotes the informational item, or infon, that $x_1, \ldots, x_n$ stand in the relation P, and

$$\langle\!\langle P, x_1, \ldots, x_n, 0 \rangle\!\rangle$$

denotes the infon that $x_1, \ldots, x_n$ do not stand in the relation P. This notation is slightly misleading in that it uses position (and often semantic knowledge) to indicate which objects fill which argument roles. A more formal notation lists the argument roles of the relation and stipulates the individual assignments of objects to those roles. Devlin (1991) describes in detail how this may be done. It should be stressed that infons are semantic objects in a mathematical theory, not sentences in some language that require interpretation.

The theory regards relations in a fairly sophisticated, realist manner in that relations are taken to be abstract objects having a definite and often intricate structure. In particular, there are in general very definite restrictions (called *appropriateness conditions*) upon what kinds of entities may and may not fill the various *argument roles* of a given relation and certain *minimality conditions* that stipulate which collection of argument roles must be filled in order to obtain an infon with that relation as head. For example, the relation *eating* has argument roles for the eater, the thing eaten, the time of the eating, and the location of the eating; the only things that are eligible to fill the role of the eater are animate individuals, the thing eaten must be some edible substance, the time role can only be filled by an appropriately sized temporal location, and the location role can only be filled by an appropriately sized spatial location. The minimality conditions require that at least one of the eater and the thing-eaten roles must be filled to produce an infon.

The class of compound infons is constructed from the infons by closing under operations of conjunction and disjunction and bounded existential and universal quantification (over parameters).

A particular infon may be true or false about a certain part of the world (a situation). Given a situation s and an infon σ,

$$s \models \sigma$$

means that the infon σ is "made factual by" the situation s, or to put it another way, that σ is an item of information that is true of s. The official name for this relation is that s *supports* σ. The facticity claim $s \models \sigma$ is referred to as a *proposition*.

TYPES

The types are defined by applying two type abstraction procedures (see presently), starting with an initial collection of *basic types*. The basic types correspond to the process of individuating or discriminating uniformities in the world at the most fundamental level. The most common basic types are as follows:

TIM: the type of temporal location;
LOC: the type of a spatial location;
IND: the type of an individual;
REL^n: the type of an n-place relation;
SIT: the type of a situation;
INF: the type of an infon;
TYP: the type of a type (see later);
PAR: the type of a *parameter* (see presently);
POL: the type of a polarity (ie, the "truth values" 0 and 1).

For each basic type T other than PAR, there is an infinite collection $T_1, T_2, T_3, \ldots$ of *basic parameters* used to denote arbitrary objects of type T. In general, the less formal notation $\dot{l}, \dot{t}, \dot{a}, \dot{s}, \ldots$ is used to denote parameters (in this case of type LOC, TIM, IND, SIT, respectively). Given an object x and a type T, the expression $x: T$ indicates that the object x is of type T.

PARAMETERS AND ANCHORS

The mechanism for assigning values to parameters is provided by *anchors*. Formally, an anchor for a set A of basic parameters is a function defined on A, which assigns to each parameter T_n in A an object of type T. If σ is a compound infon and f is an anchor for some of the parameters in σ, $\sigma[f]$ is the compound infon that results from replacing each parameter $\dot{a}$ in dom(f) by $f(a)$.

Most uses of parameters require *restricted parameters* whose range is more fine grained than the basic parameters. These are constructed as follows. Let v be a parameter. By a *condition* on v is meant any finite conjunction of infons. (At least one conjunct should involve v; otherwise the definition is degenerate.) Given such a parameter v and a condition C on v, there is a new parameter, $v \restriction C$, called a restricted parameter, that can be used to denote an object of the same type as v, that satisfies the requirements imposed by C (in any situation where this applies).

Let $\dot{r} = v \restriction C$ be a parameter. Given a situation s, a function f is said to be an anchor for $\dot{r}$ in s if:

1. f is an anchor for v and for every parameter that occurs free in C;
2. for each infon σ in C: $s \models \sigma[f]$;
3. $f(\dot{r}) = f(v)$.

TYPE ABSTRACTION

There are two kinds of type abstraction, leading to two kinds of types. First of all there are the situation types. Given a SIT parameter $\dot{s}$ and a compound infon σ, there is a corresponding situation type

$$[\dot{s} \mid \dot{s} \models \sigma]$$

the type of situation in which σ obtains.

This process of obtaining a type from a parameter $\dot{s}$ and a compound infon σ is known as (situation-) type abstraction.

For example,

$$[\text{SIT}_1 \mid \text{SIT}_1 \models \langle\!\langle \text{running}, \dot{p}, \text{LOC}_1, \text{TIM}_1, 1 \rangle\!\rangle]$$

(where $\dot{p}$ is a parameter for a person) denotes the type of situation in which someone is running at some location and at some time. (Strictly speaking, this is an example of a *parametric type*. Replacing each of the parameters $\dot{p}$, LOC$_1$, and TIM$_1$ by specific objects of the respective types would produce a *parameter-free* type.) A situation s will be of this type just in case someone is running in that situation (at some location, at some time).

As well as situation types, the theory also allows for *object types*. These include the basic types TIM, LOC, IND, REL^n, SIT, INF, TYP, PAR, and POL as well as the more fine-grained uniformities obtained as follows. Object types are determined over some initial situation. Let s be a given situation. If $\dot{x}$ is a parameter and σ is some compound infon (in general involving $\dot{x}$), then there is a type

$$[\dot{x} \mid s \models \sigma]$$

the type of all those objects x to which $\dot{x}$ may be anchored in the situation s, for which the conditions imposed by σ obtain. In many instances, the situation s is "the world" or "the environment" the agent lives in (generally denoted by w).

For example, the type of all people could be denoted by

$$[\text{IND}_1 \mid w \models \langle\!\langle \text{person}, \text{IND}_1, \dot{l}_w, \dot{t}_{\text{now}}, 1 \rangle\!\rangle]$$

Again, if s denotes Jon's environment (over a suitable time span), then

$$[\dot{e} \mid s \models \langle\!\langle \text{sees}, \text{Jon}, \dot{e}, \text{LOC}_1, \text{TIM}_1, 1 \rangle\!\rangle]$$

denotes the type of all those situations Jon sees (within s). (Again these examples are, strictly speaking, parametric types.)

Notice that situation types classify situations according to their internal structure, whereas object types classify from the outside.

CONSTRAINTS

The constraints that give rise to information flow are abstract links between situation types. They may be natural laws, conventions, logical (ie, analytic) rules, linguistic rules, empirical links, lawlike correspondences, or whatever. Their role in the information chain is quite well conveyed by the use of the word *means*. For instance, consider the following statement: *Smoke means fire*. This expresses a constraint (of the natural law variety). What it says is that there is a lawlike relation that links situations where there is smoke to situations where there is fire. If S is the type of situations where there is smoke present, and S' is the type of situations where there is a fire, then an agent (eg, a person) can pick up the information that there is a fire by observing that there is smoke (a type S situation) and being aware of, or attuned to, the constraint that links the two kinds of situation, denoted by

$$S \Rightarrow S'$$

(This is read as S *involves* S'.) Notice that any particular instance where a constraint is utilized to make an inference or modify behavior will involve specific situations (of the relevant types). Thus constraints function by relating various regularities or uniformities across actual situations.

Note that the smoke and fire example does not depend upon language. Indeed, this particular constraint is one that holds regardless of the presence or absence of any cognitive agent. For an example of a constraint that does involve language, consider the claim

"Fire" means fire.

This claim describes the constraint

$$S'' \Rightarrow S'$$

that links situations (of type S'') where someone yells the word *fire* to situations (of type S') where there is a fire. Awareness of this constraint involves knowing the meaning of the word *fire* and being familiar with the rules that govern the use of language.

The three types just introduced may be defined as follows:

$$S = [\dot{s} \mid \dot{s} \models \langle\!\langle \text{smokey}, \dot{t}, 1 \rangle\!\rangle]$$
$$S' = [\dot{s} \mid \dot{s} \models \langle\!\langle \text{firey}, \dot{t}, 1 \rangle\!\rangle]$$
$$S'' = [\dot{u} \mid \dot{u} \models \langle\!\langle \text{speaking}, \dot{a}, \dot{t}, 1 \rangle\!\rangle \wedge \langle\!\langle \text{utters}, \dot{a}, \text{FIRE}, \dot{t}, 1 \rangle\!\rangle]$$

The use of the same parameter $\dot{s}$ in the types S and S' means that the constraint

$$S \Rightarrow S'$$

functions by constraining the situation in which there is smoke to be a situation in which there is fire. The use of different parameters $\dot{u}$ and $\dot{s}$ in the types S'' and S' means that the constraint

$$S'' \Rightarrow S'$$

simply guarantees that an utterance of the word *fire* is linked to there being some situation in which there is a fire. The utterance situation and the fire situation may be quite separate. The use of the same time parameter $\dot{t}$ in all three types means that there is no time slippage in either case. The smokey and the fire are simultaneous, and so are the utterance and the fire.

In general, parameters keep track of the various informational links that are instrumental in the way constraints operate. See Devlin (1991) and Israel and Perry (1989) for details.

A good way to provide some indication of the way the situation-theoretic ontology may be used to investigate information flow is to give a brief account of some of the key ideas of situation semantics. A fuller account of the basic ideas is provided by Devlin (1991). The book by Gawron and Peters (1990) is at a more advanced level and covers some specialized issues in semantics.

SITUATION SEMANTICS

In situation semantics, the main object of study in the utterance, by some speaker, of some word, phrase, sentence, or group of sentences. For definiteness, a single listener is assumed in this account. The general framework adopted consists of the following. First of all there is the utterance situation, the situation or context in which the utterance is made and received. If Jan says to Naomi, "A man is at the door," the utterance situation u is the immediate context in which Jan utters these words and Naomi hears them. It includes both Jan and Naomi (for the duration of the utterance) and should be sufficiently rich to identify various salient factors about this utterance, such as the door to which Jan is referring. This is probably the one in her immediate environment, but if Jan utters this sentence as part of a larger discourse, the situation u could provide an alternative door. Between the utterance itself and the various objects referred to are *connections* (or *speaker's connections*). Thus,

$$u \models \langle\!\langle \text{utters, Jan, A man is at the door}, l, t, 1 \rangle\!\rangle$$
$$\wedge \langle\!\langle \text{refers-to, Jan, the door}, D, l, t, 1 \rangle\!\rangle$$

where D is a door that is fixed by u. Thus the speaker's connections link the utterance (as part of u) of the phrase *the door* to the object D. The speaker in an utterance situation u is generally denoted by a_u, the listener by b_u.

In many cases, the utterance is part of an ongoing *discourse situation* d. In cases where the utterance is made in isolation, the utterance situation and the discourse situation coincide. The discourse situation is part of a larger *embedding situation* that incorporates that part of the world of direct relevance to the discourse (in a way that can only be made clear by a complete treatment of the subject).

There may also be, a *resource situation*. For instance, if Jan says, "The man I saw running yesterday is at the door," she is making use of a situation that she witnessed the day before, the one in which a certain man was running, in order to identify the man at the door. That is, there is another situation, r, a situation that occurred the day before the utterance, and which Jan witnessed, such that

$$u \models \langle\!\langle \text{utters, Jan}, \Phi, l, t, 1 \rangle\!\rangle$$
$$\wedge \langle\!\langle \text{refers-to, Jan, the man}, M, l, t, 1 \rangle\!\rangle$$
$$\wedge \langle\!\langle \text{refers-to, Jan, the door}, D, l, t, 1 \rangle\!\rangle$$

where Φ is the sentence *The man I saw running yesterday is at the door,* and where Jan is making use of r and the fact that M is the unique man such that (for some appropriate values of l', t')

$$r \models \langle\!\langle \text{runs}, M, l', t', 1 \rangle\!\rangle$$

Resource situations can be part of the embedding situation, but they need not be. They can become available for exploitation in various ways, such as by being perceived by the speaker, by being the objects of some common knowledge about the world or some situation, by being the way the world is, or by being built up by previous discourse.

Finally, there is the *described situation,* that part of the world the utterance is about. Features of the utterance situation serve to identify the described situation. For instance, if Jan makes the preceding utterance while peering out of the upstairs window through a pair of field glasses at the house across the street, then her utterance refers to the situation s that she sees, the situation at the house across the street, and we have

$$s \models \langle\!\langle \text{present}, M, l, t, 1 \rangle\!\rangle$$

where l is the location of the door and t is the time of the utterance. It should be noted that, although cast in terms of spoken utterances, situation semantics is really a study of all forms of semantic information processing and communication, involving people, animals, or machines.

THE RELATIONAL THEORY OF MEANING

The relational theory of meaning was originally proposed to handle assertive (also known as *indicative*) sentences. For such utterances, the general idea is this. The meaning of an assertive sentence Φ is a constraint, an abstract link that connects the type of an utterance of Φ with the type of the described situation.

Sentence meaning rests upon word meaning. The meaning of a word is a relation that provides an abstract link between the utterance situation and the object (possibly an abstract object, such as a relation) in the world that the word denotes.

For example, in any utterance u the first-person singular pronoun I denotes the speaker and the meaning of I is the relation that connects u to a_u for any utterance u. So for given objects u and a,

$$u \| I \| a \quad \text{if and only if} \quad u{:}U \text{ and } a = a_u$$

where U is the type of an utterance of the word I. Thus the meaning of the pronoun I is a relation linking situations to individuals. In mathematical terms, this is expressed by saying that $\|I\|$ is a relation *on* $S \times A$, where S is the class of situations and A is the class of individuals.

Likewise, the meaning of *you* links an utterance to the listener (b_u), and the meaning of a third-person pronoun, proper name, or common noun links an utterance to some object determined by other features of the utterance. The meaning of a verb is the link between the verb and the relation it denotes. For example, the verb *runs* corresponds to the relation R of running. Verb tense is dealt with by the mechanics of situation semantics. In each case, the meaning of a word α is a relation $\|\alpha\|$ that links an utterance situation u with a certain object a, either an individual in the case where α is a pronoun or name or a relation in the case of a verb. The relation $u\|\alpha\|a$ places a constraint on the utterance situation u to supply (or contain) a suitable object.

The approach taken to language in situation semantics is an informational one. In the case of an utterance of an assertive sentence, one significant feature considered is the information intentionally conveyed by the utterance. This will consist of partial information (a compound infon) about a particular situation (the described situation). This partiality of information is a central theme in situation theory. At any instant, the agent has (in general) only partial information about a particular situation, and communication and action have to be carried out on the basis of that partial information. This is illustrated by the following abbreviated analysis of an utterance of a simple assertive sentence. Suppose u is a situation in which Jan utters the sentence

$$\Phi\text{: Keith bought a dog}$$

Then Jan is providing information about a particular described situation s_u, a situation in which someone named Keith bought some dog. Factors about the utterance situation u should (if this utterance is to succeed in imparting to the listener the information Jan wants to convey) determine a unique individual $k = c_u(\text{KEITH})$ such that for some resource situation $r_k = c_u^{\text{res}}(\text{KEITH})$,

1. $r_k \models \langle\!\langle \text{person}, k, t_k, 1 \rangle\!\rangle \wedge \langle\!\langle \text{named}, k, \text{KEITH}, t_k, 1 \rangle\!\rangle$,
2. k is the only such individual in r_k,

where, according to the overall context, either t_k includes t_u or else t_k includes the time t introduced in what follows.

The meaning of the word *bought* relates Jan's usage of this word to a relation "buys," and the usage of the past tense determines that for some time t, preceding t_u,

3. $s_u \models \langle\!\langle \text{buys}, k, p, t, 1 \rangle\!\rangle$,

where p is as follows.

Finally, for the utterance to be true, there must be an individual p and a resource situation $r_p = c_u^{\text{rec}}$ (A DOG) such that

4. $r_p \models \langle\!\langle \text{dog}, p, t, 1 \rangle\!\rangle$,
5. $s_u \models \langle\!\langle \text{buys}, k, p, t, 1 \rangle\!\rangle$.

In order for the utterance to be successful, it is not necessary that either Jan or the listener have extensive, or even the same, knowledge of the resource situation r_k. The critical information Jan needs and the listener may infer is that there is an individual k' such that

6. $r_k \models \langle\!\langle \text{person}, k', t_k, 1 \rangle\!\rangle \wedge \langle\!\langle \text{named}, k', \text{KEITH}, t_k, 1 \rangle\!\rangle$,
7. k' is the only such individual in r_k.

It is not necessary that the listener can identify the k' here with the individual k Jan is referring to, though Jan might well be assuming the listener has such knowledge. The *assumption* by Jan of a certain shared knowledge about the resource situation r_k is what enables her to use the name Keith the way she does. Though she herself may well have a very extensive stock of information about r_k, the listener's knowledge could be quite meager. It might only amount to the two items 6 and 7 in the preceding. More likely, the listener's knowledge of the rules governing English proper names would allow him to conclude in addition that

8. $r_k \models \langle\!\langle \text{male}, k', t_k, 1 \rangle\!\rangle$.

A fairly cursory knowledge of Jan's family circumstances might also provide the listener with the further information

9. $r_k \models \langle\!\langle \text{husband-of}, k', a_u, t_k, 1 \rangle\!\rangle$.

(It may also be the case that t_k includes t_u.) The listener then requires only quite minimal knowledge about r_k in order for Jan's usage of the name Keith to be informational. But notice that Jan too needs to actually draw on very little information about r_k in order to make this utterance.

Turning next to Jan's utterance of the word *bought*, assume that both the speaker and the listener associate with this word the same relation, *buys*, a complex, structured object relating a number of arguments. The usage of the past tense will be dealt with in just a moment, when the informational content of Jan's utterance is examined.

Jan's usage of the phrase *a dog* is likewise linked to a certain situation r_p, a situation associated with the dog Keith brought, a situation that supports, among other things, the fact of that dog being a dog. Notice that Jan may or may not have any direct knowledge of just which dog Keith bought. All that can be assumed is that there must be such a p and an associated resource situation r_p. The use of the indefinite article leaves aside all questions as to the identity of the dog. Thus, Jan's utterance refers to a situation in which there are two individuals, k and p. The individual k is referred to directly in the utterance, and facts about the resource situation r_k are required in order for the utterance to convey the information Jan intends of it (assuming the obvious intent, discussed below). The individual p is not referred to in the utterance, nor is the resource situation r_p. There must of course *be* such an individual, and associated with that individual there will be a resource situation r_p. But Jan's utterance does not identify them the way it does the individual k and the situation r_k.

Turning to the informational content of the utterance, in the most straightforward case, the item of information that Jan wants to convey by means of her utterance is what is referred to as the propositional content of the utterance. This is the proposition

$$s_u \models \exists \dot{p} \, \exists \dot{t} \, \langle\!\langle \text{buys}, k, \dot{p}, \dot{t}, 1 \rangle\!\rangle$$

where $\dot{p}$ is a parameter for a dog and $\dot{t}$ is a parameter for a time period prior to t_u.

Notice that this content has as constituents the described situation s_u, the individual k, and the relation *buys*. The speaker makes explicit reference both to the individual k and the relation *buys*. The described situation s_u is not referred to in the utterance. Rather the speaker's connections put s_u into the propositional content. Neither the actual time of the buying nor the actual dog bought get into the propositional content. Contrast this with an utterance of the sentence

Ψ: Keith bought the dog

Here the propositional content is

$$s_u \models \exists \dot{t} \, \langle\!\langle \text{buys}, k, p, \dot{t}, 1 \rangle\!\rangle$$

This time the particular dog, p, gets into the propositional content as an articulated constituent of the utterance. But from where does this individual come? The utterance of this one sentence alone does not serve to identify p. Rather some previous utterance, or some embedding circumstance, has to pick out the particular dog to which Jan refers. (This particular sentence would seem to force the referential use of the definite description *the dog*.) Normal language use requires that an utterance of sentence Ψ is indeed either preceded by an utterance that supplies the individual p, referred to in Ψ by the phrase *the dog*, or else the utterance is made in a circumstance where other factors serve to make this identification (such as the utterance being made while the speaker and listener are jointly viewing a scene in which there is exactly one dog).

The propositional content of the utterance of an assertive sentence is the theory's way of getting at the principal item of information that, under normal circumstances, the speaker intends to convey by the utterance. As such it is closely related to the meaning of the sentence.

The meaning of a sentence is an extrinsic feature of the sentence, independent of any particular context of utterance. For the present example, the meaning of the sentence Φ is an abstract link, $\|\Phi\|$, that connects the situation-type

$$U = [\dot{u} \mid \dot{u} \models \langle\!\langle \text{speaking-to}, \dot{a}_u, \dot{b}_u, \dot{l}_u, \dot{t}_u, 1\rangle\!\rangle$$
$$\wedge \langle\!\langle \text{utters}, \dot{a}_u, \Phi, \dot{l}_u, \dot{t}_u, 1\rangle\!\rangle$$
$$\wedge \langle\!\langle \text{refers-to}, \dot{a}_u, \text{Keith}, \dot{k}, \dot{l}_u, \dot{t}_u, 1\rangle\!\rangle]$$

and the situation type

$$E = [\dot{s} \mid \dot{s} \models \exists \dot{p}\, \exists \dot{t}\, \langle\!\langle \text{buys}, \dot{k}, \dot{p}, \dot{t}, 1\rangle\!\rangle]$$

(where $\dot{k}$ is a parameter for a person named Keith, $\dot{p}$ is a parameter for a dog, and $\dot{t}$ is a parameter for a time period preceding $\dot{t}_u$). The meaning of Φ, $\|\Phi\|$, connects any particular utterance of Φ with the fact of the world (or relevant part thereof) being the way Φ says it should be, that is to say, for appropriate situations u and v,

$$u\|\Phi\|v \text{ if and only if } [u{:}U] \text{ and } [v \supseteq s_u(\Phi)] \text{ and } [v{:}E]$$

BIBLIOGRAPHY

P. Aczel, *Non-Well-Founded Sets,* CSLI Lecture Notes 14, CSLI Publications, Stanford, Calif., 1988.

J. Barwise, *The Situation in Logic,* CSLI Lecture Notes 17, CSLI Publications, Stanford, Calif., 1989.

J. Barwise and J. Etchemendy, *The Liar: An Essay in Truth and Circularity,* Oxford University Press, New York, 1987.

J. Barwise and J. Etchemendy "Information, Infons, and Inference," in R. H. Cooper, K. Mukai, and J. Perry, eds., *Situation Theory and Its Application,* Vol. 1, Lecture Notes 22, CSLI Publications, Stanford, Calif., 1990a, pp. 33–78.

J. Barwise and J. Etchemendy, "Visual Information and Valid Reasoning," in W. Zimmerman and S. Cunningham, eds., *Visualization in Teaching and Learning Mathematics,* Mathematical Association of America, Washington, D.C., 1990b.

J. Barwise and J. Perry, *Situations and Attitudes,* Bradford Books, MIT Press, Cambridge, Mass., 1983.

R. Cooper, K. Mukai, and J. Perry, eds., *Situation Theory and its Applications,* Vol. I, CSLI Lecture Notes 22, CSLI Publications, Stanford, Calif., 1990.

K. J. Devlin, *Logic and Information,* Cambridge University Press, Cambridge, England, 1991.

M. Gawron and S. Peters, *Anaphora and Quantification in Situation Semantics,* CSLI Lecture Notes 19, CSLI Publications, Stanford, Calif., 1990.

M. Gensereth and N. Nilsson, *Logical Foundations of Artificial Intelligence,* Morgan Kaufmann, San Mateo, Calif., 1987.

D. Israel and J. Perry, "What is Information?" in *Information, Language and Cognition,* P. Hanson, ed., University of British Columbia Press, Vancouver, Canada, 1989.

H. Nakashima, H. Suzuki, P.-K. Halvorsen, and S. Peters, *Towards a Computational Interpretation of Situation Theory,* in *Proceedings of the International Conference on Fifth Generation Computer Systems 1988,* ICOT, Tokyo, Japan, 1988 pp. 489–498.

Keith J. Devlin
Colby College

SLIP

A list processing utility implemented as a FORTRAN subroutine package written by Weizenbaum in 1963, SLIP characteristically uses doubly linked lists as basic data objects and is embedded in the overt context of its host FORTRAN [see J. Weizenbaum, "Symmetric List Processing," *CACM* **6**, 524–544 (1963); N. Findler, J. Pfaltz, and H. Bernstein, *Four High Level Extensions of FORTRAN IV: SLIP, AMPPL-II, TREETRAN, and SYMBOLANG,* Spartan, New York, 1971].

A. Hanyong Yuhan
AT&T Bell Laboratories

SMALLTALK

Smalltalk is a programming language based on the properties of object-oriented technology: encapsulation, inheritance, and polymorphism. Historically, the Smalltalk language and development environment are derived from ideas in Simula-67, Sketchpad, and JOSS. Smalltalk is a graphical, interactive programming environment in which the user can store, access, and manipulate information. Details of the user interface for Smalltalk can be found in the *User Guide* to the product Objectworks for Smalltalk-80 by ParcPlace Systems. Smalltalk as a language is built on the model of communicating objects, where an object consists of some private data and a set of operations. A message is a request for an object to carry out one of its operations. The Smalltalk system is made up of many objects that provide the functions usually attributed to a computer system. (See A. Goldberg and D. Robson, *Smalltalk-80: The Language,* Addison-Wesley, Reading, Mass., 1989.) The research program that created the system is described in several articles in *Byte,* Aug. 1981.

Adele Goldberg
ParcPlace Systems

SNePS

SNePS, the Semantic Network Processing System, is a propositional semantic network (qv) knowledge representation (qv) and reasoning system. It includes SNIP, the SNePS Inference Package, which is an inference engine over rules represented in SNePS using a set of nonstandard, network-oriented propositional connectives and quantifiers (see Logic; Logic, propositional); SNeBR, the SNePS belief revision (qv) system; SNaLPS, the SNePS natural language processing System, which consists of a morphological analyzer, a morphological synthesizer, and an interpreter of generalized augmented transition network grammars that can be used to write a combined parsing and generation grammar (see Natural language understanding; Natural language generation; Morphology; Grammar, augmented transition network); and SNePSLOG, a SNePS front end that allows one to interact with SNePS in a language very close to the standard syntax of higher-order predicate calculus (see LOGIC, PREDICATE; LOGIC, HIGHER ORDER). SNIP allows for the cooperative use of path-based and node-based inference, supports bi-directional inference and default reasoning, and can use recursive rules without getting into an infinite loop (see PROCESSING, BOTTOM-UP & TOP-DOWN; RECURSION). SNePS has been used for research on knowledge representation and reasoning, natural language understanding and generation, cognitive modeling, multi-media interfaces, and applied expert diagnosis systems (see COGNITIVE MODELING; EXPERT SYSTEMS). [See S. C. Shapiro, "The SNePS Semantic Network Processing System," in N. V. Findler, ed., *Associative Networks: The Representation and Use of Knowledge by Computers,* pp. 179–203, Academic Press, New York, 1979; S. C. Shapiro and W. J. Rapaport, "SNePS Considered as a Fully Intensional Propositional Semantic Network," in N. Cercone and G. McCalla, ed., *The Knowledge Frontier,* pp. 263–315, Springer-Verlag, New York, 1987; S. C. Shapiro and W. J. Rapaport, "The SNePS Family," *Comput. Math. Applic.* (1991); S. C. Shapiro and co-workers, *SNePS-2.1 User's Manual,* Department of Computer Science, SUNY, Buffalo, N.Y., 1991.]

STUART C. SHAPIRO
SUNY at Buffalo

SNIFFER

SNIFFER is a natural deduction system completed in 1977 at SRI International by Fikes and Hendrix. SNIFFER is a manager and coordinator of deductive and problem solving processes for answering queries using knowledge stored in a partitioned semantic network representation language called K-NET. K-NET includes facilities for representing class taxonomies and context hierarchies. SNIFFER includes a logically complete set of natural deduction facilities that do not require statements to be converted into clause or prenex normal form. Using SNIFFER's coroutine-based control structure, alternative proofs may be constructed in pseudo-parallel and results shared among them. In addition, SNIFFER can also manage the application of specialist procedures that have specific knowledge about a particular domain or about the topology of the K-NET structures. (See R. Fikes and G. Hendrix, "A Network-Based Knowledge Representation and Its Natural Deduction System," *Proceedings of the Fifth International Joint Conference on Artificial Intelligence,* Cambridge, Mass., 1977, pp. 235–246.)

RICHARD FIKES
Stanford University

SNOBOL-4

SNOBOL-4 is a string- and pattern-oriented programming language. It is described in R. E. Griswold, J. F. Poage, and I. P. Polonsky, *The SNOBOL-4 Programming Language,* Prentice-Hall, Englewood Cliffs, N.J., 1971.

The superior qualities of SNOBOL-4 and its predecessors as a pattern-matching (qv) language have been used to implement several AI programs (eg, see S. C. Shapiro and G. H. Woodmansee, "A Net Structure Based Relational Question Answer: Description and Examples," in *Proceedings of the First International Joint Conference on Artificial Intelligence,* Washington, D.C., 1969, pp. 325–346). SNOBOL-4 is very different from most other programming-language families. Variables are not typed, there is no block structure, and programs are interpreted, but it is an imperative language. It permits programmer-defined data types and embodies "tables" that are arrays that can be indexed by elements of any data type, eg, by strings. Elaborate tracing mechanisms are supplied by the language.

J. GELLER
New Jersey Institute of
Technology

SOAR

Soar (Laird and co-workers, 1987) is a general symbolic architecture that has its roots in many of the early AI systems including GPS, STRIPS, and OPS5. It originated as the synthesis of the Ph.D. theses of Laird (on general problem-solving methods using subgoals) and Rosenbloom (on a learning method) (Laird and co-workers, 1986), both advised by Newell at Carnegie Mellon University. The Soar architecture is in active use worldwide and has been applied to a variety of tasks including puzzles, computer configuration, medical diagnosis, algorithm design, intelligent tutoring, natural language understanding, robotic control, and psychological modeling.

The original goal of the Soar project was to create an AI architecture that used problem spaces as the organizational framework for all types of tasks. As the architecture has evolved, the goals of the project have broadened to the following:

- Soar as an integrated intelligent system. To build a general AI system, the underlying architecture must support the integration of all of the capabilities necessary for general intelligent behavior, such as knowledge representation, problem solving, planning, learning, natural language understanding, and interaction with dynamic environments. These capabilities must be general enough to be used on a wide variety of tasks, powerful enough to provide expert-level performance, and integrated together within a single system. This goal is shared by other research projects such as PRODIGY (Minton and co-workers, 1989), THEO (Mitchell and co-workers, 1990), and Vere's basic agent (Vere and Bickmore, 1990).

- Soar as a unified theory of cognition. Most psychological theories are restricted to a narrow range of phenomena. Little or no attempt is made to create unified theories that explain broad ranges of psychological phenomena, much less all of cognition, with the possible exception of ACT* (Anderson, 1983). Many of the basic mechanisms in Soar originated in psychological research (problem spaces, production systems, chunking), and although the original design was based on functional necessities for general problem solving and learning, this same design has proven useful as the basis of a unified theory of cognition (Newell, 1990).

One of the primary assumptions of the Soar project is that the best strategy for the development of an architecture for general intelligence is to consider constraints from both psychology and artificial intelligence.

The following six dimensions characterize the structure of Soar (see Laird and co-workers, 1990).

1. *Framework for Task Formulation: Problem Spaces.* All tasks and subtasks in Soar are represented in terms of goals to be achieved within a problem space (Newell, 1980). The architecture supports problem space functions including the generation and selection of problem spaces, states, and operators. All problems and subproblems are formulated as achieving goals through the application of operators to states in a problem space.

2. *Memory: Working Memory and Long-Term Memory.* The current problem space, state, and operator for a goal are represented in a working memory. Long-term knowledge is represented in a recognition memory that matches against working memory and automatically retrieves preferences and other information relevant to the current goals, problem spaces, states, and operators. In the current implementation of Soar, a parallel production system serves as long-term memory.

3. *Control: Preference-Based Decisions.* The selections of problem spaces, states, and operators are made based on symbolic preferences for alternative selections that have been retrieved from long-term memory. The preferences are retrieved from long-term memory only when they are relevant to the current situation. The basic operation of the architecture is to fire all productions that match the contents of working memory in parallel until there are no new production matches. At this point, called quiescence, the decision procedure is run on the current preferences to select the appropriate problem space, state, and operator for a goal.

4. *Goals: Impasse-Driven Subgoaling.* Knowledge retrieved from recognition memory may be either incomplete or inconsistent so that the necessary problem space functions cannot be performed without further knowledge. Soar responds to such an impasse by creating a subgoal whose purpose is to resolve the impasse. Within the subgoal, the same problem space framework for processing is recursively applied; additional impasses within the subgoal lead to further subgoals. A subgoal terminates automatically when sufficient results are produced to resolve the impasse.

5. *Interaction with External Environments.* Input from sensors comes directly into working memory, where recognition memory can process it, either through parallel bottom-up parsing by productions or, more deliberately, through the selection and application of operators. Output is performed through the creation of working memory structures that are sent to the motor system.

6. *Learning: Chunking.* When a subgoal produces a result, Soar creates a new production that summarizes the processing in the subgoal that led to that result. This process is called chunking and is a variant of explanation-based learning (Rosenbloom and Laird, 1986). In future situations that are similar to the one that led to the subgoal, the new production will fire, producing the result directly, thus bypassing the need for the subgoal. Chunking gets its power and generality because it is based on the problem solving in subgoals, so that it can learn anything that is cast as a problem within a problem space, including declarative knowledge (Rosenbloom and co-workers, 1990).

Soar's operation on a problem evolves from where it initially encounters many impasses, possibly searching to obtain control knowledge or implement operators but continually chunking the processing in the subgoals and, thus, becoming more and more directed in its operations, to the point where it has sufficient knowledge so that it selects and applies operators based solely on direct retrievals from its long-term memory.

Current research on Soar as an integrated intelligent system is focused on natural language understanding, robotic control, task acquisition, planning, varieties of learning, and the integration of these capabilities. Research on Soar as a unified theory of cognition attempts to demonstrate the coverage of Soar by modeling psychological phenomena such as immediate reasoning, conservation learning, lexical acquisition, language comprehension, and visual attention (Lewis and co-workers, 1990).

BIBLIOGRAPHY

J. R. Anderson, *The Architecture of Cognition*, Harvard University Press, Cambridge, Mass., 1983.

J. E. Laird, P. S. Rosenbloom, and A. Newell, *Universal Subgoaling and Chunking: The Automatic Generation and Learning of Goal Hierarchies*, Kluwer Academic Publishers, Hingham, Mass., 1986.

J. E. Laird, A. Newell, and P. S. Rosenbloom, "Soar: An Architecture for General Intelligence," *Artif. Intell.* **33**(3) (1987).

J. E. Laird, C. B. Congdon, E. Altmann, and K. Swedlow, *Soar User's Manual: Version 5.2*, Technical Report CSE-TR-72-90, Electrical Engineering and Computer Science Dept., University of Michigan, Oct. 1990; also available from The Soar Group, School of Computer Science, Carnegie Mellon University, as technical report CMU-CS-90-179.

R. L. Lewis, S. B. Huffman, B. E. John, J. E. Laird, J. F. Lehman, A. Newell, P. S. Rosenbloom, T. Simon, and S. G. Tessler, "Soar as a Unified Theory of Cognition: Spring 1990," in *Pro-*

ceedings of the Twelfth Annual Conference of the Cognitive Science Society, Cambridge, Mass., 1990, pp. 1035–1042.

S. Minton, J. G. Carbonell, C. A. Knoblock, D. R. Kuokka, O. Etzioni, and Y. Gil, "Explanation-Based Learning: A Problem Solving Perspective," *Artf. Intell.,* **40**(1–3), 63–118 (1989).

T. M. Mitchell, J. Allen, P. Chalasani, J. Cheng, O. Etzionoi, M. Ringuette, and J. Schlimmer, "Theo: A Framework for Self-Improving Systems," in K. VanLehn, ed., *Architectures for Intelligence,* Erlbaum, Hillsdale, NJ, 1990.

A. Newell, "Reasoning, Problem Solving and Decision Processes: The Problem Space as a Fundamental Category," in R. Nickerson, ed., *Attention and Performance VIII,* Erlbaum, Hillsdale, N.J., 1980.

A. Newell, *Unified Theories of Cognition,* Harvard University Press, Cambridge, Mass., 1990.

P. S. Rosenblom and J. E. Laird, "Mapping Explanation-Based Generalization onto Soar," in *Proceedings of the Fifth National Conference on AI,* Philadelphia, Penn., 1986, American Association for Artificial Intelligence, Menlo Park, Calif., 1986.

P. S. Rosenbloom, A. Newell, and J. E. Laird, "Towards the Knowledge Level in Soar: The Role of the Architecture in the Use of Knowledge," in K. VanLehn, ed., *Architectures for Intelligence,* Erlbaum, Hillsdale, NJ, 1990.

S. Vere and T. Bickmore, "A Basic Agent," *Comput. Intell.* **6**(1), 41–60 (1990).

JOHN E. LAIRD
University of Michigan

SOCIETIES FOR AI

Groups of people interested in the study of artificial intelligence first formed within the context of other organizations, particularly those in computer science and electrical engineering. SIGART and AISB (1964) were among the first AI groups formed in this way. Since then, the number of associations has proliferated worldwide. Table 1 lists some of the currently active AI societies and some of the parent organizations that support work in the field. Many of these groups publish periodicals (see LITERATURE, AI) and sponsor symposia, of which a sampling is given in Table 1.

LEE WYLEGALA
John Wiley & Sons, Inc.

Table 1. Societies for AI and Related Areas

Acronym	Society Name and Contact Information	Selected Facts on Activities, Purpose, Membership
AAAI	American Association for Artificial Intelligence 445 Burgess Drive Menlo Park, CA 94025 415-328-53213	National Conference on Artificial Intelligence; proceedings (annual); Conference on Innovative Applications of Artificial Intelligence (annual); *AI Magazine* (quarterly); *AI Directory* (annual). 13,000 members.
AAR	Association for Automated Reasoning c/o William McCune, MCS-221 Argonne National Laboratory Argonne, IL 60439-4844	*AAR Newsletter* (approx. 3 per year). 350 members.

Table 1. (*continued*)

Acronym	Society Name and Contact Information	Selected Facts on Activities, Purpose, Membership
ACH	Association for Computers and the Humanities c/o Randall L. Jones Brigham Young University Dept. of German, 4096 JKHB Provo, Utah 84602 801-378-3513	*Humanities Computing* (quarterly newsletter). 300 members.
ACL	Association for Computational Linguistics c/o Donald E. Walker BELLCORE, MRE 2A379 445 South Street, Box 1910 Morristown, NJ 07960-1910 201-829-4312	*Computational Linguistics* (quarterly); *The Finite String* (quarterly newsletter); meeting and proceedings (annual); meeting of European chapter and proceedings (biennial); Conference on Applied Natural Language Processing and proceedings (occasional). 2000 members.
ACM	Association for Computing Machinery 11 West 42nd Street, 3rd Floor New York, NY 10036 212-575-1520	*Journal of the ACM; Communications of the ACM;* SIGART (Special Interest Group on Artificial Intelligence); SIGMOD (Special Interest Group on the Management of Data).
AFCET	Association Francaise pour la Cybernetique, Economique, et Technique 156, boulevard Pereire F-75017 Paris, France 1-47-662419	*AFCET Interfaces*; other journals; research reports; book series; conferences (periodic) and proceedings. 4500 members.
AFIA	Association Francaise pour l'Intelligence Artificielle Universite de Savoie Boite Postale 1104 73011-Chambery Cedex France 33-79-961062 Contact: Jean Pierre Laurent, Marc Ayel	*RIA* (quarterly); RF-IA (annual meeting, co-organized with AFCET); bulletin on conferences and seminars (quarterly). 400 members.
AISB	Society for Artificial Intelligence and Simulation of Behavior c/o Judith Dennison, AISB Admin Cognitive & Computing Sciences University of Sussex Brighton BN1 6GB UK 44-273-678379	Newsletter (quarterly); conference (biannual). 950 members.
AIST	Association for Intelligent Systems Technology 6310 Fly Road East Syracuse, NY 13057 (315)426-0929	Focus is on practical applications of intelligent systems technology.
ALLC	Association for Literary and Linguistic Computing c/o Thomas Corns University College of North Wales School of English & Linguistics Bangor, Gwynedd LL57 2DG UK	*Literary and Linguistic Computing* (quarterly); conference (annual). 500 members.
APA	American Psychological Association 1200 17th Street N.W. Washington, DC 20036 202-955-7600	Numerous periodicals; convention/meeting (annual). 70,000 members.
ASL	Association for Symbolic Logic c/o Dept. of Mathematics University of Illinois 1409 West Green Street Urbana, IL 61801 217-333-3410	*Journal of Symbolic Logic* (quarterly); newsletter (3 times yearly); conference (semiannual); meeting (annual). 1410 members.

Table 1. (continued)

Acronym	Society Name and Contact Information	Selected Facts on Activities, Purpose, Membership
ATAL	Association pour le Traitement Automatique des Langues 45, rue d'Ulm F-75005 Paris France	
BeNeLearn	Research on Machine Learning in Belgium, the Netherlands, and Luxembourg c/o Luc de Raedt Katholieke Universiteit Leuven Dept. Computerwetenschappen Celestijnenlaan 200A B-3001, Leuven Belgium 32 16 201015	Workshop (annual). 75 members.
BeNeLog	Research on and Applications of Logic Programming, BeNeLux c/o Danny De Schreye [address as for BeNeLearn]	Workshop (annual). 70 members.
CSCSI	Canadian Society for Computational Studies of Intelligence c/o Canadian Information Processing Society 243 College St., 5th floor Toronto, Ontario M5T 2Y1 Canada 416-593-4040	Publications; national CIPS congress (annual).
CSS	Cognitive Science Society c/o Alan M. Lesgold University of Pittsburgh Learning R&D Center Pittsburgh, PA 15260 412-624-7046	*Cognitive Science* (quarterly); conference (annual). 800 members.
CCAI	Communication & Cognition AI Blandijnberg 2 B-9000 Ghent Belgium 32 91 643952	*Communication & Cognition Artificial Intelligence* (quarterly). 1000 members.
ECCAI	European Coordinating Committee for AI c/o Susan Struthers, ECCAI Secretariat ISRT I-38050 Povo, Trento Italy 31 461 810105	*AICOM* (quarterly); European Conference on AI (biennial); Advanced Course on AI (biennial summer school course). 22 member societies.
IEEE	IEEE Computer Society PO Box 3014 10662 Los Vaqueros Circle Los Alamitos, CA 90720-1264 714-821-88380	*Computer* (monthly); IEEE conferences, periodicals (various). 100,000 members.
IAKE	International Association of Knowledge Engineers 11820 Parklawn Drive, Ste. 302 Rockville, MD 20852 301-231-7826	*Knowledgebase* (bimonthly newsletter); *Heuristics* (quarterly); conference (annual); seminars (occasional). 1200 members.
ICCL	International Committee on Computational Linguistics [contact same as for ACL]	International Conference on Computational Linguistics (COLING) and proceedings (biennial). 16 members.
IIA	Intelligence Industries Association PO Box 18438 Irvine, CA 92713	Commercial association; affiliates in accounting, law, research.
IFIPS	International Fuzzy Systems Association c/o Dr. James Bezdek Boeing Electronics Co. P.O. Box 24969: MS J-24 Seattle, WA 98124	*Fuzzy Sets and Systems* (bimonthly); conference (biennial). 300 members.

Table 1. (continued)

Acronym	Society Name and Contact Information	Selected Facts on Activities, Purpose, Membership
IJCAII	International Joint Conferences on Artificial Intelligence, Inc. c/o Donald E. Walker [contact same as for ACL]	International Joint Conference on Artificial Intelligence and proceedings (biennial). Not a membership organization.
NACCC	North American Computer Chess Championship c/o Monroe Newborn McGill University [or, c/o ACM]	
NAFIPS	North American Fuzzy Information Processing Society c/o Brian Schott 1916 Bayberry Road Edgewood, MD 21040 404-651-4070	*International Journal of Approximate Reasoning* (6 per year). 120 members.
RIA	Robotic Industries Association PO Box 3724 Ann Arbor, MI 48106 313-994-6088	International Robots & Vision Automation Show and Conference (biennial); National Service Robot Association (trade group). 200 member companies.
SCS	Society for Computer Simulation 4838 Ronson Court, Suite L San Diego, CA 92111 (619) 277-3888	*Simulation* (monthly); *Transactions* (quarterly); one triennial and six annual conferences. 2100 members.
SME	Society of Manufacturing Engineers One SME Drive PO Box 930 Dearborn, MI 48121	15 annual conferences; *Manufacturing Engineering* (monthly); *Robotics Today, Vision* (quarterly); Computer & Automated Systems Assoc.; Machine Vision Assoc.; Robotics International (assoc). 80,000 members.
SMI	Society for Machine Intelligence 100 Farnsworth Detroit, MI 48202	
SPIE	International Society for Optical Engineering PO Box 10 1000 20th Street Bellingham, WA 98227-0010 206-676-3290	*Optical Engineering, OE Reports* (monthly); conferences and workshops. 11,000 members.

SOPHIE

SOPHIE is a tutorial system that aids a student in troubleshooting malfunctioning equipment in an electronics laboratory and was written from 1973 to 1978 by Brown, Burton, and others at Bolt, Beranek and Newman, Inc. in Cambridge, Mass. (see J. S. Brown, R. R. Burton, and J. de Kleer, "Pedagogical, Natural Language and Knowledge Engineering Techniques in SOPHIE I, II, and III," in D. Sleeman and J. S. Brown, eds., *Intelligent Tutoring Systems*, Academic Press, New York, 1982, pp. 227–282).

M. R. TAIE
AT&T Bell Labs

SPATIAL REASONING. See REASONING, SPATIAL.

SPEECH UNDERSTANDING

Speech understanding is usually defined as a transduction from an initial acoustic representation of speech to a representation of meaning. For the purposes of practical systems, meaning can be defined operationally as that representation from which actions performed by the system are derived (Newell, 1975). Speech understanding is distinguished from speech recognition (qv), where the goal is to relate an utterance to (a sequence of) unique words in a dictionary. Until the early 1970s, most research focused on recognition. The five-year ARPA-funded speech project that began at that time made understanding, rather than recognition, the primary research goal. It was felt that a system's ability to respond intelligently to speech was a more meaningful criterion for the evaluation of speech systems. In addition, it was believed that the speech signal was an impoverished source of information, and knowledge of the context of an utterance was essential for its successful recognition and interpretation. Speech-recognition systems based on dynamic programming, pattern-matching techniques have been developed for utterances that consist solely of isolated words chosen from a small vocabulary, and to a lesser extent, the same techniques have been extended to connected sequences of words Rabiner and Levinson (1981). However, this approach, which works by finding the best match between variably pronounced words and a vocabulary of stored acoustic templates for words, is less suited to connected speech because the acoustic input in this case cannot be modeled effectively as a simple concatenation of the pronunciations of its constituent lexical items. In connected speech much of the variability that is factored out by pattern matching conveys information useful for both recognizing and interpreting the utterance. Therefore, it is necessary to start with more basic linguistic units than words, such as phonemes or distinctive features, and to preserve information concerning the timing and duration of the utterance. Once this step is taken, a knowledge-based, rather than pattern-matching, approach to speech processing becomes inevitable because to derive advantage from the recognition of a particular linguistic unit in the signal, it is necessary to know how that unit relates to the rest of the language in question.

Almost by definition, speech-understanding systems (SUSs) operate with connected, phrasal, sentential, or even paragraph-sized chunks of speech because "understanding" isolated words can only mean the essentially trivial process of associating some meaning with each word of the system's vocabulary and accessing this when the word is recognized. Understanding connected speech is a very complex task, and the design of SUSs has been influenced by research in fields as diverse as acoustic signal processing, (neuro)physiology, (psycho)linguistics, and psychology, as well as AI. SUSs can be classified along several dimensions; eg, number of speakers and dialects accepted or coverage of target language. To date, SUS have been built that understand a handful of speakers of similar dialect, producing a grammatically restricted subset of language with a vocabulary of about a thousand words. Although there are many potential applications for SUSs, their performance and reliability is still too poor for the majority of these to be practical. By contrast, speaker-dependent, isolated word-recognition systems for small vocabularies using whole-word pattern matching have been employed in a variety of applications, such as airline-baggage handling. Nevertheless, it is generally acknowledged that improvements to even this type of system, such as bigger vocabularies or greater speaker independence, will require a more knowledge-based approach.

THEORETICAL BACKGROUND

The transduction from speech to meaning must be mediated by a variety of components that utilize diverse knowledge sources (KSs) because the speech signal encodes, in a highly compressed and integrated fashion, many different types of information relevant to the recovery of meaning. This knowledge-based approach contrasts with that taken in whole-word template-matching systems; variability in the pronunciation of words in connected speech is no longer seen as a hindrance to pattern matching but rather as an important source of information, eg, concerning the location of word boundaries (Church, 1983) or of contextually important (stressed) information in the utterance. Figure 1 illustrates one possi-

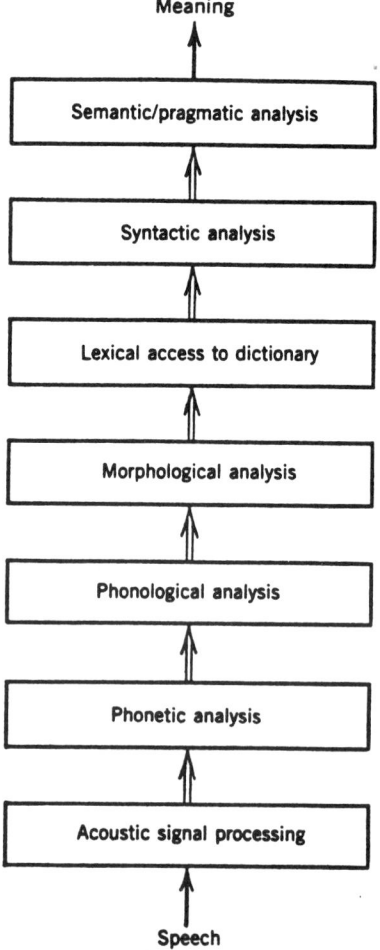

Figure 1. A typical SUS architecture.

ble organization for a SUS and the major KSs it requires to function effectively. In this organization SUS information flows upward as each component constructs intermediate representations, encoding (partial) hypotheses about the input, on the basis of the type of knowledge available to it. Acoustic signal processing digitizes the speech at a sampling rate that preserves the acoustic cues relevant to its comprehension. It also transforms the digitized signal in various ways to represent these cues in a form amenable to phonetic decoding (Flanagan, 1972; Rabiner and Schafer, 1978). For example, a spectral analysis will probably be performed and, for each analyzed frame, additional parameters, such as fundamental frequency or spectral center of gravity, computed. The parameterized signal can then be labeled as a discrete sequence of phones by searching for combinations of acoustic features. For example, if the spectral frame contains areas of "fuzziness," ie, low amplitude signals spread evenly across the spectrum, the sound is probably part of a fricative such as [f] or [v]. If the frame has a value for fundamental frequency, it must be a voiced fricative such as [v], etc. In addition, each phone is marked with suprasegmental features representing pitch, duration, and amplitude. The acoustic-phonetic transformation is crucial for the effective operation of a SUS but is still one of the least-understood aspects of speech processing. It was identified as the chief weakness in the five ARPA-funded SUSs developed in the 1970s (Klatt, 1977). Following the acoustic-phonetic transformation, a phonological analysis s performed on the phonetic representation, which identifies the linguistically important distinctions represented in the phonetic representation of the utterance, eg, levels and locations of stress, intonation contour, syllable structure, and the sequence of phonemes underlying the utterance (Lass, 1984; Ladd, 1980). Phonological analysis is essential to lexical access, which is the process of matching the phonetic form of the utterance with the canonical phonemic representations of words in a dictionary to recover the information stored there about their morphological, syntactic, and semantic properties (see MORPHOLOGY; PARSING). It undoes the effects of phonological processes such as assimilation or contraction, which apply in fluent speech; for example, the words "did" and "you" might be represented in the dictionary as the following sequence of phonemes: /dId/ and /ju:/. However, the acoustic-phonetic transformation might recover actual sounds, or phones, such as [dIjə]; to relate this phonetic sequence to the canonical phonemic representations of "did" and "you," it is necessary to recognize that palatalization has occurred at the word boundary, changing [dj] into [j], and that the unstressed vowel of "you" has been reduced to schwa. Similarly, phonological knowledge concerning allowable sequences of phonemes in syllables, often called phonotactic constraints, can be used to recognize syllable, and hence, word boundaries; for instance, in /hŏumhelp/ there must be a boundary between /m/ and the second occurrence of /h/ because no syllable in English can contain /mh/. Comparatively simple information of this type, when combined with lexical knowledge, makes the notoriously difficult task of reliably recognizing word boundaries in the acoustic signal much more tractable.

Once phonological analysis is complete, further processing of the input will be very similar to text understanding (see NATURAL LANGUAGE UNDERSTANDING). Processing will be entirely in terms of discrete symbol sets from this point upward through the SUS, and therefore, it is tempting to divide a SUS into a "recognition" phase and an "understanding" phase. However, this view is mistaken because the further morphological, syntactic, semantic, and pragmatic analysis of the utterance contributes to recognition by exploiting more of the redundancy, in the information-theoretic sense, in speech. In some of the ARPA projects, eg, there was a heavy reliance on syntactic analysis to rule out word hypotheses on the basis of syntactically inadmissable sequences. Before words hypothesized in the speech signal can be matched to lexical entries in the system's dictionary, some morphological analysis will be necessary to relate inflected variants of words to their base forms (Matthews, 1974). Apart from regular infectional morphology, such as plural /s/ or /z/, there are productive derivational morphological processes that cannot be dealt with exhaustively by expanding the number of dictionary entries; for example, there is no principled limit to the number of times "great" can be collocated with "great-grandmother" to produce a new compound noun. After morphological analysis the resulting morphophonemic representation of the speech input can be looked up in the system's dictionary to obtain syntactic and semantic information about the sequence of words hypothesized. Syntactic, semantic, and pragmatic analysis are substantially the same for speech and text understanding. However, there should be interaction between these and lower levels of analysis not only because they will contribute to correct recognition of the utterance but also because aspects of phonological analysis, particularly that relating to stress and intonation, will contribute to its interpretation. Stress, eg, is relevant to the identification of contextually new information and to finding the correct referents for pronouns. Thus, the degree of integration and interaction between different sources of information in the speech signal prevents any principled distinction between recognition and understanding. Indeed, the separation of the development of the recognition and understanding components of the SUS developed jointly by SRI International and System Development Corporation arguably explains why this major ARPA-funded SUS never worked as an integrated system (Barr and Feigenbaum, 1981).

This brief description of the contribution of different KSs to speech understanding only covers the major processes; eg, in a SUS intended to cope with several speakers, variations of voice quality, accent, and dialect must also be dealt with by the acoustic, phonetic, and phonological components. Below some issues in the design of components for the lower levels of speech analysis are discussed. The KSs deployed in speech understanding are primarily linguistic in nature, and research on them is mainly the concern of linguistic theory. However, the effectiveness of a SUS depends as much on using these KSs efficiently as on developing their content. The major contribution of AI has been to develop techniques for the representation, interpretation, and integration of KSs in a SUS. The task of speech understanding is sufficiently complex to strain the limits of current computing technology. In existing SUSs the generally errorful nature of acoustic-phonetic analysis, and the consequent unreliability of many of the specific hypotheses under consideration by a SUS at any given point, coupled with the frequent genuine ambiguity of speech with respect to any given KS, make issues of system organization and processing strategies crucial for the construction of an effective SUS capable of functioning within practical time and space constraints. Some representative solutions that have been proposed for these problems are discussed in the following sections.

ACOUSTIC-PHONETIC ANALYSIS

Undoubtedly the most crucial area in speech processing in need of more research is acoustic-phonetic analysis. If acoustic-phonetic analysis is errorful, false hypotheses will propagate through a SUS, causing much unnecessary computation and, in the worst case, an incorrect analysis. However, if the initial phonetic representation(s) derived from the acoustic signal could be guaranteed to be unique and correct, the only indeterminacies a SUS would face would be those arising from genuine linguistic ambiguities, most of which are temporary indeterminacies resolvable in terms of further information available in the speech signal. The segmentation and identification of the acoustic signal into a sequence of linguistic units has proved extremely difficult. First, speech is a code, not a cipher (Liberman and co-workers, 1967); in other words the acoustic cues associated with segments are not in a one–one relationship with those segments; rather, these cues are heavily influenced by neighboring segments and so signal the presence of several segments in parallel. For example, the spectral cues to the presence of /d/ in /di/ and /du/ are very different because they are influenced by the following vowel. Moreover, it is not possible to divide the acoustic signal into a /d/ and a following vowel in any motivated manner. These observations prompted the theory that the invariant aspect of these segments is an abstract articulatory target that is not always achieved because of the continuous motion of the vocal tract and led to accounts of speech perception as a process mediated by speech production (Liberman and co-workers, 1967; Halle and Stevens, 1964). Such analysis-by-synthesis or completely top-down models (see PROCESSING, BOTTOM-UP AND TOP-DOWN) would be, however, very computationally expensive since they require that a SUS has the capacity to generate, in principle, all possible utterances and test them against the acoustic input. More recently, it has been argued that acoustic cues to distinctive features (Lass, 1984), as opposed to phonemes or allophones, do contain invariant cues (Stevens and Blumstein, 1978), but this claim is controversial (Lisker, 1985). Second, acoustic cues are often very minimal in unstressed speech and contexts where there is more redundancy in the speech signal. This often causes many false hypotheses in systems where the acoustic-phonetic component will hypothesize a segment from a fixed inventory, say, an allophone or allophones, for every portion of the utterance. An alternative and more attractive approach is not to force an overly specific hypothesis but to iteratively refine the analysis of the acoustic signal from broad to detailed phonetic units as far as the signal allows (Johnson and co-workers, 1985). Thus, false hypotheses will not be propagated through the SUS, although at points the phonetic analysis may lack detail. Third, the acoustic cues to units vary from speaker to speaker because of physiological differences in the vocal tract, differences of characteristic voice quality, etc (Laver, 1980). Human listeners are able to compensate for these differences rapidly and fluently, but there is still little understanding of how to model this process automatically. Most commercial speech-recognition systems require lengthy training sequences with users repeating each word in the system's vocabulary several times and are therefore very speaker-dependent. In the ARPA projects several of the SUSs developed achieved a degree of speaker independence by attempting to parameterize acoustic-phonetic analysis for a new speaker on the basis of a training sentence the system knew and the user was required to speak. A mapping could then be made between portions of the utterance and a phonetic inventory.

In addition to segmentation into some inventory of units, phonetic analysis must include a representation of the prosodic, suprasegmental aspects of speech, such as stress and intonation. The acoustic cues associated with these phenomena are fundamental frequency, duration, amplitude, and pausing. Reliably measuring fundamental frequency is difficult, as is factoring out the effects of intrinsic fundamental frequency and duration of segments from genuine suprasegmental phenomena in order to recognize stressed syllables, intonational contours, and intonational phrasing. In all of the ARPA project SUSs, suprasegmental acoustic-phonetic analysis was virtually nonexistent and segmental analysis inadequate. The final performance of each system was mainly determined by the effectiveness of higher levels of analysis in correcting errors at the phonetic level. Thus, constraints on the microworld in which each SUS operated and on the range of constructions accepted were exploited in syntactic and semantic analysis to predict what was being said. More recent systems employ more sophisticated acoustic-phonetic analysis, integrating information from a variety of transformations of the acoustic signal and constructing several types of phonetic representations, but performance is still limited to an average 70% successful recognition of phonemes from utterances produced by a small number of speakers (De Mori and co-workers, 1983).

PHONOLOGICAL ANALYSIS

Phonology is concerned with the linguistically significant, meaningful patterns of sound in a particular language, including the linguistically significant aspects of suprasegmental, prosodic phenomena. A phonological component is essential for any knowledge-based connected speech-processing system because the system will require knowledge of the phonological processes active in the language, and their domain of application, to recover canonical pronunciations for words that can be matched against a dictionary entry, and to derive further cues to the syntactic and semantic/pragmatic interpretation of the utterance. Phonological components were developed for the ARPA project SUSs and other systems developed during this period (Cohen and Mercer, 1975). However, they were largely restricted to lexical, segmental processes and mostly dealt with phonologically governed variation by generating alternative pronunciations for individual lexical items and storing these in an expanded dictionary. This approach cannot deal adequately with phonological processes that span word boundaries, such as palatalization described above (Klatt, 1980). The largest domain of application for a phonological rule is the intonational phrase, which is often coextensive with a full sentence; therefore, phonology cannot be treated in terms of variant pronunciations for lexical items. Because phonological processes are rule-governed and part of the language system, a phonological analysis provides much important information for a SUS; for example, different types of phonological rule are blocked by different types of linguistic boundaries between segments, so the nonapplication of a phonological rule in an appropriate segmental environment is a clue to the presence of a boundary that blocks its application. As argued above, this is useful to aid segmentation of speech into syllables and words, but it can also provide clues for syntactic analysis; palatalization spans word boundaries but is blocked at the boundaries of major syntactic constituents (Cooper and Paccia-Cooper, 1980) so its nonoccurrence can be used to resolve an ambiguity concerning the presence of such a boundary at that point in the speech signal. Phonological rules also vary between dialects; therefore, a SUS capable of understanding speakers of different dialects would require knowledge of these differences and an ability to reconfigure itself for their speech. Palatalization, eg, occurs more frequently and more freely in dialects of American, than British, English.

At the time of the ARPA project, phonological theory was stagnant, and in particular, there was little interest in extending the domain of injury beyond segmental processes. However, since the late seventies a number of new approaches to phonology have been developed, such as autosegmental, metrical, and dependency phonology, which take as their central concern suprasegmental phenomena (Smith and van der Hulst, 1982). Few of these developments have been incorporated into SUSs, although some have been incorporated into speech-synthesis systems (Pierrehumbert, 1981; Williams, 1985) and much of this work is precise and formal enough to be suitable for machine applications. Improvements in the performance of SUSs will certainly require that these developments be incorporated into a much enhanced phonological component that can provide more than variant pronunciations for individual words.

KNOWLEDGE-SOURCE INTERPRETATION

A KS is of no use in a SUS if the knowledge it encodes cannot be represented in a way that allows its interpretation and deployment by machine. The notation employed to represent knowledge in a given field is most naturally determined by the experts in that field of knowledge; for instance phoneticians typically use the International Phonetic Alphabet for phonetic labeling. However, since choice of representation affects the application of knowledge, the representation systems of KSs in SUSs have often been a compromise between descriptive adequacy and computational efficiency. For instance, in the ARPA project every SUS, with the exception of HWIM (Woods, 1980), employed a syntactic representation thought to be unable to express all of the grammatical possibilities of English. Formal language and automata theory offer efficient algorithms for the application of KSs expressed as sets of rules with the appropriate formal properties (Aho and Ullman, 1972), and much research on representations for KSs, both in theoretical linguistics and AI, has attempted to develop descriptively adequate notations with these formal properties. For example, minimally augmented context-free notations have been argued to be descriptively adequate for English syntax (Gazdar and co-workers, 1985) and phonology (Church, 1983). Similarly, finite-state transducers have been developed for morphological analysis (Koskenniemi, 1984). However, successes of this kind do not lead automatically to computationally tractable KSs since the rule sets required to express knowledge in this form may be extremely large. In addition, it seems unlikely that all KSs employed in a SUS can be expressed within such restricted notations; therefore, more specialized and powerful techniques have also been developed, such as interpreters for production systems (McCracken, 1981) (see RULE-BASED SYSTEMS) and augmented transition networks (ATNs) (Woods, 1975) (see GRAMMAR, AUGMENTED-TRANSITION-NETWORK). Some expert-system shells (see EXPERT SYSTEMS) appear to have promising applications for the acoustic-phonetic transformation because of the more inferential and therefore principled nature of rule application (De Mori and co-workers, 1983) and the ability to factor different aspects of knowledge, which will aid parameterization of the system for different speakers (Thompson, 1984). In addition, other AI techniques associated with knowledge representation and text understanding are relevant to interpretation of KSs in a SUS. The better the understanding of a particular domain, the greater the chance of representing that knowledge both adequately and efficiently. Moreover, it is likely that different representation schemes will be most effective for different KSs; therefore, SUS architectures that impose a uniform scheme on all KSs, such as HEARSAY-II (qv) (Erman and Lesser, 1980) or HARPY (qv) (Lowerre and Reddy, 1980), are not ideal.

Choice of representation is affected by factors other than the availability of an interpretation technique for a particular scheme; for example, several SUSs do not attempt to map directly between the acoustic signal and the phonetic alphabet but construct intermediate representations, marking acoustically salient features such as nasality, to aid the process of recognizing individual phones. This reflects the difficulty, discussed above, of relating phones to distinct and invariant sets of acoustic features and a trend away from pattern matching against a continuous representation of speech toward processing of discrete symbol sets as early as possible in this process. Representations are also affected by the order in which different KSs are brought to bear on the speech signal and the overall architecture of the SUS; recently, it has been proposed that initial phonetic analysis should mark consonants, vowels, and stressed and unstressed syllables and that this simple representation should be used to derive a set of word candidates from a suitably organized dictionary (Huttenlocher and Zue, 1984). Detailed phonetic analysis would then be applied to the stressed syllable(s) to discriminate between candidates. In a SUS employing this approach, lexical constraints are applied before detailed phonetic analysis; therefore, the role of phonetic analysis is redefined quite radically.

SYSTEM ARCHITECTURE

The bulk of the AI literature on SUSc concerns intercomponent communication during processing. This issue is crucial because ambiguities need to be resolved rapidly to avoid unnecessary computation and because redundancy between KSs can be used to factor out false hypotheses caused by either system errors or genuine ambiguity in the speed signal. For example, the acoustic-phonetic component might hypothesize an aspirated /p/ or /b/ followed by a vowel and /t/, which would result at least in the word candidates "put" and "but." However, it is likely that one of these could be rejected on the basis of syntactic analysis since verbs and conjunctions do not occur in the same syntactic environments. Similarly, there might be a genuine syntactic ambiguity in an utterance, such as "He gave her dog biscuits." in which "her" may be functioning as an adjective or noun. But in this case the ambiguity can be resolved by the different stress and intonation that will accompany the two interpretations. The architectures proposed are basically hierarchical, like that of Figure 1, with a serial flow of information through a chain of component KSs, or heterarchical with no constraint, in principle, on the flow of information between components (Reddy and Erman, 1975). The advantage of the hierarchical approach is that there appears to be a natural order for the application of KSs to speech input; syntactic analysis can only proceed on the basis of lexical information, etc. Moreover, overall system control is simple. However, there are many occasions when nonserial interactions between the chain of components are useful; for example, aspects of the prosodic, suprasegmental structure of an utterance will be relevant to its phonological, syntactic, semantic, and pragmatic interpretation. Nonserial interaction can be achieved within the hierarchical model by passing up all of the possible analyses compatible with a given component to the next component, which then selects a subset of analyses, etc. But this only works if the intermediate representations passed up through the SUS are enriched to include all of the information analyzed so far that may be of use to some higher component; thus, the input to the syntactic component, in addition to syntactic information about words, must include all of the available information of potential relevance to syntactic analysis, such as prosodic information, and all information relevant to semantic/pragmatic analysis must be carried through as well. This is likely to strain representation schemes and is computationally expensive because many unnecessary, false hypotheses are computed. These false hypotheses are often avoidable, in principle, because the disambiguating information is temporally available, encoded in the part of the speech signal already analyzed by lower levels, but in the hierarchical model it is not applied until this input reaches the appropriate component in the serial chain. Heterarchical systems avoid this inefficiency by allowing components to apply in the most efficient order for a given input at the expense of a very complex flow of control within the system and considerable intercomponent communication complexities. Each component must be provided with the means to request and receive information from, or start specific processing in, any other component. This requires specialized communication channels between every component in the system. Developing an adequate control system for such a model may well be impossible because it involves envisaging all possible flows of control at the design state. Attempts at developing such models have been reduced to human simulation of each component (Woods and Makhoul, 1973). In practice, workable heterarchical models for SUSs have been restricted to uniform representations across KSs and a single global data structure, as in blackboard systems (qv).

Since the ARPA project there has been much interest in SUSs that can be run on parallel machines (Fahlman and co-workers, 1983) and the emphasis has been on hierarchical systems that still achieve interaction through selective filtering of hypotheses. Thus, a simple architecture is maintained and more powerful hardware used to cope with the extra computation. One recent major project proposes to use the chart (Kay, 1973) as a global data structure within a hierarchical architecture, employing as much parallelism as the linearized nature of speech input will allow (Thompson, 1984). This approach shares the advantage of a global data structure with the blackboard architecture but does not require a uniform representation scheme across components. None of these proposals represents a theory of nonserial interaction in speech understanding; rather, they offer general architectures that attempt to support any interaction that may be required. The designers of the blackboard specifically wanted an architecture capable of supporting arbitrary interactions and thus application to other tasks, such as vision (Erman and Lesser, 1975). An alternative approach is to specify explicitly the interactions required in a SUS and to develop a specialized architecture capable of supporting them; this approach requires a better understanding of speech than is current but offers the possibility of far more efficient and effective SUS architectures (Briscoe and Boguraev, 1984).

PROCESSING STRATEGIES

Various processing strategies have been imposed on different SUS architectures in an attempt to reduce the computation required for successful analysis in the normal case. Both hierarchical and heterarchical systems can operate bottom-up, in an essentially data-driven way, or top-down, using knowledge to produce hypotheses concerning the input (see PROCESSING, BOTTOM-UP AND TOP-DOWN). However, most recent SUSs have operated bottom-up because of the rather weak predictability of speech on the basis of the KSs that can currently be deployed effectively in a SUS. Similarly, SUSs can explore the search space in a depth-first or breadth-first manner (see SEARCH; SEARCH, DEPTH-FIRST). Most have operated breadth-first because of the uncertain and errorful nature of many hypotheses but have employed scoring techniques to keep the size of the active search space manageable. One such technique, shortfall scoring, which involves measuring the summation of individual word candidate scores against a theoretical upper bound for this score and process the hypothesis with the least difference first, guarantees that a SUS will find the best scoring complete hypothesis for the utterance first (Woods, 1982). However, this does not guarantee that the highest ranked hypothesis is correct; the effectiveness of the components that contribute to the generation of word hypotheses is still the crucial factor in the overall performance of the system. The scoring of partial hypotheses throughout a SUS in a more linguistically motivated fashion is extremely difficult. Scores must be carried across components and should reflect the differing contributions of each KS. However, the weight that should be attached to any KS must vary with context; for instance, in the recognition of an unstressed and phonetically reduced preposition, syntactic analysis should be weighted more highly relative to acoustic analysis than in recognition of a stressed syllable. In addition, analyses must be scored through time; an analysis that starts with low scores may end with the highest because redundancy in the information encoded in speech propagates both left and right through the input. Although some scoring schemes that have been used in implemented SUSs do improve performance, this is either for theoretical reasons connected with the scoring technique, as with shortfall scoring, or because they have been developed by trial and error and evaluated solely on the basis of run-time performance, as with the focus-of-attention mechanism in the HEARSAY-II blackboard system. In the former case the technique is useful but limited; in the latter case potentially valuable insights into the task of speech understanding become lost in the scoring technique (Hayes-Roth, 1983).

Analysis of the speech signal can proceed from left to right through the linearized signal or middle out in both directions from islands of greater acoustic reliability. This island-driven approach has the advantage of taking relatively error-free phonetic data as its starting point at the expense of a more complex control structure and system organization, as in HWIM (qv) (Woods, 1982). Human listeners appear to pay greater attention to stressed syllables (Cutler and Norris, 1985), which are generally more clearly enunciated and therefore more easily analyzed phonetically. In addition, the phonological structure of English vocabulary is constrained in such a way that a unique word can usually be derived from a crude phonetic analysis of syllable structure coupled with detailed analysis of its stressed syllable (Huttenlocher and Zue, 1984). Therefore, the island-driven approach is essentially correct, although it would be more effective if processing began at stressed syllables by explicitly searching for them rather than at arbitrary high scoring portions of the acoustic signal. A related approach that avoids the extra overheads in HWIM caused by middle-out analysis is to use an appropriate scoring strategy in a left-to-right system, which is able to take account of forthcoming speech events in the right context of the existing partial hypothesis (Johnstone and Altmann, 1984).

CURRENT TRENDS

Since the ARPA project in the seventies there has been a period of problem-oriented, rather than system-building, research in speech understanding. Much of this research has focused on the acoustic-phonetic transformation as a result of new evidence demonstrating the informational richness of the acoustic signal (Cole and co-workers, 1980). Now there is renewed interest in building complete systems (Thompson, 1984) incorporating this research and renewed concern with issues such as system architecture. However, the majority of the knowledge-based systems that are being developed are restricted to continuous speech recognition rather than understanding. Improvements in acoustic-phonetic analysis suggest that higher levels of analysis are not crucial for recognition of continuous speech, contrary to prevailing opinion at the time of the ARPA project. In addition, the problems of understanding, such as knowledge representation (qv) issues, the restriction to a microworld, etc, remain unsolved.

SYSTEMS

The main SUSs developed in the ARPA project were HARPY, HWIM, HEARSAY-II, and SRI/SDC. HARPY came closest to the performance criteria specified for the project (Newell and co-workers, 1973). However, HARPY's architecture required precompilation of all KSs into a single finite-state network so the language accepted by the system was more restricted than that for the other systems (Hayes-Roth, 1983). Each of these systems is briefly described by its chief designer in Lea (1980) and evaluated in Klatt (1977) and Barr and Feigenbaum (1981). A system of the same period developed at IBM but with improved performance over HARPY on the same subset of English is described in Bahl and co-workers (1976). The HEARSAY-II system is reimplemented as a production system in McCracken (1981), and extensions and improvements to the original blackboard architecture are described in Hayes-Roth (1983). Several SUSs have been developed for European languages, such as KEAL (Mercier and co-workers, 1980) and MYRTILLE-II (Pierrel and Haton, 1980) for French and EVAR (Niemann, 1982) for German. However, these systems have not surpassed the ARPA project systems in performance or design. An automated airline reservation system that incorporates continuous speech understanding is described in Levinson and Shipley (1980). This system, developed at Bell Laboratories, conducts a dialogue over a telephone to establish the appropriate reservation. It employs whole-word template-matching techniques to recognize words from a 127-word vocabulary but relies on semantic constraints deriving from this very restricted task domain and syntactic constraints imposed by a restrictive finite-state grammar to achieve robust performance.

FURTHER READING

The best introductions to speech understanding are Lea (1980) and Reddy (1975). Two further more recent collections are Cole (1980) and Simon (1980), and Fallside and Woods (1985) provide an up-to-date, advanced course. Articles on the higher levels of speech understanding can be found in the journals *Artificial Intelligence* and *Computational Linguistics*. Issues relevant to acoustic-phonetic analysis are dealt with in *Journal of the Acoustical Society of America, Journal of Phonetics* and *Language and Speech*. Many articles on whole-word template-matching techniques for isolated and connected speech and on speech signal processing can be found in the journal of the Institute of Electrical and Electronic Engineering, Acoustics, Speech and Signal Processing. Articles on the application of speech-processing systems can be found in *Speech Technology*, and *Human Factors* sometimes contains performance evaluations of systems. The *International Journal of Man-Machine Studies* also publishes articles on speech processing. Many conference proceedings also contain relevant articles, such as the *International Joint Conference on Artificial Intelligence, COLING, Association of Computational Linguistics, Acoustic Society of America, International Conference on Acoustics, Speech and Signal Processing,* and others.

BIBLIOGRAPHY

A. V. Aho and J. Ullman, *The Theory of Parsing, Translating and Compiling*, Vol. I, Prentice-Hall, Englewood Cliffs, N.J., 1972.

L. R. Bahl, J. K. Baker, P. S. Cohen, N. R. Dixon, F. Jelinek, R. L. Mercer, and H. F. Silverman, "Preliminary Results on the Performance of System for the Automatic Recognition of Continuous Speech," *International Conference on Acoustics, Speech and Signal Processing*, Philadelphia, Pa., 1976, pp. 512-514.

A. Barr and E. A. Feigenbaum, *The Handbook of Artificial Intelligence*, Vol. I, Kaufmann, Los Altos, Calif., 1981.

E. J. Briscoe and B. K. Boguraev, "Control Structures and Theories of Interaction in Speech Understanding Systems," *Proceedings of COLING84*, Stanford, Calif., 1984, pp. 259-266.

K. W. Church, *Phrase Structure Parsing: A Method for Taking Advantage of Allophonic Constraints*, Indiana University Linguistics Club, Bloomington, Ind., 1983.

P. S. Cohen and R. L. Mercer, "The Phonological Component of an Automatic Speech Recognition System," in D. R. Reddy, ed., 1975, pp. 275-320.

R. A. Cole, ed., *Perception and Production of Fluent Speech*, Erlbaum, Hillsdale, N.J., 1980.

R. A. Cole, A. I. Rudnicky, V. W. Zue, and D. R. Reddy, "Speech as Patterns on Paper," in R. A. Cole, ed., 1980, pp. 3-50.

W. E. Cooper and J. Paccia-Copper, *Syntax and Speech*, Harvard University Press, Cambridge, Mass., 1980.

A. Cutler and D. Norris, "Syllable Boundaries and Stress in Speech Segmentation," *Proceedings of the 109th Meeting of Acoustic Society of America*, Austin, Tex., 1985, pp. S39.

R. De Mori, P. Laface, G. Petrone, and M. Segnan, "Access to a Large Lexicon Using Phonetic Features," *Proceedings of EUSIPCO, Erlangen, 1983.*

L. D. Erman and V. R. Lesser, "A Multi-Level Organisation for Problem Solving Using Many, Diverse, Cooperating Sources of Knowledge," *Proceedings of the Fourth International Joint Conference of AI*, Tibilisi, Georgia, Morgan-Kaufmann, San Mateo, Calif., 1975, pp. 483-490.

L. D. Erman and V. R. Lesser, "The Hearsay-II Speech Understanding System: A Tutorial," in W. A. Lea, ed., 1980, pp. 361-381.

S. E. Fahlmann, G. E. Hinton, and T. J. Sejnowski, "Massively Parallel Architectures for AI: NETL, Thistle and Boltzmann Machines," *Proceedings of the Third National Conference for Artificial Intelligence,* Washington, D.C., AAAI, Menlo Park, Calif., 1983, pp. 109-113.

F. Fallside and W. A. Woods, eds., *Computer Speech Processing*, Prentice-Hall, Englewood Cliffs, N.J., 1985.

J. L. Flanagan, *Speech Analysis, Synthesis and Perception*, 2nd ed., Springer-Verlag, New York, 1972.

G. J. M. Gazdar, G. K. Pullum, I. A. Sag, and E. Klein, *Generalized Phrase Structure Grammar*, Blackwell, Oxford, 1985.

M. Halle and K. N. Stevens, "Speech Recognition: A Model and a Program for Research," in J. A. Fodor and J. J. Katz, eds., *The Structure of Language*, Prentice-Hall, Englewood Cliffs, N.J., 1964, pp. 604-612.

B. Hayes-Roth, *A Blackboard Model of Control*, Report No. HPP-83-38, Department of Computer Science, Stanford University, Calif., 1983.

D. P. Huttenlocher and V. W. Zue, "A Model of Lexical Access from Partial Phonetic Information," *Proceedings of the IEEE Conference on Acoustics, Speech and Signal Processing*, San Diego, Calif., Mar. 1984, pp. 2641-2644.

S. R. Johnson, J. H. Connolly, and E. A. Edmonds, "Spectrogram Analysis: A Knowledge-Based Approach to Automatic Speech Recognition," in M. A. Bramer, ed., *Research and Development in Expert Systems*, Cambridge University Press, Cambridge, UK, 1985.

A. M. Johnstone and G. Altmann, *Automated Speech Recognition: A Framework for Research*, Research Report No. 233, Edinburgh University, Department of AI, Edinburgh, 1984.

M. Kay, "The MIND System," in R. Rustin, ed., *Natural Language Processing*, Algorithmics, New York, 1973, pp. 155-188.

D. H. Klatt, "Review of the ARPA Speech Understanding Project," *J. Acoust. Soc. Am.* **62,** 1345-1366 (1977).

D. H. Klatt, "Speech Perception: A Model of Acoustic-Phonetic Analysis and Lexical Access," in R. A. Cole, ed., 1980, pp. 243-288.

K. Koskenniemi, "A General Computational Model for Word-Form Recognition and Production," *Proceedings of COLING84*, Stanford, Calif., July 1984, pp. 178-181.

D. R. Ladd, *The Structure of Intonational Meaning*, Indiana University Press, Bloomington, Ind., 1980.

R. Lass, *Phonology*, Cambridge University Press, Cambridge, UK, 1984.

J. Laver, *The Phonetic Description of Voice Quality*, Cambridge University Press, Cambridge, UK, 1980.

W. A. Lea, ed., *Trends in Speech Recognition*, Prentice-Hall, Englewood Cliffs, N.J., 1980.

S. E. Levinson and K. L. Shipley, "A Conversational-Mode Airline Information and Reservation System Using Speech Input and Output," *Bell Sys. Tech. J.* **59**, 119–137 (1980).

A. M. Liberman, F. S. Cooper, D. P. Shankweiler, and M. Studdert-Kennedy, "Perception of the Speech Code," *Psychol. Rev.* **74**, 431–461 (1967).

L. Lisker, "The Pursuit of Invariance in Speech Signals," *J. Acoust. Soc. Am.* **77**, 1199–1202 (1985).

B. T. Lowerre and D. R. Reddy, "The Harpy Speech Understanding System," in W. A. Lea, ed., 1980, pp. 340–360.

D. L. McCracken, *A Production System Version of the Hearsay-II Speech Understanding System,* UMI Research, Ann Arbor, Mich., 1981.

P. H. Matthews, *Morphology,* Cambridge University Press, Cambridge, UK, 1974.

G. Mercier, A. Nouhen, P. Qiunton, and J. Siroux, "The KEAL Speech Understanding System," in J. C. Simon, ed., 1980, pp. 525–545.

A. Newell, "A Tutorial on Speech Understanding Systems," in D. R. Reddy, ed., 1975, pp. 3–54.

A. J. Newell, J. Barnett, J. W. Forgie, C. Green, D. H. Klatt, J. C. R. Licklider, J. Munson, D. R. Reddy, and W. A. Woods, *Speech Understanding Systems: Final Report of a Study Group,* North-Holland, Amsterdam, 1973.

H. Niemann, "The Erlangen System for Recognition and Understanding of Continuous Speech," in J. Nehmer, ed., Springer-Verlag, Berlin, 1982, pp. 330–348.

J. B. Pierrehumbert, "Synthesising Intonation," *J. Acoust. Soc. Am.* **70**, 985–995 (1981).

J. M. Pierrel and J. P. Haton, "The MYRTILLE-II Speech Understanding System," in J. C. Simon, ed., 1980, pp. 553–570.

L. R. Rabiner and S. E. Levinson, "Isolated and Connected Word Recognition—Theory and Selected Applications," *IEEE Trans. Commun.* **Com-29**(5), 621–659 (1981).

L. R. Rabiner and R. W. Schafer, *Digital Processing of Speech Signals,* Prentice-Hall, Englewood Cliffs, N.J., 1978.

D. R. Reddy, ed., *Speech Recognition,* Academic Press, Inc., New York, 1975.

D. R. Reddy and L. D. Erman, "Tutorial on System Organisation for Speech Understanding," in D. R. Reddy, ed., 1975, pp. 457–480.

J. C. Simon, ed., *Spoken Language Generation and Understanding,* Reidel, Dordrecht, Holland, 1980.

N. Smith and H. van der Hulst, eds., *The Structure of Phonological Representations,* Foris, Dordrecht, Holland, 1982.

K. N. Stevens and S. E. Blumstein, "Invariant Cues for Place of Articulation in Stop Consonants," *J. Acoust. Soc. Am.* **64**, 1358–1368 (1978).

H. Thompson, "Speech Transcription: An Incremental Interactive Approach," *Proceedings of the European Conference on AI,* Pisa, Italy, Sept. 1984, Elsevier Science, New York, pp. 697–704.

B. J. Williams, "A Metrical Algorithm for Lexical Stress Assignment in English," *Proceedings of 109th Meeting of Acoustic Society of America,* Austin, Tex., 1985, p. S39.

W. A. Woods, "Syntax, Semantics and Speech," in D. R. Reddy, ed., 1975, pp. 345–400.

W. A. Woods, "Control of Syntax and Semantics in Continuous Speech Understanding," in J. C. Simon, ed., 1980, pp. 337–364.

W. A. Woods, "Optimal Search Strategies for Speech Understanding Control," *Artif. Intell.* **18**, 295–326 (1982).

W. A. Woods and J. Makhoul, "Mechanical Inference Problems in Continuous Speech Understanding," *Proceedings of the Third International Joint Conference Artificial Intelligence,* Stanford, Calif., Morgan-Kaufmann, San Mateo, Calif., 1973, pp. 200–207.

E. J. BRISCOE
University of Cambridge

SPHINX

SPHINX is the first speech recognition system that achieved high performance on a large vocabulary, speaker independent, continuous speech task. The system uses stochastic hidden Markov models (HMMs) to learn and generalize from a large multi-speaker database. SPHINX also uses techniques such as multiple codebooks, generalized triphones, and function word models. On a 1000-word task, SPHINX recognizes continuous speech from any speaker with an accuracy of 96% (see K. F. Lee, *Automatic Speech Recognition: The Development of the SPHINX System,* Kluwer Academic Publishers, Boston, Mass., 1989).

KAI-FU LEE
Apple Computer, Inc.

SSS. . .

SSS. . . (Summarization Summarization Summarization. . .) was developed to explore the utility of the encoding relationship between semantic memory and text (see R. Alterman and L. Bookman, "Reasoning About a Semantic Memory Encoding of the Connectivity of Events," *Cogn. Sci.,* in press.) An important idea developed in the work on SSS. . . was the notion of conceptual roots. Roughly, the conceptual roots correspond to the basic notions of the narrative text: the framework in the terms of which the narrative was developed. SSS. . . determined the conceptual roots from a directed acyclic graph structure that represents the coherence of the event concepts in the text as derived from the encoding provided by semantic memory. An interesting property of the conceptual roots are that they are the minimal set that covers the semantic memory-based graph encoding of the case. SSS. . . used the conceptual roots to succinctly explain the connection between any two concept coherent events in the narrative. Also implemented in SSS. . . was a measure of importance that quantifies the conceptual emphasis of the narrative. Given this measure of importance, it was shown that each of the important nodes is either a conceptual root or covered by one of the conceptual roots. Lastly, SSS. . . combined evidence from semantic memory-based coherence graph of the case, the conceptual root analysis and the importance measure, to generate a description of the basic event content of the narrative (ie, a basic summary) [see R. Alterman and L. Bookman, "Some Computation Experiments in Summarization, *Discourse Processes* **13**, 143–174 (1990)].

RICHARD ALTERMAN
Brandeis University

STEREO VISION

Two eyes or cameras looking at the same objects from different perspectives provide the means to determine three-dimensional shape and position. Scientific investigation of this effect (called variously stereo vision, stereopsis, or single vision) has a rich history in psychology, biology, and more recently, the computational modeling of perception. The human visual ability to perceive depth is both commonplace and puzzling: one perceives three-dimensional relationships effortlessly, but the means by which one does so are largely unknown and hidden from introspection. Stereo vision, however, is one way to perceive depth that is relatively well understood from a computational standpoint (see also VISUAL RECOVERY). Stereo is an important method for machine perception because it leads to relatively direct measurements and, unlike monocular techniques, does not infer depth from weak and unverifiable photometric and statistical assumptions, nor does it require specific detailed models of objects. Once two stereo images are brought into point-to-point correspondence, recovering depth by triangulation is straightforward.

We begin with a discussion of the geometrical basis for stereo vision. We then focus on three distinct computational models selected to represent both differences and common themes in approach. Next we discuss some aspects of biological stereo vision and practical applications of computational stereo. Finally, we conclude by identifying the important open questions.

STEREO GEOMETRY

The geometrical principle behind stereo vision, illustrated in Figure 1, is quite simple. Assume that two cameras form images through left and right centers of perspective **l** and **r** onto planes L and R. (In practice, these would be imperfect optical lens systems, but for this discussion we assume ideal "pinhole" projections.) Furthermore, assume that the cameras are fixed upon point **v**, which is to say that the two rays perpendicular to the image planes passing through the centers of perspective (the *principle rays*) intersect at **v**. Let θ_v be the angle between these principle rays. We say that the *absolute* disparity of **v** is θ_v. Now consider another point **p** projected onto image planes L and R as shown and let the angle between these rays be θ_p. We say that the *relative* disparity of **p** with respect to **v** is $\delta_{p|v} = \theta_p - \theta_v$. Relative disparity is the more commonly used definition.

The circle through **l**, **r**, and **v** (actually a sphere) is called the *Vieth–Müller circle* (closely related to the horopter discussed later in the section on modularity of stereo perception). Note that relative disparity $\delta_{p|v}$ is positive for points inside, negative for points outside, and zero for points on the circle. Positive and negative relative disparities are sometimes referred to as *crossed* and *uncrossed*, respectively.

Clearly, disparity is related to distance. Let $\mathbf{c} = (\mathbf{l} + \mathbf{r})/2$ be the midpoint between the focal points (the *cyclopean origin*) and **p** and **q** be two points on a line with **c**; if $|\mathbf{p} - \mathbf{c}| > |\mathbf{q} - \mathbf{c}|$ (ie, **p** is farther from the observer than **q**), then $\delta_p < \delta_q$. The two projections of a single point in the scene are called *conjugate points,* and they determine the location of the point in the scene uniquely.

This property of conjugate points establishes the importance of the *correspondence problem:* How can one determine which pairs of points in the two images correspond to actual points on surfaces in the scene? The scene is presumably made of light-reflecting surfaces, and individual markings on these surfaces will, in some sense, look about the same in the two images. In realistic imagery the correspondence problem is much harder than it may first appear, however, due to many complicating factors such as occlusion (in which some parts of the scene are seen only by one camera), periodic surface markings, surface areas with no markings at all, distortion of the surface markings in the images dues to perspective projection, sensor noise, optical distortion, etc.

Knowledge of the relative orientation of the two cameras makes the correspondence problem much more tractable by reducing the dimensionality of the search space. Any point in three-dimensional space, together with the centers of projection of the two camera systems, defines a plane called an *epipolar plane* (Figure 2). The intersection of an epipolar plane with an image plane is called an *epipolar line*. Every point on an epipolar line in one image must correspond to a point on the corresponding epipolar line in the other image. This constraint, often called the *epipolar constraint*, therefore limits the search for the match of any point in the first image to a one-dimensional neighborhood in the second image, as opposed to a two-dimensional neighborhood, with an enormous reduction in computational complexity.

COMPUTATIONAL MODELS

Many computer models of stereo vision have been proposed. In some cases these models have been offered as a theory of human stereo vision; in other cases the models

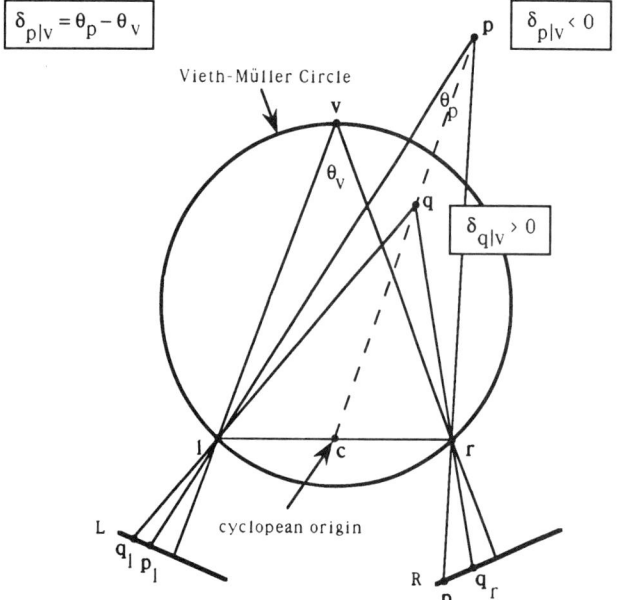

Figure 1. Basic stereo geometry.

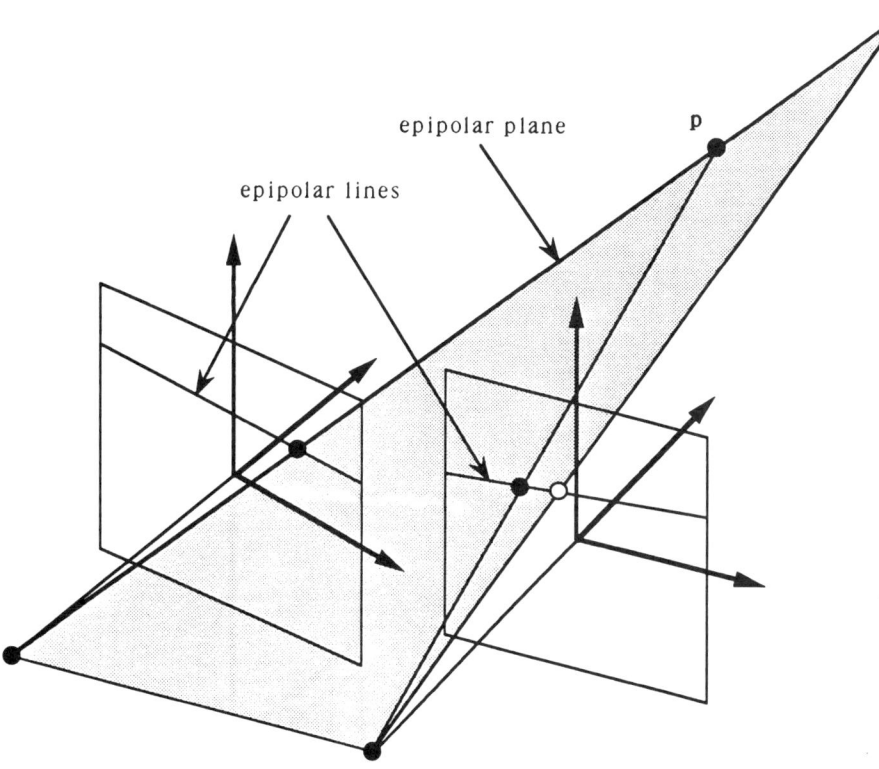

Figure 2. The epipolar constraint. Two camera systems with different orientations are shown. A point **p** in space and the two centers of projection define an epipolar plane, which intersects the images in two epipolar lines. Any other point in the epipolar plane (eg, the point shown as an open circle) must project to image locations on the epipolar lines. Therefore, searches for corresponding points in the images can be restricted to one dimension.

have been pragmatically task oriented and unconstrained by knowledge of biological vision. In this section we examine three distinct approaches illustrated by characteristic examples. We first examine the issues that confront any stereo model to a greater or lesser degree: image acquisition, camera modeling, feature acquisition, image matching (the correspondence problem), depth determination, and interpolation.

Image Acquisition. Stereoscopic images can be recorded in a large variety of ways. For example, they may be recorded either simultaneously or in a time sequence of any duration from very similar or from very different perspectives with accurate, well-calibrated instruments or with a crude hobbyist camera. The most important factor affecting image acquisition is the specific application for which the stereo computation is intended. (See the later section on practical applications.)

Camera Modeling. We have seen that knowledge of disparity allows one to calculate depth, assuming full knowledge of the geometrical arrangement of the cameras. In practice, this means one must know both the *interior orientation* of each camera (the relationship between points in the image and the coordinate system of the camera) and the *exterior orientation* of the two-camera system (the relationship between the local camera coordinate systems and an invariant world coordinate system). Exterior orientation requires knowledge of the locations of the focal points and the orientations of the cameras in the world. A stereo camera model is normally separated into an *absolute* component that specifies the transformations between a camera coordinate system and a world coordinate system and a *relative* component that specifies the transformations between two-camera coordinate systems without reference to a world coordinate system. Knowledge of the relative camera model alone is sufficient to exploit the epipolar constraint to simplify matching, as described in the section on stereo geometry. The absolute model is required to translate disparity measurements into absolute measurements of the positions of points in the world.

The derivation of a relative camera model given a large number of matched points is usually accomplished by least-squares parameter estimation. Gennery (1980) has developed such a method for finding the relative camera model in terms of azimuth, elevation, pan, tilt, roll, and focal length. From a theoretical standpoint, the minimum number of conjugate points that is necessary to derive a unique relative camera model is 5, but the solution involves three simultaneous nonlinear equations (Nagle and Neumann, 1981). If as many as eight conjugate points are available, the relative camera model can be obtained directly as the solution of a system of linear equations (Longuet-Higgins, 1981; Tsai and Huang, 1984). Fischler and Bolles (1981) provide a number of results with respect to the minimum number of points needed to obtain an absolute camera model, given a single image and a set of correspondences between points in the image and the points' locations in space; they also provide a technique for finding the complete camera model when the given set of correspondences contains a large percentage of errors.

Preprocessing. Many stereo systems perform some sort of preprocessing of the images before matching, either to set the stage for feature acquisition (see what follows) or to build image hierarchies (eg, pyramids) for coarse-to-fine matching algorithms. Preprocessing is typically a linear filtering operation in which the raw image intensities are convolved with one or more digital kernels. The three filters illustrated in Figure 3 are commonly used: the Gaussian, the difference of Gaussians (DOG), and the Laplacian of the Gaussian ($\nabla^2 G$). The Gaussian is lowpass, while the difference of Gaussians and the Laplacian of the Gaussian are bandpass. These circularly symmetric filters are parameterized by σ, the space constant of the Gaussian. By using a series of filters with different space constants, one can construct a series of images restricted to different spatial frequencies. The lower frequency images can be subsampled into smaller images to create a pyramidlike resolution hierarchy. Such hierarchies are extremely useful because the range of possible disparity values across the field of view decreases linearly with the sample spacing, which implies that the number of possible matches is relatively smaller at lower resolutions. Coarse matching can be done quickly at low resolution and the result used to initialize the search at the next finer scale.

Feature Acquisition. Clearly, some parts of the images will be easier to match than others because of the presence of characteristic surface markings. Many computational stereo models select sets of discrete features in the two images and then seek, at least, a sparse set of correspondences between these feature sets. Features can be used either as elementary tokens for matching or as "interest operators," indicating the locations of promising correlation windows. Many kinds of features have been used. Some examples are as follows:

- Isolated pointlike features can be found by a variety of methods, often modeled along the lines of Moravec's interest operator (Moravec, 1977), which selects points where there is high variance in four directions.
- Edge features can be detected by a variety of methods. One commonly used method is to select *zero crossings* in bandpassed images; that is, those contours where the bandpassed images change sign.
- Higher level features, such as line junctions, specifically shaped "primitives," and segmented regions are sometimes used.

Image Matching. The matching step—solving the correspondence problem—is clearly a critical component of any stereo model. There are three distinct approaches:

- *Area matching:* Areas of image intensity measurements (possibly after preprocessing) are the basic units to be matched. This typically involves using a feature detector to select promising areas and then using a selected "area patch" in a template search to either maximize a measure of cross-correlation or minimize root-mean-squared (RMS) error.
- *Feature matching:* Discrete features are the basic units to be matched. Once the features have been detected, no reference is made to the underlying photometry. In addition to location, features may have other properties, such as contrast sign, contrast magnitude, and directionality.
- *Variational models:* A set of matches is sought by explicitly minimizing a cost function. For example, the cost function may combine a measure of photometric error with a measure of the complexity of a dense disparity map.

In all three approaches hierarchical scale-space techniques, based on the pyramid structures described in the discussion of preprocessing, have had success.

Depth Determination. Once accurate matches have been found, the determination of distance is a relatively straightforward matter of triangulation using the absolute camera model. Nevertheless, this step can present significant difficulties if the matches are somewhat inaccurate or unreliable or if the camera model is uncertain. Figure 4 illustrates how disparity measurements are related to depth and the separation of the cameras. Suppose the cameras are fixated on point **v**. Assuming small angles, the disparity of another point **p** with respect to **v** is

$$\delta_{p|v} \approx \frac{-B \, \Delta D}{D^2}$$

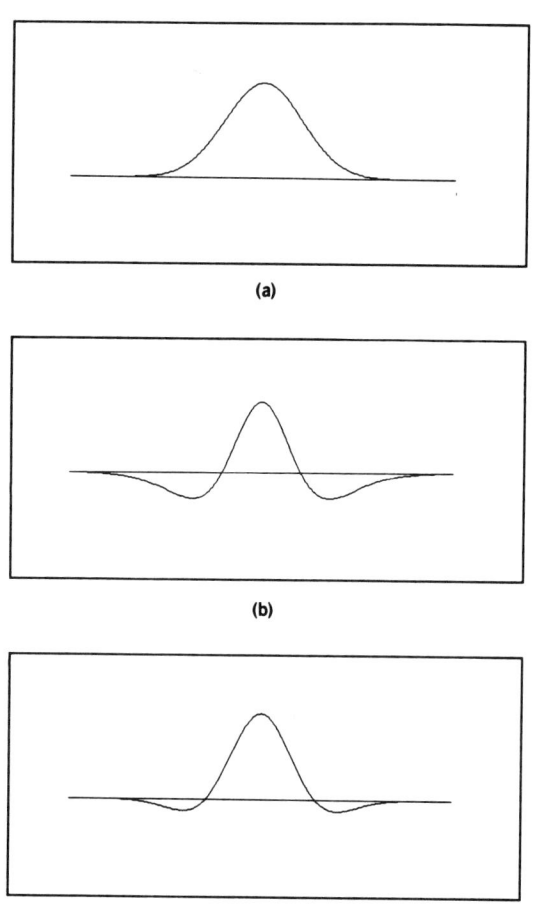

Figure 3. Three common filters for stereo preprocessing: (*a*) Gaussian (lowpass); (*b*) difference of Gaussians (bandpass); (*c*) Laplacian of Gaussian (bandpass).

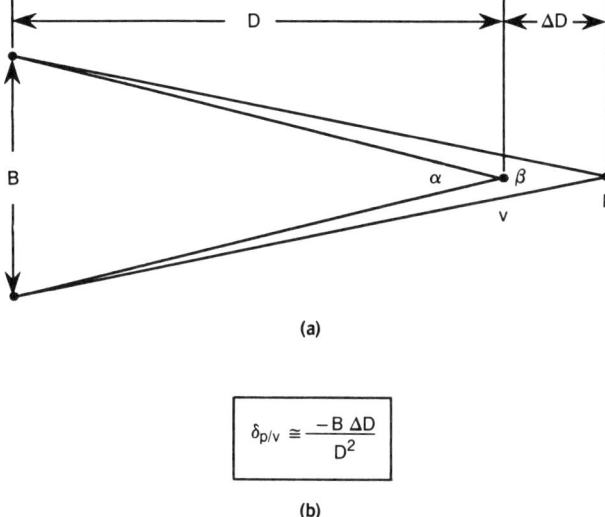

Figure 4. Disparity as a function of depth and baseline. (a) The disparity of p with respect to v is $\delta_{p|v} = \beta - \alpha$. Assuming that α and β are small: $\alpha \cong B/D, \beta \cong B/(D + \Delta D)$ and $D \gg \Delta D$, then (b) is true.

where B is the distance separating the cameras (the baseline), D is the distance from the cyclopian origin to the fixation point, and ΔD is the difference in the depths of **p** and **v**. To a first approximation, the error in stereo distance measurements is inversely proportional to the baseline and directly proportional to the square of the distance to the point being measured. Lengthening the baseline reduces error but complicates the matching problem by increasing both the disparity in the images and the difference in appearance of the areas or features being matched. Given a constant image size and sampling rate on the focal plane, increasing the focal length will decrease error proportionally, but at the cost of decreasing the field of view.

Interpolation. Stereo applications usually demand a dense array of depth estimates. The variational models can produce a dense array directly, but feature matching and area matching can only produce sparse correspondences. (This is obvious for feature matching. Area matching cannot produce correspondences unless there is significant photometric variation in the areas to be matched.) Consequently, both approaches usually require an interpolation step. The most straightforward way to derive a dense depth array from a sparse one is simply to treat the sparse array as a sampling of a continuous function using a conventional interpolation method. More elaborate and specialized methods have been proposed for interpolation when the depth may be discontinuous. An additional approach to interpolation is to fit prior geometric models to the sparse depth array.

We will now describe three stereo systems in detail. [There are many other models; see the survey articles by Barnard and Fischler (1982) and Dhond and Aggarwal (1989).] These three systems were chosen to illustrate the range of computational approaches to stereo and also to identify common themes—the use of a scale hierarchy, the use of the continuity of depth and disparity to resolve ambiguity, and the use of the epipolar constraint to limit search. These are also well-tested systems that have been used in real applications.

STEREOSYS

The goal of STEREOSYS (Hannah, 1989) is to find as many reliable point-to-point matches as possible in an approximately aligned stereo pair. Matches are determined by maximizing the cross-correlation of image intensities, normalized by mean and variance, between two rectangular areas (typically 11 × 11 pixels). STEREOSYS is an eclectic approach to area matching: several effective techniques have been combined into one system. The strategy is to use different matching algorithms in sequence, beginning with the more general algorithms to get a relatively few matches with very high confidence and then using this information to constrain further matching with more specifically tuned algorithms.

The first step is to select a set of well-scattered points in one image that indicate the centers of promising areas for which to find matches in the second image. This is done with an "interest" operator, applied over small windows, that penalizes windows with little information (ie, small variance of image intensity) or whose only information is contained in strongly linear features (both conditions that cause problems for correlation matching). The local maxima of this measure identify the set of feature points.

The first matching algorithm, *unconstrained hierarchical matching*, operates over a Gaussian image hierarchy by tracing the locations of the feature points (located in one of the full-resolution images) through the hierarchy of lower resolution, lowpass-images. Starting with the lowest resolution, this algorithm finds the best matches by searching for disparities that maximize a normalized cross-correlation of image intensity. It then uses the result to begin a more constrained search at successively higher resolutions. In this way the system bootstraps itself up to an acceptable set of matches at the highest resolution. A *back-matching* technique is used to confirm each match by repeating the search, starting with the opposite image. The next algorithm, epipolar constrained hierarchical matching, uses the highly reliable matches to derive a relative camera model. Feature points that were not matched in the first stage (perhaps because they were not promising enough) are now matched though the image hierarchy using the epipolar constraint. The third algorithm, *anchored matching*, uses the matches found so far to establish a continuity constraint for further matching.

MPG (Marr, Poggio, Grimson)

The MPG model (Marr and Poggio, 1980; Grimson, 1981, 1985) was motivated by a desire to model the human visual system, at least approximately. It has been modified since it was first proposed. Here we shall consider only the most recent description (Grimson, 1985). Briefly, the MPG model matches discrete, oriented edge features from epipolar-corrected images across a resolution hierarchy, resolving ambiguity by enforcing continuity of disparity.

The use of the epipolar constraint is justified by the effect of eye movements to align retinal images, the use of the hierarchy is justified by the existence of independent channels tuned to different spatial frequencies in the human visual system, the choice of the feature detector by the existence of similar receptive fields in neural structures, and the use of the continuity constraint by the existence of "cooperative" processes in the brain.

The first step is to preprocess both images by convolving them with a series of bandpass filters. The MPG model uses the Laplacian of a Gaussian kernal ($\nabla^2 G$). As described before in the discussion of preprocessing, the choice of the space constant of G controls the center of the passband; the MPG filters are separated by about one octave. Zero crossings are selected in the filtered images and are classified according to contrast sign.

Matching begins at the lowest frequencies, as in STEREOSYS. Each zero-crossing point in the left bandpass-filtered image is compared to all zero-crossing points in the right image within a fixed distance of the left point's coordinates, corresponding to the maximum range of disparity. (A small amount of vertical disparity is allowed to permit an approximate epipolar camera model.) Those pairs of points that have the same contrast sign are considered as matches. Next a *figural continuity* constraint is used to cull false matches from the set of possibilities. The basic idea behind figural continuity is that because zero-crossing contours are most likely to be caused by continuous features in the scene, the correct matches should lead to continuous features in space. Those subsets of matches that produce only very short linear features are discarded. In the event that only one match remains for a point, the disparity of the feature is determined, but if more than one match is found, the ambiguity is resolved by selecting the most common disparity in a local neighborhood.

CYCLOPS

CYCLOPS (Barnard, 1989) computes a dense disparity map by posing the correspondence problem as a combinatorial optimization: Find the simplest (ie, flattest) map with the least photometric error. Like STEREOSYS and MPG, CYCLOPS operates across a sequence of resolutions, in this case a Laplacian pyramid. The Laplacian pyramid is a particularly convenient structure because it is constructed of DOG filters with passbands separated by one octave, quantitatively very close to the $\nabla^2 G$ bandpass filters of MPG. Furthermore, the lower frequency images have larger sample spacings, and hence are smaller images, leading to faster search at low resolution as in STEREOSYS. The Laplacian pyramid can be computed very efficiently by exploiting the separability of the Gaussian and by using a small recursive kernel, as described by Burt (1983).

At each level of the hierarchy CYCLOPS selects a disparity map by minimizing a discretized form of the *stereo constraint equation*:

$$\mathcal{E} = \int\int \left\{ \left(\mathcal{L}\left(x - \frac{\mathcal{D}}{2}, y\right) - \mathcal{R}\left(x + \frac{\mathcal{D}}{2}, y\right) \right)^2 + \lambda |\nabla \mathcal{D}|^2 \right\} dx\, dy,$$

where $\mathcal{L}$; and $\mathcal{R}$ are the DOG-filtered image intensities, $\mathcal{D} = \mathcal{D}(x, y)$ is a cyclopean disparity map, and λ is a constant. Note that the epipolar constraint is used because only horizontal disparities are allowed. (The system uses a camera model to perform the epipolar correction if necessary.) Here $\mathcal{E}$ is a combination of two terms: the photometric error associated with the map and a measure of the first-order variation of the map.

A multigrid simulated annealing algorithm is used to minimize $\mathcal{E}$. The annealing algorithm uses random numbers to model heat. By slowly cooling the system to zero temperature, an approximation to the optimal disparity map is constructed at each level of the pyramid. Simulated annealing is more robust than a deterministic gradient-descent search because it allows "uphill" state transitions and therefore the possibility of escape from the local optima that one is likely to encounter in nonlinear objective functions such as the stereo constraint equation. Using the theory of Markov random fields, simulated annealing can be interpreted as maximum a posteriori estimation. This Bayesian interpretation shows that by minimizing $\mathcal{E}$, one finds the most probable disparity map $\mathcal{D}$ given $\mathcal{L}$ and $\mathcal{R}$, subject to a prior probability distribution of $\mathcal{D}$. The a priori distribution of $\mathcal{D}$ is given by $\lambda|\nabla\mathcal{D}|^2$, the measure of first-order variation: Disparity maps are considered to be more probable when they are flatter.

Starting with a base disparity of zero at the lowest resolution of the pyramid (typically 32×32), an incremental disparity map with values in $\{-1, 0, 1\}$ is found that minimizes $\mathcal{E}$ for the full disparity, which is the sum of the incremental and the base disparity. Note that the incremental disparity is interpreted as a correction to the base disparity, which is inherited from the previous, coarser level (or which is zero at the coarsest level). To set the base disparity for the next higher resolution, the disparity range is expanded by a factor of 2 and the values of the full disparity are doubled, reflecting the change of spatial scale. Even though the incremental disparity can only assume three values at any level of the pyramid, the full disparity can increase by a factor of 2 across levels.

Because of the Laplacian pyramid structure and the locality of the interactions in the stereo constraint equation, the CYCLOPS algorithm is ideally suited to massively parallel SIMD (single-instruction, multiple-data) architectures. The current implementation (on a Connection Machine with 4096 processors) can produce dense elevation maps of 1023×1024 aerial images in about 8 min.

ASPECTS OF BIOLOGICAL STEREO VISION

The Neuroanatomy of Stereo

Much is known about the biological and psychological basis for stereo vision, but there is currently no complete explanation for how the brain exploits binocular information. [See Kandel and Schwartz (1985) and Kuffler and co-workers (1984) for more detailed information.] The two retinas of the human visual system signal their response to visual stimuli through the optic nerves. The optic nerves partially cross in the optic chiasma, carrying information from the left half of the visual field to the right half of the brain and information from the right half of the visual field to the left half of the brain. The visual field projects to an area on the back surface of the brain called the primary visual cortex (also called striate cortex or area 17). The primary visual cortex is almost certainly the place where the first stereoptic computation is performed.

The visual cortex is a sheet of half a dozen distinct layers of cells. It is morphologically uniform across its entire expanse: Groups of cells on one part of the sheet appear essentially the same as groups of cells anywhere else on the sheet. The visual stimulus is topographically mapped to the cortex: Each part of the cortex responds to stimulation at a specific location on the retina, and there are no discontinuities except for the separation of the visual field into left and right halves.

Visual stimulation enters the cortex at one layer (layer IV) and then projects to other layers locally spreading only about 1 mm to neighboring cortical cells. The cells in layer IV (so-called simple cells) are strictly monocular: They respond exclusively to one input from one eye. The "complex" cells in the subsequent layers, however, can be stimulated by both eyes to greater or lesser degrees. Globally, the visual cortex is organized into *ocular-dominance columns*. The preference for one eye (a complete preference in layer IV) extends through the width of the cortex (ie, through a column of cells normal to the surface of the cortex), and eye preference is also highly correlated between neighboring columns. Ocular-dominance columns are thought to play an important role in stereopsis, but the mechanism is not understood. To a large degree this organization is innate, but it does undergo further elaboration and sharpening after birth. Depriving one eye of stimulation after birth causes the formation of deviant ocular-dominance columns (Hubel and Weisel, 1979) dominated by the active eye. In addition, there is a psychological effect that is probably related: the development of stereo vision passes through a critical period of postnatal development. If an animal is not exposed to stereoscopic stimulus during this relatively short period, it will never be able fully to develop stereo perception.

The Modularity of Stereo Perception

The question of whether stereopsis is inextricably linked to other modes of visual perception or whether it can stand alone as an independent mode was clarified by the invention of the random-dot stereogram (Julesz, 1971). A random-dot stereogram consists of two synthetic images of random points that are constructed to depict perspective views of the same virtual surface (Figure 5). A random-dot stereogram can be constructed as follows. The points in, say, the left image are randomly placed. The right image consists of these same points, properly displaced to provide disparity values consistent with another view of some scene model. Each image by itself usually contains no depth information because it consists only of random dots. When the pairs are viewed stereoscopically, however, the surface is readily perceived. Stereo vision is therefore capable of producing depth perception independently of any monocular cues such as size constancy, texture gradients, shading, and so on. Random-dot stereograms enable systematic comparison of human and machine performance because their parameters (such as noise, dot density, and the shape of the virtual surface) can be controlled precisely.

Limits to Stereo Fusion and Depth Perception

About 95% of people with otherwise normal vision have the ability to perform stereopsis. As discussed in the section on computational models, the accuracy of stereo measurement falls with the square of distance. At 100 ft human stereo depth perception is accurate to only about 25 ft. The maximum distance at which human stereo vision is possible is about 1500 ft.

The locality of interaction on the cortex apparently limits the fusion of the two visual fields in human stereopsis. The range over which fusion occurs is called *Panum's area* (Figure 6) (Ogle, 1950). Points inside Panum's area are seen as single points (fusion), while points outside are seen as double (diplopia). It is known that while fusion is an important feature of stereo vision, it is not absolutely necessary—even diploptic stimuli can be a cue for depth within limits. The largest disparity that still gives rise to a single, fused image varies from 6 min of arc at the center of the visual field to 20 min of arc at a peripheral angle of 6° (Fender and Julesz, 1967). The thresholds for diploptic stereo perception are about four times those for fusion. The center of Panum's area, shown in the figure as a curve passing through the fixation point, is called the *horopter*. Points on the horopter project to identical positions on the two retinas (ie, they have zero disparity). Note that the horopter does not follow the Vieth–Müller circle precisely

Figure 5. Random dot stereogram.

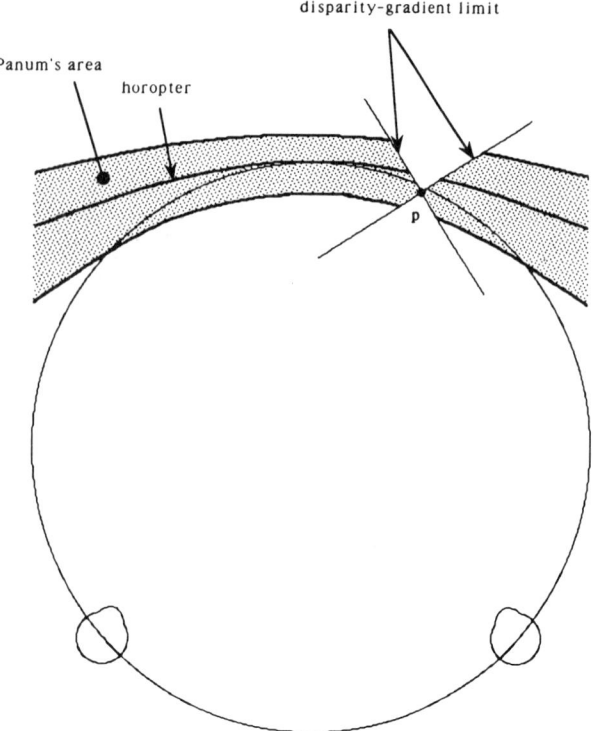

Figure 6. Limits to fusion.

because the geometry and optics of the ocular system do not quite satisfy the ideal model of Figure 1.

Experiments with stabilized images, in which the subjects were prevented from using eye movements to change vergence, have revealed that the limits to fusion are actually much more complex than Panum's area (Fender and Julesz, 1967). For example, fusion exhibits a time dependence, called *hysteresis*: as the disparity of fused, stabilized images is increased, they remain fused far beyond Panum's area until they suddenly "break away" into diplopia. Also, the limits to fusion for stimuli rich in features, such as random-dot stereograms are much greater than for simple stimuli such as individual lines.

Another limit on fusion is the *disparity-gradient limit* (Burt and Julesz, 1980), which states that for fusion to occur, the rate of change of disparity with respect to visual angle (a dimensionless number) must be bounded. Most observers have a limit of about 1. While Panum's area is an absolute limit of fusion, the disparity-gradient limit is more subtle. It implies that fusion of one point excludes the possibility of fusion of some nearby points, even if they fall within Panum's area. As shown in Figure 6, if a point **p** is fused, then no points in a cone centered on **p** can be fused simultaneously. It has been shown (Trivedi and Lloyd, 1985) that if an imaged surface has a disparity-gradient limit of less than 2, then the left and right images are topologically equivalent, that is, all points in one image are visible in the other (ie, the surface is not self-occluding), and furthermore the ordering of points is the same in both images. The disparity-gradient limit has been used to limit search for correspondences in at least one computational model (Pollard and co-workers, 1985).

Relationships between Biological and Computational Models

So far, computational models of stereo vision have addressed only some of the many phenomena associated with human stereo perception. A complete computational theory would have to include descriptions and explanations of issues such as the limits to stereo discussed in the section on the modularity of stereo perception, the relationship between fusion and diploptic depth perception, temporal effects (eg, hysteresis), the relationship to accommodation and vergence, multistable and multivalued depth perception (eg, transparency), the relationship to monocular cues for depth, the nature of the features that are matched, and the perception of depth when there are rivalrous features (eg, lines of different orientations). Nevertheless, in spite of the incomplete understanding of biological stereo vision, it is no accident that we find several analogies between computational stereo models and current knowledge of stereo vision in higher mammals. Historically, the formulation of models was often guided by biological knowledge (in particular, in the MPG model). From a pragmatic standpoint, machine models and biological neural systems may operate under similar constraints, and this is increasingly so with the introduction of massively parallel architectures.

Independent Spatial-Frequency Channels. The most immediate parallel is the use of resolution hierarchies. There is considerable evidence that the human visual system has at least four, and possibly more, independent channels tuned to different spatial frequencies separated by about one octave (Wilson and Bergen, 1979). The low-pass pyramids of STEREOSYS, the bandpass sequences of MPG, and the bandpass pyramids of CYCLOPS perform the same function. The filters used in MPG and CYCLOPS, $\nabla^2 G$ and DOG, have about the same "Mexican hat" shape as the receptive fields of cells in the early visual system (see Figure 3).

Vertical Disparity. Human stereo vision can deal with a small amount of vertical disparity, but it resorts to eye movements to align the visual fields as closely as possible (Duwaer and van den Brink, 1981a,b). The epipolar constraint allows one to use information about the camera orientation to remove vertical disparity. Because error in the camera model may cause some residual vertical disparity, the search for corresponding points must be robust enough to handle at least a small amount of error. Apparently, the search-space reduction of the epipolar constraint is so useful in biological vision that vertical disparity is to be avoided as much as possible but must be tolerated to a degree.

Three Pools of Disparity. Studies of anomolous stereo vision suggest that there are three psychophysically distinct "pools" of disparity detectors, corresponding roughly to crossed (positive), uncrossed (negative), and near-zero disparity relative to the vergence point (Richard, 1971). CYCLOPS uses the same representation, coupled with several octaves of hierarchy, to achieve efficiency without sacrificing dynamic range. At every level in the hierarchy, components of incremental disparity can assume only three local values: 1 (crossed), −1 (uncrossed), and zero. The base disparity, however, can grow by a factor of 2 across every level. The search space in any one level is therefore kept to a minimum, while the final composite disparity is allowed to have a substantial range.

Visual Cortex. The visual cortex has a remarkably uniform structure:

> Given what has been learned about the primary visual cortex, it is clear that one can consider an elementary piece of cortex to be a block about a millimeter square and two millimeters deep. To know the organization of this chunk of tissue is to know the organization for all of area 17; the whole must be mainly an iterated version of this elementary unit. (Hubel and Weisel, 1979).

As a computational substrate, the visual cortex is quite similar to a large grid of locally connected processors. Since the cortical columns appear to be anatomically and functionally equivalent, they can all be simulated by identical, locally interacting programs applied to different parts of the visual field, and therefore the visual cortex as a whole can be simulated efficiently by a fine-grained SIMD (single-instruction, multiple-data) architecture. All three systems described in the preceding have algorithmic structures that fit massively parallel SIMD architectures, and CYCLOPS is actually implemented on such a system.

PRACTICAL APPLICATIONS

There are many existing and potential applications of stereo vision, but perhaps the two most important are cartography and robot vision. The current state of the art of computational stereo is most relevant to cartographic applications, where real-time performance is not required.

In standard cartographic practice, a human analyst uses a precise stereoscopic viewing and pointing device (called a *stereoanalytic plotter*) to develop a terrain-elevation map from stereo images. As one might imagine, this work is tedious, slow, and costly. Computational methods that automate stereopsis, sometimes implemented in special-purpose hardware or on massively parallel computers, are now practical for this important application.

The most important requirements of the cartographic application are accuracy and the ability to process very large images in a reasonable amount of time. Vertical stereo images are recorded from airplanes, although satellite-based images are now being used as well. Finely calibrated, large-format, long-focal-length cameras are used, producing negatives of about 23 cm on a side, with about 60% overlap in field of view. The most common cartographic products are regular-grid terrain models, orthoimages (orthographic projections of the terrain), and contour plots. Using an absolute camera model, an automated cartographic system must convert raw disparity measurements into a dense, irregular mesh of matched-point coordinates, resample these points on a regular grid to produce a terrain-elevation model, and use the terrain model to produce a synthetic orthoimage.

Stereo vision would obviously be very useful for robots, whether as a straightforward mensuration device in a simple industrial robot or, at the other extreme, as part of an integrated perceptual system in an autonomous vehicle. The passive nature of stereo vision is highly desirable for some applications. Because these applications demand real-time performance, practical robot stereo vision awaits the development of faster, cheaper hardware. Continued improvement in the cost and performance of computer systems is bringing this important application closer.

OPEN QUESTIONS

There has been substantial progress in developing computational models of stereo vision, but many problems remain. With few exceptions, computational models have ignored such complications as transparent surfaces and occlusions. They typically produce a single-valued distance function, equivalent to a digital elevation map, sometimes with an identification of occluding contours. Such a simple representation cannot support the functions of general-purpose vision.

Computational models usually treat stereo as an independent module. While this is a useful reductionist tactic, stereo processing must ultimately be integrated into a more extensive and general perceptual (and possibly motor) framework. There is no reason why stereo processing should not be coupled with other perceptual modalities such as motion parallax and monocular perception of form and with other cognitive functions such as memory and motor control. Human stereo vision is only one part of a complex ocular-motor system; effective stereo vision for advanced applications such as intelligent robots will doubtless require a similar degree of integration.

BIBLIOGRAPHY

S. T. Barnard and M. A. Fischler, "Computational Stereo," *Comput. Surv.* **14**(4), 554–572 (December 1982).

S. T. Barnard, "Stochastic Stereo Matching over Scale," *Internat. J. Comput. Vision* **3**, 17–22 (1989).

P. Burt and B. Julesz, "A Disparity Gradient Limit for Binocular Fusion," *Science* **208**, 615–617 (1980).

P. Burt, "The Laplacian Pyramid as a Compact Image Code," *IEEE Trans. Commun.* **31**, 532–540 (1983).

U. R. Dhond and J. K. Aggarwal, "Structure from Stereo—A Review," *IEEE Trans. Sys. Man Cyber.* **19**(6) (November/December 1989).

A. L. Duwaer and G. van den Brink, "What Is the Diplopia Threshold?" *Vision Res.* **20**, 295–309 (1981a).

A. L. Duwaer and G. van den Brink, "Diplopia Thresholds and the Initiation of Vergence Eye-Movements," *Vision Res.* **21**, 1727–1737 (1981b).

D. Fender and B. Julesz, "Extension of Panum's Fusional Area in Binocularly Stabilized Vision," *J. Opt. Soc. Amer.* **57**(6), 819–830 (June 1967).

M. A. Fischler and R. C. Bolles, "Random Sample Consensus: A Paradigm for Model Fitting with Applications to Image Analysis and Automated Cartography," *CACM*, **24**(6), 381–395 (1981).

D. B. Gennery, *Modeling the Environment of an Exploring Vehicle by Means of Stereo Vision*, Ph.D. dissertation, Stanford University; Computer Science Report STAN-CS-80-805, June 1980.

W. E. L. G. Grimson, "A Computer Implementation of a Theory of Human Stereo Vision," *Phil. Trans. R. Soc. London* **B292**, 217–253 (1981).

W. E. L. G. Grimson, "Computational Experiments with a Feature-Based Stereo Algorithm," *IEEE Trans. Patt. Anal. and Mach. Intell.* **PAMI-7**(1), 17–34 (January 1985).

M. J. Hannah, "A System for Digital Stereo Image Matching," *Photogrammetric Engineering Remote Sensing* **55**(12), 1765–1770 (December 1989).

D. H. Hubel and T. S. Weisel, "Brain Mechanisms of Vision," in *The Brain*, W. H. Freeman and Co., New York, 1979.

B. Julesz, *Foundations of Cyclopean Perception*, University of Chicago Press, Chicago, 1971.

E. R. Kandel and J. H. Schwartz, *Principles of Neural Science*, 2nd ed., Elsevier Science Publishing Co., New York, 1985.

S. W. Kuffler, J. G. Nicholls, and A. R. Martin, *From Neuron to Brain*, 2nd ed., Sinaure Associates Inc., Sunderland, Mass., 1984.

H. C. Longuet-Higgens, "A Computer Algorithm for Reconstructing a Scene from Two Projections," *Nature* **293**, 133–135 (1981).

D. Marr and T. Poggio, "A Computational Theory of Human Stereo Vision," *Proc. R. Soc. London* **B207**, 187–217 (1980).

H. P. Moravec, "Towards Automatic Visual Obstacle Avoidance," *Proceedings of the Fifth IJCAI*, 1977, p. 584.

H. Nagle and B. Neumann, "On 3-D Reconstruction from Two Perspective Views," *Proceedings of the Seventh IJCAI*, Aug. 1981.

K. N. Ogle, *Researches in Binocular Vision*, Saunders, Philadelphia, Penn. 1950.

S. B. Pollard, J. E. W. Mayhew, and J. P. Frisby, "PMF: A Stereo Correspondence Algorithm Using a Disparity Gradient Limit," *Perception* **14**, 449–470 (1985).

W. Richards, "Anomalous Stereoscopic Depth Perception," *J. Opt. Soc. Amer.* **61**(3), 410–414 (March 1971).

R. Y. Tsai and T. S. Huang, "Uniqueness and Estimation of Three-Dimensional Motion Parameters of Rigid Objects with Curved Surfaces," **PAMI-6**(1), 13–27 (Jan. 1984).

H. P. Trivedi and S. A. Lloyd, "The Role of Disparity Gradient in Stereo Vision," *Perception* **14**, 685–690 (1985).

H. R. Wilson and J. R. Bergen, "A Four Mechanism Model for Threshold Spatial Vision," *Vision Res.* **19**, 19–32 (1979).

STEPHEN T. BARNARD
MARTIN A. FISCHLER
SRI International

STORY ANALYSIS

Story analysis is the subfield of discourse understanding (qv) having to do with understanding stories: coherent narratives in written form. A story analysis program may demonstrate its analysis in two ways. First, it may produce a paraphrase or summary of the story that includes information not explicitly mentioned in the text. Second, it may answer questions about the story. For example, consider the following simple story:

> The princess was asleep in the castle when a dragon came and took her away. The knight searched far and wide for the princess. Finally he found her in the dragon's den. After a mighty fight, he slew the dragon. The princess's father, the king, rewarded the knight with gold pieces and his daughter's hand.

A story analysis program might product a summary, and answer questions as follows:

Summary

A dragon kidnapped a princess. A prince rescued her, and they were married.

Q1: What happened after the knight killed the dragon?
A: He returned her to the castle.
Q2: Why did the prince kill the dragon?
A: Because he wanted to save the princess.

For both questions, the answer is not explicitly stated in the text, but it can be inferred with a high degree of confidence. There are other possible summaries and answers. Question Q2 might have been answered "Because dragons are evil, and they must be punished." This reveals a level of understanding that is sufficient for the story at hand but would not yield a complete analysis of a story in which dragons are protagonists or in which evildoers go unpunished.

Story analysis programs are interesting because they can provide insight into the structure of stories, the notion of coherence, and the interaction between events, goals, and plans. Constructing a story analysis program requires complete, explicit theories for all three of these components, and the theories can be easily tested by observing the program's responses to sample stories and questions. Improper responses can yield clues to improved theories, and proper responses serve as evidence supporting the theory.

Unfortunately, there is a vast amount of knowledge necessary to understand even a simple story. Thus, the failure of a program to properly understand any individual text might be due to a minor piece of missing information, rather than a major flaw in the theory. It is difficult to distinguish these cases. Similarly, given that a program performs well on one text, it is difficult to predict how it will perform on other texts. These difficulties place constraints on the usefulness of story analysis programs as theoretical tools.

It should be mentioned that there is a companion line of research, story generation, that makes use of much of the same theoretical tools. A story generation program takes as input a description of a situation and some characters and produces as output a story about the characters in that situation, introducing new characters and plot twists as necessary. This line of work will not be covered in this entry, but representative work includes Meehan (1975), Dehn (1981) and Lebowitz (1983).

Although there are few practical successes at this point, there is hope that discourse understanding technology may lead to practical programs that scan newswire stories, encyclopedia entries, scientific article abstracts, and other archival sources to retrieve useful information based on a thorough understanding of the texts. This could lead to a vast improvement over current techniques based on keyword search.

EARLY HISTORY

The psychological and computational study of story analysis can be said to have begun with Bartlett's *Remembering* (1932), a far-seeing study of how appropriate schemata are used in the recall of stories. Since then we have seen a number of disparate approaches to the problem, including a series of computer models that convincingly mimic human understanding capabilities on certain examples—but fail completely on others.

Another landmark analysis was by Propp (1958), who proposed certain formal properties shared by all folktales. This prompted the study of story grammars, a theory that treated stories as "big sentences"—units of text with a structure that could be parsed and hence could be grammatical or ungrammatical. The units of the grammar included settings, events, goals, attempts, and so on. The story grammar approach was introduced by Lakoff (1972) and Rummelhart (1975) and was adopted whole-heartedly by a number of psychologists. A good book-length summary is Mandler (1984).

In experiments by Mandler and Johnson (1977) and Thorndyke (1977), subjects were presented with a story and later asked to recall it. The subjects remembered goal-directed actions better than non-goal-directed actions; they remembered high-level actions better than low-level ones; and they tended to make recall errors for actions that appeared in a noncanonical position, moving the actions back in place. This was taken as evidence for a plan-based story grammar theory. The idea was that subjects formed a mental representation of the story consisting of a parse according to the story-grammatical rules.

However, a subsequent experiment by Lichtenstein and Brewer (1980) provided another explanation. They showed subjects videotapes of goal-directed activities, such as setting up a slide projector. Recall of these videotapes showed substantially the same effects as recall for stories. This suggests that the recall of stories is due at least in part to a general capacity to understand purposeful action rather than a story-specific grammar. Besides this capacity to understand actions, story analysis also depends on general language skills and on story-specific conventions. For example, it is a convention of fables that they often start with "Once upon a time." Many fables involve groups of three: the king has three children, and the third succeeds where the first two fail. It is not clear if this is just a story-telling convention or if it is routed in some more fundamental property of human cognition (perhaps there is just the right number for the memory we have).

COMPUTATIONAL VS NONCOMPUTATIONAL APPROACHES

There is a major split between story analysis researchers with different backgrounds. They disagree on the questions of methodology, theoretical assumptions, and goals. In psychology and text linguistics, the methodology is as follows: Given a story and an interpretation of that story, describe the processes that could have led to that interpretation. Many of these researchers adopt the story grammar approach. Some psychologists, following Bartlett, concentrate on the processes. For others, the goal is to describe and characterize stories, so the issue of "storyness" vs nonstoryness is often an important concern. In AI, the methodology is as follows: given a text, specify the knowledge and processes that could lead to a reasonable interpretation of that text. Many AI researchers adopt a schema interpretation approach, while others work within a more general abductive reasoning paradigm. The goal is to characterize the interpretation process and therefore often ignores the question of storyness, assuming that the program will only be presented with valid stories. Instead, the key issues are semantic and pragmatic interpretation, and the recognition of plans and other known concepts.

An example of the two camps arguing at cross-purpose is Wilensky (1983b). In this article, Wilensky attacks story grammars and suggests a theory of reasoning and interpretation in its place. Various respondents defend their position assuming their own research paradigm, and thus each side claims victory in the end.

In this entry we concentrate on the computational approach while recognizing that noncomputational work such as that by Grimes, (1975), Flammer and Kintsch (1982), van Dijk and Kintsch (1983), and Kintsch (1982, 1988) has been influential to the computationalists, in addition to being worthy work in its own right.

SCRIPT-BASED ANALYSIS

The first outline of a computational theory of story analysis was Charniak's thesis (1972). Charniak pointed out many problems but never implemented anything beyond the prototype stage. Thus Cullingford's SAM (qv) (Script Applier Mechanism) program (Schank, 1975; Cullingford, 1978, 1986) was the first real story analyzer. SAM's basic algorithm was to identify an appropriate schema, or script (see SCRIPTS), and then to interpret all subsequent information as "filling in the blanks" in that script. The following is an example of SAM's capabilities:

Input Text
John went to a restaurant. He ordered a hot dog. The waiter said they didn't have any. He asked for a hamburger. When the hamburger came, it was burnt. He left the restaurant.

Question-Answering Output
Q: Did John sit down in the restaurant?
A: Probably.

Q: Did John order a hot dog?
A: Yes.
Q: What did the waiter serve John?
A: The waiter served John a hamburger.
Q: Did John pay the check?
A: No. John was angry because the hamburger was overdone and so he left the restaurant.

The question-answering program used to demonstrate SAM's analysis was designed by Lehnert (1978).

On the surface, this seems quite impressive. First, SAM has recognized the appropriateness of the restaurant script. Second, the roles of waiter, customer, and meal have apparently been integrated into this schema. Third, steps of the script that were not explicitly mentioned in the text—sitting down, leaving without paying—were inferred by SAM. A number of subtleties are required to make this possible; for example, SAM has to match the input "the hamburger came" to the question "what did the waiter serve" to come up with the answer "the waiter served John a hamburger." This is possible because the restaurant script includes a step where the order is brought to the table, and the agent of that step is, by default, the waiter.

Unfortunately, SAM, like most AI programs, was not made available for peer review, and there was no formal experimental tests of its abilities. It performed well on preselected stories but could not handle stories that deviated from known scripts, that did not make the relevant script obvious, or that involved more than one script. SAM also had an extremely limited syntactic repertoire. Despite its limited abilities, SAM served as an early example of a working computerized story analyzer and prompted further research. Psychologists were interested in how scripts were represented and used by humans (Bower and co-workers, 1979). Other script-based programs were constructed. For example, FRUMP (qv) (DeJong, 1979) (see SCRIPTS) skimmed newspaper articles from the UPI news wire, such as the following:

Input Text:

Mount Vernon, IL (UPI) A small earthquake shook several southern Illinois counties Monday night, the National Earthquake Information Service in Goldon, CO, reported.

Spokesman Din Finley said the quake measured 3.2 on the Richter scale, "Probably not enough to do any damage or cause any injuries." The quake occurred about 7:48 pm CST and was centered about 30 miles east of Mount Vernon, Finley said. It was felt in Richland, Clay, Jasper, Effington, and Marion counties.

Small earthquakes are common in the area, Finley said.

Output:

SELECTED SKETCHY SCRIPT $EARTHQUAKE
ENGLISH SUMMARY:
THERE WAS AN EARTHQUAKE IN ILLINOIS WITH 3.2 RICHTER SCALE READING.

GOAL-BASED ANALYSIS

If SAM was a response to Bartlett's schemata, then the next program to come out of the Yale school can be seen as an answer to Propp's characterization of goal-based stories. Wilensky's (1978, 1983a) PAM (qv) (Plan Applier Mechanism) processed nonstereotypical stories by tracking character's goals, plans, and actions. For example:

Input Text

John wanted money. He got a gun and walked into a liquor store. He told the owner he wanted some money. The owner gave John the money and John left.

Question-Answering Output

Q: Why did John get a gun?
A: Because he wanted to rob a liquor store.
Q: Why did the shopkeeper give John the money?
A: Because the shopkeeper didn't want to get hurt.
Q: Why did John leave?
A: Because John didn't want to get caught.

PAM has no script for "robbing a liquor store," but it does know that people often want money, that stores have money, that a gun can be used to threaten bodily harm, that people want to avoid bodily harm, and so on. PAM attempts to explain each input as a goal for some character, as a step in a known plan, or as a substep of some intermediate plan for a known goal. This can involve a complex explanation of arbitrary length. Consider the following input: *Willa was hungry. She picked up the Michelin guide.*

For the first sentence, PAM supposes that Willa will have the goal of satisfying her hunger. This is a known goal, and so needs no further explanation. For the second sentence, PAM builds a chain of seven inferences, as follows. (1) Picking up the guide is a plan for possessing it. (2) Possessing can be a subgoal of having, so PAM hypothesizes that Willa wants to have the guide. (3) Possessing an object with a known function can be a subgoal of performing the function, in this case, reading the guide. (4) Reading is a plan for knowing new information. The Michelin guide is a source of information about restaurants (among other things), so PAM hypothesizes that Willa wants to know the location of a restaurant (and makes other hypotheses as well). (5) Knowing a restaurant's location is instrumental to going there. (6) Being at a restaurant is instrumental to eating there. (7) Eating would satisfy Willa's known hunger goal. Thus, PAM has arrived at an explanation.

PAM goes beyond SAM in being able to process nonstereotypical stories, but it suffers from brittleness in many of the same ways. Perhaps more important than the PAM program itself was the theory of goal interaction on which it was based (Wilensky, 1983). Wilensky discusses a number of relations that goals can have to one another. For example, there can be conflict (or concord) between two goals held by the same person (or by different persons). Each of these four situations gives rise to various strategies. Consider the following example:

John wanted to watch television but Mary wanted to go out to a movie. John told Mary their car should not be driven before replacing the shocks.

To understand this story, we must first understand that a limited resource—time—is in contention. We assume there is not time to both watch television and go out to a movie. Thus, John and Mary are in a goal competition situation. John has surmised that Mary has planned to drive the car, and he has constructed a counter plan to convince her not to. If Mary accepts his argument, it means that she believes he is being truthful (even though she knows that lying is a possible means of convincing) and that her goal of seeing a movie is less important than her goal of preserving the health of the car and its occupants.

The entry on FRAMES discusses Wilensky's work from another perspective.

INTEGRATED ANALYSIS

The two programs we have reviewed championed different knowledge structures: scripts for SAM and plans and goals for PAM. Both programs were successful in pointing out how important this knowledge is, but neither program was able to handle stories that strayed outside their area of expertise. SAM could not handle the liquor store or Michelin guide story because it lacked the appropriate scripts. Because it had knowledge of the character's goals and reactions, PAM could handle a simple story like "Pat hit Kim. She cried." But because the story involves no animate characters and hence no goals, it could not handle a superficially similar story like "The wind blew the vase off the table. It broke."

A more general and robust program would have to be able to handle a number of different knowledge structures. This capability was provided by Dyer's BORIS program (1982). BORIS (qv) was integrated in that it combined rules for dealing with different knowledge structures at the same time. Where SAM looked for scripts and PAM looked for plans and goals, BORIS searched for an explanation at each of four levels: scriptal, goal/plan, thematic, and role. For example, in the main example Dyer uses, two old friends meet for lunch to discuss some business. The meeting is understood by BORIS three ways: in terms of the restaurant script, the friendship theme, and the businessman role. While this approach may be a good heuristic in many cases, it will fail in others. An event could just as easily have multiple explanations at the same level. For example, in "John was hungry when it started to rain. He ducked into a restaurant," a single action can be interpreted as a plan toward two goals: staying dry and having food.

BORIS was a triumph in its coverage of disparate knowledge structures. In fact, it can be seen as primarily a theory of memory organization and access and only secondarily as a story analyzer. One of the interesting facts about BORIS is that its memory of a story can be affected by the questions it is asked. In effect, it fills in part of its representation of the story as a by-product of answering questions. This is in accord with psychological experiments by Bartlett and by Loftus.

BORIS incorporates and distinguishes 17 classes of knowledge: object primitives, scripts, settings, goals, plans, affects, themes, interpersonal relationships, physical states, events, social acts, memory organization packets, thematic abstraction units, scenes, scenarios, reasoning, and beliefs. These structures interact only in certain predefined ways. For example, inferences can be made to connect events to goals (as in PAM), but emotional affect can never be directly related to settings. Thus, if given the passage "At the restaurant Bill punched John in the mouth. John got mad" and the question "How did John feel at the restaurant?" BORIS would not be able to directly recall John's affect. Instead, it would have to first recall the restaurant setting and then the restaurant script. From that BORIS would recall that the punching event occurred as an unexpected event in the restaurant script and infer some goal of John's and finally infer his affect.

Despite—or perhaps because of—this vast and varied amount of knowledge, BORIS was in some ways even more brittle than its predecessors. Each knowledge type—indeed, each allowable combination of knowledge types—had a set of rules associated with it. Some sample rules are shown here:

IF an act at the destination setting of a transition scenario is enabled by that setting
THEN build an enables link between the goal achieved and the change of proximity goal in the scenario
IF the word just read is a pronoun
and a human is found with matching gender and case
THEN bind the concept to that human
IF the word just read is 'glass' THEN
IF it is followed by a liquid
THEN glass is used as a measure (eg, a glass of coke)
ELSE glass is used as a material (eg, a glass plate)
IF the story refers to a meal
and a human is found modified by 'with'
THEN that human is an eater in the meal

The rules were too *ad hoc* and the interactions too complicated to allow the rule base to scale up gracefully. Whereas SAM and PAM handled dozens of stories (admittedly short and contrived ones), BORIS was shown to answer questions on only two stories, both involving the same subject matter. BORIS's capabilities were deep but not broad. Clearly, we need either a sophisticated learning mechanism to acquire the knowledge BORIS needs or else an entirely new approach.

To appreciate the ramifications of continuing or abandoning the BORIS approach, one has to be aware of the tension that exists throughout AI between strong and weak methods. Strong methods are heuristics aimed at specific problems, such as the script application algorithm that embodied SAM. Weak methods are general algorithms such as exhaustive search or resolution theorem proving that can be applied to a wide variety of problems. Strong methods tend to fail when the problem at hand varies from the original target domain or when it is necessary to combine evidence from separate parts of the problem to arrive at the whole solution. Weak methods tend to fail by considering too many possible combinations and never getting to an answer. Most weak methods are provably intractable; in other words, there will always be problems for which they will take too much time to solve. BORIS was the epitome of a strong method. Every fact was encoded as a rule; every new piece of information made the algorithm more complicated. In the next two sections, we will examine approaches based on weak methods. In the last section, we show the approach that seems dominant in the 1990s. It is also based on weak methods.

UNIFIED ANALYSIS

BORIS can be seen as an attempt to deal with all the types of knowledge structures that were proposed by Schank and Abelson (1977) as well as several that were introduced since then. There is general agreement that having this knowledge is very helpful, perhaps absolutely necessary, but the knowledge would be easier to use if the ad hoc rules could be replaced with a simpler algorithm based on a unified weak method.

Norvig (1986, 1989) uses the weak method of marker passing, a spreading activation mechanism that passes markers through a network of knowledge structures, looks for relevant marker collisions, and makes inferences based on those collisions. The model stems from the TLC program of Quillian (1968, 1969), which had the ability to make some interesting inferences but suffered from a lack of maturity in both the knowledge representation and the linguistic tools available at the time. Small and Rieger (1982) and Waltz and Pollack (1984) also make use of the idea of spreading activation to do parsing and semantic interpretation, and Hendler (1985) uses marker passing to do problem solving.

Norvig's FAUSTUS program features a representation language capable of encoding a variety of knowledge structures in a uniform format. The algorithm is to pass markers from each concept in the parsed representation of the input to neighboring concepts. These markers keep track of where they came from, and so when a marker collision occurs, the paths of the two markers can be consulted to see what inference, if any, to suggest. In general, there may be contradictory suggestions, and the final interpretation consists of a coherent subset of the possible inferences. There is a measure of how coherent a set of inferences is, and the program chooses a set of inferences that tends to maximize this measure of coherence. In practice, there are too many possibilities to consider them all, so the program uses an approximation technique that looks at a small number of possibilities at a time. The important point is that coming up with an interpretation of a text is just a matter of looking for connections among the concepts mentioned. Of course, the exact connections to consider is a critical problem.

FAUSTUS looks for specific types of marker paths that suggest specific inferences. An "elaboration" path suggests a relation between two objects, and a "double-elaboration" path suggests a new object related by two separate relations to two given objects. A "reference" path suggests that one object is co-referential with another, and a "concretion" path suggests that an object should be categorized as some more specific type. These are the only paths that matter; all other marker collisions are ignored. The paths themselves are specified in terms of the primitive links that are traversed. Primitive links cover epistemological notions like taxonomic hierarchy (ISA), identity and nonidentity, and the existence of a relation that maps between two categories. Primitive links do not mention any domain concepts, such as person, buying, selling, and so on. An example follows:

Input Text
A cobbler sold a pair of boots to a hiker.

Inferences
The selling is a shoe-store-transaction.
(This is a CONCRETION inference.)

There is a walking such that it is the purpose of the boot and the hiker is the object-moved of it.
(This is a DOUBLE-ELABORATION inference.)

Rather than answer questions, FAUSTUS outputs inferences as it makes them. The program's knowledge base includes the equivalent of a script for buying and selling in a store, and it also has a more specific version of this concept, called shoe-store-transaction: a store transaction where the merchandise is shoes and the merchant is a shoe salesman. Markers from the concepts "boot" and "cobbler" intersect at shoe-store-transaction and suggest the concretion inference, that is, they suggest that the selling took place in the cobbler's shoe store. The inference is eventually accepted, since there is no evidence to contradict it. The second inference is suggested by a collision at "walking" originating at "boot" and "hiker." The markers take different paths to arrive at this collision, so a different inference is suggested, and again the inference is accepted.

FAUSTUS is able to process a variety of texts with a simple control structure coupled with a complex knowledge base. This means it can be extended by adding knowledge rather than changing the algorithm. Recall that BORIS was integrated (it used different knowledge sources in one program), while FAUSTUS is truly unified (all knowledge is in the same format). However, FAUSTUS has a difficult time deciding on a proper interpretation in the face of conflicting suggestions. There are heuristics for favoring one suggestion over another and for deciding which suggestions to consider first, but there is no provision for weighing a set of suggestions against an alternate interpretation stemming from another set. The knowledge is unified but not *commensurable*. FAUSTUS can also be seen as an abductive reasoning system; these will be discussed further below.

As an aside, note that this view of understanding as finding connections can be traced back to Bartlett (1932) (Chapt. 12, Section 1, page 227): "all the cognitive processes which have been considered, from perceiving to thinking, are ways in which some fundamental 'effort after meaning' seeks expression. Speaking very broadly, such effort is simply the attempt to connect something that is given with something other than itself."

COHERENCE-BASED ANALYSIS

Another story analyzer based on weak methods was Alterman's (1985) NEXUS program. NEXUS searched for a solution using breadth-first search while FAUSTUS used a marker-passing algorithm, but the result is much the same. The difference is that Alterman specified in advance the connections for which he was looking. Thus, his program was limited in the inferences it could make and could not be readily extended to make different ones. However, the connections chosen constitute a theory of coherence; of what makes one line of a story go with the previous lines. In particular, it is a theory of event coherence. The idea is that if each event can be hooked up to another, then the various objects will also match up appropriately. Alterman looks for taxonomic, partonomic, and temporal relations between events. The taxonomic relation says, for example, that driving is a kind of moving. Partonomic relations hold between complex events and their subparts. There are four temporal relations, representing events that necessarily (or probably) occur before (or after) another. In the following example, the event coherence structure built by NEXUS is passed to SUM (Alterman, 1986), which generates a summary.

Input Text
The pig trotted toward the stream carrying a bundle of clothes. The animal expertly soaked and scoured the laundry. The pig hung the clothes in the sun to dry. The pig gathered her laundry and trotted home.

Summarization
The pig cleaned clothes at the stream.

NEXUS misses many inferences that could be made by BORIS or FAUSTUS. However, NEXUS does capture something interesting about the notion of "storyness," or at least of coherence, in a highly compact theory involving only seven relations.

Notice that there is a difference between a paraphrase and a summarization of a story. A paraphrase uses different words to indicate that the program is capable of understanding rather than just mimicking. A summary must pick out the important points in a story. Thus, generating a summary indicates a successful understanding of the events in a story, and it also indicates that the relations between those events have been understood. Summarization returns us to the idea of storyness.

A more ambitious and complex summarization theory is Lehnert's plot unit theory. Here all events are characterized as having a positive, negative, or neutral mental state. These are connected with links denoting a motivation, actualization, termination, or equivalence. The entire text is described in these terms. The interesting part is that small groups of nodes and links group together into recognizable subgraphs. The smallest of these are the 15 primitive plot units: problem, failure, perseverance, success, etc. These fit together to form complex plot units such as nested subgoals, fortuitous problem resolution, and double-cross. Given this analysis, summarization to Lehnert is a matter of recognizing complex plot units and noticing how they fit together. The PLUGG program (Lehnert and Loiselle, 1983) was used to generate the following summary of Arnold Toynbee's synopsis of the New Testament:

> Jesus makes an appeal to the masses. The government wants to maintain authority over the masses. Jesus causes a scandal. Jesus takes the law into his own hands to avenge God. The authorities arrest Jesus. Jesus is crucified. Jesus' death is a triumph. Jesus is worshipped.

This is a satisfactory summary, but it should be noted that it was produced from a hand translation of the original synopsis into the plot unit formalism. No current program is robust enough to analyze the original text.

Both Lehnert and Alterman's models of summarization suffer from the same criticism as story grammars: They characterize events and goals solely by their connections to their effects and not by their intrinsic interest or importance. Thus, the following two texts would be assigned identical structures, while intuitively only John's plight seems like the basis of a real story:

> John had been happily married for several years.
> Then his wife contracted cancer.
>
> Fred had been happily writing for several minutes.
> Then his pen started to run out of ink.

Wilensky's theory of story points (1983) was designed to address these problems but is still open to some of the same criticisms.

Hobbs (1982) presents another attempt at defining coherence. Hobbs poses a very important question: Why should a discourse (or story) be longer than one sentence? He gives four answers. (1) It may be that more than one thing happened, and the speaker wants to convey this. However, to be a coherent discourse, the events have to be related, but they need not be related by necessary causation. Hobbs calls this the *occasion* relation; it is similar to Alterman's "probably happens after" relation. (2) The speaker may want to place an evaluative judgment on the discourse, as when a discourse is introduced with "the most remarkable thing happened." (3) The speaker needs to link what is new with what he thinks the listener knows. Thus, settings can be introduced by the "background" relation, and unusual events can be mediated by an explanation: "He was in a foul mood. He hadn't slept well that night." (4) The speaker can make his exact meaning clear by giving examples at varying levels of generality. The relations of *parallel, contrast, generalization,* and *exemplification* are used for this.

Hobbs presents a program, DIANA-2, which recognizes instances of his coherence relations. For example, consider the set of instructions *Leave the building. Turn. Go to the corner.* DIANA-2 recognizes that leaving the building is the occasion that allows turning to be appropriate, and turning then occasions going to the corner. Similar work addressing coherence in discourse is by Mann and Thompson (1986). Sperber and Wilson (1986) present a model that is based on relevance rather than coherence but is also similar (See DISCOURSE UNDERSTANDING).

COMMENSURABLE ANALYSIS

In the early 1990s, story analysis is in a period of retrenchment. We have seen some early successes that did not scale up well. We have seen tentative models of summarization in-the-small and of discourse coherence. However, we have yet to see one model that comes with a broad knowledge base, makes local coherence inferences, arrives at an overall understanding of the text's important points, themes, and moral, and distinguishes stories from nonstories. The most disheartening fact is that partial successes have not been amenable to fine-tuning and improvement. Instead, they have been discarded in favor of brand new, theoretically incompatible efforts.

In hindsight, it is easy to see why this has come about. Partly it has to do with the fact that the subject matter is complex, and there is no one established tradition for important problems like knowledge representation and linguistic formalisms. But more importantly, past research efforts were just not suitable for reuse. Single-purpose systems, like SAM and PAM, had underlying algorithms tuned to one particular knowledge structure. Thus, they could not be extended to handle other types of knowledge. Integrated systems, like BORIS, proved too complex to maintain. Unified systems, like FAUSTUS, offer hope but are still unable to make fine distinctions when there are competing interpretations. We need a methodology where evidence for competing interpretations is commensurable as well as unified. In this section we will review two systems with just that property. Both claim to be a model of semantic interpretation rather than a model of story analysis *per se*, but semantic interpretation is a large part of the battle, and the architecture of these systems should make it possible to add knowledge of story conventions.

The TACITUS project (Hobbs and co-workers, 1988) adopts a model called abductive inference, which is inference to the best explanation. They concentrate on applying knowledge to problems in local pragmatics, that is, the pragmatics of a single sentence at a time. Consider the sentence, *Disengaged compressor after lube-oil alarm.* Here the problems include finding a referent for the compressor and alarm, determining the relation between lube-oil and alarm, deciding if the prepositional phrase modifies the compressor or the disengaging, and determining that "after" refers to the time of the sounding of the alarm, not to the alarm itself. The approach is to build a logical form representation of the sentence, with certain aspects left unspecified. The next step is to specify all the variable parts of the logical expression, either by identifying variables with known objects and relations, or by just accepting new variables. To accept a new variable is to add new information, and the trick is not to add more new information than necessary; in other words, to make the sentence cohere by grounding it in known referents. New information is more likely to appear in certain linguistic constructs than in others. Hobbs assigns a "dollar" cost to each new assumption, with the costs weighted by these linguistic factors. Definite noun phrases are normally used to refer to known objects, so the cost of assuming one is high: $10 for the purposes of this example. Metonymic connections and noun compound interpretations have an even higher cost, $20, since to assume them is to fail to find a connection all together. At the other end of the scale, nonnominal propositions are often new information, so they get a low cost ($3). The logic form for the example sentence, with costs attached, is as follows:

$$\exists (e, x, c, j, k, y, a, o) \text{Past}(e)^{\$3} \wedge \text{disengage}'(e, x, c)^{\$3}$$
$$\wedge \text{ compressor}(c)^{\$5} \wedge \text{after}(j, k)^{\$3}$$
$$\wedge \text{ event}(j)^{\$10} \wedge \text{rel}(j, y)^{\$20} \wedge (y = c \vee y = e)$$
$$\wedge \text{ event}(k)^{\$10} \wedge \text{rel}(k, a)^{\$20} \wedge \text{alarm}(a)^{\$5}$$
$$\wedge \text{ noun-compound}(o, a)^{\$20} \wedge \text{lube-oil}(o)^{\$5}$$

Interpretation is now a matter of finding or assuming values for e, x, c, j, k, y, a, and o that minimize the total cost.

Charniak and Goldman (1988, 1989) propose a similar model. Instead of using costs of assumptions, Charniak and Goldman's program uses probabilities as the universal currency. Different possible interpretations are represented as logical disjunctions. The most probable interpretation is chosen, according to Bayesian probability theory. For example, given the text:

John went to the supermarket. He found the milk on the shelf. He paid for it.

the program will select as the most probable interpretation a model that has paying as a step of the supermarket shopping event, and has "it" referring to the milk rather than the shelf or the supermarket. Milk is preferred because there is additional evidence for it, stemming from the fact that in a shopping event one pays for the selected goods. Thus, the program has duplicated an inference that SAM would make using scripts. What this model has that SAM lacked, though, is the ability to rule out a script-based inference in the face of competing evidence. For example, suppose the passage was read in the context "John needed some shelving. He heard that the local supermarket was selling off some milk-damaged shelves." This context could be used to build another model, where "it" refers to the shelf. The decision between the two models would depend on the initial probabilities and on the combination rules, but the important point is that all evidence can be considered.

Schubert and Hwang (1989) present another system based on an abductive probabalistic logic. They outline how the system could be used to understand part of the Little Red Riding Hood story. However, the full system is not yet implemented. Ng and Mooney (1990) return to a coherence-based analysis, but they provide a metric for measuring coherence, so that their system can search for the interpretation that maximizes coherence. Norvig and Wilensky (1990) critically evaluate these commensurable abduction systems. They point out that maximizing a single probabilitylike measure is theoretically suspect because there is a fundamental trade-off between probability and informativeness. The more assumptions one makes, the greater the rewards of inferring something, and the greater the risk of making the mistake. If there is a single measure that can be maximized, it must be a measure of utility to the listener, not probability.

COMPOSITIONAL ANALYSIS

These last two systems have a more direct connection to formal logic than the other systems we have reviewed, so it is important to contrast them with the best-known logical formalism for semantic interpretation, Montague semantics. In Montague semantics, there is a one-to-one correspondence between syntactic and semantic forms. That is, every rule of the grammar builds a corresponding logical expression, and these are combined compositionally to form the logical interpretation of the whole sentence. Montague semantics has enjoyed a strong following in linguistics but has generally been seen as unable to cope with the pragmatic complexities necessary for story analysis. A Montague grammar interpretation of a sentence cannot be sensitive to the context, since it must be built compositionally from its components, without any provision for these components communicating with each other. Because of such problems, many AI researchers have adopted a "pragmatics first" approach, effectively ignoring syntax. While this has led to a better understanding of semantics and pragmatics, it has forced researchers to work with syntactically simple, artificial texts. The abductive approach is a major advance because it allows syntactic, semantic, and pragmatic factors to be considered on an equal footing.

There have been attempts to extend Montague's compositional approach, as in Kamp's (1981) discourse representation theory or Hirst's (1986) work on disambiguation. A more recent attempt is the Candide system (Pollack and Pereira (1988). Their solution is to use a *least commitment grammar*, which leaves undecided a number of problems, such as prepositional phrase attachment, noun–noun compound interpretation, and quantifier scopings. In effect, the syntax produces a vague parse, which corresponds to a logical form encompassing several disjunctions. These disjunctions can then be disambiguated in the presence of any context information. The interpretations must still operate within the framework of compositionality, so they are not as free to consider interactions as are Charniak and Hobbs, but they claim that the guidance offered by compositionality will make interpretation more efficient. Charniak counters by using his probability measures not only to decide the best final interpretation but also to limit search while building the interpretation: The least likely partial interpretations are discarded befoer they are fully expanded.

CONCLUSIONS

As the most recent research has shown, we are a long ways from a good model of the interpretation of a single sentence, let alone a complete story. There are basic questions to be answered in a number of fields. Despite advances in linguistics, grammatical coverage is often inadequate to handle even simple children's stories. More complete grammars and lexicons are needed (see DICTIONARY/LEXICON). It has been clearly shown that knowledge of typical plans, goals, and schemata are essential for story analysis. Cataloging these is an even larger undertaking than doing a grammar or lexicon, in the same way that producing an encyclopedia is more difficult than a dictionary. Representing even a tiny fraction of commonsense knowledge will require both painstaking work and theoretical breakthroughs. Advances in machine learning (qv) may help.

There is still room for work on the basic question of what it means to interpret a text. Most authors assume that their task is to come up with a single interpretation of each sentence, the best possible model. But many stories are intentionally ambiguous and have interpretations at multiple levels. Norvig (1988) discusses multiple interpretations. Hobbs (1990) attempts to summarize what AI and cognitive science can learn from the field of literary criticism, and vice versa. In conclusion, stories are complex entities. They rely on linguistic and literary conventions. They refer to events, characters, plans, and goals. They have morals and points, and they are conveyed by storytellers who have motives of their own. All these must be recognized before full appreciation of a text can be claimed. This makes story analysis perplexingly difficult, but it also makes it a fruitful field of research.

BIBLIOGRAPHY

R. Alterman, "A Dictionary Based on Concept Coherence," *Artif. Intell.* **25**(2), 153–186 (1985).

R. Alterman, "Summarization in the Small," in N. E. Sharkey, ed., *Advances in Cognitive Science*, Vol. 1, Wiley, Chichester, U.K., 1986, pp. 72–93.

F. C. Bartlett, *Remembering: A Study in Experimental Social Psychology*, Cambridge University Press, Cambridge, U.K., 1932.

G. H. Bower, J. B. Black, and T. Turner, "Scripts in Memory for Text," *Cogn. Psych.* **11**, 177 (1979).

E. Charniak, *Toward a Model of Children's Story Comprehension*, MIT AI Lab Technical Report AI-TR-266, Cambridge, Mass., 1972.

E. Charniak and R. Goldman, "A Logic for Semantic Interpretation," *Proceedings of the Twenty-Sixth Meeting of the ACL*, Buffalo, N.Y., 1988, pp. 87–94.

E. Charniak and R. Goldman, "A Semantics for Probabilistic Quantifier-Free First-Order Languages, with Particular Application to Story Understanding," *Proceedings of the Eleventh IJCAI*, Detroit, Mich., 1989.

R. E. Cullingford, "Script application: Computer Understanding of Newspaper Stories," Technical Report Research Report #116, Yale University, New Haven, Conn., 1978.

R. E. Cullingford, "SAM," in K. Sparck-Jones, B. J. Grosz, and B. L. Webber, eds., *Readings in Natural Language Processing*, Morgan-Kaufmann, Los Altos, Calif., 1986, pp. 627–649.

N. Dehn, "Story Generation After TALE-SPIN," *Proceedings of the Seventh IJCAI*, 1981, pp. 16–18.

G. DeJong, "Prediction and Substantiation: A New Approach to Language Processing," *Cogn. Sci.* **3**(3), 251–273 (1979).

M. G. Dyer, *In-Depth Understanding*, Technical Report Research Report #219, 1982.

A. Flammer and W. Kintsch, *Discourse Processing*, North-Holland, Amsterdam, 1982.

J. Grimes, *The Thread of Discourse*, Mouton and Co., The Hague, 1975.

J. A. Hendler, *Integrating Marker-Passing and Problem-Solving*,

Technical Report CS-85-08, Brown University, Providence, Rhode Island, 1985.

G. Hirst, *Semantic Interpretation and the Resolution of Ambiguity*, Cambridge University Press, Cambridge, U.K., 1986.

J. R. Hobbs, "Towards an Understanding of Coherence in Discourse," in W. G. Lehnert and M. H. Ringle, eds., *Strategies for Natural Language Processing*, Erlbaum, Hillsdale, N.J., 1982, pp. 223–243.

J. R. Hobbs, M. Stickel, P. Martin, and D. Edwards, "Interpretation as Abduction," *Proceedings of the Twenty-Sixth Meeting of the ACL*, Buffalo, NY, 1988, pp. 95–103.

J. R. Hobbs, *Literature and Cognition*, CSLI, Stanford, Calif., 1990.

H. Kamp, in *Formal Methods in the Study of Language*, J. A. G. Groenendijk, T. M. V. Janssen, and M. B. J. Stokhoff, eds., Mathematisch Centrum, Amsterdam, 1981, pp. 227–322.

W. Kintsch, "Aspects of Text Comprehension," in J.-F. Le Ny and W. Kintsch, eds., *Language and Comprehension*, North-Holland, Amsterdam, 1982.

W. Kintsch, "The Role of Knowledge in Discourse Comprehension: A Construction-Integration Model," *Psychol. Rev.* **95**, 163–182 (1988).

G. P. Lakoff, "Structural Complexity in Fairy Tales," *The Study of Man*, **1**, 128–150 (1972).

M. Lebowitz, "Creating a Story-Telling Universe," *Proceedings of the Eighth IJCAI*, Karlsruhe, West Germany, 1983, pp. 63–65.

W. Lehnert, *The Process of Question Answering*, Lawrence Erlbaum, Hillsdale, N.J., 1978.

W. Lehnert and C. Loiselle, *Plot Unit Recognition for Narratives*, Technical Report 83-39, University of Massachusetts, Amherst, 1983.

E. H. Lichtenstein and W. F. Brewer, "Memory for Goal-Directed Events," *Cogn. Psychol.* **12**, 412–445 (1980).

J. M. Mandler, *Stories, Scripts, and Scenes: Aspects of Schema Theory*, Lawrence Erlbaum, Hillsdale, N.J., 1984.

J. M. Mandler and N. S. Johnson, "Remembrance of Things Parsed: Story Structure and Recall," *Cogn. Psychol.* **9**, 111–151 (1977).

W. Mann and S. Thompson, "Relational Propositions in Discourse," *Discourse Processes*, **9**(1), 57–97 (1986).

M. E. Pollack and F. C. N. Pereira, "An Integrated Framework for Semantic and Pragmatic Interpertation," *Proceedings of the Twenty-Sixth Meeting of the ACL*, Buffalo, NY, 1988, pp. 75–86.

J. Meehan, "Using Planning Structures to Generate Stories," *Amer. J. Comput. Ling.* (Microfiche 33), 77–93 (1975).

H. T. Ng and R. J. Mooney, "The Role of Coherence in Constructing and Evaluating Abductive Explanations," *AAAI Spring Symposium Workshop on Automated Abduction*, Stanford, Calif., 1990.

P. Norvig, *A Unified Theory of Inference for Text Understanding*, Technical Report and Ph.D. dissertation, University of California, Berkeley, 1986.

P. Norvig, "Multiple Simultaneous Interpretations of Ambiguous Sentences," *Proceedings of the Tenth Annual Conference of the Cognitive Science Society*, 1988.

P. Norvig, "Marker Passing as a Weak Method for Text Inferencing," *Cogn. Sci.* **13**(4), 569–620 (1989).

P. Norvig and R. Wilensky, "A Critical Evaluation of Commensurable Abduction Models for Semantic Interpretation," *Thirteenth International Conference on Computational Linguistics (COLING-90)*, Helsinki, 1990.

V. Propp, *Morphology of the Folktale*, Laurence Scott, trans., Svatava Pirkova-Jakobson, ed., Indiana University Research Center in Anthropology, Folklore, and Linguistics, Bloomington, Ind., 1958.

M. Ross Quillian, "Semantic Memory," in Marvin Minsky, ed., *Semantic Information Processing*, MIT Press, Cambridge, Mass., 1968.

M. Ross Quillian, "The Teachable Language Comprehender: A Simulation Program and Theory of Language," *Communications of the ACM* **12**, 459–476 (1969).

D. Rumelhart, "Notes on a Schema for Stories," in Daniel G. Bobrow and Allan Collins, eds., *Representation and Understanding*, Academic Press, New York, 1975, pp. 211–236.

R. Schank, *SAM: A Story Understander*, Technical Report, Yale University Computer Science Research Report #43, New Haven, Conn. 1975.

R. C. Schank and R. P. Abelson, *Scripts, Plans, Goals and Understanding*, Erlbaum, Hillsdale, NJ, 1977.

L. K. Schubert and C. H. Hwang, "An Episodic Knowledge Representation for Narrative Texts," *Proceedings of the First International Conference on Principles of Knowledge Representation and Reasoning,* 1989, pp. 444–458.

S. Small and C. Rieger, "Parsing and Comprehension with Word Experts," in W. G. Lehnert and M. H. Ringle, eds., *Strategies for Natural Language Processing*, Lawrence Erlbaum, Hillsdale, N.J., 1982, pp. 89–148.

D. Sperber and D. Wilson, *Relevance*, Harvard University Press, Cambridge, Mass., 1986.

P. W. Thorndyke, "Cognitive Structures in Comprehension and Memory of Narrative Discourse," *Cogn. Psychol.* **9** (1977).

T. A. van Dijk and W. Kintsch, *Strategies of Discourse Comprehension*, Academic Press, New York, 1983.

D. L. Waltz and J. B. Pollack, "Massively Parallel Parsing: A Strongly Interactive Model of Natural Language Interpretation," *Cogn. Sci.* **9**(1), 51–74 (1984).

R. W. Wilensky, *Understanding Goal-based Stories*, Yale University Computer Science Research Report, New Haven, Conn., 1978.

R. Wilensky, *Planning and Understanding*, Addison-Wesley, Reading, Mass., 1983a.

R. Wilensky, "Story Grammars versus Story Points," *J. Behav. Brain Sci.* **6**(4), (**1983b**).

PETER NORVIG
University of California,
Berkeley

STRIPS

STRIPS is an automatic planning system that was completed by Fikes and Nilsson in 1971 at SRI International. STRIPS uses means-ends analysis to conduct a state space heuristic search in which each state is represented by a collection of predicate calculus statements. A resolution theorem power is used to answer queries about individual states. The theorem prover's partial proofs of unsatisfied goals in a given state are used by the search mechanism to generate GPS-like "differences" that are then used to select a plan operator that would "reduce" one of the differences by enabling extension or completion of a partial proof. Plan operators are represented as a set of preconditions, deletions, and additions. A key assumption (referred to as "the STRIPS assumption") in the design is that execution of a plan operator affects only those aspects of the world explicitly mentioned in the operator's deletions and additions lists. [See R. Fikes and N. Nilsson, "STRIPS: A New Approach to the Application of Theorem Proving to Problem Solving," *Artif. Intell.* **2**, 189–208 (1971).]

RICHARD FIKES
Stanford University

STUDENT

STUDENT was one of the earliest programs to explore computer understanding of natural language. STUDENT solved algebra story problems given in a subset of English (see PROBLEM SOLVING). It transformed the sentences of the problem in stages through kernel sentences to ones that directly reflected the set of simultaneous equations underlying the problem. These syntactic transformations were augmented by heuristics to identify different phrases used to refer to the same thing, or to transform phrases to appropriate semantic correspondents more useful for solving the problem. STUDENT was tested on a large set of problems adapted from textbooks (put into the limited English subset STUDENT could process), and even on the slow computers of that era, it solved the problems at speeds comparable to people. A complete description of this MIT thesis work is available (D. G. Bobrow, "Natural Language Input for a Computer Problem-Solving System," in M. Minsky, ed., *Semantic Information Processing*, MIT Press, Cambridge, Mass., 1968, pp. 146–226).

DANIEL G. BOBROW
Xerox PARC

STUF

STUF (Stuttgart Type Unification Formalism) is a feature term formalism for the representation of linguistic and other types of taxonomic knowledge [see G. Bouma, E. König and H. Uszkoreit, "A Flexible Graph-Unification Formalism and Its Application to Natural Language Processing," *IBM J. Res. Dev.* **32**, 170–184 (1988); H. Uszkoreit, "From Feature Bundles to Abstract Data Types: New Directions in the Representation of Linguistic Knowledge," in: H. Blaser, ed., *Natural Language at the Computer*, Springer, Berlin, pp. 31–64, 1989]. The formalism was developed and implemented by Uszkoreit, Seiffert, Bouma, Dörre, and others at IBM Stuttgart between 1986 and 1988 as the uniform core representation language for the integrated text understanding system LILOG (see C.-R. Rollinger, R. Studer, and H. Uszkoreit, "Text Understanding in LILOG," in: W. Brauer, ed., *Proceedings of the GI Congress in Knowledge-Based Systems*, Springer, Berlin, 1987, pp. 246–259). It is currently used for research and teaching at IBM Germany and at the Universities of Hamburg, Osnabrück, Saarbrücken, Stuttgart, and Trier.

In STUF, the feature term formalism is defined as an abstract data type (ADT). The grammar formalism uses the ADT for the representation of rules. Basic operations are unification and disjunction. The use of type names as calls to parametrized macros (templates) is permitted on all levels. Feature terms are interpreted as total functions through the introduction of a special type *undefined*. Both open (free-arity) and closed (fixed-arity) terms can be expressed. Open and closed types may even be unified if they are compatible. Knowledge can be arranged in several knowledge domains, ie, separate type lattices with specialized unification algorithms. Several slightly different versions of STUF that have been implemented in a number of PROLOG dialects run under VM and AIX. A special educational version (UNI-STUF) has been developed by Dörre for PCs running under DOS. A new version of STUF which is currently being integrated into the LILOG system also provides sorts, recursive type definitions, and negative path equations [see J. Dörre and R. Seiffert, "Sorted Feature Terms and Relational Dependencies," *IBM IWBS Report* **153** (1991)]. Because of its increased expressive power, the new STUF system can be used to implement linguistic processing fully as type inference. Grammars of all major unification grammar formalisms can be encoded and utilized for processing.

HANS USZKOREIT
University of Saarbrücken

SWALE

The SWALE project investigated a case-based approach to explanation. Developed at the Yale AI Lab by Alex Kass, David Leake, and Christopher Owens, the SWALE program developed creative hypotheses about the stories that it read by retrieving stored explanations from memory and adapting them to new situations. The new variants were then stored in memory for future use. (see R. C. Schank, *Explanation Patterns: Understanding Mechanically and Creatively*, Lawrence Earlbaum Assoc., Hillsdale, N.J.; A. M. Kass, "Adaptation-Based Explanation: Extending Script/Frame Theory to Handle Novel Input," in *Proceedings of the Eleventh Joint Conference On Artificial Intelligence*, Morgan Kaufmann, San Mateo, Calif., 1989.)

ALEX KASS
Northwestern University
Institute for the Learning
Sciences

SYMBOL PROCESSING. See LISP; LOGIC PROGRAMMING; PROGRAMMING ENVIRONMENTS.

SYNTACTIC PARSING. See PARSING.

SYSTEMIC GRAMMARS. See GRAMMAR, SYSTEMIC.

T

TACTILE SENSING. See Sensors and sensor fusion; Robotics.

TARGET TRACKING. See Military applications of AI.

TASK-ORIENTED LANGUAGE. See Robotics.

TELEOPERATORS

Current practice in robotics (qv) divides into two main areas: industrial robotics and robotic teleoperation. Industrial robots are used as an integral part of manufacturing processes and within the frame of production-engineering techniques to perform repetitive work in a structured factory environment (see Robotics). The characteristic control of industrial robots is a programmable sequence controller, typically a mini- or microcomputer that functions autonomously with only occasional human intervention, either to reprogram or retool for a new task or to correct for an interruption in the work flow. Teleoperator robots, on the other hand, serve to extend, through mechanical, sensing, and computational techniques, the human manipulative, perceptive, and cognitive abilities into an environment that is either hostile to or remote from the human operator. Teleoperator robots, or in today's nomenclature "telerobots," typically perform nonrepetitive (singular) servicing, maintenance, or repair work under a variety of environmental conditions ranging from structured to unstructured conditions. Telerobot control is characterized by a direct involvement of the human operator in the control since, by definition of task requirements, teleoperator systems extend human manipulative, perceptual, and cognitive skill which is far beyond what is obtainable with today's industrial robots.

Applications of teleoperators are numerous, in particular to the nuclear and munitions industries and in explorations that may pose danger to human life. Most teleoperators in use today are static master–slave manipulators with sole mechanical-control connection between master and slave arms, and the master arm is a replica of the slave arm. When large distances prevent a sole mechanical-control connection, the master and slave units are connected through electromechanical servo-mechanisms. Only few working systems use a digital-control communication link between master and slave arms. The master–slave-manipulator systems embody a very useful property in teleoperation: bilateral or force-reflecting control, which permits the human operator to feel the forces and moments acting on the remote slave arm and hand while manually controlling the motion of the slave arm. In this control mode the operator is kinematically and dynamically "coupled" to the remote robot arm and can command with "feel" and control with a "sense of touch."

State-of-the-art teleoperator technology, including terminology, categories of teleoperators, teleoperator design context, and teleoperator performance predictions are summarized by Book (1985). Most of the existing manipulators employed in teleoperation, together with their design features are listed in Kohler (1981), and human considerations in teleoperation are reviewed in Johnson and Corliss (1971).

Continuous human operator control in teleoperation has both advantages and disadvantages. The main advantage is that overall task control can rely on human perception, judgment, decision, dexterity, and training. The main disadvantage is that the human operator must cope with a sense of remoteness, be prepared for integration of many information and control variables, and coordinate the control of one or two mechanical arms each having many (typically six) degrees of freedom–and doing all these with limited human resources. Furthermore, in many cases, such as space and deep-sea applications, communication time delay interferes with continuous human operator control (Heer, 1973).

Modern development trends in teleoperator control technology are aimed at amplifying the advantages and alleviating the disadvantages of the human element in teleoperator control through the development and use of advanced sensing and graphics displays, intelligent computer controls, and new computer-based man–machine-interface devices and techniques in the information and control channels. The use of model-driven and sensor-data-driven automation in teleoperation offers significant new possibilities to enhance overall task performance by providing efficient means for task-level controls and displays as outlined and exemplified in Bejczy (1985) and Lee and co-workers (1985). Manipulators on a mobile base represent new demands for sensor-based automation in teleoperation as discussed and exemplified in Witkowski and co-workers (1983).

Automation in teleoperation is distinguished from other forms of automated systems by the explicit and active inclusion of the human operator in system control and information management. Such active participation by the human, interacting with automated system elements in teleoperation, is characterized by several levels of control and communication and can be conceptualized in the category of "supervisory control," as discussed in Sheridan (1977). The man–machine interaction levels in teleoperation can be considered in a hierarchic arrangement as outlined in Bejczy and Corker (1984): planning or high level algorithmic functions; motor or actuator control functions; and environmental interaction-sensing functions. These functions take place in a task context in which the level of system automation is determined by the mechanical and sensing capabilities of the telerobot system; real-time constraints on computational capabilities to deal with control, communication, and sensing; the amount, format, content, and mode of operator interaction with the telerobot system; environmental constraints, such as task complexity, and overall systems constraints, such as operator's skill or maturity of machine intelligence techniques.

Some advances have been made in teleoperator technology through the introduction of various sensors, computers, automation, and new man–machine-interface devices and techniques for remote manipulator control. The development of dexterous mechanisms, smart sensors, flexible computer controls, intelligent man–machine interfaces, and innovation system designs for advanced teleoperation is, however, far from complete and poses many interdisciplinary challenges (see HUMAN COMPUTER INTERACTION). It should also be recognized that the normal manual dexterity of humans is more a "body" skill than an intellectual one. The man–machine-interface philosophy embodied in the force-reflecting master–slave manipulator-control technology has been founded mainly on this fact. Advanced teleoperation employing sensor-referenced and computer-controlled manipulators shifts the operator–telerobot interface from the body (analog) level to a more intellectual languagelike (symbolic) level. Research efforts for developing new man–machine-interface technology for advanced teleoperation will have to render the languagelike symbolic interface between human operator and telerobot as efficient as the conventional analog interface. This remark also applies to operator-interface development for procedure-execution aids and for expert systems in teleoperator action planning and error recovery.

BIBLIOGRAPHY

A. K. Bejczy, "Sensors, Controls, and Man–Machine Interface for Advanced Teleoperation," *Science* **208**, 1327–1335 (1980).

A. K. Bejczy, "Control of Remote Manipulators," in S. Y. Nof, ed., *Handbook of Industrial Robotics,* John Wiley & Sons, Inc. New York, 1985, Chapt. 17, pp. 320–333.

A. K. Bejczy and K. Corker, "Automation in Teleoperation from a Man–Machine Interface Viewpoint," *Proceedings of AIAA/ NASA Space Systems Technology Conference,* Costa Mesa, Calif., June 5–7, 1984, pp. 87–95.

W. J. Book, "Teleoperator Arm Design," in S. Y. Nof, ed., *Handbook of Industrial Robotics,* John Wiley & Sons, Inc., 1985, Chapt. 9, pp. 138–157.

E. Heer, ed., *Remotely Manned Systems: Explorations and Operations in Space,* California Institute of Technology, Pasadena, Calif., 1973.

E. G. Johnson and W. R. Corliss, *Human Factors Applications in Teleoperator Design and Operation,* John Wiley & Sons, Inc., New York, 1971.

G. W. Kohler, *Manipulator Type Book,* Verlag Karl Thiemig, Munich, FRG, 1981.

S. Lee, G. Bekey, and A. K. Bejczy, "Computer Control of Space-Borne Teleoperators with Sensory Feedback," *Proceedings of the IEEE International Conference on Robotics and Automation,* St. Louis, Mo., March 25–28, 1985, pp. 205–214.

T. B. Sheridan, "Modeling Supervisory Control of Robots," in A. Morecki and K. Kedzior, eds., *Theory and Practice of Robots and Manipulators,* Elsevier Scientific, New York, 1977, pp. 394–406.

C. M. Witkowski, A. H. Bond, and M. Burton, "The Design of Sensors for a Mobile Teleoperator Robot," *Digital Systems for Industrial Automation* **2**(1), 85–111 (1983).

A. K. BEJCZY
Jet Propulsion Laboratory

This work has been carried out under contract with the National Aeronautics and Space Administration.

TEXT SUMMARIZATION

This article is a review of the literature on summarization. The basic idea of summarization is to take a body of information and reduce its size and content to its important points. The capacity to summarize is a fundamental property of intelligence. In our daily lives there is an overwhelming amount of information to process and much of it is not relevant or of interest. Summarization processes allow an intelligent agent to focus on the most significant aspects of a given understanding.

A pragmatic reason for studying summarization is that it provides a useful way to report back on a body of knowledge. Take a simple example. Suppose a user sits down to an information retrieval system and requests all information relevant to Japanese embargos of imports. In a given knowledge-base there might be an overwhelming number of episodes to describe. What the user does not want is a detailed description of each episode. Rather, a summary of the more important episodes would be preferred.

Summarization also serves an important function in research on cognition. One of the central issues of cognitive science (qv) is to characterize the understanding process. Summarization provides a test of a given model of understanding. Suppose a researcher claims that the thematic level of understanding plays a significant role in understanding. Summarization provides a test and a methodology for exploring this sort of claim. If thematic understandings are important, then they will be reflected in the sorts of summaries that human subjects produce for a given text and thus should also be reflected in summaries produced by computer models.

Summarization is not a single phenomena. There are a lot of different kinds of summaries. To name just a few there are: abstracts, epitomes, overviews, abridgements, digests, and recapitulations. Each style of summarization requires a slightly different viewpoint on extracting the essential content of a given text or understanding.

Different approaches to summarization emphasize alternate effects and functions of the process. Summarization is sometimes treated as a problem of memory (e.g., Kintsch and van Dijk, 1978), that is, what does the subject remember of the text after various periods of time. The point here is that, for example, as a story is read, it is not perfectly stored in memory, but only its most significant parts are retrievable; by what process does this occur? Other models of summarization are biased toward one or another implicit structure of the text. Structures that have previously been computationally tested for their contribution to the summarization process, include story schema (Rumelhart, 1975), schema narrative trees (Simmons and Correira, 1980; Correira, 1980), sketchy scripts (DeJong, 1979), plot units (Lehnert and Loiselle, 1989; Lehnert, 1981), story points (Wilensky, 1980), and generic knowledge structures (Graesser and Clark, 1985). Each of these structures presents a different point of view on the underlying understanding and summarization processes.

A first pass approximation of some important properties of a summary, includes the following:

- Does the summary reduce the workload for the interpreter–understander over the text?
- Does the summary maintain coherence?
- Does the summary maintain coverage?
- Does the summary include the important events of the story?

The issue of workload suggests that it should take less work to construct an interpretation of a summary than the original text. (A summary is not only shorter but it is also, in some manner, simpler.) The question of coherence suggests it is not good enough to just reduce the quantity of text; the summary must hold together and make sense. The third question indicates that a good summary must cover, at least implicitly, many of the events of the original text. The last issue indicates that the summary should include the important parts of the text, and where they are not necessary for reasons of coherence, exclude the unimportant parts.

The remainder of the article begins by expatiating on the axis role of representation in computational models of understanding and summarization. The bulk of the article will be concerned with sorting the available summarization frameworks and techniques. Although traditionally summarization has been studied in the context of narratives, a latter section of this article will describe why summarization research is significant for three other areas of artificial intelligence: explanation based learning, plan evaluation, and case-based reasoning.

REPRESENTATION, THE ARTIFACT OF UNDERSTANDING

What does it mean to say that a machine has modeled understanding? The traditional answer in AI models of text comprehension is to say that a program that understands produces a representation. This representation includes not only the initial elements of the text but also includes a representation of the connections among these elements. Given the text

> A peasant was chopping wood. He dropped his axe. It fell with a splash into the lake (Protter, 1961).

The task of the program is to build a representation that captures the connectiveness of the elements of the text. For example, the representation–understanding might include, in some manner, the connection between the peasant and the chopping (eg, the peasant is the agent of the chopping) or the connection between the chopping and the dropping (eg, because the peasant was chopping he was holding an axe, because he held an axe he was able to drop it). The representation–understanding might include only the notions explicitly invoked by the text or it could include also those notions invited by the text. Thus it is the task of the program–understander to take the elements of the text (phrases) and decide on a set of relationships between those elements.

Figure 1 shows the relationship between the program that constructs the representation–understanding and the summarizer. The input to the understander is typically either the text in natural language form, a syntactic parse of each of the sentences in the narrative, or each of the clauses of the input in case notation form.

Given the input, the understander uses some available knowledge source to build a representation of the coher-

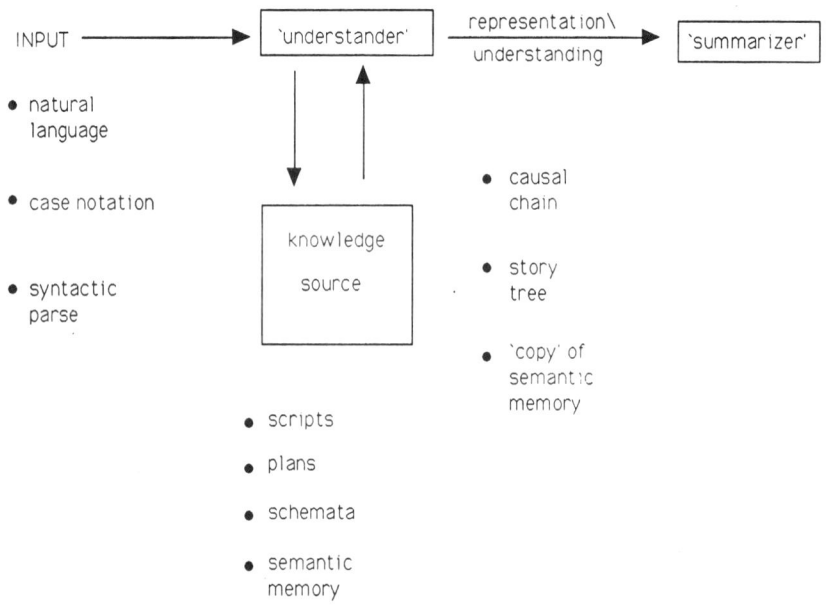

Figure 1. Understanding–representation and summarization.

ence of the text. Examples of knowledge sources are scripts and plans (Schank and Abelson, 1977; Wilensky, 1978; Cullingford, 1978), schemata (Grasser and Clark, 1985), and semantic memory (Alterman, 1985; van Dijk, 1977).

The actual form of the representation–understanding that is produced varies a great deal. In some cases it is a causal chain (Schank, 1975), in other cases a story tree (Rumelhart, 1975), a network representing the connectivity of co-referring expressions in the input text (Lockman and Klappholz, 1980), or a collection of copies of portions of semantic memory (Alterman, 1989).

There exists a tension between the ease of computing a given representation and its utility for such tasks as summarization and question answering; representations–understandings that are rich from the perspective of summarization are potentially difficult to produce. One of the reasons that summarization is important is that it can be used to evaluate the advantages, disadvantages, and differences among these various representation schemes. The representation–understanding both shapes and constrains the quality of a given summary. The summary shows the pertinence and efficacy of a given style of representation–understanding. In many cases summarization can be used to tune the knowledge source from which the understanding–representation was derived.

Given this framework for talking about understanding, each of the properties described in the introduction (coverage, coherence, importance, and workload) can be computationally grounded. Coverage and importance are tied to features of the representation–understanding. The issue now becomes: to what extent does the internal structure of the representation–understanding present methods and explanations that account for coverage and importance? So, for example, if the representation–understanding forms a tree, each level of the tree, arguably, covers the entire understanding–representation at a different level of detail (Simmons and Correira, 1980; Simmons and Chester, 1982). Or if the representation–understanding is a graph, those nodes either centrally located or maximally connected are candidates for important nodes.

The same mechanism that built the original representation–understanding can be used to build a representation–understanding of the summary. The summary lacks coherence if the understanding mechanism fails to build an adequate representation–understanding of the summary. Finally, the reduction of workload can be evaluated by attaching a quantitative measure to the understanding mechanism and comparing the effort it took to construct an interpretation of the original text with the effort for constructing an interpretation of the summary.

IN-THE-SMALL TECHNIQUES

In-the-small approaches to summarization apply local techniques. They do not require an understanding of the text as a whole, but instead preserve the test's message and proportions by means of systematic abbreviations. They consider each piece of text in relative isolation and attempt to summarize.

Consider the following piece of text from "William Tell, the Archer" (Protter, 1961).

> Just then the clatter of horses' hooves was heard. And Gessler, the governor general, galloped into the square. His military retinue followed him. He reined his horse to a stop before the pole.

An in-the-large summary would require that the importance of this passage to the message of the text as a whole be determined. An in-the-small summary applies local techniques to reduce the volume of this piece of text while maintaining its central content. A reasonable summarization-in-the-small of this text would be:

> The governor general rode into the square.

The summary includes the central event concept of this piece of text while deleting the fact that the clattering of hooves could be heard and the details of the riding. Notice that the event of riding, which is mentioned in the summary, is not explicitly mentioned in the original text.

The early macrostructure rules of van Dijk (1977) are an example of in-the-small summarization techniques. An example of a macrostructure rule is generalization; concepts are generalized by abstracting them. So "John is hitchhiking" would be generalized to "John is traveling." Another rule is deletion, which abstracts accidental properties. So "Mary was playing with the red ball" could be progressively summarized as "Mary is playing with the ball" and then just "Mary is playing." A third example of macrostructure rule is construction, which replaces the components of a concept by the concept. So "John laid the foundation. He built the walls . . ." would be summarized as "John built a house."

Techniques that are tied to a particular knowledge structure can also be seen as in-the-small techniques. For example, FRUMP (DeJong, 1979) produces representations of text by applying in a top-down fashion sketchy scripts (eg, accidents and terrorist acts). It extracts from wire-service newspaper stories just enough facts to fill in the arguments of a sketchy script. Because the stories that FRUMP works with are so stereotyped, it could summarize text by using a set of fill-in-the-blank type summarization statements attached to each sketchy script. Here is an example taken from DeJong (1979):

> The Chilean government has seized operational and financial control of the U.S. interest in the El Teniente Mining Company, one of the three big copper enterprises here. When the Kennecott Copper Company, the owners, sold a 51 percent interest in the company to the Chilean state Copper Corporation in 1967 it retained a contract to manage the mine. Robert Haldeman, Executive Vice President of El Teniente, said the contract had been "impaired" by the latest government action. After a meeting with company officials at the mine site near here, however, he said that he had instructed them to cooperate with eight administrators that the Chilean government had appointed to control all aspects of the company's operations.

FRUMP selected the NATIONALIZE sketchy script and it used it to produce the following summary: "Chile has Nationalized an American mine."

THREE APPROACHES TO IMPORTANCE

The Causal Chain and Importance

Schank (1975) suggested that the form the representation takes for narrative texts is a causal chain. There have been two broad versions of the causal chain measure of importance: those events of greatest interest lie on the causal chain that corresponds to the major narrative thread (Schank, 1975; Black and Bower, 1980); the other relates it to a count of the number of connections between a given node in the causal graph and other nodes in the causal graph (Graesser, 1981; Trabasso and Sperry, 1985; Trabasso and van den Broek, 1985). Figure 2 shows a portion of text taken from "The Father, His Son, and Their Donkey (Trabasso and Sperry, 1985). Figure 3 shows the underlying causal structure that was derived for this portion of the story. Trabasso and Sperry based this causal analysis on the Mackie (1980) test of causal necessity:

> Necessity is tested by the use of a counterfactual argument of the form: If not A then not B. That is, an event A is said to be necessary to event B if it is the case that had A not occurred then, in the circumstances, B would not have occurred.

For example, node 22 is linked to node 23 because, in the circumstances, if the boy had not gotten down from the donkey the father would not have gotten on the donkey. If critical path is interpreted as the shortest path, according to the critical path notion of importance the most important events in the passage beginning at node 21 and ending at node 34 are nodes 20, 22, 24, 32, and 34. Given the notion that the maximally connected nodes in a causal representation are the important ones, nodes 22, 24, 25, and 32 are the most important (each is connected to four other nodes in the graph).

Thematic Aspects of Representation–Understanding

Psychological evidence (Reiser and co-workers, 1985) suggests that readers do some inferencing on the thematic structure of the text. Thematic structure corresponds to a highly abstract context that is an independent representation of events (eg, competition). The Reiser and co-workers experiments were based on the plot unit analysis devel-

20. "Do you see that idle boy riding the donkey.
21. while his father has to walk?
22. You should get down
23. and let your father ride!"
24. Upon this, the son got down from the donkey,
25. and the father took his place.
26. They had not gone far
27. when they happened upon a group of women and children.
28. "Why, you lazy old fellow,
29. you should be ashamed,"
30. cried several women at once.
31. "How can you ride upon the beast,
32. when that poor little boy can hardly keep up with you?"
33. So the good-natured father hoisted his son up behind him.

Figure 2. A portion of "The Father, His Son, and Their Donkey," (Trabasso and Sperry, 1985, p. 599).

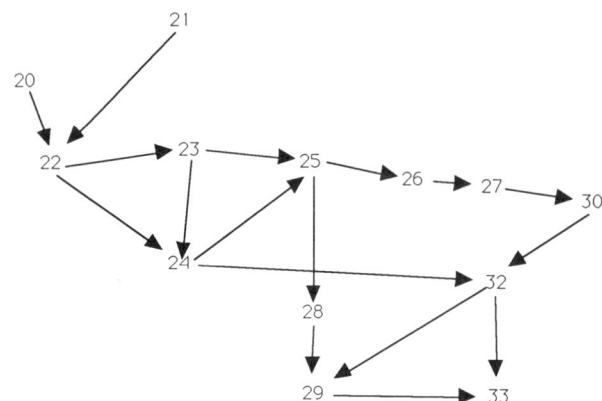

Figure 3. The causal structure.

oped by Lehnert (1981). The basic experiment was to ask a group of subjects to read a number of short texts and then sort them according to similarity. The findings of this research were that the subjects' sortings correlated to the sorting predicted by an analysis of thematic structure that was determined via a plot unit analysis. There have been several computational efforts related to the question of thematic structure, including plot units (Lehnert, 1981), points (Wilensky, 1980), TAU, and TOP. Below two theme-based approaches to the study of importance are described.

Lehnert (1981) and Lehnert and Loiselle (1989) developed a scheme for summarizing text based on plot units. Plot units represent affect-state patterns. Lehnert identified a number of primitive plot units (eg, motivation, success, perseverance) that can be combined into more complex plot units (eg, fortuitous problem resolution, fleeting success, giving up). Narrative text is represented by interconnected plot units, and summaries are based on the identification of pivotal plot units, ie, the plot units that are maximally connected. Here is an example from "The Czar's Three Daughters," (Lehnert and Loiselle, 1989; Graesser and Clark, 1985).

> Once there was a Czar who had three lovely daughters. One day the three daughters went walking in the woods. They were enjoying themselves so much that they forgot the time and stayed too long. A dragon kidnapped the three daughters. As they were being dragged off they cried for help. Three heroes came and fought the dragon and rescued the maidens. Then the heroes returned the daughters to their palace. When the Czar heard of the rescue, he rewarded the heroes.

The resulting top-level plot-unit graph is shown in Figure 4. The maximally connected nodes are (1) competition between the heroes and dragon and (2) the honored request between the daughters and the heroes.

1. Competition (Daughters and Dragon).
2. Competition (Heroes and Dragon).
3. Honored-Request (Daughters and Heroes).
4. Intentional Problem Resolution (Daughters).
5. Reward (Czar and Heroes).

Figure 4. Thematic structure.

Wilensky (1983) introduced a model of thematic structure based on a model of interacting goals. Story points (Wilensky, 1980, 1982) roughly correspond to the essential tension points of a story, ie, what the story is about. The idea was that points represent what is interesting in a story (and, therefore, likely to be included in a summary). Each story point corresponds to one of a set of point prototypes. Wilensky argued that situations where goal interactions occur are potentially dramatic and, consequently, likely candidates as story points. An example point prototype is goal subsumption termination prototype. Wilensky describes goal subsumption as referring to a situation in which a character's plan is to achieve a state that will make it easier for a character to fulfill a recurring goal. A dramatic situation occurs where a subsumption state is terminated (ie, a goal subsumption point prototype). An example of goal subsumption state termination occurs in "The Xenon Story" (Wilensky, 1983): When John loses his job he can no longer afford many of the things to which he had become accustomed.

Knowledge Triggered and Value Triggered Importance

Hidi and Baird (1986) and Ram (1989, 1990) differentiate importance and interest techniques that are derived from a particular knowledge source from those techniques that characterize the unique perspective of the individual reading the text. (Hidi and Baird use the terminology knowledge triggered versus value triggered. The value-triggered importance heuristics introduce the subjective bias of the reader.

Ram (1989) computationally modeled value-triggered importance heuristics. Examples of the subjectively important portions of a text are those that are relevant to the reader's goals or configuration of goals (or are similar to them), situations that are anomalous from the perspective of the reader, situations that contradict the reader's hypotheses, or those that present gaps in the explanation scaffolding that the reader brings to bear on the text. Conversely, those parts of the text that are uninteresting to the individual reader are those that are not relevant to the reader's goals or configurations of goals, are mundane, and have situations that are easily explained away.

Another example of value-triggered importance and interpretation can be found in the work of Gamson, who explores how the cultural context provides a background against which understanding occurs. Gamson argued that culture provides interpretive packages that frame an interpretation and function causally. He explains the following example: In the mid-1960s there was a partial meltdown in Detroit, yet it affected nuclear energy policy very little. Gamson asked the following question: Why is it that a decade later the same sort of incidence at Three Mile Island had such a major impact on nuclear energy policy? His argument is that it had to do with the interpretive packages. In the mid-1960s the sort of interpretive package available to describe the partial meltdown in Detroit was faith in progress, ie, one step back for every two steps forward. Given such an interpretive package, the important feature of the incident in Detroit is that the partial meltdown is a step back, to be followed by a step forward. By the mid-1970s when the incident at Three Mile Island occurred, there were lots of other competing interpretive packages available to interpret the same sort of event, including "small is beautiful" and public accountability. Given these sorts of interpretive packages different features of the same kind of event become important, eg, nuclear power plants are large-scale operations or failing nuclear plants are excessively dangerous to the community.

THE CONCEPTUAL ROOTS

Alterman and Bookman (in press) explore the encoding relationship between semantic memory and text [event concept coherence (Alterman, 1985, 1989)]. Semantic memory provides the basic vocabulary of concepts and practices, and their associated structure, for a given domain. The encoding relationship between semantic memory and text posits that the representation–understanding of the text is partially encoded by the vocabulary and structure is provided by semantic memory. An important feature of this is that semantic memory and the representation–understanding share the same structure; the structure of the representation–understanding is a copy of some piece of semantic memory. This copy-based notion of the representation–understanding is a characteristic of the semantic network-derived text representation schemes (Norvig, 1989; Martin and Riesbeck, 1986; Charniak, 1986, 1983; Alterman, 1985). Consider the following description of events:

> The peasant (1) took the chest of gold to the czar. He (2) walked to the czar's majestic castle. In front of the czar's chambers, he was (3) halted by a haughty general.

Figure 5 depicts the representation–understanding of the text and its copy relationship to a piece of semantic memory.

A program called SSS (qv) was developed to explore the utility of the encoding relationship between semantic memory and text. An important idea developed in the work on SSS was the notion of conceptual roots. Roughly, the conceptual roots correspond to the basic notions of the narrative text: the framework in the terms of which the narrative was developed. SSS determines the conceptual roots from a directed acyclic graph structure that represents the coherence of the event concepts in the text as derived from the encoding provided by semantic memory. An interesting property of the conceptual roots are that they are the minimal set that covers the semantic memory-based graph encoding of the case. For the piece of text shown in Figure 5 the conceptual roots are "taking a chest of gold to the czar" and "being halted in front of the czar's chambers."

With the addition of the techniques that determine the conceptual roots, SSS is able to explain succinctly the connection between any two concept coherent events in the narrative. Also implemented in SSS is a measure of importance that quantifies the conceptual emphasis of the case. Given this measure of importance, it is easy to show

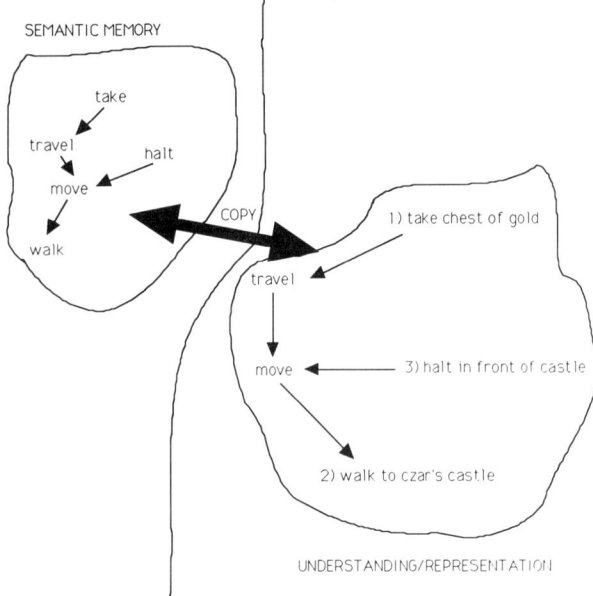

Figure 5. The encoding relationship between semantic memory and the representation–understanding (Alterman and Bookman, in press).

that each of the important nodes is either a conceptual root or covered by one of the conceptual roots. Lastly, SSS combines evidence from semantic memory-based coherence graph of the case, the conceptual root analysis and the importance measure, to generate a description of the basic event content of the narrative (ie, a basic summary). The basic summary technique developed in SSS is as follows:

1. Apply the conceptual root extraction technique to generate a list of event concepts in the story.
2. For each event in the list determine its relative importance using the coverage-based importance techniques described earlier.
3. Remove from the list of events those that have less than average importance. (Although it was not tested here, an alternate scheme would be to continue to delete important events from this list until the summary loses coherence.)

Because of the nature of the conceptual root list, this summary guarantees a fair degree of coverage: the events deleted are those that have few reachable nodes (ie, little coverage). This technique also guarantees importance. Because importance (a count of reachable nodes) correlates with the coverage, and the conceptual roots maximize coverage, the conceptual roots will include, either implicitly or explicitly, the important nodes of the text. To demonstrate coherence and test the amount of simplification Alterman and Bookman ran the summaries produced by SSS through NEXUS (Alterman, 1985), the program that produced the original interpretation. Attached to NEXUS was a workload measure (Alterman and Bookman, 1990) that was used to determine the amount of simplification in the interpretive process after summarization.

IS THE REPRESENTATION–UNDERSTANDING A TREE?

There exists a fair-sized body of work on narratives that attempt to represent part of the content of a narrative by looking at the underlying syntactic structure of the narrative. (It would be expected that the structure of a mystery is different from that of a regency romance.) Typically these types of narrative representation include story categories such as episode, or setting, and episode resolution. Overall these kinds of representations form a tree. There has been some work that has attempted to establish the primacy of certain categories as tending to be more important (Stein and Glenn, 1981; Mandler and Johnson, 1977).

There has also been some work on exploiting these treelike representations for summarization purposes. An interesting property of such representation is that each level of the tree arguably provides coverage but at a different level of detail. Rumelhart (1975), Simmons and Correira (1980), and Correira (1980) summarized text by level of the tree. Rumelhart worked with two trees, one contained the syntactic structure of the story, the other its semantic structure. His system summarized the text by simultaneously descending both trees and deleting subtrees according to a set of semantic summarization rules. Simmons and Correira worked with a single tree that represented a combination of the syntactic and semantic structure of the story; the work of Kintsch and van Dijk (1978) described a similar approach to text representation, where syntactic superstructures organize the semantic macrostructures of the text. For Simmons and Correira, any level of the tree represented a summarization of the story. No extra rewrite rules were required.

The following is a section of text from "Black and Yellow V-2 Rocket" (Simmons, 1980):

> With a great roar and burst of flame the giant rocket rose slowly and then faster and faster. Behind it trailed sixty feet of yellow flame. Soon the flame looked like a yellow star.

At one level of detail in the tree, the ascent is descibed as follows:

> The giant rocket rose with a great roar and burst of flame. It trailed sixty feet of yellow flame. Soon the flame looked like a yellow star.

This leaves out the acceleration of the rocket. At still more abstract level of detail in the tree, this segment of the story is summarized:

> The giant rocket rose with a great roar and burst of flame.

A WORKLOAD MEASURE

Alterman and Bookman (1990) developed a measure of the work associated with a program reading a particular narrative. They used this measure to characterize the difference in work before and after summarization. The workload measure characterizes the average lifetime of an inference made by the understander, while building a coherence representation of the narrative. Texts with

Table 1. The Thickness Complexity Measure

Story	Number of Input Events	Relative Thickness
Margie	6	1.0
Restaurant	8	1.5
V2-Rocket	9	1.9
Czar's daughters	13	2.3
Xenon	29	4.5
Clever peasant	93	42.1

greater durations in the life of the average inference reflect a higher complexity (greater amounts of work to read), because the reader must retain larger numbers of inferences over greater periods of time. Alterman and Bookman argue that their workload measure characterizes, along one dimension, how simple the text is in its construction.

Table 1 shows the relative thickness as compared to "The Margie Story" (Rumelhart, 1975) associated with the analysis of each of several texts. It indicates that the "The Clever Peasant and the Czar's General" is the most thick and "The Margie Story" is the least thick. "The Restaurant Story," the "V2-Rocket" story, the "Czar's Daughters" story, and "The Xenon Story" follow in increasing order of complexity. Each of the first five texts was used as a vehicle for demonstrating one or another computational theory of summarization–understanding: "The Margie Story" was used by Rumelhart (1975) for exploring story trees, "The Restaurant Story" was used by Schank and Abelson (1977) for scripts, "The Czar's Three Daughters" was used by Lehnert and Loiselle (1989) for plot units; "The Black and Yellow V-2 Rocket" was used by Simmons and Chester (1982) and de Beaugrande (1980) for schema-narrative trees, and "The Xenon Story" was used by Wilensky (1980) for story points.

OTHER APPLICATIONS OF SUMMARIZATION

Although much of the literature on summarization is concerned with the summarization of narratives, the scope of these results goes beyond narrations. Below some recent topics of interest in AI and cognitive science are listed and how summarization comes into play is described.

Explanation-Based Learning. The idea behind explanation-based learning (EBL) is that learning can occur by a process of explanation. Given some goal concept (eg, kidnapping), an EBL program operationalizes that concept by explaining a single example of that concept in terms of some domain theory (Mitchell and co-workers, 1986; DeJong and Mooney, 1986). A critical part of the EBL enterprize is to determine the relevant features of the explanation of the example, and that is a problem of summarization. A second critical part of EBL learning is to determine the goal concept behind the example and importance and suggest an approach to detect the goal concept.

Case-Based Reasoning. The idea behind case-based reasoning (CBR) is that reasoning can be supplemented, or even driven, by the use of specific previous cases or episodes. An example of a domain where CBR applies is the domain of legal reasoning, where the legal precedents act as the cases (Rissland and Ashley, 1986). Another domain where CBR has been explored is in the domain of foreign policy (Kolodner and Simpson, 1989); various international episodes play the role of cases. Summarization plays a role in CBR in a number of ways. For example, the whole question of importance, which is central to summarization, also has a significant role in CBR: the important features of a case are likely candidates for the indexing features that are used to retrieve that case during the reminding phase of CBR. Summarization techniques can also play a key role in determining the central parts of a given episode, either for storing cases or in their explanation (See REASONING, CASE-BASED).

Plan Evaluation. For large planning systems there is a problem of evaluating the utility, efficiency, and correctness of a given plan. One approach to evaluation is to run the plan in some kind of simulated environment. For larger plans, which might involve the coordination of several different large-scale plans, summarization offers an approach to evaluation. A summary of the plan allows a user to evaluate the plan rapidly at a high level, matching a proposed plan against the user's goals or circumstances that are not readily simulatable (See PLANNING.)

SUMMARY

This article is an overview of the literature on summarization. Four key features of summarization are coherence (the summary must make sense), coverage (the summary must cover the bulk of the original understanding), importance (the summary must include the important features and exclude the unimportant ones), and workload (the summary is a simplification). One approach to summarization is to nibble away at the original understanding–representation using a small arsenal of in-the-small techniques.

There have been several approaches to determining the important features of the understanding. Each approach reflects a different implicit structure in the representation–understanding. A causal chain-based representation–understanding uses notions of causal centrality and critical path to determine importance. A thematic structure analysis emphasizes the role of thematic features of the text in determining importance. Techniques that introduce the subjective bias of the reader or society also offer approaches to importance.

The notion of conceptual roots offers an approach to summarization that testably accounts for each of the four properties (coherence, coverage, importance, and simplification). The conceptual roots are derived from a semantic memory that encodes the connectivity of events in the narrative. Because of the shared structure between the semantic memory and representation–understanding, the conceptual roots are determinable.

Various researchers have proposed representation–understandings that include not only a coherence analysis of the text based on a semantic analysis but also further organizations based on the syntactic character of the text type. Generally speaking, these sorts of representation schemes result in a treelike structure. One proposed advantage of this sort of analysis is that various syntactic categories of story structure correlate in various degrees with importance. A second potential advantage is that each level of the tree provides a summary of the story at a different level of abstraction, and because of the tree form, each level arguably provides coverage.

Although much of the work in summarization has been applied to narrative summarization, many of the ideas and techniques generated in this community have wide application to other areas of research and development in artificial intelligence. Three such areas were briefly discussed: explanation-based learning, case-based reasoning, and plan evaluation.

BIBLIOGRAPHY

R. Alterman, "A Dictionary Based on Concept Coherence," *Artif. Intell.* **25**, 153–186 (1985).

R. Alterman, "Event Concept Coherence," in D. Waltz, ed., *Semantic Structures: Advances in Natural Language Processing*, Lawrence Erlbaum, Hillsdale, N.J., 1989, pp. 57–87.

R. Alterman and L. Bookman, "Some Computational Experiments in Summarization," *Discourse Proc.* **13**, 143–174 (1990).

R. Alterman and L. Bookman, "Reasoning About a Semantic Memory Encoding of the Connectivity of Events," *Cogn. Sci.*, in press.

J. Black and G. Bower, "Story Understanding as Problem Solving," *Poetics* **9**, 223–250 (1980).

E. Charniak, "Passing Markers: A Theory of Contextual Influences in Language Comprehension," *Cogn. Sci.* **7**, 171–190 (1983).

E. Charniak, "A Neat Theory of Marker Passing," in *Proceedings of the Fifth National Conference on Artificial Intelligence*, Philadelphia, Pa., AAAI, Menlo Park, Calif., 1986, pp. 584–588.

A. Correira, "Computing Story Trees," *Am. J. Computat. Ling.* **6**, 135–149 (1980).

R. Cullingford, *Script Application: Computer Understanding of Newspaper Stories*, Technical Report **116**, Yale University, New Haven, Conn., 1978.

R. de Beaugrande, *Text, Discourse, and Process: Toward a Multidisciplinary Science of Texts*, Vol. 4 of *Advances in Discourse Processes*, Ablex Publishing, Norwood, N.J., 1980.

G. DeJong, "Prediction and Substantiation: A New Approach to Natural Language Processing," *Cogn. Sci.* **3**, 251–273 (1979).

G. DeJong and R. Mooney, "Explanation-Based Learning: An Alternative View," *Machine Learning* **1**, 145–176 (1986).

A. Graesser, *Prose Comprehension Beyond the Word*, Springer-Verlag, New York, 1981.

A. Graesser and L. Clark, *Structure and Procedures of Implicit Knowledge*, Ablex Publishing, Hillsdale, N.J., 1985.

Hidi and Baird, "Interestingness—A Neglected Variable in Discourse Processing," *Cogn. Sci. J.* **10**, 179–194 (1986).

W. Kintsch and T. van Dijk, "Toward a Model of Text Comprehension and Production," *Psychol. Rev.* **85**, 363–394 (1978).

J. L. Kolodner and R. L. Simpson, "The MEDIATOR: Analysis of an Early Case-Based Problem Solver," *Cogn. Sci.* **13**, 507–549 (1989).

W. Lehnert, "Plot Units and Narrative Summarization," *Cogn. Sci.* **5**, 293–331 (1981).

W. Lehnert and C. Loiselle, "An Introduction to Plot Units," in D. Waltz, ed., *Advances in Natural Language Processing*, Lawrence Erlbaum, Hillsdale, N.J., 1989, pp. 88–111.

A. Lockman and A. D. Klappholz, "Toward a Procedural Model of Contextual Reference Resolution," *Discourse Proc.* **3**, 25–71 (1980).

J. L. Mackie, *The Cement of the Universe: A Study of Causation*, Oxford University Press (Clarendon), Oxford, UK, 1980.

J. Mandler and N. Johnson, "Remembrance of Things Parsed: Story Structure and Recall," *Cogn. Psychol.* **9**, 111–151 (1977).

C. Martin and C. Riesbeck, "Uniform Parsing and Inferencing for Learning," in *Proceedings of the Fifth National Conference on AI*, 1986, pp. 257–261.

T. Mitchell, R. Keller, and S. Kedar-Cabelli, "Explanation-Based Generalization: A Unifying View," *Machine Learning* **1**, 47–80 (1986).

P. Norvig, "Marker Passing as a Weak Method for Text Inferencing," *Cogn. Sci.* **13**(4), 569–620 (1989).

E. Protter, *A Children's Treasury of Folk and Fairy Tales*, Channel Press, 1961.

A. Ram, *Question Driven Understanding: An Integrated Theory of Story Understanding, Memory and Learning*, PhD dissertation, Yale University, New Haven, Conn., 1989.

A. Ram, "Knowledge Goals: A Theory of Interestingness," in *Proceedings of the Twelfth Annual Conference of the Cognitive Science Society*, New Haven, Conn., LEA Associates, 1990, pp. 206–214.

B. Reiser, J. Black, and W. Lehnert, "Thematic Knowledge Structures in the Understanding and Generation of Narratives," *Discourse Proc.* **8**, 357–389 (1985).

E. Rissland and K. Ashley, "Hypotheticals as Heuristic Device," in *Proceedings of the Fifth National Conference on AI*, 1986.

D. Rumelhart, "Notes on a Schema for Stories," in D. Bobrow and A. Collins, eds., *Representation and Understanding*, Academic Press, Inc., New York, 1975, pp. 211–236.

R. Schank, "The Structure of Episodes in Memory," in D. Bobrow and A. Collins, eds., *Representation and Understanding*, Academic Press, Inc., New York, 1975, pp. 237–272.

R. Schank and R. Abelson, *Scripts, Plans, Goals, and Understanding*, Lawrence Earlbaum, Hillsdale, N.J., 1977.

R. Simmons, "Rule Forms for Verse, Sentences, and Story Trees," in N. Findler, ed., *Associative Networks: The Representation and Use of Knowledge in Computers*, Academic Press, Inc., New York, 1980, pp. 363–391.

R. Simmons and D. Chester, "Relating Sentences and Semantic Networks with Procedural Logic," *CACM* **25**, 527–547 (1982).

R. Simmons and A. Correira, "Rule Forms for Verse, Sentences, and Story Trees," in N. Findler, ed., *Associative Networks: The Representation and Use of Knowledge in Computers*, Academic Press, Inc., New York, 1980, pp. 363–391.

N. Stein and C. Glenn, *An Analysis of Story Comprehension in Elementary School Children*, Vol. 2 of *Advances in Discourse Processes*, Ablex Publishing, Norwood, N.J., 1981.

T. Trabasso and L. Sperry, "Causal Relatedness and Importance of Story Events," *J. Memory Lang.* **24**, 595–611 (1985).

T. Trabasso and P. van den Broek, "Causal Thinking and Representation of Narrative Events," *J. Memory Lang.* **24**, 612–630 (1985).

T. van Dijk, "Semantic Macro-Structures and Knowledge Frames in Discourse," in M. A. Just and P. A. Carpenter, eds., *Cogni-*

tive Processes in Comprehension, Lawrence Erlbaum, Hillsdale, N.J., 1977.

R. Wilensky, *Understanding Goal-Based Stories*, Ph.D. dissertation, Yale University, New Haven, Conn., 1978.

R. Wilensky, "What's the Point?" in *Proceedings of Third National Conference of the Canadian Society for the Computational Studies of Intelligence*, 1980.

R. Wilensky, "Points: A Theory of the Structure of Stories in Memory," in W. Lehnert and M. Ringle, eds., *Strategies for Natural Language Processing*, Lawrence Erlbaum, Hillsdale, N.J., 1982.

R. Wilensky, *Planning and Understanding*, Addison-Wesley Publishing Co., Inc., Reading Mass., 1983.

General References

R. Alterman and R. Zito-Wolf, "Planning and Understanding: Revisited," in *Proceedings of the Eighth National Conference on Artificial Intelligence*, Boston, Mass., AAAI, Menlo Park, Calif., 1990.

T. van Dijk, *Macrostructures: An Interdisciplinary Study of Global Structures in Discourse, Interaction and Cognition*, Lawrence Earlbaum, Hillsdale, N.J., 1980.

T. van Dijk, "Macro-Structures and Cognition," in *Proceedings of the Twelfth Annual Carnegie Symposium on Cognition*, 1976.

T. van Dijk and W. Kintsch, *Strategies of Discourse Comprehension*, Academic Press, Inc., New York, 1983.

RICHARD ALTERMAN
Brandeis University

This work was supported in part by the Defense Advanced Research Projects Agency, administered by the U.S. Airforce Office of Scientific Research under contract #F49620-88-C-0058.

This article was reprinted from *Artificial Intelligence Review* 5(4) (1990) with permission. Intellect Ltd., copyright holder.

TEXTURE

Natural scenes are rich in texture (Fig. 1). Whatever the resolution at which a scene is imaged, the image usually contains texture. However, texture continues to be only an intuitive notion, lacking precise definition. Texture occurs at a given scale: at finer scales texture elements (texels) in large regions coalesce giving rise to a different texture than the original. There is spatial repetitiveness associated with texels, with both texel shapes and their placement showing randomness.

Texture analysis has been an active and important area of research in image understanding. In the early years, most work addressed the problem of modeling spatial gray level variation corresponding to image texture. There was some attention given to perceptually meaningful features of textures. More recently, the problem of inferring three-dimensional surface shape from texture variation across image has also been addressed. In the following sections the work done in each of these three areas will be reviewed.

The first two sections are concerned with ⟨…⟩ gray level, spatial variation in texture. Such mod⟨…⟩ traditionally been categorized as either statis⟨…⟩ structural. Statistical models characterize an im⟨…⟩ terms of its statistical properties, such as autocorr⟨…⟩ or cooccurrence. Structural models, on the other ⟨…⟩ describe an image by its structural primitives and ⟨…⟩ placement rules. This classification is not very us⟨…⟩ though, because if a structural model is not also stat⟨…⟩ cal, the images it describes are too regular to be of in⟨…⟩ est. If a statistical model cannot reveal the image's ba⟨…⟩ structure, it is too weak to be of much help. A somewh⟨…⟩ better division of image models (qv) follows.

1. *Pixel-Based Models*. These models view individual pixels as the primitives of an image. Specification of the characteristics of the spatial distribution of pixel properties (Hawkins, 1970; Muerle, 1970) constitutes the image description.

2. *Region-Based Models*. These models view an image as a set of subpatterns placed according to a given set of rules. Both the subpatterns and their arrangement may be defined statistically, and these subpatterns themselves may be hierarchically composed of smaller patterns. Again, as with pixel-based models, the objective is to model a single texture; the concept of regions is used only to capture the microstructure.

The first two sections discuss the pixel-based and region-based models. The following section reviews some work on models of textures proposed for human visual perception. The fourth section describes the work done on extracting three-dimensional shape form image texture.

PIXEL-BASED MODELS

Pixel-based models can be subdivided into two classes: one-dimensional time series models and random field models.

One-Dimensional Time Series Models

Time series analysis (Box and Jenkins, 1976) has been extensively used to model the statistical relationship between the gray level of a given pixel and of those preceding it in the raster scan (McCormick and Jayaramamurthy, 1974; Tou and Chang, 1976; Tou and co-workers, 1976). The gray level fluctuations along the raster are treated as a stochastic process that evolves over time. The future course of the process is presumed to be predictable from information about its past.

Before summarizing the models, some commonly used notation is reviewed (McCormick and Jayaramamurthy, 1974).

- Let

$$\cdots X_{t-1} X_t X_{t+1} \cdots$$

be a discrete time series where X_t is the random variable X at time i. The series is denoted by $[X]$.

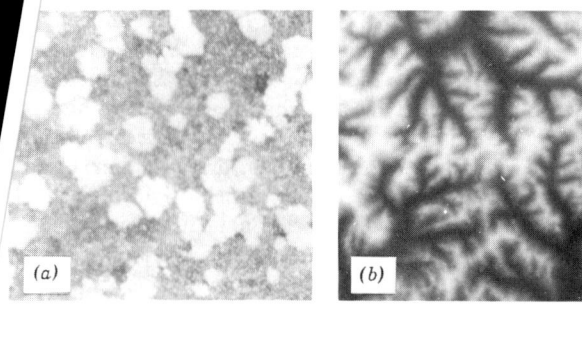
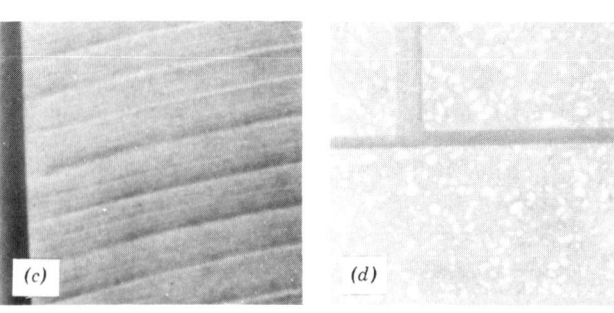

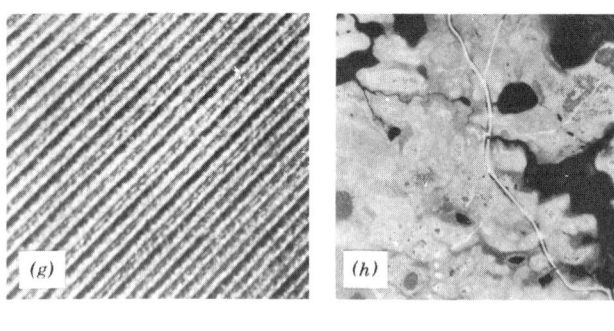
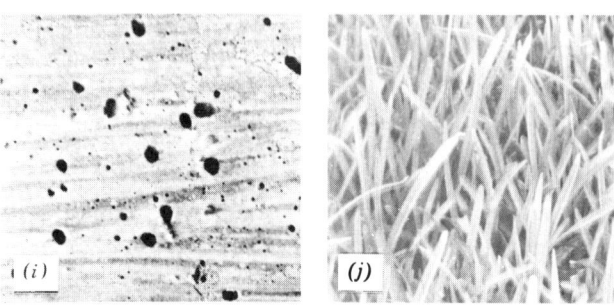

- Let μ be the mean of $[X]$, called the level of the process.
- Let $[\tilde{X}]$ denote the series of deviations about μ, that is, $\tilde{X}_i = X_i - \mu$.
- Let $[e]$ be a series of outputs from a white noise source with mean zero and variance σ^2.
- Let B be the "backward" shift operator for the deviation series such that $B\tilde{X}_t = \tilde{X}_{t-1}$; hence $B^m\tilde{X}_t = \tilde{X}_{t-m}$.
- Let ∇ be the backward difference operator for the deviation series such that

$$\nabla \tilde{X}_t = \tilde{X}_t - \tilde{X}_{t-1} = (1 - B)\tilde{X}_t.$$

Hence $\nabla^m \tilde{X}_t = (1 - B)^m \tilde{X}_t$. The dependence of the current value $\tilde{X}_t$ on the past values of $\tilde{X}$ and e can be expressed in different ways, giving rise to several different models (McCormick and Jayaramamurthy, 1974).

Autoregressive Model (AR). In this model the current $\tilde{X}$-value depends on the previous p $\tilde{X}$-values and on the current noise term

$$\tilde{X}_t = \phi_1 \tilde{X}_{t-1} + \phi_2 \tilde{X}_{t-2} + \cdots + \phi_p \tilde{X}_{t-p} + e_t \qquad (1)$$

If

$$\phi_p(B) = 1 - \phi_1 B - \phi_2 B^2 - \cdots - \phi_p B^p$$

then equation 1 becomes

$$[\phi_p(B)](\tilde{X}_t) = e_t$$

The series $[\tilde{X}]$, as defined above, is known as the autoregressive process of order p, and $\phi_p(B)$ as the autoregressive operator of order p. The name autoregressive comes from the model's similarity to regression analysis and the fact that the variable $\tilde{X}$ is being regressed on previous values of itself.

Moving Average Model (MA). In the model above, $\tilde{X}_{t-1}$ can be eliminated from the expression for $\tilde{X}_t$ by substituting

$$\tilde{X}_{t-1} = \phi_1 \tilde{X}_{t-2} + \phi_2 \tilde{X}_{t-3} + \cdots + \phi_p \tilde{X}_{t-p-1} + e_{t-1}$$

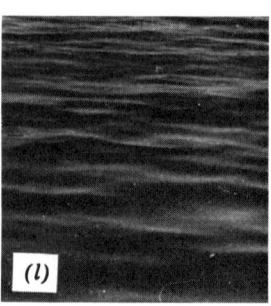

Figure 1. Some related textures. (**a**) Volcanic rock, (**b**) terrain elevations, (**c**) leaf surface, (**d**) brick wall, (**e**) straw, (**f**) orchard, (**g**) plowed field, (**h**) mud tidal flats, (**i**) concrete, (**j**) grass (in perspective), (**k**) cloud layer (in perspective), (**l**) water waves (in perspective).

This process can be repeated to eventually yield an expression for $\tilde{X}_t$ as an infinite series in the e's.

A moving average model allows a finite number q of previous e-values in the expression for $\tilde{X}_t$. This explicitly treats the series as being observations on linearly filtered Gaussian noise.

Letting

$$\theta_q(B) = 1 - \theta_1 B - \theta_2 B^2 - \cdots - \theta_q B^q$$

the following is obtained

$$\tilde{X}_t = [\theta_q(B)](e_t)$$

as the moving average process of order q.

Mixed Model: Autoregressive/Moving Average (ARMA). To achieve greater flexibility in the fitting of actual time series, this model includes both the autoregressive and the moving average terms. Thus

$$\tilde{X}_t = \phi_1 \tilde{X}_{t-1} + \phi_2 \tilde{X}_{t-2} + \cdots + \phi_p \tilde{X}_{t-p} + e_t \\ - \theta_1 e_{t-1} - \theta_2 e_{t-2} - \cdots - \theta_q e_{t-1} \quad (2)$$

that is, $[\phi_p(B)](\tilde{X}_t) = [\theta_q(B)](e_t)$.

In all three models just mentioned, the process generating the series is assumed to be in equilibrium about a constant mean level. Models characterized by this equilibrium are called stationary models.

There is another class of models, nonstationary models, in which the level μ does not remain constant. The series involved may, nevertheless, exhibit homogeneous behavior after the differences due to level drift have been accounted for. It can be shown (Box and Jenkins, 1976) that such behavior may be represented by a generalized autoregressive operator.

A time series may exhibit a repetitive pattern. For example, in a raster scanned image, the segments corresponding to rows will have similar characteristics. A model can be formulated that incorporates such seasonal effects (Bacon, 1965; McCormick and Jayaramamurthy, 1974).

All of the time series models discussed above are unilateral in that a pixel depends only on the pixels preceding it in the raster scan. Partial two-dimensional dependence among pixels can be incorporated by letting a pixel depend on a causal neighborhood (Tou and Chang, 1976; Tou and co-workers, 1976; Whittle, 1954), for example, on that part of an $n \times n$ neighborhood centered at the pixel that precedes it in the raster scan (Whittle, 1954). This does not affect the applicability of the one-dimensional time series analysis. Whittle (1954) points out that a one-dimensional approach has serious deficiencies. For example, even a finite bilateral autoregression may not always have a unilateral representation that is also a finite autoregression. Or the transformation to convert a bilateral dependence into a unilateral one may be prohibitively complex. Introduction of bilateral dependence gives rise to more complex parameter estimation problems (Bartlett, 1975; Brook, 1964). (Interestingly, a frequency domain treatment makes parameter estimation in bilateral representation much easier (Chellappa and Ahuja, 1979).

Random Field Models

The theory of stochastic processes may be extended to define models of spatial variation in two dimensions. These models can be divided into two subclasses: global models and local models.

Global Models. Global models treat an entire image as the realization of a random field. The most common approach is to view an image as an ideal signal that has been corrupted by blurring and additive noise. The blur may represent a variety of spatial degradations (Angel and Jain, 1978; Pratt, 1978; Rosenfeld and Kak, 1976). For example, in aerial reconnaissance, astronomy, and remote sensing, the pictures obtained are degraded by atmospheric turbulence, aberrations of the optical system, and relative motion between object and camera. Electron micrographs are affected by the spherical aberration of the electron lens. Additive noise represents degradations that only affect the gray levels of individual points. A common example is thermal noise occurring in photodetectors. Film grain noise, which is multiplicative, can be converted to additive noise by subjecting the image to a logarithmic transformation.

Frieden (1980) described image restoration using global models. The problem involves solving the imaging equation

$$\mathbf{D} = S\mathbf{X} + \mathbf{n}$$

for the ideal image row $\mathbf{X}$, given the image data $\mathbf{D}$ and an estimate of the point spread matrix S, despite the presence of an additive noise component $\mathbf{n}$. Here $\mathbf{X}$, $\mathbf{D}$, and $\mathbf{n}$ are column vectors of n elements each, and S is an $n \times n$ matrix. Although inversion of the image formation equation is an unstable or ill-conditioned problem, a reasonable solution can be obtained with *a priori* knowledge of the nature of the true image. This information takes the form of constraints in the restoration procedure. Frieden treats the image as a spatial distribution of photons in cells centered at the grid nodes and then defines the image model as the process most likely to have generated the given distribution.

For restoration, images have often been modeled as two-dimensional, wide sense, stationary random fields having a given mean and autocorrelation function. The following general expression has been suggested for the autocorrelation function:

$$R(\tau_1, \tau_2) = \sigma^2 \rho^{[-\alpha_1|\tau_1| - \alpha_2|\tau_2|]}$$

which is stationary and separable. Specifically, the exponential autocorrelation function ($\rho = e$) has been found to be useful for a variety of pictorial data (Franks, 1966; Habibi, 1972; Huang, 1965; Jain and Angel, 1974; Kretzmer, 1952).

Another autocorrelation function often cited as being more realistic is

$$R(\tau_1, \tau_2) = \rho^{\sqrt{\tau_1^2 + \tau_t^2}}$$

which is isotropic, but not separable, as is the case with many natural images.

Hunt (1976, 1977) pointed out that stationary Gaussian models are based on an oversimplification. Consider the vector $\mathbf{x} = (x_1, \ldots, x_n)$ formed from sample values along a raster scan, with R being the covariance matrix of the gray levels in $\mathbf{x}$. According to the Gaussian assumption, the probability density function is given by

$$f(\mathbf{x}) = k \exp\{-\tfrac{1}{2}(\mathbf{x} - \mu)^t R^{-1}(\mathbf{x} - \mu)\}$$

where $\mu = E[\mathbf{x}]$, and k is a normalizing constant. The stationarity assumption makes μ a vector of identical components, meaning that each point in the image has identical ensemble statistics. Hunt (1977) proposed a nonstationary Gaussian model that differs from the stationary model only in that the mean vector μ has unequal components. He demonstrated the appropriateness of this model by subtracting the local ensemble average from each image point and showing that the resulting image fits a stationary Gaussian model.

In a later paper, Hunt (1980) discussed three different kinds of nonstationarities:

Case 1. Nonstationary mean, nonstationary autocorrelation.

Case 2. Nonstationary mean, stationary autocorrelation.

Case 3. Stationary mean, nonstationary autocorrelation.

Because a breakdown in stationarity implies a loss of the ergodicity assumption [loosely stated, a process is called "ergodic" if its statistics can be determined from any of the sample functions in the ensemble (Assefi, 1978)], it is necessary to specify image statistics in terms of spatial averages, rather than ensemble averages. The nonstationarity in the image mean is described by the array of individual means taken over a specified neighborhood about each image point. For the autocorrelation function, the breakdown of stationarity is related to the way the correlation function changes over the image. Hunt uses three attributes of the correlation function to describe its spatial dependence: its energy, its width, and its shape. An image model consists of a specification of the parameters of a rotationally symmetric, negative exponential autocorrelation function, a set of means, and a spatial warp function to produce the autocorrelation nonstationarity.

Trussel and Kruger (1978) claim that the Laplacian density function is better suited for modeling high pass filtered imagery than the Gaussian function. Nevertheless, they contend that the basic assumptions that allow the Gaussian model to be used for image restoration purposes are still valid under a Laplacian model.

Nahi and Jahanshahi (1977) suggest modeling the image by background and foreground statistical processes. The foreground consists of regions corresponding to the objects in the image. Each type of region (foreground or background) is defined by an associated statistical process. In estimating the boundaries of horizontally convex objects in noisy binary images, Nahi and Jahanshahi assume that the two processes are statistically independent stationary random processes with known (or estimated) first two moments. The borders of the regions covered by the different statistical processes are modeled only locally. The end points of the intercepts of the given object on successive rows are assumed to form a first-order Markov process. This model thus also involves local interactions.

Using the following notation

x_i Gray level at image point i.
γ_i Binary function carrying the boundary information at point i.
b_i Sample gray level from the background process at point i.
o_t Sample gray level from the foreground process at point i.
e_i Sample gray level from the noise process at point i.

the model allows

$$x_t = \gamma_i o_i + [1 - \gamma_i] b_i + e_i$$

where γ incorporates the Markov constraints on the object boundaries.

In a subsequent paper, Nahi and Lopez-Mora (1978) use a more complex γ function. For each row, γ either indicates the absence of an object or provides a vector estimate of the object's width and geometric center in that row. Thus the two-element vector contains information about the object's size and skewness. The vectors corresponding to successive rows are assumed to define a first-order Markov process.

Cooper (1979) views the Nahi approach as too restrictive, in that it reduces the original two-dimensional problem to a one-dimensional problem. Cooper investigates the general class of images formed by a blob of constant gray level on a constant background, with additive white Gaussian noise over the entire image. He uses a Markov process to model the blob boundary and constructs a derivative field by taking the directional derivative at each pixel. He then estimates the blob boundary by maximizing the joint likelihood of a hypothetical blob boundary and of all the image data contained in the directional derivative field.

Recursive solutions based on differential (difference) equations are common in one-dimensional signal processing and have been generalized to two dimensions. Jain (1977b) investigated the applicability of three kinds of random fields to the image-modeling problem, each characterized by a different class of partial differential equations (PDE): hyperbolic, parabolic, and elliptic. A digital shape is defined by a finite difference approximation of a PDE. The class of hyperbolic PDE is shown to provide more general causal models than autoregressive moving average models. For a given spectral density (or covariance) function, parabolic PDE can provide causal, semicausal, or even noncausal representations. Elliptic PDEs provide noncausal models that represent two-dimensional discrete Markov fields and can be used to model both isotropic and anisotropic imagery. Jain argues that the PDE model is based on a well-established mathematical theory and, further, that there exists a considerable body of computer software for numerical solutions. The PDE model also obviates the need for spectral factorization, thus eliminating the restriction of a separable covariance function. System identification techniques may be used for choosing the PDE model for a given class of images. Chellappa (1980) derives convexity properties of the autocorrelation function for the PDE models. The hyperbolic (elliptic) model gives an autocorrelation function that is convex (concave) along both axes. The autocorrelation function for the parabolic model is convex along one axis and concave along the other.

Matheron's (1971) regionalized random variable approach emphasizes pixel properties whose complex mutual correlation reflects the spatial structure. He assumed weak stationarity of the gray level increments between pixels. The variogram

$$\gamma(d) = E[(\text{gray level at } i - \text{gray level } j)^2]$$

where $d = |i - j|$, is the basic analytic tool. Huijbregts (1975) gives numerous examples of regionalized variables: in geology, the ore grade and thickness, gravity, geochemical content; in forestry, the density of trees; in hydrology, the piezometric height; in meteorology, the quantity of dust and water vapor in the atmosphere. He discusses several properties of the variogram and relates them to the spatial structure of the regionalized variables. The variogram of the residuals with respect to the local mean is used for nonhomogeneous fields with locally varying mean.

Pratt and Faugeras (1978) and Gagalowicz (1978) view texture as the output of a homogeneous spatial filter excited by white, not necessarily Gaussian, noise. A texture is characterized by its mean, the histogram of the input white noise, and the transfer function of the filter. For a given texture the model parameters are obtained as follows:

1. The mean is readily estimated from the texture.
2. The autocorrelation function is computed to determine the magnitude of the transfer function.
3. Higher order moments are computed to determine the phase of the transfer function.

Inverse filtering yields the white noise image and hence its histogram and probability density. The inverse filtering of decorrelation may be done by simple operators. For example, for a first-order Markov field, decorrelation may be achieved by using a Laplacian operator (Pratt and Faugeras, 1978). The whitened field estimate of the independent, identically distributed noise process will only identify the spatial operator in terms of the autocorrelation function, which is not unique. Thus the white noise probability density and spatial filter do not, in general, make up a complete set of descriptors (Pratt and co-workers, 1978). (To generate a texture, the procedure can be reversed by generating a white noise image having the computed statistics and then applying the inverse of the whitening filter.)

A random field may represent variation in gray level, color, elevation, or temperature, among other characteristics. Several researchers have proposed models specifically for height fields. One example is the Longuet-Higgins's model (1952, 1957a, 1957b) developed for the ocean surface (Pierson, 1952). Longuet-Higgins treated the ocean surface as a random field satisfying the following assumptions:

1. The wave spectrum contains a single narrow band of frequencies.
2. The wave energy results from a large number of different sources whose phases are random.

The basic equation governing the process is

$$X_{i,j} = \sum_k A_k \cos(u_k i + v_k j + \phi_k)$$

Longuet-Higgins (1957b) obtained the statistical distribution of wave heights. He also derived the relationships governing the root-mean-square wave height, the mean height of a given highest percentage of waves, and the most likely height of the largest wave in a given region.

Longuet-Higgins (1957a, 1957b) also obtained a set of statistical relations among parameters for (1) a random moving surface and (2) a Gaussian isotropic surface. Some of the results he obtained concern the following:

1. The probability distribution of the surface elevation.
2. The probability distribution of the magnitude and orientation of the gradient.
3. The average number of zero crossings per unit distance along an arbitrarily placed line transect.
4. The average contour length per unit area.
5. The average density of maxima and minima.
6. The probability distribution of the heights of maxima and minima.

All results are expressed in terms of the two-dimensional energy spectrum. He also studied and solved the converse problem: given certain statistical properties of the surface, determine a convergent sequence of approximations to the energy spectrum.

Longuet-Higgins's treatment of images of ocean waves makes use of features and analyses that may be used for image modeling in general. Panda (1978) adopted the Longuet-Higgins approach to analyze background regions selected from forward looking infrared (FLIR) imagery (A FLIR device uses an array of heat-sensing elements to record an image. Infrared sensors are in wide use by the military, since infrared images can be made at night and do not require transmission of energy to be reflected.) He derived expressions for the density of border points and average number of connected components along a row of a thresholded image and obtained generally good agreement between observed and predicted values. (Panda,

1979) used the same approach to predict the properties of images resulting from the application of edge detectors.

Schachter (1980b) described a variation of the Longuet-Higgins model. The random field is described by the basic equation

$$X_{i,j} = \mu + \frac{1}{m} \sum_{k=1}^{m} A_k n(u_k i + v_k j + \phi_k), \quad m \leq 3$$

where $n(\cdot)$ denotes a narrow-band noise waveform of a given center frequency and bandwidth, and m denotes the number of waveforms. A narrow-band noise waveform may be thought of as an envelope function modulating a carrier frequency. Thus this model describes textures of a two-level hierarchy (Fig. 2). The model has been implemented in hardware in a real-time image-generation system for flight simulation.

Several authors describe models for the earth's surface. Freiberger and Grenander (1976) reasoned that the earth's surface is too irregular to be represented by an analytic function that has only a small number of free parameters. Nevertheless, because landscapes possess strong continuity properties, they suggested using stochastic processes derived from physical principles. Mandelbrot (1977) used a Poisson-Brown surface to give a first approximation to the earth's relief. The earth's surface is assumed to have been formed by the superimposition of very many, very small cliffs along straight faults. The positions of the faults and the heights of the cliffs are assumed random and independent. Mandelbrot suggested that the generated surface could be made to resemble some actual terrain more closely by introducing anisotropy into ridge directions. Mandelbrot's model is often used in computer graphics to generate artificial terrain scenes. Adler (1976, 1977a, 1977b, 1978a, 1978b, 1978c) and Adler and Hasoffer (1976) present a theoretical treatment of Brownian sheets and relate them to the rather esoteric mathematical concept of Hausdorff dimension. Mark (1977) discussed Brownian sheets and a number of other approaches to modeling the topological randomness of geomorphic surfaces.

Local Models. Global models characterize spatial variation in the whole image as a single random field. If neither knowledge nor hypotheses about the type of random field are available, a class of local models is used. Local models assume relationships among gray levels of pixels in small neighborhoods. Predetermined formalisms are used to describe such relationships. The modeling process consists of choosing a formalism and evaluating its parameters. Two basic categories of local models arise from the joint and conditional probability formulations of variation in a neighborhood proposed by Whittle (1963) and Bartlett (1955, 1967). Whittle's definition requires that the joint probability distribution of the variables in a given neighborhood be of the product form

$$\prod_{i,j} Q_{i,j}(x_{i,j}, x_{i-1,j}, x_{t+1,j}, x_{t,j-1}, x_{t,j+1}, \ldots)$$

where $x_{i,j}$ is a realization of the random variable $X_{i,j}$ associated with pixel (i, j) and Q is a nonnegative function. Bartlett's definition requires that the conditional probability distribution of $X_{i,j}$ depend only on the values at the neighbors of (i, j). Besag (1974b), however, described a number of difficulties with this approach. There is no obvious way to obtain a joint probability structure for a given conditional probability model; the conditional probability structure is subject to some subtle, yet highly restrictive, consistency conditions, and when these restrictions are enforced, it can be shown (Brook, 1964) that the conditional formulation is degenerate with respect to the joint formulation. Besag (1974b) found that the constraints on the conditional probability structure are so severe that they actually dictate particular models. (For example, for binary variables, the conditional probability formulation gives rise to the Ising model of statistical mechanics.)

The conditional probability approach, however, has served as the basis for a commonly used class of models, called Markov image models. Consider a finite image of n pixels with an associated collection of n random variables $\{X_i\}$. Suppose that for each pixel i, the conditional distribution of its associated random variable X_i, given all other pixel values, depends only on those pixels within a finite neighborhood $N(i)$ of pixel i. Pixel j ($\neq i$) is said to be a Markov neighbor of pixel i if and only if the functional form $\Pr(x_i | x_1, \ldots, x_{i-1}, x_{i+1}, \ldots, x_n)$ is dependent on the variable x_j. The complete set of neighborhoods $N_1, \ldots, N_n$ generate an associated class of valid probability distributions for $(X_1, \ldots, X_n)$. Any member of this class is formally called a Markov random) field. One result of the important Clifford–Hammersley theorem is that for any Markov field, the functional form

$$\Pr(X_i = x_i, X_j = x_j, \ldots,$$
$$X_s = x_s | \text{all other pixel values})$$

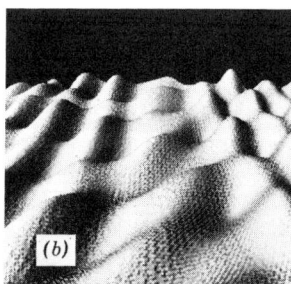

Figure 2. (a) A texture generated using a long crested narrow-band noise model, (b) the same texture displayed as a height field in perspective.

depends only on $x_i, x_j, \ldots, x_s$ and the values at neighboring sites of $i, j, \ldots, s$.

It should be noted that the use of the term Markov in a two-dimensional context is somewhat controversial. Wong (1968) for example, offered a proof that there exists no continuous two-dimensional random field that is both homogeneous and Markov. Serra (1980) also discussed the misuse of the term Markov in digital image modeling.

Different choices for the set of a pixel's neighbors give rise to different Markov models. A first-order (or nearest neighbor) Markov model lets the value at each pixel depend only upon the values at its four neighbors (two horizontal and two vertical neighbors). A second-order scheme uses an eight-adjacent neighborhood (the three × three neighborhood centered at the pixel), and so on. Let $N^m(i)$ denote the mth-order Markov neighborhood of pixel i. Second-order models are much more complex than first-order models, and unless the variables are assumed to be Gaussian, third- and higher order schemes are too cumbersome to exploit. First- and second-order schemes may be extended to other lattice structures (Besag, 1974b), nonlattice structures (Besag, 1975), higher dimensions, and the space–time domain (Besag, 1974a) as well.

The specification of the probability distribution of a pixel's gray level, given the gray levels of its neighbors, defines a strict-sense Markov field representation (Rosenfeld and Kak, 1976). Besag (1974b) described two of the more interesting models of this kind, the autobinary and the autonormal schemes. The autobinary scheme has a conditional structure of the form

$$\Pr(x_i | x_i, \ldots, x_{i-1}, x_{i+1}, \ldots, x_n)$$
$$= \frac{\exp[x_i(\alpha_i + \Sigma_{j \in N(i)} \beta_{i,j} x_j)]}{1 + \exp(\alpha_i + \Sigma_{j \in N(i)} \beta_{i,j} x_j)}$$

where x_i can take on only values of zero or one.

The autonormal scheme assumes that the joint distribution of the variables is multivariate normal. For this case, the conditional probability function is given by

$$\Pr(x_i | x_i, \ldots, x_{i-1}, x_{i+1}, \ldots, x_n)$$
$$= (2\pi\sigma^2)^{-1/2} \exp[-\tfrac{1}{2}\sigma^{-2}\{(x_i - \mu_i)^t$$
$$\times \sum_{j \in N(i)} \beta_{i,j}(x_j - \mu_j)\}^2]$$

And the joint density function is given by

$$\Pr(\mathbf{x}) = (2\pi\sigma^2)^{-n/2} |B|^{1/2} \times \exp[(\mathbf{x} - \mu)^t B(\mathbf{x} - \mu)/2\sigma^2]$$

where $\mathbf{x} = (x_i, \ldots, x_n)$, $\mu = E[\mathbf{X}]$, and B is a matrix defined as follows:

$$b_{i,j} = b_{j,i} = \begin{cases} 1, & \text{if } i = j \\ -\beta_{i,j}, & \text{if } j \in N(i), \ j \neq i \\ 0, & \text{otherwise} \end{cases}$$

Also, $E[X_i | \text{all other pixel values}] = \mu_i + \Sigma_{j \in N(i)} \beta_{i,j}(x_j - \mu_j)$. For a first-order autonormal scheme, $X_{i,j}$ (given the variety at all other pixels) is normally distributed with mean

$$\alpha + \beta_1(x_{i-1,j} + x_{i+1,j}) + \beta_2(x_{i,j-1} + x_{i,j+1})$$

and common variance σ^2.

For a discussion of other autoschemes, including the autobinomial, auto-Poisson, and autoexponential schemes, see Besag (1974b). Cross and Jain (1981) reported experiments on fitting the autobinomial model to textures from Brodatz (1966). Maximum likelihood estimates of the model parameters are used to test the hypothesis that a given texture sample is described by an autobinomial model with the estimated parameters. The model is also used to generate texture samples.

A close relative of the automodel is the simultaneous autoregressive scheme, defined by

$$X_i = \mu_i + \sum_{j \in N(i)} \beta_{i,j}(X_j - \mu_j) + e_j$$

where the error (noise) terms are independent Gaussian variables with zero mean and common variance σ^2. The joint probability density is given by

$$\Pr(\mathbf{X}) = (2\pi\sigma^2)^{-n/2} |B| \times \exp[-2\sigma^{-2}(\mathbf{X} - \mu)^t B^t B(\mathbf{X} - \mu)]$$

where B is a nonsingular matrix defined as follows:

$$b_{i,j} = \begin{cases} 0, & \text{if } i = j, \\ -\beta_{i,j}, & \text{if } j \in N(i), \ j \neq i, \\ 0, & \text{otherwise} \end{cases}$$

A first-order scheme of this type is given by

$$X_{i,j} = \beta_1 X_{i-1,j} + \beta_2 X_{i+1,j} + \beta_3 X_{i,j-1} + \beta_4 X_{i,j+1} + e_{i,j}$$

For this simple model,

$E[X_{i,j} | \text{all other pixel values}]$

$$= \alpha[(\beta_1 + \beta_2)(x_{i-1,j} + x_{i+1,j})$$
$$+ (\beta_3 + \beta_4)(x_{i,j-1} + x_{i,j+1})$$
$$- (\beta_1\beta_4 + \beta_2\beta_3)(x_{i-1,j-1} + x_{i+1,j+1})$$
$$- (\beta_1\beta_3 + \beta_2\beta_4)(x_{i-1,j+1} + x_{i+1,j-1})$$
$$- \beta_3\beta_4(x_{i,j-2} + x_{i,j+2})$$
$$- \beta_1\beta_2(x_{i-2,j} + x_{i+2,j})$$

where $\alpha = 1/(1 + \beta_1^2 + \beta_2^2 + \beta_3^2 + \beta_4^2)$ (Besag, 1974b) and $\text{Var}(X_{i,j} | \text{all other pixel values}) = \alpha\sigma^2$.

Besag (1975) noted that the symmetry requirements of the simultaneous autoregressive model (ie, $\beta_1 = \beta_2$; $\beta_3 = \beta_4$) are automatically fulfilled without the need to place prior restrictions on them. He also noted that $e_{i,j}$ and $x_{i',j'}$ are uncorrelated whenever $(i, j) \neq (i', j')$.

Techniques for estimating the unknown parameters of these models have not been covered. Good discussions of this topic can be found (Ballard and co-workers, 1977; Besag, 1974b, 1976, 1977; Box and Jenkins, 1976; Ord, 1975). The relationship between causal and noncausal

Markov neighborhoods has also been studied in two dimensions. Abend and co-workers (1965) used Markov chain methods to show that in many cases a noncausal dependence is equivalent to a causal dependence. Woods's (1972) treatment allows a larger number of equivalent pairs of causal and noncausal neighborhoods. And still other studies present additional examples and discussion of Markov models (Herin and Elliott, 1987; Deguchi and Morishita, 1976; Hassner and Sklansky, 1978; Jain and Angel, 1974; Jain, 1977a; Panda and Kak, 1977; Pickard, 1977; Strauss, 1977; Welberry and Miller, 1977; Silverman and Cooper, 1988).

Kashyap (1980) used circulant matrices to define autoregressive models for an infinite array (the array obtained by infinitely repeating a given finite image). This obviates the need for the initial conditions required by the nonperiodic and autoregressive processes. Kashyap obtained the probability density of the data and discussed the maximum likelihood estimation of the model parameters. He then gave decision rules for the choice of neighbors of a pixel (Chellappa and co-workers, 1981) and for tetsing the homogeneity of image data. For nonhomogeneous images, he used multivariate autoregressive models that are constructed as follows: an image is divided into small blocks each of which is assumed to be homogeneous; a univariate autoregressive model is then obtained for each of the windows, and the parameter vectors of these models are then viewed as data and are modeled by a multivariate random field. Finally, Kashyap (1980) obtained an expression for the probability density of the field.

Links and Biemond (1979) [along with Andrews and Hunt (1977) and Pratt (1975)] have investigated the autocorrelation-separability of image models. They consider a general model of the form

$$X_i = \sum_{j \in N(i)} \beta_{i,j} X_j + \gamma e_j$$

or in vector-matrix notation

$$\underset{n \times 1}{\mathbf{X}} = \underset{n \times n}{B} \underset{n \times 1}{\mathbf{X}} + \underset{n \times 1}{\gamma \mathbf{e}}$$

where $n = M^2$. The model autocorrelation is clearly

$$E[XX^t] = \gamma^2 B^{-1} E[\mathbf{e}\mathbf{e}^t](B^{-1})^t$$

The $n \times n$ autocorrelation matrix $E[\mathbf{XX}^t]$ may be separable into a direct product of an $M \times M$ column autocorrelation matrix B_c and an $M \times M$ row autocorrelation matrix B_r; that is,

$$E[\mathbf{XX}^t] = E[\mathbf{X}_c \mathbf{X}_c^t] \otimes E[\mathbf{X}_r \mathbf{X}_r^t]$$
$$= \gamma^2 (B_c^{-1} \otimes B_r^{-1}) E[\mathbf{e}_c \mathbf{e}_c^t]$$
$$\otimes E[\mathbf{e}_r \mathbf{e}_r^t] (B_c^{-1} \otimes (B_r^{-1})^t)$$

where $\mathbf{X}_r = (X_{i,1}, \ldots, X_{i,M})$, $\mathbf{X}_c = (X_{1,j}, \ldots, X_{M,j})^t$.

Thus, for separability of the model autocorrelation, it is only necessary that the model operator be separable into a column operator B_c and a row operator B_r and that the error autocorrelation $E[\mathbf{e}\mathbf{e}^t]$ be separable into a column autocorrelation $E[\mathbf{e}_c \mathbf{e}_c^t]$ and a row autocorrelation $E[\mathbf{e}_r \mathbf{e}_r^t]$.

If the elements of $\mathbf{e}$ are uncorrelated variables with zero mean and variance σ^2, the autocorrelation matrix $E[\mathbf{ee}^t]$ is separable: that is, $E[ee^t] = \sigma^2 I_c \otimes I_r$. The $\beta_{i,j}$ terms can be written in a matrix of the form

$$\begin{matrix} \cdot & \cdot & \cdot \\ \cdots \beta_{-1,-1} & \beta_{-1,0} & \beta_{-1,1} \cdots \\ \cdots \beta_{0,-1} & -1 & \beta_{0,1} \cdots \\ \cdots \beta_{1,-1} & \beta_{1,0} & \beta_{1,1} \cdots \\ \cdot & \cdot & \cdot \end{matrix}$$

If every two rows of the matrix are pairwise linearly independent, then the model autocorrelation is separable. Elsewhere, Kashyap and Eom (1989) have also reported the use of long correlation model for texture segmentation.

Goutsias and Mendel (1989) used a nonstationary mean, nonstationary variance model in which the mean and variance are viewed as a random field. This model is used for simultaneous optimal segmentation and model estimation. Another random field model based approach to texture segmentation and model estimation is reported in Lakshmanan and Derin (1989).

The local models discussed so far relate the gray level of a pixel to the gray levels of its neighbors, using a conditional probability formulation. The joint probability approach has also received considerable attention. Its primary difficulty, however, is the high dimensionality of the joint probability densities, even for small neighborhoods, making parameter estimation complex and cumbersome. Read and Jayaramamurthy (1972) and McCormick and Jayaramamurthy (1975) make use of switching theory techniques to reduce this intractability. They develop minimal functions for modeling local gray level patterns as follows. Suppose that each pixel is assigned one of N gray levels; then a neighborhood of M pixels may be represented by a point in an $(M \times N)$-dimensional space. Points corresponding to an aggregate of neighborhoods from a single pattern are likely to form clusters in this space. A generalization of standard switching theory, the set-covering methodology of Michalski and McCormick (1971) is used to describe the set of points in a cluster. These maximal descriptions allow coverage of empty spaces in and around clusters. The sample size need only be large enough to provide a reasonable representation. This approach has the advantage of a simple table look-up decision for classifying textures (Haralick, 1976a).

A number of investigators confine joint statistics to neighborhoods of size two. A texture is characterized in terms of its gray level cooccurrence tallies, which are the first estimate of the corresponding joint probabilities. Rosenfeld and Troy (1970), Haralick (1971, 1976a, 1976b) and Haralick and co-workers (1973) suggested the use of two-dimensional spatial dependence of gray levels for fixed distances and angular separations. Harlick and numerous other investigators apply features derived from the cooccurrence matrix to various texture classification and discrimination problems. The performance of these features as texture measures is compared with several other techniques by Weszka and co-workers (1976) and Connors and Harlow (1980). Zucker and Terzopoulos (1980) note that if a cooccurrence matrix is treated as a contingency table, then a standard chi-squared test can be used to see whether the rows and columns of the matrix are independent. (Presumably, any dependence found here is due to the structure in the image.) They use the maximum among chi-squared values corresponding to various choices of distance and orientation to identify structural characteristics of the image. Their particular approach has been used in geology for many years (Harbauch and Bonham-Carter, 1970; Vistelius and Fass, 1965; Whitten and Dacey, 1975), although in geology the classes are separate entities (mineral types), not ordered gray levels. Davis and co-workers (1979) suggest the use of a generalized cooccurrence matrix based on local features rather than gray levels.

Syntactic Models

Rosenfeld (1980) defined a procedural model as "any process that generates or recognizes images; the class that it defines consists of the images that it accepts." Grammatical (or syntactic) models fall into this category.

Conventionally, a language is defined as a set of strings over an alphabet, where the alphabet consists of the set of all symbols that can appear in the strings of the language, and a string is a finite ordered sequence of symbols. A grammar is a set of rules that define how the strings of the language are formed. Equivalently, a grammar can be used to recognize the language's strings by using the rules in reverse order. This concept can be generalized in a number of ways (Fu, 1973; Lu and Fu, 1978; Rosenfeld and Milgram, 1971; Rosenfeld, 1979) to define grammars for classes of images.

An array grammar generates images by repeatedly replacing subarrays by other subarrays. A stochastic array grammar is one in which the replacement rules are probabilistic.

In one-dimensional grammars there is no problem with replacing one string by another. But for array grammars the shapes of subarrays must be compatible so that there are no "holes" in the resulting image. Jayaramamurthy (1979) attempted to solve this problem with multilevel grammars. Here the subarrays at levels greater than zero are patterns of a specified shape, with the patterns themselves derived by a set of grammars at the next lower level. All the terminal subarrays at any level represent patterns of the same shape.

Syntactic methods have been used for locating highways and rivers in LANDSAT images and for texture modeling (Fu 1980). Although the use of subarrays in the vocabulary of array grammars poses many difficulties, it gives these models a flavor of the second major class of models, and the region-based models.

REGION-BASED MODELS

Region-based models are defined using regions, instead of pixels, as primitives. A given model specifies the shapes of the regions and gives the rules for their placement in the plane, thereby allowing increased control over some pattern characteristics. Both the shapes and the placement rules may be specified statistically.

Over the years, region-based models have received far less attention than the pixel-based models in computer image processing. But recently these models have been investigated for texture analysis and synthesis. One class studied is that of mosaic models. These models view an image as a mosaic, constructed by tessellating the plane into cells and then coloring the cells by some given process. The resultant pattern consists of color patches, each patch formed by identically colored contiguous cells. Tessellations commonly used include the regular triangular, square, and hexagonal tessellations, and random tessellations such as the following:

1. *Poisson Line.* A Poisson process chooses pairs (ρ, θ), $0 \leq \theta \leq \pi$, $-\infty < \rho < \infty$. The lines $x \cos \theta + y \sin \theta = \rho$ define a tessellation of the plane.
2. *Voronoi.* A Poisson process chooses points (nuclei) in the plane. Each nucleus defines a "Dirichlet cell" consisting of all the points in the plane nearer to it than to any other nucleus.
3. *Delaunay.* All pairs of nuclei whose Dirichlet cells are adjacent are joined by straight line segments to define the tessellation.

The coloring process most commonly used assigns one of a predetermined set of colors to a cell, according to a given probability vector. The term "color" may stand for a fixed gray level or for gray levels from a given distribution, a vector of red, green, and blue components, among other possibilities.

Another class of region-based models consists of the coverage (or "bombing") models. These models view an image as a random arrangement of a given set of colored shapes over a uniform background. Once again, the choice of shapes and placement rules specifies a particular model. Circles have often been used for the figures, placed at locations chosen by a Poisson process. Figure 3 shows some examples of random mosaics and coverage patterns.

Region-based models of the above types, mosaic and coverage, have been popular in many disciplines, including geology, forestry, biology, ecology, astronomy, crystallography, and statistics. Several properties of mosaics and coverage patterns have been obtained by researchers in these fields. Many of the point correlation properties are discussed in Matern's (1960) excellent thesis on spatial variation. Switzer (1965, 1967, 1969) and Pielou (1977) extend Matern's results. They show that a Poisson line mosaic formed from independently colored cells has the interesting property that any sequence of colors along a transect forms a Markov chain. The Markov properties of the Poisson line model have also been investigated by Scheaffer (1975a, 1975b). Switzer (1965) derived an expression for the autocorrelation function of the Poisson line mosaic, and Matern (1969, 1972) discussed some geometrical properties of the cells in random tessellations. Extensive work on estimating the geometrical characteristics of cells in Poisson line tessellations has been done by Miles (1964a, 1964b), Crain and Miles (1976) and Rich-

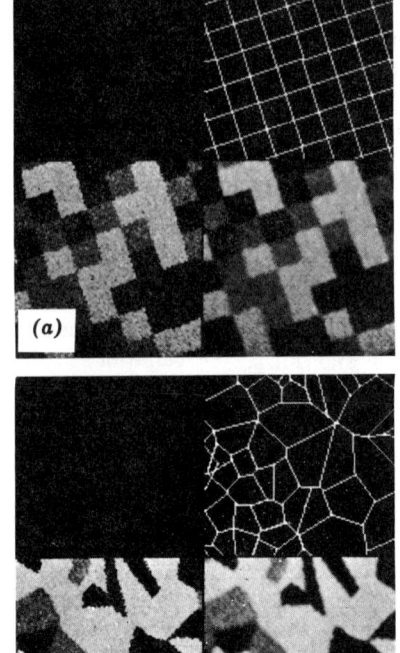
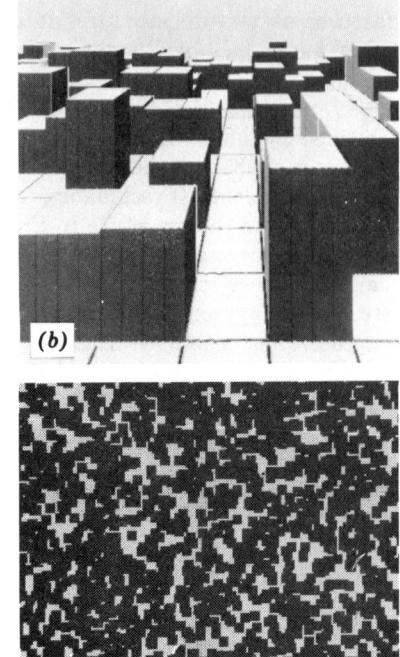

Figure 3. Examples of random mosaics and coverage patterns. (**a**) Square tessellation and mosaic, (**b**) square mosaic displayed as a height field in perspective, (**c**) Voronoi tessellation and mosaic, (**d**) square coverage pattern.

ards (1964). They estimate properties such as the expected area of a cell and the expected number of sides of a cell, the expected perimeter of a cell, and the expected number of cells meeting at a vertex. Modestino and co-workers (1979a, 1979b, 1980) discussed joint pixel properties for mosaics with correlated cell colors. Zucker (1976) viewed texture as a distortion of an ideal mosaic. The distortion is specified in terms of geometric transforms applied to the mosaic.

Ahuja (1979, 1981a, 1981c) derived extensive results on the properties of connected color components in regular mosaics (triangular, square, and hexagonal) and in random mosaics (Poisson line, Voronoi, and Delaunay). Among the properties analyzed are the expected component area, the component perimeter, the component width, the component density, and the point correlation properties. The Voronoi mosaic is of special interest because its cells mimic those formed by natural growth processes. Matern (1960) gives its autocorrelation function as a double integral equation having no elementary solution. Ahuja (1979) and Moore (1978) provide empirical estimates. The geometrical characteristics of the Voronoi tessellation are covered by Miles (1970), Gilbert (1962) and Lee (1976). Santalo (1976) is a good reference for the properties of various tessellations.

Solomon (1953) first popularized the circular coverage model. Analogous to the analysis of mosaics, Ahuja (1979, 1981b, 1981c) obtained properties of the color components and joint characteristics of pairs of points for coverage patterns. Moore (1973, 1974) investigated anisotropic random mosaics. The application of region-based models to modeling images has received very little attention. Conners and Harlow (1980) start with a real-world texture and attempt to find a set of unit patterns and placement rules which could generate the texture. Ahuja and co-workers (1980), Ahuja and Rosenfeld (1981), and Schachter and co-workers (1978) attempt fitting mosaic models to a variety of textures. Both of them choose the model and its parameters so as to provide a match between the observed and predicted expected values of component properties. Modestino and co-workers (1979b) reported experiments with texture discrimination using mosaic models. A detailed treatment of many aspects of mosaic and coverage models appears in Ahuja and Schachter (1982).

Tuceryan and Jain (1990) performed texture segmentation using shape properties of Voronoi polygons formed by the texture regions. Region-based models are further discussed by Rosenfeld and Lipkin (1970), Serra and co-workers (1973), Serra (1980), Miles (1980), Matheron (1967, 1971), Ripley (1976), Grunbaum and Shepard (1982), Haralick (1978), Schachter and Ahuja (1979), Ahuja and Rosenfeld (1981), and Davis and Mitiche (1980). Syntactic models mentioned herein have also been used as region-based models with regions instead of pixels defining the terminal symbols.

MODELS FOR HUMAN TEXTURE PERCEPTION

Mandelbrot (1983) has proposed the use of sets that have fractional dimension, or fractal sets, to model textures. A fractal set is defined as a set for which the Hausdorff-Besicovitch dimension strictly exceeds the topological dimension. Intuitively, fractal dimension characterizes the perceived roughness of an image texture of the corresponding three-dimensional surface. Pentland (1984) reports experiments that demonstrate a high correlation between perceived roughness and fractal dimension of textures. Pentland has used homogeneity of fractal dimension as a criterion to perform image segmentation (Keller and co-workers, 1989). Julesz (1962, 1975, 1981) has done extensive work on identifying characteristics of textures important in texture perception by humans. Julesz's first conjecture stated the human visual system cannot perceive differences in textures that are identical in second order gray level statistics. Gaglowicz (1981) suggested that only local second-order statistics may be used for human texture discrimination. Julesz later modified his conjecture to state that human visual system can only perceive (first-order) statistics of texture features called textons (Fig. 4). Color, line terminators, and edge segments are examples of textons.

INFERENCE OF THREE-DIMENSIONAL SHAPE FROM TEXTURE

Texture variation due to projective distortion provides important cues for recovering the three-dimensional structure of the surfaces visible in an image (Gibson, 1950).

A uniformly textured surface undergoes two types of projective distortion during the imaging process. First, an increase in the distance from the surface to the viewer causes a uniform compression of increasingly large areas of surface onto a fixed area of image. Second, foreshortening (due to the angle between the surface and the image plane) causes an anisotropic compression of the texture. These texture variations provide information about the relative distances and orientations of the textured surfaces in an image.

A major challenge in estimating shape from texture is to identify texture scale consistently. Natural surfaces exhibit a rich hierarchy of textures and subtextures. All texture measurements are prone to distortion due to the presence of subtexture, because the imaging process captures more subtexture details for close texture samples than for distant ones.

Texels and Texture Gradients

The term texel, short for texture element, denotes the repetitive unit of which a texture is composed. Texel refers to the physical texture element in the real world as well as to the appearance of the texture element in the image. In cases where the distinction must be made, the phrases physical texel versus image texel are used. Distance and foreshortening changes alter the image texel, but not the physical texel.

Projective distortion affects many texture features, and hence gives rise to a variety of texture gradients. Consider first the idealized texture of Figure 5a: a planar surface covered with nonoverlapping circular disks of constant size. The disks project as ellipses in the image. The major axis of each ellipse is perpendicular to the tilt, whereas the minor axis is parallel with the tilt. Scanning the image from bottom to top (in the direction of tilt), the apparent size of the major axes decreases linearly, due to increasing distance from the viewer (the perspective gradient). However, the apparent size of the minor axes decreases quadratically: in addition to the distance scaling, the minor axes are foreshortened. Thus the eccentricity of the ellipses increases in the tilt direction (the aspect-ratio gradient). Similarly, the area of the ellipses decreases fastest in the direction of tilt (the area gradient). This is accompanied by an increase in the density of the ellipses (the density gradient). In this idealized texture, the uniformity in the size, shape and placement of the texture elements leads to pronounced texture gradients.

Natural textures are much less regular than the idealized texture of Figure 5a; therefore the texture gradients are not as easily observed. Natural textures display considerable variability of texel size, shape, coloration and density. Physical texels are typically three-dimensional, unlike the disks portrayed in Figure 5a. Highlights, shadows, and occlusions between texels result. Also, physical texels have a complex structure. In contrast to a uniform synthetic disk, a physical texel changes in appearance as the distance to the camera decreases: more subtexture is visible for the nearby texels than for the distant texels. Supertexture regions arise when small image texels, corresponding to distant physical texels, blur into larger regions of relatively uniform gray level. These factors make it difficult to identify texture elements and extract texture gradients from real images.

The importance of various texture gradients has been studied extensively in the psychology literature (Braunstein and Payne, 1969; Phillips, 1970; Rosinski, 1974; Rosinski and Levine, 1976). Vickers (1971) was among the first to advocate an approach involving accumulation of evidence from multiple texture gradients. Cutting and Millard (1981) attempted to quantify the relative importance of various texture gradients. They tested human subjects on synthetically generated textures, which are designed to contain only a subset of the normally occurring texture gradients. Experimental results showed that for slant judgments of flat surfaces the perspective and density gradients are more important than the aspect-ratio gradient, whereas in the perception of curved surfaces the aspect-ratio gradient is dominant, with perspective and density gradients having little impact.

The Inference of Surface Shape from Texture Gradients

Blostein and Ahuja (1989) argued that correct measurement of texture gradients requires explicit identification of image texels, especially when textures show three-dimensional relief, when texels exhibit significant subtexture, or when it is unknown *a priori* which texture gradients carry surface-shape information. Texture elements cannot be identified in isolated image areas because texels are defined only by the repetitive nature of the texture as a whole. Therefore, the identification of texture elements is best done in parallel with the estimation of the shape of the textured surface.

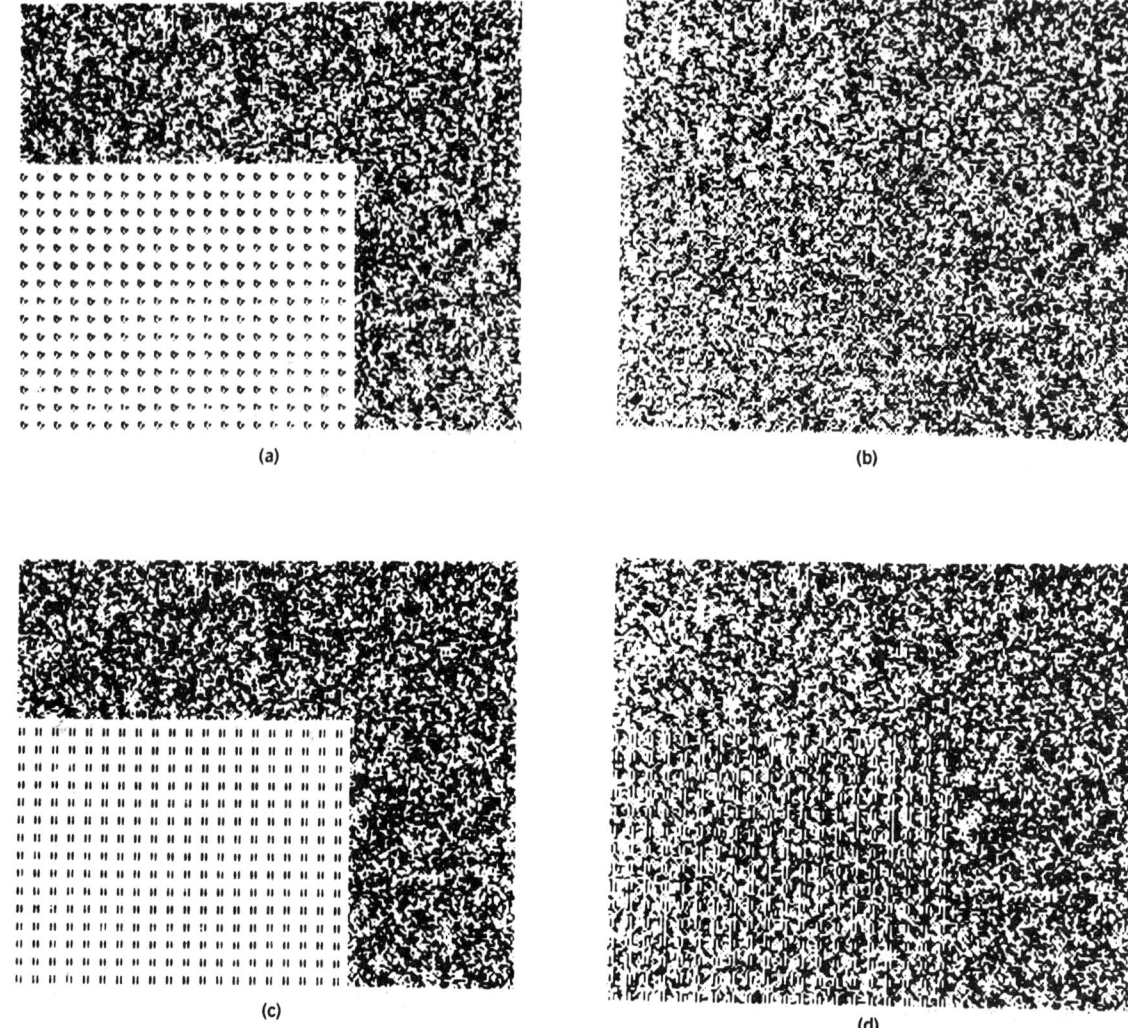

Figure 4. Demonstration that the preattentive textural system cannot process globally differences in second-order statistics, and only first-order statistics of textons yield texture discrimination. (a) Periodically repeated 4 × 4 dot micropattern that does not contain textons, flanked by randomly dotted areas, (b) same as a, except that the blank gaps between the periodic micropatterns are filled with random dots. The second-order statistics are very different between the area composed of periodic micropatterns and its random neighbor, and yet they appear indistinguishable, (c) same as a, except that the 4 × 4 dot micropattern contains textons of periodic stripes, (d) same as c, except that the noise insertion described in b is carried out. Now strong texture discrimination is experienced based on the dense occurrence of textons that are missing in the neighboring area (Julesz, 1981). Courtesy of Macmillan Magazines Ltd.

The Importance of Texel Identification. The extraction of texels is an essential step in measuring texture gradients, because it permits correct analysis of textures containing subtexture. Explicit texel identification also provides the basis for a unified treatment of the various texture gradients (area gradient, density gradient, aspect-ratio gradient) that may be present in an image. Previous researchers have avoided texel identification because it is quite difficult to do in real images. Instead, indirect methods are used to estimate texel features. Below several examples of such methods are given, and it is indicated why these methods may give erroneous results.

Most previous shape-from-texture algorithms use indirect methods to estimate texel features, by making some assumptions about the nature of texture elements. For example, texel density may be estimated by measuring edge density, under the assumption that all detected edges correspond to the borders of texture elements (Aloimonos and Swain, 1985; Aloimonos, 1986; Kanatani and Chou, 1986; Rosenfeld, 1975). Alternatively, texture elements may be assumed to have uniform edge direction histograms; surface orientation can then be estimated from any deviations from isotropy observed in the distribution of edge directions (Davis and co-workers, 1983; Kanatani, 1984; Witkin, 1981). However, the directional-isotropy assumption is very restrictive; for example, it does not hold true in images containing elongated texels such as waves. Texture coarseness and directionality may

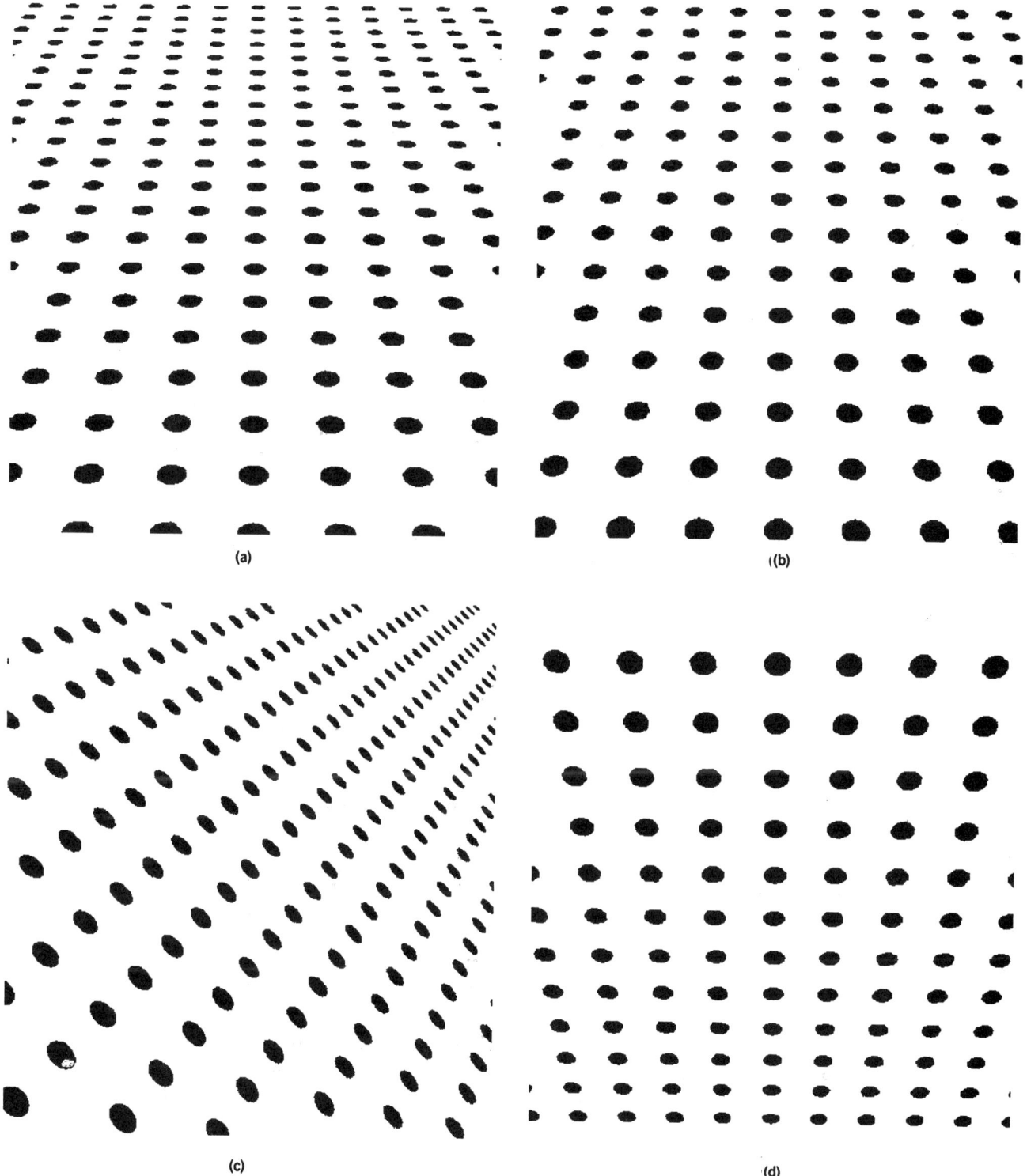

Figure 5. Synthetic textures illustrating various slants and tilts. Slant is the angle between the textured surface and the image plane. Tilt is the direction in which the surface normally projects the image. (**a**) Slant 60°, tilt 90°; (**b**) slant 50°, tilt 90°; (**c**) slant 60°, tilt 45°; (**d**) slant 45°, tilt 270°.

be characterized using Fourier domain measurements, ignoring the effect of supertextures and subtextures. Various researchers (Ikeuchi, 1980; Kender, 1980; Nakatani and co-workers, 1980) have developed algorithms to analyze textures containing parallel and perpendicular lines.

Most natural textures are too irregular to be analyzed in this way.

All of these methods may encounter problems when applied to complex natural textures seen under natural lighting conditions. Because texels are not identified and explicitly dealt with, it becomes difficult to distinguish between responses due to texels and those due to other image features, such as subtexture. It appears to be necessary to recognize the texture elements before the various measures can be computed as intended.

Explicit texel identification offers an additional advantage: texels provide a unifying framework for examination of the various texture gradients (such as gradients of apparent texel area, aspect ratio, density, etc) that may be present in an image. A given image may exhibit a combination of texture gradients. In general, the accuracy of the surface information obtainable from these gradients varies from image to image. Because it is not known in advance which texture gradients are useful for determining the three-dimensional orientation of surfaces, a shape-from-texture system should evaluate the information content of different types of gradients in a given image, and use an appropriate mix of these gradients for surface estimation.

Integration of Texel Identification and Surface-Shape Estimation. Texel identification is difficult because texels have tremendously varied shapes, sizes, and gray level characteristics. A texel cannot be identified in isolation, because texels are only defined by the repetitive nature of the texture as a whole. In order to determine if an image region is a texel, it is necessary to test if the region has properties consistent with the properties of many other image texels, ie, whether the image region is part of a texture field.

The term texture field (or field of texels) denotes a collection of image texels that exhibit one or more consistent texture gradients. Consistency is defined with respect to a perspective view of a given surface. It is not uncommon for a single image to contain several texture fields.

Texels can only be identified in the context of a texture field, where consistent texture gradients must exist across the whole field. The consistency of a texture gradient can only be evaluated for a particular surface shape and orientation. Thus texel identification must be combined with surface estimation.

Overview. The requirements for an ideal shape-from-texture algorithm will now be summarized.

Texel Identification. Texel identification is important for correct shape-from-texture analysis. In general, physical texels can give rise to complex gray level patterns. However, it is difficult to test for repetitive patterns of arbitrary gray-level configuration. In the implementation, image texels are restricted to be regions that have small gray level variation relative to a neighborhood of their size. Under this restriction, a physical texel can give rise to several image texels: often the physical repetitive unit of a texture contains both bright and dark regions.

Texture Gradients. A shape-from texture system should test each image for the presence of various texture gradients (area gradient, aspect-ratio gradient, density gradient) and combine these various sources of information to produce a surface estimation.

Surface Estimation. Ideally, a system tests for texture gradients produced by a variety of surface shapes (planar, cylindrical, spherical, etc) and is able to locate discontinuities in depth and surface orientation. Much work remains to be done in this area.

Three-Dimensional Texel Effects. For accurate image analysis, it is necessary to model the effects of three-dimensional relief on observed texture gradients. Although some theoretical treatment of the foreshortening of textures with relief exists (Kender, 1980), no one has addressed how in-plane texels could be distinguished from out-of-plane texels in real images.

Multiple Textures. A general shape-from-texture system must be able to handle images containing multiple textures; the system must perform texture segmentation as well as shape-from-texture estimation. To solve this problem it is necessary to separate texture variations due to distance and foreshortening effects from texture variations due to a boundary between different physical textures.

BIBLIOGRAPHY

R. J. Adler, "A Spectral Moment Estimation Problem in Two Dimensions," *Biometrika* **64**, 2 367–373 (1977a).

R. J. Adler, "Hausdorff Dimension and Gaussain Fields," *Ann. Prob.* **5**(1), 145–151 (1977b).

R. J. Adler, "Some Erratic Patterns Generated by the Planar Wiener Process," *Suppl. Adv. Appl. Prob.* **10**, 22–27 (1978a).

R. J. Adler, "Distribution Results for the Occupation Measures of Continuous Gaussian Fields," *Stoch. Processes Appl.* **7**, 299–310 (1978b).

R. J. Adler, "The Uniform Dimension of the Level Set of a Brownian Sheet," *Ann. Prob.* **6**, 309–315 (1978c).

R. J. Adler and A. M. Hasoffer, "Level Crossings for Random Fields," *Ann. Prob.* **4**(1), 1–12 (1976).

N. Ahuja, *Mosaic Models for Image Analysis and Synthesis,* Ph.D. Dissertation, Dept. Computer Science, University of Maryland, College Park, 1979.

N. Ahuja, "Mosaic Models for Images, 2: Geometric Properties of Components in Coverage Mosaics," *Inform. Sci.* **23**, 159–200 (April 1981).

N. Ahuja, "Mosaic Models for Images, 3: Spatial Correlation in Mosaics," *Inform. Sci.* **24**, 43–69 (June 1981a).

N. Ahuja, "Mosaic Models for Images 1: Geometric Properties of Components in Cell Structure Mosaics," *Inform. Sci.* **23**, 69–104 (March 1981b).

N. Ahuja and A. Rosenfeld, "Fitting Mosaic Models to Textures," in R. M. Haralick, ed., *Image Texture Analysis,* Plenum, New York, 1981a.

N. Ahuja and A. Rosenfeld, "Mosaic Models for Textures," *IEEE Trans. Pattern Analysis Mach. Int.* **3**, 1–11 (Jan. 1981b).

N. Ahuja and B. J. Schachter, *Pattern Models,* Wiley, New York, 1982.

N. Ahuja, T. Dubitzki, and A. Rosenfeld, "Some Experiments with Mosaic Models for Textures," *IEEE Trans. Syst. Man, Cyber.* **10**, (Nov. 1980).

J. Aloimonos, "Detection of Surface Orientation from Texture I: The Case of Planes," in *Proceedings of the IEEE Conference on*

Computer Vision and Pattern Recognition, 1986, IEEE, New York, 1986a, pp. 584–593.

J. Aloimonos and M. Swain, "Shape from Texture," in *Proceedings of 9th International Joint Conference on Artificial Intelligence,* 1985, Los Angeles, AAAI, Menlo Park, Calif., 1985, pp. 926–931.

H. C. Andrews and B. R. Hunt, *Digital Image Restoration,* Prentice-Hall, Englewood Cliffs, N.J., 1977.

E. Angel and A. K. Jain, "Frame-to-Frame Restoration of Diffusion Images," *IEEE Trans. Automat. Contr.* **AC-23,** 850–855 (1978).

T. Assefi, *Stochastic Processes, Estimation Theory, and Image Enhancement,* Jet Propulsion Laboratory, Pasadena, Calif., June 1978.

D. W. Bacon, "Seasonal Time Series," Ph.D. dissertation, University of Wisconsin, Madison, Wis., 1965.

M. S. Bartlett, *An Introduction to Stochastic Processes,* University Press, Cambridge, U.K., 1955.

M. S. Bartlett, "Inference and Stochastic Processes," *J. R. Stat. Soc.* **A 130,** 457–477 (1967).

M. S. Bartlett, *The Statistical Analysis of Spatial Pattern,* John Wiley & Sons, New York, 1975.

J. Besag, "On spatial-temporal models and Markov fields," in *Trans. 7th Prague Conf. Information Theory, Statistical Decision Function,* Vol. A, Prague, Czechoslovakia, Aug. 1974a, pp. 47–55.

J. Besag, "Spatial Interaction and the Statistical Analysis of Lattice Systems," *J. Royal Stat. Soc. Ser.* **B 36,** 192–236 (1974).

J. Besag, "Statistical Analysis of Nonlattice Data," *Statistician* **24,** 3, 175–195 (1975).

J. Besag, *Parameter Estimation for Markov Fields,* Tech. Rep. 108, Ser. 2, Dep. Statistics, Stanford University, Stanford, Calif., Feb. 1976.

J. Besag, "Errors-in-Variables Estimation for Gaussian Lattice Schemes," *J. Royal Stat. Soc. Ser.* **B 39,** 1, 73–78 (1977).

D. Blostein, and N. Ahuja, "Shape from Texture: Integrating Texture-Element Extraction and Surface Estimation" *IEEE Trans. Patt. Anal. Mach. Intell.* **PAMI-11** (12) 1233–1251 (1989).

J. E. P. Box and G. M. Jenkins, *Time Series Analysis,* Holden-Day, San Francisco, Calif., 1976.

M. L. Braunstein and J. W. Payne, "Perspective and Form Ratio as Determinants of Relative Slant Judgments," *J. Exp. Psychol.* **81**(3), 584–590 (1969).

P. Brodatz, *Textures: A Photographic Album for Artists and Designers,* Dover, New York, 1966.

D. Brook, "On the Distinction between the Conditional Probability and Joint Probability Approaches in the Specification of Nearest-Neighbor Systems," *Biometrika* **51,** 481–483 (1964).

R. Chellappa, *On the Correlation Structure of Nearest Neighbor Random Field Models of Images,* Tech. Rep. TR-912, Dept. Computer Science University of Maryland, College Park, July 1980.

R. Chellappa and N. Ahuja, *Statistical Inference Theory Applied to Image Modelling,* Tech. Rep. TR-745; Dept. Computer Science, University of Maryland, College Park, March 1979.

R. Chellappa, R. L. Kashyap, and N. Ahuja, "Decision Rules for Choice of Neighbors in Random Field Models of Images," *Comput. Gr. Image Process.* **15,** 4, 30–318 (April 1981).

R. W. Conners and C. A. Harlow, "A Theoretical Comparison of Texture Algorithms," *IEEE Trans. Pattern Anal. Mach. Intell.* **PAMI-2,** 3, 204–222 (May 1980).

D. Cooper, "Maximum Likelihood of Markov-process Blob Boundaries in Noisy Images," *IEEE Trans. Pattern Anal. Mach. Intell.* **PAMI-1,** 4, 372–384 (Oct. 1979).

L. J. Cote, *Two-Dimensional Spectral Analysis,* Mimeograph Ser. 83, Dep. Statistics, Purdue University, Lafayette, Indiana, July 1966.

I. K. Crain and R. E. Miles, "Monte Carlo Estimates of the Distribution of Random Polygons Determined by Random Lines in the Plane," *J. Stat. Comput. Simul.* **4,** 293–325 (1976).

G. R. Cross and A. K. Jain, "Markov Random Field Texture Models," in *Proceedings of the IEEE Pattern Recognition and Image Processing Conference,* Dallas, Tex., Aug. 1981.

J. E. Cutting and R. T. Millard, "Three Gradients and the Perception of Flat and Curved Surfaces," *J. Exp. Psychol.: General,* **113**(2), 198–216 (1984).

L. Davis, L. Janos, and S. Dunn, "Efficient Recovery of Shape from Texture," *IEEE Trans. Pattern Anal. Mach. Intell.,* **PAMI-5,** (5), 485–492 (Sept. 1983).

L. S. Davis, S. Johns, and J. K. Aggarwal, "Texture Analysis Using Generalized Cooccurrence Matrices," *IEEE Trans. Pattern Anal. Mach. Int.* **PAMI-1,** 3, 251–258 (July 1979).

L. S. Davis and A. Mitiche, "Edge Detection in Textures," *Comput. Gr. Image Process,* **12,** 25–39 (1980).

K. Deguchi and I. Morishita, "Texture Characterization and Texture-based Image Partitioning Using Two-dimensional Linear Estimation Techniques," in *U.S.-Japan Cooperative Science Program Seminar on Image Processing in Remote Sensing,* Washington, D.C., Nov. 1–5, 1976.

L. E. Franks, "A Model for the Random Video Process," *Bell Syst. Tech. J.* **45,** 609–630 (April 1966).

W. Freiberger and U. Grenander, *Surface Patterns in Theoretical Geography,* Rep. 41, Dept. Applied Mathematics, Brown University, Providence, Rhode Island, Sept. 1976.

B. R. Frieden, "Statistical Models for the Image Restoration Problem," *Comput. Gr. Image Process.* **12**(1), 40–59 (Jan. 1980).

K. S. Fu, "Stochastic Languages for Picture Analysis," *Comput. Gr. Image Process.* **2**(3/4), 433–453 (Dec. 1973).

K. S. Fu, "Syntactic Image Modelling Using Stochastic Tree Grammars," *Comput. Gr. Image Process.* **12,** 136–152 (Feb. 1980).

A. Gagalowicz, "Analysis of Texture Using a Stochastic Model," in *Proceedings of IAPR 4th International Joint Conference on Pattern Recognition,* Nov. 1978, pp. 541–544.

A. Gagalowicz, "A New Method for Texture Field Synthesis: Some Applications to the Study of Human Vision," *IEEE Trans. Pattern Anal. Mach. Intell.* 520–533 (Sept. 1981).

J. Gibson, *The Perception of the Visual World,* Houghton Mifflin, Boston, Mass., 1950.

E. N. Gilbert, "Random Subdivisions of Space into Crystals," *Ann. Math. Stat.* **33,** 958–972 (1962).

J. Goutsias and J. M. Mendel, "Simultaneous Optimal Segmentation and Model Estimation of Nonstationary Noisy Images," *IEEE Trans. Patt. Anal. Mach. Intell.* **PAMI-11** (9) 990–997 (1989).

B. Grunbaum and G. C. Shepard, *Tilings and Patterns,* 1982.

A. Habibi, "Two Dimensional Bayesian Estimate of Images," *Proc. IEEE* **60,** 878–883 (July 1972).

A. R. Hanson and E. M. Riseman, eds., *Computer Vision Systems,* Academic Press, New York, 1978.

R. M. Haralick, "A Texture-Context Feature Extraction Algorithm for Remotely Sensed Imagery," in *Proceedings 1971 IEEE Decision and Control Conference,* Gainesville, Fla., Dec. 1971, IEEE, New York, 1971, pp. 650–657.

R. M. Haralick, "The Table Look-up Rule," *Commun. Stat. Theor. Methods* **A5**, 12, 1163–1191 (1976a).

R. M. Haralick, "Automatic Remote Sensor Image Processing," in A. Rosenfeld, ed., *Digital Picture Analysis,* Springer, Berlin, 1976b, sect. 2.2.5, pp. 49–52.

R. M. Haralick, "Statistical and Structural Approaches to Texture," in *Proceedings 4th International Joint Conference on Pattern Recognition,* Nov. 1978, pp. 45–69.

R. M. Haralick, K. Shanmugam, and I. Dinstein, "Textural Features for Image Classification," *IEEE Trans. Syst., Man, Cybern.* **SMC-3,** 610–621 (1973).

J. Harbauch and G. Bonham-Carter, *Computer Simulation in Geology,* Wiley, New York, 1970.

J. K. Hawkins, "Textural Properties for Pattern Recognition," in B. S. Lipkin and A. Rosenfeld, eds., *Picture Processing and Psychopictorics,* Academic Press, New York, 1970, pp. 347–370.

H. Herin and H. Elliott, "Modeling and Segmentation of Noisy and Textured Images Using Gibbs Random Fields," *IEEE Trans. on Pattern Anal. and Mach. Intell.* **9**(1), 39–55 (1987).

T. S. Huang, "The Subjective Effect of Two-Dimensional Pictorial Noise," *IEEE Trans. Inform. Theory* **IT-11,** 43–53 (Jan. 1965).

C. Huijbregts, "Regionalized Variables and Quantitative Analysis of Spatial Data," in J. Davis and M. McCullagh, eds., *Display and Analysis of Spatial Data,* Wiley, New York, 1975, pp. 38–51.

B. R. Hunt, "Bayesian Methods in Nonlinear Digital Image Restoration," *IEEE Trans. Comput.* **C-26,** 219–229 (March 1977).

B. R. Hunt, "Nonstationary Statistical Image Models (and Their Application to Image Data Compression)," *Comput. Gr. Image Process.* **12,** 2, 173–186 (Feb. 1980).

B. R. Hunt and T. M. Cannon, "Nonstationary Assumptions for Gaussian Models of Images," *IEEE Trans. Syst. Man, Cybern.* **SMC-6,** 876–882 (Dec. 1976).

K. Ikeuchi, *Shape from Regular Patterns (an Example of Constraint Propagation in Vision),* MIT A.I. Memo 567, Massachusetts Institute of Technology, Cambridge, Mass., Mar. 1980.

A. K. Jain, "A Semi-Causal Model for Recursive Filtering of Two-dimensional Images," *IEEE Trans. Comput.* **C-26,** 343–350 (1977a).

A. K. Jain, "Partial Differential Equations and Finite-Difference Methods in Image Processing, Part 1: Image Representation," *J. Optimiz. Theory Appl.* **23,** 65–91 (1977b).

A. K. Jain and E. Angel, "Image Restoration, Modelling and Reduction of Dimensionality," *IEEE Trans. Comput.* **C-23,** 470–476 (May 1974).

S. N. Jayaramamurthy, "Multilevel Grammars for Generating Texture Scenes," in *Proceedings of 1979 IEEE Conference on Recognition and Image Processing,* IEEE, New York, 19779, pp. 391–398.

B. Julesz, "Visual Pattern Discrimination," *IRE Trans. Inform. Theory* **8,** 2, 84–92 (Feb. 1962).

B. Julesz, "Experiments in the Visual Perception of Texture," *Sci. Am.* **232,** 34–43 (April 1975).

B. Julesz, "Textons, and Elements of Texture Perception and Their Interactions," *Nature* (London) **290,** 91–97 (March 1981).

K. Kanatani, "Detection of Surface Orientation and Motion from Texture by a Stereological Technique," *Artif. Intell.* **23,** 213–237 (1984).

K. Kanatani and T. Chou, "Shape from Texture: General Principle," in *Proceedings of IEEE Conference on Computer Vision and Pattern Recognition,* Miami, Fla., June 1986, IEEE, New York, 1986, pp. 578–583.

R. L. Kashyap, "Random Held Models of Images," *Comput. Gr. Image Process.* **12**(3), 257–270 (March 1980).

R. L. Kashyap and K.-B. Eom, "Texture Boundary Detection Based on the Long Correlation Model," *IEEE Trans. Patt. Anal. Mach. Intell.* **PAMI-11** (1) 58–67 (1989).

J. M. Keller, S. Chen, and R. M. Crownover, "Texture Description and Segmentation through Fractal Geometry," *Computer Vision, Graphics, and Image Processing* **45**(2), 150–167 (1989).

J. R. Kender, *Shape from Texture,* Ph.D. dissertation, Carnegie-Mellon University, CMU-CS-81, Pittsburgh, Pa., November 1980.

F. R. Kretzmer, "Statistics of Television Signals," *Bell Syst. Tech. J.* **31,** 751–763 (July 1952).

S. Lakshmanan and H. Derin, "Simultaneous Parameter Estimation and Segmentation of Gibbs Random Fields Using Simulated Annealing," *IEEE Trans Patt. Anal. Mach. Intell.* **PAMI-11**(8), 799–813 (1989).

D. T. Lee, "On Finding k Nearest Neighbors in the Plane," Tech. Rep. UILU-ENG-76-2216 Coordinated Science Laboratory, University of Illinois, Urbana, Ill., May 1976.

L. H. Links and J. Biemond, "On the Nonseparability of Image Models," *IEEE Trans. Pattern Anal. Mach. Intell.* **PAMI-1,** (4) 409–411 (Oct. 1979).

M. S. Longuet-Higgins, "On the Statistical Distribution of the Heights of Sea Waves," *J. Mar. Res.* **11,** 245–266 (1952).

M. S. Longuet-Higgins, "The Statistical Analysis of a Random Moving Surface," *Phil. Trans. Roy. Soc. London* **A249,** 321–387 (Feb. 1957a).

M. S. Longuet-Higgins, "Statistical Properties of An Isotropic Random Surface," *Phil. Trans. Roy. Soc. London* **A250,** 151–171 (Oct. 1957b).

S. Y. Lu and K. S. Fu, "A Syntactic Approach to Texture Analysis," *Comput. Gr. Image Process.* **7,** 303–330 (1978).

B. H. McCormick and S. N. Jayaramamurthy, "Time Series Model for Texture Synthesis," *Int. J. Comput. Inf. Sci.* **3,** 329–343 (1974).

B. H. McCormick and S. N. Jayaramamurthy, "A Decision Theory Method for the Analysis of Texture," *Int. J. Comput. Inf. Sci.* **4,** 1–38 (1975).

B. Mandelbrot, *Fractals—Form. Chance, and Dimension,* Freeman, San Francisco, Calif., 1977.

B. B. Mandelbrot, *The Fractal Geometry of Nature,* Freeman, San Francisco, Calif., 1982.

D. M. Mark, *Topological Randomness of Geomorphic Surfaces,* Tech. Rep. 15, Dept. of Geography, Simon Fraser University, Burnaby, B.C., Canada, April 1977.

B. Matern, *Spatial Variation,* Medd Statens' Skogsforsknings Institut, Stockholm, Sweden, 1960, pp. 1–144.

B. Matern, "Stokastika Modeller for Variation in Planet (Stochastic Models for Planar Variation)," 3rd Nordic Conference on Mathematics and Statistics, Umea, Sweden, June 1969.

B. Matern, "The Analysis of Ecological Maps as Mosaics," Advanced Institute of Statistical Ecology Around the World, Pennsylvania State University, University Park, Pa., July 7, 1972.

G. Matheron, *Elements pour Une Theorie des Milieux Poreux,* Masson, Paris, 1967.

G. Matheron, "The Theory of Regionalized Variables and its Application," *Les Cahiers du Centre de Morphologie Math. de Fontainbleau* **5** (1971).

R. S. Michalski and B. H. McCormick, "Interval Generalization of Switching Theory," in *Proceedings of Third Annual Houston Conference on Computing System Science,* Houston, Tex., April 1971, pp. 213–226.

R. E. Miles, "Random Polygons Determined by Random Lines in the Plane," *Proc. Nat. Acad. Sci. USA* **52**, 901–907 (1964a).

R. E. Miles, "Random Polygons Determined by Random Lines in the Plane II," *Proc. Nat. Acad. Sci. USA* **52**, 1157–1159 (1964b).

R. E. Miles, "On the Homogeneous Planar Poisson Point Process," *Math. Biosci.* **6**, 85–127 (1970).

R. E. Miles, "A Survey of Geometrical Probability in the Plane with Emphasis on Stochastic Image Modelling," *Comput. Gr. Image Process.* **12**, 1, 1–24 (1980).

J. W. Modestino, R. W. Fries, and D. G. Daut, "Generalization of the Two-Dimensional Random Checkerboard Process," *J. Opt. Soc. Am.* **69**, 6, 897–906 (June 1979a).

J. W. Modestino, R. W. Fries, and A. L. Vickers, "Texture Discrimination Based upon an Assumed Stochastic Texture Model," Tech. Rep. 79-3, Rensselaer Polytechnic Institute, Troy, N.Y., July 1979b.

J. W. Modestino, R. W. Fries, and A. L. Vickers, "Stochastic Models Generated by Random Tessellations of the Plane," *Comput. Gr. Image Process.* **12**(1), 74–98 (Jan. 1980).

M. Moore, *The Transition Probability Function of the Occupancy Model*, Tech. Rep. 40, Ecole Polytechnique, Montreal, Canada, October 1978.

R. P. Moore, J. O. Hooper, and E. T. Hooper, "Interpretation of Microwave Radiometric Images," *Aerial Reconnaissance Systems*, vol. 79, SPIE 1976, pp. 146–153.

P. A. P. Moran, "A Gaussian Markov Process on a Square Lattice," *J. Appl. Prob.* **10**, 54–62 (1973).

J. L. Muerle, "Some Thoughts on Texture Discrimination by Computer," in B. S. Lipkin and A. Rosenfeld, eds., *Picture Processing and Psychopictorics*, Academic Press, New York, 1970, pp. 347–370.

N. E. Nahi and M. H. Jananshahi, "Image Boundary Estimation," *IEEE Trans. Comput.* **C-26**, 772–781 (Aug. 1977).

N. E. Nahi and S. Lopez-Mora, "Estimation Detection of Object Boundaries in Noisy Images," *IEEE Trans. Autom. Control* **AC-23**, 834–845 (Oct. 1978).

H. Nakatani, S. Kimura, O. Saito, and T. Kitahashi, "Extraction of Vanishing Point and its Application to Scene Analysis Based on Image Sequence," in *Proceedings of the IAPR International Conference on Pattern Recognition*, 1980, pp. 370–372.

J. K. Ord, "Estimation Methods for Models of Spatial Interaction," *J. Am. Stat. Soc.* (1975).

D. P. Panda, "Statistical Properties of Thresholded Images," *Comput. Gr. Image Process.* **8**, 334–354 (1978).

D. P. Panda and T. Dubitzki, "Statistical Analysis of Some Edge Operators," *Comput. Gr. Image Process.* **9**, 313–348 (Dec. 1979).

D. P. Panda, and A. C. Kak, "Recursive Least Squares Smoothing of Noise in Images," *IEEE Trans. Acoust. Speech, Signal Process.* **ASSP-25**, 520–524 (1977).

G. S. Patterson and S. Corrsin, "Computer Experiments on Random Walks with Both Eulerian and Langrangian Statistics," in *Dynamics of Fluids and Plasmas*, Academic Press, New York, 1966, pp. 275–307.

A. P. Pentland, Fractal-based Description of Natural Scenes, *IEEE Trans. Pattern Anal. Mach. Intell.* 661–674 (Nov. 1984).

R. J. Phillips, "Stationary Visual Texture and the Estimation of Slant Angle," *Quart. J. Psych.* **22**, 389–397 (1970).

D. K. Pickard, "A Curous Binary Lattice Process," *J. Appl. Probab.* **14**, 717–731 (1977).

E. Pielou, *Mathematical Ecology*, Wiley, New York, 1977.

W. J. Pierson, "A Unified Mathematical Theory for the Analysis, Propagation and Refraction of Storm Generated Surface Waves," Dept. of Meteorology, New York University, New York, 1952.

W. K. Pratt, "Vector Space Formulation of Two-Dimensional Signal Processing Operations," *Comput. Gr. Image Process.* **4**(1), 1–24 (March 1975).

W. K. Pratt, *Digital Image Processing*, Wiley, New York, 1978.

W. K. Pratt and O. D. Faugeras, "Development and Evaluation of Stochastic-based Visual Texture Features," in *Proceedings of the IAPR Fourth International Joint Conference on Pattern Recognition*, Nov. 1978, pp. 545–548.

W. K. Pratt, O. D. Faugeras, and A. Gagalowicz, "Visual Discrimination of Stochastic Texture Fields," *IEEE Trans. Syst. Man, Cybern.* **SMC-8**, 796–804 (1978).

J. S. Read and S. N. Jayaramamurthy, "Automatic Generation of Texture Feature Detectors," *IEEE Trans. Comput.* **C-21**, 803–812 (1972).

A. A. Requicha, "Representations for Rigid Solids: Theory, Methods, and Systems," *ACM Comput. Surv.* **12**, 4, 437–464 (Dec. 1980).

P. I. Richards, "Averages for Polygons Formed by Random Lines," *Proc. Nat. Acad. Sci. USA* **52**, 1160–1164 (1964).

B. D. Ripley, "Stochastic Geometry and the Analysis of Spatial Pattern," Ph.D. Dissertation, Churchill College, London, May 1976.

A. Rosenfeld, "A Note on Automatic Detection of Texture Gradients," *IEEE Trans. Comput.*, **C-24**, 988–991 (Oct. 1975).

A. Rosenfeld, *Picture Languages*, Academic Press, New York, 1979.

A. Rosenfeld, "Image Pattern Recognition," Tech. Rep. TR-850, Computer Science Center, University of Maryland, College Park, Md., Jan. 1980.

A. Rosenfeld and A. C. Kak, *Digital Picture Processing*, Academic Press, New York, 1976.

A. Rosenfeld and B. S. Lipkin, "Texture Synthesis," in B. S. Lipkin and A. Rosenfeld, eds., *Picture Processing and Psychopictorics*, Academic Press, New York, 1970, pp. 309–322.

A. Rosenfeld and D. L. Milgram, *Array Automata and Array Grammars 2*, Tech. Rep. 171, Dept. of Computer Science, University of Maryland, College Park, 1971.

A. Rosenfeld and E. Troy, *Visual Texture Analysis*, Tech. Rep. 70-116, Dept. of Computer Science, University of Maryland, College Park, Md., June 1970.

R. R. Rosinski, "On the Ambiguity of Visual Stimulation: A Reply to Eriksson," *Perception Psychophys.*, **16**(2), 259–263, 1974.

R. Rosinski and N. Levine, "Texture Gradient Effectiveness in the Perception of Surface Slant," *J. Exp. Child Psychol.*, **22**, 261–271 (1976).

L. A. Santalo, *Encyclopedia of Mathematics and its Applications: Integral Geometry and Geometric Probability*, Vol. 1, Addison-Wesley, Reading, Mass., 1976.

R. L. Scheaffer, "An Approximate Variance for Line Intersection Counts," (Part 3) *J. Microsc.* **103**, 343–349 (April 1975a).

R. L. Scheaffer, *Variance Approximations for Transects: the Poisson Line Model*, Tech. Rep. 86, Dept. of Statistics, University of Florida, Florida, Gainesville, Fla., Jan. 1975.

B. J. Schachter, "Model-based Texture Measures," *IEEE Pattern Anal. Mach. Intell.* **PAMI-2**(2), 169–171 (March 1980a).

B. J. Schachter, "Long Crested Wave Models for Gaussian Fields," *Comput. Gr. Image Process.* **12**, 187–201 (Feb. 1980b).

B. J. Schachter and N. Ahuja, "Random Pattern Generation Processes," *Comput. Gr. Image Process.*, **10**, 96–114 (1978).

B. J. Schachter, L. S. Davis, and A. Rosenfeld, "Random Mosaic Models for Textures," *IEEE Trans. Syst. Man, Cybern.* **SMC-8,** 694–702 (1978).

J. Serra, "The Boolean Model and Random Sets," *Comput. Gr. Image Process.* **12**(2), 99–126 (Feb. 1980).

J. Serra and G. Verchery, "Mathematical Morphology Applied to Fibre Composite Materials," *Film Sci. Technol.* **6,** 141–158 (1973).

J. F. Silverman and D. B. Cooper, "Bayesian Clustering for Unsupervised Estimation of Surface and Texture Models" *IEEE Trans. Patt. Anal. Mach. Intell.* **PAMI-10**(4), 482–495 (1988).

H. R. Solomon, "Distribution of the Measure of a Random Two-dimensional Set," *Ann. Math. Stat.* **24,** 650–656 (1953).

D. J. Strauss, "Clustering on Colored Lattices," *J. Appl. Probab.* **14,** 135–143 (1977).

P. Switzer, "A Random Set Process in the Plane with a Markovian Property," *Ann. Math. Stat.* **36**(6), 1859–1863 (Dec. 1965).

P. Switzer, "Reconstructing Patterns from Sample Data," *Ann. Math. Stat.* **38,** 138–154 (1967).

P. Switzer, *Mapping a Geographically Correlated Environment,* Tech. Rep. 145, Dept. of Statistics, Stanford University, Stanford, Calif., 1969.

W. B. Thompson, "Texture Boundary Analysis," *IEEE Trans. Comp.* **C-26,** 272–276 (1977).

J. T. Tou and Y. S. Chang, "An Approach to Texture Pattern Analysis and Recognition," in *Proceedings of 1976 IEEE Conference on Decision and Control,* Dec. 1976, pp. 398–403.

J. T. Tou, D. B. Kao, and Y. S. Chang, "Pictorial Texture Analysis and Synthesis," in *Proceedings of IAPR 3rd Joint Conference on Pattern Recognition,* Coronado, Calif., 1976.

H. J. Trussel and R. P. Kruger, "Comments on 'Nonstationary' Assumption for Gaussian Models in Images," *IEEE Trans. Syst., Man, Cybern.* **SMC-8,** 579–582 (1978).

M. Tuceryan and A. K. Jain, "Texture Segmentation Using Voronoi Polygons" *IEEE Trans. Patt. Anal. Mach. Intell.* **PAMI-12**(2), 211–215 (1990).

D. Vickers, "Perceptual Economy and the Impression of Visual Depth," *Perception and Psychophys.* **10**(1), 23–27 (1971).

A. B. Vistelius and A. U. Fass, "The Mode of Alternation of Strata in Certain Sedimentary Rock Sections," Academy Science USSR, Earth Science Section, vol. 164, 1965, pp. 629–632.

T. R. Welberry and G. H. Miller, "An Approximation to a Two-dimensional Binary Process," *J. Appl. Probab.* **14,** 862–868 (1977).

J. S. Weszka, C. R. Dyer, and A. Rosenfeld, "A Comparison of Texture Measures for Terrain Classification," *IEEE Trans. Syst., Man, Cybern.* **SMC-6,** 269–285 (April 1976).

E. H. T. Whitten and M. F. Dacey, "On the Significance of Certain Markov Features of Granite Textures," *J. Petrol.* **16**(2), 429–453 (1975).

P. Whittle, "On Stationary Processes in the Plane," *Biometrika* **41,** 434–449 (1954).

R. Whittle, "Stochastic Processes in Several Dimensions," *Bull. Inst. Int. Stat.* **40,** 974–994 (1963).

A. P. Witkin, "Recovering Surface Shape and Orientation from Texture," *Artif. Intell.* **17,** 17–45 (1981).

E. Wong, "Two-dimensional Random Fields and Representations of Images," *SIAM J. Appl. Math.* **16,** 756–770 (1968).

J. W. Woods, "Two-dimensional Discrete Markovian Fields," *IEEE Trans. Inf. Theory* **IT-18,** 232–240 (1972).

S. Zucker, "Toward a Model of Texture," *Comput. Gr. Image Process.* **5,** 190–202 (1976).

General References

H. C. Andrews, "Semiannual Technical Report," Image Processing Institute, University of Southern California, Los Angeles, Calif., Sept. 1976, secs. 2.4, 27–34.

A. Baer, C. Eastman, and M. Henrion, "A Survey of Geometric Modelling," Rep. 66, Institute of Physical Planning, Carnegie-Mellon University, Pittsburgh, Pa., March 1977.

R. Bajcsy and L. Liberman, "Texture Gradient as a Depth Cue," *Computer Graphics and Image Processing,* **5,** 52–67 (1976).

D. H. Ballard, C. M. Brown, and J. A. Feldman, "An Approach to Knowledge Directed Image Analysis," Tech. Rep. 21, Dept. of Computer Science University of Rochester, Rochester, N.Y., 1977.

H. G. Barrow and J. M. Tenenbaum, "Recovering Intrinsic Scene Characteristics from Images," in A. R. Hanson and E. M. Riseman, eds., *Computer Vision Systems,* Academic Press, New York, 1978, pp. 3–26.

M. S. Bartlett, "A Further Note on Nearest Neighbor Models," *J.R. Stat. Soc.* **A 131,** 579–580 (1968).

M. S. Bartlett, "Physical Nearest-Neighbor Models and Nonlinear Time Series," *J. Appl. Prob.* **8,** 222–232 (1977).

R. A. Brooks, R. Greineir, and T. O. Binford, "A Model Based Vision Systems," in L. S. Bauman, ed., *Proceedings of the Image Understanding Workshop,* Cambridge, Mass., May 1978; Scientific Applications, Arlington, Va.

P. C. Chen and T. Pavlidis, "Image Segmentation as an Estimation Problem." *Comput. Gr. Image Process.* **12,** 153–172 (1980).

A. D. Cliff and J. K. Ord, *Spatial Autocorrelations,* Pion Press, London, 1973.

S. Dunn, L. Davis, and H. Hakalathi, "Experiments in Recovering Surface Orientation from Texture," Computer Science Technical Report CS-TR-1399, University of Maryland, College Park, May 1984.

R. M. Haralick and W. F. Bryant, "Documentation of Procedures for Texture/Spatial Pattern Recognition Techniques," Tech. Rep. 278–1, Remote Sensing Laboratory, University of Kansas Center for Research, Lawrence, Kans., April 1976.

M. Hassner and J. Sklansky, "Markov Random Field Models of Digitized," *Pattern Recognition,* 538–540 (Nov. 1978).

R. L. Henderson, "Geometric Reference Preparation Interim Report two: the Broken Segment Matcher," Tech. Rep. RADC-TR-79-80, Control Data Corp., Minneapolis, Minn. (for Rome Air Development Center, Griffiss AFB, N.Y.), April 1979.

L. W. Hepple, "The Impact of Stochastic Process Theory upon Spatial Analysis in Human Geography," in *Progress in Geography,* vol. 5, Arnould, London, 1974, pp. 91–142.

B. K. P. Horn, "Understanding Image Intensities," *Artif. Intell.* **8,** 201–231 (1977).

K. I. Laws, "Textured Image Segmentation," Tech. Rep. 940, Image Processing Institute, University of Southern California, Los Angeles, Jan. 1980.

D. Marr, "Representing Visual Information," in *Lectures on Mathematics in the Life Sciences,* vol. 10, American Mathematics Society, 1978.

D. Marr and T. Poggio, "Cooperative Computation for Stereo Display," AI Memo 364, Artificial Intelligence Laboratory, Massachusetts Institute of Technology, Cambridge, Mass., June 1976.

R. Mead, "Models for Interplant Competition in Irregularly Distributed Populations," in *Statistical Ecology 2,* Pennsylvania State University Press, University Park, 1971, pp. 13–22.

R. Miller and J. Kahn, *Statistical Analysis in the Geological Sciences,* Wiley, New York, 1962.

O. R. Mitchell, C. R. Myers, and W. Boyne, "A Max-min Measure for Image Texture Analysis," *IEEE Trans. Comput.* **C-26,** 408–414 (1977).

M. Moore, "Non-Stationary Random Set Processes with Application to Pattern Reconstruction," *J. Appl. Prob.* **10,** 857–863 (1973).

M. Moore, "Anisotropically Random Mosaics," *J. Appl. Prob.* **11,** 374–376 (1974).

C. L. Nelson, R. L. Henderson, D. J. Panton, C. B. Grosch, and W. J. Miller, "Geometric Surface Shell Studies," Rep. F30602-79-C-008-001, Control Data Corporation, Minneapolis, Minn. (for Rome Air Development Center, Griffiss AFB, N.Y.), Aug. 1979.

R. B. Ohlander, "Analysis of Natural Scenes," Ph.D. dissertation, Carnegie Mellon University, Dept. of Computer Science, Pittsburgh, Penn., April 1975.

A. Rosenfeld, S. W. Zucker, and R. A. Hummel, "Scene Labelling by Relaxation Operations," *IEEE Trans. Syst. Man, Cybern.* **SMC-6,** 420–433 (1976).

N. L. Schult and F. Wenthen, "Advanced Weapons System Simulation II Study," Tech. Rep., General Electric Co., Daytona Beach, Fla., 1980.

A. D. Stathacopoulos and H. F. Gilmore, "Selection of Mathematical Models of Target Acquisition by Electro-Optical Systems," Naval Weapons Center Publication 5928, Science and Technology Co., Santa Barbara, Calif., June 1977.

K. Stevens, "The Information Content of Texture Gradients," *Biol. Cyber.* **42,** 95–105 (1981).

P. Switzer, *Geometrical Measures for the Smoothness of Random Functions,* Tech. Rep. 62, Dept. of Statistics, Stanford University, Stanford, Calif., 1974.

W. H. Tsai and K. S. Fu, "Image Segmentation and Recognition by Texture Discrimination: A Syntactic Approach," in *Proceedings of the Fourth International Joint Conference on Pattern Recognition,* Kyoto, Japan, Nov. 1978, pp. 560–564.

S. W. Zucker, A. Rosenfeld, and L. S. Davis, "Picture Segmentation by Texture Discrimination," *IEEE Trans. Comput.* **C-24,** 1228–1233 (1975).

NARENDRA AHUJA
University of Illinois at Urbana

THESAURUS

The term *thesaurus,* meaning "a treasury," may refer to collections of all kinds, but was early used to refer to collections of words. Its modern uses stem from Roget's (1852) *Thesaurus of English Words and Phrases.* These uses all treat a thesaurus as a classification of linguistically expressed, and especially lexical, information, which is the essential property of Roget's *Thesaurus.* But they interpret and exploit this in different ways. The three modern uses of a thesaurus are (1) as a vocabulary reference, familiar from printed forms; (2) as an information retrieval (IR) device; and (3) as a natural language processing (NLP) resource. This article focuses on uses 2 and 3, considering their common and distinct elements within the context of linguistic information processing as a proper concern of AI; but it starts with an account of Roget's *Thesaurus,* because this was a historically important stimulus to proposals for IR and NLP and also illustrates key features of a thesaurus exceptionally well.

FOUNDATION

Roget's *Thesaurus*

The *Thesaurus,* as Roget says in his introduction, was a classification of concepts: "the words and phrases of the language are here classed . . . strictly according to their *signification.*" The basic concepts, or heads of classification, approximately 1000 in number, were organized in contrasting pairs, eg, *Expansion* and *Contraction,* and were grouped hierarchically in the structure given in the table of contents. Thus *Expansion* and *Contraction* were grouped under *Dimensions,* which was in turn combined with *Form* and *Motion* under *Space,* and so forth, within a single all-embracing hierarchical scheme. Each concept had a hierarchy naming label, representing the head, and subsumed a class of words having similar meanings or topic relationships justifying their being placed together under the same head, eg, *augmentation, swelling,* and *knob* under *Expansion.* Each class was subdivided by the major parts of speech, and within each such syntactic category there were progressively finer subdivisions signaled by paragraphing and other punctuation, down to the finest classes consisting of close synonyms, subsequently called rows (Sparck Jones, 1986). Cross-references from one head to another, indeed between specific within-head locations, reflected the fact that concepts of the kind represented by the heads could not really be viewed as exclusive. Thus, for example, *knob* leads from *Expansion* to *Rotundity.*

A word could appear in as many heads as were justified by its meanings or senses (regardless of whether these distinctions were etymologically motivated or not). The display of the thesaurus information in the form of words grouped under heads, with the heads ordered according to the table of contents, was complemented by an alphabetical listing linking each word to the set of heads in which it occurred.

All of the essential properties of a thesaurus as a *semantic classification* appeared in Roget's *Thesaurus.* Each class can be seen in two complementary ways: as showing what words are similar because they stand for a common, autonomously defined notion taken as represented by the head name or, alternatively, as defining a common notion through their recognized similarity of meaning. This duality is most clearly seen in the basic heads, but also applies, although in the weaker form of shared elements of meaning, to the superclasses that combine lower-level classes under given labels; it clearly applies in principle to the subclasses as well, because these could be labeled although they are not in fact. Thus the *Thesaurus* at the same time distinguishes word senses through their thesaurus class allocations and defines, or at least characterizes, these senses in terms of the explicitly or implicitly given class concepts. However, as the head names are just ambiguous natural language words, it is better to view class concepts as implicitly defined via similarity than as explicitly defined by reference to an independent concept, because this is arbitrarily labeled and inaccessible. At the same time, describing the members of a class as similar in meaning is sometimes too strong, because other types of associative relation figure, which are more properly viewed as determining topic classes; but the basic notion of a thesaurus as founded in similarity stands.

Roget offered his *Thesaurus* as a practical aid to thinking and writing, but at the same time related this function to serious scientific need by referring to the idea of a universal character, ie, universal language, which was a significant feature of seventeenth-century scientific thought, notably among members of the Royal Society, of which Roget was later secretary. A universal character would supply a comprehensive set of distinct, basic concepts which, when applied with an appropriate combinatory grammar, would constitute at least a transparent and unambiguous, interlingual means of describing scientific phenomena or further, as envisaged by Leibniz, provide an apparatus for scientific reasoning (Sparck Jones, 1972, 1986; Knowlson, 1975; Slaughter, 1982; Large, 1985). This view of a thesaurus as a component of an interlingua has also played an important role in modern uses of a thesaurus.

Reference Thesauri

Roget thus regarded the classificatory structure of his *Thesaurus*, and particularly that supplied by the table of contents, as a central element of the whole. Many of his successors, however, failed to grasp or appreciate his intentions and, viewing the *Thesaurus* primarily as a synonym display, thought its value would be enhanced by reorganizing its body alphabetically and by providing additional entries reflecting a stricter interpretation of synonymy (Lewis, 1961). The table of contents was jettisoned as unhelpful and the index as unnecessary. There are now many different works all labeled thesaurus or even Roget's thesaurus. Dutch (1962) is a legitimate descendant, but others are very different. The range shows at once how variously the basic idea of concept characterization through classes can be interpreted and how robust this idea is. Thus while there may be no explicit relations between or ordering on classes, these are implicit in the presence of common words in different classes.

As noted earlier, the innovative modern uses of a thesaurus have been in information retrieval (IR) and in natural language processing (NLP). The Cambridge Language Research Unit (CLRU) recognized its common generic function for these purposes in the 1950s (Masterman and co-workers, 1959) and sought to give this a more substantive interpretation within a shared formal model for the semantic information processing involved in each, and in a well-founded common procedure for constructing a thesaurus. But since the 1960s there has been a divergence, and although the thesaurus has flourished in IR, it has languished in NLP. The published general-purpose reference thesauri just mentioned have not contributed to either since the first laboratory proof of concept done with the printed Roget. However, there appears to be a revival of interest now in the use of thesauri for NLP purposes, and these ordinary thesauri may, in particular, have a part to play within the general move to exploit machine-readable dictionaries to provide lexical resources for NLP.

THE THESAURUS IN IR

Development

The thesaurus as an indexing and, more important, as a retrieval device was a response to the postwar challenge presented by the rapid growth of the specialized scientific nonbook literature (Foskett, 1980; Roberts, 1984). The librarian's two traditional tools, *subject heading lists* and *subject classifications* (Library of Congress, 1986; British Standards Institute, 1985), were essentially aimed at fixed-topic characterizations and fixed-topic affiliations and were implemented in schemes suited to single-unit thumbnail descriptions for whole books. They appeared both too rigid and too coarse to meet the new needs for flexible and refined description. A thesaurus was seen as providing a set of irreducible unit *descriptors* that could be freely combined to form complex concept or topic descriptions. The constituents of a subject heading or class specification were *precoordinated,* ie, were related in a permanently fixed way. The constituents of a document description formed with a thesaurus would, in contrast, be *postcoordinated,* ie, would be freely combined in *ad hoc* document and request descriptions. Postcoordinate indexing in particular allowed arbitrary topic specifications at search time, as combinations of thesaurus descriptors, or *terms,* in requests could match subsets of those originally assigned to documents in a very flexible way. Conventional subject matching required exact request-document matching for the whole descriptions involved, or at least aimed at controlling partial matching in a systematic way, by restricting it to previously defined relationships such as those explicitly embodied in any classificatory links or implicitly permitted through the syntactic modification of a heading (Lancaster, 1972; Foskett, 1980).

It was recognized that to function effectively, thesaurus descriptors must be derived from, or at least be strongly motivated by, the particular scientific literature for which they were to be used. The literature was regarded not as an incidental expression of the autonomous underlying real state of the world, but as itself embodying that state as defined by published scientific knowledge. The set of terms for a thesaurus would thus be obtained by an examination of the literature of a field. However the crucial point at which the thesaurus approach to indexing and retrieval differed from a simple *uniterm* one (Lancaster, 1972) using text keywords, was in the provision of a lead-in vocabulary. Although the different publications in a scientific literature may share common basic concepts, these are not always conveyed in the same words. As Luhn (1957) noted, descriptors would be represented by a group of similar or closely related words, as in a conventional thesaurus like Roget's. The presence of any of these words in a document or request would justify the assignment of the corresponding descriptor. The thesaurus terms, viewed as descriptive labels, thus had an essential normalizing purpose, namely to ensure conceptual matching regardless of the surface variety or ambiguity of natural language (Lancaster, 1972).

A retrieval thesaurus is thus at once an indexing device designed to facilitate flexible topic characterization, and a searching device suited to mechanization through full or partial matching on term specifications ranging from simple term lists to more complex Boolean expressions.

It was soon found, however, that the view of thesaurus terms as a band of brothers on an equal footing was too simple, especially for a large document collection. It was necessary to allow for hierarchical relations between terms, although these were primarily local and were not seen as a means for integrating all the terms into a single unified scheme. These relations are primarily supports for searching. Although indexing and searching are complementary, the way thesauri are used to specify topics by postcoordination rather than precoordination places more emphasis on their retrieval role. Thus while it is a general rule to index with the most specific terms available, the more general ones ensure matching when used in requests.

Characteristics

A modern thesaurus (Foskett, 1980) will, therefore, consist of a term vocabulary supported by a prescriptive apparatus and amplified by a relational one. The terms themselves may be words or phrases, but will usually have a normal form, eg, singular rather than plural. The prescriptive apparatus includes scope notes (SN) indicating the meanings of terms, and leads from entry expressions to their appropriate indexing terms of the form x USE y, eg, "teenager USE adolescent" (perhaps with reciprocal y USED FOR x). The relational structure is given by links that for a given term may be to broader terms (BT), narrower terms (NT), and related terms (RT), for example, "boy BT adolescent, man," "child NT infant," "child RT pediatrics, pupil." The first two of these relations cover set relationships, the latter, in practice, a miscellany including eg, part–whole, cause–effect, action–instrument. The NT–BT relations may be exploited automatically in searching, but RTs are more likely to be offered as options to the searcher.

Current thesauri are typically large, elaborate, institutionalized structures intended for use by professional indexers and searchers and managed by large organizations, eg, the *INIS Thesaurus* (IAEA, 1987) and *Medical Subject Headings* (NLM, 1990), which despite its name is a thesaurus. Both of these have tens of thousands of descriptors. These thesauri have been constructed and applied manually, and manuals and guidelines have been developed for this purpose (UNESCO, 1973; NLIAC, 1990; Aitchison and Gilchrist, 1987); they are easier to revise than traditional classifications, but a great deal of effort goes into keeping them up to date as science and technology develop. Within the broad framework just described there are many variants, and a great deal of attention has been paid to presentation to ensure that the thesaurus content and structure is clearly and fully shown within, for example, the confines of a printed book. Automation has made maintenance, revision and use much easier, but their sheer size and intrinsic complexity makes these thesauri difficult for end users to understand and exploit.

Multilingual thesauri are very important: as thesaurus descriptors are motivated by the subject matter of a field they are in principle interlingual, so all the terms can have their associated sets of different language equivalents. Multilingual thesauri may be hard to manage in printed form, but automation makes selective operation within one language, or combined operations across languages, much easier.

Machine Indexing

Because thesauri are usually supplied with entry words or phrases, it is natural to consider automatic term assignment as a means of reducing document indexing effort: entry words occurring in the full document text or its abstract would justify indexing with their associated terms. However the available entry sets may be too limited. An entry word occurring in a document need not imply its term is legitimate, because the word may be used in another sense, or if the term is legitimate, imply that it is important. It is better to start afresh by taking the entire document vocabulary and seeing how words in it are associated with term assignments in documents that have already been indexed. If reliable correlations can be established between words, or word sets, and terms, these can be used to justify future assignment. These text items can thus be taken as entry keywords for the thesaurus terms. Even if manual checking is desirable, assignment proposals can make indexing less effort; but automatic assignment has also been implemented.

Thesaurus Construction

It is clear that in constructing a thesaurus, great care must be taken in establishing both terms and their relations. In Foskett's (1980) view, while the index descriptions of documents have many affiliations through their components, the component terms should be exclusive and univocal and should participate in only one hierarchical relation. In his view the best way of obtaining a proper classificatory structure for a thesaurus is to ground it in a facet analysis of the subject field, so individual terms are all associated with specific facets, eg, process and product, action and instrument. Aitchison's (1970) "thesaurofacet" illustrates the advantages of this approach in obtaining a well-organized structure.

It is always difficult to control individual interpretations of language in manual thesaurus construction. However, as the automatic assignment strategies just mentioned suggest, and as the definition of a retrieval thesaurus implies, a thesaurus is essentially derivative, and it should be possible to identify its terms by considering the way natural language words behave in the texts of a subject literature. Thesaurus terms are class concepts representing, or represented by, text words, which are alternative expressions or indicators of the underlying concept. In the strongest case these classes will be synonym sets like those of a conventional thesaurus. This suggests that, although the members of a retrieval thesaurus class may be viewed as a set of entry words leading to a preferred common label, the proper view is that the members of a class are directly intersubstitutable.

Automatic Techniques

The essential strategy for deriving thesaurus classes from information about the way words behave in text is then as follows. Behavior is defined in terms of occurrences and cooccurrences. Thus two words may be said to behave in the same way if they cooccur frequently with a common partner, for example a and b behave in the same way if they each cooccur with p. This implies they are strongly related, in the limiting case as synonyms in complementary distribution. The resemblance between a and b is strengthened if they also cooccur frequently with, say, q and r as well, and equally other words, say c and d may also cooccur with p, q, and r. All of a, b, c, and d may thus be treated, because their behavior is similar, as forming a class. For retrieval purposes they may then be taken as intersubstitutable so that if, for example, a document uses a and a request b, this can be taken as a match just as if both were indexed explicitly with the class concept X via its label "X". The concept label "X" is thus simply a convenience: the concept itself is implicit in, or emergent from, the word class. Taking this line further, moreover, suggests that as a and p tend to cooccur, they too can be used intersubstitutably for retrieval purposes, although the relation between them is syntagmatic rather than paradigmatic: habitual collocates are equally legitimate representatives of the underlying concept.

Thesaurus construction from cooccurrence information is formalized, and is thus potentially mechanized, through the application of statistical distribution measures. In general these are used first to define the similarity between pairs of words and then the similarities required among a set of words for these to form a class, but there are many specific ways of doing this. For example, the similarity Sij between a pair of words ij may be defined as $Cij/Oi + Oj - Cij$, where Cij is the sum of i and j's cooccurrences and Oi and Oj are the sums of their respective occurrences. An acceptable class of words may then, for instance, be defined as a set of words with high internal and low external similarities, or at least stronger internal than external similarities, which can be established by minimizing the cohesion across the boundary between a class and the rest of the objects. Thus if Saa and Sab are, respectively, the sums of similarities between the members of a putative class a and between the members and the nonmembers, and Na is the number of objects in a, it is possible to minimize the cohesion function (Sparck Jones, 1971b)

$$(Sab/Saa) \cdot ((Na^2 - Na)/Saa)$$

The precise nature of a thesaurus is determined on the one hand by the formal definitions on which it is based (Rijsbergen, 1979), and also by the algorithms actually used to find classes because, for example, it is almost always impracticable to seek all legitimate classes by testing all subsets of the universe of objects. It is determined on the other hand by the nature of the units being grouped, and by that of the text context acting as the frame within which occurrences and cooccurrences are counted.

Thus in relation to the definitions used, similarity as just defined will give a high value to directly rather than indirectly cooccurring words. But the class definition just given is an undemanding one that does not require that every member is strongly related to every other, and so can pick up indirectly cooccurring words; and it is also a definition that allows words to appear in different classes. These relatively loose and overlapping classes, reflecting text variety as well as text regularity, again appear suited to retrieval, which must be tolerant. In relation to the data elements, these may be word forms, stems, or multiword strings, and they may include all or only some of the available vocabulary: stems are often used in practice (to increase matching) and very frequent words are excluded (to inhibit matching). The occurrence context may be explicitly syntactically or simply locationally defined, and narrowly or broadly, eg, as adjective(s) plus noun or as an entire abstract. Contexts are usually defined locationally, but not just because automatic parsers are lacking, and also broadly, to obtain enough statistically reliable data.

Thus taking method and data definitions together, the view in initial work in automatic classification was that what was required were topic classes that would be much broader than synonym sets and could include both paradigmatically and syntagmatically related words. They would thus encompass both the BT-NT and the RT relationships of manual thesauri, reflecting the view that the primary function of a thesaurus is to promote recall, the retrieval of relevant documents. Sense selection and, more generally, discrimination in matching designed to promote precision, by excluding nonrelevant documents, would be achieved by postcoordination.

Retrieval Performance

Thesaurus construction was an early application of general-purpose automatic classification methods, and research in the area was concerned with many matters of detail within the broad framework just outlined (Rijsbergen, 1979; Sparck Jones, 1971a). Unfortunately, the experiments done, although they served to emphasize the complexity of IR, never established significant performance gains for automatic classification (Sparck Jones, 1981; Salton, 1975). It was possible to show that some specific approaches worked better than others, notably those confining classes to strongly related keywords, and those findings have motivated strategies for enhancing simple keyword retrieval by, eg, working with statistically related term pairs as compound terms (Salton and McGill, 1983). But if automatic classification could not be shown to be of material value, there was equally no hard evidence in favor of manually constructed and applied thesauri as opposed simply to postcoordinate keyword or phrase matching (Cleverdon, 1977; Salton, 1986). Although some investigations have been made, notably by Cleverdon (1977), operations on the scale of major IR services have never been rigorously evaluated through properly controlled comparisons, designed to establish the relative merits of different indexing languages irrespective of the many other factors involved in indexing and searching. Thus it is not clear, for example, whether a conventional thesaurus makes other factors more or less critical, especially as collection scale increases and in the context of on-line searching. The use of a retrieval thesaurus as an indexing device thus remains an act of faith, and while modern technology may make displays of conventional, or unconventional associative, thesaurus structures available for search formulation, how valuable this would be still needs to be seriously investigated.

THE THESAURUS IN NLP

Semantic Processing

Thesaurus classes in IR define generic indexing descriptors, and the thesaurus has been envisaged as having a similar function in NLP, that of providing *semantic primitives*. This connection was explicitly recognized in early work on the use of a thesaurus for NLP, and specifically for machine translation (MT). Early workers on MT, attempting general text translation, say of research papers, were immediately faced with the problem of word sense identification and, wherever direct links between input senses and their output equivalents were not, or could not be, provided, with the problem of output word (sense) selection as well. A thesaurus was seen as providing a set of general-purpose, domain-independent *semantic primitives* allowing the specification, or at least an indication, of the essential semantic concepts expressed by, or relating to, a text, and hence allowing sense determination.

The initial simple model proposed by the CLRU treated thesaurus classes (and for experimental purposes those in Roget's *Thesaurus*) as characterizing, and hence distinguishing, the senses of words, and it treated text as necessarily semantically repetitive, because it was only by the repetition of the generic concepts represented by the heads of classification that the relevant specific senses of the words in a text could be identified. Because natural language words normally have multiple senses, context (in this case established via head repetition) served to achieve correct lexical determination in text interpretation. An analogous model would work for text generation: the words shared by the heads selected for an input text would be the right output lexical items. The model in particular allowed for the fact that concept repetition is needed for sense determination, not only because lexical repetition cannot be guaranteed even for the straightforward case, because there may be synonymic variation, but because it cannot be expected for syntactically different items.

Some rudimentary MT experiments applying these ideas were successfully performed (Masterman and coworkers, 1957, 1986). These exploited Roget's *Thesaurus* supplemented for other languages, and thus used the *Thesaurus* as an interlingua. More particularly, though concept repetitions to resolve ambiguity could not always be found when searching was limited to Roget's main head set, the hierarchical table of contents could be used to extend searching: shared higher level, broad concepts could be found. Roget's *Thesaurus* was thus functioning not only as an interlingua but as a terminological knowledge base defined by class inclusion, with the subclasses within heads available if necessary as defining narrower concepts. This approach to the semantic operations required for NLP was seductively simple, and could also, it was claimed, be given a formal underpinning by lattice theory: a lattice model would represent concepts defined by equivalence classes of word senses as nodes, and semantic processes manipulating these would be implemented as lattice operations. Moreover, as with the IR thesaurus, an NLP thesaurus could in principle be built up using distributional information, thus guaranteeing objectivity for the language in question; and as with an IR thesaurus, it would be possible to form a (not necessarily exclusive) hierarchy by grouping classes.

Thesaurus Formation

Indeed in practice this derivation, while notionally directly based on a corpus of running text, could be more conveniently and realistically based directly on existing conventional dictionaries. These could be viewed as indirectly based on text, but as condensing the relevant information and providing it either in the already processed form represented by the synonym and quasi-synonym definitions that are frequently encountered, or in the readily exploitable form, suggesting related terms and supplying testing contexts, represented by descriptive definitions and their amplifying examples. Existing dictionaries, assuming they were well founded, could thus be taken as giving a helpful manual starting boost to automatic classification. The work reported in Sparck Jones (1964, 1986) represented a serious attempt to place automatic thesaurus construction for NLP purposes on a firm foundation, bootstrapping classification from minimal information about contextually subsitutable word senses. The actual experiments carried out took lexical data obtained from a dictionary and constituting rows as a starting point and then applied the clustering techniques already used for IR thesaurus construction. These tests were limited in scope, but successfully obtained Roget-style classes.

Crucial Issues

The basic model for thesaurus use in semantic processing underlying this early research was nevertheless far too simple. This became apparent when more serious tests were attempted. The model assumed a one-to-one correspondence between word senses and heads, but with heads representing broad concepts this might not be discriminating enough on senses; at the same time it assumed that at the head level, the single concept fully characterized whatever the dependent senses had in common. This raises the fundamental question as to whether a thesaurus, and hence the set of semantic primitives it embodies, is a descriptive, indeed definitional, device or is just a selective processing device. The information required for the latter may not be the same as, and may be less than, that required for the former. The problem is very clearly seen when, in an attempt to ensure repetition, more general concepts are used, because with increasing generalization the differences between word senses are reduced.

But this is not satisfactory from the processing, as well as from the descriptive, point of view: the variety of text contexts in which words are actually used places them in very different lights and correspondingly implies different selectional perspectives, so effective processing seems to require the richer characterization that the definitional view also seems to need. However it is, in turn, evident that it is difficult to capture the meaning of a word sense simply by giving an unordered list of relevant concepts. This is most clearly seen with verbs when their meaning is unpacked, because this invokes *case relationships*. It then follows that the notion of sense characterization by a simple set of concept labels must be replaced by that of characterization by a syntactically structured expression in a primitive language. This approach, which may be viewed as a fully developed application for NLP of the uses of defining basic vocabularies and entry formats made in some conventional dictionaries like LDOCE (Procter, 1978), has been advocated and investigated by Wilks (1975, 1977) and Schank (1975) in his Conceptual Dependency theory.

The second major problem area is that conceptual repetition is too crude and that it is, therefore, necessary to use semantic patterns of the kind exemplified in minimal form by conventional selection restrictions or embodied in semantic grammars. This has immediate implications for the definition of the context for semantic processing. The original simple model did not use syntactic structure to constrain matching, but the more complex requirements represented by patterns, notably those focused on verbs, imply the use of syntactic structure constraints. But these cannot be too rigid, and more generally, as Wilks's notion of preference recognizes, semantic pattern matching cannot be made absolute, or the novelty that is as characteristic of discourse as its regularity will ensure they do not work (Wilks, 1975).

The issues raised by initial work with thesauri are thus fundamental to NLP: they concern the nature of text meaning representations, and the nature of the knowledge bases required to obtain and exploit these. If semantic primitives have a key role in both, what is the status of these primitives: are they concept labels in some autonomous mental language, or are they necessarily natural language objects (Wierzbicka, 1972; Wilks, 1977; Jackendoff, 1983)? Again, how far do the functions of a thesaurus in discourse interpretation extend beyond sense selection to, say, anaphor resolution, or in response to discourse, as in question answering, to the support of inference?

THESAURUS PROPERTIES

The essential feature of a thesaurus is that it is a classification. It may thus be distinguished from a lexicon and a dictionary: from a semantic point of view a thesaurus organizes terms whereas a dictionary defines them (Scott, 1988), although it is evident that the relationship between these two is an intimate one. A thesaurus as a semantic classification deals with word meanings, which refer to the world, but it does this from a primarily linguistic point of view as a *terminological knowledge* base, complementing the direct description of the world embodied in the *assertional knowledge* base (Brachman and co-workers, 1985). A thesaurus thus characterizes word senses through their relations with others.

The elements of the thesaurus are words (or rather word senses), which characterize one another relationally at different levels of granularity, but without any difference of kind in the levels (Wilks, 1978). Semantic primitives, although they may be thought of as undefined ground elements serving as the decompositional basis for the whole structure (Mel'cuk and Polguère, 1987), are more properly thought of as words that *de facto* play a dominant role in the characterization of others, as with the basic vocabulary of a dictionary like LDOCE (Procter, 1978). But insofar as a thesaurus is a taxonomy based on lexical similarity, saying that all its classes define semantic primitives implies both that the thesaurus has a rich classificatory structure and that this can be interpreted in the sophisticated way required: it cannot simply be assumed that grouping finer classes into coarser ones will suffice to give decompositional generic primitives such as *cause*. The alternative is to identify words with a specific classificatory behavior, for example, ones with many senses figuring in many classes, as primitives, eg, *do*; this maintains the view of primitives as natural language objects but allows them a special character, reflecting a perceived distinctive functional role.

A thesaurus classification based only on similarity relations has structure; but a thesaurus may have a more complex structure. Conventional manually constructed IR thesauri, although dominated by set relationships, include others as well, like part–whole or action–instrument, and in particular make these relatively explicit where they were only implicit in the experimental automatically constructed IR thesauri. They also embody a much wider range of relations than the synonymy-based thesauri used in early NLP research. The NLP model proposed by Sparck Jones (1986) was strictly grounded in synonymy, which was essentially broadened only to likeness. Roget's *Thesaurus* and other conventional printed thesauri include both subclasses and hence class members related to one another by other relations (for example, agency), but these other relations are not treated systematically or fully, and these thesauri are dominated by sense synonymy and similarity. At the same time the hierarchical relationship is rather loosely interpreted, with set relations much more obvious in some cases (eg, as when *scabbard* and *knapsack* appear under *Receptacle*) than in others (eg, as when *Receptacle* appears under *Existence in space*). In contrast, in the application of the grammar rules for lexical definition used by Wilks (1977) and also those used by Schank (1975), other relations are explicitly involved in the form of cases and qualifiers, but there is no significant hierarchical classification of the primitives. Wilks (1978), however, recognizes the need for hierarchy and allows for multiple levels of specificity by combining Roget's levels of classification with structured definitions.

It is thus clear that a thesaurus as a serious terminological knowledge base will have to embody a case relational structure as well as a categorial taxonomic one, ie, allow for relational as well as categorial primitives. These case relationships should cover both the types of facet relationship found in conventional IR thesauri and also, insofar as these are different, linguistic case or predicate-argument type relations. These syntagmatic relations together with the paradigmatic hierarchical ones should allow for fine-grained predication constraints. Thus, for example, it is possible to envisage an associative semantic network structure encompassing frames and embedding similarity relationships. But the base must be implemented using a well-defined formalism allowing discriminating inheritance with, ideally, a proper semantics. A thesaurus with a structure like this can then meet the requirements imposed by its dual role in supporting semantic discourse processing, in sense and structure disambiguation, and in providing information about word meanings that can contribute to the further use of a text meaning representation. The scale and richness of both printed and IR thesauri suggests, however, that this computational thesaurus will not be easy to provide. In particular, it will not be easy to ensure that the thesaurus has the required openness to the lexical variety and subtlety of natural language and to ensure that it does not make inappropriate ontological commitments.

CURRENT STATE

Thesauri are standard features of operational information and especially document retrieval systems. They figure in every form, embodying varying degrees of vocabulary control and merging, on the one hand, with subject headings and, on the other, into subject classification. They remain primarily manual indexing and searching devices. They are in fact substantial instances of terminological knowledge bases, although their underlying semantics may not be fully developed, formally expressed, or explicitly indicated in a manner that would allow direct machine use: much is left to the human user's ability to interpret the natural language expressions they contain.

Some beginnings have been made, however, on applying approaches relying on NLP and AI techniques to the design and implementation of this kind of thesaurus, particularly for the purposes of text-based IR. An AI approach to knowledge representation using frames has been (manually) applied to the construction of a medical thesaurus intended to be used in conjunction with NLP applied to request and document text (Evans, 1987); and Fox and co-workers (1988) have exploited an existing machine-readable dictionary to build a thesaurus based on a well-defined semantic network formalism. This was tested with conventional indexing, but could in principle also be used to serve more sophisticated request and document text processing. The CYC work (Guha and Lenat, 1990) also has thesaural elements within its more comprehensive scope.

In recent and current NLP work, the role claimed for the thesaurus is typically filled by some combination of selection restrictions and a *sort,* ie, set, hierarchy, often of a limited and/or domain-specific kind. However more challenging applications (and particularly those involving unrestricted, large-scale text processing) have led to a new interest in the type of linguistic resource represented by thesauri. This interest has also been stimulated by the revival of MT research, which may also involve wide-ranging text material; by the growth of interest in large-scale text skimming; and, from a rather different direction, by the need to improve transportability and reduce startup costs in implementing application systems, such as database front ends, for individual domains.

In all of these cases, the concern is with broad-ranging general-purpose semantic resources and, because these are difficult and expensive to develop, with the use of existing lexical resources such as conventional dictionaries, on which a great deal of work has already been done, as starting points. This is one element in the recent growth of research on exploiting machine-readable dictionaries (Boguraev and Briscoe, 1989; Evens, 1989). Some of this work is aimed at building terminological knowledge bases with the varied relational structure represented by IR thesauri, but with a well-founded and fully explicit semantics, and some is restricted to identifying simpler taxonomic and similarity relationships. Some involves parsing, and some simply statistical operations (Fox and co-workers, 1988; Alshawi, 1989; Wilks and co-workers, 1989). Thesauric information of the narrower synonymic kind has also been seen as a necessary tool to underpin and extend dictionary analysis (Byrd and co-workers, 1987). At the same time, proposals for exploiting corpora have been made, for example, in sophisticated analysis to generate a complex base (Anick and Pustejovsky, 1990) or, by applying statistical measures to identify semantic associations, to provide an objective underpinning for lexicon development (Church and Hanks, 1990). This statistical work has not, however, so far progressed from the use of pairwise similarity measures to the full-scale automatic grouping attempted in earlier IR research.

Much of this work is based on ideas about thesauri that are not new; but it can exploit NLP techniques for text parsing and AI techniques for knowledge representation that are now available. It can also take advantage of machine resources for heavy data processing, which did not exist when these ideas were first put forward. There is, however, a manifest need for more work on applying automatic classification methods that already exist to this field and on developing relevant new methods. It is also the case that significant advances in NLP are required before detailed specifications for broad-ranging or general-purpose thesauri can be provided, because these depend, in turn, on detailed specifications for their modes of use which have themselves to be provided, and which can only be operationally established.

BIBLIOGRAPHY

J. Aitchison, "The Thesaurofacet," *J. of Documentation* **26,** 187–202 (1970).

J. Aitchison and A. Gilchrist, *Thesaurus Construction: A Practical Manual,* 2nd ed., Aslib, London, 1987.

H. Alshawi, "Analysing the Dictionary Definitions," in Boguraev and Briscoe, 1989.

P. Anick and J. Pustejovsky, "An Application of Lexical Semantics to Knowledge Acquisition from Corpora," in *COLING-90: Proceedings of the Thirteenth International Conference on Computational Linguistics,* 1990, pp. 7–12.

B. Boguraev and E. Briscoe, eds., *Computational Lexicography for Natural Language Processing,* Longman, Harlow, Essex, UK, 1989.

R. J. Brachman, R. E. Fikes, and H. J. Levesque, "KRYPTON: A Functional Approach to Knowledge Representation," in R. J. Brachman and H. J. Levesque, eds., *Readings in Knowledge Representation,* Morgan-Kaufmann, San Mateo, Calif., 1985.

British Standards Institute, *Universal Decimal Classification,* FID **571,** British Standards Institute, London, 1985.

R. J. Byrd and co-workers, "Tools and Methods for Computational Linguistics," *Comput. Ling.* **13,** 219–240 (1987).

K. W. Church and P. Hanks, "Word Association Norms, Mutual Information, and Lexicography," *Comput. Ling.* **16,** 22–29 (1990).

C. W. Cleverdon, *A Computer Evaluation of Searching by Controlled Language and Natural Language in an Experimental NASA Data Base,* Report ESA 1/**432,** European Space Agency, Frascati, Italy, 1977.

R. A. Dutch, ed., *Roget's Thesaurus of English Words and Phrases,* Longman, London, 1962.

D. A. Evans, *Final Report on the MEDSORT-II Project: Developing and Managing Medical Thesauri,* Report CMU-LCL-**87-3,** Carnegie-Mellon University, Pittsburgh, Pa., 1987.

M. Evens, "Computer-Readable Dictionaries," in M. E. Williams, ed., *Annual Review of Information Science and Technology,* Vol. 24, Elsevier Science Publishing Co., Inc., New York, 1989, pp. 85–117.

D. J. Foskett, "Thesaurus," in A. Kent, H. Lancour, and J. E. Daily, eds., *Encyclopedia of Library and Information Science,* Vol. 30, Marcel Dekker, New York, 1980.

E. A. Fox and co-workers, "Building a Large Thesaurus for Information Retrieval," in *Proceedings of the Second Conference on Applied Natural Language Processing,* Association for Computational Linguistics, 1988, pp. 101–108.

R. V. Guha and D. B. Lenat, *Building Large Knowledge Based Systems,* Addison-Wesley Publishing Co., Inc., Reading, Mass., 1990.

International Atomic Energy Agency, *INIS: Thesaurus,* International Atomic Energy Agency, Vienna, Austria, 1987.

R. Jackendoff, *Semantics and Cognition,* MIT Press, Cambridge, Mass., 1983.

J. Knowlson, *Universal Language Schemes in England and France, 1600–1800,* University of Toronto Press, Toronto, 1975.

F. W. Lancaster, *Vocabulary Control for Information Retrieval,* Information Resources Press, Washington, D.C., 1972.

A. Large, *The Artificial Language Movement,* Blackwell, Oxford, UK, 1985.

Library of Congress, *Subject Headings,* 10th ed, Library of Congress, Washington, D.C., 1986.

N. Lewis, ed., *The New Pocket Roget's Thesaurus in Dictionary Form,* Washington Square Press, New York, 1961.

H. P. Luhn, "A Statistical Approach to Mechanised Encoding and Searching of Literary Information," *IBM J. Res. Develop.* **1,** 309–317 (1957).

M. Masterman, R. M. Needham, and K. Sparck Jones, "The Analogy between Mechanical Translation and Library Retrieval," in *Proceedings of the International Conference on Scientific Information,* National Academy of Sciences, Washington, D.C., 1959, pp. 917–935.

M. Masterman and co-workers, *Agricola Incurvo Terram Dimovit Aratro,* 1957, K. Sparck Jones, ed., Computer Laboratory, University of Cambridge, Cambridge, UK, 1986.

I. Mel'cuk and A. Polguère, "A Formal Lexicon in Meaning-Text Theory (Or How to Do Lexica with Words)," *Comput. Ling.* **13,** 261–275 (1987).

National Library and Information Associations Council, *Guidelines for Thesaurus Structure, Construction, and Use,* American National Standards Institute, New York, 1990.

National Library of Medicine, *Medical Subject Headings, 1991,* 3 vols., National Library of Medicine, Bethesda, Md., 1990.

P. Procter, ed., *Longman Dictionary of Contemporary English,* Longman, Harlow, UK, 1978.

C. J. van Rijsbergen, *Information Retrieval,* 2nd ed., Butterworths, London, 1979.

N. Roberts, "The Prehistory of the Information Retrieval Thesaurus," *J. Document.* **40,** 271–285 (1984).

P. M. Roget, *A Thesaurus of English Words and Phrases,* Longman, London, 1852.

G. Salton, *Dynamic Information and Library Processing,* Prentice-Hall, Inc., Englewood Cliffs N.J., 1975.

G. Salton, "Another Look at Automatic Text Retrieval Systems," *Commun. ACM* **19,** 648–656 (1986).

G. Salton and M. J. McGill, *Introduction to Modern Information Retrieval,* McGraw-Hill Book Co., Inc., New York, 1983.

R. C. Schank, *Conceptual Information Processing,* North-Holland, Amsterdam, The Netherlands, 1975.

D. S. Scott, "Capturing Knowledge with Data Structures," in R. A. Meersman and A. C. Sernadas, eds., *Data and Knowledge (DS-2),* North-Holland, Amsterdam, The Netherlands, 1988.

M. M. Slaughter, *Universal Languages and Scientific Taxonomy,* Cambridge University Press, Cambridge, UK, 1982.

K. Sparck Jones, *Automatic Keyword Classification for Information Retrieval,* Butterworths, London, 1971a.

K. Sparck Jones, "The Theory of Clumps," in A. Kent and H. Lancour, eds., *Encyclopedia of Library and Information Science,* Vol. 5, Marcel Dekker, New York, 1971b.

K. Sparck Jones, "Some Thesauric History," *Aslib Proc.* **24,** 408–411 (1972).

K. Sparck Jones, ed., *Information Retrieval Experiment,* Butterworths, London, 1981.

K. Sparck Jones, *Synonymy and Semantic Classification,* (1964), Edinburgh University Press, Edinburgh, UK, 1986.

UNESCO, *UNISIST Guidelines for the Establishment and Development of Monologual Thesauri,* SC/WS/555, UNESCO, Paris, 1973.

A. Wierzbicka, *Semantic Primitives,* Athenaeum Verlag, Frankfurt, 1972.

Y. A. Wilks, "An Intelligent Analyser and Understander of English," *Commun. ACM* **18,** 264–274 (1975).

Y. A. Wilks, "Good and Bad Arguments about Semantic Primitives," *Commun. Cogn.* **10,** 181–221 (1977).

Y. A. Wilks, "Making Preferences More Active," *Artif. Intell.* 11, 197–223 (1978).

Y. A. Wilks and co-workers, "A Tractable Machine Dictionary as a Resource for Computational Semantics," in Boguraev and Briscoe, 1989.

KAREN SPARCK JONES
University of Cambridge

TRUTH MAINTENANCE SYSTEMS

Most computer programs constructed by researchers in artificial intelligence (AI) maintain a model of their environment, which is updated to reflect the perceived changes in the environment. This model is typically stored in a knowledge base that contains propositions about the environment (represented in some formal language, eg, first-order logic or a semantic network), and the program draws inferences from the information in the knowledge base. The set of propositions in the knowledge base under consideration at a given instant of time is called the *beliefs* of the program, that is, the set of propositions in which the program believes. New beliefs may be added to the knowledge base either through observation (propositions that are added to the knowledge and are originated outside the system) or through inference using the beliefs in the knowledge base (Figure 1). New beliefs are always added to the knowledge base.

Programs that follow this model have to face the belief revision problem, ie, the problem of changing their beliefs when some unexpected condition arises. This revision may have to be done because new observations lead to conflicts with the beliefs in the knowledge base or because new beliefs originated during inference show that some of the beliefs in the knowledge base are not plausible or are mutually inconsistent.

The study of a system with defeasible conclusions is somewhat recent in AI (eg, Ginsberg, 1987) and has drawn a considerable interest. The research carried out in this area has followed two different but complementary lines:

1. The study of logical systems in which some of the conclusions drawn can be invalidated in face of future evidence, the so-called nonmonotonic logics.
2. The study of the aspects necessary to incorporate in a computer program in order to behave nonmonotonically. These systems are called truth maintenance systems, reason maintenance systems, or belief revision systems (this article uses the first designation).

In nonmonotonic logics, additional information (ie, additional premises) entails the computation of a new theory, that is, the computation of the consequences of the new set of premises. The use of this approach in an AI program would correspond to the removal from the knowledge base of *all* derived beliefs and the start of the inference from scratch. This approach is not desirable because there are certainly many conclusions from the first set of premises that are still derivable from the second set. Instead, we would like to have a mechanism through which the *only* beliefs that are removed are those that are no longer derivable. Truth maintenance systems (TMSs) are computer systems that allow for this behavior. Although there are different kinds of TMSs they all have the following aspects in common: They keep the consistency of a set of beliefs; they only keep beliefs as long as there are reasons for it; they explain the reasons for holding a belief; they identify contradictions; they identify culprits for contradictions; and they avoid the reappearance of known contradictions.

For a TMS, the word *belief* is taken to denote *justified belief*: a proposition is believed either because the TMS was told so—this corresponds to an observation (these beliefs are called hypotheses or premises)—or because it depends on believed propositions.

An essential aspect associated with TMSs corresponds to recording dependencies between beliefs. If it would be impossible to distinguish beliefs that depend upon a premise and beliefs that do not, then any belief may be questioned when the premise is removed; if it is not possible to identify the premises that underlie a contradiction, then every premise in the knowledge base may be questioned when a contradiction occurs. Depending on the process used to record dependencies between beliefs, we can distinguish two main types of TMSs: (1) *justification-based systems*, in which each belief is associated with those beliefs that were immediately used in its derivation; and (2) *assumption-based systems*, in which each belief is associated with the premises that underlie its derivation.

A TMS extends the operations that can be performed upon the knowledge base. Typically, these systems do not have deductive capabilities [with the exception of the systems of Martins and Shapiro (1983, 1988) and McAllester (1978)], they receive information from the program that works with the application domain (the problem solver), and they supply the problem solver with information about which propositions should be believed.

The architecture of a system that uses a TMS is shown in Figure 2. This figure corresponds to a more detailed version of the architecture of Figure 1. Inference is performed by the problem solver, which receives from the TMS information about which propositions are believed and supplies the TMS with the results of the inference along with the reasons that justify the inference. Observations are also supplied to the TMS with appropriate justifications; the TMS is responsible for the revision of the beliefs in the knowledge base. Typically, a TMS explores

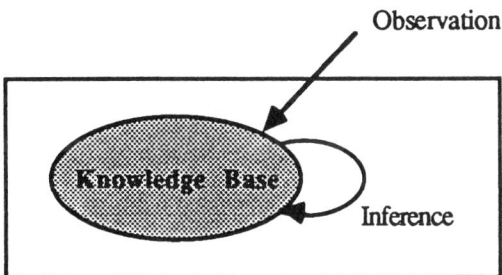

Figure 1. Typical model of an AI system.

alternatives, makes choices, explores the consequences of its choices, and compares results obtained when using different choices. If, during this process, a contradiction is detected, the TMS will revise the knowledge base, changing its beliefs in order to get rid of the contradiction.

JUSTIFICATION-BASED SYSTEMS

A justification-based TMS (JTMS) historically corresponds to the first kind of TMS developed—the result of the work of Jon Doyle (1979), the first researcher to separate the TMS from the problem solver.

In a JTMS each belief is associated with two sets of beliefs: (1) the set that should be believed for the belief to be held and (2) the set that should not be believed for the belief to be held. Let us suppose that the problem solver believes that "by default birds fly," "penguins do not fly," and "Tweety is a bird." Using auto-epistemic logic (Moore, 1985), these propositions would be represented as

$$\forall x\ ((\text{Bird}(x) \land \sim B \sim \text{Flies}(x)) \to \text{Flies}(x))$$

$$\forall x\ (\text{Penguin}(x) \to \sim \text{Flies}(x))$$

$$\text{Bird (Tweety)}$$

With this information the problem solver could be led to believe that Tweety flies and justify this belief with the belief that Tweety is a bird and the lack of belief in that Tweety does not fly. Figure 3 shows the justification of the belief that Tweety flies using the notation introduced by Goodwin (1982), which will be discussed in detail later. In this figure the word IN next to a proposition means that the proposition is believed and the word OUT next to a proposition means that the proposition is not believed.

Besides the justification for derived beliefs, as is the case for the justification to the belief that Tweety flies, there are justifications for propositions that are the result of observations (or that are told by the problem solver as basic beliefs), as is the case of "Tweety is a bird." These are called *premises*. Premises are always believed and are represented as shown in Figure 3. We should also notice that (in Figure 3) there is no justification to believe that Tweety does not fly and so this is not believed.

If we now add the premise that Tweety is a penguin, which enables the derivation that Tweety does not fly, the

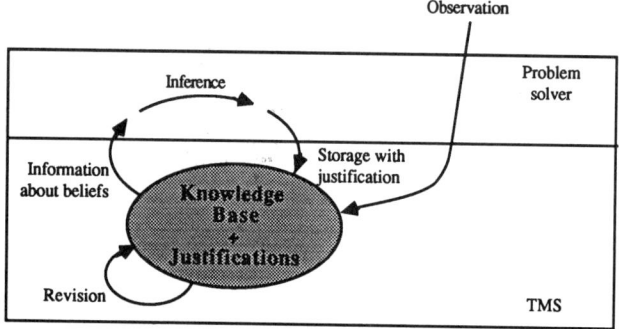

Figure 2. Architecture of a TMS-based problem solver.

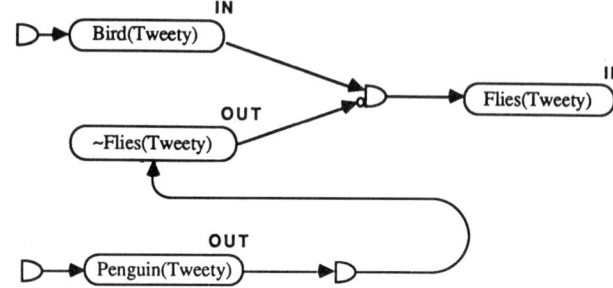

Figure 3. Justifications to believe that Tweety flies.

belief that Tweety flies is no longer held, and the justifications for this are as shown in Figure 4.

We should note the lack of representation (in Figures 3 and 4) of the beliefs $\forall x\ ((\text{Bird}(x) \land \sim B \sim \text{Flies}(x)) \to \text{Flies}(x))$ and $\forall x(\text{Penguin}(x) \to \sim \text{Flies}(x))$. In fact, a TMS only considers atomic propositions and their negation; all propositions using connectives or quantifiers ($\land, \lor, \to, \forall$) are only used by the problem solver and cannot be disbelieved [with the exception of the systems of McAllester (1978) and Martins and Shapiro (1983, 1988), in which the TMS and the problem solver are merged into a single component].

Since a TMS is only concerned about dependencies among beliefs, ignoring their contents, it is usual to replace those beliefs by identifiers (typically of the form $n_1, n_2, \ldots$), which are associated with objects called *nodes*. There is a one-to-one function T that translates between beliefs and nodes. Using the translation,

$$T\ (\text{Bird}(\text{Tweety})) = n_1$$
$$T\ (\sim\text{Flies}(\text{Tweety})) = n_2$$
$$T\ (\text{Flies}(\text{Tweety})) = n_3$$
$$T\ (\text{Penguin}(\text{Tweety})) = n_4$$

the dependencies of Figure 4 will be represented as shown in Figure 5.

In summary, a TMS works with nodes and justifications. Nodes stand for beliefs, and justifications support belief in nodes by relating them to other nodes. Associated with nodes there are labels that indicate what is the belief status of the associated node. It should be noticed that the existence of labels is due to computational efficiency since their values can always be computed given the current nodes and justifications.

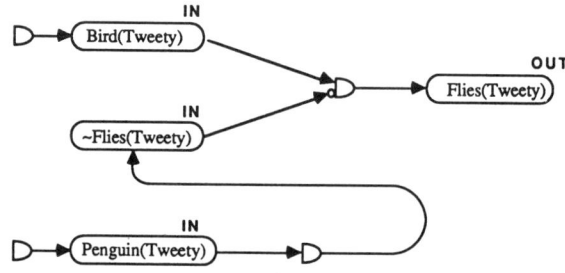

Figure 4. Justification not to believe that Tweety flies.

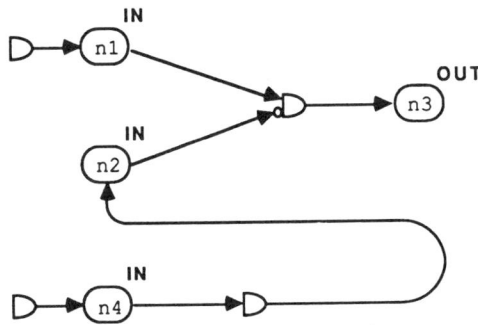

Figure 5. Dependency network, supporting the disbelief in node n_3.

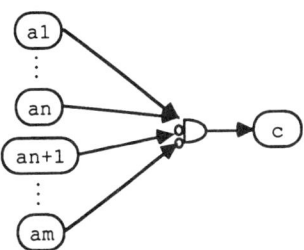

Figure 7. Representation of the justifications for c.

Dependency Networks

One of the goals of the work in TMSs is the specification of the dependencies among beliefs and, based on such specification, the computation of which beliefs do hold and which beliefs do not hold. One way of doing this is to use a formal system called dependency networks, which is described in this section. Dependency networks were first proposed by Doyle (1983) and are nicely presented in Reinfrank (1989).

Let $\mathcal{L}$ be the language used to define the identifiers for nodes. A *dependency network* is a triple $[N, C, J]$ in which $N \subset \mathcal{L}$ represents the nodes in the dependency network, $C \subset \mathcal{L}$ represents a distinguished set of nodes, the contradiction nodes, and $J \subset 2^{\mathcal{L}} \times 2^{\mathcal{L}} \times \mathcal{L}$ is a set of justifications of the form $\langle A_M | A_{NM} \Rightarrow c \rangle$ in which $A_M \subset \mathcal{L}, A_{NM} \subset \mathcal{L}$, and $c \in \mathcal{L}$ (A_M is called the set of monotonic antecedents. A_{NM} is called the set of nonmonotonic antecedents, and c is the conclusion). The justification $\langle A_M | A_{NM} \Rightarrow c \rangle$ supports the belief in c if all nodes in A_M are believed and no node in A_{NM} is believed. (We say that $\langle A_M | A_{NM} \Rightarrow c \rangle$ justifies node c). Justifications divide nodes into two categories:

1. *Premises*, which correspond to nodes for which there is a justification with no antecedents. Given the dependency network $[N, C, J]$ and a node $p \in N$, we say that p is a premise if $\langle \emptyset | \emptyset \Rightarrow p \rangle \in J$. Premises are always believed and are represented as shown in Figure 6.
2. *Conclusions*, which correspond to nodes that have a justification with at least one nonempty antecedent. In Figure 7 we represent the justification $\langle \{a_1 \cdots a_n\} | \{a_{n+1} \cdots a_m\} \Rightarrow c \rangle$. Node c is believed if nodes $a_1 \cdots a_n$ are all believed and none of the nodes $a_{n+1} \cdots a_m$ is believed.

Interaction Between JTMS and the Problem Solver

JTMS communicates with the problem solver, receiving information about new nodes and new justifications and supplying the problem solver with information about which nodes should be believed, taking into account the existing justifications (see Figure 2). The operations that can be performed by JTMS can be divided into three categories:

1. *Inspection operations:* These operations correspond to an inspection of the dependency network and are triggered by questions from the problem solver. These questions are of four types:
   a. *Should I believe in node n?* This question is answered by retrieving the label associated with node n.
   b. *Why should I believe in node n?* This question is answered by supplying the nodes that should be believed and the nodes that should not be believed so that node n is believed.
   c. *What assumptions underlie node n?* This question is answered by supplying all the premises that should be believed in order for node n to be believed.
   d. *Do I believe in a contradiction?* This question is answered by retrieving the labels associated with the contradiction nodes.
2. *Modification operations:* These operations modify the dependency network. They are originated by information supplied by the problem solver. This information can be of five types:
   a. *Add node n.* This adds a new node, with identifier n and without any justification, to the dependency network. As a result, $[N, C, J]$ is transformed into $[N \cup \{n\}, C, J]$.
   b. *Add premise p.* This adds the premise with identifier p to the dependency network. If node p already exists, it is justified as a premise. As a result, $[N, C, J]$ is transformed into $[N \cup \{p\}, C, J \cup \{\langle \emptyset | \emptyset \Rightarrow p \rangle\}]$.
   c. *Add contradiction p.* This adds the node with identifier p to the dependency network, marking it as a contradiction node. As a result, $[N, C, J]$ is transformed into $[N \cup \{p\}, C \cup \{p\}, J]$.
   d. *Justify node c based in the belief in nodes $a_1 \cdots a_n$ and in the lack of belief in nodes $a_{n+1} \cdots a_m$.* The effect of this operation is to transform $[N, C, J]$ into $[N \cup \{a_1 \cdots a_n, a_{n+1} \cdots a_m, c\}, C, J \cup \{\langle \{a_1 \cdots a_n\} | \{a_{n+1} \cdots a_m\} \Rightarrow c \rangle\}]$.
   e. *Remove premise p.* The effect of this is the removal of the justification of p as a premise. As a result, $[N, C, J]$ is transformed into $[N, C, J - \{\langle \emptyset | \emptyset \Rightarrow p \rangle\}]$.

Figure 6. Representation of the premise p.

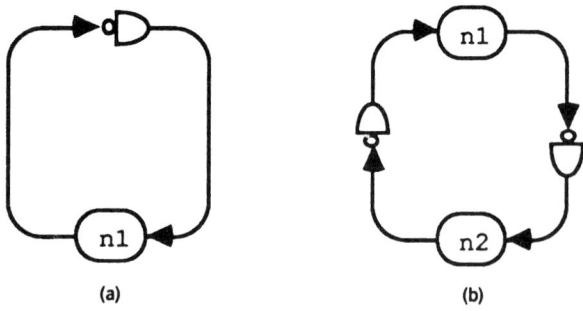

Figure 8. Odd and even loops.

3. *Updating operations:* These operations are executed whenever a change is performed upon the dependency network. Their goal is to recompute the labels associated with the nodes in the network in such a way that they are consistent with the existing justifications.

Computation of Labels for Nodes

Given the dependency network $[N, C, J]$, we want to determine sets $B \subset N$ in which it is reasonable to believe given the justifications J. The computation of reasonable beliefs is somewhat similar to the computation of an extension of a nonmonotonic logic and cannot be formalized in a constructive way. The requirements imposed upon a reasonable set of beliefs are as follows: (1) It is *well founded*, ie, the beliefs are either premises or are supported by a justification whose monotonic antecedents are all believed (using well-founded arguments) and whose nonmonotonic antecedents are all disbelieved. (2) It is closed, ie, the consequences of a justification whose monotonic antecedents are all believed and whose nonmonotonic antecedents are all disbelieved is believed. (3) It is not contradictory, that is, $B \cap C = \varnothing$.

In the process of computation of reasonable beliefs there are two kinds of loops involving justifications that are of particular importance. The *odd loop* (Figure 8a) corresponds to a belief that cannot be decided whether or not it holds; the *even loop* (Figure 8b) corresponds to two possible states of belief: if node n_1 is not believed, then node n_2 is believed, and if node n_2 is not believed, then node n_1 is believed.

Algorithms for computing labels for nodes were developed by Doyle (1979), Goodwin (1982), who developed a labeling algorithm that detects odd loops and always terminates, which is not the case with Doyle's algorithm, and Petrie (1986), who modified Doyle's labeling algorithm by eliminating the necessity of a certain type of justifications, the CP justifications.

Given the dependency network, $[N, C, J]$, labeling algorithms correspond to the computation of the values of the total function $L: N \Rightarrow \{\text{IN}, \text{OUT}\}$. It should be noticed that a labeling may not be unique, as illustrated by the dependency network of Figure 9. In this figure we show, next to each node, its two possible labels. One labeling corresponds to all labels with white background, and the other labeling corresponds to all labels with shadowed background.

Removal of Contradictions

One of the goals of a TMS is to maintain consistent sets of beliefs. Whenever the TMS discovers that its beliefs are inconsistent, ie, that $B \cap C \neq \varnothing$, it should take action in order to restore consistency. This action can be of two kinds: (1) If one choice made during the labeling of an even loop can be changed so that the inconsistency is removed, then this choice is changed and the dependency network is unchanged, or (2) if the inconsistency does not depend on choices made during the labeling process, then the dependency network has to be changed in order to remove the inconsistency. This change can either correspond to the removal of a premise or to the addition of a justification to a node that is not believed.

Suppose that we have the dependency network $[\{n_1, n_2, n_3, n_4, n_5\}, \{n_5\}, \{\langle\{\ \}|\{n_2\} \Rightarrow n_1\rangle, \langle\{\ \}|\{n_4\} \Rightarrow n_3\rangle, \langle\{n_1, n_3\}|\{\ \} \Rightarrow n_5\rangle\}]$. This dependency network and its only labeling are represented in Figure 10. According to this labeling, the nodes believed are n_1, n_3, and n_5, which include the (only) contradictory node of this network, n_5.

In order to obtain a consistent set of beliefs we should label node n_5 as OUT. This can only be achieved if one of n_1 or n_3 is labeled OUT, which, again can only be done if we label one of the nodes n_2 or n_4 as IN. Suppose that we decide to label n_4 IN (the decision of which node to label IN is taken outside the TMS; see, eg, the article on belief revision). We can only label this node in if we can provide

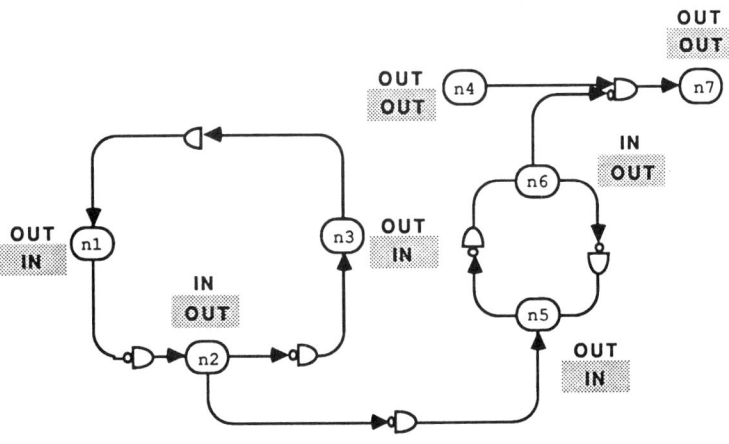

Figure 9. Two possible labelings for nodes.

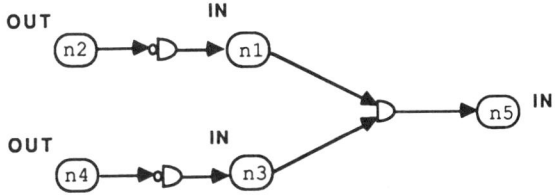

Figure 10. A contradiction is detected.

a justification for it. This is done by creating a new node, called a "nogood," that justifies the belief in n_4 based on the fact that n_1 is IN and n_5 is OUT (see Figure 11). Often more than one iteration, and the addition of a nogood, are needed in order to reach a network with a consistent set of beliefs.

Further details on the identification of possible culprits for contradictions and the removal of contradiction can be found in Stallman and Sussman (1977) which describes dependency-directed backtracking, and in Doyle (1979).

ASSUMPTION-BASED SYSTEMS

An assumption-based TMS (ATMS) associates nodes with the premises underlying their derivation. In these systems the labels of nodes are no longer IN or OUT but rather the sets of premises underlying their derivation. The term assumption-based was introduced by de Kleer (1984, 1986), although similar ideas had been investigated earlier by Martins and Shapiro (1983).

In this section we present a simplified version of de Kleer's ATMS—de Kleer considers a distinction between premises that are nodes that hold universally and assumptions made by the problem solver and that can be retracted. Since they both play a similar role in ATMS concerning the computations of the labels for the nodes that depend upon them, we will make no further distinction between them.

The big advantage of ATMS over JTMS stems from the additional flexibility it provides in dealing with multiple possible states of affairs. In fact, by labeling nodes with the sets of premises under which they hold, we no longer have a single state of belief (as is the case in JTMS, whose state of belief contains all nodes labeled IN) but rather a number of possible states that equals the cardinality of the power set of the premises introduced. This allows a comparison of the results obtained under different choices (ie, different premises), the existence of alternative solutions to a problem, the detection of the possible culprits for a contradiction, and the recovery from contradictions. The disadvantages of ATMS over JTMS are the additional difficulty involved in representing justifications with non-monotonic antecedents [most versions of the ATMS do not allow for nonmonotonic justifications; for a solution to this problem see Dressler (1988) and Cravo and Martins (1991)] and the control over the behavior of the problem solver [see de Kleer and Williams (1986), Dressler (1990), and Forbus and de Kleer (1988)].

Interaction between the ATMS and the Problem Solver

The communication between the ATMS and the problem solver is basically similar to the one described for JTMS except that with ATMS we must keep in mind that we have no longer a single state of belief. This interaction uses the following operations:

1. Inspection operations
   a. *Should I believe in node n, given the premises p_1, . . . , p_n?* This question is answered by retrieving the label associated with node n and checking whether there is in this label a set containing $\{p_1, \ldots, p_n\}$.
   b. *Why should I believe in node n?* This question is answered in the same way by JTMS and ATMS.
   c. *What assumptions underlie node n?* This question is answered by supplying the label associated with node n.
   d. *Should I believe in a contradiction given the premises $p_1, \ldots, p_n$?* This question is answered by retrieving the labels associated with the contradiction nodes and checking whether there is a label that contains $\{p_1, \ldots, p_n\}$.
2. Modification operations
   a. *Add node n.* Similar to JTMS.
   b. *Add premise p.* Similar to JTMS.
   c. *Add contradiction p.* Similar to JTMS.
   d. *Justify node c based on the belief in nodes $a_1 \ldots a_n$* (note the lack of nonmonotonic antecedents). This transforms $[N, C, J]$ into $[N \cup \{a_1 \cdots a_n, c\}, C, J \cup \{\{\{a_1 \cdots a_n\} \Rightarrow c\}\}]$.
   e. *Remove premise p.* Similar to JTMS.
3. Updating operations. These operations are executed whenever a modification operation is performed upon the dependency network. Their goal is to recompute the labels associated with the nodes in the network that are affected by the operation.

Computation of Labels for Nodes

The goal in computing ATMS labels is to find minimal sets of premises that underlie the derivation of each node.

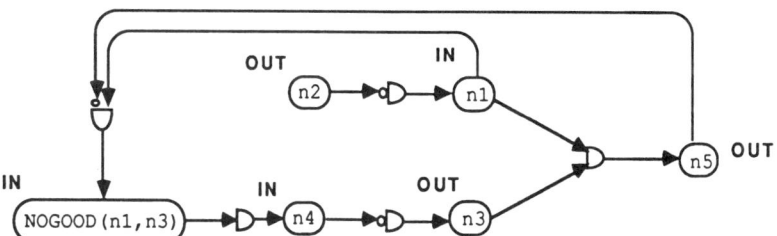

Figure 11. The contradiction is removed.

This computation is done by propagating and combining labels, starting with the labels of the premises. The premise $\langle\{\} \Rightarrow p\rangle$ is labeled with $\{\{p\}\}$. In Figure 12 we show the ATMS labels for the dependency network $[\{n_1, n_2, n_3, n_4, n_5, n_6, n_7\}, \{\}, \{\langle\{\} \Rightarrow n_1\rangle, \langle\{\} \Rightarrow n_2\rangle, \langle\{\} \Rightarrow n_4\rangle, \langle\{\} \Rightarrow n_5\rangle, \langle\{n_1, n_2\} \Rightarrow n_3\rangle, \langle\{n_3\} \Rightarrow n_7\rangle, \langle\{n_4\} \Rightarrow n_7\rangle, \langle\{n_4, n_5\} \Rightarrow n_6\rangle, \langle\{n_6\} \Rightarrow n_7\rangle\}]$. Algorithms for computing ATMS labels can be found in de Kleer (1986) and Reinfrank (1989).

The power set lattice of the premises provides a good way to visualize the space of possible combinations of premises. Figure 13 shows this lattice for the dependency network of Figure 12. The edges between sets of premises represent subset-superset relations. For example, node n_6 of Figure 12 will be believed under all sets of premises that, in the lattice, are above $\{n_4, n_5\}$.

Removal of Contradictions

In ATMS contradictions are removed by removing from the nodes' labels those sets of premises that are discovered to be inconsistent. Suppose, for example, that we have the following dependency network: $[\{n_1, n_2, n_3, n_4, n_5, n_6, n_7\}, \{n_6\}, \{\langle\{\} \Rightarrow n_1\rangle, \langle\{\} \Rightarrow n_2\rangle, \langle\{\} \Rightarrow n_4\rangle, \langle\{\} \Rightarrow n_5\rangle, \langle\{n_1, n_2\} \Rightarrow n_3\rangle, \langle\{n_3\} \Rightarrow n_7\rangle, \langle\{n_4\} \Rightarrow n_7\rangle, \langle\{n_4, n_5\} \Rightarrow n_6\rangle, \langle\{n_6\} \Rightarrow n_7\rangle\}]$. This network is similar to the one presented in Figure 12, except for the fact that node n_6 is a contradiction node.

Since the label of node n_6 is $\{\{n_4, n_5\}\}$, this set of premises is discovered to be inconsistent. When this happens, all the sets of premises that are supersets of $\{n_4, n_5\}$ are marked as nogoods (shaded areas in the lattice of Figure 14), and these sets are removed from the labels of all nodes in the dependency network. A description of the contradiction removal in ATMS can be found in de Kleer (1986).

OTHER APPROACHES

In this section we list two alternative approaches to TMS-like systems. The commonality among them is that they both support reasoning by the TMS rather than passing this task to the problem solver, as with JTMS and ATMS.

Multiple Belief Reasoner

Multiple Belief Reasoner (MBR) is an ATMS-like system in which the problem solver and the TMS are merged into one single system. MBR is based on a logic called SWM* (Martins, 1991) [a successor to SWM (Martins and Sha-

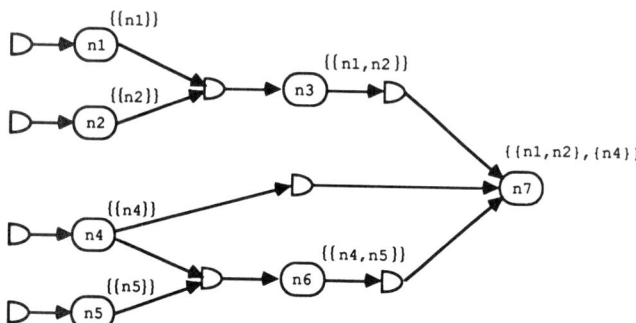

Figure 12. ATMS labeling.

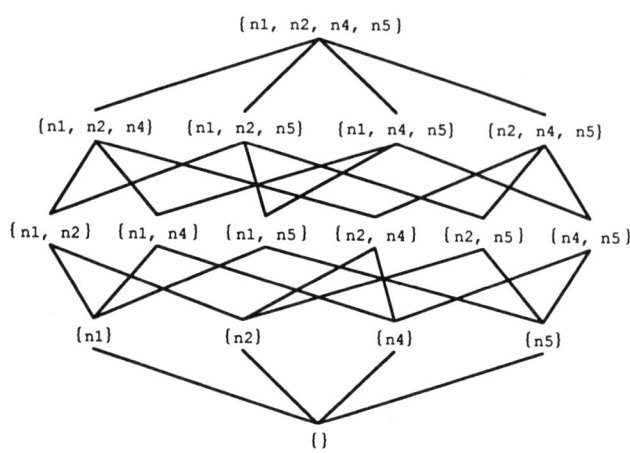

Figure 13. Environment lattice for premises n_1, n_2, n_4, and n_5.

piro, 1983, 1988)]. SWM* deals with knowledge states. A *knowledge state*, written [[KB, KIS]], is a pair containing a knowledge base (KB) and a set of known inconsistent sets (KIS). The knowledge base contains propositions (written as wffs) associated with an indication of the dependencies between a particular wff and other wffs in the knowledge base; the set of known inconsistent sets is a set containing the sets of premises in the KB known to be inconsistent.

The knowledge base is a set of supported wffs. A supported wff consists of a wff and an associated pair, its support, containing an origin tag and an origin set. The *origin tag* indicates how the supported wff was placed in the knowledge base (ie, whether it was supplied by an outside system or was generated during deduction). The *origin set* is a set of premises; it contains all and only the premises that were actually used in the derivation of that wff.

The growth of knowledge states is dictated by the rules of inference of SWM*, which are grouped into two sets:

1. *Pure logic rules* correspond to traditional inference rules. They have the effect of adding new supported wffs to the KB. This addition may be done in two

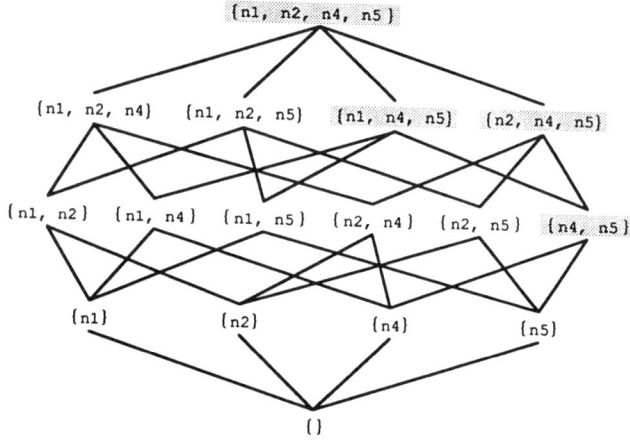

Figure 14. Inconsistent sets of premises.

different ways: a new supported wff is introduced from the outside (this corresponds to a premise, called a hypothesis in SWM*) or a supported wff is derived from other supported wffs in the KB. These rules transform [[KB, KIS]] into [[KB', KIS]] where KB ⊂ KB'.

2. *Computational rules* are rules that update the information about sets known to be inconsistent. These rules are obligatorily applied whenever a new inconsistent set is discovered, in which case a new set is added to KIS. These rules transform [[KB, KIS]] into [[KB, KIS']] in which KIS ⊂ KIS'.

Based on SWM*'s features, the behavior of an ATMS-like system called MBR is defined. MBR uses two notions: context and belief space. A *context* is defined to be a set of premises. A context determines a *belief space*, which is the set of all premises defining the context and all the wffs in the KB that were derived exclusively from them. A belief space is represented by $\langle\langle[[KB, KIS]], C\rangle\rangle$, where C is a context, ie, a set of wffs that corresponds to premises in the KB. The belief space determined by a context is the subset of all the wffs in the KB whose origin set is contained in the context. Any operation performed by MBR (query, addition, etc) is associated with a context, the *current context* that defines the *current belief space*. A proposition is said to be believed if it belongs to the current belief space.

SWM* does not consider nonmonotonic justifications, but there is an extension of it, SWMC, which does (Cravo and Martins, 1991). The language of SWMC is an extension of the language of SWM*. It contains a new quantifier, the default quantifier, which allows it to express default rules. It also has a distinguished predicate, *Applicable*, that, among other things, allows it to express exceptions to default rules.

Logic-based TMS

Logic-based TMS (LTMS) is based on the work of McAllester (1978). In this kind of TMS, relations among propositions are represented by clauses. These clauses can be used to deduce the truth value of any of the involved propositions. The description presented here is a simplification of McAllester's work. A detailed introduction to LTMS, together with a discussion of its implementation, can be found in Charniak and co-workers (1987).

LTMS works with nodes, truth states, terms, clauses, and supports. *Nodes* represent propositions supplied by problem solver. Any atomic proposition is represented by a node with no meaning to LTMS. A proposition involving logical connectives is also represented by a node, but in this case LTMS "understands" the meaning of the logical connectives that appear in the proposition. Each node has an associated *truth state*. This truth state may be TRUE (believed to be true), FALSE (believed to be false), or UNKNOWN (no belief either way). It is said that a node has a truth value when its truth state is either TRUE or FALSE; A *term* is a pair containing one node and one truth value, TRUE or FALSE. A term is true if the node has the truth value of the term. A *clause* is a set of terms one of which must be true for the clause to be true. For example, the clause ((A. FALSE) (B. TRUE)) states that either A is false or B is true. A clause represents the relationship between the truth values of the nodes appearing in the clause.

A clause may be used by LTMS to deduce a truth value for any of the nodes it contains, and in this case the clause will act as a *justification* for the deduced truth value. A clause may be given multiple interpretations. For example, the clause ((A. FALSE) (B. TRUE)) may be interpreted either as $A \rightarrow B$ or, equivalently, $\sim B \rightarrow \sim A$. If this clause were used to deduce the truth value TRUE for node B (given the truth value TRUE of node A), it would act as a justification for the truth value of B. In a JTMS the corresponding justification would be $\langle\{A\}|\varnothing \Rightarrow B\rangle$.

There are two differences worth pointing out between a JTMS justification and a LTMS clause: (1) A JTMS justification is a special kind of clause, a Horn clause. This means that only one term in the clause has TRUE as its second component. (2) A JTMS justification is not symmetrical, ie, the label (IN/OUT) of its consequent may be concluded from the labels of its antecedents, but the label of the consequent does not allow JTMS to conclude anything about the label of any one of the antecedents. In LTMS justifications are symmetrical: The truth value of any node in a clause may be computed from the truth values of the other terms in the clause.

At any time the problem solver can add a clause and supply it to LTMS. Whenever this happens, a check is immediately made to see if it is possible to derive new information. This will happen whenever all the terms of the clause are false, except for one, which is unknown. In this case, this term must be true (since the truth value of the clause is TRUE), and LTMS can conclude the truth value of this term's node. The other way a truth value can be added to a node is by deducing it from a clause. In this case the support of the truth value is the clause used to deduce it. Whenever a truth value is added, a check is made to see if this enables the deduction of some other truth value from a clause. Obviously, the only clauses that are relevant are the ones that contain a term that has been given a truth value. The procedure used to compute truth values for clauses is called *Boolean constraint propagation*.

The truth value of a node can be removed, meaning that the truth state of that node changes from TRUE or FALSE to UNKNOWN. The removal of a truth value corresponds to a removal of information. There are several ways in which the truth value of a node can be removed. One way for a truth value to be removed is when the problem solver decides to retract a premise or an assumption. This decision may be taken because the problem solver decides that a premise is no longer known or to resolve a contradiction (a contradiction is a clause whose terms are all false).

We said that LTMS "understands" the meaning of the logical connectives. To make this possible each of the logical symbols has an associated axiom set that is used to generate clausal constraints. For example, the axioms for implication are (1) ((P → Q. FALSE) (P . FALSE) (Q . TRUE)); (2) ((P → Q . TRUE) (P . TRUE)); (3) ((P → Q . TRUE) (Q . FALSE)).

THEORETICAL FOUNDATIONS

During the last few years there has been some effort in providing foundations for TMSs and relating them with other nonmonotonic formalisms: Reinfrank (1989) discussed the relationship between TMS and nonmonotonic logics. Fujiwara and Honiden (1989) and Reinfrank and co-workers (1989) have shown the equivalence between the reasonable beliefs of a dependency networks and the strongly grounded extensions of autoepistemic logic. Brown (1988) provided a formal semantics to TMS by offering a logic that characterizes some models of TMSs. Doyle (1983) was the first attempt to present a formal description of a TMS. Elkan (1990) provided a characterization of the inferences performed by a nonmonotonic TMS in terms of logic programming with stable set semantics and autoepistemic logic. Popchev and co-workers (1990) provided a logical theory of truth maintenance reasoning subsuming plausible reasoning that distinguishes between true and plausible arguments. They propose a behavior in the presence of inconsistencies that corresponds to blocking the propagation of the contradiction rather than trying to get rid of them.

APPLICATIONS

The capability of determining the source of contradictions coupled with the possibility of changing beliefs are essential features of any intelligent system. In general, any system that follows the paradigm described at the outset of this entry can use (and benefit from) TMS techniques. However, there are some problem areas in which these techniques are of paramount importance, in particular [other application areas can be found in Martins (1990)]:

1. *Reasoning based on partial information, default assumptions, and potentially inconsistent data.* This kind of reasoning is likely to produce contradictions, and a system that resorts to it should be able to recover from them. This aspect is discussed in Cravo and Martins (1991), Etherington (1987), and Morris (1987a).
2. *Constraint satisfaction.* This is a problem area that involves making choices and their retraction when a violation of constraints is detected. Again, the capability of discovering the source of the violation and its removal can be guided by TMS techniques. There is a good tradition in the application of TMSs to this area; see, for example, Dhar and Ranganathan (1990).
3. *Diagnosis.* The use of TMS techniques, in particular the recording of dependencies, is important to detect possible causes of malfunctioning. Among others, de Kleer and Williams (1987) and Struss (1988) discuss this aspect.
4. *Planning.* The application of TMSs to planning pertain to the aspect of reasoning about change, ie, reasoning about the propositions that change whenever an action is performed. Among others, the following papers discuss this aspect: Drummond (1987), Janlert (1987), Morris (1987b), and Pinto-Ferreira and Martins (1990).
5. *Search.* The ATMS introduces a new approach to search in which several alternatives are considered and switching between nodes in the search tree is done by changing the premises under consideration. Among others, Forbus and de Kleer (1988) discuss this aspect.

Tools That Use TMS Techniques

There are several commercial tools (mainly for the development of expert systems) that embody some TMS capabilities. Some of the most widely used are KEE (Filman, 1988), based on the ATMS; RUP (McAllester, 1982), based on the LTMS; and PROTEUS 2 (Petrie and co-workers, 1987) based on the JTMS.

PREHISTORY

Several papers, although not specifically addressing TMSs, were influential in their development. Their study helps in understanding the general setting under which TMSs were introduced. TMSs have their roots in the frame problem (McCarthy and Hayes, 1969), the problem of deciding which conditions change and which conditions do not change in a system when it undergoes some modification. Among the approaches to this problem, Fikes (1975) proposes a system that uses dependencies among propositions and Hayes (1975) argues about the need for TMS-style systems.

In the mid-1970s, Stallman and Sussman (1977) designed EL, a system in which dependencies of propositions are permanently recorded. The recording of dependencies has particular importance in finding faulty assumptions responsible for the generation of contradictions and for explanation of the program's beliefs. Their work had two major influences in AI: It opened a new perspective to the handling of alternatives (dependency-directed backtracking) and it influenced the creation of systems that, using dependencies, handle and can recover from contradictions. (EL was a direct influence in the development of Doyle's TMS.) At the same time, and independently from Doyle's work, London (1978) describes a planning system relying on the use of dependencies. A reasoning system, called AMORD (de Kleer and co-workers, 1977) was an influential system in the development of ATMS.

BIBLIOGRAPHY

A. L. Brown, "Logics for Justified Belief," *Proceedings of ECAI-88,* pp. 507–512, Pitman Publishing, London, 1988.

E. Charniak, C. Riesbeck, D. V. McDermott, and J. R. Meehan, *Artificial Intelligence Programming,* 2nd ed., Lawrence Erlbaum Associates, Hillsdale, N.J., 1987.

M. R. Cravo and J. P. Martins, "Being Aware of Assumptions," *Proceedings of the Österreichische Artificial Intelligence Tagung, Lecture Notes on Artificial Intelligence,* Springer-Verlag, Heidelberg, Germany, 1991.

V. Dhar and N. Ranganathan, "Integer Programming vs. Expert Systems: An Experimental Comparison," *CACM* **33**(3), 323–336 (1990).

J. Doyle, "A Truth Maintenance System," *Artif. Intell.*, **12**(3), 231–272 (1979); also in *Readings in Artificial Intelligence*, Webber and Nilsson, eds., Morgan-Kaufmann, San Mateo, Calif., 1981, pp. 496–516.

J. Doyle, "The Ins and Outs of Reason Maintenance," *Proceedings of the Eighth IJCAI*, Morgan-Kaufmann, San Mateo, Calif., 1983, pp. 349–351.

J. de Kleer, "Choices without Backtracking," *Proceedings of the Fourth National Conference on AI*, Austin, Texas, 1984, AAAI, Menlo Park, Calif., 1984, pp. 79–85.

J. de Kleer, "An Assumption-Based Truth Maintenance System," *Artif. Intell.*, **28**(2), 127–162 (1986). Also in *Readings in Nonmonotonic Reasoning*, Ginsberg, ed., Morgan-Kaufmann, San Mateo, Calif., 1987, pp. 280–297.

J. de Kleer, J. Doyle, G. Steele and G. Sussman, "AMORD: Explicit Control of Reasoning," *Proceedings of the Symposium on Artificial Intelligence and Programming Languages, SIGART Newsletter 64*, pp. 116–125, 1977. Also in Brachman and Levesque, eds., *Readings in Knowledge Representation*, Morgan-Kaufmann Publishers, Inc., San Mateo, Calif., 1985, pp. 345–355.

J. de Kleer and B. C. Williams, "Back to Backtracking: Controlling the ATMS," *Proceedings of the Fifth National Conference on AI*, Philadelphia, Penn., 1986, AAAI, Menlo Park, Calif., 1986, pp. 910–917.

J. de Kleer and B. C. Williams, "Diagnosing Multiple Faults," *Artif. Intell.* **32**(1), 97–130 (1987).

O. Dressler, "An Extended Basic ATMS," *Proceedings of The Second International Workshop on Non-Monotonic Reasoning*, Reinfrank, de Kleer, Ginsberg, and Sandewall, eds., Lecture Notes in Artificial Intelligence 346, Springer-Verlag, Heidelberg, Germany, 1988, pp. 143–163.

O. Dressler, "Problem Solving with the NM-ATMS," *Proceedings of ECAI-90*, L. C. Aiello, ed., Pitman Publishing, London, 1990, pp. 253–258.

M. E. Drummond, "A Representation of Action and Belief for Automatic Planning Systems," *Proceedings of the 1986 Workshop on Reasoning about Actions and Plans*, Georgeff and Lansky, eds., Morgan-Kaufmann, San Mateo, Calif., 1987, pp. 189–211.

C. Elkan, "A Rational Reconstruction of Nonmonotonic Truth Maintenance Systems," *Artif. Intell.* **43**(2), 219–234 (1990).

D. W. Etherington, "Formalizing Nonmonotonic Reasoning Systems," *Artif. Intell.* **31**(1), 41–85 (1987).

R. Fikes, "Deductive Retrieval Mechanisms for State Description Models," *Proc. of the Fourth IJCAI*, Morgan-Kaufmann, San Mateo, Calif., 1975, pp. 99–106.

R. E. Filman, "Reasoning with Worlds and Truth Maintenance in a Knowledge-based Programming Environment," *CACM* **31**(4), 382–401 (1988).

K. D. Forbus and J. de Kleer, "Focusing the ATMS," *Proc. of the Seventh National Conference on AI*, AAAI, Menlo Park, Calif., 1988, pp. 193–198.

Y. Fujiwara and S. Honiden, "Relating the TMS to Autoepistemic Logic," *Proceedings of the Eleventh IJCAI*, 1989, pp. 1199–1205.

M. L. Ginsberg, *Readings in Nonmonotonic Reasoning*, Morgan Kaufmann Publishers, Inc., San Mateo, Calif., 1987.

J. Goodwin, An Improved Algorithm for Nonmonotonic Dependency Network Update, Technical Report LITH-MAT-R-82-23, Linköping University, Dept. of Computer and Information Science, Linköping, Sweden, 1982.

P. J. Hayes, "A Representation for Robot Plans," *Proceedings of the Fourth IJCAI*, Morgan-Kaufmann, San Mateo, Calif., 1975, pp. 181–188.

L.-E. Janlert, "Modeling Change—The Frame Problem," in *The Robot's Dilemma: The Frame Problem in Artificial Intelligence*, Z. Pylyshyn, ed., Ablex Publishing Corporation, Norwood, N.J., 1987, pp. 1–40.

P. London, *Dependency Networks as Representation for Modelling in General Problem Solvers*, Ph.D. dissertation, Technical Report 698, University of Maryland, College Park, 1978.

J. P. Martins, "The Truth, the Whole Truth, and Nothing but the Truth: An Indexed Bibliography to the Literature on Truth Maintenance Systems," *AI Magazine* **11**(5), 7–25 (1990).

J. P. Martins, "A Structure for Epistemic States," in *New Directions for Intelligent Tutoring Systems*, Costa, ed., NATO ASI Series F, Springer-Verlag, Heidelberg, Germany, 1991.

J. P. Martins and S. C. Shapiro, "Reasoning in Multiple Belief Spaces," *Proceedings of the Eighth IJCAI*, Morgan-Kaufmann, San Mateo, Calif., 1983, pp. 370–373.

J. P. Martins and S. C. Shapiro, "A Model for Belief Revision," *Artif. Intell.* **35**(1), 25–79 (1988).

D. McAllester, "A Three-Valued Truth Maintenance System," AI Memo 473, Massachusetts Institute of Technology, AI Lab, Cambridge, Mass., 1978.

D. McAllester, "Reasoning Utility Package," AI Memo 667, Massachusetts Institute of Technology, AI Lab, Cambridge, Mass., 1982.

J. McCarthy and P. Hayes, "Some Philosophical Problems from the Standpoint of Artificial Intelligence," in *Machine Intelligence 4*, Meltzer and Michie, Eds., Edinburgh University Press, Edinburgh, 1969, pp. 463–502.

R. C. Moore, "Semantical Considerations on Non-monotonic Logic," *Artif. Intell.*, **25**(1), 75–94 (1985). Also in *Readings in Non-monotonic Reasoning*, Ginsberg, ed., Morgan-Kaufmann, San Mateo, Calif., 1987, pp. 127–136.

P. H. Morris, "Curing Anomalous Extensions," *Proceedings of the Sixth National Conference on AI*, 1987, AAAI, Menlo Park, Calif., 1987a, pp. 437–442.

P. H. Morris, "A Truth Maintenance Based Approach to the Frame Problem," *Proceedings of the 1987 Workshop on the Frame Problem in Artificial Intelligence*, Brown, ed., Morgan-Kaufmann, San Mateo, Calif., 1987b, pp. 297–307.

C. J. Petrie, "New Algorithms for Dependency-Directed Backtracking," Technical Report AI TR86-33, Artificial Intelligence Laboratory, The University of Texas at Austin, 1986.

C. J. Petrie, D. Russinoff, D. D. Steiner, and N. Ballou, "PROTEUS 2: System description," MCC Technical Report AI-136-87, Microelectronics and Computer Technology Corporation, Austin, Texas, 1987.

C. Pinto-Ferreira and J. P. Martins, "A Formal System for Reasoning about Change," *Proceedings of ECAI-90*, Aiello, ed., Pitman Publishing, London, 1990, pp. 503–508.

I. Popchev, N. Zlatareva, and M. Mircheva, "A Truth Maintenance Theory—An Alternative Approach," *Proceedings of ECAI-90*, Aiello, ed., Pitman Publishing, London, 1990, pp. 509–514.

M. Reinfrank, "Fundamentals and Logical Foundations of Truth Maintenance," Linköping Studies in Science and Technology, Dissertation 221, Linköping, Sweden, Department of Computer and Information Science, Linköping University, 1989.

M. Reinfrank, O. Dressler, and G. Brewka, "On the Relation between Truth Maintenance and Autoepistemic Logic," *Proceedings of the Eleventh IJCAI*, Morgan-Kaufmann, San Mateo, Calif., 1989, pp. 1206–1212.

R. Stallman and G. Sussman, "Forward Reasoning and Dependency-Directed Backtracking in a System for Computer-Aided Circuit Analysis," *Artif. Intell.* **9**(2), 135–196 (1977).

P. Struss, "Extensions to ATMS-based Diagnosis," in *Artificial Intelligence in Engineering: Diagnosis and Learning*, Gero, ed., Elsevier, Amsterdam, 1988, pp. 3–28.

João P. Martins
Instituto Superior Técnico,
Lisbon

This work was supported in part by JNICT under project 87-107. The author would like to thank Maria R. Cravo for her comments.

TURING MACHINES

Turing machines are named after the British mathematician who formulated their definition. They are not machines in the everyday sense but rather a mathematical construct useful in the theoretical study of the absolute limitations of computing devices (Davis and Weyuker, 1983; Lewis and Papadimitriou, 1981; Rogers, 1987; Turing, 1950). Essentially, they represent a reduction of the logical structure of any computing device that could, in principle, be constructed.

To properly convey exactly what they are and what relevance they have to AI, it is useful first to carry out an analysis of algorithmic computation similar to the one carried out by Turing himself in arriving at his definition (Turing, 1936; Minsky, 1967).

ANALYSIS

Imagine a scenario in which a clerk carefully and accurately follows a finite, precise, deterministic recipe for performing an arbitrary, discrete, symbol-manipulation task on some sheets of paper. The rules one learns with conscious effort in childhood for doing sums and products could be put in the form of such a recipe as, presumably, could the rules one learns without conscious effort for converting sentences from active to passive voice. The symbols manipulated could, eg, be numerical, textual, or the "discretized" components of a picture (pixels). Assume the recipe leaves no room for alternative interpretations. It will even have to specify exactly where to look and write on the sheets of paper. In addition, assume the sheets are carefully ruled into little squares, each capable of containing a blank space or a symbol. If the clerk had access to a discrete data space topologically more complicated than sheets of paper, the graph-theoretic (Harary, 1969) structure of that space would be representable (without overlaps) in ordinary three-dimensional Euclidean space, and, hence, on the discretized, essentially three-dimensional structure of the stack of sheets of paper with each sheet ruled into little squares—successive pages represent, then, successive two-dimensional, discretized planes. Hence, the scenario represents the most general case of algorithmic symbol manipulation.

In the next phase of the analysis certain seemingly severe restrictions are made on the forms of both the recipe and the sheets of paper. However, these restrictions do not limit the class of symbol-manipulation tasks that can be performed.

In general, the recipe could contain complex instructions that require the clerk to "parallel process," ie, to attend to and perhaps modify in one step a large number of symbols in little squares in many places on the sheets of paper. Any such complex instruction can be replaced by, perhaps, a long and tedious sequence of simpler instructions, each of which merely requires the clerk to attend to and perhaps modify (or change) the symbol in a single square. This sequence of simple instructions achieves the same symbol-manipulation effect as the complex instruction. Instructions in the recipe are restricted to this simpler type and each complex instruction is assumed to have been replaced by an appropriate sequence of these simpler instructions.

Imagine a two-dimensional configuration of symbols on one of the sheets. These symbols may be thought as forming the pixels of a scene. Imagine further a suitably wide second sheet of paper that contains, along one of its rows, the rows of the "scene" from the first sheet, laid end-to-end, with a special marker symbol between each row. Any recipe instruction for manipulating the scene on the first sheet can be converted to a suitable sequence of simple instructions for producing the analogous manipulation on the one-dimensional representation of the scene on the second sheet. (The details of such a conversion are somewhat tedious, however.) Similarly, but more generally, any recipe for performing symbol-manipulation tasks on the sheets of paper can be converted to a longer recipe for performing the analogous task on a one-dimensional paper tape. (If more tape is needed in the course of a computation, it is added to the ends.) The sheet(s) of paper are modified to consist of a single, one-dimensional, extensible tape. Assume the recipe has been appropriately converted. Some of the details of converting, such as from a two-dimensional to a one-dimensional tape, are given in Hopcroft and Ullman (1979).

The recipe may still contain instructions for traveling a large number of tape squares (from the one the clerk is looking at) to the right or left along the tape. Consider an instruction that says to travel 42 squares to the right. It can be replaced by a sequence of 42 simpler instructions each of which says to move one square to the right. Similarly, any move instruction can be replaced by a sequence of instructions each of which are instructions to move one square right (or left). Move instructions in the recipe are restricted to be of this simpler type. Assume the recipe has had any other move instructions replaced by appropriate sequences of simple move instructions.

Since the recipe is finite, it can contain only finitely many instructions. Since the recipe is precise and deterministic, it must clearly specify the instruction with which to begin. One instruction, then, is designated as the start instruction. For the same reasons, the recipe must clearly specify which instructions, under which circumstances, are to follow which other instructions. The only circumstances that need be taken into account in deciding what instruction to do next are the current instruction and the (possibly blank) symbol currently scanned: a bounded-size finite sequence of past symbols scanned can be "remembered" because this sequence can, in effect, direct the clerk to pass to an instruction that is particular to it. The recipe instructions are restricted, then, without loss of generality, each to specify the next instruction only on the basis of the symbol currently scanned.

The only other effect an instruction need achieve is the modification of the symbol currently scanned. The choice of the modification specified in an instruction is limited, again without loss of generality, to depend only on which symbol is currently scanned.

There are finitely many instructions in the recipe, one of which is the start instruction, and each of which specifies (a) a move one square right or left and/or a symbol modification and (b) a next instruction, where both (a) and (b) are a function of the symbol scanned. An instruction will, of course, specify the exact dependence on the symbol scanned. Since the recipe is finite, it can mention only a finite number of different symbols. Therefore, each instruction can involve only a finite number of symbols. Hence, it can be assumed that each instruction indicates the action to be taken and the next instruction to be carried out for each of a finite number of possible symbols scanned. Note, for instance, in the process of converting the recipe to contain only these types of instructions, an unrestricted instruction, saying to pick up a symbol **S** in one place and put it in another, would be replaced by a sequence of restricted instructions that involves changing an **S** to a blank, followed by a series of moves, followed by changing a symbol to **S**.

The conclusion of this second phase of the analysis is that recipes, operating on a one-dimension tape and containing only the restricted type of instruction of the previous paragraph, are just as general purpose at performing symbol-manipulation tasks as the unrestricted recipes operating on multiple sheets of paper with which one began: They can handle the same class of symbol-manipulation tasks although they may require more instructions to do it.

DEFINITION OF TURING MACHINES

Imagine now that each instruction in the recipe (containing the restricted type of instruction) is replaced by a uniquely corresponding, internal state of a machine. The machine is to have no states not corresponding to an instruction. Suppose this machine is connected by a read–write head to an extensible, one-dimensional tape. Suppose the machine is wired so that it begins operation in the internal state that corresponds to the start instruction. Suppose further that when, at a given time, the machine is in any one of the finitely many states corresponding to a recipe instruction, it first carries out the tape operation (moving and/or changing a symbol) specified by that recipe instruction and secondly goes into the internal state corresponding to the next recipe instruction. The choice of tape operation carried out and the next state and/or instruction, of course, depends on the symbol the machine is scanning just previously, and the particular dependence was specified in the recipe instruction itself. Clearly such a machine directly simulates the action of the clerk operating with the modified recipe on the one-dimensional tape. Hence, this machine performs essentially the same symbol-manipulation task as the original unrestricted recipe operating on the sheets of paper. One would expect, since the original algorithmic symbol-manipulation task was arbitrarily chosen, that such machines are capable of performing any algorithmic symbol-manipulation task.

The Turing machines are (by definition) the machines obtained in this way. They could actually be built out of a kind of switching network, called a McCulloch–Pitts nerve net (9). One can consider Turing-machine states also as analogous to states of mind (see PHILOSOPHICAL QUESTIONS). Careful, mathematical definitions and examples can be found in Davis and Weyuker (1983), Lewis and Papadimitriou (1981), and Rogers (1987).

APPLICATIONS

Turing's analysis, similar to the analysis above, was the crucial evidence to legitimize the definition of the algorithmic symbol-manipulation tasks as exactly those symbol-manipulation tasks performable by Turing machines (see CHURCH'S THESIS). Having such a definition enables one to rigorously, mathematically prove that certain tasks cannot be done by algorithm. The technique is to show they cannot be done by any Turing machine. The point of making all those restrictions on recipes and paper was to arrive at a simple kind of machine that would be easy to work with mathematically. The point was not to devise a kind of machine that would be useful to build; the restrictions on Turing machines make them too awkward to be practical devices for actually running computations.

An example task (about Turing machines themselves) is described that does not have a chance of algorithmic solution. Clearly any given Turing machine started on an initially blank tape either eventually prints a given symbol **S** or it does not. Consider the problem of designing an algorithm to decide from a description of any Turing machine M whether M eventually prints **S** if it is started on an initially blank tape. Turing showed that no Turing machine can correctly make this decision about arbitrary M; hence, no algorithm can be found to do it.

Turing also indicated how to construct universal Turing machines. A universal machine, given a description on its tape of any Turing machine, simulates that machine. It is generally believed that von Neumann's

(1966) idea for stored-program computers was inspired by Turing's universal machine. Stored-program computers keep one from having to rewire a computer each time a new (symbol-manipulation) task is to be performed. The computer is merely asked, in effect, to simulate a machine for the task; the "machine" to be simulated is typically described by a program.

COGNITIVE SCIENCE, MECHANISM, LEARNING, AND AI

Suppose that the highest-level brain processes to which human conscious and unconscious thoughts and/or symbol manipulations are reducible are algorithmic and that these brain processes are really produced by precise, finite, deterministic recipes somehow "wet-wired" into the human brain. Then human cognition is simulatable by Turing machines. Hence, any limitative results about Turing-machine computations apply to humans too, and perfect computer modeling of human cognition is, in principle, possible. This form of mechanism is a principal assumption of modern cognitive science (qv) and implies that *artificial* intelligence can, in principle, do anything *natural* intelligence can.

It can be argued at least at the atomic level, that brain processes are random, not deterministic. Of course, they still might be deterministic at higher levels. But suppose they are not. What, then, can be salvaged of (this form of) mechanism? It can be shown (see Allen, 1976) that if the probability distribution function of a random process is algorithmically computable, its expected or most probable behavior is, again, Turing-machine simulatable. Hence, mechanism and all its consequences apply, in this case, to expected behavior.

What about human creativity (qv)? How does mechanism account for the unbidden images that occur to people and lead to solutions of difficult problems and/or works of great beauty and significance for the human condition? The mechanist would argue that humans are not consciously aware of the brain processes that invoke such insights; hence, one has the illusion that they are not algorithmically produced. One's conscious thoughts are the mere tip of an iceberg; the curious thing is that one has any thoughts other than *unconscious*.

When one learns a list a data, such as to ride a bicycle, or even if one has had an interesting thought, one is presumably changed by the experience. A learning machine is just a machine that changes itself, perhaps in part on the basis of externally obtained information. If the changes are of bounded size, ordinary Turing machines will serve as a mathematical model—the changes are mere changes of machine state. A more interesting case allows changes of unbounded size. (Learning is thought of as a growth experience.) This can be mathematically modeled by two-tape Turing machines where one of the tapes is inside the machine. Mathematically it really makes no difference where the boundaries between inside and outside are drawn, and most of the recent theoretical literature on absolute limitations of learning machines (Case, 1986; Osherson and co-workers, 1986) (see also INDUCTIVE INFERENCE) does not bother to draw such boundaries; in fact, much of it proceeds on a level somewhat more abstract than the Turing machine model. So far, there has been very little interaction between this theoretical literature and the recent literature in AI on implementing learning machines (Michalski and co-workers, 1983) (see LEARNING, MACHINE).

FEASIBLE COMPUTATIONS AND AI

Many theoretical computer scientists investigate the inherent difficulty of useful computation tasks (Garey and Johnson, 1979). These days the standard model of feasible computation is based on resource-bounded, multitape Turing machines, Turing machines that operate a finite number of one-dimensional tapes and are required to finish before using some preset amount of time and/or paper. For example, a task that is, in principle, algorithmically performable, nonetheless, will be infeasible if any multitape Turing machine for the task, performing one operation every nanosecond, generally requires longer than the expected lifespan of the sun to complete. Unfortunately, there are results from theoretical computer science (Garey and Johnson, 1979) (see also SEARCH) to the effect that many of the tasks of importance to AI are inherently infeasible. This presumably requires AI workers to look for partial or approximately correct algorithmic solutions to such tasks (see HEURISTICS).

BIBLIOGRAPHY

M. Arbib, *Brains, Machines and Mathematics*, McGraw-Hill Book Co., Inc., New York, 1964.

J. Case, "Learning Machines," in W. Demopoulos and A. Marras, eds., *Language Learning and Concept Acquisition*, Ablex, Norwood, N.J., 1986.

M. Davis and E. Weyuker, *Computability, Complexity and Languages*, Academic Press, Inc., New York, 1983.

M. Garey and D. Johnson, *Computers and Intractability: A Guide to the Theory of NP-Completeness*, W. H. Freeman, San Francisco, Calif., 1979.

F. Harary, *Graph Theory*, Addison-Wesley Publishing Co., Inc., Reading, Mass., 1969.

J. Hopcroft and J. Ullman, *Introduction to Automata Theory, Languages, and Computation*, Addison-Wesley Publishing Co., Inc., Reading, Mass., 1979.

E. de Leeuw, C. Moore, C. Shannon, and N. Shapiro, "Computability by Probabilistic Machines," in *Automata Studies, Annals of Math. Studies*, Vol. 34, Princeton University Press, Princeton, N.J., 1956.

H. Lewis and C. Papadimitriou, *Elements of the Theory of Computation*, Prentice-Hall, Inc., Englewood Cliffs, N.J., 1981.

R. Michalski, J. Carbonell, and T. Mitchell, *Machine Learning: An Artificial Intelligence Approach*, Tioga, Palo Alto, Calif., 1983.

M. Minsky, *Computation: Finite and Infinite Machines*, Prentice-Hall, Inc., Englewood Cliffs, N.J., 1967.

D. Osherson, M. Stob, and S. Weinstein, *Systems That Learn: An Introduction for Cognitive and Computer Scientists*, MIT Press, Cambridge, Mass., 1986.

H. Rogers, *Theory of Recursive Functions and Effective Computability*, MIT Press, Cambridge, Mass., 1987.

A. M. Turing, "On Computable Numbers with an Application to the Entscheidungs Problem," *Proc. London Math. Soc.* **42**, 230–265 (1936).

A. M. Turing, "Computing Machinery and Intelligence," *Mind* **59**, 433–460 (1950).

J. von Neumann, *Theory of Self-Reproducing Automata*, A. Burks, ed., University of Illinois Perss, Urbana, Ill., 1966.

J. CASE
University of Delaware

TURING TEST

In 1637, Descartes argued that a machine can never think (Descartes, 1973). He believed that even if a machine resembled a human, there are two certain tests by which a machine can be distinguished from a rational human being. First, although a machine may utter words, a machine can never reply appropriately to everything said in its presence in the way that a human can. Second, although a machine may perform certain things as well as or even better than a human, a machine cannot have the diversity of action that a human has. Of course, many supporters of AI would challenge the inevitability of these results (see SOCIAL ISSUES OF AI). But how would one demonstrate that a machine can think? What would have to be done in AI, at least in principle, in order to show that a machine can think?

The question "Can machines think?" is difficult to answer because its wording is vague and ambiguous. What do the words "machines" and "think" mean? If humans are regarded as meat machines, then obviously machines think. On the other hand, if being a machine and thinking are incompatible concepts, thinking machines are conceptually impossible. On this interpretation, computers may think, but they would cease to be machines if they did. Even the seemingly innocuous word "can" suggests an ambiguity about the question. Is the question "Are machines able to think today?" or "Will machines eventually have the ability to think?" or "Regardless of what happens technologically, is it empirically possible that machines think?"

THE IMITATION GAME

Turing (1950) realized that the question "can machines think?" is ambiguous and sought to replace it by less ambiguous questions about a game he called "the imitation game." He introduced the imitation game by imagining a version that is played by three human beings—a man (A), a woman (B), and an interrogator. The interrogator, who is in a room apart from the other two, asks each of them questions and tries to determine from their typewritten answers which is the man and which is the woman. The object of the game for the man is to imitate a woman, and the object for the woman is to inform the interrogator about her true sex. Hence, the man tries to deceive the interrogator by giving answers that a woman would give, whereas the woman attempts to help the interrogator by giving answers that would identify her as the woman.

Turing proposed a variation of this imitation game, now known as "the Turing test," in which a computer takes the part of A in the game. An interrogator in a separate room asks questions of A and B and tries to determine from their answers which respondent is the computer. In this version of the game the computer gives deceptive answers. When asked to add 34,957 to 70,764, Turing said the computer pauses about 30 s and then gives the answer 105,621. Rather than give a correct answer quickly, the computer gives an incorrect answer slowly to imitate what a human thinker might do. Unfortunately, Turing did not carefully describe the role of B in his new version of the game. Is the computer imitating B *qua* woman, *qua* human, or *qua* thinker? Moreover, other details of the game are not given. Does one respondent know what the other respondent has said? When is the game over? How many questions can be asked? Is the winner a respondent or the interrogator? Perhaps, the programmer wins! In any event, these niggling details are probably unimportant to Turing's main claim that questions about how well a computer does in the imitation game should replace the original question "Can machines think?"

Turing's goal was to make the issue of machine thinking more objective. As he pointed out, it would be absurd to take an opinion poll to determine whether machines think. Turing wanted a more scientific approach. The imitation game is Turing's scientific test, and it has the strengths of a scientific test. The Turing test provides a format for impartially comparing the behavior of humans with the behavior of computers. The results of the Turing test are repeatable and objective. Moreover, the Turing test emphasizes evaluation of intellectual ability and eliminates prejudice based on appearance. Turing did not regard his test as a necessary condition for attributing thinking to a machine, for a machine might think but do so too quickly and accurately to play the game well. But Turing did regard the test a sufficient condition for attributing thinking to a machine. Turing, unlike Descartes, thought that machines will become quite sophisticated in their linguistic abilities. Turing (1950, p. 19) claimed that in about fifty years' time it will be possible to program computers, with a storage capacity of about 10^9, to make them play the imitation game so well that an average interrogator will not have more than 70% chance of making the right identification after five minutes of questioning.

Deep philosophical issues are not easily dismissed. When the philosophical question about machines thinking is converted into a scientific test like the Turing test, the underlying philosophical concern does not vanish but merely reappears in a new way. In this case the philosophical issue becomes "Is the Turing test a reasonable replacement for the question about machine thinking?" Turing was aware of this difficulty. On the one hand, Turing's inclination was to dismiss the question "Can machines think?" because he thought the question was "too meaningful to deserve discussion." On the other hand, he knew that questions about the adequacy of his replacement lurked in the background. Turing said, "We cannot altogether abandon the original form of the problem, for opinions will differ as to the appropriateness of the substitution and we must at least listen to what has to be said in this connexion" (Turing, 1950, p. 19). Indeed, a considerable amount has been said in this regard since Turing proposed his test.

NATURE OF THE TURING TEST

Discussions of the Turing test often assume that the test is based on some form of behaviorism or operationalism. Millar (1973) states that a virtue of the Turing test is that "it constitutes an operational definition which, given a computer terminal system, can be used as a criterion"; Searle (1980, p. 423) dismisses the Turing test on the grounds that it is "unashamedly behavioristic and operationalistic." Operationalism and behaviorism are views that claim that mental terminology, such as "thinking," should be defined in terms of overt behavior or dispositions to behave. The advantage of giving operational definitions of mental processes in terms of behavior is that overt behavior provides a deductive basis for claiming the existence of mental phenomena. If thinking is explicitly definable in terms of certain behavior and computers exhibit this behavior, then by definition computers think. But clearly a behavioral analysis of a mental concept like thinking is inadequate. Thinking is an internal activity, and fortunately for the civility of human interaction, human thinking does not have an immediate or certain manifestation in behavior or vice versa. A behavioral analysis of thinking may offer an easy justification of the Turing test, but it also makes it vulnerable to easy refutation.

Gunderson (1971) offers this kind of refutation in the form of a parody. He notes that the question "Can rocks imitate?" is perhaps "too meaningless to deserve discussion." So he imagines a toe-stepping game. In this game a person in one room puts one foot through a hole in the wall near the floor. In the next room there is a human and also a rock box apparatus that consists of a box filled with rocks coupled to an electric eye and releasing mechanism. The person with a foot through the hole in the wall must decide whether a human or rock box apparatus is pressing on his or her toe. Gunderson thinks his parody "lays bare the reason why there is no contradiction involved in saying, 'Yes, a machine can play the imitation game, but it can't think.' It is for the same reason that there is no contradiction in saying, 'Of course a rock box of such-and-such a sort can be set up, but rocks surely can't imitate'" (Gunderson, 1971, p. 44).

Gunderson's expression of his parody is misleading in that it is not the rocks alone which imitate but the rock box apparatus. Moreover, a good behaviorist would point out that imitating is a complex activity which involves different kinds of behavior beyond that described in the toe-stepping game. Nevertheless, Gunderson's basic point that neither imitation nor thinking can be completely captured by pointing to net results as correct. Thinking, after all, is primarily an internal activity.

An Inductive Interpretation

However, interpreting the Turing test in the light of operationalism or behaviorism is unnecessary. Turing himself does not say he is giving an operational definition, and he does not argue for behaviorism. Because the operational/behavioristic interpretation of the Turing test makes it so vulnerable to criticism and is not explicitly defended by Turing himself, it is reasonable to look for a more interesting interpretation of the test. Another interpretation of the Turing test is to regard it as an inductive test (Moor, 1976). On the inductive interpretation the Turing test provides a format for gathering inductive evidence that computers think. Just as in physics a subatomic target is bombarded with accelerated particles to reveal its nature, in the Turing test a target mind is probed with questions in order to reveal its nature (Hofstadter, 1981). Inductive evidence gathered from accelerator tests or Turing tests might be weak or strong, but such evidence would never be deductively certain. Inductive evidence at most provides good reasons for believing that a particular hypothesis is true or false. As with any interesting scientific hypothesis, there is no logical contradiction in saying that the evidence for it is true but the hypothesis is false. Under the inductive interpretation, Gunderson's previous objection does not apply. Inductively speaking, there is no contradiction in saying that a machine can pass the Turing test but it cannot think.

An inductive interpretation of the Turing test is aligned with a common sense as well as a scientific approach to knowledge. Ordinary knowledge that other humans think and how they think is generated by inductive inferences (qv) based on their behavior. Somebody is judged to think deeply or not so deeply about chess on the basis of that person's chess playing. On a common sense level nobody confuses thinking about a chess move with an actual move. The latter is evidence for the former. In numerous other kinds of human activities human behavior is regarded as inductive evidence for inner mental activity. An inductive approach is a natural way to investigate other human minds and seems like an equally appropriate way to investigate computer minds.

In summary, the inductive interpretation of the Turing test avoids the pitfalls of behaviorism and accords well with our scientific and common sense understanding of gathering knowledge. In addition, this interpretation provides the right framework for considering the contemporary debate about the adequacy of the test. A wide variety of objections to the Turing test have been raised over the years, and Turing himself discussed some of these objections which are based on everything from theology to ESP (Turing, 1950). But the central objections to the test are most interesting and forceful if they are understood as challenges to the inductive strength of the Turing test. Is the Turing test too easy, too narrow, or too shallow to establish that digital computers think? Here each of these objections is considered in the form of a criticism and series of replies.

Is the Test Too Easy?

Criticism. The Turing test is not a severe test. Verbal skills are rather easy to mimic with a computer, and people are easily deceived by such superficial mimicry. Therefore, the evidence gathered in the Turing test would be insufficient to justify the conclusion that computers think.

Block (1981) maintains that humans "may be too easily fooled by mindless machines." Block cites Weizenbaum's program ELIZA (qv) as an example. ELIZA contains both a language analyzer and a script, which allows it to improvise a conversation around a certain theme such as cooking eggs or managing a checking account. With a script for Rogerian psychotherapy, the program is called "DOCTOR." Weizenbaum (1976) reports, "I was startled to see how quickly and how very deeply people conversing with DOCTOR became emotionally involved with the computer and how unequivocally they anthropomorphized it" (p. 6). Weizenbaum says that even his secretary, who had watched him work on the program, wanted him to leave the room while she conversed with the computer. "What I had not realized," says Weizenbaum, "is that extremely short exposures to a relatively simple computer program could induce powerful delusional thinking in quite normal people" (p. 7). Although Block does not believe ELIZA would fool an inquisitive interrogator very long, he does think that "human gullibility being what it is, some more complex (but nonetheless unintelligent) program may be able to fool most any human judge" (Block, 1981, p. 10). Block argues that a computer might pass the Turing test if its program looked up replies from a large, but finite, set of stored conversations.

Replies. First, sophisticated language ability is not easy to model on a computer. ELIZA has a very limited ability to understand language. Although many improvements have been made in natural-language processing since ELIZA was developed, no existing computer possesses anything like the linguistic ability of a typical human being. Turing was right to see language skill as a measure of thinking, for it is sophistication in language that clearly separates humans from other animals and, at least so far, from computers.

Second, the knowledge required by a computer to pass the Turing test is enormous. In order to pass the test, a computer really needs the knowledge of a typical human. In the Turing test a computer must converse sensibly about a wide range of subjects from poetry to the weather. No existing computer system begins to have a knowledge base that is sufficient to pass the Turing test. Storing potential conversations in a computer is a logically possible, but highly improbable, method of producing a computer system that would pass the Turing test in real time.

Third, a serious interrogator would not be fooled easily. The interrogator's objective is to identify the computer and to falsify the hypothesis that a computer can imitate a human thinker. Therefore, the interrogator would ask a variety of difficult questions and would not engage in idle anthropomorphizing. Of course, an interrogator might be fooled, but this is the nature of inductive testing.

Is the Test Too Narrow?

Criticism. The Turing test may be difficult to pass but still it is a test of only one activity—playing the imitation game. Surely, if computers think, they must be able to do more than play the imitation game. Tests beyond the Turing test must be administered in order to gather adequate inductive evidence that computers think.

Gunderson (1971, pp. 53–55) compares the situation to a vacuum-cleaner salesman who claims that his vacuum cleaner is all-purpose but only demonstrates that the vacuum cleaner picks up bits of dust. To show that the vacuum cleaner is all-purpose, other kinds of abilities must be demonstrated. Similarly, the computer must do more than play one game well. As Fodor (1968) puts the point, "Turing would presumably have been dissatisfied with a device that could answer questions about how to boil water if it routinely put the kettle in the icebox when told to brew the tea."

Replies. First, characterizing the Turing test as just one test is a misleading numbers game. The Turing test is really a format for conducting many tests. By asking questions, an interrogator can test a wide range of linguistic abilities from making jokes to using foreign languages. Moreover, through language any subject matter can be discussed. An interrogator can test for thinking about urban renewal, sailing, loving, or the merits of playing Mah-Jongg in the late afternoon.

Second, a judgment about any scientific hypothesis based on a body of evidence may be overturned when additional evidence is found. Science is fallible by nature. But this does not mean that additional evidence must always be gathered before a justified inductive inference (qv) can be made. Otherwise, scientists could never gather enough evidence for any hypothesis. Thus, although evidence gathered outside the Turing test might alter a justified inductive inference that a computer can think, it does not follow from this that additional evidence is necessary in order to make a justified inductive inference that a computer thinks. A vacuum cleaner might be justifiably judged to be all-purpose if it picked up bits of dust and came with an assortment of attachments for doing other kinds of cleaning. A buyer would not have to watch the vacuum cleaner with a cobweb attachment actually suck up cobwebs before being able to reasonably infer it could to it. Similarly, one might reasonably infer from linguistic evidence that a computer played poker well without ever seeing the computer play a poker hand with traditional cards. Linguistic evidence, though fallible, is sufficient for a good inductive inference that another being thinks. For example, intelligent communication with unseen aliens on a distant planet would be a sufficient inductive basis for attributing thinking to them. Of course, such aliens might really be machines.

Third, even if further tests yielded some contrary evidence, the computer might be regarded as a thinker. Suppose that a computer that passes the Turing test routinely puts the kettle in the icebox when told to brew the tea. Perhaps the computer thinks iceboxes are funny-shaped stoves, or perhaps its motor mechanisms are malfunctioning, or perhaps the computer is playing a joke. The hypothesis that a computer thinks is compatible with some evidence that appears to refute it. Of course, if the computer acted inappropriately in lots of ways, one might indeed reject the claim that the computer thinks. But rejection is the possible fate of any scientific hypothesis.

Is the Test Too Shallow?

Criticism. The Turing test is too shallow because it provides behavioral evidence but no evidence about the internal mechanisms that produce this behavior. One's inductive inferences that other humans think are based not only on the fact that they behave similarly but on the fact that they are made similarly. Electronic computers are simply made of the wrong stuff to think. Computers might simulate but they cannot duplicate thinking. As soon as it is known that behavior is produced by a computer, one's explanation will shift to a physical account of how the behavior comes about (Stalker, 1978). Thus the Turing test is inadequate because it hides information that would lead one to reject the claim that a computer thinks.

Searle (1980) gives a version of this criticism with his Chinese-room argument. Searle offers a thought experiment in which he, who knows no Chinese, is locked in a room with a large batch of Chinese writing (a script). He is given a second batch of Chinese characters (a story) along with instructions in English that allow him to correlate the second batch with the first. Finally, he is given a third batch of Chinese characters (questions) along with more instructions in English that allow him to correlate the third batch of symbols with the first two. Searle imagines that he can identify and manipulate these symbols in a completely formal way (by shapes alone) with such care that from the point of view of somebody outside the room his answers to the questions are indistinguishable from those of a native Chinese speaker. Of course, he can also answer questions in English since he is a native English speaker. The difference, Searle claims, is that when a question is asked in English, he understands the question and his answer, but when the question is in Chinese, he understands neither the question nor the answer.

Searle thinks his example shows that there could be two systems that pass the Turing test but only one of which understands. Searle concludes that "it is no argument against this point to say that since they both pass the Turing test they must both understand, since this claim fails to meet the argument that the system in me that understands English has a great deal more than the system that merely processes Chinese" (Searle, 1980, p. 419). Searle believes that any digital electronic computer will similarly lack understanding if it operates only in a purely formal way. Searle's criticism is not about the narrowness of the Turing test. Even if the computer were inside a robot that performed many activities, such as perceiving, walking, hammering nails, and eating, the robot would still be doing it all on the basis of manipulation of formal symbols and, therefore, according to Searle, would lack understanding. Searle believes that human beings understand because of the causal powers of the human brain. Computers do not understand because "syntax alone is not sufficient for semantics, and digital computers insofar as they are computers have, by definition, a syntax alone" (Searle, 1984, p. 34).

Replies. First, although humans are biologically alike, it is simply not the case that one's inferences that others think are based on one's knowledge of their internal operation. Not even brain scientists examine the brains of their friends before attributing thinking to them. Obviously, brains are crucial for thinking; but it is easy to exaggerate one's dependence on information about our biological workings when attributing thought to others. Aristotle knew that others thought, but he also believed that the brain's function was to cool blood.

Second, Searle's Chinese-room example really is a thought experiment. No human who was truly ignorant of Chinese could really manipulate Chinese symbols in the way Searle describes in real time and pass the Turing test. From the point of view of the person in the room, of course, there is no understanding of Chinese. But the real issue is whether the whole system, including the person in the room, the English instructions, the script, the I/O mechanisms, etc, understands. Searle denies that it does or that any computer system with similar capabilities understands Chinese, but his basis for such denials is unconvincing. If neurons can be combined to form a complex system that produces understanding, why cannot electronic components be combined to produce understanding? Searle's central argument is that digital electronic computers cannot have semantics (qv). But, if biological brains have both syntax and semantics with the right causal powers, why cannot electronic brains be so endowed?

Third, computer simulation of an activity does not rule out computer duplication of the activity. A computer that simulates flight does not fly a plane. Such a computer need not leave the ground to create a good simulation. But a computer in a plane that guides the craft in flight is not simulating flying a plane; it is flying a plane. Computers today only simulate certain aspects of thinking and would not pass the Turing test. But, if the linguistic abilities of computers are greatly enhanced to rival some machines in fiction, such as HAL and C_3PO, what would be the ground or the point of insisting that such machines simulate but do not duplicate thinking?

LEGACY OF THE TURING TEST

Disagreement about how much weight to attach to a test is not uncommon in science, and disagreement about the significance of the Turing test is certainly not surprising given the controversial nature of the subject matter. Both proponents and critics of the Turing test have insights to offer. Suppose that sometime in the future a computer did pass the Turing test. Surely this would provide significant evidence that a machine thinks. Yet lingering doubts, natural curiosity, and good scientific practice would lead to further investigation. Can the computer pass more Turing tests? (Too easy?) What else can it do? (Too narrow?) How does it do it? (Too shallow?) Indeed, Turing might not be dissatisfied with this outcome, for his own goal after all was to focus questions on his test and away from the original question "Can machines think?"

Restricted Turing Tests

In addition to a particular test, Turing's approach has served as an inspiration for the methodology and goals of AI. For example, Turing-like tests have been useful in evaluating and justifying expert systems (qv) (Duda and Shortliffe, 1983). In a restricted Turing test judges compare computer behavior with human behavior in a narrow range of activity. Judges may be asked to determine which results were generated by a computer and which by a human or they may be asked simply to rank the results along some dimension. For instance, MYCIN, a program that diagnoses and recommends treatment for meningitis, was evaluated by a panel of expert judges comparing MYCIN's analyses of a series of cases with the analyses of physicians of various levels of training and experience. In this test the judges rated MYCIN's analyses to be equivalent or preferable to those of actual physicians (Yu and coworkers, 1979).

Restricted Turing-test methodology also has been useful in probing the strengths and weaknesses of computer models of human behavior. For instance, different versions of PARRY, a program that simulates paranoid behavior, have been evaluated by several restricted Turing tests (Colby and co-workers, 1972). In one test psychiatrists interviewed both an actual patient and PARRY over a teletype system, and in another test transcripts of interviews with PARRY as well as transcripts of interviews with actual patients were sent to psychiatrists and to computer scientists for discrimination and evaluation. In general, PARRY was identified as the real paranoid patient about half the time. But as Colby (Colby, 1981) stresses, the valuable information from these tests for improving the model comes from the ratings of various dimensions of the model, not from asking the more general man-machine question.

CONCLUSION

The Turing test symbolizes a long-range goal of AI, ie, the creation of a computer with general intelligence. Turing knew the best path to creating a computer that would pass the Turing test is not to program a machine with fixed knowledge but to build a child machine that can be educated. Presumably, this computer would learn from experience and would use natural language to increase its knowledge. This computer would demonstrate a practical intelligence when interacting with the everyday world. It would solve its own problems and accomplish its own goals. In effect, this computer would do just what Descartes thought a machine can never do. Whether such a computer will ever exist is an open question; but if it did, who would deny it thought?

BIBLIOGRAPHY

N. Block, "Psychologism and Behaviorism," *Philos. Rev.* **40**, 5–43 (1981).

K. M. Colby, "Modeling a Paranoid Mind," *Behav. Brain Sci.* **4**, 515–560 (1981).

K. M. Colby, F. D. Hilf, S. Weber, and H. C. Kraemer, "Turing-like Indistinguishability Tests for the Validation of a Computer Simulation of Paranoid Processes," *Artif. Intell.* **3**, 199–221 (1972).

R. Descartes, *Discourse on Method* (1637). Published in *The Philosophical Works of Descartes*, trans. by E. S. Haldane and G. R. T. Ross, Cambridge University Press, Cambridge, 1973.

R. O. Duda and E. H. Shortliffe, "Expert Systems Research," *Science* **220**, 261–268 (1983).

J. Fodor, *Psychological Explanation*, Random House, New York, pp. 126–127, 1968.

K. Gunderson, *Mentality and Machines*, Doubleday, Garden City, N.Y., 1971.

D. R. Hofstadter, "Metamagical Themas: A Coffeehouse Conversation on the Turing Test to Determine if a Machine Can Think," *Sci. Am.* **244**(5), 15–36 (1981).

P. H. Millar, "On the Point of the Imitation Game," *Mind* **82**, 595 (1973).

J. H. Moor, "An Analysis of the Turing Test," *Philos. Stud.* **30**, 249–257 (1976).

J. R. Searle, "Minds, Brains, and Programs," *Behav. Brain Sci.* **3**, 417–457 (1980).

J. R. Searle, Can Computers Think?, in *Minds, Brains and Science*, Harvard University Press, Cambridge, Mass., p. 34, 1984.

D. F. Stalker, "Why Machines Can't Think: A Reply to James Moor," *Philos. Stud.* **34**, 317–320 (1978).

A. M. Turing, "Computing Machinery and Intelligence," *Mind* **59**, 433–460 (1950).

J. Weizenbaum, *Computer Power and Human Reason*, W. H. Freeman, San Francisco, Calif., pp. 1–16, 1976.

V. L. Yu, L. M. Fagan, S. M. Wraith, W. J. Clancey, A. C. Scott, J. Hannigan, R. L. Blum, B. G. Buchanan, and S. N. Cohen, "Antimicrobial Selection by a Computer," *J. Am. Med. Assoc.* **242**, 1279–1282 (1979).

J. H. MOOR
Dartmouth College

UNCERTAINTY AND PROBABILITY. See Fuzzy and probabilistic uncertainties; Reasoning, plausible.

UNIFICATION

Unification is a matching operation that lies at the heart of many AI systems and languages. It is used most prominently in theorem proving, logic programming, and natural language processing. Abstractly, the unification problem is the following: given two descriptions x and y, find an object z that satisfies both descriptions. The unification problem is most often stated in the following context: given two terms of logic built up from function symbols, constants, and variables, find a substitution of terms for variables that will make the two terms identical. For example, consider the two terms $f(x, y)$ and $f(g(y, a), h(a))$. These two terms are said to be unifiable, because replacing x by $g(h(a), a)$ and y by $h(a)$ will transform both terms into $f(g(h(a), a), h(a))$. The nature of such unifying substitutions, as well as the means of computing them, makes up the study of unification. The next three sections briefly introduce definitions, historical remarks, data structures, and algorithms for unification. Subsequent sections explore the role unification plays in AI.

DEFINITIONS

A variable symbol is one of $\{x, y, z, \ldots\}$. A constant symbol is one of $\{a, b, c, \ldots\}$. A function symbol is one of $\{f, g, h, \ldots\}$. A term is either a variable symbol, a constant symbol, or a function symbol followed by a series of terms, separated by commas, enclosed in parentheses. Some sample terms are: $a, x, f(x, y), f(g(x, y), h(z))$. Terms are denoted by the symbols $\{s, t, u, \ldots\}$. Terms, as defined here, are not to be confused with terms of predicate logic, which include more complex expressions such as "$\forall(x)\forall(y):(f(x) \rightarrow f(y)) \leftrightarrow (\neg f(y) \rightarrow \neg f(x))$."

A substitution is a function from variables into terms. Substitutions are denoted by the symbols $\{\sigma, \tau, \theta, \ldots\}$. A substitution σ in which $\sigma(x)$ is $g(h(a), a)$ and $\sigma(y)$ is $h(a)$ can be written as a set of bindings, enclosed in curly braces, ie, $\{x \leftarrow g(h(a), a), y \leftarrow h(a)\}$. This set of bindings is usually finite. A substitution is also a function from terms to terms via its application. The application of substitution σ to term t is also written $\sigma(t)$, and denotes the term in which each variable x_i in t is replaced by $\sigma(x_i)$.

Substitutions can be composed: $\sigma\theta(t)$ denotes the term t after the application of the substitutions of θ followed by the application of the substitutions of σ. The substitution $\sigma\theta$ is a new substitution built from old substitutions σ and θ by first modifying θ by applying σ to its terms, then adding variable-term pairs in σ not found in θ. Composition of substitutions is associative, ie, $(\sigma\theta)\tau(s) = \sigma(\theta\tau)(s)$, but not in general commutative, ie, $\sigma\theta(s) \neq \theta\sigma(s)$.

Two terms s and t are unifiable if there exists a substitution σ such that $\sigma(s) = \sigma(t)$. In such a case, σ is called a unifier of s and t, and $\sigma(s)$ is called a unification of s and t. A unifier σ of terms s and t is called a most general unifier (MGU) of s and t if, for any other unifier θ, there is a substitution τ such that $\tau\sigma = \theta$. Consider, for example, the two terms $f(x)$ and $f(g(y))$. The MGU is $\{x \leftarrow g(y)\}$, but there are many non-MGU unifiers such as $\{x \leftarrow g(a), y \leftarrow a\}$. Intuitively, the MGU of two terms is the simplest of all their unifiers.

Two terms s and t are said to match if there is a substitution σ such that $\sigma(s) = t$. Matching is an important variant of unification. The word *matching* has several meanings in AI. For example, in production systems, it refers to the problem of many–many matching, in which many rules are matched against many memory elements. This article only describes the matching of single pairs of terms; for a description of many–many matching Forgy (1982).

Two terms s and t are infinitely unifiable if there is a substitution, possibly containing infinitely long terms, that is a unifier of s and t. For example, x and $f(x)$ are not unifiable, but they are infinitely unifiable under the substitution $\sigma = \{x \leftarrow f(f(f(\ldots)))\}$, since $\sigma(x)$ and $\sigma(f(x))$ are both equal to $f(f(f(\ldots)))$.

HISTORY

In his 1930 thesis, Herbrand (1971) presented a nondeterministic algorithm to compute a unifier of two terms. This work was motivated by Herbrand's interest in equation solving. The modern utility and notation of unification, however, originated with Robinson. In his pioneering paper, Robinson (1965) introduced a method of theorem proving based on resolution, a powerful inference rule. Central to the method was unification of first-order terms, as defined in the previous section. Robinson proved that two first-order terms, if unifiable, have a unique most general unifier (MGU). He gave an algorithm for computing the MGU and proved it correct.

Robinson's original algorithm was inefficient, requiring exponential time and space. A great deal of effort has gone into improving the efficiency of unification. Robinson (1971) and Boyer and Moore (1972) introduced space-efficient algorithms. Huet (1976) discovered an algorithm that runs in $O(n\alpha(n))$ time, where n is the size of the terms being unified and $\alpha(n)$ is an extremely slow-growing function. Paterson and Wegman (1978) gave the first truly linear time algorithm for unification. Martelli and Montanari (1976) independently discovered another linear algorithm for unification and later published a nonlinear algorithm (1982) that runs very fast in practice. More recent work on fast unification algorithms have been published (Aït-Kaci, 1984; Wroblewski, 1987; Godden, 1990). A more detailed historical overview is also available (Knight, 1989).

DATA STRUCTURES AND ALGORITHMS

As mentioned previously, Robinson (1965) published the first modern unification algorithm. The algorithm is recursive: two terms unify if they begin with the same function symbol, have the same number of arguments, and each pair of arguments unify with each other. Variables unify with anything, and pairs of constants unify only if they are identical. The algorithm keeps track of variable bindings to ensure that all bindings are consistent. When unifying a variable with a term, the algorithm checks to make sure that the variable appears nowhere within the term. This is called the occur check, and it prevents problems of infinite unification.

The major problem with this algorithm is one of representation. First-order terms have one obvious representation, namely the sequence of symbols used to write them down. In other words, a term can be represented as a linear array whose elements are taken from: function symbols, variables, constants, commas, and parentheses. This is called the string representation of a term. The string representation is equivalent to the tree representation, in which a function symbol stands for the root of a subtree whose children are represented by that function's arguments. Variables and constants end up as the leaves of such a tree. Figure 1 shows the tree representation of the term $f(g(f(x)), h(f(x)))$.

Now consider the terms $f(g(f(x)), h(f(x)))$ and $f(g(f(a)), h(f(a)))$. Any unification algorithm will ensure that the function symbols match and that corresponding arguments to the functions are unifiable. In this case, after processing the subterms $f(x)$ and $f(a)$, the substitution $\{x \leftarrow a\}$ will be made. However, there is no need to process the second occurences of $f(x)$ and $f(a)$, because it will mean just doing the same work over again. What is needed is a more concise representation for the terms: a graph representation. Figure 2 shows graphs for this pair of terms. The subterm $f(x)$ is shared; the work to unify it with another subterm need be done only once. If $f(x)$ were a much larger structure, the duplication of effort would be more serious, of course. In fact, if subterms are not shared, it may be necessary to generate exponentially large structures during unification. Most efficient unification algorithms (Aït-Kaci, 1984; Godden, 1990; Huet, 1976; Patterson and Wegman, 1978; Wroblewski, 1987) use some form of graph representation for terms.

THEOREM PROVING

Robinson (1965) introduced unification as part of his work on resolution theorem proving (qv). In simplest terms, res-

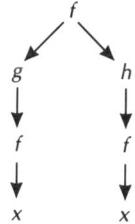

Figure 1. Tree representation of the term $f(g(f(x)), h(f(x)))$.

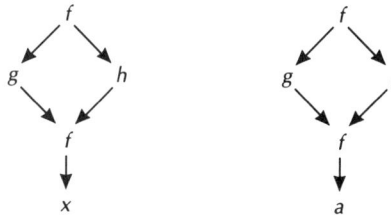

Figure 2. Term graphs for $f(g(f(x)), h(f(x)))$ and $f(g(f(a)), h(f(a)))$.

olution is a rule of inference that allows one to conclude "B or C" from the axioms "A or B" and "not-A or C." In actual theorem proving, resolution is more complex. For example, given the two facts

1. Advisors get angry when students do not take their advice.
2. If someone is angry, then he doesn't take advice.

The task is to be able to conclude a third fact

3. If a student is angry, then so is his advisor.

The first job of resolution is to put these statements into logical form.

1a. $\forall z : student(z) \rightarrow [\neg takeadvice(z, advisor(z)) \rightarrow angry(advisor(z))]$
2a. $\forall x, y : angry(x) \rightarrow \neg takesadvice(x, y)$
3a. $\forall w : student(w) \rightarrow [angry(w) \rightarrow angry(advisor(w))]$

Next, the universal quantifiers are dropped and the implication symbols are removed:

1b. $\neg student(z) \lor takesadvice(z, advisor(z)) \lor angry(advisor(z))$
2b. $\neg angry(x) \lor \neg takesadvice(x, y)$
3b. $\neg student(w) \lor \neg angry(w) \lor angry(advisor(w))$

Expressions 1b, 2b, and 3b are said to be in clausal form. Resolution is a rule of inference that will allow the last clause to be concluded from the first two. Here it is in its simplest form:

The Resolution Rule

If clause A contains some term s and clause B contains the negation of some term t, and if s and t are unifiable by a substitution σ, then a resolvent of A and B is generated by combining the clauses from A and B, removing terms s and t, and applying the substitution σ to the remaining terms. If clauses A and B have a resolvent C, then C may be inferred from A and B.

In this example, let s be $takesadvice(z, advisor(z))$, and let t be $takesadvice(x, y)$. Expression 1b contains s, and 2b contains the negation of t. Terms s and t are unifiable under the substitution $\{x \leftarrow z, y \leftarrow advisor(z)\}$. Removing s from 1b and the negation of t from 2b, and applying the substitution to the rest of the terms in 1b and 2b, we get the resolvent:

4. $\neg student(z) \lor angry(advisor(z)) \lor \neg angry(z)$

This expression is the same as 3b, subject to disjunct reordering and renaming of the unbound variable, and therefore, resolution has made the inference we intended.

Resolution is a powerful inference rule, so powerful that it is the only rule needed for a sound and complete system of logic. The simple example above illustrates the use of unification in resolution (Robinson, 1965; Nilsson, 1980). Three main lines of research grew out of the work on resolution: logic programming, higher order theorem proving, and theorem proving in equational logics.

LOGIC PROGRAMMING

The idea of programming in logic came directly out of Robinson's work: the original and still most popular logic programming (qv) language PROLOG was originally a tightly constrained resolution theorem prover. Colmerauer (1983) and Roussel turned it into a useful language, and van Emden and Kowalski (1976) provided an elegant theoretical model based on Horn clauses. Through its use of resolution, PROLOG inherited unification as a central operation. A great deal of research in logic programming focuses on efficient implementation, and unification has, therefore, received special attention.

Consider a set of four PROLOG assertions, followed by a query (Clocksin and Mellish, 1981):

likes(mary, food).
likes(mary, wine).
likes(john, wine).
likes(john, mary).

?- likes(mary, X), likes(john, X).

The query asks: Does Mary like something that John likes? PROLOG takes the first term of the query, *likes(mary, X)*, and tries to unify it with some assertion in the database. It succeeds in unifying the terms *likes(mary, X)* and *likes(mary, food)* by generating the substitution $\{X \leftarrow food\}$. PROLOG applies this substitution to every term in the query. PROLOG then moves on to the second term, which is now *likes(john, food)*. This term fails to unify with any other term in the database.

On failure, PROLOG backtracks. That is, it undoes a previous unification, in this case, the unification of *likes(mary, X)* with *likes(mary, food)*. It attempts to unify the first query term with another term in the database: the only other choice is *likes(mary, wine)*. The terms unify under the substitution $\{X \leftarrow wine\}$, which is also applied to the second query term *likes(john, X)*, to give *likes(john, wine)*. This term can now unify with a term in the database, namely *likes(john, wine)*. Done with all query terms, PROLOG outputs the substitutions it has found, in this case: "X = wine." This example shows how PROLOG makes extensive use of unification as a pattern matching facility to retrieve relevant facts from a database. Unification in PROLOG becomes nontrivial when the terms are more complex.

Colmerauer's original implementation of unification differed from Robinson's in one important respect: Colmerauer deliberately left out the occur check, allowing PROLOG to attempt unification of a variable with a term already containing that variable. For example, PROLOG will unify the terms x and $f(x)$, using the substitution $\{x \leftarrow f(f(f \ldots))\}$. Discarding the occur check corresponds to moving from unification to infinite unification. Other logic programming languages (Shapiro, 1983; Aït-Kaci and Nasr, 1986; Mukai and Yasukawa, 1985) use variants of unification specialized to handle concurrency, inheritance, and conditionals.

HIGHER ORDER UNIFICATION

First-order logic is sometimes too limited or too unwieldy to express certain facts. Second-order logic, which allows variables to range over functions (and predicates) as well as constants, can be more useful. Consider the statement, "Cats have the same annoying properties as dogs." This can be expressed in second-order logic as:

$$\forall(x)\forall(y)\forall(f):[cat(x) \land dog(y) \land annoying(f)] \to [f(x) \leftrightarrow f(y)]$$

Note that the variable f ranges over predicates, not constant values. In a more mathematical vein, here is a statement of the induction property of natural numbers:

$$\forall(f):[(f(0) \land \forall(x)\,[f(x) \to f(x+1)]) \to \forall(x)f(x)]$$

That is, for any predicate f, if f holds of 0, and if $f(x)$ implies $f(x+1)$, then f holds of all natural numbers.

For a theorem prover to deal with such statements, it is natural to work with axioms and inference rules of a higher order logic. In such a case, unification of higher order terms has great utility.

Unification in higher order logic requires some special notation for writing down higher order terms. The typed λ-calculus (Church, 1940; Henkin, 1950) is one commonly used method. Here is an example: "$\lambda(u, v)(u)$" stands for a function of two arguments, u and v, whose value is always equal to the first argument, u. It is necessary to distinguish between function constants (denoted: $A, B, C, \ldots$) and function variables (denoted: $f, g, h, \ldots$), which range over those constants. Now unification in the higher order realm can be examined.

Consider the two terms $f(x, b)$ and $A(y)$. Looking for a unifying substitution for variables f, x, and y, the following is found.

$$f \leftarrow \lambda(u, v)(u)$$
$$x \leftarrow A(y)$$
$$y \leftarrow y$$

This substitution produces the unification $A(y)$. But with further examination, another unifier is found.

$f \leftarrow \lambda(u, v)A(g(u, v))$
$x \leftarrow x$
$y \leftarrow g(x, b)$

In this case, the unification is $A(g(x, b))$. Notice that neither of the two unifying substitutions is more general than the other. A pair of higher order terms, then, may have more than one "most" general unifier. Gould (1966) was the first to demonstrate this fact. Clearly, the situation is more complex than that of first-order unification. In fact, unification in higher order logic is in general undecidable, as shown by Goldfarb (1981). There are, however, several systems for proving theorems using higher order resolution and unification (Andrews and co-workers, 1984; Darlington, 1971; Ernst, 1971; Huet, 1972; Jensen and Pietrzykowski, 1976).

EQUATIONAL THEORIES

Robinson's original algorithm unified terms without regard for the semantics of the symbols. When function symbols and constants take on certain interpretations, unification becomes more complex. Recall that at the beginning of this article, the two terms $s = f(x, y)$ and $t = f(g(y, a), h(a))$ were unified. The most general unifier σ was

$x \leftarrow g(h(a), a)$
$y \leftarrow h(a)$

From an algebraic viewpoint, this unification can be thought of as solving the equation $s = t$ by determining appropriate values for the variables x and y.

Suppose it is assumed that f denotes the function *add*, g denotes the function *multiply*, h denotes the function *successor*, and a denotes the constant *zero*. It is assumed that all the axioms of number theory hold. In this case, the equation $s = t$ is interpreted as $add(x, y) = add(mult(y, 0), successor(0))$. It turns out that there are many solutions to the equation, including the substitution τ:

$x \leftarrow h(a)$
$y \leftarrow a$

Notice that $\tau(s)$ is $f(h(a), a)$ and that $\tau(t)$ is $f(g(a, a), h(a))$. The resulting two terms are not textually identical, but under the interpretation of f, g, h, and a given above, they are certainly equivalent. The former is $successor(0) + 0$, or $successor(0)$; the latter is $(0 \cdot 0) + successor(0)$, or $successor(0)$. Therefore, it is said that τ unifies s and t under the axioms of number theory. It is clear that determining whether two terms are unifiable under the axioms of number theory is the same problem as solving equations in number theory.

Number theory has complex axioms and inference rules. Of special interest to unification are simpler equational axioms, such as:

$f(f(x, y), z) = f(x, f(y, z))$ (associativity)
$f(x, y) = f(y, x)$ (commutativity)
$f(x, x) = x$ (idempotence)

A theory is a finite collection of axioms such as the ones above. The problem of unifying two terms under theory T is written $\langle s = t \rangle_T$.

Consider the problem of unification under commutativity: $\langle s = t \rangle_C$. To unify $f(x, y)$ with $f(a, b)$ two substitutions are available: $\{x \leftarrow a, y \leftarrow b\}$ and $\{x \leftarrow b, y \leftarrow a\}$. With commutativity, the unique most general unifier of Robinson's null-theory unification is no longer obtained. Compare this situation to Gould's findings on higher order unification.

There are many applications for unification algorithms specialized for certain equational theories. A theorem prover, for example, may be asked to prove theorems about the multiplicative properties of integers, in which case it is critical to know that the multiplication function is associative. An associativity axiom could be added to the theorem prover, but it might waste precious inferences simply bracketing and rebracketing multiplication formulas. A better approach would be to build in the notion of associativity at the core of the theorem prover: the unification algorithm. Plotkin (1972) pioneered this area, and it has since been the subject of much research. Siekmann's (1989) survey of unification under equational theories is comprehensive.

FEATURE STRUCTURES

Kay (1979) introduced the idea of using unification for manipulating the syntactic structures of natural lanugages (eg, English and Japanese). He formalized the linguistic notion of features in what are now called feature structures. Feature structures resemble first-order terms, but have several restrictions lifted:

1. Substructures are labeled symbolically, not inferred by argument position; Figure 3 shows the feature structure corresponding to the term *person*(*john*, 23, 70, *spouse*(*mary*, 25)) (notice that the distinction between functions and arguments is dropped).

2. Fixed arity is not required; traditionally, feature structures have been used to represent partial information: unification combines partial structures into larger structures, assuming no conflict occurs. In other words, unification can result in new structures that are wider as well as deeper than the old structures; Figure 4 shows an example (the square cup stands for unification).

3. Variables and coreference are treated separately; variables in a term serve two purposes: they are place holders for future instantiation, and they en-

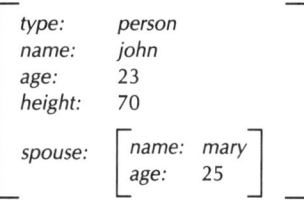

Figure 3. A feature structure.

$$\begin{bmatrix} \textit{type:} & \textit{person} \\ \textit{name:} & \textit{john} \end{bmatrix} \sqcup \begin{bmatrix} \textit{type:} & \textit{person} \\ \textit{age:} & 23 \end{bmatrix}$$

$$\Rightarrow \begin{bmatrix} \textit{type:} & \textit{person} \\ \textit{name:} & \textit{john} \\ \textit{age:} & 23 \end{bmatrix}$$

Figure 4. Unification of two feature structures.

force equality constraints among different parts of the term.

As an example, suppose the task is to express the constraint that John must marry his best friend. It may be possible to start with a term such as

$$person(john, Y, Z, spouse(W, X), bestfriend(W, X))$$

However, this is awkward and unclear; it is tedious to introduce new variables for each possible leaf node, and moreover, the term seems to imply that John can marry anyone as long as she has the same name and age as his best friend. What we really want is a variable to equate the fourth and fifth arguments, without concern for their internal structures. Figure 5 shows the feature structure formalization.

In Figure 5, and the figures to follow, the boxed number indicates coreference. Features with values marked by the same coreference label share the same value (in the sense of LISP's EQ, not EQUAL). The value itself can be placed after any one of the coreference labels, the choice of which is arbitrary. The symbol [ ] indicates a variable. A variable [ ] can unify with any other feature structure.

Like terms, feature structures can also be represented as directed graphs. Although term graphs are labeled on vertices, feature structure graphs have labels on arcs and leaves. Figure 6 shows the graph version of the feature structure of Figure 5.

Feature structures resemble other data structures used in AI. Features are very similar to slots (Minsky, 1975) and whole feature structures can easily be viewed as frames. Aït-Kaci (1984) shows how to incorporate frame-like inheritance directly into unification. The explicit labeling of Common LISP's keyword parameters (Steele, 1990) is also reminiscent of feature structures. When a function is called, the set of parameters is unified with the set sent by the caller. Notice that in LISP, variable binding occurs in only one direction; contrast this behavior to that of PROLOG, where parameters may contain uninstantiated variables.

$$\begin{bmatrix} \textit{type:} & \textit{person} \\ \textit{name:} & \textit{john} \\ \textit{age:} & [\,] \\ \textit{height:} & [\,] \\ \textit{spouse:} & \boxed{1} \begin{bmatrix} \textit{name:} & [\,] \\ \textit{age:} & [\,] \end{bmatrix} \\ \textit{bestfriend:} & \boxed{1} \end{bmatrix}$$

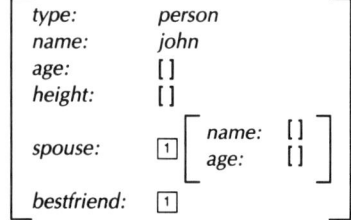

Figure 5. A feature structure with variables and coreference constraints.

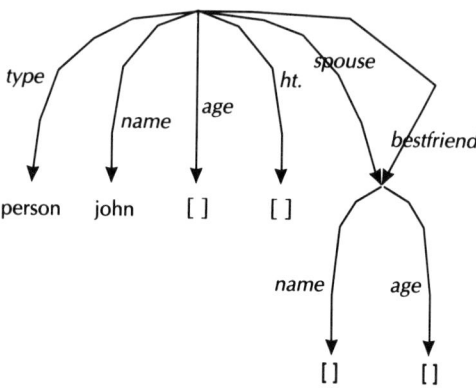

Figure 6. Graph representation of a feature structure.

NATURAL LANGUAGE PROCESSING

Unification-based parsing systems typically contain grammar rules and lexical entries. Lexical entries define words, and grammar rules define ways in which words may be combined with one another to form larger units of language, called constituents. Sample constituent types are the noun phrase (eg, "the man") and the verb phrase (eg, "eats bacon"). Grammar rules describe how smaller constituents can be put together to form larger ones.

Figure 7 shows a rule taken from a unification-based grammar. At its core is the simple context-free rule $S \Rightarrow NP\ VP$, meaning a sentence (S) can be built out of a noun phrase (NP) and a verb phrase (VP). The equations serve two purposes: to block applications of the rule under unfavorable conditions (eg, if the NP and VP have different agreement features) and to specify structures that should be created when the rule is applied. Here is how unification is used during rule application:

1. *Gather Constituent Structures.* Suppose the two structures shown in Figure 8 have already been built up. These structures represent analyses of the phrases "the man" and "eats." In parsing, the task is to combine these structures into a larger structure of category S.
2. *Temporarily Combine the Constituent Structures.* NP and VP are combined into a single structure, by way of dummy features $x1$ and $x2$ (Fig. 9).
3. *Represent the Grammar Rule Itself as a Feature Structure.* The feature structure for the sample rule

X0 ⇒ X1 X2
⟨X0 category⟩ = S
⟨X1 category⟩ = NP
⟨X2 category⟩ = VP
⟨X1 head agreement⟩ = ⟨X2 head agreement⟩
⟨X0 head subject⟩ = ⟨X1 head⟩
⟨X0 head⟩ = ⟨X2 head⟩
⟨X0 head mood⟩ = declarative

Figure 7. A grammar rule.

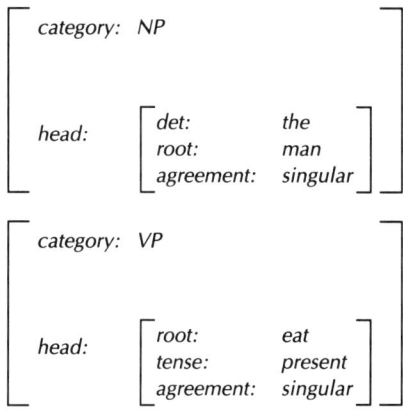

Figure 8. Feature structures representing analyses of "the man" and "eats."

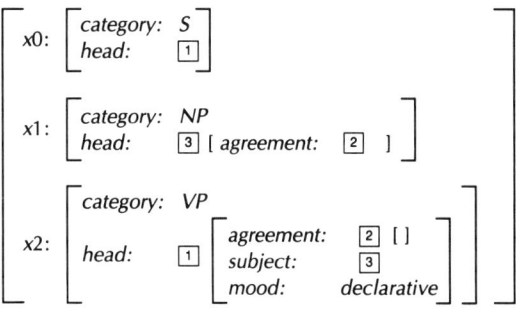

Figure 10. Feature structure representation of a grammar rule.

given above is shown in Figure 10. The boxed coreference labels enforce the equalities expressed by the rule's equations.

4. *Unify the Constituent Structure (Fig. 9) with the Rule Structure (Fig. 10).* Then the structure shown in Figure 11 is obtained. In this manner, unification builds larger syntactic constituents out of smaller ones.

5. *Retrieve the Substructure Labeled X0.* In practice, this is the only information we are interested in. The final structure is shown in Figure 12.

Notice that if the agreement feature of the original VP had been plural, unification would have failed, because the NP has the same feature with a different value, and the rule would fail to apply, blocking the parse of "the man eat."

A few issues bear discussion. First, where did the structures $X1$ and $X2$ come from? In unification-based grammar, the lexicon contains basic feature structures for individual words. Figure 13 shows a possible lexical entry for the word *man*. All higher level feature structures are built up from these lexical structures (and the grammar rules).

Second, how are the grammar rules that are applied choosen? Only a few rules can possibly apply successfully to a given set of structures. Parsing methods such as Earley's (1970) algorithm and generalized LR-parsing (Tomita, 1987) can direct the choice of grammar rules by looking at the category feature of the various constituents.

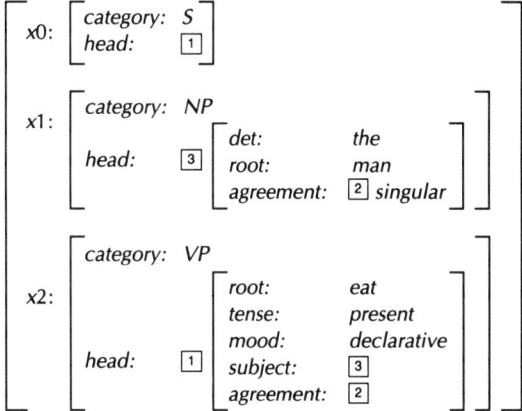

Figure 11. Result of unifying constituent and rule structures.

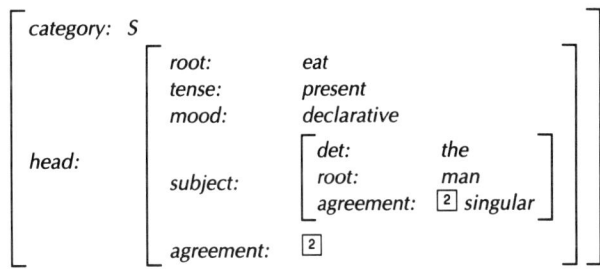

Figure 12. Feature structure analysis of "the man eats."

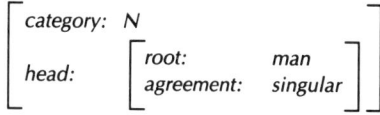

Figure 13. Sample lexical entry for the word *man*.

Finally, what are the structures used for? Feature structures can represent syntactic, semantic, or even discourse-based information. Unification provides a kind of constraint checking mechanism for merging information from various sources. The feature structure built up from the last rule application is typically the output of the parser. One advantage of using unification is that it is bidirectional. Because the equations are stated declaratively, a rule could be used to create smaller constituents from a larger one. One interesting aspect of unification-based grammars is the possibility of using the same gram-

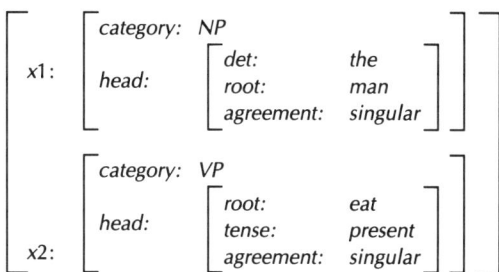

Figure 9. Combined feature structures.

mar to parse and generate natural language. See Shieber (1986) for more information on the use of unification in natural language processing.

SUMMARY

Unification is a pattern matching operation. It makes terms identical by finding bindings for variables that occur in those terms. Unification is a commutative and associative operation: the order in which unifications are applied to a series of terms does not matter. Unification is monotonic: it merges information, but never removes any. Unification is bidirectional, because variable binding may occur in both of the structures to be unified. Unification finds a number of applications in theorem proving, logic programming, and natural language processing. Related topics include parallel unification algorithms (Harland and Jaffer, 1987), disjunction and negation (Kasper, 1987), generalization (Reynolds, 1970), and type inference (Milner, 1978).

BIBLIOGRAPHY

P. Andrews, D. Miller, E. Cohen, and F. Pfenning, "Automating Higher-Order Logic," in W. Bledsoe and D. Loveland, eds., *Automated Theorem Proving: After 25 Years*, Vol. 29, American Mathematical Society, Providence, R.I., 1984.

H. Aït-Kaci, *A Lattice Theoretic Approach to Computation Based on a Calculus of Partially Ordered Type Structures*, Ph.D. dissertation, University of Pennsylvania, 1984.

H. Aït-Kaci and R. Nasr, "Login: A Logic Programming Language With Built-In Inheritance," *J. Logic Program.* **3** (1986).

R. S. Boyer and J. S. Moore, "The Sharing of Structure in Theorem-Proving Programs," *Machine Intell.* **7** (1972).

A. Church, "A Formulation of the Simple Theory of Types," *J. Symbolic Logic* **5** (1940).

W. F. Clocksin and C. S. Mellish, *Programming in Prolog*. Springer-Verlag, New York, 1981.

A. Colmerauer, "PROLOG in Ten Figures," in *Proceedings of the Eighth IJCAI*, Karlsruhe, FRG, Morgan-Kaufmann, San Mateo, Calif., 1983.

J. Darlington, "A Partial Mechanization of Second-Order Logic," *Machine Intell.* **6** (1971).

J. Earley, "An Efficient Context-Free Parsing Algorithm," *CACM* **6**(8) (1970).

G. W. Ernst, *A Matching Procedure for Type Theory*, Technical Report, Case Western Reserve University, Cleveland, Ohio, 1971.

C. L. Forgy, "Rete: A Fast Algorithm for the Many Pattern/Many Object Pattern Match Problem," *Artif. Intell.* **19**(1), 17–37 (1982).

K. Godden, "Improving the Efficiency of Graph Unification," in *Proceedings of the Twenty-eighth Annual Meeting of the Association for Computational Linguistics (ACL)*, 1990.

W. D. Goldfarb, "The Undecidability of the Second Order Unification Problem," *J. Theoret. Comput. Sci.* **13** (1981).

W. E. Gould, *A Matching Procedure for ω-Order Logic*, Ph.D. dissertation, Princeton University, Princeton, N.J., 1966.

J. Harland and J. Jaffar, "On Parallel Unification for PROLOG," *New Generation Comput.* **5** (1987).

L. Henkin, "Completeness in the Theory of Types," *J. Symbolic Logic* **15** (1950).

J. Herbrand, "Recherches sur la theorie de la demonstration," in W. Goldfarb, ed., *Logical Writings*, Harvard University Press, Cambridge, Mass., 1971.

G. Huet, *Contrained Resolution: A Complete Method for Higher Order Logic*, Ph.D. dissertation, Case Western Reserve University, Cleveland, Ohio, 1972.

G. Huet, *Resolution d'Equations dans les Langages d'Ordre 1, 2, . . . , ω.*, Ph.D. dissertation, Universite de Paris VII, France, 1976.

D. C. Jensen and T. Pietrzykowski, "Mechanizing ω-Order Type Theory Through Unification," *Theoret. Comput. Sci.* **3**(2) (1976).

R. Kasper, "A Unification Method for Disjunctive Feature Descriptions," in *Proceedings of the Twenty-fifth Annual Meeting of the Association for Computational Linguistics (ACL)*, 1987.

M. Kay, "Functional Grammar," in *Proceedings of the Fifth Annual Meeting of the Berkeley Linguistic Society*, 1979.

K. Knight, "Unification: A Multi-Disciplinary Survey," *ACM Comput. Surv.* **21**(1) (1989).

A. Martelli and U. Montanari, *Unification in Linear Time and Space: A Structured Presentation*, Internal Report B**76–16**, Ist. di Elaborazione delle Informazione, Consiglio Nazionale delle Ricerche, Pisa, Italy, 1976.

A. Martelli and U. Montanari, "An Efficient Unification Algorithm," *ACM Trans. Prog. Lang. Sys.* **4**(2) (1982).

R. Milner, "A Theory of Type Polymorphism in Programming," *J. Comput. Sys. Sci.* **17** (1978).

M. Minsky, "A Framework for Representing Knowledge," in P. Winston, ed., *The Psychology of Computer Vision*. McGraw-Hill Book Co., Inc., New York, 1975.

K. Mukai and H. Yasukawa, "Complex Indeterminates in PROLOG and Its Application to Discourse Models," *New Generation Comput.* **3** (1985).

N. J. Nilsson, *Principles of Artificial Intelligence*, Tioga, Palo Alto, Calif., 1980.

M. S. Paterson and M. N. Wegman, "Linear Unification," *J. Comput. Sys. Sci.* **16** (1978).

G. Plotkin, "Building-in Equational Theories," *Machine Intell.* **7** (1972).

J. C. Reynolds, "Transformational Systems and the Algebraic Structure of Atomic Formulas," *Machine Intell.* **5** (1970).

J. A. Robinson, "A Machine-Oriented Logic Based on the Resolution Principle," *J. ACM* **12**(1) (1965).

J. A. Robinson, "Computational Logic: The Unification Computation," *Machine Intell.* **6** (1971).

E. Shapiro, *A Subset of Concurrent PROLOG and Its Interpreter*, Technical Report TR-003, ICOT, 1983.

S. Shieber, *An Introduction to Unification-Based Approaches to Grammar*, University of Chicago, Chicago, Ill., 1986.

J. Siekmann, "Unification Theory," *J. Symbol. Comput.* **7**(3) (1989).

G. L. Steele, *Common LISP: The Language*, 2nd ed., Digital Press, Bedford, Mass., 1990.

M. Tomita, "An Efficient Augmented-Context-Free Parsing Algorithm," *Comput. Ling.* **13**(1–2) (1987).

M. H. van Emden and R. A. Kowalski, "The Semantics of Predicate Logic as a Programming Language," *J. ACM* **23**(4) (1976).

D. Wroblewski, "Nondestructive Graph Unification," in *Proceedings of the Sixth National Conference on Artificial Intelligence*, Seattle, Wash., AAAI, Menlo Park, Calif., 1987.

KEVIN KNIGHT
Carnegie Mellon University

UNIMEM

UNIMEN is a machine learning system developed by Michael Lebowitz that learns by observation [see M. Lebowitz, "Experiments with Incremental Concept Formation: UNIMEM," *Machine Learning* **2**(2), 103–138 (1987); see LEARNING, MACHINE]. It is a similarity-based learner that automatically develops a generalization hierarchy. It is a robust system designed to handle large numbers of examples, though the examples are represented very simply by feature/facet/attribute triples. It has been used in the domains of universities, Congressional voting records, U.S. state data, terrorist event descriptions, census data, and financial data, among others. It has also been used as a testbed for studying the integration of similarity-based and explanation-based learning [see M. Lebowitz, "Integrated Learning: Controlling Explanation," *Cognitive Science* **10**(2), 219–240 (1986)].

MICHAEL LEBOWITZ
Morgan Stanley and Co.

USER INTERFACE. See HUMAN–COMPUTER INTERACTION.

VISUAL MOTION ANALYSIS

When an observer moves relative to the environment, the two-dimensional (2-D) image that is projected onto the eye undergoes complex changes. These changes however, contain information regarding the relative 3-D motion and the structure of the scene in view.

There exist several representations for the pattern of movement of features in the image, containing different amounts of information related to 3-D motion and shape. The ones most studied are *optical flow, normal optical flow,* and *discrete displacements.*

OPTICAL FLOW

Optical flow (Gibson, 1950) can be represented by a 2-D field of velocity vectors as shown in Figure 1. In Figure 1a the optical flow is generated by the movement of an observer relative to a stationary environment. The "observer" is a camera mounted on an airplane that is flying over terrain. A single snapshot from a sequence of images is shown with reduced contrast. The black vectors superimposed on the image represent the optical flow, or velocity field. The direction and length of these vectors indicate the direction and speed of movement of features across the image as the airplane flies along. Optical flow is also generated by the motion of objects in the environment. Figure 1b shows three views of a three-dimensional (3-D) wire-frame object that is rotating about a central vertical axis. Figure 1c shows a snapshot of the object at a particular moment in time, with vectors superimposed that indicate the velocities of individual points on the object.

The analysis of the optical flow can be divided into two parts: The first is the measurement of optical flow from the changing image, and the second is the use of optical flow to recover important properties of the environment. The motion of features in the image is not provided to the visual system directly but must be inferred from the changing pattern of intensity that reaches the eye. Variations in the measured optical flow across the image (also known as motion parallax) can then be used to recover the movement of the observer, the 3-D shape of visible surfaces, and the locations of object boundaries. For example, from a sequence of optical flows such as that shown in Figure 1a, it is possible to recover the motion of the airplane relative to the ground. The variation in speed of movement of points on the wire-frame object of Figure 1c allows the recovery of its 3-D structure from the changing 2-D projection. Sharp changes in the optical flow field indicate the presence of object boundaries in the scene.

Computational studies offer a broad range of methods for measuring optical flow (for reviews, see Thompson and Barnard, 1981; Ullman, 1981; Ballard and Brown, 1982; Hildreth, 1984). Some methods compute the instantaneous optical-flow field directly. Methods for measuring motion also differ in the stage of image processing at which movement is first analyzed. For example, some infer movement directly from changes in the image intensities, and others first filter the image, or extract features such as edges. The range of techniques for motion measurement are reflected in a broad range of application domains, from the simple tracking of objects along a conveyor belt in an industrial setting to the analysis of more complex motions such as that of clouds in satellite weather data, heart walls in x-ray images, or cells in cell cultures. The analysis of optical flow is also becoming essential in autonomous navigation (see ROBOTS, MOBILE) and robotic assembly (see MANUFACTURING, AI IN; ROBOTICS).

The measurement of optical flow poses two fundamental problems for computer-vision systems. First, the changing pattern of image intensity provides only partial information about the true motion of features in the image due to a problem often referred to as the aperture problem. Second, when the general motion of objects is allowed, there does not exist a unique optical-flow field that is consistent with the changing image. In theory, there exist infinite possible interpretations of the motion of features in the image. Additional constraint is required to identify the most plausible interpretation from a physical viewpoint.

The aperture problem is illustrated in Figure 2. Suppose that the movement of features in the image were first detected using operations that examine only a limited area of the image. Such operations can provide only partial information about the true motion of features in the image (Thompson and Barnard, 1981; Ullman, 1981; Ballard and Brown, 1982; Hildreth, 1984; Lawton, 1983; Horn and Schunck, 1981). In Figure 2a the extended edge **E** moves across the image, and its movement is observed through a window defined by the circular aperture **A**. Through this window, it is only possible to observe the movement of the edge in the direction perpendicular to its orientation. The component of motion along the orientation of the edge is invisible through this limited aperture. Thus, it is not possible to distinguish between motions in the directions b, c, and d. This property is true of any motion detection operation that examines only a limited area of the image. As a consequence of the aperture problem, the measurement of optical flow requires two stages of analysis: The first measures components of motion in the direction perpendicular to the orientation of image features; the second combines these components of motion to compute the full 2-D pattern of movement in the image. In Figure 2b a circle undergoes pure translation to the right. The arrows along the contour represent the perpendicular components of velocity that can be measured directly from the changing image. These component measurements each provide some constraint on the possible motion of the circle. Its true motion, however, can be determined only by combining the constraints imposed by these component measurements. The movement of some features such as corners or small patches and spots can be

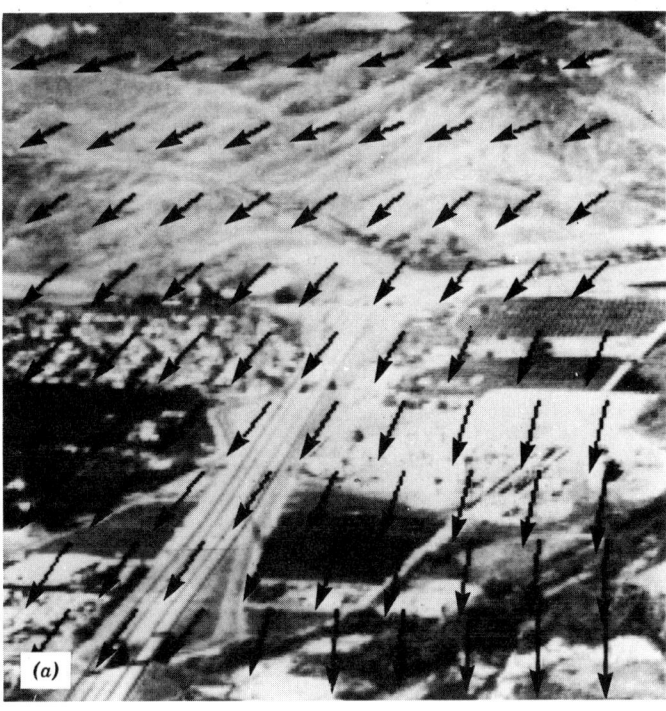

measured unambiguously in the changing image. Several methods for measuring motion rely on the tracking of such isolated features (Thompson and Barnard, 1981; Ullman, 1981; Ballard and Brown, 1982; Lawton, 1983). In general, however, the first measurements of movement provide only partial information about the true movement of features in the image and must be combined to compute the full optical-flow field.

The measurement of movement is difficult because in theory, there are infinitely many patterns of motion that are consistent with a given changing image. For example, in Figure 2c, the contour **C** rotates, translates, and deforms to yield the contour **C'** at some other time. The true motion of the point p is ambiguous. Additional constraint is required to identify a single pattern of motion. Many physical assumptions could provide this additional constraint. One possibility is the assumption of pure translation. That is, it is assumed that velocity is constant over small areas of the image. This assumption has been used both in computer-vision studies and in biological models of motion measurement (Thompson and Barnard, 1981;

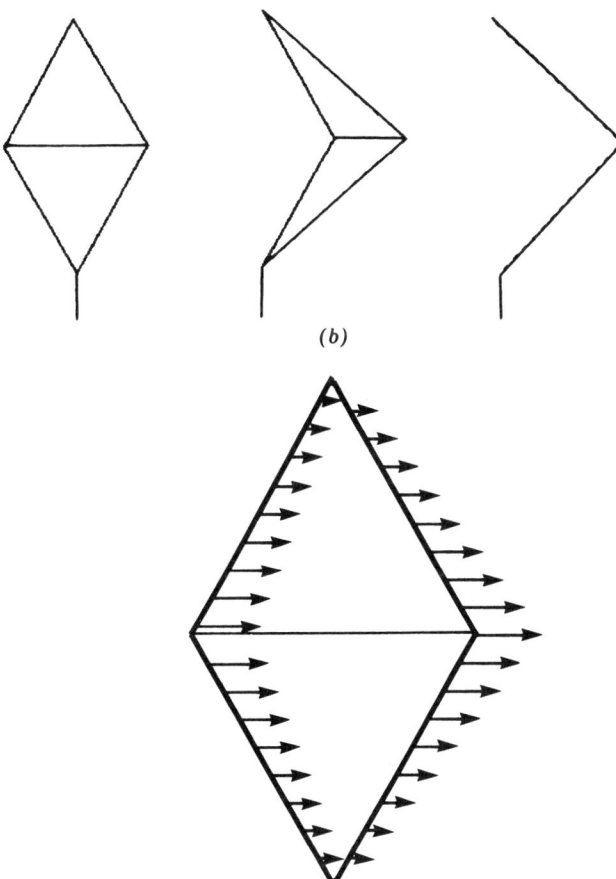

Figure 1. (a) Optical-flow field, represented by black arrows, is superimposed on a natural image that was taken from an airplane flying over terrain. (b) Three views of a wire-frame object rotating about a central vertical axis. (c) Projected pattern of velocities of individual points on the object are shown superimposed on a snapshot of the object in motion (an orthographic, or parallel projection is used).

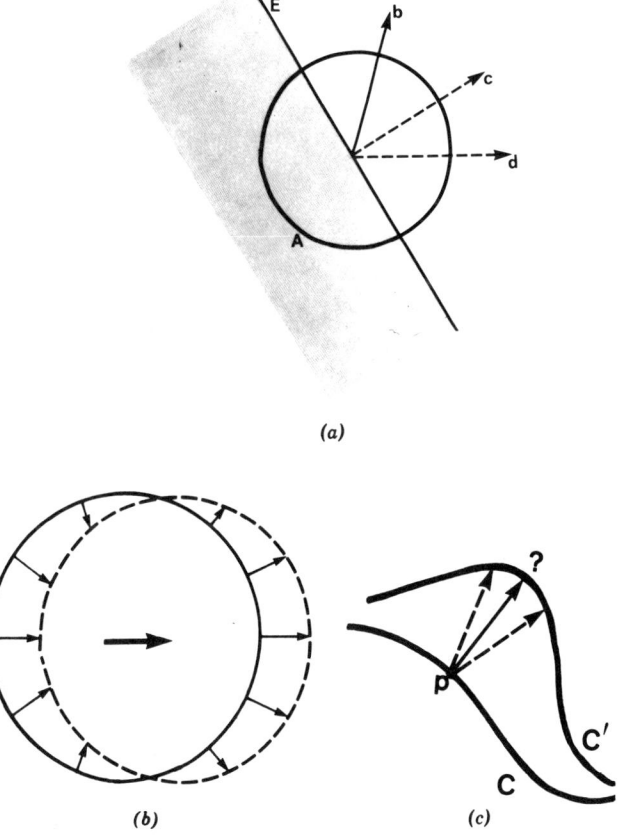

Figure 2. (a) Operation that examines the moving edge **E** through the limited aperture **A** can compute only the component of motion c in the direction perpendicular to the orientation of the edge. The true motion of the edge is ambiguous. (b) A circle undergoes pure translation to the right. The arrows along the circle represent the perpendicular components of motion that can be measured directly from the changing image. (c) A contour **C** rotates, translates, and deforms to yield the contour **C'**. The motion of the point p is ambiguous.

Ullman, 1981; Ballard and Brown, 1982; Hildreth, 1984; Lawton, 1983; Nakayama, 1985). Methods that assume pure translation are useful for detecting sudden movements and tracking objects across the visual field. These methods have led to fast algorithms for computing a rough estimate of the motion of objects, which is often sufficient in applications of motion analysis. Tasks such as the recovery of 3-D structure from motion require a more detailed measurement of relative motion in the image. The analysis of variations in motion such as those illustrated in Figure 2c requires the use of a more general physical assumption.

Other computational studies have assumed that velocity varies smoothly across the image (Hildreth, 1984; Horn and Schunck, 1981). This is motivated by the assumption that physical surfaces are generally smooth. Variations in the structure of a surface are usually small compared with the distance of the surface from the viewer. When surfaces move, nearby points tend to move with similar velocities. There exist discontinuities in movement at object boundaries, but most of the image is the projection of relatively smooth surfaces. Thus, it is assumed that image velocities vary smoothly over most of the visual field. A unique pattern of movement can be obtained by computing a velocity field that is consistent with the changing image and has the least amount of variation possible. The use of the smoothness assumption allows general motion to be analyzed and can be embodied into the optical-flow computation in a way that guarantees a unique solution (Hildreth, 1984). The optical-flow fields shown in Figure 1 were computed with an algorithm that uses the smoothness assumption (Hildreth, 1984).

NORMAL OPTICAL FLOW

An optical flow field is the vector field of the apparent velocities associated with the brightness patterns on the image plane. The scene in view is not involved in the definition of optical flow. One would hope that optical flow is equivalent to the so-called motion field (Horn, 1986), which is the perspective projection of the object's three-dimensional velocity field on the image plane. However, the optical flow field and the motion field are not equal in general. Verri and Poggio (1987) reported some general results in an attempt to quantify the difference between optical flow and the motion field. Although we do not have necessary and sufficient conditions for the equality of the two fields yet, it is clear that they are equal under specific sets of restrictive conditions.

If $I(x, y, t)$ is the image intensity function (x, y: space; t: time), the optical flow (u, v) at a point satisfies: $I_x u + I_y v + I_t = 0$, where subscripts denote partial differentiation. This equation can be written as $(I_x, I_y) \cdot (u, v) = I_t$, indicating that the projection of the optical flow (u, v) along the direction (I_x, I_y) is known. This is what is called the *normal optical flow*.

Clearly, estimating normal flow is much easier than estimating the actual optical flow. But then, how is normal flow related to the three-dimensional motion field? Is the normal optical flow field equal to the normal motion field, and under what conditions?

Let $I(x, y, t)$ denote the image intensity, and consider the optical flow field $(u, v) = \vec{v}$ and the motion field $\vec{\bar{v}} = (\bar{u}, \bar{v})$ at a point (x, y) where the local (normalized) intensity gradient is $\vec{n} = (I_x, I_y)/\sqrt{I_x^2 + I_y^2}$. The normal motion field at point (x, y) is by definition

$$\bar{u}_n = \vec{\bar{v}} \cdot \vec{n} \qquad \text{or}$$

$$\bar{u}_n = \left(\frac{dx}{dt}, \frac{dy}{dt}\right) \cdot \frac{(I_x, I_y)}{\sqrt{I_x^2 + I_y^2}} \qquad \text{or}$$

$$\bar{u}_n = \left(\frac{dx}{dt}, \frac{dy}{dt}\right) \cdot \frac{\nabla I}{\|\nabla I\|} \qquad \text{or}$$

$$\bar{u}_n = \frac{1}{\|\nabla I\|}\left(I_x \frac{dx}{dt} + I_y \frac{dy}{dt}\right)$$

Similarly, the normal optical flow is

$$u_n = -\frac{1}{\|\nabla I\|} I_t$$

Thus, when approximating the differential dI/dt by its total derivative, the result is

$$\bar{u}_n - u_n = \frac{1}{\|\nabla I\|}\frac{dI}{dt}$$

From this equation it follows that if the change of intensity of an image patch before and after its motion (dI/dt) is small enough (which is a reasonable assumption) and the local intensity gradient ∇I has a high magnitude, then the normal "optical flow" and "motion" fields are approximately equal. Thus, provided that normal flow is measured in regions where the intensity gradients are of high magnitude, it is guaranteed that the normal flow measurements can be used for inferring 3-D motion.

Clearly, the normal flow field contains less information than the optical flow field, but recent results indicate that several questions related to 3-D motion and shape can be answered solely on the basis of normal flow.

DISCRETE DISPLACEMENTS

The optical flow and normal flow representations of motion are instantaneous descriptions, ie, they are related to the velocity with which image patches move. We can consider a representation which is integrated over time, ie, we can trace features over time and thus compute a correspondence between features from one moment to the next. Features are extracted (using various operators) in several dynamic frames and points that correspond to the same point in the scene are identified through the so-called correspondence process (Ullman, 1979; Bandopadhay, 1986; Bandopadhay and Aloimonos, 1991). The latter sections will describe various approaches to the determination of three-dimensional motion of a rigid body based on time-sequential perspective views.

Determining the relative motion between an observer and his environment is a major problem in computer vision. Its applications include mobile-robot (see ROBOTS, MOBILE) navigation and monitoring dynamic industrial processes. For background material, the reader is referred to the two edited volumes of Huang (1981, 1983), the pioneering and influential book of Ullman (1979), several special journal issues and proceedings of several workshops on motion (see General References).

The next three sections describe methods that use a monocular two-dimensional sensor (such as a television camera); then methods are discussed that use a stereo pair of sensors. Finally, there is a brief discussion on numerical accuracy, multiple objects, nonrigid objects, motion prediction, and high level motion understanding. We consider as the inputs to the perceptual process of motion analysis discrete displacements (correspondences), optical flow, and normal optical flow.

TWO-VIEW MOTION ANALYSIS USING FEATURE CORRESPONDENCE

Problem Statement

The basic geometry of the problem is sketched in Figure 3. The object-space coordinates are denoted by lowercase letters and the image-space coordinates by uppercase letters. Let the two perspective views (central projections) be taken at t_1 and t_2, respectively, and $t_1 < t_2$. The coordinates at t_2 are primed, and the coordinates at t_1 are unprimed. Specifically, consider a particular physical point P on the surface of a rigid body in the scene. Let (x, y, z) be the object-space coordinates of P at time t_1, (x', y', z') the object-space coordinates of P at time t_2, (X, Y) the image-space coordinates of P at time t_1, (X', Y') the image-space coordinates of P at time t_2, and

$$\Delta X \triangleq X' - X \qquad \Delta Y \triangleq Y' - Y \qquad (1)$$

the image-space shifts (or displacements) of P from t_1 to t_2.

It is well known from kinematics that the object coordinates of P at time instants t_1 and t_2 are related by

$$\begin{bmatrix} x' \\ y' \\ z' \end{bmatrix} = R \begin{bmatrix} x \\ y \\ z \end{bmatrix} + T = \begin{bmatrix} r_{11} & r_{12} & r_{13} \\ r_{21} & r_{22} & r_{23} \\ r_{31} & r_{32} & r_{33} \end{bmatrix} \begin{bmatrix} x \\ y \\ z \end{bmatrix} + \begin{bmatrix} \Delta x \\ \Delta y \\ \Delta z \end{bmatrix} \qquad (2)$$

where R represents a rotation and T a translation. To make the representation unique, the rotation is specified around an axis passing through the origin of the coordinate system. Let $\hat{n} = (n_1, n_2, n_3)$ be a unit vector along the axis of rotation and θ be the angle of rotation from t_1 to t_2. Then the elements of R can be expressed in terms of n_1, n_2, n_3, and θ. Since $n_1^2 + n_2^2 + n_3^2 = 1$, there are six motion parameters to be determined: n_1, n_2, θ, Δx, Δy, and Δz. However, from the two perspective views, it is impossible to determine the magnitude of the translation, ie, if the object size and position as well as the translation are scaled by the same factor, one gets exactly the same two image frames. One can therefore determine the translation to only within a scale factor.

To summarize, the problem is: given two image frames at t_1 and t_2, find the motion parameters T (to within a scale factor) and R. As shown below, the equations relating the motion parameters to the image-point coordinates inevitably involve the ranges (z coordinates) of the object points. Therefore, in determining the motion parameters, one also determines the ranges of the observed object points. It will be seen that the translation vector T and the object point ranges can be determined to within a positive global scale factor. The value of this scale factor could be found if the magnitude of T or the absolute range of any observed object point is known.

Solution Using Point Correspondences

Consider a two-stage method to solve the posed problem. In the first stage, one finds point correspondences in the two perspective views (images). A point correspondence is a pair of image coordinates (X_i, Y_i), (X_i', Y_i') which are images at t_1 and t_2, respectively, of the same physical point on the object. Then, in the second stage one determines the motion parameters from these image coordinates by solving a set of equations.

Finding Point Correspondences. In order to be able to find point correspondences, the images must contain points that are distinctive in some sense. For example, images of man-made objects often contain sharp corners that are relatively easy to extract (Fang and Huang, 1982). More generally, image points where the local gray-level variations (defined in some way) are maximum can be used (Moravec, 1980). Other important approaches include Nagel (1983) and Kories and Zimmermann (1986).

In any case, in each of the two images a large number of distinctive points are extracted. Then one tries to match the two point patterns in the two images using spatial structures of the patterns (Fang and Huang, 1984). The matching will be successful only if the amount of rotation

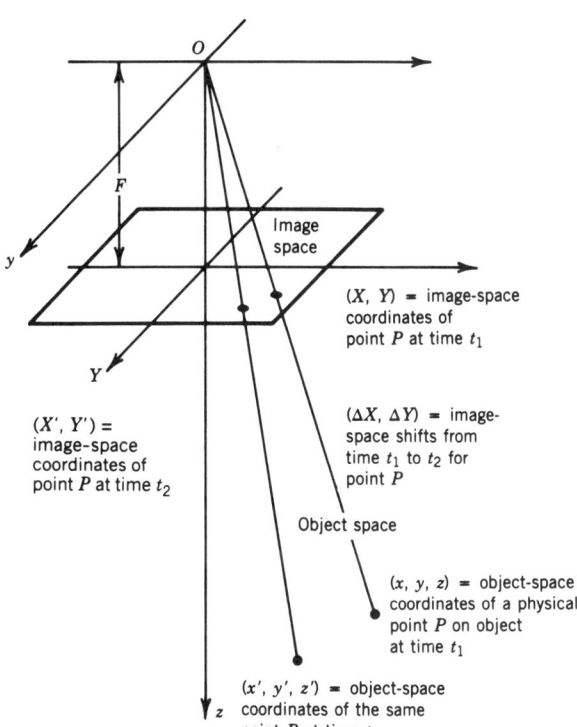

Figure 3. Basic geometry for motion analysis.

(θ) is relatively small (so that the perspective distortion is small). For example, in Fang and Huang (1982), good matching results are obtained if $\theta < 5°$. This restriction may be relaxed if there is some a priori information about the object (Gu and co-workers, 1984).

Basic Equations. From Figure 3 there is the following relationship between the image-space and the object-space coordinates:

$$X = F\frac{x}{z} \quad Y = \frac{y}{z} \quad (3)$$

For simplicity, assume throughout that $F = 1$. The motion is described by Eq. 2. From Eqs. 2 and 3,

$$X' = \frac{(r_{11}X + r_{12}Y + r_{13})z + \Delta x}{(r_{31}X + r_{32}Y + r_{33})z + \Delta z}$$

$$Y' = \frac{(r_{21}X + r_{22}Y + r_{23})z + \Delta z}{(r_{31}X + r_{32}Y + r_{33})z + \Delta z} \quad (4)$$

where the r_{ij} can be expressed in terms of n_1, n_2, n_3, and θ. By elimination of z from Eq. 4,

$$(\Delta x - X' \Delta z)\{y'(r_{31}X + r_{32}Y + r_{33}) - (r_{21}X + r_{22}Y + r_{23})\}$$
$$= (\Delta y - Y' \Delta z)\{X'(r_{31}X + r_{32}Y + r_{33}) - (r_{11}X + r_{12}Y + r_{13})\} \quad (5)$$

Also,

$$z = \frac{\Delta x - X' \Delta z}{X'(r_{31}X + r_{32}Y + r_{33}) - (r_{11}X + r_{12}Y + r_{13})}$$
$$= \frac{\Delta y - X' \Delta z}{Y'(r_{31}X + r_{32}Y + r_{33}) - (r_{21}X + r_{22}Y + r_{23})} \quad (6)$$

Equation 5 is nonlinear in the six unknowns: $\Delta x, \Delta y, \Delta z, n_1, n_2$, and θ. Also, it is homogeneous in $\Delta x, \Delta y$, and Δz. Therefore, as mentioned earlier, one can only hope to find T to within a scale factor. After finding T (to within a scale factor) and R, one can find z_i for each observed point to within the same scale factor using Eq. 6.

To fix ideas, let the translation sought after be the unit translation vector

$$\hat{T} = (\Delta \hat{x}, \Delta \hat{y}, \Delta \hat{z}) \triangleq \frac{1}{\sqrt{\Delta x^2 + \Delta y^2 + \Delta z^2}} T \quad (7)$$

Then, Eq. 5 can be considered as a nonlinear equation in the five unknowns: $\Delta \hat{x}, \Delta \hat{y}, n_1, n_2$, and θ. Thus, with 5-point correspondence, there are five equations with five unknowns. Well-known iterative techniques can then be used to find solutions. In practice, because of noise in the image data, one tries to find more than 5-point correspondences and seek a least-squares solution.

Alternative Formulation. The motion-parameter Eq. 5 was derived by eliminating z in Eq. 4. Alternatively, one can formulate equations in terms of the z coordinates of the points under consideration without containing any motion parameters (Mitchie and Aggarwal, 1985). This can be done by using the principle of distance conservation for a rigid body. Assume N point correspondences are given:

$$(X_i, Y_i) \leftrightarrow (X_i', Y_i') \ i = 1, 2, \ldots, N$$

And let (x_i, y_i, z_i) and (x_i', y_i', z_i') be the 3-D coordinates of the ith point at t_1 and t_2, respectively. Then, one has

$$(x_i - x_j)^2 + (y_i - y_j)^2 + (z_i - z_j)^2$$
$$= (x_i' - x_j')^2 + (y_i' - y_j')^2 + (z_i' - z_j')^2 \quad (8)$$

and from Eq. 3

$$(z_iX_i - z_jX_j)^2 + (z_iY_i - z_jY_j)^2 + (z_i - z_j)^2$$
$$= (z_i'X_i' - z_j'X_j')^2 + (z_i'Y_i' - z_j'Y_j')^2 + (z_i' - z_j')^2 \quad (9)$$

For each pair of points, one Eq. 9 can be written. Thus, with five-point correspondences, one can write ten equations that (if $z_1 = 1$) contain nine unknowns: $z_2, \ldots, z_5, z_1', \ldots, z_5'$. A least-squares solution for these unknowns can be found using iterative methods. Then the motion parameters are found by solving Eq. 2. Several methods for carrying out the last step are discussed under Motion from 3-D Feature Correspondences.

Disadvantage of Solving Nonlinear Equations. To find a least-squares solution of a small set of nonlinear equations 5 or 9 using iterative methods is not computationally expensive. However, unless there is a good initial-guess solution, the iteration may not coverge or it may converge to a local but not global minimum. Furthermore, with nonlinear equations it is very difficult to analyze the question of solution uniqueness.

In fact, it is an open theoretical question: what is the minimum number of point correspondences that will ensure a unique solution for the five motion parameters $\Delta \hat{x}, \Delta \hat{y}, n_1, n_2$, and θ? With 5-point correspondences the number of equations become equal to or larger than the number of unknowns. However, since the equations are nonlinear, one would expect that the solution may generally not be unique. This has indeed been verified by computer simulations in which global searches were made. The results of such simulations indicated that with 5-point correspondences there may be more than one solution; with 6-or-more-point correspondences the solution is generally unique. It is to be noted that in the case of 5-point correspondences, even though the solution may not be unique, if the iteration is started at a guess solution that is close to the true solution, one will most likely converge to it.

The conclusion is that the approach of solving nonlinear equations is viable if there is a good initial-guess solution. Otherwise, a better alternative is described in the next section: A linear algorithm that requires 8-or-more-point correspondences.

A Linear Algorithm. It turns out that by introduction of appropriate intermediate variables (which are functions of the motion parameters), Eq. 5 becomes linear (Longuet-Higgins, 1981; Tsai and Huang, 1984). Define

$$E = \begin{bmatrix} e_1 & e_2 & e_3 \\ e_4 & e_5 & e_6 \\ e_7 & e_8 & e_9 \end{bmatrix} = GR \quad (10)$$

where

$$G = \begin{bmatrix} 0 & -\Delta\hat{z} & \Delta\hat{y} \\ \Delta\hat{z} & 0 & -\Delta\hat{x} \\ -\Delta\hat{y} & \Delta\hat{x} & 0 \end{bmatrix} \quad \text{(skew symmetric)} \quad (11)$$

$\hat{T} = (\Delta\hat{x}, \Delta\hat{y}, \Delta\hat{z})$ is the unit translation vector defined in Eq. 7, and R is the orthonormal rotation matrix. Then Eq. 5 becomes

$$[X' \quad Y' \quad 1] E \begin{bmatrix} X \\ Y \\ 1 \end{bmatrix} = 0 \quad (12)$$

which is linear and homogeneous in the nine new unknowns: $e_1, \ldots, e_9$. The algorithm consists of two steps:

Step 1. From 8 or more point correspondences determine E to within an unknown scale factor k.

Step 2. decompose kE to obtain R and $\hat{T}$

Step 1 is relatively simple; it amounts to finding the least-squares solution of a set of linear equations 12. Step 2 is more complicated and is not discussed here. Several algorithms are given in other sources (Longuet-Higgins, 1981; Tsai and Huang, 1984; Yen and Huang, 1983; Zhuang and co-workers, 1986; Huang, 1985). It can be shown that, except for degenerate cases, 8 or more point correspondences yield a unique solution for R and $\hat{T}$ (Zhuang and co-workers, 1986; Huang, 1985; Longuet-Higgins, 1984).

Planar Patch Case. In many applications the points observed may all lie on a rigid planar patch in 3-D. In this case the linear algorithm shown above breaks down. One can go back to use the nonlinear equations 5 or 9. However, it turns out that a more computationally efficient, and in fact linear, algorithm exists for the planar patch case (Tsai and Huang, 1981, 1984; Tsai and co-workers, 1983). This linear algorithm, described below, also throws light on the uniqueness question for the planar case.

Let the 3-D points observed all lie on a plane whose equation at t_1 is

$$ax + by + cz = 1$$

or

$$[a, b, c] \begin{bmatrix} x \\ y \\ z \end{bmatrix} = 1 \quad (13)$$

Later, the notation $g = [a, b, c]^t$ (the superscript t denotes transportation) is used. From Eqs. 2 and 13

$$\begin{bmatrix} x' \\ y' \\ z' \end{bmatrix} = R \begin{bmatrix} x \\ y \\ z \end{bmatrix} + T = R \begin{bmatrix} x \\ y \\ z \end{bmatrix} + T[a, b, c] \begin{bmatrix} x \\ y \\ z \end{bmatrix}$$

$$= (R + T[a, b, c]) \begin{bmatrix} x \\ y \\ z \end{bmatrix}$$

or

$$\begin{bmatrix} x' \\ y' \\ z' \end{bmatrix} = A \begin{bmatrix} x \\ y \\ z \end{bmatrix} \quad (14)$$

where

$$A = \begin{bmatrix} a_1 & a_2 & a_3 \\ a_4 & a_5 & a_6 \\ a_7 & a_8 & a_9 \end{bmatrix} = R + \begin{bmatrix} \Delta x \\ \Delta y \\ \Delta z \end{bmatrix} [a, b, c] = R + Tg^t \quad (15)$$

From Eqs. 3 and 14

$$X' = \frac{a_1 X + a_2 Y + a_3}{a_7 X + a_8 Y + a_9} \quad Y' = \frac{a_4 x + a_5 Y + a_6}{a_7 X + a_8 Y + a_9} \quad (16)$$

Some other useful formulas are, from Eq. 13,

$$\frac{1}{z} = aX + bY + c \quad (17)$$

and, from Eq. 14,

$$\frac{z'}{z} = a_7 x + a_8 Y + a_9 \quad (18)$$

The two-step linear algorithm is as follows:

Step 1. From 4 or more point correspondences, a set of linear homogeneous equations 16 are solved to find A to within a scale factor.

Step 2. From A R, wT, and g/w, are determined where w is a positive scale factor.

Step 1 involves basically finding the least-squares solution of a set of linear equations. Step 2 is more complicated; an algorithm using singular-value decomposition is described in Tsai and co-workers (1983). It can be shown that, except for degenerate cases, given 4 or more point correspondences, there are generally two solutions for R, $\hat{T}$, and g. With 4 or more point correspondences over three views, the solution becomes unique (Tsai and Huang, 1985).

Solution Using Straight-Line Correspondences

In the presence of image noise and/or due to the spatial sampling, the coordinates of feature points cannot be determined accurately. This may make the estimation of motion parameters unreliable. Usually, it is easier to detect and determine the location of straight edges than feature points (Yen and Huang, 1986; Liu and Huang, 1986). Therefore, the question arises: can one estimate 3-D motion parameters by using straight-line correspondences?

Finding Straight-Line Correspondences. Images of man-made objects often contain straight edges. These straight edges can be detected using edge point detectors (such as the Sobel operator) followed by Hough transform (qv) (Duda and Hart, 1973). One first detects straight edges in both image frames and then uses structural information to match the two straight-line patterns. The algorithm of Cheng and Huang (1984) can be used to do the matching if the motion from t_1 and t_2 is small.

Two-View Nonuniqueness. By a straight-line correspondence over two frames, one knows the equations in the image plane at t_1 and t_2 of a 3-D line on the object:

$$t_1: \quad \alpha X + \beta Y = 1 \qquad (19)$$

$$t_2: \quad \alpha' X + \beta' Y = 1 \qquad (20)$$

where $(\alpha, \beta) \leftrightarrow (\alpha', \beta')$. Note that one does not assume any point correspondences on the two lines. Unfortunately, a little reflection convinces one that no matter how many straight-line correspondences are known over two frames, it is impossible to determine R and $\hat{T}$ uniquely. Heuristically, one can argue as follows: From the imaging system geometry expressions for α' and β' can be derived in terms of R, $\hat{T}$, α, β, and some additional parameters that pin down the position of the 3-D line at t_1. Given the 2-D image of a 3-D line, one needs two additional parameters (γ and δ, say) to determine the 3-D position of the line. Thus,

$$\alpha' = \alpha'(R, \hat{T}, \alpha, \beta, \gamma, \delta) \qquad (21)$$

$$\beta' = \beta'(R, \hat{T}, \alpha, \beta, \gamma, \delta) \qquad (22)$$

Each new straight-line correspondence gives two new equations 21 and 22 but also two new unknowns, γ and δ. Therefore, the number of equations is always smaller than the number of unknowns by five (the five motion parameters).

Three-View Case. With straight-line correspondences over three image frames (at $t_1 < t_2 < t_3$), it is possible to determine the motion parameters R_{12}, $\hat{T}_{12}$, (from t_1 to t_2) and R_{23}, $\hat{T}_{23}$ (from t_2 to t_3). An equation involving R_{12} and R_{23} can be obtained as follows. Let the equations in the image plane at t_1, t_2, and t_3 of a 3-D straight line be given by Eqs. 19, 20, and

$$t_3 \quad \alpha'' X + \beta'' Y = 1 \qquad (23)$$

Equation 19 implies with the help of Eq. 3, that at t_1, the 3-D straight line lies in the plane

$$\alpha x + \beta y - z = 0, \qquad (24)$$

which has a normal

$$q = (\alpha, \beta, -1) \qquad (25)$$

Similarly, at t_2 and t_3, respectively, there are the normals

$$q' = (\alpha', \beta', -1) \qquad (26)$$

$$q'' = (\alpha'', \beta'', -1) \qquad (27)$$

Then, it can be shown that the tree vectors q', $R_{12}q$, and $R_{23}^{-1}q''$ are coplanar. Thus

$$q' \cdot (R_{12}q \times R_{23}^{-1}q'') = 0 \qquad (28)$$

Here a three-element array is considered as either a vector or a column matrix from context. Equation 28 is nonlinear in the six unknown motion parameters (three from each rotation matrix). It has been found empirically that given seven or more straight-line correspondences over three frames, one can determine a unique solution to R_{12} and R_{23} by finding the least-squares solution of the set of nonlinear Eq. 28 using iterative methods. Once the rotations are found, the unit translation vectors can be obtained by solving linear equations. For a complete analysis, see Spetsakis and Aloimonos (1990).

An alternative treatment of the line correspondence case was given by Mitiche, Seida, and Aggarwal (Mitiche and co-workers, 1986).

Solution Using Planar Curve Correspondences

In some cases it may be possible to track the projection of a planar contour (eg, the boundary of a face of a polyhedron) from one image frame to the next. The change in the shape of the 2-D region (in image plane) bounded by the contour contains information on the 3-D motion parameters as well as the orientation of the plane in 3-D. More generally, if more than one region can be tracked the change in the relative positions of these regions (in image plane) can also be utilized. Gambotto and Huang (1984) have shown in a simple example how this region-based method can be used in motion analysis. However, a general methodology, even for the one-region situation, is yet to be developed. In the following, two special cases (one-region) are described.

Small-Motion Case. Kanatani (1985) has suggested a method using line (or surface) integrals. It is assumed that the amount of motion from t_1 to t_2 is small. Then

$$R \approx \begin{bmatrix} 1 & -\phi_3 & \phi_2 \\ \phi_3 & 1 & -\phi_1 \\ -\phi_2 & \phi_1 & 1 \end{bmatrix} \qquad (29)$$

where

$$\phi_i = n_i \theta \qquad (30)$$

Let C_1 and C_2 be the images at t_1 and t_2, respectively, of a 3-D planar contour. The equation of the plane at t_1 is

$$ax + by + cz = 1 \qquad (13)$$

Choose a function $F(X, Y)$ (eg, $F = X^2$), and compute

$$I(t_1) = \int_{C_1} F(X, Y) \, ds \qquad (31)$$

$$I(t_2) = \int_{C_2} F(X, Y) \, ds \qquad (32)$$

where

$$ds = \sqrt{dX^2 + dY^2} \qquad (33)$$

Then, it can be shown that

$$\begin{aligned}\Delta I \triangleq I(t_2) - I(t_2) \approx{}& K_1\,\Delta x + K_2\,\Delta y + K_3\,\Delta z + K_4\phi_1 \\ &+ K_5\phi_2 + K_6\phi_3 + K_7 a\,\Delta x + K_8 a\,\Delta y \\ &+ K_9 a\,\Delta z + K_{10}a\phi_1 + K_{11}a\phi_2 \\ &+ K_{12}a\phi_3 + K_{13}b\,\Delta x + K_{14}b\,\Delta y \\ &+ K_{15}b\,\Delta z + K_{16}b\phi_1 + K_{17}b\phi_2 \\ &+ K_{18}b\phi_3 \end{aligned} \qquad (34)$$

where the K_i are constants obtained by evaluating contour integrals around C_1 whose integrands involve F, $\partial F/\partial X$, $\partial F/\partial Y$, X, Y, dX/ds, and dY/ds and where $c = 1$ has been set to fix the global scale factor. The detailed formulas for K_i are given in Kanatani (1985). Equation 34 is nonlinear in the eight unknowns: Δx, Δy, Δz, ϕ_1, ϕ_2, ϕ_3, a, and b. To find these unknowns, eight or more different functions $F(X, Y)$ are first chosen. For each function one can calculate ΔI and the K_i to get one Eq. 34. Then one finds the least-square solution of the set of eight or more equations 34. Whether a unique solution can be obtained by this method is yet to be answered.

Orthographic Projections. For orthographic projections, instead of Eq. 3, one has

$$X = x \qquad Y = y \qquad (35)$$

Again, assume that the points observed lie on a plane in 3-D whose equation at t_1 is

$$ax + by + cz = 1 \qquad (13)$$

Then, from Eqs. 2, 35, and 13 (Young and Wang, 1984),

$$\begin{bmatrix} X' \\ Y' \end{bmatrix} = A \begin{bmatrix} X \\ Y \end{bmatrix} + D$$

where

$$A = \begin{bmatrix} a_{11} & a_{12} \\ a_{21} & a_{22} \end{bmatrix} \triangleq \begin{bmatrix} r_{11} - ar_{13} & r_{12} - br_{13} \\ r_{21} - ar_{23} & r_{22} - br_{23} \end{bmatrix}$$

and

$$D = \begin{bmatrix} d_1 \\ d_2 \end{bmatrix} \triangleq \begin{bmatrix} r_{13} + \Delta x \\ r_{23} + \Delta y \end{bmatrix}$$

($c = 1$ has been set to fix the global scale factor). Thus, the relationship between (X, Y) and (X', Y') is an affine transformation. This should be contrasted with the case of central projections where the relationship is Eq. 16.

One can attempt to find the motion and structure parameters (n_1, n_2, θ, Δx, Δy, a, and b) in two steps: first, from a contour correspondence over two frames, determine A and D in the affine transform Eq. 36 (a contour correspondence implies no point correspondences between the contour pair) and, second, determine the desired parameters from A and D. Several techniques for carrying out step 1 have been proposed. Reference 34 describe a method that relates the moment tensors of the two regions bounded by the contours at t_1 and t_2, respectively; Cyganski and Orr (1985) describes a method that relates the Fourier coefficients of the two contours after a canonic parameterization. A related work is Kanatani (1985). Un-fortunately, step 2 is generally not possible. The unknown parameters cannot be determined from A and D without additional information. This is because there are six equations:

$$\begin{aligned} r_{11} - ar_{13} &= a_{11} & r_{12} - br_{13} &= a_{12} \\ r_{21} - ar_{23} &= a_{21} & r_{22} - br_{23} &= a_{22} \\ r_{13} + \Delta x &= d_1 & r_{23} + \Delta y &= d_2 \end{aligned}$$

but seven unknowns: n_1, n_2, θ, Δx, Δy, a, and b. Solution becomes possible if one is given, eg, (a, b), ie, the orientation of the plane at t_1.

To close this section, note the classical result of Ullman (1979) for the orthographic projection case: four-point correspondence over three views determine motion/structure uniquely.

MOTION FROM OPTICAL FLOW

Problem Statement

In the two-view case, if $t_2 - t_1 = \Delta t$ is small,

$$R \approx I + S\,\Delta t \qquad (37)$$

where

$$S \triangleq \begin{bmatrix} 0 & -w_3 & w_2 \\ w_3 & 0 & -w_1 \\ -w_2 & w_1 & 0 \end{bmatrix}$$

and I is a 3×3 unity matrix.

The symbol Ω is used to denote the vector (w_1, w_2, w_3), the instantaneous angular velocities around the x, y, and z axes, respectively, at t_1. Also,

$$T \approx v\,\Delta t$$

where

$$v \triangleq \begin{bmatrix} v_x \\ v_y \\ v_z \end{bmatrix}$$

are the instantaneous translational velocities along the axes at t_1. Letting $\Delta t \to 0$, Eq. 2 becomes

$$\frac{dp(t)}{dt} = S(t)p(t) + v(t) \quad \text{(matrix equation)} \qquad (38)$$

or, equivalently,

$$\frac{dp(t)}{dt} = \Omega(t) \times p(t) + v(t) \quad \text{(vector equation)} \qquad (39)$$

where

$$p(t) \triangleq \begin{bmatrix} x(t) \\ y(t) \\ z(t) \end{bmatrix} \qquad (40)$$

As $\Delta t \to 0$, in the image plane.

$$V_x \triangleq \lim_{\Delta t \to 0} \frac{\Delta X}{\Delta t} = \frac{dX}{dt} \quad V_y \triangleq \lim_{\Delta t \to 0} \frac{\Delta Y}{\Delta t} = \frac{dY}{dt} \quad (41)$$

The image-plane velocity vector (V_x, V_y) is referred to as the optical flow. The problem of interest is to determine v (to within a scale factor) and Ω at time t_1 from optical-flow information. One takes an approach similar to that of using point correspondences in the two-view case. Specifically, it consists of two steps: Find optical-flow vectors at N image points, $[(X_i, Y_i), (Vx_i, Vy_i)]$, $i = 1, 2, \ldots, N$ and solve equations obtained from the optical-flow information to determine v and Ω.

Finding Optical Flow

Two approaches to finding optical flow are described. The first approach is to find point correspondences between two image frames at t_1 and t_2 (with $t_2 - t_1 = \Delta t$ small) using methods discussed above, and then obtain the optical-flow vectors by

$$V_x \approx \frac{\Delta X}{\Delta t} \quad V_y \approx \frac{\Delta Y}{\Delta t} \quad (42)$$

The second approach is to relate temporal and spatial differences of the image brightness. Let $f_1(X, Y)$ and $f_2(X, Y)$ be the brightness at point (X, Y) in the two successive image frames (at t_1 and t_2, respectively). At any given image point (X_0, Y_0) the time (frame) difference is

$$\Delta f(X_0, Y_0) \triangleq f_2(X_0, Y_0) - f_1(X_0, Y_0) \quad (43)$$

Assume the image point (X_0, Y_0) at t_1 and the image point (X_0', Y_0'), at t_2 correspond to the same physical point on the 3-D object, and let

$$\Delta X = X_0' - X_0 \quad \Delta Y = Y_0' - Y_0$$

Then

$$\Delta f(X_0, Y_0) = f_2(X_0, Y_0) - f_2(X_0', Y_0') \quad (44)$$

if one makes the assumption that any given point on the 3-D object appears in the two image frames with the same brightness. If the motion is small, this brightness-constancy assumption is reasonable in many situations. Then $f_2(X_0', Y_0') = f_2(X_0 + \Delta X, Y_0 + \Delta Y)$ is expanded into a Taylor series around (X_0, Y_0) and only the linear terms are kept to get

$$\Delta f(X_0, Y_0) = -\Delta X \frac{\partial f}{\partial X}(X_0, Y_0) - \Delta Y \frac{\partial f}{\partial Y}(X_0, Y_0) \quad (45)$$

This is an important equation mentioned again in the section Motion Estimation by Direct Matching of Image Intensities. Here, one can use it to find optical flow in the following way (Rocca, 1972; Limb and Murphy, 1975). If there are two or more image points (near each other) that one can assume to have the same $(\Delta X, \Delta Y)$, by calculating Δf and $[\partial f/\partial X, \partial f/\partial Y]$ (using a difference approximation) at each point, one can get a set of linear equations in the two unknowns ΔX and ΔY. Finally, the least-squares solution of these linear equations is found, and Eq. 42 is used to get V_x and V_y.

For general 3-D motion $(\Delta X, \Delta Y)$ vary with (X, Y). Therefore, it may not be reasonable to assume that $(\Delta X, \Delta Y)$ are the same at several image points. Horn and Schunck (1981) considered the case where $(\Delta X, \Delta Y)$ change slowly with (X, Y) and formulated a variational method for estimating $(\Delta X, \Delta Y)$. Other methods that are image-point-wise recursive are described (Robbins and Netravali, 1983; Cafforio and Rocca, 1983). Also, Nagel (1983) attempted to improve the estimation of $(\Delta X, \Delta Y)$ by including the second-order terms in the Taylor series expansion of $f_2(X_0 + \Delta X, Y + \Delta Y)$. For a recent insightful study on the determination of optical flow, see Hildreth (Hildreth, 1984). See also the pioneering work on optical flow by Prazdny (1980).

Basic Equations

Differentiating Eq. 3 with respect to t and using Eq. 38, one gets

$$V_x = \left\{\frac{V_x}{z} - X\frac{V_z}{z}\right\} + [-XY w_1 + (1 + X^2)w_2 - Y w_3] \quad (46)$$

$$V_y = \left\{\frac{V_y}{z} - Y\frac{V_z}{z}\right\} + [-(1 + Y^2)w_1 - XY w_2 + X w_3]$$

whence

$$z = \frac{v_x - Xv_z}{V_x + XY w_1 - (1 + X^2)w_2 + Y w_3}$$

$$= \frac{v_y - Y v_z}{V_y + (1 + Y^2)w_1 - XY w_2 + X w_3} \quad (47)$$

and

$$(v_x - Xv_z)[V_y + (1 + Y^2)w_1 - XY w_2 - X w_3]$$
$$= (v_y - Y v_z)[V_x + XY w_1 - (1 + X^2)w_2 + Y w_3] \quad (48)$$

Equation 48 is nonlinear in the six unknowns: v_x, v_y, v_z, w_1, w_2 and w_3. Also, it is homogeneous in v_x, v_y, and v_z. Therefore, $v = (v_x, v_y, v_z)$ can be determined only to within a scale factor. To fix ideas, let the sought after translation be the unit translation vector

$$\hat{v} = (\hat{v}_x, \hat{v}_y, \hat{v}_z) \triangleq \frac{v}{\sqrt{v_x^2 + v_y^2 + v_z^2}} \quad (49)$$

Then Eq. 48 contains five unknowns, eg, $\hat{v}_x$, $\hat{v}_y$, w_1, w_2, w_3. If there are optical-flow vectors at five or more image points, $[(X_i, Y_i), (Vx_i, Vy_i)]$, $i = 2, \ldots, N$, one can seek a least-squares solution to the set of N nonlinear equations 48. Note that Eq. 46 can be derived from Eq. 4 by letting $\Delta t \to 0$.

A Linear Algorithm

Similar to the two-view point-correspondence case, a linear algorithm is possible here (Zhuang and co-workers, in press). In fact, in Eq. 12, if one sets

$$G = K \, \Delta t \tag{50}$$

where

$$K \triangleq \begin{bmatrix} 0 & -v_z & v_y \\ v_z & 0 & -v_x \\ -v_y & v_x & 0 \end{bmatrix} \tag{51}$$

and

$$R = I + S \, \Delta t, \tag{37}$$

and then lets $\Delta t \to 0$, one gets

$$[V_X, V_Y, 0]K \begin{bmatrix} X \\ Y \\ 1 \end{bmatrix} + [X, Y, 1]KS \begin{bmatrix} X \\ Y \\ 1 \end{bmatrix} \tag{52}$$

Let

$$L = \begin{bmatrix} l_{11} & l_{12} & l_{13} \\ l_{21} & l_{22} & l_{23} \\ l_{31} & l_{32} & l_{33} \end{bmatrix} \triangleq KS \tag{53}$$

Then Eq. 52 is equivalent to

$$[X^2, Y^2, 1, XY, X, Y, V_y, -V_x, V_xY - V_yX]h = 0 \tag{54}$$

where

$$h = \begin{bmatrix} h_1 \\ h_2 \\ h_3 \\ h_4 \\ h_5 \\ h_6 \\ h_7 \\ h_8 \\ h_9 \end{bmatrix} \triangleq \begin{bmatrix} l_{11} \\ l_{22} \\ l_{33} \\ l_{12} + l_{21} \\ l_{13} + l_{31} \\ l_{23} + l_{32} \\ v_x \\ v_y \\ v_z \end{bmatrix} \tag{55}$$

From Eqs. 53 and 55

$$\begin{bmatrix} h_7 \\ h_8 \\ h_9 \end{bmatrix} = \begin{bmatrix} v_x \\ v_y \\ v_z \end{bmatrix} \tag{56}$$

and

$$\begin{bmatrix} h_1 \\ h_2 \\ h_3 \\ h_4 \\ h_5 \\ h_6 \end{bmatrix} = \begin{bmatrix} 0 & -w_2 & -w_3 \\ -w_1 & 0 & -w_3 \\ -w_1 & -w_2 & 0 \\ w_2 & w_1 & 0 \\ w_3 & 0 & w_1 \\ 0 & w_3 & w_2 \end{bmatrix} \begin{bmatrix} v_x \\ v_y \\ v_z \end{bmatrix} \tag{57}$$

The solution procedure is as follows. From eight or more optical-flow vectors, one determines $h_1, \ldots, h_9$ to within a scale factor from the linear Eq. 54. Then Eq. 56 gives $v = (v_x, v_y, v_z)$ to within a scale factor. Finally, Eq. 57 is used to find $\Omega = (w_1, w_2, w_3)$.

Planar Patch Case. The linear algorithm of the last section breaks down when all the image points under consideration correspond to 3-D points lying on a plane (Longuet-Higgins, 1984). However, similar to the two-view case, a different linear algorithm is available. Let the equation of the plane in 3-D be

$$ax + by + cz = 1 \tag{13}$$

Then, as before,

$$\frac{1}{z} = aX + bY + c \tag{17}$$

Substituting in Eq. 46, one gets

$$\begin{aligned} V_X &= k_1 + k_2 X + k_3 Y + k_7 X^2 + k_8 XY \\ V_Y &= k_4 + k_5 X + k_6 Y + k_7 XY + k_8 Y^2 \end{aligned} \tag{58}$$

where

$$\begin{aligned} k_1 &= cv_x + w_2 & k_2 &= av_x - cv_z & k_3 &= bv_x - w_3, \\ k_4 &= cv_y - w_1 & k_5 &= av_y + w_3 & k_6 &= bv_y - cv_z, \\ k_7 &= -av_z + w_2 & k_8 &= -bv_z - w_3 \end{aligned} \tag{59}$$

Given optical-flow vectors at four or more image points, we can determine $k_1, k_2, \ldots, k_8$ from Eq. 58. Then $\hat{v}$ and Ω can be found from the k_i as described in Longuet-Higgins (1984). Similar to the two-view case, generally there are two solutions for the motion parameters. Longuet-Higgins (1984) discusses the physical meaning of the two solutions and the fact that in many cases one of the solutions can be ruled out.

Generalized Flow Fields

Basic Equations. In the discussions of optical flow so far, only the image-point velocities V_X and V_Y have been used. A more general formulation using V_X, V_Y as well as their derivatives (with respect to X and Y) up to the second order was proposed by Waxman and Ullman. Their approach is based on studying the deformation of a small neighborhood in the image and provides much insight into the relationship between the 3-D motion/structure of a rigid body and its 2-D perspective views.

Specifically, consider the vicinity of the image origin $(X, Y) = (0, 0)$, and assume that the object surface

$$z = z(x, y) \tag{60}$$

around the point $(0, 0, z_0)$, where $z_0 = z(0, 0)$ is smooth (twice differentiable). Then 12 observables can be defined that are expressible in terms of the six motion parameters (M_1-M_6),

$$\frac{v_x}{z_0}, \frac{v_y}{z_0}, \frac{v_z}{z_0}, w_1, w_3, w_2$$

and five structure parameters (T_1-T_5),

$$\left[\frac{\partial z}{\partial x}\right]_0, \left[\frac{\partial z}{\partial y}\right]_0, z_0\left[\frac{\partial^2 z}{\partial x^2}\right]_0, z_0\left[\frac{\partial^2 z}{\partial y^2}\right]_0, z_0\left[\frac{\partial^2 z}{\partial x\, \partial y}\right]_0$$

The subscript 0 indicates that the derivative is evaluated at $(0, 0, z_0)$. Note that the five structure parameters give information on the slopes and the curvatures of the surface at $(0, 0, z_0)$.

The 12 observables are (0_1-0_{12}) V_X, V_Y, e_{11}, e_{22}, e_{12}, w, $\partial e_{11}/\partial X$, $\partial e_{11}/\partial Y$, $\partial e_{22}/\partial X$, $\partial e_{22}/\partial Y$, $\partial w/\partial X$, and $\partial w/\partial Y$, where e_{11}, e_{22}, e_{12}, and w are defined as follows: Let

$$\frac{\partial V_i}{\partial \xi_j} = \frac{1}{2}\left[\frac{\partial V_i}{\partial \xi_j} + \frac{\partial V_j}{\partial \xi_i}\right] + \frac{1}{2}\left[\frac{\partial V_i}{\partial \xi_j} - \frac{\partial V_j}{\partial \xi_i}\right] \triangleq e_{ij} + w_{ij}$$

$$i, j = 1, 2; (V_1, V_2) = (V_X, V_Y); (\xi_1, \xi_2) = (X, Y) \quad (61)$$

In terms of image deformation, e_{ij} is the rate-of-strain tensor and w_{ij} the spin tensor. The physical meaning of these quantities are e_{11} is the rate of stretch of a differential image line oriented along the X axis, e_{22} the rate of stretch of a differential image line oriented along the Y axis, e_{12} ($= e_{21}$) one-half the rate of decrease of the angle between two differential line segments along the image axes, and w_{21} ($= -w_{12} = w$) the rate of rotation (ie, the spin) of the differential neighborhood of image about the origin.

The basic flow equations relating the observables to the motion and structure parameters are derived in Waxman and Ullman (1983).

$$\begin{aligned}
0_1 &= M_1 + M_5 \\
0_2 &= M_2 - M_4 \\
0_3 &= -M_3 - M_1 T_1 \\
0_4 &= -M_3 - M_2 T_2 \\
0_5 &= -\tfrac{1}{2}(M_2 T_1 + M_1 T_2) \\
0_6 &= M_6 + \tfrac{1}{2}(M_1 T_2 - M_2 T_1) \\
0_7 &= 2(M_5 + M_3 T_1) - M_1 T_3 \\
0_8 &= -M_4 + M_3 T_2 - M_1 T_5 \\
0_9 &= M_5 + M_3 T_1 - M_2 T_5 \\
0_{10} &= 2(M_3 T_2 - M_4) - M_2 T_4 \\
0_{11} &= \tfrac{1}{2}(M_4 - M_3 T_2 - M_2 T_3 + M_1 T_5) \\
0_{12} &= \tfrac{1}{2}(M_5 + M_3 T_1 + M_1 T_4 - M_2 T_5)
\end{aligned} \quad (62)$$

These flow equations form a set of 12 coupled nonlinear algebraic equations with 11 unknowns. A method of solving these equations (given 0_1-0_{12}) is described in Waxman and Ullman (1983).

Finding the Observable. The problem remains: How does one measure the observables from the image sequence? Kanatani (1985), Waxman and Wohn (1984a,b) suggest a method based on evolving contours in the image plane. The 12 observables are in terms of $V_X^{(i,j)}$ and $V_Y^{(i,j)}$, $i, j = 0, 1, 2$ and $i - j \leq 2$, where

$$V_X^{(i,j)} \triangleq \left.\frac{\partial^{i+j} V_X}{\partial X^i\, \partial Y^j}\right|_0 \quad (63)$$

and similarly for $V_Y^{(i,j)}$. These derivatives can be obtained in the following manner. In the vicinity of $(X, Y) = (0, 0)$, one can write

$$V_X(X, Y) = \sum_{\substack{i=0\ j=0 \\ (i+j \leq 2)}}^{2}\sum^{2} V_X^{(i,j)} \frac{X^i}{i!} \frac{Y^j}{j!}$$

$$V_Y(X, Y) = \sum_{\substack{i=0\ j=0 \\ (i+j \leq 2)}}^{2}\sum^{2} V_Y^{(i,j)} \frac{X^i}{i!} \frac{Y^j}{j!} \quad (64)$$

For curved surfaces Eqs. 64 are only locally (and approximately) valid. But for planes they are globally valid—see Eqs. 58.

Assume a planar contour is tracked over two image frames separated by a small Δt. If one measures at a point (X, Y) on the contour, the normal flow velocity $V_n(X, Y)$ and the normal of the contour $n(X, Y) = (n_X, n_Y)$, one gets the equation

$$V_n(X, Y) = \sum_{\substack{i=0\ j=0 \\ (i+j \leq 2)}}^{2}\sum^{2} \frac{X^i}{i!}\frac{Y^j}{j!}\{n_X(X, Y)V_X^{(i,j)} + n_Y(X, Y)V_Y^{(i,j)}\}$$

(65)

Since there are 12 unknowns, one needs to measure the V_n and n of at least 12 points on the contour. Note that several separate contours can be used as long as they lie in the same plane in 3-D.

For curved surfaces the problem is much more difficult. Waxman and Wohn (1984b) discusses the truncation errors incurred by using the approximate Eqs. 64.

MOTION ESTIMATION BY DIRECT MATCHING OF IMAGE INTENSITIES

All the techniques for 3-D motion determination described above fall into the category of two-step methods. First, correspondences or optical-flow vectors are found, and then equations are solved to obtain the motion/structure parameters. In this section a description of a method based on direct matching of image intensities is given (also, see Finding Optical Flow, above).

Determining 2-D Translation by Displaced Frame Differences

Consider first the simple case of 2-D translation, ie, assume that $(\Delta X, \Delta Y)$ is constant for all image points corresponding to physical points on the rigid body. Again, let

$f_1(X, Y)$ = brightness of first frame (at t_1)

$f_2(X, Y)$ = brightness of second frame (at t_2)

Then the approach is to match f_1 and f_2 directly: Find $(\Delta X, \Delta Y)$ to minimize $D\{f_1(X, Y), f_2(X - \Delta X, Y + \Delta Y)\}$, where

D is a distance measure. One commonly used distance measure is

$$D = \sum_{X,Y} \{f_1(X, Y) - f_2(X + \Delta X, Y + \Delta Y]\}^2 \quad (66)$$

It is important to point out that this direct matching approach makes the tacit assumption that the two image points at t_1 and t_2, respectively, corresponding to the same physical point on the object, have the same brightness: ie, the brightness of an image point corresponding to a fixed point on the object does not change after motion. This is called the brightness-constancy assumption.

Coming back to Eq. 66, one notes that D can be minimized by using standard optimization techniques. However, the computation can be simplified in the case where the motion $(\Delta X, \Delta Y)$ is small. Then one can expand $f_2(X + \Delta X, Y + \Delta Y)$ in a Taylor series around (X, Y) and retain up to only the first-order terms. And Eq. 66 is reduced to

$$D = \sum_{X,Y} \left(\Delta f + \Delta X \frac{\partial f_2}{\partial X} + \Delta Y \frac{\partial f_2}{\partial Y} \right)^2 \quad (67)$$

where

$$\Delta f(X, Y) \triangleq f_2(X, Y) - f_1(X, Y)$$

is the frame difference at (X, Y) (Robbins and Netravali, 1983; Cafforio and Rocca, 1983).

In practice, Δf and $\partial f_2/\partial X$, $\partial f_2/\partial Y$ is calculated at N points: $(X_i, Y_i), i = 1, 2, \ldots, N$. Then the summation in Eq. 67 will be over these N points. Note that minimizing D in Eq. 67 is equivalent to finding the least-squares solution of the set of linear equations:

$$-(\Delta f)_i = \Delta X \left(\frac{\partial f_2}{\partial X} \right)_i + \Delta Y \left(\frac{\partial f_2}{\partial Y} \right)_i \quad (i = 1, 2 \ldots, N) \quad (68)$$

where a subscript i indicates that the quantity is evaluated at (X_i, Y_i). This is the same as the method described in Finding Optical Flow.

Generalization to 3-D Motion

The method of the preceding section can in principle be extended to the general case of 3-D motion. Both ΔX and ΔY are expressed in terms of the 3-D motion parameters; then D in Eq. 66 is minimized with respect to the 3-D motion parameters. In practice, there are two difficulties. The first is computational: There must be searching in a high-dimensional space. The second is that (as shown below), without further assumptions, the number of solutions is infinite. From Eqs. 1 and 4 one can get ΔX and ΔY in terms of, eg, $X, Y, z/\Delta z, n_1, n_2, \theta, \Delta x/\Delta z$, and $\Delta y/\Delta z$ (assuming $\Delta z \neq 0$). Then D in Eq. 66 is minimized with respect to these latter variables. Unfortunately, for each point (X_i, Y_i) there is a new unknown $z_i/\Delta z$. Therefore, one always has five more unknowns (the motion parameters) than the number of terms in Eq. 66, and as a result one has infinitely many solutions to the minimization problem.

One can hope to get a unique solution if one knows the form of the object surface to within a finite number of parameters. The simplest case is when the surface is a plane. Then it can be represented by

$$ax + by + cz = 1 \quad (\text{at } t_1) \quad (13)$$

and

$$\frac{z}{\Delta z} = \frac{1}{a'X + b'Y + c'} \quad (69)$$

where

$$a' \triangleq a \, \Delta z, \quad b' \triangleq b \, \Delta z \quad c' \triangleq c \, \Delta z \quad (70)$$

As a result, D in Eq. 66 can be expressed in terms of the eight unknown parameters $a', b', c', n_1, n_2, \theta, \Delta x/\Delta z$, and $\Delta y/\Delta z$ independent of how many points (X_i, Y_i) are used in the summation.

Now the computational problem: To search in an eight-dimensional space by standard optimization techniques is very time-consuming. The situation is better if the 3-D motion is small so that all $(\Delta X, \Delta Y)$ are small. Then one can use the Taylor series approach, and the problem of minimizing D is reduced to the problem of finding the least-squares solution of the set of Eq. 68, where ΔX and ΔY are now written in terms of the eight unknowns mentioned above. Note that the equations are now nonlinear (Huang and Tsai, 1981; Huang, 1985).

To summarize, the method of determining 3-D motion parameters of a rigid planar patch is to calculate Δf and $\delta f_2/\delta X$, $\delta f_2/\delta Y$ at eight or more ponts, and then find the least-squares solution (by some iterative method) of the set of eight or more nonlinear Eq. 68, where ΔX and ΔY are written in terms of the eight unknowns $a', b', c', n_1, n_2, \theta, \Delta x/\Delta z$, and $\Delta y/\Delta z$ by using Eqs. 4 and 69.

Once again, note that the method assumes brightness constancy.

Linear Algorithm for Planar Patches

The nonlinear least-squares algorithm for determining 3-D motion parameters of a rigid planar patch as described in the preceding section can be reduced to a linear least-squares problem by introducing appropriate intermediate variables (Tsai and Huang, 1981). Specifically, from Eq. 16

$$\Delta X = X' - X$$
$$= \frac{a_1 X + a_2 Y + a_3 - a_7 X^2 - a_8 XY - a_9 X}{a_7 X + a_8 Y + a_9} \quad (71)$$

$$\Delta Y = Y' - Y$$
$$= \frac{a_4 X + a_5 Y + a_6 - a_7 XY - a_8 Y^2 - a_9 Y}{a_7 X + a_8 Y + a_9}$$

Assuming the motion to be small, one can substitute Eq. 71 into Eq. 68 to get

$$(a_7 X + a_8 Y + a_9) \Delta f$$
$$= (a_1 X + a_2 Y + a_3 - a_7 X^2 - a_8 XY - a_9 X) \frac{\delta f_2}{\delta X}$$
$$+ (a_4 X + a_5 Y + a_6 - a_7 XY - a_8 Y^2 - a_9 Y) \frac{\delta f_2}{\delta Y}$$

or

$$X \frac{\delta f_2}{\delta X} a_1 + Y \frac{\delta f_2}{\delta X} a_2 + \frac{\delta f_2}{\delta X} a_3$$
$$+ X \frac{\delta f_2}{\delta Y} a_4 + Y \frac{\delta f_2}{\delta Y} a_5 + \frac{\delta f_2}{\delta Y} a_6$$
$$- \left[X^2 \frac{\delta f_2}{\delta X} + XY \frac{\delta f_2}{\delta Y} + X \Delta f \right] a_7$$
$$- \left[XY \frac{\delta f_2}{\delta X} + Y^2 \frac{\delta f_2}{\delta Y} + Y \Delta f \right] a_8$$
$$- \left[X \frac{\delta f_2}{\delta X} + Y \frac{\delta f_2}{\delta Y} + \Delta f \right] a_9 = 0 \quad (72)$$

This equation is linear and homogeneous in the nine unknowns, $a_1, \ldots, a_9$. If one calculates Δf and $\delta f_2/\delta X$, $\delta f_2/\delta Y$ at eight or more image points (X, Y), one gets a set of eight or more equations eg, Eq. 72. Then $a_1, \ldots, a_9$ can be solved to within a scale factor. Recall that the a_i are related to the motion/structure parameters by Eq. 15 and that the latter can be obtained from the former by a method described in Tsai and co-workers (1983).

MOTION FROM 3-D FEATURE CORRESPONDENCES

The motion-estimation techniques described above are based on images taken by a monocular 2-D sensor such as a single television camera. With such an arrangement the 3-D translation and the range of the object can be determined to only within a scale factor. One can determine the absolute translation velocity and ranges of object points if binocular vision (see stereo vision) is used, eg, two television cameras with known relative positions and orientations. the binocular method has several other advantages described below.

Binocular Procedure

A pair of stereo images is taken at t_1, and another pair is taken at t_2, and then the following procedure is used.

1. From the two images taken at t_1 feature points are extracted, the two point patterns are matched to find correspondences, and then by triangulation the 3-D coordinates of these points are found. The same is done for the two images taken at t_2.
2. The two 3-D point patterns at t_1 and t_2 are matched to find 3-D point correspondences.
3. A set of equations involving the motion parameters are obtained from the 3-D point correspondences.

These equations are solved to determine motion (Huang and Blostein, 1985).

Note that the matching problems in 1 and 2 are usually easier than the matching problem in the monocular two-view case (see above) because in 1, for a fixed point in one image of the stereo pair, the corresponding point in the other image is restricted to lie on the so-called epipolar line, and in 2, the distances between pairs of the 3-D points on a rigid body is invariant to motion. An algorithm for the maximal matching of two 3-D point sets is presented by Chen and Huang (1986).

Motion from 3-D Correspondences

Once one has obtained 3-D point correspondences $p_i \longleftrightarrow p'_i$, $i = 1, 2, \ldots, N$, where

$$p = \begin{bmatrix} x \\ y \\ z \end{bmatrix} \quad \text{and} \quad p' = \begin{bmatrix} x' \\ y' \\ z' \end{bmatrix}$$

how does one get the motion parameters R and T? A related question is: What is the minimum number of 3-D point correspondences needed for unique determination of R and T of a rigid body? A basic fact is that R and T are determined uniquely by three 3-D point correspondences (assuming the three points are not collinear). This becomes obvious if one notes that two points will fix a rigid body in space except for a possible rotation around the axis formed by joining the two points. A third point then fixes the rigid body completely. Once one knows three 3-D point correspondences on a rigid body, one can generate any number of other 3-D point correspondences rigid relative to the original three points.

To describe algorithms for finding R and T, Eq. 2 is rewritten as

$$p' = Rp + T \quad (73)$$

There are six unknown parameters, $n_1, n_2, \theta, \Delta x, \Delta y$, and Δz. Each 3-D point correspondence gives one matrix Eq. 73 or three scalar equations, which are nonlinear in the unknowns. An obvious method would be to find the least-squares solution (by some iterative technique) of the set of $3N$ coupled nonlinear equations obtained from the N three-dimensional point correspondences, where $N \geq 3$. However, much simpler linear algorithms are available (Blostein and Huang, 1984), one of which is described below.

Assume there are three 3-D point correspondences

$$p_i \longleftrightarrow p'_i, \quad i = 1, 2, 3.$$

Let

$$m_1 \triangleq p_1 - p_3 \quad m'_1 \triangleq p'_1 - p'_3$$
$$m_2 \triangleq p_2 - p_3 \quad m'_2 \triangleq p'_2 - p'_3 \quad (74)$$

Then, from Eq. 73,

$$m'_1 = R m_1 \quad m'_2 = R m_2 \quad (75)$$

If

$$m_3 \triangleq m_1 \times m_2 \quad m_3' \triangleq m_1' \times m_2' \quad (76)$$

(Consider m_i and m_i' as vectors.), then

$$m_3' = R m_3 \quad (77)$$

Combining Eqs. 75 and 77,

$$[m_1', m_2', m_3'] = R[m_1, m_2, m_3] \quad (78)$$

whence

$$R = [m_1', m_2', m_3'][m_1, m_2, m_3]^{-1} \quad (79)$$

and

$$T = p_i' - R p_i \quad \text{for } i = 1, 2, 3 \quad (80)$$

Note that the numerical accuracy of this algorithm is usually improved if normalized (to a magnitude of 1) versions of m_i and m_i' are used in the formulation.

Two remarks are in order. First, the above algorithm can be used not only for 3-D point correspondences but also for 3-D straight-line correspondences and surface-normal correspondences. In the latter two cases only two correspondences are needed. Second, in the pressure of noise in the data (3-D point coordinates), the matrix R obtained from the above algorithm may not be a rotation (ie, orthonormal and with a determinant equal to +1). In that case a rotation matrix R' can be found by using the algorithms in Faugeras and Hebert 91983) and Huang and co-workers (1986) to minimize

$$\|R' - R\|^2 \triangleq \sum_{i=1}^{3} \sum_{j=1}^{3} (r_{ij}' - r_{ij})^2$$

where r_{ij} and r_{ij}' are elements of R and R' respectively.

Correspondenceless Approaches

The problem of retinal correspondence is ill-defined and only partial solutions have been obtained to date. This complicates three-dimensional analysis on the basis of visual motion. Consider a set of points $A = \{(X_i, Y_i, Z_i), i = 1, \ldots, n\}$ in three dimensions that moves rigidly to a new position $A' = \{(X_i', Y_i', Z_i'), i = 1, \ldots, n\}$. Given the images $A_I = \{(x_i, y_i), i = 1, \ldots, n\}$, $A_I' = \{(x_i', y_i'), i = 1, \ldots, n\}$ (before and after the motion) and without considering individual point correspondences (only correspondences of sets of points), the problem is to recover the 3-D motion involved. Various approaches can be found (Aloimonos, 1986; Aloimonos and Rigoutsos, 1986; Aloimonos and Hervé, 1990).

Motion and Shape from Normal Flow

Although the idea of the normal optical flow field has existed in the literature for quite some time, using it to extract information about 3-D motion and structure is a rather recent activity. This is a very promising research area since normal flow fields are much easier to compute than actual flow fields. It turns out that if one employs an active observer (an observer that can control the geometric parameters of its sensory apparatus) then 3D motion and structure can be computed from normal flow. The interested reader can consult (Aloimonos, Weiss, and Bandyopadhyay (1987) and Aloimonos (1990).

ADDITIONAL TOPICS

In the preceding sections the major approaches to determining 3-D motoin/structure of a rigid body are described in some detail. This last section is a brief commend on some important additional topics. These topics also represent areas where further research is needed.

Numerical Accuracy of Algorithms

The reader should be warned that computer simulations and experiments with real images (Fang and Huang, 1984a,b) have indicated that in order to estimate motion parameters reasonably accurately (around 10% error) from two perspective views using a single camera, the image resolution has to be quite high (typically 1000 × 1000 picture elements, assuming image-point features can be measured to within one picture element). Theoretical studies or even systematic simulation studies on how the estimation errors depend on various factors are yet to be made. The situation with the two-camera case is somewhat better (Huang and Blostein, 1985). Some simulation results for the two-camera case are given below to indicate how redundant point correspondences can be used to improve estimation accuracy.

The algorithm of Motion form 3-D Correspondences (above) requires only three 3-D point correspondences. If more than three point correspondences are available, the redundancy can be used to improve estimation accuracy in several ways, two of which are adaptive least-squares (Huang and Blostein, 1985) and RANSAC (Fischler and Bolles, 1981). A hybrid of the two was used in Huang and Blostein (1985), from which some computer simulation results are quoted. The imaging geometry is as follows: Two pinhole cameras with focal length 28-mm are used, and the two image planes are coplanar; each image is 38 mm × 50 mm and has a resolution of 512 × 512 picture elements. The baseline distance between the two cameras is 400 mm.

The 3-D points are chosen randomly in a cube centered at a point 3 m from the cameras each side of which is 0.75 m long. The true motion is a rotation of 35° about an axis through the origin with direction 0.9, 0.3, and 0.316 followed by a translation of 0.8, 0.2, and 0.6 m. The simulation is done as follows. The 3-D points before and after the motion are projected onto the two images. The image coordinates of these points are quantized (with a resolution of 512 × 512). The quantized image points are then used in the method described in Motion from 3-D Feature Correspondences to estimate R and T. That is, triangulation is done using these quantized image points to obtain the 3-D coordinates of the points, which are then used in the algorithm described above. The errors in the estimated R and T are due to the inaccuracies in the 3-D coordinates of the points, which are in turn due to the quantization of the image coordinates. The results are: The average errors (in %) of θ, n_1, n_2, n_3, Δx, Δy, and Δz are, respectively: 5.2, 2.3, 14.5, 8.1, 10.1, 30.7, and 10.7 with seven 3-D point correspondences and 2.2, 1.0, 7.1, 3.1, 4.8, 14.9, and 4.4 with fifteen 3-D point correspondences. For each of the two cases the averages are computed over 100 trials.

At this point it is worth noting recent research (Spetsakis & Aloimonos, 1989) that develops algorithms that are provably optimal under assumptions about the noise that corrupts retinal correspondences. Experiments with such algorithms demonstrate that a 1% error in the input (about 4–7 pixels) can produce a 100% error in the output (3-D motion). Such results indicate that the problem of recovering 3-D motion (rotation and translation) from point correspondences in two frames might be inherently unstable.

Multiple Objects

The methods described in the earlier sections are for a single isolated rigid body. What if the scene contains several rigid bodies moving differently (this includes the special case of a single rigid body moving against a stationary but textured background)? Segmentation needs to be done somewhere along the way. If one is working with the two-view case described in Solution Using Point Correspondences (above) and if the motions of the rigid bodies are small from t_1 to t_2, the following approach can be tried.

Assuming the motions are small, one can still hope to get correct point correspondences. However, one does not know which points lie on which objects. This one attempts to find by a clustering technique. The basic ideas is to take all possible octets from the point correspondences, and for each octet compute R and $\hat{T}$ using the algorithm described above under A Linear Algorithm. Then clusters are found in the five-dimensional (n_1, n_2, θ, Δx, $\Delta \hat{y}$)-space. Ideally, each rigid body will give one cluster. To save computation, one uses heuristics (qv) to reduce the number of octets to consider and perhaps does clustering in subspaces of the five-dimensional space. Obviously, the same approach can be used in the binocular case. here, one only has to deal with triplets.

In order to handle the multiple-object case effectively, constraints on the scenario should be used wherever possible. A very impressive piece of work in that direction has been done by Adiv (1985).

Multiple Frames

Most of the approaches described up to now consider two or three dynamic frames. If several frames are used, it turns out that precision is greatly increased (due to redundancy). See Spetsakis (1989) for a survey and the treatment of the problem in its most general form.

Nonrigid Objects

Two cases are of particular interest: an articulated object (ie, an object comprising several rigid parts connected through various joints) and an elastic object. Some aspects of motion analysis of articulated objects have been studied by Asada, Yachida, and Tsuji (1984); O'Rourke and Badler (1980); and Webb and Aggarwal (1983a). In particular, Webb and Aggarwal investigated the case where the rotation axis can be assumed fixed in direction throughout the observed image sequence. The same authors (1983b) have also studied a special case of elastic objects where the object is assumed to be locally rigid, which implies an affine transformation between two image planes under local parallel projection. This approach is being extended by Chen (1985) to handle general elastic bodies. Finally Koenderink and VanDoorn (1985) are investigating the special case of bending deformation. The class of bending deformations encompasses all deformations that conserve distances along the surface but not necessarily through space.

THE ROLE OF THE VISUAL FIELD

During the development of the field of visual motion analysis it was observed that results were more accurate for wide (as opposed to narrow) visual fields. This observation led to the development of techniques for finding motion parameters from spherical flow fields. In Nelson and Aloimonos (1988), a theory is developed for determining the motion of an observer given the flow field over a full 360 degree image sphere. The method is based on the fact that the foci of expansion and contraction for an observer moving without rotation are 180 degrees opposed; and on the observation that if the flow field on the sphere is considered around three equators defining the three principal axes of rotation, then the effects of the three rotational motions decouple. The three rotational parameters can thus be determined independently by searching, in each case, for a rotational value for which the derotated equatorial flow field can be partitioned into disjoint 180 degree arcs of clockwise and counterclockwise flow. The direction of translation is obtained as a by-product of this analysis. Since this search is two dimensional in the motion parameters, it can be performed relatively efficiently. Because information is correlated over large distances, the method can be considered a pattern recognition rather than a numerical algorithm. The algorithm was shown to be robust and relatively insensitive to noise and to missing data. Both theoretical and empirical studies of the error sensitivity were presented. The theoretical analysis showed that for white noise of bounded magnitude M, the expected error is at worst linearly proportional to M. Empirical tests demonstrated negligible error for perturbations of up to 20% in the input, and errors of less than 20% for perturbations of up to 200%.

Motion Modeling and Prediction

This article has been concerned mainly with estimating the motion parameters R and T of an object between two time instants t_1 and t_2 based on image frames taken at these time instants. In most practical problems one is more interested in predicting rather than just estimating motion.

In order to predict, one needs a model of the motion that is valid over a number of image frames and contains a small number of parameters that remain constant over these frames. One can first estimate these parameters based on the first few frames and then use these estimated values to predict future motion and hence where the object will be in future frames.

One such approach is described in Huang, Weng, and Ahuja (1986), where the object has a precessional motion around its center of gravity, which is moving on a polynomial curve (eg, a parabola) in space.

High-Level Motion Understanding

In many cases the ultimate goal of motion analysis is to come up with a symbolic description of the dynamic scene under study. A complete system can conveniently be thought of as comprising two modules. The first module extracts from the observed raw data (eg, an image sequence), low/intermediate-level features such as motion and structure parameters. Then the second module arrives at a symbolic description of the dynamic scene by high-level reasoning based on the low/intermediate features as well as other a priori information about the scene.

One can find such complete dynamic scene-analysis systems in the literature in the biomedical area. Two excellent examples are Levine and co-workers, 1983, which describes a rule-based system for characterizing blood cell motion, and Tsotsos and co-workers, 1980, which describes a system for analyzing the motion of left-ventricle walls. In both cases the "scenes" are basically 2-D in nature, and therefore the task of the low/intermediate-level module is greatly simplified.

For truly 3-D scenes a complete dynamic scene-analysis system is hard to construct. The main problem is that the low/intermediate-level features the high-level module needs for its reasoning may be very difficult, if not impossible, to extract from the raw data. In fact, the low/intermediate-level module will probably need help from high-level reasoning to improve its performance. Some impressive examples of high-level modules are O'Rourke and Badler (1980), Neumann (1984), and Borchardt (1984). Neumann (1984) describes a system that observes traffic scenes and produces natural-language descriptions of them. In particular, the system will recognize and verbalize interesting occurrences (events) in the scene—eg, one car is overtaking another. Borchardt (1984) describes an expert system for event identification. The applications considered are simple assembly-line tasks. However, in both systems the low/intermediate-level features needed by the high-level modules are furnished at least in part by human operators.

Future Research

To summarize, the following are important research topics in motion analysis:

To find robust algorithms for motion estimation,

To find algorithms for estimating motion of multiple objects,

To find algorithms for estimating motion of nonrigid objects,

To find algorithms for predicting motion, and

To link and coordinate low/intermediate-level and high-level motion analysis.

BIBLIOGRAPHY

G. Adiv, "Determining 3-D Motion and Structure from Optical Flow Generated by Several Moving Objects," *IEEE Trans. PAMI* **7**(4), 384–410 (July 1985).

J. (Y.) Aloimonos, *Computing Intrinsic Images*, Ph.D. dissertation, University of Rochester, Rochester, N.Y., 1986.

J. (Y.) Aloimonos, "Purposive and Qualitative Active Vision," *Proceedings of the DARPA Image Understanding Workshop*, Pittsburgh, Pa., September 1990, pp. 816–828.

J. (Y.) Aloimonos and J. Y. Hervé, "Correspondenceless Stereo and Motion: Planar Surfaces," *IEEE Trans. PAMI* **12**, 504–510 (1990).

J. (Y.) Aloimonos and I. Rigoutsos, "Determining the 3-D Motion of a Rigid Surface Patch Without Correspondence Under Perspective Projection," *Proceedings of the Fifth National Conference on AI*, AAAI Menlo Park, Calif., 1986, pp. 681–686.

J. (Y.) Aloimonos, I. Weiss, and A. Bandyopadhyay, "Active Vision," *Intl. J. Computer Vision* **1**, 333–356 (1988).

M. Asada, M. Yachida, and S. Tsuji, "Understanding of 3-D Motions in Blocks World," *Patt. Recog.* **17**(1), 57–84 (1984).

D. H. Ballard and C. M. Brown, *Computer Vision*, Prentice-Hall, Englewood Cliffs, N.J., 1982.

A. Bandopadhay, *A Computational Study of Rigid Motion Perception*, Ph.D. dissertation, University of Rochester, Rochester, N.Y., 1986.

A Bandopadhay and J. Aloimonos, "Image Motion Estimation by Clustering," *Int'l Journal of Imaging Science and Technology* (in press).

S. D. Blostein and T. S. Huang, "Estimating Motion from Range Data," *Proceedings of the First Conference on AI Applications*, Denver, Colo., 1984.

G. C. Borchardt, *A Computer Model for the Representation and Identification of Phyical Events*. Technical Report T-142, Coordinated Science Laboratory, University of Illinois, Urbana, May 1984.

C. Cafforio and F. Rocca, "The Differential Method for Image Motion Estimation," in Huang, 1983.

S. S. Chen, "Shape and Correspondence of Nonrigid Objects," *Proceedings of the IEEE Workshop on Computer Vision*, Bellaire, Mich., 1985.

J. K. Cheng and T. S. Huang, "Image Registration by Matching Relational Structures," *Patt. Recog.* **17**(1), 149–160 (1984).

H. H. Chen and T. S. Huang, "Maximal Matching of Two 3-D Point Sets," *Proceedings of the International Conference on Pattern Recognition*, Paris, 1986.

Comput. Vis. Graph. Img. Proc., Special issues on Motion and Time-Varying Imagery **21**(1 and 2), 1–293 (Jan. and Feb. 1983).

D. Cyganski and J. A. Orr, "3-D Motion Parameters from Contours Using a Canonic Differential," *Proceedings of the ICASSP 85*, 1985, pp. 24.91–4.

R. O. Duda and P. E. Hart, *Pattern Classification and Scene Analysis*, Wiley, New York, 1973, p. 373.

J. Q. Fang and T. S. Huang, *A Corner-Finding Algorithm for*

Image Analysis and Registration, Pittsburgh, Pa., August 18–20, 1982, pp. 46–49.

J. Q. Fang and T. S. Huang, "Some Experiments on Estimating the 3-D Motion Parameters of a Rigid Body From Two Consecutive Image Frames," *IEEE Trans. PAMI* **6**(5), 547–554 (Sept. 1984).

J. Q. Fang and T. S. Huang, "Solving 3-D Small-Rotation Motion Equations," *Comput. Vis. Graph. Img. Proc.* **26**, 183–296 (1984a).

J. Q. Fang and T. S. Huang, "Some Experiments on Estimating the 3-D Motion Parameters of a Rigid Body From Two Consecutive Image Frames," *IEEE Trans. PAMI* **6**(5), 547–555 (Sept. 1984b).

O. D. Faugeras and M. Hebert, "A 3-D Recognition and Positioning Algorithm Using Geometrical Matching between Primitive Surfaces," *Proceedings of the Eighth IJCAI,* Morgan-Kaufmann, San Mateo, Calif., 1983, pp. 996–1102.

M. A. Fischler and R. C. Bolles, "Random Sample Consensus: A Paradigm for Model Fitting With Applications to Image Analysis and Automated Cartography," *CACM* **24**(6), 381–395 (June 1981).

J. P. Gambotto and T. S. Huang, "Motion Analysis of Isolated Targets in Infrared Image Sequences," *Proceedings of the Seventh ICPR,* Montreal, 1984.

J. J. Gibson, *The Perception of the Visual World,* Houghton Mifflin, Boston, Mass., 1950.

W. K. Gu, J. Y. Yang, and T. S. Huang, "Matching Perspective Views of a 3-D Object Using Composite Circuits," *Proceedings of the Seventh ICPR,* 1984.

E. C. Hildreth, *The Measurement of Visual Motion,* MIT Press, Cambridge, Mass., 1984.

B. Horn, *Robot Vision,* McGraw Hill, New York, 1986.

B. K. P. Horn and B. G. Schunck, "Determining Optical Flow," *Artif. Intell.* **17**, 185–203 (1981).

T. S. Huang, ed., *Image Sequence Analysis,* Springer-Verlag, Heidelberg, Germany, 1981.

T. S. Huang, ed., *Image Sequence Processing and Dynamic Scene Analysis,* Springer-Verlag, Heidelberg, Germany, 1983.

T. S. Huang, "Determining 3-D Motion/Structure from Two Perspective Views," in T. Y. Young and K. S. Fu, eds., *Handbook of Pattern Recognition and Image Processing,* Academic Press, New York, 1985.

T. S. Huang and R. Y. Tsai, "Image Sequence Analysis: Motion Estimation," in Huang, 1981.

T. S. Huang, "Three-Dimensional Motion Analysis by Direct Matching," *Conference Digest, Optical Society of America Topical Meeting on Computer Vision,* Incline Village, Nevada, 1985, pp. FAI-1-4.

T. S. Huang and S. D. Blostein, "Robust Algorithms for Motion Estimation Based on Two Sequential Stereo Image Pairs," *Proceedings of the Conference on Computer Vision and Pattern Recognition,* San Francisco, 1985.

T. S. Huang, J. Weng, and N. Ahuja, "3-D Motion from Image Sequences: Modeling, Understanding, and Prediction," *Proceedings of the IEEE Workshop on Motion: Representation and Analysis,* Kiawah Island, S.C., 1986, pp. 125–130.

T. S. Huang, S. D. Blostein, and E. A. Margerum, "Least-Squares Estimation of Motion Parameters from 3-D Point Correspondences," *Proceedings of the IEEE Conference on Computer Vision and Pattern Recognition,* 1986.

IEEE Comput. Mag., Special issue on Computer Analysis of Time-Varying Images **14**(8) pp. 7–69 (Aug. 1981).

IEEE Trans. PAMI, Special issue on Motion and Time-Varying Imagery **2**(6), 493–588 (Nov. 1980).

K. Kanatani, "Tracing Planar Surface Motion from a Projection Without Knowing the Correspondence," *Comput. Vis. Graph. Img. Proc.* **29**, 1–12 (1985).

K. Kanatani, "Detecting the Motion of a Planar Surface by Line and Surface Integrals," *Comput. Vis. Graph. Img. Proc.* **29**, 13–22 (1985).

J. J. Koenderink and A. J. Van Doorn, *Depth and Shape from Differential Perspective in the Presence of Bending Deformation,* Preprint, Department of Medical and Physiological Physics, Princetonpiein 5, Utrecht, The Netherlands, 1985.

R. Kories and G. Zimmermann, "A Versatile Method for the Estimation of Displacement Vector Fields from Image Sequences," *Proceedings of the IEEE Workshop on Motion,* 1986.

D. T. Lawton, "Processing Translational Motion Sequences," *Comput. Vis. Graph. Img. Proc.* **22**, 116–144 (1983).

M. D. Levine, P. B. Nobel, and Y. M. Youssef, "A Rule-Based System for Characterizing Blood Cell Motion," in Huang, 1983.

J. Limb and J. Murphy, "Estimating the Velocity of Moving Images in TV Signals," *Comput. Graph. Img. Proc.* **4**, 311–327 (1975).

Y. C. Liu and T. S. Huang, "Estimation of Rigid Body Motion Using Straight-line Correspondences," *Proceedings of the IEEE Workshop on Motion: Representation and Analysis,* 1986, pp. 47–52.

H. C. Longuet-Higgins, "A Computer Program for Reconstructing a Scene from Two Projections," *Nature* **293**, 133–135 (Sept. 1981).

H. C. Longuet-Higgins, "The Visual Ambiguity of a Moving Plane," *Proc. Roy. Soc. Series B* **223**(1), 165–170 (1984).

J. C. Longuet-Higgins, "The Reconstruction of a Scene from Two Projections-Configurations that Defeat the 8-Point Algorithm," *Proceedings of the First Conference on Artificial Intelligence Applications,* Denver, Colo., 1984, pp. 395–397.

A. Mitiche and J. K. Aggarwal, "A Computational Analysis of Time-Varying Images," in T. Y. Young and K. S. Fu, eds., *Handbook of Pattern Recognition and Image Processing,* Academic Press, New York, 1985.

A. Mitiche, S. Seida, and J. K. Aggarwal, "Line-Based Computation of Structure and Motion Using Angular Invariance," *Proceedings of the IEEE Workshop on Motion: Representation and Analysis,* 1986, pp. 175–180.

H. P. Moravec, "Obstacle Avoidance and Navigation in the Real World by a Seeing Robot Rover," Ph.D dissertation, Stanford University, September 1980.

H. H. Nagel, "Displacement Vectors Derived from 2nd-Order Intensity Variations in Image Sequences," *Comput. Vis. Graph. Img. Proc.* **21**, 85–117 (January 1983).

H. H. Nagel, "Constraints for the Estimation of Displacement Vector Fields from Image Sequences," *Proc. of the Eighth IJCAI,* Karlsruhe, FRG, Morgan-Kaufmann, San Mateo, Calif., Aug. 8–12, 1983, pp. 945–951.

K. Nakayama, "Biological Image Motion Processing: A Review," *Vis. Res.* **25**, 625–660 (1985).

R. C. Nelson and J. Aloimonos, "Finding Motion Parameters from Spherical Flow Fields (Or the Advantages of Having Eyes in the Back of Your Head)," *Biological Cybernetics* **58**, 261–273 (1988).

B. Neumann, *Natural Language Description of Time-Varying Scenes,* Bericht No. 105, FBI-HH-B-105/84, Fachberich Informatik, University of Hamburg, FRG, 1984.

J. O'Rourke and N. Badler, "Model-Based Image Analysis of Human Motion Using Constraint Propagation," *IEEE Trans. PAMI* **2**, 522–536 (1980).

J. A. Orr, D. Cyganski, and R. Vaz, "Determination of Affine Transforms from Object Contours With No Point Correspondence Information," *Proceedings of the ICASSP 85*, 1985, pp. 24.10.1–4.

K. Prazdny, "Egomotion and Relative Depth Map from Optical Flow," *Biol. Cybernet.* **36**, 87–102 (1980).

Proceedings of the ACM Workshop on Motion: Representation and Perception, Toronto, 1983.

Proceedings of the IEEE Workshop on Motion: Representation and Analysis, Kiawah Island, S.C., May 7–9, 1986.

Proceedings of the Workshop on Computer Analysis of Time-Varying Imagery, Abstracts, University of Pennsylvania, Philadelphia, Pa., 1979.

J. D. Robbins and A. N. Netravali, "Recursive Motion Compensation: A Review," in Huang, 1983.

F. Rocca, "TV Bandwidth Compression Utilizing Frame-to-Frame Correlation and Movement Compensation," in T. S. Huang and O. J. Tretiak, eds., *Picture Bandwidth Compression*, Gordon and Breach, London, 1972.

M. E. Spetsakis, "The Geometry and Statistics of Visual Motion," Ph.D. dissertation, Computer Vision Laboratory, Center for Automation Research, University of Maryland, College Park, 1989.

M. E. Spetsakis and J. Aloimonos, "Structure From Motion Using Line Correspondences," *Int'l. J. Computer Vision* **4**, 171–183 (1990).

M. E. Spetsakis and J. Aloimonos, "On Optimal Motion Algorithms," *Proceedings of the IEEE Workshop on Visual Motion*, Irvine, Calif., March 1989.

W. B. Thompson and S. T. Barnard, "Low-Level Estimation and Interpretation of Visual Motion," *IEEE Comput.* **14**, 47–56 (1981).

R. Y. Tsai and T. S. Huang, "Uniqueness and Estimation of 3-D Motion Parameters of Rigid Bodies with Curved Surfaces," *IEEE Trans. PAMI* **6**(1), 13–27 (Jan. 1984).

R. Y. Tsai and T. S. Huang, "Estimating 3-D Motion Parameters of a Rigid Planar Patch," *IEEE Trans. ASSP* **29**(7), 1147–1152 (December 1981).

R. Y. Tsai, T. S. Huang, and W. L. Zhu, "Estimating 3-D Motion Parameters of a Rigid Planar Patch. II: Singular Value Decomposition," *IEEE Trans. ASSP* **30**(4) (Aug. 1982); correction: **31**(2), 514 (April 1983).

R. Y. Tsai and T. S. Huang, "Estimating 3-D Motion Parameters of a Rigid Planar Patch. III: Finite Point Correspondences and the Three-View Problem," *IEEE Trans. ASSP* **32**(2), 213–220 (April 1984).

J. K. Tsotsos, J. Mylopoulos, H. D. Corvey, and S. W. Zucker, "A Framework for Visual Motion Understanding," *IEEE Trans. PAMI*, **2**(6), 563–573 (November 1980).

S. Ullman, *The Intepretation of Visual Motion*, MIT Press, Cambridge, Mass., 1979.

S. Ullman, "The Interpretation of Visual Motion," Ph.D. dissertation, Massachusetts Institute of Technology, Department of Electrical Engineering and Computer Science, 1979.

S. Ullman, "Analysis of Visual Motion by Biological and Computer Vision Systems," *IEEE Comput.* **14**, 57–69 (1981).

A. Verri and T. Poggio, "Against Quantitative Optic Flow," *Proc. IEEE International Conference on Computer Vision*, 1987.

A. M. Waxman and S. Ullman, *Surface Structure and 3-D Motion from Image Flow: A Kinematic Analysis*, CAR-TR-24, CS-TR-1332. Center for Automation Research, University of Maryland, College Park, October 1983.

A. M. Waxman and K. Wohn, *Contour Evolution, Neighborhood Deformation, and Global Image Flow: Planar Surface in Motion*, CAR-TR-58, CS-TR-1394, Center for Automation Research, University of Maryland, College Park, April 1984a.

A. M. Waxman and K. Wohn, "Contour Evolution, Neighborhood Deformation and Image Flow: Textured Surfaces in Motion," in W. Richards and S. Ullman, eds., *Image Understanding '84*, Ablex, Norwood, NJ, 1984b.

J. A. Webb and J. K. Aggarwal, "Structure from Motion of Rigid and Jointed Objects," *Artif. Intell.* **19**(1), 107–130 (1983a).

J. A. Webb and J. K. Aggarwal, "Shape and Correspondence," *Comput. Vis. Graph. Img. Proc.* **21**, 145–160 (1983b).

B. L. Yen and T. S. Huang, "Determining 3-D Motion and Structure of a Rigid Body Using Straight Line Correspondences," in Huang, 1983, pp. 365–394.

B. L. Yen and T. S. Huang, "Determining 3-D Motion Parameters of a Rigid Body: A Vector-Geometric Approach," *Proceedings of the ACM Workshop on Motion*, Toronto, 1983.

T. Y. Young and Y. L. Wang, "Analysis of 3-D Rotation and Linear Shape Changes," *Patt. Recog. Lett.* **2**, 239–242 (1984).

X. Zhuang, T. S. Huang, and R. M. Haralick, "Two-view Motion Analysis: A Unified Algorithm," *J. Opt. Soc. Am.* **3**(9), 1492–1500 (Sept. 1986).

X. Zhuang, R. M. Haralick, and J. S. Lee, "Rigid Body Motion and the Optic Flow Under a Small Perturbation," *IEEE Trans. PAMI* (in press).

T. S. HUANG
University of Illinois

The preparation of this article was supported by Scientific Services Program, Battelle Columbus Laboratories contract DAAG29-81-D-0100. This article is adapted and updated from the articles in the first edition entitled "Motion Analysis," by T. S. Huang, and "Optical Flow," by E. Hildreth of MIT. The help of J. (Y.) Aloimonos in carrying out the adaptation and updating of this article is gratefully acknowledged.

VISUAL PERCEPTION

The veridicality of visual perception, that is, the correspondence between the percept of the outside world and its physical features that can be verified, eg, through the sense of touch, is probably the most striking quality of vision. Despite its numerous shortcomings, catalogued and studied by psychologists as visual illusions, the visual system virtually never fails to provide information about the outside world that is of genuine behavioral importance. The three-dimensional layout of surfaces in the vicinity of the observer and the motion, compositions, and grouping of these surfaces into well-defined objects are representative examples. The resulting impression of the visual world is complete; the visual experience of the surrounding space has no gaps in it, even in those portions of it for which no input information is available (such as that part of the space projected onto the blind spot of the eye). At the same time, through fixation, attention, and scrutiny we can perceive many fine details of the environment.

QUESTIONS

Historically, reflections of the sort outlined above have led to many questions pertaining to the phenomenon of perception. These questions can be divided into distinct classes, according to the aspects of vision they address. This essay will deal with only a few of these aspects. It will survey some common features of the human perceptual performance, the processes involved in that performance and how these are studied experimentally. [Boff and co-workers (1986) is a recent comprehensive handbook on perceptual performance.] Computational accounts of vision (Marr, 1982), also offered elsewhere in the encyclopedia, will be pointed to briefly. Finally, most of the topics pertaining to the biological substrate of vision, except some of the most pervasive notions (such as receptive fields and cortical maps), will be omitted altogether. For information on the anatomy and the physiology of vision the reader is referred to other sources (e.g., Kandel and Schwartz, 1985).

Visual Performance

Gibson (1950) begins his book on visual perception with a question: "Why do things look as they do?" An obvious (but not very informative) answer to this would be: "because of the way our visual system is built." In fact, the recounting of conditions that must be fulfilled before anyone can see, which constitutes the first paragraph of Gibson's book, begs for a more constructive formulation of the basic empirical question of visual perception: how does the visual system perform under different conditions, or, what are the factors that affect the way things look? Some of the factors that influence perceptual performance, such as the basic architecture of the visual system, are internal to the observer and belong to the domain of visual neuroscience. Other factors, such as the physical characteristics of the stimulus and of the manner of its presentation, can be externally manipulated. Experimental psychological study of visual perception is aimed at understanding the outcome of the perceptual process, its building blocks, and its neural substrate, through controlled manipulation of the external stimulus.

Consider as an example Figure 1a. When asked to describe its contents, average observers usually state that it shows two overlapping triangles, of which one has its vertices at the centers of the black disks and consists predominantly of illusory contours. Why do we see this second triangle? One can make an initial step toward an answer by trying to influence the percept of the illusory triangle by manipulating the stimulus (Fig. 1b). As a by-product, this process of perceptual experimentation frequently comes up with notions that are useful for understanding other visual phenomena (in this specific example, the important notions are those of completion and filling in, to be discussed later), including the perception of natural scenes.

Visual Competence

A different angle on the problem of perception is provided by the opening lines of Marr's (1982) book on computational vision. Marr asks "What does it mean to see?" This question, which (using Chomsky's terminology) is about competence rather than performance, cannot be elaborated on much further without making a commitment to an important part of the answer. One of the two main approaches to this problem is through the notion of direct perception (Gibson, 1979). According to Gibson, perception is direct because the organism picks up relevant perceptual invariants, such as the three-dimensional shape of objects, from the visual world without intervening processing or representation. (For a long time, Gibson went so far as to deny the existence of retinal images and the relevance to perception of geometric optics involved in their formation.) In its rejection of internal representations and processes that can be described as unconscious inference, the direct perception stance is related to behaviorism. The answer of Gibson's school to the question "What does it mean to see" is "to be attuned to certain invariant qualities present in the optic array, and, potentially, to become disposed to act in certain ways, given the appropriate stimulation." Under this view, phenomena such as that illustrated in Figure 1 tend to be dismissed as unnatural and "ecologically invalid."

The other approach, called "representational" by Marr (1982), postulates that the goal of any visual system, including biological vision, is to produce representations of the environment, and that various specific visual tasks, such as recognition and navigation, are solved through inference, or computation, defined over these representations (Marr, 1982). The notion of perception as unconscious inference is usually traced back to von Helmholtz (1856/1964). In his treatise on physiological optics von Helmholtz argued that most often the information present in the visual world as projected on the eye's retina is too incomplete to support the richness of perception, which perforce must largely rely on previously or independently available data and on unconscious reasoning. According to Marr, an important source of this additional information is a knowledge of physics of the outside world and of image formation.

Consider again the example of Figure 1. A computational account of the perceived illusory triangle would indicate that (1) all contours, including the illusory ones, are explicitly represented at some stage of the visual system, and (2) the transformation between the stimulus and

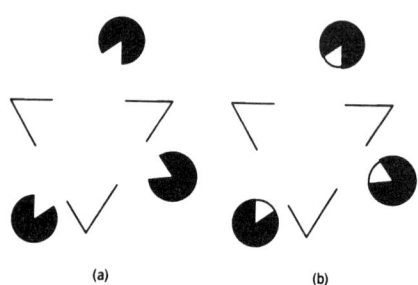

Figure 1. (a) Illusory contours, as well as some abnormal depth and lightness percepts, arise in this version of Kanizsa's triangle; (b) a modified version, in which the illusory percepts are much weaker.

the explicit representation can be computationally specified (and implemented in the hardware of the brain). A distinct advantage of computational theories of perception is that, unlike "direct" accounts, they can be made to generate concrete predictions, which, in turn, can be experimentally upheld (or refuted). Computational, psychological, and physiological investigations of illusory contours are reported in Ullman (1976), Cavanagh (1987), and von der Heydt and co-workers (1984), respectively.

To summarize, the interesting questions that can be asked about visual perception are those of performance (what conditions affect the way we see?) and of competence (what does it mean to see? how do we see?). The computational–representational paradigm proved useful in addressing all these questions. At present this approach dominates the psychology of vision, consequently; in the remainder of the article its assumptions and terminology are employed without qualification.

THE STUDY OF PERCEPTION

Goals

One way to begin investigating the basic questions mentioned above is to decide on the form into which the answers should be cast. As in other natural sciences, this calls for the formation of a mathematical framework that would encompass the existing body of data on perceptual performance and would admit generalization by successfully predicting performance under novel conditions. In relatively primitive organisms the process of perception appears indeed to be amenable to precise mathematical treatment. As Poggio and Reichardt (1976) have shown, in the fly the transfer function of the module that supplies visual motion information for the purpose of flight control can be specified by a simple expression with only a few terms. The situation in human perception is rather more complicated. Among other reasons, this is because of the sheer diversity and complexity of the human visual system, because the output representations of visual modules are as yet unknown, and because in many cases top-down influences tend to interfere with "pure" perception. A typical example of the classical mathematics of perception is Luce (1986), where one can find an exhaustive survey of the response time paradigm (see the section on methods below). The main mathematical tools of this paradigm are descriptive statistics and statistical models borrowed from signal detection theory (Green and Swets, 1966).

Shepard's proposal of a "universal law of generalization for psychological science" (Shepard, 1987) represents a more ambitious attempt at the mathematization of perception. The article, written for the occasion of the tercentenary of the publication of Newton's *Principia Mathematica*, suggests that the generalization of response from a learned to a novel stimulus depends on the distance between the stimuli in an abstract space that has the same metric structure for a wide variety of tasks, ranging from shape, size, and color judgments to auditory signal perception. While the notion of a general psychological space may apply to stimuli that themselves possess a well-defined metric structure, the chances are meager that the more cognitive perceptual processes such as object recognition would admit a similar universal law-like or nomological description. If those philosophers are right who claim that mental processes are anomalous instead of nomological (Davidson, 1980), accounts of cognition in terms of prototypes and narrow-scope or local rules should be more fitting than invocations of universal laws.

Methods

There are many ways to collect the data necessary for building a theory of perception. One may distinguish between psychological approaches, which concentrate on the perceptual capacities and experiential aspects of perception, and biological approaches, which focus on the anatomy and physiology of the sensory nervous system. Only one approach is discussed here: experimental psychology.

Experiments that quantify and measure the psychometric function (viz, the response of a subject to a controlled stimulus) have traditionally been the principal method of the psychological study of perception. This experimental paradigm, called psychophysical because it relates the magnitude of a psychological response variable such as response time to some physical quality of the stimulus, dates back to the previous century. A clear formulation, due to Jastrow (1890), states that if the process of perception is indeed structured, then different paths through this structure will yield different response times. If this is true, one may hope to infer the structure of perception from the patterns of response times obtained under different experimental conditions. Mental rotation [see Shepard and Cooper (1982) for an overview and Pylyshyn (1985) for a critique] provides an outstanding example of a phenomenon in which the dependence of response time on a characteristic of the stimulus has triggered hundreds of experiments and was incorporated into the foundations of a theory of visual representation. (In this case, the task called for a judgment of object identity between two simultaneously shown images of three-dimensional objects, and the response time was found to depend linearly on the relative misorientation of the objects with respect to one another.)

BUILDING BLOCKS

Reductionistic methods that investigate the structure of the perceptual system encourage the dissection of vision into submodalities. Some of these building blocks of perception, such as lightness, hue, texture, stereopsis, visual motion, the perception of space, and object recognition, are briefly described below. Within the scope of this article, little more than a hint can be given as to the perceptual problems solved by each module.

Lightness and Shading

Confronted with a gradient of illumination across the viewed surface, the visual system must separate the effect of illumination from the effects of surface albedo, orientation, and shape. Disentangling all the factors that contribute to the intensity of the image at a given point on the retina is probably the most complicated computational problem in vision. Thus it is not surprising that some of the more compelling illusions, such as the Mach bands and the Craik–Cornsweet–O'Brien effect [see, eg, Frisby (1979) for an overview], are caused by peculiarities of lightness perception mechanisms (one such peculiarity is illustrated in Fig. 1a, where the illusory triangle is perceived to be brighter than the background). In addressing the lightness problem, the human visual system appears to have settled for qualitative rather than quantitative solutions (Todd and Mingolla, 1983). Moreover, these solutions often seem to be based on high-level heuristics (Ramachandran, 1988) and are easily downplayed if the relevant information is available from other sources, such as the shape of the occluding contours of the surface (Koenderink, 1984) or stereopsis (Bülthoff and Mallot, 1988).

Color

In the perception of color, as in the perception of lightness, the human visual system exhibits an impressive disregard for irrelevant variables. In this case, the intensity and the spectral content of the illuminant must be factored out if a reasonable approximation to the color of the viewed surface is to be inferred [see the review in Boynton (1978)]. The mechanisms responsible for this function appear to be similar for lightness and for color in that they depend on local contrast while ignoring slow and gradual changes in image intensity and spectrum, which in many cases can be safely attributed to the influence of the illuminant (Land and McCann, 1971). Observations that are not easily accounted for by an application of such simple fixed rules were made by Gilchrist (1977), who found that global (and cognitive) factors such as the knowledge of the spatial arrangement of surfaces may affect their perceived lightness. (See also COLOR VISION.)

Texture

In the natural world, texture, along with color, is an important cue to the physical composition of visible surfaces and can be used to segment complex scenes into surface patches that have distinct origins (eg, belong to different objects). Also, texture gradients can be readily interpreted in terms of the orientation of the underlying surfaces and thus contain cues to the three-dimensional structure of the visual space (Gibson, 1950). Texture is a mass phenomenon; a surface must bear more than a few markings to be perceived as textured. The problem of texture perception can be formulated either in statistical terms, or in terms of the detection of the underlying texture elements or textons (see Julesz, 1984). An issue that was originally raised in the context of texture perception and has since been intensively studied is that of preattentive discrimination (ie, distinguishing between different stimuli without the involvement of attention or scrutiny). Presumably, features that combine into preattentively discriminable textures are processed in parallel over the entire visual field. The identification of such features provides important clues to the structure of early visual processes. An illustration of this approach may be found in recent work by Fahle (1990), who found that vernier offset stimuli in the hyperacuity range (pairs of abutting line segments displaced by an amount that is smaller than the spacing of the photoreceptors in the retina) can be detected in parallel. (See also TEXTURE.)

Stereopsis

Since the retinal image is a projection of the three-dimensional world onto a two-dimensional surface, the information on the third dimension, depth, is already lost at the very first stage of vision. The perception of depth, or stereopsis, can, however, still be attained by combining information from the two eyes. (Monocular depth cues are mentioned below in the section on space perception.) Stereopsis works because the separation between the retinal images of objects (retinal disparity) is different in the left and right eyes, depending on the separation of the objects in depth. Binocular stereo resolution is extremely fine: a difference in depth of 1 mm can be perceived at a distance of 1 meter (m). The disparity between the two eyes' views under such conditions is many times smaller than the size of a single retinal photoreceptor.

Stereopsis has received much attention in the study of vision [Julesz (1971); Poggio and Poggio (1984); see also STEREO VISION]. The behavioral importance of depth perception becomes apparent if one attempts to thread a needle, or catch a fly, with one eye closed. Stereopsis is an acquired ability: newborn babies do not perceive binocular depth until the age of 3 or 4 months. Disorders such as strabismus (the inability to fixate the same object simultaneously with both eyes) present during this period of plasticity can cause permanent stereoblindness by hampering the development of one of the two main processes underlying stereopsis: matching the two retinal images to produce the disparity field. The power of the matching process is illustrated by our ability to perceive depth in random-dot stereograms [image pairs consisting of random dots, some of which are displaced in one image with respect to the other to form a stimulus that can be perceived only through stereo vision; see Julesz (1971)]. In a random-dot stereogram, each dot in one image can match potentially any dot in the other image. Although matching is usually sufficiently selective to disambiguate such situations, in some cases people may perceive simultaneously several surfaces corresponding to multiple matchings between elements in the two images (Weinshall, 1989). Moreover, the relationship between the outcome of the matching and the perceived depth is sometimes not unequivocal. For example, the perceived depth may correspond to an average disparity rather than to one of the actual disparities derived from a possible matching (Mitchison and McKee, 1985).

The second process involved in stereopsis is surface interpolation, which fills in the gaps between those locations in the image where exact disparities are found through matching. Similar to matching, the surface interpolation subsystem possesses several distinct features that are not well understood and are not reproduced by machine vision algorithms. Two of these are simultaneous perception of multiple transparent surfaces and the integration of different depth cues in surface perception.

Motion

Visual motion contains many important cues about the outside world (see also VISUAL MOTION ANALYSIS). Moving patterns of light projected onto the retina provide information that can be used to segment the surrounding scene into objects according to their motion and to navigate in the environment while avoiding collisions with both stationary and moving obstacles. Visual motion can also be interpreted to yield the three-dimensional structure of objects (Wallach and O'Connell, 1953), even when the objects themselves are allowed to deform while moving, a common phenomenon in the motion of living things (see Johansson, 1973). The autonomy of visual motion perception is demonstrated by our ability to perceive three-dimensional structure in moving two-dimensional patterns, such as those that appear on a television screen, and even in random-dot kinematograms (Ullman, 1979). The contribution of motion to our overall impression of the world can be appreciated by anyone who has watched a film taken from the vantage point of a roller-coaster rider: the somatic illusions evoked by such stimuli are strong enough to override vestibular and somatosensory cues.

As Rock (1984) has pointed out, the presence of retinal displacement of objects is neither sufficient nor necessary for the perception of motion, despite the indisputable fact that such displacement is the starting point of neural motion processing. On one hand, moving objects that are fixated and tracked are effectively stationary with respect to the retina, but are still perceived as moving. On the other hand, we perceive the visual world as immobile when our eyes move between fixations (but not when the eyes are moved externally, eg, by gently pressing on the eyeball from the side).

Three-Dimensional Space and Shape

The perception of the three-dimensional layout of visual space and of solid objects embedded in it relies on a combined action of all the basic modules mentioned above, as well as on a variety of perceptual rules of thumb that cannot be readily attributed to one of those modules (Ramachandran, 1988). The role of shading, textural cues, retinal disparity, and motion information in seeing depth has been outlined above. Another class of depth cues is provided by the oculomotor system; depth can be estimated from convergence of the eyes and from the accommodation status of the lens. Among the pictorial cues are interposition (inferred from occlusion of some objects by others), shadows, perspective, and familiar size information (see Rock, 1984). The problem of understanding the integration process that brings the depth cues together, traditionally neglected in favor of the study of individual visual modules, has recently received increasing attention (Bülthoff and Mallot, 1988). The main aspects of the integration problem are the nature of the output representation and the relative weight given to each cue. Situations in which the cues are conflicting can be especially interesting. For example, when the contents of Figure 1a are shown stereoscopically in such a manner that the vertices of the illusory triangle appear, in conflict with the (imaginary) interposition cue, behind those of the real one, the illusion becomes weaker (Gregory, 1978).

Object Recognition

Mechanisms that support object recognition (qv) in human vision are the subject of considerable controversy among psychologists. Although most would agree that recognition involves comparison between the stimulus and an internal model or representation kept in memory, no consensus exists as to the nature of that representation. Consider the problems encountered by the visual system that attempts to identify an object present in the field of view. Assuming that the candidate object has already been detected and its approximate location estimated, the system must segment the object from the environment and factor out variations in its appearance due to changing illumination, changing viewpoint (see Fig. 2), and, possibly, changing shape of the object (as in the recognition of a moving animal; see the section on motion above).

Does the visual system represent objects in a straightforward fashion, eg, by remembering sets of two-dimensional "snapshots" taken from different vantage points, or are the object models, geometrically, three-dimensional analogs of the objects they represent? Arguments based, among other phenomena, on our ability to perceive and describe the three-dimensional shape of novel objects led many researchers [notably Marr (1982)] to postulate the formation of three-dimensional object-centered (ie, viewpoint-invariant) representations of the environment to be the ultimate goal and the final product of vision. This view amounts to much more than a theory of object recognition; it dictates the interpretation of processes of early vision in terms of the reconstruction of a replica of the visual world. Recently, this view has been disputed on philosophical, empirical and computational grounds (see Sloman, 1987; Quinlan, in press; Edelman and Weinshall, 1989; Edelman and Bülthoff, in press).

Three-dimensional object-centered models, envisaged by Marr, and other three-dimensional structural representations (eg, Biederman, 1985) are only a few of the theories competing in the field of recognition. Major alternatives (see Ullman, 1989, for a review) are template matching, description by invariant features and shape

Figure 2. The appearance of a three-dimensional object can depend strongly on the viewpoint. The image on the right is of the same object as the image on the left, rotated in depth by 90°. People find it difficult to recognize such objects from a radically unfamiliar viewpoint, even when stereo information (Rock and DiVita, 1987) or both stereo and motion cues (Edelman and Bülthoff, 1990) to the three-dimensional shape of the object are available.

normalization. Although it is clear that structural descriptions of the type suggested by Marr, Biederman, and others must be invoked to explain some perceptual phenomena, the emergence of recognition models based on interpolation among prototypical two-dimensional views (e.g., Ullman and Basri, 1990; Poggio and Edelman, 1990) indicates that memory for specific instances may be more important for recognition than previously believed.

CROSS-MODAL CHARACTERISTICS AND PROCESSES

This section lists several characteristics of perception whose common denominator is generality and pervasiveness in vision. These are grouped into two classes. The first class includes phenomena that are common to more than one of the building blocks mentioned earlier. The other class comprises dynamic processes whose scope spans several visual submodalities.

Constancy

Perceptual constancy is our tendency to see properties of objects as invariant despite perpetually changing retinal stimuli. Following is a list of the most prominent constancy phenomena. (Some of these have already been mentioned in the preceding sections.) Concrete examples of each phenomenon can be found, eg, in Rock (1984).

Lightness Constancy. The perception of the shade of a surface's lightness varies in general with the true albedo of the surface rather than with its luminance (the intensity of the light reflected by the surface, which changes, for example, because of varying illumination and shadows).

Color Constancy. When the spectral content of the illuminant undergoes a radical change, a surface will no longer reflect light that corresponds to its true color (ie, the color it reflects when illuminated with white light). Nevertheless, its perceived color will in general appear close to the true one.

Size Constancy. A given object in the world appears to be about the same size, irrespective of the variation of the size of its retinal projection (due, eg, to its varying distance from the eye).

Shape Constancy. The perceived shape of an object remains constant despite changes in the shape of its retinal projection caused by the movement of the object relative to the observer.

Space Constancy. The visual world appears to us as stable and unmoving despite continuing movement of the retinal image, caused by the movement of the eyes, as in visual tracking and saccades (see the section on attention and search below), the head and the entire body (as in locomotion).

Explanations of Constancy. The constancies of visual perception constitute an essential part of the visual experience as we know it. Imagine what a bewildering world it would be if red tomatoes turned yellow when viewed in the kitchen under incandescent light, coins appeared elliptical unless viewed from the proper vantage point, and the slightest movement of the head sent the entire surrounding scene careening about. How does the visual system achieve perceptual constancy? The stimulus-relation explanation, favored by the direct perception school, sees the stimulus itself as the sole cause of constancy. According to this account, the context in which the stimulus appears affects the way it is perceived. For example, the apparent size of an unfamiliar object may be affected by the presentation next to it of another object of known size. In many situations, however, context information is unavailable, yet size constancy still holds. To continue the preceding example, the size of a luminous object in a darkened room may be correctly judged as long as distance information is available, eg, from accommodation and convergence. If, however, the object is seen through a narrow aperture that eliminates distance cues, the constancy breaks down and the object appears to be of indeterminate size (Rock, 1984). This phenomenon prompts an alternative explanation of constancy that proposes that viewers take unconsciously into account independent or prior knowledge relevant to a given situation. As we shall see in the next section, the involvement of prior knowledge can account also for other features of vision besides constancy.

Implicit Knowledge

An example of the facilitation of perception through the use of information not available in the immediate sensory input is the visual system's superior performance in recognizing and remembering objects and scenes that make sense, as opposed to those that do not (Biederman and coworkers, 1974; Potter, 1975). Although the implicit knowledge in this case is used unconsciously, the perceiver would normally be able to identify and describe its source. In other cases the knowledge source is not so readily apparent to the observer. For example, the visual system seems to take into account the physics of specular reflection in the perception of three-dimensional shape in shaded images (Blake and Bülthoff, 1990). In another example, motion perception appears to involve implicit familiarity with the physics of transparency (Stoner and coworkers, 1990).

Illusions

The unconscious rules of thumb that are in part responsible for the incredibly rapid performance of the visual system in a wide variety of vital tasks are, necessarily, limited in scope. Certain visual stimuli produce illusory or non-veridical percepts by causing the breakdown of those perceptual processes that rely on unconscious rules. Another source of illusions is in the inherent anatomical and physiological properties and limitations of the visual system. The illusory contours of Figure 1a for which a tentative physiological mechanism has been identified (von der Heydt and co-workers, 1984) are an example of this kind (see also Gregory, 1978).

Processes

It is remarkable that a number of central parts of the process of visual perception can be described functionally in a manner that is largely independent of the particular goals they serve. What follows here is an attempt to briefly characterize these subprocesses.

Adaptation. The most common example of adaptation is the adjustment in the light sensitivity of the eye that follows any change in the ambient illumination. The dynamic range of light adaptation is very wide (at least five orders of magnitude). Only a small part of this range (a factor of 16 or so) is attributable to the changes in pupil size; the rest is supported by physiological processes that operate at the photoreceptors and in the higher levels of the retina. Presumably, some of the visual aftereffects that may be classified as adaptation phenomena happen at higher levels of the visual system. A well-known example of this type is the motion aftereffect; we tend to perceive the stationary parts of a waterfall scene as moving upward after having concentrated for sufficient time on the downward motion of the falling water. One possible explanation of the aftereffects is that the visual system represents qualities such as planarity and immobility as a dynamic balance between representations of opposites such as convexity–concavity and upward–downward motion. A fatiguelike reduction in the activity level of the representation substrate of downward motion, for example, will then cause a perception of upward motion in a stimulus that is, in fact, static. Note that this account relies on another common property of perception related to adaptation: the preferential response to temporal change and spatial contrast, as opposed to status quo and uniformity.

Attention and Search. The visual system allocates different amounts of processing resources to different portions of the visual field. Most of this nonuniformity is architectural and is due to the gradual decrease in the photoreceptor density (which entails a decrease in acuity) between the fovea and the periphery. The other part is more flexible and can be manipulated at will. The phenomenon of diverting processing resources to specified locations in the visual field or to a specified submodality is called visual attention (see, eg, Keele and Neill, 1978). Attention can be shifted to a new location overtly by executing an appropriate saccadic eye movement or covertly by a mechanism whose precise nature is not yet known. The benefit of the ability to shift attention is in the economy of processing resources required for adequate functioning. For some visual operations, such as search for compound stimuli (Treisman and Gelade, 1980), maintaining uniform processing capability over the entire field may be quite expensive. In these cases, attention provides an acceptable trade-off between resources and time.

Perceptual Organization. Perceptual organization is a collective term for a diverse set of processes that contribute to the emergence of order in the visual input. Some of the phenomena already mentioned here can be considered as particular instances of perceptual organization. Two examples that are, in reality, opposite sides of the same coin are shape constancy and visual motion. The perception of a deforming two-dimensional retinal stimulus pattern as a three-dimensional object in motion amounts to organizing the visual input so that it can be described in a simple and stable fashion. The study of perceptual organization has a long history in psychology. Palmer (1983), following Cassirer, Pitts and McCulloch, Gibson, and others, outlined a uniform framework for the study of organizational phenomena, based on the mathematical notion of invariance under transformation groups. The transformational approach allows problems of constancy and motion to be addressed in the same language as the classical issues of perceptual organization: figural goodness, grouping and frames of reference. A major attempt to understand these issues, motivated by a conviction that such understanding would shed light on perception in general, led to the formation of the Gestalt school in psychology (Köhler, 1947). Many of the laws of organization proposed by Gestalt theorists, as well as the concept of perceptual goodness (*Praegnanz*) they have introduced to account for a variety of perceptual phenomena, have been incorporated in a more rigorous formulation into the currently prevailing paradigm of visual perception [see the discussion in Marr (1982), p. 187].

Completion and Filling in. The group of phenomena that can be characterized by a tendency to optimize figural goodness includes two that have been mentioned in the section on visual competence (see also Figure 1). The first of these is contour completion: the visual system prefers to perceive a nonexistent contour forming the illusory triangle rather than see the three dented disks as unrelated to each other (in which case the missing portions of the real triangle would remain unaccounted for). It turns out that the perceived shape of the completed contour can be produced by a process that minimizes a measure of its curvature (Ullman, 1976). The second phenomenon that affects the perception of figures as wholes is that of area filling in, which may be considered a two-dimensional analog of contour completion. In Figure 1, filling in is apparent in the increased subjective lightness of the illusory triangle. Another manifestation of filling in is motion capture: our tendency to perceive stationary features that happen to fall within a moving contour as drifting along with the contour. Surface interpolation (see the section on stereopsis) is an instance of filling-in that, analogously to contour completion, can be formulated as a process of optimization (see Poggio and co-workers, 1985).

Categorization. Several illustrations of our disposition to see the environment as structured instead of chaotic were given in the previous sections, when we discussed the phenomena of object constancy and motion perception. The imposition of this kind of high-level structure on the visual world is an apotheosis of the processes of perceptual organization, linking vision to general cognition and language. Experimental evidence suggests that this connection is bilateral, and that the cognitive level can influence visual perception. The most directly relevant experiments are those in which subjects exhibit object superiority effects; an example is the facilitation of the perception of a low-level feature, such as a line segment, by virtue of its appearance as a part of the projection of a three-dimensional object (Weisstein and Harris, 1974).

In many top-down effects (including object superiority), the perceptual phenomenon is better characterized as categorization than recognition. The manner of cognitive involvement in perception is thus more flexible and more general than mere recollection of previously encountered stimulus exemplars. Experiments carried out by Rosch and her collaborators as part of a wider study of the structure of categories (see, eg, Rosch and co-workers, 1976) showed that people tend to perceive and describe objects at a certain level of detail. Importantly, this basic category level can be independently defined in terms of visual perception, language, and general cognitive development.

Some of the features of the processes involved in perceptual learning and memory are mentioned in the next section.

Perceptual Learning. Perceptual learning, or the adjustment of perception to the stimulus aspects of the environment, is sometimes distinguished from cognitive learning; the latter term is reserved for the modification of problem-solving behavior (Walk, 1978). In early vision, learning occurs in processes such as adaptation, mentioned above. The famous experiment first made by Stratton (1897/1964), in which a subject wearing inverting prisms gradually adapts to this condition, is a forceful reminder that the degree of plasticity at lower levels of the visual system should not be underestimated. (See Rock, 1984, for a discussion of the inversion experiments.)

Exactly what is learned and what is innate in vision (and in cognition in general) has been the subject of intense philosophical debate since Plato's time [see Dretske (1990) for an overview]. A century of research in visual psychophysics and neurobiology of vision shows that the basic perceptual abilities of the human visual system (such as the ability to perceive luminance contrast) are largely innate, while others (such as some varieties of object constancy) are acquired and depend on the visual experience (Spelke, 1990). Significantly, the mechanisms of perceptual organization used by infants in learning how to see seem to persist through adulthood. Thus, the study of the ontogeny of visual perception may help clarify the nature of the long-term memory representations of objects and scenes.

A similar angle on the problem of representation is provided by studies in which the subjects' perceptual performance in three-dimensional object recognition is modified merely as a result of practice or exposure to the stimuli, without any feedback from the experimenter (after all, infants acquire vision, and language, without being instructed). Normally, the subjects' response time in recognition depends monotonically on the misorientation of the stimulus with respect to some canonical attitude [Palmer and co-workers (1981); see also the discussion of mental rotation in the section on methods, above). Perceptual learning under such circumstances, inferred from the observed changes in the pattern of performance (specifically, from increasingly uniform response times for different aspects of the stimulus), can be attributed to a shift towards a more memory-intensive and less time-consuming recognition strategy (Tarr and Pinker, 1989; Edelman and Bülthoff, 1990). Indeed, such a strategy appears to be the most suitable one for a system in which memory is cheap, but time is expensive.

THE NEURAL SUBSTRATE

The architecture of the human visual system reflects the major functional constraint imposed on it, namely, the requirement of being able to recognize or classify in a few hundreds of milliseconds any object from a potentially unlimited repertoire, while taking into account a variety of visual clues (Biederman and co-workers, 1974; cf Rosenfeld, 1987). The following section contains several hints as to what the basic functional elements that constitute this architecture may be.

Vision Is Massively Parallel. The parallelism of visual information processing becomes apparent already at the level of the retina, where a separation occurs between several pathways, each of which is functionally specialized to support certain aspects of the input, such as form, motion, and color. Since eventually these have to be integrated into a coherent percept, the cortical areas fed by the different pathways are interconnected in an orderly fashion [see recent reviews in Zeki and Shipp (1988) and Kaas (1989)], so that on the whole the architecture is a heterarchy in which lateral connections and shortcuts abound, rather than a hierarchy envisaged by early visual scientists. Remarkably, in all the visual areas, as in the entire neocortex in general, information is processed by the same variety of cells, arranged in the same columnar structure (Gilbert, 1988). Thus, any comprehensive theory of brain function would have to specify, in information-processing terms, what the basic operation is that can be supported by the cortical architecture and is at the same time sufficiently powerful to address the entire range of perceptual, cognitive, and motor tasks.

Maps and Receptive Fields. Although a viable and widely accepted theory of such scope has yet to be proposed, two well-established findings in the neurobiology of perception, and in particular of vision, provide an inkling as to the basic mode of information processing in the cortex. The first of these is concerned with the notion of the receptive field of a neuron. In vision, it is defined as that region of the visual field whose stimulation affects the activity of the neuron (see, eg, Kuffler and Nicholls, 1976). Without going into the details of the taxonomy and structure of receptive fields found in the visual cortex, one may describe their function schematically as the integration of information over a finite area of the visual field and its concentration at a single point: the axon of the neuron in question, or its output terminal. Note that the axon may, in turn, connect to many (potentially, tens of thousands) other neurons at a higher level, so that as a whole this structure is as heterachical as the large-scale arrangement of cortical areas mentioned above (Fig. 3a).

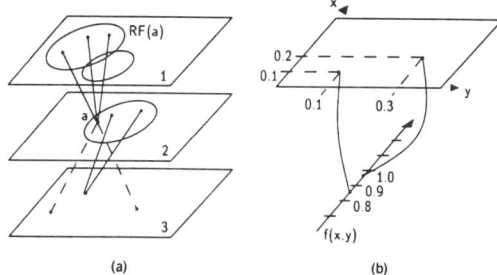

Figure 3. (a) A highly schematic illustration of the notion of a receptive field: unit a in area 2 receives input from the region marked as RF(a) in area 1, and, in turn, projects to many units in area 3; (b) computing the function $f(x) = e^{-(x^2+y^2)} \cos y$ with a two-dimensional–one dimensional (2D-to-1D) map of connections, or lookup table. Note that to find the value of the function at a point for which there in no entry in the lookup table one must resort to interpolation (see Poggio and Girosi, 1990).

The second basic notion in the architecture of vision, cortical mapping, pertains to the relationship among different receptive fields in the same visual cortical area. It turns out that many areas are interconnected by locally smooth maps (in fact, many areas are retinotopic, that is, their topology, but not necessarily their metric structure, conforms to that of the retina). Recent theoretical developments indicate that computing with maps or, equivalently, connections (Fig. 3b) is a powerful information-processing paradigm (see, eg, Ballard, 1986, for an integrative discussion). It has been suggested (Rojer and Schwartz, 1989; Mallot and co-workers, 1990; Damasio, 1989) that cortical mapping is the basic mechanism of the visual function of the brain. It remains to be seen whether this concept can be extended to encompass perception (and intelligence) in general.

CONCLUSION

The study of visual perception is bound to inspire awe, because of the recognition of the formidable problems posed by vision, and marvel, because of the appreciation of solutions developed by the brain to address these problems. Borrowing a phrase from Warren McCulloch, one can describe this study as discovering what a thing is, that a man may see it, and a man, that he may see things (McCulloch, 1965 p. 2). While looking for an answer to this question, it is worthwhile to remember that in perception, if not in intelligence, man is the measure of all things.

BIBLIOGRAPHY

D. H. Ballard, "Cortical Connections and Parallel Processing: Structure and Function," *Behav. Brain Sci.* **9,** 67–120 (1986).

I. Biederman, "Human Image Understanding: Recent Research and a Theory," *Comput. Vision, Graphics, Image Proc.* **32,** 29–73 (1985).

I. Biederman, J. C. Rabinowitz, A. L. Glass, and E. W. Stacy, "On the Information Extracted from a Glance at a Scene," *J. Exp. Psychol.* **103,** 597–600 (1974).

A. Blake and H. H. Bülthoff, "Does the Brain Know the Physics of Specular Reflection?," *Nature* **343,** 165–168 (1990).

K. R. Boff, L. Kaufman, and J. P. Thomas, eds., *Handbook of Perception and Human Performance,* Wiley, New York, 1986.

R. M. Boynton, "Color in Contour and Object Perception," in E. C. Carterette and M. P. Friedman, eds., *Handbook of Perception,* Vol. VIII, Academic Press, New York, pp. 173–199, 1978.

H. H. Bülthoff and H. A. Mallot, "Interaction of Depth Modules: Stereo and Shading," *J. Opt. Soc. Am.* **5,** 1749–1758 (1988).

P. Cavanagh, "Reconstructing the Third Dimension: Interactions between Color, Texture, Motion, Binocular Disparity and Shape," *Comput. Vision, Graphics, Image Proc.* **37,** 171–195 (1987).

A. R. Damasio, "The Brain Binds Entities and Events by Multiregional Activation from Convergence Zones," *Neural Comput.* **1,** 123–132 (1989).

D. Davidson, *Essays on Actions and Events,* Clarendon Press, Oxford, 1980.

F. Dretske, "Seeing, Believing, and Knowing," in D. N. Osherson, S. M. Kosslyn, and J. M. Hollerbach, eds., *Visual Cognition and Action,* Vol. 2, MIT Press, Cambridge, Mass., pp. 129–148, 1990.

S. Edelman and H. H. Bülthoff, *Viewpoint-Specific Representations in 3-D Object Recognition,* AI Memo No. 1239, Artif. Intelligence Lab., MIT, Cambridge, Mass., August 1990

S. Edelman and D. Weinshall, "A Self-organizing Multiple-View Representation of 3D Objects," A.I. Memo No. 1146, Artificial Intelligence Laboratory, Massachusetts Institute of Technology, Cambridge, Mass., August 1989.

S. Edelman and D. Weinshall, *Biol. Cybern.* **64,** 209–219 (1991).

J. P. Frisby, *Seeing,* Oxford University Press, Oxford, 1979.

J. J. Gibson, *The Perception of the Visual World,* Houghton Mifflin, Boston, 1950.

J. J. Gibson, *The Ecological Approach to Visual Perception,* Houghton Mifflin, Boston, 1979.

C. D. Gilbert, "Neuronal and Synaptic Organization in the Cortex," in P. Rakic and W. Singer, eds., *Neurobiology of Neucortex,* Wiley, New York, pp. 219–240, 1988.

A. L. Gilchrist, "Perceived Lightness Depends on Perceived Spatial Arrangement," *Science* **195,** 185–187 (1977).

D. M. Green and J. A. Swets, *Signal Detection Theory and Psychophysics,* Wiley, New York, 1966.

R. L. Gregory, "Illusions and Hallucinations," in E. C. Carterette and M. P. Friedman, eds., *Handbook of Perception,* Vol. IX, Academic Press, New York, pp. 337–357, 1978.

J. Jastrow, *The Time Relations of Mental Phenomena,* Hodges, New York, 1890.

G. Johansson, "Visual Perception of Biological Motion and a Model for Its Analysis," *Percept. Psychophys.* **14,** 201–211 (1973).

B. Julesz, *Foundations of Cyclopean Perception,* University of Chicago Press, Chicago, 1971.

B. Julesz, "A Brief Outline of the Texton Theory of Human Vision," *Trends Neurosci.* **7,** 41–45 (1984).

J. H. Kaas, "Why Does the Brain Have so Many Visual Areas?," *J. Cogn. Neurosci.* **1,** 121–135 (1989).

E. R. Kandel and J. H. Schwartz, *Principles of Neural Science,* Elsevier, New York, 1985.

S. W. Keele and W. T. Neill, "Mechanisms of Attention," in E. C. Carterette and M. P. Friedman, eds., *Handbook of Perception,* Vol. IX, Academic Press, New York, pp. 3–47, 1978.

J. J. Koenderink, "What Does the Occluding Contour Tell Us about Solid Shape?," *Perception* **13**, 321–330 (1984).

W. Köhler, *Gestalt Psychology*, Liveright, New York, 1947.

S. W. Kuffler and J. G. Nicholls, *From Neuron to Brain*, Sinauer, Sunderland, Mass., 1976.

E. H. Land and J. J. McCann, "Lightness and Retinex Theory," *J. Opt. Soc. Am.* **61**, 1–11 (1971).

R. D. Luce, *Response Times: Their Role in Inferring Elementary Mental Organization*, Oxford University Press, Oxford, 1986.

H. A. Mallot, W. von Seelen, and F. Giannakopoulos, "Neural Mapping and Space-Variant Image Processing," *Neural Networks*, **3**, (1990).

D. Marr, *Vision*, Freeman, San Francisco, 1982.

W. S. McCulloch, *Embodiments of Mind*, MIT Press, Cambridge, Mass., 1965.

G. J. Mitchison and S. P. McKee, "Interpolation in Stereoscopic Matching. *Nature* **315**, 402–404 (1985).

S. E. Palmer, "The Psychology of Perceptual Organization: A Transformational Approach," in J. Beck, B. Hope, and A. Rosenfeld, eds., *Human and Machine Vision*, Academic Press, New York, pp. 269–340, 1983.

S. E. Palmer, E. Rosch, and P. Chase, "Canonical Perspective and the Perception of Objects," in J. Long and A. Baddeley, eds., *Attention and Performance IX*, Erlbaum, Hillsdale, N.J., pp. 135–151, 1981.

G. F. Poggio and T. Poggio, "The Analysis of Stereopsis," *Ann. Rev. Neurosci.* **7**, 379–412 (1984).

T. Poggio and S. Edelman, "A Network That Learns to Recognize Three-Dimensional Objects," *Nature* **343**, 263–266 (1990).

T. Poggio and F. Girosi, "Regularization Algorithms for Learning That Are Equivalent to Multilayer Networks," *Science* **247**, 978–982 (1990).

T. Poggio and W. Reichardt, "Visual Control of Orientation Behavior in the Fly (Parts i and ii)," *Quart. Rev. Biophys.* **3**, 311–439 (1976).

T. Poggio, V. Torre, and C. Koch, "Computational Vision and Regularization Theory," *Nature* **317**, 314–319 (1985).

M. Potter, "Meaning in Visual Search," *Science* **187**, 965–966 (1975).

Z. Pylyshyn, *Computation and Cognition*, MIT Press, Cambridge, Mass., 1985.

P. Quinlan, "Visual Object Recognition Reconsidered," *Behav. Brain Sciences* (in press).

V. S. Ramachandran, "Perception of Shape from Shading," *Nature* **331**, 163–166 (1988).

I. Rock, *Perception*, Scientific American Books, New York, 1984.

I. Rock and J. DiVita, "A Case of Viewer-Centered Object Perception," *Cogn. Psychol.* **19**, 280–293 (1987).

A. Rojer and E. L. Schwartz, "A Multiple-Map Model for Pattern Classification," *Neural Comput.* **1**, 104–115 (1989).

E. Rosch, C. B. Mervis, W. D. Gray, D. M. Johnson, and P. Boyes-Braem, "Basic Objects in Natural Categories," *Cogn. Psychol.* **8**, 382–439 (1976).

A. Rosenfeld, "Recognizing Unexpected Objects: A Proposed Approach," *Int. J. Pattern Recogn. Artif. Intell.* **1**, 71–84 (1987).

R. N. Shepard, "Toward a Universal Law of Generalization for Psychological Science," *Science* **237**, 1317–1323 (1987).

R. N. Shepard and L. A. Cooper, *Mental Images and Their Transformations*, MIT Press, Cambridge, Mass., 1982.

A. Sloman, "What Are the Purposes of Vision?," Technical Report No. CSRP 066, University of Sussex, U.K., 1987.

E. S. Spelke, "Origins of Visual Knowledge," in D. N. Osherson, S. M. Kosslyn, and J. M. Hollerbach, eds., *Visual Cognition and Action*, Vol. 2, MIT Press, Cambridge, Mass., pp. 99–128, 1990.

G. R. Stoner, T. D. Albright, and V. S. Ramachandran, "Transparency and Coherence in Human Motion Perception," *Nature* **344**, 153–155 (1990).

G. Stratton, "Vision without Inversion of the Retinal Image," in W. N. Dember, ed., *Visual Perception: The Nineteenth Century*, Wiley, New York, pp. 143–154, 1897/1964.

M. Tarr and S. Pinker, "Mental Rotation and Orientation-Dependence in Shape Recognition," *Cogn. Psychol.* **21**, 233–282 (1989).

J. T. Todd and E. Mingolla, "Perception of Surface Curvature and Direction of Illumination from Patterns of Shading," *J. Exp. Psychol. Human Perception and Performance* **9**, 583–595 (1983).

A. Treisman and G. Gelade, "A Feature Integration Theory of Attention," *Cogn. Psychol.* **12**, 97–136 (1980).

S. Ullman, "Filling in the Gaps: The Shape of Subjective Contours and a Model for Their Generation," *Biol. Cybernet.* **25**, 1–6 (1976).

S. Ullman, *The Interpretation of Visual Motion*, MIT Press, Cambridge, Mass., 1979.

S. Ullman, "Aligning Pictorial Descriptions: An Approach to Object Recognition," *Cognition* **32**, 193–254 (1989).

S. Ullman and R. Basri, "Recognition by Linear Combinations of Models," A.I. Memo No. 1152, Artificial Intelligence Laboratory, Massachusetts Institute of Technology, Cambridge, Mass., 1990.

R. von der Heydt, E. Peterhans, and G. Baumgartner, "Illusory Contours and Cortical Neurons' Responses," *Science* **224**, 1260–1262 (1984).

H. von Helmholtz, "Unconscious Conclusions," in W. N. Dember, ed., *Visual Perception: The Nineteenth Century*, Wiley, New York, pp. 163–170, 1856/1964.

R. D. Walk, "Perceptual Learning," in E. C. Carterette and M. P. Friedman, eds., *Handbook of Perception*, Vol. IX, Academic Press, New York, pp. 257–298, 1978.

H. Wallach and D. N. O'Connell, "The Kinetic Depth Effect," *J. Exp. Psychol.* **45**, 205–217 (1953).

D. Weinshall, "Perception of Multiple Transparent Planes in Stereo Vision," *Nature* **341**, 737–739 (1989).

N. Weisstein and C. S. Harris, "Visual Detection of Line Segments: An Object-Superiority Effect," *Science* **186**, 752–755 (1974).

S. Zeki and S. Shipp, "The Functional Logic of Cortical Connections," *Nature* **335**, 311–317 (1988).

SHIMON EDELMAN
Weizmann Institute of Science

VISUAL RECOVERY

Neither objects nor properties of objects (such as shape, color, etc) exist inside our brains as such. When we see, computations are performed inside our heads which generate hypotheses about objects and their properties. To understand vision, the methods used to derive such perceptual hypotheses from visual images must be discovered.

Much of the research on computational vision over the past 35 years has concentrated on specific visual tasks, and has been concerned with how one can recover visual quantities necessary for carrying out such visual tasks as identifying and locating a known object so that a robot arm can grasp it. This research is sometimes referred to as belonging to the "recognition" school, since it deals with specific types of objects which must be identified and located. On the other hand, the "recovery" school has concentrated on the study of general visual capabilities, such as the ability to understand the shapes of general objects based on the distribution of surface markings (texture). This article reviews general visual recovery research and discusses how it relates to the recognition point of view.

Visual Problems

A very large variety of problems related to the interaction of autonomous mechanisms with their environments can potentially be solved using visual input. However, two classes of problems are commonly held to be touchstones for practical vision systems: successful navigation in a complex environment using visual information, and recognition of classes of common objects (such as people or trees) in a complex scene. A large proportion of the published papers on computer vision address, explicitly or implicitly, one or the other of these goals. If both were achieved, automatic systems would have many of the capabilities of the human visual system; but it is clear that constructing such systems presents great difficulties. These difficulties were realized during the 60s and the early 70s, after the failure of early attempts to build entire vision systems, ie, systems that exhibited some vertical integration and used knowledge at all levels, including domain-specific information. "In order to complete the construction of such systems, it is almost inevitable that corners be cut and many overly simplified assumptions be made" (Brady 1982). This results in a system capable of carrying out a limited number of tasks, but not enhancing our general understanding of vision. At about that time the recovery school of thought started to develop through the work of Marr (1982) and his colleagues. This school held that the majority of visual problems can be reduced to the following general problem: *from one or more images of a scene, derive an accurate three-dimensional description of the objects in the scene and quantitatively recover their properties (or at least those properties relevant to a given task)*. If we can recover (reconstruct) an accurate description of our environment, we can navigate, avoid obstacles, and find specific locations. If we can recover the properties of an object (shape, reflectance, color, etc), we can use them to recognize (classify) the object. Thus, the recovery school of thought in computer vision emphasized the study of visual abilities, independently of a task.

Methodology of Visual Recovery

Even if we accept that the solution to vision problems lies in the recovery of the scene, it is not obvious how to proceed. Luckily, there is a standard way to design large, complex information systems, as research in computational fields has shown (Feldman, 1985). The system is divided into functional components or subsystems which break the overall task into autonomous parts. These subsystems are analyzed and the representations of information that they use and the language of communication among them are chosen. The subsystems are then tested individually, in pairs, and all together.

This approach can be used in building a visual system, using functionally autonomous subsystems that recover specific properties of the world from images. These subsystems are called modules. Visual recovery research is devoted to the study of such modules and their integration.

There is considerable evidence for the existence of such modules in the human visual system. One source of such evidence is the study of patients with visual disabilities that result from brain lesions. In addition, psychophysicists perform experiments in which a particular module of the human visual system is seemingly isolated, for example, Julesz's (1971) work on stereoscopic fusion without monocular cues, Land's (Land and McCann, 1971) work on the computation of lightness, Gibson's (1950) work on the perception of shape from texture, etc. Thus it seems that cues such as shading (image intensity variations), texture (distribution of surface markings), contours (image discontinuities), color, motion and stereo are very helpful in recovering properties of the three-dimensional (3-D) world from images.

Marr (1982) pointed out that perceptual processes, (ie, processes underlying visual abilities), must be understood at three levels:

1. The level of *computational theory*. We must develop, through rigorous mathematical treatment, the relationship between the quantity to be computed and the observations (data = image(s)). After this computational theory is developed, we can understand whether the given problem has a unique solution.
2. The level of *algorithms and data structures*. After the computational theory has been completed, we must design algorithms and data structures that, when applied to the input (image(s)), will output the desired quantity.
3. The level of *implementation*. After the two previous levels have been developed, we must implement the algorithm in hardware (serial or parallel).

If these three levels are fully understood, then we can say that we understand the perceptual process.

What Do We Want to Recover?

What should we attempt to recover from images in order to be able to accomplish visual tasks? The answer defines the nature of research on the theory of computer vision; that is, image understanding (IU) research which is not directed towards specific applications.

It is clear that one quantity that should be recovered from images is the shapes of objects. A large amount of visual recovery research is devoted to determining the shapes of imaged objects from image cues, such as shading, texture, contour, multiple views, motion, etc. If we can recover the geometry of the environment we can perform navigational tasks such as avoiding obstacles, finding passages, etc. In addition, if we can find an appropriate representation, we can use shape information for object recognition.

Shape is not the only thing we may want to recover; for example, if we can recover the three-dimensional velocity of a moving object we can catch it, avoid it, track it, etc. Or, we may want to determine the velocity with which every image point moves, in the case of images obtained by a moving sensor (optic flow). We may also want to recover the colors of objects; to recover then pose (spatial position and orientation) of a known object; to determine the discontinuities of the image intensity that correspond to physical discontinuities; to determine a segmentation of the image that corresponds to some well-defined segmentation of the scene; or we may want to recover (or restore) the ideal image from the actual image, which is corrupted by noise, etc. Evidently, it would not be possible to review all of these topics in this paper. Most of the articles in this encyclopedia that deal with vision are devoted to general or specific recovery problems. In this article, attention will focus on the problem of recovering shape.

Since this article deals with shape recovery, shape will be defined, several commonly used shape representations will be introduced, and the different kinds of projections (imaging geometries) used in the literature will be reviewed. The modules of shape from shading, texture, contour, stereo and motion will be studied, in brief: "shape from x". The constraints relating 3-D shape to observable image data, as well as algorithms that aim to reconstruct the 3-D world from single monocular cues, will be described. After discussing the limitations of these approaches, there will be discussions on how to combine multiple cues, and an outline of the foundations for the active vision paradigm, which provides the basis for the unique and robust computation of 3-D shape, will be included.

GEOMETRIC CORRESPONDENCE BETWEEN SCENE AND IMAGE

Different imaging projections have different properties that influence the design of shape recovery modules. Described here are the most commonly used projections.

Perspective Projection

Consider an ideal pinhole at a fixed distance in front of an image plane (Fig. 1). Assume that only light coming through the pinhole can reach the image plane. Given that light travels along straight lines, each point in the image corresponds to a particular direction defined by the ray from that point through the pinhole. This is perspective projection. In the sequel, in order to simplify the equations, the nodal point of the eye (the pinhole) will be regarded as being behind the image plane, as shown in Figure 2. The optical axis is defined to be the perpendicular from the pinhole to the image plane. A Cartesian coordinate system is introduced with the origin at the nodal point and the z-axis aligned with the optical axis and pointing toward the image. Let A be any point in front of the camera. Assume that nothing lies on the ray from point A to the nodal point O. Compute the position of the image A' of A in the image plane. Let $V = (X,Y,Z)$ be the vector connecting O to A and $V' = (x,y,f)$ be the vector connecting O to A', with f the focal length, ie, the distance of the image plane from the nodal point O. Then (x,y) are the coordinates of A' on the image plane in the naturally induced coordinate system with origin the point of the intersection of the image plane with the optical axis, and axes x and y parallel to the axes of the camera coordinate system OX and OY. It is trivial to see that

$$x = \frac{fX}{Z}, y = \frac{fY}{Z} \qquad (2.1)$$

Equations 2.1 relate the world coordinates of a point to the image plane coordinates of its image. Very often, to further simplify the equations, we assume $f = 1$ without loss of generality.

Orthographic Projection

If, in the perspective projection model, we have a scene plane that lies parallel to the image plane at $Z = Z_0$, then we define the magnification, μ, as the ratio of the distance between two points measured in the image to the distance between the corresponding points in the scene plane. So, for a small interval (dX, dY, O) on the scene plane and the corresponding small interval (dx, dy) in the image, we have

$$\mu = \frac{(dx)^2 + (dy)^2}{(dX)^2 + (dY)^2} = \frac{f}{Z_0}$$

Thus a small object in the scene at average distance Z_0 will produce an image that is magnified by μ. Evidently

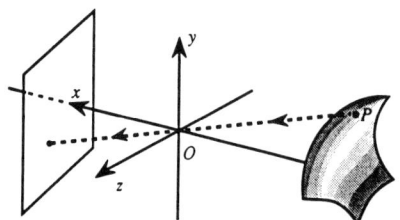

Figure 1. Perspective projection (image plane in the back).

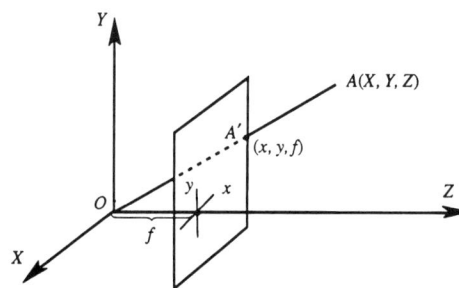

Figure 2. Perspective projection (image plane in front).

the magnification is approximately constant when the depth range of the scene is small relative to the average distance of the scene points from the camera. In this case, equations 2.1 become

$$x = \mu X, y = \mu Y \qquad (2.2)$$

with $\mu = f/Z_0$ and Z_0 the average value of the depth Z. For convenience, if $\mu = 1$, equations 2.2 further simplify to

$$x = X, y = Y \qquad (2.3)$$

Equations 2.3 define the orthographic projection model, where the rays are parallel to the optical axis (Fig. 3). The difference between orthography and perspective is small when the distance to the scene is much larger than the variation in distance among objects in the scene. A rough rule of thumb is that perspective effects are significant when a wide angle lens is used, while images taken by telephoto lenses tend to approximate orthographic projection; of course, this is not exact (Horn, 1986).

Paraperspective Projection

Orthographic projection is a very rough approximation of the projection of light on the fovea, but it is unrealistic for many machine vision applications. Perspective projection, on the other hand, involves more complicated equations and makes the analysis of some problems difficult. Paraperspective projection is a good approximation of perspective; it lies between orthography and perspective. A version of paraperspective projection was first introduced by Ohta and co-workers (1981). Let a coordinate system $OXYZ$ be fixed with respect to the camera, with Z axis pointing along the optical axis and O the nodal point of the eye. Again, we consider the image plane perpendicular to the X axis at the point $(0,0,1)$ (ie, the focal length $f = 1$, without loss of generality). Consider a small planar surface patch SP having the equation $Z = pX + qY + C$ (Fig. 4). Under perspective, any point $(X,Y,Z) \in SP$ is projected onto the point $(X/Z, Y/Z)$ on the image plane. Now consider the plane $Z = d$, where d is the Z-coordinate of the centroid C of SP. Paraperspective projection involves two steps:

1. SP is projected onto $Z = d$. This projection is performed using the rays that are parallel to the central projecting ray OC.
2. The projection of SP on $Z = d$ is projected perspectively onto the image plane. Since $Z = d$ is parallel

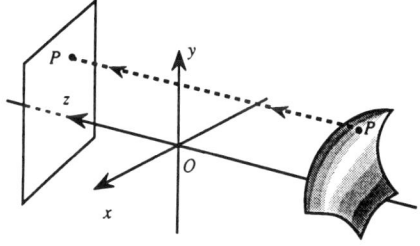

Figure 3. Orthographic projection.

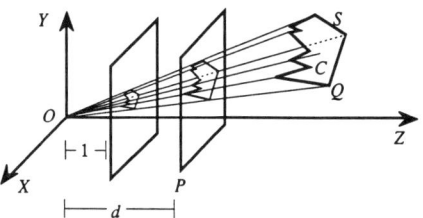

Figure 4. Paraperspective projection. Plane P is put in front of the surface S for pictorial clarity.

to the image plane, this projection is a magnification by a factor $1/d$.

Figure 5 illustrates a cross sectional view of the projection process sliced by a plane perpendicular to the XZ plane and which includes the central projecting ray. Paraperspective decomposes the projection of the scene onto the image plane into two parts. Step (a) incorporates the foreshortening distortion and part of the position effect, and step (b) incorporates both the distance and the position effects.

Paraperspective projection has nice mathematical properties, since it is an affine transformation. It has been successfully used in many areas of computer vision, such as shape from texture, shape from contour, object recognition, and the like. See Aloimonos (1990b) for applications of paraperspective projection, as well as other perspective approximations.

WHAT DO WE MEAN BY SHAPE?

A visual system analyzes images and produces descriptions of what is imaged. A description might include information about the shapes of the objects in the scene, but the shape of an object does not have a unique description; one can think of descriptions at many levels of detail and from many points of view. As Horn (1986) suggests, "we can avoid this potential philosophical snare by considering the task for which the description is intended. We don't want just any description of what is imaged, but one that allows us to take appropriate action." A reasonable first approximation to describing the shape of an object is to represent the local orientation of its surface. Only this level of description will be considered here. Global shape representations can also be used, for example the one based on superquadrics (Pentland, 1986; Bajcsy and Solina, 1987); they are appealing because they represent complex shapes using only a few numbers, but the inverse problem (finding this description from an image) still

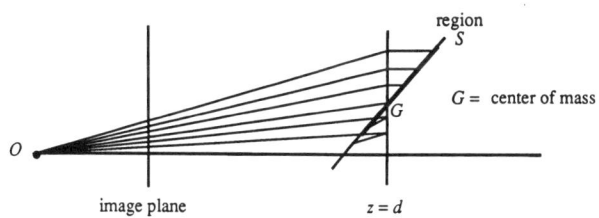

Figure 5. Cross-sectional view of paraperspective.

needs to be addressed. Various qualitative shape descriptors have been developed in the two-dimensional literature (Pavlidis, 1980), and a few in the 3-D case (Mumford, 1987), for use in object recognition; but these descriptors do not provide solutions to the general recovery task. Finding robust shape descriptions is an open research problem that will probably require advanced mathematical tools for its solution, and therefore this section is confined to the local descriptions of shape based on surface orientation.

Surface orientation is usually represented by the orientation of the surface normal vector. In the following subsections it is shown how the shape of a visible surface can be reconstructed from local orientation information.

Surface Orientation and Shape

The normal vector $\bar{n}$ to the surface $Z = Z(X,Y)$ at the point (X,Y,Z) is

$$\bar{n} = \left(\frac{\partial Z}{\partial X}, \frac{\partial Z}{\partial Y}, -1\right) \bigg/ \left[\left(\frac{\partial Z}{\partial X}\right)^2 + \left(\frac{\partial Z}{\partial Y}\right)^2 + 1\right]^{1/2}$$

Let $(x = fX/Z, y = fY/Z)$ be the image of (X,Y,Z). If (dx, dy) is a small displacement in the image, corresponding to a small displacement (dX, dY, dZ) on the surface, then

$$dX = \frac{dx \cdot Z + x \, dZ}{f}, \, dY = \frac{dy \cdot Z + y \, dZ}{f}$$

Given that $Z(X + dX, Y + dY) = Z(x + dx, y + dy)$, if we expand both sides of this equation in a Taylor series and ignore the higher order terms, we get

$$\frac{\partial Z}{\partial X} \frac{Z}{f - x\frac{\partial Z}{\partial X} - y\frac{\partial Z}{\partial Y}} dx + \frac{\partial Z}{\partial Y} \frac{Z}{f - x\frac{\partial Z}{\partial X} - y\frac{\partial Z}{\partial Y}} dy$$
$$= \frac{\partial Z}{\partial x} dx + \frac{\partial Z}{\partial y} dy$$

so that

$$\frac{\partial Z}{\partial x} = \frac{Z \frac{\partial Z}{\partial X}}{f - x\frac{\partial Z}{\partial X} - y\frac{\partial Z}{\partial Y}} \text{ and } \frac{\partial Z}{\partial y} = \frac{Z \frac{\partial Z}{\partial Y}}{f - x\frac{\partial Z}{\partial X} - y\frac{\partial Z}{\partial Y}}$$

From these equations we see that if $\partial Z/\partial X$, $\partial Z/\partial Y$ are known, the quantity

$$\frac{Z(x + dx, y + dy)}{Z(x,y)}$$

can be computed. This means that if the surface normal is known as a function of position (x,y) in the image, then the depth function $Z(x,y)$ can be computed up to a constant factor. The constant is undetermined; the surface can be small and near the camera or large and far away.

Surface Orientation and Shape Under Orthography

Under orthographic projection, the image coordinates of a point are equal to the corresponding scene coordinates, ie, $(x,y) = (X,Y)$. So

$$\left(\frac{\partial Z}{\partial X}, \frac{\partial Z}{\partial Y}\right) = \left(\frac{\partial Z}{\partial x}, \frac{\partial Z}{\partial y}\right).$$

Since

$$Z(x + dx, y + dy) - Z(x,y) = \frac{\partial Z}{\partial x} dx + \frac{\partial Z}{\partial y} dy + \text{(higher order terms)},$$

we see that $Z(x,y)$ can be computed up to a constant additive term. Thus, if we know the surface orientation under orthography, we know the surface shape, but we do not know its distance.

Other Coordinate Systems

Let $p = \partial Z/\partial X$, $q = \partial Z/\partial Y$ at the point of the surface $Z = Z(X,Y)$. We have seen that the surface normal vector is

$$\frac{(p,q,-1)}{(p^2 + q^2 + 1)^{1/2}}$$

The coordinates

$$(a,b,c) = \left(\frac{p}{k}, \frac{q}{k}, \frac{-1}{k}\right) \text{ with } k = (p^2 + q^2 + 1)^{1/2}$$

define the position of a point on the *Gaussian sphere*. This position can also be defined in terms of latitude and longitude angles. Another commonly used representation is in terms of slant and tilt, (σ, τ), where slant is the tangent of the latitude angle and tilt is the longitude angle. It is easy to see that

$$\sigma = \cos^{-1}\left(\frac{1}{\sqrt{1 + p^2 + q^2}}\right)$$

$$\tau = \tan^{-1}\left(\frac{q}{p}\right)$$

The parameterization of the local surface normal that uses the partial derivatives $p = \partial z/\partial x$, $q = \partial z/\partial y$, gives rise to the concept of gradient space (see, eg, Shafer and coworkers, 1983). The parameterization has the disadvantage that the partial derivatives can become infinite at occluding boundaries, ie, at places where the surface turns away from the viewer; a similar problem arises with the slant-tilt representation. Ikeuchi and Horn (1981) therefore used a different parameterization (f,g) of surface orientation, which they called stereographic space. f and g are related to p and q by

$$f(g) = \frac{2p(q)[\sqrt{1 + p^2 + q^2} - 1]}{p^2 + q^2}$$

Using the Gaussian sphere formalism, they showed that gradient space corresponds to projecting the Gaussian sphere from its center onto a plane tangent to the sphere at its north pole, whereas stereographic space corresponds to projecting from the south pole (see Figs. 6 and 7).

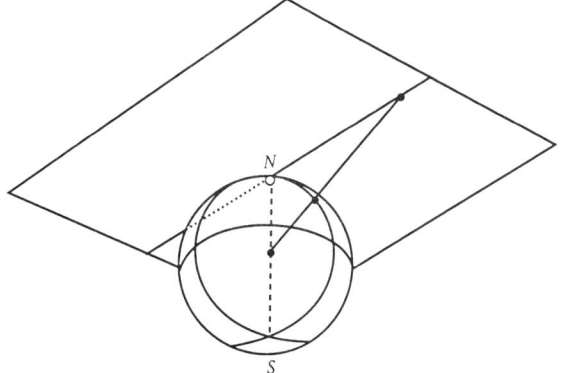

Figure 6. Projection of Gaussian sphere on gradient space. (Reproduced from Horn (1985).)

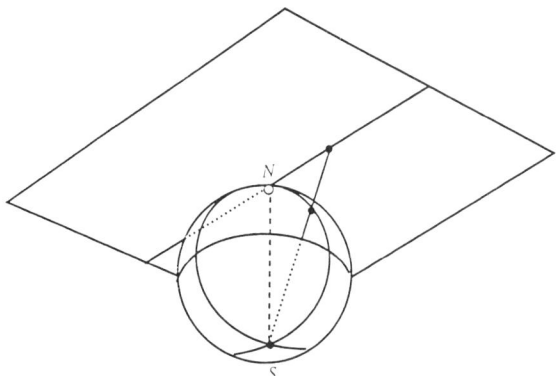

Figure 7. Stereographic projection. (Reproduced from Horn (1985).)

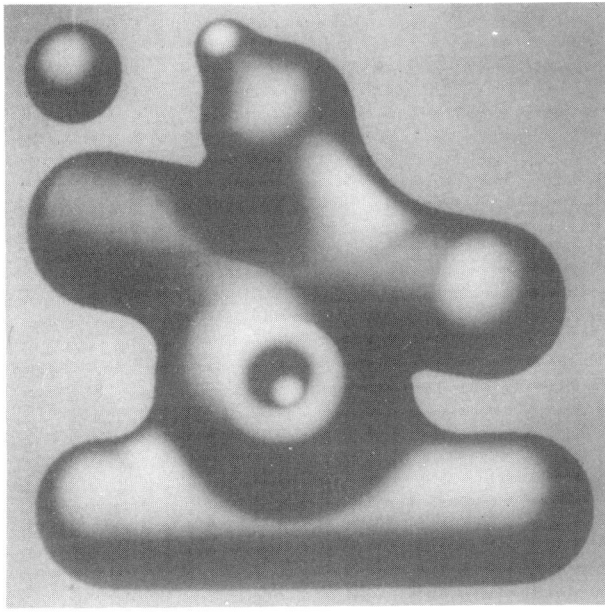

Figure 8. Shaded surface.

For a clear discussion of different shape representations, see Horn, (1986).

SHAPE FROM x

Modules that recover surface orientation from various cues in the image are called *shape from x* modules. Some of these modules operate directly on the image, while others operate on some intermediate representation created from the image. Shape from shading falls in the first category while shape from texture and contour fall in the second. As regards shape from stereo and shape from motion, some researchers put them in the first category while others put them in the second. The recovery problems defined by these modules are usually ill posed, so additional constraints must be introduced.

Shape from Shading

The recovery of surface orientation from gray level variations (shape from shading) was first studied by Horn and his colleagues at MIT. The analysis was done under orthography. Figure 8 shows an image that contains shading. Humans can easily perceive, at least qualitatively, the shape of the imaged surface. In this section we describe methods of recovering surface orientation from shading, together with other assumptions to be described later.

In general, the amount of light reflected by a surface element (the surface radiance) depends on its microstructure, on its optical properties, and on the angular distribution and state of polarization of the incident illumination. For some surfaces, the fraction of incident illumination (irradiance) reflected in a particular direction depends only on the surface orientation. The reflectance of such a surface can be represented by a function $f(i,g,e)$ of the angles i = incident, g = phase and e = emergent, as they are defined in Figure 9. For example, in perfect specular (mirror-like) reflection, the incident angle equals the emergent angle and the incident, emergent and normal vectors lie in the same plane; the phase angle is given by $g = i + e$. Thus the reflectance function is

$$f(i,e,g) = \begin{cases} 1 \text{ if } i = e \text{ and } i + e = g \\ 0 \text{ otherwise} \end{cases}$$

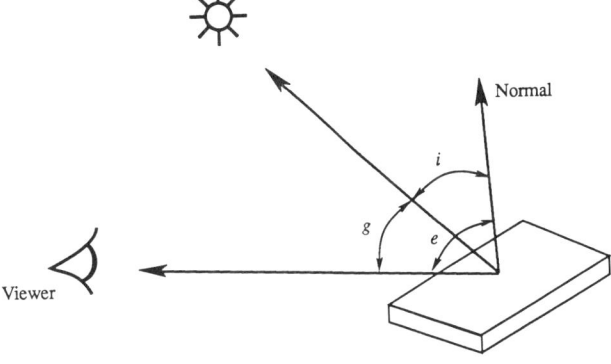

Figure 9. Geometry of reflection.

The most widely used model of surface reflectance is defined by the function $f(i,e,g) = \rho \cos i$, where ρ is constant for a given surface and is called the albedo constant. This function defines the reflectance of a perfectly diffuse (Lambertian) surface which appears equally bright from all viewing directions; the cosine of the incident angle compensates for the foreshortening of the surface as seen from the light source.

In orthographic projection, the viewing direction and hence the phase angle g are constant for all surface elements. So, for a fixed light source and viewer geometry and a given surface material, the ratio of radiance to irradiance depends only on the surface normal vector. Furthermore, suppose that each surface element receives the same irradiance. Then the surface radiance, and hence the image intensity $I(x, y)$, depends only on the surface normal vector.

When expressed in terms of the surface normal coordinates $p = \partial z/\partial x$, $q = \partial z/\partial y$, the reflectance function is called the *reflectance map* and is denoted by $R(p,q)$. This map provides a uniform representation for a given surface material for a particular light source, surface normal, and viewer geometry. A comprehensive discussion of reflectance maps for a variety of surface and light source conditions has been given by Horn (1977). A unified approach to the specification of reflectance maps has been given in Horn and Sjoberg, (1979).

Under orthographic projection, expressions for $\cos i$, $\cos e$, and $\cos g$ can be easily derived from the surface normal vector $(p, q, -1)$, the light source vector $(p_s, q_s, -1)$, and the vector $(0, 0, -1)$ that points in the direction of the viewer. For a Lambertian reflectance function these expressions give

$$R(p,q) = \frac{\rho(1 + p p_s + q q_s)}{\sqrt{(1 + p^2 + q^2)}\sqrt{(1 + p_s^2 + q_s^2)}}$$

where ρ is the albedo constant. Under perspective projection, the expressions are not known exactly, but recent results indicate that they are similar (Shafer and co-workers, 1983).

Using fixed light sources and fixed reflectance characteristics, the reflectance map associates a brightness value with each surface orientation. Figure 10 shows iso-

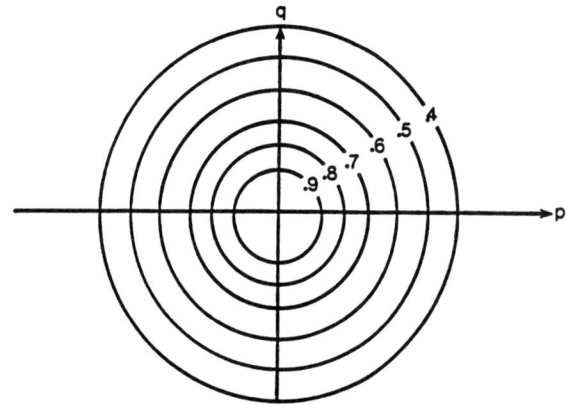

Figure 10. Isobrightness contours for a Lambertian surface when the light source is near the observer.

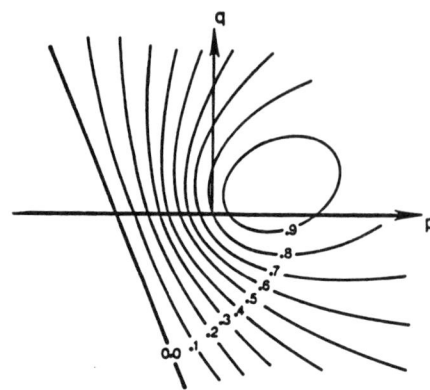

Figure 11. Isobrightness contours for a Lambertian surface when the light source is removed from the observer. (Reproduced from Horn (1977).)

brightness contours for the case of a Lambertian surface and a single light source near the viewer. Figure 11 shows the reflectance map for the same surface and a light source farther away from the viewer. Reflectance maps for non-Lambertian surfaces (constructed in a similar way) can be found in Horn, (1986).

The image irradiance equation $I(x,y) = R(p,q)$ is a nonlinear first order partial differential equation. Horn (1975) applied the characteristic strip method for solving partial differential equations to reformulate this equation as a set of ordinary differential equations. This method computes the solution surface $z = g(x,y)$ by finding a family of space curves whose local tangents all lie in the tangent plane of the solution surface. Such a curve can be specified by a one-parameter family of points $(x(s), y(s), z(s))$, where s is the distance along the curve.

Differentiating with respect to s gives

$$p\frac{dx}{ds} + q\frac{dy}{ds} - \frac{dz}{ds} = 0$$

or

$$(p,q,-1) \cdot \left(\frac{dx}{ds}, \frac{dy}{ds}, \frac{dz}{ds}\right) = 0,$$

ie, the vector $(dx/ds, dy/ds, dz/ds)$ lies in the tangent plane of the solution surface. Trivially, the vector $(R_p, R_q, pR_p + qR_q)$ also lies in that plane. From this observation, we conclude that

$$\frac{dx}{ds} = R_p \qquad (4.1)$$

$$\frac{dy}{ds} = R_q \qquad (4.2)$$

$$\frac{dz}{ds} = pR_p + qR_q \qquad (4.3)$$

where the subscripts denote partial differentiation.

Differentiating the image irradiance equation with respect to x gives $I_x = R_p p_x + R_q q_x$, and since $p_y = g_{xy} =$

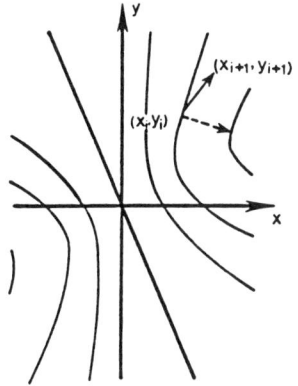 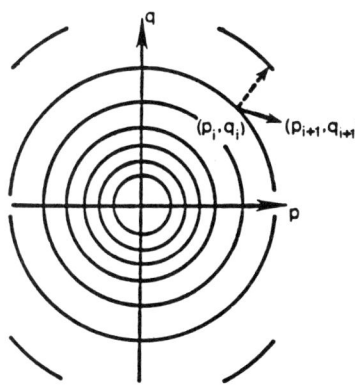

Figure 12. Isobrightness contours $(x_i, y_i) \to (p_i, q_i)$. (Reproduced from Brady (1982).)

$g_{yx} = q_x$ we have $I_x = R_p p_x + R_q p_y$, and consequently

$$I_x = \frac{dp}{ds} \quad (4.4)$$

Similarly,

$$I_y = \frac{dq}{ds} \quad (4.5)$$

Thus if we know that the image point (x_k, y_k) corresponds to a surface patch with orientation (p_i, q_i), we can extend this solution to other points. Figure 12 shows the isobrightness contours passing through (x_i, y_i) in the image and (p_i, q_i) in the reflectance map. If we take a step ds along the characteristic strip from (x_i, y_i) to (x_{i+1}, y_{i+1}), and correspondingly from (p_i, q_i) to (p_{i+1}, q_{i+1}), then the five differential equations 4.1–4.5 show that the step in the image is in direction (R_p, R_q), ie, along the normal to the isobrightness contour in the reflectance map. In the same way, the step in the reflectance map is in the direction normal to the isobrightness contour computed in the image. Thus, if we know the reflectance map we can compute the surface orientations at a sequence of points along a characteristic strip starting from a point where the surface orientation is known. Figure 13 shows the results obtained using this method.

In order to use this method we need an initial point with known surface orientation. The algorithm also depends on the assumption that the surface is locally convex at the initial point. At this stage, researchers began to be concerned about conditions under which the method works, as well as about uniqueness issues. These questions were important in subsequent research on recovery (Barrow and Tenenbaum, 1981a).

The problem is ill-posed so additional constraints will be needed. A smoothness constraint, along with boundary conditions, provides a unique solution, as described below.

Bounding or occluding contours provide boundary conditions for the shape from x problem. Ikeuchi and Horn (1981) used these conditions in conjunction with a smoothness constraint to solve the shape from shading problem. If I_{ij} is the intensity at point (i,j), and (f,g) are the stereographic coordinates of the surface orientation, we look for a surface (f_{ij}, g_{ij}), $(i,j) \in$ image that minimizes

$$e = \sum_i \sum_j (s_{ij} + \lambda r_{ij}),$$

where

$$s_{ij} = \frac{1}{4}[(f_{i+1,j} - f_{ij})^2 + (f_{i,j+1} - f_{ij})^2 + (g_{i+1,j} - g_{ij})^2 + (g_{i,j+1} - g_{ij})^2]$$

and

$$r_{ij} = (I_{ij} - R(f_{ij}, g_{ij}))$$

The first term in the sum represents departure from smoothness while the second represents departure from the constraint defined by the image irradiance equation. Thus the surface that minimizes e best satisfies the image irradiance equation and is also as smooth as possible. The parameter λ defines the relative importance of the smoothness and the irradiance constraint. We minimize e by differentiating with respect to f_{ij}, g_{ij} and setting the resulting derivatives equal to zero. This gives the follow-

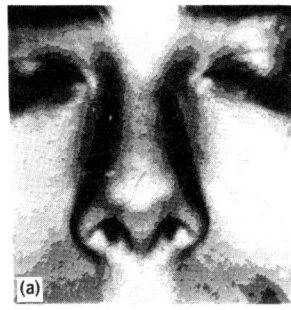 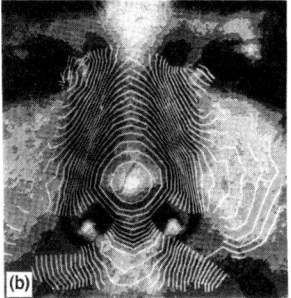

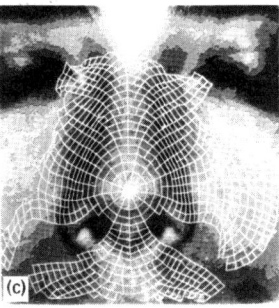

Figure 13. Reconstruction of a face. (Reproduced from Horn (1985).)

ing recurrence relations as the basis of an iterative algorithm (Ikeuchi and Horn, 1981):

$$f_{ij}^{(n+1)} = \overline{f_{ij}^{(n)}} + \lambda(I_{ij} - R(f_{ij}^{(n)}, g_{ij}^{(n)}))\frac{\partial R}{\partial f}$$

$$g_{ij}^{(n+1)} = \overline{g_{ij}^{(n)}} + \lambda(I_{ij} - R(f_{ij}^{(n)}, g_{ij}^{(n)}))\frac{\partial R}{\partial g}$$

where the superscripts in parentheses denote iterates and the bars denote local averages. Since the surface orientation at the occluding boundaries is known, this recurrence propagates information inwards and in a relaxation style computes the orientation everywhere. This algorithm works well for many images, but there is no proof that it converges. An important aspect of the algorithm is graceful degradation under errors in the placement of the light source, the surface orientation on the boundary, and the nature of the surface reflectivity. The algorithm also does not guarantee integrability of the resulting surface orientation function. Horn and Brooks (1986) attempted to remedy this deficiency; Frankot and Chellappa (1987) developed a method of enforcing integrability.

Other authors proposed smoothness constraints derived from the fact that the integral of depth around a closed path in the image is zero (Brooks, 1979; Strat, 1979). Woodham observed that the shape from shading problem can be solved uniquely if a global assumption is made about the shape of the surface, for example that it is convex, a ruled surface, or a generalized cylinder (1981).

The mathematical properties of the image irradiance equation were studied by Bruss (1980). She showed that a continuous image irradiance equation can have discontinuous solutions, and that the curvature of a surface cannot be identified in general from its image. However, Bruss proved that there is only one solution which is convex, and that bounding contours can be determined from the image only when the image irradiance equation is singular, ie, the reflectance function R and its first-order partial derivatives are continuous, while the intensity function I is discontinuous in x and/or y. Bruss studied singular image irradiance equations, called *eikonal*, of the form $p^2 + q^2 = I(x,y)$. If the intensity function $I(x,y)$ vanishes to second order at the singular point, then there is exactly one positive locally convex solution in the neighborhood of the singular point. In consequence, if there is a closed bounding contour, the solution is unique.

Most shape from shading methods require complete knowledge of the reflectance map. There have been efforts to reduce the need for such detailed knowledge. Pentland (1984) extracts information locally, but he needs strong assumptions (for example, that the surface is locally spherical). It is possible to recover the position of the light source from the image under some assumptions (Pentland, 1982; Lee and Rosenfeld, 1985; Brooks and Horn, 1985). This is important, since most research on shape from shading assumes exact knowledge of the light source position.

Horn, Woodham and Silverman developed a method for computing shape from shading using multiple (known) light sources; it is called *photometric stereo* (Woodham, 1981). Let the intensity at point (x,y) in the image obtained when only the first light source is used be $I_1(x,y)$. Then the surface orientation at (x,y) is restricted to the isobrightness contour in the reflectance map corresponding to the brightness value computed from $I_1(x,y)$. Similarly, when the second light source is used, the surface orientation is restricted to the isobrightness contour defined by $I_2(x,y)$. Thus when we use both light sources, one at a time, the surface orientation is (usually) determined by the intersection of two isobrightness contours. A third source provides complete disambiguation. Figure 14 describes the process.

One can derive useful information about surface shape without the need for a detailed solution to the image irradiance equation. For example, information from isobrightness contours might be beneficial (Koenderink and Van Doorn, 1980). The human visual system may obtain global shape information from shading without constructing a surface normal map.

Highlights in images of objects with specularly reflecting surfaces provide significant information about the surfaces. Coleman and Jain (1982) presented a method using four-source photometric stereo to identify and correct for specular reflection components. Blake (1985) assumes smooth surfaces and single point specularities and develops a computational theory for shape extraction based on the disparities of the specularities in a pair of images (specular stereo). Healey and Binford (1987) derived relationships between the properties of a specular feature in an image and local properties of the corresponding surface. Wolff (1986, 1987a, 1987b) studied shape extraction techniques from multiple images using spectral and polarization properties. Research has also begun on non-Lambertian surfaces, on illumination models due to sun and sky, etc. A comprehensive collection of papers on the topic is given in (Horn and Brooks, 1989).

Shape from Texture

Texture provides an important source of information about the orientations of surfaces. Figures 15 and 16 show the perspective images of some natural surfaces. It seems that a human can easily perceive the shapes of the surfaces. To recover shape from texture, the distorting effects of the surface orientation and the imaging geometry must be distinguished from the properties of the texture on which the distortion acts. This requires that assumptions be made about the texture. The problem of recovering the orientation of a planar surface from texture for the case of planes has been extensively studied; see (Gibson, 1950; Witkin, 1981; Stevens, 1981; Bajcsy and Lieberman, 1976; Kender, 1979, 1980; Kanatani, 1984; and Aloimonos, 1986). These studies were based on different assumptions about the texture and the imaging geometry.

The process of image formation (projection) introduces distortions into the appearance of the scene. In general, the distortions can be considered as due to two effects: the *distance* effect (objects appear larger when they are closer to the camera), and the *foreshortening* effect (the distortion depends on the angle between the surface normal and the line of sight). The orthographic projection model cap-

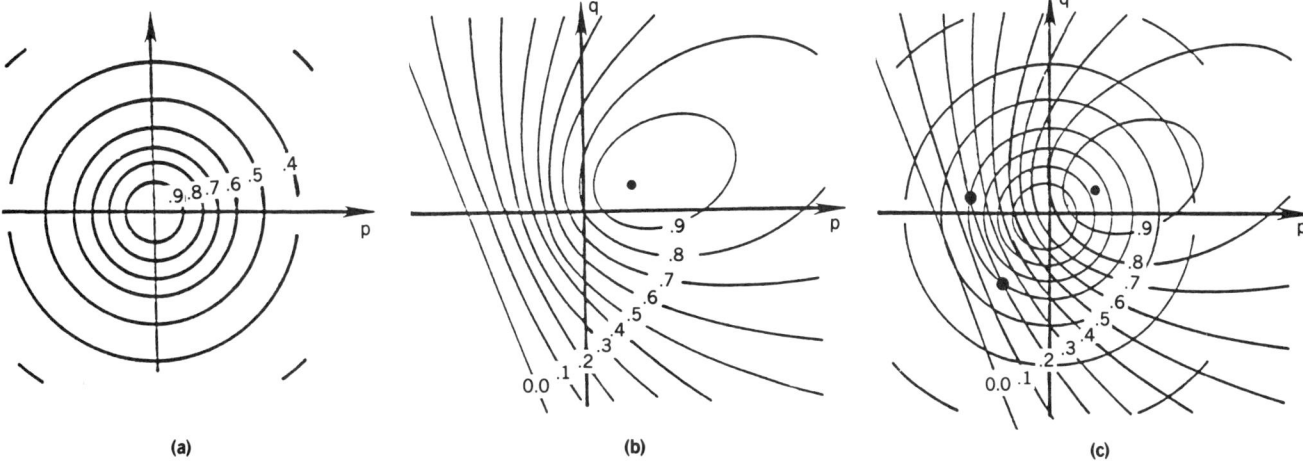

Figure 14. An illustration of photometric stereo. (Reproduced from Brady (1982).)

tures only the foreshortening effect and ignores the distance effect. Therefore, methods for shape from texture which use orthographic projection are valid only in a limited domain. The perspective projection model captures both effects, but the resulting algorithms involve the solution of nonlinear equations, and numerical errors limit their accuracy.

The first to approach the shape from texture problem was Gibson (1950). Trying to develop a theory of how humans perceive surface orientation from texture, he suggested that textures consist of small elements, which we shall call texels. Of course, these texels may be arranged very irregularly. We assume, however, that the texels are uniformly distributed on the scene plane, in the sense that each unit area on that plane contains approximately the same number of texels. In the image, however, the texel density may not be uniform; it may vary (linearly) with position. The gradient (magnitude and direction of maximum rate of change) of texture density in the image then determines the surface orientation; the magnitude depends on the surface slant, and the direction on the tilt.

Bajcsy and Lieberman (1976) used the two-dimensional Fourier power spectrum to detect the texture gradient. Their theory assumes that all the texture elements have the same size.

Witkin (1981) presented an approach that assumed directional isotropy, rather than positional uniformity. He assumed that the edges of the texels have uniformly distributed orientations. In the image, the orientations will be biased; the magnitude of the bias depends on the surface slant and its direction on the tilt. Based on an orthographic projection model, he derived maximum likelihood estimators for the slant and tilt. Witkin's work will be described in more detail in the next section since it can

Figure 15. Textured surface (gravel).

Figure 16. Textured surface (ivy).

also be used to derive surface orientation from contour. Many natural scenes do not satisfy the isotropy assumption. However, Witkin did not use the uniform density assumption because it requires detection of the texels. It will be shown later how this requirement can be eliminated.

Stevens (1980) studied the shape from texture problem under perspective projection and pointed out that texel density depends on both *scaling* (distance-position) and *foreshortening* (surface slant). He showed, however, that their effects may be (partially) separated and that the foreshortening effect can be used to compute the surface orientation.

Kender (1979, 1980) considered the computation of shape from texture as an instance of a general paradigm that derives surface orientation from each of several possible image observables. He assumes that texels are extracted from the image, and that each texel belongs to a planar surface. He defines a set of normalized texel property maps (NTPM) that generalize the reflectance map in shape from shading. If we assume that the texels all lie in a plane, and all have the same values of a given property (eg, diameter), we can derive constraints on the orientation of the plane.

Recent work (Aloimonos, 1988a) has developed a robust method of estimating the orientation of a planar surface based on the uniform density assumption. Let image regions R_1 and R_2 have areas S_1 and S_2 and contain k_1 and k_2 texels, respectively. Under paraperspective projection, the areas of the corresponding regions on the scene plane are $T_1 = S_1 c^2 \sqrt{a + p^2 + q^2}/(1 - A_1 p - B_1 q)^2$ and $T_2 = S_2 c^2 \sqrt{1 + p^2 + q^2}/(1 - A_2 p - B_2 q)^2$, respectively, where (A_1, B_1) and (A_2, B_2) are the centroids of R_1, R_2 and the scene plane has equation $Z = pX + qY + c$. By the uniform density assumption we have $k_1/T_1 = k_2/T_2$, and this can be transformed to give

$$\left[\left(\frac{k_2 S_1}{k_1 S_2}\right)^{1/3} A_2 - A_1\right] p + \left[\left(\frac{k_2 S_1}{k_1 S_2}\right)^{1/3} B_2 - B_1\right] q = \left(\frac{k_2 S_1}{k_1 S_2}\right)^{1/3} - 1$$

This equation represents a line in p-q space; thus comparing the counts of texels in two image regions constrains (p,q) to lie on a line in gradient space. Ideally, using two pairs of image regions we can solve for p and q. But be-

Figure 18. Ivy-covered wall.

cause of the errors introduced by the sampling process (image digitization and density fluctuations of the texels in the regions), this will give unreliable results. To obtain a robust result we consider many pairs of image regions. Each pair gives us a line in the gradient space, and the desired solution is the point whose sum of distances from all the lines is minimum (Fig. 17).

The above method requires that the texels be identified so they can be counted. A more realistic approach uses the total length of edges in an image region; assuming that these are texel edges, their total length should be proportional to the number of texels. Using this method one can recover the orientations of planar surfaces in real-world scenes. For example, Figure 18 shows the image of an ivy-covered wall with orientation (slant = 20°, tilt = 0°). Figure 19 shows the extracted edges; this edge image was input to an algorithm, that using the modified uniform density assumption, recovered (slant = 24.5°, tilt = 5.6°). For other examples and a theoretical treatment, see Aloimonos, (1988a). For other work using a uniform density approach, see Kanatani and Chou, (1989).

Kanatani (1984) used the second Fourier harmonics of the number of intersections between texels and parallel scan lines to find planar surface orientation, under orthographic projection, under the assumption that the texture is directionally isotropic; for other uses of the isotropy assumption see the section on Shape from Contour. Ohta and Kanade (1985) separated the image texels into types and derived surface orientation information from the area ratios of pairs of texels of the same type.

Research on shape from texture for nonplanar surfaces has been restricted to idealized domains involving sur-

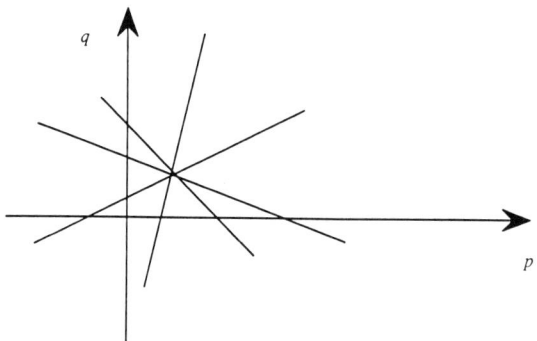

Figure 17. Intersection of lines in gradient space.

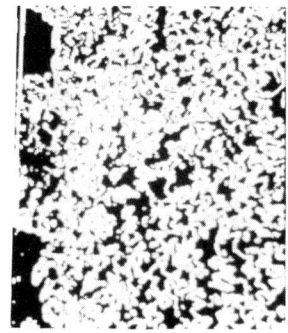

Figure 19. Edge image of the wall.

faces covered with uniformly spaced, identical texels such as the ones in Figure 20. (Kender, 1979, 1980) studied this problem under orthographic projection. He assumed the texels to be polygonal or symmetric and recovered orientation using skewed symmetry constraints (knowing the angle between two axes in space and the angle they make in the image, constraints between surface orientation and measurable image parameters can be developed). This required prior knowledge about the shapes of the texels, as well as heuristics about the orientations of some of the texels.

(Ikeuchi, 1984) studied the problem under spherical projection using texels that are known to be symmetrical; he developed constraints similar to Kender's, but in a simpler form because of the properties of the spherical projection.

(Aloimonos and Swain, 1988) proposed an approach that applies the methods used in shape from shading to the problem of shape from texture. Assume that all the texels are approximately planar and have the same area, and that we use paraperspective projection. Let S_I be the area of an image texel, S_W the area of the corresponding scene texel, (A,B) the centroid of the image texel, and d the range to the scene texel; then (assuming focal length = 1) it can be shown that

$$S_I = \frac{S_W}{d^2} \frac{1 - Ap - Bq}{\sqrt{1 + p^2 + q^2}}$$

where (p,q) is the gradient of the plane containing the scene texel. If we call S_I the "textural intensity," and S_W/d^2 the "textural albedo," the above equation is very similar to the image irradiance equation

$$I = \omega \frac{1 - Ap - Bq}{\sqrt{1 + p^2 + q^2}}$$

where I is the intensity, (p,q) is the gradient of the surface point whose image has intensity I, ω is the albedo at that point and $(A,B,-1)$ the direction of the light source (Horn, 1977; Ikeuchi and Horn, 1981). We call

$$R(p,q) = \frac{S_w}{d^2} \frac{1 - Ap - Bq}{\sqrt{1 + p^2 + q^2}}$$

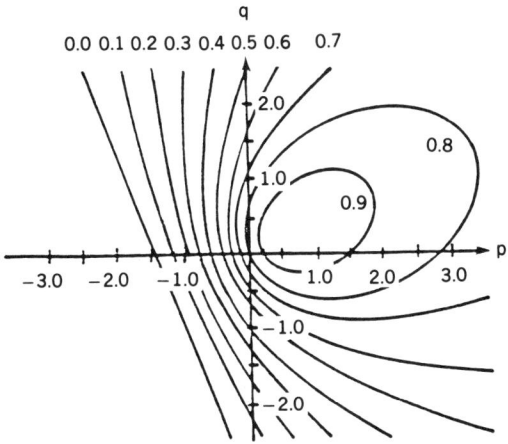

Figure 21. Textural reflectance map.

the "textural reflectance." If we fix S_w/d^2 and the position (A,B) of the texel on the image, this equation can be graphed conveniently as a series of contours of constant textural intensity. Figure 21 illustrates a simple textural reflectance map. Using $R(p,q)$, we can recover shape in a region Ω in the same way as Ikeuchi and Horn recovered shape from shading and occluding boundaries, ie, by minimizing an expression of the form

$$\int_\Omega \int \left\{ (S_I - R)^2 + \frac{\lambda}{d^2} (p_x^2 + p_y^2 + q_x^2 + q_y^2) \right\} dxdy,$$

with λ a constant weighing the relative importance of the constraint vs. smoothness. Results obtained using this method are shown in Figure 22.

Shape from Contour

"Shape from contour" refers to methods of inferring surface orientation from the shapes or orientations of planar contours (edges or lines) in the image. Perceptually, shape from contour seems to be significantly more powerful than shape from texture (Braunstein and Payne, 1969) or shape from shading (Barrow and Tenenbaum, 1981a).

Figure 20. Image of a patterned sphere.

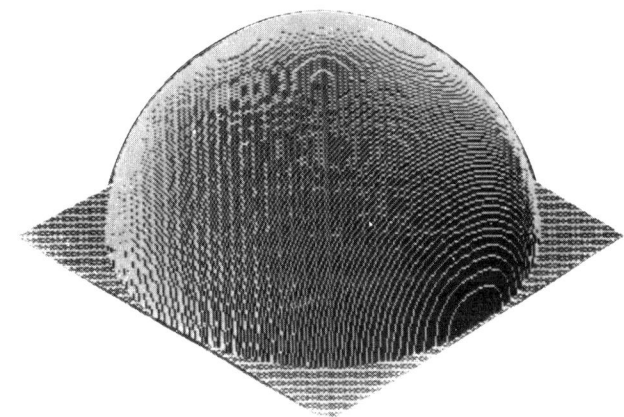

Figure 22. Reconstructed sphere (from Figure 20).

If a planar shape possesses skewed symmetry (a linear transformation of actual symmetry), it is often perceived as slanted relative to the image plane. Kanade (1981) showed that there is a one-parameter family of possible orientations of a skew-symmetric shape that lie on a hyperbola in gradient space; he suggested that we perceive the orientation that has the minimum slant.

Witkin (1981) analyzed the distribution of contour directions in the image on the assumption that they are isotropically distributed on the scene plane. Let the axes in the image and in the scene plane be parallel. If the contour direction in the image is α and the direction at the corresponding scene point is β, then

$$\tan(\alpha - \tau) = \frac{\tan\beta}{\cos\sigma}$$

where σ, τ are the slant and tilt of the scene plane. If measurements are aggregated from the whole image then a distribution of contour directions α can be constructed. One can evaluate the likelihood of this observed distribution of α, given expected distributions for β, σ, and τ. Witkin shows that the probability density function of σ is $\sin\sigma/\pi^2$. If we assume that τ and β are uniformly distributed, it can be shown that the probability of (σ, τ) given the set of measurements α_i is

$$\prod_{1 \leq i \leq n} \frac{\pi^{-2} \sin 2\sigma}{2(\cos^2(\alpha_i - \tau) + \sin^2(\alpha_i - \tau)\cos^2\sigma)}$$

The maximum likelihood estimate for surface orientation is the value (σ, τ) that maximizes this probability. Figure 23 demonstrates the results of this method applied to a variety of shapes and compares it to human estimated tilt. This method can also be applied to the problem of shape from texture under the assumption that contour directions are isotropically distributed.

Brady and Yuille (1984) proposed a general paradigm in which the assumed surface orientation is the one that extremizes some function computed on the scene contour(s). One possible function is $\oint k^2 ds$, where k is the curvature of the contour; minimization of this function has been used as a criterion for interpolating across gaps in plane curves (Horn, 1981). However, this function is not extremized when we transform an ellipse into a circle, whereas ellipses are often perceived as slanted circles. A related function proposed by Barrow and Tenenbaum (1981b) is $\oint (dk/ds)^2 ds$. However, this function is sensitive to noise, since it involves derivatives. It is also biased toward slants close to 90°.

Brady and Yuille used the function

$$m = \frac{\text{area}}{(\text{perimeter})^2}$$

Given an image contour, we choose the orientation for which the scene contour maximizes m. When this is done, an ellipse is interpreted as a slanted circle, a parallelogram as a rotated square, a triangle as a slanted equilateral triangle, and a skewed symmetric figure as symmetric. For other recent research on geometric interpretation of image contours see (Horaud and Brady, 1987).

When there is specific a priori knowledge about the scene contour (perimeter, area, etc), unique solutions for surface orientation can be obtained (Augusteijn and Dyer, 1986; Chou and co-workers, 1987). Another important topic, which has not been treated here, is the analysis of line drawings of 3-D surfaces. The interested reader can consult the papers of Malik (1987), Nalwa (1987) and Koenderink (1986) as well as their references.

Shape from Stereo and Shape (or Structure) from Motion

Given two images of a scene taken by two cameras whose relative position and orientation is known, if corresponding points can be found in the two images (ie points which are the projection of the same scene point), then by the process of triangulation the depth of the scene points can be computed. If many pairs of corresponding points that lie on the same surface can be found, the shape of this surface can be determined. This process is known as stereo (from a Greek word meaning *solid*). If the relative position and orientation of the cameras is not known, then finding the shapes of the surfaces in the scene from corresponding points in the two images is known as the problem of shape (or structure) from motion. In both cases, research has concentrated on finding correspondences between points in the two images (the disparity map for stereo, and the optic flow or displacement field for motion). In the case of motion, because of the great importance of this module in navigation, there has been extensive theoretical development. These topics will not be treated here since they are discussed in detail in separate articles in this encyclopedia which deal respectively with stereo vision and visual motion analysis.

ILL-POSEDNESS AND REGULARIZATION

All the shape from x problems treated above are ill-posed in the sense of Hadamard (1923). A problem is well-posed when its solution exists, is unique, and depends continu-

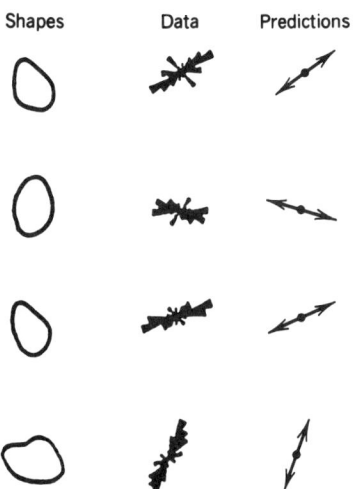

Figure 23. Results obtained by Witkin's method. (Reproduced from Witkin (1981).)

ously on the given data. Ill-posed problems fail to satisfy one or more of these criteria.

Poggio and his colleagues (Poggio and Koch, 1984; Poggio and Torre, 1984) realized that most recovery problems are ill-posed and that regularization theory (Tichonov and Arsenin, 1977; Morozov, 1984) can be used for their solution. The main approach to "solving" ill-posed problems, ie, restoring "well-posedness," is to introduce suitable constraints that restrict the space of admissible solutions. The problem of finding s (the scene) from i (the image) is ill-posed because the image is obtained from the scene by a noninvertible process, $i = Qs$. Regularization of this problem is usually done by finding the s that minimizes the function $\|Qs - i\|_D^2 + \lambda \|Ps\|_S^2$, where $\| \|_D$ and $\| \|_S$ are norms, P is a functional that usually involves smoothness, and λ is the so-called regularization parameter.

In shape from shading and shape from texture the gradient (p,q) of a surface patch is related to the data at the image point (x,y) which is the projection of that patch by an expression of the form

$$A(x,y)p^2 + B(x,y)q^2 + C(x,y)pq + D(x,y)p + E(x,y)q + F(x,y) = 0 \quad (5.1)$$

where A, B, C, D, E, F are functions of position in the image and depend on the particular physical parameters data). Indeed, in shape from shading the relationship is

$$I(x,y) = \frac{\lambda(p\, p_s + q\, q_s + 1)}{\sqrt{1 + p^2 + q^2}\sqrt{1 + p_s^2 + q_s^2}}$$

where (p_s, q_s) is the direction of the light source, λ the albedo, and $I(x,y)$ the image intensity at (x,y). In shape from texture, similarly, the relationship is

$$S_I = \frac{S_W}{d^2} \frac{1 - Ap - Bq}{\sqrt{1 + p^2 + q^2}}$$

where S_W/d^2 is the "textural albedo," and (A,B) the centroid of the texel. In such shape from x problems the constraint can be rewritten in the form $L(f,g,x,y) = 0 \ \forall (x,y)$ on the image plane, where (f,g) is the orientation of the corresponding 3-D point in stereographic coordinates whose space is bounded (Horn, 1986).

In general, suppose the surface orientation satisfies an equation of the form $L(f,g,x,y) = 0$, where x,y are the coordinates in the image plane and f,g are the stereographic coordinates of the normal to the surface patch whose image is at (x,y). Can regularization theory be used to solve for (f,g) everywhere in the image plane, perhaps with the help of boundary conditions? If this is attempted, we face the following problem:

> The equation $L = 0$ is nonlinear, but standard regularization deals with linear constraints. The situation is different if L is convex (Morozov, 1984), but it is not in the cases of shape from shading or texture.
>
> The surfaces in the scene are not all smooth, and the scene is certainly not smooth at the boundaries where one surface occludes another. If we use smoothness in our regularization process, we will obtain solutions that are not correct at discontinuities.

If we had a regularization theory that could handle discontinuities and nonlinear, nonconvex functions, then we could apply it to shape from x problems. In the next section, a general regularization method based on smoothness is presented, and in the section following, regularization in the presence of discontinuities is discussed.

A General Discrete Regularization Technique

Use will be made here of widely known techniques in the area of partial differential equations, which have already been applied to some computer vision problems (Lee, 1985). Consider the equation $L(f,g,x,y) = 0$, for $(x,y) \in D$, where D is a compact region in the x–y plane. The problem is discretized using an $m \times m$ grid and difference operators instead of differential operators and sums instead of integrals. It is assumed that the surface normals on the boundary of D are known. The desired surface is the one that minimizes an expression of the form

$$e = \sum_{i,j} (s_{ij} + \lambda l_{ij}) \quad (5.2)$$

where the sum is taken over all grid points (i,j) that do not lie on the boundary. Let (f_{ij}, g_{ij}) be the surface orientation at the grid point (i,j). If (i,j) is not a boundary point, $f_{i+1,j}, f_{i,j+1}, g_{i+1,j}$ and $g_{i,j+1}$ all exist, and we define the smoothness component of e as

$$s_{ij} = m^2\{[f_{i+1,j} - f_{ij}]^2 + [f_{i,j+1} - f_{ij}]^2 + [g_{i+1,j} - g_{ij}]^2 + [g_{i,j+1} - g_{ij}]^2\}$$

It is assumed here for simplicity that D is square; if it has a different shape a different discrete approximation to $f_x^2 + f_y^2 + g_x^2 + g_y^2$ can be used.) Similarly, we define

$$l_{ij} = [L(f_{ij}, g_{ij}, i, j)]^2$$

The minimization of e is subject to boundary conditions, since f_{ij} and g_{ij} are known if (i,j) is on the boundary.

e is defined on a compact subset K of R^2, and it is continuous in each f_{ij} and g_{ij}. Therefore, there exists a solution to the minimization problem. Furthermore, this solution is a solution of the system

$$\frac{\partial e}{\partial f_{ij}} = \frac{\partial e}{\partial g_{ij}} = 0. \quad (5.3)$$

Equations 5.3 yield

$$f_{ij} = f_{ij}^* - \frac{1}{4} \lambda m^2 [L(f_{ij}, g_{ij}, i, j)] \frac{\partial L}{\partial f}(f_{ij}, g_{ij}, i, j)$$

$$g_{ij} = g_{ij}^* - \frac{1}{4} \lambda m^2 [L(f_{ij}, g_{ij}, i, j)] \frac{\partial L}{\partial g}(f_{ij}, g_{ij}, i, j) \quad (5.4)$$

where

$$f_{ij}^* = \frac{f_{i+1,j} + f_{i,j+1} + f_{i-1,j} + f_{i,j-1}}{4} \text{ and similarly for } g_{ij}$$

This can be written compactly as

$$\Phi\xi = -\lambda m^2 \phi(\xi) \quad (5.5)$$

where

$$\xi = [f_{1,1}, \ldots, f_{1,k}, \ldots, f_{k,k}, g_{1,1}, \ldots, g_{kk}]^T$$

$$\phi = [\cdots, \{L(f_{ij}, g_{ij}, i, j)\}\frac{\partial L(f_{ij}, g_{ij}, i, j)}{\partial f}, \ldots,$$
$$\{L(f_{ij}, g_{ij}, i, j)\}\frac{\partial L(f_{ij}, g_{ij}, i, j)}{\partial g} \cdots]^T$$

and

$$\Phi = \begin{pmatrix} A & 0 \\ 0 & A \end{pmatrix} \text{ where } A = \begin{pmatrix} B & -I & & & \\ -I & B & -I & & \\ & \cdots & & & \\ & & \cdots -I & B & I \\ & & & -I & B \end{pmatrix} \in R^{n \times n}$$

$$\text{and } B = \begin{pmatrix} 4 & -1 & & & \\ -1 & 4 & -1 & & \\ & \cdots & & & \\ & & \cdots -1 & 4 & 1 \\ & & & -1 & 4 \end{pmatrix} \in R^{k \times k}.$$

Equation 5.5 is a necessary condition on the solution that minimizes 5.2.

It can be proven that equation 5.5 has a unique solution for appropriately chosen λ (Aloimonos, 1988b). Furthermore, the sequence $\xi^{(\alpha)}$ defined by

$$\xi^{(\alpha+1)} = -\lambda m^2 \Phi^{-1} \phi(\xi^{(\alpha)}), \alpha = 0, 1, 2, \cdots$$

converges to this unique solution. There thus exists a unique surface minimizing e, which is also the unique solution of equation 5.5, and the above described algorithm converges to that solution. A similar result holds even if we do not know (f,g) on the boundary, as long as we assume that "natural" smoothness conditions hold on the boundary.

Discontinuous Regularization

All the shape from x problems come under the regularization paradigm and so regularization is very appealing as a theory for all these modules. However, discontinuities appear in the world (and it is the discontinuities that make it interesting), so a theory of regularization effective in the presence of discontinuities is much needed. Most existing theories of discontinuous regularization explicitly search for boundary points: one segments the image into homogeneous regions and performs ordinary regularization in each region. This can also be done iteratively (Schunck (1984), for example, iteratively combines motion estimation and segmentation). Grimson and Pavlidis (1985) suggest not smoothing over regions where local differences of nearby points are larger than the statistics of the data as a whole would lead one to expect. Lee and Pavlidis (1987) and Lee (1986) use post-validation to find points which are likely to be boundary points. But sometimes we need to regularize over heterogeneous regions in order to take advantage of texture information or in order to attain robustness in the presence of noise by regularizing over a large enough region.

There does not exist a rigorous theory of segmentation. A rigorous discontinuous regularization theory might be the first step in the development of such a theory. A regularization paradigm due to Geman and Geman (1984) uses Bayesian statistical theory to obtain a non-convex variational measure that must be minimized. The variational condition is based on a probability distribution of a point being a boundary point. The work of Geman and Geman has been extended by Marroquin (1984, 1986) and by Mumford and Shah (1985). Geman's and Marroquin's work deals with a lattice of points whereas Mumford's work deals with a continuous domain. Geman's work deals with functions whose range is finite and small (for example, binary variables), while Marroquin's and Mumford's work deals with functions with a continuous range such as the real numbers. All these papers employ optimization procedures such as simulated annealing that seem to work reasonably well but cannot be guaranteed not to be fooled by multiple local minima. Blake and Zisserman (1987) use "graduated non-convexity" to minimize a series of variational measures which gradually approach the desired measure. Such continuation methods are certain to converge, but they are slow (Allgower and Georg, 1980; Chow and co-workers, 1978).

Standard regularization methods also smooth excessively over regions where the change is steep, but is not large enough to indicate a discontinuity. This suggests that λ, which weighs the importance of smoothing versus consistency with the data, should vary with position. Terzopoulos (1984) has pursued this idea; his smoothness term is a weighted sum of squares of first- and second-order derivatives, where the weights vary with position. However, he primarily investigated the case where the weights are constant except at a small fraction of points where they are zero. Nagel's "oriented smoothness" paradigm (Nagel and Enkelmann, 1986) is another kind of discontinuous regularization.

Shulman and Aloimonos (1988b) developed a method of regularization that does not smooth over discontinuities and does not make a rigid binary distinction between discontinuities and nondiscontinuities. It uses quadratic variational conditions, which yield linear equations.

The basic insight of this method is that we can expect the errors at nearby points to be correlated. Thus $\partial L/\partial x$ and $\partial L/\partial y$ should be small. In addition, a quadratic measure of smoothness such as $\int[(f_x)^2 + (f_y)^2 + (g_x)^2 + (g_y)^2]$ excessively penalizes large changes in orientation, and so produces large jumps in L in the vicinity of discontinuities. These jumps can be controlled by requiring smallness of the derivatives of L, and also by using a more general measure of smoothness.

The general minimization problem that our method solves has the form

$$\text{minimize } \int \left[\sum_0^\infty a_{ij} (\partial^{i+j} L / \partial x^i \partial y^j) \right]^2 dxdy$$
$$+ \int \sum_0^\infty b_{ij} (\partial^{i+j} f / \partial x^i \partial y^j)^2 + \int \sum_0^\infty c_{ij} (\partial^{i+j} g / \partial x^i \partial y^j)^2.$$

where the coefficients are parameters. Note that we impose a requirement of smallness on the derivatives of all orders. Of course, most of the coefficients can be 0. In fact, because of the noisiness of high-order derivative estimates, the coefficients should rapidly approach 0 as $i,j \to \infty$.

A problem with this approach is that computing the derivatives of L requires calculating derivatives of the data, and this calculation is numerically unstable (Poggio and co-workers 1985). As Poggio suggested in connection with the problem of edge detection, in order to differentiate numerically regularization is used. It is unnecessary to actually compute the derivatives; all one needs to know is that they can be approximated by linear functionals of L. Thus, the first integral in our condition is approximated by an expression of the form $(AL)^2$, where A is a matrix. Similarly, the second and third integrals are approximated by a polynomial that is quadratic in the f_{ij} and g_{ij}. We thus obtain Euler-Lagrange equations of the form

$$A(L)\frac{\partial A(L)}{\partial f} = -\Phi_1 \xi$$

$$A(L)\frac{\partial A(L)}{\partial g} = -\Phi_2 \xi$$

Here $A(L)$ is a sum of the form $\Sigma a_{ij} A^{ij}(L)$ where $A^{ij}(L)$ is an approximation to $\partial^{i+j} L/\partial x^i \partial y^j$. Thus, finally the following is obtained:

$$\sum a_{ij}^2 A^{ij}(L) \partial A^{ij}(L)/\partial f = \Phi_1 \xi$$

$$\sum a_{ij}^2 A^{ij}(L) \partial A^{ij}(L)/\partial g = \Phi_2 \xi$$

Write $\phi_{ij}(\xi)$ for the known function $\begin{pmatrix} A^{ij}(L)\partial A^{ij}(L)/\partial f \\ A^{ij}(L)\partial A^{ij}(L)/\partial g \end{pmatrix}$; then

$$\sum a_{ij}^2 \phi_{ij}(\xi) = \Phi \xi$$

More generally, the a_{ij}^2 could be matrices rather than constants (the constraints that the derivatives of L be small could be relaxed at certain points). If $a_{00} = I$ and $a_{ij} = 0$ for $i,j > 0$ our equations become

$$L \partial L/\partial f = -\Phi_1 \xi$$

$$L \partial L/\partial g = -\Phi_2 \xi$$

which is the usual (nondiscontinuous) regularization condition. Rewrite $\Sigma a_{ij}^2 \phi_{ij}(\xi) = -\Phi \xi$ as

$$\left(\sum \hat{a}_{ij}^2 \phi_{ij}(\xi)\right) + \Phi \xi = -\phi_{00}(\xi) \qquad (5.17)$$

where $\hat{a}_{00} = I$ and $\hat{a}_{ij} = a_{ij}$ otherwise. The first term in 5.17 represents the discontinuous correction to the usual regularization condition and we want this term to be as small as possible. To make it easier to work with, rewrite 5.17 in the form

$$\Gamma \Xi = -\phi_{00}(\xi) \qquad (5.18)$$

where Ξ is the vector $[\phi_{00}(\xi), \phi_{01}(\xi), \phi_{10}(\xi), \ldots, \phi_{mn}(\xi)]^T$ and Γ is a matrix. We choose Γ to be the least squares solution of 5.20. Computing this solution involves calculating the Moore-Penrose inverse of Ξ (Penrose, 1955; Ben-Israel and Greville, 1974). Since this is a very complex calculation, it can instead be calculated as the best solution in a restricted subspace. Note that Γ hides the regularization parameter λ. This parameter might need to vary from place to place. (We might require a different amount of smoothing near the boundary than near the center of the visual field.) Our smoothing condition might involve a combination of derivatives of different orders. Γ weights the relative importance of the various derivatives of L being small. This too can vary with position.

If Γ can be found (through adaptive estimation from examples, for instance), the resulting discontinuous regularization technique can be applied to solve various recovery problems. Since the equations involved may be nonlinear, reliable methods of solution still need to be developed. For some preliminary work on recovery tasks using discontinuous regularization see (Aloimonos and Shulman, 1989a; Hurlbert and Poggio, 1987).

MULTIPLE CUES

The methods described in the section on Shape from x are summarized in Figure 24. In each of these methods, shape is computed from a single cue; cues are not combined. Deriving shape from one cue leads to ill-posed problems, with all their associated difficulties. The situation is much improved when we try to recover shape from two or more cues. Indeed, shape can be computed uniquely from many pairs of cues. This is shown in Figure 25. Various examples of this can be found in Aloimonos (1986). Recent research along these lines includes the work of Horn (1986) on combining shading with contour, of various researchers (Richards, 1986; Huang and Blostein, 1985) on combining stereo and motion, of Grimson (1984) on combining shading and stereo, and of Milenkovic and Kanade (1985) on trinocular stereo. In this section a few examples of the use of multiple cues in shape recovery are given.

To analyze shape from shading and retinal motion, assume that the Lambertian surface of an object moves and the optic flow (displacement) field $(\Delta u(x,y), \Delta v(x,y))$ is

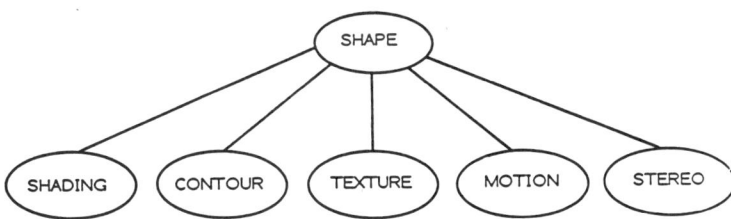

Figure 24. Previous status of shape from x research.

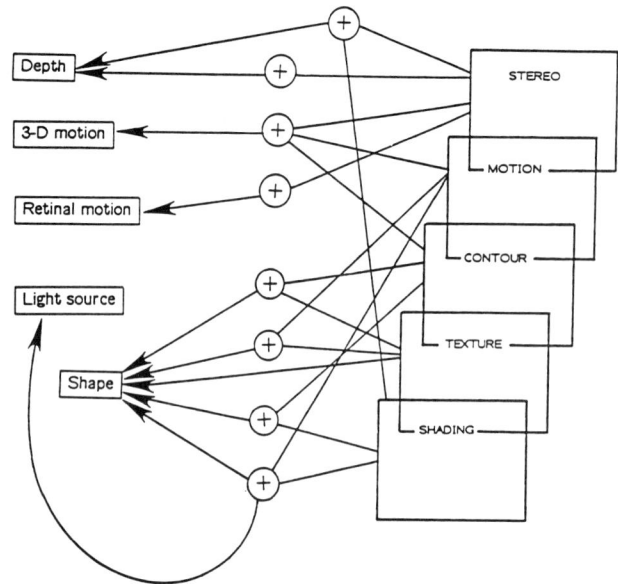

Figure 25. Combining cues.

available everywhere in the image. Then the following constraints hold (Aloimonos and Basu, 1987):

1. The image irradiance equation.
2. A constraint of the form

$$A_1 p^2 + B_1 q^2 + C_1 pq + D_1 = 0,$$

   where the coefficients are functions of the displacements.

3. A constraint due to image irradiance, light source and motion, which is of the form

$$A_2 p^2 + B_2 q^2 + C_2 pq + D_2 p + E_2 q + F_2 = 0$$

Here the coefficients are a function of the displacements, light source position and intensities. Constraints (b) and (c) are constructed on the basis of geometric and photometric invariants. Figure 26 shows a schematic description of the constraints and the solution as the point of intersection of all the constraints.

To analyze shape from contour in multiple images, let C be a contour on the scene plane with equation $Z = pX + qY + c$, and let C_l and C_r be the projections of C on the two images, using perspective projection (Fig. 27).

The difference between the areas or perimeters of C_l and C_r depends on the orientation of the scene plane. If S_L and S_R are the areas of C_l and C_r, it can be shown that

$$\frac{S_L}{S_R} = \frac{1 - A_L p - B_L q}{1 - A_R p - B_R q}, \tag{6.1}$$

where (A_L, B_L), (A_R, B_R) are the centers of mass of the left and right image contours respectively and the focal length is unity (Aloimonos and Swain, 1988). This gives a linear equation in p,q. If there are more than two images (whose centers are not collinear), we can get additional linear equations and (over)determine (p,q). Alternatively, a constraint involving perimeter can be used. For any contour C_i on the image plane, the corresponding scene plane contour has perimeter

$$\int_C \sqrt{E \, dx^2 + 2F \, dx \, dy + G \, dy^2} \tag{6.2}$$

where E, F, G are the first fundamental coefficients of the mapping from the image to the scene (Lipschutz, 1969). Expression 6.2 can be used to compute the length of the scene contour C from either of its projections C_l and C_r. Since these lengths should be the same, equating their difference to zero yields a nonlinear constraint on the parameters of the scene plane. This, together with equation

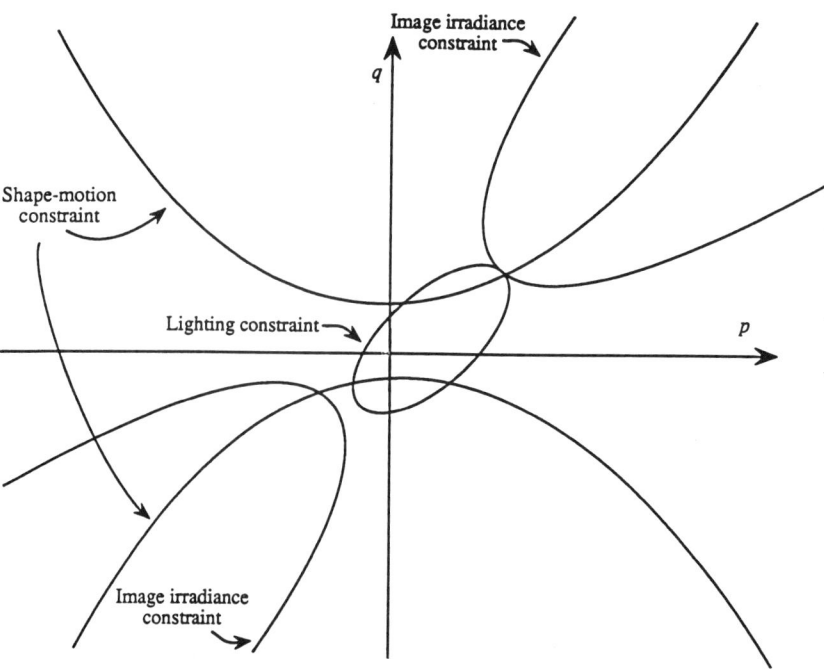

Figure 26. Intersection of constraints.

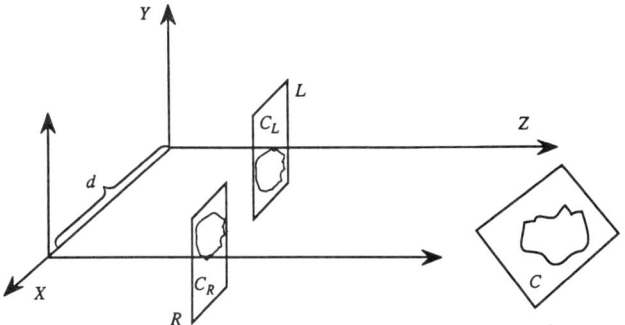

Figure 27. Contours of two images.

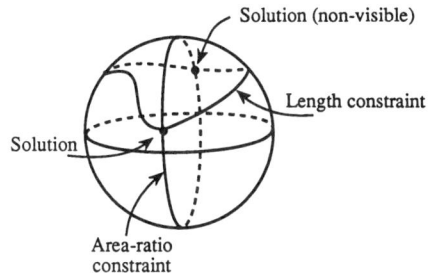

Figure 28. Constraints on the Gaussian sphere.

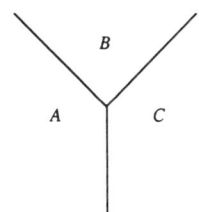

Figure 29. Trihedral vertex.

6.1, gives a finite number of solutions for the orientation (p,q) of the scene plane.

If the equation 6.1 is transformed to the coordinates of the Gaussian sphere, it represents a great circle G. We need to find which point of that great circle satisfies the perimeter constraint. Figure 28 shows the area and perimeter constraints drawn on the Gaussian sphere. It was recently shown (Aloimonos and Hervé) that there can be at most two solutions; and criteria for checking the multiplicity of the solutions have been developed.

Finally, the recovery of shape from shading and contour is illustrated with a simple example from the domain of polyhedra. Consider a trihedral vertex (three planes A, B, C intersecting at a point). Given its orthographic projection (Fig. 29) one would like to recover the orientations of the planes. If there is no other information, the only thing that can be concluded is that the gradients (p_A, q_A), (p_B, q_B) and (p_C, q_C) of A, B, and C form a triangle in gradient space, but the shape of this triangle is unknown (Shafer and co-workers, 1983). If there is also shading information (Horn, 1977), and it is assumed that the planes all have the same albedo, a finite number of solutions for the orientations can be found, using the additional constraints imposed by the image irradiance equation. If it is assumed that the dihedral angles between the planes are known, again only a finite number of solutions is possible. To find these solutions, a triangle must be found in gradient space whose vertices lie on the conic sections that result from the shading or dihedral constraints.

ACTIVE VISION

In this section the active vision paradigm is introduced, in which the observer controls the geometric parameters of the sensor—for example, its position, its orientation, its focal length, etc. This allows the observer to manipulate the constraints on the image(s) and thus provide additional information for solving recovery problems. This paradigm is partly motivated by human and animal perception, which are active. Perceptual activity is exploratory and searching. Humans do not merely see, they actively look (Bajcsy, 1985). When the activity is a known motion of the observer it has been shown (Aloimonos and co-workers, 1988) that all the shape from x problems become well-conditioned and unique solutions become possible. Some of these results are summarized in Table 1.

Table 1. Recovery Problems Are Easier to Solve for an Active Observer.

Problem	Passive Observer	Activer Observer
Shape from shading	Ill-posed problem. Needs to be regularized. Even then, unique solution is not guaranteed because of nonlinearity.	Well-posed and stable. Linear equation; unique solution.
Shape from contour	Ill-posed problem. Has not been regularized up to now in the Tichonov sense. Solvable under restrictive assumptions.	Well-posed problem. Unique solution for either monocular or binocular observer.
Shape from texture	Ill-posed problem. Needs some assumption about the texture.	Well-posed problem. No assumption required.
Structure from motion	Well-posed but unstable. Nonlinear constraints.	Well posed and stable. Quadratic constraints, simple solution methods, stability.

The basis for the active vision approach lies in being able to work in an enriched sensory domain with a partially known parametrization. As the sensor parameters are varied, the image undergoes local transformations that provide powerful constraints for computing the unknown scene parameters. Note that we do not work with a small set of discrete observations, but with continuous trajectories in the stimulus space. These trajectories are smooth, since the sensor transformations are smooth. Thus it is unnecessary to rely on the smoothness of the observed scene. Complications usually associated with multiview approaches to vision—for instance, the correspondence problem—are also avoided.

As an example, consider the active perception of shape from linear image features (texture) (Ito and Aloimonos, 1987). Suppose that a moving camera is looking at a planar surface. To simplify our analysis it is assumed, equivalently, that the surface is moving. Let $\mathbf{X} = (X,Y,Z) \in S$ be imaged onto $\mathbf{x} = (x,y)$ in the image plane R. Let the motion consist of a translation $\mathbf{T} = (T_1,T_2,T_3)$ and a rotation $\Omega = (\omega_1,\omega_2,\omega_3)$, so that $\mathbf{V}(\mathbf{X}) = T + \Omega \times \mathbf{X}$, where $\mathbf{V}(\mathbf{X})$ is the velocity of X. Then

$$\mathbf{V(X)} = \sum_{k=1}^{6} r_k V_k(X), \text{ where} \quad (7.1)$$

$r_1 = T_1, V_1(\mathbf{X}) = (1\ 0\ 0)^T;\ r_4 = \omega_1, V_4(\mathbf{X}) = (0\ -Z\ Y)^T$

$r_2 = T_2, V_1(\mathbf{X}) = (0\ 1\ 0)^T;\ r_5 = \omega_2, V_5(\mathbf{X}) = (Z\ 0\ -X)^T$

$r_3 = T_3, V_3(\mathbf{X}) = (0\ 0\ 1)^T;\ r_6 = \omega_3, V_6(\mathbf{X}) = (-Y\ X\ 0)^T$

It can be easily proved that the image velocity (u,v) at $\mathbf{x} = (x,y)$ is

$$\dot{\mathbf{x}} = \sum_{k=1}^{6} r_k \mathbf{u}_k(\mathbf{x}) = \sum_{k=1}^{6} r_k \begin{bmatrix} u_k(\mathbf{x}) \\ v_k(\mathbf{x}) \end{bmatrix},$$

where $\mathbf{u}_k$ depends on the orientation of S.

For perspective projection the parameters in equation 7.1 are $r_1 = T_1/c$, $r_2 = T_2/c$, $r_3 = T_3/c$, $r_4 = \omega_1$, $r_5 = \omega_2$, $r_6 = \omega_3$, $u_1(\mathbf{x}) = (1 - px - qy, 0)$, $u_2(\mathbf{x}) = (0, 1 - px - qy)$, $u_3(\mathbf{x}) = (-x(1 - px - qy), -y(1 - px - qy))$, $u_4(\mathbf{x}) = (xy, y^2 + 1)$, $u_5(\mathbf{x}) = (-(x^2 + 1), -xy)$ and $u_6(\mathbf{x}) = (y, -x)$, where the motion is translation $T = (T_1,T_2,T_3)$ and rotation $\Omega = (\omega_1,\omega_2,\omega_3)$ and the scene plane has equation $Z = pX + qY + c$ with respect to the camera coordinate system (Fig. 30).

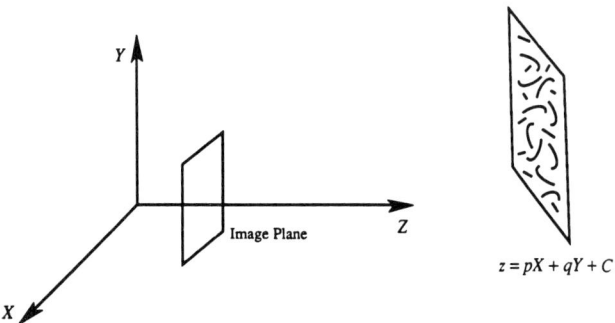

Figure 30. Imaging system and a textured surface.

Let the image intensity be $I(x,y)$. A *linear feature* (Amari, 1987) is a linear functional,

$$f = \int\int I(x,y)m(x,y)dx\,dy,$$

where m is called a measuring function.

The image velocity satisfies the following equation (Horn, 1986):

$$I_x u + I_y v + I_t = 0,$$

where (u,v) is the optic flow at a point (x,y) and I_x, I_y, I_t are the spatiotemporal derivatives of the image intensity function at the point (x,y). This equation can be written as

$$\frac{\partial I}{\partial t} = -\dot{\mathbf{x}} \cdot \nabla I.$$

The time derivative of a linear feature will be

$$\dot{f} = \int\int \frac{\partial I}{\partial t} m\,dx\,dy = -\int\int m(\dot{\mathbf{x}} \cdot \nabla I)dx\,dy$$

$$= -\sum_{k=1}^{6} r_k \int\int m(u_k I_x + v_k I_y)dx\,dy$$

$$= \sum_{k=1}^{6} r_k h_k, \text{ with } h_k = -\int\int m(u_k I_x + v_k I_y)dx\,dy$$

This equation relates linear features to shape and motion parameters. Furthermore, it is linear. If it is applied to a set of linear features, a set of linear equations in those parameters is obtained. So, a simple linear least-squares method is sufficient for the recovery of the parameters. No local correspondence has been used. The only computed quantities were the time derivatives of linear features, which involve the whole image.

It is also important to note that in this approach, the spatial derivatives of the intensity function do not need to be computed. Integration by parts avoids differentiation of the intensity function; only the derivative of the measuring function has to be computed. This avoids differentiating the image intensity, which is discrete; numerical differentiation is an ill-posed problem. More importantly, the same approach can be followed if the image is discontinuous—for example, a dot pattern or a line pattern (eg edges).

Now the algorithm can be summarized for the active detection of shape from two images $I(x,y,t)$ and $I(x,y,t + dt)$ taken by a camera with known motion.

1. Choose a set of differentiable measuring functions $\mu_i(x,y)$, $i = 1, \ldots, n$. Examples might be $x^i y^j$, $0 \le i, j \le k$, or Fourier features such as $\cos(ix + jy)$, $0 \le i, j \le k$.
2. Compute the linear features $f_i = \int\int I(x,y)\mu_i(x,y)dx\,dy$, where the integration is over any desired area of interest.
3. Estimate the time derivatives of the fs from the images $I(x,y,t)$ and $I(x,y,t + dt)$.

4. Compute $h_k = -\iint m_i(u_k I_x + v_k I_y)dxdy$ for each f.
5. Let **f** be the vector of feature values and H the matrix of hs. From equation $\mathbf{f} = Hr$ solve for p,q (and/or) c using a least squares method.

This method has been used (Aloimonos, 1989) to successfully recover the orientation of planar surfaces containing complex patterns, viewed by a moving camera.

This method involves solving a linear 3×3 system in the unknowns p, q, and c (the parameters of the plane). Let the system be $A\vec{x} = \vec{c}$, where $\vec{x} = (p \; q \; c)^T$, $A = (a_{ij})$ is a 3×3 matrix, and $\vec{c}$ is a 1×3 vector whose components are expressions involving spatiotemporal derivatives. It is possible that the system may be unstable. Since there is a discretization error as well as a slight error in the estimation of the known motion, there is some uncertainty in the elements of the matrix A and the vector c. Let the true system be $A^*\vec{x}^* = c^*$, and let

$$a_{ij}^* \in [a_{ij} - \varepsilon_{ij}, a_{ij} + \varepsilon_{ij}]$$

If there exist values of the coefficients a_{ij} in these intervals of uncertainty for which the determinant of the system becomes zero, then the system is very badly conditioned and its solution will be unreliable. It can be shown (Kuperman, 1971) that the necessary and sufficient condition for the system not to be critically ill-conditioned is

$$\sum_{i=1}^{n}\sum_{j=1}^{n}|b_{ji}|\varepsilon_{ij} < 1$$

where $(b_{ji}) = A^{-1}$. This expression can be used to test the robustness of the algorithm. Note that this represents a worst case analysis.

RESEARCH GOALS

Research on shape from x has been extensively pursued and has accomplished a great deal. The study of modules that may correspond to specific abilities of the human visual system, along with the formulation and exploitation of photometric and geometric relations, has contributed to the foundations of vision as a scientific field. Rigorous theories have been developed for deriving various intrinsic scene properties from various image characteristics. Most of these theories have found no practical applications because the theories do not result in robust algorithms. Any proposed theory explaining visual abilities must be backed up with a thorough theoretical stability analysis. A theory cannot be used for practical applications or to explain human visual capabilities if it is not robust. The algorithmic level of the Marr paradigm must be accompanied with careful theoretical error analyses. Of course, such analysis is hard. This issue is a topic of research that should be pursued; a few researchers have recently made such attempts (Aloimonos, 1986; Horn and Weldon, 1987; Adiv, 1985; Huang and Blostein, 1987).

Techniques have been developed in numerical analysis (Kuperman, 1971; Neumaier, 1984; Gay, 1981, 1982; Moore and Kioustelidis, 1980; Demmel, 1987) that may be used to study the sensitivity of vision algorithms. One could go further and do a probabilistic analysis, given assumptions about the probability distributions of the input measurements. The assumptions could be tested using statistical techniques.

Most of the shape from x modules have been studied in isolation: (shape from x and/or y). Unification of existing approaches to a given module is also of interest; some research has been done in this direction (Moerdler and Kender, 1987). But a formal theory is needed of how to combine information from different sources, especially, contradictory information. Discontinuous regularization and Markov random field methods are useful tools for this purpose (Marroquin and co-workers, 1985; Gamble and Poggio, 1987; Poggio and co-workers, 1987; Aloimonos and Shulman, 1989b).

Work on *active* vision will lead to further research on *exploratory* and *feedback* vision. Exploratory vision involves determining the activity that yields the most stable algorithm for the task at hand. Feedback vision deals with how information gathered from the environment can be used to guide future activities.

NEW DIRECTIONS

This article has dealt primarily with computer vision as a general recovery problem. Over the past 15 years many elegant mathematical theories describing various recovery modules have been formulated. Unfortunately, very few vision systems perform well in real-world environments. There seem to be several reasons for this.

One reason is that extracting useful visual information from images seems to involve a very large amount of computation. The visual cortexes of animals contain millions of neurons, which perform computations that require very large numbers of computer operations to simulate.

A second reason is the belief (Nelson, 1988) that practical results will eventually flow from a successful theory rather than vice versa. This may have more to do with the scarcity of practical systems than with philosophical conviction; historically, empirical engineering applications or unexplained observations have preceded theoretical developments at least as frequently as the reverse. If machine vision systems suddenly appeared that operated robustly in real-world domains, it is quite likely that theories explaining their commonality would soon follow.

A third reason is that the generally accepted goals for vision systems may be misplaced, or at least over-ambitious. The two commonly held touchstones for practical vision systems, recognition and navigation, are high-level objectives. If both were achieved, computer vision systems would have many of the capabilities of the human visual system. Given the lack of success in developing general systems that realize either of these goals in a robust manner, it would appear reasonable to consider simpler problems. Many researchers have gone in this direction by working on specific industrial applications. However, this work does not enhance our understanding of vision in general.

A more fruitful approach is to address specific classes of vision tasks. For example, the shape from x theories can be applied to obstacle avoidance, but we can also work on obstacle avoidance as a problem in its own right, develop a computational theory for it, design algorithms, prove that they are robust, and implement them. Nelson and Aloimonos (1987) is an example of this approach. Aloimonos and Shulman (1989b) describe this approach as working bottom-up in the Marr paradigm to find general solutions to specific problems.

If we could recover the scene we would be able to perform many tasks, but it is not always necessary to do complete recovery. What is vision for? (Ballard, 1989). Vision is needed in order to accomplish tasks that are essential for our survival: recognize mates, friends, enemies, and food, avoid danger, and so on. To carry out these tasks, it may not be necessary to recover the entire scene and all its properties. When visual abilities are studied, their purposes and their uses should be kept in mind. When vision is studied from a purposive, utilitarian (Ramachandran, 1989), or animate (Ballard, 1989) viewpoint, the problems that formulated are generally simpler, since they are relevant to specific tasks, and as a result they can often be solved by qualitative, robust techniques (Aloimonos, 1990; Zucker, 1988).

Many neuroscientists believe that the visual capabilities of animals developed (evolved) because of specific needs. Some of these abilities were based on common principles, but they may have developed at different times and may be implemented in separate hardware. The parts of the brain devoted to vision seem to implement independent processes (which of course communicate) that are devoted to the solution of specific visual tasks.

Research on recovery can continue, to try to understand why existing approaches are unstable, and try to develop provably optimal methods. A more radical idea would be to reconsider the need for the recovery paradigm. Rather, we should ask what tasks could be performed if there were adequate recovery modules. After these tasks have been identified, we can try to solve them directly, and not treat them as applications of a general recovery process. For example, to avoid obstacles it is necessary to

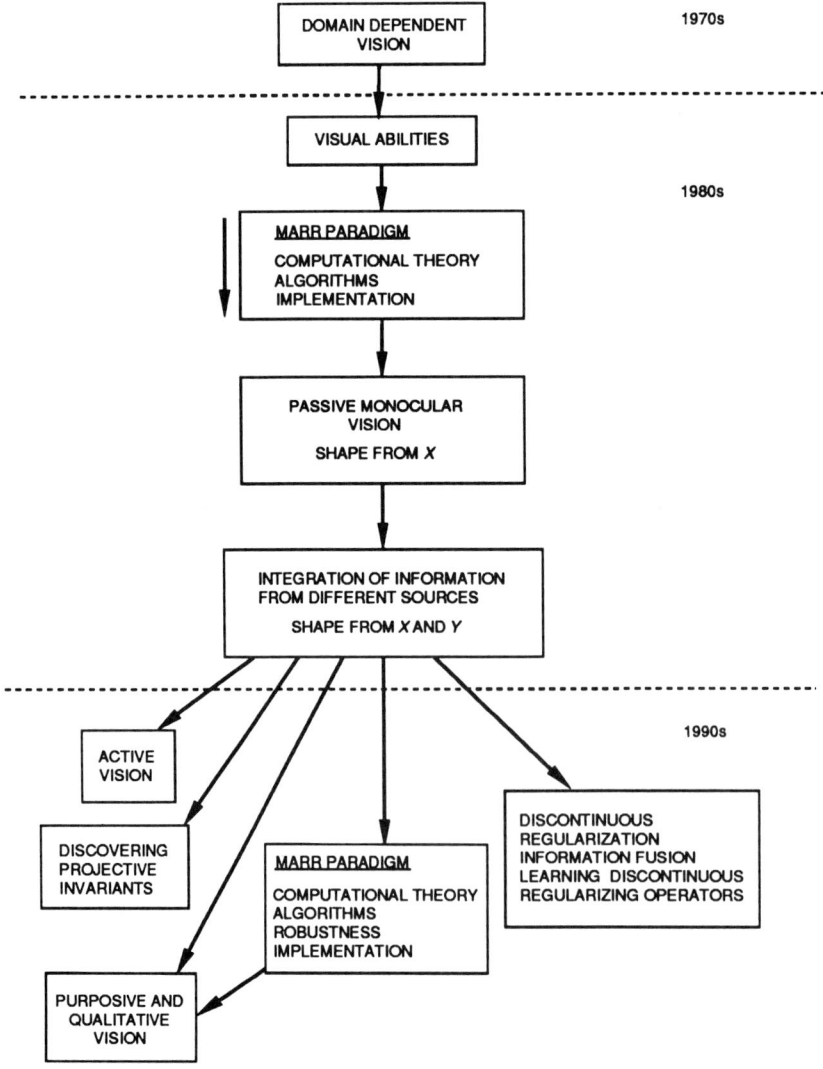

Figure 31. Research trends in visual recovery.

Table 2. Reconstructionist vs Purposive Vision.

Reconstructionist Vision	Purposive Vision
Reconstruct properties of the scene from images.	Define vision-based tasks.
Develop methods of recovering specific properties.	Develop methods of decomposing tasks into simpler subtasks.
Quantitative methods.	Qualitative methods.
General-purpose: recover the scene.	Directed (purposive).

answer a set of specific questions: Is another object present? Is it coming closer to me? If so, will it hit me? If so, how long will it take (relative to my reaction time)? If problems can be solved directly, the structure from motion module may no longer be needed. Moreover, because simple, qualitative questions that have small numbers of possible answers are being asked, it may be possible to achieve robust solutions.

In this framework, one need no longer regard vision as a collection of modules whose purpose is to reconstruct the scene and its properties and thus provide information for accomplishing various tasks. Rather, it can be regarded as a collection of processes which (individually or in groups) solve particular visual tasks. This means that vision is being considered not in isolation (as the recovery school of thought does), but as a part of a system that performs various tasks.

If we wish to study vision in general, we should study the tasks that organisms possessing vision can accomplish. If these tasks are complicated, we should decompose them into simpler tasks, and solve the simpler ones. This will then solve all the subtasks and yield a set of processes which if appropriately combined can perform the original task. This viewpoint is summarized, and contrasted with the reconstructionist viewpoint, in Table 2 (Aloimonos, 1990).

We conclude with Figure 31, which describes the evolution of research in visual recovery and our view about future directions.

BIBLIOGRAPHY

G. Adiv, "Inherent Ambiguities in Recovering 3-D Motion and Structure from a Noisy Flow Field," *Proceedings of the Conference on Computer Vision and Pattern Recognition*, 1985, pp. 70–77.

E. Allgower and K. Georg, "Simplicial and Continuation Methods of Approximating Fixed Points and Solutions to Systems of Equations," *SIAM Rev.* **22**, 28–85 (1980).

J. Aloimonos, Ph.D. thesis, Department of Computer Science, University of Rochester, 1986.

J. Aloimonos, "Shape from Texture," *Biol. Cybernetics* **58**, 345–360 (1988a).

J. Aloimonos, "Visual Shape Computation," *Proc. IEEE*, 899–916 (1988b).

J. Aloimonos, "Unifying Shading and Texture Through an Active Observer," *Proc. R. Soc. London B* **238**, 25–27 (1989).

J. Aloimonos, "Purposive and Qualitative Active Vision," *Proceedings of the DARPA Image Understanding Workshop*, 1990a, pp. 816–828.

J. Aloimonos, "Perspective Approximations," *Image and Vision Computing* **8**, 177–192 (1990b).

J. Aloimonos and A. Basu, "Combining Information in Low-level Vision," *CAR-TR-336*, Computer Vision Laboratory, Center for Automation Research, University of Maryland, College Park, 1987.

J. Aloimonos and J. Y. Hervé, "Correspondenceless Detection of Depth and Motion for a Planar Surface," *IEEE Trans. PAMI*, in press.

J. Aloimonos and D. Shulman, "Learning Early Vision Computations," *J. Opt. Soc. Am. A* **6**, 908–919 (1989a).

J. Aloimonos and D. Shulman, *Integration of Visual Modules: An Extension of the Marr Paradigm*, Academic Press, Boston, 1989b.

J. Aloimonos and M. Swain, "Shape from Patterns: Regularization," *Intl. J. Comput. Vision* **2**, 171–187 (1988).

J. Aloimonos, I. Weiss, and A. Bandopadhay, "Active Vision," *Intl. J. Comput. Vision* **2**, 333–356 (1988).

S. Amari, Personal communication, 1987.

D. Arnold, "Local Context in Matching Edges for Stereo Vision," *Proceedings of the DARPA Image Understanding Workshop*, 1978, pp. 65–72.

J. F. Augusteijn and C. R. Dyer, "Recognition and Recovery of the Three Dimensional Orientation of Planar Point Patterns," *Comput. Vision, Gr. Im. Process.* **36**, 76–99 (1986).

R. Bajcsy, "Active Perception vs. Passive Perception," *Proceedings of the Workshop on Computer Vision*, 1985, pp. 55–59.

R. Bajcsy and L. Lieberman, "Texture Gradient as a Depth Cue," *Comput. Vision, Gr., Im. Process.* **5**, 52–67 (1976).

R. Bajcsy and F. Solina, "Three Dimensional Object Representation Revisited," *Proceedings of the International Conference on Computer Vision*, 1987, pp. 231–240.

D. H. Ballard, "Reference Frames for Animate Vision," *Proceedings of the International Joint Conference on Artificial Intelligence*, Morgan Kaufmann, San Mateo, Calif., 1989, pp. 1635–1641.

H. G. Barrow and J. M. Tenenbaum, "Computational Vision," *Proc. IEEE* **69**, 572–595 (1981a).

H. G. Barrow and J. M. Tenenbaum, "Interpreting Line Drawings as Three Dimensional Surfaces," *Artif. Intell.* **17**, 75–116 (1981b).

A. Ben-Israel and T. Greville, *Generalized Inverses, Theory and Applications*, John Wiley and Sons, Inc., New York, 1974.

A. Blake, "Specular Stereo," *Proceedings of the Ninth International Joint Conference on Artificial Intelligence*, Los Angeles, Morgan-Kaufmann, San Mateo, Calif., 1985, pp. 973–976.

A. Blake and S. Zisserman, *Visual Reconstruction*, MIT Press, Cambridge, Mass., 1987.

M. Brady, "Computational Approaches to Image Understanding," *ACM Comput. Surv.* **14**, 3–71 (1982).

M. Brady and A. Yuille, "An Extremum Principle for Shape from Contour," *IEEE Trans. PAMI* **PAMI-6**, 288–301 (1984).

M. L. Braunstein and J. W. Payne, "Perspective and Form Ratio as Determinants of Relative Slant Judgments," *J. Exper. Psych.* **3**, 584–590 (1969).

M. J. Brooks, "Surface Normals from Closed Paths," *Proceedings of the Sixth International Joint Conference on Artificial Intelligence*, Tokyo, Morgan-Kaufmann, San Mateo, Calif., 1979, pp. 98–101.

M. J. Brooks and B. K. P. Horn, "Shape and Source from Shading," *Proceedings of the Ninth International Joint Conference on Artificial Intelligence,* Los Angeles, Morgan-Kaufmann, San Mateo, Calif., 1985, pp. 932–936.

A. R. Bruss, "The Image Irradiance Equation: Its Solution and Application," Ph.D. dissertation, Massachusetts Institute of Technology, Cambridge, Mass., 1980.

C. T. Chou, J. Aloimonos, and A. Rosenfeld, "Correspondenceless Model Based and Active Perception of Shape from Contour," *CAR-TR-275,* Computer Vision Laboratory, Center for Automation Research, University of Maryland, College Park, 1987.

S. N. Chow, J. Mallet-Paret, and J. A. Yorke, "Finding Zeros of Maps: Homotopy Methods that are Constructive with Probability One," *Math. Comp.* **32,** 887–899 (1978).

E. Coleman and R. Jain, "Obtaining 3D Shape of Textured and Specular Surfaces Using Four-source Photometry," *Comput. Gr., Im. Process.* **18,** 309–328 (1982).

J. Demmel, "The Geometry of Ill-conditioning," *J. Complexity* **3,** 201–299 (1987).

J. A. Feldman, "Four Frames Suffice: A Provisional Model of Vision and Space," *Behav. Brain Sci.* **8,** 265–313 (1985).

R. Frankot and R. Chellappa, "A Method for Enforcing Integrability in Shape from Shading Algorithms," *Proceedings of the International Conference on Computer Vision,* 1987, pp. 118–127.

E. Gamble and T. Poggio, "Visual Integration and Detection of Discontinuities: The Key Role of Intensity Edges," *AI Memo 970,* Artificial Intelligence Laboratory, Massachusetts Institute of Technology, Cambridge, Mass., 1987.

D. Gay, "Perturbation Bounds for Nonlinear Equations," *SIAM J. Numerical Analysis* **18,** 654–663 (1981).

D. Gay, "Solving Interval Linear Equations," *SIAM J. Numerical Analysis* **19,** 858–870 (1982).

S. Geman and D. Geman, "Stochastic Relaxation, Gibbs Distributions, and the Bayesian Restoration of Images," *IEEE Trans. PAMI* **PAM1-6,** 721–741 (1984).

J. J. Gibson, *The Perception of the Visual World,* Houghton-Mifflin, Boston, Mass., 1950.

E. Grimson, "Binocular Shading and Visual Surface Reconstruction," *Comput. Vision, Gr., Im. Process.* **28,** 19–43 (1984).

W. E. L. Grimson and T. Pavlidis, "Discontinuity Detection for Visual Surface Reconstruction," *Comput. Vision, Gr., Im. Process.* **30,** 316–330 (1985).

J. Hadamard, *Lectures on the Cauchy Problem in Linear Partial Differential Equations,* Yale, New Haven, Conn., 1923.

G. Healey and T. Binford, "Local Shape from Specularity," *Proceedings of the International Conference on Computer Vision,* 1987, pp. 151–160.

R. Horaud and M. Brady, "On the Geometric Interpretation of Image Contours," *Proceedings of the International Conference on Computer Vision,* 1987, pp. 374–382.

B. K. P. Horn, "Obtaining Shape from Shading Information," in *The Psychology of Computer Vision,* P. H. Winston, ed., McGraw-Hill, New York, 1975, pp. 115–155.

B. K. P. Horn, "Understanding Image Intensities," *Artif. Intell.* **8,** 201–231 (1977).

B. K. P. Horn, "The Curve of Least Energy," *AI Memo 610,* Artificial Intelligence Laboratory, Massachusetts Institute of Technology, Cambridge, Mass., 1981.

B. K. P. Horn, *Robot Vision,* McGraw-Hill, New York, 1986.

B. K. P. Horn and M. J. Brooks, "The Variational Approach to Shape from Shading," *Comput. Vision, Gr., Im. Process.* **33,** 174–208 (1986).

B. K. P. Horn and M. J. Brooks, *Shape from Shading,* MIT Press, Cambridge, Mass., 1989.

B. K. P. Horn and R. W. Sjoberg, "Calculating the Reflectance Map," *Applied Optics* **18,** 1770–1779 (1979).

B. K. P. Horn and E. J. Weldon, "Computationally Efficient Methods of Recovering Translational Motion," *Proceedings of the International Conference on Computer Vision,* 1987, pp. 2–11.

T. S. Huang and M. Blostein, "Robust Algorithms for Motion Estimation Based on Two Sequential Stereo Image Pairs," *Proceedings of the Conference on Computer Vision and Pattern Recognition,* 1985, pp. 518–523.

T. S. Huang and T. Blostein, "Quantization Errors in Stereo Triangulation," *Proceedings of the IEEE International Conference on Computer Vision,* 1987, pp. 325–334.

A. Hurlbert and T. Poggio, "Learning a Color Algorithm from Examples," *AI Memo 909,* Artificial Intelligence Laboratory, Massachusetts Institute of Technology, Cambridge, Mass., 1987.

K. Ikeuchi, "Shape from Regular Patterns," *Artif. Intell.* **22,** 49–75 (1984).

K. Ikeuchi and B. K. P. Horn, "Numerical Shape from Shading and Occluding Boundaries," *Artif. Intell.* **17,** 141–184 (1981).

E. Ito and J. Aloimonos, "Determining Three Dimensional Transformation Parameters from Images: Theory," *CAR-TR-318,* Computer Vision Laboratory, Center for Automation Research, University of Maryland, College Park, 1987.

B. Julesz, *Foundations of Cyclopean Perception,* University of Chicago Press, Chicago, 1971.

T. Kanade, "Determining the Shape of an Object from a Single View," *Artif. Intell.* **17,** 409–460 (1981).

K. I. Kanatani, "Detection of Surface Orientation and Motion from Texture by a Stereological Technique," *Artif. Intell.* **23,** 213–237 (1984).

K. Kanatani and T. C. Chou, "Shape from Texture: General Principle," *Artif. Intell.* **38,** 1–48 (1989).

J. R. Kender, "Shape from Texture: An Aggregation Transform that Maps a Class of Textures into Surface Orientation," *Proceedings of the Sixth International Joint Conference on Artificial Intelligence,* Tokyo, Morgan-Kaufmann, San Mateo, Calif., 1979, pp. 475–480.

J. Kender, Ph.D. thesis, Department of Computer Science, Carnegie-Mellon University, Pittsburgh, Pa., 1980.

J. J. Koenderink, "An Internal Representation for Solid Shape Based on the Topological Properties of the Apparent Contour," in W. Richards and S. Ullman, eds., *Image Understanding 1986,* Ablex, Norwood, N.J., 1986, pp. 257–285.

J. J. Koenderink and A. J. van Doorn, "Photometric Invariants Related to Solid Shape," *Acta Optica* **27,** 981–996 (1980).

I. Kuperman, *Approximate Algebraic Linear Equations,* Van Nostrand, London, 1971.

E. H. Land and J. J. McCann, "Lightness and Retinex Theory," *J. Opt. Soc. Am.* **61,** 1–11 (1971).

C. H. Lee and A. Rosenfeld, "Improved Methods of Estimating Shape from Shading Using the Light Source Coordinate System," *Artif. Intell.* **26,** 125–143 (1985).

D. Lee, "A Provably Convergent Algorithm for Shape from Shading," *Proceedings of the DARPA Image Understanding Workshop,* 1985, pp. 489–496.

D. Lee, Ph.D. thesis, Department of Computer Science, Columbia University, New York, 1986.

D. Lee and T. Pavlidis, "One-dimensional Regularization with Discontinuities," *Proceedings of the International Conference on Computer Vision,* 1987, pp. 572–577.

M. Lipschutz, "Differential Geometry," *Schaum's Outline Series*, McGraw Hill, New York, 1969.

J. Malik, "Interpreting Line Drawings of Curved Objects," *Int. J. Comput. Vision* **1**, 73–103 (1987).

D. Marr, *Vision*, W. H. Freeman, San Francisco, 1982.

J. L. Marroquin, "Surface Reconstruction Preserving Discontinuities," *AI Memo 792*, Artificial Intelligence Laboratory, Massachusetts Institute of Technology, Cambridge, Mass., 1984.

J. Marroquin, Ph.D. thesis, Artificial Intelligence Laboratory, Massachusetts Institute of Technology, Cambridge, Mass., 1986.

J. Marroquin, S. Mitter, and T. Poggio, "Probabilistic Solution of Ill-Posed Problems in Computational Vision," *Proceedings of the DARPA Image Understanding Workshop*, 1985, pp. 293–309.

V. Milenkovic and T. Kanade, "Trinocular Vision Using Photometric and Edge Orientation Constraints," *Proceedings of the DARPA Image Understanding Workshop*, 1985, pp. 163–175.

M. Moerdler and J. Kender, "An Integrated System that Unifies Multiple Shape from Texture Algorithms," *Proceedings of the DARPA Image Understanding Workshop*, 1987, pp. 574–580.

R. Moore and T. Kioustelidis, "A Simple Test for Accuracy of Approximate Solutions to (Non)linear Systems," *SIAM J. Numerical Analysis* **17**, 521–529 (1980).

V. A. Morozov, *Methods for Solving Incorrectly Posed Problems*, Springer, Berlin, 1984.

D. Mumford, "The Problem of Robust Shape Descriptions," *Proceedings of the International Conference on Computer Vision*, 1987, pp. 602–606.

D. Mumford and M. Shah, "Boundary Detection by Minimizing Functionals," *Proceedings of the IEEE Conference on Computer Vision and Pattern Recognition*, 1985, pp. 22–25.

H. H. Nagel and W. Enkelmann, "An Investigation of Smoothness Constraints for the Estimation of Displacement Vector Fields from Image Sequences," *IEEE Trans. PAMI* **PAMI-8**, 565–593 (1986).

V. Nalwa, Ph.D. thesis, Department of Computer Science, Stanford University, 1987.

R. Nelson, Ph.D. thesis, Computer Vision Laboratory, Center for Automation Research, University of Maryland, College Park, 1988.

R. Nelson and J. Aloimonos, "Using Flow Field Divergence for Obstacle Avoidance in Visual Navigation," *CAR-TR-332*, Computer Vision Laboratory, Center for Automation Research, University of Maryland, College Park, 1987.

A. Neumaier, "New Techniques for the Analysis of Linear Interval Equations," *Linear Algebra and Its Applications* **58**, 273–325 (1984).

Y. Ohta and T. Kanade, "Stereo by Intra- and Inter-scanline Search Using Dynamic Programming," *IEEE Trans. PAMI* **PAMI-7**, 139–154 (1985).

Y. Ohta, K. Maenobu, and T. Sakai, "Obtaining Surface Orientation from Texels Under Perspective Projection," *Proceedings of the Seventh International Joint Conference on Artificial Intelligence*, Vancouver, B.C., Morgan-Kaufmann, San Mateo, Calif., 1981, pp. 746–751.

T. Pavlidis, ed. "Special Memorial Issue for Professor King-Sun Fu," *IEEE Trans. PAMI* **PAMI-8**, 289–404 (1986).

R. Penrose, "A Generalized Inverse for Matrices," *Proc. Cambridge Philos. Soc.* **51**, 406–413 (1955).

A. P. Pentland, "Finding the Illuminant Direction," *J. Opt. Soc. Am.* **72**, 448–455 (1982).

A. P. Pentland, "Local Shading Analysis," *IEEE Trans. PAMI* **PAMI-6**, 170–187 (1984).

A. P. Pentland, "Perceptual Organization and the Representation of Natural Form," *Artif. Intell.* **28**, 293–331 (1986).

T. Poggio and C. Koch, "An Analog Model of Computation for the Ill-posed Problems of Early Vision," *AI Memo 783*, Artificial Intelligence Laboratory, Massachusetts Institute of Technology, Cambridge, Mass., 1984.

T. Poggio and V. Torre, "Ill-posed Problems and Regularization Analysis in Early Vision," *Proceedings of the DARPA Image Understanding Workshop*, 1984, pp. 257–263.

T. Poggio and co-workers, "MIT Progress in Understanding Images," *Proceedings of the DARPA Image Understanding Workshop*, 1985, pp. 25–39.

T. Poggio and co-workers, "MIT Progress in Understanding Images," *Proceedings of the DARPA Image Understanding Workshop*, 1987, pp. 41–54.

V. S. Ramachandran, *Proceedings of the Workshop on Visual Motion*, 1989.

W. Richards, "Structure from Stereo and Motion," *J. Opt. Soc. Am. A* **2**, 343–349 (1986).

B. Schunck, "Motion Segmentation and Estimation," Ph.D. dissertation, Massachusetts Institute of Technology, Cambridge, Mass., 1984.

S. Shafer, T. Kanade, and J. Kender, "Gradient Space Under Orthography and Perspective," *Comput. Vision, Gr., Im. Process.* **24**, 182–199 (1983).

D. Shulman and J. Aloimonos, "Boundary Preserving Regularization: Theory, Part I," *CAR-TR-340*, Computer Vision Laboratory, Center for Automation Research, University of Maryland, College Park, 1988b.

K. A. Stevens, "Surface Perception from Local Analysis of Texture and Contour," *AI Memo 512*, Artificial Intelligence Laboratory, Massachusetts Institute of Technology, Cambridge, Mass., 1980.

K. A. Stevens, "The Visual Interpretation of Surface Contours," *Artif. Intell.* **17**, 47–73 (1981).

T. M. Strat, "A Numerical Method for Shape from Shading from a Single Image," M.S. thesis, Massachusetts Institute of Technology, Cambrige, Mass., 1979.

D. Terzopoulos, Ph.D. dissertation, Massachusetts Institute of Technology, Cambridge, Mass., 1984.

A. N. Tichonov and V. Y. Arsenin, *Solution of Ill-Posed Problems*, Winston and Wiley, Washington D.C., 1977.

A. P. Witkin, "Recovering Surface Shape and Orientation from Texture," *Artif. Intell.* **17**, 17–45 (1981).

L. B. Wolff, "Physical Stereo for Combined Specular and Diffuse Reflection," *Technical Report*, Department of Computer Science, Columbia University, New York, 1986.

L. B. Wolff, "Spectral and Polarization Stereo Methods Using a Single Light Source," *Proceedings of the DARPA Image Understanding Workshop*, 1987, pp. 810–820.

L. B. Wolff, "Surface Curvature and Contour from Photometric Stereo," *Proceedings of the DARPA Image Understanding Workshop*, 1987, pp. 821–824.

R. J. Woodham, "Analyzing Images of Curved Surfaces," *Artif. Intell.* **17**, 117–141 (1981).

S. Zucker, "The Emerging Paradigm of Computational Vision," *Ann. Rev. Comput. Sci.* **2**, 69–89 (1988).

YIANNIS ALOIMONOS
AZRIEL ROSENFELD
University of Maryland

X

XCON

XCON (sometimes called R1) is a rule-based system (qv) that configures all of Digital Equipment Corp.'s computer systems. The initial version of XCON was written in 1979 by McDermott at Carnegie Mellon University [see J. McDermott, "R1: A Rule-Based Configurer of Computer Systems," *Artif. Intell.* **19,** 39–88 (1982)]. It was one of the first expert systems (qv) to do a constructive as opposed to a diagnostic task and was one of the first expert systems to be used on a regular basis in the real world [see V. Barker and D. O'Connor, "Expert Systems for Configuration at Digital: XCON and Beyond," *CACM* **33**(3) (March 1989)].

JOHN MCDERMOTT
Digital Equipment Corp.

Z

Z MODAL QUANTIFICATIONAL LOGIC

A recursively axiomatized logic designed by F.M. Brown for representing nonmonotonic reasoning. (See "A Commonsense Theory of Nonmonotonic Reasoning," *Proceedings of the Eighth International Conference on Automated Deduction*, Oxford, England, 1986, Lecture Notes in Computer Science 230, Springer-Verlag; "The Modal Logic Z," *The Frame Problem in AI, Proceedings of the 1987 AAAI Workshop*, F. Brown, ed., Morgan-Kaufmann, Los Altos, Calif.). This weak second order logic includes quantification over propositions, but not over properties. The modal structure includes S5 and additional axioms stating what is logically possible. For example, "it is logically possible that all men except Herecles are mortal" is a theorem of Z. The possibility of a proposition with respect to a theory K is represented as the logical possibility of the conjunction of K and that proposition. Nonmonotonic default sentences such as "if it is possible with respect to K for someone to be mortal then he is mortal" may be included within a conjunction of sentences which are asserted to be equivalent to K. The solutions for K in such an equivalence are essentially the nonmonotonic fixed points associated with other logics of nonmonotonic reasoning. Specific classes of equations have been found which allow for the exact simulation of all theories expressible in (R. Moore's) Autoepistemic Logic, (R. Reiter's) Default Logic, (J. McCarthy's) Parallel Circumscription, (V. Lifschitz's) Prioritized Circumscription, and (K. Clark's) closed world assumption. (See "The Modal Quantificational Logic Z Applied to the Frame Problem," P. Hayes and K. Ford, eds., *The Frame Problem in Artificial Intelligence*, JAI Press, 1992.) An automatic deduction system for Z, which is capable of nonmonotonic reasoning in all of the above theories has been implemented.

FRANK M. BROWN
University of Kansas

ZERO CROSSINGS. See EARLY VISION; EDGE AND LOCAL FEATURE DETECTION; STEREO VISION.

INDEX

A* algorithm, 1–2
  branch-and-bound search, 1471–1472
  heuristics and, 612–614, 1464–1465
  iterative-deepening (IDA*), 1464–1465
  means-ends analysis, 910
  problem solving production schema, 1222
  real-time-A*, 1465–1466
  Shakey robot and, 1527
  spatial reasoning, 1326–1327
AARON system, 52–54
Abbreviations, dictionary/lexicon construction, 344
  inter-word entry information, 348–349
Abduction, 1–3
  causal reasoning, 1285
  concept learning, 253
  logic and depiction, 854
  philosophy of AI and, 1144
  story analysis, 1574
ABDUL/ILANA system, 49–50
ABEL program
  AI in medicine (AIM) and
    causal reasoning, 920–921
    knowledge acquisition, 917
  causal reasoning and, 1281
Abelson, R. P.
  belief representation systems, 107–108
  script theory, 1443–1444
Abstraction
  early vision and, 402
  engineering and KBES, 449–450
  problem solving, 1226–1227
  search and, 1466
ABSTRIPS system
  means-ends analysis, 909, 913
  problem solving, 1227
  Shakey robot and, 1527
Access mode restriction, 1083–1084
Acoustic-phonetic analysis, 1554
ACRES system, emotion modeling, 447
ACRONYM system
  image understanding and, 649, 651–653
  knowledge system building, 488
  object recognition, 1078
Acronyms, dictionary/lexicon construction, 344
ACT system
  computational linguistics, 218
  education and AI, 438
Action
  planning and
    representations, 1160–1161
    selection, 1165–1166
  schema theory, 1434
Active design techniques, end-effector technology, 1364–1367
Active vision
  image understanding and, 645
  visual recovery, 1681–1683
ACTNET, reactive planning machines, 1175
Actor formalisms, 3–4
Actors
  defined, 3–4
  object-oriented languages, 776–777
Actuation methods, robot end-effector design, 1368
Acyclic constraint networks, 281–282
Acyclic graphs
  semantic networks, 1501
Adams, A., 468
Adaptation
  case-based reasoning, 1272
  human-computer interaction, 622–623
  perception and, 1661
Adaptive consistency, constraint networks, 278–280
Adaptive control, robotics design, 1390–1392
  arc welding, 1391

compressor-cover assembly, 1391
  modular printer-carriage assembly, 1391
  tracking, 1391
Adaptive learning algorithm, pattern recognition, 1125
Adaptive planning
  FLOABN, 11–12
  history, 5–6
  memory, 6–7
  PLEXUS system, 8–11
    abstaction hierarchy, 9–10
    core matecher, 8–10
    general problem solving (GPS), 10–11
    hierarchical planning, 10
    top-level control, 8
  retrieval, 7
  SCAVENGER, 11–12
  understanding, 6
Adaptive resonance theory (ART), 13–20
  design principles, 17–18
  distributed hypothesis testing, 14
  habituative chemical transmitters, 19–20
  hierarchical organization, 19
  neural network learning and, 13–14
  recognition and search control, 14–15
  recognition categories, 16–17
  search cycle, 15–16
Adaptive Suspension Vehicle, 1400
Adaptivity, case-based reasoning, 1267
Advanced computer science, artificial intelligence (AI), 54
Adversarial reasoning, case-based reasoning, 1275
Advice Taker, 1, 21
  history of, 832
  knowledge representation and, 744
AGE system
  blackboard system building with, 121
  domain knowledge, 389
Agenda-based systems, 21–22
  blackboard systems, 117
Agglomerative techniques, clustering analysis, 170–172
Aggregation
  logic programming, 880
  plausible reasoning and, 1308
  probabilistic networks, 1206
Agricultural chemicals, chemistry in AI and, 160
AI-complete tasks, 56–57
AILIST, as AI information source, 847
AIMDS language, law in AI and, 780
AIR-CYL system, design and, 335
Airline distance, heuristics and, 612–613
AIRPLAN system, knowledge system building, 488
AKA-WINO project, 340
ALADIN, engineering and KBES, 452–453
ALANN architecture, pattern recognition, 1125
Algebra, education and AI, 439–440
Algebraic surfaces, range data analysis, 1252
Algebraic syntax, LISP language, 822
ALGOL language, control structures, 294
Algorithms
  A*, 1–2
    see also A* algorithm
  AO*
    AND/OR graphs, 30
    see also AO* algorithm
  AQ algorithm, 256
  artificial intelligence (AI), 55
  augmented transition network (ATN) grammars, 560–561
  branch-and-bound search, 1471–1472
  branching factors, 127–128
  case-based reasoning, 1268–1269
    retrieval, 1270–1271

clustering analysis, 170
color vision systems, 196
constraint networks, 276
  graph-based, 277–284
constraint satisfaction
  backtracking and consistency, 286–289
  consistency algorithms, 285
  relaxation algorithms, 289–290
coroutines, 302
Dictionary Viterbi Algorithm (DVA), 145–146
greedy, constraint networks, 279
heuristic search, 1464–1465
learning, Boltzmann machine, 127
left-corner parsing, 1103
legged robots, rough terrain navigation, 1405–1406
logic programming and, 884–885
machine-learning and, 800–801
mathematical induction, 669–671
  termination, 670–671
minimum search, 1465–1466
model-based deduction, 935–938
  predicate calculus, 937–938
  propositional reasoning, 935–937
multipass, coroutines, 303
pattern recognition
  genetic algorithms, 1125
  SSS* algorithm, 1124
probabilistic networks, inference, 1205
problem reduction, search algorithm, 1212–1213
problem solving, production schema, 1222
program synthesis, 65–66
  enumerative algorithm, 73
  flowchart synthesis algorithm, 73
  Shapiro synthesis algorithms, 70–73
  Summers synthesis method, 73
  Turing machine, 67
range data analysis, 1250–1251
recursive-descent parsing, 1102–1103
secondary protein structure prediction, 1245–1246
simulated annealing, 1538–1540
spatial reasoning, 1332
tree-search, 84
  constraint networks, 278
unification, 1631
visual motion analysis, accuracy, 1651–1652
Viterbi algorithm, 145–146, 148
Alignment methods, object recognition, 1074–1076
All-to-all symmetric connections, Hopfield networks, 1046–1407
Allen and Perrault theory, belief representation systems, 105
ALPAC (Automatic Language Processing Advisory Committee), 204
Alpha-beta algorithm, computer chess and, 227
Alpha-beta enhancements, computer chess and, 229–235
Alpha-beta pruning, 22–24
  branching factors, 128
  checkers-playing programs, 151
    search procedures, 152
  computer chess and, 227
  game playing and, 547
  game trees, 552
  minimax procedure, 959
  minimum search, 1465–1466
ALPS languages, parallel logic programming language, 1086
ALVEN system, image understanding and, 647–648, 649, 652–653
Alvey program, 25–30
  AND/OR graphs, 28–29
  search, 30
  applications, 29–30

INDEX

history of, 25–26
ALVINN system, mobile robot sensing, 1412
AM phase shift, robot sensing and, 1384
AM system, 27
  agenda-based systems and, 22
  concept learning, 251
  creativity and, 307
  design and, 337
  problem solving, 1227
Amari, S., 1023–1024
AMBER language
  computational linguistics, 218
  language acquisition, 766–768
Ambiguity
  lexical decomposition, 806
  lexical semantics, 815–816
  natural language understanding, 998–999
  qualitative physics, 1153
AMBLER robot, 1414–1415
Amino acids, protein structure prediction, 1240
Analog semantic features, 27–28
Analog sensors, robot end-effector design, 1368
Analogy
  argument comprehension, 40–41
  concept learning, 250
  design and, 336–337
  machine-learning and, 798
  machine translation, 901
  naive physics, 1148
  problem solving, 1226–1227
Analysis techniques, natural language understanding, 999–1010
  case frame instantiation, 1006–1009
  pattern matching, 999–1001
  robust parsing, 1009–1010
  semantic grammars, 1004–1005
  syntactically driven parsing, 1001–1004
ANALYST program
  AI military applications, 950–951
Analytic learning, machine learning, 788, 795–797
Anaphora
  computational linguistics, 216
  discourse understanding, 371–372
  ellipsis and, 446
  natural language understanding, 1010
  semantic networks, 1505
Anchored matching, 1563
Anchors, in situation semantics, 1543
AND-parallel computation models
  logic programming, 1082
  machine architecture, 1089–1090
AND/OR graphs, 28–29
  Alvey program, 28–29
  applications, 29–30
  blackboard system building, 121–122
  branch-and-bound search, 1472
  game trees, 550
  image understanding and, 653
  machine learning, 795–796
  means-ends analysis, 911–912
  pattern recognition, 1123–1124
  problem reduction, 1209–1210, 1213
    algorithms, 1212–1213
    search, 1211–1213
  SAINT program, 1427
  search and, 1461
Anderson, D., 762
ANDORRA Prolog system, parallel machine architecture, 1093
ANGEL system, 1097
Anisotropically conductive silicone rubber (ACS), 1516
Annealing algorithms, image models, 632
ANON system, case-based reasoning, 1269
Antibehavioral theory, philosophy of AI and, 1138–1139
Anticomputationalist theories, 1140–1141
Antimechanism, philosophy of AI and, 1142–1143
Antonymy, lexical semantics, 815
ANYTIME algorithms
  reactive planning machines, 1177
  real-time approximation reasoning, 1319
AO* algorithm
  AND/OR graphs, 30
  branch-and-bound search, 1472
  problem reduction, 1213
AP3 system, blackboard system building, 121–122
  reactive planning machines, 1177
Apel, K., hermeneutics and, 600, 604–605
Aperture problem, optical flow analysis, 1638–1639
Apiary network architecture, 4
APPLIER system, scripts applications, 1450–1451
Appropriateness conditions
  heuristics and, 614–615
  situation semantics, 1542–1543
Approximate reasoning systems
  plausible reasoning and, 1309–1310
  real-time methods, 1319

Approximation techniques, range data analysis
  global methods, 1261
  local surface methods, 1260–1261
APRIL processor, parallel machine architecture, 1094
A priori probabilities
  pattern recognition, 1117
  decision theory, 1119
AQ algorithm, concept learning, 256
AQ11 program, concept learning, 255–256
AR-P algorithm, machine learning and, 789–790
Arbib, M. A., 1023–1024, 1172
Arc consistency algorithm, constraint satisfaction, 288
Arc reversal, probabilistic networks, 1205
Arc welding, robotics design, 1391
ARC-TEC project, 340
Area matching, stereo vision, 1562
ARGO system, design and, 336
Argonne scheduler, parallel machine architecture, 1092
ARGOS system
  image understanding and, 650
ARGOT system, computational linguistics, 212
Argument comprehension, 31–51
  argument units, 32–33, 41–46
    generality, 44–45
    realized failures, 42–43
    realized successes, 43
    unrealized failures, 43–44
    unrealized successes, 41–42
  belief systems and, 31–32
  historical background, 30–31
  meta-argument units, 46–48
  politico-economic knowledge, 36–38
  recent models, 49–50
  structure recognition and inferring beliefs, 48–49
Argument graph, argument comprehension, 33
Argument roles, situation semantics, 1542–1543
Argument units (AUs)
  argument comprehension, 41–46
  scripts and, 1453
ARIADNE system, protein structure prediction, 1248
Aristotle
  cybernetics, 310
  epistemology, 461–462
Arithmetic
  fuzzy set theory, 539
  intelligence and, 707
  qualitative physics, 1152
ARPA project
  speech understanding and, 1553
    acoustic-phonetic analysis, 1554
    phonological analysis, 1555
  Research Program, human-computer interaction, 621
ARPANET program
  as AI information source, 847–848
  LISP language and, 839
Array grammar, texture analysis, 1595
Arrays, LISP language, 830
Art, AI in, 52–54
Artificial belief systems (ABS), 106–107
Artificial intelligence (AI), 54–57
  advanced computer science, 54
  AI-complete tasking, 56–57
  applications, 57
  Church's thesis, 163
  computational philosophy, 54
  computational psychology, 54
  coroutines, 305–306
  design and, 336–337
  epistemology and, 464–466
  hermeneutics and, 605–608
  heuristic programming, 54–55
  history of, 55
  human-computer interaction, 620–623
  information retrieval, 688–689
  intellectics and, 705–706
  knowledge representation, 56
  lambda calculus, 761
  law in, 777–783
    historical background, 778–779
  learning, 56–57
  legal analysis programs, 780–781
    case-based vs. rule-based approaches, 781–782
    cognitive processes, 782–783
    Gardner's dissertation, 780–781
    TAXMAN I and II, 780
  lexical decomposition, 810–811
  logic and, 851–852
  manufacturing and, 903–908
  military applications, 947–958
  natural language, 56
  neighboring disciplines, 55–56
  problem solving, 56
  programming, 623–624
  propositional logic, 895

robotics, 57
  societies for, 1550–1551
  Turing machines and, 1624
  vision, 57
Artificial Intelligence in Model Building (AIMB) program, 160
Artificial neural networks (ANNs). See Neural networks
Artificial sequences, protein structure prediction, 1244
Aspiration search, computer chess and, 228
Assertional knowledge
  thesauri and, 1610
  semantic networks, 1504–1505
Associative disks, associative memory, 58
Associative memory, 57–58
  cognitive psychology and, 182
  memory management and hardware control, 57–58
  neural networks
    learning, 1035
    oscillatory, 1048–1049
    point attractors, 1042–1048
    temporal-pattern encoding, 1049–1050
  segmentation and, 1487
Assumption-based systems
  belief revisions and, 113–114
  truth maintenance systems (TMS), 1617–1618
ATMS (Assumption-based Truth Maintenance System), 1097
ATN parser, cognitive modeling, 180
ATOME system, blackboard systems, 123
Atomic entities,
  inductive inference, 677
  parsing, 1101–1102
Atoms, LISP language syntax, 820
ATRANS
  natural language understanding, 1007
  script structure and, 1445
Attack relationships, argument comprehension, 38–39
ATTENDING system
  AI in medicine (AIM) and, 921–922
  inference and control methods, 918
  knowledge structures, 918
Attention theory
  cognitive psychology and, 183–184
  image understanding and, 645
  perception and, 1661
Attractors
  cybernetics, 310
  neural networks, 1043
Attribute values
  dictionary/lexicon construction, 345
  machine learning and, 786
Augmented phrase structure grammar, 468
Augmented transition network (ATN)
  cognitive modeling, 179
  computational linguistics
    grammatical formalisms, 214–215
    history, 207–208
  discourse understanding, text analysis, 371
  education and AI, 437
  grammar, 552–562
    cascaded networks (CATN), 561–562
    context-free grammars and, 555–556
    factoring, 554
    formal properties, 559
    generalized transition networks and, 561
    history, 554–556
    HWIM system and, 556–557, 625
    linguistic experimentation, 558–559
    misconceptions, 560–561
    parsers, 560–561
    perspective, 559–560
    recursive transition networks (RTNs) and, 553–554
    specification, 557–558
  human-computer interaction, 621
  natural language generation, 987–988, 1003–1004
  systemic grammar, 993–994
  parsing, 1105–1106
  semantic grammar, 580–582
  semantic networks, 1508
  speech understanding and, 1555–1556
AURA program, 59
  binary resolution, 1351
  schema theory, 1437
AURORA system, parallel machine architecture, 1092
Authority triangles, argument comprehension, 34–35
Autocorrelation, texture analysis, 1589–1592
Autoepistemic reasoning
  default reasoning, 1297
  nonmonotonic reasoning and, 1304
Autogeneration, reactive planning machines, 1176
AUTOLING program, computational linguistics, 218

Automata theory, literature on, 844
Automated induction, mathematical induction, 669–671
Automated information retrieval, 685–686
Automatic guided vehicles (AGV), mobile robotics design, 1409–1410
Automatic programming, 59–81
  computational linguistics, 212–213
  historical background, 65, 73, 77
  input-output specifications, 60–65
    deductive mechanism, 62–63
    synthesizing programs, 63–64
  loop searches, 64
  mechanized assistant construction, 77–81
    automatically generating search programs, 79–81
    programmer's assistant, 78–79
  natural language dialogue, 73–77
  program synthesis, 65–73
    behavior graph factorization, 69–70
    examples, 72–73
    historical background, 73
    LISP Code, 67–68
    natural language dialogue, 73–77
    PROLOG programs, 70–72
    recurrence relations with LISP, 68–69
    trainable Turing machine, 66–67
    transformational methodologies, 64–65
Automatic test equipment (ATE), AI military applications, 954–955
Automatically generating search programs, 79–81
Automaticity, cognitive psychology and, 183–184
Autonomous Land Vehicle (ALV), 25
  AI military applications, 949
Autopoiesis, cybernetics, 311
Autoregressive (AR) models
  image models, 629
  texture analysis, 1588
Autoregressive moving average (ARMA) models, 629
  texture analysis, 1589
Axiomatic characterization, epsilon-semantics, 470
Axiomatic predicate logic, 869–870
Axiomatic propositional logic, 894
Axiomatic systems, modal logic, 862–863
Axons, neural network modeling, 1017–1018

B system, chemistry in AI and, 159
BACK system, knowledge representation and, 753
Back-drivability, robot end-effector design, 1370
Back-matching, stereo vision, 1563
Background knowledge
  adaptive planning and, 7
  discourse understanding, 372
Backjumping
  constraint networks, 277
  graph-based improvement, 283–284
Backpropagation
  machine learning and, 789
  neural networks, 1016, 1037–1040
    sequence learning, 1051–1052
    temporal-pattern encoding, 1050
  secondary protein structure prediction, 1245–1246
Backquote function, LISP language, 825–826
Backtracking, 84–88
  a-b-c example, 85–86
  advantages and disadvantages, 85
  AI in music and, 974–976
    representation and, 977–978
  AND/OR graphs, 30
  belief revisions and, 114
  chronological backtracking, 85–87
    belief revision, 110–111
    relaxation, 85
  computational linguistics, 214
  CONNIVER system, 274
  constraint networks, 276–277
    graph-based improvement, 283–284
    constraint satisfaction, 286–289
  coroutines, 302
    compilers, 304–305
    search procedures, 304
  dependency-directed, 86–88
    belief revision, 110–111
    contradictions, 86
  depth-first search, 1473
  design and, 336
  engineering and KBES, 449–450
  in programming languages, 88
  intelligent backtracking, 85–88
  knowledge representation and, 747
  logic programming, 877
    dependency-directed, 885
  natural language understanding, 1004
  planning and, 1165, 1170
  problem formulation, 84–85
  problem reduction, 1210–1211
  programming languages, 88
  reordering variables, 85–86
  variable reordering, 85–86
Backus Normal Form (BNF)
  augmented transition network (ATNs), 555
    specification, 557–558
  parsing, 1100
Backward chaining
  deductive databases, 324
  planning and, 1166
  processing, bottom-up and top-down, 1230
  rule-based systems, 1421
  see also Processing, bottom-up and top-down
Bacon, Roger, 462
BACON system
  clustering, 175–176
  concept learning, 251
  creativity and, 307
Balance
  active balance research, 1402–1404
  legged robots, 1401–1402
Bartlett, F. C., 1429–1430
BASEBALL system, 88–89
  computational linguistics, 205–206
  human-computer interaction, 621
Basic probability assumption (BPA), 1313–1314
Basic prover concept, mathematical induction, 670
Basic transition networks (BTN), parsing, 1106
BATTLE program, AI military applications, 952–953
Bayes's theorem
  AI in medicine (AIM) and, 916
  certainty-factor (CF) models, 134–135
  Dempster-Shafer theory and, 330–331
  inductive inference, 680
  modification, 1310–1312
  probabilistic reasoning, 1310
Bayesian belief networks
  AI in medicine (AIM) and, 918
  probabilistic reasoning, 1313
Bayesian decision theory
  character recognition, 148
  pattern recognition, 1119
Bayesian inference methods, 89–97
  AI in medicine (AIM) and, 918–919
  basic formulation, 89
  belief propagation in networks, 95–96
  Boltzmann machine, 126–127
  causal reasoning, 1283–1284
  certainty-factor (CF) models, 131–132
    belief networks, 137
    limits of, 133–135
  decision theory, 317
  evidence pooling, 90
  future event prediction, 93–94
  inversion formula, 89
  knowledge system techniques and, 479
  multihypothesis variables, 91–92
  multiple causes and "explaining away," 94–95
  networks, 95
  prospective and retrospective supports, 89–90
  rational decisions and quality guarantees, 96–97
  uncertain evidence (cascaded inference), 92–93
  virtual (intangible evidence), 93
Bayesian models, information retrieval, 687
Bayesian networks
  belief propagation, 95–96
  defined, 1203
  informal description, 1202–1203
  musical interactions, 1203–1204
  structure of, 95
  subjective probability, 1204
BB1 system, blackboard system building, 122
BBN Butterfly, control structures, 299
BC-Machine, parallel machine architecture, 1092
Beacons, mobile robot sensing, 1410
Beam models, image understanding and, 650
Beam search, 1467–1468
  image understanding and, 650
  machine learning, 793
Bebe hardware, computer chess with, 225
Behavioral analysis
  cognitive modeling, 177–178
  graphs, program synthesis, 69–70
  mental imagery representation, 930–931
  philosophy of AI and, 1138–1139
  reactive planning machines, 1174
BEINGS system, distributed problem solving, 379
Belief maintenance, epistemology and, 466
Belief networks
  AI in medicine (AIM) and, 920
  causal reasoning, 1283–1284
  certainty-factor (CF) models, 136–137
Belief propagation, Bayesian networks, 95–96
Belief relationships, argument comprehension, 36–41
Belief representation systems, 98–108
  argument comprehension, 37–38
  artificial belief systems, 106–107
  belief revisions and, 115
  de re and de dicto beliefs, 99, 101–102
  discourse understanding, 373
  distributed problem solving, 385–386
  epistemology and, 100, 460–461, 466
  history of, 100–101
  knowledge representation, 98
  nested beliefs, 101, 106–107
  philosophy of, 99–100
  preference semantics and, 1184
  referential opacity, 99
  subsystems, 103
  theories and systems, 98–107
    Abelson theory, 107
    Allen and Perrault theory, 105
    belief spaces, 101
    Cohen and Levesque theory, 105
    Cohen and Perrault theory, 104–105
    Colby theory, 106–107
    epistemological theories, 100–102
    fully intensional theories, 101–102
    heuristic theories, 102–105
    Konolige theory, 102–103
    Levesque theory, 103–104
    Moore theory, 102
    psychological theories, 104–108
    Kobsa and Trost theory, 102
    Konolige theory, 102
    mutual belief, 105–106
    speech act theory, 104–105
    user models, 107
    Wilks and co-workers, 106
Belief revision, 110–115
  applications, 114–115
  belief representation and, 115
  circular proofs, 112
  context-layered knowledge bases, 111
  default reasoning, 114
  EL system, 111–112
  foundation concerns, 113
  frame problem, 111
  justification-based vs. assumption based, 113–114
  machine learning, 114
  multiple belief reasoner, 113–114
  natural language understanding, 115
  origin set (OS), 113
  origin tag (OT), 113
  planning systems, 114
  qualitative reasoning, 115
  restriction set (RS), 113
  SNePS system and, 1547–1548
  suppor list (SL) justifications, 112–113
  truth maintenance systems, 112–114
Belief space, truth maintenance systems (TMS), 1619
Belief systems
  argument comprehension, 36–41
    attack relationships, 38–39
    belief representation, 37
    causal beliefs, 37
    evaluative beliefs, 37
    support relationships, 39–40
  commonsense reasoning, 1291–1292
  Dempster-Shafer theory and, 330–331
  image understanding and, 645–646
  phenomenology and, 1133–1134
  reactive planning machines, 1174–1175
  truth maintenance systems (TMS), 1613–1614
Beliefs about beliefs, argument comprehension and, 37
Believed propositions, set of, 111
BELLE chess-playing system, 111
  computer chess programs, 225
  endgame play, 236–237
Benacerraf, G.
Berkeley, C., 462
Berkeley Abstract Machine, 247
Berliner, Hans, 615–616
Bernstein polynomials, range data analysis, 1253–1254
Berry heap, in coroutines, 304
Berwick, R., 763–764
Best-first search
  branch-and-bound technique, 1470
  problem solving, 1222
  spatial reasoning, 1326–1327
Beta-structures, frame theory, 494
Beth's semantic tableaux method, 203
Bezier cubic, shape representation, 1529–1530
Bezier surface patch form, 1253–1254
Bidirectional search
  brute-force search and, 1461–1462, 1463
  processing, bottom-up and top-down, 1234
Bignums, LISP language, 830
Binary n-grams, character recognition, 144–145
Binary constraint network, constraint networks, 277
Binary features
  machine learning and, 786
  object recognition, 1066–1067
  vectors, character recognition, 144–147, 148

INDEX

Binary resolution, 1341–1352
  applications, 1351
  formal treatment, 1344–1349
  historical background, 1342–1344
  inference rules, 1346–1349
  informal treatment, 1343–1344
  reasoning programs, 1350–1351
  robot sensing and, 1385–1386
    end-effector design, 1368
  strategies, 1349–1350
  theory resolution and, 1356–1357
Binding problem, connectionism and, 271
Binocular procedures, three-dimensional feature correspondence, 1650
Biological systems
  AI in medicine (AIM) and, 917–918
  robotics design and, 1375
Blackboard systems, 116–125
  architectures, 116–118
  BB1 system, 122
  behavioral characteristics, 117
  building environments, 121–123
  cognitive psychology and, 182
  CRYSALIS system, 119–120
  current research issues, 123–124
  design and, 337
  engineering and KBES, 450
  features of, 116–117
  GBB system, 122–123
  HASP system, 119
  HEARSAY-II system, 118–119
  HEARSAY-III, 121–122
  image understanding and, 650
  objectives approach, 117–118
  OPM system, 120
  parallel machine architecture, 1096–1097
  planning and, 1166
  protein structure prediction, 1248
  schema theory, 1439–1440
Blindness concept, hermeneutics and, 607
BLISS language, coroutines, 305
Block design, intelligence and, 707
Blocks world, 395–396
  HACKER system and, 595
  planning and, 1160, 1163–1164
  reactive planning, 1172
  spatial reasoning, 1330–1331
Blum transform, shape representation, 1535–1537
Bobrow's RUS parser, cascaded augmented transition networks (CATNs), 562
Bodymotion-then-foothold paradigm, 1405
BOGART system, design and, 336–337
Boguraev, V., preference semantics and, 1188–1189
Boltzmann machine, 126–127
  constraint satisfaction, 290
  cooperative computation, 126
  Hopfield networks optimization, 1021
  learning, 127
  limits of, 127
  machine learning and, 789–790
  neural networks, 1037
  probability representation, 126
Bookkeeping, control structures, 295
Book learning, checkers-playing programs, 155
Books, as AI information source, 845–846
Boolean algebra
  belief representation, 101
  constraint logic programming, 275
  constraint satisfaction, 285–286
  fuzzy databases, 512–513
  higher-order logic, 860
  neural networks, 1038
  preference semantics and, 1188
  range data analysis, 1255
Bootstrapping
  hermeneutics, 596–597
  hermeneutic arc, 602–603
  LISP language, 841
Borders, image properties, 639
Boring, C., 706
BORIS system
  argument comprehension, 33
  discourse understanding, 373–374
  emotion modeling, 447
  integrated in-depth parsing in, 1452–1453
  integrated story analysis, 1571–1572
  memory organization packets (MOPs), 927
  OpEd reasoning scripts and, 1453–1456
Bottom-up parsing, 1231–1232
Bottom-up processing
  control structures, 296–297
  early vision and, 402
  see also Processing, bottom-up and top-down
Bound references, LISP language, 822
Boundary representation
  commonsense reasoning, 1290
  edge detection, 414
  shape representation, 1534–1535
  spatial reasoning, 1324–1325

Boyer-Moor system, mathematical induction, 671
Brain states in a box (BSB) model, 1042–1043
Brain, statistical mechanics of, 1019
Brain theory (BT), schema theory, 1427–1429
Brainstem modeling, neural networks, 1016–1017
Brainstorming, knowledge acquisition, 720
Branch-and-bound search, 1468–1472
  abstract procedures, 1469–1470
  complexity, 1471–1472
  formulation, 1469
  minimum search, 1465–1466
Branching factor, 127–128
  alpha-beta pruning, 25
  checkers-playing programs, 151
  game trees, 552
Branching inquiries, systemic grammar and, 588–590
Breadth-first search
  brute-force search and, 1461–1462
  problem solving, 1222
Breakdown concept, hermeneutics and, 607
Brentano, Franz, 1131
Bridge (card game), minimax procedure, 959
Broad, C. D., 463
Brodatz album, image models, 632–635
Brookhaven Protein Databank, 1244
Brouwer, L. E. J., 464
Brown Corpus, 128–130
  grammatical analysis, 129–130
  history of, 128–129
Brute-force search, 1461–1464
  bidirectional search, 1463
  breadth-first search, 1461–1462
  combinatorial explosion, 1463–1464
  depth-first search, 1462–1463
    iterative-deepening (DFID), 1463
  uniform-cost search, 1461–1462
Bucket brigade problem, machine learning and, 791
Built-in test (BIT), AI military applications, 955
Burton-Roberts, D., 1198
Business applications of AI
  computer-integrated manufacturing (CIM) and, 906
  literature on, 847
Butterfly LISP, parallel machine architecture, 1094

CADR system
  control structures, 298–299
  LISP machine construction and, 842
CADUCEUS system, 131
  causal reasoning and, 1281
  AI in medicine (AIM) and, 918
CAGE systems
  blackboard systems, 124
  parallel machine architecture, 1096–1097
CAIBL system, blackboard systems, 124
Calculus
  incidence, 663–668
    example, 664
    formal definitions, 664–665
    formula assignment, 667
    inference example, 666–667
    logic comparisons, 667–668
    modus ponens rule, 665–666
  lambda, 760–761
  qualitative physics, 1155
  segmentation and, 396
  situation, temporal reasoning, 1334–1336
Call-by-need mechanism, coroutines, 305
Cambridge Language Research Unit (CLRU), 1606
Cambridge Polish, LISP language, 833
Camera modeling, stereo vision, 1561
Candidate elimination algorithm, 255
Candidate states, beam search, 1467–1468
Candidate-elimination algorithm, 792–793
Cannon, 1402–1404
Canny's algorithm, edge detection, 428–429
Canonical formulas, incidence calculus, 665–666
Capture regions, neural networks, 1043
CARPS system, computational linguistics, 206
Cartesian philosophy, philosophy of AI and, 1139
Cascaded augmented transition networks (CATNs), 561–562
Cascaded inference, Bayesian inference methods, 92–93
Case-based reasoning, 1265–1277
  adaptivity, 1267
  algorithm for, 1268–1269
  applications, 1272–1276
    design, 1273
    diagnosis, 1264
    planning, 1273–1274
    problem solving, 1273–1274
  case adaptation, 1272
  classification and interpretation, 1275
  cognitive model, 1276
  design and, 336–337

dynamic memory, 392
experiential learning, 1267
indexing problem, 1269–1270
interpretive, 1274–1275
  problem-solving and, 1276
justification and adversarial reasoning, 1275
knowledge acquisition, 1266–1267
machine learning and, 786, 797–799
memory organization, 1270
memory theory, 1266
natural learning mechanism, 1267–1268
paradigm evolution, 1266–1267
projecting effects, 1275
psychological plausibility, 1267
retrieval algorithms, 1270–1271
robustness, 1266–1267
rule-based reasoning and, 1266–1267
similarity metrics, 1271–1272
system building, 1276
text summarization, 1585
Case frames, natural language understanding
  ellipsis resolution, 1011–1012
  instantiation, 1006–1009
Case grammar, 563–569
  cognitive modeling, 179
  computational linguistics, 207–208
  deep structure, 329–330
  grammatical explanation, 564–565
  meaning representation, 565–566
  Kasus element, 566–567
  lexical decomposition, 809–811
  machine translation, 901–902
  structural features, 564
  surface cases, 564
  systems, 566–569
    Celce's system, 567
    Fillmore system, 566–567
    Grimes system, 567–568
    Schank system, 568–569
  word-expert parsing (WEP), 1113
CASE system, chemistry in AI and, 159
CASEY system, 131
  indexing, 1269
CASNET program
  AI in medicine (AIM) and, 916
  causal reasoning, 920–921
  knowledge acquisition, 917–919
  causal reasoning and, 1281
  domain knowledge, 389
CASREPs, AI military applications, 956–958
Categorization, perception and, 1661–1662
Cattell, R., 709
Causal assignment, inspection systems, 702–704
Causal reasoning, 1279–1286
  AI in medicine (AIM) and, 920–921
    models, 917
  argument comprehension and, 37
  causation theories, 1283–1286
  cognitive psychology and, 185
  explicit models, 1280–1281
  implicit models, 1281–1283
  rule-based systems, 1419
Causal-temporal logic, 1284–1285
Causality
  commonsense reasoning, 1291
  knowledge representation and, 755–756
  qualitative physics, 1156–1157
  text summarization, 1582
Causation theories, 1280, 1283–1286
Cause-and-effect relationships
  Bayesian networks, 1203
  probabilistic networks, 1205–1207
Celce's deep case grammar, 567
CELIA system, case-based reasoning, 1270
CENTAUR system, agenda-based systems and, 22
Certainty
  epistemology, 461
  image understanding and, 645–646
  knowledge system techniques, 479, 481
Certainty-factor (CF) model, 131–137
  belief networks, 136–137
  belief revision and, 135–136
  correlated evidence, 134
  history of, 131
  idiot-Bayes model and, 131–132, 135
  knowledge acquisition and, 137
  limits of, 132
  mechanics, 131–132
  multiple causes for same effect, 133–134
  probabilistic reasoning, 134–135, 1312–1313
  uncertain inferences, 133–134
Certainty grid, spatial reasoning, 1324
ceteris paribus, conditional logic, 856–857
Chaos chess program
  computer chess programs, 225
  neural networks, 1020
Character recognition, 138–149
  applications, 148
  bibliographic guide, 148–149
  classifier combination, 144

contour analysis, 142–143
discriminant function classifiers, 139–140
in context, 144–146
isolated technique, 139
neural networks, 143
pattern recognition, 1127
phenomenological attributes, 143
stroke analysis, 142
structural feature vectors, 140–142
template matching, 139, 141
word recognition, 144–148
contextual postprocessing, 144–145
contextual recognition, 145–146
interactive activation model, 146–147
word shape analysis, 147–148
Character sets, LISP language, 830
Character strings, LISP language, 830
Charlie system, knowledge system building, 487–488
Chart parsing, 1104
algorithms, computational linguistics, 214
Chatham, E., 1229
Chebyshev, 1399
edge detection, 426–428
CHECKERS program, concept learning in, 249
Checkers-playing programs, 150–155
alpha-beta pruning, 25
dynamic ordering, 152
fixed ordering, 152
forward pruning, 152–153
game trees, 150–151, 550
heuristics, 155, 614
learning, 153–155
generalization, 153–155
linear polynomial approach, 153–154
rote learning, 153
signature tables, 154–155
parallel search trees, 155
phase table method, 155
phenomenology and, 1134
representation, 151–152
Samuel's work, 151
search procedures, 152–153
CHEF system, 156
case-based reasoning, 1268
case adaptation, 1272
indexing, 1269–1270
planning applications, 1274
dynamic memory, 392
memory organization packets (MOPs), 927
Chemical reaction synthesis, 157
Chemical structure language, 156–157
Chemical transmitters, adaptive resonance theory and, 19–20
CHEMICS system, chemistry in AI and, 159
Chemistry, AI in, 156–160
agricultural chemicals, 160
computer-aided education (CAE), 160
CRYSALIS system, 119–120
DENDRAL system and, 331
experimental design, 160
expert systems and, 160
future applications, 160
instrumentation, 159
chromatography, 159
infrared spectroscopy, 159
mass spectroscopy, 159
process control, 159
ultracentrifugation, 159
macromolecular structure determination, 160
natural- and chemical-language applications, 156–157
reaction synthesis, 157
structure elucidation, 157–159
candidate ranking, 158–159
enumeration, 158
fragment determination, 157–158
infrared spectroscopy, 157–158
internal consistency checks, 158
mass spectroscopy, 158
nuclear magnetic resonance, 158
X-ray powder diffraction, 158
symbolic algebra applications, 159–160
water chemistry in steam power plants, 160
Cheops program, computer chess and, 235
Chess
BELLE system, 116
minimax procedure, 959
See also Computer chess and search
Chess 4.5 program, 163
CHILD system
computational linguistics, 218
language acquisition, 766–768
CHILDES system, language acquisition and, 769
Chinese room puzzle
philosophy of AI and, 1140
Turing test, 1628
CHIP system, 163
constraint satisfaction, 291
logic programming, 888

Chomsky, Noam
AI in music and, 978–979
cognitive psychology, 182
computational linguistics, 204–205
control structures, 296–297
deep structure, 329–330
hermeneutics and, 600
inductive inference, 675
language acquisition and, 762–763
perceptrons, 1130
systemic grammar and, 583
Chooser semantics, systemic grammar and, 588–590
CHORAL system, AI in music and, 972–973, 977–980
Chordal graphs, constraint networks, 281–282
Chromatic aberration, color vision systems, 199
Chromatography, chemistry in AI and, 159
Chronological backtracking, 85–87
belief revision, 110–111
control structures, 295
planning and, 1170
Chronological ignorance, causal reasoning, 1284–1285
Chronological minimization, default reasoning, 1298
Chunk concept, rule-based systems, 1421
Church's thesis, 163–164
artificial intelligence (AI), 54
Turing machines and, 1623–1624
Church, Alonzo, 1504–1505
CIE commission (International Commission on Illumination), color vision and, 193–194
CIELUV color vision system, 195–196
Circuit analysis
constraint satisfaction, 290
dependency-directed backtracking, 87–88
Circulant matrices, texture analysis, 1594
Circular proofs, belief revisions and, 112–113
Circumscription, 164–167
applications, 167
completeness results, 166
default reasoning, 1296–1297
efficiency, 166–167
formalism, 164–165
generalization, 165
minimal models, 166
soundness, 166
theoretical basis for, 166
CK-LOG, AI military applications, 953–954
CKY grammar, 1104
speed considerations, 1107
CLASSIC system, semantic networks, 1502
Classification frameworks, knowledge acquisition, 722–723
Classifier systems, machine learning and, 791
Clause graphs, graph-based resolution, 1354–1355
Clause language, binary resolution, 1344–1346
CLAVIER system, case-based reasoning, 1273
Clifford-Hammersley theorem, texture analysis, 1592–1593
CLISP
algebraic syntax, 822
InterLisp, 836–837
Clitics, in morphology, 966–967
Clock escapement, spatial reasoning, 1331–1332
CLOS system, 168
Flavors programming, 493
frame theory and, 504–505
Closed World Assumption (CWA)
deductive databases, 323–324
inference, 683
logic programming, 878–879
normal databases, 326
Closures, LISP language, 826–827
CLUSTER/2 program, 172–173
CLUSTER/S program, 172–173
Clustering, 168–176
agglomerative techniques, 170–172
classical view, 170–172
vs. conceptual view, 168–170
color vision systems, 196–197
concept learning, 250–251
conceptual, 168–170, 172–176
attributes, 175–176
machine learning, 793–794
microcomputer problem, 173
repeated discrimination, 173–175
trains problem, 173–175
direct techniques, 172
divisive techniques, 172
machine learning and, 787
multidimensional, 170
one-dimensional, 170
pattern recognition, 1117
earth and space science, 1127
unsupervised learning, 1120
segmentation and, 1474
measurement-space guided spatial clustering, 1474–1480

multidimensional measurement-space clustering, 1479–1480
spatial clustering, 1485–1486
two-dimensional, 170
CMU WARP systolic array machine, 299
^{13}C NMR
AI in chemistry and, 156
internal consistency checks, 158
COBUILD dictionary, dictionary/lexicon construction, 361
COCCI system, semantic networks, 1500
Code-analysis, intelligence and, 711
Coding module, program synthesis, 76–77
Cognition
machine-learning and, 801
meta-knowledge and, 941–942
Cognitive mapping, commonsense reasoning, 1289–1290
Cognitive modeling, 176–180
AI and, 180
basic approaches, 178–179
case-based reasoning, 1276
computational linguistics, 217–218
concept learning, 249
cooperation, distributed problem solving, 381
education and AI, 442
evaluation, 177–178
behavioral data, 178
empirical quality, 178
theoretical quality, 177–178
language acquisition, 761, 764–770
connectionist models, 764–765
grammar acquisition, 766–769
learning and error acquisition, 769
lexicons, 765–766
psycholinguistic studies, 764
language comprehension, 180
learning, 179
memory organization and processes, 179
perception, 179
problem solving and reasoning, 180
purposes, 177
Cognitive psychology, 181–185
AI and, 182–183
artificial intelligence (AI), 55
causal reasoniong, 1285
character recognition, interactive activation model (IAM), 146–147
cognitive science and, 188, 189
epistemology, 460
future trends, 185
history and scope, 182
law in AI and, 782–783
mental imagery representation, 928–931
natural language understanding, 997–999
research areas, 183–185
attention, 183–184
language, 185
memory, 184
perception, 183
thinking, 184–185
scripts and, 1456–1457
Cognitive science, 188–192
artificial intelligence (AI), 55
causal reasoning, 1286
characteristics, 190–192
cognitive psychology and, 182
concept learning, 249
education and AI, 434
expertise and qualitative reasoning, 190
hermeneutics and, 602
human performance models, 190
interdisciplinary approach, 188–189
language acquisition, 189, 761
learning, 190
literature on, 845–846
machine translation, 899
phenomenology and, 1132
representational metapostulate, 191–192
research problems, 189–190
text summarization, 1579
Turing machines and, 1624
vision, 189–190
Cognitive-correlates research, intelligence and, 710
Cognology, 705
Cohen and Levesque theory, 105
Cohen and Perrault theory, 104–105
Cohen's model of argument comprehension, 49–50
Coherence
discourse understanding, 368
distributed problem solving, 382–384
story analysis, 1573
Coherentism, epistemology, 461
Colby, J., 446
COLING conferences, computational linguistics, 218
Collative semantics, preference semantics and, 1189

I-6 INDEX

Collocation
  dictionary/lexicon construction, 354–355
    inter-word entry information, 344–345
  lexical decomposition, 806
  lexical semantics, 813
Color
  constancy, 199–200
  perception and, 1658, 1660
  vision, 192–200
    imaging, 192–194
    optical sensor design, 1514–1515
    perceptual quantity, 199–200
    physical quantity, 198–199
    spaces and transformations, 194–196
    statistical quantity, 196–198
  segmentation and, cluster analysis, 1477–1478
Combat resource allocation, AI military applications, 952–953
Combinator Graph Reduction Multiprocessor, parallel machine architecture, 1094–1095
Combinatorial explosion, brute-force search and, 1463–1464
Command, control, communication and intelligence (C^3I) system, 948–950
Committed choice systems
  logic programming and, 887
  parallel machine architecture, 1091–1092
Common LISP
  CLOS system, 168
  data structures, 830
  history, 839
  NIL symbol, 824
  parallel machine architecture, 1095
  POPLOG systems and, 1182
Commonsense reasoning
  Advice Taker program, 21
  causal reasoning, 1283
  domain knowledge, 1288–1289
  inference, 1288–1289
  knowledge and belief, 1291–1292
  law in AI and, 781–782
  logic and depiction, 853
  physical reasoning, 1290–1291
  plans and goals, 1292–1293
  representation, 1288–1289
  spatial reasoning and, 1289–1290
  temporal reasoning and, 1289
COMMUNAL natural language system, 590–591
Communication
  education and AI, 436–437, 442–443
  knowledge system techniques and, 480
  object-oriented languages, 773
Communicative action theory, hermeneutics and, 601
Comparison, image understanding and, 644
COMPASS system, engineering and KBES, 451
Compatible Time Sharing System (CTSS), 835
Competence research, control structures, 296–297
Compiler toolkit, POPLOG systems and, 1182
Compilers
  coroutines, 304–305
  LISP 1.5, 834
  LISP language, 831–832
    separate compilation, 840
Completed Database (CDB) approach, 323
Completeness, 202–203
  education and AI, 434
  perception and, 1661
  philosophy of AI and, 1142–1143
  predicate logic, 872
  proof procedures, 202–203
Complex instruction set computer (CISC), 243
Complex sequence recognition, neural networks, 1051–1052
Complexity
  inductive inference, 678–679
  knowledge representation and, 755
  neural networks, 1037–1038
Component-based modeling, qualitative physics, 1151, 1154
Componential analysis, lexical decomposition, 807–808
Composability, qualitative physics, 1150–1151
COMPOSE Program, 979
Compounding, in morphology, 967–968
Comprehension
  intelligence and, 707
  mental models and, 933–934
Compressor-cover assembly, robotics design, 1391
Computational analysis
  artificial intelligence (AI), 54–58
  order-sorted logic, 865
  story analysis, 1569
  truth maintenance systems (TMS), 1619
Computational linguistics, 203–218
  applications, 209–213
    automatic programming, 212
    computer-aided instruction, 210–211
    database interface, 209–210

office automation, 211–212
scientific text processing, 213
artificial intelligence (AI), 56
cognitive modeling, 217–218
consultation and, 206–207
discourse understanding, 216
domain-independent implementations 213
formalism, 207–208
grammatical formalisms, 214–215
history of, 204–205
language acquisition, 218
literature sources on, 845
LUNAR system, 208–209
machine translation, 204, 213
natural language processing, 213
natural language understanding, 1006–1009
parsing, 213–214
problem solving and, 206
questioning-answering systems, 205–206
semantics and, 215
SHRDLU system, 208
speech understanding, 218
text generation, 216–217
Computational models
  education and AI, 434
  higher-order logic, 861–862
  programming styles, 1235
  stereo vision, 1560–1563
    camera modeling, 1561
    depth determination, 1562–1563
    feature acquisition, 1562
    image acquisition, 1561
    image matching, 1562
    interpolation, 1563
    preprocessing, 1561–1562
Computational semantics, 1183, 1190–1191
Computational solid geometry (CSG) models, 1534–1535
Computational systems, mental imagery representation, 931
Computational temperature, Hopfield networks optimization, 1021
Computational theory of mind (CTM)
  control structures, 296–297
  philosophy of AI and, 1140–1142
Computer and Automated Systems Association (CASA), 904
Computer-aided design (CAD)
  computer-integrated manufacturing (CIM) and, 905
  history, 332–333
  knowledge system building, 488
  robotics programming, 1394–1395
  robot sensing and, 1386–1387
  shape representation, 1532
Computer-aided education, chemistry in AI and, 160
Computer-aided engineering (CAE), shape representation, 1532
Computer-aided instruction (CAI)
  computational linguistics, 210–211
  education and AI, 435
  human-computer interaction, 621–622
Computer-aided manufacturing (CAM)
  robotics programming, 1394–1395
  shape representation, 1532
Computer-aided process planning (CAPP), 905
Computer architectures, 241–242
  control structures, 297–299
    symbolic computation, 299
  default reasoning, 1298–1299
  massive parallelism, 627
  mobile robot design, 1414–1415
  NON-VON system, 1060–1061
  parallel machine architecture, 1088–1098
    committed choice systems, 1091–1092
    concurrent processing, 1089
    conventional processing, 1089
    executable code, 1089
    knowledge-based systems, 1095–1097
    LISP and functional programming, 1094–1095
    nondeterminism, 1089
    object-oriented systems, 1095
    parallel inference machine, 1090–1091
    primitive control operations, 1089
    PROLOG and logic programming, 1089–1094
    pure parallelism systems, 1093–1094
    shared memory multiprocessors, 1092–1093
    symbolic processing, 1089
  reactive planning machines, 1173–1175
  rule-based systems, 1421–1422
Computer-assisted decision-making (CADM), 420
Computer-based knowledge acquisition systems, 728–731
Computer-based training (CBT), education and AI, 435
Computer chess and search, 224–239
  alpha-beta enhancements, 229–235
    combined enhancements, 232–234
    forward pruning, 229–230

minimal window search, 229
move ordering mechanisms, 230–231
progressive and iterative deepening, 231
transposition and refutation tables, 231–232
anatomy of, 235–239
  endgame play, 236–237
  hardware assists, 235
  knowledge errors, 238–239
  memory tables, 237–238
  selective search, 238
  software advances, 235–236
BELLE system, 116
Chess 4.5, 163
creativity and, 308
future trends, 239
game trees, 550
heuristics and, 611–612
historical perspective, 224–226
horizon effect, 616
KAISSA program, 718
phenomenology and, 1134–1136
philosophy of AI and, 1139–1140, 1143–1144
search techniques, 226–229
  alpha-beta algorithm, 227
  aspiration search, 228
  horizon effect, 229
  minimal game tree, 227–228
  minimax search, 226–227
  quiescence search, 228–229
Computer-integrated manufacturing (CIM)
  ARC-TEC project, 340
  artificial intelligence and, 903–908
    business operations system, 906
    computer-aided design, 905
    expert systems, 906–907
    future trends, 907–908
    historical background, 904–905
    production control, 905–906
    production equipment and processes, 906
    production planning, 905
  robotics design, 1395
  knowledge system building, 488
Computer systems, 241–248
  AI applications, 242–243
    instruction set, 243
    memory management, 243
  Connection machine, 246
  control strategies, 242–243
  data parallelism and, 316–317
  garbage collection, 243, 245–246
  human interface, 243
  list processing, 245–246
  PROLOG machines, 246–248
  storage management, 243–244
  Symbolics machine, 243–246
Computer understanding, conceptual dependency and, 263–264
Computer vision
  color imaging, 194
  human-computer interaction, 621
  shape representation, 1532
Concept discovery, problem solving, 1227
Concept hierarchies
  frame theory and, 499–500
  machine learning, 793–794
Concept learning, 249–257
  analogous learning, 250
  by example, 250
  classical view, 256–257
  clustering analysis, 168, 172
  data-driven, 254–255
  deductive learning, 250
  defined, 249
  exemplar view, 256–257
  extended notions, 256–257
  inductive learning, 250–256
    hypotheses generation, 251–253
    rule-based, 253
  inference classification, 249–251
    inductive, 251–253
  instance space vs. description space, 253–254
  instructional learning, 249–250
  knowledge implantation, 249
  mixed methods, 255–256
  model-driven, 255
  observation and discovery, 250–251
  probabilistic view, 256–257
  research overview, 249
  typicality, 257
  validation, 256
Concept organization, image understanding, 643
Concept writing, semantic networks, 1494
Conceptual clustering, 172–176
  attributes classification, 175–176
  conceptual cohesiveness, 170
  machine learning, 793–794
  repeated discrimination, 173–175
  vs. classical view, 168–170
Conceptual dependency (CD), 259–264
  actions (ACTs), 260–261

ATRANS, 262
ATTEND, 263
computational linguistics, 207–208
  cognitive modeling, 217–218
computer understanding, 263–264
conceptual nominals, 260–261
deep case grammar, 568–569
economy, 262
ELI system, 444–445
EXPEL, 263
GRASP, 263
hermeneutics and, 605
inferences, 264
INGEST, 263
language acquisition, 768
lexical decomposition, 811
language generation, 264
lexical decomposition
  thesaurus construction, 810
MBUILD, 263
meaning similarity, 262
MOVE, 263
MTRANS, 263
natural language understanding, 1007
object categories, 260
overview, 259
parsing, 264
picture producers (PPs), 260–261
preference semantics and, 1183–1184
primitive ACTs, 262–263
primitives, 261–262
PROPEL, 262–263
PTRANS, 262
rules, 260–261
SAM system, 1450–1451
scripts and, 1445
SPEAK, 263
stative forms, 263
structures, 259–260
Conceptual design, 334
Conceptual graphs
  logic, 1503–1504
  semantic networks, 1496–1498
Conceptual modeling, knowledge acquisition and, 725
Concurrency, knowledge representation and, 755–756
Concurrent languages, coroutines, 306
Concurrent logic programming, 291
Concurrent processing, 1089
Concurrent Prolog
  coroutines, 306
  logic programming and, 887
  parallel logic programming language
    data-level representation, 1084
    read-only annotation, 1084
    unsafeness, 1085
Conditional entailment, epsilon-semantics, 474–475
Conditional logic, 854–859
  default reasoning, 1298
  epsilon-semantics, 4668
  material implication, 854–855
  nonmonotonicity, 858–859
  proof theory, 855–857
  semantics, 857–858
Conditional probability formulation, 1593–1594
Conferences, as AI information source, 845, 847
Configuration, design and, 334–335
Confirmation theory, probabilistic reasoning, 1312–1313
Conflicts, planning and, 1164
Confluence, qualitative physics, 1152–1153
Conformal graphs, constraint networks, 281–282
CONG system, graph-based resolution, 1355
Conjugate points, stereo vision, 1560
Conjunctive normal form, propositional logic, 893–894
Connectedness, image properties, 638
Connection graphs, graph-based resolution, 1354
Connection machines, 265–266
  AI applications, 242
  algorithms, 265–266
  components and functions, 246
  computer chess and, 237
  control structures, symbolic computation, 299
  data parallelism, 315
  hardware, 265
  host machine, 265
  parallel machine architecture, 1097
  software, 265–266
Connection method, 266–268
  Gentzen's calculi, 266
  matrix reduction, 267
  order-sorted logic, 865
  predicate logic, 266
  Skolem functions, 267
Connectionism, 268–273
  AI in music and, 973, 979–980
  applications, 272–273

basic model, 269–270
Boltzmann machine, 126
cognitive modeling, 178
cognitive psychology and, 182
  memory, 184
cognitive science and, 190
distributed, 271–272
  network construction, 272
distributed problem solving, 379
localist, 270–271
  cross-talk, binding and learning, 271
  lateral inhibition and positive feedback, 270–271
  predictability and convergence, 261
motivations, 268–269
philosophy of AI and, 1141
schema theory, 1433
see also Neural networks
Connectionist learning, machine learning and, 788–790
Connectionist models
  language acquisition, 764–766
  learning and error correction, 769–770
Connectives, propositional logic, 893–894
CONNIVER system, 274
  control structures, 296
  HACKER program and, 595
  knowledge representation and, 744
CONS cells and lists
  LISP language
    run time typing, 829
    syntax, 820–821
CONS machine, LISP machine construction and, 842
CONSAT, constraint satisfaction, 290–291
Consistency
  algorithms
    constraint networks, 276–280
    constraint satisfaction, 285–289, 287–288
  constraint logic programming, 275
  epsilon-semantics, 471
  knowledge acquisition and, 725
  logic and depiction, 854
  object recognition, search techniques, 1071–1072
  proof by, mathematical induction, 671–672
Constancy, perception and, 1660
Constraint logic programming (CLP), 274–275, 887–888
Constraint networks, 276–284
  backtracking, 276–277
  consistency strategies, 276–277
  definitions, 276
  graph-based algorithms, 277–284
    acyclic networks and tree clustering, 281–282
    backtracking, 283–284
    cycle cutset scheme, 282–283
    directional and adaptive consistency, 278–280
    nonseparable component decomposition, 282
    representations, 277–278
    tree networks, 278
    w^*-based tractability, 280–281
  incidence calculus, 665–666
  subset, defined, 276
  subsumption, design and, 336
Constraint propagation
  design and, 336
  engineering and KBES, 450
Constraint satisfaction, 285–291
  applications, 289–291
  arc consistency algorithm, 288
  backtracking and consistency algorithms, 286–289
  Boolean problems, 285–286
  case-based reasoning, design applications, 1273
  computer-aided design and, 332
  constraint networks, 276
  cooperative algorithms, 290
  design and, 332, 336
  early vision and, 405, 407–408
  engineering and KBES, 450
  k-consistency, 288–289
  knowledge system techniques and, 478–481
  logic and depiction, 853
  music and AI, 977
  object recognition search techniques, 1069–1073
  path consistency, 288
  planning and, 1166
  problem solving, 1225–1226
  programs for, 290–291
  qualitative physics, 1151
  relaxation algorithms for optimization, 289–290
  robot end-effector design, 1367–1370
  search techniques and, 1460–1461
  simulated annealing, 290
  situation semantics, 1543–1544
  truth maintenance systems and, 1620
Contact force, tactile sensor design, 1516
Context
  concept learning and, 2560257
  philosophy of AI and, 1144

truth maintenance systems (TMS), 1619
Context space theory, discourse understanding, 369
Context-free grammars (CFG)
  augmented transition network (ATNs), 555–556
  computational linguistics, 215
  inductive inference, 675, 678
  natural language understanding, 1001–1002
  parsing, 1100
  phrase-structure grammars and, 574–575
Context-free language (CFL), phrase-structure grammars and, 575
Context-free phrase structure grammar (CF-PSG), 570
Context-layered knowledge bases, belief revision and, 111
Context-sensitive grammars (CSG), phrase-structure grammars and, 574–575
Contextual information
  character recognition and, 144–145
  discourse understanding, text analysis, 371
  machine translation, 899
Contiguity problem, neural networks, 1041–1042
Contingent propositions, propositional logic, 894
Continuity, heuristics and, 614–615
Contour analysis, character recognition, 142–143
Contract-net protocol, distributed problem solving, 382–383
Contradictions
  belief revision and, 111
  by negation, argument comprehension, 38–39
  dependency-directed backtracking, 86–87
  propositional logic, 894
  truth maintenance systems (TMS)
    assumption-based systems, 1618
    justification-based systems, 1616–1617
Control
  knowledge, procedural problem formulations, 1217
  parallelism, data parallelism and, 315–316
  robotics design and, 1378
    mobility, 1380
Control agreement principle (CAP), generalized phrase-structure grammar and, 571
Control structures, 293–299
  AI in medicine (AIM) and, 918
  completeness, 203
  computer architecture, 297–299
    symbolic computation, 298–299
  education and AI, 435
  history, 294
  image understanding and, 646–651
  knowledge representation and, 751–752
  knowledge system techniques and, 479
  processing, bottom-up and top-down, 1229
  programming language design, 294–296
    modularity, 294–295
    serial virtual machines, 295–296
  representation design, 296–297
    competence and performance, 296
    competence research, 296–297
    logic programming, 297
    procedural-declarative controversy, 297
  word-expert parsing (WEP), 1110
Conventional implicatures, presupposition theory, 1199
Convergence
  connectionism and, 271
  inductive inference, 674
Conversational implicatures, computational linguistics, 216
CONVERSE system, computational linguistics, 206
Convexity, image properties, 639
Conway approach, game playing and, 543
Cooccurrence matrices
  image models, 628
  lexical semantics, 813
  texture analysis, 1595
Coon's patch description, tactile sensing data fusion, 1520–1521
CO-OP system, computational linguistics, 210, 216
Cooperative algorithms
  constraint satisfaction, 290
  neural networks, 1016–1017
  schema theory, 1428
Cooperative parallelism
  neural networks and, 1018–1019
  parallel logic programming, 1082
Core matcher, adaptive planning and, 8–9
Corner detection, edge detection, 432
Coroutines, 301–306
  applications, 304–305
    compilers, 304
    operating systems, 305
    receiver-sender communication, 305
    simulation, 305
  artificial intelligence, 305–306
    concurrent languages, 306
    lazy evaluation, 305–306

object-oriented programming, 306
control structures, 295
explicit vs. implicit sequencing, 302
implementation, 303–304
   backtracking, 304
   semantic differences, 303
   spaghetti stack, 303–304
multipass algorithms and pipelines, 303
procedural relations, 302
reactivation point, 302–303, 303
symmetric vs. semisymmetric, 303
Corpus Juris Mechanicum, law in AI and, 779
Correlation, probabilistic networks, 1205–1207
Correspondence
  object recognition, 1073
  search, 1069
  stereo vision, 1560
Covariance matrix, range data analysis, 1261
CP family language, parallel logic programming language, 1086
CPL, POP-11 and, 1182
Craik, F., 932
Craik-Cornsweet-O'Brien effect, perception and, 1658
Cray Blitz, computer chess with, 225
Creativity, 307–308
  Turing machines and, 1624
Credit problem assignment, neural networks, 1033
Critical hermeneutics, 600–601
Critical temperatures, simulated annealing, 1539
Critique of ideology, 600–601, 605
CRITIQUE system
  computational linguistics, 212
  dictionary/lexicon construction, 343–344
Cross-talk, connectionism and, 271
Cryptoarithmetic problems, problem solving, 1225–1226
CRYSALIS system, 119–120
Crystallized intelligence, 709–710
CSI BATTLE PLANNER, case-based reasoning, 1274–1276
CSL system, concept learning, 255
CUBE program, LISP language and, 840
Cue Interaction Model, schema theory, 1436
Culicover, 763–764
Curie temperature, Hopfield networks, 1020
Current states, beam search, 1467–1468
Curvatures
  range data analysis, 1255–1258
  shape representation, 1528
    compound curves, 1529–1530
Curve and flow recovery, early vision, 412
CYBERNETIC COMPOSER program
  AI in music and, 972–973, 980
  representation and, 978
Cybernetics, 309–311
  CONNIVER system, 274
  epistemology, 310–311
  literature on, 844
  mechanisms of, 310
CYC project
  causal reasoning, 1283–1284
  dictionary/lexicon construction, 357
  machine translation, 900
  thesauri and, 1611
CYCL system
  dictionary/lexicon construction, 357
  knowledge representation and, 754
Cycle cutset, constraint networks, 282–283
Cyclic networks, machine learning and, 790
CYCLOPS system
  case-based reasoning, 1273
  stereo vision, 1564
CYRUS system, 312
  case-based reasoning, 1270
  dynamic memory, 392
  memory organization packets (MOPs), 927
  script acquisition and, 1457–1458

DADO system, 313–315
  parallel machine architecture, 1097
  problem definition, 313–314
Dag isomorphism, probabilistic networks, 1206
DARPA (Defense Advanced Research Projects Agency), 947–949
Dartmouth Conference, 705, 832–834
  literature on, 844
Data abstraction, LISP language, 826
Database systems
  deductive, 320–327
    alternative, 326–327
    basic axioms, 321–322
    definite databases, 322–325
    disjunctive, 327
    history and purpose, 320
    implementation, 324–325
    logic and lattice theory, 320–321
    negation, 323–324
    semantics, 322–323

stratification, 325–326
default reasoning, 1294–1295
fuzzy sets and, 508–514
  data models, 508–509, 513–514
  heterogeneous data models, 510–511
  incomplete data, 512
  information storage and retrieval models, 511
  null and range values, 509
  query evaluation, 512–513
  retrieval techniques, 511–513
  uniform data models, 509–510
information retrieval, 684
interface, computational linguistics, 209–210
logic programming and, 883–884
robotics design, programming, 1394–1395
Data Diffusion Machine, parallel machine architecture, 1093
Data-directed activation, image understanding and, 648
Data-driven processing
  incremental generalization and modification, 254–255
  processing, bottom-up and top-down, 1230
Data fusion, sensor technology, 1519–1523
  ladar and visual sensing, 1521
  range and visual sensing, 1521–1522
  tactile and visual sensing, 1520–1521
  thermal and visual sensing, 1519–1520
Data-level representation, parallel logic programming language, 1084
DATALOG program, definite databases, 322
Data parallelism, 315–317
  computer applications, 316–317
  control parallelism, 315–316
  DADO system, 313
  hardware issues, 316
  software issues, 316
Data structures
  LISP language, 830
  parallel machine architecture, 1089
  recursion and, 1340
  unification, 1631
DATR language, dictionary/lexicon construction, 352–353
DBTG network model, fuzzy databases, 508, 513–514
DDB technique, engineering and KBES, 450
DEACON system, computational linguistics, 206
Dead reckoning, mobile robot sensing, 1410
Debugging environment, LISP language, 840
Decay parameter, connectionism and, 273
Decision support systems, case-based reasoning, 1276
Decision surface, neural networks, 1036
Decision theory, 317–320
  AI in medicine (AIM) and, 919–920
  AI in music and, 974
  alternative modeling, 319–320
  Bayesian inference methods, 96–97
  cognitive psychology and, 184–185
  formal decision analysis, 317–318
  fuzzy sets and, 540
  knowledge acquisition and, 725–726
  medical applications, 318–319
  pattern recognition, 1118–1120
Decision trees
  decision theory, 318
  machine learning, 793–794
  pattern recognition, 1121
    earth and space science, 1127
  robot sensing and, 1385
Declarative knowledge, meta-knowledge and, 943
Declarative problem formulation, 1214–1216
Declarative representations, knowledge representation and, 746–747
Declarative semantics
  constraint logic programming, 274–275
  disjunctive databases, 327
  parallel logic programming language, 1083
  stratified databases, 325–326
Decomposable searching problem, DADO system, 313
Decomposition
  image properties, 639
  lexical, 806–811
  syntactic pattern recognition, 1122–1123
  theorem, fuzzy set theory, 538–539
DECTALK system, neural networks, 1040
Deduction
  algorithms, 935–938
  mental models and, 934–935
Deductive database systems, 320–327
  basic axioms, 321–322
  definite databases, 322–324
  disjunctive databases, 327
  history, 320
  implementation, 324–235
    stratified databases, 326
  logic and lattice theory, 320–321
  logic programming and, 883–884

negation, 323–324
normal databases, 326–327
semantics
  definite databases, 322–323
  stratified databases, 325–326
Deductive inference, abduction, 2–3
Deductive logic, 851
Deductive systems
  automatic programming, 62–63
  predicate logic, 869–870
  propositional logic, 894–896
    semantics, 896
    syntax, 894–895
Deep-binding, in LISP language, 823
Deep structure, 328–330
  case grammar, 563
    grammatical explanation, 564–565
    meaning representation, 565–566
  computational linguistics, 205
  lexical decomposition, 808
  meaning, 329–330
  natural language processing, 329
    fuzzy logic, 517
  parsing, 1105
  word-expert parsing (WEP), 1111–1112
Deep Thought, computer chess with, 225
Default logic (DL)
  default reasoning, 1296–1297
  nonmonotonic reasoning and, 1304
Default reasoning, 1294–1299
  architectures, 1298
  autoepistemic logic, 1297
  belief revisions and, 114–115
  circumscriptions, 1296–1297
  conditional logics, 1298
  databases, 1294–1295
  epsilon-semantics, 468, 472
  image understanding and, 646
  inheritance hierarchies, 692–693, 1295
    expressiveness limitations, 695
  knowledge representation and, 754
  logic, 852
  model preference, 1298
  negation as failure, 1295
  nonmonotonic logic, 1296–1297
  truth maintenance systems, 1295–1296
Defclass command, frame theory and, 504–505
Definite clause grammar (DCG)
  augmented transition network (ATN) grammars, 559–560
  dictionary/lexicon construction, 347
Definite databases, defined, 322
de Groot, A. D., semantic networks, 1495
Deictic representation, reactive planning machines, 1174
Deinstantiation, schema theory, 1431
Delaunay equation, texture analysis, 1595
Delay synapse networks, associative memory, 1050–1051
Delegation, object-oriented languages, 775
Delgrande, M., 859
DELPHI system
  dictionary/lexicon construction, 343
  lexical entry structure, 348, 350–351
  word senses, 354
Demodulation, binary resolution, 1350
Demon systems
  argument comprehension and, 33
  inheritance hierarchies, 698
  natural language generation, 988
  word-expert parsing (WEP), 1113
Dempster-Shafer theory, 330–331
  AI in medicine (AIM) and, 919
  engineering and KBES, 450
  fuzzy set theory, support pairs, 529
  incidence calculus, 667–668
  probabilistic reasoning, 1313–1314
DENDRAL system, 331
  agenda-based systems and, 21–22
  AI in medicine (AIM) and, 916
  chemistry in AI and, 156
    mass spectroscopy, 158–159
    structure elucidation, 159
  control structures, 296–297
  domain knowledge, 389
  law in AI and, 778–779
  problem solving
    constraint satisfaction problem, 1225–1226
    derivation-formation spectrum, 1226
    interpretation problems, 1225
Dendrites, neural network modeling, 1017–1018
Dendrogram, clustering analysis, 170–172
Dennett's scheme, philosophy of AI and, 1139–1140
Department of Defense (DOD), AI military applications, 947–949
Dependency grammar, semantic networks, 1495
Dependency networks, justification-based systems, 1615
Dependency-directed backtracking, 86–87

belief revision, 110–111
constraint networks, 284
constraint satisfaction, 287
engineering and KBES, 450
history of, 87–88
logic programming and, 885
planning and, 1170
Depiction, logic and, 853–854
Depth determination, stereo vision, 1562–1563, 1565–1566
Depth-first branch-and-bound (DFBB) search, 1473
Depth-first generation procedure
 alpha-beta pruning, 22–24
 minimax procedures, 24–25
Depth-first iterative-deepening search (DFID), 1463
Depth-first search, 1473
 branch-and-bound technique, 1470
 brute-force search and, 1462–1463
 checkers-playing programs, 151
 computer chess and, 226
 constraint satisfaction, 289
 coroutines, 304
 inheritance hierarchies, 693
 logic programming, PROLOG, 877
 object recognition, 1071–1072
 problem solving, 1222
Derivation
 dictionary/lexicon construction, 343–344
 morphology, 964–965
 problems, 1219–1220
Derivatives, qualitative physics, 1152
Descartes, René, 462
Described situation, situation semantics, 1545
Description space, concept learning, 253–254
Descriptions, predicate logic, 871–872
Design
 AI techniques in, 336–337
 approaches to, 334
 case-based reasoning, 1273
 engineering and KBES, 452–453
 history, 332–333
 knowledge-based reasoning in, 333–334
 machine learning and, 797–799
 procedures in, 335
 research in, 337
 sample systems for, 337
 theories, 331–332
 types of, 334–335
 see also Computer-aided design
Design rule systems, inspection, 702
Designer-SOAR system, design and, 336
Detail hiding, schema theory, 1431
Deterministic finite state machines, 677
Deterministic networks
 Hopfield networks optimization, 1021
 neural networks, associative memory, 1043–1044
Deterministic parser, language acquisition, 763
Detour behavior, schema theory, 1436–1437
Deutsch, Peter, 835
Dev steropsis model, schema theory, 1436
Dev, P., 1016–1017
DEVISER system, temporal planning, 1168–1169
Dextrous hand robot design, 1365–1367
DFKI organization, 339–340
 AKA-WINO project, 340
 ARC-TEC project, 340
 DISCO project, 340
 PHI systems, 340
 WIP project, 340
DFS tree, constraint networks, 283
Diagnostic techniques
 AI in medicine (AIM) and, 921
 computer-aided design and, 333
 engineering and KBES, 451
 truth maintenance systems and, 1620
DIAGRAM grammar, dictionary/lexicon construction, 350, 352
Dialogue systems
 discourse understanding, 376
 distributed problem solving, 385–386
 natural language understanding, 1010–1013
DIAMOND grammar, computational linguistics, 215
DIANA-2 system, 1573
Dichromatic reflection model, color vision systems, 198–200
Dictionary/lexicon construction, 341–362
 basic definitions, 341–342
 contrastive and complementary types, 816
 knowledge acquisition, 355–362
  machine-readable dictionaries, 358–360
  manual acquisition, 356–358
  text corpora, 360–362
 lexical decomposition, 807, 810
 lexical entry semantics, 345–347
  nominal semantics, 346–347
  verbal semantics, 345–346
 machine translation, 900

morphology, 970
organization, 347–355
 collocations and idioms, 354–355
 entry structure, 347–352
  abbreviation conventions, 348–349
  category-subcategory relations, 347–348
  morphology, 349–352
 global structure, 352–353
 lexical inheritance theories, 352–353
 mental lexicon, 353–354
 word senses, 354
 parsing lexicons, 342–345
  inter/word entry information, 343–345
  intra-entry information, 342–343
Dictionary Viterbi Algorithm (DVA), 145–146
Diday model, neural networks, 1024–1025
Differencing operations, motion-based segmentation, 1488
Differential equation metaphor, 415
Differential pulse code modulation (DPCM), 630
Differentiation
 edge detection, 397
  intensity changes, 422–426
  image understanding and, 644
Digit span, intelligence and, 707
Digit-symbol, intelligence and, 707
Digitalis Therapy Advisor, AI in medicine (AIM) and, 921
Dijkstra's algorithm
 branch-and-bound search, 1472
 brute-force search and, 1462
Dilthey, W., 597
Dimension, shape representation, 1527
Direct range measurement, robot sensing and, 1382–1385
Direct techniques, clustering analysis, 172
Directed acyclic graphs (DAGs)
 graphoids and, 593
 inheritance hierarchies, 691–692
 possibilistic reasoning, 1317
Directional consistency, constraint networks, 278–280
Directional-isotropy assumption
 texture analysis, 1598–1600
 visual recovery, shape from texture, 1673–1675
DISCO project, 340
DISCON system, clustering analysis, 172–173
Discontinuity, edge detection, 397–398
Discontinuous regularization, visual recovery, 1678–1679
Discourse constituent unit (DCU), discourse understanding, 370–371
Discourse module, program synthesis, 74–75
Discourse situation, situation semantics, 1545
Discourse understanding, 365–377
 case grammar, 565
 computational linguistics, 216
 mental models and, 933–934
 natural language modes, 376–377
 plan recognition, 374–376
  dialogue systems, 376
  speech acts, 374–375
  speech events, 376
 presupposition theory, 1199
 semantic grammar, 582
 story analysis, 1568
 structure, 366–371
  coherence, 368
  context space theory, 369
  dynamic model, 370–371
  modeling, 368–369
  pronoun resolution, 368–369
  segmentation of, 366–368
  theory, 369–371
 textual meaning, 371–374
  anaphora, 371–372
  background knowledge and plausible inference, 372–373
  logical formalisms, 371
  story summation, 373–374
  truth conditions, 371
Discourse units (DU), discourse understanding, 370–371
Discrete event simulation, planning and, 1169–1170
Discrete symbolic simulation, causal reasoning, 1282–1283
Discreteness, temporal reasoning, 1337
Discriminant function classifiers
 character recognition, 139–140
 neural networks, 1036
Discrimination nets, cognitive modeling, 180
Disjoint activities, distributed problem solving, 382
Disjunctive databases, 327
Disjunctive normal form (DNF), propositional logic, 893–894
Disparity detection, stereo vision, 1566–1567
Disparity-gradient limit, stereo vision, 1566
DISPO Advisor, AI in medicine (AIM) and, 922

Distance effect, visual recovery, 1672–1675
Distance measures, memory-based reasoning, 1300–1301
Distanciation, phenomenological hermeneutics, 601–602
Distinctiveness, memory and, 457
Distributed artificial intelligence (DAI), 1427–1429
Distributed computation studies, 626–627
Distributed connectionism, 271–272
Distributed hypothesis testing, adaptive resonance theory and, 14
Distributed interpretation, distributed problem solving, 380
Distributed planning, 380
Distributed problem solving, 379–386
 actor formalisms, 4
 AI military applications, 949–950
 applications, 380–381
 beliefs and concurrency, 385–386
 blackboard architectures, 124
 defined, 380
 functionally accurate cooperation, 383
 global coherence, 382
 incomplete and inconsistent information, 382
 local control, 384–385
 multiagent planning, 384
 negotiation, 382–383
 organizational structuring, 383–384
 task decomposition, 381–382
Distributed systems analysis, 104
Distributed Vehicle Monitoring Testbed (DVMT), 124
Distributionist approach, connectionism, 270
Divide-and-conquer algorithm
 machine learning, 793–794
 parallel logic programming, 1082
 problem solving, reduction schema, 1223–1224
Divisive techniques, clustering analysis, 172
Document retrieval, 685
Domain analyst, automatic programming, 81
Domain-dependent criteria
 backtracking, 85
 neural networks, 1019
 planning and, 1165–1166
Domain designer, automatic programming, 81
Domain expert, program synthesis, 75–76
Domain-independent systems
 computational linguistics, 213
 engineering and KBES, 451
Domain knowledge, 388–390
 commonsense reasoning, 1288
 consultation programs, 389
 design and, 332
 education and AI, 435
 first-generation expert systems, 389
 image understanding and, 642, 658–660
 knowledge acquisition and, 723–726
 ladar sensor data fusion and, 1521
 languages and environments, 389–390
 machine learning, 792
 machine translation, 899
  empiricist approach, 794–795
 protein structure prediction, 1238
Domain-specific planning, 1169
Dominance, branch-and-bound search, 1471
Domination predicate, phrase-structure grammars and, 575
DOOM system, parallel machine architecture, 1095
Dotted lists and pairs, LISP language syntax, 821
DOUBLETALK program, 979
Dreyfus, Hubert
 hermeneutics, 596
 phenomenology and, 1134
 philosophy of AI and, 1143–1144
Drilling Advisor system, 480–481, 487–488
D-SCRIPT, belief representation, 101
Dual lattice image models, 632
Dual-constraint graph, 277–278
Duration, memory and, 457
Durbin, R., 1023
DWIM program, InterLisp, 836–837
DYNA program, machine-learning and, 801
Dynamic discourse model (DDM), 370–371
Dynamic link architecture, neural networks, 1053–1055
Dynamic logic
 modal logic and, 864
 temporal reasoning, 1337–1338
Dynamic memory, 391–392
 case-based reasoning, 1266
Dynamic ordering, checkers-playing programs, 152
Dynamic programming, branch-and-bound search, 1472
Dynamic schema instantiation (DSI), 1319
Dynamic scope, LISP language, 824
Dynamic systems
 legged robots, 1401–1402
 naive physics, 1148

neural networks
  associative memories, 1042–1043
  stability, 1019–1020
DYPAR system, natural language understanding, 1005

Eager execution, logic programming and, 886
Earley's algorithm, augmented transition network (ATN) grammars, 560–561
Early vision, 394–416
  active vision research, 414–415
  as controlled hallucination, 401–402
  constraint satisfaction, 405, 408–409
  continuous relaxation labeling, 405
  cooperative processes and energy minimization, 404–405
  corners and parts, 414
  curve and flow recovery, 412
    flow patterns, 412–413
    lines vs. tangents, 412
    parallel surface contours, 412–413
  differential equation metaphor, 415
  discrete relaxation labeling, 405
  figure/ground and structural grouping, 414
  free boundary value problems, 415
  general purpose models, 409–410
  high-level vision, 415–416
  inference mechanisms, 411
  intensity discontinuities, 411–412
  intrinsic images, 407
  inverse optics, 406
  low-level and high-level vision segmentation, 395–403
    discontinuity and edge detection, 397–400
    edge detection knowledge, 400–402
    Laplacians, Mach, and edges, 396–397
    physiological optics and unconscious inference, 395
    rigidity of early systems, 402–403
    Roberts' system of segmentation and matching, 395–396
    similarities vs. differences, 396
  neural modeling, 404
  organization and complexity, 403–406
    abstraction and general purpose models, 403
    uncertainty, 403
  parallelism and, 404–405
    functional streams, 409
  primal sketches, 407
  primate visual systems, 408–409
  qualitative vs. quantitative knowledge, 409–410
  rigidity, 410
  segmentation to description, 402
  segmentation to surfaces, 406–409
  shading from shape, 406
  shape from shading, 406
  structure into function, 410–415
  surfaces, 414
  symbolism, 408
  tasks, tools, and techniques, 405–406
  texture, 413–414
Earth science, pattern recognition and, 1127
Ebcioglu, K., 978–979
Echoic memory, 455–456
Economic theory
  argument comprehension, 35–36
    trade graphs, 35–36
  conceptual dependency and, 262
  distributed problem solving, 385–386
  robotics design and, 1376
ECRC (European Computer-Industry Research Center), 420–421
  CHIP program, 163
  Knowledge System (EKS), 421
  parallel machine architecture, 1088
  structure and policies, 420–421
  technical program, 420–421
ED-JOBS system, argument comprehension, 32–34
Edge detection, 422–433
  color vision systems, 197–198
  corners and parts, 414
  curve and flow recovery, 412
  differential equation metaphor, 415
  as differentiation, 397
  discontinuity and, 397–398
  figure/ground and structural grouping, 414
  flow patterns, 412–413
  free boundary value problems, 415
  intensity changes, 422–432
    one-dimensional detection, 424–428
    two-dimensional detection, 428–432
  intensity discontinuities, 411–412
  lines vs. tangents, 412–413
  neural networks, 1054–1055
  object recognition, feature matching, 1067–1068
  parallel surface contours, 412–413
  range data analysis, 1262
  recovering properties, 432–433

robot sensing and
  intensity image processing, 1385–1386
  range image processing, 1386–1388
scale and, 398
segmentation and, 396
  hybrid linkage region growing, 1481–1482
  spatial clustering, 1485–1486
texture, 413–414
tools and techniques for, 405–406
Education, AI in, 434–443
  cognitive science and, 188
  communication reasoning, 436–437
  control issues, 435
  design criteria, 443
  engineering and KBES, 452
  example systems, 437–442
    applications, 439–440
    current trends, 437–439
    evaluation of, 441–442
    history of, 437
  expert knowledge reasonings, 435–436
  intelligence and, 709
  knowledge acquisition, 435
  knowledge representation, 435
  research issues, 442–443
  student knowledge reasoning, 436
  teaching knowledge reasoning, 435–436
  theoretical, 435–437
EES framework, explanation and, 490
Efficiency
  circumscription and, 166–167
  processing, bottom-up and top-down, 1233
Ego-motion polar transform (EMP), 1488–1489
Eidetic phenomenology
  hermeneutics and, 601–602
  meaning in, 607–608
Eigenbehavior, cybernetics, 311
Eigenorganization, cybernetics, 311
Eigenvalues
  neural networks, 1043
  range data analysis, 1257
Eigenvectors, range data analysis, 1257
Eight Puzzle
  combinatorial explosion, 1464
  search techniques and, 1460
Eight Queens Problem
  logic programming and, 886
  search techniques and, 1460–1461
EL system, belief revision and, 111–112
Elastic net algorithm, neural networks, 1022–1023
Electric actuation, robot end-effector design, 1368
Electron density map, CRYSALIS system, 119–120
Electronic Dictionary Project, 900
Electronic text, as AI information source, 847–848
ELI system, 444–445
  script application in, 1450–1451
ELIZA system, 445
  computational linguistics, 206–207
  human-computer interaction, 621
  natural language understanding, 1000
  Turing test, 1627
Ellipsis, 445–446
  context and, 446
  natural language understanding, 1010
    case frame resolution, 1011–1012
  semantic grammar, 582
  sentence structure and, 445–446
  substitution and, 445
Elman network, 1050
Elongatedness, image properties, 639
Embedding situation, situation semantics, 1545
Emergent behavior, reactive planning machines, 1179
EMI program, AI in music and, 973
E-MOPS, Cyrus system, 312
Emotion modeling, 446–448
  naive psychology, 447
  process control, 447–448
  theory testing, 446–447
Emotionality, memory and, 458
Empire State Building (ESB) network, 1175–1176
Empiricism
  cognitive modeling, 178
  epistemology and, 463–464
  language acquisition and, 762–763
  machine learning and, 792–795
    concept hierarchies, 794–795
    decision trees, 793–794
    production rules, 792–793
  philosophy of AI and, 1145–1146
EMYCIN, 448, 982
  knowledge system building, 487–488
  logic programming and, 884–885
ENCORE Multimax machines, 1095–1096
End-effector technology, robotics, 1357–1374
  active design, 1364–1367
    dextrous hands, 1365–1367
    two-fingered servo grippers, 1364–1367

design issues, 1367–1372
  actuation methods, 1368
  constraints, 1367–1370
  fixturing integration, 1371–1372
  force analysis, 1368–1371
  parts integration, 1372
  sensing, 1367–1368
  transmission systems, 1370
  versatility, 1371–1372
  wrist integration, 1371–1372
how/why diagrams, 1372–1374
human hand models, 1358–1360
passive design, 1361–1364
  soft and irregular shape grippers, 1362–1364
  two-fingered angular- and parallel-jaw grippers, 1361–1362
  vacuum and magnetic grippers, 1362
robotics research and, 1378–1379
Endgame play, computer chess and, 236–237
Endocentric terms, morphology, 968
Endorsement theory, possibilistic reasoning, 1317
Energy minimization, early vision and, 404
Engagement, adaptive planning and, 7
Engineering, knowledge-based expert systems, 448–453
  applications, 448–449, 451–453
  design, 452–453
  diagnosis-classification, 451
  education, 452
  monitoring and control, 451–452
  planning, 452
  problem-solving techniques, 449–450
  tools, 450–451
  see also Computer-aided engineering (CAE)
Entscheidungsproblem, Church's thesis, 163
Entailment analysis, presupposition theory, 1200–1201
Environment, intelligence and, 711–712
ENVISION program, naive physics, 1148
Envisioning
  qualitative physics, 1155–1156
  temporal reasoning, 1336
EP system, program synthesis, 67
EPAK system, engineering and KBES, 452
EPAM model, 179, 454
Epiphenomenal properties, mental imagery representation, 929
Epipolar constraint
  stereo vision, 1560
  tactile sensing data fusion, 1520–1521
Epipolar line, stereo vision, 1560
Epipolar plane, stereo vision, 1560
Episodic memory, 454–459
  dynamic memory, 391–392
  semantic memory and, 454–455
Epistemology, 460–466
  AI and, 464–466
  belief representation, 100–102, 461
  central problems, 460–461
  certainty, 461
  cybernetics, 310–311
  frame theory and, 500
  history of, 461–464
    classical period, 461–462
    Enlightenment, 462
    Kant and, 462–463
    twentieth century, 463–464
  justification, 461
  knowledge sources, 460–461
  philosophy of AI and, 1137, 1143–1146
EPISTLE system, 468
  computational linguistics, 212
Epsilon-semantics, 468–475
  axiomatic characterization, 470
  conditional entailment, 474–475
  consistency, 471
  definitions, 469–470
  inference rules, 470
  knowledge levels, 469
  maximum entropy (ME) approach, 474
  meta-theorems, 470
  probabilities, 468–469
  semimonotonicity, 470–471
  system Z, 472–473
Equality graphs, graph-based resolution, 1355
Equality inferencing, 475–477
Equational theories, unification, 1633
Equations, qualitative physics, 1152–1153
ERE architecture, reactive planning machines, 1177–1178
Ergodicity assumption, texture analysis, 1590
ERMA program
  computational linguistics, 217
  historical background, 987–988
  natural language generation, 987
Error backpropagation (EBP) algorithm, 1125
Error correction and detection
  error-correction rule, neural networks, 1036–1037
  robotics design and, 1376

spatial reasoning, 1328
ESPRIT I and II programs, parallel machine architecture, 1088
ETHER language, distributed problem solving, 379
Euclidean distance
  image properties, 639
  memory-based reasoning, 1301
Euclidean space
  neural networks, 1035–1036
  segmentation and, 1474
EUFID system, computational linguistics, 210
Euler-Lagrange equations, visual recovery, 1679
E-unification problem, equality inferencing, 476–477
EURISKO, 477
  concept learning, 251
  heuristics and, 614–615
European Declarative System (EDS)
  ECRC programs, 421
  parallel machine architecture, 1096
Evaluation
  AI in medicine (AIM) and, 919, 922
  game playing and, 546–547
  heuristics and, 612–614
    search, 1464
    unified view, 614
  LISP language, 820
  simple model, 828–829
Evaluative beliefs, argument comprehension and, 37
Evans's Analogy Problem Program, 1133
Evans, Thomas, 834–835
EVAR system, speech understanding and, 1557
Evidence
  Bayesian inference methods
    pooling of, 90
    uncertain (cascaded inference), 92–93
    virtual (intangible) evidence, 93
  certainty-factor (CF) models, 134
  space, probabilistic reasonig, 1315
Evidential reasoning
  Bayesian networks, 96
  fuzzy set theory, 533–535
  image understanding and, 653
  probabilistic reasoning, 1314–1315
EXCAP system, 906
Executable code, parallel machine architecture, 1089
Existence, knowledge representation and, 755–756
Existential phenomenology, 1132
EXMAT system, chemistry in AI and, 159
Exocentric terms, morphology, 968
Expectation failures, dynamic memory, 392
Expectations, image understanding and, 645
EXPEDITOR, case-based reasoning, 1274
Experience
  case-based reasoning, 1267
  machine learning and, 786
  memory and, 456–457
Experimental design, chemistry in AI and, 160
Expert Chromatography Assistance Team (ECAT), 159
Expert systems, 477–489
  AI in medicine (AIM) and, 919–920
  artificial intelligence and, 57
  Bayesian inference methods, 96–97
  case-based reasoning, 1266–1267
    rule-based reasoning and, 1266–1267
  chemistry in AI and, 156–160
  cognitive modeling, 180
  cognitive psychology and, 182
  cognitive science and, 190
  computer-aided design and, 333
  computer-integrated manufacturing (CIM) and, 906–907
  Dempster-Shafer theory and, 330
  DENDRAL system as, 331
  distributed problem solving, 380–381
  domain knowledge, 389
  hermeneutics and, 607
  inference, 683
  knowledge engineering and
    fundamentals, 481–484
    history, 478
  knowledge representation and, 745
  knowledge systems
    building tools, 486–489
    construction, 484–485
    techniques, 478–481
  literature on, 847
  logic programming and, 884–885
  machine learning, 785
  meta-knowledge and, 942–943
  phenomenology and, 1134–1136
  plausible reasoning, 1307
  PROSPECTOR system, 1238
  ROSIE system, 1416
  rule-based systems, 1417
  speech understanding and, 1555–1556

Turing test, 1629
EXPLAIN program, AI in music and, 972
Explanation, 489–492
  generation of, 491–492
  historical background, 490
  knowledge capture for, 490–491
  knowledge system techniques and, 479–480
  meta-reasoning and, 943
  natural language generation, 988–990
Explanation-based learning (EBL)
  case-based reasoning, 1270
  machine learning, 795–796
  text summarization, 1585
Explanatory schema acquisition, script acquisition and, 1457–1458
Exploratory data analysis, pattern recognition, 1117
Exploratory vision, visual recovery, 1683
Expressibility
  knowledge representation and, 755
  predicate logic, 869
Extended Herbrand Base (EHB), 327
Extensibility, object-oriented languages, 775–777
Extensions, in semantic networks, 1505–1506
Extragrammatical utterances, 1010

Face recognition system
  neural networks, 1054–1055
  robot sensing and, 1386–1387
Facet image model, 629
Facet theory of intelligence, 708–710
Factoring
  augmented transition network (ATN) grammar and, 554
  binary resolution inference rules, 1347
Facts, rule-based systems, 1419–14120
Fagin, Ronald, 104
Fahmy theory of program synthesis, 69–70
FAHQT (fully automatic high-quality translation), 204
Falk, G., 647
Falting's algorithm, spatial reasoning, 1332
FAME system, semantic networks, 1502
Family relationships, definite databases, 322
Fault Isolation System (FIS), 954–955
FAUSTUS program, story analysis, 1572–1573
FDS program, means-ends analysis, 912
Feasible computation, Turing machines and, 1624
Feature acquisition, stereo vision, 1562
Feature-based grammar, 1104
Feature cooccurrence restrictions (FCR), 570
Feature correspondence, two-view motion analysis, 1641–1645
  planar curve correspondences, 1644–1645
  point correspondences, 1641–1643
  straight-line correspondences, 1643–1644
Feature detection
  neural networks, 1026–1027
  robot sensing and, 1384–1388
  unification, 1633–1636
Feature mapping, neural networks, 1052–1503
Feature matching
  mobile robot sensing, 1412
  object recognition, 1067–1078
    alignment and hypothesis testing, 1074–1076
    components, 1068–1069
    correspondence space search, 1069
    Hough transform, 1076–1077
    parallel relaxation, 1076
    parameterized object recognition, 1077–1078
    pose space search, 1076
    post space sampling, 1077
    search alternatives, 1069–1073
    search termination, 1073–1074
  stereo vision, 1562
Feature specification defaults (FSD), 570–571
Feedback systems
  computer-integrated manufacturing (CIM), 903
  qualitative physics, 1156–1157
  vision, visual recovery, 1683
FEELER program, emotion modeling, 446–447
Feyerabend, F., hermeneutics and, 604–605
Fidelity, shape representation, 1532
Fifteen Puzzle
  combinatorial explosion, 1464
  search techniques and, 1460
Fifth Generation Computer Project
  Alvey program, 26
  DADO system, 313
  domain knowledge, 390
  generalized phrase structure grammar and, 572
  literature on, 847
Figural continuity constraint, stereo vision, 1564
Filling-in concept, perception and, 1661
Fillmore, C.,
  deep case grammar, 566–567
  lexical decomposition, 809–810
FINALE program, 973
Fingerprinting, pattern recognition, 1127

Finite element meshes (FEM), shape representation, 1532
Finite-state automation (FSA)
  inductive inference, 678–679
  morphology, 969
  parsing, 1105–1106
First-order logic, 493
  deductive databases, 320–321
  inductive inference, 677
  inheritance hierarchies, 692
  modal logic and, 863–864
  nonmonotonic reasoning and, 1304–1305
First-order predicate calculus (FOPC), 297
Fixed action patterns (FAPs), schema theory, 1435
Fixed ordering, checkers-playing programs, 152
Fixnums, LISP language, 830
Flat Concurrent Prolog, 1085–1086
Flat languages, 1085–1086
Flavors programming, 493
  control structures, 294
  frame theory and, 504–505
  LISP machine construction, 843
Flaw detection, inspection systems, 702
Flexible manufacturing systems (FMSs), 905–906
FlexP system, natural language understanding, 1010
FLOABN adaptive planner, 5–6, 11–12
Flow patterns, edge detection, 412–413
Flowcharts, program synthesis, 65–73
Fluid intelligence, 709–710
FM beat, robot sensing and, 1384
Focus, computational linguistics, 216
Focus of expansion (FOE), mobile robot sensing, 1412
Focus space, discourse understanding, 370
Focus-of-attention mechanism, 1557
Folk psychology, frame theory, 495–497
Fool's Disks puzzle, means-ends analysis, 914–915
Foot feature principle (FFP), 571
Force analysis, robot end-effector design, 1368–1371
Force sensors
  resistor (FSR), tactile sensor design, 1516
  robotics design, 1390
Foreshortening effect, visual recovery, 1672–1675
Formal decision analysis, 317–318
Formalism, computational linguistics, 207–208
Formal logic, binary resolution, 1351
Formation problems, 1220
Formula circumscription, 165
FORTRAN
  control structures, 295
  natural language generation, 983
Forward chaining
  deductive databases, 324
  processing, bottom-up and top-down, 1230
  rule-based systems, 1421
Forward looking infrared (FLIR) imagery, 1591–1592
Forward problem, robotics design and, 1377
Forward pruning
  checkers-playing programs, 152–153
  computer chess and, 229–230
Foundationalism, epistemology, 461
Fourier descriptors, object recognition, 1066
Fourier functions, color vision, 200
Fractals
  image models, 628, 631
  texture analysis, human models, 1597
Fractional models, 631
Fragility, natural language understanding, 1004
FRAIL language, frame theory and, 504
Frame axioms, planning and, 1161
Frame-based semantics, lexical decomposition, 810–811
Frame-driven recognition, 497
Frame problem
  belief revision and, 111
  frame theory, 494
Frame representation language (FRL), 501–504, 507
  inheritance hierarchies, 693
Frame systems
  cognitive psychology and, 182
  design and, 336
  natural language generation, 990–991
  semantic networks, 1493
Frame theory, 493–505
  cases, slots and predicability, 501
  concept hierarchies, 499–500
  concept subsumption, 503
  discourse understanding, 366
  epistemology, 500
  folk psychology, 495–497
  frame-driven recognition, 497
  goal-based story analysis, 1571
  history, 493–494
  image understanding and, 652
  initial categories, 499
  knowledge representation and, 745

semantic networks, 748–749
knowledge system construction and, 484–485
languages, 495, 501–504
  object-oriented languages, 504–505
manipulation, 497–499
memory organization, 497–499
misrecognition, interpretation and reinterpretation, 496–497
phenomenology and, 1134
philosophy of AI and, 1144
predicate calculus, 502–503
property inheritance formalization, 503
purpose of, 494–495
recognition
  intepretation and prediction, 495–497
  matching and indexing, 498–499
schema theory, 1429–1430
scripts and, 1448
semantic networks, 1495
slots and property inheritance, 500–501
terminology, 494
Franz LISP, 838
FREDDY system, 507
Free boundary value problems, edge detection, 415
Free energy minimization, protein structure prediction, 1248
Frege, G.
  presupposition theory, 1195–1196
  semantic networks, 1494
FRIL language, fuzzy set theory, 528–529
FRUMP system, 507
  discourse understanding, 372–373
  dynamic memory, 391
  script skimming in, 1451–1452
  text summarization, 1581
F-test, segmentation and, 1487
Full Distribution Algorithm, DADO system, 314
FUNARGS, LISP 1.5, 833
Function-oriented programming, 1236
Functional decomposition, distributed problem solving, 381–382
Functional generative description of natural language (FGD), fuzzy logic, 517–521
Functionalism, philosophy of AI and, 1139
Functionally accurate, cooperative (FA/C) problem solving, 383
Functional programming, logic programming and, 882–884
Functional unification grammar (FUG)
  generalized phrase-structure grammar and, 570
  natural language generation, 992–993
  systemic grammar and, 583, 590–591
Future event prediction, Bayesian inference methods, 93–94
Fuzzy ATO Controller, engineering and KBES, 451–452
Fuzzy cardinality, 517
Fuzzy chips, plausible reasoning, 1320
Fuzzy image subsets, 640
Fuzzy logic
  concept learning and, 257
  definitions, 537
  fundamentals, 540–541
  fuzzy truth values, 541–542
  natural language
    applications, 515–521
    semantics, 517–521
  nonfuzzy truth values, 540–541
  overview, 507–508
Fuzzy mathematical programming, 521–527
  constraints and crisp objective functions, 523–524
  extensions, 524–526
    compensatory "and," 525–526
    nonlinear membership functions, 524–525
  fuzzy parameters, 526–527
  symmetric linear programming (LP), 522–523
Fuzzy set theory
  AI in medicine (AIM) and, 919
  basic properties, 537–538
  concept learning and, 257
  databases, 508–514
  decision making, 540
  definitions, 537
  event probability, 539
  fundamentals, 537–540
  fundamentals of, 516–517
  fuzzy numbers, 539
  fuzzy relations, 539–540
  natural language applications, 515–521
  operations, 538
  overview, 507–508
  pattern recognition, 1117
  possibilistic reasoning, 1309–1310
  probabilistic uncertainties, 528–535
    evidential reasoning under uncertainty, 533–535
    fuzzy control, 535
    iterative assignment method, 533–534

    mass assignments, 528
    nonmonotonicity, 534–535
    parallel machines, 535
    probability and possibility distributions, 528
    support logic programming, 528–529
      inference, 532–533
      pairs and mass assignments, 529–532
    update interpretation, 534

Gabor functions, neural networks, 1055
Gadamer, H., 599–600
Galton, Francis (Sir), 706
Game playing, 543–549
  alpha-beta pruning, 547
  brancing factors, 128
  Conway approach, 543
  distributed problem solving, 385–386
  evaluation, 547–548
  five deep force, 549
  game graphs, 544–545
  game trees, 545
  heuristics, 547
    two-player games, 613–614
  horizon effect, 547
  inheritance hierarchies, 696–697
  Koffman-Citrenbaum technique, 546
  learning, 548–549
  literature on, 844
  mathematical formulation, 543
  minimax procedures, 545–546
    zero-sum two-person games, 960–962
  positional games, 549
  problem solving, 1215–1216
  search reduction, 545–547
    evaluations, 546–547
    kernels, 546
  search techniques and, 1460–1461
  stability, 547
  strategies, 543–545, 544–545
Game trees, 550–552
  A* algorithm, 1
  AND/OR graphs, 550–551
  branch-and-bound search, 1472
  brancing factors, 128
  checkers-playing programs, 150–151
  horizon effect, 615–616
  minimax procedure, 959
  recursion and, 1339–1340
  search and, 1461
Garbage collection
  control structures, symbolic computation, 299
  LISP machines, 839, 842
  management of, in computer systems, 243, 245–247
  word-expert parsing (WEP), 1114–1115
Gardner, A., law in AI and, 780–781
Gardner networks, 1047–1048
GARI system, planning and, 1166, 1169
Gaschnig's algorithm, constraint networks, 283
Gaussian distribution, pattern recognition, 1119
Gaussian Markov random field (GMRF) model, 631
  examples, 632–635
  texture analysis, 1590
Gaussian networks, probabilistic networks, 1207
Gaussian smoothing, edge detection, 424
Gaussian sphere, visual recovery, 1668–1669
Gazdar, G., 1199–1200
GBB system, blackboard system building, 122–124
GBPF parser, dictionary/lexicon construction, 350, 352
Gedanken experiment, programming styles, 1235
Geffner's conditional entailment, 473–474
Gelenter, Herbert, 832–833
Gelsey's algorithm, spatial reasoning, 1332
General diagnostic engine (GDE), 921
Generalization, learning and, 153–155
Generalized cones (GCs), shape representation, 1535–1537
Generalized cylinders
  robot sensing and, 1387–1388
  shape representation, 1535–1537
Generalized phrase structure grammar (GPSG), 570–573
  dictionary/lexicon construction, 345
  HPSG and, 572
  implementation, 572–573
  JPSG and, 572
  PATR and, 571–572
  revised (RGPSG), 572
  revival of, 577
  syntactic features, 570–571
  systemic grammar and, 583
Generalized transition networks (GTNs), 561
General Problem Solver (GPS), 552
  adaptive planning, 10
  cognitive modeling, 180
  engineering and KBES, 449–450
  general problem solving, 552

  means-ends analysis, 909–912
  planning and, 1170
  reduction schema, 1224
General problem-solving
  CONNIVER system, 274
  knowledge engineering, 478
General purpose programming languages, 450
Generate-and-test methods
  constraint satisfaction, 286–288
  problem reduction, 1210–1211
  procedural problem formulations, 1217–1218
Generate-recognize theory, memory and, 458–459
Generation process
  natural language generation, 983–984
  see also Natural language generation
Generation/analysis, systemic grammar and, 585
Generative grammar
  cognitive psychology, 182
  cognitive science and, 191
  language acquisition, 763
Generative semantics
  deep structure, 329–330
  lexical decomposition, 808
Genetic algorithms
  machine learning and, 790–792
    alternative uses, 791–792
    case-based reasoning and, 786
  pattern recognition, 1125
GENSYM, LISP language and, 840
Gentzen's calculi, connection method, 266
Geometry
  cognitive modeling, 179
  commonsense reasoning, 1290
  computer-aided design and, 332–333
  edge detection, 430
  image properties, 637–640
  robotics design, programming, 1394–1395
  shape representation, 1527–1529
    local to global, 1527–1529
    operations, 1532–1533
    solid geometry, volumes, 1533–1537
  stereo vision, 1560
Geometry Tutor, education and AI, 436–438
GEORGE system, chemistry in AI and, 160
Gerberich, Carl, 832–833
German Federal Computer Science Laboratory (GMD), 626–627
Gestalt psychology
  cognitive psychology and, 183
  early vision and, 404–405
  perception and, 1661
Gibbs distribution
  neural networks, 1041
  simulated annealing, 1540
Gibson, J. J., 407
GLAUBER system, clustering analysis, 172–173
Global approximation algorithm, 632
Global coherence, distributed problem solving, 382
Global object recognition, 1065–1067
  Fourier descriptors, 1066
  moments of inertia, 1066–1067
  parameter vectors, 1066
  scope of, 1067
Global positioning system (GPS), 1410
Global protein structures, 1247–1248
Global random field models, texture analysis, 1589–1592
Glymour, R., 858, philosophy of AI and, 1145–1146
Goal-based story analysis, 1570–1571
Goal-dependency network (GDN)
  clustering analysis, 170
Goal-directed activation
  image understanding and, 648
  processing, bottom-up and top-down, 1230
Goal protection, planning and, 1162–1164
Goals
  commonsense reasoning, 1292–1293
    achievement goals, 1292
    delta goals, 1293
    entertainment goals, 1293
    preservation goals, 1292
    satisfaction goals, 1292
  planning and
    avoidance goals, 1169
    hierarchies and ordering, 1167–1168
    protracted, 1169
    reactive planning machines, 1174–1175
Gödel's Incompleteness Theorem
  artificial intelligence (AI), 55
  Church's thesis, 163–164
  epistemology and, 464
  higher-order logic, 861
  knowledge representation and, 755
  mathematical induction, 669
  philosophy of AI and, 1142–1143
Government-Binding Theory, deep structure, 329
Good difference information, means-ends analysis, 914–915

GPSS simulation language, automatic programming, 77
Gradient descent algorithms, neural networks, 1039, 1041
Gradient space, edge detection, 402
Grammar
  AI in music and, 978–979
  augmented transition network (ATN), 552–562
    cascaded ATNs (CATNs), 561–562
    context-free grammars, 555–556
    factoring, 554
    formal properties, 559
    generalized transition networks, 561
    history, 554–556
    HWIM speech system, 556–557
    linguistic experimentation, 558–559
    misconceptions, 560–561
    parsing, 559–560
    recursive transition network (RTN) and, 553–554
    specification, 557–558
  Brown Corpus, 129–130
  case, 563–569
    deep cases
      grammatical explanation, 564–565
      meaning representation, 565–566
    surface cases, 564–565
    systems
      Celce system, 567
      Fillmore system, 566–567
      Grimes system, 567–568
      Schank system, 568–569
  control structures, 296–297
  dictionary/lexicon construction, 345
  formalism, computational linguistics, 214–215
  generalized phrase structure, 570–573
    controll agreement principle (CAP), 571
    feature specification defaults (FSD), 570–571
    foot feature principle (FFP), 571
    head feature convention, 571
    head-driven phrase structure grammar (HPSG), 572
    immediate dominance (ID) rules, 570–571
    implementation, 572
    Japanese phrase structure grammar (JPSG), 572
    linear precedence (LP) rules, 570
    PATR formalism, 571–572
    revised (RGPSG), 572
    syntactic features, 570–571
  least commitment, story analysis, 1575
  machine translation, 901–902
  natural language generation, 984–985, 991–994
    functional unification grammar, 992–993
    semantic grammars, 1004–1005
    surface structure, 993
    systemic grammar and ATNs, 993–994
  parsing
    Backus-Naur form (BNF), 1100
    Chomsky normal-form, 1101
    context-free grammar, 1100
    feature-based, 1104
    Greibach normal-form, 1101
    no erasing rules, 1101
    phrase-structure, 1100–1102
    transformational, 1104–1105
  pattern recognition, 1123
  phase-structure, 573–579
    as transformation grammar (TG), 576
    context-free grammars (CFG) and, 574–576
    formal properties, 575–576
    generalized (GPSG), 577–578
    head and head-driven, 578
    revival, 576–577
    terminal symbols, 576
    tree-adjoining grammars (TAG), 578–579
    trees, 573–574
  semantic, 580–582
  systemic, 583–591
    implementations and declarativity, 590–591
    metafunctionality, 585–586
    paradigmatic axis, 583–585
    semantics, 588–590
    syntactic structure, 587–588
  transformational, 1104–1105
    computational linguistics, 204–205
    deep structure, 329–330
Graph-based algorithms
  constraint networks, 277–284
    w*-tractability, 280–281
    acyclic networks and tree-clustering, 281–282
    backtracking, 283–284
    cycle cutset scheme, 282–283
    directional and adaptive consistency, 278–280
    nonseparable component decomposition, 282
    recording, 284
    representation, 277–278
    tree networks, 278
  resolution, 1353–1355
Graph factorization, program synthesis, 69–70

Graph theory
  AI in medicine (AIM) and, 919–920
  chemistry in AI and, 156
  clustering, pattern recognition, 1120
  Turing machines and, 1622
Graphics, spatial reasoning, 1324–1325
Graphoids, 592–593
  Bayesian networks, 95
  probabilistic networks, 1207
Graphs
  directed, 593
  mobile robot planning, 1413
  unidirected, 592–593
Grasp technology, robot end-effector design, 1358–1372
Gray-level imaging
  robot sensing and, 1385–1386
  segmentation and, 1473–1474
Greedy algorithms
  constraint networks, 279
  simulated annealing, 1540
Greenblatt Chess Program, 898
Grice, H. P., 463
Grid-based navigation, spatial reasoning, 1326
Grimes deep case grammar, 567–568
Gripper design
  interchangeable and universal design, 1371–1372
  for irregular shapes, 1362–1364
  robot end-effector design, 1358–1372
Group technology, robot end-effector design, 1372
Grouping, edge detection, 414
Gruber, J., lexical decomposition, 809–810
Guarded Horn Clauses (GHC)
  logic programming and, 886–887
  parallel logic programming language, 1082–1086
Guardian/BB1 Control Agent, 124
GUIDON system, 593–594
  education and AI, 437
  human–computer interaction, 622
Guilford, J., 708–709
Gurfinkel, L., legged robots, 1400
GUS system
  agenda-based systems and, 22
  computational linguistics, 212

Habermas, J., hermeneutics and, 600–601
Habitability, semantic grammar, 581–582
Habituative chemical transmitters, 19–20
HACKER system, 595
  meta-knowledge and, 946
HADES program, 595
Hallucination, vision as controlled, 401–402
HAM-ANS system, 595
  computational linguistics, 210
Hamming distance
  character recognition, 139, 141
  memory-based reasoning, 1300–1301
Handwriting, character recognition system, 138
Hardware
  associative memory and, 58|59
  computer chess and, 235
  data parallelism and, 316
Harmonic-analysis, AI in music and, 973, 975
HARPY system, 595
  human-computer interaction, 621
  image understanding and, 650
  speech understanding and, 1555–1558
Hart, Timothy, 834–835
Harvard Multi-path English Analyzer
  lexical entry structure, 347–352
  word senses, 354
Harvard Syntact Analyzer, computational linguistics, 214–215
HASP (Heuristic Adaptive Surveillance Project)
  AI military applications, 951–952
  characteristics of, 119
  knowledge system building, 488
  rule-based systems, 1425
Hatvany, J., 907–908
Haugeland, R., 1141
Hayes, Patrick, 851–852
HCVM system, blackboard systems, 123
Head feature convention, generalized phrase-structure grammar and, 571
Head grammars (HG), 578
Head, H., 1429–1430
Head-driven phrase structure grammar (HPSG), 572, 578
HEARSAY system
  domain knowledge, 389
  human-computer interaction, 621
  image understanding and, 650
  schema theory, 1429–1430
  scene interpretation, 1439–1440
HEARSAY-II, 596
  blackboard systems, 116
  characteristics of, 118–119

control structures, 295
  knowledge engineering, history of, 478
  knowledge system building, 487–488
  rule-based systems, 1425
  speech understanding and, 1555–1558
HEARSAY-III
  blackboard system building, 121–122
  knowledge system building, 488
Heart Failure Program, AI in medicine (AIM) and, 920–921
h-easy function, inductive inference, 676–677
Heat transfer, thermal sensor data fusion, 1520
Hebbian rule
  Hopfield networks, 1045–1047
  learning, 1032–1033, 1035
  neural networks
    delay synapse networks, 1051
    dynamic link architecture, 1053–1055
    plasticity, 1033–1034
Hegel, G., 599–600
Heidegger, Martin
  hermeneutics, 596, 598–600, 606
  phenomenology and, 1132–1136
Hendler's DR, reactive planning machines, 1175
Hendrix, J., temporal reasoning, 1336
Henkin's completeness, higher-order logic, 861
Herbrand base (HB), logic programming, 876–877
Herbrand instantiation, binary resolution, 1342–1344
Herbrand interpretation
  deductive databases, 321
  semantics, 322–323
  disjunctive databases, 327
  stratified databases, 325–326
  unification, 1630
Herbrand models, incidence calculus, 667–668
Herbrand theorem
  completeness, 203
  higher-order logic, 861
Herbrand universe
  binary resolution, 1345–1346
  order-sorted logic, 865
Hermeneutic arc, 602–603
Hermeneutics, 596–608
  AI and, 605–608
    eidetic phenomenology, 607–608
    natural language understanding, 605–607
    textual analysis, 605
    understanding and, 607
  as metascience, 603–605
  classic methodological, 597–598
  critical, 600–601
    strategic orientation, 600
    universal pragmatics, 600
  eidetic phenomenology, 607–608
  emancipatory science and, 605
  Gadamer's philosophical, 599–600
  Habermas-Gadamer debate, 600–601
  Heidegger's ontological, 598–599
  natural sciences and, 604–605
  origins, 597
  phenomenological, 601–603
  philosophy and, 596, 598–600
  Schleiermacher and Dilthey methodology, 597–598
  social sciences and, 603–604
Hermite cubic, shape representation, 1529–1530
Heron of Alexandria, 309
Heterarchy
  control structures, 295
  cybernetics, 310–311
  image understanding and, 649
  speech understanding and, 1556
Heterogeneous data models, fuzzy databases, 510–511
Heuristic path algorithm (HPA), heuristic search, 1465
Heuristics, 611–614
  AI in music and, 974–977
  artificial intelligence (AI), 54–55
  beam search, 1467–1468
  belief representation systems, 102–108
    Konolige's theory, 102–103
    Levesque theory, 103–104
    Moore's theories, 102
    psychological theories, 104–105
      Abelson's theories, 107
      Allen and Perrault, 105
      Cohen and Levesque, 105
      Cohen and Perrault, 104–105
      Colby, 106–107
      mutual beliefs, 105–106
      speech act theory, 104–105
      user models, 107
      Wilks and Bien, 106
  blackboard systems, 116
  checkers-playing programs, 155
    fixed ordering, 152
  cognitive psychology and, 185
  contradiction heuristics, 106

creativity and, 307
domain knowledge, 388–390
EURISKO system, 477
evaluation functions, 612–614
   learning, 614
   simplified models, 613
   single-agent problems, 612–613
   two-player games, 613–614
   unified view, 614
game playing and, 547
image understanding and, 651–652
inductive inference, 677–678
inference and, 683
knowledge acquisition, 723
knowledge engineering, 478
knowledge levels and, 742–743
knowledge system techniques and, 478–481
law in AI and, 778–779
logic programming and, 884–885
means-ends analysis, 912
meta-knowledge and, 946
object recognition, search techniques, 1073
pragmatic inference rules, 106
problem solving
   interpretation problems, 1225
   search algorithms, 1212–1213
   solution methods, 1219
protein structure prediction, 1238
relevance heuristics, 106
rule-based systems, 1418–1419
search and, 1464–1465
spatial reasoning, 1326–1327
text summarization, 1583
visual motion analysis, 1652
Hexapod legged robots, 1399–1401
Heyting, Arend, 464
h-honest function, inductive inference, 676–677
Hidden Markov Models (HMMS), 626
   SPHINX system and, 1559
Hierarchical systems
   adaptive resonance theory and, 19
   AI in music and, 974–976
   blackboard systems, control architectures, 124
   cognitive psychology and, 184
   cybernetics, 310–311
   distributed problem solving, 381–382
   frame theory and, 499
   fuzzy databases, 513–514
   image understanding and, 649–650
   inheritance, 690–700
      default reasoning, 1295, 1298
      demons, 698
      exceptions and multiple inheritance, 693–695
      expressiveness, 695
      first-order logic, 692
      inheritable relations, 698
      multiple inheritance, 691–692
      parallel-marker propagation, 698–699
      programming languages, 699–700
      properties and slots inheritance, 691
      simple exceptions, 692–693
      slot constraints, 695
      splits and partitioning, 697–698
      structured concepts, 695–697
      taxonomic hierarchies, 691
   intelligence theories and, 708–710
   logic programming, 888–889
   parallel logic programming language, 1085–1086
   planning and
      adaptive planning, 10
      distributed problem solving, 384
      goal ordering and, 1167–1168
      macro actions, 1166–1167
   reactive planning machines, 1177
   speech understanding and, 1556
   type hierarchy
      semantic networks, 1500–1501
High-level vision
   commonsense reasoning, 1289–1290
   future research, 415–416
   image understanding, 641
   schema theory, 1437–1440
      assemblages, 1437–1438
   segmentation in, 395–403
Higher order unification, 1632–1633
Higher-order logic, 860–862
   computational applications, 861–862
   proof theory, 861
   semantics, 860–861
   syntax, 860
Hilbert, David, 464
Hill's model, language acquisition, 766–769
Hill, J. C., schema theory, 1441
Hill-climbing
   design and, 335
   inductive inference, 680
   neural networks, 1034–1035
   problem solving, 1226
Hillis, W. D., tactile sensor design, 1516

Hintikka, G.
   belief representation systems, 102
   epistemology and, 466
Hintikka's logic of knowledge
   belief representation, 100
   epistemology, 100–101
Hirose, K., legged robots, 1400–1401
Histogram mode seeking, 1474–1476
HMSL program, 979–980
^{1}H NMR, chemistry in AI and, 158
HOLD actions, augmented transition network (ATN) grammars, 558
Holes, image properties, 638–639
Holism, philosophy of AI and, 1144
Holmes, G., 1429–1430
Holographic interferometry, range sensor design, 1519
Homologous proteins, protein structure prediction, 1244
HOOKUP, 979
HOPE language, logic programming and, 883
Hopfield, J. J., 1020–1024
Hopfield networks
   associative memory, 1043
   improvements, 1046–1047
   optimization and, 1020–1022
   spin representation, 1044–1045
Horizon effect, 615–616
   computer chess and, 229
   game playing and, 547
   negative-horizon effect, 616
   positive-horizon effect, 616
   terminal positions, 615
Horn, J. L., 709
Horn clauses
   inductive inference, 677
   logic programming, 874–877
      AND/OR nondeterminism, 875–876
      extensions of, 878–880
         arbitrary subgoals, 880
         metalevel programming, 880
         negation-as-failure, 878–879
         solution sets, 880
         Yale shooting problem, 879–880
      historical origins, 874–875
      minimal model semantics, 876–877
      procedural vs. declarative knowledge representation, 875
      recursive data structures, 876
   logic programming and, 886
   parallel logic programming, 1081
   problem reduction, 1210–1211
   see also Guarded Horn clauses
Horopter, stereo vision, 1565–1566
Hough transforms, 617–618
   description, 617–618
   early vision and, 400–401
   object recognition, 1076–1077
How/why diagrams, robot end-effector design, 1372–1374
Hubel-Wiesel feature detector, neural networks, 1055
Hueckel operator, edge detection, 426–428
Human cognition, meta-knowledge and, 941–942
Human-computer interaction, 618–624
   adaptation, 622–623
   AI and, 623–624
   AI applications, 620–623
   cognitive science and, 188
   computer-aided instruction (CAI), 621–622
   computer systems, 243
   design, 619–620
      styles, 619–620
      techniques and guidelines, 620
   distributed problem solving, 381
   education and AI, 435–436
   human factors engineering, 623–624
   intelligent user interfaces, 621–622
   interface design, 623
   natural language applications, 620–621
   pattern recognition, 621
   programming environments, 623
   speech, 621
   teleoperators, 1578–1579
Human intelligence, 706–714
   defined, 706–707
   facet and hierarchical theories, 708–710
   global theories, 706–707
   information processing, 710–711
   learning and, 711–713
   performance models, cognitive science and, 190
   structure of, 707–711
Humanistic machine translation, 900–901
Hume, David
   causal reasoning, 1286
   epistemology, 462
Humphreys, L. G., 706, 708–709
Husserl, Edmund
   Heidegger and, 1132
   hermeneutics and, 598, 606

   phenomenology and, 1131–1136
   philosophy of AI and, 1144
HWIM system, 625
   augmented transition network (ATNs), 556–557
   human-computer interaction, 621
   image understanding, 643
   speech understanding and, 1557
Hybrid cellular-kinematic systems, 1492
Hybrid languages, engineering and KBES, 450
Hybrid multilayer-perceptron (MLP/HMM), 627
Hybrid uncertainty management (HUM), 1319
Hydraulic power, robot end-effector design, 1368
Hypergraphs, constraint networks, 277–278
Hypermedia, knowledge acquisition and, 724
Hyperpatches, shape representation, 1534
Hyperresolution, binary resolution, 1347–1348
HYPO program
   case-based reasoning, 1268
   indexing, 1270
   interpretation, 1275
   justification, 1275
   law in AI and, 781
Hypocritical behavior, meta-argument units, 46–47
Hypotheses
   concept learning, 251–253
   hermeneutic arc and, 602–603
   image understanding, 642
      inference and, 644
   testing, object recognition
      alignment and, 1074–1076
      search techniques, 1072
Hysteresis
   neural networks, 1024–1025
   stereo vision, 1566

IBM
   801 system, control structures, 298–299
   LISP development and, 838
IC-PROLOG system
   coroutines, 305–306
   logic programming and, 886
ICAI, natural language generation, 983
ICARUS program, machine-learning and, 801
ICOT (Institute for New Generation Computer Technology)
   Alvey program, 26
   parallel machine architecture, 1088
ICSI connectionist simulator (ICSIM), 626
ID3 program, concept learning, 255
Identically distributed (IID) models, 628–629
Identification in the limit, inductive inference, 679–680
Identification problem, spatial reasoning, 1327–1328
Identity, predicate logic, 871
Idioms
   dictionary/lexicon construction, 354–355
      inter-word entry information, 345
   lexical decomposition, 806
Idiot-Bayes model, certainty-factor (CF) models, 131–133, 135–136
IF-ADDED demons, inheritance hierarchies, 698
IF-NEEDED demons, inheritance hierarchies, 698
IF-THEN rules, case-based reasoning, 1266–1267
Illiac Suite, 972, 974
ILIAD system, computational linguistics, 211
Ill-posed problems, visual recovery, 1676–1679
Illusions, perception and, 1660
Image acquisition, stereo vision, 1561
Image intensity, visual motion analysis, 1648–1650
   displaced frame differences, 1648–1649
   3-D motion, 1649
Image irradiance equation, visual recovery, 1670–1672
Image matching, stereo vision, 1562
Image models, 628–635
   fractals and fractional models, 631
   real images, 631
   region level, 632–635
   simple statistical models, 628–629
   time series models, 629
   two-dimensional
      noncausal models, 630–631
      unilateral models, 629–630
Image processing, tactile sensing, 1389
Image properties, 637–640
   geometrical properties, 638–640
      area and perimeter, 639
      borders, 639
      convexity, 639
      distance, 639
      elongatedness, 639
      extent, 639
      fuzzy subsets, 640
      holes and surroundedness, 638
      neighbors, 638
      paths and connectedness, 638

slope and curvature, 639
subset decomposition, 639
subset representation, 639–640
intrinsic
early vision, 407
range data analysis, 1251
invariant properties, 640
linear properties, 638
relations, 640
statistical and textural properties, 638
viewpoint-dependence, 640
Image segmentation, color vision systems, 196–198
Image understanding, 641–661
AI military applications, 955–956
artificial intelligence, 57
attention, 645
certainty and belief strength, 645
clustering analysis, 170
comparison and differentiation, 644
concept organization, 643
control structures, 646–651
beam models, 650
blackboard models, 650
data-directed activation, 648
failure-directed activation, 648
goal-directed activation, 648
heterarchical models, 649
hierarchical models, 649–650
model-directed activation, 648
perception cycle, 646–648
rule-based approaches, 650–651
temporally-directed activation, 648–649
examples for specific problem domains, 653–658
expectations, 645
historical perspective and techniques, 646–653
"indexing" problem, 644
inference and control requirements, 644–646
inference and goal satisfaction, 646
matching and hypothesis testing, 644–645
mobile robot sensing, 1410–1412
overview, 641–643
prototypical concepts, 643
reasoning and uncertainty, 652–653
evidential reasoning, 653
planning, 653
relaxation labeling process, 652–653
spatiotemporal reasoning, 653
representation formalisms, 651–652
frames, 652
heuristics, 652
rules, 652
semantic networks, 652
spatial representations, 651–652
representational requirements, 642–644
research issues, 658–662
domain knowledge, 658–660
early-level/high-level integration, 660
object recognition, 660
scale problem, 644
search and hypothesis activation, 644
spatial knowledge, 643–644
temporal knowledge, 644
visual recovery, 1665–1666
Imagery, spatial reasoning, 1329
Imitation game, Turing test, 1625–1626
Immediate dominance (ID) rules, generalized phrase-structure grammar and, 570
Implicit knowledge, perception and, 1660
Importance, in text summarization, 1582
Imprecision, fuzzy databases, 509–510
Improvisation, reactive planning, 1173
Incidence calculus, 663–668
definitions, 664–665
example, 664
formula assignment, 667
inference example, 666–667
logic comparisons, 667–668
modus ponens inference rule, 665–666
Incident energy distribution, optical sensor design, 1513
Incompleteness
knowledge representation and, 754–755
plausible reasoning and, 1308
Inconsistency, knowledge representation and, 754–756
Incorrect imputation theory, belief representation, 101
Incremental learning
machine learning, 787
empiricist approach, 794
Incremental refinement, in design, 335
Independence assertions, Bayesian networks, 1202–1203
Independence of the computation rule, 876
Indexical-functional representation, 1174
Indexicality, temporal reasoning, 1337
Indexing
case-based reasoning, 1269–1270
frame theory and, 498–499

information retrieval, 684
automatic indexing, 686–687
forms, 685–686
intelligent indexing, 688–689
manual indexing, 686
machine
learning and, 798
thesaurus development, 1607
object recognition, 1073
INDUCE program, concept learning, 256
Induced graphs, constraint networks, 280
INDUCT algorithm, knowledge acquisition and, 726–727
Induction
machine-learning and, 788, 799
mathematical, 668–672
algorithm termination and recursion analysis, 670–671
automated induction, 669–671
axiom computation, 669–670
basic prover, 670
completion, 671–672
implementations, 671
module, 669–670
theoretical foundations, 668–669
Induction theorem proving system (ITPS), 668
Inductive inference, 672–681
applications, 680–681
automatic programming, 59
BC (behaviorally correct) criteria, 674, 678
complexity, 678–679
direct methods, 677–678
epistemology and, 464
EX (explanatory) criteria, 674, 679–680
example, 672–673
function classification, 673–674
identification criteria, 679–680
image understanding and, 644–646
language classification, 674–675
logic and, 851
search and its variants, 675–677
efficiency, 677
h-easy method, 676
h-honest method, 676–677
more powerful search, 676–677
Turing test, 1626–1627
Industrial dynamics, cognitive science and, 191
Inertial navigation, mobile robot sensing, 1410
Inference, 682–683
AI in medicine (AIM) and, 918
binary resolution, 1344, 1346–1349
commonsense reasoning, 1288–1289
conceptual dependency and, 264
conditional logic, 855–857
decision theory, 317
deductive databases, 321
default reasoning, 1294
discourse understanding, 372
early vision, structural mechanisms, 411
engine, knowledge representation and, 743
epistemology, 461
epsilon-semantics, 470
equality, 475–477
exemplary generalization, 683
fuzzy set theory, 532–533
image understanding, 641–642, 644–646
incidence calculus, 665–667
inductive, 672–681
applications, 680–681
complexity, 678–679
concept learning, 251–253
direct methods, 677–678
epistemology and, 464
example, 672–673
functional classification, 673–674
identification criteria, 679–680
language classification, 674–675
rule-guided, 253
search and its variants, 675–677
inheritance hierarchies, 698–699
knowledge representation and, 750–751
logic and, 683, 851
mental models and, 934
meta-knowledge and, 941
modus ponens rule, 665–666
natural language understanding, 1013
negative information, 683
networks, certainty-factor (CF) models, 133–134
nonclassical logical, 683
object-oriented languages, 773
phenomenology and, 1134
predicate logic, 869–870
preference semantics and, 1187
probabilistic networks, 1204–1205
probabilistic or statistical inference, 683
processing, bottom-up and top-down, 1234
scripts and, 1448
unconscious, early vision, 395
units, computer systems, 247–248
Inflectional information

dictionary/lexicon construction, 343–344
morphology, 965–966
Influence diagrams, probabilistic networks, 1207
Information
coding, neural networks, 1026–1027
dictionary/lexicon construction
inter-word entry information, 343–345
intra-entry information, 342–343
distributed problem solving, 382
explanation and, 491
hiding, actor formalisms, 4
intelligence and, 707
negative, inference and, 683
object-oriented languages, 773
processing
cognitive-components method, 710
cognitive-content method, 710
cognitive-correlates method, 710
cognitive-training method, 710
intelligence and, 710–711
learning and, 713
retrieval, 684–689
artificial intelligence and, 688–689
automated systems, 685–686
basic elements, 684–685
computational linguistics, 205
database context, 684
document description, 685
indexing, 685–686
automatic indexing, 686–687
intelligent indexing, 688–689
manual indexing, 686
intelligent searching, 689
key problems, 685
law in AI and, 778
operations, 686
performance measurement, 684–685
system testing and evaluation, 688
law in AI and, 781
thesauri and, 1605, 1606–1610
automatic techniques, 1608
development, 1606–1607
machine indexing, 1607
performance evaluation, 1608–1609
user need and document relevance, 684
storage, fuzzy databases, 511
technology, Alvey program, 25–26
Infrared spectroscopy
chemistry in AI and
instrumentation, 159
structure elucidation, 157–158
color vision and, 193
Infrared/red ratios, 198
Inheritance
frame theory and, 500–501, 503
semantic networks, 1501–1502
Inheritance hierarchies, 690–700
default reasoning, 1295, 1298
demons, 698
dictionary/lexicon construction, 352–353
exceptions, 692–693
expressiveness, 695
first-order logic, 692
image understanding and, 646
inheritable relations, 698
multiple inheritance, 691–692
exceptions, 693–695
object-oriented languages, 775–777
parallel-marker propagation, 698–699
programming languages, 699–700
properties and slots, 691
slot constraints, 695
splits and partitioning, 697–698
structured concepts, 695–697
taxonomy, 691
INIS Thesaurus, 1607
INKA system, mathematical induction, 671
Innate releasing mechanisms (IRM), 1435
Innatism, language acquisition and, 762–763
Input guard, parallel logic programming language, 1084
Input-output specifications, 60–65
Inquiry semantics, systemic grammar and, 588–590
Inspection, 701–705
problem-solving, 701–704
causal assignment, 703–704
printed circuit boards, 702–703
visual inspection, 704
process models, 704
range data analysis, 1262–1263
INSPECTOR, LISP machine construction, 843
Instance space, concept learning, 253–254
Instance-of structure, knowledge representation and, 749
Instances, machine learning and, 787
Instantiation
constraint networks, 276
constraint satisfaction, 289
generalized phrase-structure grammar and, 570

I-16 INDEX

Herbrand, binary resolution, 1342–1344
  natural language understanding, 1006–1009
  schema theory, 1431
    scene interpretation, 1438–1439
Instruction sets, computer systems, 243
IntCAD systems
  computer-aided design and, 334
  design and, 332
Integrated circuits (ICs) design, 627
Integrated story analysis, 1571–1572
Integration, image understanding, 641–642
INTELLECT system, 705
  computational linguistics, 210
Intellectics, 705–706
Intelligence
  artificial. *See* Artificial intelligence (AI)
  fluid-crystallized intelligence distinction, 709–710
  human, 706–714
    defined, 706–707
    development of, 711–712
    facet and hierarchical theories, 708–710
    global theories, 706–707
    information processing, 710–711
    learning and, 711–713
    primary mental abilities, 707–708
    structure, 707–711
  tests, 706–707
Intelligent Automatic Test Generation (IATG), 954–955
Intelligent backtracking. *See* Dependency-directed backtracking
Intelligent execution, logic programming and, 885
Intelligent Maintenance Tutoring System (IMTS), 434, 440
Intelligent tutoring system (ITS), 434
Intellipath system, AI in medicine (AIM) and, 923–924
Intensional theories
  belief representation, 101–102
  semantic networks, 1505–1506
Intensity changes
  edge detection, 422–432
    directional or nondirectional operators, 429–430
    intensity gradient, 429
    Laplacian operator, 429–430
    multiple resolutions, 430–431
    one-dimensional detection, 424–426
    scale space filtering, 431–432
    smoothing and differentiation, 422–426
    two-dimensional detection, 428–432
  image understanding, 641–642
  robot sensing and, 1385–1386
Intensity discontinuities, early vision, 411–412
Intentional links, argument comprehension, 37
Intentional-systems theory, 1139–1140
Intentionality
  philosophy of AI and, 1141
  scripts and, 1448–1449
  phenomenology and, 1131
Interactive activation model (IAM), 146–147
Interactive explanation, agenda-based systems and, 22
Interactive maintenance, AI military applications, 955–956
Interface design, programming, 623
InterLisp, 836–837
International Computer Science Institute (ISCI), 626–627
INTERNIST system
  AI in medicine (AIM) and, 916
    diagnosis strategies, 921
    inference and control methods, 918
    knowledge acquisition, 917
    knowledge structures, 918
    Quick Medical Reference (QMR) and, 922–923
    uncertainty, 919
  CADUCEUS system and, 131
  domain knowledge, 389
  knowledge engineering, history of, 478
Interpretation
  frame theory and, 495–497, 496
  LISP language, 830–831
  problem solving, 1224–1225
  semantics
    lexical decomposition, 808, 810
    tree, object recognition, 1071–1072
Interpretation-guided segmentation (IGS) program, 647–648
Interpretive case-based reasoning, 1274–1275
  problem solving and, 1276
Interval estimation, pattern recognition, 1119
Interviewing, knowledge acquisition, 720–721
In-the-small techniques, text summarization, 1581
Intuitionism, epistemology and, 464
Invariant properties, image properties, 640
Inverse filtering, texture analysis, 1591
Inverse optics, 394
  early vision, 406, 409–410

Inverse problem, robotics design and, 1377
IPP system
  memory organization packets (MOPs), 927
  script acquisition and, 1457–1458
IQ scores, creativity and, 308
IRACQ system, dictionary/lexicon construction, 357–358
IRLIST, 847
IRUS dictionary
  knowledge acquisition, 357
  lexical entry structure, 347, 351–352
  word senses, 354
IS-A hierarchies
  dictionary/lexicon construction, 353–354
  distributed connectionism, 272
  image understanding, 643, 647–649
  inheritance hierarchies, 691
    multiple inheritance exceptions, 694–695
  knowledge representation and, 749–750
  story analysis, 1572–1573
Ising, E., 1020
ISIS system
  computer-integrated manufacturing (CIM) and, 905–906
  planning and, 1169
Islands of reliability, image understanding and, 645
Isobrightness contour, visual recovery, 1671–1672
ISWIM, POP-11 and, 1182
Iterative assignment method, fuzzy set theory, 533–534
Iterative deepening
  A* (IDA*) algorithm
    heuristic search, 1464–1465
    computer chess and, 231
Iterative redesign, 335
Iterative relaxation, range data analysis, 1261

Jackendoff's theory of decomposition, 808–809, 811
JAM FACTORY program, 973–974, 980
JANUS Master Lexicon
  knowledge acquisition, 357
  lexical entry structure, 347
  word senses, 354
Japanese phrase structure grammar (JPSG), 572
Jeffrey's updating rule
  Bayesian inference methods, 94
  fuzzy set theory, 534
Jensen, A., 706
JETS system, computational linguistics, 210
Job shop scheduling, constraint satisfaction, 290
Jobs reduction, robotics design and, 1376
JOHNNIAC machine, 832
Join graphs, constraint networks, 281–282
Joint coordinates, robotics design and, 1377
Joint probability formulation, texture analysis, 1593–1594
Joint-to-world coordinate transformation, 1377
Jordan model, neural networks, 1050
Joskowicz algorithm, spatial reasoning, 1332
Journals on AI, 844–845, 847
JPL loop-wheel vehicle, 1414
JUDGE system
  case-based reasoning, 1269
  dynamic memory, 392
  memory organization packets (MOPs), 927
JUDIS system, 717
JUDITH system, law in AI and, 779
JULIA program, 717
  case-based reasoning, 1270
  design issues, 1273
Justification-based systems
  belief revisions and, 113–114
  case-based reasoning, 1275
  epistemology, 461
  truth maintenance systems (TMS), 1613–1617
    contradiction removal, 1616–1617
    dependency networks, 1615
    premises, 1614
    problem solver interaction, 1615–1616

KAISSA program, 718
  computer chess programs, 224–225
Kalman filtering, sensor data fusion and, 1523
Kanade, image understanding and, 648
Kanisza subjective edge, 402, 409–410
Kant, Immanuel, epistemology, 462–463
Karhunen-Loève transformation
  neural networks, 1043
  segmentation and, 1477–1478
Karttunen and Peters, presupposition theory, 1199
Kasus element, deep case grammar, 566–567
Kato, I., 1403–1404
Katz's semantic theory, lexical decomposition, 810
KBMS. *See* Knowledge-based management system
KC-ONE, parallel machine architectur1090–1091e, 1090–1091
k-consistency

chronological backtracking, 85
constraint satisfaction, 288–289
KDS system, computational linguistics, 217
KEAL system, speech understanding and, 1557
KEE system, 718
Kelley, K. L., 762
Kernel systems
  binary resolution, 1351
  game playing and, 545–546
  rule-based systems, 1421
  sensor data fusion and, 1523
Keywords, information retrieval, 686
KIDS system, automatic programming, 79–81
Kinematics, robotics design and, 1377
Kirkpatrick, D., 1045
KL-ONE knowledge representation system, 718
  belief representation systems, 102
  inheritance hierarchies, 691
    demons, 698
    slot constraints, 695
    structured concepts, 695–697
  knowledge representation and characteristics, 753
  semantic networks, 749
  order-sorted logic, 866
  semantic networks, 1495, 1500
    inheritance, 1502
KL-TWO, semantic networks, 1504–1505
k-means algorithm
  clustering analysis, 170, 172
  pattern recognition, 1120
K-NET language, 1548
KNOBS program, AI military applications, 953–954
Knowing-not phenomenon, meta-knowledge and, 941–942
Knowledge acquisition, 719–731
  AI in medicine (AIM) and, 917, 919
  AI in music and, 979
  case-based reasoning, 1266–1267
  certainty-factor (CF) models, 137
  cognitive science and, 188
  dictionary/lexicon construction, 355–362
  education and AI, 435
  knowledge system construction and, 484–485
  machine learning, 786–788, 796–797
  mediating representations, 719–720
  mental models and, 934
  meta-knowledge and, 942
  modeling expertise, 719–720
  tools and techniques, 720–728
    automated methods, 726–728
    computer-based catalog, 728–731
    interactive (semiautomated) methods, 722–726
    manual methods, 720–722
    research strategies, 723–726
Knowledge-based systems (KBS)
  Alvey program, 26
  AM system, 27
  argument comprehension and, 34–36
  art and AI, 53–54
  automatic programming, 81
  Baseball systems, 88–89
  Bayesian inference methods, 96–97
  belief revision and, 111–113
  building tools, 486–489
  computer-aided design and, 333–334
  construction and design, 484–485
  edge detection, 402
  expert systems and, 478–481
  game playing and, 546
  knowledge representation and, 743, 755–756
  organization and design, 482–483
  parallel machine architecture, 1095–1097
  vision, image understanding, 641
Knowledge-based expert systems (KBES), 448–453
Knowledge-based Information Presentation project (WIP), 340
Knowledge-based management system (KBMS), 718
  ECRC program, 420–421
Knowledge-Crunching Machine (KCM), 247
  ECRC programs, 421
  logic programming, 888
Knowledge-elicitation strategies, 723–726
Knowledge engineering (KE)
  expert systems and, 477–478
  fundamentals of, 481–484
  history of, 478
  knowledge levels and, 742–743
Knowledge level, 742–743
  machine learning and, 788
Knowledge maps, certainty-factor (CF) models, 136
Knowledge organization
  knowledge acquisition, 721–722
  knowledge representation and, 749–752
Knowledge reconstruction, programming paradigms and, 123

Knowledge representation, 743–756
  argument comprehension, 30
  artificial intelligence, 56
  BACK system, 753
  checkers-playing programs, 150
  cognitive modeling, 177
  commonsense reasoning, 1288, 1291–1292
  completeness, 202
  computational linguistics, 215
  computer systems, 242
  computer-aided design and, 332, 336
  conceptual dependency, 259–264
  CycL system, 754
  education and AI, 435, 443
  epistemology, 460–466
  examples of, 752–754
  history, 744–745
  image understanding and, 651
  KL-ONE system, 718, 753
  knowledge system techniques and, 478–481
  KRL system, 753
  KRYPTON, 753
  logic and, 851–852
    procedural vs. declarative, 875
  machine learning, 785
  machine translation, 898, 899
  mathematics, 909
  meta-knowledge and, 940–941
  natural language understanding, 999
  OMEGA system, 753–754
  PLANNER system, 752
  predicate logic, 866–872
  problem solving and, 1219
  production systems, 752–753
  programming paradigms and, 1236–1237
  research issues, 754–756
    agents and actions, 756
    causality and time, 756
    entities and relationships, 756
    existence, 756
    expressiveness vs. tractability, 755
    incompleteness, 754–755
    inconsistency, 754
    knowledge base management, 756
    nonmonotonicity and defaults, 754
    ontologies, 755
    space, 756
  schema theory, 1429–1430
  SNePS, 753
  SNePS system and, 1547–1548
  systems, 745–752
    control structures, 751–752
    inference, 750–751
    instance-of structure, 749
    IS-A structure, 749–750
    knowledge organization, 749–752
    logic-based representations, 745–746
    matching, 751
    part-of mechanism, 750
    procedural representations, 746–747
    semantic networks, 747–749
Knowledge-representation language (KRL), 759
  agenda-based systems and, 22
  frame theory and, 499, 501–504
  hermeneutics and, 606
  knowledge representation and, 753
  vocabulary, 744
Knowledge source activation record (KSAR)
  BB1 system, 122
  blackboard systems, 117
  HEARSAY-II, 118–119
  HEARSAY-III, 121–122
  OPM system, 120
Knowledge sources
  AGE system, 121
  BB1 system, 122
  blackboard systems, 117
  CROSS.ARRAYRULES, 119
  CRYSALIS system, 119–120
  engineering and KBES, 449
  epistemology, 460–461
  GBB system, 122–123
  HASP system, 119
  HEARSAY-II, 118–119
  HEARSAY-III, 121–122
  MOW system, 117–118
  NOTICEPATTERN, 120
  OPM system, 120
  parallel machine architecture, 1096–1097
  planning and, 1166
  POM, 118
  PREDICT, 117–118
  REFINE-DESIGN, 120
  RPOL, 118
  SEG, 118
  SOURCE.INCORPORATIONRULES, 119
  speech understanding and, 1552–1554
    interpretation, 1555–1556
Knowledge states, truth maintenance systems (TMS), 1618–1619

Knowledge structure
  AI in medicine (AIM) and, 918
  frame theory, 494
Knuth, D., 1229–1230
Knuth-Bendix Completion Procedure, 671–672
Kobsa and Trost knowledge representation system, 102
KODIAK, frame theory and, 504
Koffman-Citrenbaum technique, 546
Kohonen's model, neural networks, 1052–1053
KOKON system, 759
Kolmogorov's axiom, Bayesian networks, 1204
Kolodner's model of adaptive planning, 7
Konolige theory
  belief representation systems, 102
  heuristics, 102–103
Konolige, Kurt, 100–104
Kriegspiel, minimax procedure, 959
Kripke model, modal logic, 963
KRITIK, case-based reasoning, 1273
Kronecker delta
  local surface approximation, 1260–1261
  range data analysis, 1255
KRYPTON system
  domain knowledge, 390
  frame theory and, 503–504
  knowledge representation and, 745, 753
  semantic networks, 1504–1505
  theory resolution and, 1356–1357
k-tails, inductive inference, 678
k-trees, constraint networks, 282
Kuhn, T. S., 604–605

Ladar
  design principles, 1516–1517
  sensor data fusion and, 1521
LADDER system, 819
  computational linguistics, 209–210
  natural language understanding, 998–999, 1011–1012
  semantic grammars, 1005
  semantic networks, 1500
Lagrangian formulation, 1377
Lambda binding, LISP language, 823
Lambda calculus, 760–761
  artificial intelligence applications, 721
  higher order unification, 1632–1633
  history, 760
  notation, 760–761
  semantic networks, 1504–1505
Lambda definability, Church's thesis, 163–164
Lambda functions
  fuzzy mathematical programming, 525–526
  InterLisp, 837
  LISP language, 832–833
    lists, 827
    machine construction, 843
  visual recovery, shape from shading, 1671–1672
Lancaster-Oslo-Bergen (LOB) corpus, 360–362
  dictionary/lexicon construction, 360–362
Landmark learning, neural networks, 1034–1035
Landmark pair boundary (LPB), spatial reasoning, 1328
Landmark values, qualitative physics, 1149–1150, 1153
Language
  cognitive modeling, 180
  cognitive psychology and, 185
  cognitive science and, 189
  coroutines, 302
  databases, Brown Corpus, 128–130
  generation, conceptual dependency and, 264
  inductive inference, 674–675
    search efficiency, 677
  intelligence and, 711–712
  models, dictionary/lexicon construction, 360–362
  morphology
    agglutinative languages, 963
    inflecting languages, 964
    isolating languages, 963
    polysynthetic language, 964
  object-oriented, 772–777
    diversity, 776–777
    history, 776
    intelligent program construction, 772–773
    knowledge sharing, 775
    medical diagnosis and, 773–775
    message-passing behavior, 775
    parallelism and, 775–776
  predicate logic, 867–869
    arguments, 867
    expressibility, 869
    semantics, 868–869
    syntax, 867–868
  preference semantics and, 1184
  programming
    parallel logic, 1081–1087
    robotics design, 1392–1394
  propositional logic, 891–894

  incidence calculus, 664
  schema theory, acquisition process, 1441
  theory, augmented transition network (ATNs), 555–556
Language acquisition, 761–770
  cognitive models, 764–770
    connectionist models, 764–765
    grammar requirements, 766–769
    lexicons, 765–766
    mearning and error correction, 769
    psycholinguistic studies, 764
  computational linguistics, 218
  future research, 769–770
  historical notes, 761–762
  innatists vs. empiricists, 762–763
  learnability models, 763–764
  taxonomy, 761–763
Language acquisition system (LAS), 762
  cognitive modeling, 179
Language-of-thought hypothesis, 1141
LapItUp program, dictionary/lexicon construction, 356–358
Laplacian equations
  density function, texture analysis, 1590
  edge detection and, 396–400, 429–430
Large processing elements (LPEs), NON-VON system, 1060–1061
Laser
  mobile robot sensing, 1411–1412
  radar design principles, 1516–1517
Last-in-first-out (LIFO) order, blackboard systems, 119
Lateral geniculate nucleus (LGN), early vision and, 399–400
Lateral inhibition
  localist connectionism, 270–271
  segmentation and, 396
Lattice structures
  semantic networks, 1501
  texture analysis, 1593
Law, AI in, 777–783
  applications, 782
  argument comprehension, 31
  cognitive processes, 782–783
  historical background, 778–779
  legal analysis programs, 780–781
    case-based vs. rule-based approaches, 781
    Gardner's dissertation, 780–781
    TAXMAN I and II, 780
  machine learning and, case-based reasoning and, 797–799
LAWGICAL program, law in AI and, 781
Lazy evaluation, coroutines, 305–306
Lazy execution, logic programming and, 886
LDL system, stratified databases, 326
LDOCE system, thesauri and, 1610
LEAP system, design and, 336
Learnability models, language acquisition and, 763–764
Learning
  algorithms, machine-learning and, 800
  artificial intelligence, 56–57
  Boltzmann machine, 127
  case-based reasoning
    experiential learning, 1267
    natural learning, 1267–1268
  checkers-playing programs, 150, 153–155
    generalization, 153–155
    linear polynomial approach, 153–154
    rote learning, 153
    signature tables, 154–155
  chemistry and machine learning, 156
  cognitive modeling, 179
  cognitive science and, 190
  concept, 249–257
    data-driven methods, 254–255
    extended notions, 256–257
    inductive inference, 251–253
    inductive learning methods, 254–256
    inference methods, 249–251
    instance space vs. description space, 253–254
    mixed methods, 255–256
    model-driven methods, 255
    rule-guided inference, 253
    validation, 256
  connectionism and, 271
  design and, 336
  game playing and, 548–549
  intelligence and, 711–713
  language acquisition and, 769
  machine, 785–801
    acquired knowledge representation, 786
    algorithms, 800
    analytic learning, 795–797
    apprentices, 787
    backpropagation, 789
    belief revisions and, 114–115
    case-based methods, 797–799
    concept hierarchies, 794–795
    connectionist learning, 788–790

INDEX

decision tree construction, 793–794
empirical methods, 792–795
experience and, 786
genetic algorithms, 790–792
incremental and nonincremental, 787
inductive and analytic, 788
integrated cognitive architectures, 801
methodology, 800–801
paradigms of, 788–800
performance tasks, 787
philosophy of AI and, 1145–1146
research dimensions, 786–788
semantic networks, 1508–1509
similarities among paradigms, 799–800
supervised and unsupervised, 787
testbeds and applications, 801
theoretical analysis of learning algorithms, 800
neural networks, 1017, 1032–1033
landmark learning, 1034–1035
statistical mechanics, 1040–1042
perception and, 1662
problem solving, 1226–1227
schema theory, 1428, 1440–1441
supervised, in neural networks, 1032
Turing machines and, 1624
unsupervised
in neural networks, 1032
pattern recognition, 1120
Least commitment grammar, story analysis, 1575
Least effort principle, preference semantics and, 1183
Least-squared error methods
Hough transforms, 618
object recognition, search techniques, 1072
Left-corner parsing, 1103
Legendre polynomials, color vision, 200
Legged robots, 1398–1407
design and mobility, 1380
dynamics and balance, 1401–1402
history, 1399–1401
running machine research, 1404–1405
LEGOL project, law in AI and, 781
Leibniz, G. W., 462
Leopard spots theory, neural networks, 1019
Let binding, LISP language, 823
Levesque theory of belief representation, 103–104
Levi-Strauss, Claude, 602
Lewis, C. I., 862
LEX project, problem solving, 1226–1227
Lexical analyzers, coroutines, 301–302
Lexical decomposition, 806–811
artificial intelligence, 810–811
frame-based semantics, 810–811
lexical items, 806
language acquisition models and, 765–766
linguistic approaches, 806–810
case grammar, 809–811
componential analysis, 807–808, 810
dictionaries and thesauri, 807, 810
field theory, 807
generative semantics, 808, 811
interpretive semantics, 808, 810
Jackendoff's theory, 808–809, 811
sense relations, 807, 810
thematic roles, 810
natural language generation, 990
Lexical entries, dictionary/lexicon construction, 341
Lexical functional grammar (LFG)
augmented transition network (ATN) grammars, 559–560
dictionary/lexicon construction, 345
generalized phrase-structure grammar and, 570
semantic networks, 1506
systemic grammar and, 587–588
Lexical inheritance theory, dictionary/lexicon construction, 352–353
Lexical knowledge acquisition, dictionary/lexicon construction, 355–362
Lexical semantics, 812–816
ambiguity and polysemy, 815–816
computational linguistics, 218
hermeneutics, 608
semantic classes, 813–815
word meaning, 813
word relations, 815
Lexical-interaction language (LIL), 1111–1112
Lexicalized tree-adjoining grammars, 578–579
Lexicon construction. *See* Dictionary/lexicon construction
LIFER system, 819
computational linguistics, 209
natural language understanding, 1011–1012
semantic grammars, 1004–1005
semantic grammar, 580–582
Lifshitz, W., 1285
Lifting Theorem, mathematical induction, 670
Light
color vision and, 193–194

perception and, 1657–1658, 1660
Lighthill, James (Sir), 25–26
Likelihood ratio parameters, 89–90
Limit analysis, qualitative physics, 1155
Limit cycles, neural networks, 1020
Line adjacency graph (LAG), 141–142
Line detectors, early vision, 412
Linear algorithms
image intensity, 1649–1650
optical flow analysis, 1646–1647
two-view motion analysis, 1642–1643
Linear equations, visual recovery, 1680–1681
Linear polynomial technique, checkers-playing programs, 153–154
Linear precedence (LP) rules, 570
Linear programming
fuzzy constraints and crisp objective functions, 523–524
symmetric fuzzy programming, 522–523
Linear properties of images, 638
Linear regression, heuristics and, 614
Linear systems, neural networks, 1020
Linear threshold units, machine learning and, 788–789
Lines of curvature, shape representation, 1528
Linguistics
augmented transition network (ATN) grammars, 558–559
Brown Corpus, 128–130
cognitive psychology, 182
cognitive science and, 191
computational, 203–218
discourse understanding, 374–376
frame theory, 493–494
lexical decomposition, 806–810
case grammar, 809–811
componential analysis, 807–808, 810
dictionaries and thesauri, 807, 810
field theory, 807
generative semantics, 808
interpretive semantics, 808, 810
Jackendoff's theory, 808–809, 811
sense relations, 807, 810
lexical semantics, 813
machine translation, 902
mental models and, 934–935
morphology, 968
natural language generation, 984–985
systemic grammars, 993–994
natural language understanding, 997–999
pattern recognition, 1116
presupposition handling, 1187–1201
quantifiers, fuzzy semantics, 520–521
semantic networks, 1495
Linking, planning and, 1161–1164
LISP 1.5 version, 833–834
compiler, 834
destructive list operation, 833
FUNARGS, 833
functions, 834
numbers, 833
program feature, 834
property lists, 833
special forms, 833
variables, 834
LISP 1.6, 837
LISP 370, 824, 838
LISP language, 819–841
automatic programming, 65–73
code synthesis, 67–68
flowchart construction, 65–66
graph factorization, 69–70
PROLOG synthesis, 70–72
recurrence relations, 68–69
trainable Turing machine, 66–67
backquote, 825–826
basics of, 820
bindings, 822–823
deep-binding, 823
free and bound references, 823
let or lambda binding, 823
let-binding, 831
low-binding, 823
shallow binding, 835
special binding, 823
blackboard system building, 121–122
closures, 826–827
cognitive modeling, 179
commercial machines, 839
compilation, 831–832
CONS cells, history, 832–833
control structures, 294
serial generalizations, 295
symbolic computation, 298–299
coroutines, 302
data abstraction, 826
dialects, 837–838
engineering and KBES, 450
explanation and, 491
extending, 839–840

Flavors programming, 493
functions, 820, 824–825
history
1956–1960, 832–834
1960–1970, 834–835
1970–1980, 835–838
1970–1985, 838–839
1980-present, 839
IBM and, 838
implementation
history, 832–833
real-time, 841
inductive inference, 673
interpretation, 830–831
knowledge representation and, 744
knowledge system techniques and, 481
lambda lists, 827
literature on, 846–847
macros, 825
mental imagery representation, 929–930
meta-interpretation, 939
object-oriented languages, 776–777
program development strengths, 840–841
debugging environment, 840
human-computer interaction, 723
separate compilation, 840
typelessness, 840
recursion and, 1339–1340
run time typing, 829–830
characters and strings, 830
data structures, 830
vectors and arrays, 830
simple evaluation model, 828–829
simple examples, 819–820
software, 839
Symbolics Machine and, 243–246
symbols, 822, 824
syntax, 820–822
algebraic syntax, 822
CONS cells and lists, 820–831
programs and data, 821–822
symbols and atoms, 820
word-expert parsing (WEP), 1110
LISP machines, 843–843
garbage collection, 842
graphical display console, 842
history - 1970–1985, 838–839
parallel machine architecture, 1094–1095
software environment, 842
virtual-address space, 842
LISP/VM, 824, 838
List processing, in computer systems, 245–26
Literature, AI in, 844–848
anti-AI literature, 846
current trends, 846–487
cybernetics, 844
future trends, 848
historical sources, 846
history of, 844–846
overview of, 846
LMA program, binary resolution, 1351
LMS procedure, machine learning and, 789
Local feature detection, 422–433
intensity changes, 422–432
one-dimensional detection, 424–428
two-dimensional detection, 428–432
recovering properties, 432–433
Local property images, 637
Local random field models, texture analysis, 1592–1595
Localist connectionism, 270–271
Locality, in qualitative physics, 1156–1157
Locke, John, 462
LOCO program, 979
Locomotion
legged robots, 1399
active balance, 1402–1404
rough terrain, 1405–1406
robotics design and, 1379–1380
Loftus effect, integrated in-depth parsing and, 1452–1453
Logic, 851–852
AI and, 851–852
causal-temporal, causal reasoning, 1284–1285
cognitive modeling, 177
commonsense reasoning, 1288
completeness, 202
conditional, 854–859
material implication, 854–855
nonmonotonicity, 858–589
proof theory, 855–857
semantics, 857–858
deductive databases, 320–321
depiction and, 853–854
epistemology, 460
formalism, text analysis, 371
higher-order, 860–862
computational applications, 861–862
proof theory, 861
semantics, 860–861

syntax, 860
incidence calculus, 667–668
inference and, 682–683
inheritance hierarchies, 692
knowledge representation and, 745–746
law in AI and, 778
modal, 862–864
    axiomatic systems, 862–863
    belief representation, 100
    dynamic logic, 864
    first-order, 863–864
    formalisms, 862–863
        Kripke models, 863
    temporal, 863
nature of, 851
neat/scruffy debate, 851–852
nonmonotonic, 1303–1305
    default reasoning, 1296–1297
object-oriented languages, 773
omniscience concept, belief representation systems, 104
order-sorted, 864–866
positivism, hermeneutics and, 604
predicate, 866–872
    deductive systems, 869–870
        axiomatic, 869–870
        natural-deduction, 870
    descriptions, 871–872
    extensions, 871–872
        identity, 871
    language, 867–869
        expressibility, 869
        semantics, 868–869
        syntax, 867–868
    metatheoretic results, 872
    second-order logic, 872
propositional, 891–896
    deductive systems, 894–896
        semantics, 896
        syntax, 894–895
    knowledge system techniques and, 478–481
    language of, 891–894
        semantics, 892–893
        syntax, 892
second-order, 872
semantic networks, 1503–1504
of general awareness, belief representation systems, 104
systems, 851
truth maintenance systems, 1619
Z modal quantification, 1689
see also Fuzzy logic
Logic programming, 873–889
    alternative execution strategies, 885–886
        dependency-directed backtracking, 885
        intelligent execution, 885
        loop detection, 886
        subgoal selection, 885–886
    alternative programming schemes, 886–888
        AND parallelism, 886
        committed-choice languages, 887
        constraint logic, 887–888
        OR parallelism, 887
        parallelism scope, 886
    binary resolution, 1343
    constraint networks, 274–276
    constraint satisfaction, 290–291
    control structures, 297
    coroutines, 302
    lazy evaluation, 305–306
    deductive databases, 320, 883–884
    dependency-directed backtracking, 87–88
    domain knowledge, 390
    ECRC program, 420
    expert systems, 884–885
        declarative input-output, 884
        heuristic vs. algorithmic programming, 884–885
        production rules, 884
    functional programming, 882–884
    Horn clauses
        AND/OR nondeterminism, 875–876
        arbitrary subgoals, 880
        extensions, 878–880
        historical origins, 874–875
        metalevel programming, 880
        minimodel semantics, 876–877
        negation-as-failure, 878–879
        procedural interpretation, 874–877
        procedural vs. declarative knowledge representation, 875
        recursive data structures, 876
        solution sets, 880
        Yale shooting problem, 879–880
    inference, 683
    knowledge representation and, 746
    literature on, 847
    meta-interpretation, 939
    parallel languages, 1081–1087
        access mode restriction, 1083–1084

AND-parallel computation model, 1082
    comparisons, 1086
    declarative semantics, 1083
    hierarchical structure and flatness, 1085–1086
    operational semantics, 1083
    OR-parallel environments, 1084–1085
    process reading, 1083
    semantics issues, 1086–1087
    syntax, 1082–1083
processing, bottom-up and top-down, 1231–1232
program derivation, 881–882
PROLOG system, 877–878
    clause addition and deletion, 878
    pruning with cut, 877–878
    sequential control, 877
semantic networks, 1493
specifications, 880–881
structuring methods, 888–889
    modules and metalevel structures, 889
    object-oriented programming, 888–889
style, 1236
unification, 1632
Logic Theory (LT) machine, 1230
LOGIX system, parallel machine architecture, 1091–1092
LOGLISP language, 883, 887
LOGO programming language, 897
Lohman, D., 709
Long-term memory (LTM)
    adaptive resonance theory and, 14–16
    schema theory, 1433–1434
        scene interpretation, 1438–1439
Look-ahead technique
    constraint networks, 277
    heuristics and, 613–614
    horizon effect, 615–616
Look-back technique, constraint networks, 277
Loop detection, logic programming and, 886
LOOPS system, 897
    automatic programming, 64
    belief revision and, 111
    domain knowledge, 390
    Flavors programming, 493
LOPS program, 897
Low-level vision
    neural networks, 1025–1028
    segmentation in, 395–403
LSP lexicon, entry structure, 349–350, 352
Lucas, J. R., 1142–1143
LUNAR system, 897
    augmented transition network (ATN) grammar, 554–555
        parsers, 560–561
    computational linguistics, 208–209
        grammatical formalisms, 214–215
    deep structure, 329
    dictionary/lexicon construction
        lexical entry structure, 347
        word senses, 354
    parsing speed, 1107
Lyapunov function, neural networks, 1020

M.1 system, rule-based systems, 1425
Mach bands
    early vision, 394, 409–410
    perception and, 1657–1658
    segmentation and, 396–397
MACHACK 6 system, 898
    computer chess programs, 224
Machine consciousness, philosophy of AI and, 1141–1142
Machine indexing, thesaurus development, 1607
Machine kinematics, spatial reasoning, 1331
Machine learning, 785–801
    acquired knowledge representation, 786
    algorithm analyses, 800–801
    analytic learning, 795–797
        macro-operators, 795–796
        preference rules, 796
        rule compilation, 795
    belief revisions and, 114–115
    case-based methods and analogy, 797–799
        indexing and memory organization, 798
        cases and abstraction, 799
    classifier systems, 791
    clustering analysis, 170
    cognitive modeling, 177
    concept learning, 249–257
    connectionist learning, 788–790
        alternative approaches, 789–790
        backpropagation in multilayer networks, 789
        perceptrons and linear threshold units, 788–789
        research issues, 790
    current research, 786–788
    empirical methods, 792–795
        concept hierarchies, 794
        decision tree construction, 793–794
        production rules, 792–793

experience representation, 786
genetic algorithms, 790–792
incremental and nonincremental, 787
induction and explanation, 799
inductive and analytic, 788
integrated cognitive architectures, 801
knowledge acquisition and, 726–728
knowledge levels and, 742–743
methodology, 800–801
performance tasks, 787
philosophy of AI and, 1145–1146
semantic networks, 1508–1509
supervised and unsupervised, 787
symbolic and subsymbolic induction, 799
testbeds and applications, 801
Machine teaching, case-based reasoning, 1276
Machine translation, 898–902
    artificial intelligence (AI), 56
    computational linguistics, 204, 213
    difficulties of, 898–899
    humanistic, 900–901
    phrase-structure and case grammars, 901–902
    scripts, 1447–1448
    semantic networks, 1493
    systemic grammar and, 591
    theories and methodologies, 899–900
    thesauri and, 1609–1610
Machine-readable dictionaries (MRDs), 355, 358–362
Mackworth, A. K., 647–648
MacLisp, history, 835–836
Macromolecular structure determination, 160
Macros
    LISP language, 825
    machine learning, 795–796
    means-ends analysis, 914
    planning and, 1166–1167
    search and, 1466
MACSYMA system, 902–903
    chemistry in AI and, 160
    domain knowledge, 389
MacWhinney's competition model, 768–769
Magnetic grippers, 1362–1364
Maintenance information, dictionary/lexicon construction, parsing lexicons, 342–345
Man-machine interface (MMI), Alvey program, 26
see also Human-computer interaction
Manchester scheduler, parallel machine architecture, 1092
Manhattan distance
    heuristics and, 612–613
    search, 1464–1465
Manipulation, robotics design and, 1377–1378
Manufacturing, AI in, 903–908
    process planning, robotics design, 1395
    see also Computer-integrated manufacturing (CIM)
Many-sorted resolution, theory resolution and, 1356–1357
Map-learning, spatial reasoning, 1328
MAPLE system, chemistry in AI and, 160
Marcus parser, language acquisition, 763
Marcus, Ruth Barcan, 864
MARGIE system
    computational linguistics, 217–218
    conceptual dependency and, 263–264
    scripts, 1447–1448
Marine Integrated Fire and Air Support System (MIFASS), 952
Markgraf Karl Refutation Procedure (MKRP), 962–963
    graph-based resolution, 1355
    HADES program, 595
    mathematics knowledge representation and, 909
    proof transformation, 1238
Markov models
    decision theory, 319–320
    texture analysis, 1592–1594
Markov random field (MRF) model, 630–631
    simulated annealing, 1540
    stereo vision, 1564
Markov rules
    probabilistic networks, 1207
    rule-based systems, 1423
Marr, David, 932–933
    image understanding and, 648–649, 652
MaRS machine, parallel machine architecture, 1094–1095
Maslov's inverse method, connection calculus, 267
Mass assignments
    fuzzy set theory, 528
    input-output pairs, 531–532
    support pairs, 529–532
Mass spectroscopy, chemistry in AI and instrumentation, 159
    structure elucidation, 158
Massive parallelism, studies in, 626–627
Masterman, Margaret, 1495
MASTERSCOPE, InterLisp, 836–837
MATCH algorithm

neural networks
  optic flow, 1027
  optimization, 1023
  schema theory, 1432
Matching techniques
  frame theory and, 498–499
  image understanding and, 644–645
  knowledge representation and, 751
Material conditional paradox, 854–855
  propositional logic, 894
Material implication, conditional logic, 854–855
Mathematics
  binary resolution, 1351
  game playing and, 543
  induction, 668–672
    algorithm termination and recursion analysis, 670–671
    automated induction, 669–671
    axiom computation, 669–670
    basic prover, 670
    completion, 671–672
    implementation, 671
    theoretical foundations, 668–669
  knowledge representation, 909
  machine learning and, 797–799
  perceptrons, 1130
  programming, fuzzy programming, 521–527
Matrix reduction, connection calculus, 267
Matrix sensors, 1368
Matsuoka, K., 1404–1405
Maximum entropy principle (MEP)
  Hopfield networks optimization, 1021
  epsilon-semantics, 474
  probabilistic reasoning, 1312
Maximum likelihood estimates
  texture analysis, 1593–1594
  visual recovery, shape from contour, 1676
McCarthy, John, 21, 832–834, 851–852
  circumscription, 166
McClelland, J., 765
McCulloch, W. S., 1430
McCulloch-Pitts neuron
  Hopfield networks optimization, 1020–1021
  neural network modeling, 1017–1018
  winner-take-all networks, 1025
McDermott, D. V., 1335–1336
MDX system
  AI in medicine (AIM) and, 918
Meaning
  deep structure, 329–330
  eidetic phenomenology, 607–608
  Gadamer's hermeneutics and, 599–600
  lexical semantics, 812–813
  memory and, 457
  representation, in case grammar, 565–566
Means-ends analysis, 909–915
  ABSTRIPS program, 913
  FDS program, 912
  good difference information, 914–915
  GPS (general problem solver), 909–912
  MPS technique, 913–914
  problem solving reduction schema, 1224
  STRIPS program, 912–913
Mechanical design
  constraint satisfaction, 290
  legged robots, 1407
Mechanized assistant
  automatic programming, 77–81
    automatically generating search programs, 79–81
    programmer's assistant, 78–79
Mediating representations, knowledge acquisition, 719–720
MEDIATOR system, 915–916
  case-based reasoning, 1270, 1273
  dynamic memory, 392
  memory organization packets (MOPs), 927
MEDIC system, 916
  case-based reasoning, 1274
Medicine, AI in, 961–924
  biomedical taxonomy and, 917–918
  case grammar, 563
  causal reasoning and, 1280–1281
  decision theory, 318–319
  evaluation functions, 919
  example systems, 922–924
    human issues, 924
    ONCOCIN, 924
    Pathfinder and Intellipath, 923–924
    Quick Medical Reference, 922–923
  inference and control methods, 918
  knowledge structure, 918
  medical knowledge base, 917
  object-oriented languages, 773–775
  overview, 916–917
  pattern recognition, 1126
  protocol analysis, 917
  research themes, 919–922
    causal reasoning, 920–921
    decision-theoretic expert systems, 919–920

diagnostic strategies, 921
explanation and critiquing, 921–922
knowledge acquisition, 919
temporal reasoning and planning, 921
validation, 922
systems
  CADUCEUS, 131
  CASEY system, 131
  certainty-factor (CF) models, 131–132
  subject headings, (MeSH) 918
    thesaurus development, 1607
  uncertainty management, 918–919
Medium-term memory (MTM), adaptive resonance theory and, 14–16
Meldman, J. A., 779
Memo functions, concept learning, 250
Memory
  associative, 57–58
  case-based reasoning
    organization, 1270
    theory, 1266
    updating and, 1268–1269
  cognitive modeling, 179
  cognitive psychology and, 184
  dynamic, 391–392
  episodic, 454–459
  events as experienced, 456–457
  frame theory and, 497–499
  machine-learning and, 798
  management of, in computer systems, 243, 245–246
  mental imagery representation, 928–931
  neural networks, 1051–1052
  primary, 455–456
  recollection, 458–459
  rule-based systems, 1419–1420
  schema theory, 1433–1434
  secondary, 456–459
  semantic, 454–455
  text summarization, 1583–1584
  see also Long-term and Short-term memory
Memory-based reasoning (MBR), 1300–1301
  data parallelism and, 316–317
  parallel machine architecture, 1097
Memory organization packets (MOPs), 926–927
  case-based reasoning, 1266
  computational linguistics, 216
  conceptual dependency and, 264
  Cyrus system, 312
  dynamic memory, 392
  E-MOPs (episodic MOPs), 1458
  integrated in-depth parsing and, 1452–1453
  law in AI and, 782–783
  S-MOPs (simple MOPs), 1457–1458
  scripts, 1449
    acquisition, 1457–1458
  semantic networks, 1508
  span, primary memory capacity and, 456
  tables, computer chess and, 237–238
MENO-II system, 622
Mental abilities, intelligence and, 707–708
Mental imagery representation, 928–931
  behavioral evidence, 930–931
  computational systems, 931
  epiphenomenality, 929
  historical background, 928
  methodology, 920
  propositional representation, 928–929
  representational debate, 929–931
Mental lexicon, dictionary/lexicon construction, 353–354
Mental models, 932–938
  algorithms for model-based deduction, 935–938
    predicate calculus, 937–938
    propositional reasoning, 935–937
  cognitive science and, 190
  comprehension and discourse models, 933–934
  deduction and, 934–935
  knowledge acquisition, 934
  machine translation, 900–901
  neural networks, 1040
  perception, 932–933
  qualitative physics, 1150
Menu-based user interface, 619
Merchant, M. E., 907–908
Merging algorithms, segmentation and, 1486–1487
Merleau-Ponty, 1132, 1134
MERLIN system, 939
Message passing
  actor formalisms, 4
  control structures, 294
  object-oriented languages, 775
Message refinement, natural language generation, 988–990
Meta-argument units, 46–48
Meta-DENDRAL program
  chemistry in AI and, 158
  concept learning, 255

Metafunctionality, systemic grammar and, 585–586
Meta-interpretation, 939–940
Meta-knowledge, 940–946
  connecting theories, 944–945
  design and, 335
  human cognition, 941–942
  knowledge and, 944
  motivations, 942–943
  rule-based systems, 1421–1422
  systems with, 945–946
Metalevel programming
  Horn-clause logic, 880
  logic programming, 889
Metalinguistic utterances, natural language understanding, 1011
Meta-MOPs, dynamic memory, 392
Metaphorical interpretation, machine translation, 901
Meta-reasoning, 940–946
  knowledge and, 944
  reasoning and, 942–944
  rule-based systems, 1421–1422
Meta-rules, 940–946
  explanation and, 490
  knowledge and, 944
  planning and, 1165–1166
  rule-based systems, 1421–1422
  TEIRESIAS system, 945–946
Metascience, hermeneutics and, 603–605
Meta-theorems
  epsilon-semantics, 470
  predicate logic, 872
Methodological hermeneutics, 604
Methodological solipsism, phenomenology and, 1132–1133
Metropolis method, simulated annealing, 1538–1540
Microfeature, distributed connectionism, 271–272
Micromanipulator, robotics research and, 1379
MICRO-PLANNER, 947
  computational linguistics, 208
  constraint satisfaction, 287
Microrelations, distributed connectionism, 271–272
MIDI program, AI in music and, 977–978
Military applications of AI, 947–958
  autonomous land vehicle (ALV), 949
  background, 947–949
  combat resource allocation, 952–953
  equipment maintenance and troubleshooting, 954–956
    automatic test equipment, 954–955
    built-in testing (BIT), 955
    interactive aids, 955–956
  HASP system, 119
  mission planning, 953–954
  natural language understanding, 956–958
  naval battle management, 949–950
  pilot's associate, 949
  sensor information integration, 950–952
  training programs, 956
MIMD parallel model, data parallelism and, 316
Minimal game tree, computer chess and, 227–228
Minimal model semantics, logic programming, 876–877
Minimal window search, computer chess and, 229
Minimality conditions, situation semantics, 1543
Minimax procedure, 959–962
  computer chess and, 226–227
  game playing and, 544–545, 959
    kernal calculations, 546
  game trees, 550
  heuristics and, 613–614
  strategies and payoffs, 959–960
  zero-sum two-person games, 960–962
Minimum search, 1465–1466
Minimum spanning trees, heuristics and, 612–613
Minsky, Marvin
  frame theory, 493–494
  knowledge representation and, 748–749
  logic, 852
  neural networks, 1037–1038
  nonmonotonic reasoning, 1302–1305
  pattern recognition, 1124–1125
  perceptrons, 1130
  programming paradigms and, 1236–1237
  schema theory, 1430, 1432–1433
MIP Expert System, engineering and KBES, 451–452
Misrecognition, frame theory and, 496
Mission planning, AI military applications, 953–954
MIT CONS machine, control structures, 298–299
Mix system, knowledge system building, 487–488
Mixed-initiative dialogue, education and AI, 435–436
ML program, POPLOG systems and, 1182
Mobile robots, 1409–1415
  architectures for, 1414–1415

design and, 1376
legged robots, 1399
mechanisms, 1413–1414
planning systems, 1412–1413
position sensing, 1410–1412
  lasar range finders, 1411–1412
  monocular vision, 1412
  passive ranging, 1412
  road following, 1412
  sonar sensing, 1410–1411
research and, 1379–1380
schema theory, 1437
visual motion analysis, 1640–1641
Modal logic, 862–864
commonsense reasoning, 1291–1292
dynamic logic, 864
first-order, 863–864
formalisms, 862–863
  axiomatic systems, 862–863
Kripke models, 863
temporal logic, 863
Z modal quantification, 1689
Mode declaration, parallel logic programming language, 1084
Model-based computer vision, 701
Model-directed learning, 255
image understanding and, 648
Model-theoretic semantics, 1184
Modeling
causation theories, 1279–1280
  explicit models, 1280–1281
  implicit models, 1281–1283
cognitive, 176–180
decision theory, 319–320
default reasoning
  model preference, 1298
discourse understanding, 368–369
education and AI, 442–443
elimination, connection calculus, 267
emotion, 446–448
human hand, robot end-effector design, 1358–1360
image modeling, 628–635
knowledge acquisition and, 725–726
mental models, 932–938
  algorithms, 935–938
  comprehension and discourse, 933–934
  knowledge acquisition, 934
  perception, 932–933
mobile robot planning, 1413
neural models, for neural networks, 1017–1018
program synthesis, 76
qualitative physics, 1151–1156
range data analysis, 1262–1264
robot sensing and, 1386–1387
shape representation, 1531–1532
spatial reasoning, 1331
Modularity
certainty-factor (CF) models, 133–135
control structures, 294–295
early vision, 407
object-oriented languages, 775
stereo vision, 1565
Modules, logic programming, 889
Modus ponens
belief representation heuristics, 102
binary resolution, 1343–1344
conditional logic, 855–857
incidence calculus, 665–666
knowledge representation and, 750–751
nonmonotonic reasoning and, 1304
possibilistic reasoning, 1315–1316
predicate logic, 869–870
programming paradigms and, 1237
Moire technology, range sensor design, 1519
Molecular biology, protein structure prediction, 1240–1245
amino acids, 1240
homologous proteins, 1244
polypeptide chains, 1240–1242
renaturation experiments, 1243
secondary structures, 1242–1243
structural levels, 1241–1242
MOLGEN system
knowledge system building, 488
meta-knowledge and, 946
planning and, 1169
  macro actions, 1166–1167
Moments of inertia, object recognition, 1066–1067
Monitoring systems, engineering and KBES, 451–452
Monochrome imaging, color vision and, 193–194
Monocular vision
design principles, 1518
mobile robot sensing, 1412
Monotonicity, conditional logic, 858
Montague grammar (MG)
dictionary/lexicon construction, 346
generalized phrase-structure grammar and, 570
story analysis, 1575

Monte Carlo simulations
decision theory, 319–320
incidence calculus, 667
Moore's theory of belief representation, 102
Moore, G. E., 463
MOPTRANS
dynamic memory, 392
memory organization packets (MOPs), 927
MORAN system, semantic networks, 1508
Morgenstern, R., minimax procedure, 959–960
Morphology, 963–970
agglutinating languages, 963
coroutines, 301–302
dictionary/lexicon construction
  inter-word entry information, 343–344
  lexical entry structure, 349–350
inflecting languages, 964
isolating languages, 963
lexical decomposition, 806
natural language generation, 983–984
natural language processing systems, 968–970
polysynthetic languages, 964
processes, 964–968
  cliticization, 966–967
  compounding, 967–968
  derivation, 964–965
  inflection, 965–966
  semi-affixes and combining forms, 965
speech understanding and, 1553
theoretical issues, 968
Most general unifier (MGU), 1630
Most nested heuristic, mathematical induction, 670
Motion analysis, cognitive science and, 189–190
Motion modeling and prediction, 1652–1653
Motion trajectories, robotics design and, 1377
Motion-based segmentation, 1487–1490
Move ordering mechanisms, computer chess and, 230–231
Moving average model, texture analysis, 1588–1589
MPG model, stereo vision, 1563–1564
MPP machines
control structures, 299
data parallelism, 315
MPS technique, means-ends analysis, 913–914
MRS language
control structures, 297
law in AI and, 781
rule-based systems, 1425
MS. Malaprop system, 972
Mu-Math, chemistry in AI and, 160
Mueller-Lyer illusion, 395
early vision, 409–410
Multiagent planning, distributed problem solving, 384
MULTIBUS program, LISP machine construction, 843
Multicausal interactions, Bayesian networks, 1203–1204
Multihypothesis variables, Bayesian inference methods, 91–92
Multipass algorithms, coroutines, 303
Multiple belief reasoner (MBR)
belief revisions and, 113–115
truth maintenance systems (TMS), 1618–1619
Multiple cues, visual recovery, 1679–1681
Multiple environments, parallel logic programming language, 1084–1085
Multiple frames, visual motion analysis, 1652
Multiple inheritance
exceptions, 693–694
inheritance hierarchies, 691–692
Multiple object recognition, visual motion analysis, 1652
Multi-PSI V1 and V2, 1090–1091
Multiresolution methods, edge detection, 430–431
Multisegment vehicles, mobile robot mechanisms, 1414
Multistage classification
pattern recognition, 1121
distributed problem solving, 383
Multivariate Gaussian model, 628–629
MUMBLE program
computational linguistics, 217
natural language generation, 988–990
Munsell system, color vision, 195–196
MUSE system
AI in music and, 979–980
parallel machine architecture, 1092
MUSIC MOUSE composition, 973
Music, AI in, 972–980
connectionism, 979–980
constrained selection, 974
exhaustive searches, 977
grammars, 978–979
heuristics, 974–976
overview, 972–974
procedural knowledge acquisition, 979
processing networks, 979

representation, 977–978
Musical distance, calculation techniques, 975–976
MUSICV program, 979
Mutual beliefs, belief representation systems, 105–106
Muybridge, Edward, 1399
MYCIN system, 982
AI in medicine (AIM) and, 916
  evaluation functions, 919
  explanation and critiquing, 921–922
  inference and control methods, 918
  knowledge acquisition, 917, 919
  knowledge structures, 918
  uncertainty, 919
certainty-factor (CF) models, 131–132
Dempster-Shafer theory and, 330
domain knowledge, 389
education and AI, 437
explanation and, 490
fuzzy set theory, 528
GUIDON system and, 593–594
knowledge engineering, history of, 478
knowledge representation and, 752–753
knowledge system building, 487
probabilistic reasoning, 1312–1313
rule-based systems, 1425
Turing test, 1629
see also EMYCIN
MYRTILLE-II, speech understanding and, 1557

NAIL! system, stratified databases, 326
Naive evaluation, deductive databases, 324
Naive physics, 1147–1148
mental models and, 934
qualitative physics, 1150
modeling, 1151–1152
spatial reasoning, 1329
temporal reasoning, 1335
Naive psychology, emotion modeling, 447
NAMER system, computational linguistics, 207
NANOKLAUS system
concept learning, 250
semantic networks, 1509
National Library of Medicine (NLM), 918
National Television System Committee (NTSC), 194
Natural language generation, 983–995
artificial intelligence (AI), 56
conceptual dependency, 259–264
current research, 985–987
grammar treatments, 991–994
  functional unification grammar (FUG), 992–993
  surface structure, 993
  systemic grammar and ATNs, 993–994
historical background, 987–988
planning, 995
procedural characteristics, 983–984
progressive message refinement, 988–990
  lexical choice, 990
  phrasal lexicons, 990–991
psycholinguistics, 995
standard components and terminology, 984–985
Natural language processing (NLP)
argument comprehension, 31
automatic programming, 59–60
computational linguistics, 203–204
commercialization of, 213
deep structure, 329
dictionary/lexicon construction, 341–342
  machine-readable dictionaries, 358–360
fuzzy logic, 515–521
hermeneutics, 596
information retrieval, 686–689
morphology, 968–970
natural language understanding, 997–999
program synthesis, 73–77
  acquisition modules, 74–76
  coding modules, 76–77
  historical background, 77
  system design, 73–74
semantic networks, 1497–1500
systemic grammar and, 583
thesauri and, 1605, 1609–1610
unification, 1634–1636
  feature structures, 1633–1634
Natural language understanding, 997–1014
analysis techniques, 999–1010
  case frame instantiation, 1006–1009
  pattern matching, 999–1001
  robust parsing, 1009–1010
  semantic grammars, 1004–1005
  syntactically driven parsing, 1001–1004
artificial intelligence (AI), 56
belief revisions and, 115
chemistry in AI and, 156–157
cognitive modeling, 177
cognitive science and, 189
computational linguistics, 215

concept learning, 252–253
conceptual dependency, 259–264
connectionism and, 273
dialogue phenomena, 1010–1013
  goal determination inference, 1013
dictionary/lexicon construction
  parsing lexicons, 342–345
discourse understanding, 376–377
domain knowledge, 389
emotion modeling, 447
epistemology and, 465–466
fuzzy logic semantics, 517–521
generation process and, 983–984
hermeneutics and, 605–606
higher-order logic, 861–862
human-computer interaction, 619
  AI applications, 620–621
information retrieval, 686–689
law in AI and, 782–783
machine translation, 898–902
meta-knowledge and, 941
military applications
  military messages, 956–958
  naval battle management, 950
  Pilot's Associate project, 949
Ms. Malaprop system, 972
natural language processing and, 997–999
nature of, 9997–999
  literalness, 998–999
  syntactic ambiguity, 998
  word sense ambiguity, 998
scripts, 1449–1456
  application, 1447–1448
semantic grammar, 580–582
SHRDLU and, 1538
speech understanding and, 1553
Natural learning
  case-based reasoning, 1267–1268
  predicate logic, 870
  see also Machine learning
Natural sciences, hermeneutics, 604–605
Naval battle management, AI military applications, 949–950
Navigation
  mobile robot sensing, inertial navigation, 1410
  range data analysis, 1263–1264
  schema theory, 1437
  spatial reasoning, 1326
Navlab Planner
  mobile robot planning, 1413
  spatial reasoning, 1328
Nearest neighbor concept
  DADO system, 313
  machine-learning and, 797–798
  robot sensing and, 1385
  segmentation and, 1481–1482
Neat-scruffy debate, logic and, 851–852
Necessity, possibilistic reasoning, 1317
Negation, deductive databases, 323–324
Negation-as-failure
  default reasoning, 1295
  logic programming, 878–879
Negation as Finite Failure (NFF), 323–324
Negative completeness, circumscription, 166
Negative-horizon effect, 616
Negotiation, distributed problem solving, 382–383
Neighbors, image properties, 638
NEOMYCIN system, explanation and, 490
NETL system
  connectionism and, 272
  frame theory and, 499
  property inheritance, 503
  inheritance hierarchies, 691–692
    structured concepts, 695–697
  knowledge representation and, 751
  semantic networks, 1495
NETtalk model, 1016
  neural networks, 1039–1040
Networks
  complexity, neural networks, 1037–1038
  connectionism and, 272
  problem solving, 381
Neural networks, 1016–1060
  adaptive resonance theory and, 13–14
  associative memories
    fixed point attractors, 1042–1048
      Gardner networks, 1047–1048
      Hopfield net spin representation, 1044–1045
      Hopfield network improvements, 1046–1047
      storage capacity, 1045–1046
    oscillatory, 1048–1049
  backpropagation, 1038–1040
  bibliographic resources, 1055–1056
  character recognition, 143, 148
  complexity, 1037–1038
  connectionism and, 272
  dynamic link architecture, 1053–1055
  early vision
    structural mechanisms, 411
  early vision and, 404

feature map self-organization, 1052–1053
Hebbian plasticity, 1033–1034
hill-climbing and landmark learning, 1034–1035
learning and self-organization, 1032–1033
machine learning and, 788–790
massive parallelism, 627
mobile robot sensing, 1412
nonadaptive, 1017–1032
  basic models, 1017–1018
  cooperative phenomena, 1018–1019
  dynamic system stability, 1019–1022
  elastic and neural optimization, 1022–1023
  low level vision models, 1025–1028
    feature detectors and information coding, 1026–1027
    optic flow MATCH algorithm, 1027
    regularization theory, 1027–1028
  oscillators and neural modulation, 1028–1032
    chain oscillator synchronization, 1031
    homogeneously coupled oscillators, 1031–1032
    rhythm generating circuitry, 1028–1030
  winner-take-all networks, 1023–1025
  statistical mechanics, 1025
pattern recognition, 1124–1125
perceptrons, 1035–1037
schema theory, 1433, 1436
  high-level vision, 1438
secondary protein structure prediction, 1245–1246
semantic networks, 1509
statistical mechanics of learning, 1040–1042
temporal-pattern encoding, 1049–1052
  complex sequence recognition, 1051–1052
  delay synapse networks, 1050–1051
  noise-driven sequence recognizer, 1051
Neural substrate, perception and, 1662–1663
Neurons
  leaky integrator, 1018
  elastic and neural optimization, 1022–1023
  structure, neural network modeling, 1017–1018
Newsletters, as AI source, 847
NEWTON program, spatial reasoning, 1329
Newton-Euler formulation, 1377
NEXPERT Object, knowledge system building, 488
NEXUS program
  story analysis, 1573
  text summarization, 1584
Neyman-Pearson scheme, pattern recognition, 1119
NIGEL system
  computational linguistics, 217
  natural language generation, 994
  systemic grammar and, 590–591
NIL LISP, 838
NLPQ program, automatic programming, 77
No-function-in-structure principle, 1151
NOAH system, 1060
  meta-reasoning and, 944
  planning and, 1161
    macro actions, 1166–1167
    problem solving, 1224
Nodes
  expansion, planning and, 1161–1164
  removal, probabilistic networks, 1205
Nogoods concept, dependency-directed backtracking, 86–87
Noise
  machine learning, 795
  range data analysis, 1251–1252
Noise-driven sequence recognizer, 1051
Nominal semantics, dictionary/lexicon construction, 346–347
NON-VON computers, 1060–1062
  applications, 1061
  architecture, 1060–1061
  benefits of, 1061
  control structures, 299
  parallel machine architecture, 1097
Nonadaptive neural networks. See Neural networks, nonadaptive
Noncompositional semantics, 345
Noncompositionality, computational linguistics, 215
Nondeterminism
  computational linguistics, 214
  finite-state automation (NFA), parsing, 1105–1106
  logic programming
    AND-OR dichotomy, 875–876
    Horn clauses, 874
  parallel machine architecture, 1089
Nonflat languages, parallel logic programming language, 1086
Nonincremental learning, machine learning and, 787
NONLIN system
  macro actions, 1166–1167
  planning and, 1161, 1169

Nonlinear systems
  membership functions, fuzzy mathematical programming, 524–525
  neural networks, stability, 1020
  two-view motion analysis, 1642
Nonmodularity, natural language understanding, 1004
Nonmonotonic justified (NMJ) rules, 1316–1317
Nonmonotonic logic (NML)
  conditional logic, 858–859
  default reasoning, 1296–1297
  fuzzy set theory, 534–535
  knowledge representation and, 754–756
  logic, 852
  nonmonotonic reasoning and, 1303–1304
Nonmonotonic reasoning, 1302–1306
  belief revision, 111
  causal reasoning, 1284
Nonnormalized fuzzy sets, 531
Nonparametric techniques, pattern recognition, 1120
Nonrigid objects, visual motion analysis, 1652
Nonseparable components, constraint networks, 282
Nonseparable graph, constraint networks, 282
Nonstationarity, image models, 632
Nonuniform rational B-splines (NURBs)
  range data analysis, 1254–1255
  shape representation, 1530
Normalized texel property maps (NTPM), 1674–1675
Noun phrases
  deep case grammar, 566–569
  generalized phrase-structure grammar and, 571
  natural language understanding, 1010
n-Parallel PROLOG, parallel machine architecture, 1093–1094
n-queens problem
  backtracking, 84
  problem formulation on search space, 85
NTT Data Flow Machine (DFM), 1094
Nuchess program, computer chess and, 238–239
Nuclear magnetic resonance (NMR)
  chemical structure elucidation, 158
  protein structure prediction, 1248
Numbers
  LISP 1.5, 833
  LISP language, 830
Numeric simulation, cognitive modeling, 178

Object assembly, intelligence and, 707
Object-oriented databases, 326–327
Object oriented data model (OODM), 513–514
Object-oriented languages, 772–777
  diversity, 776–777
  domain knowledge, 390
  frame theory and, 504–505
  history, 776
  intelligent program construction, 772–773
  knowledge-sharing, 775
  medical diagnostic applications, 773–775
  message-passing behavior, 775
  parallelism and, 775–776
Object-oriented programming
  control structures, 293
  coroutines, 306
  languages, 699–700
  logic programming, 888–889
  parallel machine architecture, 1095
  style, 1236
Object recognition, 1063–1078
  connectionism and, 273
  correspondence, 1073
  feature matching, 1067–1078
    alignment and hypothesis testing, 1074–1076
    3-D from 2-D recognition, 1076
    correspondence space search, 1069
    Hough transforms, 1076–1077
    parallel relaxation, 1076
    parameterized objects, 1077–1078
    pose space
      sampling, 1077
      search, 1076
    search alternatives, 1069–1073
      complete constrained search, 1069–1073
      exhaustive search, 1069
      heuristic search, 1073
      termination, 1073–1074
    selection or grouping methods, 1073
    system components, 1068–1069
  global methods, 1065–1067
    Fourier descriptors, 1066
    inertia moments, 1066–1067
    parameter vectors, 1066
    scope of, 1067
  image understanding and, 660–661
  indexing, 1073
  perception and, 1659–1660
  range data analysis, 1263

representation, 1063
robot sensing and, 1385–1386
scene complexity, 1064–1065
selection, 1073
sensor acquisition, 1063–1064
OBSERVER program, AI in music and, 979
OCCAM program
 causal reasoning, 1285–1286
 script acquisition and, 1457–1458
Occupancy array
 commonsense reasoning, 1290
 spatial reasoning, 1323
Octrees
 robot sensing and, 1388
 shape representation, 1533–1534
Ocular-dominance columns, stereo vision, 1565
Off-line programming, robotics design, 1394–1395
Office automation, computational linguistics, 211–212
Office of Naval Research (ONR), 947–949
OMEGA system, knowledge representation and, 753–754
ONCOCIN system, 1079
 AI in medicine (AIM) and
  flowsheet example, 923
  knowledge acquisition, 919
  temporal reasoning and planning, 921
  therapy process in, 924
One-dimensional signals, edge detection, 424–428
One-legged hopping machine, 1404–1405
Ontologies
 hermeneutics, 598–600
 knowledge acquisition and, 726
 knowledge representation and, 755–756
ONTOS project, dictionary/lexicon construction, 357–358
OPAL system, 1079–1080
 AI in medicine (AIM) and, 919
 PROTEGE system and, 1238
OpEd system, 1080
 argument comprehension, 30, 49–50
  issues, 31–34
  politico-economic knowledge, 34–36
 reasoning scripts in, 1453–1456
Open-loop control, robotics design and, 1376
Open-systems, distributed problem solving, 383
Open texture, law in AI and, 781
OPERA system, blackboard control architectures, 124
Operating systems coroutines, 305
Operational semantics, 1236
 constraint logic programming, 275
 parallel logic programming language, 1083
OPM system, characteristics of, 120
OPPLAN-CONSULTANT, 953–954
OPS program
 domain knowledge, 389–390
 knowledge system building, 488
OPS-5 language, 1080
 knowledge representation and, 752–753
 parallel machine architecture, 1097
Optic flow, neural networks, 1027
Optical character recognition (OCR). See Character recognition
Optical energy, optical sensor design, 1512
Optical flow, 1638–1640
 motion and shape, 1651
 normal flow, 1640
 visual motion analysis, 1645–1648
Optical sensors, design principles, 1512–1515
Optical spectrum, 1512
Optimal frequency domain filter, 424
Optimization
 Boltzmann machine, 126
 Hopfield networks and, 102–1022
 knowledge system techniques and, 480
 neural networks, 1022–1023
 problem solving, 1226
OR-parallelism
 machine architecture, 1089–1090
 programming language, 1084–1085
ORACLE system, parallel machine architecture, 1095–1096
Order-sorted logic, 864–866
Ordinal condition functions (OCF), 468
Organization theory
 distributed problem solving, 383–384
 memory and, 457–458
Orthographic projection
 two-view motion analysis, 1645
 visual recovery, 1666–1667
  shape from shading, 1670–1672
  surface orientation and shape, 1668
Orthographic words, dictionary/lexicon construction, 341
Oscillators, neural networks, 1028–1032
 associative memories, 1048–1049
 chain synchronization, 1031
 homogeneous coupling, 1031–1032
 neural activity, 1030–1031

OTTER system, 1080
 binary resolution, 1341–1342, 1351–1352
Outstar avalanche model, 1049–1052
Overlays, automatic programming, 78–79
OWL language, frame theory and, 504
OYSTER-CLAM system, mathematical induction, 671

PAIRS system, 159
PAM system, 1081
 discourse understanding, 373, 375–376
 dynamic memory, 391
 goal-based story analysis, 1570–1571
PANDEMONIUM
 architecture, 1081
 neural networks, 1026
 rule-based systems, 1423
Panum's area, stereo vision, 1565–1566
Papert, S.
 neural networks, 1037–1038
 pattern recognition, 1124–1125
 perceptrons, 1130
Paradigmatic axis, systemic grammar and, 583–585
Parallel computation studies, 626–627
Parallel distributed processing
 analog semantic features, 28
 see also Neural networks
Parallel Inference Machine (PIM), 247
 architecture, 1090–1091
 PIE64 architecture, 1093
Parallelism
 cognitive psychology and, 183–184
 data, 315–317
 early vision, 404–405
  functional streams, 409
 logic programming and, 886–887
 object-oriented languages, 775–776
 parallel machine architecture, 1089
 perception and, 1662
 speech understanding and, 1556
Parallel-jaw grippers, 1361–1362
Parallel logic programming languages, 1081–1087
 access mode restriction, 1083–1084
  comparison, 1084
  input guard, 1084
  mode declaration, 1084
  read-only annotation, 1084
 AND-parallel computation model, 1082
 common features, 1082–1083
  declarative semantics, 1083
  operational semantics, 1083
  process reading, 1083
  syntax, 1083
 flat languages, 1085–1086
 guard safety, 1085
 hierarchical computation structure, 1085–1086
 OR-parallel multiple environments, 1084–1085
 semantics issues, 1086–1087
Parallel machine architecture, 1088–1098
 checkers-playing programs, 150
 complex data structures, 1089
 concurrent processing, 1089
 conventional processing and, 1089
 DADO system, 313
 executable code, 1089
 fuzzy set theory, 535
 knowledge-based systems, 1095–1097
  blackboard systems, 1096–1097
  connection machines, 1097
  European declarative system, 1096
  multiuser parallelism, 1095–1096
  production systems, 1097
 LISP and functional programming, 1094–1095
 nondeterminism, 1089
 object-oriented systems, 1095
 primitive control operations, 1089
 PROLOG and logic programming systems, 1089–1094
  committed choice systems, 1091–1092
  parallel inference machine, 1090–1091
  pure parallelism systems, 1093–1094
  shared memory, 1092–1093
 symbolic processing, 1089
Parallel-marker propagation, inheritance hierarchies, 698–699
Parallel Prolog systems, 1089–1090
Parallel relaxation, object recognition, 1076
Parallel surface contours, edge detection, 412–413
Parameterization
 design, 334
 constraint satisfaction and, 332
 curvature surfaces, 1255–1256
 object recognition, 1077–1078
 range data analysis, 1255
 polynomial surface, 1253–1254
 vectors, 1066
Paramodulation
 binary resolution, 1348–1349

equality inferencing, 476–477
Paraperspective projection, visual recovery, 1667
Paraplates, preference semantics and, 1186–1187
Parlance system, dictionary/lexicon construction, 357
PARLOG
 logic programming and, 887
 parallel language, 1086
  flattening, 1085–1086
  mode declaration, 1084
 parallel machine architecture, 1092
PARRY system, 1099
 emotion modeling, 446
 natural language understanding, 1000–1001
 Turing test, 1629
Parser-interpreter system, 74–76
PARSE Program, 1230
Parse trees, natural language understanding, 1001–1002
PARSIFAL system
 augmented transition network (ATN) grammars, 559
 deep structure, 329
Parsimonious set covering, abduction, 2–3
Parsing, 1099–1108
 augmented transition networks (ATNs), 1105–1107
 context-free grammars and, 555–556
 grammars, 560–561
 Backus-Naur form grammar, 1100
 chart, 1104
 cognitive science and, 189
 computational linguistics, 213–214
 conceptual dependency and, 264, 1507
 context-free grammars, 1100
 coroutines, 301–302
 compilers, 304–305
 defined, 1099–1100
 feature-based grammars, 1104
 integrated in-depth, BORIS system, 1452–1453
 left-corner, 1103
 lexicons, dictionary/lexicon construction, 342–345
  inter-word/entry information, 343–345
  intra-entry information, 342–343
  word senses, 354
 machine translation, 898
 natural language generation, 993–994
 natural language understanding, 1004
  case frames, 1007–1009
  robust parsing, 1009–1010
  syntactically-driven, 1001–1004
 pattern recognition, 1116
 phrase-structure grammars, 1100–1102
 preference semantics and, 1183–1184, 1188–1189, 1191
 processing, bottom-up and top-down, 1230
  examples, 1230–1232
  left-corner and expectation-based parsing, 1234
 recursive-descent, 1102–1103
 semantic, 1507
  networks, 1507–1508
 speech understanding and, 1553
 speed comparisons, 1107
 syntax-directed, 1507
 top-down, pattern recognition, 1123
 transformational grammars, 1104–1105
 word-expert (WEP), 1109–1115
  abbreviated execution trace, 1114
  control mechanisms, 1113
  example analysis, 1113–1114
  formalization, 1111–1115
  message and memory objects, 1113
  model organization, 1112–1113
  principles, 1110
  program development, 1110–1111
  semantic networks and, 1507–1508
  structure, 1111–1112
  working memory after analysis, 1114–1115
Part whole descriptions, spatial reasoning, 1323
PART-OF concept
 distributed connectionism, 272
 image understanding and, 643, 647–649
 knowledge representation and, 750
 schema theory, high-level vision, 1438
Partial differential equation (PDE), texture analysis, 1590–1591
Partial global planning, distributed problem solving, 384–385
Partonomic structure
 adaptive planning and, 7
 top-level control, 8
Pask conversation theory, 311
Passive design techniques, robot end-effector technology, 1361–1364
Passive ranging
 design principles, 1517–1518
 mobile robot sensing, 1412
PATCHER program, 979

Path consistency, constraint satisfaction, 288–289
Path-finding problems, search techniques and, 1460–1461
  AI in medicine (AIM) and, 923–924
Path planning, schema theory, 1436–1437
PATR system
  dictionary/lexicon construction, 347–349, 350–351
  generalized phrase-structure grammar and, 571–572
Pattern matching
  AI in music and, 973
  knowledge representation and, 751
  natural language understanding, 999–1001
  processing, bottom-up and top-down, 1233–1234
  rule-based systems, 1421–1422
  SNOBOL-4 language, 1548
Pattern recognition, 1116–1127
  AI in chemistry and, 156
  applications, 1126–1127
    earth and space science, 1127
    fingerprint and character recognition, 1127
    medical diagnosis, 1126
    radar and sonar, 1127
    speech processing, 1126–1127
  clustering, 168
  codes, adaptive resonance theory and, 15–17
  color vision systems, 196
  game playing and, 548
  human-computer interaction, 621
  models and methodologies, 1118–1126
    artificial neural networks, 1124–1125
    decision theoretic model, 1118–1120
    genetic algorithms, 1125
    multistage classification, 1121
    nonparametric techniques, 1120
    performance assessment and feature selection, 1125–1126
    problem-reduction representations, 1123–1124
    signal processing, 1118
    state-space models, 1122
    syntactic recognition, 1122–1123
    unsupervised methods, 1120
  overview, 1116–1118
  perceptrons, 1130–1131
  segmentation and, 1474
Pattern space, neural networks, 1035–1036
PDP nets, AI in music and, 973
PDP-1 computer, LISP language development, 834–835
PDP-6 computer, 835
PDP-10 computer, 835
  control structures, 298–299
  demise of, 838
  MacLisp, 836
PDS architecture, 906
Peano arithmetic
  circumscription, 166
  first-order induction principle, 668–669
  higher-order logic, 861
Pearson Product-Moment Correlations, 707–708
Pengi program, reactive planning machines, 1173
PENMAN system, systemic grammar and, 590–591
PEPSys system, 1129
  parallel machine architecture, 1092–1093
Peptide bonds, protein structure prediction, 1240–1241
Perception, 1655–1663
  cognitive modeling, 179
  cognitive psychology and, 183
  color vision systems, 199–200, 1658
  cross-modal characteristics and processes, 1660–1662
  direct perception, 1656
  epistemology and, 463
  image understanding and, 646–648
  lightness and shading, 1657–1658
  mental models and, 932–933
  methods, 1657
  motion, 1659
  neural substrate, 1662–1663
  objection recognition, 1659–1660
  reactive planning machines, 1179
  representational, 1656
  research goals, 1657
  schema theory, 1434
    high-level vision, 1438
  spatial reasoning, 1325–1328
  steropsis, 1658–1659
  texture analysis, 1658
    human models, 1596–1597
  three-dimensional space and shape, 1659
  two-domain theory, logic and, 853–854
  visual competence, 1656–1657
Perceptrons, 1129–1131
  connectionism and, 272
  convergence theorem
    Gardner networks, 1048
    neural networks, 1037

limitations of, 1130
machine learning and, 788–789
neural networks, 1032–1033, 1035–1037
pattern recognition, 1124–1125
theoretical issues, 1130
Perceptual grouping, object recognition, 1073
Perfect information games, game trees, 551
Performance assessment
  information retrieval, 684–685
  pattern recognition, 1125–1126
  problem solving, 1215
Persistence, knowledge representation and, 755–756
Perspective, visual recovery, 1666
PERSUADER system, 1131
  case-based reasoning, 1270
  design applications, 1273
Phase-structure grammar (PSG)
  context-free grammars and, 574–576
  formal properties, 575–576
  generalized, 577–578
  head grammars, 578
  head-driven (HPSG), 578
  revival, 576–577
  terminal symbols, 576
  as transformation grammar (TG), 576
  tree-adjoining (TAG), 573–574, 578–579
Phase table method, checkers-playing programs, 155
Phase transition, Hopfield networks optimization, 1020
Phenomenology, 1131–1137
  AI and, 1132–1133
  character recognition, 143
  eidetic, 607–608
  epistemology and, 463–464
  Heidegger and, 1133–1134
  hermeneutics and, 598, 601–603
  human expertise and, 1134–1136
    competence, 1135
    proficiency, 1135
  Husserl and, 1133–1134
  philosophical overview, 1131
  philosophy of AI and, 1143–1144
  transcendental and existential, 1132
PHRED program, 1147
Philosophy, AI and, 1137–1146
  antimechanism, 1142–1143
  context and, 1144–1145
  epistemology and, 1143–1146
  functionalism, 1139–1140
  logical empiricism, 1145–1146
  of mind, 1137–1143
    computational theory, 1140–1142
    connectionism and, 1141
    semantics, 1141
    Turing test, 1137–1139
  phenomenological critique, 1143–1144
PHILOSOPHY-OF-SCIENCE mailing list, 847
PHLIQA system, computational linguistics, 210
Phonological analysis, speech understanding and, 1553, 1554–1555
Photoconduction detection, optical sensor design, 1515
Photometric stereo, visual recovery, 1672
Photopic response, optical sensor design, 1514–1515
Photorealism, shape representation, 1531–1532
PHRAN parser, 1147
  preference semantics and, 1190–1191
  semantic grammar, 582
Phrasal lexicons, natural language generation, 990–991
Phrase structure grammars (PSG)
  augmented transition network (ATN) grammar and, 554
  context-free (CP-PSG), 570
  generalized (GPSG), 570–572
  head-driven (HPSG), 572
  Japanese (JPSG), 572
  machine translation, 901–902
  parsing, 1100–1102
  revised generalized (RGPSG), 572
Phrase-structure trees
  deep structure, 329–330
  PSG and, 573–574
  revival of, 576–577
Physical reasoning, spatial reasoning, 1328–1332
Physical-symbol system hypothesis, cognitive science and, 191–192
Physicalism, philosophy of AI and, 1139
Physics
  commonsense reasoning, 1290–1291
  cooperative phenomena in, neural networks, 1019
  naive, 1147–1148
    temporal reasoning, 1335
  qualitative, 1149–1157
    ambiguities, 1153
    arithmetic, 1152

calculus, 1155
causal reasoning and, 1282
causality and feedback, 1156–1157
commonsense reasoning, 1290–1291
composability, 1150–1151
derivatives, 1152
envisioning, 1155–1156
equations, 1152–1153
modeling, 1153–1155
psychology and, 1150
quantity spaces, 1153
research issues, 1157
spatial reasoning, 1329
structure, 1151–1152
temporal reasoning, 1336–1337
quantitative vs. qualitative, 1149–1151
Physiology
  early vision, 400
  primate vision systems, 408–409
  intelligence and, 709
Piaget, Jean, 712, 762, 1130, 1285
  schema theory, 1440–1441
Picture arrangement, intelligence and, 707
Picture completion, intelligence and, 707
Picture Language Machine, computational linguistics, 207
Pierce, Charles S., semantic networks, 1494, 1504–1505
Pilot's Associate project, AI military applications, 949
PIM-R system
  control structures, 298–299
  parallel machine architecture, 1091
PIP system
  AI in medicine (AIM) and, 916
  knowledge structures, 918
Pipelining parallelism
  coroutines, 303
  parallel logic programming, 1082
Pitch analysis, AI in music and, 973, 975
Pitts, W. H., 1430
Pivot language, machine translation, 902
Pixels
  segmentation and
    color vision systems, 197–198
    measurement-space guided spatial clustering, 1474
  spatial reasoning, 1323
  texture analysis, 1587–1595
    one-dimensional time-series models, 1587–1589
    random field models, 1589–1595
  values, in color vision, 194–196
Planar curve correspondence, two-view motion analysis, 1644–1645
Planar patches
  image intensity, 1649–1650
  optical flow analysis, 1647
  two-view motion analysis, 1643
Plan-based help systems (PHI), 340
Plan-generate-test technique, DENDRAL system and, 331
Plan-oriented programming, style, 1236
Plan recognition, discourse understanding, 375–376
Plan splicing, 1168
PLANES system, 1159
  computational linguistics, 210
  natural language understanding, 1011–1012
PLANLOG system, 1159
PLANNER system, 1159
  backtracking in, CONNIVER system, 274
  belief revision and, 111
  control structures, 295–296
  dependency-directed backtracking, 88
  knowledge representation and, 744, 747
    characteristics, 752
    matching and, 751
  logic programming
    Horn clauses, 874
    negation-as-failure rule, 879
  rule-based systems, 1425
  SHRDLU and, 1538
Planner-Reactor-World system, 1178–1179
Planning, 1159–1170
  action representation, 1160–1161
  action selection, 1165–1166
  adaptive planning, 5–12
  applications, 1169
  backward chaining inhibition, 1166
  blocks world, 1160
  case-based reasoning, 1273–1274
  causal reasoning, 1283
  commonsense reasoning, 1292–1293
  constraints, 1166
  goal hierarchies and ordering, 1167–1168
  hierarchical, with macros, 1166–1167
  historical background, 1170
  image understanding and, 653
  law in AI and, 782

machine learning and, 797–799
mobile robot design, 1412–1413
natural language generation, 984, 995
operation, 1161–1165
problem solving, 1224
procedural subplanners, 1167
reactive, 1171–1180
  domain characteristics, 1172–1173
  machine architectures, 1173–1176
  reaction planning, 1176–1179
  techniques, 1173–1179
research issues, 1169–1170
schema theory
  explicit vs. implicit planning, 1440
temporal, 1168–1169
temporal reasoning, 1335
truth maintenance systems and, 1620
Planning systems
belief revisions and, 114–115
checkers-playing programs, 150
engineering and KBES, 452
text summarization, 1585
Plasticity, intellectual, intelligence and, 711–712
Plato, epistemology, 461–462
Plausible reasoning, 1307–1320. *See also* Uncertainty
approach evaluation, 1318–1319
approximate reasoning systems, 1309–1310
Boltzmann machine, 126–127
checkers-playing programs, 152–153
expert system uncertainty, 1307–1309
possibilistic approach, 1309, 1315–1317
  necessity, 1317
  PRIMO module, 1316–1317
  reasoning with uncertainty module (RUM), 1316
probabilistic reasoning, 1309–1315
  Bayes rule and modifications, 1310–1312
  Bayesian belief networks, 1313
  confirmation theory, 1312–1313
  Dempster-Shafer theory, 1313–1314
  evidence space, 13315
  evidential reasoning, 1314–1315
qualitative representation, 1317
real-time approximate reasoning systems, 1319
PLEXUS adaptive planner, 5–12
case-based reasoning, 1274
core matcher, 8–9
hierarchical planning and, 10–11
top-level control, 8
PLIDIS, dictionary/lexicon construction, 350
Plot unit theory, story analysis, 1573
Point adverbials, lexical semantics, 814
Point correspondence, two-view motion analysis, 1641–1643
Point estimation, pattern recognition, 1119
Pointer information, LISP language, 829
Poisson line, texture analysis, 1595
Poisson-Brown surfaces, texture analysis, 1592
POLIGON system
blackboard systems, 124
parallel machine architecture, 1096–1097
POLITICS system, 1181
dynamic memory, 391
Polynomial interpolation, inductive inference, 677–678
Polypeptide chains, protein structure prediction, 1240–1242
Polysemy
contrastive and complementary, 816
lexical semantics, 815–816
Polytext project, law in AI and, 782
Pong algorithm, segmentation and, 1482
POOL 1 and 2 languages, parallel machine architecture, 1095
POOMA system, parallel machine architecture, 1095
POP-11 system, 1182
POPLOG systems, 1181–1182
Popperian inference methods, inductive inference, 673
POPSYS, engineering and KBES, 452
Porphyry, 1493
Portable Standard LISP, 837
Pose space, object recognition
sampling, 1077
search of, 1076
Positional games, game playing and, 546
Positive completeness, circumscription, 166
Positive feedback, localist connectionism, 270–271
Positive-horizon effect, 616
Possibilistic reasoning, plausible reasoning and, 1309
Possibility distributions, fuzzy set theory, 528
Possible-worlds semantics
belief representation, 100
incidence calculus, 664
Potentials, mobile robot planning, 1413
PP-MEMORY, script application in, 1450–1451

P-Prolog, parallel logic programming language, 1086
Pragmatics, discourse understanding, 374–376
Prague school of linguistics, 807–808
Predicability, frame theory and, 501
Predicate calculus
clustering analysis, 172
computer systems, 242
frame theory and, 502–503
mental models and, 937–938
Predicate logic, 866–872
cognitive modeling, 179
commonsense reasoning, 1289
connection method, 266
constraint satisfaction, 286
deductive systems, 869–870
  axiomatic predicate logic, 869–870
  natural-deductive system, 870
deep structure, 329–330
extensions, 871–872
  descriptions, 871–872
  identity, 871
language, 867–869
  expressibility, 869
  semantics, 868–869
  syntax, 867–868
metatheoretic results, 872
planning and, 1161
processing, bottom-up and top-down, 1233–1234
second-order, 872
Predictability
connectionism and, 271
frame theory and, 495–497
qualitative physics, 1150
Preference rules, machine learning, 796
Preference semantics, 1182–1191
belief representations, 1184
computational semantics and, 1183, 1190–1191
extensions, 1188–1191
formulas, 1184–1185
inference rules, 1187
least effort principle, 1183
lexical decomposition, 811
linear language boundaries, 1184
paraplates, 1186–1187
parsing and, 1183–1184, 1191
preference definitions, 1188
primitives, 1184, 1191
procedural semantics and, 1183
pseudo-texts, 1187–1188
representation levels, 1184
templates, 1185–1186
thesauri, 1187
Preference values, AI in music and, 975
Preliminary design, 334
PREMO system, preference semantics and, 1189–1190
Preprocessing, stereo vision, 1561–1562
Presupposition, 1194–1201
as conventional implicatures, 1199
as discourse phenomenon, 1198–1199
Burton-Roberts definition, 1198
conventional but cancelable, 1199–1200
entailment analysis, 1200–1201
philosophical aspects, 1195–1196
projection problem, 1197
semantic theories, 1196–1199
Prey-selection models, schema theory, 1436
Price H. H., 463
PRIDE system, design and, 335
Primal-constraint graph, 277–278
Primal sketches
early vision, 407
image understanding and, 652
Primary memory, 455–456
Primate visual systems, early vision theories and, 408–409
Primitive competition model, neural networks, 1023–1024
Primitive control operations, parallel machine architecture, 1089
Primitives
computational linguistics, 215
preference semantics and, 1184–1185, 1191
syntactic pattern recognition, 1122–1123
tactile sensing data fusion, 1521
PRIMO module
evaluation, 1318–1319
possibilistic reasoning, 1316–1317
Printed circuit boards (PCBs), inspection systems, 702–704
Printer-carriage assembly, modular robotics design, 1391
Prior temporal reasoning, 1337
Probabilistic entailment, conditional logic, 858
Probabilistic inference, 683
inductive inference, 679–680
Probabilistic networks, 1201–1208
Bayesian networks, 95, 1202–1204
certainty-factor (CF) models, 134–135

correlation and causation, 1205–1207
Gaussian networks, 1207
influence diagrams, 1207
Markov networks, 1207
reasoning systems, 1201–1202
semantics and inference, 1204–1205
Probabilistic reasoning, plausible reasoning and, 1309
"Probabilistic relaxation algorithms," 290
Probabilistic uncertainties
fuzzy set theory, 528–535
  evidential reasoning, 533–535
  mass assignments, 528
  possibility distributions, 528
  support logic programming, 528–529
    inference, 532–533
  support pairs and mass assignments, 529–532
Probability
abduction, 3
Bayesian inference methods, 89
decision theory, 318
fuzzy set theory, 539
incidence calculus, 663, 665
machine learning, 795
probabilistic networks, 1201–1202
range data analysis, 1252
search and, 1466
Probably approximately correct (PAC) concept, 800
Problem acquisition, 1215
Problem reduction, 1209–1213
Alvey program, 29–30
AND/OR graphs, 29–30
applications, 1214
backtracking, 1210–1211
Horn clauses, 1210–1211
recursive formulation, 1211
representation, 1209–1210
search, 1211–1213
  algorithms, 1212–1213
  heuristic search, 1213
  solution graphs, 1211–1212
  top-down algorithm, 1213–1214
  uninformed search, 1213
strategy-seeking problems, 1210–1211
Problem solving, 1214–1227
abduction, 2
abstraction, 1226–1227
agenda-based systems, 21–22
analogy, 1226–1227
artificial intelligence, 56
backtracking, search space and, 84–85
branching factors, 127–128
case-based reasoning, 1273–1274
clustering, 168
cognitive modeling
  behavioral data, 178
  reasoning, 180
cognitive psychology and, 184–185
computational linguistics, 206
creativity and, 307
declarative formulations, 1214–1216
dependency-directed backtracking, 86–87
derivation problems, 1219–1220
distributed, 379–386
domain knowledge, 389
engineering and KBES, 449–450
expert systems, 477
FA/C approach, 383
formation problems, 1220
game playing and, 549
hybrid derivation and formation, 1224–1226
  constraint satisfaction, 1225–1226
  interpretation problems, 1224–1225
  optimization problem, 1226
inspection systems, 701–704
internal structure, 1215
interpretive case-based reasoning, 1276
learning and, 1226–1227
logic, 852–853
machine learning, 787
  preference rules, 796
machine translation, 899
means-ends analysis, 909
object-oriented languages, 773
pattern recognition, 1116
philosophy of AI and, 1144
procedural formulations, 1216–1218
processing, bottom-up and top-down, 1229
production schema, 1220–1222
protein structure prediction, 1239–1240
reduction schema, 1222–1223
relaxed reduction, 1224
representation, 1218–1219
shifts in, 1226
solution methods, 1219
temporal reasoning, 1335–1336
theory formation, 1226–1227
Problem space model, search and, 1461
Problem-reduction representation (PRR), 1123–1124

Procedural-declarative controversy, 297
Procedural problem formulations, 1216-1218
Procedural representations
    computational linguistics, 208
    knowledge representation and, 746-747
Procedural semantics
    computational linguistics, 208
    deductive databases, 324-325
    KL-ONE system, 718
    preference semantics and, 1183
    semantic grammar, 581
    semantic networks, 1509
Procedure-level representation, parallel logic programming language, 1084
Process-based modeling, qualitative physics, 1151, 1154
Process control
    chemistry in AI and, 159
    language (PCL), parallel machine architecture, 1096
Process planning, robotics design, 1395
Process reading, parallel logic programming language, 1083
Processing elements (PEs), DADO system, 313
Processing information, dictionary/lexicon construction, parsing lexicons, 342-345
Processing, bottom-up and top-down, 1229-1234
    Bayesian networks, 96
    bidirectional inference and search, 1234
    blackboard systems, 117-118
    branch-and-bound search2, 1472
    comparisons, 1233-1234
        efficiency, 1233
        pattern matching and unification, 1233-1234
    control structures, 296-297
    early vision and, 402
    examples, 1230-1233
        parsing, 1230-1232
        rule-based systems, 1232
        search, 1232-1233
    history of terms, 1229-1230
        data-driven processing, 1230
        forward vs. backward chaining, 1230
        goal-directed processing, 1230
    image understanding, 642
    knowledge system techniques and, 479
    left-corner and expectation-based parsing, 1234
    localist connectionism, 270-271
    mixed strategies, 1234
    pattern recognition, 1123
    rule-based systems, 1419
    scripts and, 1451-1452
PRODIGY program, machine-learning and, 801
Production control, computer-integrated manufacturing (CIM) and, 905-906
Production planning, computer-integrated manufacturing (CIM) and, 905
Production rules
    logic programming and, 884-885
    machine learning and, 792-793
Production schema, problem solving, 1220-1222
Production systems
    control structures, 294-295
    DADO system, 314
    domain knowledge, 389
    inference, 683
    knowledge representation and, 752-753
    parallel machine architecture, 1097
PROGRAMMAR program
    computational linguistics, 208
    SHRDLU and, 1538
Programming
    automatic, 59-81
    computer chess and, 235-239
    logic, 873-889
        alternative execution strategies, 885-886
        alternative programming strategies, 886-888
        expert systems and, 884-885
        functional programming and, 882-884
        Horn clauses, 874-877
            AND/OR nondeterminism, 875-876
            extensions, 878-880
            historical origins, 874-875
            minimal model semantics, 876-877
            procedural vs. declarative knowledge representation, 875
            recursive data structures, 876
        PROLOG, 877-878
        specification vs. program, 880-882
        structuring methods, 888-889
    paradigm, 1236-1237
    planning and, 1170
    robotics design, 1392-1395
        end-effector design, 1366-1367
        languages, 1392-1394
        off-line programming, 1394-1395
    rule-based systems, 1423
    styles of, 1234-1237
        language names, 1235-1236
Programming environment, knowledge system building, 486-489
Programming language
    control structures, 294-296
        modularity, 294-295
        serial virtual machines, 295-296
    dependency-directed backtracking, 88
    inheritance hierarchies, 691, 699-700
    knowledge acquisition, mediating representations, 720
    parallel logic, 1081-1087
    robotics design, 1392-1394
    styles of, 1235-1237
Programming Language for Natural Language Processing (PLNLP), 1508
Progressive deepening, computer chess and, 231
PROJECT2 score-generating program, 979
    AI in music and, 972
Projection
    case-based reasoning, 1275
    image understanding and, 645
Projective distortion, texture analysis, 1597
PROLOG system
    associative memory, 58
    augmented transition network (ATN) grammars, 559
    components and architectures, 246-248
    constraint satisfaction, 287
    control structures, symbolic computation, 298-299
    deductive databases, 320
    dependency-directed backtracking, 87-88
    ECRC programs, 420-421
    engineering and KBES, 450
    fuzzy set theory, 528-529
    inductive inference, 677
    law in AI and, 781
    left-corner parsing, 1103
    literature on, 847
    logic programming, 877-878
        clause addition and deletion, 878
        computation pruning, 877-878
        expert systems application, 884-885
        Horn clauses, 875
        sequential control, 877
    meta-interpretation, 939-940
    parallel logic programming, 1081-1082
    parallel machine architecture, 1090-1091
    POPLOG systems and, 1182
    rule-based systems, 1425
    synthesis, 70-72
    unification, 1632
Pronouns
    discourse understanding, 368-369
    resolution, scripts and, 1448
Proof by consistency, mathematical induction, 671-672
Proof finding, binary resolution, 1345-1346
Proof theory
    conditional logic, 855-857
    higher-order logic, 861
Proof transformation, 1238
PROP system, 451-452
Property inheritance, 692
    frame theory and, 500-501, 503
Propositional content, systemic grammar and, 585-586
Propositional language, incidence calculus, 664
Propositional logic, 891-896
    deductive systems, 894-896
        semantics, 896
        syntax, 894-895
    language, 891-894
        connective sets, 893-894
        semantics, 892-893
        syntax, 892
    mental models and, 935-937
    processing, bottom-up and top-down, 1230
Propositional networks, semantic networks, 1497-1500
Propositional representation, 928-931
PROSPECTOR system, 1238
    AI military applications, 952
    Bayesian inference methods, 96-97
    domain knowledge, 389
    probabilistic reasoning, 1310-1312
    rule-based systems, 1425
    semantic networks, 1500
Prostheses, cognitive science and, 188
PROTEAN system, knowledge system building, 488
Protectionism
    argument comprehension, 34-36
        reasoning scripts, 36-37
    politico-economic knowledge, 34-35
PROTEGE system, 1238
    AI in medicine (AIM) and, 919
    OPAL system and, 1080
Protein structure prediction, 1238-1248
    free energy minimization method, 1248
    molecular biology, 1240-1245
        amino acids, 1240
        homologous proteins, 1244
        polypeptide chains, 1240-1242
        renaturation experiments, 1243-1244
        secondary structures, 1242-1243
        structural levels, 1241-1242
    primary structure, 1241-1242
    secondary protein structures, 1241-1243, 1245-1246
        α helix, 1242-1243
        ß sheet, 1242-1243
        ß turn, 1242-1243
    global representation and prediction, 1247-1248
    protein classes, 1248
    surface residue prediction, 1248
    tertiary structure, 1241-1242
        prediction, 1248
PROTEUS system
    computational linguistics, text generation, 217
    historical background, 987-988
    natural language generation, 986-987
    systemic grammars, 994
    preference semantics and, 1190
    systemic grammar and, 590-591
Protocol analysis
    AI in medicine (AIM) and, 917
    AI in music and, 977
    knowledge acquisition, 722
Protos system, 1249
    case-based reasoning, 1274
    interpretation, 1275
Prototype
    frame theory and, 499
    image understanding, 643
PROUST system, education and AI, 437-439
Proximity, object recognition, 1074
Pruning
    alpha-beta, 22-24
    branch-and-bound technique, 1470-1471
    checkers-playing programs
        alpha-beta, 152-153
        forward pruning, 152-153
    computer chess and, forward pruning, 229-230
    sensor data fusion and, 1522
Pseudo-texts, preference semantics and, 1187-1188
PSI automatic programmer
    control structures, 298-299
    natural language dialogue, 73-77
PSL LISP, 838
Psycholinguistics
    argument comprehension, 31
    cognitive psychology, 182
    language acquisition, cognitive models, 764
    natural language generation, 995
Psychology
    case-based reasoning, 1267
    emotion modeling, 447
    hermeneutics and, 602
    heuristics
        belief representation systems, 104-106
        mutual beliefs, 105-106
        speech act theory, 104-105
    qualitative physics, 1150
    semantic networks, 1495
Psychometric research, intelligence and, 711-712
PTRANS, frame theory and, 500-501
PTTP system, 1249
PUFF system, AI in medicine (AIM) and, 924
Pulse time delay, robot sensing and, 1384

QED program, chemistry in AI and, 157
Quadrics, range data analysis, 1252
Quadtrees, shape representation, 1533-1534
Qualia structure, dictionary/lexicon construction, 353
Qualitative knowledge, early vision, 409-410
Qualitative physics, 1149-1157
    ambiguities, 1153
    arithmetic, 1152
    calculus, 1155
    causal reasoning and, 1282
    causality and feedback, 1156-1157
    commonsense reasoning, 1290-1291
    component-based, 1151
    composability, 1150-1151
    constraint-based, 1151
    derivatives, 1152
    education and AI, 443
    envisioning, 1155-1156
    equations, 1152-1153
    modeling, 1153-1155
    naive physics and, 1151-1152
    process-based, 1151
    psychology and, 1150
        mental models, 1150
        predictions, 1150
    quantity spaces, 1153

research issues, 1157
spatial reasoning, 1329
structure, 1151–1152
temporal reasoning, 1336–1337
Qualitative process theory, 1148
Qualitative reasoning
belief revisions and, 115
cognitive science and, 190
design and, 336
Quality-control (QC)
Bayesian inference methods, 96–97
inspection systems, 701
Quantitative analysis, color vision systems, 198
Quantitative knowledge, early vision, 409–410
Quantitative physics, 1149–1151
Quantum detection, optical sensor design, 1514–1515
Qubic board, game playing and, 549
Quenching thresholds, adaptive resonance theory and, 16–17
Query evaluation, fuzzy databases, 512–513
Query/Subquery (QSQ) method, deductive databases, 324–325
Question-answering systems, computational linguistics, 205–206
Quick Medical Reference (QMR), AI in medicine (AIM) and, 922–923
Quiescence search, computer chess and, 228–229, 236
Quillian models
knowledge representation and, 748–749
semantic networks, 1495
QXQ system, AI in medicine (AIM) and, 921

R1 system, 1688
knowledge system building, 487–488
history of, 478
Radar
design principles, 1516–1517
pattern recognition, 1127
Radiant flux, optical sensor design, 1512–1513
Radiation, thermal sensor data fusion, 1520
Raibert, P., 1404–1405
Rana computatrix
neural networks, 1056
schema theory, 1430, 1434–1436
Random field models
texture analysis, 1589–1595
Range data analysis, 1250–1264
applications, 1262–1264
data representations, 1252–1261
curvature-based surface description, 1255–1256
differential property estimations, 1260–1261
surface representations, 1252–1255
data sources, 1250–1251
mobile robot sensing, 1411–1412
noise modeling, 1251–1252
robot sensing and, 1386–1388
segmentation, 1261–1262
Range sensors
design principles, 1517–1519
sensor data fusion, 1521–1522
RAPIDS system, education and AI, 440
Raster displays, history, 332–333
Ratio decidendi concept, law in AI and, 779
Rayleigh quotient form, range data analysis, 1257
RDBMS systems, parallel machine architecture, 1095–1096
Reaction-diffusion equations, neural networks, 1019
Reactivation point, coroutines, 302–303
Reactive planning, 1171–1180
coupled systems, 1178–1179
domain characteristics, 1172–1173
guiding reactions, 1177–1178
hierarchical planning-reaction integration, 1177
improvisation and interaction, 1173
machine architectures, 1173–1175
behaviors and subsumption, 1174
goals and beliefs, 1174–1175
indexical-functional representation, 1174
monitoring change, 1175
machine design, 1175–1176
autogeneration, 1176
situated automata model, 1176
reactivity, 1172
time constraints, 1177
timely activity, 1172–1173
uncertainty, 1173
Reactivity, reactive planning, 1172
Read-only annotation, parallel logic programming language, 1084
Reading, character recognition and, 138
Real-time A* algorithm, minimum search, 1465–1466
Real-time learning, adaptive resonance theory, 13–14
Real-world knowledge, case grammar, 566

Realization
meta-interpretation, 939
natural language generation, 985
statements, systemic grammar and, 587–588
Reasonable belief, epistemology and, 466
Reasoned assumptions, possibilistic reasoning, 1317
Reasoning
actor models, 4
AND/OR graphs, 29–30
artificial intelligence, 56
binary resolution, 1341–1342, 1350–1351
case-based, 1265–1277
adaptation, 1272
advantages, 1267
algorithm, 1268–1269
applications, 1272–1276
as cognitive model, 1276
design and, 336–337
indexing problem, 1269–1270
interpretive, 1274–1276
memory organization, 1270
paradigm evolution, 1266–1267
problem-solving, 1273–1274
retrieval algorithms, 1270–1271
similarity metrics, 1271–1272
system construction, 1276
causal, 1279–1286
causation theories, 1283–1286
explicit causal models, 1280–1281
implicit causal models, 1281–1283
inference, 683
cognitive psychology and, 184–185
commonsense, 1288–1293
domain theory, 1288–1289
inference techniques, 1288–1289
knowledge and beliefs, 1291–1292
law in AI and, 781–782
physical reasoning, 1290–1291
plans and goals, 1292–1293
representation, 1288–1289
spatial reasoning and, 1289–1290
temporal reasoning and, 1289
default, 1294–1299
applications, 1299
architectures, 1298–1299
autoepistemic logic, 1297
belief revisions and, 114–115
circumscription, 1296–1297
conditional logic, 1298
databases, 1294–1295
image understanding and, 646
inheritance hierarchies, 1295
model preference, 1298
negation as failure, 1295
nonmonotonic logics, 1296–1297
truth maintenance systems, 1295–1296
education and AI, 435–436
epistemology and, 466
evidential, 1314–1315
image understanding and, 652–653
inheritance hierarchies, 690–691
memory-based, 1300–1301
meta-reasoning and, 942–946
nonmonotonic, 1302–1306
applications, 1305–1306
belief revision, 111
default logic, 1304
first-order logic, 1304–1305
formalisms, 1303
interconnections, 1305
limits of, 1305
logic formalisms, 1303
semantics, 1304
physical, spatial reasoning, 1328–1332
plausible, 1307–1320
applications and limitations, 1318–1319
approximate reasoning systems, 1309–1310
real-time, 1319–1320
Boltzmann machine, 126–127
distributed problem solving, 385–386
expert system uncertainty and, 1307–1309
knowledge system techniques and, 478–481
possiblistic reasoning, 1309–1310, 1315–1317
probabilistic reasoning, 1309–1315
qualitative representation, 1317
see also Uncertainty
possibilistic, 1309–1310, 1315–1317
probabilistic, 1309–1315
scripts and, 1453–1456
argument comprehension, 36–37
spatial, 1322–1332
boundary description, 1324–1325
image understanding, 643
part whole descriptions, 1323
physical reasoning, 1328–1332
route finding and exploration, 1325–1328
volumetric descriptions, 1323–1324
temporal, 1334–1338
AI applications, 1334–1336

image understanding, 644
philosophical aspects, 1337–1338
qualitative physics, 1336–1337
truth maintenance systems and, 1620
Reasoning with uncertainty module (RUM)
evaluation, 1318–1319
possibilistic reasoning, 1315–1316
RUMrunner system, 1319–1320
Rebel system, computer chess with, 225
Receiver-sender communication, 305
Receptive fields
perception and, 1662–1663
segmentation and, 397–398
Reciprocal inhibition, neural networks, 1029–1030
Recognition
adaptive resonance theory and, 14–15
frame theory and, 495–499
object recognition, search techniques, 1072
Recollection, memory and, 458–459
Recovering properties, edge detection, 432–433
Recovery Boiler Tutor (RBT), 440
Recurrence relations, LISP synthesis, 68–69
Recursion analysis, 1339–1340
AI in music and, 978–979
mathematical induction, 670–671
segmentation and, 1477–1478
Recursive data structures
logic programming, 876
problem reduction, 1211
Recursive-descent parsing, 1102–1103
Recursive-function theory, self-replication, 1492
Recursive transition networks (RTNs)
ATNS and, 553–554
augmented transition network (ATN) grammar and, 555–556
Redesign problems, 335
REDUCE system
chemistry in AI and, 160
LISP language, 837
REDUCE 3 system, 1341
Reduced instruction set computers (RISC)
architectures, 243
control structures, 298–299
Reduction schema, 1222–1224
Redundant activities, distributed problem solving, 382
REF-ARF system, 1341
constraint satisfaction, 290–291
Reference systems
inspection, 702
lexical semantics, 812–813
Reference thesauri, 1606
REFINE language, automatic programming, 78–81
Reflectance map
color vision systems, 198
visual recovery, shape from shading, 1670–1672
Reflection, robot sensing and, 1384
Refutation logics
completeness, 202
computer chess and, 231–232
Region-based modeling
image models, 632
texture analysis, 1595–1596
Region growing
color vision systems, 197
range data analysis, 1262
segmentation and, 396, 1480–1484
centroid linkage, 1482–1484
hydrid linkage, 1480–1482, 1485
single linkage, 1480
Region splitting, color vision systems, 197
Register-driven semantics, systemic grammar and, 590
Regularization theory
edge detection, 424
neural networks, 1027–1028
visual recovery, 1676–1679
Reinterpretation, frame theory and, 496–497
REL system, computational linguistics, 206, 210
Relation-based programming language, 1236
Relation-oriented programming, style, 1236
Relation selection, DADO system, 314
Relational databases
deductive databases, 320
fuzzy set theory, 508–509
logic programming and, 883–884
Relational graphs, semantic networks, 1496–1497, 1508–1509
Relational Language, 1084
Relational theory of meaning, 1545–1547
Relations
image properties, 640
inheritance hierarchies, 698
Relativity theory, schema theory, 1441–1442
RELATUS system, hermeneutics, 608
Relaxation labeling
chronological backtracking, 85
constraint satisfaction, 289–290
early vision and, 405

image understanding and, 652–653
Relaxed reduction, problem solving, 1224
Relevance
  discourse understanding, 374–376
  logic, 851
  memory and, 457
Reliability
  education and AI, 434
  inductive inference, 679–680
  plausible reasoning and, 1308
  robotics design and, 1376–1377
Remote center compliance (RCC), 1372–1374
Renaturation, Protein structure prediction, 1243–1244
RENDEZVOUS system, computational linguistics, 209–210
Representation
  AI in music and, 977–978
  binary resolution, 1344–1345
  checkers-playing programs, 151–152
  commonsense reasoning, 1288
  design, control structures, 296–297
  image understanding, 643–644
    formalisms, 651–652
  logic-based, 745–746
  machine learning and, 792
  natural language generation, 993
    phrasal lexicons, 990–991
  object recognition, 1063–1065
  preference semantics and, 1184
  problem reduction, 1209–1210
    pattern recognition, 1123–1124
  problem solving and, 1218–1219
  procedural, knowledge representation and, 746–747
  protein structure prediction, 1247–1248
  qualitative, possibilistic reasoning, 1317
  range data analysis, 1252–1261
    algebraic surfaces, 1252
    alternative curvature quantitites, 1258–1260
    Boolean sum of curves, 1255
    covariance matrix for surface normals, 1261
    curve based surface representations, 1255–1260
    global approximation methods, 1261
    iterative relaxation methods, 1261
    local surface approximation, 1260–1261
    mean and Gaussian curvature, 1257
    normal and principal curvatures, 1257–1258
    parameter requirement comparison, 1255
    parametric polynomial and spline surfaces, 1253–1254
    property estimation, 1260–1261
    rational polynomial and spline surfaces, 1254
    supertori and supperellipsoids, 1252–1253
    surface curvature from surface normals, 1261
    surface data analysis, 1252–1255
    surface smoothing splines, 1254–1255
    surface types, 1258–1260
  shape representation, 1531–1532
  speech understanding and, 1555–1556
  text summarization, 1580–1581
    tree aspects, 1584
  unification, 1631
Representational metapostulate, cognitive science and, 191–192
Repulsive potentials, mobile robot planning, 1413
Request-dependent description, information retrieval, 685
Research strategies, knowledge acquisition, 723–726
RESEARCHER system, memory organization packets (MOPs), 927
Resolution
  binary, 1341–1352
    applications, 1351
    formal treatment, 1344–1349
    historical background, 1342–1344
    inference rules, 1346–1349
    informal treatment, 1343–1344
    proof finding, 1345–1346
    reasoning programs, 1350–1351
    representation, 1344–1345
    strategies, 1349–1350
  calculi, connection method, 266
  completeness, 202–203
  framework, order-sorted logic, 865–866
  graph-based, 1353–1355
  logic and, 851–852
    Horn clauses, 874
  rule
    inference, 682–683
    unification, 1631–1632
  theory, 1356–1357
Resource situation, situation semantics, 1545
Restricted parameters, situation semantics, 1543
Result packet queue (RPQ), 1094
RESUME actions, augmented transition network (ATN) grammars, 558
RESUMETAG actions, augmented transition network (ATN) grammars, 558
RETE algorithm, parallel machine architecture, 1097
Retrieval systems
  adaptive planning and, 7
  case-based reasoning, 1270–1271
  fuzzy databases, 511–513
  information retrieval, 684
  operations, 686
Retrodictive explanation, causal reasoning, 1285
REVE software, 1357
Revised generalized phrase structure grammar (RGPSG), 572
Rewrite rules, natural language generation, 991–992
Rhythm generating circuitry, 1028–1030
Ricoeur
  interpretation theory, 602–603
  phenomenological hermeneutics, 601–602
Rigidity assumption, early vision, 410
Ring network, neural networks, 1029–1030
RITA system
  dictionary/lexicon construction, 350
  rule-based systems, 1425
RLISP, algebraic syntax, 822
RLL language
  domain knowledge, 389–390
  knowledge system building, 486
Road following tasks, mobile robot sensing, 1412
Roberts, R. B.
  control structure, 646–647
  early vision, 394, 405
  segmentation and matching, 395–396
Roberts operator, edge detection and, 397
Robinson's resolution principle, 1353–1355
Robinson's theorem, unification, 1630
Robot Schema (RS) language
  reactive planning machines, 1178
  schema theory, 1430–1431
ROBOT system, 1357
  computational linguistics, 210
  INTELLECT program, 705
Robotics, 1375–1395
  adaptive control, 1390–1392
  arc welding, 1391
  artificial intelligence and, 57
  autonomous land vehicles (ALV), 25
  characteristics, 1375–1377
  compressor-cover assembly, 1391
  control, 1378
  distributed problem solving, 381
  end-effector components, 1378–1379
  hand, 1379
  hand/tool holder, 1379
  tool, 1379
  hands and end-effectors, 1357–1374
    active hands, 1364–1367
      dextrous hands, 1365–1367
      two-fingered servo grippers, 1364–1365
    design issues, 1367–1372
      actuation methods, 1368
      constraints, 1367–1370
      fixturing, 1371–1372
      force analysis, 1368–1371
      parts integration, 1372
      sensing, 1367–1368
      transmission systems, 1370
      versatility, 1371–1372
      wrist integration, 1372
    how/why diagrams, 1372–1374
    human modeling, 1358–1360
    passive end-effectors, 1361–1364
      soft and irregular shape grippers, 1362–1364
      two-fingered angular- and parallel-jaw grippers, 1361–1362
      vacuum and magnetic grippers, 1362
  joint-to-world coordinate transformation, 1377
  kinematics, 1377
  legged machines, 1398–1407
    active balance research, 1402–1404
    applications, 1406–1407
    dynamics and balance, 1401–1402
    history, 1399–1401, 1407
    mechanical design and system integration, 1407
    rough terrain locomotion, 1405–1407
    running machines, 1404–1405
    terrain sensing, 1406
  manipulation, 1377–1378
    dynamics, 1377–1378
    machine learning and, 787
  manufacturing process planning, 1395
  micromanipulator, 1379
  mobile, 1379–1380, 1409–1415
    architectures for, 1414–1415
    control, 1380
    lasar range finders, 1411–1412
    mechanisms, 1413–1414
    monocular vision, 1412
    passive ranging, 1412
    planning systems, 1412–1413
    position sensing, 1410–1412
    road following sensing, 1412
    sonar sensing, 1410–1411
    surfaces and locomotion, 1379–1380
  modular printer-carriage assembly, 1391
  motion-planning
    spatial reasoning, 1325–1328
    trajectories, 1377
  neural networks, 1017
  planning and, 1166
  programming, 1392–1395
    languages, 1392–1394
    off-line programming, 1394–1395
  schema theory, 1437
  sensing, 1380–1381
    contact, 1388–1390
    direct range measurement, 1382–1385
    force sensors, 1390
    intensity image, 1385–1386
    noncontact, 1381–1390
    range image processing, 1386–1388
    sequence, 1380–1381
    signals, 1381
    strategy, 1381
    tactile sensors, 1388–1390
    transducers, 1388–1389
    volumetric representation, 1388
  smooth path, 1377
  teleoperators and, 1578–1579
  tracking, 1391
  workstation transforms, 1377
  world-to-joint coordinate transformation, 1377
Robustness
  case-based reasoning, 1266–1267
  image models, 632
  pattern recognition, 1125
  statistics, range data analysis, 1252
Rochester, Nathaniel, 833
Roesner's model, argument comprehension, 49–50
Roget's thesaurus, 1605–1606
Roof hypothesis, 1439
Rosenkrantz equivalent grammar, 1103
ROSIE system, 1416
  domain knowledge, 389
  knowledge system building, 486
  rule-based systems, 1418, 1425
Rote learning
  checkers-playing programs, 153
  concept learning and, 249
Rough design, 335
Rough terrain navigation, 1405–1406
ROUNDSMAN system, AI in medicine (AIM) and, 921
Route planning, 1166
  spatial reasoning, 1325–1328
Routine design, 334
  reactive planning machines, 1173–1174
Rubik's Cube, search techniques and, 1460
Rule-based systems, 1417–1426
  agenda-based systems, 21–22
  applications, 1417
  architecture, 1421–1422
  Bayesian inference methods, 96–97
  case-based reasoning, 1266–1267
  certainty-factor (CF) models, 131–132
  character recognition, stroke analysis, 142
  cognitive modeling, 180
  cognitive science and, 191–192
  computer applications, 1420
  conceptual evolution, 1423–1424
  Dempster-Shafer theory and, 330
  evolutionary system development, 1422
  functions, 1420–1421
  image understanding and, 650–652
  implementation and availability, 1425–1426
  knowledge representation and, 744–745
  knowledge system techniques and, 478–481
  law in AI and, 781
  object-oriented languages, 774
  overview of, 1418–1420
  processing, bottom-up and top-down, 1229, 1232
  programming, 1423
  reputation vs. reality in, 1426
  search and, 1422–1423
  segmentation and, 1487
  technology evoluation, 1424–1425
  XCON, 1688
Rule-learning systems, machine learning, 793
Rule-oriented programming, style, 1236
Rumelhart, D.
  language acquisition models, 765
  neural networks, 1039
RUMMAGE system, clustering analysis, 172–173
Running machines, legged robots research, 1404–1405
Run time typing, LISP language, 829–830
RUS system, natural language understanding, 1005

Russell, Bertrand, 1195–1196
Russell, Stephen, 833
Ruzzo's parsing algorithm, 1104
RX program, causal reasoning, 1283–1284

S.1 expert system
  knowledge system techniques and, 480–481
  rule-based systems, 1425
SAD SAM system, computational linguistics, 206
Saddle points, minimax procedure, 960–962
Safe languages, parallel logic programming language, 1085
SAFE synthesizer, automatic programming, 77
Safety, parallel logic programming language, 1085
SAIL language, control structures, 295
SAINT program, 1427
  artificial intelligence (AI), 54
SAL system, cognitive modeling, 179
Saliency methods, object recognition, 1073
SAM system, 1427
  discourse understanding, 372
  dynamic memory, 391
  ELI system, 444–445
  frame theory and, 496
  script application in, 1450–1451
  story analysis, 1569–1570
SAM's lemma, binary resolution, 1350–1351
Samuel, A. L.
  checkers-playing programs, 151–155
  phenomenology and, 1134
Sapir-Whorf hypothesis, hermeneutics and, 599–600
Sattley, 1229
Saunders, Robert, 834–835
Saussurean linguistics, 602
Scalability, case-based reasoning, 1268
Scalar implicatures, computational linguistics, 216
Scale problems, image understanding, 644
Scale space imaging, edge detection and, 398, 431–432
Scale space representation, edge detection, 426–428
Scaling, visual recovery, 1674–1675
SCAVENGER system, FLOABN adaptive planner, 6, 11–12
Scene analysis
  image understanding, 641
  object recognition and, 1064–1065
  schema theory, 1438–1439
Schank, Roger
  deep case grammar, 568–569
  lexical decomposition, 811
  logic, 852
  natural language understanding, 1007
  philosophy of AI and, 1140
  script theory, 1443–1444
  semantic networks, 1496–1497
SCHED system, computational linguistics, 211–212
Schema instances, 1427
  reactive planning, 1172
  Robot Schema (RS) language, 1430–1431
Schema Representation Language, 906
Schema theory, 1427–1442
  activity levels, 1428
  behavioral aspects, 1441–1442
  connectionism, 1433
  detail hiding, 1431
  explicit vs. implicit planning, 1440
  high-level vision, 1437–1440
    action-oriented perception, 1440
    scene interpretation, 1438–1440
  history and comparisons, 1429–1430
  language acquisition, 769, 1441
  learning, 1440–1441
  memory, perception and action, 1433–1434
  modulation and evolution, 1431–1433
  neural networks, 1017
  neural schema theory, 1428
  path-planning and detour behavior, 1436–1437
  probabilistic networks, 1206
  problem solving, 1220–1224
    declarative problems, 1216
    production schema, 1220–1222
    reduction schema, 1222–1224
  Rana computatrix, 1434–1436
  reactive planning machines, 1178
  Robot Schema (RS) approach, 1430–1431
  script acquisition and, 1457–1458
SCHEME language
  control structures, 294–295
    symbolic computation, 298
  LISP development and, 838
Schenker, D., 978–979
SCHEPLAN, engineering and KBES, 452
Schleiermacher, hermeneutics, 597
SCHOLAR system, 1443
  computational linguistics, 210–211
  education and AI, 437

human-computer interaction, 622
Scientific community metaphor, 384
Scientific text processing, 213
Scope notes (SN), thesaurus development, 1607
Script headers
  direct header (DH), 1446
  instrumental header (IH), 1446
  locale header (LH), 1446
  precondition header (PH), 1446
  script invocation with, 1445–1446
Scripts, 1443–1458
  acquisition, 1457–1458
  applications, 1447–1448
  BORIS system, 1452–1453
  causal reasoning and, 1280
  cognitive psychology and, 182
  computational linguistics, 217–218
  conceptual dependency and, 264
  defined, 1443–1444
  discourse understanding, 366
    textual analysis, 372–373
  dynamic memory, 391
  frame theory, 494
  frame theory and, 496
  memory organization packets (MOPs), 926–927
  natural language understanding, 1449–1456
    FRUMP system, 1451–1452
    SAM system, 1450–1451
  OpEd system, 1453–1456
  philosophy of AI and, 1140, 1144
  problems with, 1448–1449
  psychological validity of, 1456–1457
  reasoning scripts, 1453–1456
  SAM system, 1427
  schema theory, 1429–1430
  story analysis, 1569–1570
  structure, 1444–1447
    events, episodes and scenes, 1446–1447
    invocation with headers, 1445–1446
SEAC system, chemistry in AI and, 159
Search, 1460–1466
  abstraction, 1466
  adaptive resonance theory and, 14–16
    search-direct access trade-off, 17
  AND/OR graphs, 29–30
  artificial intelligence, 56
  backtracking, 84–85
  beam, 1467–1468
  bidirectional, 1463
  blackboard systems, 116
  branch-and-bound techniques, 1468–1472
  branching factor algorithm, 127–128
  breadth-first search, 1461–1462
  brute-force search, 1461–1464
  checkers-playing programs, 150
    dynamic ordering, 152
    fixed ordering, 152
    forward pruning, 152–153
  combinatorial explosion, 1463–1464
  computational linguistics, 214
  computer chess and, 226–229
    knowledge errors and, 238–239
  defined, 293
  depth-first search, 1462–1463, 1473
    iterative-deepening (DFID), 1463
  design and, 336
  execution and, 1465–1466
  forward and backward, 1232–1233
  heuristic, 612–614, 1464–1465
    A* algorithm, 1464
    evaluation functions, 1464
    iterative-deepening A* (IDA*) algorithm, 1464–1465
    optimal solutions, 1465
    path algorithm (HPA), 1465
  image understanding and, 644
  inductive inference, 675–677
    efficiency, 677
    more powerful search, 676–677
  information retrieval, intelligent search, 689
  inheritance hierarchies, 692
    multiple inheritance exceptions, 693–694
  intelligent, causal reasoning, 1282
  knowledge sources, 1466
  knowledge system techniques and, 478–481
  machine learning, 793–794
  macro-operators, 1466
  minimum, with alpha pruning, 1465–1466
  object recognition
    complete constrained search, 1069–1071
    correspondence, 1069
    exhaustive search, 1069
    feature matching components, 1069
    heuristic search, 1073
    hypothesis testing, 1072
    interpretation tree, 1071–1072
    pose space, 1076
    spurious data, 1072–1073
    termination of, 1073–1074
  perception and, 1661

probabilities, 1466
problem reduction, 1211–1213
problem solving, production schema, 1221–1222
problem space model, 1461
processing, bottom-up and top-down, 1229
  bidirectional, 1234
real-time A*, 1465–1466
recursion and, 1339–1340
rule-based systems, 1422–1423
speech understanding and, 1557
subgoaling, 1466
tree
  production schema, 1221–1222
  reduction schema, 1223
truth maintenance systems and, 1620
uniform-cost search, 1461–1462
Searle
  philosophy of AI and, 1140
  Turing test, 1628
Second-order logic, 872
Secondary memory, 456–459
Secondary protein structure
  α helix, 1241–1243, 1245–1246
  β turns and sheets, 1241–1243, 1245–1246
  prediction techniques, 1241–1243, 1245–1246
  super-secondary structures, 1247–1248
Secondary storage management, 755–756
SECS (Simulation and Evaluation of Chemical Synthesis), 157
Sedimented beliefs, phenomenology and, 1134
SEER system
  AI in medicine (AIM) and, 919
  image understanding and, 649
Segmentation, 1473–1490
  color vision systems, 196–198
  early vision and
    description and, 403
    low- and high-level vision, 395–403
    matching and, 395–396
    surfaces and, 406–409
  hybrid linkage combinations, 1485
  measurement-space guided spatial clustering, 1474–1480
    multidimensional, 1479–1480
    thresholding, 1478–1479
  motion-based, 1487–1490
  range data analysis, 1250, 1261–1262
  region growing, 1480–1484
    centroid linkage, 1482–1484
    hybrid linkage, 1480–1482
    single linkage, 1480
  rule-based, 1487
  spatial clustering, 1485–1486
  speech understanding and, 1554
  split and merge, 1486–1487
  syntactic pattern recognition, 1122–1123
  visual recovery, 1678–1679
Selection expression, systemic grammar and, 585
Selection functions
  conditional logic, 857–858
  object recognition, 1073
Selective search, computer chess and, 238
Selectivity, cognitive psychology and, 183–184
Self-organization
  feature mapping, 1052–1053
  neural networks, 1032–1033
Self-replication, 14492–1493
Selfridge, O. G., language acquisition models, 765–768
Selz, Otto, semantic networks, 1495
Semantic grammar, 580–582
  procedural, 581
Semantic networks, 1493–1509
  case grammar, 566
  character recognition, 142
  cognitive modeling, 177
  cognitive psychology and, 182
  computational linguistics, 208
  computer systems, 242
  concept learning, 254–255
  conceptual dependency, 259–264
  domain knowledge, 389
  generic and individual concepts, 1505–1506
  historical survey, 1493–1497
  image understanding and, 651–652
  inheritance hierarchies, 691, 1501–1502
  intensions and extensions and, 1505–1506
  knowledge representation and, 744–745, 747–749
  knowledge system construction and, 484–485
  language parsing and generation, 1507–1508
  law in AI and, 782
  logic, 1503–1504
  machine learning, 1508–1509
  procedural attachments, 1509
  propositional networks, 1497–1500
  relational graphs, 1496–1497
  situations, 1506–1507
  SNePS system and, 1547–1548
  taxonomic and assertional systems, 1504–1505

type hierarchy, 1500–1501
Semantic Representation Language (SRL), 1507–1508
Semantics
  adaptive planning and, 7
  analog semantic features, 27–28
  computational linguistics, 215
  conditional logic, 857–858
  constraint satisfaction, 290
  coroutines, 303
  definite databases, 322–323
  dictionary/lexicon construction
    intra-entry information, 343
    lexical entry, 345–347
    machine-readable dictionaries, 359
  discourse understanding, 366–368
    text analysis, 371–374
  disjunctive databases, 327
  epistemology and, 465
  epsilon-semantics, 468–475
    axiomatic characterization, 470
    conditional entailment, 474–475
    consistency, 471
    definitions, 469–470
    inference rules, 470
    knowledge levels, 469
    maximum entropy (ME) approach, 474
    meta-theorems, 470
    semimonotonicity, 470–471
    system Z, 472–473
  frame theory and, 501–502
  fuzzy databases, 513–514
  fuzzy set theory
    unification, 532–533
    voting model, 530–531
  higher-order logic, 860–861
  lexical, 812–816
    ambiguity and polysemy, 815–816
    field theory, 807
    frame-based, 810
    interpretive semantics, 808, 810
    semantic classes, 813–815
    word relations, 815
  memory, 454–455
  minimal model, logic programming, 876–877
  morphology, derivation, 964–965
  natural language generation, 988–991
    fuzzy logic, 517–521
  natural language understanding, 1004–1005
  nonmonotonic reasoning and, 1304
  parallel logic programming language, 1086–1087
    declarative semantics, 1083
  philosophy of AI and, 1141
  predicate logic, 868–869
  preference semantics, 1182–1191
    bare templates, 1185–1186
    belief representations, 1184
    blocks, 1187
    computational semantics and, 1183, 1190–1191
    definitions, 1188
    extensions, 1188–1191
    formulas, 1184–1185
    inference rules, 1187
    least effort principle, 1183
    linear language boundaries, 1184
    paraplates, 1186–1187
    parsing, 1183–1184, 1191
    primitives, 1184, 1191
    procedural semantics and, 1183
    pseudo-texts, 1187–1188
    representations, 1184
    thesauri, 1187
  presupposition theory, 1196–1199
  probabilistic networks, 1204–1205
  propositional logic
    deductive systems, 896
    language, 892–893
  situation, 1541–1547
    abstraction, 1543–1544
    constraints, 1544
    infons, 1542–1543
    ontology, 1542
    parameters and anchors, 1543
    relational theory of meaning, 1545–1547
    types, 1543
  stratified databases, 325–326
  systemic grammar and, 588–590
    chooser and inquiry semantics, 588–590
    register-driven semantics, 590
  text summarization, 1583–1584
  thesaurus construction, 1605–1606
    natural language processing (NLP), 1609–1610
  word-expert parsing (WEP), 1109
Semi-affixes, morphology, 965
Semijoin operations, constraint satisfaction, 287–288
Semimonotonicity, epsilon-semantics, 470–471
Sense data, epistemology and, 463
Sense frames, preference semantics and, 1189
Sense relations, lexical decomposition, 807, 810
Sense-discrimination language (SDL), 1111–1112
Sensing
  contact sensing, robotics design, 1388–1390
  force sensors, 1390
  noncontact sensing, 1381–1388
    direct range measurement, 1382–1385
    intensity image processing, 1385–1386
    range image processing, 1386–1388
    vs. tactile, 1389–1390
    volumetric representation, 1388
  robot end-effector design, 1367–1368
  robotics design, 1380–1381
    beacons, 1410
    lasar range finders, 1411–1412
    manufacturing process planning, 1395
    monocular vision, 1412
    noncontact sensing, 1381–1388
    passive ranging, 1412
    position sensing, for mobile robots, 1410
    road following example, 1412
    sonar, 1410–1411
    terrain sensing for legged robots, 1406
Sensorimotor learning, neural networks, 1040
Sensors, 1511–1523
  acquisition, object recognition and, 1063–1064
  data fusion, 1519–1523
    ladar and visual sensing, 1521
    range and visual sensing, 1521–1522
    schemes for, 1522–1523
    tactile and visual sensing, 1520–1521
    thermal and visual sensing, 1519–1520
  design principles, 1512–1519
    optical sensors, 1512–1515
    radars and ladars, 1516–1517
    range sensors, 1517–1519
    tactile sensors, 1516
    thermal sensors, 1515–1516
  information integration, 950–952
Separable graphs, constraint networks, 282
SEPIA system, ECRC programs, 420–421
SEQUENT system, 1092–1093, 1095–1096
Serial machines, control structures, 298–299
Serum Protein Diagnostic Program, 924
Set of support strategies, 1349–1350
Set search, associative memory, 58
SETHEO system, 1526–1527
Seuren, P., presupposition theory, 1198–1199
S-expressions
  LISP language, 832–833
  syntax, 820
Shading
  from shape, early vision, 406
  perception and, 1657–1658
SHAKEY robot, 1527
  planning and, 1170
Shannon, Claude, 1402–1404
Shape analysis
  connectionism and, 273
  Hough transforms, 617–618
Shape from contour, visual recovery, 1675–1676
Shape from shading algorithm
  constraint satisfaction, 290
  early vision, 406
    qualitative, 410
  visual recovery, 1669–1672
Shape from stereo, visual recovery, 1676
Shape from texture algorithm
  texture analysis, 1598–1600
  visual recovery, 1672–1675
Shape from x technique,
  range data analysis, 1251
  range sensor design, 1518
  visual recovery, 1666, 1669–1676
    shape from contour, 1675–1676
    shape from shading, 1669–1672
    shape from texture, 1672–1675
Shape representation, 1527–1537
  compound curves, 1529–1530
  compound surfaces, 1530–1531
  geometric operations, 1531–1533
  global geometry, 1528–1529
  local geometry, 1527–1529
  representation criteria, 1531–1532
  solid modeling volume elements, 1533–1537
    CSG models, 1534–1535
    generalized cylinders, 1535–1537
    voxels, 1533–1534
  spatial reasoning, 1322
    boundary description, 1324–1325
    physical reasoning, 1329
Shapiro synthesis algorithm, 71–72
Shared memory multiprocessors, 1092–1093
Shepard, R. N., 1657
Sherrington, Hopfield networks, 1045
Ship Planning System (SPS), 452
Shirai, Y., 647
Shoham, Y., 1284–1285
Short-term memory (STM)
  adaptive resonance theory and, 14–16
  stability-plasticity trade-off, 17
  schema theory, 1433–1434
Shortest-path inheritance, 693–694
SHRDLU system, 1538
  computational linguistics, 208
  text generation, 217
  hermeneutics and, 605–606
  human-computer interaction, 621
  MICRO-PLANNER and, 947
  natural language generation, 986–987
  phenomenology and, 1133
  PLANNER and, 1159
  scripts, 1447–1448
  systemic grammar and, 590–591
SIAP (Surveillance Integration Automation Project)
  AI military applications, 951–952
  knowledge system building, 488
SightPlan, design and, 335
SIGMA system, image understanding and, 653
Signal processing, pattern recognition, 1118
Signature tables, checkers-playing programs, 154–155
SIMD machine
  Connection Machine, 246
  control structures, 299
  data parallelism and, 316
  stereo vision, 1564
Simic, P. D., 1023
Similarities
  intelligence and, 707
  metrics, case-based reasoning, 1271–1272
Similarity, in meaning, 262
Simple theory of types, higher-order logic, 861
SIMULA language, 1538
  coroutines, 305
  object-oriented languages, 776
Simulated annealing, 1538–1540
  algorithm, 1538–1540
  applications, 1540
  Boltzmann machine, 126
  constraint satisfaction, 290
  history, 1538
  Hopfield networks optimization, 1021
  stereo vision, 1564
Simulation structures
  belief representation systems, 103
  coroutines, 305
  massive parallelism, 627
Single-agent functions, heuristics and, 612–613
Single-knowledge representation languages, 450
SIPE system
  macro actions, 1166–1167
  planning and, 1169
SIR system, 1541
  computational linguistics, 206
Siskind's model, language acquisition, 766
Situated activity, reactive planning machines, 1179
Situated automata, reactive planning machines, 1176
Situated control rules (SCRs), 1178
Situated plans, adaptive planning and, 7
Situation calculus
  planning and, 1161
  temporal reasoning, 1334–1336
Situation semantics, 1541–1547
  infons, 1542–1543
  ontology, 1542
  semantic networks, 1506–1507
Situation theory, 1541–1542
Skeletons, phrase-structure trees, 573–574
Skinner, B. F., 762
Skolem function
  connection calculus, 267
  higher-order logic, 861
SLD resolution
  graph-based resolution, 1354
  logic programming, 876–877
SLDNF inference, logic programming, 879
Sliding window, computer chess and, 228
Sliding-tile puzzles, search techniques and, 1460
SLIP system, 1547
Slope and curvature, image properties, 639
Slots
  frame theory and, 500–501
  inheritance hierarchies, 692
  constraints, 695
Small processing elements (SPEs), 1060–1061
Small-motion analysis, two-view motion analysis, 1644–1645
SMALLTALK language, 1538, 1547
  control structures, 294
  symbolic computation, 298
  coroutines, object-oriented programming, 306

frame theory and, 504–505
lambda calculus, 761
object-oriented languages, 776
SmartSLIM system, 906
Smithtown Economic Tutor, 439
Smoothing
  edge detection, intensity changes, 422–426
  image models, 634–635
SMP system, chemistry in AI and, 160
SNePS system, 1547–1548
  belief representation, 101–102
  graph-based resolution, 1355
  knowledge representation and, 753
  natural language generation, 994
  semantic networks, propositional networks, 1498–1500
SNIFFER system, 1548
SNOBOL-4 programming language, 1548
SOAR project, 1548–1549
  cognitive modeling, 180
  machine-learning and, 801
  problem solving, 1224
Sobel edge detector, 397–399
Social issues of AI
  natural language understanding, 1013
  robotics design and, 1375–1376
  Turing test, 1625
Social sciences, hermeneutics and, 603–604
SOCIAL system, blackboard control architectures, 124
Societies for AI, 1550–1551
Society of Manufacturing Engineers (SME), 904
Soft constraints, neural network optimization, 1022–1023
Soft grippers, 1362–1364
Software
  Alvey program, 26
  computer chess and, 235–236
  data parallelism and, 316
  LISP machines and, 839, 843
  machine translation, 899
Solid modeling, shape representation, 1533–1537
  CSG models, 1534–1535
  generalized cylinders, 1535–1537
  voxels, 1533–1534
Soloway, Elliot, 88–89
Solution grammar
  problem solving and, 1219
  procedural problem formulations, 1216–1218
Solution graphs
  problem reduction, 1211–1213
  procedural problem formulations, 1216–1218
SOME/OR graphs, pattern recognition, 1124
Sompolinsky, neural networks, 1041–1042
Sonar
  mobile robot sensing, 1410–1411
  pattern recognition, 1127
SOPHIE system, 1551
  computational linguistics, 211
  education and AI, 437
  human-computer interaction, 622
  natural language understanding, 1004–1005
  semantic grammar, 580–582
Sophisticated local control, 384–385
Soundness, circumscription, 166
Space
  knowledge representation and, 755–756
  pattern recognition, 1127
Spaghetti stack
  coroutines, 303–304
  InterLisp, 837
SPAM system, image understanding and, 651–653
SPARC system, parallel machine architecture, 1096
SPARSER system, dictionary/lexicon construction, 354
Spatial ability, intelligence and, 709
Spatial autoregressive model (SAR), 630–631
Spatial clustering, segmentation and, 1485–1486
Spatial decomposition, distributed problem solving, 381–382
Spatial filtering, edge detection, 430–431
Spatial-frequency channels, stereo vision, 1566
Spatial knowledge, image understanding, 643
Spatial proximity graph, sensor data fusion and, 1523
Spatial reasoning, 1322–1332
  boundary description, 1324–1325
  commonsense reasoning, 1289–1290
  part whole descriptions, 1323
  physical reasoning, 1328–1332
  route finding and exploration, 1325–1328
  volumetric descriptions, 1323–1324
Spatial representation, image understanding and, 651–652
Spatiotemporal reasoning, image understanding and, 653
Special pop arc (SPOP), 558
Species-specific processing, 1026

Specific heat curve, simulated annealing, 1539
Specification
  augmented transition network (ATNs), 557–558
  logic programming, 880–881
Spectral analysis, speech understanding and, 1553
Spectral power distribution (SPD), 193–200
Spectral signature analysis, 196
Specular reflection, robot sensing and, 1384
Speech acts
  belief representation systems, 104–105
  computational linguistics, 216
  discourse understanding, 374–375
  natural language understanding, 1011, 1013
Speech events, discourse understanding, 376
Speech recognition
  AI military applications, 949
  epistemology and, 465
  massive parallelism, 627
  pattern recognition, 1116
  speech understanding and, 1552
Speech synthesis
  AI military applications, 949
  neural networks, 1039–1040
Speech understanding systems (SUS), 1552–1558
  acoustic-phonetic analysis, 1554
  artificial intelligence (AI), 56
  blackboard systems, 116
  case grammer, 563
  computational linguistics, 218
  current trends, 1557
  discourse understanding, 365–366, 377
  domain knowledge, 389
  epistemology and, 465
  HARPY system, 595
  HEARSAY-II, 596
  human-computer interaction, 621
  image understanding, 642
  knowledge-source interpretation, 1555–1556
  pattern recognition, 1126–1127
  phonological analysis, 1554–1555
  processing strategies, 1556–1557
  system architecture, 1556–1558
  theoretical background, 1552–1554
Spelling corrector program, InterLisp, 836–837
Spelling errors, robust parsing, 1009–1010
Spheres system, conditional logic, 857–858
SPHINX system, 1559
  beam search, 1467–1468
Spin representation, Hopfield networks, 1044–1045
Splines
  range data analysis, 1253–1255
  shape representation, 1529–1530
Splits, inheritance hierarchies, 697–698
Splitting criterion
  range data analysis, 1262
  segmentation and, 1486–1487
Spurious data, object recognition, 1072
Spurious states, Hopfield networks, 1044–1045
SRI model
  parallel machine architecture, 1092
  vision module, robot sensing and, 1385–1386
SSS* algorithm, 1559
  pattern recognition, 1124
SSS program, text summarization, 1583–1584
Stability
  game playing and, 547
  neural networks, 1019–1020
Stable coalition, connectionism, 270
Stage-analysis, intelligence and, 711
Standard LISP, 837
Stanford Heuristic Programming project, 951
STARAN system, associative memory, 58
State evaluation function, problem solving, 1221
State selection function, 1221
State specifications, qualitative physics, 1153–1154
State-space search
  forward and backward search, 1233
  pattern recognition, 1122
  problem solving, 1221
Static crawlers, 1401
Static evaluation function, 152
Static planning, 1169
Statistical analysis
  AI in music and, 977
  image modeling, 628, 638
  inference, 683
Statistical mechanics
  inverse, Gardner networks, 1047–1048
  neural networks, 1019, 1040–1042
  winner-take-all networks, 1025
Stative conceptualizations, 263
Status labeling, game trees, 550
Steam power plants, 160
STEAMER system
  AI military applications, 956
  education and AI, 434, 440
  human-computer interaction, 619–620

Steamroller problem, order-sorted logic, 865
Steering mechanisms, mobile robot planning, 1413–1414
Stereo fusion, stereo vision, 1565–1566
Stereoscopic fusion, visual recovery, 1665
Stereosys, 1563–1564
Stereo vision, 1560–1567
  applications, 1567
  biological aspects, 1564–1567
    computational models and, 1566
    disparity pools, 1566–1567
    neuroanatomy, 1564–1565
    perception modularity, 1565
    spatial-frequency channels, 1566
    stereo fusion and depth perception limits, 1565–1566
    vertical disparity, 1566
    visual cortex, 1567
  computational models, 1560–1563
    camera modeling, 1561
    depth determination, 1562–1563
    feature acquisition, 1562
    image acquisition, 1561
    image matching, 1562
    interpolation, 1563
    preprocessing, 1561–1562
  constraint equation, 1564
  CYCLOPS system, 1564
  early vision and, 404
  edge detection, 430–431
  epistemology and, 465
  geometry, 1560
  MPG model, 1563–1564
  neural networks, 1016–1017
  perception and, 1658–1659
  range sensor design, 1518
  robot sensing and, 1384
  schema theory, 1436
  stereosys, 1563–1564
  tactile sensing data fusion, 1520–1521
Stickel's theory resolution rule, 1355
Stochastic processes
  networks, Hopfield networks optimization, 1021
  probabilistic networks, 1205
  training algorithms, neural networks, 1041
Stomatogastric ganglion network, 1029–1030
Stop lists, information retrieval, 687
Storage management
  computer systems, 243–244
  LISP language, 829
  neural networks, 1045–1046
Story analysis, 1568–1575
  causal reasoning and, 1280
  cognitive psychology and, 184
  coherence-based, 1573
  commensurability, 1574
  compositional, 1575
  computational vs. noncomputational approaches, 1569
  discourse understanding, 373–374
  early history, 1569
  frame theory and, 496–497
  goal-based, 1570–1571
  inheritance hierarchies, 695
  integrated analysis, 1571–1572
  law in AI and, 782–783
  PAM system, 1081
  philosophy of AI and, 1140
  scripts applications, 1451, 1569–1570
  unified analysis, 1572–1573
Story generation research, 1568–1569
Story points theory, story analysis, 1573
Straight-line correspondences, 1643–1644
Strange attractors, neural networks, 1020
Strategic components, natural language generation, 985
Strategic Computing Initiative (SCI), 947–949
Strategy
  binary resolution, 1349–1350
  game playing and, 543–545
  minimax procedure, 959–960
Stratified databases, defined, 325–326
Strawson, P. F., presupposition theory, 1195–1196
STREC system, chemistry in AI and, 159
Strength/threshold theory, 458–459
Stripping technique, morphology, 969
STRIPS system, 1576–1577
  belief revision and, 111
  means-ends analysis, 909, 912–913
  planning and, 1170
  Shakey robot and, 1527
  temporal reasoning, 1334–1336
STROBE system, domain knowledge, 390
Stroke analysis, character recognition, 142
Strong equivalence, parsing, 1101
Structural credit assignment problem, 1037
Structural feature vectors, 140–142
Structuralism, phenomenological hermeneutics and, 601

Structure mapping, naive physics, 1148
Structure of intellect model, 708–710
Structure-driven algorithms, 276
Structure-from-motion concept, 410
Structure light technique, 1521–1522
    robot sensing and, 1384
STUDENT system, 1577
    computational linguistics, 206
Subgoals
    problem reduction, 1210–1211
    search and, 1466
Subject headings, thesaurus development, 1606–1607
Subject probability, Bayesian networks, 1204
Subsequent reference, natural language generation, 986–987
Subsumption
    binary resolution, 1350
    frame theory and, 503
    mobile robot architecture, 1415
    reactive planning machines, 1174
Successive over-relaxation (SOR) multi-resolution, range data analysis, 1254
SUDO-PLANNER system, AI in medicine (AIM) and, 921
Summarization
    models, story analysis, 1573
    text summarization, 1579–1586
        case-based reasoning, 1585
        conceptual roots, 1583–1584
        explanation-based learning, 1585
        importance techniques, 1582–1583
        in-the-small techniques, 1581
        plan evaluation, 1585
        representation, 1580–1581
        workload measurement, 1584–1585
Summers method for LISP synthesis, 68–69, 73
SUN language, engineering and KBES2, 450–451
Superellipsoids, range data analysis, 1252–1253
Superquadrics
    high-level vision, 416
    object recognition, 1078
    visual recovery, 1667–1669
Supertori, range data analysis, 1252–1253
Supervised learning, machine learning and, 787
Supplementary images, robotics design and, 1381
Support logic programming
    fuzzy set theory, 528–529
    inference from rules, 532–533
Support relationships, argument comprehension, 39–40
Surface cases, case grammar, 564–565
Surface constraints, edge detection, 402–403
Surface elements
    compound surfaces, 1530–1531
    shape representation, 1528–1529
Surface orientation and shape, 1668
    texture analysis, 1597–1598
Surface parameters, robotics design and, 1379–1380
Surface patches, shape representation, 1528
Surface structure
    lexical decomposition, 808
    natural language generation, 993
    parsing, 1105
Surroundedness, image properties, 638–639
Susie Software system, 216
SWALE project, 1577
    case-based reasoning, 1272
Swedish Institute of Computer Science (SICS), 1088
SWM system
    belief revisions and, 113
SWM*, truth maintenance systems (TMS), 1618–1619
Symbolic computation
    chemistry in AI and, 159–160
    control structures, 298–299
Symbolic logic
    cognitive science and, 190
    semantic networks, 1502
Symbolic processing, parallel machine architecture, 1089
Symbolic relaxation algorithm, constraint satisfaction, 288
Symbolics Machine
    components and functions of, 243–246
    control structures, 298–299
    LISP machines and, 839, 843
    parallel machine architecture, 1097
Symbolism, early vision and, 408
Symbol-level learners
    knowledge levels and, 742–743
    machine learning and, 788
    analytic learning and, 795–797
Symbols
    cognitive modeling, 178

LISP language, 822, 824
    syntax, 820
Synapses, neural network modeling, 1017–1018
Synaptic coupling hypothesis, 1031
Synaptic matrices, neural networks, 1042
SYNLMA system, chemistry in AI and, 157
Synonyms
    dictionary/lexicon construction, 344
    lexical semantics, 815
Syntactic analysis
    cognitive science and, 189
    texture analysis, 1595
Syntactic pattern recognition, 1122–1123
Syntactic preference, preference semantics and, 1191
Syntactic recognition, 1117
Syntactic structure, 587–588
Syntactically-driven parsing, 1001–1004
Syntagmatic orientation
    fuzzy semantics, 518–521
    systemic grammar and, 583–585
Syntax
    conceptual dependency, 259–260
    constraint logic programming, 274–275
    dictionary/lexicon construction
        intra-entry information, 342–343
        machine-readable dictionaries, 359
    generalized phrase-structure grammar and, 570–571
    higher-order logic, 860
    language acquisition, 763
    lexical semantics, 813
    LISP language, 820–822
        algebraic syntax, 822
        CONS cells and lists, 820–821
        programs and data, 821–822
        symbols and atoms, 820
    parallel logic programming language, 1083
    predicate logic, 866–868
    propositional logic
        deductive systems, 894–895
        language, 892
Synthesis-from-example methodologies, 59
Synthesizing programs, automatic programming, 63–64
SYSCONJ action, augmented transition network (ATN) grammars, 558
Systemic-functional linguistics (SFL), 583
Systemic grammar, 583–591
    implementations and declarativity, 590–591
    metafunctionality, 585–586
    natural language generation, 993–994
    networks, 584–585
    paradigmatic axis, 583–585
    semantics, 588–590
    syntactic structure, 587–588
System integration, legged robots, 1407
System Z, epsilon-semantics, 472–473
Systems Control Technology, 951
Systems design, massive parallelism, 627

TACITUS project, story analysis, 1574
Tactile sensing
    design principles, 1516
    robotics design, 1388–1389
    sensor data fusion, 1520–1521
Tagged Brown Corpus, 129–130
Tags, LISP language, 829
Tail merging, LISP language, 825
Tail recursion, 1340
    LISP language, 825
Tautologies, propositional logic, 894
Taxadvisor program, law in AI and, 782
TAXIS project, procedural semantic networks, 1509
TAXMAN I and II, law in AI and, 779–781
Taxonomic systems
    inheritance hierarchies, 690–691
    knowledge acquisition, 722–723
    robot end-effector design, 1359–1360
    semantic networks, 1504–1505
Teachable Language Comprehender, 761–762
Teaching, case-based reasoning, 1276
TEAM system
    dictionary/lexicon construction, 357
    natural language understanding, 1005
Technical reports, as AI information source, 844
TEIRESIAS system
    AI in medicine (AIM) and, 919
    knowledge system building, 487–488
    meta-knowledge in, 945–946
    meta-reasoning and, 944
    rule-based systems, 1425
Teleoperators, 1578–1579
Template expansion algorithm, 1186

Template matching
    character recognition, 139, 141
    explanation and, 491
    preference semantics and, 1185–1186
Temporal knowledge, image understanding, 644
Temporal logic, modal logic and, 863
Temporally-directed activation, 648–649
Temporal order, qualitative physics, 1156–1157
Temporal-pattern encoding, neural networks, 1049–1052
    complex sequence recognition, 1051–1052
    delay synapse networks, 1050–1051
    noise-driven sequence recognizer, 1051
Temporal planning, 1168–1169
Temporal reasoning, 1334–1338
    AI applications, 1334–1336
    AI in medicine (AIM) and, 921
    causal reasoning, 1284
    commonsense reasoning, 1289
    engineering and KBES, 450
    knowledge representation and, 755–756
    philosophical aspects, 1337–1338
    planning and, 1159
    qualitative physics, 1336–1337
Term definition
    predicate logic, 867
    descriptions as, 871–872
Terminological knowledge base, thesauri and, 1610
Terrain navigation
    legged robots locomotion, 1405–1406
    mobile robot mechanisms, 1413–1414
Tesniére, L., semantic networks, 1495
Test collection, information retrieval, 688
Texels
    texture analysis
        identification, 1598–1600
        surface-shape estimation, 1600
        texture gradients and, 1597
    visual recovery, shape from texture, 1673–1674
Text analysis
    discourse understanding, 371–374
        anaphora, 371–372
        background knowledge and plausible inferences, 372–373
        logical formalisms, 371
        story summation, 373–374
        truth conditions, 371
    hermeneutics and, 605
    knowledge acquisition and, 726
Text comprehension principle, 498
Text corpora, dictionary/lexicon construction, 355–356, 360–362
Text generation, computational linguistics, 216–217
Text planning
    explanation and, 491
    natural language generation, 989
Text summarization, 1579–1586
    case-based reasoning, 1585
    conceptual roots, 1583–1584
    explanation-based learning, 1585
    importance techniques, 1582–1583
    in-the-small techniques, 1581
    plan evaluation, 1585
    representation, 1580–1581
    workload measurement, 1584–1585
Texture analysis, 1587–1600
    edge detection, 431–414, 432–433
    human perception models, 1596–1597
    images, 638
    perception and, 1658
    pixel-based models, 1587–1595
        autoregressive models, 1588
        autoregressive/moving average (ARMA) model, 1589
        global models, 1589–1592
        local models, 1592–1595
        moving-average model, 1588–1589
        one-dimensional time series models, 1587–1589
        random field models, 1589–1595
        syntactic models, 1595
    region-based models, 1595–1596
    segmentation, image models, 632–634
    three-dimensional shape inference, 1597–1600
        surface shape from texture gradients, 1597–1600
        texel identification and surface-shape estimation, 1600
        texels and texture gradients, 1597
    visual recovery, shape from texture, 1673–1675
Texture gradients
    surface shape inference, 1597–1598
    texels and, 1597

Thematic abstraction units (TAUs)
 computational linguistics, 216
 discourse understanding, 373–374
Thematic organization point (TOP), 392
THEO program, machine-learning and, 801
Theorem proving
 AND/OR graphs, 29–30
 binary resolution, 1343, 1349–1352
 chemistry in AI and, 157
 completeness, 202–203
 deductive databases, 320
 dependency-directed backtracking, 87–88
 engineering and KBES, 449–450
 knowledge representation and, 744, 751
 logic, 852
 MKRP system, 962–963
 search techniques and, 1460
 unification, 1631–1632
Theory formation, problem solving, 1226–1227
Theory resolution, 1356–1357
Thermal detection, optical sensor design, 1514–1515
Thermal equilibrium
 Boltzmann machine, 127
 thermal sensor data fusion, 1520
Thermal sensors
 design principles, 1515–1516
 sensor data fusion, 1519–1520
Thesaurus, 1605–1611
 foundation for, 1605–1606
 information retrieval and, 1606–1610
  automatic techniques, 1608
  characteristics, 1607
  construction, 1607–1608
  development, 1606–1607
  machine indexing, 1607
  performance evaluation, 1608–1609
  semantic processing, 1609
 lexical decomposition, 807, 810
 natural language processing, 1609–1610
 preference semantics and, 1187
 properties, 1610–1611
Theta theory, lexical decomposition, 810
Thevenin, engineering and KBES, 452
ThingLab II, constraint satisfaction, 290–291
Thinking, cognitive psychology and, 184–185
Thomason, 858
Thrashing
 backtracking, 85
 chronological backtracking, 85–87
 constraint satisfaction, 287
Three-dimensional imaging
 feature correspondence, motion analysis, 1650–1651
 object modeling, robotics programming, 1395
 range data analysis, 1250–1251
 range sensor data fusion and, 1521–1522
 texture analysis, 1597–1600
 time and space, perception and, 1659
Three-dimensional vision
 image understanding, 641–642
 object recognition, 1063–1065
 alignment, 1076
Three-valued logic, normal databases, 326
Threshold logic units (TLUs), connectionism and, 272
Thresholding techniques
 early vision and, 400–401
 segmentation and, cluster analysis, 1478–1479
Throwness concept, hermeneutics and, 607
Thurstone, L., 708
TIE routines, preference semantics and, 1186–1187
TIERS expert systems, engineering and KBES, 451–452
Time constraints, reactive planning machines, 1177
Time Map Managing System, 1337
Time series analysis
 models, 629
 texture, 1587–1589
  autoregressive model (AR), 1588
  autoregressive/moving average model, 1589
  moving average model (MA), 1588–1589
 see also Temporal reasoning
Time-of-flight (TOF) measurement, 1384–1385
Time-order relationships, Bayesian networks, 1203
Timely activity, reactive planning, 1172–1773
TLC program, story analysis, 1572–1573
Tools, robotics research and, 1379
Top-down processing
 control structures, 296–297
 early vision and, 402
 parsing, 1231
 problem reduction, 1212–1213
Topological representation, 1290

commonsense reasoning, 1290
 shape representation, 1527
TORUS system, computational linguistics, 210
TOUR program
 commonsense reasoning, 1290
 image understanding and, 652
 spatial reasoning, 1327
Tower of Hanoi puzzle
 AND/OR graphs, 29–30
 means-ends analysis, 910–911
 recursion and, 1340
TQA system
 computational linguistics, 209
 parsing speed, 1107
Trace expert, program synthesis, 75–76
Tracking, robotics design, 1391
Tractability, knowledge representation and, 755
Trade relationships, argument comprehension systems, 35–36
Trans-frame, in frame theory, 495–497, 500–501
Transcendental phenomenology, 1132
Transducers, tactile sensing, 1388–1389
Transfer, learning and intelligence, 712–713
Transformational grammar (TG)
 ATNs and, 554
 cognitive psychology and, 185
 computational linguistics, 204–205, 214–215
 deep structure, 328–330
 natural language understanding, 1002–1003
 parsing, 1104–1105
 phrase-structure grammars and, 576
Transformational methodologies, automatic programming, 64–65
Translation, machine, 898–902
Transmission systems, robot end-effector design, 1370
Transposition tables
 computer chess and, 231–232
 memory and, 237–238
Traveling salesman problem (TSP)
 heuristics and, 612
 neural network optimization, 1022–1023
 problem solving, 1226
 search techniques and, 1460
 simulated annealing, 1540
Traverse network, reactive planning machines, 1179
Tree of Porphyry, semantic networks, 1493–1494
Tree search structures
 backtracking, 84
 Bayesian inference methods, 94–95
 clustering, constraint networks, 281–282
 semantic networks, 1501
 tree-consistency algorithm, constraint networks, 278
 tree-to-tree transformation formalism, 900
Tree-adjoining grammar (TAG), 578–579
 dictionary/lexicon construction, 345
Triangular norm based reasoning systems, 1315–1316
Triangularity
 constraint networks, tree clustering, 281–282
 means-ends analysis, 915
 range sensor design, 1518–1519
 robot sensing and, 1382–1384
Trie, character recognition, 146, 148
Trimmed surfaces, shape representation, 1534–1535
TRUCKER system, case-based reasoning, 1274
Truth conditions
 discourse understanding, 371
 fuzzy logic and, 540–542
 hermeneutics and, 606
Truth functional logic, incidence calculus, 663
Truth maintenance systems (TMS), 1613–1620
 applications, 1620
 argument comprehension, 31
 belief revision and, 112–113
 constraint satisfaction, 287
 dependency-directed backtracking, 87
 default reasoning, 1295–1296
 design and, 336
 distributed problem solving, 385–386
 engineering and KBES, 450
 epistemology and, 466
 history, 1620
 justification-based systems, 1614–1617
  assumption-based systems, 1617–1618
  contradiction removal, 1616–1617
  dependency networks, 1615
  node label computations, 1616
  problem solver interactions, 1615–1616
 KEE system, 718
 knowledge representation and, 754–756
 logic-based system, 1619
 mental models and, 934

multiple belief reasoner, 1618–1619
 theoretical foundations, 1620
Truth tables
 propositional logic, 893
 semantics, 896
Tsotsos, J. K., 647–648
T-test, segmentation, 1482–1484
TUBE software, ECRC programs, 421
Turing, Alan, 844
 Alvey program, 25–26
 education and AI, 435–436
 neural network research, 1019
Turing machines, 1622–1624
 analysis, 1622
 applications, 1623–1624
 Church's thesis, 163
 defined, 1623
 inductive inference, 673
 logic programming and, 882–884
 neural network modeling, 1018
 philosophy of AI and, 1142–1143
 program synthesis, 66–67
Turing test, 1625–1629
 criticism of, 1627–1628
 imitation game, 1625–1626
 inductive interpretation, 1626–1627
 legacy of, 1628–1629
 nature of, 1626
 philosophy of AI and, 1137–1139
  antibehavioral objections to, 1138–1139
  behavioral theories, 1136
 restricted, 1629
TWEAK system, reactive planning machines, 1173
Two-and-a-half dimensional sketches, 932–933
Two-dimensional data
 Fourier power spectrum, visual recovery, 1673–1675
 image models, 628
 image understanding, 641–642
 noncausal models, 630–631
 object recognition and, 1063–1065
 shape detection, Hough transforms, 618
 signals, edge detection, 428–432
 unilateral models, 629–630
 vision, object recognition, 1076
Two-fingered angular-jaw grippers, 1361–1362
Two-fingered-servo grippers, 1364–1365
Two-player games
 heuristics and, 613–614
 horizon effect, 615–616
Two-view motion analysis, feature correspondence, 1641–1645
 planar curve correspondence, 1644–1645
 point correspondence, 1641–1643
 straight-line correspondence, 1643–1644
Type abstraction, situation semantics, 1543–1544
Type hierarchy, semantic networks, 1500–1501
Typed inheritance, dictionary/lexicon construction, 353
Typelessness, LISP language, 840
Typicality, concept learning and, 257

UC system, computational linguistics, 212
UCLA grammar, computational linguistics, 214–215
Ultracentrifugation, chemistry in AI and, 159
Umbilic point, range data analysis, 1258
Uncertainty
 AI in medicine (AIM) and, 918–919
 early vision and, 402
 engineering and KBES, 450
 fuzzy set theory
  databases, 510–511
  evidential reasoning and, 533–535
 image understanding and, 652–653
 machine learning, 795
 plausible reasoning and, 1307–1309
  comparison of approaches, 1318
  quantitative vs. qualitative approaches, 1308–1309
  sources of uncertainty and, 1307–1308
 reactive planning, 1173
Unconstrained hierarchical matching, stereo vision, 1563
Understanding
 adaptive planning and, 6–9
 existential, 598
 Gadamer's hermeneutics and, 599–600
 hermeneutic arc and, 602–603
 hermeneutics and, 597–598, 607
Ungrammaticality, computational linguistics, 215
Unichromatic reflection model, 199
Unidirected graphs, graphoids and, 592–593
Unification, 1630–1636
 data structures and algorithms, 1631
 definitions, 1630

equational theories, 1633
feature structures, 1633–1634
higher-order, 1632–1633
history, 1630
inductive inference, 677
logic programming, 1632
natural language processing, 1634–1636
processing, bottom-up and top-down, 1233–1234
theorem proving, 1631–1632
Unified Medical Language System (UMLS), 918
Unified negotiation protocol, distributed problem solving, 385–386
Unified story analysis, 1572–1573
Uniform-cost search, brute-force search and, 1461–1462
Uniform data models, fuzzy databases, 509–510
Uniformity, object-oriented languages, 776–777
UNIMEM system, 1637
Uninformed search, problem reduction, 1212
UNIRED system, parallel machine architecture, 1093
Unit preference strategy, binary resolution, 1349–1350
Unit Surface Normal Vector, range data analysis, 1256–1257
Unit-value principle, connectionism, 270
UNITS, knowledge system building, 488
Universal generalization, predicate logic, 869–870
Universal Indexing Frame (UIF), 1269–1270
Universal Plan, reactive planning machines, 1176
Universal pragmatics, hermeneutics and, 600
University Adaptive Suspension Vehicle, 1405–1406
UNIX Consultant, human-computer interaction, 622
Unreliability, blackboard systems, 117–118
Unsafe languages, parallel logic programming language, 1085
Unsupervised learning
  machine learning and, 787
  pattern recognition, 1120
UR-resolution, binary resolution, 1348
User interface management system (UIMS), 620
User interface techniques, knowledge acquisition, 722
  see also Human-computer interaction
User models, belief representation systems, 107
Utility theory
  Bayesian inference methods, 97
  decision theory, 318

Vacuum grippers, 1362
Valency theory, semantic networks, 1495
VALID language, parallel machine architecture, 1094
Validation procedures, AI in medicine (AIM) and, 922
Value anomaly, cybernetics, 311
Value cell, LISP language, 822
Value theory, AI in medicine (AIM) and, 916
Variables
  clustering analysis, 170
  multihypothesis, Bayesian inference methods, 91–92
  reordering, with chronological backtracking, 85–86
Vax computers, LISP language development and, 838
Vector models, information retrieval, 687
Vector sensors, robot end-effector design, 1368
Vectors
  LISP language, 830
  range data analysis, 1256–1257
VED, POPLOG systems and, 1182
Vehicle modeling, mobile robot planning, 1413
Verb-centered graphs, semantic networks, 1497
Verb phrases, generalized phrase-structure grammar and, 571
Verbal semantics, dictionary/lexicon construction, 345–346
VERIFY program, causal reasoning, 1282
Vertical disparity, stereo vision, 1566
Very large distributed systems
  massive parallelism, 627
  see also VLSI systems
VEXED system, design and, 337
Vieth-Muller circle
  depth perception and, 1565–1566
  stereo vision, 1560
Viewpoint-dependence, image properties, 640
VIPS system, computational linguistics, 212
Virtual arcs, augmented transition network (ATN) grammars, 558

Virtual lexicons, dictionary/lexicon construction, 347
Virtual machines
  control structures, 293
  programming language design, 294–296
  serial generalizations, 295–296
Visibility, object recognition and, 1074
Vision
  artificial intelligence, 57
  cognitive modeling, 177
  cognitive science and, 189–190
  color, 192–200
  commonsense reasoning, 1289–1290
  connectionism and, 273
  early. See Early vision
  episodic memory and, 455–456
  epistemology and, 465
  high-level, 415–416
  Hough transforms, 617–618
  image understanding, 641, 642
  inspection systems, 701–704
  low-level, neural networks, 1025–1028
  mental imagery representation, 928–931
  military applications of AI and, 955–956
  monocular, mobile robot sensing, 1412
  neural networks, face recognition system, 1054–1055
  robotics design and, 1380–1381
  schema theory, high-level vision, 1437–1440
  spatial reasoning, 1324–1332
    route finding and exploration, 1325–1328
  visual recovery, 1681–1683
  see also Object recognition; Stereo vision
VISIONS system
  image understanding and, 650–653
  schema theory, 1438–1439, 1438–1440
Visual cortex
  neural networks, 1031–1032
    Hebbian plasticity, 1033–1034
  stereo vision, 1565–1567
Visual fields, visual motion analysis, 1652–1653
Visual motion analysis, 1638–1653
  algorithm accuracy, 1651–1652
  correspondenceless approaches, 1651
  discrete displacements, 1640–1641
  high-level motion, 1653
  image intensity matching, 1648–1650
    displaced frame differences, 1648–1649
    generalized 3-D motion, 1649
    planar patch linear algorithms, 1649–1650
  multiple frames, 1652
  multiple object recognition, 1652
  optical flow, 1638–1640
    motion from, 1645–1648
    normal flow, 1640
  perception and, 1659
  3-D feature correspondences, 1650–1651
    binocular procedures, 1630
  two-view feature correspondence, 1641–1645
    nonlinear equations, 1642
    planar curve correspondences, 1644–1645
    planar patch case, 1643
    point correspondences, 1641–1643
    problem statement, 1641
    straight-line correspondence, 1643–1644
  visual field and, 1652–1653
Visual perception. See Perception
Visual programming languages, 623
Visual recovery, 1664–1685
  active vision, 1681–1683
  future trends, 1683–1685
  geometric correspondence, 1666–1667
  ill-posedness and regularization, 1676–1679
  impairment, 1665
  methodology, 1665
  multiple cues, 1679–1681
  research issues, 1683
  shape definition, 1667–1669
  shape from x technique, 1669–1676
    shape from contour, 1675–1676
    shape from shading, 1669–1672
    shape from stereo and motion, 1676
    shape from texture, 1672–1675
Visual sensing, sensor data fusion
  ladar sensing, 1521
  range sensing, 1521–1522
  tactile sensing, 1520–1521
  thermal sensing andd, 1519–1520
Viterbi algorithm, character recognition, 145–146, 148
Vividness, memory and, 457
VLSI systems
  Alvey program, 26
  associative memory, 58

computer chess and, 235
neural networks, analog implementations, 1028
parallel logic programming, 1081
tactile sensor design, 1516
VM program, AI in medicine (AIM) and, 921
Vocabulary
  intelligence and, 707
  knowledge representation and, 744
Volumetric description, spatial reasoning, 1323–1324
Volumetric representation, robot sensing and, 1388
von Helmholtz, Hermann
  cybernetics, 311
  early vision, 394, 407
  image understanding, 641
von der Malsburg, 1033–1034
von Neumann, John
  cybernetics, 309–310
  minimax procedure, 959–960
  self-replication, 1492
von Neumann architecture
  computer systems, 241–242
  connectionism, 268–269
Voronoi diagram
  shape representation, 1535–1537
  texture analysis, 1595–1596
Voting model semantics, fuzzy set theory, 530–531
Votrax speech-production system, natural language generation, 986
Voxels
  robot sensing and, 1388
  shape representation, 1533–1534
  spatial reasoning, 1323
VT system, design and, 335

Walk-through algorithm, 1188
Walking machines
  legged robots as, 1403–1404
  mobile robot mechanisms, 1414
Waltz filtering algorithm, 288
Waltz's Scene Analysis Program
  control structures, 296–297
  early vision and, 405
  phenomenology and, 1133
Wang's algorithm, propositional logic, 895
Water chemistry, AI and, 160
Wave model, neural networks, 1049–1052
Wavefront, parallel machine architecture, 1092
WAVES system, 487–488
Wechsler Adult Intelligence Scale, 707
Weight space, in neural networks, 1034–1035
Weighted quadratic regression, 1301
Weiner, Norbert, 844
  cybernetics, 309–310
Weingarten mapping, range data analysis, 1256–1257
Well-formed formula (wff), predicate logic, 867–868
Well-formed propositions (WFPs), 894
Well-founded approach
  disjunctive databases, 327
  normal databases, 326
Wexler, K., language acquisition and, 763–764
WHISPER program, spatial reasoning, 1331
Whole-task analysis, intelligence and, 711
Wilensky, G.
  frame theory and, 498
  text summarization, 1583
Willshaw, D., 1023
Winged-edge representation, 1534–1535
  shape representation, 1534–1535
Winner-take-all networks, 1023–1025
  localist connectionism, 270–271
  statistical mechanics, 1025
Winograd, Terry, 845
  hermeneutics, 596, 606
Winston's block world, concept learning, 254–255
WIP project, 340
Wireframe models, shape representation, 1535
Wiswesser line notation, 156
Wittgenstein, L., 932
  philosophy of AI and, 1144
Word recognition, character recognition and, 144–148
Word sense
  dictionary/lexicon construction, 341–342, 353–354
    inter-word entry information, 344
  disambiguation, scripts and, 1448
Word-expert parsing (WEP), 1109–1115
  abbreviated execution trace, 1114
  control mechanisms, 1113

example analysis, 1113–1114
formalization, 1111–1115
message and memory objects, 1113
model organization, 1112–1113
principles, 1110
program development, 1110–1111
structure, 1111–1112
working memory after analysis, 1114–1115
Word-shape analysis, character recognition, 144, 147–148
WordNet lexicon, 353–354
Wordtree program, lexical decomposition, 807
Working memory
 rule-based systems, 1420
 schema theory, 1434
  scene interpretation, 1438–1439
Workload measure, text summarization, 1584–1585
Workstation transforms, robotics design and, 1377
World coordinates, robotics design and, 1377
World-to-joint coordinate transformation, 1377
w^*-tractability, constraint networks, 280–281

X-Ray powder diffraction, 158
XCALIBUR project, 1011–1012
XCON system, 1688
 design and, 337
 engineering and KBES, 452–453
 knowledge system building, 488
 rule-based systems, 1425
XPLAIN system
 AI in medicine (AIM) and, 921–922
 explanation and, 490
XSEL expert system
 knowledge system building, 488
 natural language understanding, 1011–1012
XTRA system, preference semantics and, 1189

Yale shooting problem
 default reasoning, 1298
 logic programming, 879–880
Yuille, A., 1025

Z modal quantification logic, 1689
Zadeh's fuzzy set theory, 537
 AI in medicine (AIM) and, 919
ZBIE system, computational linguistics, 218
Zebra stripe theory, neural networks, 1019
Zero crossings
 edge detection, 426–428
 tactile sensing data fusion, 1520–1521
Zero moment point control, legged robots locomotion, 1406
Zero-sum two-person games, minimax procedure, 960–962
ZETALISP syste,, 843
ZMACS editor, 843